THE OXFORD PAPERBA

W9-CAE-897

German Dictionary and Grammar

JUN 09
JUL X X 2015
WITHDRAWN

REF
PF
3640
R68
1995

THE OXFORD PAPERBACK

German Dictionary and Grammar

GUNHILD PROWE
JILL SCHNEIDER
WILLIAM ROWLINSON

Oxford New York
OXFORD UNIVERSITY PRESS

Oxford University Press, Walton Street, Oxford OX2 6DP
Oxford New York
Athens Auckland Bangkok Bombay
Calcutta Cape Town Dar es Salaam Delhi
Florence Hong Kong Istanbul Karachi
Kuala Lumpur Madras Madrid Melbourne
Mexico City Nairobi Paris Singapore
Taipei Tokyo Toronto
and associated companies in
Berlin Ibadan

Oxford is a trade mark of Oxford University Press

Grammar: © Oxford University Press 1993
Dictionary: © Oxford University Press 1993
This combined edition first published 1995

All rights reserved. No part of this publication may be reproduced, stored in a retrieval system, or transmitted, in any form or by any means, without the prior permission in writing of Oxford University Press. Within the UK, exceptions are allowed in respect of any fair dealing for the purpose of research or private study, or criticism or review, as permitted under the Copyright, Designs and Patents Act, 1988, or in the case of reprographic reproduction in accordance with the terms of the licences issued by the Copyright Licensing Agency. Enquiries concerning reproduction outside these terms and in other countries should be sent to the Rights Department, Oxford University Press, at the address above

This book is sold subject to the condition that it shall not, by way of trade or otherwise, be lent, re-sold, hired out or otherwise circulated without the publisher's prior consent in any form of binding or cover other than that in which it is published and without a similar condition including this condition being imposed on the subsequent purchaser

British Library Cataloguing in Publication Data
Data available

Library of Congress Cataloguing in Publication Data
Data available

ISBN 0–19–864530–9

10 9 8 7

Printed and bound in Great Britain by
Mackays of Chatham plc, Chatham, Kent

Contents

Grammar

William Rowlinson

Dictionary

Gunhild Prowe
Jill Schneider

Grammar

Introduction

This German Grammar is more thorough, more accurate, and more practical than other pocket grammars. It is also more up to date. In the next 300 pages you will find:

- All the basic grammar of German presented clearly, comprehensively, and succinctly.
- Explanations that use everyday language, and a glossary of absolutely all the grammatical terms we have used.
- Up-to-date explanations of modern German usage not found in other grammars of this size.
- Short, simple, easy-to-follow German examples for points of basic grammar, and longer examples from modern German sources where they are needed to explain usage.
- A clear layout within a tough binding that will stand up to hard use.

This grammar is *really* comprehensive. It will explain problems met by beginners, it will be a reliable learning aid for GCSE and A level, and it will remain a first resource for quick reference and revision for German specialists who have reached university and polytechnic level. As well as covering all the grammar used in modern German, with particular stress on the difference between the spoken and the written language, it has sections on translation problems, word order, and punctuation, and verb tables with the conjugation of all the irregular verbs used in modern German. A feature of this grammar is its comprehensive reference lists of prepositions and their use, of verbs with their cases and constructions, of adverbial participles with their shades of meaning and their use. There is also a glossary of grammatical terms and an easy-to-use index.

Acknowledgements

The author wishes to thank Harry Ferrar for his meticulous reading of the manuscript and his many useful suggestions, and the editorial staff of Oxford University Press for their continued support, advice, and encouragement.

Contents

I Verbs

TENSE FORMATION

There are three types of German verb, *weak* (completely regular), *strong* (irregular, though tending to follow certain patterns), and *mixed* (partly strong, partly weak). All German verbs have infinitives ending **-en** (or occasionally just **-n**), so it is not possible to tell from the infinitive of a verb whether it is weak, strong, or mixed.

The tenses of German verbs are either simple, in which case the verb is a single word, or compound, in which case the verb is formed with part of one of the three auxiliary (helping) verbs, **haben**, **sein**, and **werden**, together with the past participle or the infinitive:

> simple tense: **ich sage**, *I say*
> compound tenses: **ich habe gesagt**, *I have said*
> **ich werde sagen**, *I shall say*

Apart from the formation of their past participles, all verbs follow the same pattern in their compound tenses.

Weak verbs

The vast majority of German verbs are weak and follow a single pattern. Their past tense is formed by adding **-te** to their stem (the infinitive minus its **-(e)n** ending), and their past participle is formed **ge . . . t**:

> **sagen**, *to say*
> **ich sage**, *I say*
> **ich sagte**, *I said*
> **ich habe gesagt**, *I have said*

▶ The complete tense formation of a weak (regular) verb is given on pp. 5–7, with the verb endings printed in bold.

▶ Some weak verbs have an infinitive ending **-eln** or **-ern** rather than **-en**. Their endings are dealt with on p. 13.

▶ Some verbs have no **ge-** in their past participle. See p. 14 (Verbs ending **-ieren** and **-eien**) and p. 34 (Inseparable Prefixes).

Strong verbs

Strong verbs change their stem vowels in the past tense and (often) in their past participle, and sometimes in parts of the present as well. They may also change the consonant after that vowel. Their past participles are formed **ge . . . en**.

> **singen,** *to sing*
> **ich singe,** *I sing*
> **ich sang,** *I sang*
> **ich habe gesungen,** *I have sung*

▶ The endings of strong verbs are regular. The complete tense formation of a strong verb is given on pp. 7–9, with the verb endings printed in bold.

▶ The modal verbs, **lassen,** and **werden** have two past participles used in differing circumstances. See pp. 66–7.

▶ There is a list of all German strong and mixed verbs showing their vowel changes on pp. 73–85.

Mixed verbs

There are only nine mixed verbs: **bringen,** *to bring,* **denken,** *to think,* **haben,** *to have,* **kennen,** *to know,* **nennen,** *to name,* **rennen,** *to run,* **senden,** *to send,* **wenden,** *to turn,* and **wissen,** *to know.* They take weak verb endings, but also change their stem vowel (and sometimes the following consonant) like strong verbs:

> **bringen**, *to bring*
> **ich bringe**, *I bring*
> **ich brachte**, *I brought*
> **ich habe gebracht**, *I have brought*

► The complete tense formation of a mixed verb is given on pp. 9–11, with the verb endings printed in bold. Mixed verbs and their vowel changes are included in the list of Irregular Verbs on pp. 73–85.

Simple-tense formation

The simple tenses are the present and past tenses and the present and past subjunctive.

To form each simple tense a fixed set of endings is added to the verb's stem. The stem is its infinitive minus **-en** (or **-n**). The ending of the verb corresponds to the subject of the verb:

> **ich sage**, *I say*
> **er sagt**, *he says*
> **wir sagen**, *we say*

The endings are different for strong verbs on the one hand and for weak and mixed verbs on the other. See conjugation tables, p. 5 onwards.

Compound-tense formation

Compound tenses are formed, as in English, from the past participle or the infinitive of the verb, used with an auxiliary verb. The auxiliary verbs in German are **haben**, *to have*, **sein**, *to be*, and **werden**, *to become*. The compound tenses and their formation are as follows:

perfect tense:
present of **haben** + PAST PARTICIPLE: **er hat gesagt,** *he has said*

pluperfect tense:
past of **haben** + PAST PARTICIPLE: **er hatte gesagt**, *he had said*

future tense:
present of **werden** + INFINITIVE: **er wird sagen**, *he will say*

conditional tense:
past subjunctive of **werden** + INFINITIVE: **er würde sagen**, *he would say*

future perfect tense:
future of **haben** + PAST PARTICIPLE: **er wird gesagt haben**, *he will have said*

conditional perfect tense:
conditional of **haben** + PAST PARTICIPLE: **er würde gesagt haben**, *he would have said*

perfect subjunctive:
present subjunctive of **haben** + PAST PARTICIPLE: **er habe gesagt**, *he has said/may have said*

pluperfect subjunctive:
past subjunctive of **haben** + PAST PARTICIPLE: **er hätte gesagt**, *he had said/might have said*

Transitive verbs form their past compound tenses with **haben**. Intransitive verbs of motion and the verbs **sein,** *to be,* **werden,** *to become,* and **bleiben,** *to remain,* use the auxiliary **sein** instead of **haben** in compound tenses:

er ist gewesen, *he has been*
er war geworden, *he had become*
er wird geblieben sein, *he will have remained*

With some verbs that use **sein** the 'motion' idea may not be immediately obvious. There is a list of these verbs on p. 16.

The past subjunctive is often substituted for the conditional, and the pluperfect subjunctive is very frequently substituted for the conditional perfect. See p. 24.

► For the position of the past participle in the sentence see pp. 217–18.

CONJUGATION OF WEAK VERBS

This is the regular pattern for the active form of most German verbs. For the forms of the passive see p. 29.

In all tenses **sie** (*she*), **es** (*it*), **man** (*one*), and singular nouns are followed by the **er** form of the verb; plural nouns are followed by the **sie** (*they*) form.

infinitive	sag**en**, *to say*
present participle	sag**end**, *saying*
past participle	**ge**sag**t**, *said*
imperative	sag(**e**), *say* (**du** *form*)
	sag**en** wir, *let's say*
	sag**t**, *say* (**ihr** form)
	sag**en** Sie, *say* (**Sie** form)

Simple tenses

present tense, *I say, I am saying*	ich sag**e**		wir sag**en**
	du sag**st**		ihr sag**t**
		Sie sag**en**[1]	
	er sag**t**		sie sag**en**
past tense, *I said, I was saying*	ich sag**te**		wir sag**ten**
	du sag**test**		ihr sag**tet**
		Sie sag**ten**[1]	
	er sag**te**		sie sag**ten**

[1] The polite form of *you* in both singular and plural is **Sie**. See p. 133.

present subjunctive,	ich sag**e**	wir sag**en**
I say, I may say	du sag**est**	ihr sag**et**
	Sie sag**en**[1]	
	er sag**e**	sie sag**en**
past subjunctive,	ich sag**te**	wir sag**ten**
I said, I might say	du sag**test**	ihr sag**tet**
	Sie sag**ten**[1]	
	er sag**te**	sie sag**ten**

Compound tenses

perfect tense,	ich **habe** gesagt	wir **haben** gesagt
I said, I have said,	du **hast** gesagt	ihr **habt** gesagt
I have been saying	Sie **haben** gesagt[1]	
	er **hat** gesagt	sie **haben** gesagt
pluperfect tense,	ich **hatte** gesagt	wir **hatten** gesagt
I had said, I had been	du **hattest** gesagt	ihr **hattet** gesagt
saying	Sie **hatten** gesagt[1]	
	er **hatte** gesagt	sie **hatten** gesagt
future tense,	ich **werde** sagen	wir **werden** sagen
I shall[2] *say, I*	du **wirst** sagen	ihr **werdet** sagen
shall[2] *be saying*	Sie **werden** sagen[1]	
	er **wird** sagen	sie **werden** sagen
conditional tense,	ich **würde** sagen	wir **würden** sagen
I should[3] *say, I*	du **würdest** sagen	ihr **würdet** sagen
should[3] *be saying*	Sie **würden** sagen[1]	
	er **würde** sagen	sie **würden** sagen
future perfect tense,	ich **werde** gesagt **haben**	wir **werden** gesagt **haben**
I shall[2] *have said,*	du **wirst** gesagt **haben**	ihr **werdet** gesagt **haben**
I shall[2] *have been*	Sie **werden** gesagt **haben**[1]	
saying	er **wird** gesagt **haben**	sie **werden** gesagt **haben**

---

[1] The polite form of *you* in both singular and plural is **Sie**. See p. 133.

[2] In English we often use *will* here.

[3] In English we often use *would* here.

conditional perfect tense, *I should*[1] *have said, I should*[1] *have been saying*	ich **würde** gesagt **haben**	wir **würden** gesagt **haben**
	du **würdest** gesagt **haben**	ihr **würdet** gesagt **haben**
	Sie **würden** gesagt **haben**[2]	
	er **würde** gesagt **haben**	sie **würden** gesagt **haben**
perfect subjunctive, *I have said, I may have said*	ich **habe** gesagt	wir **haben** gesagt
	du **habest** gesagt	ihr **habet** gesagt
	Sie **haben** gesagt[2]	
	er **habe** gesagt	sie **haben** gesagt
pluperfect subjunctive, *I had said, I might have said*	ich **hätte** gesagt	wir **hätten** gesagt
	du **hättest** gesagt	ihr **hättet** gesagt
	Sie **hätten** gesagt[2]	
	er **hätte** gesagt	sie **hätten** gesagt

CONJUGATION OF STRONG VERBS

This is the regular pattern of endings for the active form of German strong verbs. As well as adding these endings, strong verbs also change their vowel (and sometimes the following consonant) in the past participle, throughout the past tense, and (sometimes) in the **du** and **er** forms of the present and the imperative. These changes are listed in the Irregular Verb list on pp. 73–85. For the forms of the passive see p. 29.

In all tenses **sie** (*she*), **es** (*it*), **man** (*one*), and singular nouns are followed by the **er** form of the verb; plural nouns are followed by the **sie** form.

infinitive	fang**en**, *to catch*
present participle	fang**end**, *catching*
past participle	**ge**fang**en**, *caught*
imperative	fang**(e)**, *catch* (**du** form)[3]

---

[1] In English we often use *would* here.

[2] The polite form of *you* in both singular and plural is **Sie**. See page 133.

[3] Verbs like **fangen** that take an umlaut in the **du** and **er** forms of the present tense do not use it in the imperative. See p. 26.

	fangen wir, *let's catch*
	fangt, *catch* (**ihr** form)
	fangen Sie, *catch* (**Sie** form)

Simple tenses

present tense, *I catch, I am catching*	ich fang**e**		wir fang**en**
	du f**ä**ng**st**		ihr fang**t**
		Sie fang**en**[1]	
	er f**ä**ng**t**		sie fang**en**
past tense, *I caught, I was catching*	ich f**i**ng		wir f**i**ng**en**
	du f**i**ng**st**		ihr f**i**ng**t**
		Sie f**i**ng**en**[1]	
	er f**i**ng		sie f**i**ng**en**
present subjunctive, *I catch, I may catch*	ich fang**e**		wir fang**en**
	du fang**est**		ihr fang**et**
		Sie fang**en**[1]	
	er fang**e**		sie fang**en**
past subjunctive, *I caught, I might catch*	ich f**i**ng**e**		wir f**i**ng**en**
	du f**i**ng**est**		ihr f**i**ng**et**
		Sie f**i**ng**en**[1]	
	er f**i**ng**e**		sie f**i**ng**en**

Compound tenses

perfect tense, *I caught, I have caught, I have been catching*	ich **habe** gefangen		wir **haben** gefangen
	du **hast** gefangen		ihr **habt** gefangen
		Sie **haben** gefangen[1]	
	er **hat** gefangen		sie **haben** gefangen
pluperfect tense, *I had caught, I had been catching*	ich **hatte** gefangen		wir **hatten** gefangen
	du **hattest** gefangen		ihr **hattet** gefangen
		Sie **hatten** gefangen[1]	
	er **hatte** gefangen		sie **hatten** gefangen

---

[1] The polite form of *you* in both singular and plural is **Sie**. See p. 133.

future tense, *I shall[1] catch, I shall[1] be catching*	ich **werde** fangen	wir **werden** fangen
	du **wirst** fangen	ihr **werdet** fangen
	Sie **werden** fangen[2]	
	er **wird** fangen	sie **werden** fangen
conditional tense, *I should[3] catch, I should[3] be catching*	ich **würde** fangen	wir **würden** fangen
	du **würdest** fangen	ihr **würdet** fangen
	Sie **würden** fangen[2]	
	er **würde** fangen	sie **würden** fangen
future perfect tense, *I shall[1] have caught, I shall[1] have been catching*	ich **werde** gefangen **haben**	wir **werden** gefangen **haben**
	du **wirst** gefangen **haben**	ihr **werdet** gefangen **haben**
	Sie **werden** gefangen **haben**[2]	
	er **wird** gefangen **haben**	sie **werden** gefangen **haben**
conditional perfect tense, *I should[3] have caught, I should[3] have been catching*	ich **würde** gefangen **haben**	wir **würden** gefangen **haben**
	du **würdest** gefangen **haben**	ihr **würdet** gefangen **haben**
	Sie **würden** gefangen **haben**[2]	
	er **würde** gefangen **haben**	sie **würden** gefangen **haben**
perfect subjunctive, *I have caught, I may have caught*	ich **habe** gefangen	wir **haben** gefangen
	du **habest** gefangen	ihr **habet** gefangen
	Sie **haben** gefangen[2]	
	er **habe** gefangen	sie **haben** gefangen
pluperfect subjunctive, *I had caught, I might have caught*	ich **hätte** gefangen	wir **hätten** gefangen
	du **hättest** gefangen	ihr **hättet** gefangen
	Sie **hätten** gefangen[2]	
	er **hätte** gefangen	sie **hätten** gefangen

CONJUGATION OF MIXED VERBS

This is the regular pattern for the active form of mixed verbs. For the forms of the passive see p. 29.

[1] In English we often use *will* here.

[2] The polite form of *you* in both singular and plural is **Sie**. See page 133.

[3] In English we often use *would* here.

In all tenses **sie** (*she*), **es** (*it*), **man** (*one*), and singular nouns are followed by the **er** form of the verb; plural nouns are followed by the **sie** form.

infinitive	kenn**en**, *to know*
present participle	kenn**end**, *knowing*
past participle	**ge**kann**t**, *known*
imperative	kenn**(e)**, *know* (**du** form)
	kenn**en** wir, *let's know*
	kenn**t**, *know* (**ihr** form)
	kenn**en** Sie, know (**Sie** form)

Simple tenses

present tense, *I know*	ich kenn**e**		wir kenn**en**
	du kenn**st**		ihr kenn**t**
		Sie kenn**en**[1]	
	er kenn**t**		sie kenn**en**
past tense, *I knew*	ich kann**te**		wir kann**ten**
	du kann**test**		ihr kann**tet**
		Sie kann**ten**[1]	
	er kann**te**		sie kann**ten**
present subjunctive, *I know, I may know*	ich kenn**e**		wir kenn**en**
	du kenn**est**		ihr kenn**et**
		Sie kenn**en**[1]	
	er kenn**e**		sie kenn**en**
past subjunctive, *I knew, I might know*	ich kenn**te**		wir kenn**ten**
	du kenn**test**		ihr kenn**tet**
		Sie kenn**ten**[1]	
	er kenn**te**		sie kenn**ten**

[1] The polite form of *you* in both singular and plural is **Sie**. See p. 133.

Compound tenses

perfect tense, *I knew, I have known*	ich **habe** gekannt	wir **haben** gekannt
	du **hast** gekannt	ihr **habt** gekannt
	Sie **haben** gekannt[1]	
	er **hat** gekannt	sie **haben** gekannt
pluperfect tense, *I had known*	ich **hatte** gekannt	wir **hatten** gekannt
	du **hattest** gekannt	ihr **hattet** gekannt
	Sie **hatten** gekannt[1]	
	er **hatte** gekannt	sie **hatten** gekannt
future tense, *I shall know*	ich **werde** kennen	wir **werden** kennen
	du **wirst** kennen	ihr **werdet** kennen
	Sie **werden** kennen[1]	
	er **wird** kennen	sie **werden** kennen
conditional tense, *I would know*	ich **würde** kennen	wir **würden** kennen
	du **würdest** kennen	ihr **würdet** kennen
	Sie **würden** kennen[1]	
	er **würde** kennen	sie **würden** kennen
future perfect tense, *I shall have known*	ich **werde** gekannt **haben**	wir **werden** gekannt **haben**
	du **wirst** gekannt **haben**	ihr **werdet** gekannt **haben**
	Sie **werden** gekannt **haben**[1]	
	er **wird** gekannt **haben**	sie **werden** gekannt **haben**
conditional perfect tense, *I would have known*	ich **würde** gekannt **haben**	wir **würden** gekannt **haben**
	du **würdest** gekannt **haben**	ihr **würdet** gekannt **haben**
	Sie **würden** gekannt **haben**[1]	
	er **würde** gekannt **haben**	sie **würden** gekannt **haben**
perfect subjunctive, *I have known, I may have known*	ich **habe** gekannt	wir **haben** gekannt
	du **habest** gekannt	ihr **habet** gekannt
	Sie **haben** gekannt[1]	
	er **habe** gekannt	sie **haben** gekannt
pluperfect subjunctive, *I had known, I might have known*	ich **hätte** gekannt	wir **hätten** gekannt
	du **hättest** gekannt	ihr **hättet** gekannt
	Sie **hätten** gekannt[1]	
	er **hätte** gekannt	sie **hätten** gekannt

[1] The polite form of *you* in both singular and plural is **Sie**. See p. 133.

Minor irregularities in verbs

Almost all these changes are made to make the verb easier to pronounce.

■ Verbs ending **-den** or **-ten**

Weak verbs ending **-den** or **-ten** always add an extra **e** before an ending that doesn't already begin with **e**:

> **reden**, *to speak*: **du redest**, *you speak*
> **antworten**, *to answer*: **ihr antwortetet**, *you answered*
> **blenden**, *to dazzle*: **es hat geblendet**, *it has dazzled*

Strong verbs ending **-den** or **-ten** do the same, except in the **du** form of the past tense:

> **finden**, *to find*: **du findest**, *you find*
> **bitten**, *to ask*: **ihr batet**, *you asked*

but

> **du fandst**, *you found*
> **du batst**, *you asked*

In speech the **e** is often omitted in the **du** form of the present (of both weak and strong verbs):

> **du antwortst nicht!**, *you're not answering*

■ Verbs ending in **-[**CONSONANT**]men** and **-[**CONSONANT**]nen**

Verbs (they are all weak) with a consonant followed by **m** or **n** at the end of their stem add an extra **e** before an ending that doesn't already begin with **e**, but only if this would otherwise be impossible to pronounce:

> **atmen**, *to breathe*: **du atmest**, *you breathe*
> **regnen**, *to rain*: **es regnete**, *it was raining*

but

> **lernen**, *to learn*: **du lernst**, *you learn* (an extra **e** is not necessary for pronunciation)

■ Weak verbs ending **-eln** and **-ern**

The **n** is removed from the infinitive to form the stem and normal endings are then added to this; however, the **e** of the stem may be omitted with verbs ending **-eln** (usually) and **-ern** (sometimes) in the **ich** form of the present and the **du** form of the imperative:

> **angeln**, *to fish*: **ich ang(e)le gern**, *I like fishing*
> **rudern**, *to row*: **ich rud(e)re lieber**, *I prefer rowing*
> **schmeicheln**, *to flatter*: **schmeich(e)le mir nicht!**, *don't flatter me*

Plural endings of these verbs have no **e**:

> **wir angeln**, *we fish*
> **ihr rudert**, *you row*

■ Verbs whose stem ends in an **s** sound

All verbs whose stems end **-s**, **-ß**, **-z**, or **-x** lose the **s** in the ending of the **du** form of the present:

> **hexen**, *to bewitch*: **du hext**
> **heizen**, *to heat*: **du heizt**
> **schießen**, *to shoot*: **du schießt**

In strong verbs with these stems the ending of the **du** form of the past tense is **-est**:

> **du schossest**, *you shot* (in spoken German **du schoßt** is also found)

Note that none of this applies to the stem-ending **-sch**, which has quite regular verb endings after it:

> **wischen**, *to wipe*: **du wischst**

■ Verbs whose stem ends in a vowel or **h**

With both weak and strong verbs whose stems end in a vowel or **h**, the **e** of an **-en** ending disappears in spoken German (and sometimes in printed German too, especially in poetry):

> **einsehen**, *to understand* : **„Das sehn Sie nicht ein"**, *'You don't understand that'*

This also applies to infinitives, and to the **-en** ending of the past participles of strong verbs:

> **„Das wollen Sie nicht einsehn"**, *'You don't want to understand it'*
> **„Das haben Sie nicht eingesehn"**, *'You didn't understand it'*

It does not apply to the past of weak verbs, where a **t** comes before the **-en** ending:

> **bauen**, *build*: **wir bauten; sie bauten**

■ Verbs ending **-ieren** and **-eien**

Verbs ending **-ieren** and **-eien** have no **ge-** in their past participle. They are all weak:

> **ich habe ihn schon informiert**, *I've already informed him*
> **das hat sie prophezeit**, *she prophesied that*

► Inseparable verbs also form past participles without **ge-**. See p. 34.

■ Loss of **-e** endings

□ In spoken German the **-e** ending of the **ich** form of the present almost always disappears. This is shown by an apostrophe when quoting speech:

> **„Ja, ich geh' schon", sage ich**, *'Yes, all right, I'm going', I say*

□ In spoken German the **-e** ending of the **du** form of the imperative almost always disappears in both weak and strong verbs. They are written in quoted speech without an apostrophe:

> **„Komm gut nach Hause", sagte sie**, *'Get home safely', she said*

This applies also to strong verbs that simply add an umlaut to their vowel in the **du** form of the present: in the imperative they do not add the umlaut, but they may take an **e**:

> **fahren**, *to go*
> **du fährst**, *you go*
> **fahr/fahre schneller!**, *go faster!*

However, strong verbs that actually change their vowel in the **du** form of the present (as opposed to simply adding an umlaut) also change it in the **du** form of the imperative. They can never take an **e**:

> **helfen**, *to help*
> **du hilfst**, *you help*
> **hilf mir!**, *help me!*

□ The final **e** of verbs ending in **-eln**, **-ern** is never dropped if they have already dropped the **e** of their stem (see p. 13). Nor is it dropped with verbs ending **-[CONSONANT]men** or **-[CONSONANT]nen**, whose stem is unpronounceable without an ending:

> **atmen**, *to breathe*: **atme!**

□ In spoken German the **-e** of the ending of the **ich** and **er** forms of weak verbs in the past tense often disappears before a vowel. This is written with an apostrophe:

> **„Na also, ich sagt' es schon"**, *'There you are, I told you so'*

COMPOUND TENSES

▶ For the formation of the compound tenses see p. 3.

Compound tenses formed with sein

Virtually all transitive verbs and reflexive verbs form their past compound tenses with **haben**. So do most intransitive verbs.

However, three groups of intransitive verbs use **sein**:

- Verbs expressing motion, involving change of place

  er ist heute gefahren, *he left today*
  sie ist in das Zimmer getanzt, *she danced into the room*

If the verb simply expresses the action, rather than change of place, **haben** is usually used:

  ich habe heute viel geritten, *I've ridden a lot today*
  wir haben gestern abend im „Astoria" getanzt, *we went dancing at the Astoria last night*

- Verbs expressing change of state

  sie ist aufgewacht, *she woke up*
  Großmutter ist gestorben, *grandmother has died*
  du bist aber groß geworden, *you* have *got big*

In this group are included verbs meaning *to happen* (**geschehen, passieren, vorkommen, vorgehen**).

Werden, *to become*, also takes **sein** when it is used to form the passive:

  ich bin gefragt worden, *I have been asked*

See Passive, p. 29.

- The following verbs, where the idea of 'motion' or of 'change of state' seems doubtful or non-existent

  begegnen (+ DAT), *meet* (also **sich begegnen**, *meet one another*)
  bleiben, *remain*
  gelingen, *succeed* (**es ist mir gelungen**, *I succeeded*); also **mißlingen**, *fail*
  glücken, succeed (**es ist mir geglückt**, *I succeeded*); also **mißglücken**, *fail*
  sein, *be*

'Motion' verbs used transitively

Some verbs of motion that are normally intransitive and take sein can also be used transitively. They then take **haben**.

> **hat er dein Mofa gefahren?**, *has he ridden your moped?*

A very few verbs that take **sein** when used intransitively, or that are compounded from verbs that take **sein**, continue to use **sein** when they are used transitively. They are

> **loswerden**, *get rid of*
> **eingehen**, *take on*
> **Gefahr laufen**, *run a risk*
> **eine Strecke gehen**, *go some distance*

> **bist du diese Katze immer noch nicht losgeworden?**, *have you still not got rid of that cat?*

USE OF TENSES

The present tense

There is only one form of the present tense in German, corresponding to both the present simple and the present continuous in English. So **ich gehe** translates both *I go* and *I am going*. There is no possible translation of *I am going* using the present participle in German. If the continuing nature of the action needs to be stressed, **(gerade) dabeisein** is used:

> **ich bin gerade dabei, die letzten Worte zu schreiben**, *I'm just writing the last words*

General uses of the present tense

■ As in English the present is used not just to indicate what is going on at the moment:

> **ich stricke einen Pulli**, *I'm knitting a pullover*

but also what habitually occurs:

zum Frühstück esse ich nur Müsli, *I eat only muesli at breakfast*

■ It can also be used, again as in English, to indicate a future:

ich komme gleich, *I'm coming (I'll come) right away*

This use is more frequent than in English, partly because German has no equivalent to the English form *I'm going to . . .* It is especially used when an adverb already shows that the event is in the future:

kommst du morgen?, *are you coming tomorrow?* (**wirst du morgen kommen?** asks about intention: *are you going to* (*do you intend to*) *come tomorrow?*). See uses of the future tense, p. 22.

■ German uses the present as a past narrative tense (the 'historic present') at least as frequently as English:

Acht Gestalten, die Gesichter hinter Tüchern und Wollmützen versteckt, **schlendern** langsam zum Haus Nummer 128. Dann ein Krachen! Die Eingangstür **splittert**, mit einem Brecheisen **knacken** die Vermummten das Schloß. Für die Nachbarn ein klarer Fall: Hier **sind** Einbrecher am Werk. Die Polizei, die Minuten später am Tatort **erscheint, denkt** ähnlich. Großräumig **werden** die umliegenden Straßen **gesichert**, die übrigen Beamten **observieren** das Haus. Nach und nach **marschieren** immer mehr Männer in das leerstehende Haus am Gereonswall, einige **haben** sogar ihren Hund dabei.

(Express)

Eight figures with their faces hidden behind scarves and woolly hats strolled slowly up to number 128. Then came a crash. The entrance door splintered—the disguised figures were breaking the lock with a crowbar. For the neighbours it was perfectly clear—burglars were at work here. The police, who appeared at the scene of the crime moments later, thought the same thing. The surrounding streets were made secure over a wide area, the remaining officers took up watch on the house. Gradually more and more men trooped into the empty house in Gereonswall. Some even had their dogs with them.

English would be unlikely to continue with the historic present for so long, and through so many verbs. It would either use the past throughout, as above, or if the passage started in the historic present it would probably change back to the past at *'For the neighbours it was perfectly clear . . .'*

Special uses of the present tense

■ Present tense with **seit** (*for*; *since*, preposition) and **seitdem** (*since then*, adverb)

□ With the prepositions *for* and *since*, when an action or state which started in the past is still going on in the present, English uses the perfect continuous (*'I have been doing'*); German—exactly like French in these circumstances—uses a present tense.

> **sie wäscht seit anderthalb Stunden ab**, *she's been washing up for an hour and a half*
>
> **ich warte seit zwanzig nach eins**, *I've been waiting since twenty past one*

However, where a series of actions is referred to (as opposed to one continuing one), a perfect is used, as in English:

> **seit Anfang Juli hat es jeden Tag geregnet**, *it's rained every single day since the beginning of July*

and the perfect is normally always used where the statement is negative:

> **ich habe sie seit vier Wochen nicht mehr gesehen**, *I haven't seen her for four weeks*

□ Exactly the same rules apply to the adverb **seitdem**, *since (then)*:

> **und seitdem warte ich hier**, *and since then I've been waiting here*

seitdem hat es jeden Tag geregnet, *it's rained every day since*
ich habe sie seitdem nicht mehr gesehen, *I haven't seen her since*

■ Present tense with **seitdem** or **seit** (*since*, conjunction)

After the conjunction **seitdem**, *since*, the present tense in German in the **seitdem** clause *always* corresponds to the past continuous in English:

ich habe kein einziges Wort mit ihr gewechselt, seitdem sie hier wohnt, *I haven't exchanged a single word with her since she's been living here*

Seit is also used as a conjunction, though less commonly than **seitdem**.

▶ See also **seit** + past tense, p. 21.

▶ For a fuller treatment of the conjunctions **seitdem** and **seit** see pp. 199–200.

■ Present tense with **kommen**

With **kommen** + infinitive (= *come in order to do something*), German uses a present where English uses a perfect:

ich komme, euch zu warnen, *I've come to warn you*

The past tense and the perfect tense

The past tense

■ In written narrative, the German past tense corresponds exactly to the English past:

Das Transportflugzeug stürzte in der Nacht zum Mittwoch kurz nach dem Start von Ramstein nach Frankfurt über einem Wald ab und explodierte.
(Berliner Zeitung)
Shortly after leaving Ramstein for Frankfurt on Tuesday night the aircraft came down over a wood and exploded.

■ In spoken narrative, both the past tense and the perfect are used with little or no difference in meaning. See p. 22, The narrative perfect.

■ The past tense is used with **seit** (*since*; *for*) and **seitdem** (*since*, conjunction; *since then*, adverb):

> **ich wartete seit zwanzig nach eins**, *I'd been waiting since twenty past one*
>
> **seitdem sie hier wohnte, hatte ich kein einziges Wort mit ihr gewechselt**, *I hadn't exchanged a single word with her since she'd been living here*

Where English uses the pluperfect continuous (= *I had been doing*) with these expressions, German uses the past tense.

▶ See also **seit** + present tense, p. 20.

▶ For a fuller treatment of the conjunctions **seitdem** and **seit** see pp. 199–200.

The perfect tense

■ The perfect tense has two main uses in German: as a 'true' perfect and as a past narrative tense.

□ The 'true' perfect (= *I have done*)

As often in English, the true perfect is used to speak of something that happened in the past and has some bearing on what is being talked about in the present:

> **hast du meine Pralinen gegessen?**, *have you eaten my chocolates?*

However, German uses the perfect in this way much more rigorously than English does:

> **Bismarck hat die Grundlagen des heutigen deutschen Staats gelegt,** *Bismarck laid the foundations of the present German state*

Where English uses a perfect continuous, a perfect is used in German:

> **was hast du gemacht?**, *what have you been doing?*
> **ich habe gelesen; ich habe auch ferngesehen**, *I've been reading; I've been watching television too*

□ The narrative perfect

In conversation and letter-writing English usually uses the past as the narrative tense: in German the perfect is commoner. It is especially predominant in south Germany (and Austria and Switzerland). However, the past tense is also in quite common use, especially in north Germany, and especially with **haben** and **sein**, the modals, and some of the commoner strong verbs (e.g. **kommen, gehen**). Perfect and past tenses will frequently be found mixed within the same sentence, and in most cases either is entirely acceptable. If in doubt, use the perfect.

> **er kam gestern (ist gestern gekommen) und wollte wissen, was hier zu tun war — ich hab' ihm sofort die Tür gezeigt (zeigte ihm sofort die Tür)**, *he came yesterday and wanted to know what was to be done—I showed him the door straight away*

Where English uses the past continuous to describe a state of affairs, German tends to use a past tense rather than a perfect, though here too the perfect is by no means impossible:

> **es regnete, und so hab' ich meinen Schirm mitgenommen**, *it was raining, and so I took my umbrella*

The future tense

The future is used much less frequently than in English and the present is usually substituted for it if an adverb with a future meaning is used:

> **ich seh' dich morgen**, *I'll see you tomorrow*

This also applies if there is an adverb clause with a future meaning:

wenn Sie das zu Ende geschrieben haben, bin ich schon längst weg, *when you've finished writing that I'll be long gone*

■ The future may express firm intention:

ich werd' dich morgen sehen, du kannst dich darauf verlassen, *I will see you tomorrow, you can rely on it*

■ The future (and more frequently the future perfect) may express probability, as they sometimes do in English:

ich bekomme keine Antwort — er wird nicht da sein, *I'm getting no reply, he's probably not in*
sie wird den Bus wieder verpaßt haben, *she'll have missed her bus again*

■ The future (and the present) are used as alternatives to the imperative (see p. 27):

du wirst sofort nach Hause gehen! (du gehst sofort nach Hause!), *go home immediately!*

The conditional and conditional perfect tenses

■ The conditional is normally found in the main clause of an 'if' sentence ('*if he came I would go*'). The same is true of the conditional perfect. Where these tenses appear in sentences without an 'if' clause, an 'if' clause is generally to be understood:

das würde ich nicht machen! [wenn ich du wäre], *I wouldn't do that! (if I were you)*
das würde sie sonst nicht tun [wenn das nicht der Fall wäre], *otherwise she wouldn't do it (if that were not the case)*

There are three basic types of 'if' sentence:

□ 'it may happen'

wenn er anruft, fahre ich heute noch (werde ich heute noch fahren), *if he phones I'll go today*

The **wenn** clause has a present, the main clause has a present or a future.

□ 'it might happen'

> **wenn er anrufen würde, würde ich heute noch fahren**, *if he phoned I'd go today*

Both clauses have a conditional (American usage has '*would phone*' in the 'if' clause, exactly parallel to the German). In formal German the past subjunctive may be used in the 'if' clause and, if the verb is strong, in the main clause also:

> **wenn er anriefe, führe ich heute noch**

The apparently past-tense '*phoned*' in English is actually a remnant of our past subjunctive.

In spoken German **sollen** is often used in the **wenn** clause (**wenn er anrufen sollte**).

▶ For the forms of the past subjunctive see pp. 5–11.

□ 'it might have happened but it didn't'

> **wenn er angerufen hätte, wäre ich heute noch gefahren**, *if he'd phoned* (American: '*would have phoned*'), *I'd have gone today*

Both clauses normally have a pluperfect subjunctive. The conditional perfect is sometimes found in the main clause (**würde . . . gefahren sein**).

▶ For the forms of the pluperfect subjunctive see pp. 5–11.

■ In all three types normal order (rather than inversion) is occasionally found in the main clause:

> **wenn er anrufen würde, ich würde heute noch fahren**

■ In all three types, if the 'if' clause comes first, the word **wenn** may be entirely omitted, the verb placed at the head of its clause, and **so** or **dann** (*then*) inserted at the head of the main clause:

ruft er heute an, (so/dann) werde ich heute fahren
hätte er angerufen, (so/dann) wäre ich heute noch gefahren

So is more literary than **dann**. Both may be omitted and in modern journalism often are; beware of attempting to read such sentences as questions!

■ **Wer,** *anyone who*, and **wenn nicht,** *unless*

Wer is really the equivalent of '**wenn jemand**' and follows the same rules as **wenn** used in 'if' sentences:

wer das gesagt hätte, hätte gelügt, *anyone who said that would have been lying* (= **wenn jemand das gesagt hätte, hätte er gelügt**)

Wenn nicht also follows the same rules as **wenn**. Notice the position of the **nicht**:

wenn er nicht Geld genug hat, wird er zu Hause bleiben, *unless he has enough money he'll stay at home*

THE IMPERATIVE

The imperative is used to give orders or instructions or to express requests.

Formation of the imperative

The imperative has four forms, which are based on the **du, wir, ihr,** and **Sie** forms of the present tense of the verb, with the verb first and the subject always following in the case of the **wir** and **Sie** forms. The **du** form of the imperative ends in **-e** rather than **-st.**

mache (du)!, *make!*
machen wir!, *let's make!*
macht (ihr)!, *make!*
machen Sie!, *make!*

The subject is usually dropped with the **du** and **ihr** forms, unless the sense is '*you* do it, not someone else'. The final **-e** of the **du** form is often omitted, especially in speech. An apostrophe is not used in this case. The exclamation mark is much more common with the imperative in German than in English, though not absolutely obligatory.

■ Strong verbs with a complete vowel change (not just an added umlaut) in the **du** and **er** forms of the present also make this change in the **du** form of the imperative. The final **-e** is never used with these verbs:

> **geben**: **du gibst; gib!**
> **fahren**: **du fährst; fahr(e)!**

Nehmen and **treten**, which also make consonant changes in the **du** and **er** forms of the present, make the same changes in the imperative: **nimm!**; **tritt!**

Sehen (imperative normally **sieh!**) has the form **siehe!** when giving a reference:

> **siehe Kapitel 3**, *see chapter 3*

■ **Sein** has irregular imperative forms: **sei (du), seien wir, seid (ihr), seien Sie**. The **du** forms of the (highly uncommon) imperative of **werden** and **wissen** are **werde!** and **wisse!**

■ Third-person commands (*let him/her/it/them* . . .) are expressed by using the present tense of **sollen**, the imperative of **lassen**, or (more literary) the present subjunctive of the verb:

> **er soll sofort kommen! / laß ihn sofort kommen! / er komme sofort!**, *he is to to come immediately*

▶ For the present subjunctive see pp. 5–11.

Alternatives to the imperative

■ The forms **wollen wir machen, wir wollen machen**, and **laß(t) uns machen** are frequent alternatives to **machen wir**.

■ **Wollen Sie bitte . . .** is much used as a polite form of command or request:

> **wollen Sie bitte Platz nehmen!**, *would you sit down please*

■ Official language often uses an infinitive or (in military commands) a past participle for the imperative:

> **nicht hinauslehnen!**, *don't lean out*
> **stillgestanden!**, *attention!*

■ A future tense may also be used as an imperative (see p. 23), as may a present tense with future meaning:

> **du machst es gleich!**, *you'll do it now!*

■ The impersonal passive (see p. 71) may also be used with an imperative sense:

> **hier wird nicht geraucht!**, *no smoking here!*

REFLEXIVE VERBS

Reflexive verbs are verbs whose direct or indirect object is the same as their subject (*he dries himself*; *she allows herself a chocolate*). In German they consist of a simple verb followed by the reflexive pronoun in the accusative or dative.

■ The reflexive pronouns

Apart from **sich**, they are the same as the ordinary accusative and dative object pronouns. Here is the present tense of two reflexive verbs showing all the reflexive pronouns in the accusative and dative:

sich trocknen, *dry oneself*	**sich erlauben**, *allow oneself (something)*
ich trockne **mich**	ich erlaube **mir**
du trocknest **dich**	du erlaubst **dir**
er trocknet **sich**	er erlaubt **sich**
wir trocknen **uns**	wir erlauben **uns**

ihr trocknet **euch**	ihr erlaubt **euch**
Sie trocknen **sich**	Sie erlauben **sich**
sie trocknen **sich**	sie erlauben **sich**

Notice that **sich** does not have a captital letter in the **Sie** (*you*) form.

□ The reflexive pronoun corresponding to **man** is **sich**.

□ Reflexive verbs form their compound past tenses with **haben**.

□ The reflexive pronoun normally stands in the same position as other pronouns, in normal order immediately after the verb. In an infinitive phrase it comes first:

> **Sie werden gebeten, sich sofort in die Halle zu begeben,** *you are asked to make your way into the hall immediately*

■ Reciprocal pronouns (*each other*)

Reflexive pronouns in the plural—**uns, euch, sich**—as well as meaning *(to) ourselves, (to) yourselves, (to) themselves*, can also mean *(to) one another* or *(to) each other*. This includes **sich** when it refers to **man** with a plural meaning (*we, you, people*, etc.):

> **wir sehen uns übermorgen,** *we'll see each other the day after tomorrow*
> **sie begegnen sich jeden Abend,** *they bump into each other every evening*
> **man muß sich lieben,** *we must love one another*

If ambiguity might arise, **selbst** is added where the pronoun is reflexive and **gegenseitig** where it is reciprocal:

> **sie fragten sich selbst, ob . . . ,** *they asked themselves whether . . .*
> **sie fragten sich gegenseitig, ob . . . ,** *they asked each other whether . . .*

Instead of the reciprocal pronoun **einander** may be used:

wir sehen einander übermorgen, *we'll see each other the day after tomorrow*

It is less common than **sich**, except after a preposition, where it must be used. It is always written as one word with the preposition:

seid nett zueinander!, *be nice to each other*

■ A German reflexive verb may correspond to a English one:

du mußt dich waschen, *you must wash yourself*

but often it does not:

du hast dich verfahren, *you've taken the wrong road*
das bilden Sie sich ein, *you're just imagining that*

■ Reflexive verbs are occasionally used in German where English uses a passive (see p. 32):

das läßt sich machen, *that can be done*
das erklärt sich leicht, *that's easily explained*

■ The dative of the reflexive pronoun is often used with the sense of *for me* (etc.) to show involvement:

das werd' ich mir auch besorgen, *I'll get myself that too*
das mußt du dir ansehen, *you must have a look at that*
das kann ich mir denken, *I can well believe that*

► See also Pronouns, pp. 132–3.

THE PASSIVE

The passive forms of the tenses are those where the subject of the verb experiences the action rather than performs it (active: *he helped*; passive: *he was helped*).

Formation of the passive

The passive in English is formed with parts of the verb *to be* plus the past participle; in German it is formed in a similar way using parts of the verb **werden**, *to become*, plus the past participle:

> **es wird preiswert verkauft**, *it is being sold at a bargain price*
> **es wurde überall anerkannt**, *it was recognized everywhere*

■ The tenses of the passive are:

present passive	**es wird gemacht**, *it is done*
past passive	**es wurde gemacht**, *it was done*
perfect passive	**es ist gemacht worden**, *it has been done*
pluperfect passive	**es war gemacht worden**, *it had been done*
future passive	**es wird gemacht werden**, *it will be done*
conditional passive	**es würde gemacht werden**, *it would be done*

The past participle form of **werden** used when forming the passive is **worden**, not **geworden**:

> **er ist von seiner Firma belohnt worden**, *he was rewarded by his firm*

■ The following tenses and verb forms are virtually never used in the passive:

future perfect (**es wird gemacht worden sein**, *it will have been done*)
conditional perfect (**es würde gemacht worden sein**, *it would have been done*—the pluperfect subjunctive is used instead of this—see p. 24)
imperative
present participle

■ Where subjunctive forms of the passive are needed, **werden** is put into its equivalent subjunctive tense:

> **es wird gemacht** → **es werde gemacht** (present subjunctive passive)

■ With a passive verb in English *by* indicates either the 'doer' of the action or the instrument used. In German **von** is used for the person doing the action, **durch** for the instrument used:

er ist von seiner Frau ermordet worden, *he was murdered by his wife*
er ist durch Gift ermordet worden, *he was killed by poison*

but note

sie ist von einem Bus überfahren worden, *she was run over by a bus*

—in this sentence the bus is seen as the 'doer' of the action, not as an instrument.

■ The ordinary past participle of a verb when used as an adjective always has a passive meaning, as in English:

eine längst vergessene Zeit, *a long-forgotten time* (the time has *been* forgotten)

■ In English, the indirect object of an active verb may be made into the subject of the corresponding passive verb:

Adrian gave me the book→ *I was given the book by Adrian*

This is impossible in German. *I was given the book* can be translated using **man**:

man gab mir das Buch (literally: *someone gave me the book*)

but if the 'doer' is mentioned ('*by Adrian*') the active form has to be used in German:

Adrian gab mir das Buch

In the same way, verbs which take the dative in German cannot be used in the passive. *I was helped by Adrian* must become active:

Adrian hat mir geholfen

There *is* an impersonal passive equivalent:

es wurde mir von Adrian geholfen (literally: *it was helped to me by Adrian*)

—but this is clumsy and little used, and should be avoided.

▶ For the passive infinitive see p. 45.

Alternatives to the passive with werden

The passive, whilst not being largely avoided as it is in French, is used in German less frequently than in English. This is especially true of the future passive.

■ **Man** (*one, people*) is frequently used instead:

> **man hat mich angerufen**, *I was phoned up*

■ Sometimes a reflexive verb is used:

> **es hat sich als falsch erwiesen**, *it has been proved false*
> **das erklärt sich dadurch, daß . . .** , *that is explained by the fact that . . .*
> **das läßt sich machen**, *that can be done*

■ When the passive conveys a state rather than an action **sein** is used instead of **werden**:

> **sie war gut dafür geeignet**, *she was well suited to it*
> **der Brief ist auf englisch geschrieben**, *the letter is written in English* (but: **er wurde letzte Woche von mir geschrieben**, *it was written by me last week*)

COMPOUND VERBS

Compound verbs follow the same pattern of tense-endings as simple verbs. They are formed by adding a prefix to the simple verb. This prefix may be either separable (**auf-**, **an-**, **zu-**, etc.), or inseparable (**er-**, **be-**, **ver-**, etc.), or sometimes separable, sometimes inseparable according to the meaning of the verb (**um-**, **unter-**, **durch-**, etc.).

Separable prefixes

Most prefixes are separable, and most separable prefixes can also be used as parts of speech in their own right, usually prepositions (**aus**steigen), but occasionally adverbs (**davon**laufen), nouns (**teil**nehmen), adjectives (**frei**sprechen), infinitives (**stehen**bleiben). A verb with a separable prefix always has the stress on the prefix.

Position of the prefix

■ A separable prefix is found attached to its verb in the infinitive:

> **ich muß aufstehen**, *I have to get up*
> **dürfen wir weggehen?**, *may we go away?*

If the infinitive is used with **zu**, the **zu** is inserted between prefix and verb:

> **ich versuche aufzustehen**, *I'm trying to get up*

■ The prefix also remains attached in the present participle:

> **die aufgehende Sonne**, *the rising sun*

■ Once the verb is used in any of its tenses, however, the prefix separates from it and moves to the end of the clause:

> **ich stehe früh auf**, *I get up early*
> **ich stand auf**, *I got up*
> **geh sofort weg!**, *go away at once!*

If the verb itself is at the end of the clause (as is the case in subordinate order) the prefix and verb join up again:

> **ich weiß nicht, wann wir heute abfahren**, *I don't know when we're leaving today*

■ In the past participle the **ge-** appears between prefix and verb:

> **der Zug ist schon abgefahren**, *the train has already left*

Inseparable prefixes

The prefixes **be-, emp-, ent-, er-, ge-, miß-, ver-, zer-** are always inseparable. The only difference between verbs with these prefixes and simple verbs is that they have no **ge-** in their past participle:

verstehen, *to understand*: **ich habe verstanden**

Inseparable prefixes do not exist as independent words (unlike most separable prefixes). They never take the stress, which always goes on the verb itself.

Prefixes that may be either separable or inseparable

The prefixes **durch-, hinter-, über-, um-, unter-, voll-, wider-, wieder-** are separable with some verbs, inseparable with others. Whether they are being used separably or inseparably can immediately be distinguished in speech by where the main accent is—on the prefix or on the stem of the verb.

Often the same verb has different meanings according to whether the prefix is separable or inseparable. Quite frequently the separable version of the verb will have a literal meaning, the inseparable version a figurative one:

übersetzen (sep.), *ferry across*
übersetzen (insep.), *translate*

This is not, however, always the case: if in any doubt, check in the dictionary.

Double prefixes

■ A separable prefix followed by an inseparable one separates, but the verb has no **ge-** in its past participle:

zubereiten, *to prepare*
er bereitet das Mittagessen zu, *he's preparing lunch*

er versucht, das Mittagessen zuzubereiten, *he's trying to prepare lunch*
er hat das Mittagessen zubereitet, *he's prepared lunch*

■ With the verb **mißverstehen,** *to misunderstand* (which has a double inseparable prefix), the prefixes do not separate, and there is no **ge-** in the past participle; however, in the infinitive with **zu** the **miß-** behaves like a separable prefix: **mißzuverstehen,** and the stress throughout is on **miß-**:

sie miß versteht mich immer, *she always misunderstands me*
um mich nicht miß zuverstehen . . . *, so as not to misunderstand me . . .*

■ The separable prefixes **hin-** and **her-** in their literal meanings imply respectively motion away from and motion towards the speaker. As well as being added to simple verbs they may also be added to compound verbs, producing a double separable prefix. This behaves like a single separable prefix:

er kommt herauf, *he's coming up*
er ist heraufgekommen, *he came up*
er braucht nicht heraufzukommen, *he doesn't need to come up*

■ The separable prefix **wieder-** is the equivalent of the English prefix *re-*. Attached to a verb with a separable prefix, it stands alone when the prefix is separated from its verb:

wiederherstellen, *to restore*
ich stelle es wieder her, *I'm restoring it*
stell es wieder her!, *restore it*
sobald du es wiederherstellst . . . *, as soon as you restore it*
man hat es wiederhergestellt, *they've restored it*
man versucht es wiederherzustellen, *they're trying to restore it*

Somewhat similarly, compounds of **sein** and **werden** only join up in their infinitive and past participle:

> **er hofft dazusein**, *he hopes to be present*
> **sobald er da ist**, *as soon as he's there*
> **ich muß es loswerden**, *I must get rid of it*
> **wenn du es endlich los wirst . . .** , *if you're finally getting rid of it . . .*

PARTICIPLES

The present participle

Formation of the present participle

The present participle (in English, the *-ing* part of the verb) is formed in German for all verbs by adding **-d** to the infinitive:

> **machen**, *to make*: **machend**, *making*
> **gehen**, *to go*: **gehend**, *going*

Sein, *to be*, and **haben**, *to have*, have no present participles.

Uses of the present participle

The present participle is most commonly found as an adjective in German, standing immediately in front of a noun:

> **das wartende Auto**, *the waiting car*

It can, in this position, form the last element of a phrase that may be considerably longer than would be possible in front of the noun in English:

> **das reglos in der Hüppertstraße vor den großen Toren der Militärkaserne wartende Auto**, *the car, waiting motionless before the great gates of the military barracks in the Hüppertstraße*

In this position it also substitutes for the infinitive:

> **ein bei dieser Dunkelheit kaum zu sehendes Auto**, *a car scarcely to be seen in this darkness*

Note that the present participle has a passive meaning ('a car to *be* seen') in this construction.

■ Many present participles have come to be treated as adjectives and can be used after verbs such as **sein** or **werden** just as adjectives can. They can equally be used as adverbs. They include

auffallend, *striking*
aufregend, *exciting*
reizend, *charming*
empörend, *shocking*

and noun + present participle combinations such as

aufsehenerregend, *sensational*
bahnbrechend, *pioneering*
vielversprechend, *promising*

ich finde sie ganz reizend und überraschend schön,
I find her quite charming and astonishingly beautiful

The past participle

Formation of the past participle

Past participles of weak verbs are formed by adding **ge-** to the beginning and **-t** to the end of the stem of the verb:

machen, *to make*→**gemacht**, *made*
wandern, *to hike*→**gewandert**, *hiked*

There is an extra **-e** in the past-participle ending of verbs whose infinitives end **-ten** and **-den**:

antworten, *to answer*→**geantwortet**, *answered*
senden, *to send*→**gesendet**, *sent*

Past participles of strong verbs are formed by adding **ge-** to the beginning and **-en** to the end of the stem of the verb, often with a vowel change and sometimes with a consonant change as well:

braten, *to roast* →**gebraten**, *roasted*
bleiben, *to stay*→**geblieben**, *stayed*
leiden,*to suffer*→**gelitten**, *suffered*

▶ The modals and **werden** and **lassen** have two past participles. See p. 30 (**werden**) and p. 66 (modals and **lassen**).

▶ Verbs ending **-eien** and **-ieren** and verbs with inseparable prefixes have no **ge-** in the past participle. For further details see pp. 14 and 34.

▶ For all past participles of strong verbs see the Irregular Verb list, pp. 73–85.

Uses of the past participle

■ The past participle is used to form all the past compound tenses. It is always placed at the end of its clause. See pp. 217–18.

■ The past participle is used with **werden** or **sein** to form the passive. See p. 29.

■ The past participle may be used adjectivally; it then agrees with a following noun, takes an adverb qualification, etc., just like any other adjective:

ein verlorener Gegenstand, *a lost object*
ich bin völlig erschöpft, *I'm completely exhausted*

Like the present participle it may be found, with the appropriate adjective ending, standing before its noun at the end of an adjective phrase. This may sometimes be extremely long:

ich muß mich für Ihren gestern per Fax in unserem Münchener Büro erhaltenen Brief herzlich bedanken, *I must thank you cordially for your letter, received yesterday by fax in our Munich office*

This construction is extremely common in books, newspapers, and letters, but almost never found in spoken German.

■ The past participle may be used in an adjective phrase standing separately from its noun. It usually (but not necessarily) stands at the end of the phrase:

auf seinen Regenschirm gestützt, trat er ins Restaurant, *leaning on his umbrella, he came into the restaurant*
gequält von einer Schar ihrer Enkelkinder, saß die alte Dame ruhig vorm Ofen und strickte, *tormented by a crowd of her grandchildren the old lady sat by the stove calmly knitting*

■ The past participle is occasionally used as an imperative. See p. 27.

■ After the verb **kommen**, *to come*, German uses the past participle of a motion verb where English uses the present participle:

sie kommt gelaufen, *she comes running*
du kamst herbeigeeilt, *you came hurrying up*

THE SUBJUNCTIVE

The subjunctive expresses doubt, uncertainty, disagreement, and scarcely exists any longer in English (*if I were you*; *if that be so*; *would that he were* are some of the few remaining examples of it). In German, though some of its forms are literary or affected, it is still in constant use in both the written and spoken language.

Its main use is in reported matter, in order to disclaim personal responsibility for what is being said, or at least to distance oneself from it. The subjunctive is much used in newspaper reports. It is by no means obligatory when reporting speech, however, and indeed is rarely used when the reporting verb (**er sagt, er meint**, etc.) is in the present and related tenses (see p. 40).

Formation of the subjunctive

The subjunctive has four forms, present, past (sometimes called the imperfect), perfect, and pluperfect. Their grammatical names do NOT indicate their function—the past subjunctive is not a past tense.

▶ For the subjunctive forms of weak verbs see pp. 5–7.

▶ For the subjunctive forms of strong verbs see pp. 7–9.

▶ For the subjunctive forms of mixed verbs see pp. 9–11.

■ The future subjunctive is little used. It is formed with the present subjunctive of **werden** + infinitive:

ich werde gehen	**wir werden gehen**
du werdest gehen	**ihr werdet gehen**
er werde gehen	**sie werden gehen**

■ There is an almost never used future perfect subjunctive, formed with the present subjunctive of **werden** + the perfect infinitive:

ich werde gegangen sein, etc.

■ The present subjunctive of **sein** is irregular:

ich sei	**wir seien**
du sei(e)st	**ihr seiet**
er sei	**sie seien**

The subjunctive in reported speech

The subjunctive is used in indirect speech largely as a distancing device ('this is what she said, it may or may not be true, I'm not responsible for it'). It is what is said, not the 'saying' verb, that goes into the subjunctive.

If the 'saying' verb is in the present, future, or imperative, the verb that follows is not put into the subjunctive. The same applies if the 'saying' verb is in the perfect but refers to something said in the immediate past.

If it is in any past tense the following verb will normally be in the subjunctive. In German (but not in English) the tense of the subjunctive depends on the tense of the *original direct speech.*

Choice of subjunctive tense in reported speech

■ If the original speech was in the present, the present subjunctive is used to report it (or the past subjunctive, see below). This tense sequence is different from English:

sie sagte, daß er gehe, *she said he was going* (her actual words were 'er geht')

■ If the original speech was in a past tense, the perfect subjunctive is used to report it (or the pluperfect subjunctive, see below). This too does not correspond to English tenses:

sie sagte, daß er gegangen sei, *she said he had gone* (her actual words were 'er ist gegangen')

■ If the original speech was in the future or conditional, the conditional is used to report it, unless it is in the **er** form, in which case the future subjunctive may be used:

sie sagte, daß du gehen würdest, *she said you would go* (her actual words were 'du wirst gehen')

but: **sie sagte, daß er gehen werde/würde**, *she said he would go* (her actual words were 'er wird gehen')

■ Many forms of the present and perfect subjunctive are not obviously subjunctive; in such cases the past subjunctive should be used instead of the present subjunctive, and the pluperfect subjunctive instead of the perfect subjunctive:

sie sagte, daß ich es hätte, *she said I had it* (**habe** would not be obviously subjunctive)

sie sagte, daß ich es gemacht hätte, *she said I had done it* (**gemacht habe** would not be obviously subjunctive)

This substitution may sometimes be made even when the other tense is clearly subjunctive (especially in the spoken language, and especially by north Germans), and it is almost always made to avoid the **du** and **ihr** forms of the present subjunctive, which are little used in spoken German.

Also avoided are past subjunctives of strong verbs except the most common ones (e.g. **wäre, hätte, würde**, and the modals). Especially shunned are the irregular past subjunctives (see Irregular Verb list, pp. 73–85).

Dropped daß

In all the above examples the **daß** may be dropped, with normal instead of subordinate word order after the 'saying' word:

sie sagte, ich hätte es gemacht

This form without **daß** is actually the more common, except after a negative (**sie sagte nicht, daß . . .**). Newspaper reports will frequently drop the saying verb as well, after an initial indication of who was speaking. Inserts like '*he added*', '*she continued*', '*it went on*' are often necessary in English to show that reported speech continues: in German the subjunctive demonstrates this clearly:

Nach Angaben der Meteorologen in Dahlem gingen bei dem Gewitter auch bis zu fünf Zentimeter große Hagelkörner nieder. In Zehlendorf seien [not **sind**, so this is also part of the report . . .] **23 Liter Niederschlag je Quadratmeter gemessen worden.**
(Der Tagesspiegel)

According to information received from the Dahlem weather-forecasters, hailstones up to five centimetres in size also fell during this storm. In Zehlendorf precipitation of 23 litres per square metre was measured, it is claimed.

'Saying' verbs

All verbs introducing reported matter count as 'saying' verbs. The following is a list of such verbs that may not be obviously of this kind at first glance:

ahnen, *suspect*
annehmen, *assume*
denken, *think*
erklären, *explain*
erwarten, *expect*
fragen, *ask*

fühlen, *feel*
fürchten, *fear*
hoffen, *hope*
hören, *hear*
meinen, *think*
schreiben, *write*
sich einbilden, *imagine (falsely)*
sich vorstellen, *imagine*
träumen, *dream*
wünschen, *wish*
zweifeln, *doubt*

Other uses of the subjunctive

■ The past subjunctive of **werden (würde)** plus the infinitive is used to form the conditional tense; in the case of **sein**, **haben**, the modals, and some of the commoner strong verbs a past subjunctive is often used instead of a conditional:

ich würde sein / ich wäre, *I would be*

■ The past and pluperfect subjunctive are used in 'if' sentences. See Conditional, p. 24.

■ The subjunctive is used in some set third-person commands (**Gott sei Dank!**, *thank God*; **es lebe die Republik!**, *long live the Republic!*). Otherwise third-person commands are expressed by the present of **sollen** or by the imperative of **lassen**:

er soll das tun / laß ihn das tun, *let him do it*

► See Imperative, p. 25.

■ The past subjunctive is frequently used in conversation to tone down a suggestion, to make it more polite:

ich weiß, wie das zu schaffen wäre, *I know how that might be managed*
das wären dreizehn Mark fünfzig, *that will be DM 13.50*
wäre Ihnen das recht?, *would that be all right?*
wären Sie damit zufrieden?, *are you happy with that then?*

English has a variety of strategies for this ('*might*', future for present, '*would*', '*then*', etc.).

Note the similar use, when telephoning, of

ich hätte gern mit Herrn X gesprochen, *could I possibly speak to Herr X?*

■ Subjunctive after **als ob / als wenn**, *as if*

The subjunctive is correctly used after **als ob** and **als wenn** (though in casual speech it may not be). There is a difference in meaning according to the tense used:

sie sah aus, als ob sie nicht ganz vertrauenswürdig sei, *she looked as if she wasn't completely reliable* (and it turned out she wasn't!)
sie sah aus, als ob sie nicht ganz vertrauenswürdig wäre, *she looked as if she wasn't completely reliable* (but it turned out she was)

There is a similar difference between perfect and pluperfect subjunctives (both = *had been*).

The **ob** or **wenn** may be dropped, with inverted instead of subordinate word order after **als**. This is more literary:

sie sah aus, als sei sie nicht ganz vertrauenswürdig

■ The subjunctive is also found after **damit** and **(so) daß**, meaning *so that*. This is a very literary use. More usual is the addition of **können**:

halt die Leiter, damit er das Bild aufhängen kann (aufhänge), *hold the ladder, so that he can (may) hang the picture*

Similarly with **damit . . . nicht**, *lest*. Here **können** is not used:

halt die Leiter, damit sie nicht fällt (falle), *hold the ladder, so it doesn't fall*

■ The subjunctive is sometimes used after **nicht daß**, *not that*, **ohne daß**, *without*, **anstatt daß**, *instead of*, and **zu** ADJECTIVE, **als daß**, *too* ADJECTIVE *to*. It gives a less brusque meaning:

nicht, daß Sie zu alt wären . . ., *not that you're too old . . .* (rather more polite than **nicht, daß Sie zu alt sind . . .**)

The subjunctive tenses found are the past and pluperfect.

THE INFINITIVE

Infinitives of German verbs end in **-en** or occasionally just **-n**, and correspond to the English *to . . .* form of the verb:

machen, *to make*
handeln, *to act*
tun, *to do*

The infinitive is the 'name' of the verb: it is really a sort of noun and can be used as such, then being given a capital letter like all nouns. Infinitives used as nouns are neuter:

das Rauchen ist sicher gefährlich, *smoking (to smoke) is certainly dangerous*

English often uses the *-ing* form of the verb in this case.

■ Infinitives stand at the end of the clause:

ich hoffe, morgen in die Stadt zu fahren, *I hope to go into town tomorrow*

► See Word Order, p. 224.

■ When they have a dependent infinitive, the modal verbs (**dürfen, können, mögen, müssen, sollen, wollen**) use their own infinitive instead of their past participle in past compound tenses. The same applies to **lassen, sehen**, and **hören**, and a few other verbs. See pp. 66–7 and 68–9.

■ The infinitive in German has perfect and passive forms:

gemacht haben, *to have made*
gemacht werden, *to be made*
gemacht worden sein, *to have been made*

These forms are used exactly as their English equivalents are:

er hofft, bis dann den Versuch gemacht zu haben, *he hopes to have made the attempt by then*

The infinitive with and without zu

Infinitives usually follow ('depend on') another verb, and as in English they are joined to it by **zu**, *to* or by nothing at all:

ich versuche zu schwimmen, *I'm trying to swim*
ich muß schwimmen, *I must swim*

Whether **zu** is used or not depends on the head verb, not on the infinitive, and it doesn't vary—it is always **versuchen + zu** + infinitive, **müssen** + infinitive.

■ Most verbs in fact take **zu**. Only the following do not:

□ The modal verbs: **dürfen, können, mögen, müssen, sollen, wollen**. See p. 60 onwards.

□ **sehen**, *to see*
hören, *to hear*
fühlen, *to feel*
spüren, *to feel, to perceive*

ich sah ihn kommen, *I saw him coming*

Again, English uses the *-ing* form of the verb here.

With these verbs a '**wie . . .** ' clause is normally substituted if the infinitive would be in any way qualified:

ich sah, wie er langsam um die Ecke kam, *I saw him coming slowly round the corner*

□ **finden**, *to find* (only + **stehen** or **liegen**, *to find standing/lying*)

ich fand meine Socken auf dem Tisch liegen, *I found my socks lying on the table*

□ **heißen**, *to bid, to tell . . . to* (literary use)

er hieß mich gehen, *he bade me go (he told me to go)*

□ **lassen**, *to let*; *to make* (see p. 68)

■ **bleiben, gehen, kommen, schicken, haben** are used without **zu** with certain infinitives, as follows.

□ **bleiben** + 'situation' verb:

sitzen bleiben, *to stay seated*
stehen bleiben, *to remain standing*
etc.

Occasionally the verb joins up with **bleiben** and becomes a separable prefix: **bestehenbleiben**, *to continue*.

□ **gehen, kommen, schicken**, in cases where the interest is entirely focused on the dependent verb:

du gehst aber jetzt schlafen!, *you really are going to bed now!*
kommst du heute abend tanzen?, *are you coming dancing tonight?*
sie hat mich einkaufen geschickt, *she sent me shopping*

Occasionally the verb joins up with **gehen** and becomes a separable prefix: **spazierengehen**, *to go for a walk*.

□ **haben**, meaning *to have something kept or stored somewhere*:

ich habe meine Schuhe im Schrank liegen, *I've got my shoes in the cupboard*

■ Three verbs sometimes take **zu**, sometimes not: **helfen**, *to help*; **lehren**, *to teach*; **lernen**, *to learn*.

With these verbs an unqualified infinitive has no **zu**, a qualified one has **zu**:

sie hilft mir abwaschen, *she's helping me wash up*
hilf mir, dieses schmutzige Geschirr abzuwaschen, *help me wash up these dirty dishes*

With **lehren** and **lernen** a '**wie . . .** ' clause is often substituted in the latter case:

sie lehrte mich, wie man Geschirr abwäscht, *she taught me (how) to wash dishes*

■ After **sein**, **zu** + the infinitive has a passive meaning in German:

> **es war niemand zu sehen**, *there was nobody to be seen* (not '*to see*')
> **ist Herr Meyer zu sprechen, bitte?**, *can I speak to Herr Meyer please?* (*is Herr M. to be spoken to?*)

■ After parts of speech other than verbs, the infinitive is used with **zu**:

> **das ist schwer zu sagen**, *that's difficult to say*
> **ich sehe keine Möglichkeit, das zu tun**, *I can see no possibility of doing that*
> **arbeiten ist besser, als im Liegestuhl zu liegen**, *working is better than lying in a deckchair*

In the last case (after **als**) the infinitive is occasionally found without **zu**.

■ Where the sense allows it the infinitive may also be preceded by **um . . . zu**, meaning *in order to*. Notice the word order (**um** always starts the phrase):

> **ich bin hier, um meine Rechte und die meiner Mitbürger zu verlangen**, *I am here in order to demand my rights and those of my fellow citizens*

An adjective with **zu . . .**, *too*, or **. . . genug**, *enough*, is also followed by **um . . . zu** + infinitive, not just **zu**:

> **er ist alt genug (zu jung), um besser zu wissen**, *he's old enough (too young) to know better*

▶ For the use of the infinitive as an imperative see Imperative, p. 27.

▶ For the use of the comma with the infinitive see Punctuation, p. 231.

OBJECT OF THE VERB

Verbs in German may be followed by a direct (accusative) object, an indirect (dative) object, a preposition plus object, or a combination of these.

Verbs with the accusative

Most verbs taking an accusative object ('transitive' verbs) correspond exactly to English verbs and present no problems. But note

■ **sprechen** means *to speak to* and takes an accusative:

> **darf ich ihn sprechen, bitte?**, *may I speak to him please?*

(**Sprechen mit** + dative can also be used in this sense.)

■ **fragen**, **lehren**, **kosten**, and **nennen** (and its more formal equivalent, **heißen**) have two accusative objects:

> **es kostete mich 300 Mark**, *it cost me DM 300*
> **sie lehrte mich Computerwissenschaft**, *she taught me computer science*
> **frag mich das nicht!**, *don't ask me that*
> **er nannte (hieß) mich einen Dummkopf**, *he called me a fool* (the second accusative here is technically a complement)

Verbs with the dative

■ Some verbs that are transitive in English take a dative (indirect) object in German. Such verbs are

auffallen, *to strike*
begegnen, *to meet*
danken, *to thank*
dienen, *to serve*
drohen, *to threaten*
folgen, *to follow*
gefallen, *to please*
gehorchen, *to obey*
gleichen, *to equal; to resemble*
gratulieren, *to congratulate*

helfen, *to help*
imponieren, *to impress*
kündigen, *to sack*
leid tun (das tut mir leid), *to hurt*
(miß)trauen, *to (dis)trust*
nutzen/nützen, *to benefit; to help*
passen, *to suit; to fit*
raten, *to advise*
schaden, *to harm*
schmeicheln, *to flatter*
stehen, *to suit*
trotzen, *to defy*
versichern, *to assure (somebody)*
weh tun (das tut mir weh), *to hurt*

es hat mir sehr gefallen, *it pleased me a lot*
sie ist mir begegnet, *she met (= ran into) me*

Note that **begegnen** and **folgen** are verbs of motion without a direct object and so form their past compound tenses with **sein**.

■ In addition to the above list, most verbs with the following prefixes take the dative: **bei-**, **ein-**, **ent-**, **entgegen-**, **nach-**, **vor-**, **wider-**, **zu-**:

sie rief mir nach, *she called after me*
er stand mir bei, *he stood by me*

But note that **nachahmen** and **nachmachen**, both meaning *to imitate*, take the accusative.

■ The verbs **erlauben**, *to allow*, **glauben**, *to believe*, **verzeihen**, *to forgive*, **verbieten**, *to forbid*, and **befehlen**, *to order*, have an accusative if the object is a thing:

das glaube ich, *I believe that*
man erlaubt nichts, *nothing is allowed*

. . . but a dative if the object is a person:

ich glaube ihr nicht, *I don't believe her*
man erlaubte ihm, gleich zu fahren, *they allowed him to go straight away*

With **antworten**, *to answer*, a personal object is in the dative, but for an impersonal object **auf** + the accusative is used:

ich will dir sofort antworten, *I want to answer you straight away*
ich habe auf deinen Brief schon geantwortet, *I've already answered your letter*

■ A small number of reflexive verbs take a direct object that is not their reflexive pronoun; the reflexive in this case is a dative:

das kann ich mir denken, *I can imagine that*

The dative reflexive differs from the accusative only in the **mir** and **dir** forms (see p. 27).

Most such verbs are reflexive forms of verbs in the list on pp. 49–50. The following verbs, where the reflexive pronoun is dative, are not:

sich einbilden, *to imagine (wrongly)*
sich vornehmen, *to make up one's mind to*
sich vorstellen, *to imagine, to visualize*

stell dir das vor!, *just imagine that!*

► Many impersonal verbs also take a dative. See pp. 70–2.

► For dative indicating possession see p. 88.

Verbs followed by a preposition

Most prepositions may be used after verbs. Some verbs take more than one preposition, with different meanings.

The preposition that follows a German verb often differs from that used with the equivalent English verb and must be learned with the verb.

Dative or accusative?

For the case used with literal meanings of prepositions that can take either dative or accusative see pp. 159–60. The case with figurative meanings of these prepositions varies according to the preposition used:

■ **an**: meaning *in respect of, from, by, in connection with*: dative

es fehlt mir am notwendigen Geld, *I lack the necessary money*
ich leide an der Grippe, *I'm suffering from flu*
ich erkannte ihn an seiner Stimme, *I recognized him by his voice*
das hasse ich an deinem Bruder, *that's what I hate about your brother*

meaning *in the (mental) direction of*: accusative

ich erinnere mich an ihn, *I remember him*
denk an mich, *think of me*
glaubst du an Gott?, *do you believe in God?*

■ auf: normally accusative, but note **beruhen auf** + DAT, *be based on*, **bestehen auf** + DAT, *insist on*

■ **in**: dative

■ **über**: normally accusative, but note **brüten über** + DAT, *to brood on*, **stehen über** + DAT, *to have mastered (a topic)*

■ **unter:** dative

■ **vor**: dative

▶ The rules above apply equally to prepositions used after adjectives and after nouns.

▶ For the prepositions used with individual verbs see the list on pp. 53–60.

Verb + preposition + *-ing*

English often makes the *-ing* form of the verb into the object of the preposition:

I insist on them going with you
I insist on going with you

In the first type of example above, where *going* has a different subject from *insist*, German uses the preposition compounded with **da-** followed by a clause beginning **daß**:

ich bestehe darauf, daß sie mit euch mitfahren (literally: *I insist on it, that . . .*)

In the second type of example above, where both *insist* and *going* have the same subject, an infinitive phrase may be used instead of the **daß** clause:

ich bestehe darauf, mit euch mitzufahren

or: **ich bestehe darauf, daß ich mit euch mitfahre**

If the preposition begins with a vowel, as above, **dar-** and not **da-** is added.

Verbs followed by the genitive

A small number of German verbs, mostly reflexive, are followed by the genitive. They are found mainly in literary or legal language. The commonest are

anklagen, *to accuse of*
berauben, *to rob of*
sich entsinnen, *to recollect*
sich erbarmen, *to take pity on*
sich erfreuen, *to enjoy* (e.g. health)
sich erinnern, *to remember* (more commonly: **an** + ACC)
sich rühmen, *to boast*
sich schämen, *to be ashamed of* (more commonly: **wegen** + GEN)
sich vergewissern, *to make sure of*
versichern, *to assure of*
sich versichern, *to secure*

ich kann Sie meiner Hilfe versichern, *I can assure you of my help*

ALPHABETICAL LIST OF VERB CONSTRUCTIONS

The list includes the commonest verbs taking the dative and the genitive and the commonest verb + preposition constructions (with their case).

abhängen von + DAT	*be dependent on*
achten auf + ACC	*look after*
achtgeben auf + ACC	*pay attention to*
sich amüsieren über + ACC	*laugh at*
angeln nach + DAT	*fish for*
sich ängstigen um + ACC	*be anxious about*
anklagen + GEN	*accuse of*
sich anpassen + DAT	*adapt oneself to*
anspielen auf + ACC	*allude to*
antworten + DAT	*answer (somebody)*
antworten auf + ACC	*answer (something)*
anwenden auf + ACC	*apply to*
sich ärgern über + ACC	*get annoyed with*
auffallen + DAT	*strike (= occur to)*
auffallen an + DAT	*be striking about*
aufhören mit + DAT	*stop (doing)*
aufpassen auf + ACC	*keep an eye on*
ausschauen nach + DAT	*look out for*
ausweichen + DAT	*get out of the way of*
basieren auf + DAT	*be based on*
bauen auf + ACC	*build on*
sich bedanken für + ACC	*thank for*
befehlen + DAT	*order (somebody)*
befördern zu + DAT	*promote (to the post/rank of)*
begegnen + DAT	*meet*
beitragen zu + DAT	*contribute to*
sich beklagen bei + DAT	*complain to*
sich beklagen über + ACC	*complain about*
beneiden um + ACC	*envy (something)*
berauben + GEN	*rob (somebody) of*
beruhen auf + DAT	*be based on*
beruhigen über + ACC	*reassure about*
sich beschäftigen mit + DAT	*occupy oneself with*
sich beschränken auf + ACC	*restrict oneself to*
sich beschweren bei + DAT	*complain to*
sich beschweren über + ACC	*complain about*

bestehen auf + DAT	*insist on*
bestehen aus + DAT	*consist of*
bestehen in + DAT	*consist in*
sich beteiligen an + DAT	*participate in*
beten um + ACC	*pray for*
betteln um + ACC	*beg for*
sich bewerben um + ACC	*apply for*
sich beziehen auf + ACC	*refer to*
bitten um + ACC	*ask for*
danken + DAT	*thank*
denken an + ACC	*think of*
denken über + ACC or **von** + DAT	*think of (= have an opinion of)*
sich (DAT) **denken**	*imagine*
dienen + DAT	*serve*
dienen zu + DAT	*be (used) for*
drohen + DAT	*threaten*
sich drücken vor + DAT	*get out of*
dürsten nach + DAT	*thirst for*
sich (DAT) **einbilden**	*imagine (wrongly)*
eingehen auf + ACC	*agree to*
sich einsetzen für + ACC	*do what one can for*
einverstanden sein mit + DAT	*be in agreement with*
es ekelt (mich) vor + DAT	*. . . disgusts (me)*
entkommen + DAT	*escape from*
sich entscheiden für + ACC	*decide in favour of*
sich entschließen zu + DAT	*decide on*
sich entschuldigen bei + DAT	*apologize to*
sich entsinnen + GEN	*recollect*
sich erbarmen + GEN	*take pity on*
sich erfreuen + GEN	*enjoy (e.g. health)*
sich erholen von + DAT	*recover from*
erinnern an + ACC	*remind*
sich erinnern an + ACC	*remember*
erkennen an + DAT	*recognize by*
erkranken an + DAT	*become ill with*

sich erkundigen über + ACC or **nach** + DAT	*enquire about*
erlauben + DAT	*allow (somebody)*
ernennen zu + DAT	*appoint (to the post of)*
erröten über + ACC	*blush at*
erschrecken vor + DAT	*be scared by*
erschrecken über + ACC	*be shocked at*
sich erstrecken auf + ACC	*include*
erzählen über + ACC or **von** + DAT	*tell about*
es fehlt an + DAT	*there's a lack of*
fischen nach + DAT	*fish for (e.g. compliments)*
flehen um + ACC	*plead for*
fliehen vor + DAT	*flee from*
folgen + DAT	*follow*
fragen nach + DAT, **um** + ACC, or **über** + ACC	*ask for*
sich freuen auf + ACC	*look forward to*
sich freuen über + ACC	*be pleased at*
sich fürchten vor + DAT	*be afraid of*
gebrauchen zu + DAT	*use for*
gefallen + DAT	*please*
gefallen an + DAT	*be pleasing about*
gehorchen + DAT	*obey*
gehören + DAT	*belong to*
es geht um + ACC	*it's a matter of*
gelingen + DAT	*succeed*
genügen + DAT	*be enough for*
sich gewöhnen an + ACC	*get used to*
glauben + DAT	*believe (somebody)*
glauben an + ACC	*believe in*
gleichen + DAT	*equal*
graben nach + DAT	*dig for*
gratulieren + DAT	*congratulate*
greifen nach + DAT	*reach for*
halten für + ACC	*consider*

halten von + DAT	*think of; hold an opinion of*
handeln von + DAT	*be about*
es handelt sich um + ACC	*it's a question of*
hassen an + DAT	*hate about*
helfen + DAT	*help*
herrschen über + ACC	*rule over*
hinweisen auf + ACC	*refer to*
hoffen auf + ACC	*hope for*
hören über + ACC or **von** + DAT	*hear about*
sich hüten vor + DAT	*be on guard against*
imponieren + DAT	*impress*
sich interessieren für + ACC	*be interested in*
interessiert sein an + DAT	*be interested in*
sich irren in + DAT	*be mistaken about*
kämpfen um + ACC	*fight for*
kennen an + DAT	*know by*
klagen über + ACC	*grumble about*
kommen zu + DAT	*get around to*
konkurrieren um + ACC	*compete for*
sich konzentrieren auf + ACC	*concentrate on*
sich kümmern um + ACC	*care about*
kündigen + DAT	*sack*
lachen über + ACC	*laugh at*
lauern auf + ACC	*lie in wait for*
leben von + DAT	*live on*
leiden an + DAT or **unter** + DAT	*suffer from*
leid tun + DAT **(es tut mir leid)**	*be sorry*
lesen über + ACC or **von** + DAT	*read about*
mißtrauen + DAT	*distrust*
nachdenken über + ACC	*think about*
nachgeben + DAT	*give way to; give more to*
neigen zu + DAT	*be prone to*
nutzen/nützen + DAT	*benefit; help*
passen + DAT	*suit; fit*
raten + DAT	*advise*
reagieren auf + ACC	*react to*

rechnen auf + ACC	*count on*
rechnen mit + DAT	*reckon with*
reden von + DAT	*talk about*
reden über + ACC	*say unpleasant things about*
reichen + DAT	*be enough for*
retten vor + DAT	*rescue from*
riechen nach + DAT	*smell of*
sich rühmen + GEN	*boast*
sagen über + ACC or **von** + DAT	*say about*
sagen zu + DAT	*say to*
schaden + DAT	*harm*
schicken nach + DAT	*send for*
schießen auf + ACC	*shoot at*
schimpfen über + ACC	*grumble at*
schimpfen auf + ACC	*swear at*
schlagen nach + DAT	*hit out at*
schmecken + DAT	*taste good to*
schmecken nach + DAT	*taste of*
schmeicheln + DAT	*flatter*
schreiben über + ACC or **von** + DAT	*write about*
schützen vor + DAT	*protect from*
schwärmen für + ACC or **von** + DAT	*be mad/crazy about*
sehen nach + DAT	*look like*
sich sehnen nach + DAT	*long for*
sorgen für + ACC	*look after*
sich sorgen um + ACC	*worry about*
sprechen über + ACC or **von** + DAT	*speak about*
stehen + DAT	*suit*
sterben an + DAT	*die of (e.g. a disease)*
sterben vor + DAT	*be dying of (e.g. boredom)*
strahlen vor + DAT	*beam with*
streben nach + DAT	*strive for*
streiken um + ACC	*strike for*

sich streiten um + ACC	*quarrel over*
sich streiten über + ACC	*quarrel about*
sich stürzen auf + ACC	*rush at*
suchen nach + DAT	*look for*
tasten nach + DAT	*grope for*
sich täuschen über + ACC	*be mistaken about*
sich täuschen in + DAT	*be mistaken in (somebody)*
teilnehmen an + DAT	*take part in*
telefonieren mit + DAT	*telephone*
telefonieren nach + DAT	*telephone for*
trauen + DAT	*trust*
trauern um + ACC	*mourn for*
träumen von + DAT	*dream about*
trinken auf + ACC	*drink to*
trotzen + DAT	*defy*
überreden zu + DAT	*talk into having*
sich umsehen nach + DAT	*look out for*
sich unterhalten über + ACC	*talk about*
sich verabschieden von + DAT	*say goodbye to*
verbieten + DAT	*forbid (somebody)*
verfügen über + ACC	*have at one's disposal*
sich vergewissern + GEN	*make sure of*
verlangen nach + DAT	*crave for; ask to see*
verlängern um + ACC	*extend by*
sich verlassen auf + ACC	*rely on*
sich verrechnen um + ACC	*make a mistake of*
versichern + DAT	*assure (somebody)*
versichern + GEN	*assure . . . of (something)*
sich versichern + GEN	*make certain of*
sich verstecken vor + DAT	*hide from*
verstehen unter + DAT	*understand by*
sich verstehen mit + DAT	*get on with (somebody)*
vertrauen + DAT	*trust*
verzeihen + DAT	*forgive*
verzichten auf + ACC	*renounce*
vorangehen + DAT	*go ahead of*

vorbeigehen an + DAT	*go past*
sich vorbereiten auf + ACC	*prepare for*
sich (DAT) **vornehmen**	*make one's mind up*
vorstehen + DAT	*be in charge of*
sich (DAT) **vorstellen**	*imagine; visualize*
wählen zu + DAT	*elect (to the office of)*
warnen vor + DAT	*warn of*
warten auf + ACC	*wait for*
weh tun + DAT	*hurt*
sich weiden an + DAT	*gloat over*
sich wenden an + ACC	*turn to*
werben um + ACC	*court*
weitergeben an + ACC	*pass on to*
widersprechen + DAT	*contradict*
widerstehen + DAT	*resist*
wissen über + ACC or **von** + DAT	*know about*
sich wundern über + ACC	*be surprised at*
zählen auf + ACC	*count on*
zählen unter + DAT or **zu** + DAT	*number among*
sich zanken um + ACC	*quarrel over*
zielen auf + ACC	*aim at*
zittern vor + DAT	*tremble with*
zugrunde gehen an + DAT	*be ruined by*
zusehen + DAT	*watch (somebody)*
zustimmen + DAT	*agree with*

THE MODAL VERBS AND LASSEN

The modal verbs (auxiliary verbs of 'mood' like *can*, *must*, *will* in English) always have a dependent infinitive:

> **darf ich Ihnen helfen?**, *may I help you?*

Even if this infinitive is occasionally not expressed (**darf ich?**, *may I?*), it is virtually always implied. The only exception to this is some uses of **mögen**: see p. 62.

The modal verbs in German are

> **dürfen**, *may* (permission)
> **können**, *can*
> **mögen**, *may* (possibility)
> **müssen**, *must*
> **sollen**, *is to*
> **wollen**, *want*

The meanings given above are in fact not really adequate. These verbs have a number of different meanings and shades of meaning in different uses of their various tenses. These are explained below.

dürfen

■ The basic meaning of **dürfen** is *to be allowed to*; it can also express quite strong possibility. The English equivalent, in both meanings, is often *may* in the present:

> **darf ich Ihnen etwas sagen?**, *may I tell you something?*
> **das darf wohl sein**, *that may well be so*

. . . *could* in the past:

> **ich durfte zum erstenmal reisen**, *I could (= was allowed to) travel for the first time*

. . . and *might* in the past subjunctive:

> **dürfte ich noch ein Stück Torte nehmen?**, *might I possibly take another piece of flan?*
> **das dürfte wahr sein**, *that might well be true*

In the negative, English uses *mustn't* = *is not allowed to*:

> **das darf ich nicht essen**, *I mustn't (I'm not allowed to) eat that*

■ Note also:

> **was darf es sein?**, *can I help you?; what shall it be? (in shops, bars)*
> **ich darf Ihnen sagen, daß . . .**, *I am able to tell you that . . .*

können

■ Basically **können** corresponds to *can* or *is able to* in the present:

kannst du mitfahren?, *can you come with us?*

. . . and *could* or *was able to* in the past:

sie konnte nicht kommen, *she couldn't come*

■ **Können** also expresses possibility:

das kann sein, *that may be*
das kann nicht sein, *that's not possible*
sie kann jeden Moment kommen, *she may come at any moment*

The past subjunctive expresses remoter possibility:

das könnte ich vielleicht tun, *I might perhaps do that*

■ It is frequently used colloquially for **dürfen**, just as English uses *can* for *may*:

kann ich mitkommen?, *can/may I come with you?*

■ Note also:

er kann Italienisch, *he speaks Italian*
dafür kann ich nichts, *it's not my fault (I can't do anything about it)*

mögen

■ **Mögen** means both *to like*:

das mag ich nicht, *I don't like that*
ich mag nicht, *I don't like to*
möchten Sie noch Zucker?, *would you like some more sugar?*

. . . and *to be likely*, usually expressed by *may* in English:

das mag sein, *that may be*

In the past this becomes, in English, *may (well) have been* or *must have been*:

> **er mochte fünfzig sein**, *he must have been (may well have been) fifty*

■ **Mögen** also means *to want*, with a weaker, more polite sense than **wollen**:

> **ich mochte nicht,** *I didn't want to*

The past subjunctive, **ich möchte,** *I should like*, is much politer than **ich will,** *I want*:

> **ich möchte etwas länger bleiben**, *I should like to stay a little longer*
> **ich möchte Kaffee bitte**, *I should like coffee please*

This is the form of **mögen** in most frequent use.

■ The past subjunctive also expresses polite doubt or disagreement:

> **man möchte vielleicht dagegen einwenden . . .** , *one might just possibly say, on the other hand . . .*

■ The past subjunctive is also used to give polite indirect commands:

> **sagen Sie ihr, Sie möchte hereinkommen**, *tell her to please come in*

müssen

■ The basic meaning of **müssen** is *must = to have to*:

> **du mußt alles aufessen**, *you must eat everything up*

In the negative, this becomes *don't have to* in English:

> **du mußt das nicht essen**, *you don't have to eat that*

(*You mustn't eat that!* is correctly **das darfst du nicht essen!** (or **das sollst du nicht essen!**); however, in conversation **du**

mußt das nicht essen is also used in this meaning, with a weaker stress on the **mußt** than in the '*don't have to*' meaning.)

■ **Müssen** is also used to mean *must* or *to have to* expressing inevitability:

> **muß das sein?**, *is that really necessary?*
> **sie muß bald hier sein**, *she's bound to be (she has to be) here soon*

■ **Müssen** in the past subjunctive means *ought to be*, where there is no sense of duty (where there is, **sollte** is used):

> **es müßte gehen**, *it ought to be possible*
> **das Haus müßte irgendwo hier sein**, *the house ought to be somewhere around here*

■ **Haben zu** also exists, meaning *to have to*, where this means *to be in possession of something, to which something must be done*:

> **ich habe ein Auto zu verkaufen**, *I have a car to sell*

but: **ich muß mein Auto verkaufen**, *I have to sell my car*

sollen

■ The basic meaning is *is to* or *is supposed to*, expressing intention:

> **sie soll heute kommen**, *she's to come (supposed to be coming) today*
> **sie sollte gestern kommen**, *she was supposed to be coming yesterday*
> **was soll das heißen?**, *what's that supposed (intended) to mean?*
> **du sollst dein Geld bekommen**, *you're going to get (you're to get) your money*
> **ihr wißt, daß ihr das nicht tun sollt**, *you know you shouldn't (are not supposed to) be doing that*

■ **Sollen** also means *to be supposed to* in the sense of '*people say that*':

er soll reich sein, *he's supposed to be rich*
es soll bis fünf Verletzte gegeben haben, *reports say that up to five people were injured*

■ In the past and pluperfect subjunctive it means *ought to/should* and *ought to have/should have*, expressing moral duty:

das solltest du nicht machen, *you ought not to (shouldn't) do that*
das hätte er nicht tun sollen, *he ought not to (shouldn't) have done that*

■ It is used to express a command or wish, especially in the third person:

er soll ein bißchen warten, *let him wait a bit*

■ It can also be used, like **mögen** (see p. 63), in indirect commands:

sagen Sie ihr, sie soll hereinkommen, *tell her to come in*

wollen

■ The basic meaning of **wollen** is *to want* or *will*:

er will gehen, *he wants to go*
es will nicht funktionieren, *it won't (= refuses to) work*
willst du was?, *do you want something?* (much less polite than **möchtest du etwas?**)

■ **Wollen** also sometimes means *to need*:

das will sehr viel Zeit, *that needs a great deal of time*

■ It frequently means *to be about to*, expressing intention:

das will ich sofort machen, *I'll do that straight away* (stronger than '**das werde ich . . .** ')
ich wollte gerade sagen . . . , *I was just going to say . . .*

■ It can form a polite alternative to the imperative:

wollen wir gehen?, *let's go*
wollen Sie bitte Platz nehmen, *would you please take a seat*

■ It can mean *to claim*, or, in the negative, *not to admit*:

er will ein Millionär sein, *he claims to be a millionaire*
kein Mensch will es gemacht haben, *nobody admits they did it*

▶ For **lassen** + an infinitive meaning *to get something done* or *to have something done*, see p. 68.

Formation and use of the modals

▶ The modals are irregular, mixed verbs. For their conjugation see the Irregular Verb list, pp. 73–85.

■ Infinitives dependent on the modals are used without **zu**:

das will ich sofort erklären, *I'll explain that straight away*

■ The modals can also be used without a dependent infinitive:

du mußt nicht, *you don't have to*
das mag ich nicht so sehr, *I'm not too keen on that*
ganz wie du willst, *just as you like*

■ Verbs of motion are very often dropped after the modals, especially in spoken German:

ich will nach Berlin, *I want to go to Berlin*

With **mögen** this can only be done after the past subjunctive, **möchte**.

In the case of separable-prefix verbs, the prefix is not dropped:

ich muß weg (= weggehen), *I must be off*
möchtest du mit? (= mitkommen), *would you like to come with us?*

■ Past participles of the modals

The modal verbs all have two past participles, one formed **ge . . . t**, the other identical with the infinitive. The infinitive form is used where the modal has a dependent infinitive (which is more usually the case):

> **du hast nicht fahren können? — Ich habe leider nicht gekonnt**, *you weren't able to go?—I'm sorry, I couldn't*

► **Lassen** and, sometimes, **sehen** and **hören** behave similarly. See pp. 68 and 69.

■ Modals in compound tenses in subordinate clauses

When two infinitives come together at the end of a subordinate clause, an auxiliary verb stands before them, not after as you would expect. Where this happens it is usually a modal in a compound tense that is involved:

> **ich weiß, daß du nicht gestern hast fahren können**, *I know you couldn't go yesterday*

Notice that this applies not just with **haben** and **sein** used to form past compound tenses, but also with **werden** in the future and conditional tenses of modals:

> **ich hoffe, daß du nicht wirst spielen müssen**, *I hope you won't have to play*

This whole construction tends to be avoided in conversation (e.g. by using the past tense for the perfect).

■ The modals can be used with a perfect infinitive (past participle plus **haben/sein**), as they can in English. Notice the change in meaning this produces:

	sie hat es sagen müssen, *she had to say it*
but:	**sie muß es gesagt haben**, *she must have said it*
	sie haben es machen sollen, *they were supposed to do it*
but:	**sie sollen es gemacht haben**, *they're supposed to have done it*

sie haben es tun können, *they have been able to do it*

but: **sie können es getan haben**, *they may have done it*

■ A modal, as in English, may be followed by a passive infinitive (past participle plus **werden**):

es muß getan werden, *it must be done*

or by another modal:

das mußt du aber machen können, *you really must be able to do that*

Lassen and similar verbs

■ **Lassen** has two principal meanings—*to let*:

er ließ sie entkommen, *he let them escape*

. . . and *to make, to cause to, to have (something done)*:

ich lasse mir die Haare schneiden, *I'm going to have my hair cut*

sie ließ uns holen, *she sent for us (had us fetched)*

■ Like the modal verbs, **lassen** takes a following infinitive without **zu**. Also like the modals, **lassen** has two past participles. They are **gelassen** and **lassen**. The latter is used when **lassen** appears with the infinitive of another verb:

ich habe mir die Haare schneiden lassen, *I've had my hair cut*

■ The reflexive form **sich lassen** means *can be* + past participle. It is followed by an active infinitive in German, with a passive sense:

das läßt sich machen, *that can be done*

es läßt sich nicht leugnen, daß . . . , *it cannot be denied that . . .*

■ The past participles of the compounds **fallenlassen**, *to drop*, and **liegenlassen**, *to leave (lying about)*, are found both with and without **ge-**; the form without **ge-** is the more usual:

wo hast du es denn liegen(ge)lassen?, *where did you leave it then?*

Sehen, hören, heißen, fühlen

■ The rules about infinitives and past participles that apply to **lassen** (infinitives without **zu**; two past-participle forms) also apply to **sehen** and **hören**, where the construction with the infinitive form of the past participle is fairly frequent, especially in written German:

ich habe ihn kommen hören, *I heard him coming*

They also apply to the literary verb **heißen**, *to bid*:

er hieß mich eintreten, *he bade me enter*

■ **Fühlen** takes an infinitive without **zu**; it also has a second past participle in the infinitive form, but this is usually avoided by using **wie**:

ich fühlte mein Herz höher schlagen, *I felt my heart beat faster*
ich habe gefühlt, wie mein Herz höher schlug, *I felt my heart beat faster* (**ich habe mein Herz höher schlagen fühlen** is possible but stilted)

▶ For more on these and similar verbs see pp. 46–7.

▶ For **helfen, lehren**, and **lernen** with and without **zu**, see p. 47.

IMPERSONAL VERBS

Impersonal verbs are verbs whose subject is, in English, *there* or a non-specific *it*. In German this is **es**:

es ist kein Geld im Safe, *there's no money in the safe*
es regnet, *it's raining*

Impersonal verbs corresponding to English 'it . . . '

With all verbs in this group **es** is seen as a true subject, corresponding to the English *it*. If something other than **es** is put in front of the verb, the **es** is placed after the verb like any normal subject:

> **heute regnet es**, *today it's raining*
> **mich ärgert es, daß . . .** , *it annoys me that . . .*

The **es** also stays in subordinate order:

> **ich weiß nicht, ob es heute regnen wird**, *I don't know if it's going to rain today*

This group includes:

■ Most weather verbs. These have an impersonal *it* (**es**) as subject:

> **es regnet**, *it's raining*
> **es schneit**, *it's snowing*
> **es zieht**, *it's draughty*
> —and very many others

■ Verbs with an impersonal subject and a personal object, either accusative or (more often) dative, sometimes reflexive, for example:

> **es ärgert mich**, *it annoys me*
> **es ist mir recht**, *it's OK by me*
> **es scheint mir**, *it seems to me*
> **es handelt sich um**, *it's a question of*

■ **Es ist** or **es sind** + noun or pronoun. German has a fixed order: normal order with nouns, inversion with pronouns:

> **es ist meine Schwester**, *it's my sister*
> **Sie sind es!**, *it's you!*

Impersonal verbs with a postponed subject (usually corresponding to English 'there . . .')

With these verbs **es** simply functions as a substitute for the real subject, which is being held back until after the verb to give it more importance. This **es** usually corresponds to the English *there*. Very many verbs can be made impersonal in this way:

> **es bleibt jetzt sehr wenig Zeit**, *there's very little time left now*

□ If the real subject is plural, so is the verb:

> **es stehen viele Autos auf dem Parkplatz**, *there are a lot of cars (standing) in the car park*

□ If an adverb appears before the verb in this construction, the **es** simply disappears (there is no need for it, as the real subject now takes its normal third place in inverted order):

> **heute stehen viele Autos auf dem Parkplatz**, *there are many cars in the car park today* (compare: **heute regnet es**)

The **es** also disappears in subordinate order, for the same reason:

> **ich weiß schon, daß heute viele Autos auf dem Parkplatz stehen**, *I'm quite aware that there are a lot of cars in the car park today*

▶ For the appropriate translation of *there is* see pp. 72–3.

□ The real subject may be a clause. Where the real subject is a clause English uses *it* rather than *there* for the 'postponing' subject:

> **es ist wahr, daß er das nie gesagt hat**, *it is true that he never said that* (real subject: *that he never said that*)
> **wahr ist, daß er das nie gesagt hat**
> **es steht in meiner Zeitung, daß . . .** , *it says in my paper that . . .*
> **in meiner Zeitung steht, daß. . .**

□ With this construction in the passive, no real subject need be expressed at all:

> **es wird hier gebaut / hier wird gebaut**, *there's construction work taking place here*

Impersonal verbs corresponding to an English personal verb

Many German impersonal verbs are the equivalent of ordinary English personal verbs. Among the commonest verbs of this kind are:

> **es fehlt mir an** (+ DAT), *I lack*
> **es geht mir** (**gut**, etc.), *I'm* (*well*, etc.)
> **es gelingt mir**, *I succeed*
> **es tut mir leid**, *I'm sorry*
> **es freut mich**, *I'm glad*

With verbs in this group the **es** is retained after the verb if anything else is placed first in the sentence:

> **mir geht es gut heute**, *I feel well today*

But note the following exceptions, where the **es** very often disappears, especially in written German:

> **es ist mir** (**kalt**, etc.), *I'm* (*cold*, etc.)
> **es wird mir** (**kalt**, etc.), *I'm getting* (*cold*, etc.)
> **es ist mir, als ob . . . / es kommt mir vor, als ob . . .** , *I feel as if . . .*
> **es ist mir schlecht/übel**, *I feel sick*
> **es friert mich**, *I feel cold*
> **es wundert mich, daß . . .** , *I'm surprised that . . .*
> **mir ist (es) furchtbar warm hier**, *I feel terribly hot here*

In spoken German the **es** is often retained as **'s**:

> **mich friert's**, *I'm cold*

There is, there are

The English expression *there is / there are* corresponds to the German **es ist / es sind**, though German likes to substitute a more precise verb if possible (**es steht, es liegt**, etc.).

However, where existence rather than position is to be expressed, **es gibt** is used instead, meaning *there is, there are*. The **es** is always kept in this construction, the verb is always singular, and it is followed by an accusative:

> **es ist kein einziges Glas im Schrank**, *there isn't a single glass in the cupboard*
> **es gibt keine Gläser mehr**, *there aren't any glasses left*

Es ist / es sind loses the **es** in inverted or subordinate order.

ALPHABETICAL LIST OF IRREGULAR VERBS

This list includes all strong and mixed verbs in modern usage.

■ Compound verbs should be looked up under their simple form.

■ Where an irregular present-tense **er** form is given, the same irregularity will occur in the **du** form.

■ Irregular past subjunctives are given in brackets after the past tense.

■ An asterisk before the past participle indicates a verb whose past compound tenses are formed with **sein** when the verb is used intransitively.

► For the complete formation of the present and past tenses given here, see pp. 8 and 10.

► Past compound tenses and passive tenses are regular (except for the past participle form, given below). For their formation, see pp. 8 and 11 (past compound tenses) and p. 29 (passive tenses).

► Future and conditional tenses are regular. For their formation, see pp. 9 and 11.

► Present and future subjunctives are regular (except the present subjunctive of **sein**, see p. 40). For their formation see pp. 8 and 10 (present subjunctive) and p. 40 (future subjunctive).

▶ Perfect and pluperfect subjunctives are regular (except for the past participle form, given below). For their formation, see pp. 9 and 121.

▶ Past subjunctives are regular except as shown below, in brackets after the past tense. For their formation see pp. 8 and 10.

infinitive	meaning	present, **er** form, if irregular	past (**er** form; + past subjunctive if irregular)	past participle (* = **sein**)
backen	*bake*	backt/bäckt	backte	gebacken
befehlen	*command*	befiehlt	befahl (beföhle)	befohlen
beginnen	*begin*		begann	begonnen
beißen	*bite*		biß	gebissen
bergen	*save*	birgt	barg	geborgen
bersten	*burst*	birst	barst	*geborsten
biegen	*bend*		bog	gebogen
bieten	*offer*		bot	geboten
binden	*tie*		band	gebunden
bitten	*ask*		bat	gebeten
blasen	*blow*	bläst	blies	geblasen
bleiben	*stay*		blieb	*geblieben
braten	*roast*	brät	briet	gebraten
brechen	*break*	bricht	brach	gebrochen
brennen	*burn*		brannte (brennte)	gebrannt
bringen	*bring*		brachte	gebracht
denken	*think*		dachte	gedacht

infinitive	meaning	present, **er** form, if irregular	past (**er** form; + past subjunctive if irregular)	past participle (* = **sein**)
dreschen	*thresh*	drischt	drosch	gedroschen
dringen	*be urgent*		drang	gedrungen
dürfen	*be allowed*	ich/er darf	durfte	gedurft/dürfen
empfehlen	*recommend*	empfiehlt	empfahl (empföhle)	empfohlen
erlöschen	*die out*	erlischt	erlosch	*erloschen
erschrecken	*be startled*[1]	erschrickt	erschrak	*erschrocken
essen	*eat*	ißt	aß	gegessen
fahren	*travel*	fährt	fuhr	*gefahren
fallen	*fall*	fällt	fiel	*gefallen
fangen	*catch*	fängt	fing	gefangen
fechten	*fence*	ficht	focht	gefochten
finden	*find*		fand	gefunden
flechten	*plait*	flicht	flocht	geflochten
fliegen	*fly*		flog	*geflogen
fliehen	*flee*		floh	*geflohen
fließen	*flow*		floß	*geflossen
fressen	*eat (of animals)*	frißt	fraß	gefressen

frieren	*freeze*		fror	gefroren
gebären	*bear (child)*	gebärt/gebiert	gebar	geboren
geben	*give*	gibt	gab	gegeben
gedeihen	*prosper*		gedieh	*gediehen
gehen	*go*		ging	*gegangen
gelingen	*succeed*		gelang	*gelungen
gelten	*be valid*	gilt	galt (gölte)	gegolten
genesen	*recover*		genas	*genesen
genießen	*enjoy*		genoß	genossen
geschehen	*happen*	geschieht	geschah	*geschehen
gewinnen	*win*		gewann (gewönne)	gewonnen
gießen	*pour*		goß	gegossen
gleichen	*resemble*		glich	geglichen
gleiten	*slip*		glitt	*geglitten
graben	*dig*	gräbt	grub	gegraben
greifen	*grasp*		griff	gegriffen
haben	*have*	du hast; er hat	hatte	gehabt
halten	*hold*	hält	hielt	gehalten

1 In the sense of *to startle* **erschrecken** is weak.

infinitive	meaning	present, **er** form, if irregular	past (**er** form; + past subjunctive if irregular)	past participle (* = **sein**)
hauen	*hit*		haute	gehaut/ gehauen
hängen[1]	*hang*		hing	gehangen
heben	*raise*		hob	gehoben
heißen	*be called*		hieß	geheißen
helfen	*help*	hilft	half (hülfe)	geholfen
kennen	*know*		kannte (kennte)	gekannt
klingen	*sound*		klang	geklungen
kneifen	*pinch*		kniff	gekniffen
kommen	*come*		kam	*gekommen
können	*can*	ich/er kann	konnte	gekonnt/können
kriechen	*crawl*		kroch	*gekrochen
laden	*load*	lädt	lud	geladen
lassen	*let*	läßt	ließ	gelassen/lassen
laufen	*run*	läuft	lief	*gelaufen
leiden	*put up with*		litt	gelitten
leihen	*lend*		lieh	geliehen

lesen	*read*	liest	las	gelesen
liegen	*lie*		lag	gelegen
lügen	*tell lies*		log	gelogen
mahlen	*grind*		mahlte	gemahlen
meiden	*avoid*		mied	gemieden
melken[2]	*milk*	milkt	molk	gemolken
messen	*measure*	mißt	maß	gemessen
mißlingen	*fail*		mißlang	*mißlungen
mögen	*like*	ich/er mag	mochte	gemocht/mögen
müssen	*must*	ich/er muß	mußte	gemußt/müssen
nehmen	*take*	nimmt	nahm	genommen
nennen	*name*		nannte (nennte)	genannt
pfeifen	*whistle*		pfiff	gepfiffen
preisen	*praise*		pries	gepriesen
quellen	*gush*	quillt	quoll	*gequollen
raten	*advise*	rät	riet	geraten
reiben	*rub*		rieb	gerieben

1 **Hängen** is strong when intransitive, weak when transitive.

2 **Melken** is very frequently weak.

	meaning	present, **er** form, if irregular	past (**er** form; + past subjunctive if irregular)	past participle (* = **sein**)
reißen	*tear*		riß	gerissen
reiten	*ride*		ritt	*geritten
rennen	*run*		rannte (rennte)	*gerannt
riechen	*smell*		roch	gerochen
ringen	*struggle*		rang	gerungen
rinnen	*run*		rann	*geronnen
rufen	*call*		rief	gerufen
salzen	*salt*		salzte	gesalzen
saufen	*drink heavily*	säuft	soff	gesoffen
saugen[1]	*suck*		sog	gesogen
schaffen	*create*[2]		schuf	geschaffen
scheiden	*separate*		schied	*geschieden
scheinen	*seem*		schien	geschienen
scheißen	*shit*		schiß	geschissen
schelten	*scold*	schilt	schalt (schölte)	gescholten
scheren	*trim*		schor	geschoren
schieben	*push*		schob	geschoben

schießen	*shoot*		schoß	geschossen
schinden	*ill-treat*		schindete	geschunden
schlafen	*sleep*	schläft	schlief	geschlafen
schlagen	*hit*	schlägt	schlug	geschlagen
schleichen	*creep*		schlich	*geschlichen
schleifen	*sharpen*		schliff	geschliffen
schleißen[3]	*strip*		schliß	geschlissen
schließen	*shut*		schloß	geschlossen
schlingen	*loop*		schlang	geschlungen
schmeißen	*fling*		schmiß	geschmissen
schmelzen	*melt*	schmilzt	schmolz	*geschmolzen
schneiden	*cut*		schnitt	geschnitten
schreiben	*write*		schrieb	geschrieben
schreien	*shout*		schrie	geschrie(e)n
schreiten	*step*		schritt	*geschritten
schweigen	*be silent*		schwieg	geschwiegen

1 **Saugen** is usually weak.
2 In the sense of *to manage* **schaffen** is weak.
3 **Schleißen** and its compounds are often weak.

infinitive	meaning	present, **er** form, if irregular	past (**er** form; + past subjunctive if irregular)	past participle (* = **sein**)
schwellen	*swell*[1]	schwillt	schwoll	*geschwollen
schwimmen	*swim*		schwamm (schwömme)	*geschwommen
schwinden	*dwindle*		schwand	*geschwunden
schwingen	*swing*		schwang	*geschwungen
schwören	*swear*		schwor (schwüre)	geschworen
sehen	*see*	sieht	sah	gesehen
sein	*be*	ich bin; du bist; er ist; wir/sie sind; ihr seid	war	*gewesen
senden	*send*[2]		sandte (sendete)	gesandt
singen	*sing*		sang	gesungen
sinken	*sink*		sank	*gesunken
sinnen	*think*		sann	gesonnen
sitzen	*sit*		saß	gesessen
sollen	*is to*	ich/er soll	sollte	gesollt/sollen
spalten	*split*		spaltete	gespaltet/ gespalten

speien	*spew forth*		spie	gespie(e)n
spinnen	*spin*		spann (spönne)	gesponnen
sprechen	*speak*	spricht	sprach	gesprochen
sprießen	*sprout*		sproß	*gesprossen
springen	*jump*		sprang	*gesprungen
stechen	*stab*	sticht	stach	gestochen
stehen	*stand*		stand (stünde)	gestanden
stehlen	*steal*	stiehlt	stahl	gestohlen
steigen	*climb*		stieg	*gestiegen
sterben	*die*	stirbt	starb (stürbe)	*gestorben
stinken	*stink*		stank	gestunken
stoßen	*push*	stößt	stieß	gestoßen
streichen	*stroke*		strich	gestrichen
streiten	*quarrel*		stritt	gestritten
tragen	*carry*	trägt	trug	getragen
treffen	*meet*	trifft	traf	getroffen

---

1 In the transitive sense of *to fill (a sail)* **schwellen** is weak.
2 In the sense of *to broadcast* **senden** is weak.

Infinitive	meaning	present, **er** form, if irregular	past (**er** form; + past subjunctive if irregular)	past participle (* = **sein**)
treiben	*drive*		trieb	getrieben
treten	*step*	tritt	trat	*getreten
trinken	*drink*		trank	getrunken
trügen	*deceive*		trog	getrogen
tun	*do*	ich tue; du tust; er/ihr tut; wir/sie tun	tat	getan
verderben	*spoil*	verdirbt	verdarb (verdürbe)	*verdorben
verdrießen	*annoy*		verdroß	verdrossen
vergessen	*forget*	vergißt	vergaß	vergessen
verlieren	*lose*		verlor	verloren
verlöschen	*go out*	verlischt	verlosch	*verloschen
wachsen	*grow*	wächst	wuchs	*gewachsen
waschen	*wash*	wäscht	wusch	gewaschen
weben[1]	*weave*		wob	gewoben
weichen	*budge*		wich	*gewichen
weisen	*point*		wies	gewiesen

wenden[2]	*turn*		wandte (wendete)	gewandt
werben	*advertise*	wirbt	warb (würbe)	geworben
werden	*become*	du wirst; er wird	wurde	*geworden/ worden
werfen	*throw*	wirft	warf (würfe)	geworfen
wiegen	*weigh*[3]		wog	gewogen
winden	*wind*		wand	gewunden
wissen	*know*	ich/er weiß	wußte	gewußt
wollen	*want*	ich/er will	wollte	gewollt/wollen
zeihen	*indict*		zieh	geziehen
ziehen	*pull*		zog	gezogen
zwingen	*force*		zwang	gezwungen

1 **Weben** is usually weak in modern German.
2 **Wenden** may also be weak.
3 **Wiegen** is weak when it means *to rock*.

I Articles

Articles are words like *a* and *the*. In German the form of the article changes according to the gender and case of the noun following and according to whether the noun is singular or plural. For noun cases see p. 96.

FORMATION OF ARTICLES

The forms of the definite article (**der**, *the*) and indefinite article (**ein**, *a*) are as follows, shown here with a masculine noun **der Mann**, *man*, a feminine noun **die Frau**, *woman*, a neuter noun **das Buch**, *book*, and a plural noun **die Leute**, *people*:

Definite article: **der**, *the*

	SINGULAR			PLURAL
	masculine	*feminine*	*neuter*	
nominative	der Mann	die Frau	das Buch	die Leute
accusative	den Mann	die Frau	das Buch	die Leute
genitive	des Mannes	der Frau	des Buches	der Leute
dative	dem Mann	der Frau	dem Buch	den Leuten

■ Following the pattern of **der** are: **dieser**, *this/that*; **welcher**, *which*; **jener**, *that*; **jeder**, *every*; **mancher**, *many a*:

dieser, *this, that*

	SINGULAR			PLURAL
	masculine	*feminine*	*neuter*	
nominative	dieser	diese	dieses	diese
accusative	diesen	diese	dieses	diese
genitive	dieses	dieser	dieses	dieser
dative	diesem	dieser	diesem	diesen

▶ **Jener** is uncommon in modern German. For *that* **dieser** or, in speech, an emphasized **der** is used. See Demonstrative Adjectives, p.115.

▶ The definite article often compounds with certain prepositions to form a single word. So **zu + dem = zum**. See p. 161.

▶ For the noun endings in the genitive singular and dative plural, see pp. 97–9.

Indefinite article: **ein,** *a*

	SINGULAR			PLURAL
	masculine	*feminine*	*neuter*	
nominative	ein Mann	eine Frau	ein Buch	keine Leute
accusative	einen Mann	eine Frau	ein Buch	keine Leute
genitive	eines Mannes	einer Frau	eines Buches	keiner Leute
dative	einem Mann	einer Frau	einem Buch	keinen Leuten

■ Following the pattern of **ein** are: **kein,** *no* (used above for the plural forms, since **ein** has no plural) and the possessive adjectives: **mein,** *my*; **dein,** *your*; **sein,** *his/its*; **ihr,** *her/their*; **unser,** *our*; **euer,** *your*; **Ihr,** *your*.

■ **Unser** (sometimes) and **euer** (always) lose the final **e** of their stem when they have an ending: **eure Bücher**.

▶ For **kein** see p. 153.

▶ For the possessives see p. 115.

USING THE ARTICLES

Articles are used in a number of places in German where we would omit them in English.

■ The definite article is used with abstract nouns much more frequently than in English, especially when the noun is generalized:

> **die Eifersucht ist keine Tugend,** *jealousy is no virtue* (jealousy in general)

but: **das klingt wie Eifersucht**, *that sounds like jealousy* (a bit of jealousy)

Abstract nouns usually lose their definite article after the prepositions **durch**, *through*, **gegen**, *against*, **ohne**, *without*, and **über**, *about*.

■ The definite article, with added emphasis in speech, is used instead of the demonstrative **jener**, to mean *that*:

ich möchte *den* Kuchen, bitte, *I'd like that cake, please*

■ The definite article is used with a noun in the genitive where in English no article would be used:

der Klang der Musik, *the sound of music*

Spoken German usually prefers **von** to the genitive; no article is then necessary:

der Klang von Musik

■ The definite article is often used instead of the possessive with parts of the body and with clothes:

hebt die Hand!, *put your hand up!*
zieh das Hemd aus, *take your shirt off*

A dative to indicate the person concerned may be added . . .

möchtest du dir die Hände waschen?, *would you like to wash your hands?*

. . . and must be added when someone other than the subject of the sentence owns the piece of clothing or the part of the body referred to:

sie drückte mir die Hand, *she pressed my hand*

□ This construction cannot be used when the part of the body is the subject:

deine Hand ist sehr klein, *your hand is very small*

□ The alternative construction with the possessive as in English, though less frequent, is entirely possible:

zieh dein Hemd aus, *take your shirt off*

■ The definite article is used with geographical names in the following instances:

□ Before feminine names of countries:

wir fahren in die Schweiz, *we're travelling to Switzerland*

It is also used with the very few masculine and plural country names. See pp. 93 and 176. The article is dropped in addresses, however: **Schweiz** on the envelope, not **die Schweiz**.

□ Before geographical names with adjectives (English usage varies here):

das neue Deutschland, *the new Germany*
das schöne Italien, *beautiful Italy*

The same applies to proper names:

der doofe Fritz, *daft Fritz*

□ Before names of mountains, lakes, streets:

die Zugspitze; **der Comer See**, *Lake Como*; **die Bismarckstraße**

■ The definite article is used with months, seasons, parts of the day, meals:

am Vormittag, *in the morning*
der Mai ist gekommen, *May is here*
im Sommer nimmt man das Frühstück draußen, *in summer we eat breakfast outside*

■ A definite (not an indefinite) article is used in expressions of price + quantity like *seven marks a kilo*:

sieben Mark das Kilo, *seven marks a kilo*
drei Mark das Stück, *three marks apiece*

Pro, *per*, may also be used in this way. See Prepositions, p. 178.

■ A definite article may be used, familiarly, before proper names:

> **hast du den Günter gesehen?**, *have you seen Günter?*

OMISSION OF THE ARTICLES

■ The article is omitted in many prepositional phrases where we would expect it in English:

> **zu Ende**, *at an end*
> **bei Ausbruch des Krieges**, *at the outbreak of war*
> **nach längerer Zeit**, *after quite a long time*

And note **Anfang**, **Mitte**, and **Ende** with months, where both article and preposition are omitted:

> **sie kommt Anfang September**, *she's coming at the beginning of September*

■ The indefinite article is not used after **sein**, *to be* (or **werden**, *to become*, or **bleiben**, *to remain*) + a profession or nationality:

> **er wird Computerwissenschafler**, *he's going to be a computer scientist*
> **sie ist Amerikanerin**, *she's an American*

It *is* used, though, if there is an adjective in front of the noun:

> **er ist ein bekannter Schriftsteller**, *he's a well-known writer*

■ The indefinite article is not used after **als**, *as (a)*:

> **ich als Engländer weiß, daß . . .** , *I as an Englishman know that . . .*
> **er arbeitet als Maurer**, *he's working as a builder*

I Nouns

All nouns in German are spelled with a capital letter.

GENDER OF NOUNS

English has three genders: masculine, feminine, and neuter (*he, she, it*). German also has three, but whereas in English gender virtually always corresponds logically to the sex of the noun, this is not the case in German. Most nouns denoting male people and animals are in fact masculine in German, most of those denoting females are feminine; but names of inanimate objects may be masculine, feminine, or neuter. Unlike English nouns, German nouns usually make their gender obvious by means of the article and (sometimes) the adjectives in front of them.

The rules for gender in German are far from watertight—there are exceptions to most of them.

Masculine groups

■ Masculine are: names of males; days, months, seasons; points of the compass; makes of car:

> **der Mann**, *man*, **der Montag**, *Monday*, **der Januar**, *January*, **der Sommer**, *summer*, **der Norden**, *north*, **der Opel**

■ Nouns indicating a 'doer', ending **-er**, are masculine:

> **der Gärtner**, *gardener*, **der Sänger**, *singer*

By analogy, so are most 'doing' instruments: **der Computer**, *computer*, **der Wecker**, *alarm*.

■ Nouns ending **-ich**, **-ig**, **-ling** are masculine:

> **der Fittich**, *wing*, **der Honig**, *honey*, **der Lehrling**, *apprentice*

■ Nouns ending **-ismus**, **-ist**, and **-ant** are masculine. These are all of foreign origin:

> **der Kapitalismus**, *capitalism*, **der Bassist**, *bass guitarist*, **der Protestant**, *protestant*

Feminine groups

■ Feminine are: names of females; names of ships, makes of aeroplane; numbers as nouns; German rivers (exceptions: **der Rhein**, **der Main**, **der Neckar**, **der Inn**, **der Lech**). Non-German rivers ending **-a** or **-e** are also feminine; others are masculine:

> **die Frau,** *woman,* **die Scharnhorst, die Boeing, die Sieben**, *(the) seven*, **die Donau**, *Danube*, **die Wolga**, *Volga*, **die Themse**, *Thames*

■ Feminine forms of traders, workers, and many animals are made by adding **-in**:

> **die Gärtnerin**, *gardener*, **die Sängerin**, *singer*, **die Hündin**, *bitch*

Often an umlaut is added where this is possible (as in **Hund** → **Hündin** above).

■ Nouns ending **-ei**, **-ie**, **-ion**, **-heit**, **-keit**, **-schaft**, **-tät**, **-ung** are feminine (these are mostly abstract nouns):

> **die Gärtnerei**, *gardening*, **die Chemie**, *chemistry*, **die Nation**, *nation*, **die Klugheit**, *cleverness*, **die Einigkeit**, *unity*, **die Errungenschaft**, *achievement*, **die Rarität**, *rarity*, **die Regierung**, *government*

■ Nouns ending -**a** and most (though beware, not all!) nouns ending **-e** are feminine:

> **die Tuba**, *tuba*, **die Klippe**, *cliff*

Neuter groups

■ Neuter are: names of continents, countries, towns, and the German Länder (common exceptions: **die Bundesrepublik Deutschland**, *the Federal Republic*, **die Vereinigten Staaten** (pl.), *the United States*, **die Schweiz**, *Switzerland*, **die Türkei**, *Turkey*, **die Tschechoslowakei**, *Czechoslovakia*):

> **(das) Europa**, *Europe*, **(das) Deutschland**, *Germany*, **(das) Köln**, *Cologne*, **(das) Bayern**, *Bavaria*

Country names that are not neuter always have the article. *To* is **nach** with neuter countries, **in** with masculines, feminines, and plurals.

■ Neuter are names of metals (exceptions: **die Bronze**, *bronze*, **der Stahl**, *steel*); chemicals; letters of the alphabet; fractions:

> **das Eisen**, *iron*, **das Dioxin**, *dioxin*, **das A**, *A*, **das Drittel**, *third*

■ The names of the young of humans and animals are neuter:

> **das Kind**, *child*, **das Baby**, *baby*, **das Lamm**, *lamb*, **das Kalb**, *calf*, **das Junge** (adjectival noun), *cub*

■ Neuter are nouns ending **-lein** and **-chen**. These indicate diminutives:

> **das Fräulein**, *girl*, **das Mädchen**, *girl*

■ Nouns ending **-tum** and **-um** are neuter (exceptions: **der Reichtum**, *wealth*, **der Irrtum**, *mistake*):

> **das Eigentum**, *property*, **das Zentrum**, *centre*

■ Infinitives (and other parts of speech) used as nouns are neuter:

> **das Lachen**, *laughing*

■ Foreign nouns ending **-ment**, **-fon**, **-ett** are neuter:

> **das Experiment**, *experiment*, **das Mikrofon**, *microphone*, **das Parkett**, *(theatre) stalls*

■ Most (but beware, by no means all!) nouns beginning **Ge-** or ending **-nis** are neuter:

das Gebäude, *building*, **das Geheimnis**, *secret*

Gender of compound nouns

Compound nouns have the same gender as the last element of which they are composed:

die Stadt, *town* → **die Großstadt**, *city*
das Haus, *house* → **das Rathaus**, *town hall*
der Baum, *tree* → **der Apfelbaum**, *apple tree*

■ **Teil**, *part* is masculine, but some of its compounds are masculine, some neuter:

der Vorteil, *advantage*	**das Urteil**, *verdict*
der Nachteil, *disadvantage*	**das Gegenteil**, *opposite*
der Anteil, *share*	**das Abteil**, *compartment*

■ **Meter** and its metric-measurement compounds (**Kilometer**, **Zentimeter**, etc.) though officially neuter are usually treated as masculine.

Nouns with different genders, depending on meaning

der Band, *volume, book*	**die Band**, *band, group*	**das Band**, *tape, ribbon*
der Bund, *union*		**das Bund**, *bundle*
der Erbe, *heir*		**das Erbe**, *inheritance*
der Gehalt, *capacity*		**das Gehalt**, *salary*
der Golf, *gulf, bay*		**das Golf**, *golf*
der Gummi, *eraser*		**das Gummi**, *rubber*
der Heide, *heathen*	**die Heide**, *heath*	
der Hut, *hat*	**die Hut**, *protection*	
der Junge, *boy*		**das Junge**, *cub*

der Kiefer, *jaw*	**die Kiefer**, *pine*	
der Kunde, *customer*	**die Kunde**, *news*	
der Leiter, *leader, head*	**die Leiter**, *ladder*	
	die Mark, *mark (coin)*	**das Mark**, *marrow*
der Messer, *surveyor*		**das Messer**, *knife*
der Militär, *military man*		**das Militär**, *the military*
der Moment, *moment*		**das Moment**, *factor*
der Otter, *otter*	**die Otter**, *adder*	
der Pack, *package*		**das Pack**, *mob*
der Schild, *shield*		**das Schild**, *sign (board)*
der See, *lake*	**die See**, *sea*	
	die Steuer, *tax*	**das Steuer**, *rudder*
der Stift, *peg, drawing-pin*		**das Stift**, *foundation*
der Tau, *dew*		**das Tau**, *rope*
der Tor, *fool*		**das Tor**, *goal, gate*
der Verdienst, *earnings*		**das Verdienst**, *service*
der Weise, *sage*	**die Weise**, *manner, way*	

Gender traps!

The following nouns have genders that look unlikely:

das Fräulein, *girl*	**das Mitglied**, *member*
die Geisel, *hostage*	**die Person**, *person*
das Genie, *genius*	**die Wache**, *guard, sentry*
das Mädchen, *girl*	**die Waise**, *orphan*

CASE OF NOUNS

Nouns and pronouns are used in four cases in German: the nominative, the accusative, the genitive, and the dative.

■ The nominative is used for the subject of the sentence, and also for the complement of the verbs **sein**, *to be*, **werden**, *to become*, **bleiben**, *to remain*, **heißen**, *to be called*, and a few others.

> **der Hund bellte**, *the dog barked*
> **der Hund ist ein Dackel**, *the dog is a dachshund*

■ The accusative is used for the direct object, and after some prepositions (see p. 160). It is also used for definite adverbial expressions of time (see p. 212):

> **er streichelte den Hund**, *he stroked the dog*
> **er ging rund um den Hund**, *he walked around the dog*
> **sie kommt nächsten Mittwoch**, *she's coming next Wednesday*

■ The genitive is the case which shows possession. It is also used after some prepositions (see p. 160), and for indefinite adverbial expressions of time (see p. 213).

> **der Hund meines Mannes**, *my husband's dog*
> **anstatt des Hundes**, *instead of the dog*
> **eines Tages wird es passieren**, *one day it will happen*

In English a genitive may be placed in front of another noun to show possession:

> *Peter's car; my parents' house*

This is only possible in German with personal names (there is no apostrophe); otherwise the genitive follows the noun:

> **Peters Auto; das Haus meiner Eltern**

■ The dative is the indirect-object case; with some verbs the only object is in the dative (see pp. 49–50). It is also used after many prepositions (see pp. 159 and 160) and with many adjectives (see pp. 110–1):

sie gab dem Hund mein Abendessen, *she gave my supper to the dog*
mit dem Hund, *with the dog*
der Hund ist seinem Frauchen sehr gehorsam, *the dog is very obedient to his mistress*

Case changes in nouns

The case of a noun is indicated largely by the preceding article (see p. 86). Nouns also make the following case changes, however:

■ Almost all masculine nouns which form their plural in **-n** or **-en** also add this ending to all cases of the singular except the nominative:

der Russe, *Russian*

	singular	*plural*
nominative	**der Russe**	**die Russen**
accusative	**den Russen**	**die Russen**
genitive	**des Russen**	**der Russen**
dative	**dem Russen**	**den Russen**

Do not be surprised to hear these nouns used without the **-(e)n** in the singular in conversation.

□ Nouns ending **-or** add **-en** in the plural only. Their genitive singular adds **-s**. The stress moves to the **o** in the plural:

der Professor: genitive singular, **des Professors**
plural, **die Professoren**

□ **Herr** adds **-n** throughout the singular **(Herrn)**, **-en** in the plural **(Herren)**.

□ Seven masculine nouns ending **-e** add **-ns** instead of **-n** in the genitive singular:

der Name, *name*

	singular	*plural*
nominative	**der Name**	**die Namen**
accusative	**den Namen**	**die Namen**
genitive	**des Namens**	**der Namen**
dative	**dem Namen**	**den Namen**

The other nouns in this group are: **der Buchstabe**, *letter*, **der Friede**, *peace*, **der Funke**, *spark*, **der Gedanke**, *thought*, **der Glaube**, *belief*, and **der Wille**, *will*. All except **der Buchstabe** may occasionally be found with the **-n** in the nominative too:

> **der Friede** or **der Frieden**, *peace*

One neuter, **das Herz**, *heart*, also behaves in this way; it stays as **das Herz** in the accusative, however.

■ All other masculine nouns and neuter nouns add **-s** or **-es** in the genitive singular. The extra **e** is obligatory with nouns already ending in an 's' sound. It is also frequently found with monosyllables and with nouns with their stress on the last syllable:

> **der Gipfel**, *peak*: genitive singular, **des Gipfels**
> **der Schuß**, *shot*: genitive singular, **des Schusses** (for **ß** to **ss**, see p. 235)
> **der Baum**, *tree*: genitive singular, **des Baum(e)s**
> **das Geschenk**, *present*: genitive singular, **des Geschenk(e)s**

Neuter nouns ending **-nis** add **-ses** in the genitive:

> **das Gefängnis**, *prison*: genitive singular, **des Gefängnisses**

The genitive sounds rather formal in spoken German. Very frequently **von** + dative is substituted:

> **das Haus meiner Eltern** → **das Haus von meinen Eltern**, *my parents' house*

■ Personal names, both masculine and feminine, add **-s** in the genitive:

Peters Auto; Lauras Auto; Mutters Auto; Kohls Auto

If the name already ends in an 's' sound (**-s**, **-ß**, **-x**, **-z**) it simply adds an apostrophe for the genitive, or, occasionally in written German, **-ens**:

Hans' Auto or **Hansens Auto**

More frequently **von** is used:

das Auto von Hans

Titles in the genitive, except **Herr**, are not declined:

Kanzler Kohls Außenminister, *Chancellor Kohl's Foreign Minister*
Herrn Schmidts Nase, *Herr Schmidt's nose*

■ Masculine and neuter monosyllables formerly added **-e** to their dative singular. This **e** can still be found in some common expressions: **nach Hause**, *home*; **zu Hause**, *at home*; **auf dem Lande**, *in the country*.

■ All nouns except those with plural **-s** or already ending **-n** add **-n** to their dative plural:

der Mann: nominative plural, **die Männer**
dative plural, **den Männern**

■ Adjectives being used as nouns take a capital letter and the appropriate gender; they still change according to case as if they were adjectives (see Adjectives as nouns, pp. 109–10):

der Reisende, *the (male) traveller*
ein Reisender, *a (male) traveller*

■ A noun in apposition goes into the same case as the noun it stands in apposition to:

er war früher bei Robotron, der größten Firma in dieser Stadt, *he used to be with Robotron, the biggest firm in that town* (**Robotron** is in the dative—after **bei**—so **Firma** is also in the dative)

PLURAL OF NOUNS

There are no watertight rules for the formation of the plural in German. As a very general rule, most masculine nouns have plural **⸚e**, most feminines **-(e)n**, most neuters **⸚er**. However, the plural really has to learned with the noun. The following are indications of what a plural is likely to be, rather than rules: there are numerous exceptions.

Plural of masculine nouns

Basically **⸚e.**

However, about 50 just add **-e** and do not modify. Among the commonest that do not modify are:

der Arm, *arm*	**der Punkt**, *point*
der Hund, *dog*	**der Ruf**, *cry*
der Laut, *sound*	**der Schuh**, *shoe*
der Monat, *month*	**der Tag**, *day*
der Ort, *place*	**der Versuch**, *attempt*
der Pfad, *path*	

In addition:

- Nouns ending **-el**, **-en**, **-er** → no ending, some modify
- The following → **⸚er** (**-er** in the case of **Geist**)

der Geist, *spirit*	**der Rand**, *edge*
der Gott, *God*	**der Reichtum**, *wealth* (pl. *riches*)
der Irrtum, *mistake*	**der Strauch**, *shrub*
der Mann, *man*	**der Wald**, *forest*
der Mund, *mouth*	**der Wurm**, *worm*

- Nouns ending **-e** → **-n**

Many nouns in this category also add the **-n** in the singular. See pp. 97–8.

Additionally, a group of about 50 masculines not ending **-e** form their plural with **-en**. Many of these do not add the **-en** in the singular (e.g. **der Staat**, *state*, **der See**, *lake*, **der Schmerz**, *pain*, **der Vetter**, *cousin*).

Plural of feminine nouns

Basically **-(e)n**.

All feminine nouns of more than one syllable form their plural this way, except **die Mutter (¨)**, *mother*, **die Tochter (¨)**, *daughter*, and nouns ending **-nis**, which double their **s** and add **e**:

> **die Kenntnis**, *(piece of) knowledge*: plural, **die Kenntnisse**

In addition:

■ About 30 monosyllables form their plural with **¨e**. Some of the commoner are

die Frucht, *fruit*	**die Nuß**, *nut*
die Hand, *hand*	**die Stadt**, *town*
die Kuh, *cow*	**die Wand**, *wall*
die Maus, *mouse*	**die Wurst**, *sausage*
die Nacht, *night*	

■ Nouns ending **-in** double their **n** before adding **-en**:

> **die Gärtnerin**, *gardener*: plural, **die Gärtnerinnen**

Modern journalistic usage is to spell this plural with a capital **I** in the middle of the word to produce a unisex version of the otherwise strongly masculine-looking **-er** form:

> **die BürgerInnen**, *male and female citizens*

Plural of neuter nouns

Basically **¨er**.

Neuters with plural **-er** always modify if possible. In addition:

■ Neuter nouns ending **-el, -en, -er** → no change (exception: **das Kloster (¨)**, *monastery*)

- Nouns ending **-lein, -chen**→no change
- Nouns ending **-nis**→**-nisse**

    das Ereignis, *event*: plural, **die Ereignisse**

- The following five nouns→**-(e)n**

    das Auge, *eye*, **das Bett**, *bed*, **das Ende**, *end*, **das Hemd**, *shirt*, **das Ohr**, *ear*

These neuters add the **-(e)n** in the plural only.

- About 50 monosyllables→**-e**

Among the commonest are:

das Bein, *leg*
das Boot, *boat*
das Brot, *loaf*
das Fest, *festival*
das Gleis, *rail*
das Haar, *hair*
das Heft, *exercise book*
das Jahr, *year*
das Meer, *sea*
das Paar, *pair*
das Pferd, *horse*
das Recht, *right*
das Schaf, *sheep*
das Schiff, *ship*
das Schwein, *pig*
das Spiel, *game*
das Stück, *piece*
das Tier, *animal*
das Tor, *goal*
das Zelt, *tent*
das Ziel, *aim*

Plural of nouns of foreign origin

Where these have been assimilated into the language over many years they follow the rules and indications above; new and relatively new foreign nouns take **-s**. Some hover, e.g. **der Balkon**, *balcony* (pl.: **-s** or **-e**).

Most foreign nouns ending **-o** take **-s**; those ending **-a** usually change it to **-en** in the plural (**das Drama**, *drama*, **die Dramen**; **die Firma**, *firm*, **die Firmen**—but **das Komma**, *comma*, **die Kommas**).

Plural of compound nouns

Compound nouns have the same plural as the last element of which they are composed.

die Stadt (¨-e), *city*, so: **die Hauptstadt** (¨-e), *capital*

Compounds of **-mann** form their plural with **-leute**:

der Kaufmann, *merchant*: plural, **die Kaufleute**

Exceptions: **der Schneemann** (¨-er), *snowman*, **der Staatsmann** (¨-er), *statesman*. And notice **der Ehemann**, *husband*: plural, **die Ehemänner** = *husbands*; plural, **die Eheleute** = *married couples*.

Nouns with different plurals for different meanings

das Band, *bond* (**die Bande**); *tape* (**die Bänder**)
die Bank, *bench* (**die Bänke**); *bank* (**die Banken**)
der Block, *alliance* (**die Blöcke**); *pad of paper, block of flats* (**die Blocks**)
die Mutter, *mother* (**die Mütter**); (tech.) *nut* (**die Muttern**)
der Strauß, *ostrich* (**die Strauße**); *bunch of flowers* (**die Sträuße**)
das Wort, *word* (**die Worte**, *connected words*; **die Wörter**, *unconnected words*)

Nouns with no singular form

The following nouns only occur in the plural:

die Leute, *people*
die Ferien, *holidays*
die Eltern, *parents*
die Großeltern, *grandparents*

Other nouns are substituted for a singular: **die Person**, *person*; **der Ferientag**, *day off*; **der Vater**, *father*, **die Mutter**, *mother*, etc. **Der Elternteil** exists for *parent*, but is literary and clumsy.

Singular for plural

■ The following nouns are singular in German and plural in English:

die Brille, *spectacles*
der Dank, *thanks*
das Feuerwerk, *fireworks*
die Hose, *trousers*
der Inhalt, *contents*
der Lohn, *wages*
das Mittelalter, *the Middle Ages*
die Schere, *scissors*
die Treppe, *stairs*
die Umgebung, *surroundings*
die Zange, *tongs*

Many of the above have plurals with the sense of 'more than one set of':

zwei Treppen hoch, *up two flights of stairs*

■ The following nouns are singular in English and plural in German:

die Kosten, *cost*
die Möbel, *furniture*
die Noten, *(sheet) music*
die Zinsen, *interest*
(die) Weihnachten, *Christmas*
(die) Ostern, *Easter*
(die) Pfingsten, *Whitsun*

When the three in the right-hand column are the subject of a sentence, however, they are used with a singular verb:

bald kommt Weihnachten, *Christmas will soon be here*

■ Masculine and neuter nouns used as expressions of quantity do not pluralize:

zwei Glas Wein, *two glasses of wine*

Feminine expressions of quantity do:

zwei Flaschen Wein, *two bottles of wine*

Note that *of* is not translated after expressions of quantity.

I Adjectives

In German, an adjective standing in front of a noun adds endings to show whether that noun is singular or plural, what its gender is, and what case it stands in. The endings the adjective adds depend on what sort of article is standing before it. In general, the more the article tells you about the noun, the less the adjective does.

Adjectives only add an ending if they stand in front of a noun—adjectives standing after the verb remain unchanged. Where two or more adjectives stand in front of a noun they both take the same ending.

ADJECTIVE ENDINGS

Adjectives after der

The adjective endings following the definite article **der**, *the*, are as follows:

	SINGULAR		
	masculine	*feminine*	*neuter*
nom.	der rot**e** Hut, *the red hat*	die rot**e** Lampe, *the red lamp*	das rot**e** Buch, *the red book*
acc.	den rot**en** Hut	die rot**e** Lampe	das rot**e** Buch
gen.	des rot**en** Hut(e)s	der rot**en** Lampe	des rot**en** Buch(e)s
dat.	dem rot**en** Hut	der rot**en** Lampe	dem rot**en** Buch

	PLURAL
nom.	die rot**en** Autos, *the red cars*
acc.	die rot**en** Autos
gen.	der rot**en** Autos
dat.	den rot**en** Autos

■ Like adjectives after **der** are adjectives after: **welcher**, *which*; **irgendwelcher**, *some . . . or other*; **dieser**, *this/that*; **jener**, *that*; **jeder**, *every*; **mancher**, *many a*.

Adjectives after ein

The adjective endings following the indefinite article **ein**, *a*, are as follows:

	SINGULAR		
	masculine	*feminine*	*neuter*
nom.	ein rot**er** Hut, *a red hat*	eine rot**e** Lampe, *a red lamp*	ein rot**es** Buch, *a red book*
acc.	einen rot**en** Hut	eine rot**e** Lampe	ein rot**es** Buch
gen.	eines rot**en** Hut(e)s	einer rot**en** Lampe	eines rot**en** Buch(e)s
dat.	einem rot**en** Hut	einer rot**en** Lampe	einem rot**en** Buch

	PLURAL
nom.	keine rot**en** Autos, *no red cars*
acc.	keine rot**en** Autos
gen.	keiner rot**en** Autos
dat.	keinen rot**en** Autos

■ Like adjectives after **ein** are adjectives after: **kein**, *no*; **irgendein**, *some . . . or other*; and the possessives **mein**, *my*, **dein**, *your*, **sein**, *his*, *its*, **ihr**, *her*, *their*, **unser**, *our*, **euer**, *your*, **Ihr**, *your*. Do not be tempted to add **unser** and **euer** to the '**der**' group because they end in **-er**!

■ **Irgendein** has no plural form: **irgendwelche** (see p. 151) is used instead.

Adjectives without an article

Adjectives standing in front of a noun but with no preceding article take the following endings. These give much of the information about gender, case, and number that would otherwise be given by the article:

	SINGULAR		
	masculine	*feminine*	*neuter*
nom.	weiß**er** Wein, *white wine*	frisch**e** Milch, *fresh milk*	neu**es** Geld, *new money*
acc.	weiß**en** Wein	frisch**e** Milch	neu**es** Geld
gen.	weiß**en** Wein(e)s	frisch**er** Milch	neu**en** Geld(e)s
dat.	weiß**em** Wein	frisch**er** Milch	neu**em** Geld

	PLURAL
nom.	jung**e** Leute, *young people*
acc.	jung**e** Leute
gen.	jung**er** Leute
dat.	jung**en** Leuten

■ Notice the **-en** genitive form of masculine and neuter singular. In fact, the genitive forms are usually avoided if possible, often by using **von**, *of*.

■ The above endings are used on an adjective that follows an indeclinable word or phrase like

ein bißchen, *a little*
ein paar, *a few*
lauter, *nothing but*
mehr/weniger, *more/less*
-lei words such as **allerlei**, *all kinds of*, **derlei**, *such kinds of*

They are also used after names in the genitive:

Mutters neues Kleid, *mother's new dress*

and after numbers:

zwei junge Leute, *two young people*

Adjectives without endings

■ Adjectives when they do not stand before a noun do not have endings:

die Milch ist frisch, *the milk is fresh*

■ Adjectives ending in **-a** and those formed from town names by the addition of **-er** have no further endings:

eine prima Idee, *a great idea*
ein lila Sofa, *a purple sofa*
die Berliner Luft, *the Berlin air*

Adjectives after indefinites

Indefinite pronoun + adjective

After **nichts**, *nothing*, **(et)was**, *something*, **allerlei**, *all kinds of*, and other indefinite pronouns an adjective has a capital letter. It takes the ending **-es** in the nominative and accusative and the ending **-em** in the dative (the genitive is rarely found):

hier ist etwas Gutes, *here's something good*
hast du nichts Interessanteres?, *have you nothing more interesting?*
mit allerlei Gutem, *with all kinds of good things*

■ If the adjective is itself an indefinite it takes the ending but no capital:

etwas anderes, *something different*

■ With **alles** the endings differ: nominative and accusative: **alles Neue**, *everything new*; dative: **allem Neuen**.

Indefinite adjective + adjective + noun

This construction is almost always found in the plural. With the indefinite adjectives

bestimmte, *certain*
einige, *some*
einzelne, *individual*
folgende, *the following*
gewisse, *certain*
mehrere, *several*
verschiedene, *various*
viele, *many*
wenige, *few*

—and other less common indefinites—endings on both the

indefinite and the adjective are the same: they are, and behave like, two adjectives, their endings determined by what, if anything, stands in front of them:

> **viele alte Leute,** *many old people*
> **die wenigen jungen Leute**, *the few young people*

However, **alle/sämtliche**, *all*, **beide**, *both*, **solche**, *such*, and **manche**, *many*, are followed by an adjective declined as after the plural **die**:

> **alle guten Leute**, *all good people*

Adjectives losing an e

■ Adjectives ending **-el** (always) and **-en**, **-er** (sometimes) drop the **e** when they have an ending:

> **übel**: **eine üble Laune**, *a bad mood*
> **finster**: **ein finst(e)rer Mensch**, *a sinister person*

The **e** of the comparative **-er** ending is never dropped, however:

> **ein schönerer Tag als gestern**, *a finer day than yesterday*

■ An **e** preceded by **-au** or **-eu** is always dropped if the adjective has an ending:

> **sauer**: **eine saure Miene**, *a cross look*
> **teuer**: **ein teures Getränk**, *an expensive drink*

■ The adjective **hoch** loses its **c** when it has an ending:

> **ein hoher Turm**, *a high tower*

ADJECTIVES AS NOUNS

All adjectives can be used as nouns, as can present and past participles. They have a capital letter and the adjective endings they would have if they were followed, according to the sense, by **Mann**, *man*, **Frau**, *woman*, or **Ding**, *thing*:

ein Reisender, *a (male) traveller ('travelling man')*
eine Reisende, *a (female) traveller ('travelling woman')*
das Gute und das Böse, *good and evil ('good thing', 'evil thing')*

If they have a qualifying adjective it takes the same ending that they have:

mit diesem müden Reisenden, *with this tired traveller*

If the adjective has an actual noun that it can refer back to it does not take a capital:

ein kleines Glas und ein großes, *a small glass and a large one*

Der Beamte, *official*, formed from an old past participle, behaves like an adjective. **Der Junge**, *boy*, originally from the adjective **jung**, *young*, now behaves like a noun; **das Junge**, *cub*, however, still behaves as an adjective.

ADJECTIVES WITH THE DATIVE

Many adjectives can be used with a dative noun or pronoun in German, almost always corresponding to *to* + noun or pronoun in English. The dative noun or pronoun usually stands before the adjective.

The commonest such adjectives are:

ähnlich, *similar*
(un)angenehm, *(dis)agreeable*
(un)begreiflich, *(in)comprehensible*
behilflich, *helpful*
(un)bekannt, *(un)familiar, (un)known*
dankbar, *grateful*
egal, *all the same*
ergeben, *devoted*
fremd, *unknown*
gehorsam, *obedient*
(gut, übel) gesinnt, *(well, badly) disposed*
gleich, *all the same*
lästig, *troublesome*
leicht, *easy*
nah(e), *near*
nützlich, *useful*
peinlich, *embarrassing*
schuldig, *in debt*

schwer, *difficult*
(un)treu, *(un)faithful*
überlegen, *superior*
unmöglich, *impossible*
unterlegen, *inferior*
unzugänglich, *inaccessible*

das ist vielen Leuten unbegreiflich, *that is incomprehensible to many people*
wie kann ich Ihnen behilflich sein?, *how can I help (be helpful to) you?*

ADJECTIVES WITH THE GENITIVE

In literary German a few adjectives are found with a preceding genitive. **Bewußt**, *aware*, **gewiß**, *certain*, **sicher**, *sure*, **würdig**, *worthy*, are the commonest of these; in everyday German **von** + dative is used instead.

COMPARATIVE AND SUPERLATIVE OF ADJECTIVES

Formation of the comparative and superlative

There are two different ways to form the comparative and superlative of adjectives in English, according to the length of the adjective:

long: longer (comparative), *longest* (superlative)
extensive: more extensive (comparative), *most extensive* (superlative)

German forms the comparative and superlative in one way only, with the two endings **-er** (comparative) and **-(e)st** (superlative). There is no equivalent to the English use of *more*, *most* with longer adjectives.

Normal adjective endings are added to a comparative or superlative adjective standing in front of a noun.

■ Example: **leicht,** *easy*

□ Comparative: **leichter.**

> **es ist leichter, als es war,** *it's easier than it was*
> **das ist eine leichtere Aufgabe,** *that's an easier job*

□ Superlative, before a noun or an understood noun: **leichtest-.**

> **das ist die leichteste Aufgabe,** *that's the easiest job*
> **diese Aufgabe ist die leichteste,** *this job is (the) easiest (job)*

□ Superlative, standing alone: **am leichtesten**

> **das Leben ist in den Ländern des Westens am leichtesten,** *life is easiest in the countries of the West*

In the second type of superlative we are comparing aspects of one thing (here, aspects of life) rather than, as in the first one, several things (several jobs).

The extra **e** in the superlative is used (as above) where the word would be difficult or impossible to pronounce without it.

■ Comparative adjectives whose stem ends **-el, -en,** or **-er** usually drop the **e** in their stem when they have a further ending:

> **dunkel,** *dark*: **die dunkleren Abende,** *the darker evenings*

■ The adjectives listed below modify their vowel in the comparative and superlative, thus:

> **alt,** *old*: comparative: **älter,** superlative: **ältest-**

alt, *old*	**krank,** *sick*
arm, *poor*	**kurz,** *short*
dumm, *stupid*	**lang,** *long*
grob, *coarse*	**scharf,** *sharp*
hart, *hard*	**schwach,** *weak*
jung, *young*	**schwarz,** *black*
kalt, *cold*	**stark,** *strong*
klug, *clever*	**warm,** *warm*

Modification is optional for:

blaß, *pale*
fromm, *pious*
gesund, *healthy*
glatt, *smooth*
naß, *wet*
rot, *red*
schmal, *narrow*

■ The following adjectives have irregular comparatives and/or superlatives:

	comparative	*superlative*
groß, *big*	größer	größt-
gut, *good*	besser	best-
hoch, *high*	höher	höchst-
nah, *near*	näher	nächst-
viel, *much*	mehr	meist-

Mehr, *more*, and **weniger**, *less*, do not take endings:

du hast mehr Geld, er hat weniger Geld, *you have more money, he has less money*

■ The following adjectives, which are always used in front of a noun and never stand alone, have only comparative and superlative forms. In each case the superlative is formed by addng **-st** to the comparative form:

äußer-, *outer* (**äußerst-**, *outermost*)
hinter-, *back* (**hinterst-**, *hindmost*)
inner-, *inner* (**innerst-**, *innermost*)
mittler-, *middle* (**mittlerst-**, *most central*)
nieder-, *inferior* (**niederst-**, *most inferior*)
ober-, *upper* (**oberst-**, *uppermost*)
unter-, *lower* (**unterst-**, *lowest*)
vorder-, *front* (**vorderst-**, *foremost*)

■ Past participles used as adjectives form their comparative with **mehr** and their superlative with **am meisten** or **meist-**:

dies ist das am meisten gekaufte Waschpulver / das meistgekaufte Waschpulver, *this is the most (frequently) purchased washing powder*

Using the comparative and superlative

■ After a comparison *than* is **als**; after expressions of equality (and after negated expressions of equality) *as* is **wie**:

> **er ist älter als ich**, *he's older than I am*
> **er ist (nicht) so alt wie sie**, *he's (not) as old as she is*

In conversation **wie** ('**älter wie ich**') is very often also heard in the first type of sentence above.

Than ever after a comparative is **denn je**:

> **es ist teurer denn je**, *it's dearer than ever*

■ *More and more* is **immer** + comparative:

> **die Fragen werden immer schwieriger . . .** , *the questions get more and more difficult . . .*
> **. . . und immer länger**, *. . . and longer and longer*

■ *The more . . . the more* is **je . . . desto**:

> **je länger ich warte, desto kälter werd' ich**, *the longer I wait the colder I get*

The word order of the main clause is always **desto** + comparative, followed by inverted order. **Um so** may be used instead of **desto**.

■ With quite a number of common adjectives a comparative can be used to mean '*fairly . . .* ':

> **eine längere Zeit**, *a fairly long time*
> **eine jüngere Dame**, *a relatively young lady*

■ In English, *most* can mean simply '*extremely*', in which case it corresponds to the superlative adverbs **höchst** (not used with monosyllables) or **äußerst**:

> **das ist äußerst nett von Ihnen**, *that's most kind of you*
> **es war höchst unangenehm**, *it was most unpleasant*

DEMONSTRATIVE ADJECTIVES

Demonstrative adjectives (*this, that* in English) stand in exactly the same relationship to nouns as definite and indefinite articles do. They are in fact sometimes known as demonstrative articles.

The demonstrative adjectives in German are **dieser**, *this, that*, and **jener**, *that*. They both decline like **der** (see pp. 86–7).

■ **Jener** is uncommon in modern German. **Dieser** is used for both *this* and *that*. Where a differentiation has to be made an emphasized **der** is used for *that* in speech:

> **darf ich *den* Kuchen haben, bitte?**, *may I have that cake please?*

■ **Da** (or **dort**) may be added after the noun, in which case the **der** and the **da** have equal stress:

> **ja, den Kuchen da (dort)**, *yes, that cake*

▶ **Dieser**, **jener**, and **der** can also be used as pronouns (= *this one, that one*). See Demonstrative Pronouns, pp. 137–8.

POSSESSIVE ADJECTIVES

The possessive adjectives are

> **mein**, *mine*
> **dein**, *your*
> **sein**, *his; its*
> **ihr**, *her*
> **unser**, *our*
> **euer**, *your*
> **Ihr**, *your* (polite form)
> **ihr**, *your*
>
> **das ist mein Freund**, *that is my friend*

They all decline like **ein** (see p. 87); their endings are determined by the gender and case of the noun that follows them.

■ When **unser** and **euer** have an ending the **e** of the stem is frequently dropped. This is especially the case with **euer**:

> **das ist eure Mutter?**, *that's your mother?*

In the forms **unseren** and **unserem**, **eueren** and **euerem** the second **e** is often dropped instead, especially in spoken German:

> **wir kamen mit unserm Vater**, *we came with our father*

■ **Euer** with a capital is used for *Your* in titles:

> **Eure Majestät**, *Your Majesty*
> **Eure Eminenz**, *Your Eminence*

■ The genitive forms of the possessive pronoun (singular: **dessen, deren, dessen**; plural: **deren**) are used instead of the possessive adjective where it is necessary to avoid ambiguity:

> **sie fuhr mit Ilse und ihrem Freund**, *she was travelling with her friend, and with Ilse*
> **sie fuhr mit Ilse und deren Freund**, *she was travelling with Ilse and her (Ilse's) friend* (**deren** is feminine, to agree with **Ilse**)

► *My, your, his, her, our, their* are possessive adjectives and stand in front of a noun. *Mine, yours, his, hers, ours, theirs* are possessive pronouns and stand alone. Don't confuse them! For the possessive pronouns in German see pp. 135–7.

THE INTERROGATIVE ADJECTIVE

The interrogative adjective is **welcher**, *which*:

> **welche Jacke ist deine?**, *which jacket is yours?*
> **welchen Jungen meinst du?**, *which boy do you mean?*

Welcher declines like **der**. See p. 86.

■ As well as beginning a direct question, **welcher** + noun can introduce an indirect question, with subordinate order:

> **ich weiß nicht mehr, welche Jacke ich anhatte,**
> *I don't remember which jacket I had on*

■ In older and literary German **welch** without any ending is the equivalent of **was für**:

> **welch eine (was für eine) Schande!**, *what a disgrace!*

▶ **Welcher** can stand alone without a noun as an interrogative pronoun (= *which one*, see p. 144) or as a relative pronoun (= *which* or *that*, see pp. 139–40).

INDEFINITE ADJECTIVES

Indefinite adjectives, as a group, include in English such words as *several, such, each, every*. In German almost all of them can be used both as adjectives and as pronouns and so they are more conveniently grouped together. A complete alphabetical list of all common indefinites, with both their adjective and their pronoun uses, can be found on pp. 144–58.

I Adverbs

Adverbs describe or modify a verb:

sie singt schön, *she sings beautifully*

or an adjective:

sie hat eine unwahrscheinlich schöne Stimme, *she has an incredibly beautiful voice*

or another adverb:

sie singt unwahrscheinlich schön, *she sings incredibly beautifully*

or very occasionally a preposition or a conjunction:

oben im Apfelbaum, *up in the apple tree*
mitten in der Rede, *in the middle of the speech*
selbst wenn er das getan hat . . . , *even if he's done that . . .*

ADVERB FORMATION

Most adjectives in German can be used unchanged, with no endings, as adverbs. Quite a few adverbs exist only as adverbs, however (**völlig**, *completely*; **unten**, *downstairs*; **außerdem**, *besides*, etc.).

Adverbs ending -weise

Many adverbs are formed from a noun (or occasionally an adjective + **-er**) + **weise**. For example:

from nouns:

> **teilweise**, *partly*
> **zeitweise**, *temporarily*
> **beispielsweise**, *for example*
> **ausnahmsweise**, *as an exception*

from adjectives:

> **glücklicherweise**, *luckily*
> **komischerweise**, *funnily enough*

A few of them may also be used as adjectives:

> **eine teilweise Senkung**, *a partial reduction*

Gern

The adverb **gern**, *gladly*, may be used with verbs to mean '*like*':

> **ich hab' dich gern**, *I like you*
> **ich esse gern Blumenkohl**, *I like cauliflower*
> **ich bin gern in Berlin**, *I like (being in) Berlin*

With **gern haben**, **gern** goes to the end of the sentence; in the expression **ich hätte gern**, *I should like*, **gern** always follows the verb; otherwise it stands in the normal position for a 'manner' adverb. See Word Order, p. 221.

Gern may have an **-e**, **gerne**, especially when standing alone:

> **kommst du mit? — Ja, gerne**, *are you coming along?—Yes, with pleasure*

► **Gern** has an irregular comparative and superlative: see p. 121.

Hier and da

These two adverbs can only be used to mean *here* and *there* when no motion is involved. When motion is involved **hierher** and **dahin** must be used:

sie steht da, *she's standing there*
sie geht dahin, *she's going there*

er bleibt hier, *he's staying here*
er kommt hierher, *he's coming here*

The **hin** or **her** can split off like a separable prefix:

da geht sie wieder hin, *she's off there again*

The above also applies to **dort/dorthin**, *(to) there* (a more precisely localized place than **da**) and the question adverb **wo/wohin**, *(to) where*:

wo bist du?, *where are you?*
wohin gehst du? / wo gehst du hin?, *where are you going (to)?*

A similar use of **hin** for motion (though without the possibility of splitting off) is found with:

irgendwo/irgendwohin, *somewhere or other*
überall/überallhin, *everywhere*

Woher, *from where*, **irgendwoher**, *from somewhere or other*, and **überallher**, *from everywhere*, do not present a problem, since the *from* is obligatory in English.

COMPARATIVE AND SUPERLATIVE OF ADVERBS

Adverbs, like adjectives, form their comparative with the ending **-er** and their superlative with **-(e)st**.

■ Example: **leicht**, *easily*

□ Comparative: **leichter**

es läßt sich leichter machen, *it can be done more easily*

□ Superlative: **am leichtesten**

das läßt sich am leichtesten machen, *that can be done most easily*

The extra **e** in the superlative is used (as above) where the word would be difficult or impossible to pronounce without it.

The superlative adverb form is identical with that of the adjective when standing alone. See p. 112.

■ Adjectives that modify their vowel in the comparative and superlative also modify when used as adverbs. See list, p. 112.

Oft, *often*, also modifies (**öfter, am öftesten**), though **häufiger**, *more frequently*, and **am häufigsten**, *most frequently*, tend to be used instead.

■ The following adverbs have irregular comparatives and superlatives:

	comparative	*superlative*
bald, *soon*	eher	am ehesten
gern, *gladly*	lieber	am liebsten

▶ For adjectives with irregular comparatives and superlatives (most of which can also be used as adverbs), see p. 113.

■ A group of superlative adverbs ending **-stens** correspond (generally) to the English *at (the)* + superlative. The commonest are:

frühstens, *at the earliest*	**nächstens**, *soon*
höchstens, *at most*	**spätestens**, *at the latest*
letztens, *recently*	**strengstens**, *most strictly*
meistens, *mostly*	**wärmstens**, *most warmly*
mindestens, *at least*	**wenigstens**, *at least*

The common spoken form **zumindestens**, *at least*, is a mixture of **mindestens**, included above, and the adverb **zumindest**, *at least*.

▶ For **erstens**, *firstly*, etc., see Numbers, p. 206.

■ *Than* after a comparative adverb is **als**, *as* after an expression of equality is **wie**:

er macht es leichter als ich, *he does it more easily than I (do)*

er macht es genau so leicht wie früher, *he does it just as easily as he used to*

This is similar to the constructions used with adjectives (see p. 114).

▶ For the order of adverbs and their position in the sentence, see Word Order, p. 221.

ALPHABETICAL LIST OF ADVERBIAL PARTICLES

Adverbial particles—words like **mal**, **doch**, **ja**—are much used, especially in spoken German, to give flavour to the language. There are English equivalents, but English relies more on differences of intonation and emphasis and uses particles much less freely. So they can rarely be translated directly from German into English. The following list gives the main adverbial particles with their basic meaning and examples of their use in various related meanings.

aber, *but*

■ adds emphasis

das war aber ausgezeichnet, *that was really outstanding*

du hast es schon wieder verloren?—Aber nein!, *you've lost it again?—No, of course I haven't*

allerdings, *admittedly*

■ *however, though* (concedes)

ihr Auto will ich kaufen, allerdings muß der Preis vernünftiger sein, *I intend to buy her car, though the price will have to be more reasonable*

■ agrees strongly with what is seen as obvious

> **es wird schwer sein — Ja, allerdings**, *it'll be hard—Well yes, of course*

Freilich is used with the same meaning in both instances. **Zwar** (see also p. 131) can be used with the first meaning above.

auch, *also*

■ *even*

> **auch du würdest es tun können**, *even you would be able to do it*
> **auch nicht meine Mutter würde so was sagen**, *even my mother wouldn't say something like that*
> **auch wenn er schreibt, werde ich kein Wort sagen**, *even if he writes I won't say a word*

■ *either* (with a negative)

> **sie macht es auch nicht**, *she won't do it either*
> **ich auch nicht,** *me neither*

■ correcting something that should have been obvious

> **das hat er auch nicht gesagt**, *but that's not what he said*

■ concessive *-ever*, with **wer, was, wie, wann** (producing *whoever, whatever, however, whenever*)

> **wie groß es auch sein mag, werden wir es gern liefern**, *however large it may be we'll gladly deliver it*

Note the position of **auch**.

■ emphasis

> **das mußt du auch tun**, *you really will have to do that, too*

denn, *then*

■ *then* (the English concessive *then*)

gehst du denn?, *are you going, then?*

Then = if that's the case is **dann**:

dann gehe ich!, *then (in that case) I'm going*

So is *then = at that point in time* or *next:*

sie ging dann, *then she went*

In north Germany **denn** is often—confusingly—misused for **dann**.

■ in **es sei denn, daß**, *unless*, and **geschweige denn**, *much less, let alone*

ich hole ihn vom Bahnhof ab, es sei denn, daß mein Auto wieder kaputt ist, *I'll fetch him from the station, unless my car's broken down again*
radfahren kann sie nicht, geschweige denn reiten, *she can't ride a bike, let alone a horse*

doch, *yet*

■ *none the less, even so*

wir haben ihn gewarnt, aber er ist doch darauf getreten, *we warned him, but he stepped on it just the same*

Doch has stress in this use.

■ in a statement with question intonation, = **nicht wahr**

du fliegst doch heute morgen?, *your plane goes this morning, doesn't it?*

■ *surely* (with a negative)

du fliegst doch nicht mit dieser Luftlinie?, *you're surely not flying with that airline?*

■ *oh yes* (contradicting a negative statement or question, = French *si*)

> **du fliegst nicht heute — Doch!**, *you're not flying today—Oh yes I am*

It is sometimes strengthened with **ja** in this use: **ja doch!**

■ with the imperative, = *come on (now)*

> **sei doch vernünftig!**, *come on, be reasonable*

■ with **mal**, conveys encouragement

> **tu's doch mal!**, *go on, do it!*

eben, *just*

■ *just now*

> **sie ist eben angekommen**, *she has just arrived*

Gerade can be used with the same meaning; **soeben** is stronger, = *this very minute.*

■ *just = exactly*

> **eben das meinte ich**, *that's just (exactly) what I meant*
> **ja, eben**, *yes, exactly*

This is also the meaning of **eben-** in compounds: **ebensoviel,** *just as much; exactly that much.*

■ expressing resignation

> **dann eben nicht**, *well then, we won't*
> **das ist eben kalter Kaffee**, *that's just water under the bridge then*

In south Germany **halt** is used in this sense.

eigentlich, *really*

■ *in point of fact*

es ist eigentlich viel schwerer als ich gedacht habe, *really (in fact) it's much harder than I thought*

The strengthening '*really*' is **wirklich**:

es ist wirklich schwer!, *it's really difficult!*

Similarly, as adjectives **wirklich** means *real = true*, **eigentlich** means *real = fundamental*:

der wirkliche Unterschied, *the real (true) difference*
der eigentliche Unterschied, *the real difference (the actual difference, in point of fact)*

einmal, *once*

▶ See **mal**, pp. 127–83.

etwa, *about*

■ *approximately*

etwa zehn Sekunden, *approximately ten seconds*

■ *by any chance, really*

hast du etwa Geld?, *do you have money, by any chance?*
bist du etwa müde?, *are you perhaps tired?*
du willst doch nicht etwa sagen, daß . . . , *you don't really mean to say that . . .*

Don't confuse with **etwas**, *some, somewhat*:

hast du etwas Geld?, *have you some money?*
du bist etwas müde, *you're a bit tired*

freilich, *admittedly*

▶ See **allerdings**, pp. 122–3.

gerade, *just*

▶ See **eben**, p. 125.

ja, *certainly*

- *of course*

  du wirst ihn ja kennen, *you'll know him of course*
  das weißt du ja schon, *of course, you know that already*

- underlining a fact, = *why!* or *really*

  du bist ja schon da!, *why, you're here already!*
  das ist ja blöd, *that really is stupid*
  es ist ja direkt unglaublich, *it's actually totally Incredible*

- concessive *of course*

  sie ist ja furchtbar nett, aber . . . , *she's awfully nice, of course, but . . .*

- *indeed (= nay)*

  er ist wohlhabend, ja sogar reich, *he's well off, indeed you could even say (nay) rich*

mal; einmal, *once*

Mal is the more common in the spoken language in almost all cases. If **einmal** means literally *once* (i.e. *not twice*), the stress moves to the first syllable.

- *one day, some day, sometime or other*

  ich werde Sie (ein)mal in Deutschland besuchen, *I'll visit you in Germany one day*
  es war einmal ein Riese, *once upon a time there was a giant*
  irgend einmal, *some time or other*

- *for once*

    ich will mal einen Kaffee trinken, *I'll have a coffee for once*
    (ein)mal zur Abwechslung, *just once for a change*

- with an exclamation or after **wollen**, = *just*

    sei du (ein)mal ruhig!, *you just be quiet!*
    Augenblick mal!, *just a moment*
    laß mal sehen!, *let's (just) have a look*
    wir wollen mal sehen, *we'll just have a look*

- with **noch**, = *again*

    tu's noch (ein)mal, *do it again*

Noch (ein)mal implies the repetition of a specific action; **wieder**, *again*, is more general

sie ist wieder da, *she's back again*

- **nun (ein)mal** expresses resigned acceptance

    die Sache ist nun (ein)mal so, *that's the way things are*

noch, *yet*

- *still, yet* (time)

    bist du noch da?, *are you still here?*
    er ist noch nicht dreizehn, *he's not yet thirteen*

Immer is used to strengthen **noch**, before it (**immer noch**) or after (**noch immer**).

- *left*

    wieviel Geld hast du noch?, *how much money have you left?*

- *more, further*

    noch zwei Glas Wein, bitte, *two more glasses of wine, please*

noch kleiner, *even smaller*
was noch?, *what else?*

nur, *only*

■ *only*

man kann nur lachen, *you can only (you've got to) laugh*
nur einmal, *only once*

■ *just* (especially after exclamations)

nur langsam!, *just do it slowly*
sehen Sie nur!, *just look!*
wenn ich nur bitten darf, *if I may just ask*

schon, *already*

■ *already, yet*

sie ist schon da, *she's already there*
ist sie schon dagewesen?, *has she been there yet?*

■ *as early as*

er wird schon morgen hier sein, *he'll be here as early as tomorrow*

■ *even*

schon das war zuviel, *even that was too much*

■ *certainly, I'm sure*

er wird schon kommen, *he'll certainly come*
das stimmt schon, *I'm sure that's true*
ich glaube schon, *I think so*

■ with **weil** and **wegen**, = *if only because*

ich darf nicht mitkommen, schon weil es so spät anfängt, *I can't come with you, if only because it begins so late*

weiter, *further*

■ *further*

> **das Haus liegt etwas weiter entfernt**, *the house is a bit further away*

■ *else*, when **weiter** is used with **nichts** or in a question

> **und weiter nichts**, *and nothing else (nothing further)*
> **was ist weiter zu tun?**, *what else is there to do?*

Sonst is an alternative to **weiter** in this meaning.

■ *on*

> **sprich mal weiter**, *just go on speaking*

■ **weiter nicht** = *not that*

> **das ist weiter nicht schlimm**, *that doesn't matter very much (that's not that bad)*

wirklich, *really*

▶ See **eigentlich**, pp. 125–6.

wohl, *indeed*

■ *indeed, certainly*

> **das kann man wohl sagen**, *you can certainly say that*

The **wohl** is moderately stressed.

■ *probably*

> **sie wird wohl jetzt zu Hause sein**, *she's probably home by now*

The **wohl** is not stressed.

■ *full well*

> **das weißt du wohl**, *you know very well*

The **wohl** is moderately stressed.

■ *admittedly*

> **ich war wohl dafür verantwortlich, habe aber trotzdem nichts getan,** *I was indeed responsible for it, but in spite of that I did nothing*

The **wohl** is moderately stressed.

■ **wohl aber** = *but on the other hand*

> **ich kenne ihn nicht, wohl aber seinen Bruder,** *I don't know him, but I do know his brother*

The **wohl** is strongly stressed.

zwar, *admittedly*

■ *admittedly*

> **der ist zwar langsam, aber nicht faul,** *admittedly he's slow, but not lazy*

▶ For this meaning see also **allerdings**, pp. 122–3.

■ **und zwar** = *and furthermore* (introduces an extra phrase to clarify or extend)

> **er kommt immer früh an, und zwar gegen sieben,** *he always arrives early—about seven in fact*

I Pronouns

PERSONAL PRONOUNS

The basic use of the four cases of personal pronouns is similar to that of nouns. See p. 96.

Forms of the personal pronouns

The subject (nominative) pronouns are:

singular	*plural*
ich, *I*	**wir**, *we*
du, *you*	**ihr**, *you*
Sie, *you* (polite form)	
er, *he*; **sie**, *she*; **es**, *it*	**sie**, *they*

The direct object (accusative) pronouns are:

singular	*plural*
mich, *me*	**uns**, *us*
dich, *you*	**euch**, *you*
Sie, *you* (polite form)	
ihn, *him*; **sie**, *her*; **es**, *it*	**sie**, *them*

The indirect object (dative) pronouns are:

singular	*plural*
mir, *to me*	**uns**, *to us*
dir, *to you*	**euch**, *to you*
Ihnen, *to you* (polite form)	
ihm, *to him/to it*; **ihr**, *to her*	**ihnen**, *to them*

The reflexive pronouns are:

singular	*plural*
mich (accusative), *myself*; **mir** (dative), *to myself*	**uns**, *(to) ourselves*

dich (accusative), *yourself*; **dir** (dative), *to yourself* — **euch**, *(to)* yourselves

sich, *(to) yourself/-selves* (polite form)

sich, *(to) him-/her-/itself* — **sich**, *(to) themselves*

■ The polite pronoun **Sie**, *you*, is both singular and plural. It always has a capital in all forms except the reflexive **sich**. In letter-writing **du** and **ihr** are also written with a capital, in all their forms (including the possessives **dein**, **euer**).

■ The familiar forms **du** and **ihr** are used to friends, relatives, colleagues, children, and animals. The plural form **ihr** is used both for more than one '**du**' and for a mixed group of **du**'s and **Sie**'s. God is addressed as **Du** with a capital. Teachers use **Sie** to students in the last three forms of the Gymnasium, equivalent to the English sixth form. Using **du** to someone one is on **Sie** terms with, without their permission, is rude.

wollen wir uns duzen?, *shall we start using 'du' to each other?*

■ Pronouns agree in gender with the noun they refer to:

wo ist mein Bleistift? — ah, ich hab' ihn, *where's my pencil?—ah, I've got it*

However, **sie** is usually used to refer to **(das) Mädchen**, *girl*, and **(das) Fräulein**, *girl*, *Miss*.

■ The indefinite pronoun **man**, *one*, has the accusative and dative forms **einen** and **einem**. Its reflexive form is **sich**, its possessive **sein**. See pp. 153–4.

■ Genitive of the personal pronoun (*of me*, etc.).

The forms are:

meiner, *of me*; **deiner**, *of you*; **seiner**, *of him, of it*; **ihrer**, *of her, of them*; **unser**, *of us*; **euer**, *of you*

They sound literary and are usually avoided as follows:

□ Prepositions that take the genitive may be used with the dative instead.

□ Verbs that can take the genitive (e.g. **sich erinnern**) always have a preferable alternative construction (e.g. **sich erinnern an** + accusative).

□ Adjectives that take the genitive use **dessen**, *of that*, instead of **seiner**, and **derselben**, *of the same*, instead of **ihrer**.

Virtually the only time the genitive personal pronoun is used in modern German is with the adjectives **sicher**, *sure*, and **würdig**, *worthy*, which take a preceding genitive and have no alternative construction:

> **bist du seiner ganz sicher?**, *are you quite sure of him?*

Es as anticipatory object

A number of verbs insert the pronoun **es** as an anticipatory object into their main clause when they have a clause beginning **daß**, or an infinitive phrase, as their real object:

> **ich kann es nicht ertragen, daß er immer so spät kommt**, *I can't stand him always coming so late*
> **sie hat es fertiggebracht, ihr Visum zu bekommen**, *she has managed to get her visa*

This is obligatory with the following verbs:

ablehnen, *to refuse*
aushalten, *to endure*
erreichen, *to manage*
ertragen, *to endure*
fertigbringen, *to manage*
genießen, *to enjoy*
lassen, *to refrain from*
lieben, *to love*
unterlassen, *to omit*
verstehen, *to know how to*

Es is also always used with expressions such as **es eilig haben**, *to be in a hurry*, **es satt haben**, *to be sick of*, **es nötig haben**, *to need*, where the **es** forms part of the verbal phrase:

ich habe es eilig, *I'm in a hurry*
ich habe es eilig, nach Hause zu kommen, *I'm in a hurry to get home*

In addition to the list above there are many other verbs with which an anticipatory **es** may occasionally be found.

Reflexive pronouns

These are used where the direct or indirect object of the verb is the same as the subject. In addition:

■ In German a reflexive pronoun is used after a preposition to refer back to the subject of the sentence:

diese Zeit hat sie jetzt hinter sich, *she's got those days behind her now*
sie hatte nur zehn Mark bei sich, *she only had ten marks with her*

■ A dative reflexive is used in the phrase **vor sich hin**, *to oneself*, usually with a verb of speaking:

er redete vor sich hin, *he was talking to himself*

▶ See also Reflexive Verbs, p. 27.

POSSESSIVE PRONOUNS

In German there are several forms of the possessive pronoun (in English: *mine*, *yours*, *hers*, etc.). The most common form is **meiner** (etc.), declined like **dieser**:

	masculine	*feminine*	*neuter*	*plural*
nominative	meiner, *mine*	meine	mein(e)s	meine
accusative	meinen	meine	mein(e)s	meine
genitive	meines	meiner	meines	meiner
dative	meinem	meiner	meinem	meinen

The forms corresponding to **meiner** for the other persons are:

deiner, etc., *yours*
Ihrer, etc., *yours* (polite form)
seiner, etc., *his; its own*
uns(e)rer, etc., *ours*
eu(e)rer, etc., *yours*
ihrer, etc., *hers; theirs*

■ In the neuter nominative and accusative the **-e** is usually dropped in **meins, deins, seins, ihrs, Ihrs**.

■ **Eu(e)rer** (usually) and **uns(e)rer** (sometimes) lose the final **e** of their stem when they have an ending:

eure sind besser als uns(e)re, *yours are better than ours*

■ The following forms are also found:

□ **mein**, *mine*
dein, *yours*
sein, *his; its own*
unser, *ours*
euer, *yours*

These take no endings, are formal or poetic, and can only be used after the verb **sein**:

mein Herz ist dein, *my heart is yours*

They are never used after **es/das ist**. Furthermore, **'ihr'**, *hers/theirs*, and **'Ihr'**, *yours* (polite form) don't exist.

□ **der meine, die meine, das meine**, *mine*
der deine, die deine, das deine, *yours*
etc.

In this form of the possessive pronoun **mein-** etc. is treated as an adjective after the definite article. It is rather less common than the first form given above (**meiner** etc.), especially in spoken German.

□ The form **der meinige, der deinige,** etc., where **meinig-** etc. is also an adjective, is also found. It sounds a little old-fashioned.

■ The English genitive form *of mine* (etc.) is **von mir** (etc.):

> **die sind Bekannte von mir**, *they're acquaintances of mine*

DEMONSTRATIVE PRONOUNS

Demonstrative pronouns single out ('demonstrate') particular people or things. The demonstrative pronouns in German are **dieser**, *this (one)*, **der** or **jener**, *that (one)*, **derjenige**, *the one*, and **wer**, *the one who*. **Dieser** and **jener** are identical in form with the demonstrative adjectives **dieser** and **jener** (see p. 86).

Dieser, jener, der

Except in the special meaning of *the former*, **jener** has dropped out of common use. **Dieser** may be used for both *this one* and *that one*:

> **geben Sie mir dieses, bitte**, *give me that (this), please*

Frequently **der**, emphasized in speech and sometimes followed by **da**, *there*, is used for *that one* (plural: *those*):

> **stellen sie es zu denen (da), bitte**, *put it with those, please*

As a demonstrative pronoun **der** is declined like the relative pronoun **der** (see p. 139). **Dieser** and **jener** are declined like the definite article **der** (see p. 86).

The form **dies** is often found, especially in conversation, instead of **dieses** (neuter nominative and accusative):

> **dies ist aber wunderschön**, *this one is really marvellous*

■ For *this one, that one* after a preposition the compounds with **da(r)-** are used:

legen Sie es bitte darunter, *put it under that (one), please*

In this use, where **da-** = *this one/that one*, the stress in spoken German goes on the '**da**'. Compare **da-** = *it*, p. 162.

■ The demonstrative spoken without stress is often used in conversation instead of **er**, *he*, **sie**, *she/they*, and **es**, *it*. It is particularly useful to distinguish **sie**, *they*, from **Sie**, *you*:

die sind wirklich häßlich, *they're really ugly* (**sie** would be ambiguous in speech!)

The neuter forms **das** and (less common) **dies**, unstressed, are alternatives to **es** used with **sein**, *to be*, postponing the real subject; they are used with both a singular and a plural verb:

das (dies) ist meine Mutter, und das (dies) sind meine Schwestern, *that's my mother and those are my sisters*

■ **Dieser** and **jener** also mean, respectively, *the latter* and *the former*. They are used in these meanings without the rather literary sound that 'the latter' and 'the former' have in English:

was Hans und seinen Bruder betrifft: dieser ist schon bei der Bundeswehr gewesen, jener hat seinen Militärdienst noch nicht abgeleistet, *as far as Hans and his brother are concerned, the latter has (Hans's brother has) been in the army, the former has (Hans has) not yet done his national service*

Derjenige

The demonstrative pronoun **derjenige** (fem.: **diejenige**, neut.: **dasjenige**) means *the one*. Both parts of the word decline, the second part as an adjective after the definite article. **Derjenige** is usually followed by the relative **der**:

ich suche denjenigen, den er mitgebracht hat, *I'm looking for the one he brought with him*

Derjenige is literary; in conversation the demonstrative **der** is used instead:

ich suche den, den er mitgebracht hat

Wer

Wer is the equivalent of '**derjenige, der**'. It refers to people and has the general meaning of *anybody who*, *those who*, *the one who*. It always stands at the head of the sentence.

wer schon bezahlt hat, darf daran teilnehmen,
anyone who has already paid may take part

Distinguish **wer** followed by subordinate order, meaning *anybody who*, from **wer** introducing a question, meaning *who?*:

wer hat schon bezahlt?, *who's already paid?*

RELATIVE PRONOUNS

Relative pronouns introduce a subordinate clause within the sentence and usually relate it back to a noun in the main clause. In English they are *who*, *whom*, *whose*, *which*, *that*, *what*.

The relative pronouns in German are **der** and **welcher**, which are identical in meaning and can refer to either people (*who*, etc.; *that*) or things (*which*; *that*). They introduce subordinate order, sending the verb to the end of the clause.

There is a third relative, **was** (*what*), which introduces a noun clause (see pp. 141–2). **Was** is invariable; the forms of **der** and **welcher** are as follows:

der

	masculine	*feminine*	*neuter*	*plural*
nominative	der	die	das	die
accusative	den	die	das	die
genitive	dessen	deren	dessen	deren
dative	dem	der	dem	denen

welcher

	masculine	*feminine*	*neuter*	*plural*
nominative	welcher	welche	welches	welche
accusative	welchen	welche	welches	welche
dative	welchem	welcher	welchem	welchen

□ **Welcher** has no genitive forms and is less frequently used than **der**. For **welcher** as an interrogative adjective introducing a subordinate clause, see p. 117.

□ **Welcher** can't be used after indefinite pronouns referring to people (**niemand**, *nobody*, **jemand**, *somebody*, etc.):

> **kennen Sie jemand, der das tun könnte?**, *do you know anybody who could do that?*

□ Beware! Distinguish carefully the relative **das**, *that*, referring back to a neuter noun, from the conjunction **daß**, *that*, introducing a clause and not referring back to any noun.

□ Relatives can be omitted in English: *the man (that) you're speaking to*, but not in German.

■ Relatives agree in gender and number with the noun or pronoun they refer back to; but their case depends on their function in the clause they introduce. So:

> **der Mann, den Sie eingestellt haben, ist ein alter Freund von mir**, *the man that you have appointed is an old friend of mine*

Den is singular and masculine, because **der Mann**, to which it refers back, is singular and masculine. **Den** is accusative, however, because in the clause it introduces it is the object of **eingestellt haben**.

□ Exactly the same rule applies to the genitive relative:

> **der Mann, dessen Tochter Sie eingestellt haben, ist ein alter Freund von mir**, *the man whose daughter you have appointed is an old friend of mine*

Dessen is masculine because **Mann** is masculine (and in spite of the fact that it stands before the feminine word **Tochter**).

□ Where a thing rather than a person is referred to with a genitive, English often uses *of which* after the noun. German still uses **dessen/deren** and does not change the normal word order:

> **dieses Buch, dessen Anfang Sie vorgelesen haben**, *that book, the beginning of which (whose beginning) you read out*

■ A relative may follow a preposition. It stands in the case that normally follows that preposition:

> **der Herr, mit dem du sprichst . . .** , *the man you're speaking to* (literally, *with whom you're speaking*)
> **der Herr, mit dessen Frau du sprichst . . .** , *the man whose wife you're speaking to* (literally, *with whose wife you're speaking*)

In English the preposition may stand either in front of the relative (*to whose wife you're speaking*), or, less clumsily, at the end of the clause (*whose wife you're speaking to*). Only the first of these two is possible in German.

□ A less common alternative to preposition plus relative is a compound formed with **wo-** plus the preposition: **von dem→wovon**. This form can only be used to refer to things. Before a preposition beginning with a vowel an **r** is inserted: **auf dem→worauf.**

> **der Stuhl, worauf du sitzt, gehörte meinen Großeltern**, *the chair you're sitting on belonged to my grandparents*

In conversation **auf dem** would be more likely.

■ **Was** is used

□ (= *which*) to refer back to a clause:

er ist gewählt worden, was ich kaum glauben kann, *he has been elected, which (something) I can hardly believe*

□ (= *what*) at the beginning of the sentence, to introduce a noun clause:

was ich kaum glauben kann, ist die Tatsache, daß . . . , *what I can scarcely believe, is the fact that . . .*

□ (= *that; which*) as the relative after the indefinite pronouns **alles**, *everything*, **nichts**, *nothing*, **das**, *that*, **vieles**, *much*, **weniges**, *little*, and usually after **etwas**, *something*, and **folgendes**, *the following*:

fast alles, was er sagt, ist Unsinn, *nearly everything (that) he says is nonsense*

□ (= *that*) as the relative after neuter adjectival nouns:

das ist das Beste, was du je getan hast, *that's the best thing you've ever done*

Was is not used after a preposition; **wo(r)- +** preposition is substituted:

alles, woraus unsere Produkte hergestellt sind, *everything that our products are made from*

Was may of course introduce a question as well, either direct or indirect:

was meinst du?, *what do you mean?*
ich weiß nicht, was du meinst, *I don't know what you mean*

▶ For **wer** as combined demonstrative and relative (= *the one who*) see p. 139.

INTERROGATIVE PRONOUNS

The interrogative pronouns in English are *who?*, *what?*, and *which?* In German they are **wer?**, *who?*, **was?**, *what?*, and **welcher**, *which?*. **Wer** and **was** decline as follows:

nominative	wer?	was?
accusative	wen?	was?
genitive	wessen?	wessen?
dative	wem?	

They may be used in both direct and indirect questions:

wer sagt das?, *who says so?*
ich weiß nicht, was er gesagt hat, *I don't know what he said*
wessen Kugelschreiber hast du da?, *whose pen have you got there?*
ich weiß nicht, wem er gehört, *I don't know who it belongs to*

■ **Was** has no dative and its genitive is little used.

■ Both **wer** and **was** have no plural forms, though they may have a plural meaning, and with the verb **sein** they may take a plural verb form:

wer sind diese Dummköpfe?, *who are these idiots?*

With other verbs this is impossible: **alles** is added instead where a plural has to be indicated:

wer kommt denn alles?, *who is/are coming then?*

■ After a preposition **was** is not normally used, especially in written German; **wo(r)-** + preposition is substituted:

womit schreibst du?, *what are you writing with?*

The extra **-r** is used before a preposition beginning with a vowel.

The compounds **wohin** and **woher** are used to ask about motion towards and away from:

wohin gehst du?, *where are you going (to)?*
woher kommst du?, *where have you come from?*

NB: with **durch**: **wodurch** = *by what means*, **durch was** = *through what* (motion).

■ *Which (one)?* is **welcher?**, used as a pronoun:

hol mir meinen Mantel! —Welchen?, *get me my coat—Which one?*

▶ *Which* can also be an interrogative adjective (*which book?*). In this case it is **welcher**. See pp. 116–7.

ALPHABETICAL LIST OF INDEFINITE PRONOUNS AND ADJECTIVES

Indefinite pronouns (*somebody, something, anybody,* etc. in English) all take the third person (**er** form) of the verb in German, as they do in English. The forms of object pronouns, reflexives, possessives corresponding to the indefinite pronouns are also third-person masculine forms (**ihn**, **sich**, **sein**, and their plurals).

jeder erinnert sich an seine Vergangenheit, *everyone remembers his (their) past*

Indefinites all have a small letter in German. Some indefinites only function as pronouns, most can also be used as adjectives.

The genitive forms of the indefinites are in most cases rare, problematic, or unused. They are best avoided (use **von** or rephrase the sentence) except in the specific cases mentioned below.

The alphabetical list includes all common indefinite pronouns and adjectives.

■ **alles**, *everything*; *anything*; **alle**, *all*; *everybody*; **sämtlich**, *all*; *complete*

□ **Alles** and **alle** decline like **dieses** and **diese** (see p. 86). As in English, **alle**, *all*, can either itself be the subject of the sentence, or stand after the verb with a personal pronoun as subject:

> **alles ist möglich**, *everything is possible*
> **alle waren da / sie waren alle da**, *they were all there*
> **alle vier waren da / sie waren alle vier da**, *all four were there*

In the spoken language the neuter singular **alles** is used to mean *nothing but* or *entirely*:

> **das waren alles Parteimitglieder**, *they were every one of them party members*

and, also in the spoken language, **alle** is used as an adjective to mean '*all gone*':

> **das Bier ist alle**, *we've run out of beer*

□ As an adjective (*all*), **all** takes no endings and stands in front of the article (or possessive or demonstrative):

> **all die Soldaten**, *all (of) the soldiers*
> **trotz all deines Geldes**, *in spite of all your money*

If there is no article (or possessive or demonstrative) following, it declines like **dieser**:

> **alle Leute wissen das — alle intelligenten Leute**, *everybody knows that—all intelligent people*

□ The adjective **sämtlich** means *complete*:

> **Shakespeares sämtliche Werke**, *Shakespeare's complete works*

It is also very commonly used to mean *all* as an adjective, especially in the plural:

die sämtlichen Soldaten, *all the soldiers*
dein sämtliches Geld, *all your money*

Preceded by an article (or a possessive or demonstrative adjective) **sämtlich** behaves as an adjective; otherwise an adjective after it takes **-en**:

sämtliche intelligenten Leute, *all intelligent people*

□ Note that **ganz** can also translate *all* where it means *whole*:

die ganze Zeit, *all the time (= the whole time)*

■ **ander**, *other*, **ein and(e)rer**, *somebody else*, **der and(e)re**, *the other one*

Ander declines as an adjective; when it has an ending it often drops the **e** of the stem:

ein andrer wüßte das nicht, *anybody else wouldn't know that*
alles andere, *everything else*

It often follows numbers rather than standing in front of them:

die zwei anderen Kinder, *the other two children* (**die anderen zwei** is possible, however)

Where *other* means *more* it is **noch**:

eine andere Flasche Wein, *another bottle of wine* (a different one—there's something wrong with this one)
noch eine Flasche Wein, *another bottle of wine* (a further one—we've finished this one)

■ **anders**, *different(ly)*; *else*

□ **Anders** is invariable and is used after **sein** or as an adverb:

die Sache ist ganz anders, *the matter is quite different*
das mußt du anders machen, *you'll have to do that differently*

In front of a noun *different* is **ander-**:

eine andere Sache, *a different matter*

□ **Anders** is also used to mean *else* after **jemand** and **niemand**, **wer** and **wo**. It is invariable; in the case of **wo** it often joins up:

das war niemand anders als sein Onkel, *it was no one else but (none other than) his uncle*
wo kann es anders sein?, *where else can it be?*
es muß woanders sein, *it must be somewhere else*

■ **beide**, *both*; *two*

□ **Beide** declines like **dieser** (see p. 86) when it stands alone:

sie sind beide da / beide sind da, *they are both there*

After a definite article it declines as an adjective. Note the different word order: *both the* is **die beiden**:

die beiden Studenten, *both the students; the two students*

Die beiden is a very common alternative to **die zwei** for *the two*. **Beide** is the normal word used with personal pronouns:

wir beide, *the two of us*

Einer von beiden means *one or other (of them)*; **keiner von beiden** means *neither of them*:

keiner von beiden will es tun, *neither of them wants to do it*

Beide may be strengthened with **alle**: **alle beide**, *both of you*, *both of us*, etc.:

ihr seid alle beide eingeladen, *both of you are invited*

□ **Beides** can also be used as a neuter (often as an alternative to **beide**)—it is singular and invariable and is found in places where in English a plural would be used. It takes a singular verb except when used with **sein** and a plural noun:

> **ich habe beides gesehen**, *I've seen both (of them)*
> **beides wäre möglich**, *both (either) would be possible*
> **es waren beides Parteimitglieder / beides waren Parteimitglieder**, *they were both party members* (compare **alles**, p. 145)

■ **ein**, *one*; **einer**, *one*; *someone*

□ As well as being the indefinite article (see p. 87), **ein** can be a pronoun, when it declines like **dieses** (see p. 86). Its masculine form **einer** is used to refer to people when gender is not specified:

> **einer von uns muß es tun**, *one of us must do it*
> **einer muß es tun**, *someone must do it*

The **e** of the nominative and accusative **eines** is often dropped:

> **eins von beiden**, *one of the two*

Ein(e)s often means *one thing*:

> **eins muß ich sagen**, *there's one thing I've got to say*

▶ **Einen** and **einem** substitute for the non-existent accusative and dative of **man**. See p. 153.

□ **Ein**, *one*, can also be used as an adjective, when it takes adjective endings:

> **er kam in dem einen Auto an, fuhr in dem anderen ab**, *he arrived in (the) one car and left in the other*

□ The compounded form **unsereiner** means *the likes of us, people of our sort*. It declines like the pronoun **einer** and has no plural or genitive singular. The neuter **unsereins** is used in spoken German for either sex:

> **unsereins** (less colloquial: **unsereiner**) **fährt nicht erster Klasse**, *our sort don't go first class*

■ **ein bißchen**, *a bit*; *a little* (in south Germany almost always: **ein bissel**); **ein paar**, *a few*

Normally invariable:

> **er ist ein bißchen verrückt**, *he's a bit mad*
> **mit ein bißchen Geld kann man alles machen**, *with a bit of money you can do anything*
> **mit ein paar Leuten**, *with a few people*

but *the little bit* is **das bißchen**, *the few* is **die paar**, which change according to case:

> **mit dem bißchen Geld, das ich noch habe**, *with the little bit of money I still have*
> **mit den paar Leuten, die noch mit mir sprechen**, *with the few people who still speak to me*

The words **bißchen** and **paar** are always spelled with a small letter in these constructions.

▶ See also **einige**, *a few*, below, and **wenige**, *(very) few*, p. 158.

■ **einige**, *some, a few*

□ **Einige** is usually plural; it is declined like plural **diese** (see p. 86). It can be used as a pronoun or an adjective:

> **einige waren Deutsche**, *some (a few) were Germans*
> **einige Journalisten standen vorm Rathaus**, *a few journalists were standing in front of the town hall*

▶ **Einige** means *a few*; *the few* is **die wenigen** or **die paar** (see this page, above). *Few* (= *very few*) is **wenige**: see p. 158.

□ **Einige** is occasionally found in the singular: **einiger**, **einige**, **einiges**. It is used both as a pronoun and as an adjective:

> **einiges bleibt noch**, *some of it is still left*
> **vor einiger Zeit**, *some time ago*

■ **ein paar,** *a few*

► See **ein bißchen**, p. 149.

■ **etwas,** *something, anything; somewhat; some;* **nichts,** *nothing*

□ **Etwas** as a pronoun means *something* or *anything*:

> **ich muß dir etwas zeigen,** *I must show you something*

In conversation the pronoun **etwas** is very often shortened to **was:**

> **können Sie mir was zeigen?,** *can you show me anything?*

So etwas means *that sort of thing, something like that*:

> **haben Sie so etwas wie dieses, aber in Rot?,** *have you got something like this, only in red?*
> **nein, so was führen wir nicht,** *no, we don't keep that sort of thing*

So was is also used as an exclamation:

> **na, so was!,** *well, would you believe it!*

□ **Nichts** means *not . . . anything* as well as *nothing*:

> **ich kann Ihnen nichts zeigen,** *I can't show you anything*

Qualifying adverbs, e.g. **gar/durchaus,** *at all*, **sonst,** *else*, precede it:

> **hier ist gar nichts,** *there's nothing at all here*
> **ich habe sonst nichts,** *I've nothing else*

► **Nichts** and **(et)was** may be followed by a neuter adjective with a capital letter (**nichts Gutes,** *nothing good*): see p. 108.

□ **Etwas** can also be used adjectivally:

> **ich habe gerade etwas Zeit,** *I have some (a little) time at the moment*

and, often, as an adverb:

> **er ist etwas geizig,** *he's somewhat (a bit) mean*

■ **irgend etwas, irgend jemand, irgendein**, etc.

□ **Irgend** adds the sense of '*or other*' or '*at all*' to another indefinite: **irgend etwas**, *something or other, anything at all*; **irgend jemand**, *someone or other, anyone at all*:

> **hast du irgend etwas gesehen?**, *did you see anything (at all)?*
> **irgend jemand muß es getan haben**, *somebody or other (somebody) must have done it*

□ **Irgend** joins up with the following, forming adverbs:

> **wann**: **irgendwann**, *some time or other*
> **wie**: **irgendwie**, *somehow, anyhow*
> **wo**: **irgendwo**, *somewhere or other*
> **wohin**: **irgendwohin**, *(to) somewhere or other*
> **woher**: **irgendwoher**, *from somewhere or other*
>
> **wir werden uns irgendwann wiedersehen**, *we'll see each other again sometime (or other)*

□ **Irgend** joins up with **was** = **etwas**, forming a pronoun:

> **du mußt irgendwas tun**, *you must do something*

□ **Irgend** joins up with the following, forming adjectives:

> **ein**: **irgendein**, *some . . . or other*
> **welcher**: **irgendwelcher**, *some . . . or other*
>
> **das muß irgendeinen Sinn haben**, *that must have some (sort of) meaning*

Irgendein declines like **ein**, the indefinite article (see p. 87).

Irgendwelcher declines like **dieser** (see p. 86); it is mainly used before abstract nouns and as the plural of **irgendein** (**ein** has no plural):

> **habt ihr irgendwelche Schwierigkeiten damit gehabt?**, *did you have any difficulties with it?*

□ **Irgendeiner** and **irgendwelcher** are pronoun forms of **irgendein** and **irgendwelche**. They are declined like **dieser** (see p. 86) and mean *someone or other*:

irgendeiner wird da sein, *someone or other will be there*

■ **jeder**, *everyone; every, each*, **jedermann**, *everyone*

□ **Jeder** is declined like **dieser**:

jeder weiß, wie groß es ist, *everyone knows how big it is*

It is very frequently used as an adjective, declined in the same way:

jeder Zehnjährige weiß, wie groß es ist, *every ten-year-old knows how big it is*

It is occasionally used in the plural:

jede zehn Sekunden, *every ten seconds*

It can also be used after **ein**, to form **ein jeder**, *each and every one*. Here it behaves as an adjective after **ein**:

er begrüßte einen jeden persönlich, *he greeted each and every one personally*

□ **Jedermann** is an alternative to **jeder**. It is much less common, can only be used as a pronoun, is singular, and takes an ending only in the genitive:

dieses Gericht ist nicht jedermanns Sache, *this dish isn't to everyone's liking*

■ **jemand**, *somebody*; **niemand**, *nobody*

These decline as follows:

nominative	**jemand**	**niemand**
accusative	**jemand** or **jemanden**	**niemand** or **niemanden**
genitive	**(jemand(e)s)**	**(niemand(e)s)**
dative	**jemand** or **jemandem**	**niemand** or **niemandem**

Both forms of the accusative and dative are common in speech; the form with the ending is more usual in writing. The genitive is little used.

Somebody else, nobody else is **sonst jemand, sonst niemand.**

▶ For **jemand/niemand Schönes**, *someone/no one beautiful*, see Adjectives, p. 108.

▶ For **irgend jemand** see **irgend**, p. 151.

■ **keiner**, *no one*; **kein**, *no*

□ As a pronoun **keiner** declines like **dieser** (see p. 86). It is more precise than **niemand**, often being the equivalent of *none, not one*:

> **keiner weiß, wie er aussieht**, *no one knows what he looks like*
> **keiner von uns hat ihn gesehen**, *none of us (not a single one of us) has seen him*

□ As an adjective **kein** declines like **ein**: see p. 87. It is always used instead of **nicht ein** except

to stress the *one*:

> **nicht ein Pfennig Geld**, *not one penny, not a single penny*

when **nicht** and **ein** are split for stylistic emphasis:

> **einen Tiroler Hut hab' ich nicht!**, *I don't possess a Tyrolean hat*

after **wenn**:

> **ich hätte es nicht gesagt, wenn Sie nicht einen Tiroler Hut getragen hätten**, *I wouldn't have said it if you hadn't been wearing a Tyrolean hat*

before **sondern** (‘*not this but that*’):

> **das ist nicht ein Tiroler Hut, sondern ein bayrischer**, *that's not a Tyrolean hat, it's Bavarian*

■ **man**, *one, we, you, they, people in general*

Man is a subject pronoun, taking the **er** form of the verb. It corresponds to the English *one*, but whereas spoken English avoids *one* as formal (using *we*, *they*, *people* . . . instead), German uses **man** quite informally, much as French uses *on*.

Man has the reflexive **sich** and the possessive **sein**; it has no cases other than the nominative, borrowing **einen** for accusative, **einem** for dative, and avoiding the genitive.

> **man sagt, daß . . .** , *people say that*
> **man kratzt sich nicht in der Öffentlichkeit**, *one does not scratch in public*
> **dort kann es einem zu warm werden**, *it can get too hot for you there*

The possessive **sein** cannot be used to refer to **man** as part of the subject—the rather cumbersome '**das man hat**' has to be used instead:

> **die Ideen, die man hat, sind oft am Anfang nicht ganz klar**, *one's ideas are often not entirely clear to start with*

■ **manche**, *many*; **mancher**, *many a*

□ **Manche** is plural; it is declined like plural **diese** (see p. 86). It is often identical in meaning with **viele** (see pp. 156–7).

Manche . . . manche means *some (people) . . . some (people)*:

> **manche sagen ja, manche dagegen sagen nein**, *some say yes, some on the other hand say no*

The singular, **mancher**, *many a one*, is a little old-fashioned:

> **mancher wäre auch dieser Meinung**, *many a one (many people) would also be of this opinion*

□ **Mancher** is also used as an adjective, also declined like **dieser**. An adjective following it behaves like an adjective following **dieser**. **Mancher** quite often has a (meaningless) **so** in front of it:

> **manche Frauen sind nicht deiner Meinung**, *many women wouldn't agree with you*
> **so mancher brave Mann**, *many an honest man*

Manch can be used without an ending before **ein**:

manch eine Frau, *many a woman*

This too is rather old-fashioned.

■ **mehrere**, *several*

Mehrere is only found in the plural. It declines like an ordinary adjective, and a second adjective after it takes the same ending as **mehrere**:

mehrere ungewöhnliche Tatsachen, *several unusual facts*

■ **nichts**, *nothing*

▶ See **etwas**, p. 150.

■ **niemand**, *no one*

▶ See **jemand**, p. 152.

■ **sämtlich**, *all*

▶ See **alles**, p. 145.

■ **solch**, *such*; **so ein**, *such a*

□ In the singular **solch** is most frequently used as an adjective. The word order is different from the English:

ein solcher Film zieht ein großes Publikum an, *such a film attracts a large audience*

□ In conversation **so ein** is frequently substituted for **ein solcher**:

hast du je so einen Film gesehen?, *have you ever seen a film like that?*

So is always used after **kein**:

das war kein so hervorragender Film, *that wasn't such a terrific film*

□ **Solch ein** is also found, but is not common in speech:

solch ein hervorragender Film, *such an outstanding film*

In this construction **solch** is invariable.

□ The pronoun form of **solch** is **solcher**, declined like **dieser** (see p. 86):

den Film als solchen fand ich nicht so hervorragend, *I didn't find the film as such so terrific*

This form is also used as an adjective in the plural (since the **ein** of **ein solcher** and **so ein** has no plural form):

solche Filme interessieren mich nicht, *such films (films like that) don't interest me*

It is occasionally used in the singular (**so** is commoner):

bei solchem schlechten Wetter bleibe ich zu Hause, *in such bad weather I stay at home*

▶ For **so etwas** see **etwas**, p. 150.

■ **unsereiner**, *people of our sort*

▶ See **einer**, p. 148.

■ **viel**, *much*; **viele**, *many*

□ As a pronoun **viel** is declined:

	singular	*plural*
nominative	**viel** or **vieles**	**viele**
accusative	**viel** or **vieles**	**viele**
genitive		**vieler**
dative	**viel** or **vielem**	**vielen**

nicht viele denken wie du, *not many think like you*

viel(es), was du sagst, ist unverständlich, *much that (of what) you say is incomprehensible*

The form without an ending is sometimes said to be the more general, but often there seems to be little difference between the two forms. There is no genitive singular.

□ **Viel** is also used, much more commonly, as an adjective standing without an article in front of a noun. In this case it takes no endings in the singular and the endings shown above in the plural:

> **ich habe so viel Zeit**, *I've so much time*
> **nicht viele Engländer kommen zu uns**, *not many English visit us*

Viel can also be used as an adjective after an article, in which case it takes normal adjective endings:

> **die vielen guten Weine, die man hier kaufen kann**, *the many good wines one can buy here*

□ An adjective following **viel** in the singular behaves as an adjective without an article (see pp. 106–7):

> **mit sehr viel schlechtem Wein**, *with a very great deal of bad wine*

After **viele** in the plural it behaves like an adjective after another adjective (see p. 108–9):

> **viele ältere Engländer**, *many elderly English*

□ **Wieviel**, *how much* (singular) is written as one word; **wie viele**, *how many* (plural) as two; **soviel** is written as one word when it is a conjunction (= *as far as*), but as two when it means *so much*:

> **soviel ich weiß, hat er nicht so viel Theater gesehen**, *as far as I know he hasn't seen very much theatre*

► **Viel** has an irregular comparative and superlative (**mehr, meist**). See p. 113.

■ **welcher**, *some*; *any*

Welcher is declined like **dieser** (see p. 86):

> **wir haben keinen Kaffee mehr, hast du welchen?**, *we've no coffee left, have you any?*

It refers back to the last-stated noun and is especially common in spoken German.

▶ **Welcher** can also be an interrogative pronoun (see pp. 143–4), an interrogative adjective (see pp. 116–17), and a relative pronoun or adjective (see pp. 139–40).

▶ See also **irgendwelcher**, p. 151.

■ **wenig**, *little*; **wenige**, *few*

For the basic form and use of **wenig**, see **viel**, pp. 156–7: everything stated there about **viel** (except the sections on **wieviel** and the comparative and superlative) also applies to **wenig**.

□ **ein wenig**, *a little*, is invariable:

> **wir haben nur ein wenig Zeit**, *we only have a little time*

A very little is **ein klein wenig** (the **klein** is also invariable):

> **ein (ganz) klein wenig Zucker, bitte**, *(just) a very little sugar, please*

I Prepositions

Prepositions—words like *in, on, over*—stand in front of a noun or pronoun to relate it to the rest of the sentence:

> **immer singt er in seinem Bad**, *he always sings in his bath* (preposition: **in**, *in*)

Prepositions can also stand in front of a verb—*without singing*. In English this part of the verb is usually the *-ing* form. In German most prepositions cannot be followed by a verb, and the sentence has to be reconstructed (see Translation Problems, *-ing*, pp. 139–40). Those that can be followed by a verb use the infinitive with **zu**:

> **ohne zu singen**, *without singing*
> **um zu singen**, *in order to sing*

CASE WITH PREPOSITIONS

Prepositions in German are followed by nouns or pronouns in the accusative, the genitive, or the dative.

■ The dative is the case found most frequently after a preposition. In general, if you are not sure what case a preposition takes and are not in a position to look it up, use the dative. The following nine very common prepositions always take the dative, and there are many others:

> **aus**, *out of*
> **außer**, *except; outside*
> **bei**, *near; with; at the house of*
> **gegenüber**, *opposite* (follows noun)
> **mit**, *with*
> **nach**, *after; to*
> **seit**, *since*
> **von**, *from; of*
> **zu**, *to*

■ Seven prepositions always take the accusative:

bis, *until*
durch, *through*
entlang, *along* (following its noun; otherwise dative)
für, *for*
gegen, *against; towards*
ohne, *without*
um, *round*

There are also a very small number of less common prepositions that always take the accusative.

■ Four common prepositions take the genitive:

(an)statt, *instead of*
trotz, *in spite of*
während, *during*
wegen, *because of*

Prepositions ending **-seits** (e.g. **diesseits**, *this side of*) and **-halb** (e.g. **innerhalb**, *inside*) can take the genitive, but are more often found followed by **von** + the dative.

A large number of uncommon prepositions and prepositional phrases, including many legal ones, also take the genitive.

■ A group of prepositions take the accusative if motion towards is implied and the dative if not. The prepositions in this group are:

an, *on; at*
auf, *on*
in, *in*
hinter, *behind*
neben, *near; beside*
über, *over*
unter, *under; among*
vor, *in front of*
zwischen, *between*

The only prepositions outside this group that commonly imply motion towards are **zu** and **nach**, with which the case is always dative. So apart from **zu** and **nach**, if a preposition implies motion towards, as a general rule use the accusative.

■ **An, auf, über**, and **vor**, and less frequently other prepositions, can be used with a figurative meaning after verbs (e.g. **bestehen auf**, *insist on*). In such cases **vor** always takes the dative, **auf** and **über** usually take the accusative, and **an** varies (see pp. 51–2). For more detail on individual prepositions see the Alphabetical List, pp. 163–87. For preposition and case with individual verbs, Oxford Reference: *German Verbs* should be consulted.

■ Where two prepositions joined by **und** or **oder** stand before the same noun it takes the case of the last one:

> **du kommst mit oder ohne deine Schwester?**, *are you coming with or without your sister?*

CONTRACTED FORMS OF PREPOSITIONS

Many prepositions can combine with a following definite article to produce a contraction:

> **wir gehen zum (= zu *dem*) Laden**, *we're going to the shop*

■ Contractions are not used

where the article is stressed (meaning *that*):

> **wir gehen zu *dem* Laden**, *we're going to that shop*

where the noun has an adjective clause that particularizes it:

> **wir gehen zu dem Laden, wo wir immer einkaufen**, *we're going to the shop where we always shop* (i.e. that particular shop)

■ Apart from the above cases the following contracted forms are almost always preferred to the non-contracted forms:

am (an dem)	**vom (von dem)**
beim (bei dem)	**zum (zu dem)**
im (in dem)	**zur (zu der)**
ins (in das)	

In addition, the following contractions are very frequent indeed in spoken German and are very often found in modern printed German:

ans (an das)	**übern (über den)**
aufs (auf das)	**übers (über das)**
außerm (außer dem)	**ums (um das)**
durchs (durch das)	**unterm (unter dem)**
fürs (für das)	**untern (unter den)**
hinterm (hinter dem)	**unters (unter das)**
hintern (hinter den)	**vorm (vor dem)**
hinters (hinter das)	**vors (vor das)**
überm (über dem)	

Other contracted forms may be heard in spoken German:

tu's auf'n Tisch, *put it on the table*

DA + PREPOSITIONS

Da may be prefixed to most prepositions, giving the meaning 'preposition + *it*':

von, *from* → **davon**, *from it*: **was hast du davon?**, *what do you get from it?*

If the preposition begins with a vowel an extra **r** is inserted: **daraus**.

■ These combined forms are only used to refer to things.

■ The prepositions **außer, bis, gegenüber, ohne, seit** do not have **da-** forms; nor do prepositions that take the genitive.

In questions prepositions combine with **wo** in the same way to give the meaning 'preposition + *what*':

wovon?, *of what?*
worüber?, *about what?*

worüber sprichst du?, *what are you talking about?*

▶ See Interrogative Pronouns, pp. 143–4.

▶ **Wo** combinations can also be used as relatives. See Relative Pronouns, p. 141.

ALPHABETICAL LIST OF GERMAN PREPOSITIONS AND THEIR USE

The use of prepositions differs considerably from language to language. Below we give an alphabetical list of all common German prepositions, and many less common ones, with their main and subsidiary meanings, their cases, and their use. Where a preposition has a number of meanings, the principal meaning is given first, with other meanings following in alphabetical order.

In addition, on pp. 188–94 there is an alphabetical list of English prepositions with their various German equivalents, for cross-reference to the German list.

ab, *from* (time); *from . . . on* (place)

+ dative

ab morgen, *from tomorrow*
ab Mainz fuhr der Zug noch langsamer, *from Mainz on the train went even more slowly*

an, *at*

+ dative (no motion, or motion within) or accusative (motion towards)

at (dative)

es ist jemand an der Tür, *there's someone at the door*
er unterrichtet an der Kantschule, *he teaches at the Kantschule*
am Wochenende, *at the weekend*

at (accusative)

er klopfte an die Tür, *he knocked at the door*

about (dative)

das gefällt mir an ihm, *that's what I like about him*
was ist daran komisch?, *what's funny about it?*
das Schlimmste an der ganzen Sache ist . . . , *the worst thing about the whole business is . . .*

by (dative)

du erkennst mich an meinem rosa Anorak, *you'll recognize me by my pink anorak*

of; *in respect of* (dative)

ein Mangel an Geld, *a lack of money*
ein großer Aufwand an Zeit, *a great expenditure of time*
sie ist reich an Ideen, *she is rich in (= in respect of) ideas*

on (= *up against*; dative)

Frankfurt am Main, *. . . on the River Main*
am Ufer des Sees, *on the bank of the lake*
der Spiegel hängt an der langen Wand, *the mirror hangs on the long wall*
sie gingen am Strand entlang, *they walked along on the beach*

on (but not literally *on top of*, and no motion towards; dative)

er arbeitet an einem neuen Buch, *he's working on a new book*
am Sonntag, *on Sunday*
am zweiten Februar, *on the second of February*

on(to) (often, a vertical surface; accusative)

schreib es an die Tafel, *write it on the board*
er lehnte es an die Wand, *he leant it on (against) the wall*

to (accusative)

an die Arbeit!, *to work!*
sie schickte ein Weihnachtsgeschenk an ihre Mutter, *she sent a Christmas present to her mother*

(an)statt, *instead of*

+ genitive

er kam anstatt seines Sohnes, *he came instead of his son*

Sometimes takes dative instead of genitive, and must do when the noun has no article or adjective in front of it:

anstatt Protesten, *instead of protests*

auf, *on(to)*

+ dative (no motion, or motion within) or accusative (motion towards)

on (dative)

es ist so viel Verkehr auf der Straße, *there's so much traffic on the road*
sie stand eine Zeitlang auf dem Marktplatz, *she stood for a time on (in) the market square*

on(to) (accusative)

er ging auf die Straße hinaus, *he went out onto the street*
sie legte sich auf das Bett, *she lay down on the bed*

at (accusative)

sie machte es auf meinen Wunsch (meine Bitte), *she did it at my wish (my request)* *for* (+ future time; accusative)

sie kommt auf eine Woche, *she's coming for a week*

in

der Vogel saß auf einem Baum, *the bird was sitting in a tree*
auf keine Weise, *in no way*
auf englisch, *in English*
auf jeden Fall, *come what may* (= *in any possible case*)

of (accusative)

ich habe keine Hoffnung (keine Aussicht) auf eine Antwort, *I've no hope (no prospect) of an answer*
sie war immer eifersüchtig (neidisch; stolz) auf mich, *she was always jealous (envious; proud) of me*

to (accusative)

die Antwort auf meine Frage, *the answer to my question*
du hast kein Recht auf einen Paß, *you have no right to a passport*

aus, *out of*

\+ dative

out of

er stieg aus dem Auto, *he got out of the car*
trink nicht aus der Flasche!, *don't drink out of the bottle*
sie tat es aus Stolz, *she did it out of pride*

from

aus welcher Richtung kommt der Wind?, *which direction is the wind coming from?*

woher kommst du?—Aus Bremen, *where are you from?—From Bremen*

made of

ein Kaffeetisch aus Holz, *a coffee-table made of wood*

außer, *except*

+ dative

except; apart from

ich habe kein Karo außer dem As, *I haven't a diamond except (apart from) the ace*
außer uns war niemand da, *nobody was there except us*

beyond

seine Treue ist außer Zweifel, *his loyalty is beyond doubt*

out of

diese Bahn ist außer Betrieb, *this tram is out of service*
seine Kinder waren außer Kontrolle, *his children were out of control*
ich bin außer Atem, *I'm out of breath*

außerhalb, *outside*

+ genitive

er wohnt außerhalb der Stadt, *he lives outside the town*

Often takes **von** + dative instead of genitive:

er wohnt außerhalb von der Stadt

bei, *at the house of*

+ dative

at the house of

> **Sahne kannst du beim Bäcker kaufen**, *you can buy cream at the baker's*
> **bei uns (zu Hause)**, *at our house; at home*
> **wir sind bei Kaisers eingeladen**, *we're invited to the Kaisers'*

To the house of is **zu** (**bei** can't be used with a verb of motion):

> **wir gehen zu Kaisers**, *we're going to the Kaisers'*

at

> **beim Frühstück**, *at breakfast*
> **bei der Arbeit**, *at work*
> **bei der bloßen Idee**, *at the very idea*
> **bei nächster Gelegenheit**, *at the next opportunity*

by; near

> **bleib bei mir!**, *stay by me*
> **sie saß beim Feuer**, *she sat by the fire*
> **Gräfelfing bei München**, *Gräfelfing near Munich*

for (= *in spite of*)

> **bei allen seiner Tugenden ist er kein liebenswerter Mensch**, *for all his virtues he's not a lovable person*
> **bei alledem**, *for all that*

in

> **bei gutem Wetter**, *in fine weather*
> **bei schlechter Laune**, *in a bad mood*

with

> **bei Norddeutschen ist der Fall anders**, *with north Germans the case is different*

bei diesen Preisen kann man sich kaum was leisten, *with prices like these you can hardly afford anything*

beiderseits, *on both sides of*

+ genitive

beiderseits der Straße, *on both sides of the street*

Often takes **von** + dative instead of genitive:

beiderseits von der Straße

betreffend, *with regard to*

+ accusative; commercial German; less common; usually follows noun or pronoun

Ihr Fax betreffend . . . , *with regard to your fax . . .*

bis, *until; as far as*

+ accusative

until

bis jetzt habe ich nichts gesehen, *I've seen nothing until now*
warte nur bis nächsten Frühling, *just wait until next spring*
bis Sonnabend!, *see you on (= goodbye until) Saturday*

When a noun with an article follows **bis, bis zu** + dative is used:

bis zum dritten Oktober, *until the third of October*
geh bis zur Kreuzung, *go on until (go as far as) the crossroads*

The negative of **bis**, *not until*, is **erst + um, erst an**, etc.:

erst um drei Uhr, *not until three o'clock*
erst am dritten Mai, *not until the third of May*

by

bis übermorgen ist es fertig, *it'll be ready by the day after tomorrow*

bis auf, *except (for)*

\+ accusative

wir sind alle durchgefallen bis auf die drei Mädchen, *we all failed except (for) the three girls*

dank, *thanks to*

\+ dative (occasionally genitive); less common

dank Ihrer Hilfe bin ich heute noch am Leben, *thanks to your help I am still alive today*

diesseits, *on this side of*

\+ genitive

diesseits des Flusses, *on this side of the river*

Often takes **von** + dative instead of genitive:

diesseits vom Fluß

durch, *through; by*

\+ accusative

through

sie watete durch den Bach, *she waded through the stream*
sie marschierten durch die Stadt, *they marched through the town*
es kam durch das Fenster, *it came through the window*

by

> **du hast es durch deine Briefe klargemacht,** *you've made it clear by your letters*
>
> **er ist durch Schnee aufgehalten worden,** *he was held up by snow*

By is **durch** in passive constructions where a thing is referred to as the cause; where it is a person, **von** is used. See Passive, pp. 30–1.

eingerechnet, *including*

+ accusative; less common; usually follows noun or pronoun

> **die zwei Flaschen Wein (mit) eingerechnet,** *including the two bottles of wine*

entlang, *along*

+ accusative; usually follows noun or pronoun—takes dative if it precedes

> **sie schlenderte die Straße entlang,** *she strolled along the road*
>
> **entlang dem Kanal,** *along the canal*

entsprechend, *corresponding to*

+ dative; commercial German; less common; usually follows a noun or pronoun

> **unseren Erwartungen entsprechend,** *corresponding to our expectations*

für, *for*

+ accusative

> **ich habe die Blumen für dich gebracht,** *I've brought the flowers for you*

ich habe sie am Bahnhof für zehn Mark gekauft, *I bought them for ten marks at the station*
das ist sehr leicht für mich, *that's very easy for me*

Was für ein means *what sort of*. The **für** does not affect the case of **ein**: the **ein** declines according to its job in the sentence:

mit was für einem Kuli schreibst du?, *what sort of a ballpoint are you writing with?*

gegen, *against*

\+ accusative

against

er war immer gegen die EG, *he was always against the EC*
er lehnte die Leiter gegen die Mauer, *he leant the ladder against the wall*
hätten Sie etwas dagegen, wenn wir etwas später essen würden?, *would you have anything against our eating a little later?*
es geschah gegen alle unsere Hoffnungen, *it happened against all our hopes*

about (with numbers)

gegen dreihundert Soldaten, *about 300 soldiers*

compared to

gegen dich bin ich nichts, *I'm nothing compared to you*

for (= *in exchange for*)

das bekommen Sie nur gegen Bargeld, *you only get that for ready cash*

towards (usually with time)

gegen fünf Uhr, *towards five o'clock*

gegenüber, *opposite*

+ dative; follows a pronoun, usually follows a noun

opposite

die Sparkasse liegt dem Kino gegenüber (gegenüber dem Kino), *the savings bank is opposite the cinema*

compared to

dir gegenüber bin ich ein Anfänger, *I'm a beginner compared to you*

towards

unsere Haltung gegenüber den neuen Bundesländern, *our attitude towards the new federal states*

gemäß; zufolge, *in accordance with*

both: + dative; formal; less common; usually follow noun or pronoun

Ihren Befehlen gemäß / zufolge, *in accordance with your commands*

hinter, *behind; beyond*

+ dative (no motion, or motion within) or accusative (motion towards)

behind (dative)

der Garten liegt hinter dem Haus, *the garden is behind the house*

du darfst hier hinter dem Haus spielen, *you can play here behind the house*

aber nicht hinter dem Zaun!, *but not beyond the fence!*

behind (accusative)

geh schnell hinter die Mauer!, *get behind the wall quickly*

in, *in*; *into*

+ dative (no motion, or motion within) or accusative (motion towards)

in (dative)

wir essen immer im Wohnzimmer, *we always eat in the living-room*
er lief im Wohnzimmer umher, *he ran about in the living-room*
im Winter, *in winter*
im Januar, *in January*
in fünf Minuten, *in five minutes*

into (accusative)

er lief schnell ins Wohnzimmer, *he ran quickly into the living-room*
sie tanzten bis tief in die Nacht hinein, *they danced deep into the night*

to (accusative)

gehen wir in die Kirche oder ins Kino?, *shall we go to church or to the cinema?*
in die Vereinigten Staaten, *to the USA* (only non-neuter names of countries; see pp. 176–7)

innerhalb, *inside*; *within*

+ genitive

innerhalb des Schlosses, *inside the castle*

Often takes **von** + dative instead of genitive:

innerhalb vom Schloß

. . . and must take **von** when the noun has no article or adjective before it:

innerhalb von drei Stunden, *within three hours*

jenseits, *on the other side of; beyond*

+ genitive

jenseits des Todes, *beyond death*

Often takes **von** + dative instead of genitive:

jenseits vom Tod

laut, *according to*

+ dative or genitive; less common; newspaper and TV language

laut unseren (unsrer) letzten Meldungen, *according to our latest reports*

mit, *with*

+ dative

with

Obsttorte mit Schlagsahne, *fruit flan with whipped cream*

ich bin mit meinem Mann gekommen, *I'm here with my husband*

kommst du mit?, *are you coming with us/me?*

iß das mit deiner Gabel!, *eat it with your fork*

at

mit 60 km/h (= Stundenkilometern) fahren, *to travel at 60 k.p.h.*

mit 18 (Jahren), *at eighteen*

by

fährst du mit dem Bus?, *are you going by bus?*
es kam mit der Post, *it came by post*

nach, *after*

\+ dative

after

nach deinem Examen, *after your exam*
nach der Schule, *after school*
er kam uns nach, *he came after us* (**nachkommen**)
ein Tag nach dem anderen, *one day after another*
zwanzig nach vier, *twenty past* (= *after*) *four*

according to

nach Shakespeare, *according to Shakespeare*
nach Geschmack, *according to taste*
nach meiner Uhr ist es schon drei, *by* (= *according to*) *my watch it's already three*
meiner Meinung nach, *in* (= *according to*) *my opinion* (note position of **nach** in this set phrase)

for

die Sehnsucht (der Wunsch; der Verlangen; die Suche) nach politischer Macht, *the longing (the wish; the craving; the search) for political power*

to (with countries, towns, continents)

wir fahren nach England, *we're travelling to England*
eine Reise nach Berlin, *a journey to Berlin*
nächstes Jahr geht's nach Australien, *next year we're off to Australia*

But before countries used with the definite article (i.e. feminine ones, plus the very few plural or masculine ones) **in** is used:

in die Türkei, *to Turkey*
in die USA, *to the USA* (**nach** is also found)
in den Jemen, *to the Yemen*

Spoken north German extends this use of **nach** = *to* to many other places:

er ist nach der Bushaltestelle gelaufen, *he walked to the bus stop*

to the (with compass points, directions)

nach Süden (also **in den**), *to the south*
nach rechts, *to the right*
nach oben, *to the top; upstairs*

towards

sie sah nach der offenen Tür, *she looked towards the open door*
er ging langsam nach dem Fluß zu, *he went slowly towards the river*
nach Hause, *(to) home*

neben, *beside; next to*

+ dative (no motion, or motion within) or accusative (motion towards)

beside (dative)

er saß dicht neben mir, *he was sitting right beside (next to) me*
sie ging neben mir auf der Straße, *she was walking beside me on the street* (no motion relative to me)

beside (accusative)

er setzte sich dicht neben mich, *he sat down right beside me*
stell die Flasche neben die anderen, *put the bottle beside (next to) the others*

besides (dative)

> **neben den Butterbroten brauchen wir auch Wein,** *besides (as well as) the sandwiches we need wine too*

oberhalb, *above*

+ genitive; less common

> **oberhalb der Berghütte**, *above the mountain hut*

Often takes **von** + dative instead of genitive:

> **oberhalb von der Berghütte**

ohne, *without*

+ accusative

> **ohne Hoffnung**, *without hope*
> **ohne Hut**, *without a hat*
> **ohne seinen Hut,** *without his hat*

The indefinite article (but not possessives, etc.) is omitted after **ohne**.

per, *per*, *by*; pro, *per*

+ accusative; less common

> **per Luftpost**, *by airmail*
> **dreimal pro Woche**, *three times a (per) week*

Neither of these prepositions takes an article, so the accusative that follows them is usually hidden.

seit, *since*

+ dative

since

> **er ist hier seit Montag**, *he's been here since Monday*

ich habe sie seit Ostern nicht mehr gesehen, *I haven't seen her again since Easter*

for

seit zwei Monaten, *for three months*
seit einiger Zeit, *for some time*

■ Note the tenses used with **seit**:

du ißt seit einer Stunde, *you've been eating for an hour*
du ißt seit halb eins, *you've been eating since 12.30*

For an action or state starting in the past and going on to the present, **seit** + present tense is used (the English is the perfect continuous). **Seit** can have either of its two meanings.

With a negative, or a series of actions, the perfect is used, as in English:

du hast seit einer Stunde nichts gegessen, *you haven't eaten anything for an hour*
seit halb eins hast du drei Brötchen und vier Bockwürste gegessen, *since half past twelve you've eaten three rolls and four sausages*

□ The above also applies to an action starting before some point in the past and continuing to that point. This produces **seit** + the past tense:

er war seit einer Stunde dort, *he had been there for an hour*

The English tense here is the pluperfect. With a negative or a series of actions the German also uses the pluperfect:

er war seit Weihnachten dreimal in Frankfurt gewesen, *he had been to Frankfurt three times since Christmas*

statt, *instead of*

+ genitive (shortened form of **anstatt**; identical in use)

► See **anstatt**, p. 165.

trotz, *in spite of*

+ genitive

er kam trotz des Regens, *he came in spite of the rain*

Often takes dative instead of genitive, and must do when the noun has no article or adjective in front of it:

trotz Karten und Briefen, *in spite of cards and letters*

And note the datives in **trotz allem**, *in spite of everything*, and **trotzdem**, *in spite of that*.

über, *over; above*

+ dative (no motion, or motion within) or accusative (motion towards)

over; *above* (dative)

das Bild hängt über dem Fernseher, *the picture hangs over the television*
Wasservögel kreisten über dem See, *waterfowl were circling above (over) the lake*

over (accusative)

wir fahren hier über die Bahn, *here we go over the railway*
über eine halbe Stunde, *over half an hour*
über Weihnachten, *over Christmas*
ein Wettlauf über 1000 Meter, *a race over 1000 metres*

about (accusative)

> **ich muß darüber nachdenken,** *I must think about that*
> **wissen Sie etwas über Raupen?,** *do you know anything about caterpillars?*
> **er hielt einen Vortrag über Raupen,** *he gave a lecture about caterpillars*

via (accusative)

> **fahren Sie über Hamburg?,** *are you going via Hamburg?*
> **er ist über die Autobahn gekommen,** *he came via (along) the motorway*

um, *round; around*

\+ accusative

(a)round

> **sie kam um die Ecke,** *she came round the corner*
> **um 1900,** *around 1900*

Um is often strengthened by adding **rings** or **rund** before it or **herum** after it (or both):

> **rund um die Stadt herum lief eine Mauer,** *right round the town ran a wall*

at (with clock times)

> **um sieben Uhr,** *at seven o'clock*
> **um Mittag,** *at noon*

► See Time, p. 208.

by

> **ich muß den Termin um eine Woche verschieben,** *I have to postpone the appointment by a week*
> **es ist um drei Meter länger als das andere,** *it's longer by three metres than the other one*

for

der Kampf um das tägliche Brot, *the fight for one's daily bread*
wir spielen nicht um Geld, *we're not playing for money*
eine Bitte um Hilfe, *a request for help*
ich habe Angst um mein Leben, *I fear for my life*

for the sake of (**um** + genitive + **willen**)

um Himmels willen tu das nicht!, *don't do it, for heaven's sake!*

unter, *below; under*

+ dative (no motion, or motion within) or accusative (motion towards)

below; under (dative)

wir wohnen unter Schmidts, *we live below the Schmidts*
sie tanzten unter freiem Himmel, *they danced under the open sky*

below; under (accusative)

wir setzten uns unter eine Eiche, *we sat down under an oak*

among (dative)

wir sind unter Freunden, *we're among friends*

among (accusative)

du gehst nicht oft genug unter Leute in deinem Alter, *you don't mix with (go among) people of your own age enough*

given (dative)

unter diesen Umständen, *in (= given) these circumstances*
unter einer Bedingung, *on (= given) one condition*

under (= *at less than*; dative)

unter hundert Mark verkauf' ich's nicht!, *I'm not selling it under 100 DM*

unterhalb, *below*

+ genitive; less common

er wohnt irgendwo unterhalb der Kantstraße, *he lives somewhere below Kantstraße*

Sometimes takes **von** + dative instead of genitive:

unterhalb von der Kantstraße

von, *from*

+ dative

from

ich habe das Geld von meinem Vater erhalten, *I received the money from my father*

gehst du jetzt von hier weg?, *are you going away from here now?*

von Morgen bis in die Nacht, *from morning till night*

von hier aus kannst du drei Grafschaften sehen, *from (up) here you can see three counties*

von mir aus kannst du es sofort tun, *from my point of view (as far as I'm concerned) you can do it straight away*

about

was hältst du davon?, *what do you think about it?*

ich schwärme (bin begeistert) von deinem neuen Auto, *I'm mad about your new car*

by (in passive constructions)

es ist schon von der Putzfrau gemacht worden, *it has already been done by the cleaning lady* (see Passive, pp. 30–1)

of

der Geruch von Zwiebeln, *the smell of onions*
der Prinz von Dänemark, *the Prince of Denmark*
ein Kind von vier Jahren, *a child of four*
das ist furchtbar nett von Ihnen, *that's awfully kind of you*

Von (= *of*) is also very frequently used instead of the genitive in spoken German; the genitive is seen as literary or affected:

die Tante meines Freundes → die Tante von meinem Freund, *my friend's aunt*

vor, *in front of*

+ dative (no motion, or motion within) or accusative (motion towards)

in front of (dative)

draußen vorm Haus stand eine Straßenlaterne, *outside in front of the house stood a streetlamp*
er ging zwei Schritte vor mir, *he walked two paces in front of me* (no motion relative to me)

in front of (accusative)

stell dein Auto vor die Polizeiwache, *leave your car in front of the police station*

before (dative)

vor Sonnenuntergang, *before sunset*
vor dem letzten Krieg, *before the last war*
zehn Minuten vor zehn, *ten to (= before) ten*

of (= *in the face of; as a consequence of*)

sie stirbt vor Hunger, *she's dying of hunger*
ich habe Angst vor Stieren, *I'm afraid of bulls*
vor Stieren muß man immer auf der Hut sein, *you must always beware of bulls*

da war keine Warnung vor Stieren, *there was no warning of bulls*

with; for (with emotions; dative)

er strahlte vor Freude, *he beamed with joy*
ich konnte vor Aufregung nicht denken, *I couldn't think for excitement*

während, *during*

+ genitive

during

es geschah während des Kriegs, *it happened during the war*

Sometimes takes dative instead of genitive, and must do when the noun has no article or adjective in front of it:

während drei Jahren, *for three years*

wegen, *because of*

+ genitive; in literary German may follow its noun

because of

wir sind nur wegen des guten Wetters hier, *we're only here because of the fine weather*

on . . . 's account

tu das nicht wegen meines Mannes!, *don't do it on my husband's account*

Sometimes takes dative instead of genitive, and must do with a pronoun or when the noun has no article or adjective in front of it:

tu das nicht wegen mir!, *don't do it on my account!*
bloß wegen ein paar Leuten, *just because of a few people*

The compound forms **meinetwegen, deinetwegen**, etc. are also used instead of **wegen mir, wegen dir**, etc.

Von wegen + dative is used in colloquial German to mean *about*:

erzähl mir nichts von wegen Lohnsteuer!, *don't talk to me about income tax!*

wider, *against*

+ accusative; less common; literary

ich tat es wider Willen, *I did it against my will*

zu, *to*

+ dative

to

ich fahre zu meiner Tante in Ostfriesland, *I'm going to my aunt in Ostfriesland*
ich fahre zum Flughafen, *I'm driving to the airport*
du gehst zu Bett!, *you're going to bed now*
er geht zur Schule, *he goes to school*
du bist zum Abendessen eingeladen, *you're invited to supper*
kommen Sie zur Sache!, *come to the point!*

at

zu Ostern und zu Weihnachten, *at Easter and Christmas*
zu Hause, *at home*
die da zu drei Mark, bitte, *those at three marks, please*
der Römer zu Frankfurt, *the Römer (town-hall) at Frankfurt*

for

meine Neigung (Freundschaft; Liebe) zu Ihnen, *my liking (friendship; love) for you*

bist du zum Essen fertig?, *are you ready to eat (= for eating)?*
zum zweiten Mal, *for the second time*
was kriegst du zu Weihnachten (deinem Geburtstag)?, *what are you getting for Christmas (your birthday)?*

zufolge, *in accordance with*

► See **gemäß**, p. 173.

zuliebe, *for the sake of*

+ dative; less common; follows noun or pronoun

tu es mir zuliebe, *do it for my sake*

zwischen, *between*

+ dative (no motion, or motion within) or accusative (motion towards)

between (dative)

sie stand zwischen mir und ihrem Bruder, *she was standing between her brother and me*
sie ging zwischen mir und ihrem Bruder, *she was walking between her brother and me* (no motion relative to us)

between (accusative)

das Auto fuhr zwischen die Eingangssäulen und in die große Garage, *the car drove between the entrance pillars and into the big garage*

CROSS-REFERENCE LIST OF ENGLISH PREPOSITIONS

Prepositions presenting problems of translation are listed. These prepositions are cross-referenced to the list of German prepositions starting on p. 163. It is dangerous to take a German meaning from the list that follows without subsequently checking its usage in the German list.

about

an, 164
über, 181
von, 183
with numbers, **gegen**, 172

above

oberhalb, 178
über, 180

according to

laut, 175
nach, 176

after

nach, 176

against

gegen, 172
wider, 186

along

entlang, 171

among

unter, 182

apart from

außer, 167

around

um, 181

as . . . as in comparisons
so . . . wie. See p. 114.

as far as
bis, 169

as well as
neben, 178

at
an, 163
auf, 165
bei, 168
mit, 175
zu, 186
with clock times, **um**, 181

at the house of
bei, 168

because of
wegen, 185

before
vor, 184

behind
hinter, 173–4

below
unter, 182
unterhalb, 183

beside
neben, 177

besides
neben, 178

between
zwischen, 187

beyond
außer, 167
hinter, 173
jenseits, 175

by
an, 164
durch, 171
mit, 176
per, 178
= *according to*, **nach**, 176
= *near*, **bei**, 168
+ time, **bis**, 170
+ time, distance, **um**, 181
(with passive) **von**, 183

compared to
gegen, 172
gegenüber, 173

corresponding to
entsprechend, 171

during
während, 185

except
außer, 167
bis auf, 170

for
bei, 168
für, 171–2
nach, 176
um, 182
zu, 186–7
= *in exchange for*, **gegen**, 172
+ future time, **auf**, 166
+ past time continuing, **seit**, 179

+ completed past time, **während**, 182
+ emotion, **vor**, 185
See also p. 237

for the sake of
um . . . willen, see **um**, 182
zuliebe, 187

from
aus, 166–7
von, 183
time, **ab**, 163

from . . . on
place, **ab**, 163

given
unter, 182

in
auf, 166
bei, 168
in, 174
= *given*, **unter**, 182

in accordance with
gemäß; **zufolge**, 173

including
eingerechnet, 171

in front of
vor, 184

in respect of
an, 164

inside
innerhalb, 174–5

in spite of
trotz, 180

opposite
gegenüber, 173

out of
aus, 166
außer, 167

outside
außerhalb, 167

over
über, 180

per
per; **pro**, 178

round
um, 181

since
seit, 178–9
See also p. 242

thanks to
dank, 170

through
durch, 170

to
an, 165
auf, 166
in, 174
zu, 186
with countries, towns, continents, **nach**; **in** 176–7

to the (+ directions)
nach, 177

to the house of
zu, 168

I Conjunctions

Conjunctions are joining-words. They may join nouns or pronouns:

> **sie oder ihr Hund**, *she or her dog* (conjunction: **oder**)

or phrases:

> **ein sehr aufgeregter und doch noch arbeitender Beamter**, *an official, very excited and yet still working* (conjunction: **und**)

or two or more main clauses:

> **er singt, aber er kann nicht spielen**, *he sings, but he can't play* (conjunction: **aber**)

A conjunction like this that can join two main clauses together is called a coordinating conjunction.

Some conjunctions introduce subordinate clauses:

> **ich tue es, sobald ich das Geld habe**, *I'll do it as soon as I have the money* (conjunction: **sobald**)

This sort of conjunction is called a subordinating conjunction.

COORDINATING CONJUNCTIONS

In German there are six common coordinating conjunctions. When these conjunctions introduce a clause they are followed by normal word order—i.e. subject, verb, rest of sentence. See Word Order, p. 215.

They are:

- **aber**, *but*
- **allein**, *only; but*
- **denn**, *for*
- **oder**, *or*
- **sondern**, *but (on the contrary)*
- **und**, *and*

Nearly all other conjunctions are subordinating conjunctions (see p. 197).

■ **Aber** can also be an adverb, meaning *however:*

> **ihr Zug war verspätet, sie ist aber angekommen,** *her train was late; she's arrived, however,* (or, *but she's arrived*)

■ **Allein** explains why something didn't happen:

> **ich hatte mitfahren wollen, allein ich war erkältet,** *I had wanted to go with them, only (but) I had a cold*

It is rather literary: **aber** is usually used in this sense in spoken German.

■ **Oder** is also used in *either . . . or* sentences: **entweder . . . oder**:

> **entweder bezahlt er die Rechnung, oder er bekommt die Sachen nicht**, *either he pays the bill or he doesn't get the goods*
>
> **entweder Sie bezahlen, oder ich rufe die Polizei,** *either you pay or I call the police*

Note the two possible word orders in the **entweder** half of the sentence. There is a difference in tone: inversion after **entweder**, no threat; normal order after **entweder**, threat!

The opposite of **entweder . . . oder** is **weder . . . noch**, *neither . . . nor*. Both **weder** and **noch** are adverbs, and both must be followed by inversion:

> **weder bezahle ich, noch werden Sie die Polizei rufen**, *I shall neither pay, nor will you call the police*

■ **Sondern** always follows a negative and has the sense of a correction: '*not this but, on the contrary, that*'. Compare:

> **das ist nicht wahr, sondern (es ist) falsch**, *that's not true, but false*
>
> **das ist nicht wahr, aber es ist interessant**, *that's not true, but it's interesting*

Not only . . . but also is **nicht nur . . . sondern auch**:

> **nicht nur ist es furchtbar einfach, sondern man kann es jetzt auch sehr preiswert bekommen,** *not only is it very easy, but you can now also get it very cheaply*

Nicht nur is an adverb, followed by inversion; **sondern** is a coordinating conjunction followed by normal order; and the **auch** stands as an adverb later in the second clause.

SUBORDINATING CONJUNCTIONS

Apart from the conjunctions listed above all others are subordinating: they send the verb to the end of the clause. See Word Order, p. 222.

If the clause introduced by a subordinating conjunction stands first in the sentence, the main-clause verb stands immediately after it. See Word Order, p. 216.

Question words (**wo**, **wann**, etc.) can also be used as subordinating conjunctions in order to introduce indirect questions:

> **wann kommt er?**, *when is he coming?*
> **ich frage mich, wann er kommt**, *I wonder when he's coming*

Problems of some subordinating conjunctions

■ **Als, wenn, wann,** *when*

□ **Als** is only used to mean '*when, on one occasion in the past*':

> **als er anrief, wußte ich sofort, wer es war**, *when he phoned I knew straight away who it was*

□ **Wenn** means *when* in the present and future:

> **wenn er anruft, werde ich ihm die Wahrheit sagen**, *when he phones I'll tell him the truth*

However, **wenn** can also mean *if*; if there is ambiguity, use **sobald**, *as soon as*, for *when*:

> **sobald er anruft, werde ich ihm die Wahrheit sagen**

□ **Wenn** is also used to mean '*when, on more than one occasion in the past*'. If there is ambiguity in this sense of **wenn**, use **sooft**, *as often as*:

> **er rief an, wenn er konnte / sooft er konnte**, *he phoned when(ever) he could*

□ **Wann** is the question word *when*, also used in indirect questions:

> **wann ruft er an?**, *when is he phoning?*
> **ich weiß nicht, wann er anruft**, *I don't know when he's phoning*

□ After time expressions (*the day when . . . , the moment when . . .*), **als** and **wenn** may be used for *when*, but **wo** is also frequently found:

> **der Tag, als er ankam / wo er ankam**, *the day when he arrived*

■ **Bis**, *until*; **erst als, erst wenn**, *not until*

Bis is both a preposition and a subordinating conjunction:

> **bis morgen**, *until tomorrow* (preposition)
> **bis wir kommen**, *until we come* (conjunction)

► See pp. 169–70 for **bis** as a preposition.

□ The negative of **bis** the conjunction (*not until*) is **erst als** or **erst wenn** (see p. 197 for the difference between **als** and **wenn**):

> **erst wenn wir kommen, wird er fahren dürfen**, *not until we come will he be allowed to leave*
> **erst als wir kamen, durfte er fahren**, *not until we came was he allowed to leave*

Notice what happens when the 'not until' clause stands second in the sentence:

> **er wird erst fahren dürfen, wenn wir kommen,** *he will not be allowed to leave until we come*

□ **Bis** can also mean *by the time that*:

> **bis du kommst, habe ich alles aufgegessen,** *by the time you come I'll have eaten everything*

■ **Seit(dem),** *since*

Seitdem is the conjunction corresponding to the preposition **seit**, *since*. **Seit** can also be used as a conjunction, but **seitdem** is more common.

The tenses used with **seit(dem)** are the same in all respects as those used with **seit** the preposition (see Prepositions, pp. 178–9):

□ Events start in the past, continue to present . . .

Both clauses are in the present tense in German (both perfect in English):

> **seitdem ich hier wohne, bin ich viel glücklicher,** *since I've been living here I've been much happier*

With a negative main clause, the main clause is in the perfect, the **seitdem** clause in the present tense (both perfect in English):

> **seitdem ich hier wohne, habe ich keinen Menschen gesehen,** *since I've been living here I've seen no one*

□ Events start in the past, continue to the point in the past we are talking about . . .

Both clauses are in the past tense in German (both pluperfect in English):

> **seitdem ich dort wohnte, war ich viel glücklicher,** *since I'd been living there, I'd been much happier*

With a negative main clause, the main clause is in the pluperfect, the **seitdem** clause in the past tense (both pluperfect in English):

> **seitdem ich dort wohnte, hatte ich keinen Menschen gesehen**, *since I'd been living here I'd seen no one*

Numbers, Time, Measurements

CARDINAL NUMBERS

The cardinal numbers are

0	**null**	19	**neunzehn**
1	**ein** (**eins** when counting)	20	**zwanzig**
2	**zwei** (often **zwo** in speech)	21	**einundzwanzig**
3	**drei**	22	**zweiundzwanzig** . . .
4	**vier**	30	**dreißig**
5	**fünf**	40	**vierzig**
6	**sechs**	50	**fünfzig**
7	**sieben**	60	**sechzig**
8	**acht**	70	**siebzig**
9	**neun**	80	**achtzig**
10	**zehn**	90	**neunzig**
11	**elf**	100	**(ein)hundert**
12	**zwölf**	101	**(ein)hundert(und)eins** . . .
13	**dreizehn**	200	**zweihundert** . . .
14	**vierzehn**	1000	**(ein)tausend**
15	**fünfzehn**	1001	**tausendeins** . . .
16	**sechzehn**	2000	**zweitausend** . . .
17	**siebzehn**	1000 000	**eine Million** . . .
18	**achtzehn**	1000 000 000	**eine Milliarde**

■ Number punctuation

□ There are no commas between numbers in German; instead a space is left. This space is often (but not always) omitted with units of thousands:

9000 but **10 000**

Very occasionally numbers are found printed with full stops instead of spaces.

□ Telephone numbers are split up into (and spoken in) pairs:

54 78 34, vierundfünfzig achtundsiebzig vierunddreißig

□ The centuries (except millennia) are counted in hundreds:

im Jahre neunzehnhundertneunundneunzig, *in 1999*
but: **im Jahre zweitausend**, *in 2000*

□ Numbers up to but not including **eine Million** are written as a single word:

zwei Millionen dreihundertsiebentausendneunhundertneunundneunzig, *2,307,999*

Such monster written forms are avoided wherever possible; a space or hyphen is sometimes found after **-tausend**.

■ **Ein** has an **-s** when counting, in arithmetic, and when used after a noun (**Zimmer eins**, *room one*); otherwise it declines like the indefinite article. At the end of compounds, however (**hunderteins** etc.), it has the **-s** form even when standing before a noun. Unlike the indefinite article, **ein** = *one* is stressed in spoken German.

One can be a pronoun, in which case it is **einer, eine, ein(e)s,** declined like **dieser** (see Indefinites, p. 148):

nimm ein(e)s von den beiden!, *take one of the two*

■ As well as their numerical-adjective forms above, **das Hundert** and **das Tausend** are also nouns, used in such contexts as **viele Tausende von Menschen**, *many thousands of people*. **Die Million** and **die Milliarde** only have noun forms. They both take a plural **-(e)n**; this plural form is also used when counting.

■ Note the colloquial form **zig-**, *umpteen*: **zighundert**, *umpteen hundred*, **zigtausend**, *umpteen thousand*.

■ Indeclinable forms in **-er** are used in the following cases; the nouns are masculine:

> **ein Fünfziger**, *a 50-mark note*
> **ein Dreiundneunziger**, *a '93 wine*
> **in den achtziger Jahren**, *in the eighties*

ORDINAL NUMBERS

Ordinal numbers (*first, second, third,* etc.) are formed by adding **-t** to the cardinal number (up to and including **neunzehnt-**, *nineteenth*) or **-st** (from **zwanzigst-**, *twentieth,* on). **Erst-**, *first,* **dritt-**, *third,* **siebt-**, *seventh,* and **acht-**, *eighth,* are irregular.

> **erst-**
> **zweit-** (often **zwot-** in conversation, by analogy with **zwo**)
> **dritt-**
> **viert-** . . .
> **sechst-**
> **siebt-** (**siebent-** exists but sounds old-fashioned)
> **acht-**
> **neunt-** . . .
> **zwanzigst-**
> **einundzwanzigst-** . . .
> **dreißigst-** . . .
> **(ein)hundertst-**
> **(ein)hundert(und)erst-** . . .
> **millionst-**

■ Ordinals are adjectives. They always have endings.

■ Ordinals compound with superlatives:

> **das zweitkleinste Bundesland**, *the second smallest Federal State*

They also form adverbs with **-ens**:

> **drittens**, *thirdly*

See p. 206.

■ The German order with **erst-** (and **letzt-**) used with a cardinal number is often the reverse of the English:

> **die drei ersten (letzten) Wagen**, *the first (last) three coaches*

The English order (**die ersten drei**) is also possible.

■ To abbreviate ordinals a full stop or occasionally **(s)t-** is used, thus:

> **zweite**: **2.**; **II.**; **2te**
> **zwanzigste**: **20.**; **XX.**; **20ste**

Roman numerals + full stop are used for the names of kings:

> **Heinrich V.**, *Heinrich V*

■ The ordinals are used with **zu** and without any ending to mean *in . . . s*:

> **zu zweit,** *in twos*; **zu dritt**, *in threes*, etc.

In ones is **einzeln**.

FRACTIONS

Fractions are formed by adding **-el** to the ordinal. They have a small letter as (indeclinable) adjectives, a capital as (neuter) nouns. Whole number + fraction is frequently written as a single word:

> **ein achtel Liter**, *an eighth of a litre*
> **ein Viertel Leberwurst**, *a quarter of liver sausage*
> **Viertel vor eins**, *a quarter to one*
> **eineinviertel**, *one and a quarter*
>
> **das Ganze**, *the whole*
> **ein halb / die Hälfte**, ½
> **ein drittel**, ⅓
> **ein viertel**, ¼
> **ein hundertstel**, 1/100

drei siebtel, 3/7
anderthalb / ein(und)einhalb, 1½
zweieinhalb, 2½

Compounds of **-halb** (**anderthalb**, etc.) take no endings.

■ **Halb** and **Hälfte**

ein halb- = *half a*

ein halbes Dutzend Eier, *half a dozen eggs*

die Hälfte = *half (of)*

die Hälfte meines Vermögens, *half my money*

halb = *half (adverb)*

meine Arbeit is nur halb fertig, *my work is only half finished*

■ Decimals are written (and spoken) with a comma rather than a decimal point:

11,704: **elf Komma sieben null vier**, or **elfkommasiebennullvier**, *11·704*

■ The basic mathematical signs are:

+	**und; plus**	÷	**(geteilt) durch**
–	**weniger; minus**	^{2}	**hoch zwei**
×	**mal**	%	**Prozent**

zwanzig durch fünf (ist) gleich vier, *twenty divided by five equals (is) four*
drei hoch zwei (ist) gleich neun, *three squared equals (is) nine*
sieben Prozent, *seven per cent*

NUMERICAL COMPOUNDS

■ **einfach**, *simple*
zweifach, *double* (also **doppelt**)
dreifach, *triple*, etc.

These are ordinary adjectives.

- **einmal**, *once*
  zweimal, *twice*
  dreimal, *three times*, etc.
  x-mal, zigmal, *umpteen times*
- **erstens**, *firstly*
  zweitens, *secondly*
  drittens, *thirdly*, etc.
- **einerlei**, *one kind of* (also: *the same kind of; identical*)
  zweierlei, *two kinds of*
  dreierlei, *three kinds of*, etc.

These are invariable adjectives.

Note the idiomatic use of **einerlei**:

es ist mir einerlei, *it's all the same to me*

TIME AND DATE

Time of day

wie spät ist es?; wieviel Uhr ist es?, *what time is it?*
haben Sie die richtige Uhrzeit bitte?, *do you have the right time please?* (more polite)

es ist ein Uhr, one o'clock
fünf (Minuten) nach eins, *five past one*
Viertel nach eins, *quarter past one*
fünfundzwanzig (Minuten) nach eins / fünf vor halb zwei, *twenty-five past one*
halb zwei, *half past one* (NB: not '*half past two*'!)
Viertel vor zwei, *quarter to two*
eine Minute vor zwei, *a minute to two*
zwei Uhr, *two o'clock*
fünf vor (nach) zwölf, *five to (past) twelve*

Mittag, *twelve noon*
Mitternacht, *midnight*

The forms **Viertel (auf) drei** and **drei Viertel (auf) drei** for *quarter past two* and *quarter to three* (etc.) are sometimes heard in south Germany, constructed on the same look-ahead principle as **halb drei**.

■ There are no equivalents to a.m. and p.m. in German. To be specific use:

vormittags, *in the morning*
nachmittags, *in the afternoon*
abends, *in the evening*
nachts, *at night*

■ Units of clock time

die Sekunde, *second*
die Minute, *minute*
die Stunde, *hour*
eine halbe Stunde, *half an hour*
eine Viertelstunde, *a quarter of an hour,*
eine Dreiviertelstunde, *three-quarters of an hour*

The 24-hour clock

The 24-hour clock is much more common in Germany than here, being used for virtually all official and semi-official times; the 12-hour clock is standard in conversation, however.

es ist ein Uhr fünfzehn, *01.15*
ein Uhr dreißig, *01.30*
ein Uhr fünfundvierzig, *01.45*
dreizehn Uhr, *13.00*
vierundzwanzig Uhr, *24.00* (24 as opposed to 00 is only normally used for midnight exactly)
null Uhr eins, *00.01*

Expressions with time of day

- **ab**, from

  ab sieben Uhr, *from seven (on)*

- **bis**, *by*

  bis elf Uhr sind wir da, *we'll be there by eleven*

Bis also means *until*—the context makes clear which:

das Restaurant hat von Mittag bis drei auf, *the restaurant's open from twelve to three*

See Prepositions, pp. 169–70.

- **gegen**; **ungefähr um**, *at about*

  der Zug kommt ungefähr um Mittag (gegen Mittag) an, *the train comes in at about 12 o'clock*

Ungefähr um is to be preferred, since **gegen** is ambiguous—it could mean '*towards*', i.e. *just before* (clearer: **kurz vor**). **Um . . . herum**, *about*, is also common in spoken German.

- **Punkt**; **genau**; **gerade**, *exactly*

  es ist Punkt/genau/gerade eins, *it's exactly one o'clock*
  es ist genau/gerade ein Uhr zwanzig, *it's exactly twenty past one*
  es ist genau halb, *it's exactly half past*

- **um**, *at*

  um wieviel Uhr fährt der Zug?, *what time does the train go?*
  um sieben Uhr, *at seven o'clock*

Note also: **Schlag zwei**, *on (at) the stroke of two.*

- **vorbei**, *past*

  es ist Mitternacht vorbei, *it's past midnight*

Note the position of **vorbei**.

Days, months, seasons

■ **Sonntag**, *Sunday*
Montag, *Monday*
Dienstag, *Tuesday*
Mittwoch, *Wednesday*
Donnerstag, *Thursday*
Freitag, *Friday*
Sonnabend (north Germany), **Samstag** (south Germany), *Saturday*

Days of the week are masculine.

was ist heute für ein Tag?—Heute ist Montag, *what day is it?—It's Monday*

■ **Januar**, *January*
Februar, *February*
März, *March*
April, *April*
Mai, *May*
Juni, *June*
Juli, *July*
August, *August*
September, *September*
Oktober, *October*
November, *November*
Dezember, *December*

Months are masculine.

■ **der Frühling**, *spring*
der Sommer, *summer*
der Herbst, *autumn*
der Winter, *winter*

Seasons are normally used with the definite article.

■ **vorgestern**, *the day before yesterday*
gestern, *yesterday*

heute, *today*
morgen, *tomorrow*
übermorgen, *the day after tomorrow*

■ **gestern morgen, gestern früh**, *yesterday morning*
gestern nachmittag, *yesterday afternoon*
gestern abend, *last night* (= *yesterday evening*)

heute nacht, *last night* (= *during the night*)
heute früh, heute morgen, heute vormittag, *this morning*
heute nachmittag, heute mittag, *this afternoon*
heute abend, *tonight* (= *this evening*)
heute nacht, *tonight* (= *during the night*)

morgen früh, *tomorrow morning* (*tomorrow early* is **morgen ganz früh**)
morgen nachmittag, *tomorrow afternoon*
morgen abend, *tomorrow evening*

Note the ambiguity in **heute nacht**, *last night* or *tonight*. The context makes the meaning clear.

■ **vor drei Monaten**, *three months ago*
vorletzte Woche, *the week before last*
gestern vor einer Woche, gestern vor acht (NB!) **Tagen**, *a week ago yesterday*
heute in einer Woche, heute über acht Tage, *a week today*
übernächste Woche, *the week after next*
in drei Monaten, *in three months time*

■ **lange vorher**, *long before*
ein Jahr vorher, *a year before*
am Tag vorher, tags zuvor, *the day before*
am folgenden Tag, tags darauf, *the day after*
ein Jahr danach, *a year after*
lange danach, *long after*

The date

der wievielte ist heute?, den wievielten haben wir heute?, *what's the date today?*
heute ist der erste Januar, *today's the first of January*
heute ist der Erste, *today's the first*
wir fahren Sonnabend den Sechsten, *we go on Saturday the sixth*

Length of time

■ **lang(e)**, *for* (time completed, normally in the past)

wie lange war er dort?, *how long was he there?*
er war drei Wochen (lang) dort, *he was there (for) three weeks*
er war stundenlang (**tagelang, wochenlang**, etc.) **dort**, *he was there (for) hours* (*days, weeks,* etc.)

Lang(e) may be omitted, except in the question and where it forms part of the word. The **-e** is often dropped. Note **eine Zeitlang**, *for a time*.

■ **auf, für**, *for* (time intended)

(auf) wie lange ist er hier?, *how long is he here (for)?*
er ist auf drei Wochen hier, *he's here for three weeks*

Though this construction normally refers to future time, it can be set back into the past, still conveying the intention:

er war auf drei Wochen dort, *he was there for three weeks* (he intended to stay that long)

Auf is followed by the accusative. **Für** may be used instead of **auf**. It is slightly less common.

- **seit**, *for* (time started in the past, continuing into the present)

  seit wie lange ist er hier?, *how long has he been here?*
  er ist hier seit drei Wochen, *he's been here for three weeks*

▶ For tenses with **seit** see p. 179.

Definite time expressions

Definite expressions of time stand in the accusative, or take a preposition, usually **an** or **in** + dative:

den ganzen Tag (Morgen, Nachmittag, etc.), *all day* (*morning, afternoon*, etc.)
jeden Tag, *every day*
alle drei Tage, *every third day*
diesen Freitag, dieses Jahr, *this Friday, this year*
nächsten Freitag, *next Friday* (= *the coming Friday*)
den nächsten Tag, am nächsten Tag, *next day* (= *the day following*)

am Freitag, *on Friday*
im Januar, *in January*
im Frühling, *in spring*
am Abend, *in the evening*
am Tag, *by day*
dreimal am Tag (in der Woche), *three times a day* (*a week*)
in der Nacht, *by night, in the night*
im Jahre 1999, *in 1999* (or just **1999**—but NOT '**in 1999**')
im siebzehnten Jahrhundert, *in the 17th century*
n. Chr. (= nach Christus), *AD*
v. Chr. (= vor Christus), *BC*

Folgend, *following*, **letzt**, *last*, **vorig, vergangen**, *previous*, may be used in the same way as **nächst**.

No preposition is used with **Anfang, Mitte, Ende**:

er kommt Anfang (Mitte, Ende) Mai, *he's coming at the beginning (in the middle, at the end) of May*

Indefinite time expressions

Indefinite expressions of time stand in the genitive:

eines Tages, *one day*
eines Abends, *one evening*
eines Montags, *one Monday*
morgens, vormittags, *in the morning*
nachmittags, *in the afternoon*
abends, *in the evening*
wochentags, *on weekdays*
sonntags, *on Sundays*

By analogy: **eines Nachts**, *one night*, **nachts**, *at night*—in spite of the fact that **Nacht** is feminine!

MEASUREMENTS

welche Maße hat die Küche?, *what are the kitchen's measurements?*

die Küche ist 3,20 Meter (drei Meter zwanzig, or—more technically—**dreikommazweinull Meter) lang, 2,10 Meter breit und 2,20 Meter hoch**, *the kitchen is 3·2 metres long, 2·1 metres wide, and 2·2 metres high*

3,20 (Meter) mal 2,10 mal 2,20, *3·2 metres by 2·1 by 2·2*

welche Größe haben Sie (tragen Sie)?, *what size are you (do you take)?*

ich habe (trage) Größe 13, *I'm (I take) size 13*

wieviel wiegst du?, *what do you weigh?*

ich wiege einhundertdreißig Kilo, *I weigh 130 kg.*

wie groß sind Sie?, *how tall are you?*
ich bin ein Meter neunzig groß, *I'm 1·9 metres tall*
drei Meter tief, drei Meter dick, *three metres deep, three metres thick*
das Thermometer steht auf zwei (Grad), *the thermometer is at (on) two degrees*
2000 cm^3 (zweitausend Kubikzentimeter), *2000 cc*

I Word Order

WORD ORDER IN MAIN CLAUSES

There are two types of word order in main clauses in German, *normal order*, in which the subject comes first, the verb second, and then the rest of the clause third; and *inverted order*, in which something other than the subject comes first, the verb second, the subject (usually) third, and then the rest of the clause fourth.

Normal and inverted order

■ In both normal and inverted order the verb is firmly fixed as the second grammatical element in the clause. Subject, object, adverb, or adverb clause may precede the verb in a German sentence, but only one of these.

□ Normal order, subject first, verb second:

> **der junge Mann stand um halb neun sehr böse vorm Kino**, *the young man was standing outside the cinema at half past eight in a very bad temper*

□ Inverted order, verb second, subject third:

> **furchtbar böse stand der junge Mann um halb neun vorm Kino**
> **um halb neun stand der junge Mann furchtbar böse vorm Kino**
> **vorm Kino stand der junge Mann um halb neun furchtbar böse**

In each of these instances the verb is the second grammatical element in the sentence; in each instance one (and only one!) adverb phrase stands in front of it and the subject stands after it.

The first element in inverted order may be an entire subordinate clause (itself in subordinate order, see p. 222); it will be followed by a comma, with the main-clause verb next and then the main-clause subject:

> **wenn du so spät ankommst** (subordinate clause), **bin** (main-clause verb) **ich** (main-clause subject) **natürlich böse**, *if you arrive so late naturally I'm cross*

■ A coordinating conjunction may introduce a second or subsequent main clause to the sentence, followed by normal order:

> **er war furchtbar böse, denn der Film hatte schon angefangen**, *he was in a very bad temper, for the film had already started*

The coordinating conjunction **denn** (see p. 195) is here followed by normal order: subject, verb, rest of sentence.

■ There may be two or more main clauses joined by **und** or **oder** where, as in English, the subject is understood from the first:

> **er lief ins Wohnzimmer, nahm seinen Rechner in die Hand und lief wieder hinaus**, *he ran into the living room, picked up his calculator, and ran out again*

This is in fact normal order: the **er** from the first **er lief** is understood before **nahm** and again before the second **lief**.

In German the subject can be understood *only* in its normal position in front of the verb. If there is something else standing in front of the verb in the second or third clause of a sentence like the one above, the subject, in this case **er**, must be expressed:

> **er lief ins Wohnzimmer, nahm seinen Rechner in die Hand, und ohne weiteres lief er hinaus**, *. . . and without further ado ran out* (in German the subject **er** must be there if **ohne weiteres** stands before the verb)

■ The following, standing at the head of a clause, are not felt to be part of it; they have a comma after them and do not affect subsequent word order:

□ **ja** and **nein**

> **nein, das glaube ich nicht,** *no, I don't believe it*

□ exclamations (which may have either a comma or an exclamation mark)

> **ach, ich habe meinen Schlüssel vergessen**, *oh, I've forgotten my key*

□ names of people addressed

> **Günter, dich meinte ich nicht,** *Günter, I didn't mean you*

□ **er sagte**, and other verbs introducing indirect speech, but not followed by **daß**:

> **er sagte, er wollte sofort bezahlen**, *he said he wanted to pay right away*

See p. 42.

□ summing-up expressions, for example

> **das heißt**, *that is*
> **im Gegenteil**, *on the contrary*
> **ehrlich gesagt**, *to be honest*
> **unter uns**, *between ourselves*
> **wie gesagt**, *as I said*
> **wissen Sie**, *you know*

> **unter uns, ich konnte sie nie leiden**, *between ourselves, I never liked her*

Position of the parts of the verb in compound tenses

■ In past compound tenses the auxiliary verb stays in the second position, but the past participle goes to the end of the clause:

er hatte sehr lang gewartet, *he had waited for a very long time*

■ With future and conditional tenses the auxiliary verb stays in second position, and the infinitive goes to the end:

sie wird sicher bald kommen, *she's sure to turn up soon*

■ With future perfect and conditional perfect tenses the order at the end of the clause is past participle, then infinitive:

er wird sehr lange gewartet haben, *he will have been waiting a very long time*

Position of the prefix with separable verbs

■ In simple tenses of separable verbs the separable prefix goes to the end of the clause:

der Film fing vor zwanzig Minuten an, *the film started twenty minutes ago*

■ In compound tenses of such verbs the prefix and the past participle or the prefix and the infinitive both go to the end of the clause and join up:

der Film hat schon angefangen, *the film has already started*
der Film wird bald anfangen, *the film will soon start*

► See Separable Prefixes, p. 33, and Double Prefixes, pp. 34–6.

Position of the verb in direct questions

In direct questions the verb is placed either first, or, if there is a question word to introduce the question, immediately after this:

bleibst du noch lange hier vorm Kino stehen?, *are you going to stay standing here in front of the cinema for much longer?*

wo bist du denn geblieben?, *where have you been, then?*

As in English a statement with the appropriate intonation may be used as a question. The verb is then second:

du kommst rein?, *(are) you coming in?*

Position of the verb in commands

In commands the verb is usually placed first in the sentence. If the subject is expressed it follows the verb:

komm schnell rein, wir verpassen den Film!, *come on in quickly, we're missing the film*
sei du mal ruhig!, *(you) just be quiet!*

Position of the subject

■ In statements the subject is normally first or third, though object pronouns after the verb may displace a noun subject to fourth position:

noch lange ruhte sich der alte Großvater in der Küche aus, *for some time yet the old grandfather stayed resting in the kitchen*

Here the reflexive direct object is third, the noun subject fourth.

Putting something other than the subject first in a statement usually gives extra emphasis to whatever is put first.

zum allerletzten Mal wiederhole ich die Frage, *I shall repeat the question for the very last time*

■ In questions the subject is second or (if there is a question word) third, immediately after the verb. As in statements, an object pronoun after the verb may stand before a noun subject.

Position of the object

■ Objects usually come early in the sentence after the verb. In normal order a pronoun object comes directly after the verb:

> **er nahm sich schnell noch etwas von dem schmackhaften Eintopf**, *he quickly helped himself to some more of the tasty stew*

The **sich** (indirect object) comes straight after the verb; the short adverb **schnell**, however, comes before the long direct object **noch etwas von dem schmackhaften Eintopf**.

■ If there is more than one object

□ pronoun objects always precede noun objects:

> **schick mir eine Karte!**, *send me a card*

□ with two pronoun objects the accusative comes first:

> **schick sie mir!**, *send it to me*

□ with two noun objects the dative comes first:

> **schick Karen die Karte!**, *send Karen the card*

This is identical with the most common (though not the only possible) order of objects in English.

Position of the complement

The complement of such verbs as **sein**, *to be*, **werden**, *to become*, and **bleiben**, *to remain*, goes as late in the clause as possible:

> **sie ist sicher dieses Jahr zum erstenmal Karnevalsprinzessin**, *she's certainly going to be carnival princess this year, for the first time*

Position of adverbs

■ The normal order of adverbs is *time—reason—manner—place*:

er fährt sofort mit dem Auto nach Hildesheim, *he's going right away by car to Hildesheim*

er fährt heute wegen ihrer Heirat nach Hildesheim, *he's going to Hildesheim today for (because of) her wedding*

If there are two adverbs of the same kind the more general one comes first:

er fuhr letztes Jahr am einundzwanzigsten August nach Hildesheim, *last year he went to Hildesheim, on the twenty-first of August*

A time adverb will often precede a noun object:

er hat gestern sein Auto verkauft, *he sold his car yesterday*

The order and position of adverbs is, however, far from rigid: moving one to a position late in the sentence gives it additional importance:

er hat sein Auto gestern verkauft *(he sold it yesterday, he can't have sold it today, whatever you say)*

Generally speaking, in German the strong, important position in the sentence is at the end.

■ Negative adverbs (**nicht, nie**, etc.) stand in front of the word or words they are negating:

das habe ich nie wirklich gesagt, *I never really said that*

If they negate the action of the verb they stand as near the end as possible:

das habe ich wirklich nie gesagt, *I really never said that.*

► See also **kein**, p. 153.

WORD ORDER IN SUBORDINATE CLAUSES

A subordinate clause may be introduced by a subordinating conjunction (any conjunction except the six coordinating ones, see p. 195), or by a relative pronoun (see p. 139). All parts of the clause stay in main-clause order except the verb, which moves to the very end of the clause.

normal order: **ich habe nicht genug Geld**, *I haven't enough money*

subordinate order: **ich tue es, weil ich nicht genug Geld habe**, *I'm doing it because I haven't enough money*

■ In subordinate order a separable verb recombines with its prefix at the end of the clause:

normal order: **ich gehe in zwanzig Minuten fort**, *I'm going out in twenty minutes*

subordinate order: **ich tue es, weil ich in zwanzig Minuten fortgehe**, *I'm doing it because I'm going out in twenty minutes*

▶ See p. 33.

■ If there is a past participle or an infinitive at the end of the clause the verb goes beyond these, right at the end:

ein Mann muß tun, was ein Mann tun muß, *a man's got to do what a man's got to do*

However, if there are two or more infinitive forms at the end of the clause the verb will stand immediately before and not after these:

damals hat ein Mann tun müssen, was ein Mann hat tun müssen, *in those days a man had to do what a man had to do*

▶ See p. 67.

■ If there are two subordinate clauses joined by **und** (or **oder** or **sondern**), the verb goes to the end in both:

ich tue es, weil ich fortgehen muß und nicht sehr viel Zeit habe, *I'm doing it because I'm going out and (I) haven't got very much time*

If two subordinate clauses share the same verb, it goes at the end of the second one:

ich tue es, weil ich in die Stadt fahren und fürs Wochenende einkaufen muß, *I'm doing it because I have to go into town and shop for the weekend*

■ If one subordinate clause is embedded in another, they must both have subordinate order:

ich frage mich, ob das Auto, das ich letzte Woche gekauft habe, wirklich so viel wert ist, *I'm wondering if the car I bought last week is really worth that much*

Don't be tempted to say or write '**. . . ist wirklich so viel wert**'.

■ Either subordinate or inverted order may be used for exclamatory clauses:

was für blöde Sachen er geredet hat! / was hat er für blöde Sachen geredet!, *what rubbish he talked!*

■ Subordinate order is not always adhered to in spoken German: phrases tend to be added after the verb:

ich bin ganz sicher, daß alles klappen wird mit deinem Examen, *I'm quite sure everything'll go well with your exam*

There is an increasing tendency for this to occur in written German as well.

INFINITIVE PHRASES

Infinitives used in a phrase go at the end of that phrase:

seine Hoffung, am gleichen Tag nach Mannheim zu fahren, ging nicht in Erfüllung, *his hope of going to Mannheim the same day was not realized*

Position of infinitives without zu

■ Infinitives without **zu** are included in the clause, at the end:

ich muß heute fahren, *I've got to go today*

There, they go before a past participle:

er hatte an diesem Tag fahren müssen, *he had had to go on that day*

. . . before an infinitive that forms part of the future and conditional tenses:

ich werde heute fahren müssen, *I'm going to have to go today*

. . . and before the verb in subordinate order:

ich weiß, daß du fahren mußt, *I know you've got to go*

Position of infinitives with zu

■ Infinitives with **zu** are placed at the end of a clause. If they have other qualifications such as adverbs or objects they form a phrase of their own, marked off from the clause by a comma (see Punctuation, p. 231).

er versucht zu arbeiten, *he's trying to work*

sie hat versucht, ihr Auto zu verkaufen, *she's been trying to sell her car*

■ Where an infinitive depends on a separable verb the infinitive may go before or after the prefix:

er fing zu arbeiten an / er fing an zu arbeiten, *he began to work*

If the infinitive is qualified it usually goes after the prefix:

er fing an, regelmäßig an seinem Auto zu arbeiten, *he began to work on his car regularly*

■ In subordinate order with a verb in a simple tense, a short infinitive phrase with **zu** is enclosed within the clause:

> **ich weiß, daß sie es zu verkaufen versucht,** *I know she's trying to sell it*
>
> **ich weiß, daß sie ihr Auto zu verkaufen versucht**, or **. . . daß sie versucht, ihr Auto zu verkaufen**, *I know she's trying to sell her car*

A longer infinitive phrase stands outside the clause:

> **ich weiß, daß sie versucht, diesen alten, klapprigen Trabant zu verkaufen**, *I know she's trying to sell that beat-up old Trabant*

■ In subordinate order with a verb in a compound tense, the infinitive stands outside the clause:

> **ich weiß, daß sie versucht hat, es zu verkaufen,** *I know she's been trying to sell it*

■ Infinitives preceded by **um . . . zu**, *in order to*, **ohne . . . zu**, *without . . . -ing*, and **(an)statt zu**, *instead of . . . -ing*, are always placed outside the clause:

> **ich bin hier, um mein Auto zu verkaufen**, *I'm here (in order) to sell my car*

OTHER PHRASES ETC. NORMALLY STANDING OUTSIDE THE CLAUSE

■ Apart from infinitives with **zu** + further qualification, the following types of phrases usually stand outside the clause:

□ question tags, like **nicht wahr?**, **ja?**, **oder?** (corresponding to *isn't it?*, *aren't you?*, *or is it?*, etc.)

> **du bleibst hier, oder?**, *you're staying here—aren't you?* (open question)
>
> **du bleibst hier, nicht? / nicht wahr? / ja?**, *you're staying here, aren't you?* (I'm pretty sure you are)

□ phrases beginning **wie** and **als**, forming the second part of a comparison

> **du hast es genau so schwierig gefunden wie ich**, *you found it just as difficult as I did (as me)*
> **nein, ich habe es viel schwieriger gefunden als du**, *no, I found it a lot more difficult than you (did)*

Where **als** and **wie** simply mean *as* or *like*, functioning as a sort of equals sign, the phrase they introduce does not stand outside the clause:

> **das haben sie mir als Deutscher sagen wollen?**, *you meant to say that to me, as a German?*
> **das kann selbst ein Dummkopf wie ich verstehen**, *even an idiot like me can understand that*

□ phrases beginning **sondern** and **außer**

> **sie hat es nicht gemacht, sondern ich**, *it wasn't she who did it, but me (I)*
> **ich habe nichts gelesen außer einem Krimi**, *I read nothing except a detective story*

Sondern phrases have a comma before them (see Punctuation, pp. 229–30).

□ **oder nicht**, and sometimes other phrases beginning **oder**

> **wird er kommen oder nicht?**, *is he going to come or not?*
> **möchtest du Erdbeeren essen oder die Torte?**, *would you like strawberries or the flan?*

■ A relative clause stands outside the main clause when it refers back to a noun or pronoun standing immediately before a part of the verb at the end of the clause:

> **er hat schnell das Geld genommen, das ich ihm angeboten habe**, *he quickly took the money I was offering him*

but: **das Geld, das ich ihm angeboten habe, hat er schnell genommen**

I Punctuation and Spelling

CAPITAL LETTERS

■ All nouns and other words used as nouns have a capital letter:

der Mann, *the man*
das Lachen, *laughing* (verbal noun)
der Reisende, *the traveller* (present participle used as noun)

■ Pronouns:

□ The polite **Sie** and its other forms (**Ihnen, Ihr-**—but not the reflexive form **sich**) always have a capital.

□ **Du** and **ihr** and their other forms (**dich, dir, dein**; **euch, euer**) are written with a capital when writing letters.

□ **Du** (etc.) is capitalized when referring to God.

■ Adjectives made from town names by adding **-er** have a capital:

der Kölner Dom, *Cologne cathedral*

■ Adjectives in geographical and other names have a capital:

das Rote Meer, *the Red Sea*
Deutsche Bundesbahn, *German Railways*

■ Adjectives after indefinites have a capital:

etwas Grünes, *something green*

but indefinites themselves do not take a capital:

etwas anderes, *something different*
das übrige, *what's left*

► See p. 108.

■ Adjectives referring to countries take a small letter as adjectives, a capital as the name of the language:

> **die deutsche Sprache**, *the German language*
> **sie spricht Englisch**, *she speaks English*

but there is no capital for the language after **auf** = *in*:

> **auf englisch**, *in English*

■ A capital is frequently used in German in mid-sentence after a colon.

■ Cardinal numbers have a small letter, except **Million, Milliarde**, and sometimes **Hundert, Tausend** (see p. 202). Fractions are written with either a capital or a small letter (see pp. 204–5).

Ordinal numbers used as adjectives have small letters, but notice:

> **Friedrich der Zweite**, *Friedrich II*

■ Nouns not used as nouns have a small letter:

> **die Schuld**, *guilt*: **du bist daran schuld**, *it's your fault*
> **das Paar**, *pair*: **ein paar Sachen**, *a few things*
> **das Leid**, *sorrow*: **er tut mir leid**, *I'm sorry for him*

Das bißchen, *bit*, is now only ever used with a small letter:

> **ein bißchen Zucker**, *a little sugar*
> **kein bißchen Zucker**, *no sugar at all*
> **das klein bißchen Zucker**, *the small amount of sugar* (note the invariable **klein**)

THE COMMA

The use of commas is largely a matter of individual style in English. In German, however, commas are used according to fixed rules that must be followed.

■ Commas are used in lists to divide off items (but not before the **und** at the end):

> **er ist jung, schön, reich und gesund**, *he's young, handsome, rich, and healthy*

■ Commas are not used between two adjectives if the second is felt to form a single concept with its noun:

> **ein schöner, saftiger Schinken**, *a nice juicy ham*
> **ein schöner westfalischer Schinken**, *a nice Westphalian ham*

■ A comma is used before and/or after each subordinate clause to separate it from the main clause:

> **Ich weiß, daß er kommen wird**. *I know he'll come.*
> **Wenn er kommt, werden wir essen**. *When he comes we'll eat.*
> **Die Leute, die kommen werden, sind mir bekannt**. *The people who're coming are known to me.*

The comma comes before, not after, the subordinating conjunction.

■ Commas separate main clauses joined by **und** or **oder**:

> **Er kam, und wir aßen**. *He came and we ate.*

but not if an element of the first has to be understood in the second:

> **Er kommt und ißt**. (= **und er ißt**) *He comes and eats.*

This element is usually the subject, but not always:

> **Er ißt hier und die anderen zu Hause**. (= **und die anderen essen**) *He eats here and the others (eat) at home.*

■ Commas are always placed before the other coordinating conjunctions (**aber, sondern, denn, allein**—see p. 195), whether they introduce a clause or a phrase:

Ich klopfte, aber niemand antwortete. *I knocked but no one answered.*

Es ist nicht rot, sondern weiß. *It is not red, but white.*

■ Unlike English, German does not separate adverb phrases with commas:

Er stand wie immer mit Blumen vor der Tür. *He was standing, with flowers as always, at the door.*

Adjective phrases, however, are often given commas:

Er betrachtete, grün vor Neid, das Auto, das ich gerade gekauft hatte. *He looked, green with envy, at the car I had just bought.*

■ Commas are placed round appositional phrases and before a phrase beginning **und zwar**:

Herr Schmidt, unser neuer Chef, ist heute erschienen, und zwar um acht Uhr. *Herr Schmidt, our new boss, turned up today, and, would you believe it, at eight o'clock.*

■ Commas are sometimes used to join two main clauses, where the equivalent English would correctly have a semicolon. This occurs particularly where the second clause begins with **trotzdem**, *in spite of that*, **unterdessen**, *meanwhile*, and **statt dessen**, *instead*:

Es regnet, trotzdem wollen wir wandern. *It's raining; in spite of that we're still going walking.*

■ A comma is used where we would use a decimal point:

2,3 *2·3*

It is not used in large numbers, which are written with spaces where English uses commas:

1 999 777 *1,999,777*

▶ See Numbers, p. 201.

- Commas are used with infinitive phrases as follows.

□ An infinitive phrase consisting only of **zu** + infinitive has no comma before it:

> **Sie versucht zu singen**. *She tries to sing.*

□ One that is longer than just **zu** + infinitive usually has a comma:

> **Sie versucht, den ganzen Ring auswendig zu lernen.** *She's trying to learn the whole of the Ring by heart.*

□ There is always a comma where the infinitive is a complement after **sein**:

> **Ihr einiziges Streben ist, zu singen**. *Her only aspiration is to sing.*

□ There is no comma, however long the infinitive phrase, after the verbs **brauchen**, *to need*, **haben**, *to have*, **sein**, *to be*, **scheinen**, *to seem*, and **pflegen**, *to be accustomed*:

> **Jetzt brauchst du kein einziges Wort mehr zu sagen.** *Now you don't need to say a single word more.*

THE COLON

The colon marks an amplification or explanation of what has gone before. English may use a colon or a dash for this. In German the clause following a colon very frequently starts with a capital letter:

> **Etwas muß ich aber erklären**: **Das Haus ist nicht zu verkaufen**. *One thing I must make clear, however—the house is not for sale.*

The colon is also used to introduce direct speech after a verb of saying:

Sie sagte: „Komm gut nach Hause!“ *She said, 'Get home safely.'*

THE HYPHEN

A hyphen is used to represent part of a compound, to avoid clumsy repetition:

Radio- und Fernsehgeräte (= **Radiogeräte und Fernsehgeräte**), *radio and television sets*

It is also occasionally used, for clarity, to break up very long compound words.

THE DASH

This usually indicates a pause, often for thought (*dash* = **der Gedankenstrich**). It may also be used instead of three dots to suspend the sense. It is sometimes used to separate two passages of direct speech within the same paragraph.

INVERTED COMMAS

The opening set of inverted commas is placed on the line in German. Both sets are printed the opposite way round from English. German uses double inverted commas for direct speech, whereas English more and more frequently uses single:

„Das ist nicht wahr“, sagte er. *'That's not true', he said.*

French guillemets (also printed the 'wrong' way round) are sometimes found:

»Das ist nicht wahr!«

For speech within speech single inverted commas are used: **‚ ‘**.

THE EXCLAMATION MARK

The exclamation mark is used much more than in English. In none of the following cases is it obligatory, however. It is very frequently used . . .

- after exclamations

  Au! Das kann nicht sein! *Oh, that can't be true!*

- after imperatives

  Steh auf! *Stand up.*

- in public notices and admonitions, where English would not punctuate at all

  Das Betreten der Baustelle ist verboten! *Keep out*
  Nicht hinauslehnen! *Do not lean out of the window*

- sometimes at the start of letters, where English uses a comma

  Liebe Gisela! *Dear Gisela,*
  Sehr geehrte Damen und Herren! *Dear Sir or Madam,*

A comma is nowadays more common in German in this case.

FULL STOP

The full stop is used to end a sentence, and to indicate abbreviations. However, it is only used for abbreviations if what is normally said aloud for that abbreviation is the words for which it stands, not the letters of the abbreviation:

d.h. (spoken: **das heißt**), *i.e.*
but: **DB** (= **Deutsche Bundesbahn**, *German Railways*)
PKW (sometimes **Pkw**; = **Personenkraftwagen**, *passenger vehicle; car*)

Notice that **usw.** (= **und so weiter**, *etc.*) has only one full stop.

A full stop is used to abbreviate an ordinal number (including its adjective ending):

> **am 20. August (am zwanzigsten August)**, *on the 20th of August*

EMPHASIS

In older printed material this is shown by spaced printing:

> **Ich möchte d e n** . *I want that one.*

This has now been largely replaced by italics, as in English:

> **Ich möchte *den*.**

SPELLING PECULIARITIES

■ Syllable division

In German a word broken at the end of a line divides according to syllables: **kom-for-ta-bel**, *com-fort-able*. This is, however, largely a matter for printers, since we almost never split a word when writing by hand. Beware, though, of the fact that the letters **ck** divide as **k-k**, so split over two lines **Zucker** becomes **Zuk- ker**, **Bäcker** becomes **Bäk- ker**.

■ Triple consonants

In compound nouns with a sequence of three identical consonants one of the three is dropped, except

□ if the word is split between two lines:

> **das Bettuch**, *sheet*, but **Bett- tuch**

□ if a further consonant follows:

> **fetttriefend**, *dripping with fat*

□ if the first two of three **s**'s are written **ß**:

> **die Fußsohle**, *sole*

■ ß

The use of **ß** is purely a written distinction: even though it is sometimes called **'das scharfe S'**, there is *no* difference in pronunciation between **ß** and **ss**.

ß is used

□ always before another consonant:

ich mußte, *I had to*

□ always at the end of a word, and at the end of a word contained within a compound:

der Schluß, *end*; **der Schlußsatz**, *final sentence*

□ in other places, after a long vowel:

die Füße, *feet* (long **ü**)
but: **die Flüsse**, *rivers* (short **ü**)

With proper names usage varies and has to learned individually (the musicians, for instance, are Johann Strauß and Richard Strauss).

If **ß** is not available (e.g. on a keyboard) use **ss**; **sz** used for **ß** is old-fashioned. **ß** has no capital form—where a word is printed entirely in capitals **SS** is used. In Switzerland **ß** is often not used at all (the up-market **Neue Zürcher Zeitung** always uses **ss** only).

I Translation Problems

The following list is alphabetical. It includes items not treated in the body of the grammar, or treated in a number of different places and more conveniently brought together here. Reference is made throughout to the places in the body of the grammar where more detail may be found.

Translation problems not covered here should be tackled via the Index, or via the various alphabetical lists in the Grammar:

prepositions	(German),	p. 163
	(English),	p. 188
adverbial particles,		p. 122
conjunctions,		p. 197
verb constructions,		p. 53.

AS

■ As a conjunction expressing time (= *when*) *as* is **wie** or **indem**. **Wie** is the more colloquial; **indem** is only used where both actions occur literally at the same time:

> **wie ich aus dem Bus stieg, begegnete ich ihr vorm Rathaus**, *as (when) I got off the bus I ran into her in front of the town hall*
> **wie/indem ich aus dem Bus stieg, verrenkte ich mir den Fuß**, *as I got off the bus I twisted my ankle*

■ As a conjunction expressing manner (= *like*) *as* must be **wie**:

> **wie Sie sehen, habe ich mir den Fuß verrenkt**, *as you see, I've sprained my ankle*

■ In comparisons of equality (*as . . . as*), the first *as* is **so**, the second **wie**:

er ist genauso unsicher wie ich, *he's just as unsure as I (am)*

The negative of this construction is **nicht so . . . wie**, *not as . . . as*:

er ist nicht so unsicher wie ich, *he's not as unsure as I (am)*

As can also be a conjunction introducing a complete clause in a comparison of equality; it is still **wie**:

sie macht es fast so gut, wie ich es gemacht habe, *she does it almost as well as I did it*

■ As a conjunction expressing cause (= *since*), *as* is **da**:

da er nicht hier ist, werde ich es selber machen, *as he's not here I'll do it myself*

■ Meaning '*in the capacity of*', *as* is **als**:

ich als Fachmann kann Ihnen versichern, daß . . ., *I, as an expert, can assure you that . . .*

▶ *As if* is **als ob** or **als wenn**. See p. 44.

FOR

■ Conjunction, **denn**:

du mußt es tun, denn wir werden sonst keine Gelegenheit finden, *you must do it, for we shan't find any opportunity otherwise*

Denn is slightly less formal than *for* is in English. As in English the **denn** *(for)* clause can't start the sentence.

■ Preposition with time (for other prepositional uses of *for* consult pp. 190–1):

□ A completed period in the past— **lang**, or a time expression in the accusative:

er war drei Jahre lang im Jemen, *he was in the Yemen for three years*

er mußte einen ganzen Monat warten, *he had to wait for a whole month*

□ A period starting in the present or the future— **auf** + ACC or **für**:

ich bin auf/für drei Wochen hier, *I'm here for three weeks*

□ An intended period in the past— **auf** + ACC or **für**:

sie kam auf/für drei Jahre nach Deutschland, *she came to Germany for three years* (no statement of how long she stayed)

□ A period in the past stretching up to the present— **seit** + present tense:

sie ist seit drei Wochen hier, *she's been here for three weeks*

▶ See pp. 178–9 for tenses used.

□ A period in the distant past stretching up to the point in the past that we are speaking of— **seit** + past tense:

er war seit drei Jahren im Jemen, als . . . , *he had been in the Yemen for three years, when . . .*

▶ See pp. 178–9 for tenses used.

IF

■ *If* introducing a clause of possibility is **wenn**:

wenn du kommst, bring es mit, *if you come bring it with you*

It may also introduce a shortened version of this kind of clause:

wenn überhaupt, *if at all*
wenn möglich, *if possible*

■ Introducing an indirect question, *if (= whether)* is **ob**:

> **ich weiß nicht, ob ich es mitbringen kann**, *I don't know if I can bring it with me*

-ING

The *-ing* form of the verb in English corresponds basically to the present participle in German (see pp. 36–7), but it is used in ways in English that are not always paralleled in German.

■ There is no German equivalent to the English continuous tenses (*I am waiting*, etc.). The equivalent simple or compound tense must be used:

> **ich esse**, *I'm eating*
> **ich aß**, *I was eating*
> **ich habe gegessen**, *I have been eating*

■ When two actions are going on at the same time, the *-ing* phrase is translated by a clause introduced by **indem**:

> **indem sie auf das Auto wartete, dachte sie an Hans**, *waiting for the car she thought of Hans*

Auf das Auto wartend, dachte sie . . . is not impossible, but much rarer than in English.

■ When two actions occur consecutively, the *-ing* phrase is translated by a second main clause:

> **er machte die Tür auf und stieg aus dem Auto**, *opening the door, he got out of the car*

■ Where the English present participle is used as a noun, German uses a verbal noun (the infinitive with a capital letter):

> **Warten is so langweilig**, *waiting is so boring*
> **wir haben keine Zeit zum Tennisspielen**, *we've no time for playing tennis*

■ When the English *-ing* form is the equivalent of *to* + infinitive, **zu** + infinitive is used in German:

sie begann zu weinen, *she began crying (= began to cry)*
danach zu schicken, wäre das einfachste, *sending for it (= to send for it) would be easiest*

■ With the verbs *to see, to hear, to feel* (and many others) English can make a present participle depend on the object *(I hear her returning)*. A similar construction is possible in German with **hören, sehen**, and a limited number of other verbs; in German a dependent infinitive without **zu** is used:

ich höre sie zurückkommen, *I hear her returning*

▶ See pp. 46–7.

■ *Instead of* + *-ing* and *without* + *-ing* are translated by **anstatt**, *instead of*, and **ohne**, *without*, + **zu** + infinitive:

ohne zu sprechen, *without speaking*
anstatt radzufahren, *instead of cycling*

■ *By . . . -ing* is translated as **indem** + clause or **dadurch, daß** + clause:

er ist uns entkommen, indem er ein Motorboot gestohlen hat / er ist uns dadurch entkommen, daß er ein Motorboot gestohlen hat, *he got away from us by stealing a motorboat*

A similar construction to **dadurch, daß** is used when a verb that takes a preposition is followed by *-ing*:

bestehen auf, *to insist on*
ich bestehe darauf, daß ich mitkomme, *I insist on coming with you*
ich bestehe darauf, daß er mitkommt, *I insist on him coming with you*

▶ See pp. 52–3.

ONLY

■ As an adjective after an article, **einzig**:

> **das ist das einzige Geschenk, das ich bekommen habe**, *it's the only present I got*

■ As an adjective before an article, **nur**:

> **nur das Baby war da**, *only the baby was there*

■ Before a pronoun, **allein** or **nur**. **Allein** follows its pronoun, **nur** precedes it:

> **sie allein war da / nur sie war da**, *only she was there*

■ As a time adverb, **erst**:

> **erst als sie die Tür aufmachte**, *only when she opened the door*
> **erst nach dem Abendessen**, *only after supper*
> **erst jetzt verstehe ich**, *only now do I understand*
> **die Bank macht erst um zehn auf**, *the bank only opens at ten*

▶ For **erst als/wenn**, *only when*, see Until, p. 249.

■ Otherwise, as an adverb, *only* is **nur**:

> **nur langsam machte sie die Tür auf**, *she opened the door only slowly*
> **wenn sie das nur früher gesagt hätte**, *if only she had said that earlier*

■ As a conjunction, *only* is **allein** or **aber**:

> **ich hätte es getan, allein/aber ich wollte nicht**, *I'd have done it, only I didn't want to*

▶ *Not only . . . but also* is **nicht nur . . . sondern auch**. See p. 194.

PUT

The translation of the verb *to put* depends on the position in which whatever is 'put' finally ends up.

- **stellen** *(to place)*: the object stands in a vertical position

  stellen Sie die Flaschen dorthin, *put the bottles down there*

- **legen** *(to lay)*: the object lies horizontally

  legen Sie die Platte dorthin, *put the disc down there*

- **stecken** *(to stick)*: the object is put into something

  stecken Sie den Brief in den Kasten, *put the letter into the letterbox*

- **setzen** *(to set)*: the object is put into a sitting position; this is also the verb used for many non-literal meanings of *put*

  er setzte ihr das Baby auf den Schoß, *he put the baby on her lap*
  setzen Sie ihren Namen dort, bitte, *put your name there please*
  man hat den Lift außer Betrieb gesetzt, *they've put the lift out of action*

- **Tun,** *to do*, is much used in the spoken (but not the written) language for all senses of *to put*:

  tun Sie sie dorthin, *put them down there*

Observe the difference between **legen,** *to lay = to put into a lying position*, and the strong verb **liegen,** *to lie = to be in a lying position*. Similarly, **setzen,** *to set = to put into a sitting position*, and **sitzen** (strong), *to sit = to be in a sitting position.*

SINCE

- Preposition indicating time: **seit**

  seit Sonntag, *since Sunday*

er ist seit letzter Woche hier, *he's been here since last week*

▶ For tense with **seit**, preposition, see pp. 178–9.

■ Conjunction indicating time: **seitdem** or **seit**

seitdem er hier ist, habe ich nur Ärger mit ihm, *since he's been here I've been having nothing but trouble with him*

▶ For tenses with **seit(dem)**, see pp. 199–200.

■ Conjunction indicating reason: **da**

da er aber hier ist, muß ich mich irgendwie damit abfinden, *since he's here, though, I'll have to put up with it somehow*

SO

■ **So** translated **so**:

□ = *to such a degree*

ich bin so müde, daß ich nicht mehr gehen kann, *I'm so tired (that) I can't walk any further*

□ = *therefore*

er war nicht da, so mußte ich allein gehen, *he wasn't there, so I had to go alone*

□ = *thus*

so hätte man eigentlich gedacht, *so one might in fact have thought*

□ before an adjective (note the position of the article in German)

nach einer so langen Reise, *after so long a journey*

□ in a negative comparison

sie ist nicht so alt wie ich, *she's not so old as I (am)*

■ *So* translated **also**:

□ = *for that reason*

morgen hab' ich Geburtstag, also mußt du dich darauf vorbereiten, *tomorrow's my birthday, so you must get ready for it*

□ summing up (= *then*)

das ist es also, *so that's it*

■ *So* as object of verb: **es**

ich hätte es gesagt, wenn . . . *I'd have said so, if . . .*

The **es** must come after the verb. If you wish to invert, use **das**:

das hat er sehr langsam getan, *he did so very slowly*

Verbs of thinking and hoping have nothing at all:

ja, ich denke, *yes, I think so*

■ *So much the* + adjective: **um so** + adjective:

um so besser, *so much the better*

■ *So as to*: **um . . . zu**

du solltest laufen, um nicht kalt zu werden, *you should run so as not to get cold*

■ *Something so* + adjective: **so etwas** + adjectival noun

so etwas Schönes, *something so beautiful*

SO THAT

So that is **damit** or **so daß**.

■ **Damit** means '*with the intention that*':

> **ich habe den Regenschirm mitgebracht, damit du trocken bleibst**, *I've brought the umbrella, so that you'll stay dry*

In literary German the subjunctive is sometimes found after **damit**.

- **So daß** means '*with the result that*':

> **es hat furchtbar geregnet, so daß ich den Regenschirm aufspannen mußte**, *it rained dreadfully, so (that) I had to put the umbrella up*

As in English, the **so** can move into the main clause:

> **es hat so furchtbar geregnet, daß ich den Regenschirm aufspannen mußte**, *it rained so dreadfully that I had to put the umbrella up*

THAT

That has four different grammatical uses in English, each translated differently into German.

- It may be a demonstrative pronoun:

> **gib mir das dort**, *give me that*
> **das ist aber schön!**, *that's really nice*

Dies(es) could equally be used, or less commonly **jenes**. See pp. 137–8 for more detail.

- It may be a demonstrative adjective:

> **ich hätte gern *den* Kuchen, bitte**, *I should like that cake please*

Diesen Kuchen could equally be used, or less commonly **jenen Kuchen**. See p. 115 for more detail.

- It may be a relative pronoun:

> **das Geschenk, das du mitgebracht hast**, *the present that you brought*
> **der Mann, den ich geschickt habe**, *the man that I sent*

Welches, welchen would also be possible. See pp. 139–40 for more detail.

■ It may be a conjunction:

> **ich weiß, daß es nicht sehr leicht ist**, *I know that it's not very easy*

This is **daß**, with subordinate order.

Don't confuse **ich weiß, daß . . .** with **das Geschenk, das . . . . Daß** introduces a noun clause, here the object of **ich weiß**, telling us what 'I know'—**daß** is a conjunction. **Das** introduces an adjective clause, telling us more about a specific noun, here **das Geschenk**, *the present*. **Das** is neuter because **das Geschenk** is neuter—**das** is a relative pronoun.

THERE

There in German is either **da** or **dort**. **Dort** indicates a quite precise place, **da** is more general:

> **da ist jemand**, *there's somebody there*
> **er ist dort auf der Terrasse**, *he's there on the terrace*

■ *There* with a motion verb

There used with a motion verb must be **dahin** or **dorthin**, *to there*:

> **ich fahre morgen dahin**, *I'm going there tomorrow*

With other adverbs of place German makes a similar distinction between 'motion towards' and 'no motion towards', by using **nach**:

> **ich bin unten**, *I'm downstairs*
> **kommen Sie nach unten**, *come downstairs*

► See pp. 119–20.

■ *There is, there are*

There is, there are in German is **es ist, es sind**. Very often, however, German prefers a more specific verb like **es steht,** *there stands*, **es liegt**, *there lies*. These agree, as **sein** does, with the noun in the nominative that stands after them, and not with the **es**, producing the odd-looking plurals **es stehen**, *there stand*, **es liegen**, *there lie*, etc.

When existence rather than position is being spoken of **es gibt** + accusative is used for *there is, there are*. The verb stays in the singular:

> **es gibt viele Leute, die das sagen**, *there are a lot of people who say that*

▶ See pp. 72–3.

TO LIKE

The basic translation of *to like* is **gern haben** (*'to have gladly'*):

> **hast du Kinder gern?**, *do you like children?*
> **ich hätte gern zwei Stück Kuchen**, *I should like two pieces of cake*

■ Where English follows *to like* with the *-ing* form of the verb, German uses that verb + **gern**:

> **fährst du gern Ski?**, *do you like skiing?*

Especially with verbs of eating and drinking, but also with other verbs, German uses this construction where English simply uses *to like* + object:

> **sie trinkt gern Milch**, *she likes milk*
> **ißt du gern Kartoffelsalat?**, *do you like potato salad?*
> **ich höre gern Brahms**, *I like Brahms*

■ The impersonal verb **es gefällt mir** indicates an immediate rather than a lasting impression:

> **das Bild? Ja, es gefällt mir**, *that picture? Yes, I like it*

■ **Mögen** also means *to like* (amongst other things); the present tense is used particularly for people:

> **ich mag sie nicht so sehr**, *I don't like her all that much*

This construction is more common in the negative.

The past subjunctive, **möchte**, *would like*, used as a conditional, is very common indeed:

> **ich möchte noch Kaffee, bitte**, *I should like some more coffee, please*
> **möchten Sie was kaufen?**, *would you like (do you want) to buy something?*

Gern may be added to **möchte** with little if any change to the meaning. **Ich möchte gern** is particularly used when buying things in shops:

> **ich möchte gern drei Pfund Pflaumen, bitte**, *I should like three pounds of plums please*

▶ See p. 119 for the position of **gern** in the sentence, and further details.

▶ For **mögen** see pp. 62–3.

UNTIL

■ Preposition, followed by an adverb or an adverbial phrase—**bis**:

> **bis drei Uhr**, *until three o'clock*
> **bis morgen**, *until tomorrow (see you tomorrow)*

■ Preposition, followed by a noun or pronoun— **bis** + second preposition, usually **zu**:

> **bis zum Letzten des Monats**, *until the last of the month*
> **bis auf weiteres**, *until futher notice*

■ Negative preposition, *not until*— **erst** (*only*) + a preposition:

> **erst am Letzten des Monats**, *not until (only on) the last of the month*
> **erst um Mitternacht**, *not until midnight*
> **erst nach dem Krieg**, *not until after the war*

■ Conjunction— **bis**:

> **bis es repariert wird, müssen Sie irgendwie ohne auskommen**, *until it's repaired you must manage without it somehow*

■ Negative conjunction, *not until*— **erst als, erst wenn**:

> **erst wenn sie es erklären**, *not until they explain it*
> **erst als sie es erklärt hatten**, *not until they'd explained it*

The difference between **erst wenn** and **erst als** is the same as that between the simple conjunctions **wenn** and **als** (see p. 197).

► See also **bis**, pp. 198–9.

WHEN

■ *When* in German as a question word is **wann**. This is used in both direct and indirect questions:

> **wann kommt sie zurück?**, *when is she coming back?*
> **ich weiß nicht, wann sie zurückkommt**, *I don't know when she's coming back*

■ *When* as a conjunction, referring to one occasion in the past, is **als**:

> **ich war da, als sie zurückkam**, *I was there when she came back*

Referring to the present, the future, or to more than one occasion in the past, it is **wenn**:

ich war jedesmal da, wenn sie zurückkam, *I was always there when she came back*

■ **Wo** is frequently used for `when` after expressions of time:

am Tag, wo sie zurückkam, war ich da, *I was there on the day when she came back*

► See pp. 197–8 for more detail.

WHICH

`Which` is both a question word (referring to both people and things) and a relative (referring to things).

■ In questions, as an adjective used with a noun it is **welcher**:

welche Sorte möchten Sie?, *which kind would you like?*

Similarly in indirect questions:

ich weiß nicht, welche Sorte ich möchte, *I don't know which kind I want*

► See p. 116–17.

■ As a pronoun in questions it is **welcher**:

welches? Das dort im Schaufenster, *which? That one in the window*

► See p. 144.

■ As a relative pronoun it is **der** or **welcher**:

das Sofa, auf dem (auf welchem) du sitzt, *the sofa which you're sitting on*

► See pp. 139–42.

Glossary of Grammatical Terms

Abstract Noun The name of something that is not a concrete object or person. Words such as *difficulty, hope, discussion* are abstract nouns.

Accusative The direct object case in German. See Case.

Active See Passive.

Adjectival Noun An adjective used as if it were a noun: *the good, the bad, and the really horrid. Good, bad, horrid* are adjectives used as nouns (with the definite article *the*).

Adjective A word describing a noun. *A big, blue, untidy painting*—*big, blue, untidy* are adjectives describing the noun *painting*.

Adverb A word that describes or modifies (i) a verb: *he did it gracefully* (adverb: *gracefully*), or (ii) an adjective: *a disgracefully large helping* (adverb: *disgracefully*), or (iii) another adverb: *she skated extraordinarily gracefully* (adverbs: *extraordinarily, gracefully*).

Agreement In German, adjectives agree with nouns when they stand in front of them, verbs agree with subject nouns or pronouns, pronouns agree with nouns, etc. This is a way of showing that something refers to or goes with something else. Agreement is by number (showing whether something is singular or plural), by gender (showing whether something is masculine, feminine, or neuter), and by case (showing whether something is nominative, accusative, genitive, or dative). For instance: **mit diesen grünen Socken**, *with these green socks*: **mit** must be followed by the dative, so that the noun that follows it (**die Socke**, *sock*, plural **Socken**) has to be in the dative; **dies-** adds its dative plural ending **-en** to agree with **Socken**, and so does **grün**.

Apposition Two nouns or noun phrases used together, the second one giving further information about the first: *the station master, a big man with a moustache, came in. A big man with a moustache* is in apposition to *the station master.*

Articles The little words like *a* and *the* that stand in front of nouns. In English, *the* is the definite article (it defines a particular item in a category: *the hat you've got on*); *a* or *an* is the indefinite article (it doesn't specify which item in a category: *wear a hat,* any hat).

Auxiliary Verb A verb used to help form a compound tense. In *I am walking, he has walked,* the auxiliary verbs are *to be (am)* and *to have (has).*

Cardinal Number A number used in counting (*one, two, three, four,* etc.). Compare with Ordinal (Number).

Case Nouns, pronouns, adjectives, and articles show 'case' in German. This is an indication of the role they are playing within the sentence. There are four cases: the nominative, which is the case in which the subject of the sentence stands; the accusative, which is the case in which the direct object stands; the genitive, which shows possession; and the dative, which is the case in which the indirect object stands. The last three cases are also used after prepositions. Case still exists in English pronouns (nominative: *he,* accusative: *him,* genitive: *his*) but has almost disappeared otherwise.

Clause A self-contained section of a sentence containing a full verb: *He came in and was opening his mail when the lights went out*—'he came in', 'and (he) was opening his mail', 'when the lights went out' are clauses.

Comparative With adjectives and adverbs, the form produced (in English) by adding *-er* or prefixing '*more*': *bigger, more difficult, more easily.*

Complement The equivalent to an object with verbs such as *to be, to become.* The complement refers back to the subject and stands (correctly) in the nominative: *George became an engine driver. It is I. Engine driver* and *I* are complements.

Compound Noun Noun formed from two or more separate words, e.g. **das Dampfbügeleisen**, *steam-iron*—both English and German words are compound nouns. English often inserts a hyphen into compound nouns, especially if they are long. German does this only rarely, so some German compounds are very long indeed.

Compound Tense Tense of a verb formed by a part of that verb preceded by an auxiliary verb (*am, have, shall*, etc.): *am walking*; *have walked*; *shall walk.*

Compound Verb Verb formed by the addition of a prefix (*un-, over-, de-, dis-*, etc.) to another verb. Simple verbs: *wind, take*; compound verbs: *unwind, overtake*. German has many compound verbs. See Prefix.

Conditional Perfect Tense The tense used to express what might have happened (if something else had occurred) and formed in English with *should have (I should have walked, we should have walked)* or *would have (you would have walked, he would have walked, they would have walked)*.

Conditional Tense The tense used to express what might happen (if something else occurred) and formed in English with *should (I should walk, we should walk)* or *would (you would walk, he would walk, they would walk)*.

Conjugation The pattern which a type of verb follows. For instance, a regular verb in English is conjugated like this: infinitive, *to walk*; present, *I walk, he walks;* past, *he walked;* perfect, *he has walked*, etc.

Conjunction A word like *and, but, when, because* that starts a clause and joins it to the rest of the sentence.

Consonant A letter representing a sound that can only be used in conjunction with a vowel. In German, the vowels are **a, ä, e, i, o, ö, u, ü**, and (used only very occasionally) **y**. All the other letters of the alphabet are consonants.

Coordinating Conjunction A conjunction that joins two or more main clauses. Alternatively it may join two or more nouns or pronouns, or two or more phrases.

Dative The indirect object case in German. English has no dative case—we use *to* with the noun or pronoun instead. See Case.

Declension The system of endings used in German on an article, adjective, or noun to indicate case, gender, and number.

Definite Article See Articles.

Demonstrative Adjective An adjective that is used to point out a particular thing: *I'll have that cake*; *this cake is terrible*; *give me those cakes—that, this, those* are demonstrative adjectives.

Demonstrative Article Alternative name for Demonstrative Adjective.

Demonstrative Pronoun A pronoun that is used to point out a particular thing: *I'll have that*; *this is terrible*; *give me those—that, this, those* are demonstrative pronouns.

Direct Object The noun or pronoun that experiences the action of the verb: *he hits me*, direct object: *me*. See also Indirect Object.

Direct Question The simple form of the question, as put. Direct question: *Who are you?* Indirect question: *She asked me who I was. Who I was* is the indirect question. See Indirect Question.

Ending See Stem.

Feminine See Gender.

First Person See Third Person.

Future Perfect Tense The tense used to express what, at some future time, will be a past occurrence. Formed in English with *shall have (I shall have walked, we shall have walked)* and *will have (you will have walked, he will have walked, they will have walked)*.

Future Tense The tense used to express a future occurrence and formed in English with *shall (I shall walk, we shall walk)* or *will (you will walk, he will walk, they will walk)*.

Gender In German, a noun or pronoun may be masculine, feminine, or neuter: this is known as the gender of the noun or pronoun. The gender may correspond to the sex of the thing named, or may not. In English gender only shows in pronouns (*he, she, it,* etc.) and corresponds to the sex of the thing named. See Agreement.

Genitive One of the four cases in German: the genitive shows possession. The genitive is found in English, usually formed with *-s*: *Joan's book*; *his book*; *whose book*. See Case.

Historic Present Present tense used to relate past events, often in order to make the narrative more vivid: *So then I go into the kitchen and what do I see?*

Imperative The form of the verb that expresses a command. In English it is usually the same as the infinitive without *to*: infinitive, *to walk*, imperative, *walk!*

Imperfect Subjunctive In German, alternative name for the Past Subjunctive. See Subjunctive.

Imperfect Tense In German, alternative name for the Past Tense. See Past Tense.

Impersonal Verb A verb whose subject is an unspecific *it* or *there*: *it is raining*; *there's no need for that.*

Indefinite Adjective An adjective such as *each*, *such*, *some*, *other*, *every*, *several* that does not specify identifiable people or objects.

Indefinite Article See Articles.

Indefinite Pronoun A pronoun such as *somebody*, *anybody*, *something*, *anything*, *everybody*, *nobody* that does not specify identifiable people or objects.

Indirect Object The noun or pronoun at which the direct object is aimed. In English it either has or can have *to* in front of it: *I passed it (to) him,* indirect object *(to) him*; *I gave her my address (I gave my address to her),* indirect object *(to) her*. In these examples *it* and *my address* are direct objects. In German as in English some verbs take an indirect object only.

Indirect Question A question (without a question mark) in a subordinate clause. It is introduced by some such expression as *I wonder if . . . , do you know where . . . , I'll tell him when . . . , he's asking who . . .* Direct question: *When is he coming?* Indirect question: *I don't know when he's coming.*

Infinitive The basic part of the verb from which other parts are derived. In English, it is normally preceded by *to*: *to walk, to run.*

Inseparable Prefix See Prefix.

Inseparable Verb A compound verb consisting of a simple verb with an inseparable prefix. See Prefix.

Interrogative The question form of the verb.

Interrogative Adjective A question word (in English *which . . . ?* or *what . . . ?*) used adjectivally with a following noun: *which book do you mean?*

Interrogative Adverb An adverb that introduces a direct question, in English *why?, when?, how?*, etc. In indirect questions the same words function as conjunctions, joining the question to the main clause. *Why do you say that?*—direct question, *why* is an interrogative adverb; *I don't know why you say that*—indirect question, *why* is a conjunction.

Interrogative Pronoun A pronoun that asks a question, in English *who?* and *what?*

Intransitive Of verbs: having no direct object.

Irregular Verb In German, a verb that does not follow the standard pattern of a regular (also called a 'weak') verb. See Strong Verb; Mixed Verb.

Main Clause A clause within a sentence that could stand on its own and still make sense. For example: *He came in when he* *was ready. He came in* is a main clause (it makes sense standing on its own); *when he was ready* is a subordinate clause (it can't stand on its own and still make sense).

Masculine See Gender.

Mixed Verb In German, a verb that both changes its vowel in the past (like a strong verb) and also adds characteristic endings (like a weak verb). See Strong Verb; Weak Verb.

Modal Verbs (literally 'verbs of mood'). These are the auxiliary verbs (other than *have* and *be*) that always appear with a dependent infinitive: *I can walk, I must walk, I will walk—can, must, will* are modal verbs.

Neuter See Gender.

Nominative One of the four cases in German. The nominative is the case the subject of the sentence stands in. See Case.

Noun A word that names a person or thing. *Peter, box, glory, indecision* are nouns.

Noun Clause A clause that is the equivalent of a noun within the sentence: *I don't want to catch whatever you've got* (*whatever you've got* is a clause for which we might substitute a noun, e.g. *measles*).

Number With nouns, pronouns, etc.—the state of being either singular or plural. See Agreement.

Object See Direct Object; Indirect Object.

Ordinal (Number) A number such as *first, second, third, fourth*, normally used adjectivally referring to one thing in a series.

Passive The basic tenses of a verb are active. Passive tenses are the set of tenses that are used in order to make the person or thing experiencing the action of the verb (normally the object) into the subject of the verb. Active (basic tense): *I discover it*, passive: *it is discovered (by me)*; active: *he ate them*, passive: *they were eaten (by him)*.

Passive Infinitive The passive form of the infinitive, where the implied subject suffers the action of the verb. In English: active infinitive, *to eat*; passive infinitive, *to be eaten*. The perfect infinitive can also be put into the passive: perfect infinitive, active: *to have eaten*; perfect infinitive, passive, *to have been eaten.*

Past Continuous, Perfect Continuous In English, the past tenses formed using *-ing*, implying that something was or has been continuing to occur: past continuous: *I was walking*, perfect continuous: *I have been walking*.

Past Participle The part of the verb used to form compound past tenses. In English, it usually ends in *-ed*. Verb: *to walk*; past participle: *walked*; perfect tense: *I have walked.*

Past Tense In German, the tense used in written narrative and, for some verbs, in speech as well; often the equivalent to the English past tense: **ich machte**, *I made*.

Perfect Continuous See Past Continuous.

Perfect Infinitive The past form of the infinitive, formed in English from *to have* + past participle: *to have walked.*

Perfect Tense The past tense that, in English, is formed by using *have* + past participle: *I have walked*. The German perfect is usually formed in the same way (**haben** + past participle), but its use is not quite the same.

Personal Pronouns Subject and object pronouns referring to people or things (*he, him, she, her, it*, etc.).

Phrasal Verb In English, a verb made by combining a simple verb with a preposition or adverb: *run out, jump up, stand down*. English phrasal verbs often correspond to German separable verbs. See Separable Verbs.

Phrase A self-contained section of a sentence that does not contain a full verb. *Being late as usual, he arrived at a quarter past eleven*: *at a quarter past eleven* is a phrase; present and past participles are not full verbs, so *being late as usual* is also a phrase. Compare Clause.

Pluperfect Continuous In English, the equivalent tense to the pluperfect using *had been + -ing*, implying that something had been going on (when something else happened), e.g.: *I had been walking for an hour, when . . .*

Pluperfect Tense The past tense that, in English, is formed by using *had* + past participle: *I had walked.* The German pluperfect is usually formed and used in the same way (with the past tense of **haben** + past participle).

Possessive Adjective An adjective that indicates possession; in English, *my, your, her,* etc.: *that is my book.*

Possessive Article Alternative name for Possessive Adjective.

Possessive Pronoun A pronoun that indicates possession; in English, *mine, yours, hers,* etc.: *that book is mine.*

Prefix In German, a short addition to the beginning of a verb. This may form an integral part of the verb (it is then called an inseparable prefix and the verb an inseparable verb), or it may in certain circumstances separate off (it is then a separable prefix and the verb a separable verb). German separable verbs quite often correspond to English phrasal verbs: **aufstehen**, *to stand up*; **ich stehe auf,** *I stand up.*

Preposition A word like *in, over, near, across* that stands in front of a noun or pronoun relating it to the rest of the sentence.

Present Continuous See Present Tense.

Present Participle The part of the verb that in English ends in *-ing*: *to walk*: present participle, *walking.*

Present Tense The tense of the verb that refers to things now happening regularly (simple present: *I walk*), or happening at the moment (present continuous: *I am walking*).

Pronoun A word such as *he, she, which, mine* that stands instead of a noun (usually already mentioned).

Question See Direct Question; Indirect Question.

Reciprocal Pronoun A pronoun like *each other*, *one another* which implies that one inflicts the verb's action on the other member of a plural subject and not on oneself. *They shot themselves* is a reflexive verb; *they shot each other* is a reciprocal verb.

Reflexive Pronoun See Reflexive Verb.

Reflexive Verb A verb whose object is the same as its subject: *he likes himself, she can dress herself. Himself, herself* are reflexive pronouns.

Relative Pronoun A pronoun that introduces a subordinate clause and at the same time allows that clause to function as an adjective or noun. In English the relative pronouns are *who(m), which, whose, that,* and *what. Tell me what you know!*: *what you know* is a noun clause and the direct object of *tell me*. It is introduced by the relative pronoun *what. That's the lad who stole my wallet*: *who stole my wallet* is an adjectival clause describing *lad*. It is introduced by the relative pronoun *who*.

Second Person See Third Person.

Separable Prefix See Prefix.

Separable Verb A verb formed from a simple verb and a separable prefix. See Prefix.

Simple Tense A one-word tense of a verb: *I walk, I run* (as opposed to a compound tense: *I am walking, I was running*).

Stem The part of a verb to which endings indicating tense, person, etc. are added. Verb: *to walk*: stem, *walk-*: *he walk-s, he walk-ed*, etc.

Strong Verb In German, an irregular verb, showing its past tense by a vowel change.

Subject (of verb, clause, or sentence) The noun or pronoun that initiates the action of the verb: *George walked*, subject: *George*; *he hit George*, subject: *he*.

Subjunctive In German, a set of tenses that express doubt or unlikelihood. The subjunctive still exists in only a few expressions in English: *If I were you* [but I'm not], *I'd go now* (*I were* is subjunctive—the normal past tense is *I was*).

Subordinate Clause A clause in a sentence that depends, in order to make sense, on a main clause. See Main Clause.

Subordinating Conjunction A conjunction that introduces a subordinate clause.

Superlative With adjectives and adverbs, the form produced by adding *-est* or prefixing '*most*': *biggest, most difficult, most easily*.

Tense The form of a verb that indicates when the action takes place (e.g. present tense: *I walk*; past tense: *I walked*).

Third Person *He, she, it, they* (and their derivatives, like *him, his, her, their*), or any noun, or any indefinite or demonstrative pronoun. The first person is *I* or *we* (and their derivatives), the second person is *you* (and its derivatives).

Transitive Of verbs: having a direct object.

Umlaut The only accent used in German: the two dots ('diaeresis') placed over the vowels **a**, **o**, **u**, to indicate a change in the way they are pronounced.

Verb The word that tells you what the subject of the clause does: *he goes*; *she dislikes me*; *have you eaten it?*; *they know nothing*—*goes, dislikes, have eaten, know* are verbs.

Verbal Noun Part of the verb (in English, usually the present participle) used as a noun: *smoking is bad for you*: verbal noun, *smoking*.

Vowel A letter representing a sound that can be pronounced by itself without the addition of other sounds. In German, the vowels are **a**, **ä**, **e**, **i**, **o**, **ö**, **u**, **ü**, and (used only very occasionally) **y**.

Weak Verb The name given to a regular verb in German—one that follows the standard verb pattern.

Index

English prepositions should be looked up in the alphabetical list on page 188.

Irregular verbs should be looked up in the alphabetical list on page 73.

Verb constructions (preposition, case) should be looked up in the alphabetical list of verbs on page 53.

Definitions of grammatical terms will be found in the glossary on page 251.

Dictionary

Preface

This new dictionary is designed for both English and German users. It provides a handy and comprehensive reference work for tourists and business people, and covers the needs of the student for GCSE.

We should like to express our thanks to Dr Michael Clark of Oxford University Press for his advice and support, and to Roswitha and Neil Morris for reading the proofs.

G.P. & J.S.

Contents

Introduction

A swung dash ~ represents the headword or that part of the headword preceding a vertical bar |. The initial letter of a German headword is given to show whether or not it is a capital.

The vertical bar | follows the part of the headword which is not repeated in compounds or derivatives.

Square brackets [ ] are used for optional material.

Angled brackets ⟨ ⟩ are used after a verb translation to indicate the object; before a verb translation to indicate the subject; before an adjective to indicate a typical noun which it qualifies.

Round brackets ( ) are used for field or style labels (see list on page x) and for explanatory matter.

A • indicates a new part of speech within an entry.

od (oder) and *or* denote that words or portions of a phrase are synonymous. An oblique stroke / is used where there is a difference in usage or meaning.

≈ is used where no exact equivalent exists in the other language.

A dagger † indicates that a German verb is irregular and that the parts can be found in the verb table on page 551. Compound verbs are not listed there as they follow the pattern of the basic verb.

The stressed vowel is marked in a German headword by – (long) or · (short). A phonetic transcription is only given for words which do not follow the normal rules of pronunciation. These rules can be found on page 549.

Phonetics are given for all English headwords and for derivatives where there is a change of pronunciation or stress. In blocks of compounds, if no stress is shown, it falls on the first element.

A change in pronunciation or stress shown within a block of compounds applies only to that particular word (subsequent entries revert to the pronunciation and stress of the headword).

German headword nouns are followed by the gender and, with the exception of compound nouns, by the genitive and plural. These are only given at compound nouns if they present some difficulty. Otherwise the user should refer to the final element.

Nouns that decline like adjectives are entered as follows: **-e(r)** *m/f*, **-e(s)** *nt*.

Adjectives which have no undeclined form are entered in the feminine form with the masculine and neuter in brackets **-e(r,s)**.

The reflexive pronoun **sich** is accusative unless marked (*dat*).

Proprietary terms

This dictionary includes some words which are, or are asserted to be, proprietary names or trade marks. Their inclusion does not imply that they have acquired for legal purposes a non-proprietary or general significance, nor is any other judgement implied concerning their legal status. In cases where the editor has some evidence that a word is used as a proprietary name or trade mark this is indicated by the letter (P), but no judgement concerning the legal status of such words is made or implied thereby.

Abbreviations/Abkürzungen

adjective	a	Adjektiv
abbreviation	abbr	Abkürzung
accusative	acc	Akkusativ
Administration	Admin	Administration
adverb	adv	Adverb
American	Amer	amerikanisch
Anatomy	Anat	Anatomie
Archaeology	Archaeol	Archäologie
Architecture	Archit	Architektur
Astronomy	Astr	Astronomie
attributive	attrib	attributiv
Austrian	Aust	österreichisch
Motor vehicles	Auto	Automobil
Aviation	Aviat	Luftfahrt
Biology	Biol	Biologie
Botany	Bot	Botanik
Chemistry	Chem	Chemie
collective	coll	Kollektivum
Commerce	Comm	Handel
conjunction	conj	Konjunktion
Cookery	Culin	Kochkunst
dative	dat	Dativ
definite article	def art	bestimmter Artikel
demonstrative	dem	Demonstrativ-
dialect	dial	Dialekt
Electricity	Electr	Elektrizität
something	etw	etwas
feminine	f	Femininum
familiar	fam	familiär
figurative	fig	figurativ
genitive	gen	Genitiv
Geography	Geog	Geographie
Geology	Geol	Geologie
Geometry	Geom	Geometrie
Grammar	Gram	Grammatik
Horticulture	Hort	Gartenbau
impersonal	impers	unpersönlich
indefinite article	indef art	unbestimmter Artikel
indefinite pronoun	indef pron	unbestimmtes Pronomen

infinitive	inf	Infinitiv
inseparable	insep	untrennbar
interjection	int	Interjektion
invariable	inv	unveränderlich
irregular	irreg	unregelmäßig
someone	jd	jemand
someone	jdm	jemandem
someone	jdn	jemanden
someone's	jds	jemandes
Journalism	Journ	Journalismus
Law	Jur	Jura
Language	Lang	Sprache
literary	liter	dichterisch
masculine	m	Maskulinum
Mathematics	Math	Mathematik
Medicine	Med	Medizin
Meteorology	Meteorol	Meteorologie
Military	Mil	Militär
Mineralogy	Miner	Mineralogie
Music	Mus	Musik
noun	n	Substantiv
Nautical	Naut	nautisch
North German	N Ger	Norddeutsch
nominative	nom	Nominativ
neuter	nt	Neutrum
or	od	oder
Proprietary term	P	Warenzeichen
pejorative	pej	abwertend
Photography	Phot	Fotografie
Physics	Phys	Physik
plural	pl	Plural
Politics	Pol	Politik
possessive	poss	Possessiv-
past participle	pp	zweites Partizip
predicative	pred	prädikativ
prefix	pref	Präfix
preposition	prep	Präposition
present	pres	Präsens
present participle	pres p	erstes Partizip
pronoun	pron	Pronomen
Psychology	Psych	Psychologie
past tense	pt	Präteritum

Railway	Rail	Eisenbahn
reflexive	refl	reflexiv
regular	reg	regelmäßig
relative	rel	Relativ-
Religion	Relig	Religion
see	s.	siehe
School	Sch	Schule
separable	sep	trennbar
singular	sg	Singular
South German	S Ger	Süddeutsch
slang	sl	Slang
someone	s.o.	jemand
something	sth	etwas
Technical	Techn	Technik
Telephone	Teleph	Telefon
Textiles	Tex	Textilien
Theatre	Theat	Theater
Television	TV	Fernsehen
Typography	Typ	Typographie
University	Univ	Universität
auxiliary verb	v aux	Hilfsverb
intransitive verb	vi	intransitives Verb
reflexive verb	vr	reflexives Verb
transitive verb	vt	transitives Verb
vulgar	vulg	vulgär
Zoology	Zool	Zoologie

Pronunciation of the alphabet
Aussprache des Alphabets

English/Englisch		*German/Deutsch*
eɪ	a	a:
bi:	b	be:
si:	c	t͜se:
di:	d	de:
i:	e	e:
ef	f	ɛf
dʒi:	g	ge:
eɪtʃ	h	ha:
aɪ	i	i:
dʒeɪ	j	jɔt
keɪ	k	ka:
el	l	ɛl
em	m	ɛm
en	n	ɛn
əʊ	o	o:
pi:	p	pe:
kju:	q	ku:
a:(r)	r	ɛr
es	s	ɛs
ti:	t	te:
ju:	u	u:
vi:	v	fa͜u
'dʌblju:	w	ve:
eks	x	ɪks
waɪ	y	'ʏpsilɔn
zed	z	t͜sɛt
eɪ umlaut	ä	ɛ:
əʊ umlaut	ö	ø:
ju: umlaut	ü	y:
es'zed	ß	ɛs't͜sɛt

GERMAN–ENGLISH
DEUTSCH–ENGLISCH

A

Aal *m* **-[e]s,-e** eel. **a~en (sich)** *vr* laze; (*ausgestreckt*) stretch out

Aas *nt* **-es** carrion; (*sl*) swine

ạb *prep* (+ *dat*) from; **ab Montag** from Monday ● *adv* off; (*weg*) away; (*auf Fahrplan*) departs; **von jetzt ab** from now on; **ab und zu** now and then; **auf und ab** up and down

ạbändern *vt sep* alter; (*abwandeln*) modify

ạbarbeiten *vt sep* work off; **sich a~** slave away

Ạbart *f* variety. **a~ig** *a* abnormal

Ạbbau *m* dismantling; (*Kohlen-*) mining; (*fig*) reduction. **a~en** *vt sep* dismantle; mine ⟨*Kohle*⟩; (*fig*) reduce, cut

ạbbeißen† *vt sep* bite off

ạbbeizen *vt sep* strip

ạbberufen† *vt sep* recall

ạbbestellen *vt sep* cancel; **jdn a~** put s.o. off

ạbbiegen† *vi sep* (*sein*) turn off; **[nach] links a~** turn left

Ạbbild *nt* image. **a~en** *vt sep* depict, portray. **A~ung** *f* **-,-en** illustration

Ạbbitte *f* **A~ leisten** apologize

ạbblättern *vi sep* (*sein*) flake off

ạbblend|en *vt/i sep* (*haben*) **[die Scheinwerfer] a~en** dip one's headlights. **A~licht** *nt* dipped headlights *pl*

ạbbrechen† *v sep* ● *vt* break off; (*abreißen*) demolish ● *vi* (*sein/haben*) break off

ạbbrennen† *v sep* ● *vt* burn off; (*niederbrennen*) burn down; let off ⟨*Feuerwerkskörper*⟩ ● *vi* (*sein*) burn down

ạbbringen† *vt sep* dissuade (**von** from)

Ạbbruch *m* demolition; (*Beenden*) breaking off; **etw** (*dat*) **keinen A~ tun** do no harm to sth

ạbbuchen *vt sep* debit

ạbbürsten *vt sep* brush down; (*entfernen*) brush off

ạbdank|en *vi sep* (*haben*) resign; ⟨*Herrscher:*⟩ abdicate. **A~ung** *f* **-,-en** resignation; abdication

ạbdecken *vt sep* uncover; (*abnehmen*) take off; (*zudecken*) cover; **den Tisch a~** clear the table

ạbdichten *vt sep* seal

ạbdrehen *vt sep* turn off

Ạbdruck *m* (*pl* **¨e**) impression; (*Finger-*) print; (*Nachdruck*) reprint. **a~en** *vt sep* print

ạbdrücken *vt/i sep* (*haben*) fire; **sich a~** leave an impression

Abend *m* **-s,-e** evening; **am A~** in the evening. **a~** *adv* **heute a~** this evening, tonight; **gestern a~** yesterday evening, last night. **A~brot** *nt* supper. **A~essen** *nt* dinner; (*einfacher*) supper. **A~kurs[us]** *m* evening class. **A~mahl** *nt* (*Relig*) [Holy] Communion. **a~s** *adv* in the evening

Abenteuer *nt* **-s,-** adventure; (*Liebes-*) affair. **a~lich** *a* fantastic; (*gefährlich*) hazardous

Abenteurer *m* **-s,-** adventurer

aber *conj* but; **oder a~** or else ● *adv* (*wirklich*) really; **a~ ja!** but of course! **Tausende und a~ Tausende** thousands upon thousands

Aber|glaube *m* superstition. **a~gläubisch** *a* superstitious

abermals *adv* once again

ạbfahr|en† *v sep* ● *vi* (*sein*) leave; ⟨*Auto:*⟩ drive off ● *vt* take away; (*entlangfahren*) drive along; use ⟨*Fahrkarte*⟩; **abgefahrene Reifen** worn tyres. **A~t** *f* departure; (*Talfahrt*) descent; (*Piste*) run; (*Ausfahrt*) exit

Ạbfall *m* refuse, rubbish, (*Amer*) garbage; (*auf der Straße*) litter; (*Industrie-*) waste. **A~eimer** *m* rubbish-bin; litter-bin

ạbfallen† *vi sep* (*sein*) drop, fall; (*übrigbleiben*) be left (**für** for); (*sich neigen*) slope away; (*fig*) compare badly (**gegen** with); **vom Glauben a~** renounce one's faith. **a~d** *a* sloping

Abfallhaufen *m* rubbish-dump

abfällig *a* disparaging, *adv* -ly

abfangen† *vt sep* intercept; (*beherrschen*) bring under control

abfärben *vi sep* (*haben*) ⟨*Farbe:*⟩ run; ⟨*Stoff:*⟩ not be colour-fast; **a~ auf** (+*acc*) (*fig*) rub off on

abfassen *vt sep* draft

abfertigen *vt sep* attend to; (*zollamtlich*) clear; **jdn kurz a~** (*fam*) give s.o. short shrift

abfeuern *vt sep* fire

abfind|en† *vt sep* pay off; (*entschädigen*) compensate; **sich a~en mit** come to terms with. **A~ung** *f* **-,-en** compensation

abflauen *vi sep* (*sein*) decrease

abfliegen† *vi sep* (*sein*) fly off; (*Aviat*) take off

abfließen† *vi sep* (*sein*) drain *or* run away

Abflug *m* (*Aviat*) departure

Abfluß *m* drainage; (*Öffnung*) drain. **A~rohr** *nt* drain-pipe

abfragen *vt sep* **jdn** *od* **jdm Vokabeln a~** test s.o. on vocabulary

Abfuhr *f* - removal; (*fig*) rebuff

abführ|en *vt sep* take *or* lead away. **a~end** *a* laxative. **A~mittel** *nt* laxative

abfüllen *vt sep* **auf** *od* **in Flaschen a~** bottle

Abgabe *f* handing in; (*Verkauf*) sale; (*Fußball*) pass; (*Steuer*) tax

Abgang *m* departure; (*Theat*) exit; (*Schul-*) leaving

Abgase *ntpl* exhaust fumes

abgeben† *vt sep* hand in; (*abliefern*) deliver; (*verkaufen*) sell; (*zur Aufbewahrung*) leave; (*Fußball*) pass; (*ausströmen*) give off; (*abfeuern*) fire; (*verlauten lassen*) give; cast ⟨*Stimme*⟩; **jdm etw a~** give s.o. a share of sth; **sich a~ mit** occupy oneself with

abgedroschen *a* hackneyed

abgehen† *v sep* ● *vi* (*sein*) leave; (*Theat*) exit; (*sich lösen*) come off; (*abgezogen werden*) be deducted; (*abbiegen*) turn off; (*verlaufen*) go off; **ihr geht jeglicher Humor ab** she totally lacks a sense of humour ● *vt* walk along

abgehetzt *a* harassed. **abgelegen** *a* remote. **abgeneigt** *a* **etw** (*dat*) **nicht abgeneigt sein** not be averse to sth.

abgenutzt *a* worn. **Abgeordnete(r)** *m/f* deputy; (*Pol*) Member of Parliament. **abgepackt** *a* pre-packed. **abgerissen** *a* ragged

abgeschieden *a* secluded. **A~heit** *f* - seclusion

abgeschlossen *a* (*fig*) complete; ⟨*Wohnung*⟩ self-contained. **abgeschmackt** *a* (*fig*) tasteless. **abgesehen** *prep* apart (from **von**). **abgespannt** *a* exhausted. **abgestanden** *a* stale. **abgestorben** *a* dead; ⟨*Glied*⟩ numb. **abgetragen** *a* worn. **abgewetzt** *a* threadbare

abgewinnen† *vt sep* win (**jdm** from s.o.); **etw** (*dat*) **Geschmack a~** get a taste for sth

abgewöhnen *vt sep* **jdm/sich das Rauchen a~** cure s.o. of/give up smoking

abgezehrt *a* emaciated

abgießen† *vt sep* pour off; drain ⟨*Gemüse*⟩

abgleiten† *vi sep* (*sein*) slip

Abgott *m* idol

abgöttisch *adv* **a~ lieben** idolize

abgrenz|en *vt sep* divide off; (*fig*) define. **A~ung** *f* - demarcation

Abgrund *m* abyss; (*fig*) depths *pl*

abgucken *vt sep* (*fam*) copy

Abguß *m* cast

abhacken *vt sep* chop off

abhaken *vt sep* tick off

abhalten† *vt sep* keep off; (*hindern*) keep, prevent (**von** from); (*veranstalten*) hold

abhanden *adv* **a~ kommen** get lost

Abhandlung *f* treatise

Abhang *m* slope

abhängen[1] *vt sep* (*reg*) take down; (*abkuppeln*) uncouple

abhäng|en[2]† *vi sep* (*haben*) depend (**von** on). **a~ig** *a* dependent (**von** on). **A~igkeit** *f* - dependence

abhärten *vt sep* toughen up

abhauen† *v sep* ● *vt* chop off ● *vi* (*sein*) (*fam*) clear off

abheben† *v sep* ● *vt* take off; (*vom Konto*) withdraw; **sich a~** stand out (**gegen** against) ● *vi* (*haben*) (*Cards*) cut [the cards]; (*Aviat*) take off; ⟨*Rakete:*⟩ lift off

abheften *vt sep* file

abhelfen† *vt sep* (+*dat*) remedy

Abhilfe *f* remedy; **A~ schaffen** take [remedial] action

abholen *vt sep* collect; call for ⟨*Person*⟩; **jdn am Bahnhof a~** meet s.o. at the station

ạbhorchen *vt sep* (*Med*) sound
ạbhör|en *vt sep* listen to; (*überwachen*) tap; **jdn** *od* **jdm Vokabeln a∼en** test s.o. on vocabulary. **A∼gerät** *nt* bugging device
Abitu̲r *nt* **-s** ≈ A levels *pl*. **A∼iẹnt(in)** *m* **-en,-en** (*f* **-,-nen**) pupil taking the '*Abitur*'
ạbkanzeln *vt sep* (*fam*) reprimand
ạbkaufen *vt sep* buy (*dat* from)
ạbkehren (sich) *vr sep* turn away
ạbkette[l]n *vt/i sep* (*haben*) cast off
ạbklingen† *vi sep* (*sein*) die away; (*nachlassen*) subside
ạbkochen *vt sep* boil
ạbkommen† *vi sep* (*sein*) **a∼ von** stray from; (*aufgeben*) give up; **vom Thema a∼** digress. **A∼** *nt* **-s,-** agreement
ạbkömmlich *a* available
Ạbkömmling *m* **-s,-e** descendant
ạbkratzen *v sep* • *vt* scrape off • *vi* (*sein*) (*sl*) die
ạbkühlen *vt/i sep* (*sein*) cool; **sich a∼** cool [down]; ⟨*Wetter:*⟩ turn cooler
Ạbkunft *f* **-** origin
ạbkuppeln *vt sep* uncouple
ạbkürz|en *vt sep* shorten; abbreviate ⟨*Wort*⟩. **A∼ung** *f* short cut; (*Wort*) abbreviation
ạbladen† *vt sep* unload
Ạblage *f* shelf; (*für Akten*) tray
ạblager|n *vt sep* deposit; **sich a∼n** be deposited. **A∼ung** *f* **-,-en** deposit
ạblassen† *v sep* • *vt* drain [off]; let off ⟨*Dampf*⟩; (*vom Preis*) knock off • *vi* (*haben*) **a∼ von** give up; **von jdm a∼** leave s.o. alone
Ạblauf *m* drain; (*Verlauf*) course; (*Ende*) end; (*einer Frist*) expiry. **a∼en**† *v sep* • *vi* (*sein*) run *or* drain off; (*verlaufen*) go off; (*enden*) expire; ⟨*Zeit:*⟩ run out; ⟨*Uhrwerk:*⟩ run down • *vt* walk along; (*absuchen*) scour (**nach** for); (*abnutzen*) wear down
ạbleg|en *v sep* • *vt* put down; discard ⟨*Karte*⟩; (*abheften*) file; (*ausziehen*) take off; (*aufgeben*) give up; sit, take ⟨*Prüfung*⟩; **abgelegte Kleidung** cast-offs *pl* • *vi* (*haben*) take off one's coat; (*Naut*) cast off. **A∼er** *m* **-s,-** (*Bot*) cutting; (*Schößling*) shoot
ạblehn|en *vt sep* refuse; (*mißbilligen*) reject. **A∼ung** *f* **-,-en** refusal; rejection
ạbleit|en *vt sep* divert; **sich a∼en** be derived (**von/aus** from). **A∼ung** *f* derivation; (*Wort*) derivative
ạblenk|en *vt sep* deflect; divert ⟨*Aufmerksamkeit*⟩; (*zerstreuen*) distract. **A∼ung** *f* **-,-en** distraction
ạblesen† *vt sep* read; (*absuchen*) pick off
ạbleugnen *vt sep* deny
ạblicht|en *vt sep* photocopy. **A∼ung** *f* photocopy
ạbliefern *vt sep* deliver
ạblös|en *vt sep* detach; (*abwechseln*) relieve; **sich a∼en** come off; (*sich abwechseln*) take turns. **A∼ung** *f* relief
ạbmach|en *vt sep* remove; (*ausmachen*) arrange; (*vereinbaren*) agree; **abgemacht!** agreed! **A∼ung** *f* **-,-en** agreement
ạbmager|n *vi sep* (*sein*) lose weight. **A∼ungskur** *f* slimming diet
ạbmarschieren *vi sep* (*sein*) march off
ạbmelden *vt sep* cancel ⟨*Zeitung*⟩; **sich a∼** report that one is leaving; (*im Hotel*) check out
ạbmess|en† *vt sep* measure. **A∼ungen** *fpl* measurements
ạbmühen (sich) *vr sep* struggle
ạbnäh|en *vt sep* take in. **A∼er** *m* **-s,-** dart
Ạbnahme *f* **-** removal; (*Kauf*) purchase; (*Verminderung*) decrease
ạbnehm|en† *v sep* • *vt* take off, remove; pick up ⟨*Hörer*⟩; **jdm etw a∼en** take/(*kaufen*) buy sth from s.o. • *vi* (*haben*) decrease; (*nachlassen*) decline; ⟨*Person:*⟩ lose weight; ⟨*Mond:*⟩ wane. **A∼er** *m* **-s,-** buyer
Ạbneigung *f* dislike (**gegen** of)
abnọrm *a* abnormal, *adv* -ly
ạbnutz|en *vt sep* wear out; **sich a∼en** wear out. **A∼ung** *f* **-** wear [and tear]
Abon|nement /abɔnəˈmɑ̃ː/ *nt* **-s,-s** subscription. **A∼nẹnt** *m* **-en,-en** subscriber. **a∼ni̲eren** *vt* take out a subscription to
Ạbordnung *f* **-,-en** deputation
ạbpassen *vt sep* wait for; **gut a∼** time well
ạbprallen *vi sep* (*sein*) rebound; ⟨*Geschoß:*⟩ ricochet
ạbraten† *vi sep* (*haben*) **jdm von etw a∼** advise s.o. against sth
ạbräumen *vt/i* (*haben*) clear away; clear ⟨*Tisch*⟩
ạbrechn|en *v sep* • *vt* deduct • *vi* (*haben*) settle up; (*fig*) get even. **A∼ung** *f* settlement [of accounts]; (*Rechnung*) account

Abreise *f* departure. **a~n** *vi sep* (*sein*) leave

abreißen† *v sep* ● *vt* tear off; (*demolieren*) pull down ● *vi* (*sein*) come off; (*fig*) break off

abrichten *vt sep* train

abriegeln *vt sep* bolt; (*absperren*) seal off

Abriß *m* demolition; (*Übersicht*) summary

abrufen† *vt sep* call away; (*Computer*) retrieve

abrunden *vt sep* round off; **nach unten/oben a~** round down/up

abrupt *a* abrupt, *adv* -ly

abrüst|en *vi sep* (*haben*) disarm. **A~ung** *f* disarmament

abrutschen *vi sep* (*sein*) slip

Absage *f* **-,-n** cancellation; (*Ablehnung*) refusal. **a~n** *v sep* ● *vt* cancel ● *vi* (*haben*) **[jdm] a~n** cancel an appointment [with s.o.]; (*auf Einladung*) refuse [s.o.'s invitation]

absägen *vt sep* saw off; (*fam*) sack

Absatz *m* heel; (*Abschnitt*) paragraph; (*Verkauf*) sale

abschaff|en *vt sep* abolish; get rid of ⟨*Auto, Hund*⟩. **A~ung** *f* abolition

abschalten *vt/i sep* (*haben*) switch off

abschätzig *a* disparaging, *adv* -ly

Abschaum *m* (*fig*) scum

Abscheu *m* - revulsion

abscheulich *a* revolting; (*fam*) horrible, *adv* -bly

abschicken *vt sep* send off

Abschied *m* **-[e]s,-e** farewell; (*Trennung*) parting; **A~ nehmen** say goodbye (**von** to)

abschießen† *vt sep* shoot down; (*abtrennen*) shoot off; (*abfeuern*) fire; launch ⟨*Rakete*⟩

abschirmen *vt sep* shield

abschlagen† *vt sep* knock off; (*verweigern*) refuse; (*abwehren*) repel

abschlägig *a* negative; **a~e Antwort** refusal

Abschlepp|dienst *m* breakdown service. **a~en** *vt sep* tow away. **A~seil** *nt* tow-rope. **A~wagen** *m* breakdown vehicle

abschließen† *v sep* ● *vt* lock; (*beenden, abmachen*) conclude; make ⟨*Wette*⟩; balance ⟨*Bücher*⟩; **sich a~** (*fig*) cut oneself off ● *vi* (*haben*) lock up; (*enden*) end. **a~d** *adv* in conclusion

Abschluß *m* conclusion. **A~prüfung** *f* final examination. **A~zeugnis** *nt* diploma

abschmecken *vt sep* season

abschmieren *vt sep* lubricate

abschneiden† *v sep* ● *vt* cut off; **den Weg a~** take a short cut ● *vi* (*haben*) **gut/schlecht a~** do well/badly

Abschnitt *m* section; (*Stadium*) stage; (*Absatz*) paragraph; (*Kontroll-*) counterfoil

abschöpfen *vt sep* skim off

abschrauben *vt sep* unscrew

abschreck|en *vt sep* deter; (*Culin*) put in cold water ⟨*Ei*⟩. **a~end** *a* repulsive, *adv* -ly; **a~endes Beispiel** warning. **A~ungsmittel** *nt* deterrent

abschreib|en† *v sep* ● *vt* copy; (*Comm & fig*) write off ● *vi* (*haben*) copy. **A~ung** *f* (*Comm*) depreciation

Abschrift *f* copy

Abschuß *m* shooting down; (*Abfeuern*) firing; (*Raketen-*) launch

abschüssig *a* sloping; (*steil*) steep

abschwächen *vt sep* lessen; **sich a~** lessen; (*schwächer werden*) weaken

abschweifen *vi sep* (*sein*) digress

abschwellen† *vi sep* (*sein*) go down

abschwören† *vi sep* (*haben*) (+*dat*) renounce

abseh|bar *a* **in a~barer Zeit** in the foreseeable future. **a~en**† *vt/i sep* (*haben*) copy; (*voraussehen*) foresee; **a~en von** disregard; (*aufgeben*) refrain from; **es abgesehen haben auf** (+*acc*) have one's eye on; (*schikanieren*) have it in for

absein† *vi sep* (*sein*) (*fam*) have come off; (*erschöpft*) be worn out

abseits *adv* apart; (*Sport*) offside ● *prep* (+*gen*) away from. **A~** *nt* - (*Sport*) offside

absend|en† *vt sep* send off. **A~er** *m* sender

absetzen *v sep* ● *vt* put *or* set down; (*ablagern*) deposit; (*abnehmen*) take off; (*absagen*) cancel; (*abbrechen*) stop; (*entlassen*) dismiss; (*verkaufen*) sell; (*abziehen*) deduct; **sich a~** be deposited; (*fliehen*) flee ● *vi* (*haben*) pause

Absicht *f* **-,-en** intention; **mit A~** intentionally, on purpose

absichtlich *a* intentional, *adv* -ly, deliberate, *adv* -ly

absitzen† *v sep* ● *vi* (*sein*) dismount ● *vt* (*fam*) serve ⟨*Strafe*⟩

absolut *a* absolute, *adv* -ly

Absolution /-ˈtsi̯oːn/ *f* - absolution
absolvieren *vt* complete; (*bestehen*) pass
absonderlich *a* odd
absonder|n *vt sep* separate; (*ausscheiden*) secrete; **sich a~n** keep apart (**von** from). **A~ung** *f* **-,-en** secretion
absor|bieren *vt* absorb. **A~ption** /-ˈtsi̯oːn/ *f* - absorption
abspeisen *vt sep* fob off (**mit** with)
abspenstig *a* **a~ machen** take (**jdm** from s.o.)
absperr|en *vt sep* cordon off; (*abstellen*) turn off; (*SGer*) lock. **A~ung** *f* **-,-en** barrier
abspielen *vt sep* play; (*Fußball*) pass; **sich a~** take place
Absprache *f* agreement
absprechen† *vt sep* arrange; **sich a~** agree; **jdm etw a~** deny s.o. sth
abspringen† *vi sep* (*sein*) jump off; (*mit Fallschirm*) parachute; (*abgehen*) come off; (*fam: zurücktreten*) back out
Absprung *m* jump
abspülen *vt sep* rinse; (*entfernen*) rinse off
abstamm|en *vi sep* (*haben*) be descended (**von** from). **A~ung** *f* - descent
Abstand *m* distance; (*zeitlich*) interval; **A~ halten** keep one's distance; **A~ nehmen von** (*fig*) refrain from
abstatten *vt sep* **jdm einen Besuch a~** pay s.o. a visit
abstauben *vt sep* dust
abstech|en† *vi sep* (*haben*) stand out. **A~er** *m* **-s,-** detour
abstehen† *vi sep* (*haben*) stick out; **a~ von** be away from
absteigen† *vi sep* (*sein*) dismount; (*niedersteigen*) descend; (*Fußball*) be relegated
abstell|en *vt sep* put down; (*lagern*) store; (*parken*) park; (*abschalten*) turn off; (*fig: beheben*) remedy. **A~gleis** *nt* siding. **A~raum** *m* box-room
absterben† *vi sep* (*sein*) die; (*gefühllos werden*) go numb
Abstieg *m* **-[e]s,-e** descent; (*Fußball*) relegation
abstimm|en *v sep* • *vi* (*haben*) vote (**über** + *acc* on) • *vt* coordinate (**auf** + *acc* with). **A~ung** *f* vote
Abstinenz /-st-/ *f* - abstinence. **A~ler** *m* **-s,-** teetotaller
abstoßen† *vt sep* knock off; (*abschieben*) push off; (*verkaufen*) sell; (*fig: ekeln*) repel. **a~d** *a* repulsive, *adv* -ly
abstrakt /-st-/ *a* abstract
abstreifen *vt sep* remove; slip off ⟨*Kleidungsstück, Schuhe*⟩
abstreiten† *vt sep* deny
Abstrich *m* (*Med*) smear; (*Kürzung*) cut
abstufen *vt sep* grade
Absturz *m* fall; (*Aviat*) crash
abstürzen *vi sep* (*sein*) fall; (*Aviat*) crash
absuchen *vt sep* search; (*ablesen*) pick off
absurd *a* absurd
Abszeß *m* **-sses,-sse** abscess
Abt *m* **-[e]s,⸚e** abbot
abtasten *vt sep* feel; (*Techn*) scan
abtauen *vt/i sep* (*sein*) thaw; (*entfrosten*) defrost
Abtei *f* **-,-en** abbey
Abteil *nt* compartment
abteilen *vt sep* divide off
Abteilung *f* **-,-en** section; (*Admin, Comm*) department
abtragen† *vt sep* clear; (*einebnen*) level; (*abnutzen*) wear out; (*abzahlen*) pay off
abträglich *a* detrimental (*dat* to)
abtreib|en† *v sep* • *vt* (*Naut*) drive off course; **ein Kind a~en lassen** have an abortion • *vi* (*sein*) drift off course. **A~ung** *f* **-,-en** abortion
abtrennen *vt sep* detach; (*abteilen*) divide off
abtret|en† *v sep* • *vt* cede (**an** + *acc* to); **sich** (*dat*) **die Füße a~en** wipe one's feet • *vi* (*sein*) (*Theat*) exit; (*fig*) resign. **A~er** *m* **-s,-** doormat
abtrocknen *vt/i sep* (*haben*) dry; **sich a~** dry oneself
abtropfen *vi sep* (*sein*) drain
abtrünnig *a* renegade; **a~ werden** (+ *dat*) desert
abtun† *vt sep* (*fig*) dismiss
abverlangen *vt sep* demand (*dat* from)
abwägen† *vt sep* (*fig*) weigh
abwandeln *vt sep* modify
abwandern *vi sep* (*sein*) move away
abwarten *v sep* • *vt* wait for • *vi* (*haben*) wait [and see]
abwärts *adv* down[wards]
Abwasch *m* **-[e]s** washing-up; (*Geschirr*) dirty dishes *pl*. **a~en**† *v sep* • *vt* wash; wash up ⟨*Geschirr*⟩; (*entfernen*) wash off • *vi* (*haben*) wash up. **A~lappen** *m* dishcloth

Abwasser *nt* **-s,¨** sewage. **A~kanal** *m* sewer

abwechseln *vi/r sep* (*haben*) **[sich] a~** alternate; ⟨*Personen:*⟩ take turns. **a~d** *a* alternate, *adv* -ly

Abwechslung *f* **-,-en** change; **zur A~** for a change. **a~sreich** *a* varied

Abweg *m* **auf A~e geraten** (*fig*) go astray. **a~ig** *a* absurd

Abwehr *f* **-** defence; (*Widerstand*) resistance; (*Pol*) counter-espionage. **a~en** *vt sep* ward off; (*Mil*) repel; (*zurückweisen*) dismiss. **A~system** *nt* immune system

abweich|en† *vi sep* (*sein*) deviate/ (*von Regel*) depart (**von** from); (*sich unterscheiden*) differ (**von** from). **a~end** *a* divergent; (*verschieden*) different. **A~ung** *f* **-,-en** deviation; difference

abweis|en† *vt sep* turn down; turn away ⟨*Person*⟩; (*abwehren*) repel. **a~end** *a* unfriendly. **A~ung** *f* rejection; (*Abfuhr*) rebuff

abwenden† *vt sep* turn away; (*verhindern*) avert; **sich a~** turn away; **den Blick a~** look away

abwerfen† *vt sep* throw off; throw ⟨*Reiter*⟩; (*Aviat*) drop; (*Kartenspiel*) discard; shed ⟨*Haut, Blätter*⟩; yield ⟨*Gewinn*⟩

abwert|en *vt sep* devalue. **a~end** *a* pejorative, *adv* -ly. **A~ung** *f* **-,-en** devaluation

abwesen|d *a* absent; (*zerstreut*) absent-minded. **A~heit** *f* **-** absence; absent-mindedness

abwickeln *vt sep* unwind; (*erledigen*) settle

abwischen *vt sep* wipe; (*entfernen*) wipe off

abwürgen *vt sep* stall ⟨*Motor*⟩

abzahlen *vt sep* pay off

abzählen *vt sep* count

Abzahlung *f* instalment

abzapfen *vt sep* draw

Abzeichen *nt* badge

abzeichnen *vt sep* copy; (*unterzeichnen*) initial; **sich a~** stand out

Abzieh|bild *nt* transfer. **a~en**† *v sep* • *vt* pull off; take off ⟨*Laken*⟩; strip ⟨*Bett*⟩; (*häuten*) skin; (*Phot*) print; run off ⟨*Kopien*⟩; (*zurückziehen*) withdraw; (*abrechnen*) deduct • *vi* (*sein*) go away; ⟨*Rauch:*⟩ escape

abzielen *vi sep* (*haben*) **a~ auf** (+*acc*) (*fig*) be aimed at

Abzug *m* withdrawal; (*Abrechnung*) deduction; (*Phot*) print; (*Korrektur-*) proof; (*am Gewehr*) trigger; (*A~söffnung*) vent; **A~̈e** *pl* deductions

abzüglich *prep* (+*gen*) less

Abzugshaube *f* [cooker] hood

abzweig|en *v sep* • *vi* (*sein*) branch off • *vt* divert. **A~ung** *f* **-,-en** junction; (*Gabelung*) fork

ach *int* oh; **a~ je!** oh dear! **a~ so** I see; **mit A~ und Krach** (*fam*) by the skin of one's teeth

Achse *f* **-,-n** axis; (*Rad-*) axle

Achsel *f* **-,-n** shoulder; **die A~n zucken** shrug one's shoulders. **A~höhle** *f* armpit. **A~zucken** *nt* **-s** shrug

acht[1] *inv a*, **A~** *f* **-,-en** eight; **heute in a~ Tagen** a week today

acht[2] **außer a~ lassen** disregard; **sich in a~ nehmen** be careful

acht|e(r,s) *a* eighth. **a~eckig** *a* octagonal. **A~el** *nt* **-s,-** eighth. **A~elnote** *f* quaver, (*Amer*) eighth note

achten *vt* respect • *vi* (*haben*) **a~ auf** (+*acc*) pay attention to; (*aufpassen*) look after; **darauf a~, daß** take care that

ächten *vt* ban; ostracize ⟨*Person*⟩

Achter|bahn *f* roller-coaster. **a~n** *adv* (*Naut*) aft

achtgeben† *vi sep* (*haben*) be careful; **a~ auf** (+*acc*) look after

achtlos *a* careless, *adv* -ly

achtsam *a* careful, *adv* -ly

Achtung *f* **-** respect (**vor**+*dat* for); **A~!** look out! (*Mil*) attention! **'A~ Stufe'** 'mind the step'

acht|zehn *inv a* eighteen. **a~zehnte(r,s)** *a* eighteenth. **a~zig** *a inv* eighty. **a~zigste(r,s)** *a* eightieth

ächzen *vi* (*haben*) groan

Acker *m* **-s,¨** field. **A~bau** *m* agriculture. **A~land** *nt* arable land

addieren *vt/i* (*haben*) add; (*zusammenzählen*) add up

Addition /-'tsi̯o:n/ *f* **-,-en** addition

ade *int* goodbye

Adel *m* **-s** nobility

Ader *f* **-,-n** vein; **künstlerische A~** artistic bent

Adjektiv *nt* **-s,-e** adjective

Adler *m* **-s,-** eagle

adlig *a* noble. **A~e(r)** *m* nobleman

Administration /-'tsi̯o:n/ *f* **-** administration

Admiral *m* **-s,¨e** admiral

adop|tieren *vt* adopt. **A~tion** /-'tsi̯o:n/ *f* **-,-en** adoption. **A~tiveltern** *pl* adoptive parents. **A~tivkind** *nt* adopted child
Adrenalin *nt* **-s** adrenalin
Adres|se *f* **-,-n** address. **a~sieren** *vt* address
adrett *a* neat, *adv* -ly
Adria *f* **-** Adriatic
Advent *m* **-s** Advent. **A~skranz** *m* Advent wreath
Adverb *nt* **-s,-ien** /-i̯ən/ adverb
Affäre *f* **-,-n** affair
Affe *m* **-n,-n** monkey; (*Menschen-*) ape
Affekt *m* **-[e]s,-e im A~** in the heat of the moment
affektiert *a* affected. **A~heit** *f* **-** affectation
affig *a* affected; (*eitel*) vain
Afrika *nt* **-s** Africa
Afrikan|er(in) *m* **-s,-** (*f* **-,-nen**) African. **a~isch** *a* African
After *m* **-s,-** anus
Agen|t(in) *m* **-en,-en** (*f* **-,-nen**) agent. **A~tur** *f* **-,-en** agency
Aggres|sion *f* **-,-en** aggression. **a~siv** *a* aggressive, *adv* -ly. **A~sivität** *f* **-** aggressiveness
Agitation /-'tsi̯o:n/ *f* **-** agitation
Agnostiker *m* **-s,-** agnostic
Ägypt|en /ɛ'gyptən/ *nt* **-s** Egypt. **Ä~er(in)** *m* **-s,-** (*f* **-,-nen**) Egyptian. **ä~isch** *a* Egyptian
ähneln *vi* (*haben*) (*+dat*) resemble; **sich ä~** be alike
ahnen *vt* have a presentiment of; (*vermuten*) suspect
Ahnen *mpl* ancestors. **A~forschung** *f* genealogy. **A~tafel** *f* family tree
ähnlich *a* similar, *adv* -ly; **jdm ä~ sehen** resemble s.o.; (*typisch sein*) be just like s.o. **Ä~keit** *f* **-,-en** similarity; resemblance
Ahnung *f* **-,-en** premonition; (*Vermutung*) idea, hunch; **keine A~** (*fam*) no idea. **a~slos** *a* unsuspecting
Ahorn *m* **-s,-e** maple
Ähre *f* **-,-n** ear [of corn]
Aids /e:ts/ *nt* **-** Aids
Akademie *f* **-,-n** academy
Akadem|iker(in) *m* **-s,-** (*f* **-,-nen**) university graduate. **a~isch** *a* academic, *adv* -ally
akklimatisieren (sich) *vr* become acclimatized
Akkord *m* **-[e]s,-e** (*Mus*) chord; **im A~ arbeiten** be on piece-work. **A~arbeit** *f* piece-work
Akkordeon *nt* **-s,-s** accordion
Akkumulator *m* **-s,-en** /-'to:rən/ (*Electr*) accumulator
Akkusativ *m* **-s,-e** accusative. **A~objekt** *nt* direct object
Akrobat|(in) *m* **-en,-en** (*f* **-,-nen**) acrobat. **a~isch** *a* acrobatic
Akt *m* **-[e]s,-e** act; (*Kunst*) nude
Akte *f* **-,-n** file; **A~n** documents. **A~ndeckel** *m* folder. **A~nkoffer** *m* attaché case. **A~nschrank** *m* filing cabinet. **A~ntasche** *f* briefcase
Aktie /'aktsi̯ə/ *f* **-,-n** (*Comm*) share. **A~ngesellschaft** *f* joint-stock company
Aktion /ak'tsi̯o:n/ *f* **-,-en** action; (*Kampagne*) campaign. **A~är** *m* **-s,-e** shareholder
aktiv *a* active, *adv* -ly. **a~ieren** *vt* activate. **A~ität** *f* **-,-en** activity
Aktualität *f* **-,-en** topicality; **A~en** current events
aktuell *a* topical; (*gegenwärtig*) current; **nicht mehr a~** no longer relevant
Akupunktur *f* **-** acupuncture
Akust|ik *f* **-** acoustics *pl*. **a~isch** *a* acoustic, *adv* -ally
akut *a* acute
Akzent *m* **-[e]s,-e** accent
akzept|abel *a* acceptable. **a~ieren** *vt* accept
Alarm *m* **-s** alarm; (*Mil*) alert; **A~ schlagen** raise the alarm. **a~ieren** *vt* alert; (*beunruhigen*) alarm. **a~ierend** *a* alarming
albern *a* silly • *adv* in a silly way • *vi* (*haben*) play the fool
Album *nt* **-s,-ben** album
Algebra *f* **-** algebra
Algen *fpl* algae
Algerien /-i̯ən/ *nt* **-s** Algeria
Alibi *nt* **-s,-s** alibi
Alimente *pl* maintenance *sg*
Alkohol *m* **-s** alcohol. **a~frei** *a* non-alcoholic
Alkohol|iker(in) *m* **-s,-** (*f* **-,-nen**) alcoholic. **a~isch** *a* alcoholic. **A~ismus** *m* **-** alcoholism
all *inv pron* **all das/mein Geld** all the/my money; **all dies** all this
All *nt* **-s** universe
alle *pred a* finished, (*fam*) all gone; **a~ machen** finish up
all|e(r,s) *pron* all; (*jeder*) every; **a~es** everything, all; (*alle Leute*) everyone; **a~e** *pl* all; **a~es Geld** all the money; **a~e meine Freunde** all my friends; **a~e beide** both [of them/

us]; **wir a~e** we all; **a~e Tage** every day; **a~e drei Jahre** every three years; **in a~er Unschuld** in all innocence; **ohne a~en Grund** without any reason; **vor a~em** above all; **a~es in a~em** all in all; **a~es aussteigen!** all change! **a~edem** *pron* **bei/trotz a~edem** with/despite all that

Allee *f* **-,-n** avenue

Alleg|orie *f* **-,-n** allegory. **a~orisch** *a* allegorical

allein *adv* alone; (*nur*) only; **a~ der Gedanke** the mere thought; **von a~[e]** of its/⟨*Person*⟩ one's own accord; (*automatisch*) automatically; **einzig und a~** solely ● *conj* but. **A~erziehende(r)** *m/f* single parent. **a~ig** *a* sole. **a~stehend** *a* single; **A~stehende** *pl* single people

allemal *adv* every time; (*gewiß*) certainly; **ein für a~** once and for all

allenfalls *adv* at most; (*eventuell*) possibly

aller|beste(r,s) *a* very best; **am a~besten** best of all. **a~dings** *adv* indeed; (*zwar*) admittedly. **a~erste(r,s)** *a* very first

Allergie *f* **-,-n** allergy

allergisch *a* allergic (**gegen** to)

aller|hand *inv a* all sorts of ● *pron* all sorts of things; **das ist a~hand!** that's quite something! (*empört*) that's a bit much! **A~heiligen** *nt* **-s** All Saints Day. **a~höchstens** *adv* at the very most. **a~lei** *inv a* all sorts of ● *pron* all sorts of things. **a~letzte(r,s)** *a* very last. **a~liebst** *a* enchanting. **a~liebste(r,s)** *a* favourite ● *adv* **am a~liebsten** for preference; **am a~liebsten haben** like best of all. **a~meiste(r,s)** *a* most ● *adv* **am a~meisten** most of all. **A~seelen** *nt* **-s** All Souls Day. **a~seits** *adv* generally; **guten Morgen a~seits!** good morning everyone! **a~wenigste(r,s)** *a* very least ● *adv* **am a~wenigsten** least of all

alle|s *s.* **alle(r,s)**. **a~samt** *adv* all. **A~swisser** *m* **-s,-** (*fam*) know-all

allgemein *a* general, *adv* -ly; **im a~en** in general. **A~heit** *f* **-** community; (*Öffentlichkeit*) general public

Allheilmittel *nt* panacea

Allianz *f* **-,-en** alliance

Alligator *m* **-s,-en** /-'to:rən/ alligator

alliiert *a* allied; **die A~en** *pl* the Allies

all|jährlich *a* annual, *adv* -ly. **a~mächtig** *a* almighty; **der A~mächtige** the Almighty. **a~mählich** *a* gradual, *adv* -ly

Alltag *m* working day; **der A~** (*fig*) everyday life

alltäglich *a* daily; (*gewöhnlich*) everyday; ⟨*Mensch*⟩ ordinary ● *adv* daily

alltags *adv* on weekdays

allzu *adv* [far] too; **a~ vorsichtig** over-cautious. **a~bald** *adv* all too soon. **a~oft** *adv* all too often. **a~sehr** *adv* far too much. **a~viel** *adv* far too much

Alm *f* **-,-en** alpine pasture

Almosen *ntpl* alms

Alpdruck *m* nightmare

Alpen *pl* Alps. **A~veilchen** *nt* cyclamen

Alphabet *nt* **-[e]s,-e** alphabet. **a~isch** *a* alphabetical, *adv* -ly

Alptraum *m* nightmare

als *conj* as; (*zeitlich*) when; (*mit Komparativ*) than; **nichts als** nothing but; **als ob** as if *or* though; **so tun als ob** (*fam*) pretend

also *adv & conj* so; **a~ gut** all right then; **na a~!** there you are!

alt *a* (**älter, ältest**) old; (*gebraucht*) second-hand; (*ehemalig*) former; **alt werden** grow old; **alles beim a~en lassen** leave things as they are

Alt *m* **-s** (*Mus*) contralto

Altar *m* **-s,¨e** altar

Alt|e(r) *m/f* old man/woman; **die A~en** old people. **A~eisen** *nt* scrap iron. **A~enheim** *nt* old people's home

Alter *nt* **-s,-** age; (*Bejahrtheit*) old age; **im A~ von** at the age of; **im A~** in old age

älter *a* older; **mein ä~er Bruder** my elder brother

altern *vi* (*sein*) age

Alternative *f* **-,-n** alternative

Alters|grenze *f* age limit. **A~heim** *nt* old people's home. **A~rente** *f* old-age pension. **a~schwach** *a* old and infirm; ⟨*Ding*⟩ decrepit

Alter|tum *nt* **-s,¨er** antiquity. **a~tümlich** *a* old; (*altmodisch*) old-fashioned

ältest|e(r,s) *a* oldest; **der ä~e Sohn** the eldest son

althergebracht *a* traditional

altklug *a* precocious, *adv* -ly

ältlich *a* elderly

alt|modisch old-fashioned ● *adv* in an old-fashioned way. **A~papier** *nt* waste paper. **A~stadt** *f* old [part of a] town. **A~warenhändler** *m* second-hand dealer. **A~weibermärchen** *nt* old wives' tale. **A~weibersommer** *m* Indian summer; (*Spinnfäden*) gossamer

Alufolie *f* [aluminium] foil

Aluminium *nt* **-s** aluminium, (*Amer*) aluminum

am *prep* = **an dem; am Montag** on Monday; **am Morgen** in the morning; **am besten/meisten** [the] best/most; **am teuersten sein** be the most expensive

Amateur /-'tø:ɐ̯/ *m* **-s,-e** amateur

Ambition /-'tsi̯o:n/ *f* **-,-en** ambition

Amboß *m* **-sses,-sse** anvil

ambulan|t *a* out-patient ... ● *adv* **a~t behandeln** treat as an out-patient. **A~z** *f* **-,-en** out-patients' department; (*Krankenwagen*) ambulance

Ameise *f* **-,-n** ant

amen *int*, **A~** *nt* **-s** amen

Amerika *nt* **-s** America

Amerikan|er(in) *m* **-s,-** (*f* **-,-nen**) American. **a~isch** *a* American

Ami *m* **-s,-s** (*fam*) Yank

Ammoniak *nt* **-s** ammonia

Amnestie *f* **-,-n** amnesty

amoralisch *a* amoral

Ampel *f* **-,-n** traffic lights *pl*; (*Blumen-*) hanging basket

Amphib|ie /-i̯ə/ *f* **-,-n** amphibian. **a~isch** *a* amphibious

Amphitheater *nt* amphitheatre

Amput|ation /-'tsi̯o:n/ *f* **-,-en** amputation. **a~ieren** *vt* amputate

Amsel *f* **-,-n** blackbird

Amt *nt* **-[e]s,¨er** office; (*Aufgabe*) task; (*Teleph*) exchange. **a~ieren** *vi* (*haben*) hold office; **a~ierend** acting. **a~lich** *a* official, *adv* -ly. **A~szeichen** *nt* dialling tone

Amulett *nt* **-[e]s,-e** [lucky] charm

amüs|ant *a* amusing, *adv* -ly. **a~ieren** *vt* amuse; **sich a~ieren** be amused (**über** + *acc* at); (*sich vergnügen*) enjoy oneself

an *prep* (+ *dat*/*acc*) at; (*haftend, berührend*) on; (*gegen*) against; (+ *acc*) ⟨*schicken*⟩ to; **an der/die Universität** at/to university; **an dem Tag** on that day; **es ist an mir** it is up to me; **an [und für] sich** actually; **die Arbeit an sich** the work as such ● *adv* (*angeschaltet*) on; (*auf Fahrplan*) arriving; **an die zwanzig Mark/Leute** about twenty marks/people; **von heute an** from today

analog *a* analogous; (*Computer*) analog. **A~ie** *f* **-,-n** analogy

Analphabet *m* **-en,-en** illiterate person. **A~entum** *nt* **-s** illiteracy

Analy|se *f* **-,-n** analysis. **a~sieren** *vt* analyse. **A~tiker** *m* **-s,-** analyst. **a~tisch** *a* analytical

Anämie *f* **-** anaemia

Ananas *f* **-,-[se]** pineapple

Anarch|ie *f* **-** anarchy. **A~ist** *m* **-en,-en** anarchist

Anat|omie *f* **-** anatomy. **a~omisch** *a* anatomical, *adv* -ly

anbahnen (sich) *vr sep* develop

Anbau *m* cultivation; (*Gebäude*) extension. **a~en** *vt sep* build on; (*anpflanzen*) cultivate, grow

anbehalten† *vt sep* keep on

anbei *adv* enclosed

anbeißen† *v sep* ● *vt* take a bite of ● *vi* (*haben*) ⟨*Fisch:*⟩ bite; (*fig*) take the bait

anbelangen *vt sep* = **anbetreffen**

anbellen *vt sep* bark at

anbeten *vt sep* worship

Anbetracht *m* **in A~** (+ *gen*) in view of

anbetreffen† *vt sep* **was mich/das anbetrifft** as far as I am/that is concerned

Anbetung *f* **-** worship

anbiedern (sich) *vr sep* ingratiate oneself (**bei** with)

anbieten† *vt sep* offer; **sich a~** offer (**zu** to)

anbinden† *vt sep* tie up

Anblick *m* sight. **a~en** *vt sep* look at

anbrechen† *v sep* ● *vt* start on; break into ⟨*Vorräte*⟩ ● *vi* (*sein*) begin; ⟨*Tag:*⟩ break; ⟨*Nacht:*⟩ fall

anbrennen† *v sep* ● *vt* light ● *vi* (*sein*) burn; (*Feuer fangen*) catch fire

anbringen† *vt sep* bring [along]; (*befestigen*) fix

Anbruch *m* (*fig*) dawn; **A~ des Tages/der Nacht** daybreak/nightfall

anbrüllen *vt sep* (*fam*) bellow at

Andacht *f* **-,-en** reverence; (*Gottesdienst*) prayers *pl*

andächtig *a* reverent, *adv* -ly; (*fig*) rapt, *adv* -ly

andauern *vi sep* (*haben*) last; (*anhalten*) continue. **a~d** *a* persistent, *adv* -ly; (*ständig*) constant, *adv* -ly

Andenken *nt* **-s,-** memory; (*Souvenir*) souvenir; **zum A~ an** (+ *acc*) in memory of

ander|e(r,s) *a* other; (*verschieden*) different; (*nächste*) next; **ein a~er, eine a~e** another • *pron* **der a~e/die a~en** the other/others; **ein a~er** another [one]; (*Person*) someone else; **kein a~er** no one else; **einer nach dem a~en** one after the other; **alles a~e/nichts a~es** everything/nothing else; **etwas ganz a~es** something quite different; **alles a~e als** anything but; **unter a~em** among other things. **a~enfalls** *adv* otherwise. **a~erseits** *adv* on the other hand. **a~mal** *adv* **ein a~mal** another time

ändern *vt* alter; (*wechseln*) change; **sich ä~** change

andernfalls *adv* otherwise

anders *pred a* different; **a~ werden** change • *adv* differently; ⟨*riechen, schmecken*⟩ different; (*sonst*) else; **jemand/niemand/irgendwo a~** someone/no one/somewhere else

anderseits *adv* on the other hand

anders|herum *adv* the other way round. **a~wo** *adv* (*fam*) somewhere else

anderthalb *inv a* one and a half; **a~ Stunden** an hour and a half

Änderung *f* **-,-en** alteration; (*Wechsel*) change

anderweitig *a* other • *adv* otherwise; (*anderswo*) elsewhere

andeut|en *vt sep* indicate; (*anspielen*) hint at. **A~ung** *f* **-,-en** indication; hint

andicken *vt sep* (*Culin*) thicken

Andrang *m* rush (**nach** for); (*Gedränge*) crush

andre *a & pron* = **andere**

andrehen *vt sep* turn on; **jdm etw a~** (*fam*) palm sth off on s.o.

andrerseits *adv* = **andererseits**

androhen *vt sep* **jdm etw a~** threaten s.o. with sth

aneignen *vt sep* **sich** (*dat*) **a~** appropriate; (*lernen*) learn

aneinander *adv & pref* together; ⟨*denken*⟩ of one another; **a~ vorbei** past one another. **a~geraten**† *vi sep* (*sein*) quarrel

Anekdote *f* **-,-n** anecdote

anekeln *vt sep* nauseate

anerkannt *a* acknowledged

anerkenn|en† *vt sep* acknowledge, recognize; (*würdigen*) appreciate. **a~end** *a* approving, *adv* -ly. **A~ung** *f* **-** acknowledgement, recognition; appreciation

anfahren† *v sep* • *vt* deliver; (*streifen*) hit; (*schimpfen*) snap at • *vi* (*sein*) start; **angefahren kommen** drive up

Anfall *m* fit, attack. **a~en**† *v sep* • *vt* attack • *vi* (*sein*) arise; ⟨*Zinsen:*⟩ accrue

anfällig *a* susceptible (**für** to); (*zart*) delicate. **A~keit** *f* **-** susceptibility (**für** to)

Anfang *m* **-s,¨e** beginning, start; **zu** *od* **am A~** at the beginning; (*anfangs*) at first. **a~en**† *vt/i sep* (*haben*) begin, start; (*tun*) do

Anfäng|er(in) *m* **-s,-** (*f* **-,-nen**) beginner. **a~lich** *a* initial, *adv* -ly

anfangs *adv* at first. **A~buchstabe** *m* initial letter. **A~gehalt** *nt* starting salary. **A~gründe** *mpl* rudiments

anfassen *v sep* • *vt* touch; (*behandeln*) treat; tackle ⟨*Arbeit*⟩; **jdn a~** take s.o.'s hand; **sich a~** hold hands; **sich weich a~** feel soft • *vi* (*haben*) **mit a~** lend a hand

anfechten† *vt sep* contest; (*fig: beunruhigen*) trouble

anfeinden *vt sep* be hostile to

anfertigen *vt sep* make

anfeuchten *vt sep* moisten

anfeuern *vt sep* spur on

anflehen *vt sep* implore, beg

Anflug *m* (*Aviat*) approach; (*fig: Spur*) trace

anforder|n *vt sep* demand; (*Comm*) order. **A~ung** *f* demand

Anfrage *f* enquiry. **a~n** *vi sep* (*haben*) enquire, ask

anfreunden (sich) *vr sep* make friends (**mit** with); (*miteinander*) become friends

anfügen *vt sep* add

anfühlen *vt sep* feel; **sich weich a~** feel soft

anführ|en *vt sep* lead; (*zitieren*) quote; (*angeben*) give; **jdn a~en** (*fam*) have s.o. on. **A~er** *m* leader. **A~ungszeichen** *ntpl* quotation marks

Angabe *f* statement; (*Anweisung*) instruction; (*Tennis*) service; (*fam: Angeberei*) showing-off; **nähere A~n** particulars

angeb|en† *v sep* • *vt* state; give ⟨*Namen, Grund*⟩; (*anzeigen*) indicate; set ⟨*Tempo*⟩ • *vi* (*haben*) (*Tennis*) serve; (*fam: protzen*) show off. **A~er(in)** *m* **-s,-** (*f* **-,-nen**) (*fam*) show-off. **A~erei** *f* - (*fam*) showing-off

angeblich *a* alleged, *adv* -ly

angeboren *a* innate; (*Med*) congenital

Angebot *nt* offer; (*Auswahl*) range; **A~ und Nachfrage** supply and demand

angebracht *a* appropriate

angebunden *a* **kurz a~** curt

angegriffen *a* worn out; ⟨*Gesundheit*⟩ poor

angeheiratet *a* ⟨*Onkel, Tante*⟩ by marriage

angeheitert *a* (*fam*) tipsy

angehen† *v sep* ● *vi* (*sein*) begin, start; ⟨*Licht, Radio:*⟩ come on; (*anwachsen*) take root; **a~ gegen** fight ● *vt* attack; tackle ⟨*Arbeit*⟩; (*bitten*) ask (**um** for); (*betreffen*) concern; **das geht dich nichts an** it's none of your business. **a~d** *a* future; ⟨*Künstler*⟩ budding

angehör|en *vi sep* (*haben*) (+*dat*) belong to. **A~ige(r)** *m/f* relative; (*Mitglied*) member

Angeklagte(r) *m/f* accused

Angel *f* -,-**n** fishing-rod; (*Tür-*) hinge

Angelegenheit *f* matter; **auswärtige A~en** foreign affairs

Angel|haken *m* fish-hook. **a~n** *vi* (*haben*) fish (**nach** for); **a~n gehen** go fishing ● *vt* (*fangen*) catch. **A~rute** *f* fishing-rod

angelsächsisch *a* Anglo-Saxon

angemessen *a* commensurate (*dat* with); (*passend*) appropriate, *adv* -ly

angenehm *a* pleasant, *adv* -ly; (*bei Vorstellung*) **a~!** delighted to meet you!

angenommen *a* ⟨*Kind*⟩ adopted; ⟨*Name*⟩ assumed

angeregt *a* animated, *adv* -ly

angesehen *a* respected; ⟨*Firma*⟩ reputable

angesichts *prep* (+*gen*) in view of

angespannt *a* intent, *adv* -ly; ⟨*Lage*⟩ tense

Angestellte(r) *m/f* employee

angetan *a* **a~ sein von** be taken with

angetrunken *a* slightly drunk

angewandt *a* applied

angewiesen *a* dependent (**auf** +*acc* on); **auf sich selbst a~** on one's own

angewöhnen *vt sep* **jdm etw a~** get s.o. used to sth; **sich** (*dat*) **etw a~** get into the habit of doing sth

Angewohnheit *f* habit

Angina *f* - tonsillitis

angleichen† *vt sep* adjust (*dat* to)

Angler *m* -**s**,- angler

anglikanisch *a* Anglican

Anglistik *f* - English [language and literature]

Angorakatze *f* Persian cat

angreif|en† *vt sep* attack; tackle ⟨*Arbeit*⟩; (*schädigen*) damage; (*anbrechen*) break into; (*anfassen*) touch. **A~er** *m* -**s**,- attacker; (*Pol*) aggressor

angrenzen *vi sep* (*haben*) adjoin (**an etw** *acc* sth). **a~d** *a* adjoining

Angriff *m* attack; **in A~ nehmen** tackle. **a~slustig** *a* aggressive

Angst *f* -,¨**e** fear; (*Psych*) anxiety; (*Sorge*) worry (**um** about); **A~ haben** be afraid (**vor** + *dat* of); (*sich sorgen*) be worried (**um** about) ● **jdm a~ machen** frighten s.o.; **mir ist a~** I am frightened; I am worried (**um** about)

ängstigen *vt* frighten; (*Sorge machen*) worry; **sich ä~** be frightened; be worried (**um** about)

ängstlich *a* nervous, *adv* -ly; (*scheu*) timid, *adv* -ly; (*verängstigt*) frightened, scared; (*besorgt*) anxious, *adv* -ly. **Ä~keit** *f* - nervousness; timidity; anxiety

angstvoll *a* anxious, *adv* -ly; (*verängstigt*) frightened

angucken *vt sep* (*fam*) look at

angurten (sich) *vr sep* fasten one's seat-belt

anhaben† *vt sep* have on; **er/es kann mir nichts a~** (*fig*) he/it cannot hurt me

anhalt|en† *v sep* ● *vt* stop; hold ⟨*Atem*⟩; **jdn zur Arbeit/Ordnung a~en** urge s.o. to work/be tidy ● *vi* (*haben*) stop; (*andauern*) continue. **a~end** *a* persistent, *adv* -ly; ⟨*Beifall*⟩ prolonged. **A~er(in)** *m* -**s**,- (*f* -,-**nen**) hitch-hiker; **per A~er fahren** hitch-hike. **A~spunkt** *m* clue

anhand *prep* (+*gen*) with the aid of

Anhang *m* appendix; (*fam: Angehörige*) family

anhängen[1] *vt sep* (*reg*) hang up; (*befestigen*) attach; (*hinzufügen*) add

anhäng|en[2]† *vi* (*haben*) be a follower of. **A~er** *m* -**s**,- follower; (*Auto*) trailer; (*Schild*) [tie-on] label; (*Schmuck*) pendant; (*Aufhänger*) loop. **A~erin** *f* -,-**nen** follower. **A~erschaft** *f* - following, followers *pl*. **a~lich** *a* affectionate. **A~sel** *nt* -**s**,- appendage

anhäufen *vt sep* pile up; **sich a~** pile up, accumulate

anheben† *vt sep* lift; (*erhöhen*) raise

Anhieb *m* **auf A~** straight away

Anhöhe *f* hill

anhören *vt sep* listen to; **mit a~** overhear; **sich gut a~** sound good

animieren *vt* encourage (**zu** to)

Anis *m* **-es** aniseed

Anker *m* **-s,-** anchor; **vor A~ gehen** drop anchor. **a~n** *vi* (*haben*) anchor; (*liegen*) be anchored

anketten *vt sep* chain up

Anklage *f* accusation; (*Jur*) charge; (*Ankläger*) prosecution. **A~bank** *f* dock. **a~n** *vt sep* accuse (*gen* of); (*Jur*) charge (*gen* with)

Ankläger *m* accuser; (*Jur*) prosecutor

anklammern *vt sep* clip on; peg on the line ⟨*Wäsche*⟩; **sich a~** cling (**an** + *acc* to)

Anklang *m* **bei jdm A~ finden** meet with s.o.'s approval

ankleben *v sep* ● *vt* stick on ● *vi* (*sein*) stick (**an** + *dat* to)

Ankleide|kabine *f* changing cubicle; (*zur Anprobe*) fitting-room. **a~n** *vt sep* dress; **sich a~n** dress

anklopfen *vi sep* (*haben*) knock

anknipsen *vt sep* (*fam*) switch on

anknüpfen *v sep* ● *vt* tie on; (*fig*) enter into ⟨*Gespräch, Beziehung*⟩ ● *vi* (*haben*) refer (**an** + *acc* to)

ankommen† *vi sep* (*sein*) arrive; (*sich nähern*) approach; **gut a~** arrive safely; (*fig*) go down well (**bei** with); **nicht a~ gegen** (*fig*) be no match for; **a~ auf** (+*acc*) depend on; **es a~ lassen auf** (+*acc*) risk; **das kommt darauf an** it [all] depends

ankreuzen *vt sep* mark with a cross

ankündig|en *vt sep* announce. **A~ung** *f* announcement

Ankunft *f* - arrival

ankurbeln *vt sep* (*fig*) boost

anlächeln *vt sep* smile at

anlachen *vt sep* smile at

Anlage *f* **-,-n** installation; (*Industrie-*) plant; (*Komplex*) complex; (*Geld-*) investment; (*Plan*) layout; (*Beilage*) enclosure; (*Veranlagung*) aptitude; (*Neigung*) predisposition; **[öffentliche] A~n** [public] gardens; **als A~** enclosed

Anlaß *m* **-sses,⸚sse** reason; (*Gelegenheit*) occasion; **A~ geben zu** give cause for

anlass|en† *vt sep* (*Auto*) start; (*fam*) leave on ⟨*Licht*⟩, keep on ⟨*Mantel*⟩; **sich gut/schlecht a~en** start off well/badly. **A~er** *m* **-s,-** starter

anläßlich *prep* (+*gen*) on the occasion of

Anlauf *m* (*Sport*) run-up; (*fig*) attempt. **a~en**† *v sep* ● *vi* (*sein*) start; (*beschlagen*) mist up; ⟨*Metall:*⟩ tarnish; **rot a~en** go red; (*erröten*) blush; **angelaufen kommen** come running up ● *vt* (*Naut*) call at

anlegen *v sep* ● *vt* put (**an** + *acc* against); put on ⟨*Kleidung, Verband*⟩; lay back ⟨*Ohren*⟩; aim ⟨*Gewehr*⟩; (*investieren*) invest; (*ausgeben*) spend (**für** on); (*erstellen*) build; (*gestalten*) lay out; draw up ⟨*Liste*⟩; **[mit] Hand a~** lend a hand; **es darauf a~** (*fig*) aim (**zu** to); **sich a~ mit** quarrel with ● *vi* (*haben*) ⟨*Schiff:*⟩ moor; **a~ auf** (+*acc*) aim at

anlehnen *vt sep* lean (**an** + *acc* against); **sich a~** lean (**an** + *acc* on); **eine Tür angelehnt lassen** leave a door ajar

Anleihe *f* **-,-n** loan

anleinen *vt sep* put on a lead

anleit|en *vt sep* instruct. **A~ung** *f* instructions *pl*

anlernen *vt sep* train

Anliegen *nt* **-s,-** request; (*Wunsch*) desire

anlieg|en† *vi sep* (*haben*) **[eng] a~en** fit closely; **[eng] a~end** close-fitting. **A~er** *mpl* residents; **'A~er frei'** 'access for residents only'

anlocken *vt sep* attract

anlügen† *vt sep* lie to

anmachen *vt sep* (*fam*) fix; (*anschalten*) turn on; (*anzünden*) light; (*Culin*) dress ⟨*Salat*⟩

anmalen *vt sep* paint

Anmarsch *m* (*Mil*) approach

anmaß|en *vt sep* **sich** (*dat*) **a~en** presume (**zu** to); **sich** (*dat*) **ein Recht a~en** claim a right. **a~end** *a* presumptuous, *adv* -ly; (*arrogant*) arrogant, *adv* -ly. **A~ung** *f* - presumption; arrogance

anmeld|en *vt sep* announce; (*Admin*) register; **sich a~en** say that one is coming; (*Admin*) register; (*Sch*) enrol; (*im Hotel*) check in; (*beim Arzt*) make an appointment. **A~ung** *f* announcement; (*Admin*) registration; (*Sch*) enrolment; (*Termin*) appointment

anmerk|en *vt sep* mark; **sich** (*dat*) **etw a~en lassen** show sth. **A~ung** *f* **-,-en** note

Anmut *f* **-** grace; (*Charme*) charm

anmuten *vt sep* **es mutet mich seltsam/vertraut an** it seems odd/familiar to me

anmutig *a* graceful, *adv* -ly; (*lieblich*) charming, *adv* -ly

annähen *vt sep* sew on

annäher|nd *a* approximate, *adv* -ly. **A~ungsversuche** *mpl* advances

Annahme *f* **-,-n** acceptance; (*Adoption*) adoption; (*Vermutung*) assumption

annehm|bar *a* acceptable. **a~en**† *vt sep* accept; (*adoptieren*) adopt; acquire ⟨*Gewohnheit*⟩; (*sich zulegen, vermuten*) assume; **sich a~en** (+*gen*) take care of; **angenommen, daß** assuming that. **A~lichkeiten** *fpl* comforts

annektieren *vt* annex

Anno *adv* **A~ 1920** in the year 1920

Annon|ce /a'nõ:sə/ *f* **-,-n** advertisement. **a~cieren** /-'si:-/ *vt/i* (*haben*) advertise

annullieren *vt* annul; cancel ⟨*Flug*⟩

anöden *vt sep* (*fam*) bore

Anomalie *f* **-,-n** anomaly

anonym *a* anonymous, *adv* -ly

Anorak *m* **-s,-s** anorak

anordn|en *vt sep* arrange; (*befehlen*) order. **A~ung** *f* arrangement; order

anorganisch *a* inorganic

anormal *a* abnormal

anpacken *v sep* ● *vt* grasp; tackle ⟨*Arbeit, Problem*⟩ ● *vi* (*haben*) **mit a~** lend a hand

anpass|en *vt sep* try on; (*angleichen*) adapt (*dat* to); **sich a~** adapt (*dat* to). **A~ung** *f* **-** adaptation. **a~ungsfähig** *a* adaptable. **A~ungsfähigkeit** *f* adaptability

Anpfiff *m* (*Sport*) kick-off; (*fam: Rüge*) reprimand

anpflanzen *vt sep* plant; (*anbauen*) grow

Anprall *m* **-[e]s** impact. **a~en** *vi sep* (*sein*) strike (**an etw** *acc* sth)

anprangern *vt sep* denounce

anpreisen† *vt sep* commend

Anprob|e *f* fitting. **a~ieren** *vt sep* try on

anrechnen *vt sep* count (**als** as); (*berechnen*) charge for; (*verrechnen*) allow ⟨*Summe*⟩; **ich rechne ihm seine Hilfe hoch an** I very much appreciate his help

Anrecht *nt* right (**auf** + *acc* to)

Anrede *f* [form of] address. **a~n** *vt sep* address; (*ansprechen*) speak to

anreg|en *vt sep* stimulate; (*ermuntern*) encourage (**zu** to); (*vorschlagen*) suggest. **a~end** *a* stimulating. **A~ung** *f* stimulation; (*Vorschlag*) suggestion

anreichern *vt sep* enrich

Anreise *f* journey; (*Ankunft*) arrival. **a~n** *vi sep* (*sein*) arrive

Anreiz *m* incentive

anrempeln *vt sep* jostle

Anrichte *f* **-,-n** sideboard. **a~n** *vt sep* (*Culin*) prepare; (*garnieren*) garnish (**mit** with); (*verursachen*) cause

anrüchig *a* disreputable

Anruf *m* call. **A~beantworter** *m* **-s,-** answering machine. **a~en**† *v sep* ● *vt* call to; (*bitten*) call on (**um** for); (*Teleph*) ring ● *vi* (*haben*) ring (**bei jdm** s.o.)

anrühren *vt sep* touch; (*verrühren*) mix

ans *prep* = **an das**

Ansage *f* announcement. **a~n** *vt sep* announce; **sich a~n** say that one is coming. **A~r(in)** *m* **-s,-** (*f* **-,-nen**) announcer

ansamm|eln *vt sep* collect; (*anhäufen*) accumulate; **sich a~eln** collect; (*sich häufen*) accumulate; ⟨*Leute:*⟩ gather. **A~lung** *f* collection; (*Menschen-*) crowd

ansässig *a* resident

Ansatz *m* beginning; (*Haar-*) hairline; (*Versuch*) attempt; (*Techn*) extension

anschaff|en *vt sep* **[sich** *dat***] etw a~en** acquire/(*kaufen*) buy sth. **A~ung** *f* **-,-en** acquisition; (*Kauf*) purchase

anschalten *vt sep* switch on

anschau|en *vt sep* look at. **a~lich** *a* vivid, *adv* -ly. **A~ung** *f* **-,-en** (*fig*) view

Anschein *m* appearance; **den A~ haben** seem. **a~end** *adv* apparently

anschicken (sich) *vr sep* be about (**zu** to)

anschirren *vt sep* harness

Anschlag *m* notice; (*Vor-*) estimate; (*Überfall*) attack (**auf** + *acc* on); (*Mus*) touch; (*Techn*) stop; **240 A~e in der Minute** ≈ 50 words per minute. **A~brett** *nt* notice board. **a~en**† *v sep* ● *vt* put up ⟨*Aushang*⟩; strike ⟨*Note, Taste*⟩; cast on ⟨*Masche*⟩; (*beschädigen*) chip ● *vi* (*haben*) strike/(*stoßen*) knock (**an** + *acc* against); ⟨*Hund:*⟩ bark; (*wirken*) be effective ● *vi* (*sein*) knock (**an** + *acc* against); **mit dem Kopf a~en** hit one's head. **A~zettel** *m* notice

anschließen† *v sep* ● *vt* connect (**an** + *acc* to); (*zufügen*) add; **sich a~ an** (+ *acc*) (*anstoßen*) adjoin; (*folgen*) follow; (*sich anfreunden*) become friendly with; **sich jdm a~** join s.o. ● *vi* (*haben*) **a~ an** (+ *acc*) adjoin; (*folgen*) follow. **a~d** *a* adjoining; (*zeitlich*) following ● *adv* afterwards; **a~d an** (+ *acc*) after

Anschluß *m* connection; (*Kontakt*) contact; **A~ finden** make friends; **im A~ an** (+ *acc*) after

anschmieg|en (sich) *vr sep* snuggle up/⟨*Kleid:*⟩ cling (**an** + *acc* to). **a~sam** *a* affectionate

anschmieren *vt sep* smear; (*fam: täuschen*) cheat

anschnallen *vt sep* strap on; **sich a~** fasten one's seat-belt

anschneiden† *vt sep* cut into; broach ⟨*Thema*⟩

anschreiben† *vt sep* write (**an** + *acc* on); (*Comm*) put on s.o.'s account; (*sich wenden*) write to; **bei jdm gut/ schlecht angeschrieben sein** be in s.o.'s good/bad books

anschreien† *vt sep* shout at

Anschrift *f* address

anschuldig|en *vt sep* accuse. **A~ung** *f* -,-en accusation

anschwellen† *vi sep* (*sein*) swell

anschwemmen *vt sep* wash up

anschwindeln *vt sep* (*fam*) lie to

ansehen† *vt sep* look at; (*einschätzen*) regard (**als** as); **[sich** *dat*] **etw a~** look at sth; (*TV*) watch sth. **A~** *nt* **-s** respect; (*Ruf*) reputation

ansehnlich *a* considerable

ansetzen *v sep* ● *vt* join (**an** + *acc* to); (*festsetzen*) fix; (*veranschlagen*) estimate; **Rost a~** get rusty; **sich a~** form ● *vi* (*haben*) (*anbrennen*) burn; **zum Sprung a~** get ready to jump

Ansicht *f* view; **meiner A~ nach** in my view; **zur A~** (*Comm*) on approval. **A~s[post]karte** *f* picture postcard. **A~ssache** *f* matter of opinion

ansiedeln (sich) *vr sep* settle

ansonsten *adv* apart from that

anspannen *vt sep* hitch up; (*anstrengen*) strain; tense ⟨*Muskel*⟩

anspiel|en *vi sep* (*haben*) **a~en auf** (+ *acc*) allude to; (*versteckt*) hint at. **A~ung** *f* -,-en allusion; hint

Anspitzer *m* **-s,-** pencil-sharpener

Ansporn *m* (*fig*) incentive. **a~en** *vt sep* spur on

Ansprache *f* address

ansprechen† *v sep* ● *vt* speak to; (*fig*) appeal to ● *vi* (*haben*) respond (**auf** + *acc* to). **a~d** *a* attractive

anspringen† *v sep* ● *vt* jump at ● *vi* (*sein*) (*Auto*) start

Anspruch *m* claim/(*Recht*) right (**auf** + *acc* to); **A~ haben** be entitled (**auf** + *acc* to); **in A~ nehmen** make use of; (*erfordern*) demand; take up ⟨*Zeit*⟩; occupy ⟨*Person*⟩; **hohe A~e stellen** be very demanding. **a~slos** *a* undemanding; (*bescheiden*) unpretentious. **a~svoll** *a* demanding; (*kritisch*) discriminating; (*vornehm*) up-market

anspucken *vt sep* spit at

anstacheln *vt sep* (*fig*) spur on

Anstalt *f* -,-en institution; **A~en/ keine A~en machen** prepare/make no move (**zu** to)

Anstand *m* decency; (*Benehmen*) [good] manners *pl*

anständig *a* decent, *adv* -ly; (*ehrbar*) respectable, *adv* -bly; (*fam: beträchtlich*) considerable, *adv* -bly; (*richtig*) proper, *adv* -ly

Anstands|dame *f* chaperon. **a~los** *adv* without any trouble; (*bedenkenlos*) without hesitation

anstarren *vt sep* stare at

anstatt *conj & prep* (+ *gen*) instead of; **a~ zu arbeiten** instead of working

anstechen† *vt sep* tap ⟨*Faß*⟩

ansteck|en *v sep* ● *vt* pin (**an** + *acc* to/on); put on ⟨*Ring*⟩; (*anzünden*) light; (*in Brand stecken*) set fire to; (*Med*) infect; **sich a~en** catch an infection (**bei** from) ● *vi* (*haben*) be infectious. **a~end** *a* infectious, (*fam*) catching. **A~ung** *f* -,-en infection

anstehen† *vi sep* (*haben*) queue, (*Amer*) stand in line

ansteigen† *vi sep* (*sein*) climb; ⟨*Gelände, Preise:*⟩ rise

anstelle *prep* (+ *gen*) instead of

anstell|en *vt sep* put, stand (**an** + *acc* against); (*einstellen*) employ; (*anschalten*) turn on; (*tun*) do; **sich a~en** queue [up], (*Amer*) stand in line; (*sich haben*) make a fuss. **A~ung** *f* employment; (*Stelle*) job

Anstieg *m* **-[e]s,-e** climb; (*fig*) rise

anstifte|n *vt sep* cause; (*anzetteln*) instigate; **jdn a~n** put s.o. up (**zu** to). **A~r** *m* instigator

Anstoß *m* (*Anregung*) impetus; (*Stoß*) knock; (*Fußball*) kick-off; **A~ erregen/nehmen** give/take offence (**an** + *dat* at). **a~en**† *v sep* ● *vt* knock; (*mit dem Ellbogen*) nudge ● *vi* (*sein*) knock (**an** + *acc* against) ● *vi* (*haben*) adjoin (**an etw** *acc* sth); **[mit den Gläsern] a~en** clink glasses; **a~en auf** (+ *acc*) drink to; **mit der Zunge a~en** lisp

anstößig *a* offensive, *adv* -ly

anstrahlen *vt sep* floodlight; (*anlachen*) beam at

anstreiche|n† *vt sep* paint; (*anmerken*) mark. **A~r** *m* **-s,-** painter

anstreng|en *vt sep* strain; (*ermüden*) tire; **sich a~en** exert oneself; (*sich bemühen*) make an effort (**zu** to). **a~end** *a* strenuous; (*ermüdend*) tiring. **A~ung** *f* **-,-en** strain; (*Mühe*) effort

Anstrich *m* coat [of paint]

Ansturm *m* rush; (*Mil*) assault

Ansuchen *nt* **-s,-** request

Antagonismus *m* **-** antagonism

Antarktis *f* **-** Antarctic

Anteil *m* share; **A~ nehmen** take an interest (**an** + *dat* in); (*mitfühlen*) sympathize. **A~nahme** *f* **-** interest (**an** + *dat* in); (*Mitgefühl*) sympathy

Antenne *f* **-,-n** aerial

Anthologie *f* **-,-n** anthology

Anthropologie *f* **-** anthropology

Anti|alkoholiker *m* teetotaller. **A~biotikum** *nt* **-s,-ka** antibiotic

antik *a* antique. **A~e** *f* **-** [classical] antiquity

Antikörper *m* antibody

Antilope *f* **-,-n** antelope

Antipathie *f* **-** antipathy

Anti|quariat *nt* **-[e]s,-e** antiquarian bookshop. **a~quarisch** *a & adv* second-hand

Antiquitäten *fpl* antiques. **A~händler** *m* antique dealer

Antisemitismus *m* **-** anti-Semitism

Antisept|ikum *nt* **-s,-ka** antiseptic. **a~isch** *a* antiseptic

Antrag *m* **-[e]s,¨e** proposal; (*Pol*) motion; (*Gesuch*) application. **A~steller** *m* **-s,-** applicant

antreffen† *vt sep* find

antreiben† *v sep* ● *vt* urge on; (*Techn*) drive; (*anschwemmen*) wash up ● *vi* (*sein*) be washed up

antreten† *v sep* ● *vt* start; take up ⟨*Amt*⟩ ● *vi* (*sein*) line up; (*Mil*) fall in

Antrieb *m* urge; (*Techn*) drive; **aus eigenem A~** of one's own accord

antrinken† *vt sep* **sich** (*dat*) **einen Rausch a~** get drunk; **sich** (*dat*) **Mut a~** give oneself Dutch courage

Antritt *m* start; **bei A~ eines Amtes** when taking office. **A~srede** *f* inaugural address

antun† *vt sep* **jdm etw a~** do sth to s.o.; **sich** (*dat*) **etwas a~** take one's own life; **es jdm angetan haben** appeal to s.o.

Antwort *f* **-,-en** answer, reply (**auf** + *acc* to). **a~en** *vt/i* (*haben*) answer (**jdm** s.o.)

anvertrauen *vt sep* entrust/(*mitteilen*) confide (**jdm** to s.o.); **sich jdm a~** confide in s.o.

anwachsen† *vi sep* (*sein*) take root; (*zunehmen*) grow

Anwalt *m* **-[e]s,¨e**, **Anwältin** *f* **-,-nen** lawyer; (*vor Gericht*) counsel

Anwandlung *f* **-,-en** fit (**von** of)

Anwärter(in) *m*(*f*) candidate

anweis|en† *vt sep* assign (*dat* to); (*beauftragen*) instruct. **A~ung** *f* instruction; (*Geld-*) money order

anwend|en† *vt sep* apply (**auf** + *acc* to); (*gebrauchen*) use. **A~ung** *f* application; use

anwerben† *vt sep* recruit

Anwesen *nt* **-s,-** property

anwesen|d *a* present (**bei** at); **die A~den** those present. **A~heit** *f* **-** presence

anwidern *vt sep* disgust

Anwohner *mpl* residents

Anzahl *f* number

anzahl|en *vt sep* pay a deposit on; pay on account ⟨*Summe*⟩. **A~ung** *f* deposit

anzapfen *vt sep* tap

Anzeichen *nt* sign

Anzeige *f* **-,-n** announcement; (*Inserat*) advertisement; **A~ erstatten gegen jdn** report s.o. to the police. **a~n** *vt sep* announce; (*inserieren*) advertise; (*melden*) report [to the police]; (*angeben*) indicate, show. **A~r** *m* indicator

anzieh|en† *vt sep* ● *vt* attract; (*festziehen*) tighten; put on ⟨*Kleider, Bremse*⟩; draw up ⟨*Beine*⟩; (*ankleiden*) dress; **sich a~en** get dressed;

was soll ich a~en? what shall I wear? **gut angezogen** well-dressed ● *vi* (*haben*) start pulling; ⟨*Preise:*⟩ go up. **a~end** *a* attractive. **A~ung** *f* - attraction. **A~ungskraft** *f* attraction; (*Phys*) gravity

Anzug *m* suit; **im A~ sein** (*fig*) be imminent

anzüglich *a* suggestive; ⟨*Bemerkung*⟩ personal

anzünden *vt sep* light; (*in Brand stecken*) set fire to

anzweifeln *vt sep* question

apart *a* striking, *adv* -ly

Apathie *f* - apathy

apathisch *a* apathetic, *adv* -ally

Aperitif *m* **-s,-s** aperitif

Apfel *m* **-s,¨** apple. **A~mus** *nt* apple purée

Apfelsine *f* **-,-n** orange

Apostel *m* **-s,-** apostle

Apostroph *m* **-s,-e** apostrophe

Apothek|e *f* **-,-n** pharmacy. **A~er(in)** *m* **-s,-** (*f* **-,-nen**) pharmacist, [dispensing] chemist

Apparat *m* **-[e]s,-e** device; (*Phot*) camera; (*Radio, TV*) set; (*Teleph*) telephone; **am A~!** speaking! **A~ur** *f* **-,-en** apparatus

Appell *m* **-s,-e** appeal; (*Mil*) rollcall. **a~ieren** *vi* (*haben*) appeal (**an** + *acc* to)

Appetit *m* **-s** appetite; **guten A~!** enjoy your meal! **a~lich** *a* appetizing, *adv* -ly

applaudieren *vi* (*haben*) applaud

Applaus *m* **-es** applause

Aprikose *f* **-,-n** apricot

April *m* **-[s]** April; **in den A~ schicken** (*fam*) make an April fool of

Aquarell *nt* **-s,-e** water-colour

Aquarium *nt* **-s,-ien** aquarium

Äquator *m* **-s** equator

Ära *f* - era

Araber(in) *m* **-s,-** (*f* **-,-nen**) Arab

arabisch *a* Arab; (*Geog*) Arabian; ⟨*Ziffer*⟩ Arabic

Arbeit *f* **-,-en** work; (*Anstellung*) employment, job; (*Aufgabe*) task; (*Sch*) [written] test; (*Abhandlung*) treatise; (*Qualität*) workmanship; **bei der A~** at work; **zur A~ gehen** go to work; **an die A~ gehen, sich an die A~ machen** set to work; **sich** (*dat*) **viel A~ machen** go to a lot of trouble. **a~en** *v sep* ● *vi* (*haben*) work (**an** + *dat* on) ● *vt* make; **einen Anzug a~en lassen** have a suit made; **sich durch etw a~en** work one's way through sth. **A~er(in)** *m* **-s,-** (*f* **-,-nen**) worker; (*Land-, Hilfs-*) labourer. **A~erklasse** *f* working class

Arbeit|geber *m* **-s,-** employer. **A~nehmer** *m* **-s,-** employee. **a~sam** *a* industrious

Arbeits|amt *nt* employment exchange. **A~erlaubnis, A~genehmigung** *f* work permit. **A~kraft** *f* worker; **Mangel an A~kräften** shortage of labour. **a~los** *a* unemployed; **a~los sein** be out of work. **A~lose(r)** *m/f* unemployed person; **die A~losen** the unemployed *pl*. **A~losenunterstützung** *f* unemployment benefit. **A~losigkeit** *f* - unemployment

arbeitsparend *a* labour-saving

Arbeits|platz *m* job. **A~tag** *m* working day. **A~zimmer** *nt* study

Archäo|loge *m* **-n,-n** archaeologist. **A~logie** *f* - archaeology. **a~logisch** *a* archaeological

Arche *f* - **die A~ Noah** Noah's Ark

Architek|t(in) *m* **-en,-en** (*f* **-,-nen**) architect. **a~tonisch** *a* architectural. **A~tur** *f* - architecture

Archiv *nt* **-s,-e** archives *pl*

Arena *f* **-,-nen** arena

arg *a* (**ärger, ärgst**) bad; (*groß*) terrible; **sein ärgster Feind** his worst enemy ● *adv* badly; (*sehr*) terribly

Argentin|ien /-i̯ən/ *nt* **-s** Argentina. **a~isch** *a* Argentinian

Ärger *m* **-s** annoyance; (*Unannehmlichkeit*) trouble. **ä~lich** *a* annoyed; (*leidig*) annoying; **ä~lich sein** be annoyed. **ä~n** *vt* annoy; (*necken*) tease; **sich ä~n** get annoyed (**über jdn/etw** with s.o./about sth). **Ä~nis** *nt* **-ses,-se** annoyance; **öffentliches Ä~nis** public nuisance

Arglist *f* - malice. **a~ig** *a* malicious, *adv* -ly

arglos *a* unsuspecting; (*unschuldig*) innocent, *adv* -ly

Argument *nt* **-[e]s,-e** argument. **a~ieren** *vi* (*haben*) argue (**daß** that)

Argwohn *m* **-s** suspicion

argwöhn|en *vt* suspect. **a~isch** *a* suspicious, *adv* -ly

Arie /ˈaːri̯ə/ *f* **-,-n** aria

Aristo|krat *m* **-en,-en** aristocrat. **A~kratie** *f* - aristocracy. **a~kratisch** *a* aristocratic

Arithmetik *f* - arithmetic

Arkt|is *f* - Arctic. **a~isch** *a* Arctic

arm *a* (**ärmer, ärmst**) poor; **arm und reich** rich and poor

Arm *m* **-[e]s,-e** arm; **jdn auf den Arm nehmen** (*fam*) pull s.o.'s leg
Armaturenbrett *nt* instrument panel; (*Auto*) dashboard
Armband *nt* (*pl* **-bänder**) bracelet; (*Uhr-*) watch-strap. **A~uhr** *f* wrist-watch
Arm|e(r) *m/f* poor man/woman; **die A~en** the poor *pl*; **du A~e** *od* **Ärmste!** you poor thing!
Armee *f* **-,-n** army
Ärmel *m* **-s,-** sleeve. **Ä~kanal** *m* [English] Channel. **ä~los** *a* sleeveless
Arm|lehne *f* arm. **A~leuchter** *m* candelabra
ärmlich *a* poor, *adv* -ly; (*elend*) miserable, *adv* -bly
armselig *a* miserable, *adv* -bly
Armut *f* **-** poverty
Arom|a *nt* **-s,-men** & **-mas** aroma; (*Culin*) essence. **a~atisch** *a* aromatic
Arran|gement /arãʒə'mã:/ *nt* **-s,-s** arrangement. **a~gieren** /-'ʒi:rən/ *vt* arrange; **sich a~gieren** come to an arrangement
Arrest *m* **-[e]s** (*Mil*) detention
arrogan|t *a* arrogant, *adv* -ly. **A~z** *f* **-** arrogance
Arsch *m* **-[e]s,⸚e** (*vulg*) arse
Arsen *nt* **-s** arsenic
Art *f* **-,-en** manner; (*Weise*) way; (*Natur*) nature; (*Sorte*) kind; (*Biol*) species; **auf diese Art** in this way. **a~en** *vi* (*sein*) **a~en nach** take after
Arterie /-iə/ *f* **-,-n** artery
Arthritis *f* **-** arthritis
artig *a* well-behaved; (*höflich*) polite, *adv* -ly; **sei a~!** be good!
Artikel *m* **-s,-** article
Artillerie *f* **-** artillery
Artischocke *f* **-,-n** artichoke
Artist(in) *m* **-en,-en** (*f* **-,-nen**) [circus] artiste
Arznei *f* **-,-en** medicine. **A~mittel** *nt* drug
Arzt *m* **-[e]s,⸚e** doctor
Ärzt|in *f* **-,-nen** [woman] doctor. **ä~lich** *a* medical
As *nt* **-ses,-se** ace
Asbest *m* **-[e]s** asbestos
Asche *f* **-** ash. **A~nbecher** *m* ashtray. **A~rmittwoch** *m* Ash Wednesday
Asiat|(in) *m* **-en,-en** (*f* **-,-nen**) Asian. **a~isch** *a* Asian
Asien /'a:ziən/ *nt* **-s** Asia
asozial *a* antisocial
Aspekt *m* **-[e]s,-e** aspect
Asphalt *m* **-[e]s** asphalt. **a~ieren** *vt* asphalt
Assistent(in) *m* **-en,-en** (*f* **-,-nen**) assistant
Ast *m* **-[e]s,⸚e** branch
ästhetisch *a* aesthetic
Asth|ma *nt* **-s** asthma. **a~matisch** *a* asthmatic
Astro|loge *m* **-n,-n** astrologer. **A~logie** *f* **-** astrology. **A~naut** *m* **-en,-en** astronaut. **A~nom** *m* **-en,-en** astronomer. **A~nomie** *f* **-** astronomy. **a~nomisch** *a* astronomical
Asyl *nt* **-s,-e** home; (*Pol*) asylum. **A~ant** *m* **-en,-en** asylum-seeker
Atelier /-'lie:/ *nt* **-s,-s** studio
Atem *m* **-s** breath; **tief A~ holen** take a deep breath. **a~beraubend** *a* breath-taking. **a~los** *a* breathless, *adv* -ly. **A~pause** *f* breather. **A~zug** *m* breath
Atheist *m* **-en,-en** atheist
Äther *m* **-s** ether
Äthiopien /-iən/ *nt* **-s** Ethiopia
Athlet|(in) *m* **-en,-en** (*f* **-,-nen**) athlete. **a~isch** *a* athletic
Atlant|ik *m* **-s** Atlantic. **a~isch** *a* Atlantic; **der A~ische Ozean** the Atlantic Ocean
Atlas *m* **-lasses,-lanten** atlas
atmen *vt/i* (*haben*) breathe
Atmosphär|e *f* **-,-n** atmosphere. **a~isch** *a* atmospheric
Atmung *f* **-** breathing
Atom *nt* **-s,-e** atom. **a~ar** *a* atomic. **A~bombe** *f* atom bomb. **A~krieg** *m* nuclear war
Atten|tat *nt* **-[e]s,-e** assassination attempt. **A~täter** *m* [would-be] assassin
Attest *nt* **-[e]s,-e** certificate
Attrak|tion /-'tsio:n/ *f* **-,-en** attraction. **a~tiv** *a* attractive, *adv* -ly
Attrappe *f* **-,-n** dummy
Attribut *nt* **-[e]s,-e** attribute. **a~iv** *a* attributive, *adv* -ly
ätzen *vt* corrode; (*Med*) cauterize; (*Kunst*) etch. **ä~d** *a* corrosive; ⟨*Spott*⟩ caustic
au *int* ouch; **au fein!** oh good!
Aubergine /obɛr'ʒi:nə/ *f* **-,-n** aubergine
auch *adv* & *conj* also, too; (*außerdem*) what's more; (*selbst*) even; **a~ wenn** even if; **ich mag ihn—ich a~** I like him—so do I; **ich bin nicht müde—ich a~ nicht** I'm not tired—nor *or* neither am I; **sie weiß es a~ nicht** she doesn't know either; **wer/**

wie/was a~ immer whoever/however/whatever; **ist das a~ wahr?** is that really true?

Audienz *f* **-,-en** audience

audiovisuell *a* audio-visual

Auditorium *nt* **-s,-ien** (*Univ*) lecture hall

auf *prep* (+*dat*) on; (+*acc*) on [to]; (*bis*) until, till; (*Proportion*) to; **auf deutsch/englisch** in German/English; **auf einer/eine Party** at/to a party; **auf der Straße** in the street; **auf seinem Zimmer** in one's room; **auf einem Ohr taub** deaf in one ear; **auf einen Stuhl steigen** climb on [to] a chair; **auf die Toilette gehen** go to the toilet; **auf ein paar Tage verreisen** go away for a few days; **auf 10 Kilometer zu sehen** visible for 10 kilometres ● *adv* open; (*in die Höhe*) up; **auf und ab** up and down; **sich auf und davon machen** make off; **Tür auf!** open the door!

aufarbeiten *vt sep* do up; **Rückstände a~** clear arrears [of work]

aufatmen *vi sep* (*haben*) heave a sigh of relief

aufbahren *vt sep* lay out

Aufbau *m* construction; (*Struktur*) structure. **a~en** *v sep* ● *vt* construct, build; (*errichten*) erect; (*schaffen*) build up; (*arrangieren*) arrange; **sich a~en** (*fig*) be based (**auf**+*dat* on) ● *vi* (*haben*) be based (**auf**+*dat* on)

aufbäumen (sich) *vr sep* rear [up]; (*fig*) rebel

aufbauschen *vt sep* puff out; (*fig*) exaggerate

aufbehalten† *vt sep* keep on

aufbekommen† *vt sep* get open; (*Sch*) be given [as homework]

aufbessern *vt sep* improve; (*erhöhen*) increase

aufbewahr|en *vt sep* keep; (*lagern*) store. **A~ung** *f* **-** safe keeping; storage; (*Gepäck-*) left-luggage office

aufbieten† *vt sep* mobilize; (*fig*) summon up

aufblas|bar *a* inflatable. **a~en**† *vt sep* inflate; **sich a~en** (*fig*) give oneself airs

aufbleiben† *vi sep* (*sein*) stay open; ⟨*Person:*⟩ stay up

aufblenden *vt/i sep* (*haben*) (*Auto*) switch to full beam

aufblicken *vi sep* (*haben*) look up (**zu** at/(*fig*) to)

aufblühen *vi sep* (*sein*) flower; ⟨*Knospe:*⟩ open

aufbocken *vt sep* jack up

aufbraten† *vt sep* fry up

aufbrauchen *vt sep* use up

aufbrausen *vi sep* (*sein*) (*fig*) flare up. **a~d** *a* quick-tempered

aufbrechen† *v sep* ● *vt* break open ● *vi* (*sein*) ⟨*Knospe:*⟩ open; (*sich aufmachen*) set out, start

aufbringen† *vt sep* raise ⟨*Geld*⟩; find ⟨*Kraft*⟩; (*wütend machen*) infuriate

Aufbruch *m* start, departure

aufbrühen *vt sep* make ⟨*Tee*⟩

aufbürden *vt sep* **jdm etw a~** (*fig*) burden s.o. with sth

aufdecken *vt sep* (*auflegen*) put on; (*abdecken*) uncover; (*fig*) expose

aufdrängen *vt sep* force (*dat* on); **sich jdm a~** force one's company on s.o.

aufdrehen *vt sep* turn on

aufdringlich *a* persistent

aufeinander *adv* one on top of the other; ⟨*schießen*⟩ at each other; ⟨*warten*⟩ for each other. **a~folgen** *vi sep* (*sein*) follow one another. **a~folgend** *a* successive; ⟨*Tage*⟩ consecutive

Aufenthalt *m* stay; **10 Minuten A~ haben** ⟨*Zug:*⟩ stop for 10 minutes. **A~serlaubnis, A~sgenehmigung** *f* residence permit. **A~sraum** *m* recreation room; (*im Hotel*) lounge

auferlegen *vt sep* impose (*dat* on)

aufersteh|en† *vi sep* (*sein*) rise from the dead. **A~ung** *f* **-** resurrection

aufessen† *vt sep* eat up

auffahr|en† *vi sep* (*sein*) drive up; (*aufprallen*) crash, run (**auf**+*acc* into); (*aufschrecken*) start up; (*aufbrausen*) flare up. **A~t** *f* drive; (*Autobahn-*) access road, slip road; (*Bergfahrt*) ascent

auffallen† *vi sep* (*sein*) be conspicuous; **unangenehm a~** make a bad impression; **jdm a~** strike s.o. **a~d** *a* striking, *adv* -ly

auffällig *a* conspicuous, *adv* -ly; (*grell*) gaudy, *adv* -ily

auffangen† *vt sep* catch; pick up ⟨*Funkspruch*⟩

auffass|en *vt sep* understand; (*deuten*) take; **falsch a~en** misunderstand. **A~ung** *f* understanding; (*Ansicht*) view. **A~ungsgabe** *f* grasp

aufforder|n *vt sep* ask; (*einladen*) invite; **jdn zum Tanz a~n** ask s.o. to dance. **A~ung** *f* request; invitation

auffrischen *v sep* ● *vt* freshen up; revive ⟨*Erinnerung*⟩; **seine Englischkenntnisse a~** brush up one's English

aufführ|en *vt sep* perform; (*angeben*) list; **sich a~en** behave. **A~ung** *f* performance

auffüllen *vt sep* fill up; **[wieder] a~** replenish

Aufgabe *f* task; (*Rechen-*) problem; (*Verzicht*) giving up; **A~n** (*Sch*) homework *sg*

Aufgang *m* way up; (*Treppe*) stairs *pl*; (*Astr*) rise

aufgeben† *v sep* ● *vt* give up; post ⟨*Brief*⟩; send ⟨*Telegramm*⟩; place ⟨*Bestellung*⟩; register ⟨*Gepäck*⟩; put in the paper ⟨*Annonce*⟩; **jdm eine Aufgabe/ein Rätsel a~** set s.o. a task/a riddle; **jdm Suppe a~** serve s.o. with soup ● *vi* (*haben*) give up

aufgeblasen *a* (*fig*) conceited

Aufgebot *nt* contingent (**an** + *dat* of); (*Relig*) banns *pl*; **unter A~ aller Kräfte** with all one's strength

aufgebracht *a* (*fam*) angry

aufgedunsen *a* bloated

aufgehen† *vi sep* (*sein*) open; (*sich lösen*) come undone; ⟨*Teig, Sonne:*⟩ rise; ⟨*Saat:*⟩ come up; (*Math*) come out exactly; **in Flammen a~** go up in flames; **in etw** (*dat*) **a~** (*fig*) be wrapped up in sth; **ihm ging auf** (*fam*) he realized (**daß** that)

aufgelegt *a* **a~ sein zu** be in the mood for; **gut/schlecht a~ sein** be in a good/bad mood

aufgelöst *a* (*fig*) distraught; **in Tränen a~** in floods of tears

aufgeregt *a* excited, *adv* -ly; (*erregt*) agitated, *adv* -ly

aufgeschlossen *a* (*fig*) open-minded

aufgesprungen *a* chapped

aufgeweckt *a* (*fig*) bright

aufgießen† *vt sep* pour on; (*aufbrühen*) make ⟨*Tee*⟩

aufgreifen† *vt sep* pick up; take up ⟨*Vorschlag, Thema*⟩

aufgrund *prep* (+*gen*) on the strength of

Aufguß *m* infusion

aufhaben† *v sep* ● *vt* have on; **den Mund a~** have one's mouth open; **viel a~** (*Sch*) have a lot of homework ● *vi* (*haben*) be open

aufhalsen *vt sep* (*fam*) saddle with

aufhalten† *vt sep* hold up; (*anhalten*) stop; (*abhalten*) keep, detain; (*offenhalten*) hold open; hold out ⟨*Hand*⟩; **sich a~** stay; (*sich befassen*) spend one's time (**mit** on)

aufhäng|en *vt/i sep* (*haben*) hang up; (*henken*) hang; **sich a~en** hang oneself. **A~er** *m* **-s,-** loop. **A~ung** *f* - (*Auto*) suspension

aufheben† *vt sep* pick up; (*hochheben*) raise; (*aufbewahren*) keep; (*beenden*) end; (*rückgängig machen*) lift; (*abschaffen*) abolish; (*Jur*) quash ⟨*Urteil*⟩; repeal ⟨*Gesetz*⟩; (*ausgleichen*) cancel out; **sich a~** cancel each other out; **gut aufgehoben sein** be well looked after. **A~** *nt* **-s viel A~s machen** make a great fuss (**von** about)

aufheitern *vt sep* cheer up; **sich a~** ⟨*Wetter:*⟩ brighten up

aufhellen *vt sep* lighten; **sich a~** ⟨*Himmel:*⟩ brighten

aufhetzen *vt sep* incite

aufholen *v sep* ● *vt* make up ● *vi* (*haben*) catch up; (*zeitlich*) make up time

aufhorchen *vi sep* (*haben*) prick up one's ears

aufhören *vi sep* (*haben*) stop; **mit der Arbeit a~, a~ zu arbeiten** stop working

aufklappen *vt/i sep* (*sein*) open

aufklär|en *vt sep* solve; **jdn a~en** enlighten s.o.; (*sexuell*) tell s.o. the facts of life; **sich a~en** be solved; ⟨*Wetter:*⟩ clear up. **A~ung** *f* solution; enlightenment; (*Mil*) reconnaissance; **sexuelle A~ung** sex education

aufkleb|en *vt sep* stick on. **A~er** *m* **-s,-** sticker

aufknöpfen *vt sep* unbutton

aufkochen *v sep* ● *vt* bring to the boil ● *vi* (*sein*) come to the boil

aufkommen† *vi sep* (*sein*) start; ⟨*Wind:*⟩ spring up; ⟨*Mode:*⟩ come in; **a~ für** pay for

aufkrempeln *vt sep* roll up

aufladen† *vt sep* load; (*Electr*) charge

Auflage *f* impression; (*Ausgabe*) edition; (*Zeitungs-*) circulation; (*Bedingung*) condition; (*Überzug*) coating

auflassen† *vt sep* leave open; leave on ⟨*Hut*⟩

auflauern *vi sep* (*haben*) **jdm a~** lie in wait for s.o.

Auflauf *m* crowd; (*Culin*) ≈ soufflé. **a~en**† *vi sep* (*sein*) (*Naut*) run aground

auflegen *v sep* ● *vt* apply (**auf** + *acc* to); put down ⟨*Hörer*⟩; **neu a∼** reprint ● *vi* (*haben*) ring off

auflehn|en (sich) *vr sep* (*fig*) rebel. **A∼ung** *f* - rebellion

auflesen† *vt sep* pick up

aufleuchten *vi sep* (*haben*) light up

aufliegen† *vi sep* (*haben*) rest (**auf** + *dat* on)

auflisten *vt sep* list

auflockern *vt sep* break up; (*entspannen*) relax; (*fig*) liven up

auflös|en *vt sep* dissolve; close ⟨*Konto*⟩; **sich a∼en** dissolve; ⟨*Nebel:*⟩ clear. **A∼ung** *f* dissolution; (*Lösung*) solution

aufmach|en *v sep* ● *vt* open; (*lösen*) undo; **sich a∼en** set out (**nach** for); (*sich schminken*) make oneself up ● *vi* (*haben*) open; **jdm a∼en** open the door to s.o. **A∼ung** *f* -,-**en** get-up; (*Comm*) presentation

aufmerksam *a* attentive, *adv* -ly; **a∼ werden auf** (+ *acc*) notice; **jdn a∼ machen auf** (+ *acc*) draw s.o.'s attention to. **A∼keit** *f* -,-**en** attention; (*Höflichkeit*) courtesy

aufmucken *vi sep* (*haben*) rebel

aufmuntern *vt sep* cheer up

Aufnahme *f* -,-**n** acceptance; (*Empfang*) reception; (*in Klub, Krankenhaus*) admission; (*Einbeziehung*) inclusion; (*Beginn*) start; (*Foto*) photograph; (*Film-*) shot; (*Mus*) recording; (*Band-*) tape recording. **a∼fähig** *a* receptive. **A∼prüfung** *f* entrance examination

aufnehmen† *vt sep* pick up; (*absorbieren*) absorb; take ⟨*Nahrung, Foto*⟩; (*fassen*) hold; (*annehmen*) accept; (*leihen*) borrow; (*empfangen*) receive; (*in Klub, Krankenhaus*) admit; (*beherbergen, geistig erfassen*) take in; (*einbeziehen*) include; (*beginnen*) take up; (*niederschreiben*) take down; (*filmen*) film, shoot; (*Mus*) record; **auf Band a∼** tape [-record]; **etw gelassen a∼** take sth calmly; **es a∼ können mit** (*fig*) be a match for

aufopfer|n *vt sep* sacrifice; **sich a∼n** sacrifice oneself. **a∼nd** *a* devoted, *adv* -ly. **A∼ung** *f* self-sacrifice

aufpassen *vi sep* (*haben*) pay attention; (*sich vorsehen*) take care; **a∼ auf** (+ *acc*) look after

aufpflanzen (sich) *vr sep* (*fam*) plant oneself

aufplatzen *vi sep* (*sein*) split open

aufplustern (sich) *vr sep* ⟨*Vogel:*⟩ ruffle up its feathers

Aufprall *m* -[**e**]**s** impact. **a∼en** *vi sep* (*sein*) **a∼en auf** (+ *acc*) hit

aufpumpen *vt sep* pump up, inflate

aufputsch|en *vt sep* incite; **sich a∼en** take stimulants. **A∼mittel** *nt* stimulant

aufquellen† *vi sep* (*sein*) swell

aufraffen *vt sep* pick up; **sich a∼** pick oneself up; (*fig*) pull oneself together; (*sich aufschwingen*) find the energy (**zu** for)

aufragen *vi sep* (*sein*) rise [up]

aufräumen *vt/i sep* (*haben*) tidy up; (*wegräumen*) put away; **a∼ mit** (*fig*) get rid of

aufrecht *a* & *adv* upright. **a∼erhalten**† *vt sep* (*fig*) maintain

aufreg|en *vt* excite; (*beunruhigen*) upset; (*ärgern*) annoy; **sich a∼en** get excited; (*sich erregen*) get worked up. **a∼end** *a* exciting. **A∼ung** *f* excitement

aufreiben† *vt sep* chafe; (*fig*) wear down; **sich a∼** wear oneself out. **a∼d** *a* trying, wearing

aufreißen† *v sep* ● *vt* tear open; dig up ⟨*Straße*⟩; open wide ⟨*Augen, Mund*⟩ ● *vi* (*sein*) split open

aufreizend *a* provocative, *adv* -ly

aufrichten *vt sep* erect; (*fig: trösten*) comfort; **sich a∼** straighten up; (*sich setzen*) sit up

aufrichtig *a* sincere, *adv* -ly. **A∼keit** *f* - sincerity

aufriegeln *vt sep* unbolt

aufrollen *vt sep* roll up; (*entrollen*) unroll

aufrücken *vi sep* (*sein*) move up; (*fig*) be promoted

Aufruf *m* appeal (**an** + *dat* to). **a∼en**† *vt sep* call out ⟨*Namen*⟩; **jdn a∼en** call s.o.'s name; (*fig*) call on s.o. (**zu** to)

Aufruhr *m* -**s**,-**e** turmoil; (*Empörung*) revolt

aufrühr|en *vt sep* stir up. **A∼er** *m* -**s**,- rebel. **a∼erisch** *a* inflammatory; (*rebellisch*) rebellious

aufrunden *vt sep* round up

aufrüsten *vi sep* (*haben*) arm

aufs *prep* = **auf das**

aufsagen *vt sep* recite

aufsammeln *vt sep* gather up

aufsässig *a* rebellious

Aufsatz *m* top; (*Sch*) essay

aufsaugen† *vt sep* soak up

aufschauen *vi sep* (*haben*) look up (**zu** at/(*fig*) to)
aufschichten *vt sep* stack up
aufschieben† *vt sep* slide open; (*verschieben*) put off, postpone
Aufschlag *m* impact; (*Tennis*) service; (*Hosen-*) turn-up; (*Ärmel-*) upturned cuff; (*Revers*) lapel; (*Comm*) surcharge. **a~en**† *v sep* ● *vt* open; crack ⟨*Ei*⟩; (*hochschlagen*) turn up; (*errichten*) put up; (*erhöhen*) increase; cast on ⟨*Masche*⟩; **sich** (*dat*) **das Knie a~en** cut [open] one's knee ● *vi* (*haben*) hit (**auf etw** *acc*/*dat* sth); (*Tennis*) serve; (*teurer werden*) go up
aufschließen† *v sep* ● *vt* unlock ● *vi* (*haben*) unlock the door
aufschlitzen *vt sep* slit open
Aufschluß *m* **A~ geben** give information (**über**+*acc* on). **a~reich** *a* revealing; (*lehrreich*) informative
aufschneid|en† *v sep* ● *vt* cut open; (*in Scheiben*) slice; carve ⟨*Braten*⟩ ● *vi* (*haben*) (*fam*) exaggerate. **A~er** *m* **-s,-** (*fam*) show-off
Aufschnitt *m* sliced sausage, cold meat [and cheese]
aufschrauben *vt sep* screw on; (*abschrauben*) unscrew
aufschrecken *v sep* ● *vt* startle ● *vi*† (*sein*) start up; **aus dem Schlaf a~** wake up with a start
Aufschrei *m* [sudden] cry
aufschreiben† *vt sep* write down; (*fam: verschreiben*) prescribe; **jdn a~** ⟨*Polizist:*⟩ book s.o.
aufschreien† *vi sep* (*haben*) cry out
Aufschrift *f* inscription; (*Etikett*) label
Aufschub *m* delay; (*Frist*) grace
aufschürfen *vt sep* **sich** (*dat*) **das Knie a~** graze one's knee
aufschwatzen *vt sep* **jdm etw a~** talk s.o. into buying sth
aufschwingen† **(sich)** *vr sep* find the energy (**zu** for)
Aufschwung *m* (*fig*) upturn
aufsehen† *vi sep* (*haben*) look up (**zu** at/(*fig*) to). **A~** *nt* **-s A~ erregen** cause a sensation. **a~erregend** *a* sensational
Aufseher(in) *m* **-s,-** (*f* **-,-nen**) supervisor; (*Gefängnis-*) warder
aufsein† *vi sep* (*sein*) be open; ⟨*Person:*⟩ be up
aufsetzen *vt sep* put on; (*verfassen*) draw up; (*entwerfen*) draft; **sich a~** sit up
Aufsicht *f* supervision; (*Person*) supervisor. **A~srat** *m* board of directors
aufsitzen† *vi sep* (*sein*) mount
aufspannen *vt sep* put up
aufsparen *vt sep* save, keep
aufsperren *vt sep* open wide
aufspielen *v sep* ● *vi* (*haben*) play ● *vr* **sich a~** show off; **sich als Held a~** play the hero
aufspießen *vt sep* spear
aufspringen† *vi sep* (*sein*) jump up; (*aufprallen*) bounce; (*sich öffnen*) burst open; ⟨*Haut:*⟩ become chapped; **a~ auf** (+*acc*) jump on
aufspüren *vt sep* track down
aufstacheln *vt sep* incite
aufstampfen *vi sep* (*haben*) **mit dem Fuß a~** stamp one's foot
Aufstand *m* uprising, rebellion
aufständisch *a* rebellious. **A~e(r)** *m* rebel, insurgent
aufstapeln *vt sep* stack up
aufstauen *vt sep* dam [up]
aufstehen† *vi sep* (*sein*) get up; (*offen sein*) be open; (*fig*) rise up
aufsteigen† *vi sep* (*sein*) get on; ⟨*Reiter:*⟩ mount; ⟨*Bergsteiger:*⟩ climb up; (*hochsteigen*) rise [up]; (*fig: befördert werden*) rise (**zu** to); (*Sport*) be promoted
aufstell|en *vt sep* put up; (*Culin*) put on; (*postieren*) post; (*in einer Reihe*) line up; (*nominieren*) nominate; (*Sport*) select ⟨*Mannschaft*⟩; make out ⟨*Liste*⟩; lay down ⟨*Regel*⟩; make ⟨*Behauptung*⟩; set up ⟨*Rekord*⟩; **sich a~en** rise [up]; (*in einer Reihe*) line up. **A~ung** *f* nomination; (*Liste*) list
Aufstieg *m* ascent; (*fig*) rise; (*Sport*) promotion
aufstöbern *vt sep* flush out; (*fig*) track down
aufstoßen† *v sep* ● *vt* push open ● *vi* (*haben*) burp; **a~ auf** (+*acc*) strike. **A~** *nt* **-s** burping
aufstrebend *a* (*fig*) ambitious
Aufstrich *m* [sandwich] spread
aufstützen *vt sep* rest (**auf**+*acc* on); **sich a~** lean (**auf**+*acc* on)
aufsuchen *vt sep* look for; (*besuchen*) go to see
Auftakt *m* (*fig*) start
auftauchen *vi sep* (*sein*) emerge; ⟨*U-Boot:*⟩ surface; (*fig*) turn up; ⟨*Frage:*⟩ crop up
auftauen *vt*/*i sep* (*sein*) thaw
aufteil|en *vt sep* divide [up]. **A~ung** *f* division

auftischen *vt sep* serve [up]
Auftrag *m* **-[e]s, ⸚e** task; (*Kunst*) commission; (*Comm*) order; **im A~** (+*gen*) on behalf of. **a~en**† *v sep* ● *vt* apply; (*servieren*) serve; (*abtragen*) wear out; **jdm a~en** instruct s.o. (**zu** to) ● *vi* (*haben*) **dick a~en** (*fam*) exaggerate. **A~geber** *m* **-s,-** client
auftreiben† *vt sep* distend; (*fam: beschaffen*) get hold of
auftrennen *vt sep* unpick, undo
auftreten† *v sep* ● *vi* (*sein*) tread; (*sich benehmen*) behave, act; (*Theat*) appear; (*die Bühne betreten*) enter; (*vorkommen*) occur ● *vt* kick open. **A~** *nt* **-s** occurrence; (*Benehmen*) manner
Auftrieb *m* buoyancy; (*fig*) boost
Auftritt *m* (*Theat*) appearance; (*auf die Bühne*) entrance; (*Szene*) scene
auftun† *vt sep* **jdm Suppe a~** serve s.o. with soup; **sich** (*dat*) **etw a~** help oneself to sth; **sich a~** open
aufwachen *vi sep* (*sein*) wake up
aufwachsen† *vi sep* (*sein*) grow up
Aufwand *m* **-[e]s** expenditure; (*Luxus*) extravagance; (*Mühe*) trouble; **A~ treiben** be extravagant
aufwärmen *vt sep* heat up; (*fig*) rake up; **sich a~** warm oneself; (*Sport*) warm up
Aufwartefrau *f* cleaner
aufwärts *adv* upwards; (*bergauf*) uphill. **a~gehen**† *vi sep* (*sein*) **es geht a~ mit jdm/etw** s.o./sth is improving
Aufwartung *f* **-** cleaner; **jdm seine A~ machen** call on s.o.
aufwaschen† *vt/i sep* (*haben*) wash up
aufwecken *vt sep* wake up
aufweichen *v sep* ● *vt* soften ● *vi* (*sein*) become soft
aufweisen† *vt sep* have, show
aufwend|en† *vt sep* spend; **Mühe a~en** take pains. **a~ig** *a* lavish, *adv* -ly; (*teuer*) expensive, *adv* -ly
aufwerfen† *vt sep* (*fig*) raise
aufwert|en *vt sep* revalue. **A~ung** *f* revaluation
aufwickeln *vt sep* roll up; (*auswickeln*) unwrap
aufwiegeln *vt sep* stir up
aufwiegen† *vt sep* compensate for
Aufwiegler *m* **-s,-** agitator
aufwirbeln *vt sep* **Staub a~** stir up dust; (*fig*) cause a stir
aufwisch|en *vt sep* wipe up; wash ⟨*Fußboden*⟩. **A~lappen** *m* floorcloth
aufwühlen *vt sep* churn up; (*fig*) stir up
aufzähl|en *vt sep* enumerate, list. **A~ung** *f* list
aufzeichn|en *vt sep* record; (*zeichnen*) draw. **A~ung** *f* recording; **A~ungen** notes
aufziehen† *v sep* ● *vt* pull up; hoist ⟨*Segel*⟩; (*öffnen*) open; draw ⟨*Vorhang*⟩; (*auftrennen*) undo; (*großziehen*) bring up; rear ⟨*Tier*⟩; mount ⟨*Bild*⟩; thread ⟨*Perlen*⟩; wind up ⟨*Uhr*⟩; (*arrangieren*) organize; (*fam: necken*) tease ● *vi* (*sein*) approach
Aufzucht *f* rearing
Aufzug *m* hoist; (*Fahrstuhl*) lift, (*Amer*) elevator; (*Prozession*) procession; (*Theat*) act; (*fam: Aufmachung*) get-up
Augapfel *m* eyeball
Auge *nt* **-s,-n** eye; (*Punkt*) spot; **vier A~n werfen** throw a four; **gute A~n** good eyesight; **unter vier A~n** in private; **aus den A~n verlieren** lose sight of; **im A~ behalten** keep in sight; (*fig*) bear in mind
Augenblick *m* moment; **im/jeden A~** at the/at any moment; **A~!** just a moment! **a~lich** *a* immediate; (*derzeitig*) present ● *adv* immediately; (*derzeit*) at present
Augen|braue *f* eyebrow. **A~höhle** *f* eye socket. **A~licht** *nt* sight. **A~lid** *nt* eyelid. **A~schein** *m* **in A~schein nehmen** inspect. **A~zeuge** *m* eyewitness
August *m* **-[s]** August
Auktion /-'tsio:n/ *f* **-,-en** auction. **A~ator** *m* **-s,-en** /-'to:rən/ auctioneer
Aula *f* **-,-len** (*Sch*) [assembly] hall
Au-pair-Mädchen /o'pɛ:r-/ *nt* au-pair
aus *prep* (+*dat*) out of; (*von*) from; (*bestehend*) [made] of; **aus Angst** from *or* out of fear; **aus Spaß** for fun ● *adv* out; ⟨*Licht, Radio*⟩ off; **aus und ein** in and out; **nicht mehr aus noch ein wissen** be at one's wits' end; **von ... aus** from ...; **von sich aus** of one's own accord; **von mir aus** as far as I'm concerned
ausarbeiten *vt sep* work out
ausarten *vi sep* (*sein*) degenerate (**in**+*acc* into)
ausatmen *vt/i sep* (*haben*) breathe out

ausbaggern *vt sep* excavate; dredge ⟨*Fluß*⟩

ausbauen *vt sep* remove; (*vergrößern*) extend; (*fig*) expand

ausbedingen† *vt sep* **sich** (*dat*) **a~** insist on; (*zur Bedingung machen*) stipulate

ausbesser|n *vt sep* mend, repair. **A~ung** *f* repair

ausbeulen *vt sep* remove the dents from; (*dehnen*) make baggy

Ausbeut|e *f* yield. **a~en** *vt sep* exploit. **A~ung** *f* - exploitation

ausbild|en *vt sep* train; (*formen*) form; (*entwickeln*) develop; **sich a~en** train (**als/zu** as); (*entstehen*) develop. **A~er** *m* **-s,-** instructor. **A~ung** *f* training; (*Sch*) education

ausbitten† *vt sep* **sich** (*dat*) **a~** ask for; (*verlangen*) insist on

ausblasen† *vt sep* blow out

ausbleiben† *vi sep* (*sein*) fail to appear/⟨*Erfolg:*⟩ materialize; (*nicht heimkommen*) stay out; **es konnte nicht a~** it was inevitable. **A~** *nt* **-s** absence

Ausblick *m* view

ausbrech|en† *vi sep* (*sein*) break out; ⟨*Vulkan:*⟩ erupt; (*fliehen*) escape; **in Tränen a~en** burst into tears. **A~er** *m* runaway

ausbreit|en *vt sep* spread [out]; **sich a~en** spread. **A~ung** *f* - spread

ausbrennen† *v sep* ● *vt* cauterize ● *vi* (*sein*) burn out; ⟨*Haus:*⟩ be gutted [by fire]

Ausbruch *m* outbreak; (*Vulkan-*) eruption; (*Wut-*) outburst; (*Flucht*) escape, break-out

ausbrüten *vt sep* hatch

Ausbund *m* **A~ der Tugend** paragon of virtue

ausbürsten *vt sep* brush; (*entfernen*) brush out

Ausdauer *f* perseverance; (*körperlich*) stamina. **a~nd** *a* persevering; (*unermüdlich*) untiring; (*Bot*) perennial ● *adv* with perseverance; untiringly

ausdehn|en *vt sep* stretch; (*fig*) extend; **sich a~en** stretch; (*Phys & fig*) expand; (*dauern*) last. **A~ung** *f* expansion; (*Umfang*) extent

ausdenken† *vt sep* **sich** (*dat*) **a~** think up; (*sich vorstellen*) imagine

ausdrehen *vt sep* turn off

Ausdruck *m* expression; (*Fach-*) term; (*Computer*) printout. **a~en** *vt sep* print

ausdrück|en *vt sep* squeeze out; squeeze ⟨*Zitrone*⟩; stub out ⟨*Zigarette*⟩; (*äußern*) express; **sich a~en** express oneself. **a~lich** *a* express, *adv* -ly

ausdrucks|los *a* expressionless. **a~voll** *a* expressive

auseinander *adv* apart; (*entzwei*) in pieces. **a~falten** *vt sep* unfold. **a~gehen**† *vi sep* (*sein*) part; ⟨*Linien, Meinungen:*⟩ diverge; ⟨*Menge:*⟩ disperse; ⟨*Ehe:*⟩ break up; (*entzweigehen*) come apart. **a~halten**† *vt sep* tell apart. **a~nehmen**† *vt sep* take apart *or* to pieces. **a~setzen** *vt sep* explain (**jdm** to s.o.); **sich a~setzen** have it out (**mit jdm** with s.o.); come to grips (**mit einem Problem** with a problem). **A~setzung** *f* **-,-en** discussion; (*Streit*) argument

auserlesen *a* select, choice

ausfahr|en† *v sep* ● *vt* take for a drive; take out ⟨*Baby*⟩ [in the pram] ● *vi* (*sein*) go for a drive. **A~t** *f* drive; (*Autobahn , Garagen-*) exit

Ausfall *m* failure; (*Absage*) cancellation; (*Comm*) loss. **a~en**† *vi sep* (*sein*) fall out; (*versagen*) fail; (*abgesagt werden*) be cancelled; **gut/schlecht a~en** turn out to be good/poor

ausfallend, ausfällig *a* abusive

ausfertig|en *vt sep* make out. **A~ung** *f* **-,-en in doppelter/dreifacher A~ung** in duplicate/triplicate

ausfindig *a* **a~ machen** find

ausflippen *vi* (*sein*) freak out

Ausflucht *f* **-,⸚e** excuse

Ausflug *m* excursion, outing

Ausflügler *m* **-s,-** [day-]tripper

Ausfluß *m* outlet; (*Abfluß*) drain; (*Med*) discharge

ausfragen *vt sep* question

ausfransen *vi sep* (*sein*) fray

Ausfuhr *f* **-,-en** (*Comm*) export

ausführ|en *vt sep* take out; (*Comm*) export; (*durchführen*) carry out; (*erklären*) explain. **a~lich** *a* detailed ● *adv* in detail. **A~ung** *f* execution; (*Comm*) version; (*äußere*) finish; (*Qualität*) workmanship; (*Erklärung*) explanation

Ausgabe *f* issue; (*Buch-*) edition; (*Comm*) version

Ausgang *m* way out, exit; (*Flugsteig*) gate; (*Ende*) end; (*Ergebnis*) outcome, result; **A~ haben** have time off. **A~spunkt** *m* starting-point. **A~ssperre** *f* curfew

ausgeben† *vt sep* hand out; issue ⟨*Fahrkarten*⟩; spend ⟨*Geld*⟩; buy ⟨*Runde Bier*⟩; **sich a~ als** pretend to be

ausgebeult *a* baggy

ausgebildet *a* trained

ausgebucht *a* fully booked; ⟨*Vorstellung*⟩ sold out

ausgedehnt *a* extensive; (*lang*) long

ausgedient *a* worn out; ⟨*Person*⟩ retired

ausgefallen *a* unusual

ausgefranst *a* frayed

ausgeglichen *a* [well-]balanced; (*gelassen*) even-tempered

ausgeh|en† *vi sep* (*sein*) go out; ⟨*Haare:*⟩ fall out; ⟨*Vorräte, Geld:*⟩ run out; (*verblassen*) fade; (*herrühren*) come (**von** from); (*abzielen*) aim (**auf** + *acc* at); **gut/schlecht a~en** end well/badly; **leer a~en** come away empty-handed; **davon a~en, daß** assume that. **A~verbot** *nt* curfew

ausgelassen *a* high-spirited; **a~ sein** be in high spirits

ausgelernt *a* [fully] trained

ausgemacht *a* agreed; (*fam: vollkommen*) utter

ausgenommen *conj* except; **a~ wenn** unless

ausgeprägt *a* marked

ausgerechnet *adv* **a~ heute** today of all days; **a~ er/Rom** he of all people/Rome of all places

ausgeschlossen *pred a* out of the question

ausgeschnitten *a* low-cut

ausgesprochen *a* marked ● *adv* decidedly

ausgestorben *a* extinct; **[wie] a~** ⟨*Straße:*⟩ deserted

Ausgestoßene(r) *m/f* outcast

ausgewachsen *a* fully-grown

ausgewogen *a* [well-]balanced

ausgezeichnet *a* excellent, *adv* -ly

ausgiebig *a* extensive, *adv* -ly; (*ausgedehnt*) long; **a~ Gebrauch machen von** make full use of; **a~ frühstücken** have a really good breakfast

ausgießen† *vt sep* pour out; (*leeren*) empty

Ausgleich *m* **-[e]s** balance; (*Entschädigung*) compensation. **a~en**† *v sep* ● *vt* balance; even out ⟨*Höhe*⟩; (*wettmachen*) compensate for; **sich a~en** balance out ● *vi* (*haben*) (*Sport*) equalize. **A~sgymnastik** *f* keep-fit exercises *pl*. **A~streffer** *m* equalizer

ausgleiten† *vi sep* (*sein*) slip

ausgrab|en† *vt sep* dig up; (*Archaeol*) excavate. **A~ung** *f* **-,-en** excavation

Ausguck *m* **-[e]s,-e** look-out post; (*Person*) look-out

Ausguß *m* [kitchen] sink

aushaben† *vt sep* have finished ⟨*Buch*⟩; **wann habt ihr Schule aus?** when do you finish school?

aushalten† *v sep* ● *vt* bear, stand; hold ⟨*Note*⟩; (*Unterhalt zahlen für*) keep; **nicht auszuhalten, nicht zum A~** unbearable ● *vi* (*haben*) hold out

aushandeln *vt sep* negotiate

aushändigen *vt sep* hand over

Aushang *m* [public] notice

aushängen[1] *vt sep* (*reg*) display; take off its hinges ⟨*Tür*⟩

aushäng|en[2]† *vi sep* (*haben*) be displayed. **A~eschild** *nt* sign

ausharren *vi sep* (*haben*) hold out

ausheben† *vt sep* excavate; take off its hinges ⟨*Tür*⟩

aushecken *vt sep* (*fig*) hatch

aushelfen† *vi sep* (*haben*) help out (**jdm** s.o.)

Aushilf|e *f* [temporary] assistant; **zur A~e** to help out. **A~skraft** *f* temporary worker. **a~sweise** *adv* temporarily

aushöhlen *vt sep* hollow out

ausholen *vi sep* (*haben*) **[zum Schlag] a~** raise one's arm [ready to strike]

aushorchen *vt sep* sound out

auskennen† **(sich)** *vr sep* know one's way around; **sich mit/in etw** (*dat*) **a~** know all about sth

auskleiden *vt sep* undress; (*Techn*) line; **sich a~** undress

ausknipsen *vi sep* switch off

auskommen† *vi sep* (*sein*) manage (**mit/ohne** with/without); (*sich vertragen*) get on (**gut** well). **A~** *nt* **-s sein A~/ein gutes A~ haben** get by/be well off

auskosten *vt sep* enjoy [to the full]

auskugeln *vt sep* **sich** (*dat*) **den Arm a~** dislocate one's shoulder

auskühlen *vt/i sep* (*sein*) cool

auskundschaften *vt sep* spy out; (*erfahren*) find out

Auskunft *f* **-,¨e** information; (*A~sstelle*) information desk/ (*Büro*) bureau; (*Teleph*) enquiries *pl*; **eine A~** a piece of information. **A~sbüro** *nt* information bureau

auslachen *vt sep* laugh at

ausladen† *vt sep* unload; (*fam: absagen*) put off ⟨*Gast*⟩. **a~d** *a* projecting

Auslage *f* [window] display; **A~n** expenses

Ausland *nt* **im/ins A~** abroad

Ausländ|er(in) *m* **-s,-** (*f* **-,-nen**) foreigner. **a~isch** *a* foreign

Auslandsgespräch *nt* international call

auslass|en† *vt sep* let out; let down ⟨*Saum*⟩; (*weglassen*) leave out; (*versäumen*) miss; (*Culin*) melt; (*fig*) vent ⟨*Ärger*⟩ (**an** + *dat* on); **sich a~en über** (+*acc*) go on about. **A~ungszeichen** *nt* apostrophe

Auslauf *m* run. **a~en**† *vi sep* (*sein*) run out; ⟨*Farbe:*⟩ run; (*Naut*) put to sea; (*leerlaufen*) run dry; (*enden*) end; ⟨*Modell:*⟩ be discontinued

Ausläufer *m* (*Geog*) spur; (*Bot*) runner, sucker

ausleeren *vt sep* empty [out]

ausleg|en *vt sep* lay out; display ⟨*Waren*⟩; (*bedecken*) cover/(*auskleiden*) line (**mit** with); (*bezahlen*) pay; (*deuten*) interpret. **A~ung** *f* **-,-en** interpretation

ausleihen† *vt sep* lend; **sich** (*dat*) **a~** borrow

auslernen *vi sep* (*haben*) finish one's training

Auslese *f* **-** selection; (*fig*) pick; (*Elite*) elite. **a~n**† *vt sep* finish reading ⟨*Buch*⟩; (*auswählen*) pick out, select

ausliefer|n *vt sep* hand over; (*Jur*) extradite; **ausgeliefert sein** (+*dat*) be at the mercy of. **A~ung** *f* handing over; (*Jur*) extradition; (*Comm*) distribution

ausliegen† *vi sep* (*haben*) be on display

auslöschen *vt sep* extinguish; (*abwischen*) wipe off; (*fig*) erase

auslosen *vt sep* draw lots for

auslös|en *vt sep* set off, trigger; (*fig*) cause; arouse ⟨*Begeisterung*⟩; (*einlösen*) redeem; pay a ransom for ⟨*Gefangene*⟩. **A~er** *m* **-s,-** trigger; (*Phot*) shutter release

Auslosung *f* draw

auslüften *vt/i sep* (*haben*) air

ausmachen *vt sep* put out; (*abschalten*) turn off; (*abmachen*) arrange; (*erkennen*) make out; (*betragen*) amount to; (*darstellen*) represent; (*wichtig sein*) matter; **das macht mir nichts aus** I don't mind

ausmalen *vt sep* paint; (*fig*) describe; **sich** (*dat*) **a~** imagine

Ausmaß *nt* extent; **A~e** dimensions

ausmerzen *vt sep* eliminate

ausmessen† *vt sep* measure

Ausnahm|e *f* **-,-n** exception. **A~ezustand** *m* state of emergency. **a~slos** *adv* without exception. **a~sweise** *adv* as an exception

ausnehmen† *vt sep* take out; gut ⟨*Fisch*⟩; draw ⟨*Huhn*⟩; (*ausschließen*) exclude; (*fam: schröpfen*) fleece; **sich gut a~** look good. **a~d** *adv* exceptionally

ausnutz|en, ausnütz|en *vt sep* exploit; make the most of ⟨*Gelegenheit*⟩. **A~ung** *f* exploitation

auspacken *v sep* • *vt* unpack; (*auswickeln*) unwrap • *vi* (*haben*) (*fam*) talk

auspeitschen *vt sep* flog

auspfeifen *vt sep* whistle and boo

ausplaudern *vt sep* let out, blab

ausplündern *vt sep* loot; rob ⟨*Person*⟩

ausprobieren *vt sep* try out

Auspuff *m* **-s** exhaust [system]. **A~gase** *ntpl* exhaust fumes. **A~rohr** *nt* exhaust pipe

auspusten *vt sep* blow out

ausradieren *vt sep* rub out

ausrangieren *vt sep* (*fam*) discard

ausrauben *vt sep* rob

ausräuchern *vt sep* smoke out; fumigate ⟨*Zimmer*⟩

ausräumen *vt sep* clear out

ausrechnen *vt sep* work out, calculate

Ausrede *f* excuse. **a~n** *v sep* • *vi* (*haben*) finish speaking; **laß mich a~n!** let me finish! • *vt* **jdm etw a~n** talk s.o. out of sth

ausreichen *vi sep* (*haben*) be enough; **a~ mit** have enough. **a~d** *a* adequate, *adv* -ly; (*Sch*) ≈ pass

Ausreise *f* departure [from a country]. **a~n** *vi sep* (*sein*) leave the country. **A~visum** *nt* exit visa

ausreiß|en† *v sep* • *vt* pull *or* tear out • *vi* (*sein*) (*fam*) run away. **A~er** *m* (*fam*) runaway

ausrenken *vt sep* dislocate; **sich** (*dat*) **den Arm a~** dislocate one's shoulder

ausrichten *vt sep* align; (*bestellen*) deliver; (*erreichen*) achieve; **jdm a~** tell s.o. (**daß** that); **kann ich etwas**

a~? can I take a message? **ich soll Ihnen Grüße von X a~** X sends [you] his regards

ausrotten *vt sep* exterminate; (*fig*) eradicate

ausrücken *vi sep* (*sein*) (*Mil*) march off; (*fam*) run away

Ausruf *m* exclamation. **a~en**† *vt sep* exclaim; call out ⟨*Namen*⟩; (*verkünden*) proclaim; call ⟨*Streik*⟩; **jdn a~en lassen** have s.o. paged. **A~ezeichen** *nt* exclamation mark

ausruhen *vt/i sep* (*haben*) rest; **sich a~** have a rest

ausrüst|en *vt sep* equip. **A~ung** *f* equipment; (*Mil*) kit

ausrutschen *vi sep* (*sein*) slip

Aussage *f* **-,-n** statement; (*Jur*) testimony, evidence; (*Gram*) predicate. **a~n** *vt/i sep* (*haben*) state; (*Jur*) give evidence, testify

Aussatz *m* leprosy

Aussätzige(r) *m/f* leper

ausschachten *vt sep* excavate

ausschalten *vt sep* switch *or* turn off; (*fig*) eliminate

Ausschank *m* sale of alcoholic drinks; (*Bar*) bar

Ausschau *f* **- A~ halten nach** look out for. **a~en** *vi sep* (*haben*) (*SGer*) look; **a~en nach** look out for

ausscheiden† *v sep* ● *vi* (*sein*) leave; (*Sport*) drop out; (*nicht in Frage kommen*) be excluded; **aus dem Dienst a~** retire ● *vt* eliminate; (*Med*) excrete

ausschenken *vt sep* pour out; (*verkaufen*) sell

ausscheren *vi sep* (*sein*) (*Auto*) pull out

ausschildern *vt sep* signpost

ausschimpfen *vt sep* tell off

ausschlachten *vt sep* (*fig*) exploit

ausschlafen† *v sep* ● *vi/r* (*haben*) **[sich] a~** get enough sleep; (*morgens*) sleep late; **nicht ausgeschlafen haben** *od* **sein** be still tired ● *vt* sleep off ⟨*Rausch*⟩

Ausschlag *m* (*Med*) rash; **den A~ geben** (*fig*) tip the balance. **a~en**† *v sep* ● *vi* (*haben*) kick [out]; (*Bot*) sprout; ⟨*Baum:*⟩ come into leaf ● *vt* knock out; (*auskleiden*) line; (*ablehnen*) refuse. **a~gebend** *a* decisive

ausschließ|en† *vt sep* lock out; (*fig*) exclude; (*entfernen*) expel. **a~lich** *a* exclusive, *adv* -ly

ausschlüpfen *vi sep* (*sein*) hatch

Ausschluß *m* exclusion; expulsion; **unter A~ der Öffentlichkeit** in camera

ausschmücken *vt sep* decorate; (*fig*) embellish

ausschneiden† *vt sep* cut out

Ausschnitt *m* excerpt, extract; (*Zeitungs-*) cutting; (*Hals-*) neckline

ausschöpfen *vt sep* ladle out; (*Naut*) bail out; exhaust ⟨*Möglichkeiten*⟩

ausschreiben† *vt sep* write out; (*ausstellen*) make out; (*bekanntgeben*) announce; put out to tender ⟨*Auftrag*⟩

Ausschreitungen *fpl* riots; (*Exzesse*) excesses

Ausschuß *m* committee; (*Comm*) rejects *pl*

ausschütten *vt sep* tip out; (*verschütten*) spill; (*leeren*) empty; **sich vor Lachen a~** (*fam*) be in stitches

ausschweif|end *a* dissolute. **A~ung** *f* **-,-en** debauchery; **A~ungen** excesses

ausschwenken *vt sep* rinse [out]

aussehen† *vi sep* (*haben*) look; **es sieht nach Regen aus** it looks like rain; **wie sieht er/es aus?** what does he/it look like? **A~** *nt* **-s** appearance

aussein† *vi sep* (*sein*) be out; ⟨*Licht, Radio:*⟩ be off; (*zu Ende sein*) be over; **a~ auf** (+*acc*) be after; **mit ihm ist es aus** he's had it

außen *adv* [on the] outside; **nach a~** outwards. **A~bordmotor** *m* outboard motor. **A~handel** *m* foreign trade. **A~minister** *m* Foreign Minister. **A~politik** *f* foreign policy. **A~seite** *f* outside. **A~seiter** *m* **-s,-** outsider; (*fig*) misfit. **A~stände** *mpl* outstanding debts. **A~stehende(r)** *m/f* outsider

außer *prep* (+*dat*) except [for], apart from; (*außerhalb*) out of; **a~ Atem/Sicht** out of breath/sight; **a~ sich** (*fig*) beside oneself ● *conj* except; **a~ wenn** unless. **a~dem** *adv* in addition, as well ● *conj* moreover

äußer|e(r,s) *a* external; ⟨*Teil, Schicht*⟩ outer. **Ä~e(s)** *nt* exterior; (*Aussehen*) appearance

außer|ehelich *a* extramarital. **a~gewöhnlich** *a* exceptional, *adv* -ly. **a~halb** *prep* (+*gen*) outside ● *adv* **a~halb wohnen** live outside town

äußer|lich *a* external, *adv* -ly; (*fig*) outward, *adv* -ly. **ä~n** *vt* express;

sich ä~n comment; (*sich zeigen*) manifest itself
außerordentlich *a* extraordinary, *adv* -ily; (*außergewöhnlich*) exceptional, *adv* -ly
äußerst *adv* extremely
außerstande *adv* unable (**zu** to)
äußerste|(r,s) *a* outermost; (*weiteste*) furthest; (*höchste*) utmost, extreme; (*letzte*) last; (*schlimmste*) worst; **am ä~n Ende** at the very end; **aufs ä~** extremely. **Ä~(s)** *nt* **das Ä~** the limit; (*Schlimmste*) the worst; **sein Ä~s tun** do one's utmost
Äußerung *f* **-,-en** comment; (*Bemerkung*) remark
aussetzen *v sep* ● *vt* expose (*dat* to); abandon ‹*Kind, Hund*›; launch ‹*Boot*›; offer ‹*Belohnung*›; **etwas auszusetzen haben an** (+*dat*) find fault with ● *vi* (*haben*) stop; ‹*Motor:*› cut out
Aussicht *f* **-,-en** view/(*fig*) prospect (**auf** + *acc* of); **in A~ stellen** promise; **weitere A~en** (*Meteorol*) further outlook *sg*. **a~slos** *a* hopeless, *adv* -ly. **a~sreich** *a* promising
aussöhnen *vt sep* reconcile; **sich a~** become reconciled
aussortieren *vt sep* pick out; (*ausscheiden*) eliminate
ausspann|en *v sep* ● *vt* spread out; unhitch ‹*Pferd*›; (*fam: wegnehmen*) take (*dat* from) ● *vi* (*haben*) rest. **A~ung** *f* rest
aussperr|en *vt sep* lock out. **A~ung** *f* **-,-en** lock-out
ausspielen *v sep* ● *vt* play ‹*Karte*›; (*fig*) play off (**gegen** against) ● *vi* (*haben*) (*Kartenspiel*) lead
Aussprache *f* pronunciation; (*Sprechweise*) diction; (*Gespräch*) talk
aussprechen† *v sep* ● *vt* pronounce; (*äußern*) express; **sich a~** talk; come out (**für/gegen** in favour of/against) ● *vi* (*haben*) finish [speaking]
Ausspruch *m* saying
ausspucken *v sep* ● *vt* spit out ● *vi* (*haben*) spit
ausspülen *vt sep* rinse out
ausstaffieren *vt sep* (*fam*) kit out
Ausstand *m* strike; **in den A~ treten** go on strike
ausstatt|en *vt sep* equip; **mit Möbeln a~en** furnish. **A~ung** *f* **-,-en** equipment; (*Innen-*) furnishings *pl*; (*Theat*) scenery and costumes *pl*; (*Aufmachung*) get-up
ausstehen† *v sep* ● *vt* suffer; **Angst a~** be frightened; **ich kann sie nicht a~** I can't stand her ● *vi* (*haben*) be outstanding
aussteig|en† *vi sep* (*sein*) get out; (*aus Bus, Zug*) get off; (*fam: ausscheiden*) opt out; (*aus einem Geschäft*) back out; **alles a~en!** all change! **A~er(in)** *m* **-s,-** (*f* **-,-nen**) (*fam*) drop-out
ausstell|en *vt sep* exhibit; (*Comm*) display; (*ausfertigen*) make out; issue ‹*Paß*›. **A~er** *m* **-s,-** exhibitor. **A~ung** *f* exhibition; (*Comm*) display. **A~ungsstück** *nt* exhibit
aussterben† *vi sep* (*sein*) die out; (*Biol*) become extinct. **A~** *nt* **-s** extinction
Aussteuer *f* trousseau
Ausstieg *m* **-[e]s,-e** exit
ausstopfen *vt sep* stuff
ausstoßen† *vt sep* emit; utter ‹*Fluch*›; heave ‹*Seufzer*›; (*ausschließen*) expel
ausstrahl|en *vt/i sep* (*sein*) radiate, emit; (*Radio, TV*) broadcast. **A~ung** *f* radiation; (*fig*) charisma
ausstrecken *vt sep* stretch out; put out ‹*Hand*›; **sich a~** stretch out
ausstreichen† *vt sep* cross out
ausstreuen *vt sep* scatter; spread ‹*Gerüchte*›
ausströmen *v sep* ● *vi* (*sein*) pour out; (*entweichen*) escape ● *vt* emit; (*ausstrahlen*) radiate
aussuchen *vt sep* pick, choose
Austausch *m* exchange. **a~bar** *a* interchangeable. **a~en** *vt sep* exchange; (*auswechseln*) replace
austeilen *vt sep* distribute; (*ausgeben*) hand out
Auster *f* **-,-n** oyster
austoben (sich) *vr sep* ‹*Sturm:*› rage; ‹*Person:*› let off steam; ‹*Kinder:*› romp about
austragen† *vt sep* deliver; hold ‹*Wettkampf*›; play ‹*Spiel*›
Austral|ien /-i̯ən/ *nt* **-s** Australia. **A~ier(in)** *m* **-s,-** (*f* **-,-nen**) Australian. **a~isch** *a* Australian
austreiben† *v sep* ● *vt* drive out; (*Relig*) exorcize ● *vi* (*haben*) (*Bot*) sprout
austreten† *v sep* ● *vt* stamp out; (*abnutzen*) wear down ● *vi* (*sein*) come out; (*ausscheiden*) leave (**aus etw** sth); **[mal] a~** (*fam*) go to the loo; (*Sch*) be excused

austrinken† *vt/i sep* (*haben*) drink up; (*leeren*) drain
Austritt *m* resignation
austrocknen *vt/i sep* (*sein*) dry out
ausüben *vt sep* practise; carry on ⟨*Handwerk*⟩; exercise ⟨*Recht*⟩; exert ⟨*Druck, Einfluß*⟩; have ⟨*Wirkung*⟩
Ausverkauf *m* [clearance] sale. **a~t** *a* sold out; **a~tes Haus** full house
auswachsen† *vt sep* outgrow
Auswahl *f* choice, selection; (*Comm*) range; (*Sport*) team
auswählen *vt sep* choose, select
Auswander|er *m* emigrant. **a~n** *vi sep* (*sein*) emigrate. **A~ung** *f* emigration
auswärt|ig *a* non-local; (*ausländisch*) foreign. **a~s** *adv* outwards; (*Sport*) away; **a~s essen** eat out; **a~s arbeiten** not work locally. **A~sspiel** *nt* away game
auswaschen† *vt sep* wash out
auswechseln *vt sep* change; (*ersetzen*) replace; (*Sport*) substitute
Ausweg *m* (*fig*) way out. **a~los** *a* (*fig*) hopeless
ausweich|en† *vi sep* (*sein*) get out of the way; **jdm/etw a~en** avoid/(*sich entziehen*) evade s.o./sth. **a~end** *a* evasive, *adv* -ly
ausweinen *vt sep* **sich** (*dat*) **die Augen a~** cry one's eyes out; **sich a~** have a good cry
Ausweis *m* **-es,-e** pass; (*Mitglieds-, Studenten-*) card. **a~en**† *vt sep* deport; **sich a~en** prove one's identity. **A~papiere** *ntpl* identification papers. **A~ung** *f* deportation
ausweiten *vt sep* stretch; (*fig*) expand
auswendig *adv* by heart
auswerten *vt sep* evaluate; (*nutzen*) utilize
auswickeln *vt sep* unwrap
auswirk|en (sich) *vr sep* have an effect (**auf** + *acc* on). **A~ung** *f* effect; (*Folge*) consequence
auswischen *vt sep* wipe out; **jdm eins a~** (*fam*) play a nasty trick on s.o.
auswringen *vt sep* wring out
Auswuchs *m* excrescence; **Auswüchse** (*fig*) excesses
auszahlen *vt sep* pay out; (*entlohnen*) pay off; (*abfinden*) buy out; **sich a~** (*fig*) pay off
auszählen *vt sep* count; (*Boxen*) count out
Auszahlung *f* payment
auszeichn|en *vt sep* (*Comm*) price; (*ehren*) honour; (*mit einem Preis*) award a prize to; (*Mil*) decorate; **sich a~en** distinguish oneself. **A~ung** *f* honour; (*Preis*) award; (*Mil*) decoration; (*Sch*) distinction
ausziehen† *v sep* ● *vt* pull out; (*auskleiden*) undress; take off ⟨*Mantel, Schuhe*⟩; **sich a~** take off one's coat; (*sich entkleiden*) undress ● *vi* (*sein*) move out; (*sich aufmachen*) set out
Auszubildende(r) *m/f* trainee
Auszug *m* departure; (*Umzug*) move; (*Ausschnitt*) extract, excerpt; (*Bank-*) statement
authentisch *a* authentic
Auto *nt* **-s,-s** car; **A~ fahren** drive; (*mitfahren*) go in the car. **A~bahn** *f* motorway, (*Amer*) freeway
Autobiographie *f* autobiography
Auto|bus *m* bus. **A~fähre** *f* car ferry. **A~fahrer(in)** *m(f)* driver, motorist. **A~fahrt** *f* drive
Autogramm *nt* **-s,-e** autograph
autokratisch *a* autocratic
Automat *m* **-en,-en** automatic device; (*Münz-*) slot-machine; (*Verkaufs-*) vending-machine; (*Fahrkarten-*) machine; (*Techn*) robot. **A~ik** *f* - automatic mechanism; (*Auto*) automatic transmission
Auto|mation /-'tsi̯o:n/ *f* - automation. **a~matisch** *a* automatic, *adv* -ally
autonom *a* autonomous. **A~ie** *f* - autonomy
Autonummer *f* registration number
Autopsie *f* **-,-n** autopsy
Autor *m* **-s,-en** /-'to:rən/ author
Auto|reisezug *m* Motorail. **A~rennen** *nt* motor race
Autorin *f* **-,-nen** author[ess]
Autori|sation /-'tsi̯o:n/ *f* - authorization. **a~sieren** *vt* authorize. **a~tär** *a* authoritarian. **A~tät** *f* **-,-en** authority
Auto|schlosser *m* motor mechanic. **A~skooter** /-sku:tɐ/ *m* **-s,-** dodgem. **A~stopp** *m* **-s per A~stopp fahren** hitch-hike. **A~verleih** *m* car hire [firm]. **A~waschanlage** *f* car wash
autsch *int* ouch
Aversion *f* **-,-en** aversion (**gegen** to)
Axt *f* **-,¨e** axe

B

B, b /be:/ *nt* - (*Mus*) B flat
Baby /'be:bi/ *nt* **-s,-s** baby. **B~ausstattung** *f* layette. **B~sitter** /-sıtɐ/ *m* **-s,-** babysitter
Bach *m* **-[e]s,¨-e** stream
Backbord *nt* **-[e]s** port [side]
Backe *f* **-,-n** cheek
backen *v* ● *vt/i* † (*haben*) bake; (*braten*) fry ● *vi* (*reg*) (*haben*) (*kleben*) stick (**an** + *dat* to)
Backenzahn *m* molar
Bäcker *m* **-s,-** baker. **B~ei** *f* **-,-en, B~laden** *m* baker's shop
Back|form *f* baking tin. **B~obst** *nt* dried fruit. **B~ofen** *m* oven. **B~pfeife** *f* (*fam*) slap in the face. **B~pflaume** *f* prune. **B~pulver** *nt* baking-powder. **B~rohr** *nt* oven. **B~stein** *m* brick. **B~werk** *nt* cakes and pastries *pl*
Bad *nt* **-[e]s,¨-er** bath; (*im Meer*) bathe; (*Zimmer*) bathroom; (*Schwimm-*) pool; (*Ort*) spa
Bade|anstalt *f* swimming baths *pl*. **B~anzug** *m* swim-suit. **B~hose** *f* swimming trunks *pl*. **B~kappe** *f* bathing-cap. **B~mantel** *m* bathrobe. **B~matte** *f* bath-mat. **B~mütze** *f* bathing-cap. **b~n** *vi* (*haben*) have a bath; (*im Meer*) bathe ● *vt* bath; (*waschen*) bathe. **B~ort** *m* seaside resort; (*Kurort*) spa. **B~tuch** *nt* bath-towel. **B~wanne** *f* bath[-tub]. **B~zimmer** *nt* bathroom
Bagatelle *f* **-,-n** trifle; (*Mus*) bagatelle
Bagger *m* **-s,-** excavator; (*Naß-*) dredger. **b~n** *vt/i* (*haben*) excavate; dredge. **B~see** *m* flooded gravel-pit
Bahn *f* **-,-en** path; (*Astr*) orbit; (*Sport*) track; (*einzelne*) lane; (*Rodel-*) run; (*Stoff-, Papier-*) width; (*Rock-*) panel; (*Eisen-*) railway; (*Zug*) train; (*Straßen-*) tram; **auf die schiefe B~ kommen** (*fig*) get into bad ways. **b~brechend** *a* (*fig*) pioneering. **b~en** *vt* **sich** (*dat*) **einen Weg b~en** clear a way (**durch** through). **B~hof** *m* [railway] station. **B~steig** *m* **-[e]s,-e** platform. **B~übergang** *m* level crossing, (*Amer*) grade crossing
Bahre *f* **-,-n** stretcher; (*Toten-*) bier
Baiser /bɛ'ze:/ *nt* **-s,-s** meringue
Bajonett *nt* **-[e]s,-e** bayonet
Bake *f* **-,-n** (*Naut, Aviat*) beacon
Bakterien /-i̯ən/ *fpl* bacteria
Balanc|e /ba'lã:sə/ *f* - balance; **die B~e halten/verlieren** keep/lose one's balance. **b~ieren** *vt/i* (*haben/sein*) balance
bald *adv* soon; (*fast*) almost; **b~ ... b~ ...** now ... now ...
Baldachin /-xi:n/ *m* **-s,-e** canopy
bald|ig *a* early; ⟨*Besserung*⟩ speedy. **b~möglichst** *adv* as soon as possible
Balg *nt* & *m* **-[e]s,¨-er** (*fam*) brat. **b~en (sich)** *vr* tussle. **B~erei** *f* **-,-en** tussle
Balkan *m* **-s** Balkans *pl*
Balken *m* **-s,-** beam
Balkon /bal'kõ:/ *m* **-s,-s** balcony; (*Theat*) circle
Ball[1] *m* **-[e]s,¨-e** ball
Ball[2] *m* **-[e]s,¨-e** (*Tanz*) ball
Ballade *f* **-,-n** ballad
Ballast *m* **-[e]s** ballast. **B~stoffe** *mpl* roughage *sg*
ballen *vt* **die [Hand zur] Faust b~** clench one's fist; **sich b~** gather, mass. **B~** *m* **-s,-** bale; (*Anat*) ball of the hand/(*Fuß-*) foot; (*Med*) bunion
Ballerina *f* **-,-nen** ballerina
Ballett *nt* **-s,-e** ballet
Ballettänzer(in) *m(f)* ballet dancer
ballistisch *a* ballistic
Ballon /ba'lõ:/ *m* **-s,-s** balloon
Ball|saal *m* ballroom. **B~ungsgebiet** *nt* conurbation. **B~wechsel** *m* (*Tennis*) rally
Balsam *m* **-s** balm
Balt|ikum *nt* **-s** Baltic States *pl*. **b~isch** *a* Baltic
Balustrade *f* **-,-n** balustrade
Bambus *m* **-ses,-se** bamboo
banal *a* banal. **B~ität** *f* **-,-en** banality
Banane *f* **-,-n** banana
Banause *m* **-n,-n** philistine
Band[1] *nt* **-[e]s,¨-er** ribbon; (*Naht-, Ton-, Ziel-*) tape; (*Anat*) ligament; **auf B~ aufnehmen** tape; **laufendes B~** conveyor belt; **am laufenden B~** (*fam*) non-stop
Band[2] *m* **-[e]s,¨-e** volume
Band[3] *nt* **-[e]s,-e** (*fig*) bond; **B~e der Freundschaft** bonds of friendship
Band[4] /bɛnt/ *f* **-,-s** [jazz] band
Bandag|e /ban'da:ʒə/ *f* **-,-n** bandage. **b~ieren** *vt* bandage
Bande *f* **-,-n** gang
bändigen *vt* control, restrain; (*zähmen*) tame
Bandit *m* **-en,-en** bandit
Band|maß *nt* tape-measure. **B~nudeln** *fpl* noodles. **B~scheibe** *f* (*Anat*)

disc. **B~scheibenvorfall** *m* slipped disc. **B~wurm** *m* tapeworm

bang|[e] *a* **(bänger, bängst)** anxious; **jdm b~e machen** frighten s.o. **B~e** *f* **B~e haben** be afraid. **b~en** *vi* (*haben*) fear (**um** for); **mir b~t davor** I dread it

Banjo *nt* **-s,-s** banjo

Bank[1] *f* **-,⁻e** bench

Bank[2] *f* **-,-en** (*Comm*) bank. **B~einzug** *m* direct debit

Bankett *nt* **-s,-e** banquet

Bankier /baŋ'kie:/ *m* **-s,-s** banker

Bank|konto *nt* bank account. **B~note** *f* banknote

Bankrott *m* **-s,-s** bankruptcy; **B~ machen** go bankrupt. **b~** *a* bankrupt

Bankwesen *nt* banking

Bann *m* **-[e]s,-e** (*fig*) spell; **in jds B~** under s.o.'s spell. **b~en** *vt* exorcize; (*abwenden*) avert; **[wie] gebannt** spellbound

Banner *nt* **-s,-** banner

Baptist(in) *m* **-en,-en** (*f* **-,-nen**) Baptist

bar *a* (*rein*) sheer; ⟨*Gold*⟩ pure; **b~es Geld** cash; **[in] bar bezahlen** pay cash; **etw für b~e Münze nehmen** (*fig*) take sth as gospel

Bar *f* **-,-s** bar

Bär *m* **-en,-en** bear; **jdm einen B~en aufbinden** (*fam*) pull s.o.'s leg

Baracke *f* **-,-n** (*Mil*) hut

Barb|ar *m* **-en,-en** barbarian. **b~arisch** *a* barbaric

bar|fuß *adv* barefoot. **B~geld** *nt* cash

Bariton *m* **-s,-e** /-'to:nə/ baritone

Barkasse *f* **-,-n** launch

Barmann *m* (*pl* **-männer**) barman

barmherzig *a* merciful. **B~keit** *f* - mercy

barock *a* baroque. **B~** *nt* & *m* **-[s]** baroque

Barometer *nt* **-s,-** barometer

Baron *m* **-s,-e** baron. **B~in** *f* **-,-nen** baroness

Barren *m* **-s,-** (*Gold-*) bar, ingot; (*Sport*) parallel bars *pl*. **B~gold** *nt* gold bullion

Barriere *f* **-,-n** barrier

Barrikade *f* **-,-n** barricade

barsch *a* gruff, *adv* -ly; (*kurz*) curt, *adv* -ly

Barsch *m* **-[e]s,-e** (*Zool*) perch

Barschaft *f* - **meine ganze B~** all I have/had on me

Bart *m* **-[e]s,⁻e** beard; (*der Katze*) whiskers *pl*

bärtig *a* bearded

Barzahlung *f* cash payment

Basar *m* **-s,-e** bazaar

Base[1] *f* **-,-n** [female] cousin

Base[2] *f* **-,-n** (*Chem*) alkali, base

Basel *nt* **-s** Basle

basieren *vi* (*haben*) be based (**auf** +*dat* on)

Basilikum *nt* **-s** basil

Basis *f* **-,Basen** base; (*fig*) basis

basisch *a* (*Chem*) alkaline

Bask|enmütze *f* beret. **b~isch** *a* Basque

Baß *m* **-sses,⁻sse** bass; (*Kontra-*) double-bass

Bassin /ba'sɛ̃:/ *nt* **-s,-s** pond; (*Brunnen-*) basin; (*Schwimm-*) pool

Bassist *m* **-en,-en** bass player; (*Sänger*) bass

Baßstimme *f* bass voice

Bast *m* **-[e]s** raffia

basta *int* **[und damit] b~!** and that's that!

bast|eln *vt* make ● *vi* (*haben*) do handicrafts; (*herum-*) tinker (**an** +*dat* with). **B~ler** *m* **-s,-** amateur craftsman; (*Heim-*) do-it-yourselfer

Bataillon /batal'jo:n/ *nt* **-s,-e** battalion

Batterie *f* **-,-n** battery

Bau[1] *m* **-[e]s,-e** burrow; (*Fuchs-*) earth

Bau[2] *m* **-[e]s,-ten** construction; (*Gebäude*) building; (*Auf-*) structure; (*Körper-*) build; (*B~stelle*) building site; **im Bau** under construction. **B~arbeiten** *fpl* building work *sg*; (*Straßen-*) roadworks. **B~art** *f* design; (*Stil*) style

Bauch *m* **-[e]s, Bäuche** abdomen, belly; (*Magen*) stomach; (*Schmer-*) paunch; (*Bauchung*) bulge. **b~ig** *a* bulbous. **B~nabel** *m* navel. **B~redner** *m* ventriloquist. **B~schmerzen** *mpl* stomach-ache *sg*. **B~speicheldrüse** *f* pancreas. **B~weh** *nt* stomach-ache

bauen *vt* build; (*konstruieren*) construct; (*an-*) grow; **einen Unfall b~** (*fam*) have an accident ● *vi* (*haben*) build (**an etw** *dat* sth); **b~ auf** (+*acc*) (*fig*) rely on

Bauer[1] *m* **-s,-n** farmer; (*Schach*) pawn

Bauer[2] *nt* **-s,-** [bird]cage

Bäuer|in *f* **-,-nen** farmer's wife. **b~lich** *a* rustic

Bauern|haus *nt* farmhouse. **B~hof** *m* farm

bau|fällig *a* dilapidated. **B~genehmigung** *f* planning permission. **B~gerüst** *nt* scaffolding. **B~jahr** *nt* year of construction; **B~jahr 1985** (*Auto*) 1985 model. **B~kasten** *m* box of building bricks; (*Modell-*) model kit. **B~klotz** *m* building brick. **B~kunst** *f* architecture. **b~lich** *a* structural, *adv* -ly. **B~lichkeiten** *fpl* buildings

Baum *m* **-[e]s, Bäume** tree

baumeln *vi* (*haben*) dangle; **die Beine b~ lassen** dangle one's legs

bäumen (sich) *vr* rear [up]

Baum|schule *f* [tree] nursery. **B~stamm** *m* tree-trunk. **B~wolle** *f* cotton. **b~wollen** *a* cotton

Bauplatz *m* building plot

bäurisch *a* rustic; (*plump*) uncouth

Bausch *m* **-[e]s, Bäusche** wad; **in B~ und Bogen** (*fig*) wholesale. **b~en** *vt* puff out; **sich b~en** billow [out]. **b~ig** *a* puffed [out]; ⟨*Ärmel*⟩ full

Bau|sparkasse *f* building society. **B~stein** *m* building brick; (*fig*) element. **B~stelle** *f* building site; (*Straßen-*) roadworks *pl*. **B~unternehmer** *m* building contractor. **B~werk** *nt* building. **B~zaun** *m* hoarding

Bayer|(in) *m* **-s,-n** (*f* **-,-nen**) Bavarian. **B~n** *nt* **-s** Bavaria

bay[e]risch *a* Bavarian

Bazillus *m* **-,-len** bacillus; (*fam: Keim*) germ

beabsichtig|en *vt* intend. **b~t** *a* intended; (*absichtlich*) intentional

beacht|en *vt* take notice of; (*einhalten*) observe; (*folgen*) follow; **nicht b~en** ignore. **b~lich** *a* considerable. **B~ung** *f* **-** observance; **etw** (*dat*) **keine B~ung schenken** take no notice of sth

Beamte(r) *m*, **Beamtin** *f* **-,-nen** official; (*Staats-*) civil servant; (*Schalter-*) clerk

beängstigend *a* alarming

beanspruchen *vt* claim; (*erfordern*) demand; (*brauchen*) take up; (*Techn*) stress; **die Arbeit beansprucht ihn sehr** his work is very demanding

beanstand|en *vt* find fault with; (*Comm*) make a complaint about. **B~ung** *f* **-,-en** complaint

beantragen *vt* apply for

beantworten *vt* answer

bearbeiten *vt* work; (*weiter-*) process; (*behandeln*) treat (**mit** with); (*Admin*) deal with; (*redigieren*) edit; (*Theat*) adapt; (*Mus*) arrange; (*fam: bedrängen*) pester; (*fam: schlagen*) pummel

Beatmung *f* **künstliche B~** artificial respiration. **B~sgerät** *nt* ventilator

beaufsichtig|en *vt* supervise. **B~ung** *f* **-** supervision

beauftrag|en *vt* instruct; commission ⟨*Künstler*⟩; **jdn mit einer Arbeit b~en** assign a task to s.o. **B~te(r)** *m*/*f* representative

bebauen *vt* build on; (*bestellen*) cultivate

beben *vi* (*haben*) tremble

bebildert *a* illustrated

Becher *m* **-s,-** beaker; (*Henkel-*) mug; (*Joghurt-, Sahne-*) carton

Becken *nt* **-s,-** basin; (*Schwimm-*) pool; (*Mus*) cymbals *pl*; (*Anat*) pelvis

bedacht *a* careful; **b~ auf** (+*acc*) concerned about; **darauf b~** anxious (**zu** to)

bedächtig *a* careful, *adv* -ly; (*langsam*) slow, *adv* -ly

bedanken (sich) *vr* thank (**bei jdm** s.o.)

Bedarf *m* **-s** need/(*Comm*) demand (**an**+*dat* for); **bei B~** if required. **B~sartikel** *mpl* requisites. **B~shaltestelle** *f* request stop

bedauer|lich *a* regrettable. **b~licherweise** *adv* unfortunately. **b~n** *vt* regret; (*bemitleiden*) feel sorry for; **bedaure!** sorry! **B~n** *nt* **-s** regret; (*Mitgefühl*) sympathy. **b~nswert** *a* pitiful; (*bedauerlich*) regrettable

bedeck|en *vt* cover; **sich b~en** ⟨*Himmel:*⟩ cloud over. **b~t** *a* covered; ⟨*Himmel*⟩ overcast

bedenken† *vt* consider; (*überlegen*) think over; **jdn b~** give s.o. a present; **sich b~** consider. **B~** *pl* misgivings; **ohne B~** without hesitation. **b~los** *a* unhesitating, *adv* -ly

bedenklich *a* doubtful; (*verdächtig*) dubious; (*bedrohlich*) worrying; (*ernst*) serious

bedeut|en *vi* (*haben*) mean; **jdm viel/nichts b~en** mean a lot/nothing to s.o.; **es hat nichts zu b~en** it is of no significance. **b~end** *a* important; (*beträchtlich*) considerable. **b~sam** *a* = **b~ungsvoll. B~ung** *f* **-,-en** meaning; (*Wichtigkeit*) importance. **b~ungslos** *a* meaningless; (*unwichtig*) unimportant. **b~ungsvoll** *a* significant; (*vielsagend*) meaningful, *adv* -ly

bedien|en *vt* serve; (*betätigen*) operate; **sich [selbst] b~en** help oneself. **B~ung** *f* **-,-en** service; (*Betätigung*) operation; (*Kellner*) waiter; (*Kellnerin*) *f* waitress. **B~ungsgeld** *nt*, **B~ungszuschlag** *m* service charge

bedingt *a* conditional; (*eingeschränkt*) qualified

Bedingung *f* **-,-en** condition; **B~en** conditions; (*Comm*) terms. **b~slos** *a* unconditional, *adv* -ly; (*unbedingt*) unquestioning, *adv* -ly

bedrängen *vt* press; (*belästigen*) pester

bedroh|en *vt* threaten. **b~lich** *a* threatening. **B~ung** *f* threat

bedrück|en *vt* depress. **b~end** *a* depressing. **b~t** *a* depressed

bedruckt *a* printed

bedürf|en† *vi* (*haben*) (+*gen*) need. **B~nis** *nt* **-ses,-se** need. **B~nisanstalt** *f* public convenience. **b~tig** *a* needy

Beefsteak /'bi:fste:k/ *nt* **-s,-s** steak; **deutsches B~** hamburger

beeilen (sich) *vr* hurry; hasten (**zu** to); **beeilt euch!** hurry up!

beeindrucken *vt* impress

beeinflussen *vt* influence

beeinträchtigen *vt* mar; (*schädigen*) impair

beend[ig]en *vt* end

beengen *vt* restrict; **beengt wohnen** live in cramped conditions

beerben *vt* **jdn b~** inherit s.o.'s property

beerdig|en *vt* bury. **B~ung** *f* **-,-en** funeral

Beere *f* **-,-n** berry

Beet *nt* **-[e]s,-e** (*Hort*) bed

Beete *f* **-,-n rote B~** beetroot

befähig|en *vt* enable; (*qualifizieren*) qualify. **B~ung** *f* **-** qualification; (*Fähigkeit*) ability

befahr|bar *a* passable. **b~en**† *vt* drive along; **stark b~ene Straße** busy road

befallen† *vt* attack; ⟨*Angst:*⟩ seize

befangen *a* shy; (*gehemmt*) self-conscious; (*Jur*) biased. **B~heit** *f* **-** shyness; self-consciousness; bias

befassen (sich) *vr* concern oneself/ (*behandeln*) deal (**mit** with)

Befehl *m* **-[e]s,-e** order; (*Leitung*) command (**über**+*acc* of). **b~en**† *vt* **jdm etw b~en** order s.o. to do sth ● *vi* (*haben*) give the orders. **b~igen** *vt* (*Mil*) command. **B~sform** *f* (*Gram*) imperative. **B~shaber** *m* **-s,-** commander

befestig|en *vt* fasten (**an**+*dat* to); (*stärken*) strengthen; (*Mil*) fortify. **B~ung** *f* **-,-en** fastening; (*Mil*) fortification

befeuchten *vt* moisten

befinden† **(sich)** *vr* be. **B~** *nt* **-s** [state of] health

beflecken *vt* stain

beflissen *a* assiduous, *adv* -ly

befolgen *vt* follow

beförder|n *vt* transport; (*im Rang*) promote. **B~ung** *f* **-,-en** transport; promotion

befragen *vt* question

befrei|en *vt* free; (*räumen*) clear (**von** of); (*freistellen*) exempt (**von** from); **sich b~en** free oneself. **B~er** *m* **-s,-** liberator. **b~t** *a* (*erleichtert*) relieved. **B~ung** *f* **-** liberation; exemption

befremd|en *vt* disconcert. **B~en** *nt* **-s** surprise. **b~lich** *a* strange

befreunden (sich) *vr* make friends; **befreundet sein** be friends

befriedig|en *vt* satisfy. **b~end** *a* satisfying; (*zufriedenstellend*) satisfactory. **B~ung** *f* **-** satisfaction

befrucht|en *vt* fertilize. **B~ung** *f* **-** fertilization; **künstliche B~ung** artificial insemination

Befug|nis *f* **-,-se** authority. **b~t** *a* authorized

Befund *m* result

befürcht|en *vt* fear. **B~ung** *f* **-,-en** fear

befürworten *vt* support

begab|t *a* gifted. **B~ung** *f* **-,-en** gift, talent

begatten (sich) *vr* mate

begeben† **(sich)** *vr* go; (*liter: geschehen*) happen; **sich in Gefahr b~** expose oneself to danger. **B~heit** *f* **-,-en** incident

begegn|en *vi* (*sein*) **jdm/etw b~en** meet s.o./sth; **sich b~en** meet. **B~ung** *f* **-,-en** meeting; (*Sport*) encounter

begehen† *vt* walk along; (*verüben*) commit; (*feiern*) celebrate

begehr|en *vt* desire. **b~enswert** *a* desirable. **b~t** *a* sought-after

begeister|n *vt* **jdn b~n** arouse s.o.'s enthusiasm; **sich b~n** be enthusiastic (**für** about). **b~t** *a* enthusiastic,

adv -ally; (*eifrig*) keen. **B~ung** *f* - enthusiasm
Begier|de *f* -,-n desire. **b~ig** *a* eager (**auf** + *acc* for)
begießen† *vt* water; (*Culin*) baste; (*fam: feiern*) celebrate
Beginn *m* -s beginning; **zu B~** at the beginning. **b~en**† *vt/i* (*haben*) start, begin; (*anstellen*) do
beglaubigen *vt* authenticate
begleichen† *vt* settle
begleit|en *vt* accompany. **B~er** *m* -s,-, **B~erin** *f* -,-nen companion; (*Mus*) accompanist. **B~ung** *f* -,-en company; (*Gefolge*) entourage; (*Mus*) accompaniment
beglück|en *vt* make happy. **b~t** *a* happy. **b~wünschen** *vt* congratulate (**zu** on)
begnadig|en *vt* (*Jur*) pardon. **B~ung** *f* -,-en (*Jur*) pardon
begnügen (sich) *vr* content oneself (**mit** with)
Begonie /-i̯ə/ *f* -,-n begonia
begraben† *vt* bury
Begräbnis *n* -ses,-se burial; (*Feier*) funeral
begreif|en† *vt* understand; **nicht zu b~en** incomprehensible. **b~lich** *a* understandable; **jdm etw b~lich machen** make s.o. understand sth. **b~licherweise** *adv* understandably
begrenz|en *vt* form the boundary of; (*beschränken*) restrict. **b~t** *a* limited. **B~ung** *f* -,-en restriction; (*Grenze*) boundary
Begriff *m* -[e]s,-e concept; (*Ausdruck*) term; (*Vorstellung*) idea; **für meine B~e** to my mind; **im B~ sein** *od* **stehen** be about (**zu** to); **schwer von B~** (*fam*) slow on the uptake. **b~sstutzig** *a* obtuse
begründ|en *vt* give one's reason for; (*gründen*) establish. **b~et** *a* justified. **B~ung** *f* -,-en reason
begrüß|en *vt* greet; (*billigen*) welcome. **b~enswert** *a* welcome. **B~ung** *f* - greeting; welcome
begünstigen *vt* favour; (*fördern*) encourage
begutachten *vt* give an opinion on; (*fam: ansehen*) look at
begütert *a* wealthy
begütigen *vt* placate
behaart *a* hairy
behäbig *a* portly; (*gemütlich*) comfortable, *adv* -bly
behag|en *vi* (*haben*) please (**jdm** s.o.). **B~en** *nt* -s contentment; (*Genuß*) enjoyment. **b~lich** *a* comfortable, *adv* -bly. **B~lichkeit** *f* - comfort
behalten† *vt* keep; (*sich merken*) remember; **etw für sich b~** (*verschweigen*) keep sth to oneself
Behälter *m* -s,- container
behand|eln *vt* treat; (*sich befassen*) deal with. **B~lung** *f* treatment
beharr|en *vi* (*haben*) persist (**auf** + *dat* in). **b~lich** *a* persistent, *adv* -ly; (*hartnäckig*) dogged, *adv* -ly. **B~lichkeit** *f* - persistence
behaupt|en *vt* maintain; (*vorgeben*) claim; (*sagen*) say; (*bewahren*) retain; **sich b~en** hold one's own. **B~ung** *f* -,-en assertion; claim; (*Äußerung*) statement
beheben† *vt* remedy; (*beseitigen*) remove
behelf|en† **(sich)** *vr* make do (**mit** with). **b~smäßig** *a* makeshift ● *adv* provisionally
behelligen *vt* bother
behende *a* nimble, *adv* -bly
beherbergen *vt* put up
beherrsch|en *vt* rule over; (*dominieren*) dominate; (*meistern, zügeln*) control; (*können*) know; **sich b~en** control oneself. **b~t** *a* self-controlled. **B~ung** *f* - control; (*Selbst-*) self-control; (*Können*) mastery
beherz|igen *vt* heed. **b~t** *a* courageous, *adv* -ly
behilflich *a* **jdm b~ sein** help s.o.
behinder|n *vt* hinder; (*blockieren*) obstruct. **b~t** *a* handicapped; (*schwer*) disabled. **B~te(r)** *m/f* handicapped/disabled person. **B~ung** *f* -,-en obstruction; (*Med*) handicap; disability
Behörde *f* -,-n [public] authority
behüte|n *vt* protect; **Gott behüte!** heaven forbid! **b~t** *a* sheltered
behutsam *a* careful, *adv* -ly; (*zart*) gentle, *adv* -ly
bei *prep* (+ *dat*) near; (*dicht*) by; at ⟨*Firma, Veranstaltung*⟩; **bei der Hand nehmen** take by the hand; **bei sich haben** have with one; **bei mir** at my place; (*in meinem Fall*) in my case; **Herr X bei Meyer** Mr X c/o Meyer; **bei Regen** when/(*falls*) if it rains; **bei Feuer** in case of fire; **bei Tag/Nacht** by day/night; **bei der Ankunft** on arrival; **bei Tisch/der Arbeit** at table/work; **bei guter Gesundheit** in good health; **bei der hohen Miete** [what] with the high rent;

bei all seiner Klugheit for all his cleverness
beibehalten† *vt sep* keep
beibringen† *vt sep* **jdm etw b~** teach s.o. sth; (*mitteilen*) break sth to s.o.; (*zufügen*) inflict sth on s.o.
Beicht|e *f* **-,-n** confession. **b~en** *vt/i* (*haben*) confess. **B~stuhl** *m* confessional
beide *a & pron* both; **die b~n Brüder** the two brothers; **b~s** both; **dreißig b~** (*Tennis*) thirty all. **b~rseitig** *a* mutual. **b~rseits** *adv & prep* (+*gen*) on both sides (of)
beidrehen *vi sep* (*haben*) heave to
beieinander *adv* together
Beifahrer|(in) *m*(*f*) [front-seat] passenger; (*Lkw*) driver's mate; (*Motorrad*) pillion passenger. **B~sitz** *m* passenger seat
Beifall *m* **-[e]s** applause; (*Billigung*) approval; **B~ klatschen** applaud
beifällig *a* approving, *adv* -ly
beifügen *vt sep* add; (*beilegen*) enclose
beige /bɛ:ʒ/ *inv a* beige
beigeben† *v sep* ● *vt* add ● *vi* (*haben*) **klein b~** give in
Beigeschmack *m* [slight] taste
Beihilfe *f* financial aid; (*Studien-*) grant; (*Jur*) aiding and abetting
beikommen† *vi sep* (*sein*) **jdm b~** get the better of s.o.
Beil *nt* **-[e]s,-e** hatchet, axe
Beilage *f* supplement; (*Gemüse*) vegetable; **als B~ Reis** (*Culin*) served with rice
beiläufig *a* casual, *adv* -ly
beilegen *vt sep* enclose; (*schlichten*) settle
beileibe *adv* **b~ nicht** by no means
Beileid *nt* condolences *pl*. **B~sbrief** *m* letter of condolence
beiliegend *a* enclosed
beim *prep*=**bei dem; b~ Militär** in the army; **b~ Frühstück** at breakfast; **b~ Lesen** when reading; **b~ Lesen sein** be reading
beimessen† *vt sep* (*fig*) attach (*dat* to)
Bein *nt* **-[e]s,-e** leg; **jdm ein B~ stellen** trip s.o. up
beinah[e] *adv* nearly, almost
Beiname *m* epithet
beipflichten *vi sep* (*haben*) agree (*dat* with)
Beirat *m* advisory committee
beirren *vt* **sich nicht b~ lassen** not let oneself be put off
beisammen *adv* together. **b~sein**† *vi sep* (*sein*) be together. **B~sein** *nt* **-s** get-together
Beisein *nt* presence
beiseite *adv* aside; (*abseits*) apart; **b~ legen** put aside; (*sparen*) put by; **Spaß od Scherz b~** joking apart
beisetz|en *vt sep* bury. **B~ung** *f* **-,-en** funeral
Beispiel *nt* example; **zum B~** for example. **b~haft** *a* exemplary. **b~los** *a* unprecedented. **b~sweise** *adv* for example
beispringen† *vi sep* (*sein*) **jdm b~** come to s.o.'s aid
beiß|en† *vt & i* (*haben*) bite; (*brennen*) sting; **sich b~en** ⟨*Farben:*⟩ clash. **b~end** *a* (*fig*) biting; ⟨*Bemerkung*⟩ caustic. **B~zange** *f* pliers *pl*
Bei|stand *m* **-[e]s** help; **jdm B~stand leisten** help s.o. **b~stehen**† *vi sep* (*haben*) **jdm b~stehen** help s.o.
beisteuern *vt sep* contribute
beistimmen *vi sep* (*haben*) agree
Beistrich *m* comma
Beitrag *m* **-[e]s,⸚e** contribution; (*Mitglieds-*) subscription; (*Versicherungs-*) premium; (*Zeitungs-*) article. **b~en**† *vt/i sep* (*haben*) contribute
bei|treten† *vi sep* (*sein*) (+*dat*) join. **B~tritt** *m* joining
beiwohnen *vi sep* (*haben*) (+*dat*) be present at
Beize *f* **-,-n** (*Holz-*) stain; (*Culin*) marinade
beizeiten *adv* in good time
beizen *vt* stain ⟨*Holz*⟩
bejahen *vt* answer in the affirmative; (*billigen*) approve of
bejahrt *a* aged, old
bejubeln *vt* cheer
bekämpf|en *vt* fight. **B~ung** *f* **-** fight (*gen* against)
bekannt *a* well-known; (*vertraut*) familiar; **jdm b~ sein** be known to s.o.; **jdn b~ machen** introduce s.o. **B~e(r)** *m/f* acquaintance; (*Freund*) friend. **B~gabe** *f* announcement. **b~geben**† *vt sep* announce. **b~lich** *adv* as is well known. **b~machen** *vt sep* announce. **B~machung** *f* **-,-en** announcement; (*Anschlag*) notice. **B~schaft** *f* **-** acquaintance; (*Leute*) acquaintances *pl*; (*Freunde*) friends *pl*. **b~werden**† *vi sep* (*sein*) become known

bekehr|en *vt* convert; **sich b∼en** become converted. **B∼ung** *f* **-,-en** conversion

bekenn|en† *vt* confess; profess ⟨*Glauben*⟩; **sich [für] schuldig b∼en** admit one's guilt; **sich b∼en zu** confess to ⟨*Tat*⟩; profess ⟨*Glauben*⟩; (*stehen zu*) stand by. **B∼tnis** *nt* **-ses,-se** confession; (*Konfession*) denomination

beklag|en *vt* lament; (*bedauern*) deplore; **sich b∼en** complain. **b∼enswert** *a* unfortunate. **B∼te(r)** *m/f* (*Jur*) defendant

beklatschen *vt* applaud

bekleid|en *vt* hold ⟨*Amt*⟩. **b∼et** *a* dressed (**mit** in). **B∼ung** *f* clothing

Beklemmung *f* **-,-en** feeling of oppression

beklommen *a* uneasy; (*ängstlich*) anxious, *adv* -ly

bekommen† *vt* get; have ⟨*Baby*⟩; catch ⟨*Erkältung*⟩; **Angst/Hunger b∼** get frightened/hungry; **etw geliehen b∼** be lent sth ● *vi* (*sein*) **jdm gut b∼** do s.o. good; ⟨*Essen:*⟩ agree with s.o.

bekömmlich *a* digestible

beköstig|en *vt* feed; **sich selbst b∼en** cater for oneself. **B∼ung** *f* **-** board; (*Essen*) food

bekräftigen *vt* reaffirm; (*bestätigen*) confirm

bekreuzigen (sich) *vr* cross oneself

bekümmert *a* troubled; (*besorgt*) worried

bekunden *vt* show; (*bezeugen*) testify

belächeln *vt* laugh at

beladen† *vt* load ● *a* laden

Belag *m* **-[e]s,⸚e** coating; (*Fußboden-*) covering; (*Brot-*) topping; (*Zahn-*) tartar; (*Brems-*) lining

belager|n *vt* besiege. **B∼ung** *f* **-,-en** siege

Belang *m* **von/ohne B∼** of/of no importance; **B∼e** *pl* interests. **b∼en** *vt* (*Jur*) sue. **b∼los** *a* irrelevant; (*unwichtig*) trivial. **B∼losigkeit** *f* **-,-en** triviality

belassen† *vt* leave; **es dabei b∼** leave it at that

belasten *vt* load; (*fig*) burden; (*beanspruchen*) put a strain on; (*Comm*) debit; (*Jur*) incriminate

belästigen *vt* bother; (*bedrängen*) pester; (*unsittlich*) molest

Belastung *f* **-,-en** load; (*fig*) strain; (*Last*) burden; (*Comm*) debit. **B∼smaterial** *nt* incriminating evidence. **B∼szeuge** *m* prosecution witness

belaufen† **(sich)** *vr* amount (**auf** + *acc* to)

belauschen *vt* eavesdrop on

beleb|en *vt* (*fig*) revive; (*lebhaft machen*) enliven; **sich b∼en** revive; ⟨*Stadt:*⟩ come to life. **b∼t** *a* lively; ⟨*Straße*⟩ busy

Beleg *m* **-[e]s,-e** evidence; (*Beispiel*) instance (**für** of); (*Quittung*) receipt. **b∼en** *vt* cover/(*garnieren*) garnish (**mit** with); (*besetzen*) reserve; (*Univ*) enrol for; (*nachweisen*) provide evidence for; **den ersten Platz b∼en** (*Sport*) take first place. **B∼schaft** *f* **-,-en** work-force. **b∼t** *a* occupied; ⟨*Zunge*⟩ coated; ⟨*Stimme*⟩ husky; **b∼te Brote** open sandwiches; **der Platz ist b∼t** this seat is taken

belehren *vt* instruct; (*aufklären*) inform

beleibt *a* corpulent

beleidig|en *vt* offend; (*absichtlich*) insult. **B∼ung** *f* **-,-en** insult

belesen *a* well-read

beleucht|en *vt* light; (*anleuchten*) illuminate. **B∼ung** *f* **-,-en** illumination; (*elektrisch*) lighting; (*Licht*) light

Belg|ien /-i̯ən/ *nt* **-s** Belgium. **B∼ier(in)** *m* **-s,-** (*f* **-,-nen**) Belgian. **b∼isch** *a* Belgian

belicht|en *vt* (*Phot*) expose. **B∼ung** *f* **-** exposure

Belieb|en *nt* **-s nach B∼en** [just] as one likes; (*Culin*) if liked. **b∼ig** *a* **eine b∼ige Zahl/Farbe** any number/colour you like ● *adv* **b∼ig lange/oft** as long/often as one likes. **b∼t** *a* popular. **B∼theit** *f* **-** popularity

beliefern *vt* supply (**mit** with)

bellen *vi* (*haben*) bark

belohn|en *vt* reward. **B∼ung** *f* **-,-en** reward

belüften *vt* ventilate

belügen† *vt* lie to; **sich [selbst] b∼** deceive oneself

belustig|en *vt* amuse. **B∼ung** *f* **-,-en** amusement

bemächtigen (sich) *vr* (+ *gen*) seize

bemalen *vt* paint

bemängeln *vt* criticize

bemannt *a* manned

bemerk|bar *a* **sich b∼bar machen** attract attention; ⟨*Ding:*⟩ become noticeable. **b∼en** *vt* notice; (*äußern*) remark. **b~enswert** *a* remarkable, *adv* -bly. **B~ung** *f* **-,-en** remark

bemitleiden *vt* pity

bemittelt *a* well-to-do

bemüh|en *vt* trouble; **sich b~en** try (**zu** to; **um etw** to get sth); (*sich kümmern*) attend (**um** to); **b~t sein** endeavour (**zu** to). **B~ung** *f* **-,-en** effort; (*Mühe*) trouble

bemuttern *vt* mother

benachbart *a* neighbouring

benachrichtig|en *vt* inform; (*amtlich*) notify. **B~ung** *f* **-,-en** notification

benachteilig|en *vt* discriminate against; (*ungerecht sein*) treat unfairly. **B~ung** *f* **-,-en** discrimination (*gen* against)

benehmen† **(sich)** *vr* behave. **B~** *nt* **-s** behaviour

beneiden *vt* envy (**um etw** sth). **b~swert** *a* enviable

Bengel *m* **-s,-** boy; (*Rüpel*) lout

benommen *a* dazed

benötigen *vt* need

benutz|en, (*SGer*) **benütz|en** *vt* use; take ⟨*Bahn*⟩. **B~er** *m* **-s,-** user. **b~erfreundlich** *a* user-friendly. **B~ung** *f* use

Benzin *nt* **-s** petrol, (*Amer*) gasoline. **B~tank** *m* petrol tank

beobacht|en *vt* observe. **B~er** *m* **-s,-** observer. **B~ung** *f* **-,-en** observation

bepacken *vt* load (**mit** with)

bepflanzen *vt* plant (**mit** with)

bequem *a* comfortable, *adv* -bly; (*mühelos*) easy, *adv* -ily; (*faul*) lazy. **b~en (sich)** *vr* deign (**zu** to). **B~lichkeit** *f* **-,-en** comfort; (*Faulheit*) laziness

berat|en† *vt* advise; (*überlegen*) discuss; **sich b~en** confer; **sich b~en lassen** get advice ● *vi* (*haben*) discuss (**über etw** *acc* sth); (*beratschlagen*) confer. **B~er** *m* **-s,-**, **B~erin** *f* **-,-nen** adviser. **b~schlagen** *vi* (*haben*) confer. **B~ung** *f* **-,-en** guidance; (*Rat*) advice; (*Besprechung*) discussion; (*Med, Jur*) consultation. **B~ungsstelle** *f* advice centre

berauben *vt* rob (*gen* of)

berauschen *vt* intoxicate. **b~d** *a* intoxicating, heady

berechn|en *vt* calculate; (*anrechnen*) charge for; (*abfordern*) charge. **b~end** *a* (*fig*) calculating. **B~ung** *f* calculation

berechtig|en *vt* entitle; (*befugen*) authorize; (*fig*) justify. **b~t** *a* justified, justifiable. **B~ung** *f* **-,-en** authorization; (*Recht*) right; (*Rechtmäßigkeit*) justification

bered|en *vt* talk about; (*klatschen*) gossip about; (*überreden*) talk round; **sich b~en** talk. **B~samkeit** *f* - eloquence

beredt *a* eloquent, *adv* -ly

Bereich *m* **-[e]s,-e** area; (*fig*) realm; (*Fach-*) field

bereichern *vi* enrich; **sich b~** grow rich (**an** + *dat* on)

Bereifung *f* - tyres *pl*

bereinigen *vt* (*fig*) settle

bereit *a* ready. **b~en** *vt* prepare; (*verursachen*) cause; give ⟨*Überraschung*⟩. **b~halten**† *vt sep* have/ (*ständig*) keep ready. **b~legen** *vt sep* put out [ready]. **b~machen** *vt sep* get ready; **sich b~machen** get ready. **b~s** *adv* already

Bereitschaft *f* **-,-en** readiness; (*Einheit*) squad. **B~sdienst** *m* **B~sdienst haben** (*Mil*) be on standby; ⟨*Arzt:*⟩ be on call; ⟨*Apotheke:*⟩ be open for out-of-hours dispensing. **B~spolizei** *f* riot police

bereit|stehen† *vi sep* (*haben*) be ready. **b~stellen** *vt sep* put out ready; (*verfügbar machen*) make available. **B~ung** *f* - preparation. **b~willig** *a* willing, *adv* -ly. **B~willigkeit** *f* - willingness

bereuen *vt* regret

Berg *m* **-[e]s,-e** mountain; (*Anhöhe*) hill; **in den B~en** in the mountains. **b~ab** *adv* downhill. **b~an** *adv* uphill. **B~arbeiter** *m* miner. **b~auf** *adv* uphill; **es geht b~auf** (*fig*) things are looking up. **B~bau** *m* **-[e]s** mining

bergen† *vt* recover; (*Naut*) salvage; (*retten*) rescue

Berg|führer *m* mountain guide. **b~ig** *a* mountainous. **B~kette** *f* mountain range. **B~mann** *m* (*pl* **-leute**) miner. **B~steigen** *nt* **-s** mountaineering. **B~steiger(in)** *m* **-s,-** (*f* **-,-nen**) mountaineer, climber. **B~-und-Talbahn** *f* roller-coaster

Bergung *f* - recovery; (*Naut*) salvage; (*Rettung*) rescue

Berg|wacht *f* mountain rescue service. **B~werk** *nt* mine

Bericht *m* **-[e]s,-e** report; (*Reise-*) account; **B~ erstatten** report (**über** + *acc* on). **b~en** *vt/i* (*haben*) report;

(*erzählen*) tell (**von** of). **B~erstatter(in)** *m* **-s,-** (*f* **-,-nen**) reporter; (*Korrespondent*) correspondent
berichtig|en *vt* correct. **B~ung** *f* **-,-en** correction
beriesel|n *vt* irrigate. **B~ungsanlage** *f* sprinkler system
beritten *a* ⟨*Polizei*⟩ mounted
Berlin *nt* **-s** Berlin. **B~er** *m* **-s,-** Berliner; (*Culin*) doughnut ● *a* Berlin ...
Bernhardiner *m* **-s,-** St Bernard
Bernstein *m* amber
bersten† *vi* (*sein*) burst
berüchtigt *a* notorious
berückend *a* entrancing
berücksichtig|en *vt* take into consideration. **B~ung** *f* **-** consideration
Beruf *m* profession; (*Tätigkeit*) occupation; (*Handwerk*) trade. **b~en**† *vt* appoint; **sich b~en** refer (**auf** + *acc* to); (*vorgeben*) plead (**auf etw** *acc* sth) ● *a* competent; **b~en sein** be destined (**zu** to). **b~lich** *a* professional; ⟨*Ausbildung*⟩ vocational ● *adv* professionally; **b~lich tätig sein** work, have a job. **B~saussichten** *fpl* career prospects. **B~sberater(in)** *m*(*f*) careers officer. **B~sberatung** *f* vocational guidance. **b~smäßig** *adv* professionally. **B~sschule** *f* vocational school. **B~ssoldat** *m* regular soldier. **b~stätig** *a* working; **b~stätig sein** work, have a job. **B~stätige(r)** *m*/*f* working man/woman. **B~sverkehr** *m* rush-hour traffic. **B~ung** *f* **-,-en** appointment; (*Bestimmung*) vocation; (*Jur*) appeal; **B~ung einlegen** appeal. **B~ungsgericht** *nt* appeal court
beruhen *vi* (*haben*) be based (**auf** + *dat* on); **eine Sache auf sich b~ lassen** let a matter rest
beruhig|en *vt* calm [down]; (*zuversichtlich machen*) reassure; **sich b~en** calm down. **b~end** *a* calming; (*tröstend*) reassuring; (*Med*) sedative. **B~ung** *f* **-** calming; reassurance; (*Med*) sedation. **B~ungsmittel** *nt* sedative; (*bei Psychosen*) tranquillizer
berühmt *a* famous. **B~heit** *f* **-,-en** fame; (*Person*) celebrity
berühr|en *vt* touch; (*erwähnen*) touch on; (*beeindrucken*) affect; **sich b~en** touch. **B~ung** *f* **-,-en** touch; (*Kontakt*) contact
besag|en *vt* say; (*bedeuten*) mean. **b~t** *a* [afore]said
besänftigen *vt* soothe; **sich b~** calm down
Besatz *m* **-es,⸚e** trimming
Besatzung *f* **-,-en** crew; (*Mil*) occupying force
besaufen† **(sich)** *vr* (*sl*) get drunk
beschädig|en *vt* damage. **B~ung** *f* **-,-en** damage
beschaffen *vt* obtain, get ● *a* **so b~ sein, daß** be such that; **wie ist es b~ mit?** what about? **B~heit** *f* **-** consistency; (*Art*) nature
beschäftig|en *vt* occupy; ⟨*Arbeitgeber:*⟩ employ; **sich b~en** occupy oneself. **b~t** *a* busy; (*angestellt*) employed (**bei** at). **B~te(r)** *m*/*f* employee. **B~ung** *f* **-,-en** occupation; (*Anstellung*) employment. **b~ungslos** *a* unemployed. **B~ungstherapie** *f* occupational therapy
beschäm|en *vt* make ashamed. **b~end** *a* shameful; (*demütigend*) humiliating. **b~t** *a* ashamed; (*verlegen*) embarrassed
beschatten *vt* shade; (*überwachen*) shadow
beschau|en *vt* (*SGer*) [**sich** (*dat*)] **etw b~en** look at sth. **b~lich** *a* tranquil; (*Relig*) contemplative
Bescheid *m* **-[e]s** information; **jdm B~ sagen** *od* **geben** let s.o. know; **B~ wissen** know
bescheiden *a* modest, *adv* -ly. **B~heit** *f* **-** modesty
bescheinen† *vt* shine on; **von der Sonne beschienen** sunlit
bescheinig|en *vt* certify. **B~ung** *f* **-,-en** [written] confirmation; (*Schein*) certificate
beschenken *vt* give a present/presents to
bescher|en *vt* **jdn b~en** give s.o. presents; **jdm etw b~en** give s.o. sth. **B~ung** *f* **-,-en** distribution of Christmas presents; (*fam: Schlamassel*) mess
beschießen† *vt* fire at; (*mit Artillerie*) shell, bombard
beschildern *vt* signpost
beschimpf|en *vt* abuse, swear at. **B~ung** *f* **-,-en** abuse
beschirmen *vt* protect
Beschlag *m* **in B~ nehmen, mit B~ belegen** monopolize. **b~en**† *vt* shoe ● *vi* (*sein*) steam *or* mist up ● *a* steamed *or* misted up; (*erfahren*) knowledgeable (**in** + *dat* about).

B∼nahme *f* **-,-n** confiscation; (*Jur*) seizure. **b∼nahmen** *vt* confiscate; (*Jur*) seize; (*fam*) monopolize
beschleunig|en *vt* hasten; (*schneller machen*) speed up; quicken ⟨*Schritt, Tempo*⟩; **sich b∼en** speed up; quicken ● *vi* (*haben*) accelerate. **B∼ung** *f* **-** acceleration
beschließen† *vt* decide; (*beenden*) end ● *vi* (*haben*) decide (**über** +*acc* about)
Beschluß *m* decision
beschmieren *vt* smear/(*bestreichen*) spread (**mit** with)
beschmutzen *vt* make dirty; **sich b∼** get [oneself] dirty
beschneid|en† *vt* trim; (*Hort*) prune; (*fig: kürzen*) cut back; (*Relig*) circumcise. **B∼ung** *f* **-** circumcision
beschneit *a* snow-covered
beschnüffeln, beschnuppern *vt* sniff at
beschönigen *vt* (*fig*) gloss over
beschränken *vt* limit, restrict; **sich b∼ auf** (+*acc*) confine oneself to; ⟨*Sache:*⟩ be limited to
beschrankt *a* ⟨*Bahnübergang*⟩ with barrier[s]
beschränk|t *a* limited; (*geistig*) dull-witted; (*borniert*) narrow-minded. **B∼ung** *f* **-,-en** limitation, restriction
beschreib|en† *vt* describe; (*schreiben*) write on. **B∼ung** *f* **-,-en** description
beschuldig|en *vt* accuse. **B∼ung** *f* **-,-en** accusation
beschummeln *vt* (*fam*) cheat
Beschuß *m* **-sses** (*Mil*) fire; (*Artillerie-*) shelling
beschütz|en *vt* protect. **B∼er** *m* **-s,-** protector
Beschwer|de *f* **-,-n** complaint; **B∼den** (*Med*) trouble *sg*. **b∼en** *vt* weight down; **sich b∼en** complain. **b∼lich** *a* difficult
beschwichtigen *vt* placate
beschwindeln *vt* cheat (**um** out of); (*belügen*) lie to
beschwingt *a* elated; (*munter*) lively
beschwipst *a* (*fam*) tipsy
beschwören† *vt* swear to; (*anflehen*) implore; (*herauf-*) invoke
besehen† *vt* look at
beseitig|en *vt* remove. **B∼ung** *f* **-** removal
Besen *m* **-s,-** broom. **B∼ginster** *m* (*Bot*) broom. **B∼stiel** *m* broomstick
besessen *a* obsessed (**von** by)
besetz|en *vt* occupy; fill ⟨*Posten*⟩; (*Theat*) cast ⟨*Rolle*⟩; (*verzieren*) trim (**mit** with). **b∼t** *a* occupied; ⟨*Toilette, Leitung*⟩ engaged; ⟨*Zug, Bus*⟩ full up; **der Platz ist b∼t** this seat is taken; **mit Perlen b∼t** set with pearls. **B∼tzeichen** *nt* engaged tone. **B∼ung** *f* **-,-en** occupation; (*Theat*) cast
besichtig|en *vt* look round ⟨*Stadt, Museum*⟩; (*prüfen*) inspect; (*besuchen*) visit. **B∼ung** *f* **-,-en** visit; (*Prüfung*) inspection; (*Stadt-*) sightseeing
besiedelt *a* **dünn/dicht b∼** sparsely/densely populated
besiegeln *vt* (*fig*) seal
besieg|en *vt* defeat; (*fig*) overcome. **B∼te(r)** *m/f* loser
besinn|en† **(sich)** *vr* think, reflect; (*sich erinnern*) remember (**auf jdn/etw** s.o./sth); **sich anders b∼en** change one's mind. **b∼lich** *a* contemplative; (*nachdenklich*) thoughtful. **B∼ung** *f* **-** reflection; (*Bewußtsein*) consciousness; **bei/ohne B∼ung** conscious/unconscious; **zur B∼ung kommen** regain consciousness; (*fig*) come to one's senses. **b∼ungslos** *a* unconscious
Besitz *m* possession; (*Eigentum, Land-*) property; (*Gut*) estate. **b∼anzeigend** *a* (*Gram*) possessive. **b∼en**† *vt* own, possess; (*haben*) have. **B∼er(in)** *m* **-s,-** (*f* **-,-nen**) owner; (*Comm*) proprietor. **B∼ung** *f* **-,-en** [landed] property; (*Gut*) estate
besoffen *a* (*sl*) drunken; **b∼ sein** be drunk
besohlen *vt* sole
besold|en *vt* pay. **B∼ung** *f* **-** pay
besonder|e(r,s) *a* special; (*bestimmt*) particular; (*gesondert*) separate; **nichts B∼es** nothing special. **B∼heit** *f* **-,-en** peculiarity. **b∼s** *adv* [e]specially, particularly; (*gesondert*) separately
besonnen *a* calm, *adv* -ly
besorg|en *vt* get; (*kaufen*) buy; (*erledigen*) attend to; (*versorgen*) look after. **B∼nis** *f* **-,-se** anxiety; (*Sorge*) worry. **b∼niserregend** *a* worrying. **b∼t** *a* worried/(*bedacht*) concerned (**um** about). **B∼ung** *f* **-,-en** errand; **B∼ungen machen** do shopping
bespielt *a* recorded
bespitzeln *vt* spy on
besprech|en† *vt* discuss; (*rezensieren*) review; **sich b∼en** confer;

ein Tonband b~en make a tape recording. **B~ung** *f* **-,-en** discussion; review; (*Konferenz*) meeting

bespritzen *vt* splash

besser *a & adv* better. **b~n** *vt* improve; **sich b~n** get better, improve. **B~ung** *f* **-** improvement; **gute B~ung!** get well soon! **B~wisser** *m* **-s,-** know-all

Bestand *m* **-[e]s,¨e** existence; (*Vorrat*) stock (**an** + *dat* of); **B~ haben, von B~ sein** last

beständig *a* constant, *adv* -ly; ⟨*Wetter*⟩ settled; **b~ gegen** resistant to

Bestand|saufnahme *f* stock-taking. **B~teil** *m* part

bestärken *vt* (*fig*) strengthen

bestätig|en *vt* confirm; acknowledge ⟨*Empfang*⟩; **sich b~en** prove to be true. **B~ung** *f* **-,-en** confirmation

bestatt|en *vt* bury. **B~ung** *f* **-,-en** funeral. **B~ungsinstitut** *nt* [firm of] undertakers *pl*, (*Amer*) funeral home

bestäuben *vt* pollinate

bestaubt *a* dusty

Bestäubung *f* **-** pollination

bestaunen *vt* gaze at in amazement; (*bewundern*) admire

best|e(r,s) *a* best; **b~en Dank!** many thanks! **am b~en sein** be best; **zum b~en geben** recite ⟨*Gedicht*⟩; tell ⟨*Geschichte, Witz*⟩; sing ⟨*Lied*⟩; **jdn zum b~en halten** (*fam*) pull s.o.'s leg. **B~e(r,s)** *m/f/nt* best; **sein B~es tun** do one's best; **zum B~en der Armen** for the benefit of the poor

bestech|en† *vt* bribe; (*bezaubern*) captivate. **b~end** *a* captivating. **b~lich** *a* corruptible. **B~ung** *f* **-** bribery. **B~ungsgeld** *nt* bribe

Besteck *nt* **-[e]s,-e** [set of] knife, fork and spoon; (*coll*) cutlery

bestehen† *vi* (*haben*) exist; (*fortdauern*) last; (*bei Prüfung*) pass; **b~ aus** consist/(*gemacht sein*) be made of; **b~ auf** (+*dat*) insist on ● *vt* pass ⟨*Prüfung*⟩. **B~** *nt* **-s** existence

bestehlen† *vt* rob

besteig|en† *vt* climb; (*einsteigen*) board; (*aufsteigen*) mount; ascend ⟨*Thron*⟩. **B~ung** *f* ascent

bestell|en *vt* order; (*vor-*) book; (*ernennen*) appoint; (*bebauen*) cultivate; (*ausrichten*) tell; **zu sich b~en** send for; **b~t sein** have an appointment; **kann ich etwas b~en?** can I take a message? **b~en Sie Ihrer Frau Grüße von mir** give my regards to your wife. **B~schein** *m* order form. **B~ung** *f* order; (*Botschaft*) message; (*Bebauung*) cultivation

besten|falls *adv* at best. **b~s** *adv* very well

besteuer|n *vt* tax. **B~ung** *f* **-** taxation

bestialisch /-st-/ *a* bestial

Bestie /ˈbɛsti̯ə/ *f* **-,-n** beast

bestimm|en *vt* fix; (*entscheiden*) decide; (*vorsehen*) intend; (*ernennen*) appoint; (*ermitteln*) determine; (*definieren*) define; (*Gram*) qualify ● *vi* (*haben*) be in charge (**über** + *acc* of). **b~t** *a* definite, *adv* -ly; (*gewiß*) certain, *adv* -ly; (*fest*) firm, *adv* -ly. **B~theit** *f* **-** firmness; **mit B~theit** for certain. **B~ung** *f* fixing; (*Vorschrift*) regulation; (*Ermittlung*) determination; (*Definition*) definition; (*Zweck*) purpose; (*Schicksal*) destiny. **B~ungsort** *m* destination

Bestleistung *f* (*Sport*) record

bestraf|en *vt* punish. **B~ung** *f* **-,-en** punishment

bestrahl|en *vt* shine on; (*Med*) treat with radiotherapy; irradiate ⟨*Lebensmittel*⟩. **B~ung** *f* radiotherapy

Bestreb|en *nt* **-s** endeavour; (*Absicht*) aim. **b~t** *a* **b~t sein** endeavour (**zu** to). **B~ung** *f* **-,-en** effort

bestreichen† *vt* spread (**mit** with)

bestreikt *a* strike-hit

bestreiten† *vt* dispute; (*leugnen*) deny; (*bezahlen*) pay for

bestreuen *vt* sprinkle (**mit** with)

bestürmen *vt* (*fig*) besiege

bestürz|t *a* dismayed; (*erschüttert*) stunned. **B~ung** *f* **-** dismay, consternation

Bestzeit *f* (*Sport*) record [time]

Besuch *m* **-[e]s,-e** visit; (*kurz*) call; (*Schul-*) attendance; (*Gast*) visitor; (*Gäste*) visitors *pl*; **B~ haben** have a visitor/visitors; **bei jdm zu** *od* **auf B~ sein** be staying with s.o. **b~en** *vt* visit; (*kurz*) call on; (*teilnehmen*) attend; go to ⟨*Schule, Ausstellung*⟩; **gut b~t** well attended. **B~er(in)** *m* **-s,-** (*f* **-,-nen**) visitor; caller; (*Theat*) patron. **B~szeit** *f* visiting hours *pl*

betagt *a* aged, old

betasten *vt* feel

betätig|en *vt* operate; **sich b~en** work (**als** as); **sich politisch b~en** engage in politics. **B~ung** *f* **-,-en** operation; (*Tätigkeit*) activity

betäub|en *vt* stun; ⟨*Lärm:*⟩ deafen; (*Med*) anaesthetize; (*lindern*) ease; deaden ⟨*Schmerz*⟩; **wie b~t** dazed.

B~ung *f* - daze; (*Med*) anaesthesia; **unter örtlicher B~ung** under local anaesthetic. **B~ungsmittel** *nt* anaesthetic

Bete *f* **-,-n rote B~** beetroot

beteilig|en *vt* give a share to; **sich b~en** take part (**an** + *dat* in); (*beitragen*) contribute (**an** + *dat* to). **b~t** *a* **b~t sein** take part/(*an Unfall*) be involved/(*Comm*) have a share (**an** + *dat* in); **alle B~ten** all those involved. **B~ung** *f* **-,-en** participation; involvement; (*Anteil*) share

beten *vi* (*haben*) pray; (*bei Tisch*) say grace ● *vt* say

beteuer|n *vt* protest. **B~ung** *f* **-,-en** protestation

Beton /be'tɔŋ/ *m* **-s** concrete

betonen *vt* stress, emphasize

betonieren *vt* concrete

beton|t *a* stressed; (*fig*) pointed, *adv* -ly. **B~ung** *f* **-,-en** stress, emphasis

betören *vt* bewitch

betr., Betr. *abbr* (**betreffs**) re

Betracht *m* **in B~ ziehen** consider; **außer B~ lassen** disregard; **nicht in B~ kommen** be out of the question. **b~en** *vt* look at; (*fig*) regard (**als** as)

beträchtlich *a* considerable, *adv* -bly

Betrachtung *f* **-,-en** contemplation; (*Überlegung*) reflection

Betrag *m* **-[e]s,¨-e** amount. **b~en†** *vt* amount to; **sich b~en** behave. **B~en** *nt* **-s** behaviour; (*Sch*) conduct

betrauen *vt* entrust (**mit** with)

betrauern *vt* mourn

betreff|en† *vt* affect; (*angehen*) concern; **was mich betrifft** as far as I am concerned. **b~end** *a* relevant; **der b~ende Brief** the letter in question. **b~s** *prep* (+ *gen*) concerning

betreiben† *vt* (*leiten*) run; (*ausüben*) carry on; (*vorantreiben*) pursue; (*antreiben*) run (**mit** on)

betreten† *vt* step on; (*eintreten*) enter; **'B~ verboten'** 'no entry'; (*bei Rasen*) 'keep off [the grass]' ● *a* embarrassed ● *adv* in embarrassment

betreu|en *vt* look after. **B~er(in)** *m* **-s,-** (*f* **-,-nen**) helper; (*Kranken-*) nurse. **B~ung** *f* - care

Betrieb *m* business; (*Firma*) firm; (*Treiben*) activity; (*Verkehr*) traffic; **in B~** working; (*in Gebrauch*) in use; **außer B~** not in use; (*defekt*) out of order

Betriebs|anleitung, B~anweisung *f* operating instructions *pl*. **B~ferien** *pl* firm's holiday; **'B~ferien'** 'closed for the holidays'. **B~leitung** *f* management. **B~rat** *m* works committee. **B~ruhe** *f* **'montags B~ruhe'** 'closed on Mondays'. **B~störung** *f* breakdown

betrinken† (sich) *vr* get drunk

betroffen *a* disconcerted; **b~ sein** be affected (**von** by); **die B~en** those affected ● *adv* in consternation

betrüb|en *vt* sadden. **b~lich** *a* sad. **b~t** *a* sad, *adv* -ly

Betrug *m* **-[e]s** deception; (*Jur*) fraud

betrüg|en† *vt* cheat, swindle; (*Jur*) defraud; (*in der Ehe*) be unfaithful to; **sich selbst b~en** deceive oneself. **B~er(in)** *m* **-s,-** (*f* **-,-nen**) swindler. **B~erei** *f* **-,-en** fraud. **b~erisch** *a* fraudulent; ⟨*Person*⟩ deceitful

betrunken *a* drunken; **b~ sein** be drunk. **B~e(r)** *m* drunk

Bett *nt* **-[e]s,-en** bed; **im B~** in bed; **ins** *od* **zu B~ gehen** go to bed. **B~couch** *f* sofa-bed. **B~decke** *f* blanket; (*Tages-*) bedspread

bettel|arm *a* destitute. **B~ei** *f* - begging. **b~n** *vi* (*haben*) beg

bett|en *vt* lay, put; **sich b~en** lie down. **b~lägerig** *a* bedridden. **B~laken** *nt* sheet

Bettler(in) *m* **-s,-** (*f* **-,-nen**) beggar

Bettpfanne *f* bedpan

Bettuch *nt* sheet

Bett|vorleger *m* bedside rug. **B~wäsche** *f* bed linen. **B~zeug** *nt* bedding

betupfen *vt* dab (**mit** with)

beug|en *vt* bend; (*Gram*) decline; conjugate ⟨*Verb*⟩; **sich b~en** bend; (*lehnen*) lean; (*sich fügen*) submit (*dat* to). **B~ung** *f* **-,-en** (*Gram*) declension; conjugation

Beule *f* **-,-n** bump; (*Delle*) dent

beunruhig|en *vt* worry; **sich b~en** worry. **B~ung** *f* - worry

beurlauben *vt* give leave to; (*des Dienstes entheben*) suspend

beurteil|en *vt* judge. **B~ung** *f* **-,-en** judgement; (*Ansicht*) opinion

Beute *f* - booty, haul; (*Jagd-*) bag; (*B~tier*) quarry; (*eines Raubtiers*) prey

Beutel *m* **-s,-** bag; (*Geld-*) purse; (*Tabak-* & *Zool*) pouch. **B~tier** *nt* marsupial

bevölker|n *vt* populate. **B~ung** *f* **-,-en** population

bevollmächtig|en *vt* authorize. **B~te(r)** *m*/*f* [authorized] agent

bevor *conj* before; **b~ nicht** until
bevormunden *vt* treat like a child
bevorstehen† *vi sep* (*haben*) approach; (*unmittelbar*) be imminent; **jdm b~** be in store for s.o. **b~d** *a* approaching, forthcoming; **unmittelbar b~d** imminent
bevorzug|en *vt* prefer; (*begünstigen*) favour. **b~t** *a* privileged; ⟨*Behandlung*⟩ preferential; (*beliebt*) favoured
bewachen *vt* guard; **bewachter Parkplatz** car park with an attendant
bewachsen *a* covered (**mit** with)
Bewachung *f* - guard; **unter B~** under guard
bewaffn|en *vt* arm. **b~et** *a* armed. **B~ung** *f* - armament; (*Waffen*) arms *pl*
bewahren *vt* protect (**vor** + *dat* from); (*behalten*) keep; **die Ruhe b~** keep calm; **Gott bewahre!** heaven forbid!
bewähren (sich) *vr* prove one's/⟨*Ding:*⟩ its worth; (*erfolgreich sein*) prove a success
bewahrheiten (sich) *vr* prove to be true
bewähr|t *a* reliable; (*erprobt*) proven. **B~ung** *f* - (*Jur*) probation. **B~ungsfrist** *f* [period of] probation. **B~ungsprobe** *f* (*fig*) test
bewaldet *a* wooded
bewältigen *vt* cope with; (*überwinden*) overcome; (*schaffen*) manage
bewandert *a* knowledgeable
bewässer|n *vt* irrigate. **B~ung** *f* - irrigation
bewegen[1] *vt* (*reg*) move; **sich b~** move; (*körperlich*) take exercise
bewegen[2]† *vt* **jdn dazu b~, etw zu tun** induce s.o. to do sth
Beweg|grund *m* motive. **b~lich** *a* movable, mobile; (*wendig*) agile. **B~lichkeit** *f* - mobility; agility. **b~t** *a* moved; (*ereignisreich*) eventful; ⟨*See*⟩ rough. **B~ung** *f* -,-**en** movement; (*Phys*) motion; (*Rührung*) emotion; (*Gruppe*) movement; **körperliche B~ung** physical exercise; **sich in B~ung setzen** [start to] move. **B~ungsfreiheit** *f* freedom of movement/(*fig*) of action. **b~ungslos** *a* motionless
beweinen *vt* mourn
Beweis *m* -**es,-e** proof; (*Zeichen*) token; **B~e** evidence *sg*. **b~en**† *vt* prove; (*zeigen*) show; **sich b~en** prove oneself/⟨*Ding:*⟩ itself. **B~material** *nt* evidence
bewenden *vi* **es dabei b~ lassen** leave it at that
bewerb|en† **(sich)** *vr* apply (**um** for; **bei** to). **B~er(in)** *m* -**s,-** (*f* -,-**nen**) applicant. **B~ung** *f* -,-**en** application
bewerkstelligen *vt* manage
bewerten *vt* value; (*einschätzen*) rate; (*Sch*) mark, grade
bewilligen *vt* grant
bewirken *vt* cause; (*herbeiführen*) bring about; (*erreichen*) achieve
bewirt|en *vt* entertain. **B~ung** *f* - hospitality
bewohn|bar *a* habitable. **b~en** *vt* inhabit, live in. **B~er(in)** *m* -**s,-** (*f* -,-**nen**) resident, occupant; (*Einwohner*) inhabitant
bewölk|en (sich) *vr* cloud over; **b~t** cloudy. **B~ung** *f* - clouds *pl*
bewunder|n *vt* admire. **b~nswert** *a* admirable. **B~ung** *f* - admiration
bewußt *a* conscious (*gen* of); (*absichtlich*) deliberate, *adv* -ly; (*besagt*) said; **sich** (*dat*) **etw** (*gen*) **b~ sein/werden** be/become aware of sth. **b~los** *a* unconscious. **B~losigkeit** *f* - unconsciousness. **B~sein** *n* -**s** consciousness; (*Gewißheit*) awareness; **bei [vollem] B~sein** [fully] conscious; **mir kam zum B~sein** I realized (**daß** that)
bez. *abbr* (**bezahlt**) paid; (**bezüglich**) re
bezahl|en *vt/i* (*haben*) pay; pay for ⟨*Ware, Essen*⟩; **sich b~t machen** (*fig*) pay off. **B~ung** *f* - payment; (*Lohn*) pay
bezähmen *vt* control; (*zügeln*) restrain; **sich b~** restrain oneself
bezaubern *vt* enchant. **b~d** *a* enchanting
bezeichn|en *vt* mark; (*bedeuten*) denote; (*beschreiben, nennen*) describe (**als** as). **b~end** *a* typical. **B~ung** *f* marking; (*Beschreibung*) description (**als** as); (*Ausdruck*) term; (*Name*) name
bezeugen *vt* testify to
bezichtigen *vt* accuse (*gen* of)
bezieh|en† *vt* cover; (*einziehen*) move into; (*beschaffen*) obtain; (*erhalten*) get, receive; take ⟨*Zeitung*⟩; (*in Verbindung bringen*) relate (**auf** + *acc* to); **sich b~en** (*bewölken*) cloud over; **sich b~en auf** (+ *acc*) refer to; **das Bett frisch b~en** put clean sheets on the bed. **B~ung** *f*

-,-en relation; (*Verhältnis*) relationship; (*Bezug*) respect; **in dieser B~ung** in this respect; **[gute] B~ungen haben** have [good] connections. **b~ungsweise** *adv* respectively; (*vielmehr*) or rather

beziffern (sich) *vr* amount (**auf** + *acc* to)

Bezirk *m* **-[e]s,-e** district

Bezug *m* cover; (*Kissen-*) case; (*Beschaffung*) obtaining; (*Kauf*) purchase; (*Zusammenhang*) reference; **B~e** *pl* earnings; **B~ nehmen** refer (**auf** + *acc* to); **in b~ auf** (+ *acc*) regarding, concerning

bezüglich *prep* (+ *gen*) regarding, concerning ● *a* relating (**auf** + *acc* to); (*Gram*) relative

bezwecken *vt* (*fig*) aim at

bezweifeln *vt* doubt

bezwingen† *vt* conquer

BH /beːˈhaː/ *m* **-[s],-[s]** bra

bibbern *vi* (*haben*) tremble; (*vor Kälte*) shiver

Bibel *f* **-,-n** Bible

Biber[1] *m* **-s,-** beaver

Biber[2] *m* & *nt* **-s** flannelette

Biblio|graphie *f* **-,-n** bibliography. **B~thek** *f* **-,-en** library. **B~thekar(in)** *m* **-s,-** (*f* **-,-nen**) librarian

biblisch *a* biblical

bieder *a* honest, upright; (*ehrenwert*) worthy; (*einfach*) simple

bieg|en† *vt* bend; **sich b~en** bend; **sich vor Lachen b~en** (*fam*) double up with laughter ● *vi* (*sein*) curve (**nach** to); **um die Ecke b~en** turn the corner. **b~sam** *a* flexible, supple. **B~ung** *f* **-,-en** bend

Biene *f* **-,-n** bee. **B~nhonig** *m* natural honey. **B~nstock** *m* beehive. **B~nwabe** *f* honeycomb

Bier *nt* **-s,-e** beer. **B~deckel** *m* beer-mat. **B~krug** *m* beer-mug

Biest *nt* **-[e]s,-er** (*fam*) beast

bieten† *vt* offer; (*bei Auktion*) bid; (*zeigen*) present; **das lasse ich mir nicht b~** I won't stand for that

Bifokalbrille *f* bifocals *pl*

Biga|mie *f* **-** bigamy. **B~mist** *m* **-en,-en** bigamist

bigott *a* over-pious

Bikini *m* **-s,-s** bikini

Bilanz *f* **-,-en** balance sheet; (*fig*) result; **die B~ ziehen** (*fig*) draw conclusions (**aus** from)

Bild *nt* **-[e]s,-er** picture; (*Theat*) scene; **jdn ins B~ setzen** put s.o. in the picture

bilden *vt* form; (*sein*) be; (*erziehen*) educate; **sich b~** form; (*geistig*) educate oneself

Bild|erbuch *nt* picture-book. **B~ergalerie** *f* picture gallery. **B~fläche** *f* screen; **von der B~fläche verschwinden** disappear from the scene. **B~hauer** *m* **-s,-** sculptor. **B~hauerei** *f* **-** sculpture. **b~hübsch** *a* very pretty. **b~lich** *a* pictorial; (*figurativ*) figurative, *adv* -ly. **B~nis** *nt* **-ses,-se** portrait. **B~schirm** *m* (*TV*) screen. **B~schirmgerät** *nt* visual display unit, VDU. **b~schön** *a* very beautiful

Bildung *f* **-** formation; (*Erziehung*) education; (*Kultur*) culture

Billard /ˈbɪljart/ *nt* **-s** billiards *sg*. **B~tisch** *m* billiard table

Billett /bɪlˈjɛt/ *nt* **-[e]s,-e** & **-s** ticket

Billiarde *f* **-,-n** thousand million million

billig *a* cheap, *adv* -ly; (*dürftig*) poor; (*gerecht*) just; **recht und b~** right and proper. **b~en** *vt* approve. **B~ung** *f* **-** approval

Billion /bɪˈli̯oːn/ *f* **-,-en** million million, billion

bimmeln *vi* (*haben*) tinkle

Bimsstein *m* pumice stone

bin *s.* **sein; ich bin** I am

Binde *f* **-,-n** band; (*Verband*) bandage; (*Damen-*) sanitary towel. **B~hautentzündung** *f* conjunctivitis. **b~n**† *vt* tie (**an** + *acc* to); make ‹*Strauß*›; bind ‹*Buch*›; (*fesseln*) tie up; (*Culin*) thicken; **sich b~n** commit oneself. **b~nd** *a* (*fig*) binding. **B~strich** *m* hyphen. **B~wort** *nt* (*pl* **-wörter**) (*Gram*) conjunction

Bind|faden *m* string; **ein B~faden** a piece of string. **B~ung** *f* **-,-en** (*fig*) tie, bond; (*Beziehung*) relationship; (*Verpflichtung*) commitment; (*Ski-*) binding; (*Tex*) weave

binnen *prep* (+ *dat*) within; **b~ kurzem** shortly. **B~handel** *m* home trade

Binse *f* **-,-n** (*Bot*) rush. **B~nwahrheit, B~nweisheit** *f* truism

Bio- *pref* organic

Bio|chemie *f* biochemistry. **b~dynamisch** *m* organic

Bio|graphie *f* **-,-n** biography

Bio|hof *m* organic farm. **B~laden** *m* health-food store

Biolog|e *m* **-n,-n** biologist. **B~ie** *f* **-** biology. **b~isch** *a* biological, *adv* -ly;

b~ischer Anbau organic farming; **b~isch angebaut** organically grown
Birke *f* **-,-n** birch [tree]
Birm|a *nt* **-s** Burma. **b~anisch** *a* Burmese
Birn|baum *m* pear-tree. **B~e** *f* **-,-n** pear; (*Electr*) bulb
bis *prep* (+*acc*) as far as, [up] to; (*zeitlich*) until, till; (*spätestens*) by; **bis zu** up to; **bis jetzt** up to now, so far; **bis dahin** until/(*spätestens*) by then; **bis auf** (+*acc*) (*einschließlich*) [down] to; (*ausgenommen*) except [for]; **drei bis vier Mark** three to four marks; **bis morgen!** see you tomorrow! ● *conj* until
Bischof *m* **-s,¨-e** bishop
bisher *adv* so far, up to now. **b~ig** *attrib a* ⟨*Präsident*⟩ outgoing; **meine b~igen Erfahrungen** my experiences so far
Biskuit|rolle /bɪs'kvi:t-/ *f* Swiss roll. **B~teig** *m* sponge mixture
bislang *adv* so far, up to now
Biß *m* **-sses,-sse** bite
bißchen *inv pron* **ein b~** a bit, a little; **ein b~ Brot** a bit of bread; **kein b~** not a bit
Biss|en *m* **-s,-** bite, mouthful. **b~ig** *a* vicious; (*fig*) caustic
bist *s.* **sein; du b~** you are
Bistum *nt* **-s,¨-er** diocese, see
bisweilen *adv* from time to time
bitt|e *adv* please; (*nach Klopfen*) come in; (*als Antwort auf 'danke'*) don't mention it, you're welcome; **wie b~e?** pardon? (*empört*) I beg your pardon? **möchten Sie Kaffee?—Ja b~e** would you like some coffee?—yes please. **B~e** *f* **-,-n** request/(*dringend*) plea (**um** for). **b~en**† *vt/i* (*haben*) ask/(*dringend*) beg (**um** for); (*einladen*) invite, ask; **ich b~e dich!** I beg [of] you! (*empört*) I ask you! **b~end** *a* pleading, *adv* -ly
bitter *a* bitter, *adv* -ly. **B~keit** *f* - bitterness. **b~lich** *adv* bitterly
Bittschrift *f* petition
bizarr *a* bizarre, *adv* -ly
bläh|en *vt* swell; puff out ⟨*Vorhang*⟩; **sich b~en** swell; ⟨*Vorhang, Segel:*⟩ billow ● *vi* (*haben*) cause flatulence. **B~ungen** *fpl* flatulence *sg*, (*fam*) wind *sg*
Blamage /bla'ma:ʒə/ *f* **-,-n** humiliation; (*Schande*) disgrace
blamieren *vt* disgrace; **sich b~** disgrace oneself; (*sich lächerlich machen*) make a fool of oneself

blanchieren /blã'ʃi:rən/ *vt* (*Culin*) blanch
blank *a* shiny; (*nackt*) bare; **b~ sein** (*fam*) be broke. **B~oscheck** *m* blank cheque
Blase *f* **-,-n** bubble; (*Med*) blister; (*Anat*) bladder. **B~balg** *m* **-[e]s,¨-e** bellows *pl*. **b~n**† *vt/i* (*haben*) blow; play ⟨*Flöte*⟩. **B~nentzündung** *f* cystitis
Bläser *m* **-s,-** (*Mus*) wind player; **die B~** the wind section *sg*
blasiert *a* blasé
Blas|instrument *nt* wind instrument. **B~kapelle** *f* brass band
Blasphemie *f* - blasphemy
blaß *a* (**blasser, blassest**) pale; (*schwach*) faint; **b~ werden** turn pale
Blässe *f* - pallor
Blatt *nt* **-[e]s,¨-er** (*Bot*) leaf; (*Papier*) sheet; (*Zeitung*) paper; **kein B~ vor den Mund nehmen** (*fig*) not mince one's words
blätter|n *vi* (*haben*) **b~n in** (+*dat*) leaf through. **B~teig** *m* puff pastry
Blattlaus *f* greenfly
blau *a*, **B~** *nt* **-s,-** blue; **b~er Fleck** bruise; **b~es Auge** black eye; **b~ sein** (*fam*) be tight; **Fahrt ins B~e** mystery tour. **B~beere** *f* bilberry. **B~licht** *nt* blue flashing light. **b~machen** *vi sep* (*haben*) (*fam*) skive off work
Blech *nt* **-[e]s,-e** sheet metal; (*Weiß-*) tin; (*Platte*) metal sheet; (*Back-*) baking sheet; (*Mus*) brass; (*fam: Unsinn*) rubbish. **b~en** *vt/i* (*haben*) (*fam*) pay. **B~[blas]instrument** *nt* brass instrument. **B~schaden** *m* (*Auto*) damage to the bodywork
Blei *nt* **-[e]s** lead
Bleibe *f* - place to stay. **b~n**† *vi* (*sein*) remain, stay; (*übrig-*) be left; **ruhig b~n** keep calm; **bei etw b~n** (*fig*) stick to sth; **b~n Sie am Apparat** hold the line. **b~nd** *a* permanent; (*anhaltend*) lasting. **b~nlassen**† *vt sep* **etw b~nlassen** not do sth; (*aufhören*) stop doing sth
bleich *a* pale. **b~en**† *vi* (*sein*) bleach; (*ver-*) fade ● *vt* (*reg*) bleach. **B~mittel** *nt* bleach
blei|ern *a* leaden. **b~frei** *a* unleaded. **B~stift** *m* pencil. **B~stiftabsatz** *m* stiletto heel. **B~stiftspitzer** *m* **-s,-** pencil-sharpener

Blende *f* **-,-n** shade, shield; (*Sonnen-*) [sun] visor; (*Phot*) diaphragm; (*Öffnung*) aperture; (*an Kleid*) facing. **b~n** *vt* dazzle, blind. **b~nd** *a* (*fig*) dazzling; (*prima*) marvellous, *adv* -ly

Blick *m* **-[e]s,-e** look; (*kurz*) glance; (*Aussicht*) view; **auf den ersten B~** at first sight; **einen B~ für etw haben** (*fig*) have an eye for sth. **b~en** *vi* (*haben*) look/(*kurz*) glance (**auf** + *acc* at). **B~punkt** *m* (*fig*) point of view

blind *a* blind; (*trübe*) dull; **b~er Alarm** false alarm; **b~er Passagier** stowaway. **B~darm** *m* appendix. **B~darmentzündung** *f* appendicitis. **B~e(r)** *m/f* blind man/woman; **die B~en** the blind *pl*. **B~enhund** *m* guide-dog. **B~enschrift** *f* braille. **B~gänger** *m* **-s,-** (*Mil*) dud. **B~heit** *f* - blindness. **b~lings** *adv* (*fig*) blindly

blink|en *vi* (*haben*) flash; (*funkeln*) gleam; (*Auto*) indicate. **B~er** *m* **-s,-** (*Auto*) indicator. **B~licht** *nt* flashing light

blinzeln *vi* (*haben*) blink

Blitz *m* **-es,-e** [flash of] lightning; (*Phot*) flash; **ein B~ aus heiterem Himmel** (*fig*) a bolt from the blue. **B~ableiter** *m* lightning-conductor. **b~artig** *a* lightning ... • *adv* like lightning. **B~birne** *f* flashbulb. **b~en** *vi* (*haben*) flash; (*funkeln*) sparkle; **es hat geblitzt** there was a flash of lightning. **B~gerät** *nt* flash [unit]. **B~licht** *nt* (*Phot*) flash. **b~sauber** *a* spick and span. **b~schnell** *a* lightning ... • *adv* like lightning. **B~strahl** *m* flash of lightning

Block *m* **-[e]s,¨e** block • **-[e]s,-s** & **¨e** (*Schreib-*) [note-]pad; (*Häuser-*) block; (*Pol*) bloc

Blockade *f* **-,-n** blockade

Blockflöte *f* recorder

blockieren *vt* block; (*Mil*) blockade

Blockschrift *f* block letters *pl*

blöd[e] *a* feeble-minded; (*dumm*) stupid, *adv* -ly

Blödsinn *m* **-[e]s** idiocy; (*Unsinn*) nonsense. **b~ig** *a* feeble-minded; (*verrückt*) idiotic

blöken *vi* (*haben*) bleat

blond *a* fair-haired; ⟨*Haar*⟩ fair. **B~ine** *f* **-,-n** blonde

bloß *a* bare; (*alleinig*) mere; **mit b~em Auge** with the naked eye • *adv* only, just; **was mache ich b~?** whatever shall I do?

Blöße *f* **-,-n** nakedness; **sich** (*dat*) **eine B~ geben** (*fig*) show a weakness

bloß|legen *vt sep* uncover; **b~stellen** *vt sep* compromise; **sich b~stellen** show oneself up

Bluff *m* **-s,-s** bluff. **b~en** *vt/i* (*haben*) bluff

blühen *vi* (*haben*) flower; (*fig*) flourish. **b~d** *a* flowering; (*fig*) flourishing, thriving; ⟨*Phantasie*⟩ fertile

Blume *f* **-,-n** flower; (*vom Wein*) bouquet. **B~nbeet** *n* flower-bed. **B~ngeschäft** *nt* flower-shop, florist's [shop]. **B~nkohl** *m* cauliflower. **B~nmuster** *nt* floral design. **B~nstrauß** *m* bunch of flowers. **B~ntopf** *m* flowerpot; (*Pflanze*) [flowering] pot plant. **B~nzwiebel** *f* bulb

blumig *a* (*fig*) flowery

Bluse *f* **-,-n** blouse

Blut *nt* **-[e]s** blood. **b~arm** *a* anaemic. **B~bahn** *f* bloodstream. **b~befleckt** *a* blood-stained. **B~bild** *nt* blood count. **B~buche** *f* copper beech. **B~druck** *m* blood pressure. **b~dürstig** *a* bloodthirsty

Blüte *f* **-,-n** flower, bloom; (*vom Baum*) blossom; (*B~zeit*) flowering period; (*Baum-*) blossom time; (*fig*) flowering; (*Höhepunkt*) peak, prime; (*fam: Banknote*) forged note, (*fam*) dud

Blut|egel *m* **-s,-** leech. **b~en** *vi* (*haben*) bleed

Blüten|blatt *nt* petal. **B~staub** *m* pollen

Blut|er *m* **-s,-** haemophiliac. **B~erguß** *m* bruise. **B~gefäß** *nt* blood-vessel. **B~gruppe** *f* blood group. **B~hund** *m* bloodhound. **b~ig** *a* bloody. **b~jung** *a* very young. **B~körperchen** *nt* **-s,-** [blood] corpuscle. **B~probe** *f* blood test. **b~rünstig** *a* (*fig*) bloody, gory; ⟨*Person*⟩ bloodthirsty. **B~schande** *f* incest. **B~spender** *m* blood donor. **B~sturz** *m* haemorrhage. **B~sverwandte(r)** *m/f* blood relation. **B~transfusion, B~übertragung** *f* blood transfusion. **B~ung** *f* **-,-en** bleeding; (*Med*) haemorrhage; (*Regel-*) period. **b~unterlaufen** *a* bruised; ⟨*Auge*⟩ bloodshot. **B~vergießen** *nt* **-s** bloodshed. **B~vergiftung** *f* blood-poisoning. **B~wurst** *f* black pudding

Bö *f* **-,-en** gust; (*Regen-*) squall

Bob *m* **-s,-s** bob[-sleigh]

Bock *m* **-[e]s,⸚e** buck; (*Ziege*) billy goat; (*Schaf*) ram; (*Gestell*) support; **einen B~ schießen** (*fam*) make a blunder. **b~en** *vi* (*haben*) ⟨*Pferd:*⟩ buck; ⟨*Kind:*⟩ be stubborn. **b~ig** *a* (*fam*) stubborn. **B~springen** *nt* leap-frog

Boden *m* **-s,⸚** ground; (*Erde*) soil; (*Fuß-*) floor; (*Grundfläche*) bottom; (*Dach-*) loft, attic. **B~kammer** *f* attic [room]. **b~los** *a* bottomless; (*fam*) incredible. **B~satz** *m* sediment. **B~schätze** *mpl* mineral deposits. **B~see (der)** Lake Constance

Bogen *m* **-s,-** & **⸚** curve; (*Geom*) arc; (*beim Skilauf*) turn; (*Archit*) arch; (*Waffe, Geigen-*) bow; (*Papier*) sheet; **einen großen B~ um jdn/etw machen** (*fam*) give s.o./sth a wide berth. **B~gang** *m* arcade. **B~schießen** *nt* archery

Bohle *f* **-,-n** [thick] plank

Böhm|en *nt* **-s** Bohemia. **b~isch** *a* Bohemian

Bohne *f* **-,-n** bean; **grüne B~n** French beans. **B~nkaffee** *m* real coffee

bohner|n *vt* polish. **B~wachs** *nt* floor-polish

bohr|en *vt/i* (*haben*) drill (**nach** for); drive ⟨*Tunnel*⟩; sink ⟨*Brunnen*⟩; ⟨*Insekt:*⟩ bore; **in der Nase b~en** pick one's nose. **B~er** *m* **-s,-** drill. **B~insel** *f* [offshore] drilling rig. **B~maschine** *f* electric drill. **B~turm** *m* derrick

Boje *f* **-,-n** buoy

Böllerschuß *m* gun salute

Bolzen *m* **-s,-** bolt; (*Stift*) pin

bombardieren *vt* bomb; (*fig*) bombard (**mit** with)

bombastisch *a* bombastic

Bombe *f* **-,-n** bomb. **B~nangriff** *m* bombing raid. **B~nerfolg** *m* huge success. **B~r** *m* **-s,-** (*Aviat*) bomber

Bon /bɔŋ/ *m* **-s,-s** voucher; (*Kassen-*) receipt

Bonbon /bɔŋ'bɔŋ/ *m* & *nt* **-s,-s** sweet

Bonus *m* **-[sses],-[sse]** bonus

Boot *nt* **-[e]s,-e** boat. **B~ssteg** *m* landing-stage

Bord[1] *nt* **-[e]s,-e** shelf

Bord[2] *m* (*Naut*) **an B~** aboard, on board; **über B~** overboard. **B~buch** *nt* log[-book]

Bordell *nt* **-s,-e** brothel

Bord|karte *f* boarding-pass. **B~stein** *m* kerb

borgen *vt* borrow; **jdm etw b~** lend s.o. sth

Borke *f* **-,-n** bark

borniert *a* narrow-minded

Börse *f* **-,-n** purse; (*Comm*) stock exchange. **B~nmakler** *m* stockbroker

Borst|e *f* **-,-n** bristle. **b~ig** *a* bristly

Borte *f* **-,-n** braid

bösartig *a* vicious; (*Med*) malignant

Böschung *f* **-,-en** embankment; (*Hang*) slope

böse *a* wicked, evil; (*unartig*) naughty; (*schlimm*) bad, *adv* -ly; (*zornig*) cross; **jdm** *od* **auf jdn b~ sein** be cross with s.o. **B~wicht** *m* **-[e]s,-e** villain; (*Schlingel*) rascal

bos|haft *a* malicious, *adv* -ly; (*gehässig*) spiteful, *adv* -ly. **B~heit** *f* **-,-en** malice; spite; (*Handlung*) spiteful act/(*Bemerkung*) remark

böswillig *a* malicious, *adv* -ly. **B~keit** *f* **-** malice

Botani|k *f* **-** botany. **B~ker(in)** *m* **-s,-** (*f* **-,-nen**) botanist. **b~sch** *a* botanical

Bot|e *m* **-n,-n** messenger. **B~engang** *m* errand. **B~schaft** *f* **-,-en** message; (*Pol*) embassy. **B~schafter** *m* **-s,-** ambassador

Bottich *m* **-[e]s,-e** vat; (*Wasch-*) tub

Bouillon /bʊl'jɔŋ/ *f* **-,-s** clear soup. **B~würfel** *m* stock cube

Bowle /'bo:lə/ *f* **-,-n** punch

box|en *vi* (*haben*) box ● *vt* punch. **B~en** *nt* **-s** boxing. **B~er** *m* **-s,-** boxer. **B~kampf** *m* boxing match; (*Boxen*) boxing

Boykott *m* **-[e]s,-s** boycott. **b~ieren** *vt* boycott; (*Comm*) black

brachliegen† *vi sep* (*haben*) lie fallow

Branche /'brã:ʃə/ *f* **-,-n** [line of] business. **B~nverzeichnis** *nt* (*Teleph*) classified directory

Brand *m* **-[e]s,⸚e** fire; (*Med*) gangrene; (*Bot*) blight; **in B~ geraten** catch fire; **in B~ setzen** *od* **stecken** set on fire. **B~bombe** *f* incendiary bomb

branden *vi* (*haben*) surge; (*sich brechen*) break

Brand|geruch *m* smell of burning. **b~marken** *vt* (*fig*) brand. **B~stifter** *m* arsonist. **B~stiftung** *f* arson

Brandung *f* **-** surf. **B~sreiten** *nt* surfing

Brand|wunde *f* burn. **B~zeichen** *nt* brand

Branntwein *m* spirit; (*coll*) spirits *pl*. **B~brennerei** *f* distillery

bras|ilianisch *a* Brazilian. **B~ilien** /-iən/ *nt* **-s** Brazil

Brat|apfel *m* baked apple. **b~en**† *vt/i* (*haben*) roast; (*in der Pfanne*) fry. **B~en** *m* **-s,-** roast; (*B~stück*) joint. **B~ensoße** *f* gravy. **b~fertig** *a* oven-ready. **B~hähnchen, B~huhn** *nt* roast/(*zum Braten*) roasting chicken. **B~kartoffeln** *fpl* fried potatoes. **B~klops** *m* rissole. **B~pfanne** *f* frying-pan

Bratsche *f* **-,-n** (*Mus*) viola

Brat|spieß *m* spit. **B~wurst** *f* sausage for frying; (*gebraten*) fried sausage

Brauch *m* **-[e]s, Bräuche** custom. **b~bar** *a* usable; (*nützlich*) useful. **b~en** *vt* need; (*ge-, verbrauchen*) use; take ⟨*Zeit*⟩; **er b~t es nur zu sagen** he only has to say; **du b~st nicht zu gehen** you needn't go

Braue *f* **-,-n** eyebrow

brau|en *vt* brew. **B~er** *m* **-s,-** brewer. **B~erei** *f* **-,-en** brewery

braun *a*, **B~** *nt* **-s,-** brown; **b~ werden** ⟨*Person:*⟩ get a tan

Bräune *f* **-** [sun-]tan. **b~n** *vt/i* (*haben*) brown; (*in der Sonne*) tan

braungebrannt *a* [sun-]tanned

Braunschweig *nt* **-s** Brunswick

Brause *f* **-,-n** (*Dusche*) shower; (*an Gießkanne*) rose; (*B~limonade*) fizzy drink. **b~n** *vi* (*haben*) roar; (*duschen*) shower ● *vi* (*sein*) rush [along] ● *vr* **sich b~n** shower. **b~nd** *a* roaring; (*sprudelnd*) effervescent

Braut *f* **-,¨e** bride; (*Verlobte*) fiancée

Bräutigam *m* **-s,-e** bridegroom; (*Verlobter*) fiancé

Brautkleid *nt* wedding dress

bräutlich *a* bridal

Brautpaar *nt* bridal couple; (*Verlobte*) engaged couple

brav *a* good, well-behaved; (*redlich*) honest ● *adv* dutifully; (*redlich*) honestly

bravo *int* bravo!

BRD *abbr* (**Bundesrepublik Deutschland**) FRG

Brech|eisen *nt* jemmy; (*B~stange*) crowbar. **b~en**† *vt* break; (*Phys*) refract ⟨*Licht*⟩; (*erbrechen*) vomit; **sich b~en** ⟨*Wellen:*⟩ break; ⟨*Licht:*⟩ be refracted; **sich** (*dat*) **den Arm b~en** break one's arm ● *vi* (*sein*) break ● *vi* (*haben*) vomit, be sick; **mit jdm b~en** (*fig*) break with s.o. **B~er** *m* **-s,-** breaker. **B~reiz** *m* nausea. **B~stange** *f* crowbar

Brei *m* **-[e]s,-e** paste; (*Culin*) purée; (*Grieß-*) pudding; (*Hafer-*) porridge. **b~ig** *a* mushy

breit *a* wide; ⟨*Schultern, Grinsen*⟩ broad ● *adv* **b~ grinsen** grin broadly. **b~beinig** *a & adv* with legs apart. **B~e** *f* **-,-n** width; breadth; (*Geog*) latitude. **b~en** *vt* spread (**über** + *acc* over). **B~engrad** *m* [degree of] latitude. **B~enkreis** *m* parallel. **B~seite** *f* long side; (*Naut*) broadside

Bremse[1] *f* **-,-n** horsefly

Bremse[2] *f* **-,-n** brake. **b~n** *vt* slow down; (*fig*) restrain ● *vi* (*haben*) brake

Bremslicht *nt* brake-light

brenn|bar *a* combustible; **leicht b~bar** highly [in]flammable. **b~en**† *vi* (*haben*) burn; ⟨*Licht:*⟩ be on; ⟨*Zigarette:*⟩ be alight; (*weh tun*) smart, sting; **es b~t in X** there's a fire in X; **darauf b~en, etw zu tun** be dying to do sth ● *vt* burn; (*rösten*) roast; (*im Brennofen*) fire; (*destillieren*) distil. **b~end** *a* burning; (*angezündet*) lighted; (*fig*) fervent ● *adv* **ich würde b~end gern ...** I'd love to ... **B~erei** *f* **-,-en** distillery

Brennessel *f* **-,-n** stinging nettle

Brenn|holz *nt* firewood. **B~ofen** *m* kiln. **B~punkt** *m* (*Phys*) focus; **im B~punkt des Interesses stehen** be the focus of attention. **B~spiritus** *m* methylated spirits. **B~stoff** *m* fuel

brenzlig *a* (*fam*) risky; **b~er Geruch** smell of burning

Bresche *f* **-,-n** (*fig*) breach

Bretagne /bre'tanjə/ **(die)** **-** Brittany

Brett *nt* **-[e]s,-er** board; (*im Regal*) shelf; **schwarzes B~** notice board. **B~chen** *nt* **-s,-** slat; (*Frühstücks-*) small board (*used as plate*). **B~spiel** *nt* board game

Brezel *f* **-,-n** pretzel

Bridge /brɪtʃ/ *nt* **-** (*Spiel*) bridge

Brief *m* **-[e]s,-e** letter. **B~beschwerer** *m* **-s,-** paperweight. **B~block** *m* writing pad. **B~freund(in)** *m(f)* penfriend. **B~kasten** *m* letter-box, (*Amer*) mailbox. **B~kopf** *m* letterhead. **b~lich** *a & adv* by letter. **B~marke** *f* [postage] stamp. **B~öffner** *m* paper-knife. **B~papier** *nt* notepaper. **B~porto** *nt* letter rate. **B~tasche** *f* wallet. **B~träger** *m*

postman, (*Amer*) mailman. **B~umschlag** *m* envelope. **B~wahl** *f* postal vote. **B~wechsel** *m* correspondence
Brigade *f* **-,-n** brigade
Brikett *nt* **-s,-s** briquette
brillan|t /brɪl'jant/ *a* brilliant, *adv* -ly. **B~t** *m* **-en,-en** [cut] diamond. **B~z** *f* - brilliance
Brille *f* **-,-n** glasses *pl*, spectacles *pl*; (*Schutz-*) goggles *pl;* (*Klosett-*) toilet seat
bringen† *vt* bring; (*fort-*) take; (*ein-*) yield; (*veröffentlichen*) publish; (*im Radio*) broadcast; show ⟨*Film*⟩; **ins Bett b~** put to bed; **jdn nach Hause b~** take/(*begleiten*) see s.o. home; **an sich** (*acc*) **b~** get possession of; **mit sich b~** entail; **um etw b~** deprive of sth; **etw hinter sich** (*acc*) **b~** get sth over [and done] with; **jdn dazu b~, etw zu tun** get s.o. to do sth; **es weit b~** (*fig*) go far
brisant *a* explosive
Brise *f* **-,-n** breeze
Brit|e *m* **-n,-n, B~in** *f* **-,-nen** Briton. **b~isch** *a* British
Bröck|chen *nt* **-s,-** (*Culin*) crouton. **b~elig** *a* crumbly; ⟨*Gestein*⟩ friable. **b~eln** *vt/i* (*haben/sein*) crumble
Brocken *m* **-s,-** chunk; (*Erde, Kohle*) lump; **ein paar B~ Englisch** (*fam*) a smattering of English
Brokat *m* **-[e]s,-e** brocade
Brokkoli *pl* broccoli *sg*
Brombeer|e *f* blackberry. **B~strauch** *m* bramble [bush]
Bronchitis *f* - bronchitis
Bronze /'brõ:sə/ *f* **-,-n** bronze
Brosch|e *f* **-,-n** brooch. **b~iert** *a* paperback. **B~üre** *f* **-,-n** brochure; (*Heft*) booklet
Brösel *mpl* (*Culin*) breadcrumbs
Brot *n* **-[e]s,-e** bread; **ein B~** a loaf [of bread]; (*Scheibe*) a slice of bread; **sein B~ verdienen** (*fig*) earn one's living (**mit** by)
Brötchen *n* **-s,-** [bread] roll
Brot|krümel *m* breadcrumb. **B~verdiener** *m* breadwinner
Bruch *m* **-[e]s,¨e** break; (*Brechen*) breaking; (*Rohr-*) burst; (*Med*) fracture; (*Eingeweide-*) rupture, hernia; (*Math*) fraction; (*fig*) breach; (*in Beziehung*) break-up
brüchig *a* brittle
Bruch|landung *f* crash-landing. **B~rechnung** *f* fractions *pl*. **B~stück** *nt* fragment. **b~stückhaft** *a* fragmentary. **B~teil** *m* fraction
Brücke *f* **-,-n** bridge; (*Teppich*) rug
Bruder *m* **-s,¨** brother
brüderlich *a* brotherly, fraternal
Brügge *nt* **-s** Bruges
Brüh|e *f* **-,-n** broth; (*Knochen-*) stock; **klare B~e** clear soup. **b~en** *vt* scald; (*auf-*) make ⟨*Kaffee*⟩. **B~würfel** *m* stock cube
brüllen *vt/i* (*haben*) roar; ⟨*Kuh:*⟩ moo; (*fam: schreien*) bawl
brumm|eln *vt/i* (*haben*) mumble. **b~en** *vi* (*haben*) ⟨*Insekt:*⟩ buzz; ⟨*Bär:*⟩ growl; ⟨*Motor:*⟩ hum; (*murren*) grumble ● *vt* mutter. **B~er** *m* **-s,-** (*fam*) bluebottle. **b~ig** *a* (*fam*) grumpy, *adv* -ily
brünett *a* dark-haired. **B~e** *f* **-,-n** brunette
Brunnen *m* **-s,-** well; (*Spring-*) fountain; (*Heil-*) spa water. **B~kresse** *f* watercress
brüsk *a* brusque, *adv* -ly. **b~ieren** *vt* snub
Brüssel *nt* **-s** Brussels
Brust *f* **-,¨e** chest; (*weibliche, Culin: B~stück*) breast. **B~bein** *nt* breastbone. **B~beutel** *m* purse worn round the neck
brüsten (sich) *vr* boast
Brust|fellentzündung *f* pleurisy. **B~schwimmen** *nt* breast-stroke
Brüstung *f* **-,-en** parapet
Brustwarze *f* nipple
Brut *f* **-,-en** incubation; (*Junge*) brood; (*Fisch-*) fry
brutal *a* brutal, *adv* -ly. **B~ität** *f* **-,-en** brutality
brüten *vi* (*haben*) sit (*on eggs*); (*fig*) ponder (**über** + *dat* over); **b~de Hitze** oppressive heat
Brutkasten *m* (*Med*) incubator
brutto *adv*, **B~-** *pref* gross
brutzeln *vi* (*haben*) sizzle ● *vt* fry
Bub *m* **-en,-en** (*SGer*) boy. **B~e** *m* **-n,-n** (*Karte*) jack, knave
Bubikopf *m* bob
Buch *nt* **-[e]s,¨er** book; **B~ führen** keep a record (**über** + *acc* of); **die B~¨er führen** keep the accounts. **B~drucker** *m* printer
Buche *f* **-,-n** beech
buchen *vt* book; (*Comm*) enter
Bücher|bord, B~brett *nt* bookshelf. **B~ei** *f* **-,-en** library. **B~regal** *nt* bookcase, bookshelves *pl*. **B~schrank** *m* bookcase. **B~wurm** *m* bookworm

Buchfink *m* chaffinch

Buch|führung *f* bookkeeping. **B~halter(in)** *m* **-s,-** (*f* **-,-nen**) bookkeeper, accountant. **B~haltung** *f* bookkeeping, accountancy; (*Abteilung*) accounts department. **B~händler(in)** *m(f)* bookseller. **B~handlung** *f* bookshop. **B~macher** *m* **-s,-** bookmaker. **B~prüfer** *m* auditor

Büchse *f* **-,-n** box; (*Konserven-*) tin, can; (*Gewehr*) [sporting] gun. **B~nmilch** *f* evaporated milk. **B~nöffner** *m* tin *or* can opener

Buch|stabe *m* **-ns,-n** letter. **b~stabieren** *vt* spell [out]. **b~stäblich** *adv* literally

Buchstützen *fpl* book-ends

Bucht *f* **-,-en** (*Geog*) bay

Buchung *f* **-,-en** booking, reservation; (*Comm*) entry

Buckel *m* **-s,-** hump; (*Beule*) bump; (*Hügel*) hillock; **einen B~ machen** ⟨*Katze:*⟩ arch its back

bücken (sich) *vr* bend down

bucklig *a* hunchbacked. **B~e(r)** *m/f* hunchback

Bückling *m* **-s,-e** smoked herring; (*fam: Verbeugung*) bow

buddeln *vt/i* (*haben*) (*fam*) dig

Buddhis|mus *m* **-** Buddhism. **B~t(in)** *m* **-en,-en** (*f* **-,-nen**) Buddhist. **b~tisch** *a* Buddhist

Bude *f* **-,-n** hut; (*Kiosk*) kiosk; (*Markt-*) stall; (*fam: Zimmer*) room; (*Studenten-*) digs *pl*

Budget /bʏ'dʒe:/ *nt* **-s,-s** budget

Büfett *nt* **-[e]s,-e** sideboard; (*Theke*) bar; **kaltes B~** cold buffet

Büffel *m* **-s,-** buffalo. **b~n** *vt/i* (*haben*) (*fam*) swot

Bug *m* **-[e]s,-e** (*Naut*) bow[s *pl*]

Bügel *m* **-s,-** frame; (*Kleider-*) coathanger; (*Steig-*) stirrup; (*Brillen-*) sidepiece. **B~brett** *nt* ironing-board. **B~eisen** *nt* iron. **B~falte** *f* crease. **b~frei** *a* non-iron. **b~n** *vt/i* (*haben*) iron

bugsieren *vt* (*fam*) manœuvre

buhen *vi* (*haben*) (*fam*) boo

Buhne *f* **-,-n** breakwater

Bühne *f* **-,-n** stage. **B~nbild** *nt* set. **B~neingang** *m* stage door

Buhrufe *mpl* boos

Bukett *nt* **-[e]s,-e** bouquet

Bulette *f* **-,-n** [meat] rissole

Bulgarien /-i̯ən/ *nt* **-s** Bulgaria

Bull|auge *nt* (*Naut*) porthole. **B~dogge** *f* bulldog. **B~dozer** /-do:zɐ/ *m* **-s,-** bulldozer. **B~e** *m* **-n,-n** bull; (*sl: Polizist*) cop

Bumme|l *m* **-s,-** (*fam*) stroll. **B~lant** *m* **-en,-en** (*fam*) dawdler; (*Faulenzer*) loafer. **B~lei** *f* **-** (*fam*) dawdling; (*Nachlässigkeit*) carelessness

bummel|ig *a* (*fam*) slow; (*nachlässig*) careless. **b~n** *vi* (*sein*) (*fam*) stroll ● *vi* (*haben*) (*fam*) dawdle. **B~streik** *m* go-slow. **B~zug** *m* (*fam*) slow train

Bums *m* **-es,-e** (*fam*) bump, thump

Bund[1] *nt* **-[e]s,-e** bunch; (*Stroh-*) bundle

Bund[2] *m* **-[e]s,⸚e** association; (*Bündnis*) alliance; (*Pol*) federation; (*Rock-, Hosen-*) waistband; **im B~e sein** be in league (**mit** with); **der B~** the Federal Government; (*fam: Bundeswehr*) the [German] Army

Bündel *nt* **-s,-** bundle. **b~n** *vt* bundle [up]

Bundes|- *pref* Federal. **B~genosse** *m* ally. **B~kanzler** *m* Federal Chancellor. **B~land** *nt* [federal] state; (*Aust*) province. **B~liga** *f* German national league. **B~rat** *m* Upper House of Parliament. **B~regierung** *f* Federal Government. **B~republik** *f* **die B~republik Deutschland** the Federal Republic of Germany. **B~straße** *f* ≈ A road. **B~tag** *m* Lower House of Parliament. **B~wehr** *f* [Federal German] Army

bünd|ig *a & adv* **kurz und b~ig** short and to the point. **B~nis** *nt* **-sses,-sse** alliance

Bunker *m* **-s,-** bunker; (*Luftschutz-*) shelter

bunt *a* coloured; (*farbenfroh*) colourful; (*grell*) gaudy; (*gemischt*) varied; (*wirr*) confused; **b~er Abend** social evening; **b~e Platte** assorted cold meats ● *adv* **b~ durcheinander** higgledy-piggledy; **es zu b~ treiben** (*fam*) go too far. **B~stift** *m* crayon

Bürde *f* **-,-n** (*fig*) burden

Burg *f* **-,-en** castle

Bürge *m* **-n,-n** guarantor. **b~n** *vi* (*haben*) **b~n für** vouch for; (*fig*) guarantee

Bürger|(in) *m* **-s,-** (*f* **-,-nen**) citizen. **B~krieg** *m* civil war. **b~lich** *a* civil; ⟨*Pflicht*⟩ civic; (*mittelständisch*) middle-class; **b~liche Küche** plain cooking. **B~liche(r)** *m/f* commoner. **B~meister** *m* mayor. **B~rechte** *npl* civil rights. **B~steig** *m* **-[e]s,-e** pavement, (*Amer*) sidewalk

Burggraben *m* moat
Bürgschaft *f* **-,-en** surety; **B~ leisten** stand surety
Burgunder *m* **-s,-** (*Wein*) Burgundy
Burleske *f* **-,-n** burlesque
Büro *nt* **-s,-s** office. **B~angestellte(r)** *m/f* office-worker. **B~klammer** *f* paper-clip. **B~krat** *m* **-en,-en** bureaucrat. **B~kratie** *f* **-,-n** bureaucracy. **b~kratisch** *a* bureaucratic
Bursch|e *m* **-n,-n** lad, youth; (*fam: Kerl*) fellow. **b~ikos** *a* hearty; (*männlich*) mannish
Bürste *f* **-,-n** brush. **b~n** *vt* brush. **B~nschnitt** *m* crew cut
Bus *m* **-ses,-se** bus; (*Reise-*) coach. **B~bahnhof** *m* bus and coach station
Busch *m* **-[e]s,¨e** bush
Büschel *nt* **-s,-** tuft
buschig *a* bushy
Busen *m* **-s,-** bosom
Bussard *m* **-s,-e** buzzard
Buße *f* **-,-n** penance; (*Jur*) fine
büßen *vt/i* (*haben*) **[für] etw b~** atone for sth; (*fig: bezahlen*) pay for sth
buß|fertig *a* penitent. **B~geld** *nt* (*Jur*) fine
Büste *f* **-,-n** bust; (*Schneider-*) dummy. **B~nhalter** *m* **-s,-** bra
Butter *f* **-** butter. **B~blume** *f* buttercup. **B~brot** *nt* slice of bread and butter. **B~brotpapier** *nt* greaseproof paper. **B~faß** *nt* churn. **B~milch** *f* buttermilk. **b~n** *vi* (*haben*) make butter • *vt* butter
b.w. *abbr* (**bitte wenden**) PTO
bzgl. *abbr s.* **bezüglich**
bzw. *abbr s.* **beziehungsweise**

C

ca. *abbr* (**circa**) about
Café /ka'fe:/ *nt* **-s,-s** café
Cafeteria /kafete'ri:a/ *f* **-,-s** cafeteria
camp|en /'kɛmpən/ *vi* (*haben*) go camping. **C~ing** *nt* **-s** camping. **C~ingplatz** *m* campsite
Cape /ke:p/ *nt* **-s,-s** cape
Caravan /'ka[:]ravan/ *m* **-s,-s** (*Auto*) caravan; (*Kombi*) estate car
Cassette /ka'sɛtə/ *f* **-,-n** cassette. **C~nrecorder** /-rekɔrdɐ/ *m* **-s,-** cassette recorder
CD /t̮se:'de:/ *f* **-,-s** compact disc, CD
Cell|ist(in) /tʃɛ'lɪst(ɪn)/ *m* **-en,-en** (*f* **-,-nen**) cellist. **C~o** /'tʃɛlo/ *nt* **-,-los** & **-li** cello
Celsius /'t̮sɛlzi̯ʊs/ *inv* Celsius, centigrade
Cembalo /'tʃɛmbalo/ *nt* **-s,-los** & **-li** harpsichord
Champagner /ʃam'panjɐ/ *m* **-s** champagne
Champignon /'ʃampɪnjɔŋ/ *m* **-s,-s** [field] mushroom
Chance /'ʃã:s[ə]/ *f* **-,-n** chance
Chaos /'ka:ɔs/ *nt* **-** chaos
chaotisch /ka'o:tɪʃ/ *a* chaotic
Charakter /ka'raktɐ/ *m* **-s,-e** /-'te:rə/ character. **c~isieren** *vt* characterize. **c~istisch** *a* characteristic (**für** of), *adv* -ally
Charism|a /ka'rɪsma/ *nt* **-s** charisma. **c~atisch** *a* charismatic
charm|ant /ʃar'mant/ *a* charming, *adv* -ly. **C~e** /ʃarm/ *m* **-s** charm
Charter|flug /'tʃ-, 'ʃartɐ-/ *m* charter flight. **c~n** *vt* charter
Chassis /ʃa'si:/ *nt* **-,-** /-'si:[s], -'si:s/ chassis
Chauffeur /ʃɔ'fø:ɐ̯/ *m* **-s,-e** chauffeur; (*Taxi-*) driver
Chauvinis|mus /ʃovi'nɪsmʊs/ *m* **-** chauvinism. **C~t** *m* **-en,-en** chauvinist
Chef /ʃɛf/ *m* **-s,-s** head; (*fam*) boss
Chem|ie /çe'mi:/ *f* **-** chemistry. **C~ikalien** /-i̯ən/ *fpl* chemicals
Chem|iker(in) /'çe:-/ *m* **-s,-** (*f* **-,-nen**) chemist. **c~isch** *a* chemical, *adv* -ly; **c~ische Reinigung** dry-cleaning; (*Geschäft*) dry-cleaner's
Chicorée /'ʃɪkore:/ *m* **-s** chicory
Chiffr|e /'ʃɪfɐ, 'ʃɪfrə/ *f* **-,-n** cipher; (*bei Annonce*) box number. **c~iert** *a* coded
Chile /'çi:le/ *nt* **-s** Chile
Chin|a /'çi:na/ *nt* **-s** China. **C~ese** *m* **-n,-n**, **C~esin** *f* **-,-nen** Chinese. **c~esisch** *a* Chinese. **C~esisch** *nt* **-[s]** (*Lang*) Chinese
Chip /tʃɪp/ *m* **-s,-s** [micro]chip. **C~s** *pl* crisps, (*Amer*) chips
Chirurg /çi'rʊrk/ *m* **-en,-en** surgeon. **C~ie** /-'gi:/ *f* **-** surgery. **c~isch** /-g-/ *a* surgical, *adv* -ly
Chlor /klo:ɐ̯/ *nt* **-s** chlorine. **C~oform** /kloro'fɔrm/ *nt* **-s** chloroform
Choke /tʃo:k/ *m* **-s,-s** (*Auto*) choke
Cholera /'ko:lera/ *f* **-** cholera
cholerisch /ko'le:rɪʃ/ *a* irascible
Cholesterin /ço-, kolɛste'ri:n/ *nt* **-s** cholesterol

Chor /koːɐ̯/ *m* **-[e]s,¨-e** choir; (*Theat*) chorus; **im C~** in chorus
Choral /koˈraːl/ *m* **-[e]s,¨-e** chorale
Choreographie /koreograˈfiː/ *f* **-,-n** choreography
Chor|knabe /ˈkoːɐ̯-/ *m* choirboy. **C~musik** *f* choral music
Christ /krɪst/ *m* **-en,-en** Christian. **C~baum** *m* Christmas tree. **C~entum** *nt* **-s** Christianity. **C~in** *f* **-,-nen** Christian. **C~kind** *nt* Christ-child; (*als Geschenkbringer*) ≈ Father Christmas. **c~lich** *a* Christian
Christus /ˈkrɪstʊs/ *m* **-ti** Christ
Chrom /kroːm/ *nt* **-s** chromium
Chromosom /kromoˈzoːm/ *nt* **-s,-en** chromosome
Chronik /ˈkroːnɪk/ *f* **-,-en** chronicle
chron|isch /ˈkroːnɪʃ/ *a* chronic, *adv* -ally. **c~ologisch** *a* chronological, *adv* -ly
Chrysantheme /krʏzanˈteːmə/ *f* **-,-n** chrysanthemum
circa /ˈt͡sɪrka/ *adv* about
Clique /ˈklɪkə/ *f* **-,-n** clique
Clou /kluː/ *m* **-s,-s** highlight, (*fam*) high spot
Clown /klau̯n/ *m* **-s,-s** clown. **c~en** *vi* (*haben*) clown
Club /klʊp/ *m* **-s,-s** club
Cocktail /ˈkɔkteːl/ *m* **-s,-s** cocktail
Code /koːt/ *m* **-s,-s** code
Cola /ˈkoːla/ *f* **-,-** (*fam*) Coke (P)
Comic-Heft /ˈkɔmɪk-/ *nt* comic
Computer /kɔmˈpjuːtɐ/ *m* **-s,-** computer. **c~isieren** *vt* computerize
Conférencier /kõferãˈsi̯eː/ *m* **-s,-s** compère
Cord /kɔrt/ *m* **-s, C~samt** *m* corduroy. **C~[samt]hose** *f* cords *pl*
Couch /kau̯tʃ/ *f* **-,-es** settee. **C~tisch** *m* coffee-table
Coupon /kuˈpõː/ *m* **-s,-s** = **Kupon**
Cousin /kuˈzɛ̃ː/ *m* **-s,-s** [male] cousin. **C~e** /-ˈziːnə/ *f* **-,-n** [female] cousin
Creme /kreːm/ *f* **-s,-s** cream; (*Speise*) cream dessert. **c~farben** *a* cream
cremig /ˈkreːmɪç/ *a* creamy
Curry /ˈkari, ˈkœri/ *nt & m* **-s** curry powder ● *nt* **-s,-s** (*Gericht*) curry

D

da *adv* there; (*hier*) here; (*zeitlich*) then; (*in dem Fall*) in that case; **von da an** from then on ● *conj* as, since
dabehalten† *vt sep* keep there
dabei (*emphatic:* **dabei**) *adv* nearby; (*daran*) with it; (*eingeschlossen*) included; (*hinsichtlich*) about it; (*währenddem*) during this; (*gleichzeitig*) at the same time; (*doch*) and yet; **dicht d~** close by; **d~ bleiben** (*fig*) remain adamant; **was ist denn d~?** (*fam*) so what? **d~sein**† *vi sep* (*sein*) be present; (*mitmachen*) be involved; **d~sein, etw zu tun** be just doing sth
dableiben† *vi sep* (*sein*) stay there
Dach *nt* **-[e]s,¨-er** roof. **D~boden** *m* loft. **D~gepäckträger** *m* roof-rack. **D~kammer** *f* attic room. **D~luke** *f* skylight. **D~rinne** *f* gutter
Dachs *m* **-es,-e** badger
Dach|sparren *m* **-s,-** rafter. **D~ziegel** *m* [roofing] tile
Dackel *m* **-s,-** dachshund
dadurch (*emphatic:* **dadurch**) *adv* through it/them; (*Ursache*) by it; (*deshalb*) because of that; **d~, daß** because
dafür (*emphatic:* **dafür**) *adv* for it/them; (*anstatt*) instead; (*als Ausgleich*) but [on the other hand]; **d~, daß** considering that. **d~können**† *vi sep* (*haben*) **ich kann nichts dafür** it's not my fault
dagegen (*emphatic:* **dagegen**) *adv* against it/them; (*Mittel, Tausch*) for it; (*verglichen damit*) by comparison; (*jedoch*) however; **hast du was d~?** do you mind? **d~halten**† *vt sep* argue (**daß** that)
daheim *adv* at home
daher (*emphatic:* **daher**) *adv* from there; (*deshalb*) for that reason; **das kommt d~, weil** that's because; **d~ meine Eile** hence my hurry ● *conj* that is why
dahin (*emphatic:* **dahin**) *adv* there; **bis d~** up to there; (*bis dann*) until/(*Zukunft*) by then; **jdn d~ bringen, daß er etw tut** get s.o. to do sth; **d~ sein** (*fam*) be gone. **d~gehen**† *vi sep* (*sein*) walk along; 〈*Zeit:*〉 pass. **d~gestellt** *a* **d~gestellt lassen** (*fig*) leave open; **das bleibt d~gestellt** that remains to be seen
dahinten *adv* back there
dahinter (*emphatic:* **dahinter**) *adv* behind it/them. **d~kommen**† *vi sep* (*sein*) (*fig*) get to the bottom of it
Dahlie /-i̯ə/ *f* **-,-n** dahlia
dalassen† *vt sep* leave there
daliegen† *vi sep* (*haben*) lie there

damalig *a* at that time; **der d~e Minister** the then minister
damals *adv* at that time
Damast *m* **-es,-e** damask
Dame *f* **-,-n** lady; (*Karte, Schach*) queen; (*D~spiel*) draughts *sg*, (*Amer*) checkers *sg*; (*Doppelstein*) king. **D~n-** *pref* ladies'/lady's ... **d~nhaft** *a* ladylike
damit (*emphatic:* **damit**) *adv* with it/them; (*dadurch*) by it; **hör auf d~!** stop it! ● *conj* so that
dämlich *a* (*fam*) stupid, *adv* -ly
Damm *m* **-[e]s,¨e** dam; (*Insel-*) causeway; **nicht auf dem D~** (*fam*) under the weather
dämmer|ig *a* dim; **es wird d~ig** dusk is falling. **D~licht** *nt* twilight. **d~n** *vi* (*haben*) ⟨*Morgen:*⟩ dawn; **der Abend d~t** dusk is falling; **es d~t** it is getting light/(*abends*) dark. **D~ung** *f* - dawn; (*Abend-*) dusk
Dämon *m* **-s,-en** /-ˈmoːnən/ demon
Dampf *m* **-es,¨e** steam; (*Chem*) vapour. **d~en** *vi* (*haben*) steam
dämpfen *vt* (*Culin*) steam; (*fig*) muffle ⟨*Ton*⟩; lower ⟨*Stimme*⟩; dampen ⟨*Enthusiasmus*⟩
Dampf|er *m* **-s,-** steamer. **D~kochtopf** *m* pressure-cooker. **D~maschine** *f* steam engine. **D~walze** *f* steamroller
Damwild *nt* fallow deer *pl*
danach (*emphatic:* **danach**) *adv* after it/them; ⟨*suchen*⟩ for it/them; ⟨*riechen*⟩ of it; (*später*) afterwards; (*entsprechend*) accordingly; **es sieht d~ aus** it looks like it
Däne *m* **-n,-n** Dane
daneben (*emphatic:* **daneben**) *adv* beside it/them; (*außerdem*) in addition; (*verglichen damit*) by comparison. **d~gehen**† *vi sep* (*sein*) miss; (*scheitern*) fail
Dän|emark *nt* **-s** Denmark. **D~in** *f* **-,-nen** Dane. **d~isch** *a* Danish
Dank *m* **-es** thanks *pl*; **vielen D~!** thank you very much! **d~** *prep* (+*dat or gen*) thanks to. **d~bar** *a* grateful, *adv* -ly; (*erleichtert*) thankful, *adv* -ly; (*lohnend*) rewarding. **D~barkeit** *f* - gratitude. **d~e** *adv* **d~e [schön** *od* **sehr]!** thank you [very much]! **[nein] d~e!** no thank you! **d~en** *vi* (*haben*) thank (**jdm** s.o.); (*ablehnen*) decline; **ich d~e!** no thank you! **nichts zu d~en!** don't mention it!
dann *adv* then; **d~ und wann** now and then; **nur/selbst d~, wenn** only/even if
daran (*emphatic:* **daran**) *adv* on it/them; at it/them; ⟨*denken*⟩ of it; **nahe d~** on the point (**etw zu tun** of doing sth); **denkt d~!** remember! **d~gehen**† *vi sep* (*sein*), **d~machen (sich)** *vr sep* set about (**etw zu tun** doing sth). **d~setzen** *vt sep* **alles d~setzen** do one's utmost (**zu** to)
darauf (*emphatic:* **darauf**) *adv* on it/them; ⟨*warten*⟩ for it; ⟨*antworten*⟩ to it; (*danach*) after that; (*d~hin*) as a result; **am Tag d~** the day after. **d~folgend** *a* following. **d~hin** *adv* as a result
daraus (*emphatic:* **daraus**) *adv* out of *or* from it/them; **er macht sich nichts d~** he doesn't care for it; **was ist d~ geworden?** what has become of it?
Darbietung *f* **-,-en** performance; (*Nummer*) item
darin (*emphatic:* **darin**) *adv* in it/them
darlegen *vt sep* expound; (*erklären*) explain
Darlehen *nt* **-s,-** loan
Darm *m* **-[e]s,¨e** intestine; (*Wurst-*) skin. **D~grippe** *f* gastric flu
darstell|en *vt sep* represent; (*bildlich*) portray; (*Theat*) interpret; (*spielen*) play; (*schildern*) describe. **D~er** *m* **-s,-** actor. **D~erin** *f* **-,-nen** actress. **D~ung** *f* representation; interpretation; description; (*Bericht*) account
darüber (*emphatic:* **darüber**) *adv* over it/them; (*höher*) above it/them; ⟨*sprechen, lachen, sich freuen*⟩ about it; (*mehr*) more; (*inzwischen*) in the meantime; **d~ hinaus** beyond [it]; (*dazu*) on top of that
darum (*emphatic:* **darum**) *adv* round it/them; ⟨*bitten, kämpfen*⟩ for it; (*deshalb*) that is why; **d~, weil** because
darunter (*emphatic:* **darunter**) *adv* under it/them; (*tiefer*) below it/them; (*weniger*) less; (*dazwischen*) among them
das *def art & pron s.* **der**
dasein† *vi sep* (*sein*) be there/(*hier*) here; (*existieren*) exist; **wieder d~** be back; **noch nie dagewesen** unprecedented. **D~** *nt* **-s** existence
dasitzen† *vi sep* (*haben*) sit there
dasjenige *pron s.* **derjenige**
daß *conj* that; **daß du nicht fällst!** mind you don't fall!

dasselbe *pron s.* **derselbe**

dastehen† *vi sep (haben)* stand there; **allein d~** *(fig)* be alone

Daten|sichtgerät *nt* visual display unit, VDU. **D~verarbeitung** *f* data processing

datieren *vt/i (haben)* date

Dativ *m* **-s,-e** dative. **D~objekt** *nt* indirect object

Dattel *f* **-,-n** date

Datum *nt* **-s,-ten** date; **Daten** *(Angaben)* data

Dauer *f* **-** duration, length; *(Jur)* term; **von D~** lasting; **auf die D~** in the long run. **D~auftrag** *m* standing order. **d~haft** *a* lasting, enduring; *(fest)* durable. **D~karte** *f* season ticket. **D~lauf** *m* **im D~lauf** at a jog. **D~milch** *f* long-life milk. **d~n** *vi (haben)* last; **lange d~n** take a long time. **d~nd** *a* lasting; *(ständig)* constant, *adv* -ly; **d~nd fragen** keep asking. **D~stellung** *f* permanent position. **D~welle** *f* perm. **D~wurst** *f* salami-type sausage

Daumen *m* **-s,-** thumb; **jdm den D~ drücken** *od* **halten** keep one's fingers crossed for s.o.

Daunen *fpl* down *sg.* **D~decke** *f* [down-filled] duvet

davon *(emphatic:* **davon)** *adv* from it/them; *(dadurch)* by it; *(damit)* with it/them; *(darüber)* about it; *(Menge)* of it/them; **die Hälfte d~** half of it/them; **das kommt d~!** it serves you right! **d~kommen**† *vi sep (sein)* escape **(mit dem Leben** with one's life). **d~laufen**† *vi sep (sein)* run away. **d~machen (sich)** *vr sep (fam)* make off. **d~tragen**† *vt sep* carry off; *(erleiden)* suffer; *(gewinnen)* win

davor *(emphatic:* **davor)** *adv* in front of it/them; ‹*sich fürchten*› of it; *(zeitlich)* before it/them

dazu *(emphatic:* **dazu)** *adv* to it/them; *(damit)* with it/them; *(dafür)* for it; **noch d~** in addition to that; **jdn d~ bringen, etw zu tun** get s.o. to do sth; **ich kam nicht d~** I didn't get round to [doing] it. **d~gehören** *vi sep (haben)* belong to it/them; **alles, was d~gehört** everything that goes with it. **d~kommen**† *vi sep (sein)* arrive [on the scene]; *(hinzukommen)* be added; **d~ kommt, daß er krank ist** on top of that he is ill. **d~rechnen** *vt sep* add to it/them

dazwischen *(emphatic:* **dazwischen)** *adv* between them; in between; *(darunter)* among them. **d~fahren**† *vi sep (sein) (fig)* intervene. **d~kommen**† *vi sep (sein) (fig)* crop up; **wenn nichts d~kommt** if all goes well. **d~reden** *vi sep (haben)* interrupt. **d~treten**† *vi sep (sein) (fig)* intervene

DDR *f* **-** *abbr* **(Deutsche Demokratische Republik)** GDR

Debat|te *f* **-,-n** debate; **zur D~te stehen** be at issue. **d~tieren** *vt/i (haben)* debate

Debüt /de'by:/ *nt* **-s,-s** début

dechiffrieren /deʃɪ'fri:rən/ *vt* decipher

Deck *nt* **-[e]s,-s** *(Naut)* deck; **an D~** on deck. **D~bett** *nt* duvet

Decke *f* **-,-n** cover; *(Tisch-)* tablecloth; *(Bett-)* blanket; *(Reise-)* rug; *(Zimmer-)* ceiling; **unter einer D~ stecken** *(fam)* be in league

Deckel *m* **-s,-** lid; *(Flaschen-)* top; *(Buch-)* cover

decken *vt* cover; tile ‹*Dach*›; lay ‹*Tisch*›; *(schützen)* shield; *(Sport)* mark; meet ‹*Bedarf*›; **jdn d~** *(fig)* cover up for s.o.; **sich d~** *(fig)* cover oneself **(gegen** against); *(übereinstimmen)* coincide

Deck|mantel *m (fig)* pretence. **D~name** *m* pseudonym

Deckung *f* **-** *(Mil)* cover; *(Sport)* defence; *(Mann-)* marking; *(Boxen)* guard; *(Sicherheit)* security; **in D~ gehen** take cover

Defekt *m* **-[e]s,-e** defect. **d~** *a* defective

defensiv *a* defensive. **D~e** *f* **-** defensive

defilieren *vi (sein/haben)* file past

defin|ieren *vt* define. **D~ition** /-'tsi̯o:n/ *f* **-,-en** definition. **d~itiv** *a* definite, *adv* -ly

Defizit *nt* **-s,-e** deficit

Deflation /-'tsi̯o:n/ *f* **-** deflation

deformiert *a* deformed

deftig *a (fam)* ‹*Mahlzeit*› hearty; ‹*Witz*› coarse

Degen *m* **-s,-** sword; *(Fecht-)* épée

degenerier|en *vi (sein)* degenerate. **d~t** *a (fig)* degenerate

degradieren *vt (Mil)* demote; *(fig)* degrade

dehn|bar *a* elastic. **d~en** *vt* stretch; lengthen ‹*Vokal*›; **sich d~en** stretch

Deich *m* **-[e]s,-e** dike

Deichsel *f* **-,-n** pole; *(Gabel-)* shafts *pl*

dein *poss pron* your. **d~e(r,s)** *poss pron* yours; **die D~en** *pl* your family *sg.* **d~erseits** *adv* for your part. **d~etwegen** *adv* for your sake; (*wegen dir*) because of you, on your account. **d~etwillen** *adv* **um d~etwillen** for your sake. **d~ige** *poss pron* **der/die/das d~ige** yours. **d~s** *poss pron* yours

Deka *nt* **-[s],-** (*Aust*) = **Dekagramm**

dekaden|t *a* decadent. **D~z** *f* - decadence

Dekagramm *nt* (*Aust*) 10 grams; **10 D~** 100 grams

Dekan *m* **-s,-e** dean

Deklin|ation /-'tsio:n/ *f* **-,-en** declension. **d~ieren** *vt* decline

Dekolleté /dekɔl'te:/ *nt* **-s,-s** low neckline

Dekor *m & nt* **-s** decoration. **D~ateur** /-'tø:ɐ/ *m* **-s,-e** interior decorator; (*Schaufenster-*) window-dresser. **D~ation** /-'tsio:n/ *f* **-,-en** decoration; (*Schaufenster-*) window-dressing; (*Auslage*) display; **D~ationen** (*Theat*) scenery *sg.* **d~ativ** *a* decorative. **d~ieren** *vt* decorate; dress ⟨*Schaufenster*⟩

Deleg|ation /-'tsio:n/ *f* **-,-en** delegation. **d~ieren** *vt* delegate. **D~ierte(r)** *m/f* delegate

delikat *a* delicate; (*lecker*) delicious; (*taktvoll*) tactful, *adv* -ly. **D~esse** *f* **-,-n** delicacy. **D~essengeschäft** *nt* delicatessen

Delikt *nt* **-[e]s,-e** offence

Delinquent *m* **-en,-en** offender

Delirium *nt* **-s** delirium

Delle *f* **-,-n** dent

Delphin *m* **-s,-e** dolphin

Delta *nt* **-s,-s** delta

dem *def art & pron s.* **der**

Dement|i *nt* **-s,-s** denial. **d~ieren** *vt* deny

dem|entsprechend *a* corresponding; (*passend*) appropriate • *adv* accordingly; (*passend*) appropriately. **d~gemäß** *adv* accordingly. **d~nach** *adv* according to that; (*folglich*) consequently. **d~nächst** *adv* soon; (*in Kürze*) shortly

Demokrat *m* **-en,-en** democrat. **D~ie** *f* **-,-n** democracy. **d~isch** *a* democratic, *adv* -ally

demolieren *vt* wreck

Demonstr|ant *m* **-en,-en** demonstrator. **D~ation** /-'tsio:n/ *f* **-,-en** demonstration. **d~ativ** *a* pointed, *adv* -ly; (*Gram*) demonstrative. **D~ativpronomen** *nt* demonstrative pronoun. **d~ieren** *vt/i* (*haben*) demonstrate

demontieren *vt* dismantle

demoralisieren *vt* demoralize

Demoskopie *f* - opinion research

Demut *f* - humility

demütig *a* humble, *adv* -bly. **d~en** *vt* humiliate; **sich d~en** humble oneself. **D~ung** *f* **-,-en** humiliation

demzufolge *adv* = **demnach**

den *def art & pron s.* **der. d~en** *pron s.* **der**

denk|bar *a* conceivable. **d~en†** *vt/i* (*haben*) think (**an** + *acc* of); (*sich erinnern*) remember (**an etw** *acc* sth); **für jdn gedacht** meant for s.o.; **das kann ich mir d~en** I can imagine [that]; **ich d~e nicht daran** I have no intention of doing it; **d~t daran!** don't forget! **D~mal** *nt* memorial; (*Monument*) monument. **d~würdig** *a* memorable. **D~zettel** *m* **jdm einen D~zettel geben** (*fam*) teach s.o. a lesson

denn *conj* for; **besser/mehr d~ je** better/more than ever • *adv* **wie/wo d~?** but how/where? **warum d~ nicht?** why ever not? **es sei d~ [, daß]** unless

dennoch *adv* nevertheless

Denunz|iant *m* **-en,-en** informer. **d~ieren** *vt* denounce

Deodorant *nt* **-s,-s** deodorant

deplaciert /-'tsi:ɐt/ *a* (*fig*) out of place

Deponie *f* **-,-n** dump. **d~ren** *vt* deposit

deportieren *vt* deport

Depot /de'po:/ *nt* **-s,-s** depot; (*Lager*) warehouse; (*Bank-*) safe deposit

Depression *f* **-,-en** depression

deprimieren *vt* depress. **d~d** *a* depressing

Deputation /-'tsio:n/ *f* **-,-en** deputation

der, die, das, *pl* **die** *def art* (*acc* **den, die, das,** *pl* **die**; *gen* **des, der, des,** *pl* **der**; *dat* **dem, der, dem,** *pl* **den**) the; **der Mensch** man; **die Natur** nature; **das Leben** life; **das Lesen/Tanzen** reading/dancing; **sich** (*dat*) **das Gesicht/die Hände waschen** wash one's face/hands; **5 Mark das Pfund** 5 marks a pound • *pron* (*acc* **den, die, das,** *pl* **die**; *gen* **dessen, deren, dessen,** *pl* **deren**; *dat* **dem, der, dem,** *pl* **denen**) • *dem pron* that; (*pl*) those; (*substantivisch*) he, she, it; (*Ding*) it; (*betont*) that; (*d~jenige*) the one; (*pl*)

they, those; (*Dinge*) those; (*diejenigen*) the ones; **der und der** such and such; **um die und die Zeit** at such and such a time; **das waren Zeiten!** those were the days! ● *rel pron* who; (*Ding*) which, that
derart *adv* so; (*so sehr*) so much. **d~ig** *a* such ● *adv* = **derart**
derb *a* tough; (*kräftig*) strong; (*grob*) coarse, *adv* -ly; (*unsanft*) rough, *adv* -ly
deren *pron s.* **der**
dergleichen *inv a* such ● *pron* such a thing/such things; **nichts d~** nothing of the kind; **und d~** and the like
der-/die-/dasjenige, *pl* **diejenigen** *pron* the one; (*Person*) he, she; (*Ding*) it; (*pl*) those, the ones
dermaßen *adv* = **derart**
der-/die-/dasselbe, *pl* **dieselben** *pron* the same; **ein- und dasselbe** one and the same thing
derzeit *adv* at present
des *def art s.* **der**
Desert|eur /-'tø:ɐ̯/ *m* **-s,-e** deserter. **d~ieren** *vi* (*sein/haben*) desert
desgleichen *adv* likewise ● *pron* the like
deshalb *adv* for this reason; (*also*) therefore
Designer(in) /di'zai̯nɐ, -nərɪn/ *m* **-s,-** (*f* **-,-nen**) designer
Desin|fektion /dɛsˀɪnfɛk'tsi̯o:n/ *f* **-** disinfecting. **D~fektionsmittel** *nt* disinfectant. **d~fizieren** *vt* disinfect
Desodorant *nt* **-s,-s** deodorant
Despot *m* **-en,-en** despot
dessen *pron s.* **der**
Dessert /dɛ'se:ɐ̯/ *nt* **-s,-s** dessert, sweet. **D~löffel** *m* dessertspoon
Destill|ation /-'tsi̯o:n/ *f* **-** distillation. **d~ieren** *vt* distil
desto *adv* **je mehr/eher, d~ besser** the more/sooner the better
destruktiv *a* (*fig*) destructive
deswegen *adv* = **deshalb**
Detail /de'tai̯/ *nt* **-s,-s** detail
Detektiv *m* **-s,-e** detective. **D~roman** *m* detective story
Deton|ation /-'tsi̯o:n/ *f* **-,-en** explosion. **d~ieren** *vi* (*sein*) explode
deut|en *vt* interpret; predict ⟨*Zukunft*⟩ ● *vi* (*haben*) point (**auf**+*acc* at/(*fig*) to). **d~lich** *a* clear, *adv* -ly; (*eindeutig*) plain, *adv* -ly. **D~lichkeit** *f* **-** clarity
deutsch *a* German; **auf d~** in German. **D~** *nt* **-[s]** (*Lang*) German. **D~e(r)** *m/f* German. **D~land** *nt* **-s** Germany
Deutung *f* **-,-en** interpretation
Devise *f* **-,-n** motto. **D~n** *pl* foreign currency *or* exchange *sg*
Dezember *m* **-s,-** December
dezent *a* unobtrusive, *adv* -ly; (*diskret*) discreet, *adv* -ly
Dezernat *nt* **-[e]s,-e** department
Dezimal|system *nt* decimal system. **D~zahl** *f* decimal
dezimieren *vt* decimate
dgl. *abbr s.* **dergleichen**
d.h. *abbr* (**das heißt**) i.e.
Dia *nt* **-s,-s** (*Phot*) slide
Diabet|es *m* **-** diabetes. **D~iker** *m* **-s,-** diabetic
Diadem *nt* **-s,-e** tiara
Diagnos|e *f* **-,-n** diagnosis. **d~tizieren** *vt* diagnose
diagonal *a* diagonal, *adv* -ly. **D~e** *f* **-,-n** diagonal
Diagramm *nt* **-s,-e** diagram; (*Kurven-*) graph
Diakon *m* **-s,-e** deacon
Dialekt *m* **-[e]s,-e** dialect
Dialog *m* **-[e]s,-e** dialogue
Diamant *m* **-en,-en** diamond
Diameter *m* **-s,-** diameter
Diapositiv *nt* **-s,-e** (*Phot*) slide
Diaprojektor *m* slide projector
Diät *f* **-,-en** (*Med*) diet. **d~** *adv* **d~ leben** be on a diet. **D~assistent(in)** *m*(*f*) dietician
dich *pron* (*acc of* **du**) you; (*refl*) yourself
dicht *a* dense; (*dick*) thick; (*undurchlässig*) airtight; (*wasser-*) watertight ● *adv* densely; thickly; (*nahe*) close (**bei** to). **D~e** *f* **-** density. **d~en**[1] *vt* make watertight; (*ab-*) seal
dicht|en[2] *vi* (*haben*) write poetry. ● *vt* write, compose. **D~er(in)** *m* **-s,-** (*f* **-,-nen**) poet. **d~erisch** *a* poetic. **D~ung**[1] *f* **-,-en** poetry; (*Gedicht*) poem
Dichtung[2] *f* **-,-en** seal; (*Ring*) washer; (*Auto*) gasket
dick *a* thick, *adv* -ly; (*beleibt*) fat; (*geschwollen*) swollen; (*fam: eng*) close; **d~ werden** get fat; **d~ machen** be fattening; **ein d~es Fell haben** (*fam*) be thick-skinned. **D~e** *f* **-,-n** thickness; (*D~leibigkeit*) fatness. **d~fellig** *a* (*fam*) thick-skinned. **d~flüssig** *a* thick; (*Phys*) viscous. **D~kopf** *m* (*fam*) stubborn person; **einen D~kopf haben** be

stubborn. **d~köpfig** *a* (*fam*) stubborn
didaktisch *a* didactic
die *def art & pron s.* **der**
Dieb|(in) *m* **-[e]s,-e** (*f* **-,-nen**) thief. **d~isch** *a* thieving; ⟨*Freude*⟩ malicious. **D~stahl** *m* **-[e]s,¨-e** theft; (*geistiger*) plagiarism
diejenige *pron s.* **derjenige**
Diele *f* **-,-n** floorboard; (*Flur*) hall
dien|en *vi* (*haben*) serve. **D~er** *m* **-s,-** servant; (*Verbeugung*) bow. **D~erin** *f* **-,-nen** maid, servant. **d~lich** *a* helpful
Dienst *m* **-[e]s,-e** service; (*Arbeit*) work; (*Amtsausübung*) duty; **außer D~** off duty; (*pensioniert*) retired; **D~ haben** work; ⟨*Soldat, Arzt:*⟩ be on duty; **jdm einen schlechten D~ erweisen** do s.o. a disservice
Dienstag *m* Tuesday. **d~s** *adv* on Tuesdays
Dienst|alter *nt* seniority. **d~bereit** *a* obliging; ⟨*Apotheke*⟩ open. **D~bote** *m* servant. **d~eifrig** *a* zealous, *adv* -ly. **d~frei** *a* **d~freier Tag** day off; **d~frei haben** have time off; ⟨*Soldat, Arzt:*⟩ be off duty. **D~grad** *m* rank. **d~habend** *a* duty ... **D~leistung** *f* service. **d~lich** *a* official • *adv* **d~lich verreist** away on business. **D~mädchen** *nt* maid. **D~reise** *f* business trip. **D~stelle** *f* office. **D~stunden** *fpl* office hours. **D~weg** *m* official channels *pl*
dies *inv pron* this. **d~bezüglich** *a* relevant • *adv* regarding this matter. **d~e(r,s)** *pron* this; (*pl*) these; (*substantivisch*) this [one]; (*pl*) these; **d~e Nacht** tonight; (*letzte*) last night
Diesel *m* **-[s],-** (*fam*) diesel
dieselbe *pron s.* **derselbe**
Diesel|kraftstoff *m* diesel [oil]. **D~motor** *m* diesel engine
diesig *a* hazy, misty
dies|mal *adv* this time. **d~seits** *adv & prep* (+*gen*) this side (of)
Dietrich *m* **-s,-e** skeleton key
Diffam|ation /-ˈt͜si̯o:n/ *f* - defamation. **d~ierend** *a* defamatory
Differential /-ˈt͜si̯a:l/ *nt* **-s,-e** differential
Differenz *f* **-,-en** difference. **d~ieren** *vt/i* (*haben*) differentiate (**zwischen** +*dat* between)
Digital- *pref* digital. **D~uhr** *f* digital clock/watch
Dikt|at *nt* **-[e]s,-e** dictation. **D~ator** *m* **-s,-en** /-ˈto:rən/ dictator. **d~atorisch** *a* dictatorial. **D~atur** *f* **-,-en** dictatorship. **d~ieren** *vt/i* (*haben*) dictate
Dilemma *nt* **-s,-s** dilemma
Dilettant|(in) *m* **-en,-en** (*f* **-,-nen**) dilettante. **d~isch** *a* amateurish
Dill *m* **-s** dill
Dimension *f* **-,-en** dimension
Ding *nt* **-[e]s,-e** & (*fam*) **-er** thing; **guter D~e sein** be cheerful; **vor allen D~en** above all
Dinghi /ˈdɪŋgi/ *nt* **-s,-s** dinghy
Dinosaurier /-i̯ɐ/ *m* **-s,-** dinosaur
Diözese *f* **-,-n** diocese
Diphtherie *f* - diphtheria
Diplom *nt* **-s,-e** diploma; (*Univ*) degree
Diplomat *m* **-en,-en** diplomat. **D~ie** *f* - diplomacy. **d~isch** *a* diplomatic, *adv* -ally
dir *pron* (*dat of* **du**) [to] you; (*refl*) yourself; **ein Freund von dir** a friend of yours
direkt *a* direct • *adv* directly; (*wirklich*) really. **D~ion** /-ˈt͜si̯o:n/ *f* - management; (*Vorstand*) board of directors. **D~or** *m* **-s,-en** /-ˈto:rən/, **D~orin** *f* **-,-nen** director; (*Bank-, Theater-*) manager; (*Sch*) head; (*Gefängnis*) governor. **D~übertragung** *f* live transmission
Dirig|ent *m* **-en,-en** (*Mus*) conductor. **d~ieren** *vt* direct; (*Mus*) conduct
Dirndl *nt* **-s,-** dirndl [dress]
Dirne *f* **-,-n** prostitute
Diskant *m* **-s,-e** (*Mus*) treble
Diskette *f* **-,-n** floppy disc
Disko *f* **-,-s** (*fam*) disco. **D~thek** *f* **-,-en** discothèque
Diskrepanz *f* **-,-en** discrepancy
diskret *a* discreet, *adv* -ly. **D~ion** /-ˈt͜si̯o:n/ *f* - discretion
diskriminier|en *vt* discriminate against. **D~ung** *f* - discrimination
Diskus *m* **-,-se** & **Disken** discus
Disku|ssion *f* **-,-en** discussion. **d~tieren** *vt/i* (*haben*) discuss
disponieren *vi* (*haben*) make arrangements; **d~ [können] über** (+*acc*) have at one's disposal
Disput *m* **-[e]s,-e** dispute
Disqualifi|kation /-ˈt͜si̯o:n/ *f* disqualification. **d~zieren** *vt* disqualify
Dissertation /-ˈt͜si̯o:n/ *f* **-,-en** dissertation
Dissident *m* **-en,-en** dissident
Dissonanz *f* **-,-en** dissonance

Distanz *f* **-,-en** distance. **d~ieren (sich)** *vr* dissociate oneself (**von** from). **d~iert** *a* aloof

Distel *f* **-,-n** thistle

distinguiert /dɪstɪŋ'gi:ɐ̯t/ *a* distinguished

Disziplin *f* **-,-en** discipline. **d~arisch** *a* disciplinary. **d~iert** *a* disciplined

dito *adv* ditto

diverse *attrib a pl* various

Divid|ende *f* **-,-n** dividend. **d~ieren** *vt* divide (**durch** by)

Division *f* **-,-en** division

DJH *abbr* (**Deutsche Jugendherberge**) [German] youth hostel

DM *abbr* (**Deutsche Mark**) DM

doch *conj & adv* but; (*dennoch*) yet; (*trotzdem*) after all; **wenn d~ . . . !** if only . . . ! **nicht d~!** don't [do that]! **er kommt d~?** he is coming, isn't he? **kommst du nicht?— d~!** aren't you coming?—yes, I am!

Docht *m* **-[e]s,-e** wick

Dock *nt* **-s,-s** dock. **d~en** *vt/i* (*haben*) dock

Dogge *f* **-,-n** Great Dane

Dogm|a *nt* **-s,-men** dogma. **d~atisch** *a* dogmatic, *adv* -ally

Dohle *f* **-,-n** jackdaw

Doktor *m* **-s,-en** /-'to:rən/ doctor. **D~arbeit** *f* [doctoral] thesis. **D~würde** *f* doctorate

Doktrin *f* **-,-en** doctrine

Dokument *nt* **-[e]s,-e** document. **D~arbericht** *m* documentary. **D~arfilm** *m* documentary film

Dolch *m* **-[e]s,-e** dagger

doll *a* (*fam*) fantastic; (*schlimm*) awful ● *adv* beautifully; (*sehr*) very; (*schlimm*) badly

Dollar *m* **-s,-** dollar

dolmetsch|en *vt/i* (*haben*) interpret. **D~er(in)** *m* **-s,-** (*f* **-,-nen**) interpreter

Dom *m* **-[e]s,-e** cathedral

domin|ant *a* dominant. **d~ieren** *vi* (*haben*) dominate; (*vorherrschen*) predominate

Domino *nt* **-s,-s** dominoes *sg*. **D~stein** *m* domino

Dompfaff *m* **-en,-en** bullfinch

Donau *f* **-** Danube

Donner *m* **-s** thunder. **d~n** *vi* (*haben*) thunder

Donnerstag *m* Thursday. **d~s** *adv* on Thursdays

Donnerwetter *nt* (*fam*) telling-off; (*Krach*) row ● *int* /'--'--/ wow! (*Fluch*) damn it!

doof *a* (*fam*) stupid, *adv* -ly

Doppel *nt* **-s,-** duplicate; (*Tennis*) doubles *pl*. **D~bett** *nt* double bed. **D~decker** *m* **-s,-** double-decker [bus]. **d~deutig** *a* ambiguous. **D~gänger** *m* **-s,-** double. **D~kinn** *nt* double chin. **D~name** *m* double-barrelled name. **D~punkt** *m* (*Gram*) colon. **D~schnitte** *f* sandwich. **d~sinnig** *a* ambiguous. **D~stecker** *m* two-way adaptor. **d~t** *a* double; ⟨*Boden*⟩ false; **in d~ter Ausfertigung** in duplicate; **die d~te Menge** twice the amount ● *adv* doubly; (*zweimal*) twice; **d~t so viel** twice as much. **D~zimmer** *nt* double room

Dorf *nt* **-[e]s,¨er** village. **D~bewohner** *m* villager

dörflich *a* rural

Dorn *m* **-[e]s,-en** thorn. **d~ig** *a* thorny

Dörrobst *nt* dried fruit

Dorsch *m* **-[e]s,-e** cod

dort *adv* there; **d~ drüben** over there. **d~her** *adv* **[von] d~her** from there. **d~hin** *adv* there. **d~ig** *a* local

Dose *f* **-,-n** tin, can; (*Schmuck-*) box

dösen *vi* (*haben*) doze

Dosen|milch *f* evaporated milk. **D~öffner** *m* tin *or* can opener

dosieren *vt* measure out

Dosis *f* **-, Dosen** dose

Dotter *m & nt* **-s,-** [egg] yolk

Dozent(in) *m* **-en,-en** (*f* **-,-nen**) (*Univ*) lecturer

Dr. *abbr* (**Doktor**) Dr

Drache *m* **-n,-n** dragon. **D~n** *m* **-s,-** kite; (*fam: Frau*) dragon. **D~nfliegen** *nt* hang-gliding. **D~nflieger** *m* hang-glider

Draht *m* **-[e]s,¨e** wire; **auf D~** (*fam*) on the ball. **d~ig** *a* (*fig*) wiry. **D~seilbahn** *f* cable railway

drall *a* plump; ⟨*Frau*⟩ buxom

Dram|a *nt* **-s,-men** drama. **D~atik** *f* - drama. **D~atiker** *m* **-s,-** dramatist. **d~atisch** *a* dramatic, *adv* -ally. **d~atisieren** *vt* dramatize

dran *adv* (*fam*) = **daran; gut/schlecht d~ sein** be well off/in a bad way; **ich bin d~** it's my turn

Dränage /-'na:ʒə/ *f* - drainage

Drang *m* **-[e]s** urge; (*Druck*) pressure

dräng|eln *vt/i* (*haben*) push; (*bedrängen*) pester. **d~en** *vt* push; (*bedrängen*) urge; **sich d~en** crowd (**um** round) ● *vi* (*haben*) push; (*eilen*) be urgent; ⟨*Zeit:*⟩ press; **d~en auf** (+*acc*) press for

dran|halten† **(sich)** *vr sep* hurry. **d~kommen†** *vi sep* (*sein*) have one's turn; **wer kommt dran?** whose turn is it?

drapieren *vt* drape

drastisch *a* drastic, *adv* -ally

drauf *adv* (*fam*) = **darauf**; **d~ und dran sein** be on the point (**etw zu tun** of doing sth). **D~gänger** *m* **-s,-** daredevil. **d~gängerisch** *a* reckless

draus *adv* (*fam*) = **daraus**

draußen *adv* outside; (*im Freien*) out of doors

drechseln *vt* (*Techn*) turn

Dreck *m* **-s** dirt; (*Morast*) mud; (*fam: Kleinigkeit*) trifle; **in den D~ ziehen** (*fig*) denigrate. **d~ig** *a* dirty; muddy

Dreh *m* **-s** (*fam*) knack; **den D~ heraushaben** have got the hang of it. **D~bank** *f* lathe. **D~bleistift** *m* propelling pencil. **D~buch** *nt* screenplay, script. **d~en** *vt* turn; (*im Kreis*) rotate; (*verschlingen*) twist; roll ⟨*Zigarette*⟩; shoot ⟨*Film*⟩; **lauter/leiser d~en** turn up/down; **sich d~en** turn; (*im Kreis*) rotate; (*schnell*) spin; ⟨*Wind:*⟩ change; **sich d~en um** revolve around; (*sich handeln*) be about ● *vi* (*haben*) turn; ⟨*Wind:*⟩ change; **an etw** (*dat*) **d~en** turn sth. **D~orgel** *f* barrel organ. **D~stuhl** *m* swivel chair. **D~tür** *f* revolving door. **D~ung** *f* **-,-en** turn; (*im Kreis*) rotation. **D~zahl** *f* number of revolutions

drei *inv a*, **D~** *f* **-,-en** three; (*Sch*) ≈ pass. **D~eck** *nt* **-[e]s,-e** triangle. **d~eckig** *a* triangular. **D~einigkeit** *f* **- die [Heilige] D~einigkeit** the [Holy] Trinity. **d~erlei** *inv a* three kinds of ● *pron* three things. **d~fach** *a* triple; **in d~facher Ausfertigung** in triplicate. **D~faltigkeit** *f* - = **D~einigkeit. d~mal** *adv* three times. **D~rad** *nt* tricycle

dreißig *inv a* thirty. **d~ste(r,s)** *a* thirtieth

dreist *a* impudent, *adv* -ly; (*verwegen*) audacious, *adv* -ly. **D~igkeit** *f* - impudence; audacity

dreiviertel *inv a* three-quarter. **D~stunde** *f* three-quarters of an hour

dreizehn *inv a* thirteen. **d~te(r,s)** *a* thirteenth

dreschen† *vt* thresh

dress|ieren *vt* train. **D~ur** *f* - training

dribbeln *vi* (*haben*) dribble

Drill *m* **-[e]s** (*Mil*) drill. **d~en** *vt* drill

Drillinge *mpl* triplets

drin *adv* (*fam*) = **darin**; (*drinnen*) inside

dring|en† *vi* (*sein*) penetrate (**in** + *acc* into; **durch etw** sth); (*heraus-*) come (**aus** out of); **d~en auf** (+ *acc*) insist on. **d~end** *a* urgent, *adv* -ly. **d~lich** *a* urgent. **D~lichkeit** *f* - urgency

Drink *m* **-[s],-s** [alcoholic] drink

drinnen *adv* inside; (*im Haus*) indoors

dritt *adv* **zu d~** in threes; **wir waren zu d~** there were three of us. **d~e(r,s)** *a* third; **ein D~er** a third person. **D~el** *nt* **-s,-** third. **d~ens** *adv* thirdly. **d~rangig** *a* third-rate

Drog|e *f* **-,-n** drug. **D~enabhängige(r)** *m/f* drug addict. **D~erie** *f* **-,-n** chemist's shop, (*Amer*) drugstore. **D~ist** *m* **-en,-en** chemist

drohen *vi* (*haben*) threaten (**jdm** s.o.). **d~d** *a* threatening; ⟨*Gefahr*⟩ imminent

dröhnen *vi* (*haben*) resound; (*tönen*) boom

Drohung *f* **-,-en** threat

drollig *a* funny; (*seltsam*) odd

Drops *m* **-,-** [fruit] drop

Droschke *f* **-,-n** cab

Drossel *f* **-,-n** thrush

drosseln *vt* (*Techn*) throttle; (*fig*) cut back

drüb|en *adv* over there. **d~er** *adv* (*fam*) = **darüber**

Druck[1] *m* **-[e]s,⸚e** pressure; **unter D~ setzen** (*fig*) pressurize

Druck[2] *m* **-[e]s,-e** printing; (*Schrift, Reproduktion*) print. **D~buchstabe** *m* block letter

Drückeberger *m* **-s,-** shirker

drucken *vt* print

drücken *vt/i* (*haben*) press; (*aus-*) squeeze; ⟨*Schuh:*⟩ pinch; (*umarmen*) hug; (*fig: belasten*) weigh down; **Preise d~** force down prices; (*an Tür*) **d~** push; **sich d~** (*fam*) make oneself scarce; **sich d~ vor** (+ *dat*) (*fam*) shirk. **d~d** *a* heavy; (*schwül*) oppressive

Drucker *m* **-s,-** printer

Drücker *m* **-s,-** push-button; (*Tür-*) door knob

Druckerei *f* **-,-en** printing works

Druck|fehler *m* misprint. **D~knopf** *m* press-stud; (*Drücker*) push-button. **D~luft** *f* compressed air. **D~sache** *f* printed matter. **D~schrift** *f* type; (*Veröffentlichung*)

publication; **in D~schrift** in block letters *pl*

drucksen *vi* (*haben*) hum and haw

Druck|stelle *f* bruise. **D~taste** *f* push-button. **D~topf** *m* pressure-cooker

drum *adv* (*fam*) = **darum**

drunter *adv* (*fam*) = **darunter; alles geht d~ und drüber** (*fam*) everything is topsy-turvy

Drüse *f* **-,-n** (*Anat*) gland

Dschungel *m* **-s,-** jungle

du *pron* (*familiar address*) you; **auf du und du** on familiar terms

Dübel *m* **-s,-** plug

duck|en *vt* duck; (*fig: demütigen*) humiliate; **sich d~en** duck; (*fig*) cringe. **D~mäuser** *m* **-s,-** moral coward

Dudelsack *m* bagpipes *pl*

Duell *nt* **-s,-e** duel

Duett *nt* **-s,-e** [vocal] duet

Duft *m* **-[e]s,¨-e** fragrance, scent; (*Aroma*) aroma. **d~en** *vi* (*haben*) smell (**nach** of). **d~ig** *a* fine; (*zart*) delicate

duld|en *vt* tolerate; (*erleiden*) suffer ● *vi* (*haben*) suffer. **d~sam** *a* tolerant

dumm *a* **(dümmer, dümmst)** stupid, *adv* -ly; (*unklug*) foolish, *adv* -ly; (*fam: lästig*) awkward; **wie d~!** what a nuisance! **der D~e sein** (*fig*) be the loser. **d~erweise** *adv* stupidly; (*leider*) unfortunately. **D~heit** *f* **-,-en** stupidity; (*Torheit*) foolishness; (*Handlung*) folly. **D~kopf** *m* (*fam*) fool.

dumpf *a* dull, *adv* -y; (*muffig*) musty. **d~ig** *a* musty

Düne *f* **-,-n** dune

Dung *m* **-s** manure

Düng|emittel *nt* fertilizer. **d~en** *vt* fertilize. **D~er** *m* **-s,-** fertilizer

dunk|el *a* dark; (*vage*) vague, *adv* -ly; (*fragwürdig*) shady; **d~les Bier** brown ale; **im D~eln** in the dark

Dünkel *m* **-s** conceit

dunkel|blau *a* dark blue. **d~braun** *a* dark brown

dünkelhaft *a* conceited

Dunkel|heit *f* **-** darkness. **D~kammer** *f* dark-room. **d~n** *vi* (*haben*) get dark. **d~rot** *a* dark red

dünn *a* thin, *adv* -ly; ⟨*Buch*⟩ slim; (*spärlich*) sparse; (*schwach*) weak

Dunst *m* **-es,¨-e** mist, haze; (*Dampf*) vapour

dünsten *vt* steam

dunstig *a* misty, hazy

Dünung *f* **-** swell

Duo *nt* **-s,-s** [instrumental] duet

Duplikat *nt* **-[e]s,-e** duplicate

Dur *nt* **-** (*Mus*) major [key]; **in A-Dur** in A major

durch *prep* (+*acc*) through; (*mittels*) by; **[geteilt] d~** (*Math*) divided by ● *adv* **die Nacht d~** throughout the night; **sechs Uhr d~** (*fam*) gone six o'clock; **d~ und d~ naß** wet through

durcharbeiten *vt sep* work through; **sich d~** work one's way through

durchaus *adv* absolutely; **d~ nicht** by no means

durchbeißen† *vt sep* bite through

durchblättern *vt sep* leaf through

durchblicken *vi sep* (*haben*) look through; **d~ lassen** (*fig*) hint at

Durchblutung *f* circulation

durchbohren *vt insep* pierce

durchbrechen[1]† *vt/i sep* (*haben*) break [in two]

durchbrechen[2]† *vt insep* break through; break ⟨*Schallmauer*⟩

durchbrennen† *vi sep* (*sein*) burn through; ⟨*Sicherung:*⟩ blow; (*fam: weglaufen*) run away

durchbringen† *vt sep* get through; (*verschwenden*) squander; (*versorgen*) support; **sich d~ mit** make a living by

Durchbruch *m* breakthrough

durchdacht *a* **gut d~** well thought out

durchdrehen *v sep* ● *vt* mince ● *vi* (*haben/sein*) (*fam*) go crazy

durchdringen[1]† *vt insep* penetrate

durchdringen[2]† *vi sep* (*sein*) penetrate; (*sich durchsetzen*) get one's way. **d~d** *a* penetrating; ⟨*Schrei*⟩ piercing

durcheinander *adv* in a muddle; ⟨*Person*⟩ confused. **D~** *nt* **-s** muddle. **d~bringen**† *vt sep* muddle [up]; confuse ⟨*Person*⟩. **d~geraten**† *vi sep* (*sein*) get mixed up. **d~reden** *vi sep* (*haben*) all talk at once

durchfahren[1]† *vi sep* (*sein*) drive through; ⟨*Zug:*⟩ go through

durchfahren[2]† *vt insep* drive/go through; **jdn d~** ⟨*Gedanke:*⟩ flash through s.o.'s mind

Durchfahrt *f* journey/drive through; **auf der D~** passing through; **'D~ verboten'** 'no thoroughfare'

Durchfall *m* diarrhoea; (*fam: Versagen*) flop. **d~en**† *vi sep* (*sein*) fall through; (*fam: versagen*) flop; (*bei Prüfung*) fail

durchfliegen[1]† *vi sep* (*sein*) fly through; (*fam: durchfallen*) fail

durchfliegen[2]† *vt insep* fly through; (*lesen*) skim through

durchfroren *a* frozen

Durchfuhr *f* - (*Comm*) transit

durchführ|bar *a* feasible. **d~en** *vt sep* carry out

Durchgang *m* passage; (*Sport*) round; **'D~ verboten'** 'no entry'. **D~sverkehr** *m* through traffic

durchgeben† *vt sep* pass through; (*übermitteln*) transmit; (*Radio, TV*) broadcast

durchgebraten *a* **gut d~** well done

durchgehen† *v sep* ● *vi* (*sein*) go through; (*davonlaufen*) run away; ⟨*Pferd:*⟩ bolt; **jdm etw d~ lassen** let s.o. get away with sth ● *vt* go through. **d~d** *a* continuous, *adv* -ly; **d~d geöffnet** open all day; **d~der Wagen/Zug** through carriage/train

durchgreifen† *vi sep* (*haben*) reach through; (*vorgehen*) take drastic action. **d~d** *a* drastic

durchhalte|n† *v sep* (*fig*) ● *vi* (*haben*) hold out ● *vt* keep up. **D~vermögen** *nt* stamina

durchhängen† *vi sep* (*haben*) sag

durchkommen† *vi sep* (*sein*) come through; (*gelangen, am Telefon*) get through; (*bestehen*) pass; (*überleben*) pull through; (*finanziell*) get by (**mit** on)

durchkreuzen *vt insep* thwart

durchlassen† *vt sep* let through

durchlässig *a* permeable; (*undicht*) leaky

durchlaufen[1]† *v sep* ● *vi* (*sein*) run through ● *vt* wear out

durchlaufen[2]† *vt insep* pass through

Durchlauferhitzer *m* **-s,-** geyser

durchleben *vt insep* live through

durchlesen† *vt sep* read through

durchleuchten *vt insep* X-ray

durchlöchert *a* riddled with holes

durchmachen *vt sep* go through; (*erleiden*) undergo; have ⟨*Krankheit*⟩

Durchmesser *m* **-s,-** diameter

durchnäßt *a* wet through

durchnehmen† *vt sep* (*Sch*) do

durchnumeriert *a* numbered consecutively

durchpausen *vt sep* trace

durchqueren *vt insep* cross

Durchreiche *f* **-,-n** [serving] hatch. **d~n** *vt sep* pass through

Durchreise *f* journey through; **auf der D~** passing through. **d~n** *vi sep* (*sein*) pass through

durchreißen† *vt/i sep* (*sein*) tear

durchs *adv* = **durch das**

Durchsage *f* **-,-n** announcement. **d~n** *vt sep* announce

durchschauen *vt insep* (*fig*) see through

durchscheinend *a* translucent

Durchschlag *m* carbon copy; (*Culin*) colander. **d~en**[1]† *v sep* ● *vt* (*Culin*) rub through a sieve; **sich d~en** (*fig*) struggle through ● *vi* (*sein*) ⟨*Sicherung:*⟩ blow

durchschlagen[2]† *vt insep* smash

durchschlagend *a* (*fig*) effective; ⟨*Erfolg*⟩ resounding

durchschneiden† *vt sep* cut

Durchschnitt *m* average; **im D~** on average. **d~lich** *a* average ● *adv* on average. **D~s-** *pref* average

Durchschrift *f* carbon copy

durchsehen† *v sep* ● *vi* (*haben*) see through ● *vt* look through

durchseihen *vt sep* strain

durchsetzen[1] *vt sep* force through; **sich d~** assert oneself; ⟨*Mode:*⟩catch on

durchsetzen[2] *vt insep* intersperse; (*infiltrieren*) infiltrate

Durchsicht *f* check

durchsichtig *a* transparent

durchsickern *vi sep* (*sein*) seep through; ⟨*Neuigkeit:*⟩ leak out

durchsprechen† *vt sep* discuss

durchstehen† *vt sep* (*fig*) come through

durchstreichen† *vt sep* cross out

durchsuch|en *vt insep* search. **D~ung** *f* **-,-en** search

durchtrieben *a* cunning

durchwachsen *a* ⟨*Speck*⟩ streaky; (*fam: gemischt*) mixed

durchwacht *a* sleepless ⟨*Nacht*⟩

durchwählen *vi sep* (*haben*) (*Teleph*) dial direct

durchweg *adv* without exception

durchweicht *a* soggy

durchwühlen *vt insep* rummage through; ransack ⟨*Haus*⟩

durchziehen† *v sep* ● *vt* pull through ● *vi* (*sein*) pass through

durchzucken *vt insep* (*fig*) shoot through; **jdn d~** ⟨*Gedanke:*⟩ flash through s.o.'s mind

Durchzug *m* through draught

dürfen† *vt & v aux* **etw [tun] d~** be allowed to do sth; **darf ich?** may I? **sie darf es nicht sehen** she must not see it; **ich hätte es nicht tun/sagen d~** I ought not to have done/said it; **das dürfte nicht allzu schwer sein** that should not be too difficult

dürftig *a* poor; ⟨*Mahlzeit*⟩ scanty

dürr *a* dry; ⟨*Boden*⟩ arid; (*mager*) skinny. **D~e** *f* **-,-n** drought

Durst *m* **-[e]s** thirst; **D~ haben** be thirsty. **d~en** *vi* (*haben*) be thirsty. **d~ig** *a* thirsty

Dusche *f* **-,-n** shower. **d~n** *vi/r* (*haben*) **[sich] d~n** have a shower

Düse *f* **-,-n** nozzle. **D~nflugzeug** *nt* jet

düster *a* gloomy, *adv* -ily; (*dunkel*) dark

Dutzend *nt* **-s,-e** dozen. **d~weise** *adv* by the dozen

duzen *vt* **jdn d~** call s.o. 'du'

Dynam|ik *f* **-** dynamics *sg*; (*fig*) dynamism. **d~isch** *a* dynamic; ⟨*Rente*⟩ index-linked

Dynamit *nt* **-es** dynamite

Dynamo *m* **-s,-s** dynamo

Dynastie *f* **-,-n** dynasty

D-Zug /'de:-/ *m* express [train]

E

Ebbe *f* **-,-n** low tide

eben *a* level; (*glatt*) smooth; **zu e~er Erde** on the ground floor ● *adv* just; (*genau*) exactly; **e~ noch** only just; (*gerade vorhin*) just now; **das ist es e~!** that's just it! **[na] e~!** exactly! **E~bild** *nt* image. **e~bürtig** *a* equal; **jdm e~bürtig sein** be s.o.'s equal

Ebene *f* **-,-n** (*Geog*) plain; (*Geom*) plane; (*fig: Niveau*) level

eben|falls *adv* also; **danke, e~falls** thank you, [the] same to you. **E~holz** *nt* ebony. **e~mäßig** *a* regular, *adv* -ly. **e~so** *adv* just the same; (*ebensosehr*) just as much; **e~so gut/teuer** just as good/expensive. **e~sogut** *adv* just as well. **e~sosehr** *adv* just as much. **e~soviel** *adv* just as much/many. **e~sowenig** *adv* just as little/few; (*noch*) no more

Eber *m* **-s,-** boar. **E~esche** *f* rowan

ebnen *vt* level; (*fig*) smooth

Echo *nt* **-s,-s** echo. **e~en** *vt/i* (*haben*) echo

echt *a* genuine, real; (*authentisch*) authentic; ⟨*Farbe*⟩ fast; (*typisch*) typical ● *adv* (*fam*) really; typically. **E~heit** *f* **-** authenticity

Eck|ball *m* (*Sport*) corner. **E~e** *f* **-,-n** corner; **um die E~e bringen** (*fam*) bump off. **e~ig** *a* angular; ⟨*Klammern*⟩ square; (*unbeholfen*) awkward. **E~stein** *m* corner-stone. **E~stoß** *m* = **E~ball**. **E~zahn** *m* canine tooth

Ecu, ECU /e'ky:/ *m* **-[s],-[s]** ecu

edel *a* noble, *adv* -bly; (*wertvoll*) precious; (*fein*) fine. **E~mann** *m* (*pl* **-leute**) nobleman. **E~mut** *m* magnanimity. **e~mütig** *a* magnanimous, *adv* -ly. **E~stahl** *m* stainless steel. **E~stein** *m* precious stone

Efeu *m* **-s** ivy

Effekt *m* **-[e]s,-e** effect. **E~en** *pl* securities. **e~iv** *a* actual, *adv* -ly; (*wirksam*) effective, *adv* -ly. **e~voll** *a* effective

EG *f* **-** *abbr* (**Europäische Gemeinschaft**) EC

egal *a* **das ist mir e~** (*fam*) it's all the same to me ● *adv* **e~ wie/wo** no matter how/where. **e~itär** *a* egalitarian

Egge *f* **-,-n** harrow

Ego|ismus *m* **-** selfishness. **E~ist(in)** *m* **-en,-en** (*f* **-,-nen**) egoist. **e~istisch** *a* selfish, *adv* -ly. **e~zentrisch** *a* egocentric

eh *adv* (*Aust fam*) anyway; **seit eh und je** from time immemorial

ehe *conj* before; **ehe nicht** until

Ehe *f* **-,-n** marriage. **E~bett** *nt* double bed. **E~bruch** *m* adultery. **E~frau** *f* wife. **E~leute** *pl* married couple *sg*. **e~lich** *a* marital; ⟨*Recht*⟩ conjugal; ⟨*Kind*⟩ legitimate

ehemal|ig *a* former. **e~s** *adv* formerly

Ehe|mann *m* (*pl* **-männer**) husband. **E~paar** *nt* married couple

eher *adv* earlier, sooner; (*lieber, vielmehr*) rather; (*mehr*) more

Ehering *m* wedding ring

ehr|bar *a* respectable. **E~e** *f* **-,-n** honour; **jdm E~e machen** do credit to s.o. **e~en** *vt* honour. **e~enamtlich** *a* honorary ● *adv* in an honorary capacity. **E~endoktorat** *nt* honorary doctorate. **E~engast** *m* guest of honour. **e~enhaft** *a* honourable, *adv* -bly. **E~enmann** *m* (*pl*

-männer) man of honour. **E~enmitglied** *nt* honorary member. **e~enrührig** *a* defamatory. **E~enrunde** *f* lap of honour. **E~ensache** *f* point of honour. **e~enwert** *a* honourable. **E~enwort** *nt* word of honour. **e~erbietig** *a* deferential, *adv* -ly. **E~erbietung** *f* - deference. **E~furcht** *f* reverence; (*Scheu*) awe. **e~fürchtig** *a* reverent, *adv* -ly. **E~gefühl** *nt* sense of honour. **E~geiz** *m* ambition. **e~geizig** *a* ambitious. **e~lich** *a* honest, *adv* -ly; **e~lich gesagt** to be honest. **E~lichkeit** *f* - honesty. **e~los** *a* dishonourable. **e~sam** *a* respectable. **e~würdig** *a* venerable; (*als Anrede*) Reverend

Ei *nt* **-[e]s,-er** egg

Eibe *f* **-,-n** yew

Eiche *f* **-,-n** oak. **E~l** *f* **-,-n** acorn. **E~lhäher** *m* **-s,-** jay

eichen *vt* standardize

Eichhörnchen *nt* **-s,-** squirrel

Eid *m* **-[e]s,-e** oath

Eidechse *f* **-,-n** lizard

eidlich *a* sworn ● *adv* on oath

Eidotter *m & nt* egg yolk

Eier|becher *m* egg-cup. **E~kuchen** *m* pancake; (*Omelett*) omelette. **E~schale** *f* eggshell. **E~schnee** *m* beaten egg-white. **E~stock** *m* ovary. **E~uhr** *f* egg-timer

Eifer *m* **-s** eagerness; (*Streben*) zeal. **E~sucht** *f* jealousy. **e~süchtig** *a* jealous, *adv* -ly

eiförmig *a* egg-shaped; (*oval*) oval

eifrig *a* eager, *adv* -ly; (*begeistert*) keen, *adv* -ly

Eigelb *nt* **-[e]s,-e** [egg] yolk

eigen *a* own; (*typisch*) characteristic (*dat* of); (*seltsam*) odd, *adv* -ly; (*genau*) particular. **E~art** *f* peculiarity. **e~artig** *a* peculiar, *adv* -ly; (*seltsam*) odd. **E~brötler** *m* **-s,-** crank. **e~händig** *a* personal, *adv* -ly; ⟨*Unterschrift*⟩ own. **E~heit** *f* **-,-en** peculiarity. **e~mächtig** *a* high-handed; (*unbefugt*) unauthorized ● *adv* high-handedly; without authority. **E~name** *m* proper name. **E~nutz** *m* self-interest. **e~nützig** *a* selfish, *adv* -ly. **e~s** *adv* specially. **E~schaft** *f* **-,-en** quality; (*Phys*) property; (*Merkmal*) characteristic; (*Funktion*) capacity. **E~schaftswort** *nt* (*pl* **-wörter**) adjective. **E~sinn** *m* obstinacy. **e~sinnig** *a* obstinate, *adv* -ly

eigentlich *a* actual, real; (*wahr*) true ● *adv* actually, really; (*streng genommen*) strictly speaking; **wie geht es ihm e~?** by the way, how is he?

Eigen|tor *nt* own goal. **E~tum** *nt* **-s** property. **E~tümer(in)** *m* **-s,-** (*f* **-,-nen**) owner. **e~tümlich** *a* odd, *adv* -ly; (*typisch*) characteristic. **E~tumswohnung** *f* freehold flat. **e~willig** *a* self-willed; ⟨*Stil*⟩ highly individual

eign|en (sich) *vr* be suitable. **E~ung** *f* - suitability

Eil|brief *m* express letter. **E~e** *f* - hurry; **E~e haben** be in a hurry; ⟨*Sache:*⟩ be urgent. **e~en** *vi* (*sein*) hurry ● (*haben*) (*drängen*) be urgent. **e~ends** *adv* hurriedly. **e~ig** *a* hurried, *adv* -ly; (*dringend*) urgent, *adv* -ly; **es e~ig haben** be in a hurry. **E~zug** *m* semi-fast train

Eimer *m* **-s,-** bucket; (*Abfall-*) bin

ein[1] *adj* one; **e~es Tages/Abends** one day/evening; **mit jdm in einem Zimmer schlafen** sleep in the same room as s.o. ● *indef art* a, (*vor Vokal*) an; **so ein** such a; **was für ein** (*Frage*) what kind of a? (*Ausruf*) what a!

ein[2] *adv* **ein und aus** in and out; **nicht mehr ein noch aus wissen** (*fam*) be at one's wits' end

einander *pron* one another

einarbeiten *vt sep* train

einäscher|n *vt sep* reduce to ashes; cremate ⟨*Leiche*⟩. **E~ung** *f* **-,-en** cremation

einatmen *vt/i sep* (*haben*) inhale, breathe in

ein|äugig *a* one-eyed. **E~bahnstraße** *f* one-way street

einbalsamieren *vt sep* embalm

Einband *m* binding

Einbau *m* installation; (*Montage*) fitting. **e~en** *vt sep* install; (*montieren*) fit. **E~küche** *f* fitted kitchen

einbegriffen *pred a* included

einberuf|en† *vt sep* convene; (*Mil*) call up, (*Amer*) draft. **E~ung** *f* call-up, (*Amer*) draft

Einbettzimmer *nt* single room

einbeulen *vt sep* dent

einbeziehen† *vt sep* **[mit] e~** include; (*berücksichtigen*) take into account

einbiegen† *vi sep* (*sein*) turn

einbild|en *vt sep* **sich** (*dat*) **etw e~en** imagine sth; **sich** (*dat*) **viel e~en** be conceited. **E~ung** *f* imagination;

(*Dünkel*) conceit. **E~ungskraft** *f* imagination
einblenden *vt sep* fade in
einbleuen *vt sep* **jdm etw e~** (*fam*) drum sth into s.o.
Einblick *m* insight
einbrech|en† *vi sep* (*haben/sein*) break in; **bei uns ist eingebrochen worden** we have been burgled • (*sein*) set in; ⟨*Nacht:*⟩ fall. **E~er** *m* burglar
einbring|en† *vt sep* get in; bring in ⟨*Geld*⟩; **das bringt nichts ein** it's not worth while. **e~lich** *a* profitable
Einbruch *m* burglary; **bei E~ der Nacht** at nightfall
einbürger|n *vt sep* naturalize; **sich e~n** become established. **E~ung** *f* - naturalization
Ein|buße *f* loss (**an** + *dat* of). **e~büßen** *vt sep* lose
einchecken /-tʃɛkən/ *vt/i sep* (*haben*) check in
eindecken (sich) *vr sep* stock up
eindeutig *a* unambiguous; (*deutlich*) clear, *adv* -ly
eindicken *vt sep* (*Culin*) thicken
eindring|en† *vi sep* (*sein*) **e~en in** (+*acc*) penetrate into; (*mit Gewalt*) force one's/⟨*Wasser:*⟩ its way into; (*Mil*) invade; **auf jdn e~en** (*fig*) press s.o.; (*bittend*) plead with s.o. **e~lich** *a* urgent, *adv* -ly. **E~ling** *m* **-s,-e** intruder
Eindruck *m* impression; **E~ machen** impress (**auf jdn** s.o.)
eindrücken *vt sep* crush
eindrucksvoll *a* impressive
ein|e(r,s) *pron* one; (*jemand*) someone; (*man*) one, you; **e~er von uns** one of us; **es macht e~en müde** it makes you tired
einebnen *vt sep* level
eineiig *a* ⟨*Zwillinge*⟩ identical
eineinhalb *inv a* one and a half; **e~ Stunden** an hour and a half
Einelternfamilie *f* one-parent family
einengen *vt sep* restrict
Einer *m* **-s,-** (*Math*) unit. **e~** *pron s.* **eine(r,s). e~lei** *inv a* • *attrib a* one kind of; (*eintönig, einheitlich*) the same • *pred a* (*fam*) immaterial; **es ist mir e~lei** it's all the same to me. **E~lei** *nt* **-s** monotony. **e~seits** *adv* on the one hand
einfach *a* simple, *adv* -ly; ⟨*Essen*⟩ plain; ⟨*Faden, Fahrt, Fahrkarte*⟩ single; **e~er Soldat** private. **E~heit** *f* - simplicity
einfädeln *vt sep* thread; (*fig: arrangieren*) arrange; **sich e~** (*Auto*) filter in
einfahr|en† *v sep* • *vi* (*sein*) arrive; ⟨*Zug:*⟩ pull in • *vt* (*Auto*) run in; **die Ernte e~en** get in the harvest. **E~t** *f* arrival; (*Eingang*) entrance, way in; (*Auffahrt*) drive; (*Autobahn-*) access road; **keine E~t** no entry
Einfall *m* idea; (*Mil*) invasion. **e~en**† *vi sep* (*sein*) collapse; (*eindringen*) invade; (*einstimmen*) join in; **jdm e~en** occur to s.o.; **sein Name fällt mir nicht ein** I can't think of his name; **was fällt ihm ein!** what does he think he is doing! **e~sreich** *a* imaginative
Einfalt *f* - naïvety
einfältig *a* simple; (*naiv*) naïve
Einfaltspinsel *m* simpleton
einfangen† *vt sep* catch
einfarbig *a* of one colour; ⟨*Stoff, Kleid*⟩ plain
einfass|en *vt sep* edge; set ⟨*Edelstein*⟩. **E~ung** *f* border, edging
einfetten *vt sep* grease
einfinden† **(sich)** *vr sep* turn up
einfließen† *vi sep* (*sein*) flow in
einflößen *vt sep* **jdm etw e~** give s.o. sips of sth; **jdm Angst e~** (*fig*) frighten s.o.
Einfluß *m* influence. **e~reich** *a* influential
einförmig *a* monotonous, *adv* -ly. **E~keit** *f* - monotony
einfried[ig]|en *vt sep* enclose. **E~ung** *f* **-,-en** enclosure
einfrieren† *vt/i sep* (*sein*) freeze
einfügen *vt sep* insert; (*einschieben*) interpolate; **sich e~** fit in
einfühl|en (sich) *vr sep* empathize (**in** + *acc* with). **e~sam** *a* sensitive
Einfuhr *f* **-,-en** import
einführ|en *vt sep* introduce; (*einstecken*) insert; (*einweisen*) initiate; (*Comm*) import. **e~end** *a* introductory. **E~ung** *f* introduction; (*Einweisung*) initiation
Eingabe *f* petition; (*Computer*) input
Eingang *m* entrance, way in; (*Ankunft*) arrival
eingebaut *a* built-in; ⟨*Schrank*⟩ fitted
eingeben† *vt sep* hand in; (*einflößen*) give (**jdm** s.o.); (*Computer*) feed in
eingebildet *a* imaginary; (*überheblich*) conceited
Eingeborene(r) *m/f* native
Eingebung *f* **-,-en** inspiration

eingedenk *prep* (+*gen*) mindful of
eingefleischt *a* **e~er Junggeselle** confirmed bachelor
eingehakt *adv* arm in arm
eingehen† *v sep* ● *vi* (*sein*) come in; (*ankommen*) arrive; (*einlaufen*) shrink; (*sterben*) die; ⟨*Zeitung, Firma:*⟩ fold; **auf etw** (*acc*) **e~** go into sth; (*annehmen*) agree to sth ● *vt* enter into; contract ⟨*Ehe*⟩; make ⟨*Wette*⟩; take ⟨*Risiko*⟩. **e~d** *a* detailed; (*gründlich*) thorough, *adv* -ly
eingelegt *a* inlaid; (*Culin*) pickled; (*mariniert*) marinaded
eingemacht *a* (*Culin*) bottled
eingenommen *pred a* (*fig*) taken (**von** with); prejudiced (**gegen** against); **von sich e~** conceited
eingeschneit *a* snowbound
eingeschrieben *a* registered
Einge|ständnis *nt* admission. **e~stehen**† *vt sep* admit
eingetragen *a* registered
Eingeweide *pl* bowels, entrails
eingewöhnen (sich) *vr sep* settle in
eingießen† *vt sep* pour in; (*einschenken*) pour
eingleisig *a* single-track
einglieder|n *vt sep* integrate. **E~ung** *f* integration
eingraben† *vt sep* bury
eingravieren *vt sep* engrave
eingreifen† *vi sep* (*haben*) intervene. **E~** *nt* **-s** intervention
Eingriff *m* intervention; (*Med*) operation
einhaken *vt/r sep* **jdn e~** *od* **sich bei jdm e~** take s.o.'s arm
einhalten† *v sep* ● *vt* keep; (*befolgen*) observe ● *vi* (*haben*) stop
einhändigen *vt sep* hand in
einhängen *v sep* ● *vt* hang; put down ⟨*Hörer*⟩; **sich bei jdm e~** take s.o.'s arm ● *vi* (*haben*) hang up
einheimisch *a* local; (*eines Landes*) native; (*Comm*) home-produced. **E~e(r)** *m/f* local; native
Einheit *f* **-,-en** unity; (*Maß-, Mil*) unit. **e~lich** *a* uniform, *adv* -ly; (*vereinheitlicht*) standard. **E~spreis** *m* standard price; (*Fahrpreis*) flat fare
einhellig *a* unanimous, *adv* -ly
einholen *vt sep* catch up with; (*aufholen*) make up for; (*erbitten*) seek; (*einkaufen*) buy; **e~ gehen** go shopping
einhüllen *vt sep* wrap
einhundert *inv a* one hundred

einig *a* united; [**sich** (*dat*)] **e~ werden/sein** come to an/be in agreement
einig|e(r,s) *pron* some; (*ziemlich viel*) quite a lot of; (*substantivisch*) **e~e** *pl* some; (*mehrere*) several; (*ziemlich viele*) quite a lot; **e~es** *sg* some things; **vor e~er Zeit** some time ago. **e~emal** *adv* a few times
einigen *vt* unite; unify ⟨*Land*⟩; **sich e~** come to an agreement; (*ausmachen*) agree (**auf** + *acc* on)
einigermaßen *adv* to some extent; (*ziemlich*) fairly; (*ziemlich gut*) fairly well
Einig|keit *f* - unity; (*Übereinstimmung*) agreement. **E~ung** *f* - unification; (*Übereinkunft*) agreement
einjährig *a* one-year-old; (*ein Jahr dauernd*) one year's ...; **e~e Pflanze** annual
einkalkulieren *vt sep* take into account
einkassieren *vt sep* collect
Einkauf *m* purchase; (*Einkaufen*) shopping; **Einkäufe machen** do some shopping. **e~en** *vt sep* buy; **e~en gehen** go shopping. **E~skorb** *m* shopping/(*im Geschäft*) wire basket. **E~stasche** *f* shopping bag. **E~swagen** *m* shopping trolley. **E~szentrum** *nt* shopping centre
einkehren *vi sep* (*sein*) [**in einem Lokal**] **e~** stop for a meal/drink [at an inn]
einklammern *vt sep* bracket
Einklang *m* harmony; **in E~ stehen** be in accord (**mit** with)
einkleben *vt sep* stick in
einkleiden *vt sep* fit out
einklemmen *vt sep* clamp; **sich** (*dat*) **den Finger in der Tür e~** catch one's finger in the door
einkochen *v sep* ● *vi* (*sein*) boil down ● *vt* preserve, bottle
Einkommen *nt* **-s** income. **E~[s]steuer** *f* income tax
einkreisen *vt sep* encircle; **rot e~** ring in red
Einkünfte *pl* income *sg*; (*Einnahmen*) revenue *sg*
einlad|en† *vt sep* load; (*auffordern*) invite; (*bezahlen für*) treat. **e~end** *a* inviting. **E~ung** *f* invitation
Einlage *f* enclosure; (*Schuh-*) arch support; (*Zahn-*) temporary filling; (*Programm-*) interlude; (*Comm*) investment; (*Bank-*) deposit; **Suppe**

mit E~ soup with noodles/dumplings

Ein|laß *m* **-sses** admittance. **e~lassen**† *vt sep* let in; run ⟨*Bad, Wasser*⟩; **sich auf etw** (*acc*)/**mit jdm e~lassen** get involved in sth/with s.o.

einlaufen† *vi sep* (*sein*) come in; (*ankommen*) arrive; ⟨*Wasser:*⟩ run in; (*schrumpfen*) shrink; **[in den Hafen] e~** enter port

einleben (sich) *vr sep* settle in

Einlege|arbeit *f* inlaid work. **e~n** *vt sep* put in; lay in ⟨*Vorrat*⟩; lodge ⟨*Protest, Berufung*⟩; (*einfügen*) insert; (*Auto*) engage ⟨*Gang*⟩; (*verzieren*) inlay; (*Culin*) pickle; (*marinieren*) marinade; **eine Pause e~n** have a break. **E~sohle** *f* insole

einleit|en *vt sep* initiate; (*eröffnen*) begin. **e~end** *a* introductory. **E~ung** *f* introduction

einlenken *vi sep* (*haben*) (*fig*) relent

einleuchten *vi sep* (*haben*) be clear (*dat* to). **e~d** *a* convincing

einliefer|n *vt sep* take (**ins Krankenhaus** to hospital). **E~ung** *f* admission

einlösen *vt sep* cash ⟨*Scheck*⟩; redeem ⟨*Pfand*⟩; (*fig*) keep

einmachen *vt sep* preserve

einmal *adv* once; (*eines Tages*) one *or* some day; **noch/schon e~** again/before; **noch e~ so teuer** twice as expensive; **auf e~** at the same time; (*plötzlich*) suddenly; **nicht e~** not even; **es geht nun e~ nicht** it's just not possible. **E~eins** *nt* - [multiplication] tables *pl*. **e~ig** *a* single; (*einzigartig*) unique; (*fam: großartig*) fantastic, *adv* -ally

einmarschieren *vi sep* (*sein*) march in

einmisch|en (sich) *vr sep* interfere. **E~ung** *f* interference

einmütig *a* unanimous, *adv* -ly

Einnahme *f* **-,-n** taking; (*Mil*) capture; **E~n** *pl* income *sg*; (*Einkünfte*) revenue *sg*; (*Comm*) receipts; (*eines Ladens*) takings

einnehmen† *vt sep* take; have ⟨*Mahlzeit*⟩; (*Mil*) capture; take up ⟨*Platz*⟩; (*fig*) prejudice (**gegen** against); **jdn für sich e~** win s.o. over. **e~d** *a* engaging

einnicken *vi sep* (*sein*) nod off

Einöde *f* wilderness

einordnen *vt sep* put in its proper place; (*klassifizieren*) classify; **sich e~** fit in; (*Auto*) get in lane

einpacken *vt sep* pack; (*einhüllen*) wrap

einparken *vt sep* park

einpauken *vt sep* **jdm etw e~** (*fam*) drum sth into s.o.

einpflanzen *vt sep* plant; implant ⟨*Organ*⟩

einplanen *vt sep* allow for

einpräg|en *vt sep* impress (**jdm** [up]on s.o.); **sich** (*dat*) **etw e~en** memorize sth. **e~sam** *a* easy to remember; ⟨*Melodie*⟩ catchy

einquartieren *vt sep* (*Mil*) billet (**bei** on); **sich in einem Hotel e~** put up at a hotel

einrahmen *vt sep* frame

einrasten *vi sep* (*sein*) engage

einräumen *vt sep* put away; (*zugeben*) admit; (*zugestehen*) grant

einrechnen *vt sep* include

einreden *v sep* • *vt* **jdm/sich** (*dat*) **etw e~** persuade s.o./oneself of sth • *vi* (*haben*) **auf jdn e~** talk insistently to s.o.

einreib|en† *vt sep* rub (**mit** with). **E~mittel** *nt* liniment

einreichen *vt sep* submit; **die Scheidung e~** file for divorce

Einreih|er *m* **-s,-** single-breasted suit. **e~ig** *a* single-breasted

Einreise *f* entry. **e~n** *vi sep* (*sein*) enter (**nach Irland** Ireland). **E~visum** *nt* entry visa

einreißen† *v sep* • *vt* tear; (*abreißen*) pull down • *vi* (*sein*) tear; ⟨*Sitte:*⟩ become a habit

einrenken *vt sep* (*Med*) set

einricht|en *vt sep* fit out; (*möblieren*) furnish; (*anordnen*) arrange; (*Med*) set ⟨*Bruch*⟩; (*eröffnen*) set up; **sich e~en** furnish one's home; (*sich einschränken*) economize; (*sich vorbereiten*) prepare (**auf** + *acc* for). **E~ung** *f* furnishing; (*Möbel*) furnishings *pl*; (*Techn*) equipment; (*Vorrichtung*) device; (*Eröffnung*) setting up; (*Institution*) institution; (*Gewohnheit*) practice. **E~ungsgegenstand** *m* piece of equipment/(*Möbelstück*) furniture

einrollen *vt sep* roll up; put in rollers ⟨*Haare*⟩

einrosten *vi sep* (*sein*) rust; (*fig*) get rusty

einrücken *v sep* • *vi* (*sein*) (*Mil*) be called up; (*einmarschieren*) move in • *vt* indent

eins *inv a & pron* one; **noch e~** one other thing; **mir ist alles e~** (*fam*) it's all the same to me. **E～** *f* **-,-en** one; (*Sch*) ≈ A

einsam *a* lonely; (*allein*) solitary; (*abgelegen*) isolated. **E～keit** *f* - loneliness; solitude; isolation

einsammeln *vt sep* collect

Einsatz *m* use; (*Mil*) mission; (*Wett-*) stake; (*E～teil*) insert; **im E～** in action. **e～bereit** *a* ready for action

einschalt|en *vt sep* switch on; (*einschieben*) interpolate; (*fig: beteiligen*) call in; **sich e～en** (*fig*) intervene. **E～quote** *f* (*TV*) viewing figures *pl*; ≈ ratings *pl*

einschärfen *vt sep* **jdm etw e～** impress sth [up]on s.o.

einschätz|en *vt sep* assess; (*bewerten*) rate. **E～ung** *f* assessment; estimation

einschenken *vt sep* pour

einscheren *vi sep* (*sein*) pull in

einschicken *vt sep* send in

einschieben† *vt sep* push in; (*einfügen*) insert; (*fig*) interpolate

einschiff|en (sich) *vr sep* embark. **E～ung** *f* - embarkation

einschlafen† *vi sep* (*sein*) go to sleep; (*aufhören*) peter out

einschläfern *vt sep* lull to sleep; (*betäuben*) put out; (*töten*) put to sleep. **e～d** *a* soporific

Einschlag *m* impact; (*fig: Beimischung*) element. **e～en**† *v sep* ● *vt* knock in; (*zerschlagen*) smash; (*einwickeln*) wrap; (*falten*) turn up; (*drehen*) turn; take ⟨*Weg*⟩; take up ⟨*Laufbahn*⟩ ● *vi* (*haben*) hit/⟨*Blitz:*⟩ strike (**in etw** *acc* sth); (*zustimmen*) shake hands [on a deal]; (*Erfolg haben*) be a hit; **auf jdn e～en** beat s.o.

einschlägig *a* relevant

einschleusen *vt sep* infiltrate

einschließ|en† *vt sep* lock in; (*umgeben*) enclose; (*einkreisen*) surround; (*einbeziehen*) include; **sich e～en** lock oneself in; **Bedienung eingeschlossen** service included. **e～lich** *adv* inclusive ● *prep* (+ *gen*) including

einschmeicheln (sich) *vr sep* ingratiate oneself (**bei** with)

einschnappen *vi sep* (*sein*) click shut; **eingeschnappt sein** (*fam*) be in a huff

einschneiden† *vt/i sep* (*haben*) **[in] etw** *acc* **e～** cut into sth. **e～d** *a* (*fig*) drastic, *adv* -ally

Einschnitt *m* cut; (*Med*) incision; (*Lücke*) gap; (*fig*) decisive event

einschränk|en *vt sep* restrict; (*reduzieren*) cut back; **sich e～en** economize. **E～ung** *f* **-,-en** restriction; (*Reduzierung*) reduction; (*Vorbehalt*) reservation

Einschreib|[e]brief *m* registered letter. **e～en**† *vt sep* enter; register ⟨*Brief*⟩; **sich e～en** put one's name down; (*sich anmelden*) enrol. **E～en** *nt* registered letter/packet; **als** *od* **per E～en** by registered post

einschreiten† *vi sep* (*sein*) intervene

einschüchter|n *vt sep* intimidate. **E～ung** *f* - intimidation

einsegn|en *vt sep* (*Relig*) confirm. **E～ung** *f* **-,-en** confirmation

einsehen† *vt sep* inspect; (*lesen*) consult; (*begreifen*) see. **E～** *nt* **-s ein E～ haben** show some understanding; (*vernünftig sein*) see reason

einseitig *a* one-sided; (*Pol*) unilateral ● *adv* on one side; (*fig*) one-sidedly; (*Pol*) unilaterally

einsenden† *vt sep* send in

einsetzen *v sep* ● *vt* put in; (*einfügen*) insert; (*verwenden*) use; put on ⟨*Zug*⟩; call out ⟨*Truppen*⟩; (*Mil*) deploy; (*ernennen*) appoint; (*wetten*) stake; (*riskieren*) risk; **sich e～ für** support ● *vi* (*haben*) start; ⟨*Winter, Regen:*⟩ set in

Einsicht *f* insight; (*Verständnis*) understanding; (*Vernunft*) reason; **zur E～ kommen** see reason. **e～ig** *a* understanding; (*vernünftig*) sensible

Einsiedler *m* hermit

einsilbig *a* monosyllabic; ⟨*Person*⟩ taciturn

einsinken† *vi sep* (*sein*) sink in

einspannen *vt sep* harness; **jdn e～** (*fam*) rope s.o. in; **sehr eingespannt** (*fam*) very busy

einsparen *vt sep* save

einsperren *vt sep* shut/(*im Gefängnis*) lock up

einspielen (sich) *vr sep* warm up; **gut aufeinander eingespielt sein** work well together

einsprachig *a* monolingual

einspringen† *vi sep* (*sein*) step in (**für** for)

einspritzen *vt sep* inject

Einspruch *m* objection; **E～ erheben** object; (*Jur*) appeal

einspurig *a* single-track; (*Auto*) single-lane

einst *adv* once; (*Zukunft*) one day

Einstand *m* (*Tennis*) deuce

einstecken *vt sep* put in; post ⟨*Brief*⟩; (*Electr*) plug in; (*fam: behalten*) pocket; (*fam: hinnehmen*) take; suffer ⟨*Niederlage*⟩; **etw e~** put sth in one's pocket

einstehen† *vi sep* (*haben*) **e~ für** vouch for; answer for ⟨*Folgen*⟩

einsteigen† *vi sep* (*sein*) get in; (*in Bus/Zug*) get on

einstell|en *vt sep* put in; (*anstellen*) employ; (*aufhören*) stop; (*regulieren*) adjust, set; (*Optik*) focus; tune ⟨*Motor, Zündung*⟩; tune to ⟨*Sender*⟩; **sich e~en** turn up; (*ankommen*) arrive; (*eintreten*) occur; ⟨*Schwierigkeiten:*⟩ arise; **sich e~en auf** (+*acc*) adjust to; (*sich vorbereiten*) prepare for. **E~ung** *f* employment; (*Aufhören*) cessation; (*Regulierung*) adjustment; (*Optik*) focusing; (*TV, Auto*) tuning; (*Haltung*) attitude

Einstieg *m* **-[e]s,-e** entrance

einstig *a* former

einstimmen *vi sep* (*haben*) join in

einstimmig *a* unanimous, *adv* -ly. **E~keit** *f* - unanimity

einstöckig *a* single-storey

einstudieren *vt sep* rehearse

einstufen *vt sep* classify

Ein|sturz *m* collapse. **e~stürzen** *vi sep* (*sein*) collapse

einstweil|en *adv* for the time being; (*inzwischen*) meanwhile. **e~ig** *a* temporary

eintasten *vt sep* key in

eintauchen *vt/i sep* (*sein*) dip in; (*heftiger*) plunge in

eintauschen *vt sep* exchange

eintausend *inv a* one thousand

einteil|en *vt sep* divide (**in** + *acc* into); (*Biol*) classify; **sich** (*dat*) **seine Zeit gut e~en** organize one's time well. **e~ig** *a* one-piece. **E~ung** *f* division; classification

eintönig *a* monotonous, *adv* -ly. **E~keit** *f* - monotony

Eintopf *m*, **E~gericht** *nt* stew

Ein|tracht *f* - harmony. **e~trächtig** *a* harmonious • *adv* in harmony

Eintrag *m* **-[e]s,⸚e** entry. **e~en**† *vt sep* enter; (*Admin*) register; (*einbringen*) bring in; **sich e~en** put one's name down

einträglich *a* profitable

Eintragung *f* **-,-en** registration; (*Eintrag*) entry

eintreffen† *vi sep* (*sein*) arrive; (*fig*) come true; (*geschehen*) happen. **E~** *nt* **-s** arrival

eintreiben† *vt sep* drive in; (*einziehen*) collect

eintreten† *v sep* • *vi* (*sein*) enter; (*geschehen*) occur; **in einen Klub e~** join a club; **e~ für** (*fig*) stand up for • *vt* kick in

Eintritt *m* entrance; (*zu Veranstaltung*) admission; (*Beitritt*) joining; (*Beginn*) beginning. **E~skarte** *f* [admission] ticket

eintrocknen *vi sep* (*sein*) dry up

einüben *vt sep* practise

einundachtzig *inv a* eighty-one

einverleiben *vt sep* incorporate (*dat* into); **sich** (*dat*) **etw e~** (*fam*) consume sth

Einvernehmen *nt* **-s** understanding; (*Übereinstimmung*) agreement; **in bestem E~** on the best of terms

einverstanden *a* **e~ sein** agree

Einverständnis *nt* agreement; (*Zustimmung*) consent

Einwand *m* **-[e]s,⸚e** objection

Einwander|er *m* immigrant. **e~n** *vi sep* (*sein*) immigrate. **E~ung** *f* immigration

einwandfrei *a* perfect, *adv* -ly; (*untadelig*) impeccable, *adv* -bly; (*eindeutig*) indisputable, *adv* -bly

einwärts *adv* inwards

einwechseln *vt sep* change

einwecken *vt sep* preserve, bottle

Einweg- *pref* non-returnable; ⟨*Feuerzeug*⟩ throw-away

einweichen *vt sep* soak

einweih|en *vt sep* inaugurate; (*Relig*) consecrate; (*einführen*) initiate; (*fam*) use for the first time; **in ein Geheimnis e~en** let into a secret. **E~ung** *f* **-,-en** inauguration; consecration; initiation

einweisen† *vt sep* direct; (*einführen*) initiate; **ins Krankenhaus e~** send to hospital

einwenden† *vt sep* **etwas e~** object (**gegen** to); **dagegen hätte ich nichts einzuwenden** (*fam*) I wouldn't say no

einwerfen† *vt sep* insert; post ⟨*Brief*⟩; (*Sport*) throw in; (*vorbringen*) interject; (*zertrümmern*) smash

einwickeln *vt sep* wrap [up]

einwillig|en *vi sep* (*haben*) consent, agree (**in** + *acc* to). **E~ung** *f* - consent

einwirken *vi sep* (*haben*) **e~ auf** (+*acc*) have an effect on; (*beeinflussen*) influence

Einwohner|(in) *m* **-s,-** (*f* **-,-nen**) inhabitant. **E~zahl** *f* population

Einwurf *m* interjection; (*Einwand*) objection; (*Sport*) throw-in; (*Münz-*) slot

Einzahl *f* (*Gram*) singular

einzahl|en *vt sep* pay in. **E~ung** *f* payment; (*Einlage*) deposit

einzäunen *vt sep* fence in

Einzel *nt* **-s,-** (*Tennis*) singles *pl*. **E~bett** *nt* single bed. **E~fall** *m* individual/(*Sonderfall*) isolated case. **E~gänger** *m* **-s,-** loner. **E~haft** *f* solitary confinement. **E~handel** *m* retail trade. **E~händler** *m* retailer. **E~haus** *nt* detached house. **E~heit** *f* **-,-en** detail. **E~karte** *f* single ticket. **E~kind** *nt* only child

einzeln *a* single, *adv* -gly; (*individuell*) individual, *adv* -ly; (*gesondert*) separate, *adv* -ly; odd ⟨*Handschuh, Socken*⟩; **e~e Fälle** some cases. **e~e(r,s)** *pron* **der/die e~e** the individual; **ein e~er** a single one; **jeder e~e** every single one; **im e~en** in detail; **e~e** *pl* some

Einzel|person *f* single person. **E~teil** *nt* [component] part. **E~zimmer** *nt* single room

einziehen† *v sep* ● *vt* pull in; draw in ⟨*Atem, Krallen*⟩; (*Zool, Techn*) retract; indent ⟨*Zeile*⟩; (*aus dem Verkehr ziehen*) withdraw; (*beschlagnahmen*) confiscate; (*eintreiben*) collect; make ⟨*Erkundigungen*⟩; (*Mil*) call up; (*einfügen*) insert; (*einbauen*) put in; **den Kopf e~** duck [one's head] ● *vi* (*sein*) enter; (*umziehen*) move in; (*eindringen*) penetrate

einzig *a* only; (*einmalig*) unique; **eine/keine e~e Frage** a/not a single question; **ein e~es Mal** only once ● *adv* only; **e~ und allein** solely. **e~artig** *a* unique; (*unvergleichlich*) unparalleled. **e~e(r,s)** *pron* **der/die/das e~e** the only one; **ein/kein e~er** a/not a single one; **das e~e, was mich stört** the only thing that bothers me

Einzug *m* entry; (*Umzug*) move (**in** + *acc* into). **E~sgebiet** *nt* catchment area

Eis *nt* **-es** ice; (*Speise-*) ice-cream; **Eis am Stiel** ice lolly. **E~bahn** *f* ice rink. **E~bär** *m* polar bear. **E~becher** *m* ice-cream sundae. **E~bein** *nt* (*Culin*) knuckle of pork. **E~berg** *m* iceberg. **E~diele** *f* ice-cream parlour

Eisen *nt* **-s,-** iron. **E~bahn** *f* railway. **E~bahner** *m* **-s,-** railwayman

eisern *a* iron; (*fest*) resolute, *adv* -ly; **e~er Vorhang** (*Theat*) safety curtain; (*Pol*) Iron Curtain

Eis|fach *nt* freezer compartment. **e~gekühlt** *a* chilled. **e~ig** *a* icy. **E~kaffee** *m* iced coffee. **e~kalt** *a* ice cold; (*fig*) icy, *adv* -ily. **E~kunstlauf** *m* figure skating. **E~lauf** *m* skating. **e~laufen†** *vi sep* (*sein*) skate. **E~läufer(in)** *m*(*f*) skater. **E~pickel** *m* ice-axe. **E~scholle** *f* ice-floe. **E~schrank** *m* refrigerator. **E~vogel** *m* kingfisher. **E~würfel** *m* ice-cube. **E~zapfen** *m* icicle. **E~zeit** *f* ice age

eitel *a* vain; (*rein*) pure. **E~keit** *f* - vanity

Eiter *m* **-s** pus. **e~n** *vi* (*haben*) discharge pus

Eiweiß *nt* **-es,-e** egg-white; (*Chem*) protein

Ekel[1] *m* **-s** disgust; (*Widerwille*) revulsion

Ekel[2] *nt* **-s,-** (*fam*) beast

ekel|erregend *a* nauseating. **e~haft** *a* nauseating; (*widerlich*) repulsive. **e~n** *vt/i* (*haben*) **mich** *od* **mir e~t [es] davor** it makes me feel sick ● *vr* **sich e~n vor** (+ *dat*) find repulsive

eklig *a* disgusting, repulsive

Eksta|se *f* - ecstasy. **e~tisch** *a* ecstatic, *adv* -ally

Ekzem *nt* **-s,-e** eczema

elasti|sch *a* elastic; (*federnd*) springy; (*fig*) flexible. **E~zität** *f* - elasticity; flexibility

Elch *m* **-[e]s,-e** elk

Elefant *m* **-en,-en** elephant

elegan|t *a* elegant, *adv* -ly. **E~z** *f* - elegance

elektrifizieren *vt* electrify

Elektri|ker *m* **-s,-** electrician. **e~sch** *a* electric, *adv* -ally

elektrisieren *vt* electrify; **sich e~** get an electric shock

Elektrizität *f* - electricity. **E~swerk** *nt* power station

Elektr|oartikel *mpl* electrical appliances. **E~ode** *f* **-,-n** electrode. **E~oherd** *m* electric cooker. **E~on** *nt* **-s,-en** /-'tro:nən/ electron. **E~onik** *f* - electronics *sg*. **e~onisch** *a* electronic

Element *nt* **-[e]s,-e** element; (*Anbau-*) unit. **e~ar** *a* elementary

Elend *nt* **-s** misery; (*Armut*) poverty. **e~** *a* miserable, *adv* -bly, wretched, *adv* -ly; (*krank*) poorly; (*gemein*) contemptible; (*fam: schrecklich*) dreadful, *adv* -ly. **E~sviertel** *nt* slum

elf *inv a*, **E~** *f* **-,-en** eleven

Elfe *f* **-,-n** fairy

Elfenbein *nt* ivory

Elfmeter *m* (*Fußball*) penalty

elfte(r,s) *a* eleventh

eliminieren *vt* eliminate

Elite *f* **-,-n** élite

Elixier *nt* **-s,-e** elixir

Ell[en]bogen *m* elbow

Ellip|se *f* **-,-n** ellipse. **e~tisch** *a* elliptical

Elsaß *nt* **-** Alsace

elsässisch *a* Alsatian

Elster *f* **-,-n** magpie

elter|lich *a* parental. **E~n** *pl* parents. **E~nhaus** *nt* [parental] home. **e~nlos** *a* orphaned. **E~nteil** *m* parent

Email /e'mai̯/ *nt* **-s,-s**, **E~le** /e'maljə/ *f* **-,-n** enamel. **e~lieren** /ema[l]'ji:rən/ *vt* enamel

Emanzi|pation /-'t͡si̯o:n/ *f* **-** emancipation. **e~piert** *a* emancipated

Embargo *nt* **-s,-s** embargo

Emblem *nt* **-s,-e** emblem

Embryo *m* **-s,-s** embryo

Emigr|ant(in) *m* **-en,-en** (*f* **-,-nen**) emigrant. **E~ation** /-'t͡si̯o:n/ *f* **-** emigration. **e~ieren** *vi* (*sein*) emigrate

eminent *a* eminent, *adv* -ly

Emission *f* **-,-en** emission; (*Comm*) issue

Emotion /-'t͡si̯o:n/ *f* **-,-en** emotion. **e~al** *a* emotional

Empfang *m* **-[e]s,¨e** reception; (*Erhalt*) receipt; **in E~ nehmen** receive; (*annehmen*) accept. **e~en**† *vt* receive; (*Biol*) conceive

Empfäng|er *m* **-s,-** recipient; (*Post-*) addressee; (*Zahlungs-*) payee; (*Radio, TV*) receiver. **e~lich** *a* receptive/(*Med*) susceptible (**für** to). **E~nis** *f* **-** (*Biol*) conception

Empfängnisverhütung *f* contraception. **E~smittel** *nt* contraceptive

Empfangs|bestätigung *f* receipt. **E~chef** *m* reception manager. **E~dame** *f* receptionist. **E~halle** *f* [hotel] foyer

empfehl|en† *vt* recommend; **sich e~en** be advisable; (*verabschieden*) take one's leave. **e~enswert** *a* to be recommended; (*ratsam*) advisable. **E~ung** *f* **-,-en** recommendation; (*Gruß*) regards *pl*

empfind|en† *vt* feel. **e~lich** *a* sensitive (**gegen** to); (*zart*) delicate; (*wund*) tender; (*reizbar*) touchy; (*hart*) severe, *adv* -ly. **E~lichkeit** *f* **-** sensitivity; delicacy; tenderness; touchiness. **e~sam** *a* sensitive; (*sentimental*) sentimental. **E~ung** *f* **-,-en** sensation; (*Regung*) feeling

emphatisch *a* emphatic, *adv* -ally

empor *adv* (*liter*) up[wards]

empören *vt* incense; **sich e~** be indignant; (*sich auflehnen*) rebel. **e~d** *a* outrageous

Empor|kömmling *m* **-s,-e** upstart. **e~ragen** *vi sep* (*haben*) rise [up]

empör|t *a* indignant, *adv* -ly. **E~ung** *f* **-** indignation; (*Auflehnung*) rebellion

emsig *a* busy, *adv* -ily

Ende *nt* **-s,-n** end; (*eines Films, Romans*) ending; (*fam: Stück*) bit; **E~ Mai** at the end of May; **zu E~ sein/gehen** be finished/come to an end; **etw zu E~ schreiben** finish writing sth; **am E~** at the end; (*schließlich*) in the end; (*fam: vielleicht*) perhaps; (*fam: erschöpft*) at the end of one's tether

end|en *vi* (*haben*) end. **e~gültig** *a* final, *adv* -ly; (*bestimmt*) definite, *adv* -ly

Endivie /-i̯ə/ *f* **-,-n** endive

end|lich *adv* at last, finally; (*schließlich*) in the end. **e~los** *a* endless, *adv* -ly. **E~resultat** *nt* final result. **E~spiel** *nt* final. **E~spurt** *m* **-[e]s** final spurt. **E~station** *f* terminus. **E~ung** *f* **-,-en** (*Gram*) ending

Energie *f* **-** energy

energisch *a* resolute, *adv* -ly; (*nachdrücklich*) vigorous, *adv* -ly; **e~ werden** put one's foot down

eng *a* narrow; (*beengt*) cramped; (*anliegend*) tight; (*nah*) close, *adv* -ly

Enga|gement /ãgaʒə'mã:/ *nt* **-s,-s** (*Theat*) engagement; (*fig*) commitment. **e~gieren** /-'ʒi:rən/ *vt* (*Theat*) engage; **sich e~gieren** become involved; **e~giert** committed

eng|anliegend *a* tight-fitting. **E~e** *f* **-** narrowness; **in die E~e treiben** (*fig*) drive into a corner

Engel *m* **-s,-** angel. **e~haft** *a* angelic

engherzig *a* petty

England *nt* **-s** England

Engländer *m* **-s,-** Englishman; (*Techn*) monkey-wrench; **die E~** the English *pl*. **E~in** *f* **-,-nen** Englishwoman

englisch *a* English; **auf e~** in English. **E~** *nt* **-[s]** (*Lang*) English

Engpaß *m* (*fig*) bottle-neck
en gros /ã'gro:/ *adv* wholesale
engstirnig *a* (*fig*) narrow-minded
Enkel *m* **-s,-** grandson; **E~** *pl* grandchildren. **E~in** *f* **-,-nen** granddaughter. **E~kind** *nt* grandchild. **E~sohn** *m* grandson. **E~tochter** *f* granddaughter
enorm *a* enormous, *adv* -ly; (*fam: großartig*) fantastic
Ensemble /ã'sã:bəl/ *nt* **-s,-s** ensemble; (*Theat*) company
entart|en *vi* (*sein*) degenerate. **e~et** *a* degenerate
entbehr|en *vt* do without; (*vermissen*) miss. **e~lich** *a* dispensable; (*überflüssig*) superfluous. **E~ung** *f* **-,-en** privation
entbind|en† *vt* release (**von** from); (*Med*) deliver (**von** of) ● *vi* (*haben*) give birth. **E~ung** *f* delivery. **E~ungsstation** *f* maternity ward
entblöß|en *vt* bare. **e~t** *a* bare
entdeck|en *vt* discover. **E~er** *m* **-s,-** discoverer; (*Forscher*) explorer. **E~ung** *f* **-,-en** discovery
Ente *f* **-,-n** duck
entehren *vt* dishonour
enteignen *vt* dispossess; expropriate ⟨*Eigentum*⟩
enterben *vt* disinherit
Enterich *m* **-s,-e** drake
entfachen *vt* kindle
entfallen† *vi* (*sein*) not apply; **jdm e~** slip from s.o.'s hand; (*aus dem Gedächtnis*) slip s.o.'s mind; **auf jdn e~** be s.o.'s share
entfalt|en *vt* unfold; (*entwickeln*) develop; (*zeigen*) display; **sich e~en** unfold; develop. **E~ung** *f* **-** development
entfern|en *vt* remove; **sich e~en** leave. **e~t** *a* distant; (*schwach*) vague, *adv* -ly; **2 Kilometer e~t** 2 kilometres away; **e~t verwandt** distantly related; **nicht im e~testen** not in the least. **E~ung** *f* **-,-en** removal; (*Abstand*) distance; (*Reichweite*) range. **E~ungsmesser** *m* rangefinder
entfesseln *vt* (*fig*) unleash
entfliehen† *vi* (*sein*) escape
entfremd|en *vt* alienate. **E~ung** *f* **-** alienation
entfrosten *vt* defrost
entführ|en *vt* abduct, kidnap; hijack ⟨*Flugzeug*⟩. **E~er** *m* abductor, kidnapper; hijacker. **E~ung** *f* abduction, kidnapping; hijacking
entgegen *adv* towards ● *prep* (+*dat*) contrary to. **e~gehen**† *vi sep* (*sein*) (+*dat*) go to meet; (*fig*) be heading for. **e~gesetzt** *a* opposite; (*gegensätzlich*) opposing. **e~halten**† *vt sep* (*fig*) object. **e~kommen**† *vi sep* (*sein*) (+*dat*) come to meet; (*zukommen auf*) come towards; (*fig*) oblige. **E~kommen** *nt* **-s** helpfulness; (*Zugeständnis*) concession. **e~kommend** *a* approaching; ⟨*Verkehr*⟩ oncoming; (*fig*) obliging. **e~nehmen**† *vt sep* accept. **e~sehen**† *vi sep* (*haben*) (+*dat*) (*fig*) await; (*freudig*) look forward to. **e~setzen** *vt sep* **Widerstand e~setzen** (+*dat*) resist. **e~treten**† *vi sep* (*sein*) (+*dat*) (*fig*) confront; (*bekämpfen*) fight. **e~wirken** *vi sep* (*haben*) (+*dat*) counteract; (*fig*) oppose
entgegn|en *vt* reply (**auf**+*acc* to). **E~ung** *f* **-,-en** reply
entgehen† *vi sep* (*sein*) (+*dat*) escape; **jdm e~** (*unbemerkt bleiben*) escape s.o.'s notice; **sich** (*dat*) **etw e~ lassen** miss sth
entgeistert *a* flabbergasted
Entgelt *nt* **-[e]s** payment; **gegen E~** for money. **e~en** *vt* **jdn etw e~en lassen** (*fig*) make s.o. pay for sth
entgleis|en *vi* (*sein*) be derailed; (*fig*) make a gaffe. **E~ung** *f* **-,-en** derailment; (*fig*) gaffe
entgleiten† *vi* (*sein*) **jdm e~** slip from s.o.'s grasp
entgräten *vt* fillet, bone
Enthaarungsmittel *nt* depilatory
enthalt|en† *vt* contain; **in etw** (*dat*) **e~en sein** be contained/(*eingeschlossen*) included in sth; **sich der Stimme e~en** (*Pol*) abstain. **e~sam** *a* abstemious. **E~samkeit** *f* **-** abstinence. **E~ung** *f* (*Pol*) abstention
enthaupten *vt* behead
entheben† *vt* **jdn seines Amtes e~** relieve s.o. of his post
enthüll|en *vt* unveil; (*fig*) reveal. **E~ung** *f* **-,-en** revelation
Enthusias|mus *m* **-** enthusiasm. **E~t** *m* **-en,-en** enthusiast. **e~tisch** *a* enthusiastic, *adv* -ally
entkernen *vt* stone; core ⟨*Apfel*⟩
entkleid|en *vt* undress; **sich e~en** undress. **E~ungsnummer** *f* striptease [act]
entkommen† *vi* (*sein*) escape
entkorken *vt* uncork
entkräft|en *vt* weaken; (*fig*) invalidate. **E~ung** *f* **-** debility

entkrampfen *vt* relax; **sich e~** relax
entladen† *vt* unload; (*Electr*) discharge; **sich e~** discharge; ⟨*Gewitter:*⟩ break; ⟨*Zorn:*⟩ explode
entlang *adv & prep* (+*preceding acc or following dat*) along; **die Straße e~, e~ der Straße** along the road; **an etw** (*dat*) **e~** along sth. **e~fahren**† *vi sep* (*sein*) drive along. **e~gehen**† *vi sep* (*sein*) walk along
entlarven *vt* unmask
entlass|en† *vt* dismiss; (*aus Krankenhaus*) discharge; (*aus der Haft*) release; **aus der Schule e~en werden** leave school. **E~ung** *f* **-,-en** dismissal; discharge; release
entlast|en *vt* relieve the strain on; ease ⟨*Gewissen, Verkehr*⟩; relieve (**von** of); (*Jur*) exonerate. **E~ung** *f* **-** relief; exoneration. **E~ungszug** *m* relief train
entlaufen† *vi* (*sein*) run away
entledigen (sich) *vr* (+*gen*) rid oneself of; (*ausziehen*) take off; (*erfüllen*) discharge
entleeren *vt* empty
entlegen *a* remote
entleihen† *vt* borrow (**von** from)
entlocken *vt* coax (*dat* from)
entlohnen *vt* pay
entlüft|en *vt* ventilate. **E~er** *m* **-s,-** extractor fan. **E~ung** *f* ventilation
entmündigen *vt* declare incapable of managing his own affairs
entmutigen *vt* discourage
entnehmen† *vt* take (*dat* from); (*schließen*) gather (*dat* from)
Entomologie *f* **-** entomology
entpuppen (sich) *vr* (*fig*) turn out (**als etw** to be sth)
entrahmt *a* skimmed
entreißen† *vt* snatch (*dat* from)
entrichten *vt* pay
entrinnen† *vi* (*sein*) escape
entrollen *vt* unroll; unfurl ⟨*Fahne*⟩; **sich e~** unroll; unfurl
entrüst|en *vt* fill with indignation; **sich e~en** be indignant (**über** +*acc* at). **e~et** *a* indignant, *adv* -ly. **E~ung** *f* **-** indignation
entsaft|en *vt* extract the juice from. **E~er** *m* **-s,-** juice extractor
entsag|en *vi* (*haben*) (+*dat*) renounce. **E~ung** *f* **-** renunciation
entschädig|en *vt* compensate. **E~ung** *f* **-,-en** compensation
entschärfen *vt* defuse
entscheid|en† *vt/i* (*haben*) decide; **sich e~en** decide; ⟨*Sache:*⟩ be decided. **e~end** *a* decisive, *adv* -ly; (*kritisch*) crucial. **E~ung** *f* decision
entschieden *a* decided, *adv* -ly; (*fest*) firm, *adv* -ly
entschlafen† *vi* (*sein*) (*liter*) pass away
entschließen† **(sich)** *vr* decide, make up one's mind; **sich anders e~** change one's mind
entschlossen *a* determined; (*energisch*) resolute, *adv* -ly; **kurz e~** without hesitation; (*spontan*) on the spur of the moment. **E~heit** *f* **-** determination
Entschluß *m* decision; **einen E~ fassen** make a decision
entschlüsseln *vt* decode
entschuld|bar *a* excusable. **e~igen** *vt* excuse; **sich e~igen** apologize (**bei** to); **e~igen Sie [bitte]!** sorry! (*bei Frage*) excuse me. **E~igung** *f* **-,-en** apology; (*Ausrede*) excuse; **[jdn] um E~igung bitten** apologize [to s.o.]; **E~igung!** sorry! (*bei Frage*) excuse me
entsetz|en *vt* horrify. **E~en** *nt* **-s** horror. **e~lich** *a* horrible, *adv* -bly; (*schrecklich*) terrible, *adv* -bly. **e~t** *a* horrified
entsinnen† **(sich)** *vr* (+*gen*) remember
Entsorgung *f* **-** waste disposal
entspann|en *vt* relax; **sich e~en** relax; ⟨*Lage:*⟩ ease. **E~ung** *f* **-** relaxation; easing; (*Pol*) détente
entsprech|en† *vi* (*haben*) (+*dat*) correspond to; (*übereinstimmen*) agree with; (*nachkommen*) comply with. **e~end** *a* corresponding; (*angemessen*) appropriate; (*zuständig*) relevant ● *adv* correspondingly; appropriately; (*demgemäß*) accordingly ● *prep* (+*dat*) in accordance with. **E~ung** *f* **-,-en** equivalent
entspringen† *vi* (*sein*) ⟨*Fluß:*⟩ rise; (*fig*) arise, spring (*dat* from); (*entfliehen*) escape
entstammen *vi* (*sein*) come/(*abstammen*) be descended (*dat* from)
entsteh|en† *vi* (*sein*) come into being; (*sich bilden*) form; (*sich entwickeln*) develop; ⟨*Brand:*⟩ start; (*stammen*) originate/(*sich ergeben*) result (**aus** from). **E~ung** *f* **-** origin; formation; development; (*fig*) birth
entsteinen *vt* stone

entstell|en *vt* disfigure; (*verzerren*) distort. **E~ung** *f* disfigurement; distortion
entstört *a* (*Electr*) suppressed
enttäusch|en *vt* disappoint. **E~ung** *f* disappointment
entvölkern *vt* depopulate
entwaffnen *vt* disarm. **e~d** *a* (*fig*) disarming
Entwarnung *f* all-clear [signal]
entwässer|n *vt* drain. **E~ung** *f* - drainage
entweder *conj & adv* either
entweichen† *vi* (*sein*) escape
entweih|en *vt* desecrate. **E~ung** *f* - desecration
entwenden *vt* steal (*dat* from)
entwerfen† *vt* design; (*aufsetzen*) draft; (*skizzieren*) sketch
entwert|en *vt* devalue; (*ungültig machen*) cancel. **E~er** *m* **-s,-** ticket-cancelling machine. **E~ung** *f* devaluation; cancelling
entwick|eln *vt* develop; **sich e~eln** develop. **E~lung** *f* **-,-en** development; (*Biol*) evolution. **E~lungsland** *nt* developing country
entwinden† *vt* wrench (*dat* from)
entwirren *vt* disentangle; (*fig*) unravel
entwischen *vi* (*sein*) **jdm e~** (*fam*) give s.o. the slip
entwöhnen *vt* wean (*gen* from); cure ⟨*Süchtige*⟩
entwürdigend *a* degrading
Entwurf *m* design; (*Konzept*) draft; (*Skizze*) sketch
entwurzeln *vt* uproot
entzie|hen† *vt* take away (*dat* from); **jdm den Führerschein e~hen** disqualify s.o. from driving; **sich e~hen** (+ *dat*) withdraw from; (*entgehen*) evade. **E~hungskur** *f* treatment for drug/alcohol addiction
entziffern *vt* decipher
entzücken *vt* delight. **E~** *nt* **-s** delight. **e~d** *a* delightful
Entzug *m* withdrawal; (*Vorenthaltung*) deprivation. **E~serscheinungen** *fpl* withdrawal symptoms
entzünd|en *vt* ignite; (*anstecken*) light; (*fig: erregen*) inflame; **sich e~en** ignite; (*Med*) become inflamed. **e~et** *a* (*Med*) inflamed. **e~lich** *a* inflammable. **E~ung** *f* (*Med*) inflammation
entzwei *a* broken. **e~en (sich)** *vr* quarrel. **e~gehen**† *vi sep* (*sein*) break
Enzian *m* **-s,-e** gentian
Enzyklo|pädie *f* **-,-en** encyclopaedia. **e~pädisch** *a* encyclopaedic
Enzym *nt* **-s,-e** enzyme
Epidemie *f* **-,-n** epidemic
Epi|lepsie *f* - epilepsy. **E~leptiker(in)** *m* **-s,-** (*f* **-,-nen**) epileptic. **e~leptisch** *a* epileptic
Epilog *m* **-s,-e** epilogue
episch *a* epic
Episode *f* **-,-n** episode
Epitaph *nt* **-s,-e** epitaph
Epoche *f* **-,-n** epoch. **e~machend** *a* epoch-making
Epos *nt* **-,Epen** epic
er *pron* he; (*Ding, Tier*) it
erachten *vt* consider (**für nötig** necessary). **E~** *nt* **-s meines E~s** in my opinion
erbarmen (sich) *vr* have pity/⟨*Gott:*⟩ mercy (*gen* on). **E~** *nt* **-s** pity; mercy
erbärmlich *a* wretched, *adv* -ly; (*stark*) terrible, *adv* -bly
erbarmungslos *a* merciless, *adv* -ly
erbau|en *vt* build; (*fig*) edify; **sich e~en** be edified (**an** + *dat* by); **nicht e~t von** (*fam*) not pleased about. **e~lich** *a* edifying
Erbe[1] *m* **-n,-n** heir
Erbe[2] *nt* **-s** inheritance; (*fig*) heritage. **e~n** *vt* inherit
erbeuten *vt* get; (*Mil*) capture
Erbfolge *f* (*Jur*) succession
erbieten† **(sich)** *vr* offer (**zu** to)
Erbin *f* **-,-nen** heiress
erbitten† *vt* ask for
erbittert *a* bitter; (*heftig*) fierce, *adv* -ly
erblassen *vi* (*sein*) turn pale
erblich *a* hereditary
erblicken *vt* catch sight of
erblinden *vi* (*sein*) go blind
erbost *a* angry, *adv* -ily
erbrechen† *vt* vomit ● *vi/r* **[sich] e~** vomit. **E~** *nt* **-s** vomiting
Erbschaft *f* **-,-en** inheritance
Erbse *f* **-,-n** pea
Erb|stück *nt* heirloom. **E~teil** *nt* inheritance
Erd|apfel *m* (*Aust*) potato. **E~beben** *nt* **-s,-** earthquake. **E~beere** *f* strawberry. **E~boden** *m* ground
Erde *f* **-,-n** earth; (*Erdboden*) ground; (*Fußboden*) floor; **auf der E~** on earth; (*auf dem Boden*) on the ground/floor. **e~n** *vt* (*Electr*) earth
erdenklich *a* imaginable
Erd|gas *nt* natural gas. **E~geschoß** *nt* ground floor, (*Amer*) first floor.

e~ig *a* earthy. **E~kugel** *f* globe. **E~kunde** *f* geography. **E~nuß** *f* peanut. **E~öl** *nt* [mineral] oil. **E~reich** *nt* soil

erdreisten (sich) *vr* have the audacity (**zu** to)

erdrosseln *vt* strangle

erdrücken *vt* crush to death. **e~d** *a* (*fig*) overwhelming

Erd|rutsch *m* landslide. **E~teil** *m* continent

erdulden *vt* endure

ereifern (sich) *vr* get worked up

ereignen (sich) *vr* happen

Ereignis *nt* **-ses,-se** event. **e~los** *a* uneventful. **e~reich** *a* eventful

Eremit *m* **-en,-en** hermit

ererbt *a* inherited

erfahr|en† *vt* learn, hear; (*erleben*) experience ● *a* experienced. **E~ung** *f* **-,-en** experience; **in E~ung bringen** find out

erfassen *vt* seize; (*begreifen*) grasp; (*einbeziehen*) include; (*aufzeichnen*) record; **von einem Auto erfaßt werden** be struck by a car

erfind|en† *vt* invent. **E~er** *m* **-s,-** inventor. **e~erisch** *a* inventive. **E~ung** *f* **-,-en** invention

Erfolg *m* **-[e]s,-e** success; (*Folge*) result; **E~ haben** be successful. **e~en** *vi* (*sein*) take place; (*geschehen*) happen. **e~los** *a* unsuccessful, *adv* -ly. **e~reich** *a* successful, *adv* -ly. **e~versprechend** *a* promising

erforder|lich *a* required, necessary. **e~n** *vt* require, demand. **E~nis** *nt* **-ses,-se** requirement

erforsch|en *vt* explore; (*untersuchen*) investigate. **E~ung** *f* exploration; investigation

erfreu|en *vt* please; **sich guter Gesundheit e~en** enjoy good health. **e~lich** *a* pleasing, gratifying; (*willkommen*) welcome. **e~licherweise** *adv* happily. **e~t** *a* pleased

erfrier|en† *vi* (*sein*) freeze to death; ⟨*Glied:*⟩ become frostbitten; ⟨*Pflanze:*⟩ be killed by the frost. **E~ung** *f* **-,-en** frostbite

erfrisch|en *vt* refresh; **sich e~en** refresh onself. **e~end** *a* refreshing. **E~ung** *f* **-,-en** refreshment

erfüll|en *vt* fill; (*nachkommen*) fulfil; serve ⟨*Zweck*⟩; discharge ⟨*Pflicht*⟩; **sich e~en** come true. **E~ung** *f* fulfilment; **in E~ung gehen** come true

erfunden invented; (*fiktiv*) fictitious

ergänz|en *vt* complement; (*nachtragen*) supplement; (*auffüllen*) replenish; (*vervollständigen*) complete; (*hinzufügen*) add; **sich e~en** complement each other. **E~ung** *f* complement; supplement; (*Zusatz*) addition. **E~ungsband** *m* supplement

ergeb|en† *vt* produce; (*zeigen*) show, establish; **sich e~en** result; ⟨*Schwierigkeit:*⟩ arise; (*kapitulieren*) surrender; (*sich fügen*) submit; **es ergab sich** it turned out (**daß** that) ● *a* devoted, *adv* -ly; (*resigniert*) resigned, *adv* -ly. **E~enheit** *f* - devotion

Ergebnis *nt* **-ses,-se** result. **e~los** *a* fruitless, *adv* -ly

ergehen† *vi* (*sein*) be issued; **etw über sich** (*acc*) **e~ lassen** submit to sth; **wie ist es dir ergangen?** how did you get on? ● *vr* **sich e~ in** (+*dat*) indulge in

ergiebig *a* productive; (*fig*) rich

ergötzen *vt* amuse

ergreifen† *vt* seize; take ⟨*Maßnahme, Gelegenheit*⟩; take up ⟨*Beruf*⟩; (*rühren*) move; **die Flucht e~** flee. **e~d** *a* moving

ergriffen *a* deeply moved. **E~heit** *f* - emotion

ergründen *vt* (*fig*) get to the bottom of

erhaben *a* raised; (*fig*) sublime; **über etw** (*acc*) **e~ sein** (*fig*) be above sth

Erhalt *m* **-[e]s** receipt. **e~en†** *vt* receive, get; (*gewinnen*) obtain; (*bewahren*) preserve, keep; (*instandhalten*) maintain; (*unterhalten*) support; **am Leben e~en** keep alive ● *a* **gut/schlecht e~en** in good/bad condition; **e~en bleiben** survive

erhältlich *a* obtainable

Erhaltung *f* - (*s.* **erhalten**) preservation; maintenance

erhängen (sich) *vr* hang oneself

erhärten *vt* (*fig*) substantiate

erheb|en† *vt* raise; levy ⟨*Steuer*⟩; charge ⟨*Gebühr*⟩; **Anspruch e~en** lay claim (**auf**+*acc* to); **Protest e~en** protest; **sich e~en** rise; ⟨*Frage:*⟩ arise; (*sich empören*) rise up. **e~lich** *a* considerable, *adv* -bly. **E~ung** *f* **-,-en** elevation; (*Anhöhe*) rise; (*Aufstand*) uprising; (*Ermittlung*) survey

erheiter|n *vt* amuse. **E~ung** *f* - amusement

erhitzen *vt* heat; **sich e~** get hot; (*fig*) get heated

erhoffen *vt* **sich** (*dat*) **etw e~** hope for sth

erhöh|en *vt* raise; (*fig*) increase; **sich e~en** rise, increase. **E~ung** *f* **-,-en** increase. **E~ungszeichen** *nt* (*Mus*) sharp

erhol|en (sich) *vr* recover (**von** from); (*nach Krankheit*) convalesce, recuperate; (*sich ausruhen*) have a rest. **e~sam** *a* restful. **E~ung** *f* **-** recovery; convalescence; (*Ruhe*) rest. **E~ungsheim** *nt* convalescent home

erhören *vt* (*fig*) answer

erinner|n *vt* remind (**an** + *acc* of); **sich e~n** remember (**an jdn/etw** s.o./sth). **E~ung** *f* **-,-en** memory; (*Andenken*) souvenir

erkält|en (sich) *vr* catch a cold; **e~et sein** have a cold. **E~ung** *f* **-,-en** cold

erkenn|bar *a* recognizable; (*sichtbar*) visible. **e~en**† *vt* recognize; (*wahrnehmen*) distinguish; (*einsehen*) realize. **e~tlich** *a* **sich e~tlich zeigen** show one's appreciation. **E~tnis** *f* **-,-se** recognition; realization; (*Wissen*) knowledge; **die neuesten E~tnisse** the latest findings

Erker *m* **-s,-** bay

erklär|en *vt* declare; (*erläutern*) explain; **sich bereit e~en** agree (**zu** to); **ich kann es mir nicht e~en** I can't explain it. **e~end** *a* explanatory. **e~lich** *a* explicable; (*verständlich*) understandable. **e~licherweise** *adv* understandably. **e~t** *attrib a* declared. **E~ung** *f* **-,-en** declaration; explanation; **öffentliche E~ung** public statement

erklingen† *vi* (*sein*) ring out

erkrank|en *vi* (*sein*) fall ill; be taken ill (**an** + *dat* with). **E~ung** *f* **-,-en** illness

erkunden *vt* explore; (*Mil*) reconnoitre

erkundig|en (sich) *vr* enquire (**nach jdm/etw** after s.o./about sth). **E~ung** *f* **-,-en** enquiry

erlahmen *vi* (*sein*) tire; ⟨*Kraft, Eifer:*⟩ flag

erlangen *vt* attain, get

Erlaß *m* **-sses,¨sse** (*Admin*) decree; (*Befreiung*) exemption; (*Straf-*) remission

erlassen† *vt* (*Admin*) issue; **jdm etw e~** exempt s.o. from sth; let s.o. off ⟨*Strafe*⟩

erlauben *vt* allow, permit; **sich e~, etw zu tun** take the liberty of doing sth; **ich kann es mir nicht e~** I can't afford it

Erlaubnis *f* **-** permission. **E~schein** *m* permit

erläuter|n *vt* explain. **E~ung** *f* **-,-en** explanation

Erle *f* **-,-n** alder

erleb|en *vt* experience; (*mit-*) see; have ⟨*Überraschung, Enttäuschung*⟩; **etw nicht mehr e~en** not live to see sth. **E~nis** *nt* **-ses,-se** experience

erledig|en *vt* do; (*sich befassen mit*) deal with; (*beenden*) finish; (*entscheiden*) settle; (*töten*) kill; **e~t sein** be done/settled/(*fam: müde*) worn out/(*fam: ruiniert*) finished

erleichter|n *vt* lighten; (*vereinfachen*) make easier; (*befreien*) relieve; (*lindern*) ease; **sich e~n** (*fig*) unburden oneself. **e~t** *a* relieved. **E~ung** *f* **-** relief

erleiden† *vt* suffer

erlernen *vt* learn

erlesen *a* exquisite; (*auserlesen*) choice, select

erleucht|en *vt* illuminate; **hell e~et** brightly lit. **E~ung** *f* **-,-en** (*fig*) inspiration

erliegen† *vi* (*sein*) succumb (*dat* to); **seinen Verletzungen e~** die of one's injuries

erlogen *a* untrue, false

Erlös *m* **-es** proceeds *pl*

erlöschen† *vi* (*sein*) go out; (*vergehen*) die; (*aussterben*) die out; (*ungültig werden*) expire; **erloschener Vulkan** extinct volcano

erlös|en *vt* save; (*befreien*) release (**von** from); (*Relig*) redeem. **e~t** *a* relieved. **E~ung** *f* release; (*Erleichterung*) relief; (*Relig*) redemption

ermächtig|en *vt* authorize. **E~ung** *f* **-,-en** authorization

ermahn|en *vt* exhort; (*zurechtweisen*) admonish. **E~ung** *f* exhortation; admonition

ermäßig|en *vt* reduce. **E~ung** *f* **-,-en** reduction

ermatt|en *vi* (*sein*) grow weary ● *vt* weary. **E~ung** *f* **-** weariness

ermessen† *vt* judge; (*begreifen*) appreciate. **E~** *nt* **-s** discretion; (*Urteil*) judgement; **nach eigenem E~** at one's own discretion

ermitt|eln *vt* establish; (*herausfinden*) find out ● *vi* (*haben*) investigate (**gegen jdn** s.o.). **E~lungen** *fpl* investigations. **E~lungsverfahren** *nt* (*Jur*) preliminary inquiry

ermöglichen *vt* make possible

ermord|en *vt* murder. **E~ung** *f* **-,-en** murder

ermüd|en *vt* tire ● *vi* (*sein*) get tired. **E~ung** *f* - tiredness

ermunter|n *vt* encourage; **sich e~n** rouse oneself. **E~ung** *f* - encouragement

ermutigen *vt* encourage. **e~d** *a* encouraging

ernähr|en *vt* feed; (*unterhalten*) support, keep; **sich e~en von** live/ ⟨*Tier:*⟩ feed on. **E~er** *m* **-s,-** breadwinner. **E~ung** *f* - nourishment; nutrition; (*Kost*) diet

ernenn|en† *vt* appoint. **E~ung** *f* **-,-en** appointment

erneu|ern *vt* renew; (*auswechseln*) replace; change ⟨*Verband*⟩; (*renovieren*) renovate. **E~erung** *f* renewal; replacement; renovation. **e~t** *a* renewed; (*neu*) new ● *adv* again

erniedrig|en *vt* degrade; **sich e~en** lower oneself. **e~end** *a* degrading. **E~ungszeichen** *nt* (*Mus*) flat

ernst *a* serious, *adv* -ly; **e~ nehmen** take seriously. **E~** *m* **-es** seriousness; **im E~** seriously; **mit einer Drohung E~ machen** carry out a threat; **ist das dein E~?** are you serious? **E~fall** *m* **im E~fall** when the real thing happens. **e~haft** *a* serious, *adv* -ly. **e~lich** *a* serious, *adv* -ly

Ernte *f* **-,-n** harvest; (*Ertrag*) crop. **E~dankfest** *nt* harvest festival. **e~n** *vt* harvest; (*fig*) reap, win

ernüchter|n *vt* sober up; (*fig*) bring down to earth; (*enttäuschen*) disillusion. **e~nd** *a* (*fig*) sobering. **E~ung** *f* - disillusionment

Erober|er *m* **-s,-** conqueror. **e~n** *vt* conquer. **E~ung** *f* **-,-en** conquest

eröffn|en *vt* open; **jdm etw e~en** announce sth to s.o.; **sich jdm e~en** ⟨*Aussicht:*⟩ present itself to s.o. **E~ung** *f* opening; (*Mitteilung*) announcement. **E~ungsansprache** *f* opening address

erörter|n *vt* discuss. **E~ung** *f* **-,-en** discussion

Erosion *f* **-,-en** erosion

Erot|ik *f* - eroticism. **e~isch** *a* erotic

Erpel *m* **-s,-** drake

erpicht *a* **e~ auf** (+*acc*) keen on

erpress|en *vt* extort; blackmail ⟨*Person*⟩. **E~er** *m* **-s,-** blackmailer. **E~ung** *f* - extortion; blackmail

erprob|en *vt* test. **e~t** *a* proven

erquicken *vt* refresh

erraten† *vt* guess

erreg|bar *a* excitable. **e~en** *vt* excite; (*hervorrufen*) arouse; **sich e~en** get worked up. **e~end** *a* exciting. **E~er** *m* **-s,-** (*Med*) germ. **e~t** *a* agitated; (*hitzig*) heated. **E~ung** *f* - excitement; (*Erregtheit*) agitation

erreich|bar *a* within reach; ⟨*Ziel*⟩ attainable; ⟨*Person*⟩ available. **e~en** *vt* reach; catch ⟨*Zug*⟩; live to ⟨*Alter*⟩; (*durchsetzen*) achieve

erretten *vt* save

errichten *vt* erect

erringen† *vt* gain, win

erröten *vi* (*sein*) blush

Errungenschaft *f* **-,-en** achievement; (*fam: Anschaffung*) acquisition; **E~en der Technik** technical advances

Ersatz *m* **-es** replacement, substitute; (*Entschädigung*) compensation. **E~dienst** *m* = **Zivildienst**. **E~reifen** *m* spare tyre. **E~spieler(in)** *m*(*f*) substitute. **E~teil** *nt* spare part

ersäufen *vt* drown

erschaffen† *vt* create

erschallen† *vi* (*sein*) ring out

erschein|en† *vi* (*sein*) appear; ⟨*Buch:*⟩ be published; **jdm merkwürdig e~en** seem odd to s.o. **E~en** *nt* **-s** appearance; publication. **E~ung** *f* **-,-en** appearance; (*Person*) figure; (*Phänomen*) phenomenon; (*Symptom*) symptom; (*Geist*) apparition

erschieß|en† *vt* shoot [dead]. **E~ungskommando** *nt* firing squad

erschlaffen *vi* (*sein*) go limp; ⟨*Haut, Muskeln:*⟩ become flabby

erschlagen† *vt* beat to death; (*tödlich treffen*) strike dead; **vom Blitz e~ werden** be killed by lightning ● *a* (*fam*) (*erschöpft*) worn out; (*fassungslos*) stunned

erschließen† *vt* develop; (*zugänglich machen*) open up; (*nutzbar machen*) tap

erschöpf|en *vt* exhaust. **e∼end** *a* exhausting; (*fig: vollständig*) exhaustive. **e∼t** *a* exhausted. **E∼ung** *f* - exhaustion

erschreck|en† *vi* (*sein*) get a fright • *vt* (*reg*) startle; (*beunruhigen*) alarm; **du hast mich e∼t** you gave me a fright • *vr* (*reg & irreg*) **sich e∼en** get a fright. **e∼end** *a* alarming, *adv* -ly

erschrocken *a* frightened; (*erschreckt*) startled; (*bestürzt*) dismayed

erschütter|n *vt* shake; (*ergreifen*) upset deeply. **E∼ung** *f* -,**-en** shock

erschweren *vt* make more difficult

erschwinglich *a* affordable

ersehen† *vt* (*fig*) see (**aus** from)

ersetzen *vt* replace; make good ⟨*Schaden*⟩; refund ⟨*Kosten*⟩; **jdm etw e∼** compensate s.o. for sth

ersichtlich *a* obvious, apparent

erspar|en *vt* save; **jdm etw e∼en** save/(*fernhalten*) spare s.o. sth. **E∼nis** *f* -,**-se** saving; **E∼nisse** savings

erst *adv* (*zuerst*) first; (*noch nicht mehr als*) only; (*nicht vor*) not until; **e∼ dann** only then; **eben** *od* **gerade e∼** [only] just; **das machte ihn e∼ recht wütend** it made him all the more angry

erstarren *vi* (*sein*) solidify; (*gefrieren*) freeze; (*steif werden*) go stiff; (*vor Schreck*) be paralysed

erstatten *vt* (*zurück-*) refund; **Bericht e∼** report (**jdm** to s.o.)

Erstaufführung *f* first performance, première

erstaun|en *vt* amaze, astonish. **E∼en** *nt* amazement, astonishment. **e∼lich** *a* amazing, *adv* -ly. **e∼licherweise** *adv* amazingly

Erst|ausgabe *f* first edition. **e∼e(r,s)** *a* first; (*beste*) best; **E∼e Hilfe** first aid; **er kam als e∼er** he arrived first; **als e∼es** first of all; **fürs e∼e** for the time being; **der e∼e beste** the first one to come along; (*fam*) any Tom, Dick or Harry. **E∼e(r)** *m/f* best; **er ist der/sie ist die E∼e in Latein** he/she is top in Latin

erstechen† *vt* stab to death

erstehen† *vt* buy

ersteigern *vt* buy at an auction

erst|ens *adv* firstly, in the first place. **e∼ere(r,s)** *a* the former; **der/die/das e∼ere** the former

ersticken *vt* suffocate; smother ⟨*Flammen*⟩; (*unterdrücken*) suppress • *vi* (*sein*) suffocate. **E∼** *nt* **-s** suffocation; **zum E∼** stifling

erst|klassig *a* first-class. **e∼mals** *adv* for the first time

erstreben *vt* strive for. **e∼swert** *a* desirable

erstrecken (sich) *vr* stretch; **sich e∼ auf** (+*acc*) (*fig*) apply to

ersuchen *vt* ask, request. **E∼** *nt* **-s** request

ertappen *vt* (*fam*) catch

erteilen *vt* give (**jdm** s.o.)

ertönen *vi* (*sein*) sound; (*erschallen*) ring out

Ertrag *m* **-[e]s,¨-e** yield. **e∼en**† *vt* bear

erträglich *a* bearable; (*leidlich*) tolerable

ertränken *vt* drown

ertrinken† *vi* (*sein*) drown

erübrigen (sich) *vr* be unnecessary

erwachen *vi* (*sein*) awake

erwachsen *a* grown-up. **E∼e(r)** *m/f* adult, grown-up

erwäg|en† *vt* consider. **E∼ung** *f* -,**-en** consideration; **in E∼ung ziehen** consider

erwähn|en *vt* mention. **E∼ung** *f* -,**-en** mention

erwärmen *vt* warm; **sich e∼** warm up; (*fig*) warm (**für** to)

erwart|en *vt* expect; (*warten auf*) wait for. **E∼ung** *f* -,**-en** expectation. **e∼ungsvoll** *a* expectant, *adv* -ly

erwecken *vt* (*fig*) arouse; give ⟨*Anschein*⟩

erweichen *vt* soften; (*fig*) move; **sich e∼ lassen** (*fig*) relent

erweisen† *vt* prove; (*bezeigen*) do ⟨*Gefallen, Dienst, Ehre*⟩; **sich e∼ als** prove to be

erweitern *vt* widen; dilate ⟨*Pupille*⟩; (*fig*) extend, expand

Erwerb *m* **-[e]s** acquisition; (*Kauf*) purchase; (*Brot-*) livelihood; (*Verdienst*) earnings *pl*. **e∼en**† *vt* acquire; (*kaufen*) purchase; (*fig: erlangen*) gain. **e∼slos** *a* unemployed. **e∼stätig** *a* [gainfully] employed. **E∼ung** *f* -,**-en** acquisition

erwider|n *vt* reply; return ⟨*Besuch, Gruß*⟩. **E∼ung** *f* -,**-en** reply

erwirken *vt* obtain

erwischen *vt* (*fam*) catch

erwünscht *a* desired

erwürgen *vt* strangle

Erz *nt* **-es,-e** ore

erzähl|en *vt* tell (**jdm** s.o.) ● *vi* (*haben*) talk (**von** about). **E~er** *m* **-s,-** narrator. **E~ung** *f* **-,-en** story, tale

Erzbischof *m* archbishop

erzeug|en *vt* produce; (*Electr*) generate; (*fig*) create. **E~er** *m* **-s,-** producer; (*Vater*) father. **E~nis** *nt* **-ses, -se** product; **landwirtschaftliche E~nisse** farm produce *sg*. **E~ung** *f* **-** production; generation

Erz|feind *m* arch-enemy. **E~herzog** *m* archduke

erzieh|en† *vt* bring up; (*Sch*) educate. **E~er** *m* **-s,-** [private] tutor. **E~erin** *f* **-,-nen** governess. **E~ung** *f* **-** upbringing; education

erzielen *vt* achieve; score ⟨*Tor*⟩

erzogen *a* **gut/schlecht e~** well/badly brought up

erzürnt *a* angry

erzwingen† *vt* force

es *pron* it; (*Mädchen*) she; (*acc*) her; *impers* **es regnet** it is raining; **es gibt** there is/(*pl*) are; **ich hoffe es** I hope so

Esche *f* **-,-n** ash

Esel *m* **-s,-** donkey; (*fam: Person*) ass. **E~sohr** *nt* **E~sohren haben** ⟨*Buch:*⟩ be dog-eared

Eskal|ation /-'tsio:n/ *f* **-** escalation. **e~ieren** *vt/i* (*haben*) escalate

Eskimo *m* **-[s],-[s]** Eskimo

Eskort|e *f* **-,-n** (*Mil*) escort. **e~ieren** *vt* escort

eßbar *a* edible. **Eßecke** *f* dining area

essen† *vt/i* (*haben*) eat; **zu Mittag/Abend e~** have lunch/supper; **[auswärts] e~ gehen** eat out; **chinesisch e~** have a Chinese meal. **E~** *nt* **-s,-** food; (*Mahl*) meal; (*festlich*) dinner

Essenz *f* **-,-en** essence

Esser(in) *m* **-s,-** (*f* **-,-nen**) eater

Essig *m* **-s** vinegar. **E~gurke** *f* [pickled] gherkin

Eßkastanie *f* sweet chestnut. **Eßlöffel** *m* ≈ dessertspoon. **Eßstäbchen** *ntpl* chopsticks. **Eßtisch** *m* dining-table. **Eßwaren** *fpl* food *sg*; (*Vorräte*) provisions. **Eßzimmer** *nt* dining-room

Estland *nt* **-s** Estonia

Estragon *m* **-s** tarragon

etablieren (sich) *vr* establish oneself/⟨*Geschäft:*⟩ itself

Etage /e'ta:ʒə/ *f* **-,-n** storey. **E~nbett** *nt* bunk-beds *pl*. **E~nwohnung** *f* flat, (*Amer*) apartment

Etappe *f* **-,-n** stage

Etat /e'ta:/ *m* **-s,-s** budget

etepetete *a* (*fam*) fussy

Eth|ik *f* **-** ethic; (*Sittenlehre*) ethics *sg*. **e~isch** *a* ethical

Etikett *nt* **-[e]s,-e[n]** label; (*Preis-*) tag. **E~e** *f* **-,-n** etiquette; (*Aust*) = **Etikett. e~ieren** *vt* label

etlich|e(r,s) *pron* some; (*mehrere*) several; **e~es** a number of things; (*ziemlich viel*) quite a lot. **e~emal** *adv* several times

Etui /e'tvi:/ *nt* **-s,-s** case

etwa *adv* (*ungefähr*) about; (*zum Beispiel*) for instance; (*womöglich*) perhaps; **nicht e~, daß ...** not that ...; **denkt nicht e~ ...** don't imagine ...; **du hast doch nicht e~ Angst?** you're not afraid, are you? **e~ig** *a* possible

etwas *pron* something; (*fragend/verneint*) anything; (*ein bißchen*) some, a little; **ohne e~ zu sagen** without saying anything; **sonst noch e~?** anything else? **noch e~ Tee?** some more tea? **so e~ Ärgerliches!** what a nuisance! ● *adv* a bit

Etymologie *f* **-** etymology

euch *pron* (*acc of* **ihr** *pl*) you; (*dat*) [to] you; (*refl*) yourselves; (*einander*) each other; **ein Freund von e~** a friend of yours

euer *poss pron pl* your. **e~e, e~t-** *s.* **eure, euret-**

Eule *f* **-,-n** owl

Euphorie *f* **-** euphoria

eur|e *poss pron pl* your. **e~e(r,s)** *poss pron* yours. **e~erseits** *adv* for your part. **e~etwegen** *adv* for your sake; (*wegen euch*) because of you, on your account. **e~etwillen** *adv* **um e~etwillen** for your sake. **e~ige** *poss pron* **der/die/das e~ige** yours

Euro- *pref* Euro-

Europa *nt* **-s** Europe. **E~-** *pref* European

Europä|er(in) *m* **-s,-** (*f* **-,-nen**) European. **e~isch** *a* European; **E~ische Gemeinschaft** European Community

Euro|paß *m* Europassport. **E~scheck** *m* Eurocheque

Euter *nt* **-s,-** udder

evakuier|en *vt* evacuate. **E~ung** *f* **-** evacuation

evan|gelisch *a* Protestant. **E~gelist** *m* **-en,-en** evangelist. **E~gelium** *nt* **-s,-ien** gospel

evaporieren *vt/i* (*sein*) evaporate

Eventu|alität *f* **-,-en** eventuality. **e~ell** *a* possible ● *adv* possibly; (*vielleicht*) perhaps

Evolution /-'tsi̯o:n/ *f* - evolution

evtl. *abbr s.* **eventuell**

ewig *a* eternal, *adv* -ly; (*fam: ständig*) constant, *adv* -ly; (*endlos*) never-ending; **e~ dauern** (*fam*) take ages. **E~keit** *f* - eternity; **eine E~keit** (*fam*) ages

exakt *a* exact, *adv* -ly. **E~heit** *f* - exactitude

Examen *nt* **-s,- & -mina** (*Sch*) examination

Exekutive *f* - (*Pol*) executive

Exempel *nt* **-s,-** example; **ein E~ an jdm statuieren** make an example of s.o.

Exemplar *nt* **-s,-e** specimen; (*Buch*) copy. **e~isch** *a* exemplary

exerzieren *vt/i* (*haben*) (*Mil*) drill; (*üben*) practise

exhumieren *vt* exhume

Exil *nt* **-s** exile

Existenz *f* **-,-en** existence; (*Lebensgrundlage*) livelihood; (*pej: Person*) individual

existieren *vi* (*haben*) exist

exklusiv *a* exclusive. **e~e** *prep* (+*gen*) excluding

exkommunizieren *vt* excommunicate

Exkremente *npl* excrement *sg*

exotisch *a* exotic

expan|dieren *vt/i* (*haben*) expand. **E~sion** *f* - expansion

Expedition /-'tsi̯o:n/ *f* **-,-en** expedition

Experiment *nt* **-[e]s,-e** experiment. **e~ell** *a* experimental. **e~ieren** *vi* (*haben*) experiment

Experte *m* **-n,-n** expert

explo|dieren *vi* (*sein*) explode. **E~sion** *f* **-,-en** explosion. **e~siv** *a* explosive

Expor|t *m* **-[e]s,-e** export. **E~teur** /-'tø:ɐ̯/ *m* **-s,-e** exporter. **e~tieren** *vt* export

Expreß *m* **-sses,-sse** express

extra *adv* separately; (*zusätzlich*) extra; (*eigens*) specially; (*fam: absichtlich*) on purpose

Extrakt *m* **-[e]s,-e** extract

Extras *npl* (*Auto*) extras

extravagan|t *a* flamboyant, *adv* -ly; (*übertrieben*) extravagant. **E~z** *f* **-,-en** flamboyance; extravagance; (*Überspanntheit*) folly

extravertiert *a* extrovert

extrem *a* extreme, *adv* -ly. **E~** *nt* **-s,-e** extreme. **E~ist** *m* **-en,-en** extremist. **E~itäten** *fpl* extremities

Exzellenz *f* - (*title*) Excellency

Exzentr|iker *m* **-s,-** eccentric. **e~isch** *a* eccentric

Exzeß *m* **-sses,-sse** excess

F

Fabel *f* **-,-n** fable. **f~haft** *a* (*fam*) fantastic, *adv* -ally

Fabrik *f* **-,-en** factory. **F~ant** *m* **-en,-en** manufacturer. **F~at** *nt* **-[e]s,-e** product; (*Marke*) make. **F~ation** /-'tsi̯o:n/ *f* - manufacture

Facette /fa'sɛtə/ *f* **-,-n** facet

Fach *nt* **-[e]s,¨er** compartment; (*Schub-*) drawer; (*Gebiet*) field; (*Sch*) subject. **F~arbeiter** *m* skilled worker. **F~arzt** *m*, **F~ärztin** *f* specialist. **F~ausdruck** *m* technical term

fäch|eln (sich) *vr* fan oneself. **F~er** *m* **-s,-** fan

Fach|gebiet *nt* field. **f~gemäß, f~gerecht** *a* expert, *adv* -ly. **F~hochschule** *f* ≈ technical university. **f~kundig** *a* expert, *adv* -ly. **f~lich** *a* technical, *adv* -ly; (*beruflich*) professional. **F~mann** *m* (*pl* **-leute**) expert. **f~männisch** *a* expert, *adv* -ly. **F~schule** *f* technical college. **f~simpeln** *vi* (*haben*) (*fam*) talk shop. **F~werkhaus** *nt* half-timbered house. **F~wort** *nt* (*pl* **-wörter**) technical term

Fackel *f* **-,-n** torch. **F~zug** *m* torchlight procession

fade *a* insipid; (*langweilig*) dull

Faden *m* **-s,¨** thread; (*Bohnen-*) string; (*Naut*) fathom. **f~scheinig** *a* threadbare; ⟨*Grund*⟩ flimsy

Fagott *nt* **-[e]s,-e** bassoon

fähig *a* capable (**zu**/*gen* of); (*tüchtig*) able, competent. **F~keit** *f* **-,-en** ability; competence

fahl *a* pale

fahnd|en *vi* (*haben*) search (**nach** for). **F~ung** *f* **-,-en** search

Fahne *f* **-,-n** flag; (*Druck-*) galley [proof]; **eine F~ haben** (*fam*) reek of alcohol. **F~nflucht** *f* desertion. **f~nflüchtig** *a* **f~nflüchtig werden** desert

Fahr|ausweis *m* ticket. **F~bahn** *f* carriageway; (*Straße*) road. **f~bar** *a* mobile

Fähre *f* **-,-n** ferry

fahr|en† *vi* (*sein*) go, travel; ⟨*Fahrer:*⟩ drive; ⟨*Radfahrer:*⟩ ride; (*verkehren*) run; (*ab-*) leave; ⟨*Schiff:*⟩ sail; **mit dem Auto/Zug f~en** go by car/train; **in die Höhe f~en** start up; **in die Kleider f~en** throw on one's clothes; **mit der Hand über etw** (*acc*) **f~en** run one's hand over sth; **was ist in ihn gefahren?** (*fam*) what has got into him? ● *vt* drive; ride ⟨*Fahrrad*⟩; take ⟨*Kurve*⟩. **f~end** *a* moving; (*f~bar*) mobile; (*nicht seßhaft*) travelling, itinerant. **F~er** *m* **-s,-** driver. **F~erflucht** *f* failure to stop after an accident. **F~erhaus** *nt* driver's cab. **F~erin** *f* **-,-nen** woman driver. **F~gast** *m* passenger; (*im Taxi*) fare. **F~geld** *nt* fare. **F~gestell** *nt* chassis; (*Aviat*) undercarriage. **f~ig** *a* nervy; (*zerstreut*) distracted. **F~karte** *f* ticket. **F~kartenausgabe** *f*, **F~kartenschalter** *m* ticket office. **f~lässig** *a* negligent, *adv* -ly. **F~lässigkeit** *f* - negligence. **F~lehrer** *m* driving instructor. **F~plan** *m* timetable. **f~planmäßig** *a* scheduled ● *adv* according to/ (*pünktlich*) on schedule. **F~preis** *m* fare. **F~prüfung** *f* driving test. **F~rad** *nt* bicycle. **F~schein** *m* ticket

Fährschiff *nt* ferry

Fahr|schule *f* driving school. **F~schüler(in)** *m(f)* learner driver. **F~spur** *f* [traffic] lane. **F~stuhl** *m* lift, (*Amer*) elevator. **F~stunde** *f* driving lesson

Fahrt *f* **-,-en** journey; (*Auto*) drive; (*Ausflug*) trip; (*Tempo*) speed; **in voller F~** at full speed. **F~ausweis** *m* ticket

Fährte *f* **-,-n** track; (*Witterung*) scent; **auf der falschen F~** (*fig*) on the wrong track

Fahr|tkosten *pl* travelling expenses. **F~werk** *nt* undercarriage. **F~zeug** *nt* **-[e]s,-e** vehicle; (*Wasser-*) craft, vessel

fair /fɛːɐ̯/ *a* fair, *adv* -ly. **F~neß** *f* - fairness

Fakten *pl* facts

Faktor *m* **-s,-en** /-'toːrən/ factor

Fakul|tät *f* **-,-en** faculty. **f~tativ** *a* optional

Falke *m* **-n,-n** falcon

Fall *m* **-[e]s,¨e** fall; (*Jur, Med, Gram*) case; **im F~[e]** in case (*gen* of); **auf jeden F~, auf alle F¨e** in any case; (*bestimmt*) definitely; **für alle F¨e** just in case; **auf keinen F~** on no account

Falle *f* **-,-n** trap; **eine F~ stellen** set a trap (*dat* for)

fallen† *vi* (*sein*) fall; (*sinken*) go down; **[im Krieg] f~** be killed in the war; **f~ lassen** drop

fällen *vt* fell; (*fig*) pass ⟨*Urteil*⟩; make ⟨*Entscheidung*⟩

fallenlassen† *vt sep* (*fig*) drop; make ⟨*Bemerkung*⟩

fällig *a* due; ⟨*Wechsel*⟩ mature; **längst f~** long overdue. **F~keit** *f* - (*Comm*) maturity

Fallobst *nt* windfalls *pl*

falls *conj* in case; (*wenn*) if

Fallschirm *m* parachute. **F~jäger** *m* paratrooper. **F~springer** *m* parachutist

Falltür *f* trapdoor

falsch *a* wrong; (*nicht echt, unaufrichtig*) false; (*gefälscht*) forged; ⟨*Geld*⟩ counterfeit; ⟨*Schmuck*⟩ fake ● *adv* wrongly; falsely; ⟨*singen*⟩ out of tune; **f~ gehen** ⟨*Uhr:*⟩ be wrong

fälsch|en *vt* forge, fake. **F~er** *m* **-s,-** forger

Falsch|geld *nt* counterfeit money. **F~heit** *f* - falseness

fälschlich *a* wrong, *adv* -ly; (*irrtümlich*) mistaken, *adv* -ly. **f~erweise** *adv* by mistake

Falsch|meldung *f* false report; (*absichtlich*) hoax report. **F~münzer** *m* **-s,-** counterfeiter

Fälschung *f* **-,-en** forgery, fake; (*Fälschen*) forging

Falte *f* **-,-n** fold; (*Rock-*) pleat; (*Knitter-*) crease; (*im Gesicht*) line; (*Runzel*) wrinkle

falten *vt* fold; **sich f~** ⟨*Haut:*⟩ wrinkle. **F~rock** *m* pleated skirt

Falter *m* **-s,-** butterfly; (*Nacht-*) moth

faltig *a* creased; ⟨*Gesicht*⟩ lined; (*runzlig*) wrinkled

familiär *a* family ...; (*vertraut, zudringlich*) familiar; (*zwanglos*) informal

Familie /-i̯ə/ *f* **-,-n** family. **F~nanschluß** *m* **F~nanschluß haben** live as one of the family. **F~nforschung** *f* genealogy. **F~nleben** *nt* family life. **F~nname** *m* surname. **F~nplanung** *f* family planning. **F~nstand** *m* marital status

Fan /fɛn/ *m* **-s,-s** fan

Fanaltiker *m* **-s,-** fanatic. **f~tisch** *a* fanatical, *adv* -ly. **F~tismus** *m* - fanaticism

Fanfare *f* **-,-n** trumpet; (*Signal*) fanfare

Fang *m* **-[e]s,⸚e** capture; (*Beute*) catch; **F⸚e** (*Krallen*) talons; (*Zähne*) fangs. **F~arm** *m* tentacle. **f~en**† *vt* catch; (*ein-*) capture; **sich f~en** get caught (**in** + *dat* in); (*fig*) regain one's balance/(*seelisch*) composure. **F~en** *nt* **-s F~en spielen** play tag. **F~frage** *f* catch question. **F~zahn** *m* fang

fantastisch *a* = **phantastisch**

Farb|aufnahme *f* colour photograph. **F~band** *nt* (*pl* **-bänder**) typewriter ribbon. **F~e** *f* **-,-n** colour; (*Maler-*) paint; (*zum Färben*) dye; (*Karten*) suit. **f~echt** *a* colour-fast

färben *vt* colour; dye ⟨*Textilien, Haare*⟩; (*fig*) slant ⟨*Bericht*⟩; **sich [rot] f~** turn [red] ● *vi* (*haben*) not be colour-fast

farb|enblind *a* colour-blind. **f~enfroh** *a* colourful. **F~fernsehen** *nt* colour television. **F~film** *m* colour film. **F~foto** *nt* colour photo. **f~ig** *a* coloured ● *adv* in colour. **F~ige(r)** *m/f* coloured man/woman. **F~kasten** *m* box of paints. **f~los** *a* colourless. **F~stift** *m* crayon. **F~stoff** *m* dye; (*Lebensmittel-*) colouring. **F~ton** *m* shade

Färbung *f* **-,-en** colouring; (*fig: Anstrich*) bias

Farce /'farsə/ *f* **-,-n** farce; (*Culin*) stuffing

Farn *m* **-[e]s,-e, F~kraut** *nt* fern

Färse *f* **-,-n** heifer

Fasan *m* **-[e]s,-e[n]** pheasant

Faschierte(s) *nt* (*Aust*) mince

Fasching *m* **-s** (*SGer*) carnival

Faschis|mus *m* - fascism. **F~t** *m* **-en,-en** fascist. **f~tisch** *a* fascist

faseln *vt/i* (*haben*) (*fam*) **[Unsinn] f~** talk nonsense

Faser *f* **-,-n** fibre. **f~n** *vi* (*haben*) fray

Faß *nt* **-sses,⸚sser** barrel, cask; **Bier vom Faß** draught beer; **Faß ohne Boden** (*fig*) bottomless pit

Fassade *f* **-,-n** façade

faßbar *a* comprehensible; (*greifbar*) tangible

fassen *vt* take [hold of], grasp; (*ergreifen*) seize; (*fangen*) catch; (*ein-*) set; (*enthalten*) hold; (*fig: begreifen*) take in, grasp; conceive ⟨*Plan*⟩; make ⟨*Entschluß*⟩; **sich f~** compose oneself; **sich kurz/in Geduld f~** be brief/patient; **in Worte f~** put into words; **nicht zu f~** (*fig*) unbelievable ● *vi* (*haben*) **f~ an** (+ *acc*) touch; **f~ nach** reach for

faßlich *a* comprehensible

Fasson /fa'sõ:/ *f* - style; (*Form*) shape; (*Weise*) way

Fassung *f* **-,-en** mount; (*Edelstein-*) setting; (*Electr*) socket; (*Version*) version; (*Beherrschung*) composure; **aus der F~ bringen** disconcert. **f~slos** *a* shaken; (*erstaunt*) flabbergasted. **F~svermögen** *nt* capacity

fast *adv* almost, nearly; **f~ nie** hardly ever

fast|en *vi* (*haben*) fast. **F~enzeit** *f* Lent. **F~nacht** *f* Shrovetide; (*Karneval*) carnival. **F~nachtsdienstag** *m* Shrove Tuesday. **F~tag** *m* fast-day

Faszin|ation /-'tsi̯o:n/ *f* - fascination. **f~ieren** *vt* fascinate; **f~ierend** fascinating

fatal *a* fatal; (*peinlich*) embarrassing. **F~ismus** *m* - fatalism. **F~ist** *m* **-en,-en** fatalist

Fata Morgana *f* **- -/- -nen** mirage

fauchen *vi* (*haben*) spit, hiss ● *vt* snarl

faul *a* lazy; (*verdorben*) rotten, bad; ⟨*Ausrede*⟩ lame; (*zweifelhaft*) bad; (*verdächtig*) fishy

Fäule *f* - decay

faul|en *vi* (*sein*) rot; ⟨*Zahn:*⟩ decay; (*verwesen*) putrefy. **f~enzen** *vi* (*haben*) be lazy. **F~enzer** *m* **-s,-** lazybones *sg*. **F~heit** *f* - laziness. **f~ig** *a* rotting; (*Geruch*) putrid

Fäulnis *f* - decay

Faulpelz *m* (*fam*) lazy-bones *sg*

Fauna *f* - fauna

Faust *f* **-, Fäuste** fist; **auf eigene F~** (*fig*) off one's own bat. **F~handschuh** *m* mitten. **F~schlag** *m* punch

Fauxpas /fo'pa/ *m* **-,-** /-[s],-s/ gaffe

Favorit(in) /favo'ri:t(ɪn)/ *m* **-en,-en** (*f* **-,-nen**) (*Sport*) favourite

Fax *nt* **-,-[e]** fax. **f~en** *vt* fax

Faxen *fpl* (*fam*) antics; **F~ machen** fool about; **F~ schneiden** pull faces

Faxgerät *nt* fax machine

Feber *m* **-s,-** (*Aust*) February

Februar *m* **-s,-e** February

fecht|en† *vi* (*haben*) fence. **F~er** *m* **-s,-** fencer

Feder *f* **-,-n** feather; (*Schreib-*) pen; (*Spitze*) nib; (*Techn*) spring. **F~ball** *m* shuttlecock; (*Spiel*) badminton.

F∼busch *m* plume. **f∼leicht** *a* as light as a feather. **F∼messer** *nt* penknife. **f∼n** *vi* (*haben*) be springy; (*nachgeben*) give; (*hoch-*) bounce; **f∼nd** springy; (*elastisch*) elastic. **F∼ung** *f* - (*Techn*) springs *pl*; (*Auto*) suspension

Fee *f* -,-n fairy

Fegefeuer *nt* purgatory

fegen *vt* sweep • *vi* (*sein*) (*rasen*) tear

Fehde *f* -,-n feud

fehl *a* **f∼ am Platze** out of place. **F∼betrag** *m* deficit. **f∼en** *vi* (*haben*) be missing/(*Sch*) absent; (*mangeln*) be lacking; **es f∼t an** (+ *dat*) there is a shortage of; **mir f∼t die Zeit** I haven't got the time; **sie/es f∼t mir sehr** I miss her/it very much; **was f∼t ihm?** what's the matter with him? **es f∼te nicht viel und er ...** he very nearly ...; **das hat uns noch gefehlt!** that's all we need! **f∼end** *a* missing; (*Sch*) absent

Fehler *m* -s,- mistake, error; (*Sport & fig*) fault; (*Makel*) flaw. **f∼frei** *a* faultless, *adv* -ly. **f∼haft** *a* faulty. **f∼los** *a* flawless, *adv* -ly

Fehl|geburt *f* miscarriage. **f∼gehen**† *vi sep* (*sein*) go wrong; ⟨*Schuß:*⟩ miss; (*fig*) be mistaken. **F∼griff** *m* mistake. **F∼kalkulation** *f* miscalculation. **F∼schlag** *m* failure. **f∼schlagen**† *vi sep* (*sein*) fail. **F∼start** *m* (*Sport*) false start. **F∼tritt** *m* false step; (*fig*) [moral] lapse. **F∼zündung** *f* (*Auto*) misfire

Feier *f* -,-n celebration; (*Zeremonie*) ceremony; (*Party*) party. **F∼abend** *m* end of the working day; **F∼abend machen** stop work, (*fam*) knock off; **nach F∼abend** after work. **f∼lich** *a* solemn, *adv* -ly; (*förmlich*) formal, *adv* -ly. **F∼lichkeit** *f* -,-en solemnity; **F∼lichkeiten** festivities. **f∼n** *vt* celebrate; hold ⟨*Fest*⟩; (*ehren*) fête • *vi* (*haben*) celebrate; (*lustig sein*) make merry. **F∼tag** *m* [public] holiday; (*kirchlicher*) feast-day; **erster/zweiter F∼tag** Christmas Day/Boxing Day. **f∼tags** *adv* on public holidays

feige *a* cowardly; **f∼ sein** be a coward • *adv* in a cowardly way

Feige *f* -,-n fig. **F∼nbaum** *m* fig tree

Feig|heit *f* - cowardice. **F∼ling** *m* -s,-e coward

Feile *f* -,-n file. **f∼n** *vt/i* (*haben*) file

feilschen *vi* (*haben*) haggle

Feilspäne *mpl* filings

fein *a* fine, *adv* -ly; (*zart*) delicate, *adv* -ly; ⟨*Strümpfe*⟩ sheer; ⟨*Unterschied*⟩ subtle; (*scharf*) keen; (*vornehm*) refined; (*elegant*) elegant; (*prima*) great; **sich f∼ machen** dress up. **F∼arbeit** *f* precision work

Feind|(in) *m* -es,-e (*f* -,-nen) enemy. **f∼lich** *a* enemy; (*f∼selig*) hostile. **F∼schaft** *f* -,-en enmity. **f∼selig** *a* hostile. **F∼seligkeit** *f* -,-en hostility

fein|fühlig *a* sensitive. **F∼gefühl** *nt* sensitivity; (*Takt*) delicacy. **F∼heit** *f* -,-en (*s.* **fein**) fineness; delicacy; subtlety; keenness; refinement; **F∼heiten** subtleties. **F∼kostgeschäft** *nt* delicatessen [shop]. **F∼schmecker** *m* -s,- gourmet

feist *a* fat

feixen *vi* (*haben*) smirk

Feld *nt* -[e]s,-er field; (*Fläche*) ground; (*Sport*) pitch; (*Schach-*) square; (*auf Formular*) box. **F∼bau** *m* agriculture. **F∼bett** *nt* camp-bed, (*Amer*) cot. **F∼forschung** *f* fieldwork. **F∼herr** *m* commander. **F∼marschall** *m* Field Marshal. **F∼stecher** *m* -s,- field-glasses *pl*. **F∼webel** *m* (*Mil*) sergeant. **F∼zug** *m* campaign

Felge *f* -,-n [wheel] rim

Fell *nt* -[e]s,-e (*Zool*) coat; (*Pelz*) fur; (*abgezogen*) skin, pelt; **ein dickes F∼ haben** (*fam*) be thick-skinned

Fels *m* -en,-en rock. **F∼block** *m* boulder. **F∼en** *m* -s,- rock. **f∼enfest** *a* (*fig*) firm, *adv* -ly. **f∼ig** *a* rocky

feminin *a* feminine; (*weibisch*) effeminate

Femininum *nt* -s,-na (*Gram*) feminine

Feminist|(in) *m* -en,-en (*f* -,-nen) feminist. **f∼isch** *a* feminist

Fenchel *m* -s fennel

Fenster *nt* -s,- window. **F∼brett** *nt* window-sill. **F∼laden** *m* [window] shutter. **F∼leder** *nt* chamois [-leather]. **F∼putzer** *m* -s,- window-cleaner. **F∼scheibe** *f* [window-]pane

Ferien /'fe:ri̯ən/ *pl* holidays; (*Univ*) vacation *sg*; **F∼ haben** be on holiday. **F∼ort** *m* holiday resort

Ferkel *nt* -s,- piglet

fern *a* distant; **der F∼e Osten** the Far East • *adv* far away; **von f∼** from a distance • *prep* (+ *dat*) far [away] from. **F∼bedienung** *f* remote control. **f∼bleiben**† *vi sep* (*sein*) stay away (*dat* from). **F∼e** *f* - distance;

in/aus der F~e in the/from a distance; **in weiter F~e** far away; (*zeitlich*) in the distant future. **f~er** *a* further ● *adv* (*außerdem*) furthermore; (*in Zukunft*) in future. **f~gelenkt** *a* remote-controlled; ⟨*Rakete*⟩ guided. **F~gespräch** *nt* long-distance call. **f~gesteuert** *a* = **f~gelenkt**. **F~glas** *nt* binoculars *pl*. **f~halten**† *vt sep* keep away; **sich f~halten** keep away. **F~kopierer** *m* **-s,-** fax machine. **F~kurs[us]** *m* correspondence course. **F~lenkung** *f* remote control. **F~licht** *nt* (*Auto*) full beam. **F~meldewesen** *nt* telecommunications *pl*. **F~rohr** *nt* telescope. **F~schreiben** *nt* telex. **F~schreiber** *m* **-s,-** telex [machine]

Fẹrnseh|apparat *m* television set. **f~en**† *vi sep* (*haben*) watch television. **F~en** *nt* **-s** television. **F~er** *m* **-s,-** [television] viewer; (*Gerät*) television set. **F~gerät** *nt* television set

Fẹrnsprech|amt *nt* telephone exchange, (*Amer*) central. **F~er** *m* telephone. **F~nummer** *f* telephone number. **F~zelle** *f* telephone box

Fẹrnsteuerung *f* remote control

Fẹrse *f* **-,-n** heel. **F~ngeld** *nt* **F~ngeld geben** (*fam*) take to one's heels

fẹrtig *a* finished; (*bereit*) ready; (*Comm*) ready-made; ⟨*Gericht*⟩ ready-to-serve; **f~ werden mit** finish; (*bewältigen*) cope with; **f~ sein** have finished; (*fig*) be through (**mit jdm** with s.o.); (*fam: erschöpft*) be all in/(*seelisch*) shattered ● *adv* **f~ essen/lesen** finish eating/reading. **F~bau** *m* (*pl* **-bauten**) prefabricated building. **f~bringen**† *vt sep* manage to do; (*beenden*) finish; **ich bringe es nicht f~** I can't bring myself to do it. **f~en** *vt* make. **F~gericht** *nt* ready-to-serve meal. **F~haus** *nt* prefabricated house. **F~keit** *f* **-,-en** skill. **f~kriegen** *vt sep* (*fam*) = **f~bringen. f~machen** *vt sep* finish; (*bereitmachen*) get ready; (*fam: erschöpfen*) wear out; (*seelisch*) shatter; (*fam: abkanzeln*) carpet; **sich f~machen** get ready. **f~stellen** *vt sep* complete. **F~stellung** *f* completion. **F~ung** *f* - manufacture

fẹsch *a* (*fam*) attractive; (*flott*) smart; (*Aust: nett*) kind

Fẹssel *f* **-,-n** ankle

fẹsseln *vt* tie up; tie (**an** + *acc* to); (*fig*) fascinate; **ans Bett gefesselt** confined to bed. **F~** *fpl* bonds. **f~d** *a* (*fig*) fascinating; (*packend*) absorbing

fẹst *a* firm; (*nicht flüssig*) solid; (*erstarrt*) set; (*haltbar*) strong; (*nicht locker*) tight; (*feststehend*) fixed; (*ständig*) steady; ⟨*Anstellung*⟩ permanent; ⟨*Schlaf*⟩ sound; ⟨*Blick, Stimme*⟩ steady; **f~ werden** harden; ⟨*Gelee:*⟩ set; **f~e Nahrung** solids *pl* ● *adv* firmly; tightly; steadily; soundly; (*kräftig, tüchtig*) hard; **f~ schlafen** be fast asleep

Fẹst *nt* **-[e]s,-e** celebration; (*Party*) party; (*Relig*) festival; **frohes F~!** happy Christmas!

fẹst|angestellt *a* permanent. **f~binden**† *vt sep* tie (**an** + *dat* to). **f~bleiben**† *vi sep* (*sein*) (*fig*) remain firm. **f~e** *adv* (*fam*) hard. **F~essen** *nt* = **F~mahl. f~fahren**† *vi/r sep* (*sein*) **[sich] f~fahren** get stuck; ⟨*Verhandlungen:*⟩ reach deadlock. **f~halten**† *v sep* ● *vt* hold on to; (*aufzeichnen*) record; **sich f~halten** hold on ● *vi* (*haben*) **f~halten an** (+ *dat*) (*fig*) stick to; cling to ⟨*Tradition*⟩. **f~igen** *vt* strengthen; **sich f~igen** grow stronger. **F~iger** *m* **-s,-** styling lotion/(*Schaum-*) mousse. **F~igkeit** *f* - (*s.* **fest**) firmness; solidity; strength; steadiness. **f~klammern** *vt sep* clip (**an** + *dat* to); **sich f~klammern** cling (**an** + *dat* to). **F~land** *nt* mainland; (*Kontinent*) continent. **f~legen** *vt sep* (*fig*) fix, settle; lay down ⟨*Regeln*⟩; tie up ⟨*Geld*⟩; **sich f~legen** commit oneself

fẹstlich *a* festive, *adv* -ly. **F~keiten** *fpl* festivities

fẹst|liegen† *vi sep* (*haben*) be fixed, settled. **f~machen** *v sep* ● *vt* fasten/(*binden*) tie (**an** + *dat* to); (*f~legen*) fix, settle ● *vi* (*haben*) (*Naut*) moor. **F~mahl** *nt* feast; (*Bankett*) banquet. **F~nahme** *f* **-,-n** arrest. **f~nehmen**† *vt sep* arrest. **F~ordner** *m* steward. **f~setzen** *vt sep* fix, settle; (*inhaftieren*) gaol; **sich f~setzen** collect. **f~sitzen**† *vi sep* (*haben*) be firm/⟨*Schraube:*⟩ tight; (*haften*) stick; (*nicht weiterkommen*) be stuck. **F~spiele** *npl* festival *sg*. **f~stehen**† *vi sep* (*haben*) be certain. **f~stellen** *vt sep* fix; (*ermitteln*) establish; (*bemerken*) notice; (*sagen*) state. **F~stellung** *f* establishment;

(*Aussage*) statement; (*Erkenntnis*) realization. **F~tag** *m* special day

Festung *f* **-,-en** fortress

Fest|zelt *nt* marquee. **f~ziehen**† *vt sep* pull tight. **F~zug** *m* [grand] procession

Fete /'fe:tə, 'fɛ:tə/ *f* **-,-n** party

fett *a* fat; (*f~reich*) fatty; (*fettig*) greasy; (*üppig*) rich; ⟨*Druck*⟩ bold. **F~** *nt* **-[e]s,-e** fat; (*flüssig*) grease. **f~arm** *a* low-fat. **f~en** *vt* grease ● *vi* (*haben*) be greasy. **F~fleck** *m* grease mark. **f~ig** *a* greasy. **f~leibig** *a* obese. **F~näpfchen** *nt* **ins F~näpfchen treten** (*fam*) put one's foot in it

Fetzen *m* **-s,-** scrap; (*Stoff*) rag; **in F~** in shreds

feucht *a* damp, moist; ⟨*Luft*⟩ humid. **f~heiß** *a* humid. **F~igkeit** *f* **-** dampness; (*Nässe*) moisture; (*Luft-*) humidity. **F~igkeitscreme** *f* moisturizer

feudal *a* (*fam: vornehm*) sumptuous, *adv* -ly. **F~ismus** *m* **-** feudalism

Feuer *nt* **-s,-** fire; (*für Zigarette*) light; (*Begeisterung*) passion; **F~ machen** light a fire; **F~ fangen** catch fire; (*fam: sich verlieben*) be smitten; **jdm F~ geben** give s.o. a light. **F~alarm** *m* fire alarm. **F~bestattung** *f* cremation. **f~gefährlich** *a* [in]flammable. **F~leiter** *f* fire-escape. **F~löscher** *m* **-s,-** fire extinguisher. **F~melder** *m* **-s,-** fire alarm. **f~n** *vi* (*haben*) fire (**auf** + *acc* on) ● *vt* (*fam*) (*schleudern*) fling; (*entlassen*) fire. **F~probe** *f* (*fig*) test. **f~rot** *a* crimson. **f~speiend** *a* **f~speiender Berg** volcano. **F~stein** *m* flint. **F~stelle** *f* hearth. **F~treppe** *f* fire-escape. **F~wache** *f* fire station. **F~waffe** *f* firearm. **F~wehr** *f* **-,-en** fire brigade. **F~wehrauto** *nt* fire-engine. **F~wehrmann** *m* (*pl* **-männer** & **-leute**) fireman. **F~werk** *nt* firework display, fireworks *pl*. **F~werkskörper** *m* firework. **F~zeug** *nt* lighter

feurig *a* fiery; (*fig*) passionate

Fiaker *m* **-s,-** (*Aust*) horse-drawn cab

Fichte *f* **-,-n** spruce

fidel *a* cheerful

Fieber *nt* **-s** [raised] temperature; **F~ haben** have a temperature. **f~haft** *a* (*fig*) feverish, *adv* -ly. **f~n** *vi* (*haben*) be feverish. **F~thermometer** *nt* thermometer

fiebrig *a* feverish

fies *a* (*fam*) nasty, *adv* -ily

Figur *f* **-,-en** figure; (*Roman-, Film-*) character; (*Schach-*) piece

Fik|tion /-'tsi̯o:n/ *f* **-,-en** fiction. **f~tiv** *a* fictitious

Filet /fi'le:/ *nt* **-s,-s** fillet

Filial|e *f* **-,-n, F~geschäft** *nt* (*Comm*) branch

Filigran *nt* **-s** filigree

Film *m* **-[e]s,-e** film; (*Kino-*) film, (*Amer*) movie; (*Schicht*) coating. **f~en** *vt/i* (*haben*) film. **F~kamera** *f* cine/(*für Kinofilm*) film camera

Filt|er *m* & (*Techn*) *nt* **-s,-** filter; (*Zigaretten-*) filter-tip. **f~ern** *vt* filter. **F~erzigarette** *f* filter-tipped cigarette. **f~rieren** *vt* filter

Filz *m* **-es** felt. **f~en** *vi* (*haben*) become matted ● *vt* (*fam*) (*durchsuchen*) frisk; (*stehlen*) steal. **F~schreiber** *m* **-s,-, F~stift** *m* felt-tipped pen

Fimmel *m* **-s,-** (*fam*) obsession

Fina|le *nt* **-s,-** (*Mus*) finale; (*Sport*) final. **F~list(in)** *m* **-en,-en** (*f* **-,-nen**) finalist

Finanz *f* **-,-en** finance. **F~amt** *nt* tax office. **f~iell** *a* financial, *adv* -ly. **f~ieren** *vt* finance. **F~minister** *m* minister of finance

find|en† *vt* find; (*meinen*) think; **den Tod f~en** meet one's death; **wie f~est du das?** what do you think of that? **f~est du?** do you think so? **es wird sich f~en** it'll turn up; (*fig*) it'll be all right ● *vi* (*haben*) find one's way. **F~er** *m* **-s,-** finder. **F~erlohn** *m* reward. **f~ig** *a* resourceful. **F~ling** *m* **-s,-e** boulder

Finesse *f* **-,-n** (*Kniff*) trick; **F~n** (*Techn*) refinements

Finger *m* **-s,-** finger; **die F~ lassen von** (*fam*) leave alone; **etw im kleinen F~ haben** (*fam*) have sth at one's fingertips. **F~abdruck** *m* finger-mark; (*Admin*) fingerprint. **F~hut** *m* thimble. **F~nagel** *m* finger-nail. **F~ring** *m* ring. **F~spitze** *f* finger-tip. **F~zeig** *m* **-[e]s,-e** hint

fingier|en *vt* fake. **f~t** *a* fictitious

Fink *m* **-en,-en** finch

Finn|e *m* **-n,-n, F~in** *f* **-,-nen** Finn. **f~isch** *a* Finnish. **F~land** *nt* **-s** Finland

finster *a* dark; (*düster*) gloomy; (*unheildrohend*) sinister; **im F~n** in the dark. **F~nis** *f* **-** darkness; (*Astr*) eclipse

Finte *f* **-,-n** trick; (*Boxen*) feint

Firma *f* **-,-men** firm, company
firmen *vt* (*Relig*) confirm
Firmen|wagen *m* company car. **F~zeichen** *nt* trade mark, logo
Firmung *f* **-,-en** (*Relig*) confirmation
Firnis *m* **-ses,-se** varnish. **f~sen** *vt* varnish
First *m* **-[e]s,-e** [roof] ridge
Fisch *m* **-[e]s,-e** fish; **F~e** (*Astr*) Pisces. **F~dampfer** *m* trawler. **f~en** *vt/i* (*haben*) fish; **aus dem Wasser f~en** (*fam*) fish out of the water. **F~er** *m* **-s,-** fisherman. **F~erei** *f* **-**, **F~fang** *m* fishing. **F~gräte** *f* fishbone. **F~händler** *m* fishmonger. **F~otter** *m* otter. **F~reiher** *m* heron. **F~stäbchen** *nt* **-s,-** fish finger. **F~teich** *m* fish-pond
Fiskus *m* **- der F~** the Treasury
Fisole *f* **-,-n** (*Aust*) French bean
fit *a* fit. **F~neß** *f* **-** fitness
fix *a* (*fam*) quick, *adv* -ly; (*geistig*) bright; **f~e Idee** obsession; **fix und fertig** all finished; (*bereit*) all ready; (*fam: erschöpft*) shattered. **F~er** *m* **-s,-** (*sl*) junkie
fixieren *vt* stare at; (*Phot*) fix
Fjord *m* **-[e]s,-e** fiord
FKK *abbr* (**Freikörperkultur**) naturism
flach *a* flat; (*eben*) level; (*niedrig*) low; (*nicht tief*) shallow; **f~er Teller** dinner plate; **die f~e Hand** the flat of the hand
Fläche *f* **-,-n** area; (*Ober-*) surface; (*Seite*) face. **F~nmaß** *nt* square measure
Flachs *m* **-es** flax. **f~blond** *a* flaxen-haired; ⟨*Haar*⟩ flaxen
flackern *vi* (*haben*) flicker
Flagg|e *f* **-,-n** flag
flagrant *a* flagrant
Flair /flɛːɐ̯/ *nt* **-s** air, aura
Flak *f* **-,-[s]** anti-aircraft artillery/(*Geschütz*) gun
flämisch *a* Flemish
Flamme *f* **-,-n** flame; (*Koch-*) burner; **in F~n** in flames
Flanell *m* **-s** (*Tex*) flannel
Flank|e *f* **-,-n** flank. **f~ieren** *vt* flank
Flasche *f* **-,-n** bottle. **F~nbier** *nt* bottled beer. **F~nöffner** *m* bottle-opener
flatter|haft *a* fickle. **f~n** *vi* (*sein/haben*) flutter; ⟨*Segel:*⟩ flap
flau *a* (*schwach*) faint; (*Comm*) slack; **mir ist f~** I feel faint
Flaum *m* **-[e]s** down. **f~ig** *a* downy; **f~ig rühren** (*Aust Culin*) cream
flauschig *a* fleecy; ⟨*Spielzeug*⟩ fluffy
Flausen *fpl* (*fam*) silly ideas; (*Ausflüchte*) silly excuses
Flaute *f* **-,-n** (*Naut*) calm; (*Comm*) slack period; (*Schwäche*) low
fläzen (sich) *vr* (*fam*) sprawl
Flechte *f* **-,-n** (*Med*) eczema; (*Bot*) lichen; (*Zopf*) plait. **f~n**† *vt* plait; weave ⟨*Korb*⟩
Fleck *m* **-[e]s,-e[n]** spot; (*größer*) patch; (*Schmutz-*) stain, mark; **blauer F~** bruise; **nicht vom F~ kommen** (*fam*) make no progress. **f~en** *vi* (*haben*) stain. **F~en** *m* **-s,-** = **Fleck**; (*Ortschaft*) small town. **f~enlos** *a* spotless. **F~entferner** *m* **-s,-** stain remover. **f~ig** *a* stained; ⟨*Haut*⟩ blotchy
Fledermaus *f* bat
Flegel *m* **-s,-** lout. **f~haft** *a* loutish. **F~jahre** *npl* (*fam*) awkward age *sg.* **f~n (sich)** *vr* loll
flehen *vi* (*haben*) beg (**um** for). **f~tlich** *a* pleading, *adv* -ly
Fleisch *nt* **-[e]s** flesh; (*Culin*) meat; (*Frucht-*) pulp. **F~er** *m* **-s,-** butcher. **F~erei** *f* **-,-en**, **F~erladen** *m* butcher's shop. **f~fressend** *a* carnivorous. **F~fresser** *m* **-s,-** carnivore. **F~hauer** *m* **-s,-** (*Aust*) butcher. **f~ig** *a* fleshy. **f~lich** *a* carnal. **F~wolf** *m* mincer. **F~wunde** *f* flesh-wound
Fleiß *m* **-es** diligence; **mit F~** diligently; (*absichtlich*) on purpose. **f~ig** *a* diligent, *adv* -ly; (*arbeitsam*) industrious, *adv* -ly
flektieren *vt* (*Gram*) inflect
fletschen *vt* **die Zähne f~** ⟨*Tier:*⟩ bare its teeth
flex|ibel *a* flexible; ⟨*Einband*⟩ limp. **F~ibilität** *f* **-** flexibility. **F~ion** *f* **-,-en** (*Gram*) inflexion
flicken *vt* mend; (*mit Flicken*) patch. **F~** *m* **-s,-** patch
Flieder *m* **-s** lilac. **f~farben** *a* lilac
Fliege *f* **-,-n** fly; (*Schleife*) bow-tie; **zwei F~n mit einer Klappe schlagen** kill two birds with one stone. **f~n**† *vi* (*sein*) fly; (*geworfen werden*) be thrown; (*fam: fallen*) fall; (*fam: entlassen werden*) be fired/(*von der Schule*) expelled; **in die Luft f~n** blow up ● *vt* fly. **f~nd** *a* flying; ⟨*Händler*⟩ itinerant; **in f~nder Eile** in great haste. **F~r** *m* **-s,-** airman; (*Pilot*) pilot; (*fam: Flugzeug*) plane. **F~rangriff** *m* air raid
flieh|en† *vi* (*sein*) flee (**vor** + *dat* from); (*entweichen*) escape ● *vt*

shun. **f~end** *a* fleeing; ⟨*Kinn, Stirn*⟩ receding. **F~kraft** *f* centrifugal force

Fliese *f* **-,-n** tile

Fließ|band *nt* assembly line. **f~en**† *vi* (*sein*) flow; (*aus Wasserhahn*) run. **f~end** *a* flowing; ⟨*Wasser*⟩ running; ⟨*Verkehr*⟩ moving; (*geläufig*) fluent, *adv* -ly. **F~heck** *nt* fastback. **F~wasser** *nt* running water

flimmern *vi* (*haben*) shimmer; (*TV*) flicker; **es flimmert mir vor den Augen** everything is dancing in front of my eyes

flink *a* nimble, *adv* -bly; (*schnell*) quick, *adv* -ly

Flinte *f* **-,-n** shotgun

Flirt /flœɐ̯t/ *m* **-s,-s** flirtation. **f~en** *vi* (*haben*) flirt

Flitter *m* **-s** sequins *pl*; (*F~schmuck*) tinsel. **F~wochen** *fpl* honeymoon *sg*

flitzen *vi* (*sein*) (*fam*) dash; ⟨*Auto:*⟩ whizz

Flock|e *f* **-,-n** flake; (*Wolle*) tuft. **f~ig** *a* fluffy

Floh *m* **-[e]s,¨e** flea. **F~markt** *m* flea market. **F~spiel** *nt* tiddly-winks *sg*

Flor *m* **-s** gauze; (*Trauer-*) crape; (*Samt-, Teppich-*) pile

Flora *f* **-** flora

Florett *nt* **-[e]s,-e** foil

florieren *vi* (*haben*) flourish

Floskel *f* **-,-n** [empty] phrase

Floß *nt* **-es,¨e** raft

Flosse *f* **-,-n** fin; (*Seehund-, Gummi-*) flipper; (*sl: Hand*) paw

Flöt|e *f* **-,-n** flute; (*Block-*) recorder. **f~en** *vi* (*haben*) play the flute/recorder; (*fam: pfeifen*) whistle ● *vt* play on the flute/recorder. **F~ist(in)** *m* **-en,-en** (*f* **-,-nen**) flautist

flott *a* quick, *adv* -ly; (*lebhaft*) lively; (*schick*) smart, *adv* -ly; **f~ leben** live it up

Flotte *f* **-,-n** fleet

flottmachen *vt sep* **wieder f~** (*Naut*) refloat; get going again ⟨*Auto*⟩; put back on its feet ⟨*Unternehmen*⟩

Flöz *nt* **-es,-e** [coal] seam

Fluch *m* **-[e]s,¨e** curse. **f~en** *vi* (*haben*) curse, swear

Flucht[1] *f* **-,-en** (*Reihe*) line; (*Zimmer-*) suite

Flucht[2] *f* **-** flight; (*Entweichen*) escape; **die F~ ergreifen** take flight. **f~artig** *a* hasty, *adv* -ily

flücht|en *vi* (*sein*) flee (**vor** + *dat* from); (*entweichen*) escape ● *vr* **sich f~en** take refuge. **f~ig** *a* fugitive; (*kurz*) brief, *adv* -ly; ⟨*Blick, Gedanke*⟩ fleeting; ⟨*Bekanntschaft*⟩ passing; (*oberflächlich*) cursory, *adv* -ily; (*nicht sorgfältig*) careless, *adv* -ly; (*Chem*) volatile; **f~ig sein** be on the run; **f~ig kennen** know slightly. **F~igkeitsfehler** *m* slip. **F~ling** *m* **-s,-e** fugitive; (*Pol*) refugee

Fluchwort *nt* (*pl* **-wörter**) swearword

Flug *m* **-[e]s,¨e** flight. **F~abwehr** *f* anti-aircraft defence. **F~ball** *m* (*Tennis*) volley. **F~blatt** *nt* pamphlet

Flügel *m* **-s,-** wing; (*Fenster-*) casement; (*Mus*) grand piano

Fluggast *m* [air] passenger

flügge *a* fully-fledged

Flug|gesellschaft *f* airline. **F~hafen** *m* airport. **F~lotse** *m* air-traffic controller. **F~platz** *m* airport; (*klein*) airfield. **F~preis** *m* air fare. **F~schein** *m* air ticket. **F~schneise** *f* flight path. **F~schreiber** *m* **-s,-** flight recorder. **F~schrift** *f* pamphlet. **F~steig** *m* **-[e]s,-e** gate. **F~wesen** *nt* aviation. **F~zeug** *nt* **-[e]s,-e** aircraft, plane

Fluidum *nt* **-s** aura

Flunder *f* **-,-n** flounder

flunkern *vi* (*haben*) (*fam*) tell fibs; (*aufschneiden*) tell tall stories

Flunsch *m* **-[e]s,-e** pout

fluoreszierend *a* fluorescent

Flur *m* **-[e]s,-e** [entrance] hall; (*Gang*) corridor

Flusen *fpl* fluff *sg*

Fluß *m* **-sses,¨sse** river; (*Fließen*) flow; **im F~** (*fig*) in a state of flux. **f~abwärts** *adv* downstream. **f~aufwärts** *adv* upstream. **F~bett** *nt* river-bed

flüssig *a* liquid; ⟨*Lava*⟩ molten; (*fließend*) fluent, *adv* -ly; ⟨*Verkehr*⟩ freely moving. **F~keit** *f* **-,-en** liquid; (*Anat*) fluid

Flußpferd *nt* hippopotamus

flüstern *vt/i* (*haben*) whisper

Flut *f* **-,-en** high tide; (*fig*) flood; **F~en** waters. **F~licht** *nt* floodlight. **F~welle** *f* tidal wave

Föderation /-ˈtsi̯o:n/ *f* **-,-en** federation

Fohlen *nt* **-s,-** foal

Föhn *m* **-s** föhn [wind]

Folg|e *f* **-,-n** consequence; (*Reihe*) succession; (*Fortsetzung*) instalment;

(*Teil*) part; **F~e leisten** (+*dat*) accept ⟨*Einladung*⟩; obey ⟨*Befehl*⟩. **f~en** *vi* (*sein*) follow (**jdm/etw** s.o./sth); (*zuhören*) listen (*dat* to); **daraus f~t, daß** it follows that; **wie f~t** as follows ● (*haben*) (*gehorchen*) obey (**jdm** s.o.). **f~end** *a* following; **f~endes** the following. **f~endermaßen** *adv* as follows

folger|n *vt* conclude (**aus** from). **F~ung** *f* -,-en conclusion

folg|lich *adv* consequently. **f~sam** *a* obedient, *adv* -ly

Folie /'fo:li̯ə/ *f* -,-n foil; (*Plastik-*) film

Folklore *f* - folklore

Folter *f* -,-n torture; **auf die F~ spannen** (*fig*) keep on tenterhooks. **f~n** *vt* torture

Fön (P) *m* -s,-e hair-drier

Fonds /fõ:/ *m* -,- /-[s],-s/ fund

fönen *vt* [blow-]dry

Fontäne *f* -,-n jet; (*Brunnen*) fountain

Förder|band *nt* (*pl* **-bänder**) conveyor belt. **f~lich** *a* beneficial

fordern *vt* demand; (*beanspruchen*) claim; (*zum Kampf*) challenge; **gefordert werden** (*fig*) be stretched

fördern *vt* promote; (*unterstützen*) encourage; (*finanziell*) sponsor; (*gewinnen*) extract

Forderung *f* -,-en demand; (*Anspruch*) claim

Förderung *f* - (s. **fördern**) promotion; encouragement; (*Techn*) production

Forelle *f* -,-n trout

Form *f* -,-en form; (*Gestalt*) shape; (*Culin, Techn*) mould; (*Back-*) tin; **[gut] in F~** in good form

Formalität *f* -,-en formality

Format *nt* -[e]s,-e format; (*Größe*) size; (*fig: Bedeutung*) stature

Formation /-'tsi̯o:n/ *f* -,-en formation

Formel *f* -,-n formula

formell *a* formal, *adv* -ly

formen *vt* shape, mould; (*bilden*) form; **sich f~** take shape

förmlich *a* formal, *adv* -ly; (*regelrecht*) virtual, *adv* -ly. **F~keit** *f* -,-en formality

form|los *a* shapeless; (*zwanglos*) informal, *adv* -ly. **F~sache** *f* formality

Formular *nt* -s,-e [printed] form

formulier|en *vt* formulate, word. **F~ung** *f* -,-en wording

forsch *a* brisk, *adv* -ly; (*schneidig*) dashing, *adv* -ly

forsch|en *vi* (*haben*) search (**nach** for). **f~end** *a* searching. **F~er** *m* -s,- research scientist; (*Reisender*) explorer. **F~ung** *f* -,-en research. **F~ungsreisende(r)** *m* explorer

Forst *m* -[e]s,-e forest

Förster *m* -s,- forester

Forstwirtschaft *f* forestry

Forsythie /-tsi̯ə/ *f* -,-n forsythia

Fort *nt* -s,-s (*Mil*) fort

fort *adv* away; **f~ sein** be away; (*gegangen/verschwunden*) have gone; **und so f~** and so on; **in einem f~** continuously. **f~bewegen** *vt sep* move; **sich f~bewegen** move. **F~bewegung** *f* locomotion. **F~bildung** *f* further education/training. **f~bleiben**† *vi sep* (*sein*) stay away. **f~bringen**† *vt sep* take away. **f~fahren**† *vi sep* (*sein*) go away ● (*haben/sein*) continue (**zu** to). **f~fallen**† *vi sep* (*sein*) be dropped/(*ausgelassen*) omitted; (*entfallen*) no longer apply; (*aufhören*) cease. **f~führen** *vt sep* continue. **F~gang** *m* departure; (*Verlauf*) progress. **f~gehen**† *vi sep* (*sein*) leave, go away; (*ausgehen*) go out; (*andauern*) go on. **f~geschritten** *a* advanced; (*spät*) late. **F~geschrittene(r)** *m/f* advanced student. **f~gesetzt** *a* constant, *adv* -ly. **f~jagen** *vt sep* chase away. **f~lassen**† *vt sep* let go; (*auslassen*) omit. **f~laufen**† *vi sep* (*sein*) run away; (*sich f~setzen*) continue. **f~laufend** *a* consecutive, *adv* -ly. **f~nehmen**† *vt sep* take away. **f~pflanzen (sich)** *vr sep* reproduce; ⟨*Ton, Licht:*⟩ travel. **F~pflanzung** *f* - reproduction. **F~pflanzungsorgan** *nt* reproductive organ. **f~reißen**† *vt sep* carry away; (*entreißen*) tear away. **f~schaffen** *vt sep* take away. **f~schicken** *vt sep* send away; (*abschicken*) send off. **f~schreiten**† *vi sep* (*sein*) continue; (*Fortschritte machen*) progress, advance. **f~schreitend** *a* progressive; ⟨*Alter*⟩ advancing. **F~schritt** *m* progress; **F~schritte machen** make progress. **f~schrittlich** *a* progressive. **f~setzen** *vt sep* continue; **sich f~setzen** continue. **F~setzung** *f* -,-en continuation; (*Folge*) instalment; **F~setzung folgt** to be continued. **F~setzungsroman** *m* serialized novel, serial. **f~während** *a* constant, *adv* -ly. **f~werfen**† *vt sep* throw away. **f~ziehen**† *v sep* ● *vt* pull away ● *vi* (*sein*) move away

Fossil *nt* -,-ien /-i̯ən/ fossil

Foto *nt* **-s,-s** photo. **F~apparat** *m* camera. **f~gen** *a* photogenic

Fotograf|(in) *m* **-en,-en** (*f* **-,-nen**) photographer. **F~ie** *f* **-,-n** photography; (*Bild*) photograph. **f~ieren** *vt* take a photo[graph] of; **sich f~ieren lassen** have one's photo[graph] taken ● *vi* (*haben*) take photographs. **f~isch** *a* photographic

Fotokopie *f* photocopy. **f~ren** *vt* photocopy. **F~rgerät** *nt* photocopier

Fötus *m* **-,-ten** foetus

Foul /faul/ *nt* **-s,-s** (*Sport*) foul. **f~en** *vt* foul

Foyer /foa'je:/ *nt* **-s,-s** foyer

Fracht *f* **-,-en** freight. **F~er** *m* **-s,-** freighter. **F~gut** *nt* freight. **F~schiff** *nt* cargo boat

Frack *m* **-[e]s,¨e & -s** tailcoat; **im F~** in tails *pl*

Frage *f* **-,-n** question; **eine F~ stellen** ask a question; **etw in F~ stellen** question sth; (*ungewiß machen*) make sth doubtful; **ohne F~** undoubtedly; **nicht in F~ kommen** be out of the question. **F~bogen** *m* questionnaire. **f~n** *vt/i* (*haben*) ask; **sich f~n** wonder (**ob** whether). **f~nd** *a* questioning, *adv* -ly; (*Gram*) interrogative. **F~zeichen** *nt* question mark

frag|lich *a* doubtful; ⟨*Person, Sache*⟩ in question. **f~los** *adv* undoubtedly

Fragment *nt* **-[e]s,-e** fragment. **f~arisch** *a* fragmentary

fragwürdig *a* questionable; (*verdächtig*) dubious

fraisefarben /'frɛ:s-/ *a* strawberry-pink

Fraktion /-'tsio:n/ *f* **-,-en** parliamentary party

Franken[1] *m* **-s,-** (*Swiss*) franc

Franken[2] *nt* **-s** Franconia

Frankfurter *f* **-,-** frankfurter

frankieren *vt* stamp, frank

Frankreich *nt* **-s** France

Fransen *fpl* fringe *sg*

Franz|ose *m* **-n,-n** Frenchman; **die F~osen** the French *pl*. **F~ösin** *f* **-,-nen** Frenchwoman. **f~ösisch** *a* French. **F~ösisch** *nt* **-[s]** (*Lang*) French

frapp|ant *a* striking. **f~ieren** *vt* (*fig*) strike; **f~ierend** striking

fräsen *vt* (*Techn*) mill

Fraß *m* **-es** feed; (*pej: Essen*) muck

Fratze *f* **-,-n** grotesque face; (*Grimasse*) grimace; (*pej: Gesicht*) face; **F~n schneiden** pull faces

Frau *f* **-,-en** woman; (*Ehe-*) wife; **F~ Thomas** Mrs/(*unverheiratet*) Miss/(*Admin*) Ms Thomas; **Unsere Liebe F~** (*Relig*) Our Lady. **F~chen** *nt* **-s,-** mistress

Frauen|arzt *m*, **F~ärztin** *f* gynaecologist. **F~rechtlerin** *f* **-,-nen** feminist. **F~zimmer** *nt* woman

Fräulein *nt* **-s,-** single woman; (*jung*) young lady; (*Anrede*) Miss

fraulich *a* womanly

frech *a* cheeky, *adv* -ily; (*unverschämt*) impudent, *adv* -ly. **F~dachs** *m* (*fam*) cheeky monkey. **F~heit** *f* **-,-en** cheekiness; impudence; (*Äußerung, Handlung*) impertinence

frei *a* free; (*freischaffend*) freelance; ⟨*Künstler*⟩ independent; (*nicht besetzt*) vacant; (*offen*) open; (*bloß*) bare; **f~er Tag** day off; **sich** (*dat*) **f~ nehmen** take time off; **f~ machen** (*räumen*) clear; vacate ⟨*Platz*⟩; (*befreien*) liberate; (*entkleiden*) bare; **f~ lassen** leave free; **jdm f~e Hand lassen** give s.o. a free hand; **ist dieser Platz f~?** is this seat taken? **'Zimmer f~'** 'vacancies' ● *adv* freely; (*ohne Notizen*) without notes; (*umsonst*) free

Frei|bad *nt* open-air swimming pool. **f~bekommen**† *vt sep* get released; **einen Tag f~bekommen** get a day off. **f~beruflich** *a & adv* freelance. **F~e** *nt* **im F~en** in the open air, out of doors. **F~frau** *f* baroness. **F~gabe** *f* release. **f~geben**† *v sep* ● *vt* release; (*eröffnen*) open; **jdm einen Tag f~geben** give s.o. a day off ● *vi* (*haben*) **jdm f~geben** give s.o. time off. **f~gebig** *a* generous, *adv* -ly. **F~gebigkeit** *f* **-** generosity. **f~haben**† *v sep* ● *vt* **eine Stunde f~haben** have an hour off; (*Sch*) have a free period ● *vi* (*haben*) be off work/(*Sch*) school; (*beurlaubt sein*) have time off. **f~halten**† *vt sep* keep clear; (*belegen*) keep; **einen Tag/sich f~halten** keep a day/oneself free; **jdn f~halten** treat s.o. [to a meal/drink]. **F~handelszone** *f* free-trade area. **f~händig** *adv* without holding on

Freiheit *f* **-,-en** freedom, liberty; **sich** (*dat*) **F~en erlauben** take liberties. **F~sstrafe** *f* prison sentence

freiheraus *adv* frankly

Frei|herr *m* baron. **F~karte** *f* free ticket. **F~körperkultur** *f* naturism. **f~lassen**† *vt sep* release, set free.

F~lassung *f* - release. **F~lauf** *m* free-wheel. **f~legen** *vt sep* expose. **f~lich** *adv* admittedly; (*natürlich*) of course. **F~lichttheater** *nt* open-air theatre. **f~machen** *v sep* ● *vt* (*frankieren*) frank ● *vi/r* (*haben*) **[sich] f~machen** take time off. **F~marke** *f* [postage] stamp. **F~maurer** *m* Freemason. **f~mütig** *a* candid, *adv* -ly. **F~platz** *m* free seat; (*Sch*) free place. **f~schaffend** *a* freelance. **f~schwimmen**† **(sich)** *vr sep* pass one's swimming test. **f~setzen** *vt sep* release; (*entlassen*) make redundant. **f~sprechen**† *vt sep* acquit. **F~spruch** *m* acquittal. **f~stehen**† *vi sep* (*haben*) stand empty; **es steht ihm f~** (*fig*) he is free (**zu** to). **f~stellen** *vt sep* exempt (**von** from); **jdm etw f~stellen** leave sth up to s.o. **f~stempeln** *vt sep* frank. **F~stil** *m* freestyle. **F~stoß** *m* free kick. **F~stunde** *f* (*Sch*) free period

Freitag *m* Friday. **f~s** *adv* on Fridays

Frei|tod *m* suicide. **F~übungen** *fpl* [physical] exercises. **F~umschlag** *m* stamped envelope. **f~weg** *adv* freely; (*offen*) openly. **f~willig** *a* voluntary, *adv* -ily. **F~willige(r)** *m/f* volunteer. **F~zeichen** *nt* ringing tone; (*Rufzeichen*) dialling tone. **F~zeit** *f* free *or* spare time; (*Muße*) leisure; (*Tagung*) [weekend/holiday] course. **F~zeit-** *pref* leisure ... **F~zeitbekleidung** *f* casual wear. **f~zügig** *a* unrestricted; (*großzügig*) liberal; (*moralisch*) permissive

fremd *a* foreign; (*unbekannt, ungewohnt*) strange; (*nicht das eigene*) other people's; **ein f~er Mann** a stranger; **f~e Leute** strangers; **unter f~em Namen** under an assumed name; **jdm f~ sein** be unknown/(*wesens-*) alien to s.o.; **ich bin hier f~** I'm a stranger here. **f~artig** *a* strange, *adv* -ly; (*exotisch*) exotic. **F~e** *f* - **in der F~e** away from home; (*im Ausland*) in a foreign country. **F~e(r)** *m/f* stranger; (*Ausländer*) foreigner; (*Tourist*) tourist. **F~enführer** *m* [tourist] guide. **F~enverkehr** *m* tourism. **F~enzimmer** *nt* room [to let]; (*Gäste-*) guest room. **f~gehen**† *vi sep* (*sein*) (*fam*) be unfaithful. **F~körper** *m* foreign body. **f~ländisch** *a* foreign; (*exotisch*) exotic. **F~ling** *m* **-s,-e** stranger. **F~sprache** *f* foreign language. **F~wort** *nt* (*pl* **-wörter**) foreign word

frenetisch *a* frenzied

frequ|entieren *vt* frequent. **F~enz** *f* **-,-en** frequency

Freske *f* **-,-n**, **Fresko** *nt* **-s,-ken** fresco

Fresse *f* **-,-n** (*sl*) (*Mund*) gob; (*Gesicht*) mug; **halt die F~!** shut your trap! **f~n**† *vt/i* (*haben*) eat. **F~n** *nt* **-s** feed; (*sl: Essen*) grub

Freßnapf *m* feeding bowl

Freud|e *f* **-,-n** pleasure; (*innere*) joy; **mit F~en** with pleasure; **jdm eine F~e machen** please s.o. **f~ig** *a* joyful, *adv* -ly; **f~iges Ereignis** (*fig*) happy event. **f~los** *a* cheerless; (*traurig*) sad

freuen *vt* please; **sich f~** be pleased (**über** + *acc* about); **sich f~ auf** (+ *acc*) look forward to; **es freut mich, ich freue mich** I'm glad *or* pleased (**daß** that)

Freund *m* **-es,-e** friend; (*Verehrer*) boyfriend; (*Anhänger*) lover (*gen* of). **F~in** *f* **-,-nen** friend; (*Liebste*) girlfriend; (*Anhängerin*) lover (*gen* of). **f~lich** *a* kind, *adv* -ly; (*umgänglich*) friendly; (*angenehm*) pleasant; **wären Sie so f~lich?** would you be so kind? **f~licherweise** *adv* kindly. **F~lichkeit** *f* **-,-en** kindness; friendliness; pleasantness

Freundschaft *f* **-,-en** friendship; **F~ schließen** become friends. **f~lich** *a* friendly

Frevel /ˈfreːfəl/ *m* **-s,-** (*liter*) outrage. **f~haft** *a* (*liter*) wicked

Frieden *m* **-s** peace; **F~ schließen** make peace; **im F~** in peacetime; **laß mich in F~!** leave me alone! **F~srichter** *m* ≈ magistrate. **F~svertrag** *m* peace treaty

fried|fertig *a* peaceable. **F~hof** *m* cemetery. **f~lich** *a* peaceful, *adv* -ly; (*verträglich*) peaceable. **f~liebend** *a* peace-loving

frieren† *vi* (*haben*) ⟨*Person:*⟩ be cold; *impers* **es friert/hat gefroren** it is freezing/there has been a frost; **frierst du? friert [es] dich?** are you cold? ● (*sein*) (*gefrieren*) freeze

Fries *m* **-es,-e** frieze

Frikadelle *f* **-,-n** [meat] rissole

frisch *a* fresh; (*sauber*) clean; (*leuchtend*) bright; (*munter*) lively; (*rüstig*) fit; **sich f~ machen** freshen up ● *adv* freshly, newly; **f~ gelegte**

Eier new-laid eggs; **ein Bett f∼ beziehen** put clean sheets on a bed; **f∼ gestrichen!** wet paint! **F∼e** *f* - freshness; brightness; liveliness; fitness. **F∼haltepackung** *f* vacuum pack. **F∼käse** *m* ≈ cottage cheese. **f∼weg** *adv* freely

Fri|seur /fri'zø:ɐ̯/ *m* **-s,-e** hairdresser; (*Herren-*) barber. **F∼seursalon** *m* hairdressing salon. **F∼seuse** /-'zø:zə/ *f* **-,-n** hairdresser

frisier|en *vt* **jdn/sich f∼en** do s.o.'s/one's hair; **die Bilanz/einen Motor f∼en** (*fam*) fiddle the accounts/soup up an engine. **F∼kommode** *f* dressing-table. **F∼salon** *m* = **Friseursalon. F∼tisch** *m* dressing-table

Frisör *m* **-s,-e** = **Friseur**

Frist *f* **-,-en** period; (*Termin*) deadline; (*Aufschub*) time; **drei Tage F∼** three days' grace. **f∼en** *vt* **sein Leben f∼en** eke out an existence. **f∼los** *a* instant, *adv* -ly

Frisur *f* **-,-en** hairstyle

fritieren *vt* deep-fry

frivol /fri'vo:l/ *a* frivolous, *adv* -ly; (*schlüpfrig*) smutty

froh *a* happy; (*freudig*) joyful; (*erleichtert*) glad; **f∼e Ostern!** happy Easter!

fröhlich *a* cheerful, *adv* -ly; (*vergnügt*) merry, *adv* -ily; **f∼e Weihnachten!** merry Christmas! **F∼keit** *f* - cheerfulness; merriment

frohlocken *vi* (*haben*) rejoice; (*schadenfroh*) gloat

Frohsinn *m* - cheerfulness

fromm *a* (**frömmer, frömmst**) devout, *adv* -ly; (*gutartig*) docile, *adv* -ly; **f∼er Wunsch** idle wish

Frömm|igkeit *f* - devoutness, piety. **f∼lerisch** *a* sanctimonious, *adv* -ly

frönen *vi* (*haben*) indulge (*dat* in)

Fronleichnam *m* Corpus Christi

Front *f* **-,-en** front. **f∼al** *a* frontal; ⟨*Zusammenstoß*⟩ head-on ● *adv* from the front; ⟨*zusammenstoßen*⟩ head-on. **F∼alzusammenstoß** *m* head-on collision

Frosch *m* **-[e]s,⸚e** frog. **F∼laich** *m* frog-spawn. **F∼mann** *m* (*pl* **-männer**) frogman

Frost *m* **-[e]s,⸚e** frost. **F∼beule** *f* chilblain

frösteln *vi* (*haben*) shiver; **mich fröstelte [es]** I shivered/(*fror*) felt chilly

frost|ig *a* frosty, *adv* -ily. **F∼schutzmittel** *nt* antifreeze

Frottee *nt* & *m* **-s** towelling

frottier|en *vt* rub down. **F∼[hand]tuch** *nt* terry towel

frotzeln *vt/i* (*haben*) **[über] jdn f∼** make fun of s.o.

Frucht *f* **-,⸚e** fruit; **F∼ tragen** bear fruit. **f∼bar** *a* fertile; (*fig*) fruitful. **F∼barkeit** *f* - fertility. **f∼en** *vi* (*haben*) **wenig/nichts f∼en** have little/no effect. **f∼ig** *a* fruity. **f∼los** *a* fruitless, *adv* -ly. **F∼saft** *m* fruit juice

frugal *a* frugal, *adv* -ly

früh *a* early ● *adv* early; (*morgens*) in the morning; **heute/gestern/morgen f∼** this/yesterday/tomorrow morning; **von f∼ an** from an early age. **f∼auf** *adv* **von f∼auf** from an early age. **F∼aufsteher** *m* **-s,-** early riser. **F∼e** *f* - **in aller F∼e** bright and early; **in der F∼e** (*SGer*) in the morning. **f∼er** *adv* earlier; (*eher*) sooner; (*ehemals*) formerly; (*vor langer Zeit*) in the old days; **f∼er oder später** sooner or later; **ich wohnte f∼er in X** I used to live in X. **f∼ere(r,s)** *a* earlier; (*ehemalig*) former; (*vorige*) previous; **in f∼eren Zeiten** in former times. **f∼estens** *adv* at the earliest. **F∼geburt** *f* premature birth/(*Kind*) baby. **F∼jahr** *nt* spring. **F∼jahrsputz** *m* spring-cleaning. **F∼kartoffeln** *fpl* new potatoes. **F∼ling** *m* **-s,-e** spring. **f∼morgens** *adv* early in the morning. **f∼reif** *a* precocious

Frühstück *nt* breakfast. **f∼en** *vi* (*haben*) have breakfast

frühzeitig *a* & *adv* early; (*vorzeitig*) premature, *adv* -ly

Frustr|ation /-'tsi̯o:n/ *f* **-,-en** frustration. **f∼ieren** *vt* frustrate; **f∼ierend** frustrating

Fuchs *m* **-es,⸚e** fox; (*Pferd*) chestnut. **f∼en** *vt* (*fam*) annoy

Füchsin *f* **-,-nen** vixen

fuchteln *vi* (*haben*) **mit etw f∼** (*fam*) wave sth about

Fuder *nt* **-s,-** cart-load

Fuge[1] *f* **-,-n** joint; **aus den F∼n gehen** fall apart

Fuge[2] *f* **-,-n** (*Mus*) fugue

füg|en *vt* fit (**in** + *acc* into); (*an-*) join (**an** + *acc* on to); (*dazu-*) add (**zu** to); (*fig: bewirken*) ordain; **sich f∼en** fit (**in** + *acc* into); adjoin/(*folgen*) follow (**an etw** *acc* sth); (*fig: gehorchen*) submit (*dat* to); **sich in sein Schicksal f∼en** resign oneself to one's fate; **es f∼te sich** it so happened (**daß** that).

f~sam *a* obedient, *adv* -ly. **F~ung** *f* **-,-en eine F~ung des Schicksals** a stroke of fate

fühl|bar *a* noticeable. **f~en** *vt/i* (*haben*) feel; **sich f~en** feel (**krank/einsam** ill/lonely); (*fam: stolz sein*) fancy oneself; **sich [nicht] wohl f~en** [not] feel well. **F~er** *m* **-s,-** feeler. **F~ung** *f* **-** contact; **F~ung aufnehmen** get in touch

Fuhre *f* **-,-n** load

führ|en *vt* lead; guide ⟨*Tourist*⟩; (*geleiten*) take; (*leiten*) run; (*befehligen*) command; (*verkaufen*) stock; bear ⟨*Namen, Titel*⟩; keep ⟨*Liste, Bücher, Tagebuch*⟩; **bei** *od* **mit sich f~en** carry; **sich gut/schlecht f~en** conduct oneself well/badly ● *vi* (*haben*) lead; (*verlaufen*) go, run; **zu etw f~en** lead to sth. **f~end** *a* leading. **F~er** *m* **-s,-** leader; (*Fremden-*) guide; (*Buch*) guide[book]. **F~erhaus** *nt* driver's cab. **F~erschein** *m* driving licence; **den F~erschein machen** take one's driving test. **F~erscheinentzug** *m* disqualification from driving. **F~ung** *f* **-,-en** leadership; (*Leitung*) management; (*Mil*) command; (*Betragen*) conduct; (*Besichtigung*) guided tour; (*Vorsprung*) lead; **in F~ung gehen** go into the lead

Fuhr|unternehmer *m* haulage contractor. **F~werk** *nt* cart

Fülle *f* **-,-n** abundance, wealth (**an** + *dat* of); (*Körper-*) plumpness. **f~n** *vt* fill; (*Culin*) stuff; **sich f~n** fill [up]

Füllen *nt* **-s,-** foal

Füll|er *m* **-s,-** (*fam*), **F~federhalter** *m* fountain pen. **f~ig** *a* plump; ⟨*Busen*⟩ ample. **F~ung** *f* **-,-en** filling; (*Kissen-, Braten-*) stuffing; (*Pralinen-*) centre

fummeln *vi* (*haben*) fumble (**an** + *dat* with)

Fund *m* **-[e]s,-e** find

Fundament *nt* **-[e]s,-e** foundations *pl*. **f~al** *a* fundamental

Fund|büro *nt* lost-property office. **F~grube** *f* (*fig*) treasure trove. **F~sachen** *fpl* lost property *sg*

fünf *inv a*, **F~** *f* **-,-en** five; (*Sch*) ≈ fail mark. **F~linge** *mpl* quintuplets. **f~te(r,s)** *a* fifth. **f~zehn** *inv a* fifteen. **f~zehnte(r,s)** *a* fifteenth. **f~zig** *inv a* fifty. **F~ziger** *m* **-s,-** man in his fifties; (*Münze*) 50-pfennig piece. **f~zigste(r,s)** *a* fiftieth

fungieren *vi* (*haben*) act (**als** as)

Funk *m* **-s** radio; **über F~** over the radio. **F~e** *m* **-n,-n** spark. **f~eln** *vi* (*haben*) sparkle; ⟨*Stern:*⟩ twinkle. **f~elnagelneu** *a* (*fam*) brand-new. **F~en** *m* **-s,-** spark. **f~en** *vt* radio. **F~er** *m* **-s,-** radio operator. **F~sprechgerät** *nt* walkie-talkie. **F~spruch** *m* radio message. **F~streife** *f* [police] radio patrol

Funktion /-'tsi̯o:n/ *f* **-,-en** function; (*Stellung*) position; (*Funktionieren*) working; **außer F~** out of action. **F~är** *m* **-s,-e** official. **f~ieren** *vi* (*haben*) work

für *prep* (+*acc*) for; **Schritt für Schritt** step by step; **was für [ein]** what [a]! (*fragend*) what sort of [a]? **für sich** by oneself/⟨*Ding:*⟩ itself. **Für** *nt* **das Für und Wider** the pros and cons *pl*. **F~bitte** *f* intercession

Furche *f* **-,-n** furrow

Furcht *f* **-** fear (**vor** + *dat* of). **f~bar** *a* terrible, *adv* -bly

fürcht|en *vt/i* (*haben*) fear; **sich f~en** be afraid (**vor** + *dat* of); **ich f~e, das geht nicht** I'm afraid that's impossible. **f~erlich** *a* dreadful, *adv* -ly

furcht|erregend *a* terrifying. **f~los** *a* fearless, *adv* -ly. **f~sam** *a* timid, *adv* -ly

füreinander *adv* for each other

Furnier *nt* **-s,-e** veneer. **f~t** *a* veneered

fürs *prep* = **für das**

Fürsorg|e *f* care; (*Admin*) welfare; (*fam: Geld*) ≈ social security. **F~er(in)** *m* **-s,-** (*f* **-,-nen**) social worker. **f~lich** *a* solicitous

Fürsprache *f* intercession; **F~ einlegen** intercede

Fürsprecher *m* (*fig*) advocate

Fürst *m* **-en,-en** prince. **F~entum** *nt* **-s,¨er** principality. **F~in** *f* **-,-nen** princess. **f~lich** *a* princely; (*üppig*) lavish, *adv* -ly

Furt *f* **-,-en** ford

Furunkel *m* **-s,-** (*Med*) boil

Fürwort *nt* (*pl* **-wörter**) pronoun

Furz *m* **-es,-e** (*vulg*) fart. **f~en** *vi* (*haben*) (*vulg*) fart

Fusion *f* **-,-en** fusion; (*Comm*) merger. **f~ieren** *vi* (*haben*) (*Comm*) merge

Fuß *m* **-es,¨e** foot; (*Aust: Bein*) leg; (*Lampen-*) base; (*von Weinglas*) stem; **zu Fuß** on foot; **zu Fuß gehen** walk; **auf freiem Fuß** free; **auf freundschaftlichem/großem Fuß** on friendly terms/in grand style.

F~abdruck *m* footprint. **F~abtreter** *m* **-s,-** doormat. **F~bad** *nt* footbath. **F~ball** *m* football. **F~ballspieler** *m* footballer. **F~balltoto** *nt* football pools *pl.* **F~bank** *f* footstool. **F~boden** *m* floor. **F~bremse** *f* footbrake

Fussel *f* **-,-n** & *m* **-s,-[n]** piece of fluff; **F~n** fluff *sg.* **f~n** *vi* (*haben*) shed fluff

fuß|en *vi* (*haben*) be based (**auf** + *dat* on). **F~ende** *nt* foot

Fußgänger|(in) *m* **-s,-** (*f* **-,-nen**) pedestrian. **F~brücke** *f* footbridge. **F~überweg** *m* pedestrian crossing. **F~zone** *f* pedestrian precinct

Fuß|geher *m* **-s,-** (*Aust*) = **F~gänger.** **F~gelenk** *nt* ankle. **F~hebel** *m* pedal. **F~nagel** *m* toenail. **F~note** *f* footnote. **F~pflege** *f* chiropody. **F~pfleger(in)** *m(f)* chiropodist. **F~rücken** *m* instep. **F~sohle** *f* sole of the foot. **F~stapfen** *pl* **in jds F~stapfen treten** (*fig*) follow in s.o.'s footsteps. **F~tritt** *m* kick. **F~weg** *m* footpath; **eine Stunde F~weg** an hour's walk

futsch *pred a* (*fam*) gone

Futter[1] *nt* **-s** feed; (*Trocken-*) fodder

Futter[2] *nt* **-s,-** (*Kleider-*) lining

Futteral *nt* **-s,-e** case

füttern[1] *vt* feed

füttern[2] *vt* line

Futur *nt* **-s** (*Gram*) future; **zweites F~** future perfect. **f~istisch** *a* futuristic

G

Gabe *f* **-,-n** gift; (*Dosis*) dose

Gabel *f* **-,-n** fork. **g~n (sich)** *vr* fork. **G~stapler** *m* **-s,-** fork-lift truck. **G~ung** *f* **-,-en** fork (*in road*)

gackern *vi* (*haben*) cackle

gaffen *vi* (*haben*) gape, stare

Gag /gɛk/ *m* **-s,-s** (*Theat*) gag

Gage /ˈgaːʒə/ *f* **-,-n** (*Theat*) fee

gähnen *vi* (*haben*) yawn. **G~** *nt* **-s** yawn; (*wiederholt*) yawning

Gala *f* **-** ceremonial dress

galant *a* gallant, *adv* -ly

Galavorstellung *f* gala performance

Galerie *f* **-,-n** gallery

Galgen *m* **-s,-** gallows *sg.* **G~frist** *f* (*fam*) reprieve

Galionsfigur *f* figurehead

Galle *f* **-** bile; (*G~nblase*) gall-bladder. **G~nblase** *f* gall-bladder. **G~nstein** *m* gallstone

Gallert *nt* **-[e]s,-e**, **Gallerte** *f* **-,-n** [meat] jelly

Galopp *m* **-s** gallop; **im G~** at a gallop. **g~ieren** *vi* (*sein*) gallop

galvanisieren *vt* galvanize

gamm|eln *vi* (*haben*) (*fam*) loaf around. **G~ler(in)** *m* **-s,-** (*f* **-,-nen**) drop-out

Gams *f* **-,-en** (*Aust*) chamois

gang *pred a* **g~ und gäbe** quite usual

Gang *m* **-[e]s,¨e** walk; (*G~art*) gait; (*Boten-*) errand; (*Funktionieren*) running; (*Verlauf, Culin*) course; (*Durch-*) passage; (*Korridor*) corridor; (*zwischen Sitzreihen*) aisle, gangway; (*Anat*) duct; (*Auto*) gear; **in G~ bringen/halten** get/keep going; **in G~ kommen** get going/(*fig*) under way; **im G~e/in vollem G~e sein** be in progress/in full swing; **Essen mit vier G¨en** four-course meal. **G~art** *f* gait

gängig *a* common; (*Comm*) popular

Gangschaltung *f* gear change

Gangster /ˈgɛŋstɐ/ *m* **-s,-** gangster

Gangway /ˈgɛŋweː/ *f* **-,-s** gangway

Ganove *m* **-n,-n** (*fam*) crook

Gans *f* **-,¨e** goose

Gänse|blümchen *nt* **-s,-** daisy. **G~füßchen** *ntpl* inverted commas. **G~haut** *f* goose-pimples *pl.* **G~marsch** *m* **im G~marsch** in single file. **G~rich** *m* **-s,-e** gander

ganz *a* whole, entire; (*vollständig*) complete; (*fam: heil*) undamaged, intact; **die g~e Zeit** all the time, the whole time; **eine g~e Weile/Menge** quite a while/lot; **g~e zehn Mark** all of ten marks; **meine g~en Bücher** all my books; *inv* **g~ Deutschland** the whole of Germany; **g~ bleiben** (*fam*) remain intact; **wieder g~ machen** (*fam*) mend; **im g~en** in all, altogether; **im großen und g~en** on the whole • *adv* quite; (*völlig*) completely, entirely; (*sehr*) very; **nicht g~** not quite; **g~ allein** all on one's own; **ein g~ alter Mann** a very old man; **g~ wie du willst** just as you like; **es war g~ nett** it was quite nice; **g~ und gar** completely, totally; **g~ und gar nicht** not at all. **G~e(s)** *nt* whole; **es geht ums G~e** it's all or nothing. **g~jährig** *adv* all the year round

gänzlich *adv* completely, entirely

ganz|tägig *a & adv* full-time; ⟨*geöffnet*⟩ all day. **g~tags** *adv* all day; ⟨*arbeiten*⟩ full-time

gar[1] *a* done, cooked

gar[2] *adv* **gar nicht/nichts/niemand** not/nothing/no one at all; **oder gar** or even

Garage /ga'ra:ʒə/ *f* **-,-n** garage

Garantie *f* **-,-n** guarantee. **g~ren** *vt/i* (*haben*) **[für] etw g~ren** guarantee sth; **er kommt g~rt zu spät** (*fam*) he's sure to be late. **G~schein** *m* guarantee

Garbe *f* **-,-n** sheaf

Garderobe *f* **-,-n** (*Kleider*) wardrobe; (*Ablage*) cloakroom, (*Amer*) checkroom; (*Flur-*) coat-rack; (*Künstler-*) dressing-room. **G~nfrau** *f* cloakroom attendant

Gardine *f* **-,-n** curtain. **G~nstange** *f* curtain rail

garen *vt/i* (*haben*) cook

gären† *vi* (*haben*) ferment; (*fig*) seethe

Garn *nt* **-[e]s,-e** yarn; (*Näh-*) cotton

Garnele *f* **-,-n** shrimp; (*rote*) prawn

garnieren *vt* decorate; (*Culin*) garnish

Garnison *f* **-,-en** garrison

Garnitur *f* **-,-en** set; (*Wäsche*) set of matching underwear; (*Möbel-*) suite; **erste/zweite G~ sein** (*fam*) be first-rate/second best

garstig *a* nasty

Garten *m* **-s,⸚** garden; **botanischer G~** botanical gardens *pl*. **G~arbeit** *f* gardening. **G~bau** *m* horticulture. **G~haus** *nt*, **G~laube** *f* summerhouse. **G~lokal** *nt* open-air café. **G~schere** *f* secateurs *pl*

Gärtner|(in) *m* **-s,-** (*f* **-,-nen**) gardener. **G~ei** *f* **-,-en** nursery; (*fam: Gartenarbeit*) gardening

Gärung *f* **-** fermentation

Gas *nt* **-es,-e** gas; **Gas geben** (*fam*) accelerate. **G~herd** *m* gas cooker. **G~maske** *f* gas mask. **G~pedal** *nt* (*Auto*) accelerator

Gasse *f* **-,-n** alley; (*Aust*) street

Gast *m* **-[e]s,⸚e** guest; (*Hotel-, Urlaubs-*) visitor; (*im Lokal*) patron; **zum Mittag G~e haben** have people to lunch; **bei jdm zu G~ sein** be staying with s.o. **G~arbeiter** *m* foreign worker. **G~bett** *nt* spare bed

Gäste|bett *nt* spare bed. **G~buch** *nt* visitors' book. **G~zimmer** *nt* [hotel] room; (*privat*) spare room; (*Aufenthaltsraum*) residents' lounge

gast|frei, g~freundlich *a* hospitable, *adv* -bly. **G~freundschaft** *f* hospitality. **G~geber** *m* **-s,-** host. **G~geberin** *f* **-,-nen** hostess. **G~haus** *nt*, **G~hof** *m* inn, hotel

gastieren *vi* (*haben*) make a guest appearance; ⟨*Truppe, Zirkus:*⟩ perform (**in** + *dat* in)

gastlich *a* hospitable, *adv* -bly. **G~keit** *f* - hospitality

Gastro|nomie *f* - gastronomy. **g~nomisch** *a* gastronomic

Gast|spiel *nt* guest performance. **G~spielreise** *f* (*Theat*) tour. **G~stätte** *f* restaurant. **G~stube** *f* bar; (*Restaurant*) restaurant. **G~wirt** *m* landlord. **G~wirtin** *f* landlady. **G~wirtschaft** *f* restaurant

Gas|werk *nt* gasworks *sg*. **G~zähler** *m* gas-meter

Gatte *m* **-n,-n** husband

Gatter *nt* **-s,-** gate; (*Gehege*) pen

Gattin *f* **-,-nen** wife

Gattung *f* **-,-en** kind; (*Biol*) genus; (*Kunst*) genre. **G~sbegriff** *m* generic term

Gaudi *f* - (*Aust, fam*) fun

Gaul *m* **-[e]s, Gäule** [old] nag

Gaumen *m* **-s,-** palate

Gauner *m* **-s,-** crook, swindler. **G~ei** *f* **-,-en** swindle

Gaze /'ga:zə/ *f* - gauze

Gazelle *f* **-,-n** gazelle

geachtet *a* respected

geädert *a* veined

geartet *a* **gut g~** good-natured; **anders g~** different

Gebäck *nt* **-s** [cakes and] pastries *pl*; (*Kekse*) biscuits *pl*

Gebälk *nt* **-s** timbers *pl*

geballt *a* ⟨*Faust*⟩ clenched

Gebärde *f* **-,-n** gesture. **g~n (sich)** *vr* behave (**wie** like)

Gebaren *nt* **-s** behaviour

gebär|en† *vt* give birth to, bear; **geboren werden** be born. **G~mutter** *f* womb, uterus

Gebäude *nt* **-s,-** building

Gebeine *ntpl* [mortal] remains

Gebell *nt* **-s** barking

geben† *vt* give; (*tun, bringen*) put; (*Karten*) deal; (*aufführen*) perform; (*unterrichten*) teach; **etw verloren g~** give sth up as lost; **von sich g~** utter; (*fam: erbrechen*) bring up; **viel/wenig g~ auf** (+*acc*) set great/little store by; **sich g~** (*nachlassen*) wear off; (*besser werden*) get better; (*sich verhalten*) behave; **sich geschlagen g~** admit defeat • *impers* **es gibt** there is/are; **was gibt es Neues/zum Mittag/im Kino?** what's the news/for lunch/on at the cinema? **es wird Regen g~** it's going to rain; **das gibt es nicht** there's no such thing • *vi* (*haben*) (*Karten*) deal

Gebet *nt* **-[e]s,-e** prayer

Gebiet *nt* **-[e]s,-e** area; (*Hoheits-*) territory; (*Sach-*) field

gebiet|en† *vt* command; (*erfordern*) demand • *vi* (*haben*) rule. **G~er** *m* **-s,-** master; (*Herrscher*) ruler. **g~erisch** *a* imperious, *adv* -ly; ⟨*Ton*⟩ peremptory

Gebilde *nt* **-s,-** structure

gebildet *a* educated; (*kultiviert*) cultured

Gebirg|e *nt* **-s,-** mountains *pl*. **g~ig** *a* mountainous

Gebiß *nt* **-sses,-sse** teeth *pl*; (*künstliches*) false teeth *pl*, dentures *pl*; (*des Zaumes*) bit

geblümt *a* floral, flowered

gebogen *a* curved

geboren *a* born; **g~er Deutscher** German by birth; **Frau X, g~e Y** Mrs X, née Y

geborgen *a* safe, secure. **G~heit** *f* - security

Gebot *nt* **-[e]s,-e** rule; (*Relig*) commandment; (*bei Auktion*) bid

gebraten *a* fried

Gebrauch *m* use; (*Sprach-*) usage; **Gebräuche** customs; **in G~** in use; **G~ machen von** make use of. **g~en** *vt* use; **ich kann es nicht/gut g~en** I have no use for/can make good use of it; **zu nichts zu g~en** useless

gebräuchlich *a* common; ⟨*Wort*⟩ in common use

Gebrauch|sanleitung, G~sanweisung *f* directions *pl* for use. **g~t** *a* used; (*Comm*) second-hand. **G~twagen** *m* used car

gebrechlich *a* frail, infirm

gebrochen *a* broken • *adv* **g~ Englisch sprechen** speak broken English

Gebrüll *nt* **-s** roaring; (*fam: Schreien*) bawling

Gebrumm *nt* **-s** buzzing; (*Motoren-*) humming

Gebühr *f* **-,-en** charge, fee; **über G~** excessively. **g~en** *vi* (*haben*) **ihm g~t Respekt** he deserves respect; **wie es sich g~t** as is right and proper. **g~end** *a* due, *adv* duly; (*geziemend*) proper, *adv* -ly. **g~enfrei** *a* free • *adv* free of charge. **g~enpflichtig** *a & adv* subject to a charge; **g~enpflichtige Straße** toll road

gebunden *a* bound; ⟨*Suppe*⟩ thickened

Geburt *f* **-,-en** birth; **von G~** by birth. **G~enkontrolle, G~enregelung** *f* birth-control. **G~enziffer** *f* birth-rate

gebürtig *a* native (**aus** of); **g~er Deutscher** German by birth

Geburts|datum *nt* date of birth. **G~helfer** *m* obstetrician. **G~hilfe** *f* obstetrics *sg*. **G~ort** *m* place of birth. **G~tag** *m* birthday. **G~urkunde** *f* birth certificate

Gebüsch *nt* **-[e]s,-e** bushes *pl*

Gedächtnis *nt* **-ses** memory; **aus dem G~** from memory

gedämpft *a* ⟨*Ton*⟩ muffled; ⟨*Stimme*⟩ hushed; ⟨*Musik*⟩ soft; ⟨*Licht, Stimmung*⟩ subdued

Gedanke *m* **-ns,-n** thought (**an** + *acc* of); (*Idee*) idea; **sich** (*dat*) **G~n machen** worry (**über** + *acc* about). **G~nblitz** *m* brainwave. **g~nlos** *a* thoughtless, *adv* -ly; (*zerstreut*) absent-minded, *adv* -ly. **G~nstrich** *m* dash. **G~nübertragung** *f* telepathy. **g~nvoll** *a* pensive, *adv* -ly

Gedärme *ntpl* intestines; (*Tier-*) entrails

Gedeck *nt* **-[e]s,-e** place setting; (*auf Speisekarte*) set meal; **ein G~ auflegen** set a place. **g~t** *a* covered; ⟨*Farbe*⟩ muted

gedeihen† *vi* (*sein*) thrive, flourish

gedenken† *vi* (*haben*) propose (**etw zu tun** to do sth); **jds/etw g~** remember s.o./sth. **G~** *nt* **-s** memory; **zum G~ an** (+ *acc*) in memory of

Gedenk|feier *f* commemoration. **G~gottesdienst** *m* memorial service. **G~stätte** *f* memorial. **G~tafel** *f* commemorative plaque. **G~tag** *m* day of remembrance; (*Jahrestag*) anniversary

Gedicht *nt* **-[e]s,-e** poem

gediegen *a* quality . . .; (*solide*) well-made; ⟨*Charakter*⟩ upright; ⟨*Gold*⟩ pure • *adv* **g~ gebaut** well built

Gedräng|e *nt* **-s** crush, crowd. **g~t** *a* (*knapp*) concise • *adv* **g~t voll** packed

gedrückt *a* depressed

gedrungen *a* stocky

Geduld *f* - patience; **G~ haben** be patient. **g~en (sich)** *vr* be patient. **g~ig** *a* patient, *adv* -ly. **G~[s]spiel** *nt* puzzle

gedunsen *a* bloated

geehrt *a* honoured; **Sehr g~er Herr X** Dear Mr X

geeignet *a* suitable; **im g~en Moment** at the right moment

Gefahr *f* **-,-en** danger; **in/außer G~** in/out of danger; **auf eigene G~** at one's own risk; **G~ laufen** run the risk (**etw zu tun** of doing sth)

gefähr|den *vt* endanger; (*fig*) jeopardize. **g~lich** *a* dangerous, *adv* -ly; (*riskant*) risky

gefahrlos *a* safe

Gefährt *nt* **-[e]s,-e** vehicle

Gefährte *m* **-n,-n**, **Gefährtin** *f* **-,-nen** companion

gefahrvoll *a* dangerous, perilous

Gefälle *nt* **-s,-** slope; (*Straßen-*) gradient

gefallen† *vi* (*haben*) **jdm g~** please s.o.; **er/es gefällt mir** I like him/it; **sich** (*dat*) **etw g~ lassen** put up with sth

Gefallen[1] *m* **-s,-** favour

Gefallen[2] *nt* **-s** pleasure (**an** + *dat* in); **G~ finden an** (+ *dat*) like; **dir zu G~** to please you

Gefallene(r) *m* soldier killed in the war

gefällig *a* pleasing; (*hübsch*) attractive, *adv* -ly; (*hilfsbereit*) obliging; **jdm g~ sein** do s.o. a good turn; **[sonst] noch etwas g~?** will there be anything else? **G~keit** *f* **-,-en** favour; (*Freundlichkeit*) kindness. **g~st** *adv* (*fam*) kindly

Gefangen|e(r) *m/f* prisoner. **g~halten**† *vt sep* hold prisoner; keep in captivity ⟨*Tier*⟩. **G~nahme** *f* - capture. **g~nehmen**† *vt sep* take prisoner. **G~schaft** *f* - captivity; **in G~schaft geraten** be taken prisoner

Gefängnis *nt* **-ses,-se** prison; (*Strafe*) imprisonment. **G~strafe** *f* imprisonment; (*Urteil*) prison sentence. **G~wärter** *m* [prison] warder, (*Amer*) guard

Gefäß *nt* **-es,-e** container, receptacle; (*Blut-*) vessel

gefaßt *a* composed; (*ruhig*) calm, *adv* -ly; **g~ sein auf** (+ *acc*) be prepared for

Gefecht *nt* **-[e]s,-e** fight; (*Mil*) engagement; **außer G~ setzen** put out of action

gefedert *a* sprung

gefeiert *a* celebrated

Gefieder *nt* **-s** plumage. **g~t** *a* feathered

Geflecht *nt* **-[e]s,-e** network; (*Gewirr*) tangle; (*Korb-*) wickerwork

gefleckt *a* spotted

geflissentlich *adv* studiously

Geflügel *nt* **-s** poultry. **G~klein** *nt* **-s** giblets *pl*. **g~t** *a* winged; **g~tes Wort** familiar quotation

Geflüster *nt* **-s** whispering

Gefolg|e *nt* **-s** retinue, entourage. **G~schaft** *f* - followers *pl*, following; (*Treue*) allegiance

gefragt *a* popular; **g~ sein** be in demand

gefräßig *a* voracious; ⟨*Mensch*⟩ greedy

Gefreite(r) *m* lance-corporal

gefrier|en† *vi* (*sein*) freeze. **G~fach** *nt* freezer compartment. **G~punkt** *m* freezing-point. **G~schrank** *m* upright freezer. **G~truhe** *f* chest freezer

gefroren *a* frozen. **G~e(s)** *nt* (*Aust*) ice-cream

Gefüge *nt* **-s,-** structure; (*fig*) fabric

gefügig *a* compliant; (*gehorsam*) obedient

Gefühl *nt* **-[e]s,-e** feeling; (*Empfindung*) sensation; (*G~sregung*) emotion; **im G~ haben** know instinctively. **g~los** *a* insensitive; (*herzlos*) unfeeling; (*taub*) numb. **g~sbetont** *a* emotional. **g~skalt** *a* (*fig*) cold. **g~smäßig** *a* emotional, *adv* -ly; (*instinktiv*) instinctive, *adv* -ly. **G~sregung** *f* emotion. **g~voll** *a* sensitive, *adv* -ly; (*sentimental*) sentimental, *adv* -ly

gefüllt *a* filled; (*voll*) full; (*Bot*) double; (*Culin*) stuffed; ⟨*Schokolade*⟩ with a filling

gefürchtet *a* feared, dreaded

gefüttert *a* lined

gegeben *a* given; (*bestehend*) present; (*passend*) appropriate; **zu g~er Zeit** at the proper time. **g~enfalls** *adv* if need be. **G~heiten** *fpl* realities, facts

gegen *prep* (+ *acc*) against; (*Sport*) versus; (*g~über*) to[wards]; (*Vergleich*) compared with; (*Richtung, Zeit*) towards; (*ungefähr*) around; **ein Mittel g~** a remedy for ● *adv* **g~ 100 Leute** about 100 people. **G~angriff** *m* counter-attack

Gegend *f* **-,-en** area, region; (*Umgebung*) neighbourhood

gegeneinander *adv* against/ (*gegenüber*) towards one another

Gegen|fahrbahn *f* opposite carriageway. **G~gift** *nt* antidote. **G~leistung** *f* **als G~leistung** in return. **G~maßnahme** *f* countermeasure. **G~satz** *m* contrast; (*Widerspruch*) contradiction; (*G~teil*) opposite; **im G~satz zu** unlike. **g~sätzlich** *a* contrasting; (*widersprüchlich*) opposing. **g~seitig** *a* mutual, *adv* -ly; **sich g~seitig hassen** hate one another. **G~spieler** *m* opponent. **G~sprechanlage** *f* intercom. **G~stand** *m* object; (*Gram, Gesprächs-*) subject. **g~standslos** *a* unfounded; (*überflüssig*) irrelevant; (*abstrakt*) abstract. **G~stück** *nt* counterpart; (*G~teil*) opposite. **G~teil** *nt* opposite, contrary; **im G~teil** on the contrary. **g~teilig** *a* opposite

gegenüber *prep* (+*dat*) opposite; (*Vergleich*) compared with; **jdm g~ höflich sein** be polite to s.o. • *adv* opposite. **G~** *nt* **-s** person opposite. **g~liegen**† *vi sep* (*haben*) be opposite (**etw** *dat* sth). **g~liegend** *a* opposite. **g~stehen**† *vi sep* (*haben*) (+*dat*) face; **feindlich g~stehen** (+*dat*) be hostile to. **g~stellen** *vt sep* confront; (*vergleichen*) compare. **g~treten**† *vi sep* (*sein*) (+*dat*) face

Gegen|verkehr *m* oncoming traffic. **G~vorschlag** *m* counter-proposal. **G~wart** *f* - present; (*Anwesenheit*) presence. **g~wärtig** *a* present • *adv* at present. **G~wehr** *f* - resistance. **G~wert** *m* equivalent. **G~wind** *m* head wind. **g~zeichnen** *vt sep* countersign

geglückt *a* successful

Gegner|(in) *m* **-s,-** (*f* **-,-nen**) opponent. **g~isch** *a* opposing

Gehabe *nt* **-s** affected behaviour

Gehackte(s) *nt* mince, (*Amer*) ground meat

Gehalt[1] *m* **-[e]s** content

Gehalt[2] *nt* **-[e]s,¨er** salary. **G~serhöhung** *f* rise, (*Amer*) raise

gehaltvoll *a* nourishing

gehässig *a* spiteful, *adv* -ly

gehäuft *a* heaped

Gehäuse *nt* **-s,-** case; (*TV, Radio*) cabinet; (*Schnecken-*) shell; (*Kern-*) core

Gehege *nt* **-s,-** enclosure

geheim *a* secret; **im g~en** secretly. **G~dienst** *m* Secret Service. **g~halten**† *vt sep* keep secret. **G~nis** *nt* **-ses,-se** secret. **g~nisvoll** *a* mysterious, *adv* -ly. **G~polizei** *f* secret police

gehemmt *a* (*fig*) inhibited

gehen† *vi* (*sein*) go; (*zu Fuß*) walk; (*fort-*) leave; (*funktionieren*) work; ⟨*Teig:*⟩ rise; **tanzen/einkaufen g~** go dancing/shopping; **an die Arbeit g~** set to work; **in Schwarz [gekleidet] g~** dress in black; **nach Norden g~** ⟨*Fenster:*⟩ face north; **wenn es nach mir ginge** if I had my way; **über die Straße g~** cross the road; **was geht hier vor sich?** what is going on here? **das geht zu weit** (*fam*) that's going too far; *impers* **wie geht es [Ihnen]?** how are you? **es geht mir gut/besser** I am well/better; **es geht nicht/nicht anders** it's impossible/there is no other way; **es ging ganz schnell** it was very quick; **es geht um** it concerns; **es geht ihr nur ums Geld** she is only interested in the money; **es geht [so]** (*fam*) not too bad • *vt* walk. **g~lassen**† **(sich)** *vr sep* lose one's self-control; (*sich vernachlässigen*) let oneself go

geheuer *a* **nicht g~** eerie; (*verdächtig*) suspicious; **mir ist nicht g~** I feel uneasy

Geheul *nt* **-s** howling

Gehilfe *m* **-n,-n, Gehilfin** *f* **-,-nen** trainee; (*Helfer*) assistant

Gehirn *nt* **-s** brain; (*Verstand*) brains *pl*. **G~erschütterung** *f* concussion. **G~hautentzündung** *f* meningitis. **G~wäsche** *f* brainwashing

gehoben *a* (*fig*) superior; ⟨*Sprache*⟩ elevated

Gehöft *nt* **-[e]s,-e** farm

Gehölz *nt* **-es,-e** coppice, copse

Gehör *nt* **-s** hearing; **G~ schenken** (+*dat*) listen to

gehorchen *vi* (*haben*) (+*dat*) obey

gehören *vi* (*haben*) belong (*dat* to); **zu den Besten g~** be one of the best; **dazu gehört Mut** that takes courage; **sich g~** be [right and] proper; **es gehört sich nicht** it isn't done

gehörig *a* proper, *adv* -ly; **jdn g~ verprügeln** give s.o. a good hiding

gehörlos *a* deaf

Gehörn *nt* **-s,-e** horns *pl*; (*Geweih*) antlers *pl*

gehorsam *a* obedient, *adv* -ly. **G~** *m* **-s** obedience

Geh|steig *m* **-[e]s,-e** pavement, (*Amer*) sidewalk. **G~weg** *m* = **Gehsteig;** (*Fußweg*) footpath

Geier *m* **-s,-** vulture

Geig|e *f* **-,-n** violin. **g~en** *vi* (*haben*) play the violin ● *vt* play on the violin. **G~er(in)** *m* **-s,-** (*f* **-,-nen**) violinist

geil *a* lecherous; (*fam*) randy; (*fam: toll*) great

Geisel *f* **-,-n** hostage

Geiß *f* **-,-en** (*SGer*) [nanny-]goat. **G~blatt** *nt* honeysuckle

Geißel *f* **-,-n** scourge

Geist *m* **-[e]s,-er** mind; (*Witz*) wit; (*Gesinnung*) spirit; (*Gespenst*) ghost; **der Heilige G~** the Holy Ghost *or* Spirit; **im G~** in one's mind. **g~erhaft** *a* ghostly

geistes|abwesend *a* absent-minded, *adv* -ly. **G~blitz** *m* brainwave. **G~gegenwart** *f* presence of mind. **g~gegenwärtig** *adv* with great presence of mind. **g~gestört** *a* [mentally] deranged. **g~krank** *a* mentally ill. **G~krankheit** *f* mental illness. **G~wissenschaften** *fpl* arts. **G~zustand** *m* mental state

geist|ig *a* mental, *adv* -ly; (*intellektuell*) intellectual, *adv* -ly; **g~ige Getränke** spirits. **g~lich** *a* spiritual, *adv* -ly; (*religiös*) religious; ⟨*Musik*⟩ sacred; ⟨*Tracht*⟩ clerical. **G~liche(r)** *m* clergyman. **G~lichkeit** *f* - clergy. **g~los** *a* uninspired. **g~reich** *a* clever; (*witzig*) witty

Geiz *m* **-es** meanness. **g~en** *vi* (*haben*) be mean (**mit** with). **G~hals** *m* (*fam*) miser. **g~ig** *a* mean, miserly. **G~kragen** *m* (*fam*) miser

Gekicher *nt* **-s** giggling

geknickt *a* (*fam*) dejected, *adv* -ly

gekonnt *a* accomplished ● *adv* expertly

Gekrakel *nt* **-s** scrawl

gekränkt *a* offended, hurt

Gekritzel *nt* **-s** scribble

gekünstelt *a* affected, *adv* -ly

Gelächter *nt* **-s** laughter

geladen *a* loaded; (*fam: wütend*) furious

Gelage *nt* **-s,-** feast

gelähmt *a* paralysed

Gelände *nt* **-s,-** terrain; (*Grundstück*) site. **G~lauf** *m* cross-country run

Geländer *nt* **-s,-** railings *pl*; (*Treppen-*) banisters *pl*; (*Brücken-*) parapet

gelangen *vi* (*sein*) reach/(*fig*) attain (**zu etw/an etw** *acc* sth); **in jds Besitz g~** come into s.o.'s possession

gelassen *a* composed; (*ruhig*) calm, *adv* -ly. **G~heit** *f* - equanimity; (*Fassung*) composure

Gelatine /ʒela-/ *f* - gelatine

geläufig *a* common, current; (*fließend*) fluent, *adv* -ly; **jdm g~ sein** be familiar to s.o.

gelaunt *a* **gut/schlecht g~ sein** be in a good/bad mood

gelb *a* yellow; (*bei Ampel*) amber; **g~e Rübe** (*SGer*) carrot; **das G~e vom Ei** the yolk of the egg. **G~** *nt* **-s,-** yellow; **bei G~** (*Auto*) on [the] amber. **g~lich** *a* yellowish. **G~sucht** *f* jaundice

Geld *nt* **-es,-er** money; **öffentliche G~er** public funds. **G~beutel** *m*, **G~börse** *f* purse. **G~geber** *m* **-s,-** backer. **g~lich** *a* financial, *adv* -ly. **G~mittel** *ntpl* funds. **G~schein** *m* banknote. **G~schrank** *m* safe. **G~strafe** *f* fine. **G~stück** *nt* coin

Gelee /ʒe'le:/ *nt* **-s,-s** jelly

gelegen *a* situated; (*passend*) convenient; **jdm sehr g~ sein** *od* **kommen** suit s.o. well; **mir ist viel/wenig daran g~** I'm very/not keen on it; (*es ist wichtig*) it matters a lot/little to me

Gelegenheit *f* **-,-en** opportunity, chance; (*Anlaß*) occasion; (*Comm*) bargain; **bei G~** some time. **G~sarbeit** *f* casual work. **G~sarbeiter** *m* casual worker. **G~skauf** *m* bargain

gelegentlich *a* occasional ● *adv* occasionally; (*bei Gelegenheit*) some time ● *prep* (+ *gen*) on the occasion of

gelehrt *a* learned. **G~e(r)** *m/f* scholar

Geleise *nt* **-s,-** = **Gleis**

Geleit *nt* **-[e]s** escort; **freies G~** safe conduct. **g~en** *vt* escort. **G~zug** *m* (*Naut*) convoy

Gelenk *nt* **-[e]s,-e** joint. **g~ig** *a* supple; (*Techn*) flexible

gelernt *a* skilled

Geliebte(r) *m/f* lover; (*liter*) beloved

gelieren /ʒe-/ *vi* (*haben*) set

gelinde *a* mild, *adv* -ly; **g~ gesagt** to put it mildly

gelingen† *vi* (*sein*) succeed, be successful; **es gelang ihm, zu entkommen** he succeeded in escaping. **G~** *nt* **-s** success

gell *int* (*SGer*) = **gelt**

gellend *a* shrill, *adv* -y

geloben *vt* promise [solemnly]; **sich** (*dat*) **g~** vow (**zu** to); **das Gelobte Land** the Promised Land
Gelöbnis *nt* **-ses,-se** vow
gelöst *a* (*fig*) relaxed
Gelse *f* **-,-n** (*Aust*) mosquito
gelt *int* (*SGer*) **das ist schön, g~?** it's nice, isn't it? **ihr kommt doch, g~?** you are coming, aren't you?
gelten† *vi* (*haben*) be valid; ⟨*Regel:*⟩ apply; **g~ als** be regarded as; **etw nicht g~ lassen** not accept sth; **wenig/viel g~** be worth/(*fig*) count for little/a lot; **jdm g~** be meant for s.o.; **das gilt nicht** that doesn't count. **g~d** *a* valid; ⟨*Preise*⟩ current; ⟨*Meinung*⟩ prevailing; **g~d machen** assert ⟨*Recht, Forderung*⟩; bring to bear ⟨*Einfluß*⟩
Geltung *f* **-** validity; (*Ansehen*) prestige; **G~ haben** be valid; **zur G~ bringen/kommen** set off/show to advantage
Gelübde *nt* **-s,-** vow
gelungen *a* successful
Gelüst *nt* **-[e]s,-e** desire/(*stark*) craving (**nach** for)
gemächlich *a* leisurely ● *adv* in a leisurely manner
Gemahl *m* **-s,-e** husband. **G~in** *f* **-,-nen** wife
Gemälde *nt* **-s,-** painting. **G~galerie** *f* picture gallery
gemäß *prep* (+*dat*) in accordance with ● *a* **etw** (*dat*) **g~ sein** be in keeping with sth
gemäßigt *a* moderate; ⟨*Klima*⟩ temperate
gemein *a* common; (*unanständig*) vulgar; (*niederträchtig*) mean; **g~er Soldat** private; **etw g~ haben** have sth in common ● *adv* shabbily; (*fam: schrecklich*) terribly
Gemeinde *f* **-,-n** [local] community; (*Admin*) borough; (*Pfarr-*) parish; (*bei Gottesdienst*) congregation. **G~rat** *m* local council/(*Person*) councillor. **G~wahlen** *fpl* local elections
gemein|gefährlich *a* dangerous. **G~heit** *f* **-,-en** (*s.* **gemein**) commonness; vulgarity; meanness; (*Bemerkung, Handlung*) mean thing [to say/do]; **so eine G~heit!** how mean! (*wie ärgerlich*) what a nuisance! **G~kosten** *pl* overheads. **g~nützig** *a* charitable. **G~platz** *m* platitude. **g~sam** *a* common; **etw g~sam haben** have sth in common ● *adv* together
Gemeinschaft *f* **-,-en** community. **g~lich** *a* joint; ⟨*Besitz*⟩ communal ● *adv* jointly; (*zusammen*) together. **G~sarbeit** *f* team-work
Gemenge *nt* **-s,-** mixture
gemessen *a* measured; (*würdevoll*) dignified
Gemetzel *nt* **-s,-** carnage
Gemisch *nt* **-[e]s,-e** mixture. **g~t** *a* mixed
Gemme *f* **-,-n** engraved gem
Gemse *f* **-,-n** chamois
Gemurmel *nt* **-s** murmuring
Gemüse *nt* **-s,-** vegetable; (*coll*) vegetables *pl*. **G~händler** *m* greengrocer
gemustert *a* patterned
Gemüt *nt* **-[e]s,-er** nature, disposition; (*Gefühl*) feelings *pl*; (*Person*) soul
gemütlich *a* cosy; (*gemächlich*) leisurely; (*zwanglos*) informal; ⟨*Person*⟩ genial; **es sich** (*dat*) **g~ machen** make oneself comfortable ● *adv* cosily; in a leisurely manner; informally. **G~keit** *f* **-** cosiness; leisureliness
Gemüts|art *f* nature, disposition. **G~mensch** *m* (*fam*) placid person. **G~ruhe** *f* **in aller G~ruhe** (*fam*) calmly. **G~verfassung** *f* frame of mind
Gen *nt* **-s,-e** gene
genau *a* exact, *adv* -ly, precise, *adv* -ly; ⟨*Waage, Messung*⟩ accurate, *adv* -ly; (*sorgfältig*) meticulous, *adv* -ly; (*ausführlich*) detailed; **nichts G~es wissen** not know any details; **es nicht so g~ nehmen** not be too particular; **g~!** exactly! **g~genommen** *adv* strictly speaking. **G~igkeit** *f* **-** exactitude; precision; accuracy; meticulousness
genauso *adv* just the same; (*g~sehr*) just as much; **g~ gut/teuer** just as good/expensive. **g~gut** *adv* just as well. **g~sehr** *adv* just as much. **g~viel** *adv* just as much/many. **g~wenig** *adv* just as little/few; (*noch*) no more
Gendarm /ʒãˈdarm/ *m* **-en,-en** (*Aust*) policeman
Genealogie *f* **-** genealogy
genehmig|en *vt* grant; approve ⟨*Plan*⟩. **G~ung** *f* **-,-en** permission; (*Schein*) permit

geneigt *a* sloping, inclined; (*fig*) well-disposed (*dat* towards); **[nicht] g~ sein** (*fig*) [not] feel inclined (**zu** to)

General *m* **-s,¨e** general. **G~direktor** *m* managing director. **g~isieren** *vi* (*haben*) generalize. **G~probe** *f* dress rehearsal. **G~streik** *m* general strike. **g~überholen** *vt insep* (*inf & pp only*) completely overhaul

Generation /-'tsi̯o:n/ *f* **-,-en** generation

Generator *m* **-s,-en** /-'to:rən/ generator

generell *a* general, *adv* -ly

genes|en† *vi* (*sein*) recover. **G~ung** *f* **-** recovery; (*Erholung*) convalescence

Genet|ik *f* **-** genetics *sg*. **g~isch** *a* genetic, *adv* -ally

Genf *nt* **-s** Geneva. **G~er** *a* Geneva . . .; **G~er See** Lake Geneva

genial *a* brilliant, *adv* -ly; **ein g~er Mann** a man of genius. **G~ität** *f* **-** genius

Genick *nt* **-s,-e** [back of the] neck; **sich** (*dat*) **das G~ brechen** break one's neck

Genie /ʒe'ni:/ *nt* **-s,-s** genius

genieren /ʒe'ni:rən/ *vt* embarrass; **sich g~** feel *or* be embarrassed

genieß|bar *a* fit to eat/drink. **g~en**† *vt* enjoy; (*verzehren*) eat/drink. **G~er** *m* **-s,-** gourmet. **g~erisch** *a* appreciative ● *adv* with relish

Genitiv *m* **-s,-e** genitive

Genosse *m* **-n,-n** (*Pol*) comrade. **G~nschaft** *f* **-,-en** co-operative

Genre /'ʒã:rə/ *nt* **-s,-s** genre

Gentechnologie *f* genetic engineering

genug *inv a & adv* enough

Genüge *f* **zur G~** sufficiently. **g~n** *vi* (*haben*) be enough; **jds Anforderungen g~n** meet s.o.'s requirements. **g~nd** *inv a* sufficient, enough; (*Sch*) fair ● *adv* sufficiently, enough

genügsam *a* frugal, *adv* -ly; (*bescheiden*) modest, *adv* -ly

Genugtuung *f* **-** satisfaction

Genuß *m* **-sses,¨sse** enjoyment; (*Vergnügen*) pleasure; (*Verzehr*) consumption. **genüßlich** *a* pleasurable ● *adv* with relish

geöffnet *a* open

Geo|graphie *f* **-** geography. **g~graphisch** *a* geographical, *adv* -ly. **G~loge** *m* **-n,-n** geologist. **G~logie** *f* **-** geology. **g~logisch** *a* geological, *adv* -ly. **G~meter** *m* **-s,-** surveyor. **G~metrie** *f* **-** geometry. **g~metrisch** *a* geometric[al]

geordnet *a* well-ordered; (*stabil*) stable; **alphabetisch g~** in alphabetical order

Gepäck *nt* **-s** luggage, baggage. **G~ablage** *f* luggage-rack. **G~aufbewahrung** *f* left-luggage office. **G~schalter** *m* luggage office. **G~schein** *m* left-luggage ticket; (*Aviat*) baggage check. **G~stück** *nt* piece of luggage. **G~träger** *m* porter; (*Fahrrad-*) luggage carrier; (*Dach-*) roof-rack. **G~wagen** *m* luggage-van

Gepard *m* **-s,-e** cheetah

gepflegt *a* well-kept; ⟨*Person*⟩ well-groomed; ⟨*Hotel*⟩ first-class

Gepflogenheit *f* **-,-en** practice; (*Brauch*) custom

Gepolter *nt* **-s** [loud] noise

gepunktet *a* spotted

gerade *a* straight; (*direkt*) direct; (*aufrecht*) upright; (*aufrichtig*) straightforward; ⟨*Zahl*⟩ even ● *adv* straight; directly; (*eben*) just; (*genau*) exactly; (*besonders*) especially; **nicht g~ billig** not exactly cheap; **g~ erst** only just; **g~ an dem Tag** on that very day. **G~** *f* **-,-n** straight line. **g~aus** *adv* straight ahead/on

gerade|biegen† *vt sep* straighten; (*fig*) straighten out. **g~halten**† **(sich)** *vr sep* hold oneself straight. **g~heraus** *adv* (*fig*) straight out. **g~sitzen**† *vi sep* (*haben*) sit [up] straight. **g~so** *adv* just the same; **g~so gut** just as good. **g~sogut** *adv* just as well. **g~stehen**† *vi sep* (*haben*) stand up straight; (*fig*) accept responsibility (**für** for). **g~wegs** *adv* directly, straight. **g~zu** *adv* virtually; (*wirklich*) absolutely

Geranie /-i̯ə/ *f* **-,-n** geranium

Gerät *nt* **-[e]s,-e** tool; (*Acker-*) implement; (*Küchen-*) utensil; (*Elektro-*) appliance; (*Radio-, Fernseh-*) set; (*Turn-*) piece of apparatus; (*coll*) equipment

geraten† *vi* (*sein*) get; **in Brand g~** catch fire; **in Wut g~** get angry; **in Streit g~** start quarrelling; **gut/schlecht g~** turn out well/badly; **nach jdm g~** take after s.o.

Geratewohl *nt* **aufs G~** at random

geräuchert *a* smoked

geräumig *a* spacious, roomy

Geräusch *nt* **-[e]s,-e** noise. **g~los** *a* noiseless, *adv* -ly. **g~voll** *a* noisy, *adv* -ily

gerben *vt* tan

gerecht *a* just, *adv* -ly; (*fair*) fair, *adv* -ly; **g~ werden** (+*dat*) do justice to. **g~fertigt** *a* justified. **G~igkeit** *f* - justice; fairness

Gerede *nt* **-s** talk; (*Klatsch*) gossip

geregelt *a* regular

gereift *a* mature

gereizt *a* irritable, *adv* -bly. **G~heit** *f* - irritability

gereuen *vt* **es gereut mich nicht** I don't regret it

Geriatrie *f* - geriatrics *sg*

Gericht[1] *nt* **-[e]s,-e** (*Culin*) dish

Gericht[2] *nt* **-[e]s,-e** court [of law]; **vor G~** in court; **das Jüngste G~** the Last Judgement; **mit jdm ins G~ gehen** take s.o. to task. **g~lich** *a* judicial; ⟨*Verfahren*⟩ legal ● *adv* **g~lich vorgehen** take legal action. **G~sbarkeit** *f* - jurisdiction. **G~shof** *m* court of justice. **G~smedizin** *f* forensic medicine. **G~ssaal** *m* courtroom. **G~svollzieher** *m* **-s,-** bailiff

gerieben *a* grated; (*fam: schlau*) crafty

gering *a* small; (*niedrig*) low; (*g~fügig*) slight. **g~achten** *vt sep* have little regard for; (*verachten*) despise. **g~fügig** *a* slight, *adv* -ly. **g~schätzig** *a* contemptuous, *adv* -ly; ⟨*Bemerkung*⟩ disparaging. **g~ste(r,s)** *a* least; **nicht im g~sten** not in the least

gerinnen† *vi* (*sein*) curdle; ⟨*Blut:*⟩ clot

Gerippe *nt* **-s,-** skeleton; (*fig*) framework

gerissen *a* (*fam*) crafty

Germ *m* **-[e]s** & (*Aust*) *f* - yeast

German|e *m* **-n,-n** [ancient] German. **g~isch** *a* Germanic. **G~ist(in)** *m* **-en,-en** (*f* **-,-nen**) Germanist. **G~istik** *f* - German [language and literature]

gern[e] *adv* gladly; **g~ haben** like; (*lieben*) be fond of; **ich tanze/schwimme g~** I like dancing/swimming; **das kannst du g~ tun** you're welcome to do that; **willst du mit?—g~!** do you want to come?—I'd love to!

gerötet *a* red

Gerste *f* - barley. **G~nkorn** *nt* (*Med*) stye

Geruch *m* **-[e]s,¨e** smell (**von/nach** of). **g~los** *a* odourless. **G~ssinn** *m* sense of smell

Gerücht *nt* **-[e]s,-e** rumour

geruhen *vi* (*haben*) deign (**zu** to)

gerührt *a* (*fig*) moved, touched

Gerümpel *nt* **-s** lumber, junk

Gerüst *nt* **-[e]s,-e** scaffolding; (*fig*) framework

gesalzen *a* salted; (*fam: hoch*) steep

gesammelt *a* collected; (*gefaßt*) composed

gesamt *a* entire, whole. **G~ausgabe** *f* complete edition. **G~betrag** *m* total amount. **G~eindruck** *m* overall impression. **G~heit** *f* - whole. **G~schule** *f* comprehensive school. **G~summe** *f* total

Gesandte(r) *m/f* envoy

Gesang *m* **-[e]s,¨e** singing; (*Lied*) song; (*Kirchen-*) hymn. **G~buch** *nt* hymn-book. **G~verein** *m* choral society

Gesäß *nt* **-es** buttocks *pl*. **G~tasche** *f* hip pocket

Geschäft *nt* **-[e]s,-e** business; (*Laden*) shop, (*Amer*) store; (*Transaktion*) deal; (*fam: Büro*) office; **schmutzige G~e** shady dealings; **ein gutes G~ machen** do very well (**mit** out of); **sein G~ verstehen** know one's job. **g~ehalber** *adv* on business. **g~ig** *a* busy, *adv* -ily; ⟨*Treiben*⟩ bustling. **G~igkeit** *f* - activity. **g~lich** *a* business ... ● *adv* on business

Geschäfts|brief *m* business letter. **G~führer** *m* manager; (*Vereins-*) secretary. **G~mann** *m* (*pl* **-leute**) businessman. **G~reise** *f* business trip. **G~stelle** *f* office; (*Zweigstelle*) branch. **g~tüchtig** *a* **g~tüchtig sein** be a good businessman/-woman. **G~viertel** *nt* shopping area. **G~zeiten** *fpl* hours of business

geschehen† *vi* (*sein*) happen (*dat* to); **es ist ein Unglück g~** there has been an accident; **es ist um uns g~** we are done for; **das geschieht dir recht!** it serves you right! **gern g~!** you're welcome! **G~** *nt* **-s** events *pl*

gescheit *a* clever; **daraus werde ich nicht g~** I can't make head or tail of it

Geschenk *nt* **-[e]s,-e** present, gift. **G~korb** *m* gift hamper

Geschicht|e *f* **-,-n** history; (*Erzählung*) story; (*fam: Sache*) business. **g~lich** *a* historical, *adv* -ly

Geschick *nt* **-[e]s** fate; (*Talent*) skill; **G~ haben** be good (**zu** at). **G~lichkeit** *f* - skilfulness, skill. **g~t** *a* skilful, *adv* -ly; (*klug*) clever, *adv* -ly

geschieden *a* divorced. **G~e(r)** *m/f* divorcee

Geschirr *nt* **-s,-e** (*coll*) crockery; (*Porzellan*) china; (*Service*) service; (*Pferde-*) harness; **schmutziges G~** dirty dishes *pl*. **G~spülmaschine** *f* dishwasher. **G~tuch** *nt* tea-towel

Geschlecht *nt* **-[e]s,-er** sex; (*Gram*) gender; (*Familie*) family; (*Generation*) generation. **g~lich** *a* sexual, *adv* -ly. **G~skrankheit** *f* venereal disease. **G~steile** *ntpl* genitals. **G~sverkehr** *m* sexual intercourse. **G~swort** *nt* (*pl* **-wörter**) article

geschliffen *a* (*fig*) polished

geschlossen *a* closed ● *adv* unanimously; (*vereint*) in a body

Geschmack *m* **-[e]s,⸚e** taste; (*Aroma*) flavour; (*G~ssinn*) sense of taste; **einen guten G~ haben** (*fig*) have good taste; **G~ finden an** (+*dat*) acquire a taste for. **g~los** *a* tasteless, *adv* -ly; **g~los sein** (*fig*) be in bad taste. **G~ssache** *f* matter of taste. **g~voll** *a* (*fig*) tasteful, *adv* -ly

geschmeidig *a* supple; (*weich*) soft

Geschöpf *nt* **-[e]s,-e** creature

Geschoß *nt* **-sses,-sse** missile; (*Stockwerk*) storey, floor

geschraubt *a* (*fig*) stilted

Geschrei *nt* **-s** screaming; (*fig*) fuss

Geschütz *nt* **-es,-e** gun, cannon

geschützt *a* protected; ⟨*Stelle*⟩ sheltered

Geschwader *nt* **-s,-** squadron

Geschwätz *nt* **-es** talk. **g~ig** *a* garrulous

geschweift *a* curved

geschweige *conj* **g~ denn** let alone

geschwind *a* quick, *adv* -ly

Geschwindigkeit *f* **-,-en** speed; (*Phys*) velocity. **G~sbegrenzung, G~sbeschränkung** *f* speed limit

Geschwister *pl* brother[s] and sister[s]; siblings

geschwollen *a* swollen; (*fig*) pompous, *adv* -ly

Geschworene|(r) *m/f* juror; **die G~n** the jury *sg*

Geschwulst *f* **-,⸚e** swelling; (*Tumor*) tumour

geschwungen *a* curved

Geschwür *nt* **-s,-e** ulcer

Geselle *m* **-n,-n** fellow; (*Handwerks-*) journeyman

gesellig *a* sociable; (*Zool*) gregarious; (*unterhaltsam*) convivial; **g~er Abend** social evening. **G~keit** *f* **-,-en** entertaining; **die G~keit lieben** love company

Gesellschaft *f* **-,-en** company; (*Veranstaltung*) party; **die G~** society; **jdm G~ leisten** keep s.o. company. **g~lich** *a* social, *adv* -ly. **G~sreise** *f* group tour. **G~sspiel** *nt* party game

Gesetz *nt* **-es,-e** law. **G~entwurf** *m* bill. **g~gebend** *a* legislative. **G~gebung** *f* **-** legislation. **g~lich** *a* legal, *adv* -ly. **g~los** *a* lawless. **g~mäßig** *a* lawful, *adv* -ly; (*gesetzlich*) legal, *adv* -ly

gesetzt *a* staid; (*Sport*) seeded ● *conj* **g~ den Fall** supposing

gesetzwidrig *a* illegal, *adv* -ly

gesichert *a* secure

Gesicht *nt* **-[e]s,-er** face; (*Aussehen*) appearance; **zu G~ bekommen** set eyes on. **G~sausdruck** *m* [facial] expression. **G~sfarbe** *f* complexion. **G~spunkt** *m* point of view. **G~szüge** *mpl* features

Gesindel *nt* **-s** riff-raff

gesinnt *a* **gut/übel g~** well/ill disposed (*dat* towards)

Gesinnung *f* **-,-en** mind; (*Einstellung*) attitude; **politische G~** political convictions *pl*

gesittet *a* well-mannered; (*zivilisiert*) civilized

gesondert *a* separate, *adv* -ly

Gespann *nt* **-[e]s,-e** team; (*Wagen*) horse and cart/carriage

gespannt *a* taut; (*fig*) tense, *adv* -ly; ⟨*Beziehungen*⟩ strained; (*neugierig*) eager, *adv* -ly; (*erwartungsvoll*) expectant, *adv* -ly; **g~ sein, ob** wonder whether; **auf etw/jdn g~ sein** look forward eagerly to sth/to seeing s.o.

Gespenst *nt* **-[e]s,-er** ghost. **g~isch** *a* ghostly; (*unheimlich*) eerie

Gespött *nt* **-[e]s** mockery; **zum G~ werden** become a laughing-stock

Gespräch *nt* **-[e]s,-e** conversation; (*Telefon-*) call; **ins G~ kommen** get talking; **im G~ sein** be under discussion. **g~ig** *a* talkative. **G~sgegenstand** *m*, **G~sthema** *nt* topic of conversation

gesprenkelt *a* speckled

Gespür *nt* **-s** feeling; (*Instinkt*) instinct

Gestalt *f* **-,-en** figure; (*Form*) shape, form; **G~ annehmen** (*fig*) take shape. **g~en** *vt* shape; (*organisie-*

ren) arrange; (*schaffen*) create; (*entwerfen*) design; **sich g~en** turn out

geständ|ig *a* confessed; **g~ig sein** have confessed. **G~nis** *nt* **-ses,-se** confession

Gestank *m* **-s** stench, [bad] smell

gestatten *vt* allow, permit; **nicht gestattet** prohibited; **g~ Sie?** may I?

Geste /'gɛ-, 'ge:stə/ *f* **-,-n** gesture

Gesteck *nt* **-[e]s,-e** flower arrangement

gestehen† *vt/i* (*haben*) confess; confess to ⟨*Verbrechen*⟩; **offen gestanden** to tell the truth

Gestein *nt* **-[e]s,-e** rock

Gestell *nt* **-[e]s,-e** stand; (*Flaschen-*) rack; (*Rahmen*) frame

gestellt *a* **gut/schlecht g~** well/badly off; **auf sich** (*acc*) **selbst g~ sein** be thrown on one's own resources

gestelzt *a* (*fig*) stilted

gesteppt *a* quilted

gestern *adv* yesterday; **g~ nacht** last night

Gestik /'gɛstɪk/ *f* - gestures *pl*. **g~ulieren** *vi* (*haben*) gesticulate

gestrandet *a* stranded

gestreift *a* striped

gestrichelt *a* ⟨*Linie*⟩ dotted

gestrichen *a* **g~er Teelöffel** level teaspoon[ful]

gestrig /'gɛstrɪç/ *a* yesterday's; **am g~en Tag** yesterday

Gestrüpp *nt* **-s,-e** undergrowth

Gestüt *nt* **-[e]s,-e** stud [farm]

Gesuch *nt* **-[e]s,-e** request; (*Admin*) application. **g~t** *a* sought-after; (*gekünstelt*) contrived

gesund *a* healthy, *adv* -ily; **g~ sein** be in good health; ⟨*Sport, Getränk:*⟩ be good for one; **wieder g~ werden** get well again

Gesundheit *f* - health; **G~!** (*bei Niesen*) bless you! **g~lich** *a* health . . .; **g~licher Zustand** state of health ● *adv* **es geht ihm g~lich gut/schlecht** he is in good/poor health. **g~shalber** *adv* for health reasons. **g~sschädlich** *a* harmful. **G~szustand** *m* state of health

getäfelt *a* panelled

getigert *a* tabby

Getöse *nt* **-s** racket, din

getragen *a* solemn, *adv* -ly

Getränk *nt* **-[e]s,-e** drink. **G~ekarte** *f* wine-list

getrauen *vt* **sich** (*dat*) **etw g~** dare [to] do sth; **sich g~** dare

Getreide *nt* **-s** (*coll*) grain

getrennt *a* separate, *adv* -ly; **g~ leben** live apart. **g~schreiben**† *vt sep* write as two words

getreu *a* faithful, *adv* -ly ● *prep* (+*dat*) true to; **der Wahrheit g~** truthfully. **g~lich** *adv* faithfully

Getriebe *nt* **-s,-** bustle; (*Techn*) gear; (*Auto*) transmission; (*Gehäuse*) gearbox

getrost *adv* with confidence

Getto *nt* **-s,-s** ghetto

Getue *nt* **-s** (*fam*) fuss

Getümmel *nt* **-s** tumult

getüpfelt *a* spotted

geübt *a* skilled; ⟨*Auge, Hand*⟩ practised

Gewächs *nt* **-es,-e** plant; (*Med*) growth

gewachsen *a* **jdm/etw g~ sein** be a match for s.o./be equal to sth

Gewächshaus *nt* greenhouse; (*Treibhaus*) hothouse

gewagt *a* daring

gewählt *a* refined

gewahr *a* **g~ werden** become aware (*acc/gen* of)

Gewähr *f* - guarantee

gewahren *vt* notice

gewähr|en *vt* grant; (*geben*) offer; **jdn g~en lassen** let s.o. have his way. **g~leisten** *vt* guarantee

Gewahrsam *m* **-s** safekeeping; (*Haft*) custody

Gewährsmann *m* (*pl* **-männer** & **-leute**) informant, source

Gewalt *f* **-,-en** power; (*Kraft*) force; (*Brutalität*) violence; **mit G~** by force; **G~ anwenden** use force; **sich in der G~ haben** be in control of oneself. **G~herrschaft** *f* tyranny. **g~ig** *a* powerful; (*fam: groß*) enormous, *adv* -ly; (*stark*) tremendous, *adv* -ly. **g~sam** *a* forcible, *adv* -bly; ⟨*Tod*⟩ violent. **g~tätig** *a* violent. **G~tätigkeit** *f* **-,-en** violence; (*Handlung*) act of violence

Gewand *nt* **-[e]s,⸚er** robe

gewandt *a* skilful, *adv* -ly; (*flink*) nimble, *adv* -bly. **G~heit** *f* - skill; nimbleness

Gewässer *nt* **-s,-** body of water; **G~** *pl* waters

Gewebe *nt* **-s,-** fabric; (*Anat*) tissue

Gewehr *nt* **-s,-e** rifle, gun

Geweih *nt* **-[e]s,-e** antlers *pl*

Gewerb|e *nt* **-s,-** trade. **g~lich** *a* commercial, *adv* -ly. **g~smäßig** *a* professional, *adv* -ly

Gewerkschaft *f* **-,-en** trade union. **G~ler(in)** *m* **-s,-** (*f* **-,-nen**) trade unionist
Gewicht *nt* **-[e]s,-e** weight; (*Bedeutung*) importance. **G~heben** *nt* **-s** weight-lifting. **g~ig** *a* important
gewieft *a* (*fam*) crafty
gewillt *a* **g~ sein** be willing
Gewinde *nt* **-s,-** [screw] thread
Gewinn *m* **-[e]s,-e** profit; (*fig*) gain, benefit; (*beim Spiel*) winnings *pl*; (*Preis*) prize; (*Los*) winning ticket. **G~beteiligung** *f* profit-sharing. **g~bringend** *a* profitable, *adv* -bly. **g~en**† *vt* win; (*erlangen*) gain; (*fördern*) extract; **jdn für sich g~en** win s.o. over ● *vi* (*haben*) win; **g~en an** (+ *dat*) gain in. **g~end** *a* engaging. **G~er(in)** *m* **-s,-** (*f* **-,-nen**) winner
Gewirr *nt* **-s,-e** tangle; (*Straßen-*) maze; **G~ von Stimmen** hubbub of voices
gewiß *a* (**gewisser, gewissest**) certain, *adv* -ly
Gewissen *nt* **-s,-** conscience. **g~haft** *a* conscientious, *adv* -ly. **g~los** *a* unscrupulous. **G~sbisse** *mpl* pangs of conscience
gewissermaßen *adv* to a certain extent; (*sozusagen*) as it were
Gewißheit *f* **-** certainty
Gewitt|er *nt* **-s,-** thunderstorm. **g~ern** *vi* (*haben*) **es g~ert** it is thundering. **g~rig** *a* thundery
gewogen *a* (*fig*) well-disposed (*dat* towards)
gewöhnen *vt* **jdn/sich g~ an** (+*acc*) get s.o. used to/get used to; **[an] jdn/etw gewöhnt sein** be used to s.o./sth
Gewohnheit *f* **-,-en** habit. **g~smäßig** *a* habitual, *adv* -ly. **G~srecht** *nt* common law
gewöhnlich *a* ordinary, *adv* -ily; (*üblich*) usual, *adv* -ly; (*ordinär*) common
gewohnt *a* customary; (*vertraut*) familiar; (*üblich*) usual; **etw** (*acc*) **g~ sein** be used to sth
Gewöhnung *f* **-** getting used (**an** + *acc* to); (*Süchtigkeit*) addiction
Gewölb|e *nt* **-s,-** vault. **g~t** *a* curved; (*Archit*) vaulted
gewollt *a* forced
Gewühl *nt* **-[e]s** crush
gewunden *a* winding
gewürfelt *a* check[ed]
Gewürz *nt* **-es,-e** spice. **G~nelke** *f* clove
gezackt *a* serrated
gezähnt *a* serrated; ⟨*Säge*⟩ toothed
Gezeiten *fpl* tides
gezielt *a* specific; ⟨*Frage*⟩ pointed
geziemend *a* proper, *adv* -ly
geziert *a* affected, *adv* -ly
gezwungen *a* forced ● *adv* **g~ lachen** give a forced laugh. **g~ermaßen** *adv* of necessity; **etw g~ermaßen tun** be forced to do sth
Gicht *f* **-** gout
Giebel *m* **-s,-** gable
Gier *f* **-** greed (**nach** for). **g~ig** *a* greedy, *adv* -ily
gieß|en† *vt* pour; water ⟨*Blumen, Garten*⟩; (*Techn*) cast ● *v impers* **es g~t** it is pouring [with rain]. **G~erei** *f* **-,-en** foundry. **G~kanne** *f* watering-can
Gift *nt* **-[e]s,-e** poison; (*Schlangen-*) venom; (*Biol, Med*) toxin. **g~ig** *a* poisonous; ⟨*Schlange*⟩ venomous; (*Med, Chem*) toxic; (*fig*) spiteful, *adv* -ly. **G~müll** *m* toxic waste. **G~pilz** *m* poisonous fungus, toadstool. **G~zahn** *m* [poison] fang
gigantisch *a* gigantic
Gilde *f* **-,-n** guild
Gimpel *m* **-s,-** bullfinch; (*fam: Tölpel*) simpleton
Gin /dʒɪn/ *m* **-s** gin
Ginster *m* **-s** (*Bot*) broom
Gipfel *m* **-s,-** summit, top; (*fig*) peak. **G~konferenz** *f* summit conference. **g~n** *vi* (*haben*) culminate (**in** + *dat* in)
Gips *m* **-es** plaster. **G~abguß** *m* plaster cast. **G~er** *m* **-s,-** plasterer. **G~verband** *m* (*Med*) plaster cast
Giraffe *f* **-,-n** giraffe
Girlande *f* **-,-n** garland
Girokonto /ˈʒi:ro-/ *nt* current account
Gischt *m* **-[e]s** & *f* **-** spray
Gitar|re *f* **-,-n** guitar. **G~rist(in)** *m* **-en,-en** (*f* **-,-nen**) guitarist
Gitter *nt* **-s,-** bars *pl*; (*Rost*) grating, grid; (*Geländer, Zaun*) railings *pl*; (*Fenster-*) grille; (*Draht-*) wire screen; **hinter G~n** (*fam*) behind bars. **G~netz** *nt* grid
Glanz *m* **-es** shine; (*von Farbe, Papier*) gloss; (*Seiden-*) sheen; (*Politur*) polish; (*fig*) brilliance; (*Pracht*) splendour
glänzen *vi* (*haben*) shine. **g~d** *a* shining, bright; ⟨*Papier, Haar*⟩ glossy; (*fig*) brilliant, *adv* -ly
glanz|los *a* dull. **G~stück** *nt* masterpiece; (*einer Sammlung*) show-piece.

g~voll *a* (*fig*) brilliant, *adv* -ly; (*prachtvoll*) splendid, *adv* -ly. **G~zeit** *f* heyday
Glas *nt* **-es,¨er** glass; (*Brillen-*) lens; (*Fern-*) binoculars *pl*; (*Marmeladen-*) [glass] jar. **G~er** *m* **-s,-** glazier
gläsern *a* glass ...
Glashaus *nt* greenhouse
glasieren *vt* glaze; ice ⟨*Kuchen*⟩
glas|ig *a* glassy; (*durchsichtig*) transparent. **G~scheibe** *f* pane
Glasur *f* **-,-en** glaze; (*Culin*) icing
glatt *a* smooth; (*eben*) even; ⟨*Haar*⟩ straight; (*rutschig*) slippery; (*einfach*) straightforward; (*eindeutig*) downright; ⟨*Absage*⟩ flat ● *adv* smoothly; evenly; (*fam: völlig*) completely; (*gerade*) straight; (*leicht*) easily; ⟨*ablehnen*⟩ flatly; **g~ verlaufen** go off smoothly; **das ist g~ gelogen** it's a downright lie
Glätte *f* - smoothness; (*Rutschigkeit*) slipperiness
Glatteis *nt* [black] ice; **aufs G~ führen** (*fam*) take for a ride
glätten *vt* smooth; **sich g~** become smooth; ⟨*Wellen:*⟩ subside
glatt|gehen† *vi sep* (*sein*) (*fig*) go off smoothly. **g~rasiert** *a* clean-shaven. **g~streichen**† *vt sep* smooth out. **g~weg** *adv* (*fam*) outright
Glatz|e *f* **-,-n** bald patch; (*Voll-*) bald head; **eine G~e bekommen** go bald. **g~köpfig** *a* bald
Glaube *m* **-ns** belief (**an** + *acc* in); (*Relig*) faith; **in gutem G~n** in good faith; **G~n schenken** (+ *dat*) believe. **g~n** *vt/i* (*haben*) believe (**an** + *acc* in); (*vermuten*) think; **jdm g~n** believe s.o.; **nicht zu g~n** unbelievable, incredible. **G~nsbekenntnis** *nt* creed
glaubhaft *a* credible; (*überzeugend*) convincing, *adv* -ly
gläubig *a* religious; (*vertrauend*) trusting, *adv* -ly. **G~e(r)** *m/f* (*Relig*) believer; **die G~en** the faithful. **G~er** *m* **-s,-** (*Comm*) creditor
glaub|lich *a* **kaum g~lich** scarcely believable. **g~würdig** *a* credible; ⟨*Person*⟩ reliable. **G~würdigkeit** *f* - credibility; reliability
gleich *a* same; (*identisch*) identical; (*g~wertig*) equal; **2 mal 5 [ist] g~ 10** two times 5 equals 10; **das ist mir g~** it's all the same to me; **ganz g~, wo/wer** no matter where/who ● *adv* equally; (*übereinstimmend*) identically, the same; (*sofort*) immediately; (*in Kürze*) in a minute; (*fast*) nearly; (*direkt*) right; **g~ alt/schwer sein** be the same age/weight. **g~altrig** *a* [of] the same age. **g~artig** *a* similar. **g~bedeutend** *a* synonymous. **g~berechtigt** *a* equal. **G~berechtigung** *f* equality. **g~bleibend** *a* constant
gleichen† *vi* (*haben*) **jdm/etw g~** be like *or* resemble s.o./sth; **sich g~** be alike
gleich|ermaßen *adv* equally. **g~falls** *adv* also, likewise; **danke g~falls** thank you, the same to you. **g~förmig** *a* uniform, *adv* -ly; (*eintönig*) monotonous, *adv* -ly. **G~förmigkeit** *f* - uniformity; monotony. **g~gesinnt** *a* like-minded. **G~gewicht** *nt* balance; (*Phys & fig*) equilibrium. **g~gültig** *a* indifferent, *adv* -ly; (*unwichtig*) unimportant. **G~gültigkeit** *f* indifference. **G~heit** *f* - equality; (*Ähnlichkeit*) similarity. **g~machen** *vt sep* make equal; **dem Erdboden g~machen** raze to the ground. **g~mäßig** *a* even, *adv* -ly, regular, *adv* -ly; (*beständig*) constant, *adv* -ly. **G~mäßigkeit** *f* - regularity. **G~mut** *m* equanimity. **g~mütig** *a* calm, *adv* -ly
Gleichnis *nt* **-ses,-se** parable
gleich|sam *adv* as it were. **G~schritt** *m* **im G~schritt** in step. **g~sehen**† *vi sep* (*haben*) **jdm g~sehen** look like s.o.; (*fam: typisch sein*) be just like s.o. **g~setzen** *vt sep* equate/ (*g~stellen*) place on a par (*dat*/**mit** with). **g~stellen** *vt sep* place on a par (*dat* with). **G~strom** *m* direct current. **g~tun**† *vi sep* (*haben*) **es jdm g~tun** emulate s.o.
Gleichung *f* **-,-en** equation
gleich|viel *adv* no matter (**ob/wer** whether/who). **g~wertig** *a* of equal value. **g~zeitig** *a* simultaneous, *adv* -ly
Gleis *nt* **-es,-e** track; (*Bahnsteig*) platform; **G~ 5** platform 5
gleiten† *vi* (*sein*) glide; (*rutschen*) slide. **g~d** *a* sliding; **g~de Arbeitszeit** flexitime
Gleitzeit *f* flexitime
Gletscher *m* **-s,-** glacier. **G~spalte** *f* crevasse
Glied *nt* **-[e]s,-er** limb; (*Teil*) part; (*Ketten-*) link; (*Mitglied*) member;

(*Mil*) rank. **g~ern** *vt* arrange; (*einteilen*) divide; **sich g~ern** be divided (**in** + *acc* into). **G~maßen** *fpl* limbs
glimmen† *vi* (*haben*) glimmer
glimpflich *a* lenient, *adv* -ly; **g~ davonkommen** get off lightly
glitschig *a* slippery
glitzern *vi* (*haben*) glitter
global *a* global, *adv* -ly
Globus *m* - & **-busses, -ben** & **-busse** globe
Glocke *f* **-,-n** bell. **G~nturm** *m* bell-tower, belfry
glorifizieren *vt* glorify
glorreich *a* glorious
Glossar *nt* **-s,-e** glossary
Glosse *f* **-,-n** comment
glotzen *vi* (*haben*) stare
Glück *nt* **-[e]s** [good] luck; (*Zufriedenheit*) happiness; **G~/kein G~ haben** be lucky/unlucky; **zum G~** luckily, fortunately; **auf gut G~** on the off chance; (*wahllos*) at random. **g~bringend** *a* lucky. **g~en** *vi* (*sein*) succeed; **es ist mir geglückt** I succeeded
gluckern *vi* (*haben*) gurgle
glücklich *a* lucky, fortunate; (*zufrieden*) happy; (*sicher*) safe ● *adv* happily; safely; (*fam: endlich*) finally. **g~erweise** *adv* luckily, fortunately
glückselig *a* blissfully happy. **G~keit** *f* bliss
glucksen *vi* (*haben*) gurgle
Glücksspiel *nt* game of chance; (*Spielen*) gambling
Glückwunsch *m* good wishes *pl*; (*Gratulation*) congratulations *pl*; **herzlichen G~!** congratulations! (*zum Geburtstag*) happy birthday! **G~karte** *f* greetings card
Glüh|birne *f* light-bulb. **g~en** *vi* (*haben*) glow. **g~end** *a* glowing; (*rot-*) red-hot; ⟨*Hitze*⟩ scorching; (*leidenschaftlich*) fervent, *adv* -ly. **G~faden** *m* filament. **G~wein** *m* mulled wine. **G~würmchen** *nt* **-s,-** glow-worm
Glukose *f* - glucose
Glut *f* - embers *pl*; (*Röte*) glow; (*Hitze*) heat; (*fig*) ardour
Glyzinie /-i̯ə/ *f* **-,-n** wisteria
GmbH *abbr* (**Gesellschaft mit beschränkter Haftung**) ≈ plc
Gnade *f* - mercy; (*Gunst*) favour; (*Relig*) grace. **G~nfrist** *f* reprieve. **g~nlos** *a* merciless, *adv* -ly
gnädig *a* gracious, *adv* -ly; (*mild*) lenient, *adv* -ly; **g~e Frau** Madam
Gnom *m* **-en,-en** gnome
Gobelin /gobəˈlɛ̃:/ *m* **-s,-s** tapestry
Gold *nt* **-[e]s** gold. **g~en** *a* gold . . .; (*g~farben*) golden; **g~ene Hochzeit** golden wedding. **G~fisch** *m* goldfish. **G~grube** *f* gold-mine. **g~ig** *a* sweet, lovely. **G~lack** *m* wallflower. **G~regen** *m* laburnum. **G~schmied** *m* goldsmith
Golf[1] *m* **-[e]s,-e** (*Geog*) gulf
Golf[2] *nt* **-s** golf. **G~platz** *m* golf-course. **G~schläger** *m* golf-club. **G~spieler(in)** *m(f)* golfer
Gondel *f* **-,-n** gondola; (*Kabine*) cabin
Gong *m* **-s,-s** gong
gönnen *vt* **jdm etw g~** not begrudge s.o. sth; **jdm etw nicht g~** begrudge s.o. sth; **sie gönnte sich** (*dat*) **keine Ruhe** she allowed herself no rest
Gönner *m* **-s,-** patron. **g~haft** *a* patronizing, *adv* -ly
Gör *nt* **-s,-en**, **Göre** *f* **-,-n** (*fam*) kid
Gorilla *m* **-s,-s** gorilla
Gosse *f* **-,-n** gutter
Got|ik *f* - Gothic. **g~isch** *a* Gothic
Gott *m* **-[e]s,¨er** God; (*Myth*) god
Götterspeise *f* jelly
Gottes|dienst *m* service. **g~lästerlich** *a* blasphemous, *adv* -ly. **G~lästerung** *f* blasphemy
Gottheit *f* **-,-en** deity
Göttin *f* **-,-nen** goddess
göttlich *a* divine, *adv* -ly
gott|los *a* ungodly; (*atheistisch*) godless. **g~verlassen** *a* God-forsaken
Götze *m* **-n,-n**, **G~nbild** *nt* idol
Gouver|nante /guvərˈnantə/ *f* **-,-n** governess. **G~neur** /-ˈnøːɐ̯/ *m* **-s,-e** governor
Grab *nt* **-[e]s,¨er** grave
graben† *vi* (*haben*) dig
Graben *m* **-s,¨** ditch; (*Mil*) trench
Grab|mal *nt* tomb. **G~stein** *m* gravestone, tombstone
Grad *m* **-[e]s,-e** degree
Graf *m* **-en,-en** count
Grafik *f* **-,-en** graphics *sg*; (*Kunst*) graphic arts *pl*; (*Druck*) print
Gräfin *f* **-,-nen** countess
grafisch *a* graphic; **g~e Darstellung** diagram
Grafschaft *f* **-,-en** county
Gram *m* **-s** grief
grämen (sich) *vr* grieve
grämlich *a* morose, *adv* -ly
Gramm *nt* **-s,-e** gram
Gram|matik *f* **-,-en** grammar. **g~matikalisch, g~matisch** *a* grammatical, *adv* -ly

Granat *m* **-[e]s,-e** (*Miner*) garnet. **G~apfel** *m* pomegranate. **G~e** *f* **-,-n** shell; (*Hand-*) grenade

Granit *m* **-s,-e** granite

Graph|ik *f*, **g~isch** *a* = **Grafik, grafisch**

Gras *nt* **-es,¨-er** grass. **g~en** *vi* (*haben*) graze. **G~hüpfer** *m* **-s,-** grasshopper

grassieren *vi* (*haben*) be rife

gräßlich *a* dreadful, *adv* -ly

Grat *m* **-[e]s,-e** [mountain] ridge

Gräte *f* **-,-n** fishbone

Gratifikation /-'tsi̯o:n/ *f* **-,-en** bonus

gratis *adv* free [of charge]. **G~probe** *f* free sample

Gratu|lant(in) *m* **-en,-en** (*f* **-,-nen**) well-wisher. **G~lation** /-'tsi̯o:n/ *f* **-,-en** congratulations *pl*; (*Glückwünsche*) best wishes *pl*. **g~lieren** *vi* (*haben*) **jdm g~lieren** congratulate s.o. (**zu** on); (*zum Geburtstag*) wish s.o. happy birthday; **[ich] g~liere!** congratulations!

grau *a*, **G~** *nt* **-s,-** grey. **G~brot** *nt* mixed rye and wheat bread

grauen[1] *vi* (*haben*) **der Morgen** *od* **es graut** dawn is breaking

grauen[2] *v impers* **mir graut [es] davor** I dread it. **G~** *nt* **-s** dread. **g~haft, g~voll** *a* gruesome; (*gräßlich*) horrible, *adv* -bly

gräulich *a* greyish

Graupeln *fpl* soft hail *sg*

grausam *a* cruel, *adv* -ly. **G~keit** *f* **-,-en** cruelty

graus|en *v impers* **mir graust davor** I dread it. **G~en** *nt* **-s** horror, dread. **g~ig** *a* gruesome

gravieren *vt* engrave. **g~d** *a* (*fig*) serious

Grazie /'gra:tsi̯ə/ *f* **-** grace

graziös *a* graceful, *adv* -ly

greifbar *a* tangible; **in g~er Nähe** within reach

greifen† *vt* take hold of; (*fangen*) catch ● *vi* (*haben*) reach (**nach** for); **g~ zu** (*fig*) turn to; **um sich g~** (*fig*) spread. **G~** *nt* **G~ spielen** play tag

Greis *m* **-es,-e** old man. **G~enalter** *nt* extreme old age. **g~enhaft** *a* old. **G~in** *f* **-,-nen** old woman

grell *a* glaring; ‹*Farbe*› garish; (*schrill*) shrill, *adv* -y

Gremium *nt* **-s,-ien** committee

Grenz|e *f* **-,-n** border; (*Staats-*) frontier; (*Grundstücks-*) boundary; (*fig*) limit. **g~en** *vi* (*haben*) border (**an** + *acc* on). **g~enlos** *a* boundless; (*maßlos*) infinite, *adv* -ly. **G~fall** *m* borderline case

Greuel *m* **-s,-** horror. **G~tat** *f* atrocity

greulich *a* horrible, *adv* -bly

Griech|e *m* **-n,-n** Greek. **G~enland** *nt* **-s** Greece. **G~in** *f* **-,-nen** Greek woman. **g~isch** *a* Greek. **G~isch** *nt* **-[s]** (*Lang*) Greek

griesgrämig *a* (*fam*) grumpy

Grieß *m* **-es** semolina

Griff *m* **-[e]s,-e** grasp, hold; (*Hand-*) movement of the hand; (*Tür-, Messer-*) handle; (*Schwert-*) hilt. **g~bereit** *a* handy

Grill *m* **-s,-s** grill; (*Garten-*) barbecue

Grille *f* **-,-n** (*Zool*) cricket; (*fig: Laune*) whim

grill|en *vt* grill; (*im Freien*) barbecue ● *vi* (*haben*) have a barbecue. **G~fest** *nt* barbecue. **G~gericht** *nt* grill

Grimasse *f* **-,-n** grimace; **G~n schneiden** pull faces

grimmig *a* furious; ‹*Kälte*› bitter

grinsen *vi* (*haben*) grin. **G~** *nt* **-s** grin

Grippe *f* **-,-n** influenza, (*fam*) flu

grob *a* (**gröber, gröbst**) coarse, *adv* -ly; (*unsanft, ungefähr*) rough, *adv* -ly; (*unhöflich*) rude, *adv* -ly; (*schwer*) gross, *adv* -ly; ‹*Fehler*› bad; **g~e Arbeit** rough work; **g~ geschätzt** roughly. **G~ian** *m* **-s,-e** brute

gröblich *a* gross, *adv* -ly

grölen *vt/i* (*haben*) bawl

Groll *m* **-[e]s** resentment; **einen G~ gegen jdn hegen** bear s.o. a grudge. **g~en** *vi* (*haben*) be angry (*dat* with); ‹*Donner:*› rumble

Grönland *nt* **-s** Greenland

Gros[1] *nt* **-ses,-** (*Maß*) gross

Gros[2] /gro:/ *nt* **-** majority, bulk

Groschen *m* **-s,-** (*Aust*) groschen; (*fam*) ten-pfennig piece; **der G~ ist gefallen** (*fam*) the penny's dropped

groß *a* (**größer, größt**) big; ‹*Anzahl, Summe*› large; (*bedeutend, stark*) great; (*g~artig*) grand; ‹*Buchstabe*› capital; **g~e Ferien** summer holidays; **g~e Angst haben** be very frightened; **der größte Teil** the majority *or* bulk; **g~ werden** ‹*Person:*› grow up; **g~ in etw** (*dat*) **sein** be good at sth; **g~ und klein** young and old; **im g~en und ganzen** on the whole ● *adv* ‹*feiern*› in style; (*fam: viel*) much; **jdn g~ ansehen** look at s.o. in amazement

groß|artig *a* magnificent, *adv* -ly. **G~aufnahme** *f* close-up. **G~britannien** *nt* **-s** Great Britain. **G~buchstabe** *m* capital letter. **G~e(r)** *m/f* **unser G~er** our eldest; **die G~en** the grown-ups; (*fig*) the great *pl*

Größe *f* **-,-n** size; (*Ausmaß*) extent; (*Körper-*) height; (*Bedeutsamkeit*) greatness; (*Math*) quantity; (*Person*) great figure

Groß|eltern *pl* grandparents. **g~enteils** *adv* largely

Größenwahnsinn *m* megalomania

Groß|handel *m* wholesale trade. **G~händler** *m* wholesaler. **g~herzig** *a* magnanimous, *adv* -ly. **G~macht** *f* superpower. **G~mut** *f* - magnanimity. **g~mütig** *a* magnanimous, *adv* -ly. **G~mutter** *f* grandmother. **G~onkel** *m* great-uncle. **G~reinemachen** *nt* **-s** spring-clean. **G~schreibung** *f* capitalization. **g~sprecherisch** *a* boastful. **g~spurig** *a* pompous, *adv* -ly; (*überheblich*) arrogant, *adv* -ly. **G~stadt** *f* [large] city. **g~städtisch** *a* city ... **G~tante** *f* great-aunt. **G~teil** *m* large proportion; (*Hauptteil*) bulk

größtenteils *adv* for the most part

groß|tun† **(sich)** *vr sep* brag. **G~vater** *m* grandfather. **g~ziehen**† *vt sep* bring up; rear ⟨*Tier*⟩. **g~zügig** *a* generous, *adv* -ly; (*weiträumig*) spacious. **G~zügigkeit** *f* - generosity

grotesk *a* grotesque, *adv* -ly

Grotte *f* **-,-n** grotto

Grübchen *nt* **-s,-** dimple

Grube *f* **-,-n** pit

grübeln *vi* (*haben*) brood

Gruft *f* **-,⸚e** [burial] vault

grün *a* green; **im G~en** out in the country; **die G~en** the Greens. **G~** *nt* **-s,-** green; (*Laub, Zweige*) greenery

Grund *m* **-[e]s,⸚e** ground; (*Boden*) bottom; (*Hinter-*) background; (*Ursache*) reason; **auf G~** (+*gen*) on the strength of; **aus diesem G~e** for this reason; **von G~ auf** (*fig*) radically; **im G~e [genommen]** basically; **auf G~ laufen** (*Naut*) run aground. **G~begriffe** *mpl* basics. **G~besitz** *m* landed property. **G~besitzer** *m* landowner

gründ|en *vt* found, set up; start ⟨*Familie*⟩; (*fig*) base (**auf**+*acc* on); **sich g~en** be based (**auf**+*acc* on). **G~er(in)** *m* **-s,-** (*f* **-,-nen**) founder

Grund|farbe *f* primary colour. **G~form** *f* (*Gram*) infinitive. **G~gesetz** *nt* (*Pol*) constitution. **G~lage** *f* basis, foundation. **g~legend** *a* fundamental, *adv* -ly

gründlich *a* thorough, *adv* -ly. **G~keit** *f* - thoroughness

grund|los *a* bottomless; (*fig*) groundless ● *adv* without reason. **G~mauern** *fpl* foundations

Gründonnerstag *m* Maundy Thursday

Grund|regel *f* basic rule. **G~riß** *m* ground-plan; (*fig*) outline. **G~satz** *m* principle. **g~sätzlich** *a* fundamental, *adv* -ly; (*im allgemeinen*) in principle; (*prinzipiell*) on principle. **G~schule** *f* primary school. **G~stein** *m* foundation-stone. **G~stück** *nt* plot [of land]

Gründung *f* **-,-en** foundation

grün|en *vi* (*haben*) become green. **G~gürtel** *m* green belt. **G~span** *m* verdigris. **G~streifen** *m* grass verge; (*Mittel-*) central reservation, (*Amer*) median strip

grunzen *vi* (*haben*) grunt

Gruppe *f* **-,-n** group; (*Reise-*) party

gruppieren *vt* group; **sich g~** form a group/groups

Grusel|geschichte *f* horror story. **g~ig** *a* creepy

Gruß *m* **-es,⸚e** greeting; (*Mil*) salute; **einen schönen G~ an X** give my regards to X; **viele/herzliche G⸚e** regards; **Mit freundlichen G⸚en** Yours sincerely/(*Comm*) faithfully

grüßen *vt/i* (*haben*) say hallo (**jdn** to s.o.); (*Mil*) salute; **g~ Sie X von mir** give my regards to X; **jdn g~ lassen** send one's regards to s.o.; **grüß Gott!** (*SGer, Aust*) good morning/afternoon/evening!

guck|en *vi* (*haben*) (*fam*) look. **G~loch** *nt* peep-hole

Guerilla /ge'rɪlja/ *f* - guerrilla warfare. **G~kämpfer** *m* guerrilla

Gulasch *nt & m* **-[e]s** goulash

gültig *a* valid, *adv* -ly. **G~keit** *f* - validity

Gummi *m & nt* **-s,-[s]** rubber; (*Harz*) gum. **G~band** *nt* (*pl* **-bänder**) elastic *or* rubber band; (*G~zug*) elastic

gummiert *a* gummed

Gummi|knüppel *m* truncheon. **G~stiefel** *m* gumboot, wellington. **G~zug** *m* elastic

Gunst *f* - favour; **zu jds G~en** in s.o.'s favour

günstig *a* favourable, *adv* -bly; (*passend*) convenient, *adv* -ly

Günstling *m* **-s,-e** favourite

Gurgel *f* **-,-n** throat. **g~n** *vi* (*haben*) gargle. **G~wasser** *nt* gargle

Gurke *f* **-,-n** cucumber; (*Essig-*) gherkin

gurren *vi* (*haben*) coo

Gurt *m* **-[e]s,-e** strap; (*Gürtel*) belt; (*Auto*) safety-belt. **G~band** *nt* (*pl* **-bänder**) waistband

Gürtel *m* **-s,-** belt. **G~linie** *f* waistline. **G~rose** *f* shingles *sg*

GUS *abbr* **(Gemeinschaft Unabhängiger Staaten)** CIS

Guß *m* **-sses,⸚sse** (*Techn*) casting; (*Strom*) stream; (*Regen-*) downpour; (*Torten-*) icing. **G~eisen** *nt* cast iron. **g~eisern** *a* cast-iron

gut *a* **(besser, best)** good; ⟨*Gewissen*⟩ clear; (*gütig*) kind **(zu** to**)**; **jdm gut sein** be fond of s.o.; **im g~en** amicably; **zu g~er Letzt** in the end; **schon gut** that's all right ● *adv* well; ⟨*schmecken, riechen*⟩ good; (*leicht*) easily; **es gut haben** be well off; (*Glück haben*) be lucky; **gut zu sehen** clearly visible; **gut drei Stunden** a good three hours; **du hast gut reden** it's easy for you to talk

Gut *nt* **-[e]s,⸚er** possession, property; (*Land-*) estate; **Gut und Böse** good and evil; **Güter** (*Comm*) goods

Gutacht|en *nt* **-s,-** expert's report. **G~er** *m* **-s,-** expert

gut|artig *a* good-natured; (*Med*) benign. **g~aussehend** *a* good-looking. **g~bezahlt** *a* well-paid. **G~dünken** *nt* **-s nach eigenem G~dünken** at one's own discretion

Gute|(s) *nt* **etwas/nichts G~s** something/nothing good; **G~s tun** do good; **das G~ daran** the good thing about it all; **alles G~!** all the best!

Güte *f* **-,-n** goodness, kindness; (*Qualität*) quality; **du meine G~!** my goodness!

Güterzug *m* goods/(*Amer*) freight train

gut|gehen† *vi sep* (*sein*) go well; **es geht mir gut** I am well/(*geschäftlich*) doing well. **g~gehend** *a* flourishing, thriving. **g~gemeint** *a* well-meant. **g~gläubig** *a* trusting. **g~haben**† *vt sep* **fünfzig Mark g~haben** have fifty marks credit (**bei** with). **G~haben** *nt* **-s,-** [credit] balance; (*Kredit*) credit. **g~heißen**† *vt sep* approve of

gütig *a* kind, *adv* -ly

gütlich *a* amicable, *adv* -bly

gut|machen *vt sep* make up for; make good ⟨*Schaden*⟩. **g~mütig** *a* good-natured, *adv* -ly. **G~mütigkeit** *f* - good nature. **G~schein** *m* credit note; (*Bon*) voucher; (*Geschenk-*) gift token. **g~schreiben**† *vt sep* credit. **G~schrift** *f* credit

Guts|haus *nt* manor house. **G~hof** *m* manor

gut|situiert *a* well-to-do. **g~tun**† *vi sep* (*haben*) **jdm/etw g~tun** do s.o./sth good. **g~willig** *a* willing, *adv* -ly

Gymnasium *nt* **-s,-ien** ≈ grammar school

Gymnast|ik *f* - [keep-fit] exercises *pl*; (*Turnen*) gymnastics *sg*. **g~isch** *a* **g~ische Übung** exercise

Gynäko|loge *m* **-n,-n** gynaecologist. **G~logie** *f* - gynaecology. **g~logisch** *a* gynaecological

H

H, h /ha:/ *nt* **-,-** (*Mus*) B, b

Haar *nt* **-[e]s,-e** hair; **sich** (*dat*) **die Haare** *od* **das H~ waschen** wash one's hair; **um ein H~** (*fam*) very nearly. **H~bürste** *f* hairbrush. **h~en** *vi* (*haben*) shed hairs; ⟨*Tier:*⟩ moult ● *vr* **sich h~en** moult. **h~ig** *a* hairy; (*fam*) tricky. **H~klammer, H~klemme** *f* hair-grip. **H~nadel** *f* hairpin. **H~nadelkurve** *f* hairpin bend. **H~schleife** *f* bow. **H~schnitt** *m* haircut. **H~spange** *f* slide. **h~sträubend** *a* hair-raising; (*empörend*) shocking. **H~trockner** *m* **-s,-** hair-drier. **H~waschmittel** *nt* shampoo

Habe *f* - possessions *pl*

haben† *vt* have; **Angst/Hunger/Durst h~** be frightened/hungry/thirsty; **ich hätte gern** I'd like; **sich h~** (*fam*) make a fuss; **es gut/schlecht h~** be well/badly off; **etw gegen jdn h~** have sth against s.o.; **was hat er?** what's the matter with him? ● *v aux* have; **ich habe/hatte geschrieben** I have/had written; **er hätte ihr geholfen** he would have helped her

Habgier *f* greed. **h~ig** *a* greedy
Habicht *m* **-[e]s,-e** hawk
Hab|seligkeiten *fpl* belongings. **H~sucht** *f* = **Habgier**
Hachse *f* **-,-n** (*Culin*) knuckle
Hack|beil *nt* chopper. **H~braten** *m* meat loaf
Hacke[1] *f* **-,-n** hoe; (*Spitz-*) pick
Hacke[2] *f* **-,-n, Hacken** *m* **-s,-** heel
hack|en *vt* hoe; (*schlagen, zerkleinern*) chop; ⟨*Vogel:*⟩ peck; **gehacktes Rindfleisch** minced/(*Amer*) ground beef. **H~fleisch** *nt* mince, (*Amer*) ground meat
Hafen *m* **-s,¨** harbour; (*See-*) port. **H~arbeiter** *m* docker. **H~damm** *m* mole. **H~stadt** *f* port
Hafer *m* **-s** oats *pl*. **H~flocken** *fpl* [rolled] oats. **H~mehl** *nt* oatmeal
Haft *f* **-** (*Jur*) custody; (*H~strafe*) imprisonment. **h~bar** *a* (*Jur*) liable. **H~befehl** *m* warrant [of arrest]
haften *vi* (*haben*) cling; (*kleben*) stick; (*bürgen*) vouch/(*Jur*) be liable (**für** for)
Häftling *m* **-s,-e** detainee
Haftpflicht *f* (*Jur*) liability. **H~versicherung** *f* (*Auto*) third-party insurance
Haftstrafe *f* imprisonment
Haftung *f* **-** (*Jur*) liability
Hagebutte *f* **-,-n** rose-hip
Hagel *m* **-s** hail. **H~korn** *nt* hailstone. **h~n** *vi* (*haben*) hail
hager *a* gaunt
Hahn *m* **-[e]s,¨e** cock; (*Techn*) tap, (*Amer*) faucet
Hähnchen *nt* **-s,-** (*Culin*) chicken
Hai[fisch] *m* **-[e]s,-e** shark
Häkchen *nt* **-s,-** tick
häkel|n *vt/i* (*haben*) crochet. **H~nadel** *f* crochet-hook
Haken *m* **-s,-** hook; (*Häkchen*) tick; (*fam: Schwierigkeit*) snag. **h~** *vt* hook (**an** + *acc* to). **H~kreuz** *nt* swastika. **H~nase** *f* hooked nose
halb *a* half; **eine h~e Stunde** half an hour; **zum h~en Preis** at half price; **auf h~em Weg** half-way ● *adv* half; **h~ drei** half past two; **fünf [Minuten] vor/nach h~ vier** twenty-five [minutes] past three/to four; **h~ und h~** half and half; (*fast ganz*) more or less. **H~blut** *nt* half-breed. **H~dunkel** *nt* semi-darkness. **H~e(r,s)** *f/m/nt* half [a litre]
halber *prep* (+ *gen*) for the sake of; **Geschäfte h~** on business
Halb|finale *nt* semifinal. **H~heit** *f* **-,-en** (*fig*) half-measure
halbieren *vt* halve, divide in half; (*Geom*) bisect
Halb|insel *f* peninsula. **H~kreis** *m* semicircle. **H~kugel** *f* hemisphere. **h~laut** *a* low ● *adv* in an undertone. **h~mast** *adv* at half-mast. **H~messer** *m* **-s,-** radius. **H~mond** *m* half moon. **H~pension** *f* half-board. **h~rund** *a* semicircular. **H~schuh** *m* [flat] shoe. **h~stündlich** *a & adv* half-hourly. **h~tags** *adv* [for] half a day; **h~tags arbeiten** ≈ work part-time. **H~ton** *m* semitone. **h~wegs** *adv* half-way; (*ziemlich*) more or less. **h~wüchsig** *a* adolescent. **H~zeit** *f* (*Sport*) half-time; (*Spielzeit*) half
Halde *f* **-,-n** dump, tip
Hälfte *f* **-,-n** half; **zur H~** half
Halfter[1] *m & nt* **-s,-** halter
Halfter[2] *f* **-,-n** *& nt* **-s,-** holster
Hall *m* **-[e]s,-e** sound
Halle *f* **-,-n** hall; (*Hotel-*) lobby; (*Bahnhofs-*) station concourse
hallen *vi* (*haben*) resound; (*wider-*) echo
Hallen- *pref* indoor
hallo *int* hallo
Halluzination /-ˈt̮si̯oːn/ *f* **-,-en** hallucination
Halm *m* **-[e]s,-e** stalk; (*Gras-*) blade
Hals *m* **-es,¨e** neck; (*Kehle*) throat; **aus vollem H~e** at the top of one's voice; ⟨*lachen*⟩ out loud. **H~ausschnitt** *m* neckline. **H~band** *nt* (*pl* **-bänder**) collar. **H~kette** *f* necklace. **H~schmerzen** *mpl* sore throat *sg*. **h~starrig** *a* stubborn. **H~tuch** *nt* scarf
halt[1] *adv* (*SGer*) just; **es geht h~ nicht** it's just not possible
halt[2] *int* stop! (*Mil*) halt! (*fam*) wait a minute!
Halt *m* **-[e]s,-e** hold; (*Stütze*) support; (*innerer*) stability; (*Anhalten*) stop. **h~bar** *a* durable; (*Tex*) hard-wearing; (*fig*) tenable; **h~bar bis ...** (*Comm*) use by ...
halten† *vt* hold; make ⟨*Rede*⟩; give ⟨*Vortrag*⟩; (*einhalten, bewahren*) keep; **[sich** (*dat*)**] etw h~** keep ⟨*Hund*⟩; take ⟨*Zeitung*⟩; run ⟨*Auto*⟩; **warm h~** keep warm; **h~ für** regard as; **viel/nicht viel h~ von** think highly/little of; **sich h~** hold on (**an** + *dat* to); (*fig*) hold out; ⟨*Geschäft:*⟩ keep going; (*haltbar sein*) keep; ⟨*Wetter:*⟩

hold; ⟨*Blumen:*⟩ last; **sich links h~** keep left; **sich gerade h~** hold oneself upright; **sich h~ an** (+*acc*) (*fig*) keep to ● *vi* (*haben*) hold; (*haltbar sein, bestehen bleiben*) keep; ⟨*Freundschaft, Blumen:*⟩ last; (*haltmachen*) stop; **h~ auf** (+*acc*) (*fig*) set great store by; **auf sich** (*acc*) **h~** take pride in oneself; **an sich** (*acc*) **h~** contain oneself; **zu jdm h~** be loyal to s.o.

Halter *m* **-s,-** holder

Halte|stelle *f* stop. **H~verbot** *nt* waiting restriction; **'H~verbot'** 'no waiting'

halt|los *a* (*fig*) unstable; (*unbegründet*) unfounded. **h~machen** *vi sep* (*haben*) stop

Haltung *f* **-,-en** (*Körper-*) posture; (*Verhalten*) manner; (*Einstellung*) attitude; (*Fassung*) composure; (*Halten*) keeping; **H~ annehmen** (*Mil*) stand to attention

Halunke *m* **-n,-n** scoundrel

Hamburger *m* **-s,-** hamburger

hämisch *a* malicious, *adv* -ly

Hammel *m* **-s,-** ram; (*Culin*) mutton. **H~fleisch** *nt* mutton

Hammer *m* **-s,⸚** hammer

hämmern *vt/i* (*haben*) hammer; ⟨*Herz:*⟩ pound

Hämorrhoiden /hɛmɔroˈiːdən/ *fpl* haemorrhoids

Hamster *m* **-s,-** hamster. **h~n** *vt/i* (*fam*) hoard

Hand *f* **-,⸚e** hand; **jdm die H~ geben** shake hands with s.o.; **rechter/linker H~** on the right/left; **[aus] zweiter H~** second-hand; **unter der H~** unofficially; (*geheim*) secretly; **an H~ von** with the aid of; **H~ und Fuß haben** (*fig*) be sound. **H~arbeit** *f* manual work; (*handwerklich*) handicraft; (*Nadelarbeit*) needlework; (*Gegenstand*) hand-made article. **H~ball** *m* [German] handball. **H~besen** *m* brush. **H~bewegung** *f* gesture. **H~bremse** *f* handbrake. **H~buch** *nt* handbook, manual

Händedruck *m* handshake

Handel *m* **-s** trade, commerce; (*Unternehmen*) business; (*Geschäft*) deal; **H~ treiben** trade. **h~n** *vi* (*haben*) act; (*Handel treiben*) trade (**mit** in); **von etw** *od* **über etw** (*acc*) **h~n** deal with sth; **sich h~n um** be about, concern. **H~smarine** *f* merchant navy. **H~sschiff** *nt* merchant vessel. **H~sschule** *f* commercial college. **h~süblich** *a* customary. **H~sware** *f* merchandise

Hand|feger *m* **-s,-** brush. **H~fertigkeit** *f* dexterity. **h~fest** *a* sturdy; (*fig*) solid. **H~fläche** *f* palm. **h~gearbeitet** *a* hand-made. **H~gelenk** *nt* wrist. **h~gemacht** *a* handmade. **H~gemenge** *nt* **-s,-** scuffle. **H~gepäck** *nt* hand-luggage. **h~geschrieben** *a* hand-written. **H~granate** *f* hand-grenade. **h~greiflich** *a* tangible; **h~greiflich werden** become violent. **H~griff** *m* handle; **mit einem H~griff** with a flick of the wrist

handhaben *vt insep* (*reg*) handle

Handikap /ˈhɛndikɛp/ *nt* **-s,-s** handicap

Hand|kuß *m* kiss on the hand. **H~lauf** *m* handrail

Händler *m* **-s,-** dealer, trader

handlich *a* handy

Handlung *f* **-,-en** act; (*Handeln*) action; (*Roman-*) plot; (*Geschäft*) shop. **H~sweise** *f* conduct

Hand|schellen *fpl* handcuffs. **H~schlag** *m* handshake. **H~schrift** *f* handwriting; (*Text*) manuscript. **H~schuh** *m* glove. **H~schuhfach** *nt* glove compartment. **H~stand** *m* handstand. **H~tasche** *f* handbag. **H~tuch** *nt* towel. **H~voll** *f* **-,-** handful

Handwerk *nt* craft, trade; **sein H~ verstehen** know one's job. **H~er** *m* **-s,-** craftsman; (*Arbeiter*) workman

Hanf *m* **-[e]s** hemp

Hang *m* **-[e]s,⸚e** slope; (*fig*) inclination, tendency

Hänge|brücke *f* suspension bridge. **H~lampe** *f* [light] pendant. **H~matte** *f* hammock

hängen[1] *vt* (*reg*) hang

hängen[2]† *vi* (*haben*) hang; **h~ an** (+*dat*) (*fig*) be attached to. **h~bleiben**† *vi sep* (*sein*) stick (**an** + *dat* to); ⟨*Kleid:*⟩ catch (**an** + *dat* on). **h~lassen**† *vt sep* leave; **den Kopf h~lassen** be downcast

Hannover *nt* **-s** Hanover

hänseln *vt* tease

hantieren *vi* (*haben*) busy oneself

hapern *vi* (*haben*) **es hapert** there's a lack (**an** + *dat* of)

Happen *m* **-s,-** mouthful; **einen H~ essen** have a bite to eat

Harfe *f* **-,-n** harp

Harke *f* **-,-n** rake. **h~n** *vt/i* (*haben*) rake

harmlos *a* harmless; (*arglos*) innocent, *adv* -ly. **H~igkeit** *f* - harmlessness; innocence
Harmonie *f* -,-n harmony. **h~ren** *vi* (*haben*) harmonize; (*gut auskommen*) get on well
Harmonika *f* -,-s accordion; (*Mund-*) mouth-organ
harmonisch *a* harmonious, *adv* -ly
Harn *m* **-[e]s** urine. **H~blase** *f* bladder
Harpune *f* **-,-n** harpoon
hart (**härter, härtest**) *a* hard; (*heftig*) violent; (*streng*) harsh ● *adv* hard; (*streng*) harshly
Härte *f* **-,-n** hardness; (*Strenge*) harshness; (*Not*) hardship. **h~n** *vt* harden
Hart|faserplatte *f* hardboard. **h~gekocht** *a* hard-boiled. **h~herzig** *a* hard-hearted. **h~näckig** *a* stubborn, *adv* -ly; (*ausdauernd*) persistent, *adv* -ly. **H~näckigkeit** *f* - stubbornness; persistence
Harz *nt* **-es,-e** resin
Haschee *nt* **-s,-s** (*Culin*) hash
haschen *vi* (*haben*) **h~ nach** try to catch
Haschisch *nt & m* **-[s]** hashish
Hase *m* **-n,-n** hare; **falscher H~** meat loaf
Hasel *f* **-,-n** hazel. **H~maus** *f* dormouse. **H~nuß** *f* hazel-nut
Hasenfuß *m* (*fam*) coward
Haß *m* **-sses** hatred
hassen *vt* hate
häßlich *a* ugly; (*unfreundlich*) nasty, *adv* -ily. **H~keit** *f* - ugliness; nastiness
Hast *f* - haste. **h~en** *vi* (*sein*) hasten, hurry. **h~ig** *a* hasty, *adv* -ily, hurried, *adv* -ly
hast, hat, hatte, hätte *s.* **haben**
Haube *f* **-,-n** cap; (*Trocken-*) drier; (*Kühler-*) bonnet, (*Amer*) hood
Hauch *m* **-[e]s** breath; (*Luft-*) breeze; (*Duft*) whiff; (*Spur*) tinge. **h~dünn** *a* very thin; ⟨*Strümpfe*⟩ sheer. **h~en** *vt/i* (*haben*) breathe
Haue *f* **-,-n** pick; (*fam: Prügel*) beating. **h~n**† *vt* beat; (*hämmern*) knock; (*meißeln*) hew; **sich h~n** fight; **übers Ohr h~n** (*fam*) cheat ● *vi* (*haben*) bang (**auf** + *acc* on); **jdm ins Gesicht h~n** hit s.o. in the face
Haufen *m* **-s,-** heap, pile; (*Leute*) crowd
häufen *vt* heap *or* pile [up]; **sich h~** pile up; (*zunehmen*) increase
haufenweise *adv* in large numbers; **h~ Geld** pots of money
häufig *a* frequent, *adv* -ly. **H~keit** *f* - frequency
Haupt *nt* **-[e]s, Häupter** head. **H~bahnhof** *m* main station. **H~darsteller** *m*, **H~darstellerin** *f* male/female lead. **H~fach** *nt* main subject. **H~gericht** *nt* main course. **H~hahn** *m* mains tap; (*Wasser-*) stopcock
Häuptling *m* **-s,-e** chief
Haupt|mahlzeit *f* main meal. **H~mann** *m* (*pl* **-leute**) captain. **H~person** *f* most important person; (*Theat*) principal character. **H~post** *f* main post office. **H~quartier** *nt* headquarters *pl.* **H~rolle** *f* lead; (*fig*) leading role. **H~sache** *f* main thing; **in der H~sache** in the main. **h~sächlich** *a* main, *adv* -ly. **H~satz** *m* main clause. **H~schlüssel** *m* master key. **H~stadt** *f* capital. **H~straße** *f* main street. **H~verkehrsstraße** *f* main road. **H~verkehrszeit** *f* rush-hour. **H~wort** *nt* (*pl* **-wörter**) noun
Haus *nt* **-es, Häuser** house; (*Gebäude*) building; (*Schnecken-*) shell; **zu H~e** at home; **nach H~e** home. **H~angestellte(r)** *m/f* domestic servant. **H~arbeit** *f* housework; (*Sch*) homework. **H~arzt** *m* family doctor. **H~aufgaben** *fpl* homework *sg.* **H~besetzer** *m* **-s,-** squatter. **H~besuch** *m* house-call
hausen *vi* (*haben*) live; (*wüten*) wreak havoc
Haus|frau *f* housewife. **H~gehilfin** *f* domestic help. **h~gemacht** *a* home-made. **H~halt** *m* **-[e]s,-e** household; (*Pol*) budget. **h~halten**† *vi sep* (*haben*) **h~halten mit** manage carefully; conserve ⟨*Kraft*⟩. **H~hälterin** *f* **-,-nen** housekeeper. **H~haltsgeld** *nt* housekeeping [money]. **H~haltsplan** *m* budget. **H~herr** *m* head of the household; (*Gastgeber*) host. **h~hoch** *a* huge; (*fam*) big ● *adv* (*fam*) vastly; (*verlieren*) by a wide margin
hausier|en *vi* (*haben*) **h~en mit** hawk. **H~er** *m* **-s,-** hawker
Hauslehrer *m* [private] tutor. **H~in** *f* governess
häuslich *a* domestic; ⟨*Person*⟩ domesticated
Haus|meister *m* caretaker. **H~nummer** *f* house number. **H~ordnung** *f*

house rules *pl.* **H~putz** *m* cleaning. **H~rat** *m* **-[e]s** household effects *pl.* **H~schlüssel** *m* front-door key. **H~schuh** *m* slipper. **H~stand** *m* household. **H~suchung** *f* [police] search. **H~suchungsbefehl** *m* search-warrant. **H~tier** *nt* domestic animal; (*Hund, Katze*) pet. **H~tür** *f* front door. **H~wart** *m* **-[e]s,-e** caretaker. **H~wirt** *m* landlord. **H~wirtin** *f* landlady

Haut *f* **-, Häute** skin; (*Tier-*) hide; **aus der H~ fahren** (*fam*) fly off the handle. **H~arzt** *m* dermatologist

häuten *vt* skin; **sich h~** moult

haut|eng *a* skin-tight. **H~farbe** *f* colour; (*Teint*) complexion

Haxe *f* **-,-n** = **Hachse**

Hbf. *abbr s.* **Hauptbahnhof**

Hebamme *f* **-,-n** midwife

Hebel *m* **-s,-** lever. **H~kraft, H~wirkung** *f* leverage

heben† *vt* lift; (*hoch-, steigern*) raise; **sich h~** rise; ⟨*Nebel:*⟩ lift; (*sich verbessern*) improve

hebräisch *a* Hebrew

hecheln *vi* (*haben*) pant

Hecht *m* **-[e]s,-e** pike

Heck *nt* **-s,-s** (*Naut*) stern; (*Aviat*) tail; (*Auto*) rear

Hecke *f* **-,-n** hedge. **H~nschütze** *m* sniper

Heck|fenster *nt* rear window. **H~motor** *m* rear engine. **H~tür** *f* hatchback

Heer *nt* **-[e]s,-e** army

Hefe *f* **-** yeast. **H~teig** *m* yeast dough. **H~teilchen** *nt* Danish pastry

Heft[1] *nt* **-[e]s,-e** haft, handle

Heft[2] *nt* **-[e]s,-e** booklet; (*Sch*) exercise book; (*Zeitschrift*) issue. **h~en** *vt* (*nähen*) tack; (*stecken*) pin/(*klammern*) clip/(*mit Heftmaschine*) staple (**an** + *acc* to). **H~er** *m* **-s,-** file

heftig *a* fierce, *adv* -ly, violent, *adv* -ly; ⟨*Schlag, Regen*⟩ heavy, *adv* -ily; ⟨*Schmerz, Gefühl*⟩ intense, *adv* -ly; ⟨*Person*⟩ quick-tempered. **H~keit** *f* **-** fierceness, violence; intensity

Heft|klammer *f* staple; (*Büro-*) paper-clip. **H~maschine** *f* stapler. **H~pflaster** *nt* sticking plaster. **H~zwecke** *f* **-,-n** drawing-pin

hegen *vt* care for; (*fig*) cherish ⟨*Hoffnung*⟩; harbour ⟨*Verdacht*⟩

Hehl *nt & m* **kein[en] H~ machen aus** make no secret of. **H~er** *m* **-s,-** receiver, fence

Heide[1] *m* **-n,-n** heathen

Heide[2] *f* **-,-n** heath; (*Bot*) heather. **H~kraut** *nt* heather

Heidelbeere *f* bilberry, (*Amer*) blueberry

Heid|in *f* **-,-nen** heathen. **h~nisch** *a* heathen

heikel *a* difficult, tricky; (*delikat*) delicate; (*dial*) ⟨*Person*⟩ fussy

heil *a* undamaged, intact; ⟨*Person*⟩ unhurt; (*gesund*) well; **mit h~er Haut** (*fam*) unscathed

Heil *nt* **-s** salvation; **sein H~ versuchen** try one's luck

Heiland *m* **-s** (*Relig*) Saviour

Heil|anstalt *f* sanatorium; (*Nerven-*) mental hospital. **H~bad** *nt* spa. **h~bar** *a* curable

Heilbutt *m* **-[e]s,-e** halibut

heilen *vt* cure; heal ⟨*Wunde*⟩ ● *vi* (*sein*) heal

heilfroh *a* (*fam*) very relieved

Heilgymnastik *f* physiotherapy

heilig *a* holy; (*geweiht*) sacred; **der H~e Abend** Christmas Eve; **die h~e Anna** Saint Anne. **H~abend** *m* Christmas Eve. **H~e(r)** *m/f* saint. **h~en** *vt* keep, observe. **H~enschein** *m* halo. **h~halten†** *vt sep* hold sacred; keep ⟨*Feiertag*⟩. **H~keit** *f* **-** sanctity, holiness. **h~sprechen†** *vt sep* canonize. **H~tum** *nt* **-s,¨er** shrine

heil|kräftig *a* medicinal. **H~kräuter** *ntpl* medicinal herbs. **h~los** *a* unholy. **H~mittel** *nt* remedy. **H~praktiker** *m* **-s,-** practitioner of alternative medicine. **h~sam** *a* (*fig*) salutary. **H~sarmee** *f* Salvation Army. **H~ung** *f* **-** cure

Heim *nt* **-[e]s,-e** home; (*Studenten-*) hostel. **h~** *adv* home

Heimat *f* **-,-en** home; (*Land*) native land. **H~abend** *m* folk evening. **h~los** *a* homeless. **H~stadt** *f* home town

heim|begleiten *vt sep* see home. **h~bringen†** *vt sep* bring home; (*begleiten*) see home. **H~computer** *m* home computer. **h~fahren†** *v sep* ● *vi* (*sein*) go/drive home ● *vt* take/drive home. **H~fahrt** *f* way home. **h~gehen†** *vi sep* (*sein*) go home; (*sterben*) die

heimisch *a* native, indigenous; (*Pol*) domestic; **h~ sein/sich h~ fühlen** be/feel at home

Heim|kehr *f* **-** return [home]. **h~kehren** *vi sep* (*sein*) return home.

h~kommen† *vi sep* (*sein*) come home

heimlich *a* secret, *adv* -ly. **H~keit** *f* **-,-en** secrecy; **H~keiten** secrets. **H~tuerei** *f* - secretiveness

Heim|reise *f* journey home. **h~reisen** *vi sep* (*sein*) go home. **H~spiel** *nt* home game. **h~suchen** *vt sep* afflict. **h~tückisch** *a* treacherous; ⟨*Krankheit*⟩ insidious. **h~wärts** *adv* home. **H~weg** *m* way home. **H~weh** *nt* **-s** homesickness; **H~weh haben** be homesick. **H~werker** *m* **-s,-** [home] handyman. **h~zahlen** *vt sep* **jdm etw h~zahlen** (*fig*) pay s.o. back for sth

Heirat *f* **-,-en** marriage. **h~en** *vt/i* (*haben*) marry. **H~santrag** *m* proposal; **jdm einen H~santrag machen** propose to s.o. **h~sfähig** *a* marriageable

heiser *a* hoarse, *adv* -ly. **H~keit** *f* - hoarseness

heiß *a* hot, *adv* -ly; (*hitzig*) heated; (*leidenschaftlich*) fervent, *adv* -ly; **mir ist h~** I am hot

heißen† *vi* (*haben*) be called; (*bedeuten*) mean; **ich heiße ...** my name is ...; **wie h~ Sie?** what is your name? **wie heißt ... auf englisch?** what's the English for ... ? **es heißt** it says; (*man sagt*) it is said; **das heißt** that is [to say]; **was soll das h~?** what does it mean? (*empört*) what is the meaning of this? ● *vt* call; **jdn etw tun h~** tell s.o. to do sth

heiß|geliebt *a* beloved. **h~hungrig** *a* ravenous. **H~wasserbereiter** *m* **-s,-** water heater

heiter *a* cheerful, *adv* -ly; ⟨*Wetter*⟩ bright; (*amüsant*) amusing; **aus h~em Himmel** (*fig*) out of the blue. **H~keit** *f* - cheerfulness; (*Gelächter*) mirth

Heiz|anlage *f* heating; (*Auto*) heater. **H~decke** *f* electric blanket. **h~en** *vt* heat; light ⟨*Ofen*⟩ ● *vi* (*haben*) put the heating on; ⟨*Ofen:*⟩ give out heat. **H~gerät** *nt* heater. **H~kessel** *m* boiler. **H~körper** *m* radiator. **H~lüfter** *m* **-s,-** fan heater. **H~material** *nt* fuel. **H~ofen** *m* heater. **H~ung** *f* **-,-en** heating; (*Heizkörper*) radiator

Hektar *nt* & *m* **-s,-** hectare

hektisch *a* hectic

Held *m* **-en,-en** hero. **h~enhaft** *a* heroic, *adv* -ally. **H~enmut** *m* heroism. **h~enmütig** *a* heroic, *adv* -ally. **H~entum** *nt* **-s** heroism. **H~in** *f* **-,-nen** heroine

helf|en† *vi* (*haben*) help (**jdm** s.o.); (*nützen*) be effective; **sich** (*dat*) **nicht zu h~en wissen** not know what to do; **es hilft nichts** it's no use. **H~er(in)** *m* **-s,-** (*f* **-,-nen**) helper, assistant. **H~ershelfer** *m* accomplice

hell *a* light; (*Licht ausstrahlend, klug*) bright; ⟨*Stimme*⟩ clear; (*fam: völlig*) utter; **h~es Bier** ≈ lager ● *adv* brightly; **h~ begeistert** absolutely delighted. **h~hörig** *a* poorly soundproofed; **h~hörig werden** (*fig*) sit up and take notice

hellicht *a* **h~er Tag** broad daylight

Hell|igkeit *f* - brightness. **H~seher(in)** *m* **-s,-** (*f* **-,-nen**) clairvoyant. **h~wach** *a* wide awake

Helm *m* **-[e]s,-e** helmet

Hemd *nt* **-[e]s,-en** vest, (*Amer*) undershirt; (*Ober-*) shirt. **H~bluse** *f* shirt

Hemisphäre *f* **-,-n** hemisphere

hemm|en *vt* check; (*verzögern*) impede; (*fig*) inhibit. **H~ung** *f* **-,-en** (*fig*) inhibition; (*Skrupel*) scruple; **H~ungen haben** be inhibited. **h~ungslos** *a* unrestrained, *adv* -ly

Hendl *nt* **-s,-[n]** (*Aust*) chicken

Hengst *m* **-[e]s,-e** stallion. **H~fohlen** *nt* colt

Henkel *m* **-s,-** handle

henken *vt* hang

Henne *f* **-,-n** hen

her *adv* here; (*zeitlich*) ago; **her mit ...!** give me ...! **von oben/unten/Norden/weit her** from above/below/the north/far away; **vor/hinter jdm/etw her** in front of/behind s.o./sth; **von der Farbe/vom Thema her** as far as the colour/subject is concerned

herab *adv* down [here]; **von oben h~** from above; (*fig*) condescending, *adv* -ly. **h~blicken** *vi sep* (*haben*) = **h~sehen**

herablass|en† *vt sep* let down; **sich h~en** condescend (**zu** to). **h~end** *a* condescending, *adv* -ly. **H~ung** *f* - condescension

herab|sehen† *vi sep* (*haben*) look down (**auf** + *acc* on). **h~setzen** *vt sep* reduce, cut; (*fig*) belittle. **h~setzend** *a* disparaging, *adv* -ly. **h~würdigen** *vt sep* belittle, disparage

Heraldik *f* - heraldry

heran *adv* near; **[bis] h~ an** (+*acc*) up to. **h~bilden** *vt sep* train. **h~gehen**† *vi sep* (*sein*) **h~gehen an**

(+*acc*) go up to; get down to ⟨*Arbeit*⟩. **h~kommen**† *vi sep* (*sein*) approach; **h~kommen an** (+*acc*) come up to; (*erreichen*) get at; (*fig*) measure up to. **h~machen (sich)** *vr sep* **sich h~machen an** (+*acc*) approach; get down to ⟨*Arbeit*⟩. **h~reichen** *vi sep* (*haben*) **h~reichen an** (+*acc*) reach; (*fig*) measure up to. **h~wachsen**† *vi sep* (*sein*) grow up. **h~ziehen**† *v sep* ● *vt* pull up (**an**+*acc* to); (*züchten*) raise; (*h~bilden*) train; (*hinzuziehen*) call in ● *vi* (*sein*) approach

herauf *adv* up [here]; **die Treppe h~** up the stairs. **h~beschwören** *vt sep* evoke; (*verursachen*) cause. **h~kommen**† *vi sep* (*sein*) come up. **h~setzen** *vt sep* raise, increase

heraus *adv* out (**aus** of); **h~ damit** *od* **mit der Sprache!** out with it! **h~bekommen**† *vt sep* get out; (*ausfindig machen*) find out; (*lösen*) solve; **Geld h~bekommen** get change. **h~bringen**† *vt sep* bring out; (*fam*) get out. **h~finden**† *v sep* ● *vt* find out ● *vi* (*haben*) find one's way out. **H~forderer** *m* **-s,-** challenger. **h~fordern** *vt sep* provoke; challenge ⟨*Person*⟩. **H~forderung** *f* provocation; challenge. **H~gabe** *f* handing over; (*Admin*) issue; (*Veröffentlichung*) publication. **h~geben**† *vt sep* hand over; (*Admin*) issue; (*veröffentlichen*) publish; edit ⟨*Zeitschrift*⟩; **jdm Geld h~geben** give s.o. change ● *vi* (*haben*) give change (**auf**+*acc* for). **H~geber** *m* **-s,-** publisher; editor. **h~gehen**† *vi sep* (*sein*) ⟨*Fleck:*⟩ come out; **aus sich h~gehen** (*fig*) come out of one's shell. **h~halten**† **(sich)** *vr sep* (*fig*) keep out (**aus** of). **h~holen** *vt sep* get out. **h~kommen**† *vi sep* (*sein*) come out; (*aus Schwierigkeit, Takt*) get out; **auf eins** *od* **dasselbe h~kommen** (*fam*) come to the same thing. **h~lassen**† *vt sep* let out. **h~machen** *vt sep* get out; **sich gut h~machen** (*fig*) do well. **h~nehmen**† *vt sep* take out; **sich zuviel h~nehmen** (*fig*) take liberties. **h~platzen** *vi sep* (*haben*) (*fam*) burst out laughing. **h~putzen (sich)** *vr sep* doll oneself up. **h~ragen** *vi sep* (*haben*) jut out; (*fig*) stand out. **h~reden (sich)** *vr sep* make excuses. **h~rücken** *v sep* ● *vt* move out; (*hergeben*) hand over ● *vi* (*sein*) **h~rücken mit** hand over; (*fig: sagen*) come out with. **h~rutschen** *vi sep* (*sein*) slip out. **h~schlagen**† *vt sep* knock out; (*fig*) gain. **h~stellen** *vt sep* put out; **sich h~stellen** turn out (**als** to be; **daß** that). **h~suchen** *vt sep* pick out. **h~ziehen**† *vt sep* pull out

herb *a* sharp; ⟨*Wein*⟩ dry; ⟨*Landschaft*⟩ austere; (*fig*) harsh

herbei *adv* here. **h~führen** *vt sep* (*fig*) bring about. **h~lassen**† **(sich)** *vr sep* condescend (**zu** to). **h~schaffen** *vt sep* get. **h~sehnen** *vt sep* long for

Herberg|e *f* **-,-n** [youth] hostel; (*Unterkunft*) lodging. **H~svater** *m* warden

herbestellen *vt sep* summon

herbitten† *vt sep* ask to come

herbringen† *vt sep* bring [here]

Herbst *m* **-[e]s,-e** autumn. **h~lich** *a* autumnal

Herd *m* **-[e]s,-e** stove, cooker; (*fig*) focus

Herde *f* **-,-n** herd; (*Schaf-*) flock

herein *adv* in [here]; **h~!** come in! **h~bitten**† *vt sep* ask in. **h~brechen**† *vi sep* (*sein*) burst in; (*fig*) set in; ⟨*Nacht:*⟩ fall; **h~brechen über** (+*acc*) (*fig*) overtake. **h~fallen**† *vi sep* (*sein*) (*fam*) be taken in (**auf** +*acc* by). **h~kommen**† *vi sep* (*sein*) come in. **h~lassen**† *vt sep* let in. **h~legen** *vt sep* (*fam*) take for a ride. **h~rufen**† *vt sep* call in

Herfahrt *f* journey/drive here

herfallen† *vi sep* (*sein*) **h~ über** (+*acc*) attack; fall upon ⟨*Essen*⟩

hergeben† *vt sep* hand over; (*fig*) give up; **sich h~ zu** (*fig*) be a party to

hergebracht *a* traditional

hergehen† *vi sep* (*sein*) **h~ vor/neben/hinter** (+*dat*) walk along in front of/beside/behind; **es ging lustig her** (*fam*) there was a lot of merriment

herhalten† *vi sep* (*haben*) hold out; **h~ müssen** be the one to suffer

herholen *vt sep* fetch; **weit hergeholt** (*fig*) far-fetched

Hering *m* **-s,-e** herring; (*Zeltpflock*) tent-peg

her|kommen† *vi sep* (*sein*) come here; **wo kommt das her?** where does it come from? **h~kömmlich** *a* traditional. **H~kunft** *f* **-** origin

herlaufen† *vi sep* (*sein*) **h~ vor/neben/hinter** (+*dat*) run/(*gehen*) walk along in front of/beside/behind

herleiten *vt sep* derive

hermachen *vt sep* **viel/wenig h~** be impressive/unimpressive; (*wichtig nehmen*) make a lot of/little fuss (**von** of); **sich h~ über** (+*acc*) fall upon; tackle ⟨*Arbeit*⟩

Hermelin[1] *nt* **-s,-e** (*Zool*) stoat

Hermelin[2] *m* **-s,-e** (*Pelz*) ermine

hermetisch *a* hermetic, *adv* -ally

Hernie /'hɛrni̯ə/ *f* **-,-n** hernia

Heroin *nt* **-s** heroin

heroisch *a* heroic, *adv* -ally

Herr *m* **-n,-en** gentleman; (*Gebieter*) master (**über**+*acc* of); **[Gott,] der H~** the Lord [God]; **H~ Meier** Mr Meier; **Sehr geehrte H~en** Dear Sirs. **H~chen** *nt* **-s,-** master. **H~enhaus** *nt* manor [house]. **h~enlos** *a* ownerless; ⟨*Tier*⟩ stray. **H~ensitz** *m* manor

Herrgott *m* **der H~** the Lord; **H~ [noch mal]!** damn it!

herrichten *vt sep* prepare; **wieder h~** renovate

Herrin *f* **-,-nen** mistress

herrisch *a* imperious, *adv* -ly; ⟨*Ton*⟩ peremptory; (*herrschsüchtig*) overbearing

herrlich *a* marvellous, *adv* -ly; (*großartig*) magnificent, *adv* -ly. **H~keit** *f* **-,-en** splendour

Herrschaft *f* **-,-en** rule; (*Macht*) power; (*Kontrolle*) control; **meine H~en!** ladies and gentlemen!

herrsch|en *vi* (*haben*) rule; (*verbreitet sein*) prevail; **es h~te Stille/ große Aufregung** there was silence/ great excitement. **H~er(in)** *m* **-s,-** (*f* **-,-nen**) ruler. **h~süchtig** *a* domineering

herrühren *vi sep* (*haben*) stem (**von** from)

hersein† *vi sep* (*sein*) come (**von** from); **h~ hinter** (+*dat*) be after; **es ist schon lange/drei Tage her** it was a long time/three days ago

herstammen *vi sep* (*haben*) come (**aus/von** from)

herstell|en *vt sep* establish; (*Comm*) manufacture, make. **H~er** *m* **-s,-** manufacturer, maker. **H~ung** *f* **-** establishment; manufacture

herüber *adv* over [here]. **h~kommen**† *vi sep* (*sein*) come over [here]

herum *adv* **im Kreis h~** [round] in a circle; **falsch h~** the wrong way round; **um ... h~** round ...; (*ungefähr*) [round] about ... **h~albern** *vi sep* (*haben*) fool around. **h~drehen** *vt sep* turn round/(*wenden*) over; turn ⟨*Schlüssel*⟩; **sich h~drehen** turn round/over. **h~gehen**† *vi sep* (*sein*) walk around; ⟨*Zeit:*⟩ pass; **h~gehen um** go round. **h~kommen**† *vi sep* (*sein*) get about; **h~kommen um** get round; come round ⟨*Ecke*⟩; **um etw [nicht] h~kommen** (*fig*) [not] get out of sth. **h~kriegen** *vt sep* **jdn h~kriegen** (*fam*) talk s.o. round. **h~liegen**† *vi sep* (*sein*) lie around. **h~lungern** *vi sep* (*haben*) loiter. **h~schnüffeln** *vi sep* (*haben*) (*fam*) nose about. **h~sitzen**† *vi sep* (*haben*) sit around; **h~sitzen um** sit round. **h~sprechen**† **(sich)** *vr sep* ⟨*Gerücht:*⟩ get about. **h~stehen**† *vi sep* (*haben*) stand around; **h~stehen um** stand round. **h~treiben**† **(sich)** *vr sep* hang around. **h~ziehen**† *vi sep* (*sein*) move around; (*ziellos*) wander about

herunter *adv* down [here]; **die Treppe h~** down the stairs. **h~fallen**† *vi* fall off. **h~gehen**† *vi sep* (*sein*) come down; (*sinken*) go/come down. **h~gekommen** *a* (*fig*) rundown; ⟨*Gebäude*⟩ dilapidated; ⟨*Person*⟩ down-at-heel. **h~kommen**† *vi sep* (*sein*) come down; (*fig*) go to rack and ruin; ⟨*Firma, Person:*⟩ go downhill; (*gesundheitlich*) get run down. **h~lassen**† *vt sep* let down, lower. **h~machen** *vt sep* (*fam*) reprimand; (*herabsetzen*) run down. **h~spielen** *vt sep* (*fig*) play down. **h~ziehen**† *vt sep* pull down

hervor *adv* out (**aus** of). **h~bringen**† *vt sep* produce; utter ⟨*Wort*⟩. **h~gehen**† *vi sep* (*sein*) come/(*sich ergeben*) emerge/(*folgen*) follow (**aus** from). **h~heben**† *vt sep* (*fig*) stress, emphasize. **h~quellen**† *vi sep* (*sein*) stream out; (*h~treten*) bulge. **h~ragen** *vi sep* (*haben*) jut out; (*fig*) stand out. **h~ragend** *a* (*fig*) outstanding. **h~rufen**† *vt sep* (*fig*) cause. **h~stehen**† *vi sep* (*haben*) protrude. **h~treten**† *vi sep* (*sein*) protrude, bulge; (*fig*) stand out. **h~tun**† **(sich)** *vr sep* (*fig*) distinguish oneself; (*angeben*) show off

Herweg *m* way here

Herz *nt* **-ens,-en** heart; (*Kartenspiel*) hearts *pl*; **sich** (*dat*) **ein H~ fassen** pluck up courage. **H~anfall** *m* heart attack

herzeigen *vt sep* show

herz|en *vt* hug. **H~enslust** *f* **nach H~enslust** to one's heart's content. **h~haft** *a* hearty, *adv* -ily; (*würzig*) savoury

herziehen† *v sep* ● *vt* **hinter sich** (*dat*) **h~** pull along [behind one] ● *vi* (*sein*) **hinter jdm h~** follow along behind s.o.; **über jdn h~** (*fam*) run s.o. down

herz|ig *a* sweet, adorable. **H~infarkt** *m* heart attack. **H~klopfen** *nt* **-s** palpitations *pl*; **ich hatte H~klopfen** my heart was pounding

herzlich *a* cordial, *adv* -ly; (*warm*) warm, *adv* -ly; (*aufrichtig*) sincere, *adv* -ly; **h~en Dank!** many thanks! **h~e Grüße** kind regards; **h~ wenig** precious little. **H~keit** *f* - cordiality; warmth; sincerity

herzlos *a* heartless

Herzog *m* **-s,¨e** duke. **H~in** *f* **-,-nen** duchess. **H~tum** *nt* **-s,¨er** duchy

Herz|schlag *m* heartbeat; (*Med*) heart failure. **h~zerreißend** *a* heart-breaking

Hessen *nt* **-s** Hesse

heterosexuell *a* heterosexual

Hetze *f* - rush; (*Kampagne*) virulent campaign (**gegen** against). **h~n** *vt* chase; **sich h~n** hurry ● *vi* (*haben*) agitate; (*sich beeilen*) hurry ● *vi* (*sein*) rush

Heu *nt* **-s** hay; **Geld wie Heu haben** (*fam*) have pots of money

Heuchelei *f* - hypocrisy

heuch|eln *vt* feign ● *vi* (*haben*) pretend. **H~ler(in)** *m* **-s,-** (*f* **-,-nen**) hypocrite. **h~lerisch** *a* hypocritical, *adv* -ly

heuer *adv* (*Aust*) this year

Heuer *f* **-,-n** (*Naut*) pay. **h~n** *vt* hire; sign on ⟨*Matrosen*⟩

heulen *vi* (*haben*) howl; (*fam: weinen*) cry; ⟨*Sirene:*⟩ wail

Heurige(r) *m* (*Aust*) new wine

Heu|schnupfen *m* hay fever. **H~schober** *m* **-s,-** haystack. **H~schrecke** *f* **-,-n** grasshopper; (*Wander-*) locust

heut|e *adv* today; (*heutzutage*) nowadays; **h~e früh** *od* **morgen** this morning; **von h~e auf morgen** from one day to the next. **h~ig** *a* today's ...; (*gegenwärtig*) present; **der h~ige Tag** today. **h~zutage** *adv* nowadays

Hexe *f* **-,-n** witch. **h~n** *vi* (*haben*) work magic; **ich kann nicht h~n** (*fam*) I can't perform miracles. **H~njagd** *f* witch-hunt. **H~nschuß** *m* lumbago. **H~rei** *f* - witchcraft

Hieb *m* **-[e]s,-e** blow; (*Peitschen-*) lash; **H~e** hiding *sg*

hier *adv* here; **h~ und da** here and there; (*zeitlich*) now and again

Hierarchie /hi̯erar'çi:/ *f* **-,-n** hierarchy

hier|auf *adv* on this/these; (*antworten*) to this; (*zeitlich*) after this. **h~aus** *adv* out of *or* from this/these. **h~behalten**† *vt sep* keep here. **h~bleiben**† *vi sep* (*sein*) stay here. **h~durch** *adv* through this/these; (*Ursache*) as a result of this. **h~für** *adv* for this/these. **h~her** *adv* here. **h~hin** *adv* here. **h~in** *adv* in this/these. **h~lassen**† *vt sep* leave here. **h~mit** *adv* with this/these; (*Comm*) herewith; (*Admin*) hereby. **h~nach** *adv* after this/these; (*demgemäß*) according to this/these. **h~sein**† *vi sep* (*sein*) be here. **h~über** *adv* over/(*höher*) above this/these; ⟨*sprechen, streiten*⟩ about this/these. **h~unter** *adv* under/(*tiefer*) below this/these; (*dazwischen*) among these. **h~von** *adv* from this/these; (*h~über*) about this/these; (*Menge*) of this/these. **h~zu** *adv* to this/these; (*h~für*) for this/these. **h~zulande** *adv* here

hiesig *a* local. **H~e(r)** *m*/*f* local

Hilf|e *f* **-,-n** help, aid; **um H~e rufen** call for help; **jdm zu H~e kommen** come to s.o.'s aid. **h~los** *a* helpless, *adv* -ly. **H~losigkeit** *f* - helplessness. **h~reich** *a* helpful

Hilfs|arbeiter *m* unskilled labourer. **h~bedürftig** *a* needy; **h~bedürftig sein** be in need of help. **h~bereit** *a* helpful, *adv* -ly. **H~kraft** *f* helper. **H~mittel** *nt* aid. **H~verb, H~zeitwort** *nt* auxiliary verb

Himbeere *f* raspberry

Himmel *m* **-s,-** sky; (*Relig & fig*) heaven; (*Bett-*) canopy; **am H~** in the sky; **unter freiem H~** in the open air. **H~bett** *nt* four-poster [bed]. **H~fahrt** *f* Ascension; **Mariä H~fahrt** Assumption. **h~schreiend** *a* scandalous. **H~srichtung** *f* compass point; **in alle H~srichtungen** in all directions. **h~weit** *a* (*fam*) vast

himmlisch *a* heavenly

hin *adv* there; **hin und her** to and fro; **hin und zurück** there and back; (*Rail*) return; **hin und wieder** now and again; **an** (+*dat*) **... hin** along; **auf** (+*acc*) **... hin** in reply to ⟨*Brief,*

Anzeige⟩; on ⟨*jds Rat*⟩; **zu** *od* **nach ... hin** towards; **vor sich hin reden** talk to oneself

hinab *adv* down [there]

hinauf *adv* up [there]; **die Treppe/Straße h~** up the stairs/road. **h~gehen**† *vi sep* (*sein*) go up. **h~setzen** *vt sep* raise

hinaus *adv* out [there]; (*nach draußen*) outside; **zur Tür h~** out of the door; **auf Jahre h~** for years to come; **über etw** (*acc*) **h~** beyond sth; (*Menge*) [over and] above sth. **h~fliegen**† *v sep* ● *vi* (*sein*) fly out; (*fam*) get the sack ● *vt* fly out. **h~gehen**† *vi sep* (*sein*) go out; ⟨*Zimmer:*⟩ face (**nach Norden** north); **h~gehen über** (+*acc*) go beyond, exceed. **h~kommen**† *vi sep* (*sein*) get out; **h~kommen über** (+*acc*) get beyond. **h~laufen**† *vi sep* (*sein*) run out; **h~laufen auf** (+*acc*) (*fig*) amount to. **h~lehnen (sich)** *vr sep* lean out. **h~ragen** *vi sep* (*haben*) **h~ragen über** (+*acc*) project beyond; (*in der Höhe*) rise above; (*fig*) stand out above. **h~schicken** *vt sep* send out. **h~schieben**† *vt sep* push out; (*fig*) put off. **h~sehen**† *vi sep* (*haben*) look out. **h~sein**† *vi sep* (*sein*) **über etw** (*acc*) **h~sein** (*fig*) be past sth. **h~werfen**† *vt sep* throw out; (*fam: entlassen*) fire. **h~wollen**† *vi sep* (*haben*) want to go out; **h~wollen auf** (+*acc*) (*fig*) aim at; **hoch h~wollen** (*fig*) be ambitious. **h~ziehen**† *v sep* ● *vt* pull out; (*in die Länge ziehen*) drag out; (*verzögern*) delay; **sich h~ziehen** drag on; be delayed ● *vi* (*sein*) move out. **h~zögern** *vt* delay; **sich h~zögern** be delayed

Hinblick *m* **im H~ auf** (+*acc*) in view of; (*hinsichtlich*) regarding

hinbringen† *vt sep* take there; (*verbringen*) spend

hinder|lich *a* awkward; **jdm h~lich sein** hamper s.o. **h~n** *vt* hamper; (*verhindern*) prevent. **H~nis** *nt* **-ses,-se** obstacle. **H~nisrennen** *nt* steeplechase

hindeuten *vi sep* (*haben*) point (**auf**+*acc* to)

Hindu *m* **-s,-s** Hindu. **H~ismus** *m* - Hinduism

hindurch *adv* through it/them; **den Sommer h~** throughout the summer

hinein *adv* in [there]; (*nach drinnen*) inside; **h~ in** (+*acc*) into. **h~fallen**† *vi sep* (*sein*) fall in. **h~gehen**† *vi sep* (*sein*) go in, **h~gehen in** (+*acc*) go into. **h~laufen**† *vi sep* (*sein*) run in; **h~laufen in** (+*acc*) run into. **h~reden** *vi sep* (*haben*) **jdm h~reden** interrupt s.o.; (*sich einmischen*) interfere in s.o.'s affairs. **h~versetzen (sich)** *vr sep* **sich in jds Lage h~versetzen** put oneself in s.o.'s position. **h~ziehen**† *vt sep* pull in; **h~ziehen in** (+*acc*) pull into; **in etw** (*acc*) **h~gezogen werden** (*fig*) become involved in sth

hin|fahren† *v sep* ● *vi* (*sein*) go/drive there ● *vt* take/drive there. **H~fahrt** *f* journey/drive there; (*Rail*) outward journey. **h~fallen**† *vi sep* (*sein*) fall. **h~fällig** *a* (*gebrechlich*) frail; (*ungültig*) invalid. **h~fliegen**† *v sep* ● *vi* (*sein*) fly there; (*fam*) fall ● *vt* fly there. **H~flug** *m* flight there; (*Admin*) outward flight. **H~gabe** *f* - devotion; (*Eifer*) dedication

hingeb|en† *vt sep* give up; **sich h~en** (*fig*) devote oneself (**einer Aufgabe** to a task); abandon oneself (**dem Vergnügen** to pleasure). **H~ung** *f* - devotion. **h~ungsvoll** *a* devoted, *adv* -ly

hingegen *adv* on the other hand

hingehen† *vi sep* (*sein*) go/(*zu Fuß*) walk there; (*vergehen*) pass; **h~ zu** go up to; **wo gehst du hin?** where are you going? **etw h~ lassen** (*fig*) let sth pass

hingerissen *a* rapt, *adv* -ly; **h~ sein** be carried away (**von** by)

hin|halten† *vt sep* hold out; (*warten lassen*) keep waiting. **h~hocken (sich)** *vr sep* squat down. **h~kauern (sich)** *vr sep* crouch down

hinken *vi* (*haben/sein*) limp

hin|knien (sich) *vr sep* kneel down. **h~kommen**† *vi sep* (*sein*) get there; (*h~gehören*) belong, go; (*fam: auskommen*) manage (**mit** with); (*fam: stimmen*) be right. **h~länglich** *a* adequate, *adv* -ly. **h~laufen**† *vi sep* (*sein*) run/(*gehen*) walk there. **h~legen** *vt sep* lay *or* put down; **sich h~legen** lie down. **h~nehmen**† *vt sep* (*fig*) accept

hinreichen *v sep* ● *vt* hand (*dat* to) ● *vi* (*haben*) extend (**bis** to); (*ausreichen*) be adequate. **h~d** *a* adequate, *adv* -ly

Hinreise *f* journey there; (*Rail*) outward journey
hinreißen† *vt sep* (*fig*) carry away; **sich h~ lassen** get carried away. **h~d** *a* ravishing, *adv* -ly
hinricht|en *vt sep* execute. **H~ung** *f* execution
hinschicken *vt sep* send there
hinschleppen *vt sep* drag there; (*fig*) drag out; **sich h~** drag oneself along; (*fig*) drag on
hinschreiben† *vt sep* write there; (*aufschreiben*) write down
hinsehen† *vi sep* (*haben*) look
hinsein† *vi sep* (*sein*) (*fam*) be gone; (*kaputt, tot*) have had it; **[ganz] h~ von** be overwhelmed by; **es ist noch/nicht mehr lange hin** it's a long time yet/not long to go
hinsetzen *vt sep* put down; **sich h~** sit down
Hinsicht *f* - **in dieser/gewisser H~** in this respect/in a certain sense; **in finanzieller H~** financially. **h~lich** *prep* (+*gen*) regarding
hinstellen *vt sep* put *or* set down; park ⟨*Auto*⟩; (*fig*) make out (**als** to be); **sich h~** stand
hinstrecken *vt sep* hold out; **sich h~** extend
hintan|setzen, h~stellen *vt sep* ignore; (*vernachlässigen*) neglect
hinten *adv* at the back; **dort h~** back there; **nach/von h~** to the back/from behind. **h~herum** *adv* round the back; (*fam*) by devious means; ⟨*erfahren*⟩ in a roundabout way
hinter *prep* (+*dat/acc*) behind; (*nach*) after; **h~ jdm/etw herlaufen** run after s.o./sth; **h~ etw** (*dat*) **stecken** (*fig*) be behind sth; **h~ etw** (*acc*) **kommen** (*fig*) get to the bottom of sth; **etw h~ sich** (*acc*) **bringen** get sth over [and done] with. **H~bein** *nt* hind leg
Hinterbliebene *pl* (*Admin*) surviving dependants; **die H~n** the bereaved family *sg*
hinterbringen† *vt* tell (**jdm** s.o.)
hintere|(r,s) *a* back, rear; **h~s Ende** far end
hintereinander *adv* one behind/(*zeitlich*) after the other; **dreimal h~** three times in succession/(*fam*) in a row
Hintergedanke *m* ulterior motive
hintergehen† *vt* deceive
Hinter|grund *m* background. **H~halt** *m* -[e]s,-e ambush; **aus dem H~halt überfallen** ambush. **h~hältig** *a* underhand
hinterher *adv* behind, after; (*zeitlich*) afterwards. **h~gehen**† *vi sep* (*sein*) follow (**jdm** s.o.). **h~kommen**† *vi sep* (*sein*) follow [behind]. **h~laufen**† *vi sep* (*sein*) run after (**jdm** s.o.)
Hinter|hof *m* back yard. **H~kopf** *m* back of the head
hinterlassen† *vt* leave [behind]; (*Jur*) leave, bequeath (*dat* to). **H~schaft** *f* -,-en (*Jur*) estate
hinterlegen *vt* deposit
Hinter|leib *m* (*Zool*) abdomen. **H~list** *f* deceit. **h~listig** *a* deceitful, *adv* -ly. **h~m** *prep* = **hinter dem. H~mann** *m* (*pl* **-männer**) person behind. **h~n** *prep* = **hinter den. H~n** *m* **-s,-** (*fam*) bottom, backside. **H~rad** *nt* rear *or* back wheel. **h~rücks** *adv* from behind. **h~s** *prep* = **hinter das. h~ste(r,s)** *a* last; **h~ste Reihe** back row. **H~teil** *nt* (*fam*) behind
hintertreiben† *vt* (*fig*) block
Hinter|treppe *f* back stairs *pl*. **H~tür** *f* back door; (*fig*) loophole
hinterziehen† *vt* (*Admin*) evade
Hinterzimmer *nt* back room
hinüber *adv* over *or* across [there]. **h~gehen**† *vi sep* (*sein*) go over *or* across; **h~gehen über** (+*acc*) cross
hinunter *adv* down [there]; **die Treppe/Straße h~** down the stairs/road. **h~gehen**† *vi sep* (*sein*) go down. **h~schlucken** *vt sep* swallow
Hinweg *m* way there
hinweg *adv* away, off; **h~ über** (+*acc*) over; **über eine Zeit h~** over a period. **h~gehen**† *vi sep* (*sein*) **h~gehen über** (+*acc*) (*fig*) pass over. **h~kommen**† *vi sep* (*sein*) **h~kommen über** (+*acc*) (*fig*) get over. **h~sehen**† *vi sep* (*haben*) **h~sehen über** (+*acc*) see over; (*fig*) overlook. **h~setzen (sich)** *vr sep* **sich h~setzen über** (+*acc*) ignore
Hinweis *m* **-es,-e** reference; (*Andeutung*) hint; (*Anzeichen*) indication; **unter H~ auf** (+*acc*) with reference to. **h~en**† *v sep* ● *vi* (*haben*) point (**auf** + *acc* to) ● *vt* **jdn auf etw** (*acc*) **h~en** point sth out to s.o. **h~end** *a* (*Gram*) demonstrative
hin|wenden† *vt sep* turn; **sich h~wenden** turn (**zu** to). **h~werfen**† *vt sep* throw down; drop ⟨*Bemerkung*⟩; (*schreiben*) jot down; (*zeichnen*) sketch; (*fam: aufgeben*) pack in
hinwieder *adv* on the other hand

hin|zeigen *vi sep* (*haben*) point (**auf** + *acc* to). **h~ziehen**† *vt sep* pull; (*fig: in die Länge ziehen*) drag out; (*verzögern*) delay; **sich h~ziehen** drag on; be delayed; **sich h~gezogen fühlen zu** (*fig*) feel drawn to

hinzu *adv* in addition. **h~fügen** *vt sep* add. **h~kommen**† *vi sep* (*sein*) be added; (*ankommen*) arrive [on the scene]; join (**zu jdm** s.o.). **h~rechnen** *vt sep* add. **h~ziehen**† *vt sep* call in

Hiobsbotschaft *f* bad news *sg*

Hirn *nt* **-s** brain; (*Culin*) brains *pl*. **H~gespinst** *nt* **-[e]s,-e** figment of the imagination. **H~hautentzündung** *f* meningitis. **h~verbrannt** *a* (*fam*) crazy

Hirsch *m* **-[e]s,-e** deer; (*männlich*) stag; (*Culin*) venison

Hirse *f* - millet

Hirt *m* **-en,-en, Hirte** *m* **-n,-n** shepherd

hissen *vt* hoist

Histor|iker *m* **-s,-** historian. **h~isch** *a* historical; (*bedeutend*) historic

Hit *m* **-s,-s** (*Mus*) hit

Hitz|e *f* - heat. **H~ewelle** *f* heat wave. **h~ig** *a* (*fig*) heated, *adv* -ly; ⟨*Person*⟩ hot-headed; (*jähzornig*) hot-tempered. **H~kopf** *m* hothead. **H~schlag** *m* heat-stroke

H-Milch /'ha:-/ *f* long-life milk

Hobby *nt* **-s,-s** hobby

Hobel *m* **-s,-** (*Techn*) plane; (*Culin*) slicer. **h~n** *vt/i* (*haben*) plane. **H~späne** *mpl* shavings

hoch *a* (**höher, höchst**; *attrib* **hohe(r,s)**) high; ⟨*Baum, Mast*⟩ tall; ⟨*Offizier*⟩ high-ranking; ⟨*Alter*⟩ great; ⟨*Summe*⟩ large; ⟨*Strafe*⟩ heavy; **hohe Schuhe** ankle boots • *adv* high; (*sehr*) highly; **die Treppe/den Berg h~** up the stairs/hill; **sechs Mann h~** six of us/them. **H~** *nt* **-s,-s** cheer; (*Meteorol*) high

Hoch|achtung *f* high esteem. **H~achtungsvoll** *adv* Yours faithfully. **H~amt** *nt* High Mass. **h~arbeiten (sich)** *vr sep* work one's way up. **h~begabt** *attrib a* highly gifted. **H~betrieb** *m* great activity; **in den Geschäften herrscht H~betrieb** the shops are terribly busy. **H~burg** *f* (*fig*) stronghold. **H~deutsch** *nt* High German. **H~druck** *m* high pressure. **H~ebene** *f* plateau. **h~fahren**† *vi sep* (*sein*) go up; (*auffahren*) start up; (*aufbrausen*) flare up. **h~fliegend** *a* (*fig*) ambitious. **h~gehen**† *vi sep* (*sein*) go up; (*explodieren*) blow up; (*aufbrausen*) flare up. **h~gestellt** *attrib a* high-ranking; ⟨*Zahl*⟩ superior. **h~gewachsen** *a* tall. **H~glanz** *m* high gloss. **h~gradig** *a* extreme, *adv* -ly. **h~hackig** *a* high-heeled. **h~halten**† *vt sep* hold up; (*fig*) uphold. **H~haus** *nt* high-rise building. **h~heben**† *vt sep* lift up; raise ⟨*Kopf, Hand*⟩. **h~herzig** *a* magnanimous, *adv* -ly. **h~kant** *adv* on end. **h~kommen**† *vi sep* (*sein*) come up; (*aufstehen*) get up; (*fig*) get on [in the world]. **H~konjunktur** *f* boom. **h~krempeln** *vt sep* roll up. **h~leben** *vi sep* (*haben*) **h~leben lassen** give three cheers for; **... lebe hoch!** three cheers for ... ! **H~mut** *m* pride, arrogance. **h~mütig** *a* arrogant, *adv* -ly. **h~näsig** *a* (*fam*) snooty. **h~nehmen**† *vt sep* pick up; (*fam*) tease. **H~ofen** *m* blast-furnace. **h~ragen** *vi sep* rise [up]; ⟨*Turm:*⟩ soar. **H~ruf** *m* cheer. **H~saison** *f* high season. **H~schätzung** *f* high esteem. **h~schlagen**† *vt sep* turn up ⟨*Kragen*⟩. **h~schrecken**† *vi sep* (*sein*) start up. **H~schule** *f* university; (*Musik-, Kunst-*) academy. **h~sehen**† *vi sep* (*haben*) look up. **H~sommer** *m* midsummer. **H~spannung** *f* high/(*fig*) great tension. **h~spielen** *vt sep* (*fig*) magnify. **H~sprache** *f* standard language. **H~sprung** *m* high jump

höchst *adv* extremely, most

Hochstapler *m* **-s,-** confidence trickster

höchst|e(r,s) *a* highest; ⟨*Baum, Turm*⟩ tallest; (*oberste, größte*) top; **es ist h~e Zeit** it is high time. **h~ens** *adv* at most; (*es sei denn*) except perhaps. **H~fall** *m* **im H~fall** at most. **H~geschwindigkeit** *f* top *or* maximum speed. **H~maß** *nt* maximum. **h~persönlich** *adv* in person. **H~preis** *m* top price. **H~temperatur** *f* maximum temperature. **h~wahrscheinlich** *adv* most probably

hoch|trabend *a* pompous, *adv* -ly. **h~treiben**† *vt sep* push up ⟨*Preis*⟩. **H~verrat** *m* high treason. **H~wasser** *nt* high tide; (*Überschwemmung*) floods *pl*. **H~würden** *m* **-s** Reverend; (*Anrede*) Father

Hochzeit *f* **-,-en** wedding; **H~ feiern** get married. **H~skleid** *nt* wedding dress. **H~sreise** *f* honeymoon [trip]. **H~stag** *m* wedding day/(*Jahrestag*) anniversary

hochziehen† *vt sep* pull up; (*hissen*) hoist; raise ⟨*Augenbrauen*⟩

Hocke *f* - **in der H~ sitzen** squat; **in die H~ gehen** squat down. **h~n** *vi* (*haben*) squat ● *vr* **sich h~n** squat down

Hocker *m* **-s,-** stool

Höcker *m* **-s,-** bump; (*Kamel-*) hump

Hockey /'hɔki/ *nt* **-s** hockey

Hode *f* **-,-n, Hoden** *m* **-s,-** testicle

Hof *m* **-[e]s,⸚e** [court]yard; (*Bauern-*) farm; (*Königs-*) court; (*Schul-*) playground; (*Astr*) halo

hoffen *vt/i* (*haben*) hope (**auf** + *acc* for). **h~tlich** *adv* I hope, let us hope; (*als Antwort*) **h~tlich/h~tlich nicht** let's hope so/not

Hoffnung *f* **-,-en** hope. **h~slos** *a* hopeless, *adv* -ly. **h~svoll** *a* hopeful, *adv* -ly

höflich *a* polite, *adv* -ly, courteous, *adv* -ly. **H~keit** *f* **-,-en** politeness, courtesy; (*Äußerung*) civility

hohe(r,s) *a s.* **hoch**

Höhe *f* **-,-n** height; (*Aviat, Geog*) altitude; (*Niveau*) level; (*einer Summe*) size; (*An-*) hill; **in die H~ gehen** rise, go up; **nicht auf der H~** (*fam*) under the weather; **das ist die H~!** (*fam*) that's the limit!

Hoheit *f* **-,-en** (*Staats-*) sovereignty; (*Titel*) Highness. **H~sgebiet** *nt* [sovereign] territory. **H~szeichen** *nt* national emblem

Höhe|nlinie *f* contour line. **H~nsonne** *f* sun-lamp. **H~nzug** *m* mountain range. **H~punkt** *m* (*fig*) climax, peak; (*einer Vorstellung*) highlight. **h~r** *a* & *adv* higher; **h~re Schule** secondary school

hohl *a* hollow; (*leer*) empty

Höhle *f* **-,-n** cave; (*Tier-*) den; (*Hohlraum*) cavity; (*Augen-*) socket

Hohl|maß *nt* measure of capacity. **H~raum** *m* cavity

Hohn *m* **-s** scorn, derision

höhn|en *vt* deride ● *vi* (*haben*) jeer. **h~isch** *a* scornful, *adv* -ly

holen *vt* fetch, get; (*kaufen*) buy; (*nehmen*) take (**aus** from); **h~ lassen** send for; **[tief] Atem** *od* **Luft h~** take a [deep] breath; **sich** (*dat*) **etw h~** get sth; catch ⟨*Erkältung*⟩

Holland *nt* **-s** Holland

Holländ|er *m* **-s,-** Dutchman; **die H~er** the Dutch *pl.* **H~erin** *f* **-,-nen** Dutchwoman. **h~isch** *a* Dutch

Höll|e *f* - hell. **h~isch** *a* infernal; (*schrecklich*) terrible, *adv* -bly

holpern *vi* (*sein*) jolt *or* bump along ● *vi* (*haben*) be bumpy

holp[e]rig *a* bumpy

Holunder *m* **-s** (*Bot*) elder

Holz *nt* **-es,⸚er** wood; (*Nutz-*) timber. **H~blasinstrument** *nt* woodwind instrument

hölzern *a* wooden

Holz|hammer *m* mallet. **h~ig** *a* woody. **H~kohle** *f* charcoal. **H~schnitt** *m* woodcut. **H~schuh** *m* [wooden] clog. **H~wolle** *f* wood shavings *pl.* **H~wurm** *m* woodworm

homogen *a* homogeneous

Homöopathie *f* - homoeopathy

homosexuell *a* homosexual. **H~e(r)** *m/f* homosexual

Honig *m* **-s** honey. **H~wabe** *f* honeycomb

Hono|rar *nt* **-s,-e** fee. **h~rieren** *vt* remunerate; (*fig*) reward

Hopfen *m* **-s** hops *pl*; (*Bot*) hop

hopsen *vi* (*sein*) jump

Hör|apparat *m* hearing-aid. **h~bar** *a* audible, *adv* -bly

horchen *vi* (*haben*) listen (**auf** + *acc* to); (*heimlich*) eavesdrop

Horde *f* **-,-n** horde; (*Gestell*) rack

hören *vt* hear; (*an-*) listen to ● *vi* (*haben*) hear; (*horchen*) listen; (*gehorchen*) obey; **h~ auf** (+ *acc*) listen to. **H~sagen** *nt* **vom H~sagen** from hearsay

Hör|er *m* **-s,-** listener; (*Teleph*) receiver. **H~funk** *m* radio. **H~gerät** *nt* hearing-aid

Horizon|t *m* **-[e]s** horizon. **h~tal** *a* horizontal, *adv* -ly

Hormon *nt* **-s,-e** hormone

Horn *nt* **-s,⸚er** horn. **H~haut** *f* hard skin; (*Augen-*) cornea

Hornisse *f* **-,-n** hornet

Horoskop *nt* **-[e]s,-e** horoscope

Hörrohr *nt* stethoscope

Horrorfilm *m* horror film

Hör|saal *m* (*Univ*) lecture hall. **H~spiel** *nt* radio play

Hort *m* **-[e]s,-e** (*Schatz*) hoard; (*fig*) refuge. **h~en** *vt* hoard

Hortensie /-i̯ə/ *f* **-,-n** hydrangea

Hörweite *f* **in/außer H~** within/out of earshot

Hose *f* **-,-n, Hosen** *pl* trousers *pl.* **H~nrock** *m* culottes *pl.* **H~nschlitz**

m fly, flies *pl.* **H~nträger** *mpl* braces, (*Amer*) suspenders

Hostess, Hosteß *f* **-,-tessen** hostess; (*Aviat*) air hostess

Hostie /'hɔstiə/ *f* **-,-n** (*Relig*) host

Hotel *nt* **-s,-s** hotel; **H~ garni** /gar'ni:/ bed-and-breakfast hotel. **H~ier** /-'lie:/ *m* **-s,-s** hotelier

hübsch *a* pretty, *adv* -ily; (*nett*) nice, *adv* -ly; ⟨*Summe*⟩ tidy

Hubschrauber *m* **-s,-** helicopter

huckepack *adv* **jdn h~ tragen** give s.o. a piggyback

Huf *m* **-[e]s,-e** hoof. **H~eisen** *nt* horseshoe

Hüft|e *f* **-,-n** hip. **H~gürtel, H~halter** *m* **-s,-** girdle

Hügel *m* **-s,-** hill. **h~ig** *a* hilly

Huhn *nt* **-s,¨er** chicken; (*Henne*) hen

Hühn|chen *nt* **-s,-** chicken. **H~erauge** *nt* corn. **H~erbrühe** *f* chicken broth. **H~erstall** *m* henhouse, chicken-coop

huldig|en *vi* (*haben*) pay homage (*dat* to). **H~ung** *f* **-** homage

Hülle *f* **-,-n** cover; (*Verpackung*) wrapping; (*Platten-*) sleeve; **in H~ und Fülle** in abundance. **h~n** *vt* wrap

Hülse *f* **-,-n** (*Bot*) pod; (*Etui*) case. **H~nfrüchte** *fpl* pulses

human *a* humane, *adv* -ly. **h~itär** *a* humanitarian. **H~ität** *f* **-** humanity

Hummel *f* **-,-n** bumble-bee

Hummer *m* **-s,-** lobster

Hum|or *m* **-s** humour; **H~or haben** have a sense of humour. **h~oristisch** *a* humorous. **h~orvoll** *a* humorous, *adv* -ly

humpeln *vi* (*sein/haben*) hobble

Humpen *m* **-s,-** tankard

Hund *m* **-[e]s,-e** dog; (*Jagd-*) hound. **H~ehalsband** *nt* dog-collar. **H~ehütte** *f* kennel. **H~eleine** *f* dog lead

hundert *inv a* one/a hundred. **H~** *nt* **-s,-e** hundred; **H~e von** hundreds of. **H~jahrfeier** *f* centenary, (*Amer*) centennial. **h~prozentig** *a & adv* one hundred per cent. **h~ste(r,s)** *a* hundredth. **H~stel** *nt* **-s,-** hundredth

Hündin *f* **-,-nen** bitch

Hüne *m* **-n,-n** giant

Hunger *m* **-s** hunger; **H~ haben** be hungry. **h~n** *vi* (*haben*) starve; **h~n nach** (*fig*) hunger for. **H~snot** *f* famine

hungrig *a* hungry, *adv* -ily

Hupe *f* **-,-n** (*Auto*) horn. **h~n** *vi* (*haben*) sound one's horn

hüpf|en *vi* (*sein*) skip; ⟨*Vogel, Frosch:*⟩ hop; ⟨*Grashüpfer:*⟩ jump. **H~er** *m* **-s,-** skip, hop

Hürde *f* **-,-n** (*Sport & fig*) hurdle; (*Schaf-*) pen, fold

Hure *f* **-,-n** whore

hurra *int* hurray. **H~** *nt* **-s,-s** hurray; (*Beifallsruf*) cheer

Husche *f* **-,-n** [short] shower. **h~n** *vi* (*sein*) slip; ⟨*Eidechse:*⟩ dart; ⟨*Maus:*⟩ scurry; ⟨*Lächeln:*⟩ flit

hüsteln *vi* (*haben*) give a slight cough

husten *vi* (*haben*) cough. **H~** *m* **-s** cough. **H~saft** *m* cough mixture

Hut[1] *m* **-[e]s,¨e** hat; (*Pilz-*) cap

Hut[2] *f* **- auf der H~ sein** be on one's guard (**vor** + *dat* against)

hüten *vt* watch over; tend ⟨*Tiere*⟩; (*aufpassen*) look after; **das Bett h~ müssen** be confined to bed; **sich h~** be on one's guard (**vor** + *dat* against); **sich h~, etw zu tun** take care not to do sth

Hütte *f* **-,-n** hut; (*Hunde-*) kennel; (*Techn*) iron and steel works. **H~nkäse** *m* cottage cheese. **H~nkunde** *f* metallurgy

Hyäne *f* **-,-n** hyena

Hybride *f* **-,-n** hybrid

Hydrant *m* **-en,-en** hydrant

hydraulisch *a* hydraulic, *adv* -ally

hydroelektrisch /hydroˀe'lɛktrɪʃ/ *a* hydroelectric

Hygien|e /hy'gie:nə/ *f* **-** hygiene. **h~isch** *a* hygienic, *adv* -ally

hypermodern *a* ultra-modern

Hypno|se *f* **-** hypnosis. **h~tisch** *a* hypnotic. **H~tiseur** /-'zø:ɐ/ *m* **-s,-e** hypnotist. **h~tisieren** *vt* hypnotize

Hypochonder /hypo'xɔndɐ/ *m* **-s,-** hypochondriac

Hypothek *f* **-,-en** mortgage

Hypothe|se *f* **-,-n** hypothesis. **h~tisch** *a* hypothetical, *adv* -ly

Hys|terie *f* **-** hysteria. **h~terisch** *a* hysterical, *adv* -ly

I

ich *pron* I; **ich bin's** it's me. **Ich** *nt* **-[s],-[s]** self; (*Psych*) ego

IC-Zug /i'tse:-/ *m* inter-city train

ideal *a* ideal. **I~** *nt* **-s,-e** ideal. **i~isieren** *vt* idealize. **I~ismus** *m* **-** idealism. **I~ist(in)** *m* **-en,-en** (*f* **-,-nen**) idealist. **i~istisch** *a* idealistic

Idee *f* **-,-n** idea; **fixe I~** obsession; **eine I~** (*fam: wenig*) a tiny bit
identifizieren *vt* identify
identi|sch *a* identical. **I~tät** *f* **-,-en** identity
Ideo|logie *f* **-,-n** ideology. **i~logisch** *a* ideological
idiomatisch *a* idiomatic
Idiot *m* **-en,-en** idiot. **i~isch** *a* idiotic, *adv* -ally
Idol *nt* **-s,-e** idol
idyllisch /iˈdʏlɪʃ/ *a* idyllic
Igel *m* **-s,-** hedgehog
ignorieren *vt* ignore
ihm *pron* (*dat of* **er, es**) [to] him; (*Ding, Tier*) [to] it; **Freunde von ihm** friends of his
ihn *pron* (*acc of* **er**) him; (*Ding, Tier*) it. **i~en** *pron* (*dat of* **sie** *pl*) [to] them; **Freunde von i~en** friends of theirs. **I~en** *pron* (*dat of* **Sie**) [to] you; **Freunde von I~en** friends of yours
ihr *pron* (*2nd pers pl*) you ● (*dat of* **sie** *sg*) [to] her; (*Ding, Tier*) [to] it; **Freunde von ihr** friends of hers ● *poss pron* her; (*Ding, Tier*) its; (*pl*) their. **Ihr** *poss pron* your. **i~e(r,s)** *poss pron* hers; (*pl*) theirs. **I~e(r,s)** *poss pron* yours. **i~erseits** *adv* for her/(*pl*) their part. **I~erseits** *adv* on your part. **i~etwegen** *adv* for her/(*Ding, Tier*) its/(*pl*) their sake; (*wegen*) because of her/it/them, on her/its/their account. **I~etwegen** *adv* for your sake; (*wegen*) because of you, on your account. **i~etwillen** *adv* **um i~etwillen** for her/(*Ding, Tier*) its/(*pl*) their sake. **I~etwillen** *adv* **um I~etwillen** for your sake. **i~ige** *poss pron* **der/die/das i~ige** hers; (*pl*) theirs. **I~ige** *poss pron* **der/die/das I~ige** yours. **i~s** *poss pron* hers; (*pl*) theirs. **I~s** *poss pron* yours
Ikone *f* **-,-n** icon
illegal *a* illegal, *adv* -ly
Illus|ion *f* **-,-en** illusion; **sich** (*dat*) **I~ionen machen** delude oneself. **i~orisch** *a* illusory
Illustr|ation /-ˈt̮si̯o:n/ *f* **-,-en** illustration. **i~ieren** *vt* illustrate. **I~ierte** *f* **-n,-[n]** [illustrated] magazine
Iltis *m* **-ses,-se** polecat
im *prep* = **in dem; im Mai** in May; **im Kino** at the cinema
Image /ˈɪmɪdʒ/ *nt* **-[s],-s** /-ɪs/ [public] image
Imbiß *m* snack. **I~halle, I~stube** *f* snack-bar
Imit|ation /-ˈt̮si̯o:n/ *f* **-,-en** imitation. **i~ieren** *vt* imitate
Imker *m* **-s,-** bee-keeper
Immatrikul|ation /-ˈt̮si̯o:n/ *f* - (*Univ*) enrolment. **i~ieren** *vt* (*Univ*) enrol; **sich i~ieren** enrol
immer *adv* always; **für i~** for ever; (*endgültig*) for good; **i~ noch** still; **i~ mehr/weniger/wieder** more and more/less and less/again and again; **wer/was [auch] i~** whoever/whatever. **i~fort** *adv* = **i~zu. i~grün** *a* evergreen. **i~hin** *adv* (*wenigstens*) at least; (*trotzdem*) all the same; (*schließlich*) after all. **i~zu** *adv* all the time
Immobilien /-i̯ən/ *pl* real estate *sg*. **I~händler, I~makler** *m* estate agent, (*Amer*) realtor
immun *a* immune (**gegen** to). **i~isieren** *vt* immunize. **I~ität** *f* - immunity
Imperativ *m* **-s,-e** imperative
Imperfekt *nt* **-s,-e** imperfect
Imperialismus *m* - imperialism
impf|en *vt* vaccinate, inoculate. **I~stoff** *m* vaccine. **I~ung** *f* **-,-en** vaccination, inoculation
Implantat *nt* **-[e]s,-e** implant
imponieren *vi* (*haben*) impress (**jdm** s.o.)
Impor|t *m* **-[e]s,-e** import. **I~teur** /-ˈtø:ɐ̯/ *m* **-s,-e** importer. **i~tieren** *vt* import
imposant *a* imposing
impoten|t *a* (*Med*) impotent. **I~z** *f* - (*Med*) impotence
imprägnieren *vt* waterproof
Impressionismus *m* - impressionism
improvisieren *vt/i* (*haben*) improvise
Impuls *m* **-es,-e** impulse. **i~iv** *a* impulsive, *adv* -ly
imstande *pred a* able (**zu** to); capable (**etw zu tun** of doing sth)
in *prep* (+*dat*) in; (+*acc*) into, in; (*bei Bus, Zug*) on; **in der Schule/Oper** at school/the opera; **in die Schule** to school ● *a* **in sein** be in
Inbegriff *m* embodiment. **i~en** *pred a* included
Inbrunst *f* - fervour
inbrünstig *a* fervent, *adv* -ly
indem *conj* (*während*) while; (*dadurch*) by (+-ing)
Inder(in) *m* **-s,-** (*f* **-,-nen**) Indian
indessen *conj* while ● *adv* (*unterdessen*) meanwhile; (*jedoch*) however

Indian *m* **-s,-e** (*Aust*) turkey
Indianer(in) *m* **-s,-** (*f* **-,-nen**) (American) Indian. **i~isch** *a* Indian
Indien /'ɪndi̯ən/ *nt* **-s** India
indigniert *a* indignant, *adv* -ly
Indikativ *m* **-s,-e** indicative
indirekt *a* indirect, *adv* -ly
indisch *a* Indian
indiskre|t *a* indiscreet. **I~tion** /-'t͡si̯o:n/ *f* **-,-en** indiscretion
indiskutabel *a* out of the question
indisponiert *a* indisposed
Individu|alist *m* **-en,-en** individualist. **I~alität** *f* **-** individuality. **i~ell** *a* individual, *adv* -ly. **I~um** /-'vi:duʊm/ *nt* **-s,-duen** individual
Indizienbeweis /ɪn'di:t͡si̯ən-/ *m* circumstantial evidence
indoktrinieren *vt* indoctrinate
industr|ialisiert *a* industrialized. **I~ie** *f* **-,-n** industry. **i~iell** *a* industrial. **I~ielle(r)** *m* industrialist
ineinander *adv* in/into one another
Infanterie *f* **-** infantry
Infektion /-'t͡si̯o:n/ *f* **-,-en** infection. **I~skrankheit** *f* infectious disease
Infinitiv *m* **-s,-e** infinitive
infizieren *vt* infect; **sich i~** become/ ⟨*Person:*⟩ be infected
Inflation /-'t͡si̯o:n/ *f* **-** inflation. **i~är** *a* inflationary
infolge *prep* (+*gen*) as a result of. **i~dessen** *adv* consequently
Inform|atik *f* **-** information science. **I~ation** /-'t͡si̯o:n/ *f* **-,-en** information; **I~ationen** information *sg*. **i~ieren** *vt* inform; **sich i~ieren** find out (**über**+*acc* about)
infrarot *a* infra-red
Ingenieur /ɪnʒe'ni̯ø:ɐ̯/ *m* **-s,-e** engineer
Ingwer *m* **-s** ginger
Inhaber(in) *m* **-s,-** (*f* **-,-nen**) holder; (*Besitzer*) proprietor; (*Scheck-*) bearer
inhaftieren *vt* take into custody
inhalieren *vt/i* (*haben*) inhale
Inhalt *m* **-[e]s,-e** contents *pl*; (*Bedeutung, Gehalt*) content; (*Geschichte*) story. **I~sangabe** *f* summary. **I~sverzeichnis** *nt* list/(*in Buch*) table of contents
Initiale /-'t͡si̯a:lə/ *f* **-,-n** initial
Initiative /init͡si̯a'ti:və/ *f* **-,-n** initiative
Injektion /-'t͡si̯o:n/ *f* **-,-en** injection. **injizieren** *vt* inject
inklusive *prep* (+*gen*) including • *adv* inclusive
inkognito *adv* incognito
inkonsequen|t *a* inconsistent, *adv* -ly. **I~z** *f* **-,-en** inconsistency
inkorrekt *a* incorrect, *adv* -ly
Inkubationszeit /-'t͡si̯o:ns-/ *f* (*Med*) incubation period
Inland *nt* **-[e]s** home country; (*Binnenland*) interior. **I~sgespräch** *nt* inland call
inmitten *prep* (+*gen*) in the middle of; (*unter*) amongst • *adv* **i~ von** amongst, amidst
inne|haben† *vt sep* hold, have. **i~halten**† *vi sep* (*haben*) pause
innen *adv* inside; **nach i~** inwards. **I~architekt(in)** *m(f)* interior designer. **I~minister** *m* Minister of the Interior; (*in UK*) Home Secretary. **I~politik** *f* domestic policy. **I~stadt** *f* town centre
inner|e(r,s) *a* inner; (*Med, Pol*) internal. **I~e(s)** *nt* interior; (*Mitte*) centre; (*fig: Seele*) inner being. **I~eien** *fpl* (*Culin*) offal *sg*. **i~halb** *prep* (+*gen*) inside; (*zeitlich & fig*) within; (*während*) during • *adv* **i~halb von** within. **i~lich** *a* internal; (*seelisch*) inner; (*besinnlich*) introspective • *adv* internally; (*im Inneren*) inwardly. **i~ste(r,s)** innermost; **im I~sten** (*fig*) deep down
innig *a* sincere, *adv* -ly; (*tief*) deep, *adv* -ly; (*eng*) intimate, *adv* -ly
Innung *f* **-,-en** guild
inoffiziell *a* unofficial, *adv* -ly
ins *prep* = **in das; ins Kino/Büro** to the cinema/office
Insasse *m* **-n,-n** inmate; (*im Auto*) occupant; (*Passagier*) passenger
insbesondere *adv* especially
Inschrift *f* inscription
Insekt *nt* **-[e]s,-en** insect. **I~envertilgungsmittel** *nt* insecticide
Insel *f* **-,-n** island
Inser|at *nt* **-[e]s,-e** [newspaper] advertisement. **I~ent** *m* **-en,-en** advertiser. **I~ieren** *vt/i* (*haben*) advertise
insge|heim *adv* secretly. **i~samt** *adv* [all] in all
Insignien /-i̯ən/ *pl* insignia
insofern, insoweit *adv* /-'zo:-/ in this respect; **i~ als** in as much as • *conj* /-zo'fɛrn, -'vai̯t/ **i~ als** in so far as
Insp|ektion /ɪnspɛk't͡si̯o:n/ *f* **-,-en** inspection. **I~ektor** *m* **-en,-en** /-'to:rən/ inspector
Inspir|ation /ɪnspira't͡si̯o:n/ *f* **-,-en** inspiration. **i~ieren** *vt* inspire
inspizieren /-sp-/ *vt* inspect

Install|ateur /ɪnstala'tøːɐ̯/ *m* **-s,-e** fitter; (*Klempner*) plumber. **i~ieren** *vt* install

instand *adv* **i~ halten** maintain; (*pflegen*) look after; **i~ setzen** restore; (*reparieren*) repair. **I~haltung** *f* - maintenance, upkeep

inständig *a* urgent, *adv* -ly

Instandsetzung *f* - repair

Instant- /'ɪnstənt-/ *pref* instant

Instanz /-st-/ *f* **-,-en** authority

Instinkt /-st-/ *m* **-[e]s,-e** instinct. **i~iv** *a* instinctive, *adv* -ly

Institu|t /-st-/ *nt* **-[e]s,-e** institute. **I~tion** /-'tsi̯oːn/ *f* **-,-en** institution

Instrument /-st-/ *nt* **-[e]s,-e** instrument. **I~almusik** *f* instrumental music

Insulin *nt* **-s** insulin

inszenier|en *vt* (*Theat*) produce. **I~ung** *f* **-,-en** production

Integr|ation /-'tsi̯oːn/ *f* - integration. **i~ieren** *vt* integrate; **sich i~ieren** integrate. **I~ität** *f* - integrity

Intellekt *m* **-[e]s** intellect. **i~uell** *a* intellectual

intelligen|t *a* intelligent, *adv* -ly. **I~z** *f* - intelligence; (*Leute*) intelligentsia

Intendant *m* **-en,-en** director

Intens|ität *f* - intensity. **i~iv** *a* intensive, *adv* -ly. **i~ivieren** *vt* intensify. **I~ivstation** *f* intensive-care unit

inter|essant *a* interesting. **I~esse** *nt* **-s,-n** interest; **I~esse haben** be interested (**an** + *dat* in). **I~essengruppe** *f* pressure group. **I~essent** *m* **-en,-en** interested party; (*Käufer*) prospective buyer. **i~essieren** *vt* interest; **sich i~essieren** be interested (**für** in)

intern *a* (*fig*) internal, *adv* -ly

Inter|nat *nt* **-[e]s,-e** boarding school. **i~national** *a* international, *adv* -ly. **i~nieren** *vt* intern. **I~nierung** *f* - internment. **I~nist** *m* **-en,-en** specialist in internal diseases. **I~pretation** /-'tsi̯oːn/ *f* **-,-en** interpretation. **i~pretieren** *vt* interpret. **I~punktion** /-'tsi̯oːn/ *f* - punctuation. **I~rogativpronomen** *nt* interrogative pronoun. **I~vall** *nt* **-s,-e** interval. **I~vention** /-'tsi̯oːn/ *f* **-,-en** intervention

Interview /'ɪntɐvjuː/ *nt* **-s,-s** interview. **i~en** /-'vjuːən/ *vt* interview

intim *a* intimate, *adv* -ly. **I~ität** *f* **-,-en** intimacy

intoleran|t *a* intolerant. **I~z** *f* - intolerance

intransitiv *a* intransitive, *adv* -ly

intravenös *a* intravenous, *adv* -ly

Intrig|e *f* **-,-n** intrigue. **i~ieren** *vi* (*haben*) plot

introvertiert *a* introverted

Intui|tion /-'tsi̯oːn/ *f* **-,-en** intuition. **i~tiv** *a* intuitive, *adv* -ly

Invalidenrente *f* disability pension

Invasion *f* **-,-en** invasion

Inven|tar *nt* **-s,-e** furnishings and fittings *pl*; (*Techn*) equipment; (*Bestand*) stock; (*Liste*) inventory. **I~tur** *f* **-,-en** stock-taking

investieren *vt* invest

inwendig *a* & *adv* inside

inwie|fern *adv* in what way. **i~weit** *adv* how far, to what extent

Inzest *m* **-[e]s** incest

inzwischen *adv* in the meantime

Irak (der) -[s] Iraq. **i~isch** *a* Iraqi

Iran (der) -[s] Iran. **i~isch** *a* Iranian

irdisch *a* earthly

Ire *m* **-n,-n** Irishman; **die I~n** the Irish *pl*

irgend *adv* **i~ jemand/etwas** someone/something; (*fragend, verneint*) anyone/anything; **wer/was/wann i~** whoever/whatever/whenever; **wenn i~ möglich** if at all possible. **i~ein** *indef art* some/any; **i~ein anderer** someone/anyone else. **i~eine(r,s)** *pron* any one; (*jemand*) someone/anyone. **i~wann** *pron* at some time [or other]/at any time. **i~was** *pron* (*fam*) something [or other]/anything. **i~welche(r,s)** *pron* any. **i~wer** *pron* someone/anyone. **i~wie** *adv* somehow [or other]. **i~wo** *adv* somewhere/anywhere; **i~wo anders** somewhere else

Irin *f* **-,-nen** Irishwoman

Iris *f* **-,-** (*Anat, Bot*) iris

irisch *a* Irish

Irland *nt* **-s** Ireland

Ironie *f* - irony

ironisch *a* ironic, *adv* -ally

irr *a* = **irre**

irrational *a* irrational

irre *a* mad, crazy; (*fam: gewaltig*) incredible, *adv* -bly; **i~ werden** get confused. **I~(r)** *m/f* lunatic. **i~führen** *vt sep* (*fig*) mislead. **i~gehen**† *vi sep* (*sein*) lose one's way; (*sich täuschen*) be wrong

irrelevant *a* irrelevant

irre|machen *vt sep* confuse. **i~n** *vi/r* (*haben*) **[sich] i~n** be mistaken; **wenn ich mich nicht i~** if I am not

mistaken • *vi* (*sein*) wander. **I~nanstalt** *f*, **I~nhaus** *nt* lunatic asylum. **i~reden** *vi sep* (*haben*) ramble
Irr|garten *m* maze. **i~ig** *a* erroneous
irritieren *vt* irritate
Irr|sinn *m* madness, lunacy. **i~sinnig** *a* mad; (*fam: gewaltig*) incredible, *adv* -bly. **I~tum** *m* **-s,¨er** mistake. **i~tümlich** *a* mistaken, *adv* -ly
Ischias *m & nt* - sciatica
Islam **(der)** **-[s]** Islam. **islamisch** *a* Islamic
Island *nt* **-s** Iceland
Isolier|band *nt* insulating tape. **i~en** *vt* isolate; (*Phys, Electr*) insulate; (*gegen Schall*) soundproof. **I~ung** *f* - isolation; insulation; soundproofing
Isra|el /'ɪsrae:l/ *nt* **-s** Israel. **I~eli** *m* **-[s],-s** & *f* **-,-[s]** Israeli. **i~elisch** *a* Israeli
ist *s.* **sein; er ist** he is
Ital|ien /-i̯ən/ *nt* **-s** Italy. **I~iener(in)** *m* **-s,-** (*f* **-,-nen**) Italian. **i~ienisch** *a* Italian. **I~ienisch** *nt* **-[s]** (*Lang*) Italian

J

ja *adv* yes; **ich glaube ja** I think so; **'ja nicht!** not on any account! **seid 'ja vorsichtig!** whatever you do, be careful! **da seid ihr ja!** there you are! **das ist es ja** that's just it; **das mag ja wahr sein** that may well be true
Jacht *f* **-,-en** yacht
Jacke *f* **-,-n** jacket; (*Strick-*) cardigan
Jackett /ʒa'kɛt/ *nt* **-s,-s** jacket
Jade *m* **-[s]** & *f* - jade
Jagd *f* **-,-en** hunt; (*Schießen*) shoot; (*Jagen*) hunting; shooting; (*fig*) pursuit (**nach** of); **auf die J~ gehen** go hunting/shooting. **J~flugzeug** *nt* fighter aircraft. **J~gewehr** *nt* sporting gun. **J~hund** *m* gun-dog; (*Hetzhund*) hound
jagen *vt* hunt; (*schießen*) shoot; (*verfolgen, wegjagen*) chase; (*treiben*) drive; **sich j~** chase each other; **in die Luft j~** blow up • *vi* (*haben*) hunt, go hunting/shooting; (*fig*) chase (**nach** after) • *vi* (*sein*) race, dash
Jäger *m* **-s,-** hunter
jäh *a* sudden, *adv* -ly; (*steil*) steep, *adv* -ly
Jahr *nt* **-[e]s,-e** year. **J~buch** *nt* yearbook. **j~elang** *adv* for years. **J~estag** *m* anniversary. **J~eszahl** *f* year. **J~eszeit** *f* season. **J~gang** *m* year; (*Wein*) vintage. **J~hundert** *nt* century. **J~hundertfeier** *f* centenary, (*Amer*) centennial
jährlich *a* annual, yearly • *adv* annually, yearly
Jahr|markt *m* fair. **J~tausend** *nt* millennium. **J~zehnt** *nt* **-[e]s,-e** decade
Jähzorn *m* violent temper. **j~ig** *a* hot-tempered
Jalousie /ʒalu'zi:/ *f* **-,-n** venetian blind
Jammer *m* **-s** misery; (*Klagen*) lamenting; **es ist ein J~** it is a shame
jämmerlich *a* miserable, *adv* -bly; (*mitleiderregend*) pitiful, *adv* -ly
jammer|n *vi* (*haben*) lament • *vt* **jdn j~n** arouse s.o.'s pity. **j~schade** *a* **j~schade sein** (*fam*) be a terrible shame
Jänner *m* **-s,-** (*Aust*) January
Januar *m* **-s,-e** January
Jap|an *nt* **-s** Japan. **J~aner(in)** *m* **-s,-** (*f* **-,-nen**) Japanese. **j~anisch** *a* Japanese. **J~anisch** *nt* **-[s]** (*Lang*) Japanese
Jargon /ʒar'gõ:/ *m* **-s** jargon
jäten *vt/i* (*haben*) weed
jauchzen *vi* (*haben*) (*liter*) exult
jaulen *vi* (*haben*) yelp
Jause *f* **-,-n** (*Aust*) snack
jawohl *adv* yes
Jawort *nt* **jdm sein J~ geben** accept s.o.'s proposal [of marriage]
Jazz /jats, dʒɛs/ *m* - jazz
je *adv* (*jemals*) ever; (*jeweils*) each; (*pro*) per; **je nach** according to; **seit eh und je** always; **besser denn je** better than ever • *conj* **je mehr, desto** *od* **um so besser** the more the better • *prep* (+*acc*) per
Jeans /dʒi:ns/ *pl* jeans
jed|e(r,s) *pron* every; (*j~er einzelne*) each; (*j~er beliebige*) any; (*substantivisch*) everyone; each one; anyone; **ohne j~en Grund** without any reason. **j~enfalls** *adv* in any case; (*wenigstens*) at least. **j~ermann** *pron* everyone. **j~erzeit** *adv* at any time. **j~esmal** *adv* every time; **j~esmal wenn** whenever
jedoch *adv & conj* however
jeher *adv* **von** *od* **seit j~** always
jemals *adv* ever

jemand *pron* someone, somebody; (*fragend, verneint*) anyone, anybody

jen|e(r,s) *pron* that; (*pl*) those; (*substantivisch*) that one; (*pl*) those. **j~seits** *prep* (+*gen*) [on] the other side of

jetzig *a* present; ⟨*Preis*⟩ current

jetzt *adv* now. **J~zeit** *f* present

jeweil|ig *a* respective. **j~s** *adv* at a time

jiddisch *a*, **J~** *nt* **-[s]** Yiddish

Job /dʒɔp/ *m* **-s,-s** job. **j~ben** *vi* (*haben*) (*fam*) work

Joch *nt* **-[e]s,-e** yoke

Jockei, Jockey /ˈdʒɔki/ *m* **-s,-s** jockey

Jod *nt* **-[e]s** iodine

jodeln *vi* (*haben*) yodel

Joga *m & nt* **-[s]** yoga

jogg|en /ˈdʒɔgən/ *vi* (*haben/sein*) jog. **J~ing** *nt* **-[s]** jogging

Joghurt *m & nt* **-[s]** yoghurt

Johannisbeere *f* redcurrant; **schwarze J~** blackcurrant

johlen *vi* (*haben*) yell; (*empört*) jeer

Joker *m* **-s,-** (*Karte*) joker

Jolle *f* **-,-n** dinghy

Jongl|eur /ʒõˈgløːɐ̯/ *m* **-s,-e** juggler. **j~ieren** *vi* (*haben*) juggle

Joppe *f* **-,-n** [thick] jacket

Jordanien /-i̯ən/ *nt* **-s** Jordan

Journalis|mus /ʒʊrnaˈlɪsmʊs/ *m* **-** journalism. **J~t(in)** *m* **-en,-en** (*f* **-,-nen**) journalist

Jubel *m* **-s** rejoicing, jubilation. **j~n** *vi* (*haben*) rejoice

Jubil|ar(in) *m* **-s,-e** (*f* **-,-nen**) person celebrating an anniversary. **J~äum** *nt* **-s,-äen** jubilee; (*Jahrestag*) anniversary

juck|en *vi* (*haben*) itch; **sich j~en** scratch; **es j~t mich** I have an itch; (*fam: möchte*) I'm itching (**zu** to). **J~reiz** *m* itch[ing]

Jude *m* **-n,-n** Jew. **J~ntum** *nt* **-s** Judaism; (*Juden*) Jewry

Jüd|in *f* **-,-nen** Jewess. **j~isch** *a* Jewish

Judo *nt* **-[s]** judo

Jugend *f* **-** youth; (*junge Leute*) young people *pl*. **J~herberge** *f* youth hostel. **J~klub** *m* youth club. **J~kriminalität** *f* juvenile delinquency. **j~lich** *a* youthful. **J~liche(r)** *m/f* young man/woman; (*Admin*) juvenile; **J~liche** *pl* young people. **J~stil** *m* art nouveau. **J~zeit** *f* youth

Jugoslaw|ien /-i̯ən/ *nt* **-s** Yugoslavia. **j~isch** *a* Yugoslav

Juli *m* **-[s],-s** July

jung *a* (**jünger, jüngst**) young; ⟨*Wein*⟩ new ● *pron* **j~ und alt** young and old. **J~e** *m* **-n,-n** boy. **J~e(s)** *nt* young animal/bird; (*Katzen-*) kitten; (*Bären-, Löwen-*) cub; (*Hunde-, Seehund-*) pup; **die J~en** the young *pl*. **j~enhaft** *a* boyish

Jünger *m* **-s,-** disciple

Jungfer *f* **-,-n alte J~** old maid. **J~nfahrt** *f* maiden voyage

Jung|frau *f* virgin; (*Astr*) Virgo. **j~fräulich** *a* virginal. **J~geselle** *m* bachelor

Jüngling *m* **-s,-e** youth

jüngst|e(r,s) *a* youngest; (*neueste*) latest; **in j~er Zeit** recently

Juni *m* **-[s],-s** June

Junior *m* **-s,-en** /-ˈoːrən/ junior

Jura *pl* law *sg*

Jurist|(in) *m* **-en,-en** (*f* **-,-nen**) lawyer. **j~isch** *a* legal, *adv* -ly

Jury /ʒyˈriː/ *f* **-,-s** jury; (*Sport*) judges *pl*

justieren *vt* adjust

Justiz *f* **- die J~** justice. **J~irrtum** *m* miscarriage of justice. **J~minister** *m* Minister of Justice

Juwel *nt* **-s,-en** & (*fig*) **-e** jewel. **J~ier** *m* **-s,-e** jeweller

Jux *m* **-es,-e** (*fam*) joke; **aus Jux** for fun

K

Kabarett *nt* **-s,-s** & **-e** cabaret

kabbelig *a* choppy

Kabel *nt* **-s,-** cable. **K~fernsehen** *nt* cable television

Kabeljau *m* **-s,-e** & **-s** cod

Kabine *f* **-,-n** cabin; (*Umkleide-*) cubicle; (*Telefon-*) booth; (*einer K~nbahn*) car. **K~nbahn** *f* cable-car

Kabinett *nt* **-s,-e** (*Pol*) Cabinet

Kabriolett *nt* **-s,-s** convertible

Kachel *f* **-,-n** tile. **k~n** *vt* tile

Kadaver *m* **-s,-** carcass

Kadenz *f* **-,-en** (*Mus*) cadence; (*für Solisten*) cadenza

Kadett *m* **-en,-en** cadet

Käfer *m* **-s,-** beetle

Kaff *nt* **-s,-s** (*fam*) dump

Kaffee /ˈkafeː, kaˈfeː/ *m* **-s,-s** coffee; (*Mahlzeit*) afternoon coffee.

K~grund *m* = **K~satz. K~kanne** *f* coffee-pot. **K~maschine** *f* coffee-maker. **K~mühle** *f* coffee-grinder. **K~satz** *m* coffee-grounds *pl*

Käfig *m* **-s,-e** cage

kahl *a* bare; (*haarlos*) bald. **k~geschoren** *a* shaven. **k~köpfig** *a* bald-headed

Kahn *m* **-s,⸚e** boat; (*Last-*) barge

Kai *m* **-s,-s** quay

Kaiser *m* **-s,-** emperor. **K~in** *f* **-,-nen** empress. **k~lich** *a* imperial. **K~reich** *nt* empire. **K~schnitt** *m* Caesarean [section]

Kajüte *f* **-,-n** (*Naut*) cabin

Kakao /ka'kau̯/ *m* **-s** cocoa

Kakerlak *m* **-s** & **-en,-en** cockroach

Kaktee /kak'te:ə/ *f* **-,-n, Kaktus** *m* **-,-teen** /-'te:ən/ cactus

Kalb *nt* **-[e]s,⸚er** calf. **K~fleisch** *nt* veal

Kalender *m* **-s,-** calendar; (*Taschen-, Termin-*) diary

Kaliber *nt* **-s,-** calibre; (*Gewehr-*) bore

Kalium *nt* **-s** potassium

Kalk *m* **-[e]s,-e** lime; (*Kalzium*) calcium. **k~en** *vt* whitewash. **K~stein** *m* limestone

Kalkul|ation /-'t͡si̯o:n/ *f* **-,-en** calculation. **k~ieren** *vt/i* (*haben*) calculate

Kalorie *f* **-,-n** calorie

kalt *a* (**kälter, kältest**) cold; **es ist k~** it is cold; **mir ist k~** I am cold. **k~blütig** *a* cold-blooded, *adv* -ly; (*ruhig*) cool, *adv* -ly

Kälte *f* - cold; (*Gefühls-*) coldness; **10 Grad K~** 10 degrees below zero. **K~welle** *f* cold spell

kalt|herzig *a* cold-hearted. **k~schnäuzig** *a* (*fam*) cold, *adv* -ly

Kalzium *nt* **-s** calcium

Kamel *nt* **-s,-e** camel; (*fam: Idiot*) fool

Kamera *f* **-,-s** camera

Kamerad|(in) *m* **-en,-en** (*f* **-,-nen**) companion; (*Freund*) mate; (*Mil, Pol*) comrade. **K~schaft** *f* - comradeship

Kameramann *m* (*pl* **-männer** & **-leute**) cameraman

Kamille *f* - camomile

Kamin *m* **-s,-e** fireplace; (*SGer: Schornstein*) chimney. **K~feger** *m* **-s,-** (*SGer*) chimney-sweep

Kamm *m* **-[e]s,⸚e** comb; (*Berg-*) ridge; (*Zool, Wellen-*) crest

kämmen *vt* comb; **jdn/sich k~** comb s.o.'s/one's hair

Kammer *f* **-,-n** small room; (*Techn, Biol, Pol*) chamber. **K~diener** *m* valet. **K~musik** *f* chamber music

Kammgarn *nt* (*Tex*) worsted

Kampagne /kam'panjə/ *f* **-,-n** (*Pol, Comm*) campaign

Kampf *m* **-es,⸚e** fight; (*Schlacht*) battle; (*Wett-*) contest; (*fig*) struggle; **schwere K⸚e** heavy fighting *sg*; **den K~ ansagen** (+*dat*) (*fig*) declare war on

kämpf|en *vi* (*haben*) fight; **sich k~en durch** fight one's way through. **K~er(in)** *m* **-s,-** (*f* **-,-nen**) fighter

kampf|los *adv* without a fight. **K~richter** *m* (*Sport*) judge

kampieren *vi* (*haben*) camp

Kanada *nt* **-s** Canada

Kanad|ier(in) /-i̯ɐ, -i̯ərɪn/ *m* **-s,-** (*f* **-,-nen**) Canadian. **k~isch** *a* Canadian

Kanal *m* **-s,⸚e** canal; (*Abfluß-*) drain, sewer; (*Radio, TV*) channel; **der K~** the [English] Channel

Kanalis|ation /-'t͡si̯o:n/ *f* - sewerage system, drains *pl*. **k~ieren** *vt* canalize; (*fig: lenken*) channel

Kanarienvogel /-i̯ən-/ *m* canary

Kanarisch *a* **K~e Inseln** Canaries

Kandi|dat(in) *m* **-en,-en** (*f* **-,-nen**) candidate. **k~dieren** *vi* (*haben*) stand (**für** for)

kandiert *a* candied

Känguruh *nt* **-s,-s** kangaroo

Kaninchen *nt* **-s,-** rabbit

Kanister *m* **-s,-** canister; (*Benzin-*) can

Kännchen *nt* **-s,-** [small] jug; (*Kaffee-*) pot

Kanne *f* **-,-n** jug; (*Kaffee-, Tee-*) pot; (*Öl-*) can; (*große Milch-*) churn; (*Gieß-*) watering-can

Kannibal|e *m* **-n,-n** cannibal. **K~ismus** *m* - cannibalism

Kanon *m* **-s,-s** canon; (*Lied*) round

Kanone *f* **-,-n** cannon, gun; (*fig: Könner*) ace

kanonisieren *vt* canonize

Kantate *f* **-,-n** cantata

Kante *f* **-,-n** edge; **auf die hohe K~ legen** (*fam*) put by

Kanten *m* **-s,-** crust [of bread]

Kanter *m* **-s,-** canter

kantig *a* angular

Kantine *f* **-,-n** canteen

Kanton *m* **-s,-e** (*Swiss*) canton

Kantor *m* **-s,-en** /-'to:rən/ choirmaster and organist

Kanu *nt* **-s,-s** canoe

Kanzel *f* **-,-n** pulpit; (*Aviat*) cockpit

Kanzleistil *m* officialese
Kanzler *m* **-s,-** chancellor
Kap *nt* **-s,-s** (*Geog*) cape
Kapazität *f* **-,-en** capacity; (*Experte*) authority
Kapelle *f* **-,-n** chapel; (*Mus*) band
Kaper *f* **-,-n** (*Culin*) caper
kapern *vt* (*Naut*) seize
kapieren *vt* (*fam*) understand, (*fam*) get
Kapital *nt* **-s** capital; **K~ schlagen aus** (*fig*) capitalize on. **K~ismus** *m* **-** capitalism. **K~ist** *m* **-en,-en** capitalist. **k~istisch** *a* capitalist
Kapitän *m* **-s,-e** captain
Kapitel *nt* **-s,-** chapter
Kapitul|ation /-'ts̮i̯o:n/ *f* **-** capitulation. **k~ieren** *vi* (*haben*) capitulate
Kaplan *m* **-s,-e** curate
Kappe *f* **-,-n** cap. **k~n** *vt* cut
Kapsel *f* **-,-n** capsule; (*Flaschen-*) top
kaputt *a* (*fam*) broken; (*zerrissen*) torn; (*defekt*) out of order; (*ruiniert*) ruined; (*erschöpft*) worn out. **k~gehen**† *vi sep* (*sein*) (*fam*) break; (*zerreißen*) tear; (*defekt werden*) pack up; 〈*Ehe, Freundschaft:*〉 break up. **k~lachen (sich)** *vr sep* (*fam*) be in stitches. **k~machen** *vt sep* (*fam*) break; (*zerreißen*) tear; (*defekt machen*) put out of order; (*erschöpfen*) wear out; **sich k~machen** wear oneself out
Kapuze *f* **-,-n** hood
Kapuzinerkresse *f* nasturtium
Karaffe *f* **-,-n** carafe; (*mit Stöpsel*) decanter
Karambolage /karambo'la:ʒə/ *f* **-,-n** collision
Karamel *m* **-s** caramel. **K~bonbon** *m* & *nt* ≈ toffee
Karat *nt* **-[e]s,-e** carat
Karawane *f* **-,-n** caravan
Kardinal *m* **-s,¨e** cardinal. **K~zahl** *f* cardinal number
Karfiol *m* **-s** (*Aust*) cauliflower
Karfreitag *m* Good Friday
karg *a* **(kärger, kärgst)** meagre; (*frugal*) frugal; (*spärlich*) sparse; (*unfruchtbar*) barren; (*gering*) scant. **k~en** *vi* (*haben*) be sparing **(mit** with)
kärglich *a* poor, meagre; (*gering*) scant
Karibik *f* **-** Caribbean
kariert *a* check[ed]; 〈*Papier*〉 squared; **schottisch k~** tartan
Karik|atur *f* **-,-en** caricature; (*Journ*) cartoon. **k~ieren** *vt* caricature
karitativ *a* charitable
Karneval *m* **-s,-e** & **-s** carnival
Karnickel *nt* **-s,-** (*dial*) rabbit
Kärnten *nt* **-s** Carinthia
Karo *nt* **-s,-** (*Raute*) diamond; (*Viereck*) square; (*Muster*) check; (*Kartenspiel*) diamonds *pl*. **K~muster** *nt* check
Karosserie *f* **-,-n** bodywork
Karotte *f* **-,-n** carrot
Karpfen *m* **-s,-** carp
Karre *f* **-,-n** = **Karren**
Karree *nt* **-s,-s** square; **ums K~** round the block
Karren *m* **-s,-** cart; (*Hand-*) barrow. **k~** *vt* cart
Karriere /ka'ri̯e:rə/ *f* **-,-n** career; **K~ machen** get to the top
Karte *f* **-,-n** card; (*Eintritts-, Fahr-*) ticket; (*Speise-*) menu; (*Land-*) map
Kartei *f* **-,-en** card index. **K~karte** *f* index card
Karten|spiel *nt* card-game; (*Spielkarten*) pack/(*Amer*) deck of cards. **K~vorverkauf** *m* advance booking
Kartoffel *f* **-,-n** potato. **K~brei** *m*, **K~püree** *nt* mashed potatoes *pl*. **K~salat** *m* potato salad
Karton /kar'tɔŋ/ *m* **-s,-s** cardboard; (*Schachtel*) carton, cardboard box
Karussell *nt* **-s,-s** & **-e** roundabout
Karwoche *f* Holy Week
Käse *m* **-s,-** cheese. **K~kuchen** *m* cheesecake
Kaserne *f* **-,-n** barracks *pl*
Kasino *nt* **-s,-s** casino
Kasperle *nt* & *m* **-s,-** Punch. **K~theater** *nt* Punch and Judy show
Kasse *f* **-,-n** till; (*Registrier-*) cash register; (*Zahlstelle*) cash desk; (*im Supermarkt*) check-out; (*Theater-*) box-office; (*Geld*) pool [of money], (*fam*) kitty; (*Kranken-*) health insurance scheme; (*Spar-*) savings bank; **knapp/gut bei K~ sein** (*fam*) be short of cash/be flush. **K~npatient** *m* ≈ NHS patient. **K~nschlager** *m* box-office hit. **K~nwart** *m* **-[e]s,-e** treasurer. **K~nzettel** *m* receipt
Kasserolle *f* **-,-n** saucepan [with one handle]
Kassette *f* **-,-n** cassette; (*Film-, Farbband-*) cartridge; (*Schmuck-*) case; (*Geld-*) money-box. **K~nrecorder** /-rəkɔrdɐ/ *m* **-s,-** cassette recorder

kassier|en *vi* (*haben*) collect the money/(*im Bus*) the fares ● *vt* collect. **K~er(in)** *m* **-s,-** (*f* **-,-nen**) cashier

Kastagnetten /kastan'jɛtən/ *pl* castanets

Kastanie /kas'ta:ni̯ə/ *f* **-,-n** [horse] chestnut, (*fam*) conker. **k~nbraun** *a* chestnut

Kaste *f* **-,-n** caste

Kasten *m* **-s,¨** box; (*Brot-*) bin; (*Flaschen-*) crate; (*Brief-*) letter-box; (*Aust: Schrank*) cupboard; (*Kleider-*) wardrobe

kastrieren *vt* castrate; neuter ⟨*Tier*⟩

Kasus *m* **-,-** /-u:s/ (*Gram*) case.

Katalog *m* **-[e]s,-e** catalogue. **k~isieren** *vt* catalogue

Katalysator *m* **-s,-en** /-'to:rən/ catalyst; (*Auto*) catalytic converter

Katapult *nt* **-[e]s,-e** catapult. **k~ieren** *vt* catapult

Katarrh *m* **-s,-e** catarrh

katastr|ophal *a* catastrophic. **K~ophe** *f* **-,-n** catastrophe

Katechismus *m* **-** catechism

Kateg|orie *f* **-,-n** category. **k~orisch** *a* categorical, *adv* -ly

Kater *m* **-s,-** tom-cat; (*fam: Katzenjammer*) hangover

Katheder *nt* **-s,-** [teacher's] desk

Kathedrale *f* **-,-n** cathedral

Kath|olik(in) *m* **-en,-en** (*f* **-,-nen**) Catholic. **k~olisch** *a* Catholic. **K~olizismus** *m* **-** Catholicism

Kätzchen *nt* **-s,-** kitten; (*Bot*) catkin

Katze *f* **-,-n** cat. **K~njammer** *m* (*fam*) hangover. **K~nsprung** *m* **ein K~nsprung** (*fam*) a stone's throw

Kauderwelsch *nt* **-[s]** gibberish

kauen *vt/i* (*haben*) chew; bite ⟨*Nägel*⟩

kauern *vi* (*haben*) crouch; **sich k~** crouch down

Kauf *m* **-[e]s, Käufe** purchase; **guter K~** bargain; **in K~ nehmen** (*fig*) put up with. **k~en** *vt/i* (*haben*) buy; **k~en bei** shop at

Käufer(in) *m* **-s,-** (*f* **-,-nen**) buyer; (*im Geschäft*) shopper

Kauf|haus *nt* department store. **K~kraft** *f* purchasing power. **K~laden** *m* shop

käuflich *a* saleable; (*bestechlich*) corruptible; **k~ sein** be for sale; **k~ erwerben** buy

Kauf|mann *m* (*pl* **-leute**) businessman; (*Händler*) dealer; (*dial*) grocer. **k~männisch** *a* commercial. **K~preis** *m* purchase price

Kaugummi *m* chewing-gum

Kaulquappe *f* **-,-n** tadpole

kaum *adv* hardly; **k~ glaublich** *od* **zu glauben** hard to believe

kauterisieren *vt* cauterize

Kaution /-'tsi̯o:n/ *f* **-,-en** surety; (*Jur*) bail; (*Miet-*) deposit

Kautschuk *m* **-s** rubber

Kauz *m* **-es, Käuze** owl; **komischer K~** (*fam*) odd fellow

Kavalier *m* **-s,-e** gentleman

Kavallerie *f* **-** cavalry

Kaviar *m* **-s** caviare

keck *a* bold; (*frech*) cheeky

Kegel *m* **-s,-** skittle; (*Geom*) cone; **mit Kind und K~** (*fam*) with all the family. **K~bahn** *f* skittle-alley. **k~förmig** *a* conical. **k~n** *vi* (*haben*) play skittles

Kehl|e *f* **-,-n** throat; **aus voller K~e** at the top of one's voice; **etw in die falsche K~e bekommen** (*fam*) take sth the wrong way. **K~kopf** *m* larynx. **K~kopfentzündung** *f* laryngitis

Kehr|e *f* **-,-n** [hairpin] bend. **k~en** *vi* (*haben*) (*fegen*) sweep ● *vt* sweep; (*wenden*) turn; **den Rücken k~en** turn one's back (*dat* on); **sich k~en** turn; **sich nicht k~en an** (+*acc*) not care about. **K~icht** *m* **-[e]s** sweepings *pl*. **K~reim** *m* refrain. **K~seite** *f* (*fig*) drawback; **die K~seite der Medaille** the other side of the coin. **k~tmachen** *vi sep* (*haben*) turn back; (*sich umdrehen*) turn round. **K~twendung** *f* about-turn; (*fig*) U-turn

keifen *vi* (*haben*) scold

Keil *m* **-[e]s,-e** wedge

Keile *f* **-** (*fam*) hiding. **k~n (sich)** *vr* (*fam*) fight. **K~rei** *f* **-,-en** (*fam*) punch-up

Keil|kissen *nt* [wedge-shaped] bolster. **K~riemen** *m* fan belt

Keim *m* **-[e]s,-e** (*Bot*) sprout; (*Med*) germ; **im K~ ersticken** (*fig*) nip in the bud. **k~en** *vi* (*haben*) germinate; (*austreiben*) sprout. **k~frei** *a* sterile

kein *pron* no; not a; **auf k~en Fall** on no account; **k~e fünf Minuten** less than five minutes. **k~e(r,s)** *pron* no one, nobody; (*Ding*) none, not one. **k~esfalls** *adv* on no account. **k~eswegs** *adv* by no means. **k~mal** *adv* not once. **k~s** *pron* none, not one

Keks *m* **-[es],-[e]** biscuit, (*Amer*) cookie

Kelch *m* **-[e]s,-e** goblet, cup; (*Relig*) chalice; (*Bot*) calyx

Kelle *f* **-,-n** ladle; (*Maurer-, Pflanz-*) trowel

Keller *m* **-s,-** cellar. **K~ei** *f* **-,-en** winery. **K~geschoß** *nt* cellar; (*bewohnbar*) basement. **K~wohnung** *f* basement flat

Kellner *m* **-s,-** waiter. **K~in** *f* **-,-nen** waitress

keltern *vt* press

keltisch *a* Celtic

Kenia *nt* **-s** Kenya

kenn|en† *vt* know. **k~enlernen** *vt sep* get to know; (*treffen*) meet; **sich k~enlernen** meet; (*näher*) get to know one another. **K~er** *m* **-s,-, K~erin** *f* **-,-nen** connoisseur; (*Experte*) expert. **K~melodie** *f* signature tune. **k~tlich** *a* recognizable; **k~tlich machen** mark. **K~tnis** *f* **-,-se** knowledge; **zur K~tnis nehmen** take note of; **in K~tnis setzen** inform (**von** of). **K~wort** *nt* (*pl* **-wörter**) reference; (*geheimes*) password. **K~zeichen** *nt* distinguishing mark *or* feature; (*Merkmal*) characteristic; (*Markierung*) mark, marking; (*Abzeichen*) badge; (*Auto*) registration. **k~zeichnen** *vt* distinguish; (*markieren*) mark. **k~zeichnend** *a* typical (**für** of). **K~ziffer** *f* reference number

kentern *vi* (*sein*) capsize

Keramik *f* **-,-en** pottery, ceramics *sg*; (*Gegenstand*) piece of pottery

Kerbe *f* **-,-n** notch

Kerbholz *nt* **etwas auf dem K~ haben** (*fam*) have a record

Kerker *m* **-s,-** dungeon; (*Gefängnis*) prison

Kerl *m* **-s,-e** & **-s** (*fam*) fellow, bloke

Kern *m* **-s,-e** pip; (*Kirsch-*) stone; (*Nuß-*) kernel; (*Techn*) core; (*Atom-, Zell-* & *fig*) nucleus; (*Stadt-*) centre; (*einer Sache*) heart. **K~energie** *f* nuclear energy. **K~gehäuse** *nt* core. **k~gesund** *a* perfectly healthy. **k~ig** *a* robust; ⟨*Ausspruch*⟩ pithy. **k~los** *a* seedless. **K~physik** *f* nuclear physics *sg*

Kerze *f* **-,-n** candle. **k~ngerade** *a* & *adv* straight. **K~nhalter** *m* **-s,-** candlestick

keß *a* (**kesser, kessest**) pert

Kessel *m* **-s,-** kettle; (*Heiz-*) boiler. **K~stein** *m* fur

Kette *f* **-,-n** chain; (*Hals-*) necklace. **k~n** *vt* chain (**an** + *acc* to). **K~nladen** *m* chain store. **K~nraucher** *m* chain-smoker. **K~nreaktion** *f* chain reaction

Ketze|r(in) *m* **-s,-** (*f* **-,-nen**) heretic. **K~rei** *f* **-** heresy

keuch|en *vi* (*haben*) pant. **K~husten** *m* whooping cough

Keule *f* **-,-n** club; (*Culin*) leg; (*Hühner-*) drumstick

keusch *a* chaste. **K~heit** *f* **-** chastity

Kfz *abbr s.* **Kraftfahrzeug**

Khaki *nt* **-** khaki. **k~farben** *a* khaki

kichern *vi* (*haben*) giggle

Kiefer[1] *f* **-,-n** pine[-tree]

Kiefer[2] *m* **-s,-** jaw

Kiel *m* **-s,-e** (*Naut*) keel. **K~wasser** *nt* wake

Kiemen *fpl* gills

Kies *m* **-es** gravel. **K~el** *m* **-s,-, K~elstein** *m* pebble. **K~grube** *f* gravel pit

Kilo *nt* **-s,-[s]** kilo. **K~gramm** *nt* kilogram. **K~hertz** *nt* kilohertz. **K~meter** *m* kilometre. **K~meterstand** *m* ≈ mileage. **K~watt** *nt* kilowatt

Kind *nt* **-es,-er** child; **von K~ auf** from childhood

Kinder|arzt *m*, **K~ärztin** *f* paediatrician. **K~bett** *nt* child's cot. **K~ei** *f* **-,-en** childish prank. **K~garten** *m* nursery school. **K~gärtnerin** *f* nursery-school teacher. **K~geld** *nt* child benefit. **K~gottesdienst** *m* Sunday school. **K~lähmung** *f* polio. **k~leicht** *a* very easy. **k~los** *a* childless. **K~mädchen** *nt* nanny. **k~reich** *a* **k~reiche Familie** large family. **K~reim** *m* nursery rhyme. **K~spiel** *nt* children's game; **das ist ein/kein K~spiel** that is dead easy/ not easy. **K~tagesstätte** *f* day nursery. **K~teller** *m* children's menu. **K~wagen** *m* pram, (*Amer*) baby carriage. **K~zimmer** *nt* child's/ children's room; (*für Baby*) nursery

Kind|heit *f* **-** childhood. **k~isch** *a* childish, puerile. **k~lich** *a* childlike

kinetisch *a* kinetic

Kinn *nt* **-[e]s,-e** chin. **K~lade** *f* jaw

Kino *nt* **-s,-s** cinema

Kiosk *m* **-[e]s,-e** kiosk

Kippe *f* **-,-n** (*Müll-*) dump; (*fam: Zigaretten-*) fag-end; **auf der K~ stehen** (*fam*) be in a precarious position; (*unsicher sein*) hang in the balance. **k~lig** *a* wobbly. **k~ln** *vi* (*haben*) wobble. **k~n** *vt* tilt; (*schütten*) tip (**in**+*acc* into) ● *vi* (*sein*) topple

Kirch|e *f* **-,-n** church. **K~enbank** *f* pew. **K~endiener** *m* verger. **K~enlied** *nt* hymn. **K~enschiff** *nt* nave. **K~hof** *m* churchyard. **k~lich** *a* church ... ● *adv* **k~lich getraut werden** be married in church. **K~turm** *m* church tower, steeple. **K~weih** *f* **-,-en** [village] fair

Kirmes *f* **-,-sen** = **Kirchweih**

Kirsch|e *f* **-,-n** cherry. **K~wasser** *nt* kirsch

Kissen *nt* **-s,-** cushion; (*Kopf-*) pillow

Kiste *f* **-,-n** crate; (*Zigarren-*) box

Kitsch *m* **-es** sentimental rubbish; (*Kunst*) kitsch. **k~ig** *a* slushy; (*Kunst*) kitschy

Kitt *m* **-s** [adhesive] cement; (*Fenster-*) putty

Kittel *m* **-s,-** overall, smock; (*Arzt-, Labor-*) white coat

kitten *vt* stick; (*fig*) cement

Kitz *nt* **-es,-e** (*Zool*) kid

Kitz|el *m* **-s,-** tickle; (*Nerven-*) thrill. **k~eln** *vt/i* (*haben*) tickle. **k~lig** *a* ticklish

Kladde *f* **-,-n** notebook

klaffen *vi* (*haben*) gape

kläffen *vi* (*haben*) yap

Klage *f* **-,-n** lament; (*Beschwerde*) complaint; (*Jur*) action. **k~n** *vi* (*haben*) lament; (*sich beklagen*) complain; (*Jur*) sue

Kläger(in) *m* **-s,-** (*f* **-,-nen**) (*Jur*) plaintiff

kläglich *a* pitiful, *adv* -ly; (*erbärmlich*) miserable, *adv* -bly

klamm *a* cold and damp; (*steif*) stiff. **K~** *f* **-,-en** (*Geog*) gorge

Klammer *f* **-,-n** (*Wäsche-*) peg; (*Büro-*) paper-clip; (*Heft-*) staple; (*Haar-*) grip; (*für Zähne*) brace; (*Techn*) clamp; (*Typ*) bracket. **k~n (sich)** *vr* cling (**an**+*acc* to)

Klang *m* **-[e]s,⸚e** sound; (*K~farbe*) tone. **k~voll** *a* resonant; ⟨*Stimme*⟩ sonorous

Klapp|bett *nt* folding bed. **K~e** *f* **-,-n** flap; (*fam: Mund*) trap. **k~en** *vt* fold; (*hoch-*) tip up ● *vi* (*haben*) (*fam*) work out. **K~entext** *m* blurb

Klapper *f* **-,-n** rattle. **k~n** *vi* (*haben*) rattle. **K~schlange** rattlesnake

klapp|rig *a* rickety; (*schwach*) decrepit. **K~stuhl** *m* folding chair. **K~tisch** *m* folding table

Klaps *m* **-es,-e** pat; (*strafend*) smack. **k~en** *vt* smack

klar *a* clear; **sich** (*dat*) **k~** *od* **im k~en sein** realize ● *adv* clearly; (*fam: natürlich*) of course. **K~e(r)** *m* (*fam*) schnapps

klären *vt* clarify; **sich k~** clear; (*fig: sich lösen*) resolve itself

Klarheit *f* **-** clarity

Klarinette *f* **-,-n** clarinet

klar|machen *vt sep* make clear (*dat* to); **sich** (*dat*) **etw k~machen** understand sth. **K~sichtfolie** *f* transparent/(*haftend*) cling film. **k~stellen** *vt sep* clarify

Klärung *f* **-** clarification

klarwerden† *vi sep* (*sein*) (*fig*) become clear (*dat* to); **sich** (*dat*) **k~** make up one's mind; (*erkennen*) realize

Klasse *f* **-,-n** class; (*Sch*) class, form, (*Amer*) grade; (*Zimmer*) classroom; **erster/zweiter K~** first/second class. **k~** *inv a* (*fam*) super. **K~narbeit** *f* [written] test. **K~nbuch** *nt* ≈ register. **K~nkamerad(in)** *m(f)* class-mate. **K~nkampf** *m* class struggle. **K~nzimmer** *nt* classroom

klassifizier|en *vt* classify. **K~ung** *f* **-,-en** classification

Klass|ik *f* **-** classicism; (*Epoche*) classical period. **K~iker** *m* **-s,-** classical author/(*Mus*) composer. **k~isch** *a* classical; (*mustergültig, typisch*) classic

Klatsch *m* **-[e]s** gossip. **K~base** *f* (*fam*) gossip. **k~en** *vt* slap; **Beifall k~en** applaud ● *vi* (*haben*) make a slapping sound; (*im Wasser*) splash; (*tratschen*) gossip; (*applaudieren*) clap; **[in die Hände] k~en** clap one's hands ● *vi* (*haben/sein*) slap (**gegen** against). **K~maul** *nt* gossip. **k~naß** *a* (*fam*) soaking wet

klauben *vt* pick

Klaue *f* **-,-n** claw; (*fam: Schrift*) scrawl. **k~n** *vt/i* (*haben*) (*fam*) steal

Klausel *f* **-,-n** clause

Klaustrophobie *f* **-** claustrophobia

Klausur *f* **-,-en** (*Univ*) [examination] paper; (*Sch*) written test

Klaviatur *f* **-,-en** keyboard

Klavier *nt* **-s,-e** piano. **K~spieler(in)** *m(f)* pianist

kleb|en *vt* stick/(*mit Klebstoff*) glue (**an**+*acc* to) ● *vi* (*haben*) stick (**an** +*dat* to). **k~rig** *a* sticky. **K~stoff** *m* adhesive, glue. **K~streifen** *m* adhesive tape

kleckern *vi* (*haben*) (*fam*) = **klecksen**

Klecks *m* **-es,-e** stain; (*Tinten-*) blot; (*kleine Menge*) dab. **k~en** *vi* (*haben*) make a mess

Klee *m* **-s** clover. **K~blatt** *nt* clover leaf

Kleid *nt* **-[e]s,-er** dress; **K~er** dresses; (*Kleidung*) clothes. **k~en** *vt* dress; (*gut stehen*) suit; **sich k~en** dress. **K~erbügel** *m* coat-hanger. **K~erbürste** *f* clothes-brush. **K~erhaken** *m* coat-hook. **K~errock** *m* pinafore dress. **K~erschrank** *m* wardrobe, (*Amer*) clothes closet. **k~sam** *a* becoming. **K~ung** *f* **-** clothes *pl*, clothing. **K~ungsstück** *nt* garment

Kleie *f* **-** bran

klein *a* small, little; (*von kleinem Wuchs*) short; **von k~ auf** from childhood. **K~arbeit** *f* painstaking work. **K~bus** *m* minibus. **K~e(r,s)** *m/f/nt* little one. **K~geld** *nt* [small] change. **k~hacken** *vt sep* chop up small. **K~handel** *m* retail trade. **K~heit** *f* **-** smallness; (*Wuchs*) short stature. **K~holz** *nt* firewood. **K~igkeit** *f* **-,-en** trifle; (*Mahl*) snack. **K~kind** *nt* infant. **K~kram** *m* (*fam*) odds and ends *pl*; (*Angelegenheiten*) trivia *pl*. **k~laut** *a* subdued. **k~lich** *a* petty. **K~lichkeit** *f* **-** pettiness. **k~mütig** *a* faint-hearted

Kleinod *nt* **-[e]s,-e** jewel

klein|schneiden† *vt sep* cut into small pieces. **K~stadt** *f* small town. **k~städtisch** *a* provincial. **K~wagen** *m* small car

Kleister *m* **-s** paste. **k~n** *vt* paste

Klemme *f* **-,-n** [hair-]grip; **in der K~ sitzen** (*fam*) be in a fix. **k~n** *vt* jam; **sich** (*dat*) **den Finger k~n** get one's finger caught ● *vi* (*haben*) jam, stick

Klempner *m* **-s,-** plumber

Klerus (der) - the clergy

Klette *f* **-,-n** burr; **wie eine K~** (*fig*) like a limpet

kletter|n *vi* (*sein*) climb. **K~pflanze** *f* climber. **K~rose** *f* climbing rose

Klettverschluß *m* Velcro (P) fastening

klicken *vi* (*haben*) click

Klient(in) /kli'ɛnt(ɪn)/ *m* **-en,-en** (*f* **-,-nen**) (*Jur*) client

Kliff *nt* **-[e]s,-e** cliff

Klima *nt* **-s** climate. **K~anlage** *f* air-conditioning

klimat|isch *a* climatic. **k~isiert** *a* air-conditioned

klimpern *vi* (*haben*) jingle; **k~ auf** (+*dat*) tinkle on ⟨*Klavier*⟩; strum ⟨*Gitarre*⟩

Klinge *f* **-,-n** blade

Klingel *f* **-,-n** bell. **k~n** *vi* (*haben*) ring; **es k~t** there's a ring at the door

klingen† *vi* (*haben*) sound

Klini|k *f* **-,-en** clinic. **k~sch** *a* clinical, *adv* -ly

Klinke *f* **-,-n** [door] handle

klipp *pred a* **k~ und klar** quite plain, *adv* -ly

Klipp *m* **-s,-s** = **Klips**

Klippe *f* **-,-n** [submerged] rock

Klips *m* **-es,-e** clip; (*Ohr-*) clip-on ear-ring

klirren *vi* (*haben*) rattle; ⟨*Geschirr, Glas:*⟩ chink

Klischee *nt* **-s,-s** cliché

Klo *nt* **-s,-s** (*fam*) loo, (*Amer*) john

klobig *a* clumsy

klönen *vi* (*haben*) (*NGer fam*) chat

klopf|en *vi* (*haben*) knock; (*leicht*) tap; ⟨*Herz:*⟩ pound; **es k~te** there was a knock at the door ● *vt* beat; (*ein-*) knock

Klops *m* **-es,-e** meatball; (*Brat-*) rissole

Klosett *nt* **-s,-s** lavatory

Kloß *m* **-es,¨e** dumpling; **ein K~ im Hals** (*fam*) a lump in one's throat

Kloster *nt* **-s,¨** monastery; (*Nonnen-*) convent

klösterlich *a* monastic

Klotz *m* **-es,¨e** block

Klub *m* **-s,-s** club

Kluft[1] *f* **-,¨e** cleft; (*fig: Gegensatz*) gulf

Kluft[2] *f* **-,-en** outfit; (*Uniform*) uniform

klug *a* (**klüger, klügst**) intelligent, *adv* -ly; (*schlau*) clever, *adv* -ly; **nicht k~ werden aus** not understand. **K~heit** *f* **-** cleverness

Klump|en *m* **-s,-** lump. **k~en** *vi* (*haben*) go lumpy. **k~ig** *a* lumpy

knabbern *vt/i* (*haben*) nibble

Knabe *m* **-n,-n** boy. **k~nhaft** *a* boyish

Knäckebrot *nt* crispbread

knack|en *vt/i* (*haben*) crack. **K~s** *m* **-es,-e** crack; **einen K~s haben** be cracked; (*fam: verrückt sein*) be crackers

Knall *m* **-[e]s,-e** bang. **K~bonbon** *m* cracker. **k~en** *vi* (*haben*) go bang; ⟨*Peitsche:*⟩ crack ● *vt* (*fam: werfen*) chuck; **jdm eine k~en** (*fam*) clout s.o. **k~ig** *a* (*fam*) gaudy. **k~rot** *a* bright red

knapp *a* (*gering*) scant; (*kurz*) short; (*mangelnd*) scarce; (*gerade ausreichend*) bare; (*eng*) tight; **ein k~es Pfund** just under a pound. **k~halten**† *vt sep* (*fam*) keep short (**mit** of). **K~heit** *f* - scarcity

Knarre *f* -,-n rattle. **k~n** *vi* (*haben*) creak

Knast *m* -[e]s (*fam*) prison

knattern *vi* (*haben*) crackle; ⟨*Gewehr:*⟩ stutter

Knäuel *m & nt* -s,- ball

Knauf *m* -[e]s, **Knäufe** knob

knauser|ig *a* (*fam*) stingy. **k~n** *vi* (*haben*) (*fam*) be stingy

knautschen *vt* (*fam*) crumple ● *vi* (*haben*) crease

Knebel *m* -s,- gag. **k~n** *vt* gag

Knecht *m* -[e]s,-e farm-hand; (*fig*) slave. **k~en** *vt* (*fig*) enslave. **K~schaft** *f* - (*fig*) slavery

kneif|en† *vt* pinch ● *vi* (*haben*) pinch; (*fam: sich drücken*) chicken out. **K~zange** *f* pincers *pl*

Kneipe *f* -,-n (*fam*) pub, (*Amer*) bar

knet|en *vt* knead; (*formen*) mould. **K~masse** *f* Plasticine (P)

Knick *m* -[e]s,-e bend; (*im Draht*) kink; (*Kniff*) crease. **k~en** *vt* bend; (*kniffen*) fold; **geknickt sein** (*fam*) be dejected. **k~[e]rig** *a* (*fam*) stingy

Knicks *m* -es,-e curtsy. **k~en** *vi* (*haben*) curtsy

Knie *nt* -s,- /ˈkniːə/ knee. **K~bundhose** *f* knee-breeches *pl*. **K~kehle** *f* hollow of the knee

knien /ˈkniːən/ *vi* (*haben*) kneel ● *vr* **sich k~** kneel [down]

Knie|scheibe *f* kneecap. **K~strumpf** *m* knee-length sock

Kniff *m* -[e]s,-e pinch; (*Falte*) crease; (*fam: Trick*) trick. **k~en** *vt* fold. **k~[e]lig** *a* (*fam*) tricky

knipsen *vt* (*lochen*) punch; (*Phot*) photograph ● *vi* (*haben*) take a photograph/photographs

Knirps *m* -es,-e (*fam*) little chap; (**P**) (*Schirm*) telescopic umbrella

knirschen *vi* (*haben*) grate; ⟨*Schnee, Kies:*⟩ crunch; **mit den Zähnen k~** grind one's teeth

knistern *vi* (*haben*) crackle; ⟨*Papier:*⟩ rustle

Knitter|falte *f* crease. **k~frei** *a* crease-resistant. **k~n** *vi* (*haben*) crease

knobeln *vi* (*haben*) toss (**um** for); (*fam: überlegen*) puzzle

Knoblauch *m* -s garlic

Knöchel *m* -s,- ankle; (*Finger-*) knuckle

Knochen *m* -s,- bone. **K~mark** *nt* bone marrow. **k~trocken** *a* bone-dry

knochig *a* bony

Knödel *m* -s,- (*SGer*) dumpling

Knoll|e *f* -,-n tuber. **k~ig** *a* bulbous

Knopf *m* -[e]s,⸚e button; (*Kragen-*) stud; (*Griff*) knob

knöpfen *vt* button

Knopfloch *nt* buttonhole

Knorpel *m* -s gristle; (*Anat*) cartilage

knorrig *a* gnarled

Knospe *f* bud

Knötchen *nt* -s,- nodule

Knoten *m* -s,- knot; (*Med*) lump; (*Haar-*) bun, chignon. **k~** *vt* knot. **K~punkt** *m* junction

knotig *a* knotty; ⟨*Hände*⟩ gnarled

knuffen *vt* poke

knüll|en *vt* crumple ● *vi* (*haben*) crease. **K~er** *m* -s,- (*fam*) sensation

knüpfen *vt* knot; (*verbinden*) attach (**an** + *acc* to)

Knüppel *m* -s,- club; (*Gummi-*) truncheon

knurr|en *vi* (*haben*) growl; ⟨*Magen:*⟩ rumble; (*fam: schimpfen*) grumble. **k~ig** *a* grumpy

knusprig *a* crunchy, crisp

knutschen *vi* (*haben*) (*fam*) smooch

k.o. /kaˈʔoː/ *a* **k.o. schlagen** knock out; **k.o. sein** (*fam*) be worn out. **K.o.** *m* -s,-s knock-out

Koalition /koaliˈtsi̯oːn/ *f* -,-en coalition

Kobold *m* -[e]s,-e goblin, imp

Koch *m* -[e]s,⸚e cook; (*im Restaurant*) chef. **K~buch** *nt* cookery book, (*Amer*) cookbook. **k~en** *vt* cook; (*sieden*) boil; make ⟨*Kaffee, Tee*⟩ ● *vi* (*haben*) cook; (*sieden*) boil; (*fam*) seethe (**vor** + *dat* with). **K~en** *nt* -s cooking; (*Sieden*) boiling; **zum K~en bringen/kommen** bring/come to the boil. **k~end** *a* boiling ● *adv* **k~end heiß** boiling hot. **K~er** *m* -s,- cooker. **K~gelegenheit** *f* cooking facilities *pl*. **K~herd** *m* cooker, stove

Köchin *f* -,-nen [woman] cook

Koch|kunst *f* cookery. **K~löffel** *m* wooden spoon. **K~nische** *f* kitchenette. **K~platte** *f* hotplate. **K~topf** *m* saucepan

Kode /koːt/ *m* -s,-s code

Köder *m* -s,- bait

Koexist|enz /ˈkoːʔɛksɪstɛnts/ *f* coexistence. **k~ieren** *vi* (*haben*) coexist

Koffein /kɔfe'i:n/ *nt* **-s** caffeine. **k~frei** *a* decaffeinated

Koffer *m* **-s,-** suitcase. **K~kuli** *m* luggage trolley. **K~radio** *nt* portable radio. **K~raum** *m* (*Auto*) boot, (*Amer*) trunk

Kognak /'kɔnjak/ *m* **-s,-s** brandy

Kohl *m* **-[e]s** cabbage

Kohle *f* **-,-n** coal. **K~[n]hydrat** *nt* **-[e]s,-e** carbohydrate. **K~nbergwerk** *nt* coal-mine, colliery. **K~ndioxyd** *nt* carbon dioxide. **K~ngrube** *f* = **K~nbergwerk. K~nherd** *m* [kitchen] range. **K~nsäure** *f* carbon dioxide. **K~nstoff** *m* carbon. **K~papier** *nt* carbon paper

Kohl|kopf *m* cabbage. **K~rabi** *m* **-[s],-[s]** kohlrabi. **K~rübe** *f* swede

Koje *f* **-,-n** (*Naut*) bunk

Kokain /koka'i:n/ *nt* **-s** cocaine

kokett *a* flirtatious. **k~ieren** *vi* (*haben*) flirt

Kokon /ko'kõ:/ *m* **-s,-s** cocoon

Kokosnuß *f* coconut

Koks *m* **-es** coke

Kolben *m* **-s,-** (*Gewehr-*) butt; (*Mais-*) cob; (*Techn*) piston; (*Chem*) flask

Kolibri *m* **-s,-s** humming-bird

Kolik *f* **-,-en** colic

Kollabora|teur /-'tø:ɐ̯/ *m* **-s,-e** collaborator. **K~tion** /-'t͡si̯o:n/ *f* - collaboration

Kolleg *nt* **-s,-s & -ien** /-i̯ən/ (*Univ*) course of lectures

Kolleg|e *m* **-n,-n, K~in** *f* **-,-nen** colleague. **K~ium** *nt* **-s,-ien** staff

Kollek|te *f* **-,-n** (*Relig*) collection. **K~tion** /-'t͡si̯o:n/ *f* **-,-en** collection. **k~tiv** *a* collective. **K~tivum** *nt* **-s,-va** collective noun

kolli|dieren *vi* (*sein*) collide. **K~sion** *f* **-,-en** collision

Köln *nt* **-s** Cologne. **K~ischwasser, K~isch Wasser** *nt* eau-de-Cologne

Kolonialwaren *fpl* groceries

Kolon|ie *f* **-,-n** colony. **k~isieren** *vt* colonize

Kolonne *f* **-,-n** column; (*Mil*) convoy

Koloß *m* **-sses,-sse** giant

kolossal *a* enormous, *adv* -ly

Kolumne *f* **-,-n** (*Journ*) column

Koma *nt* **-s,-s** coma

Kombi *m* **-s,-s** = **K~wagen. K~nation** /-'t͡si̯o:n/ *f* **-,-en** combination; (*Folgerung*) deduction; (*Kleidung*) co-ordinating outfit. **k~nieren** *vt* combine; (*fig*) reason; (*folgern*) deduce. **K~wagen** *m* estate car, (*Amer*) station-wagon

Kombüse *f* **-,-n** (*Naut*) galley

Komet *m* **-en,-en** comet. **k~enhaft** *a* (*fig*) meteoric

Komfort /kɔm'fo:ɐ̯/ *m* **-s** comfort; (*Luxus*) luxury. **k~abel** /-'ta:bəl/ *a* comfortable, *adv* -bly; (*luxuriös*) luxurious, *adv* -ly

Komik *f* - humour. **K~er** *m* **-s,-** comic, comedian

komisch *a* funny; ⟨*Oper*⟩ comic; (*sonderbar*) odd, funny ● *adv* funnily; oddly. **k~erweise** *adv* funnily enough

Komitee *nt* **-s,-s** committee

Komma *nt* **-s,-s & -ta** comma; (*Dezimal-*) decimal point; **drei K~ fünf** three point five

Komman|dant *m* **-en,-en** commanding officer. **K~deur** /-'dø:ɐ̯/ *m* **-s,-e** commander. **k~dieren** *vt* command; (*befehlen*) order; (*fam: herum-*) order about ● *vi* (*haben*) give the orders

Kommando *nt* **-s,-s** order; (*Befehlsgewalt*) command; (*Einheit*) detachment. **K~brücke** *f* bridge

kommen† *vi* (*sein*) come; (*eintreffen*) arrive; (*gelangen*) get (**nach** to); **k~ lassen** send for; **auf/hinter etw** (*acc*) **k~** think of/find out about sth; **um/zu etw k~** lose/acquire sth; **wieder zu sich k~** come round; **wie kommt das?** why is that? **K~** *nt* **-s** coming; **K~ und Gehen** coming and going. **k~d** *a* coming; **k~den Montag** next Monday

Kommen|tar *m* **-s,-e** commentary; (*Bemerkung*) comment. **K~tator** *m* **-s,-en** /-'to:rən/ commentator. **k~tieren** *vt* comment on

kommer|zialisieren *vt* commercialize. **k~ziell** *a* commercial, *adv* -ly

Kommili|tone *m* **-n,-n, K~tonin** *f* **-,-nen** fellow student

Kommiß *m* **-sses** (*fam*) army

Kommissar *m* **-s,-e** commissioner; (*Polizei-*) superintendent

Kommission *f* **-,-en** commission; (*Gremium*) committee

Kommode *f* **-,-n** chest of drawers

Kommunalwahlen *fpl* local elections

Kommunikation /-'t͡si̯o:n/ *f* **-,-en** communication

Kommunion *f* **-,-en** [Holy] Communion

Kommuniqué /kɔmyni'ke:/ *nt* **-s,-s** communiqué

Kommun|ismus *m* **-** Communism. **K~ist(in)** *m* **-en,-en** (*f* **-,-nen**) Communist. **k~istisch** *a* Communist

kommunizieren *vi* (*haben*) receive [Holy] Communion

Komödie /ko'mø:di̯ə/ *f* **-,-n** comedy

Kompagnon /'kɔmpanjõ:/ *m* **-s,-s** (*Comm*) partner

kompakt *a* compact. **K~schallplatte** *f* compact disc

Kompanie *f* **-,-n** (*Mil*) company

Komparativ *m* **-s,-e** comparative

Komparse *m* **-n,-n** (*Theat*) extra

Kompaß *m* **-sses,-sse** compass

kompatibel *a* compatible

kompeten|t *a* competent. **K~z** *f* **-,-en** competence

komplett *a* complete, *adv* -ly

Komplex *m* **-es,-e** complex. **k~** *a* complex

Komplikation /-'t͡si̯o:n/ *f* **-,-en** complication

Kompliment *nt* **-[e]s,-e** compliment

Komplize *m* **-n,-n** accomplice

komplizier|en *vt* complicate. **k~t** *a* complicated

Komplott *nt* **-[e]s,-e** plot

kompo|nieren *vt/i* (*haben*) compose. **K~nist** *m* **-en,-en** composer. **K~sition** /-'t͡si̯o:n/ *f* **-,-en** composition

Kompositum *nt* **-s,-ta** compound

Kompost *m* **-[e]s** compost

Kompott *nt* **-[e]s,-e** stewed fruit

Kompresse *f* **-,-n** compress

komprimieren *vt* compress

Kompromiß *m* **-sses,-sse** compromise; **einen K~ schließen** compromise. **k~los** *a* uncompromising

kompromittieren *vt* compromise

Konden|sation /-'t͡si̯o:n/ *f* **-** condensation. **k~sieren** *vt* condense

Kondensmilch *f* evaporated/(*gesüßt*) condensed milk

Kondition /-'t͡si̯o:n/ *f* **-** (*Sport*) fitness; **in K~** in form. **K~al** *m* **-s,-e** (*Gram*) conditional

Konditor *m* **-s,-en** /-'to:rən/ confectioner. **K~ei** *f* **-,-en** patisserie

Kondo|lenzbrief *m* letter of condolence. **k~lieren** *vi* (*haben*) express one's condolences

Kondom *nt & m* **-s,-e** condom

Konfekt *nt* **-[e]s** confectionery; (*Pralinen*) chocolates *pl*

Konfektion /-'t͡si̯o:n/ *f* **-** ready-to-wear clothes *pl*

Konferenz *f* **-,-en** conference; (*Besprechung*) meeting

Konfession *f* **-,-en** [religious] denomination. **k~ell** *a* denominational. **k~slos** *a* non-denominational

Konfetti *nt* **-s** confetti

Konfirm|and(in) *m* **-en,-en** (*f* **-,-nen**) candidate for confirmation. **K~ation** /-'t͡si̯o:n/ *f* **-,-en** (*Relig*) confirmation. **k~ieren** *vt* (*Relig*) confirm

Konfitüre *f* **-,-n** jam

Konflikt *m* **-[e]s,-e** conflict

Konföderation /-'t͡si̯o:n/ *f* confederation

Konfront|ation /-'t͡si̯o:n/ *f* **-,-en** confrontation. **k~ieren** *vt* confront

konfus *a* confused

Kongreß *m* **-sses,-sse** congress

König *m* **-s,-e** king. **K~in** *f* **-,-nen** queen. **k~lich** *a* royal, *adv* -ly; (*hoheitsvoll*) regal, *adv* -ly; (*großzügig*) handsome, *adv* -ly; (*fam: groß*) tremendous, *adv* -ly. **K~reich** *nt* kingdom

konisch *a* conical

Konjug|ation /-'t͡si̯o:n/ *f* **-,-en** conjugation. **k~ieren** *vt* conjugate

Konjunktion /-'t͡si̯o:n/ *f* **-,-en** (*Gram*) conjunction

Konjunktiv *m* **-s,-e** subjunctive

Konjunktur *f* **-** economic situation; (*Hoch-*) boom

konkav *a* concave

konkret *a* concrete

Konkurren|t(in) *m* **-en,-en** (*f* **-,-nen**) competitor, rival. **K~z** *f* **-** competition; **jdm K~z machen** compete with s.o. **k~zfähig** *a* (*Comm*) competitive. **K~zkampf** *m* competition, rivalry

konkurrieren *vi* (*haben*) compete

Konkurs *m* **-es,-e** bankruptcy; **K~ machen** go bankrupt

können† *vt/i* (*haben*) **etw k~** be able to do sth; (*beherrschen*) know sth; **k~ Sie Deutsch?** do you know any German? **das kann ich nicht** I can't do that; **er kann nicht mehr** he can't go on; **für etw nichts k~** not be to blame for sth ● *v aux* **lesen/schwimmen k~** be able to read/swim; **er kann/konnte es tun** he can/could do it; **das kann** *od* **könnte [gut] sein** that may [well] be. **K~** *nt* **-s** ability; (*Wissen*) knowledge

Könner(in) *m* **-s,-** (*f* **-,-nen**) expert

konsequen|t *a* consistent, *adv* -ly; (*logisch*) logical, *adv* -ly. **K~z** *f* **-,-en** consequence

konservativ *a* conservative
Konserv|en *fpl* tinned *or* canned food *sg*. **K~enbüchse, K~endose** *f* tin, can. **k~ieren** *vt* preserve; (*in Dosen*) tin, can. **K~ierungsmittel** *nt* preservative
Konsistenz *f* - consistency
konsolidieren *vt* consolidate
Konsonant *m* **-en,-en** consonant
konsterniert *a* dismayed
Konstitution /-'tsi̯o:n/ *f* **-,-en** constitution. **k~ell** *a* constitutional
konstruieren *vt* construct; (*entwerfen*) design
Konstruk|tion /-'tsi̯o:n/ *f* **-,-en** construction; (*Entwurf*) design. **k~tiv** *a* constructive
Konsul *m* **-s,-n** consul. **K~at** *nt* **-[e]s,-e** consulate
Konsult|ation /-'tsi̯o:n/ *f* **-,-en** consultation. **k~ieren** *vt* consult
Konsum *m* **-s** consumption. **K~ent** *m* **-en,-en** consumer. **K~güter** *npl* consumer goods
Kontakt *m* **-[e]s,-e** contact. **K~linsen** *fpl* contact lenses. **K~person** *f* contact
kontern *vt/i* (*haben*) counter
Kontinent /'kɔn-, kɔnti'nɛnt/ *m* **-s,-e** continent
Kontingent *nt* **-[e]s,-e** (*Comm*) quota; (*Mil*) contingent
Kontinuität *f* - continuity
Konto *nt* **-s,-s** account. **K~auszug** *m* [bank] statement. **K~nummer** *f* account number. **K~stand** *m* [bank] balance
Kontrabaß *m* double-bass
Kontrast *m* **-[e]s,-e** contrast
Kontroll|abschnitt *m* counterfoil. **K~e** *f* **-,-n** control; (*Prüfung*) check. **K~eur** /-'lø:ɐ̯/ *m* **-s,-e** [ticket] inspector. **k~ieren** *vt* check; inspect ⟨*Fahrkarten*⟩; (*beherrschen*) control
Kontroverse *f* **-,-n** controversy
Kontur *f* **-,-en** contour
Konvention /-'tsi̯o:n/ *f* **-,-en** convention. **k~ell** *a* conventional, *adv* -ly
Konversation /-'tsi̯o:n/ *f* **-,-en** conversation. **K~slexikon** *nt* encyclopaedia
konvert|ieren *vi* (*haben*) (*Relig*) convert. **K~it** *m* **-en,-en** convert
konvex *a* convex
Konvoi /kɔn'vɔy/ *m* **-s,-s** convoy
Konzentration /-'tsi̯o:n/ *f* **-,-en** concentration. **K~slager** *nt* concentration camp
konzentrieren *vt* concentrate; **sich k~** concentrate (**auf** + *acc* on)
Konzept *nt* **-[e]s,-e** [rough] draft; **jdn aus dem K~ bringen** put s.o. off his stroke. **K~papier** *nt* rough paper
Konzern *m* **-s,-e** (*Comm*) group [of companies]
Konzert *nt* **-[e]s,-e** concert; (*Klavier-, Geigen-*) concerto. **K~meister** *m* leader, (*Amer*) concert-master
Konzession *f* **-,-en** licence; (*Zugeständnis*) concession
Konzil *nt* **-s,-e** (*Relig*) council
Kooperation /koˀɔpera'tsi̯o:n/ *f* co-operation
Koordin|ation /koˀɔrdina'tsi̯o:n/ *f* - co-ordination. **k~ieren** *vt* co-ordinate
Kopf *m* **-[e]s,⸚e** head; **ein K~ Kohl/Salat** a cabbage/lettuce; **aus dem K~** from memory; (*auswendig*) by heart; **auf dem K~** (*verkehrt*) upside down; **K~ an K~** neck and neck; ⟨*stehen*⟩ shoulder to shoulder; **sich** (*dat*) **den K~ waschen** wash one's hair; **sich** (*dat*) **den K~ zerbrechen** rack one's brains. **K~ball** *m* header. **K~bedeckung** *f* head-covering
Köpf|chen *nt* **-s,-** little head; **K~chen haben** (*fam*) be clever. **k~en** *vt* behead; (*Fußball*) head
Kopf|ende *nt* head. **K~haut** *f* scalp. **K~hörer** *m* headphones *pl*. **K~kissen** *nt* pillow. **K~kissenbezug** *m* pillow-case. **k~los** *a* panic-stricken. **K~nicken** *nt* **-s** nod. **K~rechnen** *nt* mental arithmetic. **K~salat** *m* lettuce. **K~schmerzen** *mpl* headache *sg*. **K~schütteln** *nt* **-s** shake of the head. **K~sprung** *m* header, dive. **K~stand** *m* headstand. **K~steinpflaster** *nt* cobble-stones *pl*. **K~stütze** *f* head-rest. **K~tuch** *nt* headscarf. **k~über** *adv* head first; (*fig*) headlong. **K~wäsche** *f* shampoo. **K~weh** *nt* headache. **K~zerbrechen** *nt* **-s sich** (*dat*) **K~zerbrechen machen** rack one's brains; (*sich sorgen*) worry
Kopie *f* **-,-n** copy. **k~ren** *vt* copy
Koppel[1] *f* **-,-n** enclosure; (*Pferde-*) paddock
Koppel[2] *nt* **-s,-** (*Mil*) belt. **k~n** *vt* couple
Koralle *f* **-,-n** coral
Korb *m* **-[e]s,⸚e** basket; **jdm einen K~ geben** (*fig*) turn s.o. down. **K~ball** *m* [kind of] netball. **K~stuhl** *m* wicker chair

Kord *m* **-s** (*Tex*) corduroy
Kordel *f* **-,-n** cord
Korinthe *f* **-,-n** currant
Kork *m* **-s** cork. **K~en** *m* **-s,-** cork. **K~enzieher** *m* **-s,-** corkscrew
Korn[1] *nt* **-[e]s,⸚er** grain; (*Samen-*) seed; (*coll: Getreide*) grain, corn; (*am Visier*) front sight
Korn[2] *m* **-[e]s,-** (*fam*) grain schnapps
Körn|chen *nt* **-s,-** granule. **k~ig** *a* granular
Körper *m* **-s,-** body; (*Geom*) solid. **K~bau** *m* build, physique. **k~behindert** *a* physically disabled. **k~lich** *a* physical, *adv* -ly; ⟨*Strafe*⟩ corporal. **K~pflege** *f* personal hygiene. **K~puder** *m* talcum powder. **K~schaft** *f* **-,-en** corporation, body. **K~strafe** *f* corporal punishment. **K~teil** *m* part of the body
Korps /ko:ɐ̯/ *nt* **-,-** /-[s],-s/ corps
korpulent *a* corpulent
korrekt *a* correct, *adv* -ly. **K~or** *m* **-s,-en** /-'to:rən/ proof-reader. **K~ur** *f* **-,-en** correction. **K~urabzug, K~urbogen** *m* proof
Korrespon|dent(in) *m* **-en,-en** (*f* **-,-nen**) correspondent. **K~denz** *f* **-,-en** correspondence. **k~dieren** *vi* (*haben*) correspond
Korridor *m* **-s,-e** corridor
korrigieren *vt* correct
Korrosion *f* **-** corrosion
korrumpieren *vt* corrupt
korrup|t *a* corrupt. **K~tion** /-'tsi̯o:n/ *f* **-** corruption
Korsett *nt* **-[e]s,-e** corset
koscher *a* kosher
Kose|name *m* pet name. **K~wort** *nt* (*pl* **-wörter**) term of endearment
Kosmet|ik *f* **-** beauty culture. **K~ika** *ntpl* cosmetics. **K~ikerin** *f* **-,-nen** beautician. **k~isch** *a* cosmetic; ⟨*Chirurgie*⟩ plastic
kosm|isch *a* cosmic. **K~onaut(in)** *m* **-en,-en** (*f* **-,-nen**) cosmonaut. **k~opolitisch** *a* cosmopolitan
Kosmos *m* **-** cosmos
Kost *f* **-** food; (*Ernährung*) diet; (*Verpflegung*) board
kostbar *a* precious. **K~keit** *f* **-,-en** treasure
kosten[1] *vt/i* (*haben*) **[von] etw k~** taste sth
kosten[2] *vt* cost; (*brauchen*) take; **wieviel kostet es?** how much is it? **K~** *pl* expense *sg*, cost *sg*; (*Jur*) costs; **auf meine K~** at my expense. **K~[vor]anschlag** *m* estimate. **k~los** *a* free • *adv* free [of charge]
Kosthappen *m* taste
köstlich *a* delicious; (*entzückend*) delightful. **K~keit** *f* **-,-en** (*fig*) gem; (*Culin*) delicacy
Kost|probe *f* taste; (*fig*) sample. **k~spielig** *a* expensive, costly
Kostüm *nt* **-s,-e** (*Theat*) costume; (*Verkleidung*) fancy dress; (*Schneider-*) suit. **K~fest** *nt* fancy-dress party. **k~iert** *a* **k~iert sein** be in fancy dress
Kot *m* **-[e]s** excrement; (*Schmutz*) dirt
Kotelett /kɔt'lɛt/ *nt* **-s,-s** chop, cutlet. **K~en** *pl* sideburns
Köter *m* **-s,-** (*pej*) dog
Kotflügel *m* (*Auto*) wing, (*Amer*) fender
kotzen *vi* (*haben*) (*sl*) throw up; **es ist zum K~** it makes you sick
Krabbe *f* **-,-n** crab; (*Garnele*) shrimp; (*rote*) prawn
krabbeln *vi* (*sein*) crawl
Krach *m* **-[e]s,⸚e** din, racket; (*Knall*) crash; (*fam: Streit*) row; (*fam: Ruin*) crash. **k~en** *vi* (*haben*) crash; **es hat gekracht** there was a bang/(*fam: Unfall*) a crash • (*sein*) break, crack; (*auftreffen*) crash (**gegen** into)
krächzen *vi* (*haben*) croak
Kraft *f* **-,⸚e** strength; (*Gewalt*) force; (*Arbeits-*) worker; **in/außer K~** in/no longer in force; **in K~ treten** come into force. **k~** *prep* (+*gen*) by virtue of. **K~ausdruck** *m* swearword. **K~fahrer** *m* driver. **K~fahrzeug** *nt* motor vehicle. **K~fahrzeugbrief** *m* [vehicle] registration document
kräftig *a* strong; (*gut entwickelt*) sturdy; (*nahrhaft*) nutritious; (*heftig*) hard • *adv* strongly; (*heftig*) hard. **k~en** *vt* strengthen
kraft|los *a* weak. **K~post** *f* post bus service. **K~probe** *f* trial of strength. **K~rad** *nt* motorcycle. **K~stoff** *m* (*Auto*) fuel. **k~voll** *a* strong, powerful. **K~wagen** *m* motor car. **K~werk** *nt* power station
Kragen *m* **-s,-** collar
Krähe *f* **-,-n** crow
krähen *vi* (*haben*) crow
krakeln *vt/i* (*haben*) scrawl
Kralle *f* **-,-n** claw. **k~n (sich)** *vr* clutch (**an jdn/etw** s.o./sth); ⟨*Katze:*⟩ dig its claws (**in** + *acc* into)

Kram *m* **-s** (*fam*) things *pl*, (*fam*) stuff; (*Angelegenheiten*) business; **wertloser K~** junk. **k~en** *vi* (*haben*) rummage about (**in** + *dat* in; **nach** for). **K~laden** *m* [small] general store

Krampf *m* **-[e]s,¨e** cramp. **K~adern** *fpl* varicose veins. **k~haft** *a* convulsive, *adv* -ly; (*verbissen*) desperate, *adv* -ly

Kran *m* **-[e]s,¨e** (*Techn*) crane

Kranich *m* **-s,-e** (*Zool*) crane

krank *a* (**kränker, kränkst**) sick; ⟨*Knie, Herz*⟩ bad; **k~ sein/werden/machen** be/fall/make ill; **sich k~ melden** report sick. **K~e(r)** *m/f* sick man/ woman, invalid; **die K~en** the sick *pl*

kränkeln *vi* (*haben*) be in poor health. **k~d** *a* ailing

kranken *vi* (*haben*) (*fig*) suffer (**an** + *dat* from)

kränken *vt* offend, hurt

Kranken|bett *nt* sick-bed. **K~geld** *nt* sickness benefit. **K~gymnast(in)** *m* **-en,-en** (*f* **-,-nen**) physiotherapist. **K~gymnastik** *f* physiotherapy. **K~haus** *nt* hospital. **K~kasse** *f* health insurance scheme/(*Amt*) office. **K~pflege** *f* nursing. **K~pfleger(in)** *m*(*f*) nurse. **K~saal** *m* [hospital] ward. **K~schein** *m* certificate of entitlement to medical treatment. **K~schwester** *f* nurse. **K~urlaub** *m* sick-leave. **K~versicherung** *f* health insurance. **K~wagen** *m* ambulance. **K~zimmer** *nt* sick-room

krank|haft *a* morbid; (*pathologisch*) pathological. **K~heit** *f* **-,-en** illness, disease

kränk|lich *a* sickly. **K~ung** *f* **-,-en** slight

Kranz *m* **-es,¨e** wreath; (*Ring*) ring

Krapfen *m* **-s,-** doughnut

kraß *a* (**krasser, krassest**) glaring; (*offensichtlich*) blatant; (*stark*) gross; rank ⟨*Außenseiter*⟩

Krater *m* **-s,-** crater

kratz|bürstig *a* (*fam*) prickly. **k~en** *vt/i* (*haben*) scratch; **sich k~en** scratch oneself/⟨*Tier:*⟩ itself. **K~er** *m* **-s,-** scratch; (*Werkzeug*) scraper

Kraul *nt* **-s** (*Sport*) crawl. **k~en**[1] *vi* (*haben/sein*) (*Sport*) do the crawl

kraulen[2] *vt* tickle; **sich am Kopf k~** scratch one's head

kraus *a* wrinkled; ⟨*Haar*⟩ frizzy; (*verworren*) muddled; **k~ ziehen** wrinkle. **K~e** *f* **-,-n** frill, ruffle; (*Haar-*) frizziness

kräuseln *vt* wrinkle; frizz ⟨*Haar*⟩; gather ⟨*Stoff*⟩; ripple ⟨*Wasser*⟩; **sich k~** wrinkle; (*sich kringeln*) curl; ⟨*Haar:*⟩ go frizzy; ⟨*Wasser:*⟩ ripple

krausen *vt* wrinkle; frizz ⟨*Haar*⟩; gather ⟨*Stoff*⟩; **sich k~** wrinkle; ⟨*Haar:*⟩ go frizzy

Kraut *nt* **-[e]s, Kräuter** herb; (*SGer*) cabbage; (*Sauer-*) sauerkraut; **wie K~ und Rüben** (*fam*) higgledy-piggledy

Krawall *m* **-s,-e** riot; (*Lärm*) row

Krawatte *f* **-,-n** [neck]tie

kraxeln *vi* (*sein*) (*fam*) clamber

krea|tiv /krea'ti:f/ *a* creative. **K~tur** *f* **-,-en** creature

Krebs *m* **-es,-e** crayfish; (*Med*) cancer; (*Astr*) Cancer. **k~ig** *a* cancerous

Kredit *m* **-s,-e** credit; (*Darlehen*) loan; **auf K~** on credit. **K~karte** *f* credit card

Kreid|e *f* **-** chalk. **k~ebleich** *a* deathly pale. **k~ig** *a* chalky

kreieren /kre'i:rən/ *vt* create

Kreis *m* **-es,-e** circle; (*Admin*) district

kreischen *vt/i* (*haben*) screech; (*schreien*) shriek

Kreisel *m* **-s,-** [spinning] top; (*fam: Kreisverkehr*) roundabout

kreis|en *vi* (*haben*) circle; revolve (**um** around). **k~förmig** *a* circular. **K~lauf** *m* cycle; (*Med*) circulation. **k~rund** *a* circular. **K~säge** *f* circular saw. **K~verkehr** *m* [traffic] roundabout, (*Amer*) traffic circle

Krem *f* **-,-s** & *m* **-s,-e** cream

Krematorium *nt* **-s,-ien** crematorium

Krempe *f* **-,-n** [hat] brim

Krempel *m* **-s** (*fam*) junk

krempeln *vt* turn (**nach oben** up)

Kren *m* **-[e]s** (*Aust*) horseradish

krepieren *vi* (*sein*) explode; (*sl: sterben*) die

Krepp *m* **-s,-s** & **-e** crêpe

Kreppapier *nt* crêpe paper

Kresse *f* **-,-n** cress; (*Kapuziner-*) nasturtium

Kreta *nt* **-s** Crete

Kreuz *nt* **-es,-e** cross; (*Kreuzung*) intersection; (*Mus*) sharp; (*Kartenspiel*) clubs *pl*; (*Anat*) small of the back; **über K~** crosswise; **das K~ schlagen** cross oneself. **k~** *adv* **k~ und quer** in all directions. **k~en** *vt* cross; **sich k~en** cross; ⟨*Straßen:*⟩

intersect; ⟨*Meinungen:*⟩ clash • *vi* (*haben/sein*) cruise; ⟨*Segelschiff:*⟩ tack. **K~er** *m* **-s,-** cruiser. **K~fahrt** *f* (*Naut*) cruise; (*K~zug*) crusade. **K~feuer** *nt* crossfire. **K~gang** *m* cloister

kreuzig|en *vt* crucify. **K~ung** *f* **-,-en** crucifixion

Kreuz|otter *f* adder, common viper. **K~ung** *f* **-,-en** intersection; (*Straßen-*) crossroads *sg*; (*Hybride*) cross. **K~verhör** *nt* cross-examination; **ins K~verhör nehmen** cross-examine. **K~weg** *m* crossroads *sg*; (*Relig*) Way of the Cross. **k~weise** *adv* crosswise. **K~worträtsel** *nt* crossword [puzzle]. **K~zug** *m* crusade

kribbel|ig *a* (*fam*) edgy. **k~n** *vi* (*haben*) tingle; (*kitzeln*) tickle

kriech|en† *vi* (*sein*) crawl; (*fig*) grovel (**vor** + *dat* to). **k~erisch** *a* grovelling. **K~spur** *f* (*Auto*) crawler lane. **K~tier** *nt* reptile

Krieg *m* **-[e]s,-e** war

kriegen *vt* (*fam*) get; **ein Kind k~** have a baby

Krieger|denkmal *nt* war memorial. **k~isch** *a* warlike; (*militärisch*) military

kriegs|beschädigt *a* war-disabled. **K~dienstverweigerer** *m* **-s,-** conscientious objector. **K~gefangene(r)** *m* prisoner of war. **K~gefangenschaft** *f* captivity. **K~gericht** *nt* court martial. **K~list** *f* stratagem. **K~rat** *m* council of war. **K~recht** *nt* martial law. **K~schiff** *nt* warship. **K~verbrechen** *nt* war crime

Krimi *m* **-s,-s** (*fam*) crime story/film. **K~nalität** *f* **-** crime; (*Vorkommen*) crime rate. **K~nalpolizei** *f* criminal investigation department. **K~nalroman** *m* crime novel. **k~nell** *a* criminal. **K~nelle(r)** *m* criminal

kringeln (sich) *vr* curl [up]; (*vor Lachen*) fall about

Kripo *f* **-** = **Kriminalpolizei**

Krippe *f* **-,-n** manger; (*Weihnachts-*) crib; (*Kinder-*) crèche. **K~nspiel** *nt* Nativity play

Krise *f* **-,-n** crisis

Kristall[1] *nt* **-s** (*Glas*) crystal; (*geschliffen*) cut glass

Kristall[2] *m* **-s,-e** crystal. **k~isieren** *vi/r* (*haben*) **[sich] k~isieren** crystallize

Kriterium *nt* **-s,-ien** criterion

Kritik *f* **-,-en** criticism; (*Rezension*) review; **unter aller K~** (*fam*) abysmal

Kriti|ker *m* **-s,-** critic; (*Rezensent*) reviewer. **k~sch** *a* critical, *adv* -ly. **k~sieren** *vt* criticize; review

kritteln *vi* (*haben*) find fault (**an** + *acc* with)

kritzeln *vt/i* (*haben*) scribble

Krokette *f* **-,-n** (*Culin*) croquette

Krokodil *nt* **-s,-e** crocodile

Krokus *m* **-,-[se]** crocus

Krone *f* **-,-n** crown; (*Baum-*) top

krönen *vt* crown

Kron|leuchter *m* chandelier. **K~prinz** *m* crown prince

Krönung *f* **-,-en** coronation; (*fig: Höhepunkt*) crowning event/(*Leistung*) achievement

Kropf *m* **-[e]s,¨e** (*Zool*) crop; (*Med*) goitre

Kröte *f* **-,-n** toad

Krücke *f* **-,-n** crutch; (*Stock-*) handle; **an K~n** on crutches

Krug *m* **-[e]s,¨e** jug; (*Bier-*) tankard

Krume *f* **-,-n** soft part [of loaf]; (*Krümel*) crumb; (*Acker-*) topsoil

Krümel *m* **-s,-** crumb. **k~ig** *a* crumbly. **k~n** *vt* crumble • *vi* (*haben*) be crumbly; ⟨*Person:*⟩ drop crumbs

krumm *a* crooked; (*gebogen*) curved; (*verbogen*) bent. **k~beinig** *a* bow-legged

krümmen *vt* bend; crook ⟨*Finger*⟩; **sich k~** bend; (*sich winden*) writhe; (*vor Schmerzen/Lachen*) double up

krummnehmen† *vt sep* (*fam*) take amiss

Krümmung *f* **-,-en** bend; (*Kurve*) curve

Krüppel *m* **-s,-** cripple

Kruste *f* **-,-n** crust; (*Schorf*) scab

Kruzifix *nt* **-es,-e** crucifix

Krypta /ˈkrʏpta/ *f* **-,-ten** crypt

Kub|a *nt* **-s** Cuba. **k~anisch** *a* Cuban

Kübel *m* **-s,-** tub; (*Eimer*) bucket; (*Techn*) skip

Kubik- *pref* cubic. **K~meter** *m & nt* cubic metre

Küche *f* **-,-n** kitchen; (*Kochkunst*) cooking; **kalte/warme K~** cold/hot food; **französische K~** French cuisine

Kuchen *m* **-s,-** cake

Küchen|herd *m* cooker, stove. **K~maschine** *f* food processor, mixer. **K~schabe** *f* **-,-n** cockroach. **K~zettel** *m* menu

Kuckuck *m* **-s,-e** cuckoo; **zum K~!** (*fam*) hang it! **K~suhr** *f* cuckoo clock

Kufe *f* **-,-n** [sledge] runner

Kugel *f* **-,-n** ball; (*Geom*) sphere; (*Gewehr-*) bullet; (*Sport*) shot. **k~förmig** *a* spherical. **K~lager** *nt* ball-bearing. **k~n** *vt/i* (*haben*) roll; **sich k~n** roll/(*vor Lachen*) fall about. **k~rund** *a* spherical; (*fam: dick*) tubby. **K~schreiber** *m* **-s,-** ballpoint [pen]. **k~sicher** *a* bullet-proof. **K~stoßen** *nt* **-s** shot-putting

Kuh *f* **-,¨e** cow

kühl *a* cool, *adv* -ly; (*kalt*) chilly. **K~box** *f* **-,-en** cool-box. **K~e** *f* **-** coolness; chilliness. **k~en** *vt* cool; refrigerate ⟨*Lebensmittel*⟩; chill ⟨*Wein*⟩. **K~er** *m* **-s,-** ice-bucket; (*Auto*) radiator. **K~erhaube** *f* bonnet, (*Amer*) hood. **K~fach** *nt* frozen-food compartment. **K~raum** *m* cold store. **K~schrank** *m* refrigerator. **K~truhe** *f* freezer. **K~ung** *f* **-** cooling; (*Frische*) coolness. **K~wasser** *nt* [radiator] water

Kuhmilch *f* cow's milk

kühn *a* bold, *adv* -ly; (*wagemutig*) daring. **K~heit** *f* **-** boldness

Kuhstall *m* cowshed

Küken *nt* **-s,-** chick; (*Enten-*) duckling

Kukuruz *m* **-[es]** (*Aust*) maize

kulant *a* obliging

Kuli *m* **-s,-s** (*fam: Kugelschreiber*) ballpoint [pen], Biro (P)

kulinarisch *a* culinary

Kulissen *fpl* (*Theat*) scenery *sg*; (*seitlich*) wings; **hinter den K~** (*fig*) behind the scenes

kullern *vt/i* (*sein*) (*fam*) roll

Kult *m* **-[e]s,-e** cult

kultivier|en *vt* cultivate. **k~t** *a* cultured

Kultur *f* **-,-en** culture; **K~en** plantations. **K~beutel** *m* toilet-bag. **k~ell** *a* cultural. **K~film** *m* documentary film

Kultusminister *m* Minister of Education and Arts

Kümmel *m* **-s** caraway; (*Getränk*) kümmel

Kummer *m* **-s** sorrow, grief; (*Sorge*) worry; (*Ärger*) trouble

kümmer|lich *a* puny; (*dürftig*) meagre; (*armselig*) wretched. **k~n** *vt* concern; **sich k~n um** look after; (*sich befassen*) concern oneself with; (*beachten*) take notice of; **ich werde mich darum k~n** I shall see to it; **k~e dich um deine eigenen Angelegenheiten!** mind your own business!

kummervoll *a* sorrowful

Kumpel *m* **-s,-** (*fam*) mate

Kunde *m* **-n,-n** customer. **K~ndienst** *m* [after-sales] service

Kund|gebung *f* **-,-en** (*Pol*) rally. **k~ig** *a* knowledgeable; (*sach-*) expert

kündig|en *vt* cancel ⟨*Vertrag*⟩; give notice of withdrawal for ⟨*Geld*⟩; give notice to quit ⟨*Wohnung*⟩; **seine Stellung k~en** give [in one's] notice ● *vi* (*haben*) give [in one's] notice; **jdm k~en** give s.o. notice [of dismissal/⟨*Vermieter:*⟩ to quit]. **K~ung** *f* **-,-en** cancellation; notice [of withdrawal/dismissal/to quit]; (*Entlassung*) dismissal. **K~ungsfrist** *f* period of notice

Kund|in *f* **-,-nen** [woman] customer. **K~machung** *f* **-,-en** (*Aust*) [public] notice. **K~schaft** *f* **-** clientele, customers *pl*

künftig *a* future ● *adv* in future

Kunst *f* **-,¨e** art; (*Können*) skill. **K~dünger** *m* artificial fertilizer. **K~faser** *f* synthetic fibre. **k~fertig** *a* skilful. **K~fertigkeit** *f* skill. **K~galerie** *f* art gallery. **k~gerecht** *a* expert, *adv* -ly. **K~geschichte** *f* history of art. **K~gewerbe** *nt* arts and crafts *pl*. **K~griff** *m* trick. **K~händler** *m* art dealer

Künstler *m* **-s,-** artist; (*Könner*) master. **K~in** *f* **-,-nen** [woman] artist. **k~isch** *a* artistic, *adv* -ally. **K~name** *m* pseudonym; (*Theat*) stage name

künstlich *a* artificial, *adv* -ly

kunst|los *a* simple. **K~maler** *m* painter. **K~stoff** *m* plastic. **K~stopfen** *nt* invisible mending. **K~stück** *nt* trick; (*große Leistung*) feat. **k~voll** *a* artistic; (*geschickt*) skilful, *adv* -ly; (*kompliziert*) elaborate, *adv* -ly. **K~werk** *nt* work of art

kunterbunt *a* multicoloured; (*gemischt*) mixed ● *adv* **k~ durcheinander** higgledy-piggledy

Kupfer *nt* **-s** copper. **k~n** *a* copper

kupieren *vt* crop

Kupon /ku'põː/ *m* **-s,-s** voucher; (*Zins-*) coupon; (*Stoff-*) length

Kuppe *f* **-,-n** [rounded] top; (*Finger-*) end, tip

Kuppel *f* **-,-n** dome

kupp|eln *vt* couple (**an**+*acc* to) ● *vi* (*haben*) (*Auto*) operate the clutch. **K~lung** *f* **-,-en** coupling; (*Auto*) clutch

Kur *f* **-,-en** course of treatment; (*im Kurort*) cure

Kür *f* **-,-en** (*Sport*) free exercise; (*Eislauf*) free programme

Kurbel *f* **-,-n** crank. **k~n** *vt* wind (**nach oben/unten** up/down). **K~welle** *f* crankshaft

Kürbis *m* **-ses,-se** pumpkin; (*Flaschen-*) marrow

Kurgast *m* health-resort visitor

Kurier *m* **-s,-e** courier

kurieren *vt* cure

kurios *a* curious, odd. **K~ität** *f* **-,-en** oddness; (*Objekt*) curiosity; (*Kunst*) curio

Kur|ort *m* health resort; (*Badeort*) spa. **K~pfuscher** *m* quack

Kurs *m* **-es,-e** course; (*Aktien-*) price. **K~buch** *nt* timetable

kursieren *vi* (*haben*) circulate

kursiv *a* italic ● *adv* in italics. **K~schrift** *f* italics *pl*

Kursus *m* **-,Kurse** course

Kurswagen *m* through carriage

Kurtaxe *f* visitors' tax

Kurve *f* **-,-n** curve; (*Straßen-*) bend

kurz *a* (**kürzer, kürzest**) short; (*knapp*) brief; (*rasch*) quick; (*schroff*) curt; **k~e Hosen** shorts; **vor k~em** a short time ago; **seit k~em** lately; **binnen k~em** shortly; **den kürzeren ziehen** get the worst of it ● *adv* briefly; quickly; curtly; **k~ vor/nach** a little way/(*zeitlich*) shortly before/after; **sich k~ fassen** be brief; **k~ und gut** in short; **über k~ oder lang** sooner or later; **zu k~ kommen** get less than one's fair share. **K~arbeit** *f* short-time working. **k~ärmelig** *a* short-sleeved. **k~atmig** *a* **k~atmig sein** be short of breath

Kürze *f* **-** shortness; (*Knappheit*) brevity; **in K~** shortly. **k~n** *vt* shorten; (*verringern*) cut

kurz|erhand *adv* without further ado. **k~fristig** *a* short-term ● *adv* at short notice. **K~geschichte** *f* short story. **k~lebig** *a* short-lived

kürzlich *adv* recently

Kurz|meldung *f* newsflash. **K~nachrichten** *fpl* news headlines. **K~schluß** *m* short circuit; (*fig*) brainstorm. **K~schrift** *f* shorthand. **k~sichtig** *a* short-sighted. **K~sichtigkeit** *f* **-** short-sightedness. **K~streckenrakete** *f* short-range missile. **k~um** *adv* in short

Kürzung *f* **-,-en** shortening; (*Verringerung*) cut (*gen* in)

Kurz|waren *fpl* haberdashery *sg*, (*Amer*) notions. **k~weilig** *a* amusing. **K~welle** *f* short wave

kuscheln (sich) *vr* snuggle (**an**+*acc* up to)

Kusine *f* **-,-n** [female] cousin

Kuß *m* **-sses,⸚sse** kiss

küssen *vt/i* (*haben*) kiss; **sich k~** kiss

Küste *f* **-,-n** coast. **K~nwache, K~nwacht** *f* coastguard

Küster *m* **-s,-** verger

Kustos *m* **-,-oden** /-'to:-/ curator

Kutsch|e *f* **-,-n** [horse-drawn] carriage/(*geschlossen*) coach. **K~er** *m* **-s,-** coachman, driver. **k~ieren** *vt/i* (*haben*) drive

Kutte *f* **-,-n** (*Relig*) habit

Kutter *m* **-s,-** (*Naut*) cutter

Kuvert /ku've:ɐ̯/ *nt* **-s,-s** envelope

KZ /ka:'tsɛt/ *nt* **-[s],-[s]** concentration camp

L

labil *a* unstable

Labo|r *nt* **-s,-s** & **-e** laboratory. **L~rant(in)** *m* **-en,-en** (*f* **-,-nen**) laboratory assistant. **L~ratorium** *nt* **-s,-ien** laboratory

Labyrinth *nt* **-[e]s,-e** maze, labyrinth

Lache *f* **-,-n** puddle; (*Blut-*) pool

lächeln *vi* (*haben*) smile. **L~** *nt* **-s** smile. **l~d** *a* smiling

lachen *vi* (*haben*) laugh. **L~** *nt* **-s** laugh; (*Gelächter*) laughter

lächerlich *a* ridiculous, *adv* -ly; **sich l~ machen** make a fool of oneself. **L~keit** *f* **-,-en** ridiculousness; (*Kleinigkeit*) triviality

lachhaft *a* laughable

Lachs *m* **-es,-e** salmon. **l~farben, l~rosa** *a* salmon-pink

Lack *m* **-[e]s,-e** varnish; (*Japan-*) lacquer; (*Auto*) paint. **l~en** *vt* varnish. **l~ieren** *vt* varnish; (*spritzen*) spray. **L~schuhe** *mpl* patent-leather shoes

Lade *f* **-,-n** drawer

laden† *vt* load; (*Electr*) charge; (*Jur: vor-*) summons

Laden *m* **-s,⸚** shop, (*Amer*) store; (*Fenster-*) shutter. **L~dieb** *m* shoplifter. **L~diebstahl** *m* shop-lifting. **L~schluß** *m* [shop] closing-time. **L~tisch** *m* counter

Laderaum *m* (*Naut*) hold

lädieren *vt* damage

Ladung *f* **-,-en** load; (*Naut, Aviat*) cargo; (*elektrische, Spreng-*) charge; (*Jur: Vor-*) summons

Lage *f* **-,-n** position; (*Situation*) situation; (*Schicht*) layer; (*fam: Runde*) round; **nicht in der L~ sein** not be in a position (**zu** to)

Lager *nt* **-s,-** camp; (*L~haus*) warehouse; (*Vorrat*) stock; (*Techn*) bearing; (*Erz-, Ruhe-*) bed; (*eines Tieres*) lair; **[nicht] auf L~** [not] in stock. **L~haus** *nt* warehouse. **l~n** *vt* store; (*legen*) lay; **sich l~n** settle; (*sich legen*) lie down ● *vi* (*haben*) camp; (*liegen*) lie; ⟨*Waren:*⟩ be stored. **L~raum** *m* store-room. **L~stätte** *f* (*Geol*) deposit. **L~ung** *f* **-** storage

Lagune *f* **-,-n** lagoon

lahm *a* lame. **l~en** *vi* (*haben*) be lame

lähmen *vt* paralyse

lahmlegen *vt sep* (*fig*) paralyse

Lähmung *f* **-,-en** paralysis

Laib *m* **-[e]s,-e** loaf

Laich *m* **-[e]s** (*Zool*) spawn. **l~en** *vi* (*haben*) spawn

Laie *m* **-n,-n** layman; (*Theat*) amateur. **l~nhaft** *a* amateurish. **L~nprediger** *m* lay preacher

Lake *f* **-,-n** brine

Laken *nt* **-s,-** sheet

lakonisch *a* laconic, *adv* -ally

Lakritze *f* **-** liquorice

lallen *vt/i* (*haben*) mumble; ⟨*Baby:*⟩ babble

Lametta *nt* **-s** tinsel

Lamm *nt* **-[e]s,⸚er** lamb

Lampe *f* **-,-n** lamp; (*Decken-, Wand-*) light; (*Glüh-*) bulb. **L~nfieber** *nt* stage fright. **L~nschirm** *m* lampshade

Lampion /lam'pi̯ɔŋ/ *m* **-s,-s** Chinese lantern

lancieren /lã'si:rən/ *vt* (*Comm*) launch

Land *nt* **-[e]s,⸚er** country; (*Fest-*) land; (*Bundes-*) state, Land; (*Aust*) province; **Stück L~** piece of land; **auf dem L~e** in the country; **an L~ gehen** (*Naut*) go ashore. **L~arbeiter** *m* agricultural worker. **L~ebahn** *f* runway. **l~einwärts** *adv* inland. **l~en** *vt/i* (*sein*) land; (*fam: gelangen*) end up

Ländereien *pl* estates

Länderspiel *nt* international

Landesteg *m* landing-stage

Landesverrat *m* treason

Land|karte *f* map. **l~läufig** *a* popular

ländlich *a* rural

Land|maschinen *fpl* agricultural machinery *sg*. **L~schaft** *f* **-,-en** scenery; (*Geog, Kunst*) landscape; (*Gegend*) country[side]. **l~schaftlich** *a* scenic; (*regional*) regional. **L~smann** *m* (*pl* **-leute**) fellow countryman, compatriot. **L~smännin** *f* **-,-nen** fellow countrywoman. **L~straße** *f* country road; (*Admin*) ≈ B road. **L~streicher** *m* **-s,-** tramp. **L~tag** *m* state/(*Aust*) provincial parliament

Landung *f* **-,-en** landing. **L~sbrücke** *f* landing-stage

Land|vermesser *m* **-s,-** surveyor. **L~weg** *m* country lane; **auf dem L~weg** overland. **L~wirt** *m* farmer. **L~wirtschaft** *f* agriculture; (*Hof*) farm. **l~wirtschaftlich** *a* agricultural

lang[1] *adv & prep* (+ *preceding acc or preceding* **an** + *dat*) along; **den** *od* **am Fluß l~** along the river

lang[2] *a* (**länger, längst**) long; (*groß*) tall; **seit l~em** for a long time ● *adv* **eine Stunde/Woche l~** for an hour/a week; **mein Leben l~** all my life. **l~ärmelig** *a* long-sleeved. **l~atmig** *a* long-winded. **l~e** *adv* a long time; ⟨*schlafen*⟩ late; **wie/zu l~e** how/too long; **schon l~e** [for] a long time; (*zurückliegend*) a long time ago; **l~e nicht** not for a long time; (*bei weitem nicht*) nowhere near

Länge *f* **-,-n** length; (*Geog*) longitude; **der L~ nach** lengthways; ⟨*liegen, fallen*⟩ full length

langen *vt* hand (*dat* to) ● *vi* (*haben*) reach (**an etw** *acc* sth; **nach** for); (*genügen*) be enough

Läng|engrad *m* degree of longitude. **L~enmaß** *nt* linear measure. **l~er** *a & adv* longer; (*längere Zeit*) [for] some time

Langeweile *f* **-** boredom; **L~ haben** be bored

lang|fristig *a* long-term; ⟨*Vorhersage*⟩ long-range. **l~jährig** *a* long-standing; ⟨*Erfahrung*⟩ long. **l~lebig** *a* long-lived

länglich *a* oblong. **l~rund** *a* oval

langmütig *a* long-suffering

längs *adv & prep* (+ *gen/dat*) along; (*der Länge nach*) lengthways

lạng|sam *a* slow, *adv* -ly. **L~samkeit** *f* - slowness. **L~schläfer(in)** *m(f)* (*fam*) late riser. **L~schrift** *f* longhand

lạ̈ngst *adv* **[schon] l~** for a long time; (*zurückliegend*) a long time ago; **l~ nicht** nowhere near

Lạng|strecken- *pref* long-distance; (*Mil, Aviat*) long-range. **l~weilen** *vt* bore; **sich l~weilen** be bored. **l~weilig** *a* boring, *adv* -ly. **L~welle** *f* long wave. **l~wierig** *a* lengthy

Lạnze *f* -,-**n** lance

Lappalie /la'pa:li̯ə/ *f* -,-**n** trifle

Lạppen *m* -**s**,- cloth; (*Anat*) lobe

lạ̈ppisch *a* silly

Lạpsus *m* -,- slip

Lạ̈rche *f* -,-**n** larch

Lạ̈rm *m* -**s** noise. **l~en** *vi* (*haben*) make a noise. **l~end** *a* noisy

Larve /'larfə/ *f* -,-**n** larva; (*Maske*) mask

lạsch *a* listless; (*schlaff*) limp; (*fade*) insipid

Lạsche *f* -,-**n** tab; (*Verschluß-*) flap; (*Zunge*) tongue

Laser /'le:-, 'la:zɐ/ *m* -**s**,- laser

lạssen† *vt* leave; (*zulassen*) let; **jdm etw l~** let s.o. keep sth; **sein Leben l~** lose one's life; **etw [sein** *od* **bleiben] l~** not do sth; (*aufhören*) stop [doing] sth; **laß das!** stop it! **jdn schlafen/gewinnen l~** let s.o. sleep/win; **jdn warten l~** keep s.o. waiting; **etw machen/reparieren l~** have sth done/repaired; **etw verschwinden l~** make sth disappear; **sich [leicht] biegen/öffnen l~** bend/open [easily]; **sich gut waschen l~** wash well; **es läßt sich nicht leugnen** it is undeniable; **laßt uns gehen!** let's go!

lạ̈ssig *a* casual, *adv* -ly. **L~keit** *f* - casualness

Lạsso *nt* -**s**,-**s** lasso

Lạst *f* -,-**en** load; (*Gewicht*) weight; (*fig*) burden; **L~en** charges; (*Steuern*) taxes; **jdm zur L~ fallen** be a burden on s.o. **L~auto** *nt* lorry. **l~en** *vi* (*haben*) weigh heavily/(*liegen*) rest (**auf** + *dat* on). **L~enaufzug** *m* goods lift

Lạster[1] *m* -**s**,- (*fam*) lorry, (*Amer*) truck

Lạster[2] *nt* -**s**,- vice. **l~haft** *a* depraved; (*zügellos*) dissolute

lạ̈ster|lich *a* blasphemous. **l~n** *vt* blaspheme ● *vi* (*haben*) make disparaging remarks (**über** + *acc* about). **L~ung** *f* -,-**en** blasphemy

lạ̈stig *a* troublesome; **l~ sein/werden** be/become a nuisance

Lạst|kahn *m* barge. **L~[kraft]wagen** *m* lorry, (*Amer*) truck. **L~zug** *m* lorry with trailer[s]

Latein *nt* -**[s]** Latin. **L~amerika** *nt* Latin America. **l~isch** *a* Latin

latẹnt *a* latent

Latẹrne *f* -,-**n** lantern; (*Straßen-*) street lamp. **L~npfahl** *m* lamp-post

latschen *vi* (*sein*) (*fam*) traipse; (*schlurfen*) shuffle

Lạtte *f* -,-**n** slat; (*Tor-, Hochsprung-*) bar

Lạtz *m* -**es**,-̈**e** bib

Lạ̈tzchen *nt* -**s**,- [baby's] bib

Lạtzhose *f* dungarees *pl*

lau *a* lukewarm; (*mild*) mild

Laub *nt* -**[e]s** leaves *pl*; (*L~werk*) foliage. **L~baum** *m* deciduous tree

Laube *f* -,-**n** summer-house; (*gewachsen*) arbour. **L~ngang** *m* pergola; (*Archit*) arcades *pl*

Laub|säge *f* fretsaw. **L~wald** *m* deciduous forest

Lauch *m* -**[e]s** leeks *pl*

Lauer *f* **auf der L~ liegen** lie in wait. **l~n** *vi* (*haben*) lurk; **l~n auf** (+ *acc*) lie in wait for

Lauf *m* -**[e]s, Läufe** run; (*Laufen*) running; (*Verlauf*) course; (*Wett-*) race; (*Sport: Durchgang*) heat; (*Gewehr-*) barrel; **im L~[e]** (+ *gen*) in the course of. **L~bahn** *f* career. **l~en**† *vi* (*sein*) run; (*zu Fuß gehen*) walk; (*gelten*) be valid; **Ski/Schlittschuh l~en** ski/skate. **l~end** *a* running; (*gegenwärtig*) current; (*regelmäßig*) regular; **l~ende Nummer** serial number; **auf dem l~enden sein/jdn auf dem l~enden halten** be/keep s.o. up to date ● *adv* continually. **l~enlassen**† *vt sep* (*fam*) let go

Läufer *m* -**s**,- (*Person, Teppich*) runner; (*Schach*) bishop

Lauf|gitter *nt* play-pen. **L~masche** *f* ladder. **L~rolle** *f* castor. **L~schritt** *m* **im L~schritt** at a run; (*Mil*) at the double. **L~stall** *m* play-pen. **L~zettel** *m* circular

Lauge *f* -,-**n** soapy water

Laun|e *f* -,-**n** mood; (*Einfall*) whim; **guter L~e sein, gute L~e haben** be in a good mood. **l~enhaft** *a* capricious. **l~isch** *a* moody

Laus *f* -, **Läuse** louse; (*Blatt-*) greenfly. **L~bub** *m* (*fam*) rascal

lauschen *vi* (*haben*) listen; (*heimlich*) eavesdrop

lausig *a* (*fam*) lousy • *adv* terribly
laut *a* loud, *adv* -ly; (*geräuschvoll*) noisy, *adv* -ily; **l~ lesen** read aloud; **l~er stellen** turn up • *prep* (+*gen*/*dat*) according to. **L~** *m* **-es,-e** sound
Laute *f* **-,-n** (*Mus*) lute
lauten *vi* (*haben*) ⟨*Text:*⟩ run, read; **auf jds Namen l~** be in s.o.'s name
läuten *vt*/*i* (*haben*) ring
lauter *a* pure; (*ehrlich*) honest; ⟨*Wahrheit*⟩ plain • *a inv* sheer; (*nichts als*) nothing but. **L~keit** *f* - integrity
läutern *vt* purify
laut|hals *adv* at the top of one's voice; ⟨*lachen*⟩ out loud. **l~los** *a* silent, *adv* -ly; ⟨*Stille*⟩ hushed. **L~schrift** *f* phonetics *pl*. **L~sprecher** *m* loudspeaker. **l~stark** *a* vociferous, *adv* -ly. **L~stärke** *f* volume
lauwarm *a* lukewarm
Lava *f* **-,-ven** lava
Lavendel *m* **-s** lavender
lavieren *vi* (*haben*) manœuvre
Lawine *f* **-,-n** avalanche
lax *a* lax. **L~heit** *f* - laxity
Lazarett *nt* **-[e]s,-e** military hospital
leasen /'li:sən/ *vt* rent
Lebehoch *nt* cheer
leben *vt*/*i* (*haben*) live (**von** on); **leb wohl!** farewell! **L~** *nt* **-s,-** life; (*Treiben*) bustle; **am L~** alive. **l~d** *a* living
lebendig *a* live; (*lebhaft*) lively; (*anschaulich*) vivid, *adv* -ly; **l~ sein** be alive. **L~keit** *f* - liveliness; vividness
Lebens|abend *m* old age. **L~alter** *nt* age. **L~art** *f* manners *pl*. **l~fähig** *a* viable. **L~gefahr** *f* mortal danger; **in L~gefahr** in mortal danger; ⟨*Patient*⟩ critically ill. **l~gefährlich** *a* extremely dangerous; ⟨*Verletzung*⟩ critical • *adv* critically. **L~größe** *f* **in L~größe** life-sized. **L~haltungskosten** *pl* cost of living *sg*. **l~lang** *a* lifelong. **l~länglich** *a* life ... • *adv* for life. **L~lauf** *m* curriculum vitae. **L~mittel** *ntpl* food *sg*. **L~mittelgeschäft** *nt* food shop. **L~mittelhändler** *m* grocer. **l~notwendig** *a* vital. **L~retter** *m* rescuer; (*beim Schwimmen*) life-guard. **L~standard** *m* standard of living. **L~unterhalt** *m* livelihood; **seinen L~unterhalt verdienen** earn one's living. **L~versicherung** *f* life assurance. **L~wandel** *m* conduct. **l~wichtig** *a* vital. **L~zeichen** *nt* sign of life. **L~zeit** *f* **auf L~zeit** for life
Leber *f* **-,-n** liver. **L~fleck** *m* mole. **L~wurst** *f* liver sausage
Lebe|wesen *nt* living being. **L~wohl** *nt* **-s,-s & -e** farewell
leb|haft *a* lively; ⟨*Farbe*⟩ vivid. **L~haftigkeit** *f* - liveliness. **L~kuchen** *m* gingerbread. **l~los** *a* lifeless. **L~tag** *m* **mein/dein L~tag** all my/your life. **L~zeiten** *fpl* **zu jds L~zeiten** in s.o.'s lifetime
leck *a* leaking. **L~** *nt* **-s,-s** leak. **l~en**[1] *vi* (*haben*) leak
lecken[2] *vt*/*i* (*haben*) lick
lecker *a* tasty. **L~bissen** *m* delicacy. **L~ei** *f* **-,-en** sweet
Leder *nt* **-s,-** leather. **l~n** *a* leather; (*wie Leder*) leathery
ledig *a* single. **l~lich** *adv* merely
Lee *f & nt* - **nach Lee** (*Naut*) to leeward
leer *a* empty; (*unbesetzt*) vacant; **l~ laufen** (*Auto*) idle. **L~e** *f* - emptiness; (*leerer Raum*) void. **l~en** *vt* empty; **sich l~en** empty. **L~lauf** *m* (*Auto*) neutral. **L~ung** *f* **-,-en** (*Post*) collection
legal *a* legal, *adv* -ly. **l~isieren** *vt* legalize. **L~ität** *f* - legality
Legas|thenie *f* - dyslexia. **L~theniker** *m* **-s,-** dyslexic
legen *vt* put; (*hin-, ver-*) lay; set ⟨*Haare*⟩; **Eier l~** lay eggs; **sich l~** lie down; ⟨*Staub:*⟩ settle; (*nachlassen*) subside
legendär *a* legendary
Legende *f* **-,-n** legend
leger /le'ʒeːɐ̯/ *a* casual, *adv* -ly
legier|en *vt* alloy; (*Culin*) thicken. **L~ung** *f* **-,-en** alloy
Legion *f* **-,-en** legion
Legislative *f* - legislature
legitim *a* legitimate, *adv* -ly. **l~ieren (sich)** *vr* prove one's identity. **L~ität** *f* - legitimacy
Lehm *m* **-s** clay. **l~ig** *a* clayey
Lehn|e *f* **-,-n** (*Rücken-*) back; (*Arm-*) arm. **l~en** *vt* lean (**an** + *acc* against); **sich l~en** lean (**an** + *acc* against) • *vi* (*haben*) be leaning (**an** + *dat* against). **L~sessel, L~stuhl** *m* armchair
Lehr|buch *nt* textbook. **L~e** *f* **-,-n** apprenticeship; (*Anschauung*) doctrine; (*Theorie*) theory; (*Wissenschaft*) science; (*Ratschlag*) advice; (*Erfahrung*) lesson; **jdm eine L~e erteilen** (*fig*) teach s.o. a lesson. **l~en** *vt*/*i* (*haben*) teach. **L~er** *m* **-s,-** teacher; (*Fahr-, Ski-*) instructor.

L~erin *f* **-,-nen** teacher. **L~erzimmer** *nt* staff-room. **L~fach** *nt* (*Sch*) subject. **L~gang** *m* course. **L~kraft** *f* teacher. **L~ling** *m* **-s,-e** apprentice; (*Auszubildender*) trainee. **L~plan** *m* syllabus. **l~reich** *a* instructive. **L~stelle** *f* apprenticeship. **L~stuhl** *m* (*Univ*) chair. **L~zeit** *f* apprenticeship

Leib *m* **-es,-er** body; (*Bauch*) belly. **L~eserziehung** *f* (*Sch*) physical education. **L~eskraft** *f* **aus L~eskräften** as hard/⟨*schreien*⟩ loud as one can. **L~gericht** *nt* favourite dish. **l~haftig** *a* **der l~haftige Satan** the devil incarnate ● *adv* in the flesh. **l~lich** *a* physical; (*blutsverwandt*) real, natural. **L~speise** *f* = **L~gericht. L~wache** *f* (*coll*) bodyguard. **L~wächter** *m* bodyguard. **L~wäsche** *f* underwear

Leiche *f* **-,-n** [dead] body; corpse. **L~nbegängnis** *nt* **-ses,-se** funeral. **L~nbestatter** *m* **-s,-** undertaker. **l~nblaß** *a* deathly pale. **L~nhalle** *f* mortuary. **L~nwagen** *m* hearse. **L~nzug** *m* funeral procession, cortège

Leichnam *m* **-s,-e** [dead] body

leicht *a* light, *adv* -ly; ⟨*Stoff, Anzug*⟩ lightweight; (*gering*) slight, *adv* -ly; (*mühelos*) easy, *adv* -ily. **L~athletik** *f* [track and field] athletics *sg*. **l~fallen**† *vi sep* (*sein*) be easy (*dat* for). **l~fertig** *a* thoughtless, *adv* -ly; (*vorschnell*) rash, *adv* -ly; (*frivol*) frivolous, *adv* -ly. **L~gewicht** *nt* (*Boxen*) lightweight. **l~gläubig** *a* gullible. **l~hin** *adv* casually. **L~igkeit** *f* - lightness; (*Mühelosigkeit*) ease; (*L~sein*) easiness; **mit L~igkeit** with ease. **l~lebig** *a* happy-go-lucky. **l~machen** *vt sep* make easy (*dat* for); **es sich** (*dat*) **l~machen** take the easy way out. **l~nehmen**† *vt sep* (*fig*) take lightly. **L~sinn** *m* carelessness; recklessness; (*Frivolität*) frivolity. **l~sinnig** *a* careless, *adv* -ly; (*unvorsichtig*) reckless, *adv* -ly; (*frivol*) frivolous, *adv* -ly

Leid *nt* **-[e]s** sorrow, grief; (*Böses*) harm. **l~** *a* **jdn/etw l~ sein/werden** be/get tired of s.o./sth; **es tut mir l~** I am sorry; **er tut mir l~** I feel sorry for him

Leide|form *f* passive. **l~n**† *vt/i* (*haben*) suffer (**an** + *dat* from); **jdn [gut] l~n können** like s.o.; **jdn/etw nicht l~n können** dislike s.o./sth. **L~n** *nt* **-s,-** suffering; (*Med*) complaint; (*Krankheit*) disease. **l~nd** *a* suffering; **l~nd sein** be in poor health. **L~nschaft** *f* **-,-en** passion. **l~nschaftlich** *a* passionate, *adv* -ly

leid|er *adv* unfortunately; **l~er ja/nicht** I'm afraid so/not. **l~ig** *a* wretched. **l~lich** *a* tolerable, *adv* -bly. **L~tragende(r)** *m/f* person who suffers; (*Trauernde*) mourner. **L~wesen** *nt* **zu meinem L~wesen** to my regret

Leier *f* **-,-n die alte L~** (*fam*) the same old story. **L~kasten** *m* barrel-organ. **l~n** *vt/i* (*haben*) wind; (*herunter-*) drone out

Leih|bibliothek, L~bücherei *f* lending library. **L~e** *f* **-,-n** loan. **l~en**† *vt* lend; **sich** (*dat*) **etw l~en** borrow sth. **L~gabe** *f* loan. **L~gebühr** *f* rental; (*für Bücher*) lending charge. **L~haus** *nt* pawnshop. **L~wagen** *m* hire-car. **l~weise** *adv* on loan

Leim *m* **-s** glue. **l~en** *vt* glue

Leine *f* **-,-n** rope; (*Wäsche-*) line; (*Hunde-*) lead, leash

Lein|en *nt* **-s** linen. **l~en** *a* linen. **L~tuch** *nt* sheet. **L~wand** *f* linen; (*Kunst*) canvas; (*Film-*) screen

leise *a* quiet, *adv* -ly; ⟨*Stimme, Musik, Berührung*⟩ soft, *adv* -ly; (*schwach*) faint, *adv* -ly; (*leicht*) light, *adv* -ly; **l~r stellen** turn down

Leiste *f* **-,-n** strip; (*Holz-*) batten; (*Zier-*) moulding; (*Anat*) groin

Leisten *m* **-s,-** [shoemaker's] last

leist|en *vt* achieve, accomplish; **sich** (*dat*) **etw l~en** treat oneself to sth; (*fam: anstellen*) get up to sth; **ich kann es mir nicht l~en** I can't afford it. **L~ung** *f* **-,-en** achievement; (*Sport, Techn*) performance; (*Produktion*) output; (*Zahlung*) payment. **l~ungsfähig** *a* efficient. **L~ungsfähigkeit** *f* efficiency

Leit|artikel *m* leader, editorial. **L~bild** *nt* (*fig*) model. **l~en** *vt* run, manage; (*an-/hinführen*) lead; (*Mus, Techn, Phys*) conduct; (*lenken, schicken*) direct. **l~end** *a* leading; ⟨*Posten*⟩ executive

Leiter[1] *f* **-,-n** ladder

Leit|er[2] *m* **-s,-** director; (*Comm*) manager; (*Führer*) leader; (*Sch*) head; (*Mus, Phys*) conductor. **L~erin** *f* **-,-nen** director; manageress; leader; head. **L~faden** *m* manual. **L~kegel** *m* [traffic] cone. **L~planke** *f* crash barrier. **L~spruch** *m* motto.

L~ung *f* **-,-en** (*Führung*) direction; (*Comm*) management; (*Aufsicht*) control; (*Electr: Schnur*) lead, flex; (*Kabel*) cable; (*Telefon-*) line; (*Rohr-*) pipe; (*Haupt-*) main. **L~ungswasser** *nt* tap water
Lektion /-'t̮sio:n/ *f* **-,-en** lesson
Lektor *m* **-s,-en** /-'to:rən/, **L~orin** *f* **-,-nen** (*Univ*) assistant lecturer; (*Verlags-*) editor. **L~üre** *f* **-,-n** reading matter; (*Lesen*) reading
Lende *f* **-,-n** loin
lenk|bar *a* steerable; (*fügsam*) tractable. **l~en** *vt* guide; (*steuern*) steer; (*Aust*) drive; (*regeln*) control; **jds Aufmerksamkeit auf sich** (*acc*) **l~en** attract s.o.'s attention. **L~er** *m* **-s,-** driver; (*L~stange*) handlebars *pl*. **L~rad** *nt* steering-wheel. **L~stange** *f* handlebars *pl*. **L~ung** *f* **-** steering
Leopard *m* **-en,-en** leopard
Lepra *f* **-** leprosy
Lerche *f* **-,-n** lark
lernen *vt/i* (*haben*) learn; (*für die Schule*) study; **schwimmen l~** learn to swim
lesbar *a* readable; (*leserlich*) legible
Lesb|ierin /'lɛsbi̯ərɪn/ *f* **-,-nen** lesbian. **l~isch** *a* lesbian
Lese *f* **-,-n** harvest. **L~buch** *nt* reader. **l~n**† *vt/i* (*haben*) read; (*Univ*) lecture ● *vt* pick, gather. **L~n** *nt* **-s** reading. **L~r(in)** *m* **-s,-** (*f* **-,-nen**) reader. **L~ratte** *f* (*fam*) bookworm. **l~rlich** *a* legible, *adv* -bly. **L~zeichen** *nt* bookmark
Lesung *f* **-,-en** reading
lethargisch *a* lethargic, *adv* -ally
Lettland *nt* **-s** Latvia
letzt|e(r,s) *a* last; (*neueste*) latest; **in l~er Zeit** recently; **l~en Endes** in the end. **l~emal** *adv* **das l~emal** the last time; **zum l~enmal** for the last time. **l~ens** *adv* recently; (*zuletzt*) lastly. **l~ere(r,s)** *a* the latter; **der/die/das l~ere** the latter
Leucht|e *f* **-,-n** light. **l~en** *vi* (*haben*) shine. **l~end** *a* shining. **L~er** *m* **-s,-** candlestick. **L~feuer** *nt* beacon. **L~kugel, L~rakete** *f* flare. **L~reklame** *f* neon sign. **L~[stoff]röhre** *f* fluorescent tube. **L~turm** *m* lighthouse. **L~zifferblatt** *nt* luminous dial
leugnen *vt* deny
Leukämie *f* **-** leukaemia
Leumund *m* **-s** reputation
Leute *pl* people; (*Mil*) men; (*Arbeiter*) workers
Leutnant *m* **-s,-s** second lieutenant
leutselig *a* affable, *adv* -bly
Levkoje /lɛf'ko:jə/ *f* **-,-n** stock
Lexikon *nt* **-s,-ka** encyclopaedia; (*Wörterbuch*) dictionary
Libanon (der) -s Lebanon
Libelle *f* **-,-n** dragonfly; (*Techn*) spirit-level; (*Haarspange*) slide
liberal *a* (*Pol*) Liberal
Libyen *nt* **-s** Libya
Licht *nt* **-[e]s,-er** light; (*Kerze*) candle; **L~ machen** turn on the light; **hinters L~ führen** (*fam*) dupe. **l~** *a* bright; (*Med*) lucid; (*spärlich*) sparse. **L~bild** *nt* [passport] photograph; (*Dia*) slide. **L~bildervortrag** *m* slide lecture. **L~blick** *m* (*fig*) ray of hope. **l~en** *vt* thin out; **den Anker l~en** (*Naut*) weigh anchor; **sich l~en** become less dense; ⟨*Haare:*⟩ thin. **L~hupe** *f* headlight flasher; **die L~hupe betätigen** flash one's headlights. **L~maschine** *f* dynamo. **L~schalter** *m* light-switch. **L~ung** *f* **-,-en** clearing
Lid *nt* **-[e]s,-er** [eye]lid. **L~schatten** *m* eye-shadow
lieb *a* dear; (*nett*) nice; (*artig*) good; **es ist mir l~** I'm glad (**daß** that); **es wäre mir l~er** I should prefer it (**wenn** if). **l~äugeln** *vi* (*haben*) **l~äugeln mit** fancy; toy with ⟨*Gedanken*⟩
Liebe *f* **-,-n** love. **L~lei** *f* **-,-en** flirtation. **l~n** *vt* love; (*mögen*) like; **sich l~n** love each other; (*körperlich*) make love. **l~nd** *a* loving ● *adv* **etw l~nd gern tun** love to do sth. **l~nswert** *a* lovable. **l~nswürdig** *a* kind. **l~nswürdigerweise** *adv* very kindly. **L~nswürdigkeit** *f* **-,-en** kindness
lieber *adv* rather; (*besser*) better; **l~ mögen** like better; **ich trinke l~ Tee** I prefer tea
Liebes|brief *m* love letter. **L~dienst** *m* favour. **L~geschichte** *f* love story. **L~kummer** *m* heartache; **L~kummer haben** be depressed over an unhappy love-affair. **L~paar** *nt* [pair of] lovers *pl*
lieb|evoll *a* loving, *adv* -ly; (*zärtlich*) affectionate, *adv* -ly. **l~gewinnen**† *vt sep* grow fond of. **l~haben**† *vt sep* be fond of; (*lieben*) love. **L~haber** *m* **-s,-** lover; (*Sammler*) collector. **L~haberei** *f* **-,-en** hobby. **l~kosen** *vt* caress. **L~kosung** *f* **-,-en** caress. **l~lich** *a* lovely; (*sanft*) gentle; (*süß*)

sweet. **L~ling** *m* **-s,-e** darling; (*Bevorzugte*) favourite. **L~lings-** *pref* favourite. **l~los** *a* loveless; ⟨*Eltern*⟩ uncaring; (*unfreundlich*) unkind ● *adv* unkindly; (*ohne Sorgfalt*) without care. **L~schaft** *f* **-,-en** [love] affair. **l~ste(r,s)** *a* dearest; (*bevorzugt*) favourite ● *adv* **am l~sten** best [of all]; **jdn/etw am l~sten mögen** like s.o./sth best [of all]; **ich hätte am l~sten geweint** I felt like crying. **L~ste(r)** *m/f* beloved; (*Schatz*) sweetheart

Lied *nt* **-[e]s,-er** song

liederlich *a* slovenly; (*unordentlich*) untidy; (*ausschweifend*) dissolute. **L~keit** *f* **-** slovenliness; untidiness; dissoluteness

Lieferant *m* **-en,-en** supplier

liefer|bar *a* (*Comm*) available. **l~n** *vt* supply; (*zustellen*) deliver; (*hervorbringen*) yield. **L~ung** *f* **-,-en** delivery; (*Sendung*) consignment; (*per Schiff*) shipment. **L~wagen** *m* delivery van

Liege *f* **-,-n** couch. **l~n**† *vi* (*haben*) lie; (*gelegen sein*) be situated; **l~n an** (+*dat*) (*fig*) be due to; (*abhängen*) depend on; **jdm [nicht] l~n** [not] suit s.o.; (*ansprechen*) [not] appeal to s.o.; **mir liegt viel/nicht daran** it is very/not important to me. **l~nbleiben**† *vi sep* (*sein*) remain lying [there]; (*im Bett*) stay in bed; ⟨*Ding:*⟩ be left; ⟨*Schnee:*⟩ settle; ⟨*Arbeit:*⟩ remain undone; (*zurückgelassen werden*) be left behind; (*Panne haben*) break down. **l~nlassen**† *vt sep* leave lying [there]; (*zurücklassen*) leave behind; (*nicht fortführen*) leave undone. **L~sitz** *m* reclining seat. **L~stuhl** *m* deck-chair. **L~stütz** *m* **-es,-e** press-up, (*Amer*) push-up. **L~wagen** *m* couchette car. **L~wiese** *f* lawn for sunbathing

Lift *m* **-[e]s,-e & -s** lift, (*Amer*) elevator

Liga *f* **-,-gen** league

Likör *m* **-s,-e** liqueur

lila *inv a* mauve; (*dunkel*) purple

Lilie /ˈliːli̯ə/ *f* **-,-n** lily

Liliputaner(in) *m* **-s,-** (*f* **-,-nen**) dwarf

Limo *f* **-,-[s]** (*fam*), **L~nade** *f* **-,-n** fizzy drink, (*Amer*) soda; (*Zitronen-*) lemonade

Limousine /limuˈziːnə/ *f* **-,-n** saloon, (*Amer*) sedan; (*mit Trennscheibe*) limousine

lind *a* mild; (*sanft*) gentle

Linde *f* **-,-n** lime tree

linder|n *vt* relieve, ease. **L~ung** *f* **-** relief

Line|al *nt* **-s,-e** ruler. **l~ar** *a* linear

Linguistik *f* **-** linguistics *sg*

Linie /-i̯ə/ *f* **-,-n** line; (*Zweig*) branch; (*Bus-*) route; **L~ 4** number 4 [bus/tram]; **in erster L~** primarily. **L~nflug** *m* scheduled flight. **L~nrichter** *m* linesman

lin[i]iert *a* lined, ruled

Link|e *f* **-n,-n** left side; (*Hand*) left hand; (*Boxen*) left; **die L~e** (*Pol*) the left; **zu meiner L~en** on my left. **l~e(r,s)** *a* left; (*Pol*) left-wing; **l~e Seite** left[-hand] side; (*von Stoff*) wrong side; **l~e Masche** purl. **l~isch** *a* awkward, *adv* -ly

links *adv* on the left; (*bei Stoff*) on the wrong side; (*verkehrt*) inside out; **von/nach l~** from/to the left; **l~ stricken** purl. **L~händer(in)** *m* **-s,-** (*f* **-,-nen**) left-hander. **l~händig** *a & adv* left-handed. **L~verkehr** *m* driving on the left

Linoleum /-leʊm/ *nt* **-s** lino[leum]

Linse *f* **-,-n** lens; (*Bot*) lentil

Lippe *f* **-,-n** lip. **L~nstift** *m* lipstick

Liquid|ation /-ˈtsi̯oːn/ *f* **-,-en** liquidation. **l~ieren** *vt* liquidate

lispeln *vt/i* (*haben*) lisp

List *f* **-,-en** trick, ruse; (*Listigkeit*) cunning

Liste *f* **-,-n** list

listig *a* cunning, crafty

Litanei *f* **-,-en** litany

Litauen *nt* **-s** Lithuania

Liter *m & nt* **-s,-** litre

liter|arisch *a* literary. **L~atur** *f* **-** literature

Litfaßsäule *f* advertising pillar

Liturgie *f* **-,-n** liturgy

Litze *f* **-,-n** braid; (*Electr*) flex

live /laif/ *adv* (*Radio, TV*) live

Lizenz *f* **-,-en** licence

Lkw /ɛlkaˈveː/ *m* **-[s],-s** = **Lastkraftwagen**

Lob *nt* **-[e]s** praise

Lobby /ˈlɔbi/ *f* **-** (*Pol*) lobby

loben *vt* praise. **l~swert** *a* praiseworthy, laudable

löblich *a* praiseworthy

Lobrede *f* eulogy

Loch *nt* **-[e]s,¨-er** hole. **l~en** *vt* punch a hole/holes in; punch ⟨*Fahrkarte*⟩. **L~er** *m* **-s,-** punch

löcher|ig *a* full of holes. **l~n** *vt* (*fam*) pester

Locke *f* **-,-n** curl. **l~n**[1] *vt* curl; **sich l~n** curl

locken² *vt* lure, entice; (*reizen*) tempt. **l~d** *a* tempting

Lockenwickler *m* **-s,-** curler; (*Rolle*) roller

locker *a* loose, *adv* -ly; ⟨*Seil*⟩ slack; ⟨*Erde, Kuchen*⟩ light; (*zwanglos*) casual; (*zu frei*) lax; (*unmoralisch*) loose. **l~n** *vt* loosen; slacken ⟨*Seil, Zügel*⟩; break up ⟨*Boden*⟩; relax ⟨*Griff*⟩; **sich l~n** become loose; ⟨*Seil:*⟩ slacken; (*sich entspannen*) relax. **L~ungsübungen** *fpl* limbering-up exercises

lockig *a* curly

Lock|mittel *nt* bait. **L~ung** *f* **-,-en** lure; (*Versuchung*) temptation. **L~vogel** *m* decoy

Loden *m* **-s** (*Tex*) loden

lodern *vi* (*haben*) blaze

Löffel *m* **-s,-** spoon; (*L~voll*) spoonful. **l~n** *vt* spoon up

Logarithmus *m* **-,-men** logarithm

Logbuch *nt* (*Naut*) log-book

Loge /'lo:ʒə/ *f* **-,-n** lodge; (*Theat*) box

Logierbesuch /lo'ʒi:ɐ̯-/ *m* house guest/guests *pl*

Log|ik *f* - logic. **l~isch** *a* logical, *adv* -ly

Logo *nt* **-s,-s** logo

Lohn *m* **-[e]s,¨e** wages *pl*, pay; (*fig*) reward. **L~empfänger** *m* wage-earner. **l~en** *vi/r* (*haben*) **[sich] l~en** be worth it *or* worth while ● *vt* be worth; **jdm etw l~en** reward s.o. for sth. **l~end** *a* worthwhile; (*befriedigend*) rewarding. **L~erhöhung** *f* [pay] rise; (*Amer*) raise. **L~steuer** *f* income tax

Lok *f* **-,-s** (*fam*) = **Lokomotive**

Lokal *nt* **-s,-e** restaurant; (*Trink-*) bar. **l~** *a* local. **l~isieren** *vt* locate; (*begrenzen*) localize

Lokomotiv|e *f* **-,-n** engine, locomotive. **L~führer** *m* engine driver

London *nt* **-s** London. **L~er** *a* London ... ● *m* **-s,-** Londoner

Lorbeer *m* **-s,-en** laurel; **echter L~** bay. **L~blatt** *nt* (*Culin*) bay-leaf

Lore *f* **-,-n** (*Rail*) truck

Los *nt* **-es,-e** lot; (*Lotterie-*) ticket; (*Schicksal*) fate; **das Große Los ziehen** hit the jackpot

los *pred a* **los sein** be loose; **jdn/etw los sein** be rid of s.o./sth; **was ist [mit ihm] los?** what's the matter [with him]? ● *adv* **los!** go on! **Achtung, fertig, los!** ready, steady, go!

lösbar *a* soluble

losbinden† *vt sep* untie

Lösch|blatt *nt* sheet of blotting-paper. **l~en¹** *vt* put out, extinguish; quench ⟨*Durst*⟩; blot ⟨*Tinte*⟩; (*tilgen*) cancel; (*streichen*) delete; erase ⟨*Aufnahme*⟩

löschen² *vt* (*Naut*) unload

Lösch|fahrzeug *nt* fire-engine. **L~gerät** *nt* fire extinguisher. **L~papier** *nt* blotting-paper

lose *a* loose, *adv* -ly

Lösegeld *nt* ransom

losen *vi* (*haben*) draw lots (**um** for)

lösen *vt* undo; (*lockern*) loosen; (*entfernen*) detach; (*klären*) solve; (*auflösen*) dissolve; cancel ⟨*Vertrag*⟩; break off ⟨*Beziehung, Verlobung*⟩; (*kaufen*) buy; **sich l~** come off; (*sich trennen*) detach oneself/itself; (*lose werden*) come undone; (*sich entspannen*) relax; (*sich klären*) resolve itself; (*sich auflösen*) dissolve

los|fahren† *vi sep* (*sein*) start; ⟨*Auto:*⟩ drive off; **l~fahren auf** (+*acc*) head for; (*fig: angreifen*) go for. **l~gehen**† *vi sep* (*sein*) set off; (*fam: anfangen*) start; (*fam: abgehen*) come off; ⟨*Bombe, Gewehr:*⟩ go off; **l~gehen auf** (+*acc*) head for; (*fig: angreifen*) go for. **l~kommen**† *vi sep* (*sein*) get away (**von** from); **l~kommen auf** (+*acc*) come towards. **l~lachen** *vi sep* (*haben*) burst out laughing. **l~lassen**† *vt sep* let go of; (*freilassen*) release

löslich *a* soluble

los|lösen *vt sep* detach; **sich l~lösen** become detached; (*fig*) break away (**von** from). **l~machen** *vt sep* detach; (*losbinden*) untie; **sich l~machen** free oneself/itself. **l~platzen** *vi sep* (*sein*) (*fam*) burst out laughing. **l~reißen**† *vt sep* tear off; **sich l~reißen** break free; (*fig*) tear oneself away. **l~sagen (sich)** *vr sep* renounce (**von etw** sth). **l~schicken** *vt sep* send off. **l~sprechen**† *vt sep* absolve (**von** from). **l~steuern** *vi sep* (*sein*) head (**auf** + *acc* for)

Losung *f* **-,-en** (*Pol*) slogan; (*Mil*) password

Lösung *f* **-,-en** solution. **L~smittel** *nt* solvent

los|werden† *vt sep* get rid of. **l~ziehen**† *vi sep* (*sein*) set off; **l~ziehen gegen** *od* **über** (+*acc*) (*beschimpfen*) run down

Lot *nt* **-[e]s,-e** perpendicular; (*Blei-*) plumb[-bob]; **im Lot sein** (*fig*) be all right. **l~en** *vt* plumb

lötlen *vt* solder. **L~lampe** *f* blow-lamp, (*Amer*) blowtorch. **L~metall** *nt* solder

lotrecht *a* perpendicular, *adv* -ly

Lotse *m* **-n,-n** (*Naut*) pilot. **l~n** *vt* (*Naut*) pilot; (*fig*) guide

Lotterie *f* **-,-n** lottery

Lotto *nt* **-s,-s** lotto; (*Lotterie*) lottery

Löwle *m* **-n,-n** lion; (*Astr*) Leo. **L~enanteil** *m* (*fig*) lion's share. **L~enzahn** *m* (*Bot*) dandelion. **L~in** *f* **-,-nen** lioness

loyal /loa'ja:l/ *a* loyal. **L~ität** *f* - loyalty

Luchs *m* **-es,-e** lynx

Lücke *f* **-,-n** gap. **L~nbüßer** *m* **-s,-** stopgap. **l~nhaft** *a* incomplete; ⟨*Wissen*⟩ patchy. **l~nlos** *a* complete; ⟨*Folge*⟩ unbroken

Luder *nt* **-s,-** (*sl*) (*Frau*) bitch; **armes L~** poor wretch

Luft *f* **-,¨e** air; **tief L~ holen** take a deep breath; **in die L~ gehen** explode. **L~angriff** *m* air raid. **L~aufnahme** *f* aerial photograph. **L~ballon** *m* balloon. **L~bild** *nt* aerial photograph. **L~blase** *f* air bubble

Lüftchen *nt* **-s,-** breeze

luftldicht *a* airtight. **L~druck** *m* atmospheric pressure

lüften *vt* air; raise ⟨*Hut*⟩; reveal ⟨*Geheimnis*⟩

Luftlfahrt *f* aviation. **L~fahrtgesellschaft** *f* airline. **L~gewehr** *nt* airgun. **L~hauch** *m* breath of air. **l~ig** *a* airy; ⟨*Kleid*⟩ light. **L~kissenfahrzeug** *nt* hovercraft. **L~krieg** *m* aerial warfare. **L~kurort** *m* climatic health resort. **l~leer** *a* **l~leerer Raum** vacuum. **L~linie** *f* **100 km L~linie** 100 km as the crow flies. **L~loch** *nt* air-hole; (*Aviat*) air pocket. **L~matratze** *f* air-bed, inflatable mattress. **L~pirat** *m* [aircraft] hijacker. **L~post** *f* airmail. **L~pumpe** *f* air pump; (*Fahrrad-*) bicycle-pump. **L~röhre** *f* windpipe. **L~schiff** *nt* airship. **L~schlange** *f* [paper] streamer. **L~schlösser** *ntpl* castles in the air. **L~schutzbunker** *m* air-raid shelter

Lüftung *f* - ventilation

Luftlveränderung *f* change of air. **L~waffe** *f* air force. **L~weg** *m* **auf dem L~weg** by air. **L~zug** *m* draught

Lügle *f* **-,-n** lie. **l~en**† *vt/i* (*haben*) lie. **L~ner(in)** *m* **-s,-** (*f* **-,-nen**) liar. **l~nerisch** *a* untrue; ⟨*Person*⟩ untruthful

Luke *f* **-,-n** hatch; (*Dach-*) skylight

Lümmel *m* **-s,-** lout; (*fam: Schelm*) rascal. **l~n (sich)** *vr* loll

Lump *m* **-en,-en** scoundrel. **L~en** *m* **-s,-** rag; **in L~en** in rags. **l~en** *vt* **sich nicht l~en lassen** be generous. **L~engesindel, L~enpack** *nt* riff-raff. **L~ensammler** *m* rag-and-bone man. **l~ig** *a* mean, shabby; (*gering*) measly

Lunchpaket /'lan[t]ʃ-/ *nt* packed lunch

Lunge *f* **-,-n** lungs *pl*; (*L~nflügel*) lung. **L~nentzündung** *f* pneumonia

lungern *vi* (*haben*) loiter

Lunte *f* **L~ riechen** (*fam*) smell a rat

Lupe *f* **-,-n** magnifying glass

Lurch *m* **-[e]s,-e** amphibian

Lust *f* **-,¨e** pleasure; (*Verlangen*) desire; (*sinnliche Begierde*) lust; **L~ haben** feel like (**auf etw** *acc* sth); **ich habe keine L~** I don't feel like it; (*will nicht*) I don't want to

Lüster *m* **-s,-** lustre; (*Kronleuchter*) chandelier

lüstern *a* greedy (**auf** + *acc* for); (*sinnlich*) lascivious; (*geil*) lecherous

lustig *a* jolly; (*komisch*) funny; **sich l~ machen über** (+ *acc*) make fun of

Lüstling *m* **-s,-e** lecher

lustllos *a* listless, *adv* -ly. **L~mörder** *m* sex killer. **L~spiel** *nt* comedy

lutherisch *a* Lutheran

lutschlen *vt/i* (*haben*) suck. **L~er** *m* **-s,-** lollipop; (*Schnuller*) dummy, (*Amer*) pacifier

lütt *a* (*NGer*) little

Lüttich *nt* **-s** Liège

Luv *f & nt* - **nach Luv** (*Naut*) to windward

luxuriös *a* luxurious, *adv* -ly

Luxus *m* - luxury. **L~artikel** *m* luxury article. **L~ausgabe** *f* de luxe edition. **L~hotel** *nt* luxury hotel

Lymphldrüse /'lʏmf-/ *f*, **L~knoten** *m* lymph gland

lynchen /'lʏnçən/ *vt* lynch

Lyrlik *f* - lyric poetry. **L~iker** *m* **-s,-** lyric poet. **l~isch** *a* lyrical; ⟨*Dichtung*⟩ lyric

M

Machlart *f* style. **m~bar** *a* feasible. **m~en** *vt* make; get ⟨*Mahlzeit*⟩; take

⟨*Foto*⟩; (*ausführen, tun, in Ordnung bringen*) do; (*Math: ergeben*) be; (*kosten*) come to; **sich** (*dat*) **etw m~en lassen** have sth made; **was m~st du da?** what are you doing? **was m~t die Arbeit?** how is work? **das m~t 6 Mark [zusammen]** that's 6 marks [altogether]; **das m~t nichts** it doesn't matter; **sich** (*dat*) **wenig/nichts m~en aus** care little/nothing for • *vr* **sich m~en** do well; **sich an die Arbeit m~en** get down to work • *vi* (*haben*) **ins Bett m~en** (*fam*) wet the bed; **schnell m~en** hurry. **M~enschaften** *fpl* machinations

Macht *f* -,⸚e power; **mit aller M~** with all one's might. **M~haber** *m* **-s,-** ruler

mächtig *a* powerful; (*groß*) enormous • *adv* (*fam*) terribly

macht|los *a* powerless. **M~wort** *nt* **ein M~wort sprechen** put one's foot down

Mädchen *nt* **-s,-** girl; (*Dienst-*) maid. **m~haft** *a* girlish. **M~name** *m* girl's name; (*vor der Ehe*) maiden name

Made *f* **-,-n** maggot

Mädel *nt* **-s,-** girl

madig *a* maggoty; **jdn m~ machen** (*fam*) run s.o. down

Madonna *f* **-,-nen** madonna

Magazin *nt* **-s,-e** magazine; (*Lager*) warehouse; (*Raum*) store-room

Magd *f* -,⸚e maid

Magen *m* **-s,⸚** stomach. **M~schmerzen** *mpl* stomach-ache *sg*. **M~verstimmung** *f* stomach upset

mager *a* thin; ⟨*Fleisch*⟩ lean; ⟨*Boden*⟩ poor; (*dürftig*) meagre. **M~keit** *f* **-** thinness; leanness. **M~sucht** *f* anorexia

Magie *f* **-** magic

Mag|ier /ˈmaːgi̯ɐ/ *m* **-s,-** magician. **m~isch** *a* magic; (*geheimnisvoll*) magical

Magistrat *m* **-s,-e** city council

Magnesia *f* **-** magnesia

Magnet *m* **-en** & **-[e]s,-e** magnet. **m~isch** *a* magnetic. **m~isieren** *vt* magnetize. **M~ismus** *m* **-** magnetism

Mahagoni *nt* **-s** mahogany

Mäh|drescher *m* **-s,-** combine harvester. **m~en** *vt/i* (*haben*) mow

Mahl *nt* **-[e]s,⸚er** meal

mahlen† *vt* grind

Mahlzeit *f* meal; **M~!** enjoy your meal!

Mähne *f* **-,-n** mane

mahn|en *vt/i* (*haben*) remind (**wegen** about); (*ermahnen*) admonish; (*auffordern*) urge (**zu** to); **zur Vorsicht/Eile m~en** urge caution/haste. **M~ung** *f* **-,-en** reminder; admonition; (*Aufforderung*) exhortation

Mai *m* **-[e]s,-e** May; **der Erste Mai** May Day. **M~glöckchen** *nt* **-s,-** lily of the valley. **M~käfer** *m* cockchafer

Mailand *nt* **-s** Milan

Mais *m* **-es** maize, (*Amer*) corn; (*Culin*) sweet corn. **M~kolben** *m* corn-cob

Majestät *f* **-,-en** majesty. **m~isch** *a* majestic, *adv* -ally

Major *m* **-s,-e** major

Majoran *m* **-s** marjoram

Majorität *f* **-,-en** majority

makaber *a* macabre

Makel *m* **-s,-** blemish; (*Defekt*) flaw; (*fig*) stain. **m~los** *a* flawless; (*fig*) unblemished

mäkeln *vi* (*haben*) grumble

Makkaroni *pl* macaroni *sg*

Makler *m* **-s,-** (*Comm*) broker

Makrele *f* **-,-n** mackerel

Makrone *f* **-,-n** macaroon

mal *adv* (*Math*) times; (*bei Maßen*) by; (*fam: einmal*) once; (*eines Tages*) one day; **schon mal** once before; (*jemals*) ever; **nicht mal** not even; **hört/seht mal!** listen!/look!

Mal[1] *nt* **-[e]s,-e** time; **zum ersten Mal** for the first time; **mit einem Mal** all at once; **ein für alle Mal** once and for all

Mal[2] *nt* **-[e]s,-e** mark; (*auf der Haut*) mole; (*Mutter-*) birthmark

Mal|buch *nt* colouring book. **m~en** *vt/i* (*haben*) paint. **M~er** *m* **-s,-** painter. **M~erei** *f* **-,-en** painting. **M~erin** *f* **-,-nen** painter. **m~erisch** *a* picturesque

Malheur /maˈløːɐ̯/ *nt* **-s,-e** & **-s** (*fam*) mishap; (*Ärger*) trouble

Mallorca /maˈlɔrka, -ˈjɔrka/ *nt* **-s** Majorca

malnehmen† *vt sep* multiply (**mit** by)

Malz *nt* **-es** malt. **M~bier** *nt* malt beer

Mama /ˈmama, maˈmaː/ *f* **-s,-s** mummy

Mammut *nt* **-s,-e** & **-s** mammoth

mampfen *vt* (*fam*) munch

man *pron* one, you; (*die Leute*) people, they; **man sagt** they say, it is said

Manager /ˈmɛnɪdʒɐ/ *m* **-s,-** manager

manch *inv pron* **m~ ein(e)** many a; **m~ einer/eine** many a man/woman. **m~e(r,s)** *pron* many a; **[so] m~es Mal** many a time; **m~e Leute** some people • (*substantivisch*) **m~er/m~e** many a man/woman; **m~e** *pl* some; (*Leute*) some people; (*viele*) many [people]; **m~es** some things; (*vieles*) many things. **m~erlei** *inv a* various • *pron* various things

manchmal *adv* sometimes

Mandant(in) *m* **-en,-en** (*f* **-,-nen**) (*Jur*) client

Mandarine *f* **-,-n** mandarin

Mandat *nt* **-[e]s,-e** mandate; (*Jur*) brief; (*Pol*) seat

Mandel *f* **-,-n** almond; (*Anat*) tonsil. **M~entzündung** *f* tonsillitis

Manege /ma'ne:ʒə/ *f* **-,-n** ring; (*Reit-*) arena

Mangel[1] *m* **-s,¨** lack; (*Knappheit*) shortage; (*Med*) deficiency; (*Fehler*) defect; **M~ leiden** go short

Mangel[2] *f* **-,-n** mangle

mangel|haft *a* faulty, defective; (*Sch*) unsatisfactory. **m~n**[1] *vi* (*haben*) **es m~t an** (+*dat*) there is a lack/(*Knappheit*) shortage of

mangeln[2] *vt* put through the mangle

mangels *prep* (+*gen*) for lack of

Mango *f* **-,-s** mango

Manie *f* **-,-n** mania; (*Sucht*) obsession

Manier *f* **-,-en** manner; **M~en** manners. **m~lich** *a* well-mannered • *adv* properly

Manifest *nt* **-[e]s,-e** manifesto. **m~ieren (sich)** *vr* manifest itself

Maniküre *f* **-,-n** manicure; (*Person*) manicurist. **m~n** *vt* manicure

Manipul|ation /-'tsi̯o:n/ *f* **-,-en** manipulation. **m~ieren** *vt* manipulate

Manko *nt* **-s,-s** disadvantage; (*Fehlbetrag*) deficit

Mann *m* **-[e]s,¨er** man; (*Ehe-*) husband

Männchen *nt* **-s,-** little man; (*Zool*) male; **M~ machen** ⟨*Hund:*⟩ sit up

Mannequin /'manəkɛ̃/ *nt* **-s,-s** model

Männerchor *m* male voice choir

Mannes|alter *nt* manhood. **M~kraft** *f* virility

mannhaft *a* manful, *adv* -ly

mannigfaltig *a* manifold; (*verschieden*) diverse

männlich *a* male; (*Gram & fig*) masculine; (*mannhaft*) manly; ⟨*Frau*⟩ mannish. **M~keit** *f* **-** masculinity; (*fig*) manhood

Mannschaft *f* **-,-en** team; (*Naut*) crew. **M~sgeist** *m* team spirit

Manöv|er *nt* **-s,-** manœuvre; (*Winkelzug*) trick. **m~rieren** *vt/i* (*haben*) manœuvre

Mansarde *f* **-,-n** attic room; (*Wohnung*) attic flat

Manschette *f* **-,-n** cuff; (*Blumentopf-*) paper frill. **M~nknopf** *m* cuff-link

Mantel *m* **-s,¨** coat; (*dick*) overcoat; (*Reifen-*) outer tyre

Manuskript *nt* **-[e]s,-e** manuscript

Mappe *f* **-,-n** folder; (*Akten-*) briefcase; (*Schul-*) bag

Marathon *m* **-s,-s** marathon

Märchen *nt* **-s,-** fairy-tale. **m~haft** *a* fairy-tale . . . ; (*phantastisch*) fabulous

Margarine *f* **-** margarine

Marienkäfer /ma'ri:ən-/ *m* ladybird, (*Amer*) ladybug

Marihuana *nt* **-s** marijuana

Marille *f* **-,-n** (*Aust*) apricot

Marinade *f* **-,-n** marinade

Marine *f* marine; (*Kriegs-*) navy. **m~blau** *a* navy [blue]. **M~infanterist** *m* marine

marinieren *vt* marinade

Marionette *f* **-,-n** puppet, marionette

Mark[1] *f* **-,-** mark; **drei M~** three marks

Mark[2] *nt* **-[e]s** (*Knochen-*) marrow; (*Bot*) pith; (*Frucht-*) pulp; **bis ins M~ getroffen** (*fig*) cut to the quick

markant *a* striking

Marke *f* **-,-n** token; (*rund*) disc; (*Erkennungs-*) tag; (*Brief-*) stamp; (*Lebensmittel-*) coupon; (*Spiel-*) counter; (*Markierung*) mark; (*Fabrikat*) make; (*Tabak-*) brand. **M~nartikel** *m* branded article

markier|en *vt* mark; (*fam: vortäuschen*) fake. **M~ung** *f* **-,-en** marking

Markise *f* **-,-n** awning

Markstück *nt* one-mark piece

Markt *m* **-[e]s,¨e** market; (*M~platz*) market-place. **M~forschung** *f* market research. **M~platz** *m* market-place

Marmelade *f* **-,-n** jam; (*Orangen-*) marmalade

Marmor *m* **-s** marble

Marokko *nt* **-s** Morocco

Marone *f* **-,-n** [sweet] chestnut

Marotte *f* **-,-n** whim

Marsch[1] *f* **-,-en** marsh

Marsch[2] *m* **-[e]s,¨e** march. **m~** *int* (*Mil*) march! **m~ ins Bett!** off to bed!

Marschall *m* **-s,¨e** marshal

marschieren *vi* (*sein*) march
Marter *f* **-,-n** torture. **m~n** *vt* torture
Martinshorn *nt* [police] siren
Märtyrer(in) *m* **-s,-** (*f* **-,-nen**) martyr
Martyrium *nt* **-s** martyrdom
Mar|xismus *m* **-** Marxism. **m~xistisch** *a* Marxist
März *m* **-,-e** March
Marzipan *nt* **-s** marzipan
Masche *f* **-,-n** stitch; (*im Netz*) mesh; (*fam: Trick*) dodge. **M~ndraht** *m* wire netting
Maschin|e *f* **-,-n** machine; (*Flugzeug*) plane; (*Schreib-*) typewriter. **m~egeschrieben** *a* typewritten, typed. **m~ell** *a* machine ... ● *adv* by machine. **M~enbau** *m* mechanical engineering. **M~engewehr** *nt* machine-gun. **M~enpistole** *f* sub-machine-gun. **M~erie** *f* **-** machinery. **M~eschreiben** *nt* typing. **M~ist** *m* **-en,-en** machinist; (*Naut*) engineer
Masern *pl* measles *sg*
Maserung *f* **-,-en** [wood] grain
Maske *f* **-,-n** mask; (*Theat*) make-up. **M~rade** *f* **-,-n** disguise; (*fig: Heuchelei*) masquerade
maskieren *vt* mask; **sich m~** dress up (**als** as)
Maskottchen *nt* **-s,-** mascot
maskulin *a* masculine
Maskulinum *nt* **-s,-na** (*Gram*) masculine
Masochis|mus /mazo'xɪsmʊs/ *m* **-** masochism. **M~t** *m* **-en,-en** masochist
Maß[1] *nt* **-es,-e** measure; (*Abmessung*) measurement; (*Grad*) degree; (*Mäßigung*) moderation; **in** *od* **mit Maß[en]** in moderation; **in hohem Maße** to a high degree
Maß[2] *f* **-,-** (*SGer*) litre [of beer]
Massage /ma'sa:ʒə/ *f* **-,-n** massage
Massaker *nt* **-s,-** massacre
Maß|anzug *m* made-to-measure suit. **M~band** *nt* (*pl* **-bänder**) tape-measure
Masse *f* **-,-n** mass; (*Culin*) mixture; (*Menschen-*) crowd; **eine M~ Arbeit** (*fam*) masses of work. **M~nartikel** *m* mass-produced article. **m~nhaft** *adv* in huge quantities. **M~nmedien** *pl* mass media. **M~nproduktion** *f* mass production. **m~nweise** *adv* in huge numbers
Masseu|r /ma'sø:ɐ̯/ *m* **-s,-e** masseur. **M~rin** *f* **-,-nen**, **M~se** /-'sø:zə/ *f* **-,-n** masseuse
maß|gebend *a* authoritative; (*einflußreich*) influential. **m~geblich** *a* decisive, *adv* -ly. **m~geschneidert** *a* made-to-measure. **m~halten**† *vi sep* (*haben*) exercise moderation
massieren[1] *vt* massage
massieren[2] **(sich)** *vr* mass
massig *a* massive
mäßig *a* moderate, *adv* -ly; (*mittelmäßig*) indifferent. **m~en** *vt* moderate; **sich m~en** moderate; (*sich beherrschen*) restrain oneself. **M~keit** *f* **-** moderation. **M~ung** *f* **-** moderation
massiv *a* solid; (*stark*) heavy
Maß|krug *m* beer mug. **m~los** *a* excessive; (*grenzenlos*) boundless; (*äußerst*) extreme, *adv* -ly. **M~nahme** *f* **-,-n** measure. **m~regeln** *vt* reprimand
Maßstab *m* scale; (*Norm & fig*) standard. **m~sgerecht, m~sgetreu** *a* scale ... ● *adv* to scale
maßvoll *a* moderate
Mast[1] *m* **-[e]s,-en** pole; (*Überland-*) pylon; (*Naut*) mast
Mast[2] *f* **-** fattening. **M~darm** *m* rectum
mästen *vt* fatten
Masturb|ation /-'tsi̯o:n/ *f* **-** masturbation. **m~ieren** *vi* (*haben*) masturbate
Material *nt* **-s,-ien** /-i̯ən/ material; (*coll*) materials *pl*. **M~ismus** *m* **-** materialism. **m~istisch** *a* materialistic
Mater|ie /ma'te:ri̯ə/ *f* **-,-n** matter; (*Thema*) subject. **m~iell** *a* material
Mathe *f* **-** (*fam*) maths *sg*
Mathe|matik *f* **-** mathematics *sg*. **M~matiker** *m* **-s,-** mathematician. **m~matisch** *a* mathematical
Matinee *f* **-,-n** (*Theat*) morning performance
Matratze *f* **-,-n** mattress
Mätresse *f* **-,-n** mistress
Matrose *m* **-n,-n** sailor
Matsch *m* **-[e]s** mud; (*Schnee-*) slush. **m~ig** *a* muddy; slushy; (*weich*) mushy
matt *a* weak; (*gedämpft*) dim; (*glanzlos*) dull; ⟨*Politur, Farbe*⟩ matt; **jdn m~ setzen** checkmate s.o. **M~** *nt* **-s** (*Schach*) mate
Matte *f* **-,-n** mat
Mattglas *nt* frosted glass
Matt|igkeit *f* **-** weakness; (*Müdigkeit*) weariness. **M~scheibe** *f* (*fam*) television screen

Matura *f* - (*Aust*) ≈ A levels *pl*

Mauer *f* **-,-n** wall. **m~n** *vt* build ● *vi* (*haben*) lay bricks. **M~werk** *nt* masonry

Maul *nt* **-[e]s, Mäuler** (*Zool*) mouth; **halt's M~!** (*fam*) shut up! **m~en** *vi* (*haben*) (*fam*) grumble. **M~korb** *m* muzzle. **M~tier** *nt* mule. **M~wurf** *m* mole. **M~wurfshaufen, M~wurfshügel** *m* molehill

Maurer *m* **-s,-** bricklayer

Maus *f* **-, Mäuse** mouse. **M~efalle** *f* mousetrap

mausern (sich) *vr* moult; (*fam*) turn (**zu** into)

Maut *f* **-,-en** (*Aust*) toll. **M~straße** *f* toll road

maximal *a* maximum

Maximum *nt* **-s,-ma** maximum

Mayonnaise /majɔ'nɛ:zə/ *f* **-,-n** mayonnaise

Mäzen *m* **-s,-e** patron

Mechan|ik /me'ça:nɪk/ *f* - mechanics *sg*; (*Mechanismus*) mechanism. **M~iker** *m* **-s,-** mechanic. **m~isch** *a* mechanical, *adv* -ly. **m~isieren** *vt* mechanize. **M~ismus** *m* **-,-men** mechanism

meckern *vi* (*haben*) bleat; (*fam: nörgeln*) grumble

Medaill|e /me'daljə/ *f* **-,-n** medal. **M~on** /-'jõ:/ *nt* **-s,-s** medallion; (*Schmuck*) locket

Medikament *nt* **-[e]s,-e** medicine

Medit|ation /-'tsi̯o:n/ *f* **-,-en** meditation. **m~ieren** *vi* (*haben*) meditate

Medium *nt* **-s,-ien** medium; **die Medien** the media

Medizin *f* **-,-en** medicine. **M~er** *m* **-s,-** doctor; (*Student*) medical student. **m~isch** *a* medical; (*heilkräftig*) medicinal

Meer *nt* **-[e]s,-e** sea. **M~busen** *m* gulf. **M~enge** *f* strait. **M~esspiegel** *m* sea-level. **M~jungfrau** *f* mermaid. **M~rettich** *m* horseradish. **M~schweinchen** *nt* **-s,-** guinea-pig

Megaphon *nt* **-s,-e** megaphone

Mehl *nt* **-[e]s** flour. **m~ig** *a* floury. **M~schwitze** *f* (*Culin*) roux. **M~speise** *f* (*Aust*) dessert; (*Kuchen*) pastry. **M~tau** *m* (*Bot*) mildew

mehr *pron & adv* more; **nicht m~** no more; (*zeitlich*) no longer; **nichts m~** no more; (*nichts weiter*) nothing else; **nie m~** never again. **m~deutig** *a* ambiguous. **m~en** *vt* increase; **sich m~en** increase. **m~ere** *pron* several. **m~eres** *pron* several things *pl*. **m~fach** *a* multiple; (*mehrmalig*) repeated ● *adv* several times. **M~fahrtenkarte** *f* book of tickets. **m~farbig** *a* [multi]coloured. **M~heit** *f* **-,-en** majority. **m~malig** *a* repeated. **m~mals** *adv* several times. **m~sprachig** *a* multilingual. **m~stimmig** *a* (*Mus*) for several voices ● *adv* **m~stimmig singen** sing in harmony. **M~wertsteuer** *f* value-added tax, VAT. **M~zahl** *f* majority; (*Gram*) plural. **M~zweck-** *pref* multi-purpose

meiden† *vt* avoid, shun

Meierei *f* **-,-en** (*dial*) dairy

Meile *f* **-,-n** mile. **M~nstein** *m* milestone. **m~nweit** *adv* [for] miles

mein *poss pron* my. **m~e(r,s)** *poss pron* mine; **die M~en** *pl* my family *sg*

Meineid *m* perjury; **einen M~ leisten** perjure oneself

meinen *vt* mean; (*glauben*) think; (*sagen*) say; **es gut m~** mean well

mein|erseits *adv* for my part. **m~etwegen** *adv* for my sake; (*wegen mir*) because of me, on my account; (*fam: von mir aus*) as far as I'm concerned. **m~etwillen** *adv* **um m~etwillen** for my sake. **m~ige** *poss pron* **der/die/das m~ige** mine. **m~s** *poss pron* mine

Meinung *f* **-,-en** opinion; **jdm die M~ sagen** give s.o. a piece of one's mind. **M~sumfrage** *f* opinion poll

Meise *f* **-,-n** (*Zool*) tit

Meißel *m* **-s,-** chisel. **m~n** *vt/i* (*haben*) chisel

meist *adv* mostly; (*gewöhnlich*) usually. **m~e** *a* **der/die/das m~e** most; **die m~en Leute** most people; **die m~e Zeit** most of the time; **am m~en** [the] most ● *pron* **das m~e** most [of it]; **die m~en** most. **m~ens** *adv* mostly; (*gewöhnlich*) usually

Meister *m* **-s,-** master craftsman; (*Könner*) master; (*Sport*) champion. **m~haft** *a* masterly ● *adv* in masterly fashion. **m~n** *vt* master. **M~schaft** *f* **-,-en** mastery; (*Sport*) championship. **M~stück, M~werk** *nt* masterpiece

Melanch|olie /melaŋko'li:/ *f* - melancholy. **m~olisch** *a* melancholy

meld|en *vt* report; (*anmelden*) register; (*ankündigen*) announce; **sich m~en** report (**bei** to); (*zum Militär*) enlist; (*freiwillig*) volunteer; (*Teleph*) answer; (*Sch*) put up one's hand; (*von sich hören lassen*) get in touch (**bei** with); **sich krank m~en** report sick. **M~ung** *f* **-,-en** report; (*Anmeldung*) registration

meliert *a* mottled; **grau m~es Haar** hair flecked with grey

melken† *vt* milk

Melod|ie *f* **-,-n** tune, melody. **m~iös** *a* melodious

melodisch *a* melodic; (*melodiös*) melodious, tuneful

melodramatisch *a* melodramatic, *adv* -ally

Melone *f* **-,-n** melon; **[schwarze] M~** (*fam*) bowler [hat]

Membran *f* **-,-en** membrane

Memoiren /me'mo̧a:rən/ *pl* memoirs

Menge *f* **-,-n** amount, quantity; (*Menschen-*) crowd; (*Math*) set; **eine M~ Geld** a lot of money. **m~n** *vt* mix

Mensa *f* **-,-sen** (*Univ*) refectory

Mensch *m* **-en,-en** human being; **der M~** man; **die M~en** people; **jeder/kein M~** everybody/nobody. **M~enaffe** *m* ape. **M~enfeind** *m* misanthropist. **m~enfeindlich** *a* antisocial. **M~enfresser** *m* **-s,-** cannibal; (*Zool*) man-eater; (*fam*) ogre. **m~enfreundlich** *a* philanthropic. **M~enleben** *nt* human life; (*Lebenszeit*) lifetime. **m~enleer** *a* deserted. **M~enmenge** *f* crowd. **M~enraub** *m* kidnapping. **M~enrechte** *ntpl* human rights. **m~enscheu** *a* unsociable. **M~enskind** *int* (*fam*) good heavens! **M~enverstand** *m* **gesunder M~enverstand** common sense. **m~enwürdig** *a* humane, *adv* -ly. **M~heit** *f* **- die M~heit** mankind, humanity. **m~lich** *a* human; (*human*) humane, *adv* -ly. **M~lichkeit** *f* **-** humanity

Menstru|ation /-'tsi̯o:n/ *f* **-** menstruation. **m~ieren** *vi* (*haben*) menstruate

Mentalität *f* **-,-en** mentality

Menü *nt* **-s,-s** menu; (*festes M~*) set meal

Menuett *nt* **-[e]s,-e** minuet

Meridian *m* **-s,-e** meridian

merk|bar *a* noticeable. **M~blatt** *nt* [explanatory] leaflet. **m~en** *vt* notice; **sich** (*dat*) **etw m~en** remember sth. **m~lich** *a* noticeable, *adv* -bly. **M~mal** *nt* feature

merkwürdig *a* odd, *adv* -ly, strange, *adv* -ly. **m~erweise** *adv* oddly enough

meß|bar *a* measurable. **M~becher** *m* (*Culin*) measure

Messe[1] *f* **-,-n** (*Relig*) mass; (*Comm*) [trade] fair

Messe[2] *f* **-,-n** (*Mil*) mess

messen† *vt/i* (*haben*) measure; (*ansehen*) look at; **[bei jdm] Fieber m~** take s.o.'s temperature; **sich m~** compete (**mit** with); **sich mit jdm m~/nicht m~ können** be a/no match for s.o.

Messer *nt* **-s,-** knife

Messias *m* **-** Messiah

Messing *nt* **-s** brass

Messung *f* **-,-en** measurement

Metabolismus *m* **-** metabolism

Metall *nt* **-s,-e** metal. **m~en** *a* metal; (*metallisch*) metallic. **m~isch** *a* metallic

Metallurgie *f* **-** metallurgy

Metamorphose *f* **-,-n** metamorphosis

Metaph|er *f* **-,-n** metaphor. **m~orisch** *a* metaphorical, *adv* -ly

Meteor *m* **-s,-e** meteor. **M~ologe** *m* **-n,-n** meteorologist. **M~ologie** *f* **-** meteorology. **m~ologisch** *a* meteorological

Meter *m & nt* **-s,-** metre, (*Amer*) meter. **M~maß** *nt* tape-measure

Method|e *f* **-,-n** method. **m~isch** *a* methodical

metrisch *a* metric

Metropole *f* **-,-n** metropolis

metzeln *vt* (*fig*) massacre

Metzger *m* **-s,-** butcher. **M~ei** *f* **-,-en** butcher's shop

Meute *f* **-,-n** pack [of hounds]; (*fig: Menge*) mob

Meuterei *f* **-,-en** mutiny

meutern *vi* (*haben*) mutiny; (*fam: schimpfen*) grumble

Mexikan|er(in) *m* **-s,-** (*f* **-,-nen**) Mexican. **m~isch** *a* Mexican

Mexiko *nt* **-s** Mexico

miauen *vi* (*haben*) mew, miaow

mich *pron* (*acc of* **ich**) me; (*refl*) myself

Mieder *nt* **-s,-** bodice; (*Korsett*) corset

Miene *f* **-,-n** expression; **M~ machen** make as if (**zu** to)

mies *a* (*fam*) lousy; **mir ist m~** I feel rotten

Miet|e *f* **-,-n** rent; (*Mietgebühr*) hire charge; **zur M~e wohnen** live in rented accommodation. **m~en** *vt* rent ⟨*Haus, Zimmer*⟩; hire ⟨*Auto, Boot, Fernseher*⟩. **M~er(in)** *m* **-s,-** (*f* **-,-nen**) tenant. **m~frei** *a & adv* rent-free. **M~shaus** *nt* block of rented flats. **M~vertrag** *m* lease. **M~wagen** *m* hire-car. **M~wohnung** *f* rented flat; (*zu vermieten*) flat to let

Mieze *f* **-,-n** (*fam*) puss[y]

Migräne *f* **-,-n** migraine

Mikrobe *f* **-,-n** microbe

Mikro|chip *m* microchip. **M~computer** *m* microcomputer. **M~film** *m* microfilm

Mikro|fon, M~phon *nt* **-s,-e** microphone. **M~prozessor** *m* **-s,-en** /-'so:rən/ microprocessor. **M~skop** *nt* **-s,-e** microscope. **m~skopisch** *a* microscopic

Mikrowelle *f* microwave. **M~ngerät** *nt*, **M~nherd** *m* microwave oven

Milbe *f* **-,-n** mite

Milch *f* **-** milk. **M~bar** *f* milk bar. **M~geschäft** *nt* dairy. **M~glas** *nt* opal glass. **m~ig** *a* milky. **M~kuh** *f* dairy cow. **M~mann** *m* (*pl* **-männer**) milkman. **M~mixgetränk** *nt* milk shake. **M~straße** *f* Milky Way

mild *a* mild; (*nachsichtig*) lenient; **m~e Gaben** alms. **M~e** *f* **-** mildness; leniency. **m~ern** *vt* make milder; (*mäßigen*) moderate; (*lindern*) alleviate, ease; **sich m~ern** become milder; (*sich mäßigen*) moderate; (*nachlassen*) abate; ⟨*Schmerz:*⟩ ease; **m~ernde Umstände** mitigating circumstances. **m~tätig** *a* charitable

Milieu /mi'li̯ø:/ *nt* **-s,-s** [social] environment

militant *a* militant

Militär *nt* **-s** army; (*Soldaten*) troops *pl*; **beim M~** in the army. **m~isch** *a* military

Miliz *f* **-,-en** militia

Milliarde /mɪ'li̯ardə/ *f* **-,-n** thousand million, billion

Milli|gramm *nt* milligram. **M~meter** *m* & *nt* millimetre. **M~meterpapier** *nt* graph paper

Million /mɪ'li̯o:n/ *f* **-,-en** million. **M~är** *m* **-s,-e** millionaire. **M~ärin** *f* **-,-nen** millionairess

Milz *f* **-** (*Anat*) spleen

mim|en *vt* (*fam: vortäuschen*) act. **M~ik** *f* **-** [expressive] gestures and facial expressions *pl*

Mimose *f* **-,-n** mimosa

minder *a* lesser • *adv* less; **mehr oder m~** more or less. **M~heit** *f* **-,-en** minority

minderjährig *a* (*Jur*) under-age; **m~ sein** be under age. **M~e(r)** *m/f* (*Jur*) minor. **M~keit** *f* **-** (*Jur*) minority

minder|n *vt* diminish; decrease ⟨*Tempo*⟩. **M~ung** *f* **-** decrease

minderwertig *a* inferior. **M~keit** *f* **-** inferiority. **M~keitskomplex** *m* inferiority complex

Mindest- *pref* minimum. **m~e** *a* & *pron* **der/die/das m~e** the least; **zum m~en** at least; **nicht im m~en** not in the least. **m~ens** *adv* at least. **M~lohn** *m* minimum wage. **M~maß** *nt* minimum

Mine *f* **-,-n** mine; (*Bleistift-*) lead; (*Kugelschreiber-*) refill. **M~nfeld** *nt* minefield. **M~nräumboot** *nt* minesweeper

Mineral *nt* **-s,-e** & **-ien** /-i̯ən/ mineral. **m~isch** *a* mineral. **M~ogie** *f* **-** mineralogy. **M~wasser** *nt* mineral water

Miniatur *f* **-,-en** miniature

Minigolf *nt* miniature golf

minimal *a* minimal

Minimum *nt* **-s,-ma** minimum

Minirock *m* miniskirt

Mini|ster *m* **-s,-** minister. **m~steriell** *a* ministerial. **M~sterium** *nt* **-s,-ien** ministry

Minorität *f* **-,-en** minority

minus *conj, adv* & *prep* (+*gen*) minus. **M~** *nt* **-** deficit; (*Nachteil*) disadvantage. **M~zeichen** *nt* minus [sign]

Minute *f* **-,-n** minute

mir *pron* (*dat of* **ich**) [to] me; (*refl*) myself; **mir nichts, dir nichts** without so much as a 'by your leave'

Misch|ehe *f* mixed marriage. **m~en** *vt* mix; blend ⟨*Tee, Kaffee*⟩; toss ⟨*Salat*⟩; shuffle ⟨*Karten*⟩; **sich m~en** mix; ⟨*Person:*⟩ mingle (**unter** | *acc* with); **sich m~en in** (+*acc*) join in ⟨*Gespräch*⟩; meddle in ⟨*Angelegenheit*⟩ • *vi* (*haben*) shuffle the cards. **M~ling** *m* **-s,-e** half-caste; (*Hund*) cross. **M~masch** *m* **-[e]s,-e** (*fam*) hotchpotch. **M~ung** *f* **-,-en** mixture; blend

miserabel *a* abominable; (*erbärmlich*) wretched

mißachten *vt* disregard

Miß|achtung *f* disregard. **M~behagen** *nt* [feeling of] unease. **M~bildung** *f* deformity

mißbilligen *vt* disapprove of

Miß|billigung *f* disapproval. **M~brauch** *m* abuse; **M~brauch treiben mit** abuse

miß|brauchen *vt* abuse; (*vergewaltigen*) rape. **m~deuten** *vt* misinterpret

missen *vt* do without; **ich möchte es nicht m~** I should not like to be without it

Miß|erfolg *m* failure. **M~ernte** *f* crop failure

Misse|tat *f* misdeed. **M~täter** *m* (*fam*) culprit

mißfallen† *vi* (*haben*) displease (**jdm** s.o.)

Miß|fallen *nt* **-s** displeasure; (*Mißbilligung*) disapproval. **m~gebildet** *a* deformed. **M~geburt** *f* freak; (*fig*) monstrosity. **M~geschick** *nt* mishap; (*Unglück*) misfortune. **m~gestimmt** *a* **m~gestimmt sein** be in a bad mood

miß|glücken *vi* (*sein*) fail. **m~gönnen** *vt* begrudge

Miß|griff *m* mistake. **M~gunst** *f* resentment. **m~günstig** *a* resentful

mißhandeln *vt* ill-treat

Miß|handlung *f* ill-treatment. **M~helligkeit** *f* **-,-en** disagreement

Mission *f* **-,-en** mission

Missionar(in) *m* **-s,-e** (*f* **-,-nen**) missionary

Miß|klang *m* discord. **M~kredit** *m* discredit; **in M~kredit bringen** discredit. **m~lich** *a* awkward. **m~liebig** *a* unpopular

mißlingen† *vi* (*sein*) fail; **es mißlang ihr** she failed. **M~** *nt* **-s** failure

Mißmut *m* ill humour. **m~ig** *a* morose, *adv* -ly

mißraten† *vi* (*sein*) turn out badly

Miß|stand *m* abuse; (*Zustand*) undesirable state of affairs. **M~stimmung** *f* discord; (*Laune*) bad mood. **M~ton** *m* discordant note

mißtrauen *vi* (*haben*) **jdm/etw m~** mistrust s.o./sth; (*Argwohn hegen*) distrust s.o./sth

Mißtrau|en *nt* **-s** mistrust; (*Argwohn*) distrust. **M~ensvotum** *nt* vote of no confidence. **m~isch** *a* distrustful; (*argwöhnisch*) suspicious

Miß|verhältnis *nt* disproportion. **M~verständnis** *nt* misunderstanding. **m~verstehen**† *vt* misunderstand. **M~wirtschaft** *f* mismanagement

Mist *m* **-[e]s** manure; (*fam*) rubbish

Mistel *f* **-,-n** mistletoe

Misthaufen *m* dungheap

mit *prep* (+*dat*) with; ⟨*sprechen*⟩ to; (*mittels*) by; (*inklusive*) including; (*bei*) at; **mit Bleistift** in pencil; **mit lauter Stimme** in a loud voice; **mit drei Jahren** at the age of three ● *adv* (*auch*) as well; **mit anfassen** (*fig*) lend a hand; **es ist mit das ärmste Land der Welt** it is among the poorest countries in the world

Mitarbeit *f* collaboration. **m~en** *vi sep* collaborate (**an**+*dat* on). **M~er(in)** *m*(*f*) collaborator; (*Kollege*) colleague; (*Betriebsangehörige*) employee

Mitbestimmung *f* co-determination

mitbring|en† *vt sep* bring [along]; **jdm Blumen m~en** bring/(*hinbringen*) take s.o. flowers. **M~sel** *nt* **-s,-** present (*brought back from holiday etc*)

Mitbürger *m* fellow citizen

miteinander *adv* with each other

miterleben *vt sep* witness

Mitesser *m* (*Med*) blackhead

mitfahren† *vi sep* (*sein*) go/come along; **mit jdm m~** go with s.o.; (*mitgenommen werden*) be given a lift by s.o.

mitfühlen *vi sep* (*haben*) sympathize. **m~d** *a* sympathetic; (*mitleidig*) compassionate

mitgeben† *vt sep* **jdm etw m~** give s.o. sth to take with him

Mitgefühl *nt* sympathy

mitgehen† *vi sep* (*sein*) **mit jdm m~** go with s.o.; **etw m~ lassen** (*fam*) pinch sth

mitgenommen *a* worn; **m~ sein** be in a sorry state; (*erschöpft*) be exhausted

Mitgift *f* **-,-en** dowry

Mitglied *nt* member. **M~schaft** *f* - membership

mithalten† *vi sep* (*haben*) join in; **mit jdm nicht m~ können** not be able to keep up with s.o.

Mithilfe *f* assistance

mitkommen† *vi sep* (*sein*) come [along] too; (*fig: folgen können*) keep up; (*verstehen*) follow

Mitlaut *m* consonant

Mitleid *nt* pity, compassion. **M~enschaft** *f* **in M~enschaft ziehen** affect. **m~erregend** *a* pitiful. **m~ig** *a* pitying; (*mitfühlend*) compassionate. **m~slos** *a* pitiless

mitmachen *v sep* ● *vt* take part in; (*erleben*) go through ● *vi* (*haben*) join in

Mitmensch *m* fellow man
mitnehmen† *vt sep* take along; (*mitfahren lassen*) give a lift to; (*fig: schädigen*) affect badly; (*erschöpfen*) exhaust; **'zum M~'** 'to take away', (*Amer*) 'to go'
mitnichten *adv* not at all
mitreden *vi sep* (*haben*) join in [the conversation]; (*mit entscheiden*) have a say (**bei** in)
mitreißen† *vt sep* sweep along; (*fig: begeistern*) carry away; **m~d** rousing
mitsamt *prep* (+*dat*) together with
mitschneiden† *vt sep* record
mitschreiben† *vt sep* (*haben*) take down
Mitschuld *f* partial blame. **m~ig** *a* **m~ig sein** be partly to blame
Mitschüler(in) *m(f)* fellow pupil
mitspiel|en *vi sep* (*haben*) join in; (*Theat*) be in the cast; (*beitragen*) play a part; **jdm übel m~en** treat s.o. badly. **M~er** *m* fellow player; (*Mitwirkender*) participant
Mittag *m* midday, noon; (*Mahlzeit*) lunch; (*Pause*) lunch-break; **[zu] M~ essen** have lunch. **m~** *adv* **heute m~** at lunch-time today. **M~essen** *nt* lunch. **m~s** *adv* at noon; (*als Mahlzeit*) for lunch; **um 12 Uhr m~s** at noon. **M~spause** *f* lunch-hour; (*Pause*) lunch-break. **M~sschlaf** *m* after-lunch nap. **M~stisch** *m* lunch table; (*Essen*) lunch. **M~szeit** *f* lunch-time
Mittäter|(in) *m(f)* accomplice. **M~schaft** *f* - complicity
Mitte *f* **-,-n** middle; (*Zentrum*) centre; **die goldene M~** the golden mean; **M~ Mai** in mid-May; **in unserer M~** in our midst
mitteil|en *vt sep* **jdm etw m~en** tell s.o. sth; (*amtlich*) inform s.o. of sth. **m~sam** *a* communicative. **M~ung** *f* **-,-en** communication; (*Nachricht*) piece of news
Mittel *nt* **-s,-** means *sg*; (*Heil-*) remedy; (*Medikament*) medicine; (*M~wert*) mean; (*Durchschnitt*) average; **M~** *pl* (*Geld-*) funds, resources. **m~** *pred a* medium; (*m~mäßig*) middling. **M~alter** *nt* Middle Ages *pl*. **m~alterlich** *a* medieval. **m~bar** *a* indirect, *adv* -ly. **M~ding** *nt* (*fig*) cross. **m~europäisch** *a* Central European. **M~finger** *m* middle finger. **m~groß** *a* medium-sized; ⟨*Person*⟩ of medium height. **M~klasse** *f* middle range. **m~los** *a* destitute. **m~mäßig** *a* middling; **[nur] m~mäßig** mediocre. **M~meer** *nt* Mediterranean. **M~punkt** *m* centre; (*fig*) centre of attention
mittels *prep* (+*gen*) by means of
Mittel|schule *f* = **Realschule. M~smann** *m* (*pl* **-männer**), **M~sperson** *f* intermediary, go-between. **M~stand** *m* middle class. **m~ste(r,s)** *a* middle. **M~streifen** *m* (*Auto*) central reservation, (*Amer*) median strip. **M~stürmer** *m* centre-forward. **M~weg** *m* (*fig*) middle course; **goldener M~weg** happy medium. **M~welle** *f* medium wave. **M~wort** *nt* (*pl* **-wörter**) participle
mitten *adv* **m~ in/auf** (*dat/acc*) in the middle of; **m~ unter** (*dat/acc*) amidst. **m~durch** *adv* [right] through the middle
Mitternacht *f* midnight
mittler|e(r,s) *a* middle; ⟨*Größe, Qualität*⟩ medium; (*durchschnittlich*) mean, average. **m~weile** *adv* meanwhile; (*seitdem*) by now
Mittwoch *m* **-s,-e** Wednesday. **m~s** *adv* on Wednesdays
mitunter *adv* now and again
mitwirk|en *vi sep* (*haben*) take part; (*helfen*) contribute. **M~ung** *f* participation
mix|en *vt* mix. **M~er** *m* **-s,-** (*Culin*) liquidizer, blender. **M~tur** *f* **-,-en** (*Med*) mixture
Möbel *pl* furniture *sg*. **M~stück** *nt* piece of furniture. **M~tischler** *m* cabinet-maker. **M~wagen** *m* removal van
mobil *a* mobile; (*fam: munter*) lively; (*nach Krankheit*) fit [and well]; **m~ machen** mobilize
Mobile *nt* **-s,-s** mobile
Mobiliar *nt* **-s** furniture
mobilisier|en *vt* mobilize. **M~ung** *f* - mobilization
Mobilmachung *f* - mobilization
möblier|en *vt* furnish; **m~tes Zimmer** furnished room
mochte, möchte *s.* **mögen**
Modalverb *nt* modal auxiliary
Mode *f* **-,-n** fashion; **M~ sein** be fashionable
Modell *nt* **-s,-e** model; **M~ stehen** pose (**jdm** for s.o.). **m~ieren** *vt* model
Modenschau *f* fashion show

Modera|tor *m* **-s,-en** /-'to:rən/, **M~torin** *f* **-,-nen** (*TV*) presenter

modern¹ *vi* (*haben*) decay

modern² *a* modern; (*modisch*) fashionable. **m~isieren** *vt* modernize

Mode|schmuck *m* costume jewellery. **M~schöpfer** *m* fashion designer

Modifi|kation /-'tsi̯o:n/ *f* **-,-en** modification. **m~zieren** *vt* modify

modisch *a* fashionable

Modistin *f* **-,-nen** milliner

modrig *a* musty

modulieren *vt* modulate

Mofa *nt* **-s,-s** moped

mogeln *vi* (*haben*) (*fam*) cheat

mögen† *vt* like; **lieber m~** prefer • *v aux* **ich möchte** I'd like; **möchtest du nach Hause?** do you want to go home? **ich mag nicht mehr** I've had enough; **ich hätte weinen m~** I could have cried; **ich mag mich irren** I may be wrong; **wer/was mag das sein?** whoever/whatever can it be? **wie mag es ihm ergangen sein?** I wonder how he got on; **[das] mag sein** that may well be; **mag kommen, was da will** come what may

möglich *a* possible; **alle m~en** all sorts of. **m~erweise** *adv* possibly. **M~keit** *f* **-,-en** possibility. **M~keitsform** *f* subjunctive. **m~st** *adv* if possible; **m~st viel/früh** as much/early as possible

Mohammedan|er(in) *m* **-s,-** (*f* **-,-nen**) Muslim. **m~isch** *a* Muslim

Mohn *m* **-s** poppy; (*Culin*) poppy-seed. **M~blume** *f* poppy

Möhre, Mohrrübe *f* **-,-n** carrot

mokieren (sich) *vr* make fun (**über** + *acc* of)

Mokka *m* **-s** mocha; (*Geschmack*) coffee

Molch *m* **-[e]s,-e** newt

Mole *f* **-,-n** (*Naut*) mole

Molekül *nt* **-s,-e** molecule

Molkerei *f* **-,-en** dairy

Moll *nt* **-** (*Mus*) minor

mollig *a* cosy; (*warm*) warm; (*rundlich*) plump

Moment *m* **-s,-e** moment; **im/jeden M~** at the/any moment; **M~ [mal]!** just a moment! **m~an** *a* momentary, *adv* -ily; (*gegenwärtig*) at the moment

Momentaufnahme *f* snapshot

Monarch *m* **-en,-en** monarch. **M~ie** *f* **-,-n** monarchy

Monat *m* **-s,-e** month. **m~elang** *adv* for months. **m~lich** *a* & *adv* monthly. **M~skarte** *f* monthly season ticket

Mönch *m* **-[e]s,-e** monk

Mond *m* **-[e]s,-e** moon

mondän *a* fashionable, *adv* -bly

Mond|finsternis *f* lunar eclipse. **m~hell** *a* moonlit. **M~sichel** *f* crescent moon. **M~schein** *m* moonlight

monieren *vt* criticize

Monitor *m* **-s,-en** /-'to:rən/ (*Techn*) monitor

Monogramm *nt* **-s,-e** monogram

Mono|log *m* **-s,-e** monologue. **M~pol** *nt* **-s,-e** monopoly. **m~polisieren** *vt* monopolize. **m~ton** *a* monotonous, *adv* -ly. **M~tonie** *f* **-** monotony

Monster *nt* **-s,-** monster

monstr|ös *a* monstrous. **M~osität** *f* **-,-en** monstrosity

Monstrum *nt* **-s,-stren** monster

Monsun *m* **-s,-e** monsoon

Montag *m* Monday

Montage /mɔn'ta:ʒə/ *f* **-,-n** fitting; (*Zusammenbau*) assembly; (*Film-*) editing; (*Kunst*) montage

montags *adv* on Mondays

Montanindustrie *f* coal and steel industry

Monteur /mɔn'tø:ɐ̯/ *m* **-s,-e** fitter. **M~anzug** *m* overalls *pl*

montieren *vt* fit; (*zusammenbauen*) assemble

Monument *nt* **-[e]s,-e** monument. **m~al** *a* monumental

Moor *nt* **-[e]s,-e** bog; (*Heide-*) moor

Moos *nt* **-es,-e** moss. **m~ig** *a* mossy

Mop *m* **-s,-s** mop

Moped *nt* **-s,-s** moped

Mops *m* **-es,¨e** pug [dog]

Moral *f* **-** morals *pl*; (*Selbstvertrauen*) morale; (*Lehre*) moral. **m~isch** *a* moral, *adv* -ly. **m~isieren** *vi* (*haben*) moralize

Morast *m* **-[e]s,-e** morass; (*Schlamm*) mud

Mord *m* **-[e]s,-e** murder; (*Pol*) assassination. **M~anschlag** *m* murder/assassination attempt. **m~en** *vt/i* (*haben*) murder, kill

Mörder *m* **-s,-** murderer; (*Pol*) assassin. **M~in** *f* **-,-nen** murderess. **m~isch** *a* murderous; (*fam: schlimm*) dreadful

Mords- *pref* (*fam*) terrific. **m~mäßig** *a* (*fam*) frightful, *adv* -ly

morgen *adv* tomorrow; **m~ früh/nachmittag** tomorrow morning/afternoon; **heute/gestern/Montag m~** this/yesterday/Monday morning
Morgen *m* **-s,-** morning; (*Maß*) ≈ acre; **am M~** in the morning. **M~dämmerung** *f* dawn. **m~dlich** *a* morning ... **M~grauen** *nt* **-s** dawn; **im M~grauen** at dawn. **M~mantel, M~rock** *m* dressing-gown. **M~rot** *nt* red sky in the morning. **m~s** *a* in the morning
morgig *a* tomorrow's; **der m~e Tag** tomorrow
Morphium *nt* **-s** morphine
morsch *a* rotten
Morsealphabet *nt* Morse code
Mörtel *m* **-s** mortar
Mosaik /moza'i:k/ *nt* **-s,-e[n]** mosaic
Moschee *f* **-,-n** mosque
Mosel *f* **-** Moselle. **M~wein** *m* Moselle [wine]
Moskau *nt* **-s** Moscow
Moskito *m* **-s,-s** mosquito
Mos|lem *m* **-s,-s** Muslim. **m~lemisch** *a* Muslim
Most *m* **-[e]s** must; (*Apfel-*) ≈ cider
Mostrich *m* **-s** (*NGer*) mustard
Motel *nt* **-s,-s** motel
Motiv *nt* **-s,-e** motive; (*Kunst*) motif. **M~ation** /-'tsi̯o:n/ *f* **-** motivation. **m~ieren** *vt* motivate
Motor /'mo:tɔr, mo'to:ɐ̯/ *m* **-s,-en** /-'to:rən/ engine; (*Elektro-*) motor. **M~boot** *nt* motor boat
motorisieren *vt* motorize
Motor|rad *nt* motor cycle. **M~radfahrer** *m* motor-cyclist. **M~roller** *m* motor scooter
Motte *f* **-,-n** moth. **M~nkugel** *f* mothball
Motto *nt* **-s,-s** motto
Möwe *f* **-,-n** gull
Mücke *f* **-,-n** gnat; (*kleine*) midge; (*Stech-*) mosquito
mucksen (sich) *vr* **sich nicht m~** (*fam*) keep quiet
müd|e *a* tired; **nicht m~e werden/es m~e sein** not tire/be tired **(etw zu tun** of doing sth). **M~igkeit** *f* **-** tiredness
Muff *m* **-s,-e** muff
muffig *a* musty; (*fam: mürrisch*) grumpy
Mühe *f* **-,-n** effort; (*Aufwand*) trouble; **sich** (*dat*) **M~ geben** make an effort; (*sich bemühen*) try; **nicht der M~ wert** not worth while; **mit M~ und Not** with great difficulty; (*gerade noch*) only just. **m~los** *a* effortless, *adv* -ly
muhen *vi* (*haben*) moo
mühe|n (sich) *vr* struggle. **m~voll** *a* laborious; (*anstrengend*) arduous
Mühl|e *f* **-,-n** mill; (*Kaffee-*) grinder. **M~stein** *m* millstone
Müh|sal *f* **-,-e** (*liter*) toil; (*Mühe*) trouble. **m~sam** *a* laborious, *adv* -ly; (*beschwerlich*) difficult, *adv* with difficulty. **m~selig** *a* laborious, *adv* -ly
Mulde *f* **-,-n** hollow
Müll *m* **-s** refuse, (*Amer*) garbage. **M~abfuhr** *f* refuse collection
Mullbinde *f* gauze bandage
Mülleimer *m* waste bin; (*Mülltonne*) dustbin, (*Amer*) garbage can
Müller *m* **-s,-** miller
Müll|halde *f* [rubbish] dump. **M~schlucker** *m* refuse chute. **M~tonne** *f* dustbin, (*Amer*) garbage can. **M~wagen** *m* dust-cart, (*Amer*) garbage truck
mulmig *a* (*fam*) dodgy; ⟨*Gefühl*⟩ uneasy; **ihm war m~ zumute** he felt uneasy/(*übel*) queasy
multi|national *a* multinational. **M~plikation** /-'tsi̯o:n/ *f* **-,-en** multiplication. **m~plizieren** *vt* multiply
Mumie /'mu:mi̯ə/ *f* **-,-n** mummy
mumifiziert *a* mummified
Mumm *m* **-s** (*fam*) energy
Mumps *m* **-** mumps
Mund *m* **-[e]s,¨er** mouth; **halt den M~!** be quiet! (*sl*) shut up! **M~art** *f* dialect. **m~artlich** *a* dialect
Mündel *nt* & *m* **-s,-** (*Jur*) ward. **m~sicher** *a* gilt-edged
münden *vi* (*sein*) flow/⟨*Straße:*⟩ lead (**in** + *acc* into)
mund|faul *a* taciturn. **M~geruch** *m* bad breath. **M~harmonika** *f* mouth-organ
mündig *a* **m~ sein/werden** (*Jur*) be/come of age. **M~keit** *f* **-** (*Jur*) majority
mündlich *a* verbal, *adv* -ly; **m~e Prüfung** oral
Mund|stück *nt* mouthpiece; (*Zigaretten-*) tip. **m~tot** *a* **m~tot machen** (*fig*) gag
Mündung *f* **-,-en** (*Fluß-*) mouth; (*Gewehr-*) muzzle
Mund|voll *m* **-,-** mouthful. **M~wasser** *nt* mouthwash. **M~werk**

nt **ein gutes M~werk haben** (*fam*) be very talkative. **M~winkel** *m* corner of the mouth

Munition /-'tsi̯o:n/ *f* - ammunition

munkeln *vt/i* (*haben*) talk (**von** of); **es wird gemunkelt** rumour has it (**daß** that)

Münster *nt* **-s,-** cathedral

munter *a* lively; (*heiter*) merry; **m~ sein** (*wach*) be wide awake/(*aufgestanden, gesund*) up and about; **gesund und m~** fit and well ● *adv* **[immer] m~** merrily

Münz|e *f* **-,-n** coin; (*M~stätte*) mint. **m~en** *vt* mint; **das war auf dich gemünzt** (*fam*) that was aimed at you. **M~fernsprecher** *m* coin-box telephone, payphone. **M~wäscherei** *f* launderette

mürbe *a* crumbly; ⟨*Obst*⟩ mellow; ⟨*Fleisch*⟩ tender; **jdn m~ machen** (*fig*) wear s.o. down. **M~teig** *m* short pastry

Murmel *f* **-,-n** marble

murmeln *vt/i* (*haben*) murmur; (*undeutlich*) mumble, mutter. **M~** *nt* **-s** murmur

Murmeltier *nt* marmot

murren *vt/i* (*haben*) grumble

mürrisch *a* surly

Mus *nt* **-es** purée

Muschel *f* **-,-n** mussel; (*Schale*) [sea] shell

Museum /mu'ze:ʊm/ *nt* **-s,-seen** /-'ze:ən/ museum

Musik *f* - music. **M~alien** /-i̯ən/ *pl* [printed] music *sg*. **m~alisch** *a* musical

Musikbox *f* juke-box

Musiker(in) *m* **-s,-** (*f* **-,-nen**) musician

Musik|instrument *nt* musical instrument. **M~kapelle** *f* band. **M~pavillon** *m* bandstand

musisch *a* artistic

musizieren *vi* (*haben*) make music

Muskat *m* **-[e]s** nutmeg

Muskel *m* **-s,-n** muscle. **M~kater** *m* stiff and aching muscles *pl*

Musku|latur *f* - muscles *pl*. **m~lös** *a* muscular

Müsli *nt* **-s** muesli

muß *s.* **müssen**. **Muß** *nt* - **ein Muß** a must

Muße *f* - leisure; **mit M~** at leis re

müssen† *v aux* **etw tun m~** have to/(*fam*) have got to do sth; **ich muß jetzt gehen** I have to *or* must go now; **ich mußte lachen** I had to laugh; **ich muß es wissen** I need to know; **du müßtest es mal versuchen** you ought to *or* should try it; **muß das sein?** is that necessary?

müßig *a* idle; (*unnütz*) futile. **M~gang** *m* - idleness

mußte, müßte *s.* **müssen**

Muster *nt* **-s,-** pattern; (*Probe*) sample; (*Vorbild*) model. **M~beispiel** *nt* typical example; (*Vorbild*) perfect example. **M~betrieb** *m* model factory. **m~gültig, m~haft** *a* exemplary. **m~n** *vt* eye; (*inspizieren*) inspect. **M~schüler(in)** *m(f)* model pupil. **M~ung** *f* **-,-en** inspection; (*Mil*) medical; (*Muster*) pattern

Mut *m* **-[e]s** courage; **jdm Mut machen** encourage s.o.

Mutation /-'tsi̯o:n/ *f* **-,-en** (*Biol*) mutation

mut|ig *a* courageous, *adv* -ly. **m~los** *a* despondent; (*entmutigt*) disheartened

mutmaß|en *vt* presume; (*Vermutungen anstellen*) speculate. **m~lich** *a* probable, *adv* -bly; **der m~liche Täter** the suspect. **M~ung** *f* **-,-en** speculation, conjecture

Mutprobe *f* test of courage

Mutter[1] *f* **-,⸚** mother; **werdende M~** mother-to-be

Mutter[2] *f* **-,-n** (*Techn*) nut

Muttergottes *f* **-,-** madonna

Mutter|land *nt* motherland. **M~leib** *m* womb

mütterlich *a* maternal; (*fürsorglich*) motherly. **m~erseits** *adv* on one's/the mother's side

Mutter|mal *nt* birthmark; (*dunkel*) mole. **M~schaft** *f* - motherhood. **m~seelenallein** *a* & *adv* all alone. **M~sprache** *f* mother tongue. **M~tag** *m* Mother's Day

Mutti *f* **-,-s** (*fam*) mummy

Mutwill|e *m* wantonness. **m~ig** *a* wanton, *adv* -ly

Mütze *f* **-,-n** cap; **wollene M~** woolly hat

MwSt. *abbr* **(Mehrwertsteuer)** VAT

mysteriös *a* mysterious, *adv* -ly

Myst|ik /'mʏstɪk/ *f* - mysticism. **m~isch** *a* mystical

myth|isch *a* mythical. **M~ologie** *f* - mythology. **M~os** *m* **-,-then** myth

N

na *int* well; **na gut** all right then; **na ja** oh well; **na und?** so what?

Nabe *f* **-,-n** hub

Nabel *m* **-s,-** navel. **N~schnur** *f* umbilical cord

nach *prep* (+*dat*) after; (*Uhrzeit*) past; (*Richtung*) to; ⟨*greifen, rufen, sich sehnen*⟩ for; (*gemäß*) according to; **meiner Meinung n~** in my opinion; **n~ oben** upwards ● *adv* **n~ und n~** gradually, bit by bit; **n~ wie vor** still

nachäffen *vt sep* mimic

nachahm|en *vt sep* imitate. **N~ung** *f* **-,-en** imitation

nacharbeiten *vt sep* make up for

nacharten *vi sep* (*sein*) **jdm n~** take after s.o.

Nachbar|(in) *m* **-n,-n** (*f* **-,-nen**) neighbour. **N~haus** *nt* house next door. **N~land** *nt* neighbouring country. **n~lich** *a* neighbourly; (*Nachbar-*) neighbouring. **N~schaft** *f* **-** neighbourhood; **gute N~schaft** neighbourliness

nachbestell|en *vt sep* reorder. **N~ung** *f* repeat order

nachbild|en *vt sep* copy, reproduce. **N~ung** *f* copy, reproduction

nachdatieren *vt sep* backdate

nachdem *conj* after; **je n~** it depends

nachdenk|en† *vi sep* (*haben*) think (**über** + *acc* about). **N~en** *nt* **-s** reflection, thought. **n~lich** *a* thoughtful, *adv* -ly

Nachdruck *m* (*pl* **-e**) reproduction; (*unveränderter*) reprint; (*Betonung*) emphasis

nachdrücklich *a* emphatic, *adv* -ally

nacheifern *vi sep* (*haben*) **jdm n~** emulate s.o.

nacheilen *vi sep* (*sein*) (+*dat*) hurry after

nacheinander *adv* one after the other

Nachfahre *m* **-n,-n** descendant

Nachfolg|e *f* succession. **n~en** *vi sep* (*sein*) (+*dat*) follow; (*im Amt*) succeed. **N~er(in)** *m* **-s,-** (*f* **-,-nen**) successor

nachforsch|en *vi sep* (*haben*) make enquiries. **N~ung** *f* enquiry; **N~ungen anstellen** make enquiries

Nachfrage *f* (*Comm*) demand. **n~n** *vi sep* (*haben*) enquire

nachfüllen *vt sep* refill ⟨*Behälter*⟩; **Wasser n~** fill up with water

nachgeben† *v sep* ● *vi* (*haben*) give way; (*sich fügen*) give in, yield ● *vt* **jdm Suppe n~** give s.o. more soup

Nachgebühr *f* surcharge

nachgehen† *vi sep* (*sein*) ⟨*Uhr:*⟩ be slow; **jdm/etw n~** follow s.o./sth; follow up ⟨*Spur, Angelegenheit*⟩; pursue ⟨*Angelegenheit, Tätigkeit*⟩; go about ⟨*Arbeit*⟩

nachgeraten† *vi sep* (*sein*) **jdm n~** take after s.o.

Nachgeschmack *m* after-taste

nachgiebig *a* indulgent; (*gefällig*) compliant. **N~keit** *f* **-** indulgence; compliance

nachgrübeln *vi sep* (*haben*) ponder (**über** + *acc* on)

nachhallen *vi sep* (*haben*) reverberate

nachhaltig *a* lasting

nachhelfen† *vi sep* (*haben*) help

nachher *adv* later; (*danach*) afterwards; **bis n~!** see you later!

Nachhilfeunterricht *m* coaching

nachhinein *adv* **im n~** afterwards

nachhinken *vi sep* (*sein*) (*fig*) lag behind

nachholen *vt sep* (*später holen*) fetch later; (*mehr holen*) get more; (*später machen*) do later; (*aufholen*) catch up on; make up for ⟨*Zeit*⟩

nachjagen *vi sep* (*haben*) (+*dat*) chase after

Nachkomme *m* **-n,-n** descendant. **n~n†** *vi sep* (*sein*) follow [later], come later; (*Schritt halten*) keep up; **etw** (*dat*) **n~n** (*fig*) comply with ⟨*Bitte, Wunsch*⟩; carry out ⟨*Versprechen, Pflicht*⟩. **N~nschaft** *f* **-** descendants *pl*, progeny

Nachkriegszeit *f* post-war period

Nachlaß *m* **-lasses,-lässe** discount; (*Jur*) [deceased's] estate

nachlassen† *v sep* ● *vi* (*haben*) decrease; ⟨*Regen, Hitze:*⟩ let up; ⟨*Schmerz:*⟩ ease; ⟨*Sturm:*⟩ abate; ⟨*Augen, Kräfte, Leistungen:*⟩ deteriorate; **er ließ nicht nach [mit Fragen]** he persisted [with his questions] ● *vt* **etw vom Preis n~** take sth off the price

nachlässig *a* careless, *adv* -ly; (*leger*) casual, *adv* -ly; (*unordentlich*) sloppy, *adv* -ily. **N~keit** *f* **-** carelessness; sloppiness

nachlaufen† *vi sep* (*sein*) (+*dat*) run after

nachlegen *vt sep* **Holz/Kohlen n~** put more wood/coal on the fire
nachlesen† *vt sep* look up
nachlöse|n *vi sep* (*haben*) pay one's fare on the train/on arrival. **N~schalter** *m* excess-fare office
nachmachen *vt sep* (*später machen*) do later; (*imitieren*) imitate, copy; (*fälschen*) forge; **jdm etw n~** copy sth from s.o.; repeat ⟨*Übung*⟩ after s.o.
Nachmittag *m* afternoon. **n~** *adv* **gestern/heute n~** yesterday/this afternoon. **n~s** *adv* in the afternoon
Nachnahme *f* **etw per N~ schicken** send sth cash on delivery *or* COD
Nachname *m* surname
Nachporto *nt* excess postage
nachprüfen *vt sep* check, verify
nachrechnen *vt sep* work out; (*prüfen*) check
Nachrede *f* **üble N~** defamation
Nachricht *f* **-,-en** [piece of] news *sg*; **N~en** news *sg*; **eine N~ hinterlassen** leave a message; **jdm N~ geben** inform, notify s.o. **N~endienst** *m* (*Mil*) intelligence service. **N~ensendung** *f* news bulletin. **N~enwesen** *nt* communications *pl*
nachrücken *vi sep* (*sein*) move up
Nachruf *m* obituary
nachsagen *vt sep* repeat (**jdm** after s.o.); **jdm Schlechtes/Gutes n~** speak ill/well of s.o.; **man sagt ihm nach, daß er geizig ist** he is said to be stingy
Nachsaison *f* late season
Nachsatz *m* postscript
nachschicken *vt sep* (*später schicken*) send later; (*hinterher-*) send after (**jdm** s.o.); send on ⟨*Post*⟩ (**jdm** to s.o.)
nachschlag|en† *v sep* • *vt* look up • *vi* (*haben*) **in einem Wörterbuch n~en** consult a dictionary; **jdm n~en** take after s.o. **N~ewerk** *nt* reference book
Nachschlüssel *m* duplicate key
Nachschrift *f* transcript; (*Nachsatz*) postscript
Nachschub *m* (*Mil*) supplies *pl*
nachsehen† *v sep* • *vt* (*prüfen*) check; (*nachschlagen*) look up; (*hinwegsehen über*) overlook • *vi* (*haben*) have a look; (*prüfen*) check; **im Wörterbuch n~** consult a dictionary; **jdm/etw n~** gaze after s.o./sth. **N~** *nt* **das N~ haben** (*fam*) go empty-handed
nachsenden† *vt sep* forward ⟨*Post*⟩ (**jdm** to s.o.); **'bitte n~'** 'please forward'
Nachsicht *f* forbearance; (*Milde*) leniency; (*Nachgiebigkeit*) indulgence. **n~ig** *a* forbearing; lenient; indulgent
Nachsilbe *f* suffix
nachsitzen† *vi sep* (*haben*) **n~ müssen** be kept in [after school]; **jdn n~ lassen** give s.o. detention. **N~** *nt* **-s** (*Sch*) detention
Nachspeise *f* dessert, sweet
Nachspiel *nt* (*fig*) sequel
nachspionieren *vi sep* (*haben*) **jdm n~** spy on s.o.
nachsprechen† *vt sep* repeat (**jdm** after s.o.)
nachspülen *vt sep* rinse
nächst /-çst/ *prep* (+*dat*) next to. **n~beste(r,s)** *a* first [available]; (*zweitbeste*) next best. **n~e(r,s)** *a* next; (*nächstgelegene*) nearest; ⟨*Verwandte*⟩ closest; **n~e Woche** next week; **in n~er Nähe** close by; **am n~en sein** be nearest *or* closest • *pron* **der/die/das n~e** the next; **der n~e bitte** next please; **als n~es** next; **fürs n~e** for the time being. **N~e(r)** *m* fellow man
nachstehend *a* following • *adv* below
nachstellen *v sep* • *vt* readjust; put back ⟨*Uhr*⟩ • *vi* (*haben*) (+*dat*) pursue
nächst|emal *adv* **das n~emal** [the] next time. **N~enliebe** *f* charity. **n~ens** *adv* shortly. **n~gelegen** *a* nearest. **n~liegend** *a* most obvious
nachstreben *vi sep* (*haben*) **jdm n~** emulate s.o.
nachsuchen *vi sep* (*haben*) search; **n~ um** request
Nacht *f* **-,¨e** night; **über/bei N~** overnight/at night. **n~** *adv* **Montag/morgen n~** Monday/tomorrow night; **heute n~** tonight; (*letzte Nacht*) last night; **gestern n~** last night; (*vorletzte Nacht*) the night before last. **N~dienst** *m* night duty
Nachteil *m* disadvantage; **zum N~** to the detriment (*gen* of). **n~ig** *a* adverse, *adv* -ly
Nacht|essen *nt* (*SGer*) supper. **N~falter** *m* moth. **N~hemd** *nt* night-dress; (*Männer-*) night-shirt
Nachtigall *f* **-,-en** nightingale
Nachtisch *m* dessert

Nacht|klub *m* night-club. **N~leben** *nt* night-life
nächtlich *a* nocturnal, night ...
Nacht|lokal *nt* night-club. **N~mahl** *nt* (*Aust*) supper
Nachtrag *m* postscript; (*Ergänzung*) supplement. **n~en**† *vt sep* add; **jdm etw n~en** walk behind s.o. carrying sth; (*fig*) bear a grudge against s.o. for sth. **n~end** *a* vindictive; **n~end sein** bear grudges
nachträglich *a* subsequent, later; (*verspätet*) belated ● *adv* later; (*nachher*) afterwards; (*verspätet*) belatedly
nachtrauern *vi sep* (*haben*) (+*dat*) mourn the loss of
Nacht|ruhe *f* night's rest; **angenehme N~ruhe!** sleep well! **n~s** *adv* at night; **2 Uhr n~s** 2 o'clock in the morning. **N~schicht** *f* night-shift. **N~tisch** *m* bedside table. **N~tischlampe** *f* bedside lamp. **N~topf** *m* chamber-pot. **N~wächter** *m* night-watchman. **N~zeit** *f* night-time
Nachuntersuchung *f* check-up
nachwachsen† *vi sep* (*sein*) grow again
Nachwahl *f* by-election
Nachweis *m* **-es,-e** proof. **n~bar** *a* demonstrable. **n~en**† *vt sep* prove; (*aufzeigen*) show; (*vermitteln*) give details of; **jdm nichts n~en können** have no proof against s.o. **n~lich** *a* demonstrable, *adv* -bly
Nachwelt *f* posterity
Nachwirkung *f* after-effect
Nachwort *nt* (*pl* **-e**) epilogue
Nachwuchs *m* new generation; (*fam: Kinder*) offspring. **N~spieler** *m* young player
nachzahlen *vt/i sep* (*haben*) pay extra; (*später zahlen*) pay later; **Steuern n~** pay tax arrears
nachzählen *vt/i sep* (*haben*) count again; (*prüfen*) check
Nachzahlung *f* extra/later payment; (*Gehalts-*) back-payment
nachzeichnen *vt sep* copy
Nachzügler *m* **-s,-** late-comer; (*Zurückgebliebener*) straggler
Nacken *m* **-s,-** nape *or* back of the neck
nackt *a* naked; (*bloß, kahl*) bare; ⟨*Wahrheit*⟩ plain. **N~baden** *nt* nude bathing. **N~heit** *f* - nakedness, nudity. **N~kultur** *f* nudism. **N~schnecke** *f* slug
Nadel *f* **-,-n** needle; (*Häkel-*) hook; (*Schmuck-, Hut-*) pin. **N~arbeit** *f* needlework. **N~baum** *m* conifer. **N~kissen** *nt* pincushion. **N~stich** *m* stitch; (*fig*) pinprick. **N~wald** *m* coniferous forest
Nagel *m* **-s,¨** nail. **N~bürste** *f* nail-brush. **N~feile** *f* nail-file. **N~haut** *f* cuticle. **N~lack** *m* nail varnish. **n~n** *vt* nail. **n~neu** *a* brand-new. **N~schere** *f* nail scissors *pl*
nagen *vt/i* (*haben*) gnaw (**an** + *dat* at); **n~d** (*fig*) nagging
Nagetier *nt* rodent
nah *a, adv & prep* = **nahe; von nah und fern** from far and wide
Näharbeit *f* sewing; **eine N~** a piece of sewing
Nahaufnahme *f* close-up
nahe *a* (**näher, nächst**) nearby; (*zeitlich*) imminent; (*eng*) close; **der N~ Osten** the Middle East; **in n~r Zukunft** in the near future; **von n~m** [from] close to; **n~ sein** be close (*dat* to); **den Tränen n~** close to tears ● *adv* near, close; ⟨*verwandt*⟩ closely; **n~ an** (+*acc/dat*) near [to], close to; **n~ daran sein, etw zu tun** nearly do sth; **jdm zu n~ treten** (*fig*) offend s.o. ● *prep* (+*dat*) near [to], close to
Nähe *f* - nearness, proximity; **aus der N~** [from] close to; **in der N~** near *or* close by; **in der N~ der Kirche** near the church
nahebei *adv* near *or* close by
nahe|gehen† *vi sep* (*sein*) **jdm n~gehen** (*fig*) affect s.o. deeply. **n~kommen**† *vi sep* (*sein*) (*fig*) come close (*dat* to); (*vertraut werden*) get close (*dat* to). **n~legen** *vt sep* recommend (*dat* to); **jdm n~legen, etw zu tun** urge s.o. to do sth. **n~liegen**† *vi sep* (*haben*) (*fig*) be highly likely. **n~liegend** *a* obvious
nahen *vi* (*sein*) (*liter*) approach
nähen *vt/i* (*haben*) sew; (*anfertigen*) make; (*Med*) stitch [up]
näher *a* closer; ⟨*Weg*⟩ shorter; ⟨*Einzelheiten*⟩ further ● *adv* closer; (*genauer*) more closely; **sich n~ erkundigen** make further enquiries; **n~ an** (+*acc/dat*) nearer [to], closer to ● *prep* (+*dat*) nearer [to], closer to. **N~e[s]** *nt* [further] details *pl*. **n~kommen**† *vi sep* (*sein*) come closer, approach; (*fig*) get closer (*dat* to). **n~n (sich)** *vr* approach
nahestehen† *vi sep* (*haben*) (*fig*) be close (*dat* to)

nahezu *adv* almost
Nähgarn *nt* [sewing] cotton
Nahkampf *m* close combat
Näh|maschine *f* sewing machine. **N~nadel** *f* sewing-needle
nähren *vt* feed; (*fig*) nurture; **sich n~ von** live on ● *vi* (*haben*) be nutritious
nahrhaft *a* nutritious
Nährstoff *m* nutrient
Nahrung *f* - food, nourishment. **N~smittel** *nt* food
Nährwert *m* nutritional value
Naht *f* -,⸚e seam; (*Med*) suture. **n~los** *a* seamless
Nahverkehr *m* local service. **N~szug** *m* local train
Nähzeug *nt* sewing; (*Zubehör*) sewing kit
naiv /na'i:f/ *a* naïve, *adv* -ly. **N~ität** /-vi'tɛ:t/ *f* - naïvety
Name *m* **-ns,-n** name; **im N~n** (+ *gen*) in the name of; ⟨*handeln*⟩ on behalf of; **das Kind beim rechten N~n nennen** (*fam*) call a spade a spade. **n~nlos** *a* nameless; (*unbekannt*) unknown, anonymous. **n~ns** *adv* by the name of ● *prep* (+ *gen*) on behalf of. **N~nstag** *m* name-day. **N~nsvetter** *m* namesake. **N~nszug** *m* signature. **n~ntlich** *adv* by name; (*besonders*) especially
namhaft *a* noted; (*ansehnlich*) considerable; **n~ machen** name
nämlich *adv* (*und zwar*) namely; (*denn*) because
nanu *int* hallo
Napf *m* **-[e]s,⸚e** bowl
Narbe *f* **-,-n** scar
Narkose *f* **-,-n** general anaesthetic. **N~arzt** *m* anaesthetist. **N~mittel** *nt* anaesthetic
Narkot|ikum *nt* **-s,-ka** narcotic; (*Narkosemittel*) anaesthetic. **n~isieren** *vt* anaesthetize
Narr *m* **-en,-en** fool; **zum N~en haben** *od* **halten** make a fool of. **n~en** *vt* fool. **n~ensicher** *a* foolproof. **N~heit** *f* **-,-en** folly
Närr|in *f* **-,-nen** fool. **n~isch** *a* foolish; (*fam: verrückt*) crazy (**auf** + *acc* about)
Narzisse *f* **-,-n** narcissus; **gelbe N~** daffodil
nasal *a* nasal
nasch|en *vt/i* (*haben*) nibble (**an** + *dat* at); **wer hat vom Kuchen genascht?** who's been at the cake? **n~haft** *a* sweet-toothed
Nase *f* **-,-n** nose; **an der N~ herumführen** (*fam*) dupe
näseln *vi* (*haben*) speak through one's nose; **n~d** nasal
Nasen|bluten *nt* **-s** nosebleed. **N~loch** *nt* nostril. **N~rücken** *m* bridge of the nose
Naseweis *m* **-es,-e** (*fam*) know-all
Nashorn *nt* rhinoceros
naß *a* (**nasser, nassest**) wet
Nässe *f* - wet; (*Naßsein*) wetness. **n~n** *vt* wet
naßkalt *a* cold and wet
Nation /na'tsi̯o:n/ *f* **-,-en** nation. **n~al** *a* national. **N~alhymne** *f* national anthem. **N~alismus** *m* - nationalism. **N~alität** *f* **-,-en** nationality. **N~alsozialismus** *m* National Socialism. **N~alspieler** *m* international
Natrium *nt* **-s** sodium
Natron *nt* **-s doppeltkohlensaures N~** bicarbonate of soda
Natter *f* **-,-n** snake; (*Gift-*) viper
Natur *f* **-,-en** nature; **von N~ aus** by nature. **N~alien** /-i̯ən/ *pl* natural produce *sg*. **n~alisieren** *vt* naturalize. **N~alisierung** *f* **-,-en** naturalization
Naturell *nt* **-s,-e** disposition
Natur|erscheinung *f* natural phenomenon. **n~farben** *a* natural-coloured. **N~forscher** *m* naturalist. **N~kunde** *f* natural history. **N~lehrpfad** *m* nature trail
natürlich *a* natural ● *adv* naturally; (*selbstverständlich*) of course. **N~keit** *f* - naturalness
natur|rein *a* pure. **N~schutz** *m* nature conservation; **unter N~schutz stehen** be protected. **N~schutzgebiet** *nt* nature reserve. **N~wissenschaft** *f* [natural] science. **N~wissenschaftler** *m* scientist. **n~wissenschaftlich** *a* scientific; (*Sch*) science . . .
nautisch *a* nautical
Navigation /-'tsi̯o:n/ *f* - navigation
Nazi *m* **-s,-s** Nazi
n.Chr. *abbr* (**nach Christus**) AD
Nebel *m* **-s,-** fog; (*leicht*) mist. **n~haft** *a* hazy. **N~horn** *nt* fog-horn. **n~ig** *a* = **neblig**
neben *prep* (+ *dat/acc*) next to, beside; (+ *dat*) (*außer*) apart from; **n~ mir** next to me. **n~an** *adv* next door
Neben|anschluß *m* (*Teleph*) extension. **N~ausgaben** *fpl* incidental expenses
nebenbei *adv* in addition; (*beiläufig*) casually; **n~ bemerkt** incidentally

Neben|bemerkung *f* passing remark. **N~beruf** *m* second job. **N~beschäftigung** *f* spare-time occupation. **N~buhler(in)** *m* **-s,-** (*f* **-,-nen**) rival

nebeneinander *adv* next to each other, side by side

Neben|eingang *m* side entrance. **N~fach** *nt* (*Univ*) subsidiary subject. **N~fluß** *m* tributary. **N~gleis** *nt* siding. **N~haus** *nt* house next door

nebenher *adv* in addition. **n~gehen**† *vi sep* (*sein*) walk alongside

nebenhin *adv* casually

Neben|höhle *f* sinus. **N~kosten** *pl* additional costs. **N~mann** *m* (*pl* **-männer**) person next to one. **N~produkt** *nt* by-product. **N~rolle** *f* supporting role; (*kleine*) minor role; **eine N~rolle spielen** (*fig*) be unimportant. **N~sache** *f* unimportant matter. **n~sächlich** *a* unimportant. **N~satz** *m* subordinate clause. **N~straße** *f* minor road; (*Seiten-*) side street. **N~verdienst** *m* additional earnings *pl.* **N~wirkung** *f* side-effect. **N~zimmer** *nt* room next door

neblig *a* foggy; (*leicht*) misty

nebst *prep* (+ *dat*) [together] with

Necessaire /nesɛ'sɛ:ɐ̯/ *nt* **-s,-s** toilet bag; (*Näh-*, *Nagel-*) set

neck|en *vt* tease. **N~erei** *f* **-** teasing. **n~isch** *a* teasing; (*keß*) saucy

nee *adv* (*fam*) no

Neffe *m* **-n,-n** nephew

negativ *a* negative. **N~** *nt* **-s,-e** (*Phot*) negative

Neger *m* **-s,-** Negro

nehmen† *vt* take (*dat* from); **sich** (*dat*) **etw n~** take sth; help oneself to ⟨*Essen*⟩; **jdn zu sich n~** have s.o. to live with one

Neid *m* **-[e]s** envy, jealousy. **n~en** *vt* **jdm den Erfolg n~en** be jealous of s.o.'s success. **n~isch** *a* envious, jealous (**auf** + *acc* of); **auf jdn n~isch sein** envy s.o.

neig|en *vt* incline; (*zur Seite*) tilt; (*beugen*) bend; **sich n~en** incline; ⟨*Boden:*⟩ slope; ⟨*Person:*⟩ bend (**über** + *acc* over) ● *vi* (*haben*) **n~en zu** (*fig*) have a tendency towards; be prone to ⟨*Krankheit*⟩; incline towards ⟨*Ansicht*⟩; **dazu n~en, etw zu tun** tend to do sth. **N~ung** *f* **-,-en** inclination; (*Gefälle*) slope; (*fig*) tendency; (*Hang*) leaning; (*Herzens-*) affection

nein *adv*, **N~** *nt* **-s** no

Nektar *m* **-s** nectar

Nelke *f* **-,-n** carnation; (*Feder-*) pink; (*Culin*) clove

nenn|en† *vt* call; (*taufen*) name; (*angeben*) give; (*erwähnen*) mention; **sich n~en** call oneself. **n~enswert** *a* significant. **N~ung** *f* **-,-en** mention; (*Sport*) entry. **N~wert** *m* face value

Neofaschismus *m* neofascism

Neon *nt* **-s** neon. **N~beleuchtung** *f* fluorescent lighting

neppen *vt* (*fam*) rip off

Nerv *m* **-s,-en** /-fən/ nerve; **die N~en verlieren** lose control of oneself. **n~en** *vt* **jdn n~en** (*sl*) get on s.o.'s nerves. **N~enarzt** *m* neurologist. **n~enaufreibend** *a* nerve-racking. **N~enbündel** *nt* (*fam*) bundle of nerves. **N~enkitzel** *m* (*fam*) thrill. **N~ensystem** *nt* nervous system. **N~enzusammenbruch** *m* nervous breakdown

nervös *a* nervy, edgy; (*Med*) nervous; **n~ sein** be on edge

Nervosität *f* **-** nerviness, edginess

Nerz *m* **-es,-e** mink

Nessel *f* **-,-n** nettle

Nest *nt* **-[e]s,-er** nest; (*fam: Ort*) small place

nesteln *vi* (*haben*) fumble (**an** + *dat* with)

Nesthäkchen *nt* **-s,-** (*fam*) baby of the family

nett *a* nice, *adv* -ly; (*freundlich*) kind, *adv* -ly

netto *adv* net. **N~gewicht** *nt* net weight

Netz *nt* **-es,-e** net; (*Einkaufs-*) string bag; (*Spinnen-*) web; (*auf Landkarte*) grid; (*System*) network; (*Electr*) mains *pl.* **N~haut** *f* retina. **N~karte** *f* area season-ticket. **N~werk** *nt* network

neu *a* new; (*modern*) modern; **wie neu** as good as new; **das ist mir neu** it's news to me; **aufs n~e** [once] again; **von n~em** all over again ● *adv* newly; (*gerade erst*) only just; (*erneut*) again; **etw neu schreiben/streichen** rewrite/repaint sth. **N~ankömmling** *m* **-s,-e** newcomer. **N~anschaffung** *f* recent acquisition. **n~artig** *a* new [kind of].

N~auflage *f* new edition; (*unverändert*) reprint. **N~bau** *m* (*pl* **-ten**) new house/building

Neu|e(r) *m/f* new person, newcomer; (*Schüler*) new boy/girl. **N~e(s)** *nt* **das N~e** the new; **etwas N~es** something new; (*Neuigkeit*) a piece of news; **was gibt's N~es?** what's the news?

neuer|dings *adv* [just] recently. **n~lich** *a* renewed, new ● *adv* again. **N~ung** *f* **-,-en** innovation

neuest|e(r,s) *a* newest; (*letzte*) latest; **seit n~em** just recently. **N~e** *nt* **das N~e** the latest thing; (*Neuigkeit*) the latest news *sg*

neugeboren *a* newborn

Neugier, Neugierde *f* **-** curiosity; (*Wißbegierde*) inquisitiveness

neugierig *a* curious (**auf** + *acc* about), *adv* -ly; (*wißbegierig*) inquisitive, *adv* -ly

Neuheit *f* **-,-en** novelty; (*Neusein*) newness; **die letzte N~** the latest thing

Neuigkeit *f* **-,-en** piece of news; **N~en** news *sg*

Neujahr *nt* New Year's Day; **über N~** over the New Year

neulich *adv* the other day

Neu|ling *m* **-s,-e** novice. **n~modisch** *a* newfangled. **N~mond** *m* new moon

neun *inv a*, **N~** *f* **-,-en** nine. **N~malkluge(r)** *m* (*fam*) clever Dick. **n~te(r,s)** *a* ninth. **n~zehn** *inv a* nineteen. **n~zehnte(r,s)** *a* nineteenth. **n~zig** *inv a* ninety. **n~zigste(r,s)** *a* ninetieth

Neuralgie *f* **-,-n** neuralgia

neureich *a* nouveau riche

Neurologe *m* **-n,-n** neurologist

Neuro|se *f* **-,-n** neurosis. **n~tisch** *a* neurotic

Neuschnee *m* fresh snow

Neuseeland *nt* **-s** New Zealand

neuste(r,s) *a* = **neueste(r,s)**

neutral *a* neutral. **n~isieren** *vt* neutralize. **N~ität** *f* **-** neutrality

Neutrum *nt* **-s,-tra** neuter noun

neu|vermählt *a* **n~vermähltes Paar** newly-weds *pl*. **N~zeit** *f* modern times *pl*

nicht *adv* not; **ich kann n~** I cannot *or* can't; **er ist n~ gekommen** he hasn't come; **n~ mehr/besser als** no more/ better than; **bitte n~!** please don't! **n~ berühren!** do not touch! **du kommst doch auch, ~ [wahr]?** you are coming too, aren't you? **du kennst ihn doch, n~?** you know him, don't you?

Nichtachtung *f* disregard; (*Geringschätzung*) disdain

Nichte *f* **-,-n** niece

nichtig *a* trivial; (*Jur*) [null and] void

Nichtraucher *m* non-smoker. **N~abteil** *nt* non-smoking compartment

nichts *pron & a* nothing; **n~ anderes/Besseres** nothing else/better; **n~ mehr** no more; **ich weiß n~** I know nothing *or* don't know anything. **N~** *nt* **-** nothingness; (*fig: Leere*) void; (*Person*) nonentity. **n~ahnend** *a* unsuspecting

Nichtschwimmer *m* non-swimmer

nichtsdesto|trotz *adv* all the same. **n~weniger** *adv* nevertheless

nichts|nutzig *a* good-for-nothing; (*fam: unartig*) naughty. **n~sagend** *a* meaningless; (*uninteressant*) nondescript. **N~tun** *nt* **-s** idleness

Nickel *nt* **-s** nickel

nicken *vi* (*haben*) nod. **N~** *nt* **-s** nod

Nickerchen *nt* **-s,-** (*fam*) nap; **ein N~ machen** have forty winks

nie *adv* never

nieder *a* low ● *adv* down. **n~brennen**† *vt/i sep* (*sein*) burn down. **N~deutsch** *nt* Low German. **N~gang** *m* (*fig*) decline. **n~gedrückt** *a* (*fig*) depressed. **n~gehen**† *vi sep* (*sein*) come down. **n~geschlagen** *a* dejected, despondent. **N~geschlagenheit** *f* **-** dejection, despondency. **N~kunft** *f* **-,⸗e** confinement. **N~lage** *f* defeat

Niederlande (die) *pl* the Netherlands

Niederländ|er *m* **-s,-** Dutchman; **die N~er** the Dutch *pl*. **N~erin** *f* **-,-nen** Dutchwoman. **n~isch** *a* Dutch

nieder|lassen† *vt sep* let down; **sich n~lassen** settle; (*sich setzen*) sit down. **N~lassung** *f* **-,-en** settlement; (*Zweigstelle*) branch. **n~legen** *vt sep* put *or* lay down; resign ⟨*Amt*⟩; **die Arbeit n~legen** go on strike; **sich n~legen** lie down. **n~machen, n~metzeln** *vt sep* massacre. **n~reißen**† *vt sep* tear down. **N~sachsen** *nt* Lower Saxony. **N~schlag** *m* precipitation; (*Regen*) rainfall; (*radioaktiver*) fall-out; (*Boxen*) knock-down. **n~schlagen**† *vt sep* knock down; lower ⟨*Augen*⟩; (*unterdrücken*) crush. **n~schmettern** *vt sep* (*fig*) shatter. **n~schreiben**† *vt sep* write down.

n~schreien† *vt sep* shout down. **n~setzen** *vt sep* put *or* set down; **sich n~setzen** sit down. **n~strecken** *vt sep* fell; (*durch Schuß*) gun down
niederträchtig *a* base, vile
Niederung *f* **-,-en** low ground
nieder|walzen *vt sep* flatten. **n~werfen**† *vt sep* throw down; (*unterdrücken*) crush; **sich n~werfen** prostrate oneself
niedlich *a* pretty; (*goldig*) sweet; (*Amer*) cute
niedrig *a* low; (*fig: gemein*) base ● *adv* low
niemals *adv* never
niemand *pron* nobody, no one
Niere *f* **-,-n** kidney; **künstliche N~** kidney machine
niesel|n *vi* (*haben*) drizzle; **es n~t** it is drizzling. **N~regen** *m* drizzle
niesen *vi* (*haben*) sneeze. **N~** *nt* **-s** sneezing; (*Nieser*) sneeze
Niet *m & nt* **-[e]s,-e, Niete**[1] *f* **-,-n** rivet; (*an Jeans*) stud
Niete[2] *f* **-,-n** blank; (*fam*) failure
nieten *vt* rivet
Nikotin *nt* **-s** nicotine
Nil *m* **-[s]** Nile. **N~pferd** *nt* hippopotamus
nimmer *adv* (*SGer*) not any more; **nie und n~** never. **n~müde** *a* tireless. **n~satt** *a* insatiable. **N~wiedersehen** *nt* **auf N~wiedersehen** (*fam*) for good
nippen *vi* (*haben*) take a sip (**an** + *dat* of)
nirgend|s, n~wo *adv* nowhere
Nische *f* **-,-n** recess, niche
nisten *vi* (*haben*) nest
Nitrat *nt* **-[e]s,-e** nitrate
Niveau /ni'vo:/ *nt* **-s,-s** level; (*geistig, künstlerisch*) standard
nix *adv* (*fam*) nothing
Nixe *f* **-,-n** mermaid
nobel *a* noble; (*fam: luxuriös*) luxurious; (*fam: großzügig*) generous
noch *adv* still; (*zusätzlich*) as well; (*mit Komparativ*) even; **n~ nicht** not yet; **gerade n~** only just; **n~ immer** *od* **immer n~** still; **n~ letzte Woche** only last week; **es ist n~ viel Zeit** there's plenty of time yet; **wer/was/wo n~?** who/what/where else? **n~ jemand/etwas** someone/something else; (*Frage*) anyone/anything else? **n~ einmal** again; **n~ ein Bier** another beer; **n~ größer** even bigger; **n~ so sehr/schön** however much/beautiful ● *conj* **weder ... n~** neither ... nor
nochmal|ig *a* further. **n~s** *adv* again
Nomad|e *m* **-n,-n** nomad. **n~isch** *a* nomadic
Nominativ *m* **-s,-e** nominative
nominell *a* nominal, *adv* -ly
nominier|en *vt* nominate. **N~ung** *f* **-,-en** nomination
nonchalant /nõʃa'lã:/ *a* nonchalant, *adv* -ly
Nonne *f* **-,-n** nun. **N~nkloster** *nt* convent
Nonstopflug *m* direct flight
Nord *m* **-[e]s** north. **N~amerika** *nt* North America. **n~deutsch** *a* North German
Norden *m* **-s** north; **nach N~** north
nordisch *a* Nordic
nördlich *a* northern; ⟨*Richtung*⟩ northerly ● *adv & prep* (+*gen*) **n~ [von] der Stadt** [to the] north of the town
Nordosten *m* north-east
Nord|pol *m* North Pole. **N~see** *f* **-** North Sea. **n~wärts** *adv* northwards. **N~westen** *m* north-west
Nörgelei *f* **-,-en** grumbling
nörgeln *vi* (*haben*) grumble
Norm *f* **-,-en** norm; (*Techn*) standard; (*Soll*) quota
normal *a* normal, *adv* -ly. **n~erweise** *adv* normally. **n~isieren** *vt* normalize; **sich n~isieren** return to normal
normen, normieren *vt* standardize
Norwe|gen *nt* **-s** Norway. **N~ger(in)** *m* **-s,-** (*f* **-,-nen**) Norwegian. **n~gisch** *a* Norwegian
Nost|algie *f* **-** nostalgia. **n~algisch** *a* nostalgic
Not *f* **-,¨-e** need; (*Notwendigkeit*) necessity; (*Entbehrung*) hardship; (*seelisch*) trouble; **Not leiden** be in need, suffer hardship; **mit knapper Not** only just; **zur Not** if need be; (*äußerstenfalls*) at a pinch
Notar *m* **-s,-e** notary public
Not|arzt *m* emergency doctor. **N~ausgang** *m* emergency exit. **N~behelf** *m* **-[e]s,-e** makeshift. **N~bremse** *f* emergency brake. **N~dienst** *m* **N~dienst haben** be on call. **n~dürftig** *a* scant; (*behelfsmäßig*) makeshift
Note *f* **-,-n** note; (*Zensur*) mark; **ganze/halbe N~** (*Mus*) semibreve/minim, (*Amer*) whole/half note; **N~n lesen** read music; **persönliche**

N~ personal touch. **N~nblatt** *nt* sheet of music. **N~nschlüssel** *m* clef. **N~nständer** *m* music-stand

Notfall *m* emergency; **im N~** in an emergency; (*notfalls*) if need be; **für den N~** just in case. **n~s** *adv* if need be

not|gedrungen *adv* of necessity. **N~groschen** *m* nest-egg

notieren *vt* note down; (*Comm*) quote; **sich** (*dat*) **etw n~** make a note of sth

nötig *a* necessary; **n~ haben** need; **das N~ste** the essentials *pl* • *adv* urgently. **n~en** *vt* force; (*auffordern*) press; **laßt euch nicht n~en** help yourselves. **n~enfalls** *adv* if need be. **N~ung** *f* - coercion

Notiz *f* -,-en note; (*Zeitungs-*) item; **[keine] N~ nehmen von** take [no] notice of. **N~buch** *nt* notebook. **N~kalender** *m* diary

Not|lage *f* plight. **n~landen** *vi* (*sein*) make a forced landing. **N~landung** *f* forced landing. **n~leidend** *a* needy. **N~lösung** *f* stopgap. **N~lüge** *f* white lie

notorisch *a* notorious

Not|ruf *m* emergency call; (*Naut, Aviat*) distress call; (*Nummer*) emergency services number. **N~signal** *nt* distress signal. **N~stand** *m* state of emergency. **N~unterkunft** *f* emergency accommodation. **N~wehr** *f* - (*Jur*) self-defence

notwendig *a* necessary; (*unerläßlich*) essential • *adv* urgently. **N~keit** *f* -,-en necessity

Notzucht *f* - (*Jur*) rape

Nougat /'nu:gat/ *m & nt* -s nougat

Novelle *f* -,-n novella; (*Pol*) amendment

November *m* -s,- November

Novität *f* -,-en novelty

Novize *m* -n,-n, **Novizin** *f* -,-nen (*Relig*) novice

Nu *m* **im Nu** (*fam*) in a flash

Nuance /'nyã:sə/ *f* -,-n nuance; (*Spur*) shade

nüchtern *a* sober; (*sachlich*) matter-of-fact; (*schmucklos*) bare; (*ohne Würze*) bland; **auf n~en Magen** on an empty stomach • *adv* soberly

Nudel *f* -,-n piece of pasta; **N~n** pasta *sg*; (*Band-*) noodles. **N~holz** *nt* rolling-pin

Nudist *m* -en,-en nudist

nuklear *a* nuclear

null *inv a* zero, nought; (*Teleph*) 0; (*Sport*) nil; (*Tennis*) love; **n~ Fehler** no mistakes; **n~ und nichtig** (*Jur*) null and void. **N~** *f* -,-en nought, zero; (*fig: Person*) nonentity; **drei Grad unter N~** three degrees below zero. **N~punkt** *m* zero

numerieren *vt* number

numerisch *a* numerical

Nummer *f* -,-n number; (*Ausgabe*) issue; (*Darbietung*) item; (*Zirkus-*) act; (*Größe*) size. **N~nschild** *nt* number-/(*Amer*) license-plate

nun *adv* now; (*na*) well; (*halt*) just; **von nun an** from now on; **nun gut!** very well then! **das Leben ist nun mal so** life's like that

nur *adv* only, just; **wo kann sie nur sein?** wherever can she be? **alles, was ich nur will** everything I could possibly want; **er soll es nur versuchen!** (*drohend*) just let him try! **könnte/hätte ich nur ...!** if only I could/had ...! **nur Geduld!** just be patient!

Nürnberg *nt* -s Nuremberg

nuscheln *vt/i* (*haben*) mumble

Nuß *f* -, **Nüsse** nut. **N~baum** *m* walnut tree. **N~knacker** *m* -s,- nutcrackers *pl*. **N~schale** *f* nutshell

Nüstern *fpl* nostrils

Nut *f* -,-en, **Nute** *f* -,-n groove

Nutte *f* -,-n (*sl*) tart (*sl*)

nutz|bar *a* usable; **n~bar machen** utilize; cultivate ⟨*Boden*⟩. **n~bringend** *a* profitable, *adv* -bly

nütze *a* **zu etwas/nichts n~ sein** be useful/useless

nutzen *vt* use, utilize; (*aus-*) take advantage of • *vi* (*haben*) = **nützen**. **N~** *m* -s benefit; (*Comm*) profit; **N~ ziehen aus** benefit from; **von N~ sein** be useful

nützen *vi* (*haben*) be useful *or* of use (*dat* to); ⟨*Mittel:*⟩ be effective; **nichts n~** be useless *or* no use; **was nützt mir das?** what good is that to me? • *vt* = **nutzen**

Nutzholz *nt* timber

nützlich *a* useful; **sich n~ machen** make oneself useful. **N~keit** *f* - usefulness

nutz|los *a* useless; (*vergeblich*) vain. **N~losigkeit** *f* - uselessness. **N~nießer** *m* -s,- beneficiary. **N~ung** *f* - use, utilization

Nylon /'nailɔn/ *nt* -s nylon

Nymphe /'nʏmfə/ *f* -,-n nymph

O

o *int* **o ja/nein!** oh yes/no! **o weh!** oh dear!

Oase *f* **-,-n** oasis

ob *conj* whether; **ob reich, ob arm** rich or poor; **ob sie wohl krank ist?** I wonder whether she is ill; **und ob!** (*fam*) you bet!

Obacht *f* **O~ geben** pay attention; **O~ geben auf** (+*acc*) look after; **O~!** look out!

Obdach *nt* **-[e]s** shelter. **o~los** *a* homeless. **O~lose(r)** *m/f* homeless person; **die O~losen** the homeless *pl*

Obduktion /-'tsio:n/ *f* **-,-en** post-mortem

O-Beine *ntpl* (*fam*) bow-legs, bandy legs. **O-beinig** *a* bandy-legged

oben *adv* at the top; (*auf der Oberseite*) on top; (*eine Treppe hoch*) upstairs; **da o~** up there; **o~ im Norden** up in the north; **siehe o~** see above; **o~ auf** (+*acc/dat*) on top of; **nach o~** up[wards]; (*die Treppe hinauf*) upstairs; **von o~** from above/upstairs; **von o~ bis unten** from top to bottom/⟨*Person*⟩ to toe; **jdn von o~ bis unten mustern** look s.o. up and down. **o~an** *adv* at the top. **o~auf** *adv* on top; **o~auf sein** (*fig*) be cheerful. **o~drein** *adv* on top of that. **o~erwähnt, o~genannt** *a* above-mentioned. **o~hin** *adv* casually

Ober *m* **-s,-** waiter

Ober|arm *m* upper arm. **O~arzt** *m* ≈ senior registrar. **O~befehlshaber** *m* commander-in-chief. **O~begriff** *m* generic term. **O~deck** *nt* upper deck. **o~e(r,s)** *a* upper; (*höhere*) higher. **O~fläche** *f* surface. **o~flächlich** *a* superficial, *adv* -ly. **O~geschoß** *nt* upper storey. **o~halb** *adv & prep* (+*gen*) above; **o~halb vom Dorf/des Dorfes** above the village. **O~hand** *f* **die O~hand gewinnen** gain the upper hand. **O~haupt** *nt* (*fig*) head. **O~haus** *nt* (*Pol*) upper house; (*in UK*) House of Lords. **O~hemd** *nt* [man's] shirt

Oberin *f* **-,-nen** matron; (*Relig*) mother superior

ober|irdisch *a* surface ... • *adv* above ground. **O~kellner** *m* head waiter. **O~kiefer** *m* upper jaw. **O~körper** *m* upper part of the body. **O~leutnant** *m* lieutenant. **O~licht** *nt* overhead light; (*Fenster*) skylight; (*über Tür*) fanlight. **O~lippe** *f* upper lip

Obers *nt* **-** (*Aust*) cream

Ober|schenkel *m* thigh. **O~schicht** *f* upper class. **O~schule** *f* grammar school. **O~schwester** *f* (*Med*) sister. **O~seite** *f* upper/(*rechte Seite*) right side

Oberst *m* **-en & -s,-en** colonel

oberste(r,s) *a* top; (*höchste*) highest; ⟨*Befehlshaber, Gerichtshof*⟩ supreme; (*wichtigste*) first

Ober|stimme *f* treble. **O~stufe** *f* upper school. **O~teil** *nt* top. **O~weite** *f* chest/(*der Frau*) bust size

obgleich *conj* although

Obhut *f* **-** care; **in guter O~ sein** be well looked after

obig *a* above

Objekt *nt* **-[e]s,-e** object; (*Haus, Grundstück*) property; **O~ der Forschung** subject of research

Objektiv *nt* **-s,-e** lens. **o~** *a* objective, *adv* -ly. **O~ität** *f* **-** objectivity

Oblate *f* **-,-n** (*Relig*) wafer

obliga|t *a* (*fam*) inevitable. **O~tion** /-'tsio:n/ *f* **-,-en** obligation; (*Comm*) bond. **o~torisch** *a* obligatory

Obmann *m* (*pl* **-männer**) [jury] foreman; (*Sport*) referee

Oboe /o'bo:ə/ *f* **-,-n** oboe

Obrigkeit *f* **-** authorities *pl*

obschon *conj* although

Observatorium *nt* **-s,-ien** observatory

obskur *a* obscure; (*zweifelhaft*) dubious

Obst *nt* **-es** (*coll*) fruit. **O~baum** *m* fruit-tree. **O~garten** *m* orchard. **O~händler** *m* fruiterer. **O~kuchen** *m* fruit flan. **O~salat** *m* fruit salad

obszön *a* obscene. **O~ität** *f* **-,-en** obscenity

O-Bus *m* trolley bus

obwohl *conj* although

Ochse *m* **-n,-n** ox. **o~n** *vi* (*haben*) (*fam*) swot. **O~nschwanzsuppe** *f* oxtail soup

öde *a* desolate; (*unfruchtbar*) barren; (*langweilig*) dull. **Öde** *f* **-** desolation; barrenness; dullness; (*Gegend*) waste

oder *conj* or; **du kennst ihn doch, o~?** you know him, don't you?

Ofen *m* **-s,¨** stove; (*Heiz-*) heater; (*Back-*) oven; (*Techn*) furnace

offen *a* open, *adv* -ly; ⟨*Haar*⟩ loose; ⟨*Flamme*⟩ naked; (*o~herzig*) frank, *adv* -ly; (*o~ gezeigt*) overt, *adv* -ly; (*unentschieden*) unsettled; **o~e Stelle** vacancy; **Tag der o~en Tür** open day; **Wein o~ verkaufen** sell wine by the glass; *adv* **o~ gesagt** *od* **gestanden** to be honest. **o~bar** *a* obvious ● *adv* apparently. **o~baren** *vt* reveal. **O~barung** *f* **-,-en** revelation. **o~bleiben**† *vi sep* (*sein*) remain open. **o~halten**† *vt sep* hold open ⟨*Tür*⟩; keep open ⟨*Mund, Augen*⟩. **O~heit** *f* - frankness, openness. **o~herzig** *a* frank, *adv* -ly. **O~herzigkeit** *f* - frankness. **o~kundig** *a* manifest, *adv* -ly. **o~lassen**† *vt sep* leave open; leave vacant ⟨*Stelle*⟩. **o~sichtlich** *a* obvious, *adv* -ly

offensiv *a* offensive. **O~e** *f* **-,-n** offensive

offenstehen† *vi sep* (*haben*) be open; ⟨*Rechnung:*⟩ be outstanding; **jdm o~** (*fig*) be open to s.o.

öffentlich *a* public, *adv* -ly. **Ö~keit** *f* - public; **an die Ö~keit gelangen** become public; **in aller Ö~keit** in public, publicly

Offerte *f* **-,-n** (*Comm*) offer

offiziell *a* official, *adv* -ly

Offizier *m* **-s,-e** (*Mil*) officer

öffn|en *vt/i* (*haben*) open; **sich ö~en** open. **Ö~er** *m* **-s,-** opener. **Ö~ung** *f* **-,-en** opening. **Ö~ungszeiten** *fpl* opening hours

oft *adv* often

öfter *adv* quite often. **ö~e(r,s)** *a* frequent; **des ö~en** frequently. **ö~s** *adv* (*fam*) quite often

oftmals *adv* often

oh *int* oh!

ohne *prep* (+*acc*) without; **o~ mich!** count me out! **oben o~** topless; **nicht o~ sein** (*fam*) be not bad; (*nicht harmlos*) be quite nasty ● *conj* **o~ zu überlegen** without thinking; **o~ daß ich es merkte** without my noticing it. **o~dies** *adv* anyway. **o~gleichen** *pred a* unparalleled; **eine Frechheit o~gleichen** a piece of unprecedented insolence. **o~hin** *adv* anyway

Ohn|macht *f* **-,-en** faint; (*fig*) powerlessness; **in O~macht fallen** faint. **o~mächtig** *a* unconscious; (*fig*) powerless; **o~mächtig werden** faint

Ohr *nt* **-[e]s,-en** ear; **übers Ohr hauen** (*fam*) cheat

Öhr *nt* **-[e]s,-e** eye

ohren|betäubend *a* deafening. **O~schmalz** *nt* ear-wax. **O~schmerzen** *mpl* earache *sg.* **O~sessel** *m* wing-chair. **O~tropfen** *mpl* ear drops

Ohrfeige *f* slap in the face; **jdm eine O~ geben** slap s.o.'s face. **o~n** *vt* **jdn o~n** slap s.o.'s face

Ohr|läppchen *nt* **-s,-** ear-lobe. **O~ring** *m* ear-ring. **O~wurm** *m* earwig

oje *int* oh dear!

okay /o'ke:/ *a & adv* (*fam*) OK

okkult *a* occult

Öko|logie *f* - ecology. **ö~logisch** *a* ecological. **Ö~nomie** *f* - economy (*Wissenschaft*) economics *sg.* **ö~nomisch** *a* economic; (*sparsam*) economical

Oktave *f* **-,-n** octave

Oktober *m* **-s,-** October

Okular *nt* **-s,-e** eyepiece

okulieren *vt* graft

ökumenisch *a* ecumenical

Öl *nt* **-[e]s,-e** oil; **in Öl malen** paint in oils. **Ölbaum** *m* olive-tree. **ölen** *vt* oil; **wie ein geölter Blitz** (*fam*) like greased lightning. **Ölfarbe** *f* oil-paint. **Ölfeld** *nt* oilfield. **Ölgemälde** *nt* oil-painting. **ölig** *a* oily

Oliv|e *f* **-,-n** olive. **O~enöl** *nt* olive oil. **o~grün** *a* olive[-green]

oll *a* (*fam*) old; (*fam: häßlich*) nasty

Ölmeßstab *m* dip-stick. **Ölsardinen** *fpl* sardines in oil. **Ölstand** *m* oil-level. **Öltanker** *m* oil-tanker. **Ölteppich** *m* oil-slick

Olympiade *f* **-,-n** Olympic Games *pl*, Olympics *pl*

Olymp|iasieger(in) /o'lʏmpi̯a-/ *m(f)* Olympic champion. **o~isch** *a* Olympic; **O~ische Spiele** Olympic Games

Ölzeug *nt* oilskins *pl*

Oma *f* **-,-s** (*fam*) granny

Omelett *nt* **-[e]s,-e** & **-s** omelette

Omen *nt* **-s,-** omen

ominös *a* ominous

Omnibus *m* bus; (*Reise-*) coach

onanieren *vi* (*haben*) masturbate

Onkel *m* **-s,-** uncle

Opa *m* **-s,-s** (*fam*) grandad

Opal *m* **-s,-e** opal

Oper *f* **-,-n** opera

Operation /-'tsi̯o:n/ *f* **-,-en** operation. **O~ssaal** *m* operating-theatre

Operette *f* **-,-n** operetta

operieren *vt* operate on ⟨*Patient, Herz*⟩; **sich o~ lassen** have an operation ● *vi* (*haben*) operate

Opern|glas *nt* opera-glasses *pl.* **O~haus** *nt* opera-house. **O~sänger(in)** *m(f)* opera-singer

Opfer *nt* **-s,-** sacrifice; (*eines Unglücks*) victim; **ein O~ bringen** make a sacrifice; **jdm/etw zum O~ fallen** fall victim to s.o./sth. **o~n** *vt* sacrifice. **O~ung** *f* **-,-en** sacrifice

Opium *nt* **-s** opium

opponieren *vi* (*haben*) **o~ gegen** oppose

Opportunist *m* **-en,-en** opportunist. **o~isch** *a* opportunist

Opposition /-'tsi̯o:n/ *f* **-** opposition. **O~spartei** *f* opposition party

Optik *f* **-** optics *sg*; (*fam: Objektiv*) lens. **O~er** *m* **-s,-** optician

optimal *a* optimum

Optimis|mus *m* **-** optimism. **O~t** *m* **-en,-en** optimist. **o~tisch** *a* optimistic, *adv* -ally

Optimum *nt* **-s,-ma** optimum

Option /ɔp'tsi̯o:n/ *f* **-,-en** option

optisch *a* optical; ⟨*Eindruck*⟩ visual

Orakel *nt* **-s,-** oracle

Orange /o'rã:ʒə/ *f* **-,-n** orange. **o~** *inv a* orange. **O~ade** /orã'ʒa:də/ *f* **-,-n** orangeade. **O~nmarmelade** *f* [orange] marmalade. **O~nsaft** *m* orange juice

Oratorium *nt* **-s,-ien** oratorio

Orchest|er /ɔr'kɛstɐ/ *nt* **-s,-** orchestra. **o~rieren** *vt* orchestrate

Orchidee /ɔrçi'de:ə/ *f* **-,-n** orchid

Orden *m* **-s,-** (*Ritter-, Kloster-*) order; (*Auszeichnung*) medal, decoration; **jdm einen O~ verleihen** decorate s.o. **O~stracht** *f* (*Relig*) habit

ordentlich *a* neat, tidy; (*anständig*) respectable; (*ordnungsgemäß, fam: richtig*) proper; ⟨*Mitglied, Versammlung*⟩ ordinary; (*fam: gut*) decent; (*fam: gehörig*) good • *adv* neatly, tidily; respectably; properly; (*fam: gut, gehörig*) well; (*sehr*) very; (*regelrecht*) really

Order *f* **-,-s & -n** order

ordinär *a* common

Ordin|ation /-'tsi̯o:n/ *f* **-,-en** (*Relig*) ordination; (*Aust*) surgery. **o~ieren** *vt* (*Relig*) ordain

ordn|en *vt* put in order; (*aufräumen*) tidy; (*an-*) arrange; **sich zum Zug o~en** form a procession. **O~er** *m* **-s,-** steward; (*Akten-*) file

Ordnung *f* **-** order; **O~ halten** keep order; **O~ machen** tidy up; **in O~ bringen** put in order; (*aufräumen*) tidy; (*reparieren*) mend; (*fig*) put right; **in O~ sein** be in order; (*ordentlich sein*) be tidy; (*fig*) be all right; **ich bin mit dem Magen** *od* **mein Magen ist nicht ganz in O~** I have a slight stomach upset; **[geht] in O~!** OK! **o~sgemäß** *a* proper, *adv* -ly. **O~sstrafe** *f* (*Jur*) fine. **o~swidrig** *a* improper, *adv* -ly

Ordonnanz *f* **-,-en** (*Mil*) orderly

Organ *nt* **-s,-e** organ; (*fam: Stimme*) voice

Organi|sation /-'tsi̯o:n/ *f* **-,-en** organization. **O~sator** *m* **-s,-en** /-'to:rən/ organizer

organisch *a* organic, *adv* -ally

organisieren *vt* organize; (*fam: beschaffen*) get [hold of]

Organismus *m* **-,-men** organism; (*System*) system

Organist *m* **-en,-en** organist

Organspenderkarte *f* donor card

Orgasmus *m* **-,-men** orgasm

Orgel *f* **-,-n** (*Mus*) organ. **O~pfeife** *f* organ-pipe

Orgie /'ɔrgi̯ə/ *f* **-,-n** orgy

Orien|t /'o:ri̯ɛnt/ *m* **-s** Orient. **o~talisch** *a* Oriental

orientier|en /ori̯ɛn'ti:rən/ *vt* inform (**über** + *acc* about); **sich o~en** get one's bearings, orientate oneself; (*unterrichten*) inform oneself (**über** + *acc* about). **O~ung** *f* **-** orientation; **die O~ung verlieren** lose one's bearings

original *a* original. **O~** *nt* **-s,-e** original; (*Person*) character. **O~ität** *f* **-** originality. **O~übertragung** *f* live transmission

originell *a* original; (*eigenartig*) unusual

Orkan *m* **-s,-e** hurricane

Ornament *nt* **-[e]s,-e** ornament

Ornat *m* **-[e]s,-e** robes *pl*

Ornithologie *f* **-** ornithology

Ort *m* **-[e]s,-e** place; (*Ortschaft*) [small] town; **am Ort** locally; **am Ort des Verbrechens** at the scene of the crime; **an Ort und Stelle** in the right place; (*sofort*) on the spot. **o~en** *vt* locate

ortho|dox *a* orthodox. **O~graphie** *f* **-** spelling. **o~graphisch** *a* spelling ... **O~päde** *m* **-n,-n** orthopaedic specialist. **o~pädisch** *a* orthopaedic

örtlich *a* local, *adv* -ly. **Ö~keit** *f* **-,-en** locality

Ortschaft *f* **-,-en** [small] town; (*Dorf*) village; **geschlossene O~** (*Auto*) built-up area

ortsǀfremd *a* **o~fremd sein** be a stranger. **O~gespräch** *nt* (*Teleph*) local call. **O~name** *m* place-name. **O~sinn** *m* sense of direction. **O~verkehr** *m* local traffic. **O~zeit** *f* local time

Öse *f* **-,-n** eyelet; (*Schlinge*) loop; **Haken und Öse** hook and eye

Ost *m* **-[e]s** east. **o~deutsch** *a* Eastern/(*Pol*) East German

Osten *m* **-s** east; **nach O~** east

ostentativ *a* pointed, *adv* -ly

Osteopath *m* **-en,-en** osteopath

Osterǀei /'o:stɐʔai̯/ *nt* Easter egg. **O~fest** *nt* Easter. **O~glocke** *f* daffodil. **O~montag** *m* Easter Monday. **O~n** *nt* **-,-** Easter; **frohe O~n!** happy Easter!

Österreich *nt* **-s** Austria. **Ö~er** *m* **-s,-, Ö~erin** *f* **-,-nen** Austrian. **ö~isch** *a* Austrian

östlich *a* eastern; ⟨*Richtung*⟩ easterly ● *adv & prep* (+*gen*) **ö~ [von] der Stadt** [to the] east of the town

Ostǀsee *f* Baltic [Sea]. **o~wärts** *adv* eastwards

oszillieren *vi* (*haben*) oscillate

Otter[1] *m* **-s,-** otter

Otter[2] *f* **-,-n** adder

Ouverture /uvɛr'ty:rə/ *f* **-,-n** overture

oval *a* oval. **O~** *nt* **-s,-e** oval

Ovation /-'t͜si̯o:n/ *f* **-,-en** ovation

Ovulation /-'t͜si̯o:n/ *f* **-,-en** ovulation

Oxid, Oxyd *nt* **-[e]s,-e** oxide

Ozean *m* **-s,-e** ocean

Ozon *nt* **-s** ozone. **O~loch** *nt* hole in the ozone layer. **O~schicht** *f* ozone layer

P

paar *pron inv* **ein p~** a few; **alle p~ Tage** every few days. **P~** *nt* **-[e]s,-e** pair; (*Ehe-, Liebes-, Tanz-*) couple. **p~en** *vt* mate; (*verbinden*) combine; **sich p~en** mate. **P~ung** *f* **-,-en** mating. **p~weise** *adv* in pairs, in twos

Pacht *f* **-,-en** lease; (*P~summe*) rent. **p~en** *vt* lease

Pächter *m* **-s,-** lessee; (*eines Hofes*) tenant

Pachtvertrag *m* lease

Pack[1] *m* **-[e]s,-e** bundle

Pack[2] *nt* **-[e]s** (*sl*) rabble

Päckchen *nt* **-s,-** package, small packet

packǀen *vt/i* (*haben*) pack; (*ergreifen*) seize; (*fig: fesseln*) grip; **p~ dich!** (*sl*) beat it! **P~en** *m* **-s,-** bundle. **p~end** *a* (*fig*) gripping. **P~papier** *nt* [strong] wrapping paper. **P~ung** *f* **-,-en** packet; (*Med*) pack

Pädagogǀe *m* **-n,-n** educationalist; (*Lehrer*) teacher. **P~ik** *f* **-** educational science. **p~isch** *a* educational

Paddel *nt* **-s,-** paddle. **P~boot** *nt* canoe. **p~n** *vt/i* (*haben/sein*) paddle. **P~sport** *m* canoeing

Page /'pa:ʒə/ *m* **-n,-n** page

Paillette /pai̯'jɛtə/ *f* **-,-n** sequin

Paket *nt* **-[e]s,-e** packet; (*Post-*) parcel

Pakistǀan *nt* **-s** Pakistan. **P~aner(in)** *m* **-s,-** (*f* **-,-nen**) Pakistani. **p~anisch** *a* Pakistani

Pakt *m* **-[e]s,-e** pact

Palast *m* **-[e]s,¨e** palace

Palästǀina *nt* **-s** Palestine. **P~inenser(in)** *m* **-s,-** (*f* **-,-nen**) Palestinian. **p~inensisch** *a* Palestinian

Palette *f* **-,-n** palette

Palmǀe *f* **-,-n** palm[-tree]; **jdn auf die P~e bringen** (*fam*) drive s.o. up the wall. **P~sonntag** *m* Palm Sunday

Pampelmuse *f* **-,-n** grapefruit

Panierǀmehl *nt* (*Culin*) breadcrumbs *pl.* **p~t** *a* (*Culin*) breaded

Panik *f* **-** panic; **in P~ geraten** panic

panisch *a* **p~e Angst** panic

Panne *f* **-,-n** breakdown; (*Reifen-*) flat tyre; (*Mißgeschick*) mishap. **P~ndienst** *m* breakdown service

Panorama *nt* **-s** panorama

panschen *vt* adulterate ● *vi* (*haben*) splash about

Pantine *f* **-,-n** [wooden] clog

Pantoffel *m* **-s,-n** slipper; (*ohne Ferse*) mule. **P~held** *m* (*fam*) henpecked husband

Pantomime[1] *f* **-,-n** mime

Pantomime[2] *m* **-n,-n** mime artist

pantschen *vt/i* = **panschen**

Panzer *m* **-s,-** armour; (*Mil*) tank; (*Zool*) shell. **p~n** *vt* armour-plate. **P~schrank** *m* safe

Papa /'papa, pa'pa:/ *m* **-s,-s** daddy

Papagei *m* **-s & -en,-en** parrot

Papier *nt* **-[e]s,-e** paper. **P~korb** *m* waste-paper basket. **P~schlange** *f* streamer. **P~waren** *fpl* stationery *sg*

Pappe *f* **-** cardboard; (*dial: Kleister*) glue

Pappel *f* **-,-n** poplar

pappen *vt/i* (*haben*) (*fam*) stick

pappig *a* (*fam*) sticky

Papp|karton *m*, **P~schachtel** *f* cardboard box
Paprika *m* **-s,-[s]** [sweet] pepper; (*Gewürz*) paprika
Papst *m* **-[e]s,⸚e** pope
päpstlich *a* papal
Parade *f* **-,-n** parade
Paradeiser *m* **-s,-** (*Aust*) tomato
Paradies *nt* **-es,-e** paradise. **p~isch** *a* heavenly
Paradox *nt* **-es,-e** paradox. **p~** *a* paradoxical
Paraffin *nt* **-s** paraffin
Paragraph *m* **-en,-en** section
parallel *a & adv* parallel. **P~e** *f* **-,-n** parallel
Paranuß *f* Brazil nut
Parasit *m* **-en,-en** parasite
parat *a* ready
Pärchen *nt* **-s,-** pair; (*Liebes-*) couple
Parcours /par'ku:ɐ̯/ *m* **-,-** /-[s],-s/ (*Sport*) course
Pardon /par'dõ:/ *int* sorry!
Parfüm *nt* **-s,-e** & **-s** perfume, scent. **p~iert** *a* perfumed, scented
parieren¹ *vt* parry
parieren² *vi* (*haben*) (*fam*) obey
Parität *f* **-** parity; (*in Ausschuß*) equal representation
Park *m* **-s,-s** park. **p~en** *vt/i* (*haben*) park. **P~en** *nt* **-s** parking; **'P~en verboten'** 'no parking'
Parkett *nt* **-[e]s,-e** parquet floor; (*Theat*) stalls *pl*
Park|haus *nt* multi-storey car park. **P~lücke** *f* parking space. **P~platz** *m* car park, (*Amer*) parking-lot; (*für ein Auto*) parking space; (*Autobahn-*) lay-by. **P~scheibe** *f* parking-disc. **P~schein** *m* car-park ticket. **P~uhr** *f* parking-meter. **P~verbot** *nt* parking ban; **'P~verbot'** 'no parking'
Parlament *nt* **-[e]s,-e** parliament. **p~arisch** *a* parliamentary
Parodie *f* **-,-n** parody. **p~ren** *vt* parody
Parole *f* **-,-n** slogan; (*Mil*) password
Part *m* **-s,-s** (*Theat, Mus*) part
Partei *f* **-,-en** (*Pol, Jur*) party; (*Miet-*) tenant; **für jdn P~ ergreifen** take s.o.'s part. **p~isch** *a* biased. **p~los** *a* independent
Parterre /par'tɛr/ *nt* **-s,-s** ground floor, (*Amer*) first floor; (*Theat*) rear stalls *pl*. **p~** *adv* on the ground floor
Partie *f* **-,-n** part; (*Tennis, Schach*) game; (*Golf*) round; (*Comm*) batch; **eine gute P~ machen** marry well
Partikel¹ *nt* **-s,-** particle
Partikel² *f* **-,-n** (*Gram*) particle
Partitur *f* **-,-en** (*Mus*) full score
Partizip *nt* **-s,-ien** /-i̯ən/ participle; **erstes/zweites P~** present/past participle
Partner|(in) *m* **-s,-** (*f* **-,-nen**) partner. **P~schaft** *f* **-,-en** partnership. **P~stadt** *f* twin town
Party /'pa:ɐ̯ti/ *f* **-,-s** party
Parzelle *f* **-,-n** plot [of ground]
Paß *m* **-sses,⸚sse** passport; (*Geog, Sport*) pass
passabel *a* passable
Passage /pa'sa:ʒə/ *f* **-,-n** passage; (*Einkaufs-*) shopping arcade
Passagier /pasa'ʒi:ɐ̯/ *m* **-s,-e** passenger
Paßamt *nt* passport office
Passant(in) *m* **-en,-en** (*f* **-,-nen**) passer-by
Paßbild *nt* passport photograph
Passe *f* **-,-n** yoke
passen *vi* (*haben*) fit; (*geeignet sein*) be right (**für** for); (*Sport*) pass the ball; (*aufgeben*) pass; **p~ zu** go [well] with; (*übereinstimmen*) match; **jdm p~** fit s.o.; (*gelegen sein*) suit s.o.; **seine Art paßt mir nicht** I don't like his manner; **[ich] passe** pass. **p~d** *a* suitable; (*angemessen*) appropriate; (*günstig*) convenient; (*übereinstimmend*) matching
passier|bar *a* passable. **p~en** *vt* pass; cross ⟨*Grenze*⟩; (*Culin*) rub through a sieve ● *vi* (*sein*) happen (**jdm** to s.o.); **es ist ein Unglück p~t** there has been an accident. **P~schein** *m* pass
Passion *f* **-,-en** passion. **p~iert** *a* very keen ⟨*Jäger, Angler*⟩
passiv *a* passive. **P~** *nt* **-s,-e** (*Gram*) passive
Paß|kontrolle *f* passport control. **P~straße** *f* pass
Paste *f* **-,-n** paste
Pastell *nt* **-[e]s,-e** pastel. **P~farbe** *f* pastel colour
Pastet|chen *nt* **-s,-** [individual] pie; (*Königin-*) vol-au-vent. **P~e** *f* **-,-n** pie; (*Gänseleber-*) pâté
pasteurisieren /pastøri'zi:rən/ *vt* pasteurize
Pastille *f* **-,-n** pastille
Pastinake *f* **-,-n** parsnip
Pastor *m* **-s,-en** /-'to:rən/ pastor
Pate *m* **-n,-n** godfather; (*fig*) sponsor; **P~n** godparents. **P~nkind** *nt* godchild. **P~nschaft** *f* **-** sponsorship. **P~nsohn** *m* godson

Patent *nt* **-[e]s,-e** patent; (*Offiziers-*) commission. **p~** *a* (*fam*) clever, *adv* -ly; ⟨*Person*⟩ resourceful. **p~ieren** *vt* patent
Patentochter *f* god-daughter
Pater *m* **-s,-** (*Relig*) Father
pathetisch *a* emotional ● *adv* with emotion
Patholog|e *m* **-n,-n** pathologist. **p~isch** *a* pathological, *adv* -ly
Pathos *nt* - emotion, feeling
Patience /pa'si̯ã:s/ *f* **-,-n** patience
Patient(in) /pa'ts̯i̯ɛnt(ɪn)/ *m* **-en,-en** (*f* **-,-nen**) patient
Patin *f* **-,-nen** godmother
Patriot|(in) *m* **-en,-en** (*f* **-,-nen**) patriot. **p~isch** *a* patriotic. **P~ismus** *m* - patriotism
Patrone *f* **-,-n** cartridge
Patrouill|e /pa'trʊljə/ *f* **-,-n** patrol. **p~ieren** /-'ji:rən/ *vi* (*haben/sein*) patrol
Patsch|e *f* **in der P~e sitzen** (*fam*) be in a jam. **p~en** *vi* (*haben/sein*) splash ● *vt* slap. **p~naß** *a* (*fam*) soaking wet
Patt *nt* **-s** stalemate
Patz|er *m* **-s,-** (*fam*) slip. **p~ig** *a* (*fam*) insolent
Pauk|e *f* **-,-n** kettledrum; **auf die P~e hauen** (*fam*) have a good time; (*prahlen*) boast. **p~en** *vt/i* (*haben*) (*fam*) swot. **P~er** *m* **-s,-** (*fam: Lehrer*) teacher
pausbäckig *a* chubby-cheeked
pauschal *a* all-inclusive; (*einheitlich*) flat-rate; (*fig*) sweeping ⟨*Urteil*⟩; **p~e Summe** lump sum ● *adv* in a lump sum; (*fig*) wholesale. **P~e** *f* **-,-n** lump sum. **P~reise** *f* package tour. **P~summe** *f* lump sum
Pause[1] *f* **-,-n** break; (*beim Sprechen*) pause; (*Theat*) interval; (*im Kino*) intermission; (*Mus*) rest; **P~ machen** have a break
Pause[2] *f* **-,-n** tracing. **p~n** *vt* trace
pausenlos *a* incessant, *adv* -ly
pausieren *vi* (*haben*) have a break; (*ausruhen*) rest
Pauspapier *nt* tracing-paper
Pavian *m* **-s,-e** baboon
Pavillon /'pavɪljõ/ *m* **-s,-s** pavilion
Pazifi|k *m* **-s** Pacific [Ocean]. **p~sch** *a* Pacific
Pazifist *m* **-en,-en** pacifist
Pech *nt* **-s** pitch; (*Unglück*) bad luck; **P~ haben** be unlucky. **p~schwarz** *a* pitch-black; ⟨*Haare, Augen*⟩ jet-black. **P~strähne** *f* run of bad luck. **P~vogel** *m* (*fam*) unlucky devil
Pedal *nt* **-s,-e** pedal
Pedant *m* **-en,-en** pedant. **p~isch** *a* pedantic, *adv* -ally
Pediküre *f* **-,-n** pedicure
Pegel *m* **-s,-** level; (*Gerät*) water-level indicator. **P~stand** *m* [water] level
peilen *vt* take a bearing on; **über den Daumen gepeilt** (*fam*) at a rough guess
Pein *f* - (*liter*) torment. **p~igen** *vt* torment
peinlich *a* embarrassing, awkward; (*genau*) scrupulous, *adv* -ly; **es war mir sehr p~** I was very embarrassed
Peitsche *f* **-,-n** whip. **p~n** *vt* whip; (*fig*) lash ● *vi* (*sein*) lash (**an** + *acc* against). **P~nhieb** *m* lash
pekuniär *a* financial, *adv* -ly
Pelikan *m* **-s,-e** pelican
Pell|e *f* **-,-n** skin. **p~en** *vt* peel; shell ⟨*Ei*⟩; **sich p~en** peel. **P~kartoffeln** *fpl* potatoes boiled in their skins
Pelz *m* **-es,-e** fur. **P~mantel** *m* fur coat
Pendel *nt* **-s,-** pendulum. **p~n** *vi* (*haben*) swing ● *vi* (*sein*) commute. **P~verkehr** *m* shuttle-service; (*für Pendler*) commuter traffic
Pendler *m* **-s,-** commuter
penetrant *a* penetrating; (*fig*) obtrusive, *adv* -ly
penibel *a* fastidious, fussy; (*pedantisch*) pedantic
Penis *m* **-,-se** penis
Penne *f* **-,-n** (*fam*) school. **p~n** *vi* (*haben*) (*fam*) sleep. **P~r** *m* **-s,-** (*sl*) tramp
Pension /pã'zi̯o:n/ *f* **-,-en** pension; (*Hotel*) guest-house; **bei voller/halber P~** with full/half board. **P~är(in)** *m* **-s,-e** (*f* **-,-nen**) pensioner. **P~at** *nt* **-[e]s,-e** boarding-school. **p~ieren** *vt* retire. **p~iert** *a* retired. **P~ierung** *f* - retirement
Pensum *nt* **-s** [allotted] work
Peperoni *f* **-,-** chilli
per *prep* (+*acc*) by; **per Luftpost** by airmail
perfekt *a* perfect, *adv* -ly; **p~ sein** ⟨*Vertrag:*⟩ be settled
Perfekt *nt* **-s** (*Gram*) perfect
Perfektion /-'ts̯i̯o:n/ *f* - perfection
perforiert *a* perforated
Pergament *nt* **-[e]s,-e** parchment. **P~papier** *nt* grease-proof paper
Period|e *f* **-,-n** period. **p~isch** *a* periodic, *adv* -ally

Perl|e *f* **-,-n** pearl; (*Glas-, Holz-*) bead; (*Sekt-*) bubble; (*fam: Hilfe*) treasure. **p~en** *vi* (*haben*) bubble. **P~mutt** *nt* **-s, P~mutter** *f* **-** & *nt* **-s** mother-of-pearl

perplex *a* (*fam*) perplexed

Perserkatze *f* Persian cat

Pers|ien /-i̯ən/ *nt* **-s** Persia. **p~isch** *a* Persian

Person *f* **-,-en** person; (*Theat*) character; **ich für meine P~** [I] for my part; **für vier P~en** for four people

Personal *nt* **-s** personnel, staff. **P~ausweis** *m* identity card. **P~chef** *m* personnel manager. **P~ien** /-i̯ən/ *pl* personal particulars. **P~mangel** *m* staff shortage. **P~pronomen** *nt* personal pronoun

Personen|kraftwagen *m* private car. **P~zug** *m* stopping train

personifizieren *vt* personify

persönlich *a* personal • *adv* personally, in person. **P~keit** *f* **-,-en** personality

Perspektive *f* **-,-n** perspective; (*Zukunfts-*) prospect

Perücke *f* **-,-n** wig

pervers *a* [sexually] perverted. **P~ion** *f* **-,-en** perversion

Pessimis|mus *m* **-** pessimism. **P~t** *m* **-en,-en** pessimist. **p~tisch** *a* pessimistic, *adv* -ally

Pest *f* **-** plague

Petersilie /-i̯ə/ *f* **-** parsley

Petroleum /-leʊm/ *nt* **-s** paraffin, (*Amer*) kerosene

Petze *f* **-,-n** (*fam*) sneak. **p~n** *vi* (*haben*) (*fam*) sneak

Pfad *m* **-[e]s,-e** path. **P~finder** *m* **-s,-** [Boy] Scout. **P~finderin** *f* **-,-nen** [Girl] Guide

Pfahl *m* **-[e]s,⸚e** stake, post

Pfalz (die) - the Palatinate

Pfand *nt* **-[e]s,⸚er** pledge; (*beim Spiel*) forfeit; (*Flaschen-*) deposit

pfänd|en *vt* (*Jur*) seize. **P~erspiel** *nt* game of forfeits

Pfand|haus *nt* pawnshop. **P~leiher** *m* **-s,-** pawnbroker

Pfändung *f* **-,-en** (*Jur*) seizure

Pfann|e *f* **-,-n** [frying-]pan. **P~kuchen** *m* pancake; **Berliner P~kuchen** doughnut

Pfarr|er *m* **-s,-** vicar, parson; (*katholischer*) priest. **P~haus** *nt* vicarage

Pfau *m* **-s,-en** peacock

Pfeffer *m* **-s** pepper. **P~kuchen** *m* gingerbread. **P~minzbonbon** *m* & *nt* [pepper]mint. **P~minze** *f* **-** (*Bot*) peppermint. **P~minztee** *m* peppermint tea. **p~n** *vt* pepper; (*fam: schmeißen*) chuck. **P~streuer** *m* **-s,-** pepper-pot

Pfeif|e *f* **-,-n** whistle; (*Tabak-, Orgel-*) pipe. **p~en**† *vt*/*i* (*haben*) whistle; (*als Signal*) blow the whistle; **ich p~e darauf!** (*fam*) I couldn't care less [about it]!

Pfeil *m* **-[e]s,-e** arrow

Pfeiler *m* **-s,-** pillar; (*Brücken-*) pier

Pfennig *m* **-s,-e** pfennig; **10 P~** 10 pfennigs

Pferch *m* **-[e]s,-e** [sheep] pen. **p~en** *vt* (*fam*) cram (**in** + *acc* into)

Pferd *nt* **-es,-e** horse; **zu P~e** on horseback; **das P~ beim Schwanz aufzäumen** put the cart before the horse. **P~erennen** *nt* horse-race; (*als Sport*) [horse-]racing. **P~eschwanz** *m* horse's tail; (*Frisur*) pony-tail. **P~estall** *m* stable. **P~estärke** *f* horsepower. **P~ewagen** *m* horse-drawn cart

Pfiff *m* **-[e]s,-e** whistle; **P~ haben** (*fam*) have style

Pfifferling *m* **-s,-e** chanterelle

pfiffig *a* smart

Pfingst|en *nt* **-s** Whitsun. **P~montag** *m* Whit Monday. **P~rose** *f* peony

Pfirsich *m* **-s,-e** peach. **p~farben** *a* peach[-coloured]

Pflanz|e *f* **-,-n** plant. **p~en** *vt* plant. **P~enfett** *nt* vegetable fat. **p~lich** *a* vegetable; ⟨*Mittel*⟩ herbal. **P~ung** *f* **-,-en** plantation

Pflaster *nt* **-s,-** pavement; (*Heft-*) plaster. **p~n** *vt* pave. **P~stein** *m* paving-stone

Pflaume *f* **-,-n** plum

Pflege *f* **-** care; (*Kranken-*) nursing; **in P~ nehmen** look after; (*Admin*) foster ⟨*Kind*⟩. **p~bedürftig** *a* in need of care. **P~eltern** *pl* foster-parents. **P~kind** *nt* foster-child. **p~leicht** *a* easy-care. **P~mutter** *f* foster-mother. **p~n** *vt* look after, care for; nurse ⟨*Kranke*⟩; cultivate ⟨*Künste, Freundschaft*⟩. **P~r(in)** *m* **-s,-** (*f* **-,-nen**) nurse; (*Tier-*) keeper

Pflicht *f* **-,-en** duty; (*Sport*) compulsory exercise/routine. **p~bewußt** *a* conscientious, *adv* -ly. **p~eifrig** *a* zealous, *adv* -ly. **P~fach** *nt* (*Sch*) compulsory subject. **P~gefühl** *nt* sense of duty. **p~gemäß** *a* due • *adv* duly

Pflock *m* **-[e]s,⸚e** peg

pflücken *vt* pick
Pflug *m* **-[e]s,¨e** plough
pflügen *vt/i* (*haben*) plough
Pforte *f* **-,-n** gate
Pförtner *m* **-s,-** porter
Pfosten *m* **-s,-** post
Pfote *f* **-,-n** paw
Pfropfen *m* **-s,-** stopper; (*Korken*) cork. **p~** *vt* graft (**auf** + *acc* on [to]); (*fam: pressen*) cram (**in** + *acc* into)
pfui *int* ugh; **p~ schäm dich!** you should be ashamed of yourself!
Pfund *nt* **-[e]s,-e** & **-** pound
Pfusch|arbeit *f* (*fam*) shoddy work. **p~en** *vi* (*haben*) (*fam*) botch one's work. **P~er** *m* **-s,-** (*fam*) shoddy worker. **P~erei** *f* **-,-en** (*fam*) botch-up
Pfütze *f* **-,-n** puddle
Phänomen *nt* **-s,-e** phenomenon. **p~al** *a* phenomenal
Phantasie *f* **-,-n** imagination; **P~n** fantasies; (*Fieber-*) hallucinations. **p~los** *a* unimaginative. **p~ren** *vi* (*haben*) fantasize; (*im Fieber*) be delirious. **p~voll** *a* imaginative, *adv* -ly
phant|astisch *a* fantastic, *adv* -ally. **P~om** *nt* **-s,-e** phantom
pharma|zeutisch *a* pharmaceutical. **P~zie** *f* **-** pharmacy
Phase *f* **-,-n** phase
Philanthrop *m* **-en,-en** philanthropist. **p~isch** *a* philanthropic
Philolo|ge *m* **-n,-n** teacher/student of language and literature. **P~gie** *f* **-** [study of] language and literature
Philosoph *m* **-en,-en** philosopher. **P~ie** *f* **-,-n** philosophy. **p~ieren** *vi* (*haben*) philosophize
philosophisch *a* philosophical, *adv* -ly
phlegmatisch *a* phlegmatic
Phobie *f* **-,-n** phobia
Phonet|ik *f* **-** phonetics *sg*. **p~isch** *a* phonetic, *adv* -ally
Phonotypistin *f* **-,-nen** audio typist
Phosphor *m* **-s** phosphorus
Photo *nt*, **Photo-** *s.* **Foto, Foto-**
Phrase *f* **-,-n** empty phrase
Physik *f* **-** physics *sg*. **p~alisch** *a* physical
Physiker(in) *m* **-s,-** (*f* **-,-nen**) physicist
Physio|logie *f* **-** physiology. **P~therapie** *f* physiotherapy
physisch *a* physical, *adv* -ly
Pianist(in) *m* **-en,-en** (*f* **-,-nen**) pianist
Pickel *m* **-s,-** pimple, spot; (*Spitzhacke*) pick. **p~ig** *a* spotty
picken *vt/i* (*haben*) peck (**nach** at); (*fam: nehmen*) pick (**aus** out of); (*Aust fam: kleben*) stick
Picknick *nt* **-s,-s** picnic. **p~en** *vi* (*haben*) picnic
piep[s]|en *vi* (*haben*) ⟨*Vogel:*⟩ cheep; ⟨*Maus:*⟩ squeak; (*Techn*) bleep. **P~er** *m* **-s,-** bleeper
Pier *m* **-s,-e** [harbour] pier
Pietät /pi̯e'tɛ:t/ *f* **-** reverence. **p~los** *a* irreverent, *adv* -ly
Pigment *nt* **-[e]s,-e** pigment. **P~ierung** *f* **-** pigmentation
Pik *nt* **-s,-s** (*Karten*) spades *pl*
pikant *a* piquant; (*gewagt*) racy
piken *vt* (*fam*) prick
pikiert *a* offended, hurt
piksen *vt* (*fam*) prick
Pilger|(in) *m* **-s,-** (*f* **-,-nen**) pilgrim. **P~fahrt** *f* pilgrimage. **p~n** *vi* (*sein*) make a pilgrimage
Pille *f* **-,-n** pill
Pilot *m* **-en,-en** pilot
Pilz *m* **-es,-e** fungus; (*eßbarer*) mushroom; **wie P~e aus dem Boden schießen** (*fig*) mushroom
pingelig *a* (*fam*) fussy
Pinguin *m* **-s,-e** penguin
Pinie /-i̯ə/ *f* **-,-n** stone-pine
pink *pred a* shocking pink
pinkeln *vi* (*haben*) (*fam*) pee
Pinsel *m* **-s,-** [paint]brush
Pinzette *f* **-,-n** tweezers *pl*
Pionier *m* **-s,-e** (*Mil*) sapper; (*fig*) pioneer. **P~arbeit** *f* pioneering work
Pirat *m* **-en,-en** pirate
pirschen *vi* (*haben*) **p~ auf** (+ *acc*) stalk ● *vr* **sich p~** creep (**an** + *acc* up to)
pissen *vi* (*haben*) (*sl*) piss
Piste *f* **-,-n** (*Ski-*) run, piste; (*Renn-*) track; (*Aviat*) runway
Pistole *f* **-,-n** pistol
pitschnaß *a* (*fam*) soaking wet
pittoresk *a* picturesque
Pizza *f* **-,-s** pizza
Pkw /'pe:kave:/ *m* **-s,-s** (= **Personenkraftwagen**) [private] car
placieren /-'t̠si:rən/ *vt* = **plazieren**
Plackerei *f* **-** (*fam*) drudgery
plädieren *vi* (*haben*) plead (**für** for); **auf Freispruch p~** (*Jur*) ask for an acquittal
Plädoyer /plɛdo̯a'je:/ *nt* **-s,-s** (*Jur*) closing speech; (*fig*) plea

Plage *f* **-,-n** [hard] labour; (*Mühe*) trouble; (*Belästigung*) nuisance. **p~n** *vt* torment, plague; (*bedrängen*) pester; **sich p~n** struggle; (*arbeiten*) work hard

Plagi|at *nt* **-[e]s,-e** plagiarism. **p~ieren** *vt* plagiarize

Plakat *nt* **-[e]s,-e** poster

Plakette *f* **-,-n** badge

Plan *m* **-[e]s,⸚e** plan

Plane *f* **-,-n** tarpaulin; (*Boden-*) groundsheet

planen *vt/i* (*haben*) plan

Planet *m* **-en,-en** planet

planier|en *vt* level. **P~raupe** *f* bulldozer

Planke *f* **-,-n** plank

plan|los *a* unsystematic, *adv* -ally. **p~mäßig** *a* systematic; ⟨*Ankunft*⟩ scheduled ● *adv* systematically; (*nach Plan*) according to plan; ⟨*ankommen*⟩ on schedule

Plansch|becken *nt* paddling pool. **p~en** *vi* (*haben*) splash about

Plantage /plan'ta:ʒə/ *f* **-,-n** plantation

Planung *f* - planning

Plapper|maul *nt* (*fam*) chatterbox. **p~n** *vi* (*haben*) chatter ● *vt* talk ⟨*Unsinn*⟩

plärren *vi* (*haben*) bawl; ⟨*Radio:*⟩ blare

Plasma *nt* **-s** plasma

Plastik[1] *f* **-,-en** sculpture

Plast|ik[2] *nt* **-s** plastic. **p~isch** *a* three-dimensional; (*formbar*) plastic; (*anschaulich*) graphic, *adv* -ally; **p~ische Chirurgie** plastic surgery

Platane *f* **-,-n** plane [tree]

Plateau /pla'to:/ *nt* **-s,-s** plateau

Platin *nt* **-s** platinum

Platitüde *f* **-,-n** platitude

platonisch *a* platonic

platschen *vi* (*sein*) splash

plätschern *vi* (*haben*) splash; ⟨*Bach:*⟩ babble ● *vi* (*sein*) ⟨*Bach:*⟩ babble along

platt *a & adv* flat; **p~ sein** (*fam*) be flabbergasted. **P~** *nt* **-[s]** (*Lang*) Low German

Plättbrett *nt* ironing-board

Platte *f* **-,-n** slab; (*Druck-*) plate; (*Metall-, Glas-*) sheet; (*Fliese*) tile; (*Koch-*) hotplate; (*Tisch-*) top; (*Auszieh-*) leaf; (*Schall-*) record, disc; (*zum Servieren*) [flat] dish, platter; **kalte P~** assorted cold meats and cheeses *pl*

Plätt|eisen *nt* iron. **p~en** *vt/i* (*haben*) iron

Plattenspieler *m* record-player

Platt|form *f* **-,-en** platform. **P~füße** *mpl* flat feet. **P~heit** *f* **-,-en** platitude

Platz *m* **-es,⸚e** place; (*von Häusern umgeben*) square; (*Sitz-*) seat; (*Sport-*) ground; (*Fußball-*) pitch; (*Tennis-*) court; (*Golf-*) course; (*freier Raum*) room, space; **P~ nehmen** take a seat; **P~ machen/lassen** make/leave room; **vom P~ stellen** (*Sport*) send off. **P~angst** *f* agoraphobia; (*Klaustrophobie*) claustrophobia. **P~anweiserin** *f* **-,-nen** usherette

Plätzchen *nt* **-s,-** spot; (*Culin*) biscuit

platzen *vi* (*sein*) burst; (*auf-*) split; (*fam: scheitern*) fall through; ⟨*Verlobung:*⟩ be off; **vor Neugier p~** be bursting with curiosity

Platz|karte *f* seat reservation ticket. **P~konzert** *nt* open-air concert. **P~mangel** *m* lack of space. **P~patrone** *f* blank. **P~regen** *m* downpour. **P~verweis** *m* (*Sport*) sending off. **P~wunde** *f* laceration

Plauderei *f* **-,-en** chat

plaudern *vi* (*haben*) chat

Plausch *m* **-[e]s,-e** (*SGer*) chat. **p~en** *vi* (*haben*) (*SGer*) chat

plausibel *a* plausible

plazieren *vt* place, put; **sich p~** (*Sport*) be placed

pleite *a* (*fam*) **p~ sein** be broke; ⟨*Firma:*⟩ be bankrupt; **p~ gehen** go bankrupt. **P~** *f* **-,-n** (*fam*) bankruptcy; (*Mißerfolg*) flop; **P~ machen** go bankrupt

plissiert *a* [finely] pleated

Plomb|e *f* **-,-n** seal; (*Zahn-*) filling. **p~ieren** *vt* seal; fill ⟨*Zahn*⟩

plötzlich *a* sudden, *adv* -ly

plump *a* plump; (*ungeschickt*) clumsy, *adv* -ily

plumpsen *vi* (*sein*) (*fam*) fall

Plunder *m* **-s** (*fam*) junk, rubbish

plündern *vt/i* (*haben*) loot

Plunderstück *nt* Danish pastry

Plural *m* **-s,-e** plural

plus *adv, conj & prep* (+*dat*) plus. **P~** *nt* - surplus; (*Gewinn*) profit; (*Vorteil*) advantage, plus. **P~punkt** *m* (*Sport*) point; (*fig*) plus. **P~quamperfekt** *nt* pluperfect. **P~zeichen** *nt* plus sign

Po *m* **-s,-s** (*fam*) bottom

Pöbel *m* **-s** mob, rabble. **p~haft** *a* loutish

pochen *vi* (*haben*) knock; ⟨*Herz:*⟩ pound; **p~ auf** (+*acc*) (*fig*) insist on

pochieren /pɔ'ʃi:rən/ *vt* poach

Pocken *pl* smallpox *sg*
Podest *nt* **-[e]s,-e** rostrum
Podium *nt* **-s,-ien** /-iən/ platform; (*Podest*) rostrum
Poesie /poe'zi:/ *f* - poetry
poetisch *a* poetic
Pointe /'pọɛ̃:tə/ *f* **-,-n** point (*of a joke*)
Pokal *m* **-s,-e** goblet; (*Sport*) cup
pökeln *vt* (*Culin*) salt
Poker *nt* **-s** poker
Pol *m* **-s,-e** pole. **p~ar** *a* polar
polarisieren *vt* polarize
Polarstern *m* pole-star
Pole *m* **-n,-n** Pole. **P~n** *nt* **-s** Poland
Police /po'li:sə/ *f* **-,-n** policy
Polier *m* **-s,-e** foreman
polieren *vt* polish
Polin *f* **-,-nen** Pole
Politesse *f* **-,-n** [woman] traffic warden
Politik *f* - politics *sg*; (*Vorgehen, Maßnahme*) policy
Polit|iker(in) *m* **-s,-** (*f* **-,-nen**) politician. **p~isch** *a* political, *adv* -ly
Politur *f* **-,-en** polish
Polizei *f* - police *pl*. **P~beamte(r)** *m* police officer. **p~lich** *a* police ... ● *adv* by the police; ⟨*sich anmelden*⟩ with the police. **P~streife** *f* police patrol. **P~stunde** *f* closing time. **P~wache** *f* police station
Polizist *m* **-en,-en** policeman. **P~in** *f* **-,-nen** policewoman
Pollen *m* **-s** pollen
polnisch *a* Polish
Polohemd *nt* polo shirt
Polster *nt* **-s,-** pad; (*Kissen*) cushion; (*Möbel-*) upholstery; (*fam: Rücklage*) reserves *pl*. **P~er** *m* **-s,-** upholsterer. **P~möbel** *pl* upholstered furniture *sg*. **p~n** *vt* pad; upholster ⟨*Möbel*⟩. **P~ung** *f* - padding; upholstery
Polter|abend *m* wedding-eve party. **p~n** *vi* (*haben*) thump, bang; (*schelten*) bawl ● *vi* (*sein*) crash down; (*gehen*) clump [along]; (*fahren*) rumble [along]
Polyäthylen *nt* **-s** polythene
Polyester *m* **-s** polyester
Polyp *m* **-en,-en** polyp; (*sl: Polizist*) copper; **P~en** adenoids *pl*
Pomeranze *f* **-,-n** Seville orange
Pommes *pl* (*fam*) French fries
Pommes frites /pɔm'fri:t/ *pl* chips; (*dünner*) French fries
Pomp *m* **-s** pomp
Pompon /põ'põ:/ *m* **-s,-s** pompon
pompös *a* ostentatious, *adv* -ly
Pony[1] *nt* **-s,-s** pony
Pony[2] *m* **-s,-s** fringe
Pop *m* **-[s]** pop. **P~musik** *f* pop music
Popo *m* **-s,-s** (*fam*) bottom
popul|är *a* popular. **P~arität** *f* - popularity
Pore *f* **-,-n** pore
Porno|graphie *f* - pornography. **p~graphisch** *a* pornographic
porös *a* porous
Porree *m* **-s** leeks *pl*; **eine Stange P~** a leek
Portal *nt* **-s,-e** portal
Portemonnaie /pɔrtmɔ'ne:/ *nt* **-s,-s** purse
Portier /pɔr'ti̯e:/ *m* **-s,-s** doorman, porter
Portion /-'t̮si̯o:n/ *f* **-,-en** helping, portion
Porto *nt* **-s** postage. **p~frei** *adv* post free, post paid
Porträ|t /pɔr'trɛ:/ *nt* **-s,-s** portrait. **p~tieren** *vt* paint a portrait of
Portugal *nt* **-s** Portugal
Portugies|e *m* **-n,-n, P~in** *f* **-,-nen** Portuguese. **p~isch** *a* Portuguese
Portwein *m* port
Porzellan *nt* **-s** china, porcelain
Posaune *f* **-,-n** trombone
Pose *f* **-,-n** pose
posieren *vi* (*haben*) pose
Position /-'t̮si̯o:n/ *f* **-,-en** position
positiv *a* positive, *adv* -ly. **P~** *nt* **-s,-e** (*Phot*) positive
Posse *f* **-,-n** (*Theat*) farce. **P~n** *m* **-s,-** prank; **P~n** *pl* tomfoolery *sg*
Possessivpronomen *nt* possessive pronoun
possierlich *a* cute
Post *f* - post office; (*Briefe*) mail, post; **mit der P~** by post
postalisch *a* postal
Post|amt *nt* post office. **P~anweisung** *f* postal money order. **P~bote** *m* postman
Posten *m* **-s,-** post; (*Wache*) sentry; (*Waren-*) batch; (*Rechnungs-*) item, entry; **P~ stehen** stand guard; **nicht auf dem P~** (*fam*) under the weather
Poster *nt & m* **-s,-** poster
Postfach *nt* post-office *or* PO box
postieren *vt* post, station; **sich p~** station oneself
Post|karte *f* postcard. **p~lagernd** *adv* poste restante. **P~leitzahl** *f* postcode, (*Amer*) Zip code. **P~scheckkonto** *nt* ≈ National Girobank account. **P~stempel** *m* postmark

postum *a* posthumous, *adv* -ly

post|wendend *adv* by return of post. **P~wertzeichen** *nt* [postage] stamp

Poten|tial /-'tsi̯a:l/ *nt* **-s,-e** potential. **p~tiell** /-'tsi̯ɛl/ *a* potential, *adv* -ly

Potenz *f* **-,-en** potency; (*Math & fig*) power

Pracht *f* **-** magnificence, splendour. **P~exemplar** *nt* magnificent specimen

prächtig *a* magnificent, *adv* -ly; (*prima*) splendid, *adv* -ly

prachtvoll *a* magnificent, *adv* -ly

Prädikat *nt* **-[e]s,-e** rating; (*Comm*) grade; (*Gram*) predicate. **p~iv** *a* (*Gram*) predicative, *adv* -ly. **P~swein** *m* high-quality wine

präge|n *vt* stamp (**auf**+*acc* on); emboss ⟨*Leder, Papier*⟩; mint ⟨*Münze*⟩; coin ⟨*Wort, Ausdruck*⟩; (*fig*) shape. **P~stempel** *m* die

pragmatisch *a* pragmatic, *adv* -ally

prägnant *a* succinct, *adv* -ly

prähistorisch *a* prehistoric

prahl|en *vi* (*haben*) boast, brag (**mit** about). **p~erisch** *a* boastful, *adv* -ly

Prakti|k *f* **-,-en** practice. **P~kant(in)** *m* **-en,-en** (*f* **-,-nen**) trainee

Prakti|kum *nt* **-s,-ka** practical training. **p~sch** *a* practical; (*nützlich*) handy; (*tatsächlich*) virtual; **p~scher Arzt** general practitioner ● *adv* practically; virtually; (*in der Praxis*) in practice; **p~sch arbeiten** do practical work. **p~zieren** *vt/i* (*haben*) practise; (*anwenden*) put into practice; (*fam: bekommen*) get

Praline *f* **-,-n** chocolate; **Schachtel P~n** box of chocolates

prall *a* bulging; (*dick*) plump; ⟨*Sonne*⟩ blazing ● *adv* **p~ gefüllt** full to bursting. **p~en** *vi* (*sein*) **p~ auf** (+*acc*)/**gegen** collide with, hit; ⟨*Sonne:*⟩ blaze down on

Prämie /-i̯ə/ *f* **-,-n** premium; (*Preis*) award

präm[i]ieren *vt* award a prize to

Pranger *m* **-s,-** pillory

Pranke *f* **-,-n** paw

Präpar|at *nt* **-[e]s,-e** preparation. **p~ieren** *vt* prepare; (*zerlegen*) dissect; (*ausstopfen*) stuff

Präposition /-'tsi̯o:n/ *f* **-,-en** preposition

Präsens *nt* **-** (*Gram*) present

präsentieren *vt* present; **sich p~** present itself/⟨*Person:*⟩ oneself

Präsenz *f* **-** presence

Präservativ *nt* **-s,-e** condom

Präsident|(in) *m* **-en,-en** (*f* **-,-nen**) president. **P~schaft** *f* **-** presidency

Präsidium *nt* **-s** presidency; (*Gremium*) executive committee; (*Polizei-*) headquarters *pl*

prasseln *vi* (*haben*) ⟨*Regen:*⟩ beat down; ⟨*Feuer:*⟩ crackle ● *vi* (*sein*) **p~ auf** (+*acc*)/**gegen** beat down on/beat against

prassen *vi* (*haben*) live extravagantly; (*schmausen*) feast

Präteritum *nt* **-s** imperfect

präventiv *a* preventive

Praxis *f* **-,-xen** practice; (*Erfahrung*) practical experience; (*Arzt-*) surgery; **in der P~** in practice

Präzedenzfall *m* precedent

präzis[e] *a* precise, *adv* -ly

Präzision *f* **-** precision

predig|en *vt/i* (*haben*) preach. **P~er** *m* **-s,-** preacher. **P~t** *f* **-,-en** sermon

Preis *m* **-es,-e** price; (*Belohnung*) prize; **um jeden/keinen P~** at any/not at any price. **P~ausschreiben** *nt* competition

Preiselbeere *f* (*Bot*) cowberry; (*Culin*) ≈ cranberry

preisen† *vt* praise; **sich glücklich p~** count oneself lucky

preisgeben† *vt sep* abandon (*dat* to); reveal ⟨*Geheimnis*⟩

preis|gekrönt *a* award-winning. **P~gericht** *nt* jury. **p~günstig** *a* reasonably priced ● *adv* at a reasonable price. **P~lage** *f* price range. **p~lich** *a* price ... ● *adv* in price. **P~richter** *m* judge. **P~schild** *nt* price-tag. **P~träger(in)** *m(f)* prizewinner. **p~wert** *a* reasonable, *adv* -bly; (*billig*) inexpensive, *adv* -ly

prekär *a* difficult; (*heikel*) delicate

Prell|bock *m* buffers *pl*. **p~en** *vt* bounce; (*verletzen*) bruise; (*fam: betrügen*) cheat. **P~ung** *f* **-,-en** bruise

Premiere /prə'mi̯e:rə/ *f* **-,-n** première

Premierminister(in) /prə'mi̯e:-/ *m(f)* Prime Minister

Presse *f* **-,-n** press. **p~n** *vt* press; **sich p~n** press (**an**+*acc* against)

pressieren *vi* (*haben*) (*SGer*) be urgent

Preßluft *f* compressed air. **P~bohrer** *m* pneumatic drill

Prestige /prɛs'ti:ʒə/ *nt* **-s** prestige

Preuß|en *nt* **-s** Prussia. **p~isch** *a* Prussian

prickeln *vi* (*haben*) tingle

Priester *m* **-s,-** priest

prima *inv a* first-class, first-rate; (*fam: toll*) fantastic, *adv* fantastically well

primär *a* primary, *adv* -ily

Primel *f* **-,-n** primula; (*Garten-*) polyanthus

primitiv *a* primitive

Prinz *m* **-en,-en** prince. **P~essin** *f* **-,-nen** princess

Prinzip *nt* **-s,-ien** /-iən/ principle; **im/aus P~** in/on principle. **p~iell** *a* ⟨*Frage*⟩ of principle ● *adv* on principle; (*im Prinzip*) in principle

Priorität *f* **-,-en** priority

Prise *f* **-,-n P~ Salz** pinch of salt

Prisma *nt* **-s,-men** prism

privat *a* private, *adv* -ly; (*persönlich*) personal. **P~adresse** *f* home address. **p~isieren** *vt* privatize

Privat|leben *nt* private life. **P~lehrer** *m* private tutor. **P~lehrerin** *f* governess. **P~patient(in)** *m(f)* private patient

Privileg *nt* **-[e]s,-ien** /-iən/ privilege. **p~iert** *a* privileged

pro *prep* (+*dat*) per. **Pro** *nt* **- das Pro und Kontra** the pros and cons *pl*

Probe *f* **-,-n** test, trial; (*Menge, Muster*) sample; (*Theat*) rehearsal; **auf die P~ stellen** put to the test. **P~fahrt** *f* test drive. **p~n** *vt/i* (*haben*) (*Theat*) rehearse. **p~weise** *adv* on a trial basis. **P~zeit** *f* probationary period

probieren *vt/i* (*haben*) try; (*kosten*) taste; (*proben*) rehearse

Problem *nt* **-s,-e** problem. **p~atisch** *a* problematic

problemlos *a* problem-free ● *adv* without any problems

Produkt *nt* **-[e]s,-e** product

Produk|tion /-'tsio:n/ *f* **-,-en** production. **p~tiv** *a* productive. **P~tivität** *f* **-** productivity

Produ|zent *m* **-en,-en** producer. **p~zieren** *vt* produce; **sich p~zieren** (*fam*) show off

professionell *a* professional, *adv* -ly

Professor *m* **-s,-en** /-'so:rən/ professor

Profi *m* **-s,-s** (*Sport*) professional

Profil *nt* **-s,-e** profile; (*Reifen-*) tread; (*fig*) image. **p~iert** *a* (*fig*) distinguished

Profit *m* **-[e]s,-e** profit. **p~ieren** *vi* (*haben*) profit (**von** from)

Prognose *f* **-,-n** forecast; (*Med*) prognosis

Programm *nt* **-s,-e** programme; (*Computer-*) program; (*TV*) channel; (*Comm: Sortiment*) range. **p~ieren** *vt/i* (*haben*) (*Computer*) program. **P~ierer(in)** *m* **-s,-** (*f* **-,-nen**) [computer] programmer

progressiv *a* progressive

Projekt *nt* **-[e]s,-e** project

Projektor *m* **-s,-en** /-'to:rən/ projector

projizieren *vt* project

Proklam|ation /-'tsio:n/ *f* **-,-en** proclamation. **p~ieren** *vt* proclaim

Prolet *m* **-en,-en** boor. **P~ariat** *nt* **-[e]s** proletariat. **P~arier** /-iɐ/ *m* **-s,-** proletarian

Prolog *m* **-s,-e** prologue

Promenade *f* **-,-n** promenade. **P~nmischung** *f* (*fam*) mongrel

Promille *pl* (*fam*) alcohol level *sg* in the blood; **zuviel P~ haben** (*fam*) be over the limit

prominen|t *a* prominent. **P~z** *f* **-** prominent figures *pl*

Promiskuität *f* **-** promiscuity

promovieren *vi* (*haben*) obtain one's doctorate

prompt *a* prompt, *adv* -ly; (*fam: natürlich*) of course

Pronomen *nt* **-s,-** pronoun

Propag|anda *f* **-** propaganda; (*Reklame*) publicity. **p~ieren** *vt* propagate

Propeller *m* **-s,-** propeller

Prophet *m* **-en,-en** prophet. **p~isch** *a* prophetic

prophezei|en *vt* prophesy. **P~ung** *f* **-,-en** prophecy

Proportion /-'tsio:n/ *f* **-,-en** proportion. **p~al** *a* proportional. **p~iert** *a* **gut p~iert** well proportioned

Prosa *f* **-** prose

prosaisch *a* prosaic, *adv* -ally

prosit *int* cheers!

Prospekt *m* **-[e]s,-e** brochure; (*Comm*) prospectus

prost *int* cheers!

Prostitu|ierte *f* **-n,-n** prostitute. **P~tion** /-'tsio:n/ *f* **-** prostitution

Protest *m* **-[e]s,-e** protest

Protestant|(in) *m* **-en,-en** (*f* **-,-nen**) (*Relig*) Protestant. **p~isch** *a* (*Relig*) Protestant

protestieren *vi* (*haben*) protest

Prothese *f* **-,-n** artificial limb; (*Zahn-*) denture

Protokoll *nt* **-s,-e** record; (*Sitzungs-*) minutes *pl*; (*diplomatisches*) protocol; (*Strafzettel*) ticket

Prototyp *m* **-s,-en** prototype

protz|en *vi* (*haben*) show off (**mit etw** sth). **p~ig** *a* ostentatious

Proviant *m* **-s** provisions *pl*
Provinz *f* **-,-en** province. **p~iell** *a* provincial
Provision *f* **-,-en** (*Comm*) commission
provisorisch *a* provisional, *adv* -ly, temporary, *adv* -ily
Provokation /-'tsi̯o:n/ *f* **-,-en** provocation
provozieren *vt* provoke. **p~d** *a* provocative, *adv* -ly
Prozedur *f* **-,-en** [lengthy] business
Prozent *nt* **-[e]s,-e** & **-** per cent; **5 P~** 5 per cent. **P~satz** *m* percentage. **p~ual** *a* percentage ...
Prozeß *m* **-sses,-sse** process; (*Jur*) lawsuit; (*Kriminal-*) trial
Prozession *f* **-,-en** procession
prüde *a* prudish
prüf|en *vt* test/(*über-*) check (**auf** + *acc* for); audit ⟨*Bücher*⟩; (*Sch*) examine; **p~ender Blick** searching look. **P~er** *m* **-s,-** inspector; (*Buch-*) auditor; (*Sch*) examiner. **P~ling** *m* **-s,-e** examination candidate. **P~ung** *f* **-,-en** examination; (*Test*) test; (*Bücher-*) audit; (*fig*) trial
Prügel *m* **-s,-** cudgel; **P~** *pl* hiding *sg*, beating *sg*. **P~ei** *f* **-,-en** brawl, fight. **p~n** *vt* beat, thrash; **sich p~n** fight, brawl
Prunk *m* **-[e]s** magnificence, splendour. **p~en** *vi* (*haben*) show off (**mit etw** sth). **p~voll** *a* magnificent, *adv* -ly
prusten *vi* (*haben*) splutter; (*schnauben*) snort
Psalm *m* **-s,-en** psalm
Pseudonym *nt* **-s,-e** pseudonym
pst *int* shush!
Psychi|ater *m* **-s,-** psychiatrist. **P~atrie** *f* **-** psychiatry. **p~atrisch** *a* psychiatric
psychisch *a* psychological, *adv* -ly; (*Med*) mental, *adv* -ly
Psycho|analyse *f* psychoanalysis. **P~loge** *m* **-n,-n** psychologist. **P~logie** *f* **-** psychology. **p~logisch** *a* psychological, *adv* -ly
Pubertät *f* **-** puberty
publik *a* **p~ werden/machen** become/make public
Publi|kum *nt* **-s** public; (*Zuhörer*) audience; (*Zuschauer*) spectators *pl*. **p~zieren** *vt* publish
Pudding *m* **-s,-s** blancmange; (*im Wasserbad gekocht*) pudding
Pudel *m* **-s,-** poodle
Puder *m* & (*fam*) *nt* **-s,-** powder; (*Körper-*) talcum [powder]. **P~dose** *f* [powder] compact. **p~n** *vt* powder. **P~zucker** *m* icing sugar
Puff[1] *m* **-[e]s,⸚e** push, poke
Puff[2] *m* & *nt* **-s,-s** (*sl*) brothel
puffen *vt* (*fam*) poke • *vi* (*sein*) puff along
Puffer *m* **-s,-** (*Rail*) buffer; (*Culin*) pancake. **P~zone** *f* buffer zone
Pull|i *m* **-s,-s** jumper. **P~over** *m* **-s,-** jumper; (*Herren-*) pullover
Puls *m* **-es** pulse. **P~ader** *f* artery. **p~ieren** *vi* (*haben*) pulsate
Pult *nt* **-[e]s,-e** desk; (*Lese-*) lectern
Pulver *nt* **-s,-** powder. **p~ig** *a* powdery. **p~isieren** *vt* pulverize
Pulver|kaffee *m* instant coffee. **P~schnee** *m* powder snow
pummelig *a* (*fam*) chubby
Pump *m* **auf P~** (*fam*) on tick
Pumpe *f* **-,-n** pump. **p~n** *vt/i* (*haben*) pump; (*fam: leihen*) lend; [**sich** (*dat*)] **etw p~n** (*fam: borgen*) borrow sth
Pumps /pœmps/ *pl* court shoes
Punkt *m* **-[e]s,-e** dot; (*Tex*) spot; (*Geom, Sport & fig*) point; (*Gram*) full stop, period; **P~ sechs Uhr** at six o'clock sharp; **nach P~en siegen** win on points. **p~iert** *a* ⟨*Linie, Note*⟩ dotted
pünktlich *a* punctual, *adv* -ly. **P~keit** *f* **-** punctuality
Punsch *m* **-[e]s,-e** [hot] punch
Pupille *f* **-,-n** (*Anat*) pupil
Puppe *f* **-,-n** doll; (*Marionette*) puppet; (*Schaufenster-, Schneider-*) dummy; (*Zool*) chrysalis
pur *a* pure; (*fam: bloß*) sheer; **Whisky pur** neat whisky
Püree *nt* **-s,-s** purée; (*Kartoffel-*) mashed potatoes *pl*
puritanisch *a* puritanical
purpurrot *a* crimson
Purzel|baum *m* (*fam*) somersault. **p~n** *vi* (*sein*) (*fam*) tumble
pusseln *vi* (*haben*) (*fam*) potter
Puste *f* **-** (*fam*) breath; **aus der P~** out of breath. **p~n** *vt/i* (*haben*) (*fam*) blow
Pute *f* **-,-n** turkey; (*Henne*) turkey hen. **P~r** *m* **-s,-** turkey cock
Putsch *m* **-[e]s,-e** coup
Putz *m* **-es** plaster; (*Staat*) finery. **p~en** *vt* clean; (*Aust*) dry-clean; (*zieren*) adorn; **sich p~en** dress up; **sich** (*dat*) **die Zähne/Nase p~en** clean one's teeth/blow one's nose. **P~frau** *f* cleaner, charwoman. **p~ig** *a* (*fam*) amusing, cute; (*seltsam*) odd. **P~macherin** *f* **-,-nen** milliner

Puzzlespiel /'pazl-/ *nt* jigsaw
Pyramide *f* **-,-n** pyramid

Q

Quacksalber *m* **-s,-** quack
Quadrat *nt* **-[e]s,-e** square. **q~isch** *a* square. **Q~meter** *m & nt* square metre
quaken *vi* (*haben*) quack; ⟨*Frosch:*⟩ croak
quäken *vi* (*haben*) screech; ⟨*Baby:*⟩ whine
Quäker(in) *m* **-s,-** (*f* **-,-nen**) Quaker
Qual *f* **-,-en** torment; (*Schmerz*) agony
quälen *vt* torment; (*foltern*) torture; (*bedrängen*) pester; **sich q~** torment oneself; (*leiden*) suffer; (*sich mühen*) struggle. **q~d** *a* agonizing
Quälerei *f* **-,-en** torture; (*Qual*) agony
Quälgeist *m* (*fam*) pest
Qualifi|kation /-'tsi̯o:n/ *f* **-,-en** qualification. **q~zieren** *vt* qualify; **sich q~zieren** qualify. **q~ziert** *a* qualified; (*fähig*) competent; ⟨*Arbeit*⟩ skilled
Qualität *f* **-,-en** quality
Qualle *f* **-,-n** jellyfish
Qualm *m* **-s** [thick] smoke. **q~en** *vi* (*haben*) smoke
qualvoll *a* agonizing
Quantität *f* **-,-en** quantity
Quantum *nt* **-s,-ten** quantity; (*Anteil*) share, quota
Quarantäne *f* **-** quarantine
Quark *m* **-s** quark, ≈ curd cheese; (*fam: Unsinn*) rubbish
Quartal *nt* **-s,-e** quarter
Quartett *nt* **-[e]s,-e** quartet
Quartier *nt* **-s,-e** accommodation; (*Mil*) quarters *pl*; **ein Q~ suchen** look for accommodation
Quarz *m* **-es** quartz
quasseln *vi* (*haben*) (*fam*) jabber
Quaste *f* **-,-n** tassel
Quatsch *m* **-[e]s** (*fam*) nonsense, rubbish; **Q~ machen** (*Unfug machen*) fool around; (*etw falsch machen*) do a silly thing. **q~en** (*fam*) *vi* (*haben*) talk; (*schwatzen*) natter; ⟨*Wasser, Schlamm:*⟩squelch ● *vt* talk. **q~naß** *a* (*fam*) soaking wet
Quecksilber *nt* mercury
Quelle *f* **-,-n** spring; (*Fluß- & fig*) source. **q~n**† *vi* (*sein*) well [up]/ (*fließen*) pour (**aus** from); (*aufquellen*) swell; (*hervortreten*) bulge
quengeln *vi* (*fam*) whine; ⟨*Baby:*⟩ grizzle
quer *adv* across, crosswise; (*schräg*) diagonally
Quere *f* **- der Q~ nach** across, crosswise; **jdm in die Q~ kommen** get in s.o.'s way
querfeldein *adv* across country
quer|gestreift *a* horizontally striped. **q~köpfig** *a* (*fam*) awkward. **Q~latte** *f* crossbar. **Q~schiff** *nt* transept. **Q~schnitt** *m* cross-section. **q~schnittsgelähmt** *a* paraplegic. **Q~straße** *f* side-street; **die erste Q~straße links** the first turning on the left. **Q~verweis** *m* cross-reference
quetsch|en *vt* squash; (*drücken*) squeeze; (*zerdrücken*) crush; (*Culin*) mash; **sich q~en in** (+*acc*) squeeze into; **sich** (*dat*) **den Arm q~en** bruise one's arm. **Q~ung** *f* **-,-en, Q~wunde** *f* bruise
Queue /kø:/ *nt* **-s,-s** cue
quicklebendig *a* very lively
quieken *vi* (*haben*) squeal; ⟨*Maus:*⟩ squeak
quietschen *vi* (*haben*) squeal; ⟨*Tür, Dielen:*⟩ creak
Quintett *nt* **-[e]s,-e** quintet
Quirl *m* **-[e]s,-e** blender with a star-shaped head. **q~en** *vt* mix
quitt *a* **q~ sein** (*fam*) be quits
Quitte *f* **-,-n** quince
quittieren *vt* receipt ⟨*Rechnung*⟩; sign for ⟨*Geldsumme, Sendung*⟩; (*reagieren auf*) greet (**mit** with); **den Dienst q~** resign
Quittung *f* **-,-en** receipt
Quiz /kvɪs/ *nt* **-,-** quiz
Quote *f* **-,-n** proportion

R

Rabatt *m* **-[e]s,-e** discount
Rabatte *f* **-,-n** (*Hort*) border
Rabattmarke *f* trading stamp
Rabbiner *m* **-s,-** rabbi
Rabe *m* **-n,-n** raven. **r~nschwarz** *a* pitch-black
rabiat *a* violent, *adv* -ly; (*wütend*) furious, *adv* -ly
Rache *f* **-** revenge, vengeance
Rachen *m* **-s,-** pharynx; (*Maul*) jaws *pl*

rächen *vt* avenge; **sich r~** take revenge (**an** + *dat* on); ⟨*Fehler, Leichtsinn:*⟩ cost s.o. dear
Racker *m* **-s,-** (*fam*) rascal
Rad *nt* **-[e]s,¨er** wheel; (*Fahr-*) bicycle, (*fam*) bike
Radar *m & nt* **-s** radar
Radau *m* **-s** (*fam*) din, racket
radebrechen *vt/i* (*haben*) **[Deutsch/Englisch] r~** speak broken German/English
radeln *vi* (*sein*) (*fam*) cycle
Rädelsführer *m* ringleader
radfahr|en† *vi sep* (*sein*) cycle; **ich fahre gern Rad** I like cycling. **R~er(in)** *m(f)* **-s,-** (*f* **-,-nen**) cyclist
radier|en *vt/i* (*haben*) rub out; (*Kunst*) etch. **R~gummi** *m* eraser, rubber. **R~ung** *f* **-,-en** etching
Radieschen /-'di:sçən/ *nt* **-s,-** radish
radikal *a* radical, *adv* -ly; (*drastisch*) drastic, *adv* -ally. **R~e(r)** *m/f* (*Pol*) radical
Radio *nt* **-s,-s** radio
radioaktiv *a* radioactive. **R~ität** *f* **-** radioactivity
Radioapparat *m* radio [set]
Radius *m* **-,-ien** /-i̯ən/ radius
Rad|kappe *f* hub-cap. **R~ler** *m* **-s,-** cyclist; (*Getränk*) shandy. **R~weg** *m* cycle track
raff|en *vt* grab; (*kräuseln*) gather; (*kürzen*) condense. **r~gierig** *a* avaricious
Raffin|ade *f* **-** refined sugar. **R~erie** *f* **-,-n** refinery. **R~esse** *f* **-,-n** refinement; (*Schlauheit*) cunning. **r~ieren** *vt* refine. **r~iert** *a* ingenious, *adv* -ly; (*durchtrieben*) crafty, *adv* -ily
Rage /'ra:ʒə/ *f* **-** (*fam*) fury
ragen *vi* (*haben*) rise [up]
Rahm *m* **-s** (*SGer*) cream
rahmen *vt* frame. **R~** *m* **-s,-** frame; (*fig*) framework; (*Grenze*) limits *pl*; (*einer Feier*) setting
Rain *m* **-[e]s,-e** grass verge
räkeln *v* = **rekeln**
Rakete *f* **-,-n** rocket; (*Mil*) missile
Rallye /'rali/ *nt* **-s,-s** rally
rammen *vt* ram
Rampe *f* **-,-n** ramp; (*Theat*) front of the stage. **R~nlicht** *nt* **im R~nlicht stehen** (*fig*) be in the limelight
ramponier|en *vt* (*fam*) damage; (*ruinieren*) ruin; **r~t** battered
Ramsch *m* **-[e]s** junk. **R~laden** *m* junk-shop
ran *adv* = **heran**

Rand *m* **-[e]s,¨er** edge; (*Teller-, Gläser-, Brillen-*) rim; (*Zier-*) border, edging; (*Buch-, Brief-*) margin; (*Stadt-*) outskirts *pl*; (*Ring*) ring; **am R~e des Ruins** on the brink of ruin; **am R~e erwähnen** mention in passing; **zu R~e kommen mit** (*fam*) cope with; **außer R~ und Band** (*fam: ausgelassen*) very boisterous
randalieren *vi* (*haben*) rampage
Rand|bemerkung *f* marginal note. **R~streifen** *m* (*Auto*) hard shoulder
Rang *m* **-[e]s,¨e** rank; (*Theat*) tier; **erster/zweiter R~** (*Theat*) dress/upper circle; **ersten R~es** first-class
rangieren /raŋ'ʒi:rən/ *vt* shunt ● *vi* (*haben*) rank (**vor** + *dat* before); **an erster Stelle r~** come first
Rangordnung *f* order of importance; (*Hierarchie*) hierarchy
Ranke *f* **-,-n** tendril; (*Trieb*) shoot
ranken (sich) *vr* (*Bot*) trail; (*in die Höhe*) climb; **sich r~ um** twine around
Ranzen *m* **-s,-** (*Sch*) satchel
ranzig *a* rancid
Rappe *m* **-n,-n** black horse
rappeln *v* (*fam*) ● *vi* (*haben*) rattle ● *vr* **sich r~** pick oneself up; (*fig*) rally
Raps *m* **-es** (*Bot*) rape
rar *a* rare; **er macht sich rar** (*fam*) we don't see much of him. **R~ität** *f* **-,-en** rarity
rasant *a* fast; (*schnittig, schick*) stylish ● *adv* fast; stylishly
rasch *a* quick, *adv* -ly
rascheln *vi* (*haben*) rustle
Rasen *m* **-s,-** lawn
rasen *vi* (*sein*) tear [along]; ⟨*Puls:*⟩ race; ⟨*Zeit:*⟩ fly; **gegen eine Mauer r~** career into a wall ● *vi* (*haben*) rave; ⟨*Sturm:*⟩ rage; **vor Begeisterung r~** go wild with enthusiasm. **r~d** *a* furious; (*tobend*) raving; ⟨*Sturm, Durst*⟩ raging; ⟨*Schmerz*⟩ excruciating; ⟨*Beifall*⟩ tumultuous ● *adv* terribly
Rasenmäher *m* lawn-mower
Raserei *f* **-** speeding; (*Toben*) frenzy
Rasier|apparat *m* razor. **r~en** *vt* shave; **sich r~en** shave. **R~klinge** *f* razor blade. **R~pinsel** *m* shaving-brush. **R~wasser** *nt* aftershave [lotion]
Raspel *f* **-,-n** rasp; (*Culin*) grater. **r~n** *vt* grate
Rasse *f* **-,-n** race. **R~hund** *m* pedigree dog

Rassel *f* **-,-n** rattle. **r~n** *vi* (*haben*) rattle; ⟨*Schlüssel:*⟩ jangle; ⟨*Kette:*⟩ clank ● *vi* (*sein*) rattle [along]

Rassen|diskriminierung *f* racial discrimination. **R~trennung** *f* racial segregation

Rassepferd *nt* thoroughbred

rassisch *a* racial

Rassis|mus *m* **-** racism. **r~tisch** *a* racist

Rast *f* **-,-en** rest. **r~en** *vi* (*haben*) rest. **R~haus** *nt* motorway restaurant. **r~los** *a* restless, *adv* -ly; (*ununterbrochen*) ceaseless, *adv* -ly. **R~platz** *m* picnic area. **R~stätte** *f* motorway restaurant [and services]

Rasur *f* **-,-en** shave

Rat[1] *m* **-[e]s** [piece of] advice; **guter Rat** good advice; **zu Rat[e] ziehen** consult; **sich** (*dat*) **keinen Rat wissen** not know what to do

Rat[2] *m* **-[e]s,⸚e** (*Admin*) council; (*Person*) councillor

Rate *f* **-,-n** instalment

raten† *vt* guess; (*empfehlen*) advise ● *vi* (*haben*) guess; **jdm r~** advise s.o.

Ratenzahlung *f* payment by instalments

Rat|geber *m* **-s,-** adviser; (*Buch*) guide. **R~haus** *nt* town hall

ratifizier|en *vt* ratify. **R~ung** *f* **-,-en** ratification

Ration /ra'tsi̯o:n/ *f* **-,-en** ration; **eiserne R~** iron rations *pl*. **r~al** *a* rational, *adv* -ly. **r~alisieren** *vt/i* (*haben*) rationalize. **r~ell** *a* efficient, *adv* -ly. **r~ieren** *vt* ration

rat|los *a* helpless, *adv* -ly; **r~los sein** not know what to do. **r~sam** *pred a* advisable; (*klug*) prudent. **R~schlag** *m* piece of advice; **R~schläge** advice *sg*

Rätsel *nt* **-s,-** riddle; (*Kreuzwort-*) puzzle; (*Geheimnis*) mystery. **r~haft** *a* puzzling, mysterious. **r~n** *vi* (*haben*) puzzle

Ratte *f* **-,-n** rat

rattern *vi* (*haben*) rattle ● *vi* (*sein*) rattle [along]

Raub *m* **-[e]s** robbery; (*Menschen-*) abduction; (*Beute*) loot, booty. **r~en** *vt* steal; abduct ⟨*Menschen*⟩; **jdm etw r~en** rob s.o. of sth

Räuber *m* **-s,-** robber

Raub|mord *m* robbery with murder. **R~tier** *nt* predator. **R~überfall** *m* robbery. **R~vogel** *m* bird of prey

Rauch *m* **-[e]s** smoke. **r~en** *vt/i* (*haben*) smoke. **R~en** *nt* **-s** smoking; **'R~en verboten'** 'no smoking'. **R~er** *m* **-s,-** smoker. **R~erabteil** *nt* smoking compartment

Räucher|lachs *m* smoked salmon. **r~n** *vt* (*Culin*) smoke

Rauch|fang *m* (*Aust*) chimney. **r~ig** *a* smoky. **R~verbot** *nt* smoking ban

räudig *a* mangy

rauf *adv* = **herauf, hinauf**

rauf|en *vt* pull; **sich** (*dat*) **die Haare r~en** (*fig*) tear one's hair ● *vr/i* (*haben*) **[sich] r~en** fight. **R~erei** *f* **-,-en** fight

rauh *a* rough, *adv* -ly; (*unfreundlich*) gruff, *adv* -ly; ⟨*Klima, Wind*⟩ harsh, raw; ⟨*Landschaft*⟩ rugged; (*heiser*) husky; ⟨*Hals*⟩ sore

Rauheit *f* **-** (*s.* **rauh**) roughness; gruffness; harshness; ruggedness

rauh|haarig *a* wire-haired. **R~reif** *m* hoar-frost

Raum *m* **-[e]s, Räume** room; (*Gebiet*) area; (*Welt-*) space

räumen *vt* clear; vacate ⟨*Wohnung*⟩; evacuate ⟨*Gebäude, Gebiet,* (*Mil*) *Stellung*⟩; (*bringen*) put (**in/auf** + *acc* into/on); (*holen*) get (**aus** out of); **beiseite r~** move/put to one side; **aus dem Weg r~** (*fam*) get rid of

Raum|fahrer *m* astronaut. **R~fahrt** *f* space travel. **R~fahrzeug** *nt* spacecraft. **R~flug** *m* space flight. **R~inhalt** *m* volume

räumlich *a* spatial. **R~keiten** *fpl* rooms

Raum|pflegerin *f* cleaner. **R~schiff** *nt* spaceship

Räumung *f* **-** (*s.* **räumen**) clearing; vacating; evacuation. **R~sverkauf** *m* clearance/closing-down sale

raunen *vt/i* (*haben*) whisper

Raupe *f* **-,-n** caterpillar

raus *adv* = **heraus, hinaus**

Rausch *m* **-[e]s, Räusche** intoxication; (*fig*) exhilaration; **einen R~ haben** be drunk

rauschen *vi* (*haben*) ⟨*Wasser, Wind:*⟩ rush; ⟨*Bäume, Blätter:*⟩ rustle ● *vi* (*sein*) rush [along]; **aus dem Zimmer r~** sweep out of the room. **r~d** *a* rushing; rustling; ⟨*Applaus*⟩ tumultuous

Rauschgift *nt* [narcotic] drug; (*coll*) drugs *pl*. **R~süchtige(r)** *m/f* drug addict

räuspern (sich) *vr* clear one's throat

rausschmeiß|en† *vt sep (fam)* throw out; *(entlassen)* sack. **R∼er** *m* **-s,-** *(fam)* bouncer

Raute *f* **-,-n** diamond

Razzia *f* **-,-ien** /-i̯ən/ [police] raid

Reagenzglas *nt* test-tube

reagieren *vi (haben)* react (**auf** + *acc* to)

Reaktion /-ˈtsi̯oːn/ *f* **-,-en** reaction. **r∼är** *a* reactionary

Reaktor *m* **-s,-en** /-ˈtoːrən/ reactor

real *a* real; *(gegenständlich)* tangible; *(realistisch)* realistic, *adv* -ally. **r∼isieren** *vt* realize

Realis|mus *m* **-** realism. **R∼t** *m* **-en,-en** realist. **r∼tisch** *a* realistic, *adv* -ally

Realität *f* **-,-en** reality

Realschule *f* ≈ secondary modern school

Rebe *f* **-,-n** vine

Rebell *m* **-en,-en** rebel. **r∼ieren** *vi (haben)* rebel. **R∼ion** *f* **-,-en** rebellion

rebellisch *a* rebellious

Rebhuhn *nt* partridge

Rebstock *m* vine

Rechen *m* **-s,-** rake. **r∼** *vt/i (haben)* rake

Rechen|aufgabe *f* arithmetical problem; *(Sch)* sum. **R∼fehler** *m* arithmetical error. **R∼maschine** *f* calculator

Rechenschaft *f* **- R∼ ablegen** give account (**über** + *acc* of); **jdn zur R∼ ziehen** call s.o. to account

recherchieren /reʃɛrˈʃiːrən/ *vt/i (haben)* investigate; *(Journ)* research

rechnen *vi (haben)* do arithmetic; *(schätzen)* reckon; *(zählen)* count (**zu** among; **auf** + *acc* on); **r∼ mit** reckon with; *(erwarten)* expect; **gut r∼ können** be good at figures ● *vt* calculate, work out; do ‹*Aufgabe*›; *(dazu-)* add (**zu** to); *(fig)* count (**zu** among). **R∼** *nt* **-s** arithmetic

Rechner *m* **-s,-** calculator; *(Computer)* computer; **ein guter R∼ sein** be good at figures

Rechnung *f* **-,-en** bill, *(Amer)* check; *(Comm)* invoice; *(Berechnung)* calculation; **R∼ führen über** (+*acc*) keep account of; **etw** *(dat)* **R∼ tragen** *(fig)* take sth into account. **R∼sjahr** *nt* financial year. **R∼sprüfer** *m* auditor

Recht *nt* **-[e]s,-e** law; *(Berechtigung)* right (**auf** + *acc* to); **im R∼ sein** be in the right; **mit** *od* **zu R∼** rightly; **von R∼s wegen** by right; *(eigentlich)* by rights

recht *a* right; *(wirklich)* real; **ich habe keine r∼e Lust** I don't really feel like it; **es jdm r∼ machen** please s.o.; **jdm r∼ sein** be all right with s.o. ● **r∼ haben/behalten** be right; **r∼ bekommen** be proved right; **jdm r∼ geben** agree with s.o. ● *adv* correctly; *(ziemlich)* quite; *(sehr)* very; **r∼ vielen Dank** many thanks

Recht|e *f* **-n,-[n]** right side; *(Hand)* right hand; *(Boxen)* right; **die R∼e** *(Pol)* the right; **zu meiner R∼en** on my right. **r∼e(r,s)** *a* right; *(Pol)* right-wing; **r∼e Masche** plain stitch. **R∼e(r)** *m/f* **der/die R∼e** the right man/woman; **du bist mir der/die R∼e!** you're a fine one! **R∼e(s)** *nt* **das R∼e** the right thing; **etwas R∼es lernen** learn something useful; **nach dem R∼en sehen** see that everything is all right

Rechteck *nt* **-[e]s,-e** rectangle. **r∼ig** *a* rectangular

rechtfertig|en *vt* justify; **sich r∼en** justify oneself. **R∼ung** *f* **-** justification

recht|haberisch *a* opinionated. **r∼lich** *a* legal, *adv* -ly. **r∼mäßig** *a* legitimate, *adv* -ly

rechts *adv* on the right; *(bei Stoff)* on the right side; **von/nach r∼** from/to the right; **zwei r∼, zwei links stricken** knit two, purl two. **R∼anwalt** *m*, **R∼anwältin** *f* lawyer

rechtschaffen *a* upright; *(ehrlich)* honest, *adv* -ly; **r∼ müde** thoroughly tired

rechtschreib|en *vi (inf only)* spell correctly. **R∼fehler** *m* spelling mistake. **R∼ung** *f* **-** spelling

Rechts|händer(in) *m* **-s,-** (*f* **-,-nen**) right-hander. **r∼händig** *a & adv* right-handed. **r∼kräftig** *a* legal, *adv* -ly. **R∼streit** *m* law suit. **R∼verkehr** *m* driving on the right. **r∼widrig** *a* illegal, *adv* -ly. **R∼wissenschaft** *f* jurisprudence

recht|winklig *a* right-angled. **r∼zeitig** *a & adv* in time

Reck *nt* **-[e]s,-e** horizontal bar

recken *vt* stretch; **sich r∼** stretch; **den Hals r∼** crane one's neck

Redakteur /redakˈtøːɐ̯/ *m* **-s,-e** editor; *(Radio, TV)* producer

Redaktion /-ˈtsi̯oːn/ *f* **-,-en** editing; *(Radio, TV)* production; *(Abteilung)*

editorial/production department. **r~ell** *a* editorial

Rede *f* **-,-n** speech; **zur R~ stellen** demand an explanation from; **davon ist keine R~** there's no question of it; **nicht der R~ wert** not worth mentioning. **r~gewandt** *a* eloquent, *adv* -ly

reden *vi* (*haben*) talk (**von** about; **mit** to); (*eine Rede halten*) speak ● *vt* talk; speak ⟨*Wahrheit*⟩; **kein Wort r~** not say a word. **R~sart** *f* saying; (*Phrase*) phrase

Redewendung *f* idiom

redigieren *vt* edit

redlich *a* honest, *adv* -ly

Red|ner *m* **-s,-** speaker. **r~selig** *a* talkative

reduzieren *vt* reduce

Reeder *m* **-s,-** shipowner. **R~ei** *f* **-,-en** shipping company

reell *a* real; (*ehrlich*) honest, *adv* -ly; ⟨*Preis, Angebot*⟩ fair

Refer|at *nt* **-[e]s,-e** report; (*Abhandlung*) paper; (*Abteilung*) section. **R~ent(in)** *m* **-en,-en** (*f* **-,-nen**) speaker; (*Sachbearbeiter*) expert. **R~enz** *f* **-,-en** reference. **r~ieren** *vi* (*haben*) deliver a paper; (*berichten*) report (**über** + *acc* on)

reflektieren *vt/i* (*haben*) reflect (**über** + *acc* on)

Reflex *m* **-es,-e** reflex; (*Widerschein*) reflection. **R~ion** *f* **-,-en** reflection. **r~iv** *a* reflexive. **R~ivpronomen** *nt* reflexive pronoun

Reform *f* **-,-en** reform. **R~ation** /-'tsi̯o:n/ *f* **-** (*Relig*) Reformation

Reform|haus *nt* health-food shop. **r~ieren** *vt* reform

Refrain /rəˈfrɛ̃:/ *m* **-s,-s** refrain

Regal *nt* **-s,-e** [set of] shelves *pl*

Regatta *f* **-,-ten** regatta

rege *a* active; (*lebhaft*) lively; (*geistig*) alert; ⟨*Handel*⟩ brisk ● *adv* actively

Regel *f* **-,-n** rule; (*Monats-*) period; **in der R~** as a rule. **r~mäßig** *a* regular, *adv* -ly. **r~n** *vt* regulate; direct ⟨*Verkehr*⟩; (*erledigen*) settle. **r~recht** *a* real, proper ● *adv* really. **R~ung** *f* **-,-en** regulation; settlement. **r~widrig** *a* irregular, *adv* -ly

regen *vt* move; **sich r~** move; (*wach werden*) stir

Regen *m* **-s,-** rain. **R~bogen** *m* rainbow. **R~bogenhaut** *f* iris

Regener|ation /-'tsi̯o:n/ *f* **-** regeneration. **r~ieren** *vt* regenerate; **sich r~ieren** regenerate

Regen|mantel *m* raincoat. **R~schirm** *m* umbrella. **R~tag** *m* rainy day. **R~tropfen** *m* raindrop. **R~wetter** *nt* wet weather. **R~wurm** *m* earthworm

Regie /reˈʒi:/ *f* **-** direction; **R~ führen** direct

regier|en *vt/i* (*haben*) govern, rule; ⟨*Monarch:*⟩ reign [over]; (*Gram*) take. **r~end** *a* ruling; reigning. **R~ung** *f* **-,-en** government; (*Herrschaft*) rule; (*eines Monarchen*) reign

Regime /reˈʒi:m/ *nt* **-s,-** /-mə/ regime

Regiment[1] *nt* **-[e]s,-er** regiment

Regiment[2] *nt* **-[e]s,-e** rule

Region *f* **-,-en** region. **r~al** *a* regional, *adv* -ly

Regisseur /reʒɪˈsø:ɐ̯/ *m* **-s,-e** director

Register *nt* **-s,-** register; (*Inhaltsverzeichnis*) index; (*Orgel-*) stop

registrier|en *vt* register; (*Techn*) record. **R~kasse** *f* cash register

Regler *m* **-s,-** regulator

reglos *a & adv* motionless

regn|en *vi* (*haben*) rain; **es r~et** it is raining. **r~erisch** *a* rainy

regul|är *a* normal, *adv* -ly; (*rechtmäßig*) legitimate, *adv* -ly. **r~ieren** *vt* regulate

Regung *f* **-,-en** movement; (*Gefühls-*) emotion. **r~slos** *a & adv* motionless

Reh *nt* **-[e]s,-e** roe-deer; (*Culin*) venison

Rehabilit|ation /-'tsi̯o:n/ *f* **-** rehabilitation. **r~ieren** *vt* rehabilitate

Rehbock *m* roebuck

Reib|e *f* **-,-n** grater. **r~en**† *vt* rub; (*Culin*) grate; **blank r~en** polish ● *vi* (*haben*) rub. **R~ereien** *fpl* (*fam*) friction *sg*. **R~ung** *f* **-** friction. **r~ungslos** *a* (*fig*) smooth, *adv* -ly

reich *a* rich (**an** + *dat* in), *adv* -ly; (*r~haltig*) abundant, *adv* -ly

Reich *nt* **-[e]s,-e** empire; (*König-*) kingdom; (*Bereich*) realm

Reich|e(r) *m/f* rich man/woman; **die R~en** the rich *pl*

reichen *vt* hand; (*anbieten*) offer ● *vi* (*haben*) be enough; (*in der Länge*) be long enough; **r~ bis zu** reach [up to]; (*sich erstrecken*) extend to; **mit dem Geld r~** have enough money; **mir reicht's!** I've had enough!

reich|haltig *a* extensive, large; ⟨*Mahlzeit*⟩ substantial. **r~lich** *a* ample; ⟨*Vorrat*⟩ abundant, plentiful;

eine r~liche Stunde a good hour ● *adv* amply; abundantly; (*fam: sehr*) very. **R~tum** *m* **-s,-tümer** wealth (**an** + *dat* of); **R~tümer** riches. **R~weite** *f* reach; (*Techn, Mil*) range

Reif *m* **-[e]s** [hoar-]frost

reif *a* ripe; (*fig*) mature; **r~ für** ready for. **R~e** *f* - ripeness; (*fig*) maturity. **r~en** *vi* (*sein*) ripen; ⟨*Wein, Käse & fig*⟩ mature

Reifen *m* **-s,-** hoop; (*Arm-*) bangle; (*Auto-*) tyre. **R~druck** *m* tyre pressure. **R~panne** *f* puncture, flat tyre

Reifeprüfung *f* ≈ A levels *pl*

reiflich *a* careful, *adv* -ly

Reihe *f* **-,-n** row; (*Anzahl & Math*) series; **der R~ nach** in turn; **außer der R~** out of turn; **wer ist an der** *od* **kommt an die R~?** whose turn is it? **r~n (sich)** *vr* **sich r~n an** (+*acc*) follow. **R~nfolge** *f* order. **R~nhaus** *nt* terraced house. **r~nweise** *adv* in rows; (*fam*) in large numbers

Reiher *m* **-s,-** heron

Reim *m* **-[e]s,-e** rhyme. **r~en** *vt* rhyme; **sich r~en** rhyme

rein¹ *a* pure; (*sauber*) clean; ⟨*Unsinn, Dummheit*⟩ sheer; **ins r~e schreiben** make a fair copy of; **ins r~e bringen** (*fig*) sort out ● *adv* purely; (*fam*) absolutely

rein² *adv* = **herein, hinein**

Reineclaude /rɛːnəˈkloːdə/ *f* **-,-n** greengage

Reinfall *m* (*fam*) let-down; (*Mißerfolg*) flop. **r~en**† *vi sep* (*sein*) fall in; (*fam*) be taken in (**auf** + *acc* by)

Rein|gewinn *m* net profit. **R~heit** *f* - purity

reinig|en *vt* clean; (*chemisch*) dry-clean. **R~ung** *f* **-,-en** cleaning; (*chemische*) dry-cleaning; (*Geschäft*) dry cleaner's

Reinkarnation /reʔɪnkarnaˈt̮si̯oːn/ *f* **-,-en** reincarnation

reinlegen *vt sep* put in; (*fam*) dupe; (*betrügen*) take for a ride

reinlich *a* clean. **R~keit** *f* - cleanliness

Rein|machefrau *f* cleaner. **R~schrift** *f* fair copy. **r~seiden** *a* pure silk

Reis *m* **-es** rice

Reise *f* **-,-n** journey; (*See-*) voyage; (*Urlaubs-, Geschäfts-*) trip. **R~andenken** *nt* souvenir. **R~büro** *nt* travel agency. **R~bus** *m* coach. **R~führer** *m* tourist guide; (*Buch*) guide. **R~gesellschaft** *f* tourist group. **R~leiter(in)** *m(f)* courier. **r~n** *vi* (*sein*) travel. **R~nde(r)** *m/f* traveller. **R~paß** *m* passport. **R~scheck** *m* traveller's cheque. **R~unternehmer, R~veranstalter** *m* **-s,-** tour operator. **R~ziel** *nt* destination

Reisig *nt* **-s** brushwood

Reißaus *m* **R~ nehmen** (*fam*) run away

Reißbrett *nt* drawing-board

reißen† *vt* tear; (*weg-*) snatch; (*töten*) kill; **Witze r~** crack jokes; **aus dem Schlaf r~** awaken rudely; **an sich** (*acc*) **r~** snatch; seize ⟨*Macht*⟩; **mit sich r~** sweep away; **sich r~ um** (*fam*) fight for; (*gern mögen*) be keen on; **hin und her gerissen sein** (*fig*) be torn ● *vi* (*sein*) tear; ⟨*Seil, Faden:*⟩ break ● *vi* (*haben*) **r~ an** (+*dat*) pull at. **r~d** *a* raging; ⟨*Tier*⟩ ferocious; ⟨*Schmerz*⟩ violent

Reißer *m* **-s,-** (*fam*) thriller; (*Erfolg*) big hit. **r~isch** *a* (*fam*) sensational

Reiß|nagel *m* = **R~zwecke. R~verschluß** *m* zip [fastener]. **R~wolf** *m* shredder. **R~zwecke** *f* **-,-n** drawing-pin, (*Amer*) thumbtack

reit|en† *vt/i* (*sein*) ride. **R~er(in)** *m* **-s,-** (*f* **-,-nen**) rider. **R~hose** *f* riding breeches *pl.* **R~pferd** *nt* saddle-horse. **R~schule** *f* riding-school. **R~weg** *m* bridle-path

Reiz *m* **-es,-e** stimulus; (*Anziehungskraft*) attraction, appeal; (*Charme*) charm. **r~bar** *a* irritable. **R~barkeit** *f* - irritability. **r~en** *vt* provoke; (*Med*) irritate; (*interessieren, locken*) appeal to, attract; arouse ⟨*Neugier*⟩; (*beim Kartenspiel*) bid. **r~end** *a* charming, *adv* -ly; (*entzückend*) delightful. **R~ung** *f* **-,-en** (*Med*) irritation. **r~voll** *a* attractive

rekapitulieren *vt/i* (*haben*) recapitulate

rekeln (sich) *vr* stretch; (*lümmeln*) sprawl

Reklamation /-ˈt̮si̯oːn/ *f* **-,-en** (*Comm*) complaint

Reklam|e *f* **-,-n** advertising, publicity; (*Anzeige*) advertisement; (*TV, Radio*) commercial; **R~e machen** advertise (**für etw** sth). **r~ieren** *vt* complain about; (*fordern*) claim ● *vi* (*haben*) complain

rekonstru|ieren *vt* reconstruct. **R~ktion** /-ˈt̮si̯oːn/ *f* **-,-en** reconstruction

Rekonvaleszenz *f* - convalescence
Rekord *m* **-[e]s,-e** record
Rekrut *m* **-en,-en** recruit. **r~ieren** *vt* recruit
Rek|tor *m* **-s,-en** /-'to:rən/ (*Sch*) head[master]; (*Univ*) vice-chancellor. **R~torin** *f* **-,-nen** head[mistress]; vice-chancellor
Relais /rə'lɛ:/ *nt* **-,-** /-s,-s/ (*Electr*) relay
relativ *a* relative, *adv* -ly. **R~pronomen** *nt* relative pronoun
relevan|t *a* relevant (**für** to). **R~z** *f* - relevance
Relief /rə'li̯ɛf/ *nt* **-s,-s** relief
Religi|on *f* **-,-en** religion; (*Sch*) religious education. **r~ös** *a* religious
Reling *f* **-,-s** (*Naut*) rail
Reliquie /re'li:kvi̯ə/ *f* **-,-n** relic
Remouladensoße /remu'la:dən-/ *f* ≈ tartar sauce
rempeln *vt* jostle; (*stoßen*) push
Ren *nt* **-s,-s** reindeer
Reneklode *f* **-,-n** greengage
Renn|auto *nt* racing car. **R~bahn** *f* race-track; (*Pferde-*) racecourse. **R~boot** *nt* speedboat. **r~en†** *vt/i* (*sein*) run; **um die Wette r~en** have a race. **R~en** *nt* **-s,-** race. **R~pferd** *nt* racehorse. **R~sport** *m* racing. **R~wagen** *m* racing car
renommiert *a* renowned; ⟨*Hotel, Firma*⟩ of repute
renovier|en *vt* renovate; redecorate ⟨*Zimmer*⟩. **R~ung** *f* - renovation; redecoration
rentabel *a* profitable, *adv* -bly
Rente *f* **-,-n** pension; **in R~ gehen** (*fam*) retire. **R~nversicherung** *f* pension scheme
Rentier *nt* reindeer
rentieren (sich) *vr* be profitable; (*sich lohnen*) be worth while
Rentner(in) *m* **-s,-** (*f* **-,-nen**) [old-age] pensioner
Reparatur *f* **-,-en** repair. **R~werkstatt** *f* repair workshop; (*Auto*) garage
reparieren *vt* repair, mend
repatriieren *vt* repatriate
Repertoire /repɛr'to̯a:ɐ̯/ *nt* **-s,-s** repertoire
Reportage /-'ta:ʒə/ *f* **-,-n** report
Reporter(in) *m* **-s,-** (*f* **-,-nen**) reporter
repräsent|ativ *a* representative (**für** of); (*eindrucksvoll*) imposing; (*Prestige verleihend*) prestigious. **r~ieren** *vt* represent ● *vi* (*haben*) perform official/social duties
Repress|alie /-li̯ə/ *f* **-,-n** reprisal. **r~iv** *a* repressive
Reprodu|ktion /-'t̮si̯o:n/ *f* **-,-en** reproduction. **r~zieren** *vt* reproduce
Reptil *nt* **-s,-ien** /-i̯ən/ reptile
Republik *f* **-,-en** republic. **r~anisch** *a* republican
requirieren *vt* (*Mil*) requisition
Requisiten *pl* (*Theat*) properties, (*fam*) props
Reservat *nt* **-[e]s,-e** reservation
Reserve *f* **-,-n** reserve; (*Mil, Sport*) reserves *pl*. **R~rad** *nt* spare wheel. **R~spieler** *m* reserve. **R~tank** *m* reserve tank
reservier|en *vt* reserve; **r~en lassen** book. **r~t** *a* reserved. **R~ung** *f* **-,-en** reservation
Reservoir /rezɛr'vo̯a:ɐ̯/ *nt* **-s,-s** reservoir
Resid|enz *f* **-,-en** residence. **r~ieren** *vi* (*haben*) reside
Resign|ation /-'t̮si̯o:n/ *f* - resignation. **r~ieren** *vi* (*haben*) (*fig*) give up. **r~iert** *a* resigned, *adv* -ly
resolut *a* resolute, *adv* -ly
Resolution /-'t̮si̯o:n/ *f* **-,-en** resolution
Resonanz *f* **-,-en** resonance; (*fig: Widerhall*) response
Respekt /-sp-, -ʃp-/ *m* **-[e]s** respect (**vor** + *dat* for). **r~abel** *a* respectable. **r~ieren** *vt* respect
respekt|los *a* disrespectful, *adv* -ly. **r~voll** *a* respectful, *adv* -ly
Ressort /rɛ'so:ɐ̯/ *nt* **-s,-s** department
Rest *m* **-[e]s,-e** remainder, rest; **R~e** remains; (*Essens-*) leftovers
Restaurant /rɛsto'rã:/ *nt* **-s,-s** restaurant
Restaur|ation /rɛstau̯ra't̮si̯o:n/ *f* - restoration. **r~ieren** *vt* restore
Rest|betrag *m* balance. **r~lich** *a* remaining. **r~los** *a* utter, *adv* -ly
Resultat *nt* **-[e]s,-e** result
Retorte *f* **-,-n** (*Chem*) retort. **R~nbaby** *nt* (*fam*) test-tube baby
rett|en *vt* save (**vor** + *dat* from); (*aus Gefahr befreien*) rescue; **sich r~en** save oneself; (*flüchten*) escape. **R~er** *m* **-s,-** rescuer; (*fig*) saviour
Rettich *m* **-s,-e** white radish
Rettung *f* **-,-en** rescue; (*fig*) salvation; **jds letzte R~** s.o.'s last hope. **R~sboot** *nt* lifeboat. **R~sdienst** *m* rescue service. **R~sgürtel** *m* lifebelt. **r~slos** *adv* hopelessly. **R~sring** *m* lifebelt. **R~swagen** *m* ambulance
retuschieren *vt* (*Phot*) retouch

Reu|e *f* - remorse; (*Relig*) repentance. **r~en** *vt* fill with remorse; **es reut mich nicht** I don't regret it. **r~ig** *a* penitent. **r~mütig** *a* contrite, *adv* -ly
Revanch|e /re'vã:ʃə/ *f* -,-**n** revenge; **R~e fordern** (*Sport*) ask for a return match. **r~ieren (sich)** *vr* take revenge; (*sich erkenntlich zeigen*) reciprocate (**mit** with); **sich für eine Einladung r~ieren** return an invitation
Revers /re've:ɐ̯/ *nt* -,- /-[s],-s/ lapel
revidieren *vt* revise; (*prüfen*) check
Revier *nt* -**s**,-**e** district; (*Zool & fig*) territory; (*Polizei-*) [police] station
Revision *f* -,-**en** revision; (*Prüfung*) check; (*Bücher-*) audit; (*Jur*) appeal
Revolte *f* -,-**n** revolt
Revolution /-'tsi̯o:n/ *f* -,-**en** revolution. **r~är** *a* revolutionary. **r~ieren** *vt* revolutionize
Revolver *m* -**s**,- revolver
Revue /rə'vy:/ *f* -,-**n** revue
Rezen|sent *m* -**en**,-**en** reviewer. **r~sieren** *vt* review. **R~sion** *f* -,-**en** review
Rezept *nt* -[**e**]**s**,-**e** prescription; (*Culin*) recipe
Rezeption /-'tsi̯o:n/ *f* -,-**en** reception
Rezession *f* -,-**en** recession
rezitieren *vt* recite
R-Gespräch *nt* reverse-charge call, (*Amer*) collect call
Rhabarber *m* -**s** rhubarb
Rhapsodie *f* -,-**n** rhapsody
Rhein *m* -**s** Rhine. **R~land** *nt* -**s** Rhineland. **R~wein** *m* hock
Rhetori|k *f* - rhetoric. **r~sch** *a* rhetorical
Rheum|a *nt* -**s** rheumatism. **r~atisch** *a* rheumatic. **R~atismus** *m* - rheumatism
Rhinozeros *nt* -[**ses**],-**se** rhinoceros
rhyth|misch /'rʏt-/ *a* rhythmic[al], *adv* -ally. **R~mus** *m* -,-**men** rhythm
Ribisel *f* -,-**n** (*Aust*) redcurrant
richten *vt* direct (**auf** + *acc* at); address ⟨*Frage, Briefe*⟩ (**an** + *acc* to); aim, train ⟨*Waffe*⟩ (**auf** + *acc* at); (*einstellen*) set; (*vorbereiten*) prepare; (*reparieren*) mend; (*hinrichten*) execute; (*SGer: ordentlich machen*) tidy; **in die Höhe r~** raise [up]; **das Wort an jdn r~** address s.o.; **sich r~** be directed (**auf** + *acc* at; **gegen** against); ⟨*Blick:*⟩ turn (**auf** + *acc* on); **sich r~ nach** comply with ⟨*Vorschrift, jds Wünschen*⟩; fit in with ⟨*jds Plänen*⟩; (*befolgen*) go by; (*abhängen*) depend on ● *vi* (*haben*) **r~ über** (+ *acc*) judge
Richter *m* -**s**,- judge
Richtfest *nt* topping-out ceremony
richtig *a* right, correct; (*wirklich, echt*) real; **das R~e** the right thing ● *adv* correctly; really; **die Uhr geht r~** the clock is right. **R~keit** *f* - correctness. **r~stellen** *vt sep* (*fig*) correct
Richtlinien *fpl* guidelines
Richtung *f* -,-**en** direction; (*fig*) trend
riechen† *vt/i* (*haben*) smell (**nach** of; **an etw** *dat* sth)
Riegel *m* -**s**,- bolt; (*Seife*) bar
Riemen *m* -**s**,- strap; (*Ruder*) oar
Riese *m* -**n**,-**n** giant
rieseln *vi* (*sein*) trickle; ⟨*Schnee:*⟩ fall lightly
Riesen|erfolg *m* huge success. **r~groß** *a* huge, enormous
riesig *a* huge; (*gewaltig*) enormous ● *adv* (*fam*) terribly
Riff *nt* -[**e**]**s**,-**e** reef
rigoros *a* rigorous, *adv* -ly
Rille *f* -,-**n** groove
Rind *nt* -**es**,-**er** ox; (*Kuh*) cow; (*Stier*) bull; (*R~fleisch*) beef; **R~er** cattle *pl*
Rinde *f* -,-**n** bark; (*Käse-*) rind; (*Brot-*) crust
Rinderbraten *m* roast beef
Rind|fleisch *nt* beef. **R~vieh** *nt* cattle *pl*; (*fam: Idiot*) idiot
Ring *m* -[**e**]**s**,-**e** ring
ringeln (sich) *vr* curl; ⟨*Schlange:*⟩ coil itself (**um** round)
ring|en† *vi* (*haben*) wrestle; (*fig*) struggle (**um/nach** for) ● *vt* wring ⟨*Hände*⟩. **R~en** *nt* -**s** wrestling. **R~er** *m* -**s**,- wrestler. **R~kampf** *m* wrestling match; (*als Sport*) wrestling. **R~richter** *m* referee
rings *adv* **r~ im Kreis** in a circle; **r~ um jdn/etw** all around s.o./sth. **r~herum, r~um** *adv* all around
Rinn|e *f* -,-**n** channel; (*Dach-*) gutter. **r~en**† *vi* (*sein*) run; ⟨*Sand:*⟩ trickle. **R~stein** *m* gutter
Rippe *f* -,-**n** rib. **R~nfellentzündung** *f* pleurisy. **R~nstoß** *m* dig in the ribs
Risiko *nt* -**s**,-**s** & -**ken** risk; **ein R~ eingehen** take a risk
risk|ant *a* risky. **r~ieren** *vt* risk
Riß *m* -**sses**,-**sse** tear; (*Mauer-*) crack; (*fig*) rift
rissig *a* cracked; ⟨*Haut*⟩ chapped
Rist *m* -[**e**]**s**,-**e** instep
Ritt *m* -[**e**]**s**,-**e** ride

Ritter *m* **-s,-** knight. **r~lich** *a* chivalrous, *adv* -ly. **R~lichkeit** *f* - chivalry
rittlings *adv* astride
Ritu|al *nt* **-s,-e** ritual. **r~ell** *a* ritual
Ritz *m* **-es,-e** scratch. **R~e** *f* **-,-n** crack; (*Fels-*) cleft; (*zwischen Betten, Vorhängen*) gap. **r~en** *vt* scratch
Rival|e *m* **-n,-n, R~in** *f* **-,-nen** rival. **r~isieren** *vi* (*haben*) compete (**mit** with). **r~isierend** *a* rival ... **R~ität** *f* **-,-en** rivalry
Robbe *f* **-,-n** seal. **r~n** *vi* (*sein*) crawl
Robe *f* **-,-n** gown; (*Talar*) robe
Roboter *m* **-s,-** robot
robust *a* robust
röcheln *vi* (*haben*) breathe stertorously
Rochen *m* **-s,-** (*Zool*) ray
Rock[1] *m* **-[e]s,¨e** skirt; (*Jacke*) jacket
Rock[2] *m* **-[s]** (*Mus*) rock
Rodel|bahn *f* toboggan run. **r~n** *vi* (*sein/haben*) toboggan. **R~schlitten** *m* toboggan
roden *vt* clear ⟨*Land*⟩; grub up ⟨*Stumpf*⟩
Rogen *m* **-s,-** [hard] roe
Roggen *m* **-s** rye
roh *a* rough; (*ungekocht*) raw; ⟨*Holz*⟩ bare; (*brutal*) brutal; **r~e Gewalt** brute force ● *adv* roughly; brutally. **R~bau** *m* **-[e]s,-ten** shell. **R~kost** *f* raw [vegetarian] food. **R~ling** *m* **-s,-e** brute. **R~material** *nt* raw material. **R~öl** *nt* crude oil
Rohr *nt* **-[e]s,-e** pipe; (*Geschütz-*) barrel; (*Bot*) reed; (*Zucker-, Bambus-*) cane
Röhr|chen *nt* **-s,-** [drinking] straw; (*Auto, fam*) breathalyser (P). **R~e** *f* **-,-n** tube; (*Radio-*) valve; (*Back-*) oven
Rohstoff *m* raw material
Rokoko *nt* **-s** rococo
Rolladen *m* roller shutter
Rollbahn *f* taxiway; (*Start-/Landebahn*) runway
Rolle *f* **-,-n** roll; (*Garn-*) reel; (*Draht-*) coil; (*Techn*) roller; (*Seil-*) pulley; (*Wäsche-*) mangle; (*Lauf-*) castor; (*Schrift-*) scroll; (*Theat*) part, role; **das spielt keine R~** (*fig*) that doesn't matter. **r~n** *vt* roll; (*auf-*) roll up; roll out ⟨*Teig*⟩; put through the mangle ⟨*Wäsche*⟩; **sich r~n** roll; (*sich ein-*) curl up ● *vi* (*sein*) roll; ⟨*Flugzeug:*⟩ taxi ● *vi* (*haben*) ⟨*Donner:*⟩ rumble. **R~r** *m* **-s,-** scooter
Roll|feld *nt* airfield. **R~kragen** *m* polo-neck. **R~mops** *m* rollmop[s] *sg*
Rollo *nt* **-s,-s** [roller] blind
Roll|schuh *m* roller-skate; **R~schuh laufen** roller-skate. **R~splitt** *m* **-s** loose chippings *pl.* **R~stuhl** *m* wheelchair. **R~treppe** *f* escalator
Rom *nt* **-s** Rome
Roman *m* **-s,-e** novel. **r~isch** *a* Romanesque; ⟨*Sprache*⟩ Romance. **R~schriftsteller(in)** *m(f)* novelist
Romant|ik *f* - romanticism. **r~isch** *a* romantic, *adv* -ally
Romanze *f* **-,-n** romance
Röm|er(in) *m* **-s,-** (*f* **-,-nen**) Roman. **r~isch** *a* Roman
Rommé /ˈrɔme:/ *nt* **-s** rummy
röntgen *vt* X-ray. **R~aufnahme** *f*, **R~bild** *nt* X-ray. **R~strahlen** *mpl* X-rays
rosa *inv a*, **R~** *nt* **-[s],-** pink
Rose *f* **-,-n** rose. **R~nkohl** *m* [Brussels] sprouts *pl.* **R~nkranz** *m* (*Relig*) rosary. **R~nmontag** *m* Monday before Shrove Tuesday
Rosette *f* **-,-n** rosette
rosig *a* rosy
Rosine *f* **-,-n** raisin
Rosmarin *m* **-s** rosemary
Roß *nt* **Rosses, Rösser** horse. **R~kastanie** *f* horse-chestnut
Rost[1] *m* **-[e]s,-e** grating; (*Kamin-*) grate; (*Brat-*) grill
Rost[2] *m* **-[e]s** rust. **r~en** *vi* (*haben*) rust
röst|en *vt* roast; toast ⟨*Brot*⟩. **R~er** *m* **-s,-** toaster
rostfrei *a* stainless
rostig *a* rusty
rot *a* (**röter, rötest**), **Rot** *nt* **-s,-** red; **rot werden** turn red; (*erröten*) go red, blush
Rotation /-ˈtsi̯o:n/ *f* **-,-en** rotation
Röte *f* - redness; (*Scham-*) blush
Röteln *pl* German measles *sg*
röten *vt* redden; **sich r~** turn red
rothaarig *a* red-haired
rotieren *vi* (*haben*) rotate
Rot|kehlchen *nt* **-s,-** robin. **R~kohl** *m* red cabbage
rötlich *a* reddish
Rot|licht *nt* red light. **R~wein** *m* red wine
Rou|lade /ruˈla:də/ *f* **-,-n** beef olive. **R~leau** /-ˈlo:/ *nt* **-s,-s** [roller] blind
Route /ˈru:tə/ *f* **-,-n** route
Routin|e /ruˈti:nə/ *f* **-,-n** routine; (*Erfahrung*) experience. **r~emäßig** *a* routine ... ● *adv* routinely. **r~iert** *a* experienced
Rowdy /ˈrau̯di/ *m* **-s,-s** hooligan

Rübe *f* **-,-n** beet; **rote R~** beetroot; **gelbe R~** (*SGer*) carrot
rüber *adv* = **herüber, hinüber**
Rubin *m* **-s,-e** ruby
Rubrik *f* **-,-en** column; (*Kategorie*) category
Ruck *m* **-[e]s,-e** jerk
Rückantwort *f* reply
ruckartig *a* jerky, *adv* -ily
rück|bezüglich *a* (*Gram*) reflexive. **R~blende** *f* flashback. **R~blick** *m* (*fig*) review (**auf** + *acc* of). **r~blickend** *adv* in retrospect. **r~datieren** *vt* (*inf & pp only*) backdate
rücken *vt/i* (*sein/haben*) move; **an etw** (*dat*) **r~** move sth
Rücken *m* **-s,-** back; (*Buch-*) spine; (*Berg-*) ridge. **R~lehne** *f* back. **R~mark** *nt* spinal cord. **R~schwimmen** *nt* backstroke. **R~wind** *m* following wind; (*Aviat*) tail wind
rückerstatten *vt* (*inf & pp only*) refund
Rückfahr|karte *f* return ticket. **R~t** *f* return journey
Rück|fall *m* relapse. **r~fällig** *a* **r~fällig werden** (*Jur*) re-offend. **R~flug** *m* return flight. **R~frage** *f* [further] query. **r~fragen** *vi* (*haben*) (*inf & pp only*) check (**bei** with). **R~gabe** *f* return. **R~gang** *m* decline; (*Preis-*) drop, fall. **r~gängig** *a* **r~gängig machen** cancel; break off ⟨*Verlobung*⟩. **R~grat** *nt* **-[e]s,-e** spine, backbone. **R~halt** *m* (*fig*) support. **R~hand** *f* backhand. **R~kehr** return. **R~lagen** *fpl* reserves. **R~licht** *nt* rear-light. **r~lings** *adv* backwards; (*von hinten*) from behind. **R~reise** *f* return journey
Rucksack *m* rucksack
Rück|schau *f* review. **R~schlag** *m* (*Sport*) return; (*fig*) set-back. **R~schluß** *m* conclusion. **R~schritt** *m* (*fig*) retrograde step. **r~schrittlich** *a* retrograde. **R~seite** *f* back; (*einer Münze*) reverse
Rücksicht *f* **-,-en** consideration; **R~ nehmen auf** (+ *acc*) show consideration for; (*berücksichtigen*) take into consideration. **R~nahme** *f* **-** consideration. **r~slos** *a* inconsiderate, *adv* -ly; (*schonungslos*) ruthless, *adv* -ly. **r~svoll** *a* considerate, *adv* -ly
Rück|sitz *m* back seat; (*Sozius*) pillion. **R~spiegel** *m* rear-view mirror. **R~spiel** *nt* return match. **R~sprache** *f* consultation; **R~sprache nehmen mit** consult. **R~stand** *m* (*Chem*) residue; (*Arbeits-*) backlog; **R~stände** arrears; **im R~stand sein** be behind. **r~ständig** *a* (*fig*) backward. **R~stau** *m* (*Auto*) tailback. **R~strahler** *m* **-s,-** reflector. **R~tritt** *m* resignation; (*Fahrrad*) back pedalling. **r~vergüten** *vt* (*inf & pp only*) refund. **R~wanderer** *m* repatriate
rückwärt|ig *a* back ..., rear ... **r~s** *adv* backwards. **R~sgang** *m* reverse [gear]
Rückweg *m* way back
ruckweise *adv* jerkily
rück|wirkend *a* retrospective, *adv* -ly. **R~wirkung** *f* retrospective force; **mit R~wirkung vom** backdated to. **R~zahlung** *f* repayment. **R~zug** *m* retreat
Rüde *m* **-n,-n** [male] dog
Rudel *nt* **-s,-** herd; (*Wolfs-*) pack; (*Löwen-*) pride
Ruder *nt* **-s,-** oar; (*Steuer-*) rudder; **am R~** (*Naut & fig*) at the helm. **R~boot** *nt* rowing boat. **R~er** *m* **-s,-** oarsman. **r~n** *vt/i* (*haben/sein*) row
Ruf *m* **-[e]s,-e** call; (*laut*) shout; (*Telefon*) telephone number; (*Ansehen*) reputation; **Künstler von Ruf** artist of repute. **r~en**† *vt/i* (*haben*) call (**nach** for); **r~en lassen** send for
Rüffel *m* **-s,-** (*fam*) telling-off. **r~n** *vt* (*fam*) tell off
Ruf|name *m* forename by which one is known. **R~nummer** *f* telephone number. **R~zeichen** *nt* dialling tone
Rüge *f* **-,-n** reprimand. **r~n** *vt* reprimand; (*kritisieren*) criticize
Ruhe *f* **-** rest; (*Stille*) quiet; (*Frieden*) peace; (*innere*) calm; (*Gelassenheit*) composure; **die R~ bewahren** keep calm; **in R~ lassen** leave in peace; **sich zur R~ setzen** retire; **R~ [da]!** quiet! **R~gehalt** *nt* [retirement] pension. **r~los** *a* restless, *adv* -ly. **r~n** *vi* (*haben*) rest (**auf** + *dat* on); ⟨*Arbeit, Verkehr:*⟩ have stopped; **hier ruht ...** here lies ... **R~pause** *f* rest, break. **R~stand** *m* retirement; **in den R~stand treten** retire; **im R~stand** retired. **R~störung** *f* disturbance of the peace. **R~tag** *m* day of rest; **'Montag R~tag'** 'closed on Mondays'
ruhig *a* quiet, *adv* -ly; (*erholsam*) restful; (*friedlich*) peaceful, *adv* -ly; (*unbewegt, gelassen*) calm, *adv* -ly; **r~ bleiben** remain calm; **sehen Sie**

sich r~ um you're welcome to look round; **man kann r~ darüber sprechen** there's no harm in talking about it

Ruhm *m* **-[e]s** fame; (*Ehre*) glory

rühmen *vt* praise; **sich r~** boast (*gen* about)

ruhmreich *a* glorious

Ruhr *f* - (*Med*) dysentery

Rühr|ei *nt* scrambled eggs *pl*. **r~en** *vt* move; (*Culin*) stir; **sich r~en** move; **zu Tränen r~en** move to tears; **r~t euch!** (*Mil*) at ease! ● *vi* (*haben*) stir; **r~en an** (+*acc*) touch; (*fig*) touch on; **r~en von** (*fig*) come from. **r~end** *a* touching, *adv* -ly

rühr|ig *a* active. **r~selig** *a* sentimental. **R~ung** *f* - emotion

Ruin *m* **-s** ruin. **R~e** *f* **-,-n** ruin; ruins *pl* (*gen* of). **r~ieren** *vt* ruin

rülpsen *vi* (*haben*) (*fam*) belch

Rum *m* **-s** rum

rum *adv* = **herum**

Rumän|ien /-i̯ən/ *nt* **-s** Romania. **r~isch** *a* Romanian

Rummel *m* **-s** (*fam*) hustle and bustle; (*Jahrmarkt*) funfair. **R~platz** *m* fairground

rumoren *vi* (*haben*) make a noise; ⟨*Magen:*⟩ rumble

Rumpel|kammer *f* junk-room. **r~n** *vi* (*haben/sein*) rumble

Rumpf *m* **-[e]s,⸚e** body, trunk; (*Schiffs-*) hull; (*Aviat*) fuselage

rümpfen *vt* **die Nase r~** turn up one's nose (**über** + *acc* at)

rund *a* round ● *adv* approximately; **r~ um** [a]round. **R~blick** *m* panoramic view. **R~brief** *m* circular [letter]

Runde *f* **-,-n** round; (*Kreis*) circle; (*eines Polizisten*) beat; (*beim Rennen*) lap; **eine R~ Bier** a round of beer. **r~n** *vt* round; **sich r~n** become round; ⟨*Backen:*⟩ fill out

Rund|fahrt *f* tour. **R~frage** *f* poll

Rundfunk *m* radio; **im R~** on the radio. **R~gerät** *nt* radio [set]

Rund|gang *m* round; (*Spaziergang*) walk (**durch** round). **r~heraus** *adv* straight out. **r~herum** *adv* all around. **r~lich** *a* rounded; (*mollig*) plump. **R~reise** *f* [circular] tour. **R~schreiben** *nt* circular. **r~um** *adv* all round. **R~ung** *f* **-,-en** curve. **r~weg** *adv* ⟨*ablehnen*⟩ flatly

runter *adv* = **herunter, hinunter**

Runzel *f* **-,-n** wrinkle. **r~n** *vt* **die Stirn r~n** frown

runzlig *a* wrinkled

Rüpel *m* **-s,-** (*fam*) lout. **r~haft** *a* (*fam*) loutish

rupfen *vt* pull out; pluck ⟨*Geflügel*⟩; (*fam: schröpfen*) fleece

ruppig *a* rude, *adv* -ly

Rüsche *f* **-,-n** frill

Ruß *m* **-es** soot

Russe *m* **-n,-n** Russian

Rüssel *m* **-s,-** (*Zool*) trunk

ruß|en *vi* (*haben*) smoke. **r~ig** *a* sooty

Russ|in *f* **-,-nen** Russian. **r~isch** *a* Russian. **R~isch** *nt* **-[s]** (*Lang*) Russian

Rußland *nt* **-s** Russia

rüsten *vi* (*haben*) prepare (**zu/für** for) ● *vr* **sich r~** get ready; **gerüstet sein** be ready

rüstig *a* sprightly

rustikal *a* rustic

Rüstung *f* **-,-en** armament; (*Harnisch*) armour. **R~skontrolle** *f* arms control

Rute *f* **-,-n** twig; (*Angel-, Wünschel-*) rod; (*zur Züchtigung*) birch; (*Schwanz*) tail

Rutsch *m* **-[e]s,-e** slide. **R~bahn** *f* slide. **R~e** *f* **-,-n** chute. **r~en** *vt* slide; (*rücken*) move ● *vi* (*sein*) slide; (*aus-, ab-*) slip; (*Auto*) skid; (*rücken*) move [along]. **r~ig** *a* slippery

rütteln *vt* shake ● *vi* (*haben*) **r~ an** (+*dat*) rattle

S

Saal *m* **-[e]s, Säle** hall; (*Theat*) auditorium; (*Kranken-*) ward

Saat *f* **-,-en** seed; (*Säen*) sowing; (*Gesätes*) crop. **S~gut** *nt* seed

sabbern *vi* (*haben*) (*fam*) slobber; ⟨*Baby:*⟩ dribble; (*reden*) jabber

Säbel *m* **-s,-** sabre

Sabo|tage /zabo'ta:ʒə/ *f* - sabotage. **S~teur** /-'tø:ɐ̯/ *m* **-s,-e** saboteur. **s~tieren** *vt* sabotage

Sach|bearbeiter *m* expert. **S~buch** *nt* non-fiction book. **s~dienlich** *a* relevant

Sache *f* **-,-n** matter, business; (*Ding*) thing; (*fig*) cause; **zur S~ kommen** come to the point

Sach|gebiet *nt* (*fig*) area, field. **s~gemäß** *a* proper, *adv* -ly. **S~kenntnis** *f* expertise. **s~kundig** *a* expert, *adv* -ly. **s~lich** *a* factual, *adv*

-ly; (*nüchtern*) matter-of-fact, *adv* -ly; (*objektiv*) objective, *adv* -ly; (*schmucklos*) functional

sächlich *a* (*Gram*) neuter

Sachse *m* **-n,-n** Saxon. **S~n** *nt* **-s** Saxony

sächsisch *a* Saxon

sacht *a* gentle, *adv* -ly

Sach|verhalt *m* **-[e]s** facts *pl.* **s~verständig** *a* expert, *adv* -ly. **S~verständige(r)** *m/f* expert

Sack *m* **-[e]s,⸚e** sack; **mit S~ und Pack** with all one's belongings

sacken *vi* (*sein*) sink; (*zusammen-*) go down; ⟨*Person:*⟩ slump

Sack|gasse *f* cul-de-sac; (*fig*) impasse. **S~leinen** *nt* sacking

Sadis|mus *m* **-** sadism. **S~t** *m* **-en,-en** sadist. **s~tisch** *a* sadistic, *adv* -ally

säen *vt/i* (*haben*) sow

Safe /ze:f/ *m* **-s,-s** safe

Saft *m* **-[e]s,⸚e** juice; (*Bot*) sap. **s~ig** *a* juicy; ⟨*Wiese*⟩ lush; ⟨*Preis, Rechnung*⟩ hefty; ⟨*Witz*⟩ coarse. **s~los** *a* dry

Sage *f* **-,-n** legend

Säge *f* **-,-n** saw. **S~mehl** *nt* sawdust

sagen *vt* say; (*mitteilen*) tell; (*bedeuten*) mean; **das hat nichts zu s~** it doesn't mean anything

sägen *vt/i* (*haben*) saw

sagenhaft *a* legendary; (*fam: unglaublich*) fantastic, *adv* -ally

Säge|späne *mpl* wood shavings. **S~werk** *nt* sawmill

Sahn|e *f* **-** cream. **S~ebonbon** *m & nt* ≈ toffee. **s~ig** *a* creamy

Saison /zɛ'zõ:/ *f* **-,-s** season

Saite *f* **-,-n** (*Mus, Sport*) string. **S~ninstrument** *nt* stringed instrument

Sakko *m & nt* **-s,-s** sports jacket

Sakrament *nt* **-[e]s,-e** sacrament

Sakrileg *nt* **-s,-e** sacrilege

Sakrist|an *m* **-s,-e** verger. **S~ei** *f* **-,-en** vestry

Salat *m* **-[e]s,-e** salad; **ein Kopf S~** a lettuce. **S~soße** *f* salad-dressing

Salbe *f* **-,-n** ointment

Salbei *m* **-s** & *f* **-** sage

salben *vt* anoint

Saldo *m* **-s,-dos & -den** balance

Salon /za'lõ:/ *m* **-s,-s** salon; (*Naut*) saloon

salopp *a* casual, *adv* -ly; ⟨*Benehmen*⟩ informal, *adv* -ly; ⟨*Ausdruck*⟩ slangy

Salto *m* **-s,-s** somersault

Salut *m* **-[e]s,-e** salute. **s~ieren** *vi* (*haben*) salute

Salve *f* **-,-n** volley; (*Geschütz-*) salvo; (*von Gelächter*) burst

Salz *nt* **-es,-e** salt. **s~en**† *vt* salt. **S~faß** *nt* salt-cellar. **s~ig** *a* salty. **S~kartoffeln** *fpl* boiled potatoes. **S~säure** *f* hydrochloric acid

Samen *m* **-s,-** seed; (*Anat*) semen, sperm

sämig *a* (*Culin*) thick

Sämling *m* **-s,-e** seedling

Sammel|becken *nt* reservoir. **S~begriff** *m* collective term. **s~n** *vt/i* (*haben*) collect; (*suchen, versammeln*) gather; **sich s~n** collect; (*sich versammeln*) gather; (*sich fassen*) collect oneself. **S~name** *m* collective noun

Samm|ler(in) *m* **-s,-** (*f* **-,-nen**) collector. **S~lung** *f* **-,-en** collection; (*innere*) composure

Samstag *m* **-s,-e** Saturday. **s~s** *adv* on Saturdays

samt *prep* (+*dat*) together with ● *adv* **s~ und sonders** without exception

Samt *m* **-[e]s** velvet. **s~ig** *a* velvety

sämtlich *indef pron inv* all. **s~e(r,s)** *indef pron* all the; **s~e Werke** complete works; **meine s~en Bücher** all my books

Sanatorium *nt* **-s,-ien** sanatorium

Sand *m* **-[e]s** sand

Sandal|e *f* **-,-n** sandal. **S~ette** *f* **-,-n** high-heeled sandal

Sand|bank *f* sandbank. **S~burg** *f* sand-castle. **s~ig** *a* sandy. **S~kasten** *m* sand-pit. **S~kuchen** *m* Madeira cake. **S~papier** *nt* sandpaper. **S~stein** *m* sandstone

sanft *a* gentle, *adv* -ly. **s~mütig** *a* meek

Sänger(in) *m* **-s,-** (*f* **-,-nen**) singer

sanieren *vt* clean up; redevelop ⟨*Gebiet*⟩; (*modernisieren*) modernize; make profitable ⟨*Industrie, Firma*⟩; **sich s~** become profitable

sanitär *a* sanitary

Sanität|er *m* **-s,-** first-aid man; (*Fahrer*) ambulance man; (*Mil*) medical orderly. **S~swagen** *m* ambulance

Sanktion /zaŋk'tsi̯o:n/ *f* **-,-en** sanction. **s~ieren** *vt* sanction

Saphir *m* **-s,-e** sapphire

Sardelle *f* **-,-n** anchovy

Sardine *f* **-,-n** sardine

Sarg *m* **-[e]s,⸚e** coffin

Sarkas|mus *m* - sarcasm. **s~tisch** *a* sarcastic, *adv* -ally
Sat|an *m* **-s** Satan; (*fam: Teufel*) devil. **s~anisch** *a* satanic
Satellit *m* **-en,-en** satellite. **S~en-fernsehen** *nt* satellite television
Satin /za'tɛŋ/ *m* **-s** satin
Satir|e *f* **-,-n** satire. **s~isch** *a* satirical, *adv* -ly
satt *a* full; ⟨*Farbe*⟩ rich; **s~ sein** have had enough [to eat]; **sich s~ essen** eat as much as one wants; **s~ machen** feed; ⟨*Speise:*⟩ be filling; **etw s~ haben** (*fam*) be fed up with sth
Sattel *m* **-s,¨** saddle. **s~n** *vt* saddle. **S~schlepper** *m* tractor unit. **S~zug** *m* articulated lorry
sättigen *vt* satisfy; (*Chem & fig*) saturate ● *vi* (*haben*) be filling. **s~d** *a* filling
Satz *m* **-es,¨e** sentence; (*Teil-*) clause; (*These*) proposition; (*Math*) theorem; (*Mus*) movement; (*Tennis, Zusammengehöriges*) set; (*Boden-*) sediment; (*Kaffee-*) grounds *pl*; (*Steuer-, Zins-*) rate; (*Druck-*) setting; (*Schrift-*) type; (*Sprung*) leap, bound. **S~aussage** *f* predicate. **S~gegenstand** *m* subject. **S~zeichen** *nt* punctuation mark
Sau *f* **-, Säue** sow; (*sl: schmutziger Mensch*) dirty pig
sauber *a* clean; (*ordentlich*) neat, *adv* -ly; (*anständig*) decent, *adv* -ly; (*fam: nicht anständig*) fine. **s~halten**† *vt sep* keep clean. **S~keit** *f* - cleanliness; neatness; decency
säuberlich *a* neat, *adv* -ly
saubermachen *vt/i sep* (*haben*) clean
säuber|n *vt* clean; (*befreien*) rid/(*Pol*) purge (**von** of). **S~ungsaktion** *f* (*Pol*) purge
Sauce /'zo:sə/ *f* **-,-n** sauce; (*Braten-*) gravy
Saudi-Arabien /-i̯ən/ *nt* **-s** Saudi Arabia
sauer *a* sour; (*Chem*) acid; (*eingelegt*) pickled; (*schwer*) hard; **saurer Regen** acid rain; **s~ sein** (*fam*) be annoyed
Sauerei *f* **-,-en** = **Schweinerei**
Sauerkraut *nt* sauerkraut
säuerlich *a* slightly sour
Sauer|stoff *m* oxygen
saufen† *vt/i* (*haben*) drink; (*sl*) booze
Säufer *m* **-s,-** (*sl*) boozer
saugen† *vt/i* (*haben*) suck; (*staub-*) vacuum, hoover; **sich voll Wasser s~** soak up water
säugen *vt* suckle
Sauger *m* **-s,-** [baby's] dummy, (*Amer*) pacifier; (*Flaschen-*) teat
Säugetier *nt* mammal
saugfähig *a* absorbent
Säugling *m* **-s,-e** infant
Säule *f* **-,-n** column
Saum *m* **-[e]s, Säume** hem; (*Rand*) edge
säumen[1] *vt* hem; (*fig*) line
säum|en[2] *vi* (*haben*) delay. **s~ig** *a* dilatory
Sauna *f* **-,-nas & -nen** sauna
Säure *f* **-,-n** acidity; (*Chem*) acid
säuseln *vi* (*haben*) rustle [softly]
sausen *vi* (*haben*) rush; ⟨*Ohren:*⟩ buzz ● *vi* (*sein*) rush [along]
Sauwetter *nt* (*sl*) lousy weather
Saxophon *nt* **-s,-e** saxophone
SB- /ɛs'be:-/ *pref* (= **Selbstbedienung**) self-service ...
S-Bahn *f* city and suburban railway
sch *int* shush! (*fort*) shoo!
Schabe *f* **-,-n** cockroach
schaben *vt/i* (*haben*) scrape
schäbig *a* shabby, *adv* -ily
Schablone *f* **-,-n** stencil; (*Muster*) pattern; (*fig*) stereotype
Schach *nt* **-s** chess; **S~!** check! **in S~ halten** (*fig*) keep in check. **S~brett** *nt* chessboard
schachern *vi* (*haben*) haggle
Schachfigur *f* chess-man
schachmatt *a* **s~ setzen** checkmate; **s~!** checkmate!
Schachspiel *nt* game of chess
Schacht *m* **-[e]s,¨e** shaft
Schachtel *f* **-,-n** box; (*Zigaretten-*) packet
Schachzug *m* move
schade *a* **s~ sein** be a pity *or* shame; **zu s~ für** too good for; **[wie] s~!** [what a] pity *or* shame!
Schädel *m* **-s,-** skull. **S~bruch** *m* fractured skull
schaden *vi* (*haben*) (+ *dat*) damage; (*nachteilig sein*) hurt; **das schadet nichts** that doesn't matter. **S~** *m* **-s,¨** damage; (*Defekt*) defect; (*Nachteil*) disadvantage; **zu S~ kommen** be hurt. **S~ersatz** *m* damages *pl*. **S~freude** *f* malicious glee. **s~froh** *a* gloating
schadhaft *a* defective
schädig|en *vt* damage, harm. **S~ung** *f* **-,-en** damage

schädlich *a* harmful

Schädling *m* **-s,-e** pest. **S~sbekämpfungsmittel** *nt* pesticide

Schaf *nt* **-[e]s,-e** sheep; (*fam: Idiot*) idiot. **S~bock** *m* ram

Schäfchen *nt* **-s,-** lamb

Schäfer *m* **-s,-** shepherd. **S~hund** *m* sheepdog; **Deutscher S~hund** German shepherd, alsatian

Schaffell *nt* sheepskin

schaffen[1]† *vt* create; (*herstellen*) establish; make ⟨*Platz*⟩; **wie geschaffen für** made for

schaffen[2] *v* (*reg*) ● *vt* manage [to do]; pass ⟨*Prüfung*⟩; catch ⟨*Zug*⟩; (*bringen*) take; **jdm zu s~ machen** trouble s.o.; **sich** (*dat*) **zu s~ machen** busy oneself (**an** + *dat* with) ● *vi* (*haben*) (*SGer: arbeiten*) work. **S~** *nt* **-s** work

Schaffner *m* **-s,-** conductor; (*Zug-*) ticket-inspector

Schaffung *f* **-** creation

Schaft *m* **-[e]s,¨e** shaft; (*Gewehr-*) stock; (*Stiefel-*) leg. **S~stiefel** *m* high boot

Schal *m* **-s,-s** scarf

schal *a* insipid; (*abgestanden*) flat; (*fig*) stale

Schale *f* **-,-n** skin; (*abgeschält*) peel; (*Eier-, Nuß-, Muschel-*) shell; (*Schüssel*) dish

schälen *vt* peel; **sich s~** peel

schalkhaft *a* mischievous, *adv* -ly

Schall *m* **-[e]s** sound. **S~dämpfer** *m* silencer. **s~dicht** *a* soundproof. **s~en** *vi* (*haben*) ring out; (*nachhallen*) resound; **s~end lachen** roar with laughter. **S~mauer** *f* sound barrier. **S~platte** *f* record, disc

schalt|en *vt* switch ● *vi* (*haben*) switch/⟨*Ampel:*⟩ turn (**auf** + *acc* to); (*Auto*) change gear; (*fam: begreifen*) catch on. **S~er** *m* **-s,-** switch; (*Post-, Bank-*) counter; (*Fahrkarten-*) ticket window. **S~hebel** *m* switch; (*Auto*) gear-lever. **S~jahr** *nt* leap year. **S~kreis** *m* circuit. **S~ung** *f* **-,-en** circuit; (*Auto*) gear change

Scham *f* **-** shame; (*Anat*) private parts *pl*; **falsche S~** false modesty

schämen (sich) *vr* be ashamed; **schämt euch!** you should be ashamed of yourselves!

scham|haft *a* modest, *adv* -ly; (*schüchtern*) bashful, *adv* -ly. **s~los** *a* shameless, *adv* -ly

Schampon *nt* **-s** shampoo. **s~ieren** *vt* shampoo

Schande *f* **-** disgrace, shame; **S~ machen** (+ *dat*) bring shame on

schänd|en *vt* dishonour; (*fig*) defile; (*Relig*) desecrate; (*sexuell*) violate. **s~lich** *a* disgraceful, *adv* -ly. **S~ung** *f* **-,-en** defilement; desecration; violation

Schanktisch *m* bar

Schanze *f* **-,-n** [ski-]jump

Schar *f* **-,-en** crowd; (*Vogel-*) flock; **in [hellen] S~en** in droves

Scharade *f* **-,-n** charade

scharen *vt* **um sich s~** gather round one; **sich s~ um** flock round. **s~weise** *adv* in droves

scharf *a* (**schärfer, schärfst**) sharp; (*stark*) strong; (*stark gewürzt*) hot; ⟨*Geruch*⟩ pungent; ⟨*Frost, Wind, Augen, Verstand*⟩ keen; (*streng*) harsh; ⟨*Galopp, Ritt*⟩ hard; ⟨*Munition*⟩ live; ⟨*Hund*⟩ fierce; **s~ einstellen** (*Phot*) focus; **s~ sein** (*Phot*) be in focus; **s~ sein auf** (+ *acc*) (*fam*) be keen on ● *adv* sharply; ⟨*hinsehen, nachdenken, bremsen, reiten*⟩ hard; (*streng*) harshly; **s~ schießen** fire live ammunition

Scharfblick *m* perspicacity

Schärfe *f* **-** (*s.* **scharf**) sharpness; strength; hotness; pungency; keenness; harshness. **s~n** *vt* sharpen

scharf|machen *vt sep* (*fam*) incite. **S~richter** *m* executioner. **S~schütze** *m* marksman. **s~sichtig** *a* perspicacious. **S~sinn** *m* astuteness. **s~sinnig** *a* astute, *adv* -ly

Scharlach *m* **-s** scarlet fever

Scharlatan *m* **-s,-e** charlatan

Scharnier *nt* **-s,-e** hinge

Schärpe *f* **-,-n** sash

scharren *vi* (*haben*) scrape; ⟨*Huhn:*⟩ scratch; ⟨*Pferd:*⟩ paw the ground ● *vt* scrape

Schart|e *f* **-,-n** nick. **s~ig** *a* jagged

Schaschlik *m* & *nt* **-s,-s** kebab

Schatten *m* **-s,-** shadow; (*schattige Stelle*) shade; **im S~** in the shade. **s~haft** *a* shadowy. **S~riß** *m* silhouette. **S~seite** *f* shady side; (*fig*) disadvantage

schattier|en *vt* shade. **S~ung** *f* **-,-en** shading; (*fig: Variante*) shade

schattig *a* shady

Schatz *m* **-es,¨e** treasure; (*Freund, Freundin*) sweetheart; (*Anrede*) darling

Schätzchen *nt* **-s,-** darling

schätzen *vt* estimate; (*taxieren*) value; (*achten*) esteem; (*würdigen*) appreciate; (*fam: vermuten*) reckon; **sich glücklich s~** consider oneself lucky

Schätzung *f* **-,-en** estimate; (*Taxierung*) valuation. **s~sweise** *adv* approximately

Schau *f* **-,-en** show; **zur S~ stellen** display. **S~bild** *nt* diagram

Schauder *m* **-s** shiver; (*vor Abscheu*) shudder. **s~haft** *a* dreadful, *adv* -ly. **s~n** *vi* (*haben*) shiver; (*vor Abscheu*) shudder; **mich s~te** I shivered/shuddered

schauen *vi* (*haben*) (*SGer, Aust*) look; **s~, daß** make sure that

Schauer *m* **-s,-** shower; (*Schauder*) shiver. **S~geschichte** *f* horror story. **s~lich** *a* ghastly. **s~n** *vi* (*haben*) shiver; **mich s~te** I shivered

Schaufel *f* **-,-n** shovel; (*Kehr-*) dustpan. **s~n** *vt* shovel; (*graben*) dig

Schaufenster *nt* shop-window. **S~bummel** *m* window-shopping. **S~puppe** *f* dummy

Schaukasten *m* display case

Schaukel *f* **-,-n** swing. **s~n** *vt* rock ● *vi* (*haben*) rock; (*auf einer Schaukel*) swing; (*schwanken*) sway. **S~pferd** *nt* rocking-horse. **S~stuhl** *m* rocking-chair

schaulustig *a* curious

Schaum *m* **-[e]s** foam; (*Seifen-*) lather; (*auf Bier*) froth; (*als Frisier-, Rasiermittel*) mousse

schäumen *vi* (*haben*) foam, froth; ⟨*Seife:*⟩ lather

Schaum|gummi *m* foam rubber. **s~ig** *a* frothy; **s~ig rühren** (*Culin*) cream. **S~krone** *f* white crest; (*auf Bier*) head. **S~speise** *f* mousse. **S~stoff** *m* [synthetic] foam. **S~wein** *m* sparkling wine

Schauplatz *m* scene

schaurig *a* dreadful, *adv* -ly; (*unheimlich*) eerie, *adv* eerily

Schauspiel *nt* play; (*Anblick*) spectacle. **S~er** *m* actor. **S~erin** *f* actress. **s~ern** *vi* (*haben*) act; (*sich verstellen*) play-act

Scheck *m* **-s,-s** cheque, (*Amer*) check. **S~buch, S~heft** *nt* cheque-book. **S~karte** *f* cheque card

Scheibe *f* **-,-n** disc; (*Schieß-*) target; (*Glas-*) pane; (*Brot-, Wurst-*) slice. **S~nwaschanlage** *f* windscreen washer. **S~nwischer** *m* **-s,-** windscreen-wiper

Scheich *m* **-s,-e & -s** sheikh

Scheide *f* **-,-n** sheath; (*Anat*) vagina

scheid|en† *vt* separate; (*unterscheiden*) distinguish; dissolve ⟨*Ehe*⟩; **sich s~en lassen** get divorced; **sich s~en** diverge; ⟨*Meinungen:*⟩ differ ● *vi* (*sein*) leave; (*voneinander*) part. **S~ung** *f* **-,-en** divorce

Schein *m* **-[e]s,-e** light; (*Anschein*) appearance; (*Bescheinigung*) certificate; (*Geld-*) note; **etw nur zum S~ tun** only pretend to do sth. **s~bar** *a* apparent, *adv* -ly. **s~en**† *vi* (*haben*) shine; (*den Anschein haben*) seem, appear; **mir s~t** it seems to me

scheinheilig *a* hypocritical, *adv* -ly. **S~keit** *f* hypocrisy

Scheinwerfer *m* **-s,-** floodlight; (*Such-*) searchlight; (*Auto*) headlight; (*Theat*) spotlight

Scheiß-, scheiß- *pref* (*vulg*) bloody. **S~e** *f* **-** (*vulg*) shit. **s~en**† *vi* (*haben*) (*vulg*) shit

Scheit *nt* **-[e]s,-e** log

Scheitel *m* **-s,-** parting. **s~n** *vt* part ⟨*Haar*⟩

scheitern *vi* (*sein*) fail

Schelle *f* **-,-n** bell. **s~n** *vi* (*haben*) ring

Schellfisch *m* haddock

Schelm *m* **-s,-e** rogue. **s~isch** *a* mischievous, *adv* -ly

Schelte *f* **-** scolding. **s~n**† *vi* (*haben*) grumble (**über** + *acc* about); **mit jdm s~n** scold s.o. ● *vt* scold; (*bezeichnen*) call

Schema *nt* **-s,-mata** model, pattern; (*Skizze*) diagram

Schemel *m* **-s,-** stool

Schenke *f* **-,-n** tavern

Schenkel *m* **-s,-** thigh; (*Geom*) side

schenken *vt* give [as a present]; **jdm Vertrauen/Glauben s~** trust/believe s.o.; **sich** (*dat*) **etw s~** give sth a miss

scheppern *vi* (*haben*) clank

Scherbe *f* **-,-n** [broken] piece

Schere *f* **-,-n** scissors *pl*; (*Techn*) shears *pl*; (*Hummer-*) claw. **s~n¹**† *vt* shear; crop ⟨*Haar*⟩; clip ⟨*Hund*⟩

scheren² *vt* (*reg*) (*fam*) bother; **sich nicht s~ um** not care about; **scher dich zum Teufel!** go to hell!

Scherenschnitt *m* silhouette

Scherereien *fpl* (*fam*) trouble *sg*

Scherz *m* **-es,-e** joke; **im/zum S~** as a joke. **s~en** *vi* (*haben*) joke. **S~frage** *f* riddle. **s~haft** *a* humorous

scheu *a* shy, *adv* -ly; ⟨*Tier*⟩ timid; **s~ werden** ⟨*Pferd:*⟩ shy; **s~ machen** startle. **S~** *f* **-** shyness; timidity; (*Ehrfurcht*) awe

scheuchen *vt* shoo

scheuen *vt* be afraid of; (*meiden*) shun; **keine Mühe/Kosten s~** spare no effort/expense; **sich s~** be afraid (**vor**+*dat* of); shrink (**etw zu tun** from doing sth) ● *vi* (*haben*) ⟨*Pferd:*⟩ shy

Scheuer|lappen *m* floor-cloth. **s~n** *vt* scrub; (*mit Scheuerpulver*) scour; (*reiben*) rub; **[wund] s~n** chafe ● *vi* (*haben*) rub, chafe. **S~tuch** *nt* floor-cloth

Scheuklappen *fpl* blinkers

Scheune *f* **-,-n** barn

Scheusal *nt* **-s,-e** monster

scheußlich *a* horrible, *adv* -bly

Schi *m* **-s,-er** ski; **S~ fahren** *od* **laufen** ski

Schicht *f* **-,-en** layer; (*Geol*) stratum; (*Gesellschafts-*) class; (*Arbeits-*) shift. **S~arbeit** *f* shift work. **s~en** *vt* stack [up]

schick *a* stylish, *adv* -ly; ⟨*Frau*⟩ chic; (*fam: prima*) great. **S~** *m* **-[e]s** style

schicken *vt/i* (*haben*) send; **s~ nach** send for; **sich s~ in** (+*acc*) resign oneself to

schicklich *a* fitting, proper

Schicksal *nt* **-s,-e** fate. **s~haft** *a* fateful. **S~sschlag** *m* misfortune

Schieb|edach *nt* (*Auto*) sun-roof. **s~en**† *vt* push; (*gleitend*) slide; (*fam: handeln mit*) traffic in; **etw s~en auf** (+*acc*) (*fig*) put sth down to; shift ⟨*Schuld, Verantwortung*⟩ on to ● *vi* (*haben*) push. **S~er** *m* **-s,-** slide; (*Person*) black marketeer. **S~etür** *f* sliding door. **S~ung** *f* **-,-en** (*fam*) illicit deal; (*Betrug*) rigging, fixing

Schieds|gericht *nt* panel of judges; (*Jur*) arbitration tribunal. **S~richter** *m* referee; (*Tennis*) umpire; (*Jur*) arbitrator

schief *a* crooked; (*unsymmetrisch*) lopsided; (*geneigt*) slanting, sloping; (*nicht senkrecht*) leaning; ⟨*Winkel*⟩ oblique; (*fig*) false; (*mißtrauisch*) suspicious ● *adv* not straight; **jdn s~ ansehen** look at s.o. askance

Schiefer *m* **-s** slate

schief|gehen† *vi sep* (*sein*) (*fam*) go wrong. **s~lachen (sich)** *vr sep* double up with laughter

schielen *vi* (*haben*) squint

Schienbein *nt* shin; (*Knochen*) shinbone

Schiene *f* **-,-n** rail; (*Gleit-*) runner; (*Med*) splint. **s~n** *vt* (*Med*) put in a splint

schier[1] *adv* almost

schier[2] *a* pure; ⟨*Fleisch*⟩ lean

Schieß|bude *f* shooting-gallery. **s~en**† *vt* shoot; fire ⟨*Kugel*⟩; score ⟨*Tor*⟩ ● *vi* (*haben*) shoot, fire (**auf** +*acc* at) ● *vi* (*sein*) shoot [along]; (*strömen*) gush; **in die Höhe s~en** shoot up. **S~erei** *f* **-,-en** shooting. **S~scheibe** *f* target. **S~stand** *m* shooting-range

Schifahr|en *nt* skiing. **S~er(in)** *m(f)* skier

Schiff *nt* **-[e]s,-e** ship; (*Kirchen-*) nave; (*Seiten-*) aisle

Schiffahrt *f* shipping

schiff|bar *a* navigable. **S~bau** *m* shipbuilding. **S~bruch** *m* shipwreck. **s~brüchig** *a* shipwrecked. **S~chen** *nt* **-s,-** small boat; (*Tex*) shuttle. **S~er** *m* **-s,-** skipper

Schikan|e *f* **-,-n** harassment; **mit allen S~en** (*fam*) with every refinement. **s~ieren** *vt* harass; (*tyrannisieren*) bully

Schi|laufen *nt* **-s** skiing. **S~läufer(in)** *m(f)* **-s,-** (*f* **-,-nen**) skier

Schild[1] *m* **-[e]s,-e** shield; **etw im S~e führen** (*fam*) be up to sth

Schild[2] *nt* **-[e]s,-er** sign; (*Namens-, Nummern-*) plate; (*Mützen-*) badge; (*Etikett*) label

Schilddrüse *f* thyroid [gland]

schilder|n *vt* describe. **S~ung** *f* **-,-en** description

Schild|kröte *f* tortoise; (*See-*) turtle. **S~patt** *nt* **-[e]s** tortoiseshell

Schilf *nt* **-[e]s** reeds *pl*

schillern *vi* (*haben*) shimmer

Schimmel *m* **-s,-** mould; (*Pferd*) white horse. **s~ig** *a* mouldy. **s~n** *vi* (*haben/sein*) go mouldy

Schimmer *m* **-s** gleam; (*Spur*) glimmer. **s~n** *vi* (*haben*) gleam

Schimpanse *m* **-n,-n** chimpanzee

schimpf|en *vi* (*haben*) grumble (**mit** at; **über**+*acc* about); scold (**mit jdm** s.o.) ● *vt* call. **S~name** *m* term of abuse. **S~wort** *nt* (*pl* **-wörter**) swear-word; (*Beleidigung*) insult

schind|en† *vt* work *or* drive hard; (*quälen*) ill-treat; **sich s~en** slave [away]; **Eindruck s~en** (*fam*) try to impress. **S~er** *m* **-s,-** slave-driver. **S~erei** *f* **-** slave-driving; (*Plackerei*) hard slog

Schinken *m* **-s,-** ham. **S~speck** *m* bacon

Schippe *f* **-,-n** shovel. **s~n** *vt* shovel

Schirm *m* **-[e]s,-e** umbrella; (*Sonnen-*) sunshade; (*Lampen-*) shade; (*Augen-*) visor; (*Mützen-*) peak; (*Ofen-, Bild-*) screen; (*fig: Schutz*) shield. **S~herr** *m* patron. **S~herrschaft** *f* patronage. **S~mütze** *f* peaked cap

schizophren *a* schizophrenic. **S~ie** *f* - schizophrenia

Schlacht *f* **-,-en** battle

schlachten *vt* slaughter, kill

Schlachter, Schlächter *m* **-s,-** (*NGer*) butcher

Schlacht|feld *nt* battlefield. **S~haus** *nt*, **S~hof** *m* abattoir. **S~platte** *f* plate of assorted cooked meats and sausages. **S~schiff** *nt* battleship

Schlacke *f* **-,-n** slag

Schlaf *m* **-[e]s** sleep; **im S~** in one's sleep. **S~anzug** *m* pyjamas *pl*, (*Amer*) pajamas *pl*. **S~couch** *f* sofa bed

Schläfe *f* **-,-n** (*Anat*) temple

schlafen† *vi* (*haben*) sleep; (*fam: nicht aufpassen*) be asleep; **s~ gehen** go to bed; **er schläft noch** he is still asleep. **S~szeit** *f* bedtime

Schläfer(in) *m* **-s,-** (*f* **-,-nen**) sleeper

schlaff *a* limp, *adv* -ly; ⟨*Seil*⟩ slack; ⟨*Muskel*⟩ flabby

Schlaf|lied *nt* lullaby. **s~los** *a* sleepless. **S~losigkeit** *f* - insomnia. **S~mittel** *nt* sleeping drug

schläfrig *a* sleepy, *adv* -ily

Schlaf|saal *m* dormitory. **S~sack** *m* sleeping-bag. **S~tablette** *f* sleeping-pill. **s~trunken** *a* [still] half asleep. **S~wagen** *m* sleeping-car, sleeper. **s~wandeln** *vi* (*haben/sein*) sleep-walk. **S~zimmer** *nt* bedroom

Schlag *m* **-[e]s,⸚e** blow; (*Faust-*) punch; (*Herz-, Puls-, Trommel-*) beat; (*einer Uhr*) chime; (*Glocken-, Gong- & Med*) stroke; (*elektrischer*) shock; (*Portion*) helping; (*Art*) type; (*Aust*) whipped cream; **S⸚e bekommen** get a beating; **S~ auf S~** in rapid succession. **S~ader** *f* artery. **S~anfall** *m* stroke. **s~artig** *a* sudden, *adv* -ly. **S~baum** *m* barrier

schlagen† *vt* hit, strike; (*fällen*) fell; knock ⟨*Loch, Nagel*⟩ (**in** + *acc* into); (*prügeln, besiegen*) beat; (*Culin*) whisk ⟨*Eiweiß*⟩; whip ⟨*Sahne*⟩; (*legen*) throw; (*wickeln*) wrap; (*hinzufügen*) add (**zu** to); **sich s~** fight; **sich geschlagen geben** admit defeat ● *vi* (*haben*) beat; ⟨*Tür:*⟩ bang; ⟨*Uhr:*⟩ strike; (*melodisch*) chime; **mit den Flügeln s~** flap its wings; **um sich s~** lash out; **es schlug sechs** the clock struck six ● *vi* (*sein*) **in etw** (*acc*) **s~** ⟨*Blitz, Kugel:*⟩ strike sth; **s~ an** (+ *acc*) knock against; **nach jdm s~** (*fig*) take after s.o. **s~d** *a* (*fig*) conclusive, *adv* -ly

Schlager *m* **-s,-** pop song; (*Erfolg*) hit

Schläger *m* **-s,-** racket; (*Tischtennis-*) bat; (*Golf-*) club; (*Hockey-*) stick; (*fam: Raufbold*) thug. **S~ei** *f* **-,-en** fight, brawl

schlag|fertig *a* quick-witted. **S~instrument** *nt* percussion instrument. **S~loch** *nt* pot-hole. **S~sahne** *f* whipped cream; (*ungeschlagen*) whipping cream. **S~seite** *f* (*Naut*) list. **S~stock** *m* truncheon. **S~wort** *nt* (*pl* **-worte**) slogan. **S~zeile** *f* headline. **S~zeug** *nt* (*Mus*) percussion. **S~zeuger** *m* **-s,-** percussionist; (*in Band*) drummer

schlaksig *a* gangling

Schlamassel *m & nt* **-s** (*fam*) mess

Schlamm *m* **-[e]s** mud. **s~ig** *a* muddy

Schlamp|e *f* **-,-n** (*fam*) slut. **s~en** *vi* (*haben*) (*fam*) be sloppy (**bei** in). **S~erei** *f* **-,-en** sloppiness; (*Unordnung*) mess. **s~ig** *a* slovenly; ⟨*Arbeit*⟩ sloppy ● *adv* in a slovenly way; sloppily

Schlange *f* **-,-n** snake; (*Menschen-, Auto-*) queue; **S~ stehen** queue, (*Amer*) stand in line

schlängeln (sich) *vr* wind; ⟨*Person:*⟩ weave (**durch** through)

Schlangen|biß *m* snakebite. **S~linie** *f* wavy line

schlank *a* slim. **S~heit** *f* slimness. **S~heitskur** *f* slimming diet

schlapp *a* tired; (*schlaff*) limp, *adv* -ly. **S~e** *f* **-,-n** (*fam*) setback

schlau *a* clever, *adv* -ly; (*gerissen*) crafty, *adv* -ily; **ich werde nicht s~ daraus** I can't make head or tail of it

Schlauch *m* **-[e]s, Schläuche** tube; (*Wasser-*) hose[pipe]. **S~boot** *nt* rubber dinghy. **s~en** *vt* (*fam*) exhaust

Schlaufe *f* **-,-n** loop

schlecht *a* bad; (*böse*) wicked; (*unzulänglich*) poor; **s~ werden** go bad; ⟨*Wetter:*⟩ turn bad; **s~er werden** get worse; **s~ aussehen** look bad/⟨*Person:*⟩ unwell; **mir ist s~** I feel sick ● *adv* badly; poorly; (*kaum*) not really. **s~gehen**† *vi sep* (*sein*) (+ *dat*) **es geht ihm s~** he's doing badly; (*gesundheitlich*) he's not well. **s~gelaunt** *attrib a* bad-tempered.

s~hin *adv* quite simply. **S~igkeit** *f* - wickedness. **s~machen** *vt sep* (*fam*) run down

schlecken *vt/i* (*haben*) lick (**an etw** *dat* sth); (*auf-*) lap up

Schlegel *m* **-s,-** mallet; (*Trommel-*) stick; (*SGer: Keule*) leg; (*Hühner-*) drumstick

schleichen† *vi* (*sein*) creep; (*langsam gehen/fahren*) crawl ● *vr* **sich s~** creep. **s~d** *a* creeping; ⟨*Krankheit*⟩ insidious

Schleier *m* **-s,-** veil; (*fig*) haze. **s~haft** *a* **es ist mir s~haft** (*fam*) it's a mystery to me

Schleife *f* **-,-n** bow; (*Fliege*) bow-tie; (*Biegung*) loop

schleifen[1] *v* (*reg*) ● *vt* drag; (*zerstören*) raze to the ground ● *vi* (*haben*) trail, drag

schleifen[2]† *vt* grind; (*schärfen*) sharpen; cut ⟨*Edelstein, Glas*⟩; (*drillen*) drill

Schleim *m* **-[e]s** slime; (*Anat*) mucus; (*Med*) phlegm. **s~ig** *a* slimy

schlemm|en *vi* (*haben*) feast ● *vt* feast on. **S~er** *m* **-s,-** gourmet

schlendern *vi* (*sein*) stroll

schlenkern *vt/i* (*haben*) swing; **s~ mit** swing; dangle ⟨*Beine*⟩

Schlepp|dampfer *m* tug. **S~e** *f* **-,-n** train. **s~en** *vt* drag; (*tragen*) carry; (*ziehen*) tow; **sich s~en** drag oneself; (*sich hinziehen*) drag on; **sich s~en mit** carry. **s~end** *a* slow, *adv* -ly. **S~er** *m* **-s,-** tug; (*Traktor*) tractor. **S~kahn** *m* barge. **S~lift** *m* T-bar lift. **S~tau** *nt* tow-rope; **ins S~tau nehmen** take in tow

Schleuder *f* **-,-n** catapult; (*Wäsche-*) spin-drier. **s~n** *vt* hurl; spin ⟨*Wäsche*⟩; extract ⟨*Honig*⟩ ● *vi* (*sein*) skid; **ins S~n geraten** skid. **S~preise** *mpl* knock-down prices. **S~sitz** *m* ejector seat

schleunigst *adv* hurriedly; (*sofort*) at once

Schleuse *f* **-,-n** lock; (*Sperre*) sluice [-gate]. **s~n** *vt* steer

Schliche *pl* tricks; **jdm auf die S~ kommen** (*fam*) get on to s.o.

schlicht *a* plain, *adv* -ly; (*einfach*) simple, *adv* -ply

schlicht|en *vt* settle ● *vi* (*haben*) arbitrate. **S~ung** *f* - settlement; (*Jur*) arbitration

Schlick *m* **-[e]s** silt

Schließe *f* **-,-n** clasp; (*Schnalle*) buckle

schließen† *vt* close; (*ab-*) lock; fasten ⟨*Kleid, Verschluß*⟩; (*stillegen*) close down; (*beenden, folgern*) conclude; enter into ⟨*Vertrag*⟩; **sich s~** close; **in die Arme s~** embrace; **etw s~ an** (+*acc*) connect sth to; **sich s~ an** (+*acc*) follow ● *vi* (*haben*) close; (*den Betrieb einstellen*) close down; (*den Schlüssel drehen*) turn the key; (*enden, folgern*) conclude; **s~ lassen auf** (+*acc*) suggest

Schließ|fach *nt* locker. **s~lich** *adv* finally, in the end; (*immerhin*) after all. **S~ung** *f* **-,-en** closure

Schliff *m* **-[e]s** cut; (*Schleifen*) cutting; (*fig*) polish; **der letzte S~** the finishing touches *pl*

schlimm *a* bad, *adv* -ly; **s~er werden** get worse; **nicht so s~!** it doesn't matter! **s~stenfalls** *adv* if the worst comes to the worst

Schlinge *f* **-,-n** loop; (*Henkers-*) noose; (*Med*) sling; (*Falle*) snare

Schlingel *m* **-s,-** (*fam*) rascal

schling|en† *vt* wind, wrap; tie ⟨*Knoten*⟩; **sich s~en um** coil around ● *vi* (*haben*) bolt one's food. **S~pflanze** *f* climber

Schlips *m* **-es,-e** tie

Schlitten *m* **-s,-** sledge; (*Rodel-*) toboggan; (*Pferde-*) sleigh; **S~ fahren** toboggan

schlittern *vi* (*haben/sein*) slide

Schlittschuh *m* skate; **S~ laufen** skate. **S~läufer(in)** *m(f)* skater

Schlitz *m* **-es,-e** slit; (*für Münze*) slot; (*Jacken-*) vent; (*Hosen-*) flies *pl*. **s~en** *vt* slit

Schloß *nt* **-sses,⸚sser** lock; (*Vorhänge-*) padlock; (*Verschluß*) clasp; (*Gebäude*) castle; (*Palast*) palace

Schlosser *m* **-s,-** locksmith; (*Auto-*) mechanic; (*Maschinen-*) fitter

Schlot *m* **-[e]s,-e** chimney

schlottern *vi* (*haben*) shake, tremble; ⟨*Kleider:*⟩ hang loose

Schlucht *f* **-,-en** ravine, gorge

schluchz|en *vi* (*haben*) sob. **S~er** *m* **-s,-** sob

Schluck *m* **-[e]s,-e** mouthful; (*klein*) sip

Schluckauf *m* **-s** hiccups *pl*

schlucken *vt/i* (*haben*) swallow. **S~** *m* **-s** hiccups *pl*

schlud|ern *vi* (*haben*) be sloppy (**bei** in). **s~rig** *a* sloppy, *adv* -ily; ⟨*Arbeit*⟩ slipshod

Schlummer *m* **-s** slumber. **s~n** *vi* (*haben*) slumber

Schlund *m* **-[e]s** [back of the] throat; (*fig*) mouth
schlüpf|en *vi* (*sein*) slip; **[aus dem Ei] s~en** hatch. **S~er** *m* **-s,-** knickers *pl*. **s~rig** *a* slippery; (*anstößig*) smutty
schlurfen *vi* (*sein*) shuffle
schlürfen *vt/i* (*haben*) slurp
Schluß *m* **-sses,¨-sse** end; (*S~folgerung*) conclusion; **zum S~** finally; **S~ machen** stop (**mit etw** sth); finish (**mit jdm** with s.o.)
Schlüssel *m* **-s,-** key; (*Schrauben-*) spanner; (*Geheim-*) code; (*Mus*) clef. **S~bein** *nt* collar-bone. **S~bund** *m & nt* bunch of keys. **S~loch** *nt* keyhole. **S~ring** *m* key-ring
Schlußfolgerung *f* conclusion
schlüssig *a* conclusive, *adv* -ly; **sich** (*dat*) **s~ werden** make up one's mind
Schluß|licht *nt* rear-light. **S~verkauf** *m* [end of season] sale
Schmach *f* - disgrace
schmachten *vi* (*haben*) languish
schmächtig *a* slight
schmackhaft *a* tasty
schmal *a* narrow; (*dünn*) thin; (*schlank*) slender; (*karg*) meagre
schmälern *vt* diminish; (*herabsetzen*) belittle
Schmalz[1] *nt* **-es** lard; (*Ohren-*) wax
Schmalz[2] *m* **-es** (*fam*) schmaltz. **s~ig** *a* (*fam*) schmaltzy, slushy
schmarotz|en *vi* (*haben*) be parasitic (**auf** + *acc* on); ⟨*Person:*⟩ sponge (**bei** on). **S~er** *m* **-s,-** parasite; (*Person*) sponger
Schmarren *m* **-s,-** (*Aust*) pancake [torn into strips]; (*fam: Unsinn*) rubbish
schmatzen *vi* (*haben*) eat noisily
schmausen *vi* (*haben*) feast
schmecken *vi* (*haben*) taste (**nach** of); **[gut] s~** taste good; **hat es dir geschmeckt?** did you enjoy it? ● *vt* taste
Schmeichelei *f* **-,-en** flattery; (*Kompliment*) compliment
schmeichel|haft *a* complimentary, flattering. **s~n** *vi* (*haben*) (+ *dat*) flatter
schmeißen† *vt/i* (*haben*) **s~ [mit]** (*fam*) chuck
Schmeißfliege *f* bluebottle
schmelz|en† *vt/i* (*sein*) melt; smelt ⟨*Erze*⟩. **S~wasser** *nt* melted snow
Schmerbauch *m* (*fam*) paunch
Schmerz *m* **-es,-en** pain; (*Kummer*) grief; **S~en haben** be in pain. **s~en** *vt* hurt; (*fig*) grieve ● *vi* (*haben*) hurt, be painful. **S~ensgeld** *nt* compensation for pain and suffering. **s~haft** *a* painful. **s~lich** *a* (*fig*) painful; (*traurig*) sad, *adv* -ly. **s~los** *a* painless, *adv* -ly. **s~stillend** *a* pain-killing; **s~stillendes Mittel** analgesic, pain-killer. **S~tablette** *f* pain-killer
Schmetterball *m* (*Tennis*) smash
Schmetterling *m* **-s,-e** butterfly
schmettern *vt* hurl; (*Tennis*) smash; (*singen*) sing; (*spielen*) blare out ● *vi* (*haben*) sound; ⟨*Trompeten:*⟩ blare
Schmied *m* **-[e]s,-e** blacksmith
Schmiede *f* **-,-n** forge. **S~eisen** *nt* wrought iron. **s~n** *vt* forge; (*fig*) hatch; **Pläne s~n** make plans
schmieg|en *vt* press; **sich s~en an** (+ *acc*) nestle *or* snuggle up to; ⟨*Kleid:*⟩ cling to. **s~sam** *a* supple
Schmier|e *f* **-,-n** grease; (*Schmutz*) mess. **s~en** *vt* lubricate; (*streichen*) spread; (*schlecht schreiben*) scrawl; (*sl: bestechen*) bribe ● *vi* (*haben*) smudge; (*schreiben*) scrawl. **S~fett** *nt* grease. **S~geld** *nt* (*fam*) bribe. **s~ig** *a* greasy; (*schmutzig*) grubby; (*anstößig*) smutty; ⟨*Person*⟩ slimy. **S~mittel** *nt* lubricant
Schminke *f* **-,-n** make-up. **s~n** *vt* make up; **sich s~n** put on make-up; **sich** (*dat*) **die Lippen s~n** put on lipstick
schmirgel|n *vt* sand down. **S~papier** *nt* emery-paper
schmökern *vt/i* (*haben*) (*fam*) read
schmollen *vi* (*haben*) sulk; (*s~d den Mund verziehen*) pout
schmor|en *vt/i* (*haben*) braise; (*fam: schwitzen*) roast. **S~topf** *m* casserole
Schmuck *m* **-[e]s** jewellery; (*Verzierung*) ornament, decoration
schmücken *vt* decorate, adorn; **sich s~** adorn oneself
schmuck|los *a* plain. **S~stück** *nt* piece of jewellery; (*fig*) jewel
schmuddelig *a* grubby
Schmuggel *m* **-s** smuggling. **s~n** *vt* smuggle. **S~ware** *f* contraband
Schmuggler *m* **-s,-** smuggler
schmunzeln *vi* (*haben*) smile
schmusen *vi* (*haben*) cuddle
Schmutz *m* **-es** dirt; **in den S~ ziehen** (*fig*) denigrate. **s~en** *vi* (*haben*) get dirty. **S~fleck** *m* dirty mark. **s~ig** *a* dirty
Schnabel *m* **-s,¨** beak, bill; (*eines Kruges*) lip; (*Tülle*) spout

Schnake *f* **-,-n** mosquito; (*Kohl-*) daddy-long-legs
Schnalle *f* **-,-n** buckle. **s~n** *vt* strap; (*zu-*) buckle; **den Gürtel enger s~n** tighten one's belt
schnalzen *vi* (*haben*) **mit der Zunge/den Fingern s~** click one's tongue/snap one's fingers
schnapp|en *vi* (*haben*) **s~en nach** snap at; gasp for ⟨*Luft*⟩ ● *vt* snatch, grab; (*fam: festnehmen*) nab. **S~schloß** *nt* spring lock. **S~schuß** *m* snapshot
Schnaps *m* **-es,¨e** schnapps
schnarchen *vi* (*haben*) snore
schnarren *vi* (*haben*) rattle; ⟨*Klingel:*⟩ buzz
schnattern *vi* (*haben*) cackle
schnauben *vi* (*haben*) snort ● *vt* **sich** (*dat*) **die Nase s~** blow one's nose
schnaufen *vi* (*haben*) puff, pant
Schnauze *f* **-,-n** muzzle; (*eines Kruges*) lip; (*Tülle*) spout
Schnecke *f* **-,-n** snail; (*Nackt-*) slug; (*Spirale*) scroll; (*Gebäck*) ≈ Chelsea bun. **S~nhaus** *nt* snail-shell
Schnee *m* **-s** snow; (*Eier-*) beaten egg-white. **S~ball** *m* snowball. **S~besen** *m* whisk. **S~brille** *f* snow-goggles *pl*. **S~fall** *m* snowfall. **S~flocke** *f* snowflake. **S~glöckchen** *nt* **-s,-** snowdrop. **S~kette** *f* snow chain. **S~mann** *m* (*pl* **-männer**) snowman. **S~pflug** *m* snow-plough. **S~schläger** *m* whisk. **S~sturm** *m* snowstorm, blizzard. **S~wehe** *f* **-,-n** snow-drift
Schneid *m* **-[e]s** (*SGer*) courage
Schneide *f* **-,-n** [cutting] edge; (*Klinge*) blade
schneiden† *vt* cut; (*in Scheiben*) slice; (*kreuzen*) cross; (*nicht beachten*) cut dead; **Gesichter s~** pull faces; **sich s~** cut oneself; (*über-*) intersect; **sich** (*dat/acc*) **in den Finger s~** cut one's finger. **s~d** *a* cutting; (*kalt*) biting
Schneider *m* **-s,-** tailor. **S~in** *f* **-,-nen** dressmaker. **s~n** *vt* make ⟨*Anzug, Kostüm*⟩
Schneidezahn *m* incisor
schneidig *a* dashing, *adv* -ly
schneien *vi* (*haben*) snow; **es schneit** it is snowing
Schneise *f* **-,-n** path; (*Feuer-*) firebreak
schnell *a* quick; ⟨*Auto, Tempo*⟩ fast ● *adv* quickly; (*in s~em Tempo*) fast; (*bald*) soon; **mach s~!** hurry up! **s~en** *vi* (*sein*) **in die Höhe s~en** shoot up. **S~igkeit** *f* - rapidity; (*Tempo*) speed. **S~imbiß** *m* snack-bar. **S~kochtopf** *m* pressure-cooker. **S~reinigung** *f* express cleaners. **s~stens** *adv* as quickly as possible. **S~zug** *m* express [train]
schnetzeln *vt* cut into thin strips
schneuzen (sich) *vr* blow one's nose
schnippen *vt* flick
schnippisch *a* pert, *adv* -ly
Schnipsel *m* & *nt* **-s,-** scrap
Schnitt *m* **-[e]s,-e** cut; (*Film-*) cutting; (*S~muster*) [paper] pattern; **im S~** (*durchschnittlich*) on average
Schnitte *f* **-,-n** slice [of bread]; (*belegt*) open sandwich
schnittig *a* stylish; (*stromlinienförmig*) streamlined
Schnitt|käse *m* hard cheese. **S~lauch** *m* chives *pl*. **S~muster** *nt* [paper] pattern. **S~punkt** *m* [point of] intersection. **S~wunde** *f* cut
Schnitzel *nt* **-s,-** scrap; (*Culin*) escalope. **s~n** *vt* shred
schnitz|en *vt/i* (*haben*) carve. **S~er** *m* **-s,-** carver; (*fam: Fehler*) blunder. **S~erei** *f* **-,-en** carving
schnodderig *a* (*fam*) brash
schnöde *a* despicable, *adv* -bly; (*verächtlich*) contemptuous, *adv* -ly
Schnorchel *m* **-s,-** snorkel
Schnörkel *m* **-s,-** flourish; (*Kunst*) scroll. **s~ig** *a* ornate
schnorren *vt/i* (*haben*) (*fam*) scrounge
schnüffeln *vi* (*haben*) sniff (**an etw** *dat* sth); (*fam: spionieren*) snoop [around]
Schnuller *m* **-s,-** [baby's] dummy, (*Amer*) pacifier
schnupf|en *vt* sniff; **Tabak s~en** take snuff. **S~en** *m* **-s,-** [head] cold. **S~tabak** *m* snuff
schnuppern *vt/i* (*haben*) sniff (**an etw** *dat* sth)
Schnur *f* **-,¨e** string; (*Kordel*) cord; (*Besatz-*) braid; (*Electr*) flex; **eine S~** a piece of string
Schnür|chen *nt* **-s,-** **wie am S~chen** (*fam*) like clockwork. **s~en** *vt* tie; lace [up] ⟨*Schuhe*⟩
schnurgerade *a* & *adv* dead straight
Schnurr|bart *m* moustache. **s~en** *vi* (*haben*) hum; ⟨*Katze:*⟩ purr
Schnür|schuh *m* lace-up shoe. **S~senkel** *m* [shoe-]lace
schnurstracks *adv* straight

Schock *m* **-[e]s,-s** shock. **s~en** *vt* (*fam*) shock; **geschockt sein** be shocked. **s~ieren** *vt* shock; **s~ierend** shocking

Schöffe *m* **-n,-n** lay judge

Schokolade *f* - chocolate

Scholle *f* **-,-n** clod [of earth]; (*Eis-*) [ice-]floe; (*Fisch*) plaice

schon *adv* already; (*allein*) just; (*sogar*) even; (*ohnehin*) anyway; **s~ einmal** before; (*jemals*) ever; **s~ immer/oft/wieder** always/often/again; **hast du ihn s~ gesehen?** have you seen him yet? **s~ der Gedanke daran** the mere thought of it; **s~ deshalb** for that reason alone; **das ist s~ möglich** that's quite possible; **ja s~, aber** well yes, but; **nun geh/komm s~!** go/come on then!

schön *a* beautiful; ⟨*Wetter*⟩ fine; (*angenehm, nett*) nice; (*gut*) good; (*fam: beträchtlich*) pretty; **s~en Dank!** thank you very much! **na s~** all right then ● *adv* beautifully; nicely; (*gut*) well; **s~ langsam** nice and slowly

schonen *vt* spare; (*gut behandeln*) look after; **sich s~** take things easy. **s~d** *a* gentle, *adv* -tly

Schönheit *f* **-,-en** beauty. **S~sfehler** *m* blemish. **S~skonkurrenz** *f*, **S~swettbewerb** *m* beauty contest

schönmachen *vt sep* smarten up; **sich s~** make oneself look nice

Schonung *f* **-,-en** gentle care; (*nach Krankheit*) rest; (*Baum-*) plantation. **s~slos** *a* ruthless, *adv* -ly

Schonzeit *f* close season

schöpf|en *vt* scoop [up]; ladle ⟨*Suppe*⟩; **Mut s~en** take heart; **frische Luft s~en** get some fresh air. **S~er** *m* **-s,-** creator; (*Kelle*) ladle. **s~erisch** *a* creative. **S~kelle** *f*, **S~löffel** *m* ladle. **S~ung** *f* **-,-en** creation

Schoppen *m* **-s,-** (*SGer*) ≈ pint

Schorf *m* **-[e]s** scab

Schornstein *m* chimney; (*Naut*) funnel. **S~feger** *m* **-s,-** chimney-sweep

Schoß *m* **-es,¨e** lap; (*Frack-*) tail

Schote *f* **-,-n** pod; (*Erbse*) pea

Schotte *m* **-n,-n** Scot, Scotsman

Schotter *m* **-s** gravel; (*für Gleise*) ballast

schott|isch *a* Scottish, Scots. **S~land** *nt* **-s** Scotland

schraffieren *vt* hatch

schräg *a* diagonal, *adv* -ly; (*geneigt*) sloping; **s~ halten** tilt. **S~e** *f* **-,-n** slope. **S~strich** *m* oblique stroke

Schramme *f* **-,-n** scratch. **s~n** *vt* scrape, scratch

Schrank *m* **-[e]s,¨e** cupboard; (*Kleider-*) wardrobe; (*Akten-, Glas-*) cabinet

Schranke *f* **-,-n** barrier

Schraube *f* **-,-n** screw; (*Schiffs-*) propeller. **s~n** *vt* screw; (*ab-*) unscrew; (*drehen*) turn; **sich in die Höhe s~n** spiral upwards. **S~nmutter** *f* nut. **S~nschlüssel** *m* spanner. **S~nzieher** *m* **-s,-** screwdriver

Schraubstock *m* vice

Schrebergarten *m* ≈ allotment

Schreck *m* **-[e]s,-e** fright; **jdm einen S~ einjagen** give s.o. a fright. **S~en** *m* **-s,-** fright; (*Entsetzen*) horror. **s~en** *vt* (*reg*) frighten; (*auf-*) startle ● *vi*† (*sein*) **in die Höhe s~en** start up

Schreck|gespenst *nt* spectre. **s~haft** *a* easily frightened; (*nervös*) jumpy. **s~lich** *a* terrible, *adv* -bly. **S~schuß** *m* warning shot

Schrei *m* **-[e]s,-e** cry, shout; (*gellend*) scream; **der letzte S~** (*fam*) the latest thing

Schreib|block *m* writing-pad. **s~en**† *vt/i* (*haben*) write; (*auf der Maschine*) type; **richtig/falsch s~en** spell right/wrong; **sich s~en** ⟨*Wort:*⟩ be spelt; (*korrespondieren*) correspond; **sich krank s~en lassen** get a doctor's certificate. **S~en** *nt* **-s,-** writing; (*Brief*) letter. **S~fehler** *m* spelling mistake. **S~heft** *nt* exercise book. **S~kraft** *f* clerical assistant; (*für Maschineschreiben*) typist. **S~maschine** *f* typewriter. **S~papier** *nt* writing-paper. **S~schrift** *f* script. **S~tisch** *m* desk. **S~ung** *f* **-,-en** spelling. **S~waren** *fpl* stationery *sg.* **S~weise** *f* spelling

schreien† *vt/i* (*haben*) cry; (*gellend*) scream; (*rufen, laut sprechen*) shout; **zum S~ sein** (*fam*) be a scream. **s~d** *a* (*fig*) glaring; (*grell*) garish

Schreiner *m* **-s,-** joiner

schreiten† *vi* (*sein*) walk

Schrift *f* **-,-en** writing; (*Druck-*) type; (*Abhandlung*) paper; **die Heilige S~** the Scriptures *pl.* **S~führer** *m* secretary. **s~lich** *a* written ● *adv* in writing. **S~sprache** *f* written language. **S~steller(in)** *m* **-s,-** (*f* **-,-nen**) writer.

S~stück *nt* document. **S~zeichen** *nt* character
schrill *a* shrill, *adv* -y
Schritt *m* **-[e]s,-e** step; (*Entfernung*) pace; (*Gangart*) walk; (*der Hose*) crotch; **im S~** in step; (*langsam*) at walking pace; **S~ halten mit** (*fig*) keep pace with. **S~macher** *m* **-s,-** pace-maker. **s~weise** *adv* step by step
schroff *a* precipitous, *adv* -ly; (*abweisend*) brusque, *adv* -ly; (*unvermittelt*) abrupt, *adv* -ly; ⟨*Gegensatz*⟩ stark
schröpfen *vt* (*fam*) fleece
Schrot *m & nt* **-[e]s** coarse meal; (*Blei-*) small shot. **s~en** *vt* grind coarsely. **S~flinte** *f* shotgun
Schrott *m* **-[e]s** scrap[-metal]; **zu S~ fahren** (*fam*) write off. **S~platz** *m* scrap-yard. **s~reif** *a* ready for the scrap-heap
schrubb|en *vt/i* (*haben*) scrub. **S~er** *m* **-s,-** [long-handled] scrubbing-brush
Schrull|e *f* **-,-n** whim; **alte S~e** (*fam*) old crone. **s~ig** *a* cranky
schrumpfen *vi* (*sein*) shrink; ⟨*Obst:*⟩ shrivel
schrump[e]lig *a* wrinkled
Schrunde *f* **-,-n** crack; (*Spalte*) crevasse
Schub *m* **-[e]s,¨e** (*Phys*) thrust; (*S~fach*) drawer; (*Menge*) batch. **S~fach** *nt* drawer. **S~karre** *f*, **S~karren** *m* wheelbarrow. **S~lade** *f* drawer
Schubs *m* **-es,-e** push, shove. **s~en** *vt* push, shove
schüchtern *a* shy, *adv* -ly; (*zaghaft*) tentative, *adv* -ly. **S~heit** *f* **-** shyness
Schuft *m* **-[e]s,-e** (*pej*) swine. **s~en** *vi* (*haben*) (*fam*) slave away
Schuh *m* **-[e]s,-e** shoe. **S~anzieher** *m* **-s,-** shoehorn. **S~band** *nt* (*pl* **-bänder**) shoe-lace. **S~creme** *f* shoe-polish. **S~löffel** *m* shoehorn. **S~macher** *m* **-s,-** shoemaker; (*zum Flicken*) [shoe] mender. **S~werk** *nt* shoes *pl*
Schul|abgänger *m* **-s,-** school-leaver. **S~arbeiten, S~aufgaben** *fpl* homework *sg*. **S~buch** *nt* school-book
Schuld *f* **-,-en** guilt; (*Verantwortung*) blame; (*Geld-*) debt; **S~en machen** get into debt; **S~ haben an** (+*dat*) be to blame for ● **s~ haben** *od* **sein** be to blame (**an** + *dat* for); **jdm s~ geben** blame s.o. **s~en** *vt* owe
schuldig *a* guilty (*gen* of); (*gebührend*) due; **jdm etw s~ sein** owe s.o. sth. **S~keit** *f* **-** duty
schuld|los *a* innocent. **S~ner** *m* **-s,-** debtor. **S~spruch** *m* guilty verdict
Schule *f* **-,-n** school; **in der/die S~** at/to school. **s~n** *vt* train
Schüler|(in) *m* **-s,-** (*f* **-,-nen**) pupil. **S~lotse** *m* pupil acting as crossing warden
schul|frei *a* **s~freier Tag** day without school; **wir haben morgen s~frei** there's no school tomorrow. **S~hof** *m* [school] playground. **S~jahr** *nt* school year; (*Klasse*) form. **S~junge** *m* schoolboy. **S~kind** *nt* schoolchild. **S~leiter(in)** *m(f)* head [teacher]. **S~mädchen** *nt* school-girl. **S~stunde** *f* lesson
Schulter *f* **-,-n** shoulder. **S~blatt** *nt* shoulder-blade. **s~n** *vt* shoulder. **S~tuch** *nt* shawl
Schulung *f* **-** training
schummeln *vi* (*haben*) (*fam*) cheat
Schund *m* **-[e]s** trash. **S~roman** *m* trashy novel
Schuppe *f* **-,-n** scale; **S~n** *pl* dandruff *sg*. **s~n (sich)** *vr* flake [off]
Schuppen *m* **-s,-** shed
Schur *f* **-** shearing
Schür|eisen *nt* poker. **s~en** *vt* poke; (*fig*) stir up
schürf|en *vt* minc; **sich** (*dat*) **das Knie s~en** graze one's knee ● *vi* (*haben*) **s~en nach** prospect for. **S~wunde** *f* abrasion, graze
Schürhaken *m* poker
Schurke *m* **-n,-n** villain
Schürze *f* **-,-n** apron. **s~n** *vt* (*raffen*) gather [up]; tie ⟨*Knoten*⟩; purse ⟨*Lippen*⟩. **S~njäger** *m* (*fam*) womanizer
Schuß *m* **-sses,¨sse** shot; (*kleine Menge*) dash
Schüssel *f* **-,-n** bowl; (*TV*) dish
schusselig *a* (*fam*) scatter-brained
Schuß|fahrt *f* (*Ski*) schuss. **S~waffe** *f* firearm
Schuster *m* **-s,-** = **Schuhmacher**
Schutt *m* **-[e]s** rubble. **S~abladeplatz** *m* rubbish dump
Schüttel|frost *m* shivering fit. **s~n** *vt* shake; **sich s~n** shake oneself/itself; (*vor Ekel*) shudder; **jdm die Hand s~n** shake s.o.'s hand
schütten *vt* pour; (*kippen*) tip; (*ver-*) spill ● *vi* (*haben*) **es schüttet** it is pouring [with rain]

Schutthaufen *m* pile of rubble

Schutz *m* **-es** protection; (*Zuflucht*) shelter; (*Techn*) guard; **S~ suchen** take refuge; **unter dem S~ der Dunkelheit** under cover of darkness. **S~anzug** *m* protective suit. **S~blech** *nt* mudguard. **S~brille** goggles *pl*

Schütze *m* **-n,-n** marksman; (*Tor-*) scorer; (*Astr*) Sagittarius; **guter S~** good shot

schützen *vt* protect/(*Zuflucht gewähren*) shelter (**vor** + *dat* from) ● *vi* (*haben*) give protection/shelter (**vor** + *dat* from). **s~d** *a* protective, *adv* -ly

Schützenfest *nt* fair with shooting competition

Schutz|engel *m* guardian angel. **S~heilige(r)** *m/f* patron saint

Schützling *m* **-s,-e** charge; (*Protegé*) protégé

schutz|los *a* defenceless, helpless. **S~mann** *m* (*pl* **-männer** & **-leute**) policeman. **S~umschlag** *m* dust-jacket

Schwaben *nt* **-s** Swabia

schwäbisch *a* Swabian

schwach *a* (**schwächer, schwächst**) weak, *adv* -ly; (*nicht gut; gering*) poor, *adv* -ly; (*leicht*) faint, *adv* -ly

Schwäche *f* **-,-n** weakness. **s~n** *vt* weaken

Schwach|heit *f* **-** weakness. **S~kopf** *m* (*fam*) idiot

schwäch|lich *a* delicate. **S~ling** *m* **-s,-e** weakling

Schwachsinn *m* mental deficiency. **s~ig** *a* mentally deficient; (*fam*) idiotic

Schwächung *f* **-** weakening

schwafeln (*fam*) *vi* (*haben*) waffle ● *vt* talk

Schwager *m* **-s,¨** brother-in-law

Schwägerin *f* **-,-nen** sister-in-law

Schwalbe *f* **-,-n** swallow

Schwall *m* **-[e]s** torrent

Schwamm *m* **-[e]s,¨e** sponge; (*SGer: Pilz*) fungus; (*eßbar*) mushroom. **s~ig** *a* spongy; (*aufgedunsen*) bloated

Schwan *m* **-[e]s,¨e** swan

schwanen *vi* (*haben*) (*fam*) **mir schwante, daß** I had a nasty feeling that

schwanger *a* pregnant

schwängern *vt* make pregnant

Schwangerschaft *f* **-,-en** pregnancy

Schwank *m* **-[e]s,¨e** (*Theat*) farce

schwank|en *vi* (*haben*) sway; ⟨*Boot:*⟩ rock; (*sich ändern*) fluctuate; (*unentschieden sein*) be undecided ● (*sein*) stagger. **S~ung** *f* **-,-en** fluctuation

Schwanz *m* **-es,¨e** tail

schwänzen *vt* (*fam*) skip; **die Schule s~** play truant

Schwarm *m* **-[e]s,¨e** swarm; (*Fisch-*) shoal; (*fam: Liebe*) idol

schwärmen *vi* (*haben*) swarm; **s~ für** (*fam*) adore; (*verliebt sein*) have a crush on; **s~ von** (*fam*) rave about

Schwarte *f* **-,-n** (*Speck-*) rind; (*fam: Buch*) tome

schwarz *a* (**schwärzer, schwärzest**) black; (*fam: illegal*) illegal, *adv* -ly; **s~er Markt** black market; **s~ gekleidet** dressed in black; **s~ auf weiß** in black and white; **ins S~e treffen** score a bull's-eye. **S~** *nt* **-[e]s,-** black. **S~arbeit** *f* moonlighting. **s~arbeiten** *vi sep* (*haben*) moonlight. **S~brot** *nt* black bread. **S~e(r)** *m/f* black

Schwärze *f* **-** blackness. **s~n** *vt* blacken

Schwarz|fahrer *m* fare-dodger. **S~handel** *m* black market (**mit** in). **S~händler** *m* black marketeer. **S~markt** *m* black market. **s~sehen**† *vi sep* (*haben*) watch television without a licence; (*fig*) be pessimistic. **S~wald** *m* Black Forest. **s~weiß** *a* black and white

Schwatz *m* **-es** (*fam*) chat

schwatzen, (*SGer*) **schwätzen** *vi* (*haben*) chat; (*klatschen*) gossip; (*Sch*) talk [in class] ● *vt* talk

schwatzhaft *a* garrulous

Schwebe *f* **- in der S~** (*fig*) undecided. **S~bahn** *f* cable railway. **s~n** *vi* (*haben*) float; (*fig*) be undecided; ⟨*Verfahren:*⟩ be pending; **in Gefahr s~n** be in danger ● (*sein*) float

Schwed|e *m* **-n,-n** Swede. **S~en** *nt* **-s** Sweden. **S~in** *f* **-,-nen** Swede. **s~isch** *a* Swedish

Schwefel *m* **-s** sulphur. **S~säure** *f* sulphuric acid

schweigen† *vi* (*haben*) be silent; **ganz zu s~ von** to say nothing of, let alone. **S~** *nt* **-s** silence; **zum S~ bringen** silence. **s~d** *a* silent, *adv* -ly

schweigsam *a* silent; (*wortkarg*) taciturn

Schwein *nt* **-[e]s,-e** pig; (*Culin*) pork; (*sl*) (*schmutziger Mensch*) dirty pig; (*Schuft*) swine; **S~ haben** (*fam*) be lucky. **S~ebraten** *m* roast pork. **S~efleisch** *nt* pork. **S~ehund** *m* (*sl*) swine. **S~erei** *f* **-,-en** (*sl*) [dirty] mess; (*Gemeinheit*) dirty trick. **S~estall** *m* pigsty. **s~isch** *a* lewd. **S~sleder** *nt* pigskin

Schweiß *m* **-es** sweat

schweiß|en *vt* weld. **S~er** *m* **-s,-** welder

Schweiz (die) - Switzerland. **S~er** *a* & *m* **-s,-, S~erin** *f* **-,-nen** Swiss. **s~erisch** *a* Swiss

schwelen *vi* (*haben*) smoulder

schwelgen *vi* (*haben*) feast; **s~ in** (+*dat*) wallow in

Schwelle *f* **-,-n** threshold; (*Eisenbahn-*) sleeper

schwell|en† *vi* (*sein*) swell. **S~ung** *f* **-,-en** swelling

Schwemme *f* **-,-n** watering-place; (*fig: Überangebot*) glut. **s~n** *vt* wash; **an Land s~n** wash up

Schwenk *m* **-[e]s** swing. **s~en** *vt* swing; (*schwingen*) wave; (*spülen*) rinse; **in Butter s~en** toss in butter • *vi* (*sein*) turn

schwer *a* heavy; (*schwierig*) difficult; (*mühsam, streng*) hard; (*ernst*) serious; (*schlimm*) bad; **3 Pfund s~ sein** weigh 3 pounds • *adv* heavily; with difficulty; (*mühsam, streng*) hard; (*schlimm, sehr*) badly, seriously; **s~ hören** be hard of hearing; **s~ arbeiten** work hard; **s~ zu sagen** difficult *or* hard to say

Schwere *f* - heaviness; (*Gewicht*) weight; (*Schwierigkeit*) difficulty; (*Ernst*) gravity. **S~losigkeit** *f* - weightlessness

schwer|fallen† *vi sep* (*sein*) be hard (*dat* for). **s~fällig** *a* ponderous, *adv* -ly; (*unbeholfen*) clumsy, *adv* -ily. **S~gewicht** *nt* heavyweight. **s~hörig** *a* **s~hörig sein** be hard of hearing. **S~kraft** *f* (*Phys*) gravity. **s~krank** *a* seriously ill. **s~lich** *adv* hardly. **s~machen** *vt sep* make difficult (*dat* for). **s~mütig** *a* melancholic. **s~nehmen**† *vt sep* take seriously. **S~punkt** *m* centre of gravity; (*fig*) emphasis

Schwert *nt* **-[e]s,-er** sword. **S~lilie** *f* iris

schwer|tun† **(sich)** *vr sep* have difficulty (**mit** with). **S~verbrecher** *m* serious offender. **s~verdaulich** *a* indigestible. **s~verletzt** *a* seriously injured. **s~wiegend** *a* weighty

Schwester *f* **-,-n** sister; (*Kranken-*) nurse. **s~lich** *a* sisterly

Schwieger|eltern *pl* parents-in-law. **S~mutter** *f* mother-in-law. **S~sohn** *m* son-in-law. **S~tochter** *f* daughter-in-law. **S~vater** *m* father-in-law

Schwiele *f* **-,-n** callus

schwierig *a* difficult. **S~keit** *f* **-,-en** difficulty

Schwimm|bad *nt* swimming-baths *pl.* **S~becken** *nt* swimming-pool. **s~en**† *vt/i* (*sein/haben*) swim; (*auf dem Wasser treiben*) float. **S~er** *m* **-s,-** swimmer; (*Techn*) float. **S~weste** *f* life-jacket

Schwindel *m* **-s** dizziness, vertigo; (*fam: Betrug*) fraud; (*Lüge*) lie. **S~anfall** *m* dizzy spell. **s~frei** *a* **s~frei sein** have a good head for heights. **s~n** *vi* (*haben*) (*lügen*) lie; **mir** *od* **mich s~t** I feel dizzy

schwinden† *vi* (*sein*) dwindle; (*vergehen*) fade; (*nachlassen*) fail

Schwindl|er *m* **-s,-** liar; (*Betrüger*) fraud, con-man. **s~ig** *a* dizzy; **mir ist** *od* **wird s~ig** I feel dizzy

schwing|en† *vi* (*haben*) swing; (*Phys*) oscillate; (*vibrieren*) vibrate • *vt* swing; wave ⟨*Fahne*⟩; (*drohend*) brandish. **S~tür** *f* swing-door. **S~ung** *f* **-,-en** oscillation; vibration

Schwips *m* **-es,-e einen S~ haben** (*fam*) be tipsy

schwirren *vi* (*haben/sein*) buzz; (*surren*) whirr

Schwitz|e *f* **-,-n** (*Culin*) roux. **s~en** *vi* (*haben*) sweat; **ich s~e** *od* **mich s~t** I am hot • *vt* (*Culin*) sweat

schwören† *vt/i* (*haben*) swear (**auf**+*acc* by); **Rache s~** swear revenge

schwul *a* (*fam: homosexuell*) gay

schwül *a* close. **S~e** *f* - closeness

schwülstig *a* bombastic, *adv* -ally

Schwung *m* **-[e]s,̈-e** swing; (*Bogen*) sweep; (*Schnelligkeit*) momentum; (*Kraft*) vigour; (*Feuer*) verve; (*fam: Anzahl*) batch; **in S~ kommen** gather momentum; (*fig*) get going. **s~haft** *a* brisk, *adv* -ly. **s~los** *a* dull. **s~voll** *a* vigorous, *adv* -ly; ⟨*Bogen, Linie*⟩ sweeping; (*mitreißend*) spirited, lively

Schwur *m* **-[e]s,̈-e** vow; (*Eid*) oath. **S~gericht** *nt* jury [court]

sechs *inv a*, **S~** *f* **-,-en** six; (*Sch*) ≈ fail mark. **s~eckig** *a* hexagonal. **s~te(r,s)** *a* sixth

sech|zehn *inv a* sixteen. **s~zehnte(r,s)** *a* sixteenth. **s~zig** *inv a* sixty. **s~zigste(r,s)** *a* sixtieth

sedieren *vt* sedate

See¹ *m* **-s,-n** /'ze:ən/ lake

See² *f* **-** sea; **an die/der See** to/at the seaside; **auf See** at sea. **S~bad** *nt* seaside resort. **S~fahrt** *f* [sea] voyage; (*Schiffahrt*) navigation. **S~gang** *m* **schwerer S~gang** rough sea. **S~hund** *m* seal. **s~krank** *a* seasick

Seele *f* **-,-n** soul. **s~nruhig** *a* calm, *adv* -ly

seelisch *a* psychological, *adv* -ly; (*geistig*) mental, *adv* -ly

Seelsorger *m* **-s,-** pastor

See|luft *f* sea air. **S~macht** *f* maritime power. **S~mann** *m* (*pl* **-leute**) seaman, sailor. **S~not** *f* **in S~not** in distress. **S~räuber** *m* pirate. **S~reise** *f* [sea] voyage. **S~rose** *f* water-lily. **S~sack** *m* kitbag. **S~stern** *m* starfish. **S~tang** *m* seaweed. **s~tüchtig** *a* seaworthy. **S~weg** *m* sea route; **auf dem S~weg** by sea. **S~zunge** *f* sole

Segel *nt* **-s,-** sail. **S~boot** *nt* sailing-boat. **S~fliegen** *nt* gliding. **S~flieger** *m* glider pilot. **S~flugzeug** *nt* glider. **s~n** *vt/i* (*sein/haben*) sail. **S~schiff** *nt* sailing-ship. **S~sport** *m* sailing. **S~tuch** *nt* canvas

Segen *m* **-s** blessing. **s~sreich** *a* beneficial; (*gesegnet*) blessed

Segler *m* **-s,-** yachtsman

Segment *nt* **-[e]s,-e** segment

segnen *vt* bless; **gesegnet mit** blessed with

sehen† *vt* see; watch ⟨*Fernsehsendung*⟩; **sich s~ lassen** show oneself ● *vi* (*haben*) see; (*blicken*) look (**auf** +*acc* at); (*ragen*) show (**aus** above); **gut/schlecht s~** have good/bad eyesight; **vom S~ kennen** know by sight; **s~ nach** keep an eye on; (*betreuen*) look after; (*suchen*) look for; **darauf s~, daß** see [to it] that. **s~swert, s~swürdig** *a* worth seeing. **S~swürdigkeit** *f* **-,-en** sight

Sehkraft *f* sight, vision

Sehne *f* **-,-n** tendon; (*eines Bogens*) string

sehnen (sich) *vr* long (**nach** for)

sehnig *a* sinewy; (*zäh*) stringy

sehn|lich[st] *a* ⟨*Wunsch*⟩ dearest ● *adv* longingly. **S~sucht** *f* **-** longing (**nach** for). **s~süchtig** *a* longing, *adv* -ly; ⟨*Wunsch*⟩ dearest

sehr *adv* very; (*mit Verb*) very much

seicht *a* shallow

seid *s.* **sein¹; ihr s~** you are

Seide *f* **-,-n** silk

Seidel *nt* **-s,-** beer-mug

seiden *a* silk ... **S~papier** *nt* tissue paper. **S~raupe** *f* silkworm. **s~weich** *a* silky-soft

seidig *a* silky

Seife *f* **-,-n** soap. **S~npulver** *nt* soap powder. **S~nschaum** *m* lather

seifig *a* soapy

seihen *vt* strain

Seil *nt* **-[e]s,-e** rope; (*Draht-*) cable. **S~bahn** *f* cable railway. **s~springen**† *vi* (*sein*) (*inf & pp only*) skip. **S~tänzer(in)** *m*(*f*) tightrope walker

sein¹† *vi* (*sein*) be; **er ist Lehrer** he is a teacher; **sei still!** be quiet! **mir ist kalt/schlecht** I am cold/feel sick; **wie dem auch sei** be that as it may ● *v aux* have; **angekommen/gestorben s~** have arrived/died; **er war/wäre gefallen** he had/would have fallen; **es ist/war viel zu tun/nichts zu sehen** there is/was a lot to be done/nothing to be seen

sein² *poss pron* his; (*Ding, Tier*) its; (*nach man*) one's; **sein Glück versuchen** try one's luck. **s~e(r,s)** *poss pron* his; (*nach man*) one's own; **das S~e tun** do one's share. **s~erseits** *adv* for his part. **s~erzeit** *adv* in those days. **s~etwegen** *adv* for his sake; (*wegen ihm*) because of him, on his account. **s~etwillen** *adv* **um s~etwillen** for his sake. **s~ige** *poss pron* **der/die/das s~ige** his

seinlassen† *vt sep* leave; (*aufhören mit*) stop

seins *poss pron* his; (*nach man*) one's own

seit *conj & prep* (+*dat*) since; **s~ wann?** since when? **s~ einiger Zeit** for some time [past]; **ich wohne s~ zehn Jahren hier** I've lived here for ten years. **s~dem** *conj* since ● *adv* since then

Seite *f* **-,-n** side; (*Buch-*) page; **S~ an S~** side by side; **zur S~ legen/treten** put/step aside; **jds starke S~** s.o.'s strong point; **von S~n** (+*gen*) on the part of; **auf der einen/anderen S~** (*fig*) on the one/other hand

seitens *prep* (+*gen*) on the part of

Seiten|schiff *nt* [side] aisle. **S~sprung** *m* infidelity; **einen S~sprung machen** be unfaithful. **S~stechen** *nt* **-s** (*Med*) stitch.

S~straße *f* side-street. **S~streifen** *m* verge; (*Autobahn-*) hard shoulder

seither *adv* since then

seit|lich *a* side ... ● *adv* at/on the side; **s~lich von** to one side of ● *prep* (+*gen*) to one side of. **s~wärts** *adv* on/to one side; (*zur Seite*) sideways

Sekret *nt* **-[e]s,-e** secretion

Sekret|är *m* **-s,-e** secretary; (*Schrank*) bureau. **S~ariat** *nt* **-[e]s,-e** secretary's office. **S~ärin** *f* **-,-nen** secretary

Sekt *m* **-[e]s** [German] sparkling wine

Sekte *f* **-,-n** sect

Sektion /-'tsi̯o:n/ *f* **-,-en** section; (*Sezierung*) autopsy

Sektor *m* **-s,-en** /-'to:rən/ sector

Sekundant *m* **-en,-en** (*Sport*) second

sekundär *a* secondary

Sekunde *f* **-,-n** second

selber *pron* (*fam*) = **selbst**

selbst *pron* oneself; **ich/du/er/sie s~** I myself/you yourself/he himself/she herself; **wir/ihr/sie s~** we ourselves/you yourselves/they themselves; **ich schneide mein Haar s~** I cut my own hair; **von s~** of one's own accord; (*automatisch*) automatically ● *adv* even. **S~achtung** *f* self-esteem, self-respect

selbständig *a* independent, *adv* -ly; self-employed ⟨*Handwerker*⟩; **sich s~ machen** set up on one's own. **S~keit** *f* - independence

Selbstaufopferung *f* self-sacrifice

Selbstbedienung *f* self-service. **S~srestaurant** *nt* self-service restaurant, cafeteria

Selbst|befriedigung *f* masturbation. **S~beherrschung** *f* self-control. **S~bestimmung** *f* self-determination. **s~bewußt** *a* self-confident. **S~bewußtsein** *nt* self-confidence. **S~bildnis** *nt* self-portrait. **S~erhaltung** *f* self-preservation. **s~gefällig** *a* self-satisfied, smug, *adv* -ly. **s~gemacht** *a* home-made. **s~gerecht** *a* self-righteous. **S~gespräch** *nt* soliloquy; **S~gespräche führen** talk to oneself. **s~haftend** *a* self-adhesive. **s~herrlich** *a* autocratic, *adv* -ally. **S~hilfe** *f* self-help. **s~klebend** *a* self-adhesive. **S~kostenpreis** *m* cost price. **S~laut** *m* vowel. **s~los** *a* selfless, *adv* -ly. **S~mitleid** *nt* self-pity. **S~mord** *m* suicide. **S~mörder(in)** *m(f)* suicide. **s~mörderisch** *a* suicidal. **S~porträt** *nt* self-portrait. **s~sicher** *a* self-assured. **S~sicherheit** *f* self-assurance. **s~süchtig** *a* selfish, *adv* -ly. **S~tanken** *nt* self-service (*for petrol*). **s~tätig** *a* automatic, *adv* -ally. **S~versorgung** *f* self-catering

selbstverständlich *a* natural, *adv* -ly; **etw für s~ halten** take sth for granted; **das ist s~** that goes without saying; **s~!** of course! **S~keit** *f* - matter of course; **das ist eine S~keit** that goes without saying

Selbst|verteidigung *f* self-defence. **S~vertrauen** *nt* self-confidence. **S~verwaltung** *f* self-government. **s~zufrieden** *a* complacent, *adv* -ly

selig *a* blissfully happy; (*Relig*) blessed; (*verstorben*) late. **S~keit** *f* - bliss

Sellerie *m* **-s,-s** & *f* **-,-** celeriac; (*Stangen-*) celery

selten *a* rare ● *adv* rarely, seldom; (*besonders*) exceptionally. **S~heit** *f* **-,-en** rarity

Selterswasser *nt* seltzer [water]

seltsam *a* odd, *adv* -ly, strange, *adv* -ly. **s~erweise** *adv* oddly/strangely enough

Semester *nt* **-s,-** (*Univ*) semester

Semikolon *nt* **-s,-s** semicolon

Seminar *nt* **-s,-e** seminar; (*Institut*) department; (*Priester-*) seminary

Semmel *f* **-,-n** [bread] roll. **S~brösel** *pl* breadcrumbs

Senat *m* **-[e]s,-e** senate. **S~or** *m* **-s,-en** /-'to:rən/ senator

senden[1]† *vt* send

sende|n[2] *vt* (*reg*) broadcast; (*über Funk*) transmit, send. **S~r** *m* **-s,-** [broadcasting] station; (*Anlage*) transmitter. **S~reihe** *f* series

Sendung *f* **-,-en** consignment, shipment; (*Auftrag*) mission; (*Radio, TV*) programme

Senf *m* **-s** mustard

sengend *a* scorching

senil *a* senile. **S~ität** *f* - senility

Senior *m* **-s,-en** /-'o:rən/ senior; **S~en** senior citizens. **S~enheim** *nt* old people's home. **S~enteller** *m* senior citizen's menu

Senke *f* **-,-n** dip, hollow

Senkel *m* **-s,-** [shoe-]lace

senken *vt* lower; bring down ⟨*Fieber, Preise*⟩; bow ⟨*Kopf*⟩; **sich s~** come down, fall; (*absinken*) subside; (*abfallen*) slope down

senkrecht *a* vertical, *adv* -ly. **S~e** *f* **-n,-n** perpendicular
Sensation /-'tsi̯o:n/ *f* **-,-en** sensation. **s~ell** *a* sensational, *adv* -ly
Sense *f* **-,-n** scythe
sensib|el *a* sensitive, *adv* -ly. **S~ilität** *f* **-** sensitivity
sentimental *a* sentimental. **S~ität** *f* **-** sentimentality
separat *a* separate, *adv* -ly
September *m* **-s,-** September
Serenade *f* **-,-n** serenade
Serie /'ze:ri̯ə/ *f* **-,-n** series; (*Briefmarken*) set; (*Comm*) range. **S~nnummer** *f* serial number
seriös *a* respectable, *adv* -bly; (*zuverlässig*) reliable, *adv* -bly; (*ernstgemeint*) serious
Serpentine *f* **-,-n** winding road; (*Kehre*) hairpin bend
Serum *nt* **-s, Sera** serum
Service[1] /zɛr'vi:s/ *nt* **-[s],-** /-'vi:s[əs], -'vi:sə/ service, set
Service[2] /'zø:ɐ̯vɪs/ *m & nt* **-s** /-vɪs[əs]/ (*Comm, Tennis*) service
servier|en *vt/i* (*haben*) serve. **S~erin** *f* **-,-nen** waitress. **S~wagen** *m* trolley
Serviette *f* **-,-n** napkin, serviette
Servus *int* (*Aust*) cheerio; (*Begrüßung*) hallo
Sessel *m* **-s,-** armchair. **S~bahn** *f*, **S~lift** *m* chair-lift
seßhaft *a* settled; **s~ werden** settle down
Set /zɛt/ *nt & m* **-[s],-s** set; (*Deckchen*) place-mat
setz|en *vt* put; (*abstellen*) set down; (*hin-*) sit down ⟨*Kind*⟩; move ⟨*Spielstein*⟩; (*pflanzen*) plant; (*schreiben, wetten*) put; **sich s~en** sit down; (*sinken*) settle ● *vi* (*sein*) leap ● *vi* (*haben*) **s~en auf** (+*acc*) back. **S~ling** *m* **-s,-e** seedling
Seuche *f* **-,-n** epidemic
seufz|en *vi* (*haben*) sigh. **S~er** *m* **-s,-** sigh
Sex /zɛks/ *m* **-[es]** sex. **s~istisch** *a* sexist
Sexu|alität *f* **-** sexuality. **s~ell** *a* sexual, *adv* -ly
sexy /'zɛksi/ *inv a* sexy
sezieren *vt* dissect
Shampoo /ʃam'pu:/, **Shampoon** /ʃam'po:n/ *nt* **-s** shampoo
siamesisch *a* Siamese
sich *refl pron* oneself; (*mit er/sie/es*) himself/herself/itself; (*mit sie pl*) themselves; (*mit Sie*) yourself; (*pl*) yourselves; (*einander*) each other; **s~ kennen** know oneself/(*einander*) each other; **s~ waschen** have a wash; **s~** (*dat*) **die Zähne putzen/die Haare kämmen** clean one's teeth/comb one's hair; **s~** (*dat*) **das Bein brechen** break a leg; **s~ wundern/schämen** be surprised/ashamed; **s~ gut lesen/verkaufen** read/sell well; **von s~ aus** of one's own accord
Sichel *f* **-,-n** sickle
sicher *a* safe; (*gesichert*) secure; (*gewiß*) certain; (*zuverlässig*) reliable; sure ⟨*Urteil, Geschmack*⟩; steady ⟨*Hand*⟩; (*selbstbewußt*) self-confident; **sich** (*dat*) **etw** (*gen*) **s~ sein** be sure of sth; **bist du s~?** are you sure? ● *adv* safely; securely; certainly; reliably; self-confidently; (*wahrscheinlich*) most probably; **er kommt s~** he is sure to come; **s~!** certainly! **s~gehen**† *vi sep* (*sein*) be sure
Sicherheit *f* **-** safety; (*Pol, Psych, Comm*) security; (*Gewißheit*) certainty; (*Zuverlässigkeit*) reliability; (*des Urteils, Geschmacks*) surety; (*Selbstbewußtsein*) self-confidence. **S~sgurt** *m* safety-belt; (*Auto*) seat-belt. **s~shalber** *adv* to be on the safe side. **S~snadel** *f* safety-pin
sicherlich *adv* certainly; (*wahrscheinlich*) most probably
sicher|n *vt* secure; (*garantieren*) safeguard; (*schützen*) protect; put the safety-catch on ⟨*Pistole*⟩; **sich** (*dat*) **etw s~n** secure sth. **s~stellen** *vt sep* safeguard; (*beschlagnahmen*) seize. **S~ung** *f* **-,-en** safeguard, protection; (*Gewehr-*) safety-catch; (*Electr*) fuse
Sicht *f* **-** view; (*S~weite*) visibility; **in S~ kommen** come into view; **auf lange S~** in the long term. **s~bar** *a* visible, *adv* -bly. **s~en** *vt* sight; (*durchsehen*) sift through. **s~lich** *a* obvious, *adv* -ly. **S~vermerk** *m* visa. **S~weite** *f* visibility; **in/außer S~weite** within/out of sight
sickern *vi* (*sein*) seep
sie *pron* (*nom*) (*sg*) she; (*Ding, Tier*) it; (*pl*) they; (*acc*) (*sg*) her; (*Ding, Tier*) it; (*pl*) them
Sie *pron* you; **gehen/warten Sie!** go/wait!
Sieb *nt* **-[e]s,-e** sieve; (*Tee-*) strainer. **s~en**[1] *vt* sieve, sift
sieben[2] *inv a*, **S~** *f* **-,-en** seven. **S~sachen** *fpl* (*fam*) belongings. **s~te(r,s)** *a* seventh

sieb|te(r,s) *a* seventh. **s~zehn** *inv a* seventeen. **s~zehnte(r,s)** *a* seventeenth. **s~zig** *inv a* seventy. **s~zigste(r,s)** *a* seventieth

siede|n† *vt/i* (*haben*) boil. **S~punkt** *m* boiling point

Siedl|er *m* **-s,-** settler. **S~ung** *f* **-,-en** [housing] estate; (*Niederlassung*) settlement

Sieg *m* **-[e]s,-e** victory

Siegel *nt* **-s,-** seal. **S~ring** *m* signet-ring

sieg|en *vi* (*haben*) win. **S~er(in)** *m* **-s,-** (*f* **-,-nen**) winner. **s~reich** *a* victorious

siezen *vt* **jdn s~** call s.o. 'Sie'

Signal *nt* **-s,-e** signal. **s~isieren** *vt* signal

signieren *vt* sign

Silbe *f* **-,-n** syllable. **S~ntrennung** *f* word-division

Silber *nt* **-s** silver. **S~hochzeit** *f* silver wedding. **s~n** *a* silver. **S~papier** *nt* silver paper

Silhouette /zɪ'lu̯ɛtə/ *f* **-,-n** silhouette

Silizium *nt* **-s** silicon

Silo *m & nt* **-s,-s** silo

Silvester *nt* **-s** New Year's Eve

simpel *a* simple, *adv* -ply; (*einfältig*) simple-minded

Simplex *nt* **-,-e** simplex

Sims *m & nt* **-es,-e** ledge; (*Kamin-*) mantelpiece

Simul|ant *m* **-en,-en** malingerer. **s~ieren** *vt* feign; (*Techn*) simulate • *vi* (*haben*) pretend; (*sich krank stellen*) malinger

simultan *a* simultaneous, *adv* -ly

sind *s.* **sein¹; wir/sie s~** we/they are

Sinfonie *f* **-,-n** symphony

singen† *vt/i* (*haben*) sing

Singular *m* **-s,-e** singular

Singvogel *m* songbird

sinken† *vi* (*sein*) sink; (*nieder-*) drop; (*niedriger werden*) go down, fall; **den Mut s~ lassen** lose courage

Sinn *m* **-[e]s,-e** sense; (*Denken*) mind; (*Zweck*) point; **im S~ haben** have in mind; **in gewissem S~e** in a sense; **es hat keinen S~** it is pointless; **nicht bei S~en sein** be out of one's mind. **S~bild** *nt* symbol. **s~en†** *vi* (*haben*) think; **auf Rache s~en** plot one's revenge

sinnlich *a* sensory; (*sexuell*) sensual; ⟨*Genüsse*⟩ sensuous. **S~keit** *f* **-** sensuality; sensuousness

sinn|los *a* senseless, *adv* -ly; (*zwecklos*) pointless, *adv* -ly. **s~voll** *a* meaningful; (*vernünftig*) sensible, *adv* -bly

Sintflut *f* flood

Siphon /'zi:fõ/ *m* **-s,-s** siphon

Sipp|e *f* **-,-n** clan. **S~schaft** *f* **-** clan; (*Pack*) crowd

Sirene *f* **-,-n** siren

Sirup *m* **-s,-e** syrup; (*schwarzer*) treacle

Sitte *f* **-,-n** custom; **S~n** manners. **s~nlos** *a* immoral

sittlich *a* moral, *adv* -ly. **S~keit** *f* **-** morality. **S~keitsverbrecher** *m* sex offender

sittsam *a* well-behaved; (*züchtig*) demure, *adv* -ly

Situ|ation /-'tsi̯o:n/ *f* **-,-en** situation. **s~iert** *a* **gut/schlecht s~iert** well/badly off

Sitz *m* **-es,-e** seat; (*Paßform*) fit

sitzen† *vi* (*haben*) sit; (*sich befinden*) be; (*passen*) fit; (*fam: treffen*) hit home; **s~ bleiben** remain seated; **[im Gefängnis] s~** (*fam*) be in jail. **s~bleiben†** *vi sep* (*sein*) (*fam*) (*Sch*) stay *or* be kept down; (*nicht heiraten*) be left on the shelf; **s~bleiben auf** (+*dat*) be left with. **s~d** *a* seated; ⟨*Tätigkeit*⟩ sedentary. **s~lassen†** *vt sep* (*fam*) (*nicht heiraten*) jilt; (*im Stich lassen*) leave in the lurch; (*Sch*) keep down

Sitz|gelegenheit *f* seat. **S~platz** *m* seat. **S~ung** *f* **-,-en** session

Sizilien /-i̯ən/ *nt* **-s** Sicily

Skala *f* **-,-len** scale; (*Reihe*) range

Skalpell *nt* **-s,-e** scalpel

skalpieren *vt* scalp

Skandal *m* **-s,-e** scandal. **s~ös** *a* scandalous

skandieren *vt* scan ⟨*Verse*⟩; chant ⟨*Parolen*⟩

Skandinav|ien /-i̯ən/ *nt* **-s** Scandinavia. **s~isch** *a* Scandinavian

Skat *m* **-s** skat

Skelett *nt* **-[e]s,-e** skeleton

Skep|sis *f* **-** scepticism. **s~tisch** *a* sceptical, *adv* -ly; (*mißtrauisch*) doubtful, *adv* -ly

Ski /ʃi:/ *m* **-s,-er** ski; **Ski fahren** *od* **laufen** ski. **S~fahrer(in), S~läufer(in)** *m(f)* skier. **S~sport** *m* skiing

Skizz|e *f* **-,-n** sketch. **s~enhaft** *a* sketchy, *adv* -ily. **s~ieren** *vt* sketch

Sklav|e *m* **-n,-n** slave. **S~erei** *f* **-** slavery. **S~in** *f* **-,-nen** slave. **s~isch** *a* slavish, *adv* -ly

Skorpion *m* **-s,-e** scorpion; (*Astr*) Scorpio

Skrupel *m* **-s,-** scruple. **s~los** *a* unscrupulous
Skulptur *f* **-,-en** sculpture
skurril *a* absurd, *adv* -ly
Slalom *m* **-s,-s** slalom
Slang /slɛŋ/ *m* **-s** slang
Slaw|e *m* **-n,-n, S~in** *f* **-,-nen** Slav. **s~isch** *a* Slav; (*Lang*) Slavonic
Slip *m* **-s,-s** briefs *pl*
Smaragd *m* **-[e]s,-e** emerald
Smoking *m* **-s,-s** dinner jacket, (*Amer*) tuxedo
Snob *m* **-s,-s** snob. **S~ismus** *m* - snobbery. **s~istisch** *a* snobbish
so *adv* so; (*so sehr*) so much; (*auf diese Weise*) like this/that; (*solch*) such; (*fam: sowieso*) anyway; (*fam: umsonst*) free; (*fam: ungefähr*) about; **nicht so schnell** not so fast; **so gut/bald wie** as good/soon as; **so ein Mann** a man like that; **so ein Zufall!** what a coincidence! **so nicht** not like that; **mir ist so, als ob** I feel as if; **so oder so** in any case; **eine Stunde oder so** an hour or so; **so um zehn Mark** (*fam*) about ten marks; **[es ist] gut so** that's fine; **so, das ist geschafft** there, that's done; **so?** really? **so kommt doch!** come on then! ● *conj* (*also*) so; (*dann*) then; **so daß** so that; **so gern ich auch käme** as much as I would like to come
sobald *conj* as soon as
Söckchen *nt* **-s,-** [ankle] sock
Socke *f* **-,-n** sock
Sockel *m* **-s,-** plinth, pedestal
Socken *m* **-s,-** sock
Soda *nt* **-s** soda. **S~wasser** *nt* soda water
Sodbrennen *nt* **-s** heartburn
soeben *adv* just [now]
Sofa *nt* **-s,-s** settee, sofa
sofern *adv* provided [that]
sofort *adv* at once, immediately; (*auf der Stelle*) instantly. **s~ig** *a* immediate
Software /ˈzɔftvɛːɐ̯/ *f* - software
sogar *adv* even
sogenannt *a* so-called
sogleich *adv* at once
Sohle *f* **-,-n** sole; (*Tal-*) bottom
Sohn *m* **-[e]s,⸗e** son
Sojabohne *f* soya bean
solange *conj* as long as
solch *inv pron* such; **s~ ein(e)** such a; **s~ einer/eine/eins** one/ (*Person*) someone like that. **s~e(r,s)** *pron* such; **ein s~er Mann/eine s~e Frau** a man/woman like that; **ich habe s~e Angst** I am so afraid ● (*substantivisch*) **ein s~er/eine s~e/ein s~es** one/ (*Person*) someone like that; **s~e** (*pl*) those; (*Leute*) people like that
Sold *m* **-[e]s** (*Mil*) pay
Soldat *m* **-en,-en** soldier
Söldner *m* **-s,-** mercenary
solidarisch *a* **s~e Handlung** act of solidarity; **sich s~ erklären** declare one's solidarity
Solidarität *f* - solidarity
solide *a* solid, *adv* -ly; (*haltbar*) sturdy, *adv* -ily; (*sicher*) sound, *adv* -ly; (*anständig*) respectable, *adv* -bly
Solist(in) *m* **-en,-en** (*f* **-,-nen**) soloist
Soll *nt* **-s** (*Comm*) debit; (*Produktions-*) quota
sollen† *v aux* **er soll warten** he is to wait; (*möge*) let him wait; **was soll ich machen?** what shall I do? **du sollst nicht lügen** you shouldn't tell lies; **du sollst nicht töten** (*liter*) thou shalt not kill; **ihr sollt jetzt still sein!** will you be quiet now! **du solltest dich schämen** you ought to *or* should be ashamed of yourself; **es hat nicht sein s~** it was not to be; **ich hätte es nicht tun s~** I ought not to *or* should not have done it; **er soll sehr nett/reich sein** he is supposed to be very nice/rich; **sollte es regnen, so ...** if it should rain then ...; **das soll man nicht [tun]** you're not supposed to [do that]; **soll ich [mal versuchen]?** shall I [try]? **soll er doch!** let him! **was soll's!** so what!
Solo *nt* **-s,-los & -li** solo. **s~** *adv* solo
somit *adv* therefore, so
Sommer *m* **-s,-** summer. **S~ferien** *pl* summer holidays. **s~lich** *a* summery; (*Sommer-*) summer ... ● *adv* **s~lich warm** as warm as summer. **S~schlußverkauf** *m* summer sale. **S~sprossen** *fpl* freckles. **s~sprossig** *a* freckled
Sonate *f* **-,-n** sonata
Sonde *f* **-,-n** probe
Sonder|angebot *nt* special offer. **s~bar** *a* odd, *adv* -ly. **S~fahrt** *f* special excursion. **S~fall** *m* special case. **s~gleichen** *adv* **eine Gemeinheit/Grausamkeit s~gleichen** unparalleled meanness/cruelty. **s~lich** *a* particular, *adv* -ly; (*sonderbar*) odd, *adv* -ly. **S~ling** *m* **-s,-e** crank. **S~marke** *f* special stamp

sondern *conj* but; **nicht nur ... s~ auch** not only ... but also

Sonder|preis *m* special price. **S~schule** *f* special school. **S~zug** *m* special train

sondieren *vt* sound out

Sonett *nt* **-[e]s,-e** sonnet

Sonnabend *m* **-s,-e** Saturday. **s~s** *adv* on Saturdays

Sonne *f* **-,-n** sun. **s~n (sich)** *vr* sun oneself; (*fig*) bask (**in** + *dat* in)

Sonnen|aufgang *m* sunrise. **s~baden** *vi* (*haben*) sunbathe. **S~bank** *f* sun-bed. **S~blume** *f* sunflower. **S~brand** *m* sunburn. **S~brille** *f* sun-glasses *pl*. **S~energie** *f* solar energy. **S~finsternis** *f* solar eclipse. **S~milch** *f* sun-tan lotion. **S~öl** *nt* sun-tan oil. **S~schein** *m* sunshine. **S~schirm** *m* sunshade. **S~stich** *m* sunstroke. **S~uhr** *f* sundial. **S~untergang** *m* sunset. **S~wende** *f* solstice

sonnig *a* sunny

Sonntag *m* **-s,-e** Sunday. **s~s** *adv* on Sundays

sonst *adv* (*gewöhnlich*) usually; (*im übrigen*) apart from that; (*andernfalls*) otherwise, or [else]; **wer/was/wie/wo s~?** who/what/how/where else? **s~ niemand/nichts** no one/nothing else; **s~ noch jemand/etwas?** anyone/anything else? **s~ noch Fragen?** any more questions? **s~ig** *a* other. **s~jemand** *pron* (*fam*) someone/(*fragend, verneint*) anyone else. **s~wer** *pron* = **s~jemand**. **s~wie** *adv* (*fam*) some/any other way. **s~wo** *adv* (*fam*) somewhere/anywhere else

sooft *conj* whenever

Sopran *m* **-s,-e** soprano

Sorge *f* **-,-n** worry (**um** about); (*Fürsorge*) care; **in S~ sein** be worried; **sich** (*dat*) **S~n machen** worry; **keine S~!** don't worry! **s~n** *vi* (*haben*) **s~n für** look after, care for; (*vorsorgen*) provide for; (*sich kümmern*) see to; **dafür s~n, daß** see [to it] *or* make sure that ● *vr* **sich s~n** worry. **s~nfrei** *a* carefree. **s~nvoll** *a* worried, *adv* -ly. **S~recht** *nt* (*Jur*) custody

Sorg|falt *f* **-** care. **s~fältig** *a* careful, *adv* -ly. **s~los** *a* careless, *adv* -ly; (*unbekümmert*) carefree. **s~sam** *a* careful, *adv* -ly

Sorte *f* **-,-n** kind, sort; (*Comm*) brand

sort|ieren *vt* sort [out]; (*Comm*) grade. **S~iment** *nt* **-[e]s,-e** range

sosehr *conj* however much

Soße *f* **-,-n** sauce; (*Braten-*) gravy; (*Salat-*) dressing

Souffl|eur /zu'flø:ɐ̯/ *m* **-s,-e**, **S~euse** /-ø:zə/ *f* **-,-n** prompter. **s~ieren** *vi* (*haben*) prompt

Souvenir /zuvə'ni:ɐ̯/ *nt* **-s,-s** souvenir

souverän /zuvə'rɛ:n/ *a* sovereign; (*fig: überlegen*) expert, *adv* -ly. **S~ität** *f* **-** sovereignty

soviel *conj* however much; **s~ ich weiß** as far as I know ● *adv* as much (**wie** as); **s~ wie möglich** as much as possible

soweit *conj* as far as; (*insoweit*) [in] so far as ● *adv* on the whole; **s~ wie möglich** as far as possible; **s~ sein** be ready; **es ist s~** the time has come

sowenig *conj* however little ● *adv* no more (**wie** than); **s~ wie möglich** as little as possible

sowie *conj* as well as; (*sobald*) as soon as

sowieso *adv* anyway, in any case

sowjet|isch *a* Soviet. **S~union** *f* **-** Soviet Union

sowohl *adv* **s~ ... als** *od* **wie auch ...** ... as well as ...; **s~ er als auch seine Frau** both he and his wife

sozial *a* social, *adv* -ly; ⟨*Einstellung, Beruf*⟩ caring. **S~arbeit** *f* social work. **S~arbeiter(in)** *m(f)* social worker. **S~demokrat** *m* social democrat. **S~hilfe** *f* social security

Sozialis|mus *m* **-** socialism. **S~t** *m* **-en,-en** socialist. **s~tisch** *a* socialist

Sozial|versicherung *f* National Insurance. **S~wohnung** *f* ≈ council flat

Soziol|oge *m* **-n,-n** sociologist. **S~ogie** *f* **-** sociology

Sozius *m* **-,-se** (*Comm*) partner; (*Beifahrersitz*) pillion

sozusagen *adv* so to speak

Spachtel *m* **-s,-** & *f* **-,-n** spatula

Spagat *m* **-[e]s,-e** (*Aust*) string; **S~ machen** do the splits *pl*

Spaghetti *pl* spaghetti *sg*

spähen *vi* (*haben*) peer

Spalier *nt* **-s,-e** trellis; **S~ stehen** line the route

Spalt *m* **-[e]s,-e** crack; (*im Vorhang*) chink

Spalt|e *f* **-,-n** crack, crevice; (*Gletscher-*) crevasse; (*Druck-*) column; (*Orangen-*) segment. **s~en**† *vt*

split; **sich s~en** split. **S~ung** *f* -,-en splitting; (*Kluft*) split; (*Phys*) fission

Span *m* -[e]s,¨e [wood] chip; (*Hobel-*) shaving

Spange *f* -,-n clasp; (*Haar-*) slide; (*Zahn-*) brace; (*Arm-*) bangle

Span|ien /-i̯ən/ *nt* -s Spain. **S~ier** *m* -s,-, **S~ierin** *f* -,-nen Spaniard. **s~isch** *a* Spanish. **S~isch** *nt* -[s] (*Lang*) Spanish

Spann *m* -[e]s instep

Spanne *f* -,-n span; (*Zeit-*) space; (*Comm*) margin

spann|en *vt* stretch; put up ⟨*Leine*⟩; (*straffen*) tighten; (*an-*) harness (**an** + *acc* to); **den Hahn s~en** cock the gun; **sich s~en** tighten ● *vi* (*haben*) be too tight. **s~end** *a* exciting. **S~er** *m* -s,- (*fam*) Peeping Tom. **S~ung** *f* -,-en tension; (*Erwartung*) suspense; (*Electr*) voltage

Spar|buch *nt* savings book. **S~büchse** *f* money-box. **s~en** *vt/i* (*haben*) save; (*sparsam sein*) economize (**mit/an** + *dat* on); **sich** (*dat*) **die Mühe s~en** save oneself the trouble. **S~er** *m* -s,- saver

Spargel *m* -s,- asparagus

Spar|kasse *f* savings bank. **S~konto** *nt* deposit account

spärlich *a* sparse, *adv* -ly; (*dürftig*) meagre; (*knapp*) scanty, *adv* -ily

Sparren *m* -s,- rafter

sparsam *a* economical, *adv* -ly; ⟨*Person*⟩ thrifty. **S~keit** *f* - economy; thrift

Sparschwein *nt* piggy bank

spartanisch *a* Spartan

Sparte *f* -,-n branch; (*Zeitungs-*) section; (*Rubrik*) column

Spaß *m* -es,¨e fun; (*Scherz*) joke; **im/aus/zum S~** for fun; **S~ machen** be fun; ⟨*Person:*⟩ be joking; **es macht mir keinen S~** I don't enjoy it; **viel S~!** have a good time! **s~en** *vi* (*haben*) joke. **s~ig** *a* amusing, funny. **S~vogel** *m* joker

Spast|iker *m* -s,- spastic. **s~isch** *a* spastic

spät *a* & *adv* late; **wie s~ ist es?** what time is it? **zu s~** too late; **zu s~ kommen** be late. **s~abends** *adv* late at night

Spatel *m* -s,- & *f* -,-n spatula

Spaten *m* -s,- spade

später *a* later; (*zukünftig*) future ● *adv* later

spätestens *adv* at the latest

Spatz *m* -en,-en sparrow

Spätzle *pl* (*Culin*) noodles

spazieren *vi* (*sein*) stroll. **s~gehen**† *vi sep* (*sein*) go for a walk

Spazier|gang *m* walk; **einen S~gang machen** go for a walk. **S~gänger(in)** *m* -s,- (*f* -,-nen) walker. **S~stock** *m* walking-stick

Specht *m* -[e]s,-e woodpecker

Speck *m* -s bacon; (*fam: Fettpolster*) fat. **s~ig** *a* greasy

Spedi|teur /ʃpedi'tøːɐ̯/ *m* -s,-e haulage/(*für Umzüge*) removals contractor. **S~tion** /-'tsi̯oːn/ *f* -,-en carriage, haulage; (*Firma*) haulage/(*für Umzüge*) removals firm

Speer *m* -[e]s,-e spear; (*Sport*) javelin

Speiche *f* -,-n spoke

Speichel *m* -s saliva

Speicher *m* -s,- warehouse; (*dial: Dachboden*) attic; (*Computer*) memory. **s~n** *vt* store

speien† *vt* spit; (*erbrechen*) vomit

Speise *f* -,-n food; (*Gericht*) dish; (*Pudding*) blancmange. **S~eis** *nt* ice-cream. **S~kammer** *f* larder. **S~karte** *f* menu. **s~n** *vi* (*haben*) eat; **zu Abend s~n** have dinner ● *vt* feed. **S~röhre** *f* oesophagus. **S~saal** *m* dining-room. **S~wagen** *m* dining-car

Spektakel *m* -s (*fam*) noise

spektakulär *a* spectacular

Spektrum *nt* -s,-tra spectrum

Spekul|ant *m* -en,-en speculator. **S~ation** /-'tsi̯oːn/ *f* -,-en speculation. **s~ieren** *vi* (*haben*) speculate; **s~ieren auf** (+*acc*) (*fam*) hope to get

Spelze *f* -,-n husk

spendabel *a* generous

Spende *f* -,-n donation. **s~n** *vt* donate; give ⟨*Blut, Schatten*⟩; **Beifall s~n** applaud. **S~r** *m* -s,- donor; (*Behälter*) dispenser

spendieren *vt* pay for; **jdm etw/ein Bier s~** treat s.o. to sth/stand s.o. a beer

Spengler *m* -s,- (*SGer*) plumber

Sperling *m* -s,-e sparrow

Sperre *f* -,-n barrier; (*Verbot*) ban; (*Comm*) embargo. **s~n** *vt* close; (*ver-*) block; (*verbieten*) ban; cut off ⟨*Strom, Telefon*⟩; stop ⟨*Scheck, Kredit*⟩; **s~n in** (+*acc*) put in ⟨*Gefängnis, Käfig*⟩; **sich s~n** balk (**gegen** at); **gesperrt gedruckt** (*Typ*) spaced

Sperr|holz *nt* plywood. **s~ig** *a* bulky. **S~müll** *m* bulky refuse. **S~stunde** *f* closing time

Spesen *pl* expenses

spezial|isieren (sich) *vr* specialize (**auf**+*acc* in). **S~ist** *m* **-en,-en** specialist. **S~ität** *f* **-,-en** speciality
speziell *a* special, *adv* -ly
spezifisch *a* specific, *adv* -ally
Sphäre /'sfɛ:rə/ *f* **-,-n** sphere
spicken *vt* (*Culin*) lard; **gespickt mit** (*fig*) full of ● *vi* (*haben*) (*fam*) crib (**bei** from)
Spiegel *m* **-s,-** mirror; (*Wasser-, Alkohol-*) level. **S~bild** *nt* reflection. **S~ei** *nt* fried egg. **s~n** *vt* reflect; **sich s~n** be reflected ● *vi* (*haben*) reflect [the light]; (*glänzen*) gleam. **S~ung** *f* **-,-en** reflection
Spiel *nt* **-[e]s,-e** game; (*Spielen*) playing; (*Glücks-*) gambling; (*Schau-*) play; (*Satz*) set; **ein S~ Karten** a pack/(*Amer*) deck of cards; **auf dem S~ stehen** be at stake; **aufs S~ setzen** risk. **S~art** *f* variety. **S~automat** *m* fruit machine. **S~bank** *f* casino. **S~dose** *f* musical box. **s~en** *vt/i* (*haben*) play; (*im Glücksspiel*) gamble; (*vortäuschen*) act; 〈*Roman:*〉 be set (**in**+*dat* in); **s~en mit** (*fig*) toy with. **s~end** *a* (*mühelos*) effortless, *adv* -ly
Spieler|(in) *m* **-s,-** (*f* **-,-nen**) player; (*Glücks-*) gambler. **S~ei** *f* **-,-en** amusement; (*Kleinigkeit*) trifle
Spiel|feld *nt* field, pitch. **S~gefährte** *m*, **S~gefährtin** *f* playmate. **S~karte** *f* playing-card. **S~marke** *f* chip. **S~plan** *m* programme. **S~platz** *m* playground. **S~raum** *m* (*fig*) scope; (*Techn*) clearance. **S~regeln** *fpl* rules [of the game]. **S~sachen** *fpl* toys. **S~verderber** *m* **-s,-** spoilsport. **S~waren** *fpl* toys. **S~warengeschäft** *nt* toyshop. **S~zeug** *nt* toy; (*S~sachen*) toys *pl*
Spieß *m* **-es,-e** spear; (*Brat-*) spit; (*für Schaschlik*) skewer; (*Fleisch-*) kebab; **den S~ umkehren** turn the tables on s.o. **S~bürger** *m* [petit] bourgeois. **s~bürgerlich** *a* bourgeois. **s~en** *vt* **etw auf etw** (*acc*) **s~en** spear sth with sth. **S~er** *m* **-s,-** [petit] bourgeois. **s~ig** *a* bourgeois. **S~ruten** *fpl* **S~ruten laufen** run the gauntlet
Spike[s]reifen /'ʃpaik[s]-/ *m* studded tyre
Spinat *m* **-s** spinach
Spind *m* & *nt* **-[e]s,-e** locker
Spindel *f* **-,-n** spindle
Spinne *f* **-,-n** spider
spinn|en† *vt/i* (*haben*) spin; **er spinnt** (*fam*) he's crazy. **S~ennetz** *nt* spider's web. **S~[en]gewebe** *nt*, **S~webe** *f* **-,-n** cobweb
Spion *m* **-s,-e** spy
Spionage /ʃpio'na:ʒə/ *f* **-** espionage, spying; **S~ treiben** spy. **S~abwehr** *f* counter-espionage
spionieren *vi* (*haben*) spy
Spionin *f* **-,-nen** [woman] spy
Spiral|e *f* **-,-n** spiral. **s~ig** *a* spiral
Spiritis|mus *m* **-** spiritualism. **s~tisch** *a* spiritualist
Spirituosen *pl* spirits
Spiritus *m* **-** alcohol; (*Brenn-*) methylated spirits *pl*. **S~kocher** *m* spirit stove
Spital *nt* **-s,¨er** (*Aust*) hospital
spitz *a* pointed; (*scharf*) sharp; (*schrill*) shrill; 〈*Winkel*〉 acute; **s~e Bemerkung** dig. **S~bube** *m* scoundrel; (*Schlingel*) rascal. **s~bübisch** *a* mischievous, *adv* -ly
Spitze *f* **-,-n** point; (*oberer Teil*) top; (*vorderer Teil*) front; (*Pfeil-, Finger-, Nasen-*) tip; (*Schuh-, Strumpf-*) toe; (*Zigarren-, Zigaretten-*) holder; (*Höchstleistung*) maximum; (*Tex*) lace; (*fam: Anspielung*) dig; **an der S~ liegen** be in the lead
Spitzel *m* **-s,-** informer
spitzen *vt* sharpen; purse 〈*Lippen*〉; prick up 〈*Ohren*〉; **sich s~ auf** (+*acc*) (*fam*) look forward to. **S~geschwindigkeit** *f* top speed
spitz|findig *a* over-subtle. **S~hacke** *f* pickaxe. **S~name** *m* nickname
Spleen /ʃpli:n/ *m* **-s,-e** obsession; **einen S~ haben** be crazy. **s~ig** *a* eccentric
Splitter *m* **-s,-** splinter. **s~n** *vi* (*sein*) shatter. **s~[faser]nackt** *a* (*fam*) stark naked
sponsern *vt* sponsor
spontan *a* spontaneous, *adv* -ly
sporadisch *a* sporadic, *adv* -ally
Spore *f* **-,-n** (*Biol*) spore
Sporn *m* **-[e]s, Sporen** spur; **einem Pferd die Sporen geben** spur a horse
Sport *m* **-[e]s** sport; (*Hobby*) hobby. **S~art** *f* sport. **S~fest** *nt* sports day. **S~ler** *m* **-s,-** sportsman. **S~lerin** *f* **-,-nen** sportswoman. **s~lich** *a* sports ...; (*fair*) sporting, *adv* -ly; (*flott, schlank*) sporty. **S~platz** *m* sports ground. **S~verein** *m* sports club. **S~wagen** *m* sports car; (*Kinder-*) push-chair, (*Amer*) stroller

Spott *m* **-[e]s** mockery. **s∼billig** *a & adv* dirt cheap

spötteln *vi* (*haben*) mock; **s∼ über** (+*acc*) poke fun at

spotten *vi* (*haben*) mock; **s∼ über** (+*acc*) make fun of; (*höhnend*) ridicule

spöttisch *a* mocking, *adv* -ly

Sprach|e *f* **-,-n** language; (*Sprechfähigkeit*) speech; **zur S∼e bringen** bring up. **S∼fehler** *m* speech defect. **S∼labor** *nt* language laboratory. **s∼lich** *a* linguistic, *adv* -ally. **s∼los** *a* speechless

Spray /ʃpre:/ *nt & m* **-s,-s** spray. **S∼dose** *f* aerosol [can]

Sprech|anlage *f* intercom. **S∼chor** *m* chorus; **im S∼chor rufen** chant

sprechen† *vi* (*haben*) speak/(*sich unterhalten*) talk (**über**+*acc*/**von** about/of); **deutsch/englisch s∼** speak German/English • *vt* speak; (*sagen, aufsagen*) say; pronounce ⟨*Urteil*⟩; **schuldig s∼** find guilty; **jdn s∼** speak to s.o.; **Herr X ist nicht zu s∼** Mr X is not available

Sprecher(in) *m* **-s,-** (*f* **-,-nen**) speaker; (*Radio, TV*) announcer; (*Wortführer*) spokesman, *f* spokeswoman

Sprechstunde *f* consulting hours *pl*; (*Med*) surgery. **S∼nhilfe** *f* (*Med*) receptionist

Sprechzimmer *nt* consulting room

spreizen *vt* spread

Sprengel *m* **-s,-** parish

spreng|en *vt* blow up; blast ⟨*Felsen*⟩; (*fig*) burst; (*begießen*) water; (*mit Sprenger*) sprinkle; dampen ⟨*Wäsche*⟩. **S∼er** *m* **-s,-** sprinkler. **S∼kopf** *m* warhead. **S∼körper** *m* explosive device. **S∼stoff** *m* explosive

Spreu *f* **-** chaff

Sprich|wort *nt* (*pl* **-wörter**) proverb. **s∼wörtlich** *a* proverbial

sprießen† *vi* (*sein*) sprout

Springbrunnen *m* fountain

spring|en† *vi* (*sein*) jump; (*Schwimmsport*) dive; ⟨*Ball:*⟩ bounce; (*spritzen*) spurt; (*zer-*) break; (*rissig werden*) crack; (*SGer: laufen*) run. **S∼er** *m* **-s,-** jumper; (*Kunst-*) diver; (*Schach*) knight. **S∼reiten** *nt* show-jumping. **S∼seil** *nt* skipping-rope

Sprint *m* **-s,-s** sprint

Sprit *m* **-s** (*fam*) petrol

Spritz|e *f* **-,-n** syringe; (*Injektion*) injection; (*Feuer-*) hose. **s∼en** *vt* spray; (*be-, ver-*) splash; (*Culin*) pipe; (*Med*) inject • *vi* (*haben*) splash; ⟨*Fett:*⟩ spit • *vi* (*sein*) splash; (*hervor-*) spurt; (*fam: laufen*) dash. **S∼er** *m* **-s,-** splash; (*Schuß*) dash. **s∼ig** *a* lively; ⟨*Wein, Komödie*⟩ sparkling. **S∼tour** *f* (*fam*) spin

spröde *a* brittle; (*trocken*) dry; (*rissig*) chapped; ⟨*Stimme*⟩ harsh; (*abweisend*) aloof

Sproß *m* **-sses,-sse** shoot

Sprosse *f* **-,-n** rung. **S∼nkohl** *m* (*Aust*) Brussels sprouts *pl*

Sprotte *f* **-,-n** sprat

Spruch *m* **-[e]s,⸚e** saying; (*Denk-*) motto; (*Zitat*) quotation. **S∼band** *nt* (*pl* **-bänder**) banner

Sprudel *m* **-s,-** sparkling mineral water. **s∼n** *vi* (*haben/sein*) bubble

Sprüh|dose *f* aerosol [can]. **s∼en** *vt* spray • *vi* (*sein*) ⟨*Funken:*⟩ fly; (*fig*) sparkle. **S∼regen** *m* fine drizzle

Sprung *m* **-[e]s,⸚e** jump, leap; (*Schwimmsport*) dive; (*fam: Katzen-*) stone's throw; (*Riß*) crack; **auf einen S∼** (*fam*) for a moment. **S∼brett** *nt* springboard. **s∼haft** *a* erratic; (*plötzlich*) sudden, *adv* -ly. **S∼schanze** *f* ski-jump. **S∼seil** *nt* skipping-rope

Spucke *f* **-** spit. **s∼n** *vt/i* (*haben*) spit; (*sich übergeben*) be sick

Spuk *m* **-[e]s,-e** [ghostly] apparition. **s∼en** *vi* (*haben*) ⟨*Geist:*⟩ walk; **in diesem Haus s∼t es** this house is haunted

Spülbecken *nt* sink

Spule *f* **-,-n** spool

Spüle *f* **-,-n** sink unit; (*Becken*) sink

spulen *vt* spool

spül|en *vt* rinse; (*schwemmen*) wash; **Geschirr s∼en** wash up • *vi* (*haben*) flush [the toilet]. **S∼kasten** *m* cistern. **S∼mittel** *nt* washing-up liquid. **S∼tuch** *nt* dishcloth

Spur *f* **-,-en** track; (*Fahr-*) lane; (*Fährte*) trail; (*Anzeichen*) trace; (*Hinweis*) lead; **keine** *od* **nicht die S∼** (*fam*) not in the least

spürbar *a* noticeable, *adv* -bly

spuren *vi* (*haben*) (*fam*) toe the line

spür|en *vt* feel; (*seelisch*) sense. **S∼hund** *m* tracker dog

spurlos *adv* without trace

spurten *vi* (*sein*) put on a spurt; (*fam: laufen*) sprint

sputen (sich) *vr* hurry

Staat *m* **-[e]s,-en** state; (*Land*) country; (*Putz*) finery. **s~lich** *a* state ... ● *adv* by the state

Staatsangehörig|e(r) *m/f* national. **S~keit** *f* - nationality

Staats|anwalt *m* state prosecutor. **S~beamte(r)** *m* civil servant. **S~besuch** *m* state visit. **S~bürger(in)** *m(f)* national. **S~mann** *m* (*pl* **-männer**) statesman. **S~streich** *m* coup

Stab *m* **-[e]s,⸚e** rod; (*Gitter-*) bar; (*Sport*) baton; (*Mitarbeiter-*) team; (*Mil*) staff

Stäbchen *ntpl* chopsticks

Stabhochsprung *m* pole-vault

stabil *a* stable; (*gesund*) robust; (*solide*) sturdy, *adv* -ily. **s~isieren** *vt* stabilize; **sich s~isieren** stabilize. **S~ität** *f* - stability

Stachel *m* **-s,-** spine; (*Gift-*) sting; (*Spitze*) spike. **S~beere** *f* gooseberry. **S~draht** *m* barbed wire. **s~ig** *a* prickly. **S~schwein** *nt* porcupine

Stadion *nt* **-s,-ien** stadium

Stadium *nt* **-s,-ien** stage

Stadt *f* **-,⸚e** town; (*Groß-*) city

Städt|chen *nt* **-s,-** small town. **s~isch** *a* urban; (*kommunal*) municipal

Stadt|mauer *f* city wall. **S~mitte** *f* town centre. **S~plan** *m* street map. **S~teil** *m* district. **S~zentrum** *nt* town centre

Staffel *f* **-,-n** team; (*S~lauf*) relay; (*Mil*) squadron

Staffelei *f* **-,-en** easel

Staffel|lauf *m* relay race. **s~n** *vt* stagger; (*abstufen*) grade

Stagn|ation /-ˈt͡si̯o:n/ *f* - stagnation. **s~ieren** *vi* (*haben*) stagnate

Stahl *m* **-s** steel. **S~beton** *m* reinforced concrete

Stall *m* **-[e]s,⸚e** stable; (*Kuh-*) shed; (*Schweine-*) sty; (*Hühner-*) coop; (*Kaninchen-*) hutch

Stamm *m* **-[e]s,⸚e** trunk; (*Sippe*) tribe; (*Kern*) core; (*Wort-*) stem. **S~baum** *m* family tree; (*eines Tieres*) pedigree

stammeln *vt/i* (*haben*) stammer

stammen *vi* (*haben*) come/(*zeitlich*) date (**von/aus** from); **das Zitat stammt von Goethe** the quotation is from Goethe

Stamm|gast *m* regular. **S~halter** *m* son and heir

stämmig *a* sturdy

Stamm|kundschaft *f* regulars *pl.* **S~lokal** *nt* favourite pub. **S~tisch** *m* table reserved for the regulars; (*Treffen*) meeting of the regulars

stampf|en *vi* (*haben*) stamp; ⟨*Maschine:*⟩ pound; **mit den Füßen s~en** stamp one's feet ● *vi* (*sein*) tramp ● *vt* pound; mash ⟨*Kartoffeln*⟩. **S~kartoffeln** *fpl* mashed potatoes

Stand *m* **-[e]s,⸚e** standing position; (*Zustand*) state; (*Spiel-*) score; (*Höhe*) level; (*gesellschaftlich*) class; (*Verkaufs-*) stall; (*Messe-*) stand; (*Taxi-*) rank; **auf den neuesten S~ bringen** update

Standard *m* **-s,-s** standard. **s~isieren** *vt* standardize

Standarte *f* **-,-n** standard

Standbild *nt* statue

Ständchen *nt* **-s,-** serenade; **jdm ein S~ bringen** serenade s.o.

Ständer *m* **-s,-** stand; (*Geschirr-, Platten-*) rack; (*Kerzen-*) holder

Standes|amt *nt* registry office. **S~beamte(r)** *m* registrar. **S~unterschied** *m* class distinction

stand|haft *a* steadfast, *adv* -ly. **s~halten**† *vi sep* (*haben*) stand firm; **etw** (*dat*) **s~halten** stand up to sth

ständig *a* constant, *adv* -ly; (*fest*) permanent, *adv* -ly

Stand|licht *nt* sidelights *pl.* **S~ort** *m* position; (*Firmen-*) location; (*Mil*) garrison. **S~pauke** *f* (*fam*) dressing-down. **S~punkt** *m* point of view. **S~spur** *f* hard shoulder. **S~uhr** *f* grandfather clock

Stange *f* **-,-n** bar; (*Holz-*) pole; (*Gardinen-*) rail; (*Hühner-*) perch; (*Zimt-*) stick; **von der S~** (*fam*) off the peg. **S~nbohne** *f* runner bean. **S~nbrot** *nt* French bread

Stanniol *nt* **-s** tin foil. **S~papier** *nt* silver paper

stanzen *vt* stamp; (*aus-*) stamp out; punch ⟨*Loch*⟩

Stapel *m* **-s,-** stack, pile; **vom S~ laufen** be launched. **S~lauf** *m* launch[ing]. **s~n** *vt* stack *or* pile up; **sich s~n** pile up

stapfen *vi* (*sein*) tramp, trudge

Star[1] *m* **-[e]s,-e** starling

Star[2] *m* **-[e]s** (*Med*) **[grauer] S~** cataract; **grüner S~** glaucoma

Star[3] *m* **-s,-s** (*Theat, Sport*) star

stark *a* (**stärker, stärkst**) strong; ⟨*Motor*⟩ powerful; ⟨*Verkehr, Regen*⟩ heavy; ⟨*Hitze, Kälte*⟩ severe; (*groß*) big; (*schlimm*) bad; (*dick*) thick;

(*korpulent*) stout ● *adv* strongly; heavily; badly; (*sehr*) very much

Stärk|e *f* **-,-n** (*s.* **stark**) strength; power; thickness; stoutness; (*Größe*) size; (*Mais-*, *Wäsche-*) starch. **S~emehl** *nt* cornflour. **s~en** *vt* strengthen; starch ⟨*Wäsche*⟩; **sich s~en** fortify oneself. **S~ung** *f* **-,-en** strengthening; (*Erfrischung*) refreshment

starr *a* rigid, *adv* -ly; (*steif*) stiff, *adv* -ly; ⟨*Blick*⟩ fixed; (*unbeugsam*) inflexible, *adv* -bly

starren *vi* (*haben*) stare; **vor Schmutz s~** be filthy

starr|köpfig *a* stubborn. **S~sinn** *m* obstinacy. **s~sinnig** *a* obstinate, *adv* -ly

Start *m* **-s,-s** start; (*Aviat*) take-off. **S~bahn** *f* runway. **s~en** *vi* (*sein*) start; (*Aviat*) take off; (*aufbrechen*) set off; (*teilnehmen*) compete ● *vt* start; (*fig*) launch

Station /-ˈtsi̯oːn/ *f* **-,-en** station; (*Haltestelle*) stop; (*Abschnitt*) stage; (*Med*) ward; **S~ machen** break one's journey; **bei freier S~** all found. **s~är** *adv* as an in-patient. **s~ieren** *vt* station

statisch *a* static

Statist(in) *m* **-en,-en** (*f* **-,-nen**) (*Theat*) extra

Statisti|k *f* **-,-en** statistics *sg*; (*Aufstellung*) statistics *pl*. **s~sch** *a* statistical, *adv* -ly

Stativ *nt* **-s,-e** (*Phot*) tripod

statt *prep* (+*gen*) instead of; **s~ dessen** instead ● *conj* **s~ etw zu tun** instead of doing sth

Stätte *f* **-,-n** place

statt|finden† *vi sep* (*haben*) take place. **s~haft** *a* permitted

stattlich *a* imposing; (*beträchtlich*) considerable

Statue /ˈʃtaːtu̯ə/ *f* **-,-n** statue

Statur *f* **-** build, stature

Status *m* **-** status. **S~symbol** *nt* status symbol

Statut *nt* **-[e]s,-en** statute

Stau *m* **-[e]s,-s** congestion; (*Auto*) [traffic] jam; (*Rück-*) tailback

Staub *m* **-[e]s** dust; **S~ wischen** dust; **S~ saugen** vacuum, hoover

Staubecken *nt* reservoir

staub|en *vi* (*haben*) raise dust; **es s~t** it's dusty. **s~ig** *a* dusty. **s~saugen** *vt/i* (*haben*) vacuum, hoover. **S~sauger** *m* vacuum cleaner, Hoover (P). **S~tuch** *nt* duster

Staudamm *m* dam

Staude *f* **-,-n** shrub

stauen *vt* dam up; **sich s~** accumulate; ⟨*Autos:*⟩ form a tailback

staunen *vi* (*haben*) be amazed *or* astonished. **S~** *nt* **-s** amazement, astonishment

Stau|see *m* reservoir. **S~ung** *f* **-,-en** congestion; (*Auto*) [traffic] jam

Steak /ʃteːk, steːk/ *nt* **-s,-s** steak

stechen† *vt* stick (**in** + *acc* in); (*verletzen*) prick; (*mit Messer*) stab; ⟨*Insekt:*⟩ sting; ⟨*Mücke:*⟩ bite; (*gravieren*) engrave ● *vi* (*haben*) prick; ⟨*Insekt:*⟩ sting; ⟨*Mücke:*⟩ bite; (*mit Stechuhr*) clock in/out; **in See s~** put to sea. **s~d** *a* stabbing; ⟨*Geruch*⟩ pungent

Stech|ginster *m* gorse. **S~kahn** *m* punt. **S~mücke** *f* mosquito. **S~palme** *f* holly. **S~uhr** *f* time clock

Steck|brief *m* 'wanted' poster. **S~dose** *f* socket. **s~en** *vt* put; (*mit Nadel, Reißzwecke*) pin; (*pflanzen*) plant ● *vi* (*haben*) be; (*fest-*) be stuck; **hinter etw** (*dat*) **s~en** (*fig*) be behind sth

Stecken *m* **-s,-** (*SGer*) stick

stecken|bleiben† *vi sep* (*sein*) get stuck. **s~lassen**† *vt sep* leave. **S~pferd** *nt* hobby-horse

Steck|er *m* **-s,-** (*Electr*) plug. **S~ling** *m* **-s,-e** cutting. **S~nadel** *f* pin. **S~rübe** *f* swede

Steg *m* **-[e]s,-e** foot-bridge; (*Boots-*) landing-stage; (*Brillen-*) bridge. **S~reif** *m* **aus dem S~reif** extempore

stehen† *vi* (*haben*) stand; (*sich befinden*) be; (*still-*) be stationary; ⟨*Maschine, Uhr:*⟩ have stopped; **vor dem Ruin s~** face ruin; **zu jdm/etw s~** (*fig*) stand by s.o./sth; **gut s~** ⟨*Getreide, Aktien:*⟩ be doing well; ⟨*Chancen:*⟩ be good; **jdm [gut] s~** suit s.o.; **sich gut s~** be on good terms; **es steht 3 zu 1** the score is 3 – 1; **es steht schlecht um ihn** he is in a bad way. **S~** *nt* **-s** standing; **zum S~ bringen/kommen** bring/come to a standstill. **s~bleiben**† *vi sep* (*sein*) stop; ⟨*Motor:*⟩ stall; ⟨*Zeit:*⟩ stand still; ⟨*Gebäude:*⟩ be left standing. **s~d** *a* standing; (*sich nicht bewegend*) stationary; ⟨*Gewässer*⟩ stagnant. **s~lassen**† *vt sep* leave; **sich** (*dat*) **einen Bart s~lassen** grow a beard

Steh|lampe *f* standard lamp. **S~leiter** *f* step-ladder

stehlen† *vt/i* (*haben*) steal; **sich s~** steal, creep

Steh|platz *m* standing place. **S~vermögen** *nt* stamina, staying-power

steif *a* stiff, *adv* -ly. **S~heit** *f* - stiffness

Steig|bügel *m* stirrup. **S~eisen** *nt* crampon

steigen† *vi* (*sein*) climb; (*hochgehen*) rise, go up; 〈*Schulden, Spannung:*〉 mount; **s~ auf** (+*acc*) climb on [to] 〈*Stuhl*〉; climb 〈*Berg, Leiter*〉; get on 〈*Pferd, Fahrrad*〉; **s~ in** (+*acc*) climb into; get in 〈*Auto*〉; get on 〈*Bus, Zug*〉; **s~ aus** climb out of; get out of 〈*Bett, Auto*〉; get off 〈*Bus, Zug*〉; **einen Drachen s~ lassen** fly a kite; **s~de Preise** rising prices

steiger|n *vt* increase; **sich s~n** increase; (*sich verbessern*) improve. **S~ung** *f* -,-en increase; improvement; (*Gram*) comparison

Steigung *f* -,-en gradient; (*Hang*) slope

steil *a* steep, *adv* -ly. **S~küste** *f* cliffs *pl*

Stein *m* -[e]s,-e stone; (*Ziegel-*) brick; (*Spiel-*) piece. **s~alt** *a* ancient. **S~bock** *m* ibex; (*Astr*) Capricorn. **S~bruch** *m* quarry. **S~garten** *m* rockery. **S~gut** *nt* earthenware. **s~hart** *a* rock-hard. **s~ig** *a* stony. **s~igen** *vt* stone. **S~kohle** *f* [hard] coal. **s~reich** *a* (*fam*) very rich. **S~schlag** *m* rock fall

Stelle *f* -,-n place; (*Fleck*) spot; (*Abschnitt*) passage; (*Stellung*) job, post; (*Büro*) office; (*Behörde*) authority; **kahle S~** bare patch; **auf der S~** immediately; **an deiner S~** in your place

stellen *vt* put; (*aufrecht*) stand; set 〈*Wecker, Aufgabe*〉; ask 〈*Frage*〉; make 〈*Antrag, Forderung, Diagnose*〉; **zur Verfügung s~** provide; **lauter/leiser s~** turn up/down; **kalt/warm s~** chill/keep hot; **sich s~** [go and] stand; give oneself up (**der Polizei** to the police); **sich tot/schlafend s~** pretend to be dead/asleep; **gut gestellt sein** be well off

Stellen|anzeige *f* job advertisement. **S~vermittlung** *f* employment agency. **s~weise** *adv* in places

Stellung *f* -,-en position; (*Arbeit*) job; **S~ nehmen** make a statement (**zu** on). **s~slos** *a* jobless. **S~suche** *f* job-hunting

stellvertret|end *a* deputy ... ● *adv* as a deputy; **s~end für jdn** on s.o.'s behalf. **S~er** *m* deputy

Stellwerk *nt* signal-box

Stelzen *fpl* stilts. **s~** *vi* (*sein*) stalk

stemmen *vt* press; lift 〈*Gewicht*〉; **sich s~ gegen** brace oneself against

Stempel *m* -s,- stamp; (*Post-*) postmark; (*Präge-*) die; (*Feingehalts-*) hallmark. **s~n** *vt* stamp; hallmark 〈*Silber*〉; cancel 〈*Marke*〉

Stengel *m* -s,- stalk, stem

Steno *f* - (*fam*) shorthand

Steno|gramm *nt* -[e]s,-e shorthand text. **S~graphie** *f* - shorthand. **s~graphieren** *vt* take down in shorthand ● *vi* (*haben*) do shorthand. **S~typistin** *f* -,-nen shorthand typist

Steppdecke *f* quilt

Steppe *f* -,-n steppe

Steptanz *m* tap-dance

sterben† *vi* (*sein*) die (**an** + *dat* of); **im S~ liegen** be dying

sterblich *a* mortal. **S~e(r)** *m/f* mortal. **S~keit** *f* - mortality

stereo *adv* in stereo. **S~anlage** *f* stereo [system]

stereotyp *a* stereotyped

steril *a* sterile. **s~isieren** *vt* sterilize. **S~ität** *f* - sterility

Stern *m* -[e]s,-e star. **S~bild** *nt* constellation. **S~chen** *nt* -s,- asterisk. **S~kunde** *f* astronomy. **S~schnuppe** *f* -,-n shooting star. **S~warte** *f* -,-n observatory

stetig *a* steady, *adv* -ily

stets *adv* always

Steuer[1] *nt* -s,- steering-wheel; (*Naut*) helm; **am S~** at the wheel

Steuer[2] *f* -,-n tax

Steuer|bord *nt* -[e]s starboard [side]. **S~erklärung** *f* tax return. **s~frei** *a* & *adv* tax-free. **S~mann** *m* (*pl* -leute) helmsman; (*beim Rudern*) cox. **s~n** *vt* steer; (*Aviat*) pilot; (*Techn*) control ● *vi* (*haben*) be at the wheel/(*Naut*) helm ● (*sein*) head (**nach** for). **s~pflichtig** *a* taxable. **S~rad** *nt* steering-wheel. **S~ruder** *nt* helm. **S~ung** *f* - steering; (*Techn*) controls *pl*. **S~zahler** *m* -s,- taxpayer

Stewardeß /'stju:ɐdɛs/ *f* -,-dessen air hostess, stewardess

Stich *m* -[e]s,-e prick; (*Messer-*) stab; (*S~wunde*) stab wound; (*Bienen-*) sting; (*Mücken-*) bite; (*Schmerz*) stabbing pain; (*Näh-*) stitch; (*Kupfer-*)

engraving; (*Kartenspiel*) trick; **S~ ins Rötliche** tinge of red; **jdn im S~ lassen** leave s.o. in the lurch; ⟨*Gedächtnis:*⟩ fail s.o. **s~eln** *vi* (*haben*) make snide remarks

Stich|flamme *f* jet of flame. **s~haltig** *a* valid. **S~probe** *f* spot check. **S~wort** *nt* (*pl* **-wörter**) headword; (*pl* **-worte**) (*Theat*) cue; **S~worte** notes

stick|en *vt/i* (*haben*) embroider. **S~erei** *f* - embroidery

stickig *a* stuffy

Stickstoff *m* nitrogen

Stiefbruder *m* stepbrother

Stiefel *m* **-s,-** boot

Stief|kind *nt* stepchild. **S~mutter** *f* stepmother. **S~mütterchen** *nt* **-s,-** pansy. **S~schwester** *f* stepsister. **S~sohn** *m* stepson. **S~tochter** *f* stepdaughter. **S~vater** *m* stepfather

Stiege *f* **-,-n** stairs *pl*

Stiel *m* **-[e]s,-e** handle; (*Blumen-, Gläser-*) stem; (*Blatt-*) stalk

Stier *m* **-[e]s,-e** bull; (*Astr*) Taurus

stieren *vi* (*haben*) stare

Stier|kampf *m* bullfight

Stift[1] *m* **-[e]s,-e** pin; (*Nagel*) tack; (*Blei-*) pencil; (*Farb-*) crayon

Stift[2] *nt* **-[e]s,-e** [endowed] foundation. **s~en** *vt* endow; (*spenden*) donate; create ⟨*Unheil, Verwirrung*⟩; bring about ⟨*Frieden*⟩. **S~er** *m* **-s,-** founder; (*Spender*) donor. **S~ung** *f* **-,-en** foundation; (*Spende*) donation

Stigma *nt* **-s** (*fig*) stigma

Stil *m* **-[e]s,-e** style; **in großem S~** in style. **s~isiert** *a* stylized. **s~istisch** *a* stylistic, *adv* -ally

still *a* quiet, *adv* -ly; (*reglos, ohne Kohlensäure*) still; (*heimlich*) secret, *adv* -ly; **der S~e Ozean** the Pacific; **im s~en** secretly; (*bei sich*) inwardly. **S~e** *f* - quiet; (*Schweigen*) silence

Stilleben *nt* still life

stilleg|en *vt sep* close down. **S~ung** *f* **-,-en** closure

stillen *vt* satisfy; quench ⟨*Durst*⟩; stop ⟨*Schmerzen, Blutung*⟩; breast-feed ⟨*Kind*⟩

stillhalten† *vi sep* (*haben*) keep still

Stillschweigen *nt* silence. **s~d** *a* silent, *adv* -ly; (*fig*) tacit, *adv* -ly

still|sitzen† *vi sep* (*haben*) sit still. **S~stand** *m* standstill; **zum S~stand bringen** stop. **s~stehen**† *vi sep* (*haben*) stand still; (*anhalten*) stop; ⟨*Verkehr:*⟩ be at a standstill

Stil|möbel *pl* reproduction furniture *sg*. **s~voll** *a* stylish, *adv* -ly

Stimm|bänder *ntpl* vocal cords. **s~berechtigt** *a* entitled to vote. **S~bruch** *m* **er ist im S~bruch** his voice is breaking

Stimme *f* **-,-n** voice; (*Wahl-*) vote

stimmen *vi* (*haben*) be right; (*wählen*) vote; **stimmt das?** is that right/ (*wahr*) true? ● *vt* tune; **jdn traurig/ fröhlich s~** make s.o. feel sad/happy

Stimm|enthaltung *f* abstention. **S~recht** *nt* right to vote

Stimmung *f* **-,-en** mood; (*Atmosphäre*) atmosphere. **s~svoll** *a* full of atmosphere

Stimmzettel *m* ballot-paper

stimulieren *vt* stimulate

stink|en† *vi* (*haben*) smell/(*stark*) stink (**nach** of). **S~tier** *nt* skunk

Stipendium *nt* **-s,-ien** scholarship; (*Beihilfe*) grant

Stirn *f* **-,-en** forehead; **die S~ bieten** (+*dat*) (*fig*) defy. **S~runzeln** *nt* **-s** frown

stöbern *vi* (*haben*) rummage

stochern *vi* (*haben*) **s~ in** (+*dat*) poke ⟨*Feuer*⟩; pick at ⟨*Essen*⟩; pick ⟨*Zähne*⟩

Stock[1] *m* **-[e]s,⸚e** stick; (*Ski-*) pole; (*Bienen-*) hive; (*Rosen-*) bush; (*Reb-*) vine

Stock[2] *m* **-[e]s,-** storey, floor. **S~bett** *nt* bunk-beds *pl*. **s~dunkel** *a* (*fam*) pitch-dark

stock|en *vi* (*haben*) stop; ⟨*Verkehr:*⟩ come to a standstill; ⟨*Person:*⟩ falter. **s~end** *a* hesitant, *adv* -ly. **s~taub** *a* (*fam*) stone-deaf. **S~ung** *f* **-,-en** hold-up

Stockwerk *nt* storey, floor

Stoff *m* **-[e]s,-e** substance; (*Tex*) fabric, material; (*Thema*) subject [matter]; (*Gesprächs-*) topic. **S~tier** *nt* soft toy. **S~wechsel** *m* metabolism

stöhnen *vi* (*haben*) groan, moan. **S~** *nt* **-s** groan, moan

stoisch *a* stoic, *adv* -ally

Stola *f* **-,-len** stole

Stollen *m* **-s,-** gallery; (*Kuchen*) stollen

stolpern *vi* (*sein*) stumble; **s~ über** (+*acc*) trip over

stolz *a* proud (**auf**+*acc* of), *adv* -ly. **S~** *m* **-es** pride

stolzieren *vi* (*sein*) strut

stopfen *vt* stuff; (*stecken*) put; (*ausbessern*) darn ● *vi* (*haben*) be constipating; (*fam: essen*) guzzle

Stopp *m* **-s,-s** stop. **s~** *int* stop!

stoppel|ig *a* stubbly. **S~n** *fpl* stubble *sg*

stopp|en *vt* stop; (*Sport*) time ● *vi* (*haben*) stop. **S~schild** *nt* stop sign. **S~uhr** *f* stop-watch

Stöpsel *m* **-s,-** plug; (*Flaschen-*) stopper

Storch *m* **-[e]s,¨e** stork

Store /ʃtoːɐ̯/ *m* **-s,-s** net curtain

stören *vt* disturb; disrupt ⟨*Rede, Sitzung*⟩; jam ⟨*Sender*⟩; (*mißfallen*) bother; **stört es Sie, wenn ich rauche?** do you mind if I smoke? ● *vi* (*haben*) be a nuisance; **entschuldigen Sie, daß ich störe** I'm sorry to bother you

stornieren *vt* cancel

störrisch *a* stubborn, *adv* -ly

Störung *f* **-,-en** (*s.* **stören**) disturbance; disruption; (*Med*) trouble; (*Radio*) interference; **technische S~** technical fault

Stoß *m* **-es,¨e** push, knock; (*mit Ellbogen*) dig; (*Hörner-*) butt; (*mit Waffe*) thrust; (*Schwimm-*) stroke; (*Ruck*) jolt; (*Erd-*) shock; (*Stapel*) stack, pile. **S~dämpfer** *m* **-s,-** shock absorber

stoßen† *vt* push, knock; (*mit Füßen*) kick; (*mit Kopf, Hörnern*) butt; (*an-*) poke, nudge; (*treiben*) thrust; **sich s~** knock oneself; **sich** (*dat*) **den Kopf s~** hit one's head ● *vi* (*haben*) push; **s~ an** (+*acc*) knock against; (*angrenzen*) adjoin ● *vi* (*sein*) **s~ gegen** knock against; bump into ⟨*Tür*⟩; **s~ auf** (+*acc*) bump into; (*entdecken*) come across; strike ⟨*Öl*⟩; (*fig*) meet with ⟨*Ablehnung*⟩

Stoß|stange *f* bumper. **S~verkehr** *m* rush-hour traffic. **S~zahn** *m* tusk. **S~zeit** *f* rush-hour

stottern *vt/i* (*haben*) stutter, stammer

Str. *abbr* (**Straße**) St

Straf|anstalt *f* prison. **S~arbeit** *f* (*Sch*) imposition. **s~bar** *a* punishable; **sich s~bar machen** commit an offence

Strafe *f* **-,-n** punishment; (*Jur & fig*) penalty; (*Geld-*) fine; (*Freiheits-*) sentence. **s~n** *vt* punish

straff *a* tight, taut. **s~en** *vt* tighten; **sich s~en** tighten

Strafgesetz *nt* criminal law

sträf|lich *a* criminal, *adv* -ly. **S~ling** *m* **-s,-e** prisoner

Straf|mandat *nt* (*Auto*) [parking/speeding] ticket. **S~porto** *nt* excess postage. **S~predigt** *f* (*fam*) lecture. **S~raum** *m* penalty area. **S~stoß** *m* penalty. **S~tat** *f* crime. **S~zettel** *m* (*fam*) = **S~mandat**

Strahl *m* **-[e]s,-en** ray; (*einer Taschenlampe*) beam; (*Wasser-*) jet. **s~en** *vi* (*haben*) shine; (*funkeln*) sparkle; (*lächeln*) beam. **S~enbehandlung** *f* radiotherapy. **s~end** *a* shining; sparkling; beaming; radiant ⟨*Schönheit*⟩. **S~entherapie** *f* radiotherapy. **S~ung** *f* - radiation

Strähn|e *f* **-,-n** strand. **s~ig** *a* straggly

stramm *a* tight, *adv* -ly; (*kräftig*) sturdy; (*gerade*) upright

Strampel|höschen *nt* **-s,-** rompers *pl.* **s~n** *vi* (*haben*) ⟨*Baby:*⟩ kick

Strand *m* **-[e]s,¨e** beach. **s~en** *vi* (*sein*) run aground; (*fig*) fail. **S~korb** *m* wicker beach-chair. **S~promenade** *f* promenade

Strang *m* **-[e]s,¨e** rope

Strapaz|e *f* **-,-n** strain. **s~ieren** *vt* be hard on; tax ⟨*Nerven, Geduld*⟩. **s~ierfähig** *a* hard-wearing. **s~iös** *a* exhausting

Straß *m* **- & -sses** paste

Straße *f* **-,-n** road; (*in der Stadt auch*) street; (*Meeres-*) strait; **auf der S~** in the road/street. **S~nbahn** *f* tram, (*Amer*) streetcar. **S~nkarte** *f* road map. **S~nlaterne** *f* street lamp. **S~nsperre** *f* road-block

Strat|egie *f* **-,-n** strategy. **s~egisch** *a* strategic, *adv* -ally

sträuben *vt* ruffle up ⟨*Federn*⟩; **sich s~** ⟨*Fell, Haar:*⟩ stand on end; (*fig*) resist

Strauch *m* **-[e]s, Sträucher** bush

straucheln *vi* (*sein*) stumble

Strauß[1] *m* **-es, Sträuße** bunch [of flowers]; (*Bukett*) bouquet

Strauß[2] *m* **-es,-e** ostrich

Strebe *f* **-,-n** brace, strut

streben *vi* (*haben*) strive (**nach** for) ● *vi* (*sein*) head (**nach/zu** for)

Streb|er *m* **-s,-** pushy person; (*Sch*) swot. **s~sam** *a* industrious

Strecke *f* **-,-n** stretch, section; (*Entfernung*) distance; (*Rail*) line; (*Route*) route

strecken *vt* stretch; (*aus-*) stretch out; (*gerade machen*) straighten; (*Culin*) thin down; **sich s~** stretch; (*sich aus-*) stretch out; **den Kopf aus**

dem Fenster s~ put one's head out of the window

Streich *m* **-[e]s,-e** prank, trick; **jdm einen S~ spielen** play a trick on s.o.

streicheln *vt* stroke

streichen† *vt* spread; (*weg-*) smooth; (*an-*) paint; (*aus-*) delete; (*kürzen*) cut ● *vi* (*haben*) **s~ über** (+*acc*) stroke

Streicher *m* **-s,-** string-player; **die S~** the strings

Streichholz *nt* match. **S~schachtel** *f* matchbox

Streich|instrument *nt* stringed instrument. **S~käse** *m* cheese spread. **S~orchester** *nt* string orchestra. **S~ung** *f* **-,-en** deletion; (*Kürzung*) cut

Streife *f* **-,-n** patrol

streifen *vt* brush against; (*berühren*) touch; (*verletzen*) graze; (*fig*) touch on ⟨*Thema*⟩; (*ziehen*) slip (**über**+*acc* over); **mit dem Blick s~** glance at ● *vi* (*sein*) roam

Streifen *m* **-s,-** stripe; (*Licht-*) streak; (*auf der Fahrbahn*) line; (*schmales Stück*) strip

Streif|enwagen *m* patrol car. **s~ig** *a* streaky. **S~schuß** *m* glancing shot; (*Wunde*) graze

Streik *m* **-s,-s** strike; **in den S~ treten** go on strike. **S~brecher** *m* strike-breaker, (*pej*) scab. **s~en** *vi* (*haben*) strike; (*fam*) refuse; (*versagen*) pack up. **S~ende(r)** *m* striker. **S~posten** *m* picket

Streit *m* **-[e]s,-e** quarrel; (*Auseinandersetzung*) dispute. **s~en†** *vr/i* (*haben*) **[sich] s~en** quarrel. **s~ig** *a* **jdm etw s~ig machen** dispute s.o.'s right to sth. **S~igkeiten** *fpl* quarrels. **S~kräfte** *fpl* armed forces. **s~süchtig** *a* quarrelsome

streng *a* strict, *adv* -ly; ⟨*Blick, Ton*⟩ stern, *adv* -ly; (*rauh, nüchtern*) severe, *adv* -ly; ⟨*Geschmack*⟩ sharp. **S~e** *f* - strictness; sternness; severity. **s~genommen** *adv* strictly speaking. **s~gläubig** *a* strict; (*orthodox*) orthodox. **s~stens** *adv* strictly

Streß *m* **-sses,-sse** stress

stressig *a* (*fam*) stressful

streuen *vt* spread; (*ver-*) scatter; sprinkle ⟨*Zucker, Salz*⟩; **die Straßen s~** grit the roads

streunen *vi* (*sein*) roam; **s~der Hund** stray dog

Strich *m* **-[e]s,-e** line; (*Feder-, Pinsel-*) stroke; (*Morse-, Gedanken-*) dash; **gegen den S~** the wrong way; (*fig*) against the grain. **S~kode** *m* bar code. **S~punkt** *m* semicolon

Strick *m* **-[e]s,-e** cord; (*Seil*) rope; (*fam: Schlingel*) rascal

strick|en *vt/i* (*haben*) knit. **S~jacke** *f* cardigan. **S~leiter** *f* rope-ladder. **S~nadel** *f* knitting-needle. **S~waren** *fpl* knitwear *sg*. **S~zeug** *nt* knitting

striegeln *vt* groom

strikt *a* strict, *adv* -ly

strittig *a* contentious

Stroh *nt* **-[e]s** straw. **S~blumen** *fpl* everlasting flowers. **S~dach** *nt* thatched roof. **s~gedeckt** *a* thatched. **S~halm** *m* straw

Strolch *m* **-[e]s,-e** (*fam*) rascal

Strom *m* **-[e]s,⸚e** river; (*Menschen-, Auto-, Blut-*) stream; (*Tränen-*) flood; (*Schwall*) torrent; (*Electr*) current, power; **gegen den S~** (*fig*) against the tide; **es regnet in Strömen** it is pouring with rain. **s~abwärts** *adv* downstream. **s~aufwärts** *adv* upstream

strömen *vi* (*sein*) flow; ⟨*Menschen, Blut:*⟩ stream, pour; **s~der Regen** pouring rain

Strom|kreis *m* circuit. **s~linienförmig** *a* streamlined. **S~sperre** *f* power cut

Strömung *f* **-,-en** current

Strophe *f* **-,-n** verse

strotzen *vi* (*haben*) be full (**vor**+*dat* of); **vor Gesundheit s~d** bursting with health

Strudel *m* **-s,-** whirlpool; (*SGer Culin*) strudel

Struktur *f* **-,-en** structure; (*Tex*) texture

Strumpf *m* **-[e]s,⸚e** stocking; (*Knie-*) sock. **S~band** *nt* (*pl* **-bänder**) suspender, (*Amer*) garter. **S~bandgürtel** *m* suspender/(*Amer*) garter belt. **S~halter** *m* = **S~band.** **S~hose** *f* tights *pl*, (*Amer*) pantyhose

Strunk *m* **-[e]s,⸚e** stalk; (*Baum-*) stump

struppig *a* shaggy

Stube *f* **-,-n** room. **s~nrein** *a* house-trained

Stuck *m* **-s** stucco

Stück *nt* **-[e]s,-e** piece; (*Zucker-*) lump; (*Seife*) tablet; (*Theater-*) play; (*Gegenstand*) item; (*Exemplar*) specimen; **20 S~ Vieh** 20 head of cattle; **ein S~** (*Entfernung*) some way; **aus freien S~en** voluntarily. **S~chen** *nt*

-s,- [little] bit. **s~weise** *adv* bit by bit; (*einzeln*) singly
Student|(in) *m* **-en,-en** (*f* **-,-nen**) student. **s~isch** *a* student ...
Studie /-iə/ *f* **-,-n** study
studier|en *vt/i* (*haben*) study. **S~zimmer** *nt* study
Studio *nt* **-s,-s** studio
Studium *nt* **-s,-ien** studies *pl*
Stufe *f* **-,-n** step; (*Treppen-*) stair; (*Raketen-*) stage; (*Niveau*) level. **s~n** *vt* terrace; (*staffeln*) grade
Stuhl *m* **-[e]s,¨-e** chair; (*Med*) stools *pl*. **S~gang** *m* bowel movement
stülpen *vt* put (**über** + *acc* over)
stumm *a* dumb; (*schweigsam*) silent, *adv* -ly
Stummel *m* **-s,-** stump; (*Zigaretten-*) butt; (*Bleistift-*) stub
Stümper *m* **-s,-** bungler. **s~haft** *a* incompetent, *adv* -ly
stumpf *a* blunt; ⟨*Winkel*⟩ obtuse; (*glanzlos*) dull; (*fig*) apathetic, *adv* -ally. **S~** *m* **-[e]s,¨-e** stump
Stumpfsinn *m* apathy; (*Langweiligkeit*) tedium. **s~ig** *a* apathetic, *adv* -ally; (*langweilig*) tedious
Stunde *f* **-,-n** hour; (*Sch*) lesson
stunden *vt* **jdm eine Schuld s~** give s.o. time to pay a debt
Stunden|kilometer *mpl* kilometres per hour. **s~lang** *adv* for hours. **S~lohn** *m* hourly rate. **S~plan** *m* timetable. **s~weise** *adv* by the hour
stündlich *a & adv* hourly
Stups *m* **-es,-e** nudge; (*Schubs*) push. **s~en** *vt* nudge; (*schubsen*) push. **S~nase** *f* snub nose
stur *a* pigheaded; (*phlegmatisch*) stolid, *adv* -ly; (*unbeirrbar*) dogged, *adv* -ly
Sturm *m* **-[e]s,¨-e** gale; (*schwer*) storm; (*Mil*) assault
stürm|en *vi* (*haben*) ⟨*Wind:*⟩ blow hard; **es s~t** it's blowing a gale • *vi* (*sein*) rush • *vt* storm; (*bedrängen*) besiege. **S~er** *m* **-s,-** forward. **s~isch** *a* stormy; ⟨*Überfahrt*⟩ rough; (*fig*) tumultuous, *adv* -ly; (*ungestüm*) tempestuous, *adv* -ly
Sturz *m* **-es,¨-e** [heavy] fall; (*Preis-, Kurs-*) sharp drop; (*Pol*) overthrow
stürzen *vi* (*sein*) fall [heavily]; (*in die Tiefe*) plunge; ⟨*Preise, Kurse:*⟩ drop sharply; ⟨*Regierung:*⟩ fall; (*eilen*) rush • *vt* throw; (*umkippen*) turn upside down; turn out ⟨*Speise, Kuchen*⟩; (*Pol*) overthrow, topple; **sich s~** throw oneself (**aus/in** + *acc* out of/into); **sich s~ auf** (+*acc*) pounce on
Sturz|flug *m* (*Aviat*) dive. **S~helm** *m* crash-helmet
Stute *f* **-,-n** mare
Stütze *f* **-,-n** support; (*Kopf-, Arm-*) rest
stutzen *vi* (*haben*) stop short • *vt* trim; (*Hort*) cut back; (*kupieren*) crop
stützen *vt* support; (*auf-*) rest; **sich s~ auf** (+*acc*) lean on; (*beruhen*) be based on
Stutzer *m* **-s,-** dandy
stutzig *a* puzzled; (*mißtrauisch*) suspicious
Stützpunkt *m* (*Mil*) base
Subjekt *nt* **-[e]s,-e** subject. **s~iv** *a* subjective, *adv* -ly
Subskription /-'tsio:n/ *f* **-,-en** subscription
Substantiv *nt* **-s,-e** noun
Substanz *f* **-,-en** substance
subtil *a* subtle, *adv* -tly
subtra|hieren *vt* subtract. **S~ktion** /-'tsio:n/ *f* **-,-en** subtraction
Subvention /-'tsio:n/ *f* **-,-en** subsidy. **s~ieren** *vt* subsidize
subversiv *a* subversive
Such|e *f* **-** search; **auf der S~e nach** looking for. **s~en** *vt* look for; (*intensiv*) search for; seek ⟨*Hilfe, Rat*⟩; **'Zimmer gesucht'** 'room wanted' • *vi* (*haben*) look, search (**nach** for). **S~er** *m* **-s,-** (*Phot*) viewfinder
Sucht *f* **-,¨-e** addiction; (*fig*) mania
süchtig *a* addicted. **S~e(r)** *m/f* addict
Süd *m* **-[e]s** south. **S~afrika** *nt* South Africa. **S~amerika** *nt* South America. **s~deutsch** *a* South German
Süden *m* **-s** south; **nach S~** south
Süd|frucht *f* tropical fruit. **s~lich** *a* southern; ⟨*Richtung*⟩ southerly • *adv & prep* (+*gen*) **s~lich [von] der Stadt** [to the] south of the town. **S~osten** *m* south-east. **S~pol** *m* South Pole. **s~wärts** *adv* southwards. **S~westen** *m* south-west
süffisant *a* smug, *adv* -ly
suggerieren *vt* suggest (*dat* to)
Suggest|ion /-'tio:n/ *f* **-,-en** suggestion. **s~iv** *a* suggestive
Sühne *f* **-,-n** atonement; (*Strafe*) penalty. **s~n** *vt* atone for
Sultanine *f* **-,-n** sultana

Sülze *f* **-,-n** [meat] jelly; (*Schweinskopf-*) brawn
Summe *f* **-,-n** sum
summ|en *vi* (*haben*) hum; ⟨*Biene:*⟩ buzz • *vt* hum. **S~er** *m* **-s,-** buzzer
summieren (sich) *vr* add up; (*sich häufen*) increase
Sumpf *m* **-[e]s,⸗e** marsh, swamp. **s~ig** *a* marshy
Sünd|e *f* **-,-n** sin. **S~enbock** *m* scapegoat. **S~er(in)** *m* **-s,-** (*f* **-,-nen**) sinner. **s~haft** *a* sinful. **s~igen** *vi* (*haben*) sin
super *inv a* (*fam*) great. **S~lativ** *m* **-s,-e** superlative. **S~markt** *m* supermarket
Suppe *f* **-,-n** soup. **S~nlöffel** *m* soup-spoon. **S~nteller** *m* soup-plate. **S~nwürfel** *m* stock cube
Surf|brett /'sø:ɐ̯f-/ *nt* surfboard. **S~en** *nt* **-s** surfing
surren *vi* (*haben*) whirr
süß *a* sweet, *adv* -ly. **S~e** *f* **-** sweetness. **s~en** *vt* sweeten. **S~igkeit** *f* **-,-en** sweet. **s~lich** *a* sweetish; (*fig*) sugary. **S~speise** *f* sweet. **S~stoff** *m* sweetener. **S~waren** *fpl* confectionery *sg*, sweets *pl*. **S~wasser-** *pref* freshwater . . .
Sylvester *nt* **-s** = **Silvester**
Symbol *nt* **-s,-e** symbol. **S~ik** *f* **-** symbolism. **s~isch** *a* symbolic, *adv* -ally. **s~isieren** *vt* symbolize
Sym|metrie *f* **-** symmetry. **s~metrisch** *a* symmetrical, *adv* -ly
Sympathie *f* **-,-n** sympathy
sympath|isch *a* agreeable; ⟨*Person*⟩ likeable. **s~isieren** *vi* (*haben*) be sympathetic (**mit** to)
Symphonie *f* **-,-n** = **Sinfonie**
Symptom *nt* **-s,-e** symptom. **s~atisch** *a* symptomatic
Synagoge *f* **-,-n** synagogue
synchronisieren /zʏnkroni'zi:rən/ *vt* synchronize; dub ⟨*Film*⟩
Syndikat *nt* **-[e]s,-e** syndicate
Syndrom *nt* **-s,-e** syndrome
synonym *a* synonymous, *adv* -ly. **S~** *nt* **-s,-e** synonym
Syntax /'zʏntaks/ *f* **-** syntax
Synthe|se *f* **-,-n** synthesis. **S~tik** *nt* **-s** synthetic material. **s~tisch** *a* synthetic, *adv* -ally
Syrien /-i̯ən/ *nt* **-s** Syria
System *nt* **-s,-e** system. **s~atisch** *a* systematic, *adv* -ally
Szene *f* **-,-n** scene. **S~rie** *f* scenery

T

Tabak *m* **-s,-e** tobacco
Tabelle *f* **-,-n** table; (*Sport*) league table
Tablett *nt* **-[e]s,-s** tray
Tablette *f* **-,-n** tablet
tabu *a* taboo. **T~** *nt* **-s,-s** taboo
Tacho *m* **-s,-s**, **Tachometer** *m* & *nt* speedometer
Tadel *m* **-s,-** reprimand; (*Kritik*) censure; (*Sch*) black mark. **t~los** *a* impeccable, *adv* -bly. **t~n** *vt* reprimand; censure. **t~nswert** *a* reprehensible
Tafel *f* **-,-n** (*Tisch, Tabelle*) table; (*Platte*) slab; (*Anschlag-, Hinweis-*) board; (*Gedenk-*) plaque; (*Schiefer-*) slate; (*Wand-*) blackboard; (*Bild-*) plate; (*Schokolade*) bar. **t~n** *vi* (*haben*) feast
Täfelung *f* **-** panelling
Tag *m* **-[e]s,-e** day; **Tag für Tag** day by day; **am T~e** in the daytime; **eines T~es** one day; **unter T~e** underground; **es wird Tag** it is getting light; **guten Tag!** good morning/afternoon! **t~aus** *adv* **t~aus, t~ein** day in, day out
Tage|buch *nt* diary. **t~lang** *adv* for days
tagen *vi* (*haben*) meet; ⟨*Gericht:*⟩ sit; **es tagt** day is breaking
Tages|anbruch *m* daybreak. **T~ausflug** *m* day trip. **T~decke** *f* bedspread. **T~karte** *f* day ticket; (*Speise-*) menu of the day. **T~licht** *nt* daylight. **T~mutter** *f* child-minder. **T~ordnung** *f* agenda. **T~rückfahrkarte** *f* day return [ticket]. **T~zeit** *f* time of the day. **T~zeitung** *f* daily [news]paper
täglich *a* & *adv* daily; **zweimal t~** twice a day
tags *adv* by day; **t~ zuvor/darauf** the day before/after
tagsüber *adv* during the day
tag|täglich *a* daily • *adv* every single day. **T~traum** *m* daydream. **T~undnachtgleiche** *f* **-,-n** equinox. **T~ung** *f* **-,-en** meeting; (*Konferenz*) conference
Taill|e /'taljə/ *f* **-,-n** waist. **t~iert** /ta'ji:ɐ̯t/ *a* fitted
Takt *m* **-[e]s,-e** tact; (*Mus*) bar; (*Tempo*) time; (*Rhythmus*) rhythm; **im T~** in time [to the music]. **T~gefühl** *nt* tact

Taktik *f* - tactics *pl.* **t~isch** *a* tactical, *adv* -ly

taktlos *a* tactless, *adv* -ly. **T~losigkeit** *f* - tactlessness. **T~stock** *m* baton. **t~voll** *a* tactful, *adv* -ly

Tal *nt* **-[e]s,¨er** valley

Talar *m* **-s,-e** robe; (*Univ*) gown

Talent *nt* **-[e]s,-e** talent. **t~iert** *a* talented

Talg *m* **-s** tallow; (*Culin*) suet

Talsperre *f* dam

Tampon /tam'põ:/ *m* **-s,-s** tampon

Tang *m* **-s** seaweed

Tangente *f* **-,-n** tangent; (*Straße*) bypass

Tank *m* **-s,-s** tank. **t~en** *vt* fill up with ⟨*Benzin*⟩ ● *vi* (*haben*) fill up with petrol; (*Aviat*) refuel; **ich muß t~en** I need petrol. **T~er** *m* **-s,-** tanker. **T~stelle** *f* petrol/(*Amer*) gas station. **T~wart** *m* **-[e]s,-e** petrol-pump attendant

Tanne *f* **-,-n** fir [tree]. **T~nbaum** *m* fir tree; (*Weihnachtsbaum*) Christmas tree. **T~nzapfen** *m* fir cone

Tante *f* **-,-n** aunt

Tantiemen /tan'ti̯e:mən/ *pl* royalties

Tanz *m* **-es,¨e** dance. **t~en** *vt/i* (*haben*) dance

Tänzer(in) *m* **-s,-** (*f* **-,-nen**) dancer

Tanzlokal *nt* dance-hall. **T~musik** *f* dance music

Tapete *f* **-,-n** wallpaper. **T~nwechsel** *m* (*fam*) change of scene

tapezieren *vt* paper. **T~er** *m* **-s,-** paperhanger, decorator

tapfer *a* brave, *adv* -ly. **T~keit** *f* - bravery

tappen *vi* (*sein*) walk hesitantly; (*greifen*) grope (**nach** for)

Tarif *m* **-s,-e** rate; (*Verzeichnis*) tariff

tarnen *vt* disguise; (*Mil*) camouflage; **sich t~en** disguise/camouflage oneself. **T~ung** *f* - disguise; camouflage

Tasche *f* **-,-n** bag; (*Hosen-, Mantel-*) pocket. **T~nbuch** *nt* paperback. **T~ndieb** *m* pickpocket. **T~ngeld** *nt* pocket-money. **T~nlampe** *f* torch, (*Amer*) flashlight. **T~nmesser** *nt* penknife. **T~ntuch** *nt* handkerchief

Tasse *f* **-,-n** cup

Tastatur *f* **-,-en** keyboard

tastbar *a* palpable. **T~e** *f* **-,-n** key; (*Druck-*) push-button. **t~en** *vi* (*haben*) feel, grope (**nach** for) ● *vt* key in ⟨*Daten*⟩; **sich t~en** feel one's way (**zu** to). **t~end** *a* tentative, *adv* -ly

Tat *f* **-,-en** action; (*Helden-*) deed; (*Straf-*) crime; **in der Tat** indeed; **auf frischer Tat ertappt** caught in the act. **t~enlos** *adv* passively

Täter(in) *m* **-s,-** (*f* **-,-nen**) culprit; (*Jur*) offender

tätig *a* active, *adv* -ly; **t~ sein** work. **T~keit** *f* **-,-en** activity; (*Funktionieren*) action; (*Arbeit*) work, job

Tatkraft *f* energy

tätlich *a* physical, *adv* -ly; **t~ werden** become violent. **T~keiten** *fpl* violence *sg*

Tatort *m* scene of the crime

tätowieren *vt* tattoo. **T~ung** *f* **-,-en** tattooing; (*Bild*) tattoo

Tatsache *f* fact. **T~nbericht** *m* documentary

tatsächlich *a* actual, *adv* -ly

tätscheln *vt* pat

Tatze *f* **-,-n** paw

Tau[1] *m* **-[e]s** dew

Tau[2] *nt* **-[e]s,-e** rope

taub *a* deaf; (*gefühllos*) numb; ⟨*Nuß*⟩ empty; ⟨*Gestein*⟩ worthless

Taube *f* **-,-n** pigeon; (*Turtel- & fig*) dove. **T~nschlag** *m* pigeon-loft

Taubheit *f* - deafness; (*Gefühllosigkeit*) numbness. **t~stumm** *a* deaf and dumb

tauchen *vt* dip, plunge; (*unter-*) duck ● *vi* (*haben/sein*) dive/(*ein-*) plunge (**in** + *acc* into); (*auf-*) appear (**aus** out of). **T~er** *m* **-s,-** diver. **T~eranzug** *m* diving-suit. **T~sieder** *m* **-s,-** [small, portable] immersion heater

tauen *vi* (*sein*) melt, thaw ● *impers* **es taut** it is thawing

Taufbecken *nt* font. **T~e** *f* **-,-n** christening, baptism. **t~en** *vt* christen, baptize. **T~pate** *m* godfather. **T~stein** *m* font

taugen *vi* (*haben*) **etwas/nichts t~n** be good/no good; **zu etw t~n/nicht t~n** be good/no good for sth. **T~nichts** *m* **-es,-e** good-for-nothing

tauglich *a* suitable; (*Mil*) fit. **T~keit** *f* - suitability; fitness

Taumel *m* **-s** daze; **wie im T~** in a daze. **t~n** *vi* (*sein*) stagger

Tausch *m* **-[e]s,-e** exchange, (*fam*) swap. **t~en** *vt* exchange/(*handeln*) barter (**gegen** for); **die Plätze t~en** change places ● *vi* (*haben*) swap (**mit etw** sth; **mit jdm** with s.o.)

täuschen *vt* deceive, fool; betray ⟨*Vertrauen*⟩; **sich t~** delude oneself; (*sich irren*) be mistaken ● *vi* (*haben*) be deceptive. **t~d** *a* deceptive; ⟨*Ähnlichkeit*⟩ striking

Tausch|geschäft *nt* exchange. **T~handel** *m* barter; (*T~geschäft*) exchange

Täuschung *f* **-,-en** deception; (*Irrtum*) mistake; (*Illusion*) delusion

tausend *inv a* one/a thousand. **T~** *nt* **-s,-e** thousand. **T~füßler** *m* **-s,-** centipede. **t~ste(r,s)** *a* thousandth. **T~stel** *nt* **-s,-** thousandth

Tau|tropfen *m* dewdrop. **T~wetter** *nt* thaw. **T~ziehen** *nt* **-s** tug of war

Taxe *f* **-,-n** charge; (*Kur-*) tax; (*Taxi*) taxi

Taxi *nt* **-s,-s** taxi, cab

taxieren *vt* estimate/(*im Wert*) value (**auf** + *acc* at); (*fam: mustern*) size up

Taxi|fahrer *m* taxi driver. **T~stand** *m* taxi rank

Teakholz /'ti:k-/ *nt* teak

Team /ti:m/ *nt* **-s,-s** team

Techni|k *f* **-,-en** technology; (*Methode*) technique. **T~ker** *m* **-s,-** technician. **t~sch** *a* technical, *adv* -ly; (*technologisch*) technological, *adv* -ly; **T~sche Hochschule** Technical University

Techno|logie *f* **-,-n** technology. **t~logisch** *a* technological

Teckel *m* **-s,-** dachshund

Teddybär *m* teddy bear

Tee *m* **-s,-s** tea. **T~beutel** *m* tea-bag. **T~kanne** *f* teapot. **T~kessel** *m* kettle. **T~löffel** *m* teaspoon

Teer *m* **-s** tar. **t~en** *vt* tar

Tee|sieb *nt* tea-strainer. **T~tasse** *f* teacup. **T~wagen** *m* [tea] trolley

Teich *m* **-[e]s,-e** pond

Teig *m* **-[e]s,-e** pastry; (*Knet-*) dough; (*Rühr-*) mixture; (*Pfannkuchen-*) batter. **T~rolle** *f*, **T~roller** *m* rolling-pin. **T~waren** *fpl* pasta *sg*

Teil *m* **-[e]s,-e** part; (*Bestand-*) component; (*Jur*) party; **der vordere T~** the front part; **zum T~** partly; **zum großen/größten T~** for the most part ● *m & nt* **-[e]s** (*Anteil*) share; **sein[en] T~ beitragen** do one's share; **ich für mein[en] T~** for my part ● *nt* **-[e]s,-e** part; (*Ersatz-*) spare part; (*Anbau-*) unit

teil|bar *a* divisible. **T~chen** *nt* **-s,-** particle. **t~en** *vt* divide; (*auf-*) share out; (*gemeinsam haben*) share; (*Pol*) partition ⟨*Land*⟩; **sich** (*dat*) **etw [mit jdm] t~en** share sth [with s.o.]; **sich t~en** divide; (*sich gabeln*) fork; ⟨*Vorhang:*⟩ open; ⟨*Meinungen:*⟩ differ ● *vi* (*haben*) share

teilhab|en† *vi sep* (*haben*) share (**an etw** *dat* sth). **T~er** *m* **-s,-** (*Comm*) partner

Teilnahm|e *f* **-** participation; (*innere*) interest; (*Mitgefühl*) sympathy. **t~slos** *a* apathetic, *adv* -ally

teilnehm|en† *vi sep* (*haben*) **t~en an** (+*dat*) take part in; (*mitfühlen*) share [in]. **T~er(in)** *m* **-s,-** (*f* **-,-nen**) participant; (*an Wettbewerb*) competitor

teil|s *adv* partly. **T~ung** *f* **-,-en** division; (*Pol*) partition. **t~weise** *a* partial ● *adv* partially, partly; (*manchmal*) in some cases. **T~zahlung** *f* part-payment; (*Rate*) instalment. **T~zeitbeschäftigung** *f* part-time job

Teint /tɛ̃:/ *m* **-s,-s** complexion

Telefax *nt* fax

Telefon *nt* **-s,-e** [tele]phone. **T~anruf** *m*, **T~at** *nt* **-[e]s,-e** [tele]phone call. **T~buch** *nt* [tele]phone book. **t~ieren** *vi* (*haben*) [tele]phone

telefon|isch *a* [tele]phone ... ● *adv* by [tele]phone. **T~ist(in)** *m* **-en,-en** (*f* **-,-nen**) telephonist. **T~karte** *f* phone card. **T~nummer** *f* [tele]phone number. **T~zelle** *f* [tele]phone box

Telegraf *m* **-en,-en** telegraph. **T~enmast** *m* telegraph pole. **t~ieren** *vi* (*haben*) send a telegram. **t~isch** *a* telegraphic ● *adv* by telegram

Telegramm *nt* **-s,-e** telegram

Telegraph *m* **-en,-en** = **Telegraf**

Teleobjektiv *nt* telephoto lens

Telepathie *f* **-** telepathy

Telephon *nt* **-s,-e** = **Telefon**

Teleskop *nt* **-s,-e** telescope. **t~isch** *a* telescopic

Telex *nt* **-,-[e]** telex. **t~en** *vt* telex

Teller *m* **-s,-** plate

Tempel *m* **-s,-** temple

Temperament *nt* **-s,-e** temperament; (*Lebhaftigkeit*) vivacity. **t~los** *a* dull. **t~voll** *a* vivacious; ⟨*Pferd*⟩ spirited

Temperatur *f* **-,-en** temperature

Tempo *nt* **-s,-s** speed; (*Mus: pl* **-pi**) tempo; **T~ [T~]!** hurry up!

Tend|enz *f* **-,-en** trend; (*Neigung*) tendency. **t~ieren** *vi* (*haben*) tend (**zu** towards)

Tennis *nt* **-** tennis. **T~platz** *m* tennis-court. **T~schläger** *m* tennis-racket

Tenor *m* **-s,⸚e** (*Mus*) tenor

Teppich *m* **-s,-e** carpet. **T~boden** *m* fitted carpet
Termin *m* **-s,-e** date; (*Arzt-*) appointment; **[letzter] T~** deadline. **T~kalender** *m* [appointments] diary
Terminologie *f* **-,-n** terminology
Terpentin *nt* **-s** turpentine
Terrain /tɛˈrɛ̃ː/ *nt* **-s,-s** terrain
Terrasse *f* **-,-n** terrace
Terrier /ˈtɛri̯ɐ/ *m* **-s,-** terrier
Terrine *f* **-,-n** tureen
Territorium *nt* **-s,-ien** territory
Terror *m* **-s** terror. **t~isieren** *vt* terrorize. **T~ismus** *m* **-** terrorism. **T~ist** *m* **-en,-en** terrorist
Terzett *nt* **-[e]s,-e** [vocal] trio
Tesafilm (**P**) *m* ≈ Sellotape (P)
Test *m* **-[e]s,-s** & **-e** test
Testament *nt* **-[e]s,-e** will; **Altes/Neues T~** Old/New Testament. **T~svollstrecker** *m* **-s,-** executor
testen *vt* test
Tetanus *m* **-** tetanus
teuer *a* expensive, *adv* -ly; (*lieb*) dear; **wie t~?** how much? **T~ung** *f* **-,-en** rise in prices
Teufel *m* **-s,-** devil; **zum T~!** (*sl*) damn [it]! **T~skreis** *m* vicious circle
teuflisch *a* fiendish
Text *m* **-[e]s,-e** text; (*Passage*) passage; (*Bild-*) caption; (*Lied-*) lyrics *pl*, words *pl*; (*Opern-*) libretto. **T~er** *m* **-s,-** copy-writer; (*Schlager-*) lyricist
Textil|ien /-i̯ən/ *pl* textiles; (*Textilwaren*) textile goods. **T~industrie** *f* textile industry
Textverarbeitungssystem *nt* word processor
TH *abbr* = **Technische Hochschule**
Theater *nt* **-s,-** theatre; (*fam: Getue*) fuss, to-do; **T~ spielen** act; (*fam*) put on an act. **T~kasse** *f* box-office. **T~stück** *nt* play
theatralisch *a* theatrical, *adv* -ly
Theke *f* **-,-n** bar; (*Ladentisch*) counter
Thema *nt* **-s,-men** subject; (*Mus*) theme
Themse *f* **-** Thames
Theolo|ge *m* **-n,-n** theologian. **T~gie** *f* **-** theology
theor|etisch *a* theoretical, *adv* -ly. **T~ie** *f* **-,-n** theory
Therapeut|(in) *m* **-en,-en** (*f* **-,-nen**) therapist. **t~isch** *a* therapeutic
Therapie *f* **-,-n** therapy
Thermal|bad *nt* thermal bath; (*Ort*) thermal spa. **T~quelle** *f* thermal spring
Thermometer *nt* **-s,-** thermometer
Thermosflasche (**P**) *f* Thermos flask (P)
Thermostat *m* **-[e]s,-e** thermostat
These *f* **-,-n** thesis
Thrombose *f* **-,-n** thrombosis
Thron *m* **-[e]s,-e** throne. **t~en** *vi* (*haben*) sit [in state]. **T~folge** *f* succession. **T~folger** *m* **-s,-** heir to the throne
Thunfisch *m* tuna
Thymian *m* **-s** thyme
Tick *m* **-s,-s** (*fam*) quirk; **einen T~ haben** be crazy
ticken *vi* (*haben*) tick
tief *a* deep; (*t~liegend, niedrig*) low; (*t~gründig*) profound; **t~er Teller** soup-plate; **im t~sten Winter** in the depths of winter ● *adv* deep; low; (*sehr*) deeply, profoundly; ⟨*schlafen*⟩ soundly. **T~** *nt* **-s,-s** (*Meteorol*) depression. **T~bau** *m* civil engineering. **T~e** *f* **-,-n** depth
Tief|ebene *f* [lowland] plain. **T~garage** *f* underground car park. **t~gekühlt** *a* [deep-]frozen. **t~greifend** *a* radical, *adv* -ly. **t~gründig** *a* (*fig*) profound
Tiefkühl|fach *nt* freezer compartment. **T~kost** *f* frozen food. **T~truhe** *f* deep-freeze
Tief|land *nt* lowlands *pl*. **T~punkt** *m* (*fig*) low. **t~schürfend** *a* (*fig*) profound. **t~sinnig** *a* (*fig*) profound; (*trübsinnig*) melancholy. **T~stand** *m* (*fig*) low
Tiefsttemperatur *f* minimum temperature
Tier *nt* **-[e]s,-e** animal. **T~arzt** *m*, **T~ärztin** *f* vet, veterinary surgeon. **T~garten** *m* zoo. **t~isch** *a* animal . . . ; (*fig: roh*) bestial. **T~kreis** *m* zodiac. **T~kreiszeichen** *nt* sign of the zodiac. **T~kunde** *f* zoology. **T~quälerei** *f* cruelty to animals
Tiger *m* **-s,-** tiger
tilgen *vt* pay off ⟨*Schuld*⟩; (*streichen*) delete; (*fig: auslöschen*) wipe out
Tinte *f* **-,-n** ink. **T~nfisch** *m* squid
Tip *m* **-s,-s** (*fam*) tip
tipp|en *vt* (*fam*) type ● *vi* (*haben*) (*berühren*) touch (**auf/an etw** *acc* sth); (*fam: maschineschreiben*) type; **t~en auf** (+*acc*) (*fam: wetten*) bet on. **T~fehler** *m* (*fam*) typing error. **T~schein** *m* pools/lottery coupon
tipptopp *a* (*fam*) immaculate, *adv* -ly
Tirol *nt* **-s** [the] Tyrol

Tisch *m* **-[e]s,-e** table; (*Schreib-*) desk; **nach T~** after the meal. **T~decke** *f* table-cloth. **T~gebet** *nt* grace. **T~ler** *m* **-s,-** joiner; (*Möbel-*) cabinet-maker. **T~rede** *f* after-dinner speech. **T~tennis** *nt* table tennis. **T~tuch** *nt* table-cloth

Titel *m* **-s,-** title. **T~rolle** *f* title-role

Toast /to:st/ *m* **-[e]s,-e** toast; (*Scheibe*) piece of toast; **einen T~ ausbringen** propose a toast (**auf** + *acc* to). **T~er** *m* **-s,-** toaster

tob|en *vi* (*haben*) rave; ⟨*Sturm:*⟩ rage; ⟨*Kinder:*⟩ play boisterously ● *vi* (*sein*) rush. **t~süchtig** *a* raving mad

Tochter *f* **-,⸚** daughter. **T~gesellschaft** *f* subsidiary

Tod *m* **-es** death. **t~ernst** *a* deadly serious, *adv* -ly

Todes|angst *f* mortal fear. **T~anzeige** *f* death announcement; (*Zeitungs-*) obituary. **T~fall** *m* death. **T~opfer** *nt* fatality, casualty. **T~strafe** *f* death penalty. **T~urteil** *nt* death sentence

Tod|feind *m* mortal enemy. **t~krank** *a* dangerously ill

tödlich *a* fatal, *adv* -ly; ⟨*Gefahr*⟩ mortal, *adv* -ly; (*groß*) deadly; **t~ gelangweilt** bored to death

tod|müde *a* dead tired. **t~sicher** *a* (*fam*) dead certain ● *adv* for sure. **T~sünde** *f* deadly sin. **t~unglücklich** *a* desperately unhappy

Toilette /tọa'lɛtə/ *f* **-,-n** toilet. **T~npapier** *nt* toilet paper

toler|ant *a* tolerant. **T~anz** *f* **-** tolerance. **t~ieren** *vt* tolerate

toll *a* crazy, mad; (*fam: prima*) fantastic; (*schlimm*) awful ● *adv* beautifully; (*sehr*) very; (*schlimm*) badly. **t~en** *vi* (*haben/sein*) romp. **t~kühn** *a* foolhardy. **T~wut** *f* rabies. **t~wütig** *a* rabid

tolpatschig *a* clumsy, *adv* -ily

Tölpel *m* **-s,-** fool

Tomate *f* **-,-n** tomato. **T~nmark** *nt* tomato purée

Tombola *f* **-,-s** raffle

Ton[1] *m* **-[e]s** clay

Ton[2] *m* **-[e]s,⸚e** tone; (*Klang*) sound; (*Note*) note; (*Betonung*) stress; (*Farb-*) shade; **der gute Ton** (*fig*) good form. **T~abnehmer** *m* **-s,-** pick-up. **t~angebend** *a* (*fig*) leading. **T~art** *f* tone [of voice]; (*Mus*) key. **T~band** *nt* (*pl* **-bänder**) tape. **T~bandgerät** *nt* tape recorder

tönen *vi* (*haben*) sound ● *vt* tint

Ton|fall *m* tone [of voice]; (*Akzent*) intonation. **T~leiter** *f* scale. **t~los** *a* toneless, *adv* -ly

Tonne *f* **-,-n** barrel, cask; (*Müll-*) bin; (*Maß*) tonne, metric ton

Topf *m* **-[e]s,⸚e** pot; (*Koch-*) pan

Topfen *m* **-s** (*Aust*) ≈ curd cheese

Töpfer|(in) *m* **-s,-** (*f* **-,-nen**) potter. **T~ei** *f* **-,-en** pottery

Töpferwaren *fpl* pottery *sg*

Topf|lappen *m* oven-cloth. **T~pflanze** *f* potted plant

Tor[1] *m* **-en,-en** fool

Tor[2] *nt* **-[e]s,-e** gate; (*Einfahrt*) gateway; (*Sport*) goal. **T~bogen** *m* archway

Torf *m* **-s** peat

Torheit *f* **-,-en** folly

Torhüter *m* **-s,-** goalkeeper

töricht *a* foolish, *adv* -ly

torkeln *vi* (*sein/haben*) stagger

Tornister *m* **-s,-** knapsack; (*Sch*) satchel

torp|edieren *vt* torpedo. **T~edo** *m* **-s,-s** torpedo

Torpfosten *m* goal-post

Torte *f* **-,-n** gâteau; (*Obst-*) flan

Tortur *f* **-,-en** torture

Torwart *m* **-s,-e** goalkeeper

tosen *vi* (*haben*) roar; ⟨*Sturm:*⟩ rage

tot *a* dead; **einen t~en Punkt haben** (*fig*) be at a low ebb

total *a* total, *adv* -ly. **t~itär** *a* totalitarian. **T~schaden** *m* ≈ write-off

Tote|(r) *m/f* dead man/woman; (*Todesopfer*) fatality; **die T~n** the dead *pl*

töten *vt* kill

toten|blaß *a* deathly pale. **T~gräber** *m* **-s,-** grave-digger. **T~kopf** *m* skull. **T~schein** *m* death certificate. **T~stille** *f* deathly silence

tot|fahren† *vt sep* run over and kill. **t~geboren** *a* stillborn. **t~lachen (sich)** *vr sep* (*fam*) be in stitches

Toto *nt* & *m* **-s** football pools *pl.* **T~schein** *m* pools coupon

tot|schießen† *vt sep* shoot dead. **T~schlag** *m* (*Jur*) manslaughter. **t~schlagen**† *vt sep* kill. **t~schweigen**† *vt sep* (*fig*) hush up. **t~stellen (sich)** *vr sep* pretend to be dead

Tötung *f* **-,-en** killing; **fahrlässige T~** (*Jur*) manslaughter

Toup|et /tu'pe:/ *nt* **-s,-s** toupee. **t~ieren** *vt* back-comb

Tour /tu:ɐ̯/ *f* **-,-en** tour; (*Ausflug*) trip; (*Auto-*) drive; (*Rad-*) ride; (*Strecke*)

distance; (*Techn*) revolution; (*fam: Weise*) way; **auf vollen T~en** at full speed; (*fam*) flat out

Touris|mus /tu'rɪsmʊs/ *m* - tourism. **T~t** *m* **-en,-en** tourist

Tournee /tʊr'ne:/ *f* **-,-n** tour

Trab *m* **-[e]s** trot

Trabant *m* **-en,-en** satellite

traben *vi* (*haben/sein*) trot

Tracht *f* **-,-en** [national] costume; **eine T~ Prügel** a good hiding

trachten *vi* (*haben*) strive (**nach** for); **jdm nach dem Leben t~** be out to kill s.o.

trächtig *a* pregnant

Tradition /-'tsi̯o:n/ *f* **-,-en** tradition. **t~ell** *a* traditional, *adv* -ly

Trafik *f* **-,-en** (*Aust*) tobacconist's

Trag|bahre *f* stretcher. **t~bar** *a* portable; ‹*Kleidung*› wearable; (*erträglich*) bearable

träge *a* sluggish, *adv* -ly; (*faul*) lazy, *adv* -ily; (*Phys*) inert

tragen† *vt* carry; (*an-/aufhaben*) wear; (*fig*) bear ● *vi* (*haben*) carry; **gut t~** ‹*Baum:*› produce a good crop; **schwer t~** carry a heavy load; (*fig*) be deeply affected (**an** + *dat* by). **t~d** *a* (*Techn*) load-bearing; (*trächtig*) pregnant

Träger *m* **-s,-** porter; (*Inhaber*) bearer; (*eines Ordens*) holder; (*Bau-*) beam; (*Stahl-*) girder; (*Achsel-*) [shoulder] strap. **T~kleid** *nt* pinafore dress

Trag|etasche *f* carrier bag. **T~fläche** *f* (*Aviat*) wing; (*Naut*) hydrofoil. **T~flächenboot, T~flügelboot** *nt* hydrofoil

Trägheit *f* - sluggishness; (*Faulheit*) laziness; (*Phys*) inertia

Trag|ik *f* - tragedy. **t~isch** *a* tragic, *adv* -ally

Tragödie /-i̯ə/ *f* **-,-n** tragedy

Tragweite *f* range; (*fig*) consequence

Train|er /'trɛ:nɐ/ *m* **-s,-** trainer; (*Tennis-*) coach. **t~ieren** *vt/i* (*haben*) train

Training /'trɛ:nɪŋ/ *nt* **-s** training. **T~sanzug** *m* tracksuit. **T~sschuhe** *mpl* trainers

Trakt *m* **-[e]s,-e** section; (*Flügel*) wing

traktieren *vi* (*haben*) **mit Schlägen/Tritten t~** hit/kick

Traktor *m* **-s,-en** /-'to:rən/ tractor

trampeln *vi* (*haben*) stamp one's feet ● *vi* (*sein*) trample (**auf** + *acc* on) ● *vt* trample

trampen /'trɛmpən/ *vi* (*sein*) (*fam*) hitch-hike

Trance /'trã:sə/ *f* **-,-n** trance

Tranchier|messer /trã'ʃi:ɐ̯-/ *nt* carving-knife. **t~en** *vt* carve

Träne *f* **-,-n** tear. **t~n** *vi* (*haben*) water. **T~ngas** *nt* tear-gas

Tränke *f* **-,-n** watering-place; (*Trog*) drinking-trough. **t~n** *vt* water ‹*Pferd*›; (*nässen*) soak (**mit** with)

Trans|aktion *f* transaction. **T~fer** *m* **-s,-s** transfer. **T~formator** *m* **-s,-en** /-'to:rən/ transformer. **T~fusion** *f* **-,-en** [blood] transfusion

Transistor *m* **-,-en** /-'to:rən/ transistor

Transit /tran'zi:t/ *m* **-s** transit

transitiv *a* transitive, *adv* -ly

Transparent *nt* **-[e]s,-e** banner; (*Bild*) transparency

transpirieren *vi* (*haben*) perspire

Transplantation /-'tsi̯o:n/ *f* **-,-en** transplant

Transport *m* **-[e]s,-e** transport; (*Güter-*) consignment. **t~ieren** *vt* transport. **T~mittel** *nt* means of transport

Trapez *nt* **-es,-e** trapeze; (*Geom*) trapezium

Tratsch *m* **-[e]s** (*fam*) gossip. **t~en** *vi* (*haben*) (*fam*) gossip

Tratte *f* **-,-n** (*Comm*) draft

Traube *f* **-,-n** bunch of grapes; (*Beere*) grape; (*fig*) cluster. **T~nzucker** *m* glucose

trauen *vi* (*haben*) (+*dat*) trust; **ich traute kaum meinen Augen** I could hardly believe my eyes ● *vt* marry; **sich t~** dare (**etw zu tun** [to] do sth); venture (**in** + *acc*/**aus** into/out of)

Trauer *f* - mourning; (*Schmerz*) grief (**um** for); **T~ tragen** be [dressed] in mourning. **T~fall** *m* bereavement. **T~feier** *f* funeral service. **T~marsch** *m* funeral march. **t~n** *vi* (*haben*) grieve; **t~n um** mourn [for]. **T~spiel** *nt* tragedy. **T~weide** *f* weeping willow

traulich *a* cosy, *adv* -ily

Traum *m* **-[e]s, Träume** dream

Trau|ma *nt* **-s,-men** trauma. **t~matisch** *a* traumatic

träumen *vt/i* (*haben*) dream

traumhaft *a* dreamlike; (*schön*) fabulous, *adv* -ly

traurig *a* sad, *adv* -ly; (*erbärmlich*) sorry. **T~keit** *f* - sadness

Trau|ring *m* wedding-ring. **T~schein** *m* marriage certificate. **T~ung** *f* **-,-en** wedding [ceremony]

Treck *m* **-s,-s** trek
Trecker *m* **-s,-** tractor
Treff *nt* **-s,-s** (*Karten*) spades *pl*
treff|en† *vt* hit; ⟨*Blitz:*⟩ strike; (*fig: verletzen*) hurt; (*zusammenkommen mit*) meet; take ⟨*Maßnahme*⟩; **sich t~en** meet (**mit jdm** s.o.); **sich gut t~en** be convenient; **es traf sich, daß** it so happened that; **es gut/schlecht t~en** be lucky/unlucky ● *vi* (*haben*) hit the target; **t~en auf** (+*acc*) meet; (*fig*) meet with. **T~en** *nt* **-s,-** meeting. **t~end** *a* apt, *adv* -ly; ⟨*Ähnlichkeit*⟩ striking. **T~er** *m* **-s,-** hit; (*Los*) winner. **T~punkt** *m* meeting-place
treiben† *vt* drive; (*sich befassen mit*) do; carry on ⟨*Gewerbe*⟩; indulge in ⟨*Luxus*⟩; get up to ⟨*Unfug*⟩; **Handel t~** trade; **Blüten/Blätter t~** come into flower/leaf; **zur Eile t~** hurry [up]; **was treibt ihr da?** (*fam*) what are you up to? ● *vi* (*sein*) drift; (*schwimmen*) float ● *vi* (*haben*) (*Bot*) sprout. **T~** *nt* **-s** activity; (*Getriebe*) bustle
Treib|haus *nt* hothouse. **T~hauseffekt** *m* greenhouse effect. **T~holz** *nt* driftwood. **T~riemen** *m* transmission belt. **T~sand** *m* quicksand. **T~stoff** *m* fuel
Trend *m* **-s,-s** trend
trenn|bar *a* separable. **t~en** *vt* separate/(*abmachen*) detach (**von** from); divide, split ⟨*Wort*⟩; **sich t~en** separate; (*auseinandergehen*) part; **sich t~en von** leave; (*fortgeben*) part with. **T~ung** *f* **-,-en** separation; (*Silben-*) division. **T~ungsstrich** *m* hyphen. **T~wand** *f* partition
trepp|ab *adv* downstairs. **t~auf** *adv* upstairs
Treppe *f* **-,-n** stairs *pl*; (*Außen-*) steps *pl*; **eine T~** a flight of stairs/steps. **T~nflur** *m* landing. **T~ngeländer** *nt* banisters *pl*. **T~nhaus** *nt* stairwell. **T~nstufe** *f* stair, step
Tresor *m* **-s,-e** safe
Tresse *f* **-,-n** braid
Treteimer *m* pedal bin
treten† *vi* (*sein/haben*) step; (*versehentlich*) tread; (*ausschlagen*) kick (**nach** at); **in Verbindung t~** get in touch ● *vt* tread; (*mit Füßen*) kick
treu *a* faithful, *adv* -ly; (*fest*) loyal, *adv* -ly. **T~e** *f* **-** faithfulness; loyalty; (*eheliche*) fidelity. **T~händer** *m* **-s,-** trustee. **t~herzig** *a* trusting, *adv* -ly; (*arglos*) innocent, *adv* -ly. **t~los** *a* disloyal, *adv* -ly; (*untreu*) unfaithful
Tribüne *f* **-,-n** platform; (*Zuschauer-*) stand
Tribut *m* **-[e]s,-e** tribute; (*Opfer*) toll
Trichter *m* **-s,-** funnel; (*Bomben-*) crater
Trick *m* **-s,-s** trick. **T~film** *m* cartoon. **t~reich** *a* clever
Trieb *m* **-[e]s,-e** drive, urge; (*Instinkt*) instinct; (*Bot*) shoot. **T~täter, T~verbrecher** *m* sex offender. **T~werk** *nt* (*Aviat*) engine; (*Uhr-*) mechanism
trief|en† *vi* (*haben*) drip; (*naß sein*) be dripping (**von/vor** + *dat* with). **t~naß** *a* dripping wet
triftig *a* valid
Trigonometrie *f* **-** trigonometry
Trikot[1] /tri'ko:/ *m* **-s** (*Tex*) jersey
Trikot[2] *nt* **-s,-s** (*Sport*) jersey; (*Fußball-*) shirt
Trimester *nt* **-s,-** term
Trimm-dich *nt* **-s** keep-fit
trimmen *vt* trim; (*fam*) train; tune ⟨*Motor*⟩; **sich t~** keep fit
trink|bar *a* drinkable. **t~en†** *vt/i* (*haben*) drink. **T~er(in)** *m* **-s,-** (*f* **-,-nen**) alcoholic. **T~geld** *nt* tip. **T~halm** *m* [drinking-]straw. **T~spruch** *m* toast. **T~wasser** *nt* drinking-water
Trio *nt* **-s,-s** trio
trippeln *vi* (*sein*) trip along
trist *a* dreary
Tritt *m* **-[e]s,-e** step; (*Fuß-*) kick. **T~brett** *nt* step. **T~leiter** *f* step-ladder
Triumph *m* **-s,-e** triumph. **t~ieren** *vi* (*haben*) rejoice; **t~ieren über** (+*acc*) triumph over. **t~ierend** *a* triumphant, *adv* -ly
trocken *a* dry, *adv* drily. **T~haube** *f* drier. **T~heit** *f* **-,-en** dryness; (*Dürre*) drought. **t~legen** *vt sep* change ⟨*Baby*⟩; drain ⟨*Sumpf*⟩. **T~milch** *f* powdered milk
trockn|en *vt/i* (*sein*) dry. **T~er** *m* **-s,-** drier
Troddel *f* **-,-n** tassel
Trödel *m* **-s** (*fam*) junk. **T~laden** *m* (*fam*) junk-shop. **T~markt** *m* (*fam*) flea market. **t~n** *vi* (*haben*) dawdle
Trödler *m* **-s,-** (*fam*) slowcoach; (*Händler*) junk-dealer
Trog *m* **-[e]s,¨e** trough
Trommel *f* **-,-n** drum. **T~fell** *nt* eardrum. **t~n** *vi* (*haben*) drum
Trommler *m* **-s,-** drummer

Trompete *f* **-,-n** trumpet. **T~r** *m* **-s,-** trumpeter
Tropen *pl* tropics
Tropf *m* **-[e]s,-e** (*Med*) drip
tröpfeln *vt/i* (*sein/haben*) drip; **es tröpfelt** it's spitting with rain
tropfen *vt/i* (*sein/haben*) drip. **T~** *m* **-s,-** drop; (*fallend*) drip. **t~weise** *adv* drop by drop
tropf|naß *a* dripping wet. **T~stein** *m* stalagmite; (*hängend*) stalactite
Trophäe /tro'fɛ:ə/ *f* **-,-n** trophy
tropisch *a* tropical
Trost *m* **-[e]s** consolation, comfort
tröst|en *vt* console, comfort; **sich t~en** console oneself. **t~lich** *a* comforting
trost|los *a* desolate; (*elend*) wretched; (*reizlos*) dreary. **T~preis** *m* consolation prize. **t~reich** *a* comforting
Trott *m* **-s** amble; (*fig*) routine
Trottel *m* **-s,-** (*fam*) idiot
trotten *vi* (*sein*) traipse; ⟨*Tier:*⟩ amble
Trottoir /trɔ'to̯a:ɐ̯/ *nt* **-s,-s** pavement, (*Amer*) sidewalk
trotz *prep* (+*gen*) despite, in spite of. **T~** *m* **-es** defiance. **t~dem** *adv* nevertheless. **t~en** *vi* (*haben*) (+*dat*) defy. **t~ig** *a* defiant, *adv* -ly; ⟨*Kind*⟩ stubborn
trübe *a* dull; ⟨*Licht*⟩ dim; ⟨*Flüssigkeit*⟩ cloudy; (*fig*) gloomy
Trubel *m* **-s** bustle
trüben *vt* dull; make cloudy ⟨*Flüssigkeit*⟩; (*fig*) spoil; strain ⟨*Verhältnis*⟩; **sich t~** ⟨*Flüssigkeit:*⟩ become cloudy; ⟨*Himmel:*⟩ cloud over; ⟨*Augen:*⟩ dim; ⟨*Verhältnis, Erinnerung:*⟩ deteriorate
Trüb|sal *f* **-** misery; **T~sal blasen** (*fam*) mope. **t~selig** *a* miserable; (*trübe*) gloomy, *adv* -ily. **T~sinn** *m* melancholy. **t~sinnig** *a* melancholy
Trugbild *nt* illusion
trüg|en† *vt* deceive ● *vi* (*haben*) be deceptive. **t~erisch** *a* false; (*täuschend*) deceptive
Trugschluß *m* fallacy
Truhe *f* **-,-n** chest
Trümmer *pl* rubble *sg*; (*T~teile*) wreckage *sg*; (*fig*) ruins. **T~haufen** *m* pile of rubble
Trumpf *m* **-[e]s,¨e** trump [card]; **T~ sein** be trumps. **t~en** *vi* (*haben*) play trumps
Trunk *m* **-[e]s** drink. **T~enbold** *m* **-[e]s,-e** drunkard. **T~enheit** *f* **-** drunkenness; **T~enheit am Steuer** drunken driving. **T~sucht** *f* alcoholism
Trupp *m* **-s,-s** group; (*Mil*) squad. **T~e** *f* **-,-n** (*Mil*) unit; (*Theat*) troupe; **T~en** troops
Truthahn *m* turkey
Tschech|e *m* **-n,-n, T~in** *f* **-,-nen** Czech. **t~isch** *a* Czech. **T~oslowakei (die) -** Czechoslovakia
tschüs *int* bye, cheerio
Tuba *f* **-,-ben** (*Mus*) tuba
Tube *f* **-,-n** tube
Tuberkulose *f* **-** tuberculosis
Tuch[1] *nt* **-[e]s,¨er** cloth; (*Hals-, Kopf-*) scarf; (*Schulter-*) shawl
Tuch[2] *nt* **-[e]s,-e** (*Stoff*) cloth
tüchtig *a* competent; (*reichlich, beträchtlich*) good; (*groß*) big ● *adv* competently; (*ausreichend*) well; ⟨*regnen, schneien*⟩ hard. **T~keit** *f* **-** competence
Tück|e *f* **-,-n** malice; **T~en haben** be temperamental; (*gefährlich sein*) be treacherous. **t~isch** *a* malicious, *adv* -ly; (*gefährlich*) treacherous
tüfteln *vi* (*haben*) (*fam*) fiddle (**an** + *dat* with); (*geistig*) puzzle (**an** + *dat* over)
Tugend *f* **-,en** virtue. **t~haft** *a* virtuous
Tülle *f* **-,-n** spout
Tulpe *f* **-,-n** tulip
tummeln (sich) *vr* romp [about]; (*sich beeilen*) hurry [up]
Tümmler *m* **-s,-** porpoise
Tumor *m* **-s,-en** /-'mo:rən/ tumour
Tümpel *m* **-s,-** pond
Tumult *m* **-[e]s,-e** commotion; (*Aufruhr*) riot
tun† *vt* do; take ⟨*Schritt, Blick*⟩; work ⟨*Wunder*⟩; (*bringen*) put (**in** + *acc* into); **sich tun** happen; **jdm etwas tun** hurt s.o.; **viel zu tun haben** have a lot to do; **das tut man nicht** it isn't done; **das tut nichts** it doesn't matter ● *vi* (*haben*) act (**als ob** as if); **überrascht tun** pretend to be surprised; **er tut nur so** he's just pretending; **zu tun haben** have things/work to do; **[es] zu tun haben mit** have to deal with; **[es] mit dem Herzen zu tun haben** have heart trouble. **Tun** *nt* **-s** actions *pl*
Tünche *f* **-,-n** whitewash; (*fig*) veneer. **t~n** *vt* whitewash
Tunesien /-i̯ən/ *nt* **-s** Tunisia
Tunke *f* **-,-n** sauce. **t~n** *vt/i* (*haben*) (*fam*) dip (**in** + *acc* into)
Tunnel *m* **-s,-** tunnel

tupf|en *vt* dab ● *vi* (*haben*) **t~en an/auf** (+*acc*) touch. **T~en** *m* **-s,-** spot. **T~er** *m* **-s,-** spot; (*Med*) swab

Tür *f* **-,-en** door

Turban *m* **-s,-e** turban

Turbine *f* **-,-n** turbine

turbulen|t *a* turbulent. **T~z** *f* **-,-en** turbulence

Türk|e *m* **-n,-n** Turk. **T~ei (die)** - Turkey. **T~in** *f* **-,-nen** Turk

türkis *inv a* turquoise. **T~** *m* **-es,-e** turquoise

türkisch *a* Turkish

Turm *m* **-[e]s,⸚e** tower; (*Schach*) rook, castle

Türm|chen *nt* **-s,-** turret. **t~en** *vt* pile [up]; **sich t~en** pile up ● *vi* (*sein*) (*fam*) escape

Turmspitze *f* spire

turn|en *vi* (*haben*) do gymnastics. **T~en** *nt* **-s** gymnastics *sg*; (*Sch*) physical education, (*fam*) gym. **T~er(in)** *m* **-s,-** (*f* **-,-nen**) gymnast. **T~halle** *f* gymnasium

Turnier *nt* **-s,-e** tournament; (*Reit-*) show

Turnschuhe *mpl* gym shoes

Türschwelle *f* doorstep, threshold

Tusch *m* **-[e]s,-e** fanfare

Tusche *f* **-,-n** [drawing] ink; (*Wasserfarbe*) watercolour

tuscheln *vt/i* (*haben*) whisper

Tüte *f* **-,-n** bag; (*Comm*) packet; (*Eis-*) cornet; **in die T~ blasen** (*fam*) be breathalysed

tuten *vi* (*haben*) hoot; ⟨*Schiff:*⟩ sound its hooter; ⟨*Sirene:*⟩ sound

TÜV *m* - ≈ MOT [test]

Typ *m* **-s,-en** type; (*fam: Kerl*) bloke. **T~e** *f* **-,-n** type; (*fam: Person*) character

Typhus *m* - typhoid

typisch *a* typical, *adv* -ly (**für** of)

Typographie *f* - typography

Typus *m* **-, Typen** type

Tyrann *m* **-en,-en** tyrant. **T~ei** *f* - tyranny. **t~isch** *a* tyrannical. **t~isieren** *vt* tyrannize

U

u.a. *abbr* (**unter anderem**) amongst other things

U-Bahn *f* underground, (*Amer*) subway

übel *a* bad; (*häßlich*) nasty, *adv* -ily; **mir ist/wird ü~** I feel sick. **Ü~** *nt* **-s,-** evil. **Ü~keit** *f* - nausea. **ü~nehmen**† *vt sep* take amiss; **jdm etw ü~nehmen** hold sth against s.o. **Ü~täter** *m* culprit

üben *vt/i* (*haben*) practise; **sich in etw** (*dat*) **ü~** practise sth

über *prep* (+*dat/acc*) over; (*höher als*) above; (*betreffend*) about; ⟨*Buch, Vortrag*⟩ on; ⟨*Scheck, Rechnung*⟩ for; (*quer ü~*) across; **ü~ Köln fahren** go via Cologne; **ü~ Ostern** over Easter; **die Woche ü~** during the week; **heute ü~ eine Woche** a week today; **Fehler ü~ Fehler** mistake after mistake ● *adv* **ü~ und ü~** all over; **jdm ü~ sein** be better/(*stärker*) stronger than s.o. ● *a* (*fam*) **ü~ sein** be left over; **etw ü~ sein** be fed up with sth

überall *adv* everywhere

überanstrengen *vt insep* overtax; strain ⟨*Augen*⟩; **sich ü~** overexert oneself

überarbeit|en *vt insep* revise; **sich ü~en** overwork. **Ü~ung** *f* - revision; overwork

überaus *adv* extremely

überbewerten *vt insep* overrate

überbieten† *vt insep* outbid; (*fig*) outdo; (*übertreffen*) surpass

Überblick *m* overall view; (*Abriß*) summary

überblicken *vt insep* overlook; (*abschätzen*) assess

überbringen† *vt insep* deliver

überbrücken *vt insep* (*fig*) bridge

überdauern *vt insep* survive

überdenken† *vt insep* think over

überdies *adv* moreover

überdimensional *a* oversized

Überdosis *f* overdose

Überdruß *m* **-sses** surfeit; **bis zum Ü~** ad nauseam

überdrüssig *a* **ü~ sein/werden** be/grow tired (*gen* of)

übereignen *vt insep* transfer

übereilt *a* over-hasty, *adv* -ily

übereinander *adv* one on top of/above the other; ⟨*sprechen*⟩ about each other. **ü~schlagen**† *vt sep* cross ⟨*Beine*⟩; fold ⟨*Arme*⟩

überein|kommen† *vi sep* (*sein*) agree. **Ü~kunft** *f* - agreement. **ü~stimmen** *vi sep* (*haben*) agree; ⟨*Zahlen:*⟩ tally; ⟨*Ansichten:*⟩ coincide; ⟨*Farben:*⟩ match. **Ü~stimmung** *f* agreement

überempfindlich *a* over-sensitive; (*Med*) hypersensitive

überfahren† *vt insep* run over
Überfahrt *f* crossing
Überfall *m* attack; (*Bank-*) raid
überfallen† *vt insep* attack; raid ⟨*Bank*⟩; (*bestürmen*) bombard (**mit** with); (*überkommen*) come over; (*fam: besuchen*) surprise
überfällig *a* overdue
überfliegen† *vt insep* fly over; (*lesen*) skim over
überflügeln *vt insep* outstrip
Überfluß *m* abundance; (*Wohlstand*) affluence
überflüssig *a* superfluous
überfluten *vt insep* flood
überfordern *vt insep* overtax
überführ|en *vt insep* transfer; (*Jur*) convict (*gen* of). **Ü~ung** *f* transfer; (*Straße*) flyover; (*Fußgänger-*) foot-bridge
überfüllt *a* overcrowded
Übergabe *f* (*s.* **übergeben**) handing over; transfer
Übergang *m* crossing; (*Wechsel*) transition. **Ü~sstadium** *nt* transitional stage
übergeben† *vt insep* hand over; (*übereignen*) transfer; **sich ü~** be sick
übergehen[1]† *vi sep* (*sein*) pass (**an** + *acc* to); (*überwechseln*) go over (**zu** to); (*werden zu*) turn (**in** + *acc* into); **zum Angriff ü~** start the attack
übergehen[2]† *vt insep* (*fig*) pass over; (*nicht beachten*) ignore; (*auslassen*) leave out
Übergewicht *nt* excess weight; (*fig*) predominance; **Ü~ haben** be overweight
übergießen† *vt insep* **mit Wasser ü~** pour water over
überglücklich *a* overjoyed
über|greifen† *vi sep* (*haben*) spread (**auf** + *acc* to). **Ü~griff** *m* infringement
über|groß *a* outsize; (*übertrieben*) exaggerated. **Ü~größe** *f* outsize
überhaben† *vt sep* have on; (*fam: satthaben*) be fed up with
überhandnehmen† *vi sep* (*haben*) increase alarmingly
überhängen *v sep* ● *vi*† (*haben*) overhang ● *vt* (*reg*) **sich** (*dat*) **etw ü~** sling over one's shoulder ⟨*Gewehr*⟩; put round one's shoulders ⟨*Jacke*⟩
überhäufen *vt insep* inundate (**mit** with)
überhaupt *adv* (*im allgemeinen*) altogether; (*eigentlich*) anyway; (*überdies*) besides; **ü~ nicht/nichts** not/nothing at all
überheblich *a* arrogant, *adv* -ly. **Ü~keit** *f* - arrogance
überhol|en *vt insep* overtake; (*reparieren*) overhaul. **ü~t** *a* outdated. **Ü~ung** *f* -,-en overhaul. **Ü~verbot** *nt* '**Ü~verbot**' 'no overtaking'
überhören *vt insep* fail to hear; (*nicht beachten*) ignore
überirdisch *a* supernatural
überkochen *vi sep* (*sein*) boil over
überladen† *vt insep* overload ● *a* over-ornate
überlassen† *vt insep* **jdm etw ü~** leave sth to s.o.; (*geben*) let s.o. have sth; **sich seinem Schmerz ü~** abandon oneself to one's grief; **sich** (*dat*) **selbst ü~ sein** be left to one's own devices
überlasten *vt insep* overload; overtax ⟨*Person*⟩
Überlauf *m* overflow
überlaufen[1]† *vi sep* (*sein*) overflow; (*Mil, Pol*) defect
überlaufen[2]† *vt insep* **jdn ü~** ⟨*Gefühl:*⟩ come over s.o. ● *a* overrun; ⟨*Kursus*⟩ over-subscribed
Überläufer *m* defector
überleben *vt/i insep* (*haben*) survive. **Ü~de(r)** *m/f* survivor
überlegen[1] *vt sep* put over
überlegen[2] *v insep* ● *vt* [**sich** *dat*] **ü~** think over, consider; **es sich** (*dat*) **anders ü~** change one's mind ● *vi* (*haben*) think, reflect, **ohne zu ü~** without thinking
überlegen[3] *a* superior; (*herablassend*) supercilious, *adv* -ly. **Ü~heit** *f* - superiority
Überlegung *f* -,-en reflection
überliefer|n *vt insep* hand down. **Ü~ung** *f* tradition
überlisten *vt insep* outwit
überm *prep* = **über dem**
Über|macht *f* superiority. **ü~mächtig** *a* superior; ⟨*Gefühl*⟩ overpowering
übermannen *vt insep* overcome
Über|maß *nt* excess. **ü~mäßig** *a* excessive, *adv* -ly
Übermensch *m* superman. **ü~lich** *a* superhuman
übermitteln *vt insep* convey; (*senden*) transmit
übermorgen *adv* the day after tomorrow

übermüdet *a* overtired
Über|mut *m* high spirits *pl.* **ü~-mütig** *a* high-spirited ● *adv* in high spirits
übern *prep* = **über den**
übernächst|e(r,s) *a* next . . . but one; **ü~es Jahr** the year after next
übernacht|en *vi insep* (*haben*) stay overnight. **Ü~ung** *f* -,-en overnight stay; **Ü~ung und Frühstück** bed and breakfast
Übernahme *f* - taking over; (*Comm*) take-over
übernatürlich *a* supernatural
übernehmen† *vt insep* take over; (*annehmen*) take on; **sich ü~** overdo things; (*finanziell*) overreach oneself
überprüf|en *vt insep* check. **Ü~ung** *f* check
überqueren *vt insep* cross
überragen *vt insep* tower above; (*fig*) surpass. **ü~d** *a* outstanding
überrasch|en *vt insep* surprise. **ü~end** *a* surprising, *adv* -ly; (*unerwartet*) unexpected, *adv* -ly. **Ü~ung** *f* -,-en surprise
überreden *vt insep* persuade
überreichen *vt insep* present
überreizt *a* overwrought
überrennen† *vt insep* overrun
Überreste *mpl* remains
überrumpeln *vt insep* take by surprise
übers *prep* = **über das**
Überschall- *pref* supersonic
überschatten *vt insep* overshadow
überschätzen *vt insep* overestimate
Überschlag *m* rough estimate; (*Sport*) somersault
überschlagen[1]† *vt sep* cross ⟨*Beine*⟩
überschlagen[2]† *vt insep* estimate roughly; (*auslassen*) skip; **sich ü~** somersault; ⟨*Ereignisse:*⟩ happen fast ● *a* tepid
überschnappen *vi sep* (*sein*) (*fam*) go crazy
überschneiden† **(sich)** *vr insep* intersect, cross; (*zusammenfallen*) overlap
überschreiben† *vt insep* entitle; (*übertragen*) transfer
überschreiten† *vt insep* cross; (*fig*) exceed
Überschrift *f* heading; (*Zeitungs-*) headline
Über|schuß *m* surplus. **ü~schüssig** *a* surplus
überschütten *vt insep* **ü~ mit** cover with; (*fig*) shower with
überschwemm|en *vt insep* flood; (*fig*) inundate. **Ü~ung** *f* -,-en flood
überschwenglich *a* effusive, *adv* -ly
Übersee in/nach Ü~ overseas; **aus/von Ü~** from overseas. **Ü~dampfer** *m* ocean liner. **ü~isch** *a* overseas
übersehen† *vt insep* look out over; (*abschätzen*) assess; (*nicht sehen*) overlook, miss; (*ignorieren*) ignore
übersenden† *vt insep* send
übersetzen[1] *vi sep* (*haben/sein*) cross [over]
übersetz|en[2] *vt insep* translate. **Ü~er(in)** *m* -s,- (*f* -,-nen) translator. **Ü~ung** *f* -,-en translation
Übersicht *f* overall view; (*Abriß*) summary; (*Tabelle*) table. **ü~lich** *a* clear, *adv* -ly
übersied|eln *vi sep* (*sein*), **übersied|eln** *vi insep* (*sein*) move (**nach** to). **Ü~lung** *f* move
übersinnlich *a* supernatural
überspannt *a* exaggerated; (*verschroben*) eccentric
überspielen *vt insep* (*fig*) cover up; **auf Band ü~** tape
überspitzt *a* exaggerated
überspringen† *vt insep* jump [over]; (*auslassen*) skip
überstehen[1]† *vi sep* (*haben*) project, jut out
überstehen[2]† *vt insep* come through; get over ⟨*Krankheit*⟩; (*überleben*) survive
übersteigen† *vt insep* climb [over]; (*fig*) exceed
überstimmen *vt insep* outvote
überstreifen *vt sep* slip on
Überstunden *fpl* overtime *sg*; **Ü~ machen** work overtime
überstürz|en *vt insep* rush; **sich ü~en** ⟨*Ereignisse:*⟩ happen fast; ⟨*Worte:*⟩ tumble out. **ü~t** *a* hasty, *adv* -ily
übertölpeln *vt insep* dupe
übertönen *vt insep* drown [out]
übertrag|bar *a* transferable; (*Med*) infectious. **ü~en**† *vt insep* transfer; (*übergeben*) assign (*dat* to); (*Techn, Med*) transmit; (*Radio, TV*) broadcast; (*übersetzen*) translate; (*anwenden*) apply (**auf** + *acc* to) ● *a* transferred, figurative. **Ü~ung** *f* -,-en transfer; transmission; broadcast; translation; application

übertreffen† *vt insep* surpass; (*übersteigen*) exceed; **sich selbst ü~** excel oneself

übertreib|en† *vt insep* exaggerate; (*zu weit treiben*) overdo. **Ü~ung** *f* **-,-en** exaggeration

übertreten[1]† *vi sep* (*sein*) step over the line; (*Pol*) go over/(*Relig*) convert (**zu** to)

übertret|en[2]† *vt insep* infringe; break ⟨*Gesetz*⟩. **Ü~ung** *f* **-,-en** infringement; breach

übertrieben *a* exaggerated; (*übermäßig*) excessive, *adv* -ly

übervölkert *a* overpopulated

übervorteilen *vt insep* cheat

überwachen *vt insep* supervise; (*kontrollieren*) monitor; (*bespitzeln*) keep under surveillance

überwachsen *a* overgrown

überwältigen *vt insep* overpower; (*fig*) overwhelm. **ü~d** *a* overwhelming

überweis|en† *vt insep* transfer; refer ⟨*Patienten*⟩. **Ü~ung** *f* transfer; (*ärztliche*) referral

überwerfen[1]† *vt sep* throw on ⟨*Mantel*⟩

überwerfen[2]† **(sich)** *vr insep* fall out (**mit** with)

überwiegen† *v insep* ● *vi* (*haben*) predominate ● *vt* outweigh. **ü~d** *a* predominant, *adv* -ly

überwind|en† *vt insep* overcome; **sich ü~en** force oneself. **Ü~ung** *f* effort

Überwurf *m* wrap; (*Bett-*) bedspread

Über|zahl *f* majority. **ü~zählig** *a* spare

überzeug|en *vt insep* convince; **sich [selbst] ü~en** satisfy oneself. **ü~end** *a* convincing, *adv* -ly. **Ü~ung** *f* **-,-en** conviction

überziehen[1]† *vt sep* put on

überziehen[2]† *vt insep* cover; overdraw ⟨*Konto*⟩

Überzug *m* cover; (*Schicht*) coating

üblich *a* usual; (*gebräuchlich*) customary

U-Boot *nt* submarine

übrig *a* remaining; (*andere*) other; **alles ü~e** [all] the rest; **im ü~en** besides; (*ansonsten*) apart from that; **ü~ sein** be left [over]; **etw ü~ haben** have sth left [over]. **ü~behalten**† *vt sep* have left [over]. **ü~bleiben**† *vi sep* (*sein*) be left [over]; **uns blieb nichts anderes ü~** we had no choice. **ü~ens** *adv* by the way. **ü~lassen**† *vt sep* leave [over]

Übung *f* **-,-en** exercise; (*Üben*) practice; **außer** *od* **aus der Ü~** out of practice

UdSSR *f* - USSR

Ufer *nt* **-s,-** shore; (*Fluß-*) bank

Uhr *f* **-,-en** clock; (*Armband-*) watch; (*Zähler*) meter; **um ein U~** at one o'clock; **wieviel U~ ist es?** what's the time? **U~armband** *nt* watch-strap. **U~macher** *m* **-s,-** watch and clockmaker. **U~werk** *nt* clock/watch mechanism. **U~zeiger** *m* [clock-/watch-]hand. **U~zeigersinn** *m* **im/entgegen dem U~zeigersinn** clockwise/anticlockwise. **U~zeit** *f* time

Uhu *m* **-s,-s** eagle owl

UKW *abbr* (**Ultrakurzwelle**) VHF

Ulk *m* **-s** fun; (*Streich*) trick. **u~en** *vi* (*haben*) joke. **u~ig** *a* funny; (*seltsam*) odd, *adv* -ly

Ulme *f* **-,-n** elm

Ultimatum *nt* **-s,-ten** ultimatum

Ultrakurzwelle *f* very high frequency

Ultraschall *m* ultrasound

ultraviolett *a* ultraviolet

um *prep* (+*acc*) [a]round; (*Uhrzeit*) at; ⟨*bitten, kämpfen*⟩ for; ⟨*streiten*⟩ over; ⟨*sich sorgen*⟩ about; ⟨*betrügen*⟩ out of; (*bei Angabe einer Differenz*) by; **um [... herum]** around, [round] about; **Tag um Tag** day after day; **einen Tag um den andern** every other day; **um seinetwillen** for his sake ● *adv* (*ungefähr*) around, about ● *conj* **um zu** to; (*Absicht*) [in order] to; **zu müde, um zu ...** too tired to ...; **um so besser** all the better

umändern *vt sep* alter

umarbeiten *vt sep* alter; (*bearbeiten*) revise

umarm|en *vt insep* embrace, hug. **U~ung** *f* **-,-en** embrace, hug

Umbau *m* rebuilding; conversion (**zu** into). **u~en** *vt sep* rebuild; convert (**zu** into)

umbild|en *vt sep* change; (*umgestalten*) reorganize; reshuffle ⟨*Kabinett*⟩. **U~ung** *f* reorganization; (*Pol*) reshuffle

umbinden† *vt sep* put on

umblättern *v sep* ● *vt* turn [over] ● *vi* (*haben*) turn the page

umblicken (sich) *vr sep* look round; (*zurück-*) look back

umbringen† *vt sep* kill; **sich u~** kill oneself
Umbruch *m* (*fig*) radical change
umbuchen *v sep* • *vt* change; (*Comm*) transfer • *vi* (*haben*) change one's booking
umdrehen *v sep* • *vt* turn round/ (*wenden*) over; turn ⟨*Schlüssel*⟩; (*umkrempeln*) turn inside out; **sich u~** turn round; (*im Liegen*) turn over • *vi* (*haben*/*sein*) turn back
Umdrehung *f* turn; (*Motor*-) revolution
umeinander *adv* around each other; **sich u~ sorgen** worry about each other
umfahren¹† *vt sep* run over
umfahren²† *vt insep* go round; bypass ⟨*Ort*⟩
umfallen† *vi sep* (*sein*) fall over; ⟨*Person:*⟩ fall down
Umfang *m* girth; (*Geom*) circumference; (*Größe*) size; (*Ausmaß*) extent; (*Mus*) range
umfangen† *vt insep* embrace; (*fig*) envelop
umfangreich *a* extensive; (*dick*) big
umfassen *vt insep* consist of, comprise; (*umgeben*) surround. **u~d** *a* comprehensive
Umfrage *f* survey, poll
umfüllen *vt sep* transfer
umfunktionieren *vt sep* convert
Umgang *m* [social] contact; (*Umgehen*) dealing (**mit** with); **U~ haben mit** associate with
umgänglich *a* sociable
Umgangs|formen *fpl* manners. **U~sprache** *f* colloquial language. **u~sprachlich** *a* colloquial, *adv* -ly
umgeb|en† *vt/i insep* (*haben*) surround • *a* **u~en von** surrounded by. **U~ung** *f* -,-en surroundings *pl*
umgehen¹† *vi sep* (*sein*) go round; **u~ mit** treat, handle; (*verkehren*) associate with; **in dem Schloß geht ein Gespenst um** the castle is haunted
umgehen²† *vt insep* avoid; (*nicht beachten*) evade; ⟨*Straße:*⟩ bypass
umgehend *a* immediate, *adv* -ly
Umgehungsstraße *f* bypass
umgekehrt *a* inverse; ⟨*Reihenfolge*⟩ reverse; **es war u~** it was the other way round • *adv* conversely; **und u~** and vice versa
umgraben† *vt sep* dig [over]
umhaben† *vt sep* have on
Umhang *m* cloak
umhauen† *vt sep* knock down; (*fällen*) chop down
umher *adv* **weit u~** all around. **u~gehen**† *vi sep* (*sein*) walk about
umhören (sich) *vr sep* ask around
Umkehr *f* - turning back. **u~en** *v sep* • *vi* (*sein*) turn back • *vt* turn round; turn inside out ⟨*Tasche*⟩; (*fig*) reverse. **U~ung** *f* - reversal
umkippen *v sep* • *vt* tip over; (*versehentlich*) knock over • *vi* (*sein*) fall over; ⟨*Boot:*⟩ capsize; (*fam: ohnmächtig werden*) faint
Umkleide|kabine *f* changing-cubicle. **u~n (sich)** *vr sep* change. **U~raum** *m* changing-room
umknicken *v sep* • *vt* bend; (*falten*) fold • *vi* (*sein*) bend; (*mit dem Fuß*) go over on one's ankle
umkommen† *vi sep* (*sein*) perish; **u~ lassen** waste ⟨*Lebensmittel*⟩
Umkreis *m* surroundings *pl*; **im U~ von** within a radius of
umkreisen *vt insep* circle; (*Astr*) revolve around; ⟨*Satellit:*⟩ orbit
umkrempeln *vt sep* turn up; (*von innen nach außen*) turn inside out; (*ändern*) change radically
Umlauf *m* circulation; (*Astr*) revolution. **U~bahn** *f* orbit
Umlaut *m* umlaut
umlegen *vt sep* lay *or* put down; flatten ⟨*Getreide*⟩; turn down ⟨*Kragen*⟩; put on ⟨*Schal*⟩; throw ⟨*Hebel*⟩; (*verlegen*) transfer; (*fam: niederschlagen*) knock down; (*töten*) kill
umleit|en *vt sep* divert. **U~ung** *f* diversion
umliegend *a* surrounding
umpflanzen *vt sep* transplant
umrahmen *vt insep* frame
umranden *vt insep* edge
umräumen *vt sep* rearrange
umrechn|en *vt sep* convert. **U~ung** *f* conversion
umreißen¹† *vt sep* tear down; knock down ⟨*Person*⟩
umreißen²† *vt insep* outline
umringen *vt insep* surround
Umriß *m* outline
umrühren *vt/i sep* (*haben*) stir
ums *pron* = **um das; u~ Leben kommen** lose one's life
Umsatz *m* (*Comm*) turnover
umschalten *vt/i sep* (*haben*) switch over; **auf Rot u~** ⟨*Ampel:*⟩ change to red

Umschau *f* **U~ halten nach** look out for. **u~en (sich)** *vr sep* look round/(*zurück*) back
Umschlag *m* cover; (*Schutz-*) jacket; (*Brief-*) envelope; (*Med*) compress; (*Hosen-*) turn-up; (*Wechsel*) change. **u~en**† *v sep* ● *vt* turn up; turn over ⟨*Seite*⟩; (*fällen*) chop down ● *vi* (*sein*) topple over; ⟨*Boot:*⟩ capsize; ⟨*Wetter:*⟩ change; ⟨*Wind:*⟩ veer
umschließen† *vt insep* enclose
umschnallen *vt sep* buckle on
umschreiben[1]† *vt sep* rewrite
umschreib|en[2]† *vt insep* define; (*anders ausdrücken*) paraphrase. **U~ung** *f* definition; paraphrase
umschulen *vt sep* retrain; (*Sch*) transfer to another school
Umschweife *pl* **keine U~ machen** come straight out with it; **ohne U~** straight out
Umschwung *m* (*fig*) change; (*Pol*) U-turn
umsehen† **(sich)** *vr sep* look round; (*zurück*) look back; **sich u~ nach** look for
umsein† *vi sep* (*sein*) (*fam*) be over; ⟨*Zeit:*⟩ be up
umseitig *a & adv* overleaf
umsetzen *vt sep* move; (*umpflanzen*) transplant; (*Comm*) sell
Umsicht *f* circumspection. **u~ig** *a* circumspect, *adv* -ly
umsied|eln *v sep* ● *vt* resettle ● *vi* (*sein*) move. **U~lung** *f* resettlement
umsonst *adv* in vain; (*grundlos*) without reason; (*gratis*) free
umspringen† *vi sep* (*sein*) change; ⟨*Wind:*⟩ veer; **übel u~ mit** treat badly
Umstand *m* circumstance; (*Tatsache*) fact; (*Aufwand*) fuss; (*Mühe*) trouble; **unter U~en** possibly; **U~e machen** make a fuss; **jdm U~e machen** put s.o. to trouble; **in andern U~en** pregnant
umständlich *a* laborious, *adv* -ly; (*kompliziert*) involved; ⟨*Person*⟩ fussy
Umstands|kleid *nt* maternity dress. **U~wort** *nt* (*pl* **-wörter**) adverb
umstehen† *vi insep* surround
Umstehende *pl* bystanders
umsteigen† *vi sep* (*sein*) change
umstellen[1] *vt insep* surround
umstell|en[2] *vt sep* rearrange; transpose ⟨*Wörter*⟩; (*anders einstellen*) reset; (*Techn*) convert; (*ändern*) change; **sich u~en** adjust. **U~ung** *f* rearrangement; transposition; resetting; conversion; change; adjustment
umstimmen *vt sep* **jdn u~** change s.o.'s mind
umstoßen† *vt sep* knock over; (*fig*) overturn; upset ⟨*Plan*⟩
umstritten *a* controversial; (*ungeklärt*) disputed
umstülpen *vt sep* turn upside down; (*von innen nach außen*) turn inside out
Um|sturz *m* coup. **u~stürzen** *v sep* ● *vt* overturn; (*Pol*) overthrow ● *vi* (*sein*) fall over
umtaufen *vt sep* rename
Umtausch *m* exchange. **u~en** *vt sep* change; exchange (**gegen** for)
umwälzend *a* revolutionary
umwandeln *vt sep* convert; (*fig*) transform
umwechseln *vt sep* change
Umweg *m* detour; **auf U~en** in a roundabout way
Umwelt *f* environment. **u~freundlich** *a* environmentally friendly. **U~schutz** *m* protection of the environment. **U~schützer** *m* environmentalist
umwenden† *vt sep* turn over; **sich u~** turn round
umwerfen† *vt sep* knock over; (*fig*) upset ⟨*Plan*⟩; (*fam*) bowl over ⟨*Person*⟩
umziehen† *v sep* ● *vi* (*sein*) move ● *vt* change; **sich u~** change
umzingeln *vt insep* surround
Umzug *m* move; (*Prozession*) procession
unabänderlich *a* irrevocable; ⟨*Tatsache*⟩ unalterable
unabhängig *a* independent, *adv* -ly; **u~ davon, ob** irrespective of whether. **U~keit** *f* - independence
unabkömmlich *pred a* busy
unablässig *a* incessant, *adv* -ly
unabsehbar *a* incalculable
unabsichtlich *a* unintentional, *adv* -ly
unachtsam *a* careless, *adv* -ly. **U~keit** *f* - carelessness
unangebracht *a* inappropriate
unangemeldet *a* unexpected, *adv* -ly
unangemessen *a* inappropriate, *adv* -ly
unangenehm *a* unpleasant, *adv* -ly; (*peinlich*) embarrassing
Unannehmlichkeiten *fpl* trouble *sg*

unansehnlich *a* shabby; ⟨*Person*⟩ plain
unanständig *a* indecent, *adv* -ly
unantastbar *a* inviolable
unappetitlich *a* unappetizing
Unart *f* **-,-en** bad habit. **u~ig** *a* naughty
unauffällig *a* inconspicuous, *adv* -ly, unobtrusive, *adv* -ly
unauffindbar *a* **u~ sein** be nowhere to be found
unaufgefordert *adv* without being asked
unauf|haltsam *a* inexorable, *adv* -bly. **u~hörlich** *a* incessant, *adv* -ly
unaufmerksam *a* inattentive
unaufrichtig *a* insincere
unausbleiblich *a* inevitable
unausgeglichen *a* unbalanced; ⟨*Person*⟩ unstable
unaus|löschlich *a* (*fig*) indelible, *adv* -bly. **u~sprechlich** *a* indescribable, *adv* -bly. **u~stehlich** *a* insufferable
unbarmherzig *a* merciless, *adv* -ly
unbeabsichtigt *a* unintentional, *adv* -ly
unbedacht *a* rash, *adv* -ly
unbedenklich *a* harmless ● *adv* without hesitation
unbedeutend *a* insignificant; (*geringfügig*) slight, *adv* -ly
unbedingt *a* absolute, *adv* -ly; **nicht u~** not necessarily
unbefangen *a* natural, *adv* -ly; (*unparteiisch*) impartial
unbefriedig|end *a* unsatisfactory. **u~t** *a* dissatisfied
unbefugt *a* unauthorized ● *adv* without authorization
unbegreiflich *a* incomprehensible
unbegrenzt *a* unlimited ● *adv* indefinitely
unbegründet *a* unfounded
Unbehag|en *nt* unease; (*körperlich*) discomfort. **u~lich** *a* uncomfortable, *adv* -bly
unbeholfen *a* awkward, *adv* -ly
unbekannt *a* unknown; (*nicht vertraut*) unfamiliar. **U~e(r)** *m|f* stranger
unbekümmert *a* unconcerned; (*unbeschwert*) carefree
unbeliebt *a* unpopular. **U~heit** *f* unpopularity
unbemannt *a* unmanned
unbemerkt *a & adv* unnoticed
unbenutzt *a* unused
unbequem *a* uncomfortable, *adv* -bly; (*lästig*) awkward
unberechenbar *a* unpredictable
unberechtigt *a* unjustified; (*unbefugt*) unauthorized
unberufen *int* touch wood!
unberührt *a* untouched; (*fig*) virgin; ⟨*Landschaft*⟩ unspoilt
unbescheiden *a* presumptuous
unbeschrankt *a* unguarded
unbeschränkt *a* unlimited ● *adv* without limit
unbeschreiblich *a* indescribable, *adv* -bly
unbeschwert *a* carefree
unbesiegbar *a* invincible
unbesiegt *a* undefeated
unbesonnen *a* rash, *adv* -ly
unbespielt *a* blank
unbeständig *a* inconsistent; ⟨*Wetter*⟩ unsettled
unbestechlich *a* incorruptible
unbestimmt *a* indefinite; ⟨*Alter*⟩ indeterminate; (*ungewiß*) uncertain; (*unklar*) vague ● *adv* vaguely
unbestreitbar *a* indisputable, *adv* -bly
unbestritten *a* undisputed ● *adv* indisputably
unbeteiligt *a* indifferent; **u~ an** (+*dat*) not involved in
unbetont *a* unstressed
unbewacht *a* unguarded
unbewaffnet *a* unarmed
unbeweglich *a & adv* motionless, still
unbewohnt *a* uninhabited
unbewußt *a* unconscious, *adv* -ly
unbezahlbar *a* priceless
unbezahlt *a* unpaid
unbrauchbar *a* useless
und *conj* and; **und so weiter** and so on; **nach und nach** bit by bit
Undank *m* ingratitude. **u~bar** *a* ungrateful; (*nicht lohnend*) thankless. **U~barkeit** *f* ingratitude
undefinierbar *a* indefinable
undenk|bar *a* unthinkable. **u~lich** *a* **seit u~lichen Zeiten** from time immemorial
undeutlich *a* indistinct, *adv* -ly; (*vage*) vague, *adv* -ly
undicht *a* leaking; **u~e Stelle** leak
Unding *nt* absurdity
undiplomatisch *a* undiplomatic, *adv* -ally
unduldsam *a* intolerant
undurch|dringlich *a* impenetrable; ⟨*Miene*⟩ inscrutable. **u~führbar** *a* impracticable

undurch|lässig *a* impermeable. **u~sichtig** *a* opaque; (*fig*) doubtful
uneben *a* uneven, *adv* -ly. **U~heit** *f* **-,-en** unevenness; (*Buckel*) bump
unecht *a* false; **u~er Schmuck/Pelz** imitation jewellery/fur
unehelich *a* illegitimate
unehr|enhaft *a* dishonourable, *adv* -bly. **u~lich** *a* dishonest, *adv* -ly. **U~lichkeit** *f* dishonesty
uneinig *a* (*fig*) divided; [**sich** (*dat*)] **u~ sein** disagree. **U~keit** *f* disagreement; (*Streit*) discord
uneins *a* **u~ sein** be at odds
unempfindlich *a* insensitive (**gegen** to); (*widerstandsfähig*) tough; (*Med*) immune
unendlich *a* infinite, *adv* -ly; (*endlos*) endless, *adv* -ly. **U~keit** *f* - infinity
unentbehrlich *a* indispensable
unentgeltlich *a* free; ⟨*Arbeit*⟩ unpaid • *adv* free of charge; ⟨*arbeiten*⟩ without pay
unentschieden *a* undecided; (*Sport*) drawn; **u~ spielen** draw. **U~** *nt* **-s,-** draw
unentschlossen *a* indecisive; (*unentschieden*) undecided. **U~heit** *f* indecision
unentwegt *a* persistent, *adv* -ly; (*unaufhörlich*) incessant, *adv* -ly
unerbittlich *a* implacable, *adv* -bly; ⟨*Schicksal*⟩ inexorable
unerfahren *a* inexperienced. **U~heit** *f* - inexperience
unerfreulich *a* unpleasant, *adv* -ly
unergründlich *a* unfathomable
unerhört *a* enormous, *adv* -ly; (*empörend*) outrageous, *adv* -ly
unerklärlich *a* inexplicable
unerläßlich *a* essential
unerlaubt *a* unauthorized • *adv* without permission
unermeßlich *a* immense, *adv* -ly
unermüdlich *a* tireless, *adv* -ly
unersättlich *a* insatiable
unerschöpflich *a* inexhaustible
unerschütterlich *a* unshakeable
unerschwinglich *a* prohibitive
unersetzlich *a* irreplaceable; ⟨*Verlust*⟩ irreparable
unerträglich *a* unbearable, *adv* -bly
unerwartet *a* unexpected, *adv* -ly
unerwünscht *a* unwanted; ⟨*Besuch*⟩ unwelcome
unfähig *a* incompetent; **u~, etw zu tun** incapable of doing sth; (*nicht in der Lage*) unable to do sth. **U~keit** *f* incompetence; inability (**zu** to)
unfair *a* unfair, *adv* -ly
Unfall *m* accident. **U~flucht** *f* failure to stop after an accident. **U~station** *f* casualty department
unfaßbar *a* incomprehensible; (*unglaublich*) unimaginable
unfehlbar *a* infallible. **U~keit** *f* - infallibility
unfolgsam *a* disobedient
unförmig *a* shapeless
unfreiwillig *a* involuntary, *adv* -ily; (*unbeabsichtigt*) unintentional, *adv* -ly
unfreundlich *a* unfriendly; (*unangenehm*) unpleasant, *adv* -ly. **U~keit** *f* unfriendliness; unpleasantness
Unfriede[n] *m* discord
unfruchtbar *a* infertile; (*fig*) unproductive. **U~keit** *f* infertility
Unfug *m* **-s** mischief; (*Unsinn*) nonsense
Ungar|(in) *m* **-n,-n** (*f* **-,-nen**) Hungarian. **u~isch** *a* Hungarian. **U~n** *nt* **-s** Hungary
ungastlich *a* inhospitable
ungeachtet *prep* (+*gen*) in spite of. **ungebärdig** *a* unruly. **ungebeugt** *a* (*Gram*) uninflected. **ungebraucht** *a* unused. **ungebührlich** *a* improper, *adv* -ly. **ungedeckt** *a* uncovered; (*Sport*) unmarked; ⟨*Tisch*⟩ unlaid
Ungeduld *f* impatience. **u~ig** *a* impatient, *adv* -ly
ungeeignet *a* unsuitable
ungefähr *a* approximate, *adv* -ly, rough, *adv* -ly
ungefährlich *a* harmless
ungehalten *a* angry, *adv* -ily
ungeheuer *a* enormous, *adv* -ly. **U~** *nt* **-s,-** monster
ungeheuerlich *a* outrageous
ungehobelt *a* uncouth
ungehörig *a* improper, *adv* -ly; (*frech*) impertinent, *adv* -ly
ungehorsam *a* disobedient. **U~** *m* disobedience
ungeklärt *a* unsolved; ⟨*Frage*⟩ unsettled; ⟨*Ursache*⟩ unknown
ungeladen *a* unloaded; ⟨*Gast*⟩ uninvited
ungelegen *a* inconvenient. **U~heiten** *fpl* trouble *sg*
ungelernt *a* unskilled. **ungemein** *a* tremendous, *adv* -ly
ungemütlich *a* uncomfortable, *adv* -bly; (*unangenehm*) unpleasant, *adv* -ly

ungenau *a* inaccurate, *adv* -ly; (*vage*) vague, *adv* -ly. **U~igkeit** *f* **-,-en** inaccuracy

ungeniert /ˈʊnʒeniːɐ̯t/ *a* uninhibited ● *adv* openly

ungenießbar *a* inedible; ⟨*Getränk*⟩ undrinkable. **ungenügend** *a* inadequate, *adv* -ly; (*Sch*) unsatisfactory. **ungepflegt** *a* neglected; ⟨*Person*⟩ unkempt. **ungerade** *a* ⟨*Zahl*⟩ odd

ungerecht *a* unjust, *adv* -ly. **U~igkeit** *f* **-,-en** injustice

ungern *adv* reluctantly

ungesalzen *a* unsalted

ungeschehen *a* **u~ machen** undo

Ungeschick|lichkeit *f* clumsiness. **u~t** *a* clumsy, *adv* -ily

ungeschminkt *a* without make-up; ⟨*Wahrheit*⟩ unvarnished. **ungeschrieben** *a* unwritten. **ungesehen** *a & adv* unseen. **ungesellig** *a* unsociable. **ungesetzlich** *a* illegal, *adv* -ly. **ungestört** *a* undisturbed. **ungestraft** *adv* with impunity. **ungestüm** *a* impetuous, *adv* -ly. **ungesund** *a* unhealthy. **ungesüßt** *a* unsweetened. **ungetrübt** *a* perfect

Ungetüm *nt* **-s,-e** monster

ungewiß *a* uncertain; **im ungewissen lassen** leave in the dark. **U~heit** *f* uncertainty

ungewöhnlich *a* unusual, *adv* -ly. **ungewohnt** *a* unaccustomed; (*nicht vertraut*) unfamiliar. **ungewollt** *a* unintentional, *adv* -ly; ⟨*Schwangerschaft*⟩ unwanted

Ungeziefer *nt* **-s** vermin

ungezogen *a* naughty, *adv* -ily

ungezwungen *a* informal, *adv* -ly; (*natürlich*) natural, *adv* -ly

ungläubig *a* incredulous

unglaublich *a* incredible, *adv* -bly, unbelievable, *adv* -bly

ungleich *a* unequal, *adv* -ly; (*verschieden*) different. **U~heit** *f* **-** inequality. **u~mäßig** *a* uneven, *adv* -ly

Unglück *nt* **-s,-e** misfortune; (*Pech*) bad luck; (*Mißgeschick*) mishap; (*Unfall*) accident; **U~ bringen** be unlucky. **u~lich** *a* unhappy, *adv* -ily; (*ungünstig*) unfortunate, *adv* -ly. **u~licherweise** *adv* unfortunately. **u~selig** *a* unfortunate. **U~sfall** *m* accident

ungültig *a* invalid; (*Jur*) void

ungünstig *a* unfavourable, *adv* -bly; (*unpassend*) inconvenient, *adv* -ly

ungut *a* ⟨*Gefühl*⟩ uneasy; **nichts für u~!** no offence!

unhandlich *a* unwieldy

Unheil *nt* **-s** disaster; **U~ anrichten** cause havoc

unheilbar *a* incurable, *adv* -bly

unheimlich *a* eerie; (*gruselig*) creepy; (*fam: groß*) terrific ● *adv* eerily; (*fam: sehr*) terribly

unhöflich *a* rude, *adv* -ly. **U~keit** *f* rudeness

unhörbar *a* inaudible, *adv* -bly

unhygienisch *a* unhygienic

Uni *f* **-,-s** (*fam*) university

uni /yˈniː/ *inv a* plain

Uniform *f* **-,-en** uniform

uninteress|ant *a* uninteresting. **u~iert** *a* uninterested; (*unbeteiligt*) disinterested

Union *f* **-,-en** union

universal *a* universal

universell *a* universal, *adv* -ly

Universität *f* **-,-en** university

Universum *nt* **-s** universe

unkennt|lich *a* unrecognizable. **U~nis** *f* ignorance

unklar *a* unclear; (*ungewiß*) uncertain; (*vage*) vague, *adv* -ly; **im u~en sein** be in the dark. **U~heit** *f* **-,-en** uncertainty

unklug *a* unwise, *adv* -ly

unkompliziert *a* uncomplicated

Unkosten *pl* expenses

Unkraut *nt* weed; (*coll*) weeds *pl*; **U~ jäten** weed. **U~vertilgungsmittel** *nt* weed-killer

unkultiviert *a* uncultured

unlängst *adv* recently

unlauter *a* dishonest; (*unfair*) unfair

unleserlich *a* illegible, *adv* -bly

unleugbar *a* undeniable, *adv* -bly

unlogisch *a* illogical, *adv* -ly

unlös|bar *a* (*fig*) insoluble. **u~lich** *a* (*Chem*) insoluble

unlustig *a* listless, *adv* -ly

unmäßig *a* excessive, *adv* -ly; (*äußerst*) extreme, *adv* -ly

Unmenge *f* enormous amount/(*Anzahl*) number

Unmensch *m* (*fam*) brute. **u~lich** *a* inhuman; (*entsetzlich*) appalling, *adv* -ly

unmerklich *a* imperceptible, *adv* -bly

unmißverständlich *a* unambiguous, *adv* -ly; (*offen*) unequivocal, *adv* -ly

unmittelbar *a* immediate, *adv* -ly; (*direkt*) direct, *adv* -ly

unmöbliert *a* unfurnished

unmodern *a* old-fashioned

unmöglich *a* impossible, *adv* -bly. **U~keit** *f* - impossibility
Unmoral *f* immorality. **u~isch** *a* immoral, *adv* -ly
unmündig *a* under-age
Unmut *m* displeasure
unnachahmlich *a* inimitable
unnachgiebig *a* intransigent
unnatürlich *a* unnatural, *adv* -ly
unnormal *a* abnormal, *adv* -ly
unnötig *a* unnecessary, *adv* -ily
unnütz *a* useless • *adv* needlessly
unord|entlich *a* untidy, *adv* -ily; (*nachlässig*) sloppy, *adv* -ily. **U~nung** *f* disorder; (*Durcheinander*) muddle
unorganisiert *a* disorganized
unorthodox *a* unorthodox • *adv* in an unorthodox manner
unparteiisch *a* impartial, *adv* -ly
unpassend *a* inappropriate, *adv* -ly; ⟨*Moment*⟩ inopportune
unpäßlich *a* indisposed
unpersönlich *a* impersonal
unpraktisch *a* impractical
unpünktlich *a* unpunctual • *adv* late
unrasiert *a* unshaven
Unrast *f* restlessness
unrealistisch *a* unrealistic, *adv* -ally
unrecht *a* wrong, *adv* -ly • *n* **u~ haben** be wrong; **jdm u~ tun** do s.o. an injustice; **jdm u~ geben** disagree with s.o. **U~** *nt* wrong; **zu U~** wrongly. **u~mäßig** *a* unlawful, *adv* -ly
unregelmäßig *a* irregular, *adv* -ly. **U~keit** *f* irregularity
unreif *a* unripe; (*fig*) immature
unrein *a* impure; ⟨*Luft*⟩ polluted; ⟨*Haut*⟩ bad; **ins u~e schreiben** make a rough draft of
unrentabel *a* unprofitable, *adv* -bly
unrichtig *a* incorrect
Unruh|e *f* -,-n restlessness; (*Erregung*) agitation; (*Besorgnis*) anxiety; **U~en** (*Pol*) unrest *sg*. **u~ig** *a* restless, *adv* -ly; ⟨*Meer*⟩ agitated; (*laut*) noisy, *adv* -ily; (*besorgt*) anxious, *adv* -ly
uns *pron* (*acc/dat of* **wir**) us; (*refl*) ourselves; (*einander*) each other; **ein Freund von uns** a friend of ours
unsagbar, unsäglich *a* indescribable, *adv* -bly
unsanft *a* rough, *adv* -ly
unsauber *a* dirty; (*nachlässig*) sloppy, *adv* -ily; (*unlauter*) dishonest, *adv* -ly
unschädlich *a* harmless
unscharf *a* blurred
unschätzbar *a* inestimable
unscheinbar *a* inconspicuous
unschicklich *a* improper, *adv* -ly
unschlagbar *a* unbeatable
unschlüssig *a* undecided
Unschuld *f* - innocence; (*Jungfräulichkeit*) virginity. **u~ig** *a* innocent, *adv* -ly
unselbständig *a* dependent • *adv* **u~ denken** not think for oneself
unser *poss pron* our. **u~e(r,s)** *poss pron* ours. **u~erseits** *adv* for our part. **u~twegen** *adv* for our sake; (*wegen uns*) because of us, on our account. **u~twillen** *adv* **um u~twillen** for our sake
unsicher *a* unsafe; (*ungewiß*) uncertain; (*nicht zuverlässig*) unreliable; ⟨*Schritte, Hand*⟩ unsteady; ⟨*Person*⟩ insecure • *adv* unsteadily. **U~heit** *f* uncertainty; unreliability; insecurity
unsichtbar *a* invisible
Unsinn *m* nonsense. **u~ig** *a* nonsensical, absurd
Unsitt|e *f* bad habit. **u~lich** *a* indecent, *adv* -ly
unsportlich *a* not sporty; (*unfair*) unsporting, *adv* -ly
uns|re(r,s) *poss pron* = **unsere(r,s)**. **u~rige** *poss pron* **der/die/das u~rige** ours
unsterblich *a* immortal. **U~keit** *f* immortality
unstet *a* restless, *adv* -ly; (*unbeständig*) unstable
Unstimmigkeit *f* -,-en inconsistency; (*Streit*) difference
Unsumme *f* vast sum
unsymmetrisch *a* not symmetrical
unsympathisch *a* unpleasant; **er ist mir u~** I don't like him
untätig *a* idle, *adv* idly. **U~keit** *f* - idleness
untauglich *a* unsuitable; (*Mil*) unfit
unteilbar *a* indivisible
unten *adv* at the bottom; (*auf der Unterseite*) underneath; (*eine Treppe tiefer*) downstairs; **hier/da u~** down here/there; **nach u~** down[wards]; (*die Treppe hinunter*) downstairs
unter *prep* (+ *dat/acc*) under; (*niedriger als*) below; (*inmitten, zwischen*) among; **u~ anderem** among other things; **u~ der Woche** during the week; **u~ sich** by themselves; **u~ uns gesagt** between ourselves

Unter|arm *m* forearm. **U~bewußtsein** *nt* subconscious
unterbieten† *vt insep* undercut; beat ⟨*Rekord*⟩
unterbinden† *vt insep* stop
unterbleiben† *vi insep* (*sein*) cease; **es hat zu u~** it must stop
unterbrech|en† *vt insep* interrupt; break ⟨*Reise*⟩. **U~ung** *f* **-,-en** interruption; break
unterbreiten *vt insep* present
unterbringen† *vt sep* put; (*beherbergen*) put up
unterdessen *adv* in the meantime
unterdrück|en *vt insep* suppress; oppress ⟨*Volk*⟩. **U~ung** *f* **-** suppression; oppression
untere(r,s) *a* lower
untereinander *adv* one below the other; (*miteinander*) among ourselves/yourselves/themselves
unterernähr|t *a* undernourished. **U~ung** *f* malnutrition
Unterfangen *nt* **-s,-** venture
Unterführung *f* underpass; (*Fußgänger-*) subway
Untergang *m* (*Astr*) setting; (*Naut*) sinking; (*Zugrundegehen*) disappearance; (*der Welt*) end
Untergebene(r) *m/f* subordinate
untergehen† *vi sep* (*sein*) (*Astr*) set; (*versinken*) go under; ⟨*Schiff:*⟩ go down, sink; (*zugrunde gehen*) disappear; ⟨*Welt:*⟩ come to an end
untergeordnet *a* subordinate
Untergeschoß *nt* basement
untergraben† *vt insep* (*fig*) undermine
Untergrund *m* foundation; (*Hintergrund*) background; (*Pol*) underground. **U~bahn** *f* underground [railway], (*Amer*) subway
unterhaken *vt sep* **jdn u~** take s.o.'s arm; **untergehakt** arm in arm
unterhalb *adv & prep* (+*gen*) below
Unterhalt *m* maintenance
unterhalt|en† *vt insep* maintain; (*ernähren*) support; (*betreiben*) run; (*erheitern*) entertain; **sich u~en** talk; (*sich vergnügen*) enjoy oneself. **u~sam** *a* entertaining. **U~ung** *f* **-,-en** maintenance; (*Gespräch*) conversation; (*Zeitvertreib*) entertainment
unterhandeln *vi insep* (*haben*) negotiate
Unter|haus *nt* (*Pol*) lower house; (*in UK*) House of Commons. **U~hemd** *nt* vest. **U~holz** *nt* undergrowth. **U~hose** *f* underpants *pl*. **u~irdisch** *a & adv* underground
unterjochen *vt insep* subjugate
Unterkiefer *m* lower jaw
unter|kommen† *vi sep* (*sein*) find accommodation; (*eine Stellung finden*) get a job. **u~kriegen** *vt sep* (*fam*) get down
Unterkunft *f* **-,-künfte** accommodation
Unterlage *f* pad; **U~n** papers
Unterlaß *m* **ohne U~** incessantly
unterlass|en† *vt insep* **etw u~en** refrain from [doing] sth; **es u~en, etw zu tun** fail *or* omit to do sth. **U~ung** *f* **-,-en** omission
unterlaufen† *vi insep* (*sein*) occur; **mir ist ein Fehler u~** I made a mistake
unterlegen[1] *vt sep* put underneath
unterlegen[2] *a* inferior; (*Sport*) losing; **zahlenmäßig u~** outnumbered (*dat* by). **U~e(r)** *m/f* loser
Unterleib *m* abdomen
unterliegen† *vi insep* (*sein*) lose (*dat* to); (*unterworfen sein*) be subject (*dat* to)
Unterlippe *f* lower lip
unterm *prep* = **unter dem**
Untermiete *f* **zur U~ wohnen** be a lodger. **U~r(in)** *m*(*f*) lodger
unterminieren *vt insep* undermine
untern *prep* = **unter den**
unternehm|en† *vt insep* undertake; take ⟨*Schritte*⟩; **etw/nichts u~en** do sth/nothing. **U~en** *nt* **-s,-** undertaking, enterprise; (*Betrieb*) concern. **u~end** *a* enterprising. **U~er** *m* **-s,-** employer; (*Bau-*) contractor; (*Industrieller*) industrialist. **U~ung** *f* **-,-en** undertaking; (*Comm*) venture. **u~ungslustig** *a* enterprising; (*abenteuerlustig*) adventurous
Unteroffizier *m* non-commissioned officer
unterordnen *vt sep* subordinate; **sich u~** accept a subordinate role
Unterredung *f* **-,-en** talk
Unterricht *m* **-[e]s** teaching; (*Privat-*) tuition; (*U~sstunden*) lessons *pl*; **U~ geben/nehmen** give/have lessons
unterrichten *vt/i insep* (*haben*) teach; (*informieren*) inform; **sich u~** inform oneself
Unterrock *m* slip
unters *prep* = **unter das**
untersagen *vt insep* forbid

Untersatz *m* mat; (*mit Füßen*) stand; (*Gläser-*) coaster

unterschätzen *vt insep* underestimate

unterscheid|en† *vt/i insep* (*haben*) distinguish; (*auseinanderhalten*) tell apart; **sich u~en** differ. **U~ung** *f* **-,-en** distinction

Unterschied *m* **-[e]s,-e** difference; (*Unterscheidung*) distinction; **im U~ zu ihm** unlike him. **u~lich** *a* different; (*wechselnd*) varying; **das ist u~lich** it varies. **u~slos** *a* equal, *adv* -ly

unterschlag|en† *vt insep* embezzle; (*verheimlichen*) suppress. **U~ung** *f* **-,-en** embezzlement; suppression

Unterschlupf *m* **-[e]s** shelter; (*Versteck*) hiding-place

unterschreiben† *vt/i insep* (*haben*) sign

Unter|schrift *f* signature; (*Bild-*) caption. **U~seeboot** *nt* submarine. **U~setzer** *m* **-s,-** = **Untersatz**

untersetzt *a* stocky

Unterstand *m* shelter

unterste(r,s) *a* lowest, bottom

unterstehen[1]† *vi sep* (*haben*) shelter

unterstehen[2]† *v insep* ● *vi* (*haben*) be answerable (*dat* to); (*unterliegen*) be subject (*dat* to) ● *vr* **sich u~** dare; **untersteh dich!** don't you dare!

unterstellen[1] *vt sep* put underneath; (*abstellen*) store; **sich u~** shelter

unterstellen[2] *vt insep* place under the control (*dat* of); (*annehmen*) assume; (*fälschlich zuschreiben*) impute (*dat* to)

unterstreichen† *vt insep* underline

unterstütz|en *vt insep* support; (*helfen*) aid. **U~ung** *f* **-,-en** support; (*finanziell*) aid; (*regelmäßiger Betrag*) allowance; (*Arbeitslosen-*) benefit

untersuch|en *vt insep* examine; (*Jur*) investigate; (*prüfen*) test; (*überprüfen*) check; (*durchsuchen*) search. **U~ung** *f* **-,-en** examination; investigation; test; check; search. **U~ungshaft** *f* detention on remand; **in U~ungshaft** on remand. **U~ungsrichter** *m* examining magistrate

Untertan *m* **-s & -en,-en** subject

Untertasse *f* saucer

untertauchen *v sep* ● *vt* duck ● *vi* (*sein*) go under; (*fig*) disappear

Unterteil *nt* bottom (part)

unterteilen *vt insep* subdivide; (*aufteilen*) divide

Untertitel *m* subtitle

Unterton *m* undertone

untervermieten *vt/i insep* (*haben*) sublet

unterwandern *vt insep* infiltrate

Unterwäsche *f* underwear

Unterwasser- *pref* underwater

unterwegs *adv* on the way; (*außer Haus*) out; (*verreist*) away

unterweisen† *vt insep* instruct

Unterwelt *f* underworld

unterwerfen† *vt insep* subjugate; **sich u~en** submit (*dat* to); **etw** (*dat*) **unterworfen sein** be subject to sth

unterwürfig *a* obsequious, *adv* -ly

unterzeichnen *vt insep* sign

unterziehen[1]† *vt sep* put on underneath; (*Culin*) fold in

unterziehen[2]† *vt insep* **etw einer Untersuchung/Überprüfung u~** examine/check sth; **sich einer Operation/Prüfung u~** have an operation/take a test

Untier *nt* monster

untragbar *a* intolerable

untrennbar *a* inseparable

untreu *a* disloyal; (*in der Ehe*) unfaithful. **U~e** *f* disloyalty; infidelity

untröstlich *a* inconsolable

untrüglich *a* infallible

Untugend *f* bad habit

unüberlegt *a* rash, *adv* -ly

unüber|sehbar *a* obvious; (*groß*) immense. **u~troffen** *a* unsurpassed

unum|gänglich *a* absolutely necessary. **u~schränkt** *a* absolute. **u~wunden** *adv* frankly

ununterbrochen *a* incessant, *adv* -ly

unveränderlich *a* invariable; (*gleichbleibend*) unchanging

unverändert *a* unchanged

unverantwortlich *a* irresponsible, *adv* -bly

unverbesserlich *a* incorrigible

unverbindlich *a* non-committal; (*Comm*) not binding ● *adv* without obligation

unverblümt *a* blunt ● *adv* -ly

unverdaulich *a* indigestible

unver|einbar *a* incompatible. **u~geßlich** *a* unforgettable. **u~gleichlich** *a* incomparable

unver|hältnismäßig *adv* disproportionately. **u~heiratet** *a* unmarried. **u~hofft** *a* unexpected, *adv* -ly. **u~hohlen** *a* undisguised ● *adv* openly. **u~käuflich** *a* not for sale; ⟨*Muster*⟩ free

unverkennbar *a* unmistakable, *adv* -bly
unverletzt *a* unhurt
unvermeidlich *a* inevitable
unver|mindert *a & adv* undiminished. **u~mittelt** *a* abrupt, *adv* -ly. **u~mutet** *a* unexpected, *adv* -ly
Unver|nunft *f* folly. **u~nünftig** *a* foolish, *adv* -ly
unverschämt *a* insolent, *adv* -ly; (*fam: ungeheuer*) outrageous, *adv* -ly. **U~heit** *f* **-,-en** insolence
unver|sehens *adv* suddenly. **u~sehrt** *a* unhurt; (*unbeschädigt*) intact. **u~söhnlich** *a* irreconcilable; ⟨*Gegner*⟩ implacable
unverständ|lich *a* incomprehensible; (*undeutlich*) indistinct. **U~nis** *nt* lack of understanding
unverträglich *a* incompatible; ⟨*Person*⟩ quarrelsome; (*unbekömmlich*) indigestible
unverwandt *a* fixed, *adv* -ly
unver|wundbar *a* invulnerable. **u~wüstlich** *a* indestructible; ⟨*Person, Humor*⟩ irrepressible; ⟨*Gesundheit*⟩ robust. **u~zeihlich** *a* unforgivable
unverzüglich *a* immediate, *adv* -ly
unvollendet *a* unfinished
unvollkommen *a* imperfect; (*unvollständig*) incomplete. **U~heit** *f* **-,-en** imperfection
unvollständig *a* incomplete
unvor|bereitet *a* unprepared. **u~eingenommen** *a* unbiased. **u~hergesehen** *a* unforeseen
unvorsichtig *a* careless, *adv* -ly. **U~keit** *f* **-** carelessness
unvorstellbar *a* unimaginable, *adv* -bly
unvorteilhaft *a* unfavourable; (*nicht hübsch*) unattractive; ⟨*Kleid, Frisur*⟩ unflattering
unwahr *a* untrue. **U~heit** *f* **-,-en** untruth. **u~scheinlich** *a* unlikely; (*unglaublich*) improbable; (*fam: groß*) incredible, *adv* -bly
unweigerlich *a* inevitable, *adv* -bly
unweit *adv & prep* (+*gen*) not far; **u~ vom Fluß/des Flusses** not far from the river
unwesentlich *a* unimportant ● *adv* slightly
Unwetter *nt* **-s,-** storm
unwichtig *a* unimportant
unwider|legbar *a* irrefutable. **u~ruflich** *a* irrevocable, *adv* -bly. **u~stehlich** *a* irresistible
Unwill|e *m* displeasure. **u~ig** *a* angry, *adv* -ily; (*widerwillig*) reluctant, *adv* -ly. **u~kürlich** *a* involuntary, *adv* -ily; (*instinktiv*) instinctive, *adv* -ly
unwirklich *a* unreal
unwirksam *a* ineffective
unwirsch *a* irritable, *adv* -bly
unwirtlich *a* inhospitable
unwirtschaftlich *a* uneconomic, *adv* -ally
unwissen|d *a* ignorant. **U~heit** *f* **-** ignorance
unwohl *a* unwell; (*unbehaglich*) uneasy. **U~sein** *nt* **-s** indisposition
unwürdig *a* unworthy (*gen* of); (*würdelos*) undignified
Unzahl *f* vast number. **unzählig** *a* innumerable, countless
unzerbrechlich *a* unbreakable
unzerstörbar *a* indestructible
unzertrennlich *a* inseparable
Unzucht *f* sexual offence; **gewerbsmäßige U~** prostitution
unzüchtig *a* indecent, *adv* -ly; ⟨*Schriften*⟩ obscene
unzufrieden *a* dissatisfied; (*innerlich*) discontented. **U~heit** *f* dissatisfaction; (*Pol*) discontent
unzulänglich *a* inadequate, *adv* -ly
unzulässig *a* inadmissible
unzumutbar *a* unreasonable
unzurechnungsfähig *a* insane. **U~keit** *f* insanity
unzusammenhängend *a* incoherent
unzutreffend *a* inapplicable; (*falsch*) incorrect
unzuverlässig *a* unreliable
unzweckmäßig *a* unsuitable, *adv* -bly
unzweideutig *a* unambiguous
unzweifelhaft *a* undoubted, *adv* -ly
üppig *a* luxuriant, *adv* -ly; (*überreichlich*) lavish, *adv* -ly; ⟨*Busen, Figur*⟩ voluptuous
uralt *a* ancient
Uran *nt* **-s** uranium
Uraufführung *f* first performance
urbar *a* **u~ machen** cultivate
Ureinwohner *mpl* native inhabitants
Urenkel *m* great-grandson; (*pl*) great-grandchildren
Urgroß|mutter *f* great-grandmother. **U~vater** *m* great-grandfather

Urheber *m* **-s,-** originator; (*Verfasser*) author. **U~recht** *nt* copyright
Urin *m* **-s,-e** urine
Urkunde *f* **-,-n** certificate; (*Dokument*) document
Urlaub *m* **-s** holiday; (*Mil, Admin*) leave; **auf U~** on holiday/leave; **U~ haben** be on holiday/leave. **U~er(in)** *m* **-s,-** (*f* **-,-nen**) holidaymaker. **U~sort** *m* holiday resort
Urne *f* **-,-n** urn; (*Wahl-*) ballot-box
Ursache *f* cause; (*Grund*) reason; **keine U~!** don't mention it!
Ursprung *m* origin
ursprünglich *a* original, *adv* -ly; (*anfänglich*) initial, *adv* -ly; (*natürlich*) natural
Urteil *nt* **-s,-e** judgement; (*Meinung*) opinion; (*U~sspruch*) verdict; (*Strafe*) sentence. **u~en** *vi* (*haben*) judge. **U~svermögen** *nt* [power of] judgement
Urwald *m* primeval forest; (*tropischer*) jungle
urwüchsig *a* natural; (*derb*) earthy
Urzeit *f* primeval times *pl*; **seit U~en** from time immemorial
USA *pl* USA *sg*
usw. *abbr* (**und so weiter**) etc.
Utensilien /-i̯ən/ *ntpl* utensils
utopisch *a* Utopian

V

vage /ˈva:gə/ *a* vague, *adv* -ly
Vakuum /ˈva:kuʊm/ *nt* **-s** vacuum. **v~verpackt** *a* vacuum-packed
Vanille /vaˈnɪljə/ *f* - vanilla
vari|abel /vaˈri̯a:bəl/ *a* variable. **V~ante** *f* **-,-n** variant. **V~ation** /-ˈt͜si̯o:n/ *f* **-,-en** variation. **v~ieren** *vt/i* (*haben*) vary
Vase /ˈva:zə/ *f* **-,-n** vase
Vater *m* **-s,⸚** father. **V~land** *nt* fatherland
väterlich *a* paternal; (*fürsorglich*) fatherly. **v~erseits** *adv* on one's/the father's side
Vater|schaft *f* - fatherhood; (*Jur*) paternity. **V~unser** *nt* **-s,-** Lord's Prayer
Vati *m* **-s,-s** (*fam*) daddy
v. Chr. *abbr* (**vor Christus**) BC
Vegetar|ier(in) /vegeˈta:ri̯ɐ, -i̯ərɪn/ *m(f)* **-s,-** (*f* **-,-nen**) vegetarian. **v~isch** *a* vegetarian
Vegetation /vegetaˈt͜si̯o:n/ *f* **-,-en** vegetation
Veilchen *nt* **-s,-** violet
Vene /ˈve:nə/ *f* **-,-n** vein
Venedig /veˈne:dɪç/ *nt* **-s** Venice
Ventil /vɛnˈti:l/ *nt* **-s,-e** valve. **V~ator** *m* **-s,-en** /-ˈto:rən/ fan
verabred|en *vt* arrange; **sich [mit jdm] v~en** arrange to meet [s.o.]. **V~ung** *f* **-,-en** arrangement; (*Treffen*) appointment
verabreichen *vt* administer
verabscheuen *vt* detest, loathe
verabschieden *vt* say goodbye to; (*aus dem Dienst*) retire; pass ⟨*Gesetz*⟩; **sich v~** say goodbye
verachten *vt* despise. **v~swert** *a* contemptible
verächtlich *a* contemptuous, *adv* -ly; (*unwürdig*) contemptible
Verachtung *f* - contempt
verallgemeiner|n *vt/i* (*haben*) generalize. **V~ung** *f* **-,-en** generalization
veralte|n *vi* (*sein*) become obsolete. **v~t** *a* obsolete
Veranda /veˈranda/ *f* **-,-den** veranda
veränder|lich *a* changeable; (*Math*) variable. **v~n** *vt* change; **sich v~n** change; (*beruflich*) change one's job. **V~ung** *f* change
verängstigt *a* frightened, scared
verankern *vt* anchor
veranlag|t *a* **künstlerisch/musikalisch v~t sein** have an artistic/a musical bent; **praktisch v~t** practically minded. **V~ung** *f* **-,-en** disposition; (*Neigung*) tendency; (*künstlerisch*) bent
veranlass|en *vt* (*reg*) arrange for; (*einleiten*) institute; **jdn v~en** prompt s.o. (**zu** to). **V~ung** *f* - reason; **auf meine V~ung** at my suggestion; (*Befehl*) on my orders
veranschaulichen *vt* illustrate
veranschlagen *vt* (*reg*) estimate
veranstalt|en *vt* organize; hold, give ⟨*Party*⟩; make ⟨*Lärm*⟩. **V~er** *m* **-s,-** organizer. **V~ung** *f* **-,-en** event
verantwort|en *vt* take responsibility for; **sich v~en** answer (**für** for). **v~lich** *a* responsible; **v~lich machen** hold responsible. **V~ung** *f* - responsibility. **v~ungsbewußt** *a* responsible, *adv* -bly. **v~ungslos** *a* irresponsible, *adv* -bly. **v~ungsvoll** *a* responsible
verarbeiten *vt* use; (*Techn*) process; (*verdauen & fig*) digest; **v~ zu** make into

verärgern *vt* annoy
verarmt *a* impoverished
verästeln (sich) *vr* branch out
verausgaben (sich) *vr* spend all one's money; (*körperlich*) wear oneself out
veräußern *vt* sell
Verb /vɛrp/ *nt* **-s,-en** verb. **v~al** /vɛr'ba:l/ *a* verbal, *adv* -ly
Verband *m* **-[e]s,¨e** association; (*Mil*) unit; (*Med*) bandage; (*Wund-*) dressing. **V~szeug** *nt* first-aid kit
verbann|en *vt* exile; (*fig*) banish. **V~ung** *f* - exile
verbarrikadieren *vt* barricade
verbeißen† *vt* suppress; **ich konnte mir kaum das Lachen v~** I could hardly keep a straight face
verbergen† *vt* hide; **sich v~** hide
verbesser|n *vt* improve; (*berichtigen*) correct. **V~ung** *f* **-,-en** improvement; correction
verbeug|en (sich) *vr* bow. **V~ung** *f* bow
verbeulen *vt* dent
verbiegen† *vt* bend; **sich v~** bend
verbieten† *vt* forbid; (*Admin*) prohibit, ban
verbillig|en *vt* reduce [in price]. **v~t** *a* reduced
verbinden† *vt* connect (**mit** to); (*zusammenfügen*) join; (*verknüpfen*) combine; (*in Verbindung bringen*) associate; (*Med*) bandage; dress ⟨*Wunde*⟩; **sich v~** combine; (*sich zusammentun*) join together; **jdm die Augen v~** blindfold s.o.; **jdm verbunden sein** (*fig*) be obliged to s.o.
verbindlich *a* friendly; (*bindend*) binding. **V~keit** *f* **-,-en** friendliness; **V~keiten** obligations; (*Comm*) liabilities
Verbindung *f* connection; (*Verknüpfung*) combination; (*Kontakt*) contact; (*Vereinigung*) association; **chemische V~** chemical compound; **in V~ stehen/sich in V~ setzen** be/get in touch
verbissen *a* grim, *adv* -ly; (*zäh*) dogged, *adv* -ly
verbitten† *vt* **sich** (*dat*) **etw v~** not stand for sth
verbitter|n *vt* make bitter. **v~t** *a* bitter. **V~ung** *f* - bitterness
verblassen *vi* (*sein*) fade
Verbleib *m* **-s** whereabouts *pl.* **v~en**† *vi* (*sein*) remain
verbleichen† *vi* (*sein*) fade
verbleit *a* ⟨*Benzin*⟩ leaded
verblüff|en *vt* amaze, astound. **V~ung** *f* - amazement
verblühen *vi* (*sein*) wither, fade
verbluten *vi* (*sein*) bleed to death
verborgen[1] *a* hidden
verborgen[2] *vt* lend
Verbot *nt* **-[e]s,-e** ban. **v~en** *a* forbidden; (*Admin*) prohibited; **'Rauchen v~en'** 'no smoking'
Verbrauch *m* **-[e]s** consumption. **v~en** *vt* use; consume ⟨*Lebensmittel*⟩; (*erschöpfen*) use up, exhaust. **V~er** *m* **-s,-** consumer. **v~t** *a* worn; ⟨*Luft*⟩ stale
verbrechen† *vt* (*fam*) perpetrate. **V~** *nt* **-s,-** crime
Verbrecher *m* **-s,-** criminal. **v~isch** *a* criminal
verbreit|en *vt* spread; **sich v~en** spread. **v~ern** *vt* widen; **sich v~ern** widen. **v~et** *a* widespread. **V~ung** *f* - spread; (*Verbreiten*) spreading
verbrenn|en† *vt/i* (*sein*) burn; cremate ⟨*Leiche*⟩. **V~ung** *f* **-,-en** burning; cremation; (*Wunde*) burn
verbringen† *vt* spend
verbrühen *vt* scald
verbuchen *vt* enter; (*fig*) notch up ⟨*Erfolg*⟩
verbünd|en (sich) *vr* form an alliance. **V~ete(r)** *m/f* ally
verbürgen *vt* guarantee; **sich v~ für** vouch for
verbüßen *vt* serve ⟨*Strafe*⟩
Verdacht *m* **-[e]s** suspicion; **in** *or* **im V~ haben** suspect
verdächtig *a* suspicious, *adv* -ly. **v~en** *vt* suspect (*gen* of). **V~te(r)** *m/f* suspect
verdamm|en *vt* condemn; (*Relig*) damn. **V~nis** *f* - damnation. **v~t** *a & adv* (*sl*) damned; **v~t!** damn!
verdampfen *vt/i* (*sein*) evaporate
verdanken *vt* owe (*dat* to)
verdau|en *vt* digest. **v~lich** *a* digestible. **V~ung** *f* - digestion
Verdeck *nt* **-[e]s,-e** hood; (*Oberdeck*) top deck. **v~en** *vt* cover; (*verbergen*) hide, conceal
verdenken† *vt* **das kann man ihm nicht v~** you can't blame him for it
verderb|en† *vi* (*sein*) spoil; ⟨*Lebensmittel:*⟩ go bad ● *vt* spoil; (*zerstören*) ruin; (*moralisch*) corrupt; **ich habe mir den Magen verdorben** I have an upset stomach. **V~en** *nt* **-s** ruin. **v~lich** *a* perishable; (*schädlich*) pernicious

verdeutlichen *vt* make clear
verdichten *vt* compress; **sich v~** ‹*Nebel:*› thicken
verdien|en *vt/i* (*haben*) earn; (*fig*) deserve. **V~er** *m* **-s,-** wage-earner
Verdienst[1] *m* **-[e]s** earnings *pl*
Verdienst[2] *nt* **-[e]s,-e** merit
verdient *a* well-deserved; ‹*Person*› of outstanding merit. **v~ermaßen** *adv* deservedly
verdoppeln *vt* double; (*fig*) redouble; **sich v~** double
verdorben *a* spoilt, ruined; ‹*Magen*› upset; (*moralisch*) corrupt; (*verkommen*) depraved
verdorren *vi* (*sein*) wither
verdrängen *vt* force out; (*fig*) displace; (*psychisch*) repress
verdreh|en *vt* twist; roll ‹*Augen*›; (*fig*) distort. **v~t** *a* (*fam*) crazy
verdreifachen *vt* treble, triple
verdreschen† *vt* (*fam*) thrash
verdrießlich *a* morose, *adv* -ly
verdrücken *vt* crumple; (*fam: essen*) polish off; **sich v~** (*fam*) slip away
Verdruß *m* **-sses** annoyance
verdunk|eln *vt* darken; black out ‹*Zimmer*›; **sich v~eln** darken. **V~[e]lung** *f* **-** black-out
verdünnen *vt* dilute; **sich v~** taper off
verdunst|en *vi* (*sein*) evaporate. **V~ung** *f* **-** evaporation
verdursten *vi* (*sein*) die of thirst
verdutzt *a* baffled
veredeln *vt* refine; (*Hort*) graft
verehr|en *vt* revere; (*Relig*) worship; (*bewundern*) admire; (*schenken*) give. **V~er(in)** *m* **-s,-** (*f* **-,-nen**) admirer. **V~ung** *f* **-** veneration; worship; admiration
vereidigen *vt* swear in
Verein *m* **-s,-e** society; (*Sport-*) club
vereinbar *a* compatible. **v~en** *vt* arrange; **nicht zu v~en** incompatible. **V~ung** *f* **-,-en** agreement
vereinen *vt* unite; **sich v~** unite
vereinfachen *vt* simplify
vereinheitlichen *vt* standardize
vereinig|en *vt* unite; merge ‹*Firmen*›; **sich v~en** unite; **V~te Staaten [von Amerika]** United States *sg* [of America]. **V~ung** *f* **-,-en** union; (*Organisation*) organization
vereinsamt *a* lonely
vereinzelt *a* isolated ● *adv* occasionally
vereist *a* frozen; ‹*Straße*› icy
vereiteln *vt* foil, thwart
vereitert *a* septic
verenden *vi* (*sein*) die
verengen *vt* restrict; **sich v~** narrow; ‹*Pupille:*› contract
vererb|en *vt* leave (*dat* to); (*Biol & fig*) pass on (*dat* to). **V~ung** *f* **-** heredity
verewigen *vt* immortalize; **sich v~** (*fam*) leave one's mark
verfahren† *vi* (*sein*) proceed; **v~ mit** deal with ● *vr* **sich v~** lose one's way ● *a* muddled. **V~** *nt* **-s,-** procedure; (*Techn*) process; (*Jur*) proceedings *pl*
Verfall *m* decay; (*eines Gebäudes*) dilapidation; (*körperlich & fig*) decline; (*Ablauf*) expiry. **v~en**† *vi* (*sein*) decay; ‹*Person, Sitten:*› decline; (*ablaufen*) expire; **v~en in** (+*acc*) lapse into; **v~en auf** (+*acc*) hit on ‹*Idee*›; **jdm/etw v~en sein** be under the spell of s.o./sth; be addicted to ‹*Alkohol*›
verfälschen *vt* falsify; adulterate ‹*Wein, Lebensmittel*›
verfänglich *a* awkward
verfärben (sich) *vr* change colour; ‹*Stoff:*› discolour
verfass|en *vt* write; (*Jur*) draw up; (*entwerfen*) draft. **V~er** *m* **-s,-** author. **V~ung** *f* (*Pol*) constitution; (*Zustand*) state
verfaulen *vi* (*sein*) rot, decay
verfechten† *vt* advocate
verfehlen *vt* miss
verfeinde|n (sich) *vr* become enemies; **v~t sein** be enemies
verfeinern *vt* refine; (*verbessern*) improve
verfilmen *vt* film
verfilzt *a* matted
verfliegen† *vi* (*sein*) evaporate; ‹*Zeit:*› fly
verflixt *a* (*fam*) awkward; (*verdammt*) blessed; **v~!** damn!
verfluch|en *vt* curse. **v~t** *a & adv* (*fam*) damned; **v~t!** damn!
verflüchtigen (sich) *vr* evaporate
verflüssigen *vt* liquefy
verfolg|en *vt* pursue; (*folgen*) follow; (*bedrängen*) pester; (*Pol*) persecute; **strafrechtlich v~en** prosecute. **V~er** *m* **-s,-** pursuer. **V~ung** *f* **-** pursuit; persecution
verfrachten *vt* ship
verfrüht *a* premature
verfügbar *a* available
verfüg|en *vt* order; (*Jur*) decree ● *vi* (*haben*) **v~en über** (+*acc*) have at one's disposal. **V~ung** *f* **-,-en** order;

(*Jur*) decree; **jdm zur V~ung stehen/stellen** be/place at s.o.'s disposal

verführ|en *vt* seduce; (*verlocken*) tempt. **V~er** *m* seducer. **v~erisch** *a* seductive; tempting. **V~ung** *f* seduction; temptation

vergammelt *a* rotten; ⟨*Gebäude*⟩ decayed; ⟨*Person*⟩ scruffy

vergangen *a* past; (*letzte*) last. **V~heit** *f* - past; (*Gram*) past tense

vergänglich *a* transitory

vergas|en *vt* gas. **V~er** *m* **-s,-** carburettor

vergeb|en† *vt* award (**an**+*dat* to); (*weggeben*) give away; (*verzeihen*) forgive. **v~ens** *adv* in vain. **v~lich** *a* futile, vain ● *adv* in vain. **V~ung** *f* - forgiveness

vergehen† *vi* (*sein*) pass; **v~ vor** (+*dat*) nearly die of; **sich v~** violate (**gegen etw** sth); (*sexuell*) sexually assault (**an jdm** s.o.). **V~** *nt* **-s,-** offence

vergelt|en† *vt* repay. **V~ung** *f* - retaliation; (*Rache*) revenge. **V~ungsmaßnahme** *f* reprisal

vergessen† *vt* forget; (*liegenlassen*) leave behind. **V~heit** *f* - oblivion; **in V~heit geraten** be forgotten

vergeßlich *a* forgetful. **V~keit** *f* - forgetfulness

vergeuden *vt* waste, squander

vergewaltig|en *vt* rape. **V~ung** *f* **-,-en** rape

vergewissern (sich) *vr* make sure (*gen* of)

vergießen† *vt* spill; shed ⟨*Tränen, Blut*⟩

vergift|en *vt* poison. **V~ung** *f* **-,-en** poisoning

Vergißmeinnicht *nt* **-[e]s,-[e]** forget-me-not

vergittert *a* barred

verglasen *vt* glaze

Vergleich *m* **-[e]s,-e** comparison; (*Jur*) settlement. **v~bar** *a* comparable. **v~en†** *vt* compare (**mit** with/to). **v~sweise** *adv* comparatively

vergnüg|en (sich) *vr* enjoy oneself. **V~en** *nt* **-s,-** pleasure; (*Spaß*) fun; **viel V~en!** have a good time! **v~lich** *a* enjoyable. **v~t** *a* cheerful, *adv* -ly; (*zufrieden*) happy, *adv* -ily; (*vergnüglich*) enjoyable. **V~ungen** *fpl* entertainments

vergolden *vt* gild; (*plattieren*) gold-plate

vergönnen *vt* grant

vergöttern *vt* idolize

vergraben† *vt* bury

vergreifen† (sich) *vr* **sich v~ an** (+*dat*) assault; (*stehlen*) steal

vergriffen *a* out of print

vergrößer|n *vt* enlarge; ⟨*Linse:*⟩ magnify; (*vermehren*) increase; (*erweitern*) extend; expand ⟨*Geschäft*⟩; **sich v~n** grow bigger; ⟨*Firma:*⟩ expand; (*zunehmen*) increase. **V~ung** *f* **-,-en** magnification; increase; expansion; (*Phot*) enlargement. **V~ungsglas** *nt* magnifying glass

Vergünstigung *f* **-,-en** privilege

vergüt|en *vt* pay for; **jdm etw v~en** reimburse s.o. for sth. **V~ung** *f* **-,-en** remuneration; (*Erstattung*) reimbursement

verhaft|en *vt* arrest. **V~ung** *f* **-,-en** arrest

verhalten† (sich) *vr* behave; (*handeln*) act; (*beschaffen sein*) be; **sich still v~** keep quiet. **V~** *nt* **-s** behaviour, conduct

Verhältnis *nt* **-ses,-se** relationship; (*Liebes-*) affair; (*Math*) ratio; **V~se** circumstances; (*Bedingungen*) conditions; **über seine V~se leben** live beyond one's means. **v~mäßig** *adv* comparatively, relatively

verhand|eln *vt* discuss; (*Jur*) try ● *vi* (*haben*) negotiate; **v~eln gegen** (*Jur*) try. **V~lung** *f* (*Jur*) trial; **V~lungen** negotiations

verhängen *vt* cover; (*fig*) impose

Verhängnis *nt* **-ses** fate, doom. **v~voll** *a* fatal, disastrous

verharmlosen *vt* play down

verharren *vi* (*haben*) remain

verhärten *vt/i* (*sein*) harden; **sich v~** harden

verhaßt *a* hated

verhätscheln *vt* spoil, pamper

verhauen† *vt* (*fam*) beat; make a mess of ⟨*Prüfung*⟩

verheerend *a* devastating; (*fam*) terrible

verhehlen *vt* conceal

verheilen *vi* (*sein*) heal

verheimlichen *vt* keep secret

verheirat|en (sich) *vr* get married (**mit** to). **v~et** *a* married

verhelfen† *vi* (*haben*) **jdm zu etw v~** help s.o. get sth

verherrlichen *vt* glorify

verhexen *vt* bewitch; **es ist wie verhext** (*fam*) there is a jinx on it

verhinder|n *vt* prevent; **v~t sein** be unable to come. **V~ung** *f* - prevention
verhöhnen *vt* deride
Verhör *nt* **-s,-e** interrogation; **ins V~ nehmen** interrogate. **v~en** *vt* interrogate; **sich v~en** mishear
verhüllen *vt* cover; (*fig*) disguise. **v~d** *a* euphemistic, *adv* -ally
verhungern *vi* (*sein*) starve
verhüt|en *vt* prevent. **V~ung** *f* - prevention. **V~ungsmittel** *nt* contraceptive
verhutzelt *a* wizened
verirren (sich) *vr* get lost
verjagen *vt* chase away
verjüngen *vt* rejuvenate; **sich v~** taper
verkalkt *a* (*fam*) senile
verkalkulieren (sich) *vr* miscalculate
Verkauf *m* sale; **zum V~** for sale. **v~en** *vt* sell; **zu v~en** for sale
Verkäufer(in) *m*(*f*) seller; (*im Geschäft*) shop assistant
Verkehr *m* **-s** traffic; (*Kontakt*) contact; (*Geschlechts-*) intercourse; **aus dem V~ ziehen** take out of circulation. **v~en** *vi* (*haben*) operate; ⟨*Bus, Zug:*⟩ run; (*Umgang haben*) associate, mix (**mit** with); (*Gast sein*) visit (**bei jdm** s.o.); frequent (**in einem Lokal** a restaurant); **brieflich v~en** correspond ● *vt* **ins Gegenteil v~en** turn round
Verkehrs|ampel *f* traffic lights *pl.* **V~büro** *nt* = **V~verein.** **V~funk** *m* [radio] traffic information. **V~unfall** *m* road accident. **V~verein** *m* tourist office. **V~zeichen** *nt* traffic sign
verkehrt *a* wrong, *adv* -ly. **v~herum** *adv* the wrong way round; (*links*) inside out
verkennen† *vt* misjudge
verklagen *vt* sue (**auf** + *acc* for)
verkleid|en *vt* disguise; (*Techn*) line; **sich v~en** disguise oneself; (*für Kostümfest*) dress up. **V~ung** *f* **-,-en** disguise; (*Kostüm*) fancy dress; (*Techn*) lining
verkleiner|n *vt* reduce [in size]. **V~ung** *f* - reduction. **V~ungsform** *f* diminutive
verklemmt *a* jammed; (*psychisch*) inhibited
verkneifen† *vt* **sich** (*dat*) **etw v~** do without sth; (*verbeißen*) suppress sth
verknittern *vt/i* (*sein*) crumple
verknüpfen *vt* knot together; (*verbinden*) connect, link; (*zugleich tun*) combine
verkommen† *vi* (*sein*) be neglected; (*sittlich*) go to the bad; (*verfallen*) decay; ⟨*Haus:*⟩ fall into disrepair; ⟨*Gegend:*⟩ become run-down; ⟨*Lebensmittel:*⟩ go bad ● *a* neglected; (*sittlich*) depraved; ⟨*Haus*⟩ dilapidated; ⟨*Gegend*⟩ run-down
verkörper|n *vt* embody, personify. **V~ung** *f* **-,-en** embodiment, personification
verkraften *vt* cope with
verkrampft *a* (*fig*) tense
verkriechen† **(sich)** *vr* hide
verkrümmt *a* crooked, bent
verkrüppelt *a* crippled; ⟨*Glied*⟩ deformed
verkühl|en (sich) *vr* catch a chill. **V~ung** *f* **-,-en** chill
verkümmer|n *vi* (*sein*) waste/ ⟨*Pflanze:*⟩ wither away. **v~t** *a* stunted
verkünd|en *vt* announce; pronounce ⟨*Urteil*⟩. **v~igen** *vt* announce; (*predigen*) preach
verkürzen *vt* shorten; (*verringern*) reduce; (*abbrechen*) cut short; while away ⟨*Zeit*⟩
verladen† *vt* load
Verlag *m* **-[e]s,-e** publishing firm
verlangen *vt* ask for; (*fordern*) demand; (*berechnen*) charge; **am Telefon verlangt werden** be wanted on the telephone. **V~** *nt* **-s** desire; (*Bitte*) request; **auf V~** on demand
verlänger|n *vt* extend; lengthen ⟨*Kleid*⟩; (*zeitlich*) prolong; renew ⟨*Paß, Vertrag*⟩; (*Culin*) thin down. **V~ung** *f* **-,-en** extension; renewal. **V~ungsschnur** *f* extension cable
verlangsamen *vt* slow down
Verlaß *m* **-sses auf ihn ist kein V~** you cannot rely on him
verlassen† *vt* leave; (*im Stich lassen*) desert; **sich v~ auf** (+ *acc*) rely *or* depend on ● *a* deserted. **V~heit** *f* - desolation
verläßlich *a* reliable
Verlauf *m* course; **im V~** (+ *gen*) in the course of. **v~en**† *vi* (*sein*) run; (*ablaufen*) go; (*zerlaufen*) melt; **gut v~en** go [off] well ● *vr* **sich v~en** lose one's way; ⟨*Menge:*⟩ disperse; ⟨*Wasser:*⟩ drain away
verleben *vt* spend

verlegen *vt* move; (*verschieben*) postpone; (*vor-*) bring forward; (*verlieren*) mislay; (*versperren*) block; (*legen*) lay ⟨*Teppich, Rohre*⟩; (*veröffentlichen*) publish; **sich v~ auf** (+*acc*) take up ⟨*Beruf, Fach*⟩; resort to ⟨*Taktik, Bitten*⟩ ● *a* embarrassed; **nie v~ um** never at a loss for. **V~heit** *f* - embarrassment

Verleger *m* **-s,-** publisher

verleihen† *vt* lend; (*gegen Gebühr*) hire out; (*überreichen*) award, confer; (*fig*) give

verleiten *vt* induce/(*verlocken*) tempt (**zu** to)

verlernen *vt* forget

verlesen[1]† *vt* read out; **ich habe mich v~** I misread it

verlesen[2]† *vt* sort out

verletz|en *vt* injure; (*kränken*) hurt; (*verstoßen gegen*) infringe; violate ⟨*Grenze*⟩. **v~end** *a* hurtful, wounding. **v~lich** *a* vulnerable. **V~te(r)** *m/f* injured person; (*bei Unfall*) casualty. **V~ung** *f* **-,-en** injury; (*Verstoß*) infringement; violation

verleugnen *vt* deny; disown ⟨*Freund*⟩

verleumd|en *vt* slander; (*schriftlich*) libel. **v~erisch** *a* slanderous; libellous. **V~ung** *f* **-,-en** slander; (*schriftlich*) libel

verlieben (sich) *vr* fall in love (**in**+*acc* with); **verliebt sein** be in love (**in**+*acc* with)

verlier|en† *vt* lose; shed ⟨*Laub*⟩; **sich v~en** disappear; ⟨*Weg:*⟩ peter out ● *vi* (*haben*) lose (**an etw** *dat* sth). **V~er** *m* **-s,-** loser

verlob|en (sich) *vr* get engaged (**mit** to); **v~t sein** be engaged. **V~te** *f* fiancée. **V~te(r)** *m* fiancé. **V~ung** *f* **-,-en** engagement

verlock|en *vt* tempt; **v~end** tempting. **V~ung** *f* **-,-en** temptation

verlogen *a* lying

verloren *a* lost; **v~e Eier** poached eggs. **v~gehen**† *vi sep* (*sein*) get lost

verlos|en *vt* raffle. **V~ung** *f* **-,-en** raffle; (*Ziehung*) draw

verlottert *a* run-down; ⟨*Person*⟩ scruffy; (*sittlich*) dissolute

Verlust *m* **-[e]s,-e** loss

vermachen *vt* leave, bequeath

Vermächtnis *nt* **-ses,-se** legacy

vermähl|en (sich) *vr* marry. **V~ung** *f* **-,-en** marriage

vermehren *vt* increase; propagate ⟨*Pflanzen*⟩; **sich v~** increase; (*sich fortpflanzen*) breed, multiply

vermeiden† *vt* avoid

vermeintlich *a* supposed, *adv* -ly

Vermerk *m* **-[e]s,-e** note. **v~en** *vt* note [down]; **übel v~en** take amiss

vermess|en† *vt* measure; survey ⟨*Gelände*⟩ ● *a* presumptuous. **V~enheit** *f* - presumption. **V~ung** *f* measurement; (*Land-*) survey

vermiet|en *vt* let, rent [out]; hire out ⟨*Boot, Auto*⟩; **zu v~en** to let; ⟨*Boot:*⟩ for hire. **V~er** *m* landlord. **V~erin** *f* landlady

verminder|n *vt* reduce, lessen. **V~ung** *f* - reduction, decrease

vermischen *vt* mix; **sich v~** mix

vermissen *vt* miss

vermißt *a* missing. **V~e(r)** *m* missing person/(*Mil*) soldier

vermittel|n *vi* (*haben*) mediate ● *vt* arrange; (*beschaffen*) find; place ⟨*Arbeitskräfte*⟩; impart ⟨*Wissen*⟩; convey ⟨*Eindruck*⟩. **v~s** *prep* (+*gen*) by means of

Vermittl|er *m* **-s,-** agent; (*Schlichter*) mediator. **V~ung** *f* **-,-en** arrangement; (*Agentur*) agency; (*Teleph*) exchange; (*Schlichtung*) mediation

vermögen† *vt* be able (**zu** to). **V~** *nt* **-s,-** fortune. **v~d** *a* wealthy

vermut|en *vt* suspect; (*glauben*) presume. **v~lich** *a* probable ● *adv* presumably. **V~ung** *f* **-,-en** supposition; (*Verdacht*) suspicion; (*Mutmaßung*) conjecture

vernachlässig|en *vt* neglect. **V~ung** *f* - neglect

vernehm|en† *vt* hear; (*verhören*) question; (*Jur*) examine. **V~ung** *f* **-,-en** questioning

verneig|en (sich) *vr* bow. **V~ung** *f* **-,-en** bow

verneinen *vt* answer in the negative; (*ablehnen*) reject. **v~end** *a* negative. **V~ung** *f* **-,-en** negative answer; (*Gram*) negative

vernicht|en *vt* destroy; (*ausrotten*) exterminate. **v~end** *a* devastating; ⟨*Niederlage*⟩ crushing. **V~ung** *f* - destruction; extermination

Vernunft *f* - reason; **V~ annehmen** see reason

vernünftig *a* reasonable, sensible; (*fam: ordentlich*) decent ● *adv* sensibly; (*fam*) properly

veröffentlich|en *vt* publish. **V~ung** *f* **-,-en** publication

verordn|en *vt* prescribe (*dat* for). **V~ung** *f* **-,-en** prescription; (*Verfügung*) decree

verpachten *vt* lease [out]

verpack|en *vt* pack; (*einwickeln*) wrap. **V~ung** *f* packaging; wrapping

verpassen *vt* miss; (*fam: geben*) give

verpfänden *vt* pawn

verpflanzen *vt* transplant

verpfleg|en *vt* feed; **sich selbst v~en** cater for oneself. **V~ung** *f* **-** board; (*Essen*) food; **Unterkunft und V~ung** board and lodging

verpflicht|en *vt* oblige; (*einstellen*) engage; (*Sport*) sign; **sich v~en** undertake/(*versprechen*) promise (**zu** to); (*vertraglich*) sign a contract; **jdm v~et sein** be indebted to s.o. **V~ung** *f* **-,-en** obligation, commitment

verpfuschen *vt* make a mess of

verpönt *a* **v~ sein** be frowned upon

verprügeln *vt* beat up, thrash

Verputz *m* **-es** plaster. **v~en** *vt* plaster; (*fam: essen*) polish off

Verrat *m* **-[e]s** betrayal, treachery. **v~en**† *vt* betray; give away ⟨*Geheimnis*⟩; (*fam: sagen*) tell; **sich v~en** give oneself away

Verräter *m* **-s,-** traitor. **v~isch** *a* treacherous; (*fig*) revealing

verräuchert *a* smoky

verrech|nen *vt* settle; clear ⟨*Scheck*⟩; **sich v~nen** make a mistake; (*fig*) miscalculate. **V~nungsscheck** *m* crossed cheque

verregnet *a* spoilt by rain; ⟨*Tag*⟩ rainy, wet

verreisen *vi* (*sein*) go away; **verreist sein** be away

verreißen† *vt* (*fam*) pan, slate

verrenken *vt* dislocate; **sich v~** contort oneself

verricht|en *vt* perform, do; say ⟨*Gebet*⟩. **V~ung** *f* **-,-en** task

verriegeln *vt* bolt

verringer|n *vt* reduce; **sich v~n** decrease. **V~ung** *f* **-** reduction; decrease

verrost|en *vi* (*sein*) rust. **v~et** *a* rusty

verrücken *vt* move

verrückt *a* crazy, mad; **v~ werden/machen** go/drive crazy. **V~e(r)** *m/f* lunatic. **V~heit** *f* **-,-en** madness; (*Torheit*) folly

Verruf *m* disrepute. **v~en** *a* disreputable

verrühren *vt* mix

verrunzelt *a* wrinkled

verrutschen *vi* (*sein*) slip

Vers /fɛrs/ *m* **-es,-e** verse

versag|en *vi* (*haben*) fail ● *vt* **jdm/sich etw v~en** deny s.o./oneself sth. **V~en** *nt* **-s,-** failure. **V~er** *m* **-s,-** failure

versalzen† *vt* put too much salt in/on; (*fig*) spoil

versamm|eln *vt* assemble; **sich v~eln** assemble, meet. **V~lung** *f* assembly, meeting

Versand *m* **-[e]s** dispatch. **V~haus** *nt* mail-order firm

versäum|en *vt* miss; lose ⟨*Zeit*⟩; (*unterlassen*) neglect; **[es] v~en, etw zu tun** fail *or* neglect to do sth. **V~nis** *nt* **-ses,-se** omission

verschaffen *vt* get; **sich** (*dat*) **v~** obtain; gain ⟨*Respekt*⟩

verschämt *a* bashful, *adv* -ly

verschandeln *vt* spoil

verschärfen *vt* intensify; tighten ⟨*Kontrolle*⟩; increase ⟨*Tempo*⟩; aggravate ⟨*Lage*⟩; **sich v~** intensify; increase; ⟨*Lage:*⟩ worsen

verschätzen (sich) *vr* **sich v~ in** (+*dat*) misjudge

verschenken *vt* give away

verscheuchen *vt* shoo/(*jagen*) chase away

verschicken *vt* send; (*Comm*) dispatch

verschieb|en† *vt* move; (*aufschieben*) put off, postpone; (*sl: handeln mit*) traffic in; **sich v~en** move, shift; (*verrutschen*) slip; (*zeitlich*) be postponed. **V~ung** *f* shift; postponement

verschieden *a* different; **v~e** (*pl*) different; (*mehrere*) various; **v~es** some things; (*dieses und jenes*) various things; **die v~sten Farben** a whole variety of colours; **das ist v~** it varies ● *adv* differently; **v~ groß/lang** of different sizes/lengths. **v~artig** *a* diverse. **V~heit** *f* **-** difference; (*Vielfalt*) diversity. **v~tlich** *adv* several times

verschimmel|n *vi* (*sein*) go mouldy. **v~t** *a* mouldy

verschlafen† *vi* (*haben*) oversleep ● *vt* sleep through ⟨*Tag*⟩; (*versäumen*) miss ⟨*Zug, Termin*⟩; **sich v~** oversleep ● *a* sleepy; **noch v~** still half asleep

Verschlag *m* **-[e]s,⸚e** shed

verschlagen† *vt* lose ⟨*Seite*⟩; **jdm die Sprache/den Atem v~** leave s.o. speechless/take s.o.'s breath away; **nach X v~ werden** end up in X ● *a* sly, *adv* -ly
verschlechter|n *vt* make worse; **sich v~n** get worse, deteriorate. **V~ung** *f* **-,-en** deterioration
verschleiern *vt* veil; (*fig*) hide
Verschleiß *m* **-es** wear and tear; (*Verbrauch*) consumption. **v~en**† *vt/i* (*sein*) wear out
verschleppen *vt* carry off; (*entführen*) abduct; spread ⟨*Seuche*⟩; neglect ⟨*Krankheit*⟩; (*hinausziehen*) delay
verschleudern *vt* sell at a loss; (*verschwenden*) squander
verschließen† *vt* close; (*abschließen*) lock; (*einschließen*) lock up
verschlimmer|n *vt* make worse; aggravate ⟨*Lage*⟩; **sich v~n** get worse, deteriorate. **V~ung** *f* **-,-en** deterioration
verschlingen† *vt* intertwine; (*fressen*) devour; (*fig*) swallow
verschlissen *a* worn
verschlossen *a* reserved. **V~heit** *f* **-** reserve
verschlucken *vt* swallow; **sich v~** choke (**an** + *dat* on)
Verschluß *m* **-sses,⸚sse** fastener, clasp; (*Fenster-, Koffer-*) catch; (*Flaschen-*) top; (*luftdicht*) seal; (*Phot*) shutter; **unter V~** under lock and key
verschlüsselt *a* coded
verschmähen *vt* spurn
verschmelzen† *vt/i* (*sein*) fuse
verschmerzen *vt* get over
verschmutz|en *vt* soil; pollute ⟨*Luft*⟩ ● *vi* (*sein*) get dirty. **V~ung** *f* **-** pollution
verschnaufen *vi/r* (*haben*) **[sich] v~** get one's breath
verschneit *a* snow-covered
verschnörkelt *a* ornate
verschnüren *vt* tie up
verschollen *a* missing
verschonen *vt* spare
verschönern *vt* brighten up; (*verbessern*) improve
verschossen *a* faded
verschrammt *a* scratched
verschränken *vt* cross
verschreiben† *vt* prescribe; **sich v~** make a slip of the pen
verschrie[e]n *a* notorious
verschroben *a* eccentric
verschrotten *vt* scrap
verschulden *vt* be to blame for. **V~** *nt* **-s** fault
verschuldet *a* **v~ sein** be in debt
verschütten *vt* spill; (*begraben*) bury
verschweigen† *vt* conceal, hide
verschwend|en *vt* waste. **v~erisch** *a* extravagant, *adv* -ly; (*üppig*) lavish, *adv* -ly. **V~ung** *f* **-** extravagance; (*Vergeudung*) waste
verschwiegen *a* discreet; ⟨*Ort*⟩ secluded. **V~heit** *f* **-** discretion
verschwimmen† *vi* (*sein*) become blurred
verschwinden† *vi* (*sein*) disappear; **[mal] v~** (*fam*) spend a penny. **V~** *nt* **-s** disappearance
verschwommen *a* blurred
verschwör|en† **(sich)** *vr* conspire. **V~ung** *f* **-,-en** conspiracy
versehen† *vt* perform; hold ⟨*Posten*⟩; keep ⟨*Haushalt*⟩; **v~ mit** provide with; **sich v~** make a mistake; **ehe man sich's versieht** before you know where you are. **V~** *nt* **-s,-** oversight; (*Fehler*) slip; **aus V~** by mistake. **v~tlich** *adv* by mistake
Versehrte(r) *m* disabled person
versenden† *vt* send [out]
versengen *vt* singe; (*stärker*) scorch
versenken *vt* sink; **sich v~ in** (+*acc*) immerse oneself in
versessen *a* keen (**auf** + *acc* on)
versetz|en *vt* move; transfer ⟨*Person*⟩; (*Sch*) move up; (*verpfänden*) pawn; (*verkaufen*) sell; (*vermischen*) blend; (*antworten*) reply; **jdn v~en** (*fam: warten lassen*) stand s.o. up; **jdm einen Stoß/Schreck v~en** give s.o. a push/fright; **jdm in Angst/Erstaunen v~en** frighten/astonish s.o.; **sich in jds Lage v~en** put oneself in s.o.'s place. **V~ung** *f* **-,-en** move; transfer; (*Sch*) move to a higher class
verseuch|en *vt* contaminate. **V~ung** *f* **-** contamination
versicher|n *vt* insure; (*bekräftigen*) affirm; **jdm v~n** assure s.o. (**daß** that). **V~ung** *f* **-,-en** insurance; assurance
versiegeln *vt* seal
versiegen *vi* (*sein*) dry up
versiert /vɛrˈziːɐ̯t/ *a* experienced
versilbert *a* silver-plated
versinken† *vi* (*sein*) sink; **in Gedanken versunken** lost in thought
Version /vɛrˈzi̯oːn/ *f* **-,-en** version
Versmaß /ˈfɛrs-/ *nt* metre

versöhn|en *vt* reconcile; **sich v~en** become reconciled. **v~lich** *a* conciliatory. **V~ung** *f* -,-en reconciliation

versorg|en *vt* provide, supply (**mit** with); provide for ⟨*Familie*⟩; (*betreuen*) look after; keep ⟨*Haushalt*⟩. **V~ung** *f* - provision, supply; (*Betreuung*) care

verspät|en (sich) *vr* be late. **v~et** *a* late; ⟨*Zug*⟩ delayed; ⟨*Dank, Glückwunsch*⟩ belated ● *adv* late; belatedly. **V~ung** *f* - lateness; **V~ung haben** be late

versperren *vt* block; bar ⟨*Weg*⟩

verspiel|en *vt* gamble away; **sich v~en** play a wrong note. **v~t** *a* playful, *adv* -ly

verspotten *vt* mock, ridicule

versprech|en† *vt* promise; **sich v~en** make a slip of the tongue; **sich** (*dat*) **viel v~en von** have high hopes of. **V~en** *nt* **-s,-** promise. **V~ungen** *fpl* promises

verspüren *vt* feel

verstaatlich|en *vt* nationalize. **V~ung** *f* - nationalization

Verstand *m* **-[e]s** mind; (*Vernunft*) reason; **den V~ verlieren** go out of one's mind. **v~esmäßig** *a* rational, *adv* -ly

verständig *a* sensible, *adv* -bly; (*klug*) intelligent, *adv* -ly. **v~en** *vt* notify, inform; **sich v~en** communicate; (*sich verständlich machen*) make oneself understood; (*sich einigen*) reach agreement. **V~ung** *f* - notification; communication; (*Einigung*) agreement

verständlich *a* comprehensible, *adv* -bly; (*deutlich*) clear, *adv* -ly; (*begreiflich*) understandable; **sich v~ machen** make oneself understood. **v~erweise** *adv* understandably

Verständnis *nt* **-ses** understanding. **v~los** *a* uncomprehending, *adv* -ly. **v~voll** *a* understanding, *adv* -ly

verstärk|en *vt* strengthen, reinforce; (*steigern*) intensify, increase; amplify ⟨*Ton*⟩; **sich v~en** intensify. **V~er** *m* **-s,-** amplifier. **V~ung** *f* reinforcement; increase; amplification; (*Truppen*) reinforcements *pl*

verstaubt *a* dusty

verstauchen *vt* sprain

verstauen *vt* stow

Versteck *nt* **-[e]s,-e** hiding-place; **V~ spielen** play hide-and-seek. **v~en** *vt* hide; **sich v~en** hide. **v~t** *a* hidden; (*heimlich*) secret; (*verstohlen*) furtive, *adv* -ly

verstehen† *vt* understand; (*können*) know; **falsch v~** misunderstand; **sich v~** understand one another; (*auskommen*) get on; **das versteht sich von selbst** that goes without saying

versteifen *vt* stiffen; **sich v~** stiffen; (*fig*) insist (**auf** + *acc* on)

versteiger|n *vt* auction. **V~ung** *f* auction

versteinert *a* fossilized

verstell|bar *a* adjustable. **v~en** *vt* adjust; (*versperren*) block; (*verändern*) disguise; **sich v~en** pretend. **V~ung** *f* - pretence

versteuern *vt* pay tax on

verstiegen *a* (*fig*) extravagant

verstimm|t *a* disgruntled; ⟨*Magen*⟩ upset; (*Mus*) out of tune. **V~ung** *f* - ill humour; (*Magen-*) upset

verstockt *a* stubborn, *adv* -ly

verstohlen *a* furtive, *adv* -ly

verstopf|en *vt* plug; (*versperren*) block; **v~t** blocked; ⟨*Person*⟩ constipated. **V~ung** *f* **-,-en** blockage; (*Med*) constipation

verstorben *a* late, deceased. **V~e(r)** *m/f* deceased

verstört *a* bewildered

Verstoß *m* infringement. **v~en**† *vt* disown ● *vi* (*haben*) **v~en gegen** contravene, infringe; offend against ⟨*Anstand*⟩

verstreichen† *vt* spread ● *vi* (*sein*) pass

verstreuen *vt* scatter

verstümmeln *vt* mutilate; garble ⟨*Text*⟩

verstummen *vi* (*sein*) fall silent; ⟨*Gespräch, Lärm:*⟩ cease

Versuch *m* **-[e]s,-e** attempt; (*Experiment*) experiment. **v~en** *vt/i* (*haben*) try; **sich v~en in** (+ *dat*) try one's hand at; **v~t sein** be tempted (**zu** to). **V~skaninchen** *nt* (*fig*) guinea-pig. **v~sweise** *adv* as an experiment. **V~ung** *f* **-,-en** temptation

versündigen (sich) *vr* sin (**an** + *dat* against)

vertagen *vt* adjourn; (*aufschieben*) postpone; **sich v~** adjourn

vertauschen *vt* exchange; (*verwechseln*) mix up

verteidig|en *vt* defend. **V~er** *m* **-s,-** defender; (*Jur*) defence counsel. **V~ung** *f* **-,-en** defence

verteil|en *vt* distribute; (*zuteilen*) allocate; (*ausgeben*) hand out; (*verstreichen*) spread; **sich v~en** spread out. **V~ung** *f* - distribution; allocation
vertief|en *vt* deepen; **v~t sein in** (+*acc*) be engrossed in. **V~ung** *f* **-,-en** hollow, depression
vertikal /vɛrti'ka:l/ *a* vertical, *adv* -ly
vertilgen *vt* exterminate; kill [off] ⟨*Unkraut*⟩; (*fam: essen*) demolish
vertippen (sich) *vr* make a typing mistake
vertonen *vt* set to music
Vertrag *m* **-[e]s,⸚e** contract; (*Pol*) treaty
vertragen† *vt* tolerate, stand; take ⟨*Kritik, Spaß*⟩; **sich v~** get on; (*passen*) go (**mit** with); **sich wieder v~** make it up ● *a* worn
vertraglich *a* contractual
verträglich *a* good-natured; (*bekömmlich*) digestible
vertrauen *vi* (*haben*) trust (**jdm/etw** s.o./sth; **auf** + *acc* in). **V~** *nt* **-s** trust, confidence (**zu** in); **im V~** in confidence. **V~smann** *m* (*pl* **-leute**) representative; (*Sprecher*) spokesman. **v~svoll** *a* trusting, *adv* -ly. **v~swürdig** *a* trustworthy
vertraulich *a* confidential, *adv* -ly; (*intim*) familiar, *adv* -ly
vertraut *a* intimate; (*bekannt*) familiar; **sich v~ machen mit** familiarize oneself with. **V~heit** *f* - intimacy; familiarity
vertreib|en† *vt* drive away; drive out ⟨*Feind*⟩; (*Comm*) sell; **sich** (*dat*) **die Zeit v~en** pass the time. **V~ung** *f* **-,-en** expulsion
vertret|en† *vt* represent; (*einspringen für*) stand in *or* deputize for; (*verfechten*) support; hold ⟨*Meinung*⟩; **sich** (*dat*) **den Fuß v~en** twist one's ankle; **sich** (*dat*) **die Beine v~en** stretch one's legs. **V~er** *m* **-s,-** representative; deputy; (*Arzt-*) locum; (*Verfechter*) supporter, advocate. **V~ung** *f* **-,-en** representation; (*Person*) deputy; (*eines Arztes*) locum; (*Handels-*) agency
Vertrieb *m* **-[e]s** (*Comm*) sale. **V~ene(r)** *m/f* displaced person
vertrocknen *vi* (*sein*) dry up
vertrösten *vt* **jdn auf später v~** put s.o. off until later
vertun† *vt* waste; **sich v~** (*fam*) make a mistake
vertuschen *vt* hush up
verübeln *vt* **jdm etw v~** hold sth against s.o.
verüben *vt* commit
verunglimpfen *vt* denigrate
verunglücken *vi* (*sein*) be involved in an accident; (*fam: mißglücken*) go wrong; **tödlich v~** be killed in an accident
verunreinigen *vt* pollute; (*verseuchen*) contaminate; (*verschmutzen*) soil
verunstalten *vt* disfigure
veruntreu|en *vt* embezzle. **V~ung** *f* - embezzlement
verursachen *vt* cause
verurteil|en *vt* condemn; (*Jur*) convict (**wegen** of); sentence (**zum Tode** to death). **V~ung** *f* - condemnation; (*Jur*) conviction
vervielfachen *vt* multiply
vervielfältigen *vt* duplicate
vervollkommnen *vt* perfect
vervollständigen *vt* complete
verwachsen *a* deformed
verwählen (sich) *vr* misdial
verwahren *vt* keep; (*verstauen*) put away; **sich v~** (*fig*) protest
verwahrlost *a* neglected; ⟨*Haus*⟩ dilapidated; (*sittlich*) depraved
Verwahrung *f* - keeping; **in V~ nehmen** take into safe keeping
verwaist *a* orphaned
verwalt|en *vt* administer; (*leiten*) manage; govern ⟨*Land*⟩. **V~er** *m* **-s,-** administrator; manager. **V~ung** *f* **-,-en** administration; management; government
verwand|eln *vt* transform, change (**in** + *acc* into); **sich v~eln** change, turn (**in** + *acc* into). **V~lung** *f* transformation
verwandt *a* related (**mit** to). **V~e(r)** *m/f* relative. **V~schaft** *f* - relationship; (*Menschen*) relatives *pl*
verwarn|en *vt* warn, caution. **V~ung** *f* warning, caution
verwaschen *a* washed out, faded
verwechs|eln *vt* mix up, confuse; (*halten für*) mistake (**mit** for). **V~lung** *f* **-,-en** mix-up
verwegen *a* audacious, *adv* -ly
Verwehung *f* **-,-en** [snow-]drift
verweichlicht *a* (*fig*) soft
verweiger|n *vt/i* (*haben*) refuse (**jdm etw** s.o sth); **den Gehorsam v~n** refuse to obey. **V~ung** *f* refusal
verweilen *vi* (*haben*) stay
Verweis *m* **-es,-e** reference (**auf** + *acc* to); (*Tadel*) reprimand. **v~en**† *vt*

refer (**auf/an** + *acc* to); (*tadeln*) reprimand; **von der Schule v~en** expel
verwelken *vi* (*sein*) wilt
verwend|en† *vt* use; spend ⟨*Zeit, Mühe*⟩. **V~ung** *f* use
verwerf|en† *vt* reject; **sich v~en** warp. **v~lich** *a* reprehensible
verwert|en *vt* utilize, use; (*Comm*) exploit. **V~ung** *f* - utilization; exploitation
verwesen *vi* (*sein*) decompose
verwick|eln *vt* involve (**in** + *acc* in); **sich v~eln** get tangled up; **in etw** (*acc*) **v~elt sein** (*fig*) be involved *or* mixed up in sth. **v~elt** *a* complicated
verwildert *a* wild; ⟨*Garten*⟩ overgrown; ⟨*Aussehen*⟩ unkempt
verwinden† *vt* (*fig*) get over
verwirken *vt* forfeit
verwirklichen *vt* realize; **sich v~** be realized
verwirr|en *vt* tangle up; (*fig*) confuse; **sich v~en** get tangled; (*fig*) become confused. **v~t** *a* confused. **V~ung** *f* - confusion
verwischen *vt* smudge
verwittert *a* weathered; ⟨*Gesicht*⟩ weather-beaten
verwitwet *a* widowed
verwöhn|en *vt* spoil. **v~t** *a* spoilt; (*anspruchsvoll*) discriminating
verworren *a* confused
verwund|bar *a* vulnerable. **v~en** *vt* wound
verwunder|lich *a* surprising. **v~n** *vt* surprise; **sich v~n** be surprised. **V~ung** *f* - surprise
Verwund|ete(r) *m* wounded soldier; **die V~eten** the wounded *pl*. **V~ung** *f* -,-**en** wound
verwünsch|en *vt* curse. **v~t** *a* confounded
verwüst|en *vt* devastate, ravage. **V~ung** *f* -,-**en** devastation
verzagen *vi* (*haben*) lose heart
verzählen (sich) *vr* miscount
verzärteln *vt* mollycoddle
verzaubern *vt* bewitch; (*fig*) enchant; **v~ in** (+*acc*) turn into
Verzehr *m* -**s** consumption. **v~en** *vt* eat; (*aufbrauchen*) use up; **sich v~en** (*fig*) pine away
verzeich|nen *vt* list; (*registrieren*) register. **V~nis** *nt* -**ses,-se** list; (*Inhalts-*) index
verzeih|en† *vt* forgive; **v~en Sie!** excuse me! **V~ung** *f* - forgiveness; **um V~ung bitten** apologize; **V~ung!** sorry! (*bei Frage*) excuse me!
verzerren *vt* distort; contort ⟨*Gesicht*⟩; pull ⟨*Muskel*⟩
Verzicht *m* -**[e]s** renunciation (**auf** + *acc* of). **v~en** *vi* (*haben*) do without; **v~en auf** (+*acc*) give up; renounce ⟨*Recht, Erbe*⟩
verziehen† *vt* pull out of shape; (*verwöhnen*) spoil; **sich v~** lose shape; ⟨*Holz:*⟩ warp; ⟨*Gesicht:*⟩ twist; (*verschwinden*) disappear; ⟨*Nebel:*⟩ disperse; ⟨*Gewitter:*⟩ pass; **das Gesicht v~** pull a face ● *vi* (*sein*) move [away]
verzier|en *vt* decorate. **V~ung** *f* -,-**en** decoration
verzinsen *vt* pay interest on
verzöger|n *vt* delay; (*verlangsamen*) slow down; **sich v~n** be delayed. **V~ung** *f* -,-**en** delay
verzollen *vt* pay duty on; **haben Sie etwas zu v~?** have you anything to declare?
verzück|t *a* ecstatic, *adv* -ally. **V~ung** *f* - rapture, ecstasy
Verzug *m* delay; **in V~** in arrears
verzweif|eln *vi* (*sein*) despair. **v~elt** *a* desperate, *adv* -ly; **v~elt sein** be in despair; (*ratlos*) be desperate. **V~lung** *f* - despair; (*Ratlosigkeit*) desperation
verzweigen (sich) *vr* branch [out]
verzwickt *a* (*fam*) tricky
Veto /ˈveːto/ *nt* -**s,-s** veto
Vetter *m* -**s,-n** cousin. **V~nwirtschaft** *f* nepotism
vgl. *abbr* (**vergleiche**) cf.
Viadukt /vi̯aˈdʊkt/ *nt* -**[e]s,-e** viaduct
vibrieren /viˈbriːrən/ *vi* (*haben*) vibrate
Video /ˈviːdeo/ *nt* -**s,-s** video. **V~kassette** *f* video cassette. **V~recorder** /-rəkɔrdɐ/ *m* -**s,-** video recorder
Vieh *nt* -**[e]s** livestock; (*Rinder*) cattle *pl*; (*fam: Tier*) creature. **v~isch** *a* brutal, *adv* -ly
viel *pron* a great deal/(*fam*) a lot of; (*pl*) many, (*fam*) a lot of; (*substantivisch*) **v~[es]** much, (*fam*) a lot; **nicht/zu v~** not/too much; **v~e** *pl* many; **das v~e Geld/Lesen** all that money/reading ● *adv* much, (*fam*) a lot; **v~ mehr/weniger** much more/less; **v~ zu groß/klein** much *or* far too big/small
viel|deutig *a* ambiguous. **v~erlei** *inv a* many kinds of ● *pron* many things. **v~fach** *a* multiple ● *adv*

many times; (*fam: oft*) frequently. **V~falt** *f* - diversity, [great] variety. **v~fältig** *a* diverse, varied

vielleicht *adv* perhaps, maybe; (*fam: wirklich*) really

vielmals *adv* very much; **danke v~!** thank you very much!

viel|mehr *adv* rather; (*im Gegenteil*) on the contrary. **v~sagend** *a* meaningful, *adv* -ly

vielseitig *a* varied; ⟨*Person*⟩ versatile ● *adv* **v~ begabt** versatile. **V~keit** *f* - versatility

vielversprechend *a* promising

vier *inv a*, **V~** *f* -,-en four; (*Sch*) ≈ fair. **V~eck** *nt* -[e]s,-e oblong, rectangle; (*Quadrat*) square. **v~eckig** *a* oblong, rectangular; square. **v~fach** *a* quadruple. **V~linge** *mpl* quadruplets

Viertel /'fɪrtəl/ *nt* -s,- quarter; (*Wein*) quarter litre; **V~ vor/nach sechs** [a] quarter to/past six; **V~ neun** [a] quarter past eight; **drei V~ neun** [a] quarter to nine. **V~finale** *nt* quarter-final. **V~jahr** *nt* three months *pl*; (*Comm*) quarter. **v~jährlich** *a & adv* quarterly. **v~n** *vt* quarter. **V~note** *f* crotchet, (*Amer*) quarter note. **V~stunde** *f* quarter of an hour

vier|zehn /'fɪr-/ *inv a* fourteen. **v~zehnte(r,s)** *a* fourteenth. **v~zig** *inv a* forty. **v~zigste(r,s)** *a* fortieth

Villa /'vɪla/ *f* -,-len villa

violett /vi̯o'lɛt/ *a* violet

Vio|line /vi̯o'li:nə/ *f* -,-n violin. **V~linschlüssel** *m* treble clef. **V~loncello** /-lɔn'tʃɛlo/ *nt* cello

Virtuose /vɪr'tu̯o:zə/ *m* -n,-n virtuoso

Virus /'vi:rʊs/ *nt* -,-ren virus

Visier /vi'zi:ɐ̯/ *nt* -s,-e visor

Vision /vi'zi̯o:n/ *f* -,-en vision

Visite /vi'zi:tə/ *f* -,-n round; **V~ machen** do one's round

visuell /vi'zu̯ɛl/ *a* visual, *adv* -ly

Visum /'vi:zʊm/ *nt* -s,-sa visa

vital /vi'ta:l/ *a* vital; ⟨*Person*⟩ energetic. **V~ität** *f* - vitality

Vitamin /vita'mi:n/ *nt* -s,-e vitamin

Vitrine /vi'tri:nə/ *f* -,-n display cabinet/(*im Museum*) case

Vizepräsident /'fi:tsə-/ *m* vice president

Vogel *m* -s,¨ bird; **einen V~ haben** (*fam*) have a screw loose. **V~scheuche** *f* -,-n scarecrow

Vokab|eln /vo'ka:bəln/ *fpl* vocabulary *sg*. **V~ular** *nt* -s,-e vocabulary

Vokal /vo'ka:l/ *m* -s,-e vowel

Volant /vo'lã:/ *m* -s,-s flounce; (*Auto*) steering-wheel

Volk *nt* -[e]s,¨er people *sg*; (*Bevölkerung*) people *pl*; (*Bienen-*) colony

Völker|kunde *f* ethnology. **V~mord** *m* genocide. **V~recht** *nt* international law

Volks|abstimmung *f* plebiscite. **V~fest** *nt* public festival. **V~hochschule** *f* adult education classes *pl*/(*Gebäude*) centre. **V~lied** *nt* folk-song. **V~tanz** *m* folk-dance. **v~tümlich** *a* popular. **V~wirt** *m* economist. **V~wirtschaft** *f* economics *sg*. **V~zählung** *f* [national] census

voll *a* full (**von** *od* **mit** of); ⟨*Haar*⟩ thick; ⟨*Erfolg, Ernst*⟩ complete; ⟨*Wahrheit*⟩ whole; **v~ machen** fill up; **die Uhr schlug v~** (*fam*) the clock struck the hour ● *adv* (*ganz*) completely; ⟨*arbeiten*⟩ full-time; ⟨*auszahlen*⟩ in full; **v~ und ganz** completely

vollauf *adv* fully, completely

Voll|beschäftigung *f* full employment. **V~blut** *nt* thoroughbred

vollbringen† *vt insep* accomplish; work ⟨*Wunder*⟩

vollende|n *vt insep* complete. **v~t** *a* perfect, *adv* -ly; **v~te Gegenwart/Vergangenheit** perfect/pluperfect

vollends *adv* completely

Vollendung *f* completion; (*Vollkommenheit*) perfection

voller *inv a* full of; **v~ Angst/Freude** filled with fear/joy; **v~ Flecken** covered with stains

Völlerei *f* - gluttony

Volleyball /'vɔli-/ *m* volleyball

vollführen *vt insep* perform

vollfüllen *vt sep* fill up

Vollgas *nt* **V~ geben** put one's foot down; **mit V~** flat out

völlig *a* complete, *adv* -ly

volljährig *a* **v~ sein** (*Jur*) be of age. **V~keit** *f* - (*Jur*) majority

Vollkaskoversicherung *f* fully comprehensive insurance

vollkommen *a* perfect, *adv* -ly; (*völlig*) complete, *adv* -ly. **V~heit** *f* - perfection

Voll|kornbrot *nt* wholemeal bread. **V~macht** *f* -,-en authority; (*Jur*) power of attorney. **V~mond** *m* full moon. **V~pension** *f* full board. **v~schlank** *a* with a fuller figure

vollständig *a* complete, *adv* -ly

vollstrecken *vt insep* execute; carry out ⟨*Urteil*⟩
volltanken *vi sep* (*haben*) (*Auto*) fill up [with petrol]
Volltreffer *m* direct hit
vollzählig *a* complete; **sind wir v~?** are we all here?
vollziehen† *vt insep* carry out; perform ⟨*Handlung*⟩; consummate ⟨*Ehe*⟩; **sich v~** take place
Volt /vɔlt/ *nt* **-[s],-** volt
Volumen /vo'lu:mən/ *nt* **-s,-** volume
vom *prep*=**von dem; vom Rauchen** from smoking
von *prep* (+*dat*) of; (*über*) about; (*Ausgangspunkt, Ursache*) from; (*beim Passiv*) by; **Musik von Mozart** music by Mozart; **einer von euch** one of you; **von hier/heute an** from here/ today; **von mir aus** I don't mind
voneinander *adv* from each other; ⟨*abhängig*⟩ on each other
vonstatten *adv* **v~ gehen** take place; **gut v~ gehen** go [off] well
vor *prep* (+*dat*/*acc*) in front of; (*zeitlich, Reihenfolge*) before; (+*dat*) (*bei Uhrzeit*) to; ⟨*warnen, sich fürchten/ schämen*⟩ of; ⟨*schützen, davonlaufen*⟩ from; ⟨*Respekt haben*⟩ for; **vor Angst/Kälte zittern** tremble with fear/cold; **vor drei Tagen/Jahren** three days/years ago; **vor sich** (*acc*) **hin murmeln** mumble to oneself; **vor allen Dingen** above all ● *adv* forward; **vor und zurück** backwards and forwards
Vor|abend *m* eve. **V~ahnung** *f* premonition
voran *adv* at the front; (*voraus*) ahead; (*vorwärts*) forward. **v~gehen**† *vi sep* (*sein*) lead the way; (*Fortschritte machen*) make progress; **jdm/etw v~gehen** precede s.o./sth. **v~kommen**† *vi sep* (*sein*) make progress; (*fig*) get on
Vor|anschlag *m* estimate. **V~anzeige** *f* advance notice. **V~arbeit** *f* preliminary work. **V~arbeiter** *m* foreman
voraus *adv* ahead (*dat* of); (*vorn*) at the front; (*vorwärts*) forward ● **im voraus** in advance. **v~bezahlen** *vt sep* pay in advance. **v~gehen**† *vi sep* (*sein*) go on ahead; **jdm/etw v~gehen** precede s.o./sth. **V~sage** *f* **-,-n** prediction. **v~sagen** *vt sep* predict. **v~sehen**† *vt sep* foresee
voraussetz|en *vt sep* take for granted; (*erfordern*) require; **vorausgesetzt, daß** provided that. **V~ung** *f* **-,-en** assumption; (*Erfordernis*) prerequisite; **unter der V~ung, daß** on condition that
Voraussicht *f* foresight; **aller V~ nach** in all probability. **v~lich** *a* anticipated, expected ● *adv* probably
Vorbehalt *m* **-[e]s,-e** reservation. **v~en**† *vt sep* **sich** (*dat*) **v~en** reserve ⟨*Recht*⟩; **jdm v~en sein/bleiben** be left to s.o. **v~los** *a* unreserved, *adv* -ly
vorbei *adv* past (**an jdm/etw** s.o./ sth); (*zu Ende*) over. **v~fahren**† *vi sep* (*sein*) drive/go past. **v~gehen**† *vi sep* (*sein*) go past; (*verfehlen*) miss; (*vergehen*) pass; (*fam: besuchen*) drop in (**bei** on). **v~kommen**† *vi sep* (*sein*) pass/(*v~können*) get past (**an jdm/etw** s.o./sth); (*fam: besuchen*) drop in (**bei** on)
vorbereit|en *vt sep* prepare; prepare for ⟨*Reise*⟩; **sich v~en** prepare [oneself] (**auf**+*acc* for). **V~ung** *f* **-,-en** preparation
vorbestellen *vt sep* order/(*im Theater, Hotel*) book in advance
vorbestraft *a* **v~ sein** have a [criminal] record
vorbeug|en *v sep* ● *vt* bend forward; **sich v~en** bend *or* lean forward ● *vi* (*haben*) prevent (**etw** *dat* sth); **v~end** preventive. **V~ung** *f* **-** prevention
Vorbild *nt* model. **v~lich** *a* exemplary, model ● *adv* in an exemplary manner
vorbringen† *vt sep* put forward; offer ⟨*Entschuldigung*⟩
vordatieren *vt sep* post-date
Vorder|bein *nt* foreleg. **v~e(r,s)** *a* front. **V~grund** *m* foreground. **V~mann** *m* (*pl* **-männer**) person in front; **auf V~mann bringen** (*fam*) lick into shape; (*aufräumen*) tidy up. **V~rad** *nt* front wheel. **V~seite** *f* front; (*einer Münze*) obverse. **v~ste(r,s)** *a* front, first. **V~teil** *nt* front
vor|drängeln (sich) *vr sep* (*fam*) jump the queue. **v~drängen (sich)** *vr sep* push forward. **v~dringen**† *vi sep* (*sein*) advance
vor|ehelich *a* pre-marital. **v~eilig** *a* rash, *adv* -ly
voreingenommen *a* biased, prejudiced. **V~heit** *f* **-** bias

vorenthalten† *vt sep* withhold
vorerst *adv* for the time being
Vorfahr *m* **-en,-en** ancestor
vorfahren† *vi sep* (*sein*) drive up; (*vorwärts-*) move forward; (*voraus-*) drive on ahead
Vorfahrt *f* right of way; **'V~ beachten'** 'give way'. **V~sstraße** *f* ≈ major road
Vorfall *m* incident. **v~en†** *vi sep* (*sein*) happen
vorfinden† *vt sep* find
Vorfreude *f* [happy] anticipation
vorführ|en *vt sep* present, show; (*demonstrieren*) demonstrate; (*aufführen*) perform. **V~ung** *f* presentation; demonstration; performance
Vor|gabe *f* (*Sport*) handicap. **V~gang** *m* occurrence; (*Techn*) process. **V~gänger(in)** *m* **-s,-** (*f* **-,-nen**) predecessor. **V~garten** *m* front garden
vorgeben† *vt sep* pretend
vor|gefaßt *a* preconceived. **v~gefertigt** *a* prefabricated
vorgehen† *vi sep* (*sein*) go forward; (*voraus-*) go on ahead; ⟨*Uhr:*⟩ be fast; (*wichtig sein*) take precedence; (*verfahren*) act, proceed; (*geschehen*) happen, go on. **V~** *nt* **-s** action
vor|geschichtlich *a* prehistoric. **V~geschmack** *m* foretaste. **V~gesetzte(r)** *m/f* superior. **v~gestern** *adv* the day before yesterday
vorhaben† *vt sep* propose, intend (**zu** to); **etw v~** have sth planned; **nichts v~** have no plans. **V~** *nt* **-s,-** plan; (*Projekt*) project
vorhalt|en† *v sep* • *vt* hold up; **jdm etw v~en** reproach s.o. for sth • *vi* (*haben*) last. **V~ungen** *fpl* **jdm V~ungen machen** reproach s.o. (**wegen** for)
Vorhand *f* (*Sport*) forehand
vorhanden *a* existing; **v~ sein** exist; (*verfügbar sein*) be available. **V~sein** *nt* **-s** existence
Vorhang *m* curtain
Vorhängeschloß *nt* padlock
vorher *adv* before[hand]
vorhergehend *a* previous
vorherig *a* prior; (*vorhergehend*) previous
Vorherrsch|aft *f* supremacy. **v~en** *vi sep* (*haben*) predominate. **v~end** *a* predominant
Vorher|sage *f* **-,-n** prediction; (*Wetter-*) forecast. **v~sagen** *vt sep* predict; forecast ⟨*Wetter*⟩. **v~sehen†** *vt sep* foresee
vorhin *adv* just now
vorige(r,s) *a* last, previous
Vor|kämpfer *m* (*fig*) champion. **V~kehrungen** *fpl* precautions. **V~kenntnisse** *fpl* previous knowledge *sg*
vorkommen† *vi sep* (*sein*) happen; (*vorhanden sein*) occur; (*nach vorn kommen*) come forward; (*hervorkommen*) come out; (*zu sehen sein*) show; **jdm bekannt/verdächtig v~** seem familiar/suspicious to s.o.; **sich** (*dat*) **dumm/alt v~** feel stupid/old. **V~** *nt* **-s,-** occurrence; (*Geol*) deposit
Vorkriegszeit *f* pre-war period
vorlad|en† *vt sep* (*Jur*) summons. **V~ung** *f* summons
Vorlage *f* model; (*Muster*) pattern; (*Gesetzes-*) bill
vorlassen† *vt sep* admit; **jdn v~** (*fam*) let s.o. pass; (*den Vortritt lassen*) let s.o. go first
Vor|lauf *m* (*Sport*) heat. **V~läufer** *m* forerunner. **v~läufig** *a* provisional, *adv* -ly; (*zunächst*) for the time being. **v~laut** *a* forward. **V~leben** *nt* past
vorleg|en *vt sep* put on ⟨*Kette*⟩; (*unterbreiten*) present; (*vorzeigen*) show; **jdm Fleisch v~en** serve s.o. with meat. **V~er** *m* **-s,-** mat; (*Bett-*) rug
vorles|en† *vt sep* read [out]; **jdm v~en** read to s.o. **V~ung** *f* lecture
vorletzt|e(r,s) *a* last ... but one; ⟨*Silbe*⟩ penultimate; **v~es Jahr** the year before last
Vorliebe *f* preference
vorliebnehmen† *vt sep* make do (**mit** with)
vorliegen† *vi sep* (*haben*) be present/(*verfügbar*) available; (*bestehen*) exist, be; **es muß ein Irrtum v~** there must be some mistake. **v~d** *a* present; ⟨*Frage*⟩ at issue
vorlügen† *vt sep* lie (*dat* to)
vorm *prep* = **vor dem**
vormachen *vt sep* put up; put on ⟨*Kette*⟩; push ⟨*Riegel*⟩; (*zeigen*) demonstrate; **jdm etwas v~** (*fam: täuschen*) kid s.o.
Vormacht *f* supremacy
vormals *adv* formerly
Vormarsch *m* (*Mil & fig*) advance

vormerken *vt sep* make a note of; (*reservieren*) reserve

Vormittag *m* morning. **v~** *adv* **gestern/heute v~** yesterday/this morning. **v~s** *adv* in the morning

Vormund *m* **-[e]s,-munde** & **-münder** guardian

vorn *adv* at the front; **nach v~** to the front; **von v~** from the front/(*vom Anfang*) beginning; **von v~ anfangen** start afresh

Vorname *m* first name

vorne *adv* = **vorn**

vornehm *a* distinguished; (*elegant*) smart, *adv* -ly

vornehmen† *vt sep* carry out; **sich** (*dat*) **v~, etw zu tun** plan/(*beschließen*) resolve to do sth

vorn|herein *adv* **von v~herein** from the start. **v~über** *adv* forward

Vor|ort *m* suburb. **V~rang** *m* priority, precedence (**vor** + *dat* over). **V~rat** *m* **-[e]s,-e** supply, stock (**an** + *dat* of). **v~rätig** *a* available; **v~rätig haben** have in stock. **V~ratskammer** *f* larder. **V~raum** *m* ante-room. **V~recht** *nt* privilege. **V~richtung** *f* device

vorrücken *vt/i sep* (*sein*) move forward; (*Mil*) advance

Vorrunde *f* qualifying round

vors *prep* = **vor das**

vorsagen *vt/i sep* (*haben*) recite; **jdm [die Antwort] v~** tell s.o. the answer

Vor|satz *m* resolution. **v~sätzlich** *a* deliberate, *adv* -ly; (*Jur*) premeditated

Vorschau *f* preview; (*Film-*) trailer

Vorschein *m* **zum V~ kommen** appear

vorschießen† *vt sep* advance ⟨*Geld*⟩

Vorschlag *m* suggestion, proposal. **v~en**† *vt sep* suggest, propose

vorschnell *a* rash, *adv* -ly

vorschreiben† *vt sep* lay down; dictate (*dat* to); **vorgeschriebene Dosis** prescribed dose

Vorschrift *f* regulation; (*Anweisung*) instruction; **jdm V~en machen** tell s.o. what to do; **Dienst nach V~** work to rule. **v~smäßig** *a* correct, *adv* -ly

Vorschule *f* nursery school

Vorschuß *m* advance

vorschützen *vt sep* plead [as an excuse]; feign ⟨*Krankheit*⟩

vorseh|en† *v sep* ● *vt* intend (**für/als** for/as); (*planen*) plan; **sich v~en** be careful (**vor** + *dat* of) ● *vi* (*haben*) peep out. **V~ung** *f* - providence

vorsetzen *vt sep* move forward; **jdm etw v~** serve s.o. sth

Vorsicht *f* - care; (*bei Gefahr*) caution; **V~!** careful! (*auf Schild*) 'caution'. **v~ig** *a* careful, *adv* -ly; cautious, *adv* -ly. **v~shalber** *adv* to be on the safe side. **V~smaßnahme** *f* precaution

Vorsilbe *f* prefix

Vorsitz *m* chairmanship; **den V~ führen** be in the chair. **v~en**† *vi sep* (*haben*) preside (*dat* over). **V~ende(r)** *m/f* chairman

Vorsorge *f* **V~ treffen** take precautions; make provisions (**für** for). **v~n** *vi sep* (*haben*) provide (**für** for). **V~untersuchung** *f* check-up

vorsorglich *adv* as a precaution

Vorspeise *f* starter

Vorspiel *nt* prelude. **v~en** *v sep* ● *vt* perform/(*Mus*) play (*dat* for) ● *vi* (*haben*) audition

vorsprechen† *v sep* ● *vt* recite; (*zum Nachsagen*) say (*dat* to) ● *vi* (*haben*) (*Theat*) audition; **bei jdm v~** call on s.o.

vorspringen† *vi sep* (*sein*) jut out; **v~des Kinn** prominent chin

Vor|sprung *m* projection; (*Fels-*) ledge; (*Vorteil*) lead (**vor** + *dat* over). **V~stadt** *f* suburb. **v~städtisch** *a* suburban. **V~stand** *m* board [of directors]; (*Vereins-*) committee; (*Partei-*) executive

vorsteh|en† *vi sep* (*haben*) project, protrude; **einer Abteilung v~en** be in charge of a department; **v~end** protruding; ⟨*Augen*⟩ bulging. **V~er** *m* **-s,-** head; (*Gemeinde-*) chairman

vorstell|bar *a* imaginable, conceivable. **v~en** *vt sep* put forward ⟨*Bein, Uhr*⟩; (*darstellen*) represent; (*bekanntmachen*) introduce; **sich v~en** introduce oneself; (*als Bewerber*) go for an interview; **sich** (*dat*) **etw v~en** imagine sth. **V~ung** *f* introduction; (*bei Bewerbung*) interview; (*Aufführung*) performance; (*Idee*) idea; (*Phantasie*) imagination. **V~ungsgespräch** *nt* interview. **V~ungskraft** *f* imagination

Vorstoß *m* advance

Vorstrafe *f* previous conviction

Vortag *m* day before

vortäuschen *vt sep* feign, fake

Vorteil *m* advantage. **v~haft** *a* advantageous, *adv* -ly; ⟨*Kleidung, Farbe*⟩ flattering

Vortrag *m* **-[e]s,¨e** talk; (*wissenschaftlich*) lecture; ⟨*Klavier-, Gedicht-*⟩ recital. **v~en**† *vt sep* perform; (*aufsagen*) recite; (*singen*) sing; (*darlegen*) present (*dat* to); express ⟨*Wunsch*⟩

vortrefflich *a* excellent, *adv* -ly

vortreten† *vi sep* (*sein*) step forward; (*hervor-*) protrude

Vortritt *m* precedence; **jdm den V~ lassen** let s.o. go first

vorüber *adv* **v~ sein** be over; **an etw** (*dat*) **v~** past sth. **v~gehen**† *vi sep* (*sein*) walk past; (*vergehen*) pass. **v~gehend** *a* temporary, *adv* -ily

Vor|urteil *nt* prejudice. **V~verkauf** *m* advance booking

vorverlegen *vt sep* bring forward

Vor|wahl[nummer] *f* dialling code. **V~wand** *m* **-[e]s,¨e** pretext; (*Ausrede*) excuse

vorwärts *adv* forward[s]. **v~kommen**† *vi sep* (*sein*) make progress; (*fig*) get on

vorweg *adv* beforehand; (*vorn*) in front; (*voraus*) ahead. **v~nehmen**† *vt sep* anticipate

vorweisen† *vt sep* show

vorwerfen† *vt sep* throw (*dat* to); **jdm etw v~** reproach s.o. with sth; (*beschuldigen*) accuse s.o. of sth

vorwiegend *adv* predominantly

Vorwort *nt* (*pl* **-worte**) preface

Vorwurf *m* reproach; **jdm Vorwürfe machen** reproach s.o. **v~svoll** *a* reproachful, *adv* -ly

Vorzeichen *nt* sign; (*fig*) omen

vorzeigen *vt sep* show

vorzeitig *a* premature, *adv* -ly

vorziehen† *vt sep* pull forward; draw ⟨*Vorhang*⟩; (*vorverlegen*) bring forward; (*lieber mögen*) prefer; (*bevorzugen*) favour

Vor|zimmer *nt* ante-room; (*Büro*) outer office. **V~zug** *m* preference; (*gute Eigenschaft*) merit, virtue; (*Vorteil*) advantage

vorzüglich *a* excellent, *adv* -ly

vorzugsweise *adv* preferably

vulgär /vʊlˈgɛːɐ̯/ *a* vulgar • *adv* in a vulgar way

Vulkan /vʊlˈkaːn/ *m* **-s,-e** volcano

W

Waage *f* **-,-n** scales *pl*; (*Astr*) Libra. **w~recht** *a* horizontal, *adv* -ly

Wabe *f* **-,-n** honeycomb

wach *a* awake; (*aufgeweckt*) alert; **w~ werden** wake up

Wach|e *f* **-,-n** guard; (*Posten*) sentry; (*Dienst*) guard duty; (*Naut*) watch; (*Polizei-*) station; **W~e halten** keep watch; **W~e stehen** stand guard. **w~en** *vi* (*haben*) be awake; **w~en über** (+*acc*) watch over. **W~hund** *m* guard-dog

Wacholder *m* **-s** juniper

Wachposten *m* sentry

Wachs *nt* **-es** wax

wachsam *a* vigilant, *adv* -ly. **W~keit** *f* - vigilance

wachsen[1]† *vi* (*sein*) grow

wachs|en[2] *vt* (*reg*) wax. **W~figur** *f* waxwork. **W~tuch** *nt* oilcloth

Wachstum *nt* **-s** growth

Wächter *m* **-s,-** guard; (*Park-*) keeper; (*Parkplatz-*) attendant

Wacht|meister *m* [police] constable. **W~posten** *m* sentry

Wachturm *m* watch-tower

wackel|ig *a* wobbly; ⟨*Stuhl*⟩ rickety; ⟨*Person*⟩ shaky. **W~kontakt** *m* loose connection. **w~n** *vi* (*haben*) wobble; (*zittern*) shake • *vi* (*sein*) totter

wacklig *a* = **wackelig**

Wade *f* **-,-n** (*Anat*) calf

Waffe *f* **-,-n** weapon; **W~n** arms

Waffel *f* **-,-n** waffle; (*Eis-*) wafer

Waffen|ruhe *f* cease-fire. **W~schein** *m* firearms licence. **W~stillstand** *m* armistice

Wagemut *m* daring. **w~ig** *a* daring, *adv* -ly

wagen *vt* risk; **es w~, etw zu tun** dare [to] do sth; **sich w~** (*gehen*) venture

Wagen *m* **-s,-** cart; (*Eisenbahn-*) carriage, coach; (*Güter-*) wagon; (*Kinder-*) pram; (*Auto*) car. **W~heber** *m* **-s,-** jack

Waggon /vaˈgõː/ *m* **-s,-s** wagon

waghalsig *a* daring, *adv* -ly

Wagnis *nt* **-ses,-se** risk

Wahl *f* **-,-en** choice; (*Pol, Admin*) election; (*geheime*) ballot; **zweite W~** (*Comm*) seconds *pl*

wähl|en *vt/i* (*haben*) choose; (*Pol, Admin*) elect; (*stimmen*) vote; (*Teleph*) dial. **W~er(in)** *m* **-s,-** (*f* **-,-nen**) voter. **w~erisch** *a* choosy, fussy

Wahl|fach *nt* optional subject. **w~frei** *a* optional. **W~kampf** *m*

election campaign. **W~kreis** *m* constituency. **W~lokal** *nt* polling-station. **w~los** *a* indiscriminate, *adv* -ly. **W~recht** *nt* [right to] vote

Wählscheibe *f* (*Teleph*) dial

Wahl|spruch *m* motto. **W~urne** *f* ballot-box

Wahn *m* **-[e]s** delusion; (*Manie*) mania

wähnen *vt* believe

Wahnsinn *m* madness. **w~ig** *a* mad, insane; (*fam: unsinnig*) crazy; (*fam: groß*) terrible; **w~ig werden** go mad ● *adv* (*fam*) terribly. **W~ige(r)** *m/f* maniac

wahr *a* true; (*echt*) real; **w~ werden** come true; **du kommst doch, nicht w~?** you are coming, aren't you?

wahren *vt* keep; (*verteidigen*) safeguard; **den Schein w~** keep up appearances

währen *vi* (*haben*) last

während *prep* (+*gen*) during ● *conj* while; (*wohingegen*) whereas. **w~dessen** *adv* in the meantime

wahrhaben *vt* **etw nicht w~ wollen** refuse to admit sth

wahrhaftig *adv* really, truly

Wahrheit *f* **-,-en** truth. **w~sgemäß** *a* truthful, *adv* -ly

wahrnehm|bar *a* perceptible. **w~en**† *vt sep* notice; (*nutzen*) take advantage of; exploit ⟨*Vorteil*⟩; look after ⟨*Interessen*⟩. **W~ung** *f* **-,-en** perception

wahrsag|en *v sep* ● *vt* predict ● *vi* (*haben*) **jdm w~en** tell s.o.'s fortune. **W~erin** *f* **-,-nen** fortune-teller

wahrscheinlich *a* probable, *adv* -bly. **W~keit** *f* **-** probability

Währung *f* **-,-en** currency

Wahrzeichen *nt* symbol

Waise *f* **-,-n** orphan. **W~nhaus** *nt* orphanage. **W~nkind** *nt* orphan

Wal *m* **-[e]s,-e** whale

Wald *m* **-[e]s,¨er** wood; (*groß*) forest. **w~ig** *a* wooded

Walis|er *m* **-s,-** Welshman. **w~isch** *a* Welsh

Wall *m* **-[e]s,¨e** mound; (*Mil*) rampart

Wallfahr|er(in) *m*(*f*) pilgrim. **W~t** *f* pilgrimage

Walnuß *f* walnut

Walze *f* **-,-n** roller. **w~n** *vt* roll

wälzen *vt* roll; pore over ⟨*Bücher*⟩; mull over ⟨*Probleme*⟩; **sich w~** roll [about]; (*schlaflos*) toss and turn

Walzer *m* **-s,-** waltz

Wand *f* **-,¨e** wall; (*Trenn-*) partition; (*Seite*) side; (*Fels-*) face

Wandel *m* **-s** change. **w~bar** *a* changeable. **w~n** *vi* (*sein*) stroll ● *vr* **sich w~n** change

Wander|er *m* **-s,-**, **W~in** *f* **-,-nen** hiker, rambler. **w~n** *vi* (*sein*) hike, ramble; (*ziehen*) travel; (*gemächlich gehen*) wander; (*ziellos*) roam. **W~schaft** *f* **-** travels *pl*. **W~ung** *f* **-,-en** hike, ramble; (*länger*) walking tour. **W~weg** *m* footpath

Wandgemälde *nt* mural

Wandlung *f* **-,-en** change, transformation

Wand|malerei *f* mural. **W~tafel** *f* blackboard. **W~teppich** *m* tapestry

Wange *f* **-,-n** cheek

wank|elmütig *a* fickle. **w~en** *vi* (*haben*) sway; ⟨*Person:*⟩ stagger; (*fig*) waver ● *vi* (*sein*) stagger

wann *adv* when

Wanne *f* **-,-n** tub

Wanze *f* **-,-n** bug

Wappen *nt* **-s,-** coat of arms. **W~kunde** *f* heraldry

war, wäre *s.* **sein**[1]

Ware *f* **-,-n** article; (*Comm*) commodity; (*coll*) merchandise; **W~n** goods. **W~nhaus** *nt* department store. **W~nprobe** *f* sample. **W~nzeichen** *nt* trademark

warm *a* (**wärmer, wärmst**) warm; ⟨*Mahlzeit*⟩ hot; **w~ machen** heat ● *adv* warmly; **w~ essen** have a hot meal

Wärm|e *f* **-** warmth; (*Phys*) heat; **10 Grad W~e** 10 degrees above zero. **w~en** *vt* warm; heat ⟨*Essen, Wasser*⟩. **W~flasche** *f* hot-water bottle

warmherzig *a* warm-hearted

Warn|blinkanlage *f* hazard [warning] lights *pl*. **w~en** *vt/i* (*haben*) warn (**vor**+*dat* of). **W~ung** *f* **-,-en** warning

Warteliste *f* waiting list

warten *vi* (*haben*) wait (**auf**+*acc* for); **auf sich** (*acc*) **w~ lassen** take one's/its time ● *vt* service

Wärter(in) *m* **-s,-** (*f* **-,-nen**) keeper; (*Museums-*) attendant; (*Gefängnis-*) warder, (*Amer*) guard; (*Kranken-*) orderly

Warte|raum, W~saal *m* waiting-room. **W~zimmer** *nt* (*Med*) waiting-room

Wartung *f* **-** (*Techn*) service

warum *adv* why

Warze *f* **-,-n** wart

was *pron* what; **was für [ein]?** what kind of [a]? **was für ein Pech!** what bad luck! **das gefällt dir, was?** you like that, don't you? ● *rel pron* that; **alles, was ich brauche** all [that] I need ● *indef pron* (*fam: etwas*) something; (*fragend, verneint*) anything; **was zu essen** something to eat; **so was Ärgerliches!** what a nuisance! ● *adv* (*fam*) (*warum*) why; (*wie*) how

wasch|bar *a* washable. **W~becken** *nt* wash-basin. **W~beutel** *m* sponge-bag

Wäsche *f* - washing; (*Unter-*) underwear; **in der W~** in the wash

waschecht *a* colour-fast; (*fam*) genuine

Wäsche|klammer *f* clothes-peg. **W~leine** *f* clothes-line

waschen† *vt* wash; **sich w~** have a wash; **sich** (*dat*) **die Hände w~** wash one's hands; **W~ und Legen** shampoo and set ● *vi* (*haben*) do the washing

Wäscherei *f* **-,-en** laundry

Wäsche|schleuder *f* spin-drier. **W~trockner** *m* tumble-drier

Wasch|küche *f* laundry-room. **W~lappen** *m* face-flannel, (*Amer*) washcloth; (*fam: Feigling*) sissy. **W~maschine** *f* washing machine. **W~mittel** *nt* detergent. **W~pulver** *nt* washing-powder. **W~raum** *m* wash-room. **W~salon** *m* launderette. **W~zettel** *m* blurb

Wasser *nt* **-s** water; (*Haar-*) lotion; **ins W~ fallen** (*fam*) fall through; **mir lief das W~ im Mund zusammen** my mouth was watering. **W~ball** *m* beach-ball; (*Spiel*) water polo. **w~dicht** *a* watertight; ⟨*Kleidung*⟩ waterproof. **W~fall** *m* waterfall. **W~farbe** *f* watercolour. **W~hahn** *m* tap, (*Amer*) faucet. **W~kasten** *m* cistern. **W~kraft** *f* water-power. **W~kraftwerk** *nt* hydroelectric power-station. **W~leitung** *f* water-main; **aus der W~leitung** from the tap. **W~mann** *m* (*Astr*) Aquarius

wässern *vt* soak; (*begießen*) water ● *vi* (*haben*) water

Wasser|scheide *f* watershed. **W~ski** *nt* **-s** water-skiing. **W~stoff** *m* hydrogen. **W~straße** *f* waterway. **W~waage** *f* spirit-level. **W~werfer** *m* **-s,-** water-cannon. **W~zeichen** *nt* watermark

wäßrig *a* watery

waten *vi* (*sein*) wade

watscheln *vi* (*sein*) waddle

Watt[1] *nt* **-[e]s** mud-flats *pl*

Watt[2] *nt* **-s,-** (*Phys*) watt

Watt|e *f* - cotton wool. **w~iert** *a* padded; (*gesteppt*) quilted

WC /ve'tse:/ *nt* **-s,-s** WC

web|en *vt/i* (*haben*) weave. **W~er** *m* **-s,-** weaver. **W~stuhl** *m* loom

Wechsel *m* **-s,-** change; (*Tausch*) exchange; (*Comm*) bill of exchange. **W~geld** *nt* change. **w~haft** *a* changeable. **W~jahre** *npl* menopause *sg*. **W~kurs** *m* exchange rate. **w~n** *vt* change; (*tauschen*) exchange ● *vi* (*haben*) change; (*ab-*) alternate; (*verschieden sein*) vary. **w~nd** *a* changing; (*verschieden*) varying. **w~seitig** *a* mutual, *adv* -ly. **W~strom** *m* alternating current. **W~stube** *f* bureau de change. **w~weise** *adv* alternately. **W~wirkung** *f* interaction

weck|en *vt* wake [up]; (*fig*) awaken ● *vi* (*haben*) ⟨*Wecker:*⟩ go off. **W~er** *m* **-s,-** alarm [clock]

wedeln *vi* (*haben*) wave; **mit dem Schwanz w~** wag its tail

weder *conj* **w~ ... noch** neither ... nor

Weg *m* **-[e]s,-e** way; (*Fuß-*) path; (*Fahr-*) track; (*Gang*) errand; **auf dem Weg** on the way (**nach** to); **sich auf den Weg machen** set off; **im Weg sein** be in the way

weg *adv* away, off; (*verschwunden*) gone; **weg sein** be away; (*gegangen/verschwunden*) have gone; (*fam: schlafen*) be asleep; **Hände weg!** hands off! **w~bleiben**† *vi sep* (*sein*) stay away. **w~bringen**† *vt sep* take away

wegen *prep* (+ *gen*) because of; (*um ... willen*) for the sake of; (*bezüglich*) about

weg|fahren† *vi sep* (*sein*) go away; (*abfahren*) leave. **w~fallen**† *vi sep* (*sein*) be dropped/(*ausgelassen*) omitted; (*entfallen*) no longer apply; (*aufhören*) cease. **w~geben**† *vt sep* give away; send to the laundry ⟨*Wäsche*⟩. **w~gehen**† *vi sep* (*sein*) leave, go away; (*ausgehen*) go out; ⟨*Fleck:*⟩ come out. **w~jagen** *vt sep* chase away. **w~kommen**† *vi sep* (*sein*) get away; (*verlorengehen*) disappear. **w~lassen**† *vt sep* let go; (*auslassen*) omit. **w~laufen**† *vi sep* (*sein*) run away. **w~machen** *vt sep* remove. **w~nehmen**† *vt sep* take away. **w~räumen** *vt sep* put away; (*entfernen*) clear away. **w~schicken** *vt sep* send away; (*abschicken*) send off. **w~tun**† *vt sep* put away; (*wegwerfen*) throw away

Wegweiser *m* **-s,-** signpost

weg|werfen† *vt sep* throw away. **w~ziehen**† *v sep* • *vt* pull away • *vi* (*sein*) move away

weh *a* sore; **weh tun** hurt; ⟨*Kopf, Rücken:*⟩ ache; **jdm weh tun** hurt s.o. • *int* **oh weh!** oh dear!

wehe *int* alas; **w~ [dir/euch]!** (*drohend*) don't you dare!

wehen *vi* (*haben*) blow; (*flattern*) flutter • *vt* blow

Wehen *fpl* contractions; **in den W~ liegen** be in labour

weh|leidig *a* soft; (*weinerlich*) whining. **W~mut** *f* - wistfulness. **w~mütig** *a* wistful, *adv* -ly

Wehr[1] *nt* **-[e]s,-e** weir

Wehr[2] *f* **sich zur W~ setzen** resist. **W~dienst** *m* military service. **W~dienstverweigerer** *m* **-s,-** conscientious objector

wehren (sich) *vr* resist; (*gegen Anschuldigung*) protest; (*sich sträuben*) refuse

wehr|los *a* defenceless. **W~macht** *f* armed forces *pl*. **W~pflicht** *f* conscription

Weib *nt* **-[e]s,-er** woman; (*Ehe-*) wife. **W~chen** *nt* **-s,-** (*Zool*) female. **W~erheld** *m* womanizer. **w~isch** *a* effeminate. **w~lich** *a* feminine; (*Biol*) female. **W~lichkeit** *f* - femininity

weich *a* soft, *adv* -ly; (*gar*) done; ⟨*Ei*⟩ soft-boiled; ⟨*Mensch*⟩ soft-hearted; **w~ werden** (*fig*) relent

Weiche *f* **-,-n** (*Rail*) points *pl*

weichen[1] *vi* (*sein*) (*reg*) soak

weichen[2]† *vi* (*sein*) give way (*dat* to); **nicht von jds Seite w~** not leave s.o.'s side

Weich|heit *f* - softness. **w~herzig** *a* soft-hearted. **w~lich** *a* soft; ⟨*Charakter*⟩ weak. **W~spüler** *m* **-s,-** (*Tex*) conditioner. **W~tier** *nt* mollusc

Weide[1] *f* **-,-n** (*Bot*) willow

Weide[2] *f* **-,-n** pasture. **w~n** *vt/i* (*haben*) graze; **sich w~n an** (+*dat*) enjoy; (*schadenfroh*) gloat over

weiger|n (sich) *vr* refuse. **W~ung** *f* **-,-en** refusal

Weihe *f* **-,-n** consecration; (*Priester-*) ordination. **w~n** *vt* consecrate; (*zum Priester*) ordain; dedicate ⟨*Kirche*⟩ (*dat* to)

Weiher *m* **-s,-** pond

Weihnacht|en *nt* **-s** & *pl* Christmas. **w~lich** *a* Christmassy. **W~sbaum** *m* Christmas tree. **W~sfest** *nt* Christmas. **W~slied** *nt* Christmas carol. **W~smann** *m* (*pl* **-männer**) Father Christmas. **W~stag** *m* **erster/zweiter W~stag** Christmas Day/ Boxing Day

Weih|rauch *m* incense. **W~wasser** *nt* holy water

weil *conj* because; (*da*) since

Weile *f* - while

Wein *m* **-[e]s,-e** wine; (*Bot*) vines *pl*; (*Trauben*) grapes *pl*. **W~bau** *m* wine-growing. **W~beere** *f* grape. **W~berg** *m* vineyard. **W~brand** *m* **-[e]s** brandy

wein|en *vt/i* (*haben*) cry, weep. **w~erlich** *a* tearful, *adv* -ly

Wein|glas *nt* wineglass. **W~karte** *f* wine-list. **W~keller** *m* wine-cellar. **W~lese** *f* grape harvest. **W~liste** *f* wine-list. **W~probe** *f* wine-tasting. **W~rebe** *f*, **W~stock** *m* vine. **W~stube** *f* wine-bar. **W~traube** *f* bunch of grapes; (*W~beere*) grape

weise *a* wise, *adv* -ly

Weise *f* **-,-n** way; (*Melodie*) tune; **auf diese W~** in this way

weisen† *vt* show; **von sich w~** (*fig*) reject • *vi* (*haben*) point (**auf**+*acc* at)

Weisheit *f* **-,-en** wisdom. **W~szahn** *m* wisdom tooth

weiß *a*, **W~** *nt* **-,-** white

weissag|en *vt/i insep* (*haben*) prophesy. **W~ung** *f* **-,-en** prophecy

Weiß|brot *nt* white bread. **W~e(r)** *m/f* white man/woman. **w~en** *vt* whitewash. **W~wein** *m* white wine

Weisung *f* **-,-en** instruction; (*Befehl*) order

weit *a* wide; (*ausgedehnt*) extensive; (*lang*) long • *adv* widely; ⟨*offen, öffnen*⟩ wide; (*lang*) far; **von w~em** from a distance; **bei w~em** by far; **w~ und breit** far and wide; **ist es noch w~?** is it much further? **ich bin so w~** I'm ready; **zu w~ gehen** (*fig*) go too far. **w~aus** *adv* far. **W~blick** *m* (*fig*) far-sightedness. **w~blickend** *a* (*fig*) far-sighted

Weite *f* **-,-n** expanse; (*Entfernung*) distance; (*Größe*) width. **w~n** *vt* widen; stretch ⟨*Schuhe*⟩; **sich w~n** widen; stretch; ⟨*Pupille*⟩ dilate

weiter *a* further ● *adv* further; (*außerdem*) in addition; (*anschließend*) then; **etw w~ tun** go on doing sth; **w~ nichts/niemand** nothing/no one else; **und so w~** and so on. **w~arbeiten** *vi sep* (*haben*) go on working

weiter|e(r,s) *a* further; **im w~en Sinne** in a wider sense; **ohne w~es** just like that; (*leicht*) easily; **bis auf w~es** until further notice; (*vorläufig*) for the time being

weiter|erzählen *vt sep* go on with; (*w~sagen*) repeat. **w~fahren**† *vi sep* (*sein*) go on. **w~geben**† *vt sep* pass on. **w~gehen**† *vi sep* (*sein*) go on. **w~hin** *adv* (*immer noch*) still; (*in Zukunft*) in future; (*außerdem*) furthermore; **etw w~hin tun** go on doing sth. **w~kommen**† *vi sep* (*sein*) get on. **w~machen** *vi sep* (*haben*) carry on. **w~sagen** *vt sep* pass on; (*verraten*) repeat

weit|gehend *a* extensive ● *adv* to a large extent. **w~hin** *adv* a long way; (*fig*) widely. **w~läufig** *a* spacious; (*entfernt*) distant, *adv* -ly; (*ausführlich*) lengthy, *adv* at length. **w~reichend** *a* far-reaching. **w~schweifig** *a* long-winded. **w~sichtig** *a* long-sighted; (*fig*) far-sighted. **W~sprung** *m* long jump. **w~verbreitet** *a* widespread

Weizen *m* **-s** wheat

welch *inv pron* what; **w~ ein(e)** what a. **w~e(r,s)** *pron* which; **um w~e Zeit?** at what time? ● *rel pron* which; (*Person*) who ● *indef pron* some; (*fragend*) any; **was für w~e?** what sort of?

welk *a* wilted; ⟨*Laub*⟩ dead. **w~en** *vi* (*haben*) wilt; (*fig*) fade

Wellblech *nt* corrugated iron

Well|e *f* **-,-n** wave; (*Techn*) shaft. **W~enlänge** *f* wavelength. **W~enlinie** *f* wavy line. **W~enreiten** *nt* surfing. **W~ensittich** *m* **-s,-e** budgerigar. **w~ig** *a* wavy

Welt *f* **-,-en** world; **auf der W~** in the world; **auf die** *od* **zur W~ kommen** be born. **W~all** *nt* universe. **w~berühmt** *a* world-famous. **w~fremd** *a* unworldly. **w~gewandt** *a* sophisticated. **W~kugel** *f* globe. **w~lich** *a* worldly; (*nicht geistlich*) secular

Weltmeister|(in) *m*(*f*) world champion. **W~schaft** *f* world championship

Weltraum *m* space. **W~fahrer** *m* astronaut

Welt|rekord *m* world record. **w~weit** *a & adv* world-wide

wem *pron* (*dat of* **wer**) to whom

wen *pron* (*acc of* **wer**) whom

Wende *f* **-,-n** change. **W~kreis** *m* (*Geog*) tropic

Wendeltreppe *f* spiral staircase

wenden[1] *vt* (*reg*) turn; **sich zum Guten w~** take a turn for the better ● *vi* (*haben*) turn [round]

wenden[2]† (*& reg*) *vt* turn; **sich w~** turn; **sich an jdn w~** turn/(*schriftlich*) write to s.o.

Wend|epunkt *m* (*fig*) turning-point. **w~ig** *a* nimble; ⟨*Auto*⟩ manœuvrable. **W~ung** *f* **-,-en** turn; (*Biegung*) bend; (*Veränderung*) change

wenig *pron* little; (*pl*) few; **w~e** *pl* few ● *adv* little; (*kaum*) not much. **w~er** *pron* less; (*pl*) fewer; **immer w~er** less and less ● *adv & conj* less. **w~ste(r,s)** least; **am w~sten** least [of all]. **w~stens** *adv* at least

wenn *conj* if; (*sobald*) when; **immer w~** whenever; **w~ nicht** *od* **außer w~** unless; **w~ auch** even though

wer *pron* who; (*fam: jemand*) someone; (*fragend*) anyone; **ist da wer?** is anyone there?

Werbe|agentur *f* advertising agency. **w~n**† *vt* recruit; attract ⟨*Kunden, Besucher*⟩ ● *vi* (*haben*) **w~n für** advertise; canvass for ⟨*Partei*⟩; **w~n um** try to attract ⟨*Besucher*⟩; court ⟨*Frau, Gunst*⟩. **W~spot** /-sp-/ *m* **-s,-s** commercial

Werbung *f* **-** advertising

werden† *vi* (*sein*) become; ⟨*müde, alt, länger*⟩ get, grow; ⟨*blind, wahnsinnig*⟩ go; **blaß w~** turn pale; **krank w~** fall ill; **es wird warm/dunkel** it is getting warm/dark; **mir wurde schlecht/schwindlig** I felt sick/dizzy; **er will Lehrer w~** he wants to be a teacher; **was ist aus ihm geworden?** what has become of him? ● *v aux* (*Zukunft*) shall; **wir w~ sehen** we shall see; **es wird bald regnen** it's going to rain soon; **würden Sie so nett sein?** would you be so kind? ● (*Passiv; pp* **worden**) be; **geliebt/geboren w~** be loved/born; **es wurde gemunkelt** it was rumoured

werfen† *vt* throw; cast ⟨*Blick, Schatten*⟩; **sich w~** ⟨*Holz:*⟩ warp ● *vi* (*haben*) **w~ mit** throw

Werft *f* **-,-en** shipyard

Werk *nt* **-[e]s,-e** work; (*Fabrik*) works *sg*, factory; (*Trieb-*) mechanism. **W~en** *nt* **-s** (*Sch*) handicraft. **W~statt** *f* **-,¨en** workshop; (*Auto-*) garage; (*Künstler-*) studio. **W~tag** *m* weekday. **w~tags** *adv* on weekdays. **w~tätig** *a* working. **W~unterricht** *m* (*Sch*) handicraft

Werkzeug *nt* tool; (*coll*) tools *pl*. **W~maschine** *f* machine tool

Wermut *m* **-s** vermouth

wert *a* **viel/50 Mark w~** worth a lot/50 marks; **nichts w~ sein** be worthless; **jds/etw** (*gen*) **w~ sein** be worthy of s.o./sth. **W~** *m* **-[e]s,-e** value; (*Nenn-*) denomination; **im W~ von** worth; **W~ legen auf** (+*acc*) set great store by. **w~en** *vt* rate

Wert|gegenstand *m* object of value; **W~gegenstände** valuables. **w~los** *a* worthless. **W~minderung** *f* depreciation. **W~papier** *nt* (*Comm*) security. **W~sachen** *fpl* valuables. **w~voll** *a* valuable

Wesen *nt* **-s,-** nature; (*Lebe-*) being; (*Mensch*) creature

wesentlich *a* essential; (*grundlegend*) fundamental; (*erheblich*) considerable; **im w~en** essentially ● *adv* considerably, much

weshalb *adv* why

Wespe *f* **-,-n** wasp

wessen *pron* (*gen of* **wer**) whose

westdeutsch *a* West German

Weste *f* **-,-n** waistcoat, (*Amer*) vest

Westen *m* **-s** west; **nach W~** west

Western *m* **-[s],-** western

Westfalen *nt* **-s** Westphalia

Westindien *nt* West Indies *pl*

west|lich *a* western; ⟨*Richtung*⟩ westerly ● *adv & prep* (+*gen*) **w~lich [von] der Stadt** [to the] west of the town. **w~wärts** *adv* westwards

weswegen *adv* why

wett *a* **w~ sein** be quits

Wett|bewerb *m* **-s,-e** competition. **W~büro** *nt* betting shop

Wette *f* **-,-n** bet; **um die W~ laufen** race (**mit jdm** s.o.)

wetteifern *vi* (*haben*) compete

wetten *vt/i* (*haben*) bet (**auf** +*acc* on); **mit jdm w~** have a bet with s.o.

Wetter *nt* **-s,-** weather; (*Un-*) storm. **W~bericht** *m* weather report. **W~hahn** *m* weathercock. **W~lage** *f* weather conditions *pl*. **W~vorhersage** *f* weather forecast. **W~warte** *f* **-,-n** meteorological station

Wett|kampf *m* contest. **W~kämpfer(in)** *m(f)* competitor. **W~lauf** *m* race. **w~machen** *vt sep* make up for. **W~rennen** *nt* race. **W~streit** *m* contest

wetzen *vt* sharpen ● *vi* (*sein*) (*fam*) dash

Whisky *m* **-s** whisky

wichsen *vt* polish

wichtig *a* important; **w~ nehmen** take seriously. **W~keit** *f* **-** importance. **w~tuerisch** *a* self-important

Wicke *f* **-,-n** sweet pea

Wickel *m* **-s,-** compress

wick|eln *vt* wind; (*ein-*) wrap; (*bandagieren*) bandage; **ein Kind frisch w~eln** change a baby. **W~ler** *m* **-s,-** curler

Widder *m* **-s,-** ram; (*Astr*) Aries

wider *prep* (+*acc*) against; (*entgegen*) contrary to; **w~ Willen** against one's will

widerfahren† *vi insep* (*sein*) **jdm w~** happen to s.o.

widerhallen *vi sep* (*haben*) echo

widerlegen *vt insep* refute

wider|lich *a* repulsive; (*unangenehm*) nasty, *adv* -ily. **w~rechtlich** *a* unlawful, *adv* -ly. **W~rede** *f* contradiction; **keine W~rede!** don't argue!

widerrufen† *vt/i insep* (*haben*) retract; revoke ⟨*Befehl*⟩

Widersacher *m* **-s,-** adversary

widersetzen (sich) *vr insep* resist (**jdm/etw** s.o./sth)

wider|sinnig *a* absurd. **w~spenstig** *a* unruly; (*störrisch*) stubborn

widerspiegeln *vt sep* reflect; **sich w~** be reflected

widersprechen† *vi insep* (*haben*) contradict (**jdm/etw** s.o./sth)

Wider|spruch *m* contradiction; (*Protest*) protest. **w~sprüchlich** *a* contradictory. **w~spruchslos** *adv* without protest

Widerstand *m* resistance; **W~ leisten** resist. **w~sfähig** *a* resistant; (*Bot*) hardy

widerstehen† *vi insep* (*haben*) resist (**jdm/etw** s.o/sth); (*anwidern*) be repugnant (**jdm** to s.o.)

widerstreben *vi insep* (*haben*) **es widerstrebt mir** I am reluctant (**zu** to). **W~** *nt* **-s** reluctance. **w~d** *a* reluctant, *adv* -ly

widerwärtig *a* disagreeable, unpleasant; (*ungünstig*) adverse

Widerwill|e *m* aversion, repugnance. **w~ig** *a* reluctant, *adv* -ly

widm|en *vt* dedicate (*dat* to); (*verwenden*) devote (*dat* to); **sich w~en** (+*dat*) devote oneself to. **W~ung** *f* **-,-en** dedication

widrig *a* adverse, unfavourable

wie *adv* how; **wie viele?** how many? **wie ist Ihr Name?** what is your name? **wie ist das Wetter?** what is the weather like? • *conj* as; (*gleich wie*) like; (*sowie*) as well as; (*als*) when, as; **genau wie du** just like you; **so gut/ reich wie** as good/rich as; **nichts wie** nothing but; **größer wie ich** (*fam*) bigger than me

wieder *adv* again; **er ist w~ da** he is back

Wiederaufbau *m* reconstruction. **w~en** *vt sep* reconstruct

wieder|aufnehmen† *vt sep* resume. **W~aufrüstung** *f* rearmament

wieder|bekommen† *vt sep* get back. **w~beleben** *vt sep* revive. **W~belebung** *f* - resuscitation. **w~bringen**† *vt sep* bring back. **w~erkennen**† *vt sep* recognize. **W~gabe** *f* (*s.* **w~geben**) return; portrayal; rendering; reproduction. **w~geben**† *vt sep* give back, return; (*darstellen*) portray; (*ausdrücken, übersetzen*) render; (*zitieren*) quote; (*Techn*) reproduce. **W~geburt** *f* reincarnation

wiedergutmach|en *vt sep* (*fig*) make up for; redress ⟨*Unrecht*⟩; (*bezahlen*) pay for. **W~ung** *f* - reparation; (*Entschädigung*) compensation

wiederher|stellen *vt sep* re-establish; restore ⟨*Gebäude*⟩; restore to health ⟨*Kranke*⟩; **w~gestellt sein** be fully recovered. **W~stellung** *f* re-establishment; restoration; (*Genesung*) recovery

wiederholen[1] *vt sep* get back

wiederhol|en[2] *vt insep* repeat; (*Sch*) revise; **sich w~en** recur; ⟨*Person:*⟩ repeat oneself. **w~t** *a* repeated, *adv* -ly. **W~ung** *f* **-,-en** repetition; (*Sch*) revision

Wieder|hören *nt* **auf W~hören!** goodbye! **W~käuer** *m* **-s,-** ruminant. **W~kehr** *f* - return; (*W~holung*) recurrence. **w~kehren** *vi sep* (*sein*) return; (*sich wiederholen*) recur. **w~kommen**† *vi sep* (*sein*) come back

wiedersehen† *vt sep* see again. **W~** *nt* **-s,-** reunion; **auf W~!** goodbye!

wiederum *adv* again; (*andererseits*) on the other hand

wiedervereinig|en *vt sep* reunify ⟨*Land*⟩. **W~ung** *f* reunification

wieder|verheiraten (sich) *vr sep* remarry. **w~verwenden**† *vt sep* reuse. **w~verwerten** *vt sep* recycle. **w~wählen** *vt sep* re-elect

Wiege *f* **-,-n** cradle

wiegen[1] † *vt/i* (*haben*) weigh

wiegen[2] *vt* (*reg*) rock; **sich w~** sway; (*schaukeln*) rock. **W~lied** *nt* lullaby

wiehern *vi* (*haben*) neigh

Wien *nt* **-s** Vienna. **W~er** *a* Viennese; **W~er Schnitzel** Wiener schnitzel • *m* **-s,-** Viennese • *f* **-,-** ≈ frankfurter. **w~erisch** *a* Viennese

Wiese *f* **-,-n** meadow

Wiesel *nt* **-s,-** weasel

wieso *adv* why

wieviel *pron* how much/(*pl*) many; **um w~ Uhr?** at what time? **w~te(r,s)** *a* which; **der W~te ist heute?** what is the date today?

wieweit *adv* how far

wild *a* wild, *adv* -ly; ⟨*Stamm*⟩ savage; **w~er Streik** wildcat strike; **w~ wachsen** grow wild. **W~** *nt* **-[e]s** game; (*Rot-*) deer; (*Culin*) venison. **W~dieb** *m* poacher. **W~e(r)** *m/f* savage

Wilder|er *m* **-s,-** poacher. **w~n** *vt/i* (*haben*) poach

wildfremd *a* totally strange; **w~e Leute** total strangers

Wild|heger, W~hüter *m* **-s,-** gamekeeper. **W~leder** *nt* suede. **w~ledern** *a* suede. **W~nis** *f* - wilderness. **W~schwein** *nt* wild boar. **W~westfilm** *m* western

Wille *m* **-ns** will; **Letzter W~** will; **seinen W~n durchsetzen** get one's [own] way; **mit W~n** intentionally

willen *prep* (+*gen*) **um . . . w~** for the sake of . . .

Willens|kraft *f* will-power. **w~stark** *a* strong-willed

willig *a* willing, *adv* -ly

willkommen *a* welcome; **w~ heißen** welcome. **W~** *nt* **-s** welcome

willkürlich *a* arbitrary, *adv* -ily

wimmeln *vi* (*haben*) swarm

wimmern *vi* (*haben*) whimper
Wimpel *m* **-s,-** pennant
Wimper *f* **-,-n** [eye]lash; **nicht mit der W~ zucken** (*fam*) not bat an eyelid. **W~ntusche** *f* mascara
Wind *m* **-[e]s,-e** wind
Winde *f* **-,-n** (*Techn*) winch
Windel *f* **-,-n** nappy, (*Amer*) diaper
winden† *vt* wind; make ⟨*Kranz*⟩; **in die Höhe w~** winch up; **sich w~** wind (**um** round); (*sich krümmen*) writhe
Wind|hund *m* greyhound. **w~ig** *a* windy. **W~mühle** *f* windmill. **W~pocken** *fpl* chickenpox *sg*. **W~schutzscheibe** *f* windscreen, (*Amer*) windshield. **w~still** *a* calm. **W~stille** *f* calm. **W~stoß** *m* gust of wind. **W~surfen** *nt* windsurfing
Windung *f* **-,-en** bend; (*Spirale*) spiral
Wink *m* **-[e]s,-e** sign; (*Hinweis*) hint
Winkel *m* **-s,-** angle; (*Ecke*) corner. **W~messer** *m* **-s,-** protractor
winken *vi* (*haben*) wave; **jdm w~** wave/(*herbei~*) beckon to s.o.
winseln *vi* (*haben*) whine
Winter *m* **-s,-** winter. **w~lich** *a* wintry; (*Winter-*) winter ... **W~schlaf** *m* hibernation; **W~schlaf halten** hibernate. **W~sport** *m* winter sports *pl*
Winzer *m* **-s,-** winegrower
winzig *a* tiny, minute
Wipfel *m* **-s,-** [tree-]top
Wippe *f* **-,-n** see-saw. **w~n** *vi* (*haben*) bounce; (*auf Wippe*) play on the see-saw
wir *pron* we; **wir sind es** it's us
Wirbel *m* **-s,-** eddy; (*Drehung*) whirl; (*Trommel-*) roll; (*Anat*) vertebra; (*Haar-*) crown; (*Aufsehen*) fuss. **w~n** *vt/i* (*sein/haben*) whirl. **W~säule** *f* spine. **W~sturm** *m* cyclone. **W~tier** *nt* vertebrate. **W~wind** *m* whirlwind
wird *s.* **werden**
wirken *vi* (*haben*) have an effect (**auf** + *acc* on); (*zur Geltung kommen*) be effective; (*tätig sein*) work; (*scheinen*) seem ● *vt* (*Tex*) knit; **Wunder w~** work miracles
wirklich *a* real, *adv* -ly. **W~keit** *f* **-,-en** reality
wirksam *a* effective, *adv* -ly. **W~keit** *f* **-** effectiveness
Wirkung *f* **-,-en** effect. **w~slos** *a* ineffective, *adv* -ly. **w~svoll** *a* effective, *adv* -ly
wirr *a* tangled; ⟨*Haar*⟩ tousled; (*verwirrt, verworren*) confused. **W~warr** *m* **-s** tangle; (*fig*) confusion; (*von Stimmen*) hubbub
Wirt *m* **-[e]s,-e** landlord. **W~in** *f* **-,-nen** landlady
Wirtschaft *f* **-,-en** economy; (*Gast-*) restaurant; (*Kneipe*) pub. **w~en** *vi* (*haben*) manage one's finances; (*sich betätigen*) busy oneself; **sie kann nicht w~en** she's a bad manager. **W~erin** *f* **-,-nen** housekeeper. **w~lich** *a* economic, *adv* -ally; (*sparsam*) economical, *adv* -ly. **W~sgeld** *nt* housekeeping [money]. **W~sprüfer** *m* auditor
Wirtshaus *nt* inn; (*Kneipe*) pub
Wisch *m* **-[e]s,-e** (*fam*) piece of paper
wisch|en *vt/i* (*haben*) wipe; wash ⟨*Fußboden*⟩ ● *vi* (*sein*) slip; ⟨*Maus:*⟩ scurry. **W~lappen** *m* cloth; (*Aufwisch-*) floor-cloth
wispern *vt/i* (*haben*) whisper
wissen† *vt/i* (*haben*) know; **weißt du noch?** do you remember? **nichts w~ wollen von** not want anything to do with. **W~** *nt* **-s** knowledge; **meines W~s** to my knowledge
Wissenschaft *f* **-,-en** science. **W~ler** *m* **-s,-** academic; (*Natur-*) scientist. **w~lich** *a* academic, *adv* -ally; scientific, *adv* -ally
wissen|swert *a* worth knowing. **w~tlich** *a* deliberate ● *adv* knowingly
witter|n *vt* scent; (*ahnen*) sense. **W~ung** *f* **-** scent; (*Wetter*) weather
Witwe *f* **-,-n** widow. **W~r** *m* **-s,-** widower
Witz *m* **-es,-e** joke; (*Geist*) wit. **W~bold** *m* **-[e]s,-e** joker. **w~ig** *a* funny; (*geistreich*) witty
wo *adv* where; (*als*) when; (*irgendwo*) somewhere; **wo immer** wherever ● *conj* seeing that; (*obwohl*) although; (*wenn*) if
woanders *adv* somewhere else
wobei *adv* how; (*relativ*) during the course of which
Woche *f* **-,-n** week. **W~nende** *nt* weekend. **W~nkarte** *f* weekly ticket. **w~nlang** *adv* for weeks. **W~ntag** *m* day of the week; (*Werktag*) weekday. **w~tags** *adv* on weekdays
wöchentlich *a* & *adv* weekly
Wodka *m* **-s** vodka

wodurch *adv* how; (*relativ*) through/ (*Ursache*) by which; (*Folge*) as a result of which

wofür *adv* what . . . for; (*relativ*) for which

Woge *f* **-,-n** wave

wogegen *adv* what . . . against; (*relativ*) against which ● *conj* whereas. **woher** *adv* where from; **woher weißt du das?** how do you know that? **wohin** *adv* where [to]; **wohin gehst du?** where are you going? **wohingegen** *conj* whereas

wohl *adv* well; (*vermutlich*) probably; (*etwa*) about; (*zwar*) perhaps; **w~ kaum** hardly; **w~ oder übel** willy-nilly; **sich w~ fühlen** feel well/ (*behaglich*) comfortable; **der ist w~ verrückt!** he must be mad! **W~** *nt* **-[e]s** welfare, well-being; **auf jds W~ trinken** drink s.o.'s health; **zum W~** (+*gen*) for the good of; **zum W~!** cheers!

wohlauf *a* **w~ sein** be well

Wohl|befinden *nt* well-being. **W~behagen** *nt* feeling of well-being. **w~behalten** *a* safe, *adv* -ly. **W~ergehen** *nt* **-s** welfare. **w~erzogen** *a* well brought-up

Wohlfahrt *f* **-** welfare. **W~sstaat** *m* Welfare State

Wohl|gefallen *nt* **-s** pleasure. **W~geruch** *m* fragrance. **w~gesinnt** *a* well disposed (*dat* towards). **w~habend** *a* prosperous, well-to-do. **w~ig** *a* comfortable, *adv* -bly. **w~klingend** *a* melodious. **w~riechend** *a* fragrant. **w~schmeckend** *a* tasty

Wohlstand *m* prosperity. **W~sgesellschaft** *f* affluent society

Wohltat *f* [act of] kindness; (*Annehmlichkeit*) treat; (*Genuß*) bliss

Wohltät|er *m* benefactor. **w~ig** *a* charitable

wohl|tuend *a* agreeable, *adv* -bly. **w~tun**† *vi sep* (*haben*) **jdm w~tun** do s.o. good. **w~verdient** *a* well-deserved. **w~weislich** *adv* deliberately

Wohlwollen *nt* **-s** goodwill; (*Gunst*) favour. **w~d** *a* benevolent, *adv* -ly

Wohn|anhänger *m* = **Wohnwagen. W~block** *m* block of flats. **w~en** *vi* (*haben*) live; (*vorübergehend*) stay. **W~gegend** *f* residential area. **w~haft** *a* resident. **W~haus** *nt* [dwelling-]house. **W~heim** *nt* hostel; (*Alten-*) home. **w~lich** *a* comfortable, *adv* -bly. **W~mobil** *nt* **-s,-e** camper. **W~ort** *m* place of residence. **W~raum** *m* living space; (*Zimmer*) living-room. **W~sitz** *m* place of residence

Wohnung *f* **-,-en** flat, (*Amer*) apartment; (*Unterkunft*) accommodation. **W~snot** *f* housing shortage

Wohn|wagen *m* caravan, (*Amer*) trailer. **W~zimmer** *nt* living-room

wölb|en *vt* curve; arch ⟨*Rücken*⟩. **W~ung** *f* **-,-en** curve; (*Archit*) vault

Wolf *m* **-[e]s,⸚e** wolf; (*Fleisch-*) mincer; (*Reiß-*) shredder

Wolk|e *f* **-,-n** cloud. **W~enbruch** *m* cloudburst. **W~enkratzer** *m* skyscraper. **w~enlos** *a* cloudless. **w~ig** *a* cloudy

Woll|decke *f* blanket. **W~e** *f* **-,-n** wool

wollen[1]† *vt/i* (*haben*) & *v aux* want; **etw tun w~** want to do sth; (*beabsichtigen*) be going to do sth; **ich will nach Hause** I want to go home; **wir wollten gerade gehen** we were just going; **ich wollte, ich könnte dir helfen** I wish I could help you; **der Motor will nicht anspringen** the engine won't start

woll|en[2] *a* woollen. **w~ig** *a* woolly. **W~sachen** *fpl* woollens

wollüstig *a* sensual, *adv* -ly

womit *adv* what . . . with; (*relativ*) with which. **womöglich** *adv* possibly. **wonach** *adv* what . . . after/⟨*suchen*⟩ for/⟨*riechen*⟩ of; (*relativ*) after/ for/of which

Wonn|e *f* **-,-n** bliss; (*Freude*) joy. **w~ig** *a* sweet

woran *adv* what . . . on/⟨*denken, sterben*⟩ of; (*relativ*) on/of which; **woran hast du ihn erkannt?** how did you recognize him? **worauf** *adv* what . . . on/⟨*warten*⟩ for; (*relativ*) on/for which; (*woraufhin*) whereupon. **woraufhin** *adv* whereupon. **woraus** *adv* what . . . from; (*relativ*) from which. **worin** *adv* what . . . in; (*relativ*) in which

Wort *nt* **-[e]s,⸚er & -e** word; **jdm ins W~ fallen** interrupt s.o.; **ein paar W~e sagen** say a few words. **w~brüchig** *a* **w~brüchig werden** break one's word

Wörterbuch *nt* dictionary

Wort|führer *m* spokesman. **w~getreu** *a* & *adv* word-for-word.

w~gewandt *a* eloquent, *adv* -ly. **w~karg** *a* taciturn. **W~laut** *m* wording

wörtlich *a* literal, *adv* -ly; (*wortgetreu*) word-for-word

wort|los *a* silent ● *adv* without a word. **W~schatz** *m* vocabulary. **W~spiel** *nt* pun, play on words. **W~wechsel** *m* exchange of words; (*Streit*) argument. **w~wörtlich** *a & adv* = **wörtlich**

worüber *adv* what ... over/⟨*lachen, sprechen*⟩ about; (*relativ*) over/about which. **worum** *adv* what ... round/⟨*bitten, kämpfen*⟩ for; (*relativ*) round/for which; **worum geht es?** what is it about? **worunter** *adv* what ... under/(*wozwischen*) among; (*relativ*) under/among which. **wovon** *adv* what ... from/⟨*sprechen*⟩ about; (*relativ*) from/about which. **wovor** *adv* what ... in front of; ⟨*sich fürchten*⟩ what ... of; (*relativ*) in front of which; of which. **wozu** *adv* what ... to/⟨*brauchen, benutzen*⟩ for; (*relativ*) to/for which; **wozu?** what for?

Wrack *nt* **-s,-s** wreck

wringen† *vt* wring

wucher|n *vi* (*haben/sein*) grow profusely. **W~preis** *m* extortionate price. **W~ung** *f* **-,-en** growth

Wuchs *m* **-es** growth; (*Gestalt*) stature

Wucht *f* **-** force. **w~en** *vt* heave. **w~ig** *a* massive

wühlen *vi* (*haben*) rummage; (*in der Erde*) burrow ● *vt* dig

Wulst *m* **-[e]s,¨e** bulge; (*Fett-*) roll. **w~ig** *a* bulging; ⟨*Lippen*⟩ thick

wund *a* sore; **w~ reiben** chafe. **W~brand** *m* gangrene

Wunde *f* **-,-n** wound

Wunder *nt* **-s,-** wonder, marvel; (*übernatürliches*) miracle; **kein W~!** no wonder! **w~bar** *a* miraculous; (*herrlich*) wonderful, *adv* -ly, marvellous, *adv* -ly. **W~kind** *nt* infant prodigy. **w~lich** *a* odd, *adv* -ly. **w~n** *vt* surprise; **sich w~n** be surprised (**über** + *acc* at). **w~schön** *a* beautiful, *adv* -ly. **w~voll** *a* wonderful, *adv* -ly

Wundstarrkrampf *m* tetanus

Wunsch *m* **-[e]s,¨e** wish; (*Verlangen*) desire; (*Bitte*) request

wünschen *vt* want; **sich** (*dat*) **etw w~** want sth; (*bitten um*) ask for sth; **jdm Glück/gute Nacht w~** wish s.o. luck/good night; **ich wünschte, ich könnte ...** I wish I could ...; **Sie w~?** can I help you? **w~swert** *a* desirable

Wunsch|konzert *nt* musical request programme. **W~traum** *m* (*fig*) dream

wurde, würde *s.* **werden**

Würde *f* **-,-n** dignity; (*Ehrenrang*) honour. **w~los** *a* undignified. **W~nträger** *m* dignitary. **w~voll** *a* dignified ● *adv* with dignity

würdig *a* dignified; (*wert*) worthy. **w~en** *vt* recognize; (*schätzen*) appreciate; **keines Blickes w~en** not deign to look at

Wurf *m* **-[e]s,¨e** throw; (*Junge*) litter

Würfel *m* **-s,-** cube; (*Spiel-*) dice; (*Zucker-*) lump. **w~n** *vi* (*haben*) throw the dice; **w~n um** play dice for ● *vt* throw; (*in Würfel schneiden*) dice. **W~zucker** *m* cube sugar

würgen *vt* choke ● *vi* (*haben*) retch; choke (**an** + *dat* on)

Wurm *m* **-[e]s,¨er** worm; (*Made*) maggot. **w~en** *vi* (*haben*) **jdn w~en** (*fam*) rankle [with s.o.]. **w~stichig** *a* worm-eaten

Wurst *f* **-,¨e** sausage; **das ist mir W~** (*fam*) I couldn't care less

Würstchen *nt* **-s,-** small sausage; **Frankfurter W~** frankfurter

Würze *f* **-,-n** spice; (*Aroma*) aroma

Wurzel *f* **-,-n** root; **W~n schlagen** take root. **w~n** *vi* (*haben*) root

würz|en *vt* season. **w~ig** *a* tasty; (*aromatisch*) aromatic; (*pikant*) spicy

wüst *a* chaotic; (*wirr*) tangled; (*öde*) desolate; (*wild*) wild, *adv* -ly; (*schlimm*) terrible, *adv* -bly

Wüste *f* **-,-n** desert

Wut *f* **-** rage, fury. **W~anfall** *m* fit of rage

wüten *vi* (*haben*) rage. **w~d** *a* furious, *adv* -ly; **w~d machen** infuriate

X

x /ɪks/ *inv a* (*Math*) x; (*fam*) umpteen. **X-Beine** *ntpl* knock-knees. **x-beinig** *a* knock-kneed. **x-beliebig** *a* (*fam*) any; **eine x-beliebige Zahl** any number [you like]. **x-mal** *adv* (*fam*) umpteen times

Y

Yoga /'jo:ga/ *m & nt* **-[s]** yoga

Z

Zack|e *f* **-,-n** point; (*Berg-*) peak; (*Gabel-*) prong. **z~ig** *a* jagged; (*gezackt*) serrated; (*fam: schneidig*) smart, *adv* -ly

zaghaft *a* timid, *adv* -ly; (*zögernd*) tentative, *adv* -ly

zäh *a* tough; (*hartnäckig*) tenacious, *adv* -ly; (*zähflüssig*) viscous; (*schleppend*) sluggish, *adv* -ly. **z~flüssig** *a* viscous; ⟨*Verkehr*⟩ slow-moving. **Z~igkeit** *f* **-** toughness; tenacity

Zahl *f* **-,-en** number; (*Ziffer, Betrag*) figure

zahl|bar *a* payable. **z~en** *vt/i* (*haben*) pay; (*bezahlen*) pay for; **bitte z~en!** the bill please!

zählen *vi* (*haben*) count; **z~ zu** (*fig*) be one/(*pl*) some of; **z~ auf** (+*acc*) count on ● *vt* count; **z~ zu** add to; (*fig*) count among; **die Stadt zählt 5000 Einwohner** the town has 5000 inhabitants

zahlenmäßig *a* numerical, *adv* -ly

Zähler *m* **-s,-** meter

Zahl|grenze *f* fare-stage. **Z~karte** *f* paying-in slip. **z~los** *a* countless. **z~reich** *a* numerous; ⟨*Anzahl, Gruppe*⟩ large ● *adv* in large numbers. **Z~ung** *f* **-,-en** payment; **in Z~ung nehmen** take in part-exchange

Zählung *f* **-,-en** count

zahlungsunfähig *a* insolvent

Zahlwort *nt* (*pl* **-wörter**) numeral

zahm *a* tame

zähmen *vt* tame; (*fig*) restrain

Zahn *m* **-[e]s,⸚e** tooth; (*am Zahnrad*) cog. **Z~arzt** *m*, **Z~ärztin** *f* dentist. **Z~belag** *m* plaque. **Z~bürste** *f* toothbrush. **z~en** *vi* (*haben*) be teething. **Z~fleisch** *nt* gums *pl*. **z~los** *a* toothless. **Z~pasta** *f* **-,-en** toothpaste. **Z~rad** *nt* cog-wheel. **Z~schmelz** *m* enamel. **Z~schmerzen** *mpl* toothache *sg*. **Z~spange** *f* brace. **Z~stein** *m* tartar. **Z~stocher** *m* **-s,-** toothpick

Zange *f* **-,-n** pliers *pl*; (*Kneif-*) pincers *pl*; (*Kohlen-, Zucker-*) tongs *pl*; (*Geburts-*) forceps *pl*

Zank *m* **-[e]s** squabble. **z~en** *vr* **sich z~en** squabble ● *vi* (*haben*) scold (**mit jdm** s.o.)

zänkisch *a* quarrelsome

Zäpfchen *nt* **-s,-** (*Anat*) uvula; (*Med*) suppository

Zapfen *m* **-s,-** (*Bot*) cone; (*Stöpsel*) bung; (*Eis-*) icicle. **z~** *vt* tap, draw. **Z~streich** *m* (*Mil*) tattoo

Zapf|hahn *m* tap. **Z~säule** *f* petrol-pump

zappel|ig *a* fidgety; (*nervös*) jittery. **z~n** *vi* (*haben*) wriggle; ⟨*Kind:*⟩ fidget

zart *a* delicate, *adv* -ly; (*weich, zärtlich*) tender, *adv* -ly; (*sanft*) gentle, *adv* -ly. **Z~gefühl** *nt* tact. **Z~heit** *f* **-** delicacy; tenderness; gentleness

zärtlich *a* tender, *adv* -ly; (*liebevoll*) loving, *adv* -ly. **Z~keit** *f* **-,-en** tenderness; (*Liebkosung*) caress

Zauber *m* **-s** magic; (*Bann*) spell. **Z~er** *m* **-s,-** magician. **z~haft** *a* enchanting. **Z~künstler** *m* conjuror. **Z~kunststück** *nt* = **Z~trick**. **z~n** *vi* (*haben*) do magic; (*Zaubertricks ausführen*) do conjuring tricks ● *vt* produce as if by magic. **Z~stab** *m* magic wand. **Z~trick** *m* conjuring trick

zaudern *vi* (*haben*) delay; (*zögern*) hesitate

Zaum *m* **-[e]s, Zäume** bridle; **im Z~ halten** (*fig*) restrain

Zaun *m* **-[e]s, Zäune** fence. **Z~könig** *m* wren

z.B. *abbr* (**zum Beispiel**) e.g.

Zebra *nt* **-s,-s** zebra. **Z~streifen** *m* zebra-crossing

Zeche *f* **-,-n** bill; (*Bergwerk*) pit

zechen *vi* (*haben*) (*fam*) drink

Zeder *f* **-,-n** cedar

Zeh *m* **-[e]s,-en** toe. **Z~e** *f* **-,-n** toe; (*Knoblauch-*) clove. **Z~ennagel** *m* toenail

zehn *inv a*, **Z~** *f* **-,-en** ten. **z~te(r,s)** *a* tenth. **Z~tel** *nt* **-s,-** tenth

Zeichen *nt* **-s,-** sign; (*Signal*) signal. **Z~setzung** *f* **-** punctuation. **Z~trickfilm** *m* cartoon [film]

zeichn|en *vt/i* (*haben*) draw; (*kenn-*) mark; (*unter-*) sign. **Z~er** *m* **-s,-** draughtsman. **Z~ung** *f* **-,-en** drawing; (*auf Fell*) markings *pl*

Zeige|finger *m* index finger. **z~n** *vt* show; **sich z~n** appear; (*sich herausstellen*) become clear; **das wird sich z~n** we shall see ● *vi* (*haben*) point (**auf**+*acc* to). **Z~r** *m* **-s,-** pointer; (*Uhr-*) hand

Zeile *f* **-,-n** line; (*Reihe*) row

zeit *prep* (+*gen*) **z~ meines/seines Lebens** all my/his life

Zeit *f* **-,-en** time; **sich** (*dat*) **Z~ lassen** take one's time; **es hat Z~** there's no hurry; **mit der Z~** in time; **in nächster Z~** in the near future; **die erste Z~** at first; **von Z~ zu Z~** from time to time; **zur Z~** at present; (*rechtzeitig*) in time; **[ach] du liebe Z~!** (*fam*) good heavens!

Zeit|alter *nt* age, era. **Z~arbeit** *f* temporary work. **Z~bombe** *f* time bomb. **z~gemäß** *a* modern, up-to-date. **Z~genosse** *m*, **Z~genossin** *f* contemporary. **z~genössisch** *a* contemporary. **z~ig** *a & adv* early. **Z~lang** *f* **eine Z~lang** for a time *or* while. **z~lebens** *adv* all one's life

zeitlich *a* ⟨*Dauer*⟩ in time; ⟨*Folge*⟩ chronological ● *adv* **z~ begrenzt** for a limited time

zeit|los *a* timeless. **Z~lupe** *f* slow motion. **Z~punkt** *m* time. **z~raubend** *a* time-consuming. **Z~raum** *m* period. **Z~schrift** *f* magazine, periodical

Zeitung *f* **-,-en** newspaper. **Z~spapier** *nt* newspaper

Zeit|verschwendung *f* waste of time. **Z~vertreib** *m* pastime; **zum Z~vertreib** to pass the time. **z~weilig** *a* temporary ● *adv* temporarily; (*hin und wieder*) at times. **z~weise** *adv* at times. **Z~wort** *nt* (*pl* **-wörter**) verb. **Z~zünder** *m* time fuse

Zelle *f* **-,-n** cell; (*Telefon-*) box

Zelt *nt* **-[e]s,-e** tent; (*Fest-*) marquee. **z~en** *vi* (*haben*) camp. **Z~en** *nt* **-s** camping. **Z~plane** *f* tarpaulin. **Z~platz** *m* campsite

Zement *m* **-[e]s** cement. **z~ieren** *vt* cement

zen|sieren *vt* (*Sch*) mark; censor ⟨*Presse, Film*⟩. **Z~sur** *f* **-,-en** (*Sch*) mark, (*Amer*) grade; (*Presse-*) censorship

Zentimeter *m & nt* centimetre. **Z~maß** *nt* tape-measure

Zentner *m* **-s,-** [metric] hundredweight (*50 kg*)

zentral *a* central, *adv* -ly. **Z~e** *f* **-,-n** central office; (*Partei-*) headquarters *pl*; (*Teleph*) exchange. **Z~heizung** *f* central heating. **z~isieren** *vt* centralize

Zentrum *nt* **-s,-tren** centre

zerbrech|en† *vt/i* (*sein*) break; **sich** (*dat*) **den Kopf z~en** rack one's brains. **z~lich** *a* fragile

zerdrücken *vt* crush; mash ⟨*Kartoffeln*⟩

Zeremonie *f* **-,-n** ceremony

Zeremoniell *nt* **-s,-e** ceremonial. **z~** *a* ceremonial, *adv* -ly

Zerfall *m* disintegration; (*Verfall*) decay. **z~en**† *vi* (*sein*) disintegrate; (*verfallen*) decay; **in drei Teile z~en** be divided into three parts

zerfetzen *vt* tear to pieces

zerfließen† *vi* (*sein*) melt; ⟨*Tinte:*⟩ run

zergehen† *vi* (*sein*) melt; (*sich auflösen*) dissolve

zergliedern *vt* dissect

zerkleinern *vt* chop/(*schneiden*) cut up; (*mahlen*) grind

zerknirscht *a* contrite

zerknüllen *vt* crumple [up]

zerkratzen *vt* scratch

zerlassen† *vt* melt

zerlegen *vt* take to pieces, dismantle; (*zerschneiden*) cut up; (*tranchieren*) carve

zerlumpt *a* ragged

zermalmen *vt* crush

zermürb|en *vt* (*fig*) wear down. **Z~ungskrieg** *m* war of attrition

zerplatzen *vi* (*sein*) burst

zerquetschen *vt* squash, crush; mash ⟨*Kartoffeln*⟩

Zerrbild *nt* caricature

zerreißen† *vt* tear; (*in Stücke*) tear up; break ⟨*Faden, Seil*⟩ ● *vi* (*sein*) tear; break

zerren *vt* drag; pull ⟨*Muskel*⟩ ● *vi* (*haben*) pull (**an**+*dat* at)

zerrinnen† *vi* (*sein*) melt

zerrissen *a* torn

zerrütten *vt* ruin, wreck; shatter ⟨*Nerven*⟩; **zerrüttete Ehe** broken marriage

zerschlagen† *vt* smash; smash up ⟨*Möbel*⟩; **sich z~** (*fig*) fall through; ⟨*Hoffnung:*⟩ be dashed ● *a* (*erschöpft*) worn out

zerschmettern *vt/i* (*sein*) smash

zerschneiden† *vt* cut; (*in Stücke*) cut up

zersetzen *vt* corrode; undermine ‹*Moral*›; **sich z~** decompose
zersplittern *vi* (*sein*) splinter; ‹*Glas:*› shatter ● *vt* shatter
zerspringen† *vi* (*sein*) shatter; (*bersten*) burst
Zerstäuber *m* **-s,-** atomizer
zerstör|en *vt* destroy; (*zunichte machen*) wreck. **Z~er** *m* **-s,-** destroyer. **Z~ung** *f* destruction
zerstreu|en *vt* scatter; disperse ‹*Menge*›; dispel ‹*Zweifel*›; **sich z~en** disperse; (*sich unterhalten*) amuse oneself. **z~t** *a* absent-minded, *adv* -ly. **Z~ung** *f* **-,-en** (*Unterhaltung*) entertainment
zerstückeln *vt* cut up into pieces
zerteilen *vt* divide up
Zertifikat *nt* **-[e]s,-e** certificate
zertreten† *vt* stamp on; (*zerdrücken*) crush
zertrümmern *vt* smash [up]; wreck ‹*Gebäude, Stadt*›
zerzaus|en *vt* tousle. **z~t** *a* dishevelled; ‹*Haar*› tousled
Zettel *m* **-s,-** piece of paper; (*Notiz*) note; (*Bekanntmachung*) notice; (*Reklame-*) leaflet
Zeug *nt* **-s** (*fam*) stuff; (*Sachen*) things *pl*; (*Ausrüstung*) gear; **dummes Z~** nonsense; **das Z~ haben zu** have the makings of
Zeuge *m* **-n,-n** witness. **z~n** *vi* (*haben*) testify; **z~n von** (*fig*) show ● *vt* father. **Z~naussage** *f* testimony. **Z~nstand** *m* witness box/ (*Amer*) stand
Zeugin *f* **-,-nen** witness
Zeugnis *nt* **-ses,-se** certificate; (*Sch*) report; (*Referenz*) reference; (*fig: Beweis*) evidence
Zickzack *m* **-[e]s,-e** zigzag
Ziege *f* **-,-n** goat
Ziegel *m* **-s,-** brick; (*Dach-*) tile. **Z~stein** *m* brick
ziehen† *vt* pull; (*sanfter; zücken; zeichnen*) draw; (*heraus-*) pull out; extract ‹*Zahn*›; raise ‹*Hut*›; put on ‹*Bremse*›; move ‹*Schachfigur*›; put up ‹*Leine, Zaun*›; (*dehnen*) stretch; make ‹*Grimasse, Scheitel*›; (*züchten*) breed; grow ‹*Rosen, Gemüse*›; **nach sich z~** (*fig*) entail ● *vr* **sich z~** (*sich erstrecken*) run; (*sich verziehen*) warp ● *vi* (*haben*) pull (**an** + *dat* on/at); ‹*Tee, Ofen:*› draw; (*Culin*) simmer; **es zieht** there is a draught; **solche Filme z~ nicht mehr** films like that are no longer popular ● *vi* (*sein*) (*um-*) move (**nach** to); ‹*Menge:*› march; ‹*Vögel:*› migrate; ‹*Wolken, Nebel:*› drift. **Z~** *nt* **-s** ache
Ziehharmonika *f* accordion
Ziehung *f* **-,-en** draw
Ziel *nt* **-[e]s,-e** destination; (*Sport*) finish; (*Z~scheibe & Mil*) target; (*Zweck*) aim, goal. **z~bewußt** *a* purposeful, *adv* -ly. **z~en** *vi* (*haben*) aim (**auf** + *acc* at). **z~end** *a* (*Gram*) transitive. **z~los** *a* aimless, *adv* -ly. **Z~scheibe** *f* target; (*fig*) butt. **z~strebig** *a* single-minded, *adv* -ly
ziemen (sich) *vr* be seemly
ziemlich *a* (*fam*) fair ● *adv* rather, fairly; (*fast*) pretty well
Zier|de *f* **-,-n** ornament. **z~en** *vt* adorn; **sich z~en** make a fuss; (*sich bitten lassen*) need coaxing
zierlich *a* dainty, *adv* -ily; (*fein*) delicate, *adv* -ly; ‹*Frau*› petite
Ziffer *f* **-,-n** figure, digit; (*Zahlzeichen*) numeral. **Z~blatt** *nt* dial
zig *inv a* (*fam*) umpteen
Zigarette *f* **-,-n** cigarette
Zigarre *f* **-,-n** cigar
Zigeuner(in) *m* **-s,-** (*f* **-,-nen**) gypsy
Zimmer *nt* **-s,-** room. **Z~mädchen** *nt* chambermaid. **Z~mann** *m* (*pl* **-leute**) carpenter. **z~n** *vt* make ● *vi* (*haben*) do carpentry. **Z~nachweis** *m* accommodation bureau. **Z~pflanze** *f* house plant
zimperlich *a* squeamish; (*wehleidig*) soft; (*prüde*) prudish
Zimt *m* **-[e]s** cinnamon
Zink *nt* **-s** zinc
Zinke *f* **-,-n** prong; (*Kamm-*) tooth
Zinn *m* **-s** tin; (*Gefäße*) pewter
Zins|en *mpl* interest *sg*; **Z~en tragen** earn interest. **Z~eszins** *m* **-es,-en** compound interest. **Z~fuß, Z~satz** *m* interest rate
Zipfel *m* **-s,-** corner; (*Spitze*) point; (*Wurst-*) [tail-]end
zirka *adv* about
Zirkel *m* **-s,-** [pair of] compasses *pl*; (*Gruppe*) circle
Zirkul|ation /-'tsio:n/ *f* - circulation. **z~ieren** *vi* (*sein*) circulate
Zirkus *m* **-,-se** circus
zirpen *vi* (*haben*) chirp
zischen *vi* (*haben*) hiss; ‹*Fett:*› sizzle ● *vt* hiss
Zit|at *nt* **-[e]s,-e** quotation. **z~ieren** *vt/i* (*haben*) quote; (*rufen*) summon
Zitr|onat *nt* **-[e]s** candied lemon-peel. **Z~one** *f* **-,-n** lemon. **Z~onenlimonade** *f* lemonade

zittern *vi* (*haben*) tremble; (*vor Kälte*) shiver; (*beben*) shake
zittrig *a* shaky, *adv* -ily
Zitze *f* **-,-n** teat
zivil *a* civilian; ⟨*Ehe, Recht, Luftfahrt*⟩ civil; (*mäßig*) reasonable. **Z~** *nt* **-s** civilian clothes *pl.* **Z~courage** /-kura:ʒə/ *f* - courage of one's convictions. **Z~dienst** *m* community service
Zivili|sation /-'tsio:n/ *f* **-,-en** civilization. **z~sieren** *vt* civilize. **z~siert** *a* civilized ● *adv* in a civilized manner
Zivilist *m* **-en,-en** civilian
zögern *vi* (*haben*) hesitate. **Z~** *nt* **-s** hesitation. **z~d** *a* hesitant, *adv* -ly
Zoll[1] *m* **-[e]s,-** inch
Zoll[2] *m* **-[e]s,¨e** [customs] duty; (*Behörde*) customs *pl.* **Z~abfertigung** *f* customs clearance. **Z~beamte(r)** *m* customs officer. **z~frei** *a & adv* duty-free. **Z~kontrolle** *f* customs check
Zone *f* **-,-n** zone
Zoo *m* **-s,-s** zoo
Zoo|loge /tsoo'lo:gə/ *m* **-n,-n** zoologist. **Z~logie** *f* - zoology. **z~logisch** *a* zoological
Zopf *m* **-[e]s,¨e** plait
Zorn *m* **-[e]s** anger. **z~ig** *a* angry, *adv* -ily
zotig *a* smutty, dirty
zottig *a* shaggy
z.T. *abbr* (**zum Teil**) partly
zu *prep* (+*dat*) to; (*dazu*) with; (*zeitlich, preislich*) at; (*Zweck*) for; (*über*) about; **zu ... hin** towards; **zu Hause** at home; **zu Fuß/Pferde** on foot/horseback; **zu beiden Seiten** on both sides; **zu Ostern** at Easter; **zu diesem Zweck** for this purpose; **zu meinem Erstaunen/Entsetzen** to my surprise/horror; **zu Dutzenden** by the dozen; **eine Marke zu 60 Pfennig** a 60-pfennig stamp; **das Stück zu zwei Mark** at two marks each; **wir waren zu dritt/viert** there were three/four of us; **es steht 5 zu 3** the score is 5–3; **zu etw werden** turn into sth ● *adv* (*allzu*) too; (*Richtung*) towards; (*geschlossen*) closed; (*an Schalter, Hahn*) off; **zu groß/weit** too big/far; **nach dem Fluß zu** towards the river; **Augen zu!** close your eyes! **Tür zu!** shut the door! **nur zu!** go on! **macht zu!** (*fam*) hurry up! ● *conj* to; **etwas zu essen** something to eat; **nicht zu glauben** unbelievable; **zu erörternde Probleme** problems to be discussed
zualler|erst *adv* first of all. **z~letzt** *adv* last of all
Zubehör *nt* **-s** accessories *pl*
zubereit|en *vt sep* prepare. **Z~ung** *f* - preparation; (*in Rezept*) method
zubilligen *vt sep* grant
zubinden† *vt sep* tie [up]
zubring|en† *vt sep* spend. **Z~er** *m* **-s,-** access road; (*Bus*) shuttle
Zucchini /tsu'ki:ni/ *pl* courgettes
Zucht *f* **-,-en** breeding; (*Pflanzen-*) cultivation; (*Art, Rasse*) breed; (*von Pflanzen*) strain; (*Z~farm*) farm; (*Pferde-*) stud; (*Disziplin*) discipline
zücht|en *vt* breed; cultivate, grow ⟨*Rosen, Gemüse*⟩. **Z~er** *m* **-s,-** breeder; grower
Zuchthaus *nt* prison
züchtigen *vt* chastise
Züchtung *f* **-,-en** breeding; (*Pflanzen-*) cultivation; (*Art, Rasse*) breed; (*von Pflanzen*) strain
zucken *vi* (*haben*) twitch; (*sich z~d bewegen*) jerk; ⟨*Blitz:*⟩ flash; ⟨*Flamme:*⟩ flicker ● *vt* **die Achseln z~** shrug one's shoulders
zücken *vt* draw ⟨*Messer*⟩
Zucker *m* **-s** sugar. **Z~dose** *f* sugar basin. **Z~guß** *m* icing. **z~krank** *a* diabetic. **Z~krankheit** *f* diabetes. **z~n** *vt* sugar. **Z~rohr** *nt* sugar cane. **Z~rübe** *f* sugar beet. **z~süß** *a* sweet; (*fig*) sugary. **Z~watte** *f* candyfloss. **Z~zange** *f* sugar tongs *pl*
zuckrig *a* sugary
zudecken *vt sep* cover up; (*im Bett*) tuck up; cover ⟨*Topf*⟩
zudem *adv* moreover
zudrehen *vt sep* turn off; **jdm den Rücken z~** turn one's back on s.o.
zudringlich *a* pushing, (*fam*) pushy
zudrücken *vt sep* press *or* push shut; close ⟨*Augen*⟩
zueinander *adv* to one another; **z~ passen** go together. **z~halten**† *vi sep* (*haben*) (*fig*) stick together
zuerkennen† *vt sep* award (*dat* to)
zuerst *adv* first; (*anfangs*) at first; **mit dem Kopf z~** head first
zufahr|en† *vi sep* (*sein*) **z~en auf** (+*acc*) drive towards. **Z~t** *f* access; (*Einfahrt*) drive
Zufall *m* chance; (*Zusammentreffen*) coincidence; **durch Z~** by chance/coincidence. **z~en**† *vi sep* (*sein*)

close, shut; **jdm z~en** ⟨*Aufgabe:*⟩ fall/⟨*Erbe:*⟩ go to s.o.

zufällig *a* chance, accidental ● *adv* by chance; **ich war z~ da** I happened to be there

Zuflucht *f* refuge; (*Schutz*) shelter. **Z~sort** *m* refuge

zufolge *prep* (+*dat*) according to

zufrieden *a* contented, *adv* -ly; (*befriedigt*) satisfied. **z~geben**† **(sich)** *vr sep* be satisfied. **Z~heit** *f* - contentment; satisfaction. **z~lassen**† *vt sep* leave in peace. **z~stellen** *vt sep* satisfy. **z~stellend** *a* satisfactory, *adv* -ily

zufrieren† *vi sep* (*sein*) freeze over

zufügen *vt sep* inflict (*dat* on); do ⟨*Unrecht*⟩ (*dat* to)

Zufuhr *f* - supply

zuführen *vt sep* ● *vt* supply ● *vi* (*haben*) **z~ auf** (+*acc*) lead to

Zug *m* **-[e]s,⸚e** train; (*Kolonne*) column; (*Um-*) procession; (*Mil*) platoon; (*Vogelschar*) flock; (*Ziehen, Zugkraft*) pull; (*Wandern, Ziehen*) migration; (*Schluck, Luft-*) draught; (*Atem-*) breath; (*beim Rauchen*) puff; (*Schach-*) move; (*beim Schwimmen, Rudern*) stroke; (*Gesichts-*) feature; (*Wesens-*) trait; **etw in vollen Zügen genießen** enjoy sth to the full; **in einem Zug[e]** at one go

Zugabe *f* (*Geschenk*) [free] gift; (*Mus*) encore

Zugang *m* access

zugänglich *a* accessible; ⟨*Mensch:*⟩ approachable; (*fig*) amenable (*dat*/**für** to)

Zugbrücke *f* drawbridge

zugeben† *vt sep* add; (*gestehen*) admit; (*erlauben*) allow. **zugegebenermaßen** *adv* admittedly

zugegen *a* **z~ sein** be present

zugehen† *vi sep* (*sein*) close; **jdm z~** be sent to s.o.; **z~ auf** (+*acc*) go towards; **dem Ende z~** draw to a close; ⟨*Vorräte:*⟩ run low; **auf der Party ging es lebhaft zu** the party was pretty lively

Zugehörigkeit *f* - membership

Zügel *m* **-s,-** rein

zugelassen *a* registered

zügel|los *a* unrestrained, *adv* -ly; (*sittenlos*) licentious. **z~n** *vt* rein in; (*fig*) curb

Zuge|ständnis *nt* concession. **z~stehen**† *vt sep* grant

zugetan *a* fond (*dat* of)

zugig *a* draughty

zügig *a* quick, *adv* -ly

Zug|kraft *f* pull; (*fig*) attraction. **z~kräftig** *a* effective; (*anreizend*) popular; ⟨*Titel*⟩ catchy

zugleich *adv* at the same time

Zug|luft *f* draught. **Z~pferd** *nt* draught-horse; (*fam*) draw

zugreifen† *vi sep* (*haben*) grab it/them; (*bei Tisch*) help oneself; (*bei Angebot*) jump at it; (*helfen*) lend a hand

zugrunde *adv* **z~ richten** destroy; **z~ gehen** be destroyed; ⟨*Ehe:*⟩ founder; (*sterben*) die; **z~ liegen** form the basis (*dat* of)

zugucken *vi sep* (*haben*) = **zusehen**

zugunsten *prep* (+*gen*) in favour of; ⟨*Sammlung*⟩ in aid of

zugute *adv* **jdm/etw z~ kommen** benefit s.o./sth; **jdm seine Jugend z~ halten** make allowances for s.o.'s youth

Zugvogel *m* migratory bird

zuhalten† *v sep* ● *vt* keep closed; (*bedecken*) cover; **sich** (*dat*) **die Nase z~** hold one's nose ● *vi* (*haben*) **z~ auf** (+*acc*) head for

Zuhälter *m* **-s,-** pimp

Zuhause *nt* **-s,-** home

zuhör|en *vi sep* (*haben*) listen (*dat* to). **Z~er(in)** *m*(*f*) listener

zujubeln *vi sep* (*haben*) **jdm z~** cheer s.o.

zukehren *vt sep* turn (*dat* to)

zukleben *vt sep* seal

zuknallen *vt/i sep* (*sein*) slam

zuknöpfen *vt sep* button up

zukommen† *vi sep* (*sein*) **z~ auf** (+*acc*) come towards; (*sich nähern*) approach; **z~ lassen** send (**jdm** s.o.); devote ⟨*Pflege*⟩ (*dat* to); **jdm z~** be s.o.'s right

Zukunft *f* - future. **zukünftig** *a* future ● *adv* in future

zulächeln *vi sep* (*haben*) smile (*dat* at)

Zulage *f* **-,-n** extra allowance

zulangen *vi sep* (*haben*) help oneself; **tüchtig z~** tuck in

zulassen† *vt sep* allow, permit; (*teilnehmen lassen*) admit; (*Admin*) license, register; (*geschlossen lassen*) leave closed; leave unopened ⟨*Brief*⟩

zulässig *a* permissible

Zulassung *f* **-,-en** admission; registration; (*Lizenz*) licence

zulaufen† *vi sep* (*sein*) **z~en auf** (+*acc*) run towards; **spitz z~en** taper to a point

zulegen *vt sep* add; **sich** (*dat*) **etw z~** get sth; grow ⟨*Bart*⟩
zuleide *adv* **jdm etwas z~ tun** hurt s.o.
zuletzt *adv* last; (*schließlich*) in the end; **nicht z~** not least
zuliebe *adv* **jdm/etw z~** for the sake of s.o./sth
zum *prep* = **zu dem; zum Spaß** for fun; **etw zum Lesen** sth to read
zumachen *v sep* ● *vt* close, shut; do up ⟨*Jacke*⟩; seal ⟨*Umschlag*⟩; turn off ⟨*Hahn*⟩; (*stillegen*) close down ● *vi* (*haben*) close, shut; (*stillgelegt werden*) close down
zumal *adv* especially ● *conj* especially since
zumeist *adv* for the most part
zumindest *adv* at least
zumutbar *a* reasonable
zumute *adv* **mir ist traurig/elend z~** I feel sad/wretched; **mir ist nicht danach z~** I don't feel like it
zumut|en *vt sep* **jdm etw z~en** ask *or* expect sth of s.o.; **sich** (*dat*) **zuviel z~en** overdo things. **Z~ung** *f* - imposition; **eine Z~ung sein** be unreasonable
zunächst *adv* first [of all]; (*anfangs*) at first; (*vorläufig*) for the moment ● *prep* (+ *dat*) nearest to
Zunahme *f* -,-n increase
Zuname *m* surname
zünd|en *vt/i* (*haben*) ignite; **z~ende Rede** rousing speech. **Z~er** *m* **-s,-** detonator, fuse. **Z~holz** *nt* match. **Z~kerze** *f* sparking-plug. **Z~schlüssel** *m* ignition key. **Z~schnur** *f* fuse. **Z~ung** *f* -,-en ignition
zunehmen† *vi sep* (*haben*) increase (**an** + *dat* in); ⟨*Mond:*⟩ wax; (*an Gewicht*) put on weight. **z~d** *a* increasing, *adv* -ly
Zuneigung *f* - affection
Zunft *f* -,**-̈e** guild
zünftig *a* proper, *adv* -ly
Zunge *f* -,-n tongue. **Z~nbrecher** *m* tongue-twister
zunichte *a* **z~ machen** wreck; **z~ werden** come to nothing
zunicken *vi sep* (*haben*) nod (*dat* to)
zunutze *a* **sich** (*dat*) **etw z~ machen** make use of sth; (*ausnutzen*) take advantage of sth
zuoberst *adv* right at the top
zuordnen *vt sep* assign (*dat* to)
zupfen *vt/i* (*haben*) pluck (**an** + *dat* at); pull out ⟨*Unkraut*⟩
zur *prep* = **zu der; zur Schule/Arbeit** to school/work; **zur Zeit** at present
zurechnungsfähig *a* of sound mind
zurecht|finden† **(sich)** *vr sep* find one's way. **z~kommen**† *vi sep* (*sein*) cope (**mit** with); (*rechtzeitig kommen*) be in time. **z~legen** *vt sep* put out ready; **sich** (*dat*) **eine Ausrede z~legen** have an excuse all ready. **z~machen** *vt sep* get ready; **sich z~machen** get ready. **z~weisen**† *vt sep* reprimand. **Z~weisung** *f* reprimand
zureden *vi sep* (*haben*) **jdm z~** try to persuade s.o.
zurichten *vt sep* prepare; (*beschädigen*) damage; (*verletzen*) injure
zuriegeln *vt sep* bolt
zurück *adv* back; **Berlin, hin und z~** return to Berlin. **z~behalten**† *vt sep* keep back; be left with ⟨*Narbe*⟩. **z~bekommen**† *vt sep* get back; **20 Pfennig z~bekommen** get 20 pfennigs change. **z~bleiben**† *vi sep* (*sein*) stay behind; (*nicht mithalten*) lag behind. **z~blicken** *vi sep* (*haben*) look back. **z~bringen**† *vt sep* bring back; (*wieder hinbringen*) take back. **z~erobern** *vt sep* recapture; (*fig*) regain. **z~erstatten** *vt sep* refund. **z~fahren**† *v sep* ● *vt* drive back ● *vi* (*sein*) return, go back; (*im Auto*) drive back; (*z~weichen*) recoil. **z~finden**† *vi sep* (*haben*) find one's way back. **z~führen** *v sep* ● *vt* take back; (*fig*) attribute (**auf** + *acc* to) ● *vi* (*haben*) lead back. **z~geben**† *vt sep* give back, return. **z~geblieben** *a* retarded. **z~gehen**† *vi sep* (*sein*) go back, return; (*abnehmen*) go down; **z~gehen auf** (+ *acc*) (*fig*) go back to
zurückgezogen *a* secluded. **Z~heit** *f* - seclusion
zurückhalt|en† *vt sep* hold back; (*abhalten*) stop; **sich z~en** restrain oneself. **z~end** *a* reserved. **Z~ung** *f* - reserve
zurück|kehren *vi sep* (*sein*) return. **z~kommen**† *vi sep* (*sein*) come back, return; (*ankommen*) get back; **z~kommen auf** (+ *acc*) (*fig*) come back to. **z~lassen**† *vt sep* leave behind; (*z~kehren lassen*) allow back. **z~legen** *vt sep* put back; (*reservieren*) keep; (*sparen*) put by; cover ⟨*Strecke*⟩. **z~lehnen (sich)** *vr sep* lean back. **z~liegen**† *vi sep* (*haben*)

be in the past; (*Sport*) be behind; **das liegt lange zurück** that was long ago. **z~melden (sich)** *vr sep* report back. **z~nehmen**† *vt sep* take back. **z~rufen**† *vt/i sep* (*haben*) call back. **z~scheuen** *vi sep* (*sein*) shrink (**vor** + *dat* from). **z~schicken** *vt sep* send back. **z~schlagen**† *v sep* ● *vi* (*haben*) hit back ● *vt* hit back; (*abwehren*) beat back; (*umschlagen*) turn back. **z~schneiden**† *vt sep* cut back. **z~schrecken**† *vi sep* (*sein*) shrink back, recoil; (*fig*) shrink (**vor** + *dat* from). **z~setzen** *v sep* ● *vt* put back; (*Auto*) reverse, back; (*herabsetzen*) reduce; (*fig*) neglect ● *vi* (*haben*) reverse, back. **z~stellen** *vt sep* put back; (*reservieren*) keep; (*fig*) put aside; (*aufschieben*) postpone. **z~stoßen**† *v sep* ● *vt* push back ● *vi* (*sein*) reverse, back. **z~treten**† *vi sep* (*sein*) step back; (*vom Amt*) resign; (*verzichten*) withdraw. **z~weichen**† *vi sep* (*sein*) draw back; (*z~schrecken*) shrink back. **z~weisen**† *vt sep* turn away; (*fig*) reject. **z~werfen**† *vt* throw back; (*reflektieren*) reflect. **z~zahlen** *vt sep* pay back. **z~ziehen**† *vt sep* draw back; (*fig*) withdraw; **sich z~ziehen** withdraw; (*vom Beruf*) retire; (*Mil*) retreat

Zuruf *m* shout. **z~en**† *vt sep* shout (*dat* to)

Zusage *f* **-,-n** acceptance; (*Versprechen*) promise. **z~n** *v sep* ● *vt* promise ● *vi* (*haben*) accept; **jdm z~n** appeal to s.o.

zusammen *adv* together; (*insgesamt*) altogether. **Z~arbeit** *f* co-operation. **z~arbeiten** *vi sep* (*haben*) co-operate. **z~bauen** *vt sep* assemble. **z~beißen**† *vt sep* **die Zähne z~beißen** clench/(*fig*) grit one's teeth. **z~bleiben**† *vi sep* (*sein*) stay together. **z~brechen**† *vi sep* (*sein*) collapse. **z~bringen**† *vt sep* bring together; (*beschaffen*) raise. **Z~bruch** *m* collapse; (*Nerven- & fig*) breakdown. **z~fahren**† *vi sep* (*sein*) collide; (*z~zucken*) start. **z~fallen**† *vi sep* (*sein*) collapse; (*zeitlich*) coincide. **z~falten** *vt sep* fold up. **z~fassen** *vt sep* summarize, sum up. **Z~fassung** *f* summary. **z~fügen** *vt sep* fit together. **z~führen** *vt sep* bring together. **z~gehören** *vi sep* (*haben*) belong together; (*z~passen*) go together. **z~gesetzt** *a* (*Gram*) compound. **z~halten**† *v sep* ● *vt* hold together; (*beisammenhalten*) keep together ● *vi* (*haben*) (*fig*) stick together. **Z~hang** *m* connection; (*Kontext*) context. **z~hängen**† *vi sep* (*haben*) be connected. **z~hanglos** *a* incoherent, *adv* -ly. **z~klappen** *v sep* ● *vt* fold up ● *vi* (*sein*) collapse. **z~kommen**† *vi sep* (*sein*) meet; (*sich sammeln*) accumulate. **Z~kunft** *f* **-,¨e** meeting. **z~laufen**† *vi sep* (*sein*) gather; ⟨*Flüssigkeit:*⟩ collect; ⟨*Linien:*⟩ converge. **z~leben** *vi sep* (*haben*) live together. **z~legen** *v sep* ● *vt* put together; (*z~falten*) fold up; (*vereinigen*) amalgamate; pool ⟨*Geld*⟩ ● *vi* (*haben*) club together. **z~nehmen**† *vt sep* gather up; summon up ⟨*Mut*⟩; collect ⟨*Gedanken*⟩; **sich z~nehmen** pull oneself together. **z~passen** *vi sep* (*haben*) go together, match; ⟨*Personen:*⟩ be well matched. **Z~prall** *m* collision. **z~prallen** *vi sep* (*sein*) collide. **z~rechnen** *vt sep* add up. **z~reißen**† **(sich)** *vr sep* (*fam*) pull oneself together. **z~rollen** *vt sep* roll up; **sich z~rollen** curl up. **z~schlagen**† *vt sep* smash up; (*prügeln*) beat up. **z~schließen**† **(sich)** *vr sep* join together; ⟨*Firmen:*⟩ merge. **Z~schluß** *m* union; (*Comm*) merger. **z~schreiben**† *vt sep* write as one word

zusammensein† *vi sep* (*sein*) be together. **Z~** *nt* **-s** get-together

zusammensetz|en *vt sep* put together; (*Techn*) assemble; **sich z~en** sit [down] together; (*bestehen*) be made up (**aus** from). **Z~ung** *f* **-,-en** composition; (*Techn*) assembly; (*Wort*) compound

zusammen|stellen *vt sep* put together; (*gestalten*) compile. **Z~stoß** *m* collision; (*fig*) clash. **z~stoßen**† *vi sep* (*sein*) collide. **z~treffen**† *vi sep* (*sein*) meet; (*zeitlich*) coincide. **Z~treffen** *nt* meeting; coincidence. **z~zählen** *vt sep* add up. **z~ziehen**† *v sep* ● *vt* draw together; (*addieren*) add up; (*konzentrieren*) mass; **sich z~ziehen** contract; ⟨*Gewitter:*⟩ gather ● *vi* (*sein*) move in together; move in (**mit** with). **z~zucken** *vi sep* (*sein*) start; (*vor Schmerz*) wince

Zusatz *m* addition; (*Jur*) rider; (*Lebensmittel-*) additive. **Z~gerät** *nt*

attachment. **zusätzlich** *a* additional ● *adv* in addition

zuschanden *adv* **z~ machen** ruin, wreck; **z~ fahren** wreck

zuschau|en *vi sep* (*haben*) watch. **Z~er(in)** *m* **-s,-** (*f* **-,-nen**) spectator; (*TV*) viewer. **Z~erraum** *m* auditorium

zuschicken *vt sep* send (*dat* to)

Zuschlag *m* surcharge; (*D-Zug-*) supplement. **z~en**† *v sep* ● *vt* shut; (*heftig*) slam; (*bei Auktion*) knock down (**jdm** to s.o.) ● *vi* (*haben*) hit out; ⟨*Feind:*⟩ strike ● *vi* (*sein*) slam shut. **z~pflichtig** *a* for which a supplement is payable

zuschließen† *v sep* ● *vt* lock ● *vi* (*haben*) lock up

zuschneiden† *vt sep* cut out; cut to size ⟨*Holz*⟩

zuschreiben† *vt sep* attribute (*dat* to); **jdm die Schuld z~** blame s.o.

Zuschrift *f* letter; (*auf Annonce*) reply

zuschulden *adv* **sich** (*dat*) **etwas z~ kommen lassen** do wrong

Zuschuß *m* contribution; (*staatlich*) subsidy

zusehen† *vi sep* (*haben*) watch; **z~, daß** see [to it] that

zusehends *adv* visibly

zusein† *vi sep* (*sein*) be closed

zusenden† *vt sep* send (*dat* to)

zusetzen *v sep* ● *vt* add; (*einbüßen*) lose ● *vi* (*haben*) **jdm z~** pester s.o.; ⟨*Hitze:*⟩ take it out of s.o.

zusicher|n *vt sep* promise. **Z~ung** *f* promise

Zuspätkommende(r) *m*/*f* latecomer

zuspielen *vt sep* (*Sport*) pass

zuspitzen (sich) *vr sep* (*fig*) become critical

zusprechen† *v sep* ● *vt* award (**jdm** s.o.); **jdm Trost/Mut z~** comfort/encourage s.o. ● *vi* (*haben*) **dem Essen z~** eat heartily

Zustand *m* condition, state

zustande *adv* **z~ bringen/kommen** bring/come about

zuständig *a* competent; (*verantwortlich*) responsible. **Z~keit** *f* - competence; responsibility

zustehen† *vi sep* (*haben*) **jdm z~** be s.o.'s right; ⟨*Urlaub:*⟩ be due to s.o.; **es steht ihm nicht zu** he is not entitled to it; (*gebührt*) it is not for him (**zu** to)

zusteigen† *vi sep* (*sein*) get on; **noch jemand zugestiegen?** tickets please; (*im Bus*) any more fares please?

zustell|en *vt sep* block; (*bringen*) deliver. **Z~ung** *f* delivery

zusteuern *v sep* ● *vi* (*sein*) head (**auf** + *acc* for) ● *vt* contribute

zustimm|en *vi sep* (*haben*) agree; (*billigen*) approve (*dat* of). **Z~ung** *f* consent; approval

zustoßen† *vi sep* (*sein*) happen (*dat* to)

Zustrom *m* influx

zutage *adv* **z~ treten** *od* **kommen/bringen** come/bring to light

Zutat *f* (*Culin*) ingredient

zuteil|en *vt sep* allocate; assign ⟨*Aufgabe*⟩. **Z~ung** *f* allocation

zutiefst *adv* deeply

zutragen† *vt sep* carry/(*fig*) report (*dat* to); **sich z~** happen

zutrau|en *vt sep* **jdm etw z~** believe s.o. capable of sth. **Z~en** *nt* **-s** confidence. **z~lich** *a* trusting, *adv* -ly; ⟨*Tier*⟩ friendly

zutreffen† *vi sep* (*haben*) be correct; **z~ auf** (+ *acc*) apply to. **z~d** *a* applicable (**auf** + *acc* to); (*richtig*) correct, *adv* -ly

zutrinken† *vi sep* (*haben*) **jdm z~** drink to s.o.

Zutritt *m* admittance

zuunterst *adv* right at the bottom

zuverlässig *a* reliable, *adv* -bly. **Z~keit** *f* - reliability

Zuversicht *f* - confidence. **z~lich** *a* confident, *adv* -ly

zuviel *pron & adv* too much; (*pl*) too many

zuvor *adv* before; (*erst*) first

zuvorkommen† *vi sep* (*sein*) (+ *dat*) anticipate; **jdm z~** beat s.o. to it. **z~d** *a* obliging, *adv* -ly

Zuwachs *m* **-es** increase

zuwege *adv* **z~ bringen** achieve

zuweilen *adv* now and then

zuweisen† *vt sep* assign; (*zuteilen*) allocate

zuwend|en† *vt sep* turn (*dat* to); **sich z~en** (+ *dat*) turn to; (*fig*) devote oneself to. **Z~ung** *f* donation; (*Fürsorge*) care

zuwenig *pron & adv* too little; (*pl*) too few

zuwerfen† *vt sep* slam ⟨*Tür*⟩; **jdm etw z~** throw s.o. sth; give s.o. ⟨*Blick, Lächeln*⟩

zuwider *adv* **jdm z~ sein** be repugnant to s.o. ● *prep* (+ *dat*) contrary to. **z~handeln** *vi sep* (*haben*) contravene (**etw** *dat* sth)

zuzahlen *vt sep* pay extra

zuziehen† *v sep* ● *vt* pull tight; draw ⟨*Vorhänge*⟩; (*hinzu-*) call in; **sich** (*dat*) **etw z~** contract ⟨*Krankheit*⟩; sustain ⟨*Verletzung*⟩; incur ⟨*Zorn*⟩ ● *vi* (*sein*) move into the area

zuzüglich *prep* (+*gen*) plus

Zwang *m* **-[e]s,-̈e** compulsion; (*Gewalt*) force; (*Verpflichtung*) obligation

zwängen *vt* squeeze

zwanglos *a* informal, *adv* -ly; ⟨*Benehmen*⟩ free and easy. **Z~igkeit** *f* - informality

Zwangs|jacke *f* straitjacket. **Z~lage** *f* predicament. **z~läufig** *a* inevitable, *adv* -bly

zwanzig *inv a* twenty. **z~ste(r,s)** *a* twentieth

zwar *adv* admittedly; **und z~** to be precise

Zweck *m* **-[e]s,-e** purpose; (*Sinn*) point; **es hat keinen Z~** there is no point. **z~dienlich** *a* appropriate; ⟨*Information*⟩ relevant. **z~los** *a* pointless. **z~mäßig** *a* suitable, *adv* -bly; (*praktisch*) functional, *adv* -ly. **z~s** *prep* (+*gen*) for the purpose of

zwei *inv a*, **Z~** *f* **-,-en** two; (*Sch*) ≈ B. **Z~bettzimmer** *nt* twinbedded room

zweideutig *a* ambiguous, *adv* -ly; (*schlüpfrig*) suggestive, *adv* -ly. **Z~keit** *f* **-,-en** ambiguity

zwei|erlei *inv a* two kinds of ● *pron* two things. **z~fach** *a* double

Zweifel *m* **-s,-** doubt. **z~haft** *a* doubtful; (*fragwürdig*) dubious. **z~los** *adv* undoubtedly. **z~n** *vi* (*haben*) doubt (**an etw** *dat* sth)

Zweig *m* **-[e]s,-e** branch. **Z~geschäft** *nt* branch. **Z~stelle** *f* branch [office]

Zwei|kampf *m* duel. **z~mal** *adv* twice. **z~reihig** *a* double-breasted. **z~sprachig** *a* bilingual

zweit *adv* **zu z~** in twos; **wir waren zu z~** there were two of us. **z~beste(r,s)** *a* second-best. **z~e(r,s)** *a* second

zwei|teilig *a* two-piece; ⟨*Film, Programm*⟩ two-part. **z~tens** *adv* secondly

zweitklassig *a* second-class

Zwerchfell *nt* diaphragm

Zwerg *m* **-[e]s,-e** dwarf

Zwetsch[g]e *f* **-,-n** quetsche

Zwickel *m* **-s,-** gusset

zwicken *vt/i* (*haben*) pinch

Zwieback *m* **-[e]s,-̈e** rusk

Zwiebel *f* **-,-n** onion; (*Blumen-*) bulb

Zwielicht *nt* half-light; (*Dämmerlicht*) twilight. **z~ig** *a* shady

Zwie|spalt *m* conflict. **z~spältig** *a* conflicting. **Z~tracht** *f* - discord

Zwilling *m* **-s,-e** twin; **Z~e** (*Astr*) Gemini

zwingen† *vt* force; **sich z~** force oneself. **z~d** *a* compelling

Zwinger *m* **-s,-** run; (*Zucht-*) kennels *pl*

zwinkern *vi* (*haben*) blink; (*als Zeichen*) wink

Zwirn *m* **-[e]s** button thread

zwischen *prep* (+*dat/acc*) between; (*unter*) among[st]. **Z~bemerkung** *f* interjection. **Z~ding** *nt* (*fam*) cross. **z~durch** *adv* in between; (*in der Z~zeit*) in the meantime; (*ab und zu*) now and again. **Z~fall** *m* incident. **Z~händler** *m* middleman. **Z~landung** *f* stop-over. **Z~raum** *m* gap, space. **Z~ruf** *m* interjection. **Z~stecker** *m* adaptor. **Z~wand** *f* partition. **Z~zeit** *f* **in der Z~zeit** in the meantime

Zwist *m* **-[e]s,-e** discord; (*Streit*) feud. **Z~igkeiten** *fpl* quarrels

zwitschern *vi* (*haben*) chirp

zwo *inv a* two

zwölf *inv a* twelve. **z~te(r,s)** *a* twelfth

zwote(r,s) *a* second

Zyklus *m* **-,-klen** cycle

Zylind|er *m* **-s,-** cylinder; (*Hut*) top hat. **z~risch** *a* cylindrical

Zyn|iker *m* **-s,-** cynic. **z~isch** *a* cynical, *adv* -ly. **Z~ismus** *m* - cynicism

Zypern *nt* **-s** Cyprus

Zypresse *f* **-,-n** cypress

Zyste /ˈt͡sʏstə/ *f* **-,-n** cyst

z.Zt. *abbr* (**zur Zeit**) at present

ENGLISH–GERMAN
ENGLISCH–DEUTSCH

A

a /ə, *betont* eɪ/ (*vor einem Vokal* **an**) *indef art* ein(e); (*each*) pro; **not a** kein(e)

aback /əˈbæk/ *adv* **be taken ~** verblüfft sein

abandon /əˈbændən/ *vt* verlassen; (*give up*) aufgeben ● *n* Hingabe *f*. **~ed** *a* verlassen; ⟨*behaviour*⟩ hemmungslos

abase /əˈbeɪs/ *vt* demütigen

abashed /əˈbæʃt/ *a* beschämt, verlegen

abate /əˈbeɪt/ *vi* nachlassen

abattoir /ˈæbətwɑː(r)/ *n* Schlachthof *m*

abb|ey /ˈæbɪ/ *n* Abtei *f*. **~ot** *n* Abt *m*

abbreviat|e /əˈbriːvɪeɪt/ *vt* abkürzen. **~ion** /-ˈeɪʃn/ *n* Abkürzung *f*

abdicat|e /ˈæbdɪkeɪt/ *vi* abdanken. **~ion** /-ˈkeɪʃn/ *n* Abdankung *f*

abdom|en /ˈæbdəmən/ *n* Unterleib *m*. **~inal** /-ˈdɒmɪnl/ *a* Unterleibs-

abduct /əbˈdʌkt/ *vt* entführen. **~ion** /-ʌkʃn/ *n* Entführung *f*. **~or** *n* Entführer *m*

aberration /æbəˈreɪʃn/ *n* Abweichung *f*; (*mental*) Verwirrung *f*

abet /əˈbet/ *vt* (*pt/pp* **abetted) aid and ~** (*Jur*) Beihilfe leisten (+ *dat*)

abeyance /əˈbeɪəns/ *n* **in ~** [zeitweilig] außer Kraft; **fall into ~** außer Kraft kommen

abhor /əbˈhɔː(r)/ *vt* (*pt/pp* **abhorred**) verabscheuen. **~rence** /-ˈhɒrəns/ *n* Abscheu *f*. **~rent** /-ˈhɒrənt/ *a* abscheulich

abid|e /əˈbaɪd/ *vt* (*pt/pp* **abided**) (*tolerate*) aushalten; ausstehen ⟨*person*⟩ ● *vi* **~e by** sich halten an (+ *acc*). **~ing** *a* bleibend

ability /əˈbɪlətɪ/ *n* Fähigkeit *f*; (*talent*) Begabung *f*

abject /ˈæbdʒekt/ *a* erbärmlich; (*humble*) demütig

ablaze /əˈbleɪz/ *a* in Flammen; **be ~** in Flammen stehen

able /ˈeɪbl/ *a* (**-r, -st**) fähig; **be ~ to do sth** etw tun können. **~ˈbodied** *a* körperlich gesund; (*Mil*) tauglich

ably /ˈeɪblɪ/ *adv* gekonnt

abnormal /æbˈnɔːml/ *a* anormal; (*Med*) abnorm. **~ity** /-ˈmælətɪ/ *n* Abnormität *f*. **~ly** *adv* ungewöhnlich

aboard /əˈbɔːd/ *adv & prep* an Bord (+ *gen*)

abode /əˈbəʊd/ *n* Wohnsitz *m*

abol|ish /əˈbɒlɪʃ/ *vt* abschaffen. **~ition** /æbəˈlɪʃn/ *n* Abschaffung *f*

abominable /əˈbɒmɪnəbl/ *a*, **-bly** *adv* abscheulich

abominate /əˈbɒmɪneɪt/ *vt* verabscheuen

aborigines /æbəˈrɪdʒəniːz/ *npl* Ureinwohner *pl*

abort /əˈbɔːt/ *vt* abtreiben. **~ion** /-ɔːʃn/ *n* Abtreibung *f*; **have an ~ion** eine Abtreibung vornehmen lassen. **~ive** /-tɪv/ *a* ⟨*attempt*⟩ vergeblich

abound /əˈbaʊnd/ *vi* reichlich vorhanden sein; **~ in** reich sein an (+ *dat*)

about /əˈbaʊt/ *adv* umher, herum; (*approximately*) ungefähr; **be ~** (*in circulation*) umgehen; (*in existence*) vorhanden sein; **be up and ~** auf den Beinen sein; **be ~ to do sth** im Begriff sein, etw zu tun; **there are a lot ~** es gibt viele; **there was no one ~** es war kein Mensch da; **run/play ~** herumlaufen/-spielen ● *prep* um (+ *acc*) [... herum]; (*concerning*) über (+ *acc*); **what is it ~?** worum geht es? ⟨*book:*⟩ wovon handelt es? **I know nothing ~ it** ich weiß nichts davon; **talk/know ~** reden/wissen von

about: ~-ˈface *n*, **-ˈturn** *n* Kehrtwendung *f*

above /əˈbʌv/ *adv* oben ● *prep* über (+ *dat/acc*); **~ all** vor allem

above: ~-ˈboard *a* legal. **~mentioned** *a* obenerwähnt

abrasion /əˈbreɪʒn/ *n* Schürfwunde *f*

abrasive /ə'breɪsɪv/ *a* Scheuer-; ⟨*remark*⟩ verletzend • *n* Scheuermittel *nt*; (*Techn*) Schleifmittel *nt*
abreast /ə'brest/ *adv* nebeneinander; **keep ~ of** Schritt halten mit
abridge /ə'brɪdʒ/ *vt* kürzen
abroad /ə'brɔ:d/ *adv* im Ausland; **go ~** ins Ausland fahren
abrupt /ə'brʌpt/ *a*, **-ly** *adv* abrupt; (*sudden*) plötzlich; (*curt*) schroff
abscess /'æbsɪs/ *n* Abszeß *m*
abscond /əb'skɒnd/ *vi* entfliehen
absence /'æbsəns/ *n* Abwesenheit *f*
absent¹ /'æbsənt/ *a*, **-ly** *adv* abwesend; **be ~** fehlen
absent² /æb'sent/ *vt* **~ oneself** fernbleiben
absentee /æbsən'ti:/ *n* Abwesende(r) *m/f*
absent-minded /æbsənt'maɪndɪd/ *a*, **-ly** *adv* geistesabwesend; (*forgetful*) zerstreut
absolute /'æbsəlu:t/ *a*, **-ly** *adv* absolut
absolution /æbsə'lu:ʃn/ *n* Absolution *f*
absolve /əb'zɒlv/ *vt* lossprechen
absorb /əb'sɔ:b/ *vt* absorbieren, aufsaugen; **~ed in** vertieft in (+ *acc*). **~ent** /-ənt/ *a* saugfähig
absorption /əb'sɔ:pʃn/ *n* Absorption *f*
abstain /əb'steɪn/ *vi* sich enthalten (**from** *gen*); **~ from voting** sich der Stimme enthalten
abstemious /əb'sti:mɪəs/ *a* enthaltsam
abstention /əb'stenʃn/ *n* (*Pol*) [Stimm]enthaltung *f*
abstinence /'æbstɪnəns/ *n* Enthaltsamkeit *f*
abstract /'æbstrækt/ *a* abstrakt • *n* (*summary*) Abriß *m*
absurd /əb'sɜ:d/ *a*, **-ly** *adv* absurd. **~ity** *n* Absurdität *f*
abundan|ce /ə'bʌndəns/ *n* Fülle *f* (**of** an + *dat*). **~t** *a* reichlich
abuse¹ /ə'bju:z/ *vt* mißbrauchen; (*insult*) beschimpfen
abus|e² /ə'bju:s/ *n* Mißbrauch *m*; (*insults*) Beschimpfungen *pl*. **~ive** /-ɪv/ ausfallend
abut /ə'bʌt/ *vi* (*pt/pp* **abutted**) angrenzen (**on to** an + *acc*)
abysmal /ə'bɪzml/ *a* (*fam*) katastrophal
abyss /ə'bɪs/ *n* Abgrund *m*
academic /ækə'demɪk/ *a*, **-ally** *adv* akademisch • *n* Akademiker(in) *m*(*f*)
academy /ə'kædəmɪ/ *n* Akademie *f*
accede /ək'si:d/ *vi* **~ to** zustimmen (+ *dat*); besteigen ⟨*throne*⟩
accelerat|e /ək'seləreɪt/ *vt* beschleunigen • *vi* die Geschwindigkeit erhöhen. **~ion** /-'reɪʃn/ *n* Beschleunigung *f*. **~or** *n* (*Auto*) Gaspedal *nt*
accent¹ /'æksənt/ *n* Akzent *m*
accent² /æk'sent/ *vt* betonen
accentuate /ək'sentjʊeɪt/ *vt* betonen
accept /ək'sept/ *vt* annehmen; (*fig*) akzeptieren • *vi* zusagen. **~able** /-əbl/ *a* annehmbar. **~ance** *n* Annahme *f*; (*of invitation*) Zusage *f*
access /'ækses/ *n* Zugang *m*; (*road*) Zufahrt *f*. **~ible** /ək'sesəbl/ *a* zugänglich
accession /ək'seʃn/ *n* (*to throne*) Thronbesteigung *f*
accessor|y /ək'sesərɪ/ *n* (*Jur*) Mitschuldige(r) *m/f*; **~ies** *pl* (*fashion*) Accessoires *pl*; (*Techn*) Zubehör *nt*
accident /'æksɪdənt/ *n* Unfall *m*; (*chance*) Zufall *m*; **by ~** zufällig; (*unintentionally*) versehentlich. **~al** /-'dentl/ *a*, **-ly** *adv* zufällig; (*unintentional*) versehentlich
acclaim /ə'kleɪm/ *n* Beifall *m* • *vt* feiern (**as** als)
acclimate /'æklɪmeɪt/ *vt* (*Amer*) = **acclimatize**
acclimatize /ə'klaɪmətaɪz/ *vt* **become ~d** sich akklimatisieren
accolade /'ækəleɪd/ *n* Auszeichnung *f*
accommodat|e /ə'kɒmədeɪt/ *vt* unterbringen; (*oblige*) entgegenkommen (+ *dat*). **~ing** *a* entgegenkommend. **~ion** /-'deɪʃn/ *n* (*rooms*) Unterkunft *f*
accompan|iment /ə'kʌmpənɪmənt/ *n* Begleitung *f*. **~ist** *n* (*Mus*) Begleiter(in) *m*(*f*)
accompany /ə'kʌmpənɪ/ *vt* (*pt/pp* **-ied**) begleiten
accomplice /ə'kʌmplɪs/ *n* Komplize/-zin *m/f*
accomplish /ə'kʌmplɪʃ/ *vt* erfüllen ⟨*task*⟩; (*achieve*) erreichen. **~ed** *a* fähig. **~ment** *n* Fertigkeit *f*; (*achievement*) Leistung *f*
accord /ə'kɔ:d/ *n* (*treaty*) Abkommen *nt*; **of one ~** einmütig; **of one's own ~** aus eigenem Antrieb • *vt* gewähren. **~ance** *n* **in ~ance with** entsprechend (+ *dat*)
according /ə'kɔ:dɪŋ/ *adv* **~ to** nach (+ *dat*). **~ly** *adv* entsprechend
accordion /ə'kɔ:dɪən/ *n* Akkordeon *nt*
accost /ə'kɒst/ *vt* ansprechen

account /ə'kaʊnt/ *n* Konto *nt*; (*bill*) Rechnung *f*; (*description*) Darstellung *f*; (*report*) Bericht *m*; **~s** *pl* (*Comm*) Bücher *pl*; **on ~ of** wegen (+ *gen*); **on no ~** auf keinen Fall; **on this ~** deshalb; **on my ~** meinetwegen; **of no ~** ohne Bedeutung; **take into ~** in Betracht ziehen, berücksichtigen ● *vi* **~ for** Rechenschaft ablegen für; (*explain*) erklären

accountant /ə'kaʊntənt/ *n* Buchhalter(in) *m*(*f*); (*chartered*) Wirtschaftsprüfer *m*; (*for tax*) Steuerberater *m*

accoutrements /ə'ku:trəmənts/ *npl* Ausrüstung *f*

accredited /ə'kredɪtɪd/ *a* akkreditiert

accrue /ə'kru:/ *vi* sich ansammeln

accumulat|e /ə'kju:mjʊleɪt/ *vt* ansammeln, anhäufen ● *vi* sich ansammeln, sich anhäufen. **~ion** /-'leɪʃn/ *n* Ansammlung *f*, Anhäufung *f*. **~or** *n* (*Electr*) Akkumulator *m*

accura|cy /'ækjʊrəsɪ/ *n* Genauigkeit *f*. **~te** /-rət/ *a*, **-ly** *adv* genau

accusation /ækju:'zeɪʃn/ *n* Anklage *f*

accusative /ə'kju:zətɪv/ *a* & *n* **~ [case]** (*Gram*) Akkusativ *m*

accuse /ə'kju:z/ *vt* (*Jur*) anklagen (**of** *gen*); **~ s.o. of doing sth** jdn beschuldigen, etw getan zu haben. **~d** *n* **the ~d** der/die Angeklagte

accustom /ə'kʌstəm/ *vt* gewöhnen (**to** an + *dat*); **grow** *or* **get ~ed to** sich gewöhnen an (+ *acc*). **~ed** *a* gewohnt

ace /eɪs/ *n* (*Cards, Sport*) As *nt*

ache /eɪk/ *n* Schmerzen *pl* ● *vi* weh tun, schmerzen

achieve /ə'tʃi:v/ *vt* leisten; (*gain*) erzielen; (*reach*) erreichen. **~ment** *n* (*feat*) Leistung *f*

acid /'æsɪd/ *a* sauer; (*fig*) beißend ● *n* Säure *f*. **~ity** /ə'sɪdətɪ/ *n* Säure *f*. **~ 'rain** *n* saurer Regen *m*

acknowledge /ək'nɒlɪdʒ/ *vt* anerkennen; (*admit*) zugeben; erwidern ⟨*greeting*⟩; **~ receipt of** den Empfang bestätigen (+ *gen*). **~ment** *n* Anerkennung *f*; (*of letter*) Empfangsbestätigung *f*

acne /'æknɪ/ *n* Akne *f*

acorn /'eɪkɔ:n/ *n* Eichel *f*

acoustic /ə'ku:stɪk/ *a*, **-ally** *adv* akustisch. **~s** *npl* Akustik *f*

acquaint /ə'kweɪnt/ *vt* **~ s.o. with** jdn bekannt machen mit; **be ~ed with** kennen; vertraut sein mit ⟨*fact*⟩. **~ance** *n* Bekanntschaft *f*; (*person*) Bekannte(r) *m*/*f*; **make s.o.'s ~ance** jdn kennenlernen

acquiesce /ækwɪ'es/ *vi* einwilligen (**to** in + *acc*). **~nce** *n* Einwilligung *f*

acquire /ə'kwaɪə(r)/ *vt* erwerben

acquisit|ion /ækwɪ'zɪʃn/ *n* Erwerb *m*; (*thing*) Erwerbung *f*. **~ive** /ə'kwɪzətɪv/ *a* habgierig

acquit /ə'kwɪt/ *vt* (*pt*/*pp* **acquitted**) freisprechen; **~ oneself well** seiner Aufgabe gerecht werden. **~tal** *n* Freispruch *m*

acre /'eɪkə(r)/ *n* ≈ Morgen *m*

acrid /'ækrɪd/ *a* scharf

acrimon|ious /ækrɪ'məʊnɪəs/ *a* bitter. **~y** /'ækrɪmənɪ/ *n* Bitterkeit *f*

acrobat /'ækrəbæt/ *n* Akrobat(in) *m*(*f*). **~ic** /-'bætɪk/ *a* akrobatisch

across /ə'krɒs/ *adv* hinüber/herüber; (*wide*) breit; (*not lengthwise*) quer; (*in crossword*) waagerecht; **come ~ sth** auf etw (*acc*) stoßen; **go ~** hinübergehen; **bring ~** herüberbringen ● *prep* über (+ *acc*); (*crosswise*) quer über (+ *acc*/*dat*); (*on the other side of*) auf der anderen Seite (+ *gen*)

act /ækt/ *n* Tat *f*; (*action*) Handlung *f*; (*law*) Gesetz *nt*; (*Theat*) Akt *m*; (*item*) Nummer *f*; **put on an ~** (*fam*) sich verstellen ● *vi* handeln; (*behave*) sich verhalten; (*Theat*) spielen; (*pretend*) sich verstellen; **~ as** fungieren als ● *vt* spielen ⟨*role*⟩. **~ing** *a* (*deputy*) stellvertretend ● *n* (*Theat*) Schauspielerei *f*. **~ing profession** *n* Schauspielerberuf *m*

action /'ækʃn/ *n* Handlung *f*; (*deed*) Tat *f*; (*Mil*) Einsatz *m*; (*Jur*) Klage *f*; (*effect*) Wirkung *f*; (*Techn*) Mechanismus *m*; **out of ~** ⟨*machine:*⟩ außer Betrieb; **take ~** handeln; **killed in ~** gefallen. **~ 'replay** *n* (*TV*) Wiederholung *f*

activate /'æktɪveɪt/ *vt* betätigen; (*Chem, Phys*) aktivieren

activ|e /'æktɪv/ *a*, **-ly** *adv* aktiv; **on ~e service** im Einsatz. **~ity** /-'tɪvətɪ/ *n* Aktivität *f*

act|or /'æktə(r)/ *n* Schauspieler *m*. **~ress** *n* Schauspielerin *f*

actual /'æktʃʊəl/ *a*, **-ly** *adv* eigentlich; (*real*) tatsächlich. **~ity** /-'ælətɪ/ *n* Wirklichkeit *f*

acumen /'ækjʊmən/ *n* Scharfsinn *m*

acupuncture /'ækjʊ-/ *n* Akupunktur *f*

acute /ə'kju:t/ *a* scharf; ⟨*angle*⟩ spitz; ⟨*illness*⟩ akut. **~ly** *adv* sehr

ad /æd/ *n* (*fam*) = **advertisement**

AD *abbr* (**Anno Domini**) n.Chr.

adamant /'ædəmənt/ *a* **be ~ that** darauf bestehen, daß

adapt /ə'dæpt/ *vt* anpassen; bearbeiten ‹*play*› ● *vi* sich anpassen. **~ability** /-ə'bɪlətɪ/ *n* Anpassungsfähigkeit *f*. **~able** /-əbl/ *a* anpassungsfähig

adaptation /ædæp'teɪʃn/ *n* (*Theat*) Bearbeitung *f*

adapter, adaptor /ə'dæptə(r)/ *n* (*Techn*) Adapter *m*; (*Electr*) (*two-way*) Doppelstecker *m*

add /æd/ *vt* hinzufügen; (*Math*) addieren ● *vi* zusammenzählen, addieren; **~ to** hinzufügen zu; (*fig: increase*) steigern; (*compound*) verschlimmern. **~ up** *vt* zusammenzählen ‹*figures*› ● *vi* zusammenzählen, addieren; **~ up to** machen; **it doesn't ~ up** (*fig*) da stimmt etwas nicht

adder /'ædə(r)/ *n* Kreuzotter *f*

addict /'ædɪkt/ *n* Süchtige(r) *m*/*f*

addict|ed /ə'dɪktɪd/ *a* süchtig; **~ed to drugs** drogensüchtig. **~ion** /-ɪkʃn/ *n* Sucht *f*. **~ive** /-ɪv/ *a* **be ~ive** zur Süchtigkeit führen

addition /ə'dɪʃn/ *n* Hinzufügung *f*; (*Math*) Addition *f*; (*thing added*) Ergänzung *f*; **in ~** zusätzlich. **~al** *a*, **-ly** *adv* zusätzlich

additive /'ædɪtɪv/ *n* Zusatz *m*

address /ə'dres/ *n* Adresse *f*, Anschrift *f*; (*speech*) Ansprache *f*; **form of ~** Anrede *f* ● *vt* adressieren (**to** an + *acc*); (*speak to*) anreden ‹*person*›; sprechen vor (+ *dat*) ‹*meeting*›. **~ee** /ædre'si:/ *n* Empfänger *m*

adenoids /'ædənɔɪdz/ *npl* [Rachen]-polypen *pl*

adept /'ædept/ *a* geschickt (**at** in + *dat*)

adequate /'ædɪkwət/ *a*, **-ly** *adv* ausreichend

adhere /əd'hɪə(r)/ *vi* kleben/(*fig*) festhalten (**to** an + *dat*). **~nce** *n* Festhalten *nt*

adhesive /əd'hi:sɪv/ *a* klebend ● *n* Klebstoff *m*

adjacent /ə'dʒeɪsnt/ *a* angrenzend

adjective /'ædʒɪktɪv/ *n* Adjektiv *nt*

adjoin /ə'dʒɔɪn/ *vt* angrenzen an (+ *acc*). **~ing** *a* angrenzend

adjourn /ə'dʒɜ:n/ *vt* vertagen (**until** auf + *acc*) ● *vi* sich vertagen. **~ment** *n* Vertagung *f*

adjudicate /ə'dʒu:dɪkeɪt/ *vi* entscheiden; (*in competition*) Preisrichter sein

adjust /ə'dʒʌst/ *vt* einstellen; (*alter*) verstellen ● *vi* sich anpassen (**to** *dat*). **~able** /-əbl/ *a* verstellbar. **~ment** *n* Einstellung *f*; Anpassung *f*

ad lib /æd'lɪb/ *adv* aus dem Stegreif ● *vi* (*pt*/*pp* **ad libbed**) (*fam*) improvisieren

administer /əd'mɪnɪstə(r)/ *vt* verwalten; verabreichen ‹*medicine*›

administrat|ion /ədmɪnɪ'streɪʃn/ *n* Verwaltung *f*; (*Pol*) Regierung *f*. **~or** /əd'mɪnɪstreɪtə(r)/ *n* Verwaltungsbeamte(r) *m*/-beamtin *f*

admirable /'ædmərəbl/ *a* bewundernswert

admiral /'ædmərəl/ *n* Admiral *m*

admiration /ædmə'reɪʃn/ *n* Bewunderung *f*

admire /əd'maɪə(r)/ *vt* bewundern. **~r** *n* Verehrer(in) *m*(*f*)

admissible /əd'mɪsəbl/ *a* zulässig

admission /əd'mɪʃn/ *n* Eingeständnis *nt*; (*entry*) Eintritt *m*

admit /əd'mɪt/ *vt* (*pt*/*pp* **admitted**) (*let in*) hereinlassen; (*acknowledge*) zugeben; **~ to sth** etw zugeben. **~tance** *n* Eintritt *m*. **~tedly** *adv* zugegebenermaßen

admoni|sh /əd'mɒnɪʃ/ *vt* ermahnen. **~tion** /ædmə'nɪʃn/ *n* Ermahnung *f*

ado /ə'du:/ *n* **without more ~** ohne weiteres

adolescen|ce /ædə'lesns/ *n* Jugend *f*, Pubertät *f*. **~t** *a* Jugend-; ‹*boy, girl*› halbwüchsig ● *n* Jugendliche(r) *m*/*f*

adopt /ə'dɒpt/ *vt* adoptieren; ergreifen ‹*measure*›; (*Pol*) annehmen ‹*candidate*›. **~ion** /-ɒpʃn/ *n* Adoption *f*. **~ive** /-ɪv/ *a* Adoptiv-

ador|able /ə'dɔ:rəbl/ *a* bezaubernd. **~ation** /ædə'reɪʃn/ *n* Anbetung *f*

adore /ə'dɔ:(r)/ *vt* (*worship*) anbeten; (*fam: like*) lieben

adorn /ə'dɔ:n/ *vt* schmücken. **~ment** *n* Schmuck *m*

adrenalin /ə'drenəlɪn/ *n* Adrenalin *nt*

Adriatic /eɪdrɪ'ætɪk/ *a* & *n* **~ [Sea]** Adria *f*

adrift /ə'drɪft/ *a* **be ~** treiben; **come ~** sich losreißen

adroit /ə'drɔɪt/ *a*, **-ly** *adv* gewandt, geschickt

adulation /ædjʊ'leɪʃn/ *n* Schwärmerei *f*

adult /'ædʌlt/ *n* Erwachsene(r) *m*/*f*

adulterate /ə'dʌltəreɪt/ *vt* verfälschen; panschen ⟨*wine*⟩

adultery /ə'dʌltərɪ/ *n* Ehebruch *m*

advance /əd'vɑ:ns/ *n* Fortschritt *m*; (*Mil*) Vorrücken *nt*; (*payment*) Vorschuß *m*; **in ~** im voraus • *vi* vorankommen; (*Mil*) vorrücken; (*make progress*) Fortschritte machen • *vt* fördern ⟨*cause*⟩; vorbringen ⟨*idea*⟩; vorschießen ⟨*money*⟩. **~ booking** *n* Kartenvorverkauf *m*. **~d** *a* fortgeschritten; (*progressive*) fortschrittlich. **~ment** *n* Förderung *f*; (*promotion*) Beförderung *f*

advantage /əd'vɑ:ntɪdʒ/ *n* Vorteil *m*; **take ~ of** ausnutzen. **~ous** /ædvən'teɪdʒəs/ *a* vorteilhaft

advent /'ædvent/ *n* Ankunft *f*; **A~** (*season*) Advent *m*

adventur|e /əd'ventʃə(r)/ *n* Abenteuer *nt*. **~er** *n* Abenteurer *m*. **~ous** /-rəs/ *a* abenteuerlich; ⟨*person*⟩ abenteuerlustig

adverb /'ædvɜ:b/ *n* Adverb *nt*

adversary /'ædvəsərɪ/ *n* Widersacher *m*

advers|e /'ædvɜ:s/ *a* ungünstig. **~ity** /əd'vɜ:sətɪ/ *n* Not *f*

advert /'ædvɜ:t/ *n* (*fam*) = **advertisement**

advertise /'ædvətaɪz/ *vt* Reklame machen für; (*by small ad*) inserieren • *vi* Reklame machen; inserieren; **~ for** per Anzeige suchen

advertisement /əd'vɜ:tɪsmənt/ *n* Anzeige *f*; (*publicity*) Reklame *f*; (*small ad*) Inserat *nt*

advertis|er /'ædvətaɪzə(r)/ *n* Inserent *m*. **~ing** *n* Werbung *f* • *attrib* Werbe-

advice /əd'vaɪs/ *n* Rat *m*. **~ note** *n* Benachrichtigung *f*

advisable /əd'vaɪzəbl/ *a* ratsam

advis|e /əd'vaɪz/ *vt* raten (**s.o.** jdm); (*counsel*) beraten; (*inform*) benachrichtigen; **~e s.o. against sth** jdm von etw abraten • *vi* raten. **~er** *n* Berater(in) *m(f)*. **~ory** *a* beratend

advocate[1] /'ædvəkət/ *n* [Rechts]anwalt *m*/-anwältin *f*; (*supporter*) Befürworter *m*

advocate[2] /'ædvəkeɪt/ *vt* befürworten

aerial /'eərɪəl/ *a* Luft- • *n* Antenne *f*

aerobics /eə'rəʊbɪks/ *n* Aerobic *nt*

aero|drome /'eərədrəʊm/ *n* Flugplatz *m*. **~plane** *n* Flugzeug *nt*

aerosol /'eərəsɒl/ *n* Spraydose *f*

aesthetic /i:s'θetɪk/ *a* ästhetisch

afar /ə'fɑ:(r)/ *adv* **from ~** aus der Ferne

affable /'æfəbl/ *a*, **-bly** *adv* freundlich

affair /ə'feə(r)/ *n* Angelegenheit *f*, Sache *f*; (*scandal*) Affäre *f*; **[love-] ~** [Liebes]verhältnis *nt*

affect /ə'fekt/ *vt* sich auswirken auf (+ *acc*); (*concern*) betreffen; (*move*) rühren; (*pretend*) vortäuschen. **~ation** /æfek'teɪʃn/ *n* Affektiertheit *f*. **~ed** *a* affektiert

affection /ə'fekʃn/ *n* Liebe *f*. **~ate** /-ət/ *a*, **-ly** *adv* liebevoll

affiliated /ə'fɪlɪeɪtɪd/ *a* angeschlossen (**to** *dat*)

affinity /ə'fɪnətɪ/ *n* Ähnlichkeit *f*; (*attraction*) gegenseitige Anziehung *f*

affirm /ə'fɜ:m/ *vt* behaupten; (*Jur*) eidesstattlich erklären

affirmative /ə'fɜ:mətɪv/ *a* bejahend • *n* Bejahung *f*

affix /ə'fɪks/ *vt* anbringen (**to** *dat*); (*stick*) aufkleben (**to** auf + *acc*); setzen ⟨*signature*⟩ (**to** unter + *acc*)

afflict /ə'flɪkt/ *vt* **be ~ed with** behaftet sein mit. **~ion** /-ɪkʃn/ *n* Leiden *nt*

affluen|ce /'æfluəns/ *n* Reichtum *m*. **~t** *a* wohlhabend. **~t society** *n* Wohlstandsgesellschaft *f*

afford /ə'fɔ:d/ *vt* (*provide*) gewähren; **be able to ~ sth** sich (*dat*) etw leisten können. **~able** /-əbl/ *a* erschwinglich

affray /ə'freɪ/ *n* Schlägerei *f*

affront /ə'frʌnt/ *n* Beleidigung *f* • *vt* beleidigen

afield /ə'fi:ld/ *adv* **further ~** weiter weg

afloat /ə'fləʊt/ *a* **be ~** ⟨*ship:*⟩ flott sein; **keep ~** ⟨*person:*⟩ sich über Wasser halten

afoot /ə'fʊt/ *a* im Gange

aforesaid /ə'fɔ:sed/ *a* (*Jur*) obenerwähnt

afraid /ə'freɪd/ *a* **be ~** Angst haben (**of** vor + *dat*); **I'm ~ not** leider nicht; **I'm ~ so** [ja] leider; **I'm ~ I can't help you** ich kann Ihnen leider nicht helfen

afresh /ə'freʃ/ *adv* von vorne

Africa /'æfrɪkə/ *n* Afrika *nt*. **~n** *a* afrikanisch • *n* Afrikaner(in) *m(f)*

after /'ɑ:ftə(r)/ *adv* danach • *prep* nach (+ *dat*); **~ that** danach; **~ all** schließlich; **the day ~ tomorrow** übermorgen; **be ~** aussein auf (+ *acc*) • *conj* nachdem

after: ~-effect *n* Nachwirkung *f*. **~math** /-mɑ:θ/ *n* Auswirkungen *pl*.

~'noon *n* Nachmittag *m*; **good ~noon!** guten Tag! **~sales service** *n* Kundendienst *m*. **~shave** *n* Rasierwasser *nt*. **~thought** *n* nachträglicher Einfall *m*. **~wards** *adv* nachher

again /ə'geɪn/ *adv* wieder; (*once more*) noch einmal; (*besides*) außerdem; **~ and ~** immer wieder

against /ə'geɪnst/ *prep* gegen (+ *acc*)

age /eɪdʒ/ *n* Alter *nt*; (*era*) Zeitalter *nt*; **~s** (*fam*) ewig; **under ~** minderjährig; **of ~** volljährig; **two years of ~** zwei Jahre alt ● *v* (*pres p* **ageing**) ● *vt* älter machen ● *vi* altern; (*mature*) reifen

aged[1] /eɪdʒd/ *a* **~ two** zwei Jahre alt

aged[2] /'eɪdʒɪd/ *a* betagt ● *n* **the ~** *pl* die Alten

ageless /'eɪdʒlɪs/ *a* ewig jung

agency /'eɪdʒənsɪ/ *n* Agentur *f*; (*office*) Büro *nt*; **have the ~ for** die Vertretung haben für

agenda /ə'dʒendə/ *n* Tagesordnung *f*; **on the ~** auf dem Programm

agent /'eɪdʒənt/ *n* Agent(in) *m(f)*; (*Comm*) Vertreter(in) *m(f)*; (*substance*) Mittel *nt*

aggravat|e /'ægrəveɪt/ *vt* verschlimmern; (*fam: annoy*) ärgern. **~ion** /-'veɪʃn/ *n* (*fam*) Ärger *m*

aggregate /'ægrɪgət/ *a* gesamt ● *n* Gesamtzahl *f*; (*sum*) Gesamtsumme *f*

aggress|ion /ə'greʃn/ *n* Aggression *f*. **~ive** /-sɪv/ *a*, **-ly** *adv* aggressiv. **~iveness** *n* Aggressivität *f*. **~or** *n* Angreifer(in) *m(f)*

aggrieved /ə'gri:vd/ *a* verletzt

aggro /'ægrəʊ/ *n* (*fam*) Ärger *m*

aghast /ə'gɑ:st/ *a* entsetzt

agil|e /'ædʒaɪl/ *a* flink, behende; ⟨*mind*⟩ wendig. **~ity** /ə'dʒɪlətɪ/ *n* Flinkheit *f*, Behendigkeit *f*

agitat|e /'ædʒɪteɪt/ *vt* bewegen; (*shake*) schütteln ● *vi* (*fig*) **~ for** agitieren für. **~ed** *a*, **-ly** *adv* erregt. **~ion** /-'teɪʃn/ *n* Erregung *f*; (*Pol*) Agitation *f*. **~or** *n* Agitator *m*

agnostic /æg'nɒstɪk/ *n* Agnostiker *m*

ago /ə'gəʊ/ *adv* vor (+ *dat*); **a month ~** vor einem Monat; **a long time ~** vor langer Zeit; **how long ~ is it?** wie lange ist es her?

agog /ə'gɒg/ *a* gespannt

agoniz|e /'ægənaɪz/ *vi* [innerlich] ringen. **~ing** *a* qualvoll

agony /'ægənɪ/ *n* Qual *f*; **be in ~** furchtbare Schmerzen haben

agree /ə'gri:/ *vt* vereinbaren; (*admit*) zugeben; **~ to do sth** sich bereit erklären, etw zu tun ● *vi* ⟨*people, figures:*⟩ übereinstimmen; (*reach agreement*) sich einigen; (*get on*) gut miteinander auskommen; (*consent*) einwilligen (**to** in + *acc*); **I ~** der Meinung bin ich auch; **~ with s.o.** jdm zustimmen; ⟨*food:*⟩ jdm bekommen; **~ with sth** (*approve of*) mit etw einverstanden sein

agreeable /ə'gri:əbl/ *a* angenehm; **be ~** einverstanden sein (**to** mit)

agreed /ə'gri:d/ *a* vereinbart

agreement /ə'gri:mənt/ *n* Übereinstimmung *f*; (*consent*) Einwilligung *f*; (*contract*) Abkommen *nt*; **reach ~** sich einigen

agricultur|al /ægrɪ'kʌltʃərəl/ *a* landwirtschaftlich. **~e** /'ægrɪkʌltʃə(r)/ *n* Landwirtschaft *f*

aground /ə'graʊnd/ *a* gestrandet; **run ~** ⟨*ship:*⟩ stranden

ahead /ə'hed/ *adv* **straight ~** geradeaus; **be ~ of s.o./sth** vor jdm/etw sein; (*fig*) voraus sein; **draw ~** nach vorne ziehen; **go on ~** vorgehen; **get ~** vorankommen; **go ~!** (*fam*) bitte! **look/plan ~** vorausblicken/-planen

aid /eɪd/ *n* Hilfe *f*; (*financial*) Unterstützung *f*; **in ~ of** zugunsten (+ *gen*) ● *vt* helfen (+ *dat*)

aide /eɪd/ *n* Berater *m*

Aids /eɪdz/ *n* Aids *nt*

ail|ing /'eɪlɪŋ/ *a* kränkelnd. **~ment** *n* Leiden *nt*

aim /eɪm/ *n* Ziel *nt*; **take ~** zielen ● *vt* richten (**at** auf + *acc*) ● *vi* zielen (**at** auf + *acc*); **~ to do sth** beabsichtigen, etw zu tun. **~less** *a*, **-ly** *adv* ziellos

air /eə(r)/ *n* Luft *f*; (*tune*) Melodie *f*; (*expression*) Miene *f*; (*appearance*) Anschein *m*; **be on the ~** ⟨*programme:*⟩ gesendet werden; ⟨*person:*⟩ senden, auf Sendung sein; **put on ~s** vornehm tun; **by ~** auf dem Luftweg; (*airmail*) mit Luftpost ● *vt* lüften; vorbringen ⟨*views*⟩

air: ~-bed *n* Luftmatratze *f*. **~-conditioned** *a* klimatisiert. **~-conditioning** *n* Klimaanlage *f*. **~craft** *n* Flugzeug *nt*. **~ fare** *n* Flugpreis *m*. **~field** *n* Flugplatz *m*. **~ force** *n* Luftwaffe *f*. **~ freshener** *n* Raumspray *nt*. **~gun** *n* Luftgewehr *nt*. **~ hostess** *n* Stewardeß *f*. **~ letter** *n*

Aerogramm *nt*. **~line** *n* Fluggesellschaft *f*. **~lock** *n* Luftblase *f*. **~mail** *n* Luftpost *f*. **~man** *n* Flieger *m*. **~plane** *n* (*Amer*) Flugzeug *nt*. **~ pocket** *n* Luftloch *nt*. **~port** *n* Flughafen *m*. **~ raid** *n* Luftangriff *m*. **~-raid shelter** *n* Luftschutzbunker *m*. **~ship** *n* Luftschiff *nt*. **~ ticket** *n* Flugschein *m*. **~tight** *a* luftdicht. **~ traffic** *n* Luftverkehr *m*. **~-traffic controller** *n* Fluglotse *m*. **~worthy** *a* flugtüchtig

airy /'eərɪ/ *a* (**-ier, -iest**) luftig; ⟨*manner*⟩ nonchalant

aisle /aɪl/ *n* Gang *m*

ajar /ə'dʒɑː(r)/ *a* angelehnt

akin /ə'kɪn/ *a* **~ to** verwandt mit; (*similar*) ähnlich (**to** *dat*)

alabaster /'æləbɑːstə(r)/ *n* Alabaster *m*

alacrity /ə'lækrətɪ/ *n* Bereitfertigkeit *f*

alarm /ə'lɑːm/ *n* Alarm *m*; (*device*) Alarmanlage *f*; (*clock*) Wecker *m*; (*fear*) Unruhe *f* ● *vt* erschrecken; alarmieren. **~ clock** *n* Wecker *m*

alas /ə'læs/ *int* ach!

album /'ælbəm/ *n* Album *nt*

alcohol /'ælkəhɒl/ *n* Alkohol *m*. **~ic** /-'hɒlɪk/ *a* alkoholisch ● *n* Alkoholiker(in) *m*(*f*). **~ism** *n* Alkoholismus *m*

alcove /'ælkəʊv/ *n* Nische *f*

alert /ə'lɜːt/ *a* aufmerksam ● *n* Alarm *m*; **on the ~** auf der Hut ● *vt* alarmieren

algae /'ældʒiː/ *npl* Algen *pl*

algebra /'ældʒɪbrə/ *n* Algebra *f*

Algeria /æl'dʒɪərɪə/ *n* Algerien *nt*

alias /'eɪlɪəs/ *n* Deckname *m* ● *adv* alias

alibi /'ælɪbaɪ/ *n* Alibi *nt*

alien /'eɪlɪən/ *a* fremd ● *n* Ausländer(in) *m*(*f*)

alienat|e /'eɪlɪəneɪt/ *vt* entfremden. **~ion** /-'neɪʃn/ *n* Entfremdung *f*

alight[1] /ə'laɪt/ *vi* aussteigen (**from** aus); ⟨*bird:*⟩ sich niederlassen

alight[2] *a* **be ~** brennen; **set ~** anzünden

align /ə'laɪn/ *vt* ausrichten. **~ment** *n* Ausrichtung *f*; **out of ~ment** nicht richtig ausgerichtet

alike /ə'laɪk/ *a & adv* ähnlich; (*same*) gleich; **look ~** sich (*dat*) ähnlich sehen

alimony /'ælɪmənɪ/ *n* Unterhalt *m*

alive /ə'laɪv/ *a* lebendig; **be ~** leben; **be ~ with** wimmeln von

alkali /'ælkəlaɪ/ *n* Base *f*, Alkali *nt*

all /ɔːl/ *a* alle *pl*; (*whole*) ganz; **~ [the] children** alle Kinder; **~ our children** alle unsere Kinder; **~ the others** alle anderen; **~ day** den ganzen Tag; **~ the wine** der ganze Wein; **for ~ that** (*nevertheless*) trotzdem; **in ~ innocence** in aller Unschuld ● *pron* alle *pl*; (*everything*) alles; **~ of you/them** Sie/sie alle; **~ of the town** die ganze Stadt; **not at ~** gar nicht; **in ~** insgesamt; **~ in ~** alles in allem; **most of ~** am meisten; **once and for ~** ein für allemal ● *adv* ganz; **~ but** fast; **~ at once** auf einmal; **~ too soon** viel zu früh; **~ the same** (*nevertheless*) trotzdem; **~ the better** um so besser; **be ~ in** (*fam*) völlig erledigt sein; **four ~** (*Sport*) vier zu vier

allay /ə'leɪ/ *vt* zerstreuen

allegation /ælɪ'geɪʃn/ *n* Behauptung *f*

allege /ə'ledʒ/ *vt* behaupten. **~d** *a*, **-ly** /-ɪdlɪ/ *adv* angeblich

allegiance /ə'liːdʒəns/ *n* Treue *f*

allegor|ical /ælɪ'gɒrɪkl/ *a* allegorisch. **~y** /'ælɪgərɪ/ *n* Allegorie *f*

allerg|ic /ə'lɜːdʒɪk/ *a* allergisch (**to** gegen). **~y** /'ælədʒɪ/ *n* Allergie *f*

alleviate /ə'liːvɪeɪt/ *vt* lindern

alley /'ælɪ/ *n* Gasse *f*; (*for bowling*) Bahn *f*

alliance /ə'laɪəns/ *n* Verbindung *f*; (*Pol*) Bündnis *nt*

allied /'ælaɪd/ *a* alliiert; (*fig: related*) verwandt (**to** mit)

alligator /'ælɪgeɪtə(r)/ *n* Alligator *m*

allocat|e /'æləkeɪt/ *vt* zuteilen; (*share out*) verteilen. **~ion** /-'keɪʃn/ *n* Zuteilung *f*

allot /ə'lɒt/ *vt* (*pt/pp* **allotted**) zuteilen (**s.o.** jdm). **~ment** *n* ≈ Schrebergarten *m*

allow /ə'laʊ/ *vt* erlauben; (*give*) geben; (*grant*) gewähren; (*reckon*) rechnen; (*agree, admit*) zugeben; **~ for** berücksichtigen; **~ s.o. to do sth** jdm erlauben, etw zu tun; **be ~ed to do sth** etw tun dürfen

allowance /ə'laʊəns/ *n* [finanzielle] Unterstützung *f*; **~ for petrol** Benzingeld *nt*; **make ~s for** berücksichtigen

alloy /'ælɔɪ/ *n* Legierung *f*

allude /ə'luːd/ *vi* anspielen (**to** auf + *acc*)

allure /ə'lʊə(r)/ *n* Reiz *m*

allusion /ə'luːʒn/ *n* Anspielung *f*

ally[1] /'ælaɪ/ *n* Verbündete(r) *m/f*; **the Allies** *pl* die Alliierten

ally² /ə'laɪ/ *vt* (*pt/pp* **-ied**) verbinden; **~ oneself with** sich verbünden mit
almighty /ɔ:l'maɪtɪ/ *a* allmächtig; (*fam: big*) Riesen- • *n* **the A~** der Allmächtige
almond /'ɑ:mənd/ *n* (*Bot*) Mandel *f*
almost /'ɔ:lməʊst/ *adv* fast, beinahe
alms /ɑ:mz/ *npl* (*liter*) Almosen *pl*
alone /ə'ləʊn/ *a & adv* allein; **leave me ~** laß mich in Ruhe; **leave that ~!** laß die Finger davon! **let ~** ganz zu schweigen von
along /ə'lɒŋ/ *prep* entlang (+ *acc*); **~ the river** den Fluß entlang • *adv* **~ with** zusammen mit; **all ~** die ganze Zeit; **come ~** komm doch; **I'll bring it ~** ich bringe es mit; **move ~** weitergehen
along'side *adv* daneben • *prep* neben (+ *dat*)
aloof /ə'lu:f/ *a* distanziert
aloud /ə'laʊd/ *adv* laut
alphabet /'ælfəbet/ *n* Alphabet *nt*. **~ical** /-'betɪkl/ *a*, **-ly** *adv* alphabetisch
alpine /'ælpaɪn/ *a* alpin; **A~** Alpen-
Alps /ælps/ *npl* Alpen *pl*
already /ɔ:l'redɪ/ *adv* schon
Alsace /æl'sæs/ *n* Elsaß *nt*
Alsatian /æl'seɪʃn/ *n* (*dog*) [deutscher] Schäferhund *m*
also /'ɔ:lsəʊ/ *adv* auch
altar /'ɔ:ltə(r)/ *n* Altar *m*
alter /'ɔ:ltə(r)/ *vt* ändern • *vi* sich verändern. **~ation** /-'reɪʃn/ *n* Änderung *f*
alternate¹ /'ɔ:ltəneɪt/ *vi* [sich] abwechseln • *vt* abwechseln
alternate² /ɔ:l'tɜ:nət/ *a*, **-ly** *adv* abwechselnd; (*Amer: alternative*) andere(r,s); **on ~ days** jeden zweiten Tag
'alternating current *n* Wechselstrom *m*
alternative /ɔ:l'tɜ:nətɪv/ *a* andere(r,s) • *n* Alternative *f*. **~ly** *adv* oder aber
although /ɔ:l'ðəʊ/ *conj* obgleich, obwohl
altitude /'æltɪtju:d/ *n* Höhe *f*
altogether /ɔ:ltə'geðə(r)/ *adv* insgesamt; (*on the whole*) alles in allem
altruistic /æltru:'ɪstɪk/ altruistisch
aluminium /æljʊ'mɪnɪəm/ *n*, (*Amer*) **aluminum** /ə'lu:mɪnəm/ *n* Aluminium *nt*
always /'ɔ:lweɪz/ *adv* immer
am /æm/ *see* **be**
a.m. *abbr* **(ante meridiem)** vormittags
amalgamate /ə'mælgəmeɪt/ *vt* vereinigen; (*Chem*) amalgamieren • *vi* sich vereinigen; (*Chem*) sich amalgamieren
amass /ə'mæs/ *vt* anhäufen
amateur /'æmətə(r)/ *n* Amateur *m* • *attrib* Amateur-; (*Theat*) Laien-. **~ish** *a* laienhaft
amaze /ə'meɪz/ *vt* erstaunen. **~d** *a* erstaunt. **~ment** *n* Erstaunen *nt*
amazing /ə'meɪzɪŋ/ *a*, **-ly** *adv* erstaunlich
ambassador /æm'bæsədə(r)/ *n* Botschafter *m*
amber /'æmbə(r)/ *n* Bernstein *m* • *a* (*colour*) gelb
ambidextrous /æmbɪ'dekstrəs/ *a* **be ~** mit beiden Händen gleich geschickt sein
ambience /'æmbɪəns/ *n* Atmosphäre *f*
ambigu|ity /æmbɪ'gju:ətɪ/ *n* Zweideutigkeit *f*. **~ous** /-'bɪgjʊəs/ *a*, **-ly** *adv* zweideutig
ambiti|on /æm'bɪʃn/ *n* Ehrgeiz *m*; (*aim*) Ambition *f*. **~ous** /-ʃəs/ *a* ehrgeizig
ambivalent /æm'bɪvələnt/ *a* zwiespältig; **be/feel ~** im Zwiespalt sein
amble /'æmbl/ *vi* schlendern
ambulance /'æmbjʊləns/ *n* Krankenwagen *m*. **~ man** *n* Sanitäter *m*
ambush /'æmbʊʃ/ *n* Hinterhalt *m* • *vt* aus dem Hinterhalt überfallen
amen /ɑ:'men/ *int* amen
amenable /ə'mi:nəbl/ *a* **~ to** zugänglich (**to** *dat*)
amend /ə'mend/ *vt* ändern. **~ment** *n* Änderung *f*. **~s** *npl* **make ~s for sth** etw wiedergutmachen
amenities /ə'mi:nətɪz/ *npl* Einrichtungen *pl*
America /ə'merɪkə/ *n* Amerika *nt*. **~n** *a* amerikanisch • *n* Amerikaner(in) *m*(*f*). **~nism** *n* Amerikanismus *m*
amiable /'eɪmɪəbl/ *a* nett
amicable /'æmɪkəbl/ *a*, **-bly** *adv* freundschaftlich; ⟨*agreement*⟩ gütlich
amid[st] /ə'mɪd[st]/ *prep* inmitten (+ *gen*)
amiss /ə'mɪs/ *a* **be ~** nicht stimmen • *adv* **not come ~** nicht unangebracht sein; **take sth ~** etw übelnehmen
ammonia /ə'məʊnɪə/ *n* Ammoniak *nt*
ammunition /æmjʊ'nɪʃn/ *n* Munition *f*
amnesia /æm'ni:zɪə/ *n* Amnesie *f*
amnesty /'æmnəstɪ/ *n* Amnestie *f*

among[st] /ə'mʌŋ[st]/ *prep* unter (+ *dat*/*acc*); **~ yourselves** untereinander
amoral /eɪ'mɒrəl/ *a* amoralisch
amorous /'æmərəs/ *a* zärtlich
amount /ə'maʊnt/ *n* Menge *f*; (*sum of money*) Betrag *m*; (*total*) Gesamtsumme *f* ● *vi* **~ to** sich belaufen auf (+ *acc*); (*fig*) hinauslaufen auf (+ *acc*)
amp /æmp/ *n* Ampere *nt*
amphibi|an /æm'fɪbɪən/ *n* Amphibie *f*. **~ous** /-ɪəs/ *a* amphibisch
amphitheatre /'æmfɪ-/ *n* Amphitheater *nt*
ample /'æmpl/ *a* (**-r, -st**), **-ly** *adv* reichlich; (*large*) füllig
amplif|ier /'æmplɪfaɪə(r)/ *n* Verstärker *m*. **~y** /-faɪ/ *vt* (*pt*/*pp* **-ied**) weiter ausführen; verstärken ⟨*sound*⟩
amputat|e /'æmpjʊteɪt/ *vt* amputieren. **~ion** /-'teɪʃn/ *n* Amputation *f*
amuse /ə'mju:z/ *vt* amüsieren, belustigen; (*entertain*) unterhalten. **~ment** *n* Belustigung *f*; Unterhaltung *f*. **~ment arcade** *n* Spielhalle *f*
amusing /ə'mju:zɪŋ/ *a* amüsant
an /ən, *betont* æn/ *see* **a**
anaem|ia /ə'ni:mɪə/ *n* Blutarmut *f*, Anämie *f*. **~ic** *a* blutarm
anaesthesia /ænəs'θi:zɪə/ *n* Betäubung *f*
anaesthetic /ænəs'θetɪk/ *n* Narkosemittel *nt*, Betäubungsmittel *nt*; **under [an] ~** in Narkose; **give s.o. an ~** jdm eine Narkose geben
anaesthet|ist /ə'ni:sθətɪst/ *n* Narkosearzt *m*. **~ize** /-taɪz/ *vt* betäuben
analog[ue] /'ænəlɒg/ *a* Analog-
analogy /ə'nælədʒɪ/ *n* Analogie *f*
analyse /'ænəlaɪz/ *vt* analysieren
analysis /ə'næləsɪs/ *n* Analyse *f*
analyst /'ænəlɪst/ *n* Chemiker(in) *m*(*f*); (*Psych*) Analytiker *m*
analytical /ænə'lɪtɪkl/ *a* analytisch
anarch|ist /'ænəkɪst/ *n* Anarchist *m*. **~y** *n* Anarchie *f*
anathema /ə'næθəmə/ *n* Greuel *m*
anatom|ical /ænə'tɒmɪkl/ *a*, **-ly** *adv* anatomisch. **~y** /ə'nætəmɪ/ *n* Anatomie *f*
ancest|or /'ænsestə(r)/ *n* Vorfahr *m*. **~ry** *n* Abstammung *f*
anchor /'æŋkə(r)/ *n* Anker *m* ● *vi* ankern ● *vt* verankern
anchovy /'æntʃəvɪ/ *n* Sardelle *f*
ancient /'eɪnʃənt/ *a* alt
ancillary /æn'sɪlərɪ/ *a* Hilfs-
and /ənd, *betont* ænd/ *conj* und; **~ so on** und so weiter; **six hundred ~ two** sechshundertzwei; **more ~ more** immer mehr; **nice ~ warm** schön warm; **try ~ come** versuche zu kommen
anecdote /'ænɪkdəʊt/ *n* Anekdote *f*
anew /ə'nju:/ *adv* von neuem
angel /'eɪndʒl/ *n* Engel *m*. **~ic** /æn'dʒelɪk/ *a* engelhaft
anger /'æŋgə(r)/ *n* Zorn *m* ● *vt* zornig machen
angle¹ /'æŋgl/ *n* Winkel *m*; (*fig*) Standpunkt *m*; **at an ~** schräg
angle² *vi* angeln; **~ for** (*fig*) fischen nach. **~r** *n* Angler *m*
Anglican /'æŋglɪkən/ *a* anglikanisch ● *n* Anglikaner(in) *m*(*f*)
Anglo-Saxon /æŋgləʊ'sæksn/ *a* angelsächsich ● *n* Angelsächsisch *nt*
angry /'æŋgrɪ/ *a* (**-ier, -iest**), **-ily** *adv* zornig; **be ~ with** böse sein auf (+ *acc*)
anguish /'æŋgwɪʃ/ *n* Qual *f*
angular /'æŋgjʊlə(r)/ *a* eckig; ⟨*features*⟩ kantig
animal /'ænɪml/ *n* Tier *nt* ● *a* tierisch
animate¹ /'ænɪmət/ *a* lebendig
animat|e² /'ænɪmeɪt/ *vt* beleben. **~ed** *a* lebhaft. **~ion** /-'meɪʃn/ *n* Lebhaftigkeit *f*
animosity /ænɪ'mɒsətɪ/ *n* Feindseligkeit *f*
aniseed /'ænɪsi:d/ *n* Anis *m*
ankle /'æŋkl/ *n* [Fuß]knöchel *m*
annex /ə'neks/ *vt* annektieren
annex[e] /'æneks/ *n* Nebengebäude *nt*; (*extension*) Anbau *m*
annihilat|e /ə'naɪəleɪt/ *vt* vernichten. **~ion** /-'leɪʃn/ *n* Vernichtung *f*
anniversary /ænɪ'vɜ:sərɪ/ *n* Jahrestag *m*
annotate /'ænəteɪt/ *vt* kommentieren
announce /ə'naʊns/ *vt* bekanntgeben; (*over loudspeaker*) durchsagen; (*at reception*) ankündigen; (*Radio, TV*) ansagen; (*in newspaper*) anzeigen. **~ment** *n* Bekanntgabe *f*, Bekanntmachung *f*; Durchsage *f*; Ansage *f*; Anzeige *f*. **~r** *n* Ansager(in) *m*(*f*)
annoy /ə'nɔɪ/ *vt* ärgern; (*pester*) belästigen; **get ~ed** sich ärgern. **~ance** *n* Ärger *m*. **~ing** *a* ärgerlich
annual /'ænjʊəl/ *a*, **-ly** *adv* jährlich ● *n* (*Bot*) einjährige Pflanze *f*; (*book*) Jahresalbum *nt*
annuity /ə'nju:ətɪ/ *n* [Leib]rente *f*

annul /ə'nʌl/ *vt* (*pt/pp* **annulled**) annullieren
anoint /ə'nɔɪnt/ *vt* salben
anomaly /ə'nɒməlɪ/ *n* Anomalie *f*
anonymous /ə'nɒnɪməs/ *a*, **-ly** *adv* anonym
anorak /'ænəræk/ *n* Anorak *m*
anorexia /ænə'reksɪə/ *n* Magersucht *f*
another /ə'nʌðə(r)/ *a & pron* ein anderer/eine andere/ein anderes; (*additional*) noch ein(e); ~ **[one]** noch einer/eine/eins; ~ **day** an einem anderen Tag; **in ~ way** auf andere Weise; ~ **time** ein andermal; **one ~** einander
answer /'ɑ:nsə(r)/ *n* Antwort *f*; (*solution*) Lösung *f* ● *vt* antworten (**s.o.** jdm); beantworten ‹*question, letter*›; ~ **the door/telephone** an die Tür/ans Telefon gehen ● *vi* antworten; (*Teleph*) sich melden; ~ **back** eine freche Antwort geben; ~ **for** verantwortlich sein für. **~able** /-əbl/ *a* verantwortlich. **~ing machine** *n* (*Teleph*) Anrufbeantworter *m*
ant /ænt/ *n* Ameise *f*
antagonis|m /æn'tægənɪzm/ *n* Antagonismus *m*. **~tic** /-'nɪstɪk/ *a* feindselig
antagonize /æn'tægənaɪz/ *vt* gegen sich aufbringen
Antarctic /ænt'ɑ:ktɪk/ *n* Antarktis *f*
antelope /'æntɪləʊp/ *n* Antilope *f*
antenatal /æntɪ'neɪtl/ *a* ~ **care** Schwangerschaftsfürsorge *f*
antenna /æn'tenə/ *n* Fühler *m*; (*Amer: aerial*) Antenne *f*
ante-room /'æntɪ-/ *n* Vorraum *m*
anthem /'ænθəm/ *n* Hymne *f*
anthology /æn'θɒlədʒɪ/ *n* Anthologie *f*
anthropology /ænθrə'pɒlədʒɪ/ *n* Anthropologie *f*
anti-'aircraft /æntɪ-/ *a* Flugabwehr-
antibiotic /æntɪbaɪ'ɒtɪk/ *n* Antibiotikum *nt*
'antibody *n* Antikörper *m*
anticipat|e /æn'tɪsɪpeɪt/ *vt* vorhersehen; (*forestall*) zuvorkommen (+ *dat*); (*expect*) erwarten. **~ion** /-'peɪʃn/ *n* Erwartung *f*
anti'climax *n* Enttäuschung *f*
anti'clockwise *a & adv* gegen den Uhrzeigersinn
antics /'æntɪks/ *npl* Mätzchen *pl*
anti'cyclone *n* Hochdruckgebiet *nt*
antidote /'æntɪdəʊt/ *n* Gegengift *nt*
'antifreeze *n* Frostschutzmittel *nt*
antipathy /æn'tɪpəθɪ/ *n* Abneigung *f*, Antipathie *f*
antiquarian /æntɪ'kweərɪən/ *a* antiquarisch. ~ **bookshop** *n* Antiquariat *nt*
antiquated /'æntɪkweɪtɪd/ *a* veraltet
antique /æn'ti:k/ *a* antik ● *n* Antiquität *f*. ~ **dealer** *n* Antiquitätenhändler *m*
antiquity /æn'tɪkwətɪ/ *n* Altertum *nt*
anti-Semitic /æntɪsɪ'mɪtɪk/ *a* antisemitisch
anti'septic *a* antiseptisch ● *n* Antiseptikum *nt*
anti'social *a* asozial; (*fam*) ungesellig
antithesis /æn'tɪθəsɪs/ *n* Gegensatz *m*
antlers /'æntləz/ *npl* Geweih *nt*
anus /'eɪnəs/ *n* After *m*
anvil /'ænvɪl/ *n* Amboß *m*
anxiety /æŋ'zaɪətɪ/ *n* Sorge *f*
anxious /'æŋkʃəs/ *a*, **-ly** *adv* ängstlich; (*worried*) besorgt; **be ~ to do sth** etw gerne machen wollen
any /'enɪ/ *a* irgendein(e); *pl* irgendwelche; (*every*) jede(r,s); *pl* alle; (*after negative*) kein(e); *pl* keine; ~ **colour/number you like** eine beliebige Farbe/Zahl; **have you ~ wine/apples?** haben Sie Wein/Äpfel? **for ~ reason** aus irgendeinem Grund ● *pron* [irgend]einer/eine/eins; *pl* [irgend]welche; (*some*) welche(r,s); *pl* welche; (*all*) alle *pl*; (*negative*) keiner/keine/keins; *pl* keine; **I don't want ~ of it** ich will nichts davon; **there aren't ~** es gibt eine; **I need wine/apples/money—have we ~?** ich brauche Wein/Äpfel/Geld—haben wir welchen/welche/welches? ● *adv* noch; ~ **quicker/slower** noch schneller/langsamer; **is it ~ better?** geht es etwas besser? **would you like ~ more?** möchten Sie noch [etwas]? **I can't eat ~ more** ich kann nichts mehr essen; **I can't go ~ further** ich kann nicht mehr weiter
'anybody *pron* [irgend] jemand; (*after negative*) niemand; ~ **can do that** das kann jeder
'anyhow *adv* jedenfalls; (*nevertheless*) trotzdem; (*badly*) irgendwie
'anyone *pron* = **anybody**
'anything *pron* [irgend] etwas; (*after negative*) nichts; (*everything*) alles
'anyway *adv* jedenfalls; (*in any case*) sowieso

'anywhere *adv* irgendwo; (*after negative*) nirgendwo; ⟨*be, live*⟩ überall; **I'd go ~** ich würde überallhin gehen

apart /ə'pɑ:t/ *adv* auseinander; **live ~** getrennt leben; **~ from** abgesehen von

apartment /ə'pɑ:tmənt/ *n* Zimmer *nt*; (*Amer: flat*) Wohnung *f*

apathy /'æpəθɪ/ *n* Apathie *f*

ape /eɪp/ *n* [Menschen]affe *m* ● *vt* nachäffen

aperitif /ə'perəti:f/ *n* Aperitif *m*

aperture /'æpətʃə(r)/ *n* Öffnung *f*; (*Phot*) Blende *f*

apex /'eɪpeks/ *n* Spitze *f*; (*fig*) Gipfel *m*

apiece /ə'pi:s/ *adv* pro Person; (*thing*) pro Stück

apologetic /əpɒlə'dʒetɪk/ *a*, **-ally** *adv* entschuldigend; **be ~** sich entschuldigen

apologize /ə'pɒlədʒaɪz/ *vi* sich entschuldigen (**to** bei)

apology /ə'pɒlədʒɪ/ *n* Entschuldigung *f*

apostle /ə'pɒsl/ *n* Apostel *m*

apostrophe /ə'pɒstrəfɪ/ *n* Apostroph *m*

appal /ə'pɔ:l/ *vt* (*pt/pp* **appalled**) entsetzen. **~ling** *a* entsetzlich

apparatus /æpə'reɪtəs/ *n* Apparatur *f*; (*Sport*) Geräte *pl*; (*single piece*) Gerät *nt*

apparel /ə'pærəl/ *n* Kleidung *f*

apparent /ə'pærənt/ *a* offenbar; (*seeming*) scheinbar. **~ly** *adv* offenbar, anscheinend

apparition /æpə'rɪʃn/ *n* Erscheinung *f*

appeal /ə'pi:l/ *n* Appell *m*, Aufruf *m*; (*request*) Bitte *f*; (*attraction*) Reiz *m*; (*Jur*) Berufung *f* ● *vi* appellieren (**to** an + *acc*); (*ask*) bitten (**for** um); (*be attractive*) zusagen (**to** *dat*); (*Jur*) Berufung einlegen. **~ing** *a* ansprechend

appear /ə'pɪə(r)/ *vi* erscheinen; (*seem*) scheinen; (*Theat*) auftreten. **~ance** *n* Erscheinen *nt*; (*look*) Aussehen *nt*; **to all ~ances** allem Anschein nach

appease /ə'pi:z/ *vt* beschwichtigen

append /ə'pend/ *vt* nachtragen; setzen ⟨*signature*⟩ (**to** unter + *acc*). **~age** /-ɪdʒ/ *n* Anhängsel *nt*

appendicitis /əpendɪ'saɪtɪs/ *n* Blinddarmentzündung *f*

appendix /ə'pendɪks/ *n* (*pl* **-ices** /-ɪsi:z/) (*of book*) Anhang *m* ● (*pl* **-es**) (*Anat*) Blinddarm *m*

appertain /æpə'teɪn/ *vi* **~ to** betreffen

appetite /'æpɪtaɪt/ *n* Appetit *m*

appetizing /'æpɪtaɪzɪŋ/ *a* appetitlich

applau|d /ə'plɔ:d/ *vt/i* Beifall klatschen (+ *dat*). **~se** *n* Beifall *m*

apple /'æpl/ *n* Apfel *m*

appliance /ə'plaɪəns/ *n* Gerät *nt*

applicable /'æplɪkəbl/ *a* anwendbar (**to** auf + *acc*); (*on form*) **not ~** nicht zutreffend

applicant /'æplɪkənt/ *n* Bewerber(in) *m*(*f*)

application /æplɪ'keɪʃn/ *n* Anwendung *f*; (*request*) Antrag *m*; (*for job*) Bewerbung *f*; (*diligence*) Fleiß *m*

applied /ə'plaɪd/ *a* angewandt

apply /ə'plaɪ/ *vt* (*pt/pp* **-ied**) auftragen ⟨*paint*⟩; anwenden ⟨*force, rule*⟩ ● *vi* zutreffen (**to** auf + *acc*); **~ for** beantragen; sich bewerben um ⟨*job*⟩

appoint /ə'pɔɪnt/ *vt* ernennen; (*fix*) festlegen; **well ~ed** gut ausgestattet. **~ment** *n* Ernennung *f*; (*meeting*) Verabredung *f*; (*at doctor's, hairdresser's*) Termin *m*; (*job*) Posten *m*; **make an ~ment** sich anmelden

apposite /'æpəzɪt/ *a* treffend

appraise /ə'preɪz/ *vt* abschätzen

appreciable /ə'pri:ʃəbl/ *a* merklich; (*considerable*) beträchtlich

appreciat|e /ə'pri:ʃɪeɪt/ *vt* zu schätzen wissen; (*be grateful for*) dankbar sein für; (*enjoy*) schätzen; (*understand*) verstehen ● *vi* (*increase in value*) im Wert steigen. **~ion** /-'eɪʃn/ *n* (*gratitude*) Dankbarkeit *f*; **in ~ion** als Dank (**of** für). **~ive** /-ətɪv/ *a* dankbar

apprehend /æprɪ'hend/ *vt* festnehmen

apprehens|ion /æprɪ'henʃn/ *n* Festnahme *f*; (*fear*) Angst *f*. **~ive** /-sɪv/ *a* ängstlich

apprentice /ə'prentɪs/ *n* Lehrling *m*. **~ship** *n* Lehre *f*

approach /ə'prəʊtʃ/ *n* Näherkommen *nt*; (*of time*) Nahen *nt*; (*access*) Zugang *m*; (*road*) Zufahrt *f* ● *vi* sich nähern; ⟨*time:*⟩ nahen ● *vt* sich nähern (+ *dat*); (*with request*) herantreten an (+ *acc*); (*set about*) sich heranmachen an (+ *acc*). **~able** /-əbl/ *a* zugänglich

approbation /æprə'beɪʃn/ *n* Billigung *f*

appropriate[1] /ə'prəʊprɪət/ *a* angebracht, angemessen

appropriate[2] /ə'prəʊprɪeɪt/ *vt* sich (*dat*) aneignen

approval /ə'pru:vl/ *n* Billigung *f*; **on ~** zur Ansicht

approv|e /ə'pru:v/ *vt* billigen ● *vi* **~e of sth/s.o.** mit etw/jdm einverstanden sein. **~ing** *a*, **-ly** *adv* anerkennend

approximate[1] /ə'prɒksɪmeɪt/ *vi* **~ to** nahekommen (+ *dat*)

approximate[2] /ə'prɒksɪmət/ *a* ungefähr. **~ly** *adv* ungefähr, etwa

approximation /əprɒksɪ'meɪʃn/ *n* Schätzung *f*

apricot /'eɪprɪkɒt/ *n* Aprikose *f*

April /'eɪprəl/ *n* April *m*; **make an ~ fool of** in den April schicken

apron /'eɪprən/ *n* Schürze *f*

apropos /'æprəpəʊ/ *adv* **~ [of]** betreffs (+ *gen*)

apt /æpt/ *a*, **-ly** *adv* passend; ⟨*pupil*⟩ begabt; **be ~ to do sth** dazu neigen, etw zu tun

aptitude /'æptɪtju:d/ *n* Begabung *f*

aqualung /'ækwəlʌŋ/ *n* Tauchgerät *nt*

aquarium /ə'kweərɪəm/ *n* Aquarium *nt*

Aquarius /ə'kweərɪəs/ *n* (*Astr*) Wassermann *m*

aquatic /ə'kwætɪk/ *a* Wasser-

Arab /'ærəb/ *a* arabisch ● *n* Araber(in) *m*(*f*). **~ian** /ə'reɪbɪən/ *a* arabisch

Arabic /'ærəbɪk/ *a* arabisch

arable /'ærəbl/ *a* **~ land** Ackerland *nt*

arbitrary /'ɑ:bɪtrərɪ/ *a*, **-ily** *adv* willkürlich

arbitrat|e /'ɑ:bɪtreɪt/ *vi* schlichten. **~ion** /-'treɪʃn/ *n* Schlichtung *f*

arc /ɑ:k/ *n* Bogen *m*

arcade /ɑ:'keɪd/ *n* Laubengang *m*; (*shops*) Einkaufspassage *f*

arch /ɑ:tʃ/ *n* Bogen *m*; (*of foot*) Gewölbe *nt* ● *vt* **~ its back** ⟨*cat:*⟩ einen Buckel machen

archaeological /ɑ:kɪə'lɒdʒɪkl/ *a* archäologisch

archaeolog|ist /ɑ:kɪ'ɒlədʒɪst/ *n* Archäologe *m*/-login *f*. **~y** *n* Archäologie *f*

archaic /ɑ:'keɪɪk/ *a* veraltet

arch'bishop /ɑ:tʃ-/ *n* Erzbischof *m*

arch-'enemy *n* Erzfeind *m*

archer /'ɑ:tʃə(r)/ *n* Bogenschütze *m*. **~y** *n* Bogenschießen *nt*

architect /'ɑ:kɪtekt/ *n* Architekt(in) *m*(*f*). **~ural** /ɑ:kɪ'tektʃərəl/ *a*, **-ly** *adv* architektonisch

architecture /'ɑ:kɪtektʃə(r)/ *n* Architektur *f*

archives /'ɑ:kaɪvz/ *npl* Archiv *nt*

archway /'ɑ:tʃweɪ/ *n* Torbogen *m*

Arctic /'ɑ:ktɪk/ *a* arktisch ● *n* **the ~** die Arktis

ardent /'ɑ:dənt/ *a*, **-ly** *adv* leidenschaftlich

ardour /'ɑ:də(r)/ *n* Leidenschaft *f*

arduous /'ɑ:djʊəs/ *a* mühsam

are /ɑ:(r)/ *see* **be**

area /'eərɪə/ *n* (*surface*) Fläche *f*; (*Geom*) Flächeninhalt *m*; (*region*) Gegend *f*; (*fig*) Gebiet *nt*. **~ code** *n* Vorwahlnummer *f*

arena /ə'ri:nə/ *n* Arena *f*

aren't /ɑ:nt/ = **are not.** *See* **be**

Argentina /ɑ:dʒən'ti:nə/ *n* Argentinien *nt*

Argentin|e /'ɑ:dʒəntaɪn/, **~ian** /-'tɪnɪən/ *a* argentinisch

argue /'ɑ:gju:/ *vi* streiten (**about** über + *acc*); ⟨*two people:*⟩ sich streiten; (*debate*) diskutieren; **don't ~!** keine Widerrede! ● *vt* (*debate*) diskutieren; (*reason*) **~ that** argumentieren, daß

argument /'ɑ:gjʊmənt/ *n* Streit *m*, Auseinandersetzung *f*; (*reasoning*) Argument *nt*; **have an ~** sich streiten. **~ative** /-'mentətɪv/ *a* streitlustig

aria /'ɑ:rɪə/ *n* Arie *f*

arid /'ærɪd/ *a* dürr

Aries /'eəri:z/ *n* (*Astr*) Widder *m*

arise /ə'raɪz/ *vi* (*pt* **arose**, *pp* **arisen**) sich ergeben (**from** aus)

aristocracy /ærɪ'stɒkrəsɪ/ *n* Aristokratie *f*

aristocrat /'ærɪstəkræt/ *n* Aristokrat(in) *m*(*f*). **~ic** /-'krætɪk/ *a* aristokratisch

arithmetic /ə'rɪθmətɪk/ *n* Rechnen *nt*

ark /ɑ:k/ *n* **Noah's A~** die Arche Noah

arm /ɑ:m/ *n* Arm *m*; (*of chair*) Armlehne *f*; **~s** *pl* (*weapons*) Waffen *pl*; (*Heraldry*) Wappen *nt*; **up in ~s** (*fam*) empört ● *vt* bewaffnen

armament /'ɑ:məmənt/ *n* Bewaffnung *f*; **~s** *pl* Waffen *pl*

'armchair *n* Sessel *m*

armed /ɑ:md/ *a* bewaffnet; **~ forces** Streitkräfte *pl*

armistice /'ɑ:mɪstɪs/ *n* Waffenstillstand *m*

armour /'ɑ:mə(r)/ *n* Rüstung *f*. **~ed** *a* Panzer-

'armpit *n* Achselhöhle *f*
army /'ɑ:mɪ/ *n* Heer *nt*; (*specific*) Armee *f*; **join the ~** zum Militär gehen
aroma /ə'rəʊmə/ *n* Aroma *nt*, Duft *m*. **~tic** /ærə'mætɪk/ *a* aromatisch
arose /ə'rəʊz/ *see* **arise**
around /ə'raʊnd/ *adv* **[all] ~** rings herum; **he's not ~** er ist nicht da; **look/turn ~** sich umsehen/umdrehen; **travel ~** herumreisen • *prep* um (+ *acc*) ... herum; (*approximately*) gegen
arouse /ə'raʊz/ *vt* aufwecken; (*excite*) erregen
arrange /ə'reɪndʒ/ *vt* arrangieren; anordnen ⟨*furniture, books*⟩; (*settle*) abmachen; **I have ~d to go there** ich habe abgemacht, daß ich dahingehe. **~ment** *n* Anordnung *f*; (*agreement*) Vereinbarung *f*; (*of flowers*) Gesteck *nt*; **make ~ments** Vorkehrungen treffen
arrears /ə'rɪəz/ *npl* Rückstände *pl*; **in ~** im Rückstand
arrest /ə'rest/ *n* Verhaftung *f*; **under ~** verhaftet • *vt* verhaften
arrival /ə'raɪvl/ *n* Ankunft *f*; **new ~s** *pl* Neuankömmlinge *pl*
arrive /ə'raɪv/ *vi* ankommen; **~ at** (*fig*) gelangen zu
arrogan|ce /'ærəgəns/ *n* Arroganz *f*. **~t** *a*, **-ly** *adv* arrogant
arrow /'ærəʊ/ *n* Pfeil *m*
arse /ɑ:s/ *n* (*vulg*) Arsch *m*
arsenic /'ɑ:sənɪk/ *n* Arsen *nt*
arson /'ɑ:sn/ *n* Brandstiftung *f*. **~ist** /-sənɪst/ *n* Brandstifter *m*
art /ɑ:t/ *n* Kunst *f*; **work of ~** Kunstwerk *nt*; **~s and crafts** *pl* Kunstgewerbe *nt*; **A~s** *pl* (*Univ*) Geisteswissenschaften *pl*
artery /'ɑ:tərɪ/ *n* Schlagader *f*, Arterie *f*
artful /'ɑ:tfl/ *a* gerissen
'art gallery *n* Kunstgalerie *f*
arthritis /ɑ:'θraɪtɪs/ *n* Arthritis *f*
artichoke /'ɑ:tɪtʃəʊk/ *n* Artischocke *f*
article /'ɑ:tɪkl/ *n* Artikel *m*; (*object*) Gegenstand *m*; **~ of clothing** Kleidungsstück *nt*
articulate¹ /ɑ:'tɪkjʊlət/ *a* deutlich; **be ~** sich gut ausdrücken können
articulate² /ɑ:'tɪkjʊleɪt/ *vt* aussprechen. **~d lorry** *n* Sattelzug *m*
artifice /'ɑ:tɪfɪs/ *n* Arglist *f*
artificial /ɑ:tɪ'fɪʃl/ *a*, **-ly** *adv* künstlich
artillery /ɑ:'tɪlərɪ/ *n* Artillerie *f*
artist /'ɑ:tɪst/ *n* Künstler(in) *m*(*f*)
artiste /ɑ:'ti:st/ *n* (*Theat*) Artist(in) *m*(*f*)
artistic /ɑ:'tɪstɪk/ *a*, **-ally** *adv* künstlerisch
artless /'ɑ:tlɪs/ *a* unschuldig
as /æz/ *conj* (*because*) da; (*when*) als; (*while*) während • *prep* als; **as a child/foreigner** als Kind/Ausländer • *adv* **as well** auch; **as soon as** sobald; **as much as** soviel wie; **as quick as you** so schnell wie du; **as you know** wie Sie wissen; **as far as I'm concerned** was mich betrifft
asbestos /æz'bestɒs/ *n* Asbest *m*
ascend /ə'send/ *vi* [auf]steigen • *vt* besteigen ⟨*throne*⟩
Ascension /ə'senʃn/ *n* (*Relig*) [Christi] Himmelfahrt *f*
ascent /ə'sent/ *n* Aufstieg *m*
ascertain /æsə'teɪn/ *vt* ermitteln
ascribe /ə'skraɪb/ *vt* zuschreiben (**to** *dat*)
ash¹ /æʃ/ *n* (*tree*) Esche *f*
ash² *n* Asche *f*
ashamed /ə'ʃeɪmd/ *a* beschämt; **be ~** sich schämen (**of** über + *acc*)
ashore /ə'ʃɔ:(r)/ *adv* an Land
ash: ~tray *n* Aschenbecher *m*. **A~'Wednesday** *n* Aschermittwoch *m*
Asia /'eɪʃə/ *n* Asien *nt*. **~n** *a* asiatisch • *n* Asiat(in) *m*(*f*). **~tic** /eɪʃɪ'ætɪk/ *a* asiatisch
aside /ə'saɪd/ *adv* beiseite; **~ from** (*Amer*) außer (+ *dat*)
ask /ɑ:sk/ *vt/i* fragen; stellen ⟨*question*⟩; (*invite*) einladen; **~ for** bitten um; verlangen ⟨*s.o.*⟩; **~ after** sich erkundigen nach; **~ s.o. in** jdn hereinbitten; **~ s.o. to do sth** jdn bitten, etw zu tun
askance /ə'skɑ:ns/ *adv* **look ~ at** schief ansehen
askew /ə'skju:/ *a & adv* schief
asleep /ə'sli:p/ *a* **be ~** schlafen; **fall ~** einschlafen
asparagus /ə'spærəgəs/ *n* Spargel *m*
aspect /'æspekt/ *n* Aspekt *m*
aspersions /ə'spɜ:ʃnz/ *npl* **cast ~ on** schlechtmachen
asphalt /'æsfælt/ *n* Asphalt *m*
asphyxia /æ'sfɪksɪə/ *n* Erstickung *f*. **~te** /æ'sfɪksɪeɪt/ *vt/i* ersticken. **~tion** /-'eɪʃn/ *n* Erstickung *f*
aspirations /æspə'reɪʃnz/ *npl* Streben *nt*
aspire /ə'spaɪə(r)/ *vi* **~ to** streben nach
ass /æs/ *n* Esel *m*
assail /ə'seɪl/ *vt* bestürmen. **~ant** *n* Angreifer(in) *m*(*f*)

assassin /ə'sæsɪn/ *n* Mörder(in) *m(f)*. **~ate** *vt* ermorden. **~ation** /-'neɪʃn/ *n* [politischer] Mord *m*
assault /ə'sɔ:lt/ *n* (*Mil*) Angriff *m*; (*Jur*) Körperverletzung *f* ● *vt* [tätlich] angreifen
assemble /ə'sembl/ *vi* sich versammeln ● *vt* versammeln; (*Techn*) montieren
assembly /ə'semblɪ/ *n* Versammlung *f*; (*Sch*) Andacht *f*; (*Techn*) Montage *f*. **~ line** *n* Fließband *nt*
assent /ə'sent/ *n* Zustimmung *f* ● *vi* zustimmen (**to** *dat*)
assert /ə'sɜ:t/ *vt* behaupten; **~ oneself** sich durchsetzen. **~ion** /-ɜ:ʃn/ *n* Behauptung *f*. **~ive** /-tɪv/ *a* **be ~ive** sich durchsetzen können
assess /ə'ses/ *vt* bewerten; (*fig & for tax purposes*) einschätzen; schätzen ⟨*value*⟩. **~ment** *n* Einschätzung *f*; (*of tax*) Steuerbescheid *m*
asset /'æset/ *n* Vorteil *m*; **~s** *pl* (*money*) Vermögen *nt*; (*Comm*) Aktiva *pl*
assiduous /ə'sɪdjʊəs/ *a*, **-ly** *adv* fleißig
assign /ə'saɪn/ *vt* zuweisen (**to** *dat*). **~ment** *n* (*task*) Aufgabe *f*
assimilate /ə'sɪmɪleɪt/ *vt* aufnehmen; (*integrate*) assimilieren
assist /ə'sɪst/ *vt/i* helfen (+ *dat*). **~ance** *n* Hilfe *f*. **~ant** *a* Hilfs- ● *n* Assistent(in) *m(f)*; (*in shop*) Verkäufer(in) *m(f)*
associat|e[1] /ə'səʊʃɪeɪt/ *vt* verbinden; (*Psych*) assoziieren ● *vi* **~ with** verkehren mit. **~ion** /-'eɪʃn/ *n* Verband *m*. **A~ion 'football** *n* Fußball *m*
associate[2] /ə'səʊʃɪət/ *a* assoziiert ● *n* Kollege *m*/-gin *f*
assort|ed /ə'sɔ:tɪd/ *a* gemischt. **~ment** *n* Mischung *f*
assum|e /ə'sju:m/ *vt* annehmen; übernehmen ⟨*office*⟩; **~ing that** angenommen, daß
assumption /ə'sʌmpʃn/ *n* Annahme *f*; **on the ~** in der Annahme (**that** daß)
assurance /ə'ʃʊərəns/ *n* Versicherung *f*; (*confidence*) Selbstsicherheit *f*
assure /ə'ʃʊə(r)/ *vt* versichern (**s.o.** jdm); **I ~ you [of that]** das versichere ich Ihnen. **~d** *a* sicher
asterisk /'æstərɪsk/ *n* Sternchen *nt*
astern /ə'stɜ:n/ *adv* achtern
asthma /'æsmə/ *n* Asthma *nt*. **~tic** /-'mætɪk/ *a* asthmatisch
astonish /ə'stɒnɪʃ/ *vt* erstaunen. **~ing** *a* erstaunlich. **~ment** *n* Erstaunen *nt*
astound /ə'staʊnd/ *vt* in Erstaunen setzen
astray /ə'streɪ/ *adv* **go ~** verlorengehen; ⟨*person:*⟩ sich verlaufen; (*fig*) vom rechten Weg abkommen; **lead ~** verleiten
astride /ə'straɪd/ *adv* rittlings ● *prep* rittlings auf (+ *dat*/*acc*)
astringent /ə'strɪndʒənt/ *a* adstringierend; (*fig*) beißend
astrolog|er /ə'strɒlədʒə(r)/ *n* Astrologe *m*/-gin *f*. **~y** *n* Astrologie *f*
astronaut /'æstrənɔ:t/ *n* Astronaut(in) *m(f)*
astronom|er /ə'strɒnəmə(r)/ *n* Astronom *m*. **~ical** /æstrə'nɒmɪkl/ *a* astronomisch. **~y** *n* Astronomie *f*
astute /ə'stju:t/ *a* scharfsinnig. **~ness** *n* Scharfsinn *m*
asylum /ə'saɪləm/ *n* Asyl *nt*; **[lunatic] ~** Irrenanstalt *f*
at /ət, *betont* æt/ *prep* an (+ *dat*/*acc*); (*with town*) in; (*price*) zu; (*speed*) mit; **at the station** am Bahnhof; **at the beginning/end** am Anfang/Ende; **at home** zu Hause; **at John's** bei John; **at work/the hairdresser's** bei der Arbeit/beim Friseur; **at school/the office** in der Schule/im Büro; **at a party/wedding** auf einer Party/Hochzeit; **at one o'clock** um ein Uhr; **at Christmas/Easter** zu Weihnachten/Ostern; **at the age of** im Alter von; **not at all** gar nicht; **at times** manchmal; **two at a time** zwei auf einmal; **good/bad at languages** gut/schlecht in Sprachen
ate /et/ *see* **eat**
atheist /'eɪθɪɪst/ *n* Atheist(in) *m(f)*
athlet|e /'æθli:t/ *n* Athlet(in) *m(f)*. **~ic** /-'letɪk/ *a* sportlich. **~ics** /-'letɪks/ *n* Leichtathletik *f*
Atlantic /ət'læntɪk/ *a* & *n* **the ~ [Ocean]** der Atlantik
atlas /'ætləs/ *n* Atlas *m*
atmospher|e /'ætməsfɪə(r)/ *n* Atmosphäre *f*. **~ic** /-'ferɪk/ *a* atmosphärisch
atom /'ætəm/ *n* Atom *nt*. **~ bomb** *n* Atombombe *f*
atomic /ə'tɒmɪk/ *a* Atom-
atone /ə'təʊn/ *vi* büßen (**for** für). **~ment** *n* Buße *f*
atrocious /ə'trəʊʃəs/ *a* abscheulich
atrocity /ə'trɒsətɪ/ *n* Greueltat *f*

attach /ə'tætʃ/ *vt* befestigen (**to** an + *dat*); beimessen ⟨*importance*⟩ (**to** *dat*); **be ~ed to** (*fig*) hängen an (+ *dat*)

attaché /ə'tæʃeɪ/ *n* Attaché *m*. **~ case** *n* Aktenkoffer *m*

attachment /ə'tætʃmənt/ *n* Bindung *f*; (*tool*) Zubehörteil *nt*; (*additional*) Zusatzgerät *nt*

attack /ə'tæk/ *n* Angriff *m*; (*Med*) Anfall *m* • *vt/i* angreifen. **~er** *n* Angreifer *m*

attain /ə'teɪn/ *vt* erreichen; (*get*) erlangen. **~able** /-əbl/ *a* erreichbar

attempt /ə'tempt/ *n* Versuch *m* • *vt* versuchen

attend /ə'tend/ *vt* anwesend sein bei; (*go regularly to*) besuchen; (*take part in*) teilnehmen an (+ *dat*); (*accompany*) begleiten; ⟨*doctor:*⟩ behandeln • *vi* anwesend sein; (*pay attention*) aufpassen; **~ to** sich kümmern um; (*in shop*) bedienen. **~ance** *n* Anwesenheit *f*; (*number*) Besucherzahl *f*. **~ant** *n* Wärter(in) *m*(*f*); (*in car park*) Wächter *m*

attention /ə'tenʃn/ *n* Aufmerksamkeit *f*; **~!** (*Mil*) stillgestanden! **pay ~** aufpassen; **pay ~ to** beachten, achten auf (+ *acc*); **need ~** reparaturbedürftig sein; **for the ~ of** zu Händen von

attentive /ə'tentɪv/ *a*, **-ly** *adv* aufmerksam

attest /ə'test/ *vt/i* **~ [to]** bezeugen

attic /'ætɪk/ *n* Dachboden *m*

attire /ə'taɪə(r)/ *n* Kleidung *f* • *vt* kleiden

attitude /'ætɪtju:d/ *n* Haltung *f*

attorney /ə'tɜ:nɪ/ *n* (*Amer: lawyer*) Rechtsanwalt *m*; **power of ~** Vollmacht *f*

attract /ə'trækt/ *vt* anziehen; erregen ⟨*attention*⟩; **~ s.o.'s attention** jds Aufmerksamkeit auf sich (*acc*) lenken. **~ion** /-ækʃn/ *n* Anziehungskraft *f*; (*charm*) Reiz *m*; (*thing*) Attraktion *f*. **~ive** /-tɪv/ *a*, **-ly** *adv* attraktiv

attribute[1] /'ætrɪbju:t/ *n* Attribut *nt*

attribut|e[2] /ə'trɪbju:t/ *vt* zuschreiben (**to** *dat*). **~ive** /-tɪv/ *a*, **-ly** *adv* attributiv

attrition /ə'trɪʃn/ *n* **war of ~** Zermürbungskrieg *m*

aubergine /'əʊbəʒi:n/ *n* Aubergine *f*

auburn /'ɔ:bən/ *a* kastanienbraun

auction /'ɔ:kʃn/ *n* Auktion *f*, Versteigerung *f* • *vt* versteigern. **~eer** /-ʃə'nɪə(r)/ *n* Auktionator *m*

audaci|ous /ɔ:'deɪʃəs/ *a*, **-ly** *adv* verwegen. **~ty** /-'dæsətɪ/ *n* Verwegenheit *f*; (*impudence*) Dreistigkeit *f*

audible /'ɔ:dəbl/ *a*, **-bly** *adv* hörbar

audience /'ɔ:dɪəns/ *n* Publikum *nt*; (*Theat, TV*) Zuschauer *pl*; (*Radio*) Zuhörer *pl*; (*meeting*) Audienz *f*

audio /'ɔ:dɪəʊ/: **~ typist** *n* Phonotypistin *f*. **~'visual** *a* audiovisuell

audit /'ɔ:dɪt/ *n* Bücherrevision *f* • *vt* (*Comm*) prüfen

audition /ɔ:'dɪʃn/ *n* (*Theat*) Vorsprechen *nt*; (*Mus*) Vorspielen *nt*; (*for singer*) Vorsingen *nt* • *vi* vorsprechen; vorspielen; vorsingen

auditor /'ɔ:dɪtə(r)/ *n* Buchprüfer *m*

auditorium /ɔ:dɪ'tɔ:rɪəm/ *n* Zuschauerraum *m*

augment /ɔ:g'ment/ *vt* vergrößern

augur /'ɔ:gə(r)/ *vi* **~ well/ill** etwas/nichts Gutes verheißen

august /ɔ:'gʌst/ *a* hoheitsvoll

August /'ɔ:gəst/ *n* August *m*

aunt /ɑ:nt/ *n* Tante *f*

au pair /əʊ'peə(r)/ *n* **~ [girl]** Au-pair-Mädchen *nt*

aura /'ɔ:rə/ *n* Fluidum *nt*

auspices /'ɔ:spɪsɪz/ *npl* (*protection*) Schirmherrschaft *f*

auspicious /ɔ:'spɪʃəs/ *a* günstig; ⟨*occasion*⟩ freudig

auster|e /ɒ'stɪə(r)/ *a* streng; (*simple*) nüchtern. **~ity** /-terətɪ/ *n* Strenge *f*; (*hardship*) Entbehrung *f*

Australia /ɒ'streɪlɪə/ *n* Australien *nt*. **~n** *a* australisch • *n* Australier(in) *m*(*f*)

Austria /'ɒstrɪə/ *n* Österreich *nt*. **~n** *a* österreichisch • *n* Österreicher(in) *m*(*f*)

authentic /ɔ:'θentɪk/ *a* echt, authentisch. **~ate** *vt* beglaubigen. **~ity** /-'tɪsətɪ/ *n* Echtheit *f*

author /'ɔ:θə(r)/ *n* Schriftsteller *m*, Autor *m*; (*of document*) Verfasser *m*

authoritarian /ɔ:θɒrɪ'teərɪən/ *a* autoritär

authoritative /ɔ:'θɒrɪtətɪv/ *a* maßgebend; **be ~** Autorität haben

authority /ɔ:'θɒrətɪ/ *n* Autorität *f*; (*public*) Behörde *f*; **in ~** verantwortlich

authorization /ɔ:θəraɪ'zeɪʃn/ *n* Ermächtigung *f*

authorize /'ɔ:θəraɪz/ *vt* ermächtigen ‹*s.o.*›; genehmigen ‹*sth*›
autobi'ography /ɔ:tə-/ *n* Autobiographie *f*
autocratic /ɔ:tə'krætɪk/ *a* autokratisch
autograph /'ɔ:tə-/ *n* Autogramm *nt*
automatic /ɔ:tə'mætɪk/ *a*, **-ally** *adv* automatisch ● *n* (*car*) Fahrzeug *nt* mit Automatikgetriebe; (*washing machine*) Waschautomat *m*
automation /ɔ:tə'meɪʃn/ *n* Automation *f*
automobile /'ɔ:təməbi:l/ *n* Auto *nt*
autonom|ous /ɔ:'tɒnəməs/ *a* autonom. **~y** *n* Autonomie *f*
autopsy /'ɔ:tɒpsɪ/ *n* Autopsie *f*
autumn /'ɔ:təm/ *n* Herbst *m*. **~al** /-'tʌmnl/ *a* herbstlich
auxiliary /ɔ:g'zɪlɪərɪ/ *a* Hilfs- ● *n* Helfer(in) *m(f)*, Hilfskraft *f*
avail /ə'veɪl/ *n* **to no ~** vergeblich ● *vi* **~ oneself of** Gebrauch machen von
available /ə'veɪləbl/ *a* verfügbar; (*obtainable*) erhältlich
avalanche /'ævəlɑ:nʃ/ *n* Lawine *f*
avaric|e /'ævərɪs/ *n* Habsucht *f*. **~ious** /-'rɪʃəs/ *a* habgierig, habsüchtig
avenge /ə'vendʒ/ *vt* rächen
avenue /'ævənju:/ *n* Allee *f*
average /'ævərɪdʒ/ *a* Durchschnitts-, durchschnittlich ● *n* Durchschnitt *m*; **on ~** im Durchschnitt, durchschnittlich ● *vt* durchschnittlich schaffen ● *vi* **~ out at** im Durchschnitt ergeben
avers|e /ə'vɜ:s/ *a* **not be ~e to sth** etw (*dat*) nicht abgeneigt sein. **~ion** /-ɜ:ʃn/ *n* Abneigung *f* (**to** gegen)
avert /ə'vɜ:t/ *vt* abwenden
aviary /'eɪvɪərɪ/ *n* Vogelhaus *nt*
aviation /eɪvɪ'eɪʃn/ *n* Luftfahrt *f*
avid /'ævɪd/ *a* gierig (**for** nach); (*keen*) eifrig
avocado /ævə'kɑ:dəʊ/ *n* Avocado *f*
avoid /ə'vɔɪd/ *vt* vermeiden; **~ s.o.** jdm aus dem Weg gehen. **~able** /-əbl/ *a* vermeidbar. **~ance** *n* Vermeidung *f*
await /ə'weɪt/ *vt* warten auf (+ *acc*)
awake /ə'weɪk/ *a* wach; **wide ~** hellwach ● *vi* (*pt* **awoke**, *pp* **awoken**) erwachen
awaken /ə'weɪkn/ *vt* wecken ● *vi* erwachen. **~ing** *n* Erwachen *nt*
award /ə'wɔ:d/ *n* Auszeichnung *f*; (*prize*) Preis *m* ● *vt* zuerkennen (**to s.o.** *dat*); verleihen ‹*prize*›
aware /ə'weə(r)/ *a* **become ~** gewahr werden (**of** *gen*); **be ~ that** wissen, daß. **~ness** *n* Bewußtsein *nt*
awash /ə'wɒʃ/ *a* **be ~** unter Wasser stehen
away /ə'weɪ/ *adv* weg, fort; (*absent*) abwesend; **be ~** nicht da sein; **far ~** weit weg; **four kilometres ~** vier Kilometer entfernt; **play ~** (*Sport*) auswärts spielen; **go/stay ~** weggehen/-bleiben. **~ game** *n* Auswärtsspiel *nt*
awe /ɔ:/ *n* Ehrfurcht *f*
awful /'ɔ:fl/ *a*, **-ly** *adv* furchtbar
awhile /ə'waɪl/ *adv* eine Weile
awkward /'ɔ:kwəd/ *a* schwierig; (*clumsy*) ungeschickt; (*embarrassing*) peinlich; (*inconvenient*) ungünstig. **~ly** *adv* ungeschickt; (*embarrassedly*) verlegen
awning /'ɔ:nɪŋ/ *n* Markise *f*
awoke(n) /ə'wəʊk(ən)/ *see* **awake**
awry /ə'raɪ/ *adv* schief
axe /æks/ *n* Axt *f* ● *vt* (*pres p* **axing**) streichen; (*dismiss*) entlassen
axis /'æksɪs/ *n* (*pl* **axes** /-si:z/) Achse *f*
axle /'æksl/ *n* (*Techn*) Achse *f*
ay[e] /aɪ/ *adv* ja ● *n* Jastimme *f*

B

B /bi:/ *n* (*Mus*) H *nt*
BA *abbr of* **Bachelor of Arts**
babble /'bæbl/ *vi* plappern; ‹*stream:*› plätschern
baboon /bə'bu:n/ *n* Pavian *m*
baby /'beɪbɪ/ *n* Baby *nt*; (*Amer, fam*) Schätzchen *nt*
baby: ~ carriage *n* (*Amer*) Kinderwagen *m*. **~ish** *a* kindisch. **~-minder** *n* Tagesmutter *f*. **~-sit** *vi* babysitten. **~-sitter** *n* Babysitter *m*
bachelor /'bætʃələ(r)/ *n* Junggeselle *m*; **B~ of Arts/Science** Bakkalaureus Artium/Scientium
bacillus /bə'sɪləs/ *n* (*pl* **-lli**) Bazillus *m*
back /bæk/ *n* Rücken *m*; (*reverse*) Rückseite *f*; (*of chair*) Rückenlehne *f*; (*Sport*) Verteidiger *m*; **at/**(*Auto*) **in the ~** hinten; **on the ~** auf der Rückseite; **~ to front** verkehrt; **at the ~ of beyond** am Ende der Welt ● *a* Hinter- ● *adv* zurück; **~ here/there** hier/da hinten; **~ at home** zu Hause; **go/pay ~** zurückgehen/-zahlen ● *vt* (*support*) unterstützen; (*with money*) finanzieren; (*Auto*)

zurücksetzen; (*Betting*) [Geld] setzen auf (+ *acc*); (*cover the back of*) mit einer Verstärkung versehen ● *vi* (*Auto*) zurücksetzen. ~ **down** *vi* klein beigeben. ~ **in** *vi* rückwärts hineinfahren. ~ **out** *vi* rückwärts hinaus-/herausfahren; (*fig*) aussteigen (**of** aus). ~ **up** *vt* unterstützen; (*confirm*) bestätigen ● *vi* (*Auto*) zurücksetzen

back: ~ache *n* Rückenschmerzen *pl*. **~biting** *n* gehässiges Gerede *nt*. **~bone** *n* Rückgrat *nt*. **~chat** *n* Widerrede *f*. **~-comb** *vt* toupieren. **~date** *vt* rückdatieren; **~dated to** rückwirkend von. **~ 'door** *n* Hintertür *f*

backer /'bækə(r)/ *n* Geldgeber *m*

back: ~'fire *vi* (*Auto*) fehlzünden; (*fig*) fehlschlagen. **~ground** *n* Hintergrund *m*; **family ~ground** Familienverhältnisse *pl*. **~hand** *n* (*Sport*) Rückhand *f*. **~'handed** *a* ⟨*compliment*⟩ zweifelhaft. **~'hander** *n* (*Sport*) Rückhandschlag *m*; (*fam: bribe*) Schmiergeld *nt*

backing /'bækɪŋ/ *n* (*support*) Unterstützung *f*; (*material*) Verstärkung *f*

back: ~lash *n* (*fig*) Gegenschlag *m*. **~log** *n* Rückstand *m* (**of** an + *dat*). **~ 'seat** *n* Rücksitz *m*. **~side** *n* (*fam*) Hintern *m*. **~stage** *adv* hinter der Bühne. **~stroke** *n* Rückenschwimmen *nt*. **~-up** *n* Unterstützung *f*; (*Amer: traffic jam*) Stau *m*

backward /'bækwəd/ *a* zurückgeblieben; ⟨*country*⟩ rückständig ● *adv* rückwärts. **~s** rückwärts; **~s and forwards** hin und her

back: ~water *n* (*fig*) unberührtes Fleckchen *nt*. **~ 'yard** *n* Hinterhof *m*; **not in my ~ yard** (*fam*) nicht vor meiner Haustür

bacon /'beɪkn/ *n* [Schinken]speck *m*

bacteria /bæk'tɪərɪə/ *npl* Bakterien *pl*

bad /bæd/ *a* (**worse, worst**) schlecht; (*serious*) schwer, schlimm; (*naughty*) unartig; **~ language** gemeine Ausdrucksweise *f*; **feel ~** sich schlecht fühlen; (*feel guilty*) ein schlechtes Gewissen haben; **go ~** schlecht werden

bade /bæd/ *see* **bid²**

badge /bædʒ/ *n* Abzeichen *nt*

badger /'bædʒə(r)/ *n* Dachs *m* ● *vt* plagen

badly /'bædlɪ/ *adv* schlecht; (*seriously*) schwer; **~ off** schlecht gestellt; **~ behaved** unerzogen; **want ~** sich (*dat*) sehnsüchtig wünschen; **need ~** dringend brauchen

bad-'mannered *a* mit schlechten Manieren

badminton /'bædmɪntən/ *n* Federball *m*

bad-'tempered *a* schlecht gelaunt

baffle /'bæfl/ *vt* verblüffen

bag /bæg/ *n* Tasche *f*; (*of paper*) Tüte *f*; (*pouch*) Beutel *m*; **~s of** (*fam*) jede Menge ● *vt* (*fam: reserve*) in Beschlag nehmen

baggage /'bægɪdʒ/ *n* [Reise]gepäck *nt*

baggy /'bægɪ/ *a* ⟨*clothes*⟩ ausgebeult

'bagpipes *npl* Dudelsack *m*

bail /beɪl/ *n* Kaution *f*; **on ~** gegen Kaution ● *vt* **~ s.o. out** jdn gegen Kaution freibekommen; (*fig*) jdm aus der Patsche helfen. **~ out** *vt* (*Naut*) ausschöpfen ● *vi* (*Aviat*) abspringen

bailiff /'beɪlɪf/ *n* Gerichtsvollzieher *m*; (*of estate*) Gutsverwalter *m*

bait /beɪt/ *n* Köder *m* ● *vt* mit einem Köder versehen; (*fig: torment*) reizen

bake /beɪk/ *vt/i* backen

baker /'beɪkə(r)/ *n* Bäcker *m*; **~'s [shop]** Bäckerei *f*. **~y** *n* Bäckerei *f*

baking /'beɪkɪŋ/ *n* Backen *nt*. **~-powder** *n* Backpulver *nt*. **~-tin** *n* Backform *f*

balance /'bæləns/ *n* (*equilibrium*) Gleichgewicht *nt*, Balance *f*; (*scales*) Waage *f*; (*Comm*) Saldo *m*; (*outstanding sum*) Restbetrag *m*; **[bank] ~** Kontostand *m*; **in the ~** (*fig*) in der Schwebe ● *vt* balancieren; (*equalize*) ausgleichen; (*Comm*) abschließen ⟨*books*⟩ ● *vi* balancieren; (*fig & Comm*) sich ausgleichen. **~d** *a* ausgewogen. **~ sheet** *n* Bilanz *f*

balcony /'bælkənɪ/ *n* Balkon *m*

bald /bɔːld/ *a* (**-er, -est**) kahl; ⟨*person*⟩ kahlköpfig; **go ~** eine Glatze bekommen

balderdash /'bɔːldədæʃ/ *n* Unsinn *m*

bald|ing /'bɔːldɪŋ/ *a* **be ~ing** eine Glatze bekommen. **~ly** *adv* unverblümt. **~ness** *n* Kahlköpfigkeit *f*

bale /beɪl/ *n* Ballen *m*

baleful /'beɪlfl/ *a*, **-ly** *adv* böse

balk /bɔːlk/ *vt* vereiteln ● *vi* **~ at** zurückschrecken vor (+ *dat*)

Balkans /'bɔːlknz/ *npl* Balkan *m*

ball¹ /bɔːl/ *n* Ball *m*; (*Billiards, Croquet*) Kugel *f*; (*of yarn*) Knäuel *m* & *nt*; **on the ~** (*fam*) auf Draht

ball[2] *n* (*dance*) Ball *m*
ballad /'bæləd/ *n* Ballade *f*
ballast /'bæləst/ *n* Ballast *m*
ball-'bearing *n* Kugellager *nt*
ballerina /bælə'ri:nə/ *n* Ballerina *f*
ballet /'bæleı/ *m* Ballett *nt*. **~ dancer** *n* Ballettänzer(in) *m(f)*
ballistic /bə'lıstık/ *a* ballistisch. **~s** *n* Ballistik *f*
balloon /bə'lu:n/ *n* Luftballon *m*; (*Aviat*) Ballon *m*
ballot /'bælət/ *n* [geheime] Wahl *f*; (*on issue*) [geheime] Abstimmung *f*. **~-box** *n* Wahlurne *f*. **~-paper** *n* Stimmzettel *m*
ball: ~-point ['pen] *n* Kugelschreiber *m*. **~room** *n* Ballsaal *m*
balm /bɑ:m/ *n* Balsam *m*
balmy /'bɑ:mı/ *a* (**-ier, -iest**) *a* sanft; (*fam: crazy*) verrückt
Baltic /'bɔ:ltık/ *a & n* **the ~ [Sea]** die Ostsee
balustrade /bælə'streıd/ *n* Balustrade *f*
bamboo /bæm'bu:/ *n* Bambus *m*
bamboozle /bæm'bu:zl/ *vt* (*fam*) übers Ohr hauen
ban /bæn/ *n* Verbot *nt* ● *vt* (*pt/pp* **banned**) verbieten
banal /bə'nɑ:l/ *a* banal. **~ity** /-'ælətı/ *n* Banalität *f*
banana /bə'nɑ:nə/ *n* Banane *f*
band /bænd/ *n* Band *nt*; (*stripe*) Streifen *m*; (*group*) Schar *f*; (*Mus*) Kapelle *f* ● *vi* **~ together** sich zusammenschließen
bandage /'bændıdʒ/ *n* Verband *m*; (*for support*) Bandage *f* ● *vt* verbinden; bandagieren ⟨*limb*⟩
b. & b. *abbr of* **bed and breakfast**
bandit /'bændıt/ *n* Bandit *m*
band: ~stand *n* Musikpavillon *m*. **~wagon** *n* **jump on the ~wagon** (*fig*) sich einer erfolgreichen Sache anschließen
bandy[1] /'bændı/ *vt* (*pt/pp* **-ied**) wechseln ⟨*words*⟩
bandy[2] *a* (**-ier, -iest**) **be ~** O-Beine haben. **~-legged** *a* O-beinig
bang /bæŋ/ *n* (*noise*) Knall *m*; (*blow*) Schlag *m* ● *adv* **go ~** knallen ● *int* bums! peng! ● *vt* knallen; (*shut noisily*) zuknallen; (*strike*) schlagen auf (+ *acc*); **~ one's head** sich (*dat*) den Kopf stoßen (**on** an + *acc*) ● *vi* schlagen; ⟨*door:*⟩ zuknallen
banger /'bæŋə(r)/ *n* (*firework*) Knallfrosch *m*; (*fam: sausage*) Wurst *f*; **old ~** (*fam: car*) Klapperkiste *f*
bangle /'bæŋgl/ *n* Armreifen *m*
banish /'bænıʃ/ *vt* verbannen
banisters /'bænıstəz/ *npl* [Treppen]geländer *nt*
banjo /'bændʒəʊ/ *n* Banjo *nt*
bank[1] /bæŋk/ *n* (*of river*) Ufer *nt*; (*slope*) Hang *m* ● *vi* (*Aviat*) in die Kurve gehen
bank[2] *n* Bank *f* ● *vt* einzahlen; **~ with** ein Konto haben bei. **~ on** *vt* sich verlassen auf (+ *acc*)
'bank account *n* Bankkonto *nt*
banker /'bæŋkə(r)/ *n* Bankier *m*
bank: ~ 'holiday *n* gesetzlicher Feiertag *m*. **~ing** *n* Bankwesen *nt*. **~note** *n* Banknote *f*
bankrupt /'bæŋkrʌpt/ *a* bankrott; **go ~** bankrott machen ● *n* Bankrotteur *m* ● *vt* bankrott machen. **~cy** *n* Bankrott *m*
banner /'bænə(r)/ *n* Banner *nt*; (*carried by demonstrators*) Transparent *nt*, Spruchband *nt*
banns /bænz/ *npl* (*Relig*) Aufgebot *nt*
banquet /'bæŋkwıt/ *n* Bankett *nt*
banter /'bæntə(r)/ *n* Spöttelei *f*
bap /bæp/ *n* weiches Brötchen *nt*
baptism /'bæptızm/ *n* Taufe *f*
Baptist /'bæptıst/ *n* Baptist(in) *m(f)*
baptize /bæp'taız/ *vt* taufen
bar /bɑ:(r)/ *n* Stange *f*; (*of cage*) [Gitter]stab *m*; (*of gold*) Barren *m*; (*of chocolate*) Tafel *f*; (*of soap*) Stück *nt*; (*long*) Riegel *m*; (*café*) Bar *f*; (*counter*) Theke *f*; (*Mus*) Takt *m*; (*fig: obstacle*) Hindernis *nt*; **parallel ~s** (*Sport*) Barren *m*; **be called to the ~** (*Jur*) als plädierender Anwalt zugelassen werden; **behind ~s** (*fam*) hinter Gittern ● *vt* (*pt/pp* **barred**) versperren ⟨*way, door*⟩; ausschließen ⟨*person*⟩ ● *prep* außer; **~ none** ohne Ausnahme
barbarian /bɑ:'beərıən/ *n* Barbar *m*
barbar|ic /bɑ:'bærık/ *a* barbarisch. **~ity** *n* Barbarei *f*. **~ous** /'bɑ:bərəs/ *a* barbarisch
barbecue /'bɑ:bıkju:/ *n* Grill *m*; (*party*) Grillfest *nt* ● *vt* [im Freien] grillen
barbed /'bɑ:bd/ *a* **~ wire** Stacheldraht *m*
barber /'bɑ:bə(r)/ *n* [Herren]friseur *m*
barbiturate /bɑ:'bıtjʊrət/ *n* Barbiturat *nt*
'bar code *n* Strichkode *m*
bare /beə(r)/ *a* (**-r, -st**) nackt, bloß; ⟨*tree*⟩ kahl; (*empty*) leer; (*mere*) bloß ● *vt* entblößen; fletschen ⟨*teeth*⟩

bare: ~back *adv* ohne Sattel. **~faced** *a* schamlos. **~foot** *adv* barfuß. **~'headed** *a* mit unbedecktem Kopf

barely /'beəlɪ/ *adv* kaum

bargain /'bɑ:gɪn/ *n* (*agreement*) Geschäft *nt*; (*good buy*) Gelegenheitskauf *m*; **into the ~** noch dazu; **make a ~** sich einigen ● *vi* handeln; (*haggle*) feilschen; **~ for** (*expect*) rechnen mit

barge /bɑ:dʒ/ *n* Lastkahn *m*; (*towed*) Schleppkahn *m* ● *vi* **~ in** (*fam*) hereinplatzen

baritone /'bærɪtəʊn/ *n* Bariton *m*

bark[1] /bɑ:k/ *n* (*of tree*) Rinde *f*

bark[2] *n* Bellen *nt* ● *vi* bellen

barley /'bɑ:lɪ/ *n* Gerste *f*

bar: ~maid *n* Schankmädchen *nt*. **~man** Barmann *m*

barmy /'bɑ:mɪ/ *a* (*fam*) verrückt

barn /bɑ:n/ *n* Scheune *f*

barometer /bə'rɒmɪtə(r)/ *n* Barometer *nt*

baron /'bærn/ *n* Baron *m*. **~ess** *n* Baronin *f*

baroque /bə'rɒk/ *a* barock ● *n* Barock *nt*

barracks /'bærəks/ *npl* Kaserne *f*

barrage /'bærɑ:ʒ/ *n* (*in river*) Wehr *nt*; (*Mil*) Sperrfeuer *nt*; (*fig*) Hagel *m*

barrel /'bærl/ *n* Faß *nt*; (*of gun*) Lauf *m*; (*of cannon*) Rohr *nt*. **~-organ** *n* Drehorgel *f*

barren /'bærn/ *a* unfruchtbar; ⟨*landscape*⟩ öde

barricade /bærɪ'keɪd/ *n* Barrikade *f* ● *vt* verbarrikadieren

barrier /'bærɪə(r)/ *n* Barriere *f*; (*across road*) Schranke *f*; (*Rail*) Sperre *f*; (*fig*) Hindernis *nt*

barring /'bɑ:rɪŋ/ *prep* **~ accidents** wenn alles gutgeht

barrister /'bærɪstə(r)/ *n* [plädierender] Rechtsanwalt *m*

barrow /'bærəʊ/ *n* Karre *f*, Karren *m*. **~ boy** *n* Straßenhändler *m*

barter /'bɑ:tə(r)/ *vt* tauschen (**for** gegen)

base /beɪs/ *n* Fuß *m*; (*fig*) Basis *f*; (*Mil*) Stützpunkt *m* ● *a* gemein; ⟨*metal*⟩ unedel ● *vt* stützen (**on** auf + *acc*); **be ~d on** basieren auf (+ *dat*)

base: ~ball *n* Baseball *m*. **~less** *a* unbegründet. **~ment** *n* Kellergeschoß *nt*. **~ment flat** *n* Kellerwohnung *f*

bash /bæʃ/ *n* Schlag *m*; **have a ~!** (*fam*) probier es mal! ● *vt* hauen; (*dent*) einbeulen; **~ed in** verbeult

bashful /'bæʃfl/ *a*, **-ly** *adv* schüchtern

basic /'beɪsɪk/ *a* Grund-; (*fundamental*) grundlegend; (*essential*) wesentlich; (*unadorned*) einfach; **the ~s** das Wesentliche. **~ally** *adv* grundsätzlich

basil /'bæzɪl/ *n* Basilikum *nt*

basilica /bə'zɪlɪkə/ *n* Basilika *f*

basin /'beɪsn/ *n* Becken *nt*; (*for washing*) Waschbecken *nt*; (*for food*) Schüssel *f*

basis /'beɪsɪs/ *n* (*pl* **-ses** /-si:z/) Basis *f*

bask /bɑ:sk/ *vi* sich sonnen

basket /'bɑ:skɪt/ *n* Korb *m*. **~ball** *n* Basketball *m*

Basle /bɑ:l/ *n* Basel *nt*

bass /beɪs/ *a* Baß-; **~ voice** Baßstimme *f* ● *n* Baß *m*; (*person*) Bassist *m*

bassoon /bə'su:n/ *n* Fagott *nt*

bastard /'bɑ:stəd/ *n* (*sl*) Schuft *m*

baste[1] /beɪst/ *vt* (*sew*) heften

baste[2] *vt* (*Culin*) begießen

bastion /'bæstɪən/ *n* Bastion *f*

bat[1] /bæt/ *n* Schläger *m*; **off one's own ~** (*fam*) auf eigene Faust ● *vt* (*pt/pp* **batted**) schlagen; **not ~ an eyelid** (*fig*) nicht mit der Wimper zucken

bat[2] *n* (*Zool*) Fledermaus *f*

batch /bætʃ/ *n* (*of people*) Gruppe *f*; (*of papers*) Stoß *m*; (*of goods*) Sendung *f*; (*of bread*) Schub *m*

bated /'beɪtɪd/ *a* **with ~ breath** mit angehaltenem Atem

bath /bɑ:θ/ *n* (*pl* **~s** /bɑ:ðz/) Bad *nt*; (*tub*) Badewanne *f*; **~s** *pl* Badeanstalt *f*; **have a ~** baden ● *vt/i* baden

bathe /beɪð/ *n* Bad *nt* ● *vt/i* baden. **~r** *n* Badende(r) *m/f*

bathing /'beɪðɪŋ/ *n* Baden *nt*. **~-cap** *n* Bademütze *f*. **~-costume** *n* Badeanzug *m*

bath: ~-mat *n* Badematte *f*. **~robe** *n* (*Amer*) Bademantel *m*. **~room** *n* Badezimmer *nt*. **~-towel** *n* Badetuch *nt*

baton /'bætn/ *n* (*Mus*) Taktstock *m*; (*Mil*) Stab *m*

battalion /bə'tælɪən/ *n* Bataillon *nt*

batten /'bætn/ *n* Latte *f*

batter /'bætə(r)/ *n* (*Culin*) flüssiger Teig *m* ● *vt* schlagen. **~ed** *a* ⟨*car*⟩ verbeult; ⟨*wife*⟩ mißhandelt

battery /'bætərɪ/ *n* Batterie *f*

battle /'bætl/ *n* Schlacht *f*; (*fig*) Kampf *m* • *vi* (*fig*) kämpfen (**for** um)

battle: ~axe *n* (*fam*) Drachen *m*. **~field** *n* Schlachtfeld *nt*. **~ship** *n* Schlachtschiff *nt*

batty /'bætɪ/ *a* (*fam*) verrückt

Bavaria /bə'veərɪə/ *n* Bayern *nt*. **~n** *a* bayrisch • *n* Bayer(in) *m*(*f*)

bawdy /'bɔ:dɪ/ *a* (**-ier, -iest**) derb

bawl /bɔ:l/ *vt*/*i* brüllen

bay[1] /beɪ/ *n* (*Geog*) Bucht *f*; (*Archit*) Erker *m*

bay[2] *n* **keep at ~** fernhalten

bay[3] *n* (*horse*) Braune(r) *m*

bay[4] *n* (*Bot*) [echter] Lorbeer *m*. **~-leaf** *n* Lorbeerblatt *nt*

bayonet /'beɪənet/ *n* Bajonett *nt*

bay 'window *n* Erkerfenster *nt*

bazaar /bə'zɑ:(r)/ *n* Basar *m*

BC *abbr* (**before Christ**) v. Chr.

be /bi:/ *vi* (*pres* **am, are, is,** *pl* **are**; *pt* **was,** *pl* **were**; *pp* **been**) sein; (*lie*) liegen; (*stand*) stehen; (*cost*) kosten; **he is a teacher** er ist Lehrer; **be quiet!** sei still! **I am cold/hot** mir ist kalt/heiß; **how are you?** wie geht es Ihnen? **I am well** mir geht es gut; **there is/are** es gibt; **what do you want to be?** was willst du werden? **I have been to Vienna** ich bin in Wien gewesen; **has the postman been?** war der Briefträger schon da? **it's hot, isn't it?** es ist heiß, nicht [wahr]? **you are coming too, aren't you?** du kommst mit, nicht [wahr]? **it's yours, is it?** das gehört also Ihnen? **yes he is/I am** ja; (*negating previous statement*) doch; **three and three are six** drei und drei macht sechs • *v aux* **~ reading/going** lesen/gehen; **I am coming/staying** ich komme/bleibe; **what is he doing?** was macht er? **I am being lazy** ich faulenze; **I was thinking of you** ich dachte an dich; **you were going to ...** du wolltest ...; **I am to stay** ich soll bleiben; **you are not to ...** du darfst nicht ...; **you are to do that immediately** das mußt du sofort machen • *passive* werden; **be attacked/deceived** überfallen/betrogen werden

beach /bi:tʃ/ *n* Strand *m*. **~wear** *n* Strandkleidung *f*

beacon /'bi:kn/ *n* Leuchtfeuer *nt*; (*Naut, Aviat*) Bake *f*

bead /bi:d/ *n* Perle *f*

beak /bi:k/ *n* Schnabel *m*

beaker /'bi:kə(r)/ *n* Becher *m*

beam /bi:m/ *n* Balken *m*; (*of light*) Strahl *m* • *vi* strahlen. **~ing** *a* [freude]strahlend

bean /bi:n/ *n* Bohne *f*; **spill the ~s** (*fam*) alles ausplaudern

bear[1] /beə(r)/ *n* Bär *m*

bear[2] *vt*/*i* (*pt* **bore**, *pp* **borne**) tragen; (*endure*) ertragen; gebären ⟨*child*⟩; **~ right** sich rechts halten. **~able** /-əbl/ *a* erträglich

beard /bɪəd/ *n* Bart *m*. **~ed** *a* bärtig

bearer /'beərə(r)/ *n* Träger *m*; (*of news, cheque*) Überbringer *m*; (*of passport*) Inhaber(in) *m*(*f*)

bearing /'beərɪŋ/ *n* Haltung *f*; (*Techn*) Lager *nt*; **have a ~ on** von Belang sein für; **get one's ~s** sich orientieren; **lose one's ~s** die Orientierung verlieren

beast /bi:st/ *n* Tier *nt*; (*fam: person*) Biest *nt*

beastly /'bi:stlɪ/ *a* (**-ier, -iest**) (*fam*) scheußlich; ⟨*person*⟩ gemein

beat /bi:t/ *n* Schlag *m*; (*of policeman*) Runde *f*; (*rhythm*) Takt *m* • *vt*/*i* (*pt* **beat**, *pp* **beaten**) schlagen; (*thrash*) verprügeln; klopfen ⟨*carpet*⟩; (*hammer*) hämmern (**on** an + *acc*); **~ a retreat** (*Mil*) sich zurückziehen; **~ it!** (*fam*) hau ab! **it ~s me** (*fam*) das begreife ich nicht. **~ up** *vt* zusammenschlagen

beat|en /'bi:tn/ *a* **off the ~en track** abseits. **~ing** *n* Prügel *pl*

beautician /bju:'tɪʃn/ *n* Kosmetikerin *f*

beauti|ful /'bju:tɪfl/ *a*, **-ly** *adv* schön. **~fy** /-faɪ/ *vt* (*pt*/*pp* **-ied**) verschönern

beauty /'bju:tɪ/ *n* Schönheit *f*. **~ parlour** *n* Kosmetiksalon *m*. **~ spot** *n* Schönheitsfleck *m*; (*place*) landschaftlich besonders reizvolle Stelle *f*

beaver /'bi:və(r)/ *n* Biber *m*

became /bɪ'keɪm/ *see* **become**

because /bɪ'kɒz/ *conj* weil • *adv* **~ of** wegen (+ *gen*)

beckon /'bekn/ *vt*/*i* **~ [to]** herbeiwinken

becom|e /bɪ'kʌm/ *vt*/*i* (*pt* **became**, *pp* **become**) werden. **~ing** *a* ⟨*clothes*⟩ kleidsam

bed /bed/ *n* Bett *nt*; (*layer*) Schicht *f*; (*of flowers*) Beet *nt*; **in ~** im Bett; **go to ~** ins *od* zu Bett gehen; **~ and breakfast** Zimmer mit Frühstück. **~clothes** *npl*, **~ding** *n* Bettzeug *nt*

bedlam /'bedləm/ *n* Chaos *nt*

'bedpan *n* Bettpfanne *f*

bedraggled /bɪ'drægld/ *a* naß und verschmutzt
bed: **~ridden** *a* bettlägerig. **~room** *n* Schlafzimmer *nt*
'bedside *n* **at his ~** an seinem Bett. **~ 'lamp** *n* Nachttischlampe *f*. **~ 'rug** *n* Bettvorleger *m*. **~ 'table** *n* Nachttisch *m*
bed: **~'sitter** *n*, **~-'sitting-room** *n* Wohnschlafzimmer *nt*. **~spread** *n* Tagesdecke *f*. **~time** *n* **at ~time** vor dem Schlafengehen
bee /bi:/ *n* Biene *f*
beech /bi:tʃ/ *n* Buche *f*
beef /bi:f/ *n* Rindfleisch *nt*. **~burger** *n* Hamburger *m*
bee: **~hive** *n* Bienenstock *m*. **~-keeper** *n* Imker(in) *m*(*f*). **~-keeping** *n* Bienenzucht *f*. **~-line** *n* **make a ~-line for** (*fam*) zusteuern auf (+ *acc*)
been /bi:n/ *see* **be**
beer /bɪə(r)/ *n* Bier *nt*
beet /bi:t/ *n* (*Amer: beetroot*) rote Bete *f*; **[sugar] ~** Zuckerrübe *f*
beetle /'bi:tl/ *n* Käfer *m*
'beetroot *n* rote Bete *f*
before /bɪ'fɔ:(r)/ *prep* vor (+ *dat/acc*); **the day ~ yesterday** vorgestern; **~ long** bald ● *adv* vorher; (*already*) schon; **never ~** noch nie; **~ that** davor ● *conj* (*time*) ehe, bevor. **~hand** *adv* vorher, im voraus
befriend /bɪ'frend/ *vt* sich anfreunden mit
beg /beg/ *v* (*pt/pp* **begged**) ● *vi* betteln ● *vt* (*entreat*) anflehen; (*ask*) bitten (**for** um)
began /bɪ'gæn/ *see* **begin**
beggar /'begə(r)/ *n* Bettler(in) *m*(*f*); (*fam*) Kerl *m*
begin /bɪ'gɪn/ *vt/i* (*pt* **began**, *pp* **begun**, *pres p* **beginning**) anfangen, beginnen; **to ~ with** anfangs. **~ner** *n* Anfänger(in) *m*(*f*). **~ning** *n* Anfang *m*, Beginn *m*
begonia /bɪ'gəʊnɪə/ *n* Begonie *f*
begrudge /bɪ'grʌdʒ/ *vt* mißgönnen
beguile /bɪ'gaɪl/ *vt* betören
begun /bɪ'gʌn/ *see* **begin**
behalf /bɪ'hɑ:f/ *n* **on ~ of** im Namen von; **on my ~** meinetwegen
behave /bɪ'heɪv/ *vi* sich verhalten; **~ oneself** sich benehmen
behaviour /bɪ'heɪvjə(r)/ *n* Verhalten *nt*; **good/bad ~** gutes/schlechtes Benehmen *nt*; **~ pattern** Verhaltensweise *f*
behead /bɪ'hed/ *vt* enthaupten
beheld /bɪ'held/ *see* **behold**
behind /bɪ'haɪnd/ *prep* hinter (+ *dat/acc*); **be ~ sth** hinter etw (*dat*) stecken ● *adv* hinten; (*late*) im Rückstand; **a long way ~** weit zurück; **in the car ~** im Wagen dahinter ● *n* (*fam*) Hintern *m*. **~hand** *adv* im Rückstand
behold /bɪ'həʊld/ *vt* (*pt/pp* **beheld**) (*liter*) sehen
beholden /bɪ'həʊldn/ *a* verbunden (**to** *dat*)
beige /beɪʒ/ *a* beige
being /'bi:ɪŋ/ *n* Dasein *nt*; **living ~** Lebewesen *nt*; **come into ~** entstehen
belated /bɪ'leɪtɪd/ *a*, **-ly** *adv* verspätet
belch /beltʃ/ *vi* rülpsen ● *vt* **~ out** ausstoßen ⟨*smoke*⟩
belfry /'belfrɪ/ *n* Glockenstube *f*; (*tower*) Glockenturm *m*
Belgian /'beldʒən/ *a* belgisch ● *n* Belgier(in) *m*(*f*)
Belgium /'beldʒəm/ *n* Belgien *nt*
belief /bɪ'li:f/ *n* Glaube *m*
believable /bɪ'li:vəbl/ *a* glaubhaft
believe /bɪ'li:v/ *vt/i* glauben (**s.o.** jdm; **in** an + *acc*). **~r** *n* (*Relig*) Gläubige(r) *m/f*
belittle /bɪ'lɪtl/ *vt* herabsetzen
bell /bel/ *n* Glocke *f*; (*on door*) Klingel *f*
belligerent /bɪ'lɪdʒərənt/ *a* kriegführend; (*aggressive*) streitlustig
bellow /'beləʊ/ *vt/i* brüllen
bellows /'beləʊz/ *npl* Blasebalg *m*
belly /'belɪ/ *n* Bauch *m*
belong /bɪ'lɒŋ/ *vi* gehören (**to** *dat*); (*be member*) angehören (**to** *dat*). **~ings** *npl* Sachen *pl*
beloved /bɪ'lʌvɪd/ *a* geliebt ● *n* Geliebte(r) *m/f*
below /bɪ'ləʊ/ *prep* unter (+ *dat/acc*) ● *adv* unten; (*Naut*) unter Deck
belt /belt/ *n* Gürtel *m*; (*area*) Zone *f*; (*Techn*) [Treib]riemen *m* ● *vi* (*fam: rush*) rasen ● *vt* (*fam: hit*) hauen
bemused /bɪ'mju:zd/ *a* verwirrt
bench /bentʃ/ *n* Bank *f*; (*work-*) Werkbank *f*; **the B~** (*Jur*) ≈ die Richter *pl*
bend /bend/ *n* Biegung *f*; (*in road*) Kurve *f*; **round the ~** (*fam*) verrückt ● *v* (*pt/pp* **bent**) ● *vt* biegen; beugen ⟨*arm, leg*⟩ ● *vi* sich bücken; ⟨*thing:*⟩ sich biegen; ⟨*road:*⟩ eine Biegung machen. **~ down** *vi* sich bücken. **~ over** *vi* sich vornüberbeugen

beneath /bɪ'ni:θ/ *prep* unter (+ *dat/acc*); **~ him** (*fig*) unter seiner Würde; **~ contempt** unter aller Würde ● *adv* darunter

benediction /benɪ'dɪkʃn/ *n* (*Relig*) Segen *m*

benefactor /'benɪfæktə(r)/ *n* Wohltäter(in) *m*(*f*)

beneficial /benɪ'fɪʃl/ *a* nützlich

beneficiary /benɪ'fɪʃərɪ/ *n* Begünstigte(r) *m/f*

benefit /'benɪfɪt/ *n* Vorteil *m*; (*allowance*) Unterstützung *f*; (*insurance*) Leistung *f*; **sickness ~** Krankengeld *nt* ● *v* (*pt/pp* **-fited**, *pres p* **-fiting**) ● *vt* nützen (+ *dat*) ● *vi* profitieren (**from** von)

benevolen|ce /bɪ'nevələns/ *n* Wohlwollen *nt*. **~t** *a*, **-ly** *adv* wohlwollend

benign /bɪ'naɪn/ *a*, **-ly** *adv* gütig; (*Med*) gutartig

bent /bent/ *see* **bend** ● *a* ⟨*person*⟩ gebeugt; (*distorted*) verbogen; (*fam: dishonest*) korrupt; **be ~ on doing sth** darauf erpicht sein, etw zu tun ● *n* Hang *m*, Neigung *f* (**for** zu); **artistic ~** künstlerische Ader *f*

be|queath /bɪ'kwi:ð/ *vt* vermachen (**to** *dat*). **~quest** /-'kwest/ *n* Vermächtnis *nt*

bereave|d /bɪ'ri:vd/ *n* **the ~d** *pl* die Hinterbliebenen. **~ment** *n* Trauerfall *m*; (*state*) Trauer *f*

bereft /bɪ'reft/ *a* **~ of** beraubt (+ *gen*)

beret /'bereɪ/ *n* Baskenmütze *f*

Berne /bɜ:n/ *n* Bern *nt*

berry /'berɪ/ *n* Beere *f*

berserk /bə'sɜ:k/ *a* **go ~** wild werden

berth /bɜ:θ/ *n* (*on ship*) [Schlaf]koje *f*; (*ship's anchorage*) Liegeplatz *m*; **give a wide ~ to** (*fam*) einen großen Bogen machen um ● *vi* anlegen

beseech /bɪ'si:tʃ/ *vt* (*pt/pp* **beseeched** *or* **besought**) anflehen

beside /bɪ'saɪd/ *prep* neben (+ *dat/acc*); **~ oneself** außer sich (*dat*)

besides /bɪ'saɪdz/ *prep* außer (+ *dat*) ● *adv* außerdem

besiege /bɪ'si:dʒ/ *vt* belagern

besought /bɪ'sɔ:t/ *see* **beseech**

bespoke /bɪ'spəʊk/ *a* ⟨*suit*⟩ maßgeschneidert

best /best/ *a & n* beste(r,s); **the ~** der/die/das Beste; **at ~** bestenfalls; **all the ~!** alles Gute! **do one's ~** sein Bestes tun; **the ~ part of a year** fast ein Jahr; **to the ~ of my knowledge** soviel ich weiß; **make the ~ of it** das Beste daraus machen ● *adv* am besten; **as ~ I could** so gut ich konnte. **~ 'man** *n* ≈ Trauzeuge *m*

bestow /bɪ'stəʊ/ *vt* schenken (**on** *dat*)

best'seller *n* Bestseller *m*

bet /bet/ *n* Wette *f* ● *v* (*pt/pp* **bet** *or* **betted**) ● *vt* **~ s.o. £5** mit jdm um £5 wetten ● *vi* wetten; **~ on** [Geld] setzen auf (+ *acc*)

betray /bɪ'treɪ/ *vt* verraten. **~al** *n* Verrat *m*

better /'betə(r)/ *a* besser; **get ~** sich bessern; (*after illness*) sich erholen ● *adv* besser; **~ off** besser dran; **~ not** lieber nicht; **all the ~** um so besser; **the sooner the ~** je eher, desto besser; **think ~ of sth** sich eines Besseren besinnen; **you'd ~ stay** du bleibst am besten hier ● *vt* verbessern; (*do better than*) übertreffen; **~ oneself** sich verbessern

'betting shop *n* Wettbüro *nt*

between /bɪ'twi:n/ *prep* zwischen (+ *dat/acc*); **~ you and me** unter uns; **~ us** (*together*) zusammen ● *adv* **[in] ~** dazwischen

beverage /'bevərɪdʒ/ *n* Getränk *nt*

bevy /'bevɪ/ *n* Schar *f*

beware /bɪ'weə(r)/ *vi* sich in acht nehmen (**of** vor + *dat*); **~ of the dog!** Vorsicht, bissiger Hund!

bewilder /bɪ'wɪldə(r)/ *vt* verwirren. **~ment** *n* Verwirrung *f*

bewitch /bɪ'wɪtʃ/ *vt* verzaubern; (*fig*) bezaubern

beyond /bɪ'jɒnd/ *prep* über (+ *acc*) ... hinaus; (*further*) weiter als; **~ reach** außer Reichweite; **~ doubt** ohne jeden Zweifel; **it's ~ me** (*fam*) das geht über meinen Horizont ● *adv* darüber hinaus

bias /'baɪəs/ *n* Voreingenommenheit *f*; (*preference*) Vorliebe *f*; (*Jur*) Befangenheit *f*; **cut on the ~** schräg geschnitten ● *vt* (*pt/pp* **biased**) (*influence*) beeinflussen. **~ed** *a* voreingenommen; (*Jur*) befangen

bib /bɪb/ *n* Lätzchen *nt*

Bible /'baɪbl/ *n* Bibel *f*

biblical /'bɪblɪkl/ *a* biblisch

bibliography /bɪblɪ'ɒgrəfɪ/ *n* Bibliographie *f*

bicarbonate /baɪ'kɑ:bəneit/ *n* **~ of soda** doppeltkohlensaures Natron *nt*

bicker /'bɪkə(r)/ *vi* sich zanken

bicycle /'baɪsɪkl/ *n* Fahrrad *nt* ● *vi* mit dem Rad fahren

bid[1] /bɪd/ *n* Gebot *nt*; (*attempt*) Versuch *m* • *vt/i* (*pt/pp* **bid**, *pres p* **bidding**) bieten (**for** auf + *acc*); (*Cards*) reizen

bid[2] *vt* (*pt* **bade** *or* **bid**, *pp* **bidden** *or* **bid**, *pres p* **bidding**) (*liter*) heißen; ~ **s.o. welcome** jdn willkommen heißen

bidder /ˈbɪdə(r)/ *n* Bieter(in) *m(f)*

bide /baɪd/ *vt* ~ **one's time** den richtigen Moment abwarten

biennial /baɪˈenɪəl/ *a* zweijährlich; (*lasting two years*) zweijährig

bier /bɪə(r)/ *n* [Toten]bahre *f*

bifocals /baɪˈfəʊklz/ *npl* **[pair of]** ~ Bifokalbrille *f*

big /bɪɡ/ *a* (**bigger, biggest**) groß • *adv* **talk** ~ (*fam*) angeben

bigam|ist /ˈbɪɡəmɪst/ *n* Bigamist *m*. ~**y** *n* Bigamie *f*

big-ˈheaded *a* (*fam*) eingebildet

bigot /ˈbɪɡət/ *n* Eiferer *m*. ~**ed** *a* engstirnig

ˈbigwig *n* (*fam*) hohes Tier *nt*

bike /baɪk/ *n* (*fam*) [Fahr]rad *nt*

bikini /bɪˈkiːnɪ/ *n* Bikini *m*

bilberry /ˈbɪlbərɪ/ *n* Heidelbeere *f*

bile /baɪl/ *n* Galle *f*

bilingual /baɪˈlɪŋɡwəl/ *a* zweisprachig

bilious /ˈbɪljəs/ *a* (*Med*) ~ **attack** verdorbener Magen *m*

bill[1] /bɪl/ *n* Rechnung *f*; (*poster*) Plakat *nt*; (*Pol*) Gesetzentwurf *m*; (*Amer: note*) Banknote *f*; ~ **of exchange** Wechsel *m* • *vt* eine Rechnung schicken (+ *dat*)

bill[2] *n* (*beak*) Schnabel *m*

billet /ˈbɪlɪt/ *n* (*Mil*) Quartier *nt* • *vt* (*pt/pp* **billeted**) einquartieren (**on** bei)

ˈbillfold *n* (*Amer*) Brieftasche *f*

billiards /ˈbɪljədz/ *n* Billard *nt*

billion /ˈbɪljən/ *n* (*thousand million*) Milliarde *f*; (*million million*) Billion *f*

billy-goat /ˈbɪlɪ-/ *n* Ziegenbock *m*

bin /bɪn/ *n* Mülleimer *m*; (*for bread*) Kasten *m*

bind /baɪnd/ *vt* (*pt/pp* **bound**) binden (**to** an + *acc*); (*bandage*) verbinden; (*Jur*) verpflichten; (*cover the edge of*) einfassen. ~**ing** *a* verbindlich • *n* Einband *m*; (*braid*) Borte *f*; (*on ski*) Bindung *f*

binge /bɪndʒ/ *n* (*fam*) **go on the** ~ eine Sauftour machen

binoculars /bɪˈnɒkjʊləz/ *npl* **[pair of]** ~ Fernglas *nt*

bio|ˈchemistry /baɪəʊ-/ *n* Biochemie *f*. ~**degradable** /-dɪˈɡreɪdəbl/ *a* biologisch abbaubar

biograph|er /baɪˈɒɡrəfə(r)/ *n* Biograph(in) *m(f)*. ~**y** *n* Biographie *f*

biological /baɪəˈlɒdʒɪkl/ *a* biologisch

biolog|ist /baɪˈɒlədʒɪst/ *n* Biologe *m*. ~**y** *n* Biologie *f*

birch /bɜːtʃ/ *n* Birke *f*; (*whip*) Rute *f*

bird /bɜːd/ *n* Vogel *m*; (*fam: girl*) Mädchen *nt*; **kill two** ~**s with one stone** zwei Fliegen mit einer Klappe schlagen

Biro (P) /ˈbaɪrəʊ/ *n* Kugelschreiber *m*

birth /bɜːθ/ *n* Geburt *f*

birth: ~ **certificate** *n* Geburtsurkunde *f*. ~**-control** *n* Geburtenregelung *f*. ~**day** *n* Geburtstag *m*. ~**mark** *n* Muttermal *nt*. ~**-rate** *n* Geburtenziffer *f*. ~**right** *n* Geburtsrecht *nt*

biscuit /ˈbɪskɪt/ *n* Keks *m*

bisect /baɪˈsekt/ *vt* halbieren

bishop /ˈbɪʃəp/ *n* Bischof *m*; (*Chess*) Läufer *m*

bit[1] /bɪt/ *n* Stückchen *nt*; (*for horse*) Gebiß *nt*; (*Techn*) Bohreinsatz *m*; **a** ~ ein bißchen; ~ **by** ~ nach und nach; **a** ~ **of bread** ein bißchen Brot; **do one's** ~ sein Teil tun

bit[2] *see* **bite**

bitch /bɪtʃ/ *n* Hündin *f*; (*sl*) Luder *nt*. ~**y** *a* gehässig

bit|e /baɪt/ *n* Biß *m*; **[insect]** ~ Stich *m*; (*mouthful*) Bissen *m* • *vt/i* (*pt* **bit**, *pp* **bitten**) beißen; ⟨*insect:*⟩ stechen; kauen ⟨*one's nails*⟩. ~**ing** *a* beißend

bitter /ˈbɪtə(r)/ *a*, **-ly** *adv* bitter; **cry** ~**ly** bitterlich weinen; ~**ly cold** bitterkalt • *n* bitteres Bier *nt*. ~**ness** *n* Bitterkeit *f*

bitty /ˈbɪtɪ/ *a* zusammengestoppelt

bizarre /bɪˈzɑː(r)/ *a* bizarr

blab /blæb/ *vi* (*pt/pp* **blabbed**) alles ausplaudern

black /blæk/ *a* (**-er, -est**) schwarz; **be** ~ **and blue** grün und blau sein • *n* Schwarz *nt*; (*person*) Schwarze(r) *m/f* • *vt* schwärzen; boykottieren ⟨*goods*⟩. ~ **out** *vt* verdunkeln • *vi* (*lose consciousness*) das Bewußtsein verlieren

black: ~**berry** *n* Brombeere *f*. ~**bird** *n* Amsel *f*. ~**board** *n* (*Sch*) [Wand]tafel *f*. ~**ˈcurrant** *n* schwarze Johannisbeere *f*

blacken *vt/i* schwärzen

black: ~ **ˈeye** *n* blaues Auge *nt*. **B**~ **ˈForest** *n* Schwarzwald *m*. ~ **ˈice** *n*

Glatteis *nt.* **~leg** *n* Streikbrecher *m.* **~list** *vt* auf die schwarze Liste setzen. **~mail** *n* Erpressung *f* ● *vt* erpressen. **~mailer** *n* Erpresser(in) *m(f).* **~ 'market** *n* schwarzer Markt *m.* **~-out** *n* Verdunkelung *f*; **have a ~-out** (*Med*) das Bewußtsein verlieren. **~ 'pudding** *n* Blutwurst *f.* **~smith** *n* [Huf]schmied *m*

bladder /'blædə(r)/ *n* (*Anat*) Blase *f*

blade /bleɪd/ *n* Klinge *f*; (*of grass*) Halm *m*

blame /bleɪm/ *n* Schuld *f* ● *vt* die Schuld geben (+ *dat*); **no one is to ~** keiner ist schuld daran. **~less** *a* schuldlos

blanch /blɑːntʃ/ *vi* blaß werden ● *vt* (*Culin*) blanchieren

blancmange /blə'mɒnʒ/ *n* Pudding *m*

bland /blænd/ *a* (**-er, -est**) mild

blank /blæŋk/ *a* leer; ⟨*look*⟩ ausdruckslos ● *n* Lücke *f*; (*cartridge*) Platzpatrone *f.* **~ 'cheque** *n* Blankoscheck *m*

blanket /'blæŋkɪt/ *n* Decke *f*; **wet ~** (*fam*) Spielverderber(in) *m(f)*

blank 'verse *n* Blankvers *m*

blare /bleə(r)/ *vt/i* schmettern

blasé /'blɑːzeɪ/ *a* blasiert

blaspheme /blæs'fiːm/ *vi* lästern

blasphem|ous /'blæsfəməs/ *a* [gottes]lästerlich. **~y** *n* [Gottes]lästerung *f*

blast /blɑːst/ *n* (*gust*) Luftstoß *m*; (*sound*) Stoß *m* ● *vt* sprengen ● *int* (*sl*) verdammt. **~ed** *a* (*sl*) verdammt

blast: ~-furnace *n* Hochofen *m.* **~-off** *n* (*of missile*) Start *m*

blatant /'bleɪtənt/ *a* offensichtlich

blaze /bleɪz/ *n* Feuer *nt* ● *vi* brennen

blazer /'bleɪzə(r)/ *n* Blazer *m*

bleach /bliːtʃ/ *n* Bleichmittel *nt* ● *vt/i* bleichen

bleak /bliːk/ *a* (**-er, -est**) öde; (*fig*) trostlos

bleary-eyed /'blɪərɪ-/ *a* mit trüben/(*on waking up*) verschlafenen Augen

bleat /bliːt/ *vi* blöken; ⟨*goat:*⟩ meckern

bleed /bliːd/ *v* (*pt/pp* **bled**) ● *vi* bluten ● *vt* entlüften ⟨*radiator*⟩

bleep /bliːp/ *n* Piepton *m* ● *vi* piepsen ● *vt* mit dem Piepser rufen. **~er** *n* Piepser *m*

blemish /'blemɪʃ/ *n* Makel *m*

blend /blend/ *n* Mischung *f* ● *vt* mischen ● *vi* sich vermischen. **~er** *n* (*Culin*) Mixer *m*

bless /bles/ *vt* segnen. **~ed** /'blesɪd/ *a* heilig; (*sl*) verflixt. **~ing** *n* Segen *m*

blew /bluː/ *see* **blow²**

blight /blaɪt/ *n* (*Bot*) Brand *m* ● *vt* (*spoil*) vereiteln

blind /blaɪnd/ *a* blind; ⟨*corner*⟩ unübersichtlich; **~ man/woman** Blinde(r) *m/f* ● *n* **[roller] ~** Rouleau *nt* ● *vt* blenden

blind: ~ 'alley *n* Sackgasse *f.* **~fold** *a* & *adv* mit verbundenen Augen ● *n* Augenbinde *f* ● *vt* die Augen verbinden (+ *dat*). **~ly** *adv* blindlings. **~ness** *n* Blindheit *f*

blink /blɪŋk/ *vi* blinzeln; ⟨*light:*⟩ blinken

blinkers /'blɪŋkəz/ *npl* Scheuklappen *pl*

bliss /blɪs/ *n* Glückseligkeit *f.* **~ful** *a* glücklich

blister /'blɪstə(r)/ *n* (*Med*) Blase *f* ● *vi* ⟨*paint:*⟩ Blasen werfen

blitz /blɪts/ *n* Luftangriff *m*; (*fam*) Großaktion *f*

blizzard /'blɪzəd/ *n* Schneesturm *m*

bloated /'bləʊtɪd/ *a* aufgedunsen

blob /blɒb/ *n* Klecks *m*

bloc /blɒk/ *n* (*Pol*) Block *m*

block /blɒk/ *n* Block *m*; (*of wood*) Klotz *m*; (*of flats*) [Wohn]block *m* ● *vt* blockieren. **~ up** *vt* zustopfen

blockade /blɒ'keɪd/ *n* Blockade *f* ● *vt* blockieren

blockage /'blɒkɪdʒ/ *n* Verstopfung *f*

block: ~head *n* (*fam*) Dummkopf *m.* **~ 'letters** *npl* Blockschrift *f*

bloke /bləʊk/ *n* (*fam*) Kerl *m*

blonde /blɒnd/ *a* blond ● *n* Blondine *f*

blood /blʌd/ *n* Blut *nt*

blood: ~ count *n* Blutbild *nt.* **~-curdling** *a* markerschütternd. **~ donor** *n* Blutspender *m.* **~ group** *n* Blutgruppe *f.* **~hound** *n* Bluthund *m.* **~-poisoning** *n* Blutvergiftung *f.* **~ pressure** *n* Blutdruck *m.* **~ relative** *n* Blutsverwandte(r) *m/f.* **~shed** *n* Blutvergießen *nt.* **~shot** *a* blutunterlaufen. **~ sports** *npl* Jagdsport *m.* **~-stained** *a* blutbefleckt. **~stream** *n* Blutbahn *f.* **~ test** *n* Blutprobe *f.* **~thirsty** *a* blutdürstig. **~ transfusion** *n* Blutübertragung *f.* **~-vessel** *n* Blutgefäß *nt*

bloody /'blʌdɪ/ *a* (**-ier, -iest**) blutig; (*sl*) verdammt. **~-'minded** *a* (*sl*) stur

bloom /blu:m/ *n* Blüte *f* ● *vi* blühen
bloom|er /'blu:mə(r)/ *n* (*fam*) Schnitzer *m*. **~ing** *a* (*fam*) verdammt
blossom /'blɒsəm/ *n* Blüte *f* ● *vi* blühen. **~ out** *vi* (*fig*) aufblühen
blot /blɒt/ *n* [Tinten]klecks *m*; (*fig*) Fleck *m* ● *vt* (*pt/pp* **blotted**) löschen. **~ out** *vt* (*fig*) auslöschen
blotch /blɒtʃ/ *n* Fleck *m*. **~y** *a* fleckig
'blotting-paper *n* Löschpapier *nt*
blouse /blaʊz/ *n* Bluse *f*
blow[1] /bləʊ/ *n* Schlag *m*
blow[2] *v* (*pt* **blew**, *pp* **blown**) ● *vt* blasen; (*fam: squander*) verpulvern; **~ one's nose** sich (*dat*) die Nase putzen ● *vi* blasen; ⟨*fuse:*⟩ durchbrennen. **~ away** *vt* wegblasen ● *vi* wegfliegen. **~ down** *vt* umwehen ● *vi* umfallen. **~ out** *vt* (*extinguish*) ausblasen. **~ over** *vi* umfallen; (*fig: die down*) vorübergehen. **~ up** *vt* (*inflate*) aufblasen; (*enlarge*) vergrößern; (*shatter by explosion*) sprengen ● *vi* explodieren
blow: ~-dry *vt* fönen. **~fly** *n* Schmeißfliege *f*. **~lamp** *n* Lötlampe *f*
blown /bləʊn/ *see* **blow**[2]
'blowtorch *n* (*Amer*) Lötlampe *f*
blowy /'bləʊɪ/ *a* windig
bludgeon /'blʌdʒn/ *vt* (*fig*) zwingen
blue /blu:/ *a* (**-r, -st**) blau; **feel ~** deprimiert sein ● *n* Blau *nt*; **have the ~s** deprimiert sein; **out of the ~** aus heiterem Himmel
blue: ~bell *n* Sternhyazinthe *f*. **~berry** *n* Heidelbeere *f*. **~bottle** *n* Schmeißfliege *f*. **~ film** *n* Pornofilm *m*. **~print** *n* (*fig*) Entwurf *m*
bluff /blʌf/ *n* Bluff *m* ● *vi* bluffen
blunder /'blʌndə(r)/ *n* Schnitzer *m* ● *vi* einen Schnitzer machen
blunt /blʌnt/ *a* stumpf; ⟨*person*⟩ geradeheraus. **~ly** *adv* unverblümt, geradeheraus
blur /blɜ:(r)/ *n* **it's all a ~** alles ist verschwommen ● *vt* (*pt/pp* **blurred**) verschwommen machen; **~red** verschwommen
blurb /blɜ:b/ *n* Klappentext *m*
blurt /blɜ:t/ *vt* **~ out** herausplatzen mit
blush /blʌʃ/ *n* Erröten *nt* ● *vi* erröten
bluster /'blʌstə(r)/ *n* Großtuerei *f*. **~y** *a* windig
boar /bɔ:(r)/ *n* Eber *m*
board /bɔ:d/ *n* Brett *nt*; (*for notices*) schwarzes Brett *nt*; (*committee*) Ausschuß *m*; (*of directors*) Vorstand *m*; **on ~** an Bord; **full ~** Vollpension *f*; **~ and lodging** Unterkunft und Verpflegung *pl*; **go by the ~** (*fam*) unter den Tisch fallen ● *vt* einsteigen in (+ *acc*); (*Naut, Aviat*) besteigen ● *vi* an Bord gehen; **~ with** in Pension wohnen bei. **~ up** *vt* mit Brettern verschlagen
boarder /'bɔ:də(r)/ *n* Pensionsgast *m*; (*Sch*) Internatsschüler(in) *m*(*f*)
board: ~-game *n* Brettspiel *nt*. **~ing-house** *n* Pension *f*. **~ing-school** *n* Internat *nt*
boast /bəʊst/ *vt* sich rühmen (+ *gen*) ● *vi* prahlen (**about** mit). **~ful** *a*, **-ly** *adv* prahlerisch
boat /bəʊt/ *n* Boot *nt*; (*ship*) Schiff *nt*. **~er** *n* (*hat*) flacher Strohhut *m*
bob /bɒb/ *n* Bubikopf *m* ● *vi* (*pt/pp* **bobbed**) (*curtsy*) knicksen; **~ up and down** sich auf und ab bewegen
bobbin /'bɒbɪn/ *n* Spule *f*
'bob-sleigh *n* Bob *m*
bode /bəʊd/ *vi* **~ well/ill** etwas/nichts Gutes verheißen
bodice /'bɒdɪs/ *n* Mieder *nt*
bodily /'bɒdɪlɪ/ *a* körperlich ● *adv* (*forcibly*) mit Gewalt
body /'bɒdɪ/ *n* Körper *m*; (*corpse*) Leiche *f*; (*corporation*) Körperschaft *f*; **the main ~** der Hauptanteil. **~guard** *n* Leibwächter *m*. **~work** *n* (*Auto*) Karosserie *f*
bog /bɒg/ *n* Sumpf *m* ● *vt* (*pt/pp* **bogged**) **get ~ged down** steckenbleiben
boggle /'bɒgl/ *vi* **the mind ~s** es ist kaum vorstellbar
bogus /'bəʊgəs/ *a* falsch
boil[1] /bɔɪl/ *n* Furunkel *m*
boil[2] *n* **bring/come to the ~** zum Kochen bringen/kommen ● *vt/i* kochen; **~ed potatoes** Salzkartoffeln *pl*. **~ down** *vi* (*fig*) hinauslaufen (**to** auf + *acc*). **~ over** *vi* überkochen. **~ up** *vt* aufkochen
boiler /'bɔɪlə(r)/ *n* Heizkessel *m*. **~suit** *n* Overall *m*
'boiling point *n* Siedepunkt *m*
boisterous /'bɔɪstərəs/ *a* übermütig
bold /bəʊld/ *a* (**-er, -est**), **-ly** *adv* kühn; (*Typ*) fett. **~ness** *n* Kühnheit *f*
bollard /'bɒlɑ:d/ *n* Poller *m*
bolster /'bəʊlstə(r)/ *n* Nackenrolle *f* ● *vt* **~ up** Mut machen (+ *dat*)
bolt /bəʊlt/ *n* Riegel *m*; (*Techn*) Bolzen *m*; **nuts and ~s** Schrauben und Muttern *pl* ● *vt* schrauben (**to** an + *acc*);

verriegeln ‹*door*›; hinunterschlingen ‹*food*› ● *vi* abhauen; ‹*horse:*› durchgehen ● *adv* ~ **upright** *adv* kerzengerade

bomb /bɒm/ *n* Bombe *f* ● *vt* bombardieren

bombard /bɒmˈbɑːd/ *vt* beschießen; (*fig*) bombardieren

bombastic /bɒmˈbæstɪk/ *a* bombastisch

bomb|er /ˈbɒmə(r)/ *n* (*Aviat*) Bomber *m*; (*person*) Bombenleger(in) *m*(*f*). **~shell** *n* **be a ~shell** (*fig*) wie eine Bombe einschlagen

bond /bɒnd/ *n* (*fig*) Band *nt*; (*Comm*) Obligation *f*; **be in ~** unter Zollverschluß stehen

bondage /ˈbɒndɪdʒ/ *n* (*fig*) Sklaverei *f*

bone /bəʊn/ *n* Knochen *m*; (*of fish*) Gräte *f* ● *vt* von den Knochen lösen ‹*meat*›; entgräten ‹*fish*›. **~-ˈdry** *a* knochentrocken

bonfire /ˈbɒn-/ *n* Gartenfeuer *nt*; (*celebratory*) Freudenfeuer *nt*

bonnet /ˈbɒnɪt/ *n* Haube *f*

bonus /ˈbəʊnəs/ *n* Prämie *f*; (*gratuity*) Gratifikation *f*; (*fig*) Plus *nt*

bony /ˈbəʊnɪ/ *a* (**-ier, -iest**) knochig; ‹*fish*› grätig

boo /buː/ *int* buh! ● *vt* ausbuhen ● *vi* buhen

boob /buːb/ *n* (*fam: mistake*) Schnitzer *m* ● *vi* (*fam*) einen Schnitzer machen

book /bʊk/ *n* Buch *nt*; (*of tickets*) Heft *nt*; **keep the ~s** (*Comm*) die Bücher führen ● *vt/i* buchen; (*reserve*) [vor]bestellen; (*for offence*) aufschreiben. **~able** /-əbl/ *a* im Vorverkauf erhältlich

book: ~case *n* Bücherregal *nt*. **~-ends** *npl* Buchstützen *pl*. **~ing-office** *n* Fahrkartenschalter *m*. **~keeping** *n* Buchführung *f*. **~let** *n* Broschüre *f*. **~maker** *n* Buchmacher *m*. **~mark** *n* Lesezeichen *nt*. **~seller** *n* Buchhändler(in) *m*(*f*). **~shop** *n* Buchhandlung *f*. **~stall** *n* Bücherstand *m*. **~worm** *n* Bücherwurm *m*

boom /buːm/ *n* (*Comm*) Hochkonjunktur *f*; (*upturn*) Aufschwung *m* ● *vi* dröhnen; (*fig*) blühen

boon /buːn/ *n* Segen *m*

boor /bʊə(r)/ *n* Flegel *m*. **~ish** *a* flegelhaft

boost /buːst/ *n* Auftrieb *m* ● *vt* Auftrieb geben (+ *dat*). **~er** *n* (*Med*) Nachimpfung *f*

boot /buːt/ *n* Stiefel *m*; (*Auto*) Kofferraum *m*

booth /buːð/ *n* Bude *f*; (*cubicle*) Kabine *f*

booty /ˈbuːtɪ/ *n* Beute *f*

booze /buːz/ *n* (*fam*) Alkohol *m* ● *vi* (*fam*) saufen

border /ˈbɔːdə(r)/ *n* Rand *m*; (*frontier*) Grenze *f*; (*in garden*) Rabatte *f* ● *vi* **~ on** grenzen an (+ *acc*). **~line** *n* Grenzlinie *f*. **~line case** *n* Grenzfall *m*

bore[1] /bɔː(r)/ *see* **bear**[2]

bore[2] *vt/i* (*Techn*) bohren

bor|e[3] *n* (*of gun*) Kaliber *nt*; (*person*) langweiliger Mensch *m*; (*thing*) langweilige Sache *f* ● *vt* langweilen; **be ~ed** sich langweilen. **~edom** *n* Langeweile *f*. **~ing** *a* langweilig

born /bɔːn/ *pp* **be ~** geboren werden ● *a* geboren

borne /bɔːn/ *see* **bear**[2]

borough /ˈbʌrə/ *n* Stadtgemeinde *f*

borrow /ˈbɒrəʊ/ *vt* [sich (*dat*)] borgen *od* leihen (**from** von)

bosom /ˈbʊzm/ *n* Busen *m*

boss /bɒs/ *n* (*fam*) Chef *m* ● *vt* herumkommandieren. **~y** *a* herrschsüchtig

botanical /bəˈtænɪkl/ *a* botanisch

botan|ist /ˈbɒtənɪst/ *n* Botaniker(in) *m*(*f*). **~y** *n* Botanik *f*

botch /bɒtʃ/ *vt* verpfuschen

both /bəʊθ/ *a & pron* beide; **~ [of] the children** beide Kinder; **~ of them** beide [von ihnen] ● *adv* **~ men and women** sowohl Männer als auch Frauen

bother /ˈbɒðə(r)/ *n* Mühe *f*; (*minor trouble*) Ärger *m* ● *int* (*fam*) verflixt! ● *vt* belästigen; (*disturb*) stören ● *vi* sich kümmern (**about** um); **don't ~** nicht nötig

bottle /ˈbɒtl/ *n* Flasche *f* ● *vt* auf Flaschen abfüllen; (*preserve*) einmachen. **~ up** *vt* (*fig*) in sich (*dat*) aufstauen

bottle: ~-neck *n* (*fig*) Engpaß *m*. **~-opener** *n* Flaschenöffner *m*

bottom /ˈbɒtəm/ *a* unterste(r,s) ● *n* (*of container*) Boden *m*; (*of river*) Grund *m*; (*of page, hill*) Fuß *m*; (*buttocks*) Hintern *m*; **at the ~** unten; **get to the ~ of sth** (*fig*) hinter etw (*acc*) kommen. **~less** *a* bodenlos

bough /baʊ/ *n* Ast *m*

bought /bɔ:t/ *see* **buy**

boulder /'bəʊldə(r)/ *n* Felsblock *m*

bounce /baʊns/ *vi* [auf]springen; ⟨*cheque:*⟩ (*fam*) nicht gedeckt sein ● *vt* aufspringen lassen ⟨*ball*⟩

bouncer /'baʊnsə(r)/ *n* (*fam*) Rausschmeißer *m*

bouncing /'baʊnsɪŋ/ *a* ~ **baby** strammer Säugling *m*

bound[1] /baʊnd/ *n* Sprung *m* ● *vi* springen

bound[2] *see* **bind** ● *a* ~ **for** ⟨*ship*⟩ mit Kurs auf (+ *acc*); **be ~ to do sth** etw bestimmt machen; (*obliged*) verpflichtet sein, etw zu machen

boundary /'baʊndərɪ/ *n* Grenze *f*

'boundless *a* grenzenlos

bounds /baʊndz/ *npl* (*fig*) Grenzen *pl*; **out of ~** verboten

bouquet /bʊ'keɪ/ *n* [Blumen]strauß *m*; (*of wine*) Bukett *nt*

bourgeois /'bʊəʒwɑ:/ *a* (*pej*) spießbürgerlich

bout /baʊt/ *n* (*Med*) Anfall *m*; (*Sport*) Kampf *m*

bow[1] /bəʊ/ *n* (*weapon & Mus*) Bogen *m*; (*knot*) Schleife *f*

bow[2] /baʊ/ *n* Verbeugung *f* ● *vi* sich verbeugen ● *vt* neigen ⟨*head*⟩

bow[3] /baʊ/ *n* (*Naut*) Bug *m*

bowel /'baʊəl/ *n* Darm *m*; **~ movement** Stuhlgang *m*. **~s** *pl* Eingeweide *pl*; (*digestion*) Verdauung *f*

bowl[1] /bəʊl/ *n* Schüssel *f*; (*shallow*) Schale *f*; (*of pipe*) Kopf *m*; (*of spoon*) Schöpfteil *m*

bowl[2] *n* (*ball*) Kugel *f* ● *vt/i* werfen. **~ over** *vt* umwerfen

bow-legged /bəʊ'legd/ *a* O-beinig

bowler[1] /'bəʊlə(r)/ *n* (*Sport*) Werfer *m*

bowler[2] *n* ~ **[hat]** Melone *f*

bowling /'bəʊlɪŋ/ *n* Kegeln *nt*. **~-alley** *n* Kegelbahn *f*

bowls /bəʊlz/ *n* Bowlsspiel *nt*

bow-'tie /bəʊ-/ *n* Fliege *f*

box[1] /bɒks/ *n* Schachtel *f*; (*wooden*) Kiste *f*; (*cardboard*) Karton *m*; (*Theat*) Loge *f*

box[2] *vt/i* (*Sport*) boxen; **~ s.o.'s ears** jdn ohrfeigen

box|er /'bɒksə(r)/ *n* Boxer *m*. **~ing** *n* Boxen *nt*. **B~ing Day** *n* zweiter Weihnachtstag *m*

box: ~-office *n* (*Theat*) Kasse *f*. **~-room** *n* Abstellraum *m*

boy /bɔɪ/ *n* Junge *m*

boycott /'bɔɪkɒt/ *n* Boykott *m* ● *vt* boykottieren

boy: ~friend *n* Freund *m*. **~ish** *a* jungenhaft

bra /brɑ:/ *n* BH *m*

brace /breɪs/ *n* Strebe *f*, Stütze *f*; (*dental*) Zahnspange *f*; **~s** *npl* Hosenträger *mpl* ● *vt* **~ oneself** sich stemmen (**against** gegen); (*fig*) sich gefaßt machen (**for** auf + *acc*)

bracelet /'breɪslɪt/ *n* Armband *nt*

bracing /'breɪsɪŋ/ *a* stärkend

bracken /'brækn/ *n* Farnkraut *nt*

bracket /'brækɪt/ *n* Konsole *f*; (*group*) Gruppe *f*; (*Typ*) **round/square ~s** runde/eckige Klammern ● *vt* einklammern

brag /bræg/ *vi* (*pt/pp* **bragged**) prahlen (**about** mit)

braid /breɪd/ *n* Borte *f*

braille /breɪl/ *n* Blindenschrift *f*

brain /breɪn/ *n* Gehirn *nt*; **~s** (*fig*) Intelligenz *f*

brain: ~child *n* geistiges Produkt *nt*. **~less** *a* dumm. **~wash** *vt* einer Gehirnwäsche unterziehen. **~wave** *n* Geistesblitz *m*

brainy /'breɪnɪ/ *a* (**-ier, -iest**) klug

braise /breɪz/ *vt* schmoren

brake /breɪk/ *n* Bremse *f* ● *vt/i* bremsen. **~-light** *n* Bremslicht *nt*

bramble /'bræmbl/ *n* Brombeerstrauch *m*

bran /bræn/ *n* Kleie *f*

branch /brɑ:ntʃ/ *n* Ast *m*; (*fig*) Zweig *m*; (*Comm*) Zweigstelle *f*; (*shop*) Filiale *f* ● *vi* sich gabeln. **~ off** *vi* abzweigen. **~ out** *vi* **~ out into** sich verlegen auf (+ *acc*)

brand /brænd/ *n* Marke *f*; (*on animal*) Brandzeichen *nt* ● *vt* mit dem Brandeisen zeichnen ⟨*animal*⟩; (*fig*) brandmarken als

brandish /'brændɪʃ/ *vt* schwingen

brand-'new *a* nagelneu

brandy /'brændɪ/ *n* Weinbrand *m*

brash /bræʃ/ *a* naßforsch

brass /brɑ:s/ *n* Messing *nt*; (*Mus*) Blech *nt*; **get down to ~ tacks** (*fam*) zur Sache kommen; **top ~** (*fam*) hohe Tiere *pl*. **~ band** *n* Blaskapelle *f*

brassiere /'bræzɪə(r)/ *n* Büstenhalter *m*

brassy /'brɑ:sɪ/ *a* (**-ier, -iest**) (*fam*) ordinär

brat /bræt/ *n* (*pej*) Balg *nt*

bravado /brə'vɑ:dəʊ/ *n* Forschheit *f*

brave /breɪv/ *a* (**-r, -st**), **-ly** *adv* tapfer ● *vt* die Stirn bieten (+ *dat*). **~ry** /-ərɪ/ *n* Tapferkeit *f*

bravo /brɑ:'vəʊ/ *int* bravo!

brawl /brɔ:l/ *n* Schlägerei *f* ● *vi* sich schlagen

brawn /brɔ:n/ *n* (*Culin*) Sülze *f*

brawny /'brɔ:nɪ/ *a* muskulös

bray /breɪ/ *vi* iahen

brazen /'breɪzn/ *a* unverschämt

brazier /'breɪzɪə(r)/ *n* Kohlenbecken *nt*

Brazil /brə'zɪl/ *n* Brasilien *nt*. **~ian** *a* brasilianisch. **~ nut** *n* Paranuß *f*

breach /bri:tʃ/ *n* Bruch *m*; (*Mil & fig*) Bresche *f*; **~ of contract** Vertragsbruch *m* ● *vt* durchbrechen; brechen ⟨*contract*⟩

bread /bred/ *n* Brot *nt*; **slice of ~ and butter** Butterbrot *nt*

bread: ~crumbs *npl* Brotkrümel *pl*; (*Culin*) Paniermehl *nt*. **~line** *n* **be on the ~line** gerade genug zum Leben haben

breadth /bredθ/ *n* Breite *f*

'bread-winner *n* Brotverdiener *m*

break /breɪk/ *n* Bruch *m*; (*interval*) Pause *f*; (*interruption*) Unterbrechung *f*; (*fam: chance*) Chance *f* ● *v* (*pt* **broke**, *pp* **broken**) ● *vt* brechen; (*smash*) zerbrechen; (*damage*) kaputtmachen (*fam*); (*interrupt*) unterbrechen; **~ one's arm** sich (*dat*) den Arm brechen ● *vi* brechen; ⟨*day:*⟩ anbrechen; ⟨*storm:*⟩ losbrechen; ⟨*thing:*⟩ kaputtgehen (*fam*); ⟨*rope, thread:*⟩ reißen; ⟨*news:*⟩ bekanntwerden; **his voice is ~ing** er ist im Stimmbruch. **~ away** *vi* sich losreißen/(*fig*) sich absetzen (**from** von). **~ down** *vi* zusammenbrechen; (*Techn*) eine Panne haben; ⟨*negotiations:*⟩ scheitern ● *vt* aufbrechen ⟨*door*⟩; aufgliedern ⟨*figures*⟩. **~ in** *vi* einbrechen. **~ off** *vt/i* abbrechen; lösen ⟨*engagement*⟩. **~ out** *vi* ausbrechen. **~ up** *vt* zerbrechen ● *vi* ⟨*crowd:*⟩ sich zerstreuen; ⟨*marriage, couple:*⟩ auseinandergehen; (*Sch*) Ferien bekommen

break|able /'breɪkəbl/ *a* zerbrechlich. **~age** /-ɪdʒ/ *n* Bruch *m*. **~down** *n* (*Techn*) Panne *f*; (*Med*) Zusammenbruch *m*; (*of figures*) Aufgliederung *f*. **~er** *n* (*wave*) Brecher *m*

breakfast /'brekfəst/ *n* Frühstück *nt*

break: ~through *n* Durchbruch *m*. **~water** *n* Buhne *f*

breast /brest/ *n* Brust *f*. **~bone** *n* Brustbein *nt*. **~-feed** *vt* stillen. **~-stroke** *n* Brustschwimmen *nt*

breath /breθ/ *n* Atem *m*; **out of ~** außer Atem; **under one's ~** vor sich (*acc*) hin

breathalyse /'breθəlaɪz/ *vt* ins Röhrchen blasen lassen. **~r (P)** *n* Röhrchen *nt*. **~r test** *n* Alcotest (P) *m*

breathe /bri:ð/ *vt/i* atmen. **~ in** *vt/i* einatmen. **~ out** *vt/i* ausatmen

breath|er /'bri:ðə(r)/ *n* Atempause *f*. **~ing** *n* Atmen *nt*

breath /'breθ-/: **~less** *a* atemlos. **~-taking** *a* atemberaubend. **~ test** *n* Alcotest (P) *m*

bred /bred/ *see* **breed**

breeches /'brɪtʃɪz/ *npl* Kniehose *f*; (*for riding*) Reithose *f*

breed /bri:d/ *n* Rasse *f* ● *v* (*pt/pp* **bred**) ● *vt* züchten; (*give rise to*) erzeugen ● *vi* sich vermehren. **~er** *n* Züchter *m*. **~ing** *n* Zucht *f*; (*fig*) [gute] Lebensart *f*

breez|e /bri:z/ *n* Lüftchen *nt*; (*Naut*) Brise *f*. **~y** *a* [leicht] windig

brevity /'brevətɪ/ *n* Kürze *f*

brew /bru:/ *n* Gebräu *nt* ● *vt* brauen; kochen ⟨*tea*⟩ ● *vi* (*fig*) sich zusammenbrauen. **~er** *n* Brauer *m*. **~ery** *n* Brauerei *f*

bribe /braɪb/ *n* (*money*) Bestechungsgeld *nt* ● *vt* bestechen. **~ry** /-ərɪ/ *n* Bestechung *f*

brick /brɪk/ *n* Ziegelstein *m*, Backstein *m* ● *vt* **~ up** zumauern

'bricklayer *n* Maurer *m*

bridal /'braɪdl/ *a* Braut-

bride /braɪd/ *n* Braut *f*. **~groom** *n* Bräutigam *m*. **~smaid** *n* Brautjungfer *f*

bridge[1] /brɪdʒ/ *n* Brücke *f*; (*of nose*) Nasenrücken *m*; (*of spectacles*) Steg *m* ● *vt* (*fig*) überbrücken

bridge[2] *n* (*Cards*) Bridge *nt*

bridle /'braɪdl/ *n* Zaum *m*. **~-path** *n* Reitweg *m*

brief[1] /bri:f/ *a* (**-er, -est**) kurz; **be ~** ⟨*person:*⟩ sich kurz fassen

brief[2] *n* Instruktionen *pl*; (*Jur: case*) Mandat *nt* ● *vt* Instruktionen geben (+ *dat*); (*Jur*) beauftragen. **~case** *n* Aktentasche *f*

brief|ing /'bri:fɪŋ/ *n* Informationsgespräch *nt*. **~ly** *adv* kurz. **~ness** *n* Kürze *f*

briefs /bri:fs/ *npl* Slip *m*

brigad|e /brɪ'geɪd/ *n* Brigade *f*. **~ier** /-ə'dɪə(r)/ *n* Brigadegeneral *m*

bright /braɪt/ *a* (**-er, -est**), **-ly** *adv* hell; ⟨*day*⟩ heiter; ~ **red** hellrot

bright|en /ˈbraɪtn/ *v* ~**en [up]** • *vt* aufheitern • *vi* sich aufheitern. ~**ness** *n* Helligkeit *f*

brilliance /ˈbrɪljəns/ *n* Glanz *m*; (*of person*) Genialität *f*

brilliant /ˈbrɪljənt/ *a*, **-ly** *adv* glänzend; ⟨*person*⟩ genial

brim /brɪm/ *n* Rand *m*; (*of hat*) Krempe *f* • *vi* (*pt/pp* **brimmed**) ~ **over** überfließen

brine /braɪn/ *n* Salzwasser *nt*; (*Culin*) [Salz]lake *f*

bring /brɪŋ/ *vt* (*pt/pp* **brought**) bringen; ~ **them with you** bring sie mit. ~ **about** *vt* verursachen. ~ **along** *vt* mitbringen. ~ **back** *vt* zurückbringen. ~ **down** *vt* herunterbringen; senken ⟨*price*⟩. ~ **off** *vt* vollbringen. ~ **on** *vt* (*cause*) verursachen. ~ **out** *vt* herausbringen. ~ **round** *vt* vorbeibringen; (*persuade*) überreden; wieder zum Bewußtsein bringen ⟨*unconscious person*⟩. ~ **up** *vt* heraufbringen; (*vomit*) erbrechen; aufziehen ⟨*children*⟩; erwähnen ⟨*question*⟩

brink /brɪŋk/ *n* Rand *m*

brisk /brɪsk/ *a* (**-er, -est**), **-ly** *adv* lebhaft; (*quick*) schnell

brist|le /ˈbrɪsl/ *n* Borste *f*. ~**ly** *a* borstig

Brit|ain /ˈbrɪtn/ *n* Großbritannien *nt*. ~**ish** *a* britisch; **the** ~**ish** die Briten *pl*. ~**on** *n* Brite *m*/Britin *f*

Brittany /ˈbrɪtənɪ/ *n* die Bretagne

brittle /ˈbrɪtl/ *a* brüchig, spröde

broach /brəʊtʃ/ *vt* anzapfen; anschneiden ⟨*subject*⟩

broad /brɔːd/ *a* (**-er, -est**) breit; ⟨*hint*⟩ deutlich; **in** ~ **daylight** am hellichten Tag. ~ **beans** *npl* dicke Bohnen *pl*

ˈ**broadcast** *n* Sendung *f* • *vt/i* (*pt/pp* **-cast**) senden. ~**er** *n* Rundfunk- und Fernsehpersönlichkeit *f*. ~**ing** *n* Funk und Fernsehen *pl*

broaden /ˈbrɔːdn/ *vt* verbreitern; (*fig*) erweitern • *vi* sich verbreitern

broadly /ˈbrɔːdlɪ/ *adv* breit; ~ **speaking** allgemein gesagt

broadˈminded *a* tolerant

brocade /brəˈkeɪd/ *n* Brokat *m*

broccoli /ˈbrɒkəlɪ/ *n inv* Brokkoli *pl*

brochure /ˈbrəʊʃə(r)/ *n* Broschüre *f*

brogue /brəʊg/ *n* (*shoe*) Wanderschuh *m*; **Irish** ~ irischer Akzent *m*

broke /brəʊk/ *see* **break** • *a* (*fam*) pleite

broken /ˈbrəʊkn/ *see* **break** • *a* zerbrochen, (*fam*) kaputt; ~ **English** gebrochenes Englisch *nt*. ~-**hearted** *a* untröstlich

broker /ˈbrəʊkə(r)/ *n* Makler *m*

brolly /ˈbrɒlɪ/ *n* (*fam*) Schirm *m*

bronchitis /brɒŋˈkaɪtɪs/ *n* Bronchitis *f*

bronze /brɒnz/ *n* Bronze *f*

brooch /brəʊtʃ/ *n* Brosche *f*

brood /bruːd/ *n* Brut *f* • *vi* brüten; (*fig*) grübeln

brook[1] /brʊk/ *n* Bach *m*

brook[2] *vt* dulden

broom /bruːm/ *n* Besen *m*; (*Bot*) Ginster *m*. ~**stick** *n* Besenstiel *m*

broth /brɒθ/ *n* Brühe *f*

brothel /ˈbrɒθl/ *n* Bordell *nt*

brother /ˈbrʌðə(r)/ *n* Bruder *m*

brother: ~-**in-law** *n* (*pl* **-s-in-law**) Schwager *m*. ~**ly** *a* brüderlich

brought /brɔːt/ *see* **bring**

brow /braʊ/ *n* Augenbraue *f*; (*forehead*) Stirn *f*; (*of hill*) [Berg]kuppe *f*

ˈ**browbeat** *vt* (*pt* **-beat**, *pp* **-beaten**) einschüchtern

brown /braʊn/ *a* (**-er, -est**) braun; ~ ˈ**paper** Packpapier *nt* • *n* Braun *nt* • *vt* bräunen • *vi* braun werden

Brownie /ˈbraʊnɪ/ *n* Wichtel *m*

browse /braʊz/ *vi* (*read*) schmökern; (*in shop*) sich umsehen

bruise /bruːz/ *n* blauer Fleck *m* • *vt* beschädigen ⟨*fruit*⟩; ~ **one's arm** sich (*dat*) den Arm quetschen

brunch /brʌntʃ/ *n* Brunch *m*

brunette /bruːˈnet/ *n* Brunette *f*

Brunswick /ˈbrʌnzwɪk/ *n* Braunschweig *nt*

brunt /brʌnt/ *n* **the** ~ **of** die volle Wucht (+ *gen*)

brush /brʌʃ/ *n* Bürste *f*; (*with handle*) Handfeger *m*; (*for paint, pastry*) Pinsel *m*; (*bushes*) Unterholz *nt*; (*fig: conflict*) Zusammenstoß *m* • *vt* bürsten; putzen ⟨*teeth*⟩; ~ **against** streifen [gegen]; ~ **aside** (*fig*) abtun. ~ **off** *vt* abbürsten; (*reject*) zurückweisen. ~ **up** *vt/i* (*fig*) ~**up [on]** auffrischen

brusque /brʊsk/ *a*, **-ly** *adv* brüsk

Brussels /ˈbrʌslz/ *n* Brüssel *nt*. ~ **sprouts** *npl* Rosenkohl *m*

brutal /ˈbruːtl/ *a*, **-ly** *adv* brutal. ~**ity** /-ˈtælətɪ/ *n* Brutalität *f*

brute /bruːt/ *n* Unmensch *m*. ~ **force** *n* rohe Gewalt *f*

B.Sc. *abbr of* **Bachelor of Science**
bubble /'bʌbl/ *n* [Luft]blase *f* • *vi* sprudeln
buck[1] /bʌk/ *n* (*deer & Gym*) Bock *m*; (*rabbit*) Rammler *m* • *vi* ⟨*horse:*⟩ bocken. **~ up** *vi* (*fam*) sich aufheitern; (*hurry*) sich beeilen
buck[2] *n* (*Amer, fam*) Dollar *m*
buck[3] *n* **pass the ~** die Verantwortung abschieben
bucket /'bʌkɪt/ *n* Eimer *m*
buckle /'bʌkl/ *n* Schnalle *f* • *vt* zuschnallen • *vi* sich verbiegen
bud /bʌd/ *n* Knospe *f* • *vi* (*pt/pp* **budded**) knospen
Buddhis|m /'bʊdɪzm/ *n* Buddhismus *m*. **~t** *a* buddhistisch • *n* Buddhist(in) *m*(*f*)
buddy /'bʌdɪ/ *n* (*fam*) Freund *m*
budge /bʌdʒ/ *vt* bewegen • *vi* sich [von der Stelle] rühren
budgerigar /'bʌdʒərɪgɑ:(r)/ *n* Wellensittich *m*
budget /'bʌdʒɪt/ *n* Budget *nt*; (*Pol*) Haushaltsplan *m*; (*money available*) Etat *m* • *vi* (*pt/pp* **budgeted**) **~ for sth** etw einkalkulieren
buff /bʌf/ *a* (*colour*) sandfarben • *n* Sandfarbe *f*; (*Amer, fam*) Fan *m* • *vt* polieren
buffalo /'bʌfələʊ/ *n* (*inv or pl* **-es**) Büffel *m*
buffer /'bʌfə(r)/ *n* (*Rail*) Puffer *m*; **old ~** (*fam*) alter Knacker *m*; **~ zone** Pufferzone *f*
buffet[1] /'bʊfeɪ/ *n* Büfett *nt*; (*on station*) Imbißstube *f*
buffet[2] /'bʌfɪt/ *vt* (*pt/pp* **buffeted**) hin und her werfen
buffoon /bə'fu:n/ *n* Narr *m*
bug /bʌg/ *n* Wanze *f*; (*fam: virus*) Bazillus *m*; (*fam: device*) Abhörgerät *nt*, (*fam*) Wanze *f* • *vt* (*pt/pp* **bugged**) (*fam*) verwanzen ⟨*room*⟩; abhören ⟨*telephone*⟩; (*Amer: annoy*) ärgern
buggy /'bʌgɪ/ *n* [Kinder]sportwagen *m*
bugle /'bju:gl/ *n* Signalhorn *m*
build /bɪld/ *n* (*of person*) Körperbau *m* • *vt/i* (*pt/pp* **built**) bauen. **~ on** *vt* anbauen (**to** an + *acc*). **~ up** *vt* aufbauen • *vi* zunehmen; ⟨*traffic:*⟩ sich stauen
builder /'bɪldə(r)/ *n* Bauunternehmer *m*
building /'bɪldɪŋ/ *n* Gebäude *nt*. **~ site** *n* Baustelle *f*. **~ society** *n* Bausparkasse *f*

built /bɪlt/ *see* **build**. **~-in** *a* eingebaut. **~-in 'cupboard** *n* Einbauschrank *m*. **~-up area** *n* bebautes Gebiet *nt*; (*Auto*) geschlossene Ortschaft *f*
bulb /bʌlb/ *n* [Blumen]zwiebel *f*; (*Electr*) [Glüh]birne *f*
bulbous /'bʌlbəs/ *a* bauchig
Bulgaria /bʌl'geərɪə/ *n* Bulgarien *nt*
bulg|e /bʌldʒ/ *n* Ausbauchung *f* • *vi* sich ausbauchen. **~ing** *a* prall; ⟨*eyes*⟩ hervorquellend; **~ing with** prall gefüllt mit
bulk /bʌlk/ *n* Masse *f*; (*greater part*) Hauptteil *m*; **in ~** en gros; (*loose*) lose. **~y** *a* sperrig; (*large*) massig
bull /bʊl/ *n* Bulle *m*, Stier *m*
'bulldog *n* Bulldogge *f*
bulldozer /'bʊldəʊzə(r)/ *n* Planierraupe *f*
bullet /'bʊlɪt/ *n* Kugel *f*
bulletin /'bʊlɪtɪn/ *n* Bulletin *nt*
'bullet-proof *a* kugelsicher
'bullfight *n* Stierkampf *m*. **~er** *n* Stierkämpfer *m*
'bullfinch *n* Dompfaff *m*
bullion /'bʊlɪən/ *n* **gold ~** Barrengold *nt*
bullock /'bʊlək/ *n* Ochse *m*
bull: ~ring *n* Stierkampfarena *f*. **~'s-eye** *n* **score a ~'s-eye** ins Schwarze treffen
bully /'bʊlɪ/ *n* Tyrann *m* • *vt* tyrannisieren
bum[1] /bʌm/ *n* (*sl*) Hintern *m*
bum[2] *n* (*Amer, fam*) Landstreicher *m*
bumble-bee /'bʌmbl-/ *n* Hummel *f*
bump /bʌmp/ *n* Bums *m*; (*swelling*) Beule *f*; (*in road*) holperige Stelle *f* • *vt* stoßen; **~ into** stoßen gegen; (*meet*) zufällig treffen. **~ off** *vt* (*fam*) um die Ecke bringen
bumper /'bʌmpə(r)/ *a* Rekord- • *n* (*Auto*) Stoßstange *f*
bumpkin /'bʌmpkɪn/ *n* **country ~** Tölpel *m*
bumptious /'bʌmpʃəs/ *a* aufgeblasen
bumpy /'bʌmpɪ/ *a* holperig
bun /bʌn/ *n* Milchbrötchen *nt*; (*hair*) [Haar]knoten *m*
bunch /bʌntʃ/ *n* (*of flowers*) Strauß *m*; (*of radishes, keys*) Bund *m*; (*of people*) Gruppe *f*; **~ of grapes** [ganze] Weintraube *f*
bundle /'bʌndl/ *n* Bündel *nt* • *vt* **~ [up]** bündeln
bung /bʌŋ/ *vt* (*fam*) (*throw*) schmeißen. **~ up** *vt* (*fam*) verstopfen

bungalow /'bʌŋgələʊ/ *n* Bungalow *m*
bungle /'bʌŋgl/ *vt* verpfuschen
bunion /'bʌnjən/ *n* (*Med*) Ballen *m*
bunk /bʌŋk/ *n* [Schlaf]koje *f*. **~-beds** *npl* Etagenbett *nt*
bunker /'bʌŋkə(r)/ *n* Bunker *m*
bunkum /'bʌŋkəm/ *n* Quatsch *m*
bunny /'bʌnɪ/ *n* (*fam*) Kaninchen *nt*
buoy /bɔɪ/ *n* Boje *f*. **~ up** *vt* (*fig*) stärken
buoyan|cy /'bɔɪənsɪ/ *n* Auftrieb *m*. **~t** *a* **be ~t** schwimmen; ⟨*water:*⟩ gut tragen
burden /'bɜ:dn/ *n* Last *f* ● *vt* belasten. **~some** /-səm/ *a* lästig
bureau /'bjʊərəʊ/ *n* (*pl* **-x** /-əʊz/ *or* **~s**) (*desk*) Sekretär *m*; (*office*) Büro *nt*
bureaucracy /bjʊə'rɒkrəsɪ/ *n* Bürokratie *f*
bureaucrat /'bjʊərəkræt/ *n* Bürokrat *m*. **~ic** /-'krætɪk/ *a* bürokratisch
burger /'bɜ:gə(r)/ *n* Hamburger *m*
burglar /'bɜ:glə(r)/ *n* Einbrecher *m*. **~ alarm** *n* Alarmanlage *f*
burglar|ize /'bɜ:gləraɪz/ *vt* (*Amer*) einbrechen in (+ *acc*). **~y** *n* Einbruch *m*
burgle /'bɜ:gl/ *vt* einbrechen in (+ *acc*); **they have been ~d** bei ihnen ist eingebrochen worden
Burgundy /'bɜ:gəndɪ/ *n* Burgund *nt*; **b~** (*wine*) Burgunder *m*
burial /'berɪəl/ *n* Begräbnis *nt*
burlesque /bɜ:'lesk/ *n* Burleske *f*
burly /'bɜ:lɪ/ *a* (**-ier, -iest**) stämmig
Burm|a /'bɜ:mə/ *n* Birma *nt*. **~ese** /-'mi:z/ *a* birmanisch
burn /bɜ:n/ *n* Verbrennung *f*; (*on skin*) Brandwunde *f*; (*on material*) Brandstelle *f* ● *v* (*pt/pp* **burnt** *or* **burned**) ● *vt* verbrennen ● *vi* brennen; ⟨*food:*⟩ anbrennen. **~ down** *vt/i* niederbrennen
burnish /'bɜ:nɪʃ/ *vt* polieren
burnt /bɜ:nt/ *see* **burn**
burp /bɜ:p/ *vi* (*fam*) aufstoßen
burrow /'bʌrəʊ/ *n* Bau *m* ● *vi* wühlen
bursar /'bɜ:sə(r)/ *n* Rechnungsführer *m*. **~y** *n* Stipendium *nt*
burst /bɜ:st/ *n* Bruch *m*; (*surge*) Ausbruch *m* ● *v* (*pt/pp* **burst**) ● *vt* platzen machen ● *vi* platzen; ⟨*bud:*⟩ aufgehen; **~ into tears** in Tränen ausbrechen
bury /'berɪ/ *vt* (*pt/pp* **-ied**) begraben; (*hide*) vergraben
bus /bʌs/ *n* [Auto]bus *m* ● *vt/i* (*pt/pp* **bussed**) mit dem Bus fahren
bush /bʊʃ/ *n* Strauch *m*; (*land*) Busch *m*. **~y** *a* (**-ier, -iest**) buschig
busily /'bɪzɪlɪ/ *adv* eifrig
business /'bɪznɪs/ *n* Angelegenheit *f*; (*Comm*) Geschäft *nt*; **on ~** geschäftlich; **he has no ~ to** er hat kein Recht, zu; **mind one's own ~** sich um seine eigenen Angelegenheiten kümmern; **that's none of your ~** das geht Sie nichts an. **~-like** *a* geschäftsmäßig. **~man** *n* Geschäftsmann *m*
busker /'bʌskə(r)/ *n* Straßenmusikant *m*
'bus-stop *n* Bushaltestelle *f*
bust[1] /bʌst/ *n* Büste *f*. **~ size** *n* Oberweite *f*
bust[2] *a* (*fam*) kaputt; **go ~** pleite machen ● *v* (*pt/pp* **busted** *or* **bust**) (*fam*) ● *vt* kaputtmachen ● *vi* kaputtgehen
bustl|e /'bʌsl/ *n* Betrieb *m*, Getriebe *nt* ● *vi* **~e about** geschäftig hin und her laufen. **~ing** *a* belebt
'bust-up *n* (*fam*) Streit *m*, Krach *m*
busy /'bɪzɪ/ *a* (**-ier, -iest**) beschäftigt; ⟨*day*⟩ voll; ⟨*street*⟩ belebt; (*with traffic*) stark befahren; (*Amer Teleph*) besetzt; **be ~** zu tun haben ● *vt* **~ oneself** sich beschäftigen (**with** mit)
'busybody *n* Wichtigtuer(in) *m*(*f*)
but /bʌt, *unbetont* bət/ *conj* aber; (*after negative*) sondern ● *prep* außer (+ *dat*); **~ for** (*without*) ohne (+ *acc*); **the last ~ one** der/die/das vorletzte; **the next ~ one** der/die/das übernächste ● *adv* nur
butcher /'bʊtʃə(r)/ *n* Fleischer *m*, Metzger *m*; **~'s [shop]** Fleischerei *f*, Metzgerei *f* ● *vt* [ab]schlachten
butler /'bʌtlə(r)/ *n* Butler *m*
butt /bʌt/ *n* (*of gun*) [Gewehr]kolben *m*; (*fig: target*) Zielscheibe *f*; (*of cigarette*) Stummel *m*; (*for water*) Regentonne *f* ● *vt* mit dem Kopf stoßen ● *vi* **~ in** unterbrechen
butter /'bʌtə(r)/ *n* Butter *f* ● *vt* mit Butter bestreichen. **~ up** *vt* (*fam*) schmeicheln (+ *dat*)
butter: ~cup *a* Butterblume *f*, Hahnenfuß *m*. **~fly** *n* Schmetterling *m*
buttocks /'bʌtəks/ *npl* Gesäß *nt*
button /'bʌtn/ *n* Knopf *m* ● *vt* **~ [up]** zuknöpfen ● *vi* geknöpft werden. **~hole** *n* Knopfloch *nt*
buttress /'bʌtrɪs/ *n* Strebepfeiler *m*; **flying ~** Strebebogen *m*
buxom /'bʌksəm/ *a* drall

buy /baɪ/ *n* Kauf *m* ● *vt* (*pt/pp* **bought**) kaufen. **~er** *n* Käufer(in) *m*(*f*)
buzz /bʌz/ *n* Summen *nt* ● *vi* summen. **~ off** *vi* (*fam*) abhauen
buzzard /'bʌzəd/ *n* Bussard *m*
buzzer /'bʌzə(r)/ *n* Summer *m*
by /baɪ/ *prep* (*close to*) bei (+ *dat*); (*next to*) neben (+ *dat/acc*); (*past*) an (+ *dat*) ... vorbei; (*to the extent of*) um (+ *acc*); (*at the latest*) bis; (*by means of*) durch; **by Mozart/Dickens** von Mozart/Dickens; **~ oneself** allein; **~ the sea** am Meer; **~ car/bus** mit dem Auto/Bus; **~ sea** mit dem Schiff; **~ day/night** bei Tag/Nacht; **~ the hour** pro Stunde; **~ the metre** meterweise; **six metres ~ four** sechs mal vier Meter; **win ~ a length** mit einer Länge Vorsprung gewinnen; **miss the train ~ a minute** den Zug um eine Minute verpassen ● *adv* **~ and ~** mit der Zeit; **~ and large** im großen und ganzen; **put ~** beiseite legen; **go/pass ~** vorbeigehen
bye /baɪ/ *int* (*fam*) tschüs
by: ~-election *n* Nachwahl *f*. **~gone** *a* vergangen. **~-law** *n* Verordnung *f*. **~pass** *n* Umgehungsstraße *f*; (*Med*) Bypass *m* ● *vt* umfahren. **~-product** *n* Nebenprodukt *m*. **~-road** *n* Nebenstraße *f*. **~stander** *n* Zuschauer(in) *m*(*f*)
Byzantine /bɪ'zæntaɪn/ *a* byzantinisch

C

cab /kæb/ *n* Taxi *nt*; (*of lorry, train*) Führerhaus *nt*
cabaret /'kæbəreɪ/ *n* Kabarett *nt*
cabbage /'kæbɪdʒ/ *n* Kohl *m*
cabin /'kæbɪn/ *n* Kabine *f*; (*hut*) Hütte *f*
cabinet /'kæbɪnɪt/ *n* Schrank *m*; **[display] ~** Vitrine *f*; (*TV, Radio*) Gehäuse *nt*; **C~** (*Pol*) Kabinett *nt*. **~-maker** *n* Möbeltischler *m*
cable /'keɪbl/ *n* Kabel *nt*; (*rope*) Tau *nt*. **~ 'railway** *n* Seilbahn *f*. **~ 'television** *n* Kabelfernsehen *nt*
cache /kæʃ/ *n* Versteck *nt*; **~ of arms** Waffenlager *nt*
cackle /'kækl/ *vi* gackern
cactus /'kæktəs/ *n* (*pl* **-ti** /-taɪ/ *or* **-tuses**) Kaktus *m*
caddie /'kædɪ/ *n* Caddie *m*
caddy /'kædɪ/ *n* **[tea-]~** Teedose *f*
cadet /kə'det/ *n* Kadett *m*
cadge /kædʒ/ *vt/i* (*fam*) schnorren
Caesarean /sɪ'zeərɪən/ *a & n* **~ [section]** Kaiserschnitt *m*
café /'kæfeɪ/ *n* Café *nt*
cafeteria /kæfə'tɪərɪə/ *n* Selbstbedienungsrestaurant *nt*
caffeine /'kæfi:n/ *n* Koffein *nt*
cage /keɪdʒ/ *n* Käfig *m*
cagey /'keɪdʒɪ/ *a* (*fam*) **be ~** mit der Sprache nicht herauswollen
cajole /kə'dʒəʊl/ *vt* gut zureden (+ *dat*)
cake /keɪk/ *n* Kuchen *m*; (*of soap*) Stück *nt*. **~d** *a* verkrustet (**with** mit)
calamity /kə'læmətɪ/ *n* Katastrophe *f*
calcium /'kælsɪəm/ *n* Kalzium *nt*
calculat|e /'kælkjʊleɪt/ *vt* berechnen; (*estimate*) kalkulieren. **~ing** *a* (*fig*) berechnend. **~ion** /-'leɪʃn/ *n* Rechnung *f*, Kalkulation *f*. **~or** *n* Rechner *m*
calendar /'kælɪndə(r)/ *n* Kalender *m*
calf¹ /kɑ:f/ *n* (*pl* **calves**) Kalb *nt*
calf² *n* (*pl* **calves**) (*Anat*) Wade *f*
calibre /'kælɪbə(r)/ *n* Kaliber *nt*
calico /'kælɪkəʊ/ *n* Kattun *m*
call /kɔ:l/ *n* Ruf *m*; (*Teleph*) Anruf *m*; (*visit*) Besuch *m*; **be on ~** ⟨*doctor:*⟩ Bereitschaftsdienst haben ● *vt* rufen; (*Teleph*) anrufen; (*wake*) wecken; ausrufen ⟨*strike*⟩; (*name*) nennen; **be ~ed** heißen ● *vi* rufen; **~ [in *or* round]** vorbeikommen. **~ back** *vt* zurückrufen ● *vi* noch einmal vorbeikommen. **~ for** *vt* rufen nach; (*demand*) verlangen; (*fetch*) abholen. **~ off** *vt* zurückrufen ⟨*dog*⟩; (*cancel*) absagen. **~ on** *vt* bitten (**for** um); (*appeal to*) appellieren an (+ *acc*); (*visit*) besuchen. **~ out** *vt* rufen; aufrufen ⟨*names*⟩ ● *vi* rufen. **~ up** *vt* (*Mil*) einberufen; (*Teleph*) anrufen
call: ~-box *n* Telefonzelle *f*. **~er** *n* Besucher *m*; (*Teleph*) Anrufer *m*. **~ing** *n* Berufung *f*
callous /'kæləs/ *a* gefühllos
'call-up *n* (*Mil*) Einberufung *f*
calm /kɑ:m/ *a* (**-er, -est**), **-ly** *adv* ruhig ● *n* Ruhe *f* ● *vt* **~ [down]** beruhigen ● *vi* **~ down** sich beruhigen. **~ness** *n* Ruhe *f*; (*of sea*) Stille *f*
calorie /'kælərɪ/ *n* Kalorie *f*
calves /kɑ:vz/ *npl see* **calf¹** & **²**
camber /'kæmbə(r)/ *n* Wölbung *f*
came /keɪm/ *see* **come**

camel /'kæml/ *n* Kamel *nt*
camera /'kæmərə/ *n* Kamera *f*. **~man** *n* Kameramann *m*
camouflage /'kæməflɑ:ʒ/ *n* Tarnung *f* ● *vt* tarnen
camp /kæmp/ *n* Lager *nt* ● *vi* campen; (*Mil*) kampieren
campaign /kæm'peɪn/ *n* Feldzug *m*; (*Comm, Pol*) Kampagne *f* ● *vi* kämpfen; (*Pol*) im Wahlkampf arbeiten
camp: ~-bed *n* Feldbett *nt*. **~er** *n* Camper *m*; (*Auto*) Wohnmobil *nt*. **~ing** *n* Camping *nt*. **~site** *n* Campingplatz *m*
campus /'kæmpəs/ *n* (*pl* **-puses**) (*Univ*) Campus *m*
can[1] /kæn/ *n* (*for petrol*) Kanister *m*; (*tin*) Dose *f*, Büchse *f*; **a ~ of beer** eine Dose Bier ● *vt* in Dosen *od* Büchsen konservieren
can[2] /kæn, *unbetont* kən/ *v aux* (*pres* **can**; *pt* **could**) können; **I cannot/can't go** ich kann nicht gehen; **he could not go** er konnte nicht gehen; **if I could go** wenn ich gehen könnte
Canad|a /'kænədə/ *n* Kanada *nt*. **~ian** /kə'neɪdɪən/ *a* kanadisch ● *n* Kanadier(in) *m(f)*
canal /kə'næl/ *n* Kanal *m*
Canaries /kə'neərɪz/ *npl* Kanarische Inseln *pl*
canary /kə'neərɪ/ *n* Kanarienvogel *m*
cancel /'kænsl/ *vt/i* (*pt/pp* **cancelled**) absagen; entwerten ‹*stamp*›; (*annul*) rückgängig machen; (*Comm*) stornieren; abbestellen ‹*newspaper*›; **be ~led** ausfallen. **~lation** /-ə'leɪʃn/ *n* Absage *f*
cancer /'kænsə(r)/ *n*, & (*Astr*) **C~** Krebs *m*. **~ous** /-rəs/ *a* krebsig
candelabra /kændə'lɑ:brə/ *n* Armleuchter *m*
candid /'kændɪd/ *a*, **-ly** *adv* offen
candidate /'kændɪdət/ *n* Kandidat(in) *m(f)*
candied /'kændɪd/ *a* kandiert
candle /'kændl/ *n* Kerze *f*. **~stick** *n* Kerzenständer *m*, Leuchter *m*
candour /'kændə(r)/ *n* Offenheit *f*
candy /'kændɪ/ *n* (*Amer*) Süßigkeiten *pl*; **[piece of] ~** Bonbon *m*. **~floss** /-flɒs/ *n* Zuckerwatte *f*
cane /keɪn/ *n* Rohr *nt*; (*stick*) Stock *m* ● *vt* mit dem Stock züchtigen
canine /'keɪnaɪn/ *a* Hunde-. **~ tooth** *n* Eckzahn *m*
canister /'kænɪstə(r)/ *n* Blechdose *f*
cannabis /'kænəbɪs/ *n* Haschisch *nt*
canned /kænd/ *a* Dosen-, Büchsen-; **~ music** (*fam*) Musik *f* aus der Konserve
cannibal /'kænɪbl/ *n* Kannibale *m*. **~ism** *n* Kannibalismus *m*
cannon /'kænən/ *n inv* Kanone *f*. **~-ball** *n* Kanonenkugel *f*
cannot /'kænɒt/ *see* **can**[2]
canny /'kænɪ/ *a* schlau
canoe /kə'nu:/ *n* Paddelboot *nt*; (*Sport*) Kanu *nt* ● *vi* paddeln; (*Sport*) Kanu fahren
canon /'kænən/ *n* Kanon *m*; (*person*) Kanonikus *m*. **~ize** /-aɪz/ *vt* kanonisieren
'can-opener *n* Dosenöffner *m*, Büchsenöffner *m*
canopy /'kænəpɪ/ *n* Baldachin *m*
cant /kænt/ *n* Heuchelei *f*
can't /kɑ:nt/ = **cannot**. *See* **can**[2]
cantankerous /kæn'tæŋkərəs/ *a* zänkisch
canteen /kæn'ti:n/ *n* Kantine *f*; **~ of cutlery** Besteckkasten *m*
canter /'kæntə(r)/ *n* Kanter *m* ● *vi* kantern
canvas /'kænvəs/ *n* Segeltuch *nt*; (*Art*) Leinwand *f*; (*painting*) Gemälde *nt*
canvass /'kænvəs/ *vi* um Stimmen werben
canyon /'kænjən/ *n* Cañon *m*
cap /kæp/ *n* Kappe *f*, Mütze *f*; (*nurse's*) Haube *f*; (*top, lid*) Verschluß *m* ● *vt* (*pt/pp* **capped**) (*fig*) übertreffen
capability /keɪpə'bɪlətɪ/ *n* Fähigkeit *f*
capable /'keɪpəbl/ *a*, **-bly** *adv* fähig; **be ~ of doing sth** fähig sein, etw zu tun
capacity /kə'pæsətɪ/ *n* Fassungsvermögen *nt*; (*ability*) Fähigkeit *f*; **in my ~ as** in meiner Eigenschaft als
cape[1] /keɪp/ *n* (*cloak*) Cape *nt*
cape[2] *n* (*Geog*) Kap *nt*
caper[1] /'keɪpə(r)/ *vi* herumspringen
caper[2] *n* (*Culin*) Kaper *f*
capital /'kæpɪtl/ *a* ‹*letter*› groß ● *n* (*town*) Hauptstadt *f*; (*money*) Kapital *nt*; (*letter*) Großbuchstabe *m*
capital|ism /'kæpɪtəlɪzm/ *n* Kapitalismus *m*. **~ist** /-ɪst/ *a* kapitalistisch ● *n* Kapitalist *m*. **~ize** /-aɪz/ *vi* **~ize on** (*fig*) Kapital schlagen aus. **~ 'letter** *n* Großbuchstabe *m*. **~ 'punishment** *n* Todesstrafe *f*
capitulat|e /kə'pɪtjʊleɪt/ *vi* kapitulieren. **~ion** /-'leɪʃn/ *n* Kapitulation *f*
capricious /kə'prɪʃəs/ *a* launisch
Capricorn /'kæprɪkɔ:n/ *n* (*Astr*) Steinbock *m*

capsize /kæp'saɪz/ *vi* kentern ● *vt* zum Kentern bringen
capsule /'kæpsjʊl/ *n* Kapsel *f*
captain /'kæptɪn/ *n* Kapitän *m*; (*Mil*) Hauptmann *m* ● *vt* anführen ⟨*team*⟩
caption /'kæpʃn/ *n* Überschrift *f*; (*of illustration*) Bildtext *m*
captivate /'kæptɪveɪt/ *vt* bezaubern
captiv|e /'kæptɪv/ *a* **hold/take ~e** gefangenhalten/-nehmen ● *n* Gefangene(r) *m/f*. **~ity** /-'tɪvətɪ/ *n* Gefangenschaft *f*
capture /'kæptʃə(r)/ *n* Gefangennahme *f* ● *vt* gefangennehmen; [ein]fangen ⟨*animal*⟩; (*Mil*) einnehmen ⟨*town*⟩
car /kɑ:(r)/ *n* Auto *nt*, Wagen *m*; **by ~** mit dem Auto *od* Wagen
carafe /kə'ræf/ *n* Karaffe *f*
caramel /'kærəmel/ *n* Karamel *m*
carat /'kærət/ *n* Karat *nt*
caravan /'kærəvæn/ *n* Wohnwagen *m*; (*procession*) Karawane *f*
carbohydrate /kɑ:bə'haɪdreɪt/ *n* Kohlenhydrat *nt*
carbon /'kɑ:bən/ *n* Kohlenstoff *m*; (*paper*) Kohlepapier *nt*; (*copy*) Durchschlag *m*
carbon: ~ copy *n* Durchschlag *m*. **~ di'oxide** *n* Kohlendioxyd *nt*; (*in drink*) Kohlensäure *f*. **~ paper** *n* Kohlepapier *nt*
carburettor /kɑ:bjʊ'retə(r)/ *n* Vergaser *m*
carcass /'kɑ:kəs/ *n* Kadaver *m*
card /kɑ:d/ *n* Karte *f*
'cardboard *n* Pappe *f*, Karton *m*. **~ 'box** *n* Pappschachtel *f*; (*large*) [Papp]karton *m*
'card-game *n* Kartenspiel *nt*
cardiac /'kɑ:dɪæk/ *a* Herz-
cardigan /'kɑ:dɪgən/ *n* Strickjacke *f*
cardinal /'kɑ:dɪnl/ *a* Kardinal-; **~ number** Kardinalzahl *f* ● *n* (*Relig*) Kardinal *m*
card 'index *n* Kartei *f*
care /keə(r)/ *n* Sorgfalt *f*; (*caution*) Vorsicht *f*; (*protection*) Obhut *f*; (*looking after*) Pflege *f*; (*worry*) Sorge *f*; **~ of** (*on letter abbr* **c/o**) bei; **take ~** vorsichtig sein; **take into ~** in Pflege nehmen; **take ~ of** sich kümmern um ● *vi* **~ about** sich kümmern um; **~ for** (*like*) mögen; (*look after*) betreuen; **I don't ~** das ist mir gleich
career /kə'rɪə(r)/ *n* Laufbahn *f*; (*profession*) Beruf *m* ● *vi* rasen
care: ~free *a* sorglos. **~ful** *a*, **-ly** *adv* sorgfältig; (*cautious*) vorsichtig. **~less** *a*, **-ly** *adv* nachlässig. **~lessness** *n* Nachlässigkeit *f*
caress /kə'res/ *n* Liebkosung *f* ● *vt* liebkosen
'caretaker *n* Hausmeister *m*
'car ferry *n* Autofähre *f*
cargo /'kɑ:gəʊ/ *n* (*pl* **-es**) Ladung *f*
Caribbean /kærɪ'bi:ən/ *n* **the ~** die Karibik
caricature /'kærɪkətjʊə(r)/ *n* Karikatur *f* ● *vt* karikieren
caring /'keərɪŋ/ *a* ⟨*parent*⟩ liebevoll; ⟨*profession, attitude*⟩ sozial
carnage /'kɑ:nɪdʒ/ *n* Gemetzel *nt*
carnal /'kɑ:nl/ *a* fleischlich
carnation /kɑ:'neɪʃn/ *n* Nelke *f*
carnival /'kɑ:nɪvl/ *n* Karneval *m*
carnivorous /kɑ:'nɪvərəs/ *a* fleischfressend
carol /'kærl/ *n* **[Christmas] ~** Weihnachtslied *nt*
carp[1] /kɑ:p/ *n inv* Karpfen *m*
carp[2] *vi* nörgeln; **~ at** herumnörgeln an (+ *dat*)
'car park *n* Parkplatz *m*; (*multi-storey*) Parkhaus *nt*; (*underground*) Tiefgarage *f*
carpent|er /'kɑ:pɪntə(r)/ *n* Zimmermann *m*; (*joiner*) Tischler *m*. **~ry** *n* Tischlerei *f*
carpet /'kɑ:pɪt/ *n* Teppich *m* ● *vt* mit Teppich auslegen
carriage /'kærɪdʒ/ *n* Kutsche *f*; (*Rail*) Wagen *m*; (*of goods*) Beförderung *f*; (*cost*) Frachtkosten *pl*; (*bearing*) Haltung *f*. **~way** *n* Fahrbahn *f*
carrier /'kærɪə(r)/ *n* Träger(in) *m(f)*; (*Comm*) Spediteur *m*; **~[-bag]** Tragetasche *f*
carrot /'kærət/ *n* Möhre *f*, Karotte *f*
carry /'kærɪ/ *vt/i* (*pt/pp* **-ied**) tragen; **be carried away** (*fam*) hingerissen sein. **~ off** *vt* wegtragen; gewinnen ⟨*prize*⟩. **~ on** *vi* weitermachen; **~ on at** (*fam*) herumnörgeln an (+ *dat*); **~ on with** (*fam*) eine Affäre haben mit ● *vt* führen; (*continue*) fortführen. **~ out** *vt* hinaus-/heraustragen; (*perform*) ausführen
'carry-cot *n* Babytragetasche *f*
cart /kɑ:t/ *n* Karren *m*; **put the ~ before the horse** das Pferd beim Schwanz aufzäumen ● *vt* karren; (*fam: carry*) schleppen
cartilage /'kɑ:tɪlɪdʒ/ *n* (*Anat*) Knorpel *m*

carton /'kɑ:tn/ *n* [Papp]karton *m*; (*for drink*) Tüte *f*; (*of cream, yoghurt*) Becher *m*

cartoon /kɑ:'tu:n/ *n* Karikatur *f*; (*joke*) Witzzeichnung *f*; (*strip*) Comic Strips *pl*; (*film*) Zeichentrickfilm *m*; (*Art*) Karton *m*. **~ist** *n* Karikaturist *m*

cartridge /'kɑ:trɪdʒ/ *n* Patrone *f*; (*for film, typewriter ribbon*) Kassette *f*; (*of record player*) Tonabnehmer *m*

carve /kɑ:v/ *vt* schnitzen; (*in stone*) hauen; (*Culin*) aufschneiden

carving /'kɑ:vɪŋ/ *n* Schnitzerei *f*. **~-knife** *n* Tranchiermesser *nt*

'car wash *n* Autowäsche *f*; (*place*) Autowaschanlage *f*

case¹ /keɪs/ *n* Fall *m*; **in any ~** auf jeden Fall; **just in ~** für alle Fälle; **in ~ he comes** falls er kommt

case² *n* Kasten *m*; (*crate*) Kiste *f*; (*for spectacles*) Etui *nt*; (*suitcase*) Koffer *m*; (*for display*) Vitrine *f*

cash /kæʃ/ *n* Bargeld *nt*; **pay [in] ~** [in] bar bezahlen; **~ on delivery** per Nachnahme ● *vt* einlösen ⟨*cheque*⟩. **~ desk** *n* Kasse *f*

cashier /kæ'ʃɪə(r)/ *n* Kassierer(in) *m(f)*

'cash register *n* Registrierkasse *f*

casino /kə'si:nəʊ/ *n* Kasino *nt*

cask /kɑ:sk/ *n* Faß *nt*

casket /'kɑ:skɪt/ *n* Kasten *m*; (*Amer: coffin*) Sarg *m*

casserole /'kæsərəʊl/ *n* Schmortopf *m*; (*stew*) Eintopf *m*

cassette /kə'set/ *n* Kassette *f*. **~ recorder** *n* Kassettenrecorder *m*

cast /kɑ:st/ *n* (*throw*) Wurf *m*; (*mould*) Form *f*; (*model*) Abguß *m*; (*Theat*) Besetzung *f*; **[plaster] ~** (*Med*) Gipsverband *m* ● *vt* (*pt/pp* **cast**) (*throw*) werfen; (*shed*) abwerfen; abgeben ⟨*vote*⟩; gießen ⟨*metal*⟩; (*Theat*) besetzen ⟨*role*⟩; **~ a glance at** einen Blick werfen auf (+ *acc*). **~ off** *vi* (*Naut*) ablegen ● *vt* (*Knitting*) abketten. **~ on** *vt* (*Knitting*) anschlagen

castanets /kæstə'nets/ *npl* Kastagnetten *pl*

castaway /'kɑ:stəweɪ/ *n* Schiffbrüchige(r) *m/f*

caste /kɑ:st/ *n* Kaste *f*

cast 'iron *n* Gußeisen *nt*

cast-'iron *a* gußeisern

castle /'kɑ:sl/ *n* Schloß *nt*; (*fortified*) Burg *f*; (*Chess*) Turm *m*

'cast-offs *npl* abgelegte Kleidung *f*

castor /'kɑ:stə(r)/ *n* (*wheel*) [Lauf]rolle *f*

'castor sugar *n* Streuzucker *m*

castrat|e /kæ'streɪt/ *vt* kastrieren. **~ion** /-eɪʃn/ *n* Kastration *f*

casual /'kæʒʊəl/ *a*, **-ly** *adv* (*chance*) zufällig; (*offhand*) lässig; (*informal*) zwanglos; (*not permanent*) Gelegenheits-; **~ wear** Freizeitbekleidung *f*

casualty /'kæʒʊəltɪ/ *n* [Todes]opfer *nt*; (*injured person*) Verletzte(r) *m/f*; **~ [department]** Unfallstation *f*

cat /kæt/ *n* Katze *f*

catalogue /'kætəlɒg/ *n* Katalog *m* ● *vt* katalogisieren

catalyst /'kætəlɪst/ *n* (*Chem & fig*) Katalysator *m*

catalytic /kætə'lɪtɪk/ *a* **~ converter** (*Auto*) Katalysator *m*

catapult /'kætəpʌlt/ *n* Katapult *nt* ● *vt* katapultieren

cataract /'kætərækt/ *n* (*Med*) grauer Star *m*

catarrh /kə'tɑ:(r)/ *n* Katarrh *m*

catastroph|e /kə'tæstrəfɪ/ *n* Katastrophe *f*. **~ic** /kætə'strɒfɪk/ *a* katastrophal

catch /kætʃ/ *n* (*of fish*) Fang *m*; (*fastener*) Verschluß *m*; (*on door*) Klinke *f*; (*fam: snag*) Haken *m* (*fam*) ● *v* (*pt/pp* **caught**) ● *vt* fangen; (*be in time for*) erreichen; (*travel by*) fahren mit; bekommen ⟨*illness*⟩; **~ a cold** sich erkälten; **~ sight of** erblicken; **~ s.o. stealing** jdn beim Stehlen erwischen; **~ one's finger in the door** sich (*dat*) den Finger in der Tür [ein]klemmen ● *vi* (*burn*) anbrennen; (*get stuck*) klemmen. **~ on** *vi* (*fam*) (*understand*) kapieren; (*become popular*) sich durchsetzen. **~ up** *vt* einholen ● *vi* aufholen; **~ up with** einholen ⟨*s.o.*⟩; nachholen ⟨*work*⟩

catching /'kætʃɪŋ/ *a* ansteckend

catch: ~-phrase *n*, **~word** *n* Schlagwort *nt*

catchy /'kætʃɪ/ *a* (**-ier, -iest**) einprägsam

catechism /'kætɪkɪzm/ *n* Katechismus *m*

categor|ical /kætɪ'gɒrɪkl/ *a*, **-ly** *adv* kategorisch. **~y** /'kætɪgərɪ/ *n* Kategorie *f*

cater /'keɪtə(r)/ *vi* **~ for** beköstigen; ⟨*firm:*⟩ das Essen liefern für ⟨*party*⟩; (*fig*) eingestellt sein auf (+ *acc*). **~ing** *n* (*trade*) Gaststättengewerbe *nt*

caterpillar /'kætəpɪlə(r)/ *n* Raupe *f*
cathedral /kə'θi:drl/ *n* Dom *m*, Kathedrale *f*
Catholic /'kæθəlɪk/ *a* katholisch ● *n* Katholik(in) *m(f)*. **C~ism** /kə'θɒlɪsɪzm/ *n* Katholizismus *m*
catkin /'kætkɪn/ *n* (*Bot*) Kätzchen *nt*
cattle /'kætl/ *npl* Vieh *nt*
catty /'kætɪ/ *a* (**-ier, -iest**) boshaft
caught /kɔ:t/ *see* **catch**
cauldron /'kɔ:ldrən/ *n* [großer] Kessel *m*
cauliflower /'kɒlɪ-/ *n* Blumenkohl *m*
cause /kɔ:z/ *n* Ursache *f*; (*reason*) Grund *m*; **good ~** gute Sache *f* ● *vt* verursachen; **~ s.o. to do sth** jdn veranlassen, etw zu tun
'causeway *n* [Insel]damm *m*
caustic /'kɔ:stɪk/ *a* ätzend; (*fig*) beißend
cauterize /'kɔ:təraɪz/ *vt* kauterisieren
caution /'kɔ:ʃn/ *n* Vorsicht *f*; (*warning*) Verwarnung *f* ● *vt* (*Jur*) verwarnen
cautious /'kɔ:ʃəs/ *a*, **-ly** *adv* vorsichtig
cavalry /'kævəlrɪ/ *n* Kavallerie *f*
cave /keɪv/ *n* Höhle *f* ● *vi* **~ in** einstürzen
cavern /'kævən/ *n* Höhle *f*
caviare /'kævɪɑ:(r)/ *n* Kaviar *m*
caving /'keɪvɪŋ/ *n* Höhlenforschung *f*
cavity /'kævətɪ/ *n* Hohlraum *m*; (*in tooth*) Loch *nt*
cavort /kə'vɔ:t/ *vi* tollen
cease /si:s/ *n* **without ~** unaufhörlich ● *vt/i* aufhören. **~-fire** *n* Waffenruhe *f*. **~less** *a*, **-ly** *adv* unaufhörlich
cedar /'si:də(r)/ *n* Zeder *f*
cede /si:d/ *vt* abtreten (**to** an + *acc*)
ceiling /'si:lɪŋ/ *n* [Zimmer]decke *f*; (*fig*) oberste Grenze *f*
celebrat|e /'selɪbreɪt/ *vt/i* feiern. **~ed** *a* berühmt (**for** wegen). **~ion** /-'breɪʃn/ *n* Feier *f*
celebrity /sɪ'lebrətɪ/ *n* Berühmtheit *f*
celery /'selərɪ/ *n* [Stangen]sellerie *m* & *f*
celiba|cy /'selɪbəsɪ/ *n* Zölibat *nt*. **~te** *a* **be ~te** im Zölibat leben
cell /sel/ *n* Zelle *f*
cellar /'selə(r)/ *n* Keller *m*
cellist /'tʃelɪst/ *n* Cellist(in) *m(f)*
cello /'tʃeləu/ *n* Cello *nt*
Celsius /'selsɪəs/ *a* Celsius
Celt /kelt/ *n* Kelte *m*/Keltin *f*. **~ic** *a* keltisch
cement /sɪ'ment/ *n* Zement *m*; (*adhesive*) Kitt *m* ● *vt* zementieren; (*stick*) kitten
cemetery /'semətrɪ/ *n* Friedhof *m*
censor /'sensə(r)/ *n* Zensor *m* ● *vt* zensieren. **~ship** *n* Zensur *f*
censure /'senʃə(r)/ *n* Tadel *m* ● *vt* tadeln
census /'sensəs/ *n* Volkszählung *f*
cent /sent/ *n* (*coin*) Cent *m*
centenary /sen'ti:nərɪ/ *n*, (*Amer*) **centennial** /sen'tenɪəl/ *n* Hundertjahrfeier *f*
center /'sentə(r)/ *n* (*Amer*) = **centre**
centi|grade /'sentɪ-/ *a* Celsius-; **5°~** 5° Celsius. **~metre** *m* Zentimeter *m* & *nt*. **~pede** /-pi:d/ *n* Tausendfüßler *m*
central /'sentrəl/ *a*, **-ly** *adv* zentral. **~ 'heating** *n* Zentralheizung *f*. **~ize** *vt* zentralisieren. **~ reser'vation** *n* (*Auto*) Mittelstreifen *m*
centre /'sentə(r)/ *n* Zentrum *nt*; (*middle*) Mitte *f* ● *v* (*pt/pp* **centred**) ● *vt* zentrieren; **~ on** (*fig*) sich drehen um. **~-'forward** *n* Mittelstürmer *m*
centrifugal /sentrɪ'fju:gl/ *a* **~ force** Fliehkraft *f*
century /'sentʃərɪ/ *n* Jahrhundert *nt*
ceramic /sɪ'ræmɪk/ *a* Keramik-. **~s** *n* Keramik *f*
cereal /'sɪərɪəl/ *n* Getreide *nt*; (*breakfast food*) Frühstücksflocken *pl*
cerebral /'serɪbrl/ *a* Gehirn-
ceremon|ial /serɪ'məʊnɪəl/ *a*, **-ly** *adv* zeremoniell, feierlich ● *n* Zeremoniell *nt*. **~ious** /-ɪəs/ *a*, **-ly** *adv* formell
ceremony /'serɪmənɪ/ *n* Zeremonie *f*, Feier *f*; **without ~** ohne weitere Umstände
certain /'sɜ:tn/ *a* sicher; (*not named*) gewiß; **for ~** mit Bestimmtheit; **make ~** (*check*) sich vergewissern (**that** daß); (*ensure*) dafür sorgen (**that** daß); **he is ~ to win** er wird ganz bestimmt siegen. **~ly** *adv* bestimmt, sicher; **~ly not!** auf keinen Fall! **~ty** *n* Sicherheit *f*, Gewißheit *f*; **it's a ~ty** es ist sicher
certificate /sə'tɪfɪkət/ *n* Bescheinigung *f*; (*Jur*) Urkunde *f*; (*Sch*) Zeugnis *nt*
certify /'sɜ:tɪfaɪ/ *vt* (*pt/pp* **-ied**) bescheinigen; (*declare insane*) für geisteskrank erklären
cessation /se'seɪʃn/ *n* Ende *nt*
cesspool /'ses-/ *n* Senkgrube *f*
cf *abbr* (*compare*) vgl
chafe /tʃeɪf/ *vt* wund reiben

chaff /tʃɑ:f/ *n* Spreu *f*
chaffinch /'tʃæfɪntʃ/ *n* Buchfink *m*
chain /tʃeɪn/ *n* Kette *f* ● *vt* ketten (**to** an + *acc*). ~ **up** *vt* anketten
chain: ~ **re'action** *n* Kettenreaktion *f*. ~**-smoker** *n* Kettenraucher *m*. ~ **store** *n* Kettenladen *m*
chair /tʃeə(r)/ *n* Stuhl *m*; (*Univ*) Lehrstuhl *m* ● *vt* den Vorsitz führen bei. ~**-lift** *n* Sessellift *m*. ~**man** *n* Vorsitzende(r) *m*/*f*
chalet /'ʃæleɪ/ *n* Chalet *nt*
chalice /'tʃælɪs/ *n* (*Relig*) Kelch *m*
chalk /tʃɔ:k/ *n* Kreide *f*. ~**y** *a* kreidig
challeng|e /'tʃælɪndʒ/ *n* Herausforderung *f*; (*Mil*) Anruf *m* ● *vt* herausfordern; (*Mil*) anrufen; (*fig*) anfechten ⟨*statement*⟩. ~**er** *n* Herausforderer *m*. ~**ing** *a* herausfordernd; (*demanding*) anspruchsvoll
chamber /'tʃeɪmbə(r)/ *n* Kammer *f*; ~**s** *pl* (*Jur*) [Anwalts]büro *nt*; **C~ of Commerce** Handelskammer *f*
chamber: ~**maid** *n* Zimmermädchen *nt*. ~ **music** *n* Kammermusik *f*. ~**-pot** *n* Nachttopf *m*
chamois[1] /'ʃæmwɑ:/ *n inv* (*animal*) Gemse *f*
chamois[2] /'ʃæmɪ/ *n* ~**[-leather]** Ledertuch *nt*
champagne /ʃæm'peɪn/ *n* Champagner *m*
champion /'tʃæmpɪən/ *n* (*Sport*) Meister(in) *m*(*f*); (*of cause*) Verfechter *m* ● *vt* sich einsetzen für. ~**ship** *n* (*Sport*) Meisterschaft *f*
chance /tʃɑ:ns/ *n* Zufall *m*; (*prospect*) Chancen *pl*; (*likelihood*) Aussicht *f*; (*opportunity*) Gelegenheit *f*; **by** ~ zufällig; **take a** ~ ein Risiko eingehen; **give s.o. a** ~ jdm eine Chance geben ● *attrib* zufällig ● *vt* ~ **it** es riskieren
chancellor /'tʃɑ:nsələ(r)/ *n* Kanzler *m*; (*Univ*) Rektor *m*; **C~ of the Exchequer** Schatzkanzler *m*
chancy /'tʃɑ:nsɪ/ *a* riskant
chandelier /ʃændə'lɪə(r)/ *n* Kronleuchter *m*
change /tʃeɪndʒ/ *n* Veränderung *f*; (*alteration*) Änderung *f*; (*money*) Wechselgeld *nt*; **for a** ~ zur Abwechslung ● *vt* wechseln; (*alter*) ändern; (*exchange*) umtauschen (**for** gegen); (*transform*) verwandeln; trocken legen ⟨*baby*⟩; ~ **one's clothes** sich umziehen; ~ **trains** umsteigen ● *vi* sich verändern; (~ *clothes*) sich umziehen; (~ *trains*) umsteigen; **all** ~! alles aussteigen!
changeable /'tʃeɪndʒəbl/ *a* wechselhaft
'changing-room *n* Umkleideraum *m*
channel /'tʃænl/ *n* Rinne *f*; (*Radio, TV*) Kanal *m*; (*fig*) Weg *m*; **the [English] C~** der Ärmelkanal; **the C~ Islands** die Kanalinseln ● *vt* (*pt*/*pp* **channelled**) leiten; (*fig*) lenken
chant /tʃɑ:nt/ *n* liturgischer Gesang *m* ● *vt* singen; ⟨*demonstrators:*⟩ skandieren
chao|s /'keɪɒs/ *n* Chaos *nt*. ~**tic** /-'ɒtɪk/ *a* chaotisch
chap /tʃæp/ *n* (*fam*) Kerl *m*
chapel /'tʃæpl/ *n* Kapelle *f*
chaperon /'ʃæpərəʊn/ *n* Anstandsdame *f* ● *vt* begleiten
chaplain /'tʃæplɪn/ *n* Geistliche(r) *m*
chapped /tʃæpt/ *a* ⟨*skin*⟩ aufgesprungen
chapter /'tʃæptə(r)/ *n* Kapitel *nt*
char[1] /tʃɑ:(r)/ *n* (*fam*) Putzfrau *f*
char[2] *vt* (*pt*/*pp* **charred**) (*burn*) verkohlen
character /'kærɪktə(r)/ *n* Charakter *m*; (*in novel, play*) Gestalt *f*; (*Typ*) Schriftzeichen *nt*; **out of** ~ uncharakteristisch; **quite a** ~ (*fam*) ein Original
characteristic /kærɪktə'rɪstɪk/ *a*, **-ally** *adv* charakteristisch (**of** für) ● *n* Merkmal *nt*
characterize /'kærɪktəraɪz/ *vt* charakterisieren
charade /ʃə'rɑ:d/ *n* Scharade *f*
charcoal /'tʃɑ:-/ *n* Holzkohle *f*
charge /tʃɑ:dʒ/ *n* (*price*) Gebühr *f*; (*Electr*) Ladung *f*; (*attack*) Angriff *m*; (*Jur*) Anklage *f*; **free of** ~ kostenlos; **be in** ~ verantwortlich sein (**of** für); **take** ~ die Aufsicht übernehmen (**of** über + *acc*) ● *vt* berechnen ⟨*fee*⟩; (*Electr*) laden; (*attack*) angreifen; (*Jur*) anklagen (**with** *gen*); ~ **s.o. for sth** jdm etw berechnen ● *vi* (*attack*) angreifen
chariot /'tʃærɪət/ *n* Wagen *m*
charisma /kə'rɪzmə/ *n* Charisma *nt*. ~**tic** /kæriz'mætɪk/ *a* charismatisch
charitable /'tʃærɪtəbl/ *a* wohltätig; (*kind*) wohlwollend
charity /'tʃærətɪ/ *n* Nächstenliebe *f*; (*organization*) wohltätige Einrichtung *f*; **for** ~ für Wohltätigkeitszwecke; **live on** ~ von Almosen leben
charlatan /'ʃɑ:lətən/ *n* Scharlatan *m*

charm /tʃɑːm/ *n* Reiz *m*; (*of person*) Charme *f*; (*object*) Amulett *nt* ● *vt* bezaubern. **~ing** *a*, **-ly** *adv* reizend; ⟨*person, smile*⟩ charmant

chart /tʃɑːt/ *n* Karte *f*; (*table*) Tabelle *f*

charter /'tʃɑːtə(r)/ *n* ~ **[flight]** Charterflug *m* ● *vt* chartern; **~ed accountant** Wirtschaftsprüfer(in) *m*(*f*)

charwoman /'tʃɑː-/ *n* Putzfrau *f*

chase /tʃeɪs/ *n* Verfolgungsjagd *f* ● *vt* jagen, verfolgen. ~ **away** *or* **off** *vt* wegjagen

chasm /'kæzm/ *n* Kluft *f*

chassis /'ʃæsɪ/ *n* (*pl* **chassis** /-sɪz/) Chassis *nt*

chaste /tʃeɪst/ *a* keusch

chastise /tʃæ'staɪz/ *vt* züchtigen

chastity /'tʃæstətɪ/ *n* Keuschheit *f*

chat /tʃæt/ *n* Plauderei *f*; **have a ~ with** plaudern mit ● *vi* (*pt/pp* **chatted**) plaudern. ~ **show** *n* Talk-Show *f*

chatter /'tʃætə(r)/ *n* Geschwätz *nt* ● *vi* schwatzen; ⟨*child:*⟩ plappern; ⟨*teeth:*⟩ klappern. **~box** *n* (*fam*) Plappermaul *nt*

chatty /'tʃætɪ/ *a* (**-ier, -iest**) geschwätzig

chauffeur /'ʃəʊfə(r)/ *n* Chauffeur *m*

chauvin|ism /'ʃəʊvɪnɪzm/ *n* Chauvinismus *m*. **~ist** *n* Chauvinist *m*; **male ~ist** (*fam*) Chauvi *m*

cheap /tʃiːp/ *a* & *adv* (**-er, -est**), **-ly** *adv* billig. **~en** *vt* entwürdigen; **~en oneself** sich erniedrigen

cheat /tʃiːt/ *n* Betrüger(in) *m*(*f*); (*at games*) Mogler *m* ● *vt* betrügen ● *vi* (*at games*) mogeln (*fam*)

check[1] /tʃek/ *a* (*squared*) kariert ● *n* Karo *nt*

check[2] *n* Überprüfung *f*; (*inspection*) Kontrolle *f*; (*Chess*) Schach *nt*; (*Amer: bill*) Rechnung *f*; (*Amer: cheque*) Scheck *m*; (*Amer: tick*) Haken *m*; **keep a ~ on** kontrollieren ● *vt* [über]prüfen; (*inspect*) kontrollieren; (*restrain*) hemmen; (*stop*) aufhalten ● *vi* **[go and] ~** nachsehen. ~ **in** *vi* sich anmelden; (*Aviat*) einchecken ● *vt* abfertigen; einchecken. ~ **out** *vi* sich abmelden. ~ **up** *vi* prüfen, kontrollieren; ~ **up on** überprüfen

check|ed /tʃekt/ *a* kariert. **~ers** *n* (*Amer*) Damespiel *nt*

check: ~mate *int* schachmatt! **~-out** *n* Kasse *f*. **~room** *n* (*Amer*) Garderobe *f*. **~-up** *n* (*Med*) [Kontroll]untersuchung *f*

cheek /tʃiːk/ *n* Backe *f*; (*impudence*) Frechheit *f*. **~y** *a*, **-ily** *adv* frech

cheep /tʃiːp/ *vi* piepen

cheer /tʃɪə(r)/ *n* Beifallsruf *m*; **three ~s** ein dreifaches Hoch (**for** auf + *acc*); **~s!** prost! (*goodbye*) tschüs! ● *vt* zujubeln (+ *dat*) ● *vi* jubeln. ~ **up** *vt* aufmuntern; aufheitern ● *vi* munterer werden. **~ful** *a*, **-ly** *adv* fröhlich. **~fulness** *n* Fröhlichkeit *f*

cheerio /tʃɪərɪ'əʊ/ *int* (*fam*) tschüs!

'cheerless *a* trostlos

cheese /tʃiːz/ *n* Käse *m*. **~cake** *n* Käsekuchen *m*

cheetah /'tʃiːtə/ *n* Gepard *m*

chef /ʃef/ *n* Koch *m*

chemical /'kemɪkl/ *a*, **-ly** *adv* chemisch ● *n* Chemikalie *f*

chemist /'kemɪst/ *n* (*pharmacist*) Apotheker(in) *m*(*f*); (*scientist*) Chemiker(in) *m*(*f*); **~'s [shop]** Drogerie *f*; (*dispensing*) Apotheke *f*. **~ry** *n* Chemie *f*

cheque /tʃek/ *n* Scheck *m*. **~-book** *n* Scheckbuch *nt*. ~ **card** *n* Scheckkarte *f*

cherish /'tʃerɪʃ/ *vt* lieben; (*fig*) hegen

cherry /'tʃerɪ/ *n* Kirsche *f* ● *attrib* Kirsch-

cherub /'tʃerəb/ *n* Engelchen *nt*

chess /tʃes/ *n* Schach *nt*

chess: ~board *n* Schachbrett *nt*. **~-man** *n* Schachfigur *f*

chest /tʃest/ *n* Brust *f*; (*box*) Truhe *f*

chestnut /'tʃesnʌt/ *n* Eßkastanie *f*, Marone *f*; (*horse-*) [Roß]kastanie *f*

chest of 'drawers *n* Kommode *f*

chew /tʃuː/ *vt* kauen. **~ing-gum** *n* Kaugummi *m*

chic /ʃiːk/ *a* schick

chick /tʃɪk/ *n* Küken *nt*

chicken /'tʃɪkɪn/ *n* Huhn *nt* ● *attrib* Hühner- ● *a* (*fam*) feige ● *vi* ~ **out** (*fam*) kneifen. **~pox** *n* Windpocken *pl*

chicory /'tʃɪkərɪ/ *n* Chicorée *f*; (*in coffee*) Zichorie *f*

chief /tʃiːf/ *a* Haupt- ● *n* Chef *m*; (*of tribe*) Häuptling *m*. **~ly** *adv* hauptsächlich

chilblain /'tʃɪlbleɪn/ *n* Frostbeule *f*

child /tʃaɪld/ *n* (*pl* **~ren**) Kind *nt*

child: ~birth *n* Geburt *f*. **~hood** *n* Kindheit *f*. **~ish** *a* kindisch. **~less** *a* kinderlos. **~like** *a* kindlich. **~-minder** *n* Tagesmutter *f*

children /'tʃɪldrən/ *npl see* **child**

Chile /'tʃɪlɪ/ *n* Chile *nt*
chill /tʃɪl/ *n* Kälte *f*; (*illness*) Erkältung *f* • *vt* kühlen
chilli /'tʃɪlɪ/ *n* (*pl* **-es**) Chili *m*
chilly /'tʃɪlɪ/ *a* kühl; **I felt ~** mich fröstelte [es]
chime /tʃaɪm/ *vi* läuten; ⟨*clock:*⟩ schlagen
chimney /'tʃɪmnɪ/ *n* Schornstein *m*. **~-pot** *n* Schornsteinaufsatz *m*. **~-sweep** *n* Schornsteinfeger *m*
chimpanzee /tʃɪmpæn'zi:/ *n* Schimpanse *m*
chin /tʃɪn/ *n* Kinn *nt*
china /'tʃaɪnə/ *n* Porzellan *nt*
Chin|a *n* China *nt*. **~ese** /-'ni:z/ *a* chinesisch • *n* (*Lang*) Chinesisch *nt*; **the ~ese** *pl* die Chinesen. **~ese 'lantern** *n* Lampion *m*
chink[1] /tʃɪŋk/ *n* (*slit*) Ritze *f*
chink[2] *n* Geklirr *nt* • *vi* klirren; ⟨*coins:*⟩ klimpern
chip /tʃɪp/ *n* (*fragment*) Span *m*; (*in china, paintwork*) angeschlagene Stelle *f*; (*Computing, Gambling*) Chip *m*; **~s** *pl* (*Culin*) Pommes frites *pl*; (*Amer: crisps*) Chips *pl* • *vt* (*pt/pp* **chipped**) (*damage*) anschlagen. **~ped** *a* angeschlagen
chiropod|ist /kɪ'rɒpədɪst/ *n* Fußpfleger(in) *m(f)*. **~y** *n* Fußpflege *f*
chirp /tʃɜ:p/ *vi* zwitschern; ⟨*cricket:*⟩ zirpen. **~y** *a* (*fam*) munter
chisel /'tʃɪzl/ *n* Meißel *m* • *vt/i* (*pt/pp* **chiselled**) meißeln
chit /tʃɪt/ *n* Zettel *m*
chival|rous /'ʃɪvlrəs/ *a*, **-ly** *adv* ritterlich. **~ry** *n* Ritterlichkeit *f*
chives /tʃaɪvz/ *npl* Schnittlauch *m*
chlorine /'klɔ:ri:n/ *n* Chlor *nt*
chloroform /'klɒrəfɔ:m/ *n* Chloroform *nt*
chocolate /'tʃɒkələt/ *n* Schokolade *f*; (*sweet*) Praline *f*
choice /tʃɔɪs/ *n* Wahl *f*; (*variety*) Auswahl *f* • *a* auserlesen
choir /'kwaɪə(r)/ *n* Chor *m*. **~boy** *n* Chorknabe *m*
choke /tʃəʊk/ *n* (*Auto*) Choke *m* • *vt* würgen; (*to death*) erwürgen • *vi* sich verschlucken; **~ on** [fast] ersticken an (+ *dat*)
cholera /'kɒlərə/ *n* Cholera *f*
cholesterol /kə'lestərɒl/ *n* Cholesterin *nt*
choose /tʃu:z/ *vt/i* (*pt* **chose**, *pp* **chosen**) wählen; (*select*) sich (*dat*) aussuchen; **~ to do/go** [freiwillig] tun/gehen; **as you ~** wie Sie wollen
choos[e]y /'tʃu:zɪ/ *a* (*fam*) wählerisch
chop /tʃɒp/ *n* (*blow*) Hieb *m*; (*Culin*) Kotelett *nt* • *vt* (*pt/pp* **chopped**) hacken. **~ down** *vt* abhacken; fällen ⟨*tree*⟩. **~ off** *vt* abhacken
chop|per /'tʃɒpə(r)/ *n* Beil *nt*; (*fam*) Hubschrauber *m*. **~py** *a* kabbelig
'chopsticks *npl* Eßstäbchen *pl*
choral /'kɔ:rəl/ *a* Chor-; **~ society** Gesangverein *m*
chord /kɔ:d/ *n* (*Mus*) Akkord *m*
chore /tʃɔ:(r)/ *n* lästige Pflicht *f*; **[household] ~s** Hausarbeit *f*
choreography /kɒrɪ'ɒgrəfɪ/ *n* Choreographie *f*
chortle /'tʃɔ:tl/ *vi* [vor Lachen] glucksen
chorus /'kɔ:rəs/ *n* Chor *m*; (*of song*) Refrain *m*
chose, chosen /tʃəʊz, 'tʃəʊzn/ *see* **choose**
Christ /kraɪst/ *n* Christus *m*
christen /'krɪsn/ *vt* taufen. **~ing** *n* Taufe *f*
Christian /'krɪstʃən/ *a* christlich • *n* Christ(in) *m(f)*. **~ity** /-stɪ'ænətɪ/ *n* Christentum *nt*. **~ name** *n* Vorname *m*
Christmas /'krɪsməs/ *n* Weihnachten *nt*. **~ card** *n* Weihnachtskarte *f*. **~ 'Day** *n* erster Weihnachtstag *m*. **~ 'Eve** *n* Heiligabend *m*. **~ tree** *n* Weihnachtsbaum *m*
chrome /krəʊm/ *n*, **chromium** /'krəʊmɪəm/ *n* Chrom *nt*
chromosome /'krəʊməsəʊm/ *n* Chromosom *nt*
chronic /'krɒnɪk/ *a* chronisch
chronicle /'krɒnɪkl/ *n* Chronik *f*
chronological /krɒnə'lɒdʒɪkl/ *a*, **-ly** *adv* chronologisch
chrysalis /'krɪsəlɪs/ *n* Puppe *f*
chrysanthemum /krɪ'sænθəməm/ *n* Chrysantheme *f*
chubby /'tʃʌbɪ/ *a* (**-ier, -iest**) mollig
chuck /tʃʌk/ *vt* (*fam*) schmeißen. **~ out** *vt* (*fam*) rausschmeißen
chuckle /'tʃʌkl/ *vi* in sich (*acc*) hineinlachen
chum /tʃʌm/ *n* Freund(in) *m(f)*
chunk /tʃʌŋk/ *n* Stück *nt*
church /tʃɜ:tʃ/ *n* Kirche *f*. **~yard** *n* Friedhof *m*
churlish /'tʃɜ:lɪʃ/ *a* unhöflich
churn /tʃɜ:n/ *n* Butterfaß *nt*; (*for milk*) Milchkanne *f* • *vt* **~ out** am laufenden Band produzieren

chute /ʃu:t/ *n* Rutsche *f*; (*for rubbish*) Müllschlucker *m*

CID *abbr* **(Criminal Investigation Department)** Kripo *f*

cider /'saɪdə(r)/ *n* Apfelwein *m*

cigar /sɪ'gɑ:(r)/ *n* Zigarre *f*

cigarette /sɪgə'ret/ *n* Zigarette *f*

cine-camera /'sɪnɪ-/ *n* Filmkamera *f*

cinema /'sɪnɪmə/ *n* Kino *nt*

cinnamon /'sɪnəmən/ *n* Zimt *m*

cipher /'saɪfə(r)/ *n* (*code*) Chiffre *f*; (*numeral*) Ziffer *f*; (*fig*) Null *f*

circle /'sɜ:kl/ *n* Kreis *m*; (*Theat*) Rang *m* ● *vt* umkreisen ● *vi* kreisen

circuit /'sɜ:kɪt/ *n* Runde *f*; (*race-track*) Rennbahn *f*; (*Electr*) Stromkreis *m*. **~ous** /sə'kju:ɪtəs/ *a* **~ route** Umweg *m*

circular /'sɜ:kjʊlə(r)/ *a* kreisförmig ● *n* Rundschreiben *nt*. **~ 'saw** *n* Kreissäge *f*. **~ 'tour** *n* Rundfahrt *f*

circulat|e /'sɜ:kjʊleɪt/ *vt* in Umlauf setzen ● *vi* zirkulieren. **~ion** /-'leɪʃn/ *n* Kreislauf *m*; (*of newspaper*) Auflage *f*

circumcis|e /'sɜ:kəmsaɪz/ *vt* beschneiden. **~ion** /-'sɪʒn/ *n* Beschneidung *f*

circumference /sə'kʌmfərəns/ *n* Umfang *m*

circumspect /'sɜ:kəmspekt/ *a*, **-ly** *adv* umsichtig

circumstance /'sɜ:kəmstəns/ *n* Umstand *m*; **~s** *pl* Umstände *pl*; (*financial*) Verhältnisse *pl*

circus /'sɜ:kəs/ *n* Zirkus *m*

CIS *abbr* **(Commonwealth of Independent States)** GUS *f*

cistern /'sɪstən/ *n* (*tank*) Wasserbehälter *m*; (*of WC*) Spülkasten *m*

cite /saɪt/ *vt* zitieren

citizen /'sɪtɪzn/ *n* Bürger(in) *m*(*f*). **~ship** *n* Staatsangehörigkeit *f*

citrus /'sɪtrəs/ *n* **~ [fruit]** Zitrusfrucht *f*

city /'sɪtɪ/ *n* [Groß]stadt *f*

civic /'sɪvɪk/ *a* Bürger-

civil /'sɪvl/ *a* bürgerlich; ⟨*aviation, defence*⟩ zivil; (*polite*) höflich. **~ engi'neering** *n* Hoch- und Tiefbau *m*

civilian /sɪ'vɪljən/ *a* Zivil-; **in ~ clothes** in Zivil ● *n* Zivilist *m*

civility /sɪ'vɪlətɪ/ *n* Höflichkeit *f*

civiliz|ation /sɪvəlaɪ'zeɪʃn/ *n* Zivilisation *f*. **~e** /'sɪvəlaɪz/ *vt* zivilisieren

civil: ~ 'servant *n* Beamte(r) *m*/Beamtin *f*. **C~ 'Service** *n* Staatsdienst *m*

clad /klæd/ *a* gekleidet (**in** in + *acc*)

claim /kleɪm/ *n* Anspruch *m*; (*application*) Antrag *m*; (*demand*) Forderung *f*; (*assertion*) Behauptung *f* ● *vt* beanspruchen; (*apply for*) beantragen; (*demand*) fordern; (*assert*) behaupten; (*collect*) abholen. **~ant** *n* Antragsteller *m*

clairvoyant /kleə'vɔɪənt/ *n* Hellseher(in) *m*(*f*)

clam /klæm/ *n* Klaffmuschel *f*

clamber /'klæmbə(r)/ *vi* klettern

clammy /'klæmɪ/ *a* (**-ier, -iest**) feucht

clamour /'klæmə(r)/ *n* Geschrei *nt* ● *vi* **~ for** schreien nach

clamp /klæmp/ *n* Klammer *f* ● *vt* [ein]spannen ● *vi* (*fam*) **~ down** durchgreifen; **~ down on** vorgehen gegen

clan /klæn/ *n* Clan *m*

clandestine /klæn'destɪn/ *a* geheim

clang /klæŋ/ *n* Schmettern *nt*. **~er** *n* (*fam*) Schnitzer *m*

clank /klæŋk/ *vi* klirren

clap /klæp/ *n* **give s.o. a ~** jdm Beifall klatschen; **~ of thunder** Donnerschlag *m* ● *vt*/*i* (*pt*/*pp* **clapped**) Beifall klatschen (+ *dat*); **~ one's hands** [in die Hände] klatschen

claret /'klærət/ *n* roter Bordeaux *m*

clari|fication /klærɪfɪ'keɪʃn/ *n* Klärung *f*. **~fy** /'klærɪfaɪ/ *vt*/*i* (*pt*/*pp* **-ied**) klären

clarinet /klærɪ'net/ *n* Klarinette *f*

clarity /'klærətɪ/ *n* Klarheit *f*

clash /klæʃ/ *n* Geklirr *nt*; (*fig*) Konflikt *m* ● *vi* klirren; ⟨*colours:*⟩ sich beißen; ⟨*events:*⟩ ungünstig zusammenfallen

clasp /klɑ:sp/ *n* Verschluß *m* ● *vt* ergreifen; (*hold*) halten

class /klɑ:s/ *n* Klasse *f*; **first/second ~** erster/zweiter Klasse ● *vt* einordnen

classic /'klæsɪk/ *a* klassisch ● *n* Klassiker *m*; **~s** *pl* (*Univ*) Altphilologie *f*. **~al** *a* klassisch

classi|fication /klæsɪfɪ'keɪʃn/ *n* Klassifikation *f*. **~fy** /'klæsɪfaɪ/ *vt* (*pt*/*pp* **-ied**) klassifizieren

'classroom *n* Klassenzimmer *nt*

classy /'klɑ:sɪ/ *a* (**-ier, -iest**) (*fam*) schick

clatter /'klætə(r)/ *n* Geklapper *nt* ● *vi* klappern

clause /klɔ:z/ *n* Klausel *f*; (*Gram*) Satzteil *m*

claustrophobia /klɔ:strə'fəʊbɪə/ *n* Klaustrophobie *f*, (*fam*) Platzangst *m*

claw /klɔ:/ *n* Kralle *f*; (*of bird of prey & Techn*) Klaue *f*; (*of crab, lobster*) Schere *f* ● *vt* kratzen

clay /kleɪ/ *n* Lehm *m*; (*pottery*) Ton *m*

clean /kli:n/ *a* (**-er, -est**) sauber ● *adv* glatt ● *vt* saubermachen; putzen ⟨*shoes, windows*⟩; **~ one's teeth** sich (*dat*) die Zähne putzen; **have sth ~ed** etw reinigen lassen. **~ up** *vt* saubermachen

cleaner /'kli:nə(r)/ *n* Putzfrau *f*; (*substance*) Reinigungsmittel *nt*; **[dry] ~'s** chemische Reinigung *f*

cleanliness /'klenlɪnɪs/ *n* Sauberkeit *f*

cleanse /klenz/ *vt* reinigen. **~r** *n* Reinigungsmittel *nt*

clean-shaven *a* glattrasiert

cleansing cream /'klenz-/ *n* Reinigungscreme *f*

clear /klɪə(r)/ *a* (**-er, -est**), **-ly** *adv* klar; (*obvious*) eindeutig; (*distinct*) deutlich; ⟨*conscience*⟩ rein; (*without obstacles*) frei; **make sth ~** etw klarmachen (**to** *dat*) ● *adv* **stand ~** zurücktreten; **keep ~ of** aus dem Wege gehen (+ *dat*) ● *vt* räumen; abräumen ⟨*table*⟩; (*acquit*) freisprechen; (*authorize*) genehmigen; (*jump over*) überspringen; **~ one's throat** sich räuspern ● *vi* ⟨*fog:*⟩ sich auflösen. **~ away** *vt* wegräumen. **~ off** *vi* (*fam*) abhauen. **~ out** *vt* ausräumen ● *vi* (*fam*) abhauen. **~ up** *vt* (*tidy*) aufräumen; (*solve*) aufklären ● *vi* ⟨*weather:*⟩ sich aufklären

clearance /'klɪərəns/ *n* Räumung *f*; (*authorization*) Genehmigung *f*; (*customs*) [Zoll]abfertigung *f*; (*Techn*) Spielraum *m*. **~ sale** *n* Räumungsverkauf *m*

clear|ing /'klɪərɪŋ/ *n* Lichtung *f*. **~way** *n* (*Auto*) Straße *f* mit Halteverbot

cleavage /'kli:vɪdʒ/ *n* Spaltung *f*; (*woman's*) Dekolleté *nt*

clef /klef/ *n* Notenschlüssel *m*

cleft /kleft/ *n* Spalte *f*

clemen|cy /'klemənsɪ/ *n* Milde *f*. **~t** *a* mild

clench /klentʃ/ *vt* **~ one's fist** die Faust ballen; **~ one's teeth** die Zähne zusammenbeißen

clergy /'klɜ:dʒɪ/ *npl* Geistlichkeit *f*. **~man** *n* Geistliche(r) *m*

cleric /'klerɪk/ *n* Geistliche(r) *m*. **~al** *a* Schreib-; (*Relig*) geistlich

clerk /klɑ:k, *Amer*: klɜ:k/ *n* Büroangestellte(r) *m*/*f*; (*Amer: shop assistant*) Verkäufer(in) *m*(*f*)

clever /'klevə(r)/ *a* (**-er, -est**), **-ly** *adv* klug; (*skilful*) geschickt

cliché /'kli:ʃeɪ/ *n* Klischee *nt*

click /klɪk/ *vi* klicken

client /'klaɪənt/ *n* Kunde *m*/Kundin *f*; (*Jur*) Klient(in) *m*(*f*)

clientele /kli:ɒn'tel/ *n* Kundschaft *f*

cliff /klɪf/ *n* Kliff *nt*

climat|e /'klaɪmət/ *n* Klima *nt*. **~ic** /-'mætɪk/ *a* klimatisch

climax /'klaɪmæks/ *n* Höhepunkt *m*

climb /klaɪm/ *n* Aufstieg *m* ● *vt* besteigen ⟨*mountain*⟩; steigen auf (+ *acc*) ⟨*ladder, tree*⟩ ● *vi* klettern; (*rise*) steigen; ⟨*road:*⟩ ansteigen. **~ down** *vi* hinunter-/herunterklettern; (*from ladder, tree*) heruntersteigen; (*fam*) nachgeben.

climber /'klaɪmə(r)/ *n* Bergsteiger *m*; (*plant*) Kletterpflanze *f*

clinch /klɪntʃ/ *vt* perfekt machen ⟨*deal*⟩ ● *vi* (*boxing*) clinchen

cling /klɪŋ/ *vi* (*pt/pp* **clung**) sich klammern (**to** an + *acc*); (*stick*) haften (**to** an + *dat*). **~ film** *n* Sichtfolie *f* mit Hafteffekt

clinic /'klɪnɪk/ *n* Klinik *f*. **~al** *a*, **-ly** *adv* klinisch

clink /klɪŋk/ *n* Klirren *nt*; (*fam: prison*) Knast *m* ● *vi* klirren

clip¹ /klɪp/ *n* Klammer *f*; (*jewellery*) Klipp *m* ● *vt* (*pt/pp* **clipped**) anklammern (**to** an + *acc*)

clip² *n* (*extract*) Ausschnitt *m* ● *vt* schneiden; knipsen ⟨*ticket*⟩. **~board** *n* Klemmbrett *nt*. **~pers** *npl* Schere *f*. **~ping** *n* (*extract*) Ausschnitt *m*

clique /kli:k/ *n* Clique *f*

cloak /kləʊk/ *n* Umhang *m*. **~room** *n* Garderobe *f*; (*toilet*) Toilette *f*

clobber /'klɒbə(r)/ *n* (*fam*) Zeug *nt* ● *vt* (*fam: hit, defeat*) schlagen

clock /klɒk/ *n* Uhr *f*; (*fam: speedometer*) Tacho *m* ● *vi* **~ in/out** stechen

clock: ~ tower *n* Uhrenturm *m*. **~wise** *a* & *adv* im Uhrzeigersinn. **~work** *n* Uhrwerk *nt*; (*of toy*) Aufziehmechanismus *m*; **like ~work** (*fam*) wie am Schnürchen

clod /klɒd/ *n* Klumpen *m*

clog /klɒg/ *n* Holzschuh *m* ● *vt*/*i* (*pt/pp* **clogged**) **~ [up]** verstopfen

cloister /'klɔɪstə(r)/ *n* Kreuzgang *m*

close¹ /kləʊs/ *a* (**-r, -st**) nah[e] (**to** *dat*); ⟨*friend*⟩ eng; ⟨*weather*⟩ schwül;

have a ~ shave (*fam*) mit knapper Not davonkommen ● *adv* nahe; **~ by** nicht weit weg ● *n* (*street*) Sackgasse *f*

close² /kləʊz/ *n* Ende *nt*; **draw to a ~** sich dem Ende nähern ● *vt* zumachen, schließen; (*bring to an end*) beenden; sperren ⟨*road*⟩ ● *vi* sich schließen; ⟨*shop:*⟩ schließen, zumachen; (*end*) enden. **~ down** *vt* schließen; stillegen ⟨*factory*⟩ ● *vi* schließen; ⟨*factory:*⟩ stillgelegt werden

closed 'shop /kləʊzd-/ *n* ≈ Gewerkschaftszwang *m*

closely /'kləʊslɪ/ *adv* eng, nah[e]; (*with attention*) genau

close season /'kləʊs-/ *n* Schonzeit *f*

closet /'klɒzɪt/ *n* (*Amer*) Schrank *m*

close-up /'kləʊs-/ *n* Nahaufnahme *f*

closure /'kləʊʒə(r)/ *n* Schließung *f*; (*of factory*) Stillegung *f*; (*of road*) Sperrung *f*

clot /klɒt/ *n* [Blut]gerinnsel *nt*; (*fam: idiot*) Trottel *m* ● *vi* (*pt/pp* **clotted**) ⟨*blood:*⟩ gerinnen

cloth /klɒθ/ *n* Tuch *nt*

clothe /kləʊð/ *vt* kleiden

clothes /kləʊðz/ *npl* Kleider *pl*. **~-brush** *n* Kleiderbürste *f*. **~-line** *n* Wäscheleine *f*

clothing /'kləʊðɪŋ/ *n* Kleidung *f*

cloud /klaʊd/ *n* Wolke *f* ● *vi* **~ over** sich bewölken. **~burst** *n* Wolkenbruch *m*

cloudy /'klaʊdɪ/ *a* (**-ier, -iest**) wolkig, bewölkt; ⟨*liquid*⟩ trübe

clout /klaʊt/ *n* (*fam*) Schlag *m*; (*influence*) Einfluß *m* ● *vt* (*fam*) hauen

clove /kləʊv/ *n* [Gewürz]nelke *f*; **~ of garlic** Knoblauchzehe *f*

clover /'kləʊvə(r)/ *n* Klee *m*. **~ leaf** *n* Kleeblatt *nt*

clown /klaʊn/ *n* Clown *m* ● *vi* **~ [about]** herumalbern

club /klʌb/ *n* Klub *m*; (*weapon*) Keule *f*; (*Sport*) Schläger *m*; **~s** *pl* (*Cards*) Kreuz *nt*, Treff *nt* ● *v* (*pt/pp* **clubbed**) ● *vt* knüppeln ● *vi* **~ together** zusammenlegen

cluck /klʌk/ *vi* glucken

clue /klu:/ *n* Anhaltspunkt *m*; (*in crossword*) Frage *f*; **I haven't a ~** (*fam*) ich habe keine Ahnung

clump /klʌmp/ *n* Gruppe *f*

clumsiness /'klʌmzɪnɪs/ *n* Ungeschicklichkeit *f*

clumsy /'klʌmzɪ/ *a* (**-ier, -iest**), **-ily** *adv* ungeschickt; (*unwieldy*) unförmig

clung /klʌŋ/ *see* **cling**

cluster /'klʌstə(r)/ *n* Gruppe *f*; (*of flowers*) Büschel *nt* ● *vi* sich scharen (**round** um)

clutch /klʌtʃ/ *n* Griff *m*; (*Auto*) Kupplung *f*; **be in s.o.'s ~es** (*fam*) in jds Klauen sein ● *vt* festhalten; (*grab*) ergreifen ● *vi* **~ at** greifen nach

clutter /'klʌtə(r)/ *n* Kram *m* ● *vt* **~ [up]** vollstopfen

c/o *abbr* (**care of**) bei

coach /kəʊtʃ/ *n* [Reise]bus *m*; (*Rail*) Wagen *m*; (*horse-drawn*) Kutsche *f*; (*Sport*) Trainer *m* ● *vt* Nachhilfestunden geben (+ *dat*); (*Sport*) trainieren

coagulate /kəʊ'ægjʊleɪt/ *vi* gerinnen

coal /kəʊl/ *n* Kohle *f*

coalition /kəʊə'lɪʃn/ *n* Koalition *f*

'coal-mine *n* Kohlenbergwerk *nt*

coarse /kɔ:s/ *a* (**-r, -st**), **-ly** *adv* grob

coast /kəʊst/ *n* Küste *f* ● *vi* (*free-wheel*) im Freilauf fahren; (*Auto*) im Leerlauf fahren. **~al** *a* Küsten-. **~er** *n* (*mat*) Untersatz *m*

coast: ~guard *n* Küstenwache *f*. **~line** *n* Küste *f*

coat /kəʊt/ *n* Mantel *m*; (*of animal*) Fell *nt*; (*of paint*) Anstrich *m*; **~ of arms** Wappen *nt* ● *vt* überziehen; (*with paint*) [an]streichen. **~-hanger** *n* Kleiderbügel *m*. **~-hook** *n* Kleiderhaken *m*

coating /'kəʊtɪŋ/ *n* Überzug *m*, Schicht *f*; (*of paint*) Anstrich *m*

coax /kəʊks/ *vt* gut zureden (+ *dat*)

cob /kɒb/ *n* (*of corn*) [Mais]kolben *m*

cobble¹ /'kɒbl/ *n* Kopfstein *m*; **~s** *pl* Kopfsteinpflaster *nt*

cobble² *vt* flicken. **~r** *m* Schuster *m*

'cobblestones *npl* = **cobbles**

cobweb /'kɒb-/ *n* Spinnengewebe *nt*

cocaine /kə'keɪn/ *n* Kokain *nt*

cock /kɒk/ *n* Hahn *m*; (*any male bird*) Männchen *nt* ● *vt* ⟨*animal:*⟩ **~ its ears** die Ohren spitzen; **~ the gun** den Hahn spannen. **~-and-'bull story** *n* (*fam*) Lügengeschichte *f*

cockerel /'kɒkərəl/ *n* [junger] Hahn *m*

cock-'eyed *a* (*fam*) schief; (*absurd*) verrückt

cockle /'kɒkl/ *n* Herzmuschel *f*

cockney /'kɒknɪ/ *n* (*dialect*) Cockney *nt*; (*person*) Cockney *m*

cock: ~pit *n* (*Aviat*) Cockpit *nt*. **~roach** /-rəʊtʃ/ *n* Küchenschabe *f*.

~tail *n* Cocktail *m.* **~-up** *n* (*sl*) **make a ~-up** Mist bauen (**of** bei)

cocky /ˈkɒkɪ/ *a* (**-ier, -iest**) (*fam*) eingebildet

cocoa /ˈkəʊkəʊ/ *n* Kakao *m*

coconut /ˈkəʊkənʌt/ *n* Kokosnuß *f*

cocoon /kəˈkuːn/ *n* Kokon *m*

cod /kɒd/ *n inv* Kabeljau *m*

COD *abbr* (**cash on delivery**) per Nachnahme

coddle /ˈkɒdl/ *vt* verhätscheln

code /kəʊd/ *n* Kode *m*; (*Computing*) Code *m*; (*set of rules*) Kodex *m.* **~d** *a* verschlüsselt

coeduˈcational /kəʊ-/ *a* gemischt. **~ school** *n* Koedukationsschule *f*

coerc|e /kəʊˈɜːs/ *vt* zwingen. **~ion** /-ˈɜːʃn/ *n* Zwang *m*

coeˈxist *vi* koexistieren. **~ence** *n* Koexistenz *f*

coffee /ˈkɒfɪ/ *n* Kaffee *m*

coffee: ~-grinder *n* Kaffeemühle *f.* **~-pot** *n* Kaffeekanne *f.* **~-table** *n* Couchtisch *m*

coffin /ˈkɒfɪn/ *n* Sarg *m*

cog /kɒg/ *n* (*Techn*) Zahn *m*

cogent /ˈkəʊdʒənt/ *a* überzeugend

cog-wheel *n* Zahnrad *nt*

cohabit /kəʊˈhæbɪt/ *vi* (*Jur*) zusammenleben

coherent /kəʊˈhɪərənt/ *a* zusammenhängend; (*comprehensible*) verständlich

coil /kɔɪl/ *n* Rolle *f*; (*Electr*) Spule *f*; (*one ring*) Windung *f* ● *vt* **~ [up]** zusammenrollen

coin /kɔɪn/ *n* Münze *f* ● *vt* prägen

coincide /kəʊɪnˈsaɪd/ *vi* zusammenfallen; (*agree*) übereinstimmen

coinciden|ce /kəʊˈɪnsɪdəns/ *n* Zufall *m.* **~tal** /-ˈdentl/ *a*, **-ly** *adv* zufällig

coke /kəʊk/ *n* Koks *m*

Coke (P) *n* (*drink*) Cola *f*

colander /ˈkʌləndə(r)/ *n* (*Culin*) Durchschlag *m*

cold /kəʊld/ *a* (**-er, -est**) kalt; **I am** *or* **feel ~** mir ist kalt ● *n* Kälte *f*; (*Med*) Erkältung *f*

cold: ~-ˈblooded *a* kaltblütig. **~-ˈhearted** *a* kaltherzig. **~ly** *adv* (*fig*) kalt, kühl. **~ness** *n* Kälte *f*

coleslaw /ˈkəʊlslɔː/ *n* Krautsalat *m*

colic /ˈkɒlɪk/ *n* Kolik *f*

collaborat|e /kəˈlæbəreɪt/ *vi* zusammenarbeiten (**with** mit); **~e on sth** mitarbeiten bei etw. **~ion** /-ˈreɪʃn/ *n* Zusammenarbeit *f*, Mitarbeit *f*; (*with enemy*) Kollaboration *f.* **~or** *n* Mitarbeiter(in) *m*(*f*); Kollaborateur *m*

collaps|e /kəˈlæps/ *n* Zusammenbruch *m*; Einsturz *m* ● *vi* zusammenbrechen; ⟨*roof, building:*⟩ einstürzen. **~ible** *a* zusammenklappbar

collar /ˈkɒlə(r)/ *n* Kragen *m*; (*for animal*) Halsband *nt.* **~-bone** *n* Schlüsselbein *nt*

colleague /ˈkɒliːg/ *n* Kollege *m*/Kollegin *f*

collect /kəˈlekt/ *vt* sammeln; (*fetch*) abholen; einsammeln ⟨*tickets*⟩; einziehen ⟨*taxes*⟩ ● *vi* sich [an]sammeln ● *adv* **call ~** (*Amer*) ein R-Gespräch führen. **~ed** /-ɪd/ *a* gesammelt; (*calm*) gefaßt

collection /kəˈlekʃn/ *n* Sammlung *f*; (*in church*) Kollekte *f*; (*of post*) Leerung *f*; (*designer's*) Kollektion *f*

collective /kəˈlektɪv/ *a* gemeinsam; (*Pol*) kollektiv. **~ ˈnoun** *n* Kollektivum *nt*

collector /kəˈlektə(r)/ *n* Sammler(in) *m*(*f*)

college /ˈkɒlɪdʒ/ *n* College *nt*

collide /kəˈlaɪd/ *vi* zusammenstoßen

colliery /ˈkɒlɪərɪ/ *n* Kohlengrube *f*

collision /kəˈlɪʒn/ *n* Zusammenstoß *m*

colloquial /kəˈləʊkwɪəl/ *a*, **-ly** *adv* umgangssprachlich. **~ism** *n* umgangssprachlicher Ausdruck *m*

Cologne /kəˈləʊn/ *n* Köln *nt*

colon /ˈkəʊlən/ *n* Doppelpunkt *m*; (*Anat*) Dickdarm *m*

colonel /ˈkɜːnl/ *n* Oberst *m*

colonial /kəˈləʊnɪəl/ *a* Kolonial-

colon|ize /ˈkɒlənaɪz/ *vt* kolonisieren. **~y** *n* Kolonie *f*

colossal /kəˈlɒsl/ *a* riesig

colour /ˈkʌlə(r)/ *n* Farbe *f*; (*complexion*) Gesichtsfarbe *f*; (*race*) Hautfarbe *f*; **~s** *pl* (*flag*) Fahne *f*; **off ~** (*fam*) nicht ganz auf der Höhe ● *vt* färben; **~ [in]** ausmalen ● *vi* (*blush*) erröten

colour: ~ bar *n* Rassenschranke *f.* **~-blind** *a* farbenblind. **~ed** *a* farbig ● *n* (*person*) Farbige(r) *m*/*f.* **~-fast** *a* farbecht. **~ film** *n* Farbfilm *m.* **~ful** *a* farbenfroh. **~less** *a* farblos. **~ photo[graph]** *n* Farbaufnahme *f.* **~ television** *n* Farbfernsehen *nt*

colt /kəʊlt/ *n* junger Hengst *m*

column /ˈkɒləm/ *n* Säule *f*; (*of soldiers, figures*) Kolonne *f*; (*Typ*) Spalte *f*; (*Journ*) Kolumne *f.* **~ist** /-nɪst/ *n* Kolumnist *m*

coma /ˈkəʊmə/ *n* Koma *nt*
comb /kəʊm/ *n* Kamm *m* ● *vt* kämmen; (*search*) absuchen; **~ one's hair** sich (*dat*) [die Haare] kämmen
combat /ˈkɒmbæt/ *n* Kampf *m* ● *vt* (*pt/pp* **combated**) bekämpfen
combination /kɒmbɪˈneɪʃn/ *n* Verbindung *f*; (*for lock*) Kombination *f*
combine[1] /kəmˈbaɪn/ *vt* verbinden ● *vi* sich verbinden; ⟨*people:*⟩ sich zusammenschließen
combine[2] /ˈkɒmbaɪn/ *n* (*Comm*) Konzern *m*. **~ [harvester]** *n* Mähdrescher *m*
combustion /kəmˈbʌstʃn/ *n* Verbrennung *f*
come /kʌm/ *vi* (*pt* **came**, *pp* **come**) kommen; (*reach*) reichen (**to** an + *acc*); **that ~s to £10** das macht £10; **~ into money** zu Geld kommen; **~ true** wahr werden; **~ in two sizes** in zwei Größen erhältlich sein; **the years to ~** die kommenden Jahre; **how ~?** (*fam*) wie das? **~ about** *vi* geschehen. **~ across** *vi* herüberkommen; (*fam*) klar werden ● *vt* stoßen auf (+ *acc*). **~ apart** *vi* sich auseinandernehmen lassen; (*accidentally*) auseinandergehen. **~ away** *vi* weggehen; ⟨*thing:*⟩ abgehen. **~ back** *vi* zurückkommen. **~ by** *vi* vorbeikommen ● *vt* (*obtain*) bekommen. **~ in** *vi* hereinkommen. **~ off** *vi* abgehen; (*take place*) stattfinden; (*succeed*) klappen (*fam*). **~ out** *vi* herauskommen; ⟨*book:*⟩ erscheinen; ⟨*stain:*⟩ herausgehen. **~ round** *vi* vorbeikommen; (*after fainting*) [wieder] zu sich kommen; (*change one's mind*) sich umstimmen lassen. **~ to** *vi* [wieder] zu sich kommen. **~ up** *vi* heraufkommen; ⟨*plant:*⟩ aufgehen; (*reach*) reichen (**to** bis); **~ up with** sich (*dat*) einfallen lassen
ˈcome-back *n* Comeback *nt*
comedian /kəˈmiːdɪən/ *n* Komiker *m*
ˈcome-down *n* Rückschritt *m*
comedy /ˈkɒmədɪ/ *n* Komödie *f*
comet /ˈkɒmɪt/ *n* Komet *m*
come-uppance /kʌmˈʌpəns/ *n* **get one's ~** (*fam*) sein Fett abkriegen
comfort /ˈkʌmfət/ *n* Bequemlichkeit *f*; (*consolation*) Trost *m* ● *vt* trösten
comfortable /ˈkʌmfətəbl/ *a*, **-bly** *adv* bequem
ˈcomfort station *n* (*Amer*) öffentliche Toilette *f*
comfy /ˈkʌmfɪ/ *a* (*fam*) bequem
comic /ˈkɒmɪk/ *a* komisch ● *n* Komiker *m*; (*periodical*) Comic-Heft *nt*. **~al** *a*, **-ly** *adv* komisch. **~ strip** *n* Comic Strips *pl*
coming /ˈkʌmɪŋ/ *a* kommend ● *n* Kommen *nt*; **~s and goings** Kommen und Gehen *nt*
comma /ˈkɒmə/ *n* Komma *nt*
command /kəˈmɑːnd/ *n* Befehl *m*; (*Mil*) Kommando *nt*; (*mastery*) Beherrschung *f* ● *vt* befehlen (+ *dat*); kommandieren ⟨*army*⟩
commandeer /kɒmənˈdɪə(r)/ *vt* beschlagnahmen
command|er /kəˈmɑːndə(r)/ *n* Befehlshaber *m*; (*of unit*) Kommandeur *m*; (*of ship*) Kommandant *m*. **~ing** *a* ⟨*view*⟩ beherrschend. **~ing officer** *n* Befehlshaber *m*. **~ment** *n* Gebot *nt*
commemorat|e /kəˈmeməreɪt/ *vt* gedenken (+ *gen*). **~ion** /-ˈreɪʃn/ *n* Gedenken *nt*. **~ive** /-ətɪv/ *a* Gedenk-
commence /kəˈmens/ *vt/i* anfangen, beginnen. **~ment** *n* Anfang *m*, Beginn *m*
commend /kəˈmend/ *vt* loben; (*recommend*) empfehlen (**to** *dat*). **~able** /-əbl/ *a* lobenswert. **~ation** /kɒmenˈdeɪʃn/ *n* Lob *nt*
commensurate /kəˈmenʃərət/ *a* angemessen; **be ~ with** entsprechen (+ *dat*)
comment /ˈkɒment/ *n* Bemerkung *f*; **no ~!** kein Kommentar! ● *vi* sich äußern (**on** zu); **~ on** (*Journ*) kommentieren
commentary /ˈkɒməntrɪ/ *n* Kommentar *m*; **[running] ~** (*Radio, TV*) Reportage *f*
commentator /ˈkɒmənteɪtə(r)/ *n* Kommentator *m*; (*Sport*) Reporter *m*
commerce /ˈkɒmɜːs/ *n* Handel *m*
commercial /kəˈmɜːʃl/ *a*, **-ly** *adv* kommerziell ● *n* (*Radio, TV*) Werbespot *m*. **~ize** *vt* kommerzialisieren
commiserate /kəˈmɪzəreit/ *vi* sein Mitleid ausdrücken (**with** *dat*)
commission /kəˈmɪʃn/ *n* (*order for work*) Auftrag *m*; (*body of people*) Kommission *f*; (*payment*) Provision *f*; (*Mil*) [Offiziers]patent *nt*; **out of ~** außer Betrieb ● *vt* beauftragen ⟨*s.o.*⟩; in Auftrag geben ⟨*thing*⟩; (*Mil*) zum Offizier ernennen
commissionaire /kəmɪʃəˈneə(r)/ *n* Portier *m*

commissioner /kə'mɪʃənə(r)/ *n* Kommissar *m*; ~ **for oaths** Notar *m*

commit /kə'mɪt/ *vt* (*pt/pp* **committed**) begehen; (*entrust*) anvertrauen (**to** *dat*); (*consign*) einweisen (**to** in + *acc*); ~ **oneself** sich festlegen; (*involve oneself*) sich engagieren; ~ **sth to memory** sich (*dat*) etw einprägen. ~**ment** *n* Verpflichtung *f*; (*involvement*) Engagement *nt*. ~**ted** *a* engagiert

committee /kə'mɪtɪ/ *n* Ausschuß *m*, Komitee *nt*

commodity /kə'mɒdətɪ/ *n* Ware *f*

common /'kɒmən/ *a* (**-er, -est**) gemeinsam; (*frequent*) häufig; (*ordinary*) gewöhnlich; (*vulgar*) ordinär ● *n* Gemeindeland *nt*; **have in** ~ gemeinsam haben; **House of C~s** Unterhaus *nt*. ~**er** *n* Bürgerliche(r) *m/f*

common: ~**'law** *n* Gewohnheitsrecht *nt*. ~**ly** *adv* allgemein. **C~ 'Market** *n* Gemeinsamer Markt *m*. ~**place** *a* häufig. ~**-room** *n* Aufenthaltsraum *m*. ~ **'sense** *n* gesunder Menschenverstand *m*

commotion /kə'məʊʃn/ *n* Tumult *m*

communal /'kɒmjʊnl/ *a* gemeinschaftlich

communicable /kə'mju:nɪkəbl/ *a* ⟨*disease*⟩ übertragbar

communicate /kə'mju:nɪkeɪt/ *vt* mitteilen (**to** *dat*); übertragen ⟨*disease*⟩ ● *vi* sich verständigen; (*be in touch*) Verbindung haben

communication /kəmju:nɪ'keɪʃn/ *n* Verständigung *f*; (*contact*) Verbindung *f*; (*of disease*) Übertragung *f*; (*message*) Mitteilung *f*; ~**s** *pl* (*technology*) Nachrichtenwesen *nt*. ~ **cord** *n* Notbremse *f*

communicative /kə'mju:nɪkətɪv/ *a* mitteilsam

Communion /kə'mju:nɪən/ *n* **[Holy]** ~ das [heilige] Abendmahl; (*Roman Catholic*) die [heilige] Kommunion

communiqué /kə'mju:nɪkeɪ/ *n* Kommuniqué *nt*

Communis|m /'kɒmjʊnɪzm/ *n* Kommunismus *m*. ~**t** /-ɪst/ *a* kommunistisch ● *n* Kommunist(in) *m(f)*

community /kə'mju:nətɪ/ *n* Gemeinschaft *f*; **local** ~ Gemeinde *f*. ~ **centre** *n* Gemeinschaftszentrum *nt*

commute /kə'mju:t/ *vi* pendeln ● *vt* (*Jur*) umwandeln. ~**r** *n* Pendler(in) *m(f)*

compact[1] /kəm'pækt/ *a* kompakt

compact[2] /'kɒmpækt/ *n* Puderdose *f*. ~ **disc** *n* CD *f*

companion /kəm'pænjən/ *n* Begleiter(in) *m(f)*. ~**ship** *n* Gesellschaft *f*

company /'kʌmpənɪ/ *n* Gesellschaft *f*; (*firm*) Firma *f*; (*Mil*) Kompanie *f*; (*fam: guests*) Besuch *m*. ~ **car** *n* Firmenwagen *m*

comparable /'kɒmpərəbl/ *a* vergleichbar

comparative /kəm'pærətɪv/ *a* vergleichend; (*relative*) relativ ● *n* (*Gram*) Komparativ *m*. ~**ly** *adv* verhältnismäßig

compare /kəm'peə(r)/ *vt* vergleichen (**with/to** mit) ● *vi* sich vergleichen lassen

comparison /kəm'pærɪsn/ *n* Vergleich *m*

compartment /kəm'pɑ:tmənt/ *n* Fach *nt*; (*Rail*) Abteil *nt*

compass /'kʌmpəs/ *n* Kompaß *m*. ~**es** *npl* **pair of** ~**es** Zirkel *m*

compassion /kəm'pæʃn/ *n* Mitleid *nt*. ~**ate** /-ʃənət/ *a* mitfühlend

compatible /kəm'pætəbl/ *a* vereinbar; ⟨*drugs*⟩ verträglich; (*Techn*) kompatibel; **be** ~ ⟨*people:*⟩ [gut] zueinander passen

compatriot /kəm'pætrɪət/ *n* Landsmann *m*/-männin *f*

compel /kəm'pel/ *vt* (*pt/pp* **compelled**) zwingen

compensat|e /'kɒmpənseɪt/ *vt* entschädigen ● *vi* ~**e for** (*fig*) ausgleichen. ~**ion** /-'seɪʃn/ *n* Entschädigung *f*; (*fig*) Ausgleich *m*

compère /'kɒmpeə(r)/ *n* Conférencier *m*

compete /kəm'pi:t/ *vi* konkurrieren; (*take part*) teilnehmen (**in** an + *dat*)

competen|ce /'kɒmpɪtəns/ *n* Tüchtigkeit *f*; (*ability*) Fähigkeit *f*; (*Jur*) Kompetenz *f*. ~**t** *a* tüchtig; fähig; (*Jur*) kompetent

competition /kɒmpə'tɪʃn/ *n* Konkurrenz *f*; (*contest*) Wettbewerb *m*; (*in newspaper*) Preisausschreiben *nt*

competitive /kəm'petətɪv/ *a* (*Comm*) konkurrenzfähig

competitor /kəm'petɪtə(r)/ *n* Teilnehmer *m*; (*Comm*) Konkurrent *m*

compile /kəm'paɪl/ *vt* zusammenstellen; verfassen ⟨*dictionary*⟩

complacen|cy /kəm'pleɪsənsɪ/ *n* Selbstzufriedenheit *f*. ~**t** *a*, **-ly** *adv* selbstzufrieden

complain /kəm'pleɪn/ *vi* klagen (**about/of** über + *acc*); (*formally*) sich beschweren. **~t** *n* Klage *f*; (*formal*) Beschwerde *f*; (*Med*) Leiden *nt*

complement¹ /'kɒmplɪmənt/ *n* Ergänzung *f*; **full ~** volle Anzahl *f*

complement² /'kɒmplɪment/ *vt* ergänzen; **~ each other** sich ergänzen. **~ary** /-'mentərɪ/ *a* sich ergänzend; **be ~ary** sich ergänzen

complete /kəm'pli:t/ *a* vollständig; (*finished*) fertig; (*utter*) völlig ● *vt* vervollständigen; (*finish*) abschließen; (*fill in*) ausfüllen. **~ly** *adv* völlig

completion /kəm'pli:ʃn/ *n* Vervollständigung *f*; (*end*) Abschluß *m*

complex /'kɒmpleks/ *a* komplex ● *n* Komplex *m*

complexion /kəm'plekʃn/ *n* Teint *m*; (*colour*) Gesichtsfarbe *f*; (*fig*) Aspekt *m*

complexity /kəm'pleksətɪ/ *n* Komplexität *f*

compliance /kəm'plaɪəns/ *n* Einverständnis *nt*; **in ~ with** gemäß (+ *dat*)

complicat|e /'kɒmplɪkeɪt/ *vt* komplizieren. **~ed** *a* kompliziert. **~ion** /-'keɪʃn/ *n* Komplikation *f*

complicity /kəm'plɪsətɪ/ *n* Mittäterschaft *f*

compliment /'kɒmplɪmənt/ *n* Kompliment *nt*; **~s** *pl* Grüße *pl* ● *vt* ein Kompliment machen (+ *dat*). **~ary** /-'mentərɪ/ *a* schmeichelhaft; (*given free*) Frei-

comply /kəm'plaɪ/ *vi* (*pt/pp* **-ied**) **~ with** nachkommen (+ *dat*)

component /kəm'pəʊnənt/ *a* & *n* **~ [part]** Bestandteil *m*, Teil *nt*

compose /kəm'pəʊz/ *vt* verfassen; (*Mus*) komponieren; **~ oneself** sich fassen; **be ~d of** sich zusammensetzen aus. **~d** *a* (*calm*) gefaßt. **~r** *n* Komponist *m*

composition /kɒmpə'zɪʃn/ *n* Komposition *f*; (*essay*) Aufsatz *m*

compost /'kɒmpɒst/ *n* Kompost *m*

composure /kəm'pəʊʒə(r)/ *n* Fassung *f*

compound¹ /kəm'paʊnd/ *vt* (*make worse*) verschlimmern

compound² /'kɒmpaʊnd/ *a* zusammengesetzt; ⟨*fracture*⟩ kompliziert ● *n* (*Chem*) Verbindung *f*; (*Gram*) Kompositum *nt*; (*enclosure*) Einfriedigung *f*. **~ 'interest** *n* Zinseszins *m*

comprehen|d /kɒmprɪ'hend/ *vt* begreifen, verstehen; (*include*) umfassen. **~sible** *a*, **-bly** *adv* verständlich. **~sion** /-'henʃn/ *n* Verständnis *nt*

comprehensive /kɒmprɪ'hensɪv/ *a* & *n* umfassend; **~ [school]** Gesamtschule *f*. **~ insurance** *n* (*Auto*) Vollkaskoversicherung *f*

compress¹ /'kɒmpres/ *n* Kompresse *f*

compress² /kəm'pres/ *vt* zusammenpressen; **~ed air** Druckluft *f*

comprise /kəm'praɪz/ *vt* umfassen, bestehen aus

compromise /'kɒmprəmaɪz/ *n* Kompromiß *m* ● *vt* kompromittieren ⟨*person*⟩ ● *vi* einen Kompromiß schließen

compuls|ion /kəm'pʌlʃn/ *n* Zwang *m*. **~ive** /-sɪv/ *a* zwanghaft; **~ive eating** Eßzwang *m*. **~ory** /-sərɪ/ *a* obligatorisch; **~ory subject** Pflichtfach *nt*

compunction /kəm'pʌŋkʃn/ *n* Gewissensbisse *pl*

comput|er /kəm'pju:tə(r)/ *n* Computer *m*. **~erize** *vt* computerisieren ⟨*data*⟩; auf Computer umstellen ⟨*firm*⟩. **~ing** *n* Computertechnik *f*

comrade /'kɒmreɪd/ *n* Kamerad *m*; (*Pol*) Genosse *m*/Genossin *f*. **~ship** *n* Kameradschaft *f*

con¹ /kɒn/ *see* **pro**

con² *n* (*fam*) Schwindel *m* ● *vt* (*pt/pp* **conned**) (*fam*) beschwindeln

concave /'kɒŋkeɪv/ *a* konkav

conceal /kən'si:l/ *vt* verstecken; (*keep secret*) verheimlichen

concede /kən'si:d/ *vt* zugeben; (*give up*) aufgeben

conceit /kən'si:t/ *n* Einbildung *f*. **~ed** *a* eingebildet

conceivable /kən'si:vəbl/ *a* denkbar

conceive /kən'si:v/ *vt* (*Biol*) empfangen; (*fig*) sich (*dat*) ausdenken ● *vi* schwanger werden. **~ of** (*fig*) sich (*dat*) vorstellen

concentrat|e /'kɒnsəntreɪt/ *vt* konzentrieren ● *vi* sich konzentrieren. **~ion** /-'treɪʃn/ *n* Konzentration *f*. **~ion camp** *n* Konzentrationslager *nt*

concept /'kɒnsept/ *n* Begriff *m*. **~ion** /kən'sepʃn/ *n* Empfängnis *f*; (*idea*) Vorstellung *f*

concern /kən'sɜ:n/ *n* Angelegenheit *f*; (*worry*) Sorge *f*; (*Comm*) Unternehmen *nt* ● *vt* (*be about, affect*) betreffen; (*worry*) kümmern; **be ~ed about** besorgt sein um; **~ oneself with** sich beschäftigen mit; **as far as I am ~ed**

was mich angeht *od* betrifft. **~ing** *prep* bezüglich (+ *gen*)

concert /'kɒnsət/ *n* Konzert *nt*; **in ~** im Chor. **~ed** /kən'sɜ:tɪd/ *a* gemeinsam

concertina /kɒnsə'ti:nə/ *n* Konzertina *f*

'concert-master *n* (*Amer*) Konzertmeister *m*

concerto /kən'tʃeətəʊ/ *n* Konzert *nt*

concession /kən'seʃn/ *n* Zugeständnis *nt*; (*Comm*) Konzession *f*; (*reduction*) Ermäßigung *f*. **~ary** *a* (*reduced*) ermäßigt

conciliation /kənsɪlɪ'eɪʃn/ *n* Schlichtung *f*

concise /kən'saɪs/ *a*, **-ly** *adv* kurz

conclude /kən'klu:d/ *vt/i* schließen

conclusion /kən'klu:ʒn/ *n* Schluß *m*; **in ~** abschließend, zum Schluß

conclusive /kən'klu:sɪv/ *a* schlüssig

concoct /kən'kɒkt/ *vt* zusammenstellen; (*fig*) fabrizieren. **~ion** /ɒkʃn/ *n* Zusammenstellung *f*; (*drink*) Gebräu *nt*

concourse /'kɒŋkɔ:s/ *n* Halle *f*

concrete /'kɒnkri:t/ *a* konkret ● *n* Beton *m* ● *vt* betonieren

concur /kən'kɜ:(r)/ *vi* (*pt/pp* **concurred**) übereinstimmen

concurrently /kən'kʌrəntlɪ/ *adv* gleichzeitig

concussion /kən'kʌʃn/ *n* Gehirnerschütterung *f*

condemn /kən'dem/ *vt* verurteilen; (*declare unfit*) für untauglich erklären. **~ation** /kɒndem'neɪʃn/ *n* Verurteilung *f*

condensation /kɒnden'seɪʃn/ *n* Kondensation *f*

condense /kən'dens/ *vt* zusammenfassen; (*Phys*) kondensieren ● *vi* sich kondensieren. **~d milk** *n* Kondensmilch *f*

condescend /kɒndɪ'send/ *vi* sich herablassen (**to** zu). **~ing** *a*, **-ly** *adv* herablassend

condiment /'kɒndɪmənt/ *n* Gewürz *nt*

condition /kən'dɪʃn/ *n* Bedingung *f*; (*state*) Zustand *m*; **~s** *pl* Verhältnisse *pl*: **on ~ that** unter der Bedingung, daß ● *vt* (*Psych*) konditionieren. **~al** *a* bedingt; **be ~al on** abhängen von ● *n* (*Gram*) Konditional *m*. **~er** *n* Haarkur *f*; (*for fabrics*) Weichspüler *m*

condolences /kən'dəʊlənsɪz/ *npl* Beileid *nt*

condom /'kɒndəm/ *n* Kondom *nt*

condominium /kɒndə'mɪnɪəm/ *n* (*Amer*) ≈ Eigentumswohnung *f*

condone /kən'dəʊn/ *vt* hinwegsehen über (+ *acc*)

conducive /kən'dju:sɪv/ *a* förderlich (**to** *dat*)

conduct[1] /'kɒndʌkt/ *n* Verhalten *nt*; (*Sch*) Betragen *nt*

conduct[2] /kən'dʌkt/ *vt* führen; (*Phys*) leiten; (*Mus*) dirigieren. **~or** *n* Dirigent *m*; (*of bus*) Schaffner *m*; (*Phys*) Leiter *m*. **~ress** *n* Schaffnerin *f*

cone /kəʊn/ *n* Kegel *m*; (*Bot*) Zapfen *m*; (*for ice-cream*) [Eis]tüte *f*; (*Auto*) Leitkegel *m*

confectioner /kən'fekʃənə(r)/ *n* Konditor *m*. **~y** *n* Süßwaren *pl*

confederation /kənfedə'reɪʃn/ *n* Bund *m*; (*Pol*) Konföderation *f*

confer /kən'fɜ:(r)/ *v* (*pt/pp* **conferred**) ● *vt* verleihen (**on** *dat*) ● *vi* sich beraten

conference /'kɒnfərəns/ *n* Konferenz *f*

confess /kən'fes/ *vt/i* gestehen; (*Relig*) beichten. **~ion** /-eʃn/ *n* Geständnis *nt*; (*Relig*) Beichte *f*. **~ional** /-eʃənəl/ *n* Beichtstuhl *m*. **~or** *n* Beichtvater *m*

confetti /kən'fetɪ/ *n* Konfetti *nt*

confide /kən'faɪd/ *vt* anvertrauen ● *vi* **~ in s.o.** sich jdm anvertrauen

confidence /'kɒnfɪdəns/ *n* (*trust*) Vertrauen *nt*; (*self-assurance*) Selbstvertrauen *nt*; (*secret*) Geheimnis *nt*; **in ~** im Vertrauen. **~ trick** *n* Schwindel *m*

confident /'kɒnfɪdənt/ *a*, **-ly** *adv* zuversichtlich; (*self assured*) selbstsicher

confidential /kɒnfɪ'denʃl/ *a*, **-ly** *adv* vertraulich

confine /kən'faɪn/ *vt* beschränken; (*keep shut up*) einsperren; **~ oneself to** sich beschränken auf (+ *acc*); **be ~d to bed** das Bett hüten müssen. **~d** *a* (*narrow*) eng. **~ment** *n* Haft *f*

confines /'kɒnfaɪnz/ *npl* Grenzen *pl*

confirm /kən'fɜ:m/ *vt* bestätigen; (*Relig*) konfirmieren; (*Roman Catholic*) firmen. **~ation** /kɒnfə'meɪʃn/ *n* Bestätigung *f*; Konfirmation *f*; Firmung *f*. **~ed** *a* **~ed bachelor** eingefleischter Junggeselle *m*

confiscat|e /'kɒnfɪskeɪt/ *vt* beschlagnahmen. **~ion** /-'keɪʃn/ *n* Beschlagnahme *f*

conflict[1] /'kɒnflɪkt/ *n* Konflikt *m*

conflict[2] /kən'flɪkt/ *vi* im Widerspruch stehen (**with** zu). **~ing** *a* widersprüchlich

conform /kən'fɔ:m/ *vi* ⟨*person:*⟩ sich anpassen; ⟨*thing:*⟩ entsprechen (**to** *dat*). **~ist** *n* Konformist *m*

confounded /kən'faʊndɪd/ *a* (*fam*) verflixt

confront /kən'frʌnt/ *vt* konfrontieren. **~ation** /kɒnfrən'teɪʃn/ *n* Konfrontation *f*

confus|e /kən'fju:z/ *vt* verwirren; (*mistake for*) verwechseln (**with** mit). **~ing** *a* verwirrend. **~ion** /-ju:ʒn/ *n* Verwirrung *f*; (*muddle*) Durcheinander *nt*

congeal /kən'dʒi:l/ *vi* fest werden; ⟨*blood:*⟩ gerinnen

congenial /kən'dʒi:nɪəl/ *a* angenehm

congenital /kən'dʒenɪtl/ *a* angeboren

congest|ed /kən'dʒestɪd/ *a* verstopft; (*with people*) überfüllt. **~ion** /-estʃn/ *n* Verstopfung *f*; Überfüllung *f*

congratulat|e /kən'grætjʊleɪt/ *vt* gratulieren (+ *dat*) (**on** zu). **~ions** /-'leɪʃnz/ *npl* Glückwünsche *pl*; **~ions!** [ich] gratuliere!

congregat|e /'kɒŋgrɪgeɪt/ *vi* sich versammeln. **~ion** /-'geɪʃn/ *n* (*Relig*) Gemeinde *f*

congress /'kɒŋgres/ *n* Kongreß *m*. **~man** *n* Kongreßabgeordnete(r) *m*

conical /'kɒnɪkl/ *a* kegelförmig

conifer /'kɒnɪfə(r)/ *n* Nadelbaum *m*

conjecture /kən'dʒektʃə(r)/ *n* Mutmaßung *f* ● *vt/i* mutmaßen

conjugal /'kɒndʒʊgl/ *a* ehelich

conjugat|e /'kɒndʒʊgeɪt/ *vt* konjugieren. **~ion** /-'geɪʃn/ *n* Konjugation *f*

conjunction /kən'dʒʌŋkʃn/ *n* Konjunktion *f*; **in ~ with** zusammen mit

conjunctivitis /kəndʒʌŋktɪ'vaɪtɪs/ *n* Bindehautentzündung *f*

conjur|e /'kʌndʒə(r)/ *vi* zaubern ● *vt* **~e up** heraufbeschwören. **~or** *n* Zauberkünstler *m*

conk /kɒŋk/ *vi* **~ out** (*fam*) ⟨*machine:*⟩ kaputtgehen; ⟨*person:*⟩ zusammenklappen

conker /'kɒŋkə(r)/ *n* (*fam*) [Roß]kastanie *f*

'con-man *n* (*fam*) Schwindler *m*

connect /kə'nekt/ *vt* verbinden (**to** mit); (*Electr*) anschließen (**to** an + *acc*) ● *vi* verbunden sein; ⟨*train:*⟩ Anschluß haben (**with** an + *acc*); **be ~ed with** zu tun haben mit; (*be related to*) verwandt sein mit

connection /kə'nekʃn/ *n* Verbindung *f*; (*Rail, Electr*) Anschluß *m*; **in ~ with** in Zusammenhang mit. **~s** *npl* Beziehungen *pl*

conniv|ance /kə'naɪvəns/ *n* stillschweigende Duldung *f*. **~e** *vi* **~e at** stillschweigend dulden

connoisseur /kɒnə'sɜ:(r)/ *n* Kenner *m*

connotation /kɒnə'teɪʃn/ *n* Assoziation *f*

conquer /'kɒŋkə(r)/ *vt* erobern; (*fig*) besiegen. **~or** *n* Eroberer *m*

conquest /'kɒŋkwest/ *n* Eroberung *f*

conscience /'kɒnʃəns/ *n* Gewissen *nt*

conscientious /kɒnʃɪ'enʃəs/ *a*, **-ly** *adv* gewissenhaft. **~ ob'jector** *n* Kriegsdienstverweigerer *m*

conscious /'kɒnʃəs/ *a*, **-ly** *adv* bewußt; **[fully] ~** bei [vollem] Bewußtsein; **be/become ~ of sth** sich (*dat*) etw (*gen*) bewußt sein/werden. **~ness** *n* Bewußtsein *nt*

conscript[1] /'kɒnskrɪpt/ *n* Einberufene(r) *m*

conscript[2] /kən'skrɪpt/ *vt* einberufen. **~ion** /-ɪpʃn/ *n* allgemeine Wehrpflicht *f*

consecrat|e /'kɒnsɪkreɪt/ *vt* weihen; einweihen ⟨*church*⟩. **~ion** /-'kreɪʃn/ *n* Weihe *f*; Einweihung *f*

consecutive /kən'sekjʊtɪv/ *a* aufeinanderfolgend. **~ly** *adv* fortlaufend

consensus /kən'sensəs/ *n* Übereinstimmung *f*

consent /kən'sent/ *n* Einwilligung *f*, Zustimmung *f* ● *vi* einwilligen (**to** in + *acc*), zustimmen (**to** *dat*)

consequen|ce /'kɒnsɪkwəns/ *n* Folge *f*; (*importance*) Bedeutung *f*. **~t** *a* daraus folgend. **~tly** *adv* folglich

conservation /kɒnsə'veɪʃn/ *n* Erhaltung *f*, Bewahrung *f*. **~ist** *n* Umweltschützer *m*

conservative /kən'sɜ:vətɪv/ *a* konservativ; ⟨*estimate*⟩ vorsichtig. **C~** (*Pol*) *a* konservativ ● *n* Konservative(r) *m/f*

conservatory /kən'sɜ:vətrɪ/ *n* Wintergarten *m*

conserve /kən'sɜ:v/ *vt* erhalten, bewahren; sparen ⟨*energy*⟩

consider /kən'sɪdə(r)/ *vt* erwägen; (*think over*) sich (*dat*) überlegen; (*take into account*) berücksichtigen; (*regard as*) betrachten als; **~ doing sth** erwägen, etw zu tun. **~able** /-əbl/ *a*, **-bly** *adv* erheblich

consider|ate /kən'sɪdərət/ *a*, **-ly** *adv* rücksichtsvoll. **~ation** /-'reɪʃn/ *n* Erwägung *f*; (*thoughtfulness*) Rücksicht *f*; (*payment*) Entgelt *nt*; **take into ~ation** berücksichtigen. **~ing** *prep* wenn man bedenkt (**that** daß); **~ing the circumstances** unter den Umständen

consign /kən'saɪn/ *vt* übergeben (**to** *dat*). **~ment** *n* Lieferung *f*

consist /kən'sɪst/ *vi* **~ of** bestehen aus

consisten|cy /kən'sɪstənsɪ/ *n* Konsequenz *f*; (*density*) Konsistenz *f*. **~t** *a* konsequent; (*unchanging*) gleichbleibend; **be ~t with** entsprechen (+ *dat*). **~tly** *adv* konsequent; (*constantly*) ständig

consolation /kɒnsə'leɪʃn/ *n* Trost *m*. **~ prize** *n* Trostpreis *m*

console /kən'səʊl/ *vt* trösten

consolidate /kən'sɒlɪdeɪt/ *vt* konsolidieren

consonant /'kɒnsənənt/ *n* Konsonant *m*

consort /'kɒnsɔ:t/ *n* Gemahl(in) *m(f)*

conspicuous /kən'spɪkjʊəs/ *a* auffällig

conspiracy /kən'spɪrəsɪ/ *n* Verschwörung *f*

conspire /kən'spaɪə(r)/ *vi* sich verschwören

constable /'kʌnstəbl/ *n* Polizist *m*

constant /'kɒnstənt/ *a*, **-ly** *adv* beständig; (*continuous*) ständig

constellation /kɒnstə'leɪʃn/ *n* Sternbild *nt*

consternation /kɒnstə'neɪʃn/ *n* Bestürzung *f*

constipat|ed /'kɒnstɪpeɪtɪd/ *a* verstopft. **~ion** /-'peɪʃn/ *n* Verstopfung *f*

constituency /kən'stɪtjʊənsɪ/ *n* Wahlkreis *m*

constituent /kən'stɪtjʊənt/ *n* Bestandteil *m*; (*Pol*) Wähler(in) *m(f)*

constitut|e /'kɒnstɪtju:t/ *vt* bilden. **~ion** /-'tju:ʃn/ *n* (*Pol*) Verfassung *f*; (*of person*) Konstitution *f*. **~ional** /-'tju:ʃənl/ *a* Verfassungs- ● *n* Verdauungsspaziergang *m*

constrain /kən'streɪn/ *vt* zwingen. **~t** *n* Zwang *m*; (*restriction*) Beschränkung *f*; (*strained manner*) Gezwungenheit *f*

constrict /kən'strɪkt/ *vt* einengen

construct /kən'strʌkt/ *vt* bauen. **~ion** /-ʌkʃn/ *n* Bau *m*; (*Gram*) Konstruktion *f*; (*interpretation*) Deutung *f*; **under ~ion** im Bau. **~ive** /-ɪv/ *a* konstruktiv

construe /kən'stru:/ *vt* deuten

consul /'kɒnsl/ *n* Konsul *m*. **~ate** /'kɒnsjʊlət/ *n* Konsulat *nt*

consult /kən'sʌlt/ *vt* [um Rat] fragen; konsultieren ⟨*doctor*⟩; nachschlagen in (+ *dat*) ⟨*book*⟩. **~ant** *n* Berater *m*; (*Med*) Chefarzt *m*. **~ation** /kɒnsl'teɪʃn/ *n* Beratung *f*; (*Med*) Konsultation *f*

consume /kɒn'sju:m/ *vt* verzehren; (*use*) verbrauchen. **~r** *n* Verbraucher *m*. **~r goods** *npl* Konsumgüter *pl*

consummat|e /'kɒnsəmeɪt/ *vt* vollziehen. **~ion** /-'meɪʃn/ *n* Vollzug *m*

consumption /kən'sʌmpʃn/ *n* Konsum *m*; (*use*) Verbrauch *m*

contact /'kɒntækt/ *n* Kontakt *m*; (*person*) Kontaktperson *f* ● *vt* sich in Verbindung setzen mit. **~ 'lenses** *npl* Kontaktlinsen *pl*

contagious /kən'teɪdʒəs/ *a* direkt übertragbar

contain /kən'teɪn/ *vt* enthalten; (*control*) beherrschen. **~er** *n* Behälter *m*; (*Comm*) Container *m*

contaminat|e /kən'tæmɪneɪt/ *vt* verseuchen. **~ion** /-'neɪʃn/ *n* Verseuchung *f*

contemplat|e /'kɒntəmpleɪt/ *vt* betrachten; (*meditate*) nachdenken über (+ *acc*); **~e doing sth** daran denken, etw zu tun. **~ion** /-'pleɪʃn/ *n* Betrachtung *f*; Nachdenken *nt*

contemporary /kən'tempərərɪ/ *a* zeitgenössisch ● *n* Zeitgenosse *m*/ -genossin *f*

contempt /kən'tempt/ *n* Verachtung *f*; **beneath ~** verabscheuungswürdig; **~ of court** Mißachtung *f* des Gerichts. **~ible** /-əbl/ *a* verachtenswert. **~uous** /-tjʊəs/ *a*, **-ly** *adv* verächtlich

contend /kən'tend/ *vi* kämpfen (**with** mit) ● *vt* (*assert*) behaupten. **~er** *n* Bewerber(in) *m(f)*; (*Sport*) Wettkämpfer(in) *m(f)*

content[1] /'kɒntent/ *n* & **contents** *pl* Inhalt *m*

content[2] /kən'tent/ *a* zufrieden ● *n* **to one's heart's ~** nach Herzenslust ● *vt* **~ oneself** sich begnügen (**with** mit). **~ed** *a*, **-ly** *adv* zufrieden

contention /kən'tenʃn/ *n* (*assertion*) Behauptung *f*

contentment /kən'tentmənt/ *n* Zufriedenheit *f*

contest[1] /'kɒntest/ *n* Kampf *m*; (*competition*) Wettbewerb *m*

contest² /kən'test/ *vt* (*dispute*) bestreiten; (*Jur*) anfechten; (*Pol*) kandidieren in (+ *dat*). **~ant** *n* Teilnehmer *m*

context /'kɒntekst/ *n* Zusammenhang *m*

continent /'kɒntɪnənt/ *n* Kontinent *m*

continental /kɒntɪ'nentl/ *a* Kontinental-. **~ breakfast** *n* kleines Frühstück *nt*. **~ quilt** *n* Daunendecke *f*

contingen|cy /kən'tɪndʒənsɪ/ *n* Eventualität *f*. **~t** *a* **be ~t upon** abhängen von ● *n* (*Mil*) Kontingent *nt*

continual /kən'tɪnjʊəl/ *a*, **-ly** *adv* dauernd

continuation /kəntɪnjʊ'eɪʃn/ *n* Fortsetzung *f*

continue /kən'tɪnju:/ *vt* fortsetzen; **~ doing** *or* **to do sth** fortfahren, etw zu tun; **to be ~d** Fortsetzung folgt ● *vi* weitergehen; (*doing sth*) weitermachen; (*speaking*) fortfahren; ⟨*weather:*⟩ anhalten

continuity /kɒntɪ'nju:ətɪ/ *n* Kontinuität *f*

continuous /kən'tɪnjʊəs/ *a*, **-ly** *adv* anhaltend, ununterbrochen

contort /kən'tɔ:t/ *vt* verzerren. **~ion** /-ɔ:ʃn/ *n* Verzerrung *f*

contour /'kɒntʊə(r)/ *n* Kontur *f*; (*line*) Höhenlinie *f*

contraband /'kɒntrəbænd/ *n* Schmuggelware *f*

contracep|tion /kɒntrə'sepʃn/ *n* Empfängnisverhütung *f*. **~tive** /-tɪv/ *a* empfängnisverhütend ● *n* Empfängnisverhütungsmittel *nt*

contract¹ /'kɒntrækt/ *n* Vertrag *m*

contract² /kən'trækt/ *vi* sich zusammenziehen ● *vt* zusammenziehen; sich (*dat*) zuziehen ⟨*illness*⟩. **~ion** /-ækʃn/ *n* Zusammenziehung *f*; (*abbreviation*) Abkürzung *f*; (*in childbirth*) Wehe *f*. **~or** *n* Unternehmer *m*

contradict /kɒntrə'dɪkt/ *vt* widersprechen (+ *dat*). **~ion** /-ɪkʃn/ *n* Widerspruch *m*. **~ory** *a* widersprüchlich

contra-flow /'kɒntrə-/ *n* Umleitung *f* [auf die entgegengesetzte Fahrbahn]

contralto /kən'træltəʊ/ *n* Alt *m*; (*singer*) Altistin *f*

contraption /kən'træpʃn/ *n* (*fam*) Apparat *m*

contrary¹ /'kɒntrərɪ/ *a* & *adv* entgegengesetzt; **~ to** entgegen (+ *dat*) ● *n* Gegenteil *nt*; **on the ~** im Gegenteil

contrary² /kən'treərɪ/ *a* widerspenstig

contrast¹ /'kɒntrɑ:st/ *n* Kontrast *m*

contrast² /kən'trɑ:st/ *vt* gegenüberstellen (**with** *dat*) ● *vi* einen Kontrast bilden (**with** zu). **~ing** *a* gegensätzlich; ⟨*colour*⟩ Kontrast-

contraven|e /kɒntrə'vi:n/ *vt* verstoßen gegen. **~tion** /-'venʃn/ *n* Verstoß *m* (**of** gegen)

contribut|e /kən'trɪbju:t/ *vt/i* beitragen; beisteuern ⟨*money*⟩; (*donate*) spenden. **~ion** /kɒntrɪ'bju:ʃn/ *n* Beitrag *m*; (*donation*) Spende *f*. **~or** *n* Beitragende(r) *m/f*

contrite /kən'traɪt/ *a* reuig

contrivance /kən'traɪvəns/ *n* Vorrichtung *f*

contrive /kən'traɪv/ *vt* verfertigen; **~ to do sth** es fertigbringen, etw zu tun

control /kən'trəʊl/ *n* Kontrolle *f*; (*mastery*) Beherrschung *f*; (*Techn*) Regler *m*; **~s** *pl* (*of car, plane*) Steuerung *f*; **get out of ~** außer Kontrolle geraten ● *vt* (*pt/pp* **controlled**) kontrollieren; (*restrain*) unter Kontrolle halten; **~ oneself** sich beherrschen

controvers|ial /kɒntrə'vɜ:ʃl/ *a* umstritten. **~y** /'kɒntrəvɜ:sɪ/ *n* Kontroverse *f*

conundrum /kə'nʌndrəm/ *n* Rätsel *nt*

conurbation /kɒnɜ:'beɪʃn/ *n* Ballungsgebiet *nt*

convalesce /kɒnvə'les/ *vi* sich erholen. **~nce** *n* Erholung *f*

convalescent /kɒnvə'lesnt/ *a* **be ~** noch erholungsbedürftig sein. **~ home** *n* Erholungsheim *nt*

convector /kən'vektə(r)/ *n* **~ [heater]** Konvektor *m*

convene /kən'vi:n/ *vt* einberufen ● *vi* sich versammeln

convenience /kən'vi:nɪəns/ *n* Bequemlichkeit *f*; **[public] ~** öffentliche Toilette *f*; **with all modern ~s** mit allem Komfort

convenient /kən'vi:nɪənt/ *a*, **-ly** *adv* günstig; **be ~ for s.o.** jdm gelegen sein *od* jdm passen; **if it is ~ [for you]** wenn es Ihnen paßt

convent /'kɒnvənt/ *n* [Nonnen]kloster *nt*

convention /kən'venʃn/ *n* (*custom*) Brauch *m*, Sitte *f*; (*agreement*) Konvention *f*; (*assembly*) Tagung *f*. **~al** *a*, **-ly** *adv* konventionell

converge /kən'vɜ:dʒ/ *vi* zusammenlaufen

conversant /kən'vɜ:sənt/ *a* ~ **with** vertraut mit

conversation /kɒnvə'seɪʃn/ *n* Gespräch *nt*; (*Sch*) Konversation *f*

converse[1] /kən'vɜ:s/ *vi* sich unterhalten

converse[2] /'kɒnvɜ:s/ *n* Gegenteil *nt*. ~**ly** *adv* umgekehrt

conversion /kən'vɜ:ʃn/ *n* Umbau *m*; (*Relig*) Bekehrung *f*; (*calculation*) Umrechnung *f*

convert[1] /'kɒnvɜ:t/ *n* Bekehrte(r) *m*/*f*, Konvertit *m*

convert[2] /kən'vɜ:t/ *vt* bekehren ⟨*person*⟩; (*change*) umwandeln (**into** in + *acc*); umbauen ⟨*building*⟩; (*calculate*) umrechnen; (*Techn*) umstellen. ~**ible** /-əbl/ *a* verwandelbar ● *n* (*Auto*) Kabriolett *nt*

convex /'kɒnveks/ *a* konvex

convey /kən'veɪ/ *vt* befördern; vermitteln ⟨*idea, message*⟩. ~**ance** *n* Beförderung *f*; (*vehicle*) Beförderungsmittel *nt*. ~**or belt** *n* Förderband *nt*

convict[1] /'kɒnvɪkt/ *n* Sträfling *m*

convict[2] /kən'vɪkt/ *vt* verurteilen (**of** wegen). ~**ion** /-ɪkʃn/ *n* Verurteilung *f*; (*belief*) Überzeugung *f*; **previous** ~**ion** Vorstrafe *f*

convinc|e /kən'vɪns/ *vt* überzeugen. ~**ing** *a*, **-ly** *adv* überzeugend

convivial /kən'vɪvɪəl/ *a* gesellig

convoluted /'kɒnvəlu:tɪd/ *a* verschlungen; (*fig*) verwickelt

convoy /'kɒnvɔɪ/ *n* Konvoi *m*

convuls|e /kən'vʌls/ *vt* **be** ~**ed** sich krümmen (**with** vor + *dat*). ~**ion** /-ʌlʃn/ *n* Krampf *m*

coo /ku:/ *vi* gurren

cook /kʊk/ *n* Koch *m*/Köchin *f* ● *vt*/*i* kochen; **is it** ~**ed?** ist es gar? ~ **the books** (*fam*) die Bilanz frisieren. ~**book** *n* (*Amer*) Kochbuch *nt*

cooker /'kʊkə(r)/ *n* [Koch]herd *m*; (*apple*) Kochapfel *m*. ~**y** *n* Kochen *nt*. ~**y book** *n* Kochbuch *nt*

cookie /'kʊkɪ/ *n* (*Amer*) Keks *m*

cool /ku:l/ *a* (**-er, -est**), **-ly** *adv* kühl ● *n* Kühle *f* ● *vt* kühlen ● *vi* abkühlen. ~**-box** *n* Kühlbox *f*. ~**ness** *n* Kühle *f*

coop /ku:p/ *n* [Hühner]stall *m* ● *vt* ~ **up** einsperren

co-operat|e /kəʊ'ɒpəreɪt/ *vi* zusammenarbeiten. ~**ion** /-'reɪʃn/ *n* Kooperation *f*

co-operative /kəʊ'ɒpərətɪv/ *a* hilfsbereit ● *n* Genossenschaft *f*

co-opt /kəʊ'ɒpt/ *vt* hinzuwählen

co-ordinat|e /kəʊ'ɔ:dɪneɪt/ *vt* koordinieren. ~**ion** /-'neɪʃn/ *n* Koordination *f*

cop /kɒp/ *n* (*fam*) Polizist *m*

cope /kəʊp/ *vi* (*fam*) zurechtkommen; ~ **with** fertig werden mit

copious /'kəʊpɪəs/ *a* reichlich

copper[1] /'kɒpə(r)/ *n* Kupfer *nt*; ~**s** *pl* Kleingeld *nt* ● *a* kupfern

copper[2] *n* (*fam*) Polizist *m*

copper 'beech *n* Blutbuche *f*

coppice /'kɒpɪs/ *n*, **copse** /kɒps/ *n* Gehölz *nt*

copulate /'kɒpjʊleɪt/ *vi* sich begatten

copy /'kɒpɪ/ *n* Kopie *f*; (*book*) Exemplar *nt* ● *vt* (*pt*/*pp* **-ied**) kopieren; (*imitate*) nachahmen; (*Sch*) abschreiben

copy: ~**right** *n* Copyright *nt*. ~**-writer** *n* Texter *m*

coral /'kɒrl/ *n* Koralle *f*

cord /kɔ:d/ *n* Schnur *f*; (*fabric*) Cordsamt *m*; ~**s** *pl* Cordhose *f*

cordial /'kɔ:dɪəl/ *a*, **-ly** *adv* herzlich ● *n* Fruchtsirup *m*

cordon /'kɔ:dn/ *n* Kordon *m* ● *vt* ~ **off** absperren

corduroy /'kɔ:dərɔɪ/ *n* Cordsamt *m*

core /kɔ:(r)/ *n* Kern *m*; (*of apple, pear*) Kerngehäuse *nt*

cork /kɔ:k/ *n* Kork *m*; (*for bottle*) Korken *m*. ~**screw** *n* Korkenzieher *m*

corn[1] /kɔ:n/ *n* Korn *nt*; (*Amer: maize*) Mais *m*

corn[2] *n* (*Med*) Hühnerauge *nt*

cornea /'kɔ:nɪə/ *n* Hornhaut *f*

corned beef /kɔ:nd'bi:f/ *n* Corned beef *nt*

corner /'kɔ:nə(r)/ *n* Ecke *f*; (*bend*) Kurve *f*; (*football*) Eckball *m* ● *vt* (*fig*) in die Enge treiben; (*Comm*) monopolisieren ⟨*market*⟩. ~**stone** *n* Eckstein *m*

cornet /'kɔ:nɪt/ *n* (*Mus*) Kornett *nt*; (*for ice-cream*) [Eis]tüte *f*

corn: ~**flour** *n*, (*Amer*) ~**starch** *n* Stärkemehl *nt*

corny /'kɔ:nɪ/ *a* (*fam*) abgedroschen

coronary /'kɒrənərɪ/ *a* & *n* ~ **[thrombosis]** Koronarthrombose *f*

coronation /kɒrə'neɪʃn/ *n* Krönung *f*

coroner /'kɒrənə(r)/ *n* Beamte(r) *m*, der verdächtige Todesfälle untersucht

coronet /'kɒrənet/ *n* Adelskrone *f*

corporal[1] /'kɔ:pərəl/ *n* (*Mil*) Stabsunteroffizier *m*
corporal[2] *a* körperlich; ~ **punishment** körperliche Züchtigung *f*
corporate /'kɔ:pərət/ *a* gemeinschaftlich
corporation /kɔ:pə'reɪʃn/ *n* Körperschaft *f*; (*of town*) Stadtverwaltung *f*
corps /kɔ:(r)/ *n* (*pl* **corps** /kɔ:z/) Korps *nt*
corpse /kɔ:ps/ *n* Leiche *f*
corpulent /'kɔ:pjʊlənt/ *a* korpulent
corpuscle /'kɔ:pʌsl/ *n* Blutkörperchen *nt*
correct /kə'rekt/ *a*, **-ly** *adv* richtig; (*proper*) korrekt ● *vt* verbessern; (*Sch, Typ*) korrigieren. **~ion** /-ekʃn/ *n* Verbesserung *f*; (*Typ*) Korrektur *f*
correlation /kɒrə'leɪʃn/ *n* Wechselbeziehung *f*
correspond /kɒrɪ'spɒnd/ *vi* entsprechen (**to** *dat*); ⟨*two things:*⟩ sich entsprechen; (*write*) korrespondieren. **~ence** *n* Briefwechsel *m*; (*Comm*) Korrespondenz *f*. **~ent** *n* Korrespondent(in) *m*(*f*). **~ing** *a*, **-ly** *adv* entsprechend
corridor /'kɒrɪdɔ:(r)/ *n* Gang *m*; (*Pol, Aviat*) Korridor *m*
corroborate /kə'rɒbəreɪt/ *vt* bestätigen
corro|de /kə'rəʊd/ *vt* zerfressen ● *vi* rosten. **~sion** /-'rəʊʒn/ *n* Korrosion *f*
corrugated /'kɒrəgeɪtɪd/ *a* gewellt. ~ **iron** *n* Wellblech *nt*
corrupt /kə'rʌpt/ *a* korrupt ● *vt* korrumpieren; (*spoil*) verderben. **~ion** /-ʌpʃn/ *n* Korruption *f*
corset /'kɔ:sɪt/ *n* & **-s** *pl* Korsett *nt*
Corsica /'kɔ:sɪkə/ *n* Korsika *nt*
cortège /kɔ:'teɪʒ/ *n* **[funeral]** ~ Leichenzug *m*
cosh /kɒʃ/ *n* Totschläger *m*
cosmetic /kɒz'metɪk/ *a* kosmetisch ● *n* **~s** *pl* Kosmetika *pl*
cosmic /'kɒzmɪk/ *a* kosmisch
cosmonaut /'kɒzmənɔ:t/ *n* Kosmonaut(in) *m*(*f*)
cosmopolitan /kɒzmə'pɒlɪtən/ *a* kosmopolitisch
cosmos /'kɒzmɒs/ *n* Kosmos *m*
cosset /'kɒsɪt/ *vt* verhätscheln
cost /kɒst/ *n* Kosten *pl*; **~s** *pl* (*Jur*) Kosten; **at all ~s** um jeden Preis; **I learnt to my ~** es ist mich teuer zu stehen gekommen ● *vt* (*pt/pp* **cost**) kosten; **it ~ me £20** es hat mich £20 gekostet ● *vt* (*pt/pp* **costed**) ~ **[out]** die Kosten kalkulieren für
costly /'kɒstlɪ/ *a* (**-ier, -iest**) teuer
cost: ~ of 'living *n* Lebenshaltungskosten *pl*. ~ **price** *n* Selbstkostenpreis *m*
costume /'kɒstju:m/ *n* Kostüm *nt*; (*national*) Tracht *f*. ~ **jewellery** *n* Modeschmuck *m*
cosy /'kəʊzɪ/ *a* (**-ier, -iest**) gemütlich ● *n* (*tea-, egg-*) Wärmer *m*
cot /kɒt/ *n* Kinderbett *nt*; (*Amer: camp-bed*) Feldbett *nt*
cottage /'kɒtɪdʒ/ *n* Häuschen *nt*. ~ **'cheese** *n* Hüttenkäse *m*
cotton /'kɒtn/ *n* Baumwolle *f*; (*thread*) Nähgarn *nt* ● *a* baumwollen ● *vi* ~ **on** (*fam*) kapieren
cotton 'wool *n* Watte *f*
couch /kaʊtʃ/ *n* Liege *f*
couchette /ku:'ʃet/ *n* (*Rail*) Liegeplatz *m*
cough /kɒf/ *n* Husten *m* ● *vi* husten. ~ **up** *vt/i* husten; (*fam: pay*) blechen
'cough mixture *n* Hustensaft *m*
could /kʊd, *unbetont* kəd/ *see* **can**[2]
council /'kaʊnsl/ *n* Rat *m*; (*Admin*) Stadtverwaltung *f*; (*rural*) Gemeindeverwaltung *f*. ~ **house** *n* ≈ Sozialwohnung *f*
councillor /'kaʊnsələ(r)/ *n* Stadtverordnete(r) *m/f*
'council tax *n* Gemeindesteuer *f*
counsel /'kaʊnsl/ *n* Rat *m*; (*Jur*) Anwalt *m* ● *vt* (*pt/pp* **counselled**) beraten. **~lor** *n* Berater(in) *m*(*f*)
count[1] /kaʊnt/ *n* Graf *m*
count[2] *n* Zählung *f*; **keep ~** zählen ● *vt/i* zählen. ~ **on** *vt* rechnen auf (+ *acc*)
countenance /'kaʊntənəns/ *n* Gesicht *nt* ● *vt* dulden
counter[1] /'kaʊntə(r)/ *n* (*in shop*) Ladentisch *m*; (*in bank*) Schalter *m*; (*in café*) Theke *f*; (*Games*) Spielmarke *f*
counter[2] *adv* ~ **to** gegen (+ *acc*) ● *a* Gegen- ● *vt/i* kontern
counter'act *vt* entgegenwirken (+ *dat*)
'counter-attack *n* Gegenangriff *m*
counter-'espionage *n* Spionageabwehr *f*
'counterfeit /-fɪt/ *a* gefälscht ● *n* Fälschung *f* ● *vt* fälschen
'counterfoil *n* Kontrollabschnitt *m*
'counterpart *n* Gegenstück *nt*
counter-pro'ductive *a* **be ~** das Gegenteil bewirken
'countersign *vt* gegenzeichnen
countess /'kaʊntɪs/ *n* Gräfin *f*

countless /ˈkaʊntlɪs/ *a* unzählig
countrified /ˈkʌntrɪfaɪd/ *a* ländlich
country /ˈkʌntrɪ/ *n* Land *nt*; (*native land*) Heimat *f*; (*countryside*) Landschaft *f*; **in the ~** auf dem Lande. **~man** *n* **[fellow] ~man** Landsmann *m*. **~side** *n* Landschaft *f*
county /ˈkaʊntɪ/ *n* Grafschaft *f*
coup /kuː/ *n* (*Pol*) Staatsstreich *m*
couple /ˈkʌpl/ *n* Paar *nt*; **a ~ of** (*two*) zwei ● *vt* verbinden; (*Rail*) koppeln
coupon /ˈkuːpɒn/ *n* Kupon *m*; (*voucher*) Gutschein *m*; (*entry form*) Schein *m*
courage /ˈkʌrɪdʒ/ *n* Mut *m*. **~ous** /kəˈreɪdʒəs/ *a*, **-ly** *adv* mutig
courgettes /kʊəˈʒets/ *npl* Zucchini *pl*
courier /ˈkʊrɪə(r)/ *n* Bote *m*; (*diplomatic*) Kurier *m*; (*for tourists*) Reiseleiter(in) *m*(*f*)
course /kɔːs/ *n* (*Naut, Sch*) Kurs *m*; (*Culin*) Gang *m*; (*for golf*) Platz *m*; **~ of treatment** (*Med*) Kur *f*; **of ~** natürlich, selbstverständlich; **in the ~ of** im Lauf[e] (+ *gen*)
court /kɔːt/ *n* Hof *m*; (*Sport*) Platz *m*; (*Jur*) Gericht *nt* ● *vt* werben um; herausfordern ⟨*danger*⟩
courteous /ˈkɜːtɪəs/ *a*, **-ly** *adv* höflich
courtesy /ˈkɜːtəsɪ/ *n* Höflichkeit *f*
court: ~ 'martial *n* (*pl* **~s martial**) Militärgericht *nt*. **~ shoes** *npl* Pumps *pl*. **~yard** *n* Hof *m*
cousin /ˈkʌzn/ *n* Vetter *m*, Cousin *m*; (*female*) Kusine *f*
cove /kəʊv/ *n* kleine Bucht *f*
cover /ˈkʌvə(r)/ *n* Decke *f*; (*of cushion*) Bezug *m*; (*of umbrella*) Hülle *f*; (*of typewriter*) Haube *f*; (*of book, lid*) Deckel *m*; (*of magazine*) Umschlag *m*; (*protection*) Deckung *f*, Schutz *m*; **take ~** Deckung nehmen; **under separate ~** mit getrennter Post ● *vt* bedecken; beziehen ⟨*cushion*⟩; decken ⟨*costs, needs*⟩; zurücklegen ⟨*distance*⟩; (*Journ*) berichten über (+ *acc*); (*insure*) versichern. **~ up** *vt* zudecken; (*fig*) vertuschen
coverage /ˈkʌvərɪdʒ/ *n* (*Journ*) Berichterstattung *f* (**of** über + *acc*)
cover: ~ charge *n* Gedeck *nt*. **~ing** *n* Decke *f*; (*for floor*) Belag *m*. **~-up** *n* Vertuschung *f*
covet /ˈkʌvɪt/ *vt* begehren
cow /kaʊ/ *n* Kuh *f*
coward /ˈkaʊəd/ *n* Feigling *m*. **~ice** /-ɪs/ *n* Feigheit *f*. **~ly** *a* feige
'cowboy *n* Cowboy *m*; (*fam*) unsolider Handwerker *m*
cower /ˈkaʊə(r)/ *vi* sich [ängstlich] ducken
'cowshed *n* Kuhstall *m*
cox /kɒks/ *n*, **coxswain** /ˈkɒksn/ *n* Steuermann *m*
coy /kɔɪ/ *a* (**-er, -est**) gespielt schüchtern
crab /kræb/ *n* Krabbe *f*. **~-apple** *n* Holzapfel *m*
crack /kræk/ *n* Riß *m*; (*in china, glass*) Sprung *m*; (*noise*) Knall *m*; (*fam: joke*) Witz *m*; (*fam: attempt*) Versuch *m* ● *a* (*fam*) erstklassig ● *vt* knacken ⟨*nut, code*⟩; einen Sprung machen in (+ *acc*) ⟨*china, glass*⟩; (*fam*) reißen ⟨*joke*⟩; (*fam*) lösen ⟨*problem*⟩ ● *vi* ⟨*china, glass:*⟩ springen; ⟨*whip:*⟩ knallen. **~ down** *vi* (*fam*) durchgreifen
cracked /krækt/ *a* gesprungen; ⟨*rib*⟩ angebrochen; (*fam: crazy*) verrückt
cracker /ˈkrækə(r)/ *n* (*biscuit*) Kräcker *m*; (*firework*) Knallkörper *m*; **[Christmas] ~** Knallbonbon *m*. **~s** *a* **be ~s** (*fam*) einen Knacks haben
crackle /ˈkrækl/ *vi* knistern
cradle /ˈkreɪdl/ *n* Wiege *f*
craft[1] /krɑːft/ *n inv* (*boat*) [Wasser]fahrzeug *nt*
craft[2] *n* Handwerk *nt*; (*technique*) Fertigkeit *f*. **~sman** *n* Handwerker *m*
crafty /ˈkrɑːftɪ/ *a* (**-ier, -iest**), **-ily** *adv* gerissen
crag /kræg/ *n* Felszacken *m*. **~gy** *a* felsig; ⟨*face*⟩ kantig
cram /kræm/ *v* (*pt/pp* **crammed**) ● *vt* hineinstopfen (**into** in + *acc*); vollstopfen (**with** mit) ● *vi* (*for exams*) pauken
cramp /kræmp/ *n* Krampf *m*. **~ed** *a* eng
crampon /ˈkræmpən/ *n* Steigeisen *nt*
cranberry /ˈkrænbərɪ/ *n* (*Culin*) Preiselbeere *f*
crane /kreɪn/ *n* Kran *m*; (*bird*) Kranich *m* ● *vt* **~ one's neck** den Hals recken
crank[1] /kræŋk/ *n* (*fam*) Exzentriker *m*
crank[2] *n* (*Techn*) Kurbel *f*. **~shaft** *n* Kurbelwelle *f*
cranky /ˈkræŋkɪ/ *a* exzentrisch; (*Amer: irritable*) reizbar
cranny /ˈkrænɪ/ *n* Ritze *f*
crash /kræʃ/ *n* (*noise*) Krach *m*; (*Auto*) Zusammenstoß *m*; (*Aviat*) Absturz *m* ● *vi* krachen (**into** gegen);

⟨*cars:*⟩ zusammenstoßen; ⟨*plane:*⟩ abstürzen ● *vt* einen Unfall haben mit ⟨*car*⟩

crash: ~ course *n* Schnellkurs *m*. **~-helmet** *n* Sturzhelm *m*. **~-landing** *n* Bruchlandung *f*

crate /kreɪt/ *n* Kiste *f*

crater /'kreɪtə(r)/ *n* Krater *m*

cravat /krə'væt/ *n* Halstuch *nt*

crav|e /kreɪv/ *vi* **~e for** sich sehnen nach. **~ing** *n* Gelüst *nt*

crawl /krɔ:l/ *n* (*Swimming*) Kraul *nt*; **do the ~** kraulen; **at a ~** im Kriechtempo ● *vi* kriechen; ⟨*baby:*⟩ krabbeln; **~ with** wimmeln von. **~er lane** *n* (*Auto*) Kriechspur *f*

crayon /'kreɪən/ *n* Wachsstift *m*; (*pencil*) Buntstift *m*

craze /kreɪz/ *n* Mode *f*

crazy /'kreɪzɪ/ *a* (**-ier, -iest**) verrückt; **be ~ about** verrückt sein nach

creak /kri:k/ *n* Knarren *nt* ● *vi* knarren

cream /kri:m/ *n* Sahne *f*; (*Cosmetic, Med, Culin*) Creme *f* ● *a* (*colour*) cremefarben ● *vt* (*Culin*) cremig rühren. **~ 'cheese** *n* ≈ Quark *m*. **~y** *a* sahnig; (*smooth*) cremig

crease /kri:s/ *n* Falte *f*; (*unwanted*) Knitterfalte *f* ● *vt* falten; (*accidentally*) zerknittern ● *vi* knittern. **~-resistant** *a* knitterfrei

creat|e /kri:'eɪt/ *vt* schaffen. **~ion** /-'eɪʃn/ *n* Schöpfung *f*. **~ive** /-tɪv/ *a* schöpferisch. **~or** *n* Schöpfer *m*

creature /'kri:tʃə(r)/ *n* Geschöpf *nt*

crèche /kreʃ/ *n* Kinderkrippe *f*

credentials /krɪ'denʃlz/ *npl* Beglaubigungsschreiben *nt*

credibility /kredə'bɪlətɪ/ *n* Glaubwürdigkeit *f*

credible /'kredəbl/ *a* glaubwürdig

credit /'kredɪt/ *n* Kredit *m*; (*honour*) Ehre *f* ● *vt* glauben; **~ s.o. with sth** (*Comm*) jdm etw gutschreiben; (*fig*) jdm etw zuschreiben. **~able** /-əbl/ *a* lobenswert

credit: ~ card *n* Kreditkarte *f*. **~or** *n* Gläubiger *m*

creed /kri:d/ *n* Glaubensbekenntnis *nt*

creek /kri:k/ *n* enge Bucht *f*; (*Amer: stream*) Bach *m*

creep /kri:p/ *vi* (*pt/pp* **crept**) schleichen ● *n* (*fam*) fieser Kerl *m*; **it gives me the ~s** es ist mir unheimlich. **~er** *n* Kletterpflanze *f*. **~y** *a* gruselig

cremat|e /krɪ'meɪt/ *vt* einäschern. **~ion** /-eɪʃn/ *n* Einäscherung *f*

crematorium /kremə'tɔ:rɪəm/ *n* Krematorium *nt*

crêpe /kreɪp/ *n* Krepp *m*. **~ paper** *n* Kreppapier *nt*

crept /krept/ *see* **creep**

crescent /'kresənt/ *n* Halbmond *m*

cress /kres/ *n* Kresse *f*

crest /krest/ *n* Kamm *m*; (*coat of arms*) Wappen *nt*

Crete /kri:t/ *n* Kreta *nt*

crevasse /krɪ'væs/ *n* [Gletscher]-spalte *f*

crevice /'krevɪs/ *n* Spalte *f*

crew /kru:/ *n* Besatzung *f*; (*gang*) Bande *f*. **~ cut** *n* Bürstenschnitt *m*

crib[1] /krɪb/ *n* Krippe *f*

crib[2] *vt/i* (*pt/pp* **cribbed**) (*fam*) abschreiben

crick /krɪk/ *n* **~ in the neck** steifes Genick *nt*

cricket[1] /'krɪkɪt/ *n* (*insect*) Grille *f*

cricket[2] *n* Kricket *nt*. **~er** *n* Kricketspieler *m*

crime /kraɪm/ *n* Verbrechen *nt*; (*rate*) Kriminalität *f*

criminal /'krɪmɪnl/ *a* kriminell, verbrecherisch; ⟨*law, court*⟩ Straf- ● *n* Verbrecher *m*

crimson /'krɪmzn/ *a* purpurrot

cringe /krɪndʒ/ *vi* sich [ängstlich] ducken

crinkle /'krɪŋkl/ *vt/i* knittern

cripple /'krɪpl/ *n* Krüppel *m* ● *vt* zum Krüppel machen; (*fig*) lahmlegen. **~d** *a* verkrüppelt

crisis /'kraɪsɪs/ *n* (*pl* **-ses** /-si:z/) Krise *f*

crisp /krɪsp/ *a* (**-er, -est**) knusprig. **~bread** *n* Knäckebrot *nt*. **~s** *npl* Chips *pl*

criss-cross /'krɪs-/ *a* schräg gekreuzt

criterion /kraɪ'tɪərɪən/ *n* (*pl* **-ria** /-rɪə/) Kriterium *nt*

critic /'krɪtɪk/ *n* Kritiker *m*. **~al** *a* kritisch. **~ally** *adv* kritisch; **~ally ill** schwer krank

criticism /'krɪtɪsɪzm/ *n* Kritik *f*

criticize /'krɪtɪsaɪz/ *vt* kritisieren

croak /krəʊk/ *vi* krächzen; ⟨*frog:*⟩ quaken

crochet /'krəʊʃeɪ/ *n* Häkelarbeit *f* ● *vt/i* häkeln. **~-hook** *n* Häkelnadel *f*

crock /krɒk/ *n* (*fam*) **old ~** (*person*) Wrack *m*; (*car*) Klapperkiste *f*

crockery /'krɒkərɪ/ *n* Geschirr *nt*

crocodile /'krɒkədaɪl/ *n* Krokodil *nt*

crocus /'krəʊkəs/ *n* (*pl* **-es**) Krokus *m*

crony /ˈkrəʊnɪ/ *n* Kumpel *m*
crook /krʊk/ *n* (*stick*) Stab *m*; (*fam: criminal*) Schwindler *m*, Gauner *m*
crooked /ˈkrʊkɪd/ *a* schief; (*bent*) krumm; (*fam: dishonest*) unehrlich
crop /krɒp/ *n* Feldfrucht *f*; (*harvest*) Ernte *f*; (*of bird*) Kropf *m* ● *v* (*pt/pp* **cropped**) ● *vt* stutzen ● *vi* ~ **up** (*fam*) zur Sprache kommen; (*occur*) dazwischenkommen
croquet /ˈkrəʊkeɪ/ *n* Krocket *nt*
croquette /krəʊˈket/ *n* Krokette *f*
cross /krɒs/ *a*, **-ly** *adv* (*annoyed*) böse (**with** auf + *acc*); **talk at ~ purposes** aneinander vorbeireden ● *n* Kreuz *nt*; (*Bot, Zool*) Kreuzung *f*; **on the ~** schräg ● *vt* kreuzen ⟨*cheque, animals*⟩; überqueren ⟨*road*⟩; **~ oneself** sich bekreuzigen; **~ one's arms** die Arme verschränken; **~ one's legs** die Beine übereinanderschlagen; **keep one's fingers ~ed for s.o.** jdm die Daumen drücken; **it ~ed my mind** es fiel mir ein ● *vi* (*go across*) hinübergehen/-fahren; ⟨*lines:*⟩ sich kreuzen. **~ out** *vt* durchstreichen
cross: ~bar *n* Querlatte *f*; (*on bicycle*) Stange *f*. **~-ˈcountry** *n* (*Sport*) Crosslauf *m*. **~-exˈamine** *vt* ins Kreuzverhör nehmen. **~-examiˈnation** *n* Kreuzverhör *nt*. **~-ˈeyed** *a* schielend; **be ~-eyed** schielen. **~fire** *n* Kreuzfeuer *nt*. **~ing** *n* Übergang *m*; (*sea journey*) Überfahrt *f*. **~-ˈreference** *n* Querverweis *m*. **~roads** *n* [Straßen]kreuzung *f*. **~-ˈsection** *n* Querschnitt *m*. **~-stitch** *n* Kreuzstich *m*. **~wise** *adv* quer. **~word** *n* **~word [puzzle]** Kreuzworträtsel *nt*
crotchet /ˈkrɒtʃɪt/ *n* Viertelnote *f*
crotchety /ˈkrɒtʃɪtɪ/ *a* griesgrämig
crouch /kraʊtʃ/ *vi* kauern
crow /krəʊ/ *n* Krähe *f*; **as the ~ flies** Luftlinie ● *vi* krähen. **~bar** *n* Brechstange *f*
crowd /kraʊd/ *n* [Menschen]menge *f* ● *vi* sich drängen. **~ed** /ˈkraʊdɪd/ *a* [gedrängt] voll
crown /kraʊn/ *n* Krone *f* ● *vt* krönen; überkronen ⟨*tooth*⟩
crucial /ˈkruːʃl/ *a* höchst wichtig; (*decisive*) entscheidend (**to** für)
crucifix /ˈkruːsɪfɪks/ *n* Kruzifix *nt*
crucif|ixion /kruːsɪˈfɪkʃn/ *n* Kreuzigung *f*. **~y** /ˈkruːsɪfaɪ/ *vt* (*pt/pp* **-ied**) kreuzigen
crude /kruːd/ *a* (**-r, -st**) (*raw*) roh
cruel /ˈkruːəl/ *a* (**crueller, cruellest**), **-ly** *adv* grausam (**to** gegen). **~ty** *n* Grausamkeit *f*; **~ty to animals** Tierquälerei *f*
cruis|e /kruːz/ *n* Kreuzfahrt *f* ● *vi* kreuzen; ⟨*car:*⟩ fahren. **~er** *n* (*Mil*) Kreuzer *m*; (*motor boat*) Kajütboot *nt*. **~ing speed** *n* Reisegeschwindigkeit *f*
crumb /krʌm/ *n* Krümel *m*
crumb|le /ˈkrʌmbl/ *vt/i* krümeln; (*collapse*) einstürzen. **~ly** *a* krümelig
crumple /ˈkrʌmpl/ *vt* zerknittern ● *vi* knittern
crunch /krʌntʃ/ *n* (*fam*) **when it comes to the ~** wenn es [wirklich] drauf ankommt ● *vt* mampfen ● *vi* knirschen
crusade /kruːˈseɪd/ *n* Kreuzzug *m*; (*fig*) Kampagne *f*. **~r** *n* Kreuzfahrer *m*; (*fig*) Kämpfer *m*
crush /krʌʃ/ *n* (*crowd*) Gedränge *nt* ● *vt* zerquetschen; zerknittern ⟨*clothes*⟩; (*fig: subdue*) niederschlagen
crust /krʌst/ *n* Kruste *f*
crutch /krʌtʃ/ *n* Krücke *f*
crux /krʌks/ *n* (*fig*) springender Punkt *m*
cry /kraɪ/ *n* Ruf *m*; (*shout*) Schrei *m*; **a far ~ from** (*fig*) weit entfernt von ● *vi* (*pt/pp* **cried**) (*weep*) weinen; ⟨*baby:*⟩ schreien; (*call*) rufen
crypt /krɪpt/ *n* Krypta *f*. **~ic** *a* rätselhaft
crystal /ˈkrɪstl/ *n* Kristall *m*; (*glass*) Kristall *nt*. **~lize** *vi* [sich] kristallisieren
cub /kʌb/ *n* (*Zool*) Junge(s) *nt*; **C~ [Scout]** Wölfling *m*
Cuba /ˈkjuːbə/ *n* Kuba *nt*
cubby-hole /ˈkʌbɪ-/ *n* Fach *nt*
cub|e /kjuːb/ *n* Würfel *m*. **~ic** *a* Kubik-
cubicle /ˈkjuːbɪkl/ *n* Kabine *f*
cuckoo /ˈkʊkuː/ *n* Kuckuck *m*. **~ clock** *n* Kuckucksuhr *f*
cucumber /ˈkjuːkʌmbə(r)/ *n* Gurke *f*
cuddl|e /ˈkʌdl/ *vt* herzen ● *vi* **~e up to** sich kuscheln an (+ *acc*). **~y** *a* kuschelig. **~y ˈtoy** *n* Plüschtier *nt*
cudgel /ˈkʌdʒl/ *n* Knüppel *m*
cue[1] /kjuː/ *n* Stichwort *nt*
cue[2] *n* (*Billiards*) Queue *nt*
cuff /kʌf/ *n* Manschette *f*; (*Amer: turn-up*) [Hosen]aufschlag *m*; (*blow*) Klaps *m*; **off the ~** (*fam*) aus dem Stegreif ● *vt* einen Klaps geben (+ *dat*). **~-link** *n* Manschettenknopf *m*

cul-de-sac /ˈkʌldəsæk/ *n* Sackgasse *f*
culinary /ˈkʌlɪnərɪ/ *a* kulinarisch
cull /kʌl/ *vt* pflücken ⟨*flowers*⟩; (*kill*) ausmerzen
culminat|e /ˈkʌlmɪneɪt/ *vi* gipfeln (**in** in + *dat*). **~ion** /-ˈneɪʃn/ *n* Gipfelpunkt *m*
culottes /kju:ˈlɒts/ *npl* Hosenrock *m*
culprit /ˈkʌlprɪt/ *n* Täter *m*
cult /kʌlt/ *n* Kult *m*
cultivate /ˈkʌltɪveɪt/ *vt* anbauen ⟨*crop*⟩; bebauen ⟨*land*⟩
cultural /ˈkʌltʃərəl/ *a* kulturell
culture /ˈkʌltʃə(r)/ *n* Kultur *f*. **~d** *a* kultiviert
cumbersome /ˈkʌmbəsəm/ *a* hinderlich; (*unwieldy*) unhandlich
cumulative /ˈkju:mjʊlətɪv/ *a* kumulativ
cunning /ˈkʌnɪŋ/ *a* listig ● *n* List *f*
cup /kʌp/ *n* Tasse *f*; (*prize*) Pokal *m*
cupboard /ˈkʌbəd/ *n* Schrank *m*
Cup 'Final *n* Pokalendspiel *nt*
Cupid /ˈkju:pɪd/ *n* Amor *m*
curable /ˈkjʊərəbl/ *a* heilbar
curate /ˈkjʊərət/ *n* Vikar *m*; (*Roman Catholic*) Kaplan *m*
curator /kjʊəˈreɪtə(r)/ *n* Kustos *m*
curb /kɜ:b/ *vt* zügeln
curdle /ˈkɜ:dl/ *vi* gerinnen
cure /kjʊə(r)/ *n* [Heil]mittel *nt* ● *vt* heilen; (*salt*) pökeln; (*smoke*) räuchern; gerben ⟨*skin*⟩
curfew /ˈkɜ:fju:/ *n* Ausgangssperre *f*
curio /ˈkjʊərɪəʊ/ *n* Kuriosität *f*
curiosity /kjʊərɪˈɒsətɪ/ *n* Neugier *f*; (*object*) Kuriosität *f*
curious /ˈkjʊərɪəs/ *a*, **-ly** *adv* neugierig; (*strange*) merkwürdig, seltsam
curl /kɜ:l/ *n* Locke *f* ● *vt* locken ● *vi* sich locken. **~ up** *vi* sich zusammenrollen
curler /ˈkɜ:lə(r)/ *n* Lockenwickler *m*
curly /ˈkɜ:lɪ/ *a* (**-ier, -iest**) lockig
currant /ˈkʌrənt/ *n* (*dried*) Korinthe *f*
currency /ˈkʌrənsɪ/ *n* Geläufigkeit *f*; (*money*) Währung *f*; **foreign ~** Devisen *pl*
current /ˈkʌrənt/ *a* augenblicklich, gegenwärtig; (*in general use*) geläufig, gebräuchlich ● *n* Strömung *f*; (*Electr*) Strom *m*. **~ affairs** *or* **events** *npl* Aktuelle(s) *nt*. **~ly** *adv* zur Zeit
curriculum /kəˈrɪkjʊləm/ *n* Lehrplan *m*. **~ vitae** /-ˈvi:taɪ/ *n* Lebenslauf *m*
curry /ˈkʌrɪ/ *n* Curry *nt & m*; (*meal*) Currygericht *nt* ● *vt* (*pt/pp* **-ied**) **~ favour** sich einschmeicheln (**with** bei)
curse /kɜ:s/ *n* Fluch *m* ● *vt* verfluchen ● *vi* fluchen
cursory /ˈkɜ:sərɪ/ *a* flüchtig
curt /kɜ:t/ *a*, **-ly** *adv* barsch
curtail /kɜ:ˈteɪl/ *vt* abkürzen
curtain /ˈkɜ:tn/ *n* Vorhang *m*
curtsy /ˈkɜ:tsɪ/ *n* Knicks *m* ● *vi* (*pt/pp* **-ied**) knicksen
curve /kɜ:v/ *n* Kurve *f* ● *vi* einen Bogen machen; **~ to the right/left** nach rechts/links biegen. **~d** *a* gebogen
cushion /ˈkʊʃn/ *n* Kissen *nt* ● *vt* dämpfen; (*protect*) beschützen
cushy /ˈkʊʃɪ/ *a* (**-ier, -iest**) (*fam*) bequem
custard /ˈkʌstəd/ *n* Vanillesoße *f*
custodian /kʌˈstəʊdɪən/ *n* Hüter *m*
custody /ˈkʌstədɪ/ *n* Obhut *f*; (*of child*) Sorgerecht *nt*; (*imprisonment*) Haft *f*
custom /ˈkʌstəm/ *n* Brauch *m*; (*habit*) Gewohnheit *f*; (*Comm*) Kundschaft *f*. **~ary** *a* üblich; (*habitual*) gewohnt. **~er** *n* Kunde *m*/Kundin *f*
customs /ˈkʌstəmz/ *npl* Zoll *m*. **~ officer** *n* Zollbeamte(r) *m*
cut /kʌt/ *n* Schnitt *m*; (*Med*) Schnittwunde *f*; (*reduction*) Kürzung *f*; (*in price*) Senkung *f*; **~ [of meat]** [Fleisch]stück *nt* ● *vt/i* (*pt/pp* **cut**, *pres p* **cutting**) schneiden; (*mow*) mähen; abheben ⟨*cards*⟩; (*reduce*) kürzen; senken ⟨*price*⟩; **~ one's finger** sich in den Finger schneiden; **~ s.o.'s hair** jdm die Haare schneiden; **~ short** abkürzen. **~ back** *vt* zurückschneiden; (*fig*) einschränken, kürzen. **~ down** *vt* fällen; (*fig*) einschränken. **~ off** *vt* abschneiden; (*disconnect*) abstellen; **be ~ off** (*Teleph*) unterbrochen werden. **~ out** *vt* ausschneiden; (*delete*) streichen; **be ~ out for** (*fam*) geeignet sein zu. **~ up** *vt* zerschneiden; (*slice*) aufschneiden
'cut-back *n* Kürzung *f*, Einschränkung *f*
cute /kju:t/ *a* (**-r, -st**) (*fam*) niedlich
cut 'glass *n* Kristall *nt*
cuticle /ˈkju:tɪkl/ *n* Nagelhaut *f*
cutlery /ˈkʌtlərɪ/ *n* Besteck *nt*
cutlet /ˈkʌtlɪt/ *n* Kotelett *nt*
'cut-price *a* verbilligt
cutting /ˈkʌtɪŋ/ *a* ⟨*remark*⟩ bissig ● *n* (*from newspaper*) Ausschnitt *m*; (*of plant*) Ableger *m*

CV *abbr of* **curriculum vitae**
cyclamen /'sɪkləmən/ *n* Alpenveilchen *nt*
cycl|e /'saɪkl/ *n* Zyklus *m*; (*bicycle*) [Fahr]rad *nt* ● *vi* mit dem Rad fahren. **~ing** *n* Radfahren *nt*. **~ist** *n* Radfahrer(in) *m(f)*
cyclone /'saɪkləʊn/ *n* Wirbelsturm *m*
cylind|er /'sɪlɪndə(r)/ *n* Zylinder *m*. **~rical** /-'lɪndrɪkl/ *a* zylindrisch
cymbals /'sɪmblz/ *npl* (*Mus*) Becken *nt*
cynic /'sɪnɪk/ *n* Zyniker *m*. **~al** *a*, **-ly** *adv* zynisch. **~ism** /-sɪzm/ *n* Zynismus *m*
cypress /'saɪprəs/ *n* Zypresse *f*
Cyprus /'saɪprəs/ *n* Zypern *nt*
cyst /sɪst/ *n* Zyste *f*. **~itis** /-'taɪtɪs/ *n* Blasenentzündung *f*
Czech /tʃek/ *a* tschechisch ● *n* Tscheche *m*/Tschechin *f*
Czechoslovak /tʃekə'sləʊvæk/ *a* tschechoslowakisch. **~ia** /-'vækɪə/ *n* die Tschechoslowakei. **~ian** /-'vækɪən/ *a* tschechoslowakisch

D

dab /dæb/ *n* Tupfer *m*; (*of butter*) Klecks *m*; **a ~ of** ein bißchen ● *vt* (*pt/pp* **dabbed**) abtupfen; betupfen (**with** mit)
dabble /'dæbl/ *vi* **~ in sth** (*fig*) sich nebenbei mit etw befassen
dachshund /'dækshʊnd/ *n* Dackel *m*
dad[dy] /'dæd[i]/ *n* (*fam*) Vati *m*
daddy-'long-legs *n* [Kohl]schnake *f*; (*Amer: spider*) Weberknecht *m*
daffodil /'dæfədɪl/ *n* Osterglocke *f*, gelbe Narzisse *f*
daft /dɑ:ft/ *a* (**-er, -est**) dumm
dagger /'dægə(r)/ *n* Dolch *m*; (*Typ*) Kreuz *nt*; **be at ~s drawn** (*fam*) auf Kriegsfuß stehen
dahlia /'deɪlɪə/ *n* Dahlie *f*
daily /'deɪlɪ/ *a* & *adv* täglich ● *n* (*newspaper*) Tageszeitung *f*; (*fam: cleaner*) Putzfrau *f*
dainty /'deɪntɪ/ *a* (**-ier, -iest**) zierlich
dairy /'deərɪ/ *n* Molkerei *f*; (*shop*) Milchgeschäft *nt*. **~ cow** *n* Milchkuh *f*. **~ products** *pl* Milchprodukte *pl*
dais /'deɪɪs/ *n* Podium *nt*
daisy /'deɪzɪ/ *n* Gänseblümchen *nt*
dale /deɪl/ *n* (*liter*) Tal *nt*
dally /'dælɪ/ *vi* (*pt/pp* **-ied**) trödeln
dam /dæm/ *n* [Stau]damm *m* ● *vt* (*pt/pp* **dammed**) eindämmen
damag|e /'dæmɪdʒ/ *n* Schaden *m* (**to** an + *dat*); **~es** *pl* (*Jur*) Schadenersatz *m* ● *vt* beschädigen; (*fig*) beeinträchtigen. **~ing** *a* schädlich
damask /'dæməsk/ *n* Damast *m*
dame /deɪm/ *n* (*liter*) Dame *f*; (*Amer sl*) Weib *nt*
damn /dæm/ *a*, *int* & *adv* (*fam*) verdammt ● *n* **I don't care or give a ~** (*fam*) ich schere mich einen Dreck darum ● *vt* verdammen. **~ation** /-'neɪʃn/ *n* Verdammnis *f* ● *int* (*fam*) verdammt!
damp /dæmp/ *a* (**-er, -est**) feucht ● *n* Feuchtigkeit *f* ● *vt* = **dampen**
damp|en *vt* anfeuchten; (*fig*) dämpfen. **~ness** *n* Feuchtigkeit *f*
dance /dɑ:ns/ *n* Tanz *m*; (*function*) Tanzveranstaltung *f* ● *vt/i* tanzen. **~-hall** *n* Tanzlokal *nt*. **~ music** *n* Tanzmusik *f*
dancer /'dɑ:nsə(r)/ *n* Tänzer(in) *m(f)*
dandelion /'dændɪlaɪən/ *n* Löwenzahn *m*
dandruff /'dændrʌf/ *n* Schuppen *pl*
Dane /deɪn/ *n* Däne *m*/Dänin *f*; **Great ~** [deutsche] Dogge *f*
danger /'deɪndʒə(r)/ *n* Gefahr *f*; **in/out of ~** in/außer Gefahr. **~ous** /-rəs/ *a*, **-ly** *adv* gefährlich; **~ously ill** schwer erkrankt
dangle /'dæŋgl/ *vi* baumeln ● *vt* baumeln lassen
Danish /'deɪnɪʃ/ *a* dänisch. **~ 'pastry** *n* Hefeteilchen *nt*, Plunderstück *nt*
dank /dæŋk/ *a* (**-er, -est**) naßkalt
Danube /'dænju:b/ *n* Donau *f*
dare /deə(r)/ *n* Mutprobe *f* ● *vt/i* (*challenge*) herausfordern (**to** zu); **~ [to] do sth** [es] wagen, etw zu tun; **I ~ say!** das mag wohl sein! **~devil** *n* Draufgänger *m*
daring /'deərɪŋ/ *a* verwegen ● *n* Verwegenheit *f*
dark /dɑ:k/ *a* (**-er, -est**) dunkel; **~ blue/brown** dunkelblau/-braun; **~ horse** (*fig*) stilles Wasser *nt*; **keep sth ~** (*fig*) etw geheimhalten ● *n* Dunkelheit *f*; **after ~** nach Einbruch der Dunkelheit; **in the ~** im Dunkeln; **keep in the ~** (*fig*) im dunkeln lassen
dark|en /'dɑ:kn/ *vt* verdunkeln ● *vi* dunkler werden. **~ness** *n* Dunkelheit *f*
'dark-room *n* Dunkelkammer *f*

darling /'dɑ:lɪŋ/ *a* allerliebst ● *n* Liebling *m*
darn /dɑ:n/ *vt* stopfen. **~ing-needle** *n* Stopfnadel *f*
dart /dɑ:t/ *n* Pfeil *m*; (*Sewing*) Abnäher *m*; **~s** *sg* (*game*) [Wurf]-pfeil *m* ● *vi* flitzen
dash /dæʃ/ *n* (*Typ*) Gedankenstrich *m*; (*in Morse*) Strich *m*; **a ~ of milk** ein Schuß Milch; **make a ~** losstürzen (**for** auf + *acc*) ● *vi* rennen ● *vt* schleudern. **~ off** *vi* losstürzen ● *vt* (*write quickly*) hinwerfen
'dashboard *n* Armaturenbrett *nt*
dashing /'dæʃɪŋ/ *a* schneidig
data /'deɪtə/ *npl & sg* Daten *pl*. **~ processing** *n* Datenverarbeitung *f*
date[1] /deɪt/ *n* (*fruit*) Dattel *f*
date[2] *n* Datum *nt*; (*fam*) Verabredung *f*; **to ~** bis heute; **out of ~** überholt; (*expired*) ungültig; **be up to ~** auf dem laufenden sein ● *vt/i* datieren; (*Amer, fam: go out with*) ausgehen mit; **~ back to** zurückgehen auf (+ *acc*)
dated /'deɪtɪd/ *a* altmodisch
'date-line *n* Datumsgrenze *f*
dative /'deɪtɪv/ *a & n* (*Gram*) **~ [case]** Dativ *m*
daub /dɔ:b/ *vt* beschmieren (**with** mit); schmieren ⟨*paint*⟩
daughter /'dɔ:tə(r)/ *n* Tochter *f*. **~-in-law** *n* (*pl* **~s-in-law**) Schwiegertochter *f*
daunt /dɔ:nt/ *vt* entmutigen; **nothing ~ed** unverzagt. **~less** *a* furchtlos
dawdle /'dɔ:dl/ *vi* trödeln
dawn /dɔ:n/ *n* Morgendämmerung *f*; **at ~** bei Tagesanbruch ● *vi* anbrechen; **it ~ed on me** (*fig*) es ging mir auf
day /deɪ/ *n* Tag *m*; **~ by ~** Tag für Tag; **~ after ~** Tag um Tag; **these ~s** heutzutage; **in those ~s** zu der Zeit; **it's had its ~** (*fam*) es hat ausgedient
day: ~break *n* **at ~break** bei Tagesanbruch *m*. **~-dream** *n* Tagtraum *m* ● *vi* [mit offenen Augen] träumen. **~light** *n* Tageslicht *nt*. **~ re'turn** *n* (*ticket*) Tagesrückfahrkarte *f*. **~time** *n* **in the ~time** am Tage
daze /deɪz/ *n* **in a ~** wie benommen. **~d** *a* benommen
dazzle /'dæzl/ *vt* blenden
deacon /'di:kn/ *n* Diakon *m*
dead /ded/ *a* tot; ⟨*flower*⟩ verwelkt; (*numb*) taub; **~ body** Leiche *f*; **be ~ on time** auf die Minute pünktlich kommen; **~ centre** genau in der Mitte ● *adv* **~ tired** todmüde; **~ slow** sehr langsam; **stop ~** stehenbleiben ● *n* **the ~** *pl* die Toten; **in the ~ of night** mitten in der Nacht
deaden /'dedn/ *vt* dämpfen ⟨*sound*⟩; betäuben ⟨*pain*⟩
dead: ~ 'end *n* Sackgasse *f*. **~ 'heat** *n* totes Rennen *nt*. **~line** *n* [letzter] Termin *m*. **~lock** *n* **reach ~lock** (*fig*) sich festfahren
deadly /'dedlɪ/ *a* (**-ier, -iest**) tödlich; (*fam: dreary*) sterbenslangweilig; **~ sins** *pl* Todsünden *pl*
deaf /def/ *a* (**-er, -est**) taub; **~ and dumb** taubstumm. **~-aid** *n* Hörgerät *nt*
deaf|en /'defn/ *vt* betäuben; (*permanently*) taub machen. **~ening** *a* ohrenbetäubend. **~ness** *n* Taubheit *f*
deal /di:l/ *n* (*transaction*) Geschäft *nt*; **whose ~?** (*Cards*) wer gibt? **a good** *or* **great ~** eine Menge; **get a raw ~** (*fam*) sehr schlecht abschneiden ● *v* (*pt/pp* **dealt** /delt/) ● *vt* (*Cards*) geben; **~ out** austeilen; **~ s.o. a blow** jdm einen Schlag versetzen ● *vi* **~ in** handeln mit; **~ with** zu tun haben mit; (*handle*) sich befassen mit; (*cope with*) fertig werden mit; (*be about*) handeln von; **that's been dealt with** das ist schon erledigt
deal|er /'di:lə(r)/ *n* Händler *m*; (*Cards*) Kartengeber *m*. **~ings** *npl* **have ~ings with** zu tun haben mit
dean /di:n/ *n* Dekan *m*
dear /dɪə(r)/ *a* (**-er, -est**) lieb; (*expensive*) teuer; (*in letter*) liebe(r,s)/(*formal*) sehr geehrte(r,s) ● *n* Liebe(r) *m/f* ● *int* **oh ~!** oje! **~ly** *adv* ⟨*love*⟩ sehr; ⟨*pay*⟩ teuer
dearth /dɜ:θ/ *n* Mangel *m* (**of** an + *dat*)
death /deθ/ *n* Tod *m*; **three ~s** drei Todesfälle. **~ certificate** *n* Sterbeurkunde *f*. **~ duty** *n* Erbschaftssteuer *f*
deathly *a* **~ silence** Totenstille *f* ● *adv* **~ pale** totenblaß
death: ~ penalty *n* Todesstrafe *f*. **~'s head** *n* Totenkopf *m*. **~-trap** *n* Todesfalle *f*
debar /dɪ'bɑ:(r)/ *vt* (*pt/pp* **debarred**) ausschließen
debase /dɪ'beɪs/ *vt* erniedrigen
debatable /dɪ'beɪtəbl/ *a* strittig
debate /dɪ'beɪt/ *n* Debatte *f* ● *vt/i* debattieren

debauchery /dɪ'bɔ:tʃərɪ/ *n* Ausschweifung *f*
debility /dɪ'bɪlətɪ/ *n* Entkräftung *f*
debit /'debɪt/ *n* Schuldbetrag *m*; **~ [side]** Soll *nt* ● *vt* (*pt/pp* **debited**) (*Comm*) belasten; abbuchen ⟨*sum*⟩
debris /'debri:/ *n* Trümmer *pl*
debt /det/ *n* Schuld *f*; **in ~** verschuldet. **~or** *n* Schuldner *m*
début /'deɪbu:/ *n* Debüt *nt*
decade /'dekeɪd/ *n* Jahrzehnt *nt*
decaden|ce /'dekədəns/ *n* Dekadenz *f*. **~t** *a* dekadent
decaffeinated /dɪ'kæfɪneɪtɪd/ *a* koffeinfrei
decant /dɪ'kænt/ *vt* umfüllen. **~er** *n* Karaffe *f*
decapitate /dɪ'kæpɪteit/ *vt* köpfen
decay /dɪ'keɪ/ *n* Verfall *m*; (*rot*) Verwesung *f*; (*of tooth*) Zahnfäule *f* ● *vi* verfallen; (*rot*) verwesen; ⟨*tooth:*⟩ schlecht werden
decease /dɪ'si:s/ *n* Ableben *nt*. **~d** *a* verstorben ● *n* **the ~d** der/die Verstorbene
deceit /dɪ'si:t/ *n* Täuschung *f*. **~ful** *a*, **-ly** *adv* unaufrichtig
deceive /dɪ'si:v/ *vt* täuschen; (*be unfaithful to*) betrügen
December /dɪ'sembə(r)/ *n* Dezember *m*
decency /'di:sənsɪ/ *n* Anstand *m*
decent /'di:sənt/ *a*, **-ly** *adv* anständig
decentralize /di:'sentrəlaɪz/ *vt* dezentralisieren
decept|ion /dɪ'sepʃn/ *n* Täuschung *f*; (*fraud*) Betrug *m*. **~ive** /-tɪv/ *a*, **-ly** *adv* täuschend
decibel /'desɪbel/ *n* Dezibel *nt*
decide /dɪ'saɪd/ *vt* entscheiden ● *vi* sich entscheiden (**on** für)
decided /dɪ'saɪdɪd/ *a*, **-ly** *adv* entschieden
deciduous /dɪ'sɪdjʊəs/ *a* **~ tree** Laubbaum *m*
decimal /'desɪml/ *a* Dezimal- ● *n* Dezimalzahl *f*. **~ 'point** *n* Komma *nt*. **~ system** *n* Dezimalsystem *nt*
decimate /'desɪmeɪt/ *vt* dezimieren
decipher /dɪ'saɪfə(r)/ *vt* entziffern
decision /dɪ'sɪʒn/ *n* Entscheidung *f*; (*firmness*) Entschlossenheit *f*
decisive /dɪ'saɪsɪv/ *a* ausschlaggebend; (*firm*) entschlossen
deck¹ /dek/ *vt* schmücken
deck² *n* (*Naut*) Deck *nt*; **on ~** an Deck; **top ~** (*of bus*) Oberdeck *nt*; **~ of cards** (*Amer*) [Karten]spiel *nt*. **~-chair** *n* Liegestuhl *m*
declaration /deklə'reɪʃn/ *n* Erklärung *f*
declare /dɪ'kleə(r)/ *vt* erklären; angeben ⟨*goods*⟩; **anything to ~?** etwas zu verzollen?
declension /dɪ'klenʃn/ *n* Deklination *f*
decline /dɪ'klaɪn/ *n* Rückgang *m*; (*in health*) Verfall *m* ● *vt* ablehnen; (*Gram*) deklinieren ● *vi* ablehnen; (*fall*) sinken; (*decrease*) nachlassen
decode /di:'kəʊd/ *vt* entschlüsseln
decompos|e /di:kəm'pəʊz/ *vi* sich zersetzen
décor /'deɪkɔ:(r)/ *n* Ausstattung *f*
decorat|e /'dekəreɪt/ *vt* (*adorn*) schmücken; verzieren ⟨*cake*⟩; (*paint*) streichen; (*wallpaper*) tapezieren; (*award medal to*) einen Orden verleihen (+ *dat*). **~ion** /-'reɪʃn/ *n* Verzierung *f*; (*medal*) Orden *m*; **~ions** *pl* Schmuck *m*. **~ive** /-rətɪv/ *a* dekorativ. **~or** *n* **painter and ~or** Maler und Tapezierer *m*
decorous /'dekərəs/ *a*, **-ly** *adv* schamhaft
decorum /dɪ'kɔ:rəm/ *n* Anstand *m*
decoy¹ /'di:kɔɪ/ *n* Lockvogel *m*
decoy² /dɪ'kɔɪ/ *vt* locken
decrease¹ /'di:kri:s/ *n* Verringerung *f*; (*in number*) Rückgang *m*; **be on the ~** zurückgehen
decrease² /dɪ'kri:s/ *vt* verringern; herabsetzen ⟨*price*⟩ ● *vi* sich verringern; ⟨*price:*⟩ sinken
decree /dɪ'kri:/ *n* Erlaß *m* ● *vt* (*pt/pp* **decreed**) verordnen
decrepit /dɪ'krepɪt/ *a* altersschwach
dedicat|e /'dedɪkeɪt/ *vt* widmen; (*Relig*) weihen. **~ed** *a* hingebungsvoll; ⟨*person*⟩ aufopfernd. **~ion** /-'keɪʃn/ *n* Hingabe *f*; (*in book*) Widmung *f*
deduce /dɪ'dju:s/ *vt* folgern (**from** aus)
deduct /dɪ'dʌkt/ *vt* abziehen
deduction /dɪ'dʌkʃn/ *n* Abzug *m*; (*conclusion*) Folgerung *f*
deed /di:d/ *n* Tat *f*; (*Jur*) Urkunde *f*
deem /di:m/ *vt* halten für
deep /di:p/ *a* (**-er, -est**), **-ly** *adv* tief; **go off the ~ end** (*fam*) auf die Palme gehen ● *adv* tief
deepen /'di:pn/ *vt* vertiefen ● *vi* tiefer werden; (*fig*) sich vertiefen
deep-'freeze *n* Gefriertruhe *f*; (*upright*) Gefrierschrank *m*
deer /dɪə(r)/ *n inv* Hirsch *m*; (*roe*) Reh *nt*

deface /dɪ'feɪs/ *vt* beschädigen
defamat|ion /defə'meɪʃn/ *n* Verleumdung *f*. **~ory** /dɪ'fæmətərɪ/ *a* verleumderisch
default /dɪ'fɔ:lt/ *n* (*Jur*) Nichtzahlung *f*; (*failure to appear*) Nichterscheinen *nt*; **win by ~** (*Sport*) kampflos gewinnen ● *vi* nicht zahlen; nicht erscheinen
defeat /dɪ'fi:t/ *n* Niederlage *f*; (*defeating*) Besiegung *f*; (*rejection*) Ablehnung *f* ● *vt* besiegen; ablehnen; (*frustrate*) vereiteln
defect[1] /dɪ'fekt/ *vi* (*Pol*) überlaufen
defect[2] /'di:fekt/ *n* Fehler *m*; (*Techn*) Defekt *m*. **~ive** /dɪ'fektɪv/ *a* fehlerhaft; (*Techn*) defekt
defence /dɪ'fens/ *n* Verteidigung *f*. **~less** *a* wehrlos
defend /dɪ'fend/ *vt* verteidigen; (*justify*) rechtfertigen. **~ant** *n* (*Jur*) Beklagte(r) *m*/*f*; (*in criminal court*) Angeklagte(r) *m*/*f*
defensive /dɪ'fensɪv/ *a* defensiv ● *n* Defensive *f*
defer /dɪ'fɜ:(r)/ *vt* (*pt*/*pp* **deferred**) (*postpone*) aufschieben; **~ to s.o.** sich jdm fügen
deferen|ce /'defərəns/ *n* Ehrerbietung *f*. **~tial** /-'renʃl/ *a*, **-ly** *adv* ehrerbietig
defian|ce /dɪ'faɪəns/ *n* Trotz *m*; **in ~ce of** zum Trotz (+ *dat*). **~t** *a*, **-ly** *adv* aufsässig
deficien|cy /dɪ'fɪʃənsɪ/ *n* Mangel *m*. **~t** *a* mangelhaft; **he is ~t in ...** ihm mangelt es an ... (*dat*)
deficit /'defɪsɪt/ *n* Defizit *nt*
defile /dɪ'faɪl/ *vt* (*fig*) schänden
define /dɪ'faɪn/ *vt* bestimmen; definieren ⟨*word*⟩
definite /'defɪnɪt/ *a*, **-ly** *adv* bestimmt; (*certain*) sicher
definition /defɪ'nɪʃn/ *n* Definition *f*; (*Phot, TV*) Schärfe *f*
definitive /dɪ'fɪnətɪv/ *a* endgültig; (*authoritative*) maßgeblich
deflat|e /dɪ'fleɪt/ *vt* die Luft auslassen aus. **~ion** /-eɪʃn/ *n* (*Comm*) Deflation *f*
deflect /dɪ'flekt/ *vt* ablenken
deform|ed /dɪ'fɔ:md/ *a* mißgebildet. **~ity** *n* Mißbildung *f*
defraud /dɪ'frɔ:d/ *vt* betrügen (**of** um)
defray /dɪ'freɪ/ *vt* bestreiten
defrost /di:'frɒst/ *vt* entfrosten; abtauen ⟨*fridge*⟩; auftauen ⟨*food*⟩
deft /deft/ *a* (**-er, -est**), **-ly** *adv* geschickt. **~ness** *n* Geschicklichkeit *f*
defunct /dɪ'fʌŋkt/ *a* aufgelöst; ⟨*law*⟩ außer Kraft gesetzt
defuse /di:'fju:z/ *vt* entschärfen
defy /dɪ'faɪ/ *vt* (*pt*/*pp* **-ied**) trotzen (+ *dat*); widerstehen (+ *dat*) ⟨*attempt*⟩
degenerate[1] /dɪ'dʒenəreɪt/ *vi* degenerieren; **~ into** (*fig*) ausarten in (+ *acc*)
degenerate[2] /dɪ'dʒenərət/ *a* degeneriert
degrading /dɪ'greɪdɪŋ/ *a* entwürdigend
degree /dɪ'gri:/ *n* Grad *m*; (*Univ*) akademischer Grad *m*; **20 ~s** 20 Grad
dehydrate /di:'haɪdreɪt/ *vt* Wasser entziehen (+ *dat*). **~d** /-ɪd/ *a* ausgetrocknet
de-ice /di:'aɪs/ *vt* enteisen
deign /deɪn/ *vi* **~ to do sth** sich herablassen, etw zu tun
deity /'di:ɪtɪ/ *n* Gottheit *f*
dejected /dɪ'dʒektɪd/ *a*, **-ly** *adv* niedergeschlagen
delay /dɪ'leɪ/ *n* Verzögerung *f*; (*of train, aircraft*) Verspätung *f*; **without ~** unverzüglich ● *vt* aufhalten; (*postpone*) aufschieben; **be ~ed** ⟨*person:*⟩ aufgehalten werden; ⟨*train, aircraft:*⟩ Verspätung haben ● *vi* zögern
delegate[1] /'delɪgət/ *n* Delegierte(r) *m*/*f*
delegat|e[2] /'delɪgeɪt/ *vt* delegieren. **~ion** /-'geɪʃn/ *n* Delegation *f*
delet|e /dɪ'li:t/ *vt* streichen. **~ion** /-i:ʃn/ *n* Streichung *f*
deliberate[1] /dɪ'lɪbərət/ *a*, **-ly** *adv* absichtlich; (*slow*) bedächtig
deliberat|e[2] /dɪ'lɪbəreɪt/ *vt*/*i* überlegen. **~ion** /-'reɪʃn/ *n* Überlegung *f*; **with ~ion** mit Bedacht
delicacy /'delɪkəsɪ/ *n* Feinheit *f*; Zartheit *f*; (*food*) Delikatesse *f*
delicate /'delɪkət/ *a* fein; ⟨*fabric, health*⟩ zart; ⟨*situation*⟩ heikel; ⟨*mechanism*⟩ empfindlich
delicatessen /delɪkə'tesn/ *n* Delikatessengeschäft *nt*
delicious /dɪ'lɪʃəs/ *a* köstlich
delight /dɪ'laɪt/ *n* Freude *f* ● *vt* entzücken ● *vi* **~ in** sich erfreuen an (+ *dat*). **~ed** *a* hocherfreut; **be ~ed** sich sehr freuen. **~ful** *a* reizend
delinquen|cy /dɪ'lɪŋkwənsɪ/ *n* Kriminalität *f*. **~t** *a* straffällig ● *n* Straffällige(r) *m*/*f*

deli|rious /dɪ'lɪrɪəs/ *a* **be ~rious** im Delirium sein. **~rium** /-rɪəm/ *n* Delirium *nt*

deliver /dɪ'lɪvə(r)/ *vt* liefern; zustellen ⟨*post, newspaper*⟩; halten ⟨*speech*⟩; überbringen ⟨*message*⟩; versetzen ⟨*blow*⟩; (*set free*) befreien; **~ a baby** ein Kind zur Welt bringen. **~ance** *n* Erlösung *f*. **~y** *n* Lieferung *f*; (*of post*) Zustellung *f*; (*Med*) Entbindung *f*; **cash on ~y** per Nachnahme

delta /'deltə/ *n* Delta *nt*

delude /dɪ'lu:d/ *vt* täuschen; **~ oneself** sich (*dat*) Illusionen machen

deluge /'delju:dʒ/ *n* Flut *f*; (*heavy rain*) schwerer Guß *m* • *vt* überschwemmen

delusion /dɪ'lu:ʒn/ *n* Täuschung *f*

de luxe /də'lʌks/ *a* Luxus-

delve /delv/ *vi* hineingreifen (**into** in + *acc*); (*fig*) eingehen (**into** auf + *acc*)

demand /dɪ'mɑ:nd/ *n* Forderung *f*; (*Comm*) Nachfrage *f*; **in ~** gefragt; **on ~** auf Verlangen • *vt* verlangen, fordern (**of/from** von). **~ing** *a* anspruchsvoll

demarcation /di:mɑ:'keɪʃn/ *n* Abgrenzung *f*

demean /dɪ'mi:n/ *vt* **~ oneself** sich erniedrigen

demeanour /dɪ'mi:nə(r)/ *n* Verhalten *nt*

demented /dɪ'mentɪd/ *a* verrückt

demise /dɪ'maɪz/ *n* Tod *m*

demister /di:'mɪstə(r)/ *n* (*Auto*) Defroster *m*

demo /'deməʊ/ *n* (*pl* **~s**) (*fam*) Demonstration *f*

demobilize /di:'məʊbɪlaɪz/ *vt* (*Mil*) entlassen

democracy /dɪ'mɒkrəsɪ/ *n* Demokratie *f*

democrat /'deməkræt/ *n* Demokrat *m*. **~ic** /-'krætɪk/ *a*, **-ally** *adv* demokratisch

demo|lish /dɪ'mɒlɪʃ/ *vt* abbrechen; (*destroy*) zerstören. **~lition** /demə'lɪʃn/ *n* Abbruch *m*

demon /'di:mən/ *n* Dämon *m*

demonstrat|e /'demənstreɪt/ *vt* beweisen; vorführen ⟨*appliance*⟩ • *vi* (*Pol*) demonstrieren. **~ion** /-'streɪʃn/ *n* Vorführung *f*; (*Pol*) Demonstration *f*

demonstrative /dɪ'mɒnstrətɪv/ *a* (*Gram*) demonstrativ; **be ~** seine Gefühle zeigen

demonstrator /'demənstreɪtə(r)/ *n* Vorführer *m*; (*Pol*) Demonstrant *m*

demoralize /dɪ'mɒrəlaɪz/ *vt* demoralisieren

demote /dɪ'məʊt/ *vt* degradieren

demure /dɪ'mjʊə(r)/ *a*, **-ly** *adv* sittsam

den /den/ *n* Höhle *f*; (*room*) Bude *f*

denial /dɪ'naɪəl/ *n* Leugnen *nt*; **official ~** Dementi *nt*

denigrate /'denɪgreɪt/ *vt* herabsetzen

denim /'denɪm/ *n* Jeansstoff *m*; **~s** *pl* Jeans *pl*

Denmark /'denmɑ:k/ *n* Dänemark *nt*

denomination /dɪnɒmɪ'neɪʃn/ *n* (*Relig*) Konfession *f*; (*money*) Nennwert *m*

denote /dɪ'nəʊt/ *vt* bezeichnen

denounce /dɪ'naʊns/ *vt* denunzieren; (*condemn*) verurteilen

dens|e /dens/ *a* (**-r, -st**), **-ly** *adv* dicht; (*fam: stupid*) blöd[e]. **~ity** *n* Dichte *f*

dent /dent/ *n* Delle *f*, Beule *f* • *vt* einbeulen; **~ed** /-ɪd/ verbeult

dental /'dentl/ *a* Zahn-; ⟨*treatment*⟩ zahnärztlich. **~ floss** /flɒs/ *n* Zahnseide *f*. **~ surgeon** *n* Zahnarzt *m*

dentist /'dentɪst/ *n* Zahnarzt *m*/-ärztin *f*. **~ry** *n* Zahnmedizin *f*

denture /'dentʃə(r)/ *n* Zahnprothese *f*; **~s** *pl* künstliches Gebiß *nt*

denude /dɪ'nju:d/ *vt* entblößen

denunciation /dɪnʌnsɪ'eɪʃn/ *n* Denunziation *f*; (*condemnation*) Verurteilung *f*

deny /dɪ'naɪ/ *vt* (*pt/pp* **-ied**) leugnen; (*officially*) dementieren; **~ s.o. sth** jdm etw verweigern

deodorant /di:'əʊdərənt/ *n* Deodorant *nt*

depart /dɪ'pɑ:t/ *vi* abfahren; (*Aviat*) abfliegen; (*go away*) weggehen/-fahren; (*deviate*) abweichen (**from** von)

department /dɪ'pɑ:tmənt/ *n* Abteilung *f*; (*Pol*) Ministerium *nt*. **~ store** *n* Kaufhaus *nt*

departure /dɪ'pɑ:tʃə(r)/ *n* Abfahrt *f*; (*Aviat*) Abflug *m*; (*from rule*) Abweichung *f*; **new ~** Neuerung *f*

depend /dɪ'pend/ *vi* abhängen (**on** von); (*rely*) sich verlassen (**on** auf + *acc*); **it all ~s** das kommt darauf an. **~able** /-əbl/ *a* zuverlässig. **~ant** *n* Abhängige(r) *m/f*. **~ence** *n* Abhängigkeit *f*. **~ent** *a* abhängig (**on** von)

depict /dɪ'pɪkt/ *vt* darstellen

depilatory /dɪ'pɪlətərɪ/ *n* Enthaarungsmittel *nt*

deplete /dɪ'pli:t/ *vt* verringern

deplor|able /dɪ'plɔ:rəbl/ *a* bedauerlich. **~e** *vt* bedauern

deploy /dɪ'plɔɪ/ *vt* (*Mil*) einsetzen • *vi* sich aufstellen

depopulate /di:'pɒpjʊleɪt/ *vt* entvölkern

deport /dɪ'pɔ:t/ *vt* deportieren, ausweisen. **~ation** /di:pɔ:'teɪʃn/ *n* Ausweisung *f*

deportment /dɪ'pɔ:tmənt/ *n* Haltung *f*

depose /dɪ'pəʊz/ *vt* absetzen

deposit /dɪ'pɒzɪt/ *n* Anzahlung *f*; (*against damage*) Kaution *f*; (*on bottle*) Pfand *nt*; (*sediment*) Bodensatz *m*; (*Geol*) Ablagerung *f* • *vt* (*pt/pp* **deposited**) legen; (*for safety*) deponieren; (*Geol*) ablagern. **~ account** *n* Sparkonto *nt*

depot /'depəʊ/ *n* Depot *nt*; (*Amer: railway station*) Bahnhof *m*

deprav|e /dɪ'preɪv/ *vt* verderben. **~ed** *a* verkommen. **~ity** /-'prævətɪ/ *n* Verderbtheit *f*

deprecate /'deprəkeɪt/ *vt* mißbilligen

depreciat|e /dɪ'pri:ʃɪeɪt/ *vi* an Wert verlieren. **~ion** /-'eɪʃn/ *n* Wertminderung *f*; (*Comm*) Abschreibung *f*

depress /dɪ'pres/ *vt* deprimieren; (*press down*) herunterdrücken. **~ed** *a* deprimiert; **~ed area** Notstandsgebiet *nt*. **~ing** *a* deprimierend. **~ion** /-eʃn/ *n* Vertiefung *f*; (*Med*) Depression *f*; (*Meteorol*) Tief *nt*

deprivation /deprɪ'veɪʃn/ *n* Entbehrung *f*

deprive /dɪ'praɪv/ *vt* entziehen; **~ s.o. of sth** jdm etw entziehen. **~d** *a* benachteiligt

depth /depθ/ *n* Tiefe *f*; **in ~** gründlich; **in the ~s of winter** im tiefsten Winter

deputation /depjʊ'teɪʃn/ *n* Abordnung *f*

deputize /'depjʊtaɪz/ *vi* **~ for** vertreten

deputy /'depjʊtɪ/ *n* Stellvertreter *m* • *attrib* stellvertretend

derail /dɪ'reɪl/ *vt* **be ~ed** entgleisen. **~ment** *n* Entgleisung *f*

deranged /dɪ'reɪndʒd/ *a* geistesgestört

derelict /'derəlɪkt/ *a* verfallen; (*abandoned*) verlassen

deri|de /dɪ'raɪd/ *vt* verhöhnen. **~sion** /-'rɪʒn/ *n* Hohn *m*

derisive /dɪ'raɪsɪv/ *a*, **-ly** *adv* höhnisch

derisory /dɪ'raɪsərɪ/ *a* höhnisch; ⟨*offer*⟩ lächerlich

derivation /derɪ'veɪʃn/ *n* Ableitung *f*

derivative /dɪ'rɪvətɪv/ *a* abgeleitet • *n* Ableitung *f*

derive /dɪ'raɪv/ *vt/i* (*obtain*) gewinnen (**from** aus); **be ~d from** ⟨*word:*⟩ hergeleitet sein aus

dermatologist /dɜ:mə'tɒlədʒɪst/ *n* Hautarzt *m*/-ärztin *f*

derogatory /dɪ'rɒgətrɪ/ *a* abfällig

derrick /'derɪk/ *n* Bohrturm *m*

derv /dɜ:v/ *n* Diesel[kraftstoff] *m*

descend /dɪ'send/ *vt/i* hinunter-/heruntergehen; ⟨*vehicle, lift:*⟩ hinunter-/herunterfahren; **be ~ed from** abstammen von. **~ant** *n* Nachkomme *m*

descent /dɪ'sent/ *n* Abstieg *m*; (*lineage*) Abstammung *f*

describe /dɪ'skraɪb/ *vt* beschreiben

descrip|tion /dɪ'skrɪpʃn/ *n* Beschreibung *f*; (*sort*) Art *f*. **~tive** /-tɪv/ *a* beschreibend; (*vivid*) anschaulich

desecrat|e /'desɪkreit/ *vt* entweihen. **~ion** /-'kreɪʃn/ *n* Entweihung *f*

desert[1] /'dezət/ *n* Wüste *f* • *a* Wüsten-; **~ island** verlassene Insel *f*

desert[2] /dɪ'zɜ:t/ *vt* verlassen • *vi* desertieren. **~ed** *a* verlassen. **~er** *n* (*Mil*) Deserteur *m*. **~ion** /-ɜ:ʃn/ *n* Fahnenflucht *f*

deserts /dɪ'zɜ:ts/ *npl* **get one's ~** seinen verdienten Lohn bekommen

deserv|e /dɪ'zɜ:v/ *vt* verdienen. **~edly** /-ɪdlɪ/ *adv* verdientermaßen. **~ing** *a* verdienstvoll; **~ing cause** guter Zweck *m*

design /dɪ'zaɪn/ *n* Entwurf *m*; (*pattern*) Muster *nt*; (*construction*) Konstruktion *f*; (*aim*) Absicht *f* • *vt* entwerfen; (*construct*) konstruieren; **be ~ed for** bestimmt sein für

designat|e /'dezɪgneɪt/ *vt* bezeichnen; (*appoint*) ernennen. **~ion** /-'neɪʃn/ *n* Bezeichnung *f*

designer /dɪ'zaɪnə(r)/ *n* Designer *m*; (*Techn*) Konstrukteur *m*; (*Theat*) Bühnenbildner *m*

desirable /dɪ'zaɪrəbl/ *a* wünschenswert; (*sexually*) begehrenswert

desire /dɪ'zaɪə(r)/ *n* Wunsch *m*; (*longing*) Verlangen *nt* (**for** nach); (*sexual*) Begierde *f* • *vt* [sich (*dat*)] wünschen; (*sexually*) begehren

desk /desk/ *n* Schreibtisch *m*; (*Sch*) Pult *nt*; (*Comm*) Kasse *f*; (*in hotel*) Rezeption *f*

desolat|e /'desələt/ *a* trostlos. **~ion** /-'leɪʃn/ *n* Trostlosigkeit *f*

despair /dɪ'speə(r)/ *n* Verzweiflung *f*; **in ~** verzweifelt ● *vi* verzweifeln

desperat|e /'despərət/ *a*, **-ly** *adv* verzweifelt; (*urgent*) dringend; **be ~e** ⟨*criminal:*⟩ zum Äußersten entschlossen sein; **be ~e for** dringend brauchen. **~ion** /-'reɪʃn/ *n* Verzweiflung *f*; **in ~ion** aus Verzweiflung

despicable /dɪ'spɪkəbl/ *a* verachtenswert

despise /dɪ'spaɪz/ *vt* verachten

despite /dɪ'spaɪt/ *prep* trotz (+ *gen*)

despondent /dɪ'spɒndənt/ *a* niedergeschlagen

despot /'despɒt/ *n* Despot *m*

dessert /dɪ'zɜ:t/ *n* Dessert *nt*, Nachtisch *m*. **~ spoon** *n* Dessertlöffel *m*

destination /destɪ'neɪʃn/ *n* [Reise]-ziel *nt*; (*of goods*) Bestimmungsort *m*

destine /'destɪn/ *vt* bestimmen

destiny /'destɪnɪ/ *n* Schicksal *nt*

destitute /'destɪtju:t/ *a* völlig mittellos

destroy /dɪ'strɔɪ/ *vt* zerstören; (*totally*) vernichten. **~er** *n* (*Naut*) Zerstörer *m*

destruc|tion /dɪ'strʌkʃn/ *n* Zerstörung *f*; Vernichtung *f*. **-tive** /-tɪv/ *a* zerstörerisch; (*fig*) destruktiv

detach /dɪ'tætʃ/ *vt* abnehmen; (*tear off*) abtrennen. **~able** /-əbl/ *a* abnehmbar. **~ed** *a* (*fig*) distanziert; **~ed house** Einzelhaus *nt*

detachment /dɪ'tætʃmənt/ *n* Distanz *f*; (*objectivity*) Abstand *m*; (*Mil*) Sonderkommando *nt*

detail /'di:teɪl/ *n* Einzelheit *f*, Detail *nt*; **in ~** ausführlich ● *vt* einzeln aufführen; (*Mil*) abkommandieren. **~ed** *a* ausführlich

detain /dɪ'teɪn/ *vt* aufhalten; ⟨*police:*⟩ in Haft behalten; (*take into custody*) in Haft nehmen. **~ee** /di:teɪ'ni:/ *n* Häftling *m*

detect /dɪ'tekt/ *vt* entdecken; (*perceive*) wahrnehmen. **~ion** /-ekʃn/ *n* Entdeckung *f*

detective /dɪ'tektɪv/ *n* Detektiv *m*. **~ story** *n* Detektivroman *m*

detector /dɪ'tektə(r)/ *n* Suchgerät *nt*; (*for metal*) Metalldetektor *m*

detention /dɪ'tenʃn/ *n* Haft *f*; (*Sch*) Nachsitzen *nt*

deter /dɪ'tɜ:(r)/ *vt* (*pt/pp* **deterred**) abschrecken; (*prevent*) abhalten

detergent /dɪ'tɜ:dʒənt/ *n* Waschmittel *nt*

deteriorat|e /dɪ'tɪərɪəreɪt/ *vi* sich verschlechtern. **~ion** /-'reɪʃn/ *n* Verschlechterung *f*

determination /dɪtɜ:mɪ'neɪʃn/ *n* Entschlossenheit *f*

determine /dɪ'tɜ:mɪn/ *vt* bestimmen; **~ to** (*resolve*) sich entschließen zu. **~d** *a* entschlossen

deterrent /dɪ'terənt/ *n* Abschreckungsmittel *nt*

detest /dɪ'test/ *vt* verabscheuen. **~able** /-əbl/ *a* abscheulich

detonat|e /'detəneɪt/ *vt* zünden ● *vi* explodieren. **~or** *n* Zünder *m*

detour /'di:tʊə(r)/ *n* Umweg *m*; (*for traffic*) Umleitung *f*

detract /dɪ'trækt/ *vi* **~ from** beeinträchtigen

detriment /'detrɪmənt/ *n* **to the ~** zum Schaden (**of** *gen*). **~al** /-'mentl/ *a* schädlich (**to** *dat*)

deuce /dju:s/ *n* (*Tennis*) Einstand *m*

devaluation /di:væljʊ'eɪʃn/ *n* Abwertung *f*

de'value *vt* abwerten ⟨*currency*⟩

devastat|e /'devəsteɪt/ *vt* verwüsten. **~ed** /-ɪd/ *a* (*fam*) erschüttert. **~ing** *a* verheerend. **~ion** /-'steɪʃn/ *n* Verwüstung *f*

develop /dɪ'veləp/ *vt* entwickeln; bekommen ⟨*illness*⟩; erschließen ⟨*area*⟩ ● *vi* sich entwickeln (**into** zu). **~er** *n* **[property] ~er** Bodenspekulant *m*

de'veloping country *n* Entwicklungsland *nt*

development /dɪ'veləpmənt/ *n* Entwicklung *f*

deviant /'di:vɪənt/ *a* abweichend

deviat|e /'di:vɪeɪt/ *vi* abweichen. **~ion** /-'eɪʃn/ *n* Abweichung *f*

device /dɪ'vaɪs/ *n* Gerät *nt*; (*fig*) Mittel *nt*; **leave s.o. to his own ~s** jdn sich (*dat*) selbst überlassen

devil /'devl/ *n* Teufel *m*. **~ish** *a* teuflisch

devious /'di:vɪəs/ *a* verschlagen; **~ route** Umweg *m*

devise /dɪ'vaɪz/ *vt* sich (*dat*) ausdenken

devoid /dɪ'vɔɪd/ *a* **~ of** ohne

devolution /di:və'lu:ʃn/ *n* Dezentralisierung *f*; (*of power*) Übertragung *f*

devot|e /dɪ'vəʊt/ *vt* widmen (**to** *dat*). **~ed** *a*, **-ly** *adv* ergeben; ⟨*care*⟩ liebevoll; **be ~ed to s.o.** sehr an jdm hängen. **~ee** /devə'ti:/ *n* Anhänger(in) *m(f)*
devotion /dɪ'vəʊʃn/ *n* Hingabe *f*; **~s** *pl* (*Relig*) Andacht *f*
devour /dɪ'vaʊə(r)/ *vt* verschlingen
devout /dɪ'vaʊt/ *a* fromm
dew /dju:/ *n* Tau *m*
dexterity /dek'sterətɪ/ *n* Geschicklichkeit *f*
diabet|es /daɪə'bi:ti:z/ *n* Zuckerkrankheit *f*. **~ic** /-'betɪk/ *a* zuckerkrank ● *n* Zuckerkranke(r) *m/f*, Diabetiker(in) *m(f)*
diabolical /daɪə'bɒlɪkl/ *a* teuflisch
diagnose /daɪəg'nəʊz/ *vt* diagnostizieren
diagnosis /daɪəg'nəʊsɪs/ *n* (*pl* **-oses** /-si:z/) Diagnose *f*
diagonal /daɪ'ægənl/ *a*, **-ly** *adv* diagonal ● *n* Diagonale *f*
diagram /'daɪəgræm/ *n* Diagramm *nt*
dial /'daɪəl/ *n* (*of clock*) Zifferblatt *nt*; (*Techn*) Skala *f*; (*Teleph*) Wählscheibe *f* ● *vt/i* (*pt/pp* **dialled**) (*Teleph*) wählen; **~ direct** durchwählen
dialect /'daɪəlekt/ *n* Dialekt *m*
dialling: ~ code *n* Vorwahlnummer *f*. **~ tone** *n* Amtszeichen *nt*
dialogue /'daɪəlɒg/ *n* Dialog *m*
'dial tone *n* (*Amer*, *Teleph*) Amtszeichen *nt*
diameter /daɪ'æmɪtə(r)/ *n* Durchmesser *m*
diametrically /daɪə'metrɪkəlɪ/ *adv* **~ opposed** genau entgegengesetzt (**to** *dat*)
diamond /'daɪəmənd/ *n* Diamant *m*; (*cut*) Brillant *m*; (*shape*) Raute *f*; **~s** *pl* (*Cards*) Karo *nt*
diaper /'daɪəpə(r)/ *n* (*Amer*) Windel *f*
diaphragm /'daɪəfræm/ *n* (*Anat*) Zwerchfell *nt*; (*Phot*) Blende *f*
diarrhoea /daɪə'ri:ə/ *n* Durchfall *m*
diary /'daɪərɪ/ *n* Tagebuch *nt*; (*for appointments*) [Termin]kalender *m*
dice /daɪs/ *n inv* Würfel *m* ● *vt* (*Culin*) in Würfel schneiden
dicey /'daɪsɪ/ *a* (*fam*) riskant
dictat|e /dɪk'teɪt/ *vt/i* diktieren. **~ion** /-eɪʃn/ *n* Diktat *nt*
dictator /dɪk'teɪtə(r)/ *n* Diktator *m*. **~ial** /-tə'tɔ:rɪəl/ *a* diktatorisch. **~ship** *n* Diktatur *f*
diction /'dɪkʃn/ *n* Aussprache *f*
dictionary /'dɪkʃənrɪ/ *n* Wörterbuch *nt*
did /dɪd/ *see* **do**
didactic /dɪ'dæktɪk/ *a* didaktisch
diddle /'dɪdl/ *vt* (*fam*) übers Ohr hauen
didn't /'dɪdnt/ = **did not**
die[1] /daɪ/ *n* (*Techn*) Prägestempel *m*; (*metal mould*) Gußform *f*
die[2] *vi* (*pres p* **dying**) sterben (**of** an + *dat*); ⟨*plant, animal:*⟩ eingehen; ⟨*flower:*⟩ verwelken; **be dying to do sth** (*fam*) darauf brennen, etw zu tun; **be dying for sth** (*fam*) sich nach etw sehnen. **~ down** *vi* nachlassen; ⟨*fire:*⟩ herunterbrennen. **~ out** *vi* aussterben
diesel /'di:zl/ *n* Diesel *m*. **~ engine** *n* Dieselmotor *m*
diet /'daɪət/ *n* Kost *f*; (*restricted*) Diät *f*; (*for slimming*) Schlankheitskur *f*; **be on a ~** diät leben; eine Schlankheitskur machen ● *vi* diät leben; eine Schlankheitskur machen
dietician /daɪə'tɪʃn/ *n* Diätassistent(in) *m(f)*
differ /'dɪfə(r)/ *vi* sich unterscheiden; (*disagree*) verschiedener Meinung sein
differen|ce /'dɪfrəns/ *n* Unterschied *m*; (*disagreement*) Meinungsverschiedenheit *f*. **~t** *a* andere(r,s); (*various*) verschiedene; **be ~t** anders sein (**from** als)
differential /dɪfə'renʃl/ *a* Differential- ● *n* Unterschied *m*; (*Techn*) Differential *nt*
differentiate /dɪfə'renʃɪeɪt/ *vt/i* unterscheiden (**between** zwischen + *dat*)
differently /'dɪfrəntlɪ/ *adv* anders
difficult /'dɪfɪkəlt/ *a* schwierig, schwer. **~y** *n* Schwierigkeit *f*
diffiden|ce /'dɪfɪdəns/ *n* Zaghaftigkeit *f*. **~t** *a* zaghaft
diffuse[1] /dɪ'fju:s/ *a* ausgebreitet; (*wordy*) langatmig
diffuse[2] /dɪ'fju:z/ *vt* (*Phys*) streuen
dig /dɪg/ *n* (*poke*) Stoß *m*; (*remark*) spitze Bemerkung *f*; (*Archaeol*) Ausgrabung *f*; **~s** *pl* (*fam*) möbliertes Zimmer *nt* ● *vt/i* (*pt/pp* **dug**, *pres p* **digging**) graben; umgraben ⟨*garden*⟩; **~ s.o. in the ribs** jdm einen Rippenstoß geben. **~ out** *vt* ausgraben. **~ up** *vt* ausgraben; umgraben ⟨*garden*⟩; aufreißen ⟨*street*⟩
digest[1] /'daɪdʒest/ *n* Kurzfassung *f*
digest[2] /dɪ'dʒest/ *vt* verdauen. **~ible** *a* verdaulich. **~ion** /-estʃn/ *n* Verdauung *f*

digger /'dɪgə(r)/ *n* (*Techn*) Bagger *m*
digit /'dɪdʒɪt/ *n* Ziffer *f*; (*finger*) Finger *m*; (*toe*) Zehe *f*
digital /'dɪdʒɪtl/ *a* Digital-; ~ **clock** Digitaluhr *f*
dignified /'dɪgnɪfaɪd/ *a* würdevoll
dignitary /'dɪgnɪtərɪ/ *n* Würdenträger *m*
dignity /'dɪgnɪtɪ/ *n* Würde *f*
digress /daɪ'gres/ *vi* abschweifen. **~ion** /-eʃn/ *n* Abschweifung *f*
dike /daɪk/ *n* Deich *m*; (*ditch*) Graben *m*
dilapidated /dɪ'læpɪdeɪtɪd/ *a* baufällig
dilate /daɪ'leɪt/ *vt* erweitern ● *vi* sich erweitern
dilatory /'dɪlətərɪ/ *a* langsam
dilemma /dɪ'lemə/ *n* Dilemma *nt*
dilettante /dɪlɪ'tæntɪ/ *n* Dilettant(in) *m*(*f*)
diligen|ce /'dɪlɪdʒəns/ *n* Fleiß *m*. **~t** *a*, **-ly** *adv* fleißig
dill /dɪl/ *n* Dill *m*
dilly-dally /'dɪlɪdælɪ/ *vi* (*pt/pp* **-ied**) (*fam*) trödeln
dilute /daɪ'lu:t/ *vt* verdünnen
dim /dɪm/ *a* (**dimmer, dimmest**), **-ly** *adv* (*weak*) schwach; (*dark*) trüb[e]; (*indistinct*) undeutlich; (*fam: stupid*) dumm, (*fam*) doof ● *v* (*pt/pp* **dimmed**) ● *vt* dämpfen ● *vi* schwächer werden
dime /daɪm/ *n* (*Amer*) Zehncentstück *nt*
dimension /daɪ'menʃn/ *n* Dimension *f*; **~s** *pl* Maße *pl*
diminish /dɪ'mɪnɪʃ/ *vt* verringern ● *vi* sich verringern
diminutive /dɪ'mɪnjʊtɪv/ *a* winzig ● *n* Verkleinerungsform *f*
dimple /'dɪmpl/ *n* Grübchen *nt*
din /dɪn/ *n* Krach *m*, Getöse *nt*
dine /daɪn/ *vi* speisen. **~r** *n* Speisende(r) *m*/*f*; (*Amer: restaurant*) Eßlokal *nt*
dinghy /'dɪŋgɪ/ *n* Dinghi *nt*; (*inflatable*) Schlauchboot *nt*
dingy /'dɪndʒɪ/ *a* (**-ier, -iest**) trübe
dining /'daɪnɪŋ/: **~-car** *n* Speisewagen *m*. **~-room** *n* Eßzimmer *nt*. **~-table** *n* Eßtisch *m*
dinner /'dɪnə(r)/ *n* Abendessen *nt*; (*at midday*) Mittagessen *nt*; (*formal*) Essen *nt*. **~-jacket** *n* Smoking *m*
dinosaur /'daɪnəsɔ:(r)/ *n* Dinosaurier *m*
dint /dɪnt/ *n* **by ~ of** durch (+ *acc*)
diocese /'daɪəsɪs/ *n* Diözese *f*
dip /dɪp/ *n* (*in ground*) Senke *f*; (*Culin*) Dip *m*; **go for a ~** kurz schwimmen gehen ● *v* (*pt/pp* **dipped**) *vt* [ein]tauchen; **~ one's headlights** (*Auto*) [die Scheinwerfer] abblenden ● *vi* sich senken
diphtheria /dɪf'θɪərɪə/ *n* Diphtherie *f*
diphthong /'dɪfθɒŋ/ *n* Diphthong *m*
diploma /dɪ'pləʊmə/ *n* Diplom *nt*
diplomacy /dɪ'pləʊməsɪ/ *n* Diplomatie *f*
diplomat /'dɪpləmæt/ *n* Diplomat *m*. **~ic** /-'mætɪk/ *a*, **-ally** *adv* diplomatisch
'dip-stick *n* (*Auto*) Ölmeßstab *m*
dire /'daɪə(r)/ *a* (**-r, -st**) bitter; ⟨*situation, consequences*⟩ furchtbar
direct /dɪ'rekt/ *a* & *adv* direkt ● *vt* (*aim*) richten (**at** auf /(*fig*) an + *acc*); (*control*) leiten; (*order*) anweisen; **~ s.o.** (*show the way*) jdm den Weg sagen; **~ a film/play** bei einem Film/Theaterstück Regie führen. **~ 'current** *n* Gleichstrom *m*
direction /dɪ'rekʃn/ *n* Richtung *f*; (*control*) Leitung *f*; (*of play, film*) Regie *f*; **~s** *pl* Anweisungen *pl*; **~s for use** Gebrauchsanweisung *f*
directly /dɪ'rektlɪ/ *adv* direkt; (*at once*) sofort ● *conj* (*fam*) sobald
director /dɪ'rektə(r)/ *n* (*Comm*) Direktor *m*; (*of play, film*) Regisseur *m*
directory /dɪ'rektərɪ/ *n* Verzeichnis *nt*; (*Teleph*) Telefonbuch *nt*
dirt /dɜ:t/ *n* Schmutz *m*; (*soil*) Erde *f*; **~ cheap** (*fam*) spottbillig
dirty /'dɜ:tɪ/ *a* (**-ier, -iest**) schmutzig ● *vt* schmutzig machen
dis|a'bility /dɪs-/ *n* Behinderung *f*. **~abled** /dɪ'seɪbld/ *a* [körper]behindert
disad'van|tage *n* Nachteil *m*; **at a ~tage** im Nachteil. **~taged** *a* benachteiligt. **~'tageous** *a* nachteilig
disaf'fected *a* unzufrieden; (*disloyal*) illoyal
disa'gree *vi* nicht übereinstimmen (**with** mit); **I ~** ich bin anderer Meinung; **we ~** wir sind verschiedener Meinung; **oysters ~ with me** Austern bekommen mir nicht
disa'greeable *a* unangenehm
disa'greement *n* Meinungsverschiedenheit *f*
disap'pear *vi* verschwinden. **~ance** *n* Verschwinden *nt*
disap'point *vt* enttäuschen. **~ment** *n* Enttäuschung *f*
disap'proval *n* Mißbilligung *f*

disap'prove *vi* dagegen sein; ~ **of** mißbilligen

dis'arm *vt* entwaffnen ● *vi* (*Mil*) abrüsten. **~ament** *n* Abrüstung *f*. **~ing** *a* entwaffnend

disar'ray *n* Unordnung *f*

disast|er /dɪ'zɑ:stə(r)/ *n* Katastrophe *f*; (*accident*) Unglück *nt*. **~rous** /-rəs/ *a* katastrophal

dis'band *vt* auflösen ● *vi* sich auflösen

disbe'lief *n* Ungläubigkeit *f*; **in ~** ungläubig

disc /dɪsk/ *n* Scheibe *f*; (*record*) [Schall]platte *f*; (*CD*) CD *f*

discard /dɪ'skɑ:d/ *vt* ablegen; (*throw away*) wegwerfen

discern /dɪ'sɜ:n/ *vt* wahrnehmen. **~ible** *a* wahrnehmbar. **~ing** *a* anspruchsvoll

'discharge¹ *n* Ausstoßen *nt*; (*Naut, Electr*) Entladung *f*; (*dismissal*) Entlassung *f*; (*Jur*) Freispruch *m*; (*Med*) Ausfluß *m*

dis'charge² *vt* ausstoßen; (*Naut, Electr*) entladen; (*dismiss*) entlassen; (*Jur*) freisprechen ‹*accused*›; **~ a duty** sich einer Pflicht entledigen

disciple /dɪ'saɪpl/ *n* Jünger *m*; (*fig*) Schüler *m*

disciplinary /'dɪsɪplɪnərɪ/ *a* disziplinarisch

discipline /'dɪsɪplɪn/ *n* Disziplin *f* ● *vt* Disziplin beibringen (+ *dat*); (*punish*) bestrafen

'disc jockey *n* Diskjockey *m*

dis'claim *vt* abstreiten. **~er** *n* Verzichterklärung *f*

dis'clos|e *vt* enthüllen. **~ure** *n* Enthüllung *f*

disco /'dɪskəʊ/ *n* (*fam*) Disko *f*

dis'colour *vt* verfärben ● *vi* sich verfärben

dis'comfort *n* Beschwerden *pl*; (*fig*) Unbehagen *nt*

disconcert /dɪskən'sɜ:t/ *vt* aus der Fassung bringen

discon'nect *vt* trennen; (*Electr*) ausschalten; (*cut supply*) abstellen

disconsolate /dɪs'kɒnsələt/ *a* untröstlich

discon'tent *n* Unzufriedenheit *f*. **~ed** *a* unzufrieden

discon'tinue *vt* einstellen; (*Comm*) nicht mehr herstellen

'discord *n* Zwietracht *f*; (*Mus & fig*) Mißklang *m*. **~ant** /dɪ'skɔ:dənt/ *a* **~ant note** Mißklang *m*

discothèque /'dɪskətek/ *n* Diskothek *f*

'discount¹ *n* Rabatt *m*

dis'count² *vt* außer acht lassen

dis'courage *vt* entmutigen; (*dissuade*) abraten (+ *dat*)

'discourse *n* Rede *f*

dis'courteous *a*, **-ly** *adv* unhöflich

discover /dɪ'skʌvə(r)/ *vt* entdecken. **~y** *n* Entdeckung *f*

dis'credit *n* Mißkredit *m* ● *vt* in Mißkredit bringen

discreet /dɪ'skri:t/ *a*, **-ly** *adv* diskret

discrepancy /dɪ'skrepənsɪ/ *n* Diskrepanz *f*

discretion /dɪ'skreʃn/ *n* Diskretion *f*; (*judgement*) Ermessen *nt*

discriminat|e /dɪ'skrɪmɪneɪt/ *vi* unterscheiden (**between** zwischen + *dat*); **~e against** diskriminieren. **~ing** *a* anspruchsvoll. **~ion** /-'neɪʃn/ *n* Diskriminierung *f*; (*quality*) Urteilskraft *f*

discus /'dɪskəs/ *n* Diskus *m*

discuss /dɪ'skʌs/ *vt* besprechen; (*examine critically*) diskutieren. **~ion** /-ʌʃn/ *n* Besprechung *f*; Diskussion *f*

disdain /dɪs'deɪn/ *n* Verachtung *f* ● *vt* verachten. **~ful** *a* verächtlich

disease /dɪ'zi:z/ *n* Krankheit *f*. **~d** *a* krank

disem'bark *vi* an Land gehen

disen'chant *vt* ernüchtern. **~ment** *n* Ernüchterung *f*

disen'gage *vt* losmachen; **~ the clutch** (*Auto*) auskuppeln

disen'tangle *vt* entwirren

dis'favour *n* Ungnade *f*; (*disapproval*) Mißfallen *nt*

dis'figure *vt* entstellen

dis'gorge *vt* ausspeien

dis'grace *n* Schande *f*; **in ~** in Ungnade ● *vt* Schande machen (+ *dat*). **~ful** *a* schändlich

disgruntled /dɪs'grʌntld/ *a* verstimmt

disguise /dɪs'gaɪz/ *n* Verkleidung *f*; **in ~** verkleidet ● *vt* verkleiden; verstellen ‹*voice*›; (*conceal*) verhehlen

disgust /dɪs'gʌst/ *n* Ekel *m*; **in ~** empört ● *vt* anekeln; (*appal*) empören. **~ing** *a* eklig; (*appalling*) abscheulich

dish /dɪʃ/ *n* Schüssel *f*; (*shallow*) Schale *f*; (*small*) Schälchen *nt*; (*food*) Gericht *nt*. **~ out** *vt* austeilen. **~ up** *vt* auftragen

'dishcloth *n* Spültuch *nt*

dis'hearten *vt* entmutigen. **~ing** *a* entmutigend
dishevelled /dɪ'ʃevld/ *a* zerzaust
dis'honest *a*, **-ly** *adv* unehrlich. **~y** *n* Unehrlichkeit *f*
dis'honour *n* Schande *f* ● *vt* entehren; nicht honorieren ⟨*cheque*⟩. **~able** *a*, **-bly** *adv* unehrenhaft
'dishwasher *n* Geschirrspülmaschine *f*
disil'lusion *vt* ernüchtern. **~ment** *n* Ernüchterung *f*
disin'fect *vt* desinfizieren. **~ant** *n* Desinfektionsmittel *nt*
disin'herit *vt* enterben
dis'integrate *vi* zerfallen
dis'interested *a* unvoreingenommen; (*uninterested*) uninteressiert
dis'jointed *a* unzusammenhängend
disk /dɪsk/ *n* = **disc**
dis'like *n* Abneigung *f* ● *vt* nicht mögen
dislocate /'dɪsləkeɪt/ *vt* ausrenken; **~ one's shoulder** sich (*dat*) den Arm auskugeln
dis'lodge *vt* entfernen
dis'loyal *a*, **-ly** *adv* illoyal. **~ty** *n* Illoyalität *f*
dismal /'dɪzməl/ *a* trüb[e]; ⟨*person*⟩ trübselig; (*fam: poor*) kläglich
dismantle /dɪs'mæntl/ *vt* auseinandernehmen; (*take down*) abbauen
dis'may *n* Bestürzung *f*. **~ed** *a* bestürzt
dis'miss *vt* entlassen; (*reject*) zurückweisen. **~al** *n* Entlassung *f*; Zurückweisung *f*
dis'mount *vi* absteigen
diso'bedien|ce *n* Ungehorsam *m*. **~t** *a* ungehorsam
diso'bey *vt/i* nicht gehorchen (+ *dat*); nicht befolgen ⟨*rule*⟩
dis'order *n* Unordnung *f*; (*Med*) Störung *f*. **~ly** *a* unordentlich; **~ly conduct** ungebührliches Benehmen *nt*
dis'organized *a* unorganisiert
dis'orientate *vt* verwirren; **be ~d** die Orientierung verloren haben
dis'own *vt* verleugnen
disparaging /dɪ'spærɪdʒɪŋ/ *a*, **-ly** *adv* abschätzig
disparity /dɪ'spærətɪ/ *n* Ungleichheit *f*
dispassionate /dɪ'spæʃənət/ *a*, **-ly** *adv* gelassen; (*impartial*) unparteiisch
dispatch /dɪ'spætʃ/ *n* (*Comm*) Versand *m*; (*Mil*) Nachricht *f*; (*report*) Bericht *m*; **with ~** prompt ● *vt* [ab]senden; (*deal with*) erledigen; (*kill*) töten. **~-rider** *n* Meldefahrer *m*
dispel /dɪ'spel/ *vt* (*pt/pp* **dispelled**) vertreiben
dispensable /dɪ'spensəbl/ *a* entbehrlich
dispensary /dɪ'spensərɪ/ *n* Apotheke *f*
dispense /dɪ'spens/ *vt* austeilen; **~ with** verzichten auf (+ *acc*). **~r** *n* Apotheker(in) *m*(*f*); (*device*) Automat *m*
dispers|al /dɪ'spɜ:sl/ *n* Zerstreuung *f*. **~e** /dɪ'spɜ:s/ *vt* zerstreuen ● *vi* sich zerstreuen
dispirited /dɪ'spɪrɪtɪd/ *a* entmutigt
dis'place *vt* verschieben; **~d person** Vertriebene(r) *m/f*
display /dɪ'spleɪ/ *n* Ausstellung *f*; (*Comm*) Auslage *f*; (*performance*) Vorführung *f* ● *vt* zeigen; ausstellen ⟨*goods*⟩
dis'please *vt* mißfallen (+ *dat*)
dis'pleasure *n* Mißfallen *nt*
disposable /dɪ'spəʊzəbl/ *a* Wegwerf-; ⟨*income*⟩ verfügbar
disposal /dɪ'spəʊzl/ *n* Beseitigung *f*; **be at s.o.'s ~** jdm zur Verfügung stehen
dispose /dɪ'spəʊz/ *vi* **~ of** beseitigen; (*deal with*) erledigen; **be well ~d** wohlgesinnt sein (**to** *dat*)
disposition /dɪspə'zɪʃn/ *n* Veranlagung *f*; (*nature*) Wesensart *f*
disproportionate /dɪsprə'pɔ:ʃənət/ *a*, **-ly** *adv* unverhältnismäßig
dis'prove *vt* widerlegen
dispute /dɪ'spju:t/ *n* Disput *m*; (*quarrel*) Streit *m* ● *vt* bestreiten
disqualifi'cation *n* Disqualifikation *f*
dis'qualify *vt* disqualifizieren; **~ s.o. from driving** jdm den Führerschein entziehen
disquieting /dɪs'kwaɪətɪŋ/ *a* beunruhigend
disre'gard *n* Nichtbeachtung *f* ● *vt* nicht beachten, ignorieren
disre'pair *n* **fall into ~** verfallen
dis'reputable *a* verrufen
disre'pute *n* Verruf *m*
disre'spect *n* Respektlosigkeit *f*. **~ful** *a*, **-ly** *adv* respektlos
disrupt /dɪs'rʌpt/ *vt* stören. **~ion** /-ʌpʃn/ *n* Störung *f*. **~ive** /-tɪv/ *a* störend
dissatis'faction *n* Unzufriedenheit *f*
dis'satisfied *a* unzufrieden
dissect /dɪ'sekt/ *vt* zergliedern; (*Med*) sezieren. **~ion** /-ekʃn/ *n* Zergliederung *f*; (*Med*) Sektion *f*

disseminat|e /dɪ'semɪneɪt/ *vt* verbreiten. **~ion** /-'neɪʃn/ *n* Verbreitung *f*

dissent /dɪ'sent/ *n* Nichtübereinstimmung *f* ● *vi* nicht übereinstimmen

dissertation /dɪsə'teɪʃn/ *n* Dissertation *f*

dis'service *n* schlechter Dienst *m*

dissident /'dɪsɪdənt/ *n* Dissident *m*

dis'similar *a* unähnlich (**to** *dat*)

dissociate /dɪ'səʊʃɪeɪt/ *vt* trennen; **~ oneself** sich distanzieren (**from** von)

dissolute /'dɪsəlu:t/ *a* zügellos; ⟨*life*⟩ ausschweifend

dissolution /dɪsə'lu:ʃn/ *n* Auflösung *f*

dissolve /dɪ'zɒlv/ *vt* auflösen ● *vi* sich auflösen

dissuade /dɪ'sweɪd/ *vt* abbringen (**from** von)

distance /'dɪstəns/ *n* Entfernung *f*; **long/short ~** lange/kurze Strecke *f*; **in the/from a ~** in/aus der Ferne

distant /'dɪstənt/ *a* fern; (*aloof*) kühl; ⟨*relative*⟩ entfernt

dis'taste *n* Abneigung *f*. **~ful** *a* unangenehm

distend /dɪ'stend/ *vi* sich [auf]blähen

distil /dɪ'stɪl/ *vt* (*pt*/*pp* **distilled**) brennen; (*Chem*) destillieren. **~lation** /-'leɪʃn/ *n* Destillation *f*. **~lery** /-ərɪ/ *n* Brennerei *f*

distinct /dɪ'stɪŋkt/ *a* deutlich; (*different*) verschieden. **~ion** /-ɪŋkʃn/ *n* Unterschied *m*; (*Sch*) Auszeichnung *f*. **~ive** /-tɪv/ *a* kennzeichnend; (*unmistakable*) unverwechselbar. **~ly** *adv* deutlich

distinguish /dɪ'stɪŋgwɪʃ/ *vt/i* unterscheiden; (*make out*) erkennen; **~ oneself** sich auszeichnen. **~ed** *a* angesehen; ⟨*appearance*⟩ distinguiert

distort /dɪ'stɔ:t/ *vt* verzerren; (*fig*) verdrehen. **~ion** /-ɔ:ʃn/ *n* Verzerrung *f*; (*fig*) Verdrehung *f*

distract /dɪ'strækt/ *vt* ablenken. **~ed** /-ɪd/ *a* [völlig] aufgelöst. **~ion** /-ækʃn/ *n* Ablenkung *f*; (*despair*) Verzweiflung *f*

distraught /dɪ'strɔ:t/ *a* [völlig] aufgelöst

distress /dɪ'stres/ *n* Kummer *m*; (*pain*) Schmerz *m*; (*poverty, danger*) Not *f* ● *vt* Kummer/Schmerz bereiten (+ *dat*); (*sadden*) bekümmern; (*shock*) erschüttern. **~ing** *a* schmerzlich; (*shocking*) erschütternd. **~ signal** *n* Notsignal *nt*

distribut|e /dɪ'strɪbju:t/ *vt* verteilen; (*Comm*) vertreiben. **~ion** /-'bju:ʃn/ *n* Verteilung *f*; Vertrieb *m*. **~or** *n* Verteiler *m*

district /'dɪstrɪkt/ *n* Gegend *f*; (*Admin*) Bezirk *m*. **~ nurse** *n* Gemeindeschwester *f*

dis'trust *n* Mißtrauen *nt* ● *vt* mißtrauen (+ *dat*). **~ful** *a* mißtrauisch

disturb /dɪ'stɜ:b/ *vt* stören; (*perturb*) beunruhigen; (*touch*) anrühren. **~ance** *n* Unruhe *f*; (*interruption*) Störung *f*. **~ed** *a* beunruhigt; **[mentally] ~ed** geistig gestört. **~ing** *a* beunruhigend

dis'used *a* stillgelegt; (*empty*) leer

ditch /dɪtʃ/ *n* Graben *m* ● *vt* (*fam: abandon*) fallenlassen ⟨*plan*⟩; wegschmeißen ⟨*thing*⟩

dither /'dɪðə(r)/ *vi* zaudern

ditto /'dɪtəʊ/ *n* dito; (*fam*) ebenfalls

divan /dɪ'væn/ *n* Polsterbett *nt*

dive /daɪv/ *n* [Kopf]sprung *m*; (*Aviat*) Sturzflug *m*; (*fam: place*) Spelunke *f* ● *vi* einen Kopfsprung machen; (*when in water*) tauchen; (*Aviat*) einen Sturzflug machen; (*fam: rush*) stürzen

diver /'daɪvə(r)/ *n* Taucher *m*; (*Sport*) [Kunst]springer *m*

diver|ge /daɪ'vɜ:dʒ/ *vi* auseinandergehen. **~gent** /-ənt/ *a* abweichend

diverse /daɪ'vɜ:s/ *a* verschieden

diversify /daɪ'vɜ:sɪfaɪ/ *vt/i* (*pt*/*pp* **-ied**) variieren; (*Comm*) diversifizieren

diversion /daɪ'vɜ:ʃn/ *n* Umleitung *f*; (*distraction*) Ablenkung *f*

diversity /daɪ'vɜ:sətɪ/ *n* Vielfalt *f*

divert /daɪ'vɜ:t/ *vt* umleiten; ablenken ⟨*attention*⟩; (*entertain*) unterhalten

divest /daɪ'vest/ *vt* sich entledigen (**of** + *gen*); (*fig*) entkleiden

divide /dɪ'vaɪd/ *vt* teilen; (*separate*) trennen; (*Math*) dividieren (**by** durch) ● *vi* sich teilen

dividend /'dɪvɪdend/ *n* Dividende *f*

divine /dɪ'vaɪn/ *a* göttlich

diving /'daɪvɪŋ/ *n* (*Sport*) Kunstspringen *nt*. **~-board** *n* Sprungbrett *nt*. **~-suit** *n* Taucheranzug *m*

divinity /dɪ'vɪnətɪ/ *n* Göttlichkeit *f*; (*subject*) Theologie *f*

divisible /dɪ'vɪzɪbl/ *a* teilbar (**by** durch)

division /dɪ'vɪʒn/ *n* Teilung *f*; (*separation*) Trennung *f*; (*Math, Mil*) Division *f*; (*Parl*) Hammelsprung *m*;

(*line*) Trennlinie *f*; (*group*) Abteilung *f*

divorce /dɪ'vɔːs/ *n* Scheidung *f* • *vt* sich scheiden lassen von. **~d** *a* geschieden; **get ~d** sich scheiden lassen

divorcee /dɪvɔː'siː/ *n* Geschiedene(r) *m/f*

divulge /daɪ'vʌldʒ/ *vt* preisgeben

DIY *abbr of* **do-it-yourself**

dizziness /'dɪzɪnɪs/ *n* Schwindel *m*

dizzy /'dɪzɪ/ *a* (**-ier, -iest**) schwindlig; **I feel ~** mir ist schwindlig

do /duː/ *n* (*pl* **dos** *or* **do's**) (*fam*) Veranstaltung *f* • *v* (*3 sg pres tense* **does**; *pt* **did**; *pp* **done**) • *vt/i* tun, machen; (*be suitable*) passen; (*be enough*) reichen, genügen; (*cook*) kochen; (*clean*) putzen; (*Sch: study*) durchnehmen; (*fam: cheat*) beschwindeln (**out of** um); **do without** auskommen ohne; **do away with** abschaffen; **be done** (*Culin*) gar sein; **well done** gut gemacht! (*Culin*) gut durchgebraten; **done in** (*fam*) kaputt, fertig; **done for** (*fam*) verloren, erledigt; **do the flowers** die Blumen arrangieren; **do the potatoes** die Kartoffeln schälen; **do the washing up** abwaschen, spülen; **do one's hair** sich frisieren; **do well/badly** gut/schlecht abschneiden; **how is he doing?** wie geht es ihm? **this won't do** das geht nicht; **are you doing anything today?** haben Sie heute etwas vor? **I could do with a spanner** ich könnte einen Schraubenschlüssel gebrauchen • *v aux* **do you speak German?** sprechen Sie deutsch? **yes, I do** ja; (*emphatic*) doch; **no, I don't** nein; **I don't smoke** ich rauche nicht; **don't you/doesn't he?** nicht [wahr]? **so do I** ich auch; **do come in** kommen Sie doch herein; **how do you do?** guten Tag. **do in** *vt* (*fam*) um die Ecke bringen. **do up** *vt* (*fasten*) zumachen; (*renovate*) renovieren; (*wrap*) einpacken

docile /'dəʊsaɪl/ *a* fügsam

dock[1] /dɒk/ *n* (*Jur*) Anklagebank *f*

dock[2] *n* Dock *nt* • *vi* anlegen, docken • *vt* docken. **~er** *n* Hafenarbeiter *m*. **~yard** *n* Werft *f*

doctor /'dɒktə(r)/ *n* Arzt *m*/Ärztin *f*; (*Univ*) Doktor *m* • *vt* kastrieren; (*spay*) sterilisieren. **~ate** /-ət/ *n* Doktorwürde *f*

doctrine /'dɒktrɪn/ *n* Lehre *f*, Doktrin *f*

document /'dɒkjʊmənt/ *n* Dokument *nt*. **~ary** /-'mentərɪ/ *a* Dokumentar- • *n* Dokumentarbericht *m*; (*film*) Dokumentarfilm *m*

doddery /'dɒdərɪ/ *a* (*fam*) tatterig

dodge /dɒdʒ/ *n* (*fam*) Trick *m*, Kniff *m* • *vt/i* ausweichen (+ *dat*); **~ out of the way** zur Seite springen

dodgems /'dɒdʒəmz/ *npl* Autoskooter *pl*

dodgy /'dɒdʒɪ/ *a* (**-ier, -iest**) (*fam*) (*awkward*) knifflig; (*dubious*) zweifelhaft

doe /dəʊ/ *n* Ricke *f*; (*rabbit*) [Kaninchen]weibchen *nt*

does /dʌz/ *see* **do**

doesn't /'dʌznt/ = **does not**

dog /dɒg/ *n* Hund *m* • *vt* (*pt/pp* **dogged**) verfolgen

dog: ~-biscuit *n* Hundekuchen *m*. **~-collar** *n* Hundehalsband *nt*; (*Relig, fam*) Kragen *m* eines Geistlichen. **~-eared** *a* **be ~-eared** Eselsohren haben

dogged /'dɒgɪd/ *a*, **-ly** *adv* beharrlich

dogma /'dɒgmə/ *n* Dogma *nt*. **~tic** /-'mætɪk/ *a* dogmatisch

'dogsbody *n* (*fam*) Mädchen *nt* für alles

doily /'dɔɪlɪ/ *n* Deckchen *nt*

do-it-yourself /duːɪtjə'self/ *n* Heimwerken *nt*. **~ shop** *n* Heimwerkerladen *m*

doldrums /'dɒldrəmz/ *npl* **be in the ~** niedergeschlagen sein; ⟨*business:*⟩ darniederliegen

dole /dəʊl/ *n* (*fam*) Stempelgeld *nt*, **be on the ~** arbeitslos sein • *vt* **~ out** austeilen

doleful /'dəʊlfl/ *a*, **-ly** *adv* trauervoll

doll /dɒl/ *n* Puppe *f* • *vt* (*fam*) **~ oneself up** sich herausputzen

dollar /'dɒlə(r)/ *n* Dollar *m*

dollop /'dɒləp/ *n* (*fam*) Klecks *m*

dolphin /'dɒlfɪn/ *n* Delphin *m*

domain /də'meɪn/ *n* Gebiet *nt*

dome /dəʊm/ *n* Kuppel *m*

domestic /də'mestɪk/ *a* häuslich; (*Pol*) Innen-; (*Comm*) Binnen-. **~ animal** *n* Haustier *nt*

domesticated /də'mestɪkeɪtɪd/ *a* häuslich; ⟨*animal*⟩ zahm

domestic: ~ flight *n* Inlandflug *m*. **~ 'servant** Hausangestellte(r) *m/f*

dominant /'dɒmɪnənt/ *a* vorherrschend

dominat|e /'dɒmɪneɪt/ *vt* beherrschen ● *vi* dominieren; **~e over** beherrschen. **~ion** /-'neɪʃn/ *n* Vorherrschaft *f*

domineer /dɒmɪ'nɪə(r)/ *vi* **~ over** tyrannisieren. **~ing** *a* herrschsüchtig

dominion /də'mɪnjən/ *n* Herrschaft *f*

domino /'dɒmɪnəʊ/ *n* (*pl* **-es**) Dominostein *m*; **~es** *sg* (*game*) Domino *nt*

don[1] /dɒn/ *vt* (*pt/pp* **donned**) (*liter*) anziehen

don[2] *n* [Universitäts]dozent *m*

donat|e /dəʊ'neɪt/ *vt* spenden. **~ion** /-eɪʃn/ *n* Spende *f*

done /dʌn/ *see* **do**

donkey /'dɒŋkɪ/ *n* Esel *m*; **~'s years** (*fam*) eine Ewigkeit. **~-work** *n* Routinearbeit *f*

donor /'dəʊnə(r)/ *n* Spender(in) *m(f)*

don't /dəʊnt/ = **do not**

doodle /'du:dl/ *vi* kritzeln

doom /du:m/ *n* Schicksal *nt*; (*ruin*) Verhängnis *nt* ● *vt* **be ~ed to failure** zum Scheitern verurteilt sein

door /dɔ:(r)/ *n* Tür *f*; **out of ~s** im Freien

door: ~man *n* Portier *m*. **~mat** *n* [Fuß]abtreter *m*. **~step** *n* Türschwelle *f*; **on the ~step** vor der Tür. **~way** *n* Türöffnung *f*

dope /dəʊp/ *n* (*fam*) Drogen *pl*; (*fam: information*) Informationen *pl*; (*fam: idiot*) Trottel *m* ● *vt* betäuben; (*Sport*) dopen

dopey /'dəʊpɪ/ *a* (*fam*) benommen; (*stupid*) blöd[e]

dormant /'dɔ:mənt/ *a* ruhend

dormer /'dɔ:mə(r)/ *n* **~ [window]** Mansardenfenster *nt*

dormitory /'dɔ:mɪtərɪ/ *n* Schlafsaal *m*

dormouse /'dɔ:-/ *n* Haselmaus *f*

dosage /'dəʊsɪdʒ/ *n* Dosierung *f*

dose /dəʊs/ *n* Dosis *f*

doss /dɒs/ *vi* (*sl*) pennen. **~er** *n* Penner *m*. **~-house** *n* Penne *f*

dot /dɒt/ *n* Punkt *m*; **on the ~** pünktlich

dote /dəʊt/ *vi* **~ on** vernarrt sein in (+ *acc*)

dotted /'dɒtɪd/ *a* **~ line** punktierte Linie *f*; **be ~ with** bestreut sein mit

dotty /'dɒtɪ/ *a* (**-ier, -iest**) (*fam*) verdreht

double /'dʌbl/ *a & adv* doppelt; ⟨*bed, chin*⟩ Doppel-; ⟨*flower*⟩ gefüllt ● *n* das Doppelte; (*person*) Doppelgänger *m*; **~s** *pl* (*Tennis*) Doppel *nt*; **at the ~** im Laufschritt ● *vt* verdoppeln; (*fold*) falten ● *vi* sich verdoppeln. **~ back** *vi* zurückgehen. **~ up** *vi* sich krümmen (**with** vor + *dat*)

double: ~-'bass *n* Kontrabaß *m*. **~-breasted** *a* zweireihig. **~-'cross** *vt* ein Doppelspiel treiben mit. **~-'decker** *n* Doppeldecker *m*. **~ 'Dutch** *n* (*fam*) Kauderwelsch *nt*. **~ 'glazing** *n* Doppelverglasung *f*. **~ 'room** *n* Doppelzimmer *nt*

doubly /'dʌblɪ/ *adv* doppelt

doubt /daʊt/ *n* Zweifel *m* ● *vt* bezweifeln. **~ful** *a*, **-ly** *adv* zweifelhaft; (*disbelieving*) skeptisch. **~less** *adv* zweifellos

dough /dəʊ/ *n* [fester] Teig *m*; (*fam: money*) Pinke *f*. **~nut** *n* Berliner [Pfannkuchen] *m*, Krapfen *m*

douse /daʊs/ *vt* übergießen; ausgießen ⟨*flames*⟩

dove /dʌv/ *n* Taube *f*. **~tail** *n* (*Techn*) Schwalbenschwanz *m*

dowdy /'daʊdɪ/ *a* (**-ier, -iest**) unschick

down[1] /daʊn/ *n* (*feathers*) Daunen *pl*

down[2] *adv* unten; (*with movement*) nach unten; **go ~** hinuntergehen; **come ~** herunterkommen; **~ there** da unten; **£50 ~** £50 Anzahlung; **~!** (*to dog*) Platz! **~ with ...!** nieder mit ...! ● *prep* **~ the road/stairs** die Straße/Treppe hinunter; **~ the river** den Fluß abwärts; **be ~ the pub** (*fam*) in der Kneipe sein ● *vt* (*fam*) (*drink*) runterkippen; **~ tools** die Arbeit niederlegen

down: ~-and-'out *n* Penner *m*. **~cast** *a* niedergeschlagen. **~fall** *n* Sturz *m*; (*ruin*) Ruin *m*. **~'grade** *vt* niedriger einstufen. **~-'hearted** *a* entmutigt. **~'hill** *adv* bergab. **~ payment** *n* Anzahlung *f*. **~pour** *n* Platzregen *m*. **~right** *a & adv* ausgesprochen. **~'stairs** *adv* unten; ⟨*go*⟩ nach unten ● *a* /'--/ im Erdgeschoß. **~'stream** *adv* stromabwärts. **~-to-'earth** *a* sachlich. **~town** *adv* (*Amer*) im Stadtzentrum. **~trodden** *a* unterdrückt. **~ward** *a* nach unten; ⟨*slope*⟩ abfallend ● *adv* & **~wards** abwärts, nach unten

downy /'daʊnɪ/ *a* (**-ier, -iest**) flaumig

dowry /'daʊrɪ/ *n* Mitgift *f*

doze /dəʊz/ *n* Nickerchen *nt* ● *vi* dösen. **~ off** *vi* einnicken

dozen /'dʌzn/ *n* Dutzend *nt*

Dr *abbr of* **doctor**

draft[1] /drɑ:ft/ *n* Entwurf *m*; (*Comm*) Tratte *f*; (*Amer Mil*) Einberufung *f*

● *vt* entwerfen; (*Amer Mil*) einberufen

draft[2] *n* (*Amer*) = **draught**

drag /dræg/ *n* (*fam*) Klotz *m* am Bein; **in ~** (*fam*) ⟨*man*⟩ als Frau gekleidet ● *vt* (*pt/pp* **dragged**) schleppen; absuchen ⟨*river*⟩. **~ on** *vi* sich in die Länge ziehen

dragon /'drægən/ *n* Drache *m*. **~-fly** *n* Libelle *f*

'drag show *n* Transvestitenshow *f*

drain /dreɪn/ *n* Abfluß *m*; (*underground*) Kanal *m*; **the ~s** die Kanalisation ● *vt* entwässern ⟨*land*⟩; ablassen ⟨*liquid*⟩; das Wasser ablassen aus ⟨*tank*⟩; abgießen ⟨*vegetables*⟩; austrinken ⟨*glass*⟩ ● *vi* **~ [away]** ablaufen; **leave sth to ~** etw abtropfen lassen

drain|age /'dreɪnɪdʒ/ *n* Kanalisation *f*; (*of land*) Dränage *f*. **~ing board** *n* Abtropfbrett *nt*. **~-pipe** *n* Abflußrohr *nt*

drake /dreɪk/ *n* Enterich *m*

drama /'drɑːmə/ *n* Drama *nt*; (*quality*) Dramatik *f*

dramatic /drə'mætɪk/ *a*, **-ally** *adv* dramatisch

dramat|ist /'dræmətɪst/ *n* Dramatiker *m*. **~ize** *vt* für die Bühne bearbeiten; (*fig*) dramatisieren

drank /dræŋk/ *see* **drink**

drape /dreɪp/ *n* (*Amer*) Vorhang *m* ● *vt* drapieren

drastic /'dræstɪk/ *a*, **-ally** *adv* drastisch

draught /drɑːft/ *n* [Luft]zug *m*; **~s** *sg* (*game*) Damespiel *nt*; **there is a ~** es zieht

draught: ~ beer *n* Bier *nt* vom Faß. **~sman** *n* technischer Zeichner *m*

draughty /'drɑːftɪ/ *a* zugig; **it's ~** es zieht

draw /drɔː/ *n* Attraktion *f*; (*Sport*) Unentschieden *nt*; (*in lottery*) Ziehung *f* ● *v* (*pt* **drew**, *pp* **drawn**) ● *vt* ziehen; (*attract*) anziehen; zeichnen ⟨*picture*⟩; abheben ⟨*money*⟩; holen ⟨*water*⟩; **~ the curtains** die Vorhänge zuziehen/(*back*) aufziehen; **~ lots** losen (**for** um) ● *vi* ⟨*tea:*⟩ ziehen; (*Sport*) unentschieden spielen. **~ back** *vt* zurückziehen ● *vi* (*recoil*) zurückweichen. **~ in** *vt* einziehen ● *vi* einfahren; ⟨*days:*⟩ kürzer werden. **~ out** *vt* herausziehen; abheben ⟨*money*⟩ ● *vi* ausfahren; ⟨*days:*⟩ länger werden. **~ up** *vt* aufsetzen ⟨*document*⟩; herrücken ⟨*chair*⟩; **~ oneself up** sich aufrichten ● *vi* [an]halten

draw: ~back *n* Nachteil *m*. **~bridge** *n* Zugbrücke *f*

drawer /drɔː(r)/ *n* Schublade *f*

drawing /'drɔːɪŋ/ *n* Zeichnung *f*

drawing: ~-board *n* Reißbrett *nt*. **~-pin** *n* Reißzwecke *f*. **~-room** *n* Wohnzimmer *nt*

drawl /drɔːl/ *n* schleppende Aussprache *f*

drawn /drɔːn/ *see* **draw**

dread /dred/ *n* Furcht *f* (**of** vor + *dat*) ● *vt* fürchten

dreadful *a*, **-ly** *adv* fürchterlich

dream /driːm/ *n* Traum *m* ● *attrib* Traum- ● *vt/i* (*pt/pp* **dreamt** /dremt/ *or* **dreamed**) träumen (**about/of** von)

dreary /'drɪərɪ/ *a* (**-ier, -iest**) trüb[e]; (*boring*) langweilig

dredge /dredʒ/ *vt/i* baggern. **~r** *n* [Naß]bagger *m*

dregs /dregz/ *npl* Bodensatz *m*

drench /drentʃ/ *vt* durchnässen

dress /dres/ *n* Kleid *nt*; (*clothing*) Kleidung *f* ● *vt* anziehen; (*decorate*) schmücken; (*Culin*) anmachen; (*Med*) verbinden; **~ oneself, get ~ed** sich anziehen ● *vi* sich anziehen. **~ up** *vi* sich schön anziehen; (*in disguise*) sich verkleiden (**as** als)

dress: ~ circle *n* (*Theat*) erster Rang *m*. **~er** *n* (*furniture*) Anrichte *f*; (*Amer: dressing-table*) Frisiertisch *m*

dressing *n* (*Culin*) Soße *f*; (*Med*) Verband *m*

dressing: ~ 'down *n* (*fam*) Standpauke *f*. **~-gown** *n* Morgenmantel *m*. **~-room** *n* Ankleidezimmer *nt*; (*Theat*) [Künstler]garderobe *f*. **~-table** *n* Frisiertisch *m*

dress: ~maker *n* Schneiderin *f*. **~making** *n* Damenschneiderei *f*. **~ rehearsal** *n* Generalprobe *f*

dressy /'dresɪ/ *a* (**-ier, -iest**) schick

drew /druː/ *see* **draw**

dribble /'drɪbl/ *vi* sabbern; (*Sport*) dribbeln

dried /draɪd/ *a* getrocknet; **~ fruit** Dörrobst *nt*

drier /'draɪə(r)/ *n* Trockner *m*

drift /drɪft/ *n* Abtrift *f*; (*of snow*) Schneewehe *f*; (*meaning*) Sinn *m* ● *vi* treiben; (*off course*) abtreiben; ⟨*snow:*⟩ Wehen bilden; (*fig*) ⟨*person:*⟩ sich treiben lassen; **~ apart**

⟨*persons:*⟩ sich auseinanderleben. **~wood** *n* Treibholz *nt*

drill /drɪl/ *n* Bohrer *m*; (*Mil*) Drill *m* ● *vt/i* bohren (**for** nach); (*Mil*) drillen

drily /'draɪlɪ/ *adv* trocken

drink /drɪŋk/ *n* Getränk *nt*; (*alcoholic*) Drink *m*; (*alcohol*) Alkohol *m*; **have a ~** etwas trinken ● *vt/i* (*pt* **drank**, *pp* **drunk**) trinken. **~ up** *vt/i* austrinken

drink|able /'drɪŋkəbl/ *a* trinkbar. **~er** *n* Trinker *m*

'drinking-water *n* Trinkwasser *nt*

drip /drɪp/ *n* Tropfen *nt*; (*drop*) Tropfen *m*; (*Med*) Tropf *m*; (*fam: person*) Niete *f* ● *vi* (*pt/pp* **dripped**) tropfen. **~-'dry** *a* bügelfrei. **~ping** *n* Schmalz *nt*

drive /draɪv/ *n* [Auto]fahrt *f*; (*entrance*) Einfahrt *f*; (*energy*) Elan *m*; (*Psych*) Trieb *m*; (*Pol*) Aktion *f*; (*Sport*) Treibschlag *m*; (*Techn*) Antrieb *m* ● *v* (*pt* **drove**, *pp* **driven**) ● *vt* treiben; fahren ⟨*car*⟩; (*Sport: hit*) schlagen; (*Techn*) antreiben; **~ s.o. mad** (*fam*) jdn verrückt machen; **what are you driving at?** (*fam*) worauf willst du hinaus? ● *vi* fahren. **~ away** *vt* vertreiben ● *vi* abfahren. **~ in** *vi* hinein-/hereinfahren. **~ off** *vt* vertreiben ● *vi* abfahren. **~ on** *vi* weiterfahren. **~ up** *vi* vorfahren

'drive-in *a* **~ cinema** Autokino *nt*

drivel /'drɪvl/ *n* (*fam*) Quatsch *m*

driven /'drɪvn/ *see* **drive**

driver /'draɪvə(r)/ *n* Fahrer(in) *m*(*f*); (*of train*) Lokführer *m*

driving /'draɪvɪŋ/ *a* ⟨*rain*⟩ peitschend; ⟨*force*⟩ treibend

driving: ~ lesson *n* Fahrstunde *f*. **~ licence** *n* Führerschein *m*. **~ school** *n* Fahrschule *f*. **~ test** Fahrprüfung *f*; **take one's ~ test** den Führerschein machen

drizzle /'drɪzl/ *n* Nieselregen *m* ● *vi* nieseln

drone /drəʊn/ *n* Drohne *f*; (*sound*) Brummen *nt*

droop /dru:p/ *vi* herabhängen; ⟨*flowers:*⟩ die Köpfe hängen lassen

drop /drɒp/ *n* Tropfen *m*; (*fall*) Fall *m*; (*in price, temperature*) Rückgang *m* ● *v* (*pt/pp* **dropped**) ● *vt* fallen lassen; abwerfen ⟨*bomb*⟩; (*omit*) auslassen; (*give up*) aufgeben ● *vi* fallen; (*fall lower*) sinken; ⟨*wind:*⟩ nachlassen. **~ in** *vi* vorbeikommen. **~ off** *vt* absetzen ⟨*person*⟩ ● *vi* abfallen; (*fall asleep*) einschlafen. **~ out** *vi* herausfallen; (*give up*) aufgeben

'drop-out *n* Aussteiger *m*

droppings /'drɒpɪŋz/ *npl* Kot *m*

drought /draʊt/ *n* Dürre *f*

drove /drəʊv/ *see* **drive**

droves /drəʊvz/ *npl* **in ~** in Scharen

drown /draʊn/ *vi* ertrinken ● *vt* ertränken; übertönen ⟨*noise*⟩; **be ~ed** ertrinken

drowsy /'draʊzɪ/ *a* schläfrig

drudgery /'drʌdʒərɪ/ *n* Plackerei *f*

drug /drʌg/ *n* Droge *f* ● *vt* (*pt/pp* **drugged**) betäuben

drug: ~ addict *n* Drogenabhängige(r) *m/f*. **~gist** *n* (*Amer*) Apotheker *m*. **~store** *n* (*Amer*) Drogerie *f*; (*dispensing*) Apotheke *f*

drum /drʌm/ *n* Trommel *f*; (*for oil*) Tonne *f* ● *v* (*pt/pp* **drummed**) ● *vi* trommeln ● *vt* **~ sth into s.o.** (*fam*) jdm etw einbleuen. **~mer** *n* Trommler *m*; (*in pop-group*) Schlagzeuger *m*. **~stick** *n* Trommelschlegel *m*; (*Culin*) Keule *f*

drunk /drʌŋk/ *see* **drink** ● *a* betrunken; **get ~** sich betrinken ● *n* Betrunkene(r) *m*

drunk|ard /'drʌŋkəd/ *n* Trinker *m*. **~en** *a* betrunken; **~en driving** Trunkenheit *f* am Steuer

dry /draɪ/ *a* (**drier, driest**) trocken ● *vt/i* trocknen; **~ one's eyes** sich *dat* die Tränen abwischen. **~ up** *vi* austrocknen; (*fig*) versiegen ● *vt* austrocknen; abtrocknen ⟨*dishes*⟩

dry: ~-'clean *vt* chemisch reinigen. **~-'cleaner's** *n* (*shop*) chemische Reinigung *f*. **~ness** *n* Trockenheit *f*

dual /'dju:əl/ *a* doppelt

dual: ~ 'carriageway *n* ≈ Schnellstraße *f*. **~-'purpose** *a* zweifach verwendbar

dub /dʌb/ *vt* (*pt/pp* **dubbed**) synchronisieren ⟨*film*⟩; kopieren ⟨*tape*⟩; (*name*) nennen

dubious /'dju:bɪəs/ *a* zweifelhaft; **be ~ about** Zweifel haben über (+ *acc*)

duchess /'dʌtʃɪs/ *n* Herzogin *f*

duck /dʌk/ *n* Ente *f* ● *vt* (*in water*) untertauchen; **~ one's head** den Kopf einziehen ● *vi* sich ducken. **~ling** *n* Entchen *nt*; (*Culin*) Ente *f*

duct /dʌkt/ *n* Rohr *nt*; (*Anat*) Gang *m*

dud /dʌd/ *a* (*fam*) nutzlos; ⟨*coin*⟩ falsch; ⟨*cheque*⟩ ungedeckt; (*forged*) gefälscht ● *n* (*fam*) (*banknote*) Blüte *f*; (*Mil: shell*) Blindgänger *m*

due /dju:/ *a* angemessen; **be ~** fällig sein; ⟨*baby:*⟩ erwartet werden; ⟨*train:*⟩ planmäßig ankommen; **~ to** (*owing to*) wegen (+ *gen*); **be ~ to** zurückzuführen sein auf (+ *acc*); **in ~ course** im Laufe der Zeit; ⟨*write*⟩ zu gegebener Zeit ● *adv* **~ west** genau westlich

duel /'dju:əl/ *n* Duell *nt*

dues /dju:z/ *npl* Gebühren *pl*

duet /dju:'et/ *n* Duo *nt*; (*vocal*) Duett *nt*

dug /dʌg/ *see* **dig**

duke /dju:k/ *n* Herzog *m*

dull /dʌl/ *a* (**-er, -est**) (*overcast, not bright*) trüb[e]; (*not shiny*) matt; ⟨*sound*⟩ dumpf; (*boring*) langweilig; (*stupid*) schwerfällig ● *vt* betäuben; abstumpfen ⟨*mind*⟩

duly /'dju:lɪ/ *adv* ordnungsgemäß

dumb /dʌm/ *a* (**-er, -est**) stumm; (*fam: stupid*) dumm. **~founded** *a* sprachlos

dummy /'dʌmɪ/ *n* (*tailor's*) [Schneider]puppe *f*; (*for baby*) Schnuller *m*; (*Comm*) Attrappe *f*

dump /dʌmp/ *n* Abfallhaufen *m*; (*for refuse*) Müllhalde *f*, Deponie *f*; (*fam: town*) Kaff *nt*; **be down in the ~s** (*fam*) deprimiert sein ● *vt* abladen; (*fam: put down*) hinwerfen (**on** auf + *acc*)

dumpling /'dʌmplɪŋ/ *n* Kloß *m*, Knödel *m*

dunce /dʌns/ *n* Dummkopf *m*

dune /dju:n/ *n* Düne *f*

dung /dʌŋ/ *n* Mist *m*

dungarees /dʌŋgə'ri:z/ *npl* Latzhose *f*

dungeon /'dʌndʒən/ *n* Verlies *nt*

dunk /dʌŋk/ *vt* eintunken

duo /'dju:əʊ/ *n* Paar *nt*; (*Mus*) Duo *nt*

dupe /dju:p/ *n* Betrogene(r) *m/f* ● *vt* betrügen

duplicate¹ /'dju:plɪkət/ *a* Zweit- ● *n* Doppel *nt*; (*document*) Duplikat *nt*; **in ~** in doppelter Ausfertigung *f*

duplicat|e² /'dju:plɪkeɪt/ *vt* kopieren; (*do twice*) zweimal machen. **~or** *n* Vervielfältigungsapparat *m*

durable /'djʊərəbl/ *a* haltbar

duration /djʊə'reɪʃn/ *n* Dauer *f*

duress /djʊə'res/ *n* Zwang *m*

during /'djʊərɪŋ/ *prep* während (+ *gen*)

dusk /dʌsk/ *n* [Abend]dämmerung *f*

dust /dʌst/ *n* Staub *m* ● *vt* abstauben; (*sprinkle*) bestäuben (**with** mit) ● *vi* Staub wischen

dust: ~bin *n* Mülltonne *f*. **~-cart** *n* Müllwagen *m*. **~er** *n* Staubtuch *nt*. **~-jacket** *n* Schutzumschlag *m*. **~man** *n* Müllmann *m*. **~pan** *n* Kehrschaufel *f*

dusty /'dʌstɪ/ *a* (**-ier, -iest**) staubig

Dutch /dʌtʃ/ *a* holländisch; **go ~** (*fam*) getrennte Kasse machen ● *n* (*Lang*) Holländisch *nt*; **the ~** *pl* die Holländer. **~man** *n* Holländer *m*

dutiable /'dju:tɪəbl/ *a* zollpflichtig

dutiful /'dju:tɪfl/ *a*, **-ly** *adv* pflichtbewußt; (*obedient*) gehorsam

duty /'dju:tɪ/ *n* Pflicht *f*; (*task*) Aufgabe *f*; (*tax*) Zoll *m*; **be on ~** Dienst haben. **~-free** *a* zollfrei

duvet /'du:veɪ/ *n* Steppdecke *f*

dwarf /dwɔ:f/ *n* (*pl* **-s** *or* **dwarves**) Zwerg *m*

dwell /dwel/ *vi* (*pt/pp* **dwelt**) (*liter*) wohnen; **~ on** (*fig*) verweilen bei. **~ing** *n* Wohnung *f*

dwindle /'dwɪndl/ *vi* abnehmen, schwinden

dye /daɪ/ *n* Farbstoff *m* ● *vt* (*pres p* **dyeing**) färben

dying /'daɪɪŋ/ *see* **die²**

dynamic /daɪ'næmɪk/ *a* dynamisch. **~s** *n* Dynamik *f*

dynamite /'daɪnəmaɪt/ *n* Dynamit *nt*

dynamo /'daɪnəməʊ/ *n* Dynamo *m*

dynasty /'dɪnəstɪ/ *n* Dynastie *f*

dysentery /'dɪsəntrɪ/ *n* Ruhr *f*

dyslex|ia /dɪs'leksɪə/ *n* Legasthenie *f*. **~ic** *a* legasthenisch; **be ~ic** Legastheniker sein

E

each /i:tʃ/ *a & pron* jede(r,s); (*per*) je; **~ other** einander; **£1~** £1 pro Person; (*for thing*) pro Stück

eager /'i:gə(r)/ *a*, **-ly** *adv* eifrig; **be ~ to do sth** etw gerne machen wollen. **~ness** *n* Eifer *m*

eagle /'i:gl/ *n* Adler *m*

ear¹ /ɪə(r)/ *n* (*of corn*) Ähre *f*

ear² *n* Ohr *nt*. **~ache** *n* Ohrenschmerzen *pl*. **~-drum** *n* Trommelfell *nt*

earl /ɜ:l/ *n* Graf *m*

early /'ɜ:lɪ/ *a & adv* (**-ier, -iest**) früh; ⟨*reply*⟩ baldig; **be ~** früh dran sein; **~ in the morning** früh am Morgen

'earmark *vt* **~ for** bestimmen für

earn /ɜ:n/ *vt* verdienen

earnest /'ɜ:nɪst/ *a*, **-ly** *adv* ernsthaft • *n* **in ~** im Ernst
earnings /'ɜ:nɪŋz/ *npl* Verdienst *m*
ear: ~phones *npl* Kopfhörer *pl*. **~-ring** *n* Ohrring *m*; (*clip-on*) Ohrklips *m*. **~shot** *n* **within/out of ~shot** in/außer Hörweite
earth /ɜ:θ/ *n* Erde *f*; (*of fox*) Bau *m*; **where/what on ~?** wo/was in aller Welt? • *vt* (*Electr*) erden
earthenware /'ɜ:θn-/ *n* Tonwaren *pl*
earthly /'ɜ:θlɪ/ *a* irdisch; **be no ~ use** (*fam*) völlig nutzlos sein
'earthquake *n* Erdbeben *nt*
earthy /'ɜ:θɪ/ *a* erdig; (*coarse*) derb
earwig /'ɪəwɪg/ *n* Ohrwurm *m*
ease /i:z/ *n* Leichtigkeit *f*; **at ~!** (*Mil*) rührt euch! **be/feel ill at ~** ein ungutes Gefühl haben • *vt* erleichtern; lindern ⟨*pain*⟩ • *vi* ⟨*pain:*⟩ nachlassen; ⟨*situation:*⟩ sich entspannen
easel /'i:zl/ *n* Staffelei *f*
easily /'i:zɪlɪ/ *adv* leicht, mit Leichtigkeit
east /i:st/ *n* Osten *m*; **to the ~ of** östlich von • *a* Ost-, ost- • *adv* nach Osten
Easter /'i:stə(r)/ *n* Ostern *nt* • *attrib* Oster-. **~ egg** *n* Osterei *nt*
east|erly /'i:stəlɪ/ *a* östlich. **~ern** *a* östlich. **~ward[s]** /-wəd[z]/ *adv* nach Osten
easy /'i:zɪ/ *a* (**-ier, -iest**) leicht; **take it ~** (*fam*) sich schonen; **take it ~!** beruhige dich! **go ~ with** (*fam*) sparsam umgehen mit
easy: ~ chair *n* Sessel *m*. **~'going** *a* gelassen; **too ~going** lässig
eat /i:t/ *vt/i* (*pt* **ate**, *pp* **eaten**) essen; ⟨*animal:*⟩ fressen. **~ up** *vt* aufessen
eat|able /'i:təbl/ *a* genießbar. **~er** *n* (*apple*) Eßapfel *m*
eau-de-Cologne /əʊdəkə'ləʊn/ *n* Kölnisch Wasser *nt*
eaves /i:vz/ *npl* Dachüberhang *m*. **~drop** *vi* (*pt/pp* **~dropped**) [heimlich] lauschen; **~drop on** belauschen
ebb /eb/ *n* (*tide*) Ebbe *f*; **at a low ~** (*fig*) auf einem Tiefstand • *vi* zurückgehen; (*fig*) verebben
ebony /'ebənɪ/ *n* Ebenholz *nt*
ebullient /ɪ'bʌlɪənt/ *a* überschwenglich
EC *abbr* (**European Community**) EG *f*
eccentric /ɪk'sentrɪk/ *a* exzentrisch • *n* Exzentriker *m*
ecclesiastical /ɪkli:zɪ'æstɪkl/ *a* kirchlich

echo /'ekəʊ/ *n* (*pl* **-es**) Echo *nt*, Widerhall *m* • *v* (*pt/pp* **echoed**, *pres p* **echoing**) • *vt* zurückwerfen; (*imitate*) nachsagen • *vi* widerhallen (**with** von)
eclipse /ɪ'klɪps/ *n* (*Astr*) Finsternis *f* • *vt* (*fig*) in den Schatten stellen
ecolog|ical /i:kə'lɒdʒɪkl/ *a* ökologisch. **~y** /i:'kɒlədʒɪ/ *n* Ökologie *f*
economic /i:kə'nɒmɪk/ *a* wirtschaftlich. **~al** *a* sparsam. **~ally** *adv* wirtschaftlich; (*thriftily*) sparsam. **~s** *n* Volkswirtschaft *f*
economist /ɪ'kɒnəmɪst/ *n* Volkswirt *m*; (*Univ*) Wirtschaftswissenschaftler *m*
economize /ɪ'kɒnəmaɪz/ *vi* sparen (**on** an + *dat*)
economy /ɪ'kɒnəmɪ/ *n* Wirtschaft *f*; (*thrift*) Sparsamkeit *f*
ecstasy /'ekstəsɪ/ *n* Ekstase *f*
ecstatic /ɪk'stætɪk/ *a*, **-ally** *adv* ekstatisch
ecu /'eɪkju:/ *n* Ecu *m*
ecumenical /i:kjʊ'menɪkl/ *a* ökumenisch
eczema /'eksɪmə/ *n* Ekzem *nt*
eddy /'edɪ/ *n* Wirbel *m*
edge /edʒ/ *n* Rand *m*; (*of table, lawn*) Kante *f*; (*of knife*) Schneide *f*; **on ~** (*fam*) nervös; **have the ~ on** (*fam*) etwas besser sein als • *vt* einfassen. **~ forward** *vi* sich nach vorn schieben
edging /'edʒɪŋ/ *n* Einfassung *f*
edgy /'edʒɪ/ *a* (*fam*) nervös
edible /'edɪbl/ *a* eßbar
edict /'i:dɪkt/ *n* Erlaß *m*
edifice /'edɪfɪs/ *n* [großes] Gebäude *nt*
edify /'edɪfaɪ/ *vt* (*pt/pp* **-ied**) erbauen. **~ing** *a* erbaulich
edit /'edɪt/ *vt* (*pt/pp* **edited**) redigieren; herausgeben ⟨*anthology, dictionary*⟩; schneiden ⟨*film, tape*⟩
edition /ɪ'dɪʃn/ *n* Ausgabe *f*; (*impression*) Auflage *f*
editor /'edɪtə(r)/ *n* Redakteur *m*; (*of anthology, dictionary*) Herausgeber *m*; (*of newspaper*) Chefredakteur *m*; (*of film*) Cutter(in) *m(f)*
editorial /edɪ'tɔ:rɪəl/ *a* redaktionell, Redaktions- • *n* (*Journ*) Leitartikel *m*
educate /'edjʊkeɪt/ *vt* erziehen; **be ~d at X** auf die X-Schule gehen. **~d** *a* gebildet
education /edjʊ'keɪʃn/ *n* Erziehung *f*; (*culture*) Bildung *f*. **~al** *a* pädagogisch; ⟨*visit*⟩ kulturell

eel /i:l/ *n* Aal *m*
eerie /'ɪərɪ/ *a* (**-ier, -iest**) unheimlich
effect /ɪ'fekt/ *n* Wirkung *f*, Effekt *m*; **in ~** in Wirklichkeit; **take ~** in Kraft treten ● *vt* bewirken
effective /ɪ'fektɪv/ *a*, **-ly** *adv* wirksam, effektiv; (*striking*) wirkungsvoll, effektvoll; (*actual*) tatsächlich. **~ness** *n* Wirksamkeit *f*
effeminate /ɪ'femɪnət/ *a* unmännlich
effervescent /efə'vesnt/ *a* sprudelnd
efficiency /ɪ'fɪʃənsɪ/ *n* Tüchtigkeit *f*; (*of machine, organization*) Leistungsfähigkeit *f*
efficient /ɪ'fɪʃənt/ *a* tüchtig; ⟨*machine, organization*⟩ leistungsfähig; ⟨*method*⟩ rationell. **~ly** *adv* gut; ⟨*function*⟩ rationell
effigy /'efɪdʒɪ/ *n* Bildnis *nt*
effort /'efət/ *n* Anstrengung *f*; **make an ~** sich (*dat*) Mühe geben. **~less** *a*, **-ly** *adv* mühelos
effrontery /ɪ'frʌntərɪ/ *n* Unverschämtheit *f*
effusive /ɪ'fju:sɪv/ *a*, **-ly** *adv* überschwenglich
e.g. *abbr* (**exempli gratia**) z.B.
egalitarian /ɪgælɪ'teərɪən/ *a* egalitär
egg¹ /eg/ *vt* **~ on** (*fam*) anstacheln
egg² *n* Ei *nt*. **~-cup** *n* Eierbecher *m*. **~shell** *n* Eierschale *f*. **~-timer** *n* Eieruhr *f*
ego /'i:gəʊ/ *n* Ich *nt*. **~centric** /-'sentrik/ *a* egozentrisch. **~ism** *n* Egoismus *m*. **~ist** *n* Egoist *m*. **~tism** *n* Ichbezogenheit *f*. **~tist** *n* ichbezogener Mensch *m*
Egypt /'i:dʒɪpt/ *n* Ägypten *nt*. **~ian** /ɪ'dʒɪpʃn/ *a* ägyptisch ● *n* Ägypter(in) *m*(*f*)
eiderdown /'aɪdə-/ *n* (*quilt*) Daunendecke *f*
eigh|t /eɪt/ *a* acht ● *n* Acht *f*; (*boat*) Achter *m*. **~'teen** *a* achtzehn. **~'teenth** *a* achtzehnte(r,s)
eighth /eɪtθ/ *a* achte(r,s) ● *n* Achtel *nt*
eightieth /'eɪtɪɪθ/ *a* achtzigste(r,s)
eighty /'eɪtɪ/ *a* achtzig
either /'aɪðə(r)/ *a* & *pron* **~ [of them]** einer von [den] beiden; (*both*) beide; **on ~ side** auf beiden Seiten ● *adv* **I don't ~** ich auch nicht ● *conj* **~... or** entweder ... oder
eject /ɪ'dʒekt/ *vt* hinauswerfen
eke /i:k/ *vt* **~ out** strecken; (*increase*) ergänzen; **~ out a living** sich kümmerlich durchschlagen
elaborate¹ /ɪ'læbərət/ *a*, **-ly** *adv* kunstvoll; (*fig*) kompliziert
elaborate² /ɪ'læbəreɪt/ *vi* ausführlicher sein; **~ on** näher ausführen
elapse /ɪ'læps/ *vi* vergehen
elastic /ɪ'læstɪk/ *a* elastisch ● *n* Gummiband *nt*. **~ 'band** *n* Gummiband *nt*
elasticity /ɪlæs'tɪsətɪ/ *n* Elastizität *f*
elated /ɪ'leɪtɪd/ *a* überglücklich
elbow /'elbəʊ/ *n* Ellbogen *m*
elder¹ /'eldə(r)/ *n* Holunder *m*
eld|er² *a* ältere(r,s) ● *n* **the ~er** der/die Ältere. **~erly** *a* alt. **~est** *a* älteste(r,s) ● *n* **the ~est** der/die Älteste
elect /ɪ'lekt/ *a* **the president ~** der designierte Präsident ● *vt* wählen; **~ to do sth** sich dafür entscheiden, etw zu tun. **~ion** /-ekʃn/ *n* Wahl *f*
elector /ɪ'lektə(r)/ *n* Wähler(in) *m*(*f*). **~al** *a* Wahl-; **~al roll** Wählerverzeichnis *nt*. **~ate** /-rət/ *n* Wählerschaft *f*
electric /ɪ'lektrɪk/ *a*, **-ally** *adv* elektrisch
electrical /ɪ'lektrɪkl/ *a* elektrisch; **~ engineering** Elektrotechnik *f*
electric: ~ 'blanket *n* Heizdecke *f*. **~ 'fire** *n* elektrischer Heizofen *m*
electrician /ɪlek'trɪʃn/ *n* Elektriker *m*
electricity /ɪlek'trɪsətɪ/ *n* Elektrizität *f*; (*supply*) Strom *m*
electrify /ɪ'lektrɪfaɪ/ *vt* (*pt/pp* **-ied**) elektrifizieren. **~ing** *a* (*fig*) elektrisierend
electrocute /ɪ'lektrəkju:t/ *vt* durch einen elektrischen Schlag töten; (*execute*) auf dem elektrischen Stuhl hinrichten
electrode /ɪ'lektrəʊd/ *n* Elektrode *f*
electron /ɪ'lektrɒn/ *n* Elektron *nt*
electronic /ɪlek'trɒnɪk/ *a* elektronisch. **~s** *n* Elektronik *f*
elegance /'elɪgəns/ *n* Eleganz *f*
elegant /'elɪgənt/ *a*, **-ly** *adv* elegant
elegy /'elɪdʒɪ/ *n* Elegie *f*
element /'elɪmənt/ *n* Element *nt*. **~ary** /-'mentərɪ/ *a* elementar
elephant /'elɪfənt/ *n* Elefant *m*
elevat|e /'elɪveɪt/ *vt* heben; (*fig*) erheben. **~ion** /-'veɪʃn/ *n* Erhebung *f*
elevator /'elɪveɪtə(r)/ *n* (*Amer*) Aufzug *m*, Fahrstuhl *m*
eleven /ɪ'levn/ *a* elf ● *n* Elf *f*. **~th** *a* elfte(r,s); **at the ~th hour** (*fam*) in letzter Minute
elf /elf/ *n* (*pl* **elves**) Elfe *f*
elicit /ɪ'lɪsɪt/ *vt* herausbekommen

eligible /'elɪdʒəbl/ *a* berechtigt; **~ young man** gute Partie *f*
eliminate /ɪ'lɪmɪneɪt/ *vt* ausschalten; (*excrete*) ausscheiden
élite /eɪ'li:t/ *n* Elite *f*
ellip|se /ɪ'lɪps/ *n* Ellipse *f*. **~tical** *a* elliptisch
elm /elm/ *n* Ulme *f*
elocution /elə'kju:ʃn/ *n* Sprecherziehung *f*
elongate /'i:lɒŋgeɪt/ *vt* verlängern
elope /ɪ'ləʊp/ *vi* durchbrennen (*fam*)
eloquen|ce /'eləkwəns/ *n* Beredsamkeit *f*. **~t** *a*, **-ly** *adv* beredt
else /els/ *adv* sonst; **who ~?** wer sonst? **nothing ~** sonst nichts; **or ~** oder; (*otherwise*) sonst; **someone/somewhere ~** jemand/irgendwo anders; **anyone ~** jeder andere; (*as question*) sonst noch jemand? **anything ~** alles andere; (*as question*) sonst noch etwas? **~where** *adv* woanders
elucidate /ɪ'lu:sɪdeɪt/ *vt* erläutern
elude /ɪ'lu:d/ *vt* entkommen (+ *dat*); (*avoid*) ausweichen (+ *dat*)
elusive /ɪ'lu:sɪv/ *a* **be ~** schwer zu fassen sein
emaciated /ɪ'meɪsɪeɪtɪd/ *a* abgezehrt
emanate /'eməneɪt/ *vi* ausgehen (**from** von)
emancipat|ed /ɪ'mænsɪpeɪtɪd/ *a* emanzipiert. **~ion** /-'peɪʃn/ *n* Emanzipation *f*; (*of slaves*) Freilassung *f*
embalm /ɪm'bɑ:m/ *vt* einbalsamieren
embankment /ɪm'bæŋkmənt/ *n* Böschung *f*; (*of railway*) Bahndamm *m*
embargo /em'bɑ:gəʊ/ *n* (*pl* **-es**) Embargo *nt*
embark /ɪm'bɑ:k/ *vi* sich einschiffen; **~ on** anfangen mit. **~ation** /embɑ:'keɪʃn/ *n* Einschiffung *f*
embarrass /ɪm'bærəs/ *vt* in Verlegenheit bringen. **~ed** *a* verlegen. **~ing** *a* peinlich. **~ment** *n* Verlegenheit *f*
embassy /'embəsɪ/ *n* Botschaft *f*
embedded /ɪm'bedɪd/ *a* **be deeply ~ in** tief stecken in (+ *dat*)
embellish /ɪm'belɪʃ/ *vt* verzieren; (*fig*) ausschmücken
embers /'embəz/ *npl* Glut *f*
embezzle /ɪm'bezl/ *vt* unterschlagen. **~ment** *n* Unterschlagung *f*
embitter /ɪm'bɪtə(r)/ *vt* verbittern
emblem /'embləm/ *n* Emblem *nt*
embodiment /ɪm'bɒdɪmənt/ *n* Verkörperung *f*
embody /ɪm'bɒdɪ/ *vt* (*pt/pp* **-ied**) verkörpern; (*include*) enthalten
emboss /ɪm'bɒs/ *vt* prägen
embrace /ɪm'breɪs/ *n* Umarmung *f* ● *vt* umarmen; (*fig*) umfassen ● *vi* sich umarmen
embroider /ɪm'brɔɪdə(r)/ *vt* besticken; sticken ⟨*design*⟩; (*fig*) ausschmücken ● *vi* sticken. **~y** *n* Stickerei *f*
embroil /ɪm'brɔɪl/ *vt* **become ~ed in sth** in etw (*acc*) verwickelt werden
embryo /'embrɪəʊ/ *n* Embryo *m*
emerald /'emərəld/ *n* Smaragd *m*
emer|ge /ɪ'mɜ:dʒ/ *vi* auftauchen (**from** aus); (*become known*) sich herausstellen; (*come into being*) entstehen. **~gence** /-əns/ *n* Auftauchen *nt*; Entstehung *f*
emergency /ɪ'mɜ:dʒənsɪ/ *n* Notfall *m*; **in an ~** im Notfall. **~ exit** *n* Notausgang *m*
emery-paper /'emərɪ-/ *n* Schmirgelpapier *nt*
emigrant /'emɪgrənt/ *n* Auswanderer *m*
emigrat|e /'emɪgreɪt/ *vi* auswandern. **~ion** /-'greɪʃn/ *n* Auswanderung *f*
eminent /'emɪnənt/ *a*, **-ly** *adv* eminent
emission /ɪ'mɪʃn/ *n* Ausstrahlung *f*; (*of pollutant*) Emission *f*
emit /ɪ'mɪt/ *vt* (*pt/pp* **emitted**) ausstrahlen ⟨*light, heat*⟩; ausstoßen ⟨*smoke, fumes, cry*⟩
emotion /ɪ'məʊʃn/ *n* Gefühl *nt*. **~al** *a* emotional; **become ~al** sich erregen
emotive /ɪ'məʊtɪv/ *a* emotional
empath|ize /'empəθaɪz/ *vi* **~ize with s.o.** sich in jdn einfühlen. **~y** *n* Einfühlungsvermögen *nt*
emperor /'empərə(r)/ *n* Kaiser *m*
emphasis /'emfəsɪs/ *n* Betonung *f*
emphasize /'emfəsaɪz/ *vt* betonen
emphatic /ɪm'fætɪk/ *a*, **-ally** *adv* nachdrücklich
empire /'empaɪə(r)/ *n* Reich *nt*
empirical /em'pɪrɪkl/ *a* empirisch
employ /ɪm'plɔɪ/ *vt* beschäftigen; (*appoint*) einstellen; (*fig*) anwenden. **~ee** /emplɔɪ'i:/ *n* Beschäftigte(r) *m/f*; (*in contrast to employer*) Arbeitnehmer *m*. **~er** *n* Arbeitgeber *m*. **~ment** *n* Beschäftigung *f*; (*work*) Arbeit *f*. **~ment agency** *n* Stellenvermittlung *f*
empower /ɪm'paʊə(r)/ *vt* ermächtigen
empress /'emprɪs/ *n* Kaiserin *f*
empties /'emptɪz/ *npl* leere Flaschen *pl*
emptiness /'emptɪnɪs/ *n* Leere *f*

empty /'emptɪ/ *a* leer ● *vt* leeren; ausleeren ⟨*container*⟩ ● *vi* sich leeren

emulate /'emjʊleɪt/ *vt* nacheifern (+ *dat*)

emulsion /ɪ'mʌlʃn/ *n* Emulsion *f*

enable /ɪ'neɪbl/ *vt* ~ **s.o. to** es jdm möglich machen, zu

enact /ɪ'nækt/ *vt* (*Theat*) aufführen

enamel /ɪ'næml/ *n* Email *nt*; (*on teeth*) Zahnschmelz *m*; (*paint*) Lack *m* ● *vt* (*pt*/*pp* **enamelled**) emaillieren

enamoured /ɪ'næməd/ *a* **be ~ of** sehr angetan sein von

enchant /ɪn'tʃɑ:nt/ *vt* bezaubern. **~ing** *a* bezaubernd. **~ment** *n* Zauber *m*

encircle /ɪn'sɜ:kl/ *vt* einkreisen

enclave /'enkleɪv/ *n* Enklave *f*

enclos|e /ɪn'kləʊz/ *vt* einschließen; (*in letter*) beilegen (**with** *dat*). **~ure** /-ʒə(r)/ *n* (*at zoo*) Gehege *nt*; (*in letter*) Anlage *f*

encompass /ɪn'kʌmpəs/ *vt* umfassen

encore /'ɒŋkɔ:(r)/ *n* Zugabe *f* ● *int* bravo!

encounter /ɪn'kaʊntə(r)/ *n* Begegnung *f*; (*battle*) Zusammenstoß *m* ● *vt* begegnen (+ *dat*); (*fig*) stoßen auf (+ *acc*)

encourag|e /ɪn'kʌrɪdʒ/ *vt* ermutigen; (*promote*) fördern. **~ement** *n* Ermutigung *f*. **~ing** *a* ermutigend

encroach /ɪn'krəʊtʃ/ *vi* ~ **on** eindringen in (+ *acc*) ⟨*land*⟩; beanspruchen ⟨*time*⟩

encumb|er /ɪn'kʌmbə(r)/ *vt* belasten (**with** mit). **~rance** /-rəns/ *n* Belastung *f*

encyclopaed|ia /ɪnsaɪklə'pi:dɪə/ *n* Enzyklopädie *f*, Lexikon *nt*. **~ic** *a* enzyklopädisch

end /end/ *n* Ende *nt*; (*purpose*) Zweck *m*; **in the ~** schließlich; **at the ~ of May** Ende Mai; **on ~** hochkant; **for days on ~** tagelang; **make ~s meet** (*fam*) [gerade] auskommen; **no ~ of** (*fam*) unheimlich viel(e) ● *vt* beenden ● *vi* enden; **~ up in** (*fam: arrive at*) landen in (+ *dat*)

endanger /ɪn'deɪndʒə(r)/ *vt* gefährden

endear|ing /ɪn'dɪərɪŋ/ *a* liebenswert. **~ment** *n* **term of ~ment** Kosewort *nt*

endeavour /ɪn'devə(r)/ *n* Bemühung *f* ● *vi* sich bemühen (**to** zu)

ending /'endɪŋ/ *n* Schluß *m*, Ende *nt*; (*Gram*) Endung *f*

endive /'endaɪv/ *n* Endivie *f*

endless /'endlɪs/ *a*, **-ly** *adv* endlos

endorse /en'dɔ:s/ *vt* (*Comm*) indossieren; (*confirm*) bestätigen. **~ment** *n* (*Comm*) Indossament *nt*; (*fig*) Bestätigung *f*; (*on driving licence*) Strafvermerk *m*

endow /ɪn'daʊ/ *vt* stiften; **be ~ed with** (*fig*) haben. **~ment** *n* Stiftung *f*

endur|able /ɪn'djʊərəbl/ *a* erträglich. **~ance** /-rəns/ *n* Durchhaltevermögen *nt*; **beyond ~ance** unerträglich

endur|e /ɪn'djʊə(r)/ *vt* ertragen ● *vi* [lange] bestehen. **~ing** *a* dauernd

enemy /'enəmɪ/ *n* Feind *m* ● *attrib* feindlich

energetic /enə'dʒetɪk/ *a* tatkräftig; **be ~** voller Energie sein

energy /'enədʒɪ/ *n* Energie *f*

enforce /ɪn'fɔ:s/ *vt* durchsetzen. **~d** *a* unfreiwillig

engage /ɪn'geɪdʒ/ *vt* einstellen ⟨*staff*⟩; (*Theat*) engagieren; (*Auto*) einlegen ⟨*gear*⟩ ● *vi* sich beteiligen (**in** an + *dat*); (*Techn*) ineinandergreifen. **~d** *a* besetzt; ⟨*person*⟩ beschäftigt; (*to be married*) verlobt; **get ~d** sich verloben (**to** mit). **~ment** *n* Verlobung *f*; (*appointment*) Verabredung *f*; (*Mil*) Gefecht *nt*

engaging /ɪn'geɪdʒɪŋ/ *a* einnehmend

engender /ɪn'dʒendə(r)/ *vt* (*fig*) erzeugen

engine /'endʒɪn/ *n* Motor *m*; (*Naut*) Maschine *f*; (*Rail*) Lokomotive *f*; (*of jet-plane*) Triebwerk *nt*. **~-driver** *n* Lokomotivführer *m*

engineer /endʒɪ'nɪə(r)/ *n* Ingenieur *m*; (*service, installation*) Techniker *m*; (*Naut*) Maschinist *m*; (*Amer*) Lokomotivführer *m* ● *vt* (*fig*) organisieren. **~ing** *n* **[mechanical] ~ing** Maschinenbau *m*

England /'ɪŋglənd/ *n* England *nt*

English /'ɪŋglɪʃ/ *a* englisch; **the ~ Channel** der Ärmelkanal ● *n* (*Lang*) Englisch *nt*; **in ~** auf englisch; **into ~** ins Englische; **the ~** *pl* die Engländer. **~man** *n* Engländer *m*. **~woman** *n* Engländerin *f*

engrav|e /ɪn'greɪv/ *vt* eingravieren. **~ing** *n* Stich *m*

engross /ɪn'grəʊs/ *vt* **be ~ed in** vertieft sein in (+ *acc*)

engulf /ɪn'gʌlf/ *vt* verschlingen

enhance /ɪn'hɑ:ns/ *vt* verschönern; (*fig*) steigern

enigma /ɪ'nɪgmə/ *n* Rätsel *nt*. **~tic** /enɪg'mætɪk/ *a* rätselhaft

enjoy /ɪn'dʒɔɪ/ *vt* genießen; **~ oneself** sich amüsieren; **~ cooking/painting** gern kochen/malen; **I ~ed it** es hat mir gut gefallen/⟨*food:*⟩ geschmeckt. **~able** /-əbl/ *a* angenehm, nett. **~ment** *n* Vergnügen *nt*

enlarge /ɪn'lɑːdʒ/ *vt* vergrößern ● *vi* **~ upon** sich näher auslassen über (+ *acc*). **~ment** *n* Vergrößerung *f*

enlighten /ɪn'laɪtn/ *vt* aufklären. **~ment** *n* Aufklärung *f*

enlist /ɪn'lɪst/ *vt* (*Mil*) einziehen; **~ s.o.'s help** jdn zur Hilfe heranziehen ● *vi* (*Mil*) sich melden

enliven /ɪn'laɪvn/ *vt* beleben

enmity /'enmətɪ/ *n* Feindschaft *f*

enormity /ɪ'nɔːmətɪ/ *n* Ungeheuerlichkeit *f*

enormous /ɪ'nɔːməs/ *a*, **-ly** *adv* riesig

enough /ɪ'nʌf/ *a, adv & n* genug; **be ~** reichen; **funnily ~** komischerweise; **I've had ~!** (*fam*) jetzt reicht's mir aber!

enquir|e /ɪn'kwaɪə(r)/ *vi* sich erkundigen (**about** nach) ● *vt* sich erkundigen nach. **~y** *n* Erkundigung *f*; (*investigation*) Untersuchung *f*

enrage /ɪn'reɪdʒ/ *vt* wütend machen

enrich /ɪn'rɪtʃ/ *vt* bereichern; (*improve*) anreichern

enrol /ɪn'rəʊl/ *v* (*pt/pp* **-rolled**) ● *vt* einschreiben ● *vi* sich einschreiben. **~ment** *n* Einschreibung *f*

ensemble /ɒn'sɒmbl/ *n* (*clothing & Mus*) Ensemble *nt*

ensign /'ensaɪn/ *n* Flagge *f*

enslave /ɪn'sleɪv/ *vt* versklaven

ensue /ɪn'sjuː/ *vi* folgen; (*result*) sich ergeben (**from** aus)

ensure /ɪn'ʃʊə(r)/ *vt* sicherstellen; **~ that** dafür sorgen, daß

entail /ɪn'teɪl/ *vt* erforderlich machen; **what does it ~?** was ist damit verbunden?

entangle /ɪn'tæŋgl/ *vt* **get ~d** sich verfangen (**in** in + *dat*); (*fig*) sich verstricken (**in** in + *acc*)

enter /'entə(r)/ *vt* eintreten/⟨*vehicle:*⟩ einfahren in (+ *acc*); einreisen in (+ *acc*) ⟨*country*⟩; (*register*) eintragen; sich anmelden zu ⟨*competition*⟩ ● *vi* eintreten; ⟨*vehicle:*⟩ einfahren; (*Theat*) auftreten; (*register as competitor*) sich anmelden; (*take part*) sich beteiligen (**in** an + *dat*)

enterpris|e /'entəpraɪz/ *n* Unternehmen *nt*; (*quality*) Unternehmungsgeist *m*. **~ing** *a* unternehmend

entertain /entə'teɪn/ *vt* unterhalten; (*invite*) einladen; (*to meal*) bewirten ⟨*guest*⟩; (*fig*) in Erwägung ziehen ● *vi* unterhalten; (*have guests*) Gäste haben. **~er** *n* Unterhalter *m*. **~ment** *n* Unterhaltung *f*

enthral /ɪn'θrɔːl/ *vt* (*pt/pp* **enthralled**) **be ~led** gefesselt sein (**by** von)

enthuse /ɪn'θjuːz/ *vi* **~ over** schwärmen von

enthusias|m /ɪn'θjuːzɪæzm/ *n* Begeisterung *f*. **~t** *n* Enthusiast *m*. **~tic** /-'æstɪk/ *a*, **-ally** *adv* begeistert

entice /ɪn'taɪs/ *vt* locken. **~ment** *n* Anreiz *m*

entire /ɪn'taɪə(r)/ *a* ganz. **~ly** *adv* ganz, völlig. **~ty** /-rətɪ/ *n* **in its ~ty** in seiner Gesamtheit

entitle /ɪn'taɪtl/ *vt* berechtigen; **~d ...** mit dem Titel ...; **be ~d to sth** das Recht auf etw (*acc*) haben. **~ment** *n* Berechtigung *f*; (*claim*) Anspruch *m* (**to** auf + *acc*)

entity /'entətɪ/ *n* Wesen *nt*

entomology /entə'mɒlədʒɪ/ *n* Entomologie *f*

entourage /'ɒntʊrɑːʒ/ *n* Gefolge *nt*

entrails /'entreɪlz/ *npl* Eingeweide *pl*

entrance[1] /ɪn'trɑːns/ *vt* bezaubern

entrance[2] /'entrəns/ *n* Eintritt *m*; (*Theat*) Auftritt *m*; (*way in*) Eingang *m*; (*for vehicle*) Einfahrt *f*. **~ examination** *n* Aufnahmeprüfung *f*. **~ fee** *n* Eintrittsgebühr *f*

entrant /'entrənt/ *n* Teilnehmer(in) *m*(*f*)

entreat /ɪn'triːt/ *vt* anflehen (**for** um)

entrench /ɪn'trentʃ/ *vt* **be ~ed in** verwurzelt sein in (+ *dat*)

entrust /ɪn'trʌst/ *vt* **~ s.o. with sth, ~ sth to s.o.** jdm etw anvertrauen

entry /'entrɪ/ *n* Eintritt *m*; (*into country*) Einreise *f*; (*on list*) Eintrag *m*; **no ~** Zutritt/(*Auto*) Einfahrt verboten. **~ form** *n* Anmeldeformular *nt*. **~ visa** *n* Einreisevisum *nt*

enumerate /ɪ'njuːməreɪt/ *vt* aufzählen

enunciate /ɪ'nʌnsɪeɪt/ *vt* [deutlich] aussprechen; (*state*) vorbringen

envelop /ɪn'veləp/ *vt* (*pt/pp* **enveloped**) einhüllen

envelope /'envələʊp/ *n* [Brief]umschlag *m*

enviable /'envɪəbl/ *a* beneidenswert

envious /ˈenvɪəs/ *a*, **-ly** *adv* neidisch (**of** auf + *acc*)
environment /ɪnˈvaɪərənmənt/ *n* Umwelt *f*
environmental /ɪnvaɪərənˈmentl/ *a* Umwelt-. **~ist** *n* Umweltschützer *m*. **~ly** *adv* **~ly friendly** umweltfreundlich
envisage /ɪnˈvɪzɪdʒ/ *vt* sich (*dat*) vorstellen
envoy /ˈenvɔɪ/ *n* Gesandte(r) *m*
envy /ˈenvɪ/ *n* Neid *m* • *vt* (*pt/pp* **-ied**) **~ s.o. sth** jdn um etw beneiden
enzyme /ˈenzaɪm/ *n* Enzym *nt*
epic /ˈepɪk/ *a* episch • *n* Epos *nt*
epidemic /epɪˈdemɪk/ *n* Epidemie *f*
epilep|sy /ˈepɪlepsɪ/ *n* Epilepsie *f*. **~tic** /-ˈleptɪk/ *a* epileptisch • *n* Epileptiker(in) *m(f)*
epilogue /ˈepɪlɒg/ *n* Epilog *m*
episode /ˈepɪsəʊd/ *n* Episode *f*; (*instalment*) Folge *f*
epistle /ɪˈpɪsl/ *n* (*liter*) Brief *m*
epitaph /ˈepɪtɑːf/ *n* Epitaph *nt*
epithet /ˈepɪθet/ *n* Beiname *m*
epitom|e /ɪˈpɪtəmɪ/ *n* Inbegriff *m*. **~ize** *vt* verkörpern
epoch /ˈiːpɒk/ *n* Epoche *f*. **~-making** *a* epochemachend
equal /ˈiːkwl/ *a* gleich (**to** *dat*); **be ~ to a task** einer Aufgabe gewachsen sein • *n* Gleichgestellte(r) *m/f* • *vt* (*pt/pp* **equalled**) gleichen (+ *dat*); (*fig*) gleichkommen (+ *dat*). **~ity** /ɪˈkwɒlətɪ/ *n* Gleichheit *f*
equalize /ˈiːkwəlaɪz/ *vt/i* ausgleichen. **~r** *n* (*Sport*) Ausgleich[streffer] *m*
equally /ˈiːkwəlɪ/ *adv* gleich; ⟨*divide*⟩ gleichmäßig; (*just as*) genauso
equanimity /ekwəˈnɪmətɪ/ *n* Gleichmut *f*
equat|e /ɪˈkweɪt/ *vt* gleichsetzen (**with** mit). **~ion** /-eɪʒn/ *n* (*Math*) Gleichung *f*
equator /ɪˈkweɪtə(r)/ *n* Äquator *m*. **~ial** /ekwəˈtɔːrɪəl/ *a* Äquator-
equestrian /ɪˈkwestrɪən/ *a* Reit-
equilibrium /iːkwɪˈlɪbrɪəm/ *n* Gleichgewicht *nt*
equinox /ˈiːkwɪnɒks/ *n* Tagundnachtgleiche *f*
equip /ɪˈkwɪp/ *vt* (*pt/pp* **equipped**) ausrüsten; (*furnish*) ausstatten. **~ment** *n* Ausrüstung *f*; Ausstattung *f*
equitable /ˈekwɪtəbl/ *a* gerecht
equity /ˈekwətɪ/ *n* Gerechtigkeit *f*
equivalent /ɪˈkwɪvələnt/ *a* gleichwertig; (*corresponding*) entsprechend • *n* Äquivalent *nt*; (*value*) Gegenwert *m*; (*counterpart*) Gegenstück *nt*
equivocal /ɪˈkwɪvəkl/ *a* zweideutig
era /ˈɪərə/ *n* Ära *f*, Zeitalter *nt*
eradicate /ɪˈrædɪkeɪt/ *vt* ausrotten
erase /ɪˈreɪz/ *vt* ausradieren; (*from tape*) löschen; (*fig*) auslöschen. **~r** *n* Radiergummi *m*
erect /ɪˈrekt/ *a* aufrecht • *vt* errichten. **~ion** /-ekʃn/ *n* Errichtung *f*; (*building*) Bau *m*; (*Biol*) Erektion *f*
ermine /ˈɜːmɪn/ *n* Hermelin *m*
ero|de /ɪˈrəʊd/ *vt* ⟨*water:*⟩ auswaschen; ⟨*acid:*⟩ angreifen. **~sion** /-əʊʒn/ *n* Erosion *f*
erotic /ɪˈrɒtɪk/ *a* erotisch. **~ism** /-tɪsɪzm/ *n* Erotik *f*
err /ɜː(r)/ *vi* sich irren; (*sin*) sündigen
errand /ˈerənd/ *n* Botengang *m*
erratic /ɪˈrætɪk/ *a* unregelmäßig; ⟨*person*⟩ unberechenbar
erroneous /ɪˈrəʊnɪəs/ *a* falsch; ⟨*belief, assumption*⟩ irrig. **~ly** *adv* fälschlich; irrigerweise
error /ˈerə(r)/ *n* Irrtum *m*; (*mistake*) Fehler *m*; **in ~** irrtümlicherweise
erudit|e /ˈerʊdaɪt/ *a* gelehrt. **~ion** /-ˈdɪʃn/ *n* Gelehrsamkeit *f*
erupt /ɪˈrʌpt/ *vi* ausbrechen. **~ion** /-ʌpʃn/ *n* Ausbruch *m*
escalat|e /ˈeskəleɪt/ *vt/i* eskalieren. **~ion** /-ˈleɪʃn/ *n* Eskalation *f*. **~or** *n* Rolltreppe *f*
escapade /ˈeskəpeɪd/ *n* Eskapade *f*
escape /ɪˈskeɪp/ *n* Flucht *f*; (*from prison*) Ausbruch *m*; **have a narrow ~** gerade noch davonkommen • *vi* flüchten; ⟨*prisoner:*⟩ ausbrechen; entkommen (**from** aus; **from s.o.** jdm); ⟨*gas:*⟩ entweichen • *vt* **~ notice** unbemerkt bleiben; **the name ~s me** der Name entfällt mir
escapism /ɪˈskeɪpɪzm/ *n* Flucht *f* vor der Wirklichkeit, Eskapismus *m*
escort[1] /ˈeskɔːt/ *n* (*of person*) Begleiter *m*; (*Mil*) Eskorte *f*; **under ~** unter Bewachung
escort[2] /ɪˈskɔːt/ *vt* begleiten; (*Mil*) eskortieren
Eskimo /ˈeskɪməʊ/ *n* Eskimo *m*
esoteric /esəˈterɪk/ *a* esoterisch
especial /ɪˈspeʃl/ *a* besondere(r,s). **~ly** *adv* besonders
espionage /ˈespɪənɑːʒ/ *n* Spionage *f*
essay /ˈeseɪ/ *n* Aufsatz *m*
essence /ˈesns/ *n* Wesen *nt*; (*Chem, Culin*) Essenz *f*; **in ~** im wesentlichen

essential /ɪ'senʃl/ *a* wesentlich; (*indispensable*) unentbehrlich ● *n* **the ~s** das Wesentliche; (*items*) das Nötigste. **~ly** *adv* im wesentlichen

establish /ɪ'stæblɪʃ/ *vt* gründen; (*form*) bilden; (*prove*) beweisen. **~ment** *n* (*firm*) Unternehmen *nt*

estate /ɪ'steɪt/ *n* Gut *nt*; (*possessions*) Besitz *m*; (*after death*) Nachlaß *m*; (*housing*) [Wohn]siedlung *f*. **~ agent** *n* Immobilienmakler *m*. **~ car** *n* Kombi[wagen] *m*

esteem /ɪ'sti:m/ *n* Achtung *f* ● *vt* hochschätzen

estimate[1] /'estɪmət/ *n* Schätzung *f*; (*Comm*) [Kosten]voranschlag *m*; **at a rough ~** grob geschätzt

estimat|e[2] /'estɪmeɪt/ *vt* schätzen. **~ion** /-'meɪʃn/ *n* Einschätzung *f*; (*esteem*) Achtung *f*; **in my ~ion** meiner Meinung nach

estuary /'estjʊərɪ/ *n* Mündung *f*

etc. /et'setərə/ *abbr* (**et cetera**) und so weiter, usw.

etching /'etʃɪŋ/ *n* Radierung *f*

eternal /ɪ'tɜ:nl/ *a*, **-ly** *adv* ewig

eternity /ɪ'tɜ:nətɪ/ *n* Ewigkeit *f*

ether /'i:θə(r)/ *n* Äther *m*

ethic /'eθɪk/ *n* Ethik *f*. **~al** *a* ethisch; (*morally correct*) moralisch einwandfrei. **~s** *n* Ethik *f*

Ethiopia /i:θɪ'əʊpɪə/ *n* Äthiopien *nt*

ethnic /'eθnɪk/ *a* ethnisch

etiquette /'etɪket/ *n* Etikette *f*

etymology /etɪ'mɒlədʒɪ/ *n* Etymologie *f*

eucalyptus /ju:kə'lɪptəs/ *n* Eukalyptus *m*

eulogy /'ju:lədʒɪ/ *n* Lobrede *f*

euphemis|m /'ju:fəmɪzm/ *n* Euphemismus *m*. **~tic** /-'mɪstɪk/ *a*, **-ally** *adv* verhüllend

euphoria /ju:'fɔ:rɪə/ *n* Euphorie *f*

Euro-: /'jʊərəʊ-/ *pref* **~cheque** *n* Euroscheck *m*. **~passport** *n* Europaß *m*

Europe /'jʊərəp/ *n* Europa *nt*

European /jʊərə'pɪən/ *a* europäisch; **~ Community** Europäische Gemeinschaft *f* ● *n* Europäer(in) *m*(*f*)

evacuat|e /ɪ'vækjʊeɪt/ *vt* evakuieren; räumen ⟨*building, area*⟩. **~ion** /-'eɪʃn/ *n* Evakuierung *f*; Räumung *f*

evade /ɪ'veɪd/ *vt* sich entziehen (+ *dat*); hinterziehen ⟨*taxes*⟩; **~ the issue** ausweichen

evaluate /ɪ'væljʊeɪt/ *vt* einschätzen

evange|lical /i:væn'dʒelɪkl/ *a* evangelisch. **~list** /ɪ'vændʒəlɪst/ *n* Evangelist *m*

evaporat|e /ɪ'væpəreɪt/ *vi* verdunsten; **~ed milk** Kondensmilch *f*, Dosenmilch *f*. **~ion** /-'reɪʃn/ *n* Verdampfung *f*

evasion /ɪ'veɪʒn/ *n* Ausweichen *nt*; **~ of taxes** Steuerhinterziehung *f*

evasive /ɪ'veɪsɪv/ *a*, **-ly** *adv* ausweichend; **be ~** ausweichen

eve /i:v/ *n* (*liter*) Vorabend *m*

even /'i:vn/ *a* (*level*) eben; (*same, equal*) gleich; (*regular*) gleichmäßig; ⟨*number*⟩ gerade; **get ~ with** (*fam*) es jdm heimzahlen ● *adv* sogar, selbst; **~ so** trotzdem; **not ~** nicht einmal ● *vt* **~ the score** ausgleichen. **~ up** *vt* ausgleichen ● *vi* sich ausgleichen

evening /'i:vnɪŋ/ *n* Abend *m*; **this ~** heute abend; **in the ~** abends, am Abend. **~ class** *n* Abendkurs *m*

evenly /'i:vnlɪ/ *adv* gleichmäßig

event /ɪ'vent/ *n* Ereignis *nt*; (*function*) Veranstaltung *f*; (*Sport*) Wettbewerb *m*; **in the ~ of** im Falle (+ *gen*); **in the ~** wie es sich ergab. **~ful** *a* ereignisreich

eventual /ɪ'ventjʊəl/ *a* **his ~ success** der Erfolg, der ihm schließlich zuteil wurde. **~ity** /-'ælətɪ/ *n* Eventualität *f*, Fall *m*. **~ly** *adv* schließlich

ever /'evə(r)/ *adv* je[mals]; **not ~** nie; **for ~** für immer; **hardly ~** fast nie; **~ since** seitdem; **~ so** (*fam*) sehr, furchtbar (*fam*)

'evergreen *n* immergrüner Strauch *m*/(*tree*) Baum *m*

ever'lasting *a* ewig

every /'evrɪ/ *a* jede(r,s); **~ one** jede(r,s) einzelne; **~ other day** jeden zweiten Tag

every: ~body *pron* jeder[mann]; alle *pl*. **~day** *a* alltäglich. **~one** *pron* jeder[mann]; alle *pl*. **~thing** *pron* alles. **~where** *adv* überall

evict /ɪ'vɪkt/ *vt* [aus der Wohnung] hinausweisen. **~ion** /-ɪkʃn/ *n* Ausweisung *f*

eviden|ce /'evɪdəns/ *n* Beweise *pl*; (*Jur*) Beweismaterial *nt*; (*testimony*) Aussage *f*; **give ~ce** aussagen. **~t** *a*, **-ly** *adv* offensichtlich

evil /'i:vl/ *a* böse ● *n* Böse *nt*

evocative /ɪ'vɒkətɪv/ *a* **be ~ of** heraufbeschwören

evoke /ɪ'vəʊk/ *vt* heraufbeschwören

evolution /i:və'lu:ʃn/ *n* Evolution *f*

evolve /ɪ'vɒlv/ *vt* entwickeln ● *vi* sich entwickeln

ewe /ju:/ *n* Schaf *nt*

exacerbate /ek'sæsəbeɪt/ *vt* verschlimmern; verschärfen ⟨*situation*⟩
exact /ɪg'zækt/ *a*, **-ly** *adv* genau; **not ~ly** nicht gerade. • *vt* erzwingen. **~ing** *a* anspruchsvoll. **~itude** /-ɪtju:d/ *n*, **~ness** *n* Genauigkeit *f*
exaggerat|e /ɪg'zædʒəreɪt/ *vt/i* übertreiben. **~ion** /-'reɪʃn/ *n* Übertreibung *f*
exalt /ɪg'zɔ:lt/ *vt* erheben; (*praise*) preisen
exam /ɪg'zæm/ *n* (*fam*) Prüfung *f*
examination /ɪgzæmɪ'neɪʃn/ *n* Untersuchung *f*; (*Sch*) Prüfung *f*
examine /ɪg'zæmɪn/ *vt* untersuchen; (*Sch*) prüfen; (*Jur*) verhören. **~r** *n* (*Sch*) Prüfer *m*
example /ɪg'zɑ:mpl/ *n* Beispiel *nt* (**of** für); **for ~** zum Beispiel; **make an ~ of** ein Exempel statuieren an (+ *dat*)
exasperat|e /ɪg'zæspəreɪt/ *vt* zur Verzweiflung treiben. **~ion** /-'reɪʃn/ *n* Verzweiflung *f*
excavat|e /'ekskəveɪt/ *vt* ausschachten; (*Archaeol*) ausgraben. **~ion** /-'veɪʃn/ *n* Ausgrabung *f*
exceed /ɪk'si:d/ *vt* übersteigen. **~ingly** *adv* äußerst
excel /ɪk'sel/ *v* (*pt/pp* **excelled**) *vi* sich auszeichnen • *vt* **~ oneself** sich selbst übertreffen
excellen|ce /'eksələns/ *n* Vorzüglichkeit *f*. **E~cy** *n* (*title*) Exzellenz *f*. **~t** *a*, **-ly** *adv* ausgezeichnet, vorzüglich
except /ɪk'sept/ *prep* außer (+ *dat*); **~ for** abgesehen von • *vt* ausnehmen. **~ing** *prep* außer (+ *dat*)
exception /ɪk'sepʃn/ *n* Ausnahme *f*; **take ~ to** Anstoß nehmen an (+ *dat*). **~al** *a*, **-ly** *adv* außergewöhnlich
excerpt /'eksɜ:pt/ *n* Auszug *m*
excess /ɪk'ses/ *n* Übermaß *nt* (**of** an + *dat*); (*surplus*) Überschuß *m*; **~es** *pl* Exzesse *pl*; **in ~ of** über (+ *dat*)
excess 'fare /'ekses-/ *n* Nachlösegebühr *f*
excessive /ɪk'sesɪv/ *a*, **-ly** *adv* übermäßig
exchange /ɪks'tʃeɪndʒ/ *n* Austausch *m*; (*Teleph*) Fernsprechamt *nt*; (*Comm*) [Geld]wechsel *m*; **[stock] ~** Börse *f*; **in ~** dafür • *vt* austauschen (**for** gegen); tauschen ⟨*places, greetings, money*⟩. **~ rate** *n* Wechselkurs *m*
exchequer /ɪks'tʃekə(r)/ *n* (*Pol*) Staatskasse *f*
excise¹ /'eksaɪz/ *n* **~ duty** Verbrauchssteuer *f*
excise² /ek'saɪz/ *vt* herausschneiden
excitable /ɪk'saɪtəbl/ *a* [leicht] erregbar
excit|e /ɪk'saɪt/ *vt* aufregen; (*cause*) erregen. **~ed** *a*, **-ly** *adv* aufgeregt; **get ~ed** sich aufregen. **~ement** *n* Aufregung *f*; Erregung *f*. **~ing** *a* aufregend; ⟨*story*⟩ spannend
exclaim /ɪk'skleɪm/ *vt/i* ausrufen
exclamation /ekskla'meɪʃn/ *n* Ausruf *m*. **~ mark** *n*, (*Amer*) **~ point** *n* Ausrufezeichen *nt*
exclu|de /ɪk'sklu:d/ *vt* ausschließen. **~ding** *prep* ausschließlich (+ *gen*). **~sion** /-ʒn/ *n* Ausschluß *m*
exclusive /ɪk'sklu:sɪv/ *a*, **-ly** *adv* ausschließlich; (*select*) exklusiv; **~ of** ausschließlich (+ *gen*)
excommunicate /ekskə'mju:nɪkeɪt/ *vt* exkommunizieren
excrement /'ekskrɪmənt/ *n* Kot *m*
excrete /ɪk'skri:t/ *vt* ausscheiden
excruciating /ɪk'skru:ʃɪeɪtɪŋ/ *a* gräßlich
excursion /ɪk'skɜ:ʃn/ *n* Ausflug *m*
excusable /ɪk'skju:zəbl/ *a* entschuldbar
excuse¹ /ɪk'skju:s/ *n* Entschuldigung *f*; (*pretext*) Ausrede *f*
excuse² /ɪk'skju:z/ *vt* entschuldigen; **~ from** freistellen von; **~ me!** Entschuldigung!
ex-di'rectory *a* **be ~** nicht im Telefonbuch stehen
execute /'eksɪkju:t/ *vt* ausführen; (*put to death*) hinrichten
execution /eksɪ'kju:ʃn/ *n* (*see* **execute**) Ausführung *f*; Hinrichtung *f*. **~er** *n* Scharfrichter *m*
executive /ɪg'zekjʊtɪv/ *a* leitend • *n* leitende(r) Angestellte(r) *m/f*; (*Pol*) Exekutive *f*
executor /ɪg'zekjʊtə(r)/ *n* (*Jur*) Testamentsvollstrecker *m*
exemplary /ɪg'zemplərɪ/ *a* beispielhaft; (*as a warning*) exemplarisch
exemplify /ɪg'zemplɪfaɪ/ *vt* (*pt/pp* **-ied**) veranschaulichen
exempt /ɪg'zempt/ *a* befreit • *vt* befreien (**from** von). **~ion** /-empʃn/ *n* Befreiung *f*
exercise /'eksəsaɪz/ *n* Übung *f*; **physical ~** körperliche Bewegung *f*; **take ~** sich bewegen • *vt* (*use*) ausüben; bewegen ⟨*horse*⟩; spazierenführen

⟨*dog*⟩ • *vi* sich bewegen. ~ **book** *n* [Schul]heft *nt*

exert /ɪg'zɜ:t/ *vt* ausüben; ~ **oneself** sich anstrengen. ~**ion** /-ɜ:ʃn/ *n* Anstrengung *f*

exhale /eks'heil/ *vt/i* ausatmen

exhaust /ɪg'zɔ:st/ *n* (*Auto*) Auspuff *m*; (*pipe*) Auspuffrohr *nt*; (*fumes*) Abgase *pl* • *vt* erschöpfen. ~**ed** *a* erschöpft. ~**ing** *a* anstrengend. ~**ion** /-ɔ:stʃn/ *n* Erschöpfung *f*. ~**ive** /-ɪv/ *a* (*fig*) erschöpfend

exhibit /ɪg'zɪbɪt/ *n* Ausstellungsstück *nt*; (*Jur*) Beweisstück *nt* • *vt* ausstellen; (*fig*) zeigen

exhibition /eksɪ'bɪʃn/ *n* Ausstellung *f*; (*Univ*) Stipendium *nt*. ~**ist** *n* Exhibitionist(in) *m*(*f*)

exhibitor /ɪg'zɪbɪtə(r)/ *n* Aussteller *m*

exhilarat|ed /ɪg'zɪləreɪtɪd/ *a* beschwingt. ~**ing** *a* berauschend. ~**ion** /-'reɪʃn/ *n* Hochgefühl *nt*

exhort /ɪg'zɔ:t/ *vt* ermahnen

exhume /ɪg'zju:m/ *vt* exhumieren

exile /'eksaɪl/ *n* Exil *nt*; (*person*) im Exil Lebende(r) *m/f* • *vt* ins Exil schicken

exist /ɪg'zɪst/ *vi* bestehen, existieren. ~**ence** /-əns/ *n* Existenz *f*; **be in** ~**ence** existieren

exit /'eksɪt/ *n* Ausgang *m*; (*Auto*) Ausfahrt *f*; (*Theat*) Abgang *m* • *vi* (*Theat*) abgehen. ~ **visa** *n* Ausreisevisum *nt*

exonerate /ɪg'zɒnəreɪt/ *vt* entlasten

exorbitant /ɪg'zɔ:bɪtənt/ *a* übermäßig hoch

exorcize /'eksɔ:saɪz/ *vt* austreiben

exotic /ɪg'zɒtɪk/ *a* exotisch

expand /ɪk'spænd/ *vt* ausdehnen; (*explain better*) weiter ausführen • *vi* sich ausdehnen; (*Comm*) expandieren; ~ **on** (*fig*) weiter ausführen

expans|e /ɪk'spæns/ *n* Weite *f*. ~**ion** /-ænʃn/ *n* Ausdehnung *f*; (*Techn, Pol, Comm*) Expansion *f*. ~**ive** /-ɪv/ *a* mitteilsam

expatriate /eks'pætrɪət/ *n* **be an** ~ im Ausland leben

expect /ɪk'spekt/ *vt* erwarten; (*suppose*) annehmen; **I** ~ **so** wahrscheinlich; **we** ~ **to arrive on Monday** wir rechnen damit, daß wir am Montag ankommen

expectan|cy /ɪk'spektənsɪ/ *n* Erwartung *f*. ~**t** *a*, **-ly** *adv* erwartungsvoll; ~**t mother** werdende Mutter *f*

expectation /ekspek'teɪʃn/ *n* Erwartung *f*; ~ **of life** Lebenserwartung *f*

expedient /ɪk'spi:dɪənt/ *a* zweckdienlich

expedite /'ekspɪdaɪt/ *vt* beschleunigen

expedition /ekspɪ'dɪʃn/ *n* Expedition *f*. ~**ary** *a* (*Mil*) Expeditions-

expel /ɪk'spel/ *vt* (*pt/pp* **expelled**) ausweisen (**from** aus); (*from school*) von der Schule verweisen

expend /ɪk'spend/ *vt* aufwenden. ~**able** /-əbl/ *a* entbehrlich

expenditure /ɪk'spendɪtʃə(r)/ *n* Ausgaben *pl*

expense /ɪk'spens/ *n* Kosten *pl*; **business** ~**s** *pl* Spesen *pl*; **at my** ~ auf meine Kosten; **at the** ~ **of** (*fig*) auf Kosten (+ *gen*)

expensive /ɪk'spensɪv/ *a*, **-ly** *adv* teuer

experience /ɪk'spɪərɪəns/ *n* Erfahrung *f*; (*event*) Erlebnis *nt* • *vt* erleben. ~**d** *a* erfahren

experiment /ɪk'sperɪmənt/ *n* Versuch *m*, Experiment *nt* • /-ment/ *vi* experimentieren. ~**al** /-'mentl/ *a* experimentell

expert /'ekspɜ:t/ *a*, **-ly** *adv* fachmännisch • *n* Fachmann *m*, Experte *m*

expertise /ekspɜ:'ti:z/ *n* Sachkenntnis *f*; (*skill*) Geschick *nt*

expire /ɪk'spaɪə(r)/ *vi* ablaufen

expiry /ɪk'spaɪərɪ/ *n* Ablauf *m*. ~ **date** *n* Verfallsdatum *nt*

explain /ɪk'spleɪn/ *vt* erklären

explana|tion /eksplə'neɪʃn/ *n* Erklärung *f*. ~**tory** /ɪk'splænətərɪ/ *a* erklärend

expletive /ɪk'spli:tɪv/ *n* Kraftausdruck *m*

explicit /ɪk'splɪsɪt/ *a*, **-ly** *adv* deutlich

explode /ɪk'spləʊd/ *vi* explodieren • *vt* zur Explosion bringen

exploit[1] /'eksplɔɪt/ *n* [Helden]tat *f*

exploit[2] /ɪk'splɔɪt/ *vt* ausbeuten. ~**ation** /eksplɔɪ'teɪʃn/ *n* Ausbeutung *f*

explora|tion /eksplə'reɪʃn/ *n* Erforschung *f*. ~**tory** /ɪk'splɒrətərɪ/ *a* Probe-

explore /ɪk'splɔ:(r)/ *vt* erforschen. ~**r** *n* Forschungsreisende(r) *m*

explos|ion /ɪk'spləʊʒn/ *n* Explosion *f*. ~**ive** /-sɪv/ *a* explosiv • *n* Sprengstoff *m*

exponent /ɪk'spəʊnənt/ *n* Vertreter *m*

export[1] /'ekspɔ:t/ *n* Export *m*, Ausfuhr *f*

export² /ɪk'spɔ:t/ *vt* exportieren, ausführen. **~er** *n* Exporteur *m*

expos|e /ɪk'spəʊz/ *vt* freilegen; (*to danger*) aussetzen (**to** *dat*); (*reveal*) aufdecken; (*Phot*) belichten. **~ure** /-ʒə(r)/ *n* Aussetzung *f*; (*Med*) Unterkühlung *f*; (*Phot*) Belichtung *f*; **24 ~ures** 24 Aufnahmen

expound /ɪk'spaʊnd/ *vt* erläutern

express /ɪk'spres/ *a* ausdrücklich; ⟨*purpose*⟩ fest ● *adv* ⟨*send*⟩ per Eilpost ● *n* (*train*) Schnellzug *m* ● *vt* ausdrücken; **~ oneself** sich ausdrücken. **~ion** /-ʃn/ *n* Ausdruck *m*. **~ive** /-ɪv/ *a* ausdrucksvoll. **~ly** *adv* ausdrücklich

expulsion /ɪk'spʌlʃn/ *n* Ausweisung *f*; (*Sch*) Verweisung *f* von der Schule

expurgate /'ekspəgeɪt/ *vt* zensieren

exquisite /ek'skwɪzɪt/ *a* erlesen

ex-'serviceman *n* Veteran *m*

extempore /ɪk'stempərɪ/ *adv* ⟨*speak*⟩ aus dem Stegreif

extend /ɪk'stend/ *vt* verlängern; (*stretch out*) ausstrecken; (*enlarge*) vergrößern ● *vi* sich ausdehnen; ⟨*table:*⟩ sich ausziehen lassen

extension /ɪk'stenʃn/ *n* Verlängerung *f*; (*to house*) Anbau *m*; (*Teleph*) Nebenanschluß *m*; **~ 7** Apparat 7

extensive /ɪk'stensɪv/ *a* weit; (*fig*) umfassend. **~ly** *adv* viel

extent /ɪk'stent/ *n* Ausdehnung *f*; (*scope*) Ausmaß *nt*, Umfang *m*; **to a certain ~** in gewissem Maße

extenuating /ɪk'stenjʊeɪtɪŋ/ *a* mildernd

exterior /ɪk'stɪərɪə(r)/ *a* äußere(r,s) ● *n* **the ~** das Äußere

exterminat|e /ɪk'stɜ:mɪneɪt/ *vt* ausrotten. **~ion** /-'neɪʃn/ *n* Ausrottung *f*

external /ɪk'stɜ:nl/ *a* äußere(r,s); **for ~ use only** (*Med*) nur äußerlich. **~ly** *adv* äußerlich

extinct /ɪk'stɪŋkt/ *a* ausgestorben; ⟨*volcano*⟩ erloschen. **~ion** /-ɪŋkʃn/ *n* Aussterben *nt*

extinguish /ɪk'stɪŋgwɪʃ/ *vt* löschen. **~er** *n* Feuerlöscher *m*

extol /ɪk'stəʊl/ *vt* (*pt/pp* **extolled**) preisen

extort /ɪk'stɔ:t/ *vt* erpressen. **~ion** /-ɔ:ʃn/ *n* Erpressung *f*

extortionate /ɪk'stɔ:ʃənət/ *a* übermäßig hoch

extra /'ekstrə/ *a* zusätzlich ● *adv* extra; (*especially*) besonders; **~ strong** extrastark ● *n* (*Theat*) Statist(in) *m*(*f*); **~s** *pl* Nebenkosten *pl*; (*Auto*) Extras *pl*

extract¹ /'ekstrækt/ *n* Auszug *m*; (*Culin*) Extrakt *m*

extract² /ɪk'strækt/ *vt* herausziehen; ziehen ⟨*tooth*⟩; (*fig*) erzwingen. **~or [fan]** *n* Entlüfter *m*

extradit|e /'ekstrədaɪt/ *vt* (*Jur*) ausliefern. **~ion** /-'dɪʃn/ *n* (*Jur*) Auslieferung *f*

extra'marital *a* außerehelich

extraordinary /ɪk'strɔ:dɪnərɪ/ *a*, **-ily** *adv* außerordentlich; (*strange*) seltsam

extravagan|ce /ɪk'strævəgəns/ *n* Verschwendung *f*; **an ~ce** ein Luxus *m*. **~t** *a* verschwenderisch; (*exaggerated*) extravagant

extrem|e /ɪk'stri:m/ *a* äußerste(r,s); (*fig*) extrem ● *n* Extrem *nt*; **in the ~e** im höchsten Grade. **~ely** *adv* äußerst. **~ist** *n* Extremist *m*

extremit|y /ɪk'stremətɪ/ *n* (*distress*) Not *f*; **the ~ies** *pl* die Extremitäten *pl*

extricate /'ekstrɪkeɪt/ *vt* befreien

extrovert /'ekstrəvɜ:t/ *n* extravertierter Mensch *m*

exuberant /ɪg'zju:bərənt/ *a* überglücklich

exude /ɪg'zju:d/ *vt* absondern; (*fig*) ausstrahlen

exult /ɪg'zʌlt/ *vi* frohlocken

eye /aɪ/ *n* Auge *nt*; (*of needle*) Öhr *nt*; (*for hook*) Öse *f*; **keep an ~ on** aufpassen auf (+ *acc*); **see ~ to ~** einer Meinung sein ● *vt* (*pt/pp* **eyed**, *pres p* **ey[e]ing**) ansehen

eye: ~ball *n* Augapfel *m*. **~brow** *n* Augenbraue *f*. **~lash** *n* Wimper *f*. **~let** /-lɪt/ *n* Öse *f*. **~lid** *n* Augenlid *nt*. **~-shadow** *n* Lidschatten *m*. **~sight** *n* Sehkraft *f*. **~sore** *n* (*fam*) Schandfleck *m*. **~-tooth** *n* Eckzahn *m*. **~witness** *n* Augenzeuge *m*

F

fable /'feɪbl/ *n* Fabel *f*

fabric /'fæbrɪk/ *n* Stoff *m*; (*fig*) Gefüge *nt*

fabrication /fæbrɪ'keɪʃn/ *n* Erfindung *f*

fabulous /'fæbjʊləs/ *a* (*fam*) phantastisch

façade /fə'sɑ:d/ *n* Fassade *f*

face /feɪs/ *n* Gesicht *nt*; (*grimace*) Grimasse *f*; (*surface*) Fläche *f*; (*of clock*) Zifferblatt *nt*; **pull ~s** Gesichter schneiden; **in the ~ of** angesichts (+ *gen*); **on the ~ of it** allem Anschein nach ● *vt/i* gegenüberstehen (+ *dat*); **~ north** ⟨*house:*⟩ nach Norden liegen; **~ me!** sieh mich an! **~ the fact that** sich damit abfinden, daß; **~ up to s.o.** jdm die Stirn bieten

face: ~-flannel *n* Waschlappen *m*. **~less** *a* anonym. **~-lift** *n* Gesichtsstraffung *f*

facet /'fæsɪt/ *n* Facette *f*; (*fig*) Aspekt *m*

facetious /fə'siːʃəs/ *a*, **-ly** *adv* spöttisch

'face value *n* Nennwert *m*

facial /'feɪʃl/ *a* Gesichts-

facile /'fæsaɪl/ *a* oberflächlich

facilitate /fə'sɪlɪteɪt/ *vt* erleichtern

facilit|y /fə'sɪlətɪ/ *n* Leichtigkeit *f*; (*skill*) Gewandtheit *f*; **~ies** *pl* Einrichtungen *pl*

facing /'feɪsɪŋ/ *n* Besatz *m*

facsimile /fæk'sɪməlɪ/ *n* Faksimile *nt*

fact /fækt/ *n* Tatsache *f*; **in ~** tatsächlich; (*actually*) eigentlich

faction /'fækʃn/ *n* Gruppe *f*

factor /'fæktə(r)/ *n* Faktor *m*

factory /'fæktərɪ/ *n* Fabrik *f*

factual /'fæktʃʊəl/ *a*, **-ly** *adv* sachlich

faculty /'fækəltɪ/ *n* Fähigkeit *f*; (*Univ*) Fakultät *f*

fad /fæd/ *n* Fimmel *m*

fade /feɪd/ *vi* verblassen; ⟨*material:*⟩ verbleichen; ⟨*sound:*⟩ abklingen; ⟨*flower:*⟩ verwelken. **~ in/out** *vt* (*Radio, TV*) ein-/ausblenden

fag /fæg/ *n* (*chore*) Plage *f*; (*fam: cigarette*) Zigarette *f*; (*Amer sl*) Homosexuelle(r) *m*

fagged /fægd/ *a* **~ out** (*fam*) völlig erledigt

Fahrenheit /'færənhaɪt/ *a* Fahrenheit

fail /feɪl/ *n* **without ~** unbedingt ● *vi* ⟨*attempt:*⟩ scheitern; (*grow weak*) nachlassen; (*break down*) versagen; (*in exam*) durchfallen; **~ to do sth** etw nicht tun; **he ~ed to break the record** es gelang ihm nicht, den Rekord zu brechen ● *vt* nicht bestehen ⟨*exam*⟩; durchfallen lassen ⟨*candidate*⟩; (*disappoint*) enttäuschen; **words ~ me** ich weiß nicht, was ich sagen soll

failing /'feɪlɪŋ/ *n* Fehler *m* ● *prep* **~ that** andernfalls

failure /'feɪljə(r)/ *n* Mißerfolg *m*; (*breakdown*) Versagen *nt*; (*person*) Versager *m*

faint /feɪnt/ *a* (**-er, -est**), **-ly** *adv* schwach; **I feel ~** mir ist schwach ● *n* Ohnmacht *f* ● *vi* ohnmächtig werden

faint: ~-'hearted *a* zaghaft. **~ness** *n* Schwäche *f*

fair[1] /feə(r)/ *n* Jahrmarkt *m*; (*Comm*) Messe *f*

fair[2] *a* (**-er, -est**) ⟨*hair*⟩ blond; ⟨*skin*⟩ hell; ⟨*weather*⟩ heiter; (*just*) gerecht, fair; (*quite good*) ziemlich gut; (*Sch*) genügend; **a ~ amount** ziemlich viel ● *adv* **play ~** fair sein. **~ly** *adv* gerecht; (*rather*) ziemlich. **~ness** *n* Blondheit *f*; Helle *f*; Gerechtigkeit *f*; (*Sport*) Fairneß *f*

fairy /'feərɪ/ *n* Elfe *f*; **good/wicked ~** gute/böse Fee *f*. **~ story, ~-tale** *n* Märchen *nt*

faith /feɪθ/ *n* Glaube *m*; (*trust*) Vertrauen *nt* (**in** zu); **in good ~** in gutem Glauben

faithful /'feɪθfl/ *a*, **-ly** *adv* treu; (*exact*) genau; **Yours ~ly** Hochachtungsvoll. **~ness** *n* Treue *f*; Genauigkeit *f*

'faith-healer *n* Gesundbeter(in) *m*(*f*)

fake /feɪk/ *a* falsch ● *n* Fälschung *f*; (*person*) Schwindler *m* ● *vt* fälschen; (*pretend*) vortäuschen

falcon /'fɔːlkən/ *n* Falke *m*

fall /fɔːl/ *n* Fall *m*; (*heavy*) Sturz *m*; (*in prices*) Fallen *nt*; (*Amer: autumn*) Herbst *m*; **have a ~** fallen ● *vi* (*pt* **fell**, *pp* **fallen**) fallen; (*heavily*) stürzen; ⟨*night:*⟩ anbrechen; **~ in love** sich verlieben; **~ back on** zurückgreifen auf (+ *acc*); **~ for s.o.** (*fam*) sich in jdn verlieben; **~ for sth** (*fam*) auf etw (*acc*) hereinfallen. **~ about** *vi* (*with laughter*) sich [vor Lachen] kringeln. **~ down** *vi* umfallen; ⟨*thing:*⟩ herunterfallen; ⟨*building:*⟩ einstürzen. **~ in** *vi* hineinfallen; (*collapse*) einfallen; (*Mil*) antreten; **~ in with** sich anschließen (+ *dat*). **~ off** *vi* herunterfallen; (*diminish*) abnehmen. **~ out** *vi* herausfallen; ⟨*hair:*⟩ ausfallen; (*quarrel*) sich überwerfen. **~ over** *vi* hinfallen. **~ through** *vi* durchfallen; ⟨*plan:*⟩ ins Wasser fallen

fallacy /'fæləsɪ/ *n* Irrtum *m*

fallible /'fæləbl/ *a* fehlbar

'fall-out *n* [radioaktiver] Niederschlag *m*

fallow /'fæləʊ/ *a* **lie ~** brachliegen

false /fɔ:ls/ *a* falsch; (*artificial*) künstlich; **~ start** (*Sport*) Fehlstart *m*. **~hood** *n* Unwahrheit *f*. **~ly** *adv* falsch. **~ness** *n* Falschheit *f*

false 'teeth *npl* [künstliches] Gebiß *nt*

falsify /'fɔ:lsɪfaɪ/ *vt* (*pt*/*pp* **-ied**) fälschen; (*misrepresent*) verfälschen

falter /'fɔ:ltə(r)/ *vi* zögern; (*stumble*) straucheln

fame /feɪm/ *n* Ruhm *m*. **~d** *a* berühmt

familiar /fə'mɪljə(r)/ *a* vertraut; (*known*) bekannt; **too ~** familiär. **~ity** /-lɪ'ærətɪ/ *n* Vertrautheit *f*. **~ize** *vt* vertraut machen (**with** mit)

family /'fæməlɪ/ *n* Familie *f*

family: ~ al'lowance *n* Kindergeld *nt*. **~ 'doctor** *n* Hausarzt *m*. **~ 'life** *n* Familienleben *nt*. **~ 'planning** *n* Familienplanung *f*. **~ 'tree** *n* Stammbaum *m*

famine /'fæmɪn/ *n* Hungersnot *f*

famished /'fæmɪʃt/ *a* sehr hungrig

famous /'feɪməs/ *a* berühmt

fan¹ /fæn/ *n* Fächer *m*; (*Techn*) Ventilator *m* ● *v* (*pt*/*pp* **fanned**) ● *vt* fächeln; **~ oneself** sich fächeln ● *vi* **~ out** sich fächerförmig ausbreiten

fan² *n* (*admirer*) Fan *m*

fanatic /fə'nætɪk/ *n* Fanatiker *m*. **~al** *a*, **-ly** *adv* fanatisch. **~ism** /-sɪzm/ *n* Fanatismus *m*

'fan belt *n* Keilriemen *m*

fanciful /'fænsɪfl/ *a* phantastisch; (*imaginative*) phantasiereich

fancy /'fænsɪ/ *n* Phantasie *f*; **have a ~ to** Lust haben, zu; **I have taken a real ~ to him** er hat es mir angetan ● *a* ausgefallen; **~ cakes and biscuits** Feingebäck *nt* ● *vt* (*believe*) meinen; (*imagine*) sich (*dat*) einbilden; (*fam: want*) Lust haben auf (+ *acc*); **~ that!** stell dir vor! (*really*) tatsächlich! **~ 'dress** *n* Kostüm *nt*

fanfare /'fænfeə(r)/ *n* Fanfare *f*

fang /fæŋ/ *n* Fangzahn *m*; (*of snake*) Giftzahn *m*

fan: ~ heater *n* Heizlüfter *m*. **~light** *n* Oberlicht *nt*

fantas|ize /'fæntəsaɪz/ *vi* phantasieren. **~tic** /-'tæstɪk/ *a* phantastisch. **~y** *n* Phantasie *f*; (*Mus*) Fantasie *f*

far /fɑ:(r)/ *adv* weit; (*much*) viel; **by ~** bei weitem; **~ away** weit weg; **as ~ as I know** soviel ich weiß; **as ~ as the church** bis zur Kirche ● *a* **at the ~ end** am anderen Ende; **the F~ East** der Ferne Osten

farc|e /fɑ:s/ *n* Farce *f*. **~ical** *a* lächerlich

fare /feə(r)/ *n* Fahrpreis *m*; (*money*) Fahrgeld *nt*; (*food*) Kost *f*; **air ~** Flugpreis *m*. **~-dodger** /-dɒdʒə(r)/ *n* Schwarzfahrer *m*

farewell /feə'wel/ *int* (*liter*) lebe wohl! ● *n* Lebewohl *nt*; **~ dinner** Abschiedsessen *nt*

far-'fetched *a* weit hergeholt; **be ~** an den Haaren herbeigezogen sein

farm /fɑ:m/ *n* Bauernhof *m* ● *vi* Landwirtschaft betreiben ● *vt* bewirtschaften ⟨*land*⟩. **~er** *n* Landwirt *m*

farm: ~house *n* Bauernhaus *nt*. **~ing** *n* Landwirtschaft *f*. **~yard** *n* Hof *m*

far: ~-'reaching *a* weitreichend. **~-'sighted** *a* (*fig*) umsichtig; (*Amer: long-sighted*) weitsichtig

fart /fɑ:t/ *n* (*vulg*) Furz *m* ● *vi* (*vulg*) furzen

farther /'fɑ:ðə(r)/ *adv* weiter; **~ off** weiter entfernt ● *a* **at the ~ end** am anderen Ende

fascinat|e /'fæsɪneɪt/ *vt* faszinieren. **~ing** *a* faszinierend. **~ion** /-'neɪʃn/ *n* Faszination *f*

fascis|m /'fæʃɪzm/ *n* Faschismus *m*. **~t** *n* Faschist *m* ● *a* faschistisch

fashion /'fæʃn/ *n* Mode *f*; (*manner*) Art *f* ● *vt* machen; (*mould*) formen. **~able** /-əbl/ *a*, **-bly** *adv* modisch; **be ~able** Mode sein

fast¹ /fɑ:st/ *a* & *adv* (**-er, -est**) schnell; (*firm*) fest; ⟨*colour*⟩ waschecht; **be ~** ⟨*clock:*⟩ vorgehen; **be ~ asleep** fest schlafen

fast² *n* Fasten *nt* ● *vi* fasten

'fastback *n* (*Auto*) Fließheck *nt*

fasten /'fɑ:sn/ *vt* zumachen; (*fix*) befestigen (**to** an + *dat*); **~ one's seatbelt** sich anschnallen. **~er** *n*, **~ing** *n* Verschluß *m*

fastidious /fə'stɪdɪəs/ *a* wählerisch; (*particular*) penibel

fat /fæt/ *a* (**fatter, fattest**) dick; ⟨*meat*⟩ fett ● *n* Fett *nt*

fatal /'feɪtl/ *a* tödlich; ⟨*error*⟩ verhängnisvoll. **~ism** /-təlɪzm/ *n* Fatalismus *m*. **~ist** /-təlist/ *n* Fatalist *m*. **~ity** /fə'tælətɪ/ *n* Todesopfer *nt*. **~ly** *adv* tödlich

fate /feɪt/ *n* Schicksal *nt*. **~ful** *a* verhängnisvoll

'fat-head *n* (*fam*) Dummkopf *m*

father /'fɑ:ðə(r)/ *n* Vater *m*; **F~ Christmas** der Weihnachtsmann ● *vt* zeugen
father: ~hood *n* Vaterschaft *f*. **~-in-law** *n* (*pl* **~s-in-law**) Schwiegervater *m*. **~ly** *a* väterlich
fathom /'fæðəm/ *n* (*Naut*) Faden *m* ● *vt* verstehen; **~ out** ergründen
fatigue /fə'ti:g/ *n* Ermüdung *f* ● *vt* ermüden
fatten /'fætn/ *vt* mästen ⟨*animal*⟩. **~ing** *a* **cream is ~ing** Sahne macht dick
fatty /'fætɪ/ *a* fett; ⟨*foods*⟩ fetthaltig
fatuous /'fætjʊəs/ *a*, **-ly** *adv* albern
faucet /'fɔ:sɪt/ *n* (*Amer*) Wasserhahn *m*
fault /fɔ:lt/ *n* Fehler *m*; (*Techn*) Defekt *m*; (*Geol*) Verwerfung *f*; **at ~** im Unrecht; **find ~ with** etwas auszusetzen haben an (+ *dat*); **it's your ~** du bist schuld ● *vt* etwas auszusetzen haben an (+ *dat*). **~less** *a*, **-ly** *adv* fehlerfrei
faulty /'fɔ:ltɪ/ *a* fehlerhaft
fauna /'fɔ:nə/ *n* Fauna *f*
favour /'feɪvə(r)/ *n* Gunst *f*; **I am in ~** ich bin dafür; **do s.o. a ~** jdm einen Gefallen tun ● *vt* begünstigen; (*prefer*) bevorzugen. **~able** /-əbl/ *a*, **-bly** *adv* günstig; ⟨*reply*⟩ positiv
favourit|e /'feɪvərɪt/ *a* Lieblings- ● *n* Liebling *m*; (*Sport*) Favorit(in) *m*(*f*). **~ism** *n* Bevorzugung *f*
fawn[1] /fɔ:n/ *a* rehbraun ● *n* Hirschkalb *nt*
fawn[2] *vi* sich einschmeicheln (**on** bei)
fax /fæks/ *n* Fax *nt* ● *vt* faxen (**s.o.** jdm). **~ machine** *n* Faxgerät *nt*
fear /fɪə(r)/ *n* Furcht *f*, Angst *f* (**of** vor + *dat*); **no ~!** (*fam*) keine Angst! ● *vt/i* fürchten
fear|ful /'fɪəfl/ *a* besorgt; (*awful*) furchtbar. **~less** *a*, **-ly** *adv* furchtlos. **~some** /-səm/ *a* furchterregend
feas|ibility /fi:zə'bɪlətɪ/ *n* Durchführbarkeit *f*. **~ible** *a* durchführbar; (*possible*) möglich
feast /fi:st/ *n* Festmahl *nt*; (*Relig*) Fest *nt* ● *vi* **~ [on]** schmausen
feat /fi:t/ *n* Leistung *f*
feather /'feðə(r)/ *n* Feder *f*
feature /'fi:tʃə(r)/ *n* Gesichtszug *m*; (*quality*) Merkmal *nt*; (*Journ*) Feature *nt* ● *vt* darstellen; ⟨*film:*⟩ in der Hauptrolle zeigen. **~ film** *n* Hauptfilm *m*
February /'febrʊərɪ/ *n* Februar *m*
feckless /'feklɪs/ *a* verantwortungslos
fed /fed/ *see* **feed** ● *a* **be ~ up** (*fam*) die Nase voll haben (**with** von)
federal /'fedərəl/ *a* Bundes-
federation /fedə'reɪʃn/ *n* Föderation *f*
fee /fi:/ *n* Gebühr *f*; (*professional*) Honorar *nt*
feeble /'fi:bl/ *a* (**-r, -st**), **-bly** *adv* schwach
feed /fi:d/ *n* Futter *nt*; (*for baby*) Essen *nt* ● *v* (*pt/pp* **fed**) ● *vt* füttern; (*support*) ernähren; (*into machine*) eingeben; speisen ⟨*computer*⟩ ● *vi* sich ernähren (**on** von)
'feedback *n* Feedback *nt*
feel /fi:l/ *v* (*pt/pp* **felt**) ● *vt* fühlen; (*experience*) empfinden; (*think*) meinen ● *vi* sich fühlen; **~ soft/hard** sich weich/hart anfühlen; **I ~ hot/ill** mir ist heiß/schlecht; **I don't ~ like it** ich habe keine Lust dazu. **~er** *n* Fühler *m*. **~ing** *n* Gefühl *nt*; **no hard ~ings** nichts für ungut
feet /fi:t/ *see* **foot**
feign /feɪn/ *vt* vortäuschen
feint /feɪnt/ *n* Finte *f*
feline /'fi:laɪn/ *a* Katzen-; (*catlike*) katzenartig
fell[1] /fel/ *vt* fällen
fell[2] *see* **fall**
fellow /'feləʊ/ *n* (*of society*) Mitglied *nt*; (*fam: man*) Kerl *m*
fellow: ~-'countryman *n* Landsmann *m*. **~ men** *pl* Mitmenschen *pl*. **~ship** *n* Kameradschaft *f*; (*group*) Gesellschaft *f*
felony /'felənɪ/ *n* Verbrechen *nt*
felt[1] /felt/ *see* **feel**
felt[2] *n* Filz *m*. **~[-tipped] 'pen** *n* Filzstift *m*
female /'fi:meɪl/ *a* weiblich ● *nt* Weibchen *nt*; (*pej: woman*) Weib *nt*
femin|ine /'femɪnɪn/ *a* weiblich ● *n* (*Gram*) Femininum *nt*. **~inity** /-'nɪnətɪ/ *n* Weiblichkeit *f*. **~ist** *a* feministisch ● *n* Feminist(in) *m*(*f*)
fenc|e /fens/ *n* Zaun *m*; (*fam: person*) Hehler *m* ● *vi* (*Sport*) fechten ● *vt* **~e in** einzäunen. **~er** *n* Fechter *m*. **~ing** *n* Zaun *m*; (*Sport*) Fechten *nt*
fend /fend/ *vi* **~ for oneself** sich allein durchschlagen. **~ off** *vt* abwehren
fender /'fendə(r)/ *n* Kaminvorsetzer *m*; (*Naut*) Fender *m*; (*Amer: wing*) Kotflügel *m*
fennel /'fenl/ *n* Fenchel *m*
ferment[1] /'fɜ:ment/ *n* Erregung *f*

ferment² /fə'ment/ *vi* gären • *vt* gären lassen. **~ation** /fɜ:men'teɪʃn/ *n* Gärung *f*
fern /fɜ:n/ *n* Farn *m*
feroc|ious /fə'rəʊʃəs/ *a* wild. **~ity** /-'rɒsətɪ/ *n* Wildheit *f*
ferret /'ferɪt/ *n* Frettchen *nt*
ferry /'ferɪ/ *n* Fähre *f* • *vt* **~ [across]** übersetzen
fertil|e /'fɜ:taɪl/ *a* fruchtbar. **~ity** /fɜ:'tɪlətɪ/ *n* Fruchtbarkeit *f*
fertilize /'fɜ:təlaɪz/ *vt* befruchten; düngen ⟨*land*⟩. **~r** *n* Dünger *m*
fervent /'fɜ:vənt/ *a* leidenschaftlich
fervour /'fɜ:və(r)/ *n* Leidenschaft *f*
fester /'festə(r)/ *vi* eitern
festival /'festɪvl/ *n* Fest *nt*; (*Mus, Theat*) Festspiele *pl*
festiv|e /'festɪv/ *a* festlich; **~e season** Festzeit *f*. **~ities** /fe'stɪvətɪz/ *npl* Feierlichkeiten *pl*
festoon /fe'stu:n/ *vt* behängen (**with** mit)
fetch /fetʃ/ *vt* holen; (*collect*) abholen; (*be sold for*) einbringen
fetching /'fetʃɪŋ/ *a* anziehend
fête /feɪt/ *n* Fest *nt* • *vt* feiern
fetish /'fetɪʃ/ *n* Fetisch *m*
fetter /'fetə(r)/ *vt* fesseln
fettle /'fetl/ *n* **in fine ~** in bester Form
feud /fju:d/ *n* Fehde *f*
feudal /'fju:dl/ *a* Feudal-
fever /'fi:və(r)/ *n* Fieber *nt*. **~ish** *a* fiebrig; (*fig*) fieberhaft
few /fju:/ *a* (**-er, -est**) wenige; **every ~ days** alle paar Tage • *n* **a ~** ein paar; **quite a ~** ziemlich viele
fiancé/ fɪ'ɒnseɪ/ *n* Verlobte(r) *m*. **fiancée** *n* Verlobte *f*
fiasco /fɪ'æskəʊ/ *n* Fiasko *nt*
fib /fɪb/ *n* kleine Lüge; **tell a ~** schwindeln
fibre /'faɪbə(r)/ *n* Faser *f*
fickle /'fɪkl/ *a* unbeständig
fiction /'fɪkʃn/ *n* Erfindung *f*; **[works of] ~** Erzählungsliteratur *f*. **~al** *a* erfunden
fictitious /fɪk'tɪʃəs/ *a* [frei] erfunden
fiddle /'fɪdl/ *n* (*fam*) Geige *f*; (*cheating*) Schwindel *m* • *vi* herumspielen (**with** mit) • *vt* (*fam*) frisieren ⟨*accounts*⟩; (*arrange*) arrangieren
fiddly /'fɪdlɪ/ *a* knifflig
fidelity /fɪ'delətɪ/ *n* Treue *f*
fidget /'fɪdʒɪt/ *vi* zappeln. **~y** *a* zappelig
field /fi:ld/ *n* Feld *nt*; (*meadow*) Wiese *f*; (*subject*) Gebiet *nt*
field: ~ events *npl* Sprung- und Wurfdisziplinen *pl*. **~-glasses** *npl* Feldstecher *m*. **F~ 'Marshal** *n* Feldmarschall *m*. **~work** *n* Feldforschung *f*
fiend /fi:nd/ *n* Teufel *m*. **~ish** *a* teuflisch
fierce /fɪəs/ *a* (**-r, -st**), **-ly** *adv* wild; (*fig*) heftig. **~ness** *n* Wildheit *f*; (*fig*) Heftigkeit *f*
fiery /'faɪərɪ/ *a* (**-ier, -iest**) feurig
fifteen /fɪf'ti:n/ *a* fünfzehn • *n* Fünfzehn *f*. **~th** *a* fünfzehnte(r,s)
fifth /fɪfθ/ *a* fünfte(r,s)
fiftieth /'fɪftɪɪθ/ *a* fünfzigste(r,s)
fifty /'fɪftɪ/ *a* fünfzig
fig /fɪg/ *n* Feige *f*
fight /faɪt/ *n* Kampf *m*; (*brawl*) Schlägerei *f*; (*between children, dogs*) Rauferei *f* • *v* (*pt/pp* **fought**) • *vt* kämpfen gegen; (*fig*) bekämpfen • *vi* kämpfen; (*brawl*) sich schlagen; ⟨*children, dogs:*⟩ sich raufen. **~er** *n* Kämpfer *m*; (*Aviat*) Jagdflugzeug *nt*. **~ing** *n* Kampf *m*
figment /'fɪgmənt/ *n* **~ of the imagination** Hirngespinst *nt*
figurative /'fɪgjərətɪv/ *a*, **-ly** *adv* bildlich, übertragen
figure /'fɪgə(r)/ *n* (*digit*) Ziffer *f*; (*number*) Zahl *f*; (*sum*) Summe *f*; (*carving, sculpture, woman's*) Figur *f*; (*form*) Gestalt *f*; (*illustration*) Abbildung *f*; **~ of speech** Redefigur *f*; **good at ~s** gut im Rechnen • *vi* (*appear*) erscheinen • *vt* (*Amer: think*) glauben. **~ out** *vt* ausrechnen
figure: ~-head *n* Galionsfigur *f*; (*fig*) Repräsentationsfigur *f*. **~ skating** *n* Eiskunstlauf *m*
filament /'fɪləmənt/ *n* Faden *m*; (*Electr*) Glühfaden *m*
filch /fɪltʃ/ *vt* (*fam*) klauen
file¹ /faɪl/ *n* Akte *f*; (*for documents*) [Akten]ordner *m* • *vt* ablegen ⟨*documents*⟩; (*Jur*) einreichen
file² *n* (*line*) Reihe *f*; **in single ~** im Gänsemarsch
file³ *n* (*Techn*) Feile *f* • *vt* feilen
filigree /'fɪlɪgri:/ *n* Filigran *nt*
filings /'faɪlɪŋz/ *npl* Feilspäne *pl*
fill /fɪl/ *n* **eat one's ~** sich satt essen • *vt* füllen; plombieren ⟨*tooth*⟩ • *vi* sich füllen. **~ in** *vt* auffüllen; ausfüllen ⟨*form*⟩. **~ out** *vt* ausfüllen ⟨*form*⟩. **~ up** *vi* sich füllen • *vt* vollfüllen; (*Auto*) volltanken; ausfüllen ⟨*form*⟩

fillet /ˈfɪlɪt/ *n* Filet *nt* ● *vt* (*pt/pp* **filleted**) entgräten
filling /ˈfɪlɪŋ/ *n* Füllung *f*; (*of tooth*) Plombe *f*. ~ **station** *n* Tankstelle *f*
filly /ˈfɪlɪ/ *n* junge Stute *f*
film /fɪlm/ *n* Film *m*; (*Culin*) **[cling]** ~ Klarsichtfolie *f* ● *vt/i* filmen; verfilmen ⟨*book*⟩. ~ **star** *n* Filmstar *m*
filter /ˈfɪltə(r)/ *n* Filter *m* ● *vt* filtern. ~ **through** *vi* durchsickern. ~ **tip** *n* Filter *m*; (*cigarette*) Filterzigarette *f*
filth /fɪlθ/ *n* Dreck *m*. ~**y** *a* (**-ier, -iest**) dreckig
fin /fɪn/ *n* Flosse *f*
final /ˈfaɪnl/ *a* letzte(r,s); (*conclusive*) endgültig; ~ **result** Endresultat *nt* ● *n* (*Sport*) Finale *nt*, Endspiel *nt*; ~**s** *pl* (*Univ*) Abschlußprüfung *f*
finale /fɪˈnɑːlɪ/ *n* Finale *nt*
final|ist /ˈfaɪnəlɪst/ *n* Finalist(in) *m*(*f*). ~**ity** /-ˈnælətɪ/ *n* Endgültigkeit *f*
final|ize /ˈfaɪnəlaɪz/ *vt* endgültig festlegen. ~**ly** *adv* schließlich
finance /faɪˈnæns/ *n* Finanz *f* ● *vt* finanzieren
financial /faɪˈnænʃl/ *a*, **-ly** *adv* finanziell
finch /fɪntʃ/ *n* Fink *m*
find /faɪnd/ *n* Fund *m* ● *vt* (*pt/pp* **found**) finden; (*establish*) feststellen; **go and** ~ holen; **try to** ~ suchen; ~ **guilty** (*Jur*) schuldig sprechen. ~ **out** *vt* herausfinden; (*learn*) erfahren ● *vi* (*enquire*) sich erkundigen
findings /ˈfaɪndɪŋz/ *npl* Ergebnisse *pl*
fine[1] /faɪn/ *n* Geldstrafe *f* ● *vt* zu einer Geldstrafe verurteilen
fine[2] *a* (**-r, -st**), **-ly** *adv* fein; ⟨*weather*⟩ schön; **he's** ~ es geht ihm gut ● *adv* gut; **cut it** ~ (*fam*) sich (*dat*) wenig Zeit lassen. ~ **arts** *npl* schöne Künste *pl*
finery /ˈfaɪnərɪ/ *n* Putz *m*, Staat *m*
finesse /fɪˈnes/ *n* Gewandtheit *f*
finger /ˈfɪŋgə(r)/ *n* Finger *m* ● *vt* anfassen
finger: ~**-mark** *n* Fingerabdruck *m*. ~**-nail** *n* Fingernagel *m*. ~**print** *n* Fingerabdruck *m*. ~**tip** *n* Fingerspitze *f*; **have sth at one's** ~**tips** etw im kleinen Finger haben
finicky /ˈfɪnɪkɪ/ *a* knifflig; (*choosy*) wählerisch
finish /ˈfɪnɪʃ/ *n* Schluß *m*; (*Sport*) Finish *nt*; (*line*) Ziel *nt*; (*of product*) Ausführung *f* ● *vt* beenden; (*use up*) aufbrauchen; ~ **one's drink** austrinken; ~ **reading** zu Ende lesen ● *vi* fertig werden; ⟨*performance:*⟩ zu Ende sein; ⟨*runner:*⟩ durchs Ziel gehen
finite /ˈfaɪnaɪt/ *a* begrenzt
Finland /ˈfɪnlənd/ *n* Finnland *nt*
Finn /fɪn/ *n* Finne *m*/Finnin *f*. ~**ish** *a* finnisch
fiord /fjɔːd/ *n* Fjord *m*
fir /fɜː(r)/ *n* Tanne *f*
fire /ˈfaɪə(r)/ *n* Feuer *nt*; (*forest, house*) Brand *m*; **be on** ~ brennen; **catch** ~ Feuer fangen; **set** ~ **to** anzünden; ⟨*arsonist:*⟩ in Brand stecken; **under** ~ unter Beschuß ● *vt* brennen ⟨*pottery*⟩; abfeuern ⟨*shot*⟩; schießen mit ⟨*gun*⟩; (*fam: dismiss*) feuern ● *vi* schießen (**at** auf + *acc*); ⟨*engine:*⟩ anspringen
fire: ~ **alarm** *n* Feueralarm *m*; (*apparatus*) Feuermelder *m*. ~**arm** *n* Schußwaffe *f*. ~ **brigade** *n* Feuerwehr *f*. ~**-engine** *n* Löschfahrzeug *nt*. ~**-escape** *n* Feuertreppe *f*. ~ **extinguisher** *n* Feuerlöscher *m*. ~**man** *n* Feuerwehrmann *m*. ~**place** *n* Kamin *m*. ~**side** *n* **by** *or* **at the** ~**side** am Kamin. ~ **station** *n* Feuerwache *f*. ~**wood** *n* Brennholz *nt*. ~**work** *n* Feuerwerkskörper *m*; ~**works** *pl* (*display*) Feuerwerk *nt*
'firing squad *n* Erschießungskommando *nt*
firm[1] /fɜːm/ *n* Firma *f*
firm[2] *a* (**-er, -est**), **-ly** *adv* fest; (*resolute*) entschlossen; (*strict*) streng
first /fɜːst/ *a & n* erste(r,s); **at** ~ zuerst; **who's** ~**?** wer ist der erste? **at** ~ **sight** auf den ersten Blick; **for the** ~ **time** zum ersten Mal; **from the** ~ von Anfang an ● *adv* zuerst; (*firstly*) erstens
first: ~ **'aid** *n* Erste Hilfe. ~**-'aid kit** *n* Verbandkasten *m*. ~**-class** *a* erstklassig; (*Rail*) erster Klasse ● /-ˈ-/ *adv* ⟨*travel*⟩ erster Klasse. ~ **e'dition** *n* Erstausgabe *f*. ~ **'floor** *n* erster Stock; (*Amer: ground floor*) Erdgeschoß *nt*. ~**ly** *adv* erstens. ~ **name** *n* Vorname *m*. ~**-rate** *a* erstklassig
fish /fɪʃ/ *n* Fisch *m* ● *vt/i* fischen; (*with rod*) angeln. ~ **out** *vt* herausfischen
fish: ~**bone** *n* Gräte *f*. ~**erman** *n* Fischer *m*. ~**-farm** *n* Fischzucht *f*. ~ **'finger** *n* Fischstäbchen *nt*

fishing /'fɪʃɪŋ/ *n* Fischerei *f*. ~ **boat** *n* Fischerboot *nt*. ~**-rod** *n* Angel[rute] *f*

fish: ~**monger** /-mʌŋgə(r)/ *n* Fischhändler *m*. ~**-slice** *n* Fischheber *m*. ~**y** *a* Fisch-; (*fam: suspicious*) verdächtig

fission /'fɪʃn/ *n* (*Phys*) Spaltung *f*

fist /fɪst/ *n* Faust *f*

fit[1] /fɪt/ *n* (*attack*) Anfall *m*

fit[2] *a* (**fitter, fittest**) (*suitable*) geeignet; (*healthy*) gesund; (*Sport*) fit; ~ **to eat** eßbar; **keep** ~ sich fit halten; **see** ~ es für angebracht halten (**to** zu)

fit[3] *n* (*of clothes*) Sitz *m*; **be a good** ~ gut passen ● *v* (*pt/pp* **fitted**) ● *vi* (*be the right size*) passen ● *vt* anbringen (**to** an + *dat*); (*install*) einbauen; ⟨*clothes:*⟩ passen (+ *dat*); ~ **with** versehen mit. ~ **in** *vi* hineinpassen; (*adapt*) sich einfügen (**with** in + *acc*) ● *vt* (*accommodate*) unterbringen

fit|ful /'fɪtfl/ *a*, **-ly** *adv* ⟨*sleep*⟩ unruhig. ~**ment** *n* Einrichtungsgegenstand *m*; (*attachment*) Zusatzgerät *nt*. ~**ness** *n* Eignung *f*; **[physical]** ~**ness** Gesundheit *f*; (*Sport*) Fitneß *f*. ~**ted** *a* eingebaut; ⟨*garment*⟩ tailliert

fitted: ~ **'carpet** *n* Teppichboden *m*. ~ **'cupboard** *n* Einbauschrank *m*. ~ **'kitchen** *n* Einbauküche *f*. ~ **'sheet** *n* Spannlaken *nt*

fitter /'fɪtə(r)/ *n* Monteur *m*

fitting /'fɪtɪŋ/ *a* passend ● *n* (*of clothes*) Anprobe *f*; (*of shoes*) Weite *f*; (*Techn*) Zubehörteil *nt*; ~**s** *pl* Zubehör *nt*. ~ **room** *n* Anprobekabine *f*

five /faɪv/ *a* fünf ● *n* Fünf *f*. ~**r** *n* Fünfpfundschein *m*

fix /fɪks/ *n* (*sl: drugs*) Fix *m*; **be in a** ~ (*fam*) in der Klemme sitzen ● *vt* befestigen (**to** an + *dat*); (*arrange*) festlegen; (*repair*) reparieren; (*Phot*) fixieren; ~ **a meal** (*Amer*) Essen machen

fixation /fɪk'seɪʃn/ *n* Fixierung *f*

fixed /'fɪkst/ *a* fest

fixture /'fɪkstʃə(r)/ *n* (*Sport*) Veranstaltung *f*; ~**s and fittings** zu einer Wohnung gehörende Einrichtungen *pl*

fizz /fɪz/ *vi* sprudeln

fizzle /'fɪzl/ *vi* ~ **out** verpuffen

fizzy /'fɪzɪ/ *a* sprudelnd. ~ **drink** *n* Brause[limonade] *f*

flabbergasted /'flæbəgɑ:stɪd/ *a* **be** ~ platt sein (*fam*)

flabby /'flæbɪ/ *a* schlaff

flag[1] /flæg/ *n* Fahne *f*; (*Naut*) Flagge *f* ● *vt* (*pt/pp* **flagged**) ~ **down** anhalten ⟨*taxi*⟩

flag[2] *vi* (*pt/pp* **flagged**) ermüden

flagon /'flægən/ *n* Krug *m*

'flag-pole *n* Fahnenstange *f*

flagrant /'fleɪgrənt/ *a* flagrant

'flagstone *n* [Pflaster]platte *f*

flair /fleə(r)/ *n* Begabung *f*

flake /fleɪk/ *n* Flocke *f* ● *vi* ~ **[off]** abblättern

flaky /'fleɪkɪ/ *a* blättrig. ~ **pastry** *n* Blätterteig *m*

flamboyant /flæm'bɔɪənt/ *a* extravagant

flame /fleɪm/ *n* Flamme *f*

flammable /'flæməbl/ *a* feuergefährlich

flan /flæn/ *n* **[fruit]** ~ Obsttorte *f*

flank /flæŋk/ *n* Flanke *f* ● *vt* flankieren

flannel /'flænl/ *n* Flanell *m*; (*for washing*) Waschlappen *m*

flannelette /flænə'let/ *n* (*Tex*) Biber *m*

flap /flæp/ *n* Klappe *f*; **in a** ~ (*fam*) aufgeregt ● *v* (*pt/pp* **flapped**) *vi* flattern; (*fam*) sich aufregen ● *vt* ~ **its wings** mit den Flügeln schlagen

flare /fleə(r)/ *n* Leuchtsignal *nt*. ● *vi* ~ **up** auflodern; (*fam: get angry*) aufbrausen. ~**d** *a* ⟨*garment*⟩ ausgestellt

flash /flæʃ/ *n* Blitz *m*; **in a** ~ (*fam*) im Nu ● *vi* blitzen; (*repeatedly*) blinken; ~ **past** vorbeirasen ● *vt* aufleuchten lassen; ~ **one's headlights** die Lichthupe betätigen

flash: ~**back** *n* Rückblende *f*. ~**bulb** *n* (*Phot*) Blitzbirne *f*. ~**er** *n* (*Auto*) Blinker *m*. ~**light** *n* (*Phot*) Blitzlicht *nt*; (*Amer: torch*) Taschenlampe *f*. ~**y** *a* auffällig

flask /flɑ:sk/ *n* Flasche *f*; (*Chem*) Kolben *m*; (*vacuum* ~) Thermosflasche (P) *f*

flat /flæt/ *a* (**flatter, flattest**) flach; ⟨*surface*⟩ eben; ⟨*refusal*⟩ glatt; ⟨*beer*⟩ schal; ⟨*battery*⟩ verbraucht/(*Auto*) leer; ⟨*tyre*⟩ platt; (*Mus*) **A** ~ As *nt*; **B** ~ B *nt* ● *n* Wohnung *f*; (*Mus*) Erniedrigungszeichen *nt*; (*fam: puncture*) Reifenpanne *f*

flat: ~ **'feet** *npl* Plattfüße *pl*. ~**-fish** *n* Plattfisch *m*. ~**ly** *adv* ⟨*refuse*⟩ glatt. ~ **rate** *n* Einheitspreis *m*

flatten /'flætn/ *vt* platt drücken
flatter /'flætə(r)/ *vt* schmeicheln (+ *dat*). **~y** *n* Schmeichelei *f*
flat 'tyre *n* Reifenpanne *f*
flatulence /'flætjʊləns/ *n* Blähungen *pl*
flaunt /flɔ:nt/ *vt* prunken mit
flautist /'flɔ:tɪst/ *n* Flötist(in) *m(f)*
flavour /'fleɪvə(r)/ *n* Geschmack *m* ● *vt* abschmecken. **~ing** *n* Aroma *nt*
flaw /flɔ:/ *n* Fehler *m*. **~less** *a* tadellos; ⟨*complexion*⟩ makellos
flax /flæks/ *n* Flachs *m*. **~en** *a* flachsblond
flea /fli:/ *n* Floh *m*. **~ market** *n* Flohmarkt *m*
fleck /flek/ *n* Tupfen *m*
fled /fled/ *see* **flee**
flee /fli:/ *v* (*pt/pp* **fled**) ● *vi* fliehen (**from** vor + *dat*) ● *vt* flüchten aus
fleec|e /fli:s/ *n* Vlies *nt* ● *vt* (*fam*) schröpfen. **~y** *a* flauschig
fleet /fli:t/ *n* Flotte *f*; (*of cars*) Wagenpark *m*
fleeting /'fli:tɪŋ/ *a* flüchtig
Flemish /'flemɪʃ/ *a* flämisch
flesh /fleʃ/ *n* Fleisch *nt*; **in the ~** (*fam*) in Person. **~y** *a* fleischig
flew /flu:/ *see* **fly²**
flex¹ /fleks/ *vt* anspannen ⟨*muscle*⟩
flex² *n* (*Electr*) Schnur *f*
flexib|ility /fleksə'bɪlətɪ/ *n* Biegsamkeit *f*; (*fig*) Flexibilität *f*. **~le** *a* biegsam; (*fig*) flexibel
'flexitime /'fleksɪ-/ *n* Gleitzeit *f*
flick /flɪk/ *vt* schnippen. **~ through** *vi* schnell durchblättern
flicker /'flɪkə(r)/ *vi* flackern
flier /'flaɪə(r)/ *n* = **flyer**
flight¹ /flaɪt/ *n* (*fleeing*) Flucht *f*; **take ~** die Flucht ergreifen
flight² *n* (*flying*) Flug *m*; **~ of stairs** Treppe *f*
flight: ~ path *n* Flugschneise *f*. **~ recorder** *n* Flugschreiber *m*
flighty /'flaɪtɪ/ *a* (**-ier, -iest**) flatterhaft
flimsy /'flɪmzɪ/ *a* (**-ier, -iest**) dünn; ⟨*excuse*⟩ fadenscheinig
flinch /flɪntʃ/ *vi* zurückzucken
fling /flɪŋ/ *n* **have a ~** (*fam*) sich austoben ● *vt* (*pt/pp* **flung**) schleudern
flint /flɪnt/ *n* Feuerstein *m*
flip /flɪp/ *vt/i* schnippen; **~ through** durchblättern
flippant /'flɪpənt/ *a*, **-ly** *adv* leichtfertig
flipper /'flɪpə(r)/ *n* Flosse *f*
flirt /flɜ:t/ *n* kokette Frau *f* ● *vi* flirten
flirtat|ion /flɜ:'teɪʃn/ *n* Flirt *m*. **~ious** /-ʃəs/ *a* kokett
flit /flɪt/ *vi* (*pt/pp* **flitted**) flattern
float /fləʊt/ *n* Schwimmer *m*; (*in procession*) Festwagen *m*; (*money*) Wechselgeld *nt* ● *vi* ⟨*thing:*⟩ schwimmen; ⟨*person:*⟩ sich treiben lassen; (*in air*) schweben; (*Comm*) floaten
flock /flɒk/ *n* Herde *f*; (*of birds*) Schwarm *m* ● *vi* strömen
flog /flɒg/ *vt* (*pt/pp* **flogged**) auspeitschen; (*fam: sell*) verkloppen
flood /flʌd/ *n* Überschwemmung *f*; (*fig*) Flut *f*; **be in ~** ⟨*river:*⟩ Hochwasser führen ● *vt* überschwemmen ● *vi* ⟨*river:*⟩ über die Ufer treten
'floodlight *n* Flutlicht *nt* ● *vt* (*pt/pp* **floodlit**) anstrahlen
floor /flɔ:(r)/ *n* Fußboden *m*; (*storey*) Stock *m* ● *vt* (*baffle*) verblüffen
floor: ~board *n* Dielenbrett *nt*. **~-cloth** *n* Scheuertuch *nt*. **~-polish** *n* Bohnerwachs *nt*. **~ show** *n* Kabarettvorstellung *f*
flop /flɒp/ *n* (*fam*) (*failure*) Reinfall *m*; (*Theat*) Durchfall *m* ● *vi* (*pt/pp* **flopped**) (*fam*) (*fail*) durchfallen; **~ down** sich plumpsen lassen
floppy /'flɒpɪ/ *a* schlapp. **~ 'disc** *n* Diskette *f*
flora /'flɔ:rə/ *n* Flora *f*
floral /'flɔ:rl/ *a* Blumen-
florid /'flɒrɪd/ *a* ⟨*complexion*⟩ gerötet; ⟨*style*⟩ blumig
florist /'flɒrɪst/ *n* Blumenhändler(in) *m(f)*
flounce /flaʊns/ *n* Volant *m* ● *vi* **~ out** hinausstolzieren
flounder¹ /'flaʊndə(r)/ *vi* zappeln
flounder² *n* (*fish*) Flunder *f*
flour /'flaʊə(r)/ *n* Mehl *nt*
flourish /'flʌrɪʃ/ *n* große Geste *f*; (*scroll*) Schnörkel *m* ● *vi* gedeihen; (*fig*) blühen ● *vt* schwenken
floury /'flaʊərɪ/ *a* mehlig
flout /flaʊt/ *vt* mißachten
flow /fləʊ/ *n* Fluß *m*; (*of traffic, blood*) Strom *m* ● *vi* fließen
flower /'flaʊə(r)/ *n* Blume *f* ● *vi* blühen
flower: ~-bed *n* Blumenbeet *nt*. **~ed** *a* geblümt. **~pot** *n* Blumentopf *m*. **~y** *a* blumig
flown /fləʊn/ *see* **fly²**
flu /flu:/ *n* (*fam*) Grippe *f*
fluctuat|e /'flʌktjʊeɪt/ *vi* schwanken. **~ion** /-'eɪʃn/ *n* Schwankung *f*

fluent /ˈfluːənt/ *a*, **-ly** *adv* fließend
fluff /flʌf/ *n* Fusseln *pl*; (*down*) Flaum *m*. **~y** *a* (**-ier, -iest**) flauschig
fluid /ˈfluːɪd/ *a* flüssig; (*fig*) veränderlich ● *n* Flüssigkeit *f*
fluke /fluːk/ *n* [glücklicher] Zufall *m*
flung /flʌŋ/ *see* **fling**
flunk /flʌŋk/ *vt/i* (*Amer, fam*) durchfallen (in + *dat*)
fluorescent /flʊəˈresnt/ *a* fluoreszierend; **~ lighting** Neonbeleuchtung *f*
fluoride /ˈflʊəraɪd/ *n* Fluor *nt*
flurry /ˈflʌrɪ/ *n* (*snow*) Gestöber *nt*; (*fig*) Aufregung *f*
flush /flʌʃ/ *n* (*blush*) Erröten *nt* ● *vi* rot werden ● *vt* spülen ● *a* in einer Ebene (**with** mit); (*fam: affluent*) gut bei Kasse
flustered /ˈflʌstəd/ *a* nervös
flute /fluːt/ *n* Flöte *f*
flutter /ˈflʌtə(r)/ *n* Flattern *nt* ● *vi* flattern
flux /flʌks/ *n* **in a state of ~** im Fluß
fly[1] /flaɪ/ *n* (*pl* **flies**) Fliege *f*
fly[2] *v* (*pt* **flew**, *pp* **flown**) ● *vi* fliegen; ⟨*flag:*⟩ wehen; (*rush*) sausen ● *vt* fliegen; führen ⟨*flag*⟩
fly[3] *n* & **flies** *pl* (*on trousers*) Hosenschlitz *m*
flyer /ˈflaɪə(r)/ *n* Flieger(in) *m(f)*; (*Amer: leaflet*) Flugblatt *nt*
flying: ~ ˈbuttress *n* Strebebogen *m*. **~ ˈsaucer** *n* fliegende Untertasse *f*. **~ ˈvisit** *n* Stippvisite *f*
fly: ~leaf *n* Vorsatzblatt *nt*. **~over** *n* Überführung *f*
foal /fəʊl/ *n* Fohlen *nt*
foam /fəʊm/ *n* Schaum *m*; (*synthetic*) Schaumstoff *m* ● *vi* schäumen. **~ ˈrubber** *n* Schaumgummi *m*
fob /fɒb/ *vt* (*pt/pp* **fobbed**) **~ sth off** etw andrehen (**on s.o.** jdm); **~ s.o. off** jdn abspeisen (**with** mit)
focal /ˈfəʊkl/ *n* Brenn-
focus /ˈfəʊkəs/ *n* Brennpunkt *m*; **in ~** scharf eingestellt ● *v* (*pt/pp* **focused** *or* **focussed**) ● *vt* einstellen (**on** auf + *acc*); (*fig*) konzentrieren (**on** auf + *acc*) ● *vi* (*fig*) sich konzentrieren (**on** auf + *acc*)
fodder /ˈfɒdə(r)/ *n* Futter *nt*
foe /fəʊ/ *n* Feind *m*
foetus /ˈfiːtəs/ *n* (*pl* **-tuses**) Fötus *m*
fog /fɒg/ *n* Nebel *m*
foggy /ˈfɒgɪ/ *a* (**foggier, foggiest**) neblig
ˈfog-horn *n* Nebelhorn *nt*
fogy /ˈfəʊgɪ/ *n* **old ~** alter Knacker *m*
foible /ˈfɔɪbl/ *n* Eigenart *f*
foil[1] /fɔɪl/ *n* Folie *f*; (*Culin*) Alufolie *f*
foil[2] *vt* (*thwart*) vereiteln
foil[3] *n* (*Fencing*) Florett *nt*
foist /fɔɪst/ *vt* andrehen (**on s.o.** jdm)
fold[1] /fəʊld/ *n* (*for sheep*) Pferch *m*
fold[2] *n* Falte *f*; (*in paper*) Kniff *m* ● *vt* falten; **~ one's arms** die Arme verschränken ● *vi* sich falten lassen; (*fail*) eingehen. **~ up** *vt* zusammenfalten; zusammenklappen ⟨*chair*⟩ ● *vi* sich zusammenfalten/-klappen lassen; (*fam*) ⟨*business:*⟩ eingehen
fold|er /ˈfəʊldə(r)/ *n* Mappe *f*. **~ing** *a* Klapp-
foliage /ˈfəʊlɪɪdʒ/ *n* Blätter *pl*; (*of tree*) Laub *nt*
folk /fəʊk/ *npl* Leute *pl*
folk: ~-dance *n* Volkstanz *m*. **~lore** *n* Folklore *f*. **~-song** *n* Volkslied *nt*
follow /ˈfɒləʊ/ *vt/i* folgen (+ *dat*); (*pursue*) verfolgen; (*in vehicle*) nachfahren (+ *dat*); **~ suit** (*fig*) dasselbe tun. **~ up** *vt* nachgehen (+ *dat*)
follow|er /ˈfɒləʊə(r)/ *n* Anhänger(in) *m(f)*. **~ing** *a* folgend ● *n* Folgende(s) *nt*; (*supporters*) Anhängerschaft *f* ● *prep* im Anschluß an (+ *acc*)
folly /ˈfɒlɪ/ *n* Torheit *f*
fond /fɒnd/ *a* (**-er, -est**), **-ly** *adv* liebevoll; **be ~ of** gern haben; gern essen ⟨*food*⟩
fondle /ˈfɒndl/ *vt* liebkosen
fondness /ˈfɒndnɪs/ *n* Liebe *f* (**for** zu)
font /fɒnt/ *n* Taufstein *m*
food /fuːd/ *n* Essen *nt*; (*for animals*) Futter *nt*; (*groceries*) Lebensmittel *pl*
food: ~ mixer *n* Küchenmaschine *f*. **~ poisoning** *n* Lebensmittelvergiftung *f*. **~ processor** *n* Küchenmaschine *f*. **~ value** *n* Nährwert *m*
fool[1] /fuːl/ *n* (*Culin*) Fruchtcreme *f*
fool[2] *n* Narr *m*; **you are a ~** du bist dumm; **make a ~ of oneself** sich lächerlich machen ● *vt* hereinlegen ● *vi* **~ around** herumalbern
ˈfool|hardy *a* tollkühn. **~ish** *a*, **-ly** *adv* dumm. **~ishness** *n* Dummheit *f*. **~proof** *a* narrensicher
foot /fʊt/ *n* (*pl* **feet**) Fuß *m*; (*measure*) Fuß *m* (*30,48 cm*); (*of bed*) Fußende *nt*; **on ~** zu Fuß; **on one's feet** auf den Beinen; **put one's ~ in it** (*fam*) ins Fettnäpfchen treten
foot: ~-and-ˈmouth disease *n* Maul- und Klauenseuche *f*. **~ball** *n* Fußball *m*. **~baller** *n* Fußballspieler *m*.

~ball pools *npl* Fußballtoto *nt*. **~-brake** *n* Fußbremse *f*. **~-bridge** *n* Fußgängerbrücke *f*. **~hills** *npl* Vorgebirge *nt*. **~hold** *n* Halt *m*. **~ing** *n* Halt *m*; (*fig*) Basis *f*. **~lights** *npl* Rampenlicht *nt*. **~man** *n* Lakai *m*. **~note** *n* Fußnote *f*. **~path** *n* Fußweg *m*. **~print** *n* Fußabdruck *m*. **~step** *n* Schritt *m*; **follow in s.o.'s ~steps** (*fig*) in jds Fußstapfen treten. **~stool** *n* Fußbank *f*. **~wear** *n* Schuhwerk *nt*

for /fə(r), *betont* fɔ:(r)/ *prep* für (+ *acc*); ⟨*send, long*⟩ nach; ⟨*ask, fight*⟩ um; **what ~?** wozu? **~ supper** zum Abendessen; **~ nothing** umsonst; **~ all that** trotz allem; **~ this reason** aus diesem Grund; **~ a month** einen Monat; **I have lived here ~ ten years** ich wohne seit zehn Jahren hier ● *conj* denn

forage /'fɒrɪdʒ/ *n* Futter *nt* ● *vi* **~ for** suchen nach

forbade /fə'bæd/ *see* **forbid**

forbear|ance /fɔ:'beərəns/ *n* Nachsicht *f*. **~ing** *a* nachsichtig

forbid /fə'bɪd/ *vt* (*pt* **forbade**, *pp* **forbidden**) verbieten (**s.o.** jdm). **~ding** *a* bedrohlich; (*stern*) streng

force /fɔ:s/ *n* Kraft *f*; (*of blow*) Wucht *f*; (*violence*) Gewalt *f*; **in ~** gültig; (*in large numbers*) in großer Zahl; **come into ~** in Kraft treten; **the ~s** *pl* die Streitkräfte *pl* ● *vt* zwingen; (*break open*) aufbrechen; **~ sth on s.o.** jdm etw aufdrängen

forced /fɔ:st/ *a* gezwungen; **~ landing** Notlandung *f*

force: ~-'feed *vt* (*pt*/*pp* **-fed**) zwangsernähren. **~ful** *a*, **-ly** *adv* energisch

forceps /'fɔ:seps/ *n inv* Zange *f*

forcibl|e /'fɔ:səbl/ *a* gewaltsam. **~y** *adv* mit Gewalt

ford /fɔ:d/ *n* Furt *f* ● *vt* durchwaten; (*in vehicle*) durchfahren

fore /fɔ:(r)/ *a* vordere(r,s) ● *n* **to the ~** im Vordergrund

fore: ~arm *n* Unterarm *m*. **~boding** /-'bəʊdɪŋ/ *n* Vorahnung *f*. **~cast** *n* Voraussage *f*; (*for weather*) Vorhersage *f* ● *vt* (*pt*/*pp* **~cast**) voraussagen, vorhersagen. **~court** *n* Vorhof *m*. **~fathers** *npl* Vorfahren *pl*. **~finger** *n* Zeigefinger *m*. **~front** *n* **be in the ~front** führend sein. **~gone** *a* **be a ~gone conclusion** von vornherein feststehen. **~ground** *n* Vordergrund *m*. **~head** /'fɒrɪd/ *n* Stirn *f*. **~hand** *n* Vorhand *f*

foreign /'fɒrən/ *a* ausländisch; ⟨*country*⟩ fremd; **he is ~** er ist Ausländer. **~ currency** *n* Devisen *pl*. **~er** *n* Ausländer(in) *m*(*f*). **~ language** *n* Fremdsprache *f*

Foreign: ~ Office *n* ≈ Außenministerium *nt*. **~ 'Secretary** *n* ≈ Außenminister *m*

fore: ~leg *n* Vorderbein *nt*. **~man** *n* Vorarbeiter *m*. **~most** *a* führend ● *adv* **first and ~most** zuallererst. **~name** *n* Vorname *m*

forensic /fə'rensɪk/ *a* **~ medicine** Gerichtsmedizin *f*

'forerunner *n* Vorläufer *m*

fore'see *vt* (*pt* **-saw**, *pp* **-seen**) voraussehen, vorhersehen. **~able** /-əbl/ *a* **in the ~able future** in absehbarer Zeit

'foresight *n* Weitblick *m*

forest /'fɒrɪst/ *n* Wald *m*. **~er** *n* Förster *m*

fore'stall *vt* zuvorkommen (+ *dat*)

forestry /'fɒrɪstrɪ/ *n* Forstwirtschaft *f*

'foretaste *n* Vorgeschmack *m*

fore'tell *vt* (*pt*/*pp* **-told**) vorhersagen

forever /fə'revə(r)/ *adv* für immer

fore'warn *vt* vorher warnen

foreword /'fɔ:wɜ:d/ *n* Vorwort *nt*

forfeit /'fɔ:fɪt/ *n* (*in game*) Pfand *nt* ● *vt* verwirken

forgave /fə'geɪv/ *see* **forgive**

forge[1] /fɔ:dʒ/ *vi* **~ ahead** (*fig*) Fortschritte machen

forge[2] *n* Schmiede *f* ● *vt* schmieden; (*counterfeit*) fälschen. **~r** *n* Fälscher *m*. **~ry** *n* Fälschung *f*

forget /fə'get/ *vt*/*i* (*pt* **-got**, *pp* **-gotten**) vergessen; verlernen ⟨*language, skill*⟩. **~ful** *a* vergeßlich. **~fulness** *n* Vergeßlichkeit *f*. **~-me-not** *n* Vergißmeinnicht *nt*

forgive /fə'gɪv/ *vt* (*pt* **-gave**, *pp* **-given**) **~ s.o. for sth** jdm etw vergeben *od* verzeihen. **~ness** *n* Vergebung *f*, Verzeihung *f*

forgo /fɔ:'gəʊ/ *vt* (*pt* **-went**, *pp* **-gone**) verzichten auf (+ *acc*)

forgot(ten) /fə'gɒt(n)/ *see* **forget**

fork /fɔ:k/ *n* Gabel *f*; (*in road*) Gabelung *f* ● *vi* ⟨*road:*⟩ sich gabeln; **~ right** rechts abzweigen. **~ out** *vt* (*fam*) blechen

fork-lift 'truck *n* Gabelstapler *m*

forlorn /fə'lɔ:n/ *a* verlassen; ⟨*hope*⟩ schwach

form /fɔ:m/ *n* Form *f*; (*document*) Formular *nt*; (*bench*) Bank *f*; (*Sch*) Klasse *f* ● *vt* formen (**into** zu);

(*create*) bilden • *vi* sich bilden; ⟨*idea:*⟩ Gestalt annehmen
formal /'fɔ:ml/ *a*, **-ly** *adv* formell, förmlich. **~ity** /-'mælətɪ/ *n* Förmlichkeit *f*; (*requirement*) Formalität *f*
format /'fɔ:mæt/ *n* Format *nt*
formation /fɔ:'meɪʃn/ *n* Formation *f*
formative /'fɔ:mətɪv/ *a* **~ years** Entwicklungsjahre *pl*
former /'fɔmə(r)/ *a* ehemalig; **the ~** der/die/das erstere. **~ly** *adv* früher
formidable /'fɔmɪdəbl/ *a* gewaltig
formula /'fɔ:mjʊlə/ *n* (*pl* **-ae** /-li:/ *or* **-s**) Formel *f*
formulate /'fɔ:mjʊleɪt/ *vt* formulieren
forsake /fə'seɪk/ *vt* (*pt* **-sook** /-sʊk/, *pp* **-saken**) verlassen
fort /fɔ:t/ *n* (*Mil*) Fort *nt*
forte /'fɔ:teɪ/ *n* Stärke *f*
forth /fɔ:θ/ *adv* **back and ~** hin und her; **and so ~** und so weiter
forth: **~'coming** *a* bevorstehend; (*fam: communicative*) mitteilsam. **~right** *a* direkt. **~'with** *adv* umgehend
fortieth /'fɔ:tɪɪθ/ *a* vierzigste(r,s)
fortification /fɔ:tɪfɪ'keɪʃn/ *n* Befestigung *f*
fortify /'fɔ:tɪfaɪ/ *vt* (*pt*/*pp* **-ied**) befestigen; (*fig*) stärken
fortitude /'fɔ:tɪtju:d/ *n* Standhaftigkeit *f*
fortnight /'fɔ:t-/ *n* vierzehn Tage *pl*. **~ly** *a* vierzehntäglich • *adv* alle vierzehn Tage
fortress /'fɔ:trɪs/ *n* Festung *f*
fortuitous /fɔ:'tju:ɪtəs/ *a*, **-ly** *adv* zufällig
fortunate /'fɔ:tʃʊnət/ *a* glücklich; **be ~** Glück haben. **~ly** *adv* glücklicherweise
fortune /'fɔ:tʃu:n/ *n* Glück *nt*; (*money*) Vermögen *nt*. **~-teller** *n* Wahrsagerin *f*
forty /'fɔ:tɪ/ *a* vierzig; **have ~ winks** (*fam*) ein Nickerchen machen • *n* Vierzig *f*
forum /'fɔ:rəm/ *n* Forum *nt*
forward /'fɔ:wəd/ *adv* vorwärts; (*to the front*) nach vorn • *a* Vorwärts-; (*presumptuous*) anmaßend • *n* (*Sport*) Stürmer *m* • *vt* nachsenden ⟨*letter*⟩. **~s** *adv* vorwärts
fossil /'fɒsl/ *n* Fossil *nt*. **~ized** *a* versteinert
foster /'fɒstə(r)/ *vt* fördern; in Pflege nehmen ⟨*child*⟩. **~-child** *n* Pflegekind *nt*. **~-mother** *n* Pflegemutter *f*
fought /fɔ:t/ *see* **fight**
foul /faʊl/ *a* (**-er, -est**) widerlich; ⟨*language*⟩ unflätig; **~ play** (*Jur*) Mord *m* • *n* (*Sport*) Foul *nt* • *vt* verschmutzen; (*obstruct*) blockieren; (*Sport*) foulen. **~-smelling** *a* übelriechend
found[1] /faʊnd/ *see* **find**
found[2] *vt* gründen
foundation /faʊn'deɪʃn/ *n* (*basis*) Grundlage *f*; (*charitable*) Stiftung *f*; **~s** *pl* Fundament *nt*. **~-stone** *n* Grundstein *m*
founder[1] /'faʊndə(r)/ *n* Gründer(in) *m*(*f*)
founder[2] *vi* ⟨*ship:*⟩ sinken; (*fig*) scheitern
foundry /'faʊndrɪ/ *n* Gießerei *f*
fountain /'faʊntɪn/ *n* Brunnen *m*. **~-pen** *n* Füllfederhalter *m*
four /fɔ:(r)/ *a* vier • *n* Vier *f*
four: **~-'poster** *n* Himmelbett *nt*. **~some** /'fɔ:səm/ *n* **in a ~some** zu viert. **~'teen** *a* vierzehn • *n* Vierzehn *f*. **~'teenth** *a* vierzehnte(r,s)
fourth /fɔ:θ/ *a* vierte(r,s)
fowl /faʊl/ *n* Geflügel *nt*
fox /fɒks/ *n* Fuchs *m* • *vt* (*puzzle*) verblüffen
foyer /'fɔɪeɪ/ *n* Foyer *nt*; (*in hotel*) Empfangshalle *f*
fraction /'frækʃn/ *n* Bruchteil *m*; (*Math*) Bruch *m*
fracture /'fræktʃə(r)/ *n* Bruch *m* • *vt*/*i* brechen
fragile /'frædʒaɪl/ *a* zerbrechlich
fragment /'frægmənt/ *n* Bruchstück *nt*, Fragment *nt*. **~ary** *a* bruchstückhaft
fragran|ce /'freɪgrəns/ *n* Duft *m*. **~t** *a* duftend
frail /freɪl/ *a* (**-er, -est**) gebrechlich
frame /freɪm/ *n* Rahmen *m*; (*of spectacles*) Gestell *nt*; (*Anat*) Körperbau *m*; **~ of mind** Gemütsverfassung *f* • *vt* einrahmen; (*fig*) formulieren; (*sl*) ein Verbrechen anhängen (+ *dat*). **~work** *n* Gerüst *nt*; (*fig*) Gerippe *nt*
franc /fræŋk/ *n* (*French, Belgian*) Franc *m*; (*Swiss*) Franken *m*
France /frɑ:ns/ *n* Frankreich *nt*
franchise /'fræntʃaɪz/ *n* (*Pol*) Wahlrecht *nt*; (*Comm*) Franchise *nt*
frank[1] /fræŋk/ *vt* frankieren
frank[2] *a*, **-ly** *adv* offen
frankfurter /'fræŋkfɜ:tə(r)/ *n* Frankfurter *f*

frantic /'fræntɪk/ *a*, **-ally** *adv* verzweifelt; **be ~** außer sich (*dat*) sein (**with** vor)
fraternal /frə'tɜ:nl/ *a* brüderlich
fraud /frɔ:d/ *n* Betrug *m*; (*person*) Betrüger(in) *m*(*f*). **~ulent** /-jʊlənt/ *a* betrügerisch
fraught /frɔ:t/ *a* **~ with danger** gefahrvoll
fray[1] /freɪ/ *n* Kampf *m*
fray[2] *vi* ausfransen
freak /fri:k/ *n* Mißbildung *f*; (*person*) Mißgeburt *f*; (*phenomenon*) Ausnahmeerscheinung *f* ● *a* anormal. **~ish** *a* anormal
freckle /'frekl/ *n* Sommersprosse *f*. **~d** *a* sommersprossig
free /fri:/ *a* (**freer, freest**) frei; ⟨*ticket, copy, time*⟩ Frei-; (*lavish*) freigebig; **~ [of charge]** kostenlos; **set ~** freilassen; (*rescue*) befreien; **you are ~ to ...** es steht Ihnen frei, zu ... ● *vt* (*pt/pp* **freed**) freilassen; (*rescue*) befreien; (*disentangle*) freibekommen
free: ~dom *n* Freiheit *f*. **~hand** *adv* aus freier Hand. **~hold** *n* [freier] Grundbesitz *m*. **~ 'kick** *n* Freistoß *m*. **~lance** *a* & *adv* freiberuflich. **~ly** *adv* frei; (*voluntarily*) freiwillig; (*generously*) großzügig. **F~mason** *n* Freimaurer *m*. **F~masonry** *n* Freimaurerei *f*. **~-range** *a* **~-range eggs** Landeier *pl*. **~ 'sample** *n* Gratisprobe *f*. **~style** *n* Freistil *m*. **~way** *n* (*Amer*) Autobahn *f*. **~-'wheel** *vi* im Freilauf fahren
freez|e /fri:z/ *vt* (*pt* **froze**, *pp* **frozen**) einfrieren; stoppen ⟨*wages*⟩ ● *vi* gefrieren; **it's ~ing** es friert
freez|er /'fri:zə(r)/ *n* Gefriertruhe *f*; (*upright*) Gefrierschrank *m*. **~ing** *a* eiskalt ● *n* **below ~ing** unter Null
freight /freɪt/ *n* Fracht *f*. **~er** *n* Frachter *m*. **~ train** *n* (*Amer*) Güterzug *m*
French /frentʃ/ *a* französisch ● *n* (*Lang*) Französisch *nt*; **the ~** *pl* die Franzosen
French: ~ 'beans *npl* grüne Bohnen *pl*. **~ 'bread** *n* Stangenbrot *nt*. **~ 'fries** *npl* Pommes frites *pl*. **~man** *n* Franzose *m*. **~ 'window** *n* Terrassentür *f*. **~woman** *n* Französin *f*
frenzied /'frenzɪd/ *a* rasend
frenzy /'frenzɪ/ *n* Raserei *f*
frequency /'fri:kwənsɪ/ *n* Häufigkeit *f*; (*Phys*) Frequenz *f*
frequent[1] /'fri:kwənt/ *a*, **-ly** *adv* häufig
frequent[2] /frɪ'kwent/ *vt* regelmäßig besuchen
fresco /'freskəʊ/ *n* Fresko *nt*
fresh /freʃ/ *a* (**-er, -est**), **-ly** *adv* frisch; (*new*) neu; (*Amer: cheeky*) frech
freshen /'freʃn/ *vi* ⟨*wind:*⟩ auffrischen. **~ up** *vt* auffrischen ● *vi* sich frisch machen
freshness /'freʃnɪs/ *n* Frische *f*
'freshwater *a* Süßwasser-
fret /fret/ *vi* (*pt/pp* **fretted**) sich grämen. **~ful** *a* weinerlich
'fretsaw *n* Laubsäge *f*
friar /'fraɪə(r)/ *n* Mönch *m*
friction /'frɪkʃn/ *n* Reibung *f*; (*fig*) Reibereien *pl*
Friday /'fraɪdeɪ/ *n* Freitag *m*
fridge /frɪdʒ/ *n* Kühlschrank *m*
fried /fraɪd/ *see* **fry**[2] ● *a* gebraten; **~ egg** Spiegelei *nt*
friend /frend/ *n* Freund(in) *m*(*f*). **~liness** *n* Freundlichkeit *f*. **~ly** *a* (**-ier, -iest**) freundlich; **~ly with** befreundet mit. **~ship** *n* Freundschaft *f*
frieze /fri:z/ *n* Fries *m*
fright /fraɪt/ *n* Schreck *m*
frighten /'fraɪtn/ *vt* angst machen (+ *dat*); (*startle*) erschrecken; **be ~ed** Angst haben (**of** vor + *dat*). **~ing** *a* angsterregend
frightful /'fraɪtfl/ *a*, **-ly** *adv* schrecklich
frigid /'frɪdʒɪd/ *a* frostig; (*Psych*) frigide. **~ity** /-'dʒɪdətɪ/ *n* Frostigkeit *f*; Frigidität *f*
frill /frɪl/ *n* Rüsche *f*; (*paper*) Manschette *f*. **~y** *a* rüschenbesetzt
fringe /frɪndʒ/ *n* Fransen *pl*; (*of hair*) Pony *m*; (*fig: edge*) Rand *m*. **~ benefits** *npl* zusätzliche Leistungen *pl*
frisk /frɪsk/ *vi* herumspringen ● *vt* (*search*) durchsuchen, (*fam*) filzen
frisky /'frɪskɪ/ *a* (**-ier, -iest**) lebhaft
fritter /'frɪtə(r)/ *vt* **~ [away]** verplempern (*fam*)
frivol|ity /frɪ'vɒlətɪ/ *n* Frivolität *f*. **~ous** /'frɪvələs/ *a*, **-ly** *adv* frivol, leichtfertig
frizzy /'frɪzɪ/ *a* kraus
fro /frəʊ/ *see* **to**
frock /frɒk/ *n* Kleid *nt*
frog /frɒg/ *n* Frosch *m*. **~man** *n* Froschmann *m*. **~-spawn** *n* Froschlaich *m*
frolic /'frɒlɪk/ *vi* (*pt/pp* **frolicked**) herumtollen

from /frɒm/ *prep* von (+ *dat*); (*out of*) aus (+ *dat*); (*according to*) nach (+ *dat*); ~ **Monday** ab Montag; ~ **that day** seit dem Tag

front /frʌnt/ *n* Vorderseite *f*; (*fig*) Fassade *f*; (*of garment*) Vorderteil *nt*; (*sea-*) Strandpromenade *f*; (*Mil, Pol, Meteorol*) Front *f*; **in** ~ **of** vor; **in** *or* **at the** ~ vorne; **to the** ~ nach vorne ● *a* vordere(r,s); ⟨*page, row*⟩ erste(r,s); ⟨*tooth, wheel*⟩ Vorder-

frontal /ˈfrʌntl/ *a* Frontal-

front: ~ **ˈdoor** *n* Haustür *f*. ~ **ˈgarden** *n* Vorgarten *m*

frontier /ˈfrʌntɪə(r)/ *n* Grenze *f*

front-wheel ˈdrive *n* Vorderradantrieb *m*

frost /frɒst/ *n* Frost *m*; (*hoar-*) Raureif *m*; **ten degrees of** ~ zehn Grad Kälte. ~**bite** *n* Erfrierung *f*. ~**bitten** *a* erfroren

frost|ed /ˈfrɒstɪd/ *a* ~**ed glass** Mattglas *nt*. ~**ing** *n* (*Amer Culin*) Zuckerguß *m*. ~**y** *a*, **-ily** *adv* frostig

froth /frɒθ/ *n* Schaum *m* ● *vi* schäumen. ~**y** *a* schaumig

frown /fraʊn/ *n* Stirnrunzeln *nt* ● *vi* die Stirn runzeln; ~ **on** mißbilligen

froze /frəʊz/ *see* **freeze**

frozen /ˈfrəʊzn/ *see* **freeze** ● *a* gefroren; (*Culin*) tiefgekühlt; **I'm** ~ (*fam*) mir ist eiskalt. ~ **food** *n* Tiefkühlkost *f*

frugal /ˈfru:gl/ *a*, **-ly** *adv* sparsam; ⟨*meal*⟩ frugal

fruit /fru:t/ *n* Frucht *f*; (*collectively*) Obst *nt*. ~ **cake** *n* englischer [Tee]kuchen *m*

fruit|erer /ˈfru:tərə(r)/ *n* Obsthändler *m*. ~**ful** *a* fruchtbar

fruition /fru:ˈɪʃn/ *n* **come to** ~ sich verwirklichen

fruit: ~ **juice** *n* Obstsaft *m*. ~**less** *a*, **-ly** *adv* fruchtlos. ~ **machine** *n* Spielautomat *m*. ~ **ˈsalad** *n* Obstsalat *m*

fruity /ˈfru:tɪ/ *a* fruchtig

frumpy /ˈfrʌmpɪ/ *a* unmodisch

frustrat|e /frʌˈstreɪt/ *vt* vereiteln; (*Psych*) frustrieren. ~**ing** *a* frustrierend. ~**ion** /-eɪʃn/ *n* Frustration *f*

fry¹ /fraɪ/ *n inv* **small** ~ (*fig*) kleine Fische *pl*

fry² *vt/i* (*pt/pp* **fried**) [in der Pfanne] braten. ~**ing-pan** *n* Bratpfanne *f*

fuck /fʌk/ *vt/i* (*vulg*) ficken. ~**ing** *a* (*vulg*) Scheiß-

fuddy-duddy /ˈfʌdɪdʌdɪ/ *n* (*fam*) verknöcherter Kerl *m*

fudge /fʌdʒ/ *n* weiche Karamellen *pl*

fuel /ˈfju:əl/ *n* Brennstoff *m*; (*for car*) Kraftstoff *m*; (*for aircraft*) Treibstoff *m*

fugitive /ˈfju:dʒətɪv/ *n* Flüchtling *m*

fugue /fju:g/ *n* (*Mus*) Fuge *f*

fulfil /fʊlˈfɪl/ *vt* (*pt/pp* **-filled**) erfüllen. ~**ment** *n* Erfüllung *f*

full /fʊl/ *a & adv* (**-er, -est**) voll; (*detailed*) ausführlich; ⟨*skirt*⟩ weit; ~ **of** voll von (+ *dat*), voller (+ *gen*); **at** ~ **speed** in voller Fahrt ● *n* **in** ~ vollständig

full: ~ **ˈmoon** *n* Vollmond *m*. ~**-scale** *a* ⟨*model*⟩ in Originalgröße; ⟨*rescue, alert*⟩ großangelegt. ~ **ˈstop** *n* Punkt *m*. ~**-time** *a* ganztägig ● *adv* ganztags

fully /ˈfʊlɪ/ *adv* völlig; (*in detail*) ausführlich

fulsome /ˈfʊlsəm/ *a* übertrieben

fumble /ˈfʌmbl/ *vi* herumfummeln (**with** an + *dat*)

fume /fju:m/ *vi* vor Wut schäumen

fumes /fju:mz/ *npl* Dämpfe *pl*; (*from car*) Abgase *pl*

fumigate /ˈfju:mɪgeɪt/ *vt* ausräuchern

fun /fʌn/ *n* Spaß *m*; **for** ~ aus *od* zum Spaß; **make** ~ **of** sich lustig machen über (+ *acc*); **have** ~**!** viel Spaß!

function /ˈfʌŋkʃn/ *n* Funktion *f*; (*event*) Veranstaltung *f* ● *vi* funktionieren; (*serve*) dienen (**as** als). ~**al** *a* zweckmäßig

fund /fʌnd/ *n* Fonds *m*; (*fig*) Vorrat *m*; ~**s** *pl* Geldmittel *pl* ● *vt* finanzieren

fundamental /fʌndəˈmentl/ *a* grundlegend; (*essential*) wesentlich

funeral /ˈfju:nərl/ *n* Beerdigung *f*; (*cremation*) Feuerbestattung *f*

funeral: ~ **directors** *pl*, (*Amer*) ~ **home** *n* Bestattungsinstitut *nt*. ~ **march** *n* Trauermarsch *m*. ~ **parlour** *n* (*Amer*) Bestattungsinstitut *nt*. ~ **service** *n* Trauergottesdienst *m*

ˈfunfair *n* Jahrmarkt *m*, Kirmes *f*

fungus /ˈfʌŋgəs/ *n* (*pl* **-gi** /-gaɪ/) Pilz *m*

funicular /fju:ˈnɪkjʊlə(r)/ *n* Seilbahn *f*

funnel /ˈfʌnl/ *n* Trichter *m*; (*on ship, train*) Schornstein *m*

funnily /ˈfʌnɪlɪ/ *adv* komisch; ~ **enough** komischerweise

funny /ˈfʌnɪ/ *a* (**-ier, -iest**) komisch. **~-bone** *n* (*fam*) Musikantenknochen *m*

fur /fɜː(r)/ *n* Fell *nt*; (*for clothing*) Pelz *m*; (*in kettle*) Kesselstein *m*. **~ 'coat** *n* Pelzmantel *m*

furious /ˈfjʊərɪəs/ *a*, **-ly** *adv* wütend (**with** auf + *acc*)

furnace /ˈfɜːnɪs/ *n* (*Techn*) Ofen *m*

furnish /ˈfɜːnɪʃ/ *vt* einrichten; (*supply*) liefern. **~ed** *a* **~ed room** möbliertes Zimmer *nt*. **~ings** *npl* Einrichtungsgegenstände *pl*

furniture /ˈfɜːnɪtʃə(r)/ *n* Möbel *pl*

furred /fɜːd/ *a* ⟨*tongue*⟩ belegt

furrow /ˈfʌrəʊ/ *n* Furche *f*

furry /ˈfɜːrɪ/ *a* ⟨*animal*⟩ Pelz-; ⟨*toy*⟩ Plüsch-

further /ˈfɜːðə(r)/ *a* weitere(r,s); **at the ~ end** am anderen Ende; **until ~ notice** bis auf weiteres ● *adv* weiter; **~ off** weiter entfernt ● *vt* fördern

further: ~ eduˈcation *n* Weiterbildung *f*. **~ˈmore** *adv* überdies

furthest /ˈfɜːðɪst/ *a* am weitesten entfernt ● *adv* am weitesten

furtive /ˈfɜːtɪv/ *a*, **-ly** *adv* verstohlen

fury /ˈfjʊərɪ/ *n* Wut *f*

fuse¹ /fjuːz/ *n* (*of bomb*) Zünder *m*; (*cord*) Zündschnur *f*

fuse² *n* (*Electr*) Sicherung *f* ● *vt/i* verschmelzen; **the lights have ~d** die Sicherung [für das Licht] ist durchgebrannt. **~-box** *n* Sicherungskasten *m*

fuselage /ˈfjuːzəlɑːʒ/ *n* (*Aviat*) Rumpf *m*

fusion /ˈfjuːʒn/ *n* Verschmelzung *f*, Fusion *f*

fuss /fʌs/ *n* Getue *nt*; **make a ~ of** verwöhnen; (*caress*) liebkosen ● *vi* Umstände machen

fussy /ˈfʌsɪ/ *a* (**-ier, -iest**) wählerisch; (*particular*) penibel

fusty /ˈfʌstɪ/ *a* moderig

futil|e /ˈfjuːtaɪl/ *a* zwecklos. **~ity** /-ˈtɪlətɪ/ *n* Zwecklosigkeit *f*

future /ˈfjuːtʃə(r)/ *a* zukünftig ● *n* Zukunft *f*; (*Gram*) [erstes] Futur *nt*; **~ perfect** zweites Futur *nt*; **in ~** in Zukunft

futuristic /fjuːtʃəˈrɪstɪk/ *a* futuristisch

fuzz /fʌz/ *n* **the ~** (*sl*) die Bullen *pl*

fuzzy /ˈfʌzɪ/ *a* (**-ier, -iest**) ⟨*hair*⟩ kraus; (*blurred*) verschwommen

G

gab /gæb/ *n* (*fam*) **have the gift of the ~** gut reden können

gabble /ˈgæbl/ *vi* schnell reden

gable /ˈgeɪbl/ *n* Giebel *m*

gad /gæd/ *vi* (*pt/pp* **gadded**) **~ about** dauernd ausgehen

gadget /ˈgædʒɪt/ *n* [kleines] Gerät *nt*

Gaelic /ˈgeɪlɪk/ *n* Gälisch *nt*

gaffe /gæf/ *n* Fauxpas *m*

gag /gæg/ *n* Knebel *m*; (*joke*) Witz *m*; (*Theat*) Gag *m* ● *vt* (*pt/pp* **gagged**) knebeln

gaiety /ˈgeɪətɪ/ *n* Fröhlichkeit *f*

gaily /ˈgeɪlɪ/ *adv* fröhlich

gain /geɪn/ *n* Gewinn *m*; (*increase*) Zunahme *f* ● *vt* gewinnen; (*obtain*) erlangen; **~ weight** zunehmen ● *vi* ⟨*clock:*⟩ vorgehen. **~ful** *a* **~ful employment** Erwerbstätigkeit *f*

gait /geɪt/ *n* Gang *m*

gala /ˈgɑːlə/ *n* Fest *nt*; **swimming ~** Schwimmfest *nt* ● *attrib* Gala-

galaxy /ˈgæləksɪ/ *n* Galaxie *f*; **the G~** die Milchstraße

gale /geɪl/ *n* Sturm *m*

gall /gɔːl/ *n* Galle *f*; (*impudence*) Frechheit *f*

gallant /ˈgælənt/ *a*, **-ly** *adv* tapfer; (*chivalrous*) galant. **~ry** *n* Tapferkeit *f*

ˈgall-bladder *n* Gallenblase *f*

gallery /ˈgælərɪ/ *n* Galerie *f*

galley /ˈgælɪ/ *n* (*ship's kitchen*) Kombüse *f*; **~ [proof]** [Druck]fahne *f*

gallivant /ˈgælɪvænt/ *vi* (*fam*) ausgehen

gallon /ˈgælən/ *n* Gallone *f* (= *4,5 l; Amer = 3,785 l*)

gallop /ˈgæləp/ *n* Galopp *m* ● *vi* galoppieren

gallows /ˈgæləʊz/ *n* Galgen *m*

ˈgallstone *n* Gallenstein *m*

galore /gəˈlɔː(r)/ *adv* in Hülle und Fülle

galvanize /ˈgælvənaɪz/ *vt* galvanisieren

gambit /ˈgæmbɪt/ *n* Eröffnungsmanöver *nt*

gamble /ˈgæmbl/ *n* (*risk*) Risiko *nt* ● *vi* [um Geld] spielen; **~ on** (*rely*) sich verlassen auf (+ *acc*). **~r** *n* Spieler(in) *m*(*f*)

game /geɪm/ *n* Spiel *nt*; (*animals, birds*) Wild *nt*; **~s** (*Sch*) Sport *m* ● *a* (*brave*) tapfer; (*willing*) bereit (**for** zu). **~keeper** *n* Wildhüter *m*

gammon /'gæmən/ *n* [geräucherter] Schinken *m*
gamut /'gæmət/ *n* Skala *f*
gander /'gændə(r)/ *n* Gänserich *m*
gang /gæŋ/ *n* Bande *f*; (*of workmen*) Kolonne *f* ● *vi* ~ **up** sich zusammenrotten (**on** gegen)
gangling /'gæŋglɪŋ/ *a* schlaksig
gangrene /'gæŋgri:n/ *n* Wundbrand *m*
gangster /'gæŋstə(r)/ *n* Gangster *m*
gangway /'gæŋweɪ/ *n* Gang *m*; (*Naut, Aviat*) Gangway *f*
gaol /dʒeɪl/ *n* Gefängnis *nt* ● *vt* ins Gefängnis sperren. **~er** *n* Gefängniswärter *m*
gap /gæp/ *n* Lücke *f*; (*interval*) Pause *f*; (*difference*) Unterschied *m*
gap|e /geɪp/ *vi* gaffen; **~e at** anstarren. **~ing** *a* klaffend
garage /'gærɑ:ʒ/ *n* Garage *f*; (*for repairs*) Werkstatt *f*; (*for petrol*) Tankstelle *f*
garb /gɑ:b/ *n* Kleidung *f*
garbage /'gɑ:bɪdʒ/ *n* Müll *m*. **~ can** *n* (*Amer*) Mülleimer *m*
garbled /'gɑ:bld/ *a* verworren
garden /'gɑ:dn/ *n* Garten *m*; **[public] ~s** *pl* [öffentliche] Anlagen *pl* ● *vi* im Garten arbeiten. **~er** *n* Gärtner(in) *m*(*f*). **~ing** *n* Gartenarbeit *f*
gargle /'gɑ:gl/ *n* (*liquid*) Gurgelwasser *nt* ● *vi* gurgeln
gargoyle /'gɑ:gɔɪl/ *n* Wasserspeier *m*
garish /'geərɪʃ/ *a* grell
garland /'gɑ:lənd/ *n* Girlande *f*
garlic /'gɑ:lɪk/ *n* Knoblauch *m*
garment /'gɑ:mənt/ *n* Kleidungsstück *nt*
garnet /'gɑ:nɪt/ *n* Granat *m*
garnish /'gɑ:nɪʃ/ *n* Garnierung *f* ● *vt* garnieren
garret /'gærɪt/ *n* Dachstube *f*
garrison /'gærɪsn/ *n* Garnison *f*
garrulous /'gærʊləs/ *a* geschwätzig
garter /'gɑ:tə(r)/ *n* Strumpfband *nt*; (*Amer: suspender*) Strumpfhalter *m*
gas /gæs/ *n* Gas *nt*; (*Amer fam: petrol*) Benzin *nt* ● *v* (*pt/pp* **gassed**) ● *vt* vergasen ● *vi* (*fam*) schwatzen. **~ cooker** *n* Gasherd *m*. **~ 'fire** *n* Gasofen *m*
gash /gæʃ/ *n* Schnitt *m*; (*wound*) klaffende Wunde *f* ● *vt* **~ one's arm** sich (*dat*) den Arm aufschlitzen
gasket /'gæskɪt/ *n* (*Techn*) Dichtung *f*
gas: ~ mask *n* Gasmaske *f*. **~-meter** *n* Gaszähler *m*
gasoline /'gæsəli:n/ *n* (*Amer*) Benzin *nt*
gasp /gɑ:sp/ *vi* keuchen; (*in surprise*) hörbar die Luft einziehen
'gas station *n* (*Amer*) Tankstelle *f*
gastric /'gæstrɪk/ *a* Magen-. **~ 'flu** *n* Darmgrippe *f*. **~ 'ulcer** *n* Magengeschwür *nt*
gastronomy /gæ'strɒnəmɪ/ *n* Gastronomie *f*
gate /geɪt/ *n* Tor *nt*; (*to field*) Gatter *nt*; (*barrier*) Schranke *f*; (*at airport*) Flugsteig *m*
gâteau /'gætəʊ/ *n* Torte *f*
gate: ~crasher *n* ungeladener Gast *m*. **~way** *n* Tor *nt*
gather /'gæðə(r)/ *vt* sammeln; (*pick*) pflücken; (*conclude*) folgern (**from** aus); (*Sewing*) kräuseln; **~ speed** schneller werden ● *vi* sich versammeln; ⟨*storm:*⟩ sich zusammenziehen. **~ing** *n* **family ~ing** Familientreffen *nt*
gaudy /'gɔ:dɪ/ *a* (**-ier, -iest**) knallig
gauge /geɪdʒ/ *n* Stärke *f*; (*Rail*) Spurweite *f*; (*device*) Meßinstrument *nt* ● *vt* messen; (*estimate*) schätzen
gaunt /gɔ:nt/ *a* hager
gauntlet /'gɔ:ntlɪt/ *n* **run the ~** Spießruten laufen
gauze /gɔ:z/ *n* Gaze *f*
gave /geɪv/ *see* **give**
gawky /'gɔ:kɪ/ *a* (**-ier, -iest**) schlaksig
gawp /gɔ:p/ *vi* (*fam*) glotzen; **~ at** anglotzen
gay /geɪ/ *a* (**-er, -est**) fröhlich; (*fam*) homosexuell, (*fam*) schwul
gaze /geɪz/ *n* [langer] Blick *m* ● *vi* sehen; **~ at** ansehen
gazelle /gə'zel/ *n* Gazelle *f*
GB *abbr of* **Great Britain**
gear /gɪə(r)/ *n* Ausrüstung *f*; (*Techn*) Getriebe *nt*; (*Auto*) Gang *m*; **in ~** mit eingelegtem Gang; **change ~** schalten ● *vt* anpassen (**to** *dat*)
gear: ~box *n* (*Auto*) Getriebe *nt*. **~-lever** *n*, (*Amer*) **~-shift** *n* Schalthebel *m*
geese /gi:s/ *see* **goose**
geezer /'gi:zə(r)/ *n* (*sl*) Typ *m*
gel /dʒel/ *n* Gel *nt*
gelatine /'dʒelətɪn/ *n* Gelatine *f*
gelignite /'dʒelɪgnaɪt/ *n* Gelatinedynamit *nt*
gem /dʒem/ *n* Juwel *nt*
Gemini /'dʒemɪnaɪ/ *n* (*Astr*) Zwillinge *pl*
gender /'dʒendə(r)/ *n* (*Gram*) Geschlecht *nt*

gene /dʒi:n/ *n* Gen *nt*
genealogy /dʒi:nɪ'ælədʒɪ/ *n* Genealogie *f*
general /'dʒenrəl/ *a* allgemein ● *n* General *m*; **in ~** im allgemeinen. **~ e'lection** *n* allgemeine Wahlen *pl*
generaliz|ation /dʒenrəlaɪ'zeɪʃn/ *n* Verallgemeinerung *f*. **~e** /'dʒenrəlaɪz/ *vi* verallgemeinern
generally /'dʒenrəlɪ/ *adv* im allgemeinen
general prac'titioner *n* praktischer Arzt *m*
generate /'dʒenəreɪt/ *vt* erzeugen
generation /dʒenə'reɪʃn/ *n* Generation *f*
generator /'dʒenəreɪtə(r)/ *n* Generator *m*
generic /dʒɪ'nerɪk/ *a* **~ term** Oberbegriff *m*
generosity /dʒenə'rɒsɪtɪ/ *n* Großzügigkeit *f*
generous /'dʒenərəs/ *a*, **-ly** *adv* großzügig
genetic /dʒɪ'netɪk/ *a* genetisch. **~ engineering** *n* Gentechnologie *f*. **~s** *n* Genetik *f*
Geneva /dʒɪ'ni:və/ *n* Genf *nt*
genial /'dʒi:nɪəl/ *a*, **-ly** *adv* freundlich
genitals /'dʒenɪtlz/ *pl* [äußere] Geschlechtsteile *pl*
genitive /'dʒenɪtɪv/ *a & n* **~ [case]** Genitiv *m*
genius /'dʒi:nɪəs/ *n* (*pl* **-uses**) Genie *nt*; (*quality*) Genialität *f*
genocide /'dʒenəsaɪd/ *n* Völkermord *m*
genre /'ʒɑ̃rə/ *n* Gattung *f*, Genre *nt*
gent /dʒent/ *n* (*fam*) Herr *m*; **the ~s** *sg* die Herrentoilette *f*
genteel /dʒen'ti:l/ *a* vornehm
gentle /'dʒentl/ *a* (**-r, -st**) sanft
gentleman /'dʒentlmən/ *n* Herr *m*; (*well-mannered*) Gentleman *m*
gent|leness /'dʒentlnɪs/ *n* Sanftheit *f*. **~ly** *adv* sanft
genuine /'dʒenjʊɪn/ *a* echt; (*sincere*) aufrichtig. **~ly** *adv* (*honestly*) ehrlich
genus /'dʒi:nəs/ *n* (*Biol*) Gattung *f*
geograph|ical /dʒɪə'græfɪkl/ *a*, **-ly** *adv* geographisch. **~y** /dʒɪ'ɒgrəfɪ/ *n* Geographie *f*, Erdkunde *f*
geological /dʒɪə'lɒdʒɪkl/ *a*, **-ly** *adv* geologisch
geolog|ist /dʒɪ'ɒlədʒɪst/ *n* Geologe *m*/-gin *f*. **~y** *n* Geologie *f*
geometr|ic(al) /dʒɪə'metrɪk(l)/ *a* geometrisch. **~y** /dʒɪ'ɒmətrɪ/ *n* Geometrie *f*
geranium /dʒə'reɪnɪəm/ *n* Geranie *f*
geriatric /dʒerɪ'ætrɪk/ *a* geriatrisch ● *n* geriatrischer Patient *m*. **~s** *n* Geriatrie *f*
germ /dʒɜ:m/ *n* Keim *m*; **~s** *pl* (*fam*) Bazillen *pl*
German /'dʒɜ:mən/ *a* deutsch ● *n* (*person*) Deutsche(r) *m*/*f*; (*Lang*) Deutsch *nt*; **in ~** auf deutsch; **into ~** ins Deutsche
Germanic /dʒə'mænɪk/ *a* germanisch
German: ~ 'measles *n* Röteln *pl*. **~ 'shepherd [dog]** *n* [deutscher] Schäferhund *m*
Germany /'dʒɜ:mənɪ/ *n* Deutschland *nt*
germinate /'dʒɜ:mɪneɪt/ *vi* keimen
gesticulate /dʒe'stɪkjʊleɪt/ *vi* gestikulieren
gesture /'dʒestʃə(r)/ *n* Geste *f*
get /get/ *v* (*pt*/*pp* **got**, *pp Amer also* **gotten**, *pres p* **getting**) ● *vt* bekommen, (*fam*) kriegen; (*procure*) besorgen; (*buy*) kaufen; (*fetch*) holen; (*take*) bringen; (*on telephone*) erreichen; (*fam: understand*) kapieren; machen ⟨*meal*⟩; **~ s.o. to do sth** jdn dazu bringen, etw zu tun ● *vi* (*become*) werden; **~ to** kommen zu/nach ⟨*town*⟩; (*reach*) erreichen; **~ dressed** sich anziehen; **~ married** heiraten. **~ at** *vt* herankommen an (+ *acc*); **what are you ~ting at?** worauf willst du hinaus? **~ away** *vi* (*leave*) wegkommen; (*escape*) entkommen. **~ back** *vi* zurückkommen ● *vt* (*recover*) zurückbekommen; **~ one's own back** sich revanchieren. **~ by** *vi* vorbeikommen; (*manage*) sein Auskommen haben. **~ down** *vi* heruntersteigen; **~ down to** sich [heran]machen an (+ *acc*) ● *vt* (*depress*) deprimieren. **~ in** *vi* einsteigen ● *vt* (*fetch*) hereinholen. **~ off** *vi* (*dismount*) absteigen; (*from bus*) aussteigen; (*leave*) wegkommen; (*Jur*) freigesprochen werden ● *vt* (*remove*) abbekommen. **~ on** *vi* (*mount*) aufsteigen; (*to bus*) einsteigen; (*be on good terms*) gut auskommen (**with** mit); (*make progress*) Fortschritte machen; **how are you ~ting on?** wie geht's? **~ out** *vi* herauskommen; (*of car*) aussteigen; **~ out of** (*avoid doing*) sich drücken

um • *vt* herausholen; herausbekommen ⟨*cork, stain*⟩. ~ **over** *vi* hinübersteigen • *vt* (*fig*) hinwegkommen über (+ *acc*). ~ **round** *vi* herumkommen; (*avoid*) umgehen; **I never ~ round to it** ich komme nie dazu • *vt* herumkriegen. ~ **through** *vi* durchkommen. ~ **up** *vi* aufstehen

get: ~**away** *n* Flucht *f*. ~**-up** *n* Aufmachung *f*

geyser /'gi:zə(r)/ *n* Durchlauferhitzer *m*; (*Geol*) Geysir *m*

ghastly /'gɑ:stlɪ/ *a* (**-ier, -iest**) gräßlich; (*pale*) blaß

gherkin /'gɜ:kɪn/ *n* Essiggurke *f*

ghetto /'getəʊ/ *n* Getto *nt*

ghost /gəʊst/ *n* Geist *m*, Gespenst *nt*. ~**ly** *a* geisterhaft

ghoulish /'gu:lɪʃ/ *a* makaber

giant /'dʒaɪənt/ *n* Riese *m* • *a* riesig

gibberish /'dʒɪbərɪʃ/ *n* Kauderwelsch *nt*

gibe /dʒaɪb/ *n* spöttische Bemerkung *f* • *vi* spotten (**at** über + *acc*)

giblets /'dʒɪblɪts/ *npl* Geflügelklein *nt*

giddiness /'gɪdɪnɪs/ *n* Schwindel *m*

giddy /'gɪdɪ/ *a* (**-ier, -iest**) schwindlig; **I feel** ~ mir ist schwindlig

gift /gɪft/ *n* Geschenk *nt*; (*to charity*) Gabe *f*; (*talent*) Begabung *f*. ~**ed** /-ɪd/ *a* begabt. ~**-wrap** *vt* als Geschenk einpacken

gig /gɪg/ *n* (*fam, Mus*) Gig *m*

gigantic /dʒaɪ'gæntɪk/ *a* riesig, riesengroß

giggle /'gɪgl/ *n* Kichern *nt* • *vi* kichern

gild /gɪld/ *vt* vergolden

gills /gɪlz/ *npl* Kiemen *pl*

gilt /gɪlt/ *a* vergoldet • *n* Vergoldung *f*. ~**-edged** *a* (*Comm*) mündelsicher

gimmick /'gɪmɪk/ *n* Trick *m*

gin /dʒɪn/ *n* Gin *m*

ginger /'dʒɪndʒə(r)/ *a* rotblond; ⟨*cat*⟩ rot • *n* Ingwer *m*. ~**bread** *n* Pfefferkuchen *m*

gingerly /'dʒɪndʒəlɪ/ *adv* vorsichtig

gipsy /'dʒɪpsɪ/ *n* = **gypsy**

giraffe /dʒɪ'rɑ:f/ *n* Giraffe *f*

girder /'gɜ:də(r)/ *n* (*Techn*) Träger *m*

girdle /'gɜ:dl/ *n* Bindegürtel *m*; (*corset*) Hüfthalter *m*

girl /gɜ:l/ *n* Mädchen *nt*; (*young woman*) junge Frau *f*. ~**friend** *n* Freundin *f*. ~**ish** *a*, **-ly** *adv* mädchenhaft

giro /'dʒaɪərəʊ/ *n* Giro *nt*; (*cheque*) Postscheck *m*

girth /gɜ:θ/ *n* Umfang *m*; (*for horse*) Bauchgurt *m*

gist /dʒɪst/ *n* **the** ~ das Wesentliche

give /gɪv/ *n* Elastizität *f* • *v* (*pt* **gave**, *pp* **given**) • *vt* geben/(*as present*) schenken (**to** *dat*); (*donate*) spenden; ⟨*lecture*⟩ halten; ⟨*one's name*⟩ angeben • *vi* geben; (*yield*) nachgeben. ~ **away** *vt* verschenken; (*betray*) verraten; (*distribute*) verteilen; ~ **away the bride** ≈ Brautführer sein. ~ **back** *vt* zurückgeben. ~ **in** *vt* einreichen • *vi* (*yield*) nachgeben. ~ **off** *vt* abgeben. ~ **up** *vt/i* aufgeben; ~ **oneself up** sich stellen. ~ **way** *vi* nachgeben; (*Auto*) die Vorfahrt beachten

given /'gɪvn/ *see* **give** • *a* ~ **name** Vorname *m*

glacier /'glæsɪə(r)/ *n* Gletscher *m*

glad /glæd/ *a* froh (**of** über + *acc*). ~**den** /'glædn/ *vt* erfreuen

glade /gleɪd/ *n* Lichtung *f*

gladly /'glædlɪ/ *adv* gern[e]

glamorous /'glæmərəs/ *a* glanzvoll; ⟨*film star*⟩ glamourös

glamour /'glæmə(r)/ *n* [betörender] Glanz *m*

glance /glɑ:ns/ *n* [flüchtiger] Blick *m* • *vi* ~ **at** einen Blick werfen auf (+ *acc*). ~ **up** *vi* aufblicken

gland /glænd/ *n* Drüse *f*

glandular /'glændjʊlə(r)/ *a* Drüsen-

glare /gleə(r)/ *n* grelles Licht *nt*; (*look*) ärgerlicher Blick *m* • *vi* ~ **at** böse ansehen

glaring /'gleərɪŋ/ *a* grell; ⟨*mistake*⟩ kraß

glass /glɑ:s/ *n* Glas *nt*; (*mirror*) Spiegel *m*; ~**es** *pl* (*spectacles*) Brille *f*. ~**y** *a* glasig

glaze /gleɪz/ *n* Glasur *f* • *vt* verglasen; (*Culin, Pottery*) glasieren

glazier /'gleɪzɪə(r)/ *n* Glaser *m*

gleam /gli:m/ *n* Schein *m* • *vi* glänzen

glean /gli:n/ *vi* Ähren lesen • *vt* (*learn*) erfahren

glee /gli:/ *n* Frohlocken *nt*. ~**ful** *a*, **-ly** *adv* frohlockend

glen /glen/ *n* [enges] Tal *nt*

glib /glɪb/ *a*, **-ly** *adv* (*pej*) gewandt

glid|e /glaɪd/ *vi* gleiten; (*through the air*) schweben. ~**er** *n* Segelflugzeug *nt*. ~**ing** *n* Segelfliegen *nt*

glimmer /'glɪmə(r)/ *n* Glimmen *nt* • *vi* glimmen

glimpse /glɪmps/ *n* **catch a ~ of** flüchtig sehen • *vt* flüchtig sehen

glint /glɪnt/ *n* Blitzen *nt* ● *vi* blitzen
glisten /ˈglɪsn/ *vi* glitzern
glitter /ˈglɪtə(r)/ *vi* glitzern
gloat /gləʊt/ *vi* schadenfroh sein; ~ **over** sich weiden an (+ *dat*)
global /ˈgləʊbl/ *a*, **-ly** *adv* global
globe /gləʊb/ *n* Kugel *f*; (*map*) Globus *m*
gloom /glu:m/ *n* Düsterkeit *f*; (*fig*) Pessimismus *m*
gloomy /ˈglu:mɪ/ *a* (**-ier, -iest**), **-ily** *adv* düster; (*fig*) pessimistisch
glorif|y /ˈglɔ:rɪfaɪ/ *vt* (*pt*/*pp* **-ied**) verherrlichen; **a ~ied waitress** eine bessere Kellnerin *f*
glorious /ˈglɔ:rɪəs/ *a* herrlich; ⟨*deed, hero*⟩ glorreich
glory /ˈglɔ:rɪ/ *n* Ruhm *m*; (*splendour*) Pracht *f* ● *vi* ~ **in** genießen
gloss /glɒs/ *n* Glanz *m* ● *a* Glanz- ● *vi* ~ **over** beschönigen
glossary /ˈglɒsərɪ/ *n* Glossar *nt*
glossy /ˈglɒsɪ/ *a* (**-ier, -iest**) glänzend
glove /glʌv/ *n* Handschuh *m*. ~ **compartment** *n* (*Auto*) Handschuhfach *nt*
glow /gləʊ/ *n* Glut *f*; (*of candle*) Schein *m* ● *vi* glühen; ⟨*candle:*⟩ scheinen. **~ing** *a* glühend; ⟨*account*⟩ begeistert
ˈglow-worm *n* Glühwürmchen *nt*
glucose /ˈglu:kəʊs/ *n* Traubenzucker *m*, Glukose *f*
glue /glu:/ *n* Klebstoff *m* ● *vt* (*pres p* **gluing**) kleben (**to** an + *acc*)
glum /glʌm/ *a* (**glummer, glummest**), **-ly** *adv* niedergeschlagen
glut /glʌt/ *n* Überfluß *m* (**of** an + *dat*); ~ **of fruit** Obstschwemme *f*
glutton /ˈglʌtn/ *n* Vielfraß *m*. **~ous** /-əs/ *a* gefräßig. **~y** *n* Gefräßigkeit *f*
gnarled /nɑ:ld/ *a* knorrig; ⟨*hands*⟩ knotig
gnash /næʃ/ *vt* ~ **one's teeth** mit den Zähnen knirschen
gnat /næt/ *n* Mücke *f*
gnaw /nɔ:/ *vt*/*i* nagen (**at** an + *dat*)
gnome /nəʊm/ *n* Gnom *m*
go /gəʊ/ *n* (*pl* **goes**) Energie *f*; (*attempt*) Versuch *m*; **on the go** auf Trab; **at one go** auf einmal; **it's your go** du bist dran; **make a go of it** Erfolg haben ● *vi* (*pt* **went**, *pp* **gone**) gehen; (*in vehicle*) fahren; (*leave*) weggehen; (*on journey*) abfahren; ⟨*time:*⟩ vergehen; (*vanish*) verschwinden; (*fail*) versagen; (*become*) werden; (*belong*) kommen; **go swimming/shopping** schwimmen/einkaufen gehen; **where are you going?** wo gehst du hin? **it's all gone** es ist nichts mehr übrig; **I am not going to** ich werde es nicht tun; **'to go'** (*Amer*) 'zum Mitnehmen'. **go away** *vi* weggehen/-fahren. **go back** *vi* zurückgehen/-fahren. **go by** *vi* vorbeigehen/-fahren; ⟨*time:*⟩ vergehen. **go down** *vi* hinuntergehen/-fahren; ⟨*sun, ship:*⟩ untergehen; ⟨*prices:*⟩ fallen; ⟨*temperature, swelling:*⟩ zurückgehen. **go for** *vt* holen; (*fam: attack*) losgehen auf (+ *acc*). **go in** *vi* hineingehen/-fahren; **go in for** teilnehmen an (+ *dat*) ⟨*competition*⟩; (*take up*) sich verlegen auf (+ *acc*). **go off** *vi* weggehen/-fahren; ⟨*alarm:*⟩ klingeln; ⟨*gun, bomb:*⟩ losgehen; (*go bad*) schlecht werden; **go off well** gut verlaufen. **go on** *vi* weitergehen/-fahren; (*continue*) weitermachen; (*talking*) fortfahren; (*happen*) vorgehen; **go on at** (*fam*) herumnörgeln an (+ *dat*). **go out** *vi* ausgehen; (*leave*) hinausgehen/-fahren. **go over** *vi* hinübergehen/-fahren ● *vt* (*check*) durchgehen. **go round** *vi* herumgehen/-fahren; (*visit*) vorbeigehen; (*turn*) sich drehen; (*be enough*) reichen. **go through** *vi* durchgehen/-fahren ● *vt* (*suffer*) durchmachen; (*check*) durchgehen. **go under** *vi* untergehen; (*fail*) scheitern. **go up** *vi* hinaufgehen/-fahren; ⟨*lift:*⟩ hochfahren; ⟨*prices:*⟩ steigen. **go without** *vt* verzichten auf (+ *acc*) ● *vi* darauf verzichten
goad /gəʊd/ *vt* anstacheln (**into** zu); (*taunt*) reizen
ˈgo-ahead *a* fortschrittlich; (*enterprising*) unternehmend ● *n* (*fig*) grünes Licht *nt*
goal /gəʊl/ *n* Ziel *nt*; (*Sport*) Tor *nt*. **~keeper** *n* Torwart *m*. **~-post** *n* Torpfosten *m*
goat /gəʊt/ *n* Ziege *f*
gobble /ˈgɒbl/ *vt* hinunterschlingen
ˈgo-between *n* Vermittler(in) *m*(*f*)
goblet /ˈgɒblɪt/ *n* Pokal *m*; (*glass*) Kelchglas *nt*
goblin /ˈgɒblɪn/ *n* Kobold *m*
God, god /gɒd/ *n* Gott *m*
god: ~child *n* Patenkind *nt*. **~-daughter** *n* Patentochter *f*. **~dess** *n* Göttin *f*. **~father** *n* Pate *m*. **G~-forsaken** *a* gottverlassen. **~mother** *n* Patin *f*. **~parents** *npl* Paten *pl*. **~send** *n* Segen *m*. **~son** *n* Patensohn *m*

goggle /'gɒgl/ *vi* (*fam*) ~ **at** anglotzen. ~**s** *npl* Schutzbrille *f*
going /'gəʊɪŋ/ *a* ⟨*price, rate*⟩ gängig; ⟨*concern*⟩ gutgehend ● *n* **it is hard** ~ es ist schwierig; **while the** ~ **is good** solange es noch geht. ~**s-'on** *npl* [seltsame] Vorgänge *pl*
gold /gəʊld/ *n* Gold *nt* ● *a* golden
golden /'gəʊldn/ *a* golden. ~ **'handshake** *n* hohe Abfindungssumme *f*. ~ **'wedding** *n* goldene Hochzeit *f*
gold: ~**fish** *n inv* Goldfisch *m*. ~**-mine** *n* Goldgrube *f*. ~**-plated** *a* vergoldet. ~**smith** *n* Goldschmied *m*
golf /gɒlf/ *n* Golf *nt*
golf: ~**-club** *n* Golfklub *m*; (*implement*) Golfschläger *m*. ~**-course** *n* Golfplatz *m*. ~**er** *m* Golfspieler(in) *m*(*f*)
gondo|la /'gɒndələ/ *n* Gondel *f*. ~**lier** /-'lɪə(r)/ *n* Gondoliere *m*
gone /gɒn/ *see* **go**
gong /gɒŋ/ *n* Gong *m*
good /gʊd/ *a* (**better, best**) gut; (*well-behaved*) brav, artig; ~ **at** gut in (+ *dat*); **a** ~ **deal** ziemlich viel; **as** ~ **as** so gut wie; (*almost*) fast; ~ **morning/evening** guten Morgen/Abend; ~ **afternoon** guten Tag; ~ **night** gute Nacht ● *n* **the** ~ das Gute; **for** ~ für immer; **do** ~ Gutes tun; **do s.o.** ~ jdm guttun; **it's no** ~ es ist nutzlos; (*hopeless*) da ist nichts zu machen; **be up to no** ~ nichts Gutes im Schilde führen
goodbye /gʊd'baɪ/ *int* auf Wiedersehen; (*Teleph, Radio*) auf Wiederhören
good: ~**-for-nothing** *a* nichtsnutzig ● *n* Taugenichts *m*. **G**~ **'Friday** *n* Karfreitag *m*. ~**-'looking** *a* gutaussehend. ~**-'natured** *a* gutmütig
goodness /'gʊdnɪs/ *n* Güte *f*; **my** ~! du meine Güte! **thank** ~! Gott sei Dank!
goods /gʊdz/ *npl* Waren *pl*. ~ **train** *n* Güterzug *m*
good'will *n* Wohlwollen *nt*; (*Comm*) Goodwill *m*
goody /'gʊdɪ/ *n* (*fam*) Gute(r) *m/f*. ~**-goody** *n* Musterkind *nt*
gooey /'gu:ɪ/ *a* (*fam*) klebrig
goof /gu:f/ *vi* (*fam*) einen Schnitzer machen
goose /gu:s/ *n* (*pl* **geese**) Gans *f*
gooseberry /'gʊzbərɪ/ *n* Stachelbeere *f*
goose /gu:s/: ~**-flesh** *n*, ~**pimples** *npl* Gänsehaut *f*
gore[1] /gɔ:(r)/ *n* Blut *nt*
gore[2] *vt* mit den Hörnern aufspießen
gorge /gɔ:dʒ/ *n* (*Geog*) Schlucht *f* ● *vt* ~ **oneself** sich vollessen
gorgeous /'gɔ:dʒəs/ *a* prachtvoll; (*fam*) herrlich
gorilla /gə'rɪlə/ *n* Gorilla *m*
gormless /'gɔ:mlɪs/ *a* (*fam*) doof
gorse /gɔ:s/ *n inv* Stechginster *m*
gory /'gɔ:rɪ/ *a* (**-ier, -iest**) blutig; ⟨*story*⟩ blutrünstig
gosh /gɒʃ/ *int* (*fam*) Mensch!
go-'slow *n* Bummelstreik *m*
gospel /'gɒspl/ *n* Evangelium *nt*
gossip /'gɒsɪp/ *n* Klatsch *m*; (*person*) Klatschbase *f* ● *vi* klatschen. ~**y** *a* geschwätzig
got /gɒt/ *see* **get**; **have** ~ haben; **have** ~ **to** müssen; **have** ~ **to do sth** etw tun müssen
Gothic /'gɒθɪk/ *a* gotisch
gotten /'gɒtn/ *see* **get**
gouge /gaʊdʒ/ *vt* ~ **out** aushöhlen
goulash /'gu:læʃ/ *n* Gulasch *nt*
gourmet /'gʊəmeɪ/ *n* Feinschmecker *m*
gout /gaʊt/ *n* Gicht *f*
govern /'gʌvn/ *vt/i* regieren; (*determine*) bestimmen. ~**ess** *n* Gouvernante *f*
government /'gʌvnmənt/ *n* Regierung *f*. ~**al** /-'mentl/ *a* Regierungs-
governor /'gʌvənə(r)/ *n* Gouverneur *m*; (*on board*) Vorstandsmitglied *nt*; (*of prison*) Direktor *m*; (*fam: boss*) Chef *m*
gown /gaʊn/ *n* [elegantes] Kleid *nt*; (*Univ, Jur*) Talar *m*
GP *abbr of* **general practitioner**
grab /græb/ *vt* (*pt/pp* **grabbed**) ergreifen; ~ **[hold of]** packen
grace /greɪs/ *n* Anmut *f*; (*before meal*) Tischgebet *nt*; (*Relig*) Gnade *f*; **with good** ~ mit Anstand; **say** ~ [vor dem Essen] beten; **three days'** ~ drei Tage Frist. ~**ful** *a*, **-ly** *adv* anmutig
gracious /'greɪʃəs/ *a* gnädig; (*elegant*) vornehm
grade /greɪd/ *n* Stufe *f*; (*Comm*) Güteklasse *f*; (*Sch*) Note *f*; (*Amer, Sch: class*) Klasse *f*; (*Amer*) = **gradient** ● *vt* einstufen; (*Comm*) sortieren. ~ **crossing** *n* (*Amer*) Bahnübergang *m*
gradient /'greɪdɪənt/ *n* Steigung *f*; (*downward*) Gefälle *nt*
gradual /'grædʒʊəl/ *a*, **-ly** *adv* allmählich

graduate¹ /ˈɡrædʒʊət/ *n* Akademiker(in) *m(f)*
graduate² /ˈɡrædʒʊeɪt/ *vi* (*Univ*) sein Examen machen. **~d** *a* abgestuft; ⟨*container*⟩ mit Maßeinteilung
graffiti /ɡrəˈfiːtiː/ *npl* Graffiti *pl*
graft /ɡrɑːft/ *n* (*Bot*) Pfropfreis *nt*; (*Med*) Transplantat *nt*; (*fam: hard work*) Plackerei *f* ● *vt* (*Bot*) aufpfropfen; (*Med*) übertragen
grain /ɡreɪn/ *n* (*sand, salt, rice*) Korn *nt*; (*cereals*) Getreide *nt*; (*in wood*) Maserung *f*; **against the ~** (*fig*) gegen den Strich
gram /ɡræm/ *n* Gramm *nt*
grammar /ˈɡræmə(r)/ *n* Grammatik *f*. **~ school** *n* ≈ Gymnasium *nt*
grammatical /ɡrəˈmætɪkl/ *a*, **-ly** *adv* grammatisch
granary /ˈɡrænərɪ/ *n* Getreidespeicher *m*
grand /ɡrænd/ *a* (**-er, -est**) großartig
grandad /ˈɡrændæd/ *n* (*fam*) Opa *m*
ˈgrandchild *n* Enkelkind *nt*
ˈgranddaughter *n* Enkelin *f*
grandeur /ˈɡrændʒə(r)/ *n* Pracht *f*
ˈgrandfather *n* Großvater *m*. **~ clock** *n* Standuhr *f*
grandiose /ˈɡrændɪəʊs/ *a* grandios
grand: ~mother *n* Großmutter *f*. **~parents** *npl* Großeltern *pl*. **~ plˈano** *n* Flügel *m*. **~son** *n* Enkel *m*. **~stand** *n* Tribüne *f*
granite /ˈɡrænɪt/ *n* Granit *m*
granny /ˈɡrænɪ/ *n* (*fam*) Oma *f*
grant /ɡrɑːnt/ *n* Subvention *f*; (*Univ*) Studienbeihilfe *f* ● *vt* gewähren; (*admit*) zugeben; **take sth for ~ed** etw als selbstverständlich hinnehmen
granular /ˈɡrænjʊlə(r)/ *a* körnig
granulated /ˈɡrænjʊleɪtɪd/ *a* **~ sugar** Kristallzucker *m*
granule /ˈɡrænjuːl/ *n* Körnchen *nt*
grape /ɡreɪp/ *n* [Wein]traube *f*; **bunch of ~s** [ganze] Weintraube *f*
grapefruit /ˈɡreɪp-/ *n inv* Grapefruit *f*, Pampelmuse *f*
graph /ɡrɑːf/ *n* Kurvendiagramm *nt*
graphic /ˈɡræfɪk/ *a*, **-ally** *adv* grafisch; (*vivid*) anschaulich. **~s** *n* (*design*) grafische Gestaltung *f*
ˈgraph paper *n* Millimeterpapier *nt*
grapple /ˈɡræpl/ *vi* ringen
grasp /ɡrɑːsp/ *n* Griff *m* ● *vt* ergreifen; (*understand*) begreifen. **~ing** *a* habgierig
grass /ɡrɑːs/ *n* Gras *nt*; (*lawn*) Rasen *m*; **at the ~ roots** an der Basis. **~hopper** *n* Heuschrecke *f*. **~land** *n* Weideland *nt*
grassy /ˈɡrɑːsɪ/ *a* grasig
grate¹ /ɡreɪt/ *n* Feuerrost *m*; (*hearth*) Kamin *m*
grate² *vt* (*Culin*) reiben; **~ one's teeth** mit den Zähnen knirschen
grateful /ˈɡreɪtfl/ *a*, **-ly** *adv* dankbar (**to** *dat*)
grater /ˈɡreɪtə(r)/ *n* (*Culin*) Reibe *f*
gratify /ˈɡrætɪfaɪ/ *vt* (*pt/pp* **-ied**) befriedigen. **~ing** *a* erfreulich
grating /ˈɡreɪtɪŋ/ *n* Gitter *nt*
gratis /ˈɡrɑːtɪs/ *adv* gratis
gratitude /ˈɡrætɪtjuːd/ *n* Dankbarkeit *f*
gratuitous /ɡrəˈtjuːɪtəs/ *a* (*uncalled for*) überflüssig
gratuity /ɡrəˈtjuːətɪ/ *n* (*tip*) Trinkgeld *nt*
grave¹ /ɡreɪv/ *a* (**-r, -st**), **-ly** *adv* ernst; **~ly ill** schwer krank
grave² *n* Grab *nt*. **~-digger** *n* Totengräber *m*
gravel /ˈɡrævl/ *n* Kies *m*
grave: ~stone *n* Grabstein *m*. **~yard** *n* Friedhof *m*
gravitate /ˈɡrævɪteɪt/ *vi* gravitieren
gravity /ˈɡrævətɪ/ *n* Ernst *m*; (*force*) Schwerkraft *f*
gravy /ˈɡreɪvɪ/ *n* [Braten]soße *f*
gray /ɡreɪ/ *a* (*Amer*) = **grey**
graze¹ /ɡreɪz/ *vi* ⟨*animal:*⟩ weiden
graze² *n* Schürfwunde *f* ● *vt* ⟨*car*⟩ streifen; ⟨*knee*⟩ aufschürfen
grease /ɡriːs/ *n* Fett *nt*; (*lubricant*) Schmierfett *nt* ● *vt* einfetten; (*lubricate*) schmieren. **~-proof ˈpaper** *n* Pergamentpapier *nt*
greasy /ˈɡriːsɪ/ *a* (**-ier, -iest**) fettig
great /ɡreɪt/ *a* (**-er, -est**) groß; (*fam: marvellous*) großartig
great: ~-ˈaunt *n* Großtante *f*. **G~ ˈBritain** *n* Großbritannien *nt*. **~-ˈgrandchildren** *npl* Urenkel *pl*. **~-ˈgrandfather** *n* Urgroßvater *m*. **~-ˈgrandmother** *n* Urgroßmutter *f*
great|ly /ˈɡreɪtlɪ/ *adv* sehr. **~ness** *n* Größe *f*
great-ˈuncle *n* Großonkel *m*
Greece /ɡriːs/ *n* Griechenland *nt*
greed /ɡriːd/ *n* [Hab]gier *f*
greedy /ˈɡriːdɪ/ *a* (**-ier, -iest**), **-ily** *adv* gierig; **don't be ~** sei nicht so unbescheiden
Greek /ɡriːk/ *a* griechisch ● *n* Grieche *m*/Griechin *f*; (*Lang*) Griechisch *nt*

green /gri:n/ *a* (**-er, -est**) grün; (*fig*) unerfahren • *n* Grün *nt*; (*grass*) Wiese *f*; **~s** *pl* Kohl *m*; **the G~s** *pl* (*Pol*) die Grünen *pl*
greenery /ˈgri:nərɪ/ *n* Grün *nt*
ˈgreenfly *n* Blattlaus *f*
greengage /ˈgri:ngeɪdʒ/ *n* Reneklode *f*
green: ~grocer *n* Obst- und Gemüsehändler *m*. **~house** *n* Gewächshaus *nt*. **~house effect** *n* Treibhauseffekt *m*
Greenland /ˈgri:nlənd/ *n* Grönland *nt*
greet /gri:t/ *vt* grüßen; (*welcome*) begrüßen. **~ing** *n* Gruß *m*; (*welcome*) Begrüßung *f*. **~ings card** *n* Glückwunschkarte *f*
gregarious /grɪˈgeərɪəs/ *a* gesellig
grenade /grɪˈneɪd/ *n* Granate *f*
grew /gru:/ *see* **grow**
grey /greɪ/ *a* (**-er, -est**) grau • *n* Grau *nt* • *vi* grau werden. **~hound** *n* Windhund *m*
grid /grɪd/ *n* Gitter *nt*; (*on map*) Gitternetz *nt*; (*Electr*) Überlandleitungsnetz *nt*
grief /gri:f/ *n* Trauer *f*; **come to ~** scheitern
grievance /ˈgri:vəns/ *n* Beschwerde *f*
grieve /gri:v/ *vt* betrüben • *vi* trauern (**for** um)
grievous /ˈgri:vəs/ *a*, **-ly** *adv* schwer
grill /grɪl/ *n* Gitter *nt*; (*Culin*) Grill *m*; **mixed ~** Gemischtes *nt* vom Grill • *vt/i* grillen; (*interrogate*) [streng] verhören
grille /grɪl/ *n* Gitter *nt*
grim /grɪm/ *a* (**grimmer, grimmest**), **-ly** *adv* ernst; ⟨*determination*⟩ verbissen
grimace /grɪˈmeɪs/ *n* Grimasse *f* • *vi* Grimassen schneiden
grime /graɪm/ *n* Schmutz *m*
grimy /ˈgraɪmɪ/ *a* (**-ier, -iest**) schmutzig
grin /grɪn/ *n* Grinsen *nt* • *vi* (*pt/pp* **grinned**) grinsen
grind /graɪnd/ *n* (*fam: hard work*) Plackerei *f* • *vt* (*pt/pp* **ground**) mahlen; (*smooth, sharpen*) schleifen; (*Amer: mince*) durchdrehen; **~ one's teeth** mit den Zähnen knirschen
grip /grɪp/ *n* Griff *m*; (*bag*) Reisetasche *f* • *vt* (*pt/pp* **gripped**) ergreifen; (*hold*) festhalten; fesseln ⟨*interest*⟩
gripe /graɪp/ *vi* (*sl: grumble*) meckern
gripping /ˈgrɪpɪŋ/ *a* fesselnd
grisly /ˈgrɪzlɪ/ *a* (**-ier, -iest**) grausig
gristle /ˈgrɪsl/ *n* Knorpel *m*
grit /grɪt/ *n* [grober] Sand *m*; (*for roads*) Streugut *nt*; (*courage*) Mut *m* • *vt* (*pt/pp* **gritted**) streuen ⟨*road*⟩; **~ one's teeth** die Zähne zusammenbeißen
grizzle /ˈgrɪzl/ *vi* quengeln
groan /grəʊn/ *n* Stöhnen *nt* • *vi* stöhnen
grocer /ˈgrəʊsə(r)/ *n* Lebensmittelhändler *m*; **~'s [shop]** Lebensmittelgeschäft *nt*. **~ies** *npl* Lebensmittel *pl*
groggy /ˈgrɒgɪ/ *a* schwach; (*unsteady*) wackelig [auf den Beinen]
groin /grɔɪn/ *n* (*Anat*) Leiste *f*
groom /gru:m/ *n* Bräutigam *m*; (*for horse*) Pferdepfleger(in) *m(f)* • *vt* striegeln ⟨*horse*⟩
groove /gru:v/ *n* Rille *f*
grope /grəʊp/ *vi* tasten (**for** nach)
gross /grəʊs/ *a* (**-er, -est**) fett; (*coarse*) derb; (*glaring*) grob; (*Comm*) brutto; ⟨*salary, weight*⟩ Brutto- • *n inv* Gros *nt*. **~ly** *adv* (*very*) sehr
grotesque /grəʊˈtesk/ *a*, **-ly** *adv* grotesk
grotto /ˈgrɒtəʊ/ *n* (*pl* **-es**) Grotte *f*
grotty /ˈgrɒtɪ/ *a* (*fam*) mies
ground[1] /graʊnd/ *see* **grind**
ground[2] *n* Boden *m*; (*terrain*) Gelände *nt*; (*reason*) Grund *m*; (*Amer, Electr*) Erde *f*; **~s** *pl* (*park*) Anlagen *pl*; (*of coffee*) Satz *m* • *vi* ⟨*ship:*⟩ auflaufen • *vt* aus dem Verkehr ziehen ⟨*aircraft*⟩; (*Amer, Electr*) erden
ground: ~ floor *n* Erdgeschoß *nt*. **~ing** *n* Grundlage *f*. **~less** *a* grundlos. **~ ˈmeat** *n* Hackfleisch *nt*. **~sheet** *n* Bodenplane *f*. **~work** *n* Vorarbeiten *pl*
group /gru:p/ *n* Gruppe *f* • *vt* gruppieren • *vi* sich gruppieren
grouse[1] /graʊs/ *n inv* schottisches Moorschneehuhn *nt*
grouse[2] *vi* (*fam*) meckern
grovel /ˈgrɒvl/ *vi* (*pt/pp* **grovelled**) kriechen. **~ling** *a* kriecherisch
grow /grəʊ/ *v* (*pt* **grew**, *pp* **grown**) • *vi* wachsen; (*become*) werden; (*increase*) zunehmen • *vt* anbauen; **~ one's hair** sich (*dat*) die Haare wachsen lassen. **~ up** *vi* aufwachsen; ⟨*town:*⟩ entstehen

growl /graʊl/ *n* Knurren *nt* ● *vi* knurren
grown /grəʊn/ *see* **grow**. **~-up** *a* erwachsen ● *n* Erwachsene(r) *m*/*f*
growth /grəʊθ/ *n* Wachstum *nt*; (*increase*) Zunahme *f*; (*Med*) Gewächs *nt*
grub /grʌb/ *n* (*larva*) Made *f*; (*fam: food*) Essen *nt*
grubby /'grʌbɪ/ *a* (**-ier, -iest**) schmuddelig
grudg|e /grʌdʒ/ *n* Groll *m*; **bear s.o. a ~e** einen Groll gegen jdn hegen ● *vt* **~e s.o. sth** jdm etw mißgönnen. **~ing** *a*, **-ly** *adv* widerwillig
gruelling /'gru:əlɪŋ/ *a* strapaziös
gruesome /'gru:səm/ *a* grausig
gruff /grʌf/ *a*, **-ly** *adv* barsch
grumble /'grʌmbl/ *vi* schimpfen (**at** mit)
grumpy /'grʌmpɪ/ *a* (**-ier, -iest**) griesgrämig
grunt /grʌnt/ *n* Grunzen *nt* ● *vi* grunzen
guarant|ee /gærən'ti:/ *n* Garantie *f*; (*document*) Garantieschein *m* ● *vt* garantieren; garantieren für ⟨*quality, success*⟩; **be ~eed** ⟨*product:*⟩ Garantie haben. **~or** *n* Bürge *m*
guard /gɑ:d/ *n* Wache *f*; (*security*) Wächter *m*; (*on train*) ≈ Zugführer *m*; (*Techn*) Schutz *m*; **be on ~** Wache stehen; **on one's ~** auf der Hut ● *vt* bewachen; (*protect*) schützen ● *vi* **~ against** sich hüten vor (+ *dat*). **~-dog** *n* Wachhund *m*
guarded /'gɑ:dɪd/ *a* vorsichtig
guardian /'gɑ:dɪən/ *n* Vormund *m*
guerrilla /gə'rɪlə/ *n* Guerillakämpfer *m*. **~ warfare** *n* Partisanenkrieg *m*
guess /ges/ *n* Vermutung *f* ● *vt* erraten ● *vi* raten; (*Amer: believe*) glauben. **~work** *n* Vermutung *f*
guest /gest/ *n* Gast *m*. **~-house** *n* Pension *f*
guffaw /gʌ'fɔ:/ *n* derbes Lachen *nt* ● *vi* derb lachen
guidance /'gaɪdəns/ *n* Führung *f*, Leitung *f*; (*advice*) Beratung *f*
guide /gaɪd/ *n* Führer(in) *m*(*f*); (*book*) Führer *m*; **[Girl] G~** Pfadfinderin *f* ● *vt* führen, leiten. **~book** *n* Führer *m*
guided /'gaɪdɪd/ *a* **~ missile** Fernlenkgeschoß *nt*; **~ tour** Führung *f*
guide: ~-dog *n* Blindenhund *m*. **~lines** *npl* Richtlinien *pl*
guild /gɪld/ *n* Gilde *f*, Zunft *f*
guile /gaɪl/ *n* Arglist *f*
guillotine /'gɪləti:n/ *n* Guillotine *f*; (*for paper*) Papierschneidemaschine *f*
guilt /gɪlt/ *n* Schuld *f*. **~ily** *adv* schuldbewußt
guilty /'gɪltɪ/ *a* (**-ier, -iest**) *a* schuldig (**of** *gen*); ⟨*look*⟩ schuldbewußt; ⟨*conscience*⟩ schlecht
guinea-pig /'gɪnɪ-/ *n* Meerschweinchen *nt*; (*person*) Versuchskaninchen *nt*
guise /gaɪz/ *n* **in the ~ of** in Gestalt (+ *gen*)
guitar /gɪ'tɑ:(r)/ *n* Gitarre *f*. **~ist** *n* Gitarrist(in) *m*(*f*)
gulf /gʌlf/ *n* (*Geog*) Golf *m*; (*fig*) Kluft *f*
gull /gʌl/ *n* Möwe *f*
gullet /'gʌlɪt/ *n* Speiseröhre *f*; (*throat*) Kehle *f*
gullible /'gʌlɪbl/ *a* leichtgläubig
gully /'gʌlɪ/ *n* Schlucht *f*; (*drain*) Rinne *f*
gulp /gʌlp/ *n* Schluck *m* ● *vi* schlucken ● *vt* **~ down** hinunterschlucken
gum[1] /gʌm/ *n* & **-s** *pl* (*Anat*) Zahnfleisch *nt*
gum[2] *n* Gummi[harz] *nt*; (*glue*) Klebstoff *m*; (*chewing-gum*) Kaugummi *m* ● *vt* (*pt*/*pp* **gummed**) kleben (**to** an + *acc*). **~boot** *n* Gummistiefel *m*
gummed /gʌmd/ *see* **gum**[2] ● *a* ⟨*label*⟩ gummiert
gumption /'gʌmpʃn/ *n* (*fam*) Grips *m*
gun /gʌn/ *n* Schußwaffe *f*; (*pistol*) Pistole *f*; (*rifle*) Gewehr *nt*; (*cannon*) Geschütz *nt* ● *vt* (*pt*/*pp* **gunned**) **~ down** niederschießen
gun: ~fire *n* Geschützfeuer *nt*. **~man** bewaffneter Bandit *m*
gunner /'gʌnə(r)/ *n* Artillerist *m*
gun: ~powder *n* Schießpulver *nt*. **~shot** *n* Schuß *m*
gurgle /'gɜ:gl/ *vi* gluckern; (*of baby*) glucksen
gush /gʌʃ/ *vi* strömen; (*enthuse*) schwärmen (**over** von). **~ out** *vi* herausströmen
gusset /'gʌsɪt/ *n* Zwickel *m*
gust /gʌst/ *n* (*of wind*) Windstoß *m*; (*Naut*) Bö *f*
gusto /'gʌstəʊ/ *n* **with ~** mit Schwung
gusty /'gʌstɪ/ *a* böig
gut /gʌt/ *n* Darm *m*; **~s** *pl* Eingeweide *pl*; (*fam: courage*) Schneid *m* ● *vt* (*pt*/*pp* **gutted**) (*Culin*) ausnehmen; **~ted by fire** ausgebrannt

gutter /'gʌtə(r)/ *n* Rinnstein *m*; (*fig*) Gosse *f*; (*on roof*) Dachrinne *f*
guttural /'gʌtərl/ *a* guttural
guy /gaɪ/ *n* (*fam*) Kerl *m*
guzzle /'gʌzl/ *vt/i* schlingen; (*drink*) schlürfen
gym /dʒɪm/ *n* (*fam*) Turnhalle *f*; (*gymnastics*) Turnen *nt*
gymnasium /dʒɪm'neɪzɪəm/ *n* Turnhalle *f*
gymnast /'dʒɪmnæst/ *n* Turner(in) *m*(*f*). **~ics** /-'næstɪks/ *n* Turnen *nt*
gym: ~ shoes *pl* Turnschuhe *pl*. **~-slip** *n* (*Sch*) Trägerkleid *nt*
gynaecolog|ist /gaɪnɪ'kɒlədʒɪst/ *n* Frauenarzt *m*/-ärztin *f*. **~y** *n* Gynäkologie *f*
gypsy /'dʒɪpsɪ/ *n* Zigeuner(in) *m*(*f*)
gyrate /dʒaɪə'reɪt/ *vi* sich drehen

H

haberdashery /'hæbədæʃərɪ/ *n* Kurzwaren *pl*; (*Amer*) Herrenmoden *pl*
habit /'hæbɪt/ *n* Gewohnheit *f*; (*Relig: costume*) Ordenstracht *f*; **be in the ~** die Angewohnheit haben (**of** zu)
habitable /'hæbɪtəbl/ *a* bewohnbar
habitat /'hæbɪtæt/ *n* Habitat *nt*
habitation /hæbɪ'teɪʃn/ *n* **unfit for human ~** für Wohnzwecke ungeeignet
habitual /hə'bɪtjʊəl/ *a* gewohnt; (*inveterate*) gewohnheitsmäßig. **~ly** *adv* gewohnheitsmäßig; (*constantly*) ständig
hack¹ /hæk/ *n* (*writer*) Schreiberling *m*; (*hired horse*) Mietpferd *nt*
hack² *vt* hacken; **~ to pieces** zerhacken
hackneyed /'hæknɪd/ *a* abgedroschen
'hacksaw *n* Metallsäge *f*
had /hæd/ *see* **have**
haddock /'hædək/ *n inv* Schellfisch *m*
haemorrhage /'hemərɪdʒ/ *n* Blutung *f*
haemorrhoids /'hemərɔɪdz/ *npl* Hämorrhoiden *pl*
hag /hæg/ *n* **old ~** alte Hexe *f*
haggard /'hægəd/ *a* abgehärmt
haggle /'hægl/ *vi* feilschen (**over** um)
hail¹ /heɪl/ *vt* begrüßen; herbeirufen ⟨*taxi*⟩ ● *vi* **~ from** kommen aus
hail² *n* Hagel *m* ● *vi* hageln. **~stone** *n* Hagelkorn *nt*
hair /heə(r)/ *n* Haar *nt*; **wash one's ~** sich (*dat*) die Haare waschen
hair: ~brush *n* Haarbürste *f*. **~cut** *n* Haarschnitt *m*; **have a ~cut** sich (*dat*) die Haare schneiden lassen. **~-do** *n* (*fam*) Frisur *f*. **~dresser** *n* Friseur *m*/Friseuse *f*. **~-drier** *n* Haartrockner *m*; (*hand-held*) Fön (P) *m*. **~-grip** *n* [Haar]klemme *f*. **~pin** *n* Haarnadel *f*. **~pin 'bend** *n* Haarnadelkurve *f*. **~-raising** *a* haarsträubend. **~-style** *n* Frisur *f*
hairy /'heərɪ/ *a* (**-ier, -iest**) behaart; (*excessively*) haarig; (*fam: frightening*) brenzlig
hake /heɪk/ *n inv* Seehecht *m*
hale /heɪl/ *a* **~ and hearty** gesund und munter
half /hɑ:f/ *n* (*pl* **halves**) Hälfte *f*; **cut in ~** halbieren; **one and a ~** eineinhalb, anderthalb; **~ a dozen** ein halbes Dutzend; **~ an hour** eine halbe Stunde ● *a & adv* halb; **~ past two** halb drei; **[at] ~ price** zum halben Preis
half: ~-board *n* Halbpension *f*. **~-caste** *n* Mischling *m*. **~-'hearted** *a* lustlos. **~-'hourly** *a & adv* halbstündlich. **~-'mast** *n* **at ~-mast** auf halbmast. **~-measure** *n* Halbheit *f*. **~-'term** *n* schulfreie Tage nach dem halben Trimester. **~-'timbered** *a* Fachwerk-. **~-'time** *n* (*Sport*) Halbzeit *f*. **~-'way** *a* **the ~-way mark/stage** die Hälfte ● *adv* auf halbem Weg; **get ~-way** den halben Weg zurücklegen; (*fig*) bis zur Hälfte kommen. **~-wit** *n* Idiot *m*
halibut /'hælɪbət/ *n inv* Heilbutt *m*
hall /hɔ:l/ *n* Halle *f*; (*room*) Saal *m*; (*Sch*) Aula *f*; (*entrance*) Flur *m*; (*mansion*) Gutshaus *nt*; **~ of residence** (*Univ*) Studentenheim *nt*
'hallmark *n* [Feingehalts]stempel *m*; (*fig*) Kennzeichen *nt* (**of** für) ● *vt* stempeln
hallo /hə'ləʊ/ *int* [guten] Tag! (*fam*) hallo!
Hallowe'en /hæləʊ'i:n/ *n* der Tag vor Allerheiligen
hallucination /həlu:sɪ'neɪʃn/ *n* Halluzination *f*
halo /'heɪləʊ/ *n* (*pl* **-es**) Heiligenschein *m*; (*Astr*) Hof *m*
halt /hɔ:lt/ *n* Halt *m*; **come to a ~** stehenbleiben; ⟨*traffic:*⟩ zum Stillstand kommen ● *vi* haltmachen; **~!** halt! **~ing** *a*, *adv* **-ly** zögernd

halve /hɑ:v/ *vt* halbieren; (*reduce*) um die Hälfte reduzieren
ham /hæm/ *n* Schinken *m*
hamburger /ˈhæmbɜ:gə(r)/ *n* Hamburger *m*
hamlet /ˈhæmlɪt/ *n* Weiler *m*
hammer /ˈhæmə(r)/ *n* Hammer *m* ● *vt/i* hämmern (**at** an + *acc*)
hammock /ˈhæmək/ *n* Hängematte *f*
hamper[1] /ˈhæmpə(r)/ *n* Picknickkorb *m*; **[gift]** ~ Geschenkkorb *m*
hamper[2] *vt* behindern
hamster /ˈhæmstə(r)/ *n* Hamster *m*
hand /hænd/ *n* Hand *f*; (*of clock*) Zeiger *m*; (*writing*) Handschrift *f*; (*worker*) Arbeiter(in) *m*(*f*); (*Cards*) Blatt *nt*; **all ~s** (*Naut*) alle Mann; **at ~** in der Nähe; **on the one/other ~** einer-/ andererseits; **out of ~** außer Kontrolle; (*summarily*) kurzerhand; **in ~** unter Kontrolle; (*available*) verfügbar; **give s.o. a ~** jdm behilflich sein ● *vt* reichen (**to** *dat*). **~ in** *vt* abgeben. **~ out** *vt* austeilen. **~ over** *vt* überreichen
hand: ~bag *n* Handtasche *f*. **~book** *n* Handbuch *nt*. **~brake** *n* Handbremse *f*. **~cuffs** *npl* Handschellen *pl*. **~ful** *n* Handvoll *f*; **be [quite] a ~ful** (*fam*) nicht leicht zu haben sein
handicap /ˈhændɪkæp/ *n* Behinderung *f*; (*Sport & fig*) Handikap *nt*. **~ped** *a* **mentally/physically ~ped** geistig/körperlich behindert
handi|craft /ˈhændɪkrɑ:ft/ *n* Basteln *nt*; (*Sch*) Werken *nt*. **~work** *n* Werk *nt*
handkerchief /ˈhæŋkətʃɪf/ *n* (*pl* **~s** & **-chieves**) Taschentuch *nt*
handle /ˈhændl/ *n* Griff *m*; (*of door*) Klinke *f*; (*of cup*) Henkel *m*; (*of broom*) Stiel *m*; **fly off the ~** (*fam*) aus der Haut fahren ● *vt* handhaben; (*treat*) umgehen mit; (*touch*) anfassen. **~bars** *npl* Lenkstange *f*
hand: ~-luggage *n* Handgepäck *nt*. **~made** *a* handgemacht. **~-out** *n* Prospekt *m*; (*money*) Unterstützung *f*. **~rail** *n* Handlauf *m*. **~shake** *n* Händedruck *m*
handsome /ˈhænsəm/ *a* gutaussehend; (*generous*) großzügig; (*large*) beträchtlich
hand: ~stand *n* Handstand *m*. **~writing** *n* Handschrift *f*. **~-ˈwritten** *a* handgeschrieben
handy /ˈhændɪ/ *a* (**-ier, -iest**) handlich; ⟨*person*⟩ geschickt; **have/keep ~** griffbereit haben/halten. **~man** *n* **[home] ~man** Heimwerker *m*
hang /hæŋ/ *vt/i* (*pt/pp* **hung**) hängen; **~ wallpaper** tapezieren ● *vt* (*pt/pp* **hanged**) hängen ⟨*criminal*⟩; **~ oneself** sich erhängen ● *n* **get the ~ of it** (*fam*) den Dreh herauskriegen. **~ about** *vi* sich herumdrücken. **~ on** *vi* sich festhalten (**to** an + *dat*); (*fam: wait*) warten. **~ out** *vi* heraushängen; (*fam: live*) wohnen ● *vt* draußen aufhängen ⟨*washing*⟩. **~ up** *vt/i* aufhängen
hangar /ˈhæŋə(r)/ *n* Flugzeughalle *f*
hanger /ˈhæŋə(r)/ *n* [Kleider]bügel *m*
hang: ~-glider *n* Drachenflieger *m*. **~-gliding** *n* Drachenfliegen *nt*. **~man** *n* Henker *m*. **~over** *n* (*fam*) Kater *m* (*fam*). **~-up** *n* (*fam*) Komplex *m*
hanker /ˈhæŋkə(r)/ *vi* **~ after sth** sich (*dat*) etw wünschen
hanky /ˈhæŋkɪ/ *n* (*fam*) Taschentuch *nt*
hanky-panky /hæŋkɪˈpæŋkɪ/ *n* (*fam*) Mauscheleien *pl*
haphazard /hæpˈhæzəd/ *a*, **-ly** *adv* planlos
happen /ˈhæpn/ *vi* geschehen, passieren; **as it ~s** zufälligerweise; **I ~ed to be there** ich war zufällig da; **what has ~ed to him?** was ist mit ihm los? (*become of*) was ist aus ihm geworden? **~ing** *n* Ereignis *nt*
happi|ly /ˈhæpɪlɪ/ *adv* glücklich; (*fortunately*) glücklicherweise. **~ness** *n* Glück *nt*
happy /ˈhæpɪ/ *a* (**-ier, -iest**) glücklich. **~-go-ˈlucky** *a* sorglos
harass /ˈhærəs/ *vt* schikanieren. **~ed** *a* abgehetzt. **~ment** *n* Schikane *f*; (*sexual*) Belästigung *f*
harbour /ˈhɑ:bə(r)/ *n* Hafen *m* ● *vt* Unterschlupf gewähren (+ *dat*); hegen ⟨*grudge*⟩
hard /hɑ:d/ *a* (**-er, -est**) hart; (*difficult*) schwer; **~ of hearing** schwerhörig ● *adv* hart; ⟨*work*⟩ schwer; ⟨*pull*⟩ kräftig; ⟨*rain, snow*⟩ stark; **think ~!** denk mal nach! **be ~ up** (*fam*) knapp bei Kasse sein; **be ~ done by** (*fam*) ungerecht behandelt werden
hard: ~back *n* gebundene Ausgabe *f*. **~board** *n* Hartfaserplatte *f*. **~-boiled** *a* hartgekocht
harden /ˈhɑ:dn/ *vi* hart werden
hard-ˈhearted *a* hartherzig

hard|ly /ˈhɑ:dlɪ/ *adv* kaum; **~ly ever** kaum [jemals]. **~ness** *n* Härte *f*. **~ship** *n* Not *f*

hard: **~ ˈshoulder** *n* (*Auto*) Randstreifen *m*. **~ware** *n* Haushaltswaren *pl*; (*Computing*) Hardware *f*. **~-ˈwearing** *a* strapazierfähig. **~-ˈworking** *a* fleißig

hardy /ˈhɑ:dɪ/ *a* (**-ier, -iest**) abgehärtet; ⟨*plant*⟩ winterhart

hare /heə(r)/ *n* Hase *m*. **~ˈlip** *n* Hasenscharte *f*

hark /hɑ:k/ *vi* **~!** hört! **~ back** *vi* **~ back to** (*fig*) zurückkommen auf (+ *acc*)

harm /hɑ:m/ *n* Schaden *m*; **out of ~'s way** in Sicherheit; **it won't do any ~** es kann nichts schaden ● *vt* **~ s.o.** jdm etwas antun. **~ful** *a* schädlich. **~less** *a* harmlos

harmonica /hɑ:ˈmɒnɪkə/ *n* Mundharmonika *f*

harmonious /hɑ:ˈməʊnɪəs/ *a*, **-ly** *adv* harmonisch

harmon|ize /ˈhɑ:mənaɪz/ *vi* (*fig*) harmonieren. **~y** *n* Harmonie *f*

harness /ˈhɑ:nɪs/ *n* Geschirr *nt*; (*of parachute*) Gurtwerk *nt* ● *vt* anschirren ⟨*horse*⟩; (*use*) nutzbar machen

harp /hɑ:p/ *n* Harfe *f* ● *vi* **~ on [about]** (*fam*) herumreiten auf (+ *dat*). **~ist** *n* Harfenist(in) *m*(*f*)

harpoon /hɑ:ˈpu:n/ *n* Harpune *f*

harpsichord /ˈhɑ:psɪkɔ:d/ *n* Cembalo *nt*

harrow /ˈhærəʊ/ *n* Egge *f*. **~ing** *a* grauenhaft

harsh /hɑ:ʃ/ *a* (**-er, -est**), **-ly** *adv* hart; ⟨*voice*⟩ rauh; ⟨*light*⟩ grell. **~ness** *n* Härte *f*; Rauheit *f*

harvest /ˈhɑ:vɪst/ *n* Ernte *f* ● *vt* ernten

has /hæz/ *see* **have**

hash /hæʃ/ *n* (*Culin*) Haschee *nt*; **make a ~ of** (*fam*) verpfuschen

hashish /ˈhæʃɪʃ/ *n* Haschisch *nt*

hassle /ˈhæsl/ *n* (*fam*) Ärger *m* ● *vt* schikanieren

hassock /ˈhæsək/ *n* Kniekissen *nt*

haste /heɪst/ *n* Eile *f*; **make ~** sich beeilen

hasten /ˈheɪsn/ *vi* sich beeilen (**to** zu); (*go quickly*) eilen ● *vt* beschleunigen

hasty /ˈheɪstɪ/ *a* (**-ier, -iest**), **-ily** *adv* hastig; ⟨*decision*⟩ voreilig

hat /hæt/ *n* Hut *m*; (*knitted*) Mütze *f*

hatch¹ /hætʃ/ *n* (*for food*) Durchreiche *f*; (*Naut*) Luke *f*

hatch² *vi* **~ [out]** ausschlüpfen ● *vt* ausbrüten

ˈhatchback *n* (*Auto*) Modell *nt* mit Hecktür

hatchet /ˈhætʃɪt/ *n* Beil *nt*

hate /heɪt/ *n* Haß *m* ● *vt* hassen. **~ful** *a* abscheulich

hatred /ˈheɪtrɪd/ *n* Haß *m*

haughty /ˈhɔ:tɪ/ *a* (**-ier, -iest**), **-ily** *adv* hochmütig

haul /hɔ:l/ *n* (*fish*) Fang *m*; (*loot*) Beute *f* ● *vt*/*i* ziehen (**on** an + *dat*). **~age** /-ɪdʒ/ *n* Transport *m*. **~ier** /-ɪə(r)/ *n* Spediteur *m*

haunt /hɔ:nt/ *n* Lieblingsaufenthalt *m* ● *vt* umgehen in (+ *dat*); **this house is ~ed** in diesem Haus spukt es

have /hæv/ *vt* (*3 sg pres tense* **has**; *pt*/*pp* **had**) haben; bekommen ⟨*baby*⟩; holen ⟨*doctor*⟩; **~ a meal/drink** etwas essen/trinken; **~ lunch** zu Mittag essen; **~ a walk** spazierengehen; **~ a dream** träumen; **~ a rest** sich ausruhen; **~ a swim** schwimmen; **~ sth done** etw machen lassen; **~ sth made** sich (*dat*) etw machen lassen; **~ to do sth** etw tun müssen; **~ it out with** zur Rede stellen; **so I ~!** tatsächlich! **he has [got] two houses** er hat zwei Häuser; **you have got the money, haven't you?** du hast das Geld, nicht [wahr]? ● *v aux* haben; (*with verbs of motion & some others*) sein; **I ~ seen him** ich habe ihn gesehen; **he has never been there** er ist nie da gewesen. **~ on** *vt* (*be wearing*) anhaben; (*dupe*) anführen

haven /ˈheɪvn/ *n* (*fig*) Zuflucht *f*

haversack /ˈhævə-/ *n* Rucksack *m*

havoc /ˈhævək/ *n* Verwüstung *f*; **play ~ with** (*fig*) völlig durcheinanderbringen

haw /hɔ:/ *see* **hum**

hawk¹ /hɔ:k/ *n* Falke *m*

hawk² *vt* hausieren mit. **~er** *n* Hausierer *m*

hawthorn /ˈhɔ:-/ *n* Hagedorn *m*

hay /heɪ/ *n* Heu *nt*. **~ fever** *n* Heuschnupfen *m*. **~stack** *n* Heuschober *m*

ˈhaywire *a* (*fam*) **go ~** verrückt spielen; ⟨*plans*:⟩ über den Haufen geworfen werden

hazard /ˈhæzəd/ *n* Gefahr *f*; (*risk*) Risiko *nt* ● *vt* riskieren. **~ous** /-əs/ *a* gefährlich; (*risky*) riskant. **~**

[warning] lights *npl* (*Auto*) Warnblinkanlage *f*
haze /heɪz/ *n* Dunst *m*
hazel /ˈheɪzl/ *n* Haselbusch *m*. **~-nut** *n* Haselnuß *f*
hazy /ˈheɪzɪ/ *a* (**-ier, -iest**) dunstig; (*fig*) unklar
he /hi:/ *pron* er
head /hed/ *n* Kopf *m*; (*chief*) Oberhaupt *nt*; (*of firm*) Chef(in) *m*(*f*); (*of school*) Schulleiter(in) *m*(*f*); (*on beer*) Schaumkrone *f*; (*of bed*) Kopfende *nt*; **20 ~ of cattle** 20 Stück Vieh; **~ first** kopfüber ● *vt* anführen; (*Sport*) köpfen ⟨*ball*⟩ ● *vi* **~ for** zusteuern auf (+ *acc*). **~ache** *n* Kopfschmerzen *pl*. **~-dress** *n* Kopfschmuck *m*
head|er /ˈhedə(r)/ *n* Kopfball *m*; (*dive*) Kopfsprung *m*. **~ing** *n* Überschrift *f*
head: ~lamp *n* (*Auto*) Scheinwerfer *m*. **~land** *n* Landspitze *f*. **~light** *n* (*Auto*) Scheinwerfer *m*. **~line** *n* Schlagzeile *f*. **~long** *adv* kopfüber. **~'master** *n* Schulleiter *m*. **~'mistress** *n* Schulleiterin *f*. **~-on** *a* & *adv* frontal. **~phones** *npl* Kopfhörer *m*. **~quarters** *npl* Hauptquartier *nt*; (*Pol*) Zentrale *f*. **~-rest** *n* Kopfstütze *f*. **~room** *n* lichte Höhe *f*. **~scarf** *n* Kopftuch *nt*. **~strong** *a* eigenwillig. **~ 'waiter** *n* Oberkellner *m*. **~way** *n* **make ~way** Fortschritte machen. **~ wind** *n* Gegenwind *m*. **~word** *n* Stichwort *nt*
heady /ˈhedɪ/ *a* berauschend
heal /hi:l/ *vt*/*i* heilen
health /helθ/ *n* Gesundheit *f*
health: ~ farm *n* Schönheitsfarm *f*. **~ foods** *npl* Reformkost *f*. **~-food shop** *n* Reformhaus *nt*. **~ insurance** *n* Krankenversicherung *f*
healthy /ˈhelθɪ/ *a* (**-ier, -iest**), **-ily** *adv* gesund
heap /hi:p/ *n* Haufen *m*; **~s** (*fam*) jede Menge ● *vt* **~ [up]** häufen; **~ed teaspoon** gehäufter Teelöffel
hear /hɪə(r)/ *vt*/*i* (*pt*/*pp* **heard**) hören; **~, ~!** hört, hört! **he would not ~ of it** er ließ es nicht zu
hearing /ˈhɪərɪŋ/ *n* Gehör *nt*; (*Jur*) Verhandlung *f*. **~-aid** *n* Hörgerät *nt*
'hearsay *n* **from ~** vom Hörensagen
hearse /hɜ:s/ *n* Leichenwagen *m*
heart /hɑ:t/ *n* Herz *nt*; (*courage*) Mut *m*; **~s** *pl* (*Cards*) Herz *nt*; **by ~** auswendig
heart: ~ache *n* Kummer *m*. **~ attack** *n* Herzanfall *m*. **~beat** *n* Herzschlag *m*. **~-break** *n* Leid *nt*. **~-breaking** *a* herzzerreißend. **~-broken** *a* untröstlich. **~burn** *n* Sodbrennen *nt*. **~en** *vt* ermutigen. **~felt** *a* herzlich[st]
hearth /hɑ:θ/ *n* Herd *m*; (*fireplace*) Kamin *m*. **~rug** *n* Kaminvorleger *m*
heart|ily /ˈhɑ:tɪlɪ/ *adv* herzlich; ⟨*eat*⟩ viel. **~less** *a*, **-ly** *adv* herzlos. **~y** *a* herzlich; ⟨*meal*⟩ groß; ⟨*person*⟩ burschikos
heat /hi:t/ *n* Hitze *f*; (*Sport*) Vorlauf *m* ● *vt* heiß machen; heizen ⟨*room*⟩. **~ed** *a* geheizt; ⟨*swimming pool*⟩ beheizt; ⟨*discussion*⟩ hitzig. **~er** *n* Heizgerät *nt*; (*Auto*) Heizanlage *f*
heath /hi:θ/ *n* Heide *f*
heathen /ˈhi:ðn/ *a* heidnisch ● *n* Heide *m*/Heidin *f*
heather /ˈheðə(r)/ *n* Heidekraut *nt*
heating /ˈhi:tɪŋ/ *n* Heizung *f*
heat: ~-stroke *n* Hitzschlag *m*. **~wave** *n* Hitzewelle *f*
heave /hi:v/ *vt*/*i* ziehen; (*lift*) heben; (*fam: throw*) schmeißen; **~ a sigh** einen Seufzer ausstoßen
heaven /ˈhevn/ *n* Himmel *m*. **~ly** *a* himmlisch
heavy /ˈhevɪ/ *a* (**-ier, -iest**), **-ily** *adv* schwer; ⟨*traffic, rain*⟩ stark; ⟨*sleep*⟩ tief. **~weight** *n* Schwergewicht *nt*
Hebrew /ˈhi:bru:/ *a* hebräisch
heckle /ˈhekl/ *vt* [durch Zwischenrufe] unterbrechen. **~r** *n* Zwischenrufer *m*
hectic /ˈhektɪk/ *a* hektisch
hedge /hedʒ/ *n* Hecke *f* ● *vi* (*fig*) ausweichen. **~hog** *n* Igel *m*
heed /hi:d/ *n* **pay ~ to** Beachtung schenken (+ *dat*) ● *vt* beachten. **~less** *a* ungeachtet (**of** *gen*)
heel[1] /hi:l/ *n* Ferse *f*; (*of shoe*) Absatz *m*; **down at ~** heruntergekommen; **take to one's ~s** (*fam*) Fersengeld geben
heel[2] *vi* **~ over** (*Naut*) sich auf die Seite legen
hefty /ˈheftɪ/ *a* (**-ier, -iest**) kräftig; (*heavy*) schwer
heifer /ˈhefə(r)/ *n* Färse *f*
height /haɪt/ *n* Höhe *f*; (*of person*) Größe *f*. **~en** *vt* (*fig*) steigern
heir /eə(r)/ *n* Erbe *m*. **~ess** *n* Erbin *f*. **~loom** *n* Erbstück *nt*
held /held/ *see* **hold**[2]
helicopter /ˈhelɪkɒptə(r)/ *n* Hubschrauber *m*
hell /hel/ *n* Hölle *f*; **go to ~!** (*sl*) geh zum Teufel! ● *int* verdammt!

hello /hə'ləʊ/ *int* [guten] Tag! (*fam*) hallo!

helm /helm/ *n* [Steuer]ruder *nt*; **at the ~** (*fig*) am Ruder

helmet /'helmɪt/ *n* Helm *m*

help /help/ *n* Hilfe *f*; (*employees*) Hilfskräfte *pl*; **that's no ~** das nützt nichts ● *vt/i* helfen (**s.o.** jdm); **~ oneself to sth** sich (*dat*) etw nehmen; **~ yourself** (*at table*) greif zu; **I could not ~ laughing** ich mußte lachen; **it cannot be ~ed** es läßt sich nicht ändern; **I can't ~ it** ich kann nichts dafür

help|er /'helpə(r)/ *n* Helfer(in) *m*(*f*). **~ful** *a*, **-ly** *adv* hilfsbereit; ‹*advice*› nützlich. **~ing** *n* Portion *f*. **~less** *a*, **-ly** *adv* hilflos

helter-skelter /heltə'skeltə(r)/ *adv* holterdiepolter ● *n* Rutschbahn *f*

hem /hem/ *n* Saum *m* ● *vt* (*pt/pp* **hemmed**) säumen; **~ in** umzingeln

hemisphere /'hemɪ-/ *n* Hemisphäre *f*

'hem-line *n* Rocklänge *f*

hemp /hemp/ *n* Hanf *m*

hen /hen/ *n* Henne *f*; (*any female bird*) Weibchen *nt*

hence /hens/ *adv* daher; **five years ~** in fünf Jahren. **~'forth** *adv* von nun an

henchman /'hentʃmən/ *n* (*pej*) Gefolgsmann *m*

'henpecked *a* **~ husband** Pantoffelheld *m*

her /hɜ:(r)/ *a* ihr ● *pron* (*acc*) sie; (*dat*) ihr; **I know ~** ich kenne sie; **give ~ the money** gib ihr das Geld

herald /'herəld/ *vt* verkünden. **~ry** *n* Wappenkunde *f*

herb /hɜ:b/ *n* Kraut *nt*

herbaceous /hɜ:'beɪʃəs/ *a* krautartig; **~ border** Staudenrabatte *f*

herd /hɜ:d/ *n* Herde *f* ● *vt* (*tend*) hüten; (*drive*) treiben. **~ together** *vi* sich zusammendrängen ● *vt* zusammentreiben

here /hɪə(r)/ *adv* hier; (*to this place*) hierher; **in ~** hier drinnen; **come/bring ~** herkommen/herbringen. **~'after** *adv* im folgenden. **~'by** *adv* hiermit

heredit|ary /hə'redɪtərɪ/ *a* erblich. **~y** *n* Vererbung *f*

here|sy /'herəsɪ/ *n* Ketzerei *f*. **~tic** *n* Ketzer(in) *m*(*f*)

here'with *adv* (*Comm*) beiliegend

heritage /'herɪtɪdʒ/ *n* Erbe *nt*

hermetic /hɜ:'metɪk/ *a*, **-ally** *adv* hermetisch

hermit /'hɜ:mɪt/ *n* Einsiedler *m*

hernia /'hɜ:nɪə/ *n* Bruch *m*, Hernie *f*

hero /'hɪərəʊ/ *n* (*pl* **-es**) Held *m*

heroic /hɪ'rəʊɪk/ *a*, **-ally** *adv* heldenhaft

heroin /'herəʊɪn/ *n* Heroin *nt*

hero|ine /'herəʊɪn/ *n* Heldin *f*. **~ism** *n* Heldentum *nt*

heron /'hern/ *n* Reiher *m*

herring /'herɪŋ/ *n* Hering *m*; **red ~** (*fam*) falsche Spur *f*. **~bone** *n* (*pattern*) Fischgrätenmuster *nt*

hers /hɜ:z/ *poss pron* ihre(r), ihrs; **a friend of ~** ein Freund von ihr; **that is ~** das gehört ihr

her'self *pron* selbst; (*refl*) sich; **by ~** allein

hesitant /'hezɪtənt/ *a*, **-ly** *adv* zögernd

hesitat|e /'hezɪteɪt/ *vi* zögern. **~ion** /-'teɪʃn/ *n* Zögern *nt*; **without ~ion** ohne zu zögern

het /het/ *a* **~ up** (*fam*) aufgeregt

hetero'sexual /hetərəʊ-/ *a* heterosexuell

hew /hju:/ *vt* (*pt* **hewed**, *pp* **hewed** *or* **hewn**) hauen

hexagonal /hek'sægənl/ *a* sechseckig

heyday /'heɪ-/ *n* Glanzzeit *f*

hi /haɪ/ *int* he! (*hallo*) Tag!

hiatus /haɪ'eɪtəs/ *n* (*pl* **-tuses**) Lücke *f*

hibernat|e /'haɪbəneɪt/ *vi* Winterschlaf halten. **~ion** /-'neɪʃn/ *n* Winterschlaf *m*

hiccup /'hɪkʌp/ *n* Hick *m*; (*fam: hitch*) Panne *f*; **have the ~s** den Schluckauf haben ● *vi* hick machen

hid /hɪd/, **hidden** *see* **hide²**

hide¹ /haɪd/ *n* (*Comm*) Haut *f*; (*leather*) Leder *nt*

hide² *v* (*pt* **hid**, *pp* **hidden**) ● *vt* verstecken; (*keep secret*) verheimlichen ● *vi* sich verstecken. **~-and-'seek** *n* **play ~-and-seek** Versteck spielen

hideous /'hɪdɪəs/ *a*, **-ly** *adv* häßlich; (*horrible*) gräßlich

'hide-out *n* Versteck *nt*

hiding¹ /'haɪdɪŋ/ *n* (*fam*) **give s.o. a ~** jdn verdreschen

hiding² *n* **go into ~** untertauchen

hierarchy /'haɪərɑ:kɪ/ *n* Hierarchie *f*

hieroglyphics /haɪərə'glɪfɪks/ *npl* Hieroglyphen *pl*

higgledy-piggledy /hɪgldɪ'pɪgldɪ/ *adv* kunterbunt durcheinander

high /haɪ/ *a* (**-er, -est**) hoch; *attrib* hohe(r,s); ‹*meat*› angegangen; ‹*wind*› stark; (*on drugs*) high; **it's ~ time** es ist höchste Zeit ● *adv* hoch;

~ and low überall • *n* Hoch *nt*; (*temperature*) Höchsttemperatur *f*

high: ~brow *a* intellektuell. **~ chair** *n* Kinderhochstuhl *m*. **~-'handed** *a* selbstherrlich. **~-'heeled** *a* hochhackig. **~ jump** *n* Hochsprung *m*

highlight *n* (*fig*) Höhepunkt *m*; **~s** *pl* (*in hair*) helle Strähnen *pl* • *vt* (*emphasize*) hervorheben

highly /'haɪlɪ/ *adv* hoch; **speak ~ of** loben; **think ~ of** sehr schätzen. **~-'strung** *a* nervös

Highness /'haɪnɪs/ *n* Hoheit *f*

high: ~-rise *a* **~-rise flats** *pl* Wohnturm *m*. **~ season** *n* Hochsaison *f*. **~ street** *n* Hauptstraße *f*. **~ 'tide** *n* Hochwasser *nt*. **~way** *n* **public ~way** öffentliche Straße *f*

hijack /'haɪdʒæk/ *vt* entführen. **~er** *n* Entführer *m*

hike /haɪk/ *n* Wanderung *f* • *vi* wandern. **~r** *n* Wanderer *m*

hilarious /hɪ'leərɪəs/ *a* sehr komisch

hill /hɪl/ *n* Berg *m*; (*mound*) Hügel *m*; (*slope*) Hang *m*

hill: ~-billy *n* (*Amer*) Hinterwäldler *m*. **~side** *n* Hang *m*. **~y** *a* hügelig

hilt /hɪlt/ *n* Griff *m*; **to the ~** (*fam*) voll und ganz

him /hɪm/ *pron* (*acc*) ihn; (*dat*) ihm; **I know ~** ich kenne ihn; **give ~ the money** gib ihm das Geld. **~'self** *pron* selbst; (*refl*) sich; **by ~self** allein

hind /haɪnd/ *a* Hinter-

hind|er /'hɪndə(r)/ *vt* hindern. **~rance** /-rəns/ *n* Hindernis *nt*

hindsight /'haɪnd-/ *n* **with ~** rückblickend

Hindu /'hɪndu:/ *n* Hindu *m* • *a* Hindu-. **~ism** *n* Hinduismus *m*

hinge /hɪndʒ/ *n* Scharnier *nt*; (*on door*) Angel *f* • *vi* **~ on** (*fig*) ankommen auf (+ *acc*)

hint /hɪnt/ *n* Wink *m*, Andeutung *f*; (*advice*) Hinweis *m*; (*trace*) Spur *f* • *vi* **~ at** anspielen auf (+ *acc*)

hip /hɪp/ *n* Hüfte *f*

hippie /'hɪpɪ/ *n* Hippie *m*

hip 'pocket *n* Gesäßtasche *f*

hippopotamus /hɪpə'pɒtəməs/ *n* (*pl* **-muses** *or* **-mi** /-maɪ/) Nilpferd *nt*

hire /'haɪə(r)/ *vt* mieten ⟨*car*⟩; leihen ⟨*suit*⟩; einstellen ⟨*person*⟩; **~ [out]** vermieten; verleihen • *n* Mieten *nt*; Leihen *nt*. **~-car** *n* Leihwagen *m*

his /hɪz/ *a* sein • *poss pron* seine(r), seins; **a friend of ~** ein Freund von ihm; **that is ~** das gehört ihm

hiss /hɪs/ *n* Zischen *nt* • *vt/i* zischen

historian /hɪ'stɔ:rɪən/ *n* Historiker(in) *m*(*f*)

historic /hɪ'stɒrɪk/ *a* historisch. **~al** *a*, **-ly** *adv* geschichtlich, historisch

history /'hɪstərɪ/ *n* Geschichte *f*

hit /hɪt/ *n* (*blow*) Schlag *m*; (*fam: success*) Erfolg *m*; **direct ~** Volltreffer *m* • *vt/i* (*pt/pp* **hit**, *pres p* **hitting**) schlagen; (*knock against, collide with, affect*) treffen; **~ the target** das Ziel treffen; **~ on** (*fig*) kommen auf (+ *acc*); **~ it off** gut auskommen (**with** mit); **~ one's head on sth** sich (*dat*) den Kopf an etw (*dat*) stoßen

hitch /hɪtʃ/ *n* Problem *nt*; **technical ~** Panne *f* • *vt* festmachen (**to** an + *dat*); **~ up** hochziehen; **~ a lift** per Anhalter fahren, (*fam*) trampen. **~-hike** *vi* per Anhalter fahren, (*fam*) trampen. **~-hiker** *n* Anhalter(in) *m*(*f*)

hither /'hɪðə(r)/ *adv* hierher; **~ and thither** hin und her. **~'to** *adv* bisher

hive /haɪv/ *n* Bienenstock *m*. **~ off** *vt* (*Comm*) abspalten

hoard /hɔ:d/ *n* Hort *m* • *vt* horten, hamstern

hoarding /'hɔ:dɪŋ/ *n* Bauzaun *m*; (*with advertisements*) Reklamewand *f*

hoar-frost /'hɔ:-/ *n* Rauhreif *m*

hoarse /hɔ:s/ *a* (**-r, -st**), **-ly** *adv* heiser. **~ness** *n* Heiserkeit *f*

hoax /həʊks/ *n* übler Scherz *m*; (*false alarm*) blinder Alarm *m*

hob /hɒb/ *n* Kochmulde *f*

hobble /'hɒbl/ *vi* humpeln

hobby /'hɒbɪ/ *n* Hobby *nt*. **~horse** *n* (*fig*) Lieblingsthema *nt*

hobnailed /'hɒb-/ *a* **~ boots** *pl* genagelte Schuhe *pl*

hock /hɒk/ *n* [weißer] Rheinwein *m*

hockey /'hɒkɪ/ *n* Hockey *nt*

hoe /həʊ/ *n* Hacke *f* • *vt* (*pres p* **hoeing**) hacken

hog /hɒg/ *n* [Mast]schwein *nt* • *vt* (*pt/pp* **hogged**) (*fam*) mit Beschlag belegen

hoist /hɔɪst/ *n* Lastenaufzug *m* • *vt* hochziehen; hissen ⟨*flag*⟩

hold[1] /həʊld/ *n* (*Naut*) Laderaum *m*

hold[2] *n* Halt *m*; (*Sport*) Griff *m*; (*fig: influence*) Einfluß *m*; **get ~ of** fassen; (*fam: contact*) erreichen • *v* (*pt/pp* **held**) • *vt* halten; ⟨*container:*⟩ fassen; (*believe*) meinen; (*possess*) haben; anhalten ⟨*breath*⟩; **~ one's tongue** den Mund halten • *vi* ⟨*rope:*⟩

halten; ⟨*weather:*⟩ sich halten; **not ~ with** (*fam*) nicht einverstanden sein mit. **~ back** *vt* zurückhalten ● *vi* zögern. **~ on** *vi* (*wait*) warten; (*on telephone*) am Apparat bleiben; **~ on to** (*keep*) behalten; (*cling to*) sich festhalten an (+ *dat*). **~ out** *vt* hinhalten ● *vi* (*resist*) aushalten. **~ up** *vt* hochhalten; (*delay*) aufhalten; (*rob*) überfallen

'hold|all *n* Reisetasche *f*. **~er** *n* Inhaber(in) *m*(*f*); (*container*) Halter *m*. **~-up** *n* Verzögerung *f*; (*attack*) Überfall *m*

hole /həʊl/ *n* Loch *nt*

holiday /'hɒlədeɪ/ *n* Urlaub *m*; (*Sch*) Ferien *pl*; (*public*) Feiertag *m*; (*day off*) freier Tag *m*; **go on ~** in Urlaub fahren. **~-maker** *n* Urlauber(in) *m*(*f*)

holiness /'həʊlɪnɪs/ *n* Heiligkeit *f*

Holland /'hɒlənd/ *n* Holland *nt*

hollow /'hɒləʊ/ *a* hohl; ⟨*promise*⟩ leer ● *n* Vertiefung *f*; (*in ground*) Mulde *f*. **~ out** *vt* aushöhlen

holly /'hɒlɪ/ *n* Stechpalme *f*

'hollyhock *n* Stockrose *f*

hologram /'hɒləgræm/ *n* Hologramm *nt*

holster /'həʊlstə(r)/ *n* Pistolentasche *f*

holy /'həʊlɪ/ *a* (**-ier, -iest**) heilig. **H~ Ghost** *or* **Spirit** *n* Heiliger Geist *m*. **~ water** *n* Weihwasser *nt*. **H~ Week** *n* Karwoche *f*

homage /'hɒmɪdʒ/ *n* Huldigung *f*; **pay ~ to** huldigen (+ *dat*)

home /həʊm/ *n* Zuhause *nt*; (*house*) Haus *nt*; (*institution*) Heim *nt*; (*native land*) Heimat *f* ● *adv* **at ~** zu Hause; **come/go ~** nach Hause kommen/gehen

home: ~ ad'dress *n* Heimatanschrift *f*. **~ com'puter** *n* Heimcomputer *m*. **~ game** *n* Heimspiel *nt*. **~ help** *n* Haushaltshilfe *f*. **~land** *n* Heimatland *nt*. **~less** *a* obdachlos

homely /'həʊmlɪ/ *a* (**-ier, -iest**) *a* gemütlich; (*Amer: ugly*) unscheinbar

home: ~-'made *a* selbstgemacht. **H~ Office** *n* Innenministerium *nt*. **H~ 'Secretary** Innenminister *m*. **~sick** *a* **be ~sick** Heimweh haben (**for** nach). **~sickness** *n* Heimweh *nt*. **~ 'town** *n* Heimatstadt *f*. **~work** *n* (*Sch*) Hausaufgaben *pl*

homicide /'hɒmɪsaɪd/ *n* Totschlag *m*; (*murder*) Mord *m*

homoeopath|ic /həʊmɪə'pæθɪk/ *a* homöopathisch. **~y** /-'ɒpəθɪ/ *n* Homöopathie *f*

homogeneous /hɒmə'dʒi:nɪəs/ *a* homogen

homo'sexual *a* homosexuell ● *n* Homosexuelle(r) *m*/*f*

honest /'ɒnɪst/ *a*, **-ly** *adv* ehrlich. **~y** *n* Ehrlichkeit *f*

honey /'hʌnɪ/ *n* Honig *m*; (*fam: darling*) Schatz *m*

honey: ~comb *n* Honigwabe *f*. **~moon** *n* Flitterwochen *pl*; (*journey*) Hochzeitsreise *f*. **~suckle** *n* Geißblatt *nt*

honk /hɒŋk/ *vi* hupen

honorary /'ɒnərərɪ/ *a* ehrenamtlich; ⟨*member, doctorate*⟩ Ehren-

honour /'ɒnə(r)/ *n* Ehre *f* ● *vt* ehren; honorieren ⟨*cheque*⟩. **~able** /-əbl/ *a*, **-bly** *adv* ehrenhaft

hood /hʊd/ *n* Kapuze *f*; (*of pram*) [Klapp]verdeck *nt*; (*over cooker*) Abzugshaube *f*; (*Auto, Amer*) Kühlerhaube *f*

hoodlum /'hu:dləm/ *n* Rowdy *m*

'hoodwink *vt* (*fam*) reinlegen

hoof /hu:f/ *n* (*pl* **~s** *or* **hooves**) Huf *m*

hook /hʊk/ *n* Haken *m*; **by ~ or by crook** mit allen Mitteln ● *vt* festhaken (**to** an + *acc*)

hook|ed /hʊkt/ *a* **~ed nose** Hakennase *f*; **~ed on** (*fam*) abhängig von; (*keen on*) besessen von. **~er** *n* (*Amer, sl*) Nutte *f*

hookey /'hʊkɪ/ *n* **play ~** (*Amer, fam*) schwänzen

hooligan /'hu:lɪgən/ *n* Rowdy *m*. **~ism** *n* Rowdytum *nt*

hoop /hu:p/ *n* Reifen *m*

hooray /hʊ'reɪ/ *int* & *n* = **hurrah**

hoot /hu:t/ *n* Ruf *m*; **~s of laughter** schallendes Gelächter *nt* ● *vi* ⟨*owl:*⟩ rufen; ⟨*car:*⟩ hupen; (*jeer*) johlen. **~er** *n* (*of factory*) Sirene *f*; (*Auto*) Hupe *f*

hoover /'hu:və(r)/ *n* **H~** (**P**) Staubsauger *m* ● *vt*/*i* [staub]saugen

hop[1] /hɒp/ *n*, & **~s** *pl* Hopfen *m*

hop[2] *n* Hüpfer *m*; **catch s.o. on the ~** (*fam*) jdm ungelegen kommen ● *vi* (*pt*/*pp* **hopped**) hüpfen; **~ it!** (*fam*) hau ab! **~ in** *vi* (*fam*) einsteigen. **~ out** *vi* (*fam*) aussteigen

hope /həʊp/ *n* Hoffnung *f*; (*prospect*) Aussicht *f* (**of** auf + *acc*) ● *vt*/*i* hoffen (**for** auf + *acc*); **I ~ so** hoffentlich

hope|ful /'həʊpfl/ *a* hoffnungsvoll; **be ~ful that** hoffen, daß. **~fully** *adv* hoffnungsvoll; (*it is hoped*) hoffentlich. **~less** *a*, **-ly** *adv* hoffnungslos; (*useless*) nutzlos; (*incompetent*) untauglich

horde /hɔ:d/ *n* Horde *f*

horizon /hə'raɪzn/ *n* Horizont *m*; **on the ~** am Horizont

horizontal /hɒrɪ'zɒntl/ *a*, **-ly** *adv* horizontal. **~ 'bar** *n* Reck *nt*

horn /hɔ:n/ *n* Horn *nt*; (*Auto*) Hupe *f*

hornet /'hɔ:nɪt/ *n* Hornisse *f*

horny /'hɔ:nɪ/ *a* schwielig

horoscope /'hɒrəskəʊp/ *n* Horoskop *nt*

horrible /'hɒrɪbl/ *a*, **-bly** *adv* schrecklich

horrid /'hɒrɪd/ *a* gräßlich

horrific /hə'rɪfɪk/ *a* entsetzlich

horrify /'hɒrɪfaɪ/ *vt* (*pt/pp* **-ied**) entsetzen

horror /'hɒrə(r)/ *n* Entsetzen *nt*. **~ film** *n* Horrorfilm *m*

hors-d'œuvre /ɔ:'dɜ:vr/ *n* Vorspeise *f*

horse /hɔ:s/ *n* Pferd *nt*

horse: ~back *n* **on ~back** zu Pferde. **~-'chestnut** *n* [Roß]kastanie *f*. **~man** *n* Reiter *m*. **~play** *n* Toben *nt*. **~power** *n* Pferdestärke *f*. **~-racing** *n* Pferderennen *nt*. **~radish** *n* Meerrettich *m*. **~shoe** *n* Hufeisen *nt*

horti'cultural /hɔ:tɪ-/ *a* Garten-

'horticulture *n* Gartenbau *m*

hose /həʊz/ *n* (*pipe*) Schlauch *m* ● *vt* **~ down** abspritzen

hosiery /'həʊʒərɪ/ *n* Strumpfwaren *pl*

hospice /'hɒspɪs/ *n* Heim *nt*; (*for the terminally ill*) Sterbeklinik *f*

hospitable /hɒ'spɪtəbl/ *a*, **-bly** *adv* gastfreundlich

hospital /'hɒspɪtl/ *n* Krankenhaus *nt*

hospitality /hɒspɪ'tælətɪ/ *n* Gastfreundschaft *f*

host[1] /həʊst/ *n* **a ~ of** eine Menge von

host[2] *n* Gastgeber *m*

host[3] *n* (*Relig*) Hostie *f*

hostage /'hɒstɪdʒ/ *n* Geisel *f*

hostel /'hɒstl/ *n* [Wohn]heim *nt*

hostess /'həʊstɪs/ *n* Gastgeberin *f*

hostile /'hɒstaɪl/ *a* feindlich; (*unfriendly*) feindselig

hostilit|y /hɒ'stɪlətɪ/ *n* Feindschaft *f*; **~ies** *pl* Feindseligkeiten *pl*

hot /hɒt/ *a* (**hotter**, **hottest**) heiß; ⟨*meal*⟩ warm; (*spicy*) scharf; **I am** *or* **feel ~** mir ist heiß

'hotbed *n* (*fig*) Brutstätte *f*

hotchpotch /'hɒtʃpɒtʃ/ *n* Mischmasch *m*

hotel /həʊ'tel/ *n* Hotel *nt*. **~ier** /-ɪə(r)/ *n* Hotelier *m*

hot: ~head *n* Hitzkopf *m*. **~'headed** *a* hitzköpfig. **~house** *n* Treibhaus *nt*. **~ly** *adv* (*fig*) heiß, heftig. **~plate** *n* Tellerwärmer *m*; (*of cooker*) Kochplatte *f*. **~ tap** *n* Warmwasserhahn *m*. **~-tempered** *a* jähzornig. **~-'water bottle** *n* Wärmflasche *f*

hound /haʊnd/ *n* Jagdhund *m* ● *vt* (*fig*) verfolgen

hour /'aʊə(r)/ *n* Stunde *f*. **~ly** *a & adv* stündlich; **~ly pay** *or* **rate** Stundenlohn *m*

house[1] /haʊs/ *n* Haus *nt*; **at my ~** bei mir

house[2] /haʊz/ *vt* unterbringen

house /haʊs/: **~boat** *n* Hausboot *nt*. **~breaking** *n* Einbruch *m*. **~hold** *n* Haushalt *m*. **~holder** *n* Hausinhaber(in) *m*(*f*). **~keeper** *n* Haushälterin *f*. **~keeping** *n* Hauswirtschaft *f*; (*money*) Haushaltsgeld *nt*. **~-plant** *n* Zimmerpflanze *f*. **~-trained** *a* stubenrein. **~-warming** *n* **have a ~-warming party** Einstand feiern. **~wife** *n* Hausfrau *f*. **~work** *n* Hausarbeit *f*

housing /'haʊzɪŋ/ *n* Wohnungen *pl*; (*Techn*) Gehäuse *nt*. **~ estate** *n* Wohnsiedlung *f*

hovel /'hɒvl/ *n* elende Hütte *f*

hover /'hɒvə(r)/ *vi* schweben; (*be undecided*) schwanken; (*linger*) herumstehen. **~craft** *n* Luftkissenfahrzeug *nt*

how /haʊ/ *adv* wie; **~ do you do?** guten Tag! **~ many** wie viele; **~ much** wieviel; **and ~!** und ob!

how'ever *adv* (*in question*) wie; (*nevertheless*) jedoch, aber; **~ small** wie klein es auch sein mag

howl /haʊl/ *n* Heulen *nt* ● *vi* heulen; ⟨*baby:*⟩ brüllen. **~er** *n* (*fam*) Schnitzer *m*

hub /hʌb/ *n* Nabe *f*; (*fig*) Mittelpunkt *m*

hubbub /'hʌbʌb/ *n* Stimmengewirr *nt*

'hub-cap *n* Radkappe *f*

huddle /'hʌdl/ *vi* **~ together** sich zusammendrängen

hue[1] /hju:/ *n* Farbe *f*

hue[2] *n* **~ and cry** Aufruhr *m*

huff /hʌf/ *n* **in a ~** beleidigt

hug /hʌg/ *n* Umarmung *f* ● *vt* (*pt/pp* **hugged**) umarmen

huge /hju:dʒ/ *a*, **-ly** *adv* riesig

hulking /ˈhʌlkɪŋ/ *a* (*fam*) ungeschlacht
hull /hʌl/ *n* (*Naut*) Rumpf *m*
hullo /həˈləʊ/ *int* = **hallo**
hum /hʌm/ *n* Summen *nt*; Brummen *nt* ● *vt/i* (*pt/pp* **hummed**) summen; ⟨*motor:*⟩brummen; **~ and haw** nicht mit der Sprache herauswollen
human /ˈhjuːmən/ *a* menschlich ● *n* Mensch *m*. **~ 'being** *n* Mensch *m*
humane /hjuːˈmeɪn/ *a*, **-ly** *adv* human
humanitarian /hjuːmænɪˈteərɪən/ *a* humanitär
humanit|y /hjuːˈmænətɪ/ *n* Menschheit *f*; **~ies** *pl* (*Univ*) Geisteswissenschaften *pl*
humble /ˈhʌmbl/ *a* (**-r, -st**), **-bly** *adv* demütig ● *vt* demütigen
'humdrum *a* eintönig
humid /ˈhjuːmɪd/ *a* feucht. **~ity** /-ˈmɪdətɪ/ *n* Feuchtigkeit *f*
humiliat|e /hjuːˈmɪlɪeɪt/ *vt* demütigen. **~ion** /-ˈeɪʃn/ *n* Demütigung *f*
humility /hjuːˈmɪlətɪ/ *n* Demut *f*
'humming-bird *n* Kolibri *m*
humorous /ˈhjuːmərəs/ *a*, **-ly** *adv* humorvoll; ⟨*story*⟩ humoristisch
humour /ˈhjuːmə(r)/ *n* Humor *m*; (*mood*) Laune *f*; **have a sense of ~** Humor haben ● *vt* **~ s.o.** jdm seinen Willen lassen
hump /hʌmp/ *n* Buckel *m*; (*of camel*) Höcker *m* ● *vt* schleppen
hunch /hʌntʃ/ *n* (*idea*) Ahnung *f*
'hunch|back *n* Bucklige(r) *m/f*. **~ed** *a* **~ed up** gebeugt
hundred /ˈhʌndrəd/ *a* **one/a ~** [ein]hundert ● *n* Hundert *nt*; (*written figure*) Hundert *f*. **~th** *a* hundertste(r,s) ● *n* Hundertstel *nt*. **~weight** *n* ≈ Zentner *m*
hung /hʌŋ/ *see* **hang**
Hungarian /hʌŋˈgeərɪən/ *a* ungarisch ● *n* Ungar(in) *m(f)*
Hungary /ˈhʌŋgərɪ/ *n* Ungarn *nt*
hunger /ˈhʌŋgə(r)/ *n* Hunger *m*. **~-strike** *n* Hungerstreik *m*
hungry /ˈhʌŋgrɪ/ *a* (**-ier, -iest**), **-ily** *adv* hungrig; **be ~** Hunger haben
hunk /hʌŋk/ *n* [großes] Stück *nt*
hunt /hʌnt/ *n* Jagd *f*; (*for criminal*) Fahndung *f* ● *vt/i* jagen; fahnden nach ⟨*criminal*⟩; **~ for** suchen. **~er** *n* Jäger *m*; (*horse*) Jagdpferd *nt*. **~ing** *n* Jagd *f*
hurdle /ˈhɜːdl/ *n* (*Sport & fig*) Hürde *f*. **~r** *n* Hürdenläufer(in) *m(f)*
hurl /hɜːl/ *vt* schleudern
hurrah /hʊˈrɑː/, **hurray** /hʊˈreɪ/ *int* hurra! ● *n* Hurra *nt*
hurricane /ˈhʌrɪkən/ *n* Orkan *m*
hurried /ˈhʌrɪd/ *a*, **-ly** *adv* eilig; (*superficial*) flüchtig
hurry /ˈhʌrɪ/ *n* Eile *f*; **be in a ~** es eilig haben ● *vi* (*pt/pp* **-ied**) sich beeilen; (*go quickly*) eilen. **~ up** *vi* sich beeilen ● *vt* antreiben
hurt /hɜːt/ *n* Schmerz *m* ● *vt/i* (*pt/pp* **hurt**) weh tun (+ *dat*); (*injure*) verletzen; (*offend*) kränken. **~ful** *a* verletzend
hurtle /ˈhɜːtl/ *vi* **~ along** rasen
husband /ˈhʌzbənd/ *n* [Ehe]mann *m*
hush /hʌʃ/ *n* Stille *f* ● *vt* **~ up** vertuschen. **~ed** *a* gedämpft. **~-'hush** *a* (*fam*) streng geheim
husk /hʌsk/ *n* Spelze *f*
husky /ˈhʌskɪ/ *a* (**-ier, -iest**) heiser; (*burly*) stämmig
hustle /ˈhʌsl/ *vt* drängen ● *n* Gedränge *nt*; **~ and bustle** geschäftiges Treiben *nt*
hut /hʌt/ *n* Hütte *f*
hutch /hʌtʃ/ *n* [Kaninchen]stall *m*
hybrid /ˈhaɪbrɪd/ *a* hybrid ● *n* Hybride *f*
hydrangea /haɪˈdreɪndʒə/ *n* Hortensie *f*
hydrant /ˈhaɪdrənt/ *n* **[fire] ~** Hydrant *m*
hydraulic /haɪˈdrɔːlɪk/ *a*, **-ally** *adv* hydraulisch
hydrochloric /haɪdrəˈklɔːrɪk/ *a* **~ acid** Salzsäure *f*
hydroe'lectric /haɪdrəʊ-/ *a* hydroelektrisch. **~ power station** *n* Wasserkraftwerk *nt*
hydrofoil /ˈhaɪdrə-/ *n* Tragflügelboot *nt*
hydrogen /ˈhaɪdrədʒən/ *n* Wasserstoff *m*
hyena /haɪˈiːnə/ *n* Hyäne *f*
hygien|e /ˈhaɪdʒiːn/ *n* Hygiene *f*. **~ic** /haɪˈdʒiːnɪk/ *a*, **-ally** *adv* hygienisch
hymn /hɪm/ *n* Kirchenlied *nt*. **~-book** *n* Gesangbuch *nt*
hyphen /ˈhaɪfn/ *n* Bindestrich *m*. **~ate** *vt* mit Bindestrich schreiben
hypno|sis /hɪpˈnəʊsɪs/ *n* Hypnose *f*. **~tic** /-ˈnɒtɪk/ *a* hypnotisch
hypno|tism /ˈhɪpnətɪzm/ *n* Hypnotik *f*. **~tist** /-tɪst/ *n* Hypnotiseur *m*. **~tize** *vt* hypnotisieren
hypochondriac /haɪpəˈkɒndrɪæk/ *a* hypochondrisch ● *n* Hypochonder *m*
hypocrisy /hɪˈpɒkrəsɪ/ *n* Heuchelei *f*

hypocrit|e /ˈhɪpəkrɪt/ *n* Heuchler(in) *m(f)*. **~ical** /-ˈkrɪtɪkl/ *a*, **-ly** *adv* heuchlerisch
hypodermic /haɪpəˈdɜːmɪk/ *a & n* **~ [syringe]** Injektionsspritze *f*
hypothe|sis /haɪˈpɒθəsɪs/ *n* Hypothese *f*. **~tical** /-əˈθetɪkl/ *a*, **-ly** *adv* hypothetisch
hyster|ia /hɪˈstɪərɪə/ *n* Hysterie *f*. **~ical** /-ˈsterɪkl/ *a*, **-ly** *adv* hysterisch. **~ics** /hɪˈsterɪks/ *npl* hysterischer Anfall *m*

I

I /aɪ/ *pron* ich
ice /aɪs/ *n* Eis *nt* ● *vt* mit Zuckerguß überziehen ⟨*cake*⟩
ice: ~ age *n* Eiszeit *f*. **~-axe** *n* Eispickel *m*. **~berg** /-bɜːg/ *n* Eisberg *m*. **~box** *n* (*Amer*) Kühlschrank *m*. **~ˈcream** *n* [Speise]eis *nt*. **~-ˈcream parlour** *n* Eisdiele *f*. **~-cube** *n* Eiswürfel *m*
Iceland /ˈaɪslənd/ *n* Island *nt*
ice: ~ ˈlolly *n* Eis *nt* am Stiel. **~ rink** *n* Eisbahn *f*
icicle /ˈaɪsɪkl/ *n* Eiszapfen *m*
icing /ˈaɪsɪŋ/ *n* Zuckerguß *m*. **~ sugar** *n* Puderzucker *m*
icon /ˈaɪkɒn/ *n* Ikone *f*
icy /ˈaɪsɪ/ *a* (**-ier, -iest**), **-ily** *adv* eisig; ⟨*road*⟩ vereist
idea /aɪˈdɪə/ *n* Idee *f*; (*conception*) Vorstellung *f*; **I have no ~!** ich habe keine Ahnung!
ideal /aɪˈdɪəl/ *a* ideal ● *n* Ideal *nt*. **~ism** *n* Idealismus *m*. **~ist** *n* Idealist(in) *m(f)*. **~istic** /-ˈlɪstɪk/ *a* idealistisch. **~ize** *vt* idealisieren. **~ly** *adv* ideal; (*in ideal circumstances*) idealerweise
identical /aɪˈdentɪkl/ *a* identisch; ⟨*twins*⟩ eineiig
identi|fication /aɪdentɪfɪˈkeɪʃn/ *n* Identifizierung *f*; (*proof of identity*) Ausweispapiere *pl*. **~fy** /aɪˈdentɪfaɪ/ *vt* (*pt/pp* **-ied**) identifizieren
identity /aɪˈdentətɪ/ *n* Identität *f*. **~ card** *n* [Personal]ausweis *m*
ideolog|ical /aɪdɪəˈlɒdʒɪkl/ *a* ideologisch. **~y** /aɪdɪˈɒlədʒɪ/ *n* Ideologie *f*
idiom /ˈɪdɪəm/ *n* [feste] Redewendung *f*. **~atic** /-ˈmætɪk/ *a*, **-ally** *adv* idiomatisch
idiosyncrasy /ɪdɪəˈsɪŋkrəsɪ/ *n* Eigenart *f*
idiot /ˈɪdɪət/ *n* Idiot *m*. **~ic** /-ˈɒtɪk/ *a* idiotisch
idle /ˈaɪdl/ *a* (**-r, -st**), **-ly** *adv* untätig; (*lazy*) faul; (*empty*) leer; ⟨*machine*⟩ nicht in Betrieb ● *vi* faulenzen; ⟨*engine:*⟩ leer laufen. **~ness** *n* Untätigkeit *f*; Faulheit *f*
idol /ˈaɪdl/ *n* Idol *nt*. **~ize** /ˈaɪdəlaɪz/ *vt* vergöttern
idyllic /ɪˈdɪlɪk/ *a* idyllisch
i.e. *abbr* (**id est**) d.h.
if /ɪf/ *conj* wenn; (*whether*) ob; **as if** als ob
ignite /ɪgˈnaɪt/ *vt* entzünden ● *vi* sich entzünden
ignition /ɪgˈnɪʃn/ *n* (*Auto*) Zündung *f*. **~ key** *n* Zündschlüssel *m*
ignoramus /ɪgnəˈreɪməs/ *n* Ignorant *m*
ignoran|ce /ˈɪgnərəns/ *n* Unwissenheit *f*. **~t** *a* unwissend; (*rude*) ungehobelt
ignore /ɪgˈnɔː(r)/ *vt* ignorieren
ilk /ɪlk/ *n* (*fam*) **of that ~** von der Sorte
ill /ɪl/ *a* krank; (*bad*) schlecht; **feel ~ at ease** sich unbehaglich fühlen ● *adv* schlecht ● *n* Schlechte(s) *nt*; (*evil*) Übel *nt*. **~-advised** *a* unklug. **~-bred** *a* schlecht erzogen
illegal /ɪˈliːgl/ *a*, **-ly** *adv* illegal
illegible /ɪˈledʒəbl/ *a*, **-bly** *adv* unleserlich
illegitima|cy /ɪlɪˈdʒɪtɪməsɪ/ *n* Unehelichkeit *f*. **~te** /-mət/ *a* unehelich; ⟨*claim*⟩ unberechtigt
illicit /ɪˈlɪsɪt/ *a*, **-ly** *adv* illegal
illitera|cy /ɪˈlɪtərəsɪ/ *n* Analphabetentum *nt*. **~te** /-rət/ *a* **be ~te** nicht lesen und schreiben können ● *n* Analphabet(in) *m(f)*
illness /ˈɪlnɪs/ *n* Krankheit *f*
illogical /ɪˈlɒdʒɪkl/ *a*, **-ly** *adv* unlogisch
ill-treat /ɪlˈtriːt/ *vt* mißhandeln. **~ment** *n* Mißhandlung *f*
illuminat|e /ɪˈluːmɪneɪt/ *vt* beleuchten. **~ing** *a* aufschlußreich. **~ion** /-ˈneɪʃn/ *n* Beleuchtung *f*
illusion /ɪˈluːʒn/ *n* Illusion *f*; **be under the ~ that** sich (*dat*) einbilden, daß
illusory /ɪˈluːsərɪ/ *a* illusorisch
illustrat|e /ˈɪləstreɪt/ *vt* illustrieren. **~ion** /-ˈstreɪʃn/ *n* Illustration *f*
illustrious /ɪˈlʌstrɪəs/ *a* berühmt
image /ˈɪmɪdʒ/ *n* Bild *nt*; (*statue*) Standbild *nt*; (*figure*) Figur *f*; (*exact likeness*) Ebenbild *nt*; **[public] ~** Image *nt*

imagin|able /ɪ'mædʒɪnəbl/ *a* vorstellbar. **~ary** /-ərɪ/ *a* eingebildet
imaginat|ion /ɪmædʒɪ'neɪʃn/ *n* Phantasie *f*; (*fancy*) Einbildung *f*. **~ive** /ɪ'mædʒɪnətɪv/ *a*, **-ly** *adv* phantasievoll; (*full of ideas*) einfallsreich
imagine /ɪ'mædʒɪn/ *vt* sich (*dat*) vorstellen; (*wrongly*) sich (*dat*) einbilden
im'balance *n* Unausgeglichenheit *f*
imbecile /'ɪmbəsi:l/ *n* Schwachsinnige(r) *m/f*; (*pej*) Idiot *m*
imbibe /ɪm'baɪb/ *vt* trinken; (*fig*) aufnehmen
imbue /ɪm'bju:/ *vt* **be ~d with** erfüllt sein von
imitat|e /'ɪmɪteɪt/ *vt* nachahmen, imitieren. **~ion** /-'teɪʃn/ *n* Nachahmung *f*, Imitation *f*
immaculate /ɪ'mækjʊlət/ *a*, **-ly** *adv* tadellos; (*Relig*) unbefleckt
imma'terial *a* (*unimportant*) unwichtig, unwesentlich
imma'ture *a* unreif
immediate /ɪ'mi:dɪət/ *a* sofortig; (*nearest*) nächste(r,s). **~ly** *adv* sofort; **~ly next to** unmittelbar neben ● *conj* sobald
immemorial /ɪmə'mɔ:rɪəl/ *a* **from time ~** seit Urzeiten
immense /ɪ'mens/ *a*, **-ly** *adv* riesig; (*fam*) enorm; (*extreme*) äußerst
immers|e /ɪ'mɜ:s/ *vt* untertauchen; **be ~ed in** (*fig*) vertieft sein in (+ *acc*). **~ion** /-ɜ:ʃn/ *n* Untertauchen *nt*. **~ion heater** *n* Heißwasserbereiter *m*
immigrant /'ɪmɪgrənt/ *n* Einwanderer *m*
immigrat|e /'ɪmɪgreɪt/ *vi* einwandern. **~ion** /-'greɪʃn/ *n* Einwanderung *f*
imminent /'ɪmɪnənt/ *a* **be ~** unmittelbar bevorstehen
immobil|e /ɪ'məʊbaɪl/ *a* unbeweglich. **~ize** /-bəlaɪz/ *vt* (*fig*) lähmen; (*Med*) ruhigstellen
immoderate /ɪ'mɒdərət/ *a* übermäßig
immodest /ɪ'mɒdɪst/ *a* unbescheiden
immoral /ɪ'mɒrəl/ *a*, **-ly** *adv* unmoralisch. **~ity** /ɪmə'rælətɪ/ *n* Unmoral *f*
immortal /ɪ'mɔ:tl/ *a* unsterblich. **~ity** /-'tælətɪ/ *n* Unsterblichkeit *f*. **~ize** *vt* verewigen
immovable /ɪ'mu:vəbl/ *a* unbeweglich; (*fig*) fest
immune /ɪ'mju:n/ *a* immun (**to/from** gegen). **~ system** *n* Abwehrsystem *nt*
immunity /ɪ'mju:nətɪ/ *n* Immunität *f*
immunize /'ɪmjʊnaɪz/ *vt* immunisieren
imp /ɪmp/ *n* Kobold *m*
impact /'ɪmpækt/ *n* Aufprall *m*; (*collision*) Zusammenprall *m*; (*of bomb*) Einschlag *m*; (*fig*) Auswirkung *f*
impair /ɪm'peə(r)/ *vt* beeinträchtigen
impale /ɪm'peɪl/ *vt* aufspießen
impart /ɪm'pɑ:t/ *vt* übermitteln (**to** *dat*); vermitteln ⟨*knowledge*⟩
im'parti|al *a* unparteiisch. **~'ality** *n* Unparteilichkeit *f*
im'passable *a* unpassierbar
impasse /æm'pɑ:s/ *n* (*fig*) Sackgasse *f*
impassioned /ɪm'pæʃnd/ *a* leidenschaftlich
im'passive *a*, **-ly** *adv* unbeweglich
im'patien|ce *n* Ungeduld *f*. **~t** *a*, **-ly** *adv* ungeduldig
impeach /ɪm'pi:tʃ/ *vt* anklagen
impeccable /ɪm'pekəbl/ *a*, **-bly** *adv* tadellos
impede /ɪm'pi:d/ *vt* behindern
impediment /ɪm'pedɪmənt/ *n* Hindernis *nt*; (*in speech*) Sprachfehler *m*
impel /ɪm'pel/ *vt* (*pt/pp* **impelled**) treiben; **feel ~led** sich genötigt fühlen (**to** zu)
impending /ɪm'pendɪŋ/ *a* bevorstehend
impenetrable /ɪm'penɪtrəbl/ *a* undurchdringlich
imperative /ɪm'perətɪv/ *a* **be ~** dringend notwendig sein ● *n* (*Gram*) Imperativ *m*, Befehlsform *f*
imper'ceptible *a* nicht wahrnehmbar
im'perfect *a* unvollkommen; (*faulty*) fehlerhaft ● *n* (*Gram*) Imperfekt *nt*. **~ion** /-'fekʃn/ *n* Unvollkommenheit *f*; (*fault*) Fehler *m*
imperial /ɪm'pɪərɪəl/ *a* kaiserlich. **~ism** *n* Imperialismus *m*
imperil /ɪm'perəl/ *vt* (*pt/pp* **imperilled**) gefährden
imperious /ɪm'pɪərɪəs/ *a*, **-ly** *adv* herrisch
im'personal *a* unpersönlich
impersonat|e /ɪm'pɜ:səneɪt/ *vt* sich ausgeben als; (*Theat*) nachahmen, imitieren. **~or** *n* Imitator *m*
impertinen|ce /ɪm'pɜ:tɪnəns/ *n* Frechheit *f*. **~t** *a* frech
imperturbable /ɪmpə'tɜ:bəbl/ *a* unerschütterlich
impervious /ɪm'pɜ:vɪəs/ *a* **~ to** (*fig*) unempfänglich für

impetuous /ɪm'petjʊəs/ *a*, **-ly** *adv* ungestüm
impetus /'ɪmpɪtəs/ *n* Schwung *m*
impish /'ɪmpɪʃ/ *a* schelmisch
implacable /ɪm'plækəbl/ *a* unerbittlich
im'plant¹ *vt* einpflanzen
'implant² *n* Implantat *nt*
implement¹ /'ɪmplɪmənt/ *n* Gerät *nt*
implement² /'ɪmplɪment/ *vt* ausführen
implicat|e /'ɪmplɪkeɪt/ *vt* verwickeln. **~ion** /-'keɪʃn/ *n* Verwicklung *f*; **~ions** *pl* Auswirkungen *pl*; **by ~ion** implizit
implicit /ɪm'plɪsɪt/ *a*, **-ly** *adv* unausgesprochen; (*absolute*) unbedingt
implore /ɪm'plɔ:(r)/ *vt* anflehen
imply /ɪm'plaɪ/ *vt* (*pt*/*pp* **-ied**) andeuten; **what are you ~ing?** was wollen Sie damit sagen?
impo'lite *a*, **-ly** *adv* unhöflich
import¹ /'ɪmpɔ:t/ *n* Import *m*, Einfuhr *f*; (*importance*) Wichtigkeit *f*; (*meaning*) Bedeutung *f*
import² /ɪm'pɔ:t/ *vt* importieren, einführen
importan|ce /ɪm'pɔ:tns/ *n* Wichtigkeit *f*. **~t** *a* wichtig
importer /ɪm'pɔ:tə(r)/ *n* Importeur *m*
impos|e /ɪm'pəʊz/ *vt* auferlegen (**on** *dat*) ● *vi* sich aufdrängen (**on** *dat*). **~ing** *a* eindrucksvoll. **~ition** /ɪmpə'zɪʃn/ *n* **be an ~ition** eine Zumutung sein
impossi'bility *n* Unmöglichkeit *f*
im'possible *a*, **-bly** *adv* unmöglich
impostor /ɪm'pɒstə(r)/ *n* Betrüger(in) *m*(*f*)
impoten|ce /'ɪmpətəns/ *n* Machtlosigkeit *f*; (*Med*) Impotenz *f*. **~t** *a* machtlos; (*Med*) impotent
impound /ɪm'paʊnd/ *vt* beschlagnahmen
impoverished /ɪm'pɒvərɪʃt/ *a* verarmt
im'practicable *a* undurchführbar
im'practical *a* unpraktisch
impre'cise *a* ungenau
impregnable /ɪm'pregnəbl/ *a* uneinnehmbar
impregnate /'ɪmpregneɪt/ *vt* tränken; (*Biol*) befruchten
im'press *vt* beeindrucken; **~ sth [up]on s.o.** jdm etw einprägen
impression /ɪm'preʃn/ *n* Eindruck *m*; (*imitation*) Nachahmung *f*; (*imprint*) Abdruck *m*; (*edition*) Auflage *f*. **~ism** *n* Impressionismus *m*
impressive /ɪm'presɪv/ *a* eindrucksvoll
'imprint¹ *n* Abdruck *m*
im'print² *vt* prägen; (*fig*) einprägen (**on** *dat*)
im'prison *vt* gefangenhalten; (*put in prison*) ins Gefängnis sperren
im'probable *a* unwahrscheinlich
impromptu /ɪm'prɒmptju:/ *a* improvisiert ● *adv* aus dem Stegreif
im'proper *a*, **-ly** *adv* inkorrekt; (*indecent*) unanständig
impro'priety *n* Unkorrektheit *f*
improve /ɪm'pru:v/ *vt* verbessern; verschönern ⟨*appearance*⟩ ● *vi* sich bessern; **~ [up]on** übertreffen. **~ment** /-mənt/ *n* Verbesserung *f*; (*in health*) Besserung *f*
improvise /'ɪmprəvaɪz/ *vt*/*i* improvisieren
im'prudent *a* unklug
impuden|ce /'ɪmpjʊdəns/ *n* Frechheit *f*. **~t** *a*, **-ly** *adv* frech
impuls|e /'ɪmpʌls/ *n* Impuls *m*; **on [an] ~e** impulsiv. **~ive** /-'pʌlsɪv/ *a*, **-ly** *adv* impulsiv
impunity /ɪm'pju:nətɪ/ *n* **with ~** ungestraft
im'pur|e *a* unrein. **~ity** *n* Unreinheit *f*; **~ities** *pl* Verunreinigungen *pl*
impute /ɪm'pju:t/ *vt* zuschreiben (**to** *dat*)
in /ɪn/ *prep* in (+ *dat*/(*into*) + *acc*); **sit in the garden** im Garten sitzen; **go in the garden** in den Garten gehen; **in May** im Mai; **in the summer/winter** im Sommer/Winter; **in 1992** [im Jahre] 1992; **in this heat** bei dieser Hitze; **in the rain/sun** im Regen/in der Sonne; **in the evening** am Abend; **in the sky** am Himmel; **in the world** auf der Welt; **in the street** auf der Straße; **deaf in one ear** auf einem Ohr taub; **in the army** beim Militär; **in English/German** auf englisch/deutsch; **in ink/pencil** mit Tinte/Bleistift; **in a soft/loud voice** mit leiser/lauter Stimme; **in doing this, he ...** indem er das tut/tat, ... er ● *adv* (*at home*) zu Hause; (*indoors*) drinnen; **he's not in yet** er ist noch nicht da; **all in** alles inbegriffen; (*fam: exhausted*) kaputt; **day in, day out** tagaus, tagein; **keep in with s.o.** sich mit jdm gut stellen; **have it in for s.o.** (*fam*) es auf jdn abgesehen haben; **let oneself in for sth** sich auf etw (*acc*) einlassen; **send/go in** hineinschicken/-gehen; **come/bring**

in hereinkommen/-bringen ● *a* (*fam: in fashion*) in ● *n* **the ins and outs** alle Einzelheiten *pl*

ina'bility *n* Unfähigkeit *f*

inac'cessible *a* unzugänglich

in'accura|cy *n* Ungenauigkeit *f*. **~te** *a*, **-ly** *adv* ungenau

in'ac|tive *a* untätig. **~'tivity** *n* Untätigkeit *f*

in'adequate *a*, **-ly** *adv* unzulänglich; **feel ~** sich der Situation nicht gewachsen fühlen

inad'missible *a* unzulässig

inadvertently /ɪnəd'vɜ:təntlɪ/ *adv* versehentlich

inad'visable *a* nicht ratsam

inane /ɪ'neɪn/ *a*, **-ly** *adv* albern

in'animate *a* unbelebt

in'applicable *a* nicht zutreffend

inap'propriate *a* unangebracht

inar'ticulate *a* undeutlich; **be ~** sich nicht gut ausdrücken können

inat'tentive *a* unaufmerksam

in'audible *a*, **-bly** *adv* unhörbar

inaugural /ɪ'nɔ:gjʊrl/ *a* Antritts-

inaugurat|e /ɪ'nɔ:gjʊreɪt/ *vt* [feierlich] in sein Amt einführen. **~ion** /-'reɪʃn/ *n* Amtseinführung *f*

inau'spicious *a* ungünstig

inborn /'ɪnbɔ:n/ *a* angeboren

inbred /ɪn'bred/ *a* angeboren

incalculable /ɪn'kælkjʊləbl/ *a* nicht berechenbar; (*fig*) unabsehbar

in'capable *a* unfähig; **be ~ of doing sth** nicht fähig sein, etw zu tun

incapacitate /ɪnkə'pæsɪteɪt/ *vt* unfähig machen

incarcerate /ɪn'kɑ:səreɪt/ *vt* einkerkern

incarnat|e /ɪn'kɑ:nət/ *a* **the devil ~e** der leibhaftige Satan. **~ion** /-'neɪʃn/ *n* Inkarnation *f*

incendiary /ɪn'sendɪərɪ/ *a* & *n* **~ [bomb]** Brandbombe *f*

incense[1] /'ɪnsens/ *n* Weihrauch *m*

incense[2] /ɪn'sens/ *vt* wütend machen

incentive /ɪn'sentɪv/ *n* Anreiz *m*

inception /ɪn'sepʃn/ *n* Beginn *m*

incessant /ɪn'sesnt/ *a*, **-ly** *adv* unaufhörlich

incest /'ɪnsest/ *n* Inzest *m*, Blutschande *f*

inch /ɪntʃ/ *n* Zoll *m* ● *vi* **~ forward** sich ganz langsam vorwärtsschieben

inciden|ce /'ɪnsɪdəns/ *n* Vorkommen *nt*. **~t** *n* Zwischenfall *m*

incidental /ɪnsɪ'dentl/ *a* nebensächlich; ⟨*remark*⟩ beiläufig; ⟨*expenses*⟩ Neben-. **~ly** *adv* übrigens

incinerat|e /ɪn'sɪnəreɪt/ *vt* verbrennen. **~or** *n* Verbrennungsofen *m*

incipient /ɪn'sɪpɪənt/ *a* angehend

incision /ɪn'sɪʒn/ *n* Einschnitt *m*

incisive /ɪn'saɪsɪv/ *a* scharfsinnig

incisor /ɪn'saɪzə(r)/ *n* Schneidezahn *m*

incite /ɪn'saɪt/ *vt* aufhetzen. **~ment** *n* Aufhetzung *f*

inci'vility *n* Unhöflichkeit *f*

in'clement *a* rauh

inclination /ɪnklɪ'neɪʃn/ *n* Neigung *f*

incline[1] /ɪn'klaɪn/ *vt* neigen; **be ~d to do sth** dazu neigen, etw zu tun ● *vi* sich neigen

incline[2] /'ɪnklaɪn/ *n* Neigung *f*

inclu|de /ɪn'klu:d/ *vt* einschließen; (*contain*) enthalten; (*incorporate*) aufnehmen (**in** in + *acc*). **~ding** *prep* einschließlich (+ *gen*). **~sion** /-u:ʒn/ *n* Aufnahme *f*

inclusive /ɪn'klu:sɪv/ *a* Inklusiv ; **~ of** einschließlich (+ *gen*) ● *adv* inklusive

incognito /ɪnkɒg'ni:təʊ/ *adv* inkognito

inco'herent *a*, **-ly** *adv* zusammenhanglos; (*incomprehensible*) unverständlich

income /'ɪnkəm/ *n* Einkommen *nt*. **~ tax** *n* Einkommensteuer *f*

'incoming *a* ankommend; ⟨*mail, call*⟩ eingehend. **~ tide** *n* steigende Flut *f*

in'comparable *a* unvergleichlich

incom'patible *a* unvereinbar; **be ~** ⟨*people:*⟩ nicht zueinander passen

in'competen|ce *n* Unfähigkeit *f*. **~t** *a* unfähig

incom'plete *a* unvollständig

incompre'hensible *a* unverständlich

incon'ceivable *a* undenkbar

incon'clusive *a* nicht schlüssig

incongruous /ɪn'kɒŋgrʊəs/ *a* unpassend

inconsequential /ɪnkɒnsɪ'kwenʃl/ *a* unbedeutend

incon'siderate *a* rücksichtslos

incon'sistent *a*, **-ly** *adv* widersprüchlich; (*illogical*) inkonsequent; **be ~** nicht übereinstimmen

inconsolable /ɪnkən'səʊləbl/ *a* untröstlich

incon'spicuous *a* unauffällig

incontinen|ce /ɪn'kɒntɪnəns/ *n* Inkontinenz *f*. **~t** *a* inkontinent

incon'venien|ce *n* Unannehmlichkeit *f*; (*drawback*) Nachteil *m*; **put s.o. to ~ce** jdm Umstände machen. **~t** *a*, **-ly** *adv* ungünstig; **be ~t for s.o.** jdm nicht passen

incorporate /ɪn'kɔ:pəreɪt/ *vt* aufnehmen; (*contain*) enthalten

incor'rect *a*, **-ly** *adv* inkorrekt

incorrigible /ɪn'kɒrɪdʒəbl/ *a* unverbesserlich

incorruptible /ɪnkə'rʌptəbl/ *a* unbestechlich

increase[1] /'ɪnkri:s/ *n* Zunahme *f*; (*rise*) Erhöhung *f*; **be on the ~** zunehmen

increas|e[2] /ɪn'kri:s/ *vt* vergrößern; (*raise*) erhöhen ● *vi* zunehmen; (*rise*) sich erhöhen. **~ing** *a*, **-ly** *adv* zunehmend

in'credible *a*, **-bly** *adv* unglaublich

incredulous /ɪn'kredjʊləs/ *a* ungläubig

increment /'ɪnkrɪmənt/ *n* Gehaltszulage *f*

incriminate /ɪn'krɪmɪneɪt/ *vt* (*Jur*) belasten

incubat|e /'ɪŋkjʊbeɪt/ *vt* ausbrüten. **~ion** /-'beɪʃn/ *n* Ausbrüten *nt*. **~ion period** *n* (*Med*) Inkubationszeit *f*. **~or** *n* (*for baby*) Brutkasten *m*

inculcate /'ɪnkʌlkeɪt/ *vt* einprägen (**in** *dat*)

incumbent /ɪn'kʌmbənt/ *a* **be ~ on s.o.** jds Pflicht sein

incur /ɪn'kɜ:(r)/ *vt* (*pt*/*pp* **incurred**) sich (*dat*) zuziehen; machen ⟨*debts*⟩

in'curable *a*, **-bly** *adv* unheilbar

incursion /ɪn'kɜ:ʃn/ *n* Einfall *m*

indebted /ɪn'detɪd/ *a* verpflichtet (**to** *dat*)

in'decent *a*, **-ly** *adv* unanständig

inde'cision *n* Unentschlossenheit *f*

inde'cisive *a* ergebnislos; ⟨*person*⟩ unentschlossen

indeed /ɪn'di:d/ *adv* in der Tat, tatsächlich; **yes ~!** allerdings! **~ I am/do** oh doch! **very much ~** sehr; **thank you very much ~** vielen herzlichen Dank

indefatigable /ɪndɪ'fætɪgəbl/ *a* unermüdlich

in'definite *a* unbestimmt. **~ly** *adv* unbegrenzt; ⟨*postpone*⟩ auf unbestimmte Zeit

indelible /ɪn'delɪbl/ *a*, **-bly** *adv* nicht zu entfernen; (*fig*) unauslöschlich

indemni|fy /ɪn'demnɪfaɪ/ *vt* (*pt*/*pp* **-ied**) versichern; (*compensate*) entschädigen. **~ty** *n* Versicherung *f*; Entschädigung *f*

indent /ɪn'dent/ *vt* (*Typ*) einrücken. **~ation** /-'teɪʃn/ *n* Einrückung *f*; (*notch*) Kerbe *f*

inde'penden|ce *n* Unabhängigkeit *f*; (*self-reliance*) Selbständigkeit *f*. **~t** *a*, **-ly** *adv* unabhängig; selbständig

indescribable /ɪndɪ'skraɪbəbl/ *a*, **-bly** *adv* unbeschreiblich

indestructible /ɪndɪ'strʌktəbl/ *a* unzerstörbar

indeterminate /ɪndɪ'tɜ:mɪnət/ *a* unbestimmt

index /'ɪndeks/ *n* Register *nt*

index: ~ card *n* Karteikarte *f*. **~ finger** *n* Zeigefinger *m*. **~-linked** *a* ⟨*pension*⟩ dynamisch

India /'ɪndɪə/ *n* Indien *nt*. **~n** *a* indisch; (*American*) indianisch ● *n* Inder(in) *m*(*f*); (*American*) Indianer(in) *m*(*f*)

Indian: ~ 'ink *n* Tusche *f*. **~ 'summer** *n* Nachsommer *m*

indicat|e /'ɪndɪkeɪt/ *vt* zeigen; (*point at*) zeigen auf (+ *acc*); (*hint*) andeuten; (*register*) anzeigen ● *vi* (*Auto*) blinken. **~ion** /-'keɪʃn/ *n* Anzeichen *nt*

indicative /ɪn'dɪkətɪv/ *a* **be ~ of** schließen lassen auf (+ *acc*) ● *n* (*Gram*) Indikativ *m*

indicator /'ɪndɪkeɪtə(r)/ *n* (*Auto*) Blinker *m*

indict /ɪn'daɪt/ *vt* anklagen. **~ment** *n* Anklage *f*

in'differen|ce *n* Gleichgültigkeit *f*. **~t** *a*, **-ly** *adv* gleichgültig; (*not good*) mittelmäßig

indigenous /ɪn'dɪdʒɪnəs/ *a* einheimisch

indi'gest|ible *a* unverdaulich; (*difficult to digest*) schwerverdaulich. **~ion** *n* Magenverstimmung *f*

indigna|nt /ɪn'dɪgnənt/ *a*, **-ly** *adv* entrüstet, empört. **~tion** /-'neɪʃn/ *n* Entrüstung *f*, Empörung *f*

in'dignity *n* Demütigung *f*

indi'rect *a*, **-ly** *adv* indirekt

indi'screet *a* indiskret

indis'cretion *n* Indiskretion *f*

indiscriminate /ɪndɪ'skrɪmɪnət/ *a*, **-ly** *adv* wahllos

indi'spensable *a* unentbehrlich

indisposed /ɪndɪ'spəʊzd/ *a* indisponiert

indisputable /ɪndɪ'spju:təbl/ *a*, **-bly** *adv* unbestreitbar

indi'stinct *a*, **-ly** *adv* undeutlich

indistinguishable /ɪndɪ'stɪŋgwɪʃəbl/ *a* **be ~** nicht zu unterscheiden sein; (*not visible*) nicht erkennbar sein

individual /ɪndɪ'vɪdjʊəl/ *a*, **-ly** *adv* individuell; (*single*) einzeln ● *n* Individuum *nt.* **~ity** /-'ælətɪ/ *n* Individualität *f*

indi'visible *a* unteilbar

indoctrinate /ɪn'dɒktrɪneɪt/ *vt* indoktrinieren

indolen|ce /'ɪndələns/ *n* Faulheit *f.* **~t** *a* faul

indomitable /ɪn'dɒmɪtəbl/ *a* unbeugsam

indoor /'ɪndɔ:(r)/ *a* Innen-; ⟨*clothes*⟩ Haus-; ⟨*plant*⟩ Zimmer-; (*Sport*) Hallen-. **~s** /-'dɔ:z/ *adv* im Haus, drinnen; **go ~s** ins Haus gehen

induce /ɪn'dju:s/ *vt* dazu bewegen (**to** zu); (*produce*) herbeiführen. **~ment** *n* (*incentive*) Anreiz *m*

indulge /ɪn'dʌldʒ/ *vt* frönen (+ *dat*); verwöhnen ⟨*child*⟩ ● *vi* **~ in** frönen (+ *dat*). **~nce** /-əns/ *n* Nachgiebigkeit *f*; (*leniency*) Nachsicht *f.* **~nt** *a* [zu] nachgiebig; nachsichtig

industrial /ɪn'dʌstrɪəl/ *a* Industrie-; **take ~ action** streiken. **~ist** *n* Industrielle(r) *m.* **~ized** *a* industrialisiert

industr|ious /ɪn'dʌstrɪəs/ *a*, **-ly** *adv* fleißig. **~y** /'ɪndəstrɪ/ *n* Industrie *f*; (*zeal*) Fleiß *m*

inebriated /ɪ'ni:brɪeɪtɪd/ *a* betrunken

in'edible *a* nicht eßbar

inef'fective *a*, **-ly** *adv* unwirksam; ⟨*person*⟩ untauglich

inef'fectual /ɪnɪ'fektʃʊəl/ *a* unwirksam; ⟨*person*⟩ untauglich

inef'ficient *a* unfähig; ⟨*organization*⟩ nicht leistungsfähig; ⟨*method*⟩ nicht rationell

in'eligible *a* nicht berechtigt

inept /ɪ'nept/ *a* ungeschickt

ine'quality *n* Ungleichheit *f*

inert /ɪ'nɜ:t/ *a* unbeweglich; (*Phys*) träge. **~ia** /ɪ'nɜ:ʃə/ *n* Trägheit *f*

inescapable /ɪnɪ'skeɪpəbl/ *a* unvermeidlich

inestimable /ɪn'estɪməbl/ *a* unschätzbar

inevitab|le /ɪn'evɪtəbl/ *a* unvermeidlich. **~ly** *adv* zwangsläufig

ine'xact *a* ungenau

inex'cusable *a* unverzeihlich

inexhaustible /ɪnɪg'zɔ:stəbl/ *a* unerschöpflich

inexorable /ɪn'eksərəbl/ *a* unerbittlich

inex'pensive *a*, **-ly** *adv* preiswert

inex'perience *n* Unerfahrenheit *f.* **~d** *a* unerfahren

inexplicable /ɪnɪk'splɪkəbl/ *a* unerklärlich

in'fallible *a* unfehlbar

infam|ous /'ɪnfəməs/ *a* niederträchtig; (*notorious*) berüchtigt. **~y** *n* Niederträchtigkeit *f*

infan|cy /'ɪnfənsɪ/ *n* frühe Kindheit *f*; (*fig*) Anfangsstadium *nt.* **~t** *n* Kleinkind *nt.* **~tile** *a* kindisch

infantry /'ɪnfəntrɪ/ *n* Infanterie *f*

infatuated /ɪn'fætʃʊeɪtɪd/ *a* vernarrt (**with** in + *acc*)

infect /ɪn'fekt/ *vt* anstecken, infizieren; **become ~ed** ⟨*wound*:⟩ sich infizieren. **~ion** /-'fekʃn/ *n* Infektion *f.* **~ious** /-'fekʃəs/ *a* ansteckend

infer /ɪn'fɜ:(r)/ *vt* (*pt*/*pp* **inferred**) folgern (**from** aus); (*imply*) andeuten. **~ence** /'ɪnfərəns/ *n* Folgerung *f*

inferior /ɪn'fɪərɪə(r)/ *a* minderwertig; (*in rank*) untergeordnet ● *n* Untergebene(r) *m*/*f*

inferiority /ɪnfɪərɪ'ɒrətɪ/ *n* Minderwertigkeit *f.* **~ complex** *n* Minderwertigkeitskomplex *m*

infern|al /ɪn'fɜ:nl/ *a* höllisch. **~o** *n* flammendes Inferno *nt*

in'fer|tile *a* unfruchtbar. **~'tility** *n* Unfruchtbarkeit *f*

infest /ɪn'fest/ *vt* **be ~ed with** befallen sein von; ⟨*place*⟩ verseucht sein mit

infi'delity *n* Untreue *f*

infighting /'ɪnfaɪtɪŋ/ *n* (*fig*) interne Machtkämpfe *pl*

infiltrate /'ɪnfɪltreɪt/ *vt* infiltrieren; (*Pol*) unterwandern

infinite /'ɪnfɪnət/ *a*, **-ly** *adv* unendlich

infinitesimal /ɪnfɪnɪ'tesɪml/ *a* unendlich klein

infinitive /ɪn'fɪnətɪv/ *n* (*Gram*) Infinitiv *m*

infinity /ɪn'fɪnətɪ/ *n* Unendlichkeit *f*

infirm /ɪn'fɜ:m/ *a* gebrechlich. **~ary** *n* Krankenhaus *nt.* **~ity** *n* Gebrechlichkeit *f*

inflame /ɪn'fleɪm/ *vt* entzünden; **become ~d** sich entzünden. **~d** *a* entzündet

in'flammable *a* feuergefährlich

inflammation /ɪnflə'meɪʃn/ *n* Entzündung *f*

inflammatory /ɪn'flæmətrɪ/ *a* aufrührerisch
inflatable /ɪn'fleɪtəbl/ *a* aufblasbar
inflat|e /ɪn'fleɪt/ *vt* aufblasen; (*with pump*) aufpumpen. **~ion** /-eɪʃn/ *n* Inflation *f*. **~ionary** /-eɪʃənərɪ/ *a* inflationär
in'flexible *a* starr; ⟨*person*⟩ unbeugsam
inflexion /ɪn'flekʃn/ *n* Tonfall *m*; (*Gram*) Flexion *f*
inflict /ɪn'flɪkt/ *vt* zufügen (**on** *dat*); versetzen ⟨*blow*⟩ (**on** *dat*)
influen|ce /'ɪnflʊəns/ *n* Einfluß *m* ● *vt* beeinflussen. **~tial** /-'enʃl/ *a* einflußreich
influenza /ɪnflʊ'enzə/ *n* Grippe *f*
influx /'ɪnflʌks/ *n* Zustrom *m*
inform /ɪn'fɔ:m/ *vt* benachrichtigen; (*officially*) informieren; **~ s.o. of sth** jdm etw mitteilen; **keep s.o. ~ed** jdn auf dem laufenden halten ● *vi* **~ against** denunzieren
in'for|mal *a*, **-ly** *adv* zwanglos; (*unofficial*) inoffiziell. **~'mality** *n* Zwanglosigkeit *f*
informant /ɪn'fɔ:mənt/ *n* Gewährsmann *m*
informat|ion /ɪnfə'meɪʃn/ *n* Auskunft *f*; **a piece of ~ion** eine Auskunft. **~ive** /ɪn'fɔ:mətɪv/ *a* aufschlußreich; (*instructive*) lehrreich
informer /ɪn'fɔ:mə(r)/ *n* Spitzel *m*; (*Pol*) Denunziant *m*
infra-'red /ɪnfrə-/ *a* infrarot
in'frequent *a*, **-ly** *adv* selten
infringe /ɪn'frɪndʒ/ *vt/i* **~ [on]** verstoßen gegen. **~ment** *n* Verstoß *m*
infuriat|e /ɪn'fjʊərɪeɪt/ *vt* wütend machen. **~ing** *a* ärgerlich; **he is ~ing** er kann einen zur Raserei bringen
infusion /ɪn'fju:ʒn/ *n* Aufguß *m*
ingenious /ɪn'dʒi:nɪəs/ *a* erfinderisch; ⟨*thing*⟩ raffiniert
ingenuity /ɪndʒɪ'nju:ətɪ/ *n* Geschicklichkeit *f*
ingenuous /ɪn'dʒenjʊəs/ *a* unschuldig
ingot /'ɪŋgət/ *n* Barren *m*
ingrained /ɪn'greɪnd/ *a* eingefleischt; **be ~** ⟨*dirt:*⟩ tief sitzen
ingratiate /ɪn'greɪʃɪeɪt/ *vt* **~ oneself** sich einschmeicheln (**with** bei)
in'gratitude *n* Undankbarkeit *f*
ingredient /ɪn'gri:dɪənt/ *n* (*Culin*) Zutat *f*
ingrowing /'ɪngrəʊɪŋ/ *a* ⟨*nail*⟩ eingewachsen
inhabit /ɪn'hæbɪt/ *vt* bewohnen. **~ant** *n* Einwohner(in) *m(f)*
inhale /ɪn'heɪl/ *vt/i* einatmen; (*Med & when smoking*) inhalieren
inherent /ɪn'hɪərənt/ *a* natürlich
inherit /ɪn'herɪt/ *vt* erben. **~ance** /-əns/ *n* Erbschaft *f*, Erbe *nt*
inhibit /ɪn'hɪbɪt/ *vt* hemmen. **~ed** *a* gehemmt. **~ion** /-'bɪʃn/ *n* Hemmung *f*
inho'spitable *a* ungastlich
in'human *a* unmenschlich
inimitable /ɪ'nɪmɪtəbl/ *a* unnachahmlich
iniquitous /ɪ'nɪkwɪtəs/ *a* schändlich; (*unjust*) ungerecht
initial /ɪ'nɪʃl/ *a* anfänglich, Anfangs- ● *n* Anfangsbuchstabe *m*; **my ~s** meine Initialen ● *vt* (*pt/pp* **initialled**) abzeichnen; (*Pol*) paraphieren. **~ly** *adv* anfangs, am Anfang
initiat|e /ɪ'nɪʃɪeɪt/ *vt* einführen. **~ion** /-'eɪʃn/ *n* Einführung *f*
initiative /ɪ'nɪʃətɪv/ *n* Initiative *f*
inject /ɪn'dʒekt/ *vt* einspritzen, injizieren. **~ion** /-ekʃn/ *n* Spritze *f*, Injektion *f*
injunction /ɪn'dʒʌŋkʃn/ *n* gerichtliche Verfügung *f*
injur|e /'ɪndʒə(r)/ *vt* verletzen. **~y** *n* Verletzung *f*
in'justice *n* Ungerechtigkeit *f*; **do s.o. an ~** jdm unrecht tun
ink /ɪŋk/ *n* Tinte *f*
inkling /'ɪŋklɪŋ/ *n* Ahnung *f*
inlaid /ɪn'leɪd/ *a* eingelegt
inland /'ɪnlənd/ *a* Binnen- ● *adv* landeinwärts. **I~ Revenue** *n* ≈ Finanzamt *nt*
in-laws /'ɪnlɔ:z/ *npl* (*fam*) Schwiegereltern *pl*
inlay /'ɪnleɪ/ *n* Einlegearbeit *f*
inlet /'ɪnlet/ *n* schmale Bucht *f*; (*Techn*) Zuleitung *f*
inmate /'ɪnmeɪt/ *n* Insasse *m*
inn /ɪn/ *n* Gasthaus *nt*
innards /'ɪnədz/ *npl* (*fam*) Eingeweide *pl*
innate /ɪ'neɪt/ *a* angeboren
inner /'ɪnə(r)/ *a* innere(r,s). **~most** *a* innerste(r,s)
'innkeeper *n* Gastwirt *m*
innocen|ce /'ɪnəsəns/ *n* Unschuld *f*. **~t** *a* unschuldig. **~tly** *adv* in aller Unschuld
innocuous /ɪ'nɒkjʊəs/ *a* harmlos
innovat|e /'ɪnəveɪt/ *vi* neu einführen. **~ion** /-'veɪʃn/ *n* Neuerung *f*. **~or** *n* Neuerer *m*

innuendo /ɪnju:'endəʊ/ *n* (*pl* **-es**) [versteckte] Anspielung *f*
innumerable /ɪ'nju:mərəbl/ *a* unzählig
inoculat|e /ɪ'nɒkjʊleɪt/ *vt* impfen. **~ion** /-'leɪʃn/ *n* Impfung *f*
inof'fensive *a* harmlos
in'operable *a* nicht operierbar
in'opportune *a* unpassend
inordinate /ɪ'nɔ:dɪnət/ *a*, **-ly** *adv* übermäßig
inor'ganic *a* anorganisch
'in-patient *n* [stationär behandelter] Krankenhauspatient *m*
input /'ɪnpʊt/ *n* Input *m* & *nt*
inquest /'ɪnkwest/ *n* gerichtliche Untersuchung *f*
inquir|e /ɪn'kwaɪə(r)/ *vi* sich erkundigen (**about** nach); **~e into** untersuchen • *vt* sich erkundigen nach. **~y** *n* Erkundigung *f*; (*investigation*) Untersuchung *f*
inquisitive /ɪn'kwɪzətɪv/ *a*, **-ly** *adv* neugierig
inroad /'ɪnrəʊd/ *n* Einfall *m*; **make ~s into sth** etw angreifen
in'sane *a* geisteskrank; (*fig*) wahnsinnig
in'sanitary *a* unhygienisch
in'sanity *n* Geisteskrankheit *f*
insatiable /ɪn'seɪʃəbl/ *a* unersättlich
inscri|be /ɪn'skraɪb/ *vt* eingravieren. **~ption** /-'skrɪpʃn/ *n* Inschrift *f*
inscrutable /ɪn'skru:təbl/ *a* unergründlich; ⟨*expression*⟩ undurchdringlich
insect /'ɪnsekt/ *n* Insekt *nt*. **~icide** /-'sektɪsaɪd/ *n* Insektenvertilgungsmittel *nt*
inse'cur|e *a* nicht sicher; (*fig*) unsicher. **~ity** *n* Unsicherheit *f*
insemination /ɪnsemɪ'neɪʃn/ *n* Besamung *f*; (*Med*) Befruchtung *f*
in'sensible *a* (*unconscious*) bewußtlos
in'sensitive *a* gefühllos; **~ to** unempfindlich gegen
in'separable *a* untrennbar; (*people*) unzertrennlich
insert[1] /'ɪnsɜ:t/ *n* Einsatz *m*
insert[2] /ɪn'sɜ:t/ *vt* einfügen, einsetzen; einstecken ⟨*key*⟩; einwerfen ⟨*coin*⟩. **~ion** /-ɜ:ʃn/ *n* (*insert*) Einsatz *m*; (*in text*) Einfügung *f*
inside /ɪn'saɪd/ *n* Innenseite *f*; (*of house*) Innere(s) *nt* • *attrib* Innen- • *adv* innen; (*indoors*) drinnen; **go ~** hineingehen; **come ~** hereinkommen; **~ out** links [herum]; **know sth ~ out** etw in- und auswendig kennen • *prep* **~ [of]** in (+ *dat*/(*into*) + *acc*)
insidious /ɪn'sɪdɪəs/ *a*, **-ly** *adv* heimtückisch
insight /'ɪnsaɪt/ *n* Einblick *m* (**into** in + *acc*); (*understanding*) Einsicht *f*
insignia /ɪn'sɪgnɪə/ *npl* Insignien *pl*
insig'nificant *a* unbedeutend
insin'cere *a* unaufrichtig
insinuat|e /ɪn'sɪnjʊeɪt/ *vt* andeuten. **~ion** /-'eɪʃn/ *n* Andeutung *f*
insipid /ɪn'sɪpɪd/ *a* fade
insist /ɪn'sɪst/ *vi* darauf bestehen; **~ on** bestehen auf (+ *dat*) • *vt* **~ that** darauf bestehen, daß. **~ence** *n* Bestehen *nt*. **~ent** *a*, **-ly** *adv* beharrlich; **be ~ent** darauf bestehen
'insole *n* Einlegesohle *f*
insolen|ce /'ɪnsələns/ *n* Unverschämtheit *f*. **~t** *a*, **-ly** *adv* unverschämt
in'soluble *a* unlöslich; (*fig*) unlösbar
in'solvent *a* zahlungsunfähig
insomnia /ɪn'sɒmnɪə/ *n* Schlaflosigkeit *f*
inspect /ɪn'spekt/ *vt* inspizieren; (*test*) prüfen; kontrollieren ⟨*ticket*⟩. **~ion** /-ekʃn/ *n* Inspektion *f*. **~or** *n* Inspektor *m*; (*of tickets*) Kontrolleur *m*
inspiration /ɪnspə'reɪʃn/ *n* Inspiration *f*
inspire /ɪn'spaɪə(r)/ *vt* inspirieren; **~ sth in s.o.** jdm etw einflößen
insta'bility *n* Unbeständigkeit *f*; (*of person*) Labilität *f*
install /ɪn'stɔ:l/ *vt* installieren; [in ein Amt] einführen ⟨*person*⟩. **~ation** /-stə'leɪʃn/ *n* Installation *f*; Amtseinführung *f*
instalment /ɪn'stɔ:lmənt/ *n* (*Comm*) Rate *f*; (*of serial*) Fortsetzung *f*; (*Radio, TV*) Folge *f*
instance /'ɪnstəns/ *n* Fall *m*; (*example*) Beispiel *nt*; **in the first ~** zunächst; **for ~** zum Beispiel
instant /'ɪnstənt/ *a* sofortig; (*Culin*) Instant- • *n* Augenblick *m*, Moment *m*. **~aneous** /-'teɪnɪəs/ *a* unverzüglich, unmittelbar; **death was ~aneous** der Tod trat sofort ein
instant 'coffee *n* Pulverkaffee *m*
instantly /'ɪnstəntlɪ/ *adv* sofort
instead /ɪn'sted/ *adv* statt dessen; **~ of** statt (+ *gen*), anstelle von; **~ of me** an meiner Stelle; **~ of going** anstatt zu gehen
'instep *n* Spann *m*, Rist *m*
instigat|e /'ɪnstɪgeɪt/ *vt* anstiften; einleiten ⟨*proceedings*⟩. **~ion** /-'geɪʃn/ *n*

Anstiftung *f*; **at his ~ion** auf seine Veranlassung. **~or** *n* Anstifter(in) *m(f)*

instil /ɪn'stɪl/ *vt* (*pt/pp* **instilled**) einprägen (**into s.o.** jdm)

instinct /'ɪnstɪŋkt/ *n* Instinkt *m*. **~ive** /ɪn'stɪŋktɪv/ *a*, **-ly** *adv* instinktiv

institut|e /'ɪnstɪtju:t/ *n* Institut *nt* ● *vt* einführen; einleiten ⟨*search*⟩. **~ion** /-'tju:ʃn/ *n* Institution *f*; (*home*) Anstalt *f*

instruct /ɪn'strʌkt/ *vt* unterrichten; (*order*) anweisen. **~ion** /-ʌkʃn/ *n* Unterricht *m*; Anweisung *f*; **~ions** *pl* **for use** Gebrauchsanweisung *f*. **~ive** /-ɪv/ *a* lehrreich. **~or** *n* Lehrer(in) *m(f)*; (*Mil*) Ausbilder *m*

instrument /'ɪnstrʊmənt/ *n* Instrument *nt*. **~al** /-'mentl/ *a* Instrumental-; **be ~al in** eine entscheidende Rolle spielen bei

insu'bordi|nate *a* ungehorsam. **~nation** /-'neɪʃn/ *n* Ungehorsam *m*; (*Mil*) Insubordination *f*

in'sufferable *a* unerträglich

insuf'ficient *a*, **-ly** *adv* nicht genügend

insular /'ɪnsjʊlə(r)/ *a* (*fig*) engstirnig

insulat|e /'ɪnsjʊleɪt/ *vt* isolieren. **~ing tape** *n* Isolierband *nt*. **~ion** /-'leɪʃn/ *n* Isolierung *f*

insulin /'ɪnsjʊlɪn/ *n* Insulin *nt*

insult¹ /'ɪnsʌlt/ *n* Beleidigung *f*

insult² /ɪn'sʌlt/ *vt* beleidigen

insuperable /ɪn'su:pərəbl/ *a* unüberwindlich

insur|ance /ɪn'ʃʊərəns/ *n* Versicherung *f*. **~e** *vt* versichern

insurrection /ɪnsə'rekʃn/ *n* Aufstand *m*

intact /ɪn'tækt/ *a* unbeschädigt; (*complete*) vollständig

'intake *n* Aufnahme *f*

in'tangible *a* nicht greifbar

integral /'ɪntɪgrl/ *a* wesentlich

integrat|e /'ɪntɪgreɪt/ *vt* integrieren ● *vi* sich integrieren. **~ion** /-'greɪʃn/ *n* Integration *f*

integrity /ɪn'tegrətɪ/ *n* Integrität *f*

intellect /'ɪntəlekt/ *n* Intellekt *m*. **~ual** /-'lektjʊəl/ *a* intellektuell

intelligen|ce /ɪn'telɪdʒəns/ *n* Intelligenz *f*; (*Mil*) Nachrichtendienst *m*; (*information*) Meldungen *pl*. **~t** *a*, **-ly** *adv* intelligent

intelligentsia /ɪntelɪ'dʒentsɪə/ *n* Intelligenz *f*

intelligible /ɪn'telɪdʒəbl/ *a* verständlich

intend /ɪn'tend/ *vt* beabsichtigen; **be ~ed for** bestimmt sein für

intense /ɪn'tens/ *a* intensiv; ⟨*pain*⟩ stark. **~ly** *adv* äußerst; ⟨*study*⟩ intensiv

intensi|fication /ɪntensɪfɪ'keɪʃn/ *n* Intensivierung *f*. **~fy** /-'tensɪfaɪ/ *v* (*pt/pp* **-ied**) ● *vt* intensivieren ● *vi* zunehmen

intensity /ɪn'tensətɪ/ *n* Intensität *f*

intensive /ɪn'tensɪv/ *a*, **-ly** *adv* intensiv; **be in ~ care** auf der Intensivstation sein

intent /ɪn'tent/ *a*, **-ly** *adv* aufmerksam; **~ on** (*absorbed in*) vertieft in (+ *acc*); **be ~ on doing sth** fest entschlossen sein, etw zu tun ● *n* Absicht *f*; **to all ~s and purposes** im Grunde

intention /ɪn'tenʃn/ *n* Absicht *f*. **~al** *a*, **-ly** *adv* absichtlich

inter /ɪn'tɜ:(r)/ *vt* (*pt/pp* **interred**) bestatten

inter'action *n* Wechselwirkung *f*

intercede /ɪntə'si:d/ *vi* Fürsprache einlegen (**on behalf of** für)

intercept /ɪntə'sept/ *vt* abfangen

'interchange¹ *n* Austausch *m*; (*Auto*) Autobahnkreuz *nt*

inter'change² *vt* austauschen. **~able** *a* austauschbar

intercom /'ɪntəkɒm/ *n* [Gegen]sprechanlage *f*

'intercourse *n* Verkehr *m*; (*sexual*) Geschlechtsverkehr *m*

interest /'ɪntrəst/ *n* Interesse *nt*; (*Comm*) Zinsen *pl*; **have an ~** (*Comm*) beteiligt sein (**in** an + *dat*) ● *vt* interessieren; **be ~ed** sich interessieren (**in** für). **~ing** *a* interessant. **~ rate** *n* Zinssatz *m*

interfere /ɪntə'fɪə(r)/ *vi* sich einmischen. **~nce** /-əns/ *n* Einmischung *f*; (*Radio, TV*) Störung *f*

interim /'ɪntərɪm/ *a* Zwischen-; (*temporary*) vorläufig ● *n* **in the ~** in der Zwischenzeit

interior /ɪn'tɪərɪə(r)/ *a* innere(r,s), Innen- ● *n* Innere(s) *nt*

interject /ɪntə'dʒekt/ *vt* einwerfen. **~ion** /-ekʃn/ *n* Interjektion *f*; (*remark*) Einwurf *m*

inter'lock *vi* ineinandergreifen

interloper /'ɪntələʊpə(r)/ *n* Eindringling *m*

interlude /'ɪntəlu:d/ *n* Pause *f*; (*performance*) Zwischenspiel *nt*

inter'marry *vi* untereinander heiraten; ⟨*different groups:*⟩ Mischehen schließen

intermediary /ɪntə'mi:dɪərɪ/ *n* Vermittler(in) *m(f)*

intermediate /ɪntə'mi:dɪət/ *a* Zwischen-

interminable /ɪn'tɜ:mɪnəbl/ *a* endlos [lang]

intermission /ɪntə'mɪʃn/ *n* Pause *f*

intermittent /ɪntə'mɪtənt/ *a* in Abständen auftretend

intern /ɪn'tɜ:n/ *vt* internieren

internal /ɪn'tɜ:nl/ *a* innere(r,s); ⟨*matter, dispute*⟩ intern. **~ly** *adv* innerlich; ⟨*deal with*⟩ intern

inter'national *a*, **-ly** *adv* international ● *n* Länderspiel *nt*; (*player*) Nationalspieler(in) *m(f)*

internist /ɪn'tɜ:nɪst/ *n* (*Amer*) Internist *m*

internment /ɪn'tɜ:nmənt/ *n* Internierung *f*

'interplay *n* Wechselspiel *nt*

interpolate /ɪn'tɜ:pəleɪt/ *vt* einwerfen

interpret /ɪn'tɜ:prɪt/ *vt* interpretieren; auslegen ⟨*text*⟩; deuten ⟨*dream*⟩; (*translate*) dolmetschen ● *vi* dolmetschen. **~ation** /-'teɪʃn/ *n* Interpretation *f*. **~er** *n* Dolmetscher(in) *m(f)*

interre'lated *a* verwandt; ⟨*facts*⟩ zusammenhängend

interrogat|e /ɪn'terəgeɪt/ *vt* verhören. **~ion** /-'geɪʃn/ *n* Verhör *nt*

interrogative /ɪntə'rɒgətɪv/ *a & n* **~ [pronoun]** Interrogativpronomen *nt*

interrupt /ɪntə'rʌpt/ *vt/i* unterbrechen; **don't ~!** red nicht dazwischen! **~ion** /-ʌpʃn/ *n* Unterbrechung *f*

intersect /ɪntə'sekt/ *vi* sich kreuzen; (*Geom*) sich schneiden. **~ion** /-ekʃn/ *n* Kreuzung *f*

interspersed /ɪntə'spɜ:st/ *a* **~ with** durchsetzt mit

inter'twine *vi* sich ineinanderschlingen

interval /'ɪntəvl/ *n* Abstand *m*; (*Theat*) Pause *f*; (*Mus*) Intervall *nt*; **at hourly ~s** alle Stunde; **bright ~s** *pl* Aufheiterungen *pl*

interven|e /ɪntə'vi:n/ *vi* eingreifen; (*occur*) dazwischenkommen. **~tion** /-'venʃn/ *n* Eingreifen *nt*; (*Mil, Pol*) Intervention *f*

interview /'ɪntəvju:/ *n* (*Journ*) Interview *nt*; (*for job*) Vorstellungsgespräch *nt*; **go for an ~** sich vorstellen ● *vt* interviewen; ein Vorstellungsgespräch führen mit. **~er** *n* Interviewer(in) *m(f)*

intestine /ɪn'testɪn/ *n* Darm *m*

intimacy /'ɪntɪməsɪ/ *n* Vertrautheit *f*; (*sexual*) Intimität *f*

intimate¹ /'ɪntɪmət/ *a*, **-ly** *adv* vertraut; ⟨*friend*⟩ eng; (*sexually*) intim

intimate² /'ɪntɪmeɪt/ *vt* zu verstehen geben; (*imply*) andeuten

intimidat|e /ɪn'tɪmɪdeɪt/ *vt* einschüchtern. **~ion** /-'deɪʃn/ *n* Einschüchterung *f*

into /'ɪntə, *vor einem Vokal* 'ɪntʊ/ *prep* in (+ *acc*); **go ~ the house** ins Haus [hinein]gehen; **be ~** (*fam*) sich auskennen mit; **7 ~ 21** 21 [geteilt] durch 7

in'tolerable *a* unerträglich

in'toleran|ce *n* Intoleranz *f*. **~t** *a* intolerant

intonation /ɪntə'neɪʃn/ *n* Tonfall *m*

intoxicat|ed /ɪn'tɒksɪkeɪtɪd/ *a* betrunken; (*fig*) berauscht. **~ion** /-'keɪʃn/ *n* Rausch *m*

intractable /ɪn'træktəbl/ *a* widerspenstig; ⟨*problem*⟩ hartnäckig

intransigent /ɪn'trænsɪdʒənt/ *a* unnachgiebig

in'transitive *a*, **-ly** *adv* intransitiv

intravenous /ɪntrə'vi:nəs/ *a*, **-ly** *adv* intravenös

intrepid /ɪn'trepɪd/ *a* kühn, unerschrocken

intricate /'ɪntrɪkət/ *a* kompliziert

intrigu|e /ɪn'tri:g/ *n* Intrige *f* ● *vt* faszinieren ● *vi* intrigieren. **~ing** *a* faszinierend

intrinsic /ɪn'trɪnsɪk/ *a* **~ value** Eigenwert *m*

introduce /ɪntrə'dju:s/ *vt* vorstellen; (*bring in, insert*) einführen

introduct|ion /ɪntrə'dʌkʃn/ *n* Einführung *f*; (*to person*) Vorstellung *f*; (*to book*) Einleitung *f*. **~ory** /-tərɪ/ *a* einleitend

introspective /ɪntrə'spektɪv/ *a* in sich (*acc*) gerichtet

introvert /'ɪntrəvɜ:t/ *n* introvertierter Mensch *m*

intru|de /ɪn'tru:d/ *vi* stören. **~der** *n* Eindringling *m*. **~sion** /-u:ʒn/ *n* Störung *f*

intuit|ion /ɪntju:'ɪʃn/ *n* Intuition *f*. **~ive** /-'tju:ɪtɪv/ *a*, **-ly** *adv* intuitiv

inundate /'ɪnəndeɪt/ *vt* überschwemmen

invade /ɪn'veɪd/ *vt* einfallen in (+ *acc*). **~r** *n* Angreifer *m*

invalid¹ /'ɪnvəlɪd/ *n* Kranke(r) *m/f*

invalid² /ɪn'vælɪd/ *a* ungültig. **~ate** *vt* ungültig machen

in'valuable *a* unschätzbar; ⟨*person*⟩ unersetzlich

in'variab|le *a* unveränderlich. **~ly** *adv* immer

invasion /ɪn'veɪʒn/ *n* Invasion *f*

invective /ɪn'vektɪv/ *n* Beschimpfungen *pl*

invent /ɪn'vent/ *vt* erfinden. **~ion** /-enʃn/ *n* Erfindung *f*. **~ive** /-tɪv/ *a* erfinderisch. **~or** *n* Erfinder *m*

inventory /'ɪnvəntrɪ/ *n* Bestandsliste *f*; **make an ~** ein Inventar aufstellen

inverse /ɪn'vɜːs/ *a*, **-ly** *adv* umgekehrt ● *n* Gegenteil *nt*

invert /ɪn'vɜːt/ *vt* umkehren. **~ed commas** *npl* Anführungszeichen *pl*

invest /ɪn'vest/ *vt* investieren, anlegen; **~ in** (*fam: buy*) sich (*dat*) zulegen

investigat|e /ɪn'vestɪgeɪt/ *vt* untersuchen. **~ion** /-'geɪʃn/ *n* Untersuchung *f*

invest|ment /ɪn'vestmənt/ *n* Anlage *f*; **be a good ~ment** (*fig*) sich bezahlt machen. **~or** *n* Kapitalanleger *m*

inveterate /ɪn'vetərət/ *a* Gewohnheits-; ⟨*liar*⟩ unverbesserlich

invidious /ɪn'vɪdɪəs/ *a* unerfreulich; (*unfair*) ungerecht

invigilate /ɪn'vɪdʒɪleɪt/ *vi* (*Sch*) Aufsicht führen

invigorate /ɪn'vɪgəreɪt/ *vt* beleben

invincible /ɪn'vɪnsəbl/ *a* unbesiegbar

inviolable /ɪn'vaɪələbl/ *a* unantastbar

in'visible *a* unsichtbar. **~ mending** *n* Kunststopfen *nt*

invitation /ɪnvɪ'teɪʃn/ *n* Einladung *f*

invit|e /ɪn'vaɪt/ *vt* einladen. **~ing** *a* einladend

invoice /'ɪnvɔɪs/ *n* Rechnung *f* ● *vt* **~ s.o.** jdm eine Rechnung schicken

invoke /ɪn'vəʊk/ *vt* anrufen

in'voluntary *a*, **-ily** *adv* unwillkürlich

involve /ɪn'vɒlv/ *vt* beteiligen; (*affect*) betreffen; (*implicate*) verwickeln; (*entail*) mit sich bringen; (*mean*) bedeuten; **be ~d in** beteiligt sein an (+ *dat*); (*implicated*) verwickelt sein in (+ *acc*); **get ~d with s.o.** sich mit jdm einlassen. **~d** *a* kompliziert

in'vulnerable *a* unverwundbar; ⟨*position*⟩ unangreifbar

inward /'ɪnwəd/ *a* innere(r,s). **~ly** *adv* innerlich. **~s** *adv* nach innen

iodine /'aɪədiːn/ *n* Jod *nt*

iota /aɪ'əʊtə/ *n* Jota *nt*; (*fam*) Funke *m*

IOU *abbr* (**I owe you**) Schuldschein *m*

Iran /ɪ'rɑːn/ *n* der Iran

Iraq /ɪ'rɑːk/ *n* der Irak

irascible /ɪ'ræsəbl/ *a* aufbrausend

irate /aɪ'reɪt/ *a* wütend

Ireland /'aɪələnd/ *n* Irland *nt*

iris /'aɪərɪs/ *n* (*Anat*) Regenbogenhaut *f*, Iris *f*; (*Bot*) Schwertlilie *f*

Irish /'aɪərɪʃ/ *a* irisch ● *n* **the ~** *pl* die Iren. **~man** *n* Ire *m*. **~woman** *n* Irin *f*

irk /ɜːk/ *vt* ärgern. **~some** /-səm/ *a* lästig

iron /'aɪən/ *a* Eisen-; (*fig*) eisern ● *n* Eisen *nt*; (*appliance*) Bügeleisen *nt* ● *vt/i* bügeln. **~ out** *vt* ausbügeln

ironic[al] /aɪ'rɒnɪk[l]/ *a* ironisch

ironing /'aɪənɪŋ/ *n* Bügeln *nt*; (*articles*) Bügelwäsche *f*; **do the ~** bügeln. **~-board** *n* Bügelbrett *nt*

ironmonger /'-mʌŋgə(r)/ *n* **~'s [shop]** Haushaltswarengeschäft *nt*

irony /'aɪərənɪ/ *n* Ironie *f*

irradiate /ɪ'reɪdɪeɪt/ *vt* bestrahlen

irrational /ɪ'ræʃənl/ *a* irrational

irreconcilable /ɪ'rekənsaɪləbl/ *a* unversöhnlich

irrefutable /ɪrɪ'fjuːtəbl/ *a* unwiderlegbar

irregular /ɪ'regjʊlə(r)/ *a*, **-ly** *adv* unregelmäßig; (*against rules*) regelwidrig. **~ity** /-'lærətɪ/ *n* Unregelmäßigkeit *f*; Regelwidrigkeit *f*

irrelevant /ɪ'reləvənt/ *a* irrelevant

irreparable /ɪ'repərəbl/ *a* unersetzlich; **be ~** nicht wiedergutzumachen sein

irreplaceable /ɪrɪ'pleɪsəbl/ *a* unersetzlich

irrepressible /ɪrɪ'presəbl/ *a* unverwüstlich; **be ~** ⟨*person:*⟩ nicht unterzukriegen sein

irresistible /ɪrɪ'zɪstəbl/ *a* unwiderstehlich

irresolute /ɪ'rezəluːt/ *a* unentschlossen

irrespective /ɪrɪ'spektɪv/ *a* **~ of** ungeachtet (+ *gen*)

irresponsible /ɪrɪ'spɒnsəbl/ *a*, **-bly** *adv* unverantwortlich; ⟨*person*⟩ verantwortungslos

irreverent /ɪ'revərənt/ *a*, **-ly** *adv* respektlos
irreversible /ɪrɪ'vɜ:səbl/ *a* unwiderruflich; (*Med*) irreversibel
irrevocable /ɪ'revəkəbl/ *a*, **-bly** *adv* unwiderruflich
irrigat|e /'ɪrɪgeɪt/ *vt* bewässern. **~ion** /-'geɪʃn/ *n* Bewässerung *f*
irritability /ɪrɪtə'bɪlətɪ/ *n* Gereiztheit *f*
irritable /'ɪrɪtəbl/ *a* reizbar
irritant /'ɪrɪtənt/ *n* Reizstoff *m*
irritat|e /'ɪrɪteɪt/ *vt* irritieren; (*Med*) reizen. **~ion** /-'teɪʃn/ *n* Ärger *m*; (*Med*) Reizung *f*
is /ɪz/ *see* **be**
Islam /'ɪzlɑ:m/ *n* der Islam. **~ic** /-'læmɪk/ *a* islamisch
island /'aɪlənd/ *n* Insel *f*. **~er** *n* Inselbewohner(in) *m*(*f*)
isle /aɪl/ *n* Insel *f*
isolat|e /'aɪsəleɪt/ *vt* isolieren. **~ed** *a* (*remote*) abgelegen; (*single*) einzeln. **~ion** /-'leɪʃn/ *n* Isoliertheit *f*; (*Med*) Isolierung *f*
Israel /'ɪzreɪl/ *n* Israel *nt*. **~i** /ɪz'reɪlɪ/ *a* israelisch ● *n* Israeli *m*/*f*
issue /'ɪʃu:/ *n* Frage *f*; (*outcome*) Ergebnis *nt*; (*of magazine, stamps*) Ausgabe *f*; (*offspring*) Nachkommen *pl*; **what is at ~?** worum geht es? **take ~ with s.o.** jdm widersprechen ● *vt* ausgeben; ausstellen ‹*passport*›; erteilen ‹*order*›; herausgeben ‹*book*›; **be ~d with sth** etw erhalten ● *vi* **~ from** herausströmen aus
isthmus /'ɪsməs/ *n* (*pl* **-muses**) Landenge *f*
it /ɪt/ *pron* es; (*m*) er; (*f*) sie; (*as direct object*) es; (*m*) ihn; (*f*) sie; (*as indirect object*) ihm; (*f*) ihr; **it is raining** es regnet; **it's me** ich bin's; **who is it?** wer ist da? **of/from it** davon; **with it** damit; **out of it** daraus
Italian /ɪ'tæljən/ *a* italienisch ● *n* Italiener(in) *m*(*f*); (*Lang*) Italienisch *nt*
italic /ɪ'tælɪk/ *a* kursiv. **~s** *npl* Kursivschrift *f*; **in ~s** kursiv
Italy /'ɪtəlɪ/ *n* Italien *nt*
itch /ɪtʃ/ *n* Juckreiz *m*; **I have an ~** es juckt mich ● *vi* jucken; **I'm ~ing** (*fam*) es juckt mich (**to** zu). **~y** *a* **be ~y** jucken
item /'aɪtəm/ *n* Gegenstand *m*; (*Comm*) Artikel *m*; (*on agenda*) Punkt *m*; (*on invoice*) Posten *m*; (*act*) Nummer *f*; **~ [of news]** Nachricht *f*. **~ize** *vt* einzeln aufführen; spezifizieren ‹*bill*›
itinerant /aɪ'tɪnərənt/ *a* Wander-
itinerary /aɪ'tɪnərərɪ/ *n* [Reise]route *f*
its /ɪts/ *poss pron* sein; (*f*) ihr
it's = **it is, it has**
itself /ɪt'self/ *pron* selbst; (*refl*) sich; **by ~** von selbst; (*alone*) allein
ivory /'aɪvərɪ/ *n* Elfenbein *nt* ● *attrib* Elfenbein-
ivy /'aɪvɪ/ *n* Efeu *m*

J

jab /dʒæb/ *n* Stoß *m*; (*fam: injection*) Spritze *f* ● *vt* (*pt*/*pp* **jabbed**) stoßen
jabber /'dʒæbə(r)/ *vi* plappern
jack /dʒæk/ *n* (*Auto*) Wagenheber *m*; (*Cards*) Bube *m* ● *vt* **~ up** (*Auto*) aufbocken
jackdaw /'dʒækdɔ:/ *n* Dohle *f*
jacket /'dʒækɪt/ *n* Jacke *f*; (*of book*) Schutzumschlag *m*. **~ po'tato** *n* in der Schale gebackene Kartoffel *f*
'jackpot *n* **hit the ~** das Große Los ziehen
jade /dʒeɪd/ *n* Jade *m*
jaded /'dʒeɪdɪd/ *a* abgespannt
jagged /'dʒægɪd/ *a* zackig
jail /dʒeɪl/ = **gaol**
jalopy /dʒə'lɒpɪ/ *n* (*fam*) Klapperkiste *f*
jam¹ /dʒæm/ *n* Marmelade *f*
jam² *n* Gedränge *nt*; (*Auto*) Stau *m*; (*fam: difficulty*) Klemme *f* ● *v* (*pt*/*pp* **jammed**) ● *vt* klemmen (**in** in + *acc*); stören ‹*broadcast*› ● *vi* klemmen
Jamaica /dʒə'meɪkə/ *n* Jamaika *nt*
jangle /'dʒæŋgl/ *vi* klimpern ● *vt* klimpern mit
janitor /'dʒænɪtə(r)/ *n* Hausmeister *m*
January /'dʒænjʊərɪ/ *n* Januar *m*
Japan /dʒə'pæn/ *n* Japan *nt*. **~ese** /dʒæpə'ni:z/ *a* japanisch ● *n* Japaner(in) *m*(*f*); (*Lang*) Japanisch *nt*
jar¹ /dʒɑ:(r)/ *n* Glas *nt*; (*earthenware*) Topf *m*
jar² *v* (*pt*/*pp* **jarred**) *vi* stören ● *vt* erschüttern
jargon /'dʒɑ:gən/ *n* Jargon *m*
jaundice /'dʒɔ:ndɪs/ *n* Gelbsucht *f*. **~d** *a* (*fig*) zynisch
jaunt /dʒɔ:nt/ *n* Ausflug *m*
jaunty /'dʒɔ:ntɪ/ *a* (**-ier, -iest**), **-ily** *adv* keck
javelin /'dʒævlɪn/ *n* Speer *m*
jaw /dʒɔ:/ *n* Kiefer *m*; **~s** *pl* Rachen *m* ● *vi* (*fam*) quatschen

jay /dʒeɪ/ *n* Eichelhäher *m*. **~-walker** *n* achtloser Fußgänger *m*

jazz /dʒæz/ *n* Jazz *m*. **~y** *a* knallig

jealous /ˈdʒeləs/ *a*, **-ly** *adv* eifersüchtig (**of** auf + *acc*). **~y** *n* Eifersucht *f*

jeans /dʒi:nz/ *npl* Jeans *pl*

jeer /dʒɪə(r)/ *n* Johlen *nt* ● *vi* johlen; **~ at** verhöhnen

jell /dʒel/ *vi* gelieren

jelly /ˈdʒelɪ/ *n* Gelee *nt*; (*dessert*) Götterspeise *f*. **~fish** *n* Qualle *f*

jemmy /ˈdʒemɪ/ *n* Brecheisen *nt*

jeopar|dize /ˈdʒepədaɪz/ *vt* gefährden. **~dy** /-dɪ/ *n* **in ~dy** gefährdet

jerk /dʒɜ:k/ *n* Ruck *m* ● *vt* stoßen; (*pull*) reißen ● *vi* rucken; ‹*limb, muscle:*› zucken. **~ily** *adv* ruckweise. **~y** *a* ruckartig

jersey /ˈdʒɜ:zɪ/ *n* Pullover *m*; (*Sport*) Trikot *nt*; (*fabric*) Jersey *m*

jest /dʒest/ *n* Scherz *m*; **in ~** im Spaß ● *vi* scherzen

jet[1] /dʒet/ *n* (*Miner*) Jett *m*

jet[2] *n* (*of water*) [Wasser]strahl *m*; (*nozzle*) Düse *f*; (*plane*) Düsenflugzeug *nt*

jet: ~-ˈblack *a* pechschwarz. **~ lag** *n* Jet-lag *nt*. **~-proˈpelled** *a* mit Düsenantrieb

jettison /ˈdʒetɪsn/ *vt* über Bord werfen

jetty /ˈdʒetɪ/ *n* Landesteg *m*; (*breakwater*) Buhne *f*

Jew /dʒu:/ *n* Jude *m*/Jüdin *f*

jewel /ˈdʒu:əl/ *n* Edelstein *m*; (*fig*) Juwel *nt*. **~ler** *n* Juwelier *m*; **~ler's [shop]** Juweliergeschäft *nt*. **~lery** *n* Schmuck *m*

Jew|ess /ˈdʒu:ɪs/ *n* Jüdin *f*. **~ish** *a* jüdisch

jib /dʒɪb/ *vi* (*pt/pp* **jibbed**) (*fig*) sich sträuben (**at** gegen)

jiffy /ˈdʒɪfɪ/ *n* (*fam*) **in a ~** in einem Augenblick

jigsaw /ˈdʒɪgsɔ:/ *n* **~ [puzzle]** Puzzlespiel *nt*

jilt /dʒɪlt/ *vt* sitzenlassen

jingle /ˈdʒɪŋgl/ *n* (*rhyme*) Verschen *nt* ● *vi* klimpern ● *vt* klimpern mit

jinx /dʒɪŋks/ *n* (*fam*) **it's got a ~ on it** es ist verhext

jitter|s /ˈdʒɪtəz/ *npl* (*fam*) **have the ~s** nervös sein. **~y** *a* (*fam*) nervös

job /dʒɒb/ *n* Aufgabe *f*; (*post*) Stelle *f*, (*fam*) Job *m*; **be a ~** (*fam*) nicht leicht sein; **it's a good ~ that** es ist [nur] gut, daß. **~centre** *n* Arbeitsvermittlungsstelle *f*. **~less** *a* arbeitslos

jockey /ˈdʒɒkɪ/ *n* Jockei *m*

jocular /ˈdʒɒkjʊlə(r)/ *a*, **-ly** *adv* spaßhaft

jog /ˈdʒɒg/ *n* Stoß *m*; **at a ~** im Dauerlauf ● *v* (*pt/pp* **jogged**) ● *vt* anstoßen; **~ s.o.'s memory** jds Gedächtnis nachhelfen ● *vi* (*Sport*) joggen. **~ging** *n* Jogging *nt*

john /dʒɒn/ *n* (*Amer, fam*) Klo *nt*

join /dʒɔɪn/ *n* Nahtstelle *f* ● *vt* verbinden (**to** mit); sich anschließen (+ *dat*) ‹*person*›; (*become member of*) beitreten (+ *dat*); eintreten in (+ *acc*) ‹*firm*› ● *vi* ‹*roads:*› sich treffen. **~ in** *vi* mitmachen. **~ up** *vi* (*Mil*) Soldat werden ● *vt* zusammenfügen

joiner /ˈdʒɔɪnə(r)/ *n* Tischler *m*

joint /dʒɔɪnt/ *a*, **-ly** *adv* gemeinsam ● *n* Gelenk *nt*; (*in wood, brickwork*) Fuge *f*; (*Culin*) Braten *m*; (*fam: bar*) Lokal *nt*

joist /dʒɔɪst/ *n* Dielenbalken *m*

jok|e /dʒəʊk/ *n* Scherz *m*; (*funny story*) Witz *m*; (*trick*) Streich *m* ● *vi* scherzen. **~er** *n* Witzbold *m*; (*Cards*) Joker *m*. **~ing** *n* **~ing apart** Spaß beiseite. **~ingly** *adv* im Spaß

jollity /ˈdʒɒlətɪ/ *n* Lustigkeit *f*

jolly /ˈdʒɒlɪ/ *a* (**-ier, -iest**) lustig ● *adv* (*fam*) sehr

jolt /dʒəʊlt/ *n* Ruck *m* ● *vt* einen Ruck versetzen (+ *dat*) ● *vi* holpern

Jordan /ˈdʒɔ:dn/ *n* Jordanien *nt*

jostle /ˈdʒɒsl/ *vt* anrempeln ● *vi* drängeln

jot /dʒɒt/ *n* Jota *nt* ● *vt* (*pt/pp* **jotted**) **~ [down]** sich (*dat*) notieren. **~ter** *n* Notizblock *m*

journal /ˈdʒɜ:nl/ *n* Zeitschrift *f*; (*diary*) Tagebuch *nt*. **~ese** /-əˈli:z/ *n* Zeitungsjargon *m*. **~ism** *n* Journalismus *m*. **~ist** *n* Journalist(in) *m*(*f*)

journey /ˈdʒɜ:nɪ/ *n* Reise *f*

jovial /ˈdʒəʊvɪəl/ *a* lustig

joy /dʒɔɪ/ *n* Freude *f*. **~ful** *a*, **-ly** *adv* freudig, froh. **~ride** *n* (*fam*) Spritztour *f* [im gestohlenen Auto]

jubil|ant /ˈdʒu:bɪlənt/ *a* überglücklich. **~ation** /-ˈleɪʃn/ *n* Jubel *m*

jubilee /ˈdʒu:bɪli:/ *n* Jubiläum *nt*

Judaism /ˈdʒu:deɪɪzm/ *n* Judentum *nt*

judder /ˈdʒʌdə(r)/ *vi* rucken

judge /dʒʌdʒ/ *n* Richter *m*; (*of competition*) Preisrichter *m* ● *vt* beurteilen; (*estimate*) [ein]schätzen ● *vi* urteilen (**by** nach). **~ment** *n* Beurteilung *f*; (*Jur*) Urteil *nt*; (*fig*) Urteilsvermögen *nt*

judic|ial /dʒu:'dɪʃl/ *a* gerichtlich. **~iary** /-ʃərɪ/ *n* Richterstand *m*. **~ious** /-ʃəs/ *a* klug

judo /'dʒu:dəʊ/ *n* Judo *nt*

jug /dʒʌg/ *n* Kanne *f*; (*small*) Kännchen *nt*; (*for water, wine*) Krug *m*

juggernaut /'dʒʌgənɔ:t/ *n* (*fam*) Riesenlaster *m*

juggle /'dʒʌgl/ *vi* jonglieren. **~r** *n* Jongleur *m*

juice /dʒu:s/ *n* Saft *m*. **~ extractor** *n* Entsafter *m*

juicy /'dʒu:sɪ/ *a* (**-ier, -iest**) saftig; (*fam*) ⟨*story*⟩ pikant

juke-box /'dʒu:k-/ *n* Musikbox *f*

July /dʒʊ'laɪ/ *n* Juli *m*

jumble /'dʒʌmbl/ *n* Durcheinander *nt* ● *vt* ~ **[up]** durcheinanderbringen. **~ sale** *n* [Wohltätigkeits]basar *m*

jumbo /'dʒʌmbəʊ/ *n* ~ **[jet]** Jumbo[-Jet] *m*

jump /dʒʌmp/ *n* Sprung *m*; (*in prices*) Anstieg *m*; (*in horse racing*) Hindernis *nt* ● *vi* springen; (*start*) zusammenzucken; **make s.o. ~** jdn erschrecken; **~ at** (*fig*) sofort zugreifen bei ⟨*offer*⟩; **~ to conclusions** voreilige Schlüsse ziehen ● *vt* überspringen; **~ the gun** (*fig*) vorschnell handeln. **~ up** *vi* aufspringen

jumper /'dʒʌmpə(r)/ *n* Pullover *m*, Pulli *m*

jumpy /'dʒʌmpɪ/ *a* nervös

junction /'dʒʌŋkʃn/ *n* Kreuzung *f*; (*Rail*) Knotenpunkt *m*

juncture /'dʒʌŋktʃə(r)/ *n* **at this ~** zu diesem Zeitpunkt

June /dʒu:n/ *n* Juni *m*

jungle /'dʒʌŋgl/ *n* Dschungel *m*

junior /'dʒu:nɪə(r)/ *a* jünger; (*in rank*) untergeordnet; (*Sport*) Junioren- ● *n* Junior *m*. **~ school** *n* Grundschule *f*

juniper /'dʒu:nɪpə(r)/ *n* Wacholder *m*

junk /dʒʌŋk/ *n* Gerümpel *nt*, Trödel *m*

junkie /'dʒʌŋkɪ/ *n* (*sl*) Fixer *m*

'junk-shop *n* Trödelladen *m*

juris|diction /dʒʊərɪs'dɪkʃn/ *n* Gerichtsbarkeit *f*. **~'prudence** *n* Rechtswissenschaft *f*

juror /'dʒʊərə(r)/ *n* Geschworene(r) *m*/*f*

jury /'dʒʊərɪ/ *n* **the ~** die Geschworenen *pl*; (*for competition*) die Jury

just /dʒʌst/ *a* gerecht ● *adv* gerade; (*only*) nur; (*simply*) einfach; (*exactly*) genau; **~ as tall** ebenso groß; **~ listen!** hör doch mal! **I'm ~ going** ich gehe schon; **~ put it down** stell es nur hin

justice /'dʒʌstɪs/ *n* Gerechtigkeit *f*; **do ~ to** gerecht werden (+ *dat*); **J~ of the Peace** ≈ Friedensrichter *m*

justifiab|le /'dʒʌstɪfaɪəbl/ *a* berechtigt. **~ly** *adv* berechtigterweise

justi|fication /dʒʌstɪfɪ'keɪʃn/ *n* Rechtfertigung *f*. **~fy** /'dʒʌstɪfaɪ/ *vt* (*pt*/*pp* **-ied**) rechtfertigen

justly /'dʒʌstlɪ/ *adv* zu Recht

jut /dʒʌt/ *vi* (*pt*/*pp* **jutted**) **~ out** vorstehen

juvenile /'dʒu:vənaɪl/ *a* jugendlich; (*childish*) kindisch ● *n* Jugendliche(r) *m*/*f*. **~ delinquency** *n* Jugendkriminalität *f*

juxtapose /dʒʌkstə'pəʊz/ *vt* nebeneinanderstellen

K

kangaroo /kæŋgə'ru:/ *n* Känguruh *nt*

karate /kə'rɑ:tɪ/ *n* Karate *nt*

kebab /kɪ'bæb/ *n* (*Culin*) Spießchen *nt*

keel /ki:l/ *n* Kiel *m* ● *vi* **~ over** umkippen; (*Naut*) kentern

keen /ki:n/ *a* (**-er, -est**) (*sharp*) scharf; (*intense*) groß; (*eager*) eifrig, begeistert; **~ on** (*fam*) erpicht auf (+ *acc*); **~ on s.o.** von jdm sehr angetan; **be ~ to do sth** etw gerne machen wollen. **~ly** *adv* tief. **~ness** *n* Eifer *m*, Begeisterung *f*

keep /ki:p/ *n* (*maintenance*) Unterhalt *m*; (*of castle*) Bergfried *m*; **for ~s** für immer ● *v* (*pt*/*pp* **kept**) ● *vt* behalten; (*store*) aufbewahren; (*not throw away*) aufheben; (*support*) unterhalten; (*detain*) aufhalten; freihalten ⟨*seat*⟩; halten ⟨*promise, animals*⟩; führen, haben ⟨*shop*⟩; einhalten ⟨*law, rules*⟩; **~ sth hot** etw warm halten; **~ s.o. from doing sth** jdn davon abhalten, etw zu tun; **~ s.o. waiting** jdn warten lassen; **~ sth to oneself** etw nicht weitersagen; **where do you ~ the sugar?** wo hast du den Zucker? ● *vi* (*remain*) bleiben; ⟨*food:*⟩ sich halten; **~ left/right** sich links/rechts halten; **~ doing sth** etw dauernd machen; **~ on doing sth** etw weitermachen; **~ in with** sich gut stellen mit. **~ up** *vi*

Schritt halten ● *vt* (*continue*) weitermachen

keep|er /'ki:pə(r)/ *n* Wärter(in) *m*(*f*). **~ing** *n* Obhut *f*; **be in ~ing with** passen zu. **~sake** *n* Andenken *nt*

keg /keg/ *n* kleines Faß *nt*

kennel /'kenl/ *n* Hundehütte *f*; **~s** *pl* (*boarding*) Hundepension *f*; (*breeding*) Zwinger *m*

Kenya /'kenjə/ *n* Kenia *nt*

kept /kept/ *see* **keep**

kerb /kɜ:b/ *n* Bordstein *m*

kernel /'kɜ:nl/ *n* Kern *m*

kerosene /'kerəsi:n/ *n* (*Amer*) Petroleum *nt*

ketchup /'ketʃʌp/ *n* Ketchup *m*

kettle /'ketl/ *n* [Wasser]kessel *m*; **put the ~ on** Wasser aufsetzen; **a pretty ~ of fish** (*fam*) eine schöne Bescherung *f*

key /ki:/ *n* Schlüssel *m*; (*Mus*) Tonart *f*; (*of piano, typewriter*) Taste *f* ● *vt* **~ in** *vt* eintasten

key: ~board *n* Tastatur *f*; (*Mus*) Klaviatur *f*. **~boarder** *n* Taster(in) *m*(*f*). **~hole** *n* Schlüsselloch *nt*. **~ring** *n* Schlüsselring *m*

khaki /'kɑ:kɪ/ *a* khakifarben ● *n* Khaki *nt*

kick /kɪk/ *n* [Fuß]tritt *m*; **for ~s** (*fam*) zum Spaß ● *vt* treten; **~ the bucket** (*fam*) abkratzen ● *vi* ⟨*animal:*⟩ ausschlagen. **~-off** *n* (*Sport*) Anstoß *m*

kid /kɪd/ *n* Kitz *nt*; (*fam: child*) Kind *nt* ● *vt* (*pt*/*pp* **kidded**) (*fam*) **~ s.o.** jdm etwas vormachen. **~ gloves** *npl* Glacéhandschuhe *pl*

kidnap /'kɪdnæp/ *vt* (*pt*/*pp* **-napped**) entführen. **~per** *n* Entführer *m*. **~ping** *n* Entführung *f*

kidney /'kɪdnɪ/ *n* Niere *f*. **~ machine** *n* künstliche Niere *f*

kill /kɪl/ *vt* töten; (*fam*) totschlagen ⟨*time*⟩; **~ two birds with one stone** zwei Fliegen mit einer Klappe schlagen. **~er** *n* Mörder(in) *m*(*f*). **~ing** *n* Tötung *f*; (*murder*) Mord *m*

'killjoy *n* Spielverderber *m*

kiln /kɪln/ *n* Brennofen *m*

kilo /'ki:ləʊ/ *n* Kilo *nt*

kilo /'kɪlə/: **~gram** *n* Kilogramm *nt*. **~hertz** /-hɜ:ts/ *n* Kilohertz *nt*. **~metre** *n* Kilometer *m*. **~watt** *n* Kilowatt *nt*

kilt /kɪlt/ *n* Schottenrock *m*

kin /kɪn/ *n* Verwandtschaft *f*; **next of ~** nächster Verwandter *m*/nächste Verwandte *f*

kind[1] /kaɪnd/ *n* Art *f*; (*brand, type*) Sorte *f*; **what ~ of car?** was für ein Auto? **~ of** (*fam*) irgendwie

kind[2] *a* (**-er, -est**) nett; **~ to animals** gut zu Tieren; **~ regards** herzliche Grüße

kindergarten /'kɪndəgɑ:tn/ *n* Vorschule *f*

kindle /'kɪndl/ *vt* anzünden

kind|ly /'kaɪndlɪ/ *a* (**-ier, -iest**) nett ● *adv* netterweise; (*if you please*) gefälligst. **~ness** *n* Güte *f*; (*favour*) Gefallen *m*

kindred /'kɪndrɪd/ *a* **~ spirit** Gleichgesinnte(r) *m*/*f*

kinetic /kɪ'netɪk/ *a* kinetisch

king /kɪŋ/ *n* König *m*; (*Draughts*) Dame *f*. **~dom** *n* Königreich *nt*; (*fig & Relig*) Reich *nt*

king: ~fisher *n* Eisvogel *m*. **~-sized** *a* extragroß

kink /kɪŋk/ *n* Knick *m*. **~y** *a* (*fam*) pervers

kiosk /'ki:ɒsk/ *n* Kiosk *m*

kip /kɪp/ *n* **have a ~** (*fam*) pennen ● *vi* (*pt*/*pp* **kipped**) (*fam*) pennen

kipper /'kɪpə(r)/ *n* Räucherhering *m*

kiss /kɪs/ *n* Kuß *m* ● *vt*/*i* küssen

kit /kɪt/ *n* Ausrüstung *f*; (*tools*) Werkzeug *nt*; (*construction ~*) Bausatz *m* ● *vt* (*pt*/*pp* **kitted**) **~ out** ausrüsten. **~bag** *n* Seesack *m*

kitchen /'kɪtʃɪn/ *n* Küche *f* ● *attrib* Küchen-. **~ette** /kɪtʃɪ'net/ *n* Kochnische *f*

kitchen: ~ 'garden *n* Gemüsegarten *m*. **~ 'sink** *n* Spülbecken *nt*

kite /kaɪt/ *n* Drachen *m*

kith /kɪθ/ *n* **with ~ and kin** mit der ganzen Verwandtschaft

kitten /'kɪtn/ *n* Kätzchen *nt*

kitty /'kɪtɪ/ *n* (*money*) [gemeinsame] Kasse *f*

kleptomaniac /kleptə'meɪnɪæk/ *n* Kleptomane *m*/-manin *f*

knack /næk/ *n* Trick *m*, Dreh *m*

knapsack /'næp-/ *n* Tornister *m*

knead /ni:d/ *vt* kneten

knee /ni:/ *n* Knie *nt*. **~cap** *n* Kniescheibe *f*

kneel /ni:l/ *vi* (*pt*/*pp* **knelt**) knien; **~ [down]** sich [nieder]knien

knelt /nelt/ *see* **kneel**

knew /nju:/ *see* **know**

knickers /'nɪkəz/ *npl* Schlüpfer *m*

knick-knacks /'nɪknæks/ *npl* Nippsachen *pl*

knife /naɪf/ *n* (*pl* **knives**) Messer *nt* ● *vt* einen Messerstich versetzen (+ *dat*); (*to death*) erstechen
knight /naɪt/ *n* Ritter *m*; (*Chess*) Springer *m* ● *vt* adeln
knit /nɪt/ *vt*/*i* (*pt*/*pp* **knitted**) stricken; **~ one, purl one** eine rechts, eine links; **~ one's brow** die Stirn runzeln. **~ting** *n* Stricken *nt*; (*work*) Strickzeug *nt*. **~ting-needle** *n* Stricknadel *f*. **~wear** *n* Strickwaren *pl*
knives /naɪvz/ *npl see* **knife**
knob /nɒb/ *n* Knopf *m*; (*on door*) Knauf *m*; (*small lump*) Beule *f*; (*small piece*) Stückchen *nt*. **~bly** *a* knorrig; (*bony*) knochig
knock /nɒk/ *n* Klopfen *nt*; (*blow*) Schlag *m*; **there was a ~ at the door** es klopfte ● *vt* anstoßen; (*at door*) klopfen an (+ *acc*); (*fam: criticize*) heruntermachen; **~ a hole in sth** ein Loch in etw (*acc*) schlagen; **~ one's head** sich (*dat*) den Kopf stoßen (**on** an + *dat*) ● *vi* klopfen. **~ about** *vt* schlagen ● *vi* (*fam*) herumkommen. **~ down** *vt* herunterwerfen; (*with fist*) niederschlagen; (*in car*) anfahren; (*demolish*) abreißen; (*fam: reduce*) herabsetzen. **~ off** *vt* herunterwerfen; (*fam: steal*) klauen; (*fam: complete quickly*) hinhauen ● *vi* (*fam: cease work*) Feierabend machen. **~ out** *vt* ausschlagen; (*make unconscious*) bewußtlos schlagen; (*Boxing*) k.o. schlagen. **~ over** *vt* umwerfen; (*in car*) anfahren
knock: ~-down *a* **~-down prices** Schleuderpreise *pl*. **~er** *n* Türklopfer *m*. **~-kneed** /-'ni:d/ *a* X-beinig. **~-out** *n* (*Boxing*) K.o. *m*
knot /nɒt/ *n* Knoten *m* ● *vt* (*pt*/*pp* **knotted**) knoten
knotty /'nɒtɪ/ *a* (**-ier, -iest**) (*fam*) verwickelt
know /nəʊ/ *vt*/*i* (*pt* **knew**, *pp* **known**) wissen; kennen ⟨*person*⟩; können ⟨*language*⟩; **get to ~** kennenlernen ● *n* **in the ~** (*fam*) im Bild
know: ~-all *n* (*fam*) Alleswisser *m*. **~-how** *n* (*fam*) [Sach]kenntnis *f*. **~ing** *a* wissend. **~ingly** *adv* wissend; (*intentionally*) wissentlich
knowledge /'nɒlɪdʒ/ *n* Kenntnis *f* (**of** von/*gen*); (*general*) Wissen *nt*; (*specialized*) Kenntnisse *pl*. **~able** /-əbl/ *a* **be ~able** viel wissen
known /nəʊn/ *see* **know** ● *a* bekannt
knuckle /'nʌkl/ *n* [Finger]knöchel *m*; (*Culin*) Hachse *f* ● *vi* **~ under** sich fügen; **~ down** sich dahinterklemmen
kosher /'kəʊʃə(r)/ *a* koscher
kowtow /kaʊ'taʊ/ *vi* Kotau machen (**to** vor + *dat*)
kudos /'kju:dɒs/ *n* (*fam*) Prestige *nt*

L

lab /læb/ *n* (*fam*) Labor *nt*
label /'leɪbl/ *n* Etikett *nt* ● *vt* (*pt*/*pp* **labelled**) etikettieren
laboratory /lə'bɒrətrɪ/ *n* Labor *nt*
laborious /lə'bɔ:rɪəs/ *a*, **-ly** *adv* mühsam
labour /'leɪbə(r)/ *n* Arbeit *f*; (*workers*) Arbeitskräfte *pl*; (*Med*) Wehen *pl*; **L~** (*Pol*) die Labourpartei ● *attrib* Labour- ● *vi* arbeiten ● *vt* (*fig*) sich lange auslassen über (+ *acc*). **~er** *n* Arbeiter *m*
'**labour-saving** *a* arbeitssparend
laburnum /lə'bɜ:nəm/ *n* Goldregen *m*
labyrinth /'læbərɪnθ/ *n* Labyrinth *nt*
lace /leɪs/ *n* Spitze *f*; (*of shoe*) Schnürsenkel *m* ● *vt* schnüren; **~d with rum** mit einem Schuß Rum
lacerate /'læsəreɪt/ *vt* zerreißen
lack /læk/ *n* Mangel *m* (**of** an + *dat*) ● *vt* **I ~ the time** mir fehlt die Zeit ● *vi* **be ~ing** fehlen
lackadaisical /lækə'deɪzɪkl/ *a* lustlos
laconic /lə'kɒnɪk/ *a*, **-ally** *adv* lakonisch
lacquer /'lækə(r)/ *n* Lack *m*; (*for hair*) [Haar]spray *m*
lad /læd/ *n* Junge *m*
ladder /'lædə(r)/ *n* Leiter *f*; (*in fabric*) Laufmasche *f*
laden /'leɪdn/ *a* beladen
ladle /'leɪdl/ *n* [Schöpf]kelle *f* ● *vt* schöpfen
lady /'leɪdɪ/ *n* Dame *f*; (*title*) Lady *f*
lady: ~bird *n*, (*Amer*) **~bug** *n* Marienkäfer *m*. **~like** *a* damenhaft
lag[1] /læg/ *vi* (*pt*/*pp* **lagged**) **~ behind** zurückbleiben; (*fig*) nachhinken
lag[2] *vt* (*pt*/*pp* **lagged**) umwickeln ⟨*pipes*⟩
lager /'lɑ:gə(r)/ *n* Lagerbier *nt*
lagoon /lə'gu:n/ *n* Lagune *f*
laid /leɪd/ *see* **lay**[3]
lain /leɪn/ *see* **lie**[2]
lair /leə(r)/ *n* Lager *nt*
laity /'leɪətɪ/ *n* Laienstand *m*

lake /leɪk/ *n* See *m*
lamb /læm/ *n* Lamm *nt*
lame /leɪm/ *a* (**-r, -st**) lahm
lament /lə'ment/ *n* Klage *f*; (*song*) Klagelied *nt* ● *vt* beklagen ● *vi* klagen. **~able** /'læməntəbl/ *a* beklagenswert
laminated /'læmɪneɪtɪd/ *a* laminiert
lamp /læmp/ *n* Lampe *f*; (*in street*) Laterne *f*. **~post** *n* Laternenpfahl *m*. **~shade** *n* Lampenschirm *m*
lance /lɑ:ns/ *n* Lanze *f* ● *vt* (*Med*) aufschneiden. **~-'corporal** *n* Gefreite(r) *m*
land /lænd/ *n* Land *nt*; **plot of ~** Grundstück *nt* ● *vt/i* landen; **~ s.o. with sth** (*fam*) jdm etw aufhalsen
landing /'lændɪŋ/ *n* Landung *f*; (*top of stairs*) Treppenflur *m*. **~-stage** *n* Landesteg *m*
land: ~lady *n* Wirtin *f*. **~-locked** *a* **~-locked country** Binnenstaat *m*. **~lord** *n* Wirt *m*; (*of land*) Grundbesitzer *m*; (*of building*) Hausbesitzer *m*. **~mark** *n* Erkennungszeichen *nt*; (*fig*) Meilenstein *m*. **~owner** *n* Grundbesitzer *m*. **~scape** /-skeɪp/ *n* Landschaft *f*. **~slide** *n* Erdrutsch *m*
lane /leɪn/ *n* kleine Landstraße *f*; (*Auto*) Spur *f*; (*Sport*) Bahn *f*; **'get in ~'** (*Auto*) 'bitte einordnen'
language /'læŋgwɪdʒ/ *n* Sprache *f*; (*speech, style*) Ausdrucksweise *f*. **~ laboratory** *n* Sprachlabor *nt*
languid /'læŋgwɪd/ *a*, **-ly** *adv* träge
languish /'læŋgwɪʃ/ *vi* schmachten
lank /læŋk/ *a* ⟨*hair*⟩ strähnig
lanky /'læŋkɪ/ *a* (**-ier, -iest**) schlaksig
lantern /'læntən/ *n* Laterne *f*
lap[1] /læp/ *n* Schoß *m*
lap[2] *n* (*Sport*) Runde *f*; (*of journey*) Etappe *f* ● *vi* (*pt/pp* **lapped**) plätschern (**against** gegen)
lap[3] *vt* (*pt/pp* **lapped**) **~ up** aufschlecken
lapel /lə'pel/ *n* Revers *nt*
lapse /læps/ *n* Fehler *m*; (*moral*) Fehltritt *m*; (*of time*) Zeitspanne *f* ● *vi* (*expire*) erlöschen; **~ into** verfallen in (+ *acc*)
larceny /'lɑ:sənɪ/ *n* Diebstahl *m*
lard /lɑ:d/ *n* [Schweine]schmalz *nt*
larder /'lɑ:də(r)/ *n* Speisekammer *f*
large /lɑ:dʒ/ *a* (**-r, -st**) & *adv* groß; **by and ~** im großen und ganzen; **at ~** auf freiem Fuß; (*in general*) im allgemeinen. **~ly** *adv* großenteils
lark[1] /lɑ:k/ *n* (*bird*) Lerche *f*
lark[2] *n* (*joke*) Jux *m* ● *vi* **~ about** herumalbern
larva /'lɑ:və/ *n* (*pl* **-vae** /-vi:/) Larve *f*
laryngitis /lærɪn'dʒaɪtɪs/ *n* Kehlkopfentzündung *f*
larynx /'lærɪŋks/ *n* Kehlkopf *m*
lascivious /lə'sɪvɪəs/ *a* lüstern
laser /'leɪzə(r)/ *n* Laser *m*
lash /læʃ/ *n* Peitschenhieb *m*; (*eyelash*) Wimper *f* ● *vt* peitschen; (*tie*) festbinden (**to** an + *acc*). **~ out** *vi* um sich schlagen; (*spend*) viel Geld ausgeben (**on** für)
lashings /'læʃɪŋz/ *npl* **~ of** (*fam*) eine Riesenmenge von
lass /læs/ *n* Mädchen *nt*
lasso /lə'su:/ *n* Lasso *nt*
last[1] /lɑ:st/ *n* (*for shoe*) Leisten *m*
last[2] *a* & *n* letzte(r,s); **~ night** heute *od* gestern nacht; (*evening*) gestern abend; **at ~** endlich; **the ~ time** das letztemal; **for the ~ time** zum letztenmal; **the ~ but one** der/die/das vorletzte; **that's the ~ straw** (*fam*) das schlägt dem Faß den Boden aus ● *adv* zuletzt; (*last time*) das letztemal; **do sth ~** etw zuletzt *od* als letztes machen; **he/she went ~** er/sie ging als letzter/letzte ● *vi* dauern; ⟨*weather:*⟩ sich halten; ⟨*relationship:*⟩ halten. **~ing** *a* dauerhaft. **~ly** *adv* schließlich, zum Schluß
latch /lætʃ/ *n* [einfache] Klinke *f*; **on the ~** nicht verschlossen
late /leɪt/ *a* & *adv* (**-r, -st**) spät; (*delayed*) verspätet; (*deceased*) verstorben; **the ~st news** die neuesten Nachrichten; **stay up ~** bis spät aufbleiben; **of ~** in letzter Zeit; **arrive ~** zu spät ankommen; **I am ~** ich komme zu spät *od* habe mich verspätet; **the train is ~** der Zug hat Verspätung. **~comer** *n* Zuspätkommende(r) *m/f*. **~ly** *adv* in letzter Zeit. **~ness** *n* Zuspätkommen *nt*; (*delay*) Verspätung *f*
latent /'leɪtnt/ *a* latent
later /'leɪtə(r)/ *a* & *adv* später; **~ on** nachher
lateral /'lætərəl/ *a* seitlich
lathe /leɪð/ *n* Drehbank *f*
lather /'lɑ:ðə(r)/ *n* [Seifen]schaum *m* ● *vt* einseifen ● *vi* schäumen
Latin /'lætɪn/ *a* lateinisch ● *n* Latein *nt*. **~ A'merica** *n* Lateinamerika *nt*
latitude /'lætɪtju:d/ *n* (*Geog*) Breite *f*; (*fig*) Freiheit *f*

latter /'lætə(r)/ *a & n* **the ~** der/die/das letztere. **~ly** *adv* in letzter Zeit
lattice /'lætɪs/ *n* Gitter *nt*
Latvia /'lætvɪə/ *n* Lettland *nt*
laudable /'lɔ:dəbl/ *a* lobenswert
laugh /lɑ:f/ *n* Lachen *nt*; **with a ~** lachend ● *vi* lachen (**at/about** über + *acc*); **~ at s.o.** (*mock*) jdn auslachen. **~able** /-əbl/ *a* lachhaft, lächerlich. **~ing-stock** *n* Gegenstand *m* des Spottes
laughter /'lɑ:ftə(r)/ *n* Gelächter *nt*
launch[1] /lɔ:ntʃ/ *n* (*boat*) Barkasse *f*
launch[2] *n* Stapellauf *m*; (*of rocket*) Abschuß *m*; (*of product*) Lancierung *f* ● *vt* vom Stapel lassen ‹*ship*›; zu Wasser lassen ‹*lifeboat*›; abschießen ‹*rocket*›; starten ‹*attack*›; (*Comm*) lancieren ‹*product*›
launder /'lɔ:ndə(r)/ *vt* waschen. **~ette** /-'dret/ *n* Münzwäscherei *f*
laundry /'lɔ:ndrɪ/ *n* Wäscherei *f*; (*clothes*) Wäsche *f*
laurel /'lɒrl/ *n* Lorbeer *m*
lava /'lɑ:və/ *n* Lava *f*
lavatory /'lævətrɪ/ *n* Toilette *f*
lavender /'lævəndə(r)/ *n* Lavendel *m*
lavish /'lævɪʃ/ *a*, **-ly** *adv* großzügig; (*wasteful*) verschwenderisch; **on a ~ scale** mit viel Aufwand ● *vt* **~ sth on s.o.** jdn mit etw überschütten
law /lɔ:/ *n* Gesetz *nt*; (*system*) Recht *nt*; **study ~** Jura studieren; **~ and order** Recht und Ordnung
law: ~-abiding *a* gesetzestreu. **~court** *n* Gerichtshof *m*. **~ful** *a* rechtmäßig. **~less** *a* gesetzlos
lawn /lɔ:n/ *n* Rasen *m*. **~-mower** *n* Rasenmäher *m*
'law suit *n* Prozeß *m*
lawyer /'lɔ:jə(r)/ *n* Rechtsanwalt *m*/-anwältin *f*
lax /læks/ *a* lax, locker
laxative /'læksətɪv/ *n* Abführmittel *nt*
laxity /'læksətɪ/ *n* Laxheit *f*
lay[1] /leɪ/ *a* Laien-
lay[2] *see* **lie**[2]
lay[3] *vt* (*pt/pp* **laid**) legen; decken ‹*table*›; **~ a trap** eine Falle stellen. **~ down** *vt* hinlegen; festlegen ‹*rules, conditions*›. **~ off** *vt* entlassen ‹*workers*› ● *vi* (*fam: stop*) aufhören. **~ out** *vt* hinlegen; aufbahren ‹*corpse*›; anlegen ‹*garden*›; (*Typ*) gestalten
lay: ~about *n* Faulenzer *m*. **~-by** *n* Parkbucht *f*; (*on motorway*) Rastplatz *m*
layer /'leɪə(r)/ *n* Schicht *f*
layette /leɪ'et/ *n* Babyausstattung *f*
lay: ~man *n* Laie *m*. **~out** *n* Anordnung *f*; (*design*) Gestaltung *f*; (*Typ*) Layout *nt*. **~ 'preacher** *n* Laienprediger *m*
laze /leɪz/ *vi* **~ [about]** faulenzen
laziness /'leɪzɪnɪs/ *n* Faulheit *f*
lazy /'leɪzɪ/ *a* (**-ier, -iest**) faul. **~-bones** *n* Faulenzer *m*
lb /paʊnd/ *abbr* (**pound**) Pfd.
lead[1] /led/ *n* Blei *nt*; (*of pencil*) [Blei-stift]mine *f*
lead[2] /li:d/ *n* Führung *f*; (*leash*) Leine *f*; (*flex*) Schnur *f*; (*clue*) Hinweis *m*, Spur *f*; (*Theat*) Hauptrolle *f*; (*distance ahead*) Vorsprung *m*; **be in the ~** in Führung liegen ● *vt/i* (*pt/pp* **led**) führen; leiten ‹*team*›; (*induce*) bringen; (*at cards*) ausspielen; **~ the way** vorangehen; **~ up to sth** (*fig*) etw (*dat*) vorangehen. **~ away** *vt* wegführen
leaded /'ledɪd/ *a* verbleit
leader /'li:də(r)/ *n* Führer *m*; (*of expedition, group*) Leiter(in) *m*(*f*); (*of orchestra*) Konzertmeister *m*; (*in newspaper*) Leitartikel *m*. **~ship** *n* Führung *f*; Leitung *f*
leading /'li:dɪŋ/ *a* führend; **~ lady** Hauptdarstellerin *f*; **~ question** Suggestivfrage *f*
leaf /li:f/ *n* (*pl* **leaves**) Blatt *nt*; (*of table*) Ausziehplatte *f* ● *vi* **~ through sth** etw durchblättern. **~let** *n* Merkblatt *nt*; (*advertising*) Reklameblatt *nt*; (*political*) Flugblatt *nt*
league /li:g/ *n* Liga *f*; **be in ~ with** unter einer Decke stecken mit
leak /li:k/ *n* (*hole*) undichte Stelle *f*; (*Naut*) Leck *nt*; (*of gas*) Gasausfluß *m* ● *vi* undicht sein; ‹*ship:*› leck sein, lecken; ‹*liquid:*› auslaufen; ‹*gas:*› ausströmen ● *vt* auslaufen lassen; **~ sth to s.o.** (*fig*) jdm etw zuspielen. **~y** *a* undicht; (*Naut*) leck
lean[1] /li:n/ *a* (**-er, -est**) mager
lean[2] *v* (*pt/pp* **leaned** *or* **leant** /lent/) ● *vt* lehnen (**against/on** an + *acc*) ● *vi* ‹*person:*› sich lehnen (**against/on** an + *acc*); (*not be straight*) sich neigen; **be ~ing against** lehnen an (+ *dat*); **~ on s.o.** (*depend*) bei jdm festen Halt finden. **~ back** *vi* sich zurücklehnen. **~ forward** *vi* sich vorbeugen. **~ out** *vi* sich hinauslehnen. **~ over** *vi* sich vorbeugen
leaning /'li:nɪŋ/ *a* schief ● *n* Neigung *f*

leap /li:p/ *n* Sprung *m* ● *vi* (*pt*/*pp* **leapt** /lept/ *or* **leaped**) springen; **he leapt at it** (*fam*) er griff sofort zu. **~-frog** *n* Bockspringen *nt*. **~ year** *n* Schaltjahr *nt*

learn /lɜ:n/ *vt*/*i* (*pt*/*pp* **learnt** *or* **learned**) lernen; (*hear*) erfahren; **~ to swim** schwimmen lernen

learn|ed /'lɜ:nɪd/ *a* gelehrt. **~er** *n* Anfänger *m*; **~er [driver]** Fahrschüler(in) *m*(*f*). **~ing** *n* Gelehrsamkeit *f*

lease /li:s/ *n* Pacht *f*; (*contract*) Mietvertrag *m*; (*Comm*) Pachtvertrag *m* ● *vt* pachten; **~ [out]** verpachten

leash /li:ʃ/ *n* Leine *f*

least /li:st/ *a* geringste(r,s); **have ~ time** am wenigsten Zeit haben ● *n* **the ~** das wenigste; **at ~** wenigstens, mindestens; **not in the ~** nicht im geringsten ● *adv* am wenigsten

leather /'leðə(r)/ *n* Leder *nt*. **~y** *a* ledern; (*tough*) zäh

leave /li:v/ *n* Erlaubnis *f*; (*holiday*) Urlaub *m*; **on ~** auf Urlaub; **take one's ~** sich verabschieden ● *v* (*pt*/*pp* **left**) ● *vt* lassen; (*go out of, abandon*) verlassen; (*forget*) liegenlassen; (*bequeath*) vermachen (**to** *dat*); **~ it to me!** überlassen Sie es mir! **there is nothing left** es ist nichts mehr übrig ● *vi* [weg]gehen/-fahren; ⟨*train, bus:*⟩ abfahren. **~ behind** *vt* zurücklassen; (*forget*) liegenlassen. **~ out** *vt* liegenlassen; (*leave outside*) draußen lassen; (*omit*) auslassen

leaves /li:vz/ *see* **leaf**

Lebanon /'lebənən/ *n* Libanon *m*

lecherous /'letʃərəs/ *a* lüstern

lectern /'lektɜ:n/ *n* [Lese]pult *nt*

lecture /'lektʃə(r)/ *n* Vortrag *m*; (*Univ*) Vorlesung *f*; (*reproof*) Strafpredigt *f* ● *vi* einen Vortrag/eine Vorlesung halten (**on** über + *acc*) ● *vt* **~ s.o.** jdm eine Strafpredigt halten. **~r** *n* Vortragende(r) *m*/*f*; (*Univ*) Dozent(in) *m*(*f*)

led /led/ *see* **lead²**

ledge /ledʒ/ *n* Leiste *f*; (*shelf, of window*) Sims *m*; (*in rock*) Vorsprung *m*

ledger /'ledʒə(r)/ *n* Hauptbuch *nt*

lee /li:/ *n* (*Naut*) Lee *f*

leech /li:tʃ/ *n* Blutegel *m*

leek /li:k/ *n* Stange *f* Porree; **~s** *pl* Porree *m*

leer /lɪə(r)/ *n* anzügliches Grinsen *nt* ● *vi* anzüglich grinsen

lee|ward /'li:wəd/ *adv* nach Lee. **~way** *n* (*fig*) Spielraum *m*

left¹ /left/ *see* **leave**

left² *a* linke(r,s) ● *adv* links; ⟨*go*⟩ nach links ● *n* linke Seite *f*; **on the ~** links; **from/to the ~** von/nach links; **the ~** (*Pol*) die Linke

left: ~-'handed *a* linkshändig. **~-'luggage [office]** *n* Gepäckaufbewahrung *f*. **~overs** *npl* Reste *pl*. **~-'wing** *a* (*Pol*) linke(r,s)

leg /leg/ *n* Bein *nt*; (*Culin*) Keule *f*; (*of journey*) Etappe *f*

legacy /'legəsɪ/ *n* Vermächtnis *nt*, Erbschaft *f*

legal /'li:gl/ *a*, **-ly** *adv* gesetzlich; ⟨*matters*⟩ rechtlich; ⟨*department, position*⟩ Rechts-; **be ~** [gesetzlich] erlaubt sein; **take ~ action** gerichtlich vorgehen

legality /lɪ'gælətɪ/ *n* Legalität *f*

legalize /'li:gəlaɪz/ *vt* legalisieren

legend /'ledʒənd/ *n* Legende *f*. **~ary** *a* legendär

legible /'ledʒəbl/ *a*, **-bly** *adv* leserlich

legion /'li:dʒn/ *n* Legion *f*

legislat|e /'ledʒɪsleɪt/ *vi* Gesetze erlassen. **~ion** /-'leɪʃn/ *n* Gesetzgebung *f*; (*laws*) Gesetze *pl*

legislat|ive /'ledʒɪslətɪv/ *a* gesetzgebend. **~ure** /-leɪtʃə(r)/ *n* Legislative *f*

legitimate /lɪ'dʒɪtɪmət/ *a* rechtmäßig; (*justifiable*) berechtigt; ⟨*child*⟩ ehelich

leisure /'leʒə(r)/ *n* Freizeit *f*; **at your ~** wenn Sie Zeit haben. **~ly** *a* gemächlich

lemon /'lemən/ *n* Zitrone *f*. **~ade** /-'neɪd/ *n* Zitronenlimonade *f*

lend /lend/ *vt* (*pt*/*pp* **lent**) leihen; **~ s.o. sth** jdm etw leihen; **~ a hand** (*fam*) helfen. **~ing library** *n* Leihbücherei *f*

length /leŋθ/ *n* Länge *f*; (*piece*) Stück *nt*; (*of wallpaper*) Bahn *f*; (*of time*) Dauer *f*; **at ~** ausführlich; (*at last*) endlich

length|en /'leŋθən/ *vt* länger machen ● *vi* länger werden. **~ways** *adv* der Länge nach, längs

lengthy /'leŋθɪ/ *a* (**-ier, -iest**) langwierig

lenien|ce /'li:nɪəns/ *n* Nachsicht *f*. **~t** *a*, **-ly** *adv* nachsichtig

lens /lenz/ *n* Linse *f*; (*Phot*) Objektiv *nt*; (*of spectacles*) Glas *nt*

lent /lent/ *see* **lend**

Lent *n* Fastenzeit *f*

lentil /'lentl/ *n* (*Bot*) Linse *f*

Leo /ˈli:əʊ/ *n* (*Astr*) Löwe *m*
leopard /ˈlepəd/ *n* Leopard *m*
leotard /ˈli:ətɑ:d/ *n* Trikot *nt*
leper /ˈlepə(r)/ *n* Leprakranke(r) *m*/*f*; *n* (*Bible & fig*) Aussätzige(r) *m*/*f*
leprosy /ˈleprəsɪ/ *n* Lepra *f*
lesbian /ˈlezbɪən/ *a* lesbisch ● *n* Lesbierin *f*
lesion /ˈli:ʒn/ *n* Verletzung *f*
less /les/ *a, adv, n & prep* weniger; **~ and ~** immer weniger; **not any the ~** um nichts weniger
lessen /ˈlesn/ *vt* verringern ● *vi* nachlassen; ⟨*value:*⟩ abnehmen
lesser /ˈlesə(r)/ *a* geringere(r,s)
lesson /ˈlesn/ *n* Stunde *f*; (*in textbook*) Lektion *f*; (*Relig*) Lesung *f*; **teach s.o. a ~** (*fig*) jdm eine Lehre erteilen
lest /lest/ *conj* (*liter*) damit ... nicht
let /let/ *vt* (*pt*/*pp* **let**, *pres p* **letting**) lassen; (*rent*) vermieten; **~ alone** (*not to mention*) geschweige denn; **'to ~'** 'zu vermieten'; **~ us go** gehen wir; **~ me know** sagen Sie mir Bescheid; **~ him do it** laß ihn das machen; **just ~ him!** soll er doch! **~ s.o. sleep/win** jdn schlafen/gewinnen lassen; **~ oneself in for sth** (*fam*) sich (*dat*) etw einbrocken. **~ down** *vt* hinunter-/herunterlassen; (*lengthen*) länger machen; **~ s.o. down** (*fam*) jdn im Stich lassen; (*disappoint*) jdn enttäuschen. **~ in** *vt* hereinlassen. **~ off** *vt* abfeuern ⟨*gun*⟩; hochgehen lassen ⟨*firework, bomb*⟩; (*emit*) ausstoßen; (*excuse from*) befreien von; (*not punish*) frei ausgehen lassen. **~ out** *vt* hinaus-/herauslassen; (*make larger*) auslassen. **~ through** *vt* durchlassen. **~ up** *vi* (*fam*) nachlassen
'let-down *n* Enttäuschung *f*, (*fam*) Reinfall *m*
lethal /ˈli:θl/ *a* tödlich
letharg|ic /lɪˈθɑ:dʒɪk/ *a* lethargisch. **~y** /ˈleθədʒɪ/ *n* Lethargie *f*
letter /ˈletə(r)/ *n* Brief *m*; (*of alphabet*) Buchstabe *m*; **by ~** brieflich. **~-box** *n* Briefkasten *m*. **~-head** *n* Briefkopf *m*. **~ing** *n* Beschriftung *f*
lettuce /ˈletɪs/ *n* [Kopf]salat *m*
'let-up *n* (*fam*) Nachlassen *nt*
leukaemia /lu:ˈki:mɪə/ *n* Leukämie *f*
level /ˈlevl/ *a* eben; (*horizontal*) waagerecht; (*in height*) auf gleicher Höhe; ⟨*spoonful*⟩ gestrichen; **draw ~ with** gleichziehen mit; **one's ~ best** sein möglichstes ● *n* Höhe *f*; (*fig*) Ebene *f*, Niveau *nt*; (*stage*) Stufe *f*; **on the ~** (*fam*) ehrlich ● *vt* (*pt*/*pp* **levelled**) einebnen; (*aim*) richten (**at** auf + *acc*)
level: ~ 'crossing *n* Bahnübergang *m*. **~-'headed** *a* vernünftig
lever /ˈli:və(r)/ *n* Hebel *m* ● *vt* **~ up** mit einem Hebel anheben. **~age** /-rɪdʒ/ *n* Hebelkraft *f*
levity /ˈlevətɪ/ *n* Heiterkeit *f*; (*frivolity*) Leichtfertigkeit *f*
levy /ˈlevɪ/ *vt* (*pt*/*pp* **levied**) erheben ⟨*tax*⟩
lewd /lju:d/ *a* (**-er, -est**) anstößig
liabilit|y /laɪəˈbɪlətɪ/ *n* Haftung *f*; **~ies** *pl* Verbindlichkeiten *pl*
liable /ˈlaɪəbl/ *a* haftbar; **be ~ to do sth** etw leicht tun können
liaise /lɪˈeɪz/ *vi* (*fam*) Verbindungsperson sein
liaison /lɪˈeɪzɒn/ *n* Verbindung *f*; (*affair*) Verhältnis *nt*
liar /ˈlaɪə(r)/ *n* Lügner(in) *m*(*f*)
libel /ˈlaɪbl/ *n* Verleumdung *f* ● *vt* (*pt*/*pp* **libelled**) verleumden. **~lous** *a* verleumderisch
liberal /ˈlɪbərl/ *a*, **-ly** *adv* tolerant; (*generous*) großzügig. **L~** *a* (*Pol*) liberal ● *n* Liberale(r) *m*/*f*
liberat|e /ˈlɪbəreɪt/ *vt* befreien. **~ed** *a* ⟨*woman*⟩ emanzipiert. **~ion** /-ˈreɪʃn/ *n* Befreiung *f*. **~or** *n* Befreier *m*
liberty /ˈlɪbətɪ/ *n* Freiheit *f*; **take the ~ of doing sth** sich (*dat*) erlauben, etw zu tun; **take liberties** sich (*dat*) Freiheiten erlauben
Libra /ˈli:brə/ *n* (*Astr*) Waage *f*
librarian /laɪˈbreərɪən/ *n* Bibliothekar(in) *m*(*f*)
library /ˈlaɪbrərɪ/ *n* Bibliothek *f*
Libya /ˈlɪbɪə/ *n* Libyen *nt*
lice /laɪs/ *see* **louse**
licence /ˈlaɪsns/ *n* Genehmigung *f*; (*Comm*) Lizenz *f*; (*for TV*) ≈ Fernsehgebühr *f*; (*for driving*) Führerschein *m*; (*for alcohol*) Schankkonzession *f*; (*freedom*) Freiheit *f*
license /ˈlaɪsns/ *vt* eine Genehmigung/(*Comm*) Lizenz erteilen (+ *dat*); **be ~d** ⟨*car:*⟩ zugelassen sein; ⟨*restaurant:*⟩ Schankkonzession haben. **~-plate** *n* Nummernschild *nt*
licentious /laɪˈsenʃəs/ *a* lasterhaft
lichen /ˈlaɪkən/ *n* (*Bot*) Flechte *f*
lick /lɪk/ *n* Lecken *nt*; **a ~ of paint** ein bißchen Farbe ● *vt* lecken; (*fam: defeat*) schlagen
lid /lɪd/ *n* Deckel *m*; (*of eye*) Lid *nt*

lie[1] /laɪ/ *n* Lüge *f*; **tell a ~** lügen ● *vi* (*pt*/*pp* **lied**, *pres p* **lying**) lügen; **~ to** belügen

lie[2] *vi* (*pt* **lay**, *pp* **lain**, *pres p* **lying**) liegen; **here ~s** ... hier ruht ... **~ down** *vi* sich hinlegen

Liège /lɪ'eɪʒ/ *n* Lüttich *nt*

'lie-in *n* **have a ~** [sich] ausschlafen

lieu /lju:/ *n* **in ~ of** statt (+ *gen*)

lieutenant /lef'tenənt/ *n* Oberleutnant *m*

life /laɪf/ *n* (*pl* **lives**) Leben *nt*; (*biography*) Biographie *f*; **lose one's ~** ums Leben kommen

life: ~belt *n* Rettungsring *m*. **~boat** *n* Rettungsboot *nt*. **~buoy** *n* Rettungsring *m*. **~-guard** *n* Lebensretter *m*. **~-jacket** *n* Schwimmweste *f*. **~less** *a* leblos. **~like** *a* naturgetreu. **~line** *n* Rettungsleine *f*. **~long** *a* lebenslang. **~ preserver** *n* (*Amer*) Rettungsring *m*. **~-size(d)** *a* ... in Lebensgröße. **~time** *n* Leben *nt*; **in s.o.'s ~time** zu jds Lebzeiten; **the chance of a ~time** eine einmalige Gelegenheit

lift /lɪft/ *n* Aufzug *m*, Lift *m*; **give s.o. a ~** jdn mitnehmen; **get a ~** mitgenommen werden ● *vt* heben; aufheben ⟨*restrictions*⟩ ● *vi* ⟨*fog:*⟩ sich lichten. **~ up** *vt* hochheben

'lift-off *n* Abheben *nt*

ligament /'lɪgəmənt/ *n* (*Anat*) Band *nt*

light[1] /laɪt/ *a* (**-er, -est**) (*not dark*) hell; **~ blue** hellblau ● *n* Licht *nt*; (*lamp*) Lampe *f*; **in the ~ of** (*fig*) angesichts (+ *gen*); **have you [got] a ~?** haben Sie Feuer? ● *vt* (*pt*/*pp* **lit** *or* **lighted**) anzünden ⟨*fire, cigarette*⟩; anmachen ⟨*lamp*⟩; (*illuminate*) beleuchten. **~ up** *vi* ⟨*face:*⟩ sich erhellen

light[2] *a* (**-er, -est**) (*not heavy*) leicht; **~ sentence** milde Strafe *f* ● *adv* **travel ~** mit wenig Gepäck reisen

'light-bulb *n* Glühbirne *f*

lighten[1] /'laɪtn/ *vt* heller machen ● *vi* heller werden

lighten[2] *vt* leichter machen ⟨*load*⟩

lighter /'laɪtə(r)/ *n* Feuerzeug *nt*

light: ~-'headed *a* benommen. **~-'hearted** *a* unbekümmert. **~house** *n* Leuchtturm *m*. **~ing** *n* Beleuchtung *f*. **~ly** *adv* leicht; (*casually*) leichthin; **get off ~ly** glimpflich davonkommen

lightning /'laɪtnɪŋ/ *n* Blitz *m*. **~-conductor** *n* Blitzableiter *m*

'lightweight *a* leicht ● *n* (*Boxing*) Leichtgewicht *nt*

like[1] /laɪk/ *a* ähnlich; (*same*) gleich ● *prep* wie; (*similar to*) ähnlich (+ *dat*); **~ this** so; **a man ~ that** so ein Mann; **what's he ~?** wie ist er denn? ● *conj* (*fam: as*) wie; (*Amer: as if*) als ob

like[2] *vt* mögen; **I should/would ~** ich möchte; **I ~ the car** das Auto gefällt mir; **I ~ chocolate** ich esse gern Schokolade; **~ dancing/singing** gern tanzen/singen; **I ~ that!** (*fam*) das ist doch die Höhe! ● *n* **~s and dislikes** *pl* Vorlieben und Abneigungen *pl*

like|able /'laɪkəbl/ *a* sympathisch. **~lihood** /-lɪhʊd/ *n* Wahrscheinlichkeit *f*. **~ly** *a* (**-ier, -iest**) & *adv* wahrscheinlich; **not ~ly!** (*fam*) auf gar keinen Fall!

'like-minded *a* gleichgesinnt

liken /'laɪkən/ *vt* vergleichen (**to** mit)

like|ness /'laɪknɪs/ *n* Ähnlichkeit *f*. **~wise** *adv* ebenso

liking /'laɪkɪŋ/ *n* Vorliebe *f*; **is it to your ~?** gefällt es Ihnen?

lilac /'laɪlək/ *n* Flieder *m* ● *a* fliederfarben

lily /'lɪlɪ/ *n* Lilie *f*. **~ of the valley** *n* Maiglöckchen *nt*

limb /lɪm/ *n* Glied *nt*

limber /'lɪmbə(r)/ *vi* **~ up** Lockerungsübungen machen

lime[1] /laɪm/ *n* (*fruit*) Limone *f*; (*tree*) Linde *f*

lime[2] *n* Kalk *m*. **~light** *n* **be in the ~light** im Rampenlicht stehen. **~stone** *n* Kalkstein *m*

limit /'lɪmɪt/ *n* Grenze *f*; (*limitation*) Beschränkung *f*; **that's the ~!** (*fam*) das ist doch die Höhe! ● *vt* beschränken (**to** auf + *acc*). **~ation** /-'teɪʃn/ *n* Beschränkung *f*. **~ed** *a* beschränkt; **~ed company** Gesellschaft *f* mit beschränkter Haftung

limousine /'lɪməzi:n/ *n* Limousine *f*

limp[1] /lɪmp/ *n* Hinken *nt*; **have a ~** hinken ● *vi* hinken

limp[2] *a* (**-er, -est**), **-ly** *adv* schlaff

limpet /'lɪmpɪt/ *n* **like a ~** (*fig*) wie eine Klette

limpid /'lɪmpɪd/ *a* klar

linctus /'lɪŋktəs/ *n* **[cough] ~** Hustensirup *m*

line[1] /laɪn/ *n* Linie *f*; (*length of rope, cord*) Leine *f*; (*Teleph*) Leitung *f*; (*of writing*) Zeile *f*; (*row*) Reihe *f*; (*wrinkle*) Falte *f*; (*of business*) Branche *f*; (*Amer: queue*) Schlange *f*;

in ~ with gemäß (+ *dat*) • *vt* säumen ⟨*street*⟩. **~ up** *vi* sich aufstellen • *vt* aufstellen

line² *vt* füttern ⟨*garment*⟩; (*Techn*) auskleiden

lineage /ˈlɪnɪɪdʒ/ *n* Herkunft *f*

linear /ˈlɪnɪə(r)/ *a* linear

lined¹ /laɪnd/ *a* (*wrinkled*) faltig; ⟨*paper*⟩ liniert

lined² *a* ⟨*garment*⟩ gefüttert

linen /ˈlɪnɪn/ *n* Leinen *nt*; (*articles*) Wäsche *f*

liner /ˈlaɪnə(r)/ *n* Passagierschiff *nt*

ˈlinesman *n* (*Sport*) Linienrichter *m*

linger /ˈlɪŋgə(r)/ *vi* [zurück]bleiben

lingerie /ˈlæ̃ʒərɪ/ *n* Damenunterwäsche *f*

linguist /ˈlɪŋgwɪst/ *n* Sprachkundige(r) *m/f*

linguistic /lɪŋˈgwɪstɪk/ *a*, **-ally** *adv* sprachlich. **~s** *n* Linguistik *f*

lining /ˈlaɪnɪŋ/ *n* (*of garment*) Futter *nt*; (*Techn*) Auskleidung *f*

link /lɪŋk/ *n* (*of chain*) Glied *nt*; (*fig*) Verbindung *f* • *vt* verbinden; **~ arms** sich unterhaken

links /lɪŋks/ *n or npl* Golfplatz *m*

lino /ˈlaɪnəʊ/ *n*, **linoleum** /lɪˈnəʊlɪəm/ *n* Linoleum *nt*

lint /lɪnt/ *n* Verbandstoff *m*

lion /ˈlaɪən/ *n* Löwe *m*; **~'s share** (*fig*) Löwenanteil *m*. **~ess** *n* Löwin *f*

lip /lɪp/ *n* Lippe *f*; (*edge*) Rand *m*; (*of jug*) Schnabel *m*

lip: ~-reading *n* Lippenlesen *nt*. **~-service** *n* **pay ~-service** ein Lippenbekenntnis ablegen (**to** zu). **~stick** *n* Lippenstift *m*

liquefy /ˈlɪkwɪfaɪ/ *vt* (*pt/pp* **-ied**) verflüssigen • *vi* sich verflüssigen

liqueur /lɪˈkjʊə(r)/ *n* Likör *m*

liquid /ˈlɪkwɪd/ *n* Flüssigkeit *f* • *a* flüssig

liquidat|e /ˈlɪkwɪdeɪt/ *vt* liquidieren. **~ion** /-ˈdeɪʃn/ *n* Liquidation *f*

liquidize /ˈlɪkwɪdaɪz/ *vt* [im Mixer] pürieren. **~r** *n* (*Culin*) Mixer *m*

liquor /ˈlɪkə(r)/ *n* Alkohol *m*; (*juice*) Flüssigkeit *f*

liquorice /ˈlɪkərɪs/ *n* Lakritze *f*

ˈliquor store *n* (*Amer*) Spirituosengeschäft *nt*

lisp /lɪsp/ *n* Lispeln *nt* • *vt/i* lispeln

list¹ /lɪst/ *n* Liste *f* • *vt* aufführen

list² *vi* ⟨*ship:*⟩ Schlagseite haben

listen /ˈlɪsn/ *vi* zuhören (**to** *dat*); **~ to the radio** Radio hören. **~er** *n* Zuhörer(in) *m(f)*; (*Radio*) Hörer(in) *m(f)*

listless /ˈlɪstlɪs/ *a*, **-ly** *adv* lustlos

lit /lɪt/ *see* **light¹**

litany /ˈlɪtənɪ/ *n* Litanei *f*

literacy /ˈlɪtərəsɪ/ *n* Lese- und Schreibfertigkeit *f*

literal /ˈlɪtərl/ *a* wörtlich. **~ly** *adv* buchstäblich

literary /ˈlɪtərərɪ/ *a* literarisch

literate /ˈlɪtərət/ *a* **be ~** lesen und schreiben können

literature /ˈlɪtrətʃə(r)/ *n* Literatur *f*; (*fam*) Informationsmaterial *nt*

lithe /laɪð/ *a* geschmeidig

Lithuania /lɪθjʊˈeɪnɪə/ *n* Litauen *nt*

litigation /lɪtɪˈgeɪʃn/ *n* Rechtsstreit *m*

litre /ˈli:tə(r)/ *n* Liter *m & nt*

litter /ˈlɪtə(r)/ *n* Abfall *m*; (*Zool*) Wurf *m* • *vt* **be ~ed with** übersät sein mit. **~-bin** *n* Abfalleimer *m*

little /ˈlɪtl/ *a* klein; (*not much*) wenig • *adv* & *n* wenig; **a ~** ein bißchen/wenig; **~ by ~** nach und nach

liturgy /ˈlɪtədʒɪ/ *n* Liturgie *f*

live¹ /laɪv/ *a* lebendig; ⟨*ammunition*⟩ scharf; **~ broadcast** Live-Sendung *f*; **be ~** (*Electr*) unter Strom stehen • *adv* (*Radio, TV*) live

live² /lɪv/ *vi* leben; (*reside*) wohnen; **~ up to** gerecht werden (+ *dat*). **~ on** *vt* leben von; (*eat*) sich ernähren von • *vi* weiterleben

liveli|hood /ˈlaɪvlɪhʊd/ *n* Lebensunterhalt *m*. **~ness** *n* Lebendigkeit *f*

lively /ˈlaɪvlɪ/ *a* (**-ier**, **-iest**) lebhaft, lebendig

liven /ˈlaɪvn/ *v* **~ up** *vt* beleben • *vi* lebhaft werden

liver /ˈlɪvə(r)/ *n* Leber *f*

lives /laɪvz/ *see* **life**

livestock /ˈlaɪv-/ *n* Vieh *nt*

livid /ˈlɪvɪd/ *a* (*fam*) wütend

living /ˈlɪvɪŋ/ *a* lebend • *n* **earn one's ~** seinen Lebensunterhalt verdienen; **the ~** *pl* die Lebenden. **~-room** *n* Wohnzimmer *nt*

lizard /ˈlɪzəd/ *n* Eidechse *f*

load /ləʊd/ *n* Last *f*; (*quantity*) Ladung *f*; (*Electr*) Belastung *f*; **~s of** (*fam*) jede Menge • *vt* laden ⟨*goods, gun*⟩; beladen ⟨*vehicle*⟩; **~ a camera** einen Film in eine Kamera einlegen. **~ed** *a* beladen; (*fam: rich*) steinreich; **~ed question** Fangfrage *f*

loaf¹ /ləʊf/ *n* (*pl* **loaves**) Brot *nt*

loaf² *vi* faulenzen

loan /ləʊn/ *n* Leihgabe *f*; (*money*) Darlehen *nt*; **on ~** geliehen • *vt* leihen (**to** *dat*)

loath /ləʊθ/ *a* **be ~ to do sth** etw ungern tun

loath|e /ləʊð/ *vt* verabscheuen. **~ing** *n* Abscheu *m*. **~some** *a* abscheulich

loaves /ləʊvz/ *see* **loaf**[1]

lobby /ˈlɒbɪ/ *n* Foyer *nt*; (*anteroom*) Vorraum *m*; (*Pol*) Lobby *f*

lobe /ləʊb/ *n* (*of ear*) Ohrläppchen *nt*

lobster /ˈlɒbstə(r)/ *n* Hummer *m*

local /ˈləʊkl/ *a* hiesig; ⟨*time, traffic*⟩ Orts-; **under ~ anaesthetic** unter örtlicher Betäubung; **I'm not ~** ich bin nicht von hier ● *n* Hiesige(r) *m*/*f*; (*fam: public house*) Stammkneipe *f*. **~ au'thority** *n* Kommunalbehörde *f*. **~ call** *n* (*Teleph*) Ortsgespräch *nt*

locality /ləʊˈkælətɪ/ *n* Gegend *f*

localized /ˈləʊkəlaɪzd/ *a* lokalisiert

locally /ˈləʊkəlɪ/ *adv* am Ort

locat|e /ləʊˈkeɪt/ *vt* ausfindig machen; **be ~ed** sich befinden. **~ion** /-ˈkeɪʃn/ *n* Lage *f*; **filmed on ~ion** als Außenaufnahme gedreht

lock[1] /lɒk/ *n* (*hair*) Strähne *f*

lock[2] *n* (*on door*) Schloß *nt*; (*on canal*) Schleuse *f* ● *vt* abschließen ● *vi* sich abschließen lassen. **~ in** *vt* einschließen. **~ out** *vt* ausschließen. **~ up** *vt* abschließen; einsperren ⟨*person*⟩ ● *vi* zuschließen

locker /ˈlɒkə(r)/ *n* Schließfach *nt*; (*Mil*) Spind *m*; (*in hospital*) kleiner Schrank *m*

locket /ˈlɒkɪt/ *n* Medaillon *nt*

lock: ~-out *n* Aussperrung *f*. **~smith** *n* Schlosser *m*

locomotion /ləʊkəˈməʊʃn/ *n* Fortbewegung *f*

locomotive /ləʊkəˈməʊtɪv/ *n* Lokomotive *f*

locum /ˈləʊkəm/ *n* Vertreter(in) *m*(*f*)

locust /ˈləʊkəst/ *n* Heuschrecke *f*

lodge /lɒdʒ/ *n* (*porter's*) Pförtnerhaus *nt*; (*masonic*) Loge *f* ● *vt* (*submit*) einreichen; (*deposit*) deponieren ● *vi* zur Untermiete wohnen (**with** bei); (*become fixed*) steckenbleiben. **~r** *n* Untermieter(in) *m*(*f*)

lodging /ˈlɒdʒɪŋ/ *n* Unterkunft *f*; **~s** *npl* möbliertes Zimmer *nt*

loft /lɒft/ *n* Dachboden *m*

lofty /ˈlɒftɪ/ *a* (**-ier, -iest**) hoch; (*haughty*) hochmütig

log /lɒg/ *n* Baumstamm *m*; (*for fire*) [Holz]scheit *nt*; **sleep like a ~** (*fam*) wie ein Murmeltier schlafen

logarithm /ˈlɒgərɪðm/ *n* Logarithmus *m*

ˈlog-book *n* (*Naut*) Logbuch *nt*

loggerheads /ˈlɒgə-/ *npl* **be at ~** (*fam*) sich in den Haaren liegen

logic /ˈlɒdʒɪk/ *n* Logik *f*. **~al** *a*, **-ly** *adv* logisch

logistics /ləˈdʒɪstɪks/ *npl* Logistik *f*

logo /ˈləʊgəʊ/ *n* Symbol *nt*, Logo *nt*

loin /lɔɪn/ *n* (*Culin*) Lende *f*

loiter /ˈlɔɪtə(r)/ *vi* herumlungern

loll /lɒl/ *vi* sich lümmeln

loll|ipop /ˈlɒlɪpɒp/ *n* Lutscher *m*. **~y** *n* Lutscher *m*; (*fam: money*) Moneten *pl*

London /ˈlʌndən/ *n* London *nt* ● *attrib* Londoner. **~er** *n* Londoner(in) *m*(*f*)

lone /ləʊn/ *a* einzeln. **~liness** *n* Einsamkeit *f*

lonely /ˈləʊnlɪ/ *a* (**-ier, -iest**) einsam

lone|r /ˈləʊnə(r)/ *n* Einzelgänger *m*. **~some** *a* einsam

long[1] /lɒŋ/ *a* (**-er** /ˈlɒŋgə(r)/, **-est** /ˈlɒŋgɪst/) lang; ⟨*journey*⟩ weit; **a ~ time** lange; **a ~ way** weit; **in the ~ run** auf lange Sicht; (*in the end*) letzten Endes ● *adv* lange; **all day ~** den ganzen Tag; **not ~ ago** vor kurzem; **before ~** bald; **no ~er** nicht mehr; **as** *or* **so ~ as** solange; **so ~!** (*fam*) tschüs! **will you be ~?** dauert es noch lange [bei dir]? **it won't take ~** es dauert nicht lange

long[2] *vi* **~ for** sich sehnen nach

long-ˈdistance *a* Fern-; (*Sport*) Langstrecken-

longevity /lɒnˈdʒevətɪ/ *n* Langlebigkeit *f*

ˈlonghand *n* Langschrift *f*

longing /ˈlɒŋɪŋ/ *a*, **-ly** *adv* sehnsüchtig ● *n* Sehnsucht *f*

longitude /ˈlɒŋgɪtju:d/ *n* (*Geog*) Länge *f*

long: ~ jump *n* Weitsprung *m*. **~-life ˈmilk** *n* H-Milch *f*. **~-lived** /-lɪvd/ *a* langlebig. **~-range** *a* (*Mil, Aviat*) Langstrecken-; ⟨*forecast*⟩ langfristig. **~-sighted** *a* weitsichtig. **~-sleeved** *a* langärmelig. **~-suffering** *a* langmütig. **~-term** *a* langfristig. **~ wave** *n* Langwelle *f*. **~-winded** /-ˈwɪndɪd/ *a* langatmig

loo /lu:/ *n* (*fam*) Klo *nt*

look /lʊk/ *n* Blick *m*; (*appearance*) Aussehen *nt*; **[good] ~s** *pl* [gutes] Aussehen *nt*; **have a ~ at** sich (*dat*) ansehen; **go and have a ~** sieh mal nach ● *vi* sehen; (*search*) nachsehen; (*seem*) aussehen; **don't ~** sieh nicht hin; **~ here!** hören Sie mal! **~**

at ansehen; ~ **for** suchen; ~ **forward to** sich freuen auf (+ *acc*); ~ **in on** vorbeischauen bei; ~ **into** (*examine*) nachgehen (+ *dat*); ~ **like** aussehen wie; ~ **on to** ⟨*room:*⟩ gehen auf (+ *acc*). ~ **after** *vt* betreuen. ~ **down** *vi* hinuntersehen; ~ **down on s.o.** (*fig*) auf jdn herabsehen. ~ **out** *vi* hinaus-/heraussehen; (*take care*) aufpassen; ~ **out for** Ausschau halten nach; ~ **out!** Vorsicht! ~ **round** *vi* sich umsehen. ~ **up** *vi* aufblicken; ~ **up to s.o.** (*fig*) zu jdm aufsehen ● *vt* nachschlagen ⟨*word*⟩

'look-out *n* Wache *f*; (*prospect*) Aussicht *f*; **be on the ~ for** Ausschau halten nach

loom[1] /lu:m/ *n* Webstuhl *m*

loom[2] *vi* auftauchen; (*fig*) sich abzeichnen

loony /'lu:nɪ/ *a* (*fam*) verrückt

loop /lu:p/ *n* Schlinge *f*; (*in road*) Schleife *f*; (*on garment*) Aufhänger *m* ● *vt* schlingen. **~hole** *n* Hintertürchen *nt*; (*in the law*) Lücke *f*

loose /lu:s/ *a* (**-r, -st**), **-ly** *adv* lose; (*not tight enough*) locker; (*inexact*) frei; **be at a ~ end** nichts zu tun haben; **set ~** freilassen; **run ~** frei herumlaufen. ~ **'change** *n* Kleingeld *nt*. ~ **'chippings** *npl* Rollsplit *m*

loosen /'lu:sn/ *vt* lockern ● *vi* sich lockern

loot /lu:t/ *n* Beute *f* ● *vt/i* plündern. **~er** *n* Plünderer *m*

lop /lɒp/ *vt* (*pt/pp* **lopped**) stutzen. ~ **off** *vt* abhacken

lop'sided *a* schief

loquacious /lə'kweɪʃəs/ *a* redselig

lord /lɔ:d/ *n* Herr *m*; (*title*) Lord *m*; **House of L~s** ≈ Oberhaus *nt*; **the L~'s Prayer** das Vaterunser; **good L~!** du liebe Zeit!

lore /lɔ:(r)/ *n* Überlieferung *f*

lorry /'lɒrɪ/ *n* Last[kraft]wagen *m*

lose /lu:z/ *v* (*pt/pp* **lost**) ● *vt* verlieren; (*miss*) verpassen ● *vi* verlieren; ⟨*clock:*⟩ nachgehen; **get lost** verlorengehen; ⟨*person:*⟩ sich verlaufen. **~r** *n* Verlierer *m*

loss /lɒs/ *n* Verlust *m*; **be at a ~** nicht mehr weiter wissen; **be at a ~ for words** nicht wissen, was man sagen soll

lost /lɒst/ *see* **lose**. ~ **'property office** *n* Fundbüro *nt*

lot[1] /lɒt/ *n* Los *nt*; (*at auction*) Posten *m*; **draw ~s** losen (**for** um)

lot[2] *n* **the ~** alle; (*everything*) alles; **a ~ [of]** viel; (*many*) viele; **~s of** (*fam*) eine Menge; **it has changed a ~** es hat sich sehr verändert

lotion /'ləʊʃn/ *n* Lotion *f*

lottery /'lɒtərɪ/ *n* Lotterie *f*. **~ ticket** *n* Los *nt*

loud /laʊd/ *a* (**-er, -est**), **-ly** *adv* laut; ⟨*colours*⟩ grell ● *adv* **[out]** ~ laut. ~**'hailer** *n* Megaphon *nt*. **~'speaker** *n* Lautsprecher *m*

lounge /laʊndʒ/ *n* Wohnzimmer *nt*; (*in hotel*) Aufenthaltsraum *m*. ● *vi* sich lümmeln. ~ **suit** *n* Straßenanzug *m*

louse /laʊs/ *n* (*pl* **lice**) Laus *f*

lousy /'laʊzɪ/ *a* (**-ier, -iest**) (*fam*) lausig

lout /laʊt/ *n* Flegel *m*, Lümmel *m*. **~ish** *a* flegelhaft

lovable /'lʌvəbl/ *a* liebenswert

love /lʌv/ *n* Liebe *f*; (*Tennis*) null; **in ~** verliebt ● *vt* lieben; **~ doing sth** etw sehr gerne machen; **I ~ chocolate** ich esse sehr gerne Schokolade. **~-affair** *n* Liebesverhältnis *nt*. ~ **letter** *n* Liebesbrief *m*

lovely /'lʌvlɪ/ *a* (**-ier, -iest**) schön; **we had a ~ time** es war sehr schön

lover /'lʌvə(r)/ *n* Liebhaber *m*

love: ~ song *n* Liebeslied *nt*. **~ story** *n* Liebesgeschichte *f*

loving /'lʌvɪŋ/ *a*, **-ly** *adv* liebevoll

low /ləʊ/ *a* (**-er, -est**) niedrig; ⟨*cloud, note*⟩ tief; ⟨*voice*⟩ leise; (*depressed*) niedergeschlagen ● *adv* niedrig; ⟨*fly, sing*⟩ tief; ⟨*speak*⟩ leise; **feel ~** deprimiert sein ● *n* (*Meteorol*) Tief *nt*; (*fig*) Tiefstand *m*

low: ~brow *a* geistig anspruchslos. **~-cut** *a* ⟨*dress*⟩ tief ausgeschnitten

lower /'ləʊə(r)/ *a & adv see* **low** ● *vt* niedriger machen; (*let down*) herunterlassen; (*reduce*) senken; **~ oneself** sich herabwürdigen

low: ~-'fat *a* fettarm. **~-'grade** *a* minderwertig. **~lands** /-ləndz/ *npl* Tiefland *nt*. ~ **'tide** *n* Ebbe *f*

loyal /'lɔɪəl/ *a*, **-ly** *adv* treu. **~ty** *n* Treue *f*

lozenge /'lɒzɪndʒ/ *n* Pastille *f*

Ltd *abbr* (**Limited**) GmbH

lubricant /'lu:brɪkənt/ *n* Schmiermittel *nt*

lubricat|e /'lu:brɪkeɪt/ *vt* schmieren. **~ion** /-'keɪʃn/ *n* Schmierung *f*

lucid /'lu:sɪd/ *a* klar. **~ity** /-'sɪdətɪ/ *n* Klarheit *f*

luck /lʌk/ *n* Glück *nt*; **bad ~** Pech *nt*; **good ~!** viel Glück! **~ily** *adv* glücklicherweise, zum Glück

lucky /ˈlʌkɪ/ *a* (**-ier, -iest**) glücklich; ⟨*day, number*⟩ Glücks-; **be ~** Glück haben; ⟨*thing:*⟩ Glück bringen. **~ ˈcharm** *n* Amulett *nt*

lucrative /ˈlu:krətɪv/ *a* einträglich

ludicrous /ˈlu:dɪkrəs/ *a* lächerlich

lug /lʌg/ *vt* (*pt/pp* **lugged**) (*fam*) schleppen

luggage /ˈlʌgɪdʒ/ *n* Gepäck *nt*

luggage: ~-rack *n* Gepäckablage *f*. **~ trolley** *n* Kofferkuli *m*. **~-van** *n* Gepäckwagen *m*

lugubrious /lu:ˈgu:brɪəs/ *a* traurig

lukewarm /ˈlu:k-/ *a* lauwarm

lull /lʌl/ *n* Pause *f* • *vt* **~ to sleep** einschläfern

lullaby /ˈlʌləbaɪ/ *n* Wiegenlied *nt*

lumbago /lʌmˈbeɪgəʊ/ *n* Hexenschuß *m*

lumber /ˈlʌmbə(r)/ *n* Gerümpel *nt*; (*Amer: timber*) Bauholz *nt* • *vt* **~ s.o. with sth** jdm etw aufhalsen. **~jack** *n* (*Amer*) Holzfäller *m*

luminous /ˈlu:mɪnəs/ *a* leuchtend; **be ~** leuchten

lump[1] /lʌmp/ *n* Klumpen *m*; (*of sugar*) Stück *nt*; (*swelling*) Beule *f*; (*in breast*) Knoten *m*; (*tumour*) Geschwulst *f*; **a ~ in one's throat** (*fam*) ein Kloß im Hals • *vt* **~ together** zusammentun

lump[2] *vt* **~ it** (*fam*) sich damit abfinden

lump: ~ sugar *n* Würfelzucker *m*. **~ ˈsum** *n* Pauschalsumme *f*

lumpy /ˈlʌmpɪ/ *a* (**-ier, -iest**) klumpig

lunacy /ˈlu:nəsɪ/ *n* Wahnsinn *m*

lunar /ˈlu:nə(r)/ *a* Mond-

lunatic /ˈlu:nətɪk/ *n* Wahnsinnige(r) *m/f*

lunch /lʌntʃ/ *n* Mittagessen *nt* • *vi* zu Mittag essen

luncheon /ˈlʌntʃn/ *n* Mittagessen *nt*. **~ meat** *n* Frühstücksfleisch *nt*. **~ voucher** *n* Essensbon *m*

lunch: ~-hour *n* Mittagspause *f*. **~-time** *n* Mittagszeit *f*

lung /lʌŋ/ *n* Lungenflügel *m*; **~s** *pl* Lunge *f*. **~ cancer** *n* Lungenkrebs *m*

lunge /lʌndʒ/ *vi* sich stürzen (**at** auf + *acc*)

lurch[1] /lɜ:tʃ/ *n* **leave in the ~** (*fam*) im Stich lassen

lurch[2] *vi* schleudern; ⟨*person:*⟩ torkeln

lure /lʊə(r)/ *n* Lockung *f*; (*bait*) Köder *m* • *vt* locken

lurid /ˈlʊərɪd/ *a* grell; (*sensational*) reißerisch

lurk /lɜ:k/ *vi* lauern

luscious /ˈlʌʃəs/ *a* lecker, köstlich

lush /lʌʃ/ *a* üppig

lust /lʌst/ *n* Begierde *f* • *vi* **~ after** gieren nach. **~ful** *a* lüstern

lustre /ˈlʌstə(r)/ *n* Glanz *m*

lusty /ˈlʌstɪ/ *a* (**-ier, -iest**) kräftig

lute /lu:t/ *n* Laute *f*

luxuriant /lʌgˈʒʊərɪənt/ *a* üppig

luxurious /lʌgˈʒʊərɪəs/ *a*, **-ly** *adv* luxuriös

luxury /ˈlʌkʃərɪ/ *n* Luxus *m* • *attrib* Luxus-

lying /ˈlaɪɪŋ/ *see* **lie**[1], **lie**[2]

lymph gland /ˈlɪmf-/ *n* Lymphdrüse *f*

lynch /lɪntʃ/ *vt* lynchen

lynx /lɪŋks/ *n* Luchs *m*

lyric /ˈlɪrɪk/ *a* lyrisch. **~al** *a* lyrisch; (*fam: enthusiastic*) schwärmerisch. **~ poetry** *n* Lyrik *f*. **~s** *npl* [Lied]text *m*

M

mac /mæk/ *n* (*fam*) Regenmantel *m*

macabre /məˈkɑ:br/ *a* makaber

macaroni /mækəˈrəʊnɪ/ *n* Makkaroni *pl*

macaroon /mækəˈru:n/ *n* Makrone *f*

mace[1] /meɪs/ *n* Amtsstab *m*

mace[2] *n* (*spice*) Muskatblüte *f*

machinations /mækɪˈneɪʃnz/ *pl* Machenschaften *pl*

machine /məˈʃi:n/ *n* Maschine *f* • *vt* (*sew*) mit der Maschine nähen; (*Techn*) maschinell bearbeiten. **~-gun** *n* Maschinengewehr *nt*

machinery /məˈʃi:nərɪ/ *n* Maschinerie *f*

machine tool *n* Werkzeugmaschine *f*

machinist /məˈʃi:nɪst/ *n* Maschinist *m*; (*on sewing machine*) Maschinennäherin *f*

mackerel /ˈmækrl/ *n inv* Makrele *f*

mackintosh /ˈmækɪntɒʃ/ *n* Regenmantel *m*

mad /mæd/ *a* (**madder, maddest**) verrückt; (*dog*) tollwütig; (*fam: angry*) böse (**at** auf + *acc*)

madam /ˈmædəm/ *n* gnädige Frau *f*

madden /ˈmædn/ *vt* (*make angry*) wütend machen

made /meɪd/ *see* **make**; ~ **to measure** maßgeschneidert

Madeira cake /mə'dɪərə-/ *n* Sandkuchen *m*

mad|ly /'mædlɪ/ *adv* (*fam*) wahnsinnig. ~**man** *n* Irre(r) *m*. ~**ness** *n* Wahnsinn *m*

madonna /mə'dɒnə/ *n* Madonna *f*

magazine /mægə'zi:n/ *n* Zeitschrift *f*; (*Mil, Phot*) Magazin *nt*

maggot /'mægət/ *n* Made *f*. ~**y** *a* madig

Magi /'meɪdʒaɪ/ *npl* **the** ~ die Heiligen Drei Könige

magic /'mædʒɪk/ *n* Zauber *m*; (*tricks*) Zauberkunst *f* ● *a* magisch; ⟨*word, wand, flute*⟩ Zauber-. ~**al** *a* zauberhaft

magician /mə'dʒɪʃn/ *n* Zauberer *m*; (*entertainer*) Zauberkünstler *m*

magistrate /'mædʒɪstreɪt/ *n* ≈ Friedensrichter *m*

magnanim|ity /mægnə'nɪmətɪ/ *n* Großmut *f*. ~**ous** /-'nænɪməs/ *a* großmütig

magnesia /mæg'ni:ʃə/ *n* Magnesia *f*

magnet /'mægnɪt/ *n* Magnet *m*. ~**ic** /-'netɪk/ *a* magnetisch. ~**ism** *n* Magnetismus *m*. ~**ize** *vt* magnetisieren

magnification /mægnɪfɪ'keɪʃn/ *n* Vergrößerung *f*

magnificen|ce /mæg'nɪfɪsəns/ *n* Großartigkeit *f*. ~**t** *a*, **-ly** *adv* großartig

magnify /'mægnɪfaɪ/ *vt* (*pt/pp* **-ied**) vergrößern; (*exaggerate*) übertreiben. ~**ing glass** *n* Vergrößerungsglas *nt*

magnitude /'mægnɪtju:d/ *n* Größe *f*; (*importance*) Bedeutung *f*

magpie /'mægpaɪ/ *n* Elster *f*

mahogany /mə'hɒgənɪ/ *n* Mahagoni *nt*

maid /meɪd/ *n* Dienstmädchen *nt*; (*liter: girl*) Maid *f*; **old** ~ (*pej*) alte Jungfer *f*

maiden /'meɪdn/ *n* (*liter*) Maid *f* ● *a* ⟨*speech, voyage*⟩ Jungfern-. ~ **'aunt** *n* unverheiratete Tante *f*. ~ **name** *n* Mädchenname *m*

mail¹ /meɪl/ *n* Kettenpanzer *m*

mail² *n* Post *f* ● *vt* mit der Post schicken; (*send off*) abschicken

mail: ~**-bag** *n* Postsack *m*. ~**box** *n* (*Amer*) Briefkasten *m*. ~**ing list** *n* Postversandliste *f*. ~**man** *n* (*Amer*) Briefträger *m*. ~**-order firm** *n* Versandhaus *nt*

maim /meɪm/ *vt* verstümmeln

main¹ /meɪn/ *n* (*water, gas, electricity*) Hauptleitung *f*

main² *a* Haupt- ● *n* **in the** ~ im großen und ganzen

main: ~**land** /-lənd/ *n* Festland *nt*. ~**ly** *adv* hauptsächlich. ~**stay** *n* (*fig*) Stütze *f*. ~ **street** *n* Hauptstraße *f*

maintain /meɪn'teɪn/ *vt* aufrechterhalten; (*keep in repair*) instandhalten; (*support*) unterhalten; (*claim*) behaupten

maintenance /'meɪntənəns/ *n* Aufrechterhaltung *f*; (*care*) Instandhaltung *f*; (*allowance*) Unterhalt *m*

maisonette /meɪzə'net/ *n* Wohnung [auf zwei Etagen]

maize /meɪz/ *n* Mais *m*

majestic /mə'dʒestɪk/ *a*, **-ally** *adv* majestätisch

majesty /'mædʒəstɪ/ *n* Majestät *f*

major /'meɪdʒə(r)/ *a* größer ● *n* (*Mil*) Major *m*; (*Mus*) Dur *nt* ● *vi* (*Amer*) ~ **in** als Hauptfach studieren

Majorca /mə'jɔ:kə/ *n* Mallorca *nt*

majority /mə'dʒɒrətɪ/ *n* Mehrheit *f*; **the** ~ in der Mehrzahl

major road *n* Hauptverkehrsstraße *f*

make /meɪk/ *n* (*brand*) Marke *f* ● (*pt/pp* **made**) ● *vt* machen; (*force*) zwingen; (*earn*) verdienen; halten ⟨*speech*⟩; treffen ⟨*decision*⟩; erreichen ⟨*destination*⟩ ● *vi* ~ **as if** Miene machen zu. ~ **do** *vi* zurechtkommen (**with** mit). ~ **for** *vi* zusteuern auf (+ *acc*). ~ **off** *vi* sich davonmachen (**with** mit). ~ **out** (*distinguish*) ausmachen; (*write out*) ausstellen; (*assert*) behaupten. ~ **over** *vt* überschreiben (**to** auf + *acc*). ~ **up** *vt* (*constitute*) bilden; (*invent*) erfinden; (*apply cosmetics to*) schminken; ~ **up one's mind** sich entschließen ● *vi* sich versöhnen; ~ **up for sth** etw wiedergutmachen; ~ **up for lost time** verlorene Zeit aufholen

'make-believe *n* Phantasie *f*

maker /'meɪkə(r)/ *n* Hersteller *m*

make: ~**shift** *a* behelfsmäßig ● *n* Notbehelf *m*. ~**-up** *n* Make-up *nt*

making /'meɪkɪŋ/ *n* **have the** ~**s** das Zeug haben zu

maladjusted /mælə'dʒʌstɪd/ *a* verhaltensgestört

malaise /mə'leɪz/ *n* (*fig*) Unbehagen *nt*

male /meɪl/ *a* männlich ● *n* Mann *m*; (*animal*) Männchen *nt*. **~ nurse** *n* Krankenpfleger *m*. **~ voice 'choir** *n* Männerchor *m*

malevolen|ce /mə'levələns/ *n* Bosheit *f*. **~t** *a* boshaft

malfunction /mæl'fʌŋkʃn/ *n* technische Störung *f*; (*Med*) Funktionsstörung *f* ● *vi* nicht richtig funktionieren

malice /'mælɪs/ *n* Bosheit *f*; **bear s.o. ~** einen Groll gegen jdn hegen

malicious /mə'lɪʃəs/ *a*, **-ly** *adv* böswillig

malign /mə'laɪn/ *vt* verleumden

malignan|cy /mə'lɪgnənsɪ/ *n* Bösartigkeit *f*. **~t** *a* bösartig

malinger /mə'lɪŋgə(r)/ *vi* simulieren, sich krank stellen. **~er** *n* Simulant *m*

malleable /'mælɪəbl/ *a* formbar

mallet /'mælɪt/ *n* Holzhammer *m*

malnu'trition /mæl-/ *n* Unterernährung *f*

mal'practice *n* Berufsvergehen *nt*

malt /mɔ:lt/ *n* Malz *nt*

mal'treat /mæl-/ *vt* mißhandeln. **~ment** *n* Mißhandlung *f*

mammal /'mæml/ *n* Säugetier *nt*

mammoth /'mæməθ/ *a* riesig ● *n* Mammut *nt*

man /mæn/ *n* (*pl* **men**) Mann *m*; (*mankind*) der Mensch; (*chess*) Figur *f*; (*draughts*) Stein *m* ● *vt* (*pt/pp* **manned**) bemannen ⟨*ship*⟩; bedienen ⟨*pump*⟩; besetzen ⟨*counter*⟩

manacle /'mænəkl/ *vt* fesseln (**to** an + *acc*); **~d** in Handschellen

manage /'mænɪdʒ/ *vt* leiten; verwalten ⟨*estate*⟩; (*cope with*) fertig werden mit; **~ to do sth** es schaffen, etw zu tun ● *vi* zurechtkommen; **~ on** auskommen mit. **~able** /-əbl/ *a* ⟨*tool*⟩ handlich; ⟨*person*⟩ fügsam. **~ment** /-mənt/ *n* **the ~ment** die Geschäftsleitung *f*

manager /'mænɪdʒə(r)/ *n* Geschäftsführer *m*; (*of bank*) Direktor *m*; (*of estate*) Verwalter *m*; (*Sport*) [Chef]trainer *m*. **~ess** *n* Geschäftsführer(in) *f*. **~ial** /-'dʒɪərɪəl/ *a* **~ial staff** Führungskräfte *pl*

managing /'mænɪdʒɪŋ/ *a* **~ director** Generaldirektor *m*

mandarin /'mændərɪn/ *n* **~ [orange]** Mandarine *f*

mandat|e /'mændeɪt/ *n* Mandat *nt*. **~ory** /-dətrɪ/ *a* obligatorisch

mane /meɪn/ *n* Mähne *f*

manful /'mænfl/ *a*, **-ly** *adv* mannhaft

manger /'meɪndʒə(r)/ *n* Krippe *f*

mangle[1] /'mæŋgl/ *n* Wringmaschine *f*; (*for smoothing*) Mangel *f*

mangle[2] *vt* (*damage*) verstümmeln

mango /'mæŋgəʊ/ *n* (*pl* **-es**) Mango *f*

mangy /'meɪndʒɪ/ *a* ⟨*dog*⟩ räudig

man: ~'handle *vt* grob behandeln ⟨*person*⟩. **~hole** *n* Kanalschacht *m*. **~hole cover** *n* Kanaldeckel *m*. **~hood** *n* Mannesalter *nt*; (*quality*) Männlichkeit *f*. **~-hour** *n* Arbeitsstunde *f*. **~-hunt** *n* Fahndung *f*

man|ia /'meɪnɪə/ *n* Manie *f*. **~iac** /-ɪæk/ *n* Wahnsinnige(r) *m/f*

manicur|e /'mænɪkjʊə(r)/ *n* Maniküre *f* ● *vt* maniküren. **~ist** *n* Maniküre *f*

manifest /'mænɪfest/ *a*, **-ly** *adv* offensichtlich ● *vt* **~ itself** sich manifestieren

manifesto /mænɪ'festəʊ/ *n* Manifest *nt*

manifold /'mænɪfəʊld/ *a* mannigfaltig

manipulat|e /mə'nɪpjʊleɪt/ *vt* handhaben; (*pej*) manipulieren. **~ion** /-'leɪʃn/ *n* Manipulation *f*

man'kind *n* die Menschheit

manly /'mænlɪ/ *a* männlich

'man-made *a* künstlich. **~ fibre** *n* Kunstfaser *f*

manner /'mænə(r)/ *n* Weise *f*; (*kind, behaviour*) Art *f*; **in this ~** auf diese Weise; **[good/bad] ~s** [gute/schlechte] Manieren *pl*. **~ism** *n* Angewohnheit *f*

mannish /'mænɪʃ/ *a* männlich

manœuvrable /mə'nu:vrəbl/ *a* manövrierfähig

manœuvre /mə'nu:və(r)/ *n* Manöver *nt* ● *vt/i* manövrieren

manor /'mænə(r)/ *n* Gutshof *m*; (*house*) Gutshaus *nt*

man: ~power *n* Arbeitskräfte *pl*. **~servant** *n* (*pl* **menservants**) Diener *m*

mansion /'mænʃn/ *n* Villa *f*

'manslaughter *n* Totschlag *m*

mantelpiece /'mæntl-/ *n* Kaminsims *m* & *nt*

manual /'mænjʊəl/ *a* Hand- ● *n* Handbuch *nt*

manufacture /mænjʊ'fæktʃə(r)/ *vt* herstellen ● *n* Herstellung *f*. **~r** *n* Hersteller *m*

manure /mə'njʊə(r)/ *n* Mist *m*

manuscript /'mænjʊskrɪpt/ *n* Manuskript *nt*

many /'menı/ *a* viele; ~ **a time** oft ● *n* **a good/great** ~ sehr viele

map /mæp/ *n* Landkarte *f*; (*of town*) Stadtplan *m* ● *vt* (*pt/pp* **mapped**) ~ **out** (*fig*) ausarbeiten

maple /'meıpl/ *n* Ahorn *m*

mar /mɑ:(r)/ *vt* (*pt/pp* **marred**) verderben

marathon /'mærəθən/ *n* Marathon *m*

marauding /mə'rɔ:dıŋ/ *a* plündernd

marble /'mɑ:bl/ *n* Marmor *m*; (*for game*) Murmel *f*

March /mɑ:tʃ/ *n* März *m*

march *n* Marsch *m* ● *vi* marschieren ● *vt* marschieren lassen; ~ **s.o. off** jdn abführen

mare /'meə(r)/ *n* Stute *f*

margarine /mɑ:dʒə'ri:n/ *n* Margarine *f*

margin /'mɑ:dʒın/ *n* Rand *m*; (*leeway*) Spielraum *m*; (*Comm*) Spanne *f*. ~**al** *a*, **-ly** *adv* geringfügig

marigold /'mærıgəuld/ *n* Ringelblume *f*

marijuana /mærı'hwɑ:nə/ *n* Marihuana *nt*

marina /mə'ri:nə/ *n* Jachthafen *m*

marinade /mærı'neıd/ *n* Marinade *f* ● *vt* marinieren

marine /mə'ri:n/ *a* Meeres- ● *n* Marine *f*; (*sailor*) Marineinfanterist *m*

marionette /mærıə'net/ *n* Marionette *f*

marital /'mærıtl/ *a* ehelich. ~ **status** *n* Familienstand *m*

maritime /'mærıtaım/ *a* See-

marjoram /'mɑ:dʒərəm/ *n* Majoran *m*

mark[1] /mɑ:k/ *n* (*currency*) Mark *f*

mark[2] *n* Fleck *m*; (*sign*) Zeichen *nt*; (*trace*) Spur *f*; (*target*) Ziel *nt*; (*Sch*) Note *f* ● *vt* markieren; (*spoil*) beschädigen; (*characterize*) kennzeichnen; (*Sch*) korrigieren; (*Sport*) decken; ~ **time** (*Mil*) auf der Stelle treten; (*fig*) abwarten; ~ **my words** das [eine] will ich dir sagen. ~ **out** *vt* markieren

marked /mɑ:kt/ *a*, ~**ly** /-kıdlı/ *adv* deutlich; (*pronounced*) ausgeprägt

marker /'mɑ:kə(r)/ *n* Marke *f*; (*of exam*) Korrektor(in) *m*(*f*)

market /'mɑ:kıt/ *n* Markt *m* ● *vt* vertreiben; (*launch*) auf den Markt bringen. ~**ing** *n* Marketing *nt*. ~ **re'search** *n* Marktforschung *f*

marking /'mɑ:kıŋ/ *n* Markierung *f*; (*on animal*) Zeichnung *f*

marksman /'mɑ:ksmən/ *n* Scharfschütze *m*

marmalade /'mɑ:məleıd/ *n* Orangenmarmelade *f*

marmot /'mɑ:mət/ *n* Murmeltier *nt*

maroon /mə'ru:n/ *a* dunkelrot

marooned /mə'ru:nd/ *a* (*fig*) von der Außenwelt abgeschnitten

marquee /mɑ:'ki:/ *n* Festzelt *nt*; (*Amer: awning*) Markise *f*

marquetry /'mɑ:kıtrı/ *n* Einlegearbeit *f*

marquis /'mɑ:kwıs/ *n* Marquis *m*

marriage /'mærıdʒ/ *n* Ehe *f*; (*wedding*) Hochzeit *f*. ~**able** /-əbl/ *a* heiratsfähig

married /'mærıd/ *see* **marry** ● *a* verheiratet. ~ **life** *n* Eheleben *nt*

marrow /'mærəʊ/ *n* (*Anat*) Mark *nt*; (*vegetable*) Kürbis *m*

marr|y /'mærı/ *vt/i* (*pt/pp* **married**) heiraten; (*unite*) trauen; **get** ~**ied** heiraten

marsh /mɑ:ʃ/ *n* Sumpf *m*

marshal /'mɑ:ʃl/ *n* Marschall *m*; (*steward*) Ordner *m* ● *vt* (*pt/pp* **marshalled**) (*Mil*) formieren; (*fig*) ordnen

marshy /'mɑ:ʃı/ *a* sumpfig

marsupial /mɑ:'su:pıəl/ *n* Beuteltier *nt*

martial /'mɑ:ʃl/ *a* kriegerisch. ~ **'law** *n* Kriegsrecht *nt*

martyr /'mɑ:tə(r)/ *n* Märtyrer(in) *m*(*f*) ● *vt* zum Märtyrer machen. ~**dom** /-dəm/ *n* Martyrium *nt*

marvel /'mɑ:vl/ *n* Wunder *nt* ● *vi* (*pt/pp* **marvelled**) staunen (**at** über + *acc*). ~**lous** /-vələs/ *a*, **-ly** *adv* wunderbar

Marxis|m /'mɑ:ksızm/ *n* Marxismus *m*. ~**t** *a* marxistisch ● *n* Marxist(in) *m*(*f*)

marzipan /'mɑ:zıpæn/ *n* Marzipan *nt*

mascara /mæ'skɑ:rə/ *n* Wimperntusche *f*

mascot /'mæskət/ *n* Maskottchen *nt*

masculin|e /'mæskjʊlın/ *a* männlich ● *n* (*Gram*) Maskulinum *nt*. ~**ity** /-'lınətı/ *n* Männlichkeit *f*

mash /mæʃ/ *n* (*fam, Culin*) Kartoffelpüree *nt* ● *vt* stampfen. ~**ed potatoes** *npl* Kartoffelpüree *nt*

mask /mɑ:sk/ *n* Maske *f* ● *vt* maskieren

masochis|m /'mæsəkızm/ *n* Masochismus *m*. ~**t** /-ıst/ *n* Masochist *m*

mason /'meısn/ *n* Steinmetz *m*

Mason *n* Freimaurer *m*. ~**ic** /mə'sɒnık/ *a* freimaurerisch

masonry /ˈmeɪsnrɪ/ *n* Mauerwerk *nt*

masquerade /mæskəˈreɪd/ *n* (*fig*) Maskerade *f* ● *vi* ~ **as** (*pose*) sich ausgeben als

mass¹ /mæs/ *n* (*Relig*) Messe *f*

mass² *n* Masse *f* ● *vi* sich sammeln; (*Mil*) sich massieren

massacre /ˈmæsəkə(r)/ *n* Massaker *nt* ● *vt* niedermetzeln

massage /ˈmæsɑːʒ/ *n* Massage *f* ● *vt* massieren

masseu|r /mæˈsɜː(r)/ *n* Masseur *m*. **~se** /-ˈsɜːz/ *n* Masseuse *f*

massive /ˈmæsɪv/ *a* massiv; (*huge*) riesig

mass: ~ **media** *npl* Massenmedien *pl*. **~-proˈduce** *vt* in Massenproduktion herstellen. ~ **proˈduction** *n* Massenproduktion *f*

mast /mɑːst/ *n* Mast *m*

master /ˈmɑːstə(r)/ *n* Herr *m*; (*teacher*) Lehrer *m*; (*craftsman, artist*) Meister *m*; (*of ship*) Kapitän *m* ● *vt* meistern; beherrschen ⟨*language*⟩

master: **~-key** *n* Hauptschlüssel *m*. **~ly** *a* meisterhaft. **~-mind** *n* führender Kopf *m* ● *vt* der führende Kopf sein von. **~piece** *n* Meisterwerk *nt*. **~y** *n* (*of subject*) Beherrschung *f*

masturbat|e /ˈmæstəbeɪt/ *vi* masturbieren. **~ion** /-ˈbeɪʃn/ *n* Masturbation *f*

mat /mæt/ *n* Matte *f*; (*on table*) Untersatz *m*

match¹ /mætʃ/ *n* Wettkampf *m*; (*in ball games*) Spiel *nt*; (*Tennis*) Match *nt*; (*marriage*) Heirat *f*; **be a good ~** ⟨*colours:*⟩ gut zusammenpassen; **be no ~ for s.o.** jdm nicht gewachsen sein ● *vt* (*equal*) gleichkommen (+ *dat*); (*be like*) passen zu; (*find sth similar*) etwas Passendes finden zu ● *vi* zusammenpassen

match² *n* Streichholz *nt*. **~box** *n* Streichholzschachtel *f*

matching /ˈmætʃɪŋ/ *a* [zusammen]passend

mate¹ /meɪt/ *n* Kumpel *m*; (*assistant*) Gehilfe *m*; (*Naut*) Maat *m*; (*Zool*) Männchen *nt*; (*female*) Weibchen *nt* ● *vi* sich paaren ● *vt* paaren

mate² *n* (*Chess*) Matt *nt*

material /məˈtɪərɪəl/ *n* Material *nt*; (*fabric*) Stoff *m*; **raw ~s** Rohstoffe *pl* ● *a* materiell

material|ism /məˈtɪərɪəlɪzm/ *n* Materialismus *m*. **~istic** /-ˈlɪstɪk/ *a* materialistisch. **~ize** /-laɪz/ *vi* sich verwirklichen

maternal /məˈtɜːnl/ *a* mütterlich

maternity /məˈtɜːnətɪ/ *n* Mutterschaft *f*. ~ **clothes** *npl* Umstandskleidung *f*. ~ **ward** *n* Entbindungsstation *f*

matey /ˈmeɪtɪ/ *a* (*fam*) freundlich

mathematic|al /mæθəˈmætɪkl/ *a*, **-ly** *adv* mathematisch. **~ian** /-məˈtɪʃn/ *n* Mathematiker(in) *m*(*f*)

mathematics /mæθəˈmætɪks/ *n* Mathematik *f*

maths /mæθs/ *n* (*fam*) Mathe *f*

matinée /ˈmætɪneɪ/ *n* (*Theat*) Nachmittagsvorstellung *f*

matriculat|e /məˈtrɪkjʊleɪt/ *vi* sich immatrikulieren. **~ion** /-ˈleɪʃn/ *n* Immatrikulation *f*

matrimon|ial /mætrɪˈməʊnɪəl/ *a* Ehe-. **~y** /ˈmætrɪmənɪ/ *n* Ehe *f*

matrix /ˈmeɪtrɪks/ *n* (*pl* **matrices** /-siːz/) *n* (*Techn: mould*) Matrize *f*

matron /ˈmeɪtrən/ *n* (*of hospital*) Oberin *f*; (*of school*) Hausmutter *f*. **~ly** *a* matronenhaft

matt /mæt/ *a* matt

matted /ˈmætɪd/ *a* verfilzt

matter /ˈmætə(r)/ *n* (*affair*) Sache *f*; (*pus*) Eiter *m*; (*Phys: substance*) Materie *f*; **money ~s** Geldangelegenheiten *pl*; **as a ~ of fact** eigentlich; **what is the ~?** was ist los? ● *vi* wichtig sein; ~ **to s.o.** jdm etwas ausmachen; **it doesn't ~** es macht nichts. **~-of-fact** *a* sachlich

matting /ˈmætɪŋ/ *n* Matten *pl*

mattress /ˈmætrɪs/ *n* Matratze *f*

matur|e /məˈtjʊə(r)/ *a* reif; (*Comm*) fällig ● *vi* reifen; ⟨*person:*⟩ reifer werden; (*Comm*) fällig werden ● *vt* reifen lassen. **~ity** *n* Reife *f*; (*Comm*) Fälligkeit *f*

maul /mɔːl/ *vt* übel zurichten

Maundy /ˈmɔːndɪ/ *n* ~ **Thursday** Gründonnerstag *m*

mauve /məʊv/ *a* lila

mawkish /ˈmɔːkɪʃ/ *a* rührselig

maxim /ˈmæksɪm/ *n* Maxime *f*

maximum /ˈmæksɪməm/ *a* maximal ● *n* (*pl* **-ima**) Maximum *nt*. ~ **speed** *n* Höchstgeschwindigkeit *f*

may /meɪ/ *v aux* (*nur Präsens*) (*be allowed to*) dürfen; (*be possible*) können; **may I come in?** darf ich reinkommen? **may he succeed** möge es ihm gelingen; **I may as well stay** am besten bleibe ich hier; **it may be true** es könnte wahr sein

May *n* Mai *m*
maybe /'meɪbi:/ *adv* vielleicht
'May Day *n* der Erste Mai
mayonnaise /meɪə'neɪz/ *n* Mayonnaise *f*
mayor /'meə(r)/ *n* Bürgermeister *m*. **~ess** *n* Bürgermeisterin *f*; (*wife of mayor*) Frau Bürgermeister *f*
maze /meɪz/ *n* Irrgarten *m*; (*fig*) Labyrinth *nt*
me /mi:/ *pron* (*acc*) mich; (*dat*) mir; **he knows ~** er kennt mich; **give ~ the money** gib mir das Geld; **it's ~** (*fam*) ich bin es
meadow /'medəʊ/ *n* Wiese *f*
meagre /'mi:gə(r)/ *a* dürftig
meal[1] /mi:l/ *n* Mahlzeit *f*; (*food*) Essen *nt*
meal[2] *n* (*grain*) Schrot *m*
mealy-mouthed /mi:lɪ'maʊðd/ *a* heuchlerisch
mean[1] /mi:n/ *a* (**-er, -est**) geizig; (*unkind*) gemein; (*poor*) schäbig
mean[2] *a* mittlere(r,s) ● *n* (*average*) Durchschnitt *m*; **the golden ~** die goldene Mitte
mean[3] *vt* (*pt/pp* **meant**) heißen; (*signify*) bedeuten; (*intend*) beabsichtigen; **I ~ it** das ist mein Ernst; **~ well** es gut meinen; **be meant for** ⟨*present:*⟩ bestimmt sein für; ⟨*remark:*⟩ gerichtet sein an (+ *acc*)
meander /mɪ'ændə(r)/ *vi* sich schlängeln; ⟨*person:*⟩ schlendern
meaning /'mi:nɪŋ/ *n* Bedeutung *f*. **~ful** *a* bedeutungsvoll. **~less** *a* bedeutungslos
means /mɪ:nz/ *n* Möglichkeit *f*, Mittel *nt*; **~ of transport** Verkehrsmittel *nt*; **by ~ of** durch; **by all ~!** aber natürlich! **by no ~** keineswegs ● *npl* (*resources*) [Geld]mittel *pl*. **~ test** *n* Bedürftigkeitsnachweis *m*
meant /ment/ *see* **mean**[3]
'meantime *n* **in the ~** in der Zwischenzeit ● *adv* inzwischen
'meanwhile *adv* inzwischen
measles /'mi:zlz/ *n* Masern *pl*
measly /'mi:zlɪ/ *a* (*fam*) mickerig
measurable /'meʒərəbl/ *a* meßbar
measure /'meʒə(r)/ *n* Maß *nt*; (*action*) Maßnahme *f* ● *vt/i* messen; **~ up to** (*fig*) herankommen an (+ *acc*). **~d** *a* gemessen. **~ment** /-mənt/ *n* Maß *nt*
meat /mi:t/ *n* Fleisch *nt*. **~ball** *n* (*Culin*) Klops *m*. **~ loaf** *n* falscher Hase *m*
mechan|ic /mɪ'kænɪk/ *n* Mechaniker *m*. **~ical** *a*, **-ly** *adv* mechanisch. **~ical engineering** Maschinenbau *m*. **~ics** *n* Mechanik *f* ● *n pl* Mechanismus *m*
mechan|ism /'mekənɪzm/ *n* Mechanismus *m*. **~ize** *vt* mechanisieren
medal /'medl/ *n* Orden *m*; (*Sport*) Medaille *f*
medallion /mɪ'dælɪən/ *n* Medaillon *nt*
medallist /'medəlɪst/ *n* Medaillengewinner(in) *m(f)*
meddle /'medl/ *vi* sich einmischen (**in** in + *acc*); (*tinker*) herumhantieren (**with** an + *acc*)
media /'mi:dɪə/ *see* **medium** ● *n pl* **the ~** die Medien *pl*
median /'mi:dɪən/ *a* **~ strip** (*Amer*) Mittelstreifen *m*
mediat|e /'mi:dɪeɪt/ *vi* vermitteln. **~or** *n* Vermittler(in) *m(f)*
medical /'medɪkl/ *a* medizinisch; ⟨*treatment*⟩ ärztlich ● *n* ärztliche Untersuchung *f*. **~ insurance** *n* Krankenversicherung *f*. **~ student** *n* Medizinstudent *m*
medicat|ed /'medɪkeɪtɪd/ *a* medizinisch. **~ion** /-'keɪʃn/ *n* (*drugs*) Medikamente *pl*
medicinal /mɪ'dɪsɪnl/ *a* medizinisch; ⟨*plant*⟩ heilkräftig
medicine /'medsən/ *n* Medizin *f*; (*preparation*) Medikament *nt*
medieval /medɪ'i:vl/ *a* mittelalterlich
mediocr|e /mi:dɪ'əʊkə(r)/ *a* mittelmäßig. **~ity** /-'ɒkrətɪ/ *n* Mittelmäßigkeit *f*
meditat|e /'medɪteɪt/ *vi* nachdenken (**on** über + *acc*); (*Relig*) meditieren. **~ion** /-'teɪʃn/ *n* Meditation *f*
Mediterranean /medɪtə'reɪnɪən/ *n* Mittelmeer *nt* ● *a* Mittelmeer-
medium /'mi:dɪəm/ *a* mittlere(r,s); ⟨*steak*⟩ medium; **of ~ size** von mittlerer Größe ● *n* (*pl* **media**) Medium *nt*; (*means*) Mittel *nt* ● (*pl* **-s**) (*person*) Medium *nt*
medium: ~-sized *a* mittelgroß. **~ wave** *n* Mittelwelle *f*
medley /'medlɪ/ *n* Gemisch *nt*; (*Mus*) Potpourri *nt*
meek /mi:k/ *a* (**-er, -est**), **-ly** *adv* sanftmütig; (*unprotesting*) widerspruchslos
meet /mi:t/ *v* (*pt/pp* **met**) ● *vt* treffen; (*by chance*) begegnen (+ *dat*); (*at station*) abholen; (*make the acquaintance of*) kennenlernen; stoßen auf (+ *acc*) ⟨*problem*⟩; bezahlen

⟨*bill*⟩; erfüllen ⟨*requirements*⟩ ● *vi* sich treffen; (*for the first time*) sich kennenlernen; ~ **with** stoßen auf (+ *acc*) ⟨*problem*⟩; sich treffen mit ⟨*person*⟩ ● *n* Jagdtreffen *nt*

meeting /'mi:tɪŋ/ *n* Treffen *nt*; (*by chance*) Begegnung *f*; (*discussion*) Besprechung *f*; (*of committee*) Sitzung *f*; (*large*) Versammlung *f*

megalomania /megələ'meɪnɪə/ *n* Größenwahnsinn *m*

megaphone /'megəfəʊn/ *n* Megaphon *nt*

melancholy /'melənkəlɪ/ *a* melancholisch ● *n* Melancholie *f*

mellow /'meləʊ/ *a* (**-er**, **-est**) ⟨*fruit*⟩ ausgereift; ⟨*sound, person*⟩ sanft ● *vi* reifer werden

melodic /mɪ'lɒdɪk/ *a* melodisch

melodious /mɪ'ləʊdɪəs/ *a* melodiös

melodrama /'melə-/ *n* Melodrama *nt*. **~tic** /-drə'mætɪk/ *a*, **-ally** *adv* melodramatisch

melody /'melədɪ/ *n* Melodie *f*

melon /'melən/ *n* Melone *f*

melt /melt/ *vt/i* schmelzen. **~ down** *vt* einschmelzen. **~ing-pot** *n* (*fig*) Schmelztiegel *m*

member /'membə(r)/ *n* Mitglied *nt*; (*of family*) Angehörige(r) *m/f*; **M~ of Parliament** Abgeordnete(r) *m/f*. **~ship** *n* Mitgliedschaft *f*; (*members*) Mitgliederzahl *f*

membrane /'membreɪn/ *n* Membran *f*

memento /mɪ'mentəʊ/ *n* Andenken *nt*

memo /'meməʊ/ *n* Mitteilung *f*

memoirs /'memwɑ:z/ *n pl* Memoiren *pl*

memorable /'memərəbl/ *a* denkwürdig

memorandum /memə'rændəm/ *n* Mitteilung *f*

memorial /mɪ'mɔ:rɪəl/ *n* Denkmal *nt*. **~ service** *n* Gedenkfeier *f*

memorize /'meməraɪz/ *vt* sich (*dat*) einprägen

memory /'memərɪ/ *n* Gedächtnis *nt*; (*thing remembered*) Erinnerung *f*; (*of computer*) Speicher *m*; **from ~** auswendig; **in ~ of** zur Erinnerung an (+ *acc*)

men /men/ *see* **man**

menac|e /'menɪs/ *n* Drohung *f*; (*nuisance*) Plage *f* ● *vt* bedrohen. **~ing** *a*, **-ly** *adv* drohend

mend /mend/ *vt* reparieren; (*patch*) flicken; ausbessern ⟨*clothes*⟩ ● *n* **on the ~** auf dem Weg der Besserung

'menfolk *n pl* Männer *pl*

menial /'mi:nɪəl/ *a* niedrig

meningitis /menɪn'dʒaɪtɪs/ *n* Hirnhautentzündung *f*, Meningitis *f*

menopause /'menə-/ *n* Wechseljahre *pl*

menstruat|e /'menstrʊeɪt/ *vi* menstruieren. **~ion** /-'eɪʃn/ *n* Menstruation *f*

mental /'mentl/ *a*, **-ly** *adv* geistig; (*fam: mad*) verrückt. **~ a'rithmetic** *n* Kopfrechnen *nt*. **~ 'illness** *n* Geisteskrankheit *f*

mentality /men'tælətɪ/ *n* Mentalität *f*

mention /'menʃn/ *n* Erwähnung *f* ● *vt* erwähnen; **don't ~ it** keine Ursache; bitte

menu /'menju:/ *n* Speisekarte *f*

mercantile /'mɜ:kəntaɪl/ *a* Handels-

mercenary /'mɜ:sɪnərɪ/ *a* geldgierig ● *n* Söldner *m*

merchandise /'mɜ:tʃəndaɪz/ *n* Ware *f*

merchant /'mɜ:tʃənt/ *n* Kaufmann *m*; (*dealer*) Händler *m*. **~ 'navy** *n* Handelsmarine *f*

merci|ful /'mɜ:sɪfl/ *a* barmherzig. **~fully** *adv* (*fam*) glücklicherweise. **~less** *a*, **-ly** *adv* erbarmungslos

mercury /'mɜ:kjʊrɪ/ *n* Quecksilber *nt*

mercy /'mɜ:sɪ/ *n* Barmherzigkeit *f*, Gnade *f*; **be at s.o.'s ~** jdm ausgeliefert sein

mere /mɪə(r)/ *a*, **-ly** *adv* bloß

merest /'mɪərɪst/ *a* kleinste(r,s)

merge /mɜ:dʒ/ *vi* zusammenlaufen; (*Comm*) fusionieren ● *vt* (*Comm*) zusammenschließen

merger /'mɜ:dʒə(r)/ *n* Fusion *f*

meridian /mə'rɪdɪən/ *n* Meridian *m*

meringue /mə'ræŋ/ *n* Baiser *nt*

merit /'merɪt/ *n* Verdienst *nt*; (*advantage*) Vorzug *m*; (*worth*) Wert *m* ● *vt* verdienen

mermaid /'mɜ:meɪd/ *n* Meerjungfrau *f*

merri|ly /'merɪlɪ/ *adv* fröhlich. **~ment** /-mənt/ *n* Fröhlichkeit *f*; (*laughter*) Gelächter *nt*

merry /'merɪ/ *a* (**-ier**, **-iest**) fröhlich; **~ Christmas!** fröhliche Weihnachten!

merry: ~-go-round *n* Karussell *nt*. **~-making** *n* Feiern *nt*

mesh /meʃ/ *n* Masche *f*; (*size*) Maschenweite *f*; (*fig: network*) Netz *nt*

mesmerize /ˈmezməraɪz/ *vt* hypnotisieren. **~d** *a* (*fig*) [wie] gebannt

mess /mes/ *n* Durcheinander *nt*; (*trouble*) Schwierigkeiten *pl*; (*something spilt*) Bescherung *f* (*fam*); (*Mil*) Messe *f*; **make a ~ of** (*botch*) verpfuschen ● *vt* **~ up** in Unordnung bringen; (*botch*) verpfuschen ● *vi* **~ about** herumalbern; (*tinker*) herumspielen (**with** mit)

message /ˈmesɪdʒ/ *n* Nachricht *f*; **give s.o. a ~** jdm etwas ausrichten

messenger /ˈmesɪndʒə(r)/ *n* Bote *m*

Messiah /mɪˈsaɪə/ *n* Messias *m*

Messrs /ˈmesəz/ *n pl see* **Mr**; (*on letter*) **~ Smith** Firma Smith

messy /ˈmesɪ/ *a* (**-ier, -iest**) schmutzig; (*untidy*) unordentlich

met /met/ *see* **meet**

metabolism /mɪˈtæbəlɪzm/ *n* Stoffwechsel *m*

metal /ˈmetl/ *n* Metall *nt* ● *a* Metall-. **~lic** /mɪˈtælɪk/ *a* metallisch. **~lurgy** /mɪˈtælədʒɪ/ *n* Metallurgie *f*

metamorphosis /metəˈmɔːfəsɪs/ *n* (*pl* **-phoses** /-siːz/) Metamorphose *f*

metaphor /ˈmetəfə(r)/ *n* Metapher *f*. **~ical** /-ˈfɒrɪkl/ *a*, **-ly** *adv* metaphorisch

meteor /ˈmiːtɪə(r)/ *n* Meteor *m*. **~ic** /-ˈɒrɪk/ *a* kometenhaft

meteorological /miːtɪərəˈlɒdʒɪkl/ *a* Wetter-

meteorolog|ist /miːtɪəˈrɒlədʒɪst/ *n* Meteorologe *m*/-gin *f*. **~y** *n* Meteorologie *f*

meter¹ /ˈmiːtə(r)/ *n* Zähler *m*

meter² *n* (*Amer*) = **metre**

method /ˈmeθəd/ *n* Methode *f*; (*Culin*) Zubereitung *f*

methodical /mɪˈθɒdɪkl/ *a*, **-ly** *adv* systematisch, methodisch

Methodist /ˈmeθədɪst/ *n* Methodist(in) *m*(*f*)

meths /meθs/ *n* (*fam*) Brennspiritus *m*

methylated /ˈmeθɪleɪtɪd/ *a* **~ spirit[s]** Brennspiritus *m*

meticulous /mɪˈtɪkjʊləs/ *a*, **-ly** *adv* sehr genau

metre /ˈmiːtə(r)/ *n* Meter *m* & *n*; (*rhythm*) Versmaß *nt*

metric /ˈmetrɪk/ *a* metrisch

metropolis /mɪˈtrɒpəlɪs/ *n* Metropole *f*

metropolitan /metrəˈpɒlɪtən/ *a* hauptstädtisch; (*international*) weltstädtisch

mettle /ˈmetl/ *n* Mut *m*

mew /mjuː/ *n* Miau *nt* ● *vi* miauen

Mexican /ˈmeksɪkən/ *a* mexikanisch ● *n* Mexikaner(in) *m*(*f*). **ˈMexico** *n* Mexiko *nt*

miaow /mɪˈaʊ/ *n* Miau *nt* ● *vi* miauen

mice /maɪs/ *see* **mouse**

microbe /ˈmaɪkrəʊb/ *n* Mikrobe *f*

micro /ˈmaɪkrəʊ/: **~chip** *n* Mikrochip *nt*. **~computer** *n* Mikrocomputer *m*. **~film** *n* Mikrofilm *m*. **~phone** *n* Mikrophon *nt*. **~processor** *n* Mikroprozessor *m*. **~scope** /-skəʊp/ *n* Mikroskop *nt*. **~scopic** /-ˈskɒpɪk/ *a* mikroskopisch. **~wave** *n* Mikrowelle *f*. **~wave [oven]** *n* Mikrowellenherd *m*

mid /mɪd/ *a* **~ May** Mitte Mai; **in ~ air** in der Luft

midday /mɪdˈdeɪ/ *n* Mittag *m*

middle /ˈmɪdl/ *a* mittlere(r,s); **the M~ Ages** das Mittelalter; **the ~ class[es]** der Mittelstand; **the M~ East** der Nahe Osten ● *n* Mitte *f*; **in the ~ of the night** mitten in der Nacht

middle: ~-aged *a* mittleren Alters. **~-class** *a* bürgerlich. **~man** *n* (*Comm*) Zwischenhändler *m*

middling /ˈmɪdlɪŋ/ *a* mittelmäßig

midge /mɪdʒ/ *n* [kleine] Mücke *f*

midget /ˈmɪdʒɪt/ *n* Liliputaner(in) *m*(*f*)

Midlands /ˈmɪdləndz/ *npl* **the ~** Mittelengland *n*

ˈmidnight *n* Mitternacht *f*

midriff /ˈmɪdrɪf/ *n* (*fam*) Taille *f*

midst /mɪdst/ *n* **in the ~ of** mitten in (+ *dat*); **in our ~** unter uns

mid: ~summer *n* Hochsommer *m*; (*solstice*) Sommersonnenwende *f*. **~way** *adv* auf halbem Wege. **~wife** *n* Hebamme *f*. **~wifery** /-wɪfrɪ/ *n* Geburtshilfe *f*. **~ˈwinter** *n* Mitte *f* des Winters

might¹ /maɪt/ *v aux* **I ~** vielleicht; **it ~ be true** es könnte wahr sein; **I ~ as well stay** am besten bleibe ich hier; **he asked if he ~ go** er fragte, ob er gehen dürfte; **you ~ have drowned** du hättest ertrinken können

might² *n* Macht *f*

mighty /ˈmaɪtɪ/ *a* (**-ier, -iest**) mächtig

migraine /ˈmiːgreɪn/ *n* Migräne *f*

migrant /ˈmaɪgrənt/ *a* Wander- ● *n* (*bird*) Zugvogel *m*

migrat|e /maɪˈgreɪt/ *vi* abwandern; ⟨*birds:*⟩ ziehen. **~ion** /-ˈgreɪʃn/ *n* Wanderung *f*; (*of birds*) Zug *m*

mike /maɪk/ *n* (*fam*) Mikrophon *nt*
mild /maɪld/ *a* (**-er**, **-est**) mild
mildew /ˈmɪldjuː/ *n* Schimmel *m*; (*Bot*) Mehltau *m*
mild|ly /ˈmaɪldlɪ/ *adv* leicht; **to put it ~ly** gelinde gesagt. **~ness** *n* Milde *f*
mile /maɪl/ *n* Meile *f* (= *1,6 km*); **~s too big** (*fam*) viel zu groß
mile|age /-ɪdʒ/ *n* Meilenzahl *f*; (*of car*) Meilenstand *m*. **~stone** *n* Meilenstein *m*
militant /ˈmɪlɪtənt/ *a* militant
military /ˈmɪlɪtrɪ/ *a* militärisch. **~ service** *n* Wehrdienst *m*
militate /ˈmɪlɪteɪt/ *vi* **~ against** sprechen gegen
militia /mɪˈlɪʃə/ *n* Miliz *f*
milk /mɪlk/ *n* Milch *f* ● *vt* melken
milk: ~man *n* Milchmann *m*. **~ shake** *n* Milchmixgetränk *nt*
milky /ˈmɪlkɪ/ *a* (**-ier**, **-iest**) milchig. **M~ Way** *n* (*Astr*) Milchstraße *f*
mill /mɪl/ *n* Mühle *f*; (*factory*) Fabrik *f* ● *vt/i* mahlen; (*Techn*) fräsen. **~ about**, **~ around** *vi* umherlaufen
millennium /mɪˈlenɪəm/ *n* Jahrtausend *nt*
miller /ˈmɪlə(r)/ *n* Müller *m*
millet /ˈmɪlɪt/ *n* Hirse *f*
milli|gram /ˈmɪlɪ-/ *n* Milligramm *nt*. **~metre** *n* Millimeter *m & nt*
milliner /ˈmɪlɪnə(r)/ *n* Modistin *f*; (*man*) Hutmacher *m*. **~y** *n* Damenhüte *pl*
million /ˈmɪljən/ *n* Million *f*; **a ~ pounds** eine Million Pfund. **~aire** /-ˈneə(r)/ *n* Millionär(in) *m*(*f*)
ˈmillstone *n* Mühlstein *m*
mime /maɪm/ *n* Pantomime *f* ● *vt* pantomimisch darstellen
mimic /ˈmɪmɪk/ *n* Imitator *m* ● *vt* (*pt/pp* **mimicked**) nachahmen. **~ry** *n* Nachahmung *f*
mimosa /mɪˈməʊzə/ *n* Mimose *f*
mince /mɪns/ *n* Hackfleisch *nt* ● *vt* (*Culin*) durchdrehen; **not ~ words** kein Blatt vor den Mund nehmen
mince: ~meat *n* Masse *f* aus Korinthen, Zitronat *usw*; **make ~meat of** (*fig*) vernichtend schlagen. **~ˈpie** *n* mit 'mincemeat' gefülltes Pastetchen *nt*
mincer /ˈmɪnsə(r)/ *n* Fleischwolf *m*
mind /maɪnd/ *n* Geist *m*; (*sanity*) Verstand *m*; **to my ~** meiner Meinung nach; **give s.o. a piece of one's ~** jdm gehörig die Meinung sagen; **make up one's ~** sich entschließen; **be out of one's ~** nicht bei Verstand sein; **have sth in ~** etw im Sinn haben; **bear sth in ~** an etw (*acc*) denken; **have a good ~ to** große Lust haben, zu; **I have changed my ~** ich habe es mir anders überlegt ● *vt* aufpassen auf (+ *acc*); **I don't ~ the noise** der Lärm stört mich nicht; **~ the step!** Achtung Stufe! ● *vi* (*care*) sich kümmern (**about** um); **I don't ~** mir macht es nichts aus; **never ~!** macht nichts! **do you ~ if?** haben Sie etwas dagegen, wenn? **~ out** *vi* aufpassen
mind|ful *a* **~ful of** eingedenk (+ *gen*). **~less** *a* geistlos
mine¹ /maɪn/ *poss pron* meine(r), meins; **a friend of ~** ein Freund von mir; **that is ~** das gehört mir
mine² *n* Bergwerk *nt*; (*explosive*) Mine *f* ● *vt* abbauen; (*Mil*) verminen. **~ detector** *n* Minensuchgerät *nt*. **~field** *n* Minenfeld *nt*
miner /ˈmaɪnə(r)/ *n* Bergarbeiter *m*
mineral /ˈmɪnərl/ *n* Mineral *nt*. **~ogy** /-ˈrælədʒɪ/ *n* Mineralogie *f*. **~ water** *n* Mineralwasser *nt*
minesweeper /ˈmaɪn-/ *n* Minenräumboot *nt*
mingle /ˈmɪŋgl/ *vi* **~ with** sich mischen unter (+ *acc*)
miniature /ˈmɪnɪtʃə(r)/ *a* Klein- ● *n* Miniatur *f*
mini|bus /ˈmɪnɪ-/ *n* Kleinbus *m*. **~cab** *n* Taxi *nt*
minim /ˈmɪnɪm/ *n* (*Mus*) halbe Note *f*
minim|al /ˈmɪnɪməl/ *a* minimal. **~ize** *vt* auf ein Minimum reduzieren. **~um** *n* (*pl* **-ima**) Minimum *nt* ● *a* Mindest-
mining /ˈmaɪnɪŋ/ *n* Bergbau *m*
miniskirt /ˈmɪnɪ-/ *n* Minirock *m*
minist|er /ˈmɪnɪstə(r)/ *n* Minister *m*; (*Relig*) Pastor *m*. **~erial** /-ˈstɪərɪəl/ *a* ministeriell
ministry /ˈmɪnɪstrɪ/ *n* (*Pol*) Ministerium *nt*; **the ~** (*Relig*) das geistliche Amt
mink /mɪŋk/ *n* Nerz *m*
minor /ˈmaɪnə(r)/ *a* kleiner; (*less important*) unbedeutend ● *n* Minderjährige(r) *m*/*f*; (*Mus*) Moll *nt*
minority /maɪˈnɒrətɪ/ *n* Minderheit *f*; (*age*) Minderjährigkeit *f*
minor road *n* Nebenstraße *f*
mint¹ /mɪnt/ *n* Münzstätte *f* ● *a* ⟨*stamp*⟩ postfrisch; **in ~ condition** wie neu ● *vt* prägen
mint² *n* (*herb*) Minze *f*; (*sweet*) Pfefferminzbonbon *m & nt*

minuet /mɪnjʊ'et/ *n* Menuett *nt*
minus /'maɪnəs/ *prep* minus, weniger; (*fam: without*) ohne ● *n* ~ **[sign]** Minuszeichen *nt*
minute[1] /'mɪnɪt/ *n* Minute *f*; **in a** ~ (*shortly*) gleich; ~**s** *pl* (*of meeting*) Protokoll *nt*
minute[2] /maɪ'nju:t/ *a* winzig; (*precise*) genau
mirac|le /'mɪrəkl/ *n* Wunder *nt*. ~**ulous** /-'rækjʊləs/ *a* wunderbar
mirage /'mɪrɑ:ʒ/ *n* Fata Morgana *f*
mire /'maɪə(r)/ *n* Morast *m*
mirror /'mɪrə(r)/ *n* Spiegel *m* ● *vt* widerspiegeln
mirth /mɜ:θ/ *n* Heiterkeit *f*
misad'venture /mɪs-/ *n* Mißgeschick *nt*
misanthropist /mɪ'zænθrəpɪst/ *n* Menschenfeind *m*
misappre'hension *n* Mißverständnis *nt*; **be under a** ~ sich irren
misbe'hav|e *vi* sich schlecht benehmen. ~**iour** *n* schlechtes Benehmen *nt*
mis'calcu|late *vt* falsch berechnen ● *vi* sich verrechnen. ~**'lation** *n* Fehlkalkulation *f*
'miscarriage *n* Fehlgeburt *f*; ~ **of justice** Justizirrtum *m*. **mis'carry** *vi* eine Fehlgeburt haben
miscellaneous /mɪsə'leɪnɪəs/ *a* vermischt
mischief /'mɪstʃɪf/ *n* Unfug *m*; (*harm*) Schaden *m*
mischievous /'mɪstʃɪvəs/ *a*, **-ly** *adv* schelmisch; (*malicious*) boshaft
miscon'ception *n* falsche Vorstellung *f*
mis'conduct *n* unkorrektes Verhalten *nt*; (*adultery*) Ehebruch *m*
miscon'strue *vt* mißdeuten
mis'deed *n* Missetat *f*
misde'meanour *n* Missetat *f*
miser /'maɪzə(r)/ *n* Geizhals *m*
miserable /'mɪzrəbl/ *a*, **-bly** *adv* unglücklich; (*wretched*) elend
miserly /'maɪzəlɪ/ *adv* geizig
misery /'mɪzərɪ/ *n* Elend *nt*; (*fam: person*) Miesepeter *m*
mis'fire *vi* fehlzünden; (*go wrong*) fehlschlagen
'misfit *n* Außenseiter(in) *m*(*f*)
mis'fortune *n* Unglück *nt*
mis'givings *npl* Bedenken *pl*
mis'guided *a* töricht
mishap /'mɪshæp/ *n* Mißgeschick *nt*
misin'form *vt* falsch unterrichten
misin'terpret *vt* mißdeuten
mis'judge *vt* falsch beurteilen; (*estimate wrongly*) falsch einschätzen
mis'lay *vt* (*pt*/*pp* **-laid**) verlegen
mis'lead *vt* (*pt*/*pp* **-led**) irreführen. ~**ing** *a* irreführend
mis'manage *vt* schlecht verwalten. ~**ment** *n* Mißwirtschaft *f*
misnomer /mɪs'nəʊmə(r)/ *n* Fehlbezeichnung *f*
'misprint *n* Druckfehler *m*
mis'quote *vt* falsch zitieren
misrepre'sent *vt* falsch darstellen
miss /mɪs/ *n* Fehltreffer *m* ● *vt* verpassen; (*fail to hit or find*) verfehlen; (*fail to attend*) versäumen; (*fail to notice*) übersehen; (*feel the loss of*) vermissen ● *vi* (*fail to hit*) nicht treffen. ~ **out** *vt* auslassen
Miss *n* (*pl* **-es**) Fräulein *nt*
misshapen /mɪs'ʃeɪpən/ *a* mißgestaltet
missile /'mɪsaɪl/ *n* [Wurf]geschoß *nt*; (*Mil*) Rakete *f*
missing /'mɪsɪŋ/ *a* fehlend; (*lost*) verschwunden; (*Mil*) vermißt; **be** ~ fehlen
mission /'mɪʃn/ *n* Auftrag *m*; (*Mil*) Einsatz *m*; (*Relig*) Mission *f*
missionary /'mɪʃənrɪ/ *n* Missionar(in) *m*(*f*)
mis'spell *vt* (*pt*/*pp* **-spelt** *or* **-spelled**) falsch schreiben
mist /mɪst/ *n* Dunst *m*; (*fog*) Nebel *m*; (*on window*) Beschlag *m* ● *vi* ~ **up** beschlagen
mistake /mɪ'steɪk/ *n* Fehler *m*; **by** ~ aus Versehen ● *vt* (*pt* **mistook**, *pp* **mistaken**) mißverstehen; ~ **for** verwechseln mit
mistaken /mɪ'steɪkən/ *a* falsch; **be** ~ sich irren; ~ **identity** Verwechslung *f*. ~**ly** *adv* irrtümlicherweise
mistletoe /'mɪsltəʊ/ *n* Mistel *f*
mistress /'mɪstrɪs/ *n* Herrin *f*; (*teacher*) Lehrerin *f*; (*lover*) Geliebte *f*
mis'trust *n* Mißtrauen *nt* ● *vt* mißtrauen (+ *dat*)
misty /'mɪstɪ/ *a* (**-ier**, **-iest**) dunstig; (*foggy*) neblig; (*fig*) unklar
misunder'stand *vt* (*pt*/*pp* **-stood**) mißverstehen. ~**ing** *n* Mißverständnis *nt*
misuse[1] /mɪs'ju:z/ *vt* mißbrauchen
misuse[2] /mɪs'ju:s/ *n* Mißbrauch *m*
mite /maɪt/ *n* (*Zool*) Milbe *f*; **little** ~ (*child*) kleines Ding *nt*

mitigat|e /ˈmɪtɪgeɪt/ *vt* mildern. **~ing** *a* mildernd

mitten /ˈmɪtn/ *n* Fausthandschuh *m*

mix /mɪks/ *n* Mischung *f* ● *vt* mischen ● *vi* sich mischen; **~ with** (*associate with*) verkehren mit. **~ up** *vt* mischen; (*muddle*) durcheinanderbringen; (*mistake for*) verwechseln (**with** mit)

mixed /mɪkst/ *a* gemischt; **be ~ up** durcheinander sein

mixer /ˈmɪksə(r)/ *n* Mischmaschine *f*; (*Culin*) Küchenmaschine *f*

mixture /ˈmɪkstʃə(r)/ *n* Mischung *f*; (*medicine*) Mixtur *f*; (*Culin*) Teig *m*

ˈmix-up *n* Durcheinander *nt*; (*confusion*) Verwirrung *f*; (*mistake*) Verwechslung *f*

moan /məʊn/ *n* Stöhnen *nt* ● *vi* stöhnen; (*complain*) jammern

moat /məʊt/ *n* Burggraben *m*

mob /mɒb/ *n* Horde *f*; (*rabble*) Pöbel *m*; (*fam: gang*) Bande *f* ● *vt* (*pt/pp* **mobbed**) herfallen über (+ *acc*); belagern ⟨*celebrity*⟩

mobile /ˈməʊbaɪl/ *a* beweglich ● *n* Mobile *nt*. **~ ˈhome** *n* Wohnwagen *m*

mobility /məˈbɪlətɪ/ *n* Beweglichkeit *f*

mobi|lization /məʊbɪlaɪˈzeɪʃn/ *n* Mobilisierung *f*. **~lize** /ˈməʊbɪlaɪz/ *vt* mobilisieren

mocha /ˈmɒkə/ *n* Mokka *m*

mock /mɒk/ *a* Schein- ● *vt* verspotten ● *vi* spotten. **~ery** *n* Spott *m*

ˈmock-up *n* Modell *nt*

modal /ˈməʊdl/ *a* **~ auxiliary** Modalverb *nt*

mode /məʊd/ *n* [Art und] Weise *f*; (*fashion*) Mode *f*

model /ˈmɒdl/ *n* Modell *nt*; (*example*) Vorbild *nt*; **[fashion] ~** Mannequin *nt* ● *a* Modell-; (*exemplary*) Muster- ● *v* (*pt/pp* **modelled**) ● *vt* formen, modellieren; vorführen ⟨*clothes*⟩ ● *vi* Mannequin sein; (*for artist*) Modell stehen

moderate¹ /ˈmɒdəreɪt/ *vt* mäßigen ● *vi* sich mäßigen

moderate² /ˈmɒdərət/ *a* mäßig; ⟨*opinion*⟩ gemäßigt ● *n* (*Pol*) Gemäßigte(r) *m/f*. **~ly** *adv* mäßig; (*fairly*) einigermaßen

moderation /mɒdəˈreɪʃn/ *n* Mäßigung *f*; **in ~** mit Maß[en]

modern /ˈmɒdn/ *a* modern. **~ize** *vt* modernisieren. **~ languages** *npl* neuere Sprachen *pl*

modest /ˈmɒdɪst/ *a* bescheiden; (*decorous*) schamhaft. **~y** *n* Bescheidenheit *f*

modicum /ˈmɒdɪkəm/ *n* **a ~ of** ein bißchen

modif|ication /mɒdɪfɪˈkeɪʃn/ *n* Abänderung *f*. **~y** /ˈmɒdɪfaɪ/ *vt* (*pt/pp* **-fied**) abändern

modulate /ˈmɒdjʊleɪt/ *vt/i* modulieren

moist /mɔɪst/ *a* (**-er, -est**) feucht

moisten /ˈmɔɪsn/ *vt* befeuchten

moistur|e /ˈmɔɪstʃə(r)/ *n* Feuchtigkeit *f*. **~izer** *n* Feuchtigkeitscreme *f*

molar /ˈməʊlə(r)/ *n* Backenzahn *m*

molasses /məˈlæsɪz/ *n* (*Amer*) Sirup *m*

mole¹ /məʊl/ *n* Leberfleck *m*

mole² *n* (*Zool*) Maulwurf *m*

mole³ *n* (*breakwater*) Mole *f*

molecule /ˈmɒlɪkjuːl/ *n* Molekül *nt*

ˈmolehill *n* Maulwurfshaufen *m*

molest /məˈlest/ *vt* belästigen

mollify /ˈmɒlɪfaɪ/ *vt* (*pt/pp* **-ied**) besänftigen

mollusc /ˈmɒləsk/ *n* Weichtier *nt*

mollycoddle /ˈmɒlɪkɒdl/ *vt* verzärteln

molten /ˈməʊltən/ *a* geschmolzen

mom /mɒm/ *n* (*Amer fam*) Mutti *f*

moment /ˈməʊmənt/ *n* Moment *m*, Augenblick *m*; **at the ~** im Augenblick, augenblicklich. **~ary** *a* vorübergehend

momentous /məˈmentəs/ *a* bedeutsam

momentum /məˈmentəm/ *n* Schwung *m*

monarch /ˈmɒnək/ *n* Monarch(in) *m(f)*. **~y** *n* Monarchie *f*

monast|ery /ˈmɒnəstrɪ/ *n* Kloster *nt*. **~ic** /məˈnæstɪk/ *a* Kloster-

Monday /ˈmʌndeɪ/ *n* Montag *m*

money /ˈmʌnɪ/ *n* Geld *nt*

money: ~-box *n* Sparbüchse *f*. **~-lender** *n* Geldverleiher *m*. **~ order** *n* Zahlungsanweisung *f*

mongrel /ˈmʌŋgrəl/ *n* Promenadenmischung *f*

monitor /ˈmɒnɪtə(r)/ *n* (*Techn*) Monitor *m* ● *vt* überwachen ⟨*progress*⟩; abhören ⟨*broadcast*⟩

monk /mʌŋk/ *n* Mönch *m*

monkey /ˈmʌŋkɪ/ *n* Affe *m*. **~-nut** *n* Erdnuß *f*. **~-wrench** *n* (*Techn*) Engländer *m*

mono /ˈmɒnəʊ/ *n* Mono *nt*

monocle /ˈmɒnəkl/ *n* Monokel *nt*

monogram /'mɒnəgræm/ *n* Monogramm *nt*
monologue /'mɒnəlɒg/ *n* Monolog *m*
monopol|ize /mə'nɒpəlaɪz/ *vt* monopolisieren. **~y** *n* Monopol *nt*
monosyll|abic /mɒnəsɪ'læbɪk/ *a* einsilbig. **~able** /'mɒnəsɪləbl/ *n* einsilbiges Wort *nt*
monotone /'mɒnətəʊn/ *n* **in a ~** mit monotoner Stimme
monoton|ous /mə'nɒtənəs/ *a*, **-ly** *adv* eintönig, monoton; (*tedious*) langweilig. **~y** *n* Eintönigkeit *f*, Monotonie *f*
monsoon /mɒn'su:n/ *n* Monsun *m*
monster /'mɒnstə(r)/ *n* Ungeheuer *nt*; (*cruel person*) Unmensch *m*
monstrosity /mɒn'strɒsətɪ/ *n* Monstrosität *f*
monstrous /'mɒnstrəs/ *a* ungeheuer; (*outrageous*) ungeheuerlich
montage /mɒn'tɑ:ʒ/ *n* Montage *f*
month /mʌnθ/ *n* Monat *m*. **~ly** *a* & *adv* monatlich ● *n* (*periodical*) Monatszeitschrift *f*
monument /'mɒnjʊmənt/ *n* Denkmal *nt*. **~al** /-'mentl/ *a* (*fig*) monumental
moo /mu:/ *n* Muh *nt* ● *vi* (*pt/pp* **mooed**) muhen
mooch /mu:tʃ/ *vi* **~ about** (*fam*) herumschleichen
mood /mu:d/ *n* Laune *f*; **be in a good/bad ~** gute/schlechte Laune haben
moody /'mu:dɪ/ *a* (**-ier, -iest**) launisch
moon /mu:n/ *n* Mond *m*; **over the ~** (*fam*) überglücklich
moon: ~light *n* Mondschein *m*. **~lighting** *n* (*fam*) ≈ Schwarzarbeit *f*. **~lit** *a* mondhell
moor¹ /mʊə(r)/ *n* Moor *nt*
moor² *vt* (*Naut*) festmachen ● *vi* anlegen. **~ings** *npl* (*chains*) Verankerung *f*; (*place*) Anlegestelle *f*
moose /mu:s/ *n* Elch *m*
moot /mu:t/ *a* **it's a ~ point** darüber läßt sich streiten ● *vt* aufwerfen ⟨*question*⟩
mop /mɒp/ *n* Mop *m*; **~ of hair** Wuschelkopf *m* ● *vt* (*pt/pp* **mopped**) wischen. **~ up** *vt* aufwischen
mope /məʊp/ *vi* Trübsal blasen
moped /'məʊped/ *n* Moped *nt*
moral /'mɒrl/ *a*, **-ly** *adv* moralisch, sittlich; (*virtuous*) tugendhaft ● *n* Moral *f*; **~s** *pl* Moral *f*
morale /mə'rɑ:l/ *n* Moral *f*
morality /mə'rælətɪ/ *n* Sittlichkeit *f*
moralize /'mɒrəlaɪz/ *vi* moralisieren
morbid /'mɔ:bɪd/ *a* krankhaft; (*gloomy*) trübe
more /mɔ:(r)/ *a*, *adv* & *n* mehr; (*in addition*) noch; **a few ~** noch ein paar; **any ~** noch etwas; **once ~** noch einmal; **~ or less** mehr oder weniger; **some ~ tea?** noch etwas Tee? **~ interesting** interessanter; **~ [and ~] quickly** [immer] schneller; **no ~, thank you**, nichts mehr, danke; **no ~ bread** kein Brot mehr; **no ~ apples** keine Äpfel mehr
moreover /mɔ:'rəʊvə(r)/ *adv* außerdem
morgue /mɔ:g/ *n* Leichenschauhaus *nt*
moribund /'mɒrɪbʌnd/ *a* sterbend
morning /'mɔ:nɪŋ/ *n* Morgen *m*; **in the ~** morgens, am Morgen; (*tomorrow*) morgen früh
Morocco /mə'rɒkəʊ/ *n* Marokko *nt*
moron /'mɔ:rɒn/ *n* (*fam*) Idiot *m*
morose /mə'rəʊs/ *a*, **-ly** *adv* mürrisch
morphine /'mɔ:fi:n/ *n* Morphium *nt*
Morse /mɔ:s/ *n* **~ [code]** Morsealphabet *nt*
morsel /'mɔ:sl/ *n* (*food*) Happen *m*
mortal /'mɔ:tl/ *a* sterblich; (*fatal*) tödlich ● *n* Sterbliche(r) *m/f*. **~ity** /mɔ:'tælətɪ/ *n* Sterblichkeit *f*. **~ly** *adv* tödlich
mortar /'mɔ:tə(r)/ *n* Mörtel *m*
mortgage /'mɔ:gɪdʒ/ *n* Hypothek *f* ● *vt* hypothekarisch belasten
mortify /'mɔ:tɪfaɪ/ *vt* (*pt/pp* **-ied**) demütigen
mortuary /'mɔ:tjʊərɪ/ *n* Leichenhalle *f*; (*public*) Leichenschauhaus *nt*; (*Amer: undertaker's*) Bestattungsinstitut *nt*
mosaic /məʊ'zeɪɪk/ *n* Mosaik *nt*
Moscow /'mɒskəʊ/ *n* Moskau *nt*
Moselle /məʊ'zel/ *n* Mosel *f*; (*wine*) Moselwein *m*
mosque /mɒsk/ *n* Moschee *f*
mosquito /mɒs'ki:təʊ/ *n* (*pl* **-es**) [Stech]mücke *f*, Schnake *f*; (*tropical*) Moskito *m*
moss /mɒs/ *n* Moos *nt*. **~y** *a* moosig
most /məʊst/ *a* der/die/das meiste; (*majority*) die meisten; **for the ~ part** zum größten Teil ● *adv* am meisten; (*very*) höchst; **the ~ interesting day** der interessanteste Tag; **~ unlikely** höchst unwahrscheinlich ● *n* das meiste; **~ of them** die meisten [von ihnen]; **at [the] ~** höchstens; **~ of the time** die meiste Zeit. **~ly** *adv* meist

MOT *n* ≈ TÜV *m*
motel /məʊ'tel/ *n* Motel *nt*
moth /mɒθ/ *n* Nachtfalter *m*; **[clothes-]~** Motte *f*
moth: ~ball *n* Mottenkugel *f*. **~-eaten** *a* mottenzerfressen
mother /'mʌðə(r)/ *n* Mutter *f*; **M~'s Day** Muttertag *m* ● *vt* bemuttern
mother: ~hood *n* Mutterschaft *f*. **~-in-law** *n* (*pl* **~s-in-law**) Schwiegermutter *f*. **~land** *n* Mutterland *nt*. **~ly** *a* mütterlich. **~-of-pearl** *n* Perlmutter *f*. **~-to-be** *n* werdende Mutter *f*. **~ tongue** *n* Muttersprache *f*
mothproof /'mɒθ-/ *a* mottenfest
motif /məʊ'ti:f/ *n* Motiv *nt*
motion /'məʊʃn/ *n* Bewegung *f*; (*proposal*) Antrag *m* ● *vt/i* **~ [to] s.o.** jdm ein Zeichen geben (**to** zu). **~less** *a*, **-ly** *adv* bewegungslos
motivat|e /'məʊtɪveɪt/ *vt* motivieren. **~ion** /-'veɪʃn/ *n* Motivation *f*
motive /'məʊtɪv/ *n* Motiv *nt*
motley /'mɒtlɪ/ *a* bunt
motor /'məʊtə(r)/ *n* Motor *m*; (*car*) Auto *nt* ● *a* Motor-; (*Anat*) motorisch ● *vi* [mit dem Auto] fahren
Motorail /'məʊtəreɪl/ *n* Autozug *m*
motor: ~ bike *n* (*fam*) Motorrad *nt*. **~ boat** *n* Motorboot *nt*. **~cade** /-keɪd/ *n* (*Amer*) Autokolonne *f*. **~ car** *n* Auto *nt*, Wagen *m*. **~ cycle** *n* Motorrad *nt*. **~cyclist** *n* Motorradfahrer *m*. **~ing** *n* Autofahren *nt*. **~ist** *n* Autofahrer(in) *m(f)*. **~ize** *vt* motorisieren. **~ vehicle** *n* Kraftfahrzeug *nt*. **~way** *n* Autobahn *f*
mottled /'mɒtld/ *a* gesprenkelt
motto /'mɒtəʊ/ *n* (*pl* **-es**) Motto *nt*
mould¹ /məʊld/ *n* (*fungus*) Schimmel *m*
mould² *n* Form *f* ● *vt* formen (**into** zu). **~ing** *n* (*Archit*) Fries *m*
mouldy /'məʊldɪ/ *a* schimmelig; (*fam: worthless*) schäbig
moult /məʊlt/ *vi* ⟨*bird:*⟩ sich mausern; ⟨*animal:*⟩ sich haaren
mound /maʊnd/ *n* Hügel *m*; (*of stones*) Haufen *m*
mount¹ /maʊnt/ *n* Berg *m*
mount² *n* (*animal*) Reittier *nt*; (*of jewel*) Fassung *f*; (*of photo, picture*) Passepartout *nt* ● *vt* (*get on*) steigen auf (+ *acc*); (*on pedestal*) montieren auf (+ *acc*); besteigen ⟨*horse*⟩; fassen ⟨*jewel*⟩; aufziehen ⟨*photo, picture*⟩ ● *vi* aufsteigen; ⟨*tension:*⟩ steigen. **~ up** *vi* sich häufen; (*add up*) sich anhäufen
mountain /'maʊntɪn/ *n* Berg *m*
mountaineer /maʊntɪ'nɪə(r)/ *n* Bergsteiger(in) *m(f)*. **~ing** *n* Bergsteigen *nt*
mountainous /'maʊntɪnəs/ *a* bergig, gebirgig
mourn /mɔ:n/ *vt* betrauern ● *vi* trauern (**for** um). **~er** *n* Trauernde(r) *m/f*. **~ful** *a*, **-ly** *adv* trauervoll. **~ing** *n* Trauer *f*
mouse /maʊs/ *n* (*pl* **mice**) Maus *f*. **~trap** *n* Mausefalle *f*
mousse /mu:s/ *n* Schaum *m*; (*Culin*) Mousse *f*
moustache /mə'stɑ:ʃ/ *n* Schnurrbart *m*
mousy /'maʊsɪ/ *a* graubraun; ⟨*person*⟩ farblos
mouth¹ /maʊð/ *vt* **~ sth** etw lautlos mit den Lippen sagen
mouth² /maʊθ/ *n* Mund *m*; (*of animal*) Maul *nt*; (*of river*) Mündung *f*
mouth: ~ful *n* Mundvoll *m*; (*bite*) Bissen *m*. **~-organ** *n* Mundharmonika *f*. **~piece** *n* Mundstück *nt*; (*fig: person*) Sprachrohr *nt*. **~wash** *n* Mundwasser *nt*
movable /'mu:vəbl/ *a* beweglich
move /mu:v/ *n* Bewegung *f*; (*fig*) Schritt *m*; (*moving house*) Umzug *m*; (*in board-game*) Zug *m*; **on the ~** unterwegs; **get a ~ on** (*fam*) sich beeilen ● *vt* bewegen; (*emotionally*) rühren; (*move along*) rücken; (*in board-game*) ziehen; (*take away*) wegnehmen; wegfahren ⟨*car*⟩; (*rearrange*) umstellen; (*transfer*) versetzen ⟨*person*⟩; verlegen ⟨*office*⟩; (*propose*) beantragen; **~ house** umziehen ● *vi* sich bewegen; (*move house*) umziehen; **don't ~!** stillhalten! (*stop*) stillstehen! **~ along** *vt/i* weiterrücken. **~ away** *vt/i* wegrücken; (*move house*) wegziehen. **~ forward** *vt/i* vorrücken; ⟨*vehicle:*⟩ vorwärts fahren. **~ in** *vi* einziehen. **~ off** *vi* ⟨*vehicle:*⟩ losfahren. **~ out** *vi* ausziehen. **~ over** *vt/i* [zur Seite] rücken. **~ up** *vi* aufrücken
movement /'mu:vmənt/ *n* Bewegung *f*; (*Mus*) Satz *m*; (*of clock*) Uhrwerk *nt*
movie /'mu:vɪ/ *n* (*Amer*) Film *m*; **go to the ~s** ins Kino gehen
moving /'mu:vɪŋ/ *a* beweglich; (*touching*) rührend

mow /məʊ/ *vt* (*pt* **mowed**, *pp* **mown** *or* **mowed**) mähen. **~ down** *vt* (*destroy*) niedermähen
mower /'məʊə(r)/ *n* Rasenmäher *m*
MP *abbr see* **Member of Parliament**
Mr /'mɪstə(r)/ *n* (*pl* **Messrs**) Herr *m*
Mrs /'mɪsɪz/ *n* Frau *f*
Ms /mɪz/ *n* Frau *f*
much /mʌtʃ/ *a*, *adv* & *n* viel; **as ~ as** soviel wie; **very ~ loved/interested** sehr geliebt/interessiert
muck /mʌk/ *n* Mist *m*; (*fam: filth*) Dreck *m*. **~ about** *vi* herumalbern; (*tinker*) herumspielen (**with** mit). **~ in** *vi* (*fam*) mitmachen. **~ out** *vt* ausmisten. **~ up** *vt* (*fam*) vermasseln; (*make dirty*) schmutzig machen
mucky /'mʌkɪ/ *a* (**-ier**, **-iest**) dreckig
mucus /'mju:kəs/ *n* Schleim *m*
mud /mʌd/ *n* Schlamm *m*
muddle /'mʌdl/ *n* Durcheinander *nt*; (*confusion*) Verwirrung *f* ● *vt* **~ [up]** durcheinanderbringen
muddy /'mʌdɪ/ *a* (**-ier**, **-iest**) schlammig; ⟨*shoes*⟩ schmutzig
'**mudguard** *n* Kotflügel *m*; (*on bicycle*) Schutzblech *nt*
muesli /'mu:zlɪ/ *n* Müsli *nt*
muff /mʌf/ *n* Muff *m*
muffle /'mʌfl/ *vt* dämpfen ⟨*sound*⟩; **~ [up]** (*for warmth*) einhüllen (**in** in + *acc*)
muffler /'mʌflə(r)/ *n* Schal *m*; (*Amer, Auto*) Auspufftopf *m*
mufti /'mʌftɪ/ *n* **in ~** in Zivil
mug[1] /mʌg/ *n* Becher *m*; (*for beer*) Bierkrug *m*; (*fam: face*) Visage *f*; (*fam: simpleton*) Trottel *m*
mug[2] *vt* (*pt*/*pp* **mugged**) überfallen. **~ger** *n* Straßenräuber *m*. **~ging** *n* Straßenraub *m*
muggy /'mʌgɪ/ *a* (**-ier**, **-iest**) schwül
mule[1] /mju:l/ *n* Maultier *nt*
mule[2] *n* (*slipper*) Pantoffel *m*
mull /mʌl/ *vt* **~ over** nachdenken über (+ *acc*)
mulled /mʌld/ *a* **~ wine** Glühwein *m*
multi /'mʌltɪ/: **~coloured** *a* vielfarbig, bunt. **~lingual** /-'lɪŋgwəl/ *a* mehrsprachig. **~'national** *a* multinational
multiple /'mʌltɪpl/ *a* vielfach; (*with pl*) mehrere ● *n* Vielfache(s) *nt*
multiplication /mʌltɪplɪ'keɪʃn/ *n* Multiplikation *f*
multiply /'mʌltɪplaɪ/ *v* (*pt*/*pp* **-ied**) ● *vt* multiplizieren (**by** mit) ● *vi* sich vermehren
multi-storey *a* **~ car park** Parkhaus *nt*
mum[1] /mʌm/ *a* **keep ~** (*fam*) den Mund halten
mum[2] *n* (*fam*) Mutti *f*
mumble /'mʌmbl/ *vt*/*i* murmeln
mummy[1] /'mʌmɪ/ *n* (*fam*) Mutti *f*
mummy[2] *n* (*Archaeol*) Mumie *f*
mumps /mʌmps/ *n* Mumps *m*
munch /mʌntʃ/ *vt*/*i* mampfen
mundane /mʌn'deɪn/ *a* banal; (*worldly*) weltlich
municipal /mju:'nɪsɪpl/ *a* städtisch
munitions /mju:'nɪʃnz/ *npl* Kriegsmaterial *nt*
mural /'mjʊərəl/ *n* Wandgemälde *nt*
murder /'mɜ:də(r)/ *n* Mord *m* ● *vt* ermorden; (*fam: ruin*) verhunzen. **~er** *n* Mörder *m*. **~ess** *n* Mörderin *f*. **~ous** /-rəs/ *a* mörderisch
murky /'mɜ:kɪ/ *a* (**-ier**, **-iest**) düster
murmur /'mɜ:mə(r)/ *n* Murmeln *nt* ● *vt*/*i* murmeln
muscle /'mʌsl/ *n* Muskel *m*
muscular /'mʌskjʊlə(r)/ *a* Muskel-; (*strong*) muskulös
muse /mju:z/ *vi* nachsinnen (**on** über + *acc*)
museum /mju:'zɪəm/ *n* Museum *nt*
mush /mʌʃ/ *n* Brei *m*
mushroom /'mʌʃrʊm/ *n* [eßbarer] Pilz *m*, *esp* Champignon *m* ● *vi* (*fig*) wie Pilze aus dem Boden schießen
mushy /'mʌʃɪ/ *a* breiig
music /'mju:zɪk/ *n* Musik *f*; (*written*) Noten *pl*; **set to ~** vertonen
musical /'mju:zɪkl/ *a* musikalisch ● *n* Musical *nt*. **~ box** *n* Spieldose *f*. **~ instrument** *n* Musikinstrument *nt*
'**music-hall** *n* Varieté *nt*
musician /mju:'zɪʃn/ *n* Musiker(in) *m*(*f*)
'**music-stand** *n* Notenständer *m*
Muslim /'mʊzlɪm/ *a* mohammedanisch ● *n* Mohammedaner(in) *m*(*f*)
muslin /'mʌzlɪn/ *n* Musselin *m*
mussel /'mʌsl/ *n* [Mies]muschel *f*
must /mʌst/ *v aux* (*nur Präsens*) müssen; (*with negative*) dürfen ● *n* **a ~** (*fam*) ein Muß *nt*
mustard /'mʌstəd/ *n* Senf *m*
muster /'mʌstə(r)/ *vt* versammeln; aufbringen ⟨*strength*⟩ ● *vi* sich versammeln
musty /'mʌstɪ/ *a* (**-ier**, **-iest**) muffig
mutation /mju:'teɪʃn/ *n* Veränderung *f*; (*Biol*) Mutation *f*
mute /mju:t/ *a* stumm

muted /'mju:tɪd/ *a* gedämpft

mutilat|e /'mju:tɪleɪt/ *vt* verstümmeln. **~ion** /-'leɪʃn/ *n* Verstümmelung *f*

mutin|ous /'mju:tɪnəs/ *a* meuterisch. **~y** *n* Meuterei *f* ● *vi* (*pt/pp* **-ied**) meutern

mutter /'mʌtə(r)/ *n* Murmeln *nt* ● *vt/i* murmeln

mutton /'mʌtn/ *n* Hammelfleisch *nt*

mutual /'mju:tjʊəl/ *a* gegenseitig; (*fam: common*) gemeinsam. **~ly** *adv* gegenseitig

muzzle /'mʌzl/ *n* (*of animal*) Schnauze *f*; (*of firearm*) Mündung *f*; (*for dog*) Maulkorb *m* ● *vt* einen Maulkorb anlegen (+ *dat*)

my /maɪ/ *a* mein

myopic /maɪ'ɒpɪk/ *a* kurzsichtig

myself /maɪ'self/ *pron* selbst; (*refl*) mich; **by ~** allein; **I thought to ~** ich habe mir gedacht

mysterious /mɪ'stɪərɪəs/ *a*, **-ly** *adv* geheimnisvoll; (*puzzling*) mysteriös, rätselhaft

mystery /'mɪstərɪ/ *n* Geheimnis *nt*; (*puzzle*) Rätsel *nt*; **~ [story]** Krimi *m*

mysti|c[al] /'mɪstɪk[l]/ *a* mystisch. **~cism** /-sɪzm/ *n* Mystik *f*

mystification /mɪstɪfɪ'keɪʃn/ *n* Verwunderung *f*

mystified /'mɪstɪfaɪd/ *a* **be ~** vor einem Rätsel stehen

mystique /mɪ'sti:k/ *n* geheimnisvoller Zauber *m*

myth /mɪθ/ *n* Mythos *m*; (*fam: untruth*) Märchen *nt*. **~ical** *a* mythisch; (*fig*) erfunden

mythology /mɪ'θɒlədʒɪ/ *n* Mythologie *f*

N

nab /næb/ *vt* (*pt/pp* **nabbed**) (*fam*) erwischen

nag[1] /næg/ *n* (*horse*) Gaul *m*

nag[2] *vt/i* (*pt/pp* **nagged**) herumnörgeln (**s.o.** an jdm). **~ging** *a* ⟨*pain*⟩ nagend ● *n* Nörgelei *f*

nail /neɪl/ *n* (*Anat, Techn*) Nagel *m*; **on the ~** (*fam*) sofort ● *vt* nageln (**to** an + *acc*). **~ down** *vt* festnageln; (*close*) zunageln

nail: ~-brush *n* Nagelbürste *f*. **~-file** *n* Nagelfeile *f*. **~ polish** *n* Nagellack *m*. **~ scissors** *npl* Nagelschere *f*. **~ varnish** *n* Nagellack *m*

naïve /naɪ'i:v/ *a*, **-ly** *adv* naiv. **~ty** /-ətɪ/ *n* Naivität *f*

naked /'neɪkɪd/ *a* nackt; ⟨*flame*⟩ offen; **with the ~ eye** mit bloßem Auge. **~ness** *n* Nacktheit *f*

name /neɪm/ *n* Name *m*; (*reputation*) Ruf *m*; **by ~** dem Namen nach; **by the ~ of** namens; **call s.o. ~s** (*fam*) jdn beschimpfen ● *vt* nennen; (*give a name to*) einen Namen geben (+ *dat*); (*announce publicly*) den Namen bekanntgeben von. **~less** *a* namenlos. **~ly** *adv* nämlich

name: ~-plate *n* Namensschild *nt*. **~sake** *n* Namensvetter *m*/Namensschwester *f*

nanny /'nænɪ/ *n* Kindermädchen *nt*. **~-goat** *n* Ziege *f*

nap /næp/ *n* Nickerchen *nt*; **have a ~** ein Nickerchen machen ● *vi* **catch s.o. ~ping** jdn überrumpeln

nape /neɪp/ *n* **~ [of the neck]** Nacken *m*

napkin /'næpkɪn/ *n* Serviette *f*; (*for baby*) Windel *f*

nappy /'næpɪ/ *n* Windel *f*

narcotic /nɑ:'kɒtɪk/ *a* betäubend ● *n* Narkotikum *nt*; (*drug*) Rauschgift *nt*

narrat|e /nə'reɪt/ *vt* erzählen. **~ion** /-eɪʃn/ *n* Erzählung *f*

narrative /'nærətɪv/ *a* erzählend ● *n* Erzählung *f*

narrator /nə'reɪtə(r)/ *n* Erzähler(in) *m(f)*

narrow /'nærəʊ/ *a* (**-er, -est**) schmal; (*restricted*) eng; ⟨*margin, majority*⟩ knapp; (*fig*) beschränkt; **have a ~ escape**, *adv* **~ly escape** mit knapper Not davonkommen ● *vi* sich verengen. **~-'minded** *a* engstirnig

nasal /'neɪzl/ *a* nasal; (*Med & Anat*) Nasen-

nastily /'nɑ:stɪlɪ/ *adv* boshaft

nasturtium /nə'stɜ:ʃəm/ *n* Kapuzinerkresse *f*

nasty /'nɑ:stɪ/ *a* (**-ier, -iest**) übel; (*unpleasant*) unangenehm; (*unkind*) boshaft; (*serious*) schlimm; **turn ~** gemein werden

nation /'neɪʃn/ *n* Nation *f*; (*people*) Volk *nt*

national /'næʃənl/ *a* national; ⟨*newspaper*⟩ überregional; ⟨*campaign*⟩ landesweit ● *n* Staatsbürger(in) *m(f)*

national: ~ 'anthem *n* Nationalhymne *f*. **N~ 'Health Service** *n* staatlicher Gesundheitsdienst *m*. **N~ In'surance** *n* Sozialversicherung *f*

nationalism /'næʃənəlɪzm/ *n* Nationalismus *m*
nationality /næʃə'nælətɪ/ *n* Staatsangehörigkeit *f*
national|ization /næʃənəlaɪ'zeɪʃn/ *n* Verstaatlichung *f*. **~ize** /'næʃənəlaɪz/ *vt* verstaatlichen. **~ly** /'næʃənəlɪ/ *adv* landesweit
'nation-wide *a* landesweit
native /'neɪtɪv/ *a* einheimisch; (*innate*) angeboren ● *n* Eingeborene(r) *m/f*; (*local inhabitant*) Einheimische(r) *m/f*; **a ~ of Vienna** ein gebürtiger Wiener
native: ~ 'land *n* Heimatland *nt*. **~ 'language** *n* Muttersprache *f*
Nativity /nə'tɪvətɪ/ *n* **the ~** Christi Geburt *f*. **~ play** *n* Krippenspiel *nt*
natter /'nætə(r)/ *n* **have a ~** (*fam*) einen Schwatz halten ● *vi* (*fam*) schwatzen
natural /'nætʃrəl/ *a*, **-ly** *adv* natürlich; **~[-coloured]** naturfarben
natural: ~ 'gas *n* Erdgas *nt*. **~ 'history** *n* Naturkunde *f*
naturalist /'nætʃrəlɪst/ *n* Naturforscher *m*
natural|ization /nætʃrəlaɪ'zeɪʃn/ *n* Einbürgerung*f*. **~ize** /'nætʃrəlaɪz/ *vt* einbürgern
nature /'neɪtʃə(r)/ *n* Natur *f*; (*kind*) Art *f*; **by ~** von Natur aus. **~ reserve** *n* Naturschutzgebiet *nt*
naturism /'neɪtʃərɪzm/ *n* Freikörperkultur *f*
naught /nɔ:t/ *n* = **nought**
naughty /'nɔ:tɪ/ *a* (**-ier**, **-iest**), **-ily** *adv* unartig; (*slightly indecent*) gewagt
nausea /'nɔ:zɪə/ *n* Übelkeit *f*
nause|ate /'nɔ:zɪeɪt/ *vt* anekeln. **~ating** *a* ekelhaft. **~ous** /-ɪəs/ *a* **I feel ~ous** mir ist übel
nautical /'nɔ:tɪkl/ *a* nautisch. **~ mile** *n* Seemeile *f*
naval /'neɪvl/ *a* Marine-
nave /neɪv/ *n* Kirchenschiff *nt*
navel /'neɪvl/ *n* Nabel *m*
navigable /'nævɪgəbl/ *a* schiffbar
navigat|e /'nævɪgeɪt/ *vi* navigieren ● *vt* befahren ⟨*river*⟩. **~ion** /-'geɪʃn/ *n* Navigation *f*. **~or** *n* Navigator *m*
navvy /'nævɪ/ *n* Straßenarbeiter *m*
navy /'neɪvɪ/ *n* [Kriegs]marine *f* ● *a* **~ [blue]** marineblau
near /nɪə(r)/ *a* (**-er**, **-est**) nah[e]; **the ~est bank** die nächste Bank ● *adv* nahe; **~ by** nicht weit weg; **~ at hand** in der Nähe; **draw ~** sich nähern ● *prep* nahe an (+ *dat*/*acc*); in der Nähe von; **~ to tears** den Tränen nahe; **go ~ [to] sth** nahe an etw (*acc*) herangehen ● *vt* sich nähern (+ *dat*)
near: ~by *a* nahegelegen. **~ly** *adv* fast, beinahe; **not ~ly** bei weitem nicht. **~ness** *n* Nähe *f*. **~ side** *n* Beifahrerseite *f*. **~-sighted** *a* (*Amer*) kurzsichtig
neat /ni:t/ *a* (**-er**, **-est**), **-ly** *adv* adrett; (*tidy*) ordentlich; (*clever*) geschickt; (*undiluted*) pur. **~ness** *n* Ordentlichkeit *f*
necessarily /'nesəserəlɪ/ *adv* notwendigerweise; **not ~** nicht unbedingt
necessary /'nesəsərɪ/ *a* nötig, notwendig
necessit|ate /nɪ'sesɪteɪt/ *vt* notwendig machen. **~y** *n* Notwendigkeit *f*; **she works from ~y** sie arbeitet, weil sie es nötig hat
neck /nek/ *n* Hals *m*; **~ and ~** Kopf an Kopf
necklace /'neklɪs/ *n* Halskette *f*
neck: ~line *n* Halsausschnitt *m*. **~tie** *n* Schlips *m*
nectar /'nektə(r)/ *n* Nektar *m*
née /neɪ/ *a* **~ Brett** geborene Brett
need /ni:d/ *n* Bedürfnis *nt*; (*misfortune*) Not *f*; **be in ~** Not leiden; **be in ~ of** brauchen; **in case of ~** notfalls; **if ~ be** wenn nötig; **there is a ~ for** es besteht ein Bedarf an (+ *dat*); **there is no ~ for that** das ist nicht nötig; **there is no ~ for you to go** du brauchst nicht zu gehen ● *vt* brauchen; **you ~ not go** du brauchst nicht zu gehen; **~ I come?** muß ich kommen? **I ~ to know** ich muß es wissen; **it ~s to be done** es muß gemacht werden
needle /'ni:dl/ *n* Nadel *f* ● *vt* (*annoy*) ärgern
needless /'ni:dlɪs/ *a*, **-ly** *adv* unnötig; **~ to say** selbstverständlich, natürlich
'needlework *n* Nadelarbeit *f*
needy /'ni:dɪ/ *a* (**-ier**, **-iest**) bedürftig
negation /nɪ'geɪʃn/ *n* Verneinung *f*
negative /'negətɪv/ *a* negativ ● *n* Verneinung *f*; (*photo*) Negativ *nt*
neglect /nɪ'glekt/ *n* Vernachlässigung *f*; **state of ~** verwahrloster Zustand *m* ● *vt* vernachlässigen; (*omit*) versäumen (**to** zu). **~ed** *a* verwahrlost. **~ful** *a* nachlässig; **be ~ful of** vernachlässigen
negligen|ce /'neglɪdʒəns/ *n* Nachlässigkeit *f*; (*Jur*) Fahrlässigkeit *f*. **~t**

a, **-ly** *adv* nachlässig; (*Jur*) fahrlässig
negligible /ˈneglɪdʒəbl/ *a* unbedeutend
negotiable /nɪˈgəʊʃəbl/ *a* ⟨*road*⟩ befahrbar; (*Comm*) unverbindlich; **not ~** nicht übertragbar
negotiat|e /nɪˈgəʊʃɪeɪt/ *vt* aushandeln; (*Auto*) nehmen ⟨*bend*⟩ ● *vi* verhandeln. **~ion** /-ˈeɪʃn/ *n* Verhandlung *f*. **~or** *n* Unterhändler(in) *m*(*f*)
Negro /ˈniːgrəʊ/ *a* Neger ● *n* (*pl* **-es**) Neger *m*
neigh /neɪ/ *vi* wiehern
neighbour /ˈneɪbə(r)/ *n* Nachbar(in) *m*(*f*). **~hood** *n* Nachbarschaft *f*; **in the ~hood of** in der Nähe von; (*fig*) um ... herum. **~ing** *a* Nachbar-. **~ly** *a* [gut]nachbarlich
neither /ˈnaɪðə(r)/ *a* & *pron* keine(r,s) [von beiden] ● *adv* **~ ... nor** weder ... noch ● *conj* auch nicht
neon /ˈniːɒn/ *n* Neon *nt*. **~ light** *n* Neonlicht *nt*
nephew /ˈnevjuː/ *n* Neffe *m*
nepotism /ˈnepətɪzm/ *n* Vetternwirtschaft *f*
nerve /nɜːv/ *n* Nerv *m*; (*fam: courage*) Mut *m*; (*fam: impudence*) Frechheit *f*; **lose one's ~** den Mut verlieren. **~-racking** *a* nervenaufreibend
nervous /ˈnɜːvəs/ *a*, **-ly** *adv* (*afraid*) ängstlich; (*highly-strung*) nervös; (*Anat, Med*) Nerven-; **be ~** Angst haben. **~ ˈbreakdown** *n* Nervenzusammenbruch *m*. **~ness** Ängstlichkeit *f*; (*Med*) Nervosität *f*
nervy /ˈnɜːvɪ/ *a* (**-ier**, **-iest**) nervös; (*Amer: impudent*) frech
nest /nest/ *n* Nest *nt* ● *vi* nisten. **~-egg** *n* Notgroschen *m*
nestle /ˈnesl/ *vi* sich schmiegen (**against** an + *acc*)
net[1] /net/ *n* Netz *nt*; (*curtain*) Store *m* ● *vt* (*pt/pp* **netted**) (*catch*) [mit dem Netz] fangen
net[2] *a* netto; ⟨*salary, weight*⟩ Netto- ● *vt* (*pt/pp* **netted**) netto einnehmen; (*yield*) einbringen
ˈnetball *n* ≈ Korbball *m*
Netherlands /ˈneðələndz/ *npl* **the ~** die Niederlande *pl*
netting /ˈnetɪŋ/ *n* **[wire] ~** Maschendraht *m*
nettle /ˈnetl/ *n* Nessel *f*
ˈnetwork *n* Netz *nt*
neuralgia /njʊəˈrældʒə/ *n* Neuralgie *f*
neurolog|ist /njʊəˈrɒlədʒɪst/ *n* Neurologe *m*/-gin *f*. **~y** *n* Neurologie *f*
neur|osis /njʊəˈrəʊsɪs/ *n* (*pl* **-oses** /-siːz/) Neurose *f*. **~otic** /-ˈrɒtɪk/ *a* neurotisch
neuter /ˈnjuːtə(r)/ *a* (*Gram*) sächlich ● *n* (*Gram*) Neutrum *nt* ● *vt* kastrieren; (*spay*) sterilisieren
neutral /ˈnjuːtrl/ *a* neutral ● *n* **in ~** (*Auto*) im Leerlauf. **~ity** /-ˈtrælətɪ/ *n* Neutralität *f*. **~ize** *vt* neutralisieren
never /ˈnevə(r)/ *adv* nie, niemals; (*fam: not*) nicht; **~ mind** macht nichts; **well I ~!** ja so was! **~-ending** *a* endlos
nevertheless /nevəðəˈles/ *adv* dennoch, trotzdem
new /njuː/ *a* (**-er**, **-est**) neu
new: ~born *a* neugeboren. **~comer** *n* Neuankömmling *m*. **~fangled** /-ˈfæŋgld/ *a* (*pej*) neumodisch. **~-laid** *a* frisch gelegt
ˈnewly *adv* frisch. **~-weds** *npl* jungverheiratetes Paar *nt*
new: ~ ˈmoon *n* Neumond *m*. **~ness** *n* Neuheit *f*
news /njuːz/ *n* Nachricht *f*; (*Radio, TV*) Nachrichten *pl*; **piece of ~** Neuigkeit *f*
news: ~agent *n* Zeitungshändler *m*. **~ bulletin** *n* Nachrichtensendung *f*. **~caster** *n* Nachrichtensprecher(in) *m*(*f*). **~flash** *n* Kurzmeldung *f*. **~letter** *n* Mitteilungsblatt *nt*. **~paper** *n* Zeitung *f*; (*material*) Zeitungspapier *nt*. **~reader** *n* Nachrichtensprecher(in) *m*(*f*)
newt /njuːt/ *n* Molch *m*
New: ~ Year's ˈDay *n* Neujahr *nt*. **~ Year's ˈEve** *n* Silvester *nt*. **~ Zealand** /ˈziːlənd/ *n* Neuseeland *nt*
next /nekst/ *a* & *n* nächste(r,s); **who's ~?** wer kommt als nächster dran? **the ~ best** das nächstbeste; **~ door** nebenan; **my ~ of kin** mein nächster Verwandter; **~ to nothing** fast gar nichts; **the week after ~** übernächste Woche ● *adv* als nächstes; **~ to** neben
NHS *abbr see* **National Health Service**
nib /nɪb/ *n* Feder *f*
nibble /ˈnɪbl/ *vt*/*i* knabbern (**at** an + *dat*)
nice /naɪs/ *a* (**-r**, **-st**) nett; ⟨*day, weather*⟩ schön; ⟨*food*⟩ gut; ⟨*distinction*⟩ fein. **~ly** *adv* nett; (*well*) gut. **~ties** /ˈnaɪsətɪz/ *npl* Feinheiten *pl*

niche /ni:ʃ/ *n* Nische *f*; (*fig*) Platz *m*
nick /nɪk/ *n* Kerbe *f*; (*fam: prison*) Knast *m*; (*fam: police station*) Revier *nt*; **in the ~ of time** (*fam*) gerade noch rechtzeitig; **in good ~** (*fam*) in gutem Zustand ● *vt* einkerben; (*steal*) klauen; (*fam: arrest*) schnappen
nickel /'nɪkl/ *n* Nickel *nt*; (*Amer*) Fünfcentstück *nt*
'nickname *n* Spitzname *m*
nicotine /'nɪkəti:n/ *n* Nikotin *nt*
niece /ni:s/ *n* Nichte *f*
Nigeria /naɪ'dʒɪərɪə/ *n* Nigeria *nt*. **~n** *a* nigerianisch ● *n* Nigerianer(in) *m*(*f*)
niggardly /'nɪgədlɪ/ *a* knauserig
niggling /'nɪglɪŋ/ *a* gering; (*petty*) kleinlich; ⟨*pain*⟩ quälend
night /naɪt/ *n* Nacht *f*; (*evening*) Abend *m*; **at ~** nachts; **Monday ~** Montag nacht/abend
night: ~cap *n* Schlafmütze *f*; (*drink*) Schlaftrunk *m*. **~-club** *n* Nachtklub *m*. **~-dress** *n* Nachthemd *nt*. **~fall** *n* **at ~fall** bei Einbruch der Dunkelheit. **~-gown** *n*, (*fam*) **~ie** /'naɪtɪ/ *n* Nachthemd *nt*
nightingale /'naɪtɪŋgeɪl/ *n* Nachtigall *f*
night: ~-life *n* Nachtleben *nt*. **~ly** *a* nächtlich ● *adv* jede Nacht. **~mare** *n* Alptraum *m*. **~shade** *n* (*Bot*) **deadly ~shade** Tollkirsche *f*. **~-time** *n* **at ~-time** bei Nacht. **~-'watchman** *n* Nachtwächter *m*
nil /nɪl/ *n* null
nimble /'nɪmbl/ *a* (**-r, -st**), **-bly** *adv* flink
nine /naɪn/ *a* neun ● *n* Neun *f*. **~'teen** *a* neunzehn. **~'teenth** *a* neunzehnte(r,s)
ninetieth /'naɪntɪɪθ/ *a* neunzigste(r,s)
ninety /'naɪntɪ/ *a* neunzig
ninth /naɪnθ/ *a* neunte(r,s)
nip /nɪp/ *n* Kniff *m*; (*bite*) Biß *m* ● *vt* kneifen; (*bite*) beißen; **~ in the bud** (*fig*) im Keim ersticken ● *vi* (*fam: run*) laufen
nipple /'nɪpl/ *n* Brustwarze *f*; (*Amer: on bottle*) Sauger *m*
nippy /'nɪpɪ/ *a* (**-ier, -iest**) (*fam*) (*cold*) frisch; (*quick*) flink
nitrate /'naɪtreɪt/ *n* Nitrat *nt*
nitrogen /'naɪtrədʒən/ *n* Stickstoff *m*
nitwit /'nɪtwɪt/ *n* (*fam*) Dummkopf *m*
no /nəʊ/ *adv* nein ● *n* (*pl* **noes**) Nein *nt* ● *a* kein(e); (*pl*) keine; **in no time** [sehr] schnell; **no parking/smoking** Parken/Rauchen verboten; **no one** = **nobody**
nobility /nəʊ'bɪlətɪ/ *n* Adel *m*
noble /'nəʊbl/ *a* (**-r, -st**) edel; (*aristocratic*) adlig. **~man** *n* Adlige(r) *m*
nobody /'nəʊbədɪ/ *pron* niemand, keiner; **he knows ~** er kennt niemanden *od* keinen ● *n* **a ~** ein Niemand *m*
nocturnal /nɒk'tɜ:nl/ *a* nächtlich; ⟨*animal, bird*⟩ Nacht-
nod /nɒd/ *n* Nicken *nt* ● *v* (*pt*/*pp* **nodded**) ● *vi* nicken ● *vt* **~ one's head** mit dem Kopf nicken. **~ off** *vi* einnicken
nodule /'nɒdju:l/ *n* Knötchen *nt*
noise /nɔɪz/ *n* Geräusch *nt*; (*loud*) Lärm *m*. **~less** *a*, **-ly** *adv* geräuschlos
noisy /'nɔɪzɪ/ *a* (**-ier, -iest**), **-ily** *adv* laut; ⟨*eater*⟩ geräuschvoll
nomad /'nəʊmæd/ *n* Nomade *m*. **~ic** /-'mædɪk/ *a* nomadisch; ⟨*life, tribe*⟩ Nomaden-
nominal /'nɒmɪnl/ *a*, **-ly** *adv* nominell
nominat|e /'nɒmɪneɪt/ *vt* nominieren, aufstellen; (*appoint*) ernennen. **~ion** /-'neɪʃn/ *n* Nominierung *f*; Ernennung *f*
nominative /'nɒmɪnətɪv/ *a* & *n* (*Gram*) **~ [case]** Nominativ *m*
nonchalant /'nɒnʃələnt/ *a*, **-ly** *adv* nonchalant; ⟨*gesture*⟩ lässig
non-com'missioned /nɒn-/ *a* **~ officer** Unteroffizier *m*
non-com'mittal *a* unverbindlich; **be ~** sich nicht festlegen
nondescript /'nɒndɪskrɪpt/ *a* unbestimmbar; ⟨*person*⟩ unscheinbar
none /nʌn/ *pron* keine(r)/keins; **~ of us** keiner von uns; **~ of it/this** nichts davon ● *adv* **~ too** nicht gerade; **~ too soon** [um] keine Minute zu früh; **~ the wiser** um nichts klüger; **~ the less** dennoch
nonentity /nɒ'nentətɪ/ *n* Null *f*
non-ex'istent *a* nichtvorhanden; **be ~** nicht vorhanden sein
non-'fiction *n* Sachliteratur *f*
non-'iron *a* bügelfrei
nonplussed /nɒn'plʌst/ *a* verblüfft
nonsens|e /'nɒnsəns/ *n* Unsinn *m*. **~ical** /-'sensɪkl/ *a* unsinnig
non-'smoker *n* Nichtraucher *m*; (*compartment*) Nichtraucherabteil *nt*
non-'stop *adv* ununterbrochen; ⟨*fly*⟩ nonstop; **~ 'flight** Nonstopflug *m*

non-'swimmer *n* Nichtschwimmer *m*

non-'violent *a* gewaltlos

noodles /'nu:dlz/ *npl* Bandnudeln *pl*

nook /nʊk/ *n* Eckchen *nt*, Winkel *m*

noon /nu:n/ *n* Mittag *m*; **at ~** um 12 Uhr mittags

noose /nu:s/ *n* Schlinge *f*

nor /nɔ:(r)/ *adv* noch ● *conj* auch nicht

Nordic /'nɔ:dɪk/ *a* nordisch

norm /nɔ:m/ *n* Norm *f*

normal /'nɔ:ml/ *a* normal. **~ity** /-'mæləti/ *n* Normalität *f*. **~ly** *adv* normal; (*usually*) normalerweise

north /nɔ:θ/ *n* Norden *m*; **to the ~ of** nördlich von ● *a* Nord-, nord- ● *adv* nach Norden

north: N~ America *n* Nordamerika *nt*. **~-east** *a* Nordost- ● *n* Nordosten *m*

norther|ly /'nɔ:ðəlɪ/ *a* nördlich. **~n** *a* nördlich. **N~n Ireland** *n* Nordirland *nt*

north: N~ 'Pole *n* Nordpol *m*. **N~ 'Sea** *n* Nordsee *f*. **~ward[s]** /-wəd[z]/ *adv* nach Norden. **~-west** *a* Nordwest- ● *n* Nordwesten *m*

Nor|way /'nɔ:weɪ/ *n* Norwegen *nt*. **~wegian** /-'wi:dʒn/ *a* norwegisch ● *n* Norweger(in) *m(f)*

nose /nəʊz/ *n* Nase *f* ● *vi* **~ about** herumschnüffeln

nose: ~bleed *n* Nasenbluten *nt*. **~dive** *n* (*Aviat*) Sturzflug *m*

nostalg|ia /nɒ'stældʒɪə/ *n* Nostalgie *f*. **~ic** *a* nostalgisch

nostril /'nɒstrəl/ *n* Nasenloch *nt*; (*of horse*) Nüster *f*

nosy /'nəʊzɪ/ *a* (**-ier, -iest**) (*fam*) neugierig

not /nɒt/ *adv* nicht; **~ a** kein(e); **if ~** wenn nicht; **~ at all** gar nicht; **~ a bit** kein bißchen; **~ even** nicht mal; **~ yet** noch nicht; **he is ~ a German** er ist kein Deutscher

notab|le /'nəʊtəbl/ *a* bedeutend; (*remarkable*) bemerkenswert. **~ly** *adv* insbesondere

notary /'nəʊtərɪ/ *n* **~ 'public** ≈ Notar *m*

notation /nəʊ'teɪʃn/ *n* Notation *f*; (*Mus*) Notenschrift *f*

notch /nɒtʃ/ *n* Kerbe *f*. **~ up** *vt* (*score*) erzielen

note /nəʊt/ *n* (*written comment*) Notiz *f*, Anmerkung *f*; (*short letter*) Briefchen *nt*, Zettel *m*; (*bank~*) Banknote *f*, Schein *m*; (*Mus*) Note *f*; (*sound*) Ton *m*; (*on piano*) Taste *f*; **eighth/quarter ~** (*Amer*) Achtel-/Viertelnote *f*; **half/whole ~** (*Amer*) halbe/ganze Note *f*; **of ~** von Bedeutung; **make a ~ of** notieren ● *vt* beachten; (*notice*) bemerken (**that** daß). **~ down** *vt* notieren

'notebook *n* Notizbuch *nt*

noted /'nəʊtɪd/ *a* bekannt (**for** für)

note: ~paper *n* Briefpapier *nt*. **~worthy** *a* beachtenswert

nothing /'nʌθɪŋ/ *n*, *pron* & *adv* nichts; **for ~** umsonst; **~ but** nichts als; **~ much** nicht viel; **~ interesting** nichts Interessantes; **it's ~ to do with you** das geht dich nichts an

notice /'nəʊtɪs/ *n* (*on board*) Anschlag *m*, Bekanntmachung *f*; (*announcement*) Anzeige *f*; (*review*) Kritik *f*; (*termination of lease, employment*) Kündigung *f*; **[advance] ~** Bescheid *m*; **give [in one's] ~** kündigen; **give s.o. ~** jdm kündigen; **take no ~ of** keine Notiz nehmen von; **take no ~!** ignoriere es! ● *vt* bemerken. **~able** /-əbl/ *a*, **-bly** *adv* merklich. **~-board** *n* Anschlagbrett *nt*

noti|fication /nəʊtɪfɪ'keɪʃn/ *n* Benachrichtigung *f*. **~fy** /'nəʊtɪfaɪ/ *vt* (*pt/pp* **-ied**) benachrichtigen

notion /'nəʊʃn/ *n* Idee *f*; **~s** *pl* (*Amer: haberdashery*) Kurzwaren *pl*

notorious /nəʊ'tɔ:rɪəs/ *a* berüchtigt

notwith'standing *prep* trotz (+ *gen*) ● *adv* trotzdem, dennoch

nought /nɔ:t/ *n* Null *f*

noun /naʊn/ *n* Substantiv *nt*

nourish /'nʌrɪʃ/ *vt* nähren. **~ing** *a* nahrhaft. **~ment** *n* Nahrung *f*

novel /'nɒvl/ *a* neu[artig] ● *n* Roman *m*. **~ist** *n* Romanschriftsteller(in) *m(f)*. **~ty** *n* Neuheit *f*; **~ties** *pl* kleine Geschenkartikel *pl*

November /nəʊ'vembə(r)/ *n* November *m*

novice /'nɒvɪs/ *n* Neuling *m*; (*Relig*) Novize *m*/Novizin *f*

now /naʊ/ *adv* & *conj* jetzt; **~ [that]** jetzt, wo; **just ~** gerade, eben; **right ~** sofort; **~ and again** hin und wieder; **now, now!** na, na!

'nowadays *adv* heutzutage

nowhere /'nəʊ-/ *adv* nirgendwo, nirgends

noxious /'nɒkʃəs/ *a* schädlich

nozzle /'nɒzl/ *n* Düse *f*

nuance /'nju:ɑ̃s/ *n* Nuance *f*

nuclear /'nju:klɪə(r)/ *a* Kern-. **~ de'terrent** *n* nukleares Abschreckungsmittel *nt*

nucleus /'nju:klɪəs/ *n* (*pl* **-lei** /-lɪaɪ/) Kern *m*
nude /nju:d/ *a* nackt ● *n* (*Art*) Akt *m*; **in the ~** nackt
nudge /nʌdʒ/ *n* Stups *m* ● *vt* stupsen
nud|ist /'nju:dɪst/ *n* Nudist *m*. **~ity** *n* Nacktheit *f*
nugget /'nʌgɪt/ *n* [Gold]klumpen *m*
nuisance /'nju:sns/ *n* Ärgernis *nt*; (*pest*) Plage *f*; **be a ~** ärgerlich sein; ⟨*person:*⟩ lästig sein; **what a ~!** wie ärgerlich!
null /nʌl/ *a* **~ and void** null und nichtig. **~ify** /'nʌlɪfaɪ/ *vt* (*pt*/*pp* **-ied**) für nichtig erklären
numb /nʌm/ *a* gefühllos, taub; **~ with cold** taub vor Kälte ● *vt* betäuben
number /'nʌmbə(r)/ *n* Nummer *f*; (*amount*) Anzahl *f*; (*Math*) Zahl *f* ● *vt* numerieren; (*include*) zählen (**among** zu). **~-plate** *n* Nummernschild *nt*
numeral /'nju:mərl/ *n* Ziffer *f*
numerate /'nju:mərət/ *a* **be ~** rechnen können
numerical /nju:'merɪkl/ *a*, **-ly** *adv* numerisch; **in ~ order** zahlenmäßig geordnet
numerous /'nju:mərəs/ *a* zahlreich
nun /nʌn/ *n* Nonne *f*
nuptial /'nʌpʃl/ *a* Hochzeits-. **~s** *npl* (*Amer*) Hochzeit *f*
nurse /nɜ:s/ *n* [Kranken]schwester *f*; (*male*) Krankenpfleger *m*; **children's ~** Kindermädchen *nt* ● *vt* pflegen. **~maid** *n* Kindermädchen *nt*
nursery /'nɜ:sərɪ/ *n* Kinderzimmer *nt*; (*Hort*) Gärtnerei *f*; **[day] ~** Kindertagesstätte *f*. **~ rhyme** *n* Kinderreim *m*. **~ school** *n* Kindergarten *m*
nursing /'nɜ:sɪŋ/ *n* Krankenpflege *f*. **~ home** *n* Pflegeheim *nt*
nurture /'nɜ:tʃə(r)/ *vt* nähren; (*fig*) hegen
nut /nʌt/ *n* Nuß *f*; (*Techn*) [Schraubenmutter *f*; (*fam: head*) Birne *f* (*fam*); **be ~s** (*fam*) spinnen (*fam*). **~crackers** *npl* Nußknacker *m*. **~meg** *n* Muskat *m*
nutrient /'nju:trɪənt/ *n* Nährstoff *m*
nutrit|ion /nju:'trɪʃn/ *n* Ernährung *f*. **~ious** /-ʃəs/ *a* nahrhaft
'nutshell *n* Nußschale *f*; **in a ~** (*fig*) kurz gesagt
nuzzle /'nʌzl/ *vt* beschnüffeln
nylon /'naɪlɒn/ *n* Nylon *nt*; **~s** *pl* Nylonstrümpfe *pl*
nymph /nɪmf/ *n* Nymphe *f*

O

O /əʊ/ *n* (*Teleph*) null
oaf /əʊf/ *n* (*pl* **oafs**) Trottel *m*
oak /əʊk/ *n* Eiche *f* ● *attrib* Eichen-
OAP *abbr* (**old-age pensioner**) Rentner(in) *m*(*f*)
oar /ɔ:(r)/ *n* Ruder *nt*. **~sman** *n* Ruderer *m*
oasis /əʊ'eɪsɪs/ *n* (*pl* **oases** /-si:z/) Oase *f*
oath /əʊθ/ *n* Eid *m*; (*swear-word*) Fluch *m*
oatmeal /'əʊt-/ *n* Hafermehl *nt*
oats /əʊts/ *npl* Hafer *m*; (*Culin*) **[rolled] ~** Haferflocken *pl*
obedien|ce /ə'bi:dɪəns/ *n* Gehorsam *m*. **~t** *a*, **-ly** *adv* gehorsam
obes|e /əʊ'bi:s/ *a* fettleibig. **~ity** *n* Fettleibigkeit *f*
obey /ə'beɪ/ *vt*/*i* gehorchen (+ *dat*); befolgen ⟨*instructions, rules*⟩
obituary /ə'bɪtjʊərɪ/ *n* Nachruf *m*; (*notice*) Todesanzeige *f*
object¹ /'ɒbdʒɪkt/ *n* Gegenstand *m*; (*aim*) Zweck *m*; (*intention*) Absicht *f*; (*Gram*) Objekt *nt*; **money is no ~** Geld spielt keine Rolle
object² /əb'dʒekt/ *vi* Einspruch erheben (**to** gegen); (*be against*) etwas dagegen haben
objection /əb'dʒekʃn/ *n* Einwand *m*; **have no ~** nichts dagegen haben. **~able** /-əbl/ *a* anstößig; ⟨*person*⟩ unangenehm
objectiv|e /əb'dʒektɪv/ *a*, **-ly** *adv* objektiv ● *n* Ziel *nt*. **~ity** /-'tɪvətɪ/ *n* Objektivität *f*
objector /əb'dʒektə(r)/ *n* Gegner *m*
obligation /ɒblɪ'geɪʃn/ *n* Pflicht *f*; **be under an ~** verpflichtet sein; **without ~** unverbindlich
obligatory /ə'blɪgətrɪ/ *a* obligatorisch; **be ~** Vorschrift sein
oblig|e /ə'blaɪdʒ/ *vt* verpflichten; (*compel*) zwingen; (*do a small service*) einen Gefallen tun (+ *dat*); **much ~ed!** vielen Dank! **~ing** *a* entgegenkommend
oblique /ə'bli:k/ *a* schräg; ⟨*angle*⟩ schief; (*fig*) indirekt. **~ stroke** *n* Schrägstrich *m*
obliterate /ə'blɪtəreɪt/ *vt* auslöschen
oblivion /ə'blɪvɪən/ *n* Vergessenheit *f*
oblivious /ə'blɪvɪəs/ *a* **be ~** sich (*dat*) nicht bewußt sein (**of** *or* **to** *gen*)
oblong /'ɒblɒŋ/ *a* rechteckig ● *n* Rechteck *nt*

obnoxious /əb'nɒkʃəs/ *a* widerlich
oboe /'əʊbəʊ/ *n* Oboe *f*
obscen|e /əb'si:n/ *a* obszön; (*atrocious*) abscheulich. **~ity** /-'senətɪ/ *n* Obszönität *f*; Abscheulichkeit *f*
obscur|e /əb'skjʊə(r)/ *a* dunkel; (*unknown*) unbekannt ● *vt* verdecken; (*confuse*) verwischen. **~ity** *n* Dunkelheit *f*; Unbekanntheit *f*
obsequious /əb'si:kwɪəs/ *a* unterwürfig
observa|nce /əb'zɜ:vns/ *n* (*of custom*) Einhaltung *f*. **~nt** *a* aufmerksam. **~tion** /ɒbzə'veɪʃn/ *n* Beobachtung *f*; (*remark*) Bemerkung *f*
observatory /əb'zɜ:vətrɪ/ *n* Sternwarte *f*; (*weather*) Wetterwarte *f*
observe /əb'zɜ:v/ *vt* beobachten; (*say, notice*) bemerken; (*keep, celebrate*) feiern; (*obey*) einhalten. **~r** *n* Beobachter *m*
obsess /əb'ses/ *vt* **be ~ed by** besessen sein von. **~ion** /-eʃn/ *n* Besessenheit *f*; (*persistent idea*) fixe Idee *f*. **~ive** /-ɪv/ *a*, **-ly** *adv* zwanghaft
obsolete /'ɒbsəli:t/ *a* veraltet
obstacle /'ɒbstəkl/ *n* Hindernis *nt*
obstetrician /ɒbstə'trɪʃn/ *n* Geburtshelfer *m*. **obstetrics** /-'stetrɪks/ *n* Geburtshilfe *f*
obstina|cy /'ɒbstɪnəsɪ/ *n* Starrsinn *m*. **~te** /-nət/ *a*, **-ly** *adv* starrsinnig; ⟨*refusal*⟩ hartnäckig
obstreperous /əb'strepərəs/ *a* widerspenstig
obstruct /əb'strʌkt/ *vt* blockieren; (*hinder*) behindern. **~ion** /-ʌkʃn/ *n* Blockierung *f*; Behinderung *f*; (*obstacle*) Hindernis *nt*. **~ive** /-ɪv/ *a* **be ~ive** Schwierigkeiten bereiten
obtain /əb'teɪn/ *vt* erhalten, bekommen ● *vi* gelten. **~able** /-əbl/ *a* erhältlich
obtrusive /əb'tru:sɪv/ *a* aufdringlich; ⟨*thing*⟩ auffällig
obtuse /əb'tju:s/ *a* (*Geom*) stumpf; (*stupid*) begriffsstutzig
obviate /'ɒbvɪeɪt/ *vt* beseitigen
obvious /'ɒbvɪəs/ *a*, **-ly** *adv* offensichtlich, offenbar
occasion /ə'keɪʒn/ *n* Gelegenheit *f*; (*time*) Mal *nt*; (*event*) Ereignis *nt*; (*cause*) Anlaß *m*, Grund *m*; **on ~** gelegentlich, hin und wieder; **on the ~ of** anläßlich (+ *gen*) ● *vt* veranlassen
occasional /ə'keɪʒənl/ *a* gelegentlich; **he has the ~ glass of wine** er trinkt gelegentlich ein Glas Wein. **~ly** *adv* gelegentlich, hin und wieder
occult /ɒ'kʌlt/ *a* okkult
occupant /'ɒkjʊpənt/ *n* Bewohner(in) *m(f)*; (*of vehicle*) Insasse *m*
occupation /ɒkjʊ'peɪʃn/ *n* Beschäftigung *f*; (*job*) Beruf *m*; (*Mil*) Besetzung *f*; (*period*) Besatzung *f*. **~al** *a* Berufs-. **~al therapy** *n* Beschäftigungstherapie *f*
occupier /'ɒkjʊpaɪə(r)/ *n* Bewohner(in) *m(f)*
occupy /'ɒkjʊpaɪ/ *vt* (*pt/pp* **occupied**) besetzen ⟨*seat*, (*Mil*) *country*⟩; einnehmen ⟨*space*⟩; in Anspruch nehmen ⟨*time*⟩; (*live in*) bewohnen; (*fig*) bekleiden ⟨*office*⟩; (*keep busy*) beschäftigen; **~ oneself** sich beschäftigen
occur /ə'kɜ:(r)/ *vi* (*pt/pp* **occurred**) geschehen; (*exist*) vorkommen, auftreten; **it ~red to me that** es fiel mir ein, daß. **occurrence** /ə'kʌrəns/ *n* Auftreten *nt*; (*event*) Ereignis *nt*
ocean /'əʊʃn/ *n* Ozean *m*
o'clock /ə'klɒk/ *adv* **[at] 7~** [um] 7 Uhr
octagonal /ɒk'tægənl/ *a* achteckig
octave /'ɒktɪv/ *n* (*Mus*) Oktave *f*
October /ɒk'təʊbə(r)/ *n* Oktober *m*
octopus /'ɒktəpəs/ *n* (*pl* **-puses**) Tintenfisch *m*
odd /ɒd/ *a* (**-er, -est**) seltsam, merkwürdig; ⟨*number*⟩ ungerade; (*not of set*) einzeln; **forty ~** über vierzig; **~ jobs** Gelegenheitsarbeiten *pl*; **the ~ one out** die Ausnahme; **at ~ moments** zwischendurch; **have the ~ glass of wine** gelegentlich ein Glas Wein trinken
odd|ity /'ɒdɪtɪ/ *n* Kuriosität *f*. **~ly** *adv* merkwürdig; **~ly enough** merkwürdigerweise. **~ment** *n* (*of fabric*) Rest *m*
odds /ɒdz/ *npl* (*chances*) Chancen *pl*; **at ~** uneinig; **~ and ends** Kleinkram *m*; **it makes no ~** es spielt keine Rolle
ode /əʊd/ *n* Ode *f*
odious /'əʊdɪəs/ *a* widerlich, abscheulich
odour /'əʊdə(r)/ *n* Geruch *m*. **~less** *a* geruchlos
oesophagus /i:'sɒfəgəs/ *n* Speiseröhre *f*
of /ɒv, *unbetont* əv/ *prep* von (+ *dat*); (*made of*) aus (+ *dat*); **the two of us** wir zwei; **a child of three** ein dreijähriges Kind; **the fourth of January** der vierte Januar; **a pound of butter** ein

Pfund Butter; **a cup of tea/coffee** eine Tasse Tee/Kaffee; **a bottle of wine** eine Flasche Wein; **half of it** die Hälfte davon; **the whole of the room** das ganze Zimmer

off /ɒf/ *prep* von (+ *dat*); **£10 ~ the price** £10 Nachlaß; **~ the coast** vor der Küste; **get ~ the ladder/bus** von der Leiter/aus dem Bus steigen; **take/leave the lid ~ the saucepan** den Topf abdecken/nicht zudecken • *adv* weg; ⟨*button, lid, handle*⟩ ab; ⟨*light*⟩ aus; ⟨*brake*⟩ los; ⟨*machine*⟩ abgeschaltet; ⟨*tap*⟩ zu; (*on appliance*) **'off'** 'aus'; **2 kilometres ~** 2 Kilometer entfernt; **a long way ~** weit weg; (*time*) noch lange hin; **~ and on** hin und wieder; **with his hat/coat ~** ohne Hut/Mantel; **with the light/lid ~** ohne Licht/Deckel; **20% ~** 20% Nachlaß; **be ~** (*leave*) [weg]gehen; (*Sport*) starten; ⟨*food:*⟩ schlecht/(*all gone*) alle sein; **be better/worse ~** besser/schlechter dran sein; **be well ~** gut dran sein; (*financially*) wohlhabend sein; **have a day ~** einen freien Tag haben; **go/drive ~** weggehen/-fahren; **turn/take sth ~** etw abdrehen/-nehmen

offal /'ɒfl/ *n* (*Culin*) Innereien *pl*

offence /ə'fens/ *n* (*illegal act*) Vergehen *nt*; **give/take ~** Anstoß erregen/nehmen (**at** an + *dat*)

offend /ə'fend/ *vt* beleidigen. **~er** *n* (*Jur*) Straftäter *m*

offensive /ə'fensɪv/ *a* anstößig; (*Mil, Sport*) offensiv • *n* Offensive *f*

offer /'ɒfə(r)/ *n* Angebot *nt*; **on special ~** im Sonderangebot • *vt* anbieten (**to** *dat*); leisten ⟨*resistance*⟩; **~ s.o. sth** jdm etw anbieten; **~ to do sth** sich anbieten, etw zu tun. **~ing** *n* Gabe *f*

off'hand *a* brüsk; (*casual*) lässig • *adv* so ohne weiteres

office /'ɒfɪs/ *n* Büro *nt*; (*post*) Amt *nt*; **in ~** im Amt; **~ hours** *pl* Dienststunden *pl*

officer /'ɒfɪsə(r)/ *n* Offizier *m*; (*official*) Beamte(r) *m*/Beamtin *f*; (*police*) Polizeibeamte(r) *m*/-beamtin *f*

official /ə'fɪʃl/ *a* offiziell, amtlich • *n* Beamte(r) *m*/Beamtin *f*; (*Sport*) Funktionär *m*. **~ly** *adv* offiziell

officiate /ə'fɪʃɪeɪt/ *vi* amtieren

officious /ə'fɪʃəs/ *a*, **-ly** *adv* übereifrig

'offing *n* **in the ~** in Aussicht

'off-licence *n* Wein- und Spirituosenhandlung *f*

off-'load *vt* ausladen

'off-putting *a* (*fam*) abstoßend

off'set *vt* (*pt/pp* **-set**, *pres p* **-setting**) ausgleichen

'offshoot *n* Schößling *m*; (*fig*) Zweig *m*

'offshore *a* offshore-. **~ rig** *n* Bohrinsel *f*

off'side *a* (*Sport*) abseits

'offspring *n* Nachwuchs *m*

off'stage *adv* hinter den Kulissen

off-'white *a* fast weiß

often /'ɒfn/ *adv* oft; **every so ~** von Zeit zu Zeit

ogle /'əʊgl/ *vt* beäugeln

ogre /'əʊgə(r)/ *n* Menschenfresser *m*

oh /əʊ/ *int* oh! ach! **oh dear!** o weh!

oil /ɔɪl/ *n* Öl *nt*; (*petroleum*) Erdöl *nt* • *vt* ölen

oil: ~cloth *n* Wachstuch *nt*. **~field** *n* Ölfeld *nt*. **~-painting** *n* Ölgemälde *nt*. **~ refinery** *n* [Erd]ölraffinerie *f*. **~skins** *npl* Ölzeug *nt*. **~-slick** *n* Ölteppich *m*. **~-tanker** *n* Öltanker *m*. **~ well** *n* Ölquelle *f*

oily /'ɔɪlɪ/ *a* (**-ier, -iest**) ölig

ointment /'ɔɪntmənt/ *n* Salbe *f*

OK /əʊ'keɪ/ *a & int* (*fam*) in Ordnung; okay • *adv* (*well*) gut • *vt* (*auch* **okay**) (*pt/pp* **okayed**) genehmigen

old /əʊld/ *a* (**-er, -est**) alt; (*former*) ehemalig

old: ~ 'age *n* Alter *nt*. **~-age 'pensioner** *n* Rentner(in) *m*(*f*). **~ boy** *n* ehemaliger Schüler. **~-'fashioned** *a* altmodisch. **~ girl** ehemalige Schülerin *f*. **~ 'maid** *n* alte Jungfer *f*

olive /'ɒlɪv/ *n* Olive *f*; (*colour*) Oliv *nt* • *a* olivgrün. **~ branch** *n* Ölzweig *m*; (*fig*) Friedensangebot *nt*. **~ 'oil** *n* Olivenöl *nt*

Olympic /ə'lɪmpɪk/ *a* olympisch • *n* **the ~s** die Olympischen Spiele *pl*

omelette /'ɒmlɪt/ *n* Omelett *nt*

omen /'əʊmən/ *n* Omen *nt*

ominous /'ɒmɪnəs/ *a* bedrohlich

omission /ə'mɪʃn/ *n* Auslassung *f*; (*failure to do*) Unterlassung *f*

omit /ə'mɪt/ *vt* (*pt/pp* **omitted**) auslassen; **~ to do sth** es unterlassen, etw zu tun

omnipotent /ɒm'nɪpətənt/ *a* allmächtig

on /ɒn/ *prep* auf (+ *dat*/(*on to*) + *acc*); (*on vertical surface*) an (+ *dat*/(*on to*) + *acc*); (*about*) über (+ *acc*); **on Monday** [am] Montag; **on Mondays**

montags; **on the first of May** am ersten Mai; **on arriving** als ich ankam; **on one's finger** am Finger; **on the right/left** rechts/links; **on the Rhine/Thames** am Rhein/an der Themse; **on the radio/television** im Radio/Fernsehen; **on the bus/train** im Bus/Zug; **go on the bus/train** mit dem Bus/Zug fahren; **get on the bus/train** in den Bus/Zug einsteigen; **on me** (*with me*) bei mir; **it's on me** (*fam*) das spendiere ich ● *adv* (*further on*) weiter; (*switched on*) an; ⟨*brake*⟩ angezogen; ⟨*machine*⟩ angeschaltet; (*on appliance*) **'on'** 'ein'; **with/without his hat/coat on** mit/ohne Hut/Mantel; **with/without the lid on** mit/ohne Deckel; **be on** ⟨*film:*⟩ laufen; ⟨*event:*⟩ stattfinden; **be on at** (*fam*) bedrängen (**zu** to); **it's not on** (*fam*) das geht nicht; **on and on** immer weiter; **on and off** hin und wieder; **and so on** und so weiter; **later on** später; **move/drive on** weitergehen/-fahren; **stick/sew on** ankleben/-nähen

once /wʌns/ *adv* einmal; (*formerly*) früher; **at ~** sofort; (*at the same time*) gleichzeitig; **~ and for all** ein für allemal ● *conj* wenn; (*with past tense*) als. **~-over** *n* (*fam*) **give s.o./sth the ~-over** sich (*dat*) jdn/etw kurz ansehen

'oncoming *a* **~ traffic** Gegenverkehr *m*

one /wʌn/ *a* ein(e); (*only*) einzig; **not ~** kein(e); **~ day/evening** eines Tages/Abends ● *n* Eins *f* ● *pron* eine(r)/eins; (*impersonal*) man; **which ~** welche(r,s); **~ another** einander; **~ by ~** einzeln; **~ never knows** man kann nie wissen

one: ~-eyed *a* einäugig. **~-parent 'family** *n* Einelternfamilie *f*. **~'self** *pron* selbst; (*refl*) sich; **by ~self** allein. **~-sided** *a* einseitig. **~-way** *a* ⟨*street*⟩ Einbahn-; ⟨*ticket*⟩ einfach

onion /'ʌnjən/ *n* Zwiebel *f*

'onlooker *n* Zuschauer(in) *m*(*f*)

only /'əʊnlɪ/ *a* einzige(r,s); **an ~ child** ein Einzelkind *nt* ● *adv & conj* nur; **~ just** gerade erst; (*barely*) gerade noch

'onset *n* Beginn *m*; (*of winter*) Einsetzen *nt*

onslaught /'ɒnslɔːt/ *n* heftiger Angriff *m*

onus /'əʊnəs/ *n* **the ~ is on me** es liegt an mir (**to** zu)

onward[s] /'ɒnwəd[z]/ *adv* vorwärts; **from then ~** von der Zeit an

ooze /uːz/ *vi* sickern

opal /'əʊpl/ *n* Opal *m*

opaque /əʊ'peɪk/ *a* undurchsichtig

open /'əʊpən/ *a*, **-ly** *adv* offen; **be ~** ⟨*shop:*⟩ geöffnet sein; **in the ~ air** im Freien ● *n* **in the ~** im Freien ● *vt* öffnen, aufmachen; (*start, set up*) eröffnen ● *vi* sich öffnen; ⟨*flower:*⟩ aufgehen; ⟨*shop:*⟩ öffnen, aufmachen; (*be started*) eröffnet werden. **~ up** *vt* öffnen, aufmachen; (*fig*) eröffnen ● *vi* sich öffnen; (*fig*) sich eröffnen

open: ~-air 'swimming pool *n* Freibad *nt*. **~ day** *n* Tag *m* der offenen Tür

opener /'əʊpənə(r)/ *n* Öffner *m*

opening /'əʊpənɪŋ/ *n* Öffnung *f*; (*beginning*) Eröffnung *f*; (*job*) Einstiegsmöglichkeit *f*. **~ hours** *npl* Öffnungszeiten *pl*

open: ~-'minded *a* aufgeschlossen. **~-plan** *a* **~-plan office** Großraumbüro *nt*. **~ 'sandwich** *n* belegtes Brot *nt*

opera /'ɒpərə/ *n* Oper *f*

operable /'ɒpərəbl/ *a* operierbar

opera: ~-glasses *npl* Opernglas *nt*. **~-house** *n* Opernhaus *nt*. **~-singer** *n* Opernsänger(in) *m*(*f*)

operate /'ɒpəreɪt/ *vt* bedienen ⟨*machine, lift*⟩; betätigen ⟨*lever, brake*⟩; (*fig: run*) betreiben ● *vi* (*Techn*) funktionieren; (*be in action*) in Betrieb sein; (*Mil & fig*) operieren; **~ [on]** (*Med*) operieren

operatic /ɒpə'rætɪk/ *a* Opern-

operation /ɒpə'reɪʃn/ *n* (*see* **operate**) Bedienung *f*; Betätigung *f*; Operation *f*; **in ~** (*Techn*) in Betrieb; **come into ~** (*fig*) in Kraft treten; **have an ~** (*Med*) operiert werden. **~al** *a* **be ~al** in Betrieb sein; ⟨*law:*⟩ in Kraft sein

operative /'ɒpərətɪv/ *a* wirksam

operator /'ɒpəreɪtə(r)/ *n* (*user*) Bedienungsperson *f*; (*Teleph*) Vermittlung *f*

operetta /ɒpə'retə/ *n* Operette *f*

opinion /ə'pɪnjən/ *n* Meinung *f*; **in my ~** meiner Meinung nach. **~ated** *a* rechthaberisch

opium /'əʊpɪəm/ *n* Opium *nt*

opponent /ə'pəʊnənt/ *n* Gegner(in) *m*(*f*)

opportun|e /ˈɒpətju:n/ *a* günstig. **~ist** /-ˈtju:nɪst/ *a* opportunistisch • *n* Opportunist *m*

opportunity /ɒpəˈtju:nətɪ/ *n* Gelegenheit *f*

oppos|e /əˈpəʊz/ *vt* Widerstand leisten (+ *dat*); (*argue against*) sprechen gegen; **be ~ed to sth** gegen etw sein; **as ~ed to** im Gegensatz zu. **~ing** *a* gegnerisch; (*opposite*) entgegengesetzt

opposite /ˈɒpəzɪt/ *a* entgegengesetzt; ⟨*house, side*⟩ gegenüberliegend; **~ number** (*fig*) Gegenstück *nt*; **the ~ sex** das andere Geschlecht • *n* Gegenteil *nt* • *adv* gegenüber • *prep* gegenüber (+ *dat*)

opposition /ɒpəˈzɪʃn/ *n* Widerstand *m*; (*Pol*) Opposition *f*

oppress /əˈpres/ *vt* unterdrücken. **~ion** /-eʃn/ *n* Unterdrückung *f*. **~ive** /-ɪv/ *a* tyrannisch; ⟨*heat*⟩ drückend. **~or** *n* Unterdrücker *m*

opt /ɒpt/ *vi* **~ for** sich entscheiden für; **~ out** ausscheiden (**of** aus)

optical /ˈɒptɪkl/ *a* optisch; **~ illusion** optische Täuschung *f*

optician /ɒpˈtɪʃn/ *n* Optiker *m*

optics /ˈɒptɪks/ *n* Optik *f*

optimis|m /ˈɒptɪmɪzm/ *n* Optimismus *m*. **~t** /-mɪst/ *n* Optimist *m*. **~tic** /-ˈmɪstɪk/ *a*, **-ally** *adv* optimistisch

optimum /ˈɒptɪməm/ *a* optimal • *n* (*pl* **-ima**) Optimum *nt*

option /ˈɒpʃn/ *n* Wahl *f*; (*Comm*) Option *f*. **~al** *a* auf Wunsch erhältlich; ⟨*subject*⟩ wahlfrei; **~al extras** *pl* Extras *pl*

opu|lence /ˈɒpjʊləns/ *n* Prunk *m*; (*wealth*) Reichtum *m*. **~lent** *a* prunkvoll; (*wealthy*) sehr reich

or /ɔ:(r)/ *conj* oder; (*after negative*) noch; **or [else]** sonst; **in a year or two** in ein bis zwei Jahren

oracle /ˈɒrəkl/ *n* Orakel *nt*

oral /ˈɔ:rl/ *a*, **-ly** *adv* mündlich; (*Med*) oral • *n* (*fam*) Mündliche(s) *nt*

orange /ˈɒrɪndʒ/ *n* Apfelsine *f*, Orange *f*; (*colour*) Orange *nt* • *a* orangefarben. **~ade** /-ˈdʒeɪd/ *n* Orangeade *f*

oration /əˈreɪʃn/ *n* Rede *f*

orator /ˈɒrətə(r)/ *n* Redner *m*

oratorio /ɒrəˈtɔ:rɪəʊ/ *n* Oratorium *nt*

oratory /ˈɒrətərɪ/ *n* Redekunst *f*

orbit /ˈɔ:bɪt/ *n* Umlaufbahn *f* • *vt* umkreisen. **~al** *a* **~al road** Ringstraße *f*

orchard /ˈɔ:tʃəd/ *n* Obstgarten *m*

orches|tra /ˈɔ:kɪstrə/ *n* Orchester *nt*. **~tral** /-ˈkestrəl/ *a* Orchester-. **~trate** *vt* orchestrieren

orchid /ˈɔ:kɪd/ *n* Orchidee *f*

ordain /ɔ:ˈdeɪn/ *vt* bestimmen; (*Relig*) ordinieren

ordeal /ɔ:ˈdi:l/ *n* (*fig*) Qual *f*

order /ˈɔ:də(r)/ *n* Ordnung *f*; (*sequence*) Reihenfolge *f*; (*condition*) Zustand *m*; (*command*) Befehl *m*; (*in restaurant*) Bestellung *f*; (*Comm*) Auftrag *m*; (*Relig, medal*) Orden *m*; **out of ~** ⟨*machine*⟩ außer Betrieb; **in ~ that** damit; **in ~ to help** um zu helfen; **take holy ~s** Geistlicher werden • *vt* (*put in ~*) ordnen; (*command*) befehlen (+ *dat*); (*Comm, in restaurant*) bestellen; (*prescribe*) verordnen

orderly /ˈɔ:dəlɪ/ *a* ordentlich; (*not unruly*) friedlich • *n* (*Mil, Med*) Sanitäter *m*

ordinary /ˈɔ:dɪnərɪ/ *a* gewöhnlich, normal; ⟨*meeting*⟩ ordentlich

ordination /ɔ:dɪˈneɪʃn/ *n* (*Relig*) Ordination *f*

ore /ɔ:(r)/ *n* Erz *nt*

organ /ˈɔ:gən/ *n* (*Biol & fig*) Organ *nt*; (*Mus*) Orgel *f*

organic /ɔ:ˈgænɪk/ *a*, **-ally** *adv* organisch; (*without chemicals*) biodynamisch; ⟨*crop*⟩ biologisch angebaut; ⟨*food*⟩ Bio-; **~ally grown** biologisch angebaut. **~ farm** *n* Biohof *m*. **~ farming** *n* biologischer Anbau *m*

organism /ˈɔ:gənɪzm/ *n* Organismus *m*

organist /ˈɔ:gənɪst/ *n* Organist *m*

organization /ɔ:gənaɪˈzeɪʃn/ *n* Organisation *f*

organize /ˈɔ:gənaɪz/ *vt* organisieren; veranstalten ⟨*event*⟩. **~r** *n* Organisator *m*; Veranstalter *m*

orgasm /ˈɔ:gæzm/ *n* Orgasmus *m*

orgy /ˈɔ:dʒɪ/ *n* Orgie *f*

Orient /ˈɔ:rɪənt/ *n* Orient *m*. **o~al** /-ˈentl/ *a* orientalisch; **~al carpet** Orientteppich *m* • *n* Orientale *m*/ Orientalin *f*

orient|ate /ˈɔ:rɪənteɪt/ *vt* **~ate oneself** sich orientieren. **~ation** /-ˈteɪʃn/ *n* Orientierung *f*

orifice /ˈɒrɪfɪs/ *n* Öffnung *f*

origin /ˈɒrɪdʒɪn/ *n* Ursprung *m*; (*of person, goods*) Herkunft *f*

original /əˈrɪdʒənl/ *a* ursprünglich; (*not copied*) original; (*new*) originell

● *n* Original *nt*. **~ity** /-ˈnælətɪ/ *n* Originalität *f*. **~ly** *adv* ursprünglich

originat|e /əˈrɪdʒɪneɪt/ *vi* entstehen ● *vt* hervorbringen. **~or** *n* Urheber *m*

ornament /ˈɔːnəmənt/ *n* Ziergegenstand *m*; (*decoration*) Verzierung *f*. **~al** /-ˈmentl/ *a* dekorativ. **~ation** /-ˈteɪʃn/ *n* Verzierung *f*

ornate /ɔːˈneɪt/ *a* reich verziert

ornithology /ɔːnɪˈθɒlədʒɪ/ *n* Vogelkunde *f*

orphan /ˈɔːfn/ *n* Waisenkind *nt*, Waise *f* ● *vt* zur Waise machen; **~ed** verwaist. **~age** /-ɪdʒ/ *n* Waisenhaus *nt*

orthodox /ˈɔːθədɒks/ *a* orthodox

orthography /ɔːˈθɒgrəfɪ/ *n* Rechtschreibung *f*

orthopaedic /ɔːθəˈpiːdɪk/ *a* orthopädisch

oscillate /ˈɒsɪleɪt/ *vi* schwingen

ostensible /ɒˈstensəbl/ *a*, **-bly** *adv* angeblich

ostentat|ion /ɒstenˈteɪʃn/ *n* Protzerei *f* (*fam*). **~ious** /-ʃəs/ *a* protzig (*fam*)

osteopath /ˈɒstɪəpæθ/ *n* Osteopath *m*

ostracize /ˈɒstrəsaɪz/ *vt* ächten

ostrich /ˈɒstrɪtʃ/ *n* Strauß *m*

other /ˈʌðə(r)/ *a, pron & n* andere(r,s); **the ~ [one]** der/die/das andere; **the ~ two** die zwei anderen; **two ~s** zwei andere; (*more*) noch zwei; **no ~s** sonst keine; **any ~ questions?** sonst noch Fragen? **every ~ day** jeden zweiten Tag; **the ~ day** neulich; **the ~ evening** neulich abends; **someone/something or ~** irgend jemand/etwas ● *adv* anders; **~ than him** außer ihm; **somehow/somewhere or ~** irgendwie/irgendwo

ˈotherwise *adv* sonst; (*differently*) anders

otter /ˈɒtə(r)/ *n* Otter *m*

ouch /aʊtʃ/ *int* autsch

ought /ɔːt/ *v aux* **I/we ~ to stay** ich sollte/wir sollten eigentlich bleiben; **he ~ not to have done it** er hätte es nicht machen sollen; **that ~ to be enough** das sollte eigentlich genügen

ounce /aʊns/ *n* Unze *f* (*28,35 g*)

our /ˈaʊə(r)/ *a* unser

ours /ˈaʊəz/ *poss pron* unsere(r,s); **a friend of ~** ein Freund von uns; **that is ~** das gehört uns

ourselves /aʊəˈselvz/ *pron* selbst; (*refl*) uns; **by ~** allein

oust /aʊst/ *vt* entfernen

out /aʊt/ *adv* (*not at home*) weg; (*outside*) draußen; (*not alight*) aus; (*unconscious*) bewußtlos; **be ~** ⟨*sun:*⟩ scheinen; ⟨*flower:*⟩ blühen; ⟨*workers:*⟩ streiken; ⟨*calculation:*⟩ nicht stimmen; (*Sport*) aus sein; (*fig: not feasible*) nicht in Frage kommen; **~ and about** unterwegs; **have it ~ with s.o.** (*fam*) jdn zur Rede stellen; **get ~!** (*fam*) raus! **~ with it!** (*fam*) heraus damit! **go/send ~** hinausgehen/-schicken; **come/bring ~** herauskommen/-bringen ● *prep* **~ of** aus (+ *dat*); **go ~ of the door** zur Tür hinausgehen; **be ~ of bed/the room** nicht im Bett/im Zimmer sein; **~ of breath/danger** außer Atem/Gefahr; **~ of work** arbeitslos; **nine ~ of ten** neun von zehn; **be ~ of sugar/bread** keinen Zucker/kein Brot mehr haben ● *prep* aus (+ *dat*); **go ~ the door** zur Tür hinausgehen

outˈbid *vt* (*pt/pp* **-bid**, *pres p* **-bidding**) überbieten

ˈoutboard *a* **~ motor** Außenbordmotor *m*

ˈoutbreak *n* Ausbruch *m*

ˈoutbuilding *n* Nebengebäude *nt*

ˈoutburst *n* Ausbruch *m*

ˈoutcast *n* Ausgestoßene(r) *m/f*

ˈoutcome *n* Ergebnis *nt*

ˈoutcry *n* Aufschrei *m* [der Entrüstung]

outˈdated *a* überholt

outˈdo *vt* (*pt* **-did**, *pp* **-done**) übertreffen, übertrumpfen

ˈoutdoor *a* ⟨*life, sports*⟩ im Freien; **~ shoes** *pl* Straßenschuhe *pl*; **~ swimming pool** Freibad *nt*

outˈdoors *adv* draußen; **go ~** nach draußen gehen

ˈouter *a* äußere(r,s)

ˈoutfit *n* Ausstattung *f*; (*clothes*) Ensemble *nt*; (*fam: organization*) Betrieb *m*; (*fam*) Laden *m*. **~ter** *n* **men's ~ter's** Herrenbekleidungsgeschäft *nt*

ˈoutgoing *a* ausscheidend; ⟨*mail*⟩ ausgehend; (*sociable*) kontaktfreudig. **~s** *npl* Ausgaben *pl*

outˈgrow *vt* (*pt* **-grew**, *pp* **-grown**) herauswachsen aus

ˈouthouse *n* Nebengebäude *nt*

outing /ˈaʊtɪŋ/ *n* Ausflug *m*

outlandish /aʊt'lændɪʃ/ *a* ungewöhnlich

'outlaw *n* Geächtete(r) *m/f* ● *vt* ächten

'outlay *n* Auslagen *pl*

'outlet *n* Abzug *m*; (*for water*) Abfluß *m*; (*fig*) Ventil *nt*; (*Comm*) Absatzmöglichkeit *f*

'outline *n* Umriß *m*; (*summary*) kurze Darstellung *f* ● *vt* umreißen

out'live *vt* überleben

'outlook *n* Aussicht *f*; (*future prospect*) Aussichten *pl*; (*attitude*) Einstellung *f*

'outlying *a* entlegen; **~ areas** *pl* Außengebiete *pl*

out'moded *a* überholt

out'number *vt* zahlenmäßig überlegen sein (+ *dat*)

'out-patient *n* ambulanter Patient *m*; **~s' department** Ambulanz *f*

'outpost *n* Vorposten *m*

'output *n* Leistung *f*, Produktion *f*

'outrage *n* Greueltat *f*; (*fig*) Skandal *m*; (*indignation*) Empörung *f* ● *vt* empören. **~ous** /-'reɪdʒəs/ *a* empörend

'outright[1] *a* völlig, total; ⟨*refusal*⟩ glatt

out'right[2] *adv* ganz; (*at once*) sofort; (*frankly*) offen

'outset *n* Anfang *m*; **from the ~** von Anfang an

'outside[1] *a* äußere(r,s); **~ wall** Außenwand *f* ● *n* Außenseite *f*; **from the ~** von außen; **at the ~** höchstens

out'side[2] *adv* außen; (*out of doors*) draußen; **go ~** nach draußen gehen ● *prep* außerhalb (+ *gen*); (*in front of*) vor (+ *dat/acc*)

out'sider *n* Außenseiter *m*

'outsize *a* übergroß

'outskirts *npl* Rand *m*

out'spoken *a* offen; **be ~** kein Blatt vor den Mund nehmen

out'standing *a* hervorragend; (*conspicuous*) bemerkenswert; (*not settled*) unerledigt; (*Comm*) ausstehend

'outstretched *a* ausgestreckt

out'strip *vt* (*pt/pp* **-stripped**) davonlaufen (+ *dat*); (*fig*) übertreffen

out'vote *vt* überstimmen

'outward /-wəd/ *a* äußerlich; **~ journey** Hinreise *f* ● *adv* nach außen; **be ~ bound** ⟨*ship:*⟩ auslaufen. **~ly** *adv* nach außen hin, äußerlich. **~s** *adv* nach außen

out'weigh *vt* überwiegen

out'wit *vt* (*pt/pp* **-witted**) überlisten

oval /'əʊvl/ *a* oval ● *n* Oval *nt*

ovary /'əʊvərɪ/ *n* (*Anat*) Eierstock *m*

ovation /əʊ'veɪʃn/ *n* Ovation *f*

oven /'ʌvn/ *n* Backofen *m*. **~-ready** *a* bratfertig

over /'əʊvə(r)/ *prep* über (+ *acc/dat*); **~ dinner** beim Essen; **~ the weekend** übers Wochenende; **~ the phone** am Telefon; **~ the page** auf der nächsten Seite; **all ~ Germany** in ganz Deutschland; ⟨*travel*⟩ durch ganz Deutschland; **all ~ the place** (*fam*) überall ● *adv* (*remaining*) übrig; (*ended*) zu Ende; **~ again** noch einmal; **~ and ~** immer wieder; **~ here/there** hier/da drüben; **all ~** (*everywhere*) überall; **it's all ~** es ist vorbei; **I ache all ~** mir tut alles weh; **go/drive ~** hinübergehen/-fahren; **come/bring ~** herüberkommen/-bringen; **turn ~** herumdrehen

overall[1] /'əʊvərɔ:l/ *n* Kittel *m*; **~s** *pl* Overall *m*

overall[2] /əʊvər'ɔ:l/ *a* gesamt; (*general*) allgemein ● *adv* insgesamt

over'awe *vt* (*fig*) überwältigen

over'balance *vi* das Gleichgewicht verlieren

over'bearing *a* herrisch

'overboard *adv* (*Naut*) über Bord

'overcast *a* bedeckt

over'charge *vt* **~ s.o.** jdm zu viel berechnen ● *vi* zu viel verlangen

'overcoat *n* Mantel *m*

over'come *vt* (*pt* **-came**, *pp* **-come**) überwinden; **be ~ by** überwältigt werden von

over'crowded *a* überfüllt

over'do *vt* (*pt* **-did**, *pp* **-done**) übertreiben; (*cook too long*) zu lange kochen; **~ it** (*fam: do too much*) sich übernehmen

'overdose *n* Überdosis *f*

'overdraft *n* [Konto]überziehung *f*; **have an ~** sein Konto überzogen haben

over'draw *vt* (*pt* **-drew**, *pp* **-drawn**) (*Comm*) überziehen

over'due *a* überfällig

over'estimate *vt* überschätzen

'overflow[1] *n* Überschuß *m*; (*outlet*) Überlauf *m*

over'flow[2] *vi* überlaufen

over'grown *a* ⟨*garden*⟩ überwachsen

'overhang[1] *n* Überhang *m*

over'hang² *vt/i* (*pt/pp* **-hung**) überhängen (über + *acc*)
'overhaul¹ *n* Überholung *f*
over'haul² *vt* (*Techn*) überholen
over'head¹ *adv* oben
'overhead² *a* Ober-; (*ceiling*) Decken-. **~s** *npl* allgemeine Unkosten *pl*
over'hear *vt* (*pt/pp* **-heard**) mit anhören ⟨*conversation*⟩; **I overheard him saying it** ich hörte zufällig, wie er das sagte
over'heat *vi* zu heiß werden ● *vt* zu stark erhitzen
over'joyed *a* überglücklich
'overland *a & adv* /--'-/ auf dem Landweg; **~ route** Landroute *f*
over'lap *v* (*pt/pp* **-lapped**) ● *vi* sich überschneiden ● *vt* überlappen
over'leaf *adv* umseitig
over'load *vt* überladen; (*Electr*) überlasten
'overlook¹ *n* (*Amer*) Aussichtspunkt *m*
over'look² *vt* überblicken; (*fail to see, ignore*) übersehen
overly /'əʊvəlɪ/ *adv* übermäßig
over'night¹ *adv* über Nacht; **stay ~** übernachten
'overnight² *a* Nacht-; **~ stay** Übernachtung *f*
'overpass *n* Überführung *f*
over'pay *vt* (*pt/pp* **-paid**) überbezahlen
over'populated *a* übervölkert
over'power *vt* überwältigen. **~ing** *a* überwältigend
over'priced *a* zu teuer
overpro'duce *vt* überproduzieren
over'rate *vt* überschätzen. **~d** *a* überbewertet
over'reach *vt* **~ oneself** sich übernehmen
overre'act *vi* überreagieren. **~ion** *n* Überreaktion *f*
over'rid|e *vt* (*pt* **-rode**, *pp* **-ridden**) sich hinwegsetzen über (+ *acc*). **~ing** *a* Haupt-
over'rule *vt* ablehnen; **we were ~d** wir wurden überstimmt
over'run *vt* (*pt* **-ran**, *pp* **-run**, *pres p* **-running**) überrennen; überschreiten ⟨*time*⟩; **be ~ with** überlaufen sein von
over'seas¹ *adv* in Übersee; **go ~** nach Übersee gehen
'overseas² *a* Übersee-
over'see *vt* (*pt* **-saw**, *pp* **-seen**) beaufsichtigen
'overseer /-sɪə(r)/ *n* Aufseher *m*
over'shadow *vt* überschatten
over'shoot *vt* (*pt/pp* **-shot**) hinausschießen über (+ *acc*)
'oversight *n* Versehen *nt*
over'sleep *vi* (*pt/pp* **-slept**) [sich] verschlafen
over'step *vt* (*pt/pp* **-stepped**) überschreiten
over'strain *vt* überanstrengen
overt /əʊ'vɜ:t/ *a* offen
over'tak|e *vt/i* (*pt* **-took**, *pp* **-taken**) überholen. **~ing** *n* Überholen *nt*; **no ~ing** Überholverbot *nt*
over'tax *vt* zu hoch besteuern; (*fig*) überfordern
'overthrow¹ *n* (*Pol*) Sturz *m*
over'throw² *vt* (*pt* **-threw**, *pp* **-thrown**) (*Pol*) stürzen
'overtime *n* Überstunden *pl* ● *adv* **work ~** Überstunden machen
over'tired *a* übermüdet
'overtone *n* (*fig*) Unterton *m*
overture /'əʊvətjʊə(r)/ *n* (*Mus*) Ouvertüre *f*; **~s** *pl* (*fig*) Annäherungsversuche *pl*
over'turn *vt* umstoßen ● *vi* umkippen
over'weight *a* übergewichtig; **be ~** Übergewicht haben
overwhelm /-'welm/ *vt* überwältigen. **~ing** *a* überwältigend
over'work *n* Überarbeitung *f* ● *vt* überfordern ● *vi* sich überarbeiten
over'wrought *a* überreizt
ovulation /ɒvjʊ'leɪʃn/ *n* Eisprung *m*
ow|e /əʊ/ *vt* schulden/(*fig*) verdanken (**[to] s.o.** jdm); **~e s.o. sth** jdm etw schuldig sein; **be ~ing** ⟨*money:*⟩ ausstehen. **'~ing to** *prep* wegen (+ *gen*)
owl /aʊl/ *n* Eule *f*
own¹ /əʊn/ *a & pron* eigen; **it's my ~** es gehört mir; **a car of my ~** mein eigenes Auto; **on one's ~** allein; **hold one's ~** sich behaupten; **get one's ~ back** (*fam*) sich revanchieren
own² *vt* besitzen; (*confess*) zugeben; **I don't ~ it** es gehört mir nicht. **~ up** *vi* es zugeben
owner /'əʊnə(r)/ *n* Eigentümer(in) *m(f)*, Besitzer(in) *m(f)*; (*of shop*) Inhaber(in) *m(f)*. **~ship** *n* Besitz *m*
ox /ɒks/ *n* (*pl* **oxen**) Ochse *m*
oxide /'ɒksaɪd/ *n* Oxyd *nt*
oxygen /'ɒksɪdʒən/ *n* Sauerstoff *m*
oyster /'ɔɪstə(r)/ *n* Auster *f*

ozone /'əʊzəʊn/ *n* Ozon *nt*. **~-'friendly** *a* ≈ ohne FCKW. **~ layer** *n* Ozonschicht *f*

P

pace /peɪs/ *n* Schritt *m*; (*speed*) Tempo *nt*; **keep ~ with** Schritt halten mit • *vi* **~ up and down** auf und ab gehen. **~-maker** *n* (*Sport & Med*) Schrittmacher *m*

Pacific /pə'sɪfɪk/ *a & n* **the ~ [Ocean]** der Pazifik

pacifier /'pæsɪfaɪə(r)/ *n* (*Amer*) Schnuller *m*

pacifist /'pæsɪfɪst/ *n* Pazifist *m*

pacify /'pæsɪfaɪ/ *vt* (*pt/pp* **-ied**) beruhigen

pack /pæk/ *n* Packung *f*; (*Mil*) Tornister *m*; (*of cards*) [Karten]spiel *nt*; (*gang*) Bande *f*; (*of hounds*) Meute *f*; (*of wolves*) Rudel *nt*; **a ~ of lies** ein Haufen Lügen • *vt/i* packen; einpacken ⟨*article*⟩; **be ~ed** (*crowded*) [gedrängt] voll sein; **send s.o. ~ing** (*fam*) jdn wegschicken. **~ up** *vt* einpacken • *vi* (*fam*) ⟨*machine:*⟩ kaputtgehen; ⟨*person:*⟩ einpacken (*fam*)

package /'pækɪdʒ/ *n* Paket *nt* • *vt* verpacken. **~ holiday** *n* Pauschalreise *f*

packed 'lunch *n* Lunchpaket *nt*

packet /'pækɪt/ *n* Päckchen *nt*; **cost a ~** (*fam*) einen Haufen Geld kosten

packing /'pækɪŋ/ *n* Verpackung *f*

pact /pækt/ *n* Pakt *m*

pad[1] /pæd/ *n* Polster *nt*; (*for writing*) [Schreib]block *m*; (*fam: home*) Wohnung *f* • *vt* (*pt/pp* **padded**) polstern

pad[2] *vi* (*pt/pp* **padded**) tappen

padding /'pædɪŋ/ *n* Polsterung *f*; (*in written work*) Füllwerk *nt*

paddle[1] /'pædl/ *n* Paddel *nt* • *vt* (*row*) paddeln

paddle[2] *vi* waten

paddock /'pædək/ *n* Koppel *f*

padlock /'pædlɒk/ *n* Vorhängeschloß *nt* • *vt* mit einem Vorhängeschloß verschließen

paediatrician /pi:dɪə'trɪʃn/ *n* Kinderarzt *m*/-ärztin *f*

pagan /'peɪgən/ *a* heidnisch • *n* Heide *m*/Heidin *f*

page[1] /peɪdʒ/ *n* Seite *f*

page[2] *n* (*boy*) Page *m* • *vt* ausrufen ⟨*person*⟩

pageant /'pædʒənt/ *n* Festzug *m*. **~ry** *n* Prunk *m*

paid /peɪd/ *see* **pay** • *a* bezahlt; **put ~ to** (*fam*) zunichte machen

pail /peɪl/ *n* Eimer *m*

pain /peɪn/ *n* Schmerz *m*; **be in ~** Schmerzen haben; **take ~s** sich (*dat*) Mühe geben; **~ in the neck** (*fam*) Nervensäge *f* • *vt* (*fig*) schmerzen

pain: ~ful *a* schmerzhaft; (*fig*) schmerzlich. **~-killer** *n* schmerzstillendes Mittel *nt*. **~less** *a*, **-ly** *adv* schmerzlos

painstaking /'peɪnzteɪkɪŋ/ *a* sorgfältig

paint /peɪnt/ *n* Farbe *f* • *vt/i* streichen; ⟨*artist:*⟩ malen. **~brush** *n* Pinsel *m*. **~er** *n* Maler *m*; (*decorator*) Anstreicher *m*. **~ing** *n* Malerei *f*; (*picture*) Gemälde *nt*

pair /peə(r)/ *n* Paar *nt*; **~ of trousers** Hose *f*; **~ of scissors** Schere *f* • *vt* paaren • *vi* **~ off** Paare bilden

pajamas /pə'dʒɑ:məz/ *npl* (*Amer*) Schlafanzug *m*

Pakistan /pɑ:kɪ'stɑ:n/ *n* Pakistan *nt*. **~i** *a* pakistanisch • *n* Pakistaner(in) *m(f)*

pal /pæl/ *n* Freund(in) *m(f)*

palace /'pælɪs/ *n* Palast *m*

palatable /'pælətəbl/ *a* schmackhaft

palate /'pælət/ *n* Gaumen *m*

palatial /pə'leɪʃl/ *a* palastartig

palaver /pə'lɑ:və(r)/ *n* (*fam: fuss*) Theater *nt* (*fam*)

pale[1] /peɪl/ *n* (*stake*) Pfahl *m*; **beyond the ~** (*fam*) unmöglich

pale[2] *a* (**-r, -st**) blaß • *vi* blaß werden. **~ness** *n* Blässe *f*

Palestin|e /'pælɪstaɪn/ *n* Palästina *nt*. **~ian** /pælə'stɪnɪən/ *a* palästinensisch • *n* Palästinenser(in) *m(f)*

palette /'pælɪt/ *n* Palette *f*

pall /pɔ:l/ *n* Sargtuch *nt*; (*fig*) Decke *f* • *vi* an Reiz verlieren

pall|id /'pælɪd/ *a* bleich. **~or** *n* Blässe *f*

palm /pɑ:m/ *n* Handfläche *f*; (*tree, symbol*) Palme *f* • *vt* **~ sth off on s.o.** jdm etw andrehen. **P~ 'Sunday** *n* Palmsonntag *m*

palpable /'pælpəbl/ *a* tastbar; (*perceptible*) spürbar

palpitat|e /'pælpɪteɪt/ *vi* klopfen. **~ions** /-'teɪʃnz/ *npl* Herzklopfen *nt*

paltry /'pɔ:ltrɪ/ *a* (**-ier, -iest**) armselig

pamper /'pæmpə(r)/ *vt* verwöhnen

pamphlet /'pæmflɪt/ *n* Broschüre *f*

pan /pæn/ *n* Pfanne *f*; (*saucepan*) Topf *m*; (*of scales*) Schale *f* ● *vt* (*pt/pp* **panned**) (*fam*) verreißen

panacea /pænə'si:ə/ *n* Allheilmittel *nt*

panache /pə'næʃ/ *n* Schwung *m*

'pancake *n* Pfannkuchen *m*

pancreas /'pæŋkrɪəs/ *n* Bauchspeicheldrüse *f*

panda /'pændə/ *n* Panda *m*. ~ **car** *n* Streifenwagen *m*

pandemonium /pændɪ'məʊnɪəm/ *n* Höllenlärm *m*

pander /'pændə(r)/ *vi* ~ **to s.o.** jdm zu sehr nachgeben

pane /peɪn/ *n* [Glas]scheibe *f*

panel /'pænl/ *n* Tafel *f*, Platte *f*; ~ **of experts** Expertenrunde *f*; ~ **of judges** Jury *f*. ~**ling** *n* Täfelung *f*

pang /pæŋ/ *n* ~**s of hunger** Hungergefühl *nt*; ~**s of conscience** Gewissensbisse *pl*

panic /'pænɪk/ *n* Panik *f* ● *vi* (*pt/pp* **panicked**) in Panik geraten. ~**-stricken** *a* von Panik ergriffen

panoram|a /pænə'rɑ:mə/ *n* Panorama *nt*. ~**ic** /-'ræmɪk/ *a* Panorama-

pansy /'pænzɪ/ *n* Stiefmütterchen *nt*

pant /pænt/ *vi* keuchen; ⟨*dog:*⟩ hecheln

pantechnicon /pæn'teknɪkən/ *n* Möbelwagen *m*

panther /'pænθə(r)/ *n* Panther *m*

panties /'pæntɪz/ *npl* [Damen]slip *m*

pantomime /'pæntəmaɪm/ *n* [zu Weihnachten aufgeführte] Märchenvorstellung *f*

pantry /'pæntrɪ/ *n* Speisekammer *f*

pants /pænts/ *npl* Unterhose *f*; (*woman's*) Schlüpfer *m*; (*trousers*) Hose *f*

'pantyhose *n* (*Amer*) Strumpfhose *f*

papal /'peɪpl/ *a* päpstlich

paper /'peɪpə(r)/ *n* Papier *nt*; (*wall*~) Tapete *f*; (*newspaper*) Zeitung *f*; (*exam* ~) Testbogen *m*; (*exam*) Klausur *f*; (*treatise*) Referat *nt*; ~**s** *pl* (*documents*) Unterlagen *pl*; (*for identification*) [Ausweis]papiere *pl*; **on** ~ schriftlich ● *vt* tapezieren

paper: ~**back** *n* Taschenbuch *nt*. ~**-clip** *n* Büroklammer *f*. ~**-knife** *n* Brieföffner *m*. ~**weight** *n* Briefbeschwerer *m*. ~**work** *n* Schreibarbeit *f*

par /pɑ:(r)/ *n* (*Golf*) Par *nt*; **on a** ~ gleichwertig (**with** *dat*); **feel below** ~ sich nicht ganz auf der Höhe fühlen

parable /'pærəbl/ *n* Gleichnis *nt*

parachut|e /'pærəʃu:t/ *n* Fallschirm *m* ● *vi* [mit dem Fallschirm] abspringen. ~**ist** *n* Fallschirmspringer *m*

parade /pə'reɪd/ *n* Parade *f*; (*procession*) Festzug *m* ● *vi* marschieren ● *vt* (*show off*) zur Schau stellen

paradise /'pærədaɪs/ *n* Paradies *nt*

paradox /'pærədɒks/ *n* Paradox *nt*. ~**ical** /-'dɒksɪkl/ paradox

paraffin /'pærəfɪn/ *n* Paraffin *nt*

paragon /'pærəgən/ *n* ~ **of virtue** Ausbund *m* der Tugend

paragraph /'pærəgrɑ:f/ *n* Absatz *m*

parallel /'pærəlel/ *a & adv* parallel ● *n* (*Geog*) Breitenkreis *m*; (*fig*) Parallele *f*

paralyse /'pærəlaɪz/ *vt* lähmen; (*fig*) lahmlegen

paralysis /pə'ræləsɪs/ *n* (*pl* **-ses** /-si:z/) Lähmung *f*

paramount /'pærəmaʊnt/ *a* überragend; **be** ~ vorgehen

paranoid /'pærənɔɪd/ *a* [krankhaft] mißtrauisch

parapet /'pærəpɪt/ *n* Brüstung *f*

paraphernalia /pærəfə'neɪlɪə/ *n* Kram *m*

paraphrase /'pærəfreɪz/ *n* Umschreibung *f* ● *vt* umschreiben

paraplegic /pærə'pli:dʒɪk/ *a* querschnittsgelähmt ● *n* Querschnittsgelähmte(r) *m/f*

parasite /'pærəsaɪt/ *n* Parasit *m*, Schmarotzer *m*

parasol /'pærəsɒl/ *n* Sonnenschirm *m*

paratrooper /'pærətru:pə(r)/ *n* Fallschirmjäger *m*

parcel /'pɑ:sl/ *n* Paket *nt*

parch /pɑ:tʃ/ *vt* austrocknen; **be** ~**ed** ⟨*person:*⟩ einen furchtbaren Durst haben

parchment /'pɑ:tʃmənt/ *n* Pergament *nt*

pardon /'pɑ:dn/ *n* Verzeihung *f*; (*Jur*) Begnadigung *f*; ~? (*fam*) bitte? **I beg your** ~ wie bitte? (*sorry*) Verzeihung! ● *vt* verzeihen; (*Jur*) begnadigen

pare /peə(r)/ *vt* (*peel*) schälen

parent /'peərənt/ *n* Elternteil *m*; ~**s** *pl* Eltern *pl*. ~**al** /pə'rentl/ *a* elterlich

parenthesis /pə'renθəsɪs/ *n* (*pl* **-ses** /-si:z/) Klammer *f*

parish /ˈpærɪʃ/ *n* Gemeinde *f*. **~ioner** /pəˈrɪʃənə(r)/ *n* Gemeindemitglied *nt*

parity /ˈpærətɪ/ *n* Gleichheit *f*

park /pɑːk/ *n* Park *m* ● *vt/i* parken

parking /ˈpɑːkɪŋ/ *n* Parken *nt*; **'no ~'** 'Parken verboten'. **~-lot** *n* (*Amer*) Parkplatz *m*. **~-meter** *n* Parkuhr *f*. **~ space** *n* Parkplatz *m*

parliament /ˈpɑːləmənt/ *n* Parlament *nt*. **~ary** /-ˈmentərɪ/ *a* parlamentarisch

parlour /ˈpɑːlə(r)/ *n* Wohnzimmer *nt*

parochial /pəˈrəʊkɪəl/ *a* Gemeinde-; (*fig*) beschränkt

parody /ˈpærədɪ/ *n* Parodie *f* ● *vt* (*pt/pp* **-ied**) parodieren

parole /pəˈrəʊl/ *n* **on ~** auf Bewährung

paroxysm /ˈpærəksɪzm/ *n* Anfall *m*

parquet /ˈpɑːkeɪ/ *n* **~ floor** Parkett *nt*

parrot /ˈpærət/ *n* Papagei *m*

parry /ˈpærɪ/ *vt* (*pt/pp* **-ied**) abwehren ⟨*blow*⟩; (*Fencing*) parieren

parsimonious /pɑːsɪˈməʊnɪəs/ *a* geizig

parsley /ˈpɑːslɪ/ *n* Petersilie *f*

parsnip /ˈpɑːsnɪp/ *n* Pastinake *f*

parson /ˈpɑːsn/ *n* Pfarrer *m*

part /pɑːt/ *n* Teil *m*; (*Techn*) Teil *nt*; (*area*) Gegend *f*; (*Theat*) Rolle *f*; (*Mus*) Part *m*; **spare ~** Ersatzteil *nt*; **for my ~** meinerseits; **on the ~ of** von Seiten (+ *gen*); **take s.o.'s ~** für jdn Partei ergreifen; **take ~ in** teilnehmen an (+ *dat*) ● *adv* teils ● *vt* trennen; scheiteln ⟨*hair*⟩ ● *vi* ⟨*people:*⟩ sich trennen; **~ with** sich trennen von

partake /pɑːˈteɪk/ *vt* (*pt* **-took**, *pp* **-taken**) teilnehmen; **~ of** (*eat*) zu sich nehmen

part-exˈchange *n* **take in ~** in Zahlung nehmen

partial /ˈpɑːʃl/ *a* Teil-; **be ~ to** mögen. **~ity** /pɑːʃɪˈælətɪ/ *n* Voreingenommenheit *f*; (*liking*) Vorliebe *f*. **~ly** *adv* teilweise

particip|ant /pɑːˈtɪsɪpənt/ *n* Teilnehmer(in) *m*(*f*). **~ate** /-peɪt/ *vi* teilnehmen (**in** an + *dat*). **~ation** /-ˈpeɪʃn/ *n* Teilnahme *f*

participle /ˈpɑːtɪsɪpl/ *n* Partizip *nt*; **present/past ~** erstes/zweites Partizip *nt*

particle /ˈpɑːtɪkl/ *n* Körnchen *nt*; (*Phys*) Partikel *nt*; (*Gram*) Partikel *f*

particular /pəˈtɪkjʊlə(r)/ *a* besondere(r,s); (*precise*) genau; (*fastidious*) penibel; **in ~** besonders. **~ly** *adv* besonders. **~s** *npl* nähere Angaben *pl*

parting /ˈpɑːtɪŋ/ *n* Abschied *m*; (*in hair*) Scheitel *m* ● *attrib* Abschieds-

partition /pɑːˈtɪʃn/ *n* Trennwand *f*; (*Pol*) Teilung *f* ● *vt* teilen. **~ off** *vt* abtrennen

partly /ˈpɑːtlɪ/ *adv* teilweise

partner /ˈpɑːtnə(r)/ *n* Partner(in) *m*(*f*); (*Comm*) Teilhaber *m*. **~ship** *n* Partnerschaft *f*; (*Comm*) Teilhaberschaft *f*

partridge /ˈpɑːtrɪdʒ/ *n* Rebhuhn *nt*

part-ˈtime *a* & *adv* Teilzeit-; **be** *or* **work ~** Teilzeitarbeit machen

party /ˈpɑːtɪ/ *n* Party *f*, Fest *nt*; (*group*) Gruppe *f*; (*Pol, Jur*) Partei *f*; **be ~ to** sich beteiligen an (+ *dat*)

ˈparty line[1] *n* (*Teleph*) Gemeinschaftsanschluß *m*

party ˈline[2] *n* (*Pol*) Parteilinie *f*

pass /pɑːs/ *n* Ausweis *m*; (*Geog*, *Sport*) Paß *m*; (*Sch*) ≈ ausreichend; **get a ~** bestehen ● *vt* vorbeigehen/-fahren an (+ *dat*); (*overtake*) überholen; (*hand*) reichen; (*Sport*) abgeben, abspielen; (*approve*) annehmen; (*exceed*) übersteigen; bestehen ⟨*exam*⟩; machen ⟨*remark*⟩; fällen ⟨*judgement*⟩; (*Jur*) verhängen ⟨*sentence*⟩; **~ water** Wasser lassen; **~ the time** sich (*dat*) die Zeit vertreiben; **~ sth off as sth** etw als etw ausgeben; **~ one's hand over sth** mit der Hand über etw (*acc*) fahren ● *vi* vorbeigehen/-fahren; (*get by*) vorbeikommen; (*overtake*) überholen; ⟨*time:*⟩ vergehen; (*in exam*) bestehen; **let sth ~** (*fig*) etw übergehen; **[I] ~!** [ich] passe! **~ away** *vi* sterben. **~ down** *vt* herunterreichen; (*fig*) weitergeben. **~ out** *vi* ohnmächtig werden. **~ round** *vt* herumreichen. **~ up** *vt* heraufreichen; (*fam: miss*) vorübergehen lassen

passable /ˈpɑːsəbl/ *a* ⟨*road*⟩ befahrbar; (*satisfactory*) passabel

passage /ˈpæsɪdʒ/ *n* Durchgang *m*; (*corridor*) Gang *m*; (*voyage*) Überfahrt *f*; (*in book*) Passage *f*

passenger /ˈpæsɪndʒə(r)/ *n* Fahrgast *m*; (*Naut*, *Aviat*) Passagier *m*; (*in car*) Mitfahrer *m*. **~ seat** *n* Beifahrersitz *m*

passer-by /pɑːsəˈbaɪ/ *n* (*pl* **-s-by**) Passant(in) *m*(*f*)

ˈpassing place *n* Ausweichstelle *f*

passion /ˈpæʃn/ *n* Leidenschaft *f*. **~ate** /-ət/ *a*, **-ly** *adv* leidenschaftlich

passive /'pæsɪv/ *a* passiv ● *n* Passiv *nt*

Passover /'pɑ:səʊvə(r)/ *n* Passah *nt*

pass: ~port *n* [Reise]paß *m*. **~word** *n* Kennwort *nt*; (*Mil*) Losung *f*

past /pɑ:st/ *a* vergangene(r,s); (*former*) ehemalig; **in the ~ few days** in den letzten paar Tagen; **that's all ~** das ist jetzt vorbei ● *n* Vergangenheit *f* ● *prep* an (+ *dat*) ... vorbei; (*after*) nach; **at ten ~ two** um zehn nach zwei ● *adv* vorbei; **go/come ~** vorbeigehen/-kommen

pasta /'pæstə/ *n* Nudeln *pl*

paste /peɪst/ *n* Brei *m*; (*dough*) Teig *m*; (*fish-, meat-*) Paste *f*; (*adhesive*) Kleister *m*; (*jewellery*) Straß *m* ● *vt* kleistern

pastel /'pæstl/ *n* Pastellfarbe *f*; (*crayon*) Pastellstift *m*; (*drawing*) Pastell *nt* ● *attrib* Pastell-

pasteurize /'pɑ:stʃəraɪz/ *vt* pasteurisieren

pastille /'pæstɪl/ *n* Pastille *f*

pastime /'pɑ:staɪm/ *n* Zeitvertreib *m*

pastoral /'pɑ:stərl/ *a* ländlich; ⟨*care*⟩ seelsorgerisch

pastr|y /'peɪstrɪ/ *n* Teig *m*; **cakes and ~ies** Kuchen und Gebäck

pasture /'pɑ:stʃə(r)/ *n* Weide *f*

pasty¹ /'pæstɪ/ *n* Pastete *f*

pasty² /'peɪstɪ/ *a* blaß, (*fam*) käsig

pat /pæt/ *n* Klaps *m*; (*of butter*) Stückchen *nt* ● *adv* **have sth off ~** etw aus dem Effeff können ● *vt* (*pt/pp* **patted**) tätscheln; **~ s.o. on the back** jdm auf die Schulter klopfen

patch /pætʃ/ *n* Flicken *m*; (*spot*) Fleck *m*; **not a ~ on** (*fam*) gar nicht zu vergleichen mit ● *vt* flicken. **~ up** *vt* [zusammen]flicken; beilegen ⟨*quarrel*⟩

patchy /'pætʃɪ/ *a* ungleichmäßig

pâté /'pæteɪ/ *n* Pastete *f*

patent /'peɪtnt/ *a*, **-ly** *adv* offensichtlich ● *n* Patent *nt* ● *vt* patentieren. **~ leather** *n* Lackleder *nt*

patern|al /pə'tɜ:nl/ *a* väterlich. **~ity** *n* Vaterschaft *f*

path /pɑ:θ/ *n* (*pl* **~s** /pɑ:ðz/) [Fuß]weg *m*, Pfad *m*; (*orbit, track*) Bahn *f*; (*fig*) Weg *m*

pathetic /pə'θetɪk/ *a* mitleiderregend; ⟨*attempt*⟩ erbärmlich

patholog|ical /pæθə'lɒdʒɪkl/ *a* pathologisch. **~ist** /pə'θɒlədʒɪst/ *n* Pathologe *m*

pathos /'peɪθɒs/ *n* Rührseligkeit *f*

patience /'peɪʃns/ *n* Geduld *f*; (*game*) Patience *f*

patient /'peɪʃnt/ *a*, **-ly** *adv* geduldig ● *n* Patient(in) *m(f)*

patio /'pætɪəʊ/ *n* Terrasse *f*

patriot /'pætrɪət/ *n* Patriot(in) *m(f)*. **~ic** /-'ɒtɪk/ *a* patriotisch. **~ism** *n* Patriotismus *m*

patrol /pə'trəʊl/ *n* Patrouille *f* ● *vt/i* patrouillieren [in (+ *dat*)]; ⟨*police:*⟩ auf Streife gehen/fahren [in (+ *dat*)]. **~ car** *n* Streifenwagen *m*

patron /'peɪtrən/ *n* Gönner *m*; (*of charity*) Schirmherr *m*; (*of the arts*) Mäzen *m*; (*customer*) Kunde *m*/Kundin *f*; (*Theat*) Besucher *m*. **~age** /'pætrənɪdʒ/ *n* Schirmherrschaft *f*

patroniz|e /'pætrənaɪz/ *vt* (*fig*) herablassend behandeln. **~ing** *a*, **-ly** *adv* gönnerhaft

patter¹ /'pætə(r)/ *n* Getrippel *nt*; (*of rain*) Plätschern *nt* ● *vi* trippeln; plätschern

patter² *n* (*speech*) Gerede *nt*

pattern /'pætn/ *n* Muster *nt*

paunch /pɔ:ntʃ/ *n* [Schmer]bauch *m*

pauper /'pɔ:pə(r)/ *n* Arme(r) *m/f*

pause /pɔ:z/ *n* Pause *f* ● *vi* innehalten

pave /peɪv/ *vt* pflastern; **~ the way** den Weg bereiten (**for** *dat*). **~ment** *n* Bürgersteig *m*

pavilion /pə'vɪljən/ *n* Pavillon *m*; (*Sport*) Klubhaus *nt*

paw /pɔ:/ *n* Pfote *f*; (*of large animal*) Pranke *f*, Tatze *f*

pawn¹ /pɔ:n/ *n* (*Chess*) Bauer *m*; (*fig*) Schachfigur *f*

pawn² *vt* verpfänden ● *n* **in ~** verpfändet. **~broker** *n* Pfandleiher *m*. **~shop** *n* Pfandhaus *nt*

pay /peɪ/ *n* Lohn *m*; (*salary*) Gehalt *nt*; **be in the ~ of** bezahlt werden von ● *v* (*pt/pp* **paid**) ● *vt* bezahlen; zahlen ⟨*money*⟩; **~ s.o. a visit** jdm einen Besuch abstatten; **~ s.o. a compliment** jdm ein Kompliment machen ● *vi* zahlen; (*be profitable*) sich bezahlt machen; (*fig*) sich lohnen; **~ for sth** etw bezahlen. **~ back** *vt* zurückzahlen. **~ in** *vt* einzahlen. **~ off** *vt* abzahlen ⟨*debt*⟩ ● *vi* (*fig*) sich auszahlen. **~ up** *vi* zahlen

payable /'peɪəbl/ *a* zahlbar; **make ~ to** ausstellen auf (+ *acc*)

payee /peɪ'i:/ *n* [Zahlungs]empfänger *m*

payment /'peɪmənt/ *n* Bezahlung *f*; (*amount*) Zahlung *f*

pay: ~ packet *n* Lohntüte *f*; **~ phone** *n* Münzfernsprecher *m*
pea /pi:/ *n* Erbse *f*
peace /pi:s/ *n* Frieden *m*; **for my ~ of mind** zu meiner eigenen Beruhigung
peace|able /'pi:səbl/ *a* friedlich. **~ful** *a*, **-ly** *adv* friedlich. **~maker** *n* Friedensstifter *m*
peach /pi:tʃ/ *n* Pfirsich *m*
peacock /'pi:kɒk/ *n* Pfau *m*
peak /pi:k/ *n* Gipfel *m*; (*fig*) Höhepunkt *m*. **~ed 'cap** *n* Schirmmütze *f*. **~ hours** *npl* Hauptbelastungszeit *f*; (*for traffic*) Hauptverkehrszeit *f*
peaky /'pi:kɪ/ *a* kränklich
peal /pi:l/ *n* (*of bells*) Glockengeläut *nt*; **~s of laughter** schallendes Gelächter *nt*
'peanut *n* Erdnuß *f*; **for ~s** (*fam*) für einen Apfel und ein Ei
pear /peə(r)/ *n* Birne *f*
pearl /pɜ:l/ *n* Perle *f*
peasant /'peznt/ *n* Bauer *m*
peat /pi:t/ *n* Torf *m*
pebble /'pebl/ *n* Kieselstein *m*
peck /pek/ *n* Schnabelhieb *m*; (*kiss*) flüchtiger Kuß *m* ● *vt/i* picken/(*nip*) hacken (**at** nach). **~ing order** *n* Hackordnung *f*
peckish /'pekɪʃ/ *a* **be ~** (*fam*) Hunger haben
peculiar /pɪ'kju:lɪə(r)/ *a* eigenartig, seltsam; **~ to** eigentümlich (+ *dat*). **~ity** /-'ærətɪ/ *n* Eigenart *f*
pedal /'pedl/ *n* Pedal *nt* ● *vt* fahren ⟨*bicycle*⟩ ● *vi* treten. **~ bin** *n* Treteimer *m*
pedantic /pɪ'dæntɪk/ *a*, **-ally** *adv* pedantisch
peddle /'pedl/ *vt* handeln mit
pedestal /'pedɪstl/ *n* Sockel *m*
pedestrian /pɪ'destrɪən/ *n* Fußgänger(in) *m*(*f*) ● *a* (*fig*) prosaisch. **~ 'crossing** *n* Fußgängerüberweg *m*. **~ 'precinct** *n* Fußgängerzone *f*
pedicure /'pedɪkjʊə(r)/ *n* Pediküre *f*
pedigree /'pedɪgri:/ *n* Stammbaum *m* ● *attrib* ⟨*animal*⟩ Rasse-
pedlar /'pedlə(r)/ *n* Hausierer *m*
pee /pi:/ *vi* (*pt/pp* **peed**) (*fam*) pinkeln
peek /pi:k/ *vi* (*fam*) gucken
peel /pi:l/ *n* Schale *f* ● *vt* schälen ● *vi* ⟨*skin:*⟩ sich schälen; ⟨*paint:*⟩ abblättern. **~ings** *npl* Schalen *pl*
peep /pi:p/ *n* kurzer Blick *m* ● *vi* gucken. **~-hole** *n* Guckloch *nt*. **P~ing 'Tom** *n* (*fam*) Spanner *m*
peer[1] /pɪə(r)/ *vi* **~ at** forschend ansehen
peer[2] *n* Peer *m*; **his ~s** *pl* seinesgleichen
peev|ed /pi:vd/ *a* (*fam*) ärgerlich. **~ish** *a* reizbar
peg /peg/ *n* (*hook*) Haken *m*; (*for tent*) Pflock *m*, Hering *m*; (*for clothes*) [Wäsche]klammer *f*; **off the ~** (*fam*) von der Stange ● *vt* (*pt/pp* **pegged**) anpflocken; anklammern ⟨*washing*⟩
pejorative /pɪ'dʒɒrətɪv/ *a*, **-ly** *adv* abwertend
pelican /'pelɪkən/ *n* Pelikan *m*
pellet /'pelɪt/ *n* Kügelchen *nt*
pelt[1] /pelt/ *n* (*skin*) Pelz *m*, Fell *nt*
pelt[2] *vt* bewerfen ● *vi* (*fam: run fast*) rasen; **~ [down]** ⟨*rain:*⟩ [hernieder]prasseln
pelvis /'pelvɪs/ *n* (*Anat*) Becken *nt*
pen[1] /pen/ *n* (*for animals*) Hürde *f*
pen[2] *n* Federhalter *m*; (*ball-point*) Kugelschreiber *m*
penal /'pi:nl/ *a* Straf-. **~ize** *vt* bestrafen; (*fig*) benachteiligen
penalty /'penltɪ/ *n* Strafe *f*; (*fine*) Geldstrafe *f*; (*Sport*) Strafstoß *m*; (*Football*) Elfmeter *m*
penance /'penəns/ *n* Buße *f*
pence /pens/ *see* **penny**
pencil /'pensɪl/ *n* Bleistift *m* ● *vt* (*pt/pp* **pencilled**) mit Bleistift schreiben. **~-sharpener** *n* Bleistiftspitzer *m*
pendant /'pendənt/ *n* Anhänger *m*
pending /'pendɪŋ/ *a* unerledigt ● *prep* bis zu
pendulum /'pendjʊləm/ *n* Pendel *nt*
penetrat|e /'penɪtreɪt/ *vt* durchdringen; **~e [into]** eindringen in (+ *acc*). **~ing** *a* durchdringend. **~ion** /-'treɪʃn/ *n* Durchdringen *nt*
'penfriend *n* Brieffreund(in) *m*(*f*)
penguin /'peŋgwɪn/ *n* Pinguin *m*
penicillin /penɪ'sɪlɪn/ *n* Penizillin *nt*
peninsula /pə'nɪnsʊlə/ *n* Halbinsel *f*
penis /'pi:nɪs/ *n* Penis *m*
peniten|ce /'penɪtəns/ *n* Reue *f*. **~t** *a* reuig ● *n* Büßer *m*
penitentiary /penɪ'tenʃərɪ/ *n* (*Amer*) Gefängnis *nt*
pen: ~knife *n* Taschenmesser *nt*. **~-name** *n* Pseudonym *nt*
pennant /'penənt/ *n* Wimpel *m*
penniless /'penɪlɪs/ *a* mittellos
penny /'penɪ/ *n* (*pl* **pence**; *single coins* **pennies**) Penny *m*; (*Amer*) Centstück *nt*; **spend a ~** (*fam*) mal

verschwinden; **the ~'s dropped** (*fam*) der Groschen ist gefallen

pension /'penʃn/ *n* Rente *f*; (*of civil servant*) Pension *f*. **~er** *n* Rentner(in) *m*(*f*); Pensionär(in) *m*(*f*)

pensive /'pensɪv/ *a* nachdenklich

Pentecost /'pentɪkɒst/ *n* Pfingsten *nt*

pent-up /'pentʌp/ *a* angestaut

penultimate /pe'nʌltɪmət/ *a* vorletzte(r,s)

penury /'penjʊrɪ/ *n* Armut *f*

peony /'pɪənɪ/ *n* Pfingstrose *f*

people /'pi:pl/ *npl* Leute *pl*, Menschen *pl*; (*citizens*) Bevölkerung *f*; **the ~** das Volk; **English ~** die Engländer; **~ say** man sagt; **for four ~** für vier Personen ● *vt* bevölkern

pep /pep/ *n* (*fam*) Schwung *m*

pepper /'pepə(r)/ *n* Pfeffer *m*; (*vegetable*) Paprika *m* ● *vt* (*Culin*) pfeffern

pepper: ~corn *n* Pfefferkorn *nt*. **~mint** *n* Pfefferminz *nt*; (*Bot*) Pfefferminze *f*. **~pot** *n* Pfefferstreuer *m*

per /pɜ:(r)/ *prep* pro; **~ cent** Prozent *nt*

perceive /pə'si:v/ *vt* wahrnehmen

percentage /pə'sentɪdʒ/ *n* Prozentsatz *m*; (*part*) Teil *m*

perceptible /pə'septəbl/ *a* wahrnehmbar

percept|ion /pə'sepʃn/ *n* Wahrnehmung *f*. **~ive** /-tɪv/ *a* feinsinnig

perch[1] /pɜ:tʃ/ *n* Stange *f* ● *vi* ⟨*bird:*⟩ sich niederlassen

perch[2] *n inv* (*fish*) Barsch *m*

percolat|e /'pɜ:kəleɪt/ *vi* durchsickern. **~or** *n* Kaffeemaschine *f*

percussion /pə'kʌʃn/ *n* Schlagzeug *nt*. **~ instrument** *n* Schlaginstrument *nt*

peremptory /pə'remptərɪ/ *a* herrisch

perennial /pə'renɪəl/ *a* ⟨*problem*⟩ immer wiederkehrend ● *n* (*Bot*) mehrjährige Pflanze *f*

perfect[1] /'pɜ:fɪkt/ *a* perfekt, vollkommen; (*fam: utter*) völlig ● *n* (*Gram*) Perfekt *nt*

perfect[2] /pə'fekt/ *vt* vervollkommnen. **~ion** /-ekʃn/ *n* Vollkommenheit *f*; **to ~ion** perfekt

perfectly /'pɜ:fɪktlɪ/ *adv* perfekt; (*completely*) vollkommen, völlig

perforate /'pɜ:fəreɪt/ *vt* perforieren; (*make a hole in*) durchlöchern. **~d** *a* perforiert

perform /pə'fɔ:m/ *vt* ausführen; erfüllen ⟨*duty*⟩; (*Theat*) aufführen ⟨*play*⟩; spielen ⟨*role*⟩ ● *vi* (*Theat*) auftreten; (*Techn*) laufen. **~ance** *n* Aufführung *f*; (*at theatre, cinema*) Vorstellung *f*; (*Techn*) Leistung *f*. **~er** *n* Künstler(in) *m*(*f*)

perfume /'pɜ:fju:m/ *n* Parfüm *nt*; (*smell*) Duft *m*

perfunctory /pə'fʌŋktərɪ/ *a* flüchtig

perhaps /pə'hæps/ *adv* vielleicht

peril /'perəl/ *n* Gefahr *f*. **~ous** /-əs/ *a* gefährlich

perimeter /pə'rɪmɪtə(r)/ *n* [äußere] Grenze *f*; (*Geom*) Umfang *m*

period /'pɪərɪəd/ *n* Periode *f*; (*Sch*) Stunde *f*; (*full stop*) Punkt *m* ● *attrib* ⟨*costume*⟩ zeitgenössisch; ⟨*furniture*⟩ antik. **~ic** /-'ɒdɪk/ *a*, **-ally** *adv* periodisch. **~ical** /-'ɒdɪkl/ *n* Zeitschrift *f*

peripher|al /pə'rɪfərl/ *a* nebensächlich. **~y** *n* Peripherie *f*

periscope /'perɪskəʊp/ *n* Periskop *nt*

perish /'perɪʃ/ *vi* ⟨*rubber:*⟩ verrotten; ⟨*food:*⟩ verderben; (*die*) ums Leben kommen. **~able** /-əbl/ *a* leicht verderblich. **~ing** *a* (*fam: cold*) eiskalt

perjur|e /'pɜ:dʒə(r)/ *vt* **~e oneself** einen Meineid leisten. **~y** *n* Meineid *m*

perk[1] /pɜ:k/ *n* (*fam*) [Sonder]vergünstigung *f*

perk[2] *vi* **~ up** munter werden

perky /'pɜ:kɪ/ *a* munter

perm /pɜ:m/ *n* Dauerwelle *f* ● *vt* **~ s.o.'s hair** jdm eine Dauerwelle machen

permanent /'pɜ:mənənt/ *a* ständig; ⟨*job, address*⟩ fest. **~ly** *adv* ständig; ⟨*work, live*⟩ dauernd, permanent; ⟨*employed*⟩ fest

permeable /'pɜ:mɪəbl/ *a* durchlässig

permeate /'pɜ:mɪeɪt/ *vt* durchdringen

permissible /pə'mɪsəbl/ *a* erlaubt

permission /pə'mɪʃn/ *n* Erlaubnis *f*

permissive /pə'mɪsɪv/ *a* ⟨*society*⟩ permissiv

permit[1] /pə'mɪt/ *vt* (*pt/pp* **-mitted**) erlauben (**s.o.** jdm); **~ me!** gestatten Sie!

permit[2] /'pɜ:mɪt/ *n* Genehmigung *f*

pernicious /pə'nɪʃəs/ *a* schädlich; (*Med*) perniziös

perpendicular /pɜ:pən'dɪkjʊlə(r)/ *a* senkrecht ● *n* Senkrechte *f*

perpetrat|e /'pɜ:pɪtreɪt/ *vt* begehen. **~or** *n* Täter *m*

perpetual /pə'petjʊəl/ *a*, **-ly** *adv* ständig, dauernd

perpetuate /pə'petjʊeɪt/ *vt* bewahren; verewigen ⟨*error*⟩
perplex /pə'pleks/ *vt* verblüffen. **~ed** *a* verblüfft. **~ity** *n* Verblüffung *f*
persecut|e /'pɜ:sɪkju:t/ *vt* verfolgen. **~ion** /-'kju:ʃn/ *n* Verfolgung *f*
perseverance /pɜ:sɪ'vɪərəns/ *n* Ausdauer *f*
persever|e /pɜ:sɪ'vɪə(r)/ *vi* beharrlich weitermachen. **~ing** *a* ausdauernd
Persia /'pɜ:ʃə/ *n* Persien *nt*
Persian /'pɜ:ʃn/ *a* persisch; ⟨*cat, carpet*⟩ Perser
persist /pə'sɪst/ *vi* beharrlich weitermachen; (*continue*) anhalten; ⟨*view:*⟩ weiter bestehen; **~ in doing sth** dabei bleiben, etw zu tun. **~ence** *n* Beharrlichkeit *f*. **~ent** *a*, **-ly** *adv* beharrlich; (*continuous*) anhaltend
person /'pɜ:sn/ *n* Person *f*; **in ~** persönlich
personal /'pɜ:sənl/ *a*, **-ly** *adv* persönlich. **~ 'hygiene** *n* Körperpflege *f*
personality /pɜ:sə'nælətɪ/ *n* Persönlichkeit *f*
personify /pə'sɒnɪfaɪ/ *vt* (*pt/pp* **-ied**) personifizieren, verkörpern
personnel /pɜ:sə'nel/ *n* Personal *nt*
perspective /pə'spektɪv/ *n* Perspektive *f*
perspicacious /pɜ:spɪ'keɪʃəs/ *a* scharfsichtig
persp|iration /pə:spɪ'reɪʃn/ *n* Schweiß *m*. **~ire** /-'spaɪə(r)/ *vi* schwitzen
persua|de /pə'sweɪd/ *vt* überreden; (*convince*) überzeugen. **~sion** /-eɪʒn/ *n* Überredung *f*; (*powers of* **~sion**) Überredungskunst *f*; (*belief*) Glaubensrichtung *f*
persuasive /pə'sweɪsɪv/ *a*, **-ly** *adv* beredsam; (*convincing*) überzeugend
pert /pɜ:t/ *a*, **-ly** *adv* keß
pertain /pə'teɪn/ *vi* **~ to** betreffen; (*belong*) gehören zu
pertinent /'pɜ:tɪnənt/ *a* relevant (**to** für)
perturb /pə'tɜ:b/ *vt* beunruhigen
peruse /pə'ru:z/ *vt* lesen
perva|de /pə'veɪd/ *vt* durchdringen. **~sive** /-sɪv/ *a* durchdringend
pervers|e /pə'vɜ:s/ *a* eigensinnig. **~ion** /-ɜ:ʃn/ *n* Perversion *f*
pervert[1] /pə'vɜ:t/ *vt* verdrehen; verführen ⟨*person*⟩
pervert[2] /'pɜ:vɜ:t/ *n* Perverse(r) *m*
perverted /pə'vɜ:tɪd/ *a* abartig
pessimis|m /'pesɪmɪzm/ *n* Pessimismus *m*. **~t** /-mɪst/ *n* Pessimist *m*. **~tic** /-'mɪstɪk/ *a*, **-ally** *adv* pessimistisch
pest /pest/ *n* Schädling *m*; (*fam: person*) Nervensäge *f*
pester /'pestə(r)/ *vt* belästigen; **~ s.o. for sth** jdm wegen etw in den Ohren liegen
pesticide /'pestɪsaɪd/ *n* Schädlingsbekämpfungsmittel *nt*
pet /pet/ *n* Haustier *nt*; (*favourite*) Liebling *m* ● *vt* (*pt/pp* **petted**) liebkosen
petal /'petl/ *n* Blütenblatt *nt*
peter /'pi:tə(r)/ *vi* **~ out** allmählich aufhören; ⟨*stream:*⟩ versickern
petite /pə'ti:t/ *a* klein und zierlich
petition /pə'tɪʃn/ *n* Bittschrift *f* ● *vt* eine Bittschrift richten an (+ *acc*)
pet 'name *n* Kosename *m*
petrif|y /'petrɪfaɪ/ *vt/i* (*pt/pp* **-ied**) versteinern; **~ied** (*frightened*) vor Angst wie versteinert
petrol /'petrl/ *n* Benzin *nt*
petroleum /pɪ'trəʊlɪəm/ *n* Petroleum *nt*
petrol: ~-pump *n* Zapfsäule *f*. **~ station** *n* Tankstelle *f*. **~ tank** *n* Benzintank *m*
'pet shop *n* Tierhandlung *f*
petticoat /'petɪkəʊt/ *n* Unterrock *m*
petty /'petɪ/ *a* (**-ier, -iest**) kleinlich. **~ 'cash** *n* Portokasse *f*
petulant /'petjʊlənt/ *a* gekränkt
pew /pju:/ *n* [Kirchen]bank *f*
pewter /'pju:tə(r)/ *n* Zinn *nt*
phantom /'fæntəm/ *n* Gespenst *nt*
pharmaceutical /fɑ:mə'sju:tɪkl/ *a* pharmazeutisch
pharmac|ist /'fɑ:məsɪst/ *n* Apotheker(in) *m(f)*. **~y** *n* Pharmazie *f*; (*shop*) Apotheke *f*
phase /feɪz/ *n* Phase *f* ● *vt* **~ in/out** allmählich einführen/abbauen
Ph.D. (*abbr of* **Doctor of Philosophy**) Dr. phil.
pheasant /'feznt/ *n* Fasan *m*
phenomen|al /fɪ'nɒmɪnl/ *a* phänomenal. **~on** *n* (*pl* **-na**) Phänomen *nt*
phial /'faɪəl/ *n* Fläschchen *nt*
philanderer /fɪ'lændərə(r)/ *n* Verführer *m*
philanthrop|ic /fɪlən'θrɒpɪk/ *a* menschenfreundlich. **~ist** /fɪ'lænθrəpɪst/ *n* Philanthrop *m*
philately /fɪ'lætəlɪ/ *n* Philatelie *f*, Briefmarkenkunde *f*
philharmonic /fɪlɑ:'mɒnɪk/ *n* (*orchestra*) Philharmoniker *pl*

Philippines /'fɪlɪpi:nz/ *npl* Philippinen *pl*
philistine /'fɪlɪstaɪn/ *n* Banause *m*
philosoph|er /fɪ'lɒsəfə(r)/ *n* Philosoph *m*. **~ical** /fɪlə'sɒfɪkl/ *a*, **-ly** *adv* philosophisch. **~y** *n* Philosophie *f*
phlegm /flem/ *n* (*Med*) Schleim *m*
phlegmatic /fleg'mætɪk/ *a* phlegmatisch
phobia /'fəʊbɪə/ *n* Phobie *f*
phone /fəʊn/ *n* Telefon *nt*; **be on the ~** Telefon haben; (*be phoning*) telefonieren ● *vt* anrufen ● *vi* telefonieren. **~ back** *vt/i* zurückrufen. **~ book** *n* Telefonbuch *nt*. **~ box** *n* Telefonzelle *f*. **~ card** *n* Telefonkarte *f*. **~-in** *n* (*Radio*) Hörersendung *f*. **~ number** *n* Telefonnummer *f*
phonetic /fə'netɪk/ *a* phonetisch. **~s** *n* Phonetik *f*
phoney /'fəʊnɪ/ *a* (**-ier, -iest**) falsch; (*forged*) gefälscht
phosphorus /'fɒsfərəs/ *n* Phosphor *m*
photo /'fəʊtəʊ/ *n* Foto *nt*, Aufnahme *f*. **~copier** *n* Fotokopiergerät *nt*. **~copy** *n* Fotokopie *f* ● *vt* fotokopieren
photogenic /fəʊtəʊ'dʒenɪk/ *a* fotogen
photograph /'fəʊtəgrɑ:f/ *n* Fotografie *f*, Aufnahme *f* ● *vt* fotografieren
photograph|er /fə'tɒgrəfə(r)/ *n* Fotograf(in) *m(f)*. **~ic** /fəʊtə'græfɪk/ *a*, **-ally** *adv* fotografisch. **~y** *n* Fotografie *f*
phrase /freɪz/ *n* Redensart *f* ● *vt* formulieren. **~-book** *n* Sprachführer *m*
physical /'fɪzɪkl/ *a*, **-ly** *adv* körperlich; ⟨*geography, law*⟩ physikalisch. **~ edu'cation** *n* Turnen *nt*
physician /fɪ'zɪʃn/ *n* Arzt *m*/Ärztin *f*
physic|ist /'fɪzɪsɪst/ *n* Physiker(in) *m(f)*. **~s** *n* Physik *f*
physiology /fɪzɪ'ɒlədʒɪ/ *n* Physiologie *f*
physio'therap|ist /fɪzɪəʊ-/ *n* Physiotherapeut(in) *m(f)*. **~y** *n* Physiotherapie *f*
physique /fɪ'zi:k/ *n* Körperbau *m*
pianist /'pɪənɪst/ *n* Klavierspieler(in) *m(f)*; (*professional*) Pianist(in) *m(f)*
piano /pɪ'ænəʊ/ *n* Klavier *nt*
pick[1] /pɪk/ *n* Spitzhacke *f*
pick[2] *n* Auslese *f*; **take one's ~** sich (*dat*) aussuchen ● *vt/i* (*pluck*) pflücken; (*select*) wählen, sich (*dat*) aussuchen; **~ and choose** wählerisch sein; **~ one's nose** in der Nase bohren; **~ a quarrel** einen Streit anfangen; **~ a hole in sth** ein Loch in etw (*acc*) machen; **~ holes in** (*fam*) kritisieren; **~ at one's food** im Essen herumstochern. **~ on** *vt* wählen; (*fam: find fault with*) herumhacken auf (+ *dat*). **~ up** *vt* in die Hand nehmen; (*off the ground*) aufheben; hochnehmen ⟨*baby*⟩; (*learn*) lernen; (*acquire*) erwerben; (*buy*) kaufen; (*Teleph*) abnehmen ⟨*receiver*⟩; auffangen ⟨*signal*⟩; (*collect*) abholen; aufnehmen ⟨*passengers*⟩; ⟨*police:*⟩ aufgreifen ⟨*criminal*⟩; sich holen ⟨*illness*⟩; (*fam*) aufgabeln ⟨*girl*⟩; **~ oneself up** aufstehen ● *vi* (*improve*) sich bessern
'pickaxe *n* Spitzhacke *f*
picket /'pɪkɪt/ *n* Streikposten *m* ● *vt* Streikposten aufstellen vor (+ *dat*). **~ line** *n* Streikpostenkette *f*
pickle /'pɪkl/ *n* (*Amer: gherkin*) Essiggurke *f*; **~s** *pl* [Mixed] Pickles *pl* ● *vt* einlegen
pick: ~pocket *n* Taschendieb *m*. **~-up** *n* (*truck*) Lieferwagen *m*; (*on record-player*) Tonabnehmer *m*
picnic /'pɪknɪk/ *n* Picknick *nt* ● *vi* (*pt/pp* **-nicked**) picknicken
pictorial /pɪk'tɔ:rɪəl/ *a* bildlich
picture /'pɪktʃə(r)/ *n* Bild *nt*; (*film*) Film *m*; **as pretty as a ~** bildhübsch; **put s.o. in the ~** (*fig*) jdn ins Bild setzen ● *vt* (*imagine*) sich (*dat*) vorstellen
picturesque /pɪktʃə'resk/ *a* malerisch
pie /paɪ/ *n* Pastete *f*; (*fruit*) Kuchen *m*
piece /pi:s/ *n* Stück *nt*; (*of set*) Teil *nt*; (*in game*) Stein *m*; (*Journ*) Artikel *m*; **a ~ of bread/paper** ein Stück Brot/Papier; **a ~ of news/advice** eine Nachricht/ein Rat; **take to ~s** auseinandernehmen ● *vt* **~ together** zusammensetzen; (*fig*) zusammenstückeln. **~meal** *adv* stückweise. **~-work** *n* Akkordarbeit *f*
pier /pɪə(r)/ *n* Pier *m*; (*pillar*) Pfeiler *m*
pierc|e /pɪəs/ *vt* durchstechen; **~e a hole in sth** ein Loch in etw (*acc*) stechen. **~ing** *a* durchdringend
piety /'paɪətɪ/ *n* Frömmigkeit *f*
piffle /'pɪfl/ *n* (*fam*) Quatsch *m*
pig /pɪg/ *n* Schwein *nt*
pigeon /'pɪdʒɪn/ *n* Taube *f*. **~-hole** *n* Fach *nt*

piggy /ˈpɪgɪ/ *n* (*fam*) Schweinchen *nt*. **~back** *n* **give s.o. a ~back** jdn huckepack tragen. **~ bank** *n* Sparschwein *nt*

pig'headed *a* (*fam*) starrköpfig

pigment /ˈpɪgmənt/ *n* Pigment *nt*. **~ation** /-menˈteɪʃn/ *n* Pigmentierung *f*

pig: ~skin *n* Schweinsleder *nt*. **~sty** *n* Schweinestall *m*. **~tail** *n* (*fam*) Zopf *m*

pike /paɪk/ *n inv* (*fish*) Hecht *m*

pilchard /ˈpɪltʃəd/ *n* Sardine *f*

pile¹ /paɪl/ *n* (*of fabric*) Flor *m*

pile² *n* Haufen *m* ● *vt* **~ sth on to sth** etw auf etw (*acc*) häufen. **~ up** *vt* häufen ● *vi* sich häufen

piles /paɪlz/ *npl* Hämorrhoiden *pl*

'pile-up *n* Massenkarambolage *f*

pilfer /ˈpɪlfə(r)/ *vt/i* stehlen

pilgrim /ˈpɪlgrɪm/ *n* Pilger(in) *m(f)*. **~age** /-ɪdʒ/ *n* Pilgerfahrt *f*, Wallfahrt *f*

pill /pɪl/ *n* Pille *f*

pillage /ˈpɪlɪdʒ/ *vt* plündern

pillar /ˈpɪlə(r)/ *n* Säule *f*. **~-box** *n* Briefkasten *m*

pillion /ˈpɪljən/ *n* Sozius[sitz] *m*

pillory /ˈpɪlərɪ/ *n* Pranger *m* ● *vt* (*pt/pp* **-ied**) anprangern

pillow /ˈpɪləʊ/ *n* Kopfkissen *nt*. **~case** *n* Kopfkissenbezug *m*

pilot /ˈpaɪlət/ *n* Pilot *m*; (*Naut*) Lotse *m* ● *vt* fliegen ⟨*plane*⟩; lotsen ⟨*ship*⟩. **~-light** *n* Zündflamme *f*

pimp /pɪmp/ *n* Zuhälter *m*

pimple /ˈpɪmpl/ *n* Pickel *m*

pin /pɪn/ *n* Stecknadel *f*; (*Techn*) Bolzen *m*, Stift *m*; (*Med*) Nagel *m*; **I have ~s and needles in my leg** (*fam*) mein Bein ist eingeschlafen ● *vt* (*pt/pp* **pinned**) anstecken (**to/on** an + *acc*); (*sewing*) stecken; (*hold down*) festhalten; **~ sth on s.o.** (*fam*) jdm etw anhängen. **~ up** *vt* hochstecken; (*on wall*) anheften, anschlagen

pinafore /ˈpɪnəfɔ:(r)/ *n* Schürze *f*. **~ dress** *n* Kleiderrock *m*

pincers /ˈpɪnsəz/ *npl* Kneifzange *f*; (*Zool*) Scheren *pl*

pinch /pɪntʃ/ *n* Kniff *m*; (*of salt*) Prise *f*; **at a ~** (*fam*) zur Not ● *vt* kneifen, zwicken; (*fam: steal*) klauen; **~ one's finger** sich (*dat*) den Finger klemmen ● *vi* ⟨*shoe:*⟩ drücken

'pincushion *n* Nadelkissen *nt*

pine¹ /paɪn/ *n* (*tree*) Kiefer *f*

pine² *vi* **~ for** sich sehnen nach; **~ away** sich verzehren

pineapple /ˈpaɪn-/ *n* Ananas *f*

ping /pɪŋ/ *n* Klingeln *nt*

'ping-pong *n* Tischtennis *nt*

pink /pɪŋk/ *a* rosa

pinnacle /ˈpɪnəkl/ *n* Gipfel *m*; (*on roof*) Turmspitze *f*

pin: ~point *vt* genau festlegen. **~stripe** *n* Nadelstreifen *m*

pint /paɪnt/ *n* Pint *nt* (*0,57 l, Amer: 0,47 l*)

'pin-up *n* Pin-up-Girl *nt*

pioneer /paɪəˈnɪə(r)/ *n* Pionier *m* ● *vt* bahnbrechende Arbeit leisten für

pious /ˈpaɪəs/ *a*, **-ly** *adv* fromm

pip¹ /pɪp/ *n* (*seed*) Kern *m*

pip² *n* (*sound*) Tonsignal *nt*

pipe /paɪp/ *n* Pfeife *f*; (*for water, gas*) Rohr *nt* ● *vt* in Rohren leiten; (*Culin*) spritzen. **~ down** *vi* (*fam*) den Mund halten

pipe: ~-dream *n* Luftschloß *nt*. **~line** *n* Pipeline *f*; **in the ~line** (*fam*) in Vorbereitung

piper /ˈpaɪpə(r)/ *n* Pfeifer *m*

piping /ˈpaɪpɪŋ/ *a* **~ hot** kochend heiß

piquant /ˈpi:kənt/ *a* pikant

pique /pi:k/ *n* **in a fit of ~** beleidigt

pirate /ˈpaɪərət/ *n* Pirat *m*

Pisces /ˈpaɪsi:z/ *n* (*Astr*) Fische *pl*

piss /pɪs/ *vi* (*sl*) pissen

pistol /ˈpɪstl/ *n* Pistole *f*

piston /ˈpɪstən/ *n* (*Techn*) Kolben *m*

pit /pɪt/ *n* Grube *f*; (*for orchestra*) Orchestergraben *m* ● *vt* (*pt/pp* **pitted**) (*fig*) messen (**against** mit)

pitch¹ /pɪtʃ/ *n* (*steepness*) Schräge *f*; (*of voice*) Stimmlage *f*; (*of sound*) [Ton]höhe *f*; (*Sport*) Feld *nt*; (*of street-trader*) Standplatz *m*; (*fig: degree*) Grad *m* ● *vt* werfen; aufschlagen ⟨*tent*⟩ ● *vi* fallen

pitch² *n* (*tar*) Pech *nt*. **~-'black** *a* pechschwarz. **~-'dark** *a* stockdunkel

pitcher /ˈpɪtʃə(r)/ *n* Krug *m*

'pitchfork *n* Heugabel *f*

piteous /ˈpɪtɪəs/ *a* erbärmlich

'pitfall *n* (*fig*) Falle *f*

pith /pɪθ/ *n* (*Bot*) Mark *nt*; (*of orange*) weiße Haut *f*; (*fig*) Wesentliche(s) *nt*

pithy /ˈpɪθɪ/ *a* (**-ier, -iest**) (*fig*) prägnant

piti|ful /ˈpɪtɪfl/ *a* bedauernswert. **~less** *a* mitleidslos

pittance /ˈpɪtns/ *n* Hungerlohn *m*

pity /ˈpɪtɪ/ *n* Mitleid *nt*, Erbarmen *nt*; **[what a] ~!** [wie] schade! **take ~ on**

sich erbarmen über (+ *acc*) ● *vt* bemitleiden

pivot /'pɪvət/ *n* Drehzapfen *m*; (*fig*) Angelpunkt *m* ● *vi* sich drehen (**on** um)

pixie /'pɪksɪ/ *n* Kobold *m*

pizza /'pi:tsə/ *n* Pizza *f*

placard /'plækɑ:d/ *n* Plakat *nt*

placate /plə'keɪt/ *vt* beschwichtigen

place /pleɪs/ *n* Platz *m*; (*spot*) Stelle *f*; (*town, village*) Ort *m*; (*fam: house*) Haus *nt*; **out of ~** fehl am Platze; **take ~** stattfinden; **all over the ~** überall ● *vt* setzen; (*upright*) stellen; (*flat*) legen; (*remember*) unterbringen (*fam*); **~ an order** eine Bestellung aufgeben; **be ~d** (*in race*) sich plazieren. **~-mat** *n* Set *nt*

placid /'plæsɪd/ *a* gelassen

plagiar|ism /'pleɪdʒərɪzm/ *n* Plagiat *nt*. **~ize** *vt* plagiieren

plague /pleɪg/ *n* Pest *f* ● *vt* plagen

plaice /pleɪs/ *n inv* Scholle *f*

plain /pleɪn/ *a* (**-er, -est**) klar; (*simple*) einfach; (*not pretty*) nicht hübsch; (*not patterned*) einfarbig; ⟨*chocolate*⟩ zartbitter; **in ~ clothes** in Zivil ● *adv* (*simply*) einfach ● *n* Ebene *f*; (*Knitting*) linke Masche *f*. **~ly** *adv* klar, deutlich; (*simply*) einfach; (*obviously*) offensichtlich

plaintiff /'pleɪntɪf/ *n* (*Jur*) Kläger(in) *m*(*f*)

plaintive /'pleɪntɪv/ *a*, **-ly** *adv* klagend

plait /plæt/ *n* Zopf *m* ● *vt* flechten

plan /plæn/ *n* Plan *m* ● *vt* (*pt/pp* **planned**) planen; (*intend*) vorhaben

plane[1] /pleɪn/ *n* (*tree*) Platane *f*

plane[2] *n* Flugzeug *nt*; (*Geom & fig*) Ebene *f*

plane[3] *n* (*Techn*) Hobel *m* ● *vt* hobeln

planet /'plænɪt/ *n* Planet *m*

plank /plæŋk/ *n* Brett *nt*; (*thick*) Planke *f*

planning /'plænɪŋ/ *n* Planung *f*. **~ permission** *n* Baugenehmigung *f*

plant /plɑ:nt/ *n* Pflanze *f*; (*Techn*) Anlage *f*; (*factory*) Werk *nt* ● *vt* pflanzen; (*place in position*) setzen; **~ oneself in front of s.o.** sich vor jdn hinstellen. **~ation** /plæn'teɪʃn/ *n* Plantage *f*

plaque /plɑ:k/ *n* [Gedenk]tafel *f*; (*on teeth*) Zahnbelag *m*

plasma /'plæzmə/ *n* Plasma *nt*

plaster /'plɑ:stə(r)/ *n* Verputz *m*; (*sticking ~*) Pflaster *nt*; **~ [of Paris]** Gips *m* ● *vt* verputzen ⟨*wall*⟩; (*cover*) bedecken mit. **~ed** *a* (*sl*) besoffen. **~er** *n* Gipser *m*

plastic /'plæstɪk/ *n* Kunststoff *m*, Plastik *nt* ● *a* Kunststoff-, Plastik-; (*malleable*) formbar, plastisch

Plasticine (P) /'plæstɪsi:n/ *n* Knetmasse *f*

plastic 'surgery *n* plastische Chirurgie *f*

plate /pleɪt/ *n* Teller *m*; (*flat sheet*) Platte *f*; (*with name, number*) Schild *nt*; (*gold and silverware*) vergoldete/versilberte Ware *f*; (*in book*) Tafel *f* ● *vt* (*with gold*) vergolden; (*with silver*) versilbern

plateau /'plætəʊ/ *n* (*pl* **~x** /-əʊz/) Hochebene *f*

platform /'plætfɔ:m/ *n* Plattform *f*; (*stage*) Podium *nt*; (*Rail*) Bahnsteig *m*; **~ 5** Gleis 5

platinum /'plætɪnəm/ *n* Platin *nt*

platitude /'plætɪtju:d/ *n* Platitüde *f*

platonic /plə'tɒnɪk/ *a* platonisch

platoon /plə'tu:n/ *n* (*Mil*) Zug *m*

platter /'plætə(r)/ *n* Platte *f*

plausible /'plɔ:zəbl/ *a* plausibel

play /pleɪ/ *n* Spiel *nt*; [Theater]stück *nt*; (*Radio*) Hörspiel *nt*; (*TV*) Fernsehspiel *nt*; **~ on words** Wortspiel *nt* ● *vt/i* spielen; ausspielen ⟨*card*⟩; **~ safe** sichergehen. **~ down** *vt* herunterspielen. **~ up** *vi* (*fam*) Mätzchen machen

play: ~boy *n* Playboy *m*. **~er** *n* Spieler(in) *m*(*f*). **~ful** *a*, **-ly** *adv* verspielt. **~ground** *n* Spielplatz *m*; (*Sch*) Schulhof *m*. **~group** *n* Kindergarten *m*

playing: ~-card *n* Spielkarte *f*. **~-field** *n* Sportplatz *m*

play: ~mate *n* Spielkamerad *m*. **~-pen** *n* Laufstall *m*, Laufgitter *nt*. **~thing** *n* Spielzeug *nt*. **~wright** /-raɪt/ *n* Dramatiker *m*

plc *abbr* (**public limited company**) ≈ GmbH

plea /pli:/ *n* Bitte *f*; **make a ~ for** bitten um

plead /pli:d/ *vt* vorschützen; (*Jur*) vertreten ⟨*case*⟩ ● *vi* flehen (**for** um); **~ guilty** sich schuldig bekennen; **~ with s.o.** jdn anflehen

pleasant /'plezənt/ *a* angenehm; ⟨*person*⟩ nett. **~ly** *adv* angenehm; ⟨*say, smile*⟩ freundlich

pleas|e /pli:z/ *adv* bitte ● *vt* gefallen (+ *dat*); **~e s.o.** jdm eine Freude machen; **~e oneself** tun, was man

will. **~ed** *a* erfreut; **be ~ed with/about sth** sich über etw (*acc*) freuen. **~ing** *a* erfreulich
pleasurable /'pleʒərəbl/ *a* angenehm
pleasure /'pleʒə(r)/ *n* Vergnügen *nt*; (*joy*) Freude *f*; **with ~** gern[e]
pleat /pli:t/ *n* Falte *f* ● *vt* fälteln. **~ed 'skirt** *n* Faltenrock *m*
plebiscite /'plebɪsɪt/ *n* Volksabstimmung *f*
pledge /pledʒ/ *n* Pfand *nt*; (*promise*) Versprechen *nt* ● *vt* verpfänden; versprechen
plentiful /'plentɪfl/ *a* reichlich; **be ~** reichlich vorhanden sein
plenty /'plentɪ/ *n* eine Menge; (*enough*) reichlich; **~ of money/people** viel Geld/viele Leute
pleurisy /'plʊərəsɪ/ *n* Rippenfellentzündung *f*
pliable /'plaɪəbl/ *a* biegsam
pliers /'plaɪəz/ *npl* [Flach]zange *f*
plight /plaɪt/ *n* [Not]lage *f*
plimsolls /'plɪmsəlz/ *npl* Turnschuhe *pl*
plinth /plɪnθ/ *n* Sockel *m*
plod /plɒd/ *vi* (*pt/pp* **plodded**) trotten; (*work hard*) sich abmühen
plonk /plɒŋk/ *n* (*fam*) billiger Wein *m*
plot /plɒt/ *n* Komplott *nt*; (*of novel*) Handlung *f*; **~ of land** Stück *nt* Land ● *vt* einzeichnen ● *vi* ein Komplott schmieden
plough /plaʊ/ *n* Pflug *m* ● *vt/i* pflügen. **~ back** *vt* (*Comm*) wieder investieren
ploy /plɔɪ/ *n* (*fam*) Trick *m*
pluck /plʌk/ *n* Mut *m* ● *vt* zupfen; rupfen ⟨*bird*⟩; pflücken ⟨*flower*⟩; **~ up courage** Mut fassen
plucky /'plʌkɪ/ *a* (**-ier, -iest**) tapfer, mutig
plug /plʌg/ *n* Stöpsel *m*; (*wood*) Zapfen *m*; (*cotton wool*) Bausch *m*; (*Electr*) Stecker *m*; (*Auto*) Zündkerze *f*; (*fam: advertisement*) Schleichwerbung *f* ● *vt* zustopfen; (*fam: advertise*) Schleichwerbung machen für. **~ in** *vt* (*Electr*) einstecken
plum /plʌm/ *n* Pflaume *f*
plumage /'plu:mɪdʒ/ *n* Gefieder *nt*
plumb /plʌm/ *n* Lot *nt* ● *adv* lotrecht ● *vt* loten. **~ in** *vt* installieren
plumb|er /'plʌmə(r)/ *n* Klempner *m*. **~ing** *n* Wasserleitungen *pl*
'plumb-line *n* [Blei]lot *nt*
plume /plu:m/ *n* Feder *f*
plummet /'plʌmɪt/ *vi* herunterstürzen
plump /plʌmp/ *a* (**-er, -est**) mollig, rundlich ● *vt* **~ for** wählen
plunder /'plʌndə(r)/ *n* Beute *f* ● *vt* plündern
plunge /plʌndʒ/ *n* Sprung *m*; **take the ~** (*fam*) den Schritt wagen ● *vt/i* tauchen
plu'perfect /plu:-/ *n* Plusquamperfekt *nt*
plural /'plʊərl/ *a* pluralisch ● *n* Mehrzahl *f*, Plural *m*
plus /plʌs/ *prep* plus (+ *dat*) ● *a* Plus- ● *n* Pluszeichen *nt*; (*advantage*) Plus *nt*
plush[y] /'plʌʃ[ɪ]/ *a* luxuriös
ply /plaɪ/ *vt* (*pt/pp* **plied**) ausüben ⟨*trade*⟩; **~ s.o. with drink** jdm ein Glas nach dem anderen eingießen. **~wood** *n* Sperrholz *nt*
p.m. *adv* (*abbr of* **post meridiem**) nachmittags
pneumatic /nju:'mætɪk/ *a* pneumatisch. **~ 'drill** *n* Preßlufthammer *m*
pneumonia /nju:'məʊnɪə/ *n* Lungenentzündung *f*
poach /pəʊtʃ/ *vt* (*Culin*) pochieren; (*steal*) wildern. **~er** *n* Wilddieb *m*
pocket /'pɒkɪt/ *n* Tasche *f*; **~ of resistance** Widerstandsnest *nt*; **be out of ~** [an einem Geschäft] verlieren ● *vt* einstecken. **~-book** *n* Notizbuch *nt*; (*wallet*) Brieftasche *f*. **~-money** *n* Taschengeld *nt*
pock-marked /'pɒk-/ *a* pockennarbig
pod /pɒd/ *n* Hülse *f*
podgy /'pɒdʒɪ/ *a* (**-ier, -iest**) dick
poem /'pəʊɪm/ *n* Gedicht *nt*
poet /'pəʊɪt/ *n* Dichter(in) *m*(*f*). **~ic** /-'etɪk/ *a* dichterisch
poetry /'pəʊɪtrɪ/ *n* Dichtung *f*
poignant /'pɔɪnjənt/ *a* ergreifend
point /pɔɪnt/ *n* Punkt *m*; (*sharp end*) Spitze *f*; (*meaning*) Sinn *m*; (*purpose*) Zweck *m*; (*Electr*) Steckdose *f*; **~s** *pl* (*Rail*) Weiche *f*; **~ of view** Standpunkt *m*; **good/bad ~s** gute/schlechte Seiten; **what is the ~?** wozu? **the ~ is** es geht darum; **I don't see the ~** das sehe ich nicht ein; **up to a ~** bis zu einem gewissen Grade; **be on the ~ of doing sth** im Begriff sein, etw zu tun ● *vt* richten (**at** auf + *acc*); ausfugen ⟨*brickwork*⟩ ● *vi* deuten (**at/to** auf + *acc*); (*with finger*) mit dem Finger zeigen. **~ out** *vt* zeigen auf (+ *acc*); **~ sth out to s.o.** jdn auf etw (*acc*) hinweisen

point-'blank *a* aus nächster Entfernung; (*fig*) rundweg

point|ed /'pɔɪntɪd/ *a* spitz; ⟨*question*⟩ gezielt. **~er** *n* (*hint*) Hinweis *m*. **~less** *a* zwecklos, sinnlos

poise /pɔɪz/ *n* Haltung *f*. **~d** *a* (*confident*) selbstsicher; **~d to** bereit zu

poison /'pɔɪzn/ *n* Gift *nt* ● *vt* vergiften. **~ous** *a* giftig

poke /pəʊk/ *n* Stoß *m* ● *vt* stoßen; schüren ⟨*fire*⟩; (*put*) stecken; **~ fun at** sich lustig machen über (+ *acc*)

poker[1] /'pəʊkə(r)/ *n* Schüreisen *nt*

poker[2] *n* (*Cards*) Poker *nt*

poky /'pəʊkɪ/ *a* (**-ier, -iest**) eng

Poland /'pəʊlənd/ *n* Polen *nt*

polar /'pəʊlə(r)/ *a* Polar-. **~ 'bear** *n* Eisbär *m*. **~ize** *vt* polarisieren

Pole /pəʊl/ *n* Pole *m*/Polin *f*

pole[1] *n* Stange *f*

pole[2] *n* (*Geog, Electr*) Pol *m*

'polecat *n* Iltis *m*

'pole-star *n* Polarstern *m*

'pole-vault *n* Stabhochsprung *m*

police /pə'li:s/ *npl* Polizei *f* ● *vt* polizeilich kontrollieren

police: ~man *n* Polizist *m*. **~ state** *n* Polizeistaat *m*. **~ station** *n* Polizeiwache *f*. **~woman** *n* Polizistin *f*

policy[1] /'pɒlɪsɪ/ *n* Politik *f*

policy[2] *n* (*insurance*) Police *f*

polio /'pəʊlɪəʊ/ *n* Kinderlähmung *f*

Polish /'pəʊlɪʃ/ *a* polnisch

polish /'pɒlɪʃ/ *n* (*shine*) Glanz *m*; (*for shoes*) [Schuh]creme *f*; (*for floor*) Bohnerwachs *m*; (*for furniture*) Politur *f*; (*for silver*) Putzmittel *nt*; (*for nails*) Lack *m*; (*fig*) Schliff *m* ● *vt* polieren; bohnern ⟨*floor*⟩. **~ off** *vt* (*fam*) verputzen ⟨*food*⟩; erledigen ⟨*task*⟩

polisher /'pɒlɪʃə(r)/ *n* (*machine*) Poliermaschine *f*; (*for floor*) Bohnermaschine *f*

polite /pə'laɪt/ *a*, **-ly** *adv* höflich. **~ness** *n* Höflichkeit *f*

politic /'pɒlɪtɪk/ *a* ratsam

politic|al /pə'lɪtɪkl/ *a*, **-ly** *adv* politisch. **~ian** /pɒlɪ'tɪʃn/ *n* Politiker(in) *m*(*f*)

politics /'pɒlətɪks/ *n* Politik *f*

polka /'pɒlkə/ *n* Polka *f*

poll /pəʊl/ *n* Abstimmung *f*; (*election*) Wahl *f*; **[opinion] ~** [Meinungs]umfrage *f*; **go to the ~s** wählen ● *vt* erhalten ⟨*votes*⟩

pollen /'pɒlən/ *n* Blütenstaub *m*, Pollen *m*

polling /'pəʊlɪŋ/: **~-booth** *n* Wahlkabine *f*. **~-station** *n* Wahllokal *nt*

'poll tax *n* Kopfsteuer *f*

pollutant /pə'lu:tənt/ *n* Schadstoff *m*

pollut|e /pə'lu:t/ *vt* verschmutzen. **~ion** /-u:ʃn/ *n* Verschmutzung *f*

polo /'pəʊləʊ/ *n* Polo *nt*. **~-neck** *n* Rollkragen *m*. **~ shirt** *n* Polohemd *nt*

polyester /pɒlɪ'estə(r)/ *n* Polyester *m*

polystyrene /pɒlɪ'staɪri:n/ *n* Polystyrol *nt*; (*for packing*) Styropor (P) *nt*

polytechnic /pɒlɪ'teknɪk/ *n* ≈ technische Hochschule *f*

polythene /'pɒlɪθi:n/ *n* Polyäthylen *nt*. **~ bag** *n* Plastiktüte *f*

polyun'saturated *a* mehrfach-ungesättigt

pomegranate /'pɒmɪgrænɪt/ *n* Granatapfel *m*

pomp /pɒmp/ *n* Pomp *m*

pompon /'pɒmpɒn/ *n* Pompon *m*

pompous /'pɒmpəs/ *a*, **-ly** *adv* großspurig

pond /pɒnd/ *n* Teich *m*

ponder /'pɒndə(r)/ *vi* nachdenken

ponderous /'pɒndərəs/ *a* schwerfällig

pong /pɒŋ/ *n* (*fam*) Mief *m*

pony /'pəʊnɪ/ *n* Pony *nt*. **~-tail** *n* Pferdeschwanz *m*. **~-trekking** *n* Ponyreiten *nt*

poodle /'pu:dl/ *n* Pudel *m*

pool[1] /pu:l/ *n* [Schwimm]becken *nt*; (*pond*) Teich *m*; (*of blood*) Lache *f*

pool[2] *n* (*common fund*) [gemeinsame] Kasse *f*; **~s** *pl* [Fußball]toto *nt* ● *vt* zusammenlegen

poor /pʊə(r)/ *a* (**-er, -est**) arm; (*not good*) schlecht; **in ~ health** nicht gesund ● *npl* **the ~** die Armen. **~ly** *a* **be ~ly** krank sein ● *adv* ärmlich; (*badly*) schlecht

pop[1] /pɒp/ *n* Knall *m*; (*drink*) Brause *f* ● *v* (*pt/pp* **popped**) ● *vt* (*fam: put*) stecken (**in** in + *acc*) ● *vi* knallen; (*burst*) platzen. **~ in** *vi* (*fam*) reinschauen. **~ out** *vi* (*fam*) kurz rausgehen

pop[2] *n* (*fam*) Popmusik *f*, Pop *m* ● *attrib* Pop-

'popcorn *n* Puffmais *m*

pope /pəʊp/ *n* Papst *m*

poplar /'pɒplə(r)/ *n* Pappel *f*

poppy /'pɒpɪ/ *n* Mohn *m*

popular /'pɒpjʊlə(r)/ *a* beliebt, populär; ⟨*belief*⟩ volkstümlich. **~ity** /-'lærətɪ/ *n* Beliebtheit *f*, Popularität *f*
populat|e /'pɒpjʊleɪt/ *vt* bevölkern. **~ion** /-'leɪʃn/ *n* Bevölkerung *f*
porcelain /'pɔ:səlɪn/ *n* Porzellan *nt*
porch /pɔ:tʃ/ *n* Vorbau *m*; (*Amer*) Veranda *f*
porcupine /'pɔ:kjʊpaɪn/ *n* Stachelschwein *nt*
pore¹ /pɔ:(r)/ *n* Pore *f*
pore² *vi* ~ **over** studieren
pork /pɔ:k/ *n* Schweinefleisch *nt*
porn /pɔ:n/ *n* (*fam*) Porno *m*
pornograph|ic /pɔ:nə'græfɪk/ *a* pornographisch. **~y** /-'nɒgrəfɪ/ *n* Pornographie *f*
porous /'pɔ:rəs/ *a* porös
porpoise /'pɔ:pəs/ *n* Tümmler *m*
porridge /'pɒrɪdʒ/ *n* Haferbrei *m*
port¹ /pɔ:t/ *n* Hafen *m*; (*town*) Hafenstadt *f*
port² *n* (*Naut*) Backbord *nt*
port³ *n* (*wine*) Portwein *m*
portable /'pɔ:təbl/ *a* tragbar
porter /'pɔ:tə(r)/ *n* Portier *m*; (*for luggage*) Gepäckträger *m*
portfolio /pɔ:t'fəʊlɪəʊ/ *n* Mappe *f*; (*Comm*) Portefeuille *nt*
'porthole *n* Bullauge *nt*
portion /'pɔ:ʃn/ *n* Portion *f*; (*part, share*) Teil *nt*
portly /'pɔ:tlɪ/ *a* (**-ier, -iest**) beleibt
portrait /'pɔ:trɪt/ *n* Porträt *nt*
portray /pɔ:'treɪ/ *vt* darstellen. **~al** *n* Darstellung *f*
Portug|al /'pɔ:tjʊgl/ *n* Portugal *nt*. **~uese** /-'gi:z/ *a* portugiesisch ● *n* Portugiese *m*/-giesin *f*
pose /pəʊz/ *n* Pose *f* ● *vt* aufwerfen ⟨*problem*⟩; stellen ⟨*question*⟩ ● *vi* posieren; (*for painter*) Modell stehen; ~ **as** sich ausgeben als
posh /pɒʃ/ *a* (*fam*) feudal
position /pə'zɪʃn/ *n* Platz *m*; (*posture*) Haltung *f*; (*job*) Stelle *f*; (*situation*) Lage *f*, Situation *f*; (*status*) Stellung *f* ● *vt* plazieren; ~ **oneself** sich stellen
positive /'pɒzətɪv/ *a*, **-ly** *adv* positiv; (*definite*) eindeutig; (*real*) ausgesprochen ● *n* Positiv *nt*
possess /pə'zes/ *vt* besitzen. **~ion** /pə'zeʃn/ *n* Besitz *m*; **~ions** *pl* Sachen *pl*
possess|ive /pə'zesɪv/ *a* Possessiv-; **be ~ive** zu sehr an jdm hängen. **~or** *n* Besitzer *m*
possibility /pɒsə'bɪlətɪ/ *n* Möglichkeit *f*
possib|le /'pɒsəbl/ *a* möglich. **~ly** *adv* möglicherweise; **not ~ly** unmöglich
post¹ /pəʊst/ *n* (*pole*) Pfosten *m* ● *vt* anschlagen ⟨*notice*⟩
post² *n* (*place of duty*) Posten *m*; (*job*) Stelle *f* ● *vt* postieren; (*transfer*) versetzen
post³ *n* (*mail*) Post *f*; **by** ~ mit der Post ● *vt* aufgeben ⟨*letter*⟩; (*send by* ~) mit der Post schicken; **keep s.o. ~ed** jdn auf dem laufenden halten
postage /'pəʊstɪdʒ/ *n* Porto *nt*. ~ **stamp** *n* Briefmarke *f*
postal /'pəʊstl/ *a* Post-. ~ **order** *n* ≈ Geldanweisung *f*
post: ~-box *n* Briefkasten *m*. **~card** *n* Postkarte *f*; (*picture*) Ansichtskarte *f*. **~code** *n* Postleitzahl *f*. **~-'date** *vt* vordatieren
poster /'pəʊstə(r)/ *n* Plakat *nt*
posterior /pɒ'stɪərɪə(r)/ *a* hintere(r,s) ● *n* (*fam*) Hintern *m*
posterity /pɒ'sterətɪ/ *n* Nachwelt *f*
posthumous /'pɒstjʊməs/ *a*, **-ly** *adv* postum
post: ~man *n* Briefträger *m*. **~mark** *n* Poststempel *m*
post-mortem /-'mɔ:təm/ *n* Obduktion *f*
'post office *n* Post *f*
postpone /pəʊst'pəʊn/ *vt* aufschieben; ~ **until** verschieben auf (+ *acc*). **~ment** *n* Verschiebung *f*
postscript /'pəʊstskrɪpt/ *n* Nachschrift *f*
posture /'pɒstʃə(r)/ *n* Haltung *f*
post-'war *a* Nachkriegs-
posy /'pəʊzɪ/ *n* Sträußchen *nt*
pot /pɒt/ *n* Topf *m*; (*for tea, coffee*) Kanne *f*; **~s of money** (*fam*) eine Menge Geld; **go to** ~ (*fam*) herunterkommen
potassium /pə'tæsɪəm/ *n* Kalium *nt*
potato /pə'teɪtəʊ/ *n* (*pl* **-es**) Kartoffel *f*
poten|cy /'pəʊtənsɪ/ *n* Stärke *f*. **~t** *a* stark
potential /pə'tenʃl/ *a*, **-ly** *adv* potentiell ● *n* Potential *nt*
pot: ~-hole *n* Höhle *f*; (*in road*) Schlagloch *nt*. **~-holer** *n* Höhlenforscher *m*. **~-shot** *n* **take a ~-shot at** schießen auf (+ *acc*)
potted /'pɒtɪd/ *a* eingemacht; (*shortened*) gekürzt. ~ **'plant** *n* Topfpflanze *f*
potter¹ /'pɒtə(r)/ *vi* ~ **[about]** herumwerkeln

potter[2] *n* Töpfer(in) *m(f)*. **~y** *n* Töpferei *f*; (*articles*) Töpferwaren *pl*
potty /'pɒtɪ/ *a* (**-ier, -iest**) (*fam*) verrückt ● *n* Töpfchen *nt*
pouch /paʊtʃ/ *n* Beutel *m*
pouffe /pu:f/ *n* Sitzkissen *nt*
poultry /'pəʊltrɪ/ *n* Geflügel *nt*
pounce /paʊns/ *vi* zuschlagen; **~ on** sich stürzen auf (+ *acc*)
pound[1] /paʊnd/ *n* (*money & 0,454 kg*) Pfund *nt*
pound[2] *vt* hämmern ● *vi* ⟨*heart:*⟩ hämmern; (*run heavily*) stampfen
pour /pɔ:(r)/ *vt* gießen; einschenken ⟨*drink*⟩ ● *vi* strömen; (*with rain*) gießen. **~ out** *vi* ausströmen ● *vt* ausschütten; einschenken ⟨*drink*⟩
pout /paʊt/ *vi* einen Schmollmund machen
poverty /'pɒvətɪ/ *n* Armut *f*
powder /'paʊdə(r)/ *n* Pulver *nt*; (*cosmetic*) Puder *m* ● *vt* pudern. **~y** *a* pulverig
power /'paʊə(r)/ *n* Macht *f*; (*strength*) Kraft *f*; (*Electr*) Strom *m*; (*nuclear*) Energie *f*; (*Math*) Potenz *f*. **~ cut** *n* Stromsperre *f*. **~ed** *a* betrieben (**by** mit); **~ed by electricity** mit Elektroantrieb. **~ful** *a* mächtig; (*strong*) stark. **~less** *a* machtlos. **~-station** *n* Kraftwerk *nt*
practicable /'præktɪkəbl/ *a* durchführbar, praktikabel
practical /'præktɪkl/ *a*, **-ly** *adv* praktisch. **~ 'joke** *n* Streich *m*
practice /'præktɪs/ *n* Praxis *f*; (*custom*) Brauch *m*; (*habit*) Gewohnheit *f*; (*exercise*) Übung *f*; (*Sport*) Training *nt*; **in ~** (*in reality*) in der Praxis; **out of ~** außer Übung; **put into ~** ausführen
practise /'præktɪs/ *vt* üben; (*carry out*) praktizieren; ausüben ⟨*profession*⟩ ● *vi* üben; ⟨*doctor:*⟩ praktizieren. **~d** *a* geübt
pragmatic /præg'mætɪk/ *a*, **~ally** *adv* pragmatisch
praise /preɪz/ *n* Lob *nt* ● *vt* loben. **~worthy** *a* lobenswert
pram /præm/ *n* Kinderwagen *m*
prance /prɑ:ns/ *vi* herumhüpfen; ⟨*horse:*⟩ tänzeln
prank /præŋk/ *n* Streich *m*
prattle /'prætl/ *vi* plappern
prawn /prɔ:n/ *n* Garnele *f*, Krabbe *f*. **~ 'cocktail** *n* Krabbencocktail *m*
pray /preɪ/ *vi* beten. **~er** /preə(r)/ *n* Gebet *nt*; **~ers** *pl* (*service*) Andacht *f*
preach /pri:tʃ/ *vt/i* predigen. **~er** *n* Prediger *m*
preamble /pri:'æmbl/ *n* Einleitung *f*
pre-ar'range /pri:-/ *vt* im 'voraus arrangieren
precarious /prɪ'keərɪəs/ *a*, **-ly** *adv* unsicher
precaution /prɪ'kɔ:ʃn/ *n* Vorsichtsmaßnahme *f*; **as a ~** zur Vorsicht. **~ary** *a* Vorsichts-
precede /prɪ'si:d/ *vt* vorangehen (+ *dat*)
preceden|ce /'presɪdəns/ *n* Vorrang *m*. **~t** *n* Präzedenzfall *m*
preceding /prɪ'si:dɪŋ/ *a* vorhergehend
precinct /'pri:sɪŋkt/ *n* Bereich *m*; (*traffic-free*) Fußgängerzone *f*; (*Amer: district*) Bezirk *m*
precious /'preʃəs/ *a* kostbar; ⟨*style*⟩ preziös ● *adv* (*fam*) **~ little** recht wenig
precipice /'presɪpɪs/ *n* Steilabfall *m*
precipitate[1] /prɪ'sɪpɪtət/ *a* voreilig
precipitat|e[2] /prɪ'sɪpɪteɪt/ *vt* schleudern; (*fig: accelerate*) beschleunigen. **~ion** /-'teɪʃn/ *n* (*Meteorol*) Niederschlag *m*
précis /'preɪsi:/ *n* (*pl* **précis** /-si:z/) Zusammenfassung *f*
precis|e /prɪ'saɪs/ *a*, **-ly** *adv* genau. **~ion** /-'sɪʒn/ *n* Genauigkeit *f*
preclude /prɪ'klu:d/ *vt* ausschließen
precocious /prɪ'kəʊʃəs/ *a* frühreif
pre|con'ceived /pri:-/ *a* vorgefaßt. **~con'ception** *n* vorgefaßte Meinung *f*
precursor /pri:'kɜ:sə(r)/ *n* Vorläufer *m*
predator /'predətə(r)/ *n* Raubtier *nt*
predecessor /'pri:dɪsesə(r)/ *n* Vorgänger(in) *m(f)*
predicament /prɪ'dɪkəmənt/ *n* Zwangslage *f*
predicat|e /'predɪkət/ *n* (*Gram*) Prädikat *nt*. **~ive** /prɪ'dɪkətɪv/ *a*, **-ly** *adv* prädikativ
predict /prɪ'dɪkt/ *vt* voraussagen. **~able** /-əbl/ *a* voraussehbar; ⟨*person*⟩ berechenbar. **~ion** /-'dɪkʃn/ *n* Voraussage *f*
pre'domin|ant /prɪ-/ *a* vorherrschend. **~antly** *adv* hauptsächlich, überwiegend. **~ate** *vi* vorherrschen
pre-'eminent /pri:-/ *a* hervorragend
pre-empt /pri:'empt/ *vt* zuvorkommen (+ *dat*)
preen /pri:n/ *vt* putzen; **~ oneself** (*fig*) selbstgefällig tun

pre|fab /'pri:fæb/ *n (fam)* [einfaches] Fertighaus *nt*. **~'fabricated** *a* vorgefertigt
preface /'prefıs/ *n* Vorwort *nt*
prefect /'pri:fekt/ *n* Präfekt *m*
prefer /prı'fɜ:(r)/ *vt (pt/pp* **preferred***)* vorziehen; **I ~ to walk** ich gehe lieber zu Fuß; **I ~ wine** ich trinke lieber Wein
prefera|ble /'prefərəbl/ *a* **be ~ble** vorzuziehen sein (**to** *dat*). **~bly** *adv* vorzugsweise
preferen|ce /'prefərəns/ *n* Vorzug *m*. **~tial** /-'renʃl/ *a* bevorzugt
prefix /'pri:fıks/ *n* Vorsilbe *f*
pregnan|cy /'pregnənsı/ *n* Schwangerschaft *f*. **~t** *a* schwanger; ⟨*animal*⟩ trächtig
prehi'storic /pri:-/ *a* prähistorisch
prejudice /'predʒʊdıs/ *n* Vorurteil *nt*; (*bias*) Voreingenommenheit *f* ● *vt* einnehmen (**against** gegen). **~d** *a* voreingenommen
preliminary /prı'lımınərı/ *a* Vor-
prelude /'prelju:d/ *n* Vorspiel *nt*
pre-'marital *a* vorehelich
premature /'premətjʊə(r)/ *a* vorzeitig; ⟨*birth*⟩ Früh-. **~ly** *adv* zu früh
pre'meditated /pri:-/ *a* vorsätzlich
premier /'premıə(r)/ *a* führend ● *n* (*Pol*) Premier[minister] *m*
première /'premıeə(r)/ *n* Premiere *f*
premises /'premısız/ *npl* Räumlichkeiten *pl*; **on the ~** im Haus
premiss /'premıs/ *n* Prämisse *f*
premium /'pri:mıəm/ *n* Prämie *f*; **be at a ~** hoch im Kurs stehen
premonition /premə'nıʃn/ *n* Vorahnung *f*
preoccupied /prı'ɒkjʊpaıd/ *a* [in Gedanken] beschäftigt
prep /prep/ *n* (*Sch*) Hausaufgaben *pl*
pre-'packed /pri:-/ *a* abgepackt
preparation /prepə'reıʃn/ *n* Vorbereitung *f*; (*substance*) Präparat *nt*
preparatory /prı'pærətrı/ *a* Vor- ● *adv* **~ to** vor (+ *dat*)
prepare /prı'peə(r)/ *vt* vorbereiten; anrichten ⟨*meal*⟩ ● *vi* sich vorbereiten (**for** auf + *acc*); **~d to** bereit zu
pre'pay /pri:-/ *vt (pt/pp* **-paid***)* im voraus bezahlen
preposition /prepə'zıʃn/ *n* Präposition *f*
prepossessing /pri:pə'zesıŋ/ *a* ansprechend
preposterous /prı'pɒstərəs/ *a* absurd
prerequisite /pri:'rekwızıt/ *n* Voraussetzung *f*
prerogative /prı'rɒgətıv/ *n* Vorrecht *nt*
Presbyterian /prezbı'tıərıən/ *a* presbyterianisch ● *n* Presbyterianer(in) *m(f)*
prescribe /prı'skraıb/ *vt* vorschreiben; (*Med*) verschreiben
prescription /prı'skrıpʃn/ *n* (*Med*) Rezept *nt*
presence /'prezns/ *n* Anwesenheit *f*, Gegenwart *f*; **~ of mind** Geistesgegenwart *f*
present[1] /'preznt/ *a* gegenwärtig; **be ~** anwesend sein; (*occur*) vorkommen ● *n* Gegenwart *f*; (*Gram*) Präsens *nt*; **at ~** zur Zeit; **for the ~** vorläufig
present[2] *n* (*gift*) Geschenk *nt*
present[3] /prı'zent/ *vt* überreichen; (*show*) zeigen; vorlegen ⟨*cheque*⟩; (*introduce*) vorstellen; **~ s.o. with sth** jdm etw überreichen. **~able** /-əbl/ *a* **be ~able** sich zeigen lassen können
presentation /prezn'teıʃn/ *n* Überreichung *f*. **~ ceremony** *n* Verleihungszeremonie *f*
presently /'prezntlı/ *adv* nachher; (*Amer: now*) zur Zeit
preservation /prezə'veıʃn/ *n* Erhaltung *f*
preservative /prı'zɜ:vətıv/ *n* Konservierungsmittel *nt*
preserve /prı'zɜ:v/ *vt* erhalten; (*Culin*) konservieren; (*bottle*) einmachen ● *n* (*Hunting & fig*) Revier *nt*; (*jam*) Konfitüre *f*
preside /prı'zaıd/ *vi* den Vorsitz haben (**over** bei)
presidency /'prezıdənsı/ *n* Präsidentschaft *f*
president /'prezıdənt/ *n* Präsident *m*; (*Amer: chairman*) Vorsitzende(r) *m/f*. **~ial** /-'denʃl/ *a* Präsidenten-; ⟨*election*⟩ Präsidentschafts-
press /pres/ *n* Presse *f* ● *vt/i* drücken; drücken auf (+ *acc*) ⟨*button*⟩; pressen ⟨*flower*⟩; (*iron*) bügeln; (*urge*) bedrängen; **~ for** drängen auf (+ *acc*); **be ~ed for time** in Zeitdruck sein. **~ on** *vi* weitergehen/-fahren; (*fig*) weitermachen
press: ~ cutting *n* Zeitungsausschnitt *m*. **~ing** *a* dringend. **~-stud** *n* Druckknopf *m*. **~-up** *n* Liegestütz *m*

pressure /'preʃə(r)/ *n* Druck *m* • *vt* = **pressurize**. **~-cooker** *n* Schnellkochtopf *m*. **~ group** *n* Interessengruppe *f*

pressurize /'preʃəraɪz/ *vt* Druck ausüben auf (+ *acc*). **~d** *a* Druck-

prestig|e /pre'sti:ʒ/ *n* Prestige *nt*. **~ious** /-'stɪdʒəs/ *a* Prestige-

presumably /prɪ'zju:məblɪ/ *adv* vermutlich

presume /prɪ'zju:m/ *vt* vermuten; **~ to do sth** sich (*dat*) anmaßen, etw zu tun • *vi* **~ on** ausnutzen

presumpt|ion /prɪ'zʌmpʃn/ *n* Vermutung *f*; (*boldness*) Anmaßung *f*. **~uous** /-'zʌmptjʊəs/ *a*, **-ly** *adv* anmaßend

presup'pose /pri:-/ *vt* voraussetzen

pretence /prɪ'tens/ *n* Verstellung *f*; (*pretext*) Vorwand *m*; **it's all ~** das ist alles gespielt

pretend /prɪ'tend/ *vt* (*claim*) vorgeben; **~ that** so tun, als ob; **~ to be** sich ausgeben als

pretentious /prɪ'tenʃəs/ *a* protzig

pretext /'pri:tekst/ *n* Vorwand *m*

pretty /'prɪtɪ/ *a* (**-ier, -iest**), **~ily** *adv* hübsch • *adv* (*fam: fairly*) ziemlich

pretzel /'pretsl/ *n* Brezel *f*

prevail /prɪ'veɪl/ *vi* siegen; 〈*custom*:〉 vorherrschen; **~ on s.o. to do sth** jdn dazu bringen, etw zu tun

prevalen|ce /'prevələns/ *n* Häufigkeit *f*. **~t** *a* vorherrschend

prevent /prɪ'vent/ *vt* verhindern, verhüten; **~ s.o. [from] doing sth** jdn daran hindern, etw zu tun. **~able** /-əbl/ *a* vermeidbar. **~ion** /-enʃn/ *n* Verhinderung *f*, Verhütung *f*. **~ive** /-ɪv/ *a* vorbeugend

preview /'pri:vju:/ *n* Voraufführung *f*

previous /'pri:vɪəs/ *a* vorhergehend; **~ to** vor (+ *dat*). **~ly** *adv* vorher, früher

pre-'war /pri:-/ *a* Vorkriegs-

prey /preɪ/ *n* Beute *f*; **bird of ~** Raubvogel *m* • *vi* **~ on** Jagd machen auf (+ *acc*); **~ on s.o.'s mind** jdm schwer auf der Seele liegen

price /praɪs/ *n* Preis *m* • *vt* (*Comm*) auszeichnen. **~less** *a* unschätzbar; (*fig*) unbezahlbar

prick /prɪk/ *n* Stich *m* • *vt/i* stechen; **~ up one's ears** die Ohren spitzen

prickl|e /'prɪkl/ *n* Stachel *m*; (*thorn*) Dorn *m*. **~y** *a* stachelig; 〈*sensation*〉 stechend

pride /praɪd/ *n* Stolz *m*; (*arrogance*) Hochmut *m*; (*of lions*) Rudel *nt* • *vt* **~ oneself on** stolz sein auf (+ *acc*)

priest /pri:st/ *n* Priester *m*

prig /prɪg/ *n* Tugendbold *m*

prim /prɪm/ *a* (**primmer, primmest**) prüde

primarily /'praɪmərɪlɪ/ *adv* hauptsächlich, in erster Linie

primary /'praɪmərɪ/ *a* Haupt-. **~ school** *n* Grundschule *f*

prime[1] /praɪm/ *a* Haupt-; (*first-rate*) erstklassig • *n* **be in one's ~** in den besten Jahren sein

prime[2] *vt* scharf machen 〈*bomb*〉; grundieren 〈*surface*〉; (*fig*) instruieren

Prime Minister /praɪ'mɪnɪstə(r)/ *n* Premierminister(in) *m(f)*

primeval /praɪ'mi:vl/ *a* Ur-

primitive /'prɪmɪtɪv/ *a* primitiv

primrose /'prɪmrəʊz/ *n* gelbe Schlüsselblume *f*

prince /prɪns/ *n* Prinz *m*

princess /prɪn'ses/ *n* Prinzessin *f*

principal /'prɪnsəpl/ *a* Haupt- • *n* (*Sch*) Rektor(in) *m(f)*

principality /prɪnsɪ'pælətɪ/ *n* Fürstentum *nt*

principally /'prɪnsəplɪ/ *adv* hauptsächlich

principle /'prɪnsəpl/ *n* Prinzip *nt*, Grundsatz *m*; **in/on ~** im/aus Prinzip

print /prɪnt/ *n* Druck *m*; (*Phot*) Abzug *m*; **in ~** gedruckt; (*available*) erhältlich; **out of ~** vergriffen • *vt* drucken; (*write in capitals*) in Druckschrift schreiben; (*Computing*) ausdrucken; (*Phot*) abziehen. **~ed matter** *n* Drucksache *f*

print|er /'prɪntə(r)/ *n* Drucker *m*. **~ing** *n* Druck *m*

'printout *n* (*Computing*) Ausdruck *m*

prior /'praɪə(r)/ *a* frühere(r,s); **~ to** vor (+ *dat*)

priority /praɪ'ɒrətɪ/ *n* Priorität *f*, Vorrang *m*; (*matter*) vordringliche Sache *f*

prise /praɪz/ *vt* **~ open/up** aufstemmen/hochstemmen

prism /'prɪzm/ *n* Prisma *nt*

prison /'prɪzn/ *n* Gefängnis *nt*. **~er** *n* Gefangene(r) *m/f*

pristine /'prɪsti:n/ *a* tadellos

privacy /'prɪvəsɪ/ *n* Privatsphäre *f*; **have no ~** nie für sich sein

private /'praɪvət/ *a*, **-ly** *adv* privat; (*confidential*) vertraulich; ⟨*car, secretary, school*⟩ Privat- • *n* (*Mil*) [einfacher] Soldat *m*; **in ~** privat; (*confidentially*) vertraulich

privation /praɪ'veɪʃn/ *n* Entbehrung *f*

privatize /'praɪvətaɪz/ *vt* privatisieren

privilege /'prɪvəlɪdʒ/ *n* Privileg *nt*. **~d** *a* privilegiert

privy /'prɪvɪ/ *a* **be ~ to** wissen

prize /praɪz/ *n* Preis *m* • *vt* schätzen. **~-giving** *n* Preisverleihung *f*. **~-winner** *n* Preisgewinner(in) *m*(*f*)

pro /prəʊ/ *n* (*fam*) Profi *m*; **the ~s and cons** das Für und Wider

probability /prɒbə'bɪlətɪ/ *n* Wahrscheinlichkeit *f*

probable /'prɒbəbl/ *a*, **-bly** *adv* wahrscheinlich

probation /prə'beɪʃn/ *n* (*Jur*) Bewährung *f*. **~ary** *a* Probe-; **~ary period** Probezeit *f*

probe /prəʊb/ *n* Sonde *f*; (*fig: investigation*) Untersuchung *f* • *vt/i* **~ [into]** untersuchen

problem /'prɒbləm/ *n* Problem *nt*; (*Math*) Textaufgabe *f*. **~atic** /-'mætɪk/ *a* problematisch

procedure /prə'si:dʒə(r)/ *n* Verfahren *nt*

proceed /prə'si:d/ *vi* gehen; (*in vehicle*) fahren; (*continue*) weitergehen/-fahren; (*speaking*) fortfahren; (*act*) verfahren • *vt* **~ to do sth** anfangen, etw zu tun

proceedings /prə'si:dɪŋz/ *npl* Verfahren *nt*; (*Jur*) Prozeß *m*

proceeds /'prəʊsi:dz/ *npl* Erlös *m*

process /'prəʊses/ *n* Prozeß *m*; (*procedure*) Verfahren *nt*; **in the ~** dabei • *vt* verarbeiten; (*Admin*) bearbeiten; (*Phot*) entwickeln

procession /prə'seʃn/ *n* Umzug *m*, Prozession *f*

proclaim /prə'kleɪm/ *vt* ausrufen

proclamation /prɒklə'meɪʃn/ *n* Proklamation *f*

procure /prə'kjʊə(r)/ *vt* beschaffen

prod /prɒd/ *n* Stoß *m* • *vt* stoßen; (*fig*) einen Stoß geben (+ *dat*)

prodigal /'prɒdɪgl/ *a* verschwenderisch

prodigious /prə'dɪdʒəs/ *a* gewaltig

prodigy /'prɒdɪdʒɪ/ *n* **[infant] ~** Wunderkind *nt*

produce[1] /'prɒdju:s/ *n* landwirtschaftliche Erzeugnisse *pl*

produce[2] /prə'dju:s/ *vt* erzeugen, produzieren; (*manufacture*) herstellen; (*bring out*) hervorholen; (*cause*) hervorrufen; inszenieren ⟨*play*⟩; (*Radio, TV*) redigieren. **~r** *n* Erzeuger *m*, Produzent *m*; Hersteller *m*; (*Theat*) Regisseur *m*; (*Radio, TV*) Redakteur(in) *m*(*f*)

product /'prɒdʌkt/ *n* Erzeugnis *nt*, Produkt *nt*. **~ion** /prə'dʌkʃn/ *n* Produktion *f*; (*Theat*) Inszenierung *f*

productiv|e /prə'dʌktɪv/ *a* produktiv; ⟨*land, talks*⟩ fruchtbar. **~ity** /-'tɪvətɪ/ *n* Produktivität *f*

profan|e /prə'feɪn/ *a* weltlich; (*blasphemous*) [gottes]lästerlich. **~ity** /-'fænətɪ/ *n* (*oath*) Fluch *m*

profess /prə'fes/ *vt* behaupten; bekennen ⟨*faith*⟩

profession /prə'feʃn/ *n* Beruf *m*. **~al** *a*, **-ly** *adv* beruflich; (*not amateur*) Berufs-; (*expert*) fachmännisch; (*Sport*) professionell • *n* Fachmann *m*; (*Sport*) Profi *m*

professor /prə'fesə(r)/ *n* Professor *m*

proficien|cy /prə'fɪʃnsɪ/ *n* Können *nt*. **~t** *a* **be ~t in** beherrschen

profile /'prəʊfaɪl/ *n* Profil *nt*; (*character study*) Porträt *nt*

profit /'prɒfɪt/ *n* Gewinn *m*, Profit *m* • *vi* **~ from** profitieren von. **~able** /-əbl/ *a*, **-bly** *adv* gewinnbringend; (*fig*) nutzbringend

profound /prə'faʊnd/ *a*, **-ly** *adv* tief

profus|e /prə'fju:s/ *a*, **-ly** *adv* üppig; (*fig*) überschwenglich. **~ion** /-ju:ʒn/ *n* **in ~ion** in großer Fülle

progeny /'prɒdʒənɪ/ *n* Nachkommenschaft *f*

program /'prəʊgræm/ *n* Programm *nt* • *vt* (*pt/pp* **programmed**) programmieren

programme /'prəʊgræm/ *n* Programm *nt*; (*Radio, TV*) Sendung *f*. **~r** *n* (*Computing*) Programmierer(in) *m*(*f*)

progress[1] /'prəʊgres/ *n* Vorankommen *nt*; (*fig*) Fortschritt *m*; **in ~** im Gange; **make ~** (*fig*) Fortschritte machen

progress[2] /prə'gres/ *vi* vorankommen; (*fig*) fortschreiten. **~ion** /-eʃn/ *n* Folge *f*; (*development*) Entwicklung *f*

progressive /prə'gresɪv/ *a* fortschrittlich; ⟨*disease*⟩ fortschreitend. **~ly** *adv* zunehmend

prohibit /prə'hɪbɪt/ *vt* verbieten (**s.o.** jdm). **~ive** /-ɪv/ *a* unerschwinglich

project¹ /'prɒdʒekt/ *n* Projekt *nt*; (*Sch*) Arbeit *f*

project² /prə'dʒekt/ *vt* projizieren ⟨*film*⟩; (*plan*) planen ● *vi* (*jut out*) vorstehen

projectile /prə'dʒektaɪl/ *n* Geschoß *nt*

projector /prə'dʒektə(r)/ *n* Projektor *m*

proletariat /prəʊlɪ'teərɪət/ *n* Proletariat *nt*

prolific /prə'lɪfɪk/ *a* fruchtbar; (*fig*) produktiv

prologue /'prəʊlɒg/ *n* Prolog *m*

prolong /prə'lɒŋ/ *vt* verlängern

promenade /prɒmə'nɑ:d/ *n* Promenade *f* ● *vi* spazierengehen

prominent /'prɒmɪnənt/ *a* vorstehend; (*important*) prominent; (*conspicuous*) auffällig; ⟨*place*⟩ gut sichtbar

promiscu|ity /prɒmɪ'skju:ətɪ/ *n* Promiskuität *f*. **~ous** /prə'mɪskjʊəs/ *a* **be ~ous** häufig den Partner wechseln

promis|e /'prɒmɪs/ *n* Versprechen *nt* ● *vt/i* versprechen (**s.o.** jdm); **the P~ed Land** das Gelobte Land. **~ing** *a* vielversprechend

promot|e /prə'məʊt/ *vt* befördern; (*advance*) fördern; (*publicize*) Reklame machen für; **be ~ed** (*Sport*) aufsteigen. **~ion** /-əʊʃn/ *n* Beförderung *f*; (*Sport*) Aufstieg *m*; (*Comm*) Reklame *f*

prompt /prɒmpt/ *a* prompt, unverzüglich; (*punctual*) pünktlich ● *adv* pünktlich ● *vt/i* veranlassen (**to** zu); (*Theat*) soufflieren (+ *dat*). **~er** *n* Souffleur *m*/Souffleuse *f*. **~ly** *adv* prompt

prone /prəʊn/ *a* **be/lie ~** auf dem Bauch liegen; **be ~ to** neigen zu; **be ~ to do sth** dazu neigen, etw zu tun

prong /prɒŋ/ *n* Zinke *f*

pronoun /'prəʊnaʊn/ *n* Fürwort *nt*, Pronomen *nt*

pronounce /prə'naʊns/ *vt* aussprechen; (*declare*) erklären. **~d** *a* ausgeprägt; (*noticeable*) deutlich. **~ment** *n* Erklärung *f*

pronunciation /prənʌnsɪ'eɪʃn/ *n* Aussprache *f*

proof /pru:f/ *n* Beweis *m*; (*Typ*) Korrekturbogen *m* ● *a* **~ against water/theft** wasserfest/diebessicher. **~-reader** *n* Korrektor *m*

prop¹ /prɒp/ *n* Stütze *f* ● *vt* (*pt/pp* **propped**) **~ open** offenhalten; **~ against** (*lean*) lehnen an (+ *acc*). **~ up** *vt* stützen

prop² *n* (*Theat*, *fam*) Requisit *nt*

propaganda /prɒpə'gændə/ *n* Propaganda *f*

propagate /'prɒpəgeɪt/ *vt* vermehren; (*fig*) verbreiten, propagieren

propel /prə'pel/ *vt* (*pt/pp* **propelled**) [an]treiben. **~ler** *n* Propeller *m*. **~ling 'pencil** *n* Drehbleistift *m*

propensity /prə'pensətɪ/ *n* Neigung *f* (**for** zu)

proper /'prɒpə(r)/ *a*, **-ly** *adv* richtig; (*decent*) anständig. **~ 'name, ~ 'noun** *n* Eigenname *m*

property /'prɒpətɪ/ *n* Eigentum *nt*; (*quality*) Eigenschaft *f*; (*Theat*) Requisit *nt*; (*land*) [Grund]besitz *m*; (*house*) Haus *nt*. **~ market** *n* Immobilienmarkt *m*

prophecy /'prɒfəsɪ/ *n* Prophezeiung *f*

prophesy /'prɒfɪsaɪ/ *vt* (*pt/pp* **-ied**) prophezeien

prophet /'prɒfɪt/ *n* Prophet *m*. **~ic** /prə'fetɪk/ *a* prophetisch

proportion /prə'pɔ:ʃn/ *n* Verhältnis *nt*; (*share*) Teil *m*; **~s** *pl* Proportionen; (*dimensions*) Maße. **~al** *a*, **-ly** *adv* proportional

proposal /prə'pəʊzl/ *n* Vorschlag *m*; (*of marriage*) [Heirats]antrag *m*

propose /prə'pəʊz/ *vt* vorschlagen; (*intend*) vorhaben; einbringen ⟨*motion*⟩; ausbringen ⟨*toast*⟩ ● *vi* einen Heiratsantrag machen

proposition /prɒpə'zɪʃn/ *n* Vorschlag *m*

propound /prə'paʊnd/ *vt* darlegen

proprietor /prə'praɪətə(r)/ *n* Inhaber(in) *m*(*f*)

propriety /prə'praɪətɪ/ *n* Korrektheit *f*; (*decorum*) Anstand *m*

propulsion /prə'pʌlʃn/ *n* Antrieb *m*

prosaic /prə'zeɪɪk/ *a* prosaisch

prose /prəʊz/ *n* Prosa *f*

prosecut|e /'prɒsɪkju:t/ *vt* strafrechtlich verfolgen. **~ion** /-'kju:ʃn/ *n* strafrechtliche Verfolgung *f*; **the ~ion** die Anklage. **~or** *n* **[Public] P~or** Staatsanwalt *m*

prospect¹ /'prɒspekt/ *n* Aussicht *f*

prospect² /prə'spekt/ *vi* suchen (**for** nach)

prospect|ive /prə'spektɪv/ *a* (*future*) zukünftig. **~or** *n* Prospektor *m*

prospectus /prə'spektəs/ *n* Prospekt *m*

prosper /'prɒspə(r)/ *vi* gedeihen, florieren; ⟨*person*⟩ Erfolg haben. **~ity** /-'sperətɪ/ *n* Wohlstand *m*

prosperous /'prɒspərəs/ *a* wohlhabend

prostitut|e /'prɒstɪtju:t/ *n* Prostituierte *f*. **~ion** /-'tju:ʃn/ *n* Prostitution *f*

prostrate /'prɒstreɪt/ *a* ausgestreckt; **~ with grief** (*fig*) vor Kummer gebrochen

protagonist /prəʊ'tægənɪst/ *n* Kämpfer *m*; (*fig*) Protagonist *m*

protect /prə'tekt/ *vt* schützen (**from** vor + *dat*); beschützen ⟨*person*⟩. **~ion** /-ekʃn/ *n* Schutz *m*. **~ive** /-ɪv/ *a* Schutz-; (*fig*) beschützend. **~or** *n* Beschützer *m*

protégé /'prɒtɪʒeɪ/ *n* Schützling *m*, Protegé *m*

protein /'prəʊti:n/ *n* Eiweiß *nt*

protest[1] /'prəʊtest/ *n* Protest *m*

protest[2] /prə'test/ *vi* protestieren

Protestant /'prɒtɪstənt/ *a* protestantisch, evangelisch ● *n* Protestant(in) *m*(*f*), Evangelische(r) *m*/*f*

protester /prə'testə(r)/ *n* Protestierende(r) *m*/*f*

protocol /'prəʊtəkɒl/ *n* Protokoll *nt*

prototype /'prəʊtə-/ *n* Prototyp *m*

protract /prə'trækt/ *vt* verlängern. **~or** *n* Winkelmesser *m*

protrude /prə'tru:d/ *vi* [her]vorstehen

proud /praʊd/ *a*, **-ly** *adv* stolz (**of** auf + *acc*)

prove /pru:v/ *vt* beweisen ● *vi* **~ to be** sich erweisen als

proverb /'prɒvɜ:b/ *n* Sprichwort *nt*. **~ial** /prə'vɜ:bɪəl/ *a* sprichwörtlich

provide /prə'vaɪd/ *vt* zur Verfügung stellen; spenden ⟨*shade*⟩; **~ s.o. with sth** jdn mit etw versorgen *od* versehen ● *vi* **~ for** sorgen für

provided /prə'vaɪdɪd/ *conj* **~ [that]** vorausgesetzt [daß]

providen|ce /'prɒvɪdəns/ *n* Vorsehung *f*. **~tial** /-'denʃl/ *a* **be ~tial** ein Glück sein

providing /prə'vaɪdɪŋ/ *conj* = **provided**

provinc|e /'prɒvɪns/ *n* Provinz *f*; (*fig*) Bereich *m*. **~ial** /prə'vɪnʃl/ *a* provinziell

provision /prə'vɪʒn/ *n* Versorgung *f* (**of** mit); **~s** *pl* Lebensmittel *pl*. **~al** *a*, **-ly** *adv* vorläufig

proviso /prə'vaɪzəʊ/ *n* Vorbehalt *m*

provocat|ion /prɒvə'keɪʃn/ *n* Provokation *f*. **~ive** /prə'vɒkətɪv/ *a*, **-ly** *adv* provozierend; (*sexually*) aufreizend

provoke /prə'vəʊk/ *vt* provozieren; (*cause*) hervorrufen

prow /praʊ/ *n* Bug *m*

prowess /'praʊɪs/ *n* Kraft *f*

prowl /praʊl/ *vi* herumschleichen ● *n* **be on the ~** herumschleichen

proximity /prɒk'sɪmətɪ/ *n* Nähe *f*

proxy /'prɒksɪ/ *n* Stellvertreter(in) *m*(*f*); (*power*) Vollmacht *f*

prude /pru:d/ *n* **be a ~** prüde sein

pruden|ce /'pru:dns/ *n* Umsicht *f*. **~t** *a*, **-ly** *adv* umsichtig; (*wise*) klug

prudish /'pru:dɪʃ/ *a* prüde

prune[1] /pru:n/ *n* Backpflaume *f*

prune[2] *vt* beschneiden

pry /praɪ/ *vi* (*pt*/*pp* **pried**) neugierig sein

psalm /sɑ:m/ *n* Psalm *m*

pseudonym /'sju:dənɪm/ *n* Pseudonym *nt*

psychiatric /saɪkɪ'ætrɪk/ *a* psychiatrisch

psychiatr|ist /saɪ'kaɪətrɪst/ *n* Psychiater(in) *m*(*f*). **~y** *n* Psychiatrie *f*

psychic /'saɪkɪk/ *a* übersinnlich; **I'm not ~** ich kann nicht hellsehen

psycho|'analyse /saɪkəʊ-/ *vt* psychoanalysieren. **~a'nalysis** *n* Psychoanalyse *f*. **~'analyst** Psychoanalytiker(in) *m*(*f*)

psychological /saɪkə'lɒdʒɪkl/ *a*, **-ly** *adv* psychologisch; ⟨*illness*⟩ psychisch

psycholog|ist /saɪ'kɒlədʒɪst/ *n* Psychologe *m*/-login *f*. **~y** *n* Psychologie *f*

psychopath /'saɪkəpæθ/ *n* Psychopath(in) *m*(*f*)

PTO *abbr* (**please turn over**) b.w.

pub /pʌb/ *n* (*fam*) Kneipe *f*

puberty /'pju:bətɪ/ *n* Pubertät *f*

public /'pʌblɪk/ *a*, **-ly** *adv* öffentlich; **make ~** publik machen ● *n* **the ~** die Öffentlichkeit; **in ~** in aller Öffentlichkeit

publican /'pʌblɪkən/ *n* [Gast]wirt *m*

publication /pʌblɪ'keɪʃn/ *n* Veröffentlichung *f*

public: ~ con'venience *n* öffentliche Toilette *f*. **~ 'holiday** *n* gesetzlicher Feiertag *m*. **~ 'house** *n* [Gast]wirtschaft *f*

publicity /pʌb'lɪsətɪ/ *n* Publicity *f*; (*advertising*) Reklame *f*

publicize /ˈpʌblɪsaɪz/ *vt* Reklame machen für

public: ~ **ˈlibrary** *n* öffentliche Bücherei *f*. ~ **ˈschool** *n* Privatschule *f*; (*Amer*) staatliche Schule *f*. ~-**ˈspirited** *a* **be** ~-**spirited** Gemeinsinn haben. ~ **ˈtransport** *n* öffentliche Verkehrsmittel *pl*

publish /ˈpʌblɪʃ/ *vt* veröffentlichen. ~**er** *n* Verleger(in) *m*(*f*); (*firm*) Verlag *m*. ~**ing** *n* Verlagswesen *nt*

pucker /ˈpʌkə(r)/ *vt* kräuseln

pudding /ˈpʊdɪŋ/ *n* Pudding *m*; (*course*) Nachtisch *m*

puddle /ˈpʌdl/ *n* Pfütze *f*

puerile /ˈpjʊəraɪl/ *a* kindisch

puff /pʌf/ *n* (*of wind*) Hauch *m*; (*of smoke*) Wölkchen *nt*; (*for powder*) Quaste *f* ● *vt* blasen, pusten; ~ **out** ausstoßen. ● *vi* keuchen; ~ **at** paffen an (+ *dat*) ⟨*pipe*⟩. ~**ed** *a* (*out of breath*) aus der Puste. ~ **pastry** *n* Blätterteig *m*

puffy /ˈpʌfɪ/ *a* geschwollen

pugnacious /pʌgˈneɪʃəs/ *a*, **-ly** *adv* aggressiv

pull /pʊl/ *n* Zug *m*; (*jerk*) Ruck *m*; (*fam: influence*) Einfluß *m* ● *vt* ziehen; ziehen an (+*dat*) ⟨*rope*⟩; ~ **a muscle** sich (*dat*) einen Muskel zerren; ~ **oneself together** sich zusammennehmen; ~ **one's weight** tüchtig mitarbeiten; ~ **s.o.'s leg** (*fam*) jdn auf den Arm nehmen. ~ **down** *vt* herunterziehen; (*demolish*) abreißen. ~ **in** *vt* hereinziehen ● *vi* (*Auto*) einscheren. ~ **off** *vt* abziehen; (*fam*) schaffen. ~ **out** *vt* herausziehen ● *vi* (*Auto*) ausscheren. ~ **through** *vt* durchziehen ● *vi* (*recover*) durchkommen. ~ **up** *vt* heraufziehen; ausziehen ⟨*plant*⟩; (*reprimand*) zurechtweisen ● *vi* (*Auto*) anhalten

pulley /ˈpʊlɪ/ *n* (*Techn*) Rolle *f*

pullover /ˈpʊləʊvə(r)/ *n* Pullover *m*

pulp /pʌlp/ *n* Brei *m*; (*of fruit*) [Frucht]fleisch *nt*

pulpit /ˈpʊlpɪt/ *n* Kanzel *f*

pulsate /pʌlˈseɪt/ *vi* pulsieren

pulse /pʌls/ *n* Puls *m*

pulses /ˈpʌlsɪz/ *npl* Hülsenfrüchte *pl*

pulverize /ˈpʌlvəraɪz/ *vt* pulverisieren

pumice /ˈpʌmɪs/ *n* Bimsstein *m*

pummel /ˈpʌml/ *vt* (*pt/pp* **pummelled**) mit den Fäusten bearbeiten

pump /pʌmp/ *n* Pumpe *f* ● *vt* pumpen; (*fam*) aushorchen. ~ **up** *vt* hochpumpen; (*inflate*) aufpumpen

pumpkin /ˈpʌmpkɪn/ *n* Kürbis *m*

pun /pʌn/ *n* Wortspiel *nt*

punch[1] /pʌntʃ/ *n* Faustschlag *m*; (*device*) Locher *m* ● *vt* boxen; lochen ⟨*ticket*⟩; stanzen ⟨*hole*⟩

punch[2] *n* (*drink*) Bowle *f*

punch: ~ **line** *n* Pointe *f*. ~-**up** *n* Schlägerei *f*

punctual /ˈpʌŋktjʊəl/ *a*, **-ly** *adv* pünktlich. ~**ity** /-ˈælətɪ/ *n* Pünktlichkeit *f*

punctuat|e /ˈpʌŋktjʊeɪt/ *vt* mit Satzzeichen versehen. ~**ion** /-ˈeɪʃn/ *n* Interpunktion *f*. ~**ion mark** *n* Satzzeichen *nt*

puncture /ˈpʌŋktʃə(r)/ *n* Loch *nt*; (*tyre*) Reifenpanne *f* ● *vt* durchstechen

pundit /ˈpʌndɪt/ *n* Experte *m*

pungent /ˈpʌndʒənt/ *a* scharf

punish /ˈpʌnɪʃ/ *vt* bestrafen. ~**able** /-əbl/ *a* strafbar. ~**ment** *n* Strafe *f*

punitive /ˈpju:nɪtɪv/ *a* Straf-

punnet /ˈpʌnɪt/ *n* Körbchen *nt*

punt /pʌnt/ *n* (*boat*) Stechkahn *m*

punter /ˈpʌntə(r)/ *n* (*gambler*) Wetter *m*; (*client*) Kunde *m*

puny /ˈpju:nɪ/ *a* (**-ier**, **-iest**) mickerig

pup /pʌp/ *n* = **puppy**

pupil /ˈpju:pl/ *n* Schüler(in) *m*(*f*); (*of eye*) Pupille *f*

puppet /ˈpʌpɪt/ *n* Puppe *f*; (*fig*) Marionette *f*

puppy /ˈpʌpɪ/ *n* junger Hund *m*

purchase /ˈpɜ:tʃəs/ *n* Kauf *m*; (*leverage*) Hebelkraft *f* ● *vt* kaufen. ~**r** *n* Käufer *m*

pure /pjʊə(r)/ *a* (**-r**, **-st**), **-ly** *adv* rein

purée /ˈpjʊəreɪ/ *n* Püree *nt*, Brei *m*

purgatory /ˈpɜ:gətrɪ/ *n* (*Relig*) Fegefeuer *nt*; (*fig*) Hölle *f*

purge /pɜ:dʒ/ *n* (*Pol*) Säuberungsaktion *f* ● *vt* reinigen; (*Pol*) säubern

puri|fication /pjʊərɪfɪˈkeɪʃn/ *n* Reinigung *f*. ~**fy** /ˈpjʊərɪfaɪ/ *vt* (*pt/pp* **-ied**) reinigen

puritanical /pjʊərɪˈtænɪkl/ *a* puritanisch

purity /ˈpjʊərɪtɪ/ *n* Reinheit *f*

purl /pɜ:l/ *n* (*Knitting*) linke Masche *f* ● *vt/i* links stricken

purple /ˈpɜ:pl/ *a* [dunkel]lila

purport /pəˈpɔ:t/ *vt* vorgeben

purpose /ˈpɜ:pəs/ *n* Zweck *m*; (*intention*) Absicht *f*; (*determination*)

Entschlossenheit *f*; **on ~** absichtlich; **to no ~** unnützerweise. **~ful** *a*, **-ly** *adv* entschlossen. **~ly** *adv* absichtlich

purr /pɜː(r)/ *vi* schnurren

purse /pɜːs/ *n* Portemonnaie *nt*; (*Amer: handbag*) Handtasche *f* ● *vt* schürzen ⟨*lips*⟩

pursue /pəˈsjuː/ *vt* verfolgen; (*fig*) nachgehen (+*dat*). **~r** /-ə(r)/ *n* Verfolger *m*

pursuit /pəˈsjuːt/ *n* Verfolgung *f*; Jagd *f*; (*pastime*) Beschäftigung *f*; **in ~** hinterher

pus /pʌs/ *n* Eiter *m*

push /pʊʃ/ *n* Stoß *m*, (*fam*) Schubs *m*; **get the ~** (*fam*) hinausfliegen ● *vt*/*i* schieben; (*press*) drücken; (*roughly*) stoßen; **be ~ed for time** (*fam*) unter Zeitdruck stehen. **~ off** *vt* hinunterstoßen ● *vi* (*fam: leave*) abhauen. **~ on** *vi* (*continue*) weitergehen/-fahren; (*with activity*) weitermachen. **~ up** *vt* hochschieben; hochtreiben ⟨*price*⟩

push: ~-button *n* Druckknopf *m*. **~-chair** *n* [Kinder]sportwagen *m*. **~-over** *n* (*fam*) Kinderspiel *nt*. **~-up** *n* (*Amer*) Liegestütz *m*

pushy /ˈpʊʃɪ/ *a* (*fam*) aufdringlich

puss /pʊs/ *n*, **pussy** /ˈpʊsɪ/ *n* Mieze *f*

put /pʊt/ *vt* (*pt*/*pp* **put**, *pres p* **putting**) tun; (*place*) setzen; (*upright*) stellen; (*flat*) legen; (*express*) ausdrücken; (*say*) sagen; (*estimate*) schätzen (**at** auf + *acc*); **~ aside** *or* **by** beiseite legen; **~ one's foot down** (*fam*) energisch werden; (*Auto*) Gas geben ● *vi* **~ to sea** auslaufen ● *a* **stay ~** dableiben. **~ away** *vt* wegräumen. **~ back** *vt* wieder hinsetzen/-stellen/-legen; zurückstellen ⟨*clock*⟩. **~ down** *vt* hinsetzen/-stellen/-legen; (*suppress*) niederschlagen; (*kill*) töten; (*write*) niederschreiben; (*attribute*) zuschreiben (**to** *dat*). **~ forward** *vt* vorbringen; vorstellen ⟨*clock*⟩. **~ in** *vt* hineinsetzen/-stellen/-legen; (*insert*) einstecken; (*submit*) einreichen ● *vi* **~ in for** beantragen. **~ off** *vt* ausmachen ⟨*light*⟩; (*postpone*) verschieben; **~ s.o. off** jdn abbestellen; (*disconcert*) jdn aus der Fassung bringen; **~ s.o. off sth** jdm etw verleiden. **~ on** *vt* anziehen ⟨*clothes, brake*⟩; sich (*dat*) aufsetzen ⟨*hat*⟩; (*Culin*) aufsetzen; anmachen ⟨*light*⟩; aufführen ⟨*play*⟩; annehmen ⟨*accent*⟩; **~ on weight** zunehmen. **~ out** *vt* hinaussetzen/-stellen/-legen; ausmachen ⟨*fire, light*⟩; ausstrecken ⟨*hand*⟩; (*disconcert*) aus der Fassung bringen; **~ s.o./oneself out** jdm/sich Umstände machen. **~ through** *vt* durchstecken; (*Teleph*) verbinden (**to** mit). **~ up** *vt* errichten ⟨*building*⟩; aufschlagen ⟨*tent*⟩; aufspannen ⟨*umbrella*⟩; anschlagen ⟨*notice*⟩; erhöhen ⟨*price*⟩; unterbringen ⟨*guest*⟩; **~ s.o. up to sth** jdn zu etw anstiften ● *vi* (*at hotel*) absteigen in (+ *dat*); **~ up with sth** sich (*dat*) etw bieten lassen

putrefy /ˈpjuːtrɪfaɪ/ *vi* (*pt*/*pp* **-ied**) verwesen

putrid /ˈpjuːtrɪd/ faulig

putty /ˈpʌtɪ/ *n* Kitt *m*

put-up /ˈpʊtʌp/ *a* **a ~ job** ein abgekartetes Spiel *nt*

puzzl|e /ˈpʌzl/ *n* Rätsel *nt*; (*jig-saw*) Puzzlespiel *nt* ● *vt* **it ~es me** es ist mir rätselhaft ● *vi* **~e over** sich (*dat*) den Kopf zerbrechen über (+ *acc*). **~ing** *a* rätselhaft

pyjamas /pəˈdʒɑːməz/ *npl* Schlafanzug *m*

pylon /ˈpaɪlən/ *n* Mast *m*

pyramid /ˈpɪrəmɪd/ *n* Pyramide *f*

python /ˈpaɪθn/ *n* Pythonschlange *f*

Q

quack[1] /kwæk/ *n* Quaken *nt* ● *vi* quaken

quack[2] *n* (*doctor*) Quacksalber *m*

quad /kwɒd/ *n* (*fam: court*) Hof *m*; **~s** *pl* = **quadruplets**

quadrangle /ˈkwɒdræŋgl/ *n* Viereck *nt*; (*court*) Hof *m*

quadruped /ˈkwɒdrʊped/ *n* Vierfüßer *m*

quadruple /ˈkwɒdrʊpl/ *a* vierfach ● *vt* vervierfachen ● *vi* sich vervierfachen. **~ts** /-plɪts/ *npl* Vierlinge *pl*

quagmire /ˈkwɒgmaɪə(r)/ *n* Sumpf *m*

quaint /kweɪnt/ *a* (**-er, -est**) malerisch; (*odd*) putzig

quake /kweɪk/ *n* (*fam*) Erdbeben *nt* ● *vi* beben; (*with fear*) zittern

Quaker /ˈkweɪkə(r)/ *n* Quäker(in) *m*(*f*)

qualif|ication /kwɒlɪfɪˈkeɪʃn/ *n* Qualifikation *f*; (*reservation*) Einschränkung *f*. **~ied** /-faɪd/ *a* qualifiziert; (*trained*) ausgebildet; (*limited*) bedingt

qualify /'kwɒlɪfaɪ/ *v* (*pt/pp* **-ied**) ● *vt* qualifizieren; (*entitle*) berechtigen; (*limit*) einschränken ● *vi* sich qualifizieren

quality /'kwɒlətɪ/ *n* Qualität *f*; (*characteristic*) Eigenschaft *f*

qualm /kwɑ:m/ *n* Bedenken *pl*

quandary /'kwɒndərɪ/ *n* Dilemma *nt*

quantity /'kwɒntətɪ/ *n* Quantität *f*, Menge *f*; **in ~** in großen Mengen

quarantine /'kwɒrənti:n/ *n* Quarantäne *f*

quarrel /'kwɒrl/ *n* Streit *m* ● *vi* (*pt/pp* **quarrelled**) sich streiten. **~some** *a* streitsüchtig

quarry[1] /'kwɒrɪ/ *n* (*prey*) Beute *f*

quarry[2] *n* Steinbruch *m*

quart /kwɔ:t/ *n* Quart *nt*

quarter /'kwɔ:tə(r)/ *n* Viertel *nt*; (*of year*) Vierteljahr *nt*; (*Amer*) 25-Cent-Stück *nt*; **~s** *pl* Quartier *nt*; **at [a] ~ to six** um Viertel vor sechs; **from all ~s** aus allen Richtungen ● *vt* vierteln; (*Mil*) einquartieren (**on** bei). **~-'final** *n* Viertelfinale *nt*

quarterly /'kwɔ:təlɪ/ *a & adv* vierteljährlich

quartet /kwɔ:'tet/ *n* Quartett *nt*

quartz /kwɔ:ts/ *n* Quarz *m*. **~ watch** *n* Quarzuhr *f*

quash /kwɒʃ/ *vt* aufheben; niederschlagen ⟨*rebellion*⟩

quaver /'kweɪvə(r)/ *n* (*Mus*) Achtelnote *f* ● *vi* zittern

quay /ki:/ *n* Kai *m*

queasy /'kwi:zɪ/ *a* **I feel ~** mir ist übel

queen /kwi:n/ *n* Königin *f*; (*Cards, Chess*) Dame *f*

queer /kwɪə(r)/ *a* (**-er, -est**) eigenartig; (*dubious*) zweifelhaft; (*ill*) unwohl; (*fam: homosexual*) schwul ● *n* (*fam*) Schwule(r) *m*

quell /kwel/ *vt* unterdrücken

quench /kwentʃ/ *vt* löschen

query /'kwɪərɪ/ *n* Frage *f*; (*question mark*) Fragezeichen *nt* ● *vt* (*pt/pp* **-ied**) in Frage stellen; reklamieren ⟨*bill*⟩

quest /kwest/ *n* Suche *f* (**for** nach)

question /'kwestʃn/ *n* Frage *f*; (*for discussion*) Thema *nt*; **out of the ~** ausgeschlossen; **without ~** ohne Frage; **the person in ~** die fragliche Person ● *vt* in Frage stellen; **~ s.o.** jdn ausfragen; ⟨*police:*⟩ jdn verhören. **~able** /-əbl/ *a* zweifelhaft. **~ mark** *n* Fragezeichen *nt*

questionnaire /kwestʃə'neə(r)/ *n* Fragebogen *m*

queue /kju:/ *n* Schlange *f* ● *vi* **~ [up]** Schlange stehen, sich anstellen (**for** nach)

quibble /'kwɪbl/ *vi* Haarspalterei treiben

quick /kwɪk/ *a* (**-er, -est**), **-ly** *adv* schnell; **be ~!** mach schnell! **have a ~ meal** schnell etwas essen ● *adv* schnell ● *n* **cut to the ~** (*fig*) bis ins Mark getroffen. **~en** *vt* beschleunigen ● *vi* sich beschleunigen

quick: ~sand *n* Treibsand *m*. **~-tempered** *a* aufbrausend

quid /kwɪd/ *n inv* (*fam*) Pfund *nt*

quiet /'kwaɪət/ *a* (**-er, -est**), **-ly** *adv* still; (*calm*) ruhig; (*soft*) leise; **keep ~ about** (*fam*) nichts sagen von ● *n* Stille *f*; Ruhe *f*; **on the ~** heimlich

quiet|en /'kwaɪətn/ *vt* beruhigen ● *vi* **~en down** ruhig werden. **~ness** *n* (*see* **quiet**) Stille *f*; Ruhe *f*

quill /kwɪl/ *n* Feder *f*; (*spine*) Stachel *m*

quilt /kwɪlt/ *n* Steppdecke *f*. **~ed** *a* Stepp-

quince /kwɪns/ *n* Quitte *f*

quins /kwɪnz/ *npl* (*fam*) = **quintuplets**

quintet /kwɪn'tet/ *n* Quintett *nt*

quintuplets /'kwɪntjʊplɪts/ *npl* Fünflinge *pl*

quip /kwɪp/ *n* Scherz *m* ● *vi* (*pt/pp* **quipped**) scherzen

quirk /kwɜ:k/ *n* Eigenart *f*

quit /kwɪt/ *v* (*pt/pp* **quitted** *or* **quit**) ● *vt* verlassen; (*give up*) aufgeben; **~ doing sth** aufhören, etw zu tun ● *vi* gehen; **give s.o. notice to ~** jdm die Wohnung kündigen

quite /kwaɪt/ *adv* ganz; (*really*) wirklich; **~ [so]!** genau! **~ a few** ziemlich viele

quits /kwɪts/ *a* quitt

quiver /'kwɪvə(r)/ *vi* zittern

quiz /kwɪz/ *n* Quiz *nt* ● *vt* (*pt/pp* **quizzed**) ausfragen. **~zical** *a*, **-ly** *adv* fragend

quorum /'kwɔ:rəm/ *n* **have a ~** beschlußfähig sein

quota /'kwəʊtə/ *n* Anteil *m*; (*Comm*) Kontingent *nt*

quotation /kwəʊ'teɪʃn/ *n* Zitat *nt*; (*price*) Kostenvoranschlag *m*; (*of shares*) Notierung *f*. **~ marks** *npl* Anführungszeichen *pl*

quote /kwəʊt/ *n* (*fam*) = **quotation; in ~s** in Anführungszeichen ● *vt/i* zitieren

R

rabbi /'ræbaɪ/ *n* Rabbiner *m*; (*title*) Rabbi *m*
rabbit /'ræbɪt/ *n* Kaninchen *nt*
rabble /'ræbl/ *n* **the ~** der Pöbel
rabid /'ræbɪd/ *a* fanatisch; ⟨*animal*⟩ tollwütig
rabies /'reɪbi:z/ *n* Tollwut *f*
race¹ /reɪs/ *n* Rasse *f*
race² *n* Rennen *nt*; (*fig*) Wettlauf *m* ● *vi* [am Rennen] teilnehmen; ⟨*athlete, horse:*⟩ laufen; (*fam: rush*) rasen ● *vt* um die Wette laufen mit; an einem Rennen teilnehmen lassen ⟨*horse*⟩
race: ~course *n* Rennbahn *f*. **~horse** *n* Rennpferd *nt*. **~-track** *n* Rennbahn *f*
racial /'reɪʃl/ *a*, **-ly** *adv* rassisch; ⟨*discrimination, minority*⟩ Rassen-
racing /'reɪsɪŋ/ *n* Rennsport *m*; (*horse-*) Pferderennen *nt*. **~ car** *n* Rennwagen *m*. **~ driver** *n* Rennfahrer *m*
racis|m /'reɪsɪzm/ *n* Rassismus *m*. **~t** /-ɪst/ *a* rassistisch ● *n* Rassist *m*
rack¹ /ræk/ *n* Ständer *m*; (*for plates*) Gestell *nt* ● *vt* **~ one's brains** sich (*dat*) den Kopf zerbrechen
rack² *n* **go to ~ and ruin** verfallen; (*fig*) herunterkommen
racket¹ /'rækɪt/ *n* (*Sport*) Schläger *m*
racket² *n* (*din*) Krach *m*; (*swindle*) Schwindelgeschäft *nt*
racy /'reɪsɪ/ *a* (**-ier, -iest**) schwungvoll; (*risqué*) gewagt
radar /'reɪdɑ:(r)/ *n* Radar *m*
radian|ce /'reɪdɪəns/ *n* Strahlen *nt*. **~t** *a*, **-ly** *adv* strahlend
radiat|e /'reɪdɪeɪt/ *vt* ausstrahlen ● *vi* ⟨*heat:*⟩ ausgestrahlt werden; ⟨*roads:*⟩ strahlenförmig ausgehen. **~ion** /-'eɪʃn/ *n* Strahlung *f*
radiator /'reɪdɪeɪtə(r)/ *n* Heizkörper *m*; (*Auto*) Kühler *m*
radical /'rædɪkl/ *a*, **-ly** *adv* radikal ● *n* Radikale(r) *m/f*
radio /'reɪdɪəʊ/ *n* Radio *nt*; **by ~** über Funk ● *vt* funken ⟨*message*⟩
radio|'active *a* radioaktiv. **~ac'tivity** *n* Radioaktivität *f*
radiography /reɪdɪ'ɒgrəfɪ/ *n* Röntgenographie *f*
'radio ham *n* Hobbyfunker *m*
radio'therapy *n* Strahlenbehandlung *f*
radish /'rædɪʃ/ *n* Radieschen *nt*
radius /'reɪdɪəs/ *n* (*pl* **-dii** /-dɪaɪ/) Radius *m*, Halbmesser *m*
raffle /'ræfl/ *n* Tombola *f* ● *vt* verlosen
raft /rɑ:ft/ *n* Floß *nt*
rafter /'rɑ:ftə(r)/ *n* Dachsparren *m*
rag¹ /ræg/ *n* Lumpen *m*; (*pej: newspaper*) Käseblatt *nt*; **in ~s** in Lumpen
rag² *vt* (*pt/pp* **ragged**) (*fam*) aufziehen
rage /reɪdʒ/ *n* Wut *f*; **all the ~** (*fam*) der letzte Schrei ● *vi* rasen; ⟨*storm:*⟩ toben
ragged /'rægɪd/ *a* zerlumpt; ⟨*edge*⟩ ausgefranst
raid /reɪd/ *n* Überfall *m*; (*Mil*) Angriff *m*; (*police*) Razzia *f* ● *vt* überfallen; (*Mil*) angreifen; ⟨*police:*⟩ eine Razzia durchführen in (+ *dat*); (*break in*) eindringen in (+ *acc*). **~er** *n* Eindringling *m*; (*of bank*) Bankräuber *m*
rail /reɪl/ *n* Schiene *f*; (*pole*) Stange *f*; (*hand~*) Handlauf *m*; (*Naut*) Reling *f*; **by ~** mit der Bahn
railings /'reɪlɪŋz/ *npl* Geländer *nt*
'railroad *n* (*Amer*) = **railway**
'railway *n* [Eisen]bahn *f*. **~man** *n* Eisenbahner *m*. **~ station** *n* Bahnhof *m*
rain /reɪn/ *n* Regen *m* ● *vi* regnen
rain: ~bow *n* Regenbogen *m*. **~check** *n* (*Amer*) **take a ~check on** aufschieben. **~coat** *n* Regenmantel *m*. **~fall** *n* Niederschlag *m*
rainy /'reɪnɪ/ *a* (**-ier, -iest**) regnerisch
raise /reɪz/ *n* (*Amer*) Lohnerhöhung *f* ● *vt* erheben; (*upright*) aufrichten; (*make higher*) erhöhen; (*lift*) [hoch]heben; lüften ⟨*hat*⟩; [auf]ziehen ⟨*children, animals*⟩; aufwerfen ⟨*question*⟩; aufbringen ⟨*money*⟩
raisin /'reɪzn/ *n* Rosine *f*
rake /reɪk/ *n* Harke *f*, Rechen *m* ● *vt* harken, rechen. **~ up** *vt* zusammenharken; (*fam*) wieder aufrühren
'rake-off *n* (*fam*) Prozente *pl*
rally /'rælɪ/ *n* Versammlung *f*; (*Auto*) Rallye *f*; (*Tennis*) Ballwechsel *m* ● *vt* sammeln ● *vi* sich sammeln; (*recover strength*) sich erholen
ram /ræm/ *n* Schafbock *m*; (*Astr*) Widder *m* ● *vt* (*pt/pp* **rammed**) rammen
rambl|e /'ræmbl/ *n* Wanderung *f* ● *vi* wandern; (*in speech*) irrereden. **~er** *n* Wanderer *m*; (*rose*) Kletterrose *f*.

~ing *a* weitschweifig; ⟨*club*⟩ Wander-
ramp /ræmp/ *n* Rampe *f*; (*Aviat*) Gangway *f*
rampage[1] /ˈræmpeɪdʒ/ *n* **be/go on the ~** randalieren
rampage[2] /ræmˈpeɪdʒ/ *vi* randalieren
rampant /ˈræmpənt/ *a* weit verbreitet; (*in heraldry*) aufgerichtet
rampart /ˈræmpɑːt/ *n* Wall *m*
ramshackle /ˈræmʃækl/ *a* baufällig
ran /ræn/ *see* **run**
ranch /rɑːntʃ/ *n* Ranch *f*
rancid /ˈrænsɪd/ *a* ranzig
rancour /ˈræŋkə(r)/ *n* Groll *m*
random /ˈrændəm/ *a* willkürlich; **a ~ sample** eine Stichprobe ● *n* **at ~** aufs Geratewohl; ⟨*choose*⟩ willkürlich
randy /ˈrændɪ/ *a* (**-ier, -iest**) (*fam*) geil
rang /ræŋ/ *see* **ring**[2]
range /reɪndʒ/ *n* Serie *f*, Reihe *f*; (*Comm*) Auswahl *f*, Angebot *nt* (**of** an + *dat*); (*of mountains*) Kette *f*; (*Mus*) Umfang *m*; (*distance*) Reichweite *f*; (*for shooting*) Schießplatz *m*; (*stove*) Kohlenherd *m*; **at a ~ of** auf eine Entfernung von ● *vi* reichen; **~ from ... to** gehen von ... bis. **~r** *n* Aufseher *m*
rank[1] /ræŋk/ *n* (*row*) Reihe *f*; (*Mil*) Rang *m*; (*social position*) Stand *m*; **the ~ and file** die breite Masse; **the ~s** *pl* die gemeinen Soldaten ● *vt/i* einstufen; **~ among** zählen zu
rank[2] *a* (*bad*) übel; ⟨*plants*⟩ üppig; (*fig*) kraß
ransack /ˈrænsæk/ *vt* durchwühlen; (*pillage*) plündern
ransom /ˈrænsəm/ *n* Lösegeld *nt*; **hold s.o. to ~** Lösegeld für jdn fordern
rant /rænt/ *vi* rasen
rap /ræp/ *n* Klopfen *nt*; (*blow*) Schlag *m* ● *v* (*pt/pp* **rapped**) ● *vt* klopfen auf (+ *acc*) ● *vi* **~ at/on** klopfen an/auf (+ *acc*)
rape[1] /reɪp/ *n* (*Bot*) Raps *m*
rape[2] *n* Vergewaltigung *f* ● *vt* vergewaltigen
rapid /ˈræpɪd/ *a*, **-ly** *adv* schnell. **~ity** /rəˈpɪdətɪ/ *n* Schnelligkeit *f*
rapids /ˈræpɪdz/ *npl* Stromschnellen *pl*
rapist /ˈreɪpɪst/ *n* Vergewaltiger *m*
rapport /ræˈpɔː(r)/ *n* [innerer] Kontakt *m*
rapt /ræpt/ *a*, **-ly** *adv* gespannt; ⟨*look*⟩ andächtig; **~ in** versunken in (+ *acc*)
raptur|e /ˈræptʃə(r)/ *n* Entzücken *nt*. **~ous** /-rəs/ *a*, **-ly** *adv* begeistert
rare[1] /reə(r)/ *a* (**-r, -st**), **-ly** *adv* selten
rare[2] *a* (*Culin*) englisch gebraten
rarefied /ˈreərɪfaɪd/ *a* dünn
rarity /ˈreərətɪ/ *n* Seltenheit *f*
rascal /ˈrɑːskl/ *n* Schlingel *m*
rash[1] /ræʃ/ *n* (*Med*) Ausschlag *m*
rash[2] *a* (**-er, -est**), **-ly** *adv* voreilig
rasher /ˈræʃə(r)/ *n* Speckscheibe *f*
rasp /rɑːsp/ *n* Raspel *f*
raspberry /ˈrɑːzbərɪ/ *n* Himbeere *f*
rat /ræt/ *n* Ratte *f*; (*fam: person*) Schuft *m*; **smell a ~** (*fam*) Lunte riechen
rate /reɪt/ *n* Rate *f*; (*speed*) Tempo *nt*; (*of payment*) Satz *m*; (*of exchange*) Kurs *m*; **~s** *pl* (*taxes*) ≈ Grundsteuer *f*; **at any ~** auf jeden Fall; **at this ~** auf diese Weise ● *vt* einschätzen; **~ among** zählen zu ● *vi* **~ as** gelten als
rather /ˈrɑːðə(r)/ *adv* lieber; (*fairly*) ziemlich; **~!** und ob!
rati|fication /rætɪfɪˈkeɪʃn/ *n* Ratifizierung *f*. **~fy** /ˈrætɪfaɪ/ *vt* (*pt/pp* **-ied**) ratifizieren
rating /ˈreɪtɪŋ/ *n* Einschätzung *f*; (*class*) Klasse *f*; (*sailor*) [einfacher] Matrose *m*; **~s** *pl* (*Radio, TV*) ≈ Einschaltquote *f*
ratio /ˈreɪʃɪəʊ/ *n* Verhältnis *nt*
ration /ˈræʃn/ *n* Ration *f* ● *vt* rationieren
rational /ˈræʃənl/ *a*, **-ly** *adv* rational. **~ize** *vt/i* rationalisieren
'rat race *n* (*fam*) Konkurrenzkampf *m*
rattle /ˈrætl/ *n* Rasseln *nt*; (*of china, glass*) Klirren *nt*; (*of windows*) Klappern *nt*; (*toy*) Klapper *f* ● *vi* rasseln; klirren; klappern ● *vt* rasseln mit; (*shake*) schütteln. **~ off** *vt* herunterrasseln
'rattlesnake *n* Klapperschlange *f*
raucous /ˈrɔːkəs/ *a* rauh
ravage /ˈrævɪdʒ/ *vt* verwüsten, verheeren
rave /reɪv/ *vi* toben; **~ about** schwärmen von
raven /ˈreɪvn/ *n* Rabe *m*
ravenous /ˈrævənəs/ *a* heißhungrig
ravine /rəˈviːn/ *n* Schlucht *f*
raving /ˈreɪvɪŋ/ *a* **~ mad** (*fam*) total verrückt
ravishing /ˈrævɪʃɪŋ/ *a* hinreißend

raw /rɔ:/ *a* (**-er, -est**) roh; (*not processed*) Roh-; ⟨*skin*⟩ wund; ⟨*weather*⟩ naßkalt; (*inexperienced*) unerfahren; **get a ~ deal** (*fam*) schlecht wegkommen. **~ ma'terials** *npl* Rohstoffe *pl*

ray /reɪ/ *n* Strahl *m*; **~ of hope** Hoffnungsschimmer *m*

raze /reɪz/ *vt* **~ to the ground** dem Erdboden gleichmachen

razor /'reɪzə(r)/ *n* Rasierapparat *m*. **~ blade** *n* Rasierklinge *f*

re /ri:/ *prep* betreffs (+ *gen*)

reach /ri:tʃ/ *n* Reichweite *f*; (*of river*) Strecke *f*; **within/out of ~** in/außer Reichweite; **within easy ~** leicht erreichbar ● *vt* erreichen; (*arrive at*) ankommen in (+ *dat*); (**~** *as far as*) reichen bis zu; kommen zu ⟨*decision, conclusion*⟩; (*pass*) reichen ● *vi* reichen (**to** bis zu); **~ for** greifen nach; **I can't ~** ich komme nicht daran

re'act /rɪ-/ *vi* reagieren (**to** auf + *acc*)

re'action /rɪ-/ *n* Reaktion *f*. **~ary** *a* reaktionär

reactor /rɪ'æktə(r)/ *n* Reaktor *m*

read /ri:d/ *vt/i* (*pt/pp* **read** /red/) lesen; (*aloud*) vorlesen (**to** *dat*); (*Univ*) studieren; ablesen ⟨*meter*⟩. **~ out** *vt* vorlesen

readable /'ri:dəbl/ *a* lesbar

reader /'ri:də(r)/ *n* Leser(in) *m*(*f*); (*book*) Lesebuch *nt*

readi|ly /'redɪlɪ/ *adv* bereitwillig; (*easily*) leicht. **~ness** *n* Bereitschaft *f*; **in ~ness** bereit

reading /'ri:dɪŋ/ *n* Lesen *nt*; (*Pol, Relig*) Lesung *f*

rea'djust /ri:-/ *vt* neu einstellen ● *vi* sich umstellen (**to** auf + *acc*)

ready /'redɪ/ *a* (**-ier, -iest**) fertig; (*willing*) bereit; (*quick*) schnell; **get ~** sich fertigmachen; (*prepare to*) sich bereitmachen

ready: ~-'made *a* fertig. **~ 'money** *n* Bargeld *nt*. **~-to-'wear** *a* Konfektions-

real /rɪəl/ *a* wirklich; (*genuine*) echt; (*actual*) eigentlich ● *adv* (*Amer, fam*) echt. **~ estate** *n* Immobilien *pl*

realis|m /'rɪəlɪzm/ *n* Realismus *m*. **~t** /-lɪst/ *n* Realist *m*. **~tic** /-'lɪstɪk/ *a*, **-ally** *adv* realistisch

reality /rɪ'ælətɪ/ *n* Wirklichkeit *f*, Realität *f*

realization /rɪəlaɪ'zeɪʃn/ *n* Erkenntnis *f*

realize /'rɪəlaɪz/ *vt* einsehen; (*become aware*) gewahr werden; verwirklichen ⟨*hopes, plans*⟩; (*Comm*) realisieren; einbringen ⟨*price*⟩; **I didn't ~** das wußte ich nicht

really /'rɪəlɪ/ *adv* wirklich; (*actually*) eigentlich

realm /relm/ *n* Reich *nt*

realtor /'ri:əltə(r)/ *n* (*Amer*) Immobilienmakler *m*

reap /ri:p/ *vt* ernten

reap'pear /ri:-/ *vi* wiederkommen

rear[1] /rɪə(r)/ *a* Hinter-; (*Auto*) Heck- ● *n* **the ~** der hintere Teil; **from the ~** von hinten

rear[2] *vt* aufziehen ● *vi* **~ [up]** ⟨*horse:*⟩ sich aufbäumen

'rear-light *n* Rücklicht *nt*

re'arm /ri:-/ *vi* wieder aufrüsten

rear'range /ri:-/ *vt* umstellen

rear-view 'mirror *n* (*Auto*) Rückspiegel *m*

reason /'ri:zn/ *n* Grund *m*; (*good sense*) Vernunft *f*; (*ability to think*) Verstand *m*; **within ~** in vernünftigen Grenzen ● *vi* argumentieren; **~ with** vernünftig reden mit. **~able** /-əbl/ *a* vernünftig; (*not expensive*) preiswert. **~ably** /-əblɪ/ *adv* (*fairly*) ziemlich

reas'sur|ance /ri:-/ *n* Beruhigung *f*; Versicherung *f*. **~e** *vt* beruhigen; **~e s.o. of sth** jdm etw (*gen*) versichern

rebate /'ri:beɪt/ *n* Rückzahlung *f*; (*discount*) Nachlaß *m*

rebel[1] /'rebl/ *n* Rebell *m*

rebel[2] /rɪ'bel/ *vi* (*pt/pp* **rebelled**) rebellieren. **~lion** /-ɪən/ *n* Rebellion *f*. **~lious** /-ɪəs/ *a* rebellisch

re'bound[1] /rɪ-/ *vi* abprallen

'rebound[2] /ri:-/ *n* Rückprall *m*

rebuff /rɪ'bʌf/ *n* Abweisung *f* ● *vt* abweisen; eine Abfuhr erteilen (**s.o.** jdm)

re'build /ri:-/ *vt* (*pt/pp* **-built**) wieder aufbauen; (*fig*) wiederaufbauen

rebuke /rɪ'bju:k/ *n* Tadel *m* ● *vt* tadeln

rebuttal /rɪ'bʌtl/ *n* Widerlegung *f*

re'call /rɪ-/ *n* Erinnerung *f*; **beyond ~** unwiderruflich ● *vt* zurückrufen; abberufen ⟨*diplomat*⟩; vorzeitig einberufen ⟨*parliament*⟩; (*remember*) sich erinnern an (+ *acc*)

recant /rɪ'kænt/ *vi* widerrufen

recap /'ri:kæp/ *vt/i* (*fam*) = **recapitulate**

recapitulate /ri:kə'pɪtjʊleɪt/ *vt/i* zusammenfassen; rekapitulieren

re'capture /ri:-/ *vt* wieder gefangennehmen ⟨*person*⟩; wieder einfangen ⟨*animal*⟩

reced|e /rɪ'si:d/ *vi* zurückgehen. **~ing** *a* ⟨*forehead, chin*⟩ fliehend; **~ing hair** Stirnglatze *f*

receipt /rɪ'si:t/ *n* Quittung *f*; (*receiving*) Empfang *m*; **~s** *pl* (*Comm*) Einnahmen *pl*

receive /rɪ'si:v/ *vt* erhalten, bekommen; empfangen ⟨*guests*⟩. **~r** *n* (*Teleph*) Hörer *m*; (*Radio, TV*) Empfänger *m*; (*of stolen goods*) Hehler *m*

recent /'ri:sənt/ *a* kürzlich erfolgte(r,s). **~ly** *adv* in letzter Zeit; (*the other day*) kürzlich, vor kurzem

receptacle /rɪ'septəkl/ *n* Behälter *m*

reception /rɪ'sepʃn/ *n* Empfang *m*; **~ [desk]** (*in hotel*) Rezeption *f*. **~ist** *n* Empfangsdame *f*

receptive /rɪ'septɪv/ *a* aufnahmefähig; **~ to** empfänglich für

recess /rɪ'ses/ *n* Nische *f*; (*holiday*) Ferien *pl*; (*Amer, Sch*) Pause *f*

recession /rɪ'seʃn/ *n* Rezession *f*

re'charge /ri:-/ *vt* [wieder] aufladen

recipe /'resəpɪ/ *n* Rezept *nt*

recipient /rɪ'sɪpɪənt/ *n* Empfänger *m*

recipro|cal /rɪ'sɪprəkl/ *a* gegenseitig. **~cate** /-keɪt/ *vt* erwidern

recital /rɪ'saɪtl/ *n* (*of poetry, songs*) Vortrag *m*; (*on piano*) Konzert *nt*

recite /rɪ'saɪt/ *vt* aufsagen; (*before audience*) vortragen; (*list*) aufzählen

reckless /'reklɪs/ *a*, **-ly** *adv* leichtsinnig; (*careless*) rücksichtslos. **~ness** *n* Leichtsinn *m*; Rücksichtslosigkeit *f*

reckon /'rekən/ *vt* rechnen; (*consider*) glauben ● *vi* **~ on/with** rechnen mit

re'claim /rɪ-/ *vt* zurückfordern; zurückgewinnen ⟨*land*⟩

reclin|e /rɪ'klaɪn/ *vi* liegen. **~ing seat** *n* Liegesitz *m*

recluse /rɪ'klu:s/ *n* Einsiedler(in) *m*(*f*)

recognition /rekəg'nɪʃn/ *n* Erkennen *nt*; (*acknowledgement*) Anerkennung *f*; **in ~** als Anerkennung (**of** *gen*); **be beyond ~** nicht wiederzuerkennen sein

recognize /'rekəgnaɪz/ *vt* erkennen; (*know again*) wiedererkennen; (*acknowledge*) anerkennen

re'coil /rɪ-/ *vi* zurückschnellen; (*in fear*) zurückschrecken

recollect /rekə'lekt/ *vt* sich erinnern an (+ *acc*). **~ion** /-ekʃn/ *n* Erinnerung *f*

recommend /rekə'mend/ *vt* empfehlen. **~ation** /-'deɪʃn/ *n* Empfehlung *f*

recompense /'rekəmpens/ *n* Entschädigung *f* ● *vt* entschädigen

recon|cile /'rekənsaɪl/ *vt* versöhnen; **~cile oneself to** sich abfinden mit. **~ciliation** /-sɪlɪ'eɪʃn/ *n* Versöhnung *f*

recon'dition /ri:-/ *vt* generalüberholen. **~ed engine** *n* Austauschmotor *m*

reconnaissance /rɪ'kɒnɪsns/ *n* (*Mil*) Aufklärung *f*

reconnoitre /rekə'nɔɪtə(r)/ *vi* (*pres p* **-tring**) auf Erkundung ausgehen

recon'sider /ri:-/ *vt* sich (*dat*) noch einmal überlegen

recon'struct /ri:-/ *vt* wieder aufbauen; rekonstruieren ⟨*crime*⟩. **~ion** *n* Wiederaufbau *m*; Rekonstruktion *f*

record¹ /rɪ'kɔ:d/ *vt* aufzeichnen; (*register*) registrieren; (*on tape*) aufnehmen

record² /'rekɔ:d/ *n* Aufzeichnung *f*; (*Jur*) Protokoll *nt*; (*Mus*) [Schall]-platte *f*; (*Sport*) Rekord *m*; **~s** *pl* Unterlagen *pl*; **keep a ~ of** sich (*dat*) notieren; **off the ~** inoffiziell; **have a [criminal] ~** vorbestraft sein

recorder /rɪ'kɔ:də(r)/ *n* (*Mus*) Blockflöte *f*

recording /rɪ'kɔ:dɪŋ/ *n* Aufzeichnung *f*, Aufnahme *f*

'record-player *n* Plattenspieler *m*

recount /rɪ'kaʊnt/ *vt* erzählen

re-'count¹ /ri:-/ *vt* nachzählen

're-count² /ri:-/ *n* (*Pol*) Nachzählung *f*

recoup /rɪ'ku:p/ *vt* wiedereinbringen; ausgleichen ⟨*losses*⟩

recourse /rɪ'kɔ:s/ *n* **have ~ to** Zuflucht nehmen zu

re-'cover /ri:-/ *vt* neu beziehen

recover /rɪ'kʌvə(r)/ *vt* zurückbekommen; bergen ⟨*wreck*⟩ ● *vi* sich erholen. **~y** *n* Wiedererlangung *f*; Bergung *f*; (*of health*) Erholung *f*

recreation /rekrɪ'eɪʃn/ *n* Erholung *f*; (*hobby*) Hobby *nt*. **~al** *a* Freizeit-; **be ~al** erholsam sein

recrimination /rɪkrɪmɪ'neɪʃn/ *n* Gegenbeschuldigung *f*

recruit /rɪ'kru:t/ *n* (*Mil*) Rekrut *m*; **new ~** (*member*) neues Mitglied *nt*; (*worker*) neuer Mitarbeiter *m* ● *vt* rekrutieren; anwerben ⟨*staff*⟩.

~ment *n* Rekrutierung *f*; Anwerbung *f*
rectang|le /'rektæŋgl/ *n* Rechteck *nt*. **~ular** /-'tæŋgjʊlə(r)/ *a* rechteckig
rectify /'rektɪfaɪ/ *vt* (*pt/pp* **-ied**) berichtigen
rector /'rektə(r)/ *n* Pfarrer *m*; (*Univ*) Rektor *m*. **~y** *n* Pfarrhaus *nt*
recuperat|e /rɪ'kju:pəreɪt/ *vi* sich erholen. **~ion** /-'reɪʃn/ *n* Erholung *f*
recur /rɪ'kɜ:(r)/ *vi* (*pt/pp* **recurred**) sich wiederholen; ⟨*illness:*⟩ wiederkehren
recurren|ce /rɪ'kʌrəns/ *n* Wiederkehr *f*. **~t** *a* wiederkehrend
recycle /ri:'saɪkl/ *vt* wiederverwerten. **~d paper** *n* Umweltschutzpapier *nt*
red /red/ *a* (**redder, reddest**) rot ● *n* Rot *nt*. **~'currant** *n* rote Johannisbeere *f*
redd|en /'redn/ *vt* röten ● *vi* rot werden. **~ish** *a* rötlich
re'decorate /ri:-/ *vt* renovieren; (*paint*) neu streichen; (*wallpaper*) neu tapezieren
redeem /rɪ'di:m/ *vt* einlösen; (*Relig*) erlösen
redemption /rɪ'dempʃn/ *n* Erlösung *f*
rede'ploy /ri:-/ *vt* an anderer Stelle einsetzen
red: ~-haired *a* rothaarig. **~-'handed** *a* **catch s.o. ~-handed** jdn auf frischer Tat ertappen. **~ 'herring** *n* falsche Spur *f*. **~-hot** *a* glühend heiß. **R~ 'Indian** *n* Indianer(in) *m*(*f*)
redi'rect /ri:-/ *vt* nachsenden ⟨*letter*⟩; umleiten ⟨*traffic*⟩
red: ~ 'light *n* (*Auto*) rote Ampel *f*. **~ness** *n* Röte *f*
re'do /ri:-/ *vt* (*pt* **-did**, *pp* **-done**) noch einmal machen
re'double /ri:-/ *vt* verdoppeln
redress /rɪ'dres/ *n* Entschädigung *f* ● *vt* wiedergutmachen; wiederherstellen ⟨*balance*⟩
red 'tape *n* (*fam*) Bürokratie *f*
reduc|e /rɪ'dju:s/ *vt* verringern, vermindern; (*in size*) verkleinern; ermäßigen ⟨*costs*⟩; herabsetzen ⟨*price, goods*⟩; (*Culin*) einkochen lassen. **~tion** /-'dʌkʃn/ *n* Verringerung *f*; (*in price*) Ermäßigung *f*; (*in size*) Verkleinerung *f*
redundan|cy /rɪ'dʌndənsɪ/ *n* Beschäftigungslosigkeit *f*; (*payment*) Abfindung *f*. **~t** *a* überflüssig; **make ~t** entlassen; **be made ~t** beschäftigungslos werden
reed /ri:d/ *n* [Schilf]rohr *nt*; **~s** *pl* Schilf *nt*
reef /ri:f/ *n* Riff *nt*
reek /ri:k/ *vi* riechen (**of** nach)
reel /ri:l/ *n* Rolle *f*, Spule *f* ● *vi* (*stagger*) taumeln ● *vt* **~ off** (*fig*) herunterrasseln
refectory /rɪ'fektərɪ/ *n* Refektorium *nt*; (*Univ*) Mensa *f*
refer /rɪ'fɜ:(r)/ *v* (*pt/pp* **referred**) ● *vt* verweisen (**to** an + *acc*); übergeben, weiterleiten ⟨*matter*⟩ (**to** an + *acc*) ● *vi* **~ to** sich beziehen auf (+ *acc*); (*mention*) erwähnen; (*concern*) betreffen; (*consult*) sich wenden an (+ *acc*); nachschlagen in (+ *dat*) ⟨*book*⟩; **are you ~ring to me?** meinen Sie mich?
referee /refə'ri:/ *n* Schiedsrichter *m*; (*Boxing*) Ringrichter *m*; (*for job*) Referenz *f* ● *vt/i* (*pt/pp* **refereed**) Schiedsrichter/Ringrichter sein (bei)
reference /'refərəns/ *n* Erwähnung *f*; (*in book*) Verweis *m*; (*for job*) Referenz *f*; (*Comm*) **'your ~'** 'Ihr Zeichen'; **with ~ to** in bezug auf (+ *acc*); (*in letter*) unter Bezugnahme auf (+ *acc*); **make [a] ~ to** erwähnen. **~ book** *n* Nachschlagewerk *nt*. **~ number** *n* Aktenzeichen *nt*
referendum /refə'rendəm/ *n* Volksabstimmung *f*
re'fill[1] /ri:-/ *vt* nachfüllen
'refill[2] /ri:-/ *n* (*for pen*) Ersatzmine *f*
refine /rɪ'faɪn/ *vt* raffinieren. **~d** *a* fein, vornehm. **~ment** *n* Vornehmheit *f*; (*Techn*) Verfeinerung *f*. **~ry** /-ərɪ/ *n* Raffinerie *f*
reflect /rɪ'flekt/ *vt* reflektieren; ⟨*mirror:*⟩ [wider]spiegeln; **be ~ed in** sich spiegeln in (+ *dat*) ● *vi* nachdenken (**on** über + *acc*); **~ badly upon s.o.** (*fig*) jdn in ein schlechtes Licht stellen. **~ion** /-ekʃn/ *n* Reflexion *f*; (*image*) Spiegelbild *nt*; **on ~ion** nach nochmaliger Überlegung. **~ive** /-ɪv/ *a*, **-ly** *adv* nachdenklich. **~or** *n* Rückstrahler *m*
reflex /'ri:fleks/ *n* Reflex *m* ● *attrib* Reflex-
reflexive /rɪ'fleksɪv/ *a* reflexiv
reform /rɪ'fɔ:m/ *n* Reform *f* ● *vt* reformieren ● *vi* sich bessern. **R~ation** /refə'meɪʃn/ *n* (*Relig*) Reformation *f*. **~er** *n* Reformer *m*; (*Relig*) Reformator *m*

refract /rɪ'frækt/ *vt* (*Phys*) brechen

refrain[1] /rɪ'freɪn/ *n* Refrain *m*

refrain[2] *vi* ~ **from doing sth** etw nicht tun

refresh /rɪ'freʃ/ *vt* erfrischen. **~ing** *a* erfrischend. **~ments** *npl* Erfrischungen *pl*

refrigerat|e /rɪ'frɪdʒəreɪt/ *vt* kühlen. **~or** *n* Kühlschrank *m*

re'fuel /riː-/ *v* (*pt/pp* **-fuelled**) *vt/i* auftanken

refuge /'refjuːdʒ/ *n* Zuflucht *f*; **take ~ in** Zuflucht nehmen in (+ *dat*)

refugee /refjʊ'dʒiː/ *n* Flüchtling *m*

'refund[1] /riː-/ **get a ~** sein Geld zurückbekommen

re'fund[2] /rɪ-/ *vt* zurückerstatten

refurbish /riː'fɜːbɪʃ/ *vt* renovieren

refusal /rɪ'fjuːzl/ *n* (*see* **refuse**[1]) Ablehnung *f*; Weigerung *f*

refuse[1] /rɪ'fjuːz/ *vt* ablehnen; (*not grant*) verweigern; **~ to do sth** sich weigern, etw zu tun ● *vi* ablehnen; sich weigern

refuse[2] /'refjuːs/ *n* Müll *m*, Abfall *m*. **~ collection** *n* Müllabfuhr *f*

refute /rɪ'fjuːt/ *vt* widerlegen

re'gain /rɪ-/ *vt* wiedergewinnen

regal /'riːgl/ *a*, **-ly** *adv* königlich

regalia /rɪ'geɪlɪə/ *npl* Insignien *pl*

regard /rɪ'gɑːd/ *n* (*heed*) Rücksicht *f*; (*respect*) Achtung *f*; **~s** *pl* Grüße *pl*; **with ~ to** in bezug auf (+ *acc*) ● *vt* ansehen, betrachten (**as** als); **as ~s** in bezug auf (+ *acc*). **~ing** *prep* bezüglich (+ *gen*). **~less** *adv* ohne Rücksicht (**of** auf + *acc*)

regatta /rɪ'gætə/ *n* Regatta *f*

regenerate /rɪ'dʒenəreɪt/ *vt* regenerieren ● *vi* sich regenerieren

regime /reɪ'ʒiːm/ *n* Regime *nt*

regiment /'redʒɪmənt/ *n* Regiment *nt*. **~al** /-'mentl/ *a* Regiments-. **~ation** /-'teɪʃn/ *n* Reglementierung *f*

region /'riːdʒən/ *n* Region *f*; **in the ~ of** (*fig*) ungefähr. **~al** *a*, **-ly** *adv* regional

register /'redʒɪstə(r)/ *n* Register *nt*; (*Sch*) Anwesenheitsliste *f* ● *vt* registrieren; (*report*) anmelden; einschreiben ⟨*letter*⟩; aufgeben ⟨*luggage*⟩ ● *vi* (*report*) sich anmelden; **it didn't ~** (*fig*) ich habe es nicht registriert

registrar /redʒɪ'strɑː(r)/ *n* Standesbeamte(r) *m*

registration /redʒɪ'streɪʃn/ *n* Registrierung *f*; Anmeldung *f*. **~ number** *n* Autonummer *f*

registry office /'redʒɪstrɪ-/ *n* Standesamt *nt*

regret /rɪ'gret/ *n* Bedauern *nt* ● *vt* (*pt/pp* **regretted**) bedauern. **~fully** *adv* mit Bedauern

regrettab|le /rɪ'gretəbl/ *a* bedauerlich. **~ly** *adv* bedauerlicherweise

regular /'regjʊlə(r)/ *a*, **-ly** *adv* regelmäßig; (*usual*) üblich; (*Mil*) Berufs- ● *n* Berufssoldat *m*; (*in pub*) Stammgast *m*; (*in shop*) Stammkunde *m*. **~ity** /-'lærətɪ/ *n* Regelmäßigkeit *f*

regulat|e /'regjʊleɪt/ *vt* regulieren. **~ion** /-'leɪʃn/ *n* (*rule*) Vorschrift *f*

rehabilitat|e /riːhə'bɪlɪteɪt/ *vt* rehabilitieren. **~ion** /-'teɪʃn/ *n* Rehabilitation *f*

rehears|al /rɪ'hɜːsl/ *n* (*Theat*) Probe *f*. **~e** *vt* proben

reign /reɪn/ *n* Herrschaft *f* ● *vi* herrschen, regieren

reimburse /riːɪm'bɜːs/ *vt* **~ s.o. for sth** jdm etw zurückerstatten

rein /reɪn/ *n* Zügel *m*

reincarnation /riːɪnkɑː'neɪʃn/ *n* Reinkarnation *f*, Wiedergeburt *f*

reindeer /'reɪndɪə(r)/ *n inv* Rentier *nt*

reinforce /riːɪn'fɔːs/ *vt* verstärken. **~d 'concrete** *n* Stahlbeton *m*. **~ment** *n* Verstärkung *f*; **send ~ments** Verstärkung schicken

reinstate /riːɪn'steɪt/ *vt* wiedereinstellen; (*to office*) wiedereinsetzen

reiterate /riː'ɪtəreɪt/ *vt* wiederholen

reject /rɪ'dʒekt/ *vt* ablehnen. **~ion** /-ekʃn/ *n* Ablehnung *f*

rejects /'riːdʒekts/ *npl* (*Comm*) Ausschußware *f*

rejoic|e /rɪ'dʒɔɪs/ *vi* (*liter*) sich freuen. **~ing** *n* Freude *f*

re'join /rɪ-/ *vt* sich wieder anschließen (+ *dat*); wieder beitreten (+ *dat*) ⟨*club, party*⟩; (*answer*) erwidern

rejuvenate /rɪ'dʒuːvəneɪt/ *vt* verjüngen

relapse /rɪ'læps/ *n* Rückfall *m* ● *vi* einen Rückfall erleiden

relate /rɪ'leɪt/ *vt* (*tell*) erzählen; (*connect*) verbinden ● *vi* zusammenhängen (**to** mit). **~d** *a* verwandt (**to** mit)

relation /rɪ'leɪʃn/ *n* Beziehung *f*; (*person*) Verwandte(r) *m/f*. **~ship** *n* Beziehung *f*; (*link*) Verbindung *f*; (*blood tie*) Verwandtschaft *f*; (*affair*) Verhältnis *nt*

relative /'relətɪv/ *n* Verwandte(r) *m/f* ● *a* relativ; (*Gram*) Relativ-. **~ly** *adv* relativ, verhältnismäßig

relax /rɪ'læks/ *vt* lockern, entspannen ● *vi* sich lockern, sich entspannen. **~ation** /-'seɪʃn/ *n* Entspannung *f.* **~ing** *a* entspannend

relay[1] /ri:'leɪ/ *vt* (*pt/pp* **-layed**) weitergeben; (*Radio, TV*) übertragen

relay[2] /'ri:leɪ/ *n* (*Electr*) Relais *nt*; **work in ~s** sich bei der Arbeit ablösen. **~ [race]** *n* Staffel *f*

release /rɪ'li:s/ *n* Freilassung *f*, Entlassung *f*; (*Techn*) Auslöser *m* ● *vt* freilassen; (*let go of*) loslassen; (*Techn*) auslösen; veröffentlichen ⟨*information*⟩

relegate /'relɪgeɪt/ *vt* verbannen; **be ~d** (*Sport*) absteigen

relent /rɪ'lent/ *vi* nachgeben. **~less** *a*, **-ly** *adv* erbarmungslos; (*unceasing*) unaufhörlich

relevan|ce /'reləvəns/ *n* Relevanz *f.* **~t** *a* relevant (**to** für)

reliab|ility /rɪlaɪə'bɪlətɪ/ *n* Zuverlässigkeit *f.* **~le** /-'laɪəbl/ *a*, **-ly** *adv* zuverlässig

relian|ce /rɪ'laɪəns/ *n* Abhängigkeit *f* (**on** von). **~t** *a* angewiesen (**on** auf + *acc*)

relic /'relɪk/ *n* Überbleibsel *nt*; (*Relig*) Reliquie *f*

relief /rɪ'li:f/ *n* Erleichterung *f*; (*assistance*) Hilfe *f*; (*distraction*) Abwechslung *f*; (*replacement*) Ablösung *f*; (*Art*) Relief *nt*; **in ~** im Relief. **~ map** *n* Reliefkarte *f.* **~ train** *n* Entlastungszug *m*

relieve /rɪ'li:v/ *vt* erleichtern; (*take over from*) ablösen; **~ of** entlasten von

religion /rɪ'lɪdʒən/ *n* Religion *f*

religious /rɪ'lɪdʒəs/ *a* religiös. **~ly** *adv* (*conscientiously*) gewissenhaft

relinquish /rɪ'lɪŋkwɪʃ/ *vt* loslassen; (*give up*) aufgeben

relish /'relɪʃ/ *n* Genuß *m*; (*Culin*) Würze *f* ● *vt* genießen

relo'cate /ri:-/ *vt* verlegen

reluctan|ce /rɪ'lʌktəns/ *n* Widerstreben *nt.* **~t** *a* widerstrebend; **be ~t** zögern (**to** zu). **~tly** *adv* ungern, widerstrebend

rely /rɪ'laɪ/ *vi* (*pt/pp* **-ied**) **~ on** sich verlassen auf (+ *acc*); (*be dependent on*) angewiesen sein auf (+ *acc*)

remain /rɪ'meɪn/ *vi* bleiben; (*be left*) übrigbleiben. **~der** *n* Rest *m.* **~ing** *a* restlich. **~s** *npl* Reste *pl*; **[mortal] ~s** [sterbliche] Überreste *pl*

remand /rɪ'mɑ:nd/ *n* **on ~** in Untersuchungshaft ● *vt* **~ in custody** in Untersuchungshaft schicken

remark /rɪ'mɑ:k/ *n* Bemerkung *f* ● *vt* bemerken. **~able** /-əbl/ *a*, **-bly** *adv* bemerkenswert

re'marry /ri:-/ *vi* wieder heiraten

remedial /rɪ'mi:dɪəl/ *a* Hilfs-; (*Med*) Heil-

remedy /'remədɪ/ *n* [Heil]mittel *nt* (**for** gegen); (*fig*) Abhilfe *f* ● *vt* (*pt/pp* **-ied**) abhelfen (+ *dat*); beheben ⟨*fault*⟩

rememb|er /rɪ'membə(r)/ *vt* sich erinnern an (+ *acc*); **~er to do sth** daran denken, etw zu tun; **~er me to him** grüßen Sie ihn von mir ● *vi* sich erinnern. **~rance** *n* Erinnerung *f*

remind /rɪ'maɪnd/ *vt* erinnern (**of** an + *acc*). **~er** *n* Andenken *nt*; (*letter, warning*) Mahnung *f*

reminisce /remɪ'nɪs/ *vi* sich seinen Erinnerungen hingeben. **~nces** /-ənsɪs/ *npl* Erinnerungen *pl.* **~nt** *a* **be ~nt of** erinnern an (+ *acc*)

remiss /rɪ'mɪs/ *a* nachlässig

remission /rɪ'mɪʃn/ *n* Nachlaß *m*; (*of sentence*) [Straf]erlaß *m*; (*Med*) Remission *f*

remit /rɪ'mɪt/ *vt* (*pt/pp* **remitted**) überweisen ⟨*money*⟩. **~tance** *n* Überweisung *f*

remnant /'remnənt/ *n* Rest *m*

remonstrate /'remənstreɪt/ *vi* protestieren; **~ with s.o.** jdm Vorhaltungen machen

remorse /rɪ'mɔ:s/ *n* Reue *f.* **~ful** *a*, **-ly** *adv* reumütig. **~less** *a*, **-ly** *adv* unerbittlich

remote /rɪ'məʊt/ *a* fern; (*isolated*) abgelegen; (*slight*) gering. **~ con'trol** *n* Fernsteuerung *f*; (*for TV*) Fernbedienung *f.* **~-con'trolled** *a* ferngesteuert; fernbedient

remotely /rɪ'məʊtlɪ/ *adv* entfernt; **not ~** nicht im entferntesten

re'movable /rɪ-/ *a* abnehmbar

removal /rɪ'mu:vl/ *n* Entfernung *f*; (*from house*) Umzug *m.* **~ van** *n* Möbelwagen *m*

remove /rɪ'mu:v/ *vt* entfernen; (*take off*) abnehmen; (*take out*) herausnehmen

remunerat|e /rɪ'mju:nəreɪt/ *vt* bezahlen. **~ion** /-'reɪʃn/ *n* Bezahlung *f.* **~ive** /-ətɪv/ *a* einträglich

render /'rendə(r)/ *vt* machen; erweisen ⟨*service*⟩; (*translate*) wiedergeben; (*Mus*) vortragen

renegade /'renɪgeɪd/ *n* Abtrünnige(r) *m/f*
renew /rɪ'nju:/ *vt* erneuern; verlängern ⟨*contract*⟩. **~al** *n* Erneuerung *f*; Verlängerung *f*
renounce /rɪ'naʊns/ *vt* verzichten auf (+ *acc*); (*Relig*) abschwören (+ *dat*)
renovat|e /'renəveɪt/ *vt* renovieren. **~ion** /-'veɪʃn/ *n* Renovierung *f*
renown /rɪ'naʊn/ *n* Ruf *m*. **~ed** *a* berühmt
rent /rent/ *n* Miete *f* ● *vt* mieten; (*hire*) leihen; **~ [out]** vermieten; verleihen. **~al** *n* Mietgebühr *f*; Leihgebühr *f*
renunciation /rɪnʌnsɪ'eɪʃn/ *n* Verzicht *m*
re'open /ri:-/ *vt/i* wieder aufmachen
re'organize /ri:-/ *vt* reorganisieren
rep /rep/ *n* (*fam*) Vertreter *m*
repair /rɪ'peə(r)/ *n* Reparatur *f*; **in good/bad ~** in gutem/schlechtem Zustand ● *vt* reparieren
repartee /repɑ:'ti:/ *n* **piece of ~** schlagfertige Antwort *f*
repatriat|e /ri:'pætrɪeɪt/ *vt* repatriieren. **~ion** /-'eɪʃn/ *n* Repatriierung *f*
re'pay /ri:-/ *vt* (*pt/pp* **-paid**) zurückzahlen; **~ s.o. for sth** jdm etw zurückzahlen. **~ment** *n* Rückzahlung *f*
repeal /rɪ'pi:l/ *n* Aufhebung *f* ● *vt* aufheben
repeat /rɪ'pi:t/ *n* Wiederholung *f* ● *vt/i* wiederholen; **~ after me** sprechen Sie mir nach. **~ed** *a*, **-ly** *adv* wiederholt
repel /rɪ'pel/ *vt* (*pt/pp* **repelled**) abwehren; (*fig*) abstoßen. **~lent** *a* abstoßend
repent /rɪ'pent/ *vi* Reue zeigen. **~ance** *n* Reue *f*. **~ant** *a* reuig
repercussions /ri:pə'kʌʃnz/ *npl* Auswirkungen *pl*
repertoire /'repətwɑ:(r)/ *n* Repertoire *nt*
repertory /'repətrɪ/ *n* Repertoire *nt*
repetit|ion /repɪ'tɪʃn/ *n* Wiederholung *f*. **~ive** /rɪ'petɪtɪv/ *a* eintönig
re'place /rɪ-/ *vt* zurücktun; (*take the place of*) ersetzen; (*exchange*) austauschen, auswechseln. **~ment** *n* Ersatz *m*. **~ment part** *n* Ersatzteil *nt*
'replay /ri:-/ *n* (*Sport*) Wiederholungsspiel *nt*; **[action] ~** Wiederholung *f*
replenish /rɪ'plenɪʃ/ *vt* auffüllen ⟨*stocks*⟩; (*refill*) nachfüllen
replete /rɪ'pli:t/ *a* gesättigt
replica /'replɪkə/ *n* Nachbildung *f*
reply /rɪ'plaɪ/ *n* Antwort *f* (**to** auf + *acc*) ● *vt/i* (*pt/pp* **replied**) antworten
report /rɪ'pɔ:t/ *n* Bericht *m*; (*Sch*) Zeugnis *nt*; (*rumour*) Gerücht *nt*; (*of gun*) Knall *m* ● *vt* berichten; (*notify*) melden; **~ s.o. to the police** jdn anzeigen ● *vi* berichten (**on** über + *acc*); (*present oneself*) sich melden (**to** bei). **~er** *n* Reporter(in) *m(f)*
repose /rɪ'pəʊz/ *n* Ruhe *f*
repos'sess /ri:-/ *vt* wieder in Besitz nehmen
reprehensible /reprɪ'hensəbl/ *a* tadelnswert
represent /reprɪ'zent/ *vt* darstellen; (*act for*) vertreten, repräsentieren. **~ation** /-'teɪʃn/ *n* Darstellung *f*; **make ~ations to** vorstellig werden bei
representative /reprɪ'zentətɪv/ *a* repräsentativ (**of** für) ● *n* Bevollmächtigte(r) *m/f*; (*Comm*) Vertreter(in) *m(f)*; (*Amer, Pol*) Abgeordnete(r) *m/f*
repress /rɪ'pres/ *vt* unterdrücken. **~ion** /-eʃn/ *n* Unterdrückung *f*. **~ive** /-ɪv/ *a* repressiv
reprieve /rɪ'pri:v/ *n* Begnadigung *f*; (*postponement*) Strafaufschub *m*; (*fig*) Gnadenfrist *f* ● *vt* begnadigen
reprimand /'reprɪmɑ:nd/ *n* Tadel *m* ● *vt* tadeln
'reprint[1] /ri:-/ *n* Nachdruck *m*
re'print[2] /ri:-/ *vt* neu auflegen
reprisal /rɪ'praɪzl/ *n* Vergeltungsmaßnahme *f*
reproach /rɪ'prəʊtʃ/ *n* Vorwurf *m* ● *vt* Vorwürfe *pl* machen (+ *dat*). **~ful** *a*, **-ly** *adv* vorwurfsvoll
repro'duc|e /ri:-/ *vt* wiedergeben, reproduzieren ● *vi* sich fortpflanzen. **~tion** /-'dʌkʃn/ *n* Reproduktion *f*; (*Biol*) Fortpflanzung *f*. **~tion furniture** *n* Stilmöbel *pl*. **~tive** /-'dʌktɪv/ *a* Fortpflanzungs-
reprove /rɪ'pru:v/ *vt* tadeln
reptile /'reptaɪl/ *n* Reptil *nt*
republic /rɪ'pʌblɪk/ *n* Republik *f*. **~an** *a* republikanisch ● *n* Republikaner(in) *m(f)*
repudiate /rɪ'pju:dɪeɪt/ *vt* zurückweisen
repugnan|ce /rɪ'pʌgnəns/ *n* Widerwille *m*. **~t** *a* widerlich

repuls|e /rɪ'pʌls/ *vt* abwehren; (*fig*) abweisen. **~ion** /-ʌlʃn/ *n* Widerwille *m*. **~ive** /-ɪv/ *a* abstoßend, widerlich
reputable /'repjʊtəbl/ *a* ⟨*firm*⟩ von gutem Ruf; (*respectable*) anständig
reputation /repjʊ'teɪʃn/ *n* Ruf *m*
repute /rɪ'pju:t/ *n* Ruf *m*. **~d** /-ɪd/ *a*, **-ly** *adv* angeblich
request /rɪ'kwest/ *n* Bitte *f* ● *vt* bitten. **~ stop** *n* Bedarfshaltestelle *f*
require /rɪ'kwaɪə(r)/ *vt* (*need*) brauchen; (*demand*) erfordern; **be ~d to do sth** etw tun müssen. **~ment** *n* Bedürfnis *nt*; (*condition*) Erfordernis *nt*
requisite /'rekwɪzɪt/ *a* erforderlich ● *n* **toilet/travel ~s** *pl* Toiletten-/Reiseartikel *pl*
requisition /rekwɪ'zɪʃn/ *n* **~ [order]** Anforderung *f* ● *vt* anfordern
re'sale /ri:-/ *n* Weiterverkauf *m*
rescind /rɪ'sɪnd/ *vt* aufheben
rescue /'reskju:/ *n* Rettung *f* ● *vt* retten. **~r** *n* Retter *m*
research /rɪ'sɜ:tʃ/ *n* Forschung *f* ● *vt* erforschen; (*Journ*) recherchieren ● *vi* **~ into** erforschen. **~er** *n* Forscher *m*; (*Journ*) Rechercheur *m*
resem|blance /rɪ'zembləns/ *n* Ähnlichkeit *f*. **~ble** /-bl/ *vt* ähneln (+ *dat*)
resent /rɪ'zent/ *vt* übelnehmen; einen Groll hegen gegen ⟨*person*⟩. **~ful** *a*, **-ly** *adv* verbittert. **~ment** *n* Groll *m*
reservation /rezə'veɪʃn/ *n* Reservierung *f*; (*doubt*) Vorbehalt *m*; (*enclosure*) Reservat *nt*
reserve /rɪ'zɜ:v/ *n* Reserve *f*; (*for animals*) Reservat *nt*; (*Sport*) Reservespieler(in) *m*(*f*) ● *vt* reservieren; ⟨*client:*⟩ reservieren lassen; (*keep*) aufheben; sich (*dat*) vorbehalten ⟨*right*⟩. **~d** *a* reserviert
reservoir /'rezəvwɑ:(r)/ *n* Reservoir *nt*
re'shape /ri:-/ *vt* umformen
re'shuffle /ri:-/ *n* (*Pol*) Umbildung *f* ● *vt* (*Pol*) umbilden
reside /rɪ'zaɪd/ *vi* wohnen
residence /'rezɪdəns/ *n* Wohnsitz *m*; (*official*) Residenz *f*; (*stay*) Aufenthalt *m*. **~ permit** *n* Aufenthaltsgenehmigung *f*
resident /'rezɪdənt/ *a* ansässig (**in** in + *dat*); ⟨*housekeeper, nurse*⟩ im Haus wohnend ● *n* Bewohner(in) *m*(*f*); (*of street*) Anwohner *m*. **~ial** /-'denʃl/ *a* Wohn-
residue /'rezɪdju:/ *n* Rest *m*; (*Chem*) Rückstand *m*
resign /rɪ'zaɪn/ *vt* **~ oneself to** sich abfinden mit ● *vi* kündigen; (*from public office*) zurücktreten. **~ation** /rezɪg'neɪʃn/ *n* Resignation *f*; (*from job*) Kündigung *f*; Rücktritt *m*. **~ed** *a*, **-ly** *adv* resigniert
resilient /rɪ'zɪlɪənt/ *a* federnd; (*fig*) widerstandsfähig
resin /'rezɪn/ *n* Harz *nt*
resist /rɪ'zɪst/ *vt/i* sich widersetzen (+ *dat*); (*fig*) widerstehen (+ *dat*). **~ance** *n* Widerstand *m*. **~ant** *a* widerstandsfähig
resolut|e /'rezəlu:t/ *a*, **-ly** *adv* entschlossen. **~ion** /-'lu:ʃn/ *n* Entschlossenheit *f*; (*intention*) Vorsatz *m*; (*Pol*) Resolution *f*
resolve /rɪ'zɒlv/ *n* Entschlossenheit *f*; (*decision*) Beschluß *m* ● *vt* beschließen; (*solve*) lösen. **~d** *a* entschlossen
resonan|ce /'rezənəns/ *n* Resonanz *f*. **~t** *a* klangvoll
resort /rɪ'zɔ:t/ *n* (*place*) Urlaubsort *m*; **as a last ~** wenn alles andere fehlschlägt ● *vi* **~ to** (*fig*) greifen zu
resound /rɪ'zaʊnd/ *vi* widerhallen. **~ing** *a* widerhallend; (*loud*) laut; (*notable*) groß
resource /rɪ'sɔ:s/ *n* **~s** *pl* Ressourcen *pl*. **~ful** *a* findig. **~fulness** *n* Findigkeit *f*
respect /rɪ'spekt/ *n* Respekt *m*, Achtung *f* (**for** vor + *dat*); (*aspect*) Hinsicht *f*; **with ~ to** in bezug auf (+ *acc*) ● *vt* respektieren, achten
respectability /rɪspektə'bɪlətɪ/ *n* (*see* **respectable**) Ehrbarkeit *f*; Anständigkeit *f*
respect|able /rɪ'spektəbl/ *a*, **-bly** *adv* ehrbar; (*decent*) anständig; (*considerable*) ansehnlich. **~ful** *a*, **-ly** *adv* respektvoll
respective /rɪ'spektɪv/ *a* jeweilig. **~ly** *adv* beziehungsweise
respiration /respə'reɪʃn/ *n* Atmung *f*
respite /'respaɪt/ *n* [Ruhe]pause *f*; (*delay*) Aufschub *m*
resplendent /rɪ'splendənt/ *a* glänzend
respond /rɪ'spɒnd/ *vi* antworten; (*react*) reagieren (**to** auf + *acc*); ⟨*patient:*⟩ ansprechen (**to** auf + *acc*)
response /rɪ'spɒns/ *n* Antwort *f*; Reaktion *f*

responsibility /rɪspɒnsɪ'bɪlətɪ/ *n* Verantwortung *f*; (*duty*) Verpflichtung *f*

responsib|le /rɪ'spɒnsəbl/ *a* verantwortlich; (*trustworthy*) verantwortungsvoll. **~ly** *adv* verantwortungsbewußt

responsive /rɪ'spɒnsɪv/ *a* **be ~** reagieren

rest¹ /rest/ *n* Ruhe *f*; (*holiday*) Erholung *f*; (*interval & Mus*) Pause *f*; **have a ~** eine Pause machen; (*rest*) sich ausruhen ● *vt* ausruhen; (*lean*) lehnen (**on** an/auf + *acc*) ● *vi* ruhen; (*have a rest*) sich ausruhen

rest² *n* **the ~** der Rest; (*people*) die Übrigen *pl* ● *vi* **it ~s with you** es ist an Ihnen (**to** zu)

restaurant /'restərɒnt/ *n* Restaurant *nt*, Gaststätte *f*. **~ car** *n* Speisewagen *m*

restful /'restfl/ *a* erholsam

restitution /restɪ'tju:ʃn/ *n* Entschädigung *f*; (*return*) Rückgabe *f*

restive /'restɪv/ *a* unruhig

restless /'restlɪs/ *a*, **-ly** *adv* unruhig

restoration /restə'reɪʃn/ *n* (*of building*) Restaurierung *f*

restore /rɪ'stɔ:(r)/ *vt* wiederherstellen; restaurieren ⟨*building*⟩; (*give back*) zurückgeben

restrain /rɪ'streɪn/ *vt* zurückhalten; **~ oneself** sich beherrschen. **~ed** *a* zurückhaltend. **~t** *n* Zurückhaltung *f*

restrict /rɪ'strɪkt/ *vt* einschränken; **~ to** beschränken auf (+ *acc*). **~ion** /-ɪkʃn/ *n* Einschränkung *f*; Beschränkung *f*. **~ive** /-ɪv/ *a* einschränkend

'rest room *n* (*Amer*) Toilette *f*

result /rɪ'zʌlt/ *n* Ergebnis *nt*, Resultat *nt*; (*consequence*) Folge *f*; **as a ~** als Folge (**of** *gen*) ● *vi* sich ergeben (**from** aus); **~ in** enden in (+ *dat*); (*lead to*) führen zu

resume /rɪ'zju:m/ *vt* wiederaufnehmen; wieder einnehmen ⟨*seat*⟩ ● *vi* wieder beginnen

résumé /'rezʊmeɪ/ *n* Zusammenfassung *f*

resumption /rɪ'zʌmpʃn/ *n* Wiederaufnahme *f*

resurgence /rɪ'sɜ:dʒəns/ *n* Wiederaufleben *nt*

resurrect /rezə'rekt/ *vt* (*fig*) wiederbeleben. **~ion** /-ekʃn/ *n* **the R~ion** (*Relig*) die Auferstehung

resuscitat|e /rɪ'sʌsɪteɪt/ *vt* wiederbeleben. **~ion** /-'teɪʃn/ *n* Wiederbelebung *f*

retail /'ri:teɪl/ *n* Einzelhandel *m* ● *a* Einzelhandels- ● *adv* im Einzelhandel ● *vt* im Einzelhandel verkaufen ● *vi* **~ at** im Einzelhandel kosten. **~er** *n* Einzelhändler *m*. **~ price** *n* Ladenpreis *m*

retain /rɪ'teɪn/ *vt* behalten

retaliat|e /rɪ'tælɪeɪt/ *vi* zurückschlagen. **~ion** /-'eɪʃn/ *n* Vergeltung *f*; **in ~ion** als Vergeltung

retarded /rɪ'tɑ:dɪd/ *a* zurückgeblieben

retentive /rɪ'tentɪv/ *a* ⟨*memory*⟩ gut

reticen|ce /'retɪsns/ *n* Zurückhaltung *f*. **~t** *a* zurückhaltend

retina /'retɪnə/ *n* Netzhaut *f*

retinue /'retɪnju:/ *n* Gefolge *nt*

retire /rɪ'taɪə(r)/ *vi* in den Ruhestand treten; (*withdraw*) sich zurückziehen. **~d** *a* im Ruhestand. **~ment** *n* Ruhestand *m*; **since my ~ment** seit ich nicht mehr arbeite

retiring /rɪ'taɪərɪŋ/ *a* zurückhaltend

retort /rɪ'tɔ:t/ *n* scharfe Erwiderung *f*; (*Chem*) Retorte *f* ● *vt* scharf erwidern

re'touch /ri:-/ *vt* (*Phot*) retuschieren

re'trace /rɪ-/ *vt* zurückverfolgen; **~ one's steps** denselben Weg zurückgehen

retract /rɪ'trækt/ *vt* einziehen; zurücknehmen ⟨*remark*⟩ ● *vi* widerrufen

re'train /ri:-/ *vt* umschulen ● *vi* umgeschult werden

retreat /rɪ'tri:t/ *n* Rückzug *m*; (*place*) Zufluchtsort *m* ● *vi* sich zurückziehen

re'trial /ri:-/ *n* Wiederaufnahmeverfahren *nt*

retribution /retrɪ'bju:ʃn/ *n* Vergeltung *f*

retrieve /rɪ'tri:v/ *vt* zurückholen; (*from wreckage*) bergen; (*Computing*) wiederauffinden; ⟨*dog:*⟩ apportieren

retrograde /'retrəgreɪd/ *a* rückschrittlich

retrospect /'retrəspekt/ *n* **in ~** rückblickend. **~ive** /-ɪv/ *a*, **-ly** *adv* rückwirkend; (*looking back*) rückblickend

return /rɪ'tɜ:n/ *n* Rückkehr *f*; (*giving back*) Rückgabe *f*; (*Comm*) Ertrag *m*; (*ticket*) Rückfahrkarte *f*; (*Aviat*) Rückflugschein *m*; **by ~ [of post]**

postwendend; **in ~** dafür; **in ~ for** für; **many happy ~s!** herzlichen Glückwunsch zum Geburtstag! ● *vi* zurückgehen/-fahren; (*come back*) zurückkommen ● *vt* zurückgeben; (*put back*) zurückstellen/-legen; (*send back*) zurückschicken; (*elect*) wählen

return: ~ flight *n* Rückflug *m*. **~ match** *n* Rückspiel *nt*. **~ ticket** *n* Rückfahrkarte *f*; (*Aviat*) Rückflugschein *m*

reunion /ri:'ju:nɪən/ *n* Wiedervereinigung *f*; (*social gathering*) Treffen *nt*

reunite /ri:ju:'naɪt/ *vt* wiedervereinigen ● *vi* sich wiedervereinigen

re'us|able /ri:-/ *a* wiederverwendbar. **~e** *vt* wiederverwenden

rev /rev/ *n* (*Auto, fam*) Umdrehung *f* ● *vt/i* **~ [up]** den Motor auf Touren bringen

reveal /rɪ'vi:l/ *vt* zum Vorschein bringen; (*fig*) enthüllen. **~ing** *a* (*fig*) aufschlußreich

revel /'revl/ *vi* (*pt/pp* **revelled**) **~ in sth** etw genießen

revelation /revə'leɪʃn/ *n* Offenbarung *f*, Enthüllung *f*

revelry /'revlrɪ/ *n* Lustbarkeit *f*

revenge /rɪ'vendʒ/ *n* Rache *f*; (*fig & Sport*) Revanche *f* ● *vt* rächen

revenue /'revənju:/ *n* [Staats]einnahmen *pl*

reverberate /rɪ'vɜ:bəreɪt/ *vi* nachhallen

revere /rɪ'vɪə(r)/ *vt* verehren. **~nce** /'revərəns/ *n* Ehrfurcht *f*

Reverend /'revərənd/ *a* **the ~ X** Pfarrer X; (*Catholic*) Hochwürden X

reverent /'revərənt/ *a*, **-ly** *adv* ehrfürchtig

reverie /'revərɪ/ *n* Träumerei *f*

revers /rɪ'vɪə/ *n* (*pl* **revers** /-z/) Revers *nt*

reversal /rɪ'vɜ:sl/ *n* Umkehrung *f*

reverse /rɪ'vɜ:s/ *a* umgekehrt ● *n* Gegenteil *nt*; (*back*) Rückseite *f*; (*Auto*) Rückwärtsgang *m* ● *vt* umkehren; (*Auto*) zurücksetzen; **~ the charges** (*Teleph*) ein R-Gespräch führen ● *vi* zurücksetzen

revert /rɪ'vɜ:t/ *vi* **~ to** zurückfallen an (+ *acc*); zurückkommen auf (+ *acc*) ⟨*topic*⟩

review /rɪ'vju:/ *n* Rückblick *m* (**of** auf + *acc*); (*re-examination*) Überprüfung *f*; (*Mil*) Truppenschau *f*; (*of book, play*) Kritik *f*, Rezension *f* ● *vt* zurückblicken auf (+ *acc*); überprüfen ⟨*situation*⟩; (*Mil*) besichtigen; kritisieren, rezensieren ⟨*book, play*⟩. **~er** *n* Kritiker *m*, Rezensent *m*

revile /rɪ'vaɪl/ *vt* verunglimpfen

revis|e /rɪ'vaɪz/ *vt* revidieren; (*for exam*) wiederholen. **~ion** /-'vɪʒn/ *n* Revision *f*; Wiederholung *f*

revival /rɪ'vaɪvl/ *n* Wiederbelebung *f*

revive /rɪ'vaɪv/ *vt* wiederbeleben; (*fig*) wieder aufleben lassen ● *vi* wieder aufleben

revoke /rɪ'vəʊk/ *vt* aufheben; widerrufen ⟨*command, decision*⟩

revolt /rɪ'vəʊlt/ *n* Aufstand *m* ● *vi* rebellieren ● *vt* anwidern. **~ing** *a* widerlich, eklig

revolution /revə'lu:ʃn/ *n* Revolution *f*; (*Auto*) Umdrehung *f*. **~ary** /-ərɪ/ *a* revolutionär. **~ize** *vt* revolutionieren

revolve /rɪ'vɒlv/ *vi* sich drehen; **~ around** kreisen um

revolv|er /rɪ'vɒlvə(r)/ *n* Revolver *m*. **~ing** *a* Dreh-

revue /rɪ'vju:/ *n* Revue *f*; (*satirical*) Kabarett *nt*

revulsion /rɪ'vʌlʃn/ *n* Abscheu *m*

reward /rɪ'wɔ:d/ *n* Belohnung *f* ● *vt* belohnen. **~ing** *a* lohnend

re'write /ri:-/ *vt* (*pt* **rewrote**, *pp* **rewritten**) noch einmal [neu] schreiben; (*alter*) umschreiben

rhapsody /'ræpsədɪ/ *n* Rhapsodie *f*

rhetoric /'retərɪk/ *n* Rhetorik *f*. **~al** /rɪ'tɒrɪkl/ *a* rhetorisch

rheuma|tic /ru:'mætɪk/ *a* rheumatisch. **~tism** /'ru:mətɪzm/ *n* Rheumatismus *m*, Rheuma *nt*

Rhine /raɪn/ *n* Rhein *m*

rhinoceros /raɪ'nɒsərəs/ *n* Nashorn *nt*, Rhinozeros *nt*

rhubarb /'ru:bɑ:b/ *n* Rhabarber *m*

rhyme /raɪm/ *n* Reim *m* ● *vt* reimen ● *vi* sich reimen

rhythm /'rɪðm/ *n* Rhythmus *m*. **~ic[al]** *a*, **-ally** *adv* rhythmisch

rib /rɪb/ *n* Rippe *f* ● *vt* (*pt/pp* **ribbed**) (*fam*) aufziehen (*fam*)

ribald /'rɪbld/ *a* derb

ribbon /'rɪbən/ *n* Band *nt*; (*for typewriter*) Farbband *nt*; **in ~s** in Fetzen

rice /raɪs/ *n* Reis *m*

rich /rɪtʃ/ *a* (**-er, -est**), **-ly** *adv* reich; ⟨*food*⟩ gehaltvoll; (*heavy*) schwer ● *n* **the ~** *pl* die Reichen; **~es** *pl* Reichtum *m*

rickets /'rɪkɪts/ *n* Rachitis *f*

rickety /'rɪkətɪ/ *a* wackelig

ricochet /'rɪkəʃeɪ/ *vi* abprallen

rid /rɪd/ *vt* (*pt/pp* **rid**, *pres p* **ridding**) befreien (**of** von); **get ~ of** loswerden

riddance /'rɪdns/ *n* **good ~!** auf Nimmerwiedersehen!

ridden /'rɪdn/ *see* **ride**

riddle /'rɪdl/ *n* Rätsel *nt*

riddled /'rɪdld/ *a* **~ with** durchlöchert mit

ride /raɪd/ *n* Ritt *m*; (*in vehicle*) Fahrt *f*; **take s.o. for a ~** (*fam*) jdn reinlegen ● *v* (*pt* **rode**, *pp* **ridden**) ● *vt* reiten ⟨*horse*⟩; fahren mit ⟨*bicycle*⟩ ● *vi* reiten; (*in vehicle*) fahren. **~r** *n* Reiter(in) *m(f)*; (*on bicycle*) Fahrer(in) *m(f)*; (*in document*) Zusatzklausel *f*

ridge /rɪdʒ/ *n* Erhebung *f*; (*on roof*) First *m*; (*of mountain*) Grat *m*, Kamm *m*; (*of high pressure*) Hochdruckkeil *m*

ridicule /'rɪdɪkju:l/ *n* Spott *m* ● *vt* verspotten, spotten über (+ *acc*)

ridiculous /rɪ'dɪkjʊləs/ *a*, **-ly** *adv* lächerlich

riding /'raɪdɪŋ/ *n* Reiten *nt* ● *attrib* Reit-

rife /raɪf/ *a* **be ~** weit verbreitet sein

riff-raff /'rɪfræf/ *n* Gesindel *nt*

rifle /'raɪfl/ *n* Gewehr *nt* ● *vt* plündern; **~ through** durchwühlen

rift /rɪft/ *n* Spalt *m*; (*fig*) Riß *m*

rig[1] /rɪg/ *n* Ölbohrturm *m*; (*at sea*) Bohrinsel *f* ● *vt* (*pt/pp* **rigged**) **~ out** ausrüsten; **~ up** aufbauen

rig[2] *vt* (*pt/pp* **rigged**) manipulieren

right /raɪt/ *a* richtig; (*not left*) rechte(r,s); **be ~** ⟨*person:*⟩ recht haben; ⟨*clock:*⟩ richtig gehen; **put ~** wieder in Ordnung bringen; (*fig*) richtigstellen; **that's ~!** das stimmt! ● *adv* richtig; (*directly*) direkt; (*completely*) ganz; (*not left*) rechts; ⟨*go*⟩ nach rechts; **~ away** sofort ● *n* Recht *nt*; (*not left*) rechte Seite *f*; **on the ~** rechts; **from/to the ~** von/nach rechts; **be in the ~** recht haben; **by ~s** eigentlich; **the R~** (*Pol*) die Rechte. **~ angle** *n* rechter Winkel *m*

righteous /'raɪtʃəs/ *a* rechtschaffen

rightful /'raɪtfl/ *a*, **-ly** *adv* rechtmäßig

right: ~-'handed *a* rechtshändig. **~-hand 'man** *n* (*fig*) rechte Hand *f*

rightly /'raɪtlɪ/ *adv* mit Recht

right: ~ of way *n* Durchgangsrecht *nt*; (*path*) öffentlicher Fußweg *m*; (*Auto*) Vorfahrt *f*. **~-'wing** *a* (*Pol*) rechte(r,s)

rigid /'rɪdʒɪd/ *a* starr; (*strict*) streng. **~ity** /-'dʒɪdətɪ/ *n* Starrheit *f*; Strenge *f*

rigmarole /'rɪgmərəʊl/ *n* Geschwätz *nt*; (*procedure*) Prozedur *f*

rigorous /'rɪgərəs/ *a*, **-ly** *adv* streng

rigour /'rɪgə(r)/ *n* Strenge *f*

rile /raɪl/ *vt* (*fam*) ärgern

rim /rɪm/ *n* Rand *m*; (*of wheel*) Felge *f*

rind /raɪnd/ *n* (*on fruit*) Schale *f*; (*on cheese*) Rinde *f*; (*on bacon*) Schwarte *f*

ring[1] /rɪŋ/ *n* Ring *m*; (*for circus*) Manege *f*; **stand in a ~** im Kreis stehen ● *vt* umringen; **~ in red** rot einkreisen

ring[2] *n* Klingeln *nt*; **give s.o. a ~** (*Teleph*) jdn anrufen ● *v* (*pt* **rang**, *pp* **rung**) ● *vt* läuten; **~ [up]** (*Teleph*) anrufen ● *vi* läuten, klingeln. **~ back** *vt/i* (*Teleph*) zurückrufen. **~ off** *vi* (*Teleph*) auflegen

ring: ~leader *n* Rädelsführer *m*. **~ road** *n* Umgehungsstraße *f*

rink /rɪŋk/ *n* Eisbahn *f*

rinse /rɪns/ *n* Spülung *f*; (*hair colour*) Tönung *f* ● *vt* spülen; tönen ⟨*hair*⟩. **~ off** *vt* abspülen

riot /'raɪət/ *n* Aufruhr *m*; **~s** *pl* Unruhen *pl*; **~ of colours** bunte Farbenpracht *f*; **run ~** randalieren ● *vi* randalieren. **~er** *n* Randalierer *m*. **~ous** /-əs/ *a* aufrührerisch; (*boisterous*) wild

rip /rɪp/ *n* Riß *m* ● *vt/i* (*pt/pp* **ripped**) zerreißen; **~ open** aufreißen. **~ off** *vt* (*fam*) neppen

ripe /raɪp/ *a* (**-r, -st**) reif

ripen /'raɪpn/ *vi* reifen ● *vt* reifen lassen

ripeness /'raɪpnɪs/ *n* Reife *f*

'rip-off *n* (*fam*) Nepp *m*

ripple /'rɪpl/ *n* kleine Welle *f* ● *vt* kräuseln ● *vi* sich kräuseln

rise /raɪz/ *n* Anstieg *m*; (*fig*) Aufstieg *m*; (*increase*) Zunahme *f*; (*in wages*) Lohnerhöhung *f*; (*in salary*) Gehaltserhöhung *f*; **give ~ to** Anlaß geben zu ● *vi* (*pt* **rose**, *pp* **risen**) steigen; ⟨*ground:*⟩ ansteigen; ⟨*sun, dough:*⟩ aufgehen; ⟨*river:*⟩ entspringen; (*get up*) aufstehen; (*fig*) aufsteigen (**to** zu); (*rebel*) sich erheben; ⟨*court:*⟩ sich vertagen. **~r** *n* **early ~r** Frühaufsteher *m*

rising /ˈraɪzɪŋ/ *a* steigend; ⟨*sun*⟩ aufgehend; **the ~ generation** die heranwachsende Generation ● *n* (*revolt*) Aufstand *m*
risk /rɪsk/ *n* Risiko *nt*; **at one's own ~** auf eigene Gefahr ● *vt* riskieren
risky /ˈrɪskɪ/ *a* (**-ier, -iest**) riskant
risqué /ˈrɪskeɪ/ *a* gewagt
rissole /ˈrɪsəʊl/ *n* Frikadelle *f*
rite /raɪt/ *n* Ritus *m*; **last ~s** Letzte Ölung *f*
ritual /ˈrɪtjʊəl/ *a* rituell ● *n* Ritual *nt*
rival /ˈraɪvl/ *a* rivalisierend ● *n* Rivale *m*/Rivalin *f*; **~s** *pl* (*Comm*) Konkurrenten *pl* ● *vt* (*pt/pp* **rivalled**) gleichkommen (+ *dat*); (*compete with*) rivalisieren mit. **~ry** *n* Rivalität *f*; (*Comm*) Konkurrenzkampf *m*
river /ˈrɪvə(r)/ *n* Fluß *m*. **~-bed** *n* Flußbett *nt*
rivet /ˈrɪvɪt/ *n* Niete *f* ● *vt* [ver]nieten; **~ed by** (*fig*) gefesselt von
road /rəʊd/ *n* Straße *f*; (*fig*) Weg *m*
road: ~-block *n* Straßensperre *f*. **~-hog** *n* (*fam*) Straßenschreck *m*. **~-map** *n* Straßenkarte *f*. **~ safety** *n* Verkehrssicherheit *f*. **~ sense** *n* Verkehrssinn *m*. **~side** *n* Straßenrand *m*. **~way** *n* Fahrbahn *f*. **~-works** *npl* Straßenarbeiten *pl*. **~worthy** *a* verkehrssicher
roam /rəʊm/ *vi* wandern
roar /rɔ:(r)/ *n* Gebrüll *nt*; **~s of laughter** schallendes Gelächter *nt* ● *vi* brüllen; (*with laughter*) schallend lachen. **~ing** *a* ⟨*fire*⟩ prasselnd; **do a ~ing trade** (*fam*) ein Bombengeschäft machen
roast /rəʊst/ *a* gebraten, Brat-; **~ beef/pork** Rinder-/Schweinebraten *m* ● *n* Braten *m* ● *vt/i* braten; rösten ⟨*coffee, chestnuts*⟩
rob /rɒb/ *vt* (*pt/pp* **robbed**) berauben (**of** *gen*); ausrauben ⟨*bank*⟩. **~ber** *n* Räuber *m*. **~bery** *n* Raub *m*
robe /rəʊb/ *n* Robe *f*; (*Amer: bathrobe*) Bademantel *m*
robin /ˈrɒbɪn/ *n* Rotkehlchen *nt*
robot /ˈrəʊbɒt/ *n* Roboter *m*
robust /rəʊˈbʌst/ *a* robust
rock[1] /rɒk/ *n* Fels *m*; **stick of ~** Zuckerstange *f*; **on the ~s** ⟨*ship*⟩ aufgelaufen; ⟨*marriage*⟩ kaputt; ⟨*drink*⟩ mit Eis
rock[2] *vt/i* schaukeln
rock[3] *n* (*Mus*) Rock *m*
rock-ˈbottom *n* Tiefpunkt *m*
rockery /ˈrɒkərɪ/ *n* Steingarten *m*
rocket /ˈrɒkɪt/ *n* Rakete *f* ● *vi* in die Höhe schießen
rocking: ~-chair *n* Schaukelstuhl *m*. **~-horse** *n* Schaukelpferd *nt*
rocky /ˈrɒkɪ/ *a* (**-ier, -iest**) felsig; (*unsteady*) wackelig
rod /rɒd/ *n* Stab *m*; (*stick*) Rute *f*; (*for fishing*) Angel[rute] *f*
rode /rəʊd/ *see* **ride**
rodent /ˈrəʊdnt/ *n* Nagetier *nt*
roe[1] /rəʊ/ *n* Rogen *m*; (*soft*) Milch *f*
roe[2] *n* (*pl* **roe** *or* **roes**) **~[-deer]** Reh *nt*
rogue /rəʊg/ *n* Gauner *m*
role /rəʊl/ *n* Rolle *f*
roll /rəʊl/ *n* Rolle *f*; (*bread*) Brötchen *nt*; (*list*) Liste *f*; (*of drum*) Wirbel *m* ● *vi* rollen; **be ~ing in money** (*fam*) Geld wie Heu haben ● *vt* rollen; walzen ⟨*lawn*⟩; ausrollen ⟨*pastry*⟩. **~ over** *vi* sich auf die andere Seite rollen. **~ up** *vt* aufrollen; hochkrempeln ⟨*sleeves*⟩ ● *vi* (*fam*) auftauchen
ˈroll-call *n* Namensaufruf *m*; (*Mil*) Appell *m*
roller /ˈrəʊlə(r)/ *n* Rolle *f*; (*lawn, road*) Walze *f*; (*hair*) Lockenwickler *m*. **~ blind** *n* Rollo *nt*. **~-coaster** *n* Berg-und-Talbahn *f*. **~-skate** *n* Rollschuh *m*
ˈrolling-pin *n* Teigrolle *f*
Roman /ˈrəʊmən/ *a* römisch ● *n* Römer(in) *m*(*f*)
romance /rəˈmæns/ *n* Romantik *f*; (*love-affair*) Romanze *f*; (*book*) Liebesgeschichte *f*
Romania /rəʊˈmeɪnɪə/ *n* Rumänien *nt*. **~n** *a* rumänisch ● *n* Rumäne *m*/-nin *f*
romantic /rəʊˈmæntɪk/ *a*, **-ally** *adv* romantisch. **~ism** /-tɪsɪzm/ *n* Romantik *f*
Rome /rəʊm/ *n* Rom *nt*
romp /rɒmp/ *n* Tollen *nt* ● *vi* [herum]tollen. **~ers** *npl* Strampelhöschen *nt*
roof /ru:f/ *n* Dach *nt*; (*of mouth*) Gaumen *m* ● *vt* **~ over** überdachen. **~-rack** *n* Dachgepäckträger *m*. **~-top** *n* Dach *nt*
rook /rʊk/ *n* Saatkrähe *f*; (*Chess*) Turm *m* ● *vt* (*fam: swindle*) schröpfen
room /ru:m/ *n* Zimmer *nt*; (*for functions*) Saal *m*; (*space*) Platz *m*. **~y** *a* geräumig
roost /ru:st/ *n* Hühnerstange *f* ● *vi* schlafen

root[1] /ru:t/ *n* Wurzel *f*; **take ~** anwachsen ● *vi* Wurzeln schlagen. **~ out** *vt* (*fig*) ausrotten

root[2] *vi* **~ about** wühlen; **~ for s.o.** (*Amer, fam*) für jdn sein

rope /rəʊp/ *n* Seil *nt*; **know the ~s** (*fam*) sich auskennen. **~ in** *vt* (*fam*) einspannen

rope-'ladder *n* Strickleiter *f*

rosary /'rəʊzərɪ/ *n* Rosenkranz *m*

rose[1] /rəʊz/ *n* Rose *f*; (*of watering-can*) Brause *f*

rose[2] *see* **rise**

rosemary /'rəʊzmərɪ/ *n* Rosmarin *m*

rosette /rəʊ'zet/ *n* Rosette *f*

roster /'rɒstə(r)/ *n* Dienstplan *m*

rostrum /'rɒstrəm/ *n* Podest *nt*, Podium *nt*

rosy /'rəʊzɪ/ *a* (**-ier, -iest**) rosig

rot /rɒt/ *n* Fäulnis *f*; (*fam: nonsense*) Quatsch *m* ● *vi* (*pt/pp* **rotted**) [ver]faulen

rota /'rəʊtə/ *n* Dienstplan *m*

rotary /'rəʊtərɪ/ *a* Dreh-; (*Techn*) Rotations-

rotat|e /rəʊ'teɪt/ *vt* drehen; im Wechsel anbauen ⟨*crops*⟩ ● *vi* sich drehen; (*Techn*) rotieren. **~ion** /-eɪʃn/ *n* Drehung *f*; (*of crops*) Fruchtfolge *f*; **in ~ion** im Wechsel

rote /rəʊt/ *n* **by ~** auswendig

rotten /'rɒtn/ *a* faul; (*fam*) mies; ⟨*person*⟩ fies

rotund /rəʊ'tʌnd/ *a* rundlich

rough /rʌf/ *a* (**-er, -est**) rauh; (*uneven*) uneben; (*coarse, not gentle*) grob; (*brutal*) roh; (*turbulent*) stürmisch; (*approximate*) ungefähr ● *adv* **sleep ~** im Freien übernachten; **play ~** holzen ● *n* **do sth in ~** etw ins unreine schreiben ● *vt* **~ it** primitiv leben. **~ out** *vt* im Groben entwerfen

roughage /'rʌfɪdʒ/ *n* Ballaststoffe *pl*

rough 'draft *n* grober Entwurf *m*

rough|ly /'rʌflɪ/ *adv* (*see* **rough**) rauh; grob; roh; ungefähr. **~ness** *n* Rauheit *f*

'rough paper *n* Konzeptpapier *nt*

round /raʊnd/ *a* (**-er, -est**) rund ● *n* Runde *f*; (*slice*) Scheibe *f*; **do one's ~s** seine Runde machen ● *prep* um (+ *acc*); **~ the clock** rund um die Uhr ● *adv* **all ~** ringsherum; **~ and ~** im Kreis; **ask s.o. ~** jdn einladen; **turn/look ~** sich umdrehen/umsehen ● *vt* biegen um ⟨*corner*⟩ ● *vi* **~ on s.o.** jdn anfahren. **~ off** *vt* abrunden. **~ up** *vt* aufrunden; zusammentreiben ⟨*animals*⟩; festnehmen ⟨*criminals*⟩

roundabout /'raʊndəbaʊt/ *a* **~ route** Umweg *m* ● *n* Karussell *nt*; (*for traffic*) Kreisverkehr *m*

round: ~-'shouldered *a* mit einem runden Rücken. **~ 'trip** *n* Rundreise *f*

rous|e /raʊz/ *vt* wecken; (*fig*) erregen. **~ing** *a* mitreißend

route /ru:t/ *n* Route *f*; (*of bus*) Linie *f*

routine /ru:'ti:n/ *a*, **-ly** *adv* routinemäßig ● *n* Routine *f*; (*Theat*) Nummer *f*

roux /ru:/ *n* Mehlschwitze *f*

rove /rəʊv/ *vi* wandern

row[1] /rəʊ/ *n* (*line*) Reihe *f*; **in a ~** (*one after the other*) nacheinander

row[2] *vt/i* rudern

row[3] /raʊ/ *n* (*fam*) Krach *m* ● *vi* (*fam*) sich streiten

rowan /'rəʊən/ *n* Eberesche *f*

rowdy /'raʊdɪ/ *a* (**-ier, -iest**) laut

rowing boat /'rəʊɪŋ-/ *n* Ruderboot *nt*

royal /'rɔɪəl/ *a*, **-ly** *adv* königlich

royalt|y /'rɔɪəltɪ/ *n* Königtum *nt*; (*persons*) Mitglieder *pl* der königlichen Familie; **-ies** *pl* (*payments*) Tantiemen *pl*

rub /rʌb/ *n* **give sth a ~** etw reiben/(*polish*) polieren ● *vt* (*pt/pp* **rubbed**) reiben; (*polish*) polieren; **don't ~ it in** (*fam*) reib es mir nicht unter die Nase. **~ off** *vt* abreiben ● *vi* abgehen; **~ off on** abfärben auf (+ *acc*). **~ out** *vt* ausradieren

rubber /'rʌbə(r)/ *n* Gummi *m*; (*eraser*) Radiergummi *m*. **~ band** *n* Gummiband *nt*. **~y** *a* gummiartig

rubbish /'rʌbɪʃ/ *n* Abfall *m*, Müll *m*; (*fam: nonsense*) Quatsch *m*; (*fam: junk*) Plunder *m*, Kram *m* ● *vt* (*fam*) schlechtmachen. **~ bin** *n* Mülleimer *m*, Abfalleimer *m*. **~ dump** *n* Abfallhaufen *m*; (*official*) Müllhalde *f*

rubble /'rʌbl/ *n* Trümmer *pl*, Schutt *m*

ruby /'ru:bɪ/ *n* Rubin *m*

rucksack /'rʌksæk/ *n* Rucksack *m*

rudder /'rʌdə(r)/ *n* [Steuer]ruder *nt*

ruddy /'rʌdɪ/ *a* (**-ier, -iest**) rötlich; (*sl*) verdammt

rude /ru:d/ *a* (**-r, -st**), **-ly** *adv* unhöflich; (*improper*) unanständig. **~ness** *n* Unhöflichkeit *f*

rudiment /'ru:dımənt/ *n* **~s** *pl* Anfangsgründe *pl.* **~ary** /-'mentərı/ *a* elementar; (*Biol*) rudimentär
rueful /'ru:fl/ *a*, **-ly** *adv* reumütig
ruffian /'rʌfıən/ *n* Rüpel *m*
ruffle /'rʌfl/ *n* Rüsche *f* ● *vt* zerzausen
rug /rʌg/ *n* Vorleger *m*, [kleiner] Teppich *m*; (*blanket*) Decke *f*
rugged /'rʌgıd/ *a* ⟨*coastline*⟩ zerklüftet
ruin /'ru:ın/ *n* Ruine *f*; (*fig*) Ruin *m* ● *vt* ruinieren. **~ous** /-əs/ *a* ruinös
rule /ru:l/ *n* Regel *f*; (*control*) Herrschaft *f*; (*government*) Regierung *f*; (*for measuring*) Lineal *nt*; **as a ~** in der Regel ● *vt* regieren, herrschen über (+ *acc*); (*fig*) beherrschen; (*decide*) entscheiden; ziehen ⟨*line*⟩ ● *vi* regieren, herrschen. **~ out** *vt* ausschließen
ruled /ru:ld/ *a* ⟨*paper*⟩ liniert
ruler /'ru:lə(r)/ *n* Herrscher(in) *m(f)*; (*measure*) Lineal *nt*
ruling /'ru:lıŋ/ *a* herrschend; ⟨*factor*⟩ entscheidend; (*Pol*) regierend ● *n* Entscheidung *f*
rum /rʌm/ *n* Rum *m*
rumble /'rʌmbl/ *n* Grollen *nt* ● *vi* grollen; ⟨*stomach:*⟩ knurren
ruminant /'ru:mınənt/ *n* Wiederkäuer *m*
rummage /'rʌmıdʒ/ *vi* wühlen; **~ through** durchwühlen
rummy /'rʌmı/ *n* Rommé *nt*
rumour /'ru:mə(r)/ *n* Gerücht *nt* ● *vt* **it is ~ed that** es geht das Gerücht, daß
rump /rʌmp/ *n* Hinterteil *nt*. **~ steak** *n* Rumpsteak *nt*
rumpus /'rʌmpəs/ *n* (*fam*) Spektakel *m*
run /rʌn/ *n* Lauf *m*; (*journey*) Fahrt *f*; (*series*) Serie *f*, Reihe *f*; (*Theat*) Laufzeit *f*; (*Skiing*) Abfahrt *f*; (*enclosure*) Auslauf *m*; (*Amer: ladder*) Laufmasche *f*; **at a ~** im Laufschritt; **~ of bad luck** Pechsträhne *f*; **be on the ~** flüchtig sein; **have the ~ of sth** etw zu seiner freien Verfügung haben; **in the long ~** auf lange Sicht ● *v* (*pt* **ran**, *pp* **run**, *pres p* **running**) ● *vi* laufen; (*flow*) fließen; ⟨*eyes:*⟩ tränen; ⟨*bus:*⟩ verkehren, fahren; ⟨*butter, ink:*⟩ zerfließen; ⟨*colours:*⟩ [ab]färben; (*in election*) kandidieren; **~ across s.o./sth** auf jdn/etw stoßen ● *vt* laufen lassen; einlaufen lassen ⟨*bath*⟩; (*manage*) führen, leiten; (*drive*) fahren; eingehen ⟨*risk*⟩; (*Journ*) bringen ⟨*article*⟩; **~ one's hand over sth** mit der Hand über etw (*acc*) fahren. **~ away** *vi* weglaufen. **~ down** *vi* hinunter-/herunterlaufen; ⟨*clockwork:*⟩ ablaufen; ⟨*stocks:*⟩ sich verringern ● *vt* (*run over*) überfahren; (*reduce*) verringern; (*fam: criticize*) heruntermachen. **~ in** *vi* hinein-/hereinlaufen. **~ off** *vi* weglaufen ● *vt* abziehen ⟨*copies*⟩. **~ out** *vi* hinaus-/herauslaufen; ⟨*supplies, money:*⟩ ausgehen; **I've ~ out of sugar** ich habe keinen Zucker mehr. **~ over** *vi* hinüber-/herüberlaufen; (*overflow*) überlaufen ● *vt* überfahren. **~ through** *vi* durchlaufen. **~ up** *vi* hinauf-/herauflaufen; (*towards*) hinlaufen ● *vt* machen ⟨*debts*⟩; auflaufen lassen ⟨*bill*⟩; (*sew*) schnell nähen
'runaway *n* Ausreißer *m*
run-'down *a* ⟨*area*⟩ verkommen
rung[1] /rʌŋ/ *n* (*of ladder*) Sprosse *f*
rung[2] *see* **ring**[2]
runner /'rʌnə(r)/ *n* Läufer *m*; (*Bot*) Ausläufer *m*; (*on sledge*) Kufe *f*. **~ bean** *n* Stangenbohne *f*. **~-up** *n* Zweite(r) *m/f*
running /'rʌnıŋ/ *a* laufend; ⟨*water*⟩ fließend; **four times ~** viermal nacheinander ● *n* Laufen *nt*; (*management*) Führung *f*, Leitung *f*; **be/not be in the ~** eine/keine Chance haben. **~ 'commentary** *n* fortlaufender Kommentar *m*
runny /'rʌnı/ *a* flüssig
run: ~-of-the-'mill *a* gewöhnlich. **~-up** *n* (*Sport*) Anlauf *m*; (*to election*) Zeit *f* vor der Wahl. **~way** *n* Start- und Landebahn *f*, Piste *f*
rupture /'rʌptʃə(r)/ *n* Bruch *m* ● *vt/i* brechen; **~ oneself** sich (*dat*) einen Bruch heben
rural /'rʊərəl/ *a* ländlich
ruse /ru:z/ *n* List *f*
rush[1] /rʌʃ/ *n* (*Bot*) Binse *f*
rush[2] *n* Hetze *f*; **in a ~** in Eile ● *vi* sich hetzen; (*run*) rasen; ⟨*water:*⟩ rauschen ● *vt* hetzen, drängen; **~ s.o. to hospital** jdn schnellstens ins Krankenhaus bringen. **~-hour** *n* Hauptverkehrszeit *f*, Stoßzeit *f*
rusk /rʌsk/ *n* Zwieback *m*

Russia /'rʌʃə/ *n* Rußland *nt.* **~n** *a* russisch ● *n* Russe *m*/Russin *f*; (*Lang*) Russisch *nt*

rust /rʌst/ *n* Rost *m* ● *vi* rosten

rustic /'rʌstɪk/ *a* bäuerlich; ⟨*furniture*⟩ rustikal

rustle /'rʌsl/ *vi* rascheln ● *vt* rascheln mit; (*Amer*) stehlen ⟨*cattle*⟩. **~ up** *vt* (*fam*) improvisieren

'**rustproof** *a* rostfrei

rusty /'rʌstɪ/ *a* (**-ier, -iest**) rostig

rut /rʌt/ *n* Furche *f*; **be in a ~** (*fam*) aus dem alten Trott nicht herauskommen

ruthless /'ru:θlɪs/ *a*, **-ly** *adv* rücksichtslos. **~ness** *n* Rücksichtslosigkeit *f*

rye /raɪ/ *n* Roggen *m*

S

sabbath /'sæbəθ/ *n* Sabbat *m*

sabbatical /sə'bætɪkl/ *n* (*Univ*) Forschungsurlaub *m*

sabot|age /'sæbətɑ:ʒ/ *n* Sabotage *f* ● *vt* sabotieren. **~eur** /-'tɜ:(r)/ *n* Saboteur *m*

sachet /'sæʃeɪ/ *n* Beutel *m*; (*scented*) Kissen *nt*

sack[1] /sæk/ *vt* (*plunder*) plündern

sack[2] *n* Sack *m*; **get the ~** (*fam*) rausgeschmissen werden ● *vt* (*fam*) rausschmeißen. **~ing** *n* Sackleinen *nt*; (*fam: dismissal*) Rausschmiß *m*

sacrament /'sækrəmənt/ *n* Sakrament *nt*

sacred /'seɪkrɪd/ *a* heilig

sacrifice /'sækrɪfaɪs/ *n* Opfer *nt* ● *vt* opfern

sacrilege /'sækrɪlɪdʒ/ *n* Sakrileg *nt*

sad /sæd/ *a* (**sadder, saddest**) traurig; ⟨*loss, death*⟩ schmerzlich. **~den** *vt* traurig machen

saddle /'sædl/ *n* Sattel *m* ● *vt* satteln; **~ s.o. with sth** (*fam*) jdm etw aufhalsen

sadis|m /'seɪdɪzm/ *n* Sadismus *m*. **~t** /-dɪst/ *n* Sadist *m*. **~tic** /sə'dɪstɪk/ *a*, **-ally** *adv* sadistisch

sad|ly /'sædlɪ/ *adv* traurig; (*unfortunately*) leider. **~ness** *n* Traurigkeit *f*

safe /seɪf/ *a* (**-r, -st**) sicher; ⟨*journey*⟩ gut; (*not dangerous*) ungefährlich; **~ and sound** gesund und wohlbehalten ● *n* Safe *m*. **~guard** *n* Schutz *m* ● *vt* schützen. **~ly** *adv* sicher; ⟨*arrive*⟩ gut

safety /'seɪftɪ/ *n* Sicherheit *f*. **~-belt** *n* Sicherheitsgurt *m*. **~-pin** *n* Sicherheitsnadel *f*. **~-valve** *n* [Sicherheits]ventil *nt*

sag /sæg/ *vi* (*pt/pp* **sagged**) durchhängen

saga /'sɑ:gə/ *n* Saga *f*; (*fig*) Geschichte *f*

sage[1] /seɪdʒ/ *n* (*herb*) Salbei *m*

sage[2] *a* weise ● *n* Weise(r) *m*

Sagittarius /sædʒɪ'teərɪəs/ *n* (*Astr*) Schütze *m*

said /sed/ *see* **say**

sail /seɪl/ *n* Segel *nt*; (*trip*) Segelfahrt *f* ● *vi* segeln; (*on liner*) fahren; (*leave*) abfahren (**for** nach) ● *vt* segeln mit

'**sailboard** *n* Surfbrett *nt*. **~ing** *n* Windsurfen *nt*

sailing /'seɪlɪŋ/ *n* Segelsport *m*. **~-boat** *n* Segelboot *nt*. **~-ship** *n* Segelschiff *nt*

sailor /'seɪlə(r)/ *n* Seemann *m*; (*in navy*) Matrose *m*

saint /seɪnt/ *n* Heilige(r) *m/f*. **~ly** *a* heilig

sake /seɪk/ *n* **for the ~ of ...** um ... (*gen*) willen; **for my/your ~** um meinet-/deinetwillen

salad /'sæləd/ *n* Salat *m*. **~ cream** *n* ≈ Mayonnaise *f*. **~-dressing** *n* Salatsoße *f*

salary /'sælərɪ/ *n* Gehalt *nt*

sale /seɪl/ *n* Verkauf *m*; (*event*) Basar *m*; (*at reduced prices*) Schlußverkauf *m*; **for ~** zu verkaufen

sales|man *n* Verkäufer *m*. **~woman** *n* Verkäuferin *f*

salient /'seɪlɪənt/ *a* wichtigste(r,s)

saliva /sə'laɪvə/ *n* Speichel *m*

sallow /'sæləʊ/ *a* (**-er, -est**) bleich

salmon /'sæmən/ *n* Lachs *m*. **~-pink** *a* lachsrosa

saloon /sə'lu:n/ *n* Salon *m*; (*Auto*) Limousine *f*; (*Amer: bar*) Wirtschaft *f*

salt /sɔ:lt/ *n* Salz *nt* ● *a* salzig; ⟨*water, meat*⟩ Salz- ● *vt* salzen; (*cure*) pökeln; streuen ⟨*road*⟩. **~-cellar** *n* Salzfaß *nt*. **~ 'water** *n* Salzwasser *nt*. **~y** *a* salzig

salutary /'sæljʊtərɪ/ *a* heilsam

salute /sə'lu:t/ *n* (*Mil*) Gruß *m* ● *vt/i* (*Mil*) grüßen

salvage /'sælvɪdʒ/ *n* (*Naut*) Bergung *f* ● *vt* bergen

salvation /sæl'veɪʃn/ *n* Rettung *f*; (*Relig*) Heil *nt*. **S~ 'Army** *n* Heilsarmee *f*

salvo /'sælvəʊ/ *n* Salve *f*

same /seɪm/ *a & pron* **the ~** der/die/das gleiche; (*pl*) die gleichen; (*identical*) der-/die-/dasselbe; (*pl*) dieselben ● *adv* **the ~** gleich; **all the ~** trotzdem; **the ~ to you** gleichfalls
sample /'sɑ:mpl/ *n* Probe *f*; (*Comm*) Muster *nt* ● *vt* probieren, kosten
sanatorium /sænə'tɔ:rɪəm/ *n* Sanatorium *nt*
sanctify /'sæŋktɪfaɪ/ *vt* (*pt/pp* **-fied**) heiligen
sanctimonious /sæŋktɪ'məʊnɪəs/ *a*, **-ly** *adv* frömmlerisch
sanction /'sæŋkʃn/ *n* Sanktion *f* ● *vt* sanktionieren
sanctity /'sæŋktətɪ/ *n* Heiligkeit *f*
sanctuary /'sæŋktjʊərɪ/ *n* (*Relig*) Heiligtum *nt*; (*refuge*) Zuflucht *f*; (*for wildlife*) Tierschutzgebiet *nt*
sand /sænd/ *n* Sand *m* ● *vt* **~ [down]** [ab]schmirgeln
sandal /'sændl/ *n* Sandale *f*
sand: ~bank *n* Sandbank *f*. **~paper** *n* Sandpapier *nt* ● *vt* [ab]schmirgeln. **~-pit** *n* Sandkasten *m*
sandwich /'sænwɪdʒ/ *n* ≈ belegtes Brot *nt*; Sandwich *m* ● *vt* **~ed between** eingeklemmt zwischen
sandy /'sændɪ/ *a* (**-ier, -iest**) sandig; ⟨*beach, soil*⟩ Sand-; ⟨*hair*⟩ rotblond
sane /seɪn/ *a* (**-r, -st**) geistig normal; (*sensible*) vernünftig
sang /sæŋ/ *see* **sing**
sanitary /'sænɪtərɪ/ *a* hygienisch; ⟨*system*⟩ sanitär. **~ napkin** *n* (*Amer*), **~ towel** *n* [Damen]binde *f*
sanitation /sænɪ'teɪʃn/ *n* Kanalisation und Abfallbeseitigung *pl*
sanity /'sænətɪ/ *n* [gesunder] Verstand *m*
sank /sæŋk/ *see* **sink**
sap /sæp/ *n* (*Bot*) Saft *m* ● *vt* (*pt/pp* **sapped**) schwächen
sapphire /'sæfaɪə(r)/ *n* Saphir *m*
sarcas|m /'sɑ:kæzm/ *n* Sarkasmus *m*. **~tic** /-'kæstɪk/ *a*, **-ally** *adv* sarkastisch
sardine /sɑ:'di:n/ *n* Sardine *f*
Sardinia /sɑ:'dɪnɪə/ *n* Sardinien *nt*
sardonic /sɑ:'dɒnɪk/ *a*, **-ally** *adv* höhnisch; ⟨*smile*⟩ sardonisch
sash /sæʃ/ *n* Schärpe *f*
sat /sæt/ *see* **sit**
satanic /sə'tænɪk/ *a* satanisch
satchel /'sætʃl/ *n* Ranzen *m*
satellite /'sætəlaɪt/ *n* Satellit *m*. **~ dish** *n* Satellitenschüssel *f*. **~ television** *n* Satellitenfernsehen *nt*
satin /'sætɪn/ *n* Satin *m*
satire /'sætaɪə(r)/ *n* Satire *f*
satirical /sə'tɪrɪkl/ *a*, **-ly** *adv* satirisch
satir|ist /'sætərɪst/ *n* Satiriker(in) *m(f)*. **~ize** *vt* satirisch darstellen; ⟨*book:*⟩ eine Satire sein auf (+ *acc*)
satisfaction /sætɪs'fækʃn/ *n* Befriedigung *f*; **to my ~** zu meiner Zufriedenheit
satisfactory /sætɪs'fæktərɪ/ *a*, **-ily** *adv* zufriedenstellend
satisf|y /'sætɪsfaɪ/ *vt* (*pt/pp* **-fied**) befriedigen; zufriedenstellen ⟨*customer*⟩; (*convince*) überzeugen; **be ~ied** zufrieden sein. **~ying** *a* befriedigend; ⟨*meal*⟩ sättigend
saturat|e /'sætʃəreɪt/ *vt* durchtränken; (*Chem & fig*) sättigen. **~ed** *a* durchnäßt; ⟨*fat*⟩ gesättigt
Saturday /'sætədeɪ/ *n* Samstag *m*, Sonnabend *m*
sauce /sɔ:s/ *n* Soße *f*; (*cheek*) Frechheit *f*. **~pan** *n* Kochtopf *m*
saucer /'sɔ:sə(r)/ *n* Untertasse *f*
saucy /'sɔ:sɪ/ *a* (**-ier, -iest**) frech
Saudi Arabia /saʊdɪə'reɪbɪə/ *n* Saudi-Arabien *nt*
sauna /'sɔ:nə/ *n* Sauna *f*
saunter /'sɔ:ntə(r)/ *vi* schlendern
sausage /'sɒsɪdʒ/ *n* Wurst *f*
savage /'sævɪdʒ/ *a* wild; (*fierce*) scharf; (*brutal*) brutal ● *n* Wilde(r) *m/f* ● *vt* anfallen. **~ry** *n* Brutalität *f*
save /seɪv/ *n* (*Sport*) Abwehr *f* ● *vt* retten (**from** vor + *dat*); (*keep*) aufheben; (*not waste*) sparen; (*collect*) sammeln; (*avoid*) ersparen; (*Sport*) verhindern ⟨*goal*⟩ ● *vi* **~ [up]** sparen ● *prep* außer (+ *dat*), mit Ausnahme (+ *gen*)
saver /'seɪvə(r)/ *n* Sparer *m*
saving /'seɪvɪŋ/ *n* (*see* **save**) Rettung *f*; Sparen *nt*; Ersparnis *f*; **~s** *pl* (*money*) Ersparnisse *pl*. **~s account** *n* Sparkonto *nt*. **~s bank** *n* Sparkasse *f*
saviour /'seɪvjə(r)/ *n* Retter *m*
savour /'seɪvə(r)/ *n* Geschmack *m* ● *vt* auskosten. **~y** *a* herzhaft, würzig; (*fig*) angenehm
saw[1] /sɔ:/ *see* **see**[1]
saw[2] *n* Säge *f* ● *vt/i* (*pt* **sawed**, *pp* **sawn** *or* **sawed**) sägen. **~dust** *n* Sägemehl *nt*
saxophone /'sæksəfəʊn/ *n* Saxophon *nt*
say /seɪ/ *n* Mitspracherecht *nt*; **have one's ~** seine Meinung sagen ● *vt/i* (*pt/pp* **said**) sagen; sprechen ⟨*prayer*⟩; **that is to ~** das heißt; **that**

goes without ~ing das versteht sich von selbst; **when all is said and done** letzten Endes; **I ~!** (*attracting attention*) hallo! **~ing** *n* Redensart *f*

scab /skæb/ *n* Schorf *m*; (*pej*) Streikbrecher *m*

scaffold /'skæfəld/ *n* Schafott *nt*. **~ing** *n* Gerüst *nt*

scald /skɔ:ld/ *vt* verbrühen

scale¹ /skeɪl/ *n* (*of fish*) Schuppe *f*

scale² *n* Skala *f*; (*Mus*) Tonleiter *f*; (*ratio*) Maßstab *m*; **on a grand ~** in großem Stil ● *vt* (*climb*) erklettern. **~ down** *vt* verkleinern

scales /skeɪlz/ *npl* (*for weighing*) Waage *f*

scalp /skælp/ *n* Kopfhaut *f* ● *vt* skalpieren

scalpel /'skælpl/ *n* Skalpell *nt*

scam /skæm/ *n* (*fam*) Schwindel *m*

scamper /'skæmpə(r)/ *vi* huschen

scan /skæn/ *n* (*Med*) Szintigramm *nt* ● *v* (*pt/pp* **scanned**) ● *vt* absuchen; (*quickly*) flüchtig ansehen; (*Med*) szintigraphisch untersuchen ● *vi* ⟨*poetry:*⟩ das richtige Versmaß haben

scandal /'skændl/ *n* Skandal *m*; (*gossip*) Skandalgeschichten *pl*. **~ize** /-dəlaɪz/ *vt* schockieren. **~ous** /-əs/ *a* skandalös

Scandinavia /skændɪ'neɪvɪə/ *n* Skandinavien *nt*. **~n** *a* skandinavisch ● *n* Skandinavier(in) *m(f)*

scant /skænt/ *a* wenig

scanty /'skæntɪ/ *a* (**-ier, -iest**), **-ily** *adv* spärlich; ⟨*clothing*⟩ knapp

scapegoat /'skeɪp-/ *n* Sündenbock *m*

scar /skɑ:(r)/ *n* Narbe *f* ● *vt* (*pt/pp* **scarred**) eine Narbe hinterlassen auf (+ *dat*)

scarc|e /skeəs/ *a* (**-r, -st**) knapp; **make oneself ~e** (*fam*) sich aus dem Staub machen. **~ely** *adv* kaum. **~ity** *n* Knappheit *f*

scare /skeə(r)/ *n* Schreck *m*; (*panic*) [allgemeine] Panik *f*; (*bomb ~*) Bombendrohung *f* ● *vt* Angst machen (+ *dat*); **be ~d** Angst haben (**of** vor + *dat*)

'scarecrow *n* Vogelscheuche *f*

scarf /skɑ:f/ *n* (*pl* **scarves**) Schal *m*; (*square*) Tuch *nt*

scarlet /'skɑ:lət/ *a* scharlachrot. **~ 'fever** *n* Scharlach *m*

scary /'skeərɪ/ *a* unheimlich

scathing /'skeɪðɪŋ/ *a* bissig

scatter /'skætə(r)/ *vt* verstreuen; (*disperse*) zerstreuen ● *vi* sich zerstreuen. **~-brained** *a* (*fam*) schusselig. **~ed** *a* verstreut; ⟨*showers*⟩ vereinzelt

scatty /'skætɪ/ *a* (**-ier, -iest**) (*fam*) verrückt

scavenge /'skævɪndʒ/ *vi* [im Abfall] Nahrung suchen; ⟨*animal:*⟩ Aas fressen. **~r** *n* Aasfresser *m*

scenario /sɪ'nɑ:rɪəʊ/ *n* Szenario *nt*

scene /si:n/ *n* Szene *f*; (*sight*) Anblick *m*; (*place of event*) Schauplatz *m*; **behind the ~s** hinter den Kulissen; **~ of the crime** Tatort *m*

scenery /'si:nərɪ/ *n* Landschaft *f*; (*Theat*) Szenerie *f*

scenic /'si:nɪk/ *a* landschaftlich schön; (*Theat*) Bühnen-

scent /sent/ *n* Duft *m*; (*trail*) Fährte *f*; (*perfume*) Parfüm *nt*. **~ed** *a* parfümiert

sceptic|al /'skeptɪkl/ *a*, **-ly** *adv* skeptisch. **~ism** /-tɪsɪzm/ *n* Skepsis *f*

schedule /'ʃedju:l/ *n* Programm *nt*; (*of work*) Zeitplan *m*; (*timetable*) Fahrplan *m*; **behind ~** im Rückstand; **according to ~** planmäßig ● *vt* planen. **~d flight** *n* Linienflug *m*

scheme /ski:m/ *n* Programm *nt*; (*plan*) Plan *m*; (*plot*) Komplott *nt* ● *vi* Ränke schmieden

schizophren|ia /skɪtsə'fri:nɪə/ *n* Schizophrenie *f*. **~ic** /-'frenɪk/ *a* schizophren

scholar /'skɒlə(r)/ *n* Gelehrte(r) *m/f*. **~ly** *a* gelehrt. **~ship** *n* Gelehrtheit *f*; (*grant*) Stipendium *nt*

school /sku:l/ *n* Schule *f*; (*Univ*) Fakultät *f* ● *vt* schulen; dressieren ⟨*animal*⟩

school: ~boy *n* Schüler *m*. **~girl** *n* Schülerin *f*. **~ing** *n* Schulbildung *f*. **~master** *n* Lehrer *m*. **~mistress** *n* Lehrerin *f*. **~teacher** *n* Lehrer(in) *m(f)*

sciatica /saɪ'ætɪkə/ *n* Ischias *m*

scien|ce /'saɪəns/ *n* Wissenschaft *f*. **~tific** /-'tɪfɪk/ *a* wissenschaftlich. **~tist** *n* Wissenschaftler *m*

scintillating /'sɪntɪleɪtɪŋ/ *a* sprühend

scissors /'sɪzəz/ *npl* Schere *f*; **a pair of ~** eine Schere

scoff¹ /skɒf/ *vi* **~ at** spotten über (+ *acc*)

scoff² *vt* (*fam*) verschlingen

scold /skəʊld/ *vt* ausschimpfen

scoop /sku:p/ *n* Schaufel *f*; (*Culin*) Portionierer *m*; (*Journ*) Exklusivmeldung *f* • *vt* ~ **out** aushöhlen; (*remove*) auslöffeln; ~ **up** schaufeln; schöpfen ⟨*liquid*⟩

scoot /sku:t/ *vi* (*fam*) rasen. ~**er** *n* Roller *m*

scope /skəʊp/ *n* Bereich *m*; (*opportunity*) Möglichkeiten *pl*

scorch /skɔ:tʃ/ *vt* versengen. ~**ing** *a* glühend heiß

score /skɔ:(r)/ *n* [Spiel]stand *m*; (*individual*) Punktzahl *f*; (*Mus*) Partitur *f*; (*Cinema*) Filmmusik *f*; **a** ~ **[of]** (*twenty*) zwanzig; **keep [the]** ~ zählen; (*written*) aufschreiben; **on that** ~ was das betrifft • *vt* erzielen; schießen ⟨*goal*⟩; (*cut*) einritzen • *vi* Punkte erzielen; (*Sport*) ein Tor schießen; (*keep score*) Punkte zählen. ~**r** *n* Punktezähler *m*; (*of goals*) Torschütze *m*

scorn /skɔ:n/ *n* Verachtung *f* • *vt* verachten. ~**ful** *a*, **-ly** *adv* verächtlich

Scorpio /'skɔ:pɪəʊ/ *n* (*Astr*) Skorpion *m*

scorpion /'skɔ:pɪən/ *n* Skorpion *m*

Scot /skɒt/ *n* Schotte *m*/Schottin *f*

Scotch /skɒtʃ/ *a* schottisch • *n* (*whisky*) Scotch *m*

scotch *vt* unterbinden

scot-'free *a* **get off** ~ straffrei ausgehen

Scot|land /'skɒtlənd/ *n* Schottland *nt*. ~**s**, ~**tish** *a* schottisch

scoundrel /'skaʊndrl/ *n* Schurke *m*

scour[1] /'skaʊə(r)/ *vt* (*search*) absuchen

scour[2] *vt* (*clean*) scheuern

scourge /skɜ:dʒ/ *n* Geißel *f*

scout /skaʊt/ *n* (*Mil*) Kundschafter *m* • *vi* ~ **for** Ausschau halten nach

Scout *n* **[Boy]** ~ Pfadfinder *m*

scowl /skaʊl/ *n* böser Gesichtsausdruck *m* • *vi* ein böses Gesicht machen

scraggy /'skrægɪ/ *a* (**-ier, -iest**) (*pej*) dürr, hager

scram /skræm/ *vi* (*fam*) abhauen

scramble /'skræmbl/ *n* Gerangel *nt* • *vi* klettern; ~ **for** sich drängen nach • *vt* (*Teleph*) verschlüsseln. ~**d 'egg[s]** *n*[*pl*] Rührei *nt*

scrap[1] /skræp/ *n* (*fam: fight*) Rauferei *f* • *vi* sich raufen

scrap[2] *n* Stückchen *nt*; (*metal*) Schrott *m*; ~**s** *pl* Reste; **not a** ~ kein bißchen • *vt* (*pt/pp* **scrapped**) aufgeben

'scrap-book *n* Sammelalbum *nt*

scrape /skreɪp/ *vt* schaben; (*clean*) abkratzen; (*damage*) [ver]schrammen. ~ **through** *vi* gerade noch durchkommen. ~ **together** *vt* zusammenkriegen

scraper /'skreɪpə(r)/ *n* Kratzer *m*

'scrap iron *n* Alteisen *nt*

scrappy /'skræpɪ/ *a* lückenhaft

'scrap-yard *n* Schrottplatz *m*

scratch /skrætʃ/ *n* Kratzer *m*; **start from** ~ von vorne anfangen; **not be up to** ~ zu wünschen übriglassen • *vt/i* kratzen; (*damage*) zerkratzen

scrawl /skrɔ:l/ *n* Gekrakel *nt* • *vt/i* krakeln

scrawny /'skrɔ:nɪ/ *a* (**-ier, -iest**) (*pej*) dürr, hager

scream /skri:m/ *n* Schrei *m* • *vt/i* schreien

screech /skri:tʃ/ *n* Kreischen *nt* • *vt/i* kreischen

screen /skri:n/ *n* Schirm *m*; (*Cinema*) Leinwand *f*; (*TV*) Bildschirm *m* • *vt* schützen; (*conceal*) verdecken; vorführen ⟨*film*⟩; (*examine*) überprüfen; (*Med*) untersuchen. ~**ing** *n* (*Med*) Reihenuntersuchung *f*. ~**play** *n* Drehbuch *nt*

screw /skru:/ *n* Schraube *f* • *vt* schrauben. ~ **up** *vt* festschrauben; (*crumple*) zusammenknüllen; zusammenkneifen ⟨*eyes*⟩; (*sl: bungle*) vermasseln; ~ **up one's courage** seinen Mut zusammennehmen

'screwdriver *n* Schraubenzieher *m*

screwy /'skru:ɪ/ *a* (**-ier, -iest**) (*fam*) verrückt

scribble /'skrɪbl/ *n* Gekritzel *nt* • *vt/i* kritzeln

script /skrɪpt/ *n* Schrift *f*; (*of speech, play*) Text *m*; (*Radio, TV*) Skript *nt*; (*of film*) Drehbuch *nt*

Scripture /'skrɪptʃə(r)/ *n* (*Sch*) Religion *f*; **the** ~**s** *pl* die Heilige Schrift *f*

scroll /skrəʊl/ *n* Schriftrolle *f*; (*decoration*) Volute *f*

scrounge /skraʊndʒ/ *vt/i* schnorren. ~**r** *n* Schnorrer *m*

scrub[1] /skrʌb/ *n* (*land*) Buschland *nt*, Gestrüpp *nt*

scrub[2] *vt/i* (*pt/pp* **scrubbed**) schrubben; (*fam: cancel*) absagen; fallenlassen ⟨*plan*⟩

scruff /skrʌf/ *n* **by the** ~ **of the neck** beim Genick

scruffy /'skrʌfɪ/ *a* (**-ier, -iest**) vergammelt
scrum /skrʌm/ *n* Gedränge *nt*
scruple /'skru:pl/ *n* Skrupel *m*
scrupulous /'skru:pjʊləs/ *a*, **-ly** *adv* gewissenhaft
scrutin|ize /'skru:tɪnaɪz/ *vt* [genau] ansehen. **~y** *n* (*look*) prüfender Blick *m*
scuff /skʌf/ *vt* abstoßen
scuffle /'skʌfl/ *n* Handgemenge *nt*
scullery /'skʌlərɪ/ *n* Spülküche *f*
sculpt|or /'skʌlptə(r)/ *n* Bildhauer(in) *m(f)*. **~ure** /-tʃə(r)/ *n* Bildhauerei *f*; (*piece of work*) Skulptur *f*, Plastik *f*
scum /skʌm/ *n* Schmutzschicht *f*; (*people*) Abschaum *m*
scurrilous /'skʌrɪləs/ *a* niederträchtig
scurry /'skʌrɪ/ *vi* (*pt/pp* **-ied**) huschen
scuttle[1] /'skʌtl/ *n* Kohleneimer *m*
scuttle[2] *vt* versenken ⟨*ship*⟩
scuttle[3] *vi* schnell krabbeln
scythe /saɪð/ *n* Sense *f*
sea /si:/ *n* Meer *nt*, See *f*; **at ~** auf See; **by ~** mit dem Schiff. **~board** *n* Küste *f*. **~food** *n* Meeresfrüchte *pl*. **~gull** *n* Möwe *f*
seal[1] /si:l/ *n* (*Zool*) Seehund *m*
seal[2] *n* Siegel *nt*; (*Techn*) Dichtung *f* ● *vt* versiegeln; (*Techn*) abdichten; (*fig*) besiegeln. **~ off** *vt* abriegeln
'sea-level *n* Meeresspiegel *m*
seam /si:m/ *n* Naht *f*; (*of coal*) Flöz *nt*
'seaman *n* Seemann *m*; (*sailor*) Matrose *m*
seamless /'si:mlɪs/ *a* nahtlos
seance /'seɪɑ:ns/ *n* spiritistische Sitzung *f*
sea: ~plane *n* Wasserflugzeug *nt*. **~port** *n* Seehafen *m*
search /sɜ:tʃ/ *n* Suche *f*; (*official*) Durchsuchung *f* ● *vt* durchsuchen; absuchen ⟨*area*⟩ ● *vi* suchen (**for** nach). **~ing** *a* prüfend, forschend
search: ~light *n* [Such]scheinwerfer *m*. **~-party** *n* Suchmannschaft *f*
sea: ~sick *a* seekrank. **~side** *n* **at/to the ~side** am/ans Meer
season /'si:zn/ *n* Jahreszeit *f*; (*social, tourist, sporting*) Saison *f* ● *vt* (*flavour*) würzen. **~able** /-əbl/ *a* der Jahreszeit gemäß. **~al** *a* Saison-. **~ing** *n* Gewürze *pl*
'season ticket *n* Dauerkarte *f*
seat /si:t/ *n* Sitz *m*; (*place*) Sitzplatz *m*; (*bottom*) Hintern *m*; **take a ~** Platz nehmen ● *vt* setzen; (*have seats for*) Sitzplätze bieten (+ *dat*); **remain ~ed** sitzen bleiben. **~-belt** *n* Sicherheitsgurt *m*; **fasten one's ~-belt** sich anschnallen
sea: ~weed *n* [See]tang *m*. **~worthy** *a* seetüchtig
secateurs /sekə'tɜ:z/ *npl* Gartenschere *f*
seclu|de /sɪ'klu:d/ *vt* absondern. **~ded** *a* abgelegen. **~sion** /-ʒn/ *n* Zurückgezogenheit *f*
second[1] /sɪ'kɒnd/ *vt* (*transfer*) [vorübergehend] versetzen
second[2] /'sekənd/ *a* zweite(r,s); **on ~ thoughts** nach weiterer Überlegung ● *n* Sekunde *f*; (*Sport*) Sekundant *m*; **~s** *pl* (*goods*) Waren zweiter Wahl; **the ~** der/die/das zweite ● *adv* (*in race*) an zweiter Stelle ● *vt* unterstützen ⟨*proposal*⟩
secondary /'sekəndrɪ/ *a* zweitrangig; (*Phys*) Sekundär-. **~ school** *n* höhere Schule *f*
second: ~-best *a* zweitbeste(r,s). **~ 'class** *adv* ⟨*travel, send*⟩ zweiter Klasse. **~-class** *a* zweitklassig
'second hand *n* (*on clock*) Sekundenzeiger *m*
second-'hand *a* gebraucht ● *adv* aus zweiter Hand
secondly /'sekəndlɪ/ *adv* zweitens
second-'rate *a* zweitklassig
secrecy /'si:krəsɪ/ *n* Heimlichkeit *f*
secret /'si:krɪt/ *a* geheim; ⟨*agent, police*⟩ Geheim-; ⟨*drinker, lover*⟩ heimlich ● *n* Geheimnis *nt*
secretarial /sekrə'teərɪəl/ *a* Sekretärinnen-; ⟨*work, staff*⟩ Sekretariats-
secretary /'sekrətərɪ/ *n* Sekretär(in) *m(f)*
secret|e /sɪ'kri:t/ *vt* absondern. **~ion** /-i:ʃn/ *n* Absonderung *f*
secretive /'si:krətɪv/ *a* geheimtuerisch. **~ness** *n* Heimlichtuerei *f*
secretly /'si:krɪtlɪ/ *adv* heimlich
sect /sekt/ *n* Sekte *f*
section /'sekʃn/ *n* Teil *m*; (*of text*) Abschnitt *m*; (*of firm*) Abteilung *f*; (*of organization*) Sektion *f*
sector /'sektə(r)/ *n* Sektor *m*
secular /'sekjʊlə(r)/ *a* weltlich
secure /sɪ'kjʊə(r)/ *a*, **-ly** *adv* sicher; (*firm*) fest; (*emotionally*) geborgen ● *vt* sichern; (*fasten*) festmachen; (*obtain*) sich (*dat*) sichern
securit|y /sɪ'kjʊərətɪ/ *n* Sicherheit *f*; (*emotional*) Geborgenheit *f*; **~ies** *pl* Wertpapiere *pl*; (*Fin*) Effekten *pl*
sedan /sɪ'dæn/ *n* (*Amer*) Limousine *f*

sedate[1] /sɪ'deɪt/ *a*, **-ly** *adv* gesetzt
sedate[2] *vt* sedieren
sedation /sɪ'deɪʃn/ *n* Sedierung *f*; **be under ~** sediert sein
sedative /'sedətɪv/ *a* beruhigend ● *n* Beruhigungsmittel *nt*
sedentary /'sedəntərɪ/ *a* sitzend
sediment /'sedɪmənt/ *n* [Boden]satz *m*
seduce /sɪ'dju:s/ *vt* verführen
seduct|ion /sɪ'dʌkʃn/ *n* Verführung *f*. **~ive** /-tɪv/ *a*, **-ly** *adv* verführerisch
see[1] /si:/ *v* (*pt* **saw**, *pp* **seen**) ● *vt* sehen; (*understand*) einsehen; (*imagine*) sich (*dat*) vorstellen; (*escort*) begleiten; **go and ~** nachsehen; (*visit*) besuchen; **~ you later!** bis nachher! **~ing that** da ● *vi* sehen; (*check*) nachsehen; **~ about** sich kümmern um. **~ off** *vt* verabschieden; (*chase away*) vertreiben. **~ through** *vi* durchsehen ● *vt* (*fig*) **~ through s.o.** jdn durchschauen
see[2] *n* (*Relig*) Bistum *nt*
seed /si:d/ *n* Samen *m*; (*of grape*) Kern *m*; (*fig*) Saat *f*; (*Tennis*) gesetzter Spieler *m*; **go to ~** Samen bilden; (*fig*) herunterkommen. **~ed** *a* (*Tennis*) gesetzt. **~ling** *n* Sämling *m*
seedy /'si:dɪ/ *a* (**-ier, -iest**) schäbig; ⟨*area*⟩ heruntergekommen
seek /si:k/ *vt* (*pt/pp* **sought**) suchen
seem /si:m/ *vi* scheinen. **~ingly** *adv* scheinbar
seemly /'si:mlɪ/ *a* schicklich
seen /si:n/ *see* **see**[1]
seep /si:p/ *vi* sickern
see-saw /'si:sɔ:/ *n* Wippe *f*
seethe /si:ð/ *vi* **~ with anger** vor Wut schäumen
'see-through *a* durchsichtig
segment /'segmənt/ *n* Teil *m*; (*of worm*) Segment *nt*; (*of orange*) Spalte *f*
segregat|e /'segrɪgeɪt/ *vt* trennen. **~ion** /-'geɪʃn/ *n* Trennung *f*
seize /si:z/ *vt* ergreifen; (*Jur*) beschlagnahmen; **~ s.o. by the arm** jdn am Arm packen. **~ up** *vi* (*Techn*) sich festfressen
seizure /'si:ʒə(r)/ *n* (*Jur*) Beschlagnahme *f*; (*Med*) Anfall *m*
seldom /'seldəm/ *adv* selten
select /sɪ'lekt/ *a* ausgewählt; (*exclusive*) exklusiv ● *vt* auswählen; aufstellen ⟨*team*⟩. **~ion** /-ekʃn/ *n* Auswahl *f*. **~ive** /-ɪv/ *a*, **-ly** *adv* selektiv; (*choosy*) wählerisch
self /self/ *n* (*pl* **selves**) Ich *nt*
self: ~-ad'dressed *a* adressiert. **~-ad'hesive** *a* selbstklebend. **~-as'surance** *n* Selbstsicherheit *f*. **~-as'sured** *a* selbstsicher. **~-'catering** *n* Selbstversorgung *f*. **~-'centred** *a* egozentrisch. **~-'confidence** *n* Selbstbewußtsein *nt*, Selbstvertrauen *nt*. **~-'confident** *a* selbstbewußt. **~-'conscious** *a* befangen. **~-con'tained** *a* ⟨*flat*⟩ abgeschlossen. **~-con'trol** *n* Selbstbeherrschung *f*. **~-de'fence** *n* Selbstverteidigung *f*; (*Jur*) Notwehr *f*. **~-de'nial** *n* Selbstverleugnung *f*. **~-determi'nation** *n* Selbstbestimmung *f*. **~-em'ployed** selbständig. **~-e'steem** *n* Selbstachtung *f*. **~-'evident** *a* offensichtlich. **~-'governing** *a* selbstverwaltet. **~-'help** *n* Selbsthilfe *f*. **~-in'dulgent** *a* maßlos. **~-'interest** *n* Eigennutz *m*
self|ish /'selfɪʃ/ *a*, **-ly** *adv* egoistisch, selbstsüchtig. **~less** *a*, **-ly** *adv* selbstlos
self: ~-'pity *n* Selbstmitleid *nt*. **~-'portrait** *n* Selbstporträt *nt*. **~-pos'sessed** *a* selbstbeherrscht. **~-preser'vation** *n* Selbsterhaltung *f*. **~-re'spect** *n* Selbstachtung *f*. **~-'righteous** *a* selbstgerecht. **~-'sacrifice** *n* Selbstaufopferung *f*. **~-'satisfied** *a* selbstgefällig. **~-'service** *n* Selbstbedienung *f* ● *attrib* Selbstbedienungs-. **~-suf'ficient** *a* selbständig. **~-'willed** *a* eigenwillig
sell /sel/ *v* (*pt/pp* **sold**) ● *vt* verkaufen; **be sold out** ausverkauft sein ● *vi* sich verkaufen. **~ off** *vt* verkaufen
seller /'selə(r)/ *n* Verkäufer *m*
Sellotape (P) /'seləʊ-/ *n* ≈ Tesafilm (P) *m*
'sell-out *n* **be a ~** ausverkauft sein; (*fam: betrayal*) Verrat sein
selves /selvz/ *see* **self**
semblance /'sembləns/ *n* Anschein *m*
semen /'si:mən/ *n* (*Anat*) Samen *m*
semester /sɪ'mestə(r)/ *n* (*Amer*) Semester *nt*
semi|breve /'semɪbri:v/ *n* (*Mus*) ganze Note *f*. **~circle** *n* Halbkreis *m*. **~'circular** *a* halbkreisförmig. **~'colon** *n* Semikolon *nt*. **~-de'tached** *a* & *n* **~-detached [house]** Doppelhaushälfte *f*. **~'final** *n* Halbfinale *nt*
seminar /'semɪnɑ:(r)/ *n* Seminar *nt*. **~y** /-nərɪ/ *n* Priesterseminar *nt*
'semitone *n* (*Mus*) Halbton *m*
semolina /semə'li:nə/ *n* Grieß *m*

senat|e /ˈsenət/ *n* Senat *m*. **~or** *n* Senator *m*
send /send/ *vt/i* (*pt/pp* **sent**) schicken; **~ one's regards** grüßen lassen; **~ for** kommen lassen ⟨*person*⟩; sich (*dat*) schicken lassen ⟨*thing*⟩. **~er** *n* Absender *m*. **~-off** *n* Verabschiedung *f*
senil|e /ˈsi:naɪl/ *a* senil. **~ity** /sɪˈnɪlətɪ/ *n* Senilität *f*
senior /ˈsi:nɪə(r)/ *a* älter; (*in rank*) höher • *n* Ältere(r) *m/f*; (*in rank*) Vorgesetzte(r) *m/f*. **~ ˈcitizen** *n* Senior(in) *m(f)*
seniority /si:nɪˈɒrətɪ/ *n* höheres Alter *nt*; (*in rank*) höherer Rang *m*
sensation /senˈseɪʃn/ *n* Sensation *f*; (*feeling*) Gefühl *nt*. **~al** *a*, **-ly** *adv* sensationell
sense /sens/ *n* Sinn *m*; (*feeling*) Gefühl *nt*; (*common ~*) Verstand *m*; **in a ~** in gewisser Hinsicht; **make ~** Sinn ergeben • *vt* spüren. **~less** *a*, **-ly** *adv* sinnlos; (*unconscious*) bewußtlos
sensible /ˈsensəbl/ *a*, **-bly** *adv* vernünftig; ⟨*suitable*⟩ zweckmäßig
sensitiv|e /ˈsensətɪv/ *a*, **-ly** *adv* empfindlich; (*understanding*) einfühlsam. **~ity** /-ˈtɪvətɪ/ Empfindlichkeit *f*
sensory /ˈsensərɪ/ *a* Sinnes-
sensual /ˈsensjʊəl/ *a* sinnlich. **~ity** /-ˈælətɪ/ *n* Sinnlichkeit *f*
sensuous /ˈsensjʊəs/ *a* sinnlich
sent /sent/ *see* **send**
sentence /ˈsentəns/ *n* Satz *m*; (*Jur*) Urteil *nt*; (*punishment*) Strafe *f* • *vt* verurteilen
sentiment /ˈsentɪmənt/ *n* Gefühl *nt*; (*opinion*) Meinung *f*; (*sentimentality*) Sentimentalität *f*. **~al** /-ˈmentl/ *a* sentimental. **~ality** /-ˈtælətɪ/ *n* Sentimentalität *f*
sentry /ˈsentrɪ/ *n* Wache *f*
separable /ˈsepərəbl/ *a* trennbar
separate[1] /ˈsepərət/ *a*, **-ly** *adv* getrennt, separat
separat|e[2] /ˈsepəreɪt/ *vt* trennen • *vi* sich trennen. **~ion** /-ˈreɪʃn/ *n* Trennung *f*
September /sepˈtembə(r)/ *n* September *m*
septic /ˈseptɪk/ *a* vereitert; **go ~** vereitern
sequel /ˈsi:kwl/ *n* Folge *f*; (*fig*) Nachspiel *nt*
sequence /ˈsi:kwəns/ *n* Reihenfolge *f*
sequin /ˈsi:kwɪn/ *n* Paillette *f*
serenade /serəˈneɪd/ *n* Ständchen *nt* • *vt* **~ s.o.** jdm ein Ständchen bringen
seren|e /sɪˈri:n/ *a*, **-ly** *adv* gelassen. **~ity** /-ˈrenətɪ/ *n* Gelassenheit *f*
sergeant /ˈsɑ:dʒənt/ *n* (*Mil*) Feldwebel *m*; (*in police*) Polizeimeister *m*
serial /ˈsɪərɪəl/ *n* Fortsetzungsgeschichte *f*; (*Radio, TV*) Serie *f*. **~ize** *vt* in Fortsetzungen veröffentlichen/ (*Radio, TV*) senden
series /ˈsɪəri:z/ *n inv* Serie *f*
serious /ˈsɪərɪəs/ *a*, **-ly** *adv* ernst; ⟨*illness, error*⟩ schwer. **~ness** *n* Ernst *m*
sermon /ˈsɜ:mən/ *n* Predigt *f*
serpent /ˈsɜ:pənt/ *n* Schlange *f*
serrated /seˈreɪtɪd/ *a* gezackt
serum /ˈsɪərəm/ *n* Serum *nt*
servant /ˈsɜ:vənt/ *n* Diener(in) *m(f)*
serve /sɜ:v/ *n* (*Tennis*) Aufschlag *m* • *vt* dienen (+ *dat*); bedienen ⟨*customer, guest*⟩; servieren ⟨*food*⟩; (*Jur*) zustellen (**on s.o.** jdm); verbüßen ⟨*sentence*⟩; **~ its purpose** seinen Zweck erfüllen; **it ~s you right!** das geschieht dir recht! **~s two** für zwei Personen • *vi* dienen; (*Tennis*) aufschlagen
service /ˈsɜ:vɪs/ *n* Dienst *m*; (*Relig*) Gottesdienst *m*; (*in shop, restaurant*) Bedienung *f*; (*transport*) Verbindung *f*; (*maintenance*) Wartung *f*; (*set of crockery*) Service *nt*; (*Tennis*) Aufschlag *m*; **~s** *pl* Dienstleistungen *pl*; (*on motorway*) Tankstelle und Raststätte *f*; **in the ~s** beim Militär; **be of ~** nützlich sein; **out of/in ~** ⟨*machine:*⟩ außer/in Betrieb • *vt* (*Techn*) warten. **~able** /-əbl/ *a* nützlich; (*durable*) haltbar
service: ~ area *n* Tankstelle und Raststätte *f*. **~ charge** *n* Bedienungszuschlag *m*. **~man** *n* Soldat *m*. **~ station** *n* Tankstelle *f*
serviette /sɜ:vɪˈet/ *n* Serviette *f*
servile /ˈsɜ:vaɪl/ *a* unterwürfig
session /ˈseʃn/ *n* Sitzung *f*; (*Univ*) Studienjahr *nt*
set /set/ *n* Satz *m*; (*of crockery*) Service *nt*; (*of cutlery*) Garnitur *f*; (*TV, Radio*) Apparat *m*; (*Math*) Menge *f*; (*Theat*) Bühnenbild *nt*; (*Cinema*) Szenenaufbau *m*; (*of people*) Kreis *m*; **shampoo and ~** Waschen und Legen • *a* (*ready*) fertig, bereit; (*rigid*) fest; ⟨*book*⟩ vorgeschrieben; **be ~ on doing sth** entschlossen sein, etw zu tun; **be ~ in one's ways** in seinen

Gewohnheiten festgefahren sein • *v* (*pt/pp* **set**, *pres p* **setting**) • *vt* setzen; (*adjust*) einstellen; stellen ⟨*task, alarm clock*⟩; festsetzen, festlegen ⟨*date, limit*⟩; aufgeben ⟨*homework*⟩; zusammenstellen ⟨*questions*⟩; [ein]fassen ⟨*gem*⟩; einrichten ⟨*bone*⟩; legen ⟨*hair*⟩; decken ⟨*table*⟩ • *vi* ⟨*sun:*⟩ untergehen; (*become hard*) fest werden; **~ about sth** sich an etw (*acc*) machen; **~ about doing sth** sich daranmachen, etw zu tun. **~ back** *vt* zurücksetzen; (*hold up*) aufhalten; (*fam: cost*) kosten. **~ off** *vi* losgehen; (*in vehicle*) losfahren • *vt* auslösen ⟨*alarm*⟩; explodieren lassen ⟨*bomb*⟩. **~ out** *vi* losgehen; (*in vehicle*) losfahren; **~ out to do sth** sich vornehmen, etw zu tun • *vt* auslegen; (*state*) darlegen. **~ up** *vt* aufbauen; (*fig*) gründen

set 'meal *n* Menü *nt*

settee /se'ti:/ *n* Sofa *nt*, Couch *f*

setting /'setɪŋ/ *n* Rahmen *m*; (*surroundings*) Umgebung *f*; (*of sun*) Untergang *m*; (*of jewel*) Fassung *f*

settle /'setl/ *vt* (*decide*) entscheiden; (*agree*) regeln; (*fix*) festsetzen; (*calm*) beruhigen; (*pay*) bezahlen • *vi* sich niederlassen; ⟨*snow, dust:*⟩ liegenbleiben; (*subside*) sich senken; ⟨*sediment:*⟩ sich absetzen. **~ down** *vi* sich beruhigen; (*permanently*) seßhaft werden. **~ up** *vi* abrechnen

settlement /'setlmənt/ *n* (*see* **settle**) Entscheidung *f*; Regelung *f*; Bezahlung *f*; (*Jur*) Vergleich *m*; (*colony*) Siedlung *f*

settler /'setlə(r)/ *n* Siedler *m*

'set-to *n* (*fam*) Streit *m*

'set-up *n* System *nt*

seven /'sevn/ *a* sieben. **~'teen** *a* siebzehn. **~'teenth** *a* siebzehnte(r,s)

seventh /'sevnθ/ *a* siebte(r,s)

seventieth /'sevntɪɪθ/ *a* siebzigste(r,s)

seventy /'sevntɪ/ *a* siebzig

sever /'sevə(r)/ *vt* durchtrennen; abbrechen ⟨*relations*⟩

several /'sevrl/ *a & pron* mehrere, einige

sever|e /sɪ'vɪə(r)/ *a* (**-r, -st**), **-ly** *adv* streng; ⟨*pain*⟩ stark; ⟨*illness*⟩ schwer. **~ity** /-'verətɪ/ *n* Strenge *f*; Schwere *f*

sew /səʊ/ *vt/i* (*pt* **sewed**, *pp* **sewn** *or* **sewed**) nähen. **~ up** *vt* zunähen

sewage /'su:ɪdʒ/ *n* Abwasser *nt*

sewer /'su:ə(r)/ *n* Abwasserkanal *m*

sewing /'səʊɪŋ/ *n* Nähen *nt*; (*work*) Näharbeit *f*. **~ machine** *n* Nähmaschine *f*

sewn /səʊn/ *see* **sew**

sex /seks/ *n* Geschlecht *nt*; (*sexuality, intercourse*) Sex *m*. **~ist** *a* sexistisch. **~ offender** *n* Triebverbrecher *m*

sexual /'seksjʊəl/ *a*, **-ly** *adv* sexuell. **~ 'intercourse** *n* Geschlechtsverkehr *m*

sexuality /seksjʊ'ælətɪ/ *n* Sexualität *f*

sexy /'seksɪ/ *a* (**-ier, -iest**) sexy

shabby /'ʃæbɪ/ *a* (**-ier, -iest**), **-ily** *adv* schäbig

shack /ʃæk/ *n* Hütte *f*

shackles /'ʃæklz/ *npl* Fesseln *pl*

shade /ʃeɪd/ *n* Schatten *m*; (*of colour*) [Farb]ton *m*; (*for lamp*) [Lampen]schirm *m*; (*Amer: window-blind*) Jalousie *f* • *vt* beschatten; (*draw lines on*) schattieren

shadow /'ʃædəʊ/ *n* Schatten *m* • *vt* (*follow*) beschatten. **~y** *a* schattenhaft

shady /'ʃeɪdɪ/ *a* (**-ier, -iest**) schattig; (*fam: disreputable*) zwielichtig

shaft /ʃɑ:ft/ *n* Schaft *m*; (*Techn*) Welle *f*; (*of light*) Strahl *m*; (*of lift*) Schacht *m*; **~s** *pl* (*of cart*) Gabeldeichsel *f*

shaggy /'ʃægɪ/ *a* (**-ier, -iest**) zottig

shake /ʃeɪk/ *n* Schütteln *nt* • *v* (*pt* **shook**, *pp* **shaken**) • *vt* schütteln; (*cause to tremble, shock*) erschüttern; **~ hands with s.o.** jdm die Hand geben • *vi* wackeln; (*tremble*) zittern. **~ off** *vt* abschütteln

shaky /'ʃeɪkɪ/ *a* (**-ier, -iest**) wackelig; ⟨*hand, voice*⟩ zittrig

shall /ʃæl/ *v aux* **I ~ go** ich werde gehen; **we ~ see** wir werden sehen; **what ~ I do?** was soll ich machen? **I'll come too, ~ I?** ich komme mit, ja? **thou shalt not kill** (*liter*) du sollst nicht töten

shallow /'ʃæləʊ/ *a* (**-er, -est**) seicht; ⟨*dish*⟩ flach; (*fig*) oberflächlich

sham /ʃæm/ *a* unecht • *n* Heuchelei *f*; (*person*) Heuchler(in) *m(f)* • *vt* (*pt/pp* **shammed**) vortäuschen

shambles /'ʃæmblz/ *n* Durcheinander *nt*

shame /ʃeɪm/ *n* Scham *f*; (*disgrace*) Schande *f*; **be a ~** schade sein; **what a ~!** wie schade! **~-faced** *a* betreten

shame|ful /'ʃeɪmfl/ *a*, **-ly** *adv* schändlich. **~less** *a*, **-ly** *adv* schamlos

shampoo /ʃæm'pu:/ *n* Shampoo *nt* ● *vt* schamponieren

shandy /'ʃændɪ/ *n* Radler *m*

shan't /ʃɑ:nt/ = **shall not**

shape /ʃeɪp/ *n* Form *f*; (*figure*) Gestalt *f*; **take ~** Gestalt annehmen ● *vt* formen (**into** zu) ● *vi* **~ up** sich entwickeln. **~less** *a* formlos; ⟨*clothing*⟩ unförmig

shapely /'ʃeɪplɪ/ *a* (**-ier, -iest**) wohlgeformt

share /ʃeə(r)/ *n* [An]teil *m*; (*Comm*) Aktie *f* ● *vt/i* teilen. **~holder** *n* Aktionär(in) *m(f)*

shark /ʃɑ:k/ *n* Hai[fisch] *m*

sharp /ʃɑ:p/ *a* (**-er, -est**), **-ly** *adv* scharf; (*pointed*) spitz; (*severe*) heftig; (*sudden*) steil; (*alert*) clever; (*unscrupulous*) gerissen ● *adv* scharf; (*Mus*) zu hoch; **at six o'clock ~** Punkt sechs Uhr; **look ~!** beeil dich! ● *n* (*Mus*) Kreuz *nt*. **~en** *vt* schärfen; [an]spitzen ⟨*pencil*⟩

shatter /'ʃætə(r)/ *vt* zertrümmern; (*fig*) zerstören; **be ~ed** ⟨*person:*⟩ erschüttert sein ● *vi* zersplittern

shave /ʃeɪv/ *n* Rasur *f*; **have a ~** sich rasieren ● *vt* rasieren ● *vi* sich rasieren. **~r** *n* Rasierapparat *m*

shaving /'ʃeɪvɪŋ/ *n* Rasieren *nt*. **~-brush** *n* Rasierpinsel *m*

shawl /ʃɔ:l/ *n* Schultertuch *nt*

she /ʃi:/ *pron* sie

sheaf /ʃi:f/ *n* (*pl* **sheaves**) Garbe *f*; (*of papers*) Bündel *nt*

shear /ʃɪə(r)/ *vt* (*pt* **sheared**, *pp* **shorn** *or* **sheared**) scheren

shears /ʃɪəz/ *npl* [große] Schere *f*

sheath /ʃi:θ/ *n* (*pl* **~s** /ʃi:ðz/) Scheide *f*

sheaves /ʃi:vz/ *see* **sheaf**

shed[1] /ʃed/ *n* Schuppen *m*; (*for cattle*) Stall *m*

shed[2] *vt* (*pt/pp* **shed**, *pres p* **shedding**) verlieren; vergießen ⟨*blood, tears*⟩; **~ light on** Licht bringen in (+ *acc*)

sheen /ʃi:n/ *n* Glanz *m*

sheep /ʃi:p/ *n inv* Schaf *nt*. **~-dog** *n* Hütehund *m*

sheepish /'ʃi:pɪʃ/ *a*, **-ly** *adv* verlegen

'sheepskin *n* Schaffell *nt*

sheer /ʃɪə(r)/ *a* rein; (*steep*) steil; (*transparent*) hauchdünn ● *adv* steil

sheet /ʃi:t/ *n* Laken *nt*, Bettuch *nt*; (*of paper*) Blatt *nt*; (*of glass, metal*) Platte *f*

sheikh /ʃeɪk/ *n* Scheich *m*

shelf /ʃelf/ *n* (*pl* **shelves**) Brett *nt*, Bord *nt*; (*set of shelves*) Regal *nt*

shell /ʃel/ *n* Schale *f*; (*of snail*) Haus *nt*; (*of tortoise*) Panzer *m*; (*on beach*) Muschel *f*; (*of unfinished building*) Rohbau *m*; (*Mil*) Granate *f* ● *vt* pellen; enthülsen ⟨*peas*⟩; (*Mil*) [mit Granaten] beschießen. **~ out** *vi* (*fam*) blechen

'shellfish *n inv* Schalentiere *pl*; (*Culin*) Meeresfrüchte *pl*

shelter /'ʃeltə(r)/ *n* Schutz *m*; (*air-raid ~*) Luftschutzraum *m* ● *vt* schützen (**from** vor + *dat*) ● *vi* sich unterstellen. **~ed** *a* geschützt; ⟨*life*⟩ behütet

shelve /ʃelv/ *vt* auf Eis legen; (*abandon*) aufgeben ● *vi* ⟨*slope:*⟩ abfallen

shelves /ʃelvz/ *see* **shelf**

shelving /'ʃelvɪŋ/ *n* (*shelves*) Regale *pl*

shepherd /'ʃepəd/ *n* Schäfer *m*; (*Relig*) Hirte *m* ● *vt* führen. **~ess** *n* Schäferin *f*. **~'s pie** *n* Auflauf *m* aus mit Kartoffelbrei bedecktem Hackfleisch

sherry /'ʃerɪ/ *n* Sherry *m*

shield /ʃi:ld/ *n* Schild *m*; (*for eyes*) Schirm *m*; (*Techn & fig*) Schutz *m* ● *vt* schützen (**from** vor + *dat*)

shift /ʃɪft/ *n* Verschiebung *f*; (*at work*) Schicht *f*; **make ~** sich (*dat*) behelfen (**with** mit) ● *vt* rücken; (*take away*) wegnehmen; (*rearrange*) umstellen; schieben ⟨*blame*⟩ (**on to** auf + *acc*) ● *vi* sich verschieben; (*fam: move quickly*) rasen

'shift work *n* Schichtarbeit *f*

shifty /'ʃɪftɪ/ *a* (**-ier, -iest**) (*pej*) verschlagen

shilly-shally /'ʃɪlɪʃælɪ/ *vi* fackeln (*fam*)

shimmer /'ʃɪmə(r)/ *n* Schimmer *m* ● *vi* schimmern

shin /ʃɪn/ *n* Schienbein *nt*

shine /ʃaɪn/ *n* Glanz *m* ● *v* (*pt/pp* **shone**) ● *vi* leuchten; (*reflect light*) glänzen; ⟨*sun:*⟩ scheinen ● *vt* **~ a light on** beleuchten

shingle /'ʃɪŋgl/ *n* (*pebbles*) Kiesel *pl*

shingles /'ʃɪŋglz/ *n* (*Med*) Gürtelrose *f*

shiny /'ʃaɪnɪ/ *a* (**-ier, -iest**) glänzend

ship /ʃɪp/ *n* Schiff *nt* ● *vt* (*pt/pp* **shipped**) verschiffen

ship: ~building *n* Schiffbau *m*. **~ment** *n* Sendung *f*. **~per** *n* Spediteur *m*. **~ping** *n* Versand *m*; (*traffic*)

Schiffahrt *f*. **~shape** *a & adv* in Ordnung. **~wreck** *n* Schiffbruch *m*. **~wrecked** *a* schiffbrüchig. **~yard** *n* Werft *f*

shirk /ʃɜ:k/ *vt* sich drücken vor (+ *dat*). **~er** *n* Drückeberger *m*

shirt /ʃɜ:t/ *n* [Ober]hemd *nt*; (*for woman*) Hemdbluse *f*

shit /ʃɪt/ *n* (*vulg*) Scheiße *f* ● *vi* (*pt/pp* **shit**) (*vulg*) scheißen

shiver /ˈʃɪvə(r)/ *n* Schauder *m* ● *vi* zittern

shoal /ʃəʊl/ *n* (*of fish*) Schwarm *m*

shock /ʃɒk/ *n* Schock *m*; (*Electr*) Schlag *m*; (*impact*) Erschütterung *f* ● *vt* einen Schock versetzen (+ *dat*); (*scandalize*) schockieren. **~ing** *a* schockierend; (*fam: dreadful*) fürchterlich

shod /ʃɒd/ *see* **shoe**

shoddy /ˈʃɒdɪ/ *a* (**-ier, -iest**) minderwertig

shoe /ʃu:/ *n* Schuh *m*; (*of horse*) Hufeisen *nt* ● *vt* (*pt/pp* **shod**, *pres p* **shoeing**) beschlagen ⟨*horse*⟩

shoe: ~horn *n* Schuhanzieher *m*. **~-lace** *n* Schnürsenkel *m*. **~maker** *n* Schuhmacher *m*. **~-string** *n* **on a ~-string** (*fam*) mit ganz wenig Geld

shone /ʃɒn/ *see* **shine**

shoo /ʃu:/ *vt* scheuchen ● *int* sch!

shook /ʃʊk/ *see* **shake**

shoot /ʃu:t/ *n* (*Bot*) Trieb *m*; (*hunt*) Jagd *f* ● *v* (*pt/pp* **shot**) ● *vt* schießen; (*kill*) erschießen; drehen ⟨*film*⟩ ● *vi* schießen. **~ down** *vt* abschießen. **~ out** *vi* (*rush*) herausschießen. **~ up** *vi* (*grow*) in die Höhe schießen; ⟨*prices:*⟩ schnellen

'shooting-range *n* Schießstand *m*

shop /ʃɒp/ *n* Laden *m*, Geschäft *nt*; (*workshop*) Werkstatt *f*; **talk ~** (*fam*) fachsimpeln ● *vi* (*pt/pp* **shopped**, *pres p* **shopping**) einkaufen; **go ~ping** einkaufen gehen

shop: ~ assistant *n* Verkäufer(in) *m(f)*. **~keeper** *n* Ladenbesitzer(in) *m(f)*. **~-lifter** *n* Ladendieb *m*. **~-lifting** *n* Ladendiebstahl *m*

shopping /ˈʃɒpɪŋ/ *n* Einkaufen *nt*; (*articles*) Einkäufe *pl*; **do the ~** einkaufen. **~ bag** *n* Einkaufstasche *f*. **~ centre** *n* Einkaufszentrum *nt*. **~ trolley** *n* Einkaufswagen *m*

shop: ~ 'steward *n* [gewerkschaftlicher] Vertrauensmann *m*. **~-'window** *n* Schaufenster *nt*

shore /ʃɔ:(r)/ *n* Strand *m*; (*of lake*) Ufer *nt*

shorn /ʃɔ:n/ *see* **shear**

short /ʃɔ:t/ *a* (**-er, -est**) kurz; ⟨*person*⟩ klein; (*curt*) schroff; **a ~ time ago** vor kurzem; **be ~ of ...** zuwenig ... haben; **be in ~ supply** knapp sein ● *adv* kurz; (*abruptly*) plötzlich; (*curtly*) kurz angebunden; **in ~** kurzum; **~ of** (*except*) außer; **go ~** Mangel leiden; **stop ~ of doing sth** davor zurückschrecken, etw zu tun

shortage /ˈʃɔ:tɪdʒ/ *n* Mangel *m* (**of** an + *dat*); (*scarcity*) Knappheit *f*

short: ~bread *n* ≈ Mürbekekse *pl*. **~ 'circuit** *n* Kurzschluß *m*. **~coming** *n* Fehler *m*. **~ 'cut** *n* Abkürzung *f*

shorten /ˈʃɔ:tn/ *vt* [ab]kürzen; kürzer machen ⟨*garment*⟩

short: ~hand *n* Kurzschrift *f*, Stenographie *f*. **~-'handed** *a* **be ~-handed** zuwenig Personal haben. **~hand 'typist** *n* Stenotypistin *f*. **~ list** *n* engere Auswahl *f*. **~-lived** /-lɪvd/ *a* kurzlebig

short|ly /ˈʃɔ:tlɪ/ *adv* in Kürze; **~ly before/after** kurz vorher/danach. **~ness** *n* Kürze *f*; (*of person*) Kleinheit *f*

shorts /ʃɔ:ts/ *npl* kurze Hose *f*, Shorts *pl*

short: ~-'sighted *a* kurzsichtig. **~-sleeved** *a* kurzärmelig. **~-'staffed** *a* **be ~-staffed** zuwenig Personal haben. **~ 'story** *n* Kurzgeschichte *f*. **~-'tempered** *a* aufbrausend. **~-term** *a* kurzfristig. **~ wave** *n* Kurzwelle *f*

shot /ʃɒt/ *see* **shoot** ● *n* Schuß *m*; (*pellets*) Schrot *m*; (*person*) Schütze *m*; (*Phot*) Aufnahme *f*; (*injection*) Spritze *f*; (*fam: attempt*) Versuch *m*; **like a ~** (*fam*) sofort. **~gun** *n* Schrotflinte *f*. **~-putting** *n* (*Sport*) Kugelstoßen *nt*

should /ʃʊd/ *v aux* **you ~ go** du solltest gehen; **I ~ have seen him** ich hätte ihn sehen sollen; **I ~ like** ich möchte; **this ~ be enough** das müßte eigentlich reichen; **if he ~ be there** falls er da sein sollte

shoulder /ˈʃəʊldə(r)/ *n* Schulter *f* ● *vt* schultern; (*fig*) auf sich (*acc*) nehmen. **~-blade** *n* Schulterblatt *nt*. **~-strap** *n* Tragriemen *m*; (*on garment*) Träger *m*

shout /ʃaʊt/ *n* Schrei *m* ● *vt/i* schreien. **~ down** *vt* niederschreien

shouting /ˈʃaʊtɪŋ/ *n* Geschrei *nt*

shove /ʃʌv/ *n* Stoß *m*; (*fam*) Schubs *m* ● *vt* stoßen; (*fam*) schubsen;

(*fam: put*) tun ● *vi* drängeln. **~ off** *vi* (*fam*) abhauen

shovel /'ʃʌvl/ *n* Schaufel *f* ● *vt* (*pt/pp* **shovelled**) schaufeln

show /ʃəʊ/ *n* (*display*) Pracht *f*; (*exhibition*) Ausstellung *f*, Schau *f*; (*performance*) Vorstellung *f*; (*Theat, TV*) Show *f*; **on ~** ausgestellt ● *v* (*pt* **showed**, *pp* **shown**) ● *vt* zeigen; (*put on display*) ausstellen; vorführen ⟨*film*⟩ ● *vi* sichtbar sein; ⟨*film:*⟩ gezeigt werden. **~ in** *vt* hereinführen. **~ off** *vi* (*fam*) angeben ● *vt* vorführen; (*flaunt*) angeben mit. **~ up** *vi* [deutlich] zu sehen sein; (*fam: arrive*) auftauchen ● *vt* deutlich zeigen; (*fam: embarrass*) blamieren

'show-down *n* Entscheidungskampf *m*

shower /'ʃaʊə(r)/ *n* Dusche *f*; (*of rain*) Schauer *m*; **have a ~** duschen ● *vt* **~ with** überschütten mit ● *vi* duschen. **~proof** *a* regendicht. **~y** *a* regnerisch

'show-jumping *n* Springreiten *nt*

shown /ʃəʊn/ *see* **show**

show: ~-off *n* Angeber(in) *m*(*f*). **~-piece** *n* Paradestück *nt*. **~room** *n* Ausstellungsraum *m*

showy /'ʃəʊɪ/ *a* protzig

shrank /ʃræŋk/ *see* **shrink**

shred /ʃred/ *n* Fetzen *m*; (*fig*) Spur *f* ● *vt* (*pt/pp* **shredded**) zerkleinern; (*Culin*) schnitzeln. **~der** *n* Reißwolf *m*; (*Culin*) Schnitzelwerk *nt*

shrewd /ʃru:d/ *a* (**-er, -est**), **-ly** *adv* klug. **~ness** *n* Klugheit *f*

shriek /ʃri:k/ *n* Schrei *m* ● *vt/i* schreien

shrift /ʃrɪft/ *n* **give s.o. short ~** jdn kurz abfertigen

shrill /ʃrɪl/ *a*, **-y** *adv* schrill

shrimp /ʃrɪmp/ *n* Garnele *f*, Krabbe *f*

shrine /ʃraɪn/ *n* Heiligtum *nt*

shrink /ʃrɪŋk/ *vi* (*pt* **shrank**, *pp* **shrunk**) schrumpfen; ⟨*garment:*⟩ einlaufen; (*draw back*) zurückschrecken (**from** vor + *dat*)

shrivel /'ʃrɪvl/ *vi* (*pt/pp* **shrivelled**) verschrumpeln

shroud /ʃraʊd/ *n* Leichentuch *nt*; (*fig*) Schleier *m*

Shrove /ʃrəʊv/ *n* **~ 'Tuesday** Fastnachtsdienstag *m*

shrub /ʃrʌb/ *n* Strauch *m*

shrug /ʃrʌg/ *n* Achselzucken *nt* ● *vt/i* (*pt/pp* **shrugged**) **~ [one's shoulders]** die Achseln zucken

shrunk /ʃrʌŋk/ *see* **shrink. ~en** *a* geschrumpft

shudder /'ʃʌdə(r)/ *n* Schauder *m* ● *vi* schaudern; (*tremble*) zittern

shuffle /'ʃʌfl/ *vi* schlurfen ● *vt* mischen ⟨*cards*⟩

shun /ʃʌn/ *vt* (*pt/pp* **shunned**) meiden

shunt /ʃʌnt/ *vt* rangieren

shush /ʃʊʃ/ *int* sch!

shut /ʃʌt/ *v* (*pt/pp* **shut**, *pres p* **shutting**) ● *vt* zumachen, schließen; **~ one's finger in the door** sich (*dat*) den Finger in der Tür einklemmen ● *vi* sich schließen; ⟨*shop:*⟩ schließen, zumachen. **~ down** *vt* schließen; stillegen ⟨*factory*⟩ ● *vi* schließen; ⟨*factory:*⟩ stillgelegt werden. **~ up** *vt* abschließen; (*lock in*) einsperren ● *vi* (*fam*) den Mund halten

'shut-down *n* Stillegung *f*

shutter /'ʃʌtə(r)/ *n* [Fenster]laden *m*; (*Phot*) Verschluß *m*

shuttle /'ʃʌtl/ *n* (*Tex*) Schiffchen *nt* ● *vi* pendeln

shuttle: ~cock *n* Federball *m*. **~ service** *n* Pendelverkehr *m*

shy /ʃaɪ/ *a* (**-er, -est**), **-ly** *adv* schüchtern; (*timid*) scheu ● *vi* (*pt/pp* **shied**) ⟨*horse:*⟩ scheuen. **~ness** *n* Schüchternheit *f*

Siamese /saɪə'mi:z/ *a* siamesisch

siblings /'sɪblɪŋz/ *npl* Geschwister *pl*

Sicily /'sɪsɪlɪ/ *n* Sizilien *nt*

sick /sɪk/ *a* krank; ⟨*humour*⟩ makaber; **be ~** (*vomit*) sich übergeben; **be ~ of sth** (*fam*) etw satt haben; **I feel ~** mir ist schlecht

sicken /'sɪkn/ *vt* anwidern ● *vi* **be ~ing for something** krank werden

sickle /'sɪkl/ *n* Sichel *f*

sick|ly /'sɪklɪ/ *a* (**-ier, -iest**) kränklich. **~ness** *n* Krankheit *f*; (*vomiting*) Erbrechen *nt*

'sick-room *n* Krankenzimmer *nt*

side /saɪd/ *n* Seite *f*; **on the ~** (*as sideline*) nebenbei; **~ by ~** nebeneinander; (*fig*) Seite an Seite; **take ~s** Partei ergreifen (**with** für); **to be on the safe ~** vorsichtshalber ● *attrib* Seiten- ● *vi* **~ with** Partei ergreifen für

side: ~board *n* Anrichte *f*. **~burns** *npl* Koteletten *pl*. **~-effect** *n* Nebenwirkung *f*. **~lights** *npl* Standlicht *nt*. **~line** *n* Nebenbeschäftigung *f*. **~-show** *n* Nebenattraktion *f*. **~-step** *vt* ausweichen (+ *dat*). **~-track** *vt* ablenken. **~walk** *n* (*Amer*) Bürgersteig *m*. **~ways** *adv* seitwärts

siding /'saɪdɪŋ/ *n* Abstellgleis *nt*

sidle /'saɪdl/ *vi* sich heranschleichen (**up to** an + *acc*)

siege /si:dʒ/ *n* Belagerung *f*; (*by police*) Umstellung *f*

sieve /sɪv/ *n* Sieb *nt* ● *vt* sieben

sift /sɪft/ *vt* sieben; (*fig*) durchsehen

sigh /saɪ/ *n* Seufzer *m* ● *vi* seufzen

sight /saɪt/ *n* Sicht *f*; (*faculty*) Sehvermögen *nt*; (*spectacle*) Anblick *m*; (*on gun*) Visier *nt*; **~s** *pl* Sehenswürdigkeiten *pl*; **at first ~** auf den ersten Blick; **within/out of ~** in/außer Sicht; **lose ~ of** aus dem Auge verlieren; **know by ~** vom Sehen kennen; **have bad ~** schlechte Augen haben ● *vt* sichten

'sightseeing *n* **go ~** die Sehenswürdigkeiten besichtigen

sign /saɪn/ *n* Zeichen *nt*; (*notice*) Schild *nt* ● *vt/i* unterschreiben; ⟨*author, artist:*⟩ signieren. **~ on** *vi* (*as unemployed*) sich arbeitslos melden; (*Mil*) sich verpflichten

signal /'sɪgnl/ *n* Signal *nt* ● *vt/i* (*pt/pp* **signalled**) signalisieren; **~ to s.o.** jdm ein Signal geben (**to** zu). **~-box** *n* Stellwerk *nt*

signature /'sɪgnətʃə(r)/ *n* Unterschrift *f*; (*of artist*) Signatur *f*. **~ tune** *n* Kennmelodie *f*

signet-ring /'sɪgnɪt-/ *n* Siegelring *m*

significan|ce /sɪg'nɪfɪkəns/ *n* Bedeutung *f*. **~t** *a*, **-ly** *adv* bedeutungsvoll; (*important*) bedeutend

signify /'sɪgnɪfaɪ/ *vt* (*pt/pp* **-ied**) bedeuten

signpost /'saɪn-/ *n* Wegweiser *m*

silence /'saɪləns/ *n* Stille *f*; (*of person*) Schweigen *nt* ● *vt* zum Schweigen bringen. **~r** *n* (*on gun*) Schalldämpfer *m*; (*Auto*) Auspufftopf *m*

silent /'saɪlənt/ *a*, **-ly** *adv* still; (*without speaking*) schweigend; **remain ~** schweigen. **~ film** *n* Stummfilm *m*

silhouette /sɪlu:'et/ *n* Silhouette *f*; (*picture*) Schattenriß *m* ● *vt* **be ~d** sich als Silhouette abheben

silicon /'sɪlɪkən/ *n* Silizium *nt*

silk /sɪlk/ *n* Seide *f* ● *attrib* Seiden-. **~worm** *n* Seidenraupe *f*

silky /'sɪlkɪ/ *a* (**-ier, -iest**) seidig

sill /sɪl/ *n* Sims *m & nt*

silly /'sɪlɪ/ *a* (**-ier, -iest**) dumm, albern

silo /'saɪləʊ/ *n* Silo *m*

silt /sɪlt/ *n* Schlick *m*

silver /'sɪlvə(r)/ *a* silbern; ⟨*coin, paper*⟩ Silber- ● *n* Silber *nt*

silver: ~-plated *a* versilbert. **~ware** *n* Silber *nt*. **~ 'wedding** *n* Silberhochzeit *f*

similar /'sɪmɪlə(r)/ *a*, **-ly** *adv* ähnlich. **~ity** /-'lærətɪ/ *n* Ähnlichkeit *f*

simile /'sɪmɪlɪ/ *n* Vergleich *m*

simmer /'sɪmə(r)/ *vi* leise kochen, ziehen ● *vt* ziehen lassen

simple /'sɪmpl/ *a* (**-r, -st**) einfach; ⟨*person*⟩ einfältig. **~-'minded** *a* einfältig. **~ton** /'sɪmpltən/ *n* Einfaltspinsel *m*

simplicity /sɪm'plɪsətɪ/ *n* Einfachheit *f*

simpli|fication /sɪmplɪfɪ'keɪʃn/ *n* Vereinfachung *f*. **~fy** /'sɪmplɪfaɪ/ *vt* (*pt/pp* **-ied**) vereinfachen

simply /'sɪmplɪ/ *adv* einfach

simulat|e /'sɪmjʊleɪt/ *vt* vortäuschen; (*Techn*) simulieren. **~ion** /-'leɪʃn/ *n* Vortäuschung *f*; Simulation *f*

simultaneous /sɪml'teɪnɪəs/ *a*, **-ly** *adv* gleichzeitig; ⟨*interpreting*⟩ Simultan-

sin /sɪn/ *n* Sünde *f* ● *vi* (*pt/pp* **sinned**) sündigen

since /sɪns/ *prep* seit (+ *dat*) ● *adv* seitdem ● *conj* seit; (*because*) da

sincere /sɪn'sɪə(r)/ *a* aufrichtig; (*heartfelt*) herzlich. **~ly** *adv* aufrichtig; **Yours ~ly** Mit freundlichen Grüßen

sincerity /sɪn'serətɪ/ *n* Aufrichtigkeit *f*

sinew /'sɪnju:/ *n* Sehne *f*

sinful /'sɪnfl/ *a* sündhaft

sing /sɪŋ/ *vt/i* (*pt* **sang**, *pp* **sung**) singen

singe /sɪndʒ/ *vt* (*pres p* **singeing**) versengen

singer /'sɪŋə(r)/ *n* Sänger(in) *m*(*f*)

single /'sɪŋgl/ *a* einzeln; (*one only*) einzig; (*unmarried*) ledig; ⟨*ticket*⟩ einfach; ⟨*room, bed*⟩ Einzel- ● *n* (*ticket*) einfache Fahrkarte *f*; (*record*) Single *f*; **~s** *pl* (*Tennis*) Einzel *nt* ● *vt* **~ out** auswählen

single: ~-breasted *a* einreihig. **~-handed** *a & adv* allein. **~-minded** *a* zielstrebig. **~ 'parent** *n* Alleinerziehende(r) *m/f*

singlet /'sɪŋglɪt/ *n* Unterhemd *nt*

singly /'sɪŋglɪ/ *adv* einzeln

singular /'sɪŋgjʊlə(r)/ *a* eigenartig; (*Gram*) im Singular ● *n* Singular *m*. **~ly** *adv* außerordentlich

sinister /'sɪnɪstə(r)/ *a* finster

sink /sɪŋk/ *n* Spülbecken *nt* ● *v* (*pt* **sank**, *pp* **sunk**) ● *vi* sinken ● *vt* versenken ⟨*ship*⟩; senken ⟨*shaft*⟩. **~ in** *vi* einsinken; (*fam: be understood*) kapiert werden

'sink unit *n* Spüle *f*

sinner /'sɪnə(r)/ *n* Sünder(in) *m*(*f*)

sinus /'saɪnəs/ *n* Nebenhöhle *f*

sip /sɪp/ *n* Schlückchen *nt* ● *vt* (*pt*/*pp* **sipped**) in kleinen Schlucken trinken

siphon /'saɪfn/ *n* (*bottle*) Siphon *m*. **~ off** *vt* mit einem Saugheber ablassen

sir /sɜ:(r)/ *n* mein Herr; **S~** (*title*) Sir; **Dear S~s** Sehr geehrte Herren

siren /'saɪrən/ *n* Sirene *f*

sissy /'sɪsɪ/ *n* Waschlappen *m*

sister /'sɪstə(r)/ *n* Schwester *f*; (*nurse*) Oberschwester *f*. **~-in-law** *n* (*pl* **~s-in-law**) Schwägerin *f*. **~ly** *a* schwesterlich

sit /sɪt/ *v* (*pt*/*pp* **sat**, *pres p* **sitting**) ● *vi* sitzen; (*sit down*) sich setzen; ⟨*committee:*⟩ tagen ● *vt* setzen; machen ⟨*exam*⟩. **~ back** *vi* sich zurücklehnen. **~ down** *vi* sich setzen. **~ up** *vi* [aufrecht] sitzen; (*rise*) sich aufsetzen; (*not slouch*) gerade sitzen; (*stay up*) aufbleiben

site /saɪt/ *n* Gelände *nt*; (*for camping*) Platz *m*; (*Archaeol*) Stätte *f* ● *vt* legen

sitting /'sɪtɪŋ/ *n* Sitzung *f*; (*for meals*) Schub *m*

situat|e /'sɪtjʊeɪt/ *vt* legen; **be ~ed** liegen. **~ion** /-'eɪʃn/ *n* Lage *f*; (*circumstances*) Situation *f*; (*job*) Stelle *f*

six /sɪks/ *a* sechs. **~teen** *a* sechzehn. **~teenth** *a* sechzehnte(r,s)

sixth /sɪksθ/ *a* sechste(r,s)

sixtieth /'sɪkstɪɪθ/ *a* sechzigste(r,s)

sixty /'sɪkstɪ/ *a* sechzig

size /saɪz/ *n* Größe *f* ● *vt* **~ up** (*fam*) taxieren

sizeable /'saɪzəbl/ *a* ziemlich groß

sizzle /'sɪzl/ *vi* brutzeln

skate[1] /skeɪt/ *n inv* (*fish*) Rochen *m*

skate[2] *n* Schlittschuh *m*; (*roller-*) Rollschuh *m* ● *vi* Schlittschuh/Rollschuh laufen. **~r** *n* Eisläufer(in) *m*(*f*); Rollschuhläufer(in) *m*(*f*)

skating /'skeɪtɪŋ/ *n* Eislaufen *nt*. **~-rink** *n* Eisbahn *f*

skeleton /'skelɪtn/ *n* Skelett *nt*. **~ 'key** *n* Dietrich *m*. **~ 'staff** *n* Minimalbesetzung *f*

sketch /sketʃ/ *n* Skizze *f*; (*Theat*) Sketch *m* ● *vt* skizzieren

sketchy /'sketʃɪ/ *a* (**-ier, -iest**), **-ily** *adv* skizzenhaft

skew /skju:/ *n* **on the ~** schräg

skewer /'skjʊə(r)/ *n* [Brat]spieß *m*

ski /ski:/ *n* Ski *m* ● *vi* (*pt*/*pp* **skied**, *pres p* **skiing**) Ski fahren *or* laufen

skid /skɪd/ *n* Schleudern *nt* ● *vi* (*pt*/*pp* **skidded**) schleudern

skier /'ski:ə(r)/ *n* Skiläufer(in) *m*(*f*)

skiing /'ski:ɪŋ/ *n* Skilaufen *nt*

skilful /'skɪlfl/ *a*, **-ly** *adv* geschickt

skill /skɪl/ *n* Geschick *nt*. **~ed** *a* geschickt; (*trained*) ausgebildet

skim /skɪm/ *vt* (*pt*/*pp* **skimmed**) entrahmen ⟨*milk*⟩. **~ off** *vt* abschöpfen. **~ through** *vt* überfliegen

skimp /skɪmp/ *vt* sparen an (+ *dat*)

skimpy /'skɪmpɪ/ *a* (**-ier, -iest**) knapp

skin /skɪn/ *n* Haut *f*; (*on fruit*) Schale *f* ● *vt* (*pt*/*pp* **skinned**) häuten; schälen ⟨*fruit*⟩

skin: ~-deep *a* oberflächlich. **~-diving** *n* Sporttauchen *nt*

skinflint /'skɪnflɪnt/ *n* Geizhals *m*

skinny /'skɪnɪ/ *a* (**-ier, -iest**) dünn

skip[1] /skɪp/ *n* Container *m*

skip[2] *n* Hüpfer *m* ● *v* (*pt*/*pp* **skipped**) *vi* hüpfen; (*with rope*) seilspringen ● *vt* überspringen

skipper /'skɪpə(r)/ *n* Kapitän *m*

'skipping-rope *n* Sprungseil *nt*

skirmish /'skɜ:mɪʃ/ *n* Gefecht *nt*

skirt /skɜ:t/ *n* Rock *m* ● *vt* herumgehen um

skit /skɪt/ *n* parodistischer Sketch *m*

skittle /'skɪtl/ *n* Kegel *m*

skive /skaɪv/ *vi* (*fam*) blaumachen

skulk /skʌlk/ *vi* lauern

skull /skʌl/ *n* Schädel *m*

skunk /skʌŋk/ *n* Stinktier *nt*

sky /skaɪ/ *n* Himmel *m*. **~light** *n* Dachluke *f*. **~scraper** *n* Wolkenkratzer *m*

slab /slæb/ *n* Platte *f*; (*slice*) Scheibe *f*; (*of chocolate*) Tafel *f*

slack /slæk/ *a* (**-er, -est**) schlaff, locker; ⟨*person*⟩ nachlässig; (*Comm*) flau ● *vi* bummeln

slacken /'slækn/ *vi* sich lockern; (*diminish*) nachlassen; ⟨*speed:*⟩ sich verringern ● *vt* lockern; (*diminish*) verringern

slacks /slæks/ *npl* Hose *f*

slag /slæg/ *n* Schlacke *f*

slain /sleɪn/ *see* **slay**

slake /sleɪk/ *vt* löschen

slam /slæm/ *v* (*pt*/*pp* **slammed**) ● *vt* zuschlagen; (*put*) knallen (*fam*);

(*fam: criticize*) verreißen • *vi* zuschlagen

slander /'slɑ:ndə(r)/ *n* Verleumdung *f* • *vt* verleumden. **~ous** /-rəs/ *a* verleumderisch

slang /slæŋ/ *n* Slang *m*. **~y** *a* salopp

slant /slɑ:nt/ *n* Schräge *f*; **on the ~** schräg • *vt* abschrägen; (*fig*) färben ⟨*report*⟩ • *vi* sich neigen

slap /slæp/ *n* Schlag *m* • *vt* (*pt/pp* **slapped**) schlagen; (*put*) knallen (*fam*) • *adv* direkt

slap: ~dash *a* (*fam*) schludrig. **~-up** *a* (*fam*) toll

slash /slæʃ/ *n* Schlitz *m* • *vt* aufschlitzen; [drastisch] reduzieren ⟨*prices*⟩

slat /slæt/ *n* Latte *f*

slate /sleɪt/ *n* Schiefer *m* • *vt* (*fam*) heruntermachen; verreißen ⟨*performance*⟩

slaughter /'slɔ:tə(r)/ *n* Schlachten *nt*; (*massacre*) Gemetzel *nt* • *vt* schlachten; abschlachten. **~house** *n* Schlachthaus *nt*

Slav /slɑ:v/ *a* slawisch • *n* Slawe *m*/Slawin *f*

slave /sleɪv/ *n* Sklave *m*/Sklavin *f* • *vi* **~ [away]** schuften. **~-driver** *n* Leuteschinder *m*

slav|ery /'sleɪvərɪ/ *n* Sklaverei *f*. **~ish** *a*, **-ly** *adv* sklavisch

Slavonic /slə'vɒnɪk/ *a* slawisch

slay /sleɪ/ *vt* (*pt* **slew**, *pp* **slain**) ermorden

sleazy /'sli:zɪ/ *a* (**-ier, -iest**) schäbig

sledge /sledʒ/ *n* Schlitten *m*. **~-hammer** *n* Vorschlaghammer *m*

sleek /sli:k/ *a* (**-er, -est**) seidig; (*well-fed*) wohlgenährt

sleep /sli:p/ *n* Schlaf *m*; **go to ~** einschlafen; **put to ~** einschläfern • *v* (*pt/pp* **slept**) • *vi* schlafen • *vt* (*accommodate*) Unterkunft bieten für. **~er** *n* Schläfer(in) *m*(*f*); (*Rail*) Schlafwagen *m*; (*on track*) Schwelle *f*

sleeping: ~-bag *n* Schlafsack *m*. **~-car** *n* Schlafwagen *m*. **~-pill** *n* Schlaftablette *f*

sleep: ~less *a* schlaflos. **~-walking** *n* Schlafwandeln *nt*

sleepy /'sli:pɪ/ *a* (**-ier, -iest**), **-ily** *adv* schläfrig

sleet /sli:t/ *n* Schneeregen *m* • *vi* **it is ~ing** es gibt Schneeregen

sleeve /sli:v/ *n* Ärmel *m*; (*for record*) Hülle *f*. **~less** *a* ärmellos

sleigh /sleɪ/ *n* [Pferde]schlitten *m*

sleight /slaɪt/ *n* **~ of hand** Taschenspielerei *f*

slender /'slendə(r)/ *a* schlank; (*fig*) gering

slept /slept/ *see* **sleep**

sleuth /slu:θ/ *n* Detektiv *m*

slew[1] /slu:/ *vi* schwenken

slew[2] *see* **slay**

slice /slaɪs/ *n* Scheibe *f* • *vt* in Scheiben schneiden; **~d bread** Schnittbrot *nt*

slick /slɪk/ *a* clever • *n* (*of oil*) Ölteppich *m*

slid|e /slaɪd/ *n* Rutschbahn *f*; (*for hair*) Spange *f*; (*Phot*) Dia *nt* • *v* (*pt/pp* **slid**) • *vi* rutschen • *vt* schieben. **~ing** *a* gleitend; ⟨*door, seat*⟩ Schiebe-

slight /slaɪt/ *a* (**-er, -est**), **-ly** *adv* leicht; ⟨*importance*⟩ gering; ⟨*acquaintance*⟩ flüchtig; (*slender*) schlank; **not in the ~est** nicht im geringsten; **~ly better** ein bißchen besser • *vt* kränken, beleidigen • *n* Beleidigung *f*

slim /slɪm/ *a* (**slimmer, slimmest**) schlank; ⟨*volume*⟩ schmal; (*fig*) gering • *vi* eine Schlankheitskur machen

slim|e /slaɪm/ *n* Schleim *m*. **~y** *a* schleimig

sling /slɪŋ/ *n* (*Med*) Schlinge *f* • *vt* (*pt/pp* **slung**) (*fam*) schmeißen

slip /slɪp/ *n* (*mistake*) Fehler *m*, (*fam*) Patzer *m*; (*petticoat*) Unterrock *m*; (*for pillow*) Bezug *m*; (*paper*) Zettel *m*; **give s.o. the ~** (*fam*) jdm entwischen; **~ of the tongue** Versprecher *m* • *v* (*pt/pp* **slipped**) • *vi* rutschen; (*fall*) ausrutschen; (*go quickly*) schlüpfen; (*decline*) nachlassen • *vt* schieben; **~ s.o.'s mind** jdm entfallen. **~ away** *vi* sich fortschleichen; ⟨*time:*⟩ verfliegen. **~ up** *vi* (*fam*) einen Schnitzer machen

slipped 'disc *n* (*Med*) Bandscheibenvorfall *m*

slipper /'slɪpə(r)/ *n* Hausschuh *m*

slippery /'slɪpərɪ/ *a* glitschig; ⟨*surface*⟩ glatt

slipshod /'slɪpʃɒd/ *a* schludrig

'slip-up *n* (*fam*) Schnitzer *m*

slit /slɪt/ *n* Schlitz *m* • *vt* (*pt/pp* **slit**) aufschlitzen

slither /'slɪðə(r)/ *vi* rutschen

sliver /'slɪvə(r)/ *n* Splitter *m*

slobber /'slɒbə(r)/ *vi* sabbern

slog /slɒg/ *n* **[hard] ~** Schinderei *f* • *v* (*pt/pp* **slogged**) • *vi* schuften • *vt* schlagen

slogan /ˈsləʊgən/ *n* Schlagwort *nt*; (*advertising*) Werbespruch *m*

slop /slɒp/ *v* (*pt/pp* **slopped**) ● *vt* verschütten ● *vi* ~ **over** überschwappen. **~s** *npl* Schmutzwasser *nt*

slop|e /sləʊp/ *n* Hang *m*; (*inclination*) Neigung *f* ● *vi* sich neigen. **~ing** *a* schräg

sloppy /ˈslɒpɪ/ *a* (**-ier, -iest**) schludrig; (*sentimental*) sentimental

slosh /slɒʃ/ *vi* (*fam*) platschen; ⟨*water:*⟩ schwappen ● *vt* (*fam: hit*) schlagen

slot /slɒt/ *n* Schlitz *m*; (*TV*) Sendezeit *f* ● *v* (*pt/pp* **slotted**) ● *vt* einfügen ● *vi* sich einfügen (**in** in + *acc*)

sloth /sləʊθ/ *n* Trägheit *f*

'slot-machine *n* Münzautomat *m*; (*for gambling*) Spielautomat *m*

slouch /slaʊtʃ/ *vi* sich schlecht halten

slovenly /ˈslʌvnlɪ/ *a* schlampig

slow /sləʊ/ *a* (**-er, -est**), **-ly** *adv* langsam; **be** ~ ⟨*clock:*⟩ nachgehen; **in** ~ **motion** in Zeitlupe ● *adv* langsam ● *vt* verlangsamen ● *vi* ~ **down,** ~ **up** langsamer werden

slow: ~coach *n* (*fam*) Trödler *m*. **~ness** *n* Langsamkeit *f*

sludge /slʌdʒ/ *n* Schlamm *m*

slug /slʌg/ *n* Nacktschnecke *f*

sluggish /ˈslʌgɪʃ/ *a*, **-ly** *adv* träge

sluice /slu:s/ *n* Schleuse *f*

slum /slʌm/ *n* (*house*) Elendsquartier *nt*; **~s** *pl* Elendsviertel *nt*

slumber /ˈslʌmbə(r)/ *n* Schlummer *m* ● *vi* schlummern

slump /slʌmp/ *n* Sturz *m* ● *vi* fallen; (*crumple*) zusammensacken; ⟨*prices:*⟩ stürzen; ⟨*sales:*⟩ zurückgehen

slung /slʌŋ/ *see* **sling**

slur /slɜ:(r)/ *n* (*discredit*) Schande *f* ● *vt* (*pt/pp* **slurred**) undeutlich sprechen

slurp /slɜ:p/ *vt/i* schlürfen

slush /slʌʃ/ *n* [Schnee]matsch *m*; (*fig*) Kitsch *m*. ~ **fund** *n* Fonds *m* für Bestechungsgelder

slushy /ˈslʌʃɪ/ *a* matschig; (*sentimental*) kitschig

slut /slʌt/ *n* Schlampe *f* (*fam*)

sly /slaɪ/ *a* (**-er, -est**), **-ly** *adv* verschlagen ● *n* **on the** ~ heimlich

smack¹ /smæk/ *n* Schlag *m*, Klaps *m* ● *vt* schlagen; ~ **one's lips** mit den Lippen schmatzen ● *adv* (*fam*) direkt

smack² *vi* ~ **of** (*fig*) riechen nach

small /smɔ:l/ *a* (**-er, -est**) klein; **in the** ~ **hours** in den frühen Morgenstunden ● *adv* **chop up** ~ kleinhacken ● *n* ~ **of the back** Kreuz *nt*

small: ~ **ads** *npl* Kleinanzeigen *pl*. ~ **'change** *n* Kleingeld *nt*. **~-holding** *n* landwirtschaftlicher Kleinbetrieb *m*. **~pox** *n* Pocken *pl*. ~ **talk** *n* leichte Konversation *f*

smarmy /ˈsmɑ:mɪ/ *a* (**-ier, -iest**) (*fam*) ölig

smart /smɑ:t/ *a* (**-er, -est**), **-ly** *adv* schick; (*clever*) schlau, clever; (*brisk*) flott; (*Amer fam: cheeky*) frech ● *vi* brennen

smarten /ˈsmɑ:tn/ *vt* ~ **oneself up** mehr auf sein Äußeres achten

smash /smæʃ/ *n* Krach *m*; (*collision*) Zusammenstoß *m*; (*Tennis*) Schmetterball *m* ● *vt* zerschlagen; (*strike*) schlagen; (*Tennis*) schmettern ● *vi* zerschmettern; (*crash*) krachen (**into** gegen). **~ing** *a* (*fam*) toll

smattering /ˈsmætərɪŋ/ *n* **a** ~ **of German** ein paar Brocken Deutsch

smear /smɪə(r)/ *n* verschmierter Fleck *m*; (*Med*) Abstrich *m*; (*fig*) Verleumdung *f* ● *vt* schmieren; (*coat*) beschmieren (**with** mit); (*fig*) verleumden ● *vi* schmieren

smell /smel/ *n* Geruch *m*; (*sense*) Geruchssinn *m* ● *v* (*pt/pp* **smelt** *or* **smelled**) ● *vt* riechen; (*sniff*) riechen an (+ *dat*) ● *vi* riechen (**of** nach)

smelly /ˈsmelɪ/ *a* (**-ier, -iest**) übelriechend

smelt¹ /smelt/ *see* **smell**

smelt² *vt* schmelzen

smile /smaɪl/ *n* Lächeln *nt* ● *vi* lächeln; ~ **at** anlächeln

smirk /smɜ:k/ *vi* feixen

smith /smɪθ/ *n* Schmied *m*

smithereens /smɪðəˈri:nz/ *npl* **smash to** ~ in tausend Stücke schlagen

smitten /ˈsmɪtn/ *a* ~ **with** sehr angetan von

smock /smɒk/ *n* Kittel *m*

smog /smɒg/ *n* Smog *m*

smoke /sməʊk/ *n* Rauch *m* ● *vt/i* rauchen; (*Culin*) räuchern. **~less** *a* rauchfrei; ⟨*fuel*⟩ rauchlos

smoker /ˈsməʊkə(r)/ *n* Raucher *m*; (*Rail*) Raucherabteil *nt*

'smoke-screen *n* [künstliche] Nebelwand *f*

smoking /ˈsməʊkɪŋ/ *n* Rauchen *nt*; **'no** ~**'** 'Rauchen verboten'

smoky /ˈsməʊkɪ/ *a* (**-ier**, **-iest**) verraucht; ⟨*taste*⟩ rauchig

smooth /smu:ð/ *a* (**-er**, **-est**), **-ly** *adv* glatt ● *vt* glätten. **~ out** *vt* glattstreichen

smother /ˈsmʌðə(r)/ *vt* ersticken; (*cover*) bedecken; (*suppress*) unterdrücken

smoulder /ˈsməʊldə(r)/ *vi* schwelen

smudge /smʌdʒ/ *n* Fleck *m* ● *vt* verwischen ● *vi* schmieren

smug /smʌg/ *a* (**smugger**, **smuggest**), **-ly** *adv* selbstgefällig

smuggl|e /ˈsmʌgl/ *vt* schmuggeln. **~er** *n* Schmuggler *m*. **~ing** *n* Schmuggel *m*

smut /smʌt/ *n* Rußflocke *f*; (*mark*) Rußfleck *m*; (*fig*) Schmutz *m*

smutty /ˈsmʌtɪ/ *a* (**-ier**, **-iest**) schmutzig

snack /snæk/ *n* Imbiß *m*. **~-bar** *n* Imbißstube *f*

snag /snæg/ *n* Schwierigkeit *f*, (*fam*) Haken *m*

snail /sneɪl/ *n* Schnecke *f*; **at a ~'s pace** im Schneckentempo

snake /sneɪk/ *n* Schlange *f*

snap /snæp/ *n* Knacken *nt*; (*photo*) Schnappschuß *m* ● *attrib* ⟨*decision*⟩ plötzlich ● *v* (*pt*/*pp* **snapped**) ● *vi* [entzwei]brechen; **~ at** (*bite*) schnappen nach; (*speak sharply*) [scharf] anfahren ● *vt* zerbrechen; (*say*) fauchen; (*Phot*) knipsen. **~ up** *vt* wegschnappen

snappy /ˈsnæpɪ/ *a* (**-ier**, **-iest**) bissig; (*smart*) flott; **make it ~!** ein bißchen schnell!

ˈsnapshot *n* Schnappschuß *m*

snare /sneə(r)/ *n* Schlinge *f*

snarl /snɑ:l/ *vi* [mit gefletschten Zähnen] knurren

snatch /snætʃ/ *n* (*fragment*) Fetzen *pl*; (*theft*) Raub *m*; **make a ~ at** greifen nach ● *vt* schnappen; (*steal*) klauen; entführen ⟨*child*⟩; **~ sth from s.o.** jdm etw entreißen

sneak /sni:k/ *n* (*fam*) Petze *f* ● *vi* schleichen; (*fam: tell tales*) petzen ● *vt* (*take*) mitgehen lassen ● *vi* **~ in/out** sich hinein-/hinausschleichen

sneakers /ˈsni:kəz/ *npl* (*Amer*) Turnschuhe *pl*

sneaking /ˈsni:kɪŋ/ *a* heimlich; ⟨*suspicion*⟩ leise

sneaky /ˈsni:kɪ/ *a* hinterhältig

sneer /snɪə(r)/ *vi* höhnisch lächeln; (*mock*) spotten

sneeze /sni:z/ *n* Niesen *nt* ● *vi* niesen

snide /snaɪd/ *a* (*fam*) abfällig

sniff /snɪf/ *vi* schnüffeln ● *vt* schnüffeln an (+ *dat*); schnüffeln ⟨*glue*⟩

snigger /ˈsnɪgə(r)/ *vi* [boshaft] kichern

snip /snɪp/ *n* Schnitt *m*; (*fam: bargain*) günstiger Kauf *m* ● *vt*/*i* **~ [at]** schnippeln an (+ *dat*)

snipe /snaɪp/ *vi* **~ at** aus dem Hinterhalt schießen auf (+ *acc*); (*fig*) anschießen. **~r** *n* Heckenschütze *m*

snippet /ˈsnɪpɪt/ *n* Schnipsel *m*; (*of information*) Bruchstück *nt*

snivel /ˈsnɪvl/ *vi* (*pt*/*pp* **snivelled**) flennen

snob /snɒb/ *n* Snob *m*. **~bery** *n* Snobismus *m*. **~bish** *a* snobistisch

snoop /snu:p/ *vi* (*fam*) schnüffeln

snooty /ˈsnu:tɪ/ *a* (*fam*) hochnäsig

snooze /snu:z/ *n* Nickerchen *nt* ● *vi* dösen

snore /snɔ:(r)/ *vi* schnarchen

snorkel /ˈsnɔ:kl/ *n* Schnorchel *m*

snort /snɔ:t/ *vi* schnauben

snout /snaʊt/ *n* Schnauze *f*

snow /snəʊ/ *n* Schnee *m* ● *vi* schneien; **~ed under with** (*fig*) überhäuft mit

snow: ~ball *n* Schneeball *m* ● *vi* lawinenartig anwachsen. **~drift** *n* Schneewehe *f*. **~drop** *n* Schneeglöckchen *nt*. **~fall** *n* Schneefall *m*. **~flake** *n* Schneeflocke *f*. **~ flurry** *n* Schneegestöber *nt*. **~man** *n* Schneemann *m*. **~plough** *n* Schneepflug *m*. **~storm** *n* Schneesturm *m*

snub /snʌb/ *n* Abfuhr *f* ● *vt* (*pt*/*pp* **snubbed**) brüskieren

ˈsnub-nosed *a* stupsnasig

snuff[1] /snʌf/ *n* Schnupftabak *m*

snuff[2] *vt* **~ [out]** löschen

snuffle /ˈsnʌfl/ *vi* schnüffeln

snug /snʌg/ *a* (**snugger**, **snuggest**) behaglich, gemütlich

snuggle /ˈsnʌgl/ *vi* sich kuscheln (**up to** an + *acc*)

so /səʊ/ *adv* so; **not so fast** nicht so schnell; **so am I** ich auch; **so does he** er auch; **so I see** das sehe ich; **that is so** das stimmt; **so much the better** um so besser; **so it is** tatsächlich; **if so** wenn ja; **so as to** um zu; **so long!** (*fam*) tschüs! ● *pron* **I hope so** hoffentlich; **I think so** ich glaube schon; **I told you so** ich hab's dir gleich gesagt; **because I say so** weil ich es sage; **I'm afraid so** leider ja; **so saying/doing, he/she ...** indem er/sie das sagte/tat, . . .; **an hour or so** eine Stunde oder so; **very much so** durchaus ● *conj* (*therefore*) also; **so that** damit; **so there!** fertig! **so what!** na und! **so you see** wie du siehst; **so where have you been?** wo warst du denn?

soak /səʊk/ *vt* naß machen; (*steep*) einweichen; (*fam: fleece*) schröpfen ● *vi* weichen; ⟨*liquid:*⟩ sickern. **~ up** *vt* aufsaugen

soaking /ˈsəʊkɪŋ/ *a & adv* **~ [wet]** patschnaß (*fam*)

soap /səʊp/ *n* Seife *f*. **~ opera** *n* Seifenoper *f*. **~ powder** *n* Seifenpulver *nt*

soapy /ˈsəʊpɪ/ *a* (**-ier, -iest**) seifig

soar /sɔː(r)/ *vi* aufsteigen; ⟨*prices:*⟩ in die Höhe schnellen

sob /sɒb/ *n* Schluchzer *m* ● *vi* (*pt/pp* **sobbed**) schluchzen

sober /ˈsəʊbə(r)/ *a*, **-ly** *adv* nüchtern; (*serious*) ernst; ⟨*colour*⟩ gedeckt. **~ up** *vi* nüchtern werden

ˈso-called *a* sogenannt

soccer /ˈsɒkə(r)/ *n* (*fam*) Fußball *m*

sociable /ˈsəʊʃəbl/ *a* gesellig

social /ˈsəʊʃl/ *a* gesellschaftlich; (*Admin, Pol, Zool*) sozial

socialis|m /ˈsəʊʃəlɪzm/ *n* Sozialismus *m*. **~t** /-ɪst/ *a* sozialistisch ● *n* Sozialist *m*

socialize /ˈsəʊʃəlaɪz/ *vi* [gesellschaftlich] verkehren

socially /ˈsəʊʃəlɪ/ *adv* gesellschaftlich; **know ~** privat kennen

social: ~ seˈcurity *n* Sozialhilfe *f*. **~ work** *n* Sozialarbeit *f*. **~ worker** *n* Sozialarbeiter(in) *m*(*f*)

society /səˈsaɪətɪ/ *n* Gesellschaft *f*; (*club*) Verein *m*

sociolog|ist /səʊsɪˈɒlədʒɪst/ *n* Soziologe *m*. **~y** *n* Soziologie *f*

sock[1] /sɒk/ *n* Socke *f*; (*knee-length*) Kniestrumpf *m*

sock[2] *n* (*fam*) Schlag *m* ● *vt* (*fam*) hauen

socket /ˈsɒkɪt/ *n* (*of eye*) Augenhöhle *f*; (*of joint*) Gelenkpfanne *f*; (*wall plug*) Steckdose *f*; (*for bulb*) Fassung *f*

soda /ˈsəʊdə/ *n* Soda *nt*; (*Amer*) Limonade *f*. **~ water** *n* Sodawasser *nt*

sodden /ˈsɒdn/ *a* durchnäßt

sodium /ˈsəʊdɪəm/ *n* Natrium *nt*

sofa /ˈsəʊfə/ *n* Sofa *nt*. **~ bed** *n* Schlafcouch *f*

soft /sɒft/ *a* (**-er, -est**), **-ly** *adv* weich; (*quiet*) leise; (*gentle*) sanft; (*fam: silly*) dumm; **have a ~ spot for s.o.** jdn mögen. **~ drink** *n* alkoholfreies Getränk *nt*

soften /ˈsɒfn/ *vt* weich machen; (*fig*) mildern ● *vi* weich werden

soft: ~ toy *n* Stofftier *nt*. **~ware** *n* Software *f*

soggy /ˈsɒgɪ/ *a* (**-ier, -iest**) aufgeweicht

soil[1] /sɔɪl/ *n* Erde *f*, Boden *m*

soil[2] *vt* verschmutzen

solace /ˈsɒləs/ *n* Trost *m*

solar /ˈsəʊlə(r)/ *a* Sonnen-

sold /səʊld/ *see* **sell**

solder /ˈsəʊldə(r)/ *n* Lötmetall *nt* ● *vt* löten

soldier /ˈsəʊldʒə(r)/ *n* Soldat *m* ● *vi* **~ on** [unbeirrbar] weitermachen

sole[1] /səʊl/ *n* Sohle *f*

sole[2] *n* (*fish*) Seezunge *f*

sole[3] *a* einzig. **~ly** *adv* einzig und allein

solemn /ˈsɒləm/ *a*, **-ly** *adv* feierlich; (*serious*) ernst. **~ity** /səˈlemnətɪ/ *n* Feierlichkeit *f*; Ernst *m*

solicit /səˈlɪsɪt/ *vt* bitten um ● *vi* ⟨*prostitute:*⟩ sich an Männer heranmachen

solicitor /səˈlɪsɪtə(r)/ *n* Rechtsanwalt *m*/-anwältin *f*

solicitous /səˈlɪsɪtəs/ *a* besorgt

solid /ˈsɒlɪd/ *a* fest; (*sturdy*) stabil; (*not hollow, of same substance*) massiv; (*unanimous*) einstimmig; (*complete*) ganz ● *n* (*Geom*) Körper *m*; **~s** *pl* (*food*) feste Nahrung *f*

solidarity /sɒlɪˈdærətɪ/ *n* Solidarität *f*

solidify /səˈlɪdɪfaɪ/ *vi* (*pt/pp* **-ied**) fest werden

soliloquy /səˈlɪləkwɪ/ *n* Selbstgespräch *nt*

solitary /ˈsɒlɪtərɪ/ *a* einsam; (*sole*) einzig. **~ conˈfinement** *n* Einzelhaft *f*

solitude /ˈsɒlɪtjuːd/ *n* Einsamkeit *f*

solo /ˈsəʊləʊ/ *n* Solo *nt* ● *a* Solo-; ⟨*flight*⟩ Allein- ● *adv* solo. **~ist** *n* Solist(in) *m*(*f*)

solstice /ˈsɒlstɪs/ *n* Sonnenwende *f*

soluble /ˈsɒljʊbl/ *a* löslich; (*solvable*) lösbar

solution /səˈluːʃn/ *n* Lösung *f*

solvable /ˈsɒlvəbl/ *a* lösbar

solve /sɒlv/ *vt* lösen

solvent /ˈsɒlvənt/ *a* zahlungsfähig; (*Chem*) lösend ● *n* Lösungsmittel *nt*

sombre /ˈsɒmbə(r)/ *a* dunkel; ⟨*mood*⟩ düster

some /sʌm/ *a & pron* etwas; (*a little*) ein bißchen; (*with pl noun*) einige; (*a *few*) ein paar; (*certain*) manche(r,s); (*one or the other*) [irgend]ein; ~ **day** eines Tages; **I want** ~ ich möchte etwas/(*pl*) welche; **will you have** ~ **wine?** möchten Sie Wein? **I need** ~ **money/books** ich brauche Geld/Bücher; **do** ~ **shopping** einkaufen

some: ~**body** /-bədɪ/ *pron & n* jemand; (*emphatic*) irgend jemand. ~**how** *adv* irgendwie. ~**one** *pron & n* = **somebody**

somersault /'sʌməsɔ:lt/ *n* Purzelbaum *m* (*fam*); (*Sport*) Salto *m*; **turn a** ~ einen Purzelbaum schlagen/einen Salto springen

'**something** *pron & adv* etwas; (*emphatic*) irgend etwas; ~ **different** etwas anderes; ~ **like** so etwas wie; **see** ~ **of s.o.** jdn mal sehen

some: ~**time** *adv* irgendwann • *a* ehemalig. ~**times** *adv* manchmal. ~**what** *adv* ziemlich. ~**where** *adv* irgendwo; ⟨*go*⟩ irgendwohin

son /sʌn/ *n* Sohn *m*

sonata /sə'nɑ:tə/ *n* Sonate *f*

song /sɒŋ/ *n* Lied *nt*. ~**bird** *n* Singvogel *m*

sonic /'sɒnɪk/ *a* Schall-. ~ '**boom** *n* Überschallknall *m*

'**son-in-law** *n* (*pl* ~**s-in-law**) Schwiegersohn *m*

soon /su:n/ *adv* (**-er, -est**) bald; (*quickly*) schnell; **too** ~ zu früh; **as** ~ **as** sobald; **as** ~ **as possible** so bald wie möglich; ~**er or later** früher oder später; **no** ~**er had I arrived than ...** kaum war ich angekommen, da ...; **I would** ~**er stay** ich würde lieber bleiben

soot /sʊt/ *n* Ruß *m*

sooth|e /su:ð/ *vt* beruhigen; lindern ⟨*pain*⟩. ~**ing** *a*, **-ly** *adv* beruhigend; lindernd

sooty /'sʊtɪ/ *a* rußig

sop /sɒp/ *n* Beschwichtigungsmittel *nt*

sophisticated /sə'fɪstɪkeɪtɪd/ *a* weltgewandt; (*complex*) hochentwickelt

soporific /sɒpə'rɪfɪk/ *a* einschläfernd

sopping /'sɒpɪŋ/ *a & adv* ~ **[wet]** durchnäßt

soppy /'sɒpɪ/ *a* (**-ier, -iest**) (*fam*) rührselig

soprano /sə'prɑ:nəʊ/ *n* Sopran *m*; (*woman*) Sopranistin *f*

sordid /'sɔ:dɪd/ *a* schmutzig

sore /sɔ:(r)/ *a* (**-r, -st**) wund; (*painful*) schmerzhaft; **have a** ~ **throat** Halsschmerzen haben • *n* wunde Stelle *f*. ~**ly** *adv* sehr

sorrow /'sɒrəʊ/ *n* Kummer *m*, Leid *nt*. ~**ful** *a* traurig

sorry /'sɒrɪ/ *a* (**-ier, -iest**) (*sad*) traurig; (*wretched*) erbärmlich; **I am** ~ es tut mir leid; **she is** *or* **feels** ~ **for him** er tut ihr leid; **I am** ~ **to say** leider; ~! Entschuldigung!

sort /sɔ:t/ *n* Art *f*; (*brand*) Sorte *f*; **he's a good** ~ (*fam*) er ist in Ordnung; **be out of** ~**s** (*fam*) nicht auf der Höhe sein • *vt* sortieren. ~ **out** *vt* sortieren; (*fig*) klären

sought /sɔ:t/ *see* **seek**

soul /səʊl/ *n* Seele *f*. ~**ful** *a* gefühlvoll

sound[1] /saʊnd/ *a* (**-er, -est**) gesund; (*sensible*) vernünftig; (*secure*) solide; (*thorough*) gehörig • *adv* **be** ~ **asleep** fest schlafen

sound[2] *vt* (*Naut*) loten. ~ **out** *vt* (*fig*) aushorchen

sound[3] *n* (*strait*) Meerenge *f*

sound[4] *n* Laut *m*; (*noise*) Geräusch *nt*; (*Phys*) Schall *m*; (*Radio, TV*) Ton *m*; (*of bells, music*) Klang *m*; **I don't like the** ~ **of it** (*fam*) das hört sich nicht gut an • *vi* [er]tönen; (*seem*) sich anhören • *vt* (*pronounce*) aussprechen; schlagen ⟨*alarm*⟩; (*Med*) abhorchen ⟨*chest*⟩. ~ **barrier** *n* Schallmauer *f*. ~**less** *a*, **-ly** *adv* lautlos

soundly /'saʊndlɪ/ *adv* solide; ⟨*sleep*⟩ fest; ⟨*defeat*⟩ vernichtend

'**soundproof** *a* schalldicht

soup /su:p/ *n* Suppe *f*. ~**ed-up** *a* (*fam*) ⟨*engine*⟩ frisiert

soup: ~**-plate** *n* Suppenteller *m*. ~**-spoon** *n* Suppenlöffel *m*

sour /'saʊə(r)/ *a* (**-er, -est**) sauer; (*bad-tempered*) griesgrämig, verdrießlich

source /sɔ:s/ *n* Quelle *f*

south /saʊθ/ *n* Süden *m*; **to the** ~ **of** südlich von • *a* Süd-, süd- • *adv* nach Süden

south: S~ '**Africa** *n* Südafrika *nt*. **S**~ **A'merica** *n* Südamerika *nt*. ~**-'east** *n* Südosten *m*

southerly /'sʌðəlɪ/ *a* südlich

southern /'sʌðən/ *a* südlich

South 'Pole *n* Südpol *m*

'**southward[s]** /-wəd[z]/ *adv* nach Süden

souvenir /su:və'nɪə(r)/ *n* Andenken *nt*, Souvenir *nt*

sovereign /'sɒvrɪn/ *a* souverän • *n* Souverän *m*. ~**ty** *n* Souveränität *f*

Soviet /'səʊvɪət/ *a* sowjetisch; ~ **Union** Sowjetunion *f*
sow[1] /saʊ/ *n* Sau *f*
sow[2] /səʊ/ *vt* (*pt* **sowed**, *pp* **sown** *or* **sowed**) säen
soya /'sɔɪə/ *n* ~ **bean** Sojabohne *f*
spa /spɑ:/ *n* Heilbad *nt*
space /speɪs/ *n* Raum *m*; (*gap*) Platz *m*; (*Astr*) Weltraum *m*; **leave/clear a** ~ Platz lassen/schaffen ● *vt* ~ **[out]** [in Abständen] verteilen
space: ~**craft** *n* Raumfahrzeug *nt*. ~**ship** *n* Raumschiff *nt*
spacious /'speɪʃəs/ *a* geräumig
spade /speɪd/ *n* Spaten *m*; (*for child*) Schaufel *f*; ~**s** *pl* (*Cards*) Pik *nt*; **call a** ~ **a** ~ das Kind beim rechten Namen nennen. ~**work** *n* Vorarbeit *f*
Spain /speɪn/ *n* Spanien *nt*
span[1] /spæn/ *n* Spanne *f*; (*of arch*) Spannweite *f* ● *vt* (*pt*/*pp* **spanned**) überspannen; umspannen ⟨*time*⟩
span[2] *see* **spick**
Span|iard /'spænjəd/ *n* Spanier(in) *m*(*f*). ~**ish** *a* spanisch ● *n* (*Lang*) Spanisch *nt*; **the** ~**ish** *pl* die Spanier
spank /spæŋk/ *vt* verhauen
spanner /'spænə(r)/ *n* Schraubenschlüssel *m*
spar /spɑ:(r)/ *vi* (*pt*/*pp* **sparred**) (*Sport*) sparren; (*argue*) sich zanken
spare /speə(r)/ *a* (*surplus*) übrig; (*additional*) zusätzlich; ⟨*seat, time*⟩ frei; ⟨*room*⟩ Gäste-; ⟨*bed, cup*⟩ Extra- ● *n* (*part*) Ersatzteil *nt* ● *vt* ersparen; (*not hurt*) verschonen; (*do without*) entbehren; (*afford to give*) erübrigen; **to** ~ (*surplus*) übrig. ~ **'wheel** *n* Reserverad *nt*
sparing /'speərɪŋ/ *a*, **-ly** *adv* sparsam
spark /spɑ:k/ *n* Funke *m* ● *vt* ~ **off** zünden; (*fig*) auslösen. ~**ing-plug** *n* (*Auto*) Zündkerze *f*
sparkl|e /'spɑ:kl/ *n* Funkeln *nt* ● *vi* funkeln. ~**ing** *a* funkelnd; ⟨*wine*⟩ Schaum-
sparrow /'spærəʊ/ *n* Spatz *m*
sparse /spɑ:s/ *a* spärlich. ~**ly** *adv* spärlich; ⟨*populated*⟩ dünn
Spartan /'spɑ:tn/ *a* spartanisch
spasm /'spæzm/ *n* Anfall *m*; (*cramp*) Krampf *m*. ~**odic** /-'mɒdɪk/ *a*, **-ally** *adv* sporadisch; (*Med*) krampfartig
spastic /'spæstɪk/ *a* spastisch [gelähmt] ● *n* Spastiker(in) *m*(*f*)
spat /spæt/ *see* **spit**[2]
spate /speɪt/ *n* Flut *f*; (*series*) Serie *f*; **be in full** ~ Hochwasser führen
spatial /'speɪʃl/ *a* räumlich
spatter /'spætə(r)/ *vt* spritzen; ~ **with** bespritzen mit
spatula /'spætjʊlə/ *n* Spachtel *m*; (*Med*) Spatel *m*
spawn /spɔ:n/ *n* Laich *m* ● *vi* laichen ● *vt* (*fig*) hervorbringen
spay /speɪ/ *vt* sterilisieren
speak /spi:k/ *v* (*pt* **spoke**, *pp* **spoken**) ● *vi* sprechen (**to** mit); ~**ing!** (*Teleph*) am Apparat! ● *vt* sprechen; sagen ⟨*truth*⟩. ~ **up** *vi* lauter sprechen; ~ **up for oneself** seine Meinung äußern
speaker /'spi:kə(r)/ *n* Sprecher(in) *m*(*f*); (*in public*) Redner(in) *m*(*f*); (*loudspeaker*) Lautsprecher *m*
spear /spɪə(r)/ *n* Speer *m* ● *vt* aufspießen. ~**head** *vt* (*fig*) anführen
spec /spek/ *n* **on** ~ (*fam*) auf gut Glück
special /'speʃl/ *a* besondere(r,s), speziell. ~**ist** *n* Spezialist *m*; (*Med*) Facharzt *m*/-ärztin *f*. ~**ity** /-ʃɪ'ælətɪ/ *n* Spezialität *f*
special|ize /'speʃəlaɪz/ *vi* sich spezialisieren (**in** auf + *acc*). ~**ly** *adv* speziell; (*particularly*) besonders
species /'spi:ʃi:z/ *n* Art *f*
specific /spə'sɪfɪk/ *a* bestimmt; (*precise*) genau; (*Phys*) spezifisch. ~**ally** *adv* ausdrücklich
specification /spesɪfɪ'keɪʃn/ *n* & ~**s** *pl* genaue Angaben *pl*
specify /'spesɪfaɪ/ *vt* (*pt*/*pp* **-ied**) [genau] angeben
specimen /'spesɪmən/ *n* Exemplar *nt*; (*sample*) Probe *f*; (*of urine*) Urinprobe *f*
speck /spek/ *n* Fleck *m*; (*particle*) Teilchen *nt*
speckled /'spekld/ *a* gesprenkelt
specs /speks/ *npl* (*fam*) Brille *f*
spectacle /'spektəkl/ *n* (*show*) Schauspiel *nt*; (*sight*) Anblick *m*. ~**s** *npl* Brille *f*
spectacular /spek'tækjʊlə(r)/ *a* spektakulär
spectator /spek'teɪtə(r)/ *n* Zuschauer(in) *m*(*f*)
spectre /'spektə(r)/ *n* Gespenst *nt*; (*fig*) Schreckgespenst *nt*
spectrum /'spektrəm/ *n* (*pl* **-tra**) Spektrum *nt*
speculat|e /'spekjʊleɪt/ *vi* spekulieren. ~**ion** /-'leɪʃn/ *n* Spekulation *f*. ~**or** *n* Spekulant *m*
sped /sped/ *see* **speed**

speech /spi:tʃ/ *n* Sprache *f*; (*address*) Rede *f*. **~less** *a* sprachlos

speed /spi:d/ *n* Geschwindigkeit *f*; (*rapidity*) Schnelligkeit *f*; (*gear*) Gang *m*; **at ~** mit hoher Geschwindigkeit • *vi* (*pt/pp* **sped**) schnell fahren • (*pt/pp* **speeded**) (*go too fast*) zu schnell fahren. **~ up** (*pt/pp* **speeded up**) • *vt* beschleunigen • *vi* schneller werden; ⟨*vehicle:*⟩ schneller fahren

speed: ~boat *n* Rennboot *nt*. **~ing** *n* Geschwindigkeitsüberschreitung *f*. **~ limit** *n* Geschwindigkeitsbeschränkung *f*

speedometer /spi:'dɒmɪtə(r)/ *n* Tachometer *m*

speedy /'spi:dɪ/ *a* (**-ier, -iest**), **-ily** *adv* schnell

spell[1] /spel/ *n* Weile *f*; (*of weather*) Periode *f*

spell[2] *v* (*pt/pp* **spelled** *or* **spelt**) • *vt* schreiben; (*aloud*) buchstabieren; (*fig: mean*) bedeuten • *vi* richtig schreiben; (*aloud*) buchstabieren. **~ out** *vt* buchstabieren; (*fig*) genau erklären

spell[3] *n* Zauber *m*; (*words*) Zauberspruch *m*. **~bound** *a* wie verzaubert

spelling /'spelɪŋ/ *n* Schreibweise *f*; (*orthography*) Rechtschreibung *f*

spelt /spelt/ *see* **spell**[2]

spend /spend/ *vt/i* (*pt/pp* **spent**) ausgeben; verbringen ⟨*time*⟩

spent /spent/ *see* **spend**

sperm /spɜ:m/ *n* Samen *m*

spew /spju:/ *vt* speien

spher|e /sfɪə(r)/ *n* Kugel *f*; (*fig*) Sphäre *f*. **~ical** /'sferɪkl/ *a* kugelförmig

spice /spaɪs/ *n* Gewürz *nt*; (*fig*) Würze *f*

spick /spɪk/ *a* **~ and span** blitzsauber

spicy /'spaɪsɪ/ *a* würzig, pikant

spider /'spaɪdə(r)/ *n* Spinne *f*

spik|e /spaɪk/ *n* Spitze *f*; (*Bot, Zool*) Stachel *m*; (*on shoe*) Spike *m*. **~y** *a* stachelig

spill /spɪl/ *v* (*pt/pp* **spilt** *or* **spilled**) • *vt* verschütten; vergießen ⟨*blood*⟩ • *vi* überlaufen

spin /spɪn/ *v* (*pt/pp* **spun**, *pres p* **spinning**) • *vt* drehen; spinnen ⟨*wool*⟩; schleudern ⟨*washing*⟩ • *vi* sich drehen. **~ out** *vt* in die Länge ziehen

spinach /'spɪnɪdʒ/ *n* Spinat *m*

spinal /'spaɪnl/ *a* Rückgrat-. **~ 'cord** *n* Rückenmark *nt*

spindl|e /'spɪndl/ *n* Spindel *f*. **~y** *a* spindeldürr

spin-'drier *n* Wäscheschleuder *f*

spine /spaɪn/ *n* Rückgrat *nt*; (*of book*) [Buch]rücken *m*; (*Bot, Zool*) Stachel *m*. **~less** *a* (*fig*) rückgratlos

spinning /'spɪnɪŋ/ *n* Spinnen *nt*. **~-wheel** *n* Spinnrad *nt*

'spin-off *n* Nebenprodukt *nt*

spinster /'spɪnstə(r)/ *n* ledige Frau *f*

spiral /'spaɪrl/ *a* spiralig • *n* Spirale *f* • *vi* (*pt/pp* **spiralled**) sich hochwinden; ⟨*smoke:*⟩ in einer Spirale aufsteigen. **~ 'staircase** *n* Wendeltreppe *f*

spire /'spaɪə(r)/ *n* Turmspitze *f*

spirit /'spɪrɪt/ *n* Geist *m*; (*courage*) Mut *m*; **~s** *pl* (*alcohol*) Spirituosen *pl*; **in high ~s** in gehobener Stimmung; **in low ~s** niedergedrückt. **~ away** *vt* verschwinden lassen

spirited /'spɪrɪtɪd/ *a* lebhaft; (*courageous*) beherzt

spirit: ~-level *n* Wasserwaage *f*. **~ stove** *n* Spirituskocher *m*

spiritual /'spɪrɪtjʊəl/ *a* geistig; (*Relig*) geistlich. **~ism** /-ɪzm/ *n* Spiritismus *m*. **~ist** /-ɪst/ *a* spiritistisch • *n* Spiritist *m*

spit[1] /spɪt/ *n* (*for roasting*) [Brat]spieß *m*

spit[2] *n* Spucke *f* • *vt/i* (*pt/pp* **spat**, *pres p* **spitting**) spucken; ⟨*cat:*⟩ fauchen; ⟨*fat:*⟩ spritzen; **it's ~ting with rain** es tröpfelt; **be the ~ting image of s.o.** jdm wie aus dem Gesicht geschnitten sein

spite /spaɪt/ *n* Boshaftigkeit *f*; **in ~ of** trotz (+ *gen*) • *vt* ärgern. **~ful** *a*, **-ly** *adv* gehässig

spittle /'spɪtl/ *n* Spucke *f*

splash /splæʃ/ *n* Platschen *nt*; (*fam: drop*) Schuß *m*; **~ of colour** Farbfleck *m* • *vt* spritzen; **~ s.o. with sth** jdn mit etw bespritzen • *vi* spritzen. **~ about** *vi* planschen

spleen /spli:n/ *n* Milz *f*

splendid /'splendɪd/ *a* herrlich, großartig

splendour /'splendə(r)/ *n* Pracht *f*

splint /splɪnt/ *n* (*Med*) Schiene *f*

splinter /'splɪntə(r)/ *n* Splitter *m* • *vi* zersplittern

split /splɪt/ *n* Spaltung *f*; (*Pol*) Bruch *m*; (*tear*) Riß *m* • *v* (*pt/pp* **split**, *pres p* **splitting**) • *vt* spalten; (*share*) teilen; (*tear*) zerreißen; **~ one's sides** sich kaputtlachen • *vi* sich spalten; (*tear*) zerreißen; **~ on s.o.** (*fam*) jdn verpfeifen. ~ **up** *vt* aufteilen • *vi* ⟨*couple:*⟩ sich trennen

splutter /'splʌtə(r)/ *vi* prusten

spoil /spɔɪl/ *n* ~**s** *pl* Beute *f* • *v* (*pt*/*pp* **spoilt** *or* **spoiled**) • *vt* verderben; verwöhnen ⟨*person*⟩ • *vi* verderben. ~**sport** *n* Spielverderber *m*

spoke[1] /spəʊk/ *n* Speiche *f*

spoke[2], **spoken** /'spəʊkn/ *see* **speak**

'spokesman *n* Sprecher *m*

sponge /spʌndʒ/ *n* Schwamm *m* • *vt* abwaschen • *vi* ~ **on** schmarotzen bei. ~**-bag** *n* Waschbeutel *m*. ~**-cake** *n* Biskuitkuchen *m*

spong|er /'spʌndʒə(r)/ *n* Schmarotzer *m*. ~**y** *a* schwammig

sponsor /'spɒnsə(r)/ *n* Sponsor *m*; (*god-parent*) Pate *m*/Patin *f*; (*for membership*) Bürge *m* • *vt* sponsern; bürgen für

spontaneous /spɒn'teɪnɪəs/ *a*, **-ly** *adv* spontan

spoof /spu:f/ *n* (*fam*) Parodie *f*

spooky /'spu:kɪ/ *a* (**-ier, -iest**) (*fam*) gespenstisch

spool /spu:l/ *n* Spule *f*

spoon /spu:n/ *n* Löffel *m* • *vt* löffeln. ~**-feed** *vt* (*pt*/*pp* **-fed**) (*fig*) alles vorkauen (+ *dat*). ~**ful** *n* Löffel *m*

sporadic /spə'rædɪk/ *a*, **-ally** *adv* sporadisch

sport /spɔ:t/ *n* Sport *m*; (*amusement*) Spaß *m* • *vt* [stolz] tragen. ~**ing** *a* sportlich; **a ~ing chance** eine faire Chance

sports: ~ **car** *n* Sportwagen *m*. ~ **coat** *n*, ~ **jacket** *n* Sakko *m*. ~**man** *n* Sportler *m*. ~**woman** *n* Sportlerin *f*

sporty /'spɔ:tɪ/ *a* (**-ier, -iest**) sportlich

spot /spɒt/ *n* Fleck *m*; (*place*) Stelle *f*; (*dot*) Punkt *m*; (*drop*) Tropfen *m*; (*pimple*) Pickel *m*; ~**s** *pl* (*rash*) Ausschlag *m*; **a ~ of** (*fam*) ein bißchen; **on the ~** auf der Stelle; **be in a tight ~** (*fam*) in der Klemme sitzen • *vt* (*pt*/*pp* **spotted**) entdecken

spot: ~ **'check** *n* Stichprobe *f*. ~**less** *a* makellos; (*fam: very clean*) blitzsauber. ~**light** *n* Scheinwerfer *m*; (*fig*) Rampenlicht *nt*

spotted /'spɒtɪd/ *a* gepunktet

spotty /'spɒtɪ/ *a* (**-ier, -iest**) fleckig; (*pimply*) pickelig

spouse /spaʊz/ *n* Gatte *m*/Gattin *f*

spout /spaʊt/ *n* Schnabel *m*, Tülle *f* • *vi* schießen (**from** aus)

sprain /spreɪn/ *n* Verstauchung *f* • *vt* verstauchen

sprang /spræŋ/ *see* **spring**[2]

sprat /spræt/ *n* Sprotte *f*

sprawl /sprɔ:l/ *vi* sich ausstrecken; (*fall*) der Länge nach hinfallen

spray[1] /spreɪ/ *n* (*of flowers*) Strauß *m*

spray[2] *n* Sprühnebel *m*; (*from sea*) Gischt *m*; (*device*) Spritze *f*; (*container*) Sprühdose *f*; (*preparation*) Spray *nt* • *vt* spritzen; (*with aerosol*) sprühen

spread /spred/ *n* Verbreitung *f*; (*paste*) Aufstrich *m*; (*fam: feast*) Festessen *nt* • *v* (*pt*/*pp* **spread**) • *vt* ausbreiten; streichen ⟨*butter, jam*⟩; bestreichen ⟨*bread, surface*⟩; streuen ⟨*sand, manure*⟩; verbreiten ⟨*news, disease*⟩; verteilen ⟨*payments*⟩ • *vi* sich ausbreiten. ~ **out** *vt* ausbreiten; (*space out*) verteilen • *vi* sich verteilen

spree /spri:/ *n* (*fam*) **go on a shopping ~** groß einkaufen gehen

sprig /sprɪg/ *n* Zweig *m*

sprightly /'spraɪtlɪ/ *a* (**-ier, -iest**) rüstig

spring[1] /sprɪŋ/ *n* Frühling *m* • *attrib* Frühlings-

spring[2] *n* (*jump*) Sprung *m*; (*water*) Quelle *f*; (*device*) Feder *f*; (*elasticity*) Elastizität *f* • *v* (*pt* **sprang**, *pp* **sprung**) • *vi* springen; (*arise*) entspringen (**from** *dat*) • *vt* ~ **sth on s.o.** jdn mit etw überfallen

spring: ~**board** *n* Sprungbrett *nt*. ~**-'cleaning** *n* Frühjahrsputz *m*. ~**time** *n* Frühling *m*

sprinkl|e /'sprɪŋkl/ *vt* sprengen; (*scatter*) streuen; bestreuen ⟨*surface*⟩. ~**er** *n* Sprinkler *m*; (*Hort*) Sprenger *m*. ~**ing** *n* dünne Schicht *f*

sprint /sprɪnt/ *n* Sprint *m* • *vi* rennen; (*Sport*) sprinten. ~**er** *n* Kurzstreckenläufer(in) *m*(*f*)

sprout /spraʊt/ *n* Trieb *m*; **[Brussels] ~s** *pl* Rosenkohl *m* • *vi* sprießen

spruce /spru:s/ *a* gepflegt • *n* Fichte *f*

sprung /sprʌŋ/ *see* **spring**[2] • *a* gefedert

spry /spraɪ/ *a* (**-er, -est**) rüstig

spud /spʌd/ *n* (*fam*) Kartoffel *f*

spun /spʌn/ *see* **spin**

spur /spɜ:(r)/ *n* Sporn *m*; (*stimulus*) Ansporn *m*; (*road*) Nebenstraße *f*; **on the ~ of the moment** ganz spontan • *vt* (*pt*/*pp* **spurred**) ~ **[on]** (*fig*) anspornen

spurious /'spjʊərɪəs/ *a*, **-ly** *adv* falsch

spurn /spɜ:n/ *vt* verschmähen

spurt /spɜ:t/ *n* Strahl *m*; (*Sport*) Spurt *m*; **put on a ~** spurten • *vi* spritzen

spy /spaɪ/ *n* Spion(in) *m(f)* ● *vi* spionieren; ~ **on s.o.** jdm nachspionieren ● *vt* (*fam: see*) sehen. ~ **out** *vt* auskundschaften

spying /'spaɪɪŋ/ *n* Spionage *f*

squabble /'skwɒbl/ *n* Zank *m* ● *vi* sich zanken

squad /skwɒd/ *n* Gruppe *f*; (*Sport*) Mannschaft *f*

squadron /'skwɒdrən/ *n* (*Mil*) Geschwader *nt*

squalid /'skwɒlɪd/ *a*, **-ly** *adv* schmutzig

squall /skwɔːl/ *n* Bö *f* ● *vi* brüllen

squalor /'skwɒlə(r)/ *n* Schmutz *m*

squander /'skwɒndə(r)/ *vt* vergeuden

square /skweə(r)/ *a* quadratisch; ⟨*metre, mile*⟩ Quadrat-; ⟨*meal*⟩ anständig; **all** ~ (*fam*) quitt ● *n* Quadrat *nt*; (*area*) Platz *m*; (*on chessboard*) Feld *nt* ● *vt* (*settle*) klären; (*Math*) quadrieren ● *vi* (*agree*) übereinstimmen

squash /skwɒʃ/ *n* Gedränge *nt*; (*drink*) Fruchtsaftgetränk *nt*; (*Sport*) Squash *nt* ● *vt* zerquetschen; (*suppress*) niederschlagen. ~**y** *a* weich

squat /skwɒt/ *a* gedrungen ● *n* (*fam*) besetztes Haus *nt* ● *vi* (*pt/pp* **squatted**) hocken; ~ **in a house** ein Haus besetzen. ~**ter** *n* Hausbesetzer *m*

squawk /skwɔːk/ *vi* krächzen

squeak /skwiːk/ *n* Quieken *nt*; (*of hinge, brakes*) Quietschen *nt* ● *vi* quieken; quietschen

squeal /skwiːl/ *n* Schrei *m*; (*screech*) Kreischen *nt* ● *vi* schreien; kreischen

squeamish /'skwiːmɪʃ/ *a* empfindlich

squeeze /skwiːz/ *n* Druck *m*; (*crush*) Gedränge *nt* ● *vt* drücken; (*to get juice*) ausdrücken; (*force*) zwängen; (*fam: extort*) herauspressen (**from** aus) ● *vi* ~ **in/out** sich hinein-/hinauszwängen

squelch /skweltʃ/ *vi* quatschen

squid /skwɪd/ *n* Tintenfisch *m*

squiggle /'skwɪgl/ *n* Schnörkel *m*

squint /skwɪnt/ *n* Schielen *nt* ● *vi* schielen

squire /'skwaɪə(r)/ *n* Gutsherr *m*

squirm /skwɜːm/ *vi* sich winden

squirrel /'skwɪrl/ *n* Eichhörnchen *nt*

squirt /skwɜːt/ *n* Spritzer *m* ● *vt/i* spritzen

St *abbr* (**Saint**) St.; (**Street**) Str.

stab /stæb/ *n* Stich *m*; (*fam: attempt*) Versuch *m* ● *vt* (*pt/pp* **stabbed**) stechen; (*to death*) erstechen

stability /stə'bɪlətɪ/ *n* Stabilität *f*

stabilize /'steɪbɪlaɪz/ *vt* stabilisieren ● *vi* sich stabilisieren

stable[1] /'steɪbl/ *a* (**-r, -st**) stabil

stable[2] *n* Stall *m*; (*establishment*) Reitstall *m*

stack /stæk/ *n* Stapel *m*; (*of chimney*) Schornstein *m*; (*fam: large quantity*) Haufen *m* ● *vt* stapeln

stadium /'steɪdɪəm/ *n* Stadion *nt*

staff /stɑːf/ *n* (*stick & Mil*) Stab *m* ● (& *pl*) (*employees*) Personal *nt*; (*Sch*) Lehrkräfte *pl* ● *vt* mit Personal besetzen. ~**-room** *n* (*Sch*) Lehrerzimmer *nt*

stag /stæg/ *n* Hirsch *m*

stage /steɪdʒ/ *n* Bühne *f*; (*in journey*) Etappe *f*; (*in process*) Stadium *nt*; **by** *or* **in** ~**s** in Etappen ● *vt* aufführen; (*arrange*) veranstalten

stage: ~ **door** *n* Bühneneingang *m*. ~ **fright** *n* Lampenfieber *nt*

stagger /'stægə(r)/ *vi* taumeln ● *vt* staffeln ⟨*holidays*⟩; versetzt anordnen ⟨*seats*⟩; **I was** ~**ed** es hat mir die Sprache verschlagen. ~**ing** *a* unglaublich

stagnant /'stægnənt/ *a* stehend; (*fig*) stagnierend

stagnat|e /stæg'neɪt/ *vi* (*fig*) stagnieren. ~**ion** /-'neɪʃn/ *n* Stagnation *f*

staid /steɪd/ *a* gesetzt

stain /steɪn/ *n* Fleck *m*; (*for wood*) Beize *f* ● *vt* farben; beizen ⟨*wood*⟩; (*fig*) beflecken; ~**ed glass** farbiges Glas *nt*. ~**less** *a* fleckenlos; ⟨*steel*⟩ rostfrei. ~ **remover** *n* Fleckentferner *m*

stair /steə(r)/ *n* Stufe *f*; ~**s** *pl* Treppe *f*. ~**case** *n* Treppe *f*

stake /steɪk/ *n* Pfahl *m*; (*wager*) Einsatz *m*; (*Comm*) Anteil *m*; **be at** ~ auf dem Spiel stehen ● *vt* [an einem Pfahl] anbinden; (*wager*) setzen; ~ **a claim to sth** Anspruch auf etw (*acc*) erheben

stale /steɪl/ *a* (**-r, -st**) alt; ⟨*air*⟩ verbraucht. ~**mate** *n* Patt *nt*

stalk[1] /stɔːk/ *n* Stiel *m*, Stengel *m*

stalk[2] *vt* pirschen auf (+ *acc*) ● *vi* stolzieren

stall /stɔːl/ *n* Stand *m*; ~**s** *pl* (*Theat*) Parkett *nt* ● *vi* ⟨*engine:*⟩ stehenbleiben; (*fig*) ausweichen ● *vt* abwürgen ⟨*engine*⟩

stallion /ˈstæljən/ *n* Hengst *m*
stalwart /ˈstɔːlwət/ *a* treu ● *n* treuer Anhänger *m*
stamina /ˈstæmɪnə/ *n* Ausdauer *f*
stammer /ˈstæmə(r)/ *n* Stottern *nt* ● *vt/i* stottern
stamp /stæmp/ *n* Stempel *m*; (*postage* ~) [Brief]marke *f* ● *vt* stempeln; (*impress*) prägen; (*put postage on*) frankieren; ~ **one's feet** mit den Füßen stampfen ● *vi* stampfen. ~ **out** *vt* [aus]stanzen; (*fig*) ausmerzen
stampede /stæmˈpiːd/ *n* wilde Flucht *f*; (*fam*) Ansturm *m* ● *vi* in Panik fliehen
stance /stɑːns/ *n* Haltung *f*
stand /stænd/ *n* Stand *m*; (*rack*) Ständer *m*; (*pedestal*) Sockel *m*; (*Sport*) Tribüne *f*; (*fig*) Einstellung *f* ● *v* (*pt/pp* **stood**) ● *vi* stehen; (*rise*) aufstehen; (*be candidate*) kandidieren; (*stay valid*) gültig bleiben; ~ **still** stillstehen; ~ **firm** (*fig*) festbleiben; ~ **together** zusammenhalten; ~ **to lose/gain** gewinnen/verlieren können; ~ **to reason** logisch sein; ~ **in for** vertreten; ~ **for** (*mean*) bedeuten; **I won't** ~ **for that** das lasse ich mir nicht bieten ● *vt* stellen; (*withstand*) standhalten (+ *dat*); (*endure*) ertragen; vertragen ⟨*climate*⟩; (*put up with*) aushalten; haben ⟨*chance*⟩; ~ **one's ground** nicht nachgeben; ~ **the test of time** sich bewähren; ~ **s.o. a beer** jdm ein Bier spendieren; **I can't** ~ **her** (*fam*) ich kann sie nicht ausstehen. ~ **by** *vi* danebenstehen; (*be ready*) sich bereithalten ● *vt* ~ **by s.o.** (*fig*) zu jdm stehen. ~ **down** *vi* (*retire*) zurücktreten. ~ **out** *vi* hervorstehen; (*fig*) herausragen. ~ **up** *vi* aufstehen; ~ **up for** eintreten für; ~ **up to** sich wehren gegen
standard /ˈstændəd/ *a* Normal-; **be** ~ **practice** allgemein üblich sein ● *n* Maßstab *m*; (*Techn*) Norm *f*; (*level*) Niveau *nt*; (*flag*) Standarte *f*; ~**s** *pl* (*morals*) Prinzipien *pl*; ~ **of living** Lebensstandard *m*. ~**ize** *vt* standardisieren; (*Techn*) normen
ˈstandard lamp *n* Stehlampe *f*
ˈstand-in *n* Ersatz *m*
standing /ˈstændɪŋ/ *a* (*erect*) stehend; (*permanent*) ständig ● *n* Rang *m*; (*duration*) Dauer *f*. ~ **ˈorder** *n* Dauerauftrag *m*. ~**-room** *n* Stehplätze *pl*
stand: ~**-offish** /stændˈɒfɪʃ/ *a* distanziert. ~**point** *n* Standpunkt *m*. ~**still** *n* Stillstand *m*; **come to a** ~**still** zum Stillstand kommen
stank /stæŋk/ *see* **stink**
staple[1] /ˈsteɪpl/ *a* Grund- ● *n* (*product*) Haupterzeugnis *nt*
staple[2] *n* Heftklammer *f* ● *vt* heften. ~**r** *n* Heftmaschine *f*
star /stɑː(r)/ *n* Stern *m*; (*asterisk*) Sternchen *nt*; (*Theat, Sport*) Star *m* ● *vi* (*pt/pp* **starred**) die Hauptrolle spielen
starboard /ˈstɑːbəd/ *n* Steuerbord *nt*
starch /stɑːtʃ/ *n* Stärke *f* ● *vt* stärken. ~**y** *a* stärkehaltig; (*fig*) steif
stare /steə(r)/ *n* Starren *nt* ● *vi* starren; ~ **at** anstarren
ˈstarfish *n* Seestern *m*
stark /stɑːk/ *a* (**-er, -est**) scharf; ⟨*contrast*⟩ kraß ● *adv* ~ **naked** splitternackt
starling /ˈstɑːlɪŋ/ *n* Star *m*
ˈstarlit *a* sternhell
starry /ˈstɑːrɪ/ *a* sternklar
start /stɑːt/ *n* Anfang *m*, Beginn *m*; (*departure*) Aufbruch *m*; (*Sport*) Start *m*; **from the** ~ von Anfang an; **for a** ~ erstens ● *vi* anfangen, beginnen; (*set out*) aufbrechen; ⟨*engine:*⟩ anspringen; (*Auto, Sport*) starten; (*jump*) aufschrecken; **to** ~ **with** zuerst ● *vt* anfangen, beginnen; (*cause*) verursachen; (*found*) gründen; starten ⟨*car, race*⟩; in Umlauf setzen ⟨*rumour*⟩. ~**er** *n* (*Culin*) Vorspeise *f*; (*Auto, Sport*) Starter *m*. ~**ing-point** *n* Ausgangspunkt *m*
startle /ˈstɑːtl/ *vt* erschrecken
starvation /stɑːˈveɪʃn/ *n* Verhungern *nt*
starve /stɑːv/ *vi* hungern; (*to death*) verhungern ● *vt* verhungern lassen
stash /stæʃ/ *vt* (*fam*) ~ **[away]** beiseite schaffen
state /steɪt/ *n* Zustand *m*; (*grand style*) Prunk *m*; (*Pol*) Staat *m*; ~ **of play** Spielstand *m*; **be in a** ~ ⟨*person:*⟩ aufgeregt sein; **lie in** ~ feierlich aufgebahrt sein ● *attrib* Staats-, staatlich ● *vt* erklären; (*specify*) angeben. ~**-aided** *a* staatlich gefördert. ~**less** *a* staatenlos
stately /ˈsteɪtlɪ/ *a* (**-ier, -iest**) stattlich. ~ **ˈhome** *n* Schloß *nt*
statement /ˈsteɪtmənt/ *n* Erklärung *f*; (*Jur*) Aussage *f*; (*Banking*) Auszug *m*
ˈstatesman *n* Staatsmann *m*

static /'stætɪk/ *a* statisch; **remain ~** unverändert bleiben
station /'steɪʃn/ *n* Bahnhof *m*; (*police*) Wache *f*; (*radio*) Sender *m*; (*space, weather*) Station *f*; (*Mil*) Posten *m*; (*status*) Rang *m* ● *vt* stationieren; (*post*) postieren. **~ary** /-ərɪ/ *a* stehend; **be ~ary** stehen
stationer /'steɪʃənə(r)/ *n* **~'s [shop]** Schreibwarengeschäft *nt*. **~y** *n* Briefpapier *nt*; (*writing-materials*) Schreibwaren *pl*
'station-wagon *n* (*Amer*) Kombi[wagen] *m*
statistic /stə'tɪstɪk/ *n* statistische Tatsache *f*. **~al** *a*, **-ly** *adv* statistisch. **~s** *n & pl* Statistik *f*
statue /'stætju:/ *n* Statue *f*
stature /'stætʃə(r)/ *n* Statur *f*; (*fig*) Format *nt*
status /'steɪtəs/ *n* Status *m*, Rang *m*. **~ symbol** *n* Statussymbol *nt*
statut|e /'stætju:t/ *n* Statut *nt*. **~ory** *a* gesetzlich
staunch /stɔ:ntʃ/ *a* (**-er, -est**), **-ly** *adv* treu
stave /steɪv/ *vt* **~ off** abwenden
stay /steɪ/ *n* Aufenthalt *m* ● *vi* bleiben; (*reside*) wohnen; **~ the night** übernachten; **~ put** dableiben ● *vt* **~ the course** durchhalten. **~ away** *vi* wegbleiben. **~ behind** *vi* zurückbleiben. **~ in** *vi* zu Hause bleiben; (*Sch*) nachsitzen. **~ up** *vi* oben bleiben; (*upright*) stehen bleiben; (*on wall*) hängen bleiben; ⟨*person:*⟩ aufbleiben
stead /sted/ *n* **in his ~** an seiner Stelle; **stand s.o. in good ~** jdm zustatten kommen. **~fast** *a*, **-ly** *adv* standhaft
steadily /'stedɪlɪ/ *adv* fest; (*continually*) stetig
steady /'stedɪ/ *a* (**-ier, -iest**) fest; (*not wobbly*) stabil; ⟨*hand*⟩ ruhig; (*regular*) regelmäßig; (*dependable*) zuverlässig
steak /steɪk/ *n* Steak *nt*
steal /sti:l/ *vt/i* (*pt* **stole**, *pp* **stolen**) stehlen (**from** *dat*). **~ in/out** *vi* sich hinein-/hinausstehlen
stealth /stelθ/ *n* Heimlichkeit *f*; **by ~** heimlich. **~y** *a* heimlich
steam /sti:m/ *n* Dampf *m*; **under one's own ~** (*fam*) aus eigener Kraft ● *vt* (*Culin*) dämpfen, dünsten ● *vi* dampfen. **~ up** *vi* beschlagen
'steam-engine *n* Dampfmaschine *f*; (*Rail*) Dampflokomotive *f*
steamer /'sti:mə(r)/ *n* Dampfer *m*
'steamroller *n* Dampfwalze *f*
steamy /'sti:mɪ/ *a* dampfig
steel /sti:l/ *n* Stahl *m* ● *vt* **~ oneself** allen Mut zusammennehmen
steep[1] /sti:p/ *vt* (*soak*) einweichen
steep[2] *a*, **-ly** *adv* steil; (*fam: exorbitant*) gesalzen
steeple /'sti:pl/ *n* Kirchturm *m*. **~chase** *n* Hindernisrennen *nt*
steer /stɪə(r)/ *vt/i* steuern; **~ clear of s.o./sth** jdm/etw aus dem Weg gehen. **~ing** *n* (*Auto*) Steuerung *f*. **~ing-wheel** *n* Lenkrad *nt*
stem[1] /stem/ *n* Stiel *m*; (*of word*) Stamm *m* ● *vi* (*pt/pp* **stemmed**) **~ from** zurückzuführen sein auf (+ *acc*)
stem[2] *vt* (*pt/pp* **stemmed**) eindämmen; stillen ⟨*bleeding*⟩
stench /stentʃ/ *n* Gestank *m*
stencil /'stensl/ *n* Schablone *f*; (*for typing*) Matrize *f*
step /step/ *n* Schritt *m*; (*stair*) Stufe *f*; **~s** *pl* (*ladder*) Trittleiter *f*; **in ~** im Schritt; **~ by ~** Schritt für Schritt; **take ~s** (*fig*) Schritte unternehmen ● *vi* (*pt/pp* **stepped**) treten; **~ in** (*fig*) eingreifen; **~ into s.o.'s shoes** an jds Stelle treten; **~ out of line** aus der Reihe tanzen. **~ up** *vi* hinaufsteigen ● *vt* (*increase*) erhöhen, steigern; verstärken ⟨*efforts*⟩
step: ~brother *n* Stiefbruder *m*. **~child** *n* Stiefkind *nt*. **~daughter** *n* Stieftochter *f*. **~father** *n* Stiefvater *m*. **~-ladder** *n* Trittleiter *f*. **~mother** *n* Stiefmutter *f*
'stepping-stone *n* Trittstein *m*; (*fig*) Sprungbrett *nt*
step: ~sister *n* Stiefschwester *f*. **~son** *n* Stiefsohn *m*
stereo /'sterɪəʊ/ *n* Stereo *nt*; (*equipment*) Stereoanlage *f*; **in ~** stereo. **~phonic** /-'fɒnɪk/ *a* stereophon
stereotype /'sterɪətaɪp/ *n* stereotype Figur *f*. **~d** *a* stereotyp
steril|e /'steraɪl/ *a* steril. **~ity** /stə'rɪlətɪ/ *n* Sterilität *f*
steriliz|ation /sterəlaɪ'zeɪʃn/ *n* Sterilisation *f*. **~e** *vt* sterilisieren
sterling /'stɜ:lɪŋ/ *a* Sterling-; (*fig*) gediegen ● *n* Sterling *m*
stern[1] /stɜ:n/ *a* (**-er, -est**), **-ly** *adv* streng
stern[2] *n* (*of boat*) Heck *nt*
stew /stju:/ *n* Eintopf *m*; **in a ~** (*fam*) aufgeregt ● *vt/i* schmoren; **~ed fruit** Kompott *nt*

steward /'stju:əd/ *n* Ordner *m*; (*on ship, aircraft*) Steward *m*. **~ess** *n* Stewardeß *f*

stick[1] /stɪk/ *n* Stock *m*; (*of chalk*) Stück *nt*; (*of rhubarb*) Stange *f*; (*Sport*) Schläger *m*

stick[2] *v* (*pt/pp* **stuck**) ● *vt* stecken; (*stab*) stechen; (*glue*) kleben; (*fam: put*) tun; (*fam: endure*) aushalten ● *vi* stecken; (*adhere*) kleben, haften (**to** an + *dat*); (*jam*) klemmen; **~ to sth** (*fig*) bei etw bleiben; **~ at it** (*fam*) dranbleiben; **~ at nothing** (*fam*) vor nichts zurückschrecken; **~ up for** (*fam*) eintreten für; **be stuck** nicht weiterkönnen; ⟨*vehicle:*⟩ festsitzen, festgefahren sein; ⟨*drawer:*⟩ klemmen; **be stuck with sth** (*fam*) etw am Hals haben. **~ out** *vi* abstehen; (*project*) vorstehen ● *vt* (*fam*) hinausstrecken; herausstrecken ⟨*tongue*⟩

sticker /'stɪkə(r)/ *n* Aufkleber *m*

'sticking plaster *n* Heftpflaster *nt*

stickler /'stɪklə(r)/ *n* **be a ~ for** es sehr genau nehmen mit

sticky /'stɪkɪ/ *a* (**-ier, -iest**) klebrig; (*adhesive*) Klebe-

stiff /stɪf/ *a* (**-er, -est**), **-ly** *adv* steif; ⟨*brush*⟩ hart; ⟨*dough*⟩ fest; (*difficult*) schwierig; ⟨*penalty*⟩ schwer; **be bored ~** (*fam*) sich zu Tode langweilen. **~en** *vt* steif machen ● *vi* steif werden. **~ness** *n* Steifheit *f*

stifl|e /'staɪfl/ *vt* ersticken; (*fig*) unterdrücken. **~ing** *a* **be ~ing** zum Ersticken sein

stigma /'stɪgmə/ *n* Stigma *nt*

stile /staɪl/ *n* Zauntritt *m*

stiletto /stɪ'letəʊ/ *n* Stilett *nt*; (*heel*) Bleistiftabsatz *m*

still[1] /stɪl/ *n* Destillierapparat *m*

still[2] *a* still; ⟨*drink*⟩ ohne Kohlensäure; **keep ~** stillhalten; **stand ~** stillstehen ● *n* Stille *f* ● *adv* noch; (*emphatic*) immer noch; (*nevertheless*) trotzdem; **~ not** immer noch nicht

'stillborn *a* totgeboren

still 'life *n* Stilleben *nt*

stilted /'stɪltɪd/ *a* gestelzt, geschraubt

stilts /stɪlts/ *npl* Stelzen *pl*

stimulant /'stɪmjʊlənt/ *n* Anregungsmittel *nt*

stimulat|e /'stɪmjʊleɪt/ *vt* anregen. **~ion** /-'leɪʃn/ *n* Anregung *f*

stimulus /'stɪmjʊləs/ *n* (*pl* **-li** /-laɪ/) Reiz *m*

sting /stɪŋ/ *n* Stich *m*; (*from nettle, jellyfish*) Brennen *nt*; (*organ*) Stachel *m* ● *v* (*pt/pp* **stung**) ● *vt* stechen ● *vi* brennen; ⟨*insect:*⟩ stechen. **~ing nettle** *n* Brennessel *f*

stingy /'stɪndʒɪ/ *a* (**-ier, -iest**) geizig, (*fam*) knauserig

stink /stɪŋk/ *n* Gestank *m* ● *vi* (*pt* **stank**, *pp* **stunk**) stinken (**of** nach)

stint /stɪnt/ *n* Pensum *nt* ● *vi* **~ on** sparen an (+ *dat*)

stipulat|e /'stɪpjʊleɪt/ *vt* vorschreiben. **~ion** /-'leɪʃn/ *n* Bedingung *f*

stir /stɜ:(r)/ *n* (*commotion*) Aufregung *f* ● *v* (*pt/pp* **stirred**) *vt* rühren ● *vi* sich rühren

stirrup /'stɪrəp/ *n* Steigbügel *m*

stitch /stɪtʃ/ *n* Stich *m*; (*Knitting*) Masche *f*; (*pain*) Seitenstechen *nt*; **be in ~es** (*fam*) sich kaputtlachen ● *vt* nähen

stoat /stəʊt/ *n* Hermelin *nt*

stock /stɒk/ *n* Vorrat *m* (**of** an + *dat*); (*in shop*) [Waren]bestand *m*; (*livestock*) Vieh *nt*; (*lineage*) Abstammung *f*; (*Finance*) Wertpapiere *pl*; (*Culin*) Brühe *f*; (*plant*) Levkoje *f*; **in/out of ~** vorrätig/nicht vorrätig; **take ~** (*fig*) Bilanz ziehen ● *a* Standard ● *vt* ⟨*shop:*⟩ führen; auffüllen ⟨*shelves*⟩. **~ up** *vi* sich eindecken (**with** mit)

stock: ~broker *n* Börsenmakler *m*. **~ cube** *n* Brühwürfel *m*. **S~ Exchange** *n* Börse *f*

stocking /'stɒkɪŋ/ *n* Strumpf *m*

stockist /'stɒkɪst/ *n* Händler *m*

stock: ~ market *n* Börse *f*. **~pile** *vt* horten; anhäufen ⟨*weapons*⟩. **~-'still** *a* bewegungslos. **~taking** *n* (*Comm*) Inventur *f*

stocky /'stɒkɪ/ *a* (**-ier, -iest**) untersetzt

stodgy /'stɒdʒɪ/ *a* pappig [und schwer verdaulich]

stoical /'stəʊɪkl/ *a*, **-ly** *adv* stoisch

stoke /stəʊk/ *vt* heizen

stole[1] /stəʊl/ *n* Stola *f*

stole[2], **stolen** /'stəʊln/ *see* **steal**

stolid /'stɒlɪd/ *a*, **-ly** *adv* stur

stomach /'stʌmək/ *n* Magen *m* ● *vt* vertragen. **~-ache** *n* Magenschmerzen *pl*

stone /stəʊn/ *n* Stein *m*; (*weight*) 6,35 kg ● *a* steinern; ⟨*wall, Age*⟩ Stein- ● *vt* mit Steinen bewerfen; entsteinen ⟨*fruit*⟩. **~-cold** *a* eiskalt. **~-'deaf** *n* (*fam*) stocktaub

stony /'stəʊnɪ/ *a* steinig

stood /stʊd/ *see* **stand**

stool /stu:l/ *n* Hocker *m*

stoop /stu:p/ *n* **walk with a ~** gebeugt gehen ● *vi* sich bücken; (*fig*) sich erniedrigen

stop /stɒp/ *n* Halt *m*; (*break*) Pause *f*; (*for bus*) Haltestelle *f*; (*for train*) Station *f*; (*Gram*) Punkt *m*; (*on organ*) Register *nt*; **come to a ~** stehenbleiben; **put a ~ to sth** etw unterbinden ● *v* (*pt/pp* **stopped**) ● *vt* anhalten, stoppen; (*switch off*) abstellen; (*plug, block*) zustopfen; (*prevent*) verhindern; **~ s.o. doing sth** jdn daran hindern, etw zu tun; **~ doing sth** aufhören, etw zu tun; **~ that!** hör auf damit! laß das sein! ● *vi* anhalten; (*cease*) aufhören; ⟨*clock:*⟩ stehenbleiben; (*fam: stay*) bleiben (**with** bei) ● *int* halt! stopp!

stop: ~gap *n* Notlösung *f*. **~-over** *n* Zwischenaufenthalt *m*; (*Aviat*) Zwischenlandung *f*

stoppage /'stɒpɪdʒ/ *n* Unterbrechung *f*; (*strike*) Streik *m*; (*deduction*) Abzug *m*

stopper /'stɒpə(r)/ *n* Stöpsel *m*

stop: ~-press *n* letzte Meldungen *pl*. **~-watch** *n* Stoppuhr *f*

storage /'stɔ:rɪdʒ/ *n* Aufbewahrung *f*; (*in warehouse*) Lagerung *f*; (*Computing*) Speicherung *f*

store /stɔ:(r)/ *n* (*stock*) Vorrat *m*; (*shop*) Laden *m*; (*department ~*) Kaufhaus *nt*; (*depot*) Lager *nt*; **in ~** auf Lager; **put in ~** lagern; **set great ~ by** großen Wert legen auf (+ *acc*); **be in ~ for s.o.** (*fig*) jdm bevorstehen ● *vt* aufbewahren; (*in warehouse*) lagern; (*Computing*) speichern. **~-room** *n* Lagerraum *m*

storey /'stɔ:rɪ/ *n* Stockwerk *nt*

stork /stɔ:k/ *n* Storch *m*

storm /stɔ:m/ *n* Sturm *m*; (*with thunder*) Gewitter *nt* ● *vt/i* stürmen. **~y** *a* stürmisch

story /'stɔ:rɪ/ *n* Geschichte *f*; (*in newspaper*) Artikel *m*; (*fam: lie*) Märchen *nt*

stout /staʊt/ *a* (**-er, -est**) beleibt; (*strong*) fest

stove /stəʊv/ *n* Ofen *m*; (*for cooking*) Herd *m*

stow /stəʊ/ *vt* verstauen. **~away** *n* blinder Passagier *m*

straddle /'strædl/ *vt* rittlings sitzen auf (+ *dat*); (*standing*) mit gespreizten Beinen stehen über (+ *dat*)

straggl|e /'strægl/ *vi* hinterherhinken. **~er** *n* Nachzügler *m*. **~y** *a* strähnig

straight /streɪt/ *a* (**-er, -est**) gerade; (*direct*) direkt; (*clear*) klar; ⟨*hair*⟩ glatt; ⟨*drink*⟩ pur; **be ~** (*tidy*) in Ordnung sein ● *adv* gerade; (*directly*) direkt, geradewegs; (*clearly*) klar; **~ away** sofort; **~ on** *or* **ahead** geradeaus; **~ out** (*fig*) geradeheraus; **go ~** (*fam*) ein ehrliches Leben führen; **put sth ~** etw in Ordnung bringen; **sit/stand up ~** geradesitzen/-stehen

straighten /'streɪtn/ *vt* gerademachen; (*put straight*) geraderichten ● *vi* gerade werden; **~ [up]** ⟨*person:*⟩ sich aufrichten. **~ out** *vt* geradebiegen

straight'forward *a* offen; (*simple*) einfach

strain¹ /streɪn/ *n* Rasse *f*; (*Bot*) Sorte *f*; (*of virus*) Art *f*

strain² *n* Belastung *f*; **~s** *pl* (*of music*) Klänge *pl* ● *vt* belasten; (*overexert*) überanstrengen; (*injure*) zerren ⟨*muscle*⟩; (*Culin*) durchseihen; abgießen ⟨*vegetables*⟩ ● *vi* sich anstrengen. **~ed** *a* ⟨*relations*⟩ gespannt. **~er** *n* Sieb *nt*

strait /streɪt/ *n* Meerenge *f*; **in dire ~s** in großen Nöten. **~-jacket** *n* Zwangsjacke *f*. **~-'laced** *a* puritanisch

strand¹ /strænd/ *n* (*of thread*) Faden *m*; (*of beads*) Kette *f*; (*of hair*) Strähne *f*

strand² *vt* **be ~ed** festsitzen

strange /streɪndʒ/ *a* (**-r, -st**) fremd; (*odd*) seltsam, merkwürdig. **~r** *n* Fremde(r) *m/f*

strangely /'streɪndʒlɪ/ *adv* seltsam, merkwürdig; **~ enough** seltsamerweise

strangle /'stræŋgl/ *vt* erwürgen; (*fig*) unterdrücken

strangulation /strængjʊ'leɪʃn/ *n* Erwürgen *nt*

strap /stræp/ *n* Riemen *m*; (*for safety*) Gurt *m*; (*to grasp in vehicle*) Halteriemen *m*; (*of watch*) Armband *nt*; (*shoulder-*) Träger *m* ● *vt* (*pt/pp* **strapped**) schnallen; **~ in** *or* **down** festschnallen

strapping /'stræpɪŋ/ *a* stramm

strata /'strɑ:tə/ *npl see* **stratum**

stratagem /'strætədʒəm/ *n* Kriegslist *f*

strategic /strəˈtiːdʒɪk/ *a*, **-ally** *adv* strategisch
strategy /ˈstrætədʒɪ/ *n* Strategie *f*
stratum /ˈstrɑːtəm/ *n* (*pl* **strata**) Schicht *f*
straw /strɔː/ *n* Stroh *nt*; (*single piece, drinking*) Strohhalm *m*; **that's the last ~** jetzt reicht's aber
strawberry /ˈstrɔːbərɪ/ *n* Erdbeere *f*
stray /streɪ/ *a* streunend ● *n* streunendes Tier *nt* ● *vi* sich verirren; (*deviate*) abweichen
streak /striːk/ *n* Streifen *m*; (*in hair*) Strähne *f*; (*fig: trait*) Zug *m* ● *vi* flitzen. **~y** *a* streifig; ⟨*bacon*⟩ durchwachsen
stream /striːm/ *n* Bach *m*; (*flow*) Strom *m*; (*current*) Strömung *f*; (*Sch*) Parallelzug *m* ● *vi* strömen; **~ in/out** hinaus-/herausströmen
streamer /ˈstriːmə(r)/ *n* Luftschlange *f*; (*flag*) Wimpel *m*
ˈstreamline *vt* (*fig*) rationalisieren. **~d** *a* stromlinienförmig
street /striːt/ *n* Straße *f*. **~car** *n* (*Amer*) Straßenbahn *f*. **~ lamp** *n* Straßenlaterne *f*
strength /streŋθ/ *n* Stärke *f*; (*power*) Kraft *f*; **on the ~ of** auf Grund (+ *gen*). **~en** *vt* stärken; (*reinforce*) verstärken
strenuous /ˈstrenjʊəs/ *a* anstrengend
stress /stres/ *n* (*emphasis*) Betonung *f*; (*strain*) Belastung *f*; (*mental*) Streß *m* ● *vt* betonen; (*put a strain on*) belasten. **~ful** *a* stressig (*fam*)
stretch /stretʃ/ *n* (*of road*) Strecke *f*; (*elasticity*) Elastizität *f*; **at a ~** ohne Unterbrechung; **a long ~** eine lange Zeit; **have a ~** sich strecken ● *vt* strecken; (*widen*) dehnen; (*spread*) ausbreiten; fordern ⟨*person*⟩; **~ one's legs** sich (*dat*) die Beine vertreten ● *vi* sich erstrecken; (*become wider*) sich dehnen; ⟨*person:*⟩ sich strecken. **~er** *n* Tragbahre *f*
strew /struː/ *vt* (*pp* **strewn** *or* **strewed**) streuen
stricken /ˈstrɪkn/ *a* betroffen; **~ with** heimgesucht von
strict /strɪkt/ *a* (**-er, -est**), **-ly** *adv* streng; **~ly speaking** strenggenommen
stride /straɪd/ *n* [großer] Schritt *m*; **make great ~s** (*fig*) große Fortschritte machen; **take sth in one's ~** mit etw gut fertig werden ● *vi* (*pt* **strode**, *pp* **stridden**) [mit großen Schritten] gehen
strident /ˈstraɪdnt/ *a*, **-ly** *adv* schrill; ⟨*colour*⟩ grell
strife /straɪf/ *n* Streit *m*
strike /straɪk/ *n* Streik *m*; (*Mil*) Angriff *m*; **be on ~** streiken ● *v* (*pt/pp* **struck**) ● *vt* schlagen; (*knock against, collide with*) treffen; prägen ⟨*coin*⟩; anzünden ⟨*match*⟩; stoßen auf (+ *acc*) ⟨*oil, gold*⟩; abbrechen ⟨*camp*⟩; (*delete*) streichen; (*impress*) beeindrucken; (*occur to*) einfallen (+ *dat*); (*Mil*) angreifen; **~ s.o. a blow** jdm einen Schlag versetzen ● *vi* treffen; ⟨*lightning:*⟩ einschlagen; ⟨*clock:*⟩ schlagen; (*attack*) zuschlagen; ⟨*workers:*⟩ streiken; **~ lucky** Glück haben. **~-breaker** *n* Streikbrecher *m*
striker /ˈstraɪkə(r)/ *n* Streikende(r) *m/f*
striking /ˈstraɪkɪŋ/ *a* auffallend
string /strɪŋ/ *n* Schnur *f*; (*thin*) Bindfaden *m*; (*of musical instrument, racket*) Saite *f*; (*of bow*) Sehne *f*; (*of pearls*) Kette *f*; **the ~s** (*Mus*) die Streicher *pl*; **pull ~s** (*fam*) seine Beziehungen spielen lassen, Fäden ziehen ● *vt* (*pt/pp* **strung**) (*thread*) aufziehen ⟨*beads*⟩. **~ed** *a* (*Mus*) Saiten-; (*played with bow*) Streich-
stringent /ˈstrɪndʒnt/ *a* streng
strip /strɪp/ *n* Streifen *m* ● *v* (*pt/pp* **stripped**) ● *vt* ablösen; ausziehen ⟨*clothes*⟩; abziehen ⟨*bed*⟩; abbeizen ⟨*wood, furniture*⟩; auseinandernehmen ⟨*machine*⟩; (*deprive*) berauben (**of** *gen*); **~ sth off sth** etw von etw entfernen ● *vi* (*undress*) sich ausziehen. **~ club** *n* Stripteaselokal *nt*
stripe /straɪp/ *n* Streifen *m*. **~d** *a* gestreift
ˈstriplight *n* Neonröhre *f*
stripper /ˈstrɪpə(r)/ *n* Stripperin *f*; (*male*) Stripper *m*
strip-ˈtease *n* Striptease *m*
strive /straɪv/ *vi* (*pt* **strove**, *pp* **striven**) sich bemühen (**to** zu); **~ for** streben nach
strode /strəʊd/ *see* **stride**
stroke[1] /strəʊk/ *n* Schlag *m*; (*of pen*) Strich *m*; (*Swimming*) Zug *m*; (*style*) Stil *m*; (*Med*) Schlaganfall *m*; **~ of luck** Glücksfall *m*; **put s.o. off his ~** jdn aus dem Konzept bringen
stroke[2] ● *vt* streicheln
stroll /strəʊl/ *n* Spaziergang *m*, (*fam*) Bummel *m* ● *vi* spazieren, (*fam*) bummeln. **~er** *n* (*Amer: push-chair*) [Kinder]sportwagen *m*

strong /strɒŋ/ *a* (**-er** /-gə(r)/, **-est** /-gɪst/), **-ly** *adv* stark; (*powerful, healthy*) kräftig; (*severe*) streng; (*sturdy*) stabil; (*convincing*) gut

strong: ~-box *n* Geldkassette *f*. **~hold** *n* Festung *f*; (*fig*) Hochburg *f*. **~-'minded** *a* willensstark. **~-room** *n* Tresorraum *m*

stroppy /'strɒpɪ/ *a* widerspenstig

strove /strəʊv/ *see* **strive**

struck /strʌk/ *see* **strike**

structural /'strʌktʃərl/ *a*, **-ly** *adv* baulich

structure /'strʌktʃə(r)/ *n* Struktur *f*; (*building*) Bau *m*

struggle /'strʌgl/ *n* Kampf *m*; **with a ~** mit Mühe ● *vi* kämpfen; **~ for breath** nach Atem ringen; **~ to do sth** sich abmühen, etw zu tun; **~ to one's feet** mühsam aufstehen

strum /strʌm/ *v* (*pt/pp* **strummed**) ● *vt* klimpern auf (+ *dat*) ● *vi* klimpern

strung /strʌŋ/ *see* **string**

strut¹ /strʌt/ *n* Strebe *f*

strut² *vi* (*pt/pp* **strutted**) stolzieren

stub /stʌb/ *n* Stummel *m*; (*counterfoil*) Abschnitt *m* ● *vt* (*pt/pp* **stubbed**) **~ one's toe** sich (*dat*) den Zeh stoßen (**on** an + *dat*). **~ out** *vt* ausdrücken ⟨*cigarette*⟩

stubb|le /'stʌbl/ *n* Stoppeln *pl*. **~ly** *a* stoppelig

stubborn /'stʌbən/ *a*, **-ly** *adv* starrsinnig; ⟨*refusal*⟩ hartnäckig

stubby /'stʌbɪ/ *a* (**-ier, -iest**) kurz und dick

stucco /'stʌkəʊ/ *n* Stuck *m*

stuck /stʌk/ *see* **stick²**. **~-'up** *a* (*fam*) hochnäsig

stud¹ /stʌd/ *n* Nagel *m*; (*on clothes*) Niete *f*; (*for collar*) Kragenknopf *m*; (*for ear*) Ohrstecker *m*

stud² *n* (*of horses*) Gestüt *nt*

student /'stju:dnt/ *n* Student(in) *m(f)*; (*Sch*) Schüler(in) *m(f)*. **~ nurse** *n* Lernschwester *f*

studied /'stʌdɪd/ *a* gewollt

studio /'stju:dɪəʊ/ *n* Studio *nt*; (*for artist*) Atelier *nt*

studious /'stju:dɪəs/ *a* lerneifrig; (*earnest*) ernsthaft

stud|y /'stʌdɪ/ *n* Studie *f*; (*room*) Studierzimmer *nt*; (*investigation*) Untersuchung *f*; **~ies** *pl* Studium *nt* ● *v* (*pt/pp* **studied**) ● *vt* studieren; (*examine*) untersuchen ● *vi* lernen; (*at university*) studieren

stuff /stʌf/ *n* Stoff *m*; (*fam: things*) Zeug *nt* ● *vt* vollstopfen; (*with padding, Culin*) füllen; ausstopfen ⟨*animal*⟩; **~ sth into sth** etw in etw (*acc*) [hinein]stopfen. **~ing** *n* Füllung *f*

stuffy /'stʌfɪ/ *a* (**-ier, -iest**) stickig; (*old-fashioned*) spießig

stumbl|e /'stʌmbl/ *vi* stolpern; **~e across** zufällig stoßen auf (+ *acc*). **~ing-block** *n* Hindernis *nt*

stump /stʌmp/ *n* Stumpf *m* ● **~ up** *vt/i* (*fam*) blechen. **~ed** *a* (*fam*) überfragt

stun /stʌn/ *vt* (*pt/pp* **stunned**) betäuben; **~ned by** (*fig*) wie betäubt von

stung /stʌŋ/ *see* **sting**

stunk /stʌŋk/ *see* **stink**

stunning /'stʌnɪŋ/ *a* (*fam*) toll

stunt¹ /stʌnt/ *n* (*fam*) Kunststück *nt*

stunt² *vt* hemmen. **~ed** *a* verkümmert

stupendous /stju:'pendəs/ *a*, **-ly** *adv* enorm

stupid /'stju:pɪd/ *a* dumm. **~ity** /-'pɪdətɪ/ *n* Dummheit *f*. **~ly** *adv* dumm; **~ly [enough]** dummerweise

stupor /'stju:pə(r)/ *n* Benommenheit *f*

sturdy /'stɜ:dɪ/ *a* (**-ier, -iest**) stämmig; ⟨*furniture*⟩ stabil; ⟨*shoes*⟩ fest

stutter /'stʌtə(r)/ *n* Stottern *nt* ● *vt/i* stottern

sty¹ /staɪ/ *n* (*pl* **sties**) Schweinestall *m*

sty², **stye** *n* (*pl* **styes**) (*Med*) Gerstenkorn *nt*

style /staɪl/ *n* Stil *m*; (*fashion*) Mode *f*; (*sort*) Art *f*; (*hair~*) Frisur *f*; **in ~** in großem Stil

stylish /'staɪlɪʃ/ *a*, **-ly** *adv* stilvoll

stylist /'staɪlɪst/ *n* Friseur *m*/Friseuse *f*. **~ic** /-'lɪstɪk/ *a*, **-ally** *adv* stilistisch

stylized /'staɪlaɪzd/ *a* stilisiert

stylus /'staɪləs/ *n* (*on record-player*) Nadel *f*

suave /swɑ:v/ *a* (*pej*) gewandt

sub'conscious /sʌb-/ *a*, **-ly** *adv* unterbewußt ● *n* Unterbewußtsein *nt*

subcon'tract *vt* [vertraglich] weitervergeben (**to** an + *acc*)

'subdivi|de *vt* unterteilen. **~sion** *n* Unterteilung *f*

subdue /səb'dju:/ *vt* unterwerfen; (*make quieter*) beruhigen. **~d** *a* gedämpft; ⟨*person*⟩ still

subject¹ /'sʌbdʒɪkt/ *a* **be ~ to sth** etw (*dat*) unterworfen sein ● *n* Staatsbürger(in) *m(f)*; (*of ruler*) Untertan *m*; (*theme*) Thema *nt*; (*of investigation*) Gegenstand *m*; (*Sch*) Fach *nt*; (*Gram*) Subjekt *nt*

subject[2] /səb'dʒekt/ *vt* unterwerfen (**to** *dat*); (*expose*) aussetzen (**to** *dat*)

subjective /səb'dʒektɪv/ *a*, **-ly** *adv* subjektiv

subjugate /'sʌbdʒʊgeɪt/ *vt* unterjochen

subjunctive /səb'dʒʌŋktɪv/ *n* Konjunktiv *m*

sub'let *vt* (*pt*/*pp* **-let**) untervermieten

sublime /sə'blaɪm/ *a*, **-ly** *adv* erhaben

subliminal /sʌ'blɪmɪnl/ *a* unterschwellig

sub-ma'chine-gun *n* Maschinenpistole *f*

subma'rine *n* Unterseeboot *nt*

submerge /səb'mɜ:dʒ/ *vt* untertauchen; **be ~d** unter Wasser stehen ● *vi* tauchen

submiss|ion /səb'mɪʃn/ *n* Unterwerfung *f*. **~ive** /-sɪv/ *a* gehorsam; (*pej*) unterwürfig

submit /səb'mɪt/ *v* (*pt*/*pp* **-mitted**, *pres p* **-mitting**) ● *vt* vorlegen (**to** *dat*); (*hand in*) einreichen ● *vi* sich unterwerfen (**to** *dat*)

subordinate[1] /sə'bɔ:dɪnət/ *a* untergeordnet ● *n* Untergebene(r) *m*/*f*

subordinate[2] /sə'bɔ:dɪneɪt/ *vt* unterordnen (**to** *dat*)

subscribe /səb'skraɪb/ *vi* spenden; **~ to** (*fig*) sich anschließen (+ *dat*); abonnieren ⟨*newspaper*⟩. **~r** *n* Spender *m*; Abonnent *m*

subscription /səb'skrɪpʃn/ *n* (*to club*) [Mitglieds]beitrag *m*; (*to newspaper*) Abonnement *nt*; **by ~** mit Spenden

subsequent /'sʌbsɪkwənt/ *a*, **-ly** *adv* folgend; (*later*) später

subservient /səb'sɜ:vɪənt/ *a*, **-ly** *adv* untergeordnet; (*servile*) unterwürfig

subside /səb'saɪd/ *vi* sinken; ⟨*ground:*⟩ sich senken; ⟨*storm:*⟩ nachlassen

subsidiary /səb'sɪdɪərɪ/ *a* untergeordnet ● *n* Tochtergesellschaft *f*

subsid|ize /'sʌbsɪdaɪz/ *vt* subventionieren. **~y** *n* Subvention *f*

subsist /səb'sɪst/ *vi* leben (**on** von). **~ence** *n* Existenz *f*

substance /'sʌbstəns/ *n* Substanz *f*

sub'standard *a* unzulänglich; ⟨*goods*⟩ minderwertig

substantial /səb'stænʃl/ *a* solide; ⟨*meal*⟩ reichhaltig; (*considerable*) beträchtlich. **~ly** *adv* solide; (*essentially*) im wesentlichen

substantiate /səb'stænʃɪeɪt/ *vt* erhärten

substitut|e /'sʌbstɪtju:t/ *n* Ersatz *m*; (*Sport*) Ersatzspieler(in) *m*(*f*) ● *vt* **~e A for B** B durch A ersetzen ● *vi* **~e for s.o.** jdn vertreten. **~ion** /-'tju:ʃn/ *n* Ersetzung *f*

subterfuge /'sʌbtəfju:dʒ/ *n* List *f*

subterranean /sʌbtə'reɪnɪən/ *a* unterirdisch

'subtitle *n* Untertitel *m*

subtle /'sʌtl/ *a* (**-r**, **-st**), **-tly** *adv* fein; (*fig*) subtil

subtract /səb'trækt/ *vt* abziehen, subtrahieren. **~ion** /-ækʃn/ *n* Subtraktion *f*

suburb /'sʌbɜ:b/ *n* Vorort *m*; **in the ~s** am Stadtrand. **~an** /sə'bɜ:bən/ *a* Vorort-; (*pej*) spießig. **~ia** /sə'bɜ:bɪə/ *n* die Vororte *pl*

subversive /səb'vɜ:sɪv/ *a* subversiv

'subway *n* Unterführung *f*; (*Amer: railway*) U-Bahn *f*

succeed /sək'si:d/ *vi* Erfolg haben; ⟨*plan:*⟩ gelingen; (*follow*) nachfolgen (+*dat*); **I ~ed** es ist mir gelungen; **he ~ed in escaping** es gelang ihm zu entkommen ● *vt* folgen (+*dat*). **~ing** *a* folgend

success /sək'ses/ *n* Erfolg *m*. **~ful** *a*, **-ly** *adv* erfolgreich

succession /sək'seʃn/ *n* Folge *f*; (*series*) Serie *f*; (*to title, office*) Nachfolge *f*; (*to throne*) Thronfolge *f*; **in ~** hintereinander

successive /sək'sesɪv/ *a* aufeinanderfolgend. **~ly** *adv* hintereinander

successor /sək'sesə(r)/ *n* Nachfolger(in) *m*(*f*)

succinct /sək'sɪŋkt/ *a*, **-ly** *adv* prägnant

succulent /'sʌkjʊlənt/ *a* saftig

succumb /sə'kʌm/ *vi* erliegen (**to** *dat*)

such /sʌtʃ/ *a* solche(r,s); **~ a book** ein solches *od* solch ein Buch; **~ a thing** so etwas; **~ a long time** so lange; **there is no ~ thing** das gibt es gar nicht; **there is no ~ person** eine solche Person gibt es nicht ● *pron* **as ~** als solche(r,s); (*strictly speaking*) an sich; **~ as** wie [zum Beispiel]; **and ~** und dergleichen. **~like** *pron* (*fam*) dergleichen

suck /sʌk/ *vt*/*i* saugen; lutschen ⟨*sweet*⟩. **~ up** *vt* aufsaugen ● *vi* **~ up to s.o.** (*fam*) sich bei jdm einschmeicheln

sucker /'sʌkə(r)/ *n* (*Bot*) Ausläufer *m*; (*fam: person*) Dumme(r) *m*/*f*
suckle /'sʌkl/ *vt* säugen
suction /'sʌkʃn/ *n* Saugwirkung *f*
sudden /'sʌdn/ *a*, **-ly** *adv* plötzlich; (*abrupt*) jäh ● *n* **all of a ~** auf einmal
sue /su:/ *vt* (*pres p* **suing**) verklagen (**for** auf + *acc*) ● *vi* klagen
suede /sweɪd/ *n* Wildleder *nt*
suet /'su:ɪt/ *n* [Nieren]talg *m*
suffer /'sʌfə(r)/ *vi* leiden (**from** an + *dat*) ● *vt* erleiden; (*tolerate*) dulden. **~ance** /-əns/ *n* **on ~ance** bloß geduldet. **~ing** *n* Leiden *nt*
suffice /sə'faɪs/ *vi* genügen
sufficient /sə'fɪʃnt/ *a*, **-ly** *adv* genug, genügend; **be ~** genügen
suffix /'sʌfɪks/ *n* Nachsilbe *f*
suffocat|e /'sʌfəkeɪt/ *vt*/*i* ersticken. **~ion** /-'keɪʃn/ *n* Ersticken *nt*
sugar /'ʃʊgə(r)/ *n* Zucker *m* ● *vt* zuckern; (*fig*) versüßen. **~ basin, ~-bowl** *n* Zuckerschale *f*. **~y** *a* süß; (*fig*) süßlich
suggest /sə'dʒest/ *vt* vorschlagen; (*indicate, insinuate*) andeuten. **~ion** /-estʃn/ *n* Vorschlag *m*; Andeutung *f*; (*trace*) Spur *f*. **~ive** /-ɪv/ *a*, **-ly** *adv* anzüglich; **be ~ive of** schließen lassen auf (+ *acc*)
suicidal /su:ɪ'saɪdl/ *a* selbstmörderisch
suicide /'su:ɪsaɪd/ *n* Selbstmord *m*
suit /su:t/ *n* Anzug *m*; (*woman's*) Kostüm *nt*; (*Cards*) Farbe *f*; (*Jur*) Prozeß *m*; **follow ~** (*fig*) das Gleiche tun ● *vt* (*adapt*) anpassen (**to** *dat*); (*be convenient for*) passen (+ *dat*); (*go with*) passen zu; ⟨*clothing:*⟩ stehen (**s.o.** jdm); **be ~ed for** geeignet sein für; **~ yourself!** wie du willst!
suit|able /'su:təbl/ *a* geeignet; (*convenient*) passend; (*appropriate*) angemessen; (*for weather, activity*) zweckmäßig. **~ably** *adv* angemessen; zweckmäßig
'suitcase *n* Koffer *m*
suite /swi:t/ *n* Suite *f*; (*of furniture*) Garnitur *f*
sulk /sʌlk/ *vi* schmollen. **~y** *a* schmollend
sullen /'sʌlən/ *a*, **-ly** *adv* mürrisch
sulphur /'sʌlfə(r)/ *n* Schwefel *f*. **~ic** /-'fjʊərɪk/ *a* **~ic acid** Schwefelsäure *f*
sultana /sʌl'tɑ:nə/ *n* Sultanine *f*
sultry /'sʌltrɪ/ *a* (**-ier, -iest**) ⟨*weather*⟩ schwül
sum /sʌm/ *n* Summe *f*; (*Sch*) Rechenaufgabe *f* ● *vt*/*i* (*pt*/*pp* **summed**) **~ up** zusammenfassen; (*assess*) einschätzen
summar|ize /'sʌməraɪz/ *vt* zusammenfassen. **~y** *n* Zusammenfassung *f* ● *a*, **-ily** *adv* summarisch; ⟨*dismissal*⟩ fristlos
summer /'sʌmə(r)/ *n* Sommer *m*. **~-house** *n* [Garten]laube *f*. **~time** *n* Sommer *m*
summery /'sʌmərɪ/ *a* sommerlich
summit /'sʌmɪt/ *n* Gipfel *m*. **~ conference** *n* Gipfelkonferenz *f*
summon /'sʌmən/ *vt* rufen; holen ⟨*help*⟩; (*Jur*) vorladen. **~ up** *vt* aufbringen
summons /'sʌmənz/ *n* (*Jur*) Vorladung *f* ● *vt* vorladen
sump /sʌmp/ *n* (*Auto*) Ölwanne *f*
sumptuous /'sʌmptjʊəs/ *a*, **-ly** *adv* prunkvoll; ⟨*meal*⟩ üppig
sun /sʌn/ *n* Sonne *f* ● *vt* (*pt*/*pp* **sunned**) **~ oneself** sich sonnen
sun: ~bathe *vi* sich sonnen. **~-bed** *n* Sonnenbank *f*. **~burn** *n* Sonnenbrand *m*
sundae /'sʌndeɪ/ *n* Eisbecher *m*
Sunday /'sʌndeɪ/ *n* Sonntag *m*
'sundial *n* Sonnenuhr *f*
sundry /'sʌndrɪ/ *a* verschiedene *pl*; **all and ~** alle *pl*
'sunflower *n* Sonnenblume *f*
sung /sʌŋ/ *see* **sing**
'sun-glasses *npl* Sonnenbrille *f*
sunk /sʌŋk/ *see* **sink**
sunken /'sʌŋkn/ *a* gesunken; ⟨*eyes*⟩ eingefallen
sunny /'sʌnɪ/ *a* (**-ier, -iest**) sonnig
sun: ~rise *n* Sonnenaufgang *m*. **~-roof** *n* (*Auto*) Schiebedach *nt*. **~set** *n* Sonnenuntergang *m*. **~shade** *n* Sonnenschirm *m*. **~shine** *n* Sonnenschein *m*. **~stroke** *n* Sonnenstich *m*. **~-tan** *n* [Sonnen]bräune *f*. **~-tanned** *a* braun[gebrannt]. **~-tan oil** *n* Sonnenöl *nt*
super /'su:pə(r)/ *a* (*fam*) prima, toll
superb /sʊ'pɜ:b/ *a* erstklassig
supercilious /su:pə'sɪlɪəs/ *a* überlegen
superficial /su:pə'fɪʃl/ *a*, **-ly** *adv* oberflächlich
superfluous /sʊ'pɜ:flʊəs/ *a* überflüssig
super'human *a* übermenschlich
superintendent /su:pərɪn'tendənt/ *n* (*of police*) Kommissar *m*
superior /su:'pɪərɪə(r)/ *a* überlegen; (*in rank*) höher ● *n* Vorgesetzte(r) *m*/*f*. **~ity** /-'ɒrətɪ/ *n* Überlegenheit *f*

superlative /su:'pɜ:lətɪv/ *a* unübertrefflich ● *n* Superlativ *m*
'superman *n* Übermensch *m*
'supermarket *n* Supermarkt *m*
super'natural *a* übernatürlich
'superpower *n* Supermacht *f*
supersede /su:pə'si:d/ *vt* ersetzen
super'sonic *a* Überschall-
superstiti|on /su:pə'stɪʃn/ *n* Aberglaube *m*. **~ous** /-'stɪʃəs/ *a*, **-ly** *adv* abergläubisch
supervis|e /'su:pəvaɪz/ *vt* beaufsichtigen; überwachen ⟨*work*⟩. **~ion** /-'vɪʒn/ *n* Aufsicht *f*; Überwachung *f*. **~or** *n* Aufseher(in) *m(f)*
supper /'sʌpə(r)/ *n* Abendessen *nt*
supple /'sʌpl/ *a* geschmeidig
supplement /'sʌplɪmənt/ *n* Ergänzung *f*; (*addition*) Zusatz *m*; (*to fare*) Zuschlag *m*; (*book*) Ergänzungsband *m*; (*to newspaper*) Beilage *f* ● *vt* ergänzen. **~ary** /-'mentərɪ/ *a* zusätzlich
supplier /sə'plaɪə(r)/ *n* Lieferant *m*
supply /sə'plaɪ/ *n* Vorrat *m*; **supplies** *pl* (*Mil*) Nachschub *m* ● *vt* (*pt/pp* **-ied**) liefern; **~ s.o. with sth** jdn mit etw versorgen
support /sə'pɔ:t/ *n* Stütze *f*; (*fig*) Unterstützung *f* ● *vt* stützen; (*bear weight of*) tragen; (*keep*) ernähren; (*give money to*) unterstützen; (*speak in favour of*) befürworten; (*Sport*) Fan sein von. **~er** *n* Anhänger(in) *m(f)*; (*Sport*) Fan *m*. **~ive** /-ɪv/ *a* **be ~ive [to s.o.]** [jdm] eine große Stütze sein
suppose /sə'pəʊz/ *vt* annehmen; (*presume*) vermuten; (*imagine*) sich (*dat*) vorstellen; **be ~d to do sth** etw tun sollen; **not be ~d to** (*fam*) nicht dürfen; **I ~ so** vermutlich. **~dly** /-ɪdlɪ/ *adv* angeblich
supposition /sʌpə'zɪʃn/ *n* Vermutung *f*
suppository /sʌ'pɒzɪtrɪ/ *n* Zäpfchen *nt*
suppress /sə'pres/ *vt* unterdrücken. **~ion** /-eʃn/ *n* Unterdrückung *f*
supremacy /su:'preməsɪ/ *n* Vorherrschaft *f*
supreme /su:'pri:m/ *a* höchste(r,s); ⟨*court*⟩ oberste(r,s)
surcharge /'sɜ:tʃɑ:dʒ/ *n* Zuschlag *m*
sure /ʃʊə(r)/ *a* (**-r, -st**) sicher; **make ~** sich vergewissern (**of** *gen*); (*check*) nachprüfen; **be ~ to do it** sieh zu, daß du es tust ● *adv* (*Amer, fam*) klar; **~ enough** tatsächlich. **~ly** *adv* sicher; (*for emphasis*) doch; (*Amer: gladly*) gern
surety /'ʃʊərətɪ/ *n* Bürgschaft *f*; **stand ~ for** bürgen für
surf /sɜ:f/ *n* Brandung *f*
surface /'sɜ:fɪs/ *n* Oberfläche *f* ● *vi* (*emerge*) auftauchen. **~ mail** *n* **by ~ mail** auf dem Land-/Seeweg
'surfboard *n* Surfbrett *nt*
surfeit /'sɜ:fɪt/ *n* Übermaß *nt*
surfing /'sɜ:fɪŋ/ *n* Surfen *nt*
surge /sɜ:dʒ/ *n* (*of sea*) Branden *nt*; (*fig*) Welle *f* ● *vi* branden; **~ forward** nach vorn drängen
surgeon /'sɜ:dʒən/ *n* Chirurg(in) *m(f)*
surgery /'sɜ:dʒərɪ/ *n* Chirurgie *f*; (*place*) Praxis *f*; (*room*) Sprechzimmer *nt*; (*hours*) Sprechstunde *f*; **have ~** operiert werden
surgical /'sɜ:dʒɪkl/ *a*, **-ly** *adv* chirurgisch
surly /'sɜ:lɪ/ *a* (**-ier, -iest**) mürrisch
surmise /sə'maɪz/ *vt* mutmaßen
surmount /sə'maʊnt/ *vt* überwinden
surname /'sɜ:neɪm/ *n* Nachname *m*
surpass /sə'pɑ:s/ *vt* übertreffen
surplus /'sɜ:pləs/ *a* überschüssig; **be ~ to requirements** nicht benötigt werden ● *n* Überschuß *m* (**of** an + *dat*)
surpris|e /sə'praɪz/ *n* Überraschung *f* ● *vt* überraschen; **be ~ed** sich wundern (**at** über + *acc*). **~ing** *a*, **-ly** *adv* überraschend
surrender /sə'rendə(r)/ *n* Kapitulation *f* ● *vi* sich ergeben; (*Mil*) kapitulieren ● *vt* aufgeben
surreptitious /sʌrəp'tɪʃəs/ *a*, **-ly** *adv* heimlich, verstohlen
surrogate /'sʌrəgət/ *n* Ersatz *m*. **~ 'mother** *n* Leihmutter *f*
surround /sə'raʊnd/ *vt* umgeben; (*encircle*) umzingeln; **~ed by** umgeben von. **~ing** *a* umliegend. **~ings** *npl* Umgebung *f*
surveillance /sə'veɪləns/ *n* Überwachung *f*; **be under ~** überwacht werden
survey[1] /'sɜ:veɪ/ *n* Überblick *m*; (*poll*) Umfrage *f*; (*investigation*) Untersuchung *f*; (*of land*) Vermessung *f*; (*of house*) Gutachten *nt*
survey[2] /sə'veɪ/ *vt* betrachten; vermessen ⟨*land*⟩; begutachten ⟨*building*⟩. **~or** *n* Landvermesser *m*; Gutachter *m*
survival /sə'vaɪvl/ *n* Überleben *nt*; (*of tradition*) Fortbestand *m*

surviv|e /sə'vaɪv/ *vt* überleben ● *vi* überleben; ⟨*tradition:*⟩ erhalten bleiben. **~or** *n* Überlebende(r) *m/f*; **be a ~or** (*fam*) nicht unterzukriegen sein

susceptible /sə'septəbl/ *a* empfänglich/(*Med*) anfällig (**to** für)

suspect¹ /sə'spekt/ *vt* verdächtigen; (*assume*) vermuten; **he ~s nothing** er ahnt nichts

suspect² /'sʌspekt/ *a* verdächtig ● *n* Verdächtige(r) *m/f*

suspend /sə'spend/ *vt* aufhängen; (*stop*) [vorläufig] einstellen; (*from duty*) vorläufig beurlauben. **~er belt** *n* Strumpfbandgürtel *m*. **~ers** *npl* Strumpfbänder *pl*; (*Amer: braces*) Hosenträger *pl*

suspense /sə'spens/ *n* Spannung *f*

suspension /sə'spenʃn/ *n* (*Auto*) Federung *f*. **~ bridge** *n* Hängebrücke *f*

suspici|on /sə'spɪʃn/ *n* Verdacht *m*; (*mistrust*) Mißtrauen *nt*; (*trace*) Spur *f*. **~ous** /-ɪʃəs/ *a*, **-ly** *adv* mißtrauisch; (*arousing suspicion*) verdächtig

sustain /sə'steɪn/ *vt* tragen; (*fig*) aufrechterhalten; erhalten ⟨*life*⟩; erleiden ⟨*injury*⟩

sustenance /'sʌstɪnəns/ *n* Nahrung *f*

swab /swɒb/ *n* (*Med*) Tupfer *m*; (*specimen*) Abstrich *m*

swagger /'swægə(r)/ *vi* stolzieren

swallow¹ /'swɒləʊ/ *vt/i* schlucken. **~ up** *vt* verschlucken; verschlingen ⟨*resources*⟩

swallow² *n* (*bird*) Schwalbe *f*

swam /swæm/ *see* **swim**

swamp /swɒmp/ *n* Sumpf *m* ● *vt* überschwemmen. **~y** *a* sumpfig

swan /swɒn/ *n* Schwan *m*

swank /swæŋk/ *vi* (*fam*) angeben

swap /swɒp/ *n* (*fam*) Tausch *m* ● *vt/i* (*pt/pp* **swapped**) (*fam*) tauschen (**for** gegen)

swarm /swɔ:m/ *n* Schwarm *m* ● *vi* schwärmen; **be ~ing with** wimmeln von

swarthy /'swɔ:ðɪ/ *a* (**-ier, -iest**) dunkel

swastika /'swɒstɪkə/ *n* Hakenkreuz *nt*

swat /swɒt/ *vt* (*pt/pp* **swatted**) totschlagen

sway /sweɪ/ *n* (*fig*) Herrschaft *f* ● *vi* schwanken; (*gently*) sich wiegen ● *vt* wiegen; (*influence*) beeinflussen

swear /sweə(r)/ *v* (*pt* **swore**, *pp* **sworn**) ● *vt* schwören ● *vi* schwören (**by** auf + *acc*); (*curse*) fluchen. **~-word** *n* Kraftausdruck *m*

sweat /swet/ *n* Schweiß *m* ● *vi* schwitzen

sweater /'swetə(r)/ *n* Pullover *m*

sweaty /'swetɪ/ *a* verschwitzt

swede /swi:d/ *n* Kohlrübe *f*

Swed|e *n* Schwede *m*/-din *f*. **~en** *n* Schweden *nt*. **~ish** *a* schwedisch

sweep /swi:p/ *n* Schornsteinfeger *m*; (*curve*) Bogen *m*; (*movement*) ausholende Bewegung *f*; **make a clean ~** (*fig*) gründlich aufräumen ● *v* (*pt/pp* **swept**) ● *vt* fegen, kehren ● *vi* (*go swiftly*) rauschen; ⟨*wind:*⟩ fegen. **~ up** *vt* zusammenfegen/-kehren

sweeping /'swi:pɪŋ/ *a* ausholend; ⟨*statement*⟩ pauschal; ⟨*changes*⟩ weitreichend

sweet /swi:t/ *a* (**-er, -est**) süß; **have a ~ tooth** gern Süßes mögen ● *n* Bonbon *m & nt*; (*dessert*) Nachtisch *m*. **~ corn** *n* [Zucker]mais *m*

sweeten /'swi:tn/ *vt* süßen. **~er** *n* Süßstoff *m*; (*fam: bribe*) Schmiergeld *nt*

sweet: ~heart *n* Schatz *m*. **~-shop** *n* Süßwarenladen *m*. **~ness** *n* Süße *f*. **~ 'pea** *n* Wicke *f*

swell /swel/ *n* Dünung *f* ● *v* (*pt* **swelled**, *pp* **swollen** *or* **swelled**) ● *vi* [an]schwellen; ⟨*sails:*⟩ sich blähen; ⟨*wood:*⟩ aufquellen ● *vt* anschwellen lassen; (*increase*) vergrößern. **~ing** *n* Schwellung *f*

swelter /'sweltə(r)/ *vi* schwitzen

swept /swept/ *see* **sweep**

swerve /swɜ:v/ *vi* einen Bogen machen

swift /swɪft/ *a* (**-er, -est**), **-ly** *adv* schnell

swig /swɪg/ *n* (*fam*) Schluck *m*, Zug *m* ● *vt* (*pt/pp* **swigged**) (*fam*) [herunter]kippen

swill /swɪl/ *n* (*for pigs*) Schweinefutter *nt* ● *vt* **~ [out]** [aus]spülen

swim /swɪm/ *n* **have a ~** schwimmen ● *vi* (*pt* **swam**, *pp* **swum**) schwimmen; **my head is ~ming** mir dreht sich der Kopf. **~mer** *n* Schwimmer(in) *m(f)*

swimming /'swɪmɪŋ/ *n* Schwimmen *nt*. **~-baths** *npl* Schwimmbad *nt*. **~-pool** *n* Schwimmbecken *nt*; (*private*) Swimmingpool *m*

'swim-suit *n* Badeanzug *m*

swindle /'swɪndl/ *n* Schwindel *m*, Betrug *m* ● *vt* betrügen. **~r** *n* Schwindler *m*

swine /swaɪn/ *n* Schwein *nt*
swing /swɪŋ/ *n* Schwung *m*; (*shift*) Schwenk *m*; (*seat*) Schaukel *f*; **in full ~** in vollem Gange ● *v* (*pt/pp* **swung**) ● *vi* schwingen; (*on swing*) schaukeln; (*sway*) schwanken; (*dangle*) baumeln; (*turn*) schwenken ● *vt* schwingen; (*influence*) beeinflussen. **~-'door** *n* Schwingtür *f*
swingeing /'swɪndʒɪŋ/ *a* hart; (*fig*) drastisch
swipe /swaɪp/ *n* (*fam*) Schlag *m* ● *vt* (*fam*) knallen; (*steal*) klauen
swirl /swɜ:l/ *n* Wirbel *m* ● *vt/i* wirbeln
swish /swɪʃ/ *a* (*fam*) schick ● *vi* zischen
Swiss /swɪs/ *a* Schweizer, schweizerisch ● *n* Schweizer(in) *m*(*f*); **the ~** *pl* die Schweizer. **~ 'roll** *n* Biskuitrolle *f*
switch /swɪtʃ/ *n* Schalter *m*; (*change*) Wechsel *m*; (*Amer, Rail*) Weiche *f* ● *vt* wechseln; (*exchange*) tauschen ● *vi* wechseln; **~ to** umstellen auf (+ *acc*). **~ off** *vt* ausschalten; abschalten ⟨*engine*⟩. **~ on** *vt* einschalten, anschalten
switch: ~back *n* Achterbahn *f*. **~board** *n* [Telefon]zentrale *f*
Switzerland /'swɪtsələnd/ *n* die Schweiz
swivel /'swɪvl/ *v* (*pt/pp* **swivelled**) ● *vt* drehen ● *vi* sich drehen
swollen /'swəʊlən/ *see* **swell** ● *a* geschwollen. **~-'headed** *a* eingebildet
swoop /swu:p/ *n* Sturzflug *m*; (*by police*) Razzia *f* ● *vi* **~ down** herabstoßen
sword /sɔ:d/ *n* Schwert *nt*
swore /swɔ:(r)/ *see* **swear**
sworn /swɔ:n/ *see* **swear**
swot /swɒt/ *n* (*fam*) Streber *m* ● *vt/i* (*pt/pp* **swotted**) (*fam*) büffeln
swum /swʌm/ *see* **swim**
swung /swʌŋ/ *see* **swing**
syllable /'sɪləbl/ *n* Silbe *f*
syllabus /'sɪləbəs/ *n* Lehrplan *m*; (*for exam*) Studienplan *m*
symbol /'sɪmbəl/ *n* Symbol *nt* (**of** für). **~ic** /-'bɒlɪk/ *a*, **-ally** *adv* symbolisch. **~ism** /-ɪzm/ *n* Symbolik *f*. **~ize** *vt* symbolisieren
symmetr|ical /sɪ'metrɪkl/ *a*, **-ly** *adv* symmetrisch. **~y** /'sɪmətrɪ/ *n* Symmetrie *f*
sympathetic /sɪmpə'θetɪk/ *a*, **-ally** *adv* mitfühlend; (*likeable*) sympathisch
sympathize /'sɪmpəθaɪz/ *vi* mitfühlen. **~r** *n* (*Pol*) Sympathisant *m*
sympathy /'sɪmpəθɪ/ *n* Mitgefühl *nt*; (*condolences*) Beileid *nt*
symphony /'sɪmfənɪ/ *n* Sinfonie *f*
symptom /'sɪmptəm/ *n* Symptom *nt*. **~atic** /-'mætɪk/ *a* symptomatisch (**of** für)
synagogue /'sɪnəgɒg/ *n* Synagoge *f*
synchronize /'sɪŋkrənaɪz/ *vt* synchronisieren
syndicate /'sɪndɪkət/ *n* Syndikat *nt*
syndrome /'sɪndrəʊm/ *n* Syndrom *nt*
synonym /'sɪnənɪm/ *n* Synonym *nt*. **~ous** /-'nɒnɪməs/ *a*, **-ly** *adv* synonym
synopsis /sɪ'nɒpsɪs/ *n* (*pl* **-opses** /-si:z/) Zusammenfassung *f*; (*of opera, ballet*) Inhaltsangabe *f*
syntax /'sɪntæks/ *n* Syntax *f*
synthesis /'sɪnθəsɪs/ *n* (*pl* **-ses** /-si:z/) Synthese *f*
synthetic /sɪn'θetɪk/ *a* synthetisch ● *n* Kunststoff *m*
Syria /'sɪrɪə/ *n* Syrien *nt*
syringe /sɪ'rɪndʒ/ *n* Spritze *f* ● *vt* spritzen; ausspritzen ⟨*ears*⟩
syrup /'sɪrəp/ *n* Sirup *m*
system /'sɪstəm/ *n* System *nt*. **~atic** /-'mætɪk/ *a*, **-ally** *adv* systematisch

T

tab /tæb/ *n* (*projecting*) Zunge *f*; (*with name*) Namensschild *nt*; (*loop*) Aufhänger *m*; **keep ~s on** (*fam*) [genau] beobachten; **pick up the ~** (*fam*) bezahlen
tabby /'tæbɪ/ *n* getigerte Katze *f*
table /'teɪbl/ *n* Tisch *m*; (*list*) Tabelle *f*; **at [the] ~** bei Tisch ● *vt* einbringen. **~-cloth** *n* Tischdecke *f*, Tischtuch *nt*. **~spoon** *n* Servierlöffel *m*
tablet /'tæblɪt/ *n* Tablette *f*; (*of soap*) Stück *nt*; (*slab*) Tafel *f*
'table tennis *n* Tischtennis *nt*
tabloid /'tæblɔɪd/ *n* kleinformatige Zeitung *f*; (*pej*) Boulevardzeitung *f*
taboo /tə'bu:/ *a* tabu ● *n* Tabu *nt*
tacit /'tæsɪt/ *a*, **-ly** *adv* stillschweigend
taciturn /'tæsɪtɜ:n/ *a* wortkarg

tack /tæk/ *n* (*nail*) Stift *m*; (*stitch*) Heftstich *m*; (*Naut & fig*) Kurs *m* ● *vt* festnageln; (*sew*) heften ● *vi* (*Naut*) kreuzen

tackle /ˈtækl/ *n* Ausrüstung *f* ● *vt* angehen

tacky /ˈtækɪ/ *a* klebrig

tact /tækt/ *n* Takt *m*, Taktgefühl *nt*. **~ful** *a*, **-ly** *adv* taktvoll

tactic|al /ˈtæktɪkl/ *a*, **-ly** *adv* taktisch. **~s** *npl* Taktik *f*

tactless /ˈtæktlɪs/ *a*, **-ly** *adv* taktlos. **~ness** *n* Taktlosigkeit *f*

tadpole /ˈtædpəʊl/ *n* Kaulquappe *f*

tag¹ /tæg/ *n* (*label*) Schild *nt* ● *vi* (*pt*/*pp* **tagged**) **~ along** mitkommen

tag² *n* (*game*) Fangen *nt*

tail /teɪl/ *n* Schwanz *m*; **~s** *pl* (*tailcoat*) Frack *m*; **heads or ~s?** Kopf oder Zahl? ● *vt* (*fam: follow*) beschatten ● *vi* **~ off** zurückgehen

tail: ~back *n* Rückstau *m*. **~coat** *n* Frack *m*. **~-end** *n* Ende *nt*. **~ light** *n* Rücklicht *nt*

tailor /ˈteɪlə(r)/ *n* Schneider *m*. **~-made** *a* maßgeschneidert

ˈtail wind *n* Rückenwind *m*

taint /teɪnt/ *vt* verderben

take /teɪk/ *v* (*pt* **took**, *pp* **taken**) ● *vt* nehmen; (*with one*) mitnehmen; (*take to a place*) bringen; (*steal*) stehlen; (*win*) gewinnen; (*capture*) einnehmen; (*require*) brauchen; (*last*) dauern; (*teach*) geben; machen ⟨*exam, subject, holiday, photograph*⟩; messen ⟨*pulse, temperature*⟩; **~ s.o. home** jdn nach Hause bringen; **~ sth to the cleaner's** etw in die Reinigung bringen; **~ s.o. prisoner** jdn gefangennehmen; **be ~n ill** krank werden; **~ sth calmly** etw gelassen aufnehmen ● *vi* ⟨*plant:*⟩ angehen; **~ after s.o.** jdm nachschlagen; (*in looks*) jdm ähnlich sehen; **~ to** (*like*) mögen; (*as a habit*) sich (*dat*) angewöhnen. **~ away** *vt* wegbringen; (*remove*) wegnehmen; (*subtract*) abziehen; **'to ~ away'** 'zum Mitnehmen'. **~ back** *vt* zurücknehmen; (*return*) zurückbringen. **~ down** *vt* herunternehmen; (*remove*) abnehmen; (*write down*) aufschreiben. **~ in** *vt* hineinbringen; (*bring indoors*) hereinholen; (*to one's home*) aufnehmen; (*understand*) begreifen; (*deceive*) hereinlegen; (*make smaller*) enger machen. **~ off** *vt* abnehmen; ablegen ⟨*coat*⟩; sich (*dat*) ausziehen ⟨*clothes*⟩; (*deduct*) abziehen; (*mimic*) nachmachen; **~ time off** sich (*dat*) frei nehmen; **~ oneself off** [fort]gehen ● *vi* (*Aviat*) starten. **~ on** *vt* annehmen; (*undertake*) übernehmen; (*engage*) einstellen; (*as opponent*) antreten gegen. **~ out** *vt* hinausbringen; (*for pleasure*) ausgehen mit; ausführen ⟨*dog*⟩; (*remove*) herausnehmen; (*withdraw*) abheben ⟨*money*⟩; (*from library*) ausleihen; **~ out a subscription to sth** etw abonnieren; **~ it out on s.o.** (*fam*) seinen Ärger an jdm auslassen. **~ over** *vt* hinüberbringen; übernehmen ⟨*firm, control*⟩ ● *vi* **~ over from s.o.** jdn ablösen. **~ up** *vt* hinaufbringen; annehmen ⟨*offer*⟩; ergreifen ⟨*profession*⟩; sich (*dat*) zulegen ⟨*hobby*⟩; in Anspruch nehmen ⟨*time*⟩; einnehmen ⟨*space*⟩; aufreißen ⟨*floorboards*⟩; **~ sth up with s.o.** mit jdm über etw (*acc*) sprechen ● *vi* **~ up with s.o.** sich mit jdm einlassen

take: ~-away *n* Essen *nt* zum Mitnehmen; (*restaurant*) Restaurant *nt* mit Straßenverkauf. **~-off** *n* (*Aviat*) Start *m*, Abflug *m*. **~-over** *n* Übernahme *f*

takings /ˈteɪkɪŋz/ *npl* Einnahmen *pl*

talcum /ˈtælkəm/ *n* **~ [powder]** Körperpuder *m*

tale /teɪl/ *n* Geschichte *f*

talent /ˈtælənt/ *n* Talent *nt*. **~ed** *a* talentiert

talk /tɔːk/ *n* Gespräch *nt*; (*lecture*) Vortrag *m*; **make small ~** Konversation machen ● *vi* reden, sprechen (**to/with** mit) ● *vt* reden; **~ s.o. into sth** jdn zu etw überreden. **~ over** *vt* besprechen

talkative /ˈtɔːkətɪv/ *a* gesprächig

ˈtalking-to *n* Standpauke *f*

tall /tɔːl/ *a* (**-er, -est**) groß; ⟨*building, tree*⟩ hoch; **that's a ~ order** das ist ziemlich viel verlangt. **~boy** *n* hohe Kommode *f*. **~ ˈstory** *n* übertriebene Geschichte *f*

tally /ˈtælɪ/ *n* **keep a ~ of** Buch führen über (+ *acc*) ● *vi* übereinstimmen

talon /ˈtælən/ *n* Klaue *f*

tambourine /tæmbəˈriːn/ *n* Tamburin *nt*

tame /teɪm/ *a* (**-r, -st**), **-ly** *adv* zahm; (*dull*) lahm (*fam*) ● *vt* zähmen. **~r** *n* Dompteur *m*

tamper /ˈtæmpə(r)/ *vi* **~ with** sich (*dat*) zu schaffen machen an (+ *dat*)

tampon /ˈtæmpɒn/ *n* Tampon *m*

tan /tæn/ *a* gelbbraun ● *n* Gelbbraun *nt*; (*from sun*) Bräune *f* ● *v* (*pt/pp* **tanned**) ● *vt* gerben ⟨*hide*⟩ ● *vi* braun werden

tang /tæŋ/ *n* herber Geschmack *m*; (*smell*) herber Geruch *m*

tangent /ˈtændʒənt/ *n* Tangente *f*; **go off at a ~** (*fam*) vom Thema abschweifen

tangible /ˈtændʒɪbl/ *a* greifbar

tangle /ˈtæŋgl/ *n* Gewirr *nt*; (*in hair*) Verfilzung *f* ● *vt* **~ [up]** verheddern ● *vi* sich verheddern

tango /ˈtæŋgəʊ/ *n* Tango *m*

tank /tæŋk/ *n* Tank *m*; (*Mil*) Panzer *m*

tankard /ˈtæŋkəd/ *n* Krug *m*

tanker /ˈtæŋkə(r)/ *n* Tanker *m*; (*lorry*) Tank[last]wagen *m*

tantaliz|e /ˈtæntəlaɪz/ *vt* quälen. **~ing** *a* verlockend

tantamount /ˈtæntəmaʊnt/ *a* **be ~ to** gleichbedeutend sein mit

tantrum /ˈtæntrəm/ *n* Wutanfall *m*

tap /tæp/ *n* Hahn *m*; (*knock*) Klopfen *nt*; **on ~** zur Verfügung ● *v* (*pt/pp* **tapped**) ● *vt* klopfen an (+ *acc*); anzapfen ⟨*barrel, tree*⟩; erschließen ⟨*resources*⟩; abhören ⟨*telephone*⟩ ● *vi* klopfen. **~dance** *n* Step[tanz] *m* ● *vi* Step tanzen, steppen

tape /teɪp/ *n* Band *nt*; (*adhesive*) Klebstreifen *m*; (*for recording*) Tonband *nt* ● *vt* mit Klebstreifen zukleben; (*record*) auf Band aufnehmen

ˈtape-measure *n* Bandmaß *nt*

taper /ˈteɪpə(r)/ *n* dünne Wachskerze *f* ● *vi* sich verjüngen

ˈtape recorder *n* Tonbandgerät *nt*

tapestry /ˈtæpɪstrɪ/ *n* Gobelinstickerei *f*

ˈtapeworm *n* Bandwurm *m*

ˈtap water *n* Leitungswasser *nt*

tar /tɑː(r)/ *n* Teer *m* ● *vt* (*pt/pp* **tarred**) teeren

tardy /ˈtɑːdɪ/ *a* (**-ier, -iest**) langsam; (*late*) spät

target /ˈtɑːgɪt/ *n* Ziel *nt*; (*board*) [Ziel]scheibe *f*

tariff /ˈtærɪf/ *n* Tarif *m*; (*duty*) Zoll *m*

tarnish /ˈtɑːnɪʃ/ *vi* anlaufen

tarpaulin /tɑːˈpɔːlɪn/ *n* Plane *f*

tarragon /ˈtærəgən/ *n* Estragon *m*

tart¹ /tɑːt/ *a* (**-er, -est**) sauer; (*fig*) scharf

tart² *n* ≈ Obstkuchen *m*; (*individual*) Törtchen *nt*; (*sl: prostitute*) Nutte *f* ● *vt* **~ oneself up** (*fam*) sich auftakeln

tartan /ˈtɑːtn/ *n* Schottenmuster *nt*; (*cloth*) Schottenstoff *m* ● *attrib* schottisch kariert

tartar /ˈtɑːtə(r)/ *n* (*on teeth*) Zahnstein *m*

tartar ˈsauce /tɑːtə-/ *n* ≈ Remouladensoße *f*

task /tɑːsk/ *n* Aufgabe *f*; **take s.o. to ~** jdm Vorhaltungen machen. **~ force** *n* Sonderkommando *nt*

tassel /ˈtæsl/ *n* Quaste *f*

taste /teɪst/ *n* Geschmack *m*; (*sample*) Kostprobe *f* ● *vt* kosten, probieren; schmecken ⟨*flavour*⟩ ● *vi* schmecken (**of** nach). **~ful** *a*, **-ly** *adv* (*fig*) geschmackvoll. **~less** *a*, **-ly** *adv* geschmacklos

tasty /ˈteɪstɪ/ *a* (**-ier, -iest**) lecker, schmackhaft

tat /tæt/ *see* **tit²**

tatter|ed /ˈtætəd/ *a* zerlumpt; ⟨*pages*⟩ zerfleddert. **~s** *npl* **in ~s** in Fetzen

tattoo¹ /təˈtuː/ *n* Tätowierung *f* ● *vt* tätowieren

tattoo² *n* (*Mil*) Zapfenstreich *m*

tatty /ˈtætɪ/ *a* (**-ier, -iest**) schäbig; ⟨*book*⟩ zerfleddert

taught /tɔːt/ *see* **teach**

taunt /tɔːnt/ *n* höhnische Bemerkung *f* ● *vt* verhöhnen

Taurus /ˈtɔːrəs/ *n* (*Astr*) Stier *m*

taut /tɔːt/ *a* straff

tavern /ˈtævən/ *n* (*liter*) Schenke *f*

tawdry /ˈtɔːdrɪ/ *a* (**-ier, -iest**) billig und geschmacklos

tawny /ˈtɔːnɪ/ *a* gelbbraun

tax /tæks/ *n* Steuer *f* ● *vt* besteuern; (*fig*) strapazieren; **~ with** beschuldigen (+ *gen*). **~able** /-əbl/ *a* steuerpflichtig. **~ation** /-ˈseɪʃn/ *n* Besteuerung *f*. **~-free** *a* steuerfrei

taxi /ˈtæksɪ/ *n* Taxi *nt* ● *vi* (*pt/pp* **taxied**, *pres p* **taxiing**) ⟨*aircraft:*⟩ rollen. **~ driver** *n* Taxifahrer *m*. **~ rank** *n* Taxistand *m*

ˈtaxpayer *n* Steuerzahler *m*

tea /tiː/ *n* Tee *m*. **~-bag** *n* Teebeutel *m*. **~-break** *n* Teepause *f*

teach /tiːtʃ/ *vt/i* (*pt/pp* **taught**) unterrichten; **~ s.o. sth** jdm etw beibringen. **~er** *n* Lehrer(in) *m*(*f*)

tea: ~-cloth *n* (*for drying*) Geschirrtuch *nt*. **~cup** *n* Teetasse *f*

teak /tiːk/ *n* Teakholz *nt*

team /tiːm/ *n* Mannschaft *f*; (*fig*) Team *nt*; (*of animals*) Gespann *nt* ● *vi* **~ up** sich zusammentun

'team-work *n* Teamarbeit *f*
'teapot *n* Teekanne *f*
tear¹ /teə(r)/ *n* Riß *m* ● *v* (*pt* **tore**, *pp* **torn**) ● *vt* reißen; (*damage*) zerreißen; ~ **open** aufreißen; ~ **oneself away** sich losreißen ● *vi* [zer]reißen; (*run*) rasen. ~ **up** *vt* zerreißen
tear² /tɪə(r)/ *n* Träne *f*. ~**ful** *a* weinend. ~**fully** *adv* unter Tränen. ~**-gas** *n* Tränengas *nt*
tease /ti:z/ *vt* necken
tea: ~**-set** *n* Teeservice *nt*. ~ **shop** *n* Café *nt*. ~**spoon** *n* Teelöffel *m*. ~**-strainer** *n* Teesieb *nt*
teat /ti:t/ *n* Zitze *f*; (*on bottle*) Sauger *m*
'tea-towel *n* Geschirrtuch *nt*
technical /'teknɪkl/ *a* technisch; (*specialized*) fachlich. ~**ity** /-'kælətɪ/ *n* technisches Detail *nt*; (*Jur*) Formfehler *m*. ~**ly** *adv* technisch; (*strictly*) streng genommen. ~ **term** *n* Fachausdruck *m*
technician /tek'nɪʃn/ *n* Techniker *m*
technique /tek'ni:k/ *n* Technik *f*
technological /teknə'lɒdʒɪkl/ *a*, **-ly** *adv* technologisch
technology /tek'nɒlədʒɪ/ *n* Technologie *f*
teddy /'tedɪ/ *n* ~ **[bear]** Teddybär *m*
tedious /'ti:dɪəs/ *a* langweilig
tedium /'ti:dɪəm/ *n* Langeweile *f*
teem /ti:m/ *vi* (*rain*) in Strömen gießen; **be ~ing with** (*full of*) wimmeln von
teenage /'ti:neɪdʒ/ *a* Teenager-; ~ **boy/girl** Junge *m*/Mädchen *nt* im Teenageralter. ~**r** *n* Teenager *m*
teens /ti:nz/ *npl* **the** ~ dic Teenagerjahre *pl*
teeny /'ti:nɪ/ *a* (**-ier, -iest**) winzig
teeter /'ti:tə(r)/ *vi* schwanken
teeth /ti:θ/ *see* **tooth**
teeth|e /ti:ð/ *vi* zahnen. ~**ing troubles** *npl* (*fig*) Anfangsschwierigkeiten *pl*
teetotal /ti:'təʊtl/ *a* abstinent. ~**ler** *n* Abstinenzler *m*
telecommunications /telɪkəmju:nɪ'keɪʃnz/ *npl* Fernmeldewesen *nt*
telegram /'telɪgræm/ *n* Telegramm *nt*
telegraph /'telɪgrɑ:f/ *n* Telegraf *m*. ~**ic** /-'græfɪk/ *a* telegrafisch. ~ **pole** *n* Telegrafenmast *m*
telepathy /tɪ'lepəθɪ/ *n* Telepathie *f*; **by** ~ telepathisch
telephone /'telɪfəʊn/ *n* Telefon *nt*; **be on the** ~ Telefon haben; (*be telephoning*) telefonieren ● *vt* anrufen ● *vi* telefonieren
telephone: ~ **book** *n* Telefonbuch *nt*. ~ **booth** *n*, ~ **box** *n* Telefonzelle *f*. ~ **directory** *n* Telefonbuch *nt*. ~ **number** *n* Telefonnummer *f*
telephonist /tɪ'lefənɪst/ *n* Telefonist(in) *m*(*f*)
tele'photo /telɪ-/ *a* ~ **lens** Teleobjektiv *nt*
teleprinter /'telɪ-/ *n* Fernschreiber *m*
telescop|e /'telɪskəʊp/ *n* Teleskop *nt*, Fernrohr *nt*. ~**ic** /-'skɒpɪk/ *a* teleskopisch; (*collapsible*) ausziehbar
televise /'telɪvaɪz/ *vt* im Fernsehen übertragen
television /'telɪvɪʒn/ *n* Fernsehen *nt*; **watch** ~ fernsehen. ~ **set** *n* Fernsehapparat *m*, Fernseher *m*
telex /'teleks/ *n* Telex *nt* ● *vt* telexen
tell /tel/ *vt/i* (*pt/pp* **told**) sagen (**s.o.** jdm); (*relate*) erzählen; (*know*) wissen; (*distinguish*) erkennen; ~ **the time** die Uhr lesen; **time will** ~ das wird man erst sehen; **his age is beginning to** ~ sein Alter macht sich bemerkbar; **don't ~ me** sag es mir nicht; **you musn't** ~ du darfst nichts sagen. ~ **off** *vt* ausschimpfen
teller /'telə(r)/ *n* (*cashier*) Kassierer(in) *m*(*f*)
telly /'telɪ/ *n* (*fam*) = **television**
temerity /tɪ'merətɪ/ *n* Kühnheit *f*
temp /temp/ *n* (*fam*) Aushilfssekretärin *f*
temper /'tempə(r)/ *n* (*disposition*) Naturell *nt*, (*mood*) Laune *f*; (*anger*) Wut *f*; **lose one's** ~ wütend werden ● *vt* (*fig*) mäßigen
temperament /'temprəmənt/ *n* Temperament *nt*. ~**al** /-'mentl/ *a* temperamentvoll; (*moody*) launisch
temperance /'tempərəns/ *n* Mäßigung *f*; (*abstinence*) Abstinenz *f*
temperate /'tempərət/ *a* gemäßigt
temperature /'temprətʃə(r)/ *n* Temperatur *f*; **have** *or* **run a** ~ Fieber haben
tempest /'tempɪst/ *n* Sturm *m*. ~**uous** /-'pestjʊəs/ *a* stürmisch
template /'templɪt/ *n* Schablone *f*
temple¹ /'templ/ *n* Tempel *m*
temple² *n* (*Anat*) Schläfe *f*
tempo /'tempəʊ/ *n* Tempo *nt*
temporary /'tempərərɪ/ *a*, **-ily** *adv* vorübergehend; ⟨*measure, building*⟩ provisorisch

tempt /tempt/ *vt* verleiten; (*Relig*) versuchen; herausfordern ⟨*fate*⟩; (*entice*) [ver]locken; **be ~ed** versucht sein (**to** zu); **I am ~ed by it** es lockt mich. **~ation** /-'teɪʃn/ *n* Versuchung *f*. **~ing** *a* verlockend

ten /ten/ *a* zehn

tenable /'tenəbl/ *a* (*fig*) haltbar

tenaci|ous /tɪ'neɪʃəs/ *a*, **-ly** *adv* hartnäckig. **~ty** /-'næsətɪ/ *n* Hartnäckigkeit *f*

tenant /'tenənt/ *n* Mieter(in) *m(f)*; (*Comm*) Pächter(in) *m(f)*

tend¹ /tend/ *vt* (*look after*) sich kümmern um

tend² *vi* **~ to do sth** dazu neigen, etw zu tun

tendency /'tendənsɪ/ *n* Tendenz *f*; (*inclination*) Neigung *f*

tender¹ /'tendə(r)/ *n* (*Comm*) Angebot *nt*; **legal ~** gesetzliches Zahlungsmittel *nt* ● *vt* anbieten; einreichen ⟨*resignation*⟩

tender² *a* zart; (*loving*) zärtlich; (*painful*) empfindlich. **~ly** *adv* zärtlich. **~ness** *n* Zartheit *f*; Zärtlichkeit *f*

tendon /'tendən/ *n* Sehne *f*

tenement /'tenəmənt/ *n* Mietshaus *nt*

tenet /'tenɪt/ *n* Grundsatz *m*

tenner /'tenə(r)/ *n* (*fam*) Zehnpfundschein *m*

tennis /'tenɪs/ *n* Tennis *nt*. **~-court** *n* Tennisplatz *m*

tenor /'tenə(r)/ *n* Tenor *m*

tense¹ /tens/ *n* (*Gram*) Zeit *f*

tense² *a* (**-r, -st**) gespannt ● *vt* anspannen ⟨*muscle*⟩

tension /'tenʃn/ *n* Spannung *f*

tent /tent/ *n* Zelt *nt*

tentacle /'tentəkl/ *n* Fangarm *m*

tentative /'tentətɪv/ *a*, **-ly** *adv* vorläufig; (*hesitant*) zaghaft

tenterhooks /'tentəhʊks/ *npl* **be on ~** wie auf glühenden Kohlen sitzen

tenth /tenθ/ *a* zehnte(r,s) ● *n* Zehntel *nt*

tenuous /'tenjʊəs/ *a* (*fig*) schwach

tepid /'tepɪd/ *a* lauwarm

term /tɜ:m/ *n* Zeitraum *m*; (*Sch*) ≈ Halbjahr *nt*; (*Univ*) ≈ Semester *nt*; (*expression*) Ausdruck *m*; **~s** *pl* (*conditions*) Bedingungen *pl*; **~ of office** Amtszeit *f*; **in the short/long ~** kurz-/langfristig; **be on good/bad ~s** gut/nicht gut miteinander auskommen; **come to ~s with** sich abfinden mit

terminal /'tɜ:mɪnl/ *a* End-; (*Med*) unheilbar ● *n* (*Aviat*) Terminal *m*; (*of bus*) Endstation *f*; (*on battery*) Pol *m*; (*Computing*) Terminal *nt*

terminat|e /'tɜ:mɪneɪt/ *vt* beenden; lösen ⟨*contract*⟩; unterbrechen ⟨*pregnancy*⟩ ● *vi* enden. **~ion** /-'neɪʃn/ *n* Beendigung *f*; (*Med*) Schwangerschaftsabbruch *m*

terminology /tɜ:mɪ'nɒlədʒɪ/ *n* Terminologie *f*

terminus /'tɜ:mɪnəs/ *n* (*pl* **-ni** /-naɪ/) Endstation *f*

terrace /'terəs/ *n* Terrasse *f*; (*houses*) Häuserreihe *f*; **the ~s** (*Sport*) die [Steh]ränge *pl*. **~d house** *n* Reihenhaus *nt*

terrain /te'reɪn/ *n* Gelände *nt*

terrible /'terəbl/ *a*, **-bly** *adv* schrecklich

terrier /'terɪə(r)/ *n* Terrier *m*

terrific /tə'rɪfɪk/ *a* (*fam*) (*excellent*) sagenhaft; (*huge*) riesig

terri|fy /'terɪfaɪ/ *vt* (*pt/pp* **-ied**) angst machen (+ *dat*); **be ~fied** Angst haben. **~fying** *a* furchterregend

territorial /terɪ'tɔ:rɪəl/ *a* Territorial-

territory /'terɪtərɪ/ *n* Gebiet *nt*

terror /'terə(r)/ *n* [panische] Angst *f*; (*Pol*) Terror *m*. **~ism** /-ɪzm/ *n* Terrorismus *m*. **~ist** /-ɪst/ *n* Terrorist *m*. **~ize** *vt* terrorisieren

terse /tɜ:s/ *a*, **-ly** *adv* kurz, knapp

test /test/ *n* Test *m*; (*Sch*) Klassenarbeit *f*; **put to the ~** auf die Probe stellen ● *vt* prüfen; (*examine*) untersuchen (**for** auf + *acc*)

testament /'testəmənt/ *n* Testament *nt*; **Old/New T~** Altes/Neues Testament *nt*

testicle /'testɪkl/ *n* Hoden *m*

testify /'testɪfaɪ/ *v* (*pt/pp* **-ied**) ● *vt* beweisen; **~ that** bezeugen, daß ● *vi* aussagen; **~ to** bezeugen

testimonial /testɪ'məʊnɪəl/ *n* Zeugnis *nt*

testimony /'testɪmənɪ/ *n* Aussage *f*

'test-tube *n* Reagenzglas *nt*. **~ 'baby** *n* (*fam*) Retortenbaby *nt*

testy /'testɪ/ *a* gereizt

tetanus /'tetənəs/ *n* Tetanus *m*

tetchy /'tetʃɪ/ *a* gereizt

tether /'teðə(r)/ *n* **be at the end of one's ~** am Ende seiner Kraft sein ● *vt* anbinden

text /tekst/ *n* Text *m*. **~book** *n* Lehrbuch *nt*

textile /'tekstaɪl/ *a* Textil- ● *n* **~s** *pl* Textilien *pl*

texture /'tekstʃə(r)/ *n* Beschaffenheit *f*; (*Tex*) Struktur *f*

Thai /taɪ/ *a* thailändisch. **~land** *n* Thailand *nt*

Thames /temz/ *n* Themse *f*

than /ðən, *betont* ðæn/ *conj* als; **older ~ me** älter als ich

thank /θæŋk/ *vt* danken (+ *dat*); **~ you [very much]** danke [schön]. **~ful** *a*, **-ly** *adv* dankbar. **~less** *a* undankbar

thanks /θæŋks/ *npl* Dank *m*; **~!** (*fam*) danke! **~ to** dank (+ *dat or gen*)

that /ðæt/ *a & pron* (*pl* **those**) der/die/das; (*pl*) die; **~ one** der/die/das da; **I'll take ~** ich nehme den/die/das; **I don't like those** die mag ich nicht; **~ is** das heißt; **is ~ you?** bist du es? **who is ~?** wer ist da? **with/after ~** damit/danach; **like ~** so; **a man like ~** so ein Mann; **~ is why** deshalb; **~'s it!** genau! **all ~ I know** alles was ich weiß; **the day ~ I saw him** an dem Tag, als ich ihn sah ● *adv* so; **~ good/hot** so gut/heiß ● *conj* daß

thatch /θætʃ/ *n* Strohdach *nt*. **~ed** *a* strohgedeckt

thaw /θɔ:/ *n* Tauwetter *nt* ● *vt/i* auftauen; **it's ~ing** es taut

the /ðə, *vor einem Vokal* ðɪ:/ *def art* der/die/das; (*pl*) die; **play ~ piano/violin** Klavier/Geige spielen ● *adv* **~ more ~ better** je mehr, desto besser; **all ~ better** um so besser

theatre /'θɪətə(r)/ *n* Theater *nt*; (*Med*) Operationssaal *m*

theatrical /θɪ'ætrɪkl/ *a* Theater-; (*showy*) theatralisch

theft /θeft/ *n* Diebstahl *m*

their /ðeə(r)/ *a* ihr

theirs /ðeəz/ *poss pron* ihre(r), ihrs; **a friend of ~** ein Freund von ihnen; **those are ~** die gehören ihnen

them /ðem/ *pron* (*acc*) sie; (*dat*) ihnen; **I know ~** ich kenne sie; **give ~ the money** gib ihnen das Geld

theme /θi:m/ *n* Thema *nt*

them'selves *pron* selbst; (*refl*) sich; **by ~** allein

then /ðen/ *adv* dann; (*at that time in past*) damals; **by ~** bis dahin; **since ~** seitdem; **before ~** vorher; **from ~ on** von da an; **now and ~** dann und wann; **there and ~** auf der Stelle ● *a* damalig

theolog|ian /θɪə'ləʊdʒɪən/ *n* Theologe *m*. **~y** /-'ɒlədʒɪ/ *n* Theologie *f*

theorem /'θɪərəm/ *n* Lehrsatz *m*

theoretical /θɪə'retɪkl/ *a*, **-ly** *adv* theoretisch

theory /'θɪərɪ/ *n* Theorie *f*; **in ~** theoretisch

therapeutic /θerə'pju:tɪk/ *a* therapeutisch

therap|ist /'θerəpɪst/ *n* Therapeut(in) *m*(*f*). **~y** *n* Therapie *f*

there /ðeə(r)/ *adv* da; (*with movement*) dahin, dorthin; **down/up ~** da unten/oben; **~ is/are** da ist/sind; (*in existence*) es gibt; **~ he/she is** da ist er/sie; **send/take ~** hinschicken/-bringen ● *int* **there, there!** nun, nun!

there: ~abouts *adv* da [in der Nähe]; **or ~abouts** (*roughly*) ungefähr. **~'after** *adv* danach. **~by** *adv* dadurch. **~fore** /-fɔ:(r)/ *adv* deshalb, also

thermal /'θɜ:ml/ *a* Thermal-; **~ 'underwear** *n* Thermowäsche *f*

thermometer /θə'mɒmɪtə(r)/ *n* Thermometer *nt*

Thermos (P) /'θɜ:məs/ *n* **~ [flask]** Thermosflasche (P) *f*

thermostat /'θɜ:məstæt/ *n* Thermostat *m*

these /ði:z/ *see* **this**

thesis /'θi:sɪs/ *n* (*pl* **-ses** /-si:z/) Dissertation *f*; (*proposition*) These *f*

they /ðeɪ/ *pron* sie; **~ say** (*generalizing*) man sagt

thick /θɪk/ *a* (**-er, -est**), **-ly** *adv* dick; (*dense*) dicht; ⟨*liquid*⟩ dickflüssig; (*fam: stupid*) dumm ● *adv* dick ● *n* **in the ~ of** mitten in (+ *dat*). **~en** *vt* dicker machen; eindicken ⟨*sauce*⟩ ● *vi* dicker werden; ⟨*fog:*⟩ dichter werden; ⟨*plot:*⟩ kompliziert werden. **~ness** *n* Dicke *f*; Dichte *f*; Dickflüssigkeit *f*

thick: ~set *a* untersetzt. **~-'skinned** *a* (*fam*) dickfellig

thief /θi:f/ *n* (*pl* **thieves**) Dieb(in) *m*(*f*)

thieving /'θi:vɪŋ/ *a* diebisch ● *n* Stehlen *nt*

thigh /θaɪ/ *n* Oberschenkel *m*

thimble /'θɪmbl/ *n* Fingerhut *m*

thin /θɪn/ *a* (**thinner, thinnest**), **-ly** *adv* dünn ● *adv* dünn ● *v* (*pt/pp* **thinned**) ● *vt* verdünnen ⟨*liquid*⟩ ● *vi* sich lichten. **~ out** *vt* ausdünnen

thing /θɪŋ/ *n* Ding *nt*; (*subject, affair*) Sache *f*; **~s** *pl* (*belongings*) Sachen *pl*; **for one ~** erstens; **the right ~** das Richtige; **just the ~!** genau das Richtige! **how are ~s?** wie geht's? **the latest ~** (*fam*) der letzte Schrei; **the best ~ would be** am besten wäre es

think /θɪŋk/ *vt/i* (*pt/pp* **thought**) denken (**about/of** an + *acc*); (*believe*) meinen; (*consider*) nachdenken; (*regard as*) halten für; **I ~ so** ich glaube schon; **what do you ~?** was meinen Sie? **what do you ~ of it?** was halten Sie davon? **~ better of it** es sich (*dat*) anders überlegen. **~ over** *vt* sich (*dat*) überlegen. **~ up** *vt* sich (*dat*) ausdenken

third /θɜ:d/ *a* dritte(r,s) ● *n* Drittel *nt*. **~ly** *adv* drittens. **~-rate** *a* drittrangig

thirst /θɜ:st/ *n* Durst *m*. **~y** *a*, **-ily** *adv* durstig; **be ~y** Durst haben

thirteen /θɜ:'ti:n/ *a* dreizehn. **~th** *a* dreizehnte(r,s)

thirtieth /'θɜ:tɪɪθ/ *a* dreißigste(r,s)

thirty /'θɜ:tɪ/ *a* dreißig

this /ðɪs/ *a* (*pl* **these**) diese(r,s); (*pl*) diese; **~ one** diese(r,s) da; **I'll take ~** ich nehme diesen/diese/dieses; **~ evening/morning** heute abend/morgen; **these days** heutzutage ● *pron* (*pl* **these**) das, dies[es]; (*pl*) die, diese; **~ and that** dies und das; **~ or that** dieses oder das da; **like ~** so; **~ is Peter** das ist Peter; (*Teleph*) hier [spricht] Peter; **who is ~ ?** wer ist das? (*Teleph, Amer*) wer ist am Apparat?

thistle /'θɪsl/ *n* Distel *f*

thorn /θɔ:n/ *n* Dorn *m*. **~y** *a* dornig

thorough /'θʌrə/ *a* gründlich

thorough: ~bred *n* reinrassiges Tier *nt*; (*horse*) Rassepferd *nt*. **~fare** *n* Durchfahrtsstraße *f*; **'no ~fare'** 'keine Durchfahrt'

thorough|ly /'θʌrəlɪ/ *adv* gründlich; (*completely*) völlig; (*extremely*) äußerst. **~ness** *n* Gründlichkeit *f*

those /ðəʊz/ *see* **that**

though /ðəʊ/ *conj* obgleich, obwohl; **as ~** als ob ● *adv* (*fam*) doch

thought /θɔ:t/ *see* **think** ● *n* Gedanke *m*; (*thinking*) Denken *nt*. **~ful** *a*, **-ly** *adv* nachdenklich; (*considerate*) rücksichtsvoll. **~less** *a*, **-ly** *adv* gedankenlos

thousand /'θaʊznd/ *a* **one/a ~** [ein]tausend ● *n* Tausend *nt*; **~s of** Tausende von. **~th** *a* tausendste(r,s) ● *n* Tausendstel *nt*

thrash /θræʃ/ *vt* verprügeln; (*defeat*) [vernichtend] schlagen. **~ about** *vi* sich herumwerfen; ⟨*fish:*⟩ zappeln. **~ out** *vt* ausdiskutieren

thread /θred/ *n* Faden *m*; (*of screw*) Gewinde *nt* ● *vt* einfädeln; auffädeln ⟨*beads*⟩; **~ one's way through** sich schlängeln durch. **~bare** *a* fadenscheinig

threat /θret/ *n* Drohung *f*; (*danger*) Bedrohung *f*

threaten /'θretn/ *vt* drohen (+ *dat*); (*with weapon*) bedrohen; **~ to do sth** drohen, etw zu tun; **~ s.o. with sth** jdm etw androhen ● *vi* drohen. **~ing** *a*, **-ly** *adv* drohend; (*ominous*) bedrohlich

three /θri:/ *a* drei. **~fold** *a & adv* dreifach. **~some** /-səm/ *n* Trio *nt*

thresh /θreʃ/ *vt* dreschen

threshold /'θreʃəʊld/ *n* Schwelle *f*

threw /θru:/ *see* **throw**

thrift /θrɪft/ *n* Sparsamkeit *f*. **~y** *a* sparsam

thrill /θrɪl/ *n* Erregung *f*; (*fam*) Nervenkitzel *m* ● *vt* (*excite*) erregen; **be ~ed with** sich sehr freuen über (+ *acc*). **~er** *n* Thriller *m*. **~ing** *a* erregend

thrive /θraɪv/ *vi* (*pt* **thrived** *or* **throve**, *pp* **thrived** *or* **thriven** /'θrɪvn/) gedeihen (**on** bei); ⟨*business:*⟩ florieren

throat /θrəʊt/ *n* Hals *m*; **sore ~** Halsschmerzen *pl*; **cut s.o.'s ~** jdm die Kehle durchschneiden

throb /θrɒb/ *n* Pochen *nt* ● *vi* (*pt/pp* **throbbed**) pochen; (*vibrate*) vibrieren

throes /θrəʊz/ *npl* **in the ~ of** (*fig*) mitten in (+ *dat*)

thrombosis /θrɒm'bəʊsɪs/ *n* Thrombose *f*

throne /θrəʊn/ *n* Thron *m*

throng /θrɒŋ/ *n* Menge *f*

throttle /'θrɒtl/ *vt* erdrosseln

through /θru:/ *prep* durch (+ *acc*); (*during*) während (+ *gen*); (*Amer: up to & including*) bis einschließlich ● *adv* durch; **all ~** die ganze Zeit; **~ and ~** durch und durch; **wet ~** durch und durch naß; **read sth ~** etw durchlesen; **let/walk ~** durchlassen/-gehen ● *a* ⟨*train*⟩ durchgehend; **be ~** (*finished*) fertig sein; (*Teleph*) durch sein

throughout /θru:'aʊt/ *prep* **~ the country** im ganzen Land; **~ the night** die Nacht durch ● *adv* ganz; (*time*) die ganze Zeit

throve /θrəʊv/ *see* **thrive**

throw /θrəʊ/ *n* Wurf *m* ● *vt* (*pt* **threw**, *pp* **thrown**) werfen; schütten ⟨*liquid*⟩; betätigen ⟨*switch*⟩; abwerfen ⟨*rider*⟩; (*fam: disconcert*) aus der Fassung bringen; (*fam*) geben

⟨*party*⟩; **~ sth to s.o.** jdm etw zuwerfen; **~ sth at s.o.** etw nach jdm werfen; (*pelt with*) jdn mit etw bewerfen. **~ away** *vt* wegwerfen. **~ out** *vt* hinauswerfen; (**~** *away*) wegwerfen; verwerfen ⟨*plan*⟩. **~ up** *vt* hochwerfen ● *vi* (*fam*) sich übergeben

'throw-away *a* Wegwerf-

thrush /θrʌʃ/ *n* Drossel *f*

thrust /θrʌst/ *n* Stoß *m*; (*Phys*) Schub *m* ● *vt* (*pt/pp* **thrust**) stoßen; (*insert*) stecken; **~ [up]on** aufbürden (**s.o.** jdm)

thud /θʌd/ *n* dumpfer Schlag *m*

thug /θʌg/ *n* Schläger *m*

thumb /θʌm/ *n* Daumen *m*; **rule of ~** Faustregel *f*; **under s.o.'s ~** unter jds Fuchtel ● *vt* **~ a lift** (*fam*) per Anhalter fahren. **~-index** *n* Daumenregister *nt*. **~tack** *n* (*Amer*) Reißzwecke *f*

thump /θʌmp/ *n* Schlag *m*; (*noise*) dumpfer Schlag *m* ● *vt* schlagen ● *vi* hämmern (**on** an/auf + *acc*); ⟨*heart:*⟩ pochen

thunder /'θʌndə(r)/ *n* Donner *m* ● *vi* donnern. **~clap** *n* Donnerschlag *m*. **~storm** *n* Gewitter *nt*. **~y** *a* gewittrig

Thursday /'θɜːzdeɪ/ *n* Donnerstag *m*

thus /ðʌs/ *adv* so

thwart /θwɔːt/ *vt* vereiteln; **~ s.o.** jdm einen Strich durch die Rechnung machen

thyme /taɪm/ *n* Thymian *m*

thyroid /'θaɪrɔɪd/ *n* Schilddrüse *f*

tiara /tɪ'ɑːrə/ *n* Diadem *nt*

tick[1] /tɪk/ *n* **on ~** (*fam*) auf Pump

tick[2] *n* (*sound*) Ticken *nt*; (*mark*) Häkchen *nt*; (*fam: instant*) Sekunde *f* ● *vi* ticken ● *vt* abhaken. **~ off** *vt* abhaken; (*fam*) rüffeln. **~ over** *vi* ⟨*engine:*⟩ im Leerlauf laufen

ticket /'tɪkɪt/ *n* Karte *f*; (*for bus, train*) Fahrschein *m*; (*Aviat*) Flugschein *m*; (*for lottery*) Los *nt*; (*for article deposited*) Schein *m*; (*label*) Schild *nt*; (*for library*) Lesekarte *f*; (*fine*) Strafzettel *m*. **~-collector** *n* Fahrkartenkontrolleur *m*. **~-office** *n* Fahrkartenschalter *m*; (*for entry*) Kasse *f*

tick|le /'tɪkl/ *n* Kitzeln *nt* ● *vt/i* kitzeln. **~lish** /'tɪklɪʃ/ *a* kitzlig

tidal /'taɪdl/ *a* ⟨*river, harbour*⟩ Tide-. **~ wave** *n* Flutwelle *f*

tiddly-winks /'tɪdlɪwɪŋks/ *n* Flohspiel *nt*

tide /taɪd/ *n* Gezeiten *pl*; (*of events*) Strom *m*; **the ~ is in/out** es ist Flut/Ebbe ● *vt* **~ s.o. over** jdm über die Runden helfen

tidiness /'taɪdɪnɪs/ *n* Ordentlichkeit *f*

tidy /'taɪdɪ/ *a* (**-ier, -iest**), **-ily** *adv* ordentlich ● *vt* **~ [up]** aufräumen; **~ oneself up** sich zurechtmachen

tie /taɪ/ *n* Krawatte *f*, Schlips *m*; (*cord*) Schnur *f*; (*fig: bond*) Band *nt*; (*restriction*) Bindung *f*; (*Sport*) Unentschieden *nt*; (*in competition*) Punktgleichheit *f* ● *v* (*pres p* **tying**) ● *vt* binden; machen ⟨*knot*⟩ ● *vi* (*Sport*) unentschieden spielen; (*have equal scores, votes*) punktgleich sein; **~ in with** passen zu. **~ up** *vt* festbinden; verschnüren ⟨*parcel*⟩; fesseln ⟨*person*⟩; **be ~d up** (*busy*) beschäftigt sein

tier /tɪə(r)/ *n* Stufe *f*; (*of cake*) Etage *f*; (*in stadium*) Rang *m*

tiff /tɪf/ *n* Streit *m*, (*fam*) Krach *m*

tiger /'taɪgə(r)/ *n* Tiger *m*

tight /taɪt/ *a* (**-er, -est**), **-ly** *adv* fest; (*taut*) straff; ⟨*clothes*⟩ eng; ⟨*control*⟩ streng; (*fam: drunk*) blau; **in a ~ corner** (*fam*) in der Klemme ● *adv* fest

tighten /'taɪtn/ *vt* festerziehen; straffen ⟨*rope*⟩; anziehen ⟨*screw*⟩; verschärfen ⟨*control*⟩ ● *vi* sich spannen

tight: ~-'fisted *a* knauserig. **~rope** *n* Hochseil *nt*

tights /taɪts/ *npl* Strumpfhose *f*

tile /taɪl/ *n* Fliese *f*; (*on wall*) Kachel *f*; (*on roof*) [Dach]ziegel *m* ● *vt* mit Fliesen auslegen; kacheln ⟨*wall*⟩; decken ⟨*roof*⟩

till[1] /tɪl/ *prep & conj* = **until**

till[2] *n* Kasse *f*

tiller /'tɪlə(r)/ *n* Ruderpinne *f*

tilt /tɪlt/ *n* Neigung *f*; **at full ~** mit voller Wucht ● *vt* kippen; [zur Seite] neigen ⟨*head*⟩ ● *vi* sich neigen

timber /'tɪmbə(r)/ *n* [Nutz]holz *nt*

time /taɪm/ *n* Zeit *f*; (*occasion*) Mal *nt*; (*rhythm*) Takt *m*; **~s** (*Math*) mal; **at any ~** jederzeit; **this ~** dieses Mal, diesmal; **at ~s** manchmal; **~ and again** immer wieder; **two at a ~** zwei auf einmal; **on ~** pünktlich; **in ~** rechtzeitig; (*eventually*) mit der Zeit; **in no ~** im Handumdrehen; **in a year's ~** in einem Jahr; **behind ~** verspätet; **behind the ~s** rückständig; **for the ~ being** vorläufig; **what is the ~?** wie spät ist es? wieviel Uhr ist es? **by the ~ we arrive** bis wir ankommen; **did you have a nice ~?** hat es dir gut gefallen? **have a good ~!** viel Vergnügen! ● *vt* stoppen ‹*race*›; **be well ~d** gut abgepaßt sein

time: ~ bomb *n* Zeitbombe *f*. **~-lag** *n* Zeitdifferenz *f*. **~less** *a* zeitlos. **~ly** *a* rechtzeitig. **~-switch** *n* Zeitschalter *m*. **~table** *n* Fahrplan *m*; (*Sch*) Stundenplan *m*

timid /'tɪmɪd/ *a*, **-ly** *adv* scheu; (*hesitant*) zaghaft

timing /'taɪmɪŋ/ *n* Wahl *f* des richtigen Zeitpunkts; (*Sport, Techn*) Timing *nt*

tin /tɪn/ *n* Zinn *nt*; (*container*) Dose *f* ● *vt* (*pt/pp* **tinned**) in Dosen *od* Büchsen konservieren. **~ foil** *n* Stanniol *nt*; (*Culin*) Alufolie *f*

tinge /tɪndʒ/ *n* Hauch *m* ● *vt* **~d with** mit einer Spur von

tingle /'tɪŋgl/ *vi* kribbeln

tinker /'tɪŋkə(r)/ *vi* herumbasteln (**with** an + *dat*)

tinkle /'tɪŋkl/ *n* Klingeln *nt* ● *vi* klingeln

tinned /tɪnd/ *a* Dosen-, Büchsen-

'tin opener *n* Dosen-/Büchsenöffner *m*

'tinpot *a* (*pej*) ‹*firm*› schäbig

tinsel /'tɪnsl/ *n* Lametta *nt*

tint /tɪnt/ *n* Farbton *m* ● *vt* tönen

tiny /'taɪnɪ/ *a* (**-ier, -iest**) winzig

tip[1] /tɪp/ *n* Spitze *f*

tip[2] *n* (*money*) Trinkgeld *nt*; (*advice*) Rat *m*, (*fam*) Tip *m*; (*for rubbish*) Müllhalde *f* ● *v* (*pt/pp* **tipped**) ● *vt* (*tilt*) kippen; (*reward*) Trinkgeld geben (**s.o.** jdm) ● *vi* kippen. **~ off** *vt* **~ s.o. off** jdm einen Hinweis geben. **~ out** *vt* auskippen. **~ over** *vt/i* umkippen

'tip-off *n* Hinweis *m*

tipped /tɪpt/ *a* Filter-

tipsy /'tɪpsɪ/ *a* (*fam*) beschwipst

tiptoe /'tɪptəʊ/ *n* **on ~** auf Zehenspitzen

tiptop /tɪp'tɒp/ *a* (*fam*) erstklassig

tire /'taɪə(r)/ *vt/i* ermüden. **~d** *a* müde; **be ~d of sth** etw satt haben; **~d out** [völlig] erschöpft. **~less** *a*, **-ly** *adv* unermüdlich. **~some** /-səm/ *a* lästig

tiring /'taɪrɪŋ/ *a* ermüdend

tissue /'tɪʃu:/ *n* Gewebe *nt*; (*handkerchief*) Papiertaschentuch *nt*. **~-paper** *n* Seidenpapier *nt*

tit[1] /tɪt/ *n* (*bird*) Meise *f*

tit[2] *n* **~ for tat** wie du mir, so ich dir

'titbit *n* Leckerbissen *m*

titillate /'tɪtɪleɪt/ *vt* erregen

title /'taɪtl/ *n* Titel *m*. **~-role** *n* Titelrolle *f*

tittle-tattle /'tɪtltætl/ *n* Klatsch *m*

titular /'tɪtjʊlə(r)/ *a* nominell

to /tu:, *unbetont* tə/ *prep* zu (+ *dat*); (*with place, direction*) nach; (*to cinema, theatre*) in (+ *acc*); (*to wedding, party*) auf (+ *acc*); ‹*address, send, fasten*› an (+ *acc*); (*per*) pro; (*up to, until*) bis; **to the station** zum Bahnhof; **to Germany/Switzerland** nach Deutschland/in die Schweiz; **to the toilet/one's room** auf die Toilette/sein Zimmer; **to the office/an exhibition** ins Büro/in eine Ausstellung; **to university** auf die Universität; **twenty/quarter to eight** zwanzig/Viertel vor acht; **5 to 6 pounds** 5 bis 6 Pfund; **to the end** bis zum Schluß; **to this day** bis heute; **to the best of my knowledge** nach meinem besten Wissen; **give/say sth to s.o.** jdm etw geben/sagen; **go/come to s.o.** zu jdm gehen/kommen; **I've never been to Berlin** ich war noch nie in Berlin; **there's nothing to it** es ist nichts dabei ● *verbal constructions* **to go** gehen; **to stay** bleiben; **learn to swim** schwimmen lernen; **want to/have to go** gehen wollen/müssen; **be easy/difficult to forget** leicht/schwer zu vergessen sein; **too ill/tired to go** zu krank/müde, um zu gehen; **he did it to annoy me** er tat es, um mich zu ärgern; **you have to** du mußt; **I don't want to** ich will nicht; **I'd love to** gern; **I forgot to** ich habe es vergessen; **he wants to be a teacher** er will Lehrer werden; **live to be 90** 90 werden; **he was the last to arrive** er kam als letzter; **to be honest** ehrlich gesagt ● *adv* **pull to** anlehnen; **to and fro** hin und her

toad /təʊd/ *n* Kröte *f*. **~stool** *n* Giftpilz *m*

toast /təʊst/ *n* Toast *m* ● *vt* toasten ‹*bread*›; (*drink a ~ to*) trinken auf (+ *acc*). **~er** *n* Toaster *m*

tobacco /tə'bækəʊ/ *n* Tabak *m*. **~nist's [shop]** *n* Tabakladen *m*

toboggan /tə'bɒgən/ *n* Schlitten *m* ● *vi* Schlitten fahren

today /tə'deɪ/ *n & adv* heute; **~ week** heute in einer Woche; **~'s paper** die heutige Zeitung

toddler /'tɒdlə(r)/ *n* Kleinkind *nt*

to-do /tə'du:/ *n* (*fam*) Getue *nt*, Theater *nt*
toe /təʊ/ *n* Zeh *m*; (*of footwear*) Spitze *f* ● *vt* ~ **the line** spuren. ~**nail** *n* Zehennagel *m*
toffee /'tɒfɪ/ *n* Karamelbonbon *m* & *nt*
together /tə'geðə(r)/ *adv* zusammen; (*at the same time*) gleichzeitig
toil /tɔɪl/ *n* [harte] Arbeit *f* ● *vi* schwer arbeiten
toilet /'tɔɪlɪt/ *n* Toilette *f*. ~ **bag** *n* Kulturbeutel *m*. ~ **paper** *n* Toilettenpapier *nt*
toiletries /'tɔɪlɪtrɪz/ *npl* Toilettenartikel *pl*
toilet: ~ **roll** *n* Rolle *f* Toilettenpapier. ~ **water** *n* Toilettenwasser *nt*
token /'təʊkən/ *n* Zeichen *nt*; (*counter*) Marke *f*; (*voucher*) Gutschein *m* ● *attrib* symbolisch
told /təʊld/ *see* **tell** ● *a* **all** ~ insgesamt
tolerable /'tɒlərəbl/ *a*, **-bly** *adv* erträglich; (*not bad*) leidlich
toleran|ce /'tɒlərəns/ *n* Toleranz *f*. ~**t** *a*, **-ly** *adv* tolerant
tolerate /'tɒləreɪt/ *vt* dulden, tolerieren; (*bear*) ertragen
toll[1] /təʊl/ *n* Gebühr *f*; (*for road*) Maut *f* (*Aust*); **death** ~ Zahl *f* der Todesopfer; **take a heavy** ~ einen hohen Tribut fordern
toll[2] *vi* läuten
tom /tɒm/ *n* (*cat*) Kater *m*
tomato /tə'mɑ:təʊ/ *n* (*pl* **-es**) Tomate *f*. ~ **purée** *n* Tomatenmark *nt*
tomb /tu:m/ *n* Grabmal *nt*
'tomboy *n* Wildfang *m*
'tombstone *n* Grabstein *m*
'tom-cat *n* Kater *m*
tome /təʊm/ *n* dicker Band *m*
tomfoolery /tɒm'fu:lərɪ/ *n* Blödsinn *m*
tomorrow /tə'mɒrəʊ/ *n* & *adv* morgen; ~ **morning** morgen früh; **the day after** ~ übermorgen; **see you** ~**!** bis morgen!
ton /tʌn/ *n* Tonne *f*; ~**s of** (*fam*) jede Menge
tone /təʊn/ *n* Ton *m*; (*colour*) Farbton *m* ● *vt* ~ **down** dämpfen; (*fig*) mäßigen. ~ **up** *vt* kräftigen; straffen ⟨*muscles*⟩
tongs /tɒŋz/ *npl* Zange *f*
tongue /tʌŋ/ *n* Zunge *f*; ~ **in cheek** (*fam*) nicht ernst. ~**-twister** *n* Zungenbrecher *m*
tonic /'tɒnɪk/ *n* Tonikum *nt*; (*for hair*) Haarwasser *nt*; (*fig*) Wohltat *f*; ~ **[water]** Tonic *nt*
tonight /tə'naɪt/ *n* & *adv* heute nacht; (*evening*) heute abend
tonne /tʌn/ *n* Tonne *f*
tonsil /'tɒnsl/ *n* (*Anat*) Mandel *f*. ~**litis** /-sə'laɪtɪs/ *n* Mandelentzündung *f*
too /tu:/ *adv* zu; (*also*) auch; ~ **much/little** zuviel/zuwenig
took /tʊk/ *see* **take**
tool /tu:l/ *n* Werkzeug *nt*; (*for gardening*) Gerät *nt*
toot /tu:t/ *n* Hupsignal *nt* ● *vi* tuten; (*Auto*) hupen
tooth /tu:θ/ *n* (*pl* **teeth**) Zahn *m*
tooth: ~**ache** *n* Zahnschmerzen *pl*. ~**brush** *n* Zahnbürste *f*. ~**less** *a* zahnlos. ~**paste** *n* Zahnpasta *f*. ~**pick** *n* Zahnstocher *m*
top[1] /tɒp/ *n* (*toy*) Kreisel *m*
top[2] *n* oberer Teil *m*; (*apex*) Spitze *f*; (*summit*) Gipfel *m*; (*Sch*) Erste(r) *m/f*; (*top part or half*) Oberteil *nt*; (*head*) Kopfende *nt*; (*of road*) oberes Ende *nt*; (*upper surface*) Oberfläche *f*; (*lid*) Deckel *m*; (*of bottle*) Verschluß *m*; (*garment*) Top *nt*; **at the/on** ~ oben; **on** ~ **of** oben auf (+ *dat/acc*); **on** ~ **of that** (*besides*) obendrein; **from** ~ **to bottom** von oben bis unten ● *a* oberste(r,s); (*highest*) höchste(r,s); (*best*) beste(r,s) ● *vt* (*pt/pp* **topped**) an erster Stelle stehen auf (+ *dat*) ⟨*list*⟩; (*exceed*) übersteigen; (*remove the* ~ *of*) die Spitze abschneiden von. ~ **up** *vt* nachfüllen, auffüllen
top: ~ **'hat** *n* Zylinder[hut] *m*. ~**-heavy** *a* kopflastig
topic /'tɒpɪk/ *n* Thema *nt*. ~**al** *a* aktuell
top: ~**less** *a* & *adv* oben ohne. ~**most** *a* oberste(r,s)
topple /'tɒpl/ *vt/i* umstürzen. ~ **off** *vi* stürzen
top-'secret *a* streng geheim
topsy-turvy /tɒpsɪ'tɜ:vɪ/ *adv* völlig durcheinander
torch /tɔ:tʃ/ *n* Taschenlampe *f*; (*flaming*) Fackel *f*
tore /tɔ:(r)/ *see* **tear**[1]
torment[1] /'tɔ:ment/ *n* Qual *f*
torment[2] /tɔ:'ment/ *vt* quälen
torn /tɔ:n/ *see* **tear**[1] ● *a* zerrissen
tornado /tɔ:'neɪdəʊ/ *n* (*pl* **-es**) Wirbelsturm *m*

torpedo /tɔ:ˈpi:dəʊ/ *n* (*pl* **-es**) Torpedo *m* ● *vt* torpedieren

torrent /ˈtɒrənt/ *n* reißender Strom *m*. **~ial** /təˈrenʃl/ *a* ⟨*rain*⟩ wolkenbruchartig

torso /ˈtɔ:səʊ/ *n* Rumpf *m*; (*Art*) Torso *m*

tortoise /ˈtɔ:təs/ *n* Schildkröte *f*. **~shell** *n* Schildpatt *nt*

tortuous /ˈtɔ:tjʊəs/ *a* verschlungen; (*fig*) umständlich

torture /ˈtɔ:tʃə(r)/ *n* Folter *f*; (*fig*) Qual *f* ● *vt* foltern; (*fig*) quälen

toss /tɒs/ *vt* werfen; (*into the air*) hochwerfen; (*shake*) schütteln; (*unseat*) abwerfen; mischen ⟨*salad*⟩; wenden ⟨*pancake*⟩; **~ a coin** mit einer Münze losen ● *vi* **~ and turn** (*in bed*) sich [schlaflos] im Bett wälzen. **~ up** *vi* [mit einer Münze] losen

tot¹ /tɒt/ *n* kleines Kind *nt*; (*fam: of liquor*) Gläschen *nt*

tot² *vt* (*pt/pp* **totted**) **~ up** (*fam*) zusammenzählen

total /ˈtəʊtl/ *a* gesamt; (*complete*) völlig, total ● *n* Gesamtzahl *f*; (*sum*) Gesamtsumme *f* ● *vt* (*pt/pp* **totalled**) zusammenzählen; (*amount to*) sich belaufen auf (+ *acc*)

totalitarian /təʊtælɪˈteərɪən/ *a* totalitär

totally /ˈtəʊtəlɪ/ *adv* völlig, total

totter /ˈtɒtə(r)/ *vi* taumeln; (*rock*) schwanken. **~y** *a* wackelig

touch /tʌtʃ/ *n* Berührung *f*; (*sense*) Tastsinn *m*; (*Mus*) Anschlag *m*; (*contact*) Kontakt *m*; (*trace*) Spur *f*; (*fig*) Anflug *m*; **get/be in ~** sich in Verbindung setzen/in Verbindung stehen (**with** mit) ● *vt* berühren; (*get hold of*) anfassen; (*lightly*) tippen auf/an (+ *acc*); (*brush against*) streifen [gegen]; (*reach*) erreichen; (*equal*) herankommen an (+ *acc*); (*fig: move*) rühren; anrühren ⟨*food, subject*⟩; **don't ~ that!** faß das nicht an! ● *vi* sich berühren; **~ on** (*fig*) berühren. **~ down** *vi* (*Aviat*) landen. **~ up** *vt* ausbessern

touch|ing /ˈtʌtʃɪŋ/ *a* rührend. **~y** *a* empfindlich; ⟨*subject*⟩ heikel

tough /tʌf/ *a* (**-er, -est**) zäh; (*severe, harsh*) hart; (*difficult*) schwierig; (*durable*) strapazierfähig

toughen /ˈtʌfn/ *vt* härten; **~ up** abhärten

tour /tʊə(r)/ *n* Reise *f*, Tour *f*; (*of building, town*) Besichtigung *f*; (*Theat, Sport*) Tournee *f*; (*of duty*) Dienstzeit *f* ● *vt* fahren durch; besichtigen ⟨*building*⟩ ● *vi* herumreisen

touris|m /ˈtʊərɪzm/ *n* Tourismus *m*, Fremdenverkehr *m*. **~t** /-rɪst/ *n* Tourist(in) *m*(*f*) ● *attrib* Touristen-. **~t office** *n* Fremdenverkehrsbüro *nt*

tournament /ˈtʊənəmənt/ *n* Turnier *nt*

ˈtour operator *n* Reiseveranstalter *m*

tousle /ˈtaʊzl/ *vt* zerzausen

tout /taʊt/ *n* Anreißer *m*; (*ticket ~*) Kartenschwarzhändler *m* ● *vi* **~ for customers** Kunden werben

tow /təʊ/ *n* **give s.o./a car a ~** jdn/ein Auto abschleppen; **'on ~'** 'wird geschleppt'; **in ~** (*fam*) im Schlepptau ● *vt* schleppen; ziehen ⟨*trailer*⟩. **~ away** *vt* abschleppen

toward[s] /təˈwɔ:d(z)/ *prep* zu (+ *dat*); (*with time*) gegen (+ *acc*); (*with respect to*) gegenüber (+ *dat*)

towel /ˈtaʊəl/ *n* Handtuch *nt*. **~ling** *n* (*Tex*) Frottee *nt*

tower /ˈtaʊə(r)/ *n* Turm *m* ● *vi* **~ above** überragen. **~ block** *n* Hochhaus *nt*. **~ing** *a* hochragend

town /taʊn/ *n* Stadt *f*. **~ ˈhall** *n* Rathaus *nt*

tow: ~-path *n* Treidelpfad *m*. **~-rope** *n* Abschleppseil *nt*

toxic /ˈtɒksɪk/ *a* giftig. **~ ˈwaste** *n* Giftmüll *m*

toxin /ˈtɒksɪn/ *n* Gift *nt*

toy /tɔɪ/ *n* Spielzeug *nt* ● *vi* **~ with** spielen mit; stochern in (+ *dat*) ⟨*food*⟩. **~shop** *n* Spielwarengeschäft *nt*

trac|e /treɪs/ *n* Spur *f* ● *vt* folgen (+ *dat*); (*find*) finden; (*draw*) zeichnen; (*with tracing-paper*) durchpausen. **~ing-paper** *n* Pauspapier *nt*

track /træk/ *n* Spur *f*; (*path*) [unbefestigter] Weg *m*; (*Sport*) Bahn *f*; (*Rail*) Gleis *nt*; **keep ~ of** im Auge behalten ● *vt* verfolgen. **~ down** *vt* aufspüren; (*find*) finden

ˈtracksuit *n* Trainingsanzug *m*

tract¹ /trækt/ *n* (*land*) Gebiet *nt*

tract² *n* (*pamphlet*) [Flug]schrift *f*

tractor /ˈtræktə(r)/ *n* Traktor *m*

trade /treɪd/ *n* Handel *m*; (*line of business*) Gewerbe *nt*; (*business*) Geschäft *nt*; (*craft*) Handwerk *nt*; **by ~** von Beruf ● *vt* tauschen; **~ in** (*give in part exchange*) in Zahlung geben ● *vi* handeln (**in** mit)

'trade mark *n* Warenzeichen *nt*
trader /'treɪdə(r)/ *n* Händler *m*
trade: ~ 'union *n* Gewerkschaft *f*. **~ 'unionist** *n* Gewerkschaftler(in) *m(f)*
trading /'treɪdɪŋ/ *n* Handel *m*. **~ estate** *n* Gewerbegebiet *nt*. **~ stamp** *n* Rabattmarke *f*
tradition /trə'dɪʃn/ *n* Tradition *f*. **~al** *a*, **-ly** *adv* traditionell
traffic /'træfɪk/ *n* Verkehr *m*; (*trading*) Handel *m* • *vi* handeln (**in** mit)
traffic: ~ circle *n* (*Amer*) Kreisverkehr *m*. **~ jam** *n* [Verkehrs]stau *m*. **~ lights** *npl* [Verkehrs]ampel *f*. **~ warden** *n* ≈ Hilfspolizist *m*; (*woman*) Politesse *f*
tragedy /'trædʒədɪ/ *n* Tragödie *f*
tragic /'trædʒɪk/ *a*, **-ally** *adv* tragisch
trail /treɪl/ *n* Spur *f*; (*path*) Weg *m*, Pfad *m* • *vi* schleifen; ⟨*plant:*⟩ sich ranken; **~ [behind]** zurückbleiben; (*Sport*) zurückliegen • *vt* verfolgen, folgen (+ *dat*); (*drag*) schleifen
trailer /'treɪlə(r)/ *n* (*Auto*) Anhänger *m*; (*Amer: caravan*) Wohnwagen *m*; (*film*) Vorschau *f*
train /treɪn/ *n* Zug *m*; (*of dress*) Schleppe *f*; **~ of thought** Gedankengang *m* • *vt* ausbilden; (*Sport*) trainieren; (*aim*) richten auf (+ *acc*); erziehen ⟨*child*⟩; abrichten/(*to do tricks*) dressieren ⟨*animal*⟩; ziehen ⟨*plant*⟩ • *vi* eine Ausbildung machen; (*Sport*) trainieren. **~ed** *a* ausgebildet
trainee /treɪ'ni:/ *n* Auszubildende(r) *m/f*; (*Techn*) Praktikant(in) *m(f)*
train|er /'treɪnə(r)/ *n* (*Sport*) Trainer *m*; (*in circus*) Dompteur *m*; **~ers** *pl* Trainingsschuhe *pl*. **~ing** *n* Ausbildung *f*; (*Sport*) Training *nt*; (*of animals*) Dressur *f*
traipse /treɪps/ *vi* (*fam*) latschen
trait /treɪt/ *n* Eigenschaft *f*
traitor /'treɪtə(r)/ *n* Verräter *m*
tram /træm/ *n* Straßenbahn *f*. **~-lines** *npl* Straßenbahnschienen *pl*
tramp /træmp/ *n* Landstreicher *m*; (*hike*) Wanderung *f* • *vi* stapfen; (*walk*) marschieren
trample /'træmpl/ *vt/i* trampeln (**on** auf + *acc*)
trampoline /'træmpəli:n/ *n* Trampolin *nt*
trance /trɑ:ns/ *n* Trance *f*
tranquil /'træŋkwɪl/ *a* ruhig. **~lity** /-'kwɪlətɪ/ *n* Ruhe *f*
tranquillizer /'træŋkwɪlaɪzə(r)/ *n* Beruhigungsmittel *nt*
transact /træn'zækt/ *vt* abschließen. **~ion** /-ækʃn/ *n* Transaktion *f*
transcend /træn'send/ *vt* übersteigen
transcript /'trænskrɪpt/ *n* Abschrift *f*; (*of official proceedings*) Protokoll *nt*. **~ion** /-'skrɪpʃn/ *n* Abschrift *f*
transept /'trænsept/ *n* Querschiff *nt*
transfer¹ /'trænsfɜ:(r)/ *n* (*see* **transfer²**) Übertragung *f*; Verlegung *f*; Versetzung *f*; Überweisung *f*; (*Sport*) Transfer *m*; (*design*) Abziehbild *nt*
transfer² /træns'fɜ:(r)/ *v* (*pt/pp* **transferred**) • *vt* übertragen; verlegen ⟨*firm, prisoners*⟩; versetzen ⟨*employee*⟩; überweisen ⟨*money*⟩; (*Sport*) transferieren • *vi* [über]wechseln; (*when travelling*) umsteigen. **~able** /-əbl/ *a* übertragbar
transform /træns'fɔ:m/ *vt* verwandeln. **~ation** /-fə'meɪʃn/ *n* Verwandlung *f*. **~er** *n* Transformator *m*
transfusion /træns'fju:ʒn/ *n* Transfusion *f*
transient /'trænzɪənt/ *a* kurzlebig; ⟨*life*⟩ kurz
transistor /træn'zɪstə(r)/ *n* Transistor *m*
transit /'trænsɪt/ *n* Transit *m*; (*of goods*) Transport *m*; **in ~** ⟨*goods*⟩ auf dem Transport
transition /træn'sɪʒn/ *n* Übergang *m*. **~al** *a* Übergangs-
transitive /'trænsɪtɪv/ *a*, **-ly** *adv* transitiv
transitory /'trænsɪtərɪ/ *a* vergänglich; ⟨*life*⟩ kurz
translat|e /træns'leɪt/ *vt* übersetzen. **~ion** /-'leɪʃn/ *n* Übersetzung *f*. **~or** *n* Übersetzer(in) *m(f)*
translucent /trænz'lu:snt/ *a* durchscheinend
transmission /trænz'mɪʃn/ *n* Übertragung *f*
transmit /trænz'mɪt/ *vt* (*pt/pp* **transmitted**) übertragen. **~ter** *n* Sender *m*
transparen|cy /træns'pærənsɪ/ *n* (*Phot*) Dia *nt*. **~t** *a* durchsichtig
transpire /træn'spaɪə(r)/ *vi* sich herausstellen; (*fam: happen*) passieren
transplant¹ /'trænsplɑ:nt/ *n* Verpflanzung *f*, Transplantation *f*
transplant² /træns'plɑ:nt/ *vt* umpflanzen; (*Med*) verpflanzen

transport[1] /'trænspɔ:t/ *n* Transport *m*

transport[2] /træn'spɔ:t/ *vt* transportieren. **~ation** /-'teɪʃn/ *n* Transport *m*

transpose /træns'pəʊz/ *vt* umstellen

transvestite /træns'vestaɪt/ *n* Transvestit *m*

trap /træp/ *n* Falle *f*; (*fam: mouth*) Klappe *f*; **pony and ~** Einspänner *m* • *vt* (*pt/pp* **trapped**) [mit einer Falle] fangen; (*jam*) einklemmen; **be ~ped** festsitzen; (*shut in*) eingeschlossen sein; (*cut off*) abgeschnitten sein. **~'door** *n* Falltür *f*

trapeze /trə'pi:z/ *n* Trapez *nt*

trash /træʃ/ *n* Schund *m*; (*rubbish*) Abfall *m*; (*nonsense*) Quatsch *m*. **~can** *n* (*Amer*) Mülleimer *m*. **~y** *a* Schund-

trauma /'trɔ:mə/ *n* Trauma *nt*. **~tic** /-'mætɪk/ *a* traumatisch

travel /'trævl/ *n* Reisen *nt* • *v* (*pt/pp* **travelled**) • *vi* reisen; (*go in vehicle*) fahren; ⟨*light, sound:*⟩ sich fortpflanzen; (*Techn*) sich bewegen • *vt* bereisen; fahren ⟨*distance*⟩. **~ agency** *n* Reisebüro *nt*. **~ agent** *n* Reisebürokaufmann *m*

traveller /'trævələ(r)/ *n* Reisende(r) *m/f*; (*Comm*) Vertreter *m*; **~s** *pl* (*gypsies*) Zigeuner *pl*. **~'s cheque** *n* Reisescheck *m*

trawler /'trɔ:lə(r)/ *n* Fischdampfer *m*

tray /treɪ/ *n* Tablett *nt*; (*for baking*) [Back]blech *nt*; (*for documents*) Ablagekorb *m*

treacher|ous /'tretʃərəs/ *a* treulos; (*dangerous, deceptive*) tückisch. **~y** *n* Verrat *m*

treacle /'tri:kl/ *n* Sirup *m*

tread /tred/ *n* Schritt *m*; (*step*) Stufe *f*; (*of tyre*) Profil *nt* • *v* (*pt* **trod**, *pp* **trodden**) • *vi* (*walk*) gehen; **~ on/in** treten auf/in (+ *acc*) • *vt* treten

treason /'tri:zn/ *n* Verrat *m*

treasure /'treʒə(r)/ *n* Schatz *m* • *vt* in Ehren halten. **~r** *n* Kassenwart *m*

treasury /'treʒərɪ/ *n* Schatzkammer *f*; **the T~** das Finanzministerium

treat /tri:t/ *n* [besonderes] Vergnügen *nt*; **give s.o. a ~** jdm etwas Besonderes bieten • *vt* behandeln; **~ s.o. to sth** jdm etw spendieren

treatise /'tri:tɪz/ *n* Abhandlung *f*

treatment /'tri:tmənt/ *n* Behandlung *f*

treaty /'tri:tɪ/ *n* Vertrag *m*

treble /'trebl/ *a* dreifach; **~ the amount** dreimal soviel • *n* (*Mus*) Diskant *m*; (*voice*) Sopran *m* • *vt* verdreifachen • *vi* sich verdreifachen. **~ clef** *n* Violinschlüssel *m*

tree /tri:/ *n* Baum *m*

trek /trek/ *n* Marsch *m* • *vi* (*pt/pp* **trekked**) latschen

trellis /'trelɪs/ *n* Gitter *nt*

tremble /'trembl/ *vi* zittern

tremendous /trɪ'mendəs/ *a*, **-ly** *adv* gewaltig; (*fam: excellent*) großartig

tremor /'tremə(r)/ *n* Zittern *nt*; **[earth] ~** Beben *nt*

trench /trentʃ/ *n* Graben *m*; (*Mil*) Schützengraben *m*

trend /trend/ *n* Tendenz *f*; (*fashion*) Trend *m*. **~y** *a* (**-ier, -iest**) (*fam*) modisch

trepidation /trepɪ'deɪʃn/ *n* Beklommenheit *f*

trespass /'trespəs/ *vi* **~ on** unerlaubt betreten. **~er** *n* Unbefugte(r) *m/f*

trial /'traɪəl/ *n* (*Jur*) [Gerichts]verfahren *nt*, Prozeß *m*; (*test*) Probe *f*; (*ordeal*) Prüfung *f*; **be on ~** auf Probe sein; (*Jur*) angeklagt sein (**for** wegen); **by ~ and error** durch Probieren

triang|le /'traɪæŋgl/ *n* Dreieck *nt*; (*Mus*) Triangel *m*. **~ular** /-'æŋgjʊlə(r)/ *a* dreieckig

tribe /traɪb/ *n* Stamm *m*

tribulation /trɪbjʊ'leɪʃn/ *n* Kummer *m*

tribunal /traɪ'bju:nl/ *n* Schiedsgericht *nt*

tributary /'trɪbjʊtərɪ/ *n* Nebenfluß *m*

tribute /'trɪbju:t/ *n* Tribut *m*; **pay ~** Tribut zollen (**to** *dat*)

trice /traɪs/ *n* **in a ~** im Nu

trick /trɪk/ *n* Trick *m*; (*joke*) Streich *m*; (*Cards*) Stich *m*; (*feat of skill*) Kunststück *nt*; **that should do the ~** (*fam*) damit dürfte es klappen • *vt* täuschen, (*fam*) hereinlegen

trickle /'trɪkl/ *vi* rinnen

trick|ster /'trɪkstə(r)/ *n* Schwindler *m*. **~y** *a* (**-ier, -iest**) *a* schwierig

tricycle /'traɪsɪkl/ *n* Dreirad *nt*

tried /traɪd/ *see* **try**

trifl|e /'traɪfl/ *n* Kleinigkeit *f*; (*Culin*) Trifle *nt*. **~ing** *a* unbedeutend

trigger /'trɪgə(r)/ *n* Abzug *m*; (*fig*) Auslöser *m* • *vt* **~ [off]** auslösen

trigonometry /trɪgə'nɒmɪtrɪ/ *n* Trigonometrie *f*

trim /trɪm/ *a* (**trimmer, trimmest**) gepflegt • *n* (*cut*) Nachschneiden *nt*;

(*decoration*) Verzierung *f*; (*condition*) Zustand *m* • *vt* schneiden; (*decorate*) besetzen; (*Naut*) trimmen. **~ming** *n* Besatz *m*; **~mings** *pl* (*accessories*) Zubehör *nt*; (*decorations*) Verzierungen *pl*; **with all the ~mings** mit allem Drum und Dran

Trinity /ˈtrɪnətɪ/ *n* **the [Holy] ~** die [Heilige] Dreieinigkeit *f*

trinket /ˈtrɪŋkɪt/ *n* Schmuckgegenstand *m*

trio /ˈtri:əʊ/ *n* Trio *nt*

trip /trɪp/ *n* Reise *f*; (*excursion*) Ausflug *m* • *v* (*pt/pp* **tripped**) • *vt* **~ s.o. up** jdm ein Bein stellen • *vi* stolpern (**on/over** über + *acc*)

tripe /traɪp/ *n* Kaldaunen *pl*; (*nonsense*) Quatsch *m*

triple /ˈtrɪpl/ *a* dreifach • *vt* verdreifachen • *vi* sich verdreifachen

triplets /ˈtrɪplɪts/ *npl* Drillinge *pl*

triplicate /ˈtrɪplɪkət/ *n* **in ~** in dreifacher Ausfertigung

tripod /ˈtraɪpɒd/ *n* Stativ *nt*

tripper /ˈtrɪpə(r)/ *n* Ausflügler *m*

trite /traɪt/ *a* banal

triumph /ˈtraɪʌmf/ *n* Triumph *m* • *vi* triumphieren (**over** über + *acc*). **~ant** /-ˈʌmfnt/ *a*, **-ly** *adv* triumphierend

trivial /ˈtrɪvɪəl/ *a* belanglos. **~ity** /-ˈælətɪ/ *n* Belanglosigkeit *f*

trod, trodden /trɒd, ˈtrɒdn/ *see* **tread**

trolley /ˈtrɒlɪ/ *n* (*for serving food*) Servierwagen *m*; (*for shopping*) Einkaufswagen *m*; (*for luggage*) Kofferkuli *m*; (*Amer: tram*) Straßenbahn *f*. **~ bus** *n* O-Bus *m*

trombone /trɒmˈbəʊn/ *n* Posaune *f*

troop /tru:p/ *n* Schar *f*; **~s** *pl* Truppen *pl* • *vi* **~ in/out** hinein-/hinausströmen

trophy /ˈtrəʊfɪ/ *n* Trophäe *f*; (*in competition*) ≈ Pokal *m*

tropic /ˈtrɒpɪk/ *n* Wendekreis *m*; **~s** *pl* Tropen *pl*. **~al** *a* tropisch; ⟨*fruit*⟩ Süd-

trot /trɒt/ *n* Trab *m* • *vi* (*pt/pp* **trotted**) traben

trouble /ˈtrʌbl/ *n* Ärger *m*; (*difficulties*) Schwierigkeiten *pl*; (*inconvenience*) Mühe *f*; (*conflict*) Unruhe *f*; (*Med*) Beschwerden *pl*; (*Techn*) Probleme *pl*; **get into ~** Ärger bekommen; **take ~** sich (*dat*) Mühe geben • *vt* (*disturb*) stören; (*worry*) beunruhigen • *vi* sich bemühen. **~maker** *n* Unruhestifter *m*. **~some** /-səm/ *a* schwierig; ⟨*flies, cough*⟩ lästig

trough /trɒf/ *n* Trog *m*

trounce /traʊns/ *vt* vernichtend schlagen; (*thrash*) verprügeln

troupe /tru:p/ *n* Truppe *f*

trousers /ˈtraʊzəz/ *npl* Hose *f*

trousseau /ˈtru:səʊ/ *n* Aussteuer *f*

trout /traʊt/ *n inv* Forelle *f*

trowel /ˈtraʊəl/ *n* Kelle *f*; (*for gardening*) Pflanzkelle *f*

truant /ˈtru:ənt/ *n* **play ~** die Schule schwänzen

truce /tru:s/ *n* Waffenstillstand *m*

truck /trʌk/ *n* Last[kraft]wagen *m*; (*Rail*) Güterwagen *m*

truculent /ˈtrʌkjʊlənt/ *a* aufsässig

trudge /trʌdʒ/ *n* [mühseliger] Marsch *m* • *vi* latschen

true /tru:/ *a* (**-r, -st**) wahr; (*loyal*) treu; (*genuine*) echt; **come ~** in Erfüllung gehen; **is that ~?** stimmt das?

truism /ˈtru:ɪzm/ *n* Binsenwahrheit *f*

truly /ˈtru:lɪ/ *adv* wirklich; (*faithfully*) treu; **Yours ~** Hochachtungsvoll

trump /trʌmp/ *n* (*Cards*) Trumpf *m* • *vt* übertrumpfen. **~ up** *vt* (*fam*) erfinden

trumpet /ˈtrʌmpɪt/ *n* Trompete *f*. **~er** *n* Trompeter *m*

truncheon /ˈtrʌntʃn/ *n* Schlagstock *m*

trundle /ˈtrʌndl/ *vt/i* rollen

trunk /trʌŋk/ *n* [Baum]stamm *m*; (*body*) Rumpf *m*; (*of elephant*) Rüssel *m*; (*for travelling*) [Übersee]koffer *m*; (*for storage*) Truhe *f*; (*Amer: of car*) Kofferraum *m*; **~s** *pl* Badehose *f*

truss /trʌs/ *n* (*Med*) Bruchband *nt*

trust /trʌst/ *n* Vertrauen *nt*; (*group of companies*) Trust *m*; (*organization*) Treuhandgesellschaft *f*; (*charitable*) Stiftung *f* • *vt* trauen (+ *dat*), vertrauen (+ *dat*); (*hope*) hoffen • *vi* vertrauen (**in/to** auf + *acc*)

trustee /trʌsˈti:/ *n* Treuhänder *m*

ˈtrust|ful /ˈtrʌstfl/ *a*, **-ly** *adv* vertrauensvoll. **~ing** *a* vertrauensvoll. **~worthy** *a* vertrauenswürdig

truth /tru:θ/ *n* (*pl* **-s** /tru:ðz/) Wahrheit *f*. **~ful** *a*, **-ly** *adv* ehrlich

try /traɪ/ *n* Versuch *m* • *v* (*pt/pp* **tried**) • *vt* versuchen; (*sample, taste*) probieren; (*be a strain on*) anstrengen; (*Jur*) vor Gericht stellen; verhandeln ⟨*case*⟩ • *vi* versuchen; (*make an* *effort*) sich bemühen. ~ **on** *vt* anprobieren; aufprobieren ⟨*hat*⟩. ~ **out** *vt* ausprobieren

trying /'traɪɪŋ/ *a* schwierig

T-shirt /'ti:-/ *n* T-Shirt *nt*

tub /tʌb/ *n* Kübel *m*; (*carton*) Becher *m*; (*bath*) Wanne *f*

tuba /'tju:bə/ *n* (*Mus*) Tuba *f*

tubby /'tʌbɪ/ *a* (**-ier, -iest**) rundlich

tube /tju:b/ *n* Röhre *f*; (*pipe*) Rohr *nt*; (*flexible*) Schlauch *m*; (*of toothpaste*) Tube *f*; (*Rail, fam*) U-Bahn *f*

tuber /'tju:bə(r)/ *n* Knolle *f*

tuberculosis /tju:bɜ:kjʊ'ləʊsɪs/ *n* Tuberkulose *f*

tubing /'tju:bɪŋ/ *n* Schlauch *m*

tubular /'tju:bjʊlə(r)/ *a* röhrenförmig

tuck /tʌk/ *n* Saum *m*; (*decorative*) Biese *f* • *vt* (*put*) stecken. ~ **in** *vt* hineinstecken; ~ **s.o. in** jdn zudecken • *vi* (*fam: eat*) zulangen. ~ **up** *vt* hochkrempeln ⟨*sleeves*⟩; (*in bed*) zudecken

Tuesday /'tju:zdeɪ/ *n* Dienstag *m*

tuft /tʌft/ *n* Büschel *nt*

tug /tʌg/ *n* Ruck *m*; (*Naut*) Schleppdampfer *m* • *v* (*pt/pp* **tugged**) • *vt* ziehen • *vi* zerren (**at** an + *dat*). ~ **of war** *n* Tauziehen *nt*

tuition /tju:'ɪʃn/ *n* Unterricht *m*

tulip /'tju:lɪp/ *n* Tulpe *f*

tumble /'tʌmbl/ *n* Sturz *m* • *vi* fallen; ~ **to sth** (*fam*) etw kapieren. ~**down** *a* verfallen. ~**-drier** *n* Wäschetrockner *m*

tumbler /'tʌmblə(r)/ *n* Glas *nt*

tummy /'tʌmɪ/ *n* (*fam*) Magen *m*; (*abdomen*) Bauch *m*

tumour /'tju:mə(r)/ *n* Geschwulst *f*, Tumor *m*

tumult /'tju:mʌlt/ *n* Tumult *m*. ~**uous** /-'mʌltjʊəs/ *a* stürmisch

tuna /'tju:nə/ *n* Thunfisch *m*

tune /tju:n/ *n* Melodie *f*; **out of** ~ ⟨*instrument*⟩ verstimmt; **to the** ~ **of** (*fam*) in Höhe von • *vt* stimmen; (*Techn*) einstellen. ~ **in** *vt* einstellen • *vi* ~ **in to a station** einen Sender einstellen. ~ **up** *vi* (*Mus*) stimmen

tuneful /'tju:nfl/ *a* melodisch

tunic /'tju:nɪk/ *n* (*Mil*) Uniformjacke *f*; (*Sch*) Trägerkleid *nt*

Tunisia /tju:'nɪzɪə/ *n* Tunesien *nt*

tunnel /'tʌnl/ *n* Tunnel *m* • *vi* (*pt/pp* **tunnelled**) einen Tunnel graben

turban /'tɜ:bən/ *n* Turban *m*

turbine /'tɜ:baɪn/ *n* Turbine *f*

turbot /'tɜ:bət/ *n* Steinbutt *m*

turbulen|ce /'tɜ:bjʊləns/ *n* Turbulenz *f*. ~**t** *a* stürmisch

tureen /tjʊə'ri:n/ *n* Terrine *f*

turf /tɜ:f/ *n* Rasen *m*; (*segment*) Rasenstück *nt*. ~ **out** *vt* (*fam*) rausschmeißen

'**turf accountant** *n* Buchmacher *m*

Turk /tɜ:k/ *n* Türke *m*/Türkin *f*

turkey /'tɜ:kɪ/ *n* Pute *f*, Truthahn *m*

Turk|ey *n* die Türkei. ~**ish** *a* türkisch

turmoil /'tɜ:mɔɪl/ *n* Aufruhr *m*; (*confusion*) Durcheinander *nt*

turn /tɜ:n/ *n* (*rotation*) Drehung *f*; (*in road*) Kurve *f*; (*change of direction*) Wende *f*; (*short walk*) Runde *f*; (*Theat*) Nummer *f*; (*fam: attack*) Anfall *m*; **do s.o. a good** ~ jdm einen guten Dienst erweisen; **take** ~**s** sich abwechseln; **in** ~ der Reihe nach; **out of** ~ außer der Reihe; **it's your** ~ du bist an der Reihe • *vt* drehen; (~ *over*) wenden; (*reverse*) umdrehen; (*Techn*) drechseln ⟨*wood*⟩; ~ **the page** umblättern; ~ **the corner** um die Ecke biegen • *vi* sich drehen; (~ *round*) sich umdrehen; ⟨*car:*⟩ wenden; ⟨*leaves:*⟩ sich färben; ⟨*weather:*⟩ umschlagen; (*become*) werden; ~ **right/left** nach rechts/links abbiegen; ~ **to s.o.** sich an jdn wenden; **have** ~**ed against s.o.** gegen jdn sein. ~ **away** *vt* abweisen • *vi* sich abwenden. ~ **down** *vt* herunterschlagen ⟨*collar*⟩; herunterdrehen ⟨*heat, gas*⟩; leiser stellen ⟨*sound*⟩; (*reject*) ablehnen; abweisen ⟨*person*⟩. ~ **in** *vt* einschlagen ⟨*edges*⟩ • *vi* ⟨*car:*⟩ einbiegen; (*fam: go to bed*) ins Bett gehen. ~ **off** *vt* zudrehen ⟨*tap*⟩; ausschalten ⟨*light, radio*⟩; abstellen ⟨*water, gas, engine, machine*⟩ • *vi* abbiegen. ~ **on** *vt* aufdrehen ⟨*tap*⟩; einschalten ⟨*light, radio*⟩; anstellen ⟨*water, gas, engine, machine*⟩. ~ **out** *vt* (*expel*) vertreiben, (*fam*) hinauswerfen; ausschalten ⟨*light*⟩; abdrehen ⟨*gas*⟩; (*produce*) produzieren; (*empty*) ausleeren; [gründlich] aufräumen ⟨*room, cupboard*⟩ • *vi* (*go out*) hinausgehen; (*transpire*) sich herausstellen; ~ **out well/badly** gut/schlecht gehen. ~ **over** *vt* umdrehen • *vi* sich umdrehen. ~ **up** *vt* hochschlagen ⟨*collar*⟩; aufdrehen ⟨*heat, gas*⟩; lauter stellen ⟨*sound, radio*⟩ • *vi* auftauchen

turning /'tɜ:nɪŋ/ *n* Abzweigung *f*. ~**-point** *n* Wendepunkt *m*

turnip /'tɜ:nɪp/ *n* weiße Rübe *f*

turn: **~-out** *n* (*of people*) Teilnahme *f*, Beteiligung *f*; (*of goods*) Produktion *f*. **~over** *n* (*Comm*) Umsatz *m*; (*of staff*) Personalwechsel *m*. **~pike** *n* (*Amer*) gebührenpflichtige Autobahn *f*. **~stile** *n* Drehkreuz *nt*. **~table** *n* Drehscheibe *f*; (*on record-player*) Plattenteller *m*. **~-up** *n* [Hosen]aufschlag *m*

turpentine /'tɜ:pəntaɪn/ *n* Terpentin *nt*

turquoise /'tɜ:kwɔɪz/ *a* türkis[farben] ● *n* (*gem*) Türkis *m*

turret /'tʌrɪt/ *n* Türmchen *nt*

turtle /'tɜ:tl/ *n* Seeschildkröte *f*

tusk /tʌsk/ *n* Stoßzahn *m*

tussle /'tʌsl/ *n* Balgerei *f*; (*fig*) Streit *m* ● *vi* sich balgen

tutor /'tju:tə(r)/ *n* [Privat]lehrer *m*

tuxedo /tʌk'si:dəʊ/ *n* (*Amer*) Smoking *m*

TV *abbr of* **television**

twaddle /'twɒdl/ *n* Geschwätz *nt*

twang /twæŋ/ *n* (*in voice*) Näseln *nt* ● *vt* zupfen

tweed /twi:d/ *n* Tweed *m*

tweezers /'twi:zəz/ *npl* Pinzette *f*

twelfth /twelfθ/ *a* zwölfte(r,s)

twelve /twelv/ *a* zwölf

twentieth /'twentɪɪθ/ *a* zwanzigste(r,s)

twenty /'twentɪ/ *a* zwanzig

twerp /twɜ:p/ *n* (*fam*) Trottel *m*

twice /twaɪs/ *adv* zweimal

twiddle /'twɪdl/ *vt* drehen an (+ *dat*)

twig[1] /twɪg/ *n* Zweig *m*

twig[2] *vt/i* (*pt/pp* **twigged**) (*fam*) kapieren

twilight /'twaɪ-/ *n* Dämmerlicht *nt*

twin /twɪn/ *n* Zwilling *m* ● *attrib* Zwillings-. **~ beds** *npl* zwei Einzelbetten *pl*

twine /twaɪn/ *n* Bindfaden *m* ● *vi* sich winden; ⟨*plant:*⟩ sich ranken

twinge /twɪndʒ/ *n* Stechen *nt*; **~ of conscience** Gewissensbisse *pl*

twinkle /'twɪŋkl/ *n* Funkeln *nt* ● *vi* funkeln

twin 'town *n* Partnerstadt *f*

twirl /twɜ:l/ *vt/i* herumwirbeln

twist /twɪst/ *n* Drehung *f*; (*curve*) Kurve *f*; (*unexpected occurrence*) überraschende Wendung *f* ● *vt* drehen; (*distort*) verdrehen; (*fam: swindle*) beschummeln; **~ one's ankle** sich (*dat*) den Knöchel verrenken ● *vi* sich drehen; ⟨*road:*⟩ sich winden. **~er** *n* (*fam*) Schwindler *m*

twit /twɪt/ *n* (*fam*) Trottel *m*

twitch /twɪtʃ/ *n* Zucken *nt* ● *vi* zucken

twitter /'twɪtə(r)/ *n* Zwitschern *nt* ● *vi* zwitschern

two /tu:/ *a* zwei

two: **~-faced** *a* falsch. **~-piece** *a* zweiteilig. **~some** /-səm/ *n* Paar *nt*. **~-way** *a* **~-way traffic** Gegenverkehr *m*

tycoon /taɪ'ku:n/ *n* Magnat *m*

tying /'taɪɪŋ/ *see* **tie**

type /taɪp/ *n* Art *f*, Sorte *f*; (*person*) Typ *m*; (*printing*) Type *f* ● *vt* mit der Maschine schreiben, (*fam*) tippen ● *vi* maschineschreiben, (*fam*) tippen. **~writer** *n* Schreibmaschine *f*. **~written** *a* maschinegeschrieben

typhoid /'taɪfɔɪd/ *n* Typhus *m*

typical /'tɪpɪkl/ *a*, **-ly** *adv* typisch (**of** für)

typify /'tɪpɪfaɪ/ *vt* (*pt/pp* **-ied**) typisch sein für

typing /'taɪpɪŋ/ *n* Maschineschreiben *nt*. **~ paper** *n* Schreibmaschinenpapier *nt*

typist /'taɪpɪst/ *n* Schreibkraft *f*

typography /taɪ'pɒgrəfɪ/ *n* Typographie *f*

tyrannical /tɪ'rænɪkl/ *a* tyrannisch

tyranny /'tɪrənɪ/ *n* Tyrannei *f*

tyrant /'taɪrənt/ *n* Tyrann *m*

tyre /'taɪə(r)/ *n* Reifen *m*

U

ubiquitous /ju:'bɪkwɪtəs/ *a* allgegenwärtig; **be ~** überall zu finden sein

udder /'ʌdə(r)/ *n* Euter *nt*

ugl|iness /'ʌglɪnɪs/ *n* Häßlichkeit *f*. **~y** *a* (**-ier, -iest**) häßlich; (*nasty*) übel

UK *abbr see* **United Kingdom**

ulcer /'ʌlsə(r)/ *n* Geschwür *nt*

ulterior /ʌl'tɪərɪə(r)/ *a* **~ motive** Hintergedanke *m*

ultimate /'ʌltɪmət/ *a* letzte(r,s); (*final*) endgültig; (*fundamental*) grundlegend, eigentlich. **~ly** *adv* schließlich

ultimatum /ʌltɪ'meɪtəm/ *n* Ultimatum *nt*

ultrasound /'ʌltrə-/ *n* (*Med*) Ultraschall *m*

ultra'violet *a* ultraviolett

umbilical /ʌm'bɪlɪkl/ *a* **~ cord** Nabelschnur *f*

umbrella /ʌmˈbrelə/ *n* [Regen]schirm *m*
umpire /ˈʌmpaɪə(r)/ *n* Schiedsrichter *m* ● *vt/i* Schiedsrichter sein (bei)
umpteen /ʌmpˈtiːn/ *a* (*fam*) zig. **~th** *a* (*fam*) zigste(r,s); **for the ~th time** zum zigsten Mal
un'able /ʌn-/ *a* **be ~ to do sth** etw nicht tun können
una'bridged *a* ungekürzt
unac'companied *a* ohne Begleitung; ⟨*luggage*⟩ unbegleitet
unac'countabl|e *a* unerklärlich. **~y** *adv* unerklärlicherweise
unac'customed *a* ungewohnt; **be ~ to sth** etw nicht gewohnt sein
una'dulterated *a* unverfälscht, rein; (*utter*) völlig
un'aided *a* ohne fremde Hilfe
unalloyed /ʌnəˈlɔɪd/ *a* (*fig*) ungetrübt
unanimity /juːnəˈnɪmətɪ/ *n* Einstimmigkeit *f*
unanimous /juːˈnænɪməs/ *a*, **-ly** *adv* einmütig; ⟨*vote, decision*⟩ einstimmig
un'armed *a* unbewaffnet; **~ combat** Kampf *m* ohne Waffen
unas'suming *a* bescheiden
unat'tached *a* nicht befestigt; ⟨*person*⟩ ungebunden
unat'tended *a* unbeaufsichtigt
un'authorized *a* unbefugt
una'voidable *a* unvermeidlich
una'ware *a* **be ~ of sth** sich (*dat*) etw (*gen*) nicht bewußt sein. **~s** /-eəz/ *adv* **catch s.o. ~s** jdn überraschen
un'balanced *a* unausgewogen; (*mentally*) unausgeglichen
un'bearable *a*, **-bly** *adv* unerträglich
unbeat|able /ʌnˈbiːtəbl/ *a* unschlagbar. **~en** *a* ungeschlagen; ⟨*record*⟩ ungebrochen
unbeknown /ʌnbɪˈnəʊn/ *a* (*fam*) **~ to me** ohne mein Wissen
unbe'lievable *a* unglaublich
un'bend *vi* (*pt/pp* **-bent**) (*relax*) aus sich herausgehen
un'biased *a* unvoreingenommen
un'block *vt* frei machen
un'bolt *vt* aufriegeln
un'breakable *a* unzerbrechlich
unbridled /ʌnˈbraɪdld/ *a* ungezügelt
un'burden *vt* **~ oneself** (*fig*) sich aussprechen
un'button *vt* aufknöpfen
uncalled-for /ʌnˈkɔːldfɔː(r)/ *a* unangebracht
un'canny *a* unheimlich
un'ceasing *a* unaufhörlich
uncere'monious *a*, **-ly** *adv* formlos; (*abrupt*) brüsk
un'certain *a* (*doubtful*) ungewiß; ⟨*origins*⟩ unbestimmt; **be ~** nicht sicher sein; **in no ~ terms** ganz eindeutig. **~ty** *n* Ungewißheit *f*
un'changed *a* unverändert
un'charitable *a* lieblos
uncle /ˈʌŋkl/ *n* Onkel *m*
un'comfortable *a*, **-bly** *adv* unbequem; **feel ~** (*fig*) sich nicht wohl fühlen
un'common *a* ungewöhnlich
un'compromising *a* kompromißlos
uncon'ditional *a*, **-ly** *adv* bedingungslos
un'conscious *a* bewußtlos; (*unintended*) unbewußt; **be ~ of sth** sich (*dat*) etw (*gen*) nicht bewußt sein. **~ly** *adv* unbewußt
uncon'ventional *a* unkonventionell
unco'operative *a* nicht hilfsbereit
un'cork *vt* entkorken
uncouth /ʌnˈkuːθ/ *a* ungehobelt
un'cover *vt* aufdecken
unctuous /ˈʌŋktjʊəs/ *a*, **-ly** *adv* salbungsvoll
unde'cided *a* unentschlossen; (*not settled*) nicht entschieden
undeniable /ʌndɪˈnaɪəbl/ *a*, **-bly** *adv* unbestreitbar
under /ˈʌndə(r)/ *prep* unter (+ *dat/acc*); **~ it** darunter; **~ there** da drunter; **~ repair** in Reparatur; **~ construction** im Bau; **~ age** minderjährig; **~ way** unterwegs; (*fig*) im Gange ● *adv* darunter
'undercarriage *n* (*Aviat*) Fahrwerk *nt*, Fahrgestell *nt*
'underclothes *npl* Unterwäsche *f*
under'cover *a* geheim
'undercurrent *n* Unterströmung *f*; (*fig*) Unterton *m*
under'cut *vt* (*pt/pp* **-cut**) (*Comm*) unterbieten
'underdog *n* Unterlegene(r) *m*
under'done *a* nicht gar; (*rare*) nicht durchgebraten
under'estimate *vt* unterschätzen
under'fed *a* unterernährt
under'foot *adv* am Boden; **trample ~** zertrampeln
under'go *vt* (*pt* **-went**, *pp* **-gone**) durchmachen; sich unterziehen (+ *dat*) ⟨*operation, treatment*⟩; **~ repairs** repariert werden
under'graduate *n* Student(in) *m(f)*
under'ground[1] *adv* unter der Erde; ⟨*mining*⟩ unter Tage

'underground² *a* unterirdisch; (*secret*) Untergrund- ● *n* (*railway*) U-Bahn *f*. ~ **car park** *n* Tiefgarage *f*
'undergrowth *n* Unterholz *nt*
'underhand *a* hinterhältig
'underlay *n* Unterlage *f*
under'lie *vt* (*pt* **-lay**, *pp* **-lain**, *pres p* **-lying**) (*fig*) zugrundeliegen (+ *dat*)
under'line *vt* unterstreichen
underling /'ʌndəlɪŋ/ *n* (*pej*) Untergebene(r) *m*/*f*
under'lying *a* (*fig*) eigentlich
under'mine *vt* (*fig*) unterminieren, untergraben
underneath /ʌndə'ni:θ/ *prep* unter (+ *dat*/*acc*); ~ **it** darunter ● *adv* darunter
'underpants *npl* Unterhose *f*
'underpass *n* Unterführung *f*
under'privileged *a* unterprivilegiert
under'rate *vt* unterschätzen
'underseal *n* (*Auto*) Unterbodenschutz *m*
'undershirt *n* (*Amer*) Unterhemd *nt*
understaffed /-'stɑ:ft/ *a* unterbesetzt
under'stand *vt*/*i* (*pt*/*pp* **-stood**) verstehen; **I** ~ **that** ... (*have heard*) ich habe gehört, daß ... ~**able** /-əbl/ *a* verständlich. ~**ably** /-əblɪ/ *adv* verständlicherweise
under'standing *a* verständnisvoll ● *n* Verständnis *nt*; (*agreement*) Vereinbarung *f*; **reach an** ~ sich verständigen; **on the** ~ **that** unter der Voraussetzung, daß
'understatement *n* Untertreibung *f*
'understudy *n* (*Theat*) Ersatzspieler(in) *m*(*f*)
under'take *vt* (*pt* **-took**, *pp* **-taken**) unternehmen; ~ **to do sth** sich verpflichten, etw zu tun
'undertaker *n* Leichenbestatter *m*; **[firm of]** ~**s** Bestattungsinstitut *nt*
under'taking *n* Unternehmen *nt*; (*promise*) Versprechen *nt*
'undertone *n* (*fig*) Unterton *m*; **in an** ~ mit gedämpfter Stimme
under'value *vt* unterbewerten
'underwater¹ *a* Unterwasser-
under'water² *adv* unter Wasser
'underwear *n* Unterwäsche *f*
under'weight *a* untergewichtig; **be** ~ Untergewicht haben
'underworld *n* Unterwelt *f*
'underwriter *n* Versicherer *m*
unde'sirable *a* unerwünscht
undies /'ʌndɪz/ *npl* (*fam*) [Damen]unterwäsche *f*
un'dignified *a* würdelos
un'do *vt* (*pt* **-did**, *pp* **-done**) aufmachen; (*fig*) ungeschehen machen; (*ruin*) zunichte machen
un'done *a* offen; (*not accomplished*) unerledigt
un'doubted *a* unzweifelhaft. ~**ly** *adv* zweifellos
un'dress *vt* ausziehen; **get** ~**ed** sich ausziehen ● *vi* sich ausziehen
un'due *a* übermäßig
undulating /'ʌndjʊleɪtɪŋ/ *a* Wellen-; ⟨*country*⟩ wellig
un'duly *adv* übermäßig
un'dying *a* ewig
un'earth *vt* ausgraben; (*fig*) zutage bringen. ~**ly** *a* unheimlich; **at an** ~**ly hour** (*fam*) in aller Herrgottsfrühe
un'eas|e *n* Unbehagen *nt*. ~**y** *a* unbehaglich; **I feel** ~**y** mir ist unbehaglich zumute
un'eatable *a* ungenießbar
uneco'nomic *a*, **-ally** *adv* unwirtschaftlich
uneco'nomical *a* verschwenderisch
unem'ployed *a* arbeitslos ● *npl* **the** ~ die Arbeitslosen
unem'ployment *n* Arbeitslosigkeit *f*. ~ **benefit** *n* Arbeitslosenunterstützung *f*
un'ending *a* endlos
un'equal *a* unterschiedlich; ⟨*struggle*⟩ ungleich; **be** ~ **to a task** einer Aufgabe nicht gewachsen sein. ~**ly** *adv* ungleichmäßig
unequivocal /ʌnɪ'kwɪvəkl/ *a*, **-ly** *adv* eindeutig
unerring /ʌn'ɜ:rɪŋ/ *a* unfehlbar
un'ethical *a* unmoralisch; **be** ~ gegen das Berufsethos verstoßen
un'even *a* uneben; (*unequal*) ungleich; (*not regular*) ungleichmäßig; ⟨*number*⟩ ungerade. ~**ly** *adv* ungleichmäßig
unex'pected *a*, **-ly** *adv* unerwartet
un'failing *a* nie versagend
un'fair *a*, **-ly** *adv* ungerecht, unfair. ~**ness** *n* Ungerechtigkeit *f*
un'faithful *a* untreu
unfa'miliar *a* ungewohnt; (*unknown*) unbekannt
un'fasten *vt* aufmachen; (*detach*) losmachen
un'favourable *a* ungünstig
un'feeling *a* gefühllos
un'finished *a* unvollendet; ⟨*business*⟩ unerledigt

un'fit *a* ungeeignet; (*incompetent*) unfähig; (*Sport*) nicht fit; ~ **for work** arbeitsunfähig

unflinching /ʌn'flɪntʃɪŋ/ *a* unerschrocken

un'fold *vt* auseinanderfalten, entfalten; (*spread out*) ausbreiten ● *vi* sich entfalten

unfore'seen *a* unvorhergesehen

unforgettable /ʌnfə'getəbl/ *a* unvergeßlich

unforgivable /ʌnfə'gɪvəbl/ *a* unverzeihlich

un'fortunate *a* unglücklich; (*unfavourable*) ungünstig; (*regrettable*) bedauerlich; **be** ~ ⟨*person:*⟩ Pech haben. **~ly** *adv* leider

un'founded *a* unbegründet

unfurl /ʌn'fɜ:l/ *vt* entrollen ● *vi* sich entrollen

un'furnished *a* unmöbliert

ungainly /ʌn'geɪnlɪ/ *a* unbeholfen

ungodly /ʌn'gɒdlɪ/ *a* gottlos; **at an ~ hour** (*fam*) in aller Herrgottsfrühe

un'grateful *a*, **-ly** *adv* undankbar

un'happi|ly *adv* unglücklich; (*unfortunately*) leider. **~ness** *n* Kummer *m*

un'happy *a* unglücklich; (*not content*) unzufrieden

un'harmed *a* unverletzt

un'healthy *a* ungesund

un'hook *vt* vom Haken nehmen; aufhaken ⟨*dress*⟩

un'hurt *a* unverletzt

unhy'gienic *a* unhygienisch

unicorn /'ju:nɪkɔ:n/ *n* Einhorn *nt*

unification /ju:nɪfɪ'keɪʃn/ *n* Einigung *f*

uniform /'ju:nɪfɔ:m/ *a*, **-ly** *adv* einheitlich ● *n* Uniform *f*

unify /'ju:nɪfaɪ/ *vt* (*pt*/*pp* **-ied**) einigen

uni'lateral /ju:nɪ-/ *a*, **-ly** *adv* einseitig

uni'maginable *a* unvorstellbar

unim'portant *a* unwichtig

unin'habited *a* unbewohnt

unin'tentional *a*, **-ly** *adv* unabsichtlich

union /'ju:nɪən/ *n* Vereinigung *f*; (*Pol*) Union *f*; (*trade* ~) Gewerkschaft *f*. **~ist** *n* (*Pol*) Unionist *m*

unique /ju:'ni:k/ *a* einzigartig. **~ly** *adv* einmalig

unison /'ju:nɪsn/ *n* **in** ~ einstimmig

unit /'ju:nɪt/ *n* Einheit *f*; (*Math*) Einer *m*; (*of furniture*) Teil *nt*, Element *nt*

unite /ju:'naɪt/ *vt* vereinigen ● *vi* sich vereinigen

united /ju:'naɪtɪd/ *a* einig. **U~ 'Kingdom** *n* Vereinigtes Königreich *nt*. **U~ 'Nations** *n* Vereinte Nationen *pl*. **U~ States [of America]** *n* Vereinigte Staaten *pl* [von Amerika]

unity /'ju:nətɪ/ *n* Einheit *f*; (*harmony*) Einigkeit *f*

universal /ju:nɪ'vɜ:sl/ *a*, **-ly** *adv* allgemein

universe /'ju:nɪvɜ:s/ *n* [Welt]all *nt*, Universum *nt*

university /ju:nɪ'vɜ:sətɪ/ *n* Universität *f* ● *attrib* Universitäts-

un'just *a*, **-ly** *adv* ungerecht

unkempt /ʌn'kempt/ *a* ungepflegt

un'kind *a*, **-ly** *adv* unfreundlich; (*harsh*) häßlich. **~ness** *n* Unfreundlichkeit *f*; Häßlichkeit *f*

un'known *a* unbekannt

un'lawful *a*, **-ly** *adv* gesetzwidrig

unleaded /ʌn'ledɪd/ *a* bleifrei

un'leash *vt* (*fig*) entfesseln

unless /ən'les/ *conj* wenn ... nicht; **~ I am mistaken** wenn ich mich nicht irre

un'like *a* nicht ähnlich, unähnlich; (*not the same*) ungleich ● *prep* im Gegensatz zu (+ *dat*)

un'likely *a* unwahrscheinlich

un'limited *a* unbegrenzt

un'load *vt* entladen; ausladen ⟨*luggage*⟩

un'lock *vt* aufschließen

un'lucky *a* unglücklich; ⟨*day, number*⟩ Unglücks-; **be** ~ Pech haben; ⟨*thing:*⟩ Unglück bringen

un'manned *a* unbemannt

un'married *a* unverheiratet. **~ 'mother** *n* ledige Mutter *f*

un'mask *vt* (*fig*) entlarven

unmistakable /ʌnmɪ'steɪkəbl/ *a*, **-bly** *adv* unverkennbar

un'mitigated *a* vollkommen

un'natural *a*, **-ly** *adv* unnatürlich; (*not normal*) nicht normal

un'necessary *a*, **-ily** *adv* unnötig

un'noticed *a* unbemerkt

unob'tainable *a* nicht erhältlich

unob'trusive *a*, **-ly** *adv* unaufdringlich; ⟨*thing*⟩ unauffällig

unof'ficial *a*, **-ly** *adv* inoffiziell

un'pack *vt*/*i* auspacken

un'paid *a* unbezahlt

un'palatable *a* ungenießbar

un'paralleled *a* beispiellos

un'pick *vt* auftrennen

un'pleasant *a*, **-ly** *adv* unangenehm. **~ness** *n* (*bad feeling*) Ärger *m*

un'plug *vt* (*pt/pp* **-plugged**) den Stecker herausziehen von
un'popular *a* unbeliebt
un'precedented *a* beispiellos
unpre'dictable *a* unberechenbar
unpre'meditated *a* nicht vorsätzlich
unpre'pared *a* nicht vorbereitet
unprepos'sessing *a* wenig attraktiv
unpre'tentious *a* bescheiden
un'principled *a* skrupellos
unpro'fessional *a* **be ~** gegen das Berufsethos verstoßen; (*Sport*) unsportlich sein
un'profitable *a* unrentabel
un'qualified *a* unqualifiziert; (*fig: absolute*) uneingeschränkt
un'questionable *a* unbezweifelbar; ⟨*right*⟩ unbestreitbar
unravel /ʌn'rævl/ *vt* (*pt/pp* **-ravelled**) entwirren; (*Knitting*) aufziehen
un'real *a* unwirklich
un'reasonable *a* unvernünftig; **be ~** zuviel verlangen
unre'lated *a* unzusammenhängend; **be ~** nicht verwandt sein; ⟨*events:*⟩ nicht miteinander zusammenhängen
unre'liable *a* unzuverlässig
unrequited /ʌnrɪ'kwaɪtɪd/ *a* unerwidert
unreservedly /ʌnrɪ'zɜ:vɪdlɪ/ *adv* uneingeschränkt; (*frankly*) offen
un'rest *n* Unruhen *pl*
un'rivalled *a* unübertroffen
un'roll *vt* aufrollen • *vi* sich aufrollen
unruly /ʌn'ru:lɪ/ *a* ungebärdig
un'safe *a* nicht sicher
un'said *a* ungesagt
un'salted *a* ungesalzen
unsatis'factory *a* unbefriedigend
un'savoury *a* unangenehm; (*fig*) unerfreulich
unscathed /ʌn'skeɪðd/ *a* unversehrt
un'screw *vt* abschrauben
un'scrupulous *a* skrupellos
un'seemly *a* unschicklich
un'selfish *a* selbstlos
un'settled *a* ungeklärt; ⟨*weather*⟩ unbeständig; ⟨*bill*⟩ unbezahlt
unshakeable /ʌn'ʃeɪkəbl/ *a* unerschütterlich
unshaven /ʌn'ʃeɪvn/ *a* unrasiert
unsightly /ʌn'saɪtlɪ/ *a* unansehnlich
un'skilled *a* ungelernt; ⟨*work*⟩ unqualifiziert
un'sociable *a* ungesellig
unso'phisticated *a* einfach
un'sound *a* krank, nicht gesund; ⟨*building*⟩ nicht sicher; ⟨*advice*⟩ unzuverlässig; ⟨*reasoning*⟩ nicht stichhaltig; **of ~ mind** unzurechnungsfähig
unspeakable /ʌn'spi:kəbl/ *a* unbeschreiblich
un'stable *a* nicht stabil; (*mentally*) labil
un'steady *a*, **-ily** *adv* unsicher; (*wobbly*) wackelig
un'stuck *a* **come ~** sich lösen; (*fam: fail*) scheitern
unsuc'cessful *a*, **-ly** *adv* erfolglos; **be ~** keinen Erfolg haben
un'suitable *a* ungeeignet; (*inappropriate*) unpassend; (*for weather, activity*) unzweckmäßig
unsu'specting *a* ahnungslos
un'sweetened *a* ungesüßt
unthinkable /ʌn'θɪŋkəbl/ *a* unvorstellbar
un'tidiness *n* Unordentlichkeit *f*
un'tidy *a*, **-ily** *adv* unordentlich
un'tie *vt* aufbinden; losbinden ⟨*person, boat, horse*⟩
until /ən'tɪl/ *prep* bis (+ *acc*); **not ~** erst; **~ the evening** bis zum Abend; **~ his arrival** bis zu seiner Ankunft • *conj* bis; **not ~** erst wenn; (*in past*) erst als
untimely /ʌn'taɪmlɪ/ *a* ungelegen; (*premature*) vorzeitig
un'tiring *a* unermüdlich
un'told *a* unermeßlich
unto'ward *a* ungünstig; (*unseemly*) ungehörig; **if nothing ~ happens** wenn nichts dazwischenkommt
un'true *a* unwahr; **that's ~** das ist nicht wahr
unused[1] /ʌn'ju:zd/ *a* unbenutzt; (*not utilized*) ungenutzt
unused[2] /ʌn'ju:st/ *a* **be ~ to sth** etw nicht gewohnt sein
un'usual *a*, **-ly** *adv* ungewöhnlich
un'veil *vt* enthüllen
un'versed *a* nicht bewandert (**in** in + *dat*)
un'wanted *a* unerwünscht
un'warranted *a* ungerechtfertigt
un'welcome *a* unwillkommen
un'well *a* **be** *or* **feel ~** sich nicht wohl fühlen
unwieldy /ʌn'wi:ldɪ/ *a* sperrig
un'willing *a*, **-ly** *adv* widerwillig; **be ~ to do sth** etw nicht tun wollen
un'wind *v* (*pt/pp* **unwound**) • *vt* abwickeln • *vi* sich abwickeln; (*fam: relax*) sich entspannen

un'wise *a*, **-ly** *adv* unklug
unwitting /ʌn'wɪtɪŋ/ *a*, **-ly** *adv* unwissentlich
un'worthy *a* unwürdig
un'wrap *vt* (*pt/pp* **-wrapped**) auswickeln; auspacken ⟨*present*⟩
un'written *a* ungeschrieben
up /ʌp/ *adv* oben; (*with movement*) nach oben; (*not in bed*) auf; ⟨*collar*⟩ hochgeklappt; ⟨*road*⟩ aufgerissen; ⟨*price*⟩ gestiegen; ⟨*curtains*⟩ aufgehängt; ⟨*shelves*⟩ angebracht; ⟨*notice*⟩ angeschlagen; ⟨*tent*⟩ aufgebaut; ⟨*building*⟩ gebaut; **be up for sale** zu verkaufen sein; **up there** da oben; **up to** (*as far as*) bis; **time's up** die Zeit ist um; **what's up?** (*fam*) was ist los? **what's he up to?** (*fam*) was hat er vor? **I don't feel up to it** ich fühle mich dem nicht gewachsen; **be one up on s.o.** (*fam*) jdm etwas voraushaben; **go up** hinaufgehen; **come up** heraufkommen ● *prep* **be up on sth** [oben] auf etw (*dat*) sein; **up the mountain** oben am Berg; (*movement*) den Berg hinauf; **be up the tree** oben im Baum sein; **up the road** die Straße entlang; **up the river** stromaufwärts; **go up the stairs** die Treppe hinaufgehen; **be up the pub** (*fam*) in der Kneipe sein
'upbringing *n* Erziehung *f*
up'date *vt* auf den neuesten Stand bringen
up'grade *vt* aufstufen
upheaval /ʌp'hi:vl/ *n* Unruhe *f*; (*Pol*) Umbruch *m*
up'hill *a* (*fig*) mühsam ● *adv* bergauf
up'hold *vt* (*pt/pp* **upheld**) unterstützen; bestätigen ⟨*verdict*⟩
upholster /ʌp'həʊlstə(r)/ *vt* polstern. **~er** *n* Polsterer *m*. **~y** *n* Polsterung *f*
'upkeep *n* Unterhalt *m*
up-'market *a* anspruchsvoll
upon /ə'pɒn/ *prep* auf (+ *dat/acc*)
upper /'ʌpə(r)/ *a* obere(r,s); ⟨*deck, jaw, lip*⟩ Ober-; **have the ~ hand** die Oberhand haben ● *n* (*of shoe*) Obermaterial *nt*
upper: ~ circle *n* zweiter Rang *m*. **~ class** *n* Oberschicht *f*. **~most** *a* oberste(r,s)
'upright *a* aufrecht ● *n* Pfosten *m*
'uprising *n* Aufstand *m*
'uproar *n* Aufruhr *m*
up'root *vt* entwurzeln
up'set[1] *vt* (*pt/pp* **upset**, *pres p* **upsetting**) umstoßen; (*spill*) verschütten; durcheinanderbringen ⟨*plan*⟩; (*distress*) erschüttern; ⟨*food:*⟩ nicht bekommen (+ *dat*); **get ~ about sth** sich über etw (*acc*) aufregen; **be very ~** sehr bestürzt sein
'upset[2] *n* Aufregung *f*; **have a stomach ~** einen verdorbenen Magen haben
'upshot *n* Ergebnis *nt*
upside 'down *adv* verkehrt herum; **turn ~** umdrehen
up'stairs[1] *adv* oben; ⟨*go*⟩ nach oben
'upstairs[2] *a* im Obergeschoß
'upstart *n* Emporkömmling *m*
up'stream *adv* stromaufwärts
'upsurge *n* Zunahme *f*
'uptake *n* **slow on the ~** schwer von Begriff; **be quick on the ~** schnell begreifen
up'tight *a* nervös
'upturn *n* Aufschwung *m*
upward /'ʌpwəd/ *a* nach oben; ⟨*movement*⟩ Aufwärts-; **~ slope** Steigung *f* ● **~[s]** aufwärts, nach oben
uranium /jʊ'reɪnɪəm/ *n* Uran *nt*
urban /'3:bən/ *a* städtisch
urbane /3:'beɪn/ *a* weltmännisch
urge /3:dʒ/ *n* Trieb *m*, Drang *m* ● *vt* drängen; **~ on** antreiben
urgen|cy /'3:dʒənsɪ/ *n* Dringlichkeit *f*. **~t** *a*, **-ly** *adv* dringend
urinate /'jʊərɪneɪt/ *vi* urinieren
urine /'jʊərɪn/ *n* Urin *m*, Harn *m*
urn /3:n/ *n* Urne *f*; (*for tea*) Teemaschine *f*
us /ʌs/ *pron* uns; **it's us** wir sind es
US[A] *abbr* USA *pl*
usable /'ju:zəbl/ *a* brauchbar
usage /'ju:zɪdʒ/ *n* Brauch *m*; (*of word*) [Sprach]gebrauch *m*
use[1] /ju:s/ *n* (*see* **use**[2]) Benutzung *f*; Verwendung *f*; Gebrauch *m*; **be of ~** nützlich sein; **be of no ~** nichts nützen; **make ~ of** Gebrauch machen von; (*exploit*) ausnutzen; **it is no ~** es hat keinen Zweck; **what's the ~?** wozu?
use[2] /ju:z/ *vt* benutzen ⟨*implement, room, lift*⟩; verwenden ⟨*ingredient, method, book, money*⟩; gebrauchen ⟨*words, force, brains*⟩; **~ [up]** aufbrauchen
used[1] /ju:zd/ *a* benutzt; ⟨*car*⟩ Gebraucht-
used[2] /ju:st/ *pt/pp* **be ~ to sth** an etw (*acc*) gewöhnt sein; **get ~ to** sich gewöhnen an (+ *acc*); **he ~ to say** er hat immer gesagt; **he ~ to live here** er hat früher hier gewohnt

useful /'ju:sfl/ *a* nützlich. **~ness** *n* Nützlichkeit *f*

useless /'ju:slɪs/ *a* nutzlos; (*not usable*) unbrauchbar; (*pointless*) zwecklos

user /'ju:zə(r)/ *n* Benutzer(in) *m*(*f*). **~-'friendly** *a* benutzerfreundlich

usher /'ʌʃə(r)/ *n* Platzanweiser *m*; (*in court*) Gerichtsdiener *m* ● *vt* **~ in** hineinführen

usherette /ʌʃə'ret/ *n* Platzanweiserin *f*

USSR *abbr* UdSSR *f*

usual /'ju:ʒʊəl/ *a* üblich. **~ly** *adv* gewöhnlich

usurp /ju:'zɜ:p/ *vt* sich (*dat*) widerrechtlich aneignen

utensil /ju:'tensl/ *n* Gerät *nt*

uterus /'ju:tərəs/ *n* Gebärmutter *f*

utilitarian /ju:tɪlɪ'teərɪən/ *a* zweckmäßig

utility /ju:'tɪlətɪ/ *a* Gebrauchs- ● *n* Nutzen *m*. **~ room** *n* ≈ Waschküche *f*

utiliz|ation /ju:tɪlaɪ'zeɪʃn/ *n* Nutzung *f*. **~e** /'ju:tɪlaɪz/ *vt* nutzen

utmost /'ʌtməʊst/ *a* äußerste(r,s), größte(r,s) ● *n* **do one's ~** sein möglichstes tun

utter[1] /'ʌtə(r)/ *a*, **-ly** *adv* völlig

utter[2] *vt* von sich geben ⟨*sigh, sound*⟩; sagen ⟨*word*⟩. **~ance** /-əns/ *n* Äußerung *f*

U-turn /'ju:-/ *n* (*fig*) Kehrtwendung *f*; **'no ~s'** (*Auto*) 'Wenden verboten'

V

vacan|cy /'veɪkənsɪ/ *n* (*job*) freie Stelle *f*; (*room*) freies Zimmer *nt*; **'no ~cies'** 'belegt'. **~t** *a* frei; ⟨*look*⟩ [gedanken]leer

vacate /və'keɪt/ *vt* räumen

vacation /və'keɪʃn/ *n* (*Univ & Amer*) Ferien *pl*

vaccinat|e /'væksɪneɪt/ *vt* impfen. **~ion** /-'neɪʃn/ *n* Impfung *f*

vaccine /'væksi:n/ *n* Impfstoff *m*

vacuum /'vækjʊəm/ *n* Vakuum *nt*, luftleerer Raum *m* ● *vt* saugen. **~ cleaner** *n* Staubsauger *m*. **~ flask** *n* Thermosflasche (P) *f*. **~-packed** *a* vakuumverpackt

vagaries /'veɪgərɪz/ *npl* Launen *pl*

vagina /və'dʒaɪnə/ *n* (*Anat*) Scheide *f*

vagrant /'veɪgrənt/ *n* Landstreicher *m*

vague /veɪg/ *a* (**-r, -st**), **-ly** *adv* vage; ⟨*outline*⟩ verschwommen

vain /veɪn/ *a* (**-er, -est**) eitel; ⟨*hope, attempt*⟩ vergeblich; **in ~** vergeblich. **~ly** *adv* vergeblich

vale /veɪl/ *n* (*liter*) Tal *nt*

valet /'væleɪ/ *n* Kammerdiener *m*

valiant /'vælɪənt/ *a*, **-ly** *adv* tapfer

valid /'vælɪd/ *a* gültig; ⟨*claim*⟩ berechtigt; ⟨*argument*⟩ stichhaltig; ⟨*reason*⟩ triftig. **~ate** *vt* (*confirm*) bestätigen. **~ity** /və'lɪdətɪ/ *n* Gültigkeit *f*

valley /'vælɪ/ *n* Tal *nt*

valour /'vælə(r)/ *n* Tapferkeit *f*

valuable /'væljʊəbl/ *a* wertvoll. **~s** *npl* Wertsachen *pl*

valuation /væljʊ'eɪʃn/ *n* Schätzung *f*

value /'vælju:/ *n* Wert *m*; (*usefulness*) Nutzen *m* ● *vt* schätzen. **~ 'added tax** *n* Mehrwertsteuer *f*

valve /vælv/ *n* Ventil *nt*; (*Anat*) Klappe *f*; (*Electr*) Röhre *f*

vampire /'væmpaɪə(r)/ *n* Vampir *m*

van /væn/ *n* Lieferwagen *m*

vandal /'vændl/ *n* Rowdy *m*. **~ism** /-ɪzm/ *n* mutwillige Zerstörung *f*. **~ize** *vt* demolieren

vanilla /və'nɪlə/ *n* Vanille *f*

vanish /'vænɪʃ/ *vi* verschwinden

vanity /'vænətɪ/ *n* Eitelkeit *f*. **~ bag** *n* Kosmetiktäschchen *nt*

vantage-point /'vɑ:ntɪdʒ-/ *n* Aussichtspunkt *m*

vapour /'veɪpə(r)/ *n* Dampf *m*

variable /'veərɪəbl/ *a* unbeständig; (*Math*) variabel; (*adjustable*) regulierbar

variance /'veərɪəns/ *n* **be at ~** nicht übereinstimmen

variant /'veərɪənt/ *n* Variante *f*

variation /veərɪ'eɪʃn/ *n* Variation *f*; (*difference*) Unterschied *m*

varicose /'værɪkəʊs/ *a* **~ veins** *pl* Krampfadern *pl*

varied /'veərɪd/ *a* vielseitig; ⟨*diet*⟩ abwechslungsreich

variety /və'raɪətɪ/ *n* Abwechslung *f*; (*quantity*) Vielfalt *f*; (*Comm*) Auswahl *f*; (*type*) Art *f*; (*Bot*) Abart *f*; (*Theat*) Varieté *nt*

various /'veərɪəs/ *a* verschiedene. **~ly** *adv* unterschiedlich

varnish /'vɑ:nɪʃ/ *n* Lack *m* ● *vt* lackieren

vary /'veərɪ/ *v* (*pt/pp* **-ied**) ● *vi* sich ändern; (*be different*) verschieden sein ● *vt* [ver]ändern; (*add variety to*) abwechslungsreicher gestalten.

~ing *a* wechselnd; (*different*) unterschiedlich
vase /vɑ:z/ *n* Vase *f*
vast /vɑ:st/ *a* riesig; ⟨*expanse*⟩ weit. **~ly** *adv* gewaltig
vat /væt/ *n* Bottich *m*
VAT /vi:eɪ'ti:, væt/ *abbr* (**value added tax**) Mehrwertsteuer *f*, MwSt.
vault¹ /vɔ:lt/ *n* (*roof*) Gewölbe *nt*; (*in bank*) Tresor *m*; (*tomb*) Gruft *f*
vault² *n* Sprung *m* ● *vt/i* ~ **[over]** springen über
VDU *abbr* (**visual display unit**) Bildschirmgerät *nt*
veal /vi:l/ *n* Kalbfleisch *nt* ● *attrib* Kalbs-
veer /vɪə(r)/ *vi* sich drehen; (*Naut*) abdrehen; (*Auto*) ausscheren
vegetable /'vedʒtəbl/ *n* Gemüse *nt*; **~s** *pl* Gemüse *nt* ● *attrib* Gemüse-; ⟨*oil, fat*⟩ Pflanzen-
vegetarian /vedʒɪ'teərɪən/ *a* vegetarisch ● *n* Vegetarier(in) *m(f)*
vegetat|e /'vedʒɪteɪt/ *vi* dahinvegetieren. **~ion** /-'teɪʃn/ *n* Vegetation *f*
vehemen|ce /'vi:əməns/ *n* Heftigkeit *f*. **~t** *a*, **-ly** *adv* heftig
vehicle /'vi:ɪkl/ *n* Fahrzeug *nt*; (*fig: medium*) Mittel *nt*
veil /veɪl/ *n* Schleier *m* ● *vt* verschleiern
vein /veɪn/ *n* Ader *f*; (*mood*) Stimmung *f*; (*manner*) Art *f*; **~s and arteries** Venen und Arterien. **~ed** *a* geädert
Velcro (P) /'velkrəʊ/ *n* ~ **fastening** Klettverschluß *m*
velocity /vɪ'lɒsətɪ/ *n* Geschwindigkeit *f*
velvet /'velvɪt/ *n* Samt *m*. **~y** *a* samtig
vending-machine /'vendɪŋ-/ *n* [Verkaufs]automat *m*
vendor /'vendə(r)/ *n* Verkäufer(in) *m(f)*
veneer /və'nɪə(r)/ *n* Furnier *nt*; (*fig*) Tünche *f*. **~ed** *a* furniert
venerable /'venərəbl/ *a* ehrwürdig
venereal /vɪ'nɪərɪəl/ *a* ~ **disease** Geschlechtskrankheit *f*
Venetian /və'ni:ʃn/ *a* venezianisch. **v~ blind** *n* Jalousie *f*
vengeance /'vendʒəns/ *n* Rache *f*; **with a ~** (*fam*) gewaltig
Venice /'venɪs/ *n* Venedig *nt*
venison /'venɪsn/ *n* (*Culin*) Wild *nt*
venom /'venəm/ *n* Gift *nt*; (*fig*) Haß *m*. **~ous** /-əs/ *a* giftig
vent¹ /vent/ *n* Öffnung *f*; (*fig*) Ventil *nt*; **give ~ to** Luft machen (+*dat*) ● *vt* Luft machen (+*dat*)
vent² *n* (*in jacket*) Schlitz *m*
ventilat|e /'ventɪleɪt/ *vt* belüften. **~ion** /-'leɪʃn/ *n* Belüftung *f*; (*installation*) Lüftung *f*. **~or** *n* Lüftungsvorrichtung *f*; (*Med*) Beatmungsgerät *nt*
ventriloquist /ven'trɪləkwɪst/ *n* Bauchredner *m*
venture /'ventʃə(r)/ *n* Unternehmung *f* ● *vt* wagen ● *vi* sich wagen
venue /'venju:/ *n* Treffpunkt *m*; (*for event*) Veranstaltungsort *m*
veranda /və'rændə/ *n* Veranda *f*
verb /vɜ:b/ *n* Verb *nt*. **~al** *a*, **-ly** *adv* mündlich; (*Gram*) verbal
verbatim /vɜ:'beɪtɪm/ *a* & *adv* [wort]wörtlich
verbose /vɜ:'bəʊs/ *a* weitschweifig
verdict /'vɜ:dɪkt/ *n* Urteil *nt*
verge /vɜ:dʒ/ *n* Rand *m*; **be on the ~ of doing sth** im Begriff sein, etw zu tun ● *vi* ~ **on** (*fig*) grenzen an (+ *acc*)
verger /'vɜ:dʒə(r)/ *n* Küster *m*
verify /'verɪfaɪ/ *vt* (*pt/pp* **-ied**) überprüfen; (*confirm*) bestätigen
vermin /'vɜ:mɪn/ *n* Ungeziefer *nt*
vermouth /'vɜ:məθ/ *n* Wermut *m*
vernacular /və'nækjʊlə(r)/ *n* Landessprache *f*
versatil|e /'vɜ:sətaɪl/ *a* vielseitig. **~ity** /-'tɪlətɪ/ *n* Vielseitigkeit *f*
verse /vɜ:s/ *n* Strophe *f*; (*of Bible*) Vers *m*; (*poetry*) Lyrik *f*
version /'vɜ:ʃn/ *n* Version *f*; (*translation*) Übersetzung *f*; (*model*) Modell *nt*
versus /'vɜ:səs/ *prep* gegen (+ *acc*)
vertebra /'vɜ:tɪbrə/ *n* (*pl* **-brae** /-bri:/) (*Anat*) Wirbel *m*
vertical /'vɜ:tɪkl/ *a*, **-ly** *adv* senkrecht ● *n* Senkrechte *f*
vertigo /'vɜ:tɪgəʊ/ *n* (*Med*) Schwindel *m*
verve /vɜ:v/ *n* Schwung *m*
very /'verɪ/ *adv* sehr; **~ much** sehr; (*quantity*) sehr viel; **~ little** sehr wenig; **~ probably** höchstwahrscheinlich; **at the ~ most** allerhöchstens ● *a* (*mere*) bloß; **the ~ first** der/die/das allererste; **the ~ thing** genau das Richtige; **at the ~ end/beginning** ganz am Ende/Anfang; **only a ~ little** nur ein ganz kleines bißchen

vessel /ˈvesl/ *n* Schiff *nt*; (*receptacle & Anat*) Gefäß *nt*

vest /vest/ *n* [Unter]hemd *nt*; (*Amer: waistcoat*) Weste *f* • *vt* ~ **sth in s.o.** jdm etw verleihen; **have a ~ed interest in sth** ein persönliches Interesse an etw (*dat*) haben

vestige /ˈvestɪdʒ/ *n* Spur *f*

vestment /ˈvestmənt/ *n* (*Relig*) Gewand *nt*

vestry /ˈvestrɪ/ *n* Sakristei *f*

vet /vet/ *n* Tierarzt *m*/-ärztin *f* • *vt* (*pt*/*pp* **vetted**) überprüfen

veteran /ˈvetərən/ *n* Veteran *m*. **~ car** *n* Oldtimer *m*

veterinary /ˈvetərɪnərɪ/ *a* tierärztlich. **~ surgeon** *n* Tierarzt *m*/-ärztin *f*

veto /ˈviːtəʊ/ *n* (*pl* **-es**) Veto *nt* • *vt* sein Veto einlegen gegen

vex /veks/ *vt* ärgern. **~ation** /-ˈseɪʃn/ *n* Ärger *m*. **~ed** *a* verärgert; **~ed question** vieldiskutierte Frage *f*

VHF *abbr* (**very high frequency**) UKW

via /ˈvaɪə/ *prep* über (+ *acc*)

viable /ˈvaɪəbl/ *a* lebensfähig; (*fig*) realisierbar; ⟨*firm*⟩ rentabel

viaduct /ˈvaɪədʌkt/ *n* Viadukt *nt*

vibrant /ˈvaɪbrənt/ *a* (*fig*) lebhaft

vibrat|e /vaɪˈbreɪt/ *vi* vibrieren. **~ion** /-ˈbreɪʃn/ *n* Vibrieren *nt*

vicar /ˈvɪkə(r)/ *n* Pfarrer *m*. **~age** /-rɪdʒ/ *n* Pfarrhaus *nt*

vicarious /vɪˈkeərɪəs/ *a* nachempfunden

vice¹ /vaɪs/ *n* Laster *nt*

vice² *n* (*Techn*) Schraubstock *m*

vice ˈchairman *n* stellvertretender Vorsitzender *m*

vice ˈpresident *n* Vizepräsident *m*

vice versa /vaɪsɪˈvɜːsə/ *adv* umgekehrt

vicinity /vɪˈsɪnətɪ/ *n* Umgebung *f*; **in the ~ of** in der Nähe von

vicious /ˈvɪʃəs/ *a*, **-ly** *adv* boshaft; ⟨*animal*⟩ bösartig. **~ ˈcircle** *n* Teufelskreis *m*

victim /ˈvɪktɪm/ *n* Opfer *nt*. **~ize** *vt* schikanieren

victor /ˈvɪktə(r)/ *n* Sieger *m*

victor|ious /vɪkˈtɔːrɪəs/ *a* siegreich. **~y** /ˈvɪktərɪ/ *n* Sieg *m*

video /ˈvɪdɪəʊ/ *n* Video *nt*; (*recorder*) Videorecorder *m* • *attrib* Video- • *vt* [auf Videoband] aufnehmen

video: ~ casˈsette *n* Videokassette *f*. **~ game** *n* Videospiel *nt*. **~ ˈnasty** *n* Horrorvideo *nt*. **~ recorder** *n* Videorecorder *m*

vie /vaɪ/ *vi* (*pres p* **vying**) wetteifern

Vienn|a /vɪˈenə/ *n* Wien *nt*. **~ese** /vɪəˈniːz/ *a* Wiener

view /vjuː/ *n* Sicht *f*; (*scene*) Aussicht *f*, Blick *m*; (*picture, opinion*) Ansicht *f*; **in my ~** meiner Ansicht nach; **in ~ of** angesichts (+ *gen*); **keep/have sth in ~** etw im Auge behalten/haben; **be on ~** besichtigt werden können • *vt* sich (*dat*) ansehen; besichtigen ⟨*house*⟩; (*consider*) betrachten • *vi* (*TV*) fernsehen. **~er** *n* (*TV*) Zuschauer(in) *m*(*f*); (*Phot*) Diabetrachter *m*

view: ~finder *n* (*Phot*) Sucher *m*. **~point** *n* Standpunkt *m*

vigil /ˈvɪdʒɪl/ *n* Wache *f*

vigilan|ce /ˈvɪdʒɪləns/ *n* Wachsamkeit *f*. **~t** *a*, **-ly** *adv* wachsam

vigorous /ˈvɪgərəs/ *a*, **-ly** *adv* kräftig; (*fig*) heftig

vigour /ˈvɪgə(r)/ *n* Kraft *f*; (*fig*) Heftigkeit *f*

vile /vaɪl/ *a* abscheulich

villa /ˈvɪlə/ *n* (*for holidays*) Ferienhaus *nt*

village /ˈvɪlɪdʒ/ *n* Dorf *nt*. **~r** *n* Dorfbewohner(in) *m*(*f*)

villain /ˈvɪlən/ *n* Schurke *m*; (*in story*) Bösewicht *m*

vim /vɪm/ *n* (*fam*) Schwung *m*

vindicat|e /ˈvɪndɪkeɪt/ *vt* rechtfertigen. **~ion** /-ˈkeɪʃn/ *n* Rechtfertigung *f*

vindictive /vɪnˈdɪktɪv/ *a* nachtragend

vine /vaɪn/ *n* Weinrebe *f*

vinegar /ˈvɪnɪgə(r)/ *n* Essig *m*

vineyard /ˈvɪnjɑːd/ *n* Weinberg *m*

vintage /ˈvɪntɪdʒ/ *a* erlesen • *n* (*year*) Jahrgang *m*. **~ ˈcar** *n* Oldtimer *m*

viola /vɪˈəʊlə/ *n* (*Mus*) Bratsche *f*

violat|e /ˈvaɪəleɪt/ *vt* verletzen; (*break*) brechen; (*disturb*) stören; (*defile*) schänden. **~ion** /-ˈleɪʃn/ *n* Verletzung *f*; Schändung *f*

violen|ce /ˈvaɪələns/ *n* Gewalt *f*; (*fig*) Heftigkeit *f*. **~t** *a* gewalttätig; (*fig*) heftig. **~tly** *adv* brutal; (*fig*) heftig

violet /ˈvaɪələt/ *a* violett • *n* (*flower*) Veilchen *nt*

violin /vaɪəˈlɪn/ *n* Geige *f*, Violine *f*. **~ist** *n* Geiger(in) *m*(*f*)

VIP *abbr* (**very important person**) Prominente(r) *m*/*f*

viper /ˈvaɪpə(r)/ *n* Kreuzotter *f*; (*fig*) Schlange *f*

virgin /ˈvɜːdʒɪn/ *a* unberührt • *n* Jungfrau *f*. **~ity** /-ˈdʒɪnətɪ/ *n* Unschuld *f*

Virgo /ˈvɜːgəʊ/ *n* (*Astr*) Jungfrau *f*

viril|e /ˈvɪraɪl/ *a* männlich. **~ity** /-ˈrɪlətɪ/ *n* Männlichkeit *f*

virtual /ˈvɜːtjʊəl/ *a* **a ~**… praktisch ein… **~ly** *adv* praktisch

virtu|e /ˈvɜːtjuː/ *n* Tugend *f*; (*advantage*) Vorteil *m*; **by** *or* **in ~e of** auf Grund (+ *gen*)

virtuoso /vɜːtjʊˈəʊzəʊ/ *n* (*pl* **-si** /-ziː/) Virtuose *m*

virtuous /ˈvɜːtjʊəs/ *a* tugendhaft

virulent /ˈvɪrʊlənt/ *a* bösartig; ⟨*poison*⟩ stark; (*fig*) scharf

virus /ˈvaɪərəs/ *n* Virus *nt*

visa /ˈviːzə/ *n* Visum *nt*

vis-à-vis /viːzɑːˈviː/ *adv & prep* gegenüber (+ *dat*)

viscous /ˈvɪskəs/ *a* dickflüssig

visibility /vɪzəˈbɪlətɪ/ *n* Sichtbarkeit *f*; (*Meteorol*) Sichtweite *f*

visible /ˈvɪzəbl/ *a*, **-bly** *adv* sichtbar

vision /ˈvɪʒn/ *n* Vision *f*; (*sight*) Sehkraft *f*; (*foresight*) Weitblick *m*

visit /ˈvɪzɪt/ *n* Besuch *m* ● *vt* besuchen; besichtigen ⟨*town, building*⟩. **~ing hours** *npl* Besuchszeiten *pl*. **~or** *n* Besucher(in) *m*(*f*); (*in hotel*) Gast *m*; **have ~ors** Besuch haben

visor /ˈvaɪzə(r)/ *n* Schirm *m*; (*on helmet*) Visier *nt*; (*Auto*) [Sonnen]blende *f*

vista /ˈvɪstə/ *n* Aussicht *f*

visual /ˈvɪzjʊəl/ *a*, **-ly** *adv* visuell; **~ly handicapped** sehbehindert. **~ aids** *npl* Anschauungsmaterial *nt*. **~ disˈplay unit** *n* Bildschirmgerät *nt*

visualize /ˈvɪzjʊəlaɪz/ *vt* sich (*dat*) vorstellen

vital /ˈvaɪtl/ *a* unbedingt notwendig; (*essential to life*) lebenswichtig. **~ity** /vaɪˈtælətɪ/ *n* Vitalität *f*. **~ly** /ˈvaɪtəlɪ/ *adv* äußerst

vitamin /ˈvɪtəmɪn/ *n* Vitamin *nt*

vitreous /ˈvɪtrɪəs/ *a* glasartig; ⟨*enamel*⟩ Glas-

vivaci|ous /vɪˈveɪʃəs/ *a*, **-ly** *adv* lebhaft. **~ty** /-ˈvæsətɪ/ *n* Lebhaftigkeit *f*

vivid /ˈvɪvɪd/ *a*, **-ly** *adv* lebhaft; ⟨*description*⟩ lebendig

vixen /ˈvɪksn/ *n* Füchsin *f*

vocabulary /vəˈkæbjʊlərɪ/ *n* Wortschatz *m*; (*list*) Vokabelverzeichnis *nt*; **learn ~** Vokabeln lernen

vocal /ˈvəʊkl/ *a*, **-ly** *adv* stimmlich; (*vociferous*) lautstark. **~ cords** *npl* Stimmbänder *pl*

vocalist /ˈvəʊkəlɪst/ *n* Sänger(in) *m*(*f*)

vocation /vəˈkeɪʃn/ *n* Berufung *f*. **~al** *a* Berufs-

vociferous /vəˈsɪfərəs/ *a* lautstark

vodka /ˈvɒdkə/ *n* Wodka *m*

vogue /vəʊg/ *n* Mode *f*; **in ~** in Mode

voice /vɔɪs/ *n* Stimme *f* ● *vt* zum Ausdruck bringen

void /vɔɪd/ *a* leer; (*not valid*) ungültig; **~ of** ohne ● *n* Leere *f*

volatile /ˈvɒlətaɪl/ *a* flüchtig; ⟨*person*⟩ sprunghaft

volcanic /vɒlˈkænɪk/ *a* vulkanisch

volcano /vɒlˈkeɪnəʊ/ *n* Vulkan *m*

volition /vəˈlɪʃn/ *n* **of one's own ~** aus eigenem Willen

volley /ˈvɒlɪ/ *n* (*of gunfire*) Salve *f*; (*Tennis*) Volley *m*

volt /vəʊlt/ *n* Volt *nt*. **~age** /-ɪdʒ/ *n* (*Electr*) Spannung *f*

voluble /ˈvɒljʊbl/ *a*, **-bly** *adv* redselig; ⟨*protest*⟩ wortreich

volume /ˈvɒljuːm/ *n* (*book*) Band *m*; (*Geom*) Rauminhalt *m*; (*amount*) Ausmaß *nt*; (*Radio, TV*) Lautstärke *f*. **~ control** *n* Lautstärkeregler *m*

voluntary /ˈvɒləntərɪ/ *a*, **-ily** *adv* freiwillig

volunteer /vɒlənˈtɪə(r)/ *n* Freiwillige(r) *m*/*f* ● *vt* anbieten; geben ⟨*information*⟩ ● *vi* sich freiwillig melden

voluptuous /vəˈlʌptjʊəs/ *a* sinnlich

vomit /ˈvɒmɪt/ *n* Erbrochene(s) *nt* ● *vt* erbrechen ● *vi* sich übergeben

voracious /vəˈreɪʃəs/ *a* gefräßig; ⟨*appetite*⟩ unbändig

vot|e /vəʊt/ *n* Stimme *f*; (*ballot*) Abstimmung *f*; (*right*) Wahlrecht *nt*; **take a ~e on** abstimmen über (+ *acc*) ● *vi* abstimmen; (*in election*) wählen ● *vt* **~e s.o. president** jdn zum Präsidenten wählen. **~er** *n* Wähler(in) *m*(*f*)

vouch /vaʊtʃ/ *vi* **~ for** sich verbürgen für. **~er** *n* Gutschein *m*

vow /vaʊ/ *n* Gelöbnis *nt*; (*Relig*) Gelübde *nt* ● *vt* geloben

vowel /ˈvaʊəl/ *n* Vokal *m*

voyage /ˈvɔɪɪdʒ/ *n* Seereise *f*; (*in space*) Reise *f*, Flug *m*

vulgar /ˈvʌlgə(r)/ *a* vulgär, ordinär. **~ity** /-ˈgærətɪ/ *n* Vulgarität *f*

vulnerable /ˈvʌlnərəbl/ *a* verwundbar

vulture /ˈvʌltʃə(r)/ *n* Geier *m*

vying /ˈvaɪɪŋ/ *see* **vie**

W

wad /wɒd/ *n* Bausch *m*; (*bundle*) Bündel *nt*. **~ding** *n* Wattierung *f*
waddle /'wɒdl/ *vi* watscheln
wade /weɪd/ *vi* waten; **~ through** (*fam*) sich durchackern durch ⟨*book*⟩
wafer /'weɪfə(r)/ *n* Waffel *f*; (*Relig*) Hostie *f*
waffle¹ /'wɒfl/ *vi* (*fam*) schwafeln
waffle² *n* (*Culin*) Waffel *f*
waft /wɒft/ *vt*/*i* wehen
wag /wæg/ *v* (*pt*/*pp* **wagged**) ● *vt* wedeln mit; **~ one's finger at s.o.** jdm mit dem Finger drohen ● *vi* wedeln
wage¹ /weɪdʒ/ *vt* führen
wage² *n*, & **~s** *pl* Lohn *m*. **~ packet** *n* Lohntüte *f*
wager /'weɪdʒə(r)/ *n* Wette *f*
waggle /'wægl/ *vt* wackeln mit ● *vi* wackeln
wagon /'wægən/ *n* Wagen *m*; (*Rail*) Waggon *m*
wail /weɪl/ *n* [klagender] Schrei *m* ● *vi* heulen; (*lament*) klagen
waist /weɪst/ *n* Taille *f*. **~coat** /'weɪskəʊt/ *n* Weste *f*. **~line** *n* Taille *f*
wait /weɪt/ *n* Wartezeit *f*; **lie in ~ for** auflauern (+ *dat*) ● *vi* warten (**for** auf + *acc*); (*at table*) servieren; **~ on** bedienen ● *vt* **~ one's turn** warten, bis man an der Reihe ist
waiter /'weɪtə(r)/ *n* Kellner *m*; **~!** Herr Ober!
waiting: ~-list *n* Warteliste *f*. **~-room** *n* Warteraum *m*; (*doctor's*) Wartezimmer *nt*
waitress /'weɪtrɪs/ *n* Kellnerin *f*
waive /weɪv/ *vt* verzichten auf (+ *acc*)
wake¹ /weɪk/ *n* Totenwache *f* ● *v* (*pt* **woke**, *pp* **woken**) **~ [up]** ● *vt* [auf]wecken ● *vi* aufwachen
wake² *n* (*Naut*) Kielwasser *nt*; **in the ~ of** im Gefolge (+ *gen*)
waken /'weɪkn/ *vt* [auf]wecken ● *vi* aufwachen
Wales /weɪlz/ *n* Wales *nt*
walk /wɔːk/ *n* Spaziergang *m*; (*gait*) Gang *m*; (*path*) Weg *m*; **go for a ~** spazierengehen ● *vi* gehen; (*not ride*) laufen, zu Fuß gehen; (*ramble*) wandern; **learn to ~** laufen lernen ● *vt* ausführen ⟨*dog*⟩. **~ out** *vi* hinausgehen; ⟨*workers*:⟩ in den Streik treten; **~ out on s.o.** jdn verlassen
walker /'wɔːkə(r)/ *n* Spaziergänger(in) *m*(*f*); (*rambler*) Wanderer *m*/Wanderin *f*
walking /'wɔːkɪŋ/ *n* Gehen *nt*; (*rambling*) Wandern *nt*. **~-stick** *n* Spazierstock *m*
walk: ~-out *n* Streik *m*. **~-over** *n* (*fig*) leichter Sieg *m*
wall /wɔːl/ *n* Wand *f*; (*external*) Mauer *f*; **go to the ~** (*fam*) eingehen; **drive s.o. up the ~** (*fam*) jdn auf die Palme bringen ● *vt* **~ up** zumauern
wallet /'wɒlɪt/ *n* Brieftasche *f*
'wallflower *n* Goldlack *m*
wallop /'wɒləp/ *n* (*fam*) Schlag *m* ● *vt* (*pt*/*pp* **walloped**) (*fam*) schlagen
wallow /'wɒləʊ/ *vi* sich wälzen; (*fig*) schwelgen
'wallpaper *n* Tapete *f* ● *vt* tapezieren
walnut /'wɔːlnʌt/ *n* Walnuß *f*
waltz /wɔːlts/ *n* Walzer *m* ● *vi* Walzer tanzen; **come ~ing up** (*fam*) angetanzt kommen
wan /wɒn/ *a* bleich
wand /wɒnd/ *n* Zauberstab *m*
wander /'wɒndə(r)/ *vi* umherwandern, (*fam*) bummeln; (*fig: digress*) abschweifen. **~ about** *vi* umherwandern. **~lust** *n* Fernweh *nt*
wane /weɪn/ *n* **be on the ~** schwinden; ⟨*moon*:⟩ abnehmen ● *vi* schwinden; abnehmen
wangle /'wæŋgl/ *vt* (*fam*) organisieren
want /wɒnt/ *n* Mangel *m* (**of** an + *dat*); (*hardship*) Not *f*; (*desire*) Bedürfnis *nt* ● *vt* wollen; (*need*) brauchen; **~ [to have] sth** etw haben wollen; **~ to do sth** etw tun wollen; **we ~ to stay** wir wollen bleiben; **I ~ you to go** ich will, daß du gehst; **it ~s painting** es müßte gestrichen werden; **you ~ to learn to swim** du solltest schwimmen lernen ● *vi* **he doesn't ~ for anything** ihm fehlt es an nichts. **~ed** *a* gesucht. **~ing** *a* **be ~ing** fehlen; **he is ~ing in** ihm fehlt es an (+ *dat*)
wanton /'wɒntən/ *a*, **-ly** *adv* mutwillig
war /wɔː(r)/ *n* Krieg *m*; **be at ~** sich im Krieg befinden
ward /wɔːd/ *n* [Kranken]saal *m*; (*unit*) Station *f*; (*of town*) Wahlbezirk *m*; (*child*) Mündel *nt* ● *vt* **~ off** abwehren

warden /ˈwɔːdn/ *n* Heimleiter(in) *m(f)*; (*of youth hostel*) Herbergsvater *m*; (*supervisor*) Aufseher(in) *m(f)*
warder /ˈwɔːdə(r)/ *n* Wärter(in) *m(f)*
wardrobe /ˈwɔːdrəʊb/ *n* Kleiderschrank *m*; (*clothes*) Garderobe *f*
warehouse /ˈweəhaʊs/ *n* Lager *nt*; (*building*) Lagerhaus *nt*
wares /weəz/ *npl* Waren *pl*
war: ~fare *n* Krieg *m*. **~head** *n* Sprengkopf *m*. **~like** *a* kriegerisch
warm /wɔːm/ *a* (**-er, -est**), **-ly** *adv* warm; ⟨*welcome*⟩ herzlich; **I am ~** mir ist warm ● *vt* wärmen. **~ up** *vt* aufwärmen ● *vi* warm werden; (*Sport*) sich aufwärmen. **~-hearted** *a* warmherzig
warmth /wɔːmθ/ *n* Wärme *f*
warn /wɔːn/ *vt* warnen (**of** vor + *dat*). **~ing** *n* Warnung *f*; (*advance notice*) Vorwarnung *f*; (*caution*) Verwarnung *f*
warp /wɔːp/ *vt* verbiegen ● *vi* sich verziehen
ˈwar-path *n* **on the ~** auf dem Kriegspfad
warrant /ˈwɒrənt/ *n* (*for arrest*) Haftbefehl *m*; (*for search*) Durchsuchungsbefehl *m* ● *vt* (*justify*) rechtfertigen; (*guarantee*) garantieren
warranty /ˈwɒrəntɪ/ *n* Garantie *f*
warrior /ˈwɒrɪə(r)/ *n* Krieger *m*
ˈwarship *n* Kriegsschiff *nt*
wart /wɔːt/ *n* Warze *f*
ˈwartime *n* Kriegszeit *f*
wary /ˈweərɪ/ *a* (**-ier, -iest**), **-ily** *adv* vorsichtig; (*suspicious*) mißtrauisch
was /wɒz/ *see* **be**
wash /wɒʃ/ *n* Wäsche *f*; (*Naut*) Wellen *pl*; **have a ~** sich waschen ● *vt* waschen; spülen ⟨*dishes*⟩; aufwischen ⟨*floor*⟩; (*flow over*) bespülen; **~ one's hands** sich (*dat*) die Hände waschen ● *vi* sich waschen; ⟨*fabric:*⟩ sich waschen lassen. **~ out** *vt* auswaschen; ausspülen ⟨*mouth*⟩. **~ up** *vt* abwaschen, spülen ● *vi* (*Amer*) sich waschen
washable /ˈwɒʃəbl/ *a* waschbar
wash: ~-basin *n* Waschbecken *nt*. **~cloth** *n* (*Amer*) Waschlappen *m*
washed ˈout *a* (*faded*) verwaschen; (*tired*) abgespannt
washer /ˈwɒʃə(r)/ *n* (*Techn*) Dichtungsring *m*; (*machine*) Waschmaschine *f*
washing /ˈwɒʃɪŋ/ *n* Wäsche *f*. **~-machine** *n* Waschmaschine *f*. **~-powder** *n* Waschpulver *nt*. **~-ˈup** *n* Abwasch *m*; **do the ~-up** abwaschen, spülen. **~-ˈup liquid** *n* Spülmittel *nt*
wash: ~-out *n* Pleite *f*; (*person*) Niete *f*. **~-room** *n* Waschraum *m*
wasp /wɒsp/ *n* Wespe *f*
wastage /ˈweɪstɪdʒ/ *n* Schwund *m*
waste /weɪst/ *n* Verschwendung *f*; (*rubbish*) Abfall *m*; **~s** *pl* Öde *f*; **~ of time** Zeitverschwendung *f* ● *a* ⟨*product*⟩ Abfall-; **lay ~** verwüsten ● *vt* verschwenden ● *vi* **~ away** immer mehr abmagern
waste: ~-diˈsposal unit *n* Müllzerkleinerer *m*. **~ful** *a* verschwenderisch. **~land** *n* Ödland *nt*. **~ ˈpaper** *n* Altpapier *nt*. **~-ˈpaper basket** *n* Papierkorb *m*
watch /wɒtʃ/ *n* Wache *f*; (*timepiece*) [Armband]uhr *f*; **be on the ~** aufpassen ● *vt* beobachten; sich (*dat*) ansehen ⟨*film, match*⟩; (*be careful of, look after*) achten auf (+ *acc*); **~ television** fernsehen ● *vi* zusehen. **~ out** *vi* Ausschau halten (**for** nach); (*be careful*) aufpassen
watch: ~-dog *n* Wachhund *m*. **~ful** *a*, **-ly** *adv* wachsam. **~maker** *n* Uhrmacher *m*. **~man** *n* Wachmann *m*. **~-strap** *n* Uhrarmband *nt*. **~-tower** *n* Wachturm *m*. **~word** *n* Parole *f*
water /ˈwɔːtə(r)/ *n* Wasser *nt*; **~s** *pl* Gewässer *nt* ● *vt* gießen ⟨*garden, plant*⟩; (*dilute*) verdünnen; (*give drink to*) tränken ● *vi* ⟨*eyes:*⟩ tränen; **my mouth was ~ing** mir lief das Wasser im Munde zusammen. **~ down** *vt* verwässern
water: ~-colour *n* Wasserfarbe *f*; (*painting*) Aquarell *nt*. **~cress** *n* Brunnenkresse *f*. **~fall** *n* Wasserfall *m*
ˈwatering-can *n* Gießkanne *f*
water: ~-lily *n* Seerose *f*. **~logged** *a* **be ~logged** ⟨*ground:*⟩ unter Wasser stehen. **~-main** *n* Hauptwasserleitung *f*. **~mark** *n* Wasserzeichen *nt*. **~ polo** *n* Wasserball *m*. **~-power** *n* Wasserkraft *f*. **~proof** *a* wasserdicht. **~shed** *n* Wasserscheide *f*; (*fig*) Wendepunkt *m*. **~-skiing** *n* Wasserskilaufen *nt*. **~tight** *a* wasserdicht. **~way** *n* Wasserstraße *f*
watery /ˈwɔːtərɪ/ *a* wäßrig
watt /wɒt/ *n* Watt *nt*

wave /weɪv/ *n* Welle *f*; (*gesture*) Handbewegung *f*; (*as greeting*) Winken *nt* ● *vt* winken mit; (*brandish*) schwingen; (*threateningly*) drohen mit; wellen ⟨*hair*⟩; ~ **one's hand** winken ● *vi* winken (**to** *dat*); ⟨*flag:*⟩ wehen. **~length** *n* Wellenlänge *f*

waver /ˈweɪvə(r)/ *vi* schwanken

wavy /ˈweɪvɪ/ *a* wellig

wax[1] /wæks/ *vi* ⟨*moon:*⟩ zunehmen; (*fig: become*) werden

wax[2] *n* Wachs *nt*; (*in ear*) Schmalz *nt* ● *vt* wachsen. **~works** *n* Wachsfigurenkabinett *nt*

way /weɪ/ *n* Weg *m*; (*direction*) Richtung *f*; (*respect*) Hinsicht *f*; (*manner*) Art *f*; (*method*) Art und Weise *f*; **~s** *pl* Gewohnheiten *pl*; **in the ~** im Weg; **on the ~** auf dem Weg (**to** nach/zu); (*under way*) unterwegs; **a little/long ~** ein kleines/ganzes Stück; **a long ~ off** weit weg; **this ~** hierher; (*like this*) so; **which ~** in welche Richtung; (*how*) wie; **by the ~** übrigens; **in some ~s** in gewisser Hinsicht; **either ~** so oder so; **in this ~** auf diese Weise; **in a ~** in gewisser Weise; **in a bad ~** ⟨*person*⟩ in schlechter Verfassung; **lead the ~** vorausgehen; **make ~** Platz machen (**for** *dat*); **'give ~'** (*Auto*) 'Vorfahrt beachten'; **go out of one's ~** (*fig*) sich (*dat*) besondere Mühe geben (**to** zu); **get one's [own] ~** seinen Willen durchsetzen ● *adv* weit; **~ behind** weit zurück. **~ 'in** *n* Eingang *m*

way'lay *vt* (*pt/pp* **-laid**) überfallen; (*fam: intercept*) abfangen

way 'out *n* Ausgang *m*; (*fig*) Ausweg *m*

way-'out *a* (*fam*) verrückt

wayward /ˈweɪwəd/ *a* eigenwillig

WC *abbr* WC *nt*

we /wiː/ *pron* wir

weak /wiːk/ *a* (**-er, -est**), **-ly** *adv* schwach; ⟨*liquid*⟩ dünn. **~en** *vt* schwächen ● *vi* schwächer werden. **~ling** *n* Schwächling *m*. **~ness** *n* Schwäche *f*

wealth /welθ/ *n* Reichtum *m*; (*fig*) Fülle *f* (**of** an + *dat*). **~y** *a* (**-ier, -iest**) reich

wean /wiːn/ *vt* entwöhnen

weapon /ˈwepən/ *n* Waffe *f*

wear /weə(r)/ *n* (*clothing*) Kleidung *f*; **~ and tear** Abnutzung *f*, Verschleiß *m* ● *v* (*pt* **wore**, *pp* **worn**) ● *vt* tragen; (*damage*) abnutzen; **~ a hole in sth** etw durchwetzen; **what shall I ~?** was soll ich anziehen? ● *vi* sich abnutzen; (*last*) halten. **~ off** *vi* abgehen; ⟨*effect:*⟩ nachlassen. **~ out** *vt* abnutzen; (*exhaust*) erschöpfen ● *vi* sich abnutzen

wearable /ˈweərəbl/ *a* tragbar

weary /ˈwɪərɪ/ *a* (**-ier, -iest**), **-ily** *adv* müde ● *v* (*pt/pp* **wearied**) ● *vt* ermüden ● *vi* **~ of sth** etw (*gen*) überdrüssig werden

weasel /ˈwiːzl/ *n* Wiesel *nt*

weather /ˈweðə(r)/ *n* Wetter *nt*; **in this ~** bei diesem Wetter; **under the ~** (*fam*) nicht ganz auf dem Posten ● *vt* abwettern ⟨*storm*⟩; (*fig*) überstehen

weather: ~-beaten *a* verwittert; wettergegerbt ⟨*face*⟩. **~cock** *n* Wetterhahn *m*. **~ forecast** *n* Wettervorhersage *f*. **~-vane** *n* Wetterfahne *f*

weave[1] /wiːv/ *vi* (*pt/pp* **weaved**) sich schlängeln (**through** durch)

weave[2] *n* (*Tex*) Bindung *f* ● *vt* (*pt* **wove**, *pp* **woven**) weben; (*plait*) flechten; (*fig*) einflechten (**in** in + *acc*). **~r** *n* Weber *m*

web /web/ *n* Netz *nt*. **~bed feet** *npl* Schwimmfüße *pl*

wed /wed/ *vt/i* (*pt/pp* **wedded**) heiraten. **~ding** *n* Hochzeit *f*; (*ceremony*) Trauung *f*

wedding: ~ day *n* Hochzeitstag *m*. **~ dress** *n* Hochzeitskleid *nt*. **~-ring** *n* Ehering *m*, Trauring *m*

wedge /wedʒ/ *n* Keil *m*; (*of cheese*) [keilförmiges] Stück *nt* ● *vt* festklemmen

wedlock /ˈwedlɒk/ *n* (*liter*) Ehe *f*; **in/out of ~** ehelich/unehelich

Wednesday /ˈwenzdeɪ/ *n* Mittwoch *m*

wee /wiː/ *a* (*fam*) klein ● *vi* Pipi machen

weed /wiːd/ *n* & **~s** *pl* Unkraut *nt* ● *vt/i* jäten. **~ out** *vt* (*fig*) aussieben

'weed-killer *n* Unkrautvertilgungsmittel *nt*

weedy /ˈwiːdɪ/ *a* (*fam*) spillerig

week /wiːk/ *n* Woche *f*. **~day** *n* Wochentag *m*. **~end** *n* Wochenende *nt*

weekly /ˈwiːklɪ/ *a* & *adv* wöchentlich ● *n* Wochenzeitschrift *f*

weep /wiːp/ *vi* (*pt/pp* **wept**) weinen. **~ing 'willow** *n* Trauerweide *f*

weigh /weɪ/ *vt/i* wiegen; **~ anchor** den Anker lichten. **~ down** *vt* (*fig*) niederdrücken. **~ up** *vt* (*fig*) abwägen

weight /weɪt/ *n* Gewicht *nt*; **put on/lose ~** zunehmen/abnehmen. **~ing** *n* (*allowance*) Zulage *f*

weight: ~lessness *n* Schwerelosigkeit *f*. **~-lifting** *n* Gewichtheben *nt*

weighty /ˈweɪtɪ/ *a* (**-ier, -iest**) schwer; (*important*) gewichtig

weir /wɪə(r)/ *n* Wehr *nt*

weird /wɪəd/ *a* (**-er, -est**) unheimlich; (*bizarre*) bizarr

welcome /ˈwelkəm/ *a* willkommen; **you're ~!** nichts zu danken! **you're ~ to have it** das können Sie gerne haben ● *n* Willkommen *nt* ● *vt* begrüßen

weld /weld/ *vt* schweißen. **~er** *n* Schweißer *m*

welfare /ˈwelfeə(r)/ *n* Wohl *nt*; (*Admin*) Fürsorge *f*. **W~ State** *n* Wohlfahrtsstaat *m*

well[1] /wel/ *n* Brunnen *m*; (*oil ~*) Quelle *f*; (*of staircase*) Treppenhaus *nt*

well[2] *adv* (**better, best**) gut; **as ~** auch; **as ~ as** (*in addition*) sowohl ... als auch; **~ done!** gut gemacht! ● *a* gesund; **he is not ~** es geht ihm nicht gut; **get ~ soon!** gute Besserung! ● *int* nun, na

well: ~-behaved *a* artig. **~-being** *n* Wohl *nt*. **~-bred** *a* wohlerzogen. **~-heeled** *a* (*fam*) gut betucht

wellingtons /ˈwelɪŋtənz/ *npl* Gummistiefel *pl*

well: ~-known *a* bekannt. **~-meaning** *a* wohlmeinend. **~-meant** *a* gutgemeint. **~-off** *a* wohlhabend; **be ~-off** gut dran sein. **~-read** *a* belesen. **~-to-do** *a* wohlhabend

Welsh /welʃ/ *a* walisisch ● *n* (*Lang*) Walisisch *nt*; **the ~** *pl* die Waliser. **~man** *n* Waliser *m*. **~ rabbit** *n* überbackenes Käsebrot *nt*

went /went/ *see* **go**

wept /wept/ *see* **weep**

were /wɜː(r)/ *see* **be**

west /west/ *n* Westen *m*; **to the ~ of** westlich von ● *a* West-, west- ● *adv* nach Westen; **go ~** (*fam*) flötengehen. **~erly** *a* westlich. **~ern** *a* westlich ● *n* Western *m*

West: ~ ˈGermany *n* Westdeutschland *nt*. **~ ˈIndian** *a* westindisch ● *n* Westinder(in) *m(f)*. **~ ˈIndies** /-ˈɪndɪz/ *npl* Westindische Inseln *pl*

ˈwestward[s] /-wəd[z]/ *adv* nach Westen

wet /wet/ *a* (**wetter, wettest**) naß; ⟨*fam: person*⟩ weichlich, lasch; **'~ paint'** 'frisch gestrichen' ● *vt* (*pt/pp* **wet** *or* **wetted**) naß machen. **~ ˈblanket** *n* Spaßverderber *m*

whack /wæk/ *n* (*fam*) Schlag *m* ● *vt* (*fam*) schlagen. **~ed** *a* (*fam*) kaputt

whale /weɪl/ *n* Wal *m*; **have a ~ of a time** (*fam*) sich toll amüsieren

wharf /wɔːf/ *n* Kai *m*

what /wɒt/ *pron & int* was; **~ for?** wozu? **~ is it like?** wie ist es? **~ is your name?** wie ist Ihr Name? **~ is the weather like?** wie ist das Wetter? **~'s he talking about?** wovon redet er? ● *a* welche(r,s); **~ kind of a** was für ein(e); **at ~ time?** um wieviel Uhr?

whatˈever *a* [egal] welche(r,s) ● *pron* was ... auch; **~ is it?** was ist das bloß? **~ he does** was er auch tut; **~ happens** was auch geschieht; **nothing ~** überhaupt nichts

whatsoˈever *pron & a* ≈ **whatever**

wheat /wiːt/ *n* Weizen *m*

wheedle /ˈwiːdl/ *vt* gut zureden (+ *dat*); **~ sth out of s.o.** jdm etw ablocken

wheel /wiːl/ *n* Rad *nt*; (*pottery*) Töpferscheibe *f*; (*steering ~*) Lenkrad *nt*; **at the ~** am Steuer ● *vt* (*push*) schieben ● *vi* kehrtmachen; (*circle*) kreisen

wheel: ~barrow *n* Schubkarre *f*. **~chair** *n* Rollstuhl *m*. **~-clamp** *n* Parkkralle *f*

wheeze /wiːz/ *vi* keuchen

when /wen/ *adv* wann; **the day ~** der Tag, an dem ● *conj* wenn; (*in the past*) als; (*although*) wo ... doch; **~ swimming/reading** beim Schwimmen/Lesen

whence /wens/ *adv* (*liter*) woher

whenˈever *conj & adv* [immer] wenn; (*at whatever time*) wann immer; **~ did it happen?** wann ist das bloß passiert?

where /weə(r)/ *adv & conj* wo; **~ [to]** wohin; **~ [from]** woher

whereabouts[1] /weərəˈbaʊts/ *adv* wo

ˈwhereabouts[2] *n* Verbleib *m*; (*of person*) Aufenthaltsort *m*

whereˈas *conj* während; (*in contrast*) wohingegen

whereˈby *adv* wodurch

whereuˈpon *adv* worauf[hin]

wherˈever *conj & adv* wo immer; (*to whatever place*) wohin immer; (*from *whatever place*) woher immer; (*everywhere*) überall wo; ~ **is he?** wo ist er bloß? ~ **possible** wenn irgend möglich

whet /wet/ *vt* (*pt/pp* **whetted**) wetzen; anregen ⟨*appetite*⟩

whether /'weðə(r)/ *conj* ob

which /wɪtʃ/ *a & pron* welche(r,s); ~ **one** welche(r,s) ● *rel pron* der/die/das, (*pl*) die; (*after clause*) was; **after** ~ wonach; **on** ~ worauf

which'ever *a & pron* [egal] welche(r, s); ~ **it is** was es auch ist

whiff /wɪf/ *n* Hauch *m*

while /waɪl/ *n* Weile *f*; **a long** ~ lange; **be worth** ~ sich lohnen; **it's worth my** ~ es lohnt sich für mich ● *conj* während; (*as long as*) solange; (*although*) obgleich ● *vt* ~ **away** sich (*dat*) vertreiben

whilst /waɪlst/ *conj* während

whim /wɪm/ *n* Laune *f*

whimper /'wɪmpə(r)/ *vi* wimmern; ⟨*dog:*⟩ winseln

whimsical /'wɪmzɪkl/ *a* skurril

whine /waɪn/ *n* Winseln *nt* ● *vi* winseln

whip /wɪp/ *n* Peitsche *f*; (*Pol*) Einpeitscher *m* ● *vt* (*pt/pp* **whipped**) peitschen; (*Culin*) schlagen; (*snatch*) reißen; (*fam: steal*) klauen. ~ **up** *vt* (*incite*) anheizen; (*fam*) schnell hinzaubern ⟨*meal*⟩. ~**ped 'cream** *n* Schlagsahne *f*

whirl /wɜːl/ *n* Wirbel *m*; **I am in a** ~ mir schwirrt der Kopf ● *vt/i* wirbeln. ~**pool** *n* Strudel *m*. ~**wind** *n* Wirbelwind *m*

whirr /wɜː(r)/ *vi* surren

whisk /wɪsk/ *n* (*Culin*) Schneebesen *m* ● *vt* (*Culin*) schlagen. ~ **away** *vt* wegreißen

whisker /'wɪskə(r)/ *n* Schnurrhaar *nt*; ~**s** *pl* (*on man's cheek*) Backenbart *m*

whisky /'wɪskɪ/ *n* Whisky *m*

whisper /'wɪspə(r)/ *n* Flüstern *nt*; (*rumour*) Gerücht *nt*; **in a** ~ im Flüsterton ● *vt/i* flüstern

whistle /'wɪsl/ *n* Pfiff *m*; (*instrument*) Pfeife *f* ● *vt/i* pfeifen

white /waɪt/ *a* (**-r, -st**) weiß ● *n* Weiß *nt*; (*of egg*) Eiweiß *nt*; (*person*) Weiße(r) *m/f*

white: ~ **'coffee** *n* Kaffee *m* mit Milch. ~**-'collar worker** *n* Angestellte(r) *m*. ~ **'lie** *n* Notlüge *f*

whiten /'waɪtn/ *vt* weiß machen ● *vi* weiß werden

whiteness /'waɪtnɪs/ *n* Weiß *nt*

'whitewash *n* Tünche *f*; (*fig*) Schönfärberei *f* ● *vt* tünchen

Whitsun /'wɪtsn/ *n* Pfingsten *nt*

whittle /'wɪtl/ *vt* ~ **down** reduzieren; kürzen ⟨*list*⟩

whiz[z] /wɪz/ *vi* (*pt/pp* **whizzed**) zischen. ~**-kid** *n* (*fam*) Senkrechtstarter *m*

who /huː/ *pron* wer; (*acc*) wen; (*dat*) wem ● *rel pron* der/die/das, (*pl*) die

who'ever *pron* wer [immer]; ~ **he is** wer er auch ist; ~ **is it?** wer ist das bloß?

whole /həʊl/ *a* ganz; ⟨*truth*⟩ voll ● *n* Ganze(s) *nt*; **as a** ~ als Ganzes; **on the** ~ im großen und ganzen; **the** ~ **lot** alle; (*everything*) alles; **the** ~ **of Germany** ganz Deutschland; **the** ~ **time** die ganze Zeit

whole: ~**food** *n* Vollwertkost *f*. ~**'hearted** *a* rückhaltlos. ~**meal** *a* Vollkorn-

'wholesale *a* Großhandels- ● *adv* en gros; (*fig*) in Bausch und Bogen. ~**r** *n* Großhändler *m*

wholesome /'həʊlsəm/ *a* gesund

wholly /'həʊlɪ/ *adv* völlig

whom /huːm/ *pron* wen; **to** ~ wem ● *rel pron* den/die/das, (*pl*) die; (*dat*) dem/der/dem, (*pl*) denen

whooping cough /'huːpɪŋ-/ *n* Keuchhusten *m*

whopping /'wɒpɪŋ/ *a* (*fam*) Riesen-

whore /hɔː(r)/ *n* Hure *f*

whose /huːz/ *pron* wessen; ~ **is that?** wem gehört das? ● *rel pron* dessen/deren/dessen, (*pl*) deren

why /waɪ/ *adv* warum; (*for what purpose*) wozu; **that's** ~ darum ● *int* na

wick /wɪk/ *n* Docht *m*

wicked /'wɪkɪd/ *a* böse; (*mischievous*) frech, boshaft

wicker /'wɪkə(r)/ *n* Korbgeflecht *nt* ● *attrib* Korb-

wide /waɪd/ *a* (**-r, -st**) weit; (*broad*) breit; (*fig*) groß; **be** ~ (*far from target*) danebengehen ● *adv* weit; (*off target*) daneben; ~ **awake** hellwach; **far and** ~ weit und breit. ~**ly** *adv* weit; ⟨*known, accepted*⟩ weithin; ⟨*differ*⟩ stark

widen /'waɪdn/ *vt* verbreitern; (*fig*) erweitern ● *vi* sich verbreitern

'widespread *a* weitverbreitet

widow /'wɪdəʊ/ *n* Witwe *f*. ~**ed** *a* verwitwet. ~**er** *n* Witwer *m*

width /wɪdθ/ *n* Weite *f*; (*breadth*) Breite *f*
wield /wi:ld/ *vt* schwingen; ausüben ⟨*power*⟩
wife /waɪf/ *n* (*pl* **wives**) [Ehe]frau *f*
wig /wɪg/ *n* Perücke *f*
wiggle /'wɪgl/ *vi* wackeln ● *vt* wackeln mit
wild /waɪld/ *a* (**-er, -est**), **-ly** *adv* wild; ⟨*animal*⟩ wildlebend; ⟨*flower*⟩ wildwachsend; (*furious*) wütend; **be ~ about** (*keen on*) wild sein auf (+ *acc*) ● *adv* wild; **run ~** frei herumlaufen ● *n* **in the ~** wild; **the ~s** *pl* die Wildnis *f*
'wildcat strike *n* wilder Streik *m*
wilderness /'wɪldənɪs/ *n* Wildnis *f*; (*desert*) Wüste *f*
wild: ~-'goose chase *n* aussichtslose Suche *f*. **~life** *n* Tierwelt *f*
wilful /'wɪlfl/ *a*, **-ly** *adv* mutwillig; (*self-willed*) eigenwillig
will[1] /wɪl/ *v aux* wollen; (*forming future tense*) werden; **he ~ arrive tomorrow** er wird morgen kommen; **~ you go?** gehst du? **you ~ be back soon, won't you?** du kommst doch bald wieder, nicht? **he ~ be there, won't he?** er wird doch da sein? **she ~ be there by now** sie wird jetzt schon da sein; **~ you be quiet!** willst du wohl ruhig sein! **~ you have some wine?** möchten Sie Wein? **the engine won't start** der Motor will nicht anspringen
will[2] *n* Wille *m*; (*document*) Testament *nt*
willing /'wɪlɪŋ/ *a* willig; (*eager*) bereitwillig; **be ~** bereit sein. **~ly** *adv* bereitwillig; (*gladly*) gern. **~ness** *n* Bereitwilligkeit *f*
willow /'wɪləʊ/ *n* Weide *f*
'will-power *n* Willenskraft *f*
willy-'nilly *adv* wohl oder übel
wilt /wɪlt/ *vi* welk werden, welken
wily /'waɪlɪ/ *a* (**-ier, -iest**) listig
wimp /wɪmp/ *n* Schwächling *m*
win /wɪn/ *n* Sieg *m*; **have a ~** gewinnen ● *v* (*pt/pp* **won**; *pres p* **winning**) ● *vt* gewinnen; bekommen ⟨*scholarship*⟩ ● *vi* gewinnen; (*in battle*) siegen. **~ over** *vt* auf seine Seite bringen
wince /wɪns/ *vi* zusammenzucken
winch /wɪntʃ/ *n* Winde *f* ● *vt* **~ up** hochwinden
wind[1] /wɪnd/ *n* Wind *m*; (*breath*) Atem *m*; (*fam: flatulence*) Blähungen *pl*; **have the ~ up** (*fam*) Angst haben ● *vt* **~ s.o.** jdm den Atem nehmen
wind[2] /waɪnd/ *v* (*pt/pp* **wound**) ● *vt* (*wrap*) wickeln; (*move by turning*) kurbeln; aufziehen ⟨*clock*⟩ ● *vi* ⟨*road:*⟩ sich winden. **~ up** *vt* aufziehen ⟨*clock*⟩; schließen ⟨*proceedings*⟩
wind /wɪnd/: **~fall** *n* unerwarteter Glücksfall *m*; **~falls** *pl* (*fruit*) Fallobst *nt*. **~ instrument** *n* Blasinstrument *nt*. **~mill** *n* Windmühle *f*
window /'wɪndəʊ/ *n* Fenster *nt*; (*of shop*) Schaufenster *nt*
window: ~-box *n* Blumenkasten *m*. **~-cleaner** *n* Fensterputzer *m*. **~-dresser** *n* Schaufensterdekorateur(in) *m*(*f*). **~-dressing** *n* Schaufensterdekoration *f*; (*fig*) Schönfärberei *f*. **~-pane** *n* Fensterscheibe *f*. **~-shopping** *n* Schaufensterbummel *m*. **~-sill** *n* Fensterbrett *nt*
'windpipe *n* Luftröhre *f*
'windscreen *n*, (*Amer*) **'windshield** *n* Windschutzscheibe *f*. **~ washer** *n* Scheibenwaschanlage *f*. **~-wiper** *n* Scheibenwischer *m*
wind: ~surfing *n* Windsurfen *nt*. **~swept** *a* windgepeitscht; ⟨*person*⟩ zersaust
windy /'wɪndɪ/ *a* (**-ier, -iest**) windig; **be ~** (*fam*) Angst haben
wine /waɪn/ *n* Wein *m*
wine: ~-bar *n* Weinstube *f*. **~glass** *n* Weinglas *nt*. **~-list** *n* Weinkarte *f*
winery /'waɪnərɪ/ *n* (*Amer*) Weingut *nt*
'wine-tasting *n* Weinprobe *f*
wing /wɪŋ/ *n* Flügel *m*; (*Auto*) Kotflügel *m*; **~s** *pl* (*Theat*) Kulissen *pl*
wink /wɪŋk/ *n* Zwinkern *nt*; **not sleep a ~** kein Auge zutun ● *vi* zwinkern; ⟨*light:*⟩ blinken
winner /'wɪnə(r)/ *n* Gewinner(in) *m*(*f*); (*Sport*) Sieger(in) *m*(*f*)
winning /'wɪnɪŋ/ *a* siegreich; ⟨*smile*⟩ gewinnend. **~-post** *n* Zielpfosten *m*. **~s** *npl* Gewinn *m*
wint|er /'wɪntə(r)/ *n* Winter *m*. **~ry** *a* winterlich
wipe /waɪp/ *n* **give sth a ~** etw abwischen ● *vt* abwischen; aufwischen ⟨*floor*⟩; (*dry*) abtrocknen. **~ off** *vt* abwischen; (*erase*) auslöschen. **~ out** *vt* (*cancel*) löschen; (*destroy*) ausrotten. **~ up** *vt* aufwischen; abtrocknen ⟨*dishes*⟩
wire /'waɪə(r)/ *n* Draht *m*. **~-haired** *a* rauhhaarig

wireless /'waɪəlɪs/ *n* Radio *nt*
wire 'netting *n* Maschendraht *m*
wiring /'waɪərɪŋ/ *n* [elektrische] Leitungen *pl*
wiry /'waɪərɪ/ *a* **(-ier, -iest)** drahtig
wisdom /'wɪzdəm/ *n* Weisheit *f*; (*prudence*) Klugheit *f*. **~ tooth** *n* Weisheitszahn *m*
wise /waɪz/ *a* **(-r, -st)**, **-ly** *adv* weise; (*prudent*) klug
wish /wɪʃ/ *n* Wunsch *m* ● *vt* wünschen; **~ s.o. well** jdm alles Gute wünschen; **I ~ you could stay** ich wünschte, du könntest hierbleiben ● *vi* sich (*dat*) etwas wünschen. **~ful** *a* **~ful thinking** Wunschdenken *nt*
wishy-washy /'wɪʃɪwɒʃɪ/ *a* labberig; ⟨*colour*⟩ verwaschen; ⟨*person*⟩ lasch
wisp /wɪsp/ *n* Büschel *nt*; (*of hair*) Strähne *f*; (*of smoke*) Fahne *f*
wisteria /wɪs'tɪərɪə/ *n* Glyzinie *f*
wistful /'wɪstfl/ *a*, **-ly** *adv* wehmütig
wit /wɪt/ *n* Geist *m*, Witz *m*; (*intelligence*) Verstand *m*; (*person*) geistreicher Mensch *m*; **be at one's ~s' end** sich (*dat*) keinen Rat mehr wissen; **scared out of one's ~s** zu Tode erschrocken
witch /wɪtʃ/ *n* Hexe *f*. **~craft** *n* Hexerei *f*. **~-hunt** *n* Hexenjagd *f*
with /wɪð/ *prep* mit (+ *dat*); **~ fear/cold** vor Angst/Kälte; **~ it** damit; **I'm going ~ you** ich gehe mit; **take it ~ you** nimm es mit; **I haven't got it ~ me** ich habe es nicht bei mir; **I'm not ~ you** (*fam*) ich komme nicht mit
with'draw *v* (*pt* **-drew**, *pp* **-drawn**) ● *vt* zurückziehen; abheben ⟨*money*⟩ ● *vi* sich zurückziehen. **~al** *n* Zurückziehen *nt*; (*of money*) Abhebung *f*; (*from drugs*) Entzug *m*. **~al symptoms** *npl* Entzugserscheinungen *pl*
with'drawn *see* **withdraw** ● *a* ⟨*person*⟩ verschlossen
wither /'wɪðə(r)/ *vi* [ver]welken
with'hold *vt* (*pt/pp* **-held**) vorenthalten (**from s.o.** jdm)
with'in *prep* innerhalb (+ *gen*); **~ the law** im Rahmen des Gesetzes ● *adv* innen
with'out *prep* ohne (+ *acc*); **~ my noticing it** ohne daß ich es merkte
with'stand *vt* (*pt/pp* **-stood**) standhalten (+ *dat*)
witness /'wɪtnɪs/ *n* Zeuge *m*/Zeugin *f*; (*evidence*) Zeugnis *nt* ● *vt* Zeuge/Zeugin sein (+ *gen*); bestätigen ⟨*signature*⟩. **~-box** *n*, (*Amer*) **~-stand** *n* Zeugenstand *m*
witticism /'wɪtɪsɪzm/ *n* geistreicher Ausspruch *m*
wittingly /'wɪtɪŋlɪ/ *adv* wissentlich
witty /'wɪtɪ/ *a* **(-ier, -iest)** witzig, geistreich
wives /waɪvz/ *see* **wife**
wizard /'wɪzəd/ *n* Zauberer *m*. **~ry** *n* Zauberei *f*
wizened /'wɪznd/ *a* verhutzelt
wobb|le /'wɒbl/ *vi* wackeln. **~ly** *a* wackelig
woe /wəʊ/ *n* (*liter*) Jammer *m*; **~ is me!** wehe mir!
woke, woken /wəʊk, 'wəʊkn/ *see* **wake**[1]
wolf /wʊlf/ *n* (*pl* **wolves** /wʊlvz/) Wolf *m* ● *vt* **~ [down]** hinunterschlingen
woman /'wʊmən/ *n* (*pl* **women**) Frau *f*. **~izer** *n* Schürzenjäger *m*. **~ly** *a* fraulich
womb /wu:m/ *n* Gebärmutter *f*
women /'wɪmɪn/ *npl see* **woman**; **W~'s Libber** /'lɪbə(r)/ *n* Frauenrechtlerin *f*. **W~'s Liberation** *n* Frauenbewegung *f*
won /wʌn/ *see* **win**
wonder /'wʌndə(r)/ *n* Wunder *nt*; (*surprise*) Staunen *nt* ● *vt/i* sich fragen; (*be surprised*) sich wundern; **I ~** da frage ich mich; **I ~ whether she is ill** ob sie wohl krank ist? **~ful** *a*, **-ly** *adv* wunderbar
won't /wəʊnt/ = **will not**
woo /wu:/ *vt* (*liter*) werben um; (*fig*) umwerben
wood /wʊd/ *n* Holz *nt*; (*forest*) Wald *m*; **touch ~!** unberufen!
wood: ~cut *n* Holzschnitt *m*. **~ed** /-ɪd/ *a* bewaldet. **~en** *a* Holz-; (*fig*) hölzern. **~pecker** *n* Specht *m*. **~wind** *n* Holzbläser *pl*. **~work** *n* (*wooden parts*) Holzteile *pl*; (*craft*) Tischlerei *f*. **~worm** *n* Holzwurm *m*. **~y** *a* holzig
wool /wʊl/ *n* Wolle *f* ● *attrib* Woll-. **~len** *a* wollen. **~lens** *npl* Wollsachen *pl*
woolly /'wʊlɪ/ *a* **(-ier, -iest)** wollig; (*fig*) unklar
word /wɜ:d/ *n* Wort *nt*; (*news*) Nachricht *f*; **by ~ of mouth** mündlich; **have a ~ with** sprechen mit; **have ~s** einen Wortwechsel haben. **~ing** *n* Wortlaut *m*. **~ processor** *n* Textverarbeitungssystem *nt*
wore /wɔ:(r)/ *see* **wear**

work /wɜ:k/ *n* Arbeit *f*; (*Art, Literature*) Werk *nt*; **~s** *pl* (*factory, mechanism*) Werk *nt*; **at ~** bei der Arbeit; **out of ~** arbeitslos ● *vi* arbeiten; ⟨*machine, system:*⟩ funktionieren; (*have effect*) wirken; (*study*) lernen; **it won't ~** (*fig*) es klappt nicht ● *vt* arbeiten lassen; bedienen ⟨*machine*⟩; betätigen ⟨*lever*⟩; **~ one's way through sth** sich durch etw hindurcharbeiten. **~ off** *vt* abarbeiten. **~ out** *vt* ausrechnen; (*solve*) lösen ● *vi* gutgehen, (*fam*) klappen. **~ up** *vt* aufbauen; sich (*dat*) holen ⟨*appetite*⟩; **get ~ed up** sich aufregen

workable /'wɜ:kəbl/ *a* (*feasible*) durchführbar

workaholic /wɜ:kə'hɒlɪk/ *n* arbeitswütiger Mensch *m*

worker /'wɜ:kə(r)/ *n* Arbeiter(in) *m*(*f*)

working /'wɜ:kɪŋ/ *a* berufstätig; ⟨*day, clothes*⟩ Arbeits-; **be in ~ order** funktionieren. **~ 'class** *n* Arbeiterklasse *f*. **~-class** *a* Arbeiter-; **be ~-class** zur Arbeiterklasse gehören

work: ~man *n* Arbeiter *m*; (*craftsman*) Handwerker *m*. **~manship** *n* Arbeit *f*. **~-out** *n* [Fitneß]training *nt*. **~shop** *n* Werkstatt *f*

world /wɜ:ld/ *n* Welt *f*; **in the ~** auf der Welt; **a ~ of difference** ein himmelweiter Unterschied; **think the ~ of s.o.** große Stücke auf jdn halten. **~ly** *a* weltlich; ⟨*person*⟩ weltlich gesinnt. **~-wide** *a & adv* /-'-/ weltweit

worm /wɜ:m/ *n* Wurm *m* ● *vt* **~ one's way into s.o.'s confidence** sich in jds Vertrauen einschleichen. **~-eaten** *a* wurmstichig

worn /wɔ:n/ *see* **wear** ● *a* abgetragen. **~-out** *a* abgetragen; ⟨*carpet*⟩ abgenutzt; ⟨*person*⟩ erschöpft

worried /'wʌrɪd/ *a* besorgt

worry /'wʌrɪ/ *n* Sorge *f* ● *v* (*pt/pp* **worried**) ● *vt* beunruhigen, Sorgen machen (+ *dat*); (*bother*) stören ● *vi* sich beunruhigen, sich (*dat*) Sorgen machen. **~ing** *a* beunruhigend

worse /wɜ:s/ *a & adv* schlechter; (*more serious*) schlimmer ● *n* Schlechtere(s) *nt*; Schlimmere(s) *nt*

worsen /'wɜ:sn/ *vt* verschlechtern ● *vi* sich verschlechtern

worship /'wɜ:ʃɪp/ *n* Anbetung *f*; (*service*) Gottesdienst *m*; **Your/His W~** Euer/Seine Ehren ● *v* (*pt/pp* **-shipped**) ● *vt* anbeten ● *vi* am Gottesdienst teilnehmen

worst /wɜ:st/ *a* schlechteste(r,s); (*most serious*) schlimmste(r,s) ● *adv* am schlechtesten; am schlimmsten ● *n* **the ~** das Schlimmste; **get the ~ of it** den kürzeren ziehen

worsted /'wʊstɪd/ *n* Kammgarn *m*

worth /wɜ:θ/ *n* Wert *m*; **£10's ~ of petrol** Benzin für £10 ● *a* **be ~ £5** £5 wert sein; **be ~ it** (*fig*) sich lohnen. **~less** *a* wertlos. **~while** *a* lohnend

worthy /'wɜ:ðɪ/ *a* würdig

would /wʊd/ *v aux* **I ~ do it** ich würde es tun, ich täte es; **~ you go?** würdest du gehen? **he said he ~n't** er sagte, er würde es nicht tun; **what ~ you like?** was möchten Sie?

wound[1] /wu:nd/ *n* Wunde *f* ● *vt* verwunden

wound[2] /waʊnd/ *see* **wind**[2]

wove, woven /wəʊv, 'wəʊvn/ *see* **weave**[2]

wrangle /'ræŋgl/ *n* Streit *m* ● *vi* sich streiten

wrap /ræp/ *n* Umhang *m* ● *vt* (*pt/pp* **wrapped**) **~ [up]** wickeln; einpacken ⟨*present*⟩ ● *vi* **~ up warmly** sich warm einpacken; **be ~ped up in** (*fig*) aufgehen in (+ *dat*). **~per** *n* Hülle *f*. **~ping** *n* Verpackung *f*. **~ping paper** *n* Einwickelpapier *nt*

wrath /rɒθ/ *n* Zorn *m*

wreak /ri:k/ *vt* **~ havoc** Verwüstungen anrichten

wreath /ri:θ/ *n* (*pl* **~s** /-ðz/) Kranz *m*

wreck /rek/ *n* Wrack *nt* ● *vt* zerstören; zunichte machen ⟨*plans*⟩; zerrütten ⟨*marriage*⟩. **~age** /-ɪdʒ/ *n* Wrackteile *pl*; (*fig*) Trümmer *pl*

wren /ren/ *n* Zaunkönig *m*

wrench /rentʃ/ *n* Ruck *m*; (*tool*) Schraubenschlüssel *m*; **be a ~** (*fig*) weh tun ● *vt* reißen; **~ sth from s.o.** jdm etw entreißen

wrest /rest/ *vt* entwinden **(from s.o.** jdm)

wrestl|e /'resl/ *vi* ringen. **~er** *n* Ringer *m*. **~ing** *n* Ringen *nt*

wretch /retʃ/ *n* Kreatur *f*. **~ed** /-ɪd/ *a* elend; (*very bad*) erbärmlich

wriggle /'rɪgl/ *n* Zappeln *nt* ● *vi* zappeln; (*move forward*) sich schlängeln; **~ out of sth** (*fam*) sich vor etw (*dat*) drücken

wring /rɪŋ/ *vt* (*pt/pp* **wrung**) wringen; (**~ out**) auswringen; umdrehen ⟨*neck*⟩; ringen ⟨*hands*⟩; **be ~ing wet** tropfnaß sein

wrinkle /'rɪŋkl/ *n* Falte *f*; (*on skin*) Runzel *f* • *vt* kräuseln • *vi* sich kräuseln, sich falten. **~d** *a* runzlig
wrist /rɪst/ *n* Handgelenk *nt*. **~-watch** *n* Armbanduhr *f*
writ /rɪt/ *n* (*Jur*) Verfügung *f*
write /raɪt/ *vt/i* (*pt* **wrote**, *pp* **written**, *pres p* **writing**) schreiben. **~ down** *vt* aufschreiben. **~ off** *vt* abschreiben; zu Schrott fahren ⟨*car*⟩
'write-off *n* ≈ Totalschaden *m*
writer /'raɪtə(r)/ *n* Schreiber(in) *m*(*f*); (*author*) Schriftsteller(in) *m*(*f*)
'write-up *n* Bericht *m*; (*review*) Kritik *f*
writhe /raɪð/ *vi* sich winden
writing /'raɪtɪŋ/ *n* Schreiben *nt*; (*handwriting*) Schrift *f*; **in ~** schriftlich. **~-paper** *n* Schreibpapier *nt*
written /'rɪtn/ *see* **write**
wrong /rɒŋ/ *a*, **-ly** *adv* falsch; (*morally*) unrecht; (*not just*) ungerecht; **be ~** nicht stimmen; ⟨*person:*⟩ unrecht haben; **what's ~?** was ist los? • *adv* falsch; **go ~** ⟨*person:*⟩ etwas falsch machen; ⟨*machine:*⟩ kaputtgehen; ⟨*plan:*⟩ schiefgehen • *n* Unrecht *nt* • *vt* Unrecht tun (+ *dat*). **~ful** *a* ungerechtfertigt. **~fully** *adv* ⟨*accuse*⟩ zu Unrecht
wrote /rəʊt/ *see* **write**
wrought 'iron /rɔ:t-/ *n* Schmiedeeisen *nt* • *attrib* schmiedeeisern
wrung /rʌŋ/ *see* **wring**
wry /raɪ/ *a* (**-er, -est**) ironisch; ⟨*humour*⟩ trocken

X

xerox (P) /'zɪərɒks/ *vt* fotokopieren
Xmas /'krɪsməs, 'eksməs/ *n* (*fam*) Weihnachten *nt*
'X-ray *n* (*picture*) Röntgenaufnahme *f*; **~s** *pl* Röntgenstrahlen *pl*; **have an ~** geröntgt werden • *vt* röntgen; durchleuchten ⟨*luggage*⟩

Y

yacht /jɒt/ *n* Jacht *f*; (*for racing*) Segelboot *nt*. **~ing** *n* Segeln *nt*
yank /jæŋk/ *vt* (*fam*) reißen
Yank *n* (*fam*) Amerikaner(in) *m*(*f*), (*fam*) Ami *m*
yap /jæp/ *vi* (*pt/pp* **yapped**) ⟨*dog:*⟩ kläffen
yard[1] /jɑ:d/ *n* Hof *m*; (*for storage*) Lager *nt*
yard[2] *n* Yard *nt* (= *0,91 m*). **~stick** *n* (*fig*) Maßstab *m*
yarn /jɑ:n/ *n* Garn *nt*; (*fam: tale*) Geschichte *f*
yawn /jɔ:n/ *n* Gähnen *nt* • *vi* gähnen. **~ing** *a* gähnend
year /jɪə(r)/ *n* Jahr *nt*; (*of wine*) Jahrgang *m*; **for ~s** jahrelang. **~-book** *n* Jahrbuch *nt*. **~ly** *a & adv* jährlich
yearn /jɜ:n/ *vi* sich sehnen (**for** nach). **~ing** *n* Sehnsucht *f*
yeast /ji:st/ *n* Hefe *f*
yell /jel/ *n* Schrei *m* • *vi* schreien
yellow /'jeləʊ/ *a* gelb • *n* Gelb *nt*. **~ish** *a* gelblich
yelp /jelp/ *vi* jaulen
yen /jen/ *n* Wunsch *m* (**for** nach)
yes /jes/ *adv* ja; (*contradicting*) doch • *n* Ja *nt*
yesterday /'jestədeɪ/ *n & adv* gestern; **~'s paper** die gestrige Zeitung; **the day before ~** vorgestern
yet /jet/ *adv* noch; (*in question*) schon; (*nevertheless*) doch; **as ~** bisher; **not ~** noch nicht; **the best ~** das bisher beste • *conj* doch
yew /ju:/ *n* Eibe *f*
Yiddish /'jɪdɪʃ/ *n* Jiddisch *nt*
yield /ji:ld/ *n* Ertrag *m* • *vt* bringen; abwerfen ⟨*profit*⟩ • *vi* nachgeben; (*Amer, Auto*) die Vorfahrt beachten
yodel /'jəʊdl/ *vi* (*pt/pp* **yodelled**) jodeln
yoga /'jəʊgə/ *n* Yoga *m*
yoghurt /'jɒgət/ *n* Joghurt *m*
yoke /jəʊk/ *n* Joch *nt*; (*of garment*) Passe *f*
yokel /'jəʊkl/ *n* Bauerntölpel *m*
yolk /jəʊk/ *n* Dotter *m*, Eigelb *nt*
yonder /'jɒndə(r)/ *adv* (*liter*) dort drüben
you /ju:/ *pron* du; (*acc*) dich; (*dat*) dir; (*pl*) ihr; (*acc, dat*) euch; (*formal*) (*nom & acc, sg & pl*) Sie; (*dat, sg & pl*) Ihnen; (*one*) man; (*acc*) einen; (*dat*) einem; **all of ~** ihr/Sie alle; **I know ~** ich kenne dich/euch/Sie; **I'll give ~ the money** ich gebe dir/euch/Ihnen das Geld; **it does ~ good** es tut gut; **it's bad for ~** es ist ungesund
young /jʌŋ/ *a* (**-er** /-gə(r)/, **-est** /-gɪst/) jung • *npl* (*animals*) Junge *pl*; **the ~** die Jugend *f*. **~ster** *n* Jugendliche(r) *m/f*; (*child*) Kleine(r) *m/f*

your /jɔ:(r)/ *a* dein; (*pl*) euer; (*formal*) Ihr
yours /jɔ:z/ *poss pron* deine(r), deins; (*pl*) eure(r), euers; (*formal, sg & pl*) Ihre(r), Ihr[e]s; **a friend of ~** ein Freund von dir/Ihnen/euch; **that is ~** das gehört dir/Ihnen/euch
your'self *pron* (*pl* **-selves**) selbst; (*refl*) dich; (*dat*) dir; (*pl*) euch; (*formal*) sich; **by ~** allein
youth /ju:θ/ *n* (*pl* **youths** /-ðz/ Jugend *f*; (*boy*) Jugendliche(r) *m*. **~ful** *a* jugendlich. **~ hostel** *n* Jugendherberge *f*
Yugoslav /'ju:gəslɑ:v/ *a* jugoslawisch. **~ia** /-'slɑ:vɪə/ *n* Jugoslawien *nt*

Z

zany /'zeɪnɪ/ *a* (**-ier, -iest**) närrisch, verrückt
zeal /zi:l/ *n* Eifer *m*
zealous /'zeləs/ *a*, **-ly** *adv* eifrig
zebra /'zebrə/ *n* Zebra *nt*. **~'crossing** *n* Zebrastreifen *m*
zenith /'zenɪθ/ *n* Zenit *m*; (*fig*) Gipfel *m*
zero /'zɪərəʊ/ *n* Null *f*
zest /zest/ *n* Begeisterung *f*
zigzag /'zɪgzæg/ *n* Zickzack *m* ● *vi* (*pt/pp* **-zagged**) im Zickzack laufen/(*in vehicle*) fahren
zinc /zɪŋk/ *n* Zink *nt*
zip /zɪp/ *n* **~ [fastener]** Reißverschluß *m* ● *vt* **~ [up]** den Reißverschluß zuziehen an (+ *dat*)
'Zip code *n* (*Amer*) Postleitzahl *f*
zipper /'zɪpə(r)/ *n* Reißverschluß *m*
zither /'zɪðə(r)/ *n* Zither *f*
zodiac /'zəʊdɪæk/ *n* Tierkreis *m*
zombie /'zɒmbɪ/ *n* (*fam*) **like a ~** ganz benommen
zone /zəʊn/ *n* Zone *f*
zoo /zu:/ *n* Zoo *m*
zoological /zəʊə'lɒdʒɪkl/ *a* zoologisch
zoolog|ist /zəʊ'ɒlədʒɪst/ *n* Zoologe *m*/-gin *f*. **~y** Zoologie *f*
zoom /zu:m/ *vi* sausen. **~ lens** *n* Zoomobjektiv *nt*

Englische unregelmäßige Verben

Ein Sternchen (*) weist darauf hin, daß die korrekte Form von der jeweiligen Bedeutung abhängt.

Infinitive *Infinitiv*	Past Tense *Präteritum*	Past Participle *2. Partizip*
arise	arose	arisen
awake	awoke	awoken
be	was *sg*, were *pl*	been
bear	bore	borne
beat	beat	beaten
become	became	become
begin	began	begun
behold	beheld	beheld
bend	bent	bent
beseech	beseeched, besought	beseeched, besought
bet	bet, betted	bet, betted
bid	*bade, bid	*bidden, bid
bind	bound	bound
bite	bit	bitten
bleed	bled	bled
blow	blew	blown
break	broke	broken
breed	bred	bred
bring	brought	brought
build	built	built
burn	burnt, burned	burnt, burned
burst	burst	burst
bust	busted, bust	busted, bust
buy	bought	bought
cast	cast	cast
catch	caught	caught
choose	chose	chosen
cling	clung	clung
come	came	come
cost	*cost, costed	*cost, costed
creep	crept	crept
cut	cut	cut
deal	dealt	dealt
dig	dug	dug
do	did	done
draw	drew	drawn
dream	dreamt, dreamed	dreamt, dreamed
drink	drank	drunk
drive	drove	driven
dwell	dwelt	dwelt
eat	ate	eaten
fall	fell	fallen
feed	fed	fed
feel	felt	felt
fight	fought	fought
find	found	found

Infinitive *Infinitiv*	Past Tense *Präteritum*	Past Participle *2. Partizip*
flee	fled	fled
fling	flung	flung
fly	flew	flown
forbid	forbade	forbidden
forget	forgot	forgotten
forgive	forgave	forgiven
forsake	forsook	forsaken
freeze	froze	frozen
get	got	got, (*Amer also*) gotten
give	gave	given
go	went	gone
grind	ground	ground
grow	grew	grown
hang	*hung, hanged	*hung, hanged
have	had	had
hear	heard	heard
hew	hewed	hewed, hewn
hide	hid	hidden
hit	hit	hit
hold	held	held
hurt	hurt	hurt
keep	kept	kept
kneel	knelt	knelt
know	knew	known
lay	laid	laid
lead	led	led
lean	leaned, lent	leaned, lent
leap	leapt, leaped	leapt, leaped
learn	learnt, learned	learnt, learned
leave	left	left
lend	lent	lent
let	let	let
lie[2]	lay	lain
light	lit, lighted	lit, lighted
lose	lost	lost
make	made	made
mean	meant	meant
meet	met	met
mow	mowed	mown, mowed
overhang	overhung	overhung
pay	paid	paid
put	put	put
quit	quitted, quit	quitted, quit
read /ri:d/	read /red/	read /red/
rid	rid	rid
ride	rode	ridden
ring[2]	rang	rung
rise	rose	risen
run	ran	run
saw	sawed	sawn, sawed

Infinitive *Infinitiv*	Past Tense *Präteritum*	Past Participle *2. Partizip*
say	said	said
see	saw	seen
seek	sought	sought
sell	sold	sold
send	sent	sent
set	set	set
sew	sewed	sewn, sewed
shake	shook	shaken
shear	sheared	shorn, sheared
shed	shed	shed
shine	shone	shone
shit	shit	shit
shoe	shod	shod
shoot	shot	shot
show	showed	shown
shrink	shrank	shrunk
shut	shut	shut
sing	sang	sung
sink	sank	sunk
sit	sat	sat
slay	slew	slain
sleep	slept	slept
slide	slid	slid
sling	slung	slung
slit	slit	slit
smell	smelt, smelled	smelt, smelled
sow	sowed	sown, sowed
speak	spoke	spoken
speed	*sped, speeded	*sped, speeded
spell	spelled, spelt	spelled, spelt
spend	spent	spent
spill	spilt, spilled	spilt, spilled
spin	spun	spun
spit	spat	spat
split	split	split
spoil	spoilt, spoiled	spoilt, spoiled
spread	spread	spread
spring	sprang	sprung
stand	stood	stood
steal	stole	stolen
stick	stuck	stuck
sting	stung	stung
stink	stank	stunk
strew	strewed	strewn, strewed
stride	strode	stridden
strike	struck	struck
string	strung	strung
strive	strove	striven
swear	swore	sworn
sweep	swept	swept
swell	swelled	swollen, swelled

Infinitive *Infinitiv*	Past Tense *Präteritum*	Past Participle *2. Partizip*
swim	swam	swum
swing	swung	swung
take	took	taken
teach	taught	taught
tear	tore	torn
tell	told	told
think	thought	thought
thrive	thrived, throve	thrived, thriven
throw	threw	thrown
thrust	thrust	thrust
tread	trod	trodden
understand	understood	understood
undo	undid	undone
wake	woke	woken
wear	wore	worn
weave[2]	wove	woven
weep	wept	wept
wet	wet, wetted	wet, wetted
win	won	won
wind[2] /waɪnd/	wound /waʊnd/	wound /waʊnd/
wring	wrung	wrung
write	wrote	written

Phonetic symbols used for German words

a	Hand	hant	ŋ	lang	laŋ
a:	Bahn	ba:ɳ	o	moral	mo'ra:l
ɐ	Ober	'o:bɐ	o:	Boot	bo:t
ɐ̯	Uhr	u:ɐ̯	o̯	Foyer	fo̯a'je:
ã	Conférencier	kõferã'si̯e:	õ	Konkurs	kõ'kʊrs
ã:	Abonnement	abɔnə'mã:	õ:	Ballon	ba'lõ:
ai̯	weit	vai̯t	ɔ	Post	pɔst
au̯	Haut	hau̯t	ø	Ökonom	øko'no:m
b	Ball	bal	ø:	Öl	ø:l
ç	ich	ɪç	œ	göttlich	'gœtlɪç
d	dann	dan	ɔ̯y	heute	'hɔ̯ytə
d͜ʒ	Gin	d͜ʒɪn	p	Pakt	pakt
e	Metall	me'tal	r	Rast	rast
e:	Beet	be:t	s	Hast	hast
ɛ	mästen	'mɛstən	ʃ	Schal	ʃa:l
ɛ:	wählen	'vɛ:lən	t	Tal	ta:l
ɛ̃:	Cousin	ku'zɛ̃:	t͜s	Zahl	t͜sa:l
ə	Nase	'na:zə	tʃ	Couch	kau̯tʃ
f	Faß	fas	u	kulant	ku'lant
g	Gast	gast	u:	Hut	hu:t
h	haben	'ha:bən	u̯	aktuell	ak'tu̯ɛl
i	Rivale	ri'va:lə	ʊ	Pult	pʊlt
i:	viel	fi:l	v	was	vas
i̯	Aktion	ak't͜si̯o:n	x	Bach	bax
ɪ	Birke	'bɪrkə	y	Physik	fy'zi:k
j	ja	ja:	y:	Rübe	'ry:bə
k	kalt	kalt	y̆	Nuance	'ny̆ã:sə
l	Last	last	ʏ	Fülle	'fʏlə
m	Mast	mast	z	Nase	'na:zə
n	Naht	na:t	ʒ	Regime	re'ʒi:m

ˀ Glottal stop, e.g. Koordination /koˀɔrdina't͜si̯o:n/.

: Length sign after a vowel, e.g. Chrom /kro:m/.

' Stress mark before stressed syllable, e.g. Balkon /bal'kõ:/.

Die für das Englische verwendeten Zeichen der Lautschrift

ɑ:	barn	bɑ:n	l	lot	lɒt
ɑ̃	nuance	'nju:ɑ̃s	m	mat	mæt
æ	fat	fæt	n	not	nɒt
æ̃	lingerie	'læ̃ʒərɪ	ŋ	sing	sɪŋ
aɪ	fine	faɪn	ɒ	got	gɒt
aʊ	now	naʊ	ɔ:	paw	pɔ:
b	bat	bæt	ɔɪ	boil	bɔɪl
d	dog	dɒg	p	pet	pet
dʒ	jam	dʒæm	r	rat	ræt
e	met	met	s	sip	sɪp
eɪ	fate	feɪt	ʃ	ship	ʃɪp
eə	fairy	'feərɪ	t	tip	tɪp
əʊ	goat	gəʊt	tʃ	chin	tʃɪn
ə	ago	ə'gəʊ	θ	thin	θɪn
ɜ:	fur	fɜ:(r)	ð	the	ðə
f	fat	fæt	u:	boot	bu:t
g	good	gʊd	ʊ	book	bʊk
h	hat	hæt	ʊə	tourism	'tʊərɪzm
ɪ	bit, happy	bɪt, 'hæpɪ	ʌ	dug	dʌg
ɪə	near	nɪə(r)	v	van	væn
i:	meet	mi:t	w	win	wɪn
j	yet	jet	z	zip	zɪp
k	kit	kɪt	ʒ	vision	'vɪʒn

: bezeichnet Länge des vorhergehenden Vokals, z. B. boot [bu:t].

' Betonung, steht unmittelbar vor einer betonten Silbe, z. B. ago [ə'gəʊ].

(r) Ein „r" in runden Klammern wird nur gesprochen, wenn im Textzusammenhang ein Vokal unmittelbar folgt, z. B. fire /'faɪə(r)/; fire at /'faɪər æt/.

Guide to German pronunciation

Consonants are pronounced as in English with the following exceptions:

b	as	p	*at the end of a word or syllable*
d	as	t	
g	as	k	
ch	as in Scottish loch *after a, o, u, au*		
	like an exaggerated h as in huge		*after i, e, ä, ö, ü, eu, ei*
-chs	as	x	(as in box)
-ig	as	-ich /ıç/	*when a suffix*
j	as	y	(as in yes)
ps, pn			the p is pronounced
qu	as	k + v	
s	as	z	(as in zero) *at the beginning of a word*
	as	s	(as in bus) *at the end of a word or syllable, before a consonant, or when doubled*
sch	as	sh	
sp	as	shp	*at the beginning of a word*
st	as	sht	
v	as	f	(as in for)
	as	v	(as in very) *within a word*
w	as	v	(as in very)
z	as	ts	

Vowels are approximately as follows:

a	short	as	u	(as in but)
	long	as	a,	(as in car)
e	short	as	e	(as in pen)
	long	as	a	(as in paper)
i	short	as	i	(as in bit)
	long	as	ee	(as in queen)
o	short	as	o	(as in hot)
	long	as	o	(as in pope)

u	short	as	oo	(as in foot)
	long	as	oo	(as in boot)

Vowels are always short before a double consonant, and long when followed by an h or when double

ie	is pronounced ee	(as in keep)

Diphthongs

au	as	ow	(as in how)
ei ai	as	y	(as in my)
eu äu	as	oy	(as in boy)

German irregular verbs

1st, 2nd and 3rd person present are given after the infinitive, and past subjunctive after the past indicative, where there is a change of vowel or any other irregularity.

Compound verbs are only given if they do not take the same forms as the corresponding simple verb, e.g. *befehlen*, or if there is no corresponding simple verb, e.g. *bewegen*.

An asterisk (*) indicates a verb which is also conjugated regularly.

Infinitive *Infinitiv*	Past Tense *Präteritum*	Past Participle *2. Partizip*
abwägen	wog (wöge) ab	abgewogen
ausbedingen	bedang (bedänge) aus	ausbedungen
*backen (du bäckst, er bäckt)	buk (büke)	gebacken
befehlen (du befiehlst, er befiehlt)	befahl (beföhle, befähle)	befohlen
beginnen	begann (begänne)	begonnen
beißen (du/er beißt)	biß (bisse)	gebissen
bergen (du birgst, er birgt)	barg (bärge)	geborgen
bersten (du/er birst)	barst (bärste)	geborsten
bewegen[2]	bewog (bewöge)	bewogen
biegen	bog (böge)	gebogen
bieten	bot (böte)	geboten
binden	band (bände)	gebunden
bitten	bat (bäte)	gebeten
blasen (du/er bläst)	blies	geblasen
bleiben	blieb	geblieben
*bleichen	blich	geblichen
braten (du brätst, er brät)	briet	gebraten
brechen (du brichst, er bricht)	brach (bräche)	gebrochen
brennen	brannte (brennte)	gebrannt
bringen	brachte (brächte)	gebracht
denken	dachte (dächte)	gedacht
dreschen (du drischst, er drischt)	drosch (drösche)	gedroschen
dringen	drang (dränge)	gedrungen
dürfen (ich/er darf, du darfst)	durfte (dürfte)	gedurft
empfehlen (du empfiehlst, er empfiehlt)	empfahl (empföhle)	empfohlen
erlöschen (du erlischst, er erlischt)	erlosch (erlösche)	erloschen
*erschallen	erscholl (erschölle)	erschollen
*erschrecken (du erschrickst, er erschrickt)	erschrak (erschräke)	erschrocken

Infinitive *Infinitiv*	Past Tense *Präteritum*	Past Participle *2. Partizip*
erwägen	erwog (erwöge)	erwogen
essen (du/er ißt)	aß (äße)	gegessen
fahren (du fährst, er fährt)	fuhr (führe)	gefahren
fallen (du fällst, er fällt)	fiel	gefallen
fangen (du fängst, er fängt)	fing	gefangen
fechten (du fichtst, er ficht)	focht (föchte)	gefochten
finden	fand (fände)	gefunden
flechten (du flichtst, er flicht)	flocht (flöchte)	geflochten
fliegen	flog (flöge)	geflogen
fliehen	floh (flöhe)	geflohen
fließen (du/er fließt)	floß (flösse)	geflossen
fressen (du/er frißt)	fraß (fräße)	gefressen
frieren	fror (fröre)	gefroren
*gären	gor (göre)	gegoren
gebären (du gebierst, sie gebiert)	gebar (gebäre)	geboren
geben (du gibst, er gibt)	gab (gäbe)	gegeben
gedeihen	gedieh	gediehen
gehen	ging	gegangen
gelingen	gelang (gelänge)	gelungen
gelten (du giltst, er gilt)	galt (gölte, gälte)	gegolten
genesen (du/er genest)	genas (genäse)	genesen
genießen (du/er genießt)	genoß (genösse)	genossen
geschehen (es geschieht)	geschah (geschähe)	geschehen
gewinnen	gewann (gewönne, gewänne)	gewonnen
gießen (du/er gießt)	goß (gösse)	gegossen
gleichen	glich	geglichen
gleiten	glitt	geglitten
glimmen	glomm (glömme)	geglommen
graben (du gräbst, er gräbt)	grub (grübe)	gegraben
greifen	griff	gegriffen
haben (du hast, er hat)	hatte (hätte)	gehabt
halten (du hältst, er hält)	hielt	gehalten
hängen[2]	hing	gehangen
hauen	haute	gehauen
heben	hob (höbe)	gehoben
heißen (du/er heißt)	hieß	geheißen
helfen (du hilfst, er hilft)	half (hülfe)	geholfen
kennen	kannte (kennte)	gekannt
klingen	klang (klänge)	geklungen
kneifen	kniff	gekniffen
kommen	kam (käme)	gekommen
können (ich/er kann, du kannst)	konnte (könnte)	gekonnt
kriechen	kroch (kröche)	gekrochen
laden (du lädst, er lädt)	lud (lüde)	geladen
lassen (du/er läßt)	ließ	gelassen
laufen (du läufst, er läuft)	lief	gelaufen

Infinitive *Infinitiv*	Past Tense *Präteritum*	Past Participle *2. Partizip*
leiden	litt	gelitten
leihen	lieh	geliehen
lesen (du/er liest)	las (läse)	gelesen
liegen	lag (läge)	gelegen
lügen	log (löge)	gelogen
mahlen	mahlte	gemahlen
meiden	mied	gemieden
melken	molk (mölke)	gemolken
messen (du/er mißt)	maß (mäße)	gemessen
mißlingen	mißlang (mißlänge)	mißlungen
mögen (ich/er mag, du magst)	mochte (möchte)	gemocht
müssen (ich/er muß, du mußt)	mußte (müßte)	gemußt
nehmen (du nimmst, er nimmt)	nahm (nähme)	genommen
nennen	nannte (nennte)	genannt
pfeifen	pfiff	gepfiffen
preisen (du/er preist)	pries	gepriesen
quellen (du quillst, er quillt)	quoll (quölle)	gequollen
raten (du rätst, er rät)	riet	geraten
reiben	rieb	gerieben
reißen (du/er reißt)	riß	gerissen
reiten	ritt	geritten
rennen	rannte (rennte)	gerannt
riechen	roch (röche)	gerochen
ringen	rang (ränge)	gerungen
rinnen	rann (ränne)	geronnen
rufen	rief	gerufen
*salzen (du/er salzt)	salzte	gesalzen
saufen (du säufst, er säuft)	soff (söffe)	gesoffen
*saugen	sog (söge)	gesogen
schaffen[1]	schuf (schüfe)	geschaffen
scheiden	schied	geschieden
scheinen	schien	geschienen
scheißen (du/er scheißt)	schiß	geschissen
schelten (du schiltst, er schilt)	schalt (schölte)	gescholten
scheren[1]	schor (schöre)	geschoren
schieben	schob (schöbe)	geschoben
schießen (du/er schießt)	schoß (schösse)	geschossen
schinden	schindete	geschunden
schlafen (du schläfst, er schläft)	schlief	geschlafen
schlagen (du schlägst, er schlägt)	schlug (schlüge)	geschlagen
schleichen	schlich	geschlichen
schleifen[2]	schliff	geschliffen
schließen (du/er schließt)	schloß (schlösse)	geschlossen
schlingen	schlang (schlänge)	geschlungen

Infinitive *Infinitiv*	Past Tense *Präteritum*	Past Participle *2. Partizip*
schmeißen (du/er schmeißt)	schmiß (schmisse)	geschmissen
schmelzen (du/er schmilzt)	schmolz (schmölze)	geschmolzen
schneiden	schnitt	geschnitten
*schrecken (du schrickst, er schrickt)	schrak (schräke)	geschreckt
schreiben	schrieb	geschrieben
schreien	schrie	geschrie[e]n
schreiten	schritt	geschritten
schweigen	schwieg	geschwiegen
schwellen (du schwillst, er schwillt)	schwoll (schwölle)	geschwollen
schwimmen	schwamm (schwömme)	geschwommen
schwinden	schwand (schwände)	geschwunden
schwingen	schwang (schwänge)	geschwungen
schwören	schwor (schwüre)	geschworen
sehen (du siehst, er sieht)	sah (sähe)	gesehen
sein (ich bin, du bist, er ist, wir sind, ihr seid, sie sind)	war (wäre)	gewesen
senden[1]	sandte (sendete)	gesandt
sieden	sott (sötte)	gesotten
singen	sang (sänge)	gesungen
sinken	sank (sänke)	gesunken
sinnen	sann (sänne)	gesonnen
sitzen (du/er sitzt)	saß (säße)	gesessen
sollen (ich/er soll, du sollst)	sollte	gesollt
*spalten	spaltete	gespalten
speien	spie	gespie[e]n
spinnen	spann (spönne, spänne)	gesponnen
sprechen (du sprichst, er spricht)	sprach (spräche)	gesprochen
sprießen (du/er sprießt)	sproß (sprösse)	gesprossen
springen	sprang (spränge)	gesprungen
stechen (du stichst, er sticht)	stach (stäche)	gestochen
stehen	stand (stünde, stände)	gestanden
stehlen (du stiehlst, er stiehlt)	stahl (stähle)	gestohlen
steigen	stieg	gestiegen
sterben (du stirbst, er stirbt)	starb (stürbe)	gestorben
stinken	stank (stänke)	gestunken
stoßen (du/er stößt)	stieß	gestoßen
streichen	strich	gestrichen
streiten	stritt	gestritten
tragen (du trägst, er trägt)	trug (trüge)	getragen
treffen (du triffst, er trifft)	traf (träfe)	getroffen
treiben	trieb	getrieben
treten (du trittst, er tritt)	trat (träte)	getreten

Infinitive *Infinitiv*	Past Tense *Präteritum*	Past Participle *2. Partizip*
*triefen	troff (tröffe)	getroffen
trinken	trank (tränke)	getrunken
trügen	trog (tröge)	getrogen
tun (du tust, er tut)	tat (täte)	getan
verderben (du verdirbst, er verdirbt)	verdarb (verdürbe)	verdorben
vergessen (du/er vergißt)	vergaß (vergäße)	vergessen
verlieren	verlor (verlöre)	verloren
verschleißen (du/er verschleißt)	verschliß	verschlissen
verzeihen	verzieh	verziehen
wachsen[1] (du/er wächst)	wuchs (wüchse)	gewachsen
waschen (du wäschst, er wäscht)	wusch (wüsche)	gewaschen
weichen[2]	wich	gewichen
weisen (du/er weist)	wies	gewiesen
*wenden[2]	wandte (wendete)	gewandt
werben (du wirbst, er wirbt)	warb (würbe)	geworben
werden (du wirst, er wird)	wurde (würde)	geworden
werfen (du wirfst, er wirft)	warf (würfe)	geworfen
wiegen[1]	wog (wöge)	gewogen
winden	wand (wände)	gewunden
wissen (ich/er weiß, du weißt)	wußte (wüßte)	gewußt
wollen (ich/er will, du willst)	wollte	gewollt
wringen	wrang (wränge)	gewrungen
ziehen	zog (zöge)	gezogen
zwingen	zwang (zwänge)	gezwungen